Nazi
Germany

A NEW HISTORY

Nazi Germany

A NEW HISTORY

Klaus P.
Fischer

CONTINUUM · NEW YORK

1995

The Continuum Publishing Company
370 Lexington Avenue, New York, NY 10017

Copyright © 1995 by Klaus P. Fischer

Printed in the United States of America

Library of Congress Cataloging-in-Publication Data
Fischer, Klaus P., 1942–
    Nazi Germany : a new history / Klaus P. Fischer
      p.   cm.
    Includes bibliographical references and index.
    ISBN 0-8264-0797-8 (alk. paper)
    1. Germany—History—1933–1945. 2. National socialism—Germany.
  3. Hitler, Adolf, 1889–1945.   I. Title.
  DD256.5.F55 1995
  943.086–dc20
                                 94–41796
                                     CIP

c. 1

Contents

Acknowledgments

This book could not have been written without the support of my family, especially my wife, Ann; my students, who patiently listened and contributed to this subject over the past fifteen years; and a number of close friends and helpful critics. I am especially indebted to Dr. Roger Lydon, whose knowledge of German culture is both extensive and profound. Throughout the writing of this book, he was an invaluable editor and alter ego who kept me on track, moderated my judgments, and corrected various oversights. Thanks are also due to Dr. Jeannine Schmid, who encouraged me to explore the personalities of the Third Reich from the perspectives opened up by recent research in developmental and social psychology. I would also like to thank Professors Gerhart Hoffmeister and Leonard Marsak, both of the University of California, Santa Barbara, for having scrutinized the manuscript and offered valuable suggestions. Professor Robert G. L. Waite, to whom I am indebted for much of my analysis of Adolf Hitler, alerted me to several factual and substantive problems; his generous and gracious remarks are much appreciated. My mother, who grew up in Nazi Germany and served in the German navy during World War II, provided a living link to certain aspects of the period; I am grateful for her insights, realizing that many of them brought back painful memories. Finally, a debt of gratitude is due to Sheila and Jim Harmon for deciphering my handwriting, typing the manuscript, and putting up with my eccentricities. It goes without saying that whatever shortcomings remain are entirely my own.

Part One

THE ROOTS
1870-1933

Chapter 1

The Origins of Totalitarianism

The European Background

A nation, like an individual, has a past that conditions the present. Every human condition, good or evil, is the sum total of past actions and inherited characteristics. By carefully tracing the significant events that have shaped a nation's history, we can understand its present condition and chart its future possibilities. In this sense knowledge of things past is the key to things to come. Human events in time and place are not inexplicable occurrences, wholly unexpected and unconnected to past forms of behavior. Adolf Hitler did not fall on the Germans out of a blue sky; his coming was prepared by the political and ideological climate of postwar cynicism, extremism, and despair. Hitler and his movement were the outcome of certain historical forces that we can retrodict; but in so doing, we must be careful to avoid three common fallacies: the error of *post hoc, ergo propter hoc* analysis, the danger of infinite causal regress, and the imposition of deterministic explanations on the historical process.

As to the first of these fallacies, which involves assigning inappropriate causes to account for the occurrence of certain effects, it is important to remember that just because a given event happened before Hitler does not necessarily mean that it was a cause of Hitler's rise to power. The second fallacy — that of infinite causal regress — would lead us, if we accepted it, to the belief that Hitler was the product of German history as a whole. The fallacy can be countered by understanding that the sum of causes of a particular event cannot be infinite, for otherwise nothing could happen in history. If the causes of the Hitler movement were infinite, we would still be waiting for its occurrence. The causes of National Socialism must be finite and limited to a manageable, circumambient historical space. It is fruitless to analyze the Hitler movement, located in the 1930s, as the logical product of German history as a whole. German history, like the history of other European nations, is infinitely rich in many great events, some of which are causally related to each other and some of which are not.

The third fallacy, involving the deterministic belief that events happen by a kind of predetermined necessity, is the result of a dangerous tendency to view secular events in teleological terms as inexorable manifestations of immanent psychological, political, or economic circumstances. Theologians may base their explanations on transcendental principles and speak of inevitability and final ends, but historians, who deal with variegated, mutable, and often causally unrelated events, can never speak with certainty about the past or the future. Their accounts of the past are memory pictures, imaginative but not scientific reconstructions of bygone events. The fact that something happened is no logical proof that it must have happened or that it will happen again. It is true that events recur in clearly recognizable patterns, allowing us to retrodict the past and to predict the future with a modest degree of probability. At the same time, the contingencies are so vast, the facts so infinite in number, that no event, however well known, can be understood with complete certainty. Hitler happened to the Germans for good reasons, but there were equally good reasons why he should have never come to power in the first place. As historians, however, we must concentrate on what actually happened and not on what might have happened. Reasons that may account for what did not happen are irrelevant as explanations for what did happen.

In order to understand the political and cultural roots of Nazi Germany, it is therefore necessary to trace the real chain of causes and effects that culminated in Hitler's seizure of power in 1933. To do so, it is especially important to view the Nazi revolution in a larger historical perspective. In other words, it is essential to ask: What was it about the Nazi movement that made it a distinctly European phenomenon and what elements were there in it that made it a uniquely German event? Further, what did Hitler bring to those preexisting forces that made the Nazi movement such a great success in Germany? In answering such questions, we are attempting to raise the larger metahistorical issues of historical causation and the role of the individual within the historical process.

It is the contention of this work that National Socialism represents the right-wing variant of modern totalitarianism, the ideological counterpart of Communism, or left-wing totalitarianism. Totalitarianism may be defined as the monopolizing of human activities, private and public, by a modern technocratic state. The term *totalitarian* must be understood as an ideal type, not as a historical reality; and the fact that Germany fell far short of being totalitarian does not invalidate the use of the term nor our major claim that National Socialism "aimed" at the total control of a citizen's life. No concept can explain the multiplicity of social life in the modern world, but the term *totalitarian* captures the essence of certain twentieth-century movements much better than most others.[1]

The historical roots of National Socialism are embedded in the period 1871–1933, a period of great upheavals and disruptions within German society. This included the establishment of imperial Germany, World War I, the German defeat and its aftermath (the fall of the monarchy, revolution, the impact of the Versailles Treaty, and catastrophic inflation), Germany's ill-fated experience with democracy under the Weimar Republic, the Great Depression, and the rise of Adolf Hitler. During these six seminal decades, German society underwent such a series of violent disruptions that a breaking point had been reached in 1933. National Socialism may be viewed as Germany's response to conditions of extreme stress caused by specific historical circumstances.[2] Other nations, of course, were also afflicted by chaotic conditions during the postwar period, but they did not resort to totalitarianism as a means of coping with their socioeconomic problems. What made Germany different?

The major reason why Germany and several other countries turned to totalitarianism resides in their failure to integrate traditional institutions with the requirements of modern industrial civilization. In Germany or Italy, for example, the social fabric was far more fragile than it was in England or France, where decades of socioeconomic conflicts had forced traditional institutions into more successful accommodations with modern industrial civilization. In addition, neither Germany nor Italy became a unified nation until the last quarter of the nineteenth century; and while both grappled with the psychological problem of identity, powerful industrial changes eroded ancient traditions and institutions that were needed as a stable foundation for the future.

All totalitarian movements in modern times must be seen against the background of the great demographic and political changes that occurred as a result of the dual revolutions of the eighteenth century — the Industrial and the French Revolutions. Educated Europeans asked themselves how a rapidly growing and restless population could be controlled and brought within the traditional orbit of European culture. The democratic revolutions of the period 1776–1848 had already provided a clue: popular sovereignty based on democratic consent. Within the democratic tradition, however, resided two variants — the libertarian and the collectivist, the former embodying the individualistic premises of the Lockean-Puritan conscience, and the latter the communal-coercive notions of Rousseau and Jacobinism. Libertarianism and its various permutations gave rise to the Anglo-American style of thought with its emphasis on representative government, freedom, equality, and human rights, while collectivism informed the rising Socialist and Communist movements and their demands for the abolition of private property, the communal ownership of goods, and "true" equality. Both movements, however, were an outgrowth of the eighteenth-century Enlightenment, having been imbued with the secular and antireligious message of human fulfillment through economic affluence and the pursuit of happiness. The good life was seen to be the goods life; the two branches of democracy differed only on the specific means by which the goods life might be attained. The libertarian tradition favored individualism and a free-market approach, while the collectivist tradition advocated communal organization of resources and ownership as the only viable means of implementing the common good.

The implementation of democratic approaches, however, foundered on the resistance of authoritarian-monarchical traditions that were still very strong and prevented either of the two democratic solutions from being fully attained. In some cases, as in Germany, Italy, Spain, Russia, and several southern European nations, the rising democratic style was often preempted by the conservative feudal establishment. In these less developed and still half-feudal societies the collectivist branch of democracy was regarded as the lesser of two evils because its emphasis on the general will and the identity of ruler and ruled could be reconciled with traditional notions of monarchy. It was also within the collectivist branch of democracy that some of the chief causes of twentieth-century totalitarianism resided. Among these causes are the messianic political impulse, born of displaced religiosity, which holds that politics is redemptive (Jacobinism and Marxism), and the communal approach to politics that insists that the individual must bow obediently to the common good.

In the second half of the nineteenth century, all political movements were subject to the influence of three powerful currents: nationalism, imperialism, and racism. In the eighteenth century, nationalism had been largely cultural; it was a kind of generous romantic outlook that respected the distinct cultural contributions of each nation and favored the growth of each nation within the context of political independence and constitutional government.[3] By the 1870s, however, nationalism had changed from an attitude of pride in one's country to a quasi-religious, millenarian movement. It inspired the most divergent passions and seized entire populations in frenzied excitements and seething emotions. It was invoked by statesmen under the banner of national self-determination, but it was also used by imperialists as a smoke screen for conquest and subjugation. In fact, nationalism and imperialism are essentially the expression of a dominant economic order that has succeeded in mobilizing a nation for the purpose of political and economic expansion. In the nineteenth century that dominant economic order was the commercial middle class. This is why imperialism in modern times is coextensive with capitalism — both are based on unlimited expansion. Now capitalism presupposes a dynamic economy, but markets are not infinitely elastic; they contract sooner or later under the impact of inherent obstacles to growth such as competition, overproduction, shortages, and lack of purchasing power. When the home markets began to shrink in the late nineteenth century, capitalists looked to new markets they could exploit, turning to overseas expansion for goods and profits. Unlike earlier forms of colonialism, which rested on a kind of "cash and carry" basis by which European merchants bought goods from colonial people, the new imperialism (1870–1914) involved the systematic exploitation of overseas colonies. In practical terms, this meant investing vast amounts of capital in overseas ventures and in setting up the instruments of production and exchange: mines, factories, docks, warehouses, refineries, railroads, steamboats, and banks. Moreover, since the technological and managerial skills required for the efficient operation of such tasks were still beyond the capacity of the natives, it became necessary to export the experts. These technical managers expected a high standard of living abroad to justify the sacrifice involved in moving to distant and often inhospitable areas. They insisted on regal mansions, resort clubs, and splendid offices.

The affluent and sometimes sybaritic lifestyles of the white colonial elite were often gained at a heavy price: the shameless exploitation of the native population. European nations introduced class systems into their colonies that they had long abandoned at home as unjust and oppressive. Such "legalized inequality," in turn, was often justified by racist arguments preaching the superiority of the white man. In many cases, these blatant attempts to subjugate the natives boomeranged in the form of desperate colonial revolts. Economic control, therefore, necessitated political control by the home government: the flag followed trade. This is why imperialism and nationalism were indissolubly linked to each other — territorial expansion on land or on sea usually involved the nation-state. Without active government support the long-range mobilization of resources necessary to control colonial acquisitions would have been impossible.

The characteristics that imperialism imparted to totalitarianism may be summed up as follows: imperialism reinforced aggressive habits and encouraged the militarization of everyday life; stimulated racial and ethnic conflicts at home and abroad; encouraged a kind of messianic sense among the imperial elites that revitalized the habit of arrogant authority; infused brutal and callous attitudes, acquired from the mistreatment of "inferior breeds," into the fabric of European society; and led to a dangerous web of diplomatic entanglements that helped prepare the way for World War I.

In the late nineteenth century nationalism and imperialism not only stimulated overseas conquests but also inflamed tribal animosities between ethnic groups at home. These tribal conflicts manifested themselves in the proliferating ethnic movements such as pan-Slavism, pan-Anglo-Saxonism, pan-Germanism, or pan-Hispanism. The aim of these intensely xenophobic groups was to heighten feelings of ethnic superiority and to create stronger ties between the mother country and scattered ethnic groups living outside its territorial jurisdiction. Since the European continent was a confused hodgepodge of widely scattered ethnic groups, it proved impossible to merge all Germans into a larger Germany or all Slavs into a larger Slavic state. Every nation could claim some of its own nationals residing in other nations; similarly, every nation had alien groups living within its own borders. The most acute ethnic tensions existed between Germans and Slavs, particularly in that part of Europe lying within the long, wide belt from the Baltic to the Black Sea, where centuries of shifting conquests had splintered these areas into a multiracial, multilinguistic, and multireligious confusion.[4] The growth of nationalism in these areas served as a strong force in breaking up supranational empires and in reviving imperialistic dreams among the ruling elites. There was another insidious influence that ethnic conflicts invariably encouraged — racism.

In the nineteenth century, racism also evolved from a personal or even a social bias to an all-embracing ideology claiming to possess a master key to world history. In this sense racism was the eschatological counterpart to Communism because both claimed to possess the ultimate interpretation of the historical process. In extolling the racial superiority of their tribe, racists adduced a variety of different rationalizations. Since the last quarter of the nineteenth century was dominated intellectually by Darwinian biology, public discussion was intensely preoccupied with such magical phrases as natural selection, heredity, struggle for existence, and the survival of the fittest. A veritable flood of printed material was devoted to racial stocks, racial behavior, and racial breeding, creating the impression that racial issues could be reduced to the level of scientific animal husbandry. In his study of Houston Stewart Chamberlain, who was considered the evangelist of racism, Geoffrey Field captured the mood of this intensely race-conscious age when he wrote that "scores of researchers, clutching complicated calipers, craniometers, spirometers, and other sundry gauges that measured scientific ingenuity more than anatomy, scoured the countryside weighing skulls, examining bones, classifying hair and eye color and skin pigmentation, and measuring noses, ears, heads, and every other attribute of the physical frame. From the data accumulated, large numbers of racial taxonomies were invented."[5]

In the light of Darwin's discoveries, the public wanted to know who was fittest and why; and invariably ethnocentric researchers jumped to the hasty conclusion that skin color was the chief determinant of biological and, therefore, social superiority. It was merely a question of elucidating the racial traits of the strongest (fittest) and the weakest (least fit) nations and demonstrating, by way of comparative anthropology or physiology, which qualities promoted survival and which did not. The general consensus was that competition, boldness, bravery, and other assertive qualities made for survival, while weakness, compromise, pacifism, altruism, in short, passive traits, were sociobiologically undesirable.

Sir Francis Galton, Darwin's cousin, was in the vanguard of such sociobiological speculation. He was convinced that heredity rather than environment molded individual characteristics, and he called for a concerted national effort to regulate heredity. By appropriate eugenic methods, he believed, it should be possible to breed a superior race of people; it was just a matter of encouraging the fittest to procreate and discouraging — by sterilization if necessary — the procreation of the feeble, incompetent, and sickly types. Galton's friend, Karl Pearson, described the nation on the analogy of an individual organism and warned that no nation could survive in the struggle for existence unless it was a homogeneous whole. Class conflicts are, therefore, utterly divisive and must be rooted out with vigor. The best homogeneous whole, Pearson believed, was a Socialist state in which every individual, regardless of station or rank, cooperated with others for the common good. Pearson saw socialism as an instinct for national greatness, and his celebration of the state earned him the title "National Socialist."[6] Galton and Pearson were not alone in their fascination with racial characteristics and racial improvement. A host of anthropologists, biologists, psychologists, and similar behavioral "scientists" were busy classifying races, elucidating racial gestalts, and delivering weighty pronouncements on the future of the white man. The classification of races on the basis of certain behavioral characteristics was undertaken by a group of social psychologists, including Gustav Le Bon (the famous analyst of crowd psychology), Vacher de Lapouge, Anders Retzius, and a host of minor lights.

Of all these racial theorists, the two most persuasive evangelists of racism were Arthur de Gobineau and Houston Stewart Chamberlain. Gobineau, a French count, is often seen as the founding father of white or "Aryan" superiority in the nineteenth century, and his four-volume essay entitled *Inequality of Races* (1853–54) is also considered, along with Houston Stewart Chamberlain's *Foundations of the Nineteenth Century,* as one of the major ideological capstones of twentieth-century fascism. Much cited, but little understood, the count's essay represented an ambitious attempt to explain the rise and fall of civilizations in racial terms. Just as Marx singled out economic factors as constituting the substructure of any given society, Gobineau focused on racial characteristics as the chief determinants of historical events. A man of decided conservative and even reactionary leanings, ill at ease in a petit bourgeois environment, Gobineau longed for a restoration of a more exciting and heroic age. However, he was by no means a knee-jerk reactionary, but rather was a deeply disturbed cultural conservative who left behind an immensely polished and broad-ranging literary output amounting to some forty volumes, including political essays, novels, travel books, Oriental studies, and letters. In addition, he was a widely traveled man, a sparkling conversationalist, and an experienced statesman who served as cabinet secretary to Alexis de Tocqueville in 1849 and who was entrusted with various diplomatic missions that took him to Switzerland, Germany, Persia, Greece, Newfoundland, Brazil, and Sweden.

Despite his cosmopolitan experiences, Gobineau not only held strong racial prejudices but intellectualized them into a sweeping philosophy of history. He divided the human race into three racial types — white, yellow, and black — and linked special racial characteristics to each type. Whites, for example, exhibit the most noble qualities of the human race such as leadership, energy, and superiority, while the yellow or black races display fertility and sensuality, respectively. Oddly enough, Gobineau was convinced that great civilizations required a mixture of races because each race possessed an innate superiority in one area of human achievement. At the same time, a great civilization requires a dominant race that provides the intellectual leadership. France, he believed, had been governed by an Aryan-Nordic aristocracy, but was now becoming bastardized by inferior blood, chiefly Gallic, Semitic, and Latin. He lamented the fact that inferior black and yellow races had infected the whole Mediterranean basin with their "nigridity" and that France had suffered a degree of cultural decline that might be irreversible.

Gobineau's racial theories were promoted with great success by the composer Richard Wagner; in fact, the two men struck up a close friendship after discovering that their aesthetic sensibilities were much the same. In the Wagner circle at Bayreuth, Gobineau's racial doctrines were enthusiastically promoted. In 1894, Ludwig Scheemann, who translated Gobineau's work into German, founded the Gobineau Vereinigung in Freiburg. In 1899, Houston Stewart Chamberlain, a Germanophile who used Gobineau as a cornerstone of his own system, raised racism to an even higher power.

Chamberlain (1855–1927), a transplanted Englishman and scion of a wealthy, aristocratic family of scholars, explorers, and soldiers of the British Empire, became one of the great trailblazers of Aryan supremacy and Germanic ethnocentrism. Attracted to Richard Wagner's music and aesthetic philosophy of life, he settled in Germany, married one of Wagner's daughters, and became the focal point of radical Germanism and violent antimodernism. Chamberlain belonged to that class of intellectuals who saw themselves uprooted by the urban industrial movement and its egalitarian principles. Like Nietzsche, he was a solitary wanderer and aesthetic dandy, immersing himself in the cultural heritage of the past until, at length, he found his true mission — that of spreading the gospel of Aryan superiority. As a member of Wagner's inner circle, he participated in Wagner's dream of regenerating both German art and German greatness. His stupendous and encyclopedic knowledge, often inchoate and dilettantish, was subsequently directed toward spreading the German gospel, culminating in his major work, *Foundations of the Nineteenth Century*. This rambling, highly intuitive, and impressionistic work, written with real flashes of insight along with many fatuous observations, was designed to be a cultural history of Europe from the ancient world to 1800. In actuality, the book's scholarly facade represented merely the scaffolding for a racist interpretation of culture in general and German culture in particular. The book represented an emerging literary genre that was made up of texts pretending to be rigorous works of academic scholarship while belonging more properly in the demimonde of popular advocacy.[7] The purpose of such works was not to bore educated readers with scholarly jargon but to excite them into action through highly partisan accounts of the past.

The defining characteristic of Chamberlain's works was the racial interpretation of history. In attempting to explain the chief forces that had molded the nineteenth century, Chamberlain singled out Hellenic art and philosophy; Roman administration and jurisprudence; the Christian revelation; the destructive power of the Jews; and the redemptive mission of the Aryan race. The leitmotif of his whole work is the conviction that race is the ultimate determinant of cultural greatness and that the Aryan race had always represented a regenerative element in societies threatened by degeneration; conversely, the existence of lesser blood types, such as the Slavs and the Semites, always signified impending degeneration of societies.

All that was great in the history of Western culture, Chamberlain believed, must be attributed to the contributions of the Teutonic race, whereas all (or nearly all) that was mean, petty, and disruptive was the handiwork of the Jews. If the Teutons are culture creators, the Jews are culture destroyers. Once the Jew has put his stamp on any movement, its vital force is sapped. Christianity is a case in point because of its Janus-like physiognomy — half Jewish and half Aryan. Its Aryan face is profoundly rich in symbolism and mythology, while its Jewish face is strongly colored by rigid adherence to ritual and law. Thus, what was best in Christianity — its primitive vigor and childlike faith — became distorted by Jewish elements into an intolerant creed emphasizing sin, guilt, and punishment rather than redemption, love, and divine grace. In the course of these ruminations, Chamberlain also came to the curious conclusion that Jesus could not really have been Jewish given his heroic qualities. Chamberlain's work sold well over a hundred thousand copies by the outbreak of World War I, and various pan-German groups enthusiastically endorsed its beliefs. The book was translated into several languages, including English, and caused a storm of controversy. Moreover, since Chamberlain moved in highly influential circles, counting the German kaiser, among others, as his friend, his ideas were sanctioned by people who had a vested interest in spreading racial doctrines. Chamberlain himself participated in World War I as an ideological soldier who promoted the superiority of the German cause. During the 1920s, he actively supported the Nazis, who considered him one of their own. In 1927, Alfred Rosenberg, the Nazi racial philosopher, called Chamberlain's work a *Kampfbuch* (book of struggle), a beacon lighting the way to victory for the party.

In the late nineteenth century, racism cross-fertilized with several other disturbing attitudes; in fact, the period from 1890 to 1914 witnessed several disconcerting dissonances in the consciousness of Europe. A decisive reaction set in against formal, classical, and rationalistic modes of thought, a reaction that profoundly undermined the equilibrium of Western culture.[8] The primacy of reason, which had been the hallmark of the Enlightenment and much of the nineteenth century, was increasingly challenged by speculative writers who emphasized the preeminent role of will, the irrational, the subjective, the intuitive, or the unconscious in human life. Historians have characterized this intellectual reorientation as "vitalism," "irrationalism," "neoromanticism," or simply "neomysticism" — labels that are suggestive but also misleading. The revolt against reason was primarily directed against the spirit of industrial civilization, and this involved a profound dissatisfaction with urbanism, technical rationality, and the generally tame, unexciting, and unglamorous routine of bourgeois life. By some instinctual logic there was a sudden convergence of archaic patterns that, from diverse literary and philosophical quarters, began to challenge axiomatic assumptions about the rationality of the human being and the perfectibility of the social order through science, capitalism, and parliamentary democracy.

Decrying the dehumanization of technology, the rapacity of capitalism, the danger of lower-class politics, and the decline in aesthetic taste, many intellectuals and young people adopted a profoundly antidemocratic, elitist attitude, which only further served to alienate them from the forces of modernity. Thus, what has been termed the "politics of cultural despair"[9] strongly reinforced patterns of authoritarianism in European societies. It is well to remember that the political background of modern totalitarianism was the existence of strong authoritarian traditions and unrepresentative forms of government in many parts of Europe. This is why totalitarianism succeeded in Italy, Germany, Russia, and east-central Europe — in short, in countries where authoritarian habits were still deeply entrenched. Even in more democratic societies, however, the authoritarian style was never wholly absent because all European societies had evolved from long-standing feudal, monarchical, and elitist backgrounds. In times of socioeconomic pressures, many European societies tended to revert to the authoritarian style; they became impatient with the democratic approach because it seemed cumbersome and ineffective.

In Italy, for example, there was a mounting tide of dissatisfaction with the democratic process in the late nineteenth century. Under a series of ineffective parliamentary regimes the country was sinking deeper and deeper into a political morass. Italy fell into the hands of clever political trimmers who transformed parliamentary government into a Machiavellian chess game of unscrupulous deals and makeshift alliances. The most astute of these political trimmers was Giovanni Giolitti, aptly called the Minister of the Underworld, who imposed on Italian politics a thinly disguised parliamentary dictatorship that seriously blemished responsible government and indirectly encouraged the rise of political extremism.

On the political left this extremism resulted in the defection of the radicals from the majority revisionist wing of the Socialist movement. Led by Benito Mussolini, Ettore Cicotti, and Constantino Lazzari, these radicals denounced the cautious gradualism of the party revisionists and demanded the true aim of socialism should be the destruction of capitalism. The radicals also linked capitalism with democracy and therefore called for the destruction of bourgeois democracy. On the political right, Giolitti's cynical policy of *combinazione* evoked widespread revulsion against parliamentary democracy and loud demands for inspired charismatic leadership based on military force. Behind these antidemocratic tendencies were also increasingly popular theories, embodied in the works of Gaetano Mosca, Vilfredo Pareto, and Robert Michels, that debunked the democratic ideal as illusory and urged charismatic rule by a strong-willed elite or "creative minority."

Italy was not an isolated example of this widespread impatience with the politics of liberalism. There was a growing conviction that parliamentary democracy encouraged social conflict and party strife more than it did efficient government or decisive leadership. In Germany and Austria the crown continued to justify its authoritarian style by claiming that it represented the only bulwark against the anarchy of the democratic process. This was also true to some extent in France, where Louis Napoleon (1851–70) had already set an example of a "post-liberal authoritarian regime."[10] It was also in France that the first modern Fascist movement, Action Française, was born in 1899. Action Française modernized the monarchical-authoritarian tradition by grafting itself on more vital movements such as nationalism and even socialism. In the hands of Charles Maurras, the chief ideologue of Action Française, royalism no longer spoke the language of feudal absolutism but rather spoke of popular sovereignty with the king being transformed into a reflection of the general will, conducting the well-being of the whole without regard to the petty self-interest of either classes or masses.

As the nineteenth century drew to a close, astute observers noticed a strong undercurrent of revolt against bourgeois civilization and the values on which it was anchored — parliamentary democracy, scientific rationality, and capitalism. These values presupposed the existence of a stable, predictable universe, but that universe was being undermined steadily by some of the leading intellectuals of Europe who displaced the axis of social thought from the objectively verifiable world of physical experience to the subjective and only partially accessible world of unconscious motivation, as in the works of Sigmund Freud.[11] Reason appeared increasingly as a feeble veneer entirely at the mercy of instinctual forces. Arthur Schopenhauer had already rejected the primacy of reason as an "ancient and universal radical error," insisting instead that the "real" determinant of all life-forms was the unconscious will, a will of "imperious desire."[12] Schopenhauer's intellectual heir, Friedrich Nietzsche, consecrated this instinctual "will to power" by insisting that it was equivalent to "the will to grow" and that happiness consisted in a surging feeling that power was growing and that resistance was overcome.[13] Nietzsche also suggested that "where the will to power is lacking there is decline";[14] he warned that European civilization was rapidly enervating under the paralyzing influence of technical rationality. The more we depart from our vital roots, from our instinctual and archaic heritage, the more enfeebled and therefore the more decadent we will become. Nietzsche's contempt of bourgeois civilization, whose egalitarian and materialistic values he abhorred, prompted him into a tragic, Don Quixote–like crusade aimed at celebrating the redemptive value of the Dionysian life force and the rule of a noble caste of supermen "without pity for the degenerate."

Nietzsche's explorations of unconscious and primeval instincts were later developed at length by the great pioneers of psychology, most notably by Sigmund Freud and Carl Jung. These writers broadened the gulf that was developing between intellect and instinct, the conscious and the unconscious in human life; they reduced conscious motives to disguised or repressed unconscious desires, thus unwittingly reviving the archaic superstition that most surface phenomena are oblique manifestations of subterranean forces beyond our control. The topography of a bicameral mind at war with itself raised another ancient fear: the dilemma of being controlled by invisible and therefore potentially more powerful forces. If the within is not coextensive with the without, the human soul remains tragically divided. This amounted to the grafting of a biological and psychological dimension on the old theological dichotomy of spirit and flesh, except that in the modernized version of the dual nature of the human being the head speaks the language of technical civilization while the body speaks a more archaic, at times a more frightening, language.

The recovery of the unconscious and the encounter with the primitive had many positive consequences: they stimulated renewed interest in humankind's archaic past, and they also led to a deeper understanding of the symbolic language by which this archaic heritage had been passed on through legend, myth, and ritual.[15] Moreover, the encounter with the primitive and the archaic served as a fruitful corrective to modern patterns of life, reminding anxiety-ridden city-dwellers that important lessons might be derived from inveterate customs and archaic patterns of social life.

On the other hand, preoccupation with atavistic forces could also foster the recrudescence of ancient cruelties and tribal prejudices. Worship of primitivism, far from healing the split in the human psyche, could just as easily turn into a savage attack on respectable society and disrupt the order of civilization itself. The "will to power" could easily be adulterated from Nietzsche's belief in "spiritual transcendence" or self-overcoming into brutal domination and unbridled aggression. The belief in myth, rather than linking us to a communal past, could turn into collective delusion and incitement to revolution. Breeding a higher type

of man, the *Übermensch,* far from assuring the education and maturation of "a Caesar with the heart of Christ," could, under the influence of
crude Darwinian biology and racial doctrines, result in the establishment
of human stud farms controlled by dangerous deviants. Finally, the cult
of youth and nature could be perverted into collective indoctrination
and twist genuine youthful idealism into warlike aggressive ends.

World War I was just such an atavistic eruption of tribal hatreds;
and when it was all over, close to ten million young men had bled
to death on the battlefields of Europe. If the convergence of nationalism, ideological fanaticism, and imperialism furnished the seedbed of
twentieth-century totalitarianism, World War I and its aftermath provided the real catalyst that made totalitarianism possible in the interwar
period. The war had greatly strengthened the power of the state in almost every European country because national survival depended on
group cohesion and government control of resources. Throughout the
course of the war, European nations systematically controlled their
human and natural resources; they managed their economies in open
violation of the principles of free enterprise. Government planners rationalized this departure from nineteenth-century liberalism by arguing
that a free economy, though crucial for the existence of capitalism, was
too wasteful in times of national emergency. Those who persisted in
following their own entrepreneurial interests were denounced as "profiteers"; and the profit motive itself, the very hallmark of capitalism, was
often condemned as unpatriotic. The planned economy, the nightmare
of nineteenth-century libertarians, became an everyday reality during
the war as government planners regulated wages and prices, allocated
resources, and coerced workers into needed occupations.

John Stuart Mill had warned that the increase of state power is
usually accompanied by a decrease in individual power and that state
control invariably undermines individual liberty. Nineteenth-century libertarians had also drawn attention to the fact that individual liberty is
closely allied with economic autonomy; and if the state is the primary
determinant of a citizen's means of livelihood, individuals are deprived
of free choice and therefore of their liberty.

World War I, in fact, deprived millions of their right to choose. Governments decided who should live and who should die, who should
work and why. The specter of "Big Brother" began to rear its head
by subverting selfhood, restricting choice, and undermining liberty. The
state, of course, had always demanded sacrifices from its citizens in
the past by claiming the right of administering justice, providing for
the common defense, imposing taxes, regulating schools and churches,
and dispensing welfare. World War I, however, greatly accelerated this
tendency toward state control in the industrialized nations of Europe.

Another legacy World War I imparted to totalitarianism was institutionalized lying in the form of wartime propaganda. Psychological
warfare, of course, is as old as warfare itself, but the systematic prac-

tice of the black arts of war by specialists in deception is the product of World War I. The war produced in embryonic form George Orwell's nightmare vision of "Newspeak" — that is to say, official double-talk aimed at controlling public information. Psychological warriors on the home front became the auxiliaries of the soldiers in the trenches, the former fighting with the pen while the latter battled with guns. In both cases the results were poisonous.

Although the term *propaganda* first came into being when Pope Gregory XV founded the Congregation for the Propagation of the Faith in 1622, the extensive use of propaganda in wartime was first orchestrated by the British in September 1914. The brain behind the English propaganda effort was Charles Masterman, a Cambridge professor who was appointed by Prime Minister Asquith to head a new office of propaganda. Throughout the war Masterman and his clever associates churned out a steady stream of propaganda that showed the Germans to be naked aggressors without traces of humanity, as savage "Huns" who delighted in cruelty. His *pièce de résistance* was the Bryce report on the bestial conduct of German soldiers in Belgium. The report was printed in over thirty languages and recounted hair-raising stories of German atrocities in Belgium.[16]

Much of Masterman's work was later taken over by a new Ministry of Information headed by the press mogul Lord Beaverbrook, a man of enormous resources who also brought together other leaders of the press such as Lord Rothermere and Lord Northcliff in an effort to pool the most persuasive talents. It is generally agreed that the Anglo-American side produced "better" propaganda, perhaps for the simple reason that it proved more difficult to persuade people to fight in an open-society where freedom of thought might successfully question government propaganda. When America entered the war, President Wilson established the Committee of Public Information, headed by George Creel, a well-known journalist, with sole responsibility for waging propaganda.

Similar organizations were founded in other countries. Most of these propaganda organizations worked hand in glove with their military commands, intelligence services, and police departments. In addition, they enlisted patriotic writers to promote the cause of war just as advertising departments would later promote products endorsed by famous personalities. The consequences of this cordial symbiosis between the government and the fifth estate was pernicious because the propagandists deceived not just others but themselves as well. Tragically, the war and its aftermath unleashed hatreds that had been easily aroused but were not so easily controlled. Mutual lying had set the stage for decades of mistrust out of which future aggression would be hatched.

In summarizing the main features of the emerging totalitarian style and mentality, several characteristics must be highlighted. In the first place, totalitarianism was a response to the rapid industrial changes that were taking place in the late nineteenth century. It was an effort, still embryonic and somewhat inchoate before World War I, of recapturing political wholeness and of restoring fragmented people and antagonistic social groups to some kind of political consensus. The Fascist approach to unity made use of biological conceptions of organic life as a means of healing the sickness of the divided social system, while the Communist approach still looked to a revolutionary transformation of society based on leveling and equality as the only source of human redemption. The emerging Fascist movement, still dormant before World War I, pitted the vitality of nature against the enervated spirit produced by the grinding discipline of modern industry; it called for a transformation of human-kind and society through obedience to a higher feeling, imagination, and will. In short, it sought to heal the inner schism by reverting to primitivism, by indicting modernity for its subversion of archaic truth. It was for this reason that proto-Fascist writers constantly invoked the values of a preindustrial world, pleaded for a restoration of social hierarchy, and vehemently rejected democratic and egalitarian values.

In the second place, totalitarianism represents the twentieth-century version of traditional religiosity; it is in many ways the secular equivalent of the religious life. Unless this crucial point is captured, the quintessential nature of totalitarianism will elude us. For millions of people who live and have lived under totalitarian control, there is only one style of governance — enforced commitment to a "normative" way of life without the possibility of choice and individual liberty. It implies the ultimate violation of selfhood by institutionalized coercion. This enforced "consensus," however, does not rest on any transcendental spiritual reality, but on naked force claiming to be its own justification. Not even the absolute regimes of the past, however repressive they may have been in practice, ever claimed to be beyond the control of supernatural authority. Only the systematic destruction of holiness and piety, which the late nineteenth century consummated in various secular ideologies, could have made this surrender to such organized oppression possible.

In the third place, totalitarianism cut across ideological boundaries: Communism arose on the left and fascism on the right, but in practice there was little difference between them. As Friedrich and Brzezinski have pointed out, the basic traits of totalitarianism, whether of the left or the right, are essentially the same, to wit: an all-embracing ideology; a single mass party generally led by one man; a terroristic police; a communications monopoly; a weapons monopoly; and a centrally directed economy.[17] There are, of course, major differences relating to class affiliations. Totalitarianism of the left is primarily a working-class movement that speaks the language of the eighteenth century, emphasizing economic and social equality, while totalitarianism of the right is largely a middle-class movement that resolutely opposes all presumptions toward equality. Totalitarianism of the right spoke the language of social

Darwinism and racism, denouncing equality as a poisonous influence in politics. Both types of totalitarianism, however, relied upon mass support by camouflaging their ultimate intentions under the smoke screen of historical inevitability; both movements also cynically preempted, amalgamated, and distorted the positions of their moderate opponents, promising their followers political redemption in "a worker's paradise" or "a thousand-year Reich." Additionally, both fascism and Communism denied the possibility of an open universe of choice and of free will. Every citizen was forced to make an ultimate commitment to a political way of life that claimed to be normative and exclusive.

If the totalitarian movements revealed many similar patterns, the dynamics of socioeconomic control were different. Totalitarianism of the left was the radicalization of the working class, while totalitarianism of the right was the radicalization of the middle class. It is true that the vanguard of both types of totalitarianism was often in the hands of classless or free-floating intellectuals who appealed to ideological abstractions and thus displayed no firm allegiance to any class. Still, the ultimate socioeconomic impetus of both movements resided in different socioeconomic groups. Fascism or its German variant, National Socialism, was the desperation of the middle class; it was the totalitarianism of the right responding to the totalitarianism of the left. As Ernst Nolte observed, "Fascism is an anti-Marxism that seeks to destroy the enemy by the evolvement of a radically opposed, yet related ideology and by the use of almost identical and typically modified methods, always, however, within the unyielding framework of national self-assertion and autonomy."[18]

For a time, Europe became an ideological, political, and ultimately a military battlefield between these two types of totalitarianism, illustrating the poverty of political life in the twentieth century. The German version of totalitarianism was a form of fascism called National Socialism. This type of fascism, as we shall see, assumed basically three distinct features: the reliance on a charismatic leader and the military to browbeat opponents into line; the invention of shared enemies (Jews, Communists, liberals, pacifists, Freemasons, Gypsies, Jehovah's Witnesses, and so on); and the co-option of working-class radicalism by way of certain integrative social policies such as extreme nationalism, welfare statism, racism, artificially contrived enthusiasms, and war.

The German Background

One way of understanding the full scope of the Nazi movement is to ask a prospective question in hopes that it will yield a retrospective answer, namely: Could it happen again? In order to answer this question, we have to identify the preconditions that would have to be duplicated before National Socialism could reappear in roughly the same form.

Five major preconditions would probably be essential in producing a movement similar to National Socialism:

1. The existence of a hybrid society, half-feudal and half-industrial with long-standing militaristic and authoritarian traditions.

2. The nationalization of the masses as an instrument of social control and international aggression.

3. The respectability of biological-racial beliefs.

4. The traumatic effect of extreme stress caused by military defeat and economic ruin.

5. The convergence of sociopathic personalities and xenophobic movements.

Three of these causes were rooted in prewar conditions, but by themselves they would not have been able to produce the rise of Adolf Hitler. In fact, it could be argued that prewar Germany, though exhibiting certain disturbing signs of social maladjustment, could well have developed into a modern, stable, and humane society. The immediate causes leading to the rise of Hitler were triggered by Germany's defeat in war and the tragic corollaries resulting from it — revolution, the Versailles Treaty, reparations, inflation, political extremism, and economic collapse. If it had not been for World War I, German society would probably have been able to make a more successful adjustment to the challenges of modern industrial civilization. Defeat in war and the inability to cope realistically with a series of postwar calamities both exacerbated and rekindled previously unresolved social tensions. The convergence of these symptoms of social maladjustment in the 1920s produced an acute social and cultural crisis that is not likely to repeat itself in the same form, although it is conceivable that traditional and underdeveloped societies, threatened by vast industrial changes from within and war from without, may regress to totalitarian tactics to solve their problems. How this happened in Germany is the subject of the following discussion and the focus of the next two chapters.

A Hybrid Social System: The Second Reich, 1871–1914

One of the major leitmotifs of German history is the problem of political fragmentation (*Zerissenheit*), the inability of the German people to develop a united nation-state. Unlike other European people, the Germans attained nationhood very late in their history, and when they did so it was not the result of a broad democratic consensus but the consequence of military victory by force of superior Prussian arms. For centuries, Germany had been a political and geographic expression, a fragmented patchwork of independent feudal territories; but within that "carnival jacket" of states, as Germany was mockingly referred to by its foreign detractors, one state, the feudal-military state of Prussia, gradually achieved supremacy. Aided by the military weaknesses of its enemies, the centrifugal forces within German politics, and its own inveterate militaristic traditions, the Kingdom of Prussia gradually extended its territory and its power. Between 1864 and 1871, the Prussian state, led by its "Iron Chancellor" Otto von Bismarck, unified Germany and then imposed the militaristic-authoritarian character of its institutions on the rest of Germany. The Hohenzollern king of Prussia became the German emperor; the Prussian capital of Berlin became the German capital; and Prussian institutions and habits of mind began to pervade all aspects of the national consciousness.

The new Prussianized Germany possessed many good qualities. Even Prussia's most hostile critic, Friedrich Nietzsche, always stressed the positive aspects of the Prussian spirit: a respect for authority, a strong dedication to duty and hard work, and an ingrained sense of good order. At the same time, the militaristic traditions of Prussia, which elevated the second lieutenant over the highest civilian in the social order, were not always compatible with civilized values. Friedrich Meinecke, one of the great German historians of the twentieth century and himself a Prussian, sadly acknowledged in his old age that there had always existed two souls in the Prussian personality — one capable of culture, the other hostile to it.[19] One was humane and individualistic, the outgrowth of Protestant conscience; the other was brutal and collectivist, the product of a long and rigid tradition of militarism. During the newly created German Empire (1871–1918), the Prussian spirit of subservience to authority, symbolized by the semidivine status still accorded the emperor, penetrated many aspects of German life.

The new Prussianized Germany was militaristic in the highest sense, closely approximating Alfred Vagts's classic definition of militarism as "the domination of the military man over the civilian, an emphasis on military considerations, spirit, and ideals and scales of value, ... the imposition of heavy burdens on a people for military purposes, to the neglect of welfare and culture, and the waste of the nation's best man power in unproductive army service."[20] In short, the new Germany institutionalized and perpetuated archaic military-feudal values in a way that no other European country was doing; it indoctrinated young Germans with the idea that to be "German" meant, above all, to be a courageous and loyal soldier. The only other country in the world that idolized the warrior as a cultural role model was Japan.

In fact, in imperial Germany the military establishment stood sovereignly aloof from all other institutions, enjoying the sort of reputation accorded only to ecclesiastical orders in former times. The officers' corps was venerated like an idol, as evidenced by the popular saying that "the human race begins with the lieutenant." Anyone who put on the *Kaiserrock,* the kaiser's coat, was instantly elevated above ordinary mortals. As a member of an exclusive caste, every German officer was immune from civilian control; his obedience was, first and foremost, to the emperor. The military caste had its own code of honor and its own code of law — the military court of honor; but since the military was not subject to civilian control, it represented a law unto itself. Sir Wheeler-Bennett justly remarked that the German officers' corps stood to the kaiser in the relation of the Praetorian guard to the Roman emperor.[21]

The young emperor, William II, epitomized the Prussian delight in military affairs. Contemptuous of civilians, to whom he disparagingly referred as *schlappe Zivilisten* (slovenly civilians), the kaiser put his trust in the army rather than in the Reichstag or the constitution. His rhetoric always tended toward the grandiloquent and belligerent, and to foreigners it seemed intolerably provocative. Addressing the German contingent of troops detailed to help in suppressing the Boxer Rebellion in China, the kaiser ordered them to take no prisoners and conduct themselves like Huns — a phrase that was later used with great effect by Allied propagandists to characterize all Germans as fiendish. William's saber-rattling rhetoric was replete with such words as "smash," "war to the knife," "unbending will," and so on. He loved to impress his people with inflated expressions of regal authority, coupled with menacing threats that he would not tolerate opposition to his sovereignty. Those who knew the emperor realized that most of these statements were hyperbole designed for public consumption; at the same time, it is significant that martial language was considered to be the best language for public consumption. Martial art also underscored this militaristic atmosphere in the Second Reich. The kaiser's official portraits always showed him in full military regalia with his head thrust aggressively forward and his twirled mustache bristling with tense excitement. A particularly bellicose portrait of him once prompted a French general to exclaim: "That is not a portrait. It is a declaration of war!"[22]

Yet the aura of authority that was conveyed by this new martial empire was basically illusory. Beneath the grandeur of Hohenzollern power lurked many social forces that were incompatible with the pretensions of a feudal monarchy. In times of rapid industrial growth, the German monarchy adhered to the traditional values of its preindustrial past. The social perpetuation of an obsolete feudal regime in the midst of rising capitalism had caused the downfall of the *ancien régime* in France less than a century before. Was there any reason to assume that Germany was going to escape from the dire consequences of a similar cultural lag? Prewar Germany, like prerevolutionary France, was a hybrid society that saw the persistence of feudal political institutions within the context of modern capitalism and machine technology.

Politically, the new Reich contained a number of anomalies and discordant voices. Bismarck's constitution established a thinly veiled autocracy in which the emperor, as the chief executive officer, was empowered to appoint and dismiss the chancellor and other officials; to control the whole of foreign policy; to serve as commander in chief of the armed forces; to declare martial law in case of domestic unrest; to deprive dissident member states of their territorial sovereignty; to summon, prorogue, and dismiss the Reichstag; to publish and supervise the execution of all federal laws; and to interpret the constitution.[23]

These sweeping discretionary powers, which may have been more appropriate in the Age of Absolutism, were not suited to an industrial age in which shared power or, at the very least, countervailing powers proved more effective in blunting social conflicts. Countervailing powers, no doubt, existed in the form of a bicameral parliament (Bundesrat, or upper house, and Reichstag, or lower house), the growth of political parties, the rise of the trade-union movement, powerful business cartels, and so on. Unfortunately, neither Bismarck nor his successors trained the German people for political democracy, opting instead for makeshift pragmatic alliances and the formation of special-interest groups in solving political problems. Under Bismarck and his successors the Reichstag was largely excluded from decision making because the ruling conservative elite succeeded in maintaining and even enlarging its preponderant Prussian influence in the new Reich. Despite appearances to the contrary, the political reality of the new Reich consisted of a powerful Prussian state with a virtual monopoly on military power, a predominant role in the upper house (Bundesrat), and an illiberal state electoral process that favored the wealthier classes.

Germany, of course, did not escape the pressures of popular sovereignty, but genuine demands for democratic participation were either blunted or co-opted by the feudal-monarchical establishment. That such tactics succeeded may be explained, in part, by centuries of subservience on the part of many Germans to higher authority and the rationalizations of the sacredness of the powers-that-be by religious or philosophical spokesmen (Luther, Fichte, Hegel, Treitschke). Opposition to the ruling autocracy remained relatively ineffective also because the best elements of the nation chose not to serve in parliament and because most political parties evolved into narrow economic interest groups rather than national parties that could successfully address the grave issues of the day — the widening gulf between the feudal elites and the working population, the diplomatic role of Germany in the European community of nations, and the arrogant exclusivity of a military establishment that saw itself as standing above the law of the land.

Although in practice political life in imperial Germany was relatively free and social democracy made steady progress, as evidenced by the fact that the Social Democratic Party became the largest party in the Reichstag in 1912, the sad fact was that meaningful participation in politics was still exclusively controlled by a narrow and often arrogant elite bent upon perpetuating its rule into the twentieth century. Those who had created the Second Reich, though acknowledging the importance of popular sovereignty, made it unmistakably clear that power was to remain in the hands of the old dynastic order. It did not escape the notice of vigilant Germans of ordinary backgrounds that their constitution made no mention of fundamental civil rights in the form of a "Bill of Rights" or a "Declaration of the Rights of Man and Citizen."

Economically, the autocratic spirit of the new Prussianized Germany manifested itself, as Ralf Dahrendorf perceptively noticed, in a "fruitful misalliance" between industry and the feudal state.[24] As soon as Germany was unified, the state managed the industrial process from above by granting loans without interest; tolerating large syndicates, trusts, and cartels; and owning vast property and enterprises (coal mines, blast furnaces, utilities, and so on). The state also administered these enterprises through an intricate network of capable and obedient civil servants. Thus, in Germany free enterprise was displaced by state enterprise; industrial expansion, the most dynamic in Europe at the time, was the result of government control. Even the odious consequences of industrialization — unemployment, sickness, accident, poor working conditions — fell under the protective mantle of the state. Having traditionally displayed a paternalistic attitude toward the average citizen, the state now perpetuated this role into the industrial age by instituting progressive social welfare measures. In Ralf Dahrendorf's judgment, the German state was therefore both socialistic and capitalistic:

> From almost the earliest beginnings of industrialization a kind of state socialism corresponded to the prevailing system of state capitalism. In contrast to the applied Social Darwinism of publicly tolerated misery of industrial workers, their wives and children in England, which Marx took as the emotional point of departure in his demand for state action, public agencies in Germany consistently felt responsible for the welfare of workers. There was poverty, illness, and misery in industrializing Germany as elsewhere; but the official attitude to the social question strikingly documents the pre-industrial combination of a severe and benevolent paternal authority.[25]

Paternalism conditions a population to obedience and dependency; it fosters the illusion that nothing great can be accomplished without state intervention and that the individual is insignificant apart from the state. This is what Oswald Spengler later referred to as the Prussian instinct that prompts the good citizen to work for the common good rather than for his or her own private or selfish good.[26] In this sense, the Prussian goal aims at promoting both nationalism and socialism; it is in a curious way a prefiguration of National Socialism. Unquestionable obedience and loyalty to the state are expected of every citizen; in return, the state rewards such total commitment with generous social benefits such as old age pensions, unemployment insurance, disability protection, and health care. The good citizen should strive to become an integral part of a well-organized civil service community in which people are measured by performance, talent, and loyalty to the state.

Yet these beliefs remained pure theory because in practice the ruling elite was not willing to include the majority in a larger share of the expanding resources, and no amount of paternalism could gloss over the disparities in distributive justice in the new Reich. Class conflicts therefore abounded; and instead of building bridges to the growing working class, the imperial elite preferred to build moats.[27] Moreover, the imperial leadership increasingly expressed its insecurity in strident and insensitive rhetoric. The ascension of the politically immature and in many ways clownish Emperor Wilhelm II (1888) symbolized the weaknesses of the new Germany; his bellicose and boisterous pronouncements never really concealed the inferiority and lack of assurance that prompted them. The kaiser was Germany writ large, for he represented a nation that had not found a stable identity, trying, instead, to cover up its weaknesses by irritating posturing and dogmatic self-assertion.

The intellectual community also mirrored the tensions and anomalies embodied in the institutions of the new Reich. Bismarck had forged the new Germany by "blood and iron"; and in so doing, he had flung a challenge to the German intellectuals. How did the nation of "poets and thinkers," as Germany had been seen until the creation of the new Reich, respond to the idea of a martial empire? Surprisingly, many of Bismarck's former critics surrendered to his success; they even performed an astonishing *volte-face* after the triumph of Prussian arms and abandoned their peaceful democratic ideals as unrealistic pipe dreams. The Germany of Goethe and the romantic poets was gone; the Germany of hard-boiled realists, saluting "General Doktor von Staat," as Thomas Mann dubbed the new idol, was now at hand. Impressed by the successes of Prussian military might, many intellectuals became convinced that the essence of life resided in power. Even Friedrich Nietzsche, who warned his fellow Germans that power politics, unaccompanied by spiritual depth, would stupefy and brutalize the German people, nevertheless consecrated his own life to what he termed "the will to power" — a phrase later used with much fanfare by the Nazis. In a famous passage, Nietzsche asked rhetorically, "What is good?" He answered: "everything that heightens the feeling of power in man, the will to power, power itself." Conversely, "What is bad?" Answer: "everything that is born of weakness." Finally, "What is happiness?" Answer: "the feeling that power is growing, that resistance is overcome."[28]

Nietzsche's spiritualization of power differed only in kind from others that were generally less subtle and more aggressive. Many German thinkers increasingly viewed power as the ultimate source and sanction of reality rather than as a pragmatic tool for the attainment of certain specific political goals. Similarly, the state was now seen by many in Hegelian terms as the manifestation of the divine will on earth rather than a conventional set of human institutions. This being the case, it would seem to follow that every citizen must submit himself to a pious devotion to the state.

Among the German intellectual community of the prewar period we can detect a strong antidemocratic prejudice and a preference for political absolutism, attitudes that were often at odds with moderation or compromise. On the other hand, the German intelligentsia made concerted efforts to find a solution to the social problem, articulating a set of values often referred to as "the ideas of 1914." The term was coined by Johann Plenge, a professor of sociology at the University of Münster, who lined up a galaxy of famous intellectuals in an effort to spell out the difference between German Kultur and decadent Western materialism at the outset of World War I.[29] Among the men who pledged themselves to "the ideas of 1914" were Thomas Mann, Ernst Troeltsch, Friedrich Meinecke, Walther Rathenau, Max Scheler, Werner Sombart, and Friedrich Naumann. Despite many differences, these men generally agreed that Anglo-American liberalism was without a real moral spine and wittingly or unwittingly reinforced various forces of social decay with its easy-going gospel of moral relativity, affluence, and universal happiness. In place of bourgeois liberalism and its materialistic values they stressed a more conservative way of life in which a sense of tradition, honor, love of country, and consciousness of the past would be highly prized. In social terms this meant an organic community without class divisions, a society in which each individual or group worked for the common good. German sociologists such as Max Weber, Werner Sombart, and Ernst Troeltsch hoped that German society would not become as atomistic and rootless as Anglo-Saxon societies; they stressed the importance of *Gemeinschaft* rather than *Gesellschaft*, an organically integrated folk community rather than an agglomeration of selfish individuals pursuing their hedonistic desires. Laissez-faire individualism, untempered by a sense of ordered liberty, they argued, would undermine the very fabric of German society. These ideas also figured prominently in Thomas Mann's novels and essays. Mann believed that the liberal values of 1789 had been corrupted by bourgeois materialism and that only a national regeneration, touching the real spiritual roots of the German past, could serve as a corrective to the decadent values of the *fin de siècle*. Perhaps the most influential voice of these conservative nationalists was that of Friedrich Naumann, who proposed an international order in central Europe under the political umbrella of Germany. In a highly influential book, *Mitteleuropa* (1915), he provided the most articulate statement of Germany's war aims. Naumann envisioned a loose economic union between Germany and the various ethnic groups residing in the Habsburg dominions; he believed that such a union would finally bring economic and political stability to this historically troubled part of Europe. As a conservative German nationalist, Naumann wanted Germany to assume a dominant role in this new central European order; in fact, he felt strongly that only a German preponderance could maintain ordered liberty in this part of the world.

The "men of 1914" were also acutely conscious of the "social question" — that is, the problem of class conflict and distributive justice. Like Bismarck, they realized that socialism was a force to be reckoned with in politics; and for this reason, they tried to build bridges to the working classes because they realized that the working classes could not be permanently excluded from meaningful participation in politics. A number of these intellectuals were "Revisionary Socialists" who stressed gradual change and peaceful cooperation among all social groups. They wanted to exorcise the specter of Marx from political theory in general and socialism in particular because Marxism delighted in conflict theory and relished the idea of inciting one class against another for no better reason, it seemed, than narrow class interests. The men of 1914 believed that class warfare meant the death of society; instead of class conflict, they favored the integration of the working people into the conservative order. The best way of accomplishing this task, they believed, was to win the working class over to the monarchy and the nation. There was much talk during this period of a "National Socialism" in order to avert social disruption, national weakness, and alienation among classes. When Adolf Hitler spoke a similar language in the 1920s, he simply repeated, perhaps in more strident language, a message that had been taught by many prewar "Tory democrats."[30]

The Nationalization of the Masses

In order to integrate the hitherto disenfranchised masses into the conservative social order, the ruling classes of the German Empire envisioned a strong central Europe under German hegemony, an expansionist policy in the east, and the acquisition of a colonial empire abroad. As previously noted, rapid industrialization had fostered deep social divisions in German society, polarizing the nation into opposing ideological camps. This made it imperative to narrow the "gap of tragedy," the widening disparity between those who were benefiting from the military-industrial complex and those who were not protected by this corporate umbrella. Unfortunately, the social gap was not narrowed through genuine reforms, but through stopgap measures aimed at blunting or even co-opting radical demands. Thus, Bismarck approached domestic politics in the same way he had approached foreign policy: he cleverly manipulated parties or interest groups. His objective was not so much to bring about a lasting harmony of social orders, which would have required the abolition of privileges on the part of the old order, but short-range alliances, makeshift rapprochements, or artificially contrived crusades such as the *Kulturkampf* (cultural battle) or the battle against the Socialists.

Although Bismarck carefully avoided overseas entanglements on the assumption that the new Reich had not been politically stabilized, his successors, who faced more serious social problems, began to invoke tribal nationalism and imperialism in order to gain the support of the working classes. In the Wilhelmine era, the German people were exposed to the white heat of deliberately stocked enthusiasms in the form of popular imperialism, the naval race, and the rise of patriotic associations or interest groups. A succession of influential leaders such as Johannes Miquel, Alfred Tirpitz, Karl Bülow, and the kaiser himself advocated policies of internal mobilization and external expansion prefiguring the Nazi crusades in everything except emotional intensity.

The German kaiser, who saw himself as a reincarnated Caesar, wanted to transform his country into a world power surpassing even the British Empire. He knew that such objectives would probably put him on a collision course with Great Britain and other major powers. He was, by birth, half English and half German; his mother, Princess Victoria, was the daughter of Queen Victoria of England and Albert of Saxe-Coburg. When he came to the throne in 1888, the year before Adolf Hitler was born, he was eager to chart a new course for Germany. Steeped in the literature of late nineteenth-century imperialism, he dreamed of a greater German Empire whose future lay in its overseas colonies. The kaiser admired imperialistic authors and adventurers such as Rudyard Kipling, Cecil Rhodes, Admiral Mahan, and, above all, Houston Stewart Chamberlain, whose theories of Teutonic superiority captured his imagination and greatly stimulated his aggressive rhetoric.

The kaiser, in turn, galvanized others to the imperial call. Alfred von Tirpitz, secretary of the navy, was instrumental in building the second most powerful navy in the world and in orchestrating a brilliant public relations campaign on behalf of imperialistic policies. He also propounded the popular conservative "risk theory" that called for a powerful German fleet that could challenge the English navy and serve as a real deterrent to any interference with German colonial aims. These imperialistic views were disseminated by a host of popular associations, most notably the Pan-German League, the Naval League, the Colonial Society, and the *Wehrverein* — organizations that popularized war as a noble cause, celebrated the struggle for existence, demanded *Lebensraum* (living space) for the German people, and proclaimed the Germans as the *Herrenvolk* (master race) of the future.[31]

Among these social imperialists, who were the intellectual precursors of fascism, we find some interesting supporters or fellow travelers of the later Hitler movement, including Alfred Hugenberg (1865–1951), the cofounder of the Pan-German League; Gustav Krupp von Bohlen und Halbach (1870–1950), industrialist and arms mogul; court councillor Dr. Heinrich Class (1868–1953), a student of Treitschke and a confirmed anti-Semite who later opened the door of the Pan-German League to Hitler; Fritz Thyssen (1873–1951), the wealthy industrialist who extended financial assistance to the Nazi Party; and Emil Kirdorf (1847–1938), another wealthy iron and coal magnate who poured money into the Nazi coffers. The Pan-German League later championed wild annexationist policies in World War I, proclaimed the superiority of the Nordic race, called for *Lebensraum* in the east, and anxiously awaited the coming of a messianic führer who would deliver Germany from the

Jewish menace. Although the Pan-German League only counted about twenty-five thousand members, its influence was far-reaching because its membership was drawn from the most influential sections of German society — leading writers, industrialists, landowners, scientists, and military officers.[32]

The imperialistic policies of the Second Reich thus furnish the background to the foreign policy of the Third Reich.[33] There is a basic continuity between the policies of the ruling elites of the old prewar establishment and the Nazi leaders of the 1930s. Hitler had a clear-cut mandate from the old ruling classes who approved his nationalization of the masses and his conquests, but who ultimately were forced to oppose him when he tried to replace them with a new "racial" elite. By then it was too late because the old ruling class had committed itself too deeply to be able to extricate itself from a head-on rush into catastrophe.

There is, of course, no direct causal link between these German industrialists, military leaders, or intellectuals and the Hitler movement, except for two important factors. Fostering a fond attachment to paternalistic authority, many prewar intellectuals later rejected the democratic Weimar Republic, and by so doing, they contributed, if only by default, to the destruction of German democracy. Yet when the deed was done, many looked aghast at the alternative that Nazism represented. A second factor that serves as a remote causal link between the Nazi movement and these prewar conservatives was the idea of National Socialism. There is a vast difference, however, in style and temperament between the prewar intellectuals and Adolf Hitler and his brownshirted minions. The generation of 1914 still believed in honor and country; it was restrained by both religious conscience and scientific intellect. By contrast, the generation of 1933, scarred by war and economic ruin, subordinated intellect to emotion and surrendered its political destiny to a group of dangerous deviants marching to the sounds of a racist drummer. Yet the seeds of racism, too, were sown in the prewar period.

The Respectability of Racism

Although tribal hatreds were as intense in German-speaking territories as they were in other parts of Europe, the most virulent form of racism in Germany was undoubtedly anti-Semitism. For centuries the Jews had been treated as pariahs, as dreaded "Christ-killers," who had to be excluded from Christian communities by every conceivable means, including extermination. Being excluded and seeing themselves as exclusive, the Jews refused to participate in the cultural life of the national communities in which they resided. Not until the eighteenth century did a substantial number of Jews participate in the cultural life of European societies, but by then patterns of racism were deeply entrenched. The roots of hate between Gentile and Jew were indeed deep and broad;

they involved on both sides centuries-old religious, socioeconomic, and psychological antipathies.

It is one of the supreme ironies of history that close affinities often breed the greatest animosities and that among the many different pairings of Gentiles and Jews, it was the German-Jewish relationship that was the closest and therefore the most explosive. It is widely agreed that the mentalities of these two peoples have often converged and interpenetrated in the last two centuries. Erich Kahler, for example, argued that both peoples shared a peculiar affinity, an "interpenetration of dispositions and destinies, which in both peoples, through accordances and discordances, touched the nerves of existence."[34] The poet Heinrich Heine, himself both a German and a Jew, also drew attention to this "intimate elective affinity," claiming that this special relationship began when the two peoples first met as outsiders in the struggle against the Romans.[35] More recently, Friedrich Sieburg, a German cultural historian, described both Germans and Jews as two peoples who are

> admired and hated,...both equally unable to make themselves liked, equally ambivalent between servility and arrogance, equally indispensable as well as troublesome to the world, equally aggressive, equally inclined to self-pity, equally vilified without distinction and admired for the boldness of their thinking; musical, talented for speculative thinking, but hopelessly different in one point: in their attitude toward violence. How deeply they were interwoven with our life![36]

When two different peoples, separated by religion, ethnicity, and linguistic origins, exhibit loosely similar traits, it may be because they have shared similar historical experiences. Again, Erich Kahler believed that both Germans and Jews have never fully defined their character in political terms because they were both transnational peoples who, until recently, have failed to integrate themselves into a cohesive national community.[37] Buffeted by historical setbacks, both peoples compensated for their lack of political identity by cultivating spiritual rather than political pursuits. Until the middle of the nineteenth century, German intellectual life was largely preoccupied with metaphysical questions: the meaning of existence, the relationship between man and god, the problem of evil and suffering in the world, and the role of the transcendent in art, literature, philosophy, and history. Madame de Staël's description of Germany as a land of poets and philosophers, though overdrawn, was essentially accurate. Germany was indeed a land of poets and thinkers because the repressive feudal system made it difficult to direct creative energies into political channels. Thus, just as the Jews found the only outlet to their abilities in a few officially sanctioned fields, the German intellectuals tended to express their creative abilities in the "safe" realm of abstract speculation.

Germans and Jews, therefore, were forced to displace vital energies, and it so happened that they directed those energies into similar pursuits, often speculative or academic. In the unpolitical German of the eighteenth century, the Jew encountered a sympathetic partner and explored the possibility of cultural dialogue. The friendship between Gotthold Lessing, the epitome of the German Enlightenment, and Moses Mendelssohn, the chief representative of the German-Jewish Enlightenment, furnishes the highest exemplar of this interpenetration. Lessing's great drama, *Nathan der Weise,* one of the great panegyrics to human brotherhood, reflects not only the common meeting ground of German and Jew in the humane values of the Enlightenment, but also the lack of concrete experience that informed its noble rhetoric. Being apolitical, both German and Jew could conceptualize a new heaven and a new earth; they could project religious-philosophical abstractions against concrete reality; but it was left up to others to apply such abstractions in revolutionary practice.

German and Jew thus found a common meeting ground on the plane of philosophical abstraction. Until the late nineteenth century, they also shared a distaste of politics, an attitude no doubt nourished by political failure, inexperience, and a widely shared belief that politics profanes the spiritual life. Walter Laqueur draws attention to this Jewish inexperience with politics when he says that the Jews "have shown great ability on the level of abstract thought, but politics also involves instinct, common sense, wisdom, and foresight, and in this respect their record has not been impressive" — a judgment that has also been made about the Germans.[38] Even when both peoples have concerned themselves with politics, they did so more in abstract than in practical ways, viewing the political process in teleological terms as the inevitable manifestation of immanent principles, laws, or revelations. Much of nineteenth-century thought, for example, centers around the philosophical systems of Hegel, the archetypal German philosopher, and Marx, the product of both German idealism and Judeo-Christian millenarianism.

Germans and Jews not only shared certain thought patterns but also expressed themselves in the same language. Most Jewish writers, including the Zionists, had assimilated German culture and wrote their major works in German. Leo Baeck, one of the greatest and most learned rabbis of modern times, wrote in German, as did Martin Buber, commonly regarded as the greatest Jewish philosopher of the twentieth century. Theodor Herzl, one of the spiritual founding fathers of the state of Israel and leader of the Zionist movement, wrote his book *Der Judenstaat* in German. Eastern European Jews eagerly assimilated German culture and expressed their innermost thoughts in the German language. According to one account:

> The writings and thoughts of the representatives of German intellectual life were widely spread among the Jews of the East. The ideal of many young Jews was to sit at the feet of German professors, to learn their language, and to enjoy Germany's freedom and culture.... Even those who could not travel felt attracted by Germany.... And when my heart longed

for the spirit of the people, I was driven toward Germany — I might almost say, to the mother country of my language.[39]

The close linguistic kinship between German and Jew is embodied in Yiddish dialect, the language of many lower-class Jews of eastern Europe. Yiddish is an offspring of medieval High German dialects with additional words drawn from Hebrew and Slavic languages; it is written in Hebrew characters and is widely spoken by Jewish communities in eastern and western Europe. Most Germans have little difficulty in understanding or appreciating Yiddish, though as animosities between the two peoples intensified, the Yiddish dialect became a stigma to the person who used it in German society.

These points of "interpenetration" between German and Jew tended to foster some fundamental distortions concerning the real nature of both ethnic groups. Jews themselves tended to contribute to this distortion by believing in the ideal of the humane, tolerant, and civilized German. We may call this idealized image the "Weimar stereotype." This involved the belief that Germany, at its highest, exemplified the spirit of Goethe, Schiller, Herder, and the classical *paideia*. Such views were unrealistic because Weimar culture did not exist outside the small and unpolitical circles of poets and writers who created a brief, but ephemeral, enclave of civilized refinement in the early part of the nineteenth century. The larger Germany, as it crystallized by the end of the century, was the Prussianized Germany of Bismarck, the land of "blood and iron," not the country of poets and philosophers. Yet many Jews continued to believe in Weimar Germany as the "real" Germany, the country of their idealized hopes. This is why many Jews enthusiastically supported the Weimar Republic after World War I, for the new government had been expressly established in order to revitalize the humane values of Goethe's Weimar rather than the militaristic values of Frederick the Great's Potsdam.

Unfortunately, the other Germany was still present, rearing its authoritarian head and threatening to crush the new democracy. As the antidemocratic pressures against the Weimar Republic intensified, many Jewish intellectuals increasingly began to feel like outsiders looking in on a society that had failed to conform to their expectations. Some even became unrelenting critics, sneering at many German rituals, values, or attitudes. Walter Laqueur has labeled this type of criticism as the "Tucholsky syndrome," a phrase that refers to the German-Jewish critic and journalist Kurt Tucholsky (1890–1935), who poured out a stream of venomous essays on the German character.[40] Charged by his opponents with unpatriotic behavior, he nonchalantly brushed aside such criticism by saying that "the country which I am supposedly betraying is not my country; this state is not my state; and this legal order is not my legal order. I am indifferent to the color of their flag as I am to their provincially limited ideals. I have nothing to betray here because no one has entrusted me with anything."[41] In 1928 he stated publicly that "there is no secret of the German Army which I would not deliver to a foreign power, if this seemed necessary for the preservation of peace.... We are high traitors. But we betray a country which we repudiate, in favor of a country which we love, for the sake of peace and for our true fatherland: Europe."[42]

Although Tucholsky was not representative of Jewish feelings in Germany, his outraged disenchantment with German conditions undoubtedly struck a responsive chord in some quarters. Many Germans overreacted to Tucholsky's malicious and biting criticisms; they saw in him the stereotype of the cosmopolitan or "un-German" Jewish intellectual who delighted in undermining German culture. It is difficult to estimate how or to what extent the "Tucholsky syndrome" helped in reinforcing German stereotypes about Jewish intellectuals. It is equally difficult to establish whether the "Tucholsky syndrome" was merely the disguised expression of Jewish ambiguity and perhaps even self-hatred, leading to further negative self-stereotypes in the Jewish character.

Much has been written, and not always in a sensitive vein, about Jewish self-hatred and self-destructiveness. Some have attributed this tendency to Jewish fundamentalism and its self-righteous and exclusive doctrines. Buttressing themselves behind self-righteous doctrines, this argument contends, the Jews inspired little affection and provoked bitter resentments in many parts of the world. Jews generally kept themselves isolated from the national communities in which they resided, thereby perpetuating certain unique spiritual and even physical traits. Anthropologists generally reject the notion that the Jew represents a distinct racial type, but as Horst von Maltitz observed, "It was a fact that the Jews in Germany constituted a group within which, whether as a result of inbreeding or for other reasons, large numbers of a similar type occurred — a type which showed easily recognizable characteristics in physical appearance, voice quality, mentality, behavior, and temperament."[43]

It was perhaps the influx of eastern Jews (Ostjuden) into Germany that accentuated these perceived cultural and physical differences between German and Jew. Speaking Yiddish, wearing unfamiliar ghetto attire, and forming clannish communities, the eastern Jew created the impression in the minds of many Germans, including, ironically, the assimilated German Jew, that an alien body amounting to a state within a state was being implanted in the midst of German society. To many Germans, these eastern Jews presented an unpleasant sight as they scurried the pavements of Vienna or Berlin in search of some business. Walter Rathenau, himself an assimilated German Jew, could say with apparent sincerity that the Jews were becoming a "foreign organism in the German people's body,"[44] thus expressing, as Karl Marx had done before him, a deep-seated ambiguity toward the Jewish heritage within himself.

If Walter Rathenau, himself a Jew, was offended by the sight of certain Jews, how much greater must have been Adolf Hitler's antipathies when he first encountered these beings clad in caftan, wearing black curls, and smelling offensively. Suddenly Walter Rathenau's foreign organism became a "poisonous abscess," a "ferment of decomposition," a "bacillus," and the battle to be waged against such a deadly virus required heroic measures comparable to those used by Louis Pasteur and Robert Koch.[45] In short, a perception of Jews as alien organisms created its own dreadful consequences — extermination. Only psychopathology can adequately explain the sequential steps that led from a perception of Jews as socially offensive to a willingness to exterminate the entire race on the ground that they were not human but deadly bacilli, so that by warding off the Jews one would be doing the Lord's work.

If the Jew at times stood out as a physical type, he stood out even more as an intellectual type. The evidence is overwhelming that Jews have displayed equal, if not superior, intelligence whenever they have competed freely with other people. Jews have constituted a high percentage among professionals in such fields as law, medicine, science, education, industry, and publishing; they have also consistently garnered more Nobel prizes than any other group. Of the total of 183 Nobel prizes awarded up until 1939, 9 percent were granted to German Jews and 11 percent were given to Jews throughout the rest of the world — a total of 20 percent of Nobel prizes awarded thus went to Jews.[46] It is also common knowledge that many of the leading intellects of the period under consideration (1870–1933) were of Jewish origin: Karl Marx, Sigmund Freud, Albert Einstein, Ernst Cassirer, Herman Cohen, Arthur Schnitzler, Georg Simmel, Walter Rathenau, Max Reinhardt, and many other outstanding talents.

Such disproportionate representation of Jews among the intellectual elite has given rise to intense speculation about the possible causes of this embarrassing superiority. Some attribute it to centuries of exegetical learning that gave Jews a distinct advantage over preliterate communities, while others point to genetic factors. As to the first argument, it must be remembered that the Jews were an ancient cultured people who, during the Middle Ages, found themselves living among primitive Western people who were repelled by their superior intelligence and their clever business acumen. There was mutual contempt and hate, due not to race thinking, but to a difference of cultural phase. In other words, the two peoples were living geographically alongside each other, but they were immersed in different cultural stages. As to the second or genetic argument, few have seriously defended it because it would amount, in essence, to the endorsement of at least a variant of racism itself, namely, that there is something in the Jewish race that promotes a greater degree of intelligence. Whatever factor is singled out in explaining Jewish differences, the result was often the same: Jews, because of their Jewishness, were forced to bear the brunt of ethnic prejudices.

It was especially in turbulent times that the Jew became the focal point of converging ethnic prejudices. These anti-Semitic feelings were often reinforced in authoritarian societies by Jewish participation in radical causes. Many Jews enthusiastically joined liberal or left-wing movements, while shunning conservative or right-wing causes. In fact, some of the leading spokesmen of radical movements in Europe were Jewish: Karl Marx, Ferdinand Lassalle, Karl Liebknecht, Rosa Luxemburg, Eduard Bernstein, Klara Zetkin, Gustav Landauer, Kurt Eisner, Ernst Toller, and so on. When German Communists attempted to emulate their Russian compatriots by setting up subversive "soviets" within the German army and navy shortly before the end of World War I, their opponents almost immediately drew a mental connection between Communism and Jewishness because so many members of these subversive groups were in fact Jewish or led by Jewish agitators. It was in this volatile atmosphere that the infamous "stab-in-the-back" (*Dolchstoss*) legend was born. In the confused minds of many Germans, especially that of Hitler, the Jews were co-responsible for the German defeat in the war because along with other "traitors" and "criminals" they undermined the war effort from within, robbing the front-line soldier of the victory he would have surely achieved if it had not been for such sneaky subversives. Along with pacifists, liberals, and Bolsheviks, the Jew became a convenient scapegoat (*Sündenbock*) absorbing the failures that should have been realistically faced by the Germans themselves.

It is commonly agreed that organized anti-Semitism in Germany did not break out until the last two decades of the nineteenth century. One of the first spokesmen for anti-Semitism in Germany was Court Chaplain Adolf Stöcker, who founded the Christian Social Party (Christlich-Soziale Partei) in 1878 in order to rescue the lower social classes from the clutches of Marxian socialism. Sensing the importance of mass appeal, Stöcker hoped to create a right-wing counterpoise to the threat of left-wing politics. As a chaplain of the imperial court, he enjoyed the unofficial blessing of Hohenzollern authority, and his close relations with the conservative newspaper *Kreuzzeitung* gave him access to the molders of public opinion. Additionally, he cultivated a close contact with the lower classes in his capacity as director of the Berlin City Mission, a charitable organization of the Protestant church. Stöcker's anti-Semitism was essentially opportunistic rather than the product of intellectual conviction. Representing an economically displaced lower middle class, threatened by an increasingly well-organized proletariat from below and by feudal interests from above, he used the Jews as a convenient scapegoat for the ills of widespread economic problems caused by the depression of 1873 and by a series of financial scandals that rocked Germany in the 1870s. Stöcker also insinuated that "Jewish capital" supported big corporate interests but not small German business owners. He identified himself with the common complaint of small business owners who claimed that they were ruined by corporations and banks; and since these institutions were in the hands of Jews, all their misfortunes were caused by Jews. There was just enough credibility in this fallacious way of reasoning to make it attractive to the half-educated. As Hannah Arendt observed, many of the bankers were Jews, and, even more important, the general figure of the banker bore definite Jewish traits for historical reasons.[47]

Stöcker failed in founding a mass movement, but his anti-Semitic rhetoric was widely accepted among conservative circles, notably among such conservative newspapers as the *Kreuzzeitung* and *Germania*. In a series of highly charged articles, the *Kreuzzeitung* attacked the government's fiscal policies by dubbing them bankers' policies made by and for Jews. It singled out Bismarck's close financial confidant, the Jewish banker Gerson Bleichröder, as the chief culprit of economic distress in Germany.[48] The same sentiments were voiced by the leading Catholic paper, *Germania,* which embarrassed Bismarck by reprinting a speech he had delivered against Jewish emancipation a quarter of a century earlier. *Germania* also cast aspersions on the motives of German Jews, insisting that Jews were overrepresented in lucrative businesses and underrepresented in "productive" enterprises, and advising good Catholics that the disproportionate number of wealthy Jews in Germany might be offset by a boycott of Jewish businesses.

The pattern of anti-Semitism in Germany was similar to that in other European countries; it was essentially the resentful expression of displaced social groups who suffered most from economic depressions and blamed Bismarck or Jewish liberalism for their problems. One of the most articulate spokesmen of these pent-up frustrations and resentments, besides Stöcker, was Wilhelm Marr (1819–1904), who wrote two influential books, *Der Sieg des Judentums über das Germanentum* (The victory of Jewry over Germandom) and *Der Judenspiegel* (Jewish mirror). Marr's psychological approach was to insinuate scare tactics into the anti-Jewish campaign by suggesting that the Jews, far from being weak or politically impotent, were in fact formidable and even insidious people, bent upon sapping the racial strength of the German people as a prelude to the establishment of a New Palestine in Germany. Marr's anti-Semitism already bore definite apocalyptic and millenarian features; he saw Germans and Jews locked in mortal combat, warning that the hour was late and that only a concerted counterattack against world Jewry could stay the doom of the German race.

Wilhelm Marr's shrill message was by no means an aberrant exception. In 1874, *Die Gartenlaube*, a literary magazine catering to middle-class readers, published a series of anti-Semitic articles on the stock exchange and speculation frauds in Berlin. Written by Otto Glagau (1834–92), these articles reflected the grievances of the lower middle class — artisans, small businessmen, merchants, minor civil servants — who blamed Jewish bankers and politicians for their plight. The chief recipient of their paranoid fears more often than not was Bismarck's

friend and confidant, the Jewish banker Gerson Bleichröder. As Fritz
Stern puts it:

> He embodied all that the socially aggrieved came to detest: he was a
> Jew with legendary wealth and power, a parvenu and plutocrat unset-
> tling the traditional order of rank. He seemed to fit all the stereotypes of
> the anti-Semites: the Jew as promoter and plotter, as corrupter and per-
> petual wire-puller, the Jew, in short, as a man of devious power — and
> it was Jewish power that made gentiles uneasy and anti-Semites frantic.
> He had amassed his fortune by stockjobbing, in defiance of that sacred
> principle that a man should earn his daily bread. There was a violent ant-
> icapitalist element in the new anti-Semitism; Bleichröder, the international
> banker, the respectable usurer, was proof of all the iniquities of Jews and
> capitalists.[49]

Germans who thought this way were more likely to belong to the
Mittelstand, to the petit bourgeois order that felt especially threatened
by the recurring economic fluctuations under capitalism. Such groups
felt unrepresented and neglected, scarcely knowing which way to turn.
As Paul W. Massing points out, liberalism had nothing to offer them but
noble rhetoric about free enterprise; conservatism was too remote and
too elitist to persuade them; and socialism wrote them off the books as
doomed by the laws of history. It took National Socialism to mobilize
their frustrations.[50]

These heterogeneous efforts eventually found a common focal point:
politicized anti-Semitism. In 1879 Wilhelm Marr founded the League
of Anti-Semites (Bund der Antisemiten); in 1880 two new parties, the
Social Reich Party and the German Reform Party, came into being;
both relied on anti-Semitism as their chief platform. In 1881 Max
Liebermann von Sonnenberg, a minor aristocrat, and Bernhard Förster,
Nietzsche's brother-in-law, founded the German People's League. Förster
later emigrated to Paraguay with the intention of founding a pure Aryan
colony called New Germania. His bizarre experiment failed, and Förster
committed suicide in 1889.

Meanwhile, Germany was inundated by a proliferation of anti-
Semitic parties, magazines, books, and public speeches. The German
Anti-Semitic League was expressly formed to lobby for anti-Semitic
laws, and one of its founders, Theodor Fritsch (1852–1934), published
a highly influential reference guide entitled *Handbuch der Judenfrage*
(Handbook of the Jewish question). Fritsch founded his own publishing
house in Leipzig, the Hammer Publishing Company, which promoted a
steady stream of anti-Semitic books and deftly exploited popular racial
prejudices through its periodical magazine called *Hammer.* The theme in
these publications was always the same: the Jews, in connivance with
other conspiratorial groups such as Freemasons, Catholics, Jehovah's
Witnesses, were secretly planning to gain control over the reins of power
throughout the world. A tone of urgency and paranoia rang throughout
most of Fritsch's writings; and in his *Handbook,* Fritsch went so far

as to append a detailed list of Jews he considered responsible for major crimes such as murder, treason, forgery, and rape. Such Jew-baiting was much appreciated later by the two greatest Jew-baiters in the Nazi movement — Hitler and Streicher.

In 1887, Otto Böckel, the author of a notorious anti-Semitic tract entitled *The Jews: The Kings of Our Times,* became the first "official" anti-Semite to be elected as an Independent to the Reichstag. His platform called for a radical separation of German and Jew along with treating Jews as foreigners with limited rights. Although Böckel eventually lost his seat and faded from public view, he left behind him the seeds from which future anti-Semitism could sprout. In 1889, the year of Hitler's birth, Liebermann von Sonnenberg founded the German Social Anti-Semitic Party in Bochum; and in cooperation with Böckel's new party, the Anti-Semitic People's Party, Sonnenberg's group managed to elect five members to the Reichstag. Although these anti-Semitic parties were relatively small, they all claimed to stand above narrow party interests on account of their broad national goals.

This theme of representing national rather than provincial interests was even more pronounced in Austria, where ethnic conflicts were far more intense than in Germany. Habsburg Austria was a multiracial and multilinguistic society in which the German population saw itself in imminent danger of being displaced by other ethnic groups. The result was the growth of xenophobic Germanism with strident anti-Semitic overtones.[51]

When Adolf Hitler arrived in Vienna in 1907, the city was governed by the anti-Semitic mayor Dr. Karl Lueger (1844–1910), whom Hitler later called "the mightiest mayor of all times."[52] Lueger was a Christian Socialist who had been swept into office by his lower-middle-class constituency during a period of economic hardships and financial scandals. Lueger was a romantic reactionary who favored a return to a more organic racial community untainted by the vices of finance capitalism. His aim was to remove Jews from influential professions and from public life in general.

Lueger's political rival was Georg Ritter von Schönerer (1842–1921), a landowner, member of the Austrian House of Delegates, and one of the founders of the Pan-German Nationalist Party. Schönerer also founded the Los von Rom (Break with Rome) movement, which called for an end to the cultural and religious domination by Roman Catholicism. Schönerer's creed of annexation to Germany, his rabid anti-Semitism, and his conservative nationalism made a deep impression on the young Hitler.

It is commonly admitted that these anti-Semitic parties and movements were politically ineffective. In Germany, there were few serious anti-Semitic disturbances before World War I. Although some of the racial groups and parties previously mentioned incited latent prejudices, and even managed to elect a few members to the Reichstag, their overall influence on public life was negligible. Jewish emancipation continued without serious political obstructions. Although it is true that anti-Semitism represented an ugly residue of archaic tribal hatreds, managing to flare up in times of socioeconomic distress, it was not until Adolf Hitler organized such tribal hatreds in the form of a single mass party that the full extent of its barbarity was revealed.

Before World War I blatant anti-Semitic prejudices were generally rare and limited largely to the lunatic fringe of various racial cults. Yet these cultist movements and the cranks who dominated them played a significant role in the shaping of future policy. A case in point was Georg Lanz von Liebenfels (a pseudonym for Adolf Josef Lanz), a man who gave Hitler many of his racial ideas. In 1905 Liebenfels (1874–1954) founded the Order of the Temple (Ordensburg Werfenstein), whose membership was restricted to fair-haired, blue-eyed men, who, mating with equally endowed Aryan women, were expected to produce a new racial order in Germany. Liebenfels disseminated his racial ideas in his periodical *Ostara,* a magazine usually adorned with a swastika on its front page. Copies of *Ostara* sold briskly in both Austria and Germany; in fact, circulation reached over one hundred thousand for the fall issue of 1908. In that year, Liebenfels produced his major work, entitled *Theozoology; or, the Science of Sodom's Apelings and the Divine Electron: An Introduction to the Earliest and Most Recent Worldview and a Vindication of Royalty and the Nobility* — a rambling work that tried to show that history was a perennial conflict between the children of darkness (Sodom's Apelings) and the children of light (Aryans or Heldlinge). Liebenfels claimed that the heroic Aryans possessed electric organs and built-in electric transmitters, but their energies had been dissipated by centuries of accumulated racial impurities. He hoped to revitalize the heroic qualities within the Aryan race by means of purifying eugenics, thus helping the Aryans to rekindle their electromagnetic-radiological organs and become all-knowing, all-wise, and all-powerful.

Liebenfels was not only a crank but also an imposter; as mentioned above, his real name was Adolf Josef Lanz, and he was a former Cistercian monk in the Heiligenkreuz monastery. In 1899 he left the monastery, called himself "Baron," awarded himself a doctoral title, and otherwise obscured his origin. In addition to his literary activities, Liebenfels also gathered like-minded cultists in a ruined castle in upper Austria at Werfenstein. Here he hoisted a swastika and chanted magical incantations to the Teutonic spirits. According to Wilfried Daim, Hitler actually met Liebenfels on one occasion, asking him for some back issues of *Ostara.*[53] In fact, the swastika symbol, the racial theory of history, the Holy Grail of Aryan purity, the extermination of apelike humans (*Tiermenschen*) — all these mental aberrations were prefabricated for Hitler by Liebenfels.

It would be a grave mistake, however, to single out Hitler or the racial lunatic fringe as the only avid purveyors of racial theories. There was

considerable cross-fertilization of racial ideas and even personal contacts between very respected academics, on the one hand, and racial popularizers, on the other. In 1900, for example, the arms manufacturer Friedrich Albert Krupp sponsored an essay competition on the subject, "What can we learn from the principles of Darwinism and its application to the inner political development and the laws of the state?" The panel of judges was chaired by the social Darwinist Ernst Haeckel, and the majority of the contestants were believers in Aryan superiority and endorsed some form of anti-Semitism. First prize in the competition went to a Munich physician by the name of Wilhelm Schallmeyer, who colored all human activities with the crude social Darwinian brush of survival of the fittest and recommended benign neglect of the racially weak specimens. Schallmeyer strongly believed that the Aryan race represented the apex of human achievement and that stringent eugenic efforts, preferably state supported, would be required to keep the Aryan race pure and predominant.

Another contestant in Krupp's competition, Ludwig Woltman, who was awarded the third prize, later received much renown by publishing a racial journal called *Politisch-Anthropologische Revue* (1902). Woltman's journal, however, was only one of several scholarly journals dedicated to racial studies. One of the most "respectable" was the *Archiv für Rassen und Gesellschaftsbiologie,* published by Alfred Ploetz, the founder of the eugenic movement in Germany. Ploetz's publication became a forum for avant-garde racial ideas. Ploetz later coined the phrase "race Hygiene," founded a secret Nordic society, and was lavishly rewarded for his racial contributions with a university chair by Adolf Hitler. As Leon Poliakov points out, some of the chief eugenicists and geneticists of the next generation — the scientists, in other words, who flourished under the protective mantle of National Socialism — were influenced by Woltman and Ploetz.[54] Among this group we find Eugen Fischer, Fritz Lenz, and Otmar Verschuer, the man who served as a mentor to the future "Angel of Death" at Auschwitz, Dr. Josef Mengele. The most influential of these men was Eugen Fischer, who applied Mendel's laws to racial hygiene. In 1934 he boasted that he was the first scientist to promote Woltman's ideas within the academic community and to have "inflamed young hearts with enthusiasm for racial science."[55] Fischer's colleague, Fritz Lenz, was a disciple of Alfred Ploetz and a frequent contributor to his racial journal. Before the outbreak of World War I, Ploetz's *Revue* was avidly read by many German academics; it became a clearinghouse for all sorts of racial doctrines, including the pseudoscientific rantings and ruminations of Fritsch and Lanz von Liebenfels.

Thus, by a circuitous route we return to Adolf Hitler, whose racial image of the world was not the product of his own delusion but the result of the findings of "respectable" science. When Hitler read Fritsch or Liebenfels, he merely absorbed ideas that were widely entertained

in both academic and popular circles. The message embodied in these doctrines was unmistakable: any living organism is engaged in a cease-less struggle for existence and is doomed to extinction if it does not fight. Nations, like individuals, are also engaged in a ceaseless conflict in which only the fittest can hope to survive. The fighting quality of a nation depends upon its racial purity and its ability to breed the fittest specimens in the form of productive workers, savage fighters, and charis-matic leaders. Those who defile a race of people — Jews, Gypsies, Asiatic inferiors — must be eliminated through appropriate state measures. Of all the human racial stocks, the Aryan race clearly represents the apex of human achievement; and since Germany is the homeland of the Aryan race, the German people are charged with a sacred mission — to prop-agate the Aryan race and dominate the world. Racial mongrelization, however, has gone so far that the hour may be late indeed. Only state intervention can protect the Aryan race from further infections by in-ferior races. In 1913 Eugen Fischer boldly prophesied "with absolute certainty" that all Europeans would become extinct unless govern-ments, especially the German government, developed and implemented a coherent racial policy.[56] Adolf Hitler provided that policy.

The Trauma of Military Defeat and Economic Ruin, 1919–23

The End of the Second Reich

The German people were ecstatic when war was declared in August 1914, and many soldiers shared Adolf Hitler's euphoria about the impending thrill of combat. The parties of the left joined with their political antagonists by pledging themselves to suspend civil dissent until victory was achieved. The emperor proudly proclaimed a *Burgfrieden* (cessation of party strife) and said: "I no longer recognize parties; I recognize only Germans."[1] Intoxicated by this mood of nationalistic fervor, most Germans looked upon the war as a pleasant diversion from the boredom of civilian life and expected it to be all over by Christmas.

However, the war was not won by Christmas of 1914; it had turned, instead, into a seesaw battle of attrition with such staggering losses in men and materiel that even cold-hearted militarists gasped when they saw the casualty lists. The home front increasingly began to show cracks. The parties on the left, having voted for war credits, expected significant social and political concessions from the ruling elite; but when these were not forthcoming, political dissension reopened with a vengeance. It is still remarkable, however, that support for the war continued as long as it did, a fact that could only be attributed to an excessive delight in war, official insensitivity to suffering, and a misguided belief on the part of the German people that their leadership would richly reward them with the fruits of military victory.

The stark geopolitical and military reality pointed inevitably toward ignominious defeat. This should have been apparent to the German high command from the beginning. Germany was fighting on two major fronts against an enemy of decided numerical and productive superiority — an enemy, moreover, who possessed the geopolitical means of strangling Germany's tenuous lifeline by imposing a crippling economic blockade. Such a deadly threat required careful coordination of overall strategic policy, especially with Germany's partners in the alliance, and close cooperation between civilian and military authorities. Neither of these essential factors for success existed.² Not only did the German high command lack a strategic plan for coordinating the war, but it increasingly began to subvert the power of the civilian government. This became especially serious when Paul von Hindenburg and Erich Ludendorff assumed supreme command of the German war effort in August 1916. Having crippled the Russians at Tannenberg and the Masurian Lakes, Hindenburg and Ludendorff became superhuman heroes in the eyes of the German public, and their reputations so dwarfed that of the emperor or any civilian that few dared to question the wisdom of their policies. Neither the emperor nor the chancellor, Bethmann Hollweg, was able to control Germany's military autocrats — first Field Marshal von Moltke, then General Falkenhayn, and finally the team of Hindenburg and Ludendorff. As early as the winter of 1914, the emperor had already complained that "the General Staff tells me nothing and never asks me advice. If people in Germany think that I am the Supreme Commander, they are gravely mistaken. I drink tea, saw wood, and go for walks, which pleases the gentlemen."³

The generals not only reduced the emperor to a position of political impotence but also rode roughshod over the chancellor, the cabinet, the Reichstag, industrialists, and trade unionists. All this proved highly popular with most Germans, provided, of course, that the military could hoodwink them into believing that victory was just around the corner.

The truth was that these military geniuses bungled from one disaster into another. In 1914 their much-vaunted Schlieffen Plan had failed to deliver the knockout blow in the west; in 1915 and 1916 they sacrificed a million men in futile battles on the western front; in 1916 their effort to challenge Britain's fleet failed off Jutland; in 1917 they committed three blunders that almost certainly guaranteed defeat: they threw away whatever chances they had to conclude a moderate peace with the Western powers, authorized unlimited submarine warfare and thus made inevitable the entrance of the United States into the war, and foolishly shipped Lenin from Switzerland into Russia to engineer the Russian Revolution. Finally, in 1918 they committed Germany's last reserves in a series of futile battles, and, facing certain defeat, they appointed civilians to arrange for a cease-fire and later blamed civilians for having "stabbed" the German army in the back.⁴

The defeat of a proud and arrogant nation, which up to the very last months of the war believed that final victory was within its grasp, is bound to cause a collective trauma with far-ranging consequences. Having been conditioned by four years of wartime propaganda to believe that victory was inevitable, most Germans refused to accept the reality of defeat. The generals subsequently blamed their failures on defeatism and sabotage at home, while others with political ambitions preferred to blame the defeat on conspiratorial forces — Communists, pacifists, Jews. Adolf Hitler later referred to these amorphous forces as the "November

Criminals"; they were supposed to have stabbed the German army in the back and thus produced all subsequent calamities.

In the fall of 1918, however, most Germans were too numbed by four years of bloody war to think about who was responsible for it all. The war had devoured almost two million young lives and permanently crippled as many more. A generation of young people had bled to death on the battlefields of western and eastern Europe; and those who survived were permanently scarred by their wartime experiences, lacking the psychological resources needed to build a stable and peaceful society. Four ancient empires had collapsed: the German, Austro-Hungarian, Russian, and Ottoman. With the collapse of these ancient monarchies disappeared old symbols of authority that were not so easily replaced. The trauma of defeat and the collapse of ancient authorities opened the floodgates to years of violence, revolution, and extremism. It is against this postwar chaos, which extended into the 1920s and was later rekindled by the Great Depression, that the growth of political pathology must be seen. In Germany, as elsewhere in Europe, a generation of political extremists roamed the political landscape in search of a messianic leader who could redeem them from meaningless sacrifices on the battlefield and restore a collective sense of purpose that had disappeared with the old authorities.

When Germany faced inevitable defeat, those who had been most responsible for the disaster — the leaders of the military establishment — deftly stepped aside and let the new democratic leaders take the blame. As early as September 29, 1918, the day the Hindenburg line cracked, the German high command finally awoke to the reality of defeat. The Second Reich was drawing to a close. The emperor was by now a virtual nonentity, as he had been during most of the war; and when the military high command asked Chancellor Hertling to open negotiations for an armistice, it became painfully obvious even to die-hard supporters of the monarchy that President Woodrow Wilson and the Western allies did not want to negotiate with the kaiser and his military autocrats. The old order had become a diplomatic liability because Woodrow Wilson, enamored by lofty democratic sentiments, insisted that he would not bargain with the emperor or the military but only with the true representatives of the German people. This amounted in some way to an incitement to revolt or, at the very least, to a strong expectation, backed up by menacing threats, that the German people replace the monarchy with a more acceptable democratic government.[5]

The Allied powers, of course, were not the only catalysts of sweeping changes in Germany. By the middle of 1918, the Allied blockade was exacting a grim toll in the form of widespread starvation, food riots, political strikes, and plain lawlessness, made all the more serious by a worldwide influenza epidemic that killed twenty million people. In Munich, a young scholar named Oswald Spengler summed up much of this apocalyptic mood by finishing the last chapter of his *Decline of the West* by candlelight, often sitting atop a chair he had put on his desk because it was warmer near the ceiling. In Berlin, banks were failing, food rations were reduced even further, people died of the influenza virus, and the kaiser's credibility had reached rock bottom. Although the emperor dismissed Chancellor Hertling, who was widely regarded as a stooge of the military, the appointment of Max von Baden, his liberal cousin, did not improve his popularity.

Meanwhile, the generals left military headquarters at Spa for Berlin, where the major decisions were being made. Before they departed Spa, they issued a strident proclamation calling for the end of negotiations because President Wilson's terms, they felt, were unacceptable. A turbulent conference between the government and the military followed. This time the military lost. Ludendorff tendered his resignation and was replaced by General Groener. Max von Baden now sent his final note to Wilson, informing him that the German military was now fully subject to civilian control. The American president replied on November 5, stating that peace could be made in accordance with his Fourteen Points although he made one important reservation: Germany, he insisted, would be held liable for all damage done to Allied property. This was an ominous indication of what was in store for Germany: the imposition of "war guilt," reparations payments, and territorial losses.

On November 8, 1918, the German armistice commission, led by Matthias Erzberger, a leading Catholic Center politician and a catalyst of the peace resolutions in the Reichstag, arrived in the French village of Rethondes in the forest of Compiègne to parley with Marshal Ferdinand Foch, the supreme generalissimo of the Allied armies on the western front. Negotiating in a railroad car, later used by Hitler to dictate peace to the French in 1940, Foch presented several tough conditions to the German side before fighting would cease. The Germans were given two days, November 9 and 10, to respond to the Allied proposals. This presented a real problem to the German delegation because during the course of these two days the German emperor resigned, a republic was proclaimed, and Max von Baden handed over all of his authority to an interim president, Friedrich Ebert. In view of these events, the French wondered whether they were really dealing with the legal representatives of Germany. However, on November 10, Ebert sent a message agreeing to the armistice terms. The next day, November 11, the armistice was signed.

The terms of the armistice were anything but lenient. Germany was given two weeks to withdraw from Alsace-Lorraine and from all other invaded territory. All German territory west of the Rhine was to be occupied by Allied troops. The Germans were to evacuate East Africa. Germany also forfeited an enormous amount of cannons, machine guns, planes, and trucks. All submarines were to be surrendered, and the whole German fleet was to be put into Allied hands. The treaties of Brest Litovsk and Bucharest, made with Russia and Rumania respectively, were declared null and void. Finally, Germany was to free Allied prisoners even though the Allies were not required to free German prisoners. The armistice was clearly designed to convince the Germans that they had lost the war. All was now quiet on the western front.

Inside Germany, however, all was not quiet on any front. While the German delegation agonized over the terms of the armistice in their railroad car in the forest of Compiègne, total confusion broke out in Germany. On November 9, Kaiser William abdicated his throne and a republic was proclaimed by the Social Democrat Phillip Scheidemann. The kaiser's hasty departure for exile in Holland left a political vacuum that several factions, including the Communists, attempted to fill. The Russian defeat in war had brought the Bolsheviks to power, and there were good reasons to suspect that similar developments might occur in Germany. This is certainly how Lenin perceived the situation from his vantage point in Moscow in November 1918. The Bolshevik autocrat spoke of Russia and Germany as twins and looked to the more industrialized Germany as his advanced outpost in the coming struggle with capitalism. Directly and indirectly, the Russian Communists gave enthusiastic support to their German comrades in hopes that a communized Germany would be the catalyst for a communized Europe.

Lenin's euphoria seemed confirmed by the events taking place in Germany in the fall of 1918. Even before the kaiser's government collapsed on November 9, 1918, councils of workers and soldiers had sprouted all over Germany. On October 28, 1918, mutinous sailors in Kiel refused to obey an order to steam out into the North Sea for another encounter with the British navy. Instead of launching their ships, the sailors turned their hoses on the fires in the boiler rooms, sang revolutionary songs, hoisted red flags over their ships, and then proceeded to take over the city of Kiel. The sailors' mutiny, in turn, inspired a rash of revolts throughout Germany that the government, paralyzed by defeat and general demobilization of troops, was unable to control. Besides Kiel, other north German ports soon fell into the hands of left-wing radicals who were not so much interested in revolution as they were in ending the war and improving working conditions within the navy.

The mutiny of the German sailors was the beginning of the end for the old imperial order. On November 8, the Independent Socialist Kurt Eisner, supported by councils of workers, soldiers, and peasants, overthrew the royal government in Bavaria and proclaimed a Socialist republic. Two days later, all eyes turned to the German capital, where a six-man council of people's commissars proclaimed itself the executive branch of the new German government.

Thus, in the first two weeks of November 1918 a reenactment of the Russian Revolution seemed to be taking place in Germany. This is certainly how a temporarily blinded young corporal by the name of Adolf Hitler, who was recovering from a poison gas attack at Pasewalk in Pomerania, perceived the political situation. In reality, the fear of a

Communist revolution was much exaggerated because the German situation did not resemble the Russian. In Russia, the urban working class was proportionally much smaller than the German working force; it was also less disciplined along formal union lines and lacked the tradition of skilled craftsmanship that predisposed the German worker toward a more conservative political outlook. Both the Russian peasants and workers hated the tsarist regime and longed for its violent overthrow. Under the impact of a disastrous war, an elite cadre of revolutionaries skillfully mobilized these seething resentments and, taking advantage of the blunders of the first or moderate revolution of March 1917, staged a second revolution that put an end to the traditional order in Russia. The Bolsheviks imposed a one-party dictatorship on Russia and gradually assembled the instruments of mass control that such a rule inevitably necessitates: a revolutionary army (the Red Army), a secret police (Cheka), forced labor camps for political opponents, and a pliant cadre of government officials executing the will of the reigning autocracy.

By contrast, in Germany there was only one revolution, and that one left the traditional social structure essentially undisturbed.[6] The decisive political shift of power in Germany had taken place during the last month of the war when the ruling elites, composed of the aristocracy, the upper middle class, and the High Command of the Armed Forces, were politically displaced for the moment by the forces of social democracy, especially by the parties in the Reichstag that commanded the loyalties of the workers and portions of the middle classes.

The largest of these left-wing parties was the Social Democratic Party. Founded in 1875, the party had gone through a hectic period of external persecution and internal dissension. In 1914 the party had reluctantly voted to support the war effort; but in doing so, it had spread further dissent into the rank and file, precipitating a walkout by the dissidents who formed a new party in 1917 called the Independent Socialist Party. The aim of this new radical party was to establish genuine socialism in Germany and bring an immediate halt to the despised war. The Independent Socialists were supported by the more radical Communists who had been organized into the Spartacist League by two remarkable revolutionaries — Rosa Luxemburg and Karl Liebknecht. Supported by many disenchanted workers, particularly the shop stewards, these Spartacists, named after the ill-fated Roman slave leader Spartacus, called for a Communist regime modeled on Bolshevik rule in Russia; they favored immediate revolution, expropriation of industry and landed estates, and the establishment of "soviets" or workers' councils. Their leader, Karl Liebknecht, was the son of Wilhelm Liebknecht, friend of Karl Marx and one of the founding fathers of the Social Democratic Party. Karl Liebknecht broke with the party in 1914 because he could not go along with its support of the war. Liebknecht was a short, slender man who wore a pince-nez, sported a military moustache, and gave the overall impression of a minor clerk in the civil service rather than a dangerous subversive. Yet Liebknecht was a man of unshakable determination and revolutionary zeal; his hatred of the Prussian military caste had earned him a jail sentence before the war for maligning the military establishment. After he voted against further war credits, his own party disavowed him and ultimately expelled him from its ranks. The military also retaliated against him by drafting him into a punishment battalion; but since he was a member of the Reichstag, he enjoyed certain immunities that allowed him to spread propaganda against the war.

In the Reichstag, Liebknecht was one of the few courageous deputies who frequently attacked Germany's military autocrats for their conduct of the war. He also published a radical newsletter called *Spartacus* and recruited disenchanted workers for his Spartacist League. On May 1, 1916, he organized a demonstration against the war at the Potzdammer Platz in Berlin, denouncing the war-mongers in the government and calling for a violent overthrow of the government. This seditious activity promptly earned him a four-year jail sentence. In October 1918, however, Liebknecht was released from prison as a result of a general amnesty and quickly returned to Berlin to resume his revolutionary activities. When he arrived in Berlin, he was welcomed by huge crowds and celebrated like a conquering hero. One government minister, startled by this remarkable change in public opinion, observed: "Liebknecht has been carried shoulder-high by soldiers who have been decorated with the Iron Cross. Who could have dreamt of such a thing happening three weeks ago?"[7]

With a sizeable part of the German left rallying around Liebknecht and his second-in-command, the gifted ideologue Rosa Luxemburg — a stout, crippled, but combative agitator in her middle forties — the Majority Socialists (Social Democrats) struggled to maintain their control over the German workers. Ostensibly Marxist in their orientation, the Majority Socialists showed little interest in ideology and even less in subverting the social order for Communism. In their lifestyles, the Majority Socialists were *petit bourgeois;* they wanted to raise the general standard of living for the working people in the context of a modern democratic society. Their leader, Friedrich Ebert, typified these relatively moderate expectations. Born in 1871, the son of a humble Catholic tailor, Ebert was apprenticed as a journeyman saddlemaker and, by dint of hard work, gradually rose to the chairmanship of the saddlers' union in Bremen. His good sense, jovial character, and pragmatic outlook made him popular among the rank and file and led to his election to the Bremen city council before he was thirty. In 1904 he became cochairman of his party's convention; and a year later, he was appointed secretary to the central committee of the party in Berlin. In 1912 Ebert became a deputy of his party to the Reichstag; in 1913 he succeeded August Bebel as head of the German Social Democratic Party (SPD).

The Majority Socialists admired Ebert's tact and diplomatic aplomb; they liked his flexibility on ideological issues. In fact, Ebert was not doctrinaire on ideological questions; he was, by conviction and temperament, a revisionary Socialist who strongly believed in parliamentary democracy, preferably in republican but under certain conditions also in monarchical form. His bête noire was lack of organization and lack of good order. He believed that everything should be done according to some acceptable protocol and that decisions should never be forced on constituted authorities by the irrational actions of crowds and rabble-rousers.[8] This is why Ebert threw his authority behind the government of Prince Max von Baden in October 1918, because he genuinely feared a social revolution that would lead, as in Russia, to a Bolshevik coup. The prospect of a Bolshevik revolution filled Ebert and his colleagues, including his right-hand man, Philipp Scheidemann (1863–1939), with horror.

The center of political gravity was thus shifting in the fall of 1918 from the imperial elites to the Majority Socialists. The crucial day was November 9, 1918. In order to prevent the Independent Socialists and the radical Spartacists from gaining control over the working population of Berlin, the Majority Socialists demanded the abdication of Kaiser William, who had moved to army headquarters at Spa for his own protection.

Berliners were in a state of nervous tension on November 9, 1918, sensing that something historic was about to happen. The streets were filled on this day because the Independent Socialists, backed by the Spartacists, had called a general strike. Although crowds milled about in expectation of some major event, relatively little violence occurred. There were some ugly scenes, however, of enlisted soldiers attacking their officers and tearing off their insignia of rank. What most Berliners expected on that day was the abdication of the emperor. Although this was a foregone conclusion, it seemed to drag on interminably. When the Majority Socialists, after repeated inquiries to the chancellery, did not receive definitive news of the emperor's abdication — for William was still toying with the idea of reasserting his control — they made good on their earlier threat of withdrawing their representatives from Max's cabinet. The man who now forced everybody's hands and decided the fate of postwar German politics was Max von Baden. On his own authority, he announced the kaiser's abdication and called for elections to a constituent assembly and the establishment of a regency. Max von Baden then resigned in favor of Friedrich Ebert. The emperor, who was still at Spa with his high-ranking military leaders, referred to this decision by his cousin as "bare-faced, outrageous treason," but his support among the German people had eroded to such an extent that even Groener had to remind him that, with no army behind him, the oath his soldiers had sworn to him was now meaningless. After a final but fruitless argument with his generals, William boarded a special train that carried him into exile in Holland. He never saw Germany again.

Germany in Revolutionary Turmoil

At noon on November 9, 1919, while Philipp Scheidemann was eating a bowl of potato soup in the Reichstag dining hall, a crowd of soldiers rushed into the hall and accosted him with the ominous news that Liebknecht was already speaking from the balcony of the imperial palace and was ready to proclaim the Soviet Republic of Germany. Recalling his horrified reaction, Scheidemann later wrote:

> Now I clearly saw what was afoot. I knew his [Liebknecht's] slogan — supreme authority for the workers' councils. Germany to be therefore a Russian province, a branch of the Soviet. No, no, a thousand times no![9]

Scheidemann then rushed to one of the large windows of the Reichstag and addressed a throng of cheering Berliners with the startling news that "the accursed war is at an end.... The emperor has abdicated.... Long live the new! Long live the German Republic!"[10]

When Scheidemann made this startling announcement, the news of the emperor's abdication had not been released, and even Liebknecht had not fully marshaled his forces. Thus, when Friedrich Ebert heard that his second-in-command had proclaimed a republic, "His face turned livid with wrath," as Scheidemann later recalled. Ebert banged his fist on a table and yelled at the embarrassed culprit: "You have no right to proclaim a Republic!"[11] Germany had received a republic by accident; and the fact that it was proclaimed by a Socialist would stigmatize it from the moment of its birth.

Later that day, Liebknecht's troops managed to occupy the deserted imperial palace, and it was from there that Liebknecht proclaimed a free Socialist republic, promising "to build a new order of the proletariat." By nightfall no one knew who was really in power in Berlin because two republics had been proclaimed successively. The issue, however, was actually decided on that very evening. As Friedrich Ebert tried to work out the implications of the day's events in his mind in the chancellor's private office, one of the office phones, which turned out to be a secret line to military headquarters at Spa, began to ring. Unaware of this secret line, Ebert was startled to hear General Groener, Ludendorff's successor, on the other end of the line. The general briefly recapitulated the day's events at Spa: he informed Ebert that the emperor had abdicated and was on his way to Holland and that an orderly withdrawal of Germany's front-line armies would commence immediately. In response to Ebert's question as to where the army stood in the present crisis, the general replied that the army would support Ebert's government if, in turn, the new government would support the officers' corps, maintain strict discipline in the army, and oppose Communism. Much reassured, Ebert agreed to these friendly overtures; by doing so, he concluded that much criticized marriage of convenience between the fledgling democratic republic and the traditional military-industrial complex. Although this pact saved both parties from the extreme elements of the revolution, it also, as John Wheeler-Bennett has pointed out, doomed the Weimar Republic from the start.[12] By agreeing not to tamper with the traditional structure of the German army, Ebert and his Majority Socialists unwittingly helped to perpetuate a military establishment that despised the democratic process. Throughout the Weimar Republic the military became a frequent rallying point for right-wing extremists who wanted to destroy the democratic republic.

Yet without the support of the army Ebert's government would probably not have survived the attacks launched against it by the extreme revolutionary left. By Christmas of 1918, Ebert was skating on very thin ice indeed; his cooperation with the military had exposed him to charges of counterrevolutionary activities. Playing for time, he invited three Independent Socialists to join his newly formed cabinet and temporarily endorsed the radicals' claim that all sovereignty resided in the council of soldiers and workers. Privately, he made it clear that he abhorred government by councils of workers and soldiers. The present situation, as he saw it, called for a sound constitutional method by which power would be transferred to a publicly elected constituent assembly that would then proceed to frame a constitution acceptable to the nation.

Ebert's hopes of a peaceful and orderly transition to parliamentary government required the restoration of law and order, and the most effective means of bringing this about still resided in Germany's armed forces. Unfortunately, many army units were melting away quickly in the wake of the general withdrawal from enemy territories and the impending plans to demobilize most of the units. Even in defeat, however, the army managed to preserve its dignity. General Groener succeeded so brilliantly in marching almost two million troops home to Germany that it created the illusion, especially in Berlin, that the German army had not really been defeated at all. On November 11, the day the armistice was signed in France, the vanguard of eleven army divisions staged a spectacular parade by marching up Unter den Linden to the sounds of cheers and hurrahs, with the band striking up "Deutschland, Deutschland, über Alles." Ebert himself reviewed the troops from a specially erected platform, declaring, "I salute you who return unvanquished from the field of battle."[13] The aura of militarism was still so powerful that not even a Socialist could admit publicly that the German army had been defeated.

In the general confusion following the tenuous transfer of power from the old ruling elites to the make-shift cabinet assembled by Friedrich Ebert, the ingrained German sense of order had prevented not only a complete political breakdown but a possible Communist seizure of power as well. Moreover, in order to avoid the collapse of German industry, representatives of employers sat down with trade unionist leaders and worked out mutually beneficial agreements that recognized the existence of independent trade unions and their right to collective bargaining. Finally, to safeguard the integrity of the civil service system, Ebert called upon all state officials to remain at their posts, a measure for which he was much criticized because the managerial elite of the old civil service was bound to be hostile to democracy. Yet only a small minority of Socialists, consisting largely of radicalized shop stewards and Spartacists, resisted these stabilizing policies set forth by Ebert and his Majority Socialists. Even within the councils of workers and soldiers there was determined opposition to following the Russian example of violent or "root-and-branch" revolution.

Despite such determined opposition to Communist radicalism, Ebert and his Majority Socialist experienced some apprehensive moments. While the National Congress of Workers' and Soldiers' Councils was deliberating, an ugly crowd intimidated the delegates and pressured them to repudiate Ebert's plan for national elections, the convening of a national constituent assembly, and the drafting of a democratic constitution for all of Germany. However, the delegates refused to cave in to these threats and overwhelmingly voted for the government's plan, designating January 19, 1919, as the date for the coming national election. Although the congress voted for a potentially revolutionary program that would have included a democratic civil guard (*Freiwillige Volkswehr*), subordination of the military to the cabinet, the election of officers by the troops, abolition of insignia of rank, elimination of slavish military obedience (*Kadavergehorsam*), and elimination of a regular standing army, subsequent resistance by the army and Ebert's own growing power effectively prevented the implementation of these radical proposals.

Ebert's opponents on the left watched his increasing dependence on the military with alarm and contempt, particularly after the government requested help from the army in squelching a revolt by mutinous sailors who had entrenched themselves in the imperial palace and refused to evacuate it. The troops dispatched to Berlin, however, proved to be so unreliable that, after only a few skirmishes on Christmas Eve, they simply threw down their arms and ran away, forcing the humiliated government to give in to the sailors' demands for higher pay.

Ebert's reliance on the army convinced the Independent Socialists that the revolution they envisioned had been compromised. On December 27, the three Independent Socialists who had joined Ebert's cabinet resigned, though the party itself still shied away from the use of force. However, the Spartacists, who had allied themselves for tactical reasons with the Independent Socialists, repudiated their former partners and formally created a new party called the German Communist Party (January 1, 1919). This set the stage for revolutionary insurrection.

If the fighting on Christmas Eve had proved anything, it was that the regular army was not a reliable tool for dealing with insurgents and that a more effective force was needed to deal with such emergencies. Exclusive reliance on war-weary troops had turned out to be self-defeating. General Groener believed that what was needed was a resilient, highly mobile force of volunteers — the Free Corps (Freikorps). As early as December 12, 1918, General Ludwig Maercker had submitted a proposal to his superiors urging the creation of a volunteer rifle corps that could be used to maintain law and order. After receiving permission by his superiors, the general put together a respectable force that consisted largely of dyed-in-the-wool professionals who regarded soldiering as their life's oxygen, hated left-wing radicals, and found the idea of a peaceful civilian life distasteful. It was in this way that the infamous political shock troops for-hire, the Free Corps, came into existence, destined to plague the democratic Weimar Republic throughout its existence.[14] The Free Corps would play an important role in the wake of the general chaos following World War I, and it would also furnish the esprit de corps as well as the manpower for the Nazi movement.

The backbone of the Free Corps units consisted of declassed imperial officers who were frightened by the prospect of giving up their privileged positions in German society. Having lost the war along with their warlord, they faced a bleak prospect under a Socialist regime that was known to be hostile to the old military establishment. It is estimated that there were some 270,000 officers in 1919, many of them coming from the ranks of the nobility.[15] They had enjoyed virtual immunity from civilian control, exercising a degree of social influence that was the envy of ordinary Germans. Stunned by the shock of defeat and the prospect of a dreary life under socialism or even Communism, they became outraged elitist reactionaries, desperately searching for a new imperial banner under which they could continue to enjoy their privileges.

Thus, when the struggling government of Fritz Ebert found it necessary and expedient to call upon the army for support, a large number of officers and men stepped forward to do their duty. Despite defeat in war, the martial spirit was still remarkably strong, especially among the remnants of the elite imperial shock troops (*Stosstruppen*). These mobile units had served as advanced battering rams against the enemy's front line, and their officers and men had acquired a legendary reputation for bravery under murderous fire. Some *Stosstruppen* leaders would later sanctify their experiences in quasi-religious terms, as Ernst Jünger did in his compelling accounts of the war front experience (*Fronterlebnis*).[16]

In reality, these Free Corps soldiers were often little more than trained killers, although they would sometimes justify their brutalities by telling the world that they were fighting against Bolshevism, safeguarding the fatherland, or simply making men out of boys. On the eastern front, some of the Free Corps units saw themselves as latter-day versions of the Teutonic Knights; and the lure of "free estates" in the east served as an attractive incentive for recruiting fresh young men to the banner of the anti-Bolshevik crusade. In the end, the Free Corps became little more than roving bands of hired killers, more loyal to their unit commanders than to the government they were supposed to protect.

General Ludwig von Maercker's example inspired other commanders to establish Free Corps units. On December 26, 1918, Colonel Wilhelm Reinhard organized a Free Corps in Berlin, soon joined by the Suppe Free Corps that had defended the chancellery on Christmas Eve. At Potsdam a Free Corps was organized by Major von Stephani; it consisted of the remnants of the old First Regiment of foot guards and the Imperial Potsdam Regiment, but Stephani bolstered its strength by soliciting volunteers from former officers, professional men, cadets, and university students. All of these emerging units, still small in December 1918, were placed under the command of General Walther von Lüttwitz, who would later distinguish himself by using Free Corps units to overthrow the government in the Kapp Putsch.

In the meantime, Ebert was frantically trying to build up his own sagging support in Berlin, where the streets were now largely in the hands of insurgents after the army's ignominious defeat on Christmas Eve. The new year opened on a depressing note: Ebert's government had no army to support it; the police force was in the hands of Emil Eickhorn, an Independent Socialist who despised Ebert; the tireless Liebknecht was fomenting disorder by organizing strikes and demonstrations; and Russian revolutionaries, notably Karl Radek, were inciting the still cautious workers to unleash a red terror against their bourgeois oppressors. On January 6, 1919, the radical Socialists launched their attack on the Ebert government with a massive general strike, followed by the seizure of railroad stations, public buildings, and newspapers. At his wit's end, Ebert called Groener and suggested that the seat of government be moved from Berlin to Potsdam. "I shall go away," the harassed Ebert told Groener; he continued: "I shall disappear utterly from the chancellor's palace and go to sleep....If the Liebknecht crowd takes this opportunity to seize power, there will be nothing here...and then we shall be in a position to set up our government somewhere else in a few day's time, possibly in Potsdam."[17]

Ebert's depression was a reflection of his insecurity and his lack of charismatic leadership. Although a shrewd political infighter, he lacked decisive leadership abilities. The same was true of his fellow Socialists, who had been brought up to feel socially inferior in sight of their upperclass betters; they secretly wished that someone else would take the reins of power. In Richard Watt's judgment, "A lifetime in the Socialist movement had conditioned them for a role of opposition. They had been neither trained nor emotionally prepared for a Socialist victory; in truth, they had not really expected that it would come in their lifetime."[18]

If Ebert lacked the ability to launch a decisive counterblow against the radicals, there were others who knew exactly what was needed to

crush the revolutionary left. Once more the quick-witted Quartermaster General Groener came to Ebert's aid by telling him to hold out and
rely on the army and its affiliated Free Corps units. Groener had also
persuaded Ebert in late December to call on Gustav Noske, the man
who had restored law and order in Kiel in the wake of the sailors'
mutiny. Noske, who had a reputation as a "rightist" and a nationalist among the Majority Socialists, was one of the few men of the left
whom the military trusted. When Ebert appointed him minister of defense, Noske made it unmistakably clear that he would not hesitate
to become the bloodhound who would carry out his responsibility in
restoring law and order.[19] Moving out of the center of the city to a
girls' school in the wealthy suburb of Dahlem, Noske proceeded with
methodical skill in raising reliable troops and coordinating his activities with General von Lüttwitz. On January 11, 1919, the beginning
of "Spartacist Week," Noske moved against the radicals with his Free
Corps. In several days of bloody fighting, the soldiers of the Free Corps
took vengeance against the hated Communists and indiscriminately massacred hundreds, including Karl Liebknecht and Rosa Luxemburg, who
were killed on January 15, 1919, while "trying to escape."

From Berlin, the Spartacist revolt spread to other parts of Germany,
but Free Corps units ruthlessly crushed the insurgents. In Bavaria, the
future home of the Nazi movement, the Socialist revolution of Kurt Eisner was short-lived, giving way after Eisner's assassination to a second
revolution and a Communist takeover of Munich in April 1919. Again,
Free Corps units, some of them flying swastika banners, mercilessly massacred the opposition and restored "law and order," turning Bavaria
into a right-wing citadel against Communism as well as the emerging
democratic Weimar Republic.

Weimar and Versailles

Between 1919 and 1933, Germany was subject to two major documents:
the Treaty of Versailles, which determined how Germans responded
to foreign powers, and the Weimar Constitution, which regulated the
political life of Germans until Adolf Hitler decided to tear up both
documents. Although the Weimar Constitution was one of the most
democratic constitutions in the world in 1919, Richard Watt's clever
judgment that the constitution began and ended as a document in search
of a people remains a sad and tragic fact.[20] By the same token, one
could argue that the Treaty of Versailles was also a document that began and ended in search of a single people willing to accept all of its
provisions. Neither of these documents proved to be acceptable to the
German people, and the fourteen-year history of the Weimar Republic
(1919–33) witnessed persistent attempts, especially by the parties of the
extreme ends of the political spectrum, to repudiate both.

On January 19, 1919, the German people went to the polls to elect 421 deputies to the National Constituent Assembly. The task of the assembly was to appoint a new government, write a constitution, and conclude peace with the Allied powers. The Social Democratic Party (SPD) gained the largest number of votes (11.5 million), but they did not receive a majority of seats in the assembly, polling just 163 out of 421 seats. Consequently, without a mandate to rule by themselves, the Social Democrats found it necessary to form a coalition government with the moderate bourgeois center parties (the Democratic Party and Center Party) in order to obtain a workable majority. In view of the fact that the first postwar election came on the heels of the bloody Spartacist Week, it was surprising that the Social Democrats (Majority Socialists) garnered as many votes as they did. At the same time, the conservative parties staged a remarkable recovery from the trauma caused by the fall of the monarchy. Although they registered their determined opposition to the republic, making no secret of their monarchist leanings, the conservatives grudgingly accepted the new democratic facts of life and appeared willing to work for their objectives through the democratic process. Out of deference to the new democratic spirit, some of the prewar conservative parties even renamed themselves by incorporating the term "people" in their official labels. Thus, the prewar Conservative Party reemerged as the German National People's Party (DNVP). Yet despite its democratic sounding title, it was still the party of wealthy landowners, industrialists, and influential members of the traditional military-industrial complex. In the election, it came in fourth, polling about three million votes and receiving forty-four seats in the assembly. Working in concert with other parties of the right, such as Gustav Stresemann's German People's Party (DVP), the DNVP controlled almost 15 percent of the seats in the assembly.

The results of the January elections harbored several positive signs: the German people had clearly decided in favor of moderation and appeared to be willing to experiment with social democracy, though few Germans understood what democracy entailed in practice. In addition, the parties on the extreme ends of the political spectrum had suffered a noticeable setback. As a result of the Spartacist defeat, the Communist Party abstained from participating in the January 19 elections. On the political right, the shock that had accompanied the fall of the monarchy had not yet worn off, allowing the parties of the center to consolidate their position. Despite these positive indications, one could also detect certain long-range problems. The elections had revealed that the voters did not show overwhelming support or enthusiasm for any party. This meant that no single party was able to claim a clear mandate for governing and that the only way in which the democratic process could be made to work was to form coalition cabinets. Such makeshift arrangements, however, threatened to produce internally divided governments since the policy makers represented different ideological views and reported to different constituencies. Indeed, throughout the life of the Weimar Republic, stable democratic government was constantly undermined by unpopular minority cabinets and internally weak grand coalitions.[21] Finally, when even these flawed democratic processes no longer worked, German politicians reverted to authoritarian solutions by setting up extraparliamentary authoritarian cabinets and rule by executive fiat, thus paving the way for outright totalitarianism.

On Thursday, February 6, 1919, the National Constituent Assembly began its work in the New National Theater in Weimar. Located on the river Ilm about 150 miles southwest of Berlin, the city of Weimar had been picked by the government as a meeting place of the assembly because it offered a safer environment than the volatile capital. Weimar also occupied a special place in the hearts of Germans because it was the city of Goethe, Schiller, and Herder, the cynosure of the "good" Germany of humane poets and philosophers. Psychologically, therefore, Weimar was not a bad choice for a new democratic beginning.

Since the middle of November 1918, Hugo Preuss (1860–1925), the minister of the interior in the Ebert-Scheidemann government, had been working on a new democratic constitution for the German people. Being Jewish and liberal, Hugo Preuss had been unsuccessful in securing a traditional university post and had to settle for teaching constitutional law at the Berlin School of Business Administration. Preuss also served in the Berlin city parliament as a left progressive. A student of the famous legal historian Otto von Gierke, he was a subtle theorist as well as a shrewd tactician, but as Hajo Holborn points out, Preuss suffered the bane of most intellectual experts in politics by having only as much power over the men in actual control as his personal persuasiveness might win.[22] In his single-minded effort to find the best constitutional arrangement for the wartorn country, Preuss picked eclectically from several sources — the American Constitution, the best features of European parliamentarianism, and even the abortive constitution of the Frankfurt Assembly of 1848. Having to work with antagonistic parties and social interest groups, Preuss was necessarily forced to compromise; and the final document, after being meticulously revised several times, was in many ways a mirror image of the social dissonances of German society. The Weimar Constitution was a hodge-podge of principles drawn from Socialist and liberal agendas; it represented so much confusion in regard to economic objectives and unresolved class conflicts that German democracy was stymied from the beginning.[23]

Although an impressive democratic document, the Weimar Constitution contained a number of provisions that could be construed autocratically as well as democratically. To begin with, Hugo Preuss was a strong believer in the unitary state (*Einheitsstaat*), and he pushed to reduce the power of the individual states vis-à-vis the central government to a much weaker level than it had been under the monarchy. Although the opposition to this proved strong and federalism was retained in principle, the central government still emerged as much more powerful than it had been under the monarchy. The central government gained sole control over the armed forces; directed all matters pertaining to foreign policy; raised and levied taxes as required; and made all civil servants, formerly subject to the states, directly responsible to Berlin. In addition, the central government assumed ownership of the national railroad system and claimed responsibility for a multitude of duties previously exercised by either state or private institutions, including control of relief to the poor, health care, labor relations, communications (the press, cinema, theater), banking, commerce, and civil and criminal law.[24] It is true that the individual states (*Länder*) were allowed to exercise authority over their internal affairs through their own miniature parliaments, but the power of the central government was deemed preeminent over state governments; and in the event that any state defied the will of the central government, military action could be taken against the offending state.

Thus, the newly emerging government contained at its core a strong basis for absolute sovereignty for anyone who cared to exercise it. Even the name of the new nation did not differ from the old one, for the framers of the constitution, in their eagerness to preserve a sense of historical continuity, retained the word *Reich* in referring to the new republic. It was not clear just how the idea of empire, with all the imperial symbols it evoked, and the idea of a democratic republic could be harmonized. The truth was that the contradictions inherent in such efforts caused psychic dissonances that were made all the more acute by the pressures of economic hardship and national humiliation. Throughout the life of the republic, the average German was treated to frequent public spectacles in which the feudal classes, dressed in their resplendent uniforms, medals, and ribbons, strutted up and down the streets of German cities taunting the democratic establishment. Funerals and patriotic meetings invariably prompted gaudy displays of aristocratic splendor and created the impression, first, that nothing had changed since the fall of the monarchy, and, second, that the traditional classes somehow had a monopoly on patriotism.

The framers of the constitution were sensitive to the fact that strong executive leadership was required in order to unify the divided nation. It was for this reason that the president of the republic was endowed with more power than was customary under other parliamentary systems. The office of the Presidency was a compromise between a constitutional monarch and a parliamentary president. He was to be elected by the German people for a period of seven years (Article 41). The constitution specified that the president had to be elected by a majority of the voters, and that runoff elections, during which different candidates could be appointed, had to be arranged if no candidate achieved a clear majority. The president's powers were extensive: he appointed the chancellor; served as commander in chief; appointed and removed all military officers; possessed the right to dissolve the Reichstag; and in times of national emergency, he was empowered to suspend civil liberties and intervene with the help of the armed forces to restore public safety and order. This innocuous article (Article 48) gave little concern in 1919 because the constitution also specified that the Reichstag could repeal a president's emergency decree. In addition, the constitution also provided for countervailing powers by insisting that every order or decree issued by the president had to be countersigned by the chancellor.

The chancellor and his ministers formed the government of the Reich. The chancellor himself was appointed and could be dismissed by the president, and the ministers he chose also had to be approved by the president. The chancellor's government had to have the confidence of the Reichstag; and if the Reichstag chose to withdraw its confidence in the chancellor or any of his ministers, the particular individual had to resign. Furthermore, should any member of the government violate the constitution, the culprit could be brought before the Supreme Court (Staatsgerichthof) for trial.

Legislative power was vested in a bicameral house composed of the Reichstag and Reichsrat. Members of the Reichstag or lower house were elected for four years by universal suffrage (female and male citizens of twenty years and over) and in accordance with a new principle of representation called "proportional representation."[25] This meant that voters cast their votes for a party and not for individual candidates. Each party drew up lists of names and waited for the election results to see how many candidates on the list were eligible for the Reichstag. For each sixty thousand votes a party was guaranteed one seat in the Reichstag. Although this system of proportional representation seemed to represent the popular will more closely than any other, it also fragmented the political process into a host of different and mutually antagonistic parties. Since most parties stood a good chance of garnering sixty thousand votes, even the smallest parties could gain a handful of seats in the Reichstag. The result of the first Reichstag election confirms this tendency toward fragmentation and the distasteful consequences it would entail in the future — political horse trading, inter- and intraparty factionalism, noisy grandstanding and obstructionism by small parties, and lack of common purpose. Beyond the tiny parties, there were already seven major parties in the new government. By the end of the Weimar period there were forty groups represented in the Reichstag; in Schleswig-Holstein voters were confounded by no less than twenty-one parties, most of them reflecting very narrowly focused interests. Such proliferation of parties created a very unfortunate impression of the democratic process in the minds of most Germans who saw the resulting confusion as a validation of their authoritarian prejudices, namely, that democracy spells chaos and corruption.

Besides causing political fragmentation, the system of proportional representation also undermined the one-on-one relationship between the citizen and his delegate, and it put undue power into the hands of party managers, who often chose lackluster candidates for their party lists. This effectively debarred outstanding candidates from declaring their candidacy and deprived the republic of the talent it sorely needed to survive.[26] All in all, the system of proportional representation, favored by the Social Democrats, who hoped to gain the most by it, merely magnified the social divisions in the German political system. Being the embodiment of national sovereignty, the Reichstag possessed extensive powers of initiating and passing laws; and since the cabinet was responsible to the Reichstag, parliamentary control over executive decisions was possible for the first time in German politics. Unfortunately, the divided Reichstags of the Weimar period did not effectively exercise their constitutional prerogatives, thereby further undermining the democratic process.

The Reichsrat, or upper house, consisted of appointed members who primarily represented the German states (*Länder*). Although the Reichsrat possessed the power to protest any legislation by sending it back to the Reichstag, the lower house could override such protests by a two-thirds majority. The Reichsrat was limited in its operations to issues pertaining to the individual states, but even in this area its role was strictly circumscribed. For example, the question of whether a local state law conflicted with a law enacted by the central government was to be decided by the Reich Supreme Court.

In a separate section, the Weimar Constitution guaranteed the rights of citizens by declaring all Germans to be equal before the law and by specifying an impressive array of liberties, including freedom of speech, press, and assembly; religious toleration; the right to own private property; the right to free public education; the right to travel freely; and the right of habeas corpus (due process). These impressive democratic features, along with the referendum and the initiative by which the electorate could participate in legislation and remove public officials from office, made the Weimar Constitution one of the most democratic documents in the world. In 1919, however, it was doubtful whether such a democratic constitution could work in the hands of a people that was neither psychologically nor historically prepared for self-government. Even Hugo Preuss wondered aloud whether such a system should be given to a people that resisted it with every sinew of its body.[27]

On January 18, 1919, one day before the German people went to the polls to elect members to the National Constituent Assembly, the peace conference assembled in Paris to make the world safe for democracy, a phrase that had been coined by H. G. Wells in August 1914 to explain the meaning of the Allied cause. Unfortunately, after months of bitter wrangling, the conference succeeded in the opposite: it made the world safe from democracy.[28] The peace treaty, supposed to create a just and lasting world, was not made among coequal powers, but was summarily imposed upon the vanquished with menacing threats that left no doubt that war would be resumed if they failed to sign. Unlike the Treaty of Vienna of 1815, which was the product of a fraternity of European aristocrats, the Treaty of Paris was a punitive action imposed on the vanquished and their people by democratic politicians who were less guided by principles than by the highly charged emotions of their constituencies. It had been easier for the monarchs of 1815 to forget national animosities than for the democratic leaders to set aside their hatreds and design a lasting peace. The statesmen who gathered at Paris were subject to the passions they had inflamed in their constituents; they were satisfied with nothing less than the humiliation of their opponents, though publicly they spoke in lofty terms about "peace without victory."

The discrepancy between noble rhetoric and vindictive punishment caused a savage backlash to the treaty. The Germans had sued for peace with the expectation that the treaty would be based on Woodrow Wilson's Fourteen Points. Briefly summarized, these points envisioned: an end to secret treaties and secret diplomacy; absolute freedom of the seas; removal of barriers and inequalities in international trade; reduction of armaments; equitable readjustments of colonial claims; evacuation of occupied territories; national self-determination; and the establishment of an international organization to prevent future wars. The major assumption behind Woodrow Wilson's Fourteen Points was to make an entirely different treaty based on humane and liberal principles. The American president was convinced that the old diplomacy, mired in power politics and secret diplomatic deals, was incompatible with the open spirit of democracy, and that negotiations should take place in an atmosphere of mutual confidence and trust.

Since Woodrow Wilson decided to journey to Paris himself, accompanied by a large staff of experts, the other Allied statesmen also felt obliged to attend in person. France was represented by Georges Clemenceau (1841–1929), England by David Lloyd George (1863–1945), and Italy by Vittorio Orlando (1860–1952). Although there were representatives from other nations, including Belgium, Greece, Poland, Czechoslovakia, Australia, and Japan, the real source of power resided in the Council of Four, consisting of the statesmen from the United States, Great Britain, France, and Italy (Wilson, Lloyd George, Clemenceau, and Orlando).

The statesmen from the Council of Four, supported by several committees, faced two incompatible tasks: on the one hand, they were expected to rebuild the world on a just foundation, and, on the other, they were supposed to satisfy the bitter resentments that had accumulated during four years of savage fighting. President Woodrow Wilson, the self-appointed apostle of international morality, had sailed to France with his staff of experts in hope of converting the old autocratic Europe to the blessings of democracy. Wilson represented an idealistic, naive, and powerful America — a nation for which, as one historian has observed, "the war had been fun."[29] Armed with his lofty ideals, he encountered in the French prime minister Georges Clemenceau, aptly called the "Old Tiger," a determined pessimist who had no illusions about either democracy or Germany. Clemenceau represented an exhausted France whose territory had borne the brunt of the war. The French people expected Clemenceau to make the Boche pay for the deaths of 1,315,000 Frenchmen and for the enormous material destruction that had rendered France's most advanced industrial areas a "nightmarish sight of scorched earth strewn with the skeletons of trees and blackened ruins...as far as the eye could see."[30] The Old Tiger had been reared on revanche, and his overriding aim was to redeem French sacrifices by permanently crippling Germany. This vengeful attitude was deeply at odds with the Wilsonian spirit of constructing a just and lasting peace. As Golo Mann has pointed out, "The product of this clash of attitudes was repulsive: a close-knit mesh of regulations intended to be 'just' and unquestionably so in many details, but allowing injustice inspired by malice, hatred and the intoxication with victory to slip in wherever possible; so much so that the whole, in spite of individual examples of justice, seemed an enormous instrument for the suppression, exploitation, and permanent humiliation of Germany."[31]

Although the Big Four drew up peace terms with all the Central Powers, its chief task consisted in settling the German problem. On May 5, 1919, after three months of work, the Allied powers concluded their treaty with Germany and expected a prompt German ratification. The German delegation to Versailles was led by Count Ulrich von Brockdorff-Rantzau (1869–1928), a capable diplomat of the old school who unfortunately reinforced in the Allied statesmen ancient stereotypes of the arrogant, monocled Prussian official. Brockdorff-Rantzau and his large professional staff had been held incommunicado behind barbed wire in a Paris hotel without being allowed to negotiate face-to-face with the peacemakers. When the delegation was presented with the treaty, which Clemenceau referred to as "the weighty settlement of our account," the Germans were aghast by its punitive terms.[32] They were also shocked to learn that the terms of the treaty were not subject to negotiation and that if they did not sign, hostilities would be resumed. It has been suggested that if the German delegation in Paris had not been so precipitous in publishing the terms of the treaty — for its provisions were still unknown to the public — secret negotiations could have been initiated that might have altered some of the harsher features of the treaty. The Germans, however, panicked and rushed to the presses to tell the world how unjustly they were being treated.[33] The public reaction in Germany can only be described as a profusion of public fury. Germans had not experienced such a sense of unity since the opening of the war; they felt betrayed and humiliated. The new democratic government, which had to bear the onus of the treaty, even contemplated armed resistance. Chancellor Scheidemann went on record by telling the nation that the intent of the proposed treaty was to make Germans "slaves and helots . . . doing forced labour behind barbed wire and prison bars" and that it was dishonorable to accept the treaty.[34] Despite the German reaction, the Allied powers refused to budge, giving the Germans one week to sign the treaty. This, in turn, caused a government crisis in Germany, with Scheidemann and his entire cabinet resigning in protest. The new government, headed by Gustav Bauer, another Social Democrat, realized that resistance was fruitless and urged the National Assembly to sign the document. On June 22, following bitter and acrimonious debates, the National Assembly finally yielded. The formal signing took place on June 28 in the same Hall of Mirrors in the Versailles Palace where Bismarck had proclaimed the German Empire in 1871.

The provisions of the Versailles Treaty can be seen as treating three basic themes: territorial losses, reparations, and punitive actions aimed at reducing Germany to the level of a minor power. Concerning outright territorial losses, Alsace-Lorraine, as expected, reverted to France, and all German overseas possessions were parceled out among the victors. Acrimonious discussions occurred over the fate of the Rhineland, with the French demanding that the left bank of the Rhine be detached from the rest of Germany and set up as an independent state. Although this extreme proposal was rejected, the peacemakers did agree to detach the left bank of the Rhine along with fifty kilometers of territory on the right bank of the river. Such territory was designated a neutral zone; within that zone Germany was prohibited from establishing any military presence. Moreover, this "demilitarized zone" was to be occupied by Allied troops for a period of fifteen years. The Saar Valley, with its rich coal deposits, was to be placed in French hands for the same period of time; its citizens would then be given a choice whether they wanted to join Germany or France.

To the east, the Allied powers wanted to set up strong buffer states against Bolshevism. As a result, those parts of the former German Empire that had been populated by Poles were assigned to the new state of Poland, and those parts that had been populated by Czechs or Slovaks were given to the new state of Czechoslovakia. Unfortunately, large numbers of Germans would now find themselves living in Poland and Czechoslovakia. In the case of Poland, the peacemakers decided to give the new state access to the Baltic Sea, but by cutting a "corridor" to that sea, they cut off East Prussia from the rest of Germany. The city of Danzig, located at the end of the corridor, became a "free city," politically independent but economically available to Poland. The problem of Danzig and the corridor, involving disputed territory and ethnic conflicts, would poison the relationship between Germany and Poland in the inter-war period, ultimately providing Hitler with a pretext for triggering World War II.

The fate of other territories, east or west, was to be decided by democratic plebiscites. Upper Silesia, a rich mining area, was annexed by Poland after a disputed plebiscite, while the rest of Silesia went to

Germany. Although plebiscites were regarded by the Allies as an expression of national self-determination, they were not always honored when the decision was likely to run counter to the expected outcome of the victors. Thus, when the Austrians wanted to join Germany, the peacemakers set aside self-determination in favor of national self-interest, prohibiting the *Anschluss* on the grounds that this would add too much territory and too many people to Germany. The same argument was made in respect to the Sudetenland and the Tyrol. Over four million Germans lived in the mountainous provinces of Bohemia and Moravia — two regions that the peacemakers had given to the new state of Czechoslovakia, ostensibly to provide the Czechs with more defensible frontiers. The Germans who lived in these regions were called Sudeten Germans after the mountain belt separating Bohemia and Silesia. Strictly speaking, these Germans had formerly belonged to the Habsburg Empire, but now found themselves as a minority within the new Czechoslovakian state. The same was true of those Germans living in the South Tyrol, for when the Brenner Pass was given to the Italians for strategic military reasons, the Germans in the South Tyrol now suddenly found themselves living in Italy.

The clauses of the Versailles Treaty dealing with reparations were the most punitive because they were based on the self-serving belief that Germany was solely responsible for having caused the war. The peacemakers' claim that Germany was responsible for the war was summed up in Article 231 of the treaty, subsequently referred to by the Germans as the "war guilt" clause:

> The Allied and Associated Governments affirm and Germany accepts the responsibility of Germany and her allies for causing all the loss and damage to which the Allied and Associated Governments and their nationals have been subjected as a consequence of the war imposed upon them by the aggression of Germany and her Allies.[35]

In practice, this statement declaring Germany guilty of having caused all the damage and suffering of World War I was intended to be a moral justification for reparations. The peacemakers were determined to hold Germany liable for all the material damage caused by four years of devastating warfare; but since they could not translate this claim into a measurable or sensible amount of money, the treaty remained silent on the full amount of payments the Germans were expected to dole out to the victors. In the meantime, the treaty forced Germany to pay five billion dollars in gold before May 1, 1921, and to relinquish extensive deliveries of coal, chemicals, river barges, and most of the German merchant marine fleet. The German delegation at Versailles was further informed that a special Inter-Allied Reparations Commission would be convened to settle Germany's final obligations. The German counterargument that this amounted to a blank check, obligating Germany in advance to pay any amount the victors wanted to impose, was categorically rejected by the Allies without explanation.

No other provisions of the Versailles Treaty poisoned the postwar period as much as the articles of the treaty that concerned reparations; and when the Inter-Allied Reparations Committee finally announced the total bill in 1921, a staggering sum of thirty-five billion dollars in gold, even Allied statesmen doubted that Germany could afford such exorbitant obligations. No Hitlerian demagogue was required to point out that such vindictive measures would cripple Germany's economy. Similar arguments were already being made on the Allied side, notably by John Maynard Keynes, then a young Cambridge economist and a member of the British delegation to the Paris Peace Conference. In a dispassionate work of analytical reasoning entitled *The Economic Consequences of the War* (1921), Keynes persuasively argued that reparations really aimed at the destruction of economic life in Germany and that by doing so, they would ironically also threaten the health and prosperity of the Allies themselves.[36] He argued that already before the war, German trade had shown a large deficit because imports far exceeded exports, but he added that Germany had balanced its international trade account by "invisible exports" such as selling rights to the use of German shipping, selling interest in German investments abroad, selling insurance premiums, and so on. The treaty, however, impaired payments to Germany from abroad, thus in turn making it impossible for the Germans to pay off the vast reparations demanded of them. This was made all the more difficult now by

> the almost total loss of her colonies, her overseas connections, her mercantile marine; and her foreign properties; by the cession of ten percent of her territory and population, of one third of her coal and of three-quarters of her iron ore; by two million casualties among men in the prime of life; by the starvation of her people for four years; by the burden of a vast war debt; by the depreciation of her currency to less than one-seventh its former value; by the disruption of her allies and their territories; by revolution at home and Bolshevism on her borders; and by all the unmeasured ruin in strength and hope of four years of all-swallowing war and final defeat.[37]

Keynes denounced the peacemakers as hypocrites and political opportunists whose pious promises of a just and lasting peace had led only to "the weaving of that web of sophistries and Jesuitical exegesis that was finally to clothe with insincerity the language and substance of the whole treaty."[38] He recommended the reconstruction of the German economy as a precondition to a general European recovery. Helping the Germans back on their feet, however, would require a scaling down of reparations, cancellation of war debts, reduction of inflation, and massive reinvigoration of German industry through international loans. Keynes even proposed an extensive free common market under the aegis of the League of Nations. His immensely stimulating and controversial ideas were roundly condemned by the defenders of the Versailles Treaty because they amounted, in essence, to a repudiation of the treaty at the moment of its birth.

Equally as shattering as the economic provisions of the Versailles Treaty were the terms relating to the future of the Germany military. The German army was to be reduced in size to a volunteer force of one hundred thousand men. Of these one hundred thousand, no more than four thousand could be officers, and their term of service was limited to twenty-five years, while that of the enlisted personnel was limited to twelve years. The strength of this small volunteer force was to be further impaired by depriving it of tanks, aircraft, and other "offensive" weapons. Similarly, the German navy was to be dismantled except for a token surface-vessel force not exceeding ten thousand tons. The German battle fleet was to be delivered into Allied hands, but when the German officers who had taken the fleet to the naval harbor of Scapa Flow in the Orkney Islands learned of the fate that was in store for their ships, they cheated the Allies of their prize by scuttling fifty of the sixty-eight ships.[39]

Finally, with an eye toward the heart of the German military establishment, the treaty called for the abolition of the general staff, the war college, and all cadet schools. Adding insult to injury, the peacemakers also demanded that Germany hand over the kaiser and other war leaders for trial on charges of violating the laws of war.

Political Chaos, Putsches, and the End of Money

The immediate impact of the Versailles Treaty on Germany was twofold: it led to the first cabinet crisis within the new democratic government, and it inspired a soldiers' revolt against the republic. The first of these events occurred when the Scheidemann cabinet received the terms of the treaty, found the provisions unacceptable, and resigned on June 20, 1919. More serious was the military's reaction to the treaty. As previously noted, the provisions dealing with the future of the German military were devastating, especially on the German officers' corps. When the implications of the treaty had been fully recognized, several leaders of the German military, notably General Walter Reinhardt, commander of the provisional Reichswehr, began to think seriously about armed resistance. These still inchoate plans, however, did not immediately come to fruition because even the most die-hard generals realized that opposition to the Allies was hopeless. Some military leaders now shifted their rage to the hapless republican government, blaming it for being pliantly submissive to the will of the Allied powers.

The republican government, in the meantime, was under intense pressure from the Allied powers to reduce the German army to a peacetime force of one hundred thousand men and to disband all paramilitary

(Free Corps) forces that were still roaming the country. This only served to fuel the military's resentments, resulting in a series of mutinous acts aimed at overthrowing the government. The most serious of these acts came in March 1920 when several army officers conspired to overthrow the Weimar Republic.

The chief characters in this plot were General Walther von Lüttwitz, commander of the Berlin army district; Captain Hermann Erhardt, commander of the Second Marine Brigade, which had helped in crushing the Communists but was now itself singled out for dissolution; and Wolfgang Kapp, an undistinguished Prussian civil servant. Lüttwitz's plan was crude and simple: march on Berlin, expel the hated Ebert government, and establish a military dictatorship with Kapp as a pliant figurehead.[40] The general sounded out various prominent military leaders, including Reinhardt, General Hans von Seeckt, and Ludendorff. Although they were noncommittal, Lüttwitz came away with the unmistakable impression that the army would not fire on its own soldiers.

The immediate cause of the Kapp Putsch was the government's policy of demobilizing the army to bring it in line with the one hundred thousand volunteer force dictated by the Versailles Treaty. When Ebert rejected Lüttwitz's demands for the reinstatement of two Free Corps units, including one that was commanded by Captain Hermann Erhardt, the general gave orders to Erhardt to march on Berlin. The government asked General von Seeckt, the army's chief of staff, whether the military could be counted on in the present crisis. Seeckt, a brilliant but Sphinxlike oracle, replied laconically that the army could not fire on its own soldiers. Seeckt then gingerly stepped aside, waiting to support the winner.[41]

Abandoned by its own army, the republican government had little choice but to leave the capital, fleeing first to Dresden and then to Stuttgart. Before leaving Berlin, however, the government appealed to all German workers to support a general strike in order to thwart the putschists from gaining political control. On the morning of March 13, 1920, shortly after the Ebert government had abandoned Berlin, the men of the Erhardt and Baltikum brigades, helmets gleaming with swastikas, marched jubilantly into the German capital. At the Brandenburg Gate they were met by the chief conspirators — Lüttwitz, Ludendorff, and Kapp — and marched in solidarity to the Wilhelmstrasse, where they proceeded to take over the abandoned government buildings.

It was one thing to seize empty government buildings and quite another to rule the country. The new leaders were singularly inexperienced in the art of government, and they discovered quickly that they had little support. Their incompetent bungling even prevented the coup from being announced in the Sunday newspapers because Fräulein Kapp had trouble in finding a typewriter in the chancellery. Worse, banks refused to make loans; fraternal right-wing organizations remained noncommittal; the army continued its wait-and-see attitude; and the general strike was so successful that most economic activity came to a standstill throughout Germany. On March 20, it was all over. Lüttwitz and Kapp resigned and the republican government returned to Berlin.

In retrospect, the Kapp Putsch revealed, among other things, how unreliable the military turned out to be in the defense of the republic, especially when attacks against it were launched by right-wing forces. The army would suppress left-wing revolts with great alacrity; it was thoroughly unreliable, however, when it was called upon to defend the republic from right-wing extremists. In fact, the military increasingly became a rallying point of right-wing fanatics throughout the Weimar Republic.

A case in point was the takeover of the Ruhr by a Red army of eighty thousand in the wake of the Kapp Putsch. The hapless Ebert regime was now put in the uncomfortable position of having to call upon the very forces that had proved so unreliable just a week before. Yet this time Seeckt had no qualms in putting down the revolt. The army had weathered another crisis, and Ebert's hopes of dismantling the officers' corps and rebuilding a new republican army were disappointed for good.[42]

The Kapp Putsch had two further results: it brought right-wing reactionaries to power in Bavaria, and it forced the German government to call the first regular election. While the Kapp Putsch was unfolding, General Arnold von Möhl, who commanded the armed forces in the Munich area, decided to launch an insurrection of his own. He informed the Bavarian prime minister, Johannes Hoffmann, that he could no longer guarantee the safety of the government and suggested that all authority should be vested in his own hands. Hoffmann convened his cabinet and urged rejection of Möhl's presumptuous proposal, but most cabinet members did not support Hoffmann. They favored, instead, another plan by which Möhl would exercise complete military control, while Gustav von Kahr, the governor of Upper Bavaria, would administer all civil affairs in the state. Hoffmann resigned along with his entire cabinet. On March 16, 1920, Gustav von Kahr was elected prime minister by the Bavarian diet. Bavaria now became the land of the extreme right, spearheading the opposition against Berlin democracy.[43]

The election of June 6, 1920, saw a decided shift to the right, a disappointing setback to the supporters of the republic. The parties of the coalition suffered heavy losses, the most damaging being sustained by the Democrats, who lost over 3,000,000 votes and saw their mandates in the Reichstag shrink from 75 to 41. The other two parties of the Weimar coalition, the Center Party and the Social Democratic Party (SPD), also lost seats. The Center Party lost 27 of its 91 seats and saw its popular vote melt from 5,641,800 to 2,333,700, a loss that was to some extent offset by the fact that Bavarian voters had shifted their allegiance from the Center Party to its Bavarian counterpart, the Bavarian People's Party. The Social Democrats held on to only 102 of their 163 seats and took a devastating beating in the popular polls, dropping from 11,500,000 to 6,100,000. The Independent Socialists, on the other hand, picked up 84 seats in the Reichstag, many of them undoubtedly at the expense of the SPD. The parties to the right of center staged a strong comeback. The German National People's Party (DNVP) increased its following from 2,873,523 to 3,736,778 votes and increased its mandates in the Reichstag from 42 to 71 seats. Gustav Stresemann's German People's Party (DVP) also gained in standing, increasing its following by 2,000,000 and sending 65 deputies to the Reichstag.

Controlling only 205 out of 452 mandates, the parties of the Weimar coalition had effectively lost control over the Reichstag. Moreover, forces unfriendly to the republic were now outnumbering its supporters. This being the case, Chancellor Müller and his Social Democrats made a dreadful decision: they withdrew from the governance of the republic because they refused to serve in a coalition in which there was a preponderance of bourgeois representation. Although the SPD was later represented in the Stresemann cabinet of 1923 and the second Müller cabinet of 1928–30, its active participation in governing had come to an end in 1920. By resigning itself to a place of opposition, the SPD yielded the field to those parties that had shown, at best, a lukewarm support for the republic.[44]

The new government that finally emerged from the shambles of the original Weimar coalition was a bourgeois coalition backed by the German People's Party, the Center, and the Democrats. It was headed by Konstantin Fehrenbach, a prominent leader of the Center Party and a strong supporter of the republic. However, the Fehrenbach cabinet fell soon after the Inter-Allied Reparations Commission announced on April 27, 1921, that the final reparations bill, which, as mentioned above, had been left a blank in the Versailles Treaty, would come to 35 billion dollars in gold (132 billion gold marks). On May 5, one day after the Fehrenbach government fell, the commission gave Germany a six-day ultimatum to accept the reparations bill unconditionally and warned that failure to do so would result in an invasion of the Ruhr. After a universal outcry, the Weimar coalition assumed responsibility, counseling a policy of fulfillment rather than resistance, as the nationalists had urged. The new chancellor, Josef Wirth, was a left-wing member of the Center Party who strongly believed in social reform, a policy warmly applauded by the left but vehemently opposed by right-wing members of his own party. Wirth now faced the unenviable task of accepting yet another Allied ultimatum. When his government accepted the ultimatum, the nationalists, who had shrouded themselves in the mantle of noble patriotism, immediately screamed treason and sellout. They were especially infuriated by Wirth's appointment of Walter Rathenau to the post of minister of reconstruction and later minister of foreign affairs. Rathenau, a Jew, was universally despised by right-wing nationalists whose hatred of him was expressed in a popular couplet: "Knallt ab den Walter Rathenau / Die gottverfluchte Juden-sau — Shoot down that Walter Rathenau / That cursed, goddamned Jewish sow."[45]

Both Wirth and Rathenau rejected the idea of resisting the Allies; they favored a policy of fulfillment, hoping to persuade the Allies of Germany's good intentions. To do so in a highly charged atmosphere of political rancor, however, proved practically impossible. Vicious attacks were now launched by right-wing nationalists against those who supported this policy of fulfillment. The more extreme nationalists formed conspiratorial societies vowing vengeance against traitors, Jews, liberals — in short, against anyone who counseled cooperation with the Allies. The most notorious of these societies was called Organization "C" (*Consul*), founded by none other than Captain Hermann Erhardt of Kapp Putsch fame. Its purpose was to combat the antinational Weimar Constitution, to set up secret "Vehm" tribunals to try and execute "traitors," and to eradicate the whole array of evils besetting the fatherland — parliamentary democracy, Social Democrats, Communists, pacifists, and Jews.[46] On August 2, 1921, two ex-officers and members of Organization "C" murdered Matthias Erzberger, managed to escape abroad, and were celebrated as heroes by many Germans.

The task of the Wirth government, which was exposed to a constant chorus of right-wing denunciations, was not made any easier by having its policy of fulfillment repeatedly undercut by the Allies themselves. On March 20, 1921, a plebiscite was held in Upper Silesia that resulted in a two-to-one victory for Germany. Nevertheless, in October 1921 the Allies partitioned the area, awarding the most valuable industrial districts to Poland. Wirth resigned in protest but was persuaded by Ebert to form a new government. Several months later Wirth made one of his most controversial decisions by appointing Walter Rathenau as foreign minister.

Rathenau's appointment was a courageous but also a politically explosive decision. Rathenau, the son of a wealthy German-Jewish industrialist, possessed a brilliant grasp of organizing economic resources, a skill that led to his appointment in 1916 as head of the "war material" section. In this capacity, Rathenau instituted a kind of "war socialism," systematically subordinating all production to state needs. After the war, he helped found the Democratic Party and dedicated his service to the economic recovery of Germany. Author of two best-sellers, urbane cosmopolitan, technocrat, gifted musician and painter, Rathenau embodied qualities that incited narrow-minded reactionaries to homicidal fury.

Under Rathenau's leadership, Weimar Germany scored its first success in foreign policy. Rathenau tried to parry France's thrust of isolating Germany through alliances with eastern European powers by turning to the Soviet Union, the other isolated pariah besides Germany after World War I. In April 1922, Wirth and Rathenau attended an international economic conference at Genoa; at nearby Rapallo, they concluded a treaty of friendship with the Soviet Union. By the terms of this agreement, the two countries agreed to establish diplomatic relations, consented not to ask reparations of each other, and entered into close economic relations. In a secret provision, subsequently concluded between General von Seeckt and the Russian general staff, the two countries established close military relations.

The Treaty of Rapallo caused considerable consternation abroad, especially in France where Raymond Poincaré had been advocating a strong anti-German position for some time. Inside Germany, the treaty did little to raise the prestige of the government. On the contrary, the pervasive atmosphere of hysterical opposition to the republic was intensifying, culminating on June 24, 1922, in the assassination of Walter Rathenau by right-wing terrorists hatched by Organization "C." Chancellor Josef Wirth, in paying homage to the memory of Rathenau in an emotional Reichstag address, cried out that "the enemy is on the right."

The political repercussions of Rathenau's murder only temporarily lowered the emotional tensions that were still polarizing German politics. Although a law in "defense of the republic," passed shortly after Rathenau's murder, prescribed heavy punishment for terrorists, conspiratorial activities against the government continued unabated and criminal actions, especially when perpetrated by the right, were treated very leniently. For example, of Rathenau's assassins, one was killed by the police, another committed suicide, and a third was given a prison sentence of fifteen years but only served seven. During the period 1918–22, right-wing groups committed 354 political murders as compared to 22 murders committed by left-wing groups. Of the 354 murders committed by the right, 326 went unpunished, whereas 17 of the 22 murders perpetrated by the left were punished severely, 10 by execution.[47] The conclusion is inescapable: the German legal system, backed by a substantial majority of the German upper and middle classes, sympathized with the opponents of the republic.

In the meantime, the republic still found itself in a political quagmire. Josef Wirth had attempted to broaden his government by including members of the Conservative People's Party, but the Social Democrats refused to serve in such a government. On November 14, 1922, Wirth resigned; he was replaced by Wilhelm Cuno, head of the Hamburg-America Steamship Line. Cuno was an ebullient executive with a shrewd business sense, qualities that were shortly to be put to a severe test.

Germany's economic position was deteriorating daily as a result of runaway inflation. These inflationary difficulties stemmed primarily from a series of imprudent government fiscal policies that originated in World War I.[48] The German government did not try to finance the war by taxation but rather by floating internal bonds. In addition, the government also removed restrictions on the circulation of notes not covered by gold reserves; it further authorized the establishment of Loan Banks with the right to extend credit on collateral that had not previously been approved for Reichsbank loans under existing regulations. These Loan Banks extended liberal credits to a variety of borrowers — the federal states, municipalities, and newly founded war corporations. Funds were simply provided by printing paper money.

As war costs increased, the government resorted more and more to the printing presses, driving up the amount of currency in circulation and devaluing the mark. By 1918 the mark stood at half the gold parity of 1914. The war hid the problem of inflation, but the pressures of defeat, coupled with the economic burdens imposed on Germany by the Versailles Treaty, brought the problem to the surface in dramatic terms. The whole German economy was now cracking under the impact of years of deficit spending and burdensome obligations imposed by the Allies.

The immediate cause of the collapse of the German economy was the invasion of the Ruhr by the French on January 11, 1923. The French prime minister, Raymond Poincaré, was a Germanophobe who strongly believed that the Germans were willfully deceiving the Allies that they could not faithfully meet their financial obligations. The French had already spent billions of francs in restoring their wartorn areas, expecting the Germans to pay for every penny of it. Poincaré adamantly rejected Cuno's request for a moratorium on reparations payments and then tried to galvanize other Allied powers into supporting military intervention. Neither the British nor the Americans, however, believed that an Allied invasion of the Ruhr was justified. Poincaré pressed on regardless, merely waiting for a legal pretext. This came when the Reparations Commission declared Germany in default on the delivery of 140,000 telegraph poles.

On January 11, 1923, a French-Belgian force invaded the Ruhr, seized its industries and mines, and stirred up separatist feelings aimed at further weakening the unity of the Reich.[49] French occupying troops acted harshly and brutally. Bloody clashes were the order of the day. The German government responded to the French invasion with a policy of "passive resistance," which meant that all economic activity came to a standstill in the Ruhr. The German economy now became unglued because the government, in an effort to subsidize the Ruhr workers who had gone on strike, resorted to printing more and more paper money. Inflation reached fantastic heights; unemployment soared. Even with the best intentions, the German government simply could not meet all of its social obligations; it was already chaffing under the weight of its obligations to the Allies, to its war veterans, to the unemployed, to the aged.

Germans were caught in a vortex from which there seemed no escape. The world was upside-down: a simple penny postage stamp cost 5 million marks, an egg 80 million, a pound of meat 3.2 billion, a pound of butter 6 billion, a pound of potatoes 50 million, a glass of beer 150 million. Prices changed from day to day, prompting people to rush to the stores armed with satchels of worthless money to buy simple necessities.

To many Germans this period seemed like an economic apocalypse. Konrad Heiden has referred to it as the "end of money,"[50] the end of roseate visions of material affluence, and the end of all secular faiths in progress. We might add that it also seemed like the end of faith in government, its good word, and its assurance that the savings of ordinary citizens would be protected. For nine years, Germans had sacrificed their lives and their savings to the government. In return, the government had squandered a third of the national wealth in a futile war as a result of which war loans, savings, and investments were now worthless. The savings of thrifty middle-class Germans were wiped out. It was not uncommon for German savers to receive polite letters from bank managers informing them that "the bank deeply regrets that it can no longer administer your deposit of sixty-eight thousand marks, since the costs are all out of proportion to the capital. We are therefore taking the liberty of returning your capital. Since we have no bank-notes of small enough denominations at our disposal, we have rounded out the sum to one million marks. Enclosure: one 1,000,000 mark bill."[51] To add insult to injury, the envelope was adorned by a canceled five million mark postage stamp.

While the majority of middle-class Germans were ruined by the collapse of 1923, never fully regaining their trust in the government, a few clever financial manipulators grew fabulously wealthy by securing massive bank credits, promptly investing in "physical values" (real estate, businesses), and repaying the debts with devalued money. It was in this manner that Hugo Stinnes, already a wealthy man before 1923, bought up at random large numbers of businesses, including banks, hotels, newspapers, paper mills, and so on.

Stinnes was a stuffed shirt and not given to lavish displays of money, but there were hundreds like him who spent garishly and contributed much to the growing atmosphere of moral decadence and cynicism, an atmosphere that has been so vividly captured in the music, art, and popular entertainment of the 1920s. While a few grew rich, the country as a whole steadily deteriorated. Unemployment increased, farmers hoarded their produce, manufacturing dropped, and millions of thrifty savers lost all of their savings.

Since Cuno did not offer a solution to the crisis, the Social Democrats withdrew their support and called for stronger leadership. On August 12, 1923, Ebert appointed Gustav Stresemann, leader of the German People's Party, as chancellor of the new government. The new chancellor, destined to become one of the most important statesmen of the Weimar Republic, faced staggering problems: the Ruhr was occupied by the French; Communist-Socialist regimes had taken power in Thuringia and Saxony; Communist insurrections plagued Hamburg; Bavaria had fallen into the hands of right-wing reactionaries who threatened to secede from the Reich; Germany's eastern borders were threatened by the Poles; and the mark stood at 4.6 million to the dollar. It was in this volatile atmosphere that an obscure corporal of World War I, leader of a growing right-wing party, determined to overthrow the Weimar Republic. His name was Adolf Hitler.

Chapter 3

The Rise of Adolf Hitler

Ancestral Roots

In July 1938, two months after Hitler annexed Austria, the Austrian Land Registries received an order to conduct a land survey of Döllersheim and surrounding areas in order to determine whether the terrain was suitable for army maneuvers. In 1939 the citizens of Döllersheim were forcibly evacuated, and the village, along with its heavily wooded countryside, was blasted beyond recognition by mortar shells and thoroughly ploughed over by army tanks. The village of Döllersheim was part of the poverty-stricken Waldviertel, a section of Austria lying between the Danube and the Bohemian border. It was also the birthplace of Hitler's ancestors. Why is it that the triumphant conqueror of his native Austria encouraged the obliteration of his ancestral roots, rendering the birthplace of his father and the site of his grandmother's grave all but unrecognizable?[1] The answers to this question, leading us toward the mystery of Hitler's roots and of his subsequent actions to obscure his beginnings, represent the first clue to his character.

In 1837, a forty-one-year-old maid by the name of Maria Anna Schickelgruber (1796–1847) returned to her native village of Strones, pregnant and unmarried. Her family treated her as a moral leper and refused to have anything to do with her. A tenant farmer named Trummelschlager finally took pity on her and gave her food and shelter. On June 7, 1837, Maria Anna Schickelgruber gave birth to a baby boy. Since Strones was too small to be a parish, the child was baptized in nearby Döllersheim as Aloys (later spelled Alois) Schickelgruber, "illegitimate." The space for the father's name was left blank, a common practice in an area where inbreeding was as frequent as it was notorious. The only difference was that this illegitimate child was no ordinary bastard but the father of the future leader of the German Reich — Adolf Hitler.

Three major candidates have been suggested as Alois Schickelgruber's real father: a wealthy Graz Jew by the name of Frankenberger; Johann Georg Hiedler, the man Maria Anna married five years after giving birth to Alois; and Johann Nepomuk Hiedler, the brother of Johann Georg and the effective foster father of Alois.[2]

Frankenberger was the first and most spectacular of these candidates. While awaiting execution for war crimes at Nuremberg, Hitler's former Reich minister, Hans Frank, produced a sensational revelation about Hitler's ancestral roots. In a dramatic autobiography entitled *Im Angesicht des Galgens* (In sight of the gallows), Frank revealed that a highly agitated Hitler called on him in 1930 to look into allegations that he had Jewish blood in his veins, a potentially devastating revelation because it would have jeopardized Hitler's whole ideological position.[3] Frank stated that he promptly went to work and supposedly discovered that Hitler's father was the illegitimate child of Maria Anna Schickelgruber, who, at the time her baby was conceived, had been employed as a cook in the household of a Jewish family in Graz by the name of Frankenberger. Frank even claimed that "starting on the day the child was born and continuing right up to its fourteenth year, Frankenberger Senior paid maintenance to the mother on behalf of his nineteen year old son."[4] The Frankenbergers, we are told, continued to correspond with Maria Anna Schickelgruber for many years, and underlying everything they said in their letters was the tacit understanding that the baby had been begotten in circumstances that made it a duty of the Frankenbergers to pay for its maintenance.[5]

When confronted with this uncorroborated account, Hitler is said to have denounced this story as a blatant lie, insisting that his grandmother had personally assured him that the story was false and that she only took the money from the Jew because she was so poor.[6] If Hitler really made this statement to Frank, he was obviously lying — his grandmother had died more than forty-two years before he was born! Frank's account was probably based on hearsay, but if Frank actually reported this information to Hitler, the German dictator had cause to be alarmed. We know that he was dismayed by reports insinuating that his family contained Jewish blood. His own stepnephew, William Patrick Hitler, made sensational statements to the effect that his famous uncle had a Jewish grandfather. Since Hitler had made anti-Semitism the motivating force of his ideology, the revelation that his own grandfather might have been a Jew would have had a devastating impact on the rising Nazi movement. Although no shred of evidence has yet surfaced proving that Hitler was one-quarter Jewish, the evidence indirectly suggests that Hitler suspected that he might have been poisoned by Jewish blood — a terrible knowledge to a man who was so obsessed with paranoid fear of Jews.[7]

Near to Alois's familial orbit there are two other obvious paternal candidates — the brothers Johann Georg and Johann Nepomuk Hiedler. Johann Georg Hiedler, who married Maria Anna Schickelgruber after the birth of her son, was an unemployed journeyman-miller who seems never to have held a full-time job in his life. According to one source, Johann Georg and his wife were so impoverished that at one point they did not even possess a bed and had to sleep in a feeding trough for cattle.[8] It was for this reason that Maria Anna turned her son over to

Johann Nepomuk Hiedler, her husband's brother, who took the boy to his farm in Spital and raised him as his son. Alois never saw his mother and his stepfather again.

At the age of thirteen the boy left the home of his foster father to be apprenticed as a shoemaker in Vienna. Later he managed to enter the Imperial Board of Revenue and, by dint of hard work and dedication, rose to the highest position that was open to a man of his background and education. Johann Nepomuk Hiedler, his foster father, was so proud of Alois's achievements that he urged him to change his name from Schickelgruber to Hiedler. Alois himself probably felt the need to erase his illegitimacy by adopting an honorable ("legitimate") name befitting his new station in life. Accordingly, on June 6, 1876, Johann Nepomuk Hiedler and three other relatives traveled to the town of Weitra and swore before the local notary that Johann Nepomuk's brother, whose name they misspelled as Johann Georg "Hitler," was the real father of Alois Schickelgruber. The next day the same group journeyed to Döllersheim, where the official birth records of Alois Schickelgruber were kept, and persuaded the elderly parish priest to alter the birth register. The priest then changed the item "illegitimate" to "legitimate," crossed out Schickelgruber, filled in Hitler, and added the following marginal note: "The undersigned confirm that Georg Hitler, registered as the father, who is well known to the undersigned witnesses, admits to being the father of the child Alois as stated by the child's mother Maria Anna Schickelgruber, and has requested the entry of his name in the present baptismal register."[9]

After nearly half a century of research, Hitler's biographers still have not been able to pinpoint Alois's real father, though one historian, Werner Maser, has claimed that Johann Nepomuk is the most likely candidate.[10] The truth is that we simply do not know who the real father was, and, since we do not know much about the men in the life of Maria Anna Schickelgruber, the truth will probably never emerge.

Adolf Hitler himself left his origins deliberately obscured, partly because he feared that his grandfather might have been tainted by Jewish blood, partly because his ancestors were illiterate peasants who intermarried and produced illegitimate offspring. A shadowy ancestral past was actually an asset to the future führer because it enabled him to fabricate stories about his legendary origins. In *Mein Kampf*, he merely tells us that his father was an imperial customs official, the "son of a poor cottager," while his mother is idealized as a loving and devoted housewife.[11] The fact is that Adolf Hitler was born on April 20, 1889, in the Austro-German border town of Braunau on the River Inn. Adolf was the fourth child of his father's third marriage. Klara Pölzl, Alois's third wife, was a domestic servant from Spital; she was also the granddaughter of Johann Nepomuk Hiedler. If the latter was the real father of Alois Hitler, this would mean that Adolf Hitler's paternal grandfather and his maternal great-grandfather were one and the same — Johann Nepomuk

Hiedler. It would also mean, as Werner Maser points out, that Klara was the niece of Alois Hitler and the daughter of his half-sister.[12] This tangled web of inbreeding furnishes ample reason why Hitler, eager to portray himself as a messianic leader, did not want to reveal too much about his actual origin. Similarly, Hitler rarely revealed much about his half-brother Alois, his half-sister Angela, or even his sister Paula.

His half-brother Alois married an Irish woman, Bridget Dowling, who later fabricated a story about Adolf Hitler's visit to England in 1912–13.[13] Her son Patrick had traveled to Germany in the 1930s in hopes of extracting money and favors from his famous uncle, but was turned away with a few marks and stern advice about settling down to work. Adolf's half-sister Angela, who had married Leo Raubal, remained much closer to him than his other relatives because he fell deeply in love with her daughter Geli, whose subsequent suicide almost wrecked his career. Angela's son Leo also faded in and out of his orbit. Adolf was fond of Leo, and when the young man, who was a second lieutenant in the engineers, was captured at Stalingrad, Hitler vainly sought to exchange Stalin's son Jakob, who was then in German captivity, for his nephew Leo. As to Hitler's youngest sister, Paula, the only other surviving member of the family, there is compelling evidence that Hitler was very attached to her and saw to it that her needs were met. From 1936 onward she was in charge of his household, using the name Paula Wolf.

Childhood Fixations

Hitler's childhood appeared outwardly normal; the boy was loved and spoiled by his parents, especially after two of his brothers, Gustav and Otto, and his sister Ida died within a span of only two years. Moreover, Hitler's father was a proud and self-made man who had risen in the Imperial Customs Service and left his family well off. Those who knew him described Alois Hitler as a loyal, punctilious bureaucrat, proud of his status, sure of his judgments, and shrewd in his business affairs. His associates also agreed about his terrible temper, his lack of humor, and his officious behavior toward subordinates who risked stern rebuke if they did not address him by his correct title of "Herr Senior Official Hitler."[14] Hitler's father was the type of man who commanded respect and respected command — the authoritarian type who expected the awe, if not the love, of the family he ruled. Although there is evidence to support the claim that Hitler was beaten and, by today's standards, possibly abused as a child, there is little evidence to show that Alois Hitler was any more "abusive" than other fathers of his time or social class.[15] Authoritarian households (which were the norm at this time) can be warm and protective, save on those occasions when children assert their own will and spirit. This was certainly the case with Adolf. As hot-tempered as his father, he began to resist his father's wishes about a choice of career, but since this conflict did not occur until Adolf was twelve or thirteen, it is reasonable to assume that there were few serious domestic conflicts between father and son until that time. Even if we accept Hitler's own story about his father's violent opposition to his artistic goals, we should keep in mind that his half-brother Alois, a good-for-nothing, disappointed his father terribly and left the family when he was fourteen. Later he was imprisoned twice, left Germany for Paris, and ended up in Ireland where he married Bridget Dowling. From Ireland Alois moved to Liverpool, where Patrick was born. In the 1920s he moved back to Germany, opened a restaurant in Berlin called "Alois," was arrested for bigamy, and finally returned to England, much to Adolf's relief. Alois Hitler probably compounded his failure with Alois Jr. by constantly nagging Adolf, thereby alienating his younger son just as he had his older one.

The conflict between Adolf and his father never reached a breaking point because Alois died of a heart attack in January 1903. It is probably true that Adolf's attitude toward his father was extremely ambivalent, but it is doubtful, as one historian has claimed, that this flawed father and son relationship could serve as a textbook description of the Oedipal conflict.[16] Alois Hitler certainly left an indelible mark on his son's character; like the father the son displayed a stubborn will, a groveling awe for authority, a quick and calculating intelligence, and a terrible temper that could be easily aroused but not so easily suppressed.

Hitler's mother, Klara Pölzl, was his father's third wife. She had come to Braunau at the age of sixteen when Alois Hitler was still married to his first wife, Anna Glassl. At that time Alois had affairs with both Klara and Franziska (Fanni) Matzelberger, who became his second wife. When Alois separated from his first wife, he took Fanni to live with him and sent Klara to Vienna so that she would not be a threat to Fanni. In 1883 he married Fanni and had two children by her — Alois Jr. and Angela. However, Fanni contracted tuberculosis and was bedridden for several years. In the meantime, Klara Pölzl returned to Braunau, selflessly took care of Fanni, but also carelessly allowed Alois to make her pregnant. As soon as Fanni died, Alois married Klara. On a grey and damp winter morning in January 1885, Alois, then forty-eight years old, walked down the aisle of the parish church in Braunau with his pregnant bride and married for the third time. Klara was a dutiful, self-effacing young woman who suffered much in her lifetime. Her first three children, Gustav, Ida, and Otto, all died; two of them, Gustav and Ida, tragically passed away after contracting diphtheria. Obviously, Klara showered all her tender care on her fourth child, Adolf.

Since the boy was a sickly looking child, Klara smothered him with care because she feared that he, too, would not be able to survive to adulthood. Adolf was, therefore, overprotected, pampered, and sheltered by his mother, inviting the conclusion that some of Hitler's subsequent tendencies — his obsessive need for self-indulgence, his excessive demands, even his needs for oral gratifications — stemmed from the impaired mother-child relationship.[17]

Numerous attempts have been made to reconstruct Hitler's childhood from psychological perspectives. Although these heuristic aids to historical understanding are indispensable in shedding light on Hitler's childhood, they are largely speculative because they are not based on clinical evidence, so that the conclusions drawn from such unverifiable material, though perhaps sound, are inferential but not scientifically compelling.[18] At the same time psychological approaches to Hitler are necessary because Adolf Hitler was not a "normal" person. Hitler's phobias, abnormalities, and irrationalities cannot be omitted from any historical account of the Nazi period because they later became public policy. In other words, Hitler and his deranged henchmen, some of whom mirrored his pathologies, imposed their characters on German public life; and in so doing, they twisted the shape of normal human behavior. Without some understanding of psychopathology, much of the Hitler movement would be inexplicable.

One thing seems certain about Hitler's childhood: no one who exhibited his later character traits could have enjoyed a happy childhood. We know that the combination of overcrowding, moving, and the deaths of several children made life in the Hitler family less than idyllic. Besides Adolf, there were Alois and Angela; later came Edmund, who died at the age of six, and his sister Paula — all in all there were five children who lived with their parents in relatively crowded conditions. Whether young Adolf witnessed his rough father making love to his wife and interpreted it as rape or assault, as some biographers believe, cannot be known but is entirely conceivable given the circumstances.[19]

Therefore, we suspect that the atmosphere in the parental home was not as idyllic as Hitler would like us to believe. The family also moved frequently. In 1892 the Hitlers moved from Braunau to Passau, then to Hafeld near Lambach on Traun, where Alois bought a house and nine acres of land (1895). It was at Fischlam near Lambach that Adolf entered the first grade of primary school (*Volksschule*), giving no signs of future problems with his studies. In 1896 Alois retired after forty years of service; in the same year Adolf entered the second grade of the denominational school of the ancient Benedictine foundation at Lambach. He received high grades and enjoyed going to school. He also served as a choirboy and admired the Catholic priesthood, especially the abbot Hagen, whose "coat of arms, like the ring of his finger, contained a stylized swastika which he had also carved on the pulpit."[20]

Adolf's father, who now had plenty of leisure time, kept his bees, visited local taverns, and nagged his children. Although father and son now drew closer, they also quarreled frequently. The atmosphere in the home worsened. In 1896 Hitler's half-brother Alois, who could no longer endure the father's bad temper, ran away from home. As a result,

Adolf now became the recipient of his father's well-meaning but often ill-founded moral judgments.

In 1897 the family moved again, this time to Lambach itself, where Alois had bought a new house; a year later they moved for the last time, buying a home in Leonding near Linz on the Danube. Since his father had singled him out for a technical career, Adolf was sent to a state secondary school (*Realschule*) at Linz, but Adolf's interest in school now began to flag and his grades dropped markedly, a fact he later rationalized by saying that he deliberately neglected his studies in order to thwart his father's wishes to turn him into a civil servant.[21] When his father died in 1903, Adolf's performance in school grew even worse. He became increasingly lazy and uncooperative in class. Liberated from his father's tight control, he now did exactly what he pleased because there was no one who had a will to oppose him. At home in Leonding he was the only man living with four women — his mother, aunt, a female lodger, and his sister Paula.

In September 1904, Hitler transferred to another school in Steyr, about fifteen miles from his home, where his mother had rented a room for him. In the absence of tight parental control, his grades now slipped badly. His midterm report indicated failing grades in German, French, mathematics, and stenography; it was such a bad report card that Adolf decided to get drunk and used the document for toilet paper.[22] When the final grade report still showed no improvement, indicating failing grades in mathematics and German, Hitler dropped out of school for good. Throughout his year at Steyr, Hitler was mildly depressed, withdrawn, and periodically ill. Except for his history professor, Dr. Leopold Pötsch, he disliked most of his teachers because "they had no sympathy with youth: their one objective was to stuff our brains and turn us into erudite apes like themselves."[23] His teachers returned the compliment: one of them, Professor Eduard Hümer, who testified at his trial in 1924, had this to say about his former pupil:

> I can recall the gaunt, pale-faced youth pretty well. He had definite talent, though in a narrow field. But he lacked self-discipline, being notoriously cantankerous, willful, arrogant, and irascible. He had obvious difficulty in fitting in at school. Moreover, he was lazy; otherwise, with his gifts, he would have done very much better....But his enthusiasm for hard work evaporated all too quickly. He reacted with ill-concealed hostility to advice or reproof; at the same time, he demanded of his fellow pupils their unqualified subservience, fancying himself in the role of leader.[24]

The death of his father removed the only strong hand that could have guided the sickly looking, self-absorbed, and morose adolescent toward realistic goals. Unfortunately, Adolf now adopted a "negative identity" — the opposite of what his father expected him to be. Rather than continue in school, Adolf persuaded his weak-willed mother to let him quit school. The pretext for this was a pulmonary illness that, as

Adolf himself admitted, suddenly "came to his aid" and settled the issue in his favor.[25]

Adolescent Fantasies

For almost two years (fall of 1905 until 1907) Hitler spent his time in idleness and self-absorption in Linz, the city to which his mother had moved in June 1905. During these two years he fantasized about becoming a great painter and architect; and with his friend August ("Gustl") Kubizek, an upholsterer's son and an eager sounding board for Hitler's fantasies, he visited the opera and the museums. He also read voraciously and indiscriminately, as his friend Gustl later attested:

> That's how my friend was. It was always books and more books! I cannot imagine Adolf without books. At home he would have them piled up all round him. If he was really interested in a book he always had to have it with him.... Books were his whole world.[26]

What sort of books or magazines did the young Hitler read in Linz or Vienna during his most formative and impressionable years? Although he claimed to have read many serious academic works, he read only skin-deep in order to appear sophisticated. There is no reason to doubt Kubizek's testimony that Hitler read in the works of Schopenhauer, Nietzsche, Schiller, Lessing, or Ibsen, but his cognitive development was such that he could not have understood much of what he read. In *Mein Kampf* Hitler himself later admitted that

> by reading I may possibly mean something entirely different from the great average of our so-called intelligentsia! I know people who endlessly "read" a lot, book after book, letter for letter, yet I would not call them "well read." ... They lack the ability to distinguish in a book that which is of value and that which is of no value to them; to keep the one in mind forever, and to overlook, if possible, the other; instead of carrying it with them as so much unnecessary ballast. Reading, furthermore, is not a purpose in itself, but a means to an end. It should serve, first of all, to fill in the frame which is formed by the talents and abilities of the individual;... secondly, reading has to give a general picture of the world.[27]

The fact is that Hitler had a pigeon-hole mind, turning to the printed page for confirmation of already existing biases or beliefs. Since his mind was not formally trained, it habitually lacked what José Ortega y Gasset has called the faculty of ideation — the ability to examine ideas impartially and to refer them to a higher authority of reason and of logic.[28] Hitler's ideas, like those of the uncritical mass to whom he appealed, were little more than "appetites in words," highly charged incentives for action.

Hitler's two years of drifting in Linz already revealed certain future traits: his intense but unorganized enthusiasms; his penchant for fantasy;

his inability to form loving ties. His only friend in Linz, Gustl Kubizek, reports that Adolf enjoyed speechifying for him while the two friends were walking through deserted fields, punctuating his orations with violent movements and vivid gestures. One night, after listening to Wagner's *Rienzi,* Hitler led his friend atop a steep hill, where with feverish excitement he began speaking in a strange raspy voice that did not seem to belong to him. According to Kubizek, Hitler seemed possessed by his own daimon; and in a state of complete ecstasy and rapture, he transferred the character of Rienzi with visionary power to the plane of his own ambitions. This was the first time that Kubizek had seen this aspect of Hitler's developing personality. Adolf's belief that he was singled out to play a providential role in world history must have sounded strange to his young friend.[29]

Hitler's penchant for the grandiose was also reflected in his artistic efforts. The experts agree that Hitler had genuine talent but that his impatient temperament prevented him from developing his craft systematically, thus causing him to fail as a serious artist. He painted numerous landscapes, but his heart and his emotions were in designing monumental buildings and in reorganizing whole cities. Kubizek, who was often his reluctant companion, reports that Hitler would roam through the city of Linz and point out to his friend what would have to be changed and precisely how it would have to be done. The town hall, he told his friend, would have to be removed, and in its place he envisioned a stately modern structure. As to the castle, it had to be completely renovated; the railroad tracks would have to be placed underground because they marred the city. Placing the railroad tracks underground, of course, meant placing the railroad station itself on the edge of town. In addition, he envisioned a railroad running atop the Lichtenberg hill where he would build a sumptuous hotel and erect a nine-hundred-foot steel tower from which one could look down on a high-level bridge spanning the Danube.[30]

It is remarkable that such addictions to fantasy, so characteristic of his later career, were already crystalizing at this time. Most adolescents, of course, daydream, but by adulthood most people cease stubbornly projecting grandiose fantasies against reality. Hitler's tendency to prefer fantasy for reality may be further illustrated by the famous episode of the lottery ticket. Adolf persuaded his friend Gustl to invest in a state lottery ticket, not only convincing him that they would win but already planning how they would spend their prize money. They would rent the entire second floor of a large mansion overlooking the Danube and devote their lives to art:

> There we would make music, study, read — above all, learn; the field of German art was so wide, said my friend, that there could be no end to the study of it....A lady of exquisite culture would preside over the household as a "chatelaine," but this educated lady would have to be

sedate in temperament and years in order that no expectations should be aroused of a kind unwelcome to us.[31]

The sedate and educated lady alluded to in Hitler's description to Gustl represents anticipations of the well-to-do ladies of the upper classes who would later gravitate into the orbit of the young Munich rabble-rouser. In his adolescent years we hear of only one young lady, by the name of Stephanie, to whom Adolf was romantically attracted. Stephanie, however, was more of a romantic abstraction; she was Hitler's unattainable ideal of Nordic beauty. Kubizek tells us that Hitler frequently stalked her through the streets of Linz, but that he was too shy to approach her openly, telling Kubizek that eventually everything would be clear between them without so much as a word being exchanged. When the young lady, who did not even know that Hitler existed, continued to ignore his presence as he shadowed her through Linz, Hitler devised a suicide scenario replete with dialogue and spectators.[32]

Stephanie, like Gustl and all the lofty blueprints, was a means to Hitler's romantic ends. As Werner Maser has said, "Genuine interest in others was totally alien to him — the man who could inflame the masses and identify himself with their longings as few others, never bothered to find out what his friends — let alone strangers — thought and felt."[33] Already in his adolescence, Hitler was well on his way to becoming Shakespeare's self-contained man; like Richard the Third, he could exclaim: "I am myself alone." According to Joachim Fest, Hitler virtually "created everything out of himself and was himself everything at once: his own teacher, organizer of a party and author of its ideology, tactician and demagogic savior, leader, statesman, and for a decade the 'axis' of the world."[34]

Since Hitler wanted to make his mark as a great artist in the world, he looked to Vienna rather than to Linz as a more suitable place for his artistic training. Not even his mother's operation for breast cancer in January 1907 could deflect him from his single-minded pursuit of artistic greatness. In the summer of 1907 his mother gave him seven hundred Kronen from his father's inheritance so that he could support himself for one year as an art student in Vienna.

A young man who pins all his hopes on the fulfillment of artistic greatness, as Adolf Hitler did, is bound to be crushed by failure. When Hitler failed his entrance examination to the Academy of Fine Arts, he was shaken to the depths of his being, and his dream of artistic glory, which he had nourished so tenaciously, seemed to dissipate before his eyes. The rector of the academy, whom he consulted about his failure, supposedly told him that he had no aptitude for painting and that his real talent was in architecture.[35] Hitler's sample paintings were judged below standards because they lacked one quality that he never acquired — the appreciation of the human form. His drawings were technically accomplished but devoid of human feelings. Human figures were afterthoughts or decorative fringes; and in many of his pictures, they stand stiffly and unnaturally like marionettes in a puppet theater. However, despite his failure Hitler did not give up his plans to study at the Academy of Fine Arts. He swore to retake the examination in the fall of 1908, hoping to improve his techniques and his portfolio by the time of his reexamination.

In the meantime, his mother was dying of incurable cancer; and the iodoform treatment recommended by Dr. Eduard Bloch, her Jewish physician, was costly, painful, and futile. A radical mastectomy, performed in January 1907, had not arrested Klara's cancer; and in October of that year, her condition rapidly deteriorated. The treatment that Dr. Bloch prescribed consisted of excruciatingly painful applications of iodoform gauzes onto the suppurating wound. In the words of one expert, "Iodoform absorbed into the system quickens the pulse and attacks the nerves and the brain, inducing restlessness, headaches, insomnia, fever, and — in severe cases — delirium with hallucinations."[36] The stench emitted by Dr. Bloch's treatments infested the tiny rooms in which Adolf, now temporarily returned from Vienna, lovingly took care of his dying mother. It was all to no avail. On a dark gloomy morning, December 21, 1907, Klara died in the glow of a lighted Christmas tree. "In all my career," recalled Dr. Bloch, "I never saw anyone so prostrate with grief as Adolf Hitler."[37]

The death of his mother and the failure at the academy left deep scars on Hitler's personality, setting in motion a set of responses to life that would never leave him. His father and mother were now gone, and he felt utterly alone, helpless, and exposed to capricious forces beyond his control. In self-defense, he withdrew into his shell and conditioned himself for survival in a cruel world. In short, he developed negative survival skills — manipulative, callous, exploitive rather than positive means of adaptation. After his mother's funeral he returned to Vienna with enough money from her inheritance to continue his studies. Werner Maser, who has painstakingly examined Hitler's circumstances at the time, reports that Adolf's share from his father's inheritance, together with his orphan's pension, amounted to a respectable sum, the equivalent of a lawyer's salary, and that the hard fate so often referred to by Hitler did not occur until the young man had squandered most of his inheritance.[38] He returned to Vienna and shared an apartment with his friend Kubizek, who was studying at the Conservatory of Music. Kubizek tells us that his friend had not changed his mode of living at all, but continued to act like a debonair artist in pursuit of his destiny, although he made a half-hearted effort to prepare himself for his second examination. In the autumn of 1908 he sat for the examination and failed again. When Kubizek returned from a brief spell in the military, he discovered that his friend had moved out without leaving a forwarding address.

The Homeless Outsider, 1908–13

Between 1908 and 1913 Hitler's movements become obscured. Having exhausted his legacy, he was forced to live in men's hostels and cheap apartments, eking out a marginal existence as a dispensable member of Viennese society. Looking back on this period, Hitler later wrote that "at that time I formed an image of the world and a view of life which became the granite foundation for my actions. I have had to add but little to that which I had learned then and I have had to change nothing....Vienna was and remained for me the hardest, but also the most thorough, school of my life."[39]

After Adolf Hitler moved out of the apartment he had been sharing with his friend Kubizek, his financial and psychological condition steadily deteriorated as he sank lower and lower into the ranks of rejected humanity. His only source of income was the orphan's pension that he shared with his sister Paula, but since this amounted to only twenty-five kronen, hardly enough to buy food, he was forced to become a *Bettgeher,* a lodger who rented beds in private homes or, at the last resort, sought shelter in squalid mass quarters (*Massenquartiere*). In the summer he would sometimes sleep in the open, either on a park bench or under an archway, but when the weather turned cold, he sought refuge in the hostel for the homeless in the Meidling district. The asylum housed a quarter of a million homeless people in 1909 and was run by a private philanthropic society whose major donations came from a wealthy Jewish family.[40]

From the beginning of 1910 until his move to Munich in May 1913, Hitler lived in this hostel for the homeless on 27 Meldemannstrasse, renting a private sleeping cubicle for three kronen a week. The rules of the hostel specified that a lodger could not occupy his bed until nine o'clock at night and had to vacate it by nine in the morning. The hostel, however, offered several amenities: a day reading room, a smoking room, and a canteen. Not all the occupants of the hostel were vagrants; quite a number of residents, in fact, came from respectable backgrounds, found themselves in dire circumstances, and simply waited for a change in their fortunes.[41]

The young Hitler now began to mingle with desperate and hardened characters who saw life as a jungle in which only the most ruthless had a chance of surviving. In late 1909 Hitler teamed up with a vagabond from Germany named Reinhold Hanisch, a garrulous and dishonest good-for-nothing who saw in Hitler a man he could use for his own profit. Appealing to Hitler's weakest side — his vanity and self-importance — Hanisch offered himself to Hitler as a sales agent, promising him that he would sell his artistic masterpieces. Clinging to his dream of artistic greatness, which had surprisingly withstood his recent rejection by the Academy of Fine Arts, Hitler now produced a steady stream of small pictures, most of them copies of postcards and old prints. This arrangement proved eminently suitable to Hitler's Bohemian temperament. Since he was too lazy to draw or paint scenes from life, he preferred to turn out quick reproductions whenever it struck his fancy. Hanisch managed to hawk quite a number of Hitler's pictures to good-hearted Viennese citizens and art dealers.

Hanisch's attempts to prod the lazy artist into a steady and reliable routine, which would have meant self-discipline and hard work, were to no avail, and in the summer of 1910 their partnership came to an abrupt end. In August, Hitler signed a written complaint at Brigittenau police station, accusing Hanisch of defrauding him of two pictures — a complaint that resulted in his partner's arrest and eight-day jail sentence. Hanisch later took revenge by spreading libelous and largely untrue stories about Hitler's private life to the press. After annexing Austria in 1938, Hitler struck back at Hanisch by having him tracked down and killed, thus erasing another embarrassing reminder of his Viennese past.[42]

The "granite foundation" that Hitler developed during his poverty-ridden years in Vienna was based on three interrelated attitudes — social Darwinism, anti-Communism, and anti-Semitism. These three convictions, it should be noted, were psychological expressions of Hitler's inner conflicts; they were not, as he would like us to believe, the result of studious reading habits or objective studies of current events. Hitler's convictions were either rationalizations of personal weaknesses or powerful projections of unrealistic fantasies. The truth is that Hitler intellectualized his deep-seated resentments; and by claiming that his hatred of Jews or Communists was motivated by intellectual reasons, he deliberately clouded the true source of his prejudices.

Looking back on this period Hitler observed, "Vienna, the city that to so many represents the idea of harmless gaiety, the festive place for merry-making, is to me only the living memory of the most miserable time of my life."[43] Reduced to poverty, stripped of his self-esteem, and envious of the "festive place of merry-making," he found himself among the dregs of society, but for that reason uniquely qualified, he thought, to report what the world was really like. In *Mein Kampf* the language he used to describe the real Vienna was colored by jarring images taken from scatology or venereal disease. If we bid farewell to the glittering facade of the Ringstrasse and descend into the real Vienna, he later wrote, we will encounter the wretched hovels of the impoverished, a world of "repugnant filth," criminality, prostitution, drunkenness, and sexual abuse. "Those who have never felt the grip of this murderous viper," Hitler declared in a particularly ill-chosen but highly revealing outburst, "will never know its poisonous fangs."[44]

These wild expressions are the revelations of a desperate youth whose squalid existence taught him that life was a perpetual struggle for survival and that only the fittest — that is, the most brutal and callous — stood a chance of emerging victoriously from it. Romantic notions of love and affection, of peace and cooperation, are, therefore, so much sentimental claptrap and bourgeois hypocrisy. If the world had treated him with cold indifference and brutality, why should he treat the world with love and kindness? For Hitler it followed that "he who wants to live should fight, therefore, and he who does not want to battle in this world of eternal struggle does not deserve to be alive."[45] He acquired the belief that everything born of gentleness or love somehow reeked of weakness and decadence and that the strong man would rise above such enervating weaknesses. It was probably for this reason that Hitler despised both socialism and Christianity — he regarded these movements as rationalizations of biological weaknesses, as noble rhetorical ideas disguising cowardly motives.

The psychological dimensions of failure are directed either toward the self or toward external forces; the former can involve critical self-examination or self-reproaches, while the latter seeks to ascribe blame by projecting responsibility onto larger and often amorphous forces beyond one's control. These are coping mechanisms, each involving varying degrees of social adjustment or further maladjustments. It is not surprising that Hitler's failures involved externalization of conflict or feelings of victimization; but it is interesting to note that his reaction to the presumed oppressor was one of admiration. Despite his position as a social failure, which should have moved him in the direction of left-wing movements, Hitler admired the strength and power that had placed the dominant elite into positions of superiority. He may have resented their place and status, but he desired what they possessed — power and authority. Even the capitalists, he later told Otto Strasser, "have worked their way to the top through their capacity, and on the basis of this selection, which again only proves their higher race, they have a right to lead."[46]

The key to much of Hitler's behavior resides in this attitude toward dominant authority, which Wilhelm Reich has described as one of ambivalence, alternating between awed submission and resentful opposition.[47] In this sense, Hitler's outlook was to some extent a reflection of the lower middle class, whose precarious social position, wedged between the feudal elites at the top and the growing working population at the bottom, made a definite social commitment very difficult. The German and Austrian middle class, however, still acknowledged its dependence on the old ruling classes, finding it difficult to develop an autonomous bourgeois lifestyle. In Austria and Germany the middle class mimicked the attitudes of the ruling classes, while at the same time dreading contamination by proletarian tastes. Similarly, young Hitler also identified with the charisma of power, while at the same time regarding the workers as inferior types, as a dismal, gruesome mass. Kubizek reports that the young Hitler clung to the pretense of refinement and social polish, wearing a decent suit, a dark, good-quality overcoat, a dark hat and carrying a walking stick with an ivory handle, while at the same time inveighing against the outrageous suggestion that he should accept a "mere bread-and-butter job."[48]

Sinking into the grey bleakness of proletarian life represented the greatest fear to the middle class in general and Adolf Hitler in particular. In 1923 and then again in 1929, when this fear threatened to became reality, Adolf Hitler knew how to exploit it because it had been a permanent part of his psychological frame of mind since his Vienna years. Like Hitler, the German middle class could not be pulled in the direction of socialism or Communism because the authoritarian conscience was too deeply embedded in the collective psyche of the German people. The young Hitler did not defect to the enemy on the left; instead, he preferred to identify himself with the conservative establishment in Germany. A man who lived the English equivalent of the conservative style of life, Winston Churchill, instinctively recognized this attitude in Hitler and even called such an identification with conservative German authority "an honorable inversion of loyalties."[49]

The fact is that Hitler epitomized the feelings of the German *Mittelstand* and its admiration, however grudgingly, of the old feudal values. As a declassed outsider, a failed artist in a social no-man's-land, he preferred to identify himself with the heroic and manly virtues of the aristocracy rather than the vulgar tastes of the proletariat. Hitler's reaction to proletarian ideology, Marxist or social democratic, was one of unbridled condemnation. In his mind, even democratic socialism was tantamount to Communism. The Marxist inspired ideology of the working people was a living obscenity, a "pestilential whore covered with the mask of social virtue and brotherly love."[50] He despised its cosmopolitanism and its commitment to class ties at the exclusion of national ties. He also believed that by uplifting the weakest link in the social scale, social democratic politicians had violated the law of nature, a law that always favors the strongest race, nation, or class.

As Hitler listened to the noisy and somewhat chaotic proceedings of the Austrian Reichsrat, he came away with a lasting antipathy toward the democratic process. Parliamentary democracy, he became convinced, was nothing more than endless haggling and cheap compromising, and its much vaunted principle of majority rule made robust decision making difficult. All the great deeds of history, he believed, had been accomplished by exceptional geniuses who often swam against the stream of majority opinion. Since the "masses' aversion to every superior genius is an instinctive one," he avowed, "one cannot contradict too sharply the absurd opinion that men of genius are born out of general elections."[51]

Besides contempt for various working-class social ideologies and a preference for crude social Darwinian ideas, Hitler also acquired a virulent hatred of Jews during his Vienna years. According to Werner Maser, "Despite the wealth of information gained from an analysis of all the available data on Hitler's medical, intellectual and social backgrounds, there is still no satisfactory explanation of his anti-Semitism."[52] Maser's judgment is still fundamentally correct except for one important omission: Hitler's anti-Semitism was not merely a prejudice or an aberration but a pathology.

Millions of Germans, Frenchmen, Englishmen, and Americans were prejudiced against the Jews, having been brought up on long-standing stereotypical images of negative Jewish personality traits. Such prejudices, as we have seen, were deeply ingrained in Western consciousness and in Western institutions; but they did not result in organized "assembly-line" techniques of mass murder. Hitler's anti-Semitism went beyond prejudice; it was a psychopathology of the sort that must be ranked with witchcraft and demonology in the history of the human race. If seen in this light, how did it come about that Adolf Hitler integrated anti-Semitic prejudices into a delusional system of thought?

Although we lack the clinical evidence, we possess a wealth of data, much of it gleaned from Hitler's own words, that clearly points toward a developing psychopathology. Anti-Semitism, in fact, was the oxygen of Hitler's political life. Once it had crystallized, it remained a permanent feature of his character, increasing steadily in virulence up to his final moments in his underground tomb beneath the Reich chancellery. Although few historians now doubt that Hitler was subject to a serious delusion, it is still not clear when or how he acquired his morbid fear and virulent hatred of Jews. Hitler may have been mildly exposed to anti-Semitic prejudices in Linz, but as he admits in *Mein Kampf,* he encountered few Jews there who fit the stereotypes of his later obsessions. His mother's physician, Dr. Eduard Bloch, had been Jewish, as had been a number of people with whom he had some personal contact. At the hostel for the homeless, Hitler was on close terms with Josef Neumann, a Jewish companion who was also down on his luck.[53] Such personal contacts with Jews seem to have had little influence in shaping his growing anti-Semitism. The origin of Hitler's anti-Semitism appears to have been rooted more in ideological conviction than in personal experience; it was the result of his exposure to noxious anti-Semitic literature during his Vienna period reinforced by the traumatic effects associated with the German defeat in World War I. When Hitler lived on Felberstrasse in Vienna, he would often buy copies of Lanz von Liebenfels's anti-Semitic magazine *Ostara,* which was on sale at a nearby tobacco shop. On one occasion, as mentioned above, he even sought out the cranky editor to obtain some of the back issues that he had missed.[54] He also steeped himself in the various tabloids, most notably the *Deutsches Volksblatt,* that dished up nauseating articles on Jews, sex, and other prejudices aimed at tantalizing a gullible public. Hitler also fell under the influence of political demagogues such as Viennese mayor Karl Lueger and the pan-German nationalist Georg Ritter von Schönerer.

In conjunction with his contact with these anti-Semitic ideas and personalities, Hitler became personally aware of the growing presence of Jews on the streets of Vienna. Several statistics may be helpful in this

connection: in 1857 a mere 6,217 Jews made up slightly more than 2
percent of Vienna's population; by 1910, however, the Jewish population had risen to 175,318, or 8.6 percent.[55] The proportion of Jewish
students at the higher schools (*Mittelschulen,* gymnasiums, or universities) rose spectacularly. By 1913, 27.6 percent of those enrolled at
the *Mittelschulen* were Jewish; and by 1914, just before the outbreak
of World War I, Jews constituted 27.6 percent of the total enrollment
at the University of Vienna, most of them clustering in such professional fields as medicine, law, and administration.[56] Demographically,
larger and larger numbers of Jews lived in the Leopoldstadt, the poor
section of Vienna, where Hitler had his first fateful encounter with
alien-looking Jews.

The presence of these Jews reinforced latent anti-Semitic prejudices
everywhere, but it caused special alarm among the ranks of the unemployed and the disaffected. Adolf Hitler was the paradigm of the
disaffected outsider who was beginning to see in the Jew the source of all
his problems. He was steeping himself in the anti-Semitic tabloids readily available in every coffeehouse, and his impressionable mind, haunted
by fears of inadequacy, was focusing increasingly on the Jews as the chief
cause of all evils. A few personal experiences seemed to bring the whole
problem into clear focus for Hitler. One day, he later recounted in *Mein
Kampf,* his abstraction of the leering Jew took on flesh and blood as
he came face-to-face with a foreign-looking Jew on the pavements of
Vienna:

> One day when I was walking through the inner city, I suddenly came
> upon a being clad in long caftan, with black curls. Is this also a Jew?
> was my first thought. At Linz they certainly did not look like that. Se-
> cretly and cautiously I watched the man, but the longer I stared at this
> strange face and scrutinized one feature after the other, the more my mind
> reshaped the first question into another form: Is this also a German?[57]

For Hitler the answer was a resounding no. Jews can never be
German because they are racially and religiously different; and their difference is so vast, their character so alien, that they must be removed
from German society by every possible means. Hitler's perception of
the Jews as alien beings was emotionally heightened by his belief that
they smelled differently, that, perhaps, their whole olfactory system was
putrid and offensive — a common reaction of primitive ethnocentricity:

> The moral and physical cleanliness of this race was a point in itself. It
> was externally apparent that these were not water-loving people, and un-
> fortunately one could frequently tell that even with eyes closed. Later the
> smell of these caftan wearers often made me ill. Added to this were their
> dirty clothes and their none too heroic appearance. Perhaps all this was
> not very attractive; aside from the physical uncleanliness, it was repelling
> suddenly to discover the moral blemishes of the chosen people.[58]

The scales seemed to fall from Hitler's eyes: Vienna's foul-smelling Jews were merely the tip of the iceberg, the most visible sign of a deeper malaise that afflicted the whole social organism. Like leeches, the Jews graft themselves on a social body and suck out its blood. Thus, whenever we cut open a social sore, Hitler maliciously observed, we always "find a little Jew, blinded by the sudden light, like a maggot in a rotten corpse."[59] Jewish influence, Hitler believed, was particularly poisonous in the press, the theater, the fine arts, and literature. Jews also have a stranglehold on the economic life of a nation; they exploit shamelessly without replenishing anything. Since they have no commitment to the society in which they reside, they care nothing about its basic values. This is why nothing is sacred to Jews, except their own Jewishness. For this reason, Hitler even claimed to have discovered a connection between Jewishness and prostitution: "When walking at night through the streets and alleys of the Leopoldstadt," Hitler warned, "with every step one could witness things which were unknown to the greater part of the German nation until the war gave the soldiers on the eastern front an opportunity to see similar things.... An icy shudder ran down my spine when seeing for the first time the Jew as a cool, shameless, and calculating manager of this shocking vice, the outcome of the scum of the big city."[60]

The Jew, in Hitler's eyes, was the common denominator of all the negative sides of the social equation. Everything repulsive and offensive, every quality Hitler hated in himself and others, was inevitably projected onto the Jew. When speaking of Jews, Hitler habitually used words drawn from scatology or parasitology, claiming that anything touched by Jewish hands reeked of syphilis, filth, decomposition, maggots, germs, poisoning, bacilli, and so on. In the alley as well as in the haunts of the mighty we always find a leering Jew who wants to exploit and ultimately subvert Aryan purity. In the alley it is the "black-haired Jew boy, diabolic joy in his face, [who] waits in ambush for the unsuspecting girl whom he defiles with his blood and thus robs her from her people."[61] In the haunts of the mighty — the press, the theater, the big corporation, the government itself — the Jew also conspires to defile the nation by means of such powerful corrosive agents as Communism, liberalism, pacifism, and parliamentary democracy.

Robert G. L. Waite probably came close to identifying the real nature of Hitler's anti-Semitism when he observed that Hitler felt "Jewishness to be an evil within himself, a poison to be purged, a demon to be exorcised."[62] Waite's conclusion is that Hitler's anti-Semitism was the product of his psychopathology, the expression of a personality disorder that began in childhood, solidified in adolescence and early adulthood, and was powerfully reinforced and normalized in a society Hitler ultimately shaped to his own personality traits. Hitler's personality traits, according to Waite, are typical of the "borderline personality."[63] Such personalities are paranoid, fantasize about their magical omnipotence,

suffer from unresolved Oedipal conflicts, behave in selfish and narcissistic ways, display marked phobias about dirt, feces, and contamination,
and are prone to gross forms of sexual perversion involving filth. Additionally, borderline personalities are divided selves with dramatically
opposing traits; and since their egos are so shallow, these opposing traits, if left to operate freely, will often give the impression of
double personality. Borderline personalities also tend to reinforce the
divided self by "introjecting" admired qualities (Aryan toughness, will,
masculinity, creativity) while at the same time "projecting" despised
characteristics (degeneracy, softness, femininity) onto outer scapegoats.
Finally, borderline personalities see the world in sharp dichotomies —
in terms of sublime good or radical evil, heroic strength or cowardly
weakness.

Young Hitler certainly displayed some of these traits, and there is no
doubt, judging by his later personality development, that he exhibited
a good many other of these borderline symptoms. On the other hand,
this disorder is often accompanied by many features of other personality
disorders, such as schizotypal, histrionic, narcissistic, and antisocial personality. For this reason, more than one diagnosis is warranted.[64] It is
the contention of this work that Hitler probably suffered from multiple
personality disorders, including borderline personality, but if a leitmotif
can be detected in the chaotic dissonances of his mind, it would probably be that of the sociopathic or antisocial personality disorder.[65] It is,
of course, difficult to perform retroactive psychological evaluations, but
any historian who glosses over Hitler's many written, public, and private
utterances about little Jews in rotting corpses or repulsive, crooked-
legged Jew bastards lusting to rape Aryan girls is neglecting important
psychological evidence. It is impossible to determine the stage of Hitler's personality disorder during his flophouse years in Vienna, but it
seems reasonably certain that the foundation of his anti-Semitism and
his antisocial tendencies was established in those years.

Hitler in Munich, 1913-14

In May 1913 Adolf Hitler arrived in Munich and rented a small attic
room in the home of a tailor called Josef Popp, at 34 Schleissheimerstrasse in the district of Schwabing. He was now twenty-four years old
and still without a sense of direction in his life, continuing the hermitlike
existence he had adopted in Vienna. He was also penniless and lonely,
though psychologically euphoric about the prospect of living in a German city. Vienna, he later wrote, had repelled him because of its ethnic
impurity: that is, its many minorities such as Czechs, Poles, Hungarians,
Ruthenians, Serbs, Croats, and, above all, "the eternal parasitic fungi of
mankind — Jews and more Jews."[66] Munich, he believed, was infinitely

superior in this regard, and he hoped that the light-hearted atmosphere (*Gemütlichkeit*) in Bavaria would stimulate his artistic abilities.

In contrast to Berlin, which many Germans saw as a kind of Sparta on the Spree, Munich was widely perceived as "the Athens on the Isar," a far more mellow and uninhibited city than the imperial Prussian capital. Although Munich was the seat of the Catholic Wittelsbach monarchy, the style of government was paternalistic and unobtrusive. Müncheners were especially tolerant toward eccentrics; and in Schwabing, the Bohemian section of the city, a colorful array of odd characters would congregate and spout unconventional ideas in numerous cafés and beerhalls. Munich, like Vienna, prized its *Gemütlichkeit*, its sausages, beers, wines, and rich pastries.

Culturally, the city was in the forefront of major developments in art, music, and literature.[67] Richard Wagner's *Tristan und Isolde, Die Meistersinger,* and *Das Rheingold* were first performed in Munich. Richard Strauss was born there and found the atmosphere congenial to his musical talents. The lifestyle of the painter was regarded in Munich as the most legitimate of all, which explains why even a minor artist like Adolf Hitler was treated with a degree of deference that was equaled only by Paris. In fact, a revolution in painting associated with Vassily Kandinsky (1866–1944) occurred in Munich before World War I. Kandinsky was the leading member of a group of Munich artists called Der Blaue Reiter (the Blue Rider), after a picture of that name by Kandinsky. Members of that group, including besides Kandinsky such innovators as Paul Klee (1879–1940) and Franz Marc (1880–1916), carried modern art in entirely new directions by exploring the emotional and psychological properties of color, line, and shape. The result was a completely nonobjective type of art in which form and color have become abstracted of their physical content and raised to a higher spiritual reality.

Munich poets also experimented with new symbols and modes of literary representation. Germany's greatest modern poets, Rainer Maria Rilke (1875–1926) and Stefan George (1868–1934), lived in Munich and wrote their best works there. A whole literary cult centered around Stefan George, who taught his talented followers to abandon bourgeois civilization and cultivate instead the austere life of poetic beauty. He also celebrated the primacy of instinct and emotion over reason and longed for the appearance of an artistic superman who would revitalize decaying German society. Alfred Schuler, one of George's disciples, practiced the occult arts in the drawing rooms of the wealthy, rediscovered the swastika, and taught a murky theory of Nordic racial superiority.

The great German novelist Thomas Mann (1875–1955), though north German by birth, also chose Munich as his home and wrote some of his best works there. Revolutionary dramas by Bertold Brecht (1898–1956) were first performed on Munich stages, as were the disturbing dramas of Franz Wedekind (1864–1918), such as *Pandora's Box* and *Earth Spirit.*

By some historical fluke several great historical personalities lived in Munich's Schwabing district before the Great War. Ilych Ulyanov, known to the Russian underground as Lenin, lived at 106 Schleissheimerstrasse, on the same street as Hitler; and at 54 Agnesstrasse, only four streets up from Lenin's flat, resided Oswald Spengler, a young and still obscure writer who was collecting material for his great historical work, *The Decline of the West*. These three men, so unlike each other in many respects, nevertheless shared a strong sense of foreboding and contempt for the present; they saw decadence and decline in most parts of the Western tradition. Eventually, they became the grave diggers of nineteenth-century bourgeois civilization.

The pessimism of Munich's intellectuals stood in apparent contrast to the happy *Gemütlichkeit* of its fun-loving citizens. In reality, the gaiety of Munich was only skin-deep, concealing a pervasive sense of pessimism among intellectuals and ordinary citizens alike. Such pessimism, though more prevalent among the political right, was no respecter of ideological affiliation. The patrician Thomas Mann was as preoccupied with morbid images of corruption and degeneration as the working-class dramatist Franz Wedekind or the aloof retired schoolteacher Oswald Spengler. Schwabing coffeehouse intellectuals lived not only on coffee or beer but on social criticisms as well. Coffeehouses and beerhalls resounded with ambitious projects aimed at social reconstruction.

Two famous *Kaffeehausliteraten* (coffeehouse highbrows) who commanded a large following before World War I were Erich Mühsam and Kurt Eisner.[68] Mühsam, a small and disheveled man with a provocative red beard, periodically frightened the citizens of Munich with his grandiose rhetoric aimed at liberating the downtrodden masses from the shackles of capitalism. His headquarter was Café Stefanie, where he loved to play chess and hold forth on the inequalities of life in the modern world. Yet his acerbic wit and charm blunted the radical fervor of his somewhat vague ideology. Like Prince Peter Kropotkin, Mühsam was really a gentle man with a genuine sense of empathy for the poor, hoping to initiate a revolution that would not hurt anyone. However, Mühsam's belligerent political style, though impractical and utopian, frightened the respectable burghers of Munich who wanted nothing better than to see him hang from the nearest lamppost.

Another prominent coffeehouse radical, destined to play a leading role during the postwar chaos, was Kurt Eisner. Perhaps more than Mühsam, Kurt Eisner seemed to fit the stereotype of the unwashed, unkempt radical, the type every respectable and law-abiding German loved to hate. Walking on the street, he gave the impression of a shaggy dog; he was small and spindly, sported an unruly grey beard that covered most of his face, peered over a pair of thick eyeglasses, draped his body in a long coat, and hid most of his face in a curious-looking floppy hat. Yet behind this almost comical appearance resided an intelligent, if impractical, interior. The son of a prosperous Jewish shop owner in

Berlin, Eisner had studied philosophy at the University of Berlin before becoming a journalist. In 1897 he was sentenced to prison for satirizing the king of Prussia in a magazine article. This brought him to the attention of Karl Liebknecht Sr., who persuaded him to join the Social Democratic Party and made him the editor of *Vorwärts,* the party's official newspaper. However, Eisner's eccentric character and his visionary style put him at odds with many of his party comrades, especially the die-hard radicals. Dismissed from his job because of his revisionary leanings, he abandoned his wife and five children and came to Bavaria, first to Nuremberg and then to Munich, where he served as theater critic for the Socialist newspaper *Münchener Post* and dabbled in local politics. Disparagingly referred to as a "Schwabing Bolshevist," Eisner had in fact a large following beyond Schwabing's left-wing literary coterie that included many working-class people, but he lacked clear-cut principles and, as subsequent events would reveal, he had little talent in organizing mass discontent into a successful political cause. His failures as a political activist probably resided in his lack of seriousness and his inability to judge human character other than by vague ideological abstractions.

Adolf Hitler moved through the excitement and glitter of prewar Munich like a shadow, unloved and unattached. His reaction to the world around him, especially to some of the avant-garde experiments in the fine arts, was one of hostility and contempt. Since he had not matured as a person, he also had not developed as an artist, for his paintings were the same pedestrian watercolors that he had produced in Vienna. Only the themes were different: instead of Viennese sights he now painted Munich scenes. Moreover, his financial situation was as bleak in Munich as it had been in Vienna. He lived from hand-to-mouth, often supplementing the money he made from selling his pictures by doing odd jobs for his landlord.

Hitler's monotonous existence in Munich was rudely interrupted in January 1914 when he was arrested by the criminal police on charges of evading military service in his native Austria.[69] On January 19, 1914, he was taken to the Austrian consulate to explain his actions and to inform the Austrian authorities why he should not report for military service in Linz on January 20. Hitler became so unhinged by these actions that he must have presented a pitiful sight to the police; but cleverly playing on their sympathies, he composed a lengthy letter, full of grammatical errors and sentimental appeals, in which he pleaded for mercy and asked for a reprieve before reporting for service. The Austrian consul recommended that he be allowed to report for service two weeks later in nearby Salzburg. On February 5, 1914, Hitler went to Salzburg, was examined by the medical authorities, and due to his run-down physical condition was found "unfit for military and auxiliary service; too weak. Incapable of bearing arms."[70]

It is ironic that the man who was declared unfit for military service by the Austrian government in February 1914 could hardly wait to join the

German army when war was declared on August 1, 1914. Like many men of his generation, Hitler was jubilant when he heard the news that Germany was at war; he was overcome, as he later recalled, with "impassionate enthusiasm," falling on his knees and thanking heaven that he was granted the good fortune to live in such times.[71] By some incredible fluke of fate, Hitler's euphoria on that day was actually captured by Heinrich Hoffmann, Hitler's private photographer, who had snapped a picture of a large crowd in the Odeonsplatz where the declaration of war was read to the public. When Hitler told Hoffmann many years later that he had been in the crowd that day, a microscopic search revealed him standing close to one of the stone lions of the Feldherrnhalle (Hall of Field Marshals) that overlook the square. The enlarged picture represents one of the most revealing moments in his life; it shows him in a state of ecstasy. Swept away by the excitement of the moment his half open mouth and shimmering eyes indicate a fleeting premonition that destiny was beckoning him to greatness. As Richard Hanser has written, "The picture freezes forever the precise instant at which the career of Adolf Hitler became possible. The war that was being proclaimed as the photo was taken would produce the social chaos indispensable to his rise."[72]

Redeemed by War, 1914–18

Hitler was swept away by the excitement of war; he sat down in feverish anticipation in his little attic room and penned a letter to the government requesting permission to serve in the German army. On August 4, 1914, he received notification from the government that he was accepted as a volunteer. Two weeks later, he went through basic training; and after barely ten weeks, his regiment, the Sixteenth Bavarian Infantry Regiment (the List Regiment), was sent into combat on the western front.

Hitler spent most of the war in the frontline trenches, serving as a courier between the regimental staff in the rear and the fighting units in the advanced positions near the battlefield. According to most reliable sources, Hitler was an intrepid and highly dependable soldier who never complained and obediently followed orders.[73] His comrades in the trenches respected and trusted him; but his overly zealous attitude was also resented. Apparently, he was so grateful for having found a kind of surrogate home that he overcompensated for his gratitude by undue brown-nosing. While his comrades relaxed, he would often busy himself with gratuitous tasks such as cleaning his rifle or polishing his bayonet. One man who served with him later recalled that Hitler never relaxed and always acted "as if we'd lose the war if he weren't on the job every minute."[74] He received no letters and no packages, never grumbled, stoically accepted his lot, and — to the chagrin of his comrades — rarely joined in the antics common to most ordinary soldiers. Although the war forged extraordinary bonds among the fighting men, Hitler always remained the solitary outsider. This probably accounted for the fact that he was not promoted above the rank of corporal. The adjutant of the List Regiment, Fritz Wiedemann (1891–1970), later testified at Nuremberg that Hitler's promotion to the rank of noncommissioned officer had been denied because "we could discover no leadership qualities in him."[75] In addition, despite his willingness to please his superiors, Hitler found it difficult to shed his Bohemian habits and unconventional mannerisms. His bearing, according to Wiedemann, was exceedingly unmilitary; he was slovenly dressed, slouching in his movements, and sometimes annoyingly taciturn, save on those occasions when some irritating remark would stir him into delivering impassioned harangues.[76] At the same time, those who knew him fairly well — Fritz Wiedemann, Max Amann (his sergeant), and his three closest comrades (Hans Mend, Ernst Schmidt, and Ignaz Westenkircher) — report that he was not only a brave soldier but also a loyal friend.

For Hitler, as for most young Germans, World War I was the pivot around which the future would revolve. Four years of savage fighting, involving gruesome and heart-wrenching personal experiences, fundamentally remolded the personalities of men in the prime of their lives. Psychologically, many young Germans permanently lost their youthful innocence and their idealism under the duress of war. Many could only go on by trying to find some noble meaning in the endless carnage. The poet Ernst Jünger spoke for many of his comrades when he tried to extract sublimity from unspeakable horrors:

> The war had entered into us like wine. We had set out in a rain of flowers to seek the death of heroes. The war was our dream of greatness, power and glory. It was a man's work, a duel on fields whose flowers would be stained with blood. There is no lovelier death in the world.[77]

Hitler, too, entered into this "spirit of the trenches." It seemed to him, as it did to Jünger, that the trenches were holy ground, that the fighting front was the sacred altar of German honor, and that it was a privilege to sacrifice oneself to the fatherland. A heroic death under enemy fire was infinitely preferable to a long and dreary life as a civilian. Although the zeal for self-sacrifice quickly faded under the pall of death and destruction, many German soldiers continued to believe in the nobility of warfare. Their ultimate disillusionment was not with war itself but with the way it had been fought and betrayed.

Hitler was redeemed by World War I for several reasons. The war ended his aimless life and enabled him to find his mission. He found a surrogate home in the List Regiment, a sense of belonging that he had not experienced since the death of his mother. In the company of his fellow soldiers, he felt genuinely at home. Even after he became a prominent leader, politician, and warlord, Hitler always idealized the military over the civilian way of life, although his slovenly artistic temperament was frequently at odds with his admiration for military discipline. Still, he felt most at home at military headquarters, in the trenches, or in dugouts at the front.[78] World War I also validated his Germanism as well as his perception that to be German one would have to accept the virtues of the martial arts. As a politician, Hitler always wanted to re-create the psychological conditions of the beleaguered nation-under-arms, to re-capture that ecstatic moment of August 1914 when, as a young man, he stood in a vast crowd at the Odeonsplatz and heard the jubilant cries as a government official announced that war had been declared. To per-petuate the feeling of soldierly fraternity into peacetime, to extinguish class differences, and to infuse the spirit of the trenches into everyday politics — these were Adolf Hitler's deepest wishes.

The List Regiment suffered appalling losses, but Hitler miraculously escaped death, raising suspicion among his comrades that fate was somehow protecting him, and that to be around him was to be out of harm's way.[79] However, on October 5, 1916, Hitler was hit in the upper thigh of his left leg by a shell fragment and was temporarily hos-pitalized near Berlin. This was the first time he had left the front since joining the army in 1914, and he was shocked by what he heard on the home front. The war was no longer popular; the mood had changed to "anger, grumbling, and cursing." Hitler regarded this attitude of de-featism as a personal attack as well as an insult to the honor of the German army.[80] His short reassignment to a replacement battalion in Munich, where disgust with war was even stronger, reinforced his grow-ing conviction that the war was being lost on the home front and not on the battlefield. He specifically blamed pacifists, left-wing subversives, Jews, and poor propaganda for Germany's cracking morale. After the war, he rationalized the defeat by accepting the stab-in-the-back leg-end (*Dolchstosslegende*) that had taken root among many Germans. As previously noted, this myth held that the German army had never been defeated in the field, but was stabbed in the back at home by traitors — pacifists, Communists, liberals, Jews.

As the tide of battle turned against Germany, Hitler became increas-ingly despondent. The army had given him a new home and validated his Germanism. In December 1914 and again in August 1918, he was decorated for bravery with the Iron Cross First and Second Class, re-spectively. It is still not clear how he earned these decorations, but most of the reliable accounts, though conflicting and anecdotal, would indicate that he richly deserved them.[81]

The shock of defeat, therefore, affected Hitler deeply, perhaps as trag-ically as his mother's death. The impact of defeat was further heightened by Hitler's personal injury just one month before the armistice. On Oc-tober 13, 1918, the British launched a poison gas attack just south of Ypres. Hitler was personally caught in this attack and temporarily blinded. He was shipped back home to Pasewalk hospital in Pomerania.

While lying in his hospital bunk, blind and depressed, Hitler was informed by the hospital pastor that Germany had quit the war, signed an armistice, and rid itself of the emperor. This was too much for him. "I could stand it no more," he later recalled, "it was impossible to stay any longer. While everything went black before my eyes, stumbling, I groped my way back to the dormitory, threw myself on the cot and buried my burning head in the covers and pillows. I had not wept since the day I had stood at the grave of my mother."[82] He added with grim determination that, if he could help it, he would personally avenge Germany's humiliation by punishing the originators of this dastardly crime.[83]

The Vision Is Born

We will never know what went on in Hitler's mind while he was recuperating from his blindness at Pasewalk, but we do have enough indirect evidence to suggest that he experienced a powerful revelation that compelled him to dedicate the rest of his life to the redemption of Germany's honor. Hitler himself dated the beginning of his political career to this experience, claiming that he became increasingly aware of his destiny, namely redeeming Germany's honor by destroying the Jews.[84] While still suffering from the effects of the mustard gas attack, his mind appears to have snapped. It is suspected that he lapsed into a prolonged hysterical condition that seems to have triggered a number of insights of such power that he attributed them to a higher spiritual source.

Rudolph Binion argues that the mustard gas that temporarily blinded Hitler in the fall of 1918 reminded him of the iodoform administered to his dying mother in 1907.[85] Both mustard gas and iodoform are sharp-scented liquids that burn through the skin and leave a lingering and foul-smelling odor behind them. As previously noted, Hitler knew this sickening smell very well because it had infested his mother's house during her final illness. Dr. Bloch, his mother's physician, was a Jew, and subconsciously Hitler may well have blamed him for torturing and killing his mother.

Lying prostrate in his hospital bed, Hitler relived his mother's martyrdom, except that this time Germany, his surrogate mother, was being defiled. Once he had made the connection that in both cases the Jews had been responsible, Hitler had discovered the solution to his problem.[86] Dr. Bloch had been right in treating one poison with another; the time had come to apply the same treatment to Germany's disease — to poison the poisoners, or Jews. In Binion's judgment, "Hitler repeated his mother's terminal treatment — applied it to Germany, that is — while also taking it out on Bloch alias the Jew."[87] His hallucinated mandate was to gas the Jews in order to avenge both his mother and his defiled country.

After his discharge from the hospital in Pasewalk at the end of November 1918, Hitler returned to Munich to report to the reserve battalion of his regiment. Although momentous developments were tearing apart the fabric of Bavaria and the Reich, Hitler himself was still politically uninvolved. In February 1919, he volunteered for guard duty in a prisoner-of-war camp at Traunstein near the Austrian frontier, but after only a month he returned to Munich because the camp had been closed. He still remained with the army, taking quarters in the barracks at Oberwiesenfeld. The army was still his island of institutional safety, his only family; but now that family was subjected to the winds of new left-wing ideologies. Bavaria, as discussed above, fell into the hands of left-wing radicals under the madcap leadership of Kurt Eisner, whose assassination in February 1919 ushered in a period of even greater confusion, culminating in the establishment of a soviet-style republic in early April of that year. On May 1, 1919, Free Corps formations overthrew this soviet republic and massacred its leaders.

As a strong nationalist, Hitler found himself in a precarious position during the rule of this soviet republic; but when the red terror was over, he eagerly offered his services to a board of inquiry set up to examine traitorous activities within the ranks of the army. He did his job of snitching on his fellow soldiers so well that the army sent him to a training course in "civic thinking." The man in charge of this course was Captain Karl Mayr, head of the Department of Press and Propaganda in Reichswehr Group Headquarters No. 4 (Bavaria). It was Mayr and some of Hitler's instructors, notably the historian Alexander von Müller, who discovered Hitler's remarkably compelling powers as a public speaker.[88] In fact, Hitler's big mouth so impressed his superiors that they made him an instructional officer (*Bildungsoffizier*) charged with the responsibility of indoctrinating the men with correct nationalistic ideas and of insulating them from the perils of socialism, pacifism, and democracy.

Up until now Hitler had enjoyed only a limited audience, consisting largely of reluctant hearers; but now, with the help of the army, he was given the opportunity of addressing much larger groups. His reputation as a natural orator grew. In the words of one observer, "Hitler is a born demagogue; at a meeting his fanaticism and popular appeal compel his audience to listen to him."[89] In September 1919, Mayr instructed Hitler to investigate an obscure new party called the German Workers' Party (Deutsche Arbeiterpartei — DAP) whose nationalistic, anti-Semitic, and antidemocratic ideas might be an appropriate reflection of current army thinking. Hitler basically liked what he heard, joined the party, became a frequent popular speaker for the party, and eventually left the army in order to devote his full energies to the new party.[90] He had found his mission and the instrument by which he would proclaim it.

Summary

The young Hitler who returned to Munich in November 1918 carried within himself the raging turmoil of a divided personality. He was seething with pent-up hatreds, paranoid fears, and twisted visions of reality. The chaos of the postwar period in Germany made it possible for him to normalize his pathology within a growing circle of like-minded believers. By looking at Hitler in 1918 we can already see the disturbing traits of the future dictator with remarkable clarity. These traits, representing permanent aspects of his habitual style, changed little over time except in intensity or further distortion. The unknown soldier who suddenly stepped out of the shadow of war in 1919 and began to mesmerize an ever-increasing number of people exhibited a syndrome of alarming characteristics, involving:

1. A paranoid fear of Jews.

2. A pigeon-hole mind dividing the world into sharp and unambiguous opposites.

3. A habitual need to project or externalize inner failings onto outer scapegoats — Jews, pacifists, democrats, Communists, and so on.

4. An inability to form loving ties, especially with women, and corresponding attitudes of callousness and manipulation in all interpersonal relationships.

5. Extreme self-absorption in unrealistic fantasies and grand illusions.

6. Admiration for brutal strength and success.

Chapter 4

The Rise of the Nazi Party, 1919-23

From Red Revolution to White Counterrevolution, 1918-19

Between November 1918 and May 1919, a series of unprecedented events transformed Munich and much of the rest of Bavaria from a land of amiable, if sometimes raucous, *Gemütlichkeit* and Roman Catholic conservatism into a seething cauldron of political agitation. In the span of six months, Bavaria passed through sweeping political changes that involved the fall of the Wittelsbach monarchy, the establishment of a Socialist republic under Kurt Eisner, the rule of the Schwabing coffeehouse anarchists, a reign of terror under a soviet regime, and a counterrevolution by right-wing forces that would eventually prepare the ground for the incipient Nazi movement. By studying the shrill political contrasts of postwar Bavaria, we can already make out the faint outlines of Germany's violent future under National Socialism.

In Bavaria, as in the rest of Germany, the political breakdown following the war produced a power vacuum that opened the possibility of a government takeover by the forces of the left. Except for the differences in local temperament and custom, the revolution in Bavaria appears in retrospect like a dress rehearsal for the revolution that would take place a day later in Berlin. In both cases, power had shifted from conservative and liberal bourgeois parties to the various groupings on the political left (Social Democrats, Independent Socialists, Communists). The largest of these left-wing groups in Bavaria, as in the rest of Germany, was the Social Democratic Party (SPD). These Social Democrats (also called Majority Socialists) in Bavaria were the same cautious trade unionists as those led by Ebert and Scheidemann. Erich Auer, the leader of the Bavarian Social Democrats, shared with Ebert a strong preference for a gradual and peaceful transition to social democracy; like Ebert, he was by temperament a party functionary rather than a forceful leader.[1] Auer, like Ebert, also faced stubborn opposition to his moderate reform proposals from a minority of increasingly vocal radicals on the extreme left. The difference between Munich and Berlin, however, was that in Munich the radicals actually managed, for a short period of time, to seize the reins of power; but they exploited the instruments of power so ineptly that they ended up undermining the cause of moderate social democracy and virtually guaranteeing the triumph of right-wing military forces, notably in the form of National Socialism.

The unlikely personality on the political left who galvanized the radical forces into seizing power was Kurt Eisner, Bavaria's soft-hearted version of Karl Liebknecht. Eisner, like Liebknecht, had spent almost nine months in prison for his vocal opposition to the war, earning the reputation of a political martyr.[2] Upon his release from Stadelheim Prison, Eisner was nominated to lead the Independent Socialist Party, which had been formed out of a small dissident faction within the Social Democratic Party. On the occasion of his first public appearance on October 23, 1918, Eisner made it quite clear, as Auer had not, that he favored an overthrow of the monarchy and the establishment of a Socialist republic. Although the government had already made substantial democratic concessions, which would have transformed Bavaria into a democratic republic, the winds of radical change proved to be stronger than the proposed democratic changes.

On November 7, 1918, Eisner and Auer staged a mass peace demonstration on the Theresienwiese, a huge grassy field that was used for the annual Oktoberfest. November 7 was a beautiful day: sunny, warm, and clear, a perfect day for an open-air rally. Not surprisingly, a huge crowd turned out to listen to the speeches of various Socialist speakers. The audience was in a festive mood; it consisted of workers from the larger war industry plants, soldiers, a contingent of landlocked sailors, an assortment of beerhall perennials, Bohemians from Schwabing, students, and various curiosity seekers, including some women and children.[3] It was a carnival atmosphere with little indication of major disruptions. Auer gave a well-received speech on the planned democratic reorganization of the Bavarian government and then proposed a peaceful march on the city, having hired a band beforehand to lead the march. As Auer's group marched off eastward into the city, Eisner continued to harangue his followers on the far northwest corner of the Theresienwiese, urging the soldiers in the crowd to "scatter throughout the city, occupy the barracks, seize weapons and ammunitions, win over the rest of the troops, and make yourselves masters of the government."[4] This is precisely what Eisner and his followers proceeded to do as they seized a temporary munitions depot at the Guldstein School and took over the city's military barracks, hoisting red flags. While these events transpired, Eisner went to the Mathäser Beerhall, the largest and rowdiest beerhall in the city, to consult with the city's first council of workers and soldiers. The council appointed him as its first chairman, and Eisner jubilantly proclaimed the Bavarian Republic. Later, sinking down dead tired but elated into a plush sofa in the Landtag (diet) building, Eisner remarked to Felix Fehrenbach, his secretary, "Isn't it wonderful, we have made a revolution without spilling a drop of blood! Something like this has never happened in history."[5]

King Ludwig III, who heard about the revolution while on his daily constitutional in the Hofgarten, left the city along with his family the same evening for his private estate in the mountains of Wildenwart. Although the king never formally abdicated his throne and, in fact, hoped for a restoration of the monarchy from his later Hungarian exile, he publicly released his civil servants, officers, and soldiers from their personal oath to the monarchy. Eisner interpreted this statement by the king as being tantamount to an abdication and officially proclaimed the end of the thousand-year-old Wittelsbach dynasty.[6]

How a minority of *Zugroaste Schlawiner* (alien rascals) could have orchestrated such a bizarre and curiously unopposed coup d'état struck many Bavarians as incomprehensible at the time. The truth was that Eisner's bloodless coup was the result of a temporary disintegration of military authority and a complete failure of nerve of the Bavarian state bureaucracy. Eisner had taken power because it was there for the taking; unlike Friedrich Ebert, who was designated to head a provisional government until national elections to a constituent assembly could be held, Kurt Eisner swept into office with no pretension of representing the will of the Bavarian people. His authority rested on no popular consensus; its only real source resided in the make-shift council of workers and soldiers — a council that, in turn, had not been elected by anyone.[7] Although Eisner put together a short-lived coalition with Auer and the Majority Socialists, his inept leadership, along with a strong resurgence of Catholic, conservative, and military forces, made the "First Bavarian Revolution" doomed from the start.

Most Bavarians later recoiled with horror from the antics of the first Socialist government, regarding it as the work of a few Schwabing Bolsheviks; but the truth, not usually perceived in times of radical change, is that Eisner was not a Bolshevik in the Russian sense, and his regime was not an instrument of mass terror. Personally, Eisner was a witty and acerbic eccentric, but he was also a political utopian who was totally out of line with the wishes of the majority of the Bavarian people. While in office, he conducted government affairs in a curiously freewheeling, eccentric, and open manner. His office, located in the regal apartments of former imperial chancellor Count von Hertling, who had been minister president of Bavaria before becoming imperial chancellor, was open to anyone who cared to drop in. Visitors were free to inspect any of the documents, even the most secret, which were strewn across his untidy desk or piled on various chairs throughout his office. Surrounded by a clutter of desks behind which various secretaries banged out his innumerable memos and proclamations, the eccentric leader seemed to conduct the business of state almost entirely out of his own head and heart.[8]

At first Eisner's bizarre rule enjoyed a measure of popular support among a population traditionally receptive to outlandish behavior. But while Eisner indulged himself in dreams about transforming souls and in staging spectacular revolutionary *fetes* at the national theater with Bruno Walter conducting the orchestra, Bavaria's fragile economic and political fabric was being torn apart. In Bavaria, as in the rest of Germany, problems of demobilization and the conversion of wartime industries into peacetime enterprises caused severe economic strains. These strains were exacerbated by the fact that Munich was a major processing center for those who were being mustered out of the armed forces.[9] Although the government had foreseen the problem of potential crowding and had requisitioned school buildings, hotels, and beerhalls, its efforts fell woefully short of what was needed to accommodate everybody. The result was that the city became inundated by returning soldiers, many of whom were looking for entertainment or trouble or both. Every night thousands of demobilized and unemployed soldiers crowded the dance halls and abandoned themselves to a raucous atmosphere "evocative of the *lieber Augustin* and the Black Death."[10]

Unemployment, in the meantime, steadily rose under the impact of such idle manpower and the cessation of wartime production. Curiously enough, the Eisner government continued some of the manufacture of munitions well into January because it calculated that a minimum of eight thousand workers would have lost their jobs if these industries had stopped all production.[11] This well-meaning policy, however, was simply a palliative measure that invited further problems since it violated the disarmament provisions of November 11, exposed Eisner's regime to charges of encouraging the continuation of militarism, and added to the proliferation of weapons in a city already charged with incendiary potential. Furthermore, Munich and Bavaria faced a serious shortage of fuel, especially coal, a shortage made all the more dangerous by a deteriorating and bankrupt transportation system. Nor was transportation the only bankrupt system. In order to compensate the unemployed and to maintain a growing Socialist welfare state, the government literally spent itself into bankruptcy.

It could be argued that Eisner's political and diplomatic skills were also bankrupt. Politically, Eisner never fused the network of council bodies that had sprouted up all over Bavaria; nor did he know how to reconcile government by traditional processes with the rule of revolutionary councils. It was not even clear to him how parliamentary democracy could coexist with a council system in which members were neither elected by nor responsible to the will of the Bavarian people. In the meantime, he simply allowed the traditional civil service to function under the aegis of the councils, which created much confusion and duplication of effort. As to the political future of Bavaria, Eisner did finally bow to the will of the Majority Socialists that a general election should be held to select members for a new sovereign parliament.

Eisner's rule began to collapse at the polls. On January 12, 1919, elections were held to pick members to the Bavarian Landtag, the future sovereign power of the new Bavarian republic. Over three million voters, including a large percentage of women (53 percent), turned out and gave their approval to the idea of a unicameral legislature based on a multiparty system and directed by a responsible cabinet of ministers.[12] The conservative Bavarian People's Party came in first, polling 35 percent of the votes and gaining sixty-six seats in the new Landtag, followed by the Majority Socialists, who received 33 percent of the total vote and sixty-one seats. Eisner's Independent Socialist Party came in fifth after the German Democratic Party and the Peasants' League (Bauernbund); it gained only 2.5 percent of the total vote and three seats in the Landtag. Although Eisner tried to put a good face on the outcome by saying that Bavaria now had a clear choice between Socialist and bourgeois rule, the election results represented a stunning defeat to Eisner and the rule by councils of workers, peasants, and soldiers. Until the new parliament assembled and drafted a constitution, Eisner continued in office based on an interim constitution of January 4 that held, among other things, that until a final constitutional settlement had been drafted, "the revolutionary [i.e., Eisner's] regime exercises legislative and executive power."[13]

Eisner's last desperate appeal to the Majority Socialists to join him in a united front failed. Only a small group around Ernst Niekisch, a young teacher who spearheaded the Augsburg council of workers and soldiers and who later chaired the Bavarian central council (*Zentralrat*), contemplated a united front with Eisner's Independent Socialists. In the meantime, groups to the left of Eisner were planning to subvert the will of the electorate by another spontaneous coup. Erich Mühsam expressed their feelings: "The revolution will not allow itself to be voted down."[14]

Although the extreme left made good on its threat to resort to bullets rather than ballots, the trigger on the revolutionary gun was pulled by the counterrevolutionary right. For some time now, the opposition to Eisner's regime had gradually crystallized on the political right. Initially caught off balance by the fall of the monarchy, conservative and Roman Catholic forces soon staged a counterattack. The major focal point of counterrevolutionary activities was army headquarters in Munich, where Colonel Ritter von Epp commanded the remnants of the Royal Bavarian Life Guard and later, as major general, the Seventh District Command of the Reichswehr.

Franz Ritter von Epp (1868–1947), who became one of the legendary heroes of the Nazi movement, was born in Munich in 1868, the son of a painter. He entered the army at the age of eighteen and acquired his first military experience by fighting overseas, first in the Boxer Rebellion in China (1901–2) and then in German Southwest Africa, where he participated in the genocidal annihilation of the rebellious Hereros.[15] During World War I, Epp was appointed to command the famed Royal Bavarian Life Guard, an elite unit whose daring commando exploits inculcated in its members a special sense of mission and superiority. Epp himself received the highest Bavarian medal, the Max-Josef Ritterorden, which also elevated him into the ranks of the nobility.

During the revolutionary upheavals of 1918–19, Epp and his fellow officers became a rallying point of opposition to Eisner's Socialist republic. When Munich itself became too unstable for the safe operation of his counterrevolutionary activity, Epp transferred his theater of operations outside Bavaria. Since Eisner's regime had prohibited Free Corps units on Bavarian soil, Epp set up a Free Corps in Ohrdruf, Thuringia, just a few miles beyond the Bavarian state border. This Free Corps was financed by the Reich government and was under the overall direction of Gustav Noske, Reich minister of defense.

With Epp at Ohrdruf was Captain Ernst Röhm, the future SA (Sturmabteilung, or Storm Detachment = storm troopers) leader and mentor of the young rabble-rouser Adolf Hitler. Röhm (1887–1934), like Ritter von Epp, belonged to a military caste whose very existence was threatened by the radical course of events. The class enemy to both Röhm and Epp was the revolutionary left, and the only proper tactical approach to dealing with it, they believed, was annihilation. Both men also feared the possibility that the German middle class might become infected by liberal and democratic ideals, which they regarded as a mortal threat to the militaristic structure of German society in general and their own careers in particular.

Ernst Röhm came from an old family of Bavarian civil servants, but by temperament and experience he grew into a risk-taking soldier who rose to the rank of captain during the war as a result of his leadership abilities and daredevil feats. In the course of four years of fighting, he was wounded numerous times. The upper part of his nose had been shot away, and a bullet had left a deep scar in one cheek. Röhm was a short and stocky man with closely cropped hair, a ruddy complexion, a swashbuckling manner, and a fondness for good-looking young men. Like many of his fellow officers, especially those in the junior ranks, he was deeply affected by the outcome of the war.[16] Hardened by four years of trench warfare and leaving the battlefield with the belief that the German army had never been defeated, Röhm felt betrayed and subsequently blamed the "November Criminals" for Germany's defeat.

As officers of the Reichswehr, both Röhm and Epp wanted to avenge the shame of defeat and revolution, to redeem the honor of the German army by ridding the country of left-wing radicals. Röhm now transformed himself into an equally risk-taking and thrill-seeking political soldier opposing the left-wing government in Munich. Later, like Epp, he supported and joined the Nazi Party. During the period 1919–23, both Epp and Röhm were instrumental in launching the Nazi Party.

Another major focus of the counterrevolution, often working closely with Epp and the military, was the Thule Society, a *völkisch* (ethnocentric) conspiratorial organization that some have seen as the real midwife of the Nazi movement. The society grew out of a *völkisch* sect called the Germanic Order (Germanenorden), founded in Munich in 1913 and reorganized as the Thule Society in 1918.[17] Its headquarters was in the fashionable Hotel Vierjahreszeiten, where the group had its club rooms. Admission to the Thule Society required filling out a form indicating the degree of hairiness of various parts of the body and leaving the mark of a footprint on a separate sheet of paper as proof of Aryan descent.[18]

Although the Thule Society fronted as a literary club dedicated to the study of Germanic culture, its members had more on their minds than studying the legendary kingdom where the German race had supposedly originated. The society became a focal point for right-wing, nationalistic, and anti-Semitic agitators who enjoyed substantial backing from wealthy and influential citizens of Munich. The society's official mouthpiece was the *Münchener Beobachter* (Munich observer), founded in 1868 and published since 1900 by the Franz Eher Verlag, later one of the Nazi Party's official publishing houses.

The Thule Society hatched the early pioneers of the Nazi movement, giving them a platform for their racial ideas and furthering their political ambitions. The men who congregated there included, among others, Dietrich Eckart, poet, editor of an anti-Semitic journal *Auf Gut Deutsch* (In plain German), and mentor of the young Hitler; Alfred Rosenberg, destined to become the official philosopher of the Nazi Party; Gottfried Feder, the wooly fiscal expert of the rising Nazi Party; Hans Frank, Hitler's future lawyer and later governor-general (and butcher) of occupied Poland; Rudolf Hess, Hitler's private secretary and later deputy führer; and Father Bernhard Stempfle, who helped Hitler write *Mein Kampf* and was later eliminated because he knew too much about the führer's seedy past.

Although the Thule Society was one of the spiritual sources of the Nazi movement, its own future was short-lived because it could never rise above the role of a small conspiratorial sect with elitist pretensions. The personality of its leader, Freiherr (Baron) Rudolf von Sebattendorf, illustrates these inherent limitations.

The man who called himself Baron Rudolf von Sebattendorf was really one Rudolf Glauer, the son of a Silesian locomotive engineer; his background and ultimate fate are still shrouded in mystery. We do know that in 1909 he was convicted and sentenced to prison as a forger, only to reappear four years later as "Baron von Sebattendorf," a title he had gained by persuading an Austrian by that name to adopt him. After his participation in the Bavarian upheavals of 1918–19, he moved to Istanbul, traveled to Mexico and possibly the United States, and reappeared in Germany in 1933 in hopes of reviving the Thule Society. Shortly after Hitler's seizure of power, he published his own version of the origins of the Nazi movement under the intriguing title *Bevor Hitler kam* (Before Hitler came). Since the content of the book did not fit the official myth-encrusted version of the origin of the Nazi Party, the book was banned in 1934 and its author mysteriously vanished, presumably one of the many victims of the "Night of the Long Knives."[19]

Sebattendorf has been described as the archetype of the shady and mysterious adventurer who grafts himself on extreme nationalistic causes.[20] An unpublished account of his life portrays him as a short and corpulent man with slightly protruding eyes; he described himself as "an artist rather than a pedant, a sybarite rather than a Platonist."[21] (We might add that sybarites [Danton, Röhm, Sebattendorf] do not generally survive the stern rule of the Platonists [Robespierre, Lenin, or Hitler]). Sebattendorf is also an important piece in the *völkisch* mosaic because he was directly influenced by the whole array of racially inspired theories associated with Theodor Fritsch and Lanz von Liebenfels, the same theories that bolstered Hitler's Weltanschauung. In fact, the Germanic Order, later the Thule Society, was founded in 1912 in Leipzig and was in close contact with Fritsch's anti-Semitic Hammer League and similar *völkisch* organizations. Sebattendorf's career as right-wing intriguer is therefore highly instructive, especially since it symbolizes the convergence of similar sociopathic personalities and rising xenophobic movements.

The Thule Society was directly responsible for Eisner's death because one of its prospective applicants, a young aristocrat and World War I veteran by the name of Count Arco-Valley, whose mother was Jewish, was informed by the society that he could be admitted only if he performed an act that would prove him to be a worthy member. On February 21, 1919, he performed his worthy act by pumping two bullets into Eisner's head, killing him instantly. Ironically, Eisner was on his way to the Landtag in order to tender his resignation as minister president. The twenty-two-year-old assassin, who had blamed Eisner and his Socialists for all of Germany's troubles, was in turn shot in the neck, mouth, and chest by Eisner's bodyguards, but was later miraculously saved by one of Germany's legendary surgeons, Dr. Ferdinand Sauerbruch.

Just one hour after Eisner's assassination, Alois Lindner, a butcher's apprentice and close follower of Eisner, walked into the chamber of the Landtag, where the deputies were still stunned by the news of Eisner's murder. He walked unnoticed down the aisle toward Auer's seat, took out his pistol, placed it on a railing just in front of Auer's seat to get a better aim, and in full view of the horrified members of the Landtag literally shot Auer out of his seat, leaving him writhing in agony on the floor.[22] After firing several shots at the other ministers, he calmly made his way up the aisles. An army officer who tried to block his way was cut down by another shot from Lindner's pistol. Lindner then left the building unmolested and disappeared into the crowd. Meanwhile, pandemonium broke out in the chamber. A hail of bullets rained down from the spectators' gallery, killing another deputy and sending the rest diving for cover or dashing to the exits; some deputies even jumped out of the windows. The Landtag broke up in total confusion. Law and order had collapsed in Munich.

The radicals in the council of workers and soldiers, suspecting a nationwide conspiracy by right-wing reactionaries, imposed a state of emergency on Bavaria and called for a general strike. Red army soldiers seized banks and public buildings, took hostages, and instituted tight censorship and public curfews. For almost a month, power was exercised by a central council (*Zentralrat*) headed by Ernst Niekisch. On March 17–18 parliament was reconvened and the Social Democrat Johannes Hoffmann was appointed to the premiership. However, by that time the extreme left, emboldened by the apparent success of Bolshevism in Hungary under Bela Kun, believed that Germany was now ripe for Communism and proclaimed a soviet republic.

Eisner's death triggered a belated wave of sentimental affection for the fallen leader of the revolution. Workers set up framed portraits of their martyr throughout the city, and armed soldiers forced passers-by to salute them. The spot where Eisner was assassinated was turned into a shrine and guarded by devoted and armed folowers. Eisner's funeral, marked by the ringing of all of Munich's church bells, attracted a hundred thousand mourners. Thomas Mann's renegade brother, the novelist Heinrich Mann, hailed Eisner in a memorial address as the first truly spiritual man ever to head a German state. However, there were also many people who were jubilant at the news of Eisner's death. Students at the University of Munich burst into cheers when they heard of Eisner's death. Many Munich burghers, sensing that a further and even more radical shift to the left was in the offing, looked to military or paramilitary groups for the restoration of law and order. On the right, the irrational revulsion against Eisner, even in death, reached an all-time low when members of the Thule Society mixed the scent of bitches in heat into bags of flour and scattered it all over Eisner's assassination site. For days, packs of dogs desecrated the site into a foul-smelling spot.[23] Such hateful acts made dialogue or compromise impossible. Munich degenerated into an armed camp.

The immediate political consequence of Eisner's assassination was that the radical left was able to seize power in Munich in late February 1919. As early as November 1918, Erich Mühsam, an anarchist, had founded the Union of Revolutionary Bavarian Internationalists; at the beginning of 1919, Max Levien, a Russian-born follower of Lenin, established the Munich branch of the Communist Party. Mühsam was the spokesman of the Schwabing radicals; their meeting place, Café Stefanie, which was also known as "Café Megalomania," became the center of left-wing projects for the salvation of humanity. Mühsam's two closest partners were Gustav Landauer and Ernst Toller. Landauer, scion of a wealthy Jewish family, had broken off a promising academic career in order to dedicate his life to a nonviolent type of socialism based on the principles of Prince Peter Kropotkin, whom he met personally and whose writings he translated into German. Landauer had come to Munich on Eisner's urgent plea to help redeem lost souls; and his decision to do so would cost him his life.

Ernst Toller, a young poet, Utopian Socialist, and disabled war veteran, came from a Jewish family in Polish Prussia. After being discharged from the army, he resumed his university studies at Heidelberg and Munich. Toller was a poet-politician whose visionary speeches strongly appealed to working-class audiences. The trio of Mühsam, Landauer, and Toller represented a definite type abhorrent to the *völkisch* right: the abstract, compassionate "Jewish litterateur" who feels compelled to liberate the down-trodden masses from the yoke of capitalism, militarism, and imperialism.

This motley group of Jewish Bohemians was joined by various emissaries of the new Bolshevik regime in Russia, specifically the trio of Max Levien, Eugen Levine, and Towia Axelrod. Together these radicals seized power in the wake of Eisner's assassination and proclaimed in Munich and parts of Upper Bavaria a soviet republic (*Räterepublik*). Hoffmann and the Majority Socialists fled north to the city of Bamberg and proclaimed a Bavarian government in exile that pledged its loyalty to the central government in Berlin.

The new Bavarian Soviet Republic went through two phases — an ephemeral one-week rule by the Schwabing anarchists Mühsam, Toller, and Landauer (*Scheinräterepublik*) and a Bolshevik reign of terror conducted by the Russian Jews Levien, Levine, and Axelrod.[24] A "Red Army," consisting largely of radical workers from the Munich Krupp, Krauss, and Maffei factories, was placed under the command of Rudolf Egelhofer, a twenty-six-year-old sailor who had participated in the November 18 sailors' mutiny in Kiel.

The madcap rule of the "coffeehouse anarchists" exceeded that of Eisner's in the sheer magnitude of its antics. Toller and Mühsam announced that they would transform the world "into a meadow full of flowers in which each man can pick his share."[25] The regime's "commissar for public instruction" announced that admission to the University of Munich was now open to anyone and that the study of history, the "enemy of civilization," was officially terminated. Other commissars experimented with "free money" and new housing accommodations that specified that homes could have no more than three rooms, with the living room having to be situated above the kitchen and bedroom.[26] One commissar, Dr. Franz Lipp, turned out to be an outright madman who dispatched embarrassingly incoherent telegrams to Lenin and the pope. To Lenin, he cabled that "the proletariat of Upper Bavaria is happily united. Socialists plus Communists plus Independents fused together like a hammer. However, the hairy gorilla hands of Gustav Noske are dripping with blood. We want peace forever. Immanuel Kant, *Vom Ewigen Frieden, 1795, Theses 2–5*."[27] To "Comrade Pope," Lipp complained that the cowardly Hoffmann had absconded with the key to the ministry toilet, and to the transport minister he announced that he had declared war on Württemberg and Switzerland because "these dogs did not send me 60 locomotives immediately. I am certain of victory. Moreover, I have just sent a supplication to the Pope — a very good friend of mine — begging him to bless our arms."[28]

It is not surprising that such a madcap team lasted for hardly a week and was replaced by a more professional cadre of revolutionaries led by Levien, Levine, and Axelrod. For about three weeks (April 12–May 1, 1919), a red terror descended on Munich, an experience that many Müncheners, especially members of the middle and upper classes, would always cite as an example of what would be in store for all Germans if the Communists ever seized power nationwide. In their eagerness to set up a dictatorship of the proletariat, the Munich reds rounded up scores of middle-class hostages and incarcerated them at Stadelheim Prison, closed schools, instituted censorship, confiscated houses and personal valuables, and withheld food from middle-class families.

After an unsuccessful attempt to take Munich with a force of Bavarian troops, the Hoffmann government at Bamberg had no choice but to swallow its pride and ask the central government in Berlin for help. Noske mobilized several experienced Free Corps units, including Epp's Free Corps at Ohrdruf in Thuringia. While the various Free Corps units tightened the noose around Munich, the Communists murdered about twenty hostages at the Luitpold Gymnasium, mutilating the bodies of the victims so badly that they could not be positively identified later. The victims, some of them members of the Thule Society, included prominent figures from the city's social elite such as Countess Hella von Westarp, Prince Maria von Thurn und Taxis, Baron von Sydlitz, Baron von Teikert, and a Professor Ernst Berger.

On May 1, 1919, Noske's troops took the city and exacted a gruesome toll, not only killing Communists but indiscriminately murdering innocent people who happened to be in the wrong place at the wrong time.[29] Both Levien and Axelrod managed to make their way back to Russia. Egelhofer was pulled out of his car by the Whites and beaten to death; Landauer was beaten, shot, and trampled to death by soldiers while he was in "protective" custody. Levine was caught, tried, and then summarily executed. Mühsam was tried and sentenced to fifteen years in prison, but his sentence was commuted in 1924. He was later rearrested by the Nazis and brutally murdered in a concentration camp in 1934. Toller received a five-year sentence, owing largely to the intercession on his behalf by prominent German writers, including Thomas Mann. Ernst Niekisch, the nominal head of the first soviet republic, received a prison sentence of two years.

The Bavarian revolution of 1919 had poisonous consequences for both Bavaria and the Reich. The liberation of Munich at first seemed to signal the restoration of parliamentary government and the end of the council system. However, given the fact that the Majority Socialists had been restored to power by force of right-wing bayonets, it was just a matter of time before the piper began to insist on a right-wing tune that would relegate the Social Democrats to the political wilderness. Like the Ebert regime in Berlin, the Bavarian Social Democrats were accused of betraying their fellow Socialists when they terminated the basic institution on which their revolution had rested — the councils of workers, soldiers, and peasants. Furthermore the Social Democrats undermined their credibility with their own constituency by calling upon Free Corps units to save them from the excesses of their comrades. The political left had failed on all counts. The moderate Social Democrats were now seen by the radicals on the left as loathsome creatures and by their military protectors as feeble amateurs. The extreme left revealed its pronounced weakness in Bavarian and German politics. It stood revealed as a hollow and entirely visionary movement whose leaders had no real understanding of power and popular opinion. The German middle class, initially caught off balance by left-wing radicalism, regained confidence in its ability to control working-class radicalism by exposing its ideology as subversive and un-German and by countering left-wing radicalism with a patriotic and populist message of its own — a message that National Socialism would articulate most successfully.

Another major consequence of the Bavarian revolution was the transformation of the city of Munich from a place of easy-going tolerance to a seething cauldron of mass disaffection, a city in which almost every group nursed some kind of bitter grievance. Political intrigue abounded amid the proliferation of conspiratorial groups. A brood of extremist councils, defensive and defiance leagues, associations, and home and citizens' guards inundated the city with hate slogans and held interminable public meetings. Most of these groups had their own paramilitary forces, commanded, in some cases, a frightening array of secret arms, and sent out their most asocial bullies to disrupt the meetings of their opponents.

In this highly charged political atmosphere, civilized dialogue between right and left became impossible. A sizeable majority, rightly or wrongly, came to view the political left as an assortment of lunatics and criminals. This explains, in part, the sheer delight in the cruelty inflicted on the failures of the revolution, as well as the gratuitous slights and humiliations visited upon the survivors. The needle on the political compass pointed unmistakably to the right, especially when we look at public perceptions of who was right or wrong, good or bad during the revolutionary upheavals. Radicals on the left were condemned as vicious agents of international Communism and world Jewry, while the radicals on the right were celebrated as patriotic heroes who were motivated by a pure love of the fatherland. The White "liberators" who had indiscriminately tortured and killed their victims were bathed in public admiration; and in the few cases where some were tried for crimes, the sentences meted out were embarrassingly lenient. Count Arco-Valley's death sentence for murdering Eisner was quickly commuted to life imprisonment, but he actually served only a few years in a minimum security camp.[30] The murderers of Landauer, including the commanding officer involved in the case, Count von Gagern, received insultingly lenient sentences: von Gagern was sentenced to a five hundred mark fine, and the soldier who stole Landauer's watch was sentenced to five weeks in prison.[31]

It should also be noted that Landauer's gruesome death was widely applauded as entirely deserved, all the more so since he had been a mere Jew as well as a Communist. In fact, many Bavarians, already anti-Semitic before the revolution, became convinced more than ever that the revolution, in Sebattendorf's words, had been "made by a lower race to corrupt the Germans." Sebattendorf continued: "In place of our blood-related princes we are now governed by our mortal enemy: Juda. From now on it must be an eye for an eye and a tooth for a tooth."[32] Since almost every leader of the revolutionary left had been a Jew, many Bavarians concluded that Bolshevism and Jewry must be identical, a message Adolf Hitler would later pound into the head of every German.

In conclusion, the Bavarian revolution as well as the revolution in Berlin proved that Germans were still a conservative people with a strong preference for the military style of life. A strong authoritarian government continued to be the preferred political choice of many Germans, while republicanism was never fully accepted emotionally, except by a few liberal intellectuals. Despite visiting untold miseries on the German people, the military was still venerated by the solid citizens of Germany; in fact, its reputation grew in the wake of the failed revolution because it could now claim to have delivered the country from Bolshevism. On May 1, 1919, Thomas Mann, who spoke for many educated Germans, wrote in his diary that "the Munich communist episode is over; there will scarcely be much desire left to try it again. I too cannot resist a feeling of liberation and cheerfulness. The pressure was abominable. I hope those scoundrelly heroes of the masses, who have on their conscience the brazen, criminal stupidity of murdering hostages, can be seized and given over to exemplary justice."[33]

In retrospect, the real beneficiaries of the upheavals of 1918–19 were those groups that associated themselves with the conservative politics of the military or the various paramilitary forces. Following the liberation of Munich on May 1, 1919, Bavaria was militarily integrated into a countrywide command structure as District Seven of the Reichswehr, commanded by General Franz Ritter von Epp. The Bavarian military command and its associated paramilitary units became a magnet attracting extreme right-wing groups from all over Germany, particularly after the failed Kapp Putsch of 1920. In fact, it was in the wake of the Kapp Putsch that the Bavarian army placed a right-wing government under Gustav von Kahr in power. From that moment on, Bavaria would pursue policies that were diametrically opposed to the Social Democratic government in Berlin, and Munich became the *Sammelbecken* (collecting vessel) of conspiratorial groups that plotted to overthrow the Weimar Republic. The Bavarian authorities turned a blind eye to all sorts of right-wing groups, including refractory Free Corps units that operated freely under the protection of the Reichswehr. The Erhardt Brigade found refuge in Bavaria after the Kapp Putsch, and here, too, extremists instigated the political assassinations of Erzberger and Rathenau. The leading officers of the army district command in Munich openly sympathized with the Nazi cause, and some, like Ernst Röhm, would often roam the beer cellars of Munich or scour the ranks of the Free Corps and similar ex-servicemen's associations for new recruits for the Nazi Party. These men saw themselves as harbingers of a revitalized Germany and as crusading knights against Communism. In retrospect, we now know that Communism had discredited itself without much help from its strident opponents. What these militant men of the right succeeded in doing was to plant an incubus in Bavaria that was to weigh upon the humane conscience of the German people well beyond their own lifetimes.

The Origin and Growth of the Nazi Party (NSDAP)

In the winter of 1918, Rudolf von Sebattendorf, the founder of the Thule Society, became interested in a new group called the Free Workers' Committee for a Good Peace (Freier Arbeiterauschuss für einen guten Frieden).[34] This informal group of workers had been founded in March 1918 by Anton Drexler (1884–1942), a toolmaker in the Munich railroad works. Sebattendorf saw an opportunity in using this small circle of workers as a catalyst to convert other German workers to the cause of his own *völkisch* movement. He suspected that many German workers would not defect to Communism because their loyalty to the nation was stronger than their allegiance to class, and that all Germans — workers, soldiers, merchants, farmers — could be integrated into a *völkisch* state.

In October 1918 Sebattendorf instructed Karl Harrer (1890–1926), a sports journalist and member of the Thule Society, to combine forces with Drexler, and the result was the establishment of the Political Workers' Circle (Politische Arbeiterzirkel), a small group of machinists from Drexler's workshop that met informally, in *Stammtisch* (reserved beer table) fashion, to discuss political issues.[35] On January 5, 1918, the Political Workers' Circle renamed itself the German Workers' Party (Deutsche Arbeiterpartei [DAP]). During its first meeting at the Fürstenfelder-Hof in Munich, Drexler set forth his political agenda, later circulated in his pamphlet *Mein politisches Erwachen* (My political awakening). Drexler was a somewhat slow-witted but well-intentioned do-gooder who wanted to save the German working class from the clutches of international Communism. Equally opposed to Communism and capitalism, he envisioned a *völkisch* state, purged of all alien forces (Jews, foreigners, pacifists) that rested primarily on a broad middle class, including skilled workers, and exhibited a sound social conscience. The social and economic welfare of the whole German people was to be the spinal principle of such a regenerated German *Volk* community.

A few days after its first meeting at the Fürstenfelder-Hof, the German Workers' Party met again, this time in the Hotel Vierjahreszeiten, where the Thule Society had its headquarters, and elected Karl Harrer national chairman and Anton Drexler as his second-in-command with primary responsibility for leading the local (Munich) branch of the party.

The new "party" was little more than a beerhall debating society, and for some time its members had to keep an extremely low profile in order to avoid being shot by the radicals of the left, especially during the chaotic days of the *Räterepublik*. In fact, Drexler barely escaped being stood in front of a firing squad by Egelhofer's red guards; he was saved when one Communist called out to his comrades: "You can't shoot this one; he's crazy."[36] The defeat of the Communists by the forces of the right, however, enabled the DAP to surface publicly and work aggressively to recruit new members.

Originally, the party drew upon four diverse groups for its membership: petit bourgeois nationalists with strong racist predilections, amateur intellectuals with bizarre panaceas for Germany's salvation, military men with decided conservative and authoritarian attitudes, and asocial characters with shadowy pasts who used the party for their own opportunistic purposes. Among the first group were Harrer and Drexler; among the second group were Gottfried Feder, Dietrich Eckart, Alfred Rosenberg, and Max Erwin von Scheubner-Richter; among the prominent military men were Ritter von Epp, Ernst Röhm, and Alfred Ludendorff; and among the growing group of asocial bullies or con men was Hermann Esser, who epitomized the type before Adolf Hitler replaced him in that role.

Next to Drexler and Harrer, Gottfried Feder (1883–1941) could claim to be one of the original pioneers of the Nazi Party. A construction engineer from Würzburg who settled in Munich and took to political pamphleteering in the wake of Germany's collapse, Feder initially approached the Eisner government with his unorthodox economic remedies, but when he was ignored he turned to more congenial right-wing groups and eventually became the Nazi Party's murky financial expert. Among the various unorthodox financial panaceas offered by Feder was a plan to abolish all interest rates; the plan was based on his belief that Germany's economic plight, especially that suffered by the workers, was the result of financial speculators of Jewish extraction who had ruined the country by charging usurious interest rates. Feder therefore demanded that the slavery of interest rates must be broken by the government, and he proposed a new plan by which the government would finance projects by issuing state treasury certificates that represented the actual value of whatever was to be produced. The assumption behind this idea was that real value resided in actual physical assets rather than in the abstractions of finance capitalism. Feder also supported inflationary fiscal policies, interest-free state credits, nationalization of all banks, socialization of large department stores, and the abolition of trusts. His vision was a curious hybrid of medieval communalism and modern state socialism; it tried to blend ideas of the thrifty, homogeneous *Volk* community with state sponsored industrialization and socialization.

What attracted Hitler and others to these ideas was the monocausal explanation they provided about Germany's economic crisis. Feder had identified the Jews as the real financial malefactors of Germany's economic collapse, an explanation that, to Hitler and others, seemed like a revelation and reinforced the rising paranoid style among the recent converts to various right-wing ideologies.

Feder has been aptly called a kind of "central European William Jennings Bryan," a populist with a quick-fix solution to complex economic problems.[37] He spoke for the economic little man, the Drexlers of this world, who felt betrayed and sold out by both big business and big labor, who clung nostalgically to a preindustrial vision of a harmonious *Volk* community in which burghers, workers, and soldiers cooperated for the good of the fatherland. This message, which Hitler would later promote as long as it suited him politically, found widespread support among many Germans, chiefly among marginal economic groups (handicraftsmen, small business proprietors, agricultural laborers, domestics, semiskilled workers) who felt alienated, displaced, and unrepresented. Buffeted by seemingly irrational events, these groups increasingly regressed mentally to what Richard Hofstadter has termed, in another context, the "paranoid style" in politics.[38] Feder and his cohorts believed that Germany had been taken away from them by scheming and sinister types who were the real wire-pullers of modern times, unhinging the normal course of events and deliberately causing crises, runs on banks, depressions — all for their own profit and enjoyment. These stereotypical images of sybaritic malefactors centered, above all, on the Jews, the real agents of historical causation, immune themselves from historical change unless unmasked in all their stark evil by charismatically gifted prophets.

Hitler saw "enormous theoretical truth"[39] in Feder's economic doctrines and subsequently permitted embodying some of his anticapitalist views into the party program (Points 11, 19, 25). Feder became an important liaison man to certain economic groups, especially members of the lower middle classes; but he later became a liability when Hitler needed the support of big business. When this became obvious, Hitler fobbed him off by giving him minor sinecures and generally ignoring him. By that time, he had become, if not a victim, a kind of respectable nonentity and died in obscurity in 1941.

Another amateur intellectual of the German Workers' Party was Dietrich Eckart (1868–1923), a lawyer's son from Neumarkt in Bavaria. After abandoning his medical studies, Eckart pursued a career in journalism and the theater, gaining a reputation as a talented dramatist whose ornate and flowery patriotic plays proved popular among nationalistic Germans. His personality was a cross between self-inflated poseur and cheap huckster. In Bavarian circles, he was arguably seen as the archetypal Bavarian — bon vivant, womanizer, and spouter of outlandish beliefs. He was also unstable, having spent time in a mental institution and gradually becoming addicted to alcohol and morphine. At the same time, Eckart was a persuasive and ingratiating conversationalist who built up a large circle of social connections that included some very influential people. From 1918 to 1920, Eckart published the highly inflammatory paper called *Auf Gut Deutsch* (In plain German), which specialized in anti-Semitic and anti-Communist propaganda. Eckart was also a prominent member of the Thule Society and thus a midwife to the Nazi Party. His social connections enabled the German Workers' Party to acquire the *Münchener Beobachter* in December 1920. Edited by Eckart, this paper was later renamed *Völkischer Beobachter* (Ethnic observer) and became the Nazi Party's ideological mouthpiece; its subtitle, "Broadside of the National-Socialist Movement of Greater Germany," reflected Eckart's belief, expressed in an earlier poem, that Germany must be awakened with a philosophical (Nietzschean) hammer if it was to survive its calamities. Eckart saw in Hitler Germany's redeemer, took the young inexperienced rabble-rouser under his wing, and furthered his political career. Hitler, in turn, looked up to Eckart as a role model and spiritual godfather of the Nazi movement, later dedicating *Mein Kampf* to his memory.

Eckart was a crucial figure in the early days of the Nazi Party as a propagandist, fund-raiser, and talent scout. One of the various "talents," besides Hitler, that he furthered was Alfred Rosenberg (1893–1946), a Baltic German who appeared one day in Eckart's office and inquired whether Eckart could use "a fighter against Jerusalem." The delighted editor supposedly responded by saying: "Certainly."[40] This launched Rosenberg on his infamous career as an expert on "the Jewish question," Bolshevism, and Nazi ideology. What would later impress Hitler was Rosenberg's identification of Communism with world Jewry, which eventually helped the Nazi leader in closing his paranoid ideological circle in which anti-Semitism and Communism were identified as monocausal explanations for all of Germany's problems.

Rosenberg was born in Reval, Estonia, son of an Estonian mother and a Lithuanian father. Intellectually, Rosenberg belonged to the Auslandsdeutsche, to those persons of German ethnicity who lived in German communities in the Baltic states, Russia, or elsewhere in Europe or overseas. These "little Germanies" often cultivated an exaggerated sense of Germanism with strong nationalistic and racial coloration. Although Rosenberg had pursued a technical career, studying architecture at Riga and Moscow, he had steeped himself so well in the intellectual demimonde of racist philosophy that when he met Adolf Hitler, the two men immediately recognized each other as soul mates. Rosenberg was a brooding, pedantic, and intolerant ideologue who has been termed "a profoundly half-educated man."[41] Like Hitler's, his knowledge of the world was culled primarily from ethnic-racial tracts and countless apocryphal sources and theories; and out of this mesh of self-serving doctrines of Aryan superiority, he had constructed a Weltanschauung that he would subsequently launch upon the world in such works as *Die Spur des Juden im Wandel der Zeiten* (The trace of the Jew in changing times [1920]), *Unmoral im Talmud* (Immorality in the Talmud [1920]), and his magnum opus, *Der Mythus des 20. Jahrhunderts* (The myth of the 20th century [1930]).

In 1918, Rosenberg fled from the Bolsheviks and came to Munich, where he joined the Thule Society and subsequently the DAP. He became chief editor of the *Völkischer Beobachter* in 1921, a post he was to hold throughout his career. His role in the formative years of the party was very important because he exercised a profound influence over the mind of Adolf Hitler. Otto Strasser and others have even argued that, during the years 1919–23, Hitler was largely the mouthpiece of Alfred Rosenberg,[42] a judgement that erroneously assumes that Hitler's racial views were molded primarily by Rosenberg. The truth is that Hitler adopted some of Rosenberg's racial views to his already firmly held anti-Semitic biases. Rosenberg may have been a catalyst in helping Hitler formulate a consistent anti-Semitic philosophy, but in other respects Rosenberg's influence was minimal. Hitler greatly respected Rosenberg in the early years of the movement and even appointed him interim leader of the party while he served his prison sentence at Landsberg. Later, when their contacts became less frequent, Hitler continued to regard Rosenberg as a valued member and pioneer of the party, but he never sought him out as a close comrade-in-arms and generally excluded him from his inner circle. This was also partly due to the fact that Rosenberg was a ponderous and utterly humorless man without visible social skills. As Rosenberg himself summed up his relationship with Hitler: "He valued me very much, but he did not like me."[43]

Another Baltic German, Max Erwin von Scheubner-Richter (1884–1923), was brought into the party by Rosenberg and played an important role in its early history. Rosenberg had met Scheubner-Richter in Riga and was impressed by his background. Scheubner-Richter had studied engineering at Riga, Dresden, and Munich, graduating with a doctoral degree from the Technical University of Munich. During World War I he served both as an officer and as a member of the German diplomatic corps in various capacities in far-flung theaters of war like eastern Europe and Turkey. A man of learning and impressive diplomatic skills, Scheubner-Richter had built up a diverse circle of prominent people, including members of the house of Wittelsbach, captains of industry, high prelates, Russian emigrants, and officers of the armed forces. Scheubner-Richter had a knack for political intrigue as well as for raising money from his circle of acquaintances, and he was to serve as an important liaison between the new Nazi Party and the traditional military-industrial complex.

One of Scheubner-Richter's most important contacts was General Ludendorff, legendary war hero to the Germans and reviled war criminal to the Allies.[44] Ludendorff had briefly escaped from Germany and had gone to Sweden in order to avoid the wrath of the radical left; but when the Spartacists were defeated in January 1919, he felt secure enough to return to Germany the following month. While in Sweden, he had feverishly written his war memoirs almost entirely from memory within just three months; and armed with this remarkable document, which combined a vivid reconstruction of events with an obvious desire to exculpate himself from their tragic consequences, Ludendorff returned to Berlin not only to rehabilitate himself but also to further his political ambitions. In many quarters he was still celebrated as a great war hero and a national treasure. For some time he lived entirely rent-free in the fashionable Adlon Hotel under the assumed name of Karl Neumann. Since the Allied Disarmament Commission also had its seat in the Adlon Hotel, the management of the hotel had even conveniently given Ludendorff a suite with a private exit onto the Wilhelmstrasse, thus saving him from the embarrassment of being recognized and possibly arrested as a war criminal. Although Ludendorff had been a brilliant military tactician, blessed with a remarkably quick mind and seemingly boundless energy, he was entirely lacking in a sense of proportion and a broad understanding of the world. This became even more apparent after he launched into right-wing political causes after his return to Germany. In 1920, as previously noted, he associated himself with the Kapp conspiracy to overthrow the Weimar Republic. When the Putsch failed, he moved out of harm's way and settled in the more congenial right-wing atmosphere of Munich, where a sympathetic baron generously placed a spacious villa at his disposal. His political judgments, which never equaled his military acumen, steadily deteriorated, particularly after he divorced his wife Margarethe and married Mathilde Kemnitz, a sinister and pseudointellectual quack who poisoned his mind with racist, pagan, and anti-Semitic ideas. Scheubner-Richter and most of the leaders of the new German Workers' Party saw Ludendorff as a convenient front man whose reputation would be useful in enhancing the party's popularity.

Both Rosenberg and Scheubner-Richter were also in touch with exiles from Bolshevism, with Russians who had formed sizeable colonies in some of the major German cities, notably Berlin and Munich. These exiles were sworn enemies of Communism, and they spent their waking hours spewing propaganda and plotting revenge. Their influence on fascistic movements has still not been fully appreciated, but there is enough evidence that it was far more powerful than is commonly supposed.[45] In Berlin, for example, Fyodor Vinberg, a former tsarist officer, published a daily Russian-language newspaper called *Prizyv* (The call) in which, among other things, he advocated as "the final solution" to the Jewish problem the actual extermination of all Jews. In support of this monstrous proposal, Vinberg disseminated the first copies in Germany of *The Protocols of the Elders of Zion,* an anti-Semitic hate document that had been fabricated by the tsarist secret police and was widely circulated in Russia before World War I. The document purported to be the record of secret meetings of Zionist leaders who pledged themselves to overthrow Western Christian civilization by infecting it with the subversive forces of democracy, liberalism, and socialism. *The Protocols* also described the technical means by which the establishment of a world Jewish state could be accomplished. Many exiles from Bolshevism carried copies of this document with them; one of them was Alfred Rosenberg, who had been exposed to it while he was a student in Moscow. A German version of *The Protocols* appeared as early as 1920, later supplemented by Rosenberg's own edited version in 1923.

What was required to bring these heterogeneous elements together and fuse them into one party was a man of organizational genius and great rhetorical abilities. Some members of the German Workers' Party at first thought that Hermann Esser (1900–1981), a "demon speech-maker" and rabble-rouser, might be the spark that would ignite the incendiary feelings of disaffected Germans. Born in Roormohs, near Dachau in Bavaria, Esser came from a middle-class family, attended a humanistic gymnasium, and volunteered, while still an adolescent, for service in the army during World War I. He returned to Munich after the war as a confirmed Socialist and became one of the cofounders of the German Workers' Party (member no. 2). Esser was intelligent, cunning, and utterly unscrupulous. Konrad Heiden described him as the prototypical Nazi — crude, brutal, without moral inhibitions, and callous in his interpersonal relationships, especially with women.[46] He had a gift for vivid phrases and excelled in dishing up nauseous stories about Jews in the pages of the *Völkischer Beobachter.* Although Hitler valued his doglike devotion, he privately admitted that Esser was a scoundrel and a potential liability; but he also knew that Esser was perfectly capable, when pushed against the wall, of divulging the most embarrassing secrets about the inner machinations of the Nazi Party. For this reason, Esser was fobbed off with various assignments and minor posts in later years; in return, he kept his mouth shut and managed to survive the capricious terrors he himself helped to inspire.

What disqualified Esser from building up a mass party and inspiring it with a sense of mission and purpose was his selfish opportunism and his lack of true ideological conviction. An incident that illustrates his inability to inspire devoted followers or to be taken seriously as a man of unswerving loyalty to the party occurred when he threatened to walk out of the party and go over to the Communists because he had not received his salary punctually. He even intimated on that occasion that he might reveal some embarrassing secrets to the opposition if he did not receive satisfaction.

Mass movements may attract such selfish opportunists as Esser, but they are led by dedicated and utterly single-minded fanatics, by what Bruce Mazlish has termed "revolutionary ascetics."[47] Such political zealots, once they have seen the light, are transfigured by a special kind of energy and charisma that may appear to many as a gift of God. Displacing their selfishness onto abstractions with which they totally identify, these ascetics become catalysts of converting millions to their own ideological beliefs. They mesmerize their followers with a power that flows from an inner conviction, a power made all the more credible in the eyes of the followers because of its assumed purity. The leader's power compels because it appears to spring from self-denying or ascetic sources. As Bruce Mazlish puts it, "All-powerful, all-knowing, immune (especially if asceticism is added to displaced libido) to the vagaries of the flesh, the leader is perceived as godlike — and just as impersonal."[48] It was Adolf Hitler rather than Esser who carried within himself some of these qualities, projected them onto a fertile political landscape, and thus produced one of the most dynamic political movements of the twentieth century.

When Adolf Hitler joined the German Workers' Party as board member number 7 in September 1919 and was given responsibility for recruitment and propaganda, he was shocked by the Bavarian *Schlamperei* (slovenliness) that characterized the party's day-to-day business procedures. He was disturbed by not only the lack of vision displayed by the party's leaders but also the easy-going democratic spirit that seemed to motivate the proceedings. Hitler was determined to reorganize the party along military lines; and only three months after he joined the party, he suggested sweeping changes aimed at creating the framework for a mass party. Both Drexler and Harrer were content with the idea of running a small party, but Hitler rightly perceived that by thinking small, the leaders of the party would condemn the fledgling organization to political impotence. With his penchant for grandiose visions, Hitler dreamed of transforming the DAP into a mass party by means of skillfully orchestrated mass rallies and protests. He saw himself as a soldier-politician who would create the most awe-inspiring organization and then launch it against the hated Weimar Republic. With feverish energy, he began networking among like-minded believers, sending out invitations to meetings, building up lists of potential members, and personally soliciting support. At first the seven-man party committee met informally at Café Gasteig, but Hitler persuaded the party to rent the vaultlike cellar of the Sternecker Beerhall as the party's new headquarters. These moves struck the old guard as pretentiously unrealistic, and some of them, notably Harrer and Drexler, began to accuse the young rabble-rouser of being *grössenwahnsinnig* (deluded by grandeur).[49]

In his effort to reorganize the party along military lines, Hitler's immediate aim was to attract recruits with military backgrounds who would be more loyal to him than they would be to the more cautious and conservative old guard. In time, these Hitler supporters would constitute a kind of shadow leadership corps, waiting to spring into action against the stodgy old leaders.[50] Harrer, who had staunchly resisted Hitler's propaganda plans, was the first to go. The executive committee then gave in to Hitler's proposal to stage mass rallies and issued a call for its first mass meeting in the *Festsaal* (banquet hall) of the Hofbräuhaus on February 24, 1920.

According to later party hagiography, this mass meeting represented the historical equivalent of Martin Luther's nailing of the Ninety-Five Theses on the church door at Wittenberg because, on that evening, Adolf Hitler revealed the twenty-five theses of the new party platform to a crowd of almost two thousand, many of whom, much to Hitler's delight, were Independent Socialists and Communists who might be converted on the spot.[51] In reality the meeting was a curious combination of raucous buffoonery and political demagoguery. The main speaker of the evening was not Adolf Hitler but Dr. Johannes Dingfelder, a homeopathic physician who wrote cranky racist articles in right-wing journals under the pseudonym Germanus Agricola. On that evening he held forth on the causes of Germany's political disease and ended with hopeful and pious platitudes, supported by quotations from Shakespeare and Schiller.

When Hitler rose to his feet and delivered his impassioned address on the current political situation, the atmosphere in the hall changed abruptly. Unlike Dingfelder, Hitler engaged the audience as coactors who either thrilled to his incendiary rhetoric or reacted to it with hostile catcalls or provocative heckling; and far from being perturbed by such audience disruptions, Hitler seemed to be energized by them. He knew intuitively that indifference was the kiss of death to any politician, especially in an age of mass politics and at a time of national despair. Such times called for a leader who could articulate mass disaffections, identify himself with the suffering of ordinary people, and convert the masses to his redemptive vision. The aim was not so much to tell the truth but to appear credible, to persuade and convert the masses to a definitive political position. Given the extreme polarization of German politics, Hitler expected vocal and derisive opposition, and on that evening, as he himself admitted, he was frequently interrupted by shouts that "came down like showers of hail,"[52] threatening to disrupt the whole proceeding. Party bruisers had to spring into action with rubber truncheons and riding whips, hustling troublemakers out of the hall. Such scenes of provocative demagoguery, marked by ecstatic cries and thundering applause but also by vigorous opposition in the form of catcalls, flying beer mugs, and even physical assaults, would become the hallmark of many of Hitler's speeches.

The same can be said of the quality of Hitler's rhetoric and the general format in which it was usually delivered. The speech of February 24 was in many ways a prototype for thousands of Hitler's speeches to come. Delivered at night to a packed audience that would often be kept anxiously waiting, a typical Hitler speech would play upon a mood of tension and keyed-up expectations. Hitler would begin by recapitulating a chain of events that had led to the current national crisis. This portion of the speech, as J. P. Stern has observed, would contain an element of information; the audience, however, was to be informed only for the purpose of participating in a performance that would make history.[53] An important part of this performance was for Hitler to identify himself with the suffering of the audience and to portray himself as an ordinary veteran and patriot who put the good of the country over the good of narrow self-interest groups. Being a veteran himself, he could share in the bitter disappointments and shattered illusions of many ex-servicemen in the audience. The speech next proceeded to an unmasking of malefactors who had brought ruin and humiliation on the German people. Hitler now opened up his clever arsenal of rhetorical devices aimed at identifying the culprits. He would make sly and then more blatant, even libelous, charges against Weimar politicians, evoking angry responses from members of the audience demanding that such rascals be thrown out of office, thrashed, or hanged. He would castigate the "November Criminals," war profiteers, pacifists, liberals, Communists, and, above all, the Jews. The pace of the speech would now accelerate in emotional intensity as Hitler warmed up to the growing rapport with his audience. His rhetoric would become more and more belligerent and menacing. He left no doubt in anyone's mind what would happen when the party seized power: heads would roll. At this point the audience would become transfigured, both by his message and the brilliantly effective gestures, tone of voice, and rhetorical devices of the speaker.

German audiences seemed particularly mesmerized by Hitler's voice. There was something mysterious about it to many Germans because it did not seem to be rooted in any local dialect or class other than being south German or Austrian. In J. P. Stern's suggestive phrase, it was the voice of no one and all,[54] the voice of the ordinary German expressing exactly what ordinary Germans thought and felt. Hitler's speeches would invariably end with rousing affirmations of German national greatness and reassurances that such greatness would be rejuvenated under the banner of National Socialism. At this point most of the audience would fasten on his every word and spontaneously burst out in frenzied cheering, hand-clapping, and table-pounding. There would even be wild cries and uncontrolled sobs by some members of the audience, especially women.

Hitler's harangue on February 24 began with a recapitulation of Germany's desperate economic plight and the inability of the government to deal with it. He castigated government leaders for being too cowardly to tell the truth and for spouting pious phrases about working harder.[55] He proclaimed that by working harder, the German people were only contributing to the benefit of their enemies. He blamed the peace treaty for creating new and untold miseries, not the least of which were those brought about by the printing of worthless paper money. There was a time, he said, when German civil servants were known for their reliability and honor, but how could one expect honorable behavior from the likes of Erzberger (stormy applause), whose misconduct had been such that it was incomprehensible that he wasn't already sitting in prison (lively applause)? These aspersions of criminal malfeasance in high office were followed by sly insinuations of Jewish culpability, prompting loud howls from the audience of "Down with the Jewish Press" and "Throw'em out!"[56] This is exactly what Hitler himself felt, for in the next breath he proceeded to identify the Jews as the real culprits and demanded that they be thrown out of Germany as a prerequisite for internal chimney-sweeping (lively applause). When it comes to criminal profiteers and usurers, he exclaimed, it is useless to assess monetary fines. The audience suggested a more effective form of punishment for such types — thrashing and hanging. When he asked rhetorically what should be done with such blood-sucking leeches, the howling crowd replied lustily, "Hang them."[57]

Hitler then called upon all Germans to draw together into a solid *Volk* community; and with an eye toward those who might be counting on international class solidarity, he reminded his listeners that anyone who counted on international goodwill was lost. Finally, amid a highly charged atmosphere in the hall, marked by warm applause but also ugly catcalls, Hitler proceeded to read the party program. The hallmark of this program, which Hitler never regarded as anything but a propaganda tool, consisted of a clever mixture of nationalistic and socialistic ideas for the obvious purpose of attracting the largest number of followers. Although for some the terms *nationalism* and *socialism* stood for incompatible goals, for Hitler they were little more than symbolic or even mystical slogans by which to invoke positive impressions or feelings in different groups. Unconsciously he saw in these mystical slogans a way of integrating diverse groups and giving them a sense that they could believe in the same ideological convictions. Socialism, in Hitler's mind, was not to be taken in its "degenerate" Marxist sense of class struggle and proletarian equality but in Oswald Spengler's meaning of "Prussian socialism" based on class harmony, hard work, obedience, and service to the state. Some party ideologues like the Strassers did not seem to understand that by the term *socialism* Hitler was not referring to a specific economic system but to an instinct for national self-preservation. Hitler's socialism, they learned to their great disappointment, was driven

by nationalism, for Hitler believed that only in that form could socialism promote the common good over the private good (*Gemeinnutz vor
Eigennutz*), preserve social tranquility, and promote the reestablishment
of a healthy folk community.

Socialism was thus intimately linked with nationalism because a homogeneous and prosperous whole requires the love and commitment of
its members; but that commitment is also reciprocal: the whole must
care for the individual parts. Germans must be taught that they work
not just for their own selfish ends but for the good of the nation; and
by working for the collective, Germans should be secure in the knowledge that the state, in turn, works on their behalf by guaranteeing them
a good livelihood, conducive working conditions, unemployment benefits, old-age pensions, free education, and other social benefits. The
party platform therefore demanded that "the state make it its primary
duty to provide a livelihood for its citizens" (Article 7); and in a series of bold socialistic proposals, it called for "the nationalization of all
business enterprises that have been organized into corporations" (Article
13); "profit-sharing in large industrial enterprises" (Article 14); "generous development of old age insurance" (Article 15); and "the immediate
socialization of the huge department stores and their lease, at low rates,
to small tradesmen" (Article 16).[58]

There were equally strong nationalistic and racist provisions in the
party program, beginning with the demand, based on the principle of
national self-determination, that all Germans be united into a Greater
Germany. In practice this meant that German nationals who were living
outside German territorial borders in 1920 — in Austria, Italy, Poland,
or Czechoslovakia — should be reunited with the fatherland. This territorial question, in turn, raised a number of racial and imperialistic
issues, the most ominous being the demand for "living space" (*Lebensraum*). Thus, Article 3 spoke of the demand for colonies to feed the
German people, and those who had been listening to Hitler before knew
that he looked to Russia as a field of German colonization. In a speech
given to an earlier DAP meeting on December 10, 1919, entitled "Germany in Her Deepest Humiliation," he had pointedly asked whether it
was right that one Russian owned eighteen times as much land as a
German.[59]

Hatred of foreigners and Jews also played a prominent role in the
1920 program. Article 4, for example, argues syllogistically that "only
a racial comrade can be a citizen; only a person of German blood, irre-
spective of religious denomination, can be a racial comrade; therefore,
no Jew can be a racial comrade."[60] Hitler had made it abundantly clear
before that Jews belonged to a racial rather than a religious community,
and that a rational policy of anti-Semitism must aim at the legalization
of racial discrimination and the eventual elimination of all Jews from
German soil.[61] Overall, the party program appeared to be more negative than positive; it was a document searching to define itself by what

was hated — foreigners, Jews, parliamentary government, the Western powers, usury, and profiteers. However, beginning with its first major meeting in the Hofbräuhaus on February 24, the party had a platform and a mission. On that day, as Joachim Fest observes, "began the evolution of Drexler's beer-drinking racist club into Adolf Hitler's mass party."[62]

A week after this meeting the German Workers' Party (DAP) changed its name to the National Socialist German Workers' Party (NSDAP). On March 31, 1920, Hitler mustered out of the army in order to dedicate himself heart and soul to the party. His unflagging efforts, spellbinding oratory, and ability to attract large crowds enabled the party to expand its membership and its base of operation. In April 1920 the first branch of the party outside Munich was founded at Rosenheim; by the end of the year the party had established branches in ten provincial areas outside Munich and one locale outside Bavaria (Mannheim).[63] This expansion required a change in the party's legal status, and on October 20, 1920, the party incorporated itself as the Nationalsozialistischer Deutscher Arbeiterverein, eingetragener Verein (NSDAV e.v.). German law specified that in order to be a registered club, an organization had to establish bylaws. Accordingly, the party vested control in a board of directors, consisting of two chairmen, two secretaries, and two treasurers. As chief of propaganda, Hitler was not part of this ruling body and thus was ostensibly excluded from the decision-making process. However, since new party members were required to attend periodic indoctrination sessions, Hitler was able to exercise a remarkable degree of influence over the rank and file. As mentioned above, in December 1920 the party acquired what became the official party newspaper, the *Völkischer Beobachter*, whose editorial policy fell under the purview of the propaganda chief, thus giving Hitler another important lever of power. By controlling the editorial policy of the *Völkischer Beobachter*, Hitler would be able to shape party policy and to scrutinize the ideological commitments of its members. In this way, he gradually built up a cadre of followers who were pledged to him by personal loyalty.

On January 22, 1921, the party assembled for its first national congress in Munich. Hitler had every reason to be proud of his accomplishments: his personal charisma was largely undisputed, and the party, now three thousand strong, had become a respectable force in Bavarian right-wing circles. Of course, it was still only one of many similar right-wing nationalistic organizations. Rival groups operated elsewhere: in Nuremberg, Julius Streicher led a branch of the Deutschsozialistische Partei (German Socialist Party), while Otto Dickel headed a branch of the same party in Augsburg. In the Sudetenland, now in Czechoslovakia, as well as in Austria, pan-German workers' parties had been active for some time. One of them, the Deutsche Arbeiterpartei (German Workers' Party), led by an Austrian lawyer, Walther Riehl, and a railway employee, Rudolf Jung, appeared to be an almost exact copy of Drexler's group except that it already had greater political experience because it dated back to the prewar period. The Austrian DAP subsequently changed its name from the German Workers' Party to the German National Socialist Workers' Party, began using the swastika as its party symbol, and tried to establish fraternal connections with similar organizations, culminating in an interstate conference at Salzburg in August 1920. Although Hitler attended the Salzburg conference, he discouraged members of the Nazi Party from cooperating too closely because it might splinter the loyalties of the rank and file, dilute its program, and weaken its political strength.

Hitler's ultimate aim was to create a homogeneous party that would be organized like a superb military force and subject to a clear-cut chain of command. As he gained confidence in his own leadership abilities, he increasingly tried to mold the party to fit his own visions. The old guard naturally resented his heavy-handed methods, rightly suspecting that Hitler wanted to seize control of the party and make himself its absolute leader. The issue that brought about an open breach between Hitler and the old guard was a plan by the Augsburg local of the NS-DAP to negotiate a merger with the German Socialist Party. Outwardly, a fusion between the two parties seemed practical and logical because both organizations were much alike. By pooling their financial resources and talents, the proponents of this plan argued, the Nazi Party would be greatly strengthened. Since the merger was backed by the anti-Hitler forces in the party, Hitler smelled ulterior motives. He suspected that, just as he had built up his own following by diluting support for the old guard through new recruits, the old guard was now trying to turn the tables on him by swelling the party with raw recruits of uncertain loyalties from a different organization. In addition, by proposing to transfer party headquarters from Munich to Berlin, the old guard hoped to isolate Hitler's followers in Bavaria from the real source of power.

Hitler's response was as swift as it was daring: he resigned from the party on July 12, 1921. Caught completely off guard by this radical step, the executive committee made a major blunder by maligning Hitler in a hastily contrived broadside, accusing him of dictatorial intentions, which was true, and being in the pay of Jews and the emperor of Austria, which was manifestly absurd.[64] He was still interested in rejoining the party, he indicated to his detractors, but only on condition of being invested with dictatorial powers. He demanded to be elected as first chairman of the party, replacement of the old executive committee by a new three-man action committee chosen by himself, and the convening of a party congress to settle these issues.

The man who was instrumental at this point in roping Hitler back into the party was Anton Drexler. Like most members of the old guard, Drexler was suspicious of Hitler's intentions and his unconventional Bohemian lifestyle, but he was perceptive enough to realize that Hitler's exclusion from the party would seriously jeopardize its future. He knew that the party's growing strength was largely the result of Hitler's organizational talent, the sort of talent that was indispensable to the party at this crucial juncture in its formative stages. For these reasons he counseled moderation and persuaded the other members of the committee to accede to Hitler's demands. The party congress, held on July 29, 1921, was a personal triumph for Hitler and a complete defeat for the old guard. By a constitutional amendment, the old guard gave Hitler dictatorial powers to mold the party as he saw fit.

The new executive branch of the party now consisted of a three-man action committee dominated by Hitler. All policy matters originated with this group, while the details of party organization were turned over to six subcommittees: propaganda, finance, youth organization, sports, investigation, and mediation. Hitler made sure that his personal loyalists were appointed to leadership posts on these subcommittees. Hermann Esser was put in charge of propaganda, while Eckart was appointed editor of the *Völkischer Beobachter.* Gustav Adolf Lenk, a young admirer of Hitler, became chairman of the party's youth organization, the Jungsturm, the precursor of the Hitler Youth. The subcommittee on sports and athletics was quickly transformed into the Sturmabteilung (SA), the storm troopers, destined to become the notorious paramilitary branch of the Nazi Party. We do not know who headed the section on investigation, but as Dietrich Orlow has pointed out, Hitler probably dominated much of its proceedings because it controlled admission and expulsion of party members.[65] Of the old guard, only Drexler was given a voice in the party; he became chairman of the subcommittee on mediation and honorary member for life in the party. Although this title was largely honorific, it reflects Hitler's desire to prevent further party strife.

One of Hitler's chief aims was to impose a tight structure on the party, especially in fiscal matters. For that purpose, Hitler appointed his former company sergeant, Max Amann (1891–1957), a blunt, capable, and totally loyal friend, to the post of business manager. In this post, which involved administrative as well as fiscal responsibilities, Amann eventually built up a powerful administrative empire that included besides his fiscal duties the supervision of Nazi publications, the management of Hitler's personal wealth, and eventually the coordination of the whole Reich Press Chamber.

Another feature of the new centralizing efforts involved sending out circular letters (*Rundschreiben*) to all local branches of the party, instructing them on the acquisition of flags and insignia and urging them to report local developments in a prompt manner and to submit lists of all new members for screening purposes. Hitler placed great emphasis on the need for symbols and myths in party organization. As early as August 1920, he approved of the swastika as the party's prime symbol. As previously mentioned, the swastika had been used by a variety of *völkisch* groups and paramilitary organizations, but as a symbol it dates back to ancient times. In Sanskrit the word *swastika* originally meant "good luck," and in the pictorial records of various religions (Egyptian, Greek, Chinese, Japanese, and Persian) the swastika denoted an object of veneration.

The final swastika emblem, although approved by Hitler, was not Hitler's idea but came from a design by Dr. Friedrich Krohn, who designed it for the founding of the Ortsgruppe Starnberg. At the founding meeting of the Starnberg local, the speaker's lectern was draped with a flag with a background of red, a white circle, and a black swastika in the white center. Hitler approved this design except for one modification — namely, that the arms of the swastika extended in right rather than in left angles.[66] He later explained the symbolic meaning of this design by saying that "in the red we see the social ideal of the movement, in the white the national idea, in the swastika the mission of the fight for the victory of Aryan man, and at the same time also the victory of the idea of creative work which in itself is and always will be anti-Semitic."[67]

Although Hitler did not originate the use of many symbols, he possessed a keen psychological and aesthetic appreciation of the unifying power of symbols in political life. He would spend hours on end thumbing through art magazines and the heraldic departments of the Munich State Library to find the right eagle for the standard rubber stamp of the party.[68] About the same time that the swastika became the official symbol of the party, Josef Fuess, a jeweler, was commissioned by Hitler to design the party's official badge.[69] Party armbands, displaying the swastika in the same manner depicted on flags, came into being shortly afterward, and Hitler insisted that all party members wear such insignia during duty hours. By the end of 1922, Hitler had also designed the NSDAP standards as banners for the SA. These standards were adorned with an eagle perched atop an encircled swastika; below that was a rectangular party shield (or local party shield) to which was affixed the party banner with swastika and the slogan, "Germany Awaken."

The greeting "Heil Hitler" was not officially used in the early 1920s but some individual members addressed each other in this manner even before the Putsch.[70] The word *Heil* was an acclamation reserved for the highest dignitaries in German history such as princes, but it also has a religious-medical connotation in German meaning "healed" or "saved." The name for savior in German is *Heiland;* and various compound nouns that include *Heil* denote healing processes or institutions — *Heilanstalt* (sanatorium or asylum), *Heilbad* (mineral bath), *Heilkraft* (healing power), *Heilkraut* (medicinal herb), *Heilkunde* (medical science), *Heilmittel* (remedy), *heilsam* (wholesome), *Heilsarmee* (salvation army).

Hitler had an uncanny ability to find such mystical symbols and adapt them to Nazi purposes. He was willing to learn and borrow even from institutions he hated such as the Communist Party or the Roman Catholic Church. The Communists taught him the importance of rank and file discipline, ideological commitment, and revolutionary zeal. The Catholic Church taught him the secret of psychic control, the art of binding the members of a group in the mysteries of communal fellowship. It is striking how much religious symbolism found in the Catholic Church was redirected to the rituals and ceremonies of the Nazi Party. The cross became the swastika; church liturgy found its counterpart in Nazi greetings, commands, and incantations; clerical robes, miters, and rosaries were transformed into resplendent Nazi uniforms, standards, medals, badges, and batons; and rituals of worship, as in the Mass, found their Nazi equivalents in party rallies, where later in the 1930s huge masses of devoted followers prayed to their savior, Adolf Hitler, under Speer's cathedrals of light.

In all matters of party organization, Hitler insisted on the strictest military discipline, decor, and protocol. He agonized over the minutest detail of ceremony: the acoustics and ventilation of meeting halls, the mood of crowds, the size and appeal of campaign posters, the arrangement of seats, and the attire of party members. He wondered whether the Hackerbräu called for a louder voice than the Kindl-Keller, and he issued detailed guidelines specifying, among other things, that halls should always be too small, that at least a third of the audience should consist of party members, and that party attire, though clean and attractive, should be egalitarian enough in order to make ordinary working people feel at ease.[71]

Such scrupulous attention to detail, together with an intense effort regarding propaganda and public spectacles, led to a steady increase in party membership. By the beginning of 1922 the NSDAP had six thousand registered voters. Since the proclamation of the twenty-five-point party program in February 1920, the NSDAP had staged eighty-one public meetings.[72] Some of these meetings, especially those held in large settings like the massive tent of the Circus Krone, foreshadowed the superspectacles of the 1930s. What sort of audience did the party attract, how did it finance its operations, and what role did Hitler envision for the growing paramilitary arm of the party, the SA?

Party Membership, Finance, and Paramilitary Organizations

Although the party name and program emphasized a basic commitment to socialism, the class structure of the party was predominantly lower middle class, which meant that loyalty to nation assumed a greater importance than loyalty to class or to a socialistic agenda. The party leadership was motivated by nationalistic and militaristic values. In fact, Hitler's aim was to strengthen ties with the right-wing Bavarian government and the Reichswehr. He wanted to depict the party as a new force in German politics, demonstrating not only that it could gain the support of the middle classes but also that it could build bridges to the urban working classes by mouthing the language of socialism.

As a sociological phenomenon, the Nazi movement had its root causes in the socioeconomically disenfranchised classes of the postwar period — beleaguered members of the lower middle classes, of course, but also demobilized and declassed military men, alienated students and intellectuals, upper-middle-class professionals or business owners who had been frightened by the prospect of Communism, and failed outsiders without marketable skills or with deviant tendencies. These generalizations can be supported in two ways: statistically and biographically.

According to the statistical information available to us, the NSDAP attracted a disproportionately large number of lower-middle-class members, especially from merchant and master-craftsmen backgrounds.[73] From the time of Hitler's involvement in the Nazi Party the number of master craftsmen in the Munich local rose from 7 percent in 1919 to 10.6 percent in 1922, while the number of merchants rose from 16 percent in 1920 to 19.2 percent in 1921. In several branches outside Munich the figures are similar and in some cases even higher. For example, 12.6 percent of the new members of the Rosenheim NSDAP in 1922 were master craftsmen; in Landshut the figure for the same year was 13 percent. In 1922, 35 percent of the new membership of the Mannheim NSDAP consisted of merchants.[74]

Although the plight of these groups was not as dire as has previously been assumed, these occupational groups were indeed heavily affected by postwar inflation, credit restrictions, shortages of raw materials, and competition from large corporations or chain stores. The proliferation of small business proprietors, specializing in small tobacco shops, grocery stores, delicatessens, or clothing stores, had been a response to the explosive growth of cities in the late nineteenth century. These merchants were poorly trained and inadequately prepared to compete with the larger department stores. Yet the number of small retailers continued to increase dramatically, from 695,800 in 1907 to 847,900 in 1925 — an increase of about 22 percent.[75] In the 1920s many of these small-business owners lived on the economic margin, on essentially proletarian incomes. Socially, however, these business owners saw themselves as solid members of the middle class and were terrified of sinking down socially to the level of the urban workers. The same could be said of master craftsmen, whose special skills and talents had traditionally given them a higher social status than most members of the urban working class. Anti-Semitism was strong among both groups, perhaps stronger among the small-business proprietors because they came more frequently in contact with Jews in the retail business and often blamed Jews for their economic hardship.

Lower-middle-class membership in the Munich local of the Nazi Party for the year 1920 was 51 percent. In the fall of 1923, at the time of the Hitler Putsch, lower-middle-class representation for the whole Reich was 52.1 percent. Yet the figures also indicate surprising strengths among the upper classes (managers, higher civil servants, academics, students, entrepreneurs). Although the figures are sparse for this group, the 1920–21 data for Munich reveal that 20.4 percent of its new members came from elite backgrounds, many of them being student recruits. This remarkably high figure may have been the result of the greater disenchantment of the Bavarian elites with the Berlin government and the more effective mobilization of that discontent by the still largely Bavarian-based NSDAP. This is borne out by the fact that elite representation for the whole Reich in 1923 was 11.9 percent.[76]

Inconclusive as our figures for the period 1919–23 undoubtedly are, they do, in part, confirm the traditional "lower-middle-class" thesis propounded in the 1960s by Seymour Lipset and subsequently restated by many historians;[77] but such figures also reveal that the Nazi Party's influence cut across class lines and occupations, making it a genuinely populist party. This judgment is also confirmed by taking a closer biographical look at some of the new active and influential members who joined the party between 1920 and 1923. What motivated people of such diverse social and educational backgrounds to join the Nazi Party?

Two brothers, Otto and Gregor Strasser, were attracted to National Socialism because they were looking for a German-oriented socialism and thought they found it in the new Nazi Party. Gregor, the older brother, was a pharmacist by profession who had served as a lieutenant in World War I. After the war, he settled in his native Landshut as an apothecary, but his real energies went into organizing a Free Corps–type of private army, the Sturmbataillon Niederbayern (Storm Battalion Lower Bavaria). One day in the autumn of 1920 his younger brother, Otto, came to see him to discuss the future of German socialism. Otto had just left the Independent Socialist Party in disgust because it had opted for world revolution and was tying itself too closely to Russian Bolshevism. When Otto arrived at his brother's house for a heart-to-heart talk, Gregor was visited by Ludendorff and Hitler, who managed to persuade Gregor to join the party, thus gaining another energetic and valuable member.[78] Otto at first stayed aloof, but then joined the party and helped edit his brother's newspaper, *Berliner Arbeiter Zeitung* (Berlin workers' gazette). The two brothers would fight emotional see-saw battles with Hitler over the party's social direction, later accusing Hitler of betraying socialism for the sake of power. Both eventually left or were drummed out of the party; Gregor was liquidated in the wake of the Röhm purge of 1934, and Otto bolted the party, organized a "Black Front" of disillusioned former Nazis and Communists, and after Hitler's seizure of power fled Germany.

Ernst Röhm, Rudolf Hess, and Hermann Göring joined the party because they saw in it an extension of the German army and a means of furthering their own ambitions. Röhm dreamed of using the paramilitary branch of the party, the SA, as an elite force in whose image the whole German army would be remolded. He visualized a permanent nation-under-arms with himself as the führer's chief condottiere. Rudolf Hess (1894–1987), who became Hitler's doting secretary and later his deputy führer, saw in Hitler the fulfillment of a dream he had expressed in an essay at the University of Munich on the subject "How must the man be constituted who will lead Germany back to her old heights?" Hess was born in Alexandria, Egypt, the son of a German importer. In World War I he served at first on the western front as a lieutenant in the infantry and then joined the more glamorous flying branch of the service. After the war, he attended the University of Munich, studying under Professor Karl Haushofer (1869–1946), a former general who taught geopolitical theories that later impressed Adolf Hitler. In Munich, Hess was quickly drawn into the maelstrom of right-wing politics, first joining the Thule Society and then giving his heart and soul to Hitler and the Nazi Party. Hess was a political simpleton but also a doggedly devoted loyalist who idolized Hitler and craved his company.

Hermann Göring (1893–1946), a hero of the famed Richthofen flying squadron, joined the Nazi Party for the same reasons that Röhm or Hess had joined. After spending two years as a barnstorming stunt pilot in Sweden following World War I, the highly decorated Göring returned to Germany in 1921 with his Swedish wife, Karin, attended the University of Munich, dabbled in politics and joined the Nazi Party after he heard Hitler speak in the fall of 1922. A man of driving ambition, Göring possessed great organizational talent and leadership abilities. Utterly ruthless in his single-minded pursuit of power and glory, he could also be extremely charming and personally attractive. His cunning sociopathic personality proved to be of decisive importance to the Nazi Party.

Dietrich Eckart, Alfred Rosenberg, and Julius Streicher, the anti-Semitic trio, followed later by Heinrich Himmler and Joseph Goebbels, joined the party primarily out of ideological convictions. Eckart, as previously mentioned, was a debauched poet and romantic revolutionary with a flair for the dramatic. A man of learning, he was also an alcoholic and a drug addict, thus speaking the language of the gutter as well as that of the parlor. He bridged two worlds without belonging to either of them. Moreover, he was a cynic who harbored a malicious delight in besting his superiors and showing disdain for the masses. Until his death from a heart attack in 1923, Eckart was inseparable from Hitler. The older man brushed up his younger friend's manners and grammar, taught him how to dress, took him to the better-class restaurants, and introduced him to influential people.

Alfred Rosenberg joined the party out of ideological-racist convictions, but his bond to Hitler, as previously noted, was never very close personally. It was quite different with a new, up-and-coming figure in the party by the name of Julius Streicher (1885–1946), who has been called by many the "world's Jew-baiter No. 1."[79] Like Rosenberg, he joined the Nazi Party because he saw in its anti-Semitism the reflections of his own prejudices and in Adolf Hitler the future savior of Germany. When he heard Hitler speak for the first time in 1922, he was so mesmerized that afterward he made his way to the podium and said to Hitler: "I am Julius Streicher. At this moment I know that I can only be a follower. But you are a leader! I give to you the popular movement which I have built in Franconia."[80] Born in Fleinhausen near Augsburg in 1885, Julius Streicher had followed his father in becoming a school teacher. He then served with great distinction in World War I, relishing the camaraderie of the trenches and often taking inordinate risks. After the war, he resumed his teaching career in Nuremberg while at the same time getting involved in right-wing politics, heading the Nuremberg branch of the Deutschsozialistische Partei (German Socialist Party), a party he would merge with the Nazi Party after his personal encounter with Hitler. In 1923, Streicher founded what would ultimately become the world's most notorious anti-Semitic tabloid — *Der Stürmer* (The stormer).

In his personal life, Streicher was a sexual deviate and a bully, habitually strutting about with a riding whip and later taking great pleasure in beating up political prisoners. It has been suggested that the leering, sexually obsessed Jew he conjured up in the pages of *Der Stürmer* was really a reflection of his own conduct,[81] a form of conduct that was by most standards crude and uncivilized. In fact, it can be said of Streicher and many other members of Hitler's inner circle that they were shabby little bigots who delighted in each other's company, thought of women as sex objects, enjoyed a brawling fight with their political opponents, and resented what was "respectable" or "refined." The Nazi movement authenticated the brutal impulses of such asocial characters and allowed the Streichers of Germany to "normalize" their deviancy.

For over twenty years, Streicher dished up a steady stream of nauseating anti-Semitic articles in the pages of *Der Stürmer*. Never before or since have the black arts of racist prejudice reached such a perfection of rottenness. In its heyday, *Der Stürmer* reached close to half a million people per issue and thrilled its anti-Semitic readers with hair-raising stories about Jewish misconduct or crimes such as ritual child murder, rape, financial machinations, sinister political plots, and so on. Philippe Rupprecht (pseud. FIPS), the paper's cartoonist, usually drew Jews as short, fat, ugly, unshaven, drooling, slouching, sexually perverted, bent-nosed, with pig-like eye and protruding lips. In order to dehumanize the Jews, he also depicted them as toads, vampires, vultures, insects, spiders, bacteria, and toadstools.[82] Other tactics of desensitizing the reader consisted of showing that Jews did not possess any real human qualities such as love, laughter, loyalty, friendship, sympathy; portraying them as physically repulsive; insinuating that, therefore, they were morally tainted; and advocating, as a corollary of the above, that they were not worthy to live in the company of decent Germans. These anti-Semitic tactics, subsequently pounded into the heads of millions of

Germans, would constitute an important psychological prerequisite for removing the civilized restraints that stood in the way of the unthinkable — the extermination of a whole group of people simply because they were Jews.

Besides these major Nazi personalities in the early days of the party, there were two other major groups who joined the party or served as fellow travelers or financial backers. One group, sometimes referred to as the *alte Kämpfer* (old fighters), constituted the quintessential Fascist core of the party. These members were often asocial characters from semiskilled, working-class backgrounds who had severe difficulties in adjusting to peacetime conditions, finding neither capitalism nor Communism attractive and looking for a new militant German ideology under which they could continue to fight. Hitler's private entourage, what has sometimes been called "a collection of little Hitlers,"[83] consisted largely of such types. This group included Heinrich Hoffmann (1885–1957), Hitler's official photographer and court jester who had a pretty shop assistant, Eva Braun, who would later become the führer's mistress; Max Amann (1891–1957), the führer's former sergeant-in-arms and his trusted business manager; Ulrich Graf (1898–1945), a butcher by trade who became one of Hitler's loyal bodyguards and probably saved his chief's life during the Putsch by shielding him and taking eleven bullets himself; Emil Maurice (1897–1979), a former clockmaker turned chauffeur and intimate confidant of the führer's innermost secrets, including the later Geli Raubal affair and the executions surrounding the Röhm purge of 1934; Christian Weber (1883–1945), a burly former horse-trader and ex-barroom bouncer with a fondness for whips and beating up Communists who was content to serve as an errand boy for Hitler; Julius Schaub (1898–?), member of the Stosstrupp Hitler who later became Hitler's bodyguard and personal adjutant; and Hermann Esser, previously mentioned, a gifted speaker, Jew-baiter, and scoundrel.

Yet behind this collection of little Hitlers were more solid and respectable people with impeccable social pedigrees. One of the most important in the early years of the party was Ernst (Putzi) Hanfstaengl (1887–1975), a burly, 6'4" bon vivant with a large head, pugnacious jaw, and thick hair. Of German-American descent, Hanfstaengl's family was well known for being connoisseurs and patrons of the arts. His mother came from a well-known New England family, the Sedgwicks, who produced two Civil War generals. Hanfstaengl's grandfather had established a flourishing art reproduction and photography business in Munich, and his father had set up a branch of the family business on Fifth Avenue in New York. "Putzi" (little fellow) Hanfstaengl, as he was affectionately called, thus grew up in a patrician atmosphere in which education and the fine arts were highly prized. In order to learn the business and eventually to take over the American branch of the business, Hanfstaengl was sent to Harvard University, where he made a number of important contacts, including T. S. Eliot, Walter Lippman, Hendrick van Loon, Hans von Kaltenborn, Robert Benchley, and John Reed. Through Theodore Roosevelt's eldest son, also a Harvard student, he even received an invitation to the White House, where he displayed his prowess on the piano. In fact, his piano playing also endeared him to the Harvard football team, which he used to pep up before their games. Later, he would thrill Hitler with American football marches and convince the führer to apply American entertainment and advertising techniques to politics, especially the practice of whipping up the enthusiasms of crowds through cheerleaders. Hanfstaengl also became a close friend of Franklin Roosevelt, then a rising senator from New York.

Marooned in America during World War I, Hanfstaengl did not return to Germany until 1921, entering the University of Munich to work on his Ph.D. in history. In 1922 a young military attaché, who was familiarizing himself with Bavarian politics, informed Hanfstaengl that he had met a remarkable fellow by the name of Adolf Hitler, a rising politician who was destined to play a big role in German politics. He gave Hanfstaengl a ticket to one of his political meetings; and after being exposed to a vintage Hitler speech, Hanfstaengl was so impressed by his oratory that he sought him out immediately and became a dedicated follower. Moreover, Hanfstaengl used his family connections to give Hitler an entrée into Munich high society; he introduced the still socially inept Hitler to a variety of influential people, especially to wealthy matrons and donated some of his personal wealth to the party.[84] Hitler was a frequent guest at the Hanfstaengl home; he was probably smitten by Hanfstaengl's beautiful blond American wife, who may have done the world a grave disservice by saving Hitler from suicide after the failed Putsch when she wrested, in jujitsu fashion, Hitler's Browning pistol from his hand just as he was about to turn it on himself and pull the trigger.[85] Hanfstaengl soon became a member of Hitler's inner circle, serving as a kind of adviser, a comedian, and a piano player. Although serving briefly in Hitler's government after the seizure of power in 1933, Hanfstaengl became increasingly disenchanted with the Nazi regime and fled for his life in 1937, not to return to his homeland until after World War II.

Behind Hanfstaengl were other well-placed society figures. These included Winifred Wagner, the daughter-in-law of the famed composer; the author Houston Stuart Chamberlain, who had married the composer's daughter Eva and saw in Hitler Germany's future savior; the Bruckmanns, a major Munich publishing family; and the Bechsteins, a well-known family of piano manufacturers. The women involved in these haute bourgeoisie contacts were particularly captivated by Hitler. Most of these women were doting matrons who were tantalized by the führer's primitive manners, thrilled by seeing him enter their refined parlors with riding whip, cartridge belt, and revolver. Some of the older ladies took him under their wing like surrogate mothers, showering him with rich pastries and rapt attention. Even forty years after his death, Frau Wilhelmine Kallenbach recalls what a "perfect gentleman" Hitler had been when he visited them for tea and pastries. Before one Hitler visit, she later reminisced, she had been so nervous that she baked her cake with salt rather than sugar, but Hitler was such a perfect gentleman, she said, that he specifically asked for another piece of cake.[86] Frau Helene Bechstein, another Hitler worshiper, was so smitten by Hitler that she confessed that she wished that he was her son, later visiting him in prison under the guise of being his adoptive mother. Frau Elsa Bruckmann felt the same way, as did another motherly type, Carola Hoffmann, a retired schoolteacher, who was later affectionately referred to as "Hitler Mutti" by the führer's private entourage.

These upper-middle-class contacts were undoubtedly important in Hitler's design to transform a local party into a national mass party, but what the party needed was a much broader financial base than the relatively limited resources of a few Bavarian capitalists. Hitler would have to cast his net much wider if he wanted to catch the big fish — that is, the industrial magnates of the north. In December 1922, rumors circulated in Bavaria that the Nazi Party was heavily subsidized by big business, rumors that continued throughout the 1920s and 1930s because they seemed to reinforce Marxist stereotypes about the symbiosis of fascism and capitalism. Although some historians still propound the thesis that the Nazis were heavily financed by big business, the truth is that the Nazi Party received only marginal support from big business during the period 1919–23; even as regards the later years of the 1920s and the early 1930s, the actual financial contributions of big business have been greatly exaggerated.[87]

This is not to say that Hitler did not seek financial support from big business; on the contrary, as early as 1921–22 he tried to raise money from northern capitalists in order to expand his party in that area. His contact man in this effort was Emil Gansser, a chemist and former employee of the electric firm of Siemens, who was an active member of the conservative National Club of high-ranking civil servants, military men, and big businessmen. Gansser arranged for Hitler to address the National Club on May 29, 1922; and according to the reports of those who heard him on that day, Hitler made a very positive impression on this elite audience. He depicted his party as the only effective counterpoise to the Marxist-based parties on the left and argued that it was the sole instrument of genuine reform because it was a national party untainted by those international forces that threatened Germany — Jews, Freemasons, and political Catholics.[88] He ended by depicting himself as a mere drummer for a national freedom movement.

In June 1922 Hitler was invited again to the National Club, which led to further invitations to various business-sponsored meetings. Hermann Augst, an executive of a Munich malt-coffee firm who had heard him speak in Berlin, was so impressed by Hitler that he put him in touch with members of the League of Bavarian Industrialists. He received speaking engagements at the exclusive conservative Herrenklub (Gentlemen's Club) and at other elite groups in Bavaria. However, these contacts did not yield big money because most of his donors were tight-fisted Munich merchants, tradesmen, or artisans. Only a few of these early donors are known today because the records containing the financial transactions of the party between 1919 and 1923 were destroyed when the party was dissolved after the Beerhall Putsch.

Among the more substantial donors were Gottfried Grandel, an Augsburg spice and cooking-oil processor who at one point provided security for a key loan to the NSDAP and made good for it when the party subsequently defaulted on it. Another donor was Richard Franck, heir to a Ludwigsburg coffee-processing work, who contributed sixty thousand Swiss francs in order to keep the *Völkischer Beobachter* afloat in 1923. There was also Heinrich Becker, a Swabian undergarment manufacturer who contributed funds that stood out among the rest. As previously noted, Hanfstaengl donated his valuable dollar resources, and the Bechsteins or Bruckmanns came through with needed resources at crucial moments. However, as Henry Turner points out, what Hitler owed to these Bavarian contacts was an entrée into the upper classes; their sponsorship would make him *gesellschaftsfähig* (acceptable to polite society).[89]

Only two northern industrialists stand out as significant contributors to the Nazi Party between 1919 and 1923 — Ernst von Borsig and Fritz Thyssen. Borsig was the head of an old Berlin firm that manufactured locomotives, boilers, and heavy industrial equipment. Although his business was dwarfed by new emerging giants, he wielded a lot of influence over the German business community as chairman of the Vereinigung der Deutschen Arbeitergeberverbände (Alliance of German Employers' Associations), which defended the interests of industrial employers. After he heard Hitler speak, Borsig believed that he found the "man who could, through his movement, make a contribution toward bridging the cleft between the social classes by reviving the national sentiment of the working class."[90] Borsig had a private meeting with Hitler and advanced some of his own money to help establish a Berlin branch of the party. However, the results were disappointing. This may have been due, in part, to the chaotic effects of inflation and the Ruhr crisis, but there was also the fact that Borsig did not succeed in persuading other businessmen to contribute financially to the NSDAP because they still perceived the Nazis as enemies of capitalism.[91]

The other major northern industrialist who donated money to the Nazi cause was Fritz Thyssen, at that time the heir-in-waiting to the gigantic steel firm that he would inherit in 1926 and then reorganize as the Vereinigte Stahlwerke AG. According to his later account in *I Paid Hitler* (1941), Thyssen donated one hundred thousand gold marks to the NSDAP, though he later indicated that he meant the money to go to Ludendorff rather than Hitler.

It would appear therefore that the Nazi Party was not fueled by big business; its resources were derived from membership dues, from party publications, and from the money collected at mass meetings.[92] Large donations such as Thyssen's were the rare exception, though Hitler sent his agents everywhere, including abroad, in order to find needed revenues. Kurt Lüdecke, a young playboy with international connections, hit various foreign luminaries such as Mussolini and Henry Ford for donations. In the fall of 1923 Hitler himself went to Zurich and purportedly returned with a "steamer trunk stuffed with Swiss francs and American dollars."[93] Yet when everything is taken into account, the Nazi Party succeeded not because it was financed by the moguls of capitalism but because it was a genuinely populist movement whose appeal cut across class lines and occupations.

What united these diverse groups and individuals was a strong sense of nationalism, a fear of Communism, a distrust of the democratic Weimar Republic, and a pervasive anti-Semitism. All saw in the Nazi Party a reflection of their own visions and prejudices. To the old fighters (*alte Kämpfer*), the party was a populist, egalitarian organization that allowed them to unite nationalism and the gutter.[94] To Hanfstaengl, the Bechsteins, or the Bruckmanns, the Nazis offered themselves as the vanguard of the masses on the side of the middle class. To the militarists, the Nazi Party was a revival of the old wartime Vaterland Party, which would do the bidding of the military-industrial complex. The ideologues saw in National Socialism a counterpoise to the two dominant and largely suspect movements of the twentieth century — capitalism and Communism. They saw in the Nazi organization a third force, a dialectical synthesis of all previous social ideologies. Finally, most saw in Adolf Hitler the best hope of Germany's salvation.

It was during this period (1920–23) that Hitler, gradually and haltingly, discovered his political style and his remarkable energy as a leader. In attempting to explain how an obscure and rootless outsider without social skills and the barest educational training could have risen to the highest peaks of power, Alan Bullock sadly confesses that "the more I learn about Adolf Hitler, the harder I find it to explain and accept what followed. Somehow, the causes are inadequate to account for the size of the effects."[95] Indeed, it was a phenomenal achievement, coming as it did from a lazy, apparently good-for-nothing Austrian outsider who, by sheer will power, transformed himself publicly from a shy, neurotically compulsive, and insecure man into the image of a heroic leader. It did not come easy. Privately, Hitler was extremely self-conscious of his lowly origins, felt habitually ill at ease in the company of men like Ludendorff, and for several years saw himself more as a drummer than a leader. As Joachim Fest has observed, the reek of the home for the homeless still clung to his clothing; he even continued to live as he had before, renting a tiny one-room flat in the Thierstrasse, keeping eccentric hours, and trying to escape from solitude by surrounding himself with camp followers with whom he would spend hours at various beerhalls or coffeehouses. His private life and his habits were unchanged; he alternated between solitary brooding and hysterically charged energy, between periods of idleness and frenzied activities. Hitler was all of a piece; he never changed. Instead, he compelled the world to change to his perception of reality.

"My whole life," he once confessed, "was nothing but constant cajolings (*überreden*)."[96] Without his remarkable gift of persuasion, Hitler would have never reached such heights of power; and given the nature of his aberrant fantasies, it required a genius to make them plausible to millions of people. We must, therefore, acknowledge his rhetorical genius and also his uncanny ability to appeal to people of diverse backgrounds. Hitler was a consummate actor who could play with many mirrors. This is why hundreds of different perceptions of him are recorded, all of them by eye-witness observers who saw in him what they wanted him to be and what he, in turn, reinforced in their own self-serving perceptions. He could play like a "virtuoso on the well-tempered piano of lower-middle-class hearts";[97] and to extend this analogy, he could also play equally well on upper-class or working-class hearts. Further, in an age of mass democracy, he could claim that he had truly risen from the people.

Hitler instinctively sensed that the real source of his power resided in the masses, so that his aim was to organize mass affections, mass disaffections, mass prejudices or hatreds. Given his histrionic personality and his persuasive powers, this proved easier than it did for most politicians. In fact, he needed crowds in order to authenticate himself and to recharge his energy. In the dynamics of Hitler and his audiences can be found the key to Nazi success. Those who observed him over time — Hanfstaengl or Professor Alexander von Müller, for example — noticed the remarkable strength he gained in the act of seducing crowds. Some have even suggested that Hitler's speeches were really orgiastic performances, heralded by alluring atmospheric enticements, followed by frenzied movements of seduction during which the members of the audience, especially women, would moan, sob, shriek, and ultimately explode in a climax of devotional ecstasy.

Mixing politics with entertainment, Hitler managed to put on such an array of gaudy happenings that all of Munich was beginning to refer to him as "the king of Munich." This king of Munich, however, did not preach a humane and peaceful gospel; on the contrary, his speeches and demonstrations were so outrageously provocative, the antics of his storm troopers so incendiary, that the whole city was periodically torn apart by violent incidents. His rowdy followers would also inject themselves into the meetings of their opponents and cause frequent disruptions leading to scuffles and escalating into public brawls that left people seriously injured. The police monitored these meetings

on a regular basis and repeatedly warned Hitler to keep his followers in check. Party leaflets, pamphlets, posters, or billboards were often
censored because of their venomous and libelous messages.

On January 12, 1922, Hitler was sentenced to three months in prison
for disrupting a meeting at the Löwenbräukeller of an opposition group,
the Bavarian League (Bayernbund), and severely injuring its leader, Otto
Ballerstedt. Serving only four weeks, he was celebrated upon his release like a conquering hero, "the most popular and the most hated
man in Munich."[98] His party managed repeatedly to top the opposition in the sheer magnitude of its outrages. The NSDAP flooded Munich
and a large part of Bavaria with political meetings, mass protests, and
demonstrations. His brawling storm troopers, making themselves look
deliberately savage and martial, staged noisy marches, posted slogans
on the walls of houses and factories, fought their opponents, tore down
flags, and organized commando raids against presumed enemies.[99]

These provocative tactics, as Hitler predicted, were popular among
many Bavarians, who enjoyed mixing fun with a bit of coarseness and
called it a jolly good time or *Gaudi*. To take in one of Hitler's gaudy
performances, marked by the guzzling of stout beer, speechifying, stirring marching songs, and a bit of rowdiness in the form of flying beer
mugs, overturned tables, and perhaps some hand-to-hand fighting — all
this was an exciting pastime to many people. Despite its excesses, the
Nazi Party became to many an affectionate household word; in fact, the
word NAZI, an acronym formed from the first syllable of NAtional and
the second syllable SoZIalist, also sounded in Bavarian like the nickname for Ignaz, thus giving it a kind of homey and familiar ring. The
party worked hard to strengthen the image of rootedness in folk and
soil, so that even the figure of the tough storm trooper would become as
publicly acceptable as that of the street-corner policeman.

Those who joined the paramilitary branch of the party, the SA
(Sturmabteilung), did so because they found in it an extension of the
armed forces, an outlet for aggressive tendencies, or perhaps a substitute
family that could provide them with a sense of security and direction.[100]
Important social bonds were forged within this tight-knit company of
garrulous and assertive manhood. These bonds were strengthened by
maintaining a sense of cozy exclusivity and by encouraging such ritualistic practices as weekly talk sessions, group outings, concerts, cookouts,
singing evenings, and salutings.

The development of the paramilitary organization, the SA, dates to
the summer of 1921 when Emil Maurice's somewhat unorganized band
of "armed Bohemians," charged to keep order at party functions, was
transformed into a more tightly organized fighting unit. In August 1921
this paramilitary group disguised itself as the Gymnastics and Sports Division of the party, although its real function, as a party proclamation
made quite clear, was to serve as an offensive force at the disposal of
the movement.[101] In October 1921 it changed its name to Sturmabtei-

lung (Storm Detachment), or SA for short. Those who commanded this section saw in it a germ cell for a revitalized German army of the future; they intended it to serve not just as a defensive organization designed to keep order at political meetings but as an instrument to gain political control.

The original members of the SA were largely recruited from members of the Free Corps, particularly from Captain Erhardt's Number 2 Naval Brigade. After the Kapp Putsch, Erhardt and some of his men had fled to Munich, where they reorganized under the name "Consul Organization," a conspiratorial racist order sworn to eliminate traitors, Jews, liberals, pacifists, democrats — in short, anyone who failed the litmus test of the extreme political right. In August 1921 members of this organization assassinated Matthias Erzberger. It may have been to find a better camouflage that Erhardt reluctantly agreed to lend some of his best officers to the SA. Thus, the Erhardt Brigade, formerly fighting Bolshevism in the Baltic regions and conspiring to overthrow the Weimar Republic, was now reborn in Munich in the summer of 1921 as "Sturmabteilung Hitler." Even the brigade's fighting song needed only slight revision:

Hakenkreuz am Stahlhelm	The Swastika on our helmet
Schwarzweissrotes Band,	Black-white-red armband
Sturmabteilung Hitler	Storm Detachment Hitler
Werden wir genannt	Is our name.[102]

The storm troopers were as good as their word: from now on the battle for the streets and the meeting halls began to intensify. On November 4, 1921, the "myth of the SA" was born in the so-called Hofbräuhaus Battle when Hitler's foot soldiers flung themselves "like wolves in packs of eight to ten, again and again,...on their opponents" and beat them out of the hall.[103] Frequent "hall battles" (*Saalschlachten*) followed. Organizing itself in groups of one hundred men, the SA grew by leaps and bounds during 1922. In October 1922, Hitler went to Coburg on a special train with eight hundred storm troopers to attend a patriotic demonstration to which the city had invited him. Although he was asked not to march into Coburg in closed formation, he refused and his boisterous followers caused a street riot, cleared the streets of opponents, and literally held the city under siege. This act of bravado seems to have emboldened Hitler to believe that he could challenge the Bavarian authorities with relative impunity. It also enhanced the reputation of the Nazi Party and its paramilitary fighting force. Between February and November 1922, the party enrolled thirty-five thousand new members, and the SA grew to nearly fifteen thousand members.[104]

Although the members of the SA were sworn to render willing obedience to its leader, Hitler realized that their loyalties were often divided between the Nazi Party and Erhardt and his officers. There was also

a problem concerning the primary role to be played by the SA. Unlike
Röhm, who saw it as a catalyst for a new radical army, Hitler viewed
it as a propaganda weapon, subservient to the political branch of the
party and answerable to his command. Between 1922 and 1923, however, the SA began to take on a life of its own, as it would again after
the 1929 economic depression. Hitler had the feeling that it was being
manipulated too much by outside forces.[105]

In order to counteract this influence, Hitler replaced Erhardt's man,
Hans Ulrich Klintsch, the first SA leader, with a man he thought
he could trust — Hermann Göring. Although a wise move, this appointment changed little in the short-run because the gulf between the
leadership of the NSDAP and its paramilitary formations was and would
continue to be a source of friction. It was perhaps to safeguard himself
against unruly SA leaders that Hitler built up his own Praetorian guard.
In March 1923, a few of the "old fighters" formed a personal bodyguard
(the Stabswache) to protect their leader against potential harm. This was
the first appearance of the future SS (Schutzstaffel, or Protective Squad).
In order to distinguish themselves from the regular SA, members of the
Stabswache took to wearing grey field overcoats, black ski caps with a
silver death's head button, and black-bordered swastika armbands.[106]

Hitler's first bodyguard broke up in May 1923 when Captain Erhardt severed his partnership with Hitler and recalled his men from
the SA. Shortly afterward, Hitler formed a new guard, the Stosstruppe
Adolf Hitler, whose members came from quite a different strata than
Captain Erhardt's men. The leader of the Stosstrupp was Julius Schreck
(1898–1936), who superficially looked like Hitler and later served as his
double. Along with Josef Berchtold, Schreck organized a mobile assault
squad that would spring into action to carry out the führer's personal
orders. The mentality of these political foot soldiers has been faithfully recorded by Hans Kallenbach (1897–1966), a machine-gun troop
leader, in his book *Mit Hitler auf Festung Landsberg,* a much-neglected
Baron von Münchhausen account in which he attempted to glamorize
his comrades as noble warriors in the service of a holy cause. The tone
of the book, which probably represents a fair approximation of historical verisimilitude, is a mixture of patriotic piety and Mafialike brutality.
The men of the Stosstrupp described themselves as real he-men, tough
as Krupp steel and brutally honest (often an excuse for bad manners).
They rationalized their lawless activities as acts of noble patriotism and
branded their opponents as cowardly supporters of the democratic Jew
republic. Kallenbach later recalled:

> Hard and rough and sometimes quite uncouth were the customs, the
> habits, and the appearance of the Stosstrupp. They did not know false
> respect and groveling. They clung to the right of the stronger, the old
> right of the fist. In an emergency they knew no commandment.... When
> the whistling signal of Berchtold or his deputy Julius Schreck sounded
> and the Stosstrupp commando called us into action — to attack right and

left — march, march! — then things were torn to shreds [*flogen die Fetzen durch die Gegend*] and in minutes streets and squares were swept clean of enemies.... Soon we were known in village and town, up and down the country. The provocations of the Reds became less frequent and more docile whenever the Stosstrupp appeared on the scene. We earned respect and love from friends. The enemy pursued us with hatred and scorn.[107]

Most members of the Stosstrupp came from lower-middle-class or working-class backgrounds. Julius Schreck was an SA man with a seedy past who later became Hitler's chauffeur; the diminutive Berchtold, a former lieutenant, ran a stationary store; as previously mentioned, Ulrich Graf, Hitler's first bodyguard, was a butcher, local amateur boxer, and beerhall brawler; Emil Maurice, another of Hitler's bosom buddies (*Duzfreund*), was a watchmaker who had been convicted of embezzlement; and Christian Weber was a hulky former horse dealer with a fondness for whips who eked out a living at the Blaue Bock in Munich as a bouncer. The few officers among them carried ranks no higher than second lieutenant on the reserve.[108] Hitler felt most at home in the company of these toughs because they validated his own asocial, resentful, and aggressive tendencies. In his mind, these old fighters could do no wrong, and he would be willing later to excuse them for all kinds of debaucheries and illegalities. On his small dresser in the Berlin bunker, where he would commit suicide in April 1945, Hitler displayed only two photographs — that of his mother and that of Emil Maurice. The few surviving pictures that show Hitler in the company of the old fighters are highly revealing because they illustrate, in the brutal physiognomies visually frozen for our inspection, the type of men who would constitute the essence of Nazi power.

Although Hitler had transformed the Nazi Party into a rallying point of opposition to the Berlin government, his leadership decisions in 1922–23 committed the party to an almost fatal goal — that of seizing the state by force rather than by constitutional means. In October 1922 Mussolini grabbed power by marching on Rome; Hitler was increasingly convinced that a similar march on Berlin was feasible, perhaps not by his own forces alone but by a combined effort of conservative military groups who would line up behind a national symbol such as Field Marshal Ludendorff. Hitler still did not see himself as the sole leader of the revolutionary right; in fact, from time to time he wondered out loud whether he was just a John the Baptist or the Messiah himself.

As the party continued to grow, Hitler stepped up his aggressive rhetoric and his plans for a coup. In January 1923, amidst the chaos of the Ruhr crisis, six thousand SA men assembled in Munich for the first Reich party rally. Rumors of an impending coup were rampant in Munich as Hitler harangued his storm troopers and called for a national dictatorship to save Germany from impending collapse. In February, Hitler formed that fatal alliance with other right-wing paramilitary forces that would almost wreck his career. He agreed to combine forces with such right-wing organizations as the Reichsflagge (Reich Banner) led by Captain Adolf Heiss; Lieutenant Alfred Hoffmann's Kampfverband Niederbayern (Lower Bavarian Fighting League); Alfred Zeller's Vaterländische Vereine München (Patriotic Leagues of Munich); and Mulzer's Bund Oberland (Oberland League). A joint committee was set up and Lieutenant Colonel Hermann Kriebel was appointed as the military leader of this Arbeitsgemeinschaft der Vaterländischen Kampfverbände (Working Union of the Patriotic Fighting Associations). Hitler and Röhm tried to cajole other right-wing groups into joining the new organization, and they also tried to solidify a political role for Hitler that would be the equal to Kriebel's in the military field.[109]

In the following months, as Germany was reeling from one crisis to another, rumors of a coup intensified. It was at this point that Hitler devised a plan to squash left-wing Labor Day demonstrations and thereby convince the authorities that he was, in fact, "the king of Munich." However, on May 1, 1923, his loyalists and sympathizers in the government left him in the lurch; and to his great embarrassment, his thousands of SA men, who were poised in battle readiness for hours on the Oberwiesenfeld, had to return their guns to Reichswehr arsenals from which they had earlier been borrowed by a ruse. After spending much of the summer incommunicado at Berchtesgaden, Hitler returned much invigorated, participating in a paramilitary rally in Nuremberg (September 1–2) that was intended to commemorate "German Day." The leaders of the various paramilitary groups renewed their February agreement and announced a new Deutsche Kampfbund (German Fighting League), including Bund Oberland, Reichsflagge, and the Nazi Party. On September 25 the leaders of the Kampfbund met to discuss strategy for a Putsch. Hitler put his fifteen thousand storm troopers in a state of military readiness and announced over a dozen mass meetings in Munich alone. The following day, the alarmed Bavarian minister president, Eugen von Knilling (1865–1927), persuaded the cabinet to invoke a state of emergency and appoint Dr. Gustav von Kahr, former prime minister and reactionary conservative separatist, as state commissioner with dictatorial powers. Kahr's power rested largely on the support of General Otto von Lassow, head of the Seventh Division of the Reichswehr, and Colonel Hans Ritter von Seisser, commander of the Bavarian state police. Kahr immediately prohibited all mass demonstrations, but at the same time conspired with Lassow and Seisser to get rid of the hated Berlin government. In these conspiratorial plans by Kahr, Lassow, and Seisser, only a marginal role was envisioned for Hitler and the Nazi Party. The conservative establishment, however, soon found out that Hitler would go far beyond drumming up opposition to actually instigating a coup in which they themselves would also be deeply implicated.

Chapter 5

The Beerhall Putsch and Its Aftermath

The Hitler Putsch of November 8-9, 1923

On November 7, 1923, the major leaders of Bavaria's right-wing organizations finalized their plans for a coup d'état against the Weimar Republic. Although much divided them from one another, including political motives and personal ambitions, they were solidly united against the hated republic. This is why they had formed the Kampfbund (Battle League) to destroy the republic and to punish the November Criminals who had supposedly betrayed Germany and rendered it *ehrlos und wehrlos* (dishonored and defenseless). The chief conspirators, meeting in the Munich apartment of retired Lieutenant Colonel Hermann Kriebel, the Kampfbund leader who hosted the gathering, were General Ludendorff, who was accompanied by his personal adjutant, Major Hans Streck; Dr. Friedrich Weber, leader of the Oberland League; and Adolf Hitler, flanked on that evening by Hermann Göring and Scheubner-Richter.

These conspirators planned to enmesh the right-wing government in Bavaria in a coup against the Reich government in Berlin. Given the fact that relations between Berlin and Munich had deteriorated to the point of armed hostilities on both sides, the Kampfbund leaders judged that the time had come to strike. As previously mentioned, an open conflict between Bavaria and the Reich government had been building up for some time. On September 26, the Bavarian cabinet had appointed Dr. Gustav von Kahr as general state commissioner with dictatorial powers. On the next day, and partly in response to the Bavarian crisis, President Ebert invoked Article 48 of the Weimar Constitution and invested Defense Minister Otto Gessler and General Hans von Seeckt, commander of the Reichswehr, with executive authority to maintain law and order and to crush any insurrection against the Reich. It was on this occasion that General Seeckt purportedly delivered his famous oracular pronouncement in response to President Ebert's question: "Where does the Reichswehr stand?" Seeckt's reply was: "Die Reichswehr, Herr Reichspresident, steht hinter mir" (The Reichswehr, Mr. President, stands behind me).[1] Although President Ebert justified invoking this emergency measure by arguing that it was sanctioned by the constitution, what it meant in practice was that from September 26, 1923, until February 1924, when the emergency decree of the constitution was rescinded, the country was effectively ruled by General von Seeckt and his local commanders. Two dictatorial governments, one national and the other regional, were bound to clash given their profound political differences.

There can be no doubt that Hitler was eager to exploit such differences between the Reich and the Bavarian governments. On September 27, a scurrilous article in the *Völkischer Beobachter,* entitled "Stresemann und Seeckt," accused the two men of betraying Germany to the French and of plotting to create a dictatorship under the aegis of international Jewry, which should hardly be surprising, the article intimated, since the wives of both Stresemann and Seeckt were Jewish.[2] Berlin ordered Lassow to ban the *Völkischer Beobachter* and also demanded the arrest of three Free Corps leaders — Rossbach, Heiss, and Erhardt. Both orders were ignored. In the case of von Lassow, his actions amounted to rank insubordination. To complicate matters, on October 4, Kahr banned the *Völkischer Beobachter* because it had published an article — "Artillerymen! Prepare to Fire!" — which called upon all patriotic artillerymen to report for action by joining the SA and even conveniently provided an address for that purpose.[3] Now that his own authority was being challenged, Kahr sprang into action, having shown no such inclination when Stresemann and Seeckt had been maligned. The *Völkischer Beobachter* was to be banned October 6–14 not because it had offended Berlin but because it had displeased Munich, the implication being that it was all right to insult Berlin but not Munich.

On October 19, Kahr addressed high-ranking military officers, including Lassow, of the Seventh District Command and told them that Berlin had exaggerated a purely local political affair into a military crisis of national proportions. The real issue, he said, involved "a great battle of two worldviews which will decide the destiny of the German people — the international Marxist-Jewish and the national Germanic."[4] Bavaria, he urged, must take the lead in promoting the nationalist cause, and he left no doubt in his sympathetic audience that he would actively work to undermine the "un-German" Weimar Constitution and replace it with a better and more German one.[5]

Hitler could not have said it any better. Nor was Kahr the only one who voiced such openly seditious remarks against the Berlin government. Lassow and Seisser, the other members of the triumvirate, felt the same way; in fact, Lassow's attitude changed from passive resistance to open defiance when he was fired by General von Seeckt on October 20 for dereliction of office and conduct unbecoming an officer in the German army. Lassow's dismissal was almost immediately countermanded by Kahr, who promptly reinstated him as commander of the army of

Bavaria and exacted a personal oath to the Bavarian government from the officers and enlisted men of the Seventh District Command, an act that the Berlin government denounced as a flagrant violation of the Weimar Constitution.[6]

On October 24, General Lassow delivered an address to the commanding officers of the Bavarian army, officials of the state police, and leaders of the Kampfbund (except the Nazis) and proposed three possible approaches to the current crisis: (1) marching on Berlin and proclaiming a national dictatorship; (2) muddling along, with Bavaria dangling on the hook; or (3) secession of Bavaria from the Reich.[7] He made it unmistakably clear that he favored a march on Berlin; and by so doing, put himself squarely on the side of the conspirators. In John Wheeler-Bennett's words, "He had now become merely a petty conspirator, and from then on must consort with other conspirators equally petty."[8] The triumvirate now agreed in principle to march on Berlin, and they set in motion the preliminary military plans to implement their grand design. This included inviting Captain Erhardt from his Salzburg hiding place, where he had gone to escape a warrant for his arrest by the federal court, to Munich in order to assist in preparing for the coup. It also included massing troops on Bavaria's northern border for an invasion of Thuringia and Saxony, where the Communists were poised to seize power.

Kahr was a stodgy reactionary monarchist who was not normally given to rash actions. His apparently decisive moves against Berlin were just that — apparently decisive, for they depended on his current popularity among right-wing nationalists and on the fact that the Stresemann government was unlikely to intervene in Bavaria since it was facing multiple crises, including run-away inflation, separatism in the Rhineland, the resurgence of left-wing extremism in Thuringia, Saxony, and other parts of northern Germany, and an internal cabinet crisis involving Social Democrats and conservatives.

The political winds, however, had a way of shifting quickly during those crisis-ridden years of the republic, and they did so again at the very moment the triumvirate was scheming to march on Berlin. On October 23, a Communist uprising was successfully broken up in Hamburg. By the end of October the Reichswehr, now legally empowered by Article 48 of the Weimar Constitution, invaded Saxony and Thuringia and drove the Communists from the governments of both states, thus giving the Munich plotters even less excuse for using the danger of Communism in both of these states as a pretext for marching on Berlin. Although the Social Democrats in Stresemann's cabinet bolted the government in protest against what they considered an illegal military interference by the federal government in the internal affairs of two German states, their departure was hailed by many conservatives as a step in the right direction — that is, the formation of a strong, conservative, authoritarian regime. Kahr now began to develop second thoughts about an immediate march on Berlin. Preparing to compromise, he sent Colonel Seisser to Berlin to test the political waters. When Seisser returned to Munich with a sobering report that northern Germany was unlikely to join a Bavarian uprising against Berlin, the triumvirate became less urgent in their conspiratorial deliberations. By the first week of November, the atmosphere of crisis that had characterized the plotting of the triumvirate began to dissipate noticeably and, to Hitler's way of thinking, alarmingly.

Yet to Hitler and the other conspirators who were meeting at Kriebel's apartment on November 7, the chances for staging a successful coup were still regarded as excellent, provided, of course, that the vacillating triumvirate could be compromised into participating in the Putsch. Kriebel initially suggested a coup for the night of November 10–11 to coincide with the fifth anniversary of the armistice of 1918. On that evening, bivouac and training exercises had been planned by the Kampfbund on a heath north of Munich. Instead of putting the troops through training exercises, the plan called for marching them on Munich, overpowering the authorities, and proclaiming a new national government headed by Ludendorff, Hitler, and others loyal to the cause.[9] Hitler objected to this plan because it contained too many uncertainties and suggested instead that the conspirators strike on the very next day, November 8, when most of the prominent leaders of Munich would be attending a major address by Gustav von Kahr at the Bürgerbräukeller, one of the largest beerhalls in Munich. Kampfbund troops, Hitler reasoned, could easily seal off the building, allowing the conspirators to seize their hostages and persuade them to participate in a national revolution against the Berlin government. Hitler's rhetorical persuasion turned the trick as the seven conspirators approved this alternative plan and then proceeded to discuss the technical details of implementing it.

Although the plot was not unrealistic, its chances of success were greatly weakened by the fact that there were too many suspicious plotters who distrusted not only each other but also the triumvirate they hoped to implicate in the coup. As Alan Bullock observes, there were at least four groups involved in the Beerhall Putsch: Hitler and his associated right-wing formations, the Bavarian authorities, the central government in Berlin, and the Reichswehr.[10] Only Hitler's aim was clear in its simplicity: he demanded a march on Berlin in cooperation with the political and military forces in Bavaria, followed by the establishment of a new dictatorial government. However, Hitler did not lead a unified or cohesive force; he could count on the loyalty of only the SA, not on the loyalty of other associated formations that were under the overall control of Hermann Kriebel, a Ludendorff loyalist.

As to the Bavarian authorities, civil as well as military, there was only a confusion of conflicting motives and personal ambitions. Gustav von Kahr, the state commissioner, was a reactionary monarchist who toyed with the idea of using the military resources of Bavaria in order to topple the Berlin government and replace it with a restored German monarchy under the leadership of Kaiser Rupprecht, the heir apparent to the Wittelsbach throne. Alternatively, he also toyed with the idea of a restored independent Bavarian monarchy that would be loosely allied with a south German or Danubian federation. Such ideas were anathema to both Hitler and Ludendorff, let alone the majority of the German people. Kahr was not only a muddle-headed politician but also a colorless and flat personality. As his subsequent actions would reveal, he had few organizational talents and fewer leadership qualities.

Kahr's military counterpart, General Otto Hermann von Lassow, appeared to be the archetype of the German general staff officer: trim, dignified, with close-cropped hair, grey mustache, and pince-nez. Although judged to be a cold-blooded realist, he was in actual fact a vacillating political intriguer who listened to too many different factions without being able to make a definitive commitment to any of them. Lassow was not a Bavarian separatist; he supported the prevailing view that the Berlin government should be replaced by a national dictatorship.

The third member of the Bavarian triumvirate, Colonel Hans von Seisser, head of the Bavarian state police, was a brilliant and energetic general staff officer who had almost single-handedly created an impressive ten-thousand-man state police force out of the remnant of the old Royal Bavarian Army.[11] Like Kahr, he was a strong Bavarian loyalist who had contempt for Prussians like Ludendorff, but who was in all other respects made out of the same reactionary cloth. Seisser's sympathies leaned toward Captain Erhardt's brigade, which he deputized, armed, and then assigned to Bavaria's northern frontier as a "state police force."[12] Seisser's relations with Hitler were cordial and pragmatic, depending on the prevailing political atmosphere. Seisser and the other triumvirs had too much to lose by staking their careers on a risky venture; they would commit themselves only if the odds were overwhelming. When this did not happen, they preferred to sit on the fence, waiting to support the winner. Hitler would sorely regret his decision to involve them in the coup, as he would regret involving any group other than his own in such high stakes.

As to the Berlin government, now headed by Gustav Stresemann, the immediate goal was to prevent the civil war that was looming on the political horizon; and to stave off civil war, Stresemann needed the support of the Reichswehr and its commanding officer, General Hans von Seeckt. The key to the political future of the republic, therefore, resided with the army. By the end of September 1923, there were already unmistakable signs that the leadership of the Reichswehr and the government, despite profound political differences, was agreed on one essential aim — the protection of the current government from the centrifugal forces threatening to tear it apart. Although both Stresemann and Seeckt were still monarchists at heart, they realized that Germany could not recover its status as a great power unless law and order had been reestablished at home and a measure of goodwill had been secured abroad. In order to achieve these aims, both the chancellor and the general decided to work through the legitimate institutions of the republic; both had also abandoned as unrealistic any idea either of restoring the monarchy or of establishing a conservative dictatorship. Moreover, both had reached the conclusion that extremists on the left or the right who still harbored such illusions had to be stopped by all possible means.[13]

General Seeckt believed that the army should be above politics, acting as the guardian of the state.[14] In surveying the political situation, he came to the conclusion that the integrity of the Reich could be protected only by the army, although he was by no means completely convinced that the army must necessarily support the democratic republic. Some of his actions in the six months preceding the coup were sufficiently ambiguous to arouse suspicions that he was toying with the idea of throwing in his lot with the antirepublican forces on the right.[15] Given his inscrutable and sometimes ambiguous statements, there was ample justification for calling him the "Sphinx." However, Seeckt seems to have formed at least one firm position, and that was to keep the German army above politics — a position that was to haunt the army during the Nazi period, especially when it became clear that the army was serving a criminal leadership. In Seeckt's view, the army must obey legitimate authority, distasteful as that authority might be to the ideological convictions of those who happened to serve it. He squirmed on the hooks of this dilemma because it would have been personally unacceptable to him to serve a regime that acted contrary to the traditions of the German army. By 1923 Seeckt had reached the conclusion that the republic, despite its democratic drawbacks, was no longer a threat to the army. Accordingly, he decided to oppose anyone who threatened the republic with armed insurrection. Thus, when Heinrich Class, the pan-German fanatic, approached him to take the lead in forming a national dictatorship, Seeckt warned him that he would have no part in such seditious plots; he would "fight to the last shot against the revolutionaries of the right as well as against those of the left."[16]

By the time the Munich crisis came to a head, General von Seeckt had already shown on two occasions that he would defend the constitution of the republic against insurrectionists of any political persuasion. During the first week of October he suppressed a mutiny by members of the Black Reichswehr, a secret paramilitary force within the armed forces, and had their leaders condemned on charges of high treason. He then moved on the Communists in Thuringia and Saxony. Given this show of support for the republic, what made Hitler or Ludendorff think that their projected revolt against the republic would not be met by the same stern countermeasures? Whether it was the result of ideological wishful

thinking or political miscalculation, Hitler and the leaders of the Kampfbund decided to forge ahead with their plan to overthrow the republic
by announcing a new national government at the Bürgerbräukeller on
November 8, followed by a march on Berlin.

The scene of the Munich Beerhall Putsch of November 8–9 was the
Bürgerbräukeller, a large beer cellar located on the south bank of the
Isar River and roughly half a mile from the center of the city. Although
it was called a beerhall, the Bürgerbräukeller was actually a large restaurant complex surrounded by outside gardens and containing a variety of
dining rooms and bars. On the evening of November 8, 1923, the main
hall was jam-packed with high dignitaries, the political and social elite
of Bavaria, who came to listen to what was touted as a major address
by State Commissioner Gustav von Kahr. In the main hall, chairs and
tables were pushed so closely together that the buxom waitresses, clutching scores of heavy beer steins, could hardly make their way through the
smoke-filled room.[17]

Shortly before 8:00 P.M., Adolf Hitler drove up to the Bürgerbräukeller in his red Mercedes Benz and piled out of the car along with
Amann, Rosenberg, and Graf. He was met there by Putzi Hanfstaengl,
who was supposed to act as the Nazi liaison with the foreign press.
When the group finally got through the police cordon that blocked
the entrance to unauthorized visitors, they were joined by several other
Putschists in the lobby. Through the connecting door to the auditorium
they could hear Kahr speaking to the audience in a dull, monotone
voice, droning on interminably on the subject "Vom Volk zur Nation"
(From people to nation). Hanfstaengl eased the tense waiting period by
buying three-liter-jugs of beer for everyone. He later recalled that he paid
a billion marks apiece.[18]

Just as Kahr said the words, "And now I come to the consideration
of ...," which Hanfstaengl sarcastically referred to as probably the high
point of his speech, the door behind the conspirators flew open and in
burst Göring, "looking like Wallenstein on the march, with all his orders
clinking," followed by about twenty-five of his SA men with pistols and
machine-guns.[19] Other SA troops were cordoning off the whole building, blocking access and occupying the facilities. When Göring and his
troops burst through the swinging door into the main hall, the packed
crowd went into an uproar. Tables with beer mugs were overturned.
Some frightened spectators crawled under tables for cover, while other
climbed on top of chairs or tables to get a better view of what was going on. Women screamed and even fainted at the sight of passing steel
helmets and machine-guns.[20]

Hitler and his entourage then ploughed through the crowd and
mounted the speaker's platform. Hitler climbed on a chair and shouted,
"Ruhe! Ruhe!" (Quiet! Quiet!), but when this had no effect whatsoever,
he fired a single shot at the ceiling. The crowd froze in silence. Hitler
then barked out his famous announcement:

The national revolution has broken out in the whole of Germany. This
hall is occupied by six hundred armed men, and no one may leave it.
Reichswehr and State Police are marching under our banner from their
barracks; a national German and Bavarian government is being formed;
the government of Knilling and the Reich government are deposed.[21]

Hitler then shoved Kahr, Lassow, and Seisser into a side room, wildly
brandishing his pistol in an effort to look heroic, but only managing
to look more like a poor little waiter (*armes Kellnerlein*) in the ridiculous cutaway coat he had chosen to wear for this special occasion.[22]
"Komödie spielen" (Put on an act), Lassow purportedly mumbled to
Kahr and Seisser as they were being led to the side room.[23] When the
door to the side room slammed shut, a screeching and wildly gestic-
ulating Hitler, pistol still in hand, informed the captive trio that the
Bavarian government was deposed and that they would be part of a
new Reich government. Kahr was amazed to learn that he was the new
regent for Bavaria serving along with Ernst Pöhner, the new prime minister, with dictatorial powers. As to the other new appointments, Hitler
barked: "The Reich government, that will be me. The national army
is Ludendorff. Lassow is Reichswehr minister, and Seisser, Reich police
minister."[24]

Such wild histrionics, including menacing threats that he would shoot
everyone and reserve the last bullet for himself if they did not cooperate, did not overly impress the three men; nor did they thrill to Hitler's
grand announcement that they had been anointed as leading partners in
a new Reich government. However, Hitler could be a brilliant persuader;
and after talking to the triumvirate in a more reasoned tone, the mood
gradually changed, especially after Hitler announced that "His Excellency Ludendorff" himself was part of the coup and would join them
presently.

While the reluctant hostages were waiting in the side room for Ludendorff, Hitler stepped back into the main hall, where the audience
had become noticeably restless and impatient, and gave one of the
most compelling performances of his life — so compelling that Professor Alexander von Müller, who was in the audience that night, referred
to it as "a rhetorical masterpiece" and confessed that "never before have
I seen the mood of a mass audience change so quickly and dramatically.
It was almost as if a sorcerer were casting a magic spell over them."[25]
Even the triumvirate was impressed to the point of believing that Hitler
must have a special mandate from the crowd that could not be so easily
defied. Moreover, when Ludendorff himself finally arrived and appealed
to their patriotic consciences, their objections seemed to melt away and
they gave their guarded approval to the plans proposed to them. Although Kahr, Lassow, and Seisser still harbored inner doubts about
throwing in their lot with Hitler, they gave no such signs when they
came back from their confinement and publicly pledged their support to
the coup in front of the cheering crowd in the main hall about 9:40.

While one scene of the drama was unfolding inside the Bürgerbräukeller, another was being staged in the city of Munich, where out-of-control SA thugs were acting out a reign of terror directed at political opponents and Jews. The home of the Social Democrat Erich Auer, who had wisely gone into hiding on that evening, was broken into twice by SA storm troopers. Auer's grey-haired wife was harassed, the home ransacked, and Auer's son-in-law was kidnapped. In the Bürgerbräukeller and elsewhere throughout the city hostages were being taken by these self-appointed guardians of Aryan law and order. Rudolf Hess and his storm troopers practically "arrested" the whole Bavarian cabinet, including Prime Minister Knilling and Interior Minister Schweyer, and later took them into the country where they mistreated and threatened them with death. It was a portent of things to come.

While some SA troopers hounded Jews and tortured political opponents, Hitler's Stosstrupp unit, headed by Maurice and Kallenbach, broke into the Socialist *Münchener Post* and indiscriminately vandalized editorial offices and the press room. Their rage was stopped only by a "police official" wearing a swastika armband who prevented them from doing further damage by suggesting that perhaps they should preserve some of the equipment and furniture for the future nationalist cause.[26]

In the meantime, back at the Bürgerbräukeller, Hitler made a fatal mistake by leaving his post to take care of unsuccessful efforts by the Putschists to take over several military barracks. By leaving his command post, he relinquished control over the key players in the plot — Kahr, Lassow, and Seisser. While Hitler was gone, the three reluctant hostages persuaded Ludendorff to let them go on the pretext that they could fulfill the functions assigned to them much better at their respective headquarters. Ludendorff let them go after they pledged, on their word of honor as German officers, that they would abide by the terms of the agreement reached earlier that evening.

When Hitler returned to the Bürgerbräukeller, he was appalled to learn that the triumvirate had been allowed to slip away, but the general brushed aside his objections by rebuking him with the curt remark: "I forbid you to doubt the word of honor of a German officer."[27] Hitler's trust in German officers, however, was already wearing thin because his mission to help capture various barracks had failed precisely when the Reichswehr officers in charge had refused to hand over their facilities to civilians without specific orders from their superiors.

The Putschists could boast of at least one spectacular success, and that came when the cadets from the Infantry Officers' Training School put their commanding officer under house arrest because he refused to support the coup and then marched, about a thousand strong and well armed, to the Bürgerbräukeller to help the Putschists. They were led by none other than Lieutenant Gerhard Rossbach, the notorious Free Corps leader who had fought in the Baltic, had supported the abortive Kapp Putsch, and had lately cultivated the cadet corps as a potential Free

Corps within the Reichswehr. He had led the cadets to believe that they would become the nucleus of an elite corps, the Ludendorff regiment, within a reborn German national army. No wonder that the cadets arrived in great fettle at the Bürgerbräukeller, where they stood at proud attention while Ludendorff reviewed them.

Although thousands of SA and paramilitary troops were swarming all over Munich on the night of November 8, only one major military objective was actually attained, and that was the seizure by Ernst Röhm's men of Military District Headquarters. The seizure was the result of a series of steps. Röhm and his two thousand SA, Oberland, and Reichskriegsflagge storm troopers had been assembled at the Löwenbräu, another prominent beerhall, where they awaited instructions from the Bürgerbräukeller; and when at last they received the code words *glücklich entbunden* (successfully delivered), pandemonium broke out in the beerhall. A beaming Röhm told the assembled storm troopers that the Bavarian government had been deposed and a new government under the leadership of Hitler had been formed. Röhm ordered his men to march to the Bürgerbräukeller in support of the coup, but when the formation set off it was overtaken by a courier who ordered it to seize and hold Military District Headquarters instead. In front of the formation was a near-sighted, spindly, and somewhat oafish-looking young man by the name of Heinrich Himmler.

By this time, however, the Putsch was already unraveling. Once the triumvirate had been allowed to slip away from the Bürgerbräukeller, the Putsch was lost. Lassow established a command post in the intelligence section of the Nineteenth Infantry Barracks, where his own troops were in complete control. He declared a general military alarm and ordered outlying Reichswehr units into Munich. At 2:55 A.M., he issued the following message to all German radio stations:

> State Commissioner General v. Kahr, Col. v. Seisser and General v. Lassow repudiate the Hitler Putsch. Expressions of support extracted by gunpoint invalid. Caution is urged against misuse of the above names.[28]

Although Kahr seems to have agonized a bit longer about his position, by 1:00 A.M. he, too, had made up his mind to resist the coup with all the powers at his command. He drafted a strongly worded proclamation to the people of Munich:

> Deception and breach of faith by certain ambitious characters turned a demonstration for Germany's reawakening into a scene of repulsive force and violence. Declarations extorted from me, General Lassow and Colonel von Seisser by pistol point are null and void. Had the senseless and purposeless attempt at revolt succeeded, Germany would have been plunged into the abyss and Bavaria with it.[29]

Kahr then ordered the dissolution of the Nazi Party and the two fighting forces associated with it — Bund Oberland and Reichskriegsflagge. He also announced that the government would move for the time being from Munich to Regensburg. Munich was not going to march on Berlin after all. If anything, Berlin was now seriously considering marching on Munich. In a hastily convened Reich cabinet meeting in the early hours of November 9 at the chancellor's office, von Seeckt was once more invested with absolute authority to put down the revolt. In a sharply worded telegraph to Lassow, Seeckt ordered the Bavarian commander to suppress the revolt at once, adding: "You do it — or I will."[30] A general proclamation by President Ebert to the people of Germany spoke in the same decisive tone, condemning the Putschists as being guilty of high treason and warning the German people that the government's efforts to restore economic well-being would be undermined if this "mad attempt in Munich" succeeded.[31]

As the morning hours passed, the Putschists gradually discovered that they had been betrayed by the triumvirate. The Reichswehr units, though sympathetic to the coup, were not going to defect after all. Most of the important centers of authority in the city, except for Military District Headquarters, captured earlier by Röhm's forces, were still in the hands of the government. Pöhner and Frick, Hitler's fifth columnists in the Bavarian government, were arrested by Lassow's men at police headquarters. The Putsch, in fact, had hardly spread beyond the Bürgerbräukeller, where the plotters were now becoming increasingly alarmed and depressed, asking themselves what they should do next.

Poor coordination and lack of trust now exacted a heavy price. Part of the blame must also rest on Hitler personally. Although he could not be faulted as a superb propagandist, his leadership qualities on this evening were less than impressive.[32] He could easily stir people into action, but his secretiveness and lack of trust proved to be a great liability in an effort that called for coordinated strategy and careful planning. Hitler's supporters did not even hear about the coup until the day it was supposed to take place. Gregor Strasser was informed about it so late that he barely managed to assemble his 350 men and drive them to Munich in the morning hours of November 9. Party members in Berlin heard about the coup after it had already failed. Hitler's secretiveness, combined with his volatile histrionic and paranoid temperament, would undermine more than one operation in his lifetime. Moreover, whenever failure threatened, Hitler would plunge into the deepest despair followed by convulsions and rages. Thus, when the Putsch began to go awry, he remarked to his followers: "If it comes off, all's well, if not we'll hang ourselves."[33] Neither Hitler nor his followers, of course, hanged themselves, but their revolt against the government certainly was a hanging offense; and as failure began to stare them in the face, they undoubtedly ruminated about the consequences of their action. On General Ludendorff's insistence, they finally decided on a march on the city in order to stir the people and the Reichswehr into supporting their uprising.

Toward noon on November 9, a miserably cold and gloomy day, a column of about two thousand men, some looking smart and combat-ready, others sadly ragamuffin in their improvised uniforms, set out for the center of the city. One of the marchers himself later admitted that the column hardly inspired confidence, looking like "a defeated army that hadn't fought anybody."[34] The main column marched eight a breast, with the leaders of the Putsch in the front rows. Hitler and Ludendorff were in the center of the first rank, along with Göring, Kriebel, Scheubner-Richter, Dr. Weber, Graf, and the commander of the Munich storm troop regiment, Wilhelm Brückner. To Hitler's right was Ludendorff, and to his left Scheubner-Richter, who had earlier confided to Hitler that he had a premonition that this would be their last walk together.

When the column reached the Ludwig Bridge, which led over the Isar River to the center of the city, it encountered a detachment of the state police that had been sent there to block the protesters. However, the relatively small "Green Police" were confused about their exact duties and were easily overwhelmed by the marchers. This seemed to invigorate the column as it resumed its march on the city, the men singing as they went along. They went through the Isar Gate, proceeded along the broad thoroughfare called the Tal, and entered the Marienplatz (St. Mary's Square), the heart of the city, where the swastika was fluttering from the neo-Gothic town hall. Storm troopers had captured the hall and were holding the city council, including the mayor, captive. The Marienplatz was packed with enthusiastic supporters of the coup, having been whipped up to a frenzy by several Nazi agitators like Julius Streicher.

Although the procession was jubilantly received at the Marienplatz, it got itself hopelessly tangled up in the unwieldy crowd. No one seemed to know where to march next, some suggesting a return to the Bürgerbräukeller, others urging that they continue northward toward Military District Headquarters, where Röhm's men were now virtual prisoners of the Reichswehr. The decision to press forward was made almost at the spur of the moment by Ludendorff. It sealed the doom of the procession. In order to reach Röhm, the column had to pass through Odeon Square. As the marchers bored their way toward Odeon Square, their progress was slowed by a heavy congestion of civilians; they approached the Residenzstrasse, passing the Wittelsbach palace on their right and drawing close to the Feldherrnhalle (Hall of Field Marshals) from the rear. The Residenzstrasse ran past the east side of the Feldherrnhalle and led into Odeon Square. It was at the point where the Residenzstrasse led into Odeon Square that the Green Police, armed with carbines, pistols, and rubber truncheons, had formed a cordon to block the procession.

The commander of the Green Police, a tough young lieutenant by the name of Baron Michael von Godin, was determined to stop the approaching column, particularly after he saw what was coming at him, men well armed with fixed bayonets and pistols. As the column drew within a few feet of the Green Police, Ulrich Graf, Hitler's bulky bodyguard, reportedly shouted: "No shooting. Excellency Ludendorff is coming. Don't shoot!"[35] It was a futile cry, probably heard by just a few. A single shot then rang out, no one to this day knowing where it came from, followed by a fusillade of shots fired from both sides. Hitler, who had been locking arms with Scheubner-Richter, was pulled to the ground when the latter was mortally wounded by a bullet in the heart. Although not hit by a bullet, Hitler dislocated his shoulders as he was being pulled to the ground by Scheubner-Richter. Ulrich Graf flung himself over Hitler and probably saved his life: Graf was hit by eleven bullets in the chest, stomach, arms, and thighs.[36] Near Hitler was a large man in a dark overcoat lying in a pool of blood; Hitler mistakenly assumed him to be General Ludendorff. Elsewhere other Nazis were struck by police bullets. All in all, sixteen Nazis were killed and scores were wounded. Hermann Göring was shot in the groin and crawled out of harm's way, later to be cared for by a Jewish physician and then escaping across the border into Austria. As for Hitler, he hurriedly abandoned his dying and wounded comrades, a rather unheroic deed that was later touched up by Nazi myth-makers, and scrambled into a party car driven by Dr. Walther Schultze, the chief SA doctor. Two days later, Hitler was arrested in Hanfstaengl's home at Uffing on Staffel Lake, about thirty six miles from Munich. Of all the conspirators who marched on Munich that day, only Ludendorff and his adjutant marched straight through the police cordon and into protective custody. The Putsch had failed.

The Hitler Trial

When Hitler was arrested at the country home of Putzi Hanfstaengl, he was in a state of utter despondency. Taken by the police to the fortress of Landsberg am Lech, he even expected to be shot at any moment; but when he found out that he would be tried on charges of high treason (*Hochverrat*) along with the other major Putschists, including Ludendorff, his spirits revived almost immediately because he realized that he might still be able to salvage some credibility for his cause in a public forum. Perhaps there was a chance after all of appealing to the nation at large, of showing that the Putsch was not a criminal act against legitimate authority but a noble deed of resistance against the government of the "November Criminals." Hitler knew that the tactics he had chosen to accomplish his goal were wrong; he also knew that he had allied himself with unreliable partners outside his own party whose motives had been ambiguous and at odds with his own, except for one aim — the overthrow of the republic. He swore that such mistakes would not be repeated again. But would there be another chance to gain political power? Like a desperado, Hitler braced himself for his impending trial, hoping to rehabilitate himself and his movement in front of the nation.

On February 24, 1924, exactly four years after Hitler had called his first mass meeting in the Hofbräuhaus and revealed the party program, the "Hitler trial" for high treason opened before a special court in one of Munich's former infantry schools in Blutenburgstrasse. Besides Hitler, the defendants included Ludendorff, Röhm, Frick, Pöhner, Kriebel, Weber, several leaders of the Kampfbund, and three active leaders of the storm troopers (Wilhelm Brückner, Robert Wagner, and Heinz Pernet). Three other trials, completely overshadowed by the Hitler trial, dealt with the members of the Stosstrupp Hitler for their vandalization of the *Münchener Post,* and with various Putschists who were accused of stealing banknotes from a government printing press or seizing weapons without authorization.

The trial was bound to be high political drama, and, given the equivocal atmosphere in Bavaria, it was perhaps also made for a real *Gaudi* (good time). After all, assembled right there in court were two of the most controversial figures in German politics: Ludendorff and Hitler, the great war hero of World War I and the greatest living demagogue, respectively. Moreover, the witnesses testifying for the prosecution — Kahr, Lassow, and Seisser — had themselves been implicated in the Putsch and could, therefore, hardly be counted upon to step forward as impartial witnesses. If the right-wing authorities in Bavaria had their druthers, they would have preferred to hush up the whole distasteful business.[37] Hitler knew this only too well, and he was ready to exploit his moral advantage to the hilt by trying to show his starched-collared accusers that the judgment of history resided with his cause.

Hitler's prospects were, therefore, far from hopeless. Public sentiment favored the conspirators; even behind the scenes, in the justice department, there was strong support for the Putschists. The minister of justice, Franz Gürtner, was openly sympathetic to the Nazi cause and would later be rewarded for his support by being appointed Reich minister of justice. The presiding judge, Georg Neithardt, was a fervent nationalist who regarded Ludendorff as a national treasure and believed that the coup was a "national deed."[38] The lay judges, as it turned out, would be even more blatantly in favor of the Putschists. Although these advantages were not known to Hitler before the trial began, he had an intuitive sense that the climate of opinion in and out of the courtroom would be favorable to his cause. It is for this reason that he took the offensive from the moment the trial opened. Unlike Ludendorff, who tried to prove that his role in the Putsch was that of an unwitting and innocent participant, Hitler took full responsibility for his actions and deftly turned the tables on the witnesses for the prosecution by showing that Kahr, Lassow, and Seisser were equally culpable:

> The fact was that for that whole time Seisser and Kahr shared the same goal with us; namely, the removal of the Reich government ... and its replacement by an absolute, nationalistic, antiparliamentary government — a dictatorship. If they declare that they did not want to use force, that they did not want to force a coup d'état but rather something like a coup d'état just using pressure, I regret that I have no records, no information,

on this kind of coup. Revolution is the destruction of a government by the former opposition; a coup is the disposal of a government by a former ruling group.... If in fact our whole undertaking was high treason, then Kahr, Lassow, and Seisser also must have committed high treason because for months on end they agitated for nothing other than that for which we sit in the dock.[39]

The truth of the matter, Hitler expostulated, was that both the accusers and the defendants really pursued the same goal — that of overthrowing a criminal regime. His conscience, he said, was clear on the question of criminal involvement because how could one commit "high treason" against the traitors of 1918?[40] He added pointedly that "if I am really supposed to have committed high treason, then I am amazed not to see in the dock the officials whom the prosecution is obliged to indict since they strove for the same end."[41]

The officials Hitler was referring to were visibly dumbstruck by these brilliant rhetorical flourishes, all the more so since Hitler's remarks were couched in such noble sentiments that they tended to forestall objective examination of the real issue at hand — criminal wrongdoing on the part of the defendants. It is true that Lassow delivered an angry and very effective riposte, accusing Hitler of lacking any sense of reality and fancying himself a kind of German Mussolini when in fact he was little more than a political drummer.[42] Lassow also drew a very accurate picture of Hitler's histrionic personality, but he undermined his credibility by telling the court that the only reason he listened to Hitler's "overpowering suggestive eloquence" was because he saw "a healthy kernel" in his movement.[43] Moreover, in cross-examination Hitler made him lose his temper several times by insinuating that the general was either a coward or a vacillating weakling who could not make up his mind whether he should support or oppose the coup. Speaking in a loud and agitated manner, Hitler had to be warned several times to lower his voice and restrain himself; his parting shot, accusing Lassow of being a turncoat, was such a low blow that the judge reprimanded him for inexcusable, scandalous, and impertinent behavior.[44]

In his closing remarks, Hitler once more depicted himself as a man of destiny who wanted to undo the shame of defeat and treason. The Putsch, he pointed out, had not been a defeat but a successful stepping stone to ultimate victory; and addressing himself to a larger audience beyond the courtroom, he pointedly reminded the members of the court that they were not truly qualified to pass judgment in this case, a case so special that only the "eternal court of history" could render a fair verdict:

> Gentlemen, judgment will not be passed on us by you; judgment will be passed on us by the eternal court of history. This court will judge the accusations that have been made against us. That other court, however, will not ask: "Did you or did you not commit high treason?" That court

will pass judgment on us, on the General in command of the Quartermaster Corps of the old Army, on his officers and soldiers, who as Germans wanted the best for their people and their country, who were willing to fight and die for it. Even if you find us guilty a thousand times over, the goddess of the eternal tribunal of history will smilingly tear apart the proposal of the Prosecutor and the sentence of the Court, because she will acquit us.[45]

Given the friendly attitude of the Bavarian judicial system, Hitler did not need the help of "the eternal court of history." On April 1, 1924, the People's Court in Munich, packed with sympathetic spectators, handed down what some considered to be a real *Aprilscherz* (April fool's joke) in the form of ridiculously lenient sentences. In Hitler's case, the court prefaced its verdict by stressing the "pure patriotic motives and honorable intentions" of the defendant and then sentenced him to five years in prison with the possibility of parole after six months. The court dismissed the prosecution's demand that Hitler be extradited as an undesirable alien on the grounds that this did not apply to a man "who thinks and feels in such German terms as Hitler."[46]

The sentences of the other conspirators were equally lenient. Kriebel, Pöhner, and Weber also received five years, while Brückner, Frick, Röhm, Pernet, and Wagner received fifteen months, but were released immediately on parole. Ludendorff was acquitted altogether. There were loud shouts of "bravos" in the courtroom. Acknowledging the cheers of his elated followers, Hitler then left the courtroom to return to his cell at Landsberg Prison. He had won a moral victory, while the democratic republic had received a stunning rebuke. In right-wing Bavaria, a plot against the government had merited only a slap on the wrist. As Alan Bullock observes, "Such were the penalties of high treason in a state where disloyalty to the regime was the surest recommendation to mercy."[47]

Landsberg and *Mein Kampf*

From November 11, 1923, to December 20, 1924, Adolf Hitler served his time for high treason in the minimum prison fortress of Landsberg, located about fifty miles west of Munich in the wooded valley of the river Lech. Imprisoned with him were some forty Nazi conspirators, including Rudolf Hess, Hermann Kriebel, Dr. Friedrich Weber, Max Amann, and members of the Stosstrupp (Berchtold, Hermann Fobke, Walter Hewel, Kallenbach, Maurice). Although the prison was housed in a former castle and gave the appearance of being like a dungeon, the whole facility had been substantially modernized around the turn of the century, providing some inmates with comfortable cells and, in Hitler's case, with beautiful views of the surrounding countryside. The food, eaten by both inmates and guards, was better than average. Inmates were also allowed to consume either half a pint (*Schoppen*) of wine or half a liter of beer a day; on hot days, the prison authorities would generously double the daily beer allotment. Hans Kallenbach, who suffered from occasional bouts of malaria, was permitted a glass of schnapps (brandy) for medicinal purposes, a concession that prompted the arrival of a whole battery of brandy bottles and Kallenbach's generous sharing of brandy with his comrades, especially after one guard was persuaded that the term "glass" meant a half-liter glass.[48]

Morale at Landsberg was very high. The whole place was quickly transformed into a beehive of party activity. Cells were decorated with party emblems and personal pictures. At mealtimes, the Nazis would gather in the common room like a family, taking their seats at a special table that was presided over by their führer and the prominent display of a swastika banner behind his seat. While not busy working on various prison details, Nazi inmates would spend their time playing cards, engaging in team sports, or taking walks in the prison garden. They organized an orchestra, a cabaret, a fortress newspaper, and otherwise amused themselves by socializing. A flood of mail, most of it very supportive, and a steady influx of food parcels also boosted the prisoners' morale. Hitler's cell, according to Hanfstaengl, looked "like a delicatessen store. You could have opened up a flower and fruit and a wine shop with all the stuff stacked there."[49]

In contrast to the somewhat rowdy behavior of his followers, Hitler used his time more productively to reflect upon the past and to chart some direction for the future. The conditions for this sort of stock-taking were extremely conducive at Landsberg. Thanks to the government, he had plenty of time to reflect on his future; and with some justice, he would later refer to his incarceration as "a university education at government expense."[50] During the course of a typical day he would rise at six and breakfast with fellow inmates.[51] Upon returning to his cell, he would find everything neatly tidied up by a crew of inmates. Since he had dislocated his shoulder during the Putsch and still suffered occasional pain, the warden had exempted him from all prison work. After breakfast, he would spend his time reading or writing or sometimes watching the activities of fellow prisoners. Lunch was a shared ritual, with Hitler presiding over the table and usually delivering weighty pronouncements. In the afternoon, he would answer additional mail, meet visitors, and take his daily constitutional. After dinner, he watched various athletic contests by Nazi inmates, returned to his cell at eight, and went to bed at ten. This routine seems to have suited him so well that he gained a lot of weight and found enough time to write a personal account of his past struggles and his future visions.

Although convinced that all great movements in history were shaped more successfully by persuasive oratory than by the printed word, Hitler was eager to establish his intellectual credentials, trying to prove that, despite his lack of formal education, he was a serious thinker in his own right. Starting in the summer of 1924, he spent several hours every day dictating his thoughts first to Maurice and then to his personal secretary Rudolf Hess, who would type his running account into a portable Remington typewriter. Originally, Hitler chose a long and clumsy title for his magnum opus, *Four and a Half Years of Struggle against Lies, Stupidity, and Cowardice,* but his business manager and publisher, Max Amann, wisely shortened it to *Mein Kampf* (My battle). He finished the first part of the book in under four months, claiming later that his rapid progress was prompted by a strong need to get things off his chest. Amann had hoped that Hitler would write an exposé on the recent Putsch, but Hitler studiously avoided being drawn into past controversies or indulging in recriminations against recent political opponents, especially at a time when he was still a prisoner and therefore vulnerable to official reprisals. This is why he chose the high-minded road of philosophical formulations and inoffensive autobiographical impressions.

Hitler's book was substantially finished by the time he left prison in December 1924, but the somewhat inchoate manuscript had to be pruned and corrected by several editors, notably by Father Stempfle (the publisher of the anti-Semitic *Miesbacher Anzeiger*), by Putzi Hanfstaengl, and by Professor Haushofer. The final product was still so rough and turgid that even Hitler later admitted that, had he known he would became German chancellor, he would not have published the book in its original form. Some party wags poked fun at it by suggesting that Hitler should have called the book *Mein Krampf* (My cramp or My fit) rather than *Mein Kampf.*[52] Polished or not, the first volume of *Mein Kampf,* subtitled *Eine Abrechnung* (A settlement of accounts), was published on July 18, 1925, by Franz Eher Publications in Munich. The second volume, subtitled *Die nationalsozialistische Bewegung* (The National Socialist movement), followed on December 11, 1926. Until 1930, *Mein Kampf* appeared in two separate volumes, but then it was combined into a one-volume, Biblelike people's edition at eight marks per copy. Before the Nazi seizure of power, 287,000 copies were sold in Germany. By 1945, roughly 10 million copies had been sold overall, and the book had been translated into sixteen languages, making it one of the best known books in the world.[53] An American edition of *Mein Kampf,* published by Houghton, Mifflin and Company in 1933, sold briskly during Hitler's reign of power, especially during the war years. Even after World War II, *Mein Kampf* intermittently found a good market in the United States.[54] Between 1925 and 1945, Hitler earned over eight million marks from *Mein Kampf,* making him a very wealthy man. After 1945, publication rights of the book reverted to the state of Bavaria, whose official position has been to prohibit publication of the book in any new edition. As a result, *Mein Kampf* has been unavailable to German readers through bookstores or public libraries. Only researchers have had access to the book through academic libraries.

The rhetorical style of *Mein Kampf* is intensely aggressive and propagandistic. The tone is pleading and urgent, leaving steadfast readers gasping for air and oppressing them with apocalyptic warnings about sinister forces defiling Aryan blood, poisoning society, and destroying the world. Hitler's prose is overwrought, repetitive, pompous, pretentious, and verbose. Mixed metaphors and awkward reifications abound. The syntax is clumsy and convoluted, made all the more turgid by the author's needless repetitions, abrupt changes of direction, and dissociated thoughts. One German literary critic has counted 164,000 errors in grammar and syntax.[55] From the point of view of critical thinking, there are also many fallacies in reasoning, the most prominent being those of bifurcation ("the all or nothing" fallacy), reification, amphiboly, the false dilemma, *post hoc, ergo propter hoc,* hasty and unrepresentative generalizations, false analogies, dicto simpliciters, and countless *ad hominem* attacks.

It is tempting to infer from this overwrought style a definite psychological frame of mind. After all, style is an emblem of thought that expresses the character of its author. Hitler's mental style reveals several disturbing features: a tendency to rationalize personal failures or weaknesses; a marked preference for aberrant fantasies based on distorted ego projections; a paranoid fear of being defiled by malignant forces; and a deplorable habit of stating uninformed opinions, based on nothing more than self-serving prejudices, as absolute certainties.

Tragically, Hitler's turgid style and his blatant prejudices have misled many contemporaries into underrating the importance of *Mein Kampf.* Even historians, repelled by its tone and content, have not always appreciated the importance of this book. It is, of course, perfectly correct to describe *Mein Kampf* as verbose, difficult to read, dull, the product of thwarted intellectual ambition, and therefore full of pretentious tricks of the half-educated man.[56] This judgment, however, obscures the fact that the style and substance of *Mein Kampf* became public policy. Moreover, the book is not unreadable or devoid of content or even continuity.[57] It reveals a brilliantly negative force by which the author manages to twist lies or half-truths into plausible realities. In short, the book illustrates the nature of a superb demagogue who skillfully tried to inspire his readers to share in his hatreds and to project them onto the world at large. Hitler wrote *Mein Kampf* to fabricate a certain image of his life and to articulate a consistent racial view of the world. His autobiographical impressions are primarily aimed at creating the mythology of a common man who rose from humble yet respectable circumstances and reluctantly abandoned his artistic career in favor of saving Germany from its enemies. The glimpses he gives us of his childhood, adolescence, and struggling years in Vienna are valuable not as objective truths but as psychological data we can use in order to understand his character or his prejudices.

Of greater importance is the author's effort to articulate a coherent Weltanschauung for the Nazi Party. Before describing its essential elements, it is important to realize that Hitler's worldview was not based on formal academic traditions, but was primarily rooted in pseudohistory and mythology. It was a pervasive mood based on atavistic forces rather than on formal systems or logically articulated concepts. Its dynamic force, in other words, resided in myths and tribal prejudices. This is why all attempts to construct a formal lineage of intellectual precursors to Nazism — Fichte, Hegel, Treitschke, Wagner, Nietzsche — have been simplistic and reductionist. Hitler and other spokesmen of Nazi ideology were anti-intellectuals who were motivated largely by propagandistic purposes. Their affinity was closer to those minds that dwelled in the demimonde of popular prejudices and cranky opinions (racists, occultists, health faddists, and so on). It was from *völkisch* racial tracts that Hitler derived much of his information about the world. Although *Mein Kampf* makes reference to a few famous German authors, these references are invariably misleading and distorted. The ideas he derived from them are generally altered to fit the Procrustean bed of his own hate-filled mentality.

In sum, Hitler's Weltanschauung was a system of prejudices rather than a philosophy based on well-warranted premises, objective truth-testing, and logically derived conclusions. Hitler was well aware of this. In politics, he believed, there is greater cognitive value in myths and feelings than in science or reason. Approaching *Mein Kampf* from this perspective, we can readily identify four major prejudices: a racist interpretation of history, a social Darwinist view of life and nature, a preference for the militaristic style of life, and a belief in transforming Germany into a world power.

The bedrock of Hitler's worldview, what he called his "granite foundation," was the belief in the biological and cultural superiority of the Aryan race. This belief formed the basis of his philosophy of history and his political ideology. Hitler was a crude naturalist who explained human nature on the analogy of nature. His concept of nature, however, was not the benign view of the eighteenth-century Enlightenment but the cruel Darwinian view that nature is red in tooth and claw and always favors the strongest or fittest. Moreover, he assumed a law of nature that promotes what he termed "higher breeding." In order to promote human progress, nature encourages the stronger specimen to mate with the stronger, while discouraging the propagation of the weak. By interfering in this process, we sin against the natural order of things.

Hitler actually believed that nature was endowed with an intelligible design; he was convinced, for example, that "nature thinks aristocratically,"[58] makes "certain corrective decisions about the racial purity of mortal beings" (603), does not like bastards, and "inexorably revenges the transgressions of her laws" (84). Hitler seems to have based these sweeping generalizations on little more than uninformed prejudices about higher forces. In fact, throughout *Mein Kampf* he is preoccupied with abstract forces such as nature, fate (*Schicksal*), providence (*Vorsehung*), the Goddess of Misery, the Goddess of History, and so on. It goes without saying that these forces support the truth of his convictions.

He assumes that the strength and weakness of man rest solely in the blood (469). There is superior blood and inferior blood; unless we artificially interfere in nature's aristocratic design, the superior blood will inevitably overcome the inferior blood. In Hitler's view the best blood is obtained when animals mate solely with representatives of their own species — titmouse seeking titmouse, the finch the finch, the stork the stork, the fieldmouse the fieldmouse, the wolf the wolf (389). Any crossing between beings of not quite the same type produces inherently weaker or infertile types. Strength, resilience, and intelligence are the result of racial purity, struggle, and the mating of superior types with each other.

Since human nature is part of nature, the same biological laws of racial purity are applicable. Here, too, nature encourages sharp separations between the racial groups, while also promoting uniform characteristics within each group. Thus the white, black, or yellow person seeks his or her own kind. Since human racial groups are qualitatively different, it follows that cross-breeding undermines racial purity and produces inferior offspring. The worst blood defiling occurs when the Jew mates with the Aryan. Hitler seems to feel that this almost amounts to mating across species, a biological absurdity because no human group has speciated.

Hitler divided the human race into three distinct and qualitatively different groups: Aryan culture-founders, culture-bearers, and culture-destroyers (389). This taxonomy rested on two essential criteria — self-serving ethnocentrism and the racist belief that skin pigmentation is a primary determinant of cultural achievement. Only the Aryan creates culture; he is the Prometheus of mankind "out of whose bright forehead springs the divine spark of genius at all times" (389). Asiatic people, Hitler conceded, possess high culture, but only because the Aryan has provided the creative impetus for it. In the absence of Aryan influences, the Japanese, for example, would fall back into the sleep from which the Aryans aroused them in the nineteenth century. Other racial groups are equally uncreative, and Africans are incapable of even being culture-bearers. In an obviously irritated mood, Hitler denounced all well-meaning efforts to raise primitive blacks to the level of culture-bearers, arguing that this would have to be at the expense of retarding the progress of able Aryans, an effort that would be as self-defeating as it would be unnatural (640).

As to the Jew, he is without genuine culture because he is not capable of creating one. The Jew merely exploits what others have created; he is a pure parasite feeding on the body of healthy cultures, "a sponger who, like a harmful bacillus, spreads out more and more if only a favorable medium invites him to do so" (419–20). The Jew has always lived a furtive existence in other people's communities, where he secretly built up his own state under the guise of a religious community. His great lie, Hitler insisted, is that he is only religiously different, while in other respects being as German as a German or as English as an Englishman. On the contrary, Hitler was convinced that the Jews are "always a people with definite racial qualities and never a religion" (421).

Moreover, Hitler also believed in the existence of a Jewish world conspiracy, as foretold in *The Protocols of the Elders of Zion*. In his lengthy survey of the secret machinations of the Jews over the ages, Hitler revealed that he passionately believed in a conspiratorial view of history according to which the Jews are the real causal forces behind events. In other words, the great changes in European society are not directly the result of great economic transformations, revolutions, or wars — the sort of events covered by ordinary historians — but the result of secret connivings by malicious Jews behind the scenes. Thus, every destructive event is unmasked by Hitler's paranoid mind as being plotted by a scheming Jew, whether it is the rapacious money-lending Jew, the Jew as court Svengali, the Jew as bleeding-heart liberal, the Jew as parliamentary democrat, the Jew as pacifist, or the Jew as Bolshevik. The end result is the same: the Jew incites social divisiveness, hollows out a healthy community from within, and thus prepares the way for the final takeover of the world.

The irrational logic of this argument led Hitler to conclude that the Jew must be the personification of the devil, the spirit who always subverts (447). As a consequence of his delusional system of ideas, Hitler could literally envision "bow-legged Jew bastards" lurking behind the corners of dark alleys in order to rape and therefore defile young Aryan girls (448). This and other passages in *Mein Kampf*, especially the long section in chapter 10 of book 1 dealing with syphilis, clearly point to a potentially malignant pathology. The whole book reverberates with dark ruminations about blood-defiling and blood-poisoning by demonic Jews. The author rants and raves about nature-abhorring bastards and appeals to our sacred obligation to keep the blood pure. Here are only a few samples (with corresponding page numbers) of Hitler's prejudiced epithets, describing the Jews as:

- Personifications of the devil (447)
- Defilers of Aryan blood (448, 826–27)
- Ferment of decomposition (666, 952)
- Blood-suckers and vampires (426–27, 451)
- Purveyors of prostitution and syphilis (78)
- Rapists of Aryan women (448, 826)
- Harmful bacillus (420)
- Maggots (75)
- Poisoners (76, 312)
- Pestilence (76)

- Bow-legged bastards (619)
- Foul-smelling creatures (75)
- Spongers (420)
- Fungi (160)
- Regents of the stock exchange (930)
- Great masters of lying (313, 412)
- Members of a different race (74)
- Wire-pullers (772, 911)

Hitler was passionately convinced that a people's historical greatness depended upon the purity of its blood. Whenever a people permits itself to become bastardized, it *"sins against the will of eternal Providence"* (452; emphasis added). Elsewhere, he called race pollution the original sin (928). Although the Jew has seriously undermined the German blood and spirit, the German people can recover its racial purity by ruthlessly weeding out inferior types from within and by preventing alien races from poisoning the group from without.

The *völkisch* state, therefore, has a clear-cut mission: to breed the most racially pure, fertile, and healthy specimens, so that, at length, the entire national group participates in the blessing of a "high-bred racial treasure" (609). From these strictures it is only a short step to Himmler's racial stud farms, the SS elite, and the extermination of inferior breeds (Gypsies, Asiatic inferiors, cripples, the mentally retarded, and Jews). The antidote to what Hitler perceived to be a clear and present danger of race pollution was to keep the blood pure and to eliminate the Jew before the Jew destroyed the German. To Hitler, this was an "all or nothing" proposition because the Jew is the "great agitator for the complete destruction of Germany. Wherever in the world we read about attacks on Germany, Jews are their fabricators" (906). Germany must therefore devise a state policy in order to eliminate the Jew; and in one ominous passage, which could have served as the lever for the "final solution to the Jewish problem," Hitler even suggested the most effective means by which the Jews could be eradicated — poison gas:

> If, at the beginning of the War and during the War, twelve or fifteen thousand of these Hebraic corrupters of the nation had been subjected to poison gas such as had to be endured in the field by hundreds of thousands of our very best German workers of all classes and professions, then the sacrifice of millions at the front would not have been in vain. On the contrary: twelve thousand scoundrels opportunely eliminated and perhaps a million orderly, worth-while Germans had been saved for the future. (984)

In sketching the future Nazi state, Hitler made it clear at the outset that the *völkisch* state must be based on the principle of personality rather than the decisions of majorities. In other words, the state must be organized like a military chain of command culminating in one man who decides for the whole (669–70). Effective organizations, whether political, economic, or educational, are governed best when they are governed by strong leaders. Men of genius are never born out of general elections; they are bred. Hitler believed that it was easier for a camel to go through the eye of a needle than for a great man to be discovered in a general election. The Western democratic process, he argued, encouraged mediocrity, lack of responsibility, and habitual obstructionism. He rejected the idea that every individual had a constitutional right to participate in shared governance; only the select few have or ever will exercise meaningful power in any system, even in those systems that are ostensibly based on majority rule. The masses must not be deluded into believing that they can actually exercise power. This must be done for them by gifted leaders who rise from their midst and express their longings while also expressing the good of the nation. The interest of the people is not always synonymous with the good of the nation; in fact, the masses often crave selfishly, so that by giving them rights without corresponding responsibilities, they will tend to take from the state rather than give to it.

In opposition to what he termed decadent Western democracy, Hitler proposed to establish a "German type of democracy" by which a leader is freely chosen by the people and then given full responsibilities to do what he has to do (116). There would be no obstructionist parties, state institutions, or special-interest groups to thwart the mandate that has been given to the leader by the *Volk* — in short, there would be no cumbersome countervailing powers to executive leadership at all. That such unlimited executive power has historically resulted in tyranny is conveniently ignored. The fact is that Hitler had no conception of the state at all, other than in the form of the personal dictatorship he craved for himself. In his racially pure state, power would be exercised by a charismatically gifted leader who ruled through a one-party system and delegated dictatorial power to his subordinates. It would be a vertical system of dictatorial empowerment, starting with the führer at the top of the pyramid and extending downward by way of intermediate führers right down to the father führer in each German family.

The executive leaders of the German people, of course, have to rely on the advice given to them by appropriate councils of experts in their given fields. These councils, however, are not subject to popular control; their function is largely advisory. Hitler acknowledged the importance of some representative body, but only within the framework of the one-party state. Such a representative body, he argued, should be divided into political and professional chambers, with ultimate authority once more residing in their respective chairmen. In order to guarantee cooperation between these chambers, Hitler proposed to subordinate them to a kind of mediatory senate with purely advisory powers.

Hitler's discussion of the processes that should govern the Nazi state is vague and perfunctory. Other than the concept that "one man decides," Hitler had nothing specific to say about how a modern industrial state should be governed. There is some evidence that he was vaguely familiar with Mussolini's corporate state in which the socioeconomic sectors of society are organized into a limited number of state controlled corporations. However, he made no attempt in *Mein Kampf* or even later in his career to spell out the precise organizational structure of the Nazi state, causing much confusion, duplication of effort, intramural rivalry, and lack of coordination in what appeared otherwise to be a tightly structured totalitarian state.

In his remarks on foreign policy, Hitler took a strident pan-German position, arguing that the future of Germany resided in the conquest of living space. He differed with many prewar imperialists, however, in rejecting the acquisition of overseas colonies on the grounds that Germany was not a traditional sea power and should not become entangled again in a major conflict with the British Empire. Imperial Germany had been right in pursuing an expansionist policy, but wrong in pursuing it overseas. No sacrifice should have been too great to gain England's favor because England is a great Germanic nation with as equal a claim to territorial expansion as Germany. Hitler believed that England and Germany were natural allies, provided they left each other alone to pursue their territorial ambitions in different parts of the world. It is not entirely clear how or why Hitler expected the English to support German dominance on the Continent, especially since he was well aware of the traditional British policy of favoring a balance of power on the Continent. His views of England consisted of a combination of wishful thinking and misinformation. He assumed that the English regarded the French as a greater threat than they did the Germans because the war had made them the strongest power on the Continent and also because the French, like the English, were a colonial power, and thus a serious overseas competitor to English imperial interests. He realized that the English did not want to see any continental state rise to the position of a world power, but he also believed that the English would probably support a German world power whose economic and territorial interests did not infringe upon England's overseas empire.

As to the French, they are "the German people's irreconcilable mortal enemy" (902). The English might not want Germany to be a world power, but the French desire that Germany have no power at all. The French, he thought, posed a mortal danger because Jewish financial interests there were working hand in glove with rabid chauvinists to destroy Germany as a nation. He also saw the French people becoming more and more "negrofied," thereby also posing a profound racial threat to Germany (907–8). He strongly believed that French policy toward Germany had not changed since Louis XIV, namely to encourage the balkanization of Germany into small states and to build up a solid hegemony over the Continent. In order to dwarf France's grand design, Germany must search for powerful allies, regain its military greatness, and find new soil and territory in order to support its population. In *Mein Kampf,* he was quite explicit about all three: Germany, he argued, should align itself with England and Italy against France, break the shackles of Versailles, and search for *Lebensraum* (living space) in that part of the world where its ancestors had traditionally pursued their imperial ambitions — eastern Europe.[59]

Germany's natural sphere of interest, Hitler believed, was in eastern Europe and the vast spaces of Russia (179, 892). A growing race requires space in order to achieve national greatness and attain the status of a world power. If Germany confined itself to the limited space allotted to it by the Versailles Treaty, it would cease to be a great power in the world. Hitler was a believer in the conventional Eurocentric mythology that European powers could rule the world provided that they pursued a ruthless policy of territorial expansion and economic growth. In fact, he assumed a direct causal connection between territorial expansion by force of arms and economic growth, rejecting the liberal democratic view that nations could also be great by pursuing a peaceful policy of free enterprise, as was subsequently proved by postwar Germany and Japan.

Hitler rationalized these blatantly imperialistic views in purely Machiavellian and frequently crude social Darwinian terms, holding that "might alone makes right" (949), that "one makes alliances only for fighting" (959), that nature does not know political borders, and that conquering the vast spaces of Russia is racially and geopolitically right because the area is populated only by the "scum of humanity" — Jews, Asiatic inferiors, and Communists (959–60). In fighting Russia, Hitler believed, one would be able to reduce two of the deadliest poisons in one full swoop — Jews and Communists.

Hitler's aims, then, were crystal-clear: domestically, he proposed to breed a higher race, weeding out "impurities of the blood" and "unGerman" attitudes (liberal, democratic, pacifistic, Communistic, and so on), while internationally promising to elevate Germany to the ranks of a world power. In fact, in the chapter on future alliances after the war, Hitler delivered both a prophecy and a deadly threat to Germans and to the world by saying that "Germany will be either a world power or will not be at all" (950).

Hitler was also quite explicit on the means by which these grand visions were to be attained — that is, how he would mold a relatively small nation, limited in resources and manpower, and transform it into the strongest power in the world. He would nationalize and fanaticize the masses through unrelenting propaganda until, at last, shaped into a superbly organized fighting force, the German masses would carry out their sacred racial mission. The chief strategy in Hitler's arsenal of gaining, maintaining, and expanding power was propaganda. Without propaganda, it is impossible to reach the heart of the people and imbue them with a sense of purpose or mission. Effective propaganda, Hitler believed, did not rest on logic or reason but rather on faith and emotions. The masses are not comfortable with ambiguities or skeptical habits of mind; they crave certainty. In order to reach their hearts, where the deeper convictions are always rooted, it is necessary to teach them a fanatically one-sided doctrine; for once the masses have found a political faith, it is very difficult to undermine it. Knowledge is more easily undermined than faith. History teaches us, Hitler insisted, that the "driving force of the most important changes in this world has been found less in a scientific knowledge animating the masses, but rather in a fanaticism dominating them and in a hysteria which drove them forward" (968).

The success of a movement, Hitler felt, did not depend on enlightening the voters but rather on the manipulation of mass affections or disaffections. Hitler, therefore, made no distinction between education and propaganda; the two were virtually synonymous in his mind. However, propaganda is simply a means to an end rather than an end in itself. The end of politics, of course, is power — the alpha and omega of life itself. Propaganda can be effective only if it promotes a firm set of ideological positions. Any technique, no matter how reprehensible, is justified in promoting such ideological convictions. Since politics in the modern age has become largely quantitative by appealing to the largest number of voters, the propagandist must always address the capacities inherent in the group mind or mentality, which is just another way of saying that the masses are inherently limited in their mental capacities and can understand only simple ideas:

> All propaganda has to be popular and has to adapt its spiritual level to the perception of the least intelligent of those toward whom it intends to direct itself. Therefore its spiritual level has to be screwed the lower, the greater the mass of people which one wants to attract.... The more modest, then, its scientific ballast is, and the more it exclusively considers the feelings of the masses, the more striking will be its success. (232–33)

It is another function of propaganda to hammer home, by endless repetition if necessary, a few clearly articulated notions, preferably in vivid pictorial images. Moreover, since propaganda aims at persuasion rather than instruction, it is far more effective to appeal to the emotions than to the rational capacities of crowds. This can always be done more effectively through the spoken word and in settings where masses of people can be reached. The heart assents more easily than the mind, especially when a demon speech maker unleashes the seductive powers of emotionality. Hitler believed that crowds are more impressionable and gullible than individuals; they are apt to believe the unbelievable. In fact, they swallow the big lie more easily than the small lie, which would suggest that the biggest promises or claims are more persuasive than the humbler truths. Hitler also held that "people, in an overwhelming majority, are so feminine in their nature and attitude that their activities and thoughts are motivated less by sober consideration than by feeling and sentiment" (237).

In the end, people are persuaded effectively only when the last vestiges of doubt have been removed from their minds. This cannot be accomplished by objective presentation of all sides of an issue, but rather by the insistence that only one side is the absolute truth. The task of propaganda, Hitler insisted, is to stress exclusively the doctrine one is advocating and to contrast it sharply with its false alternative. In political discourse there are no shades of grey but only the positive or the negative, love or hate, right or wrong, truth or the lie (236–37).

Propaganda made and destroyed the Third Reich. In Hitler's world, it became an end in itself, an evolving form of institutionalized deception that proved to be unresponsive to criticism, self-correction, and effective reality-testing. Critical or analytical habits of mind, at any rate, were dismissed by Hitler as Jewish or intellectual and thus unwanted in the *völkisch* state. In several appallingly anti-intellectual passages, Hitler let it be known that he would change the whole direction of German education by getting rid of intellectuals and by emphasizing the education of the will rather than the brain. Intellectuals are a source of grave danger to group cohesion because they lack the will to believe by instinct. They are overeducated apes "stuffed with knowledge and intellect, but bare of any sound instinct and devoid of all energy and courage" (642–43). Their theoretical knowledge estranges them from the healthy folk below, so that what is required in the *völkisch* state is a periodic infusion of healthy blood from the masses into the ranks of enervated intellectuals. In actual practice, this crude prejudice that the lower levels of society were healthier than the upper levels was later translated by the Nazis into a government practice of recruiting and promoting people on the basis of race and political correctness rather than individual merit.

Such attitudes were undoubtedly based on Hitler's own failures in the Austrian school system, but they also expressed widespread resentments with an elitist and authoritarian school system in general. Although Hitler's rhetoric against the German-Austrian school system contained an undertone of crude egalitarianism, it was in actual fact elitist to the core, except with a different emphasis: instead of promoting a caste of intellectual mandarins recruited from the upper classes, Hitler proposed to groom a classless elite from the ranks of the racially pure and politically correct candidates. Among themselves, the chosen elite would practice a kind of democratic camaraderie, the sort of fraternal experience that Hitler associated with the trenches in World War I. In fact, the education of the trenches should serve as a model for the education of the new army-state.

It does not require hindsight to understand the implications of Hitler's ideas. Anyone who bothered to study *Mein Kampf* with an open mind before Hitler's seizure of power could not have had any doubts as to what would be in store for Germany if this man were entrusted with absolute power.

The Disintegration of the Nazi Party

While Hitler served his prison term at Landsberg, the Nazi Party was falling to pieces "like a pile of chaff."[60] The blame for this must rest largely on Hitler himself. Although many leaders in the past had successfully led their movements from behind prison bars, Hitler decided to go into temporary hibernation rather than waste his time in trying to hold his scattered forces together. As long as he could not exercise direct control, he preferred to see the party in disarray. This "all or nothing" syndrome, so typical of his mentality, probably also accounted for the fact that he chose the weakest and least threatening follower to carry on in his place — Alfred Rosenberg.

Although Rosenberg tried to hold the movement together under a new umbrella called the Greater German People's Community, his uninspiring leadership only hastened the process of dissolution already in progress. In the absence of Hitler's highly personal and charismatic leadership style, the movement disintegrated into a host of squabbling cliques, each vying with the others for power and appealing their differences to an imprisoned leader who seemed to enjoy dividing his potential opposition by never issuing clear guidelines. Accordingly, the strong personalities in the movement followed their own drummers: Röhm ran himself ragged trying to reorganize the SA under a new name, the Frontbann, and actually managed to recruit thirty thousand new members all over Germany;[61] Ludendorff tried to galvanize the *völkisch* wing of the party, and with the help of Albrecht von Graefe, Gregor Strasser, and Röhm, he organized the National Socialist Freedom Party; Julius Streicher and Hermann Esser joined forces in founding the Nuremberg chapter of the Greater German People's Community and undermining the work of Rosenberg.

A major source of disagreement between Rosenberg and his detractors centered around the party's future direction in German politics. Rosenberg, supported by Gregor Strasser, Ernst Pöhner, and Erich Ludendorff, favored cooperation with other right-wing groups and participation in the 1924 spring elections. Although Hitler came around to the position that the party's only hope of success in the future resided in following a path of legality and participating in the democratic process, he was adamantly opposed to weakening the party again by forming alliances with outside elements. He rightly perceived that such alliances would split and therefore weaken the movement. Already there were two major heirs to the former Nazi Party — the Greater German People's Community with its largely Bavarian base of operation and the National Socialist Freedom Party with its more extensive northern sphere of influence. True, both parties pledged loyalty to Hitler but also accused each other of betraying him. A unity conference, meeting in Weimar in August, failed to resolve these lingering differences. The northern group turned to Ludendorff as a substitute leader and looked with suspicion upon the southern group. This ongoing feud not only weakened the radical right but also reopened traditional suspicions, especially in the north, that the Nazis were a Bavarian and southern German rather than a national party.[62]

Yet despite Hitler's opposition to fraternal ties with other *völkisch* groups, Rosenberg continued to cooperate with such groups, most notably with the Völkisch Bloc, and worked hard to field various candidates for the state and national elections of April and May 1924. In the April state elections, the Völkisch Bloc, now running as the Völkisch Social Bloc, finished a surprising third behind the Bavarian People's Party and the Socialists, an impressive showing that was largely the result of Bavarian voters' widespread sympathy with Hitler's position at his trial.[63] One month later, the Völkisch Social Bloc polled almost two million votes in the Reichstag elections. This meant that 32 seats out of 472 went to Völkisch Bloc candidates; but unlike the Bavarian state elections, in which most of the Völkisch Bloc members had been former Nazis, only ten members of the former Nazi Party now running under the banner of the National Socialist German Freedom Movement were elected to the Reichstag.[64] Among the Nazis elected were Strasser, Röhm, Feder, Frick, and Ludendorff.

Hitler looked at these developments with grave concern because they threatened his own leadership position. With some of his followers now in the Reichstag, enjoying parliamentary immunity and a legislative salary, he felt himself increasingly isolated and powerless as he looked suspiciously upon the activities of his followers from his prison cell at Landsberg. The party had split into contentious factions, and its internal cohesion was being threatened by makeshift alliances with outside forces. Moreover, Hitler's absence had created a leadership vacuum, which, as previously mentioned, was being filled by others — by Röhm, Ludendorff, Streicher, and by new interlopers such as Albrecht von Graefe, Alexander Glaser, Rudolf Buttmann, and Ludolf Haase.

In the face of such mounting dissension, Hitler at first tried to steer a diplomatic middle course, patiently listening to a constant litany of complaints by various emissaries who came to see him at Landsberg but refusing to side with any one group. However, in the summer of 1924 he decided to divest himself of the whole albatross by making a startling announcement to those who had sought his mediation:

> It is no longer possible for me under such circumstances to intervene from here in any way or even to assume responsibility. I have therefore decided to withdraw from active politics until my restored freedom offers me the possibility of being a real leader. I must therefore inform you that from now on nobody possesses the right to act on my behalf, to appeal to my authority, or to deliver explanations in my name. I also request that from now on no political letters are sent to me.[65]

Like Hitler's dramatic resignation from the party in 1921, this declaration of withdrawal from politics involved substantial risks as well as benefits. Its short-range consequence, of course, was that it effectively removed Hitler from further involvement in active party politics, even from the sidelines. This disadvantage, however, was offset by the fact that Hitler had made a clean sweep of his liabilities, namely, the potential failures of his followers, the divisive influence of various splinter groups, and the suspicions of the authorities regarding his continued participation in politics. Hitler was acutely aware that his parole, set for October 1, could be seriously jeopardized by his involvement in current controversies. Indeed, in September, the Bavarian authorities moved against the Frontbann, which had grown alarmingly, and arrested most of its leadership. Although Hitler was not directly linked to the Frontbann, the police recommended that Hitler be deported upon his release, which was now delayed until the end of the year. Given these uncertainties, Hitler was more than willing to divest himself temporarily of party business and prove himself to be a model prisoner.

On December 7, 1924, Reichstag elections were held in Germany. Voting was especially heavy because state parliamentary elections were also held on this day in various German states such as Prussia, Hesse, Braunschweig, and Bremen, while in Bavaria there were local community elections. The results indicated a shift away from the extreme left (Communist) and extreme right (*völkisch* parties) of the political spectrum toward a more moderate middle. The *völkisch* right lost votes in every electoral district in Germany, with the heaviest losses occurring in Bavaria, where the Völkisch Bloc received only 5.1 percent of the votes as opposed to 16 percent in May.[66]

This setback to extremism was largely the result of economic stabilization in Germany and a much improved atmosphere on the international scene. The Stresemann government had ended passive resistance in the Ruhr and at the same time eliminated the immediate threat of revolution throughout Germany. Under the leadership of Hjalmar Schacht, a shrewd financial realist, the printing presses stopped churning out worthless money, and Schacht issued a new currency, the Rentenmark, based on the total resources of the nation. Stability gradually returned, reinforced in the spring of 1924 by major favorable changes in international relations, as moderates began to replace hardliners in France and England. The Allied powers also arranged for easier reparations payments. Under the terms of the Dawes Plan, named after the American banker Charles G. Dawes, annual reparations payments were reduced and foreign loans were made available so that Germany could meet its treaty obligations. By the summer of 1924 a measure of political stability had also returned to German domestic politics. Although the Stresemann government had been replaced in November 1923 for being too soft on right-wing radicals, the two cabinets that governed Germany from November 1923 to December 1924 had Stresemann serving as foreign minister and were led on both occasions by the centrist Wilhelm Marx. The Marx government was replaced in December by a moderately conservative cabinet headed by the civil servant Hans Luther, with Stresemann again serving as foreign minister.

Given these developments, especially the devastating defeat of the *völkisch* right in the December 7, 1924, election, the Bavarian authorities concluded that Hitler, with his now-defunct Nazi Party, was no longer a threat to the security of the state and should therefore be released on parole. The possibility of deporting him was no longer an issue because the Austrian government had informed the Bavarian authorities that it did not want him back in Austria. On December 20, 1924, the photographer Heinrich Hoffman, a friend of Hitler, drove out to Landsberg to pick him up. Posing next to Hoffmann's car in front of one of Landsberg's ancient town gates, a shivering Hitler, hat in hand and raincoat covering his Lederhosen, struck a defiant pose and then departed for Munich and an uncertain future.

Chapter 6

The Years in the Political Wilderness, 1924–29

The Cracks in the Weimar Republic

The middle years of the Weimar Republic (1924–29), sometimes referred to as the Roaring or Golden Twenties, saw a temporary return of domestic prosperity and a concurrent relaxation in international relations. With the benefit of hindsight, we now know that peace and prosperity in Germany were made possible primarily by huge American loans, amounting to over twenty billion dollars, and by a far more conciliatory attitude on the part of the Western powers toward Germany's financial obligations. In 1924 Germany negotiated the Dawes Plan, mentioned above, which recommended the evacuation of the Ruhr by the French, reduced reparations payments, and made arrangements by which Germany could borrow extensive capital from abroad. In the following years many Western loans were made to Germany, creating an impressive boom that persuaded many that the crisis of 1923 had been resolved. Germany used the borrowed capital in two profitable ways: financing a program of public works and investing in the modernization of industry. In 1923 German industrial output had fallen to 47 percent of 1913 levels, but by 1929 it surpassed 1913 levels by 4 percent.[1]

The return of prosperity brought with it a corresponding improvement in international relations, partly because the Western powers recognized that their economic well-being in an increasingly interconnected economic order rested on cooperation rather than on conflict and partly because a group of more moderate and capable statesmen now took the helm in foreign policy in the major Western nations — Gustav Stresemann in Germany, Aristide Briand in France, and Ramsey McDonald in Great Britain. In 1925 Germany signed several treaties at Locarno pledging to renounce force as a means of adjusting disputed frontiers with Belgium, France, Poland, and Czechoslovakia. In 1926 Germany joined the League of Nations, and in 1928 it signed, along with sixty-four other nations, the Kellogg-Briand Pact, which called for peaceful arbitration of international problems and condemned the recourse to war.

This relaxed atmosphere in international relations, combined with the return to prosperity, also lowered the political temperature in Germany. As previously mentioned, the December elections of 1924, during which both the Nazis on the right and the Communists on the left sustained heavy losses, produced a more moderate Reichstag, although the new cabinet headed by the independent Hans Luther leaned to the right and did not enjoy the support of the Social Democrats. In 1925, following the death of Friedrich Ebert, the Weimar Republic gained new respectability with the election as president of the venerable Paul von Hindenburg, who would painstakingly observe his oath to the republic despite his monarchist convictions.

The political life of the republic, of course, still had not stabilized or matured. Between 1924 and 1929 governments were glued together by tenuous coalitions of center to moderate right-wing parties — three Marx cabinets, two Luther cabinets, and a lackluster cabinet headed by the Social Democrat Hermann Müller. In the May 1928 Reichstag elections the Social Democrats and other parties loyal to the republic appeared to gain new life, while the Communists and nationalists lost important seats. The Nazis were almost annihilated, gaining only 810,000 popular votes and a mere twelve seats in the Reichstag. Press headlines triumphantly announced that "Hitler Is Finished," that it was "The End of the Nazis," or that "The Drummer Has Drummed Badly."

Indeed, Hitler's national career seemed to have come to a grinding halt by 1925. In Munich the Nazi Party had little more than seven hundred members. Between 1925 and 1928, Hitler lived largely in semiretirement, spending most of his time at Berchtesgaden. In 1928 he leased and later purchased a comfortable villa, Haus Wachenfeld, on the slope of the Obersalzberg, a house he later remodeled on a grander scale and renamed the Berghof.[2] He built a wall around himself, socialized only with party cronies or doting matrons, and indulged his growing passion for his niece Geli Raubal.

Although Hitler may have been relegated to the political wilderness during these years, the conditions that had made his rise in politics possible in the first place had not changed. On the surface, the republic appeared to be prosperous and stable, but there were unmistakable signs of fault lines below the surface that if aggravated could pull apart the republic's tenuous lifeline. The most serious of these faults were political divisiveness, extreme cultural and generational polarizations, and what we shall call the dark underside of German society.

The republic had come into being as a *Zufallsrepublik,* an accidental republic, with a democratic constitution that few Germans understood or appreciated. Tarnished by its opponents with the stigma of Versailles and saddled with staggering socioeconomic problems, the republic found few passionate supporters — so few, in fact, that cynics were perhaps justified in calling the new government a republic without republicans.

With the fall of the monarchy, which had provided a sense of unity and historical continuity, the Germans became an orphaned people, splintering into a host of antagonistic parties, groups, and associations. A conservative people, many Germans would have been more apt to support a constitutional monarchy than a republic. Even those who reluctantly came around in support of the republic — *Vernunftrepublikaner* such as Gustav Stresemann, Friedrich Meinecke, Max Weber, or Thomas Mann — did so only out of good sense (*Vernunft*) rather than out of a passionate commitment to republican principles. What really tied them to the republic was their objection to all existing alternatives. Since this was also true of many politically involved Germans, one would have thought that the republican government constituted the least objectionable government to everyone concerned. The growing antirepublican groups hated each other with far greater intensity than they did the republic. Recognition of this fact could have made the republic the least divisive choice for all Germans. Unfortunately, this fact was not widely recognized or appreciated as Germans began to embrace extreme and one-dimensional ideologies and abandoned political cooperation in favor of more militant solutions. This polarization was particularly evident in the field of party politics.

Political parties reflected the traditional social, religious, and regional cleavages that had divided the German people from each other in the past.[3] Even parties located close to each other on the political spectrum found greater strengths in their differences than in their similarities. On the political left, Socialists fought internecine wars with each other over the direction of both party and state. The militant left (Communists and Independent Socialists) accused the Majority Socialists (SPD) of betraying the revolution to the German military-industrial elite and refused to cooperate with them throughout the course of the republic, even when the life of the republic itself was at stake. The Majority Socialists, in turn, accused the militant left of trying to destroy parliamentary democracy in favor of soviet totalitarianism.

As long as there was a viable democratic center, working coalitions could be formed among those parties claiming a commitment to the republic — the Social Democrats (SPD), the Democratic Party, and the Center Party. However, the predominantly south German and Catholic Center Party, itself subject to internal divisions, often found it difficult to cooperate with the Majority Socialists because they projected neither a strong nationalist nor a strong middle-class position. Moreover, their Marxist ideology was offensive to middle-class interests in general and to middle-class religious convictions in particular.

Right-of-center parties such as the German People's Party (DVP) and the German National People's Party (DNVP) were even less inclined to cooperate with the SPD or the Center Party. The DVP, founded in 1919 by Gustav Stresemann, stood firmly for *Besitz und Bildung* (property and education) and looked upon the SPD as a Marxist party that still had not successfully abandoned its revolutionary principles. Although Stresemann had hoped that the DVP would become a party of vital and realistic liberalism, capable of forming alliances with the center and moderate left, the party steadily moved to the right, finding more in common with the reactionary DNVP. The DNVP was an enlarged prewar conservative party, predominantly west German, urban, upper-middle-class, and strongly reactionary in outlook. Originally led, before his death, by Karl Helfferich, the former imperial treasury secretary, the party fell into the hands of the stiff-necked press mogul Alfred Hugenberg, who used his considerable influence and fortune not only to move his party in the direction of strident nationalism but also to aid and abet the Nazi movement. The DNVP consisted of a collection of disgruntled conservative nationalists who drifted through the political confusion of the Weimar Republic without a strong leader or a strong platform but were forever receptive to either a restored monarchy or a conservative dictatorship.

In surveying the polarized German party system, one fact, above all, stands out in sharp relief: out of some ten major parties, none displayed a passionate commitment to the republic. Its strongest support came from the SPD and the DDP, followed by lukewarm support from the Center Party and the DVP. The parties on the extreme ends of the political spectrum, gaining steadily at the expense of the more moderate parties, especially after the 1929 depression, were on public record that they favored the destruction of the republic. The number of viable working combinations of parties willing to support the republic was essentially limited to three possibilities: the SPD and the strong parties to the left of the DNVP; the parties of the bourgeois coalition, including the DNVP; and the parties to the right of the SPD. By 1930 such combinations had been made nearly impossible as a result of further ideological infighting, heavy losses sustained by the republican parties, and startling increases in the voting strength of extreme parties on both the left (Communists) and the right (Nazis).

The political foundation of the republic was also under attack by Germany's elite institutions and groups — the legal profession, universities, the military, and leaders of heavy industry. The overwhelming majority of judges were unsympathetic to the republic, often expounded blatantly biased right-wing views, and handed down sentences that favored conservative causes. Moreover, the punishment meted out by German judges in political cases was usually more lenient or nonexistent when it came to right-wing offenders and Draconian when it came to left-wing offenders.[4] The lenient sentence given to Hitler, who should have been deported to Austria, is a case in point. What was true of the German judiciary was equally true of Germany's law enforcement agencies, whose leaders were generally conservative, if not reactionary, in their political persuasions.[5]

The universities were bastions of institutionalized conservatism and elitism. Access was still restricted to the upper classes and to graduates of the elite gymnasia, while the overall control of the system remained in the hands of state authorities with decidedly conservative and authoritarian tendencies. The emphasis during the years of the republic, as before, was on discipline, order, and obedience to authority. There was also considerable anti-Semitism in academia, exacerbated by the fact that academic positions, and jobs in general, were extremely scarce in the 1920s. Students were particularly vulnerable to the appeals of National Socialism, as indicated by the astonishing successes the Nazis scored in student council elections.[6]

The military, of course, was the most powerful bulwark against democratization. Under the leadership of the monocled and fishy-eyed General Hans von Seeckt, the Reichswehr had managed to preserve its traditional structure and conservative ethos, though officially it pretended to stay above politics. When Seeckt fell from power in 1926, the Reichswehr increasingly abandoned its avowed neutrality in favor of more active involvement in politics. The new thinking was epitomized by General Kurt von Schleicher, head of the political bureau of the Reichswehr, who called for revision of the Versailles Treaty, rearmament, and political cooperation by the Reichswehr with those parties that shared its conservative and authoritarian tendencies. Schleicher himself looked favorably upon an autocratic, presidential regime that would bypass what he considered to be the cumbersome and self-defeating process of parliamentary democracy. Since this was also one of the major goals of the Nazis, Schleicher and the military saw in the Nazi movement certain elements they thought they could exploit for their own purposes, but to do so implied active involvement and cooperation with the Nazis. In practice, this was almost calculated to turn the military into one of the grave diggers of the republic as well as making it a participant in the rise of Nazi totalitarianism. The Reichswehr was never able to extricate itself from that fatal embrace with National Socialism because its mentality, if not always its leadership, was strongly colored by authoritarian values that were also shared by the Nazis. Although the Reichswehr was numerically small as an institution during the Weimar Republic, it was a powerful and cohesive force: it was largely a non-working-class army because its recruits came from rural and conservative districts and its officers predominantly from officers' families, thus making it a virtually "Socialist-free" army.[7] It must be remembered that out of its wartime ranks emerged the most vocal and powerful insurgents against democracy. The front generation was acculturated into the military ethos, reinforced in that mentality during service in the Free Corps years of 1919–23, and subsequently fine-tuned its antidemocratic attitudes in the SA.

The leaders of heavy industry also wanted to dismantle the Weimar system because it supported the costly welfare state. The Weimar Constitution had guaranteed every German a living through productive work (Article 163), specifying that if no opportunity for work could be found, the state would provide the means necessary for a worker's livelihood. The democratic founders had even attached a naive shopping-list of generous benefits.[8] Although the republic had been launched socioeconomically by a shared agreement between labor and management (the Stinnes-Legien Agreement) to promote economic democracy by way of codetermination, collective bargaining, and compulsory arbitration, German big business gradually mounted a counterattack against labor by trying to reduce wages and benefits.

Temperamentally, leaders of big business clung to certain feudal-elitist values that were fundamentally out of tune with postwar realities. Big business directors still saw themselves as *Herrn-im-Hause* (lords-of-the-household) and expected respect and obedience from their employees in the same way that officers demanded obedience from their enlisted men. In return, business owners were willing to treat their employees in a paternalistic manner. The removal of the monarchy in 1918 did not alter these authoritarian habits. Although Henry Turner is undoubtedly right in arguing that the military rather than big business spearheaded the assault on the republic, big business had no love for the republic and its whole social politics (*Sozialpolitik*).[9]

In addition to these political and institutional cleavages, the Weimar Republic also faced intense cultural divisions stemming from what sociologists call the process of "modernization." The Weimar Republic experienced the impact of modernization with a far greater force than the Second Reich and with far fewer stable defenses. Historically, modernization refers to a profound shift in both the methods and the systems used in the process by which societies collectively make a living. Sociologically, this shift involved complex patterns of bureaucracy, rapid urbanization, and mass education. Culturally, it involved the search for new forms of expression suitable to a mass audience rather than a small cultural elite. The pull of modernization was in the direction of the new rather than the old, usually at the expense of ancient traditions and inherited patterns of life. Even under normal conditions this process is accompanied by widespread anxiety, but coming in the wake of a lost war and its chaotic aftermath the impact was far more acute in Germany than in most other parts of Europe.

Although Germany had experienced the impact of modernity during the imperial period, the floodgates did not really open up until the Weimar Republic. This is why the republic, certainly in the eyes of cultural conservatives, became causally associated with every threatening wind of change in fashion, mores, or intellectual attitudes. Intellectually, the 1920s were characterized by the impact of Einstein's theory of relativity and Heisenberg's principle of uncertainty. Both theories postulated a

universe of flux and taught that all "facts" are simply fleeting perceptions of different possibilities. Truth now appeared to be a function of
subjective perception and morality just an expression of individual or
group choice. Objective truth thus gave way to cultural relativism; it
was in the eye of the individual beholder. The Roaring Twenties ushered in a new age of moral uncertainty, made all the more disturbing by
the fact that a whole generation had been brutalized by four years of
war and now seemed deprived of the moral standards that had guided
the *Gründerzeit* generation. Many young people, especially those who
had been traumatized by war, exhibited disturbing symptoms of psychological maladjustment: depression, scapegoating, paranoid fears, and
aggressive behavior. Some sought refuge in nihilistic lifestyles, others
searched for a messianic leader who would redeem their sacrifices and
lead them into a glorious future. A Nietzschean mood of smashing
old idols, including parental authority, pervaded the postwar climate
of opinion. In a world that was no longer stable or predictable, pious
pronouncements about "the good old days" or self-righteous appeals
to Christian morality now seemed somehow hypocritical, platitudinous,
and hollow. This being the case, why not just live and party for today?
After all, "Man lebt ja nur so kurze Zeit und ist so lange tot" (One
lives but such a short time and is dead for so very long). Such attitudes,
captured so well in the cabaret songs of Berlin, also expressed a simple
human need to enjoy life after years of morbid fear, suffering, and death.

For ten years, until Hitler wrung down the curtain on the Roaring
Twenties, many Germans enjoyed a temporary triumph of eros over
thanatos, experiencing a sense of liberation hitherto unknown in a land
where strong discipline and public conformity had held sway for generations. The country was gripped by a veritable dance fever, and sex
emerged from the hidden domain of taboo morality. Sexual expression ranged from quasi-scientific research institutes to nude shows and
hard-core pornography, with Berlin becoming the capital of liberated
sexuality where cabarets and bordellos enticed people with such titles as "Nights in a Harem," "The White Slave Traffic," or "Women
with Whips."[10] Although cultural conservatives pretended to be shocked
by these libidinal vulgarities and delivered blanket condemnations, the
vice industry was not as malignant or ubiquitous as it seemed. As
Walter Laqueur reminds us, a great deal of traditional piety and self-
restraint continued to operate, even in sinful Berlin, where the famous
"Tiller girls" traveled with both a chaperon and a clergyman and had
to say their prayers every night.[11] However, the perception of many
conservative-oriented Germans was of a world out of joint, a Sodom
and Gomorrah of rampant wickedness, an outcome, they believed, of
the permissive republic and its liberal policies.

What some historians have called the first "modern" culture was
in fact a curious hybrid of conservative tradition and creative experimentation.[12] In the 1920s German intellectuals formed the vanguard

of modernity and articulated the patterns of consciousness we still use in such diverse fields as psychology, philosophy, sociology, the fine arts, and the natural sciences. Avant-garde movements proliferated: psychoanalysis, the sociology of knowledge, expressionism, atonal music, Bauhaus architecture, existential philosophy, and quantum physics. The Psychoanalytical Institute in Berlin, founded by Max Eitington and supported by Hanns Sachs and Karl Abraham, trained a host of brilliant analysts who would make important contributions to psychology — Karen Horney, Franz Alexander, Wilhelm Reich, and Melanie Klein. In the field of sociology, the Institute of Social Research, founded in 1923, espoused a critical Marxist humanism, and the scholars associated with the institute — Max Horkheimer, Theodor Adorno, Walter Benjamin, Erich Fromm, and Franz Neumann — would provide the theoretical impetus in the social sciences for decades to come, particularly after the institute relocated to New York in the 1930s. In literature, a whole galaxy of bright stars, some traditional and some smartly avant-garde, lit the postwar sky, including the brothers Thomas and Heinrich Mann, Hermann Hesse, Bertolt Brecht, Robert Musil, Rainer Maria Rilke, Stefan George, Gottfried Benn, and Alfred Döblin. In music, too, there were new and novel approaches, many expressing a sense of disquiet, as in the discordant sounds of artists like Arnold Schönberg, Paul Hindemith, and Kurt Weill. Architecture and art, now more closely related than ever, also experimented with new ideas and symbolic forms of expression. Walter Gropius and the Bauhaus school stressed the union of art and technology and experimented with steel, glass, reinforced concrete, and plastic in order to achieve the ideal of pure form and function. Finally, out of theoretical physics and existential philosophy would emerge an indistinct, largely subjective, and ideational universe that reinforced an already pervasive feeling about the anxiety (angst), uncertainty, and ambiguity of modern life.

Many traditional artists, craftsmen, writers, and cultural commentators condemned these avant-garde movements as a betrayal of the classical canons of the past. Their opposition, however, was not merely aesthetic but also political. When they saw painters apparently revelling in incoherent forms and ugliness, musicians throwing harmony overboard in favor of a cacophony of dissonant sounds, writers taking their readers to the brink of the social abyss, sociologists and psychologists denouncing German institutions as inherently unjust and repressive, they mounted vocal protests and delivered blanket indictments against the culture of modernity as a whole.

Invariably, the critique of the new, taking the form of a profound cultural pessimism (*Kulturpessimismus*), came from the political right. In the works of Oswald Spengler, Arthur Moeller van den Bruck, Ernst Jünger, and Edgar Jung the emerging mass consumption culture was variously denounced as vulgar, soulless, materialistic, decadent, and American.[13] Although these critics scored some valid objections to modernity by exposing its weaknesses, they often marred their criticism by needless and shrill exaggerations. However, the same charge could also be brought against the cultural critics on the left and their mindless denunciations of capitalism and bourgeois life. In what would become paradigmatic of German intellectual discourse, both left and right not only talked past each other but also mindlessly attacked the republic and what it stood for — with the left attacking capitalism and the right attacking democracy.[14]

In the field of culture, as in so many other fields, Germany became radically polarized between the traditionalists, who preached the unity of a German style in all the expressions of culture, and the cultural pluralists, who welcomed the existence of divergent, even contradictory, styles because it meant a more vibrant and creative spirit. It was a profound cultural split with important political overtones because the Nazis would subsequently use the cultural criticism of the conservative right as a stalking horse to power. As one historian has rightly observed, "The most consistent electoral support for the Nazi Party was concentrated in those social and occupational groups that harbored the greatest reservations about the development of modern industrial society."[15]

An important aspect of Germany's cultural fragmentation involved profound generational problems, most of which stemmed from World War I and its chaotic aftermath. Throughout the 1920s, Germany was plagued by the vexing problem of what to do with a lot of superfluous young men who often could not find work and had to go through the rites of passage at a time of constant crisis. Women, too, found themselves facing new and often difficult choices. World War I had given German women a sense of empowerment and self-esteem because the nation looked upon them for the first time as vital element in the nation's workforce; but now that the war was over and jobs were scarce, many women were torn by the contradictory demands of returning to the home as wives and mothers or competing with men in the marketplace. The position of women in German society was still marked by legal and social inequalities; their problems were also intergenerational as well as generational since they were exposed to condescending and discriminatory practices by parents, grandparents, and male siblings alike.

Parents, schools, churches, and social organizations persisted in seeing the youth problem in the Weimar period as one of control.[16] Most of these groups and institutions still clung stubbornly to authoritarian traditions. Out of some nine million young people, 4.3 million belonged to various youth organizations such as the Workers Youth movement, the Young Communists, the Young German Order (Jungdo), various church organizations, and the Bund movement deriving from the hiking groups (Wandervögel) of the nineteenth century. Most of these movements were opposed to the new democratic changes of the Weimar period and displayed marked preferences for völkisch ideas and traditions. Young

Germans in general were restless, disoriented, and alienated; they tried to forge, if only in a haphazard fashion, closer emotional bonds with each other. Unfortunately, these coping mechanisms were often reactionary and escapist and contained, in embryonic form, certain features that the Nazi movement was to exploit and pervert shamelessly. These features were in the form of innocent attitudes and vague longings such as a pantheistic love of nature, a mystical love of fatherland, homoerotic friendships, romanticized longings for a world without asphalt and money, a strong need for group affiliation, and a cult of hero worship. In 1932, a pastor of the Marienkirche in Berlin lamented that

> never have generational differences been more important in German politics.... Our youth is anti-reason.... The new generation also knows nothing of liberalism and can hardly be expected to.... From the tradition of the "nests" of young boys and girls, from their nature hikes and wanderings there came the *idea of a leader*...and of a *Bund* of many like-minded youth groups...and of regional *ethnic culture* (*Volkstum*). ... Because of the bitter experiences of unemployment of many of these youths, however, political radicalism got a hold of them by tying itself to all their favorite ideas. The idea of the leader became the promotion of the dictatorship of an unstable Austrian, the warm affection for the people became ice-cold anti-Semitism, the sticking together of the youth group turned into a vicious struggle against those who dare to disagree with them.[17]

Deviance and crime also tore at the seams of the Weimar Republic. The postwar period witnessed the most dramatic increase in crime since the compilation of crime statistics.[18] There was also a corresponding decline in ethical standards, giving rise to what one historian has called a "racketeering mentality."[19] Stories about Berlin in the 1920s usually contain accounts of dope peddlers and prostitutes, homicidal maniacs and notorious robbers.[20] Endemic crime and political violence plagued the major German cities throughout the Weimar Republic:

> Berlin was in a state of civil war. Hate exploded suddenly, without warning, out of nowhere; at street corners, in restaurants, cinemas, dance halls, swimming-baths; at midnight, after breakfast, in the middle of the afternoon. Knives were whipped out, blows were dealt with spiked rings, beer mugs, chair-legs or leaded clubs; bullets slashed the advertisements on the poster-columns; rebounded from the iron roofs of latrines. In the middle of a crowded street a young man would be attacked, stripped, thrashed and left bleeding on the pavement; in fifteen seconds it was all over and the assailants had disappeared.[21]

We need to understand these darker corners of German life in order to discover the clues to the Nazi future. Drawing on certain preexisting pathologies, the Nazis not only committed criminal acts but also tried to normalize them in the culture. Since the Nazis, in Allan Bullock's words, "turned the law inside out and made illegality legal,"[22] it is important to gain some understanding of the underside of German life. Crime often provides a mirror image of society; and we might add that the type of criminal a society produces will be an indication of the type of crimes committed on a large scale when the leadership of that society has itself become criminal.

World War I and five years of civil unrest, marked by senseless deaths on the battlefield and followed by equally senseless murders and assassinations, left its imprint on the German scene. These experiences cheapened the value of human life to such a degree that the public became desensitized to brutality and violence. Besides a widespread acceptance of violence there was also a disturbing toleration, even glorification, of the *Hochstapler* (confidence man). This preoccupation with swindlers and criminals, as Gordon Craig reminds us, figured prominently in the novels and plays of the Weimar period — in Hans J. Rehfisch's *Das Duell am Lido,* Thomas Mann's *Felix Krull,* Vicki Baum's *Menschen im Hotel,* Bertolt Brecht's *Dreigroschenoper,* and Frank Wedekind's *Marquis von Keith.*[23] Brecht's *Three Penny Opera* is basically an anarchist play that glorifies the gangster. We are meant to sympathize with the gangster, Macheath, because he preys on a rotten social system. Interestingly enough, in the *Three Penny* novel, which appeared six years after the *Three Penny Opera,* Macheath has become the director of a bourgeois bank — an appropriate place for a crook in the eyes of many Germans who were ruined by the inflation of 1923!

Criminality also featured prominently on the silver screen. In some of Fritz Lang's motion pictures, especially *M,* the world of the police and that of the criminal are often interchangeable, so that it is quite unclear to the viewer who is really good or bad. In *M,* the police and the criminal underground actually cooperate to bring the child murderer, played by Peter Lorre, to justice. The police, in fact, tolerated ex-convict associations called *Ringvereine,* whose ostensible purpose was to take care of recently released convicts and help them in making a smooth transition to law-abiding life. In reality, the *Ringvereine* often became dens of iniquity rather than centers of rehabilitation. The police tolerated them on the grounds that this was one way of keeping a tab on criminal activity. Although this strange symbiosis of police and gangster often had its humorous side, it unfortunately illustrates a disturbing social trend in some of Germany's major urban centers — that of normalizing and even glorifying the abnormal. As Gordon Craig aptly remarks, "A society that glorifies the criminal is implicitly saying that the system he is preying on is not worth defending."[24]

The movies portrayed, in part, a world that was out of joint. Films such as *Das Cabinet des Dr. Caligari, Dr. Marbuse,* or *M* brought viewers face to face with insane authority, sex murders, prostitution, and insatiable lust for cruelty.[25] In *M,* based on the Düsseldorf child-murderer Kürten, the murderer (the character called "M") has no rational explanation for his heinous crimes other than pathetically crying out that he could not help himself. M was in appearance the prototype of the petit bourgeois — pudgy, submissive, and fastidious. He was also perhaps symbolically and prophetically the prototype of the future desk murderers of the Third Reich.

German filmmakers did not have to look hard to find manifestations of pathology in German society. In the 1920s several grisly serial murders were committed, some even implicating unsuspecting Germans in mass cannibalism.[26] Shortly before Christmas of 1924, Karl Denke, a shopkeeper in Münsterberg near Breslau, was discovered as having killed thirty people and sold their flesh as "smoked pork," keeping a neat record that included the dates and weights of his victims. In Berlin, Carl Wilhelm Grossmann, an unemployed, kindly looking, middle-aged butcher who tried to make a living as a door-to-door Fuller Brush man, preyed on penniless and helpless young peasant girls from the country, enticing them to his home, chopping them into pieces, and selling the usable parts to local butchers while discarding the rest in the nearby Luisenstädter Canal. Meanwhile, in Hannover, another relatively innocuous, soft-spoken, and apparently mild little man by the name of Georg Haarmann preyed on young boys who needed help. He would befriend these boys by offering them food and drink, then invite them to stay overnight in his home. After tucking them into bed, he would sexually assault them and then kill them by tearing out their throats with his teeth. Haarmann could not remember anything relating to these attacks other than experiencing a violent rage and afterward finding himself in bed with another dead boy the next morning. Haarmann disposed of his corpses in the same tidy manner as Denke and Grossmann: he would do a brisk business selling their clothes and reducing their bodies to nicely boiled, potted meat. Such corpses, attractively packaged as pork or veal, would fetch good prices on the black market.

When Haarmann was arrested he showed no feelings at all, not even at the prospect of his execution. In fact, an acrimonious public debate occurred over his impending execution, with liberals, who had been opposing the death penalty, pleading for a life sentence or incarceration in a mental institution. However, the possibility that Haarmann might not be found guilty by virtue of insanity enraged those Germans who had been demanding his immediate execution. When Haarmann was finally executed, people began singing songs about his wicked deeds. One particularly sick ditty, undoubtedly meant as a warning to naughty children, had this to say:

> Warte, warte nur ein Weilchen
> Bald kommt Haarmann auch zu dir.
> Mit dem kleinen Hackelbeilchen
> Macht er Pöckelfleisch aus dir.
>
> [Wait, wait just a little while,
> And soon Haarmann will come to you.

With his little hatchet
He'll make smoked meat out of you.][27]

Such sick expressions are common in societies that have become desensitized by violence, societies in which brutality is often accepted in
the form of callous remarks, malicious snickers, or foul jokes. Public tolerance of brutality was, in fact, disconcertingly high in postwar
Germany — the result, no doubt, of years of bloody war, domestic upheavals, and mass hunger. Yet German society had long harbored within
itself dark corners, attitudes expressed in a fascination with morbid, demonic, putrid, and brutal themes. Even German fairy tales reflected this
disturbing underside of the collective unconscious. Although everybody
loves and admires the fairy tales of the Grimm brothers, it is appalling
to learn, as Robert Waite reminds us, how much bizarre physical and
psychic cruelty they contain:

> A queen boils and eats her own children; a young man is required to
> sleep with a corpse and keep it warm; a king's daughter is torn apart by
> bears and her mother is roasted alive; a wicked step-mother ... is put into
> a barrel filled with venomous snakes; a little girl's tongue and eyes are cut
> out; a pretty young girl is hacked to pieces and thrown into a vat filled
> with putrefying human remains; a little boy is chopped up, put into a
> pan, and made into a pudding which is eaten by his father; a stepmother
> plans to eat the lungs and liver of her children; an old woman cuts off
> the head of her beautiful stepdaughter, whereupon drops of blood from
> the girl's head carry on a conversation.... The fate that awaited Hansel
> and Gretel, it will be recalled, was to be roasted and eaten.[28]

The lessons young Germans were taught to derive from such tales
included obedience to authority, discipline, and distrust of strangers
(foreigners and Jews). Willful disobedience would result in dire consequences such as being spooked to death or having one's limbs cut off.

Fairy tales are not only the expression of the mythmaking function of the collective psyche; they are also powerful tools for shaping
young minds because they are used as educative devices by parents. The
predominant themes in these German fairy tales and legends are the glorification of force and authority and the condemnation of everything
that is weak or "un-German." Nourished by a stream of high- and low-
brow romantic literature, such attitudes were taught to young Germans
by their nurturing mothers and their authoritarian fathers and were later
reinforced by the public schools, the army, and the workplace.

In an effort to explain Auschwitz, Ralf Dahrendorf pointed an accusing finger at these "dark corners" of German society, particularly the
role accorded to the nonmember of the German tribe. Whoever did not
conform to established rituals and beliefs or fell short of ideal physical
expectations — the deformed, the handicapped, the foreigner — was immediately suspect.[29] According to Dahrendorf, German social life was
characterized by an "extreme narrowness of permitted actions."[30] In

every society, of course, there is a line that demarcates what is permissible, specifying what individuals are allowed to do and what society is allowed to stop them from doing. In Germany this line was drawn overwhelmingly in favor of collective or authoritarian mores or expectations. Outsiders, including Germans who fell short of rigid expectations, were often humiliated, rejected, ostracized, and, under the Nazis, arrested, tortured, and annihilated. That this could take place in an otherwise civilized country whose people were, in general, religious, law-abiding, and friendly, has puzzled historians to this very day. It may be that the Germans, at certain points in their history, have displayed arrogant, supercilious, and aggressive cultural traits, made all the more destructive because they were motivated by closed systems of thought, religious or political, and reinforced institutionally in family, school, and work until they became habitual in everyday life. Would it then not be conceivable that even a Haarmann could be considered normal, provided that he externalized his lust for cruelty on outsiders such as Jews?

When Klaus Mann, son of the novelist, was sitting in the Carlton Tea Room in Munich, he saw Hitler, who was sitting at another table, devouring three strawberry tarts in succession. As he scrutinized the führer's face, he thought that the Nazi leader reminded him of someone whose picture he had recently seen in the newspapers, but it took him some time to make the connection:

> There was nothing but dim rosy light, soft music and heaps of cookies; and in the midst of this sugary idyll, a moustached little man with veiled eyes and a stubborn forehead, chatting with some colorless henchmen. ...While I called the waitress to pay for my cup of coffee, I suddenly remembered whom Herr Hitler resembled. It was that sex murderer in Hannover, whose case had such huge headlines....His name was Haarmann....The likeness between him and Hitler was striking. The sightless eyes, the moustache, the brutal and nervous mouth, even the unspeakable vulgarity of the fleshy nose; it was, indeed, precisely the same physiognomy.[31]

Hitler Reconstructs the Party, 1924-29

When Adolf Hitler returned to Munich after spending eight months at Landsberg Prison, he was determined to rebuild the party into a highly centralized yet flexible institution that would carry out his commands with unconditional obedience. He realized that his tactics of seizing power by a military coup in cooperation with fraternal paramilitary groups had been a fatal blunder. From now on the mission of the party was to work within the democratic system, using the methods of democracy to destroy democracy. Strict legality was to be the order of the day. Hitler also began to visualize the reborn party as a state within a state, a sort of shadow organization ready to undermine the government and then take its place without missing a beat.[32] And once having gained power, the party would then set aside democracy in favor of a one-party dictatorship under his control.

In short, what Hitler thought he needed was a broadly based political party that could attract a mass following, not an elite military organization wasting its time in hatching conspiratorial plots against the government. Already at Landsberg, he had told Lüdecke, who had come to visit him:

> When I resume active work it will be necessary to pursue a new policy. Instead of working to achieve power by an armed *coup,* we shall have to hold our noses and enter the Reichstag against the Catholic and Marxist deputies. If out-voting them takes longer than out-shooting them, at least the result will be guaranteed by their own Constitution. Any lawful process is slow.... Sooner or later we shall have a majority — and after that, Germany.[33]

Only fourteen days after his release from prison, Hitler followed Pöhner's advice and arranged a personal interview with Dr. Heinrich Held, the new Bavarian prime minister, and gave him sanctimonious assurances that he would respect the constitution and never resort to force again. Although Held was skeptical about Hitler's overly pious declarations, he was reluctantly persuaded by Dr. Franz Gürtner to lift the ban on the Nazi Party and its official newspaper, the *Völkischer Beobachter.* Held later rationalized his generous decision by lamely arguing that "the beast has been tamed."[34]

After having received permission from the Bavarian government to reopen the party, Hitler formally celebrated the happy occasion by staging a party rally at the Bürgerbräukeller on February 27, 1925. Addressing an enthusiastic and wildly cheering crowd of four thousand loyalists, he made it crystal-clear that he alone intended to lead the movement, asked for a year's probationary period, and promised that he would resign his office if things turned out badly. In the meantime, however, he told his followers, "I alone lead the movement, and no one sets me conditions as long as I personally bear the responsibility for everything that happens in the movement."[35]

Hitler's sudden reappearance into the political limelight and the zeal by which he was supported by his noisy followers stirred the Bavarian government into taking precautionary measures. On March 9, 1925, the Bavarian authorities prohibited Hitler from speaking publicly until further notice. Most other German states, with the exception of Thuringia, Brunswick, Württemberg, and Mecklenburg-Schwerin, also imposed a speaking ban on him. Bavaria did not rescind the speaking ban until March 5, 1927.

Officially muzzled by most German states, Hitler decided to work vigorously behind the scenes. He began by reestablishing his network of personal loyalists in Munich and the south. Although some party members wanted him to relocate party headquarters in the north, there were more compelling reasons for him to keep it where it was. After all, it all began in Munich. The core membership, business affairs, and the party newspaper were located there. In addition, the city of Munich had acquired a special psychological aura as *the* capital of the movement, evoking most of the memorable symbols of the party — Bürgerbräukeller, Zirkus Krone, Feldherrnhalle, Odeonsplatz.[36]

Once he had outlined a general goal for the future direction of the party, Hitler threw himself into his task with renewed vigor. Between 1925 and 1927 he was preoccupied with three interrelated problems — divesting himself of people he thought had become a liability to the movement, building up a strong core of loyalists in Munich and the south, and neutralizing growing dissensions in the party.

Hitler's first steps in reorganizing the party appeared to be aimed more toward alienating some of its shrinking membership than healing divisions. In reality, he was deliberately provoking confrontations to test loyalties, thus separating the chaff from the wheat.[37] Independent-minded nationalists who insisted on a different course from his own were unceremoniously dropped from the ranks. Former supporters as well as stalwarts who did not acknowledge his absolute control were also rejected. Two personalities who had played a major role in the rise of the NSDAP, Ludendorff and Röhm, no longer seemed to fit into the new order and had therefore become a liability. Under the influence of his second wife, Mathilde Kemnitz, Ludendorff had become increasingly cranky and quarrelsome, devoting much of his time to the propagation of bizarre racial and pagan obsessions, which reminded Hitler of Lanz von Liebenfels and the conspiratorial atmosphere of the Thule Society. The general's anti-Catholic and antisouthern views, spouted with uninhibited abandon in Catholic Bavaria, also raised grave doubts in Hitler's mind about Ludendorff's political usefulness. As previously mentioned, Hitler's feeling about Ludendorff had always been equivocal, undoubtedly reflecting the deep-seated insecurities of the former corporal who still thought that he could never hope to rise to the exalted level of the famous warlord. Upon his release from Landsberg, Hitler had several acrimonious meetings with the general that confirmed their mutual differences. The two men subsequently went their own ways.[38]

Röhm, too, had become a liability to Hitler because he asserted too much independence and strength of will. Hitler had watched Röhm's activities with great suspicion from Landsberg Prison; he was particularly critical of Röhm's new Frontbann organization, which struck him as nothing but a warmed-over version of those diverse and unpredictable forces that had made up the former Kampfbund. Röhm had obviously not learned the lesson of November 9, 1923, for he still toyed with the idea of staging a military coup in cooperation with the Reichswehr. He even considered subordinating the SA to his Frontbann organization. Hitler would have nothing to do with such tactics and bluntly confronted Röhm with a simple choice: submit or resign. On April 17, 1925, Röhm chose to resign his position as head of the SA; shortly afterward, he also stepped down from his post as head of the Frontbann. After spending four years in semiretirement, which he likened to the life of a sick animal, Röhm left Germany for Bolivia as an adviser to the Bolivian army.

Ludendorff and Röhm were prima donnas who had been difficult to handle, but closer to his own personal circle there were dedicated cronies who could be more easily trusted and controlled. These were the men who constituted his narrow social circle and the men who managed the day-to-day business activities of the party at Munich central headquarters in the Schellingstrasse. As party manager, Hitler chose the owlish-looking Philipp Bouhler (1899–1945), a diffident and punctilious bureaucrat who could be trusted to carry out any order, no matter how outlandish, that Hitler might choose to issue, proving it later by carrying out Hitler's euthanasia order (September 1, 1939) that led to the gassing of over one hundred thousand men, women, and children who did not fit the image of healthy racial Aryans (the mentally handicapped and the physically deformed). Bouhler was flanked at party headquarters by the equally unimaginative but competent Franz Xaver Schwarz (1875–1947), who had spent most of his working life as an accountant at Munich city hall and now scrupulously watched over every incoming penny at party headquarters. The third major personality associated closely with party headquarters was Hitler's regimental sergeant, Max Amann, who had served six months with Hitler at Landsberg and now resumed his post as director of the Eher publishing house and all other Nazi press organs. Other loyalists who had proved their mettle in 1923 were rewarded with key posts: Esser was appointed as propaganda chief, Feder as the party's ideological spokesman, while Julius Streicher and Artur Dinter were given control of the party in Franconia and Thuringia, respectively. Hess continued to serve as Hitler's loyal secretary, later becoming his chief deputy; Rosenberg was carried on, after the disbanding of the GDVG (Grossdeutsche Volksgemeinschaft [Greater German People's Community]) that he had led, as chief editor of the *Völkischer Beobachter* and trusted pawn in Hitler's internal party chess games; Göring was still in exile, not to return to Germany until 1927. Several trusted friends of Hitler such as Eckart and Pöhner had recently died, but the cronies of his inner circle, consisting of Maurice, Graf, and Hoffmann, were still loyal and supportive. Hitler lived in a small, poorly furnished room in the Thierschstrasse and socialized only with his cronies or the Hanfstaengls, Bruckmanns, or Essers. Although chronically short of money, royalties from *Mein Kampf,* augmented by party funds, made him reasonably solvent, enough to be able to lease and then purchase Haus Wachenfeld on the Obersalzberg. It was here that he would later withdraw into the company of his new housekeeper, his widowed half-sister Angela

Raubal, who brought along her seventeen-year-old daughter, Geli, the love of his life.

Although the Bavarian loyalists instinctively rallied behind Hitler, party unity was seriously threatened in 1925 when dissident members in various north and west German affiliates objected to the growing führer cult in the south and criticized the apparent lip service the southern group paid to the Socialist provisions in the party program. The northern groups, to whom the initiative in the party now appeared to turn, suspected that Bavaria, a conservative and Catholic state, was not as fertile a ground as the more industrial north.[39] These northern groups insisted, however, that in order to gain electoral support in the industrial north, where the Nazis had to compete with the SPD and the Communists, the party would have to develop an effective and vital social program for the working population.[40]

This is why the northern groups took the party's commitment to socialism far more seriously than their southern counterparts. The northerners also saw themselves as "soldier-revolutionaries" and advocated a syndicalist strategy of seizing political power by paralyzing the country's economy through strikes and street terror.[41] Since Hitler had opted for ballots rather than bullets, he rejected this approach as a primary tactic on the grounds that it would alienate the electorate. He was also uneasy about the vague economic remedies the radical Socialists proposed; they seemed to combine Mussolini's notions of the corporate state with equally murky ideas of "German democracy."

Among these dissidents in the north was a group of Socialists who had managed to capture control of the Rhineland-North *Gau* (a *Gau* [pl. *Gaue*] = a Nazi administrative district; a *Gauleiter* = a leader of a *Gau*; for full discussion of the terms, see below p. 205). Their business manager was Joseph Goebbels, a diminutive, clubfooted intellectual with a Ph.D. and a sharp tongue. Destined to become the Svengali behind the Nazi propaganda machine, Goebbels was at that time a confused, young intellectual searching for the political holy grail, a search that had led him, after a series of failures as a journalist, novelist, and stock-exchange crier, into the fold of National Socialism. Already in 1924, when he found his way into the Nazi Party, Goebbels discovered that he possessed a talent for political propaganda — the ability, which would later become his stock-in-trade, of elevating manifest falsehoods into credible truths and manufacturing political mythologies out of ordinary events.

Besides Goebbels, the most prominent leaders of these northern dissidents were Karl Kaufmann (1900–1969), a young Free Corps fighter and *Gauleiter* of Rhineland-North, and Franz von Pfeffer (1888–?), World War I army officer, Free Corps leader, and Kapp Putschist. Based at Elberfeld in the Ruhr, this group was defining itself as the major center of opposition to the Bavarian loyalists who had rallied around Hitler. Goebbels and Kaufmann managed to oust Axel Ripke, the former *Gau-*

leiter of Rhineland-North, ostensibly on charges of embezzling party funds but in fact because he was not radical enough.[42]

The man who really organized this discontent and became its chief spokesman was Gregor Strasser. The indefatigable Strasser had been elected Reichstag deputy in 1924 and was now vigorously at work promoting his own brand of National Socialism. Leaving his own *Gau* of Lower Bavaria to his deputy Heinrich Himmler, Strasser spent most of his time recruiting new members in the industrial areas of north-central Germany. Strasser, flanked by his even more dogmatic brother Otto, favored the nationalization of banks and heavy industry as a prerequisite for social justice. His vision of the good society was an ethnically harmonious community based on "German" rather than Marxian socialism. Neither Gregor nor Otto ever spelled out very clearly what they meant by socialism, but both felt that Hitler and the southern group had little commitment to socialism other than in a purely rhetorical or opportunistic sense. The Strassers believed that the NSDAP was turning into a radical anti-Semitic and petit bourgeois party, betraying its promises to the industrial workers. To counteract this perceived trend, they blanketed northern Germany with Socialist propaganda.

Gregor Strasser's passion for national regeneration and social justice, combined with his outgoing and jovial personality, made a great impression on those who came in contact with him, including Joseph Goebbels, who noted in his diary of August 21, 1925:

> Strasser was here for the whole of yesterday afternoon. A splendid fellow. A massive Bavarian. With a wonderful sense of humour. Brought much sad news from Munich. About that abominable and wretched management of the central office. Hitler is surrounded with the wrong people. I believe Hermann Esser is his undoing. With Strasser we shall now organize the entire West.... That will give us a weapon against those sclerotic bosses in Munich. I am sure we shall convince Hitler.[43]

Strasser and the northern dissidents formed a working committee (Arbeitsgemeinschaft) comprising the north and west German *Gaue* and began to disseminate their views in Strasser's new journal, edited by Goebbels, entitled *NS-Briefe* (NS-Letters). Many of the views expressed in this free-wheeling magazine criticized the Munich people for being soft on capitalism and short on organizational skills. The perception of many contributors was that the Munich leadership, perhaps not Hitler himself but certainly the men who were advising him, intended to transform a genuine working-class party into a radical bourgeois party with violent anti-Semitic overtones. Their disenchantment with Munich openly erupted for the first time in a meeting of disgruntled *Gauleiter* on November 22, 1925.

Near the end of 1925, Gregor Strasser submitted a draft for a new program that he believed would strengthen the Socialist provisions of the party program of 1920. Strasser's thinking at this time was influenced by Oswald Spengler's book *Prussianism and Socialism;* in fact, the oracle of *The Decline of the West,* although rejecting Strasser's offer to become a contributor to a proposed monthly magazine, *Nazionalsozial-istische Monatshefte,* saw in Strasser "the most clever man next to Hugo Stinnes that I have met in my life,"[44] and supported his idea of a German state socialism as a far more realistic approach than that proposed by the wooly anti-Semitic and *völkisch* wing of the emerging Nazi Party.

If Spengler had actually seen Strasser's draft, he might have revised his perception of Strasser's realism, for the draft was such a confusing mixture of utopian and anticapitalist elements that it provoked acrimonious debates even within the Arbeitsgemeinschaft itself. Strasser's draft called for nationalization of all land, to be held in lease by the state; the breakup of estates over one thousand acres into smaller units to be farmed by peasants; public ownership of 51 percent of all "vital" industries and 49 percent of all "nonvital" industries, with 10 percent reserved for the benefit of employees; managerial control of industry to remain in private hands; expulsion of Jews who had entered Germany after August 1, 1914; and restoration of all former German territories.[45] Some members of the Arbeitsgemeinschaft saw the document as being too socialistic or Bolshevist, as Pfeffer did, while others criticized it for not being radical enough in a *völkisch* sense. Gottfried Feder, the author of the original twenty-five-point party program, who had received a copy of Strasser's draft through an indiscretion, was angry that Hitler had not been officially notified of its existence.

In an effort to iron out the disagreements the members of the Arbeitsgemeinschaft had with each other and with their Munich counterparts, another conference was convened on January 25, 1926, at Hannover in the house of Gauleiter Bernhard Rust. Besides Rust, the major participants were Joseph Goebbels, Franz von Pfeffer, Robert Ley, and Gottfried Feder. Three topics dominated the agenda: whether to support a proposal advanced by Communist deputies in the Reichstag that the property of the nobility be expropriated by the states; the status of Strasser's draft program; and the organizational problems of the party. With the exception of Robert Ley, *Gauleiter* of Cologne, the northerners supported the proposal to expropriate the property of the nobility, while Hitler and the Munich group were on record that they did not. In a subsequent national plebiscite, the German voters approved expropriation, but since less than half of the eligible electorate had voted on the proposal, the plebiscite was not ratified by the Reichstag. The Strasser program was shelved, and the writing of a revised draft was delegated to a small group.[46] Discussions centering on the future leadership of the party, however, revealed what the tenor of the meeting was really like. Some delegates wondered about Hitler's suitability given the fact that he was a Catholic, an Austrian, and, since April 27, 1925, actually a "stateless" person.[47] Alternative leaders were mentioned, as were alternative models of organization—a directorate rather than a single leader and an interest group or association rather than a party. Goebbels purportedly went so far as to demand that "the petit bourgeois Adolf Hitler be excluded from the National Socialist Party."[48] In the end, however, the group decided that a leader was vital and that Hitler was probably preferable to other leaders; but these agreements were voiced with little enthusiasm.

Once Feder had fully briefed Hitler on the Hannover meeting, there was no doubt in Hitler's mind that decisive action was required before further disagreements completely wrecked party unity. He invited the dissident members to a meeting at Bamberg on February 14, 1926 — not to explore the possibility of a genuine compromise but to reestablish his complete dictatorial control. The conference was a vintage Hitler production of pomp and circumstance, designed to teach the poor cousins from the north where the real power actually resided. The northerners were impressed by the fact that the Bamberg local had managed to sign up a sizable percentage of the town's eligible voters when they could barely manage to rope in twenty or thirty members in the most populous areas in the north.[49] Hitler spoke to them for several hours in a very cutting and uncompromising tone. He bluntly deflated their most cherished radical ideas, shocked Goebbels especially by insisting that the party should look to Britain and Italy for allies, and indicated that he did not appreciate divisive discussions about the future direction of the party. He also made it unmistakably clear that party unity required undisputed leadership and centralized control.[50]

Although the dissidents did not completely cave in on that day — in fact, they briefly toyed with the idea of challenging Hitler's rigid party line during the week following the Bamberg meeting — they were too divided among themselves to resist Hitler's will. Strasser had already convinced himself that if he bolted a divided party, he would probably be unable to carry many members with him. Shortly afterward, on March 10, he was badly injured in a car accident, which deprived him of whatever energy he would have needed to put up a determined stand against Hitler.

In the meantime, Goebbels was going through a process of rapid conversion. He had been in the depths of despair when he heard Hitler dismantle some of his fondest illusions, especially his belief that Germany should follow the Bolshevik example, writing in his diary that he was stunned and beaten by Hitler's reactionary comments. But Hitler had a keen eye for disciples, and he saw in Goebbels certain qualities that could be highly useful to the party. For this reason, he decided to woo him. He invited Goebbels to Munich (April 7–8), wined and dined him, generously let him use his personal automobile, and allowed him to speak to a large meeting at the Bürgerbräukeller. Before sending the dazed Goebbels home to Elberfeld, he surprised him further by appointing him co-*Gauleiter* of the Ruhr and graciously forgave his previous indiscretions against the Munich leadership.[51] After another personal meeting at Berchtesgaden, during which Hitler submitted Goebbels to

some additional brainwashing, all remaining doubts in Goebbel's mind
began to melt away. Goebbels's diary records the process of seduction
in embarrassing detail:

> February 15, 1926: Hitler speaks for two hours. I am almost beaten.
> What kind of Hitler? A reactionary? Amazingly clumsy and uncertain.
> Russian question: altogether beside the point. Italy and Britain the natural
> allies. Horrible! It is our job to smash Bolshevism. Bolshevism is a Jewish
> creation! We must become Russia's heirs! Hundred and eighty millions'!
> I cannot say a word. I am stunned.[52]

> March 13, 1926: Reading: Adolf Hitler, *The South German Question
> and the Problem of German Alliances*. An amazingly lucid pamphlet with
> a grand perspective. What a man he is...the chief! Once again he has
> removed many a doubt from my mind![53]

> April 13, 1926: At eight pm by car to the Bürgerbräu. Hitler is there al-
> ready. My heart beats to breaking-point. Into the hall. Roaring welcome.
> Packed. Streicher opens. And then I speak for two and a half hours. I go
> all out. Roaring and tumult. Hitler embraces me at the end. He has tears
> in his eyes. I feel something like happy....Office. Hitler comes....He
> speaks for three hours. Brilliant. Could make one uncertain....We are
> moving closer. We ask. He gives brilliant replies. I love him....He has
> thought it all out. I am reassured all round. Taken all round he is a man.
> With this sparkling mind he can be my leader. I bow to his greatness, his
> political genius.[54]

In this way began one of the most successful partnerships in the black
arts of propaganda, for Hitler had discovered the "spin doctor" who
would help him merchandize the führer cult. Joseph Goebbels (1897–
1945) was born in Rheydt, an industrial town in the Rhineland, of
Catholic, middle-class parents. The boy was loved and pampered as a
child, but his dwarfish size and his physical deformity fundamentally
affected his self-image and his perception of the world around him.
Goebbels was either born with a congenital deformity (clubfoot) or
contracted a childhood disease such as polio or osteomyelitis — the result being that his left leg was shorter than his right one, forcing him
to limp all of his life and making it necessary to wear special shoes
and braces. In childhood, as in later life, his deformity exposed him to
pitying glances, malicious jokes, and painful slights.[55]

Ironically, the future minister of propaganda, evoking the Aryan ideal
of perfect beauty and strength, was himself a small cripple and the recipient of some painful discrimination. And it is highly revealing that
these unfortunate experiences, far from humanizing him, actually hardened his character and reinforced his determination to prove himself,
to apply his superior intellect in order to dominate the roughnecks he
would often seek out as henchmen or the many women he slept with. In
short, Goebbels's deformity constitutes the key to his misanthropy and
his frequent disparaging remarks about life being "shit" and man being
a "canaille." Helmut Heiber summarizes:

The malice with which he destroyed his personal enemies; the suspicion which he would suddenly bring to bear on people who were close to him; the lacerating acuity with which he could dissect human weaknesses, as long as it wasn't his own; his emotional antipathy toward any large and especially handsome man; his hectic women chasing...all arose from his ever conscious, ever-present feeling of physical inferiority.[56]

Despite his deformity and his size, Goebbels was in fact a good-looking man, a man of great intelligence, energy, and talent. Expected by his parents to go into the priesthood, young Goebbels devoted himself instead to the study of German literature, receiving a Ph.D. from the University of Heidelberg in 1922 and then promptly joining the ranks of the many desperate job-seekers during the early 1920s. His efforts to conquer the literary world by storm failed miserably not only because times were bad but also because his writings had not matured beyond schmaltzy romantic stories dripping with sentimental patriotism. Yet instead of honest self-criticism, Goebbels externalized his weaknesses by blaming outside forces, especially Jewish publishers and literati, for his own shortcomings as a writer.

Before he found his way to Hitler and the Nazi movement, Goebbels was a torn and rootless man without a faith and a cause. Having rejected his Catholic faith, which alarmed his devout parents, he desperately looked for a new one — for "it is almost immaterial," he confessed, "what we believe in, so long as we believe in something."[57] When, at length, he found his new faith, it was really in a man, Adolf Hitler, rather than a doctrine; but the merchandizing of this personal faith now became his sacred mission in life.

His diaries are living testimonies to his ongoing self-deception, which he failed to appreciate, and to his remarkable success in deceiving others, which he fully acknowledged. He was a brilliant propagandist with a lucid, Latin-type of mind and a superb melodious voice powerful enough in range to resound throughout the largest hall.[58] In the words of his best biographer, he was also "one of the most technically adept speakers to have used the German language."[59] Unlike Hitler's speeches, which were "ejaculations of sensuality," Goebbels's speeches were artistically crafted and lucidly presented arguments. The little doctor would subsequently put his propagandistic skills to great use, almost single-handedly fabricating the mythic image of the führer and feeding on it to replace the inner void in his own heart.

With the conversion of Joseph Goebbels, Hitler had effectively neutralized the dissensions within the party; but having gained a convert in Goebbels, Hitler had no intention of dropping the valuable Strasser. In fact, Hitler continued to rely heavily on Strasser's expertise and even appointed him to the posts of Reich propaganda leader (*Reichspropagandaleiter,* 1926) and Reich organization leader (*Reichsorganisationsleiter,* 1927). Some historians have wondered whether Hitler's overly solicitous treatment of Strasser was motivated by a keen sense of tactical shrewdness or by regressions to former insecurities.[60] The answer is that probably both motives figured in Hitler's decision not only to retain Strasser but also to invest him with additional powers. Hitler probably calculated that Strasser's popularity, with both the rank and file and the public at large, combined with his organizational talents, outweighed the potentially divisive force that left-wing "Strasserism" represented within the Nazi Party. Hitler was right in the short run, wrong in the long run. Strasser proved to be supremely useful to the party during its reconstruction years, but when he persisted in following his own drummer and eventually began to see through the web of deceptions and dishonesties Hitler was spinning in politics, he objected, resisted, and resigned, paying the ultimate price that such actions inevitably merited in Hitler's Germany — liquidation. Strasser had always been able to separate the idea of a leader from the idea of National Socialism, arguing that the latter should have preeminence.[61] On this issue, more than on any other, would subsequently depend most high-ranking careers in Nazi Germany, for the ultimate test in the Nazi scheme of things was a person's loyalty to the führer rather than his competence, honesty, or integrity.

By the summer of 1926 Hitler had regained complete dictatorial control of the party. Moreover, the party's financial picture also improved, enabling Hitler to stage an impressive party congress at Weimar in Thuringia, one of the few states where Hitler was allowed to speak publicly. All of the major party leaders from the north and south attended the meeting and paid homage to Adolf Hitler, who for the first time saluted them with outstretched arm patterned after the fashion of the Italian Fascists.[62]

Between 1926 and 1928 Hitler and Strasser imposed a uniform structure on the party by dividing the country into *Gaue,* solidifying top leadership positions, preparing party conventions, and organizing Reich conferences for *Gauleiter.* From a tactical point of view, Hitler approved Strasser's plan of establishing a strong beachhead in urban industrial areas. By this plan the Nazis hoped to win the allegiance of industrial workers by promoting the Socialist provisions in the party program. For several years Hitler reluctantly chose not to notice some party spokesmen, chiefly from the Strasser left wing, who seem to have made it a practice to "pour propagandistic venom on the capitalist and decadent bourgeoisie."[63]

The chief organizational and electoral focus during these two years (1926–28) was therefore largely concentrated on the industrial Ruhr, Berlin, Hamburg, and Thuringia-Saxony — areas where the Social Democrats and Communists enjoyed the overwhelming support of the working population. The weakest links in the Nazi organizational chain in these areas were Berlin and Hamburg. In both cities the party was in disarray; and in a shrewd tactical move, designed to secure the party's flank position, Hitler appointed Joseph Goebbels as *Gauleiter* of Berlin and entrusted him with the daunting task of turning "red" Berlin into a strong Nazi outpost. Hitler's gamble succeeded to the extent that Goebbels was able to take a noisy, poorly organized, and brawling number of brown shirts and transform them into a cohesive and ideologically committed vanguard of Nazism. But his *Kampf um Berlin* (battle for Berlin), marked by incendiary slogans, mass meetings, and violence, took on such menacing proportions that the party was banned by the authorities in Berlin and the Province of Brandenburg (May 1927–April 1928). Unfazed, Goebbels continued as an *agent provocateur*, spewing his venom on the opposition, particularly through his newspaper *Der Angriff* (The attack), which specialized in the art of abuse, character assassination, innuendo, and sensationalism. On the assumption that the public was too dim-witted to appreciate complexities, and that it was not the task of journalism to provide objective truth, Goebbels followed Hitler's belief that the primary task of journalism was to convert rather than to inform the reader. It followed that a good newspaper article was therefore a soap-box speech put down on paper, ideally conveying the impression in the reader's mind that the speaker was literally standing next to the reader and trying to convert him or her.[64] In one issue, dated April 30, 1928, Goebbels provided the bluntest explanation to date on where the party stood vis-à-vis the Weimar Republic:

> We are an anti-parliamentary party and reject for good reasons the Weimar Republic and its established republican institutions.... What, then, do we want in the Reichstag? ... We go into the Reichstag in order to acquire the weapons of democracy from its arsenal. We become Reichstag deputies in order to paralyze the Weimar mentality with its own assistance. If democracy is stupid enough to give us free travel privileges and per diem allowances for this service, that is its affair. We do not worry our heads about this. We will take any legal means to revolutionize the existing situation.[65]

The urban plan of 1926–28 did not succeed in its broad aim of converting the working masses to National Socialism in Germany's industrial areas. One major reason for this failure resided in Hitler's stubborn refusal to establish National Socialist unions, thus severely reducing the party's urban appeal.[66] Although factory cell organizations developed spontaneously in the Berlin area and were later enlarged nationwide into the National Socialist Factory Cell Organization (NSBO), headed by Walther Schuhmann, Hitler opposed the idea of Nazi unions competing with more established unions. He was also ideologically opposed to the development of powerful unions on the grounds that they were instruments of class divisiveness and therefore a deadly threat to the economy. The most he was willing to concede to the party's left wing was propaganda activity aimed at infiltrating already established unions. Such activities of infiltration, even after they were greatly accelerated in 1931 under the slogan "Hinein in die Betriebe" (Into the factories), generally failed in making inroads into the strongholds of Christian or

Marxist labor unions. Another reason the party was not able to produce mass defections among the working population was that the Nazi Party, in its broad membership and political appeal, was still primarily oriented toward the middle class and expressed the socioeconomic and cultural values of the political right rather than the political left. However, the party's appeal went far beyond the lower middle class, and its breakthrough in 1929 did not reside, as some historians still believe, in its class affiliation but rather in its organizational superiority over any other party in the political system.[67]

What ultimately undermined the urban plan was the dismal showing of the Nazi Party in the May 1928 elections, which revealed that the Nazis had neither gained a footing among the workers in urban areas nor made substantial inroads anywhere else. The party polled only 810,000 votes (2.6 percent) and therefore received just 12 out of 491 mandates in the Reichstag. The 12 men who represented the party in the Reichstag were predominantly middle-aged, professional men with considerable charismatic appeal: 5 retired military officers (Walter Buch, Franz Ritter von Epp, Hermann Göring, Count Ernst Reventlow, Werner Willikens), 5 professional men (Gottfried Feder, Wilhelm Frick, Joseph Goebbels, Gregor Strasser, Josef Wagner), a union official (Franz Stöhr), and a mechanic (Dreher).[68]

After analyzing the results of the May 1928 elections, Hitler and the *Reichsleitung* (Reich directorate) decided to shift the party's electoral focus from urban areas, where it had performed very poorly, to rural districts, where it had gained steady support across the board, especially in Schleswig-Holstein, rural Hannover, and Bavaria. Hitler sensed that rural, nationalistic, and middle-class voters would be more receptive to National Socialist appeals. Most Germans still lived in small villages and towns in 1928; most Germans were also strongly nationalistic and conservative in outlook. The party therefore decided to tailor its appeal to this broad constituency. The *Völkischer Beobachter* (May 31, 1928) pointed out another major reason why the rural areas offered a distinct advantage over urban centers, namely, that with a smaller expenditure of energy, money, and time much better results could be achieved in the rural areas than in the big cities. Moreover, mass meetings were likely to have a far greater impact in rural areas, where they represented a real novelty and were talked about for weeks afterward, than they would in large cities, where they would have to compete with many other events. Although Hitler did not completely abandon the urban plan, for it was to his political advantage to maintain the illusion that the NSDAP was a working-class party, he did order a major change of direction in order to tap the real locus of political power in Germany, and that was the broad middle class, the conservative countryside, and the military.

The new nationalistic-conservative strategy involved further administrative changes in the organization of the party. Even before 1928, Hitler and Strasser had put in place a highly effective and flexible organization that was structured like a military institution while at the same time projecting a broad populist appeal. The Bamberg meeting had convinced Hitler that a national party, though encouraging a degree of regional autonomy, required a strong centralized direction. It also required a mechanism of internal correction in case of inner conflicts and outer pressures. As early as 1921, when Hitler reorganized the party and took dictatorial control, he had set up a subcommittee on internal investigation and empowered delegates to oversee the activities of various local branches of the party in specific regions. This system was now greatly enlarged with the reestablishment of a party arbitration tribunal (Untersuchungs-und Schlichtungsausschuss [Uschla]) designed to control the loyalty and political correctness of party subleaders. Hitler himself appointed and dismissed the members of this tribunal and expected them to follow his policies. As head of the tribunal, he picked Walter Buch (1883–1949), retired army officer, early party member, and SA leader who later furthered the career of his son-in-law Martin Bohrmann, the future *éminence grise* behind the führer's throne.

As early as 1925, the party had encouraged an "organic" development of *Gaue* in those parts of Germany where strong organizational talents could recruit a successful following. The term *Gau* comes from an old Germanic custom of dividing land and people into specific regions. Although the term fell into disuse in modern times, it was revived by Nazi gymnastics and youth organizations in their efforts to recruit on a national level. The Nazi Party began to use the word extensively after 1925 to refer to its highest political units (*Hoheitsgebiete*). Each *Gau* was managed by a *Gauleiter* who served as the party's chief political officer in a given region. Between 1925 and 1928 the *Gaue* developed spontaneously and did not correspond to already existing state or electoral boundaries. After the party's abysmal showing in the election of May 1928, Hitler decided to revamp his organizational structure in order to bring it into line with his goal of scoring electoral victories. The *Gaue* were now far more closely tailored to the electoral districts of the Weimar Republic. In turn, they were further divided into *Kreise* (districts), these into *Ortsgruppen* (local groups), which, in the larger cities, were further subdivided into *Zellen* (cells) and *Blocks* (blocks).

It was characteristic of Hitler's inspirational and romantic leadership style that no written document or manual was ever formulated to outline the specific policies pertaining to the *Gaue* or *Gauleiter*. Hitler seems to have modeled his ideal of subordinates on the medieval-feudal relationship between knight and vassal. In return for receiving his *Gau* or fief from his "knight," the vassal owed specific obligations to his Nazi overlord in the form of recruiting party members, raising funds, and in general educating the people to the truth of Nazi doctrines. The *Gauleiter* was invested by Hitler, served at his pleasure, and could be dismissed only by him.[69] Given considerable autonomy within his region, subject to periodic visitations by roving inspectors from Munich, the *Gauleiter* was the personal executive agent of Adolf Hitler, his political general on the local level. Although the Nazi Party evolved increasingly into a modern-style bureaucracy, with *apparatchiki* replacing military adventurers, it never lost what Dietrich Orlow called its "bureaucratized romanticism" — that is, its personalized style of leadership in the form of a charismatic führer who inspired and empowered his followers but who also demanded their fealty, obedience, and homage.[70]

In the years 1928–29 Hitler not only reorganized the *Gaue,* bringing them into line with the electoral districts of the republic, but he also expanded the party structure and modeled it on the institutions of the German government. At the top of the party hierarchy was the *Reichsleitung* (Reich directorate), headed by Hitler and supported by a secretary (Rudolf Hess), a treasurer (Franz Xaver Schwarz), and a secretary general (Philipp Bouhler), along with several subcommittees. Before July 1930, party offices were located in relatively dingy rooms in the Schellingstrasse and Corneliusstrasse, but after the party received substantial contributions from big business, party headquarters moved to the former Barlow-Palais, a more spacious neoclassical building in the Briennerstrasse, dubbed by the locals as the Brown House because of the brown uniforms of the party members who worked there.

The *Reichsleitung* presided over two main branches of the party: the first one (*Angriff*) was concerned with organizing the party for electoral victories, a task placed in the hands of Gregor Strasser, who was appointed Reich organization leader, while the other (*Aufbau*) was charged with developing the institutional mechanisms by which the party could transform itself into a new state, a position assigned to Colonel Konstantin Hierl (1875–1955), a former general staff officer, Free Corps leader, and Ludendorff follower. The first branch was composed of three divisions: foreign (Hans Nieland), press (Otto Dietrich), and infiltration and party-cell building (Walther Schuhmann). The second branch consisted of agriculture (Walther Darré), economics (Otto Wagener), race and culture (Hanno von Konopath), work of the ministry of interior (Helmut Nicolai), legal questions (Hans Frank), technical questions (Gottfried Feder), and labor service (Paul Schulz). Propaganda was kept a separate department under Hitler's control; it was headed until his appointment to Reich organization leader by Gregor Strasser and then ended up permanently in the hands of Joseph Goebbels.

By looking at the 1928–30 organizational chart, we can already catch a glimpse at the future leadership of the Third Reich. Among the newcomers who would play an important part in the Third Reich were Otto Dietrich (1877–1952), the future press chief of the NSDAP; Hans Frank (1900–1946), Hitler's personal attorney and chief of the party's legal division; and Walther Darré (1895–1953), an agricultural expert of Argentinean-German background who became the party's apostle of "blood and soil" ideology promoting soil-bound callings as culturally and racially superior to industrial or technical pursuits. Not directly involved in the day-to-day operation of the party, but nevertheless working actively on behalf of the NSDAP, were two important figures: Hermann Göring and Wilhelm Frick. After an absence of almost four years, which he had spent in exile in Austria and Sweden, Hermann Göring returned to Germany to resume his connection with the Nazi Party. Without a penny to his name, the garrulous and clever Göring soon established himself in Berlin as a sales representative for BMW, built up an extensive social circle, and wormed his way back into the party, being appointed in 1928 as one of the twelve NSDAP Reichstag deputies. His rise to power in the party was steady: in 1932 he became president of the Reichstag, in 1933 minister without portfolio in Hitler's new cabinet and minister president for Prussia, in 1935 reich minister for aviation and commander in chief of the air force, and in 1940 Reich marshal and successor-designate to Adolf Hitler. Dr. Wilhelm Frick (1877–1946), a lawyer and civil servant by profession, was one of Hitler's earliest followers. Despite his involvement in the 1923 Putsch, Frick was able to avoid a fifteen-month prison term when the National Socialist Freedom Party picked him as one of its representatives to the Reichstag in 1924. In 1928 he became a Nazi delegate to the Reichstag; in 1930 he became minister of the interior and minister of education for the state of Thuringia, using these powerful offices to subvert the state's law enforcement and educational institutions. In his role as education minister, Frick inveighed against "nigger and jazz culture," introduced nationalistic prayers into the public schools, and appointed the racial philosopher Hans F. K. Günther (1891–1968) to the position of professor of social anthropology at the University of Jena. Frick was Hitler's trusted adviser and favorite bureaucrat. As minister of the interior in 1933, he was also a key player in transforming Germany into a one party dictatorial state.

The newly restructured NSDAP was based on a vertical chain of command. At the top was Hitler and the *Reichsleitung,* followed by the *Gaue* and the locals at the bottom of the pyramid. Each level was subordinate to the one above. Hitler communicated only general directives down the chain, usually abstaining from micromanaging the system. In the day-to-day operations, the *Reichsleitung* communicated directly with the *Gaue,* expecting the local *Gauleiter* to implement policies in their areas and holding them accountable by way of monthly reports and periodic audits. Local branches of the party sometimes resented the heavy hand of their *Gauleiter,* but their protests to the *Reichsleitung* were rejected and routinely rerouted to the appropriate *Gauleiter.*

Between 1928–29 the party also expanded its horizontal structure through the development of new ancillary and front organizations. In line with Hitler's totalitarian ideal of monopolizing the lives of all Germans by engulfing them in National Socialism, there came into being various party organizations (*Gliederungen*) and associated leagues (*Verbände*). Hitler believed that a resilient mass party could literally capture the hearts and minds of its citizens by persuading or forcing them to join appropriate party organizations at various stages of their lives and their careers, so that ideally no person under National Socialism would ever escape the vigilant attention of the party throughout his or her lifetime. As previously mentioned, the party had already created a Youth Association (Jugendbund der NSDAP), which now ripened into the Hitler Youth (Hitlerjugend [HJ]) with branches for both boys and girls. There also developed a National Socialist German Student League (NS-Deutscher Studentenbund) under the leadership of Baldur von Schirach (1907–74), a young Hitler zealot who became head of the Hitler Youth in 1931 and later Reich youth leader. Another organization for the young was the National Socialist Pupils' League (NS-Schülerbund) for grammar-school boys.

Specific professional organizations were also created, including the National Socialist Teachers' League (NS-Lehrerbund [NSLB]), headed by Hans Schemm and located at Bayreuth; the National Socialist Physicians' League (NS-Ärztebund [NSDÄB]), founded at the fourth party congress in 1929 and later also opened up to veterinarians and pharmacists; and the National Socialist Women's Organization (NS-Frauenschaft [NSF]), a token concession to women that did not become a *Gliederung* until 1935 and was then headed by Gertrud Scholtz-Klink, the Reich women's leader (*Reichfrauenführerin*). Closely associated leagues, encompassing most professions and trades, would evolve over the next ten years, notably the German Labor Front (Deutsche Arbeitsfront [DAF]), the Reich League for Civil Servants (Reichsbund der Deutschen Beamten [RDB]), and the National Socialist Law Officers' League (NS-Rechtswahrerbund [NSRB]).

The image of the party Hitler wanted to project to the majority of the German people was that of a disciplined and uniformed force, resolutely led by its führer. Hitler made sure that this image would become ingrained in the minds of Germans by visually assaulting them with Nazi uniforms, marches, rallies, and party congresses. In 1927 he staged the first of the famous Nuremberg party congresses, which would evolve over time into gigantic rituals of mass intoxication, featuring blood rituals, funereal orations, marches, torchlight parades, and sacred chants to victory ("Sieg Heil") or to the führer ("Heil Hitler"). Hitler also flung his storm troopers on the streets of Germany as a daily reminder of the party's determination and power. He expected his political foot soldiers to convey a more credible impression than the less disciplined and poorly dressed supporters of the political left, for he knew that how the representatives of any kind of authority dressed or walked or talked would determine how many Germans voted for them at the ballot box.

The soldiers of the party continued to come out of the SA. Between 1926 and 1928 the SA also underwent significant changes. In July 1926 Hitler appointed retired army captain Franz von Pfeffer as Reich SA-führer (Osaf). Son of a Düsseldorf privy councillor, Pfeffer had served as an army officer in World War I on the western front and was highly decorated for bravery. After the war he founded his own Free Corps unit and participated in various conflicts in the Baltic, Upper Silesia, and Lithuania, while also being drawn into the Kapp Putsch of 1920. Arrested for his role in the Kapp Putsch, he was subsequently cleared of all charges by a general amnesty and released to continue his subversive activities against the republic. In 1923 he was active in the Ruhr upheavals and joined the Völkisch Social Bloc, and in 1925 he found his way into the NSDAP. His fortunes in the party began to improve after being appointed both *Gauleiter* and SA leader for Westphalia. After a brief stint as joint *Gauleiter*, along with Kaufmann and Goebbels, of a "Greater Ruhr *Gau*," which quickly dissolved as a result of internal bickering, Pfeffer was asked by Hitler to help in reorganizing the SA.

Pfeffer was made out of essentially the same reactionary right-wing cloth as most Free Corps leaders; he was a strict disciplinarian and a ploddingly methodical administrator with a fondness for annoying acronyms and abbreviations (Osaf, SABE, GRUSA, Bez, Gru, Gruf, Sturmf, Tr, Sta, and so on). Pfeffer's mission was to create a disciplined army of political foot soldiers. A lingering question was still whether such a force should be subordinate to the party or separate from it. With the debacle of 1923 still fresh in his mind, Hitler chose to make the SA a subordinate branch of the movement; his hope was that it would become an auxiliary force that could stand on its own rather than the driving force of the movement itself. The SA was to be his instrument under his control, subject to his political guidelines and strictly keeping to the path of legality.

In actual practice, however, the SA would turn out to be a grassroots organization that would prove difficult to control, especially once it had been allowed to develop independently in the hands of an SA leader who was empowered to organize it as he saw fit. Partly out of a sense of insecurity, partly out of a shrewd recognition that he was not administratively competent in overseeing such an organization himself, Hitler once more turned to proven personnel from the traditional military elite. Pfeffer was given carte blanche to structure the organization as he saw fit, which meant that he controlled its composition and its leadership.[71] As führer of the SA he also controlled the SS, then still a token force, the youth association, and assorted student associations. The potential for real trouble was therefore obvious because too much power in the hands of an independent SA leader who was in charge of a growing army of brownshirts could seriously jeopardize Hitler's own leadership position. That Hitler sensed such a possibility could account for his choice of Pfeffer, a man of integrity and loyalty but otherwise an undistinguished little man who was unlikely to threaten the führer's personal authority. When Hitler replaced Pfeffer and eventually picked the more independent-minded Ernst Röhm, the dual-track dilemma of party and SA would resurface, ultimately culminating in the Night of the Long Knives of June 30, 1934.

In the meantime Pfeffer went to work in reorganizing the SA into a flexible instrument of Nazi propaganda. Using the Free Corps as his model, he divided the SA into various units. The smallest was the *Schar* (band) of three to thirteen men, followed by a *Trupp* (troop), a *Sturm* (storm), a *Standarte* (standard), and a *Brigade* (brigade). The leaders were simply named after their units — *Truppenführer, Sturmführer, Standartenführer, Brigadeführer*. Their brown uniforms originally came from left-over khaki uniforms worn by German soldiers in the colonial services in Africa; later, the brown color of the shirts was associated with the wholesomeness of earth and soil (*Scholle und Boden*).

Hitler directed that only party members could belong to the SA, a move that was designed to produce a homogeneous organization free from outside interference by related paramilitary forces. Hitler had attempted to integrate the various veterans organizations (*Wehrverbände*) such as Stahlhelm and Wehrwolf, but with disappointing results; and while this may have slightly affected recruiting efforts, there were other forces at work that led to a steady increase in the size of the SA.

In the first place, the smallest local of the party in any area of Germany could found an SA unit since only a few men were required to form a *Schar*. In the second place, the movement also encouraged individual initiative and turned a blind eye to various leadership squabbles on the Darwinian assumption that the fittest leaders would naturally emerge and recruit larger and larger units. In the third place, the SA increasingly acquired an aura of political potency and thus authenticated for many recruits a sense of manliness, camaraderie, and excitement. For many young Germans, especially for those who were unemployed, the SA would become a surrogate family, the uniform with its insignia would build up the esteem of its members, and the jackboots reinforced in some the lust for power and domination. Finally, the SA was no ordinary traditional army cultivating a narrow elitist or Prussian spirit. Under Pfeffer, and later Röhm, the SA avoided strict rank consciousness; instead, the men adopted an easy-going camaraderie and even put together their own groups. Pfeffer wanted his troops to be young and revolutionary, and he allowed considerable decision making among the lower ranks. Only top positions were staffed by Pfeffer himself, and these were recruited from former army officers such as Viktor Lutze, Walther Stennes, August Schneidhuber, and Paul Dincklade. In all other respects, the SA was becoming an army of youthful militants, idealists, as well as asocial bullies. Of the Berlin SA, 70 percent were younger than twenty-six and almost 90 percent were under thirty.[72]

Between 1926 and 1929 the SA grew steadily, and its visibility on the streets became a daily experience for many Germans. At party rallies Hitler would involve his storm troopers in mystical rituals replete with loyalty oaths and presentation of standards. Over thirty thousand boisterous storm troopers converged on the Nuremberg party congress of 1929 to hear Hitler tell them that their brown shirts were a badge of honor and expressing the hope that millions would soon long to put them on.[73]

Hitler could hardly have imagined that millions would soon flock to the banner of the Nazi Party, which was still small and politically insignificant. By the summer of 1929, however, Hitler had completed the party's reconstruction. Although the party and its auxiliary institutions were still small and its electoral successes meager, at best, Hitler had succeeded in laying the foundation for a well-organized party whose members were more militant and committed than the members of any other party in Germany. Problems, of course, remained. Internal party divisions, triggered by Strasser and his loyalists, continued under the surface. The SA was running on a parallel track that could threaten at some point to change direction and cross the aims of the party. Funds were still appallingly meager and electoral prospects dim. However, by the summer of 1929 the party had successfully reorganized itself and shed its image of a failed putschist party. Two events would transform it into a formidable threat to the republic: one was the nationalistic agitation centering around the Young Plan; and the other, more important, event was the onset of the Great Depression.

The Young Plan and the Coming of the Great Depression

In February 1929 a conference of international fiscal experts, chaired by the American banker Owen D. Young, met in Paris to find a satisfactory solution to Germany's reparations problems. The conference had been the brainchild of Gustav Stresemann, Germany's foreign minister, who was working tirelessly on a plan to reduce reparations payments and to persuade the Allied powers to evacuate the Rhineland. After intensive bargaining, an agreement was reached on June 7, 1929, that obligated Germany to pay roughly two billion marks per year for thirty-seven years, with lesser additional payments over a twenty-two-year period earmarked for covering the Inter-Allied war debt. The method of meeting the annual payments was made more flexible than that of the previous Dawes Plan, for only a portion of the payment was mandatory, while the other portion could be postponed. There were also no harsh provisions concerning foreign interference, possible arbitrary actions by reparations agents, cost-of-living increases, and the like. Another international conference, meeting at The Hague in August 1929, legalized the Paris agreement and approved Stresemann's proposal to link the lowering of reparations payments with an Allied withdrawal from the Rhineland to begin in September 1929. This was Stresemann's last victory. Seriously ill from six years of overwork and political vilification by his enemies, he died in October 1929, a time when the republic needed him most.

Right-wing nationalists who had reviled Stresemann for years, carping mercilessly at every step he took to bring about international understanding, now combined forces to defeat the Young Plan and to crucify anyone who supported it. On July 9, 1929, Stahlhelm leaders formed a national committee for a plebiscite against the Young Plan. The committee was headed by the pig-headed mass-media mogul Alfred Hugenberg, whose party, the DNVP, was increasingly turning into a kind of "bourgeois caricature" of the Nazi Party.[74] The aroused Hugenberg managed to galvanize most of the political right, including the Nazis, into defeating the Young Plan. Cranking up his media resources — newspapers, wire services, UFA (Universum-Film Aktiengesellschaft [Universal-Film Joint-Stock Company]) newsreels — he unleashed a campaign of such chauvinistic and demagogic intensity that even Hitler was impressed by it. In fact, Hitler was delighted to be associated with this campaign because it gave the Nazi Party a national forum free of charge.

The Weimar Constitution specified that a referendum could be submitted to the voters if 10 percent of the electorate petitioned for it. Hugenberg's committee proceeded to formulate the referendum, entitled "Law against the Enslavement of the German People," and gathered the requisite number of signatures. Drafted by Wilhelm Frick, the proposed law called on the government to renounce the moral grounds on which reparations had been anchored, namely, Article 231 of the Versailles Treaty, and to reject any further reparations payments. It also insisted on the immediate evacuation of the Rhineland and demanded that any public official who had signed "tribute payments" be tried for treason.

Although the nationalists unleashed a Blitzkrieg campaign in support of their referendum, the Reichstag decisively rejected it on November 30, 1929, by a vote of 318 to 82. However, the defeat was really a victory for the Nazis. For almost five months Hugenberg had given Hitler free publicity through his newspaper chain and news agencies, thus introducing him to many people who had never heard of him or the party he led. In addition, the conservative circles in which Hugenberg moved opened up new and powerful contacts for Hitler.

One of the most important contacts, next to Fritz Thyssen, who had supported the Nazi Party since the early 1920s, was Emil Kirdorf, one of the founding fathers of German industry and the man who controlled the Gelsenkirchen Mine Company, the political funds of the mining union, and the famous "Ruhr Treasury" of the North-West Iron Association. Kirdorf had heard Hitler speak to an audience of businessmen in Essen in 1927 and was impressed by his nationalistic orientation. In the summer of 1927 Elsa Bruckmann served as a go-between and brought the two men together in her Munich residence. The result was that Kirdorf fell under Hitler's spell, financed publication (in pamphlet form) of the remarks Hitler had made to him during their meeting at the Bruck-manns, and subsequently joined the Nazi Party.[75] It is interesting to note that Kirdorf later changed his mind about the Nazi Party because of its apparent hostility toward capitalism. In August 1928, he bolted the party and returned to the DNVP. Hitler's cooperation with Hugenberg and the nationalists, however, brought Kirdorf back into the Nazi orbit. Kirdorf's attitude was probably fairly typical among conservative busi-nessmen who were suffering from a kind of cognitive dissonance as a result of being exposed simultaneously to Nazi anticapitalist as well as traditional nationalistic slogans.

Hitler's political genius consisted in cultivating divergent sections of German society with essentially incompatible ideas. Thus, when he played down the radical anticapitalist and anti-Semitic ideas of the party and mimicked the role of a respectable, middle-class politician, Kirdorf and many other businessmen were tricked into believing that Hitler could be won over to the conservative-nationalistic side. In 1929 very few people knew what Hitler was really like. Different audiences heard different things and believed them. The businessmen who listened to his ingratiating remarks, free of all anticapitalist or anti-Semitic references, did not suspect that they were dealing with a murderous anti-Semite and a brutal sociopath who would do anything to gain dictatorial power. The Young campaign and the resulting alliance with the conservative nationalists provided an important impetus to the attainment of Hitler's goals. The most important catalyst, however, was the beginning of the Great Depression, without which Hitler would have never been more than the leader of a small extremist party.

The Weimar Republic had been plagued from its beginning by severe economic problems. Many of these economic woes were the result of World War I. As previously mentioned, the war was financed largely by dubious loans and bonds rather than by taxes, which fueled post-war inflation and set the stage for the 1923 fiscal collapse. However, the German economy, after three decades of expansion (1884–1914), was already showing signs of stagnation before the impact of the war was felt. The major reason for the sluggishness of the German econ-omy was not the war but rather certain internal or structural flaws in the German economy itself. The Achilles heel of the German economy was its noncompetitive and highly state-dominated orientation.[76] Decision making did not reside in the hands of risk-taking entrepreneurs, willing to experiment with new ideas, but in the hands of cautious state civil servants, large feudal landowners, and industrialists who depended too heavily on state support. The system was further saddled by too many small and unproductive farmers who lacked the technological expertise and sufficient capital to mechanize their operations. In addition, the Ger-man economy was weighed down by an inflated urban petit bourgeoisie in the form of small shopkeepers and a growing white-collar class who were equally noncompetitive, resistant to change, and often reactionary in their political persuasion.

Behind these economic problems lurked concomitant social cleavages. The stabilization of the currency in 1924 and the massive infusion of foreign loans simply masked the underlying weaknesses. In 1925 Germany's industrial output had returned to only 95 percent of 1913 levels; its shares in world exports had fallen from 13.2 percent in 1913 to 9.1 percent in 1927,[77] a sluggishness attributable to the defeat in war, the economic burden imposed by the Versailles Treaty, the loss of Germany's merchant fleet, territorial losses, and financial liabilities.

From 1914 to 1934 the German economy stagnated. Poor economic growth, in turn, resulted in chronic unemployment. Even before the onset of the Great Depression in 1929, unemployment remained disconcertingly high, at one point (1926) reaching 10 percent.[78] At the same time, the general standard of living for most ordinary Germans was worse in the 1920s than it had been before the war. Although the capacity for industrial output had been greatly improved due to new technologies and automation, this trend was not accompanied by greater consumer purchasing power, which further weakened an already sluggish expansion. Compared to the managerial elite and well-paid public employees, who took the lion's share of wages and profits, many ordinary German workers received less than a balanced share, which accounts for the increasingly divisive struggles between labor and management over wages. As previously noted, the republic had been founded on an economic partnership between labor and management to support the mission of a welfare state. This partnership, however, did not survive the adverse economic forces just cited. Even under the best of circumstances — steady economic growth, new markets, technological innovations, low labor costs, and high productivity — it is difficult to maintain extensive welfare and entitlement programs. By the late 1920s, especially beginning with the worldwide depression, it was becoming increasingly obvious that the republic could no longer afford to maintain, let alone increase, past levels of welfare spending. This is certainly how the business community viewed the situation, attributing the republic's economic problems to unreasonably generous social benefits, to reparations, and to the scarcity of investment capital. The Social Democrats, on the other hand, blamed the economic crisis on insufficient consumer purchasing power, arguing that the appropriate remedy was to pay the workers higher salaries, which, along with better training and benefits, would turn them into better producers *and* better consumers. Both sides argued from rigid premises that did not allow them to address economic complexities that exceeded the limited capacities of their Procrustean models. Thus, the stage was set for further and more damaging polarizations and at a time of worsening economic crisis.

In the meantime, an invisible depression had already been gnawing on the German economy long before the financial crisis of 1929, and that was an ongoing agricultural malaise that spread through Germany's rural provinces and towns. The agricultural problem was worldwide, but it hit Germany harder than most countries. Especially hard hit were the East Elbian landowners. Having been deprived of their markets by the war and losing the protection they had enjoyed under the Hohenzollern monarchy, the large East Elbian landowners, lacking capital as well as government protection, were in dire economic straits. By the middle 1920s, a mood of political radicalism had spread throughout the German countryside, infecting both owners and farmworkers alike. Although the agrarian elites put considerable pressure on President Hindenburg, who himself had recently joined the ranks of the Prussian landowners, and managed to receive a steady stream of subsidies (*Osthilfe*) from the government, the crisis continued unabated. The Nazis were the chief beneficiaries of this agricultural crisis, especially after they refocused their electoral appeals from the urban to the rural plan and exploited the social and cultural roots behind the agricultural crisis.

The Germany economy was essentially a house of cards. What made it fall was the Great Crash of 1929 in the United States. Since the late nineteenth century, an interlocking world economy had come into being. This involved, among other things, an international monetary system that allowed the free convertibility of currencies one into the other, the free exchange of goods in the international market, and investments of capital into foreign securities. Although World War I had seriously distorted this picture, as nations began to erect high tariff walls and tried to move toward self-sufficiency (autarky), the interlocking system generally prevailed throughout the 1920s. Germany in particular was deeply enmeshed in it during the postwar years because of its financial obligations and its overdependence on foreign loans to meet them.

The kingpin in this interlocking world economy was the United States. The American economy in the 1920s was outwardly booming, but behind the impressive facade there were serious structural problems. In the first place, the U.S. economy was poorly diversified, overspecializing in the construction and automobile industries. When these industries began to contract in the mid-1920s, a "ripple effect" developed that spread to related industries such as steel, glass, and rubber. In the second place, the U.S. economy was fueled by dubious methods of credit, borrowing, and investment. In the third place, it was an economy that concealed widespread inequalities in wealth and poverty, with some twenty-four thousand families at the top of the economic pyramid reaping an average income greater than that of six million families at the bottom. In the fourth place, workers received less than a balanced share, so that purchasing power was relatively weak, making it difficult to absorb the volume of goods produced. In the fifth place, the

U.S. economy was inconsistently managed by several republican administrations that navigated uncertainly between hands-off (laissez-faire) policies in fiscal areas (control of banks and the stock exchange) and interventionist policies in favor of high tariffs (Hawley-Smoot Bill). Finally, and most importantly, America had been on a speculative binge since the early 1920s, for the shortest way to riches, it was said, was to speculate in stocks and bonds. By the mid-1920s prices were climbing far out of proportion to their real value. In September 1929 the market "broke," and prices tumbled. One month later, the market crashed as frightened speculators, many of whom had borrowed money from banks to "play" the market, suddenly unloaded their "insecurities." An orgy of selling followed. On "Black Tuesday," October 29, 1929, over sixteen million shares were sold in an atmosphere of utter panic. Wall Street turned into a monetary necropolis as bankers and investors went broke and sometimes jumped out of skyscrapers to commit suicide. By the end of 1929 American stockholders had lost forty billion dollars in paper values, a sum that was higher than the total cost of World War I.

The stock market crash provided the psychological impetus for a panic mentality, and it also exposed deep-seated economic weaknesses, triggering the longest-lasting depression in American history. By the end of 1929 more than three million people were out of work; a year later, that figure had doubled. A thousand banks failed, factories closed, millions of unemployed loitered the streets desperately looking for work. The crisis passed from finance to industry and from the United States to Europe. American investments and loans to Europe abruptly stopped, pulling the rug from under the postwar prosperity, especially in Germany. Thus, when the American stock market collapsed in October 1929, the economic shock waves reached Germany in a matter of weeks because American loans had in large part propped up the sluggish German economy. The result was a deep depression, comparable in economic scope to that in the United States but far more serious in its political implications.

The withdrawal of foreign capital set in motion a vicious downward spiral: trade and production fell off dramatically, wages and prices decreased, businesses and factories closed, banks failed, and the cancer of unemployment spread. Before the stock market crash in the United States, there were three million unemployed in Germany. This figure now increased steadily, reaching 4.35 million by September 1931, 5.1 million by September 1932, and 6 million during the winter of 1932–33.[79] Not counted in these appalling statistics were unregistered and part-time workers. In human terms, what these statistics reveal is that one out of two German families was affected. By 1933 many Germans could look back on five years without work.[80] Almost all sections of German society were affected, especially blue- and white-collar workers. Even white-collar public employees, though retaining their jobs, saw their salaries slashed repeatedly. Shopkeepers and tradesmen suffered from the fall in prices and purchasing power, while agrarian workers were laid off in droves as a result of the ongoing agricultural depression. As in the United States, the streets of Germany were overrun by an army of dispirited and increasingly enraged unemployed workers. The stage was set for the final drama that would sweep Adolf Hitler into power.

Chapter 7

The Nazi Seizure of Power

The Breakdown of Parliamentary Democracy

In December 1929 the German government was in a tailspin of financial calamities, facing a shortfall of 1.5 billion marks in anticipated revenues while at the same time trying to finance an unemployment insurance program whose annual cost, calculated in 1928 on the basis of 800,000 unemployed, had now more than tripled under the impact of 2.8 million idle workers. The financial crisis, in turn, triggered a political crisis that went far beyond the issue of unemployment insurance to the very breakdown of parliamentary democracy itself. The controversy over unemployment insurance, which split the great coalition government of Hermann Müller, was just the opening round in a lengthy and divisive battle of political self-destruction. When the government ran out of money by the end of 1929, the Reich finance minister, Rudolf Hilferding, proposed a tax on tobacco and an increase in insurance premiums from 3 to 3.5 percent.[1] Although a Social Democrat, Hilferding resorted to strict conservative fiscal policies of raising taxes and slashing spending, measures that caused an immediate howl of protest from diverse interest groups and led to a humiliating defeat of his program in the Reichstag.

However, the republic was not threatened, as a current joke had it, by a half-percentage increase in insurance rates; rather, the threat came from the renewed outbreak of political extremism on both the left and the right. If the German people had possessed confidence in the republic and its leaders, the flood of economic bad news that now began to inundate them might have been more bearable; but the sad fact was that even before the Great Depression, as previously stated, the German people displayed little trust in their democratic institutions. The initial assault on democracy, however, was not orchestrated by Adolf Hitler, who certainly benefited from it, but by political intriguers in the German military.[2] A few powerful military schemers, notably General Schleicher, undermined the Müller government in two ways: first, by persuading Hindenburg not to empower the chancellor to pass his fiscal program by emergency decree, thus almost certainly assuring his downfall, and, second, by actively promoting Heinrich Brüning as Müller's successor.

The military chiefs had criticized the Müller government for not aggressively pushing their rearmament program, but their real fear in the bleak winter of 1929–30 was that the government was too weak to deal resolutely with the potentially explosive social consequences of Germany's economic crisis. In fact, sitting in Müller's cabinet was one man, General Groener, who still had a very vivid recollection of the civil war that had engulfed Germany in 1918–19, a disaster he was determined to prevent with the same methods he had used eleven years ago, namely, using the military to quell civil unrest. As minister of defense, Groener worked closely with his "adopted son" and "cardinal in politics" General Schleicher, trying to replace the Müller cabinet with a professional team of experts from the political right — a team that would bypass the Reichstag, if necessary, and resolve the nation's crisis by presidential fiat.

Of the handful of men who would determine the course of German history for the next three years, none was more perniciously influential than the scheming General Kurt von Schleicher, a man whose name (Schleicher suggests creeper or crawler in German) was in many ways an index to his character. The bald-headed and outwardly jovial-looking general was a highly gifted and intelligent officer who had advanced rapidly through the ranks of the armed forces. Born in 1882 in Brandenburg, Schleicher came from an old Prussian military family, graduated from a military academy with a distinguished record, and then joined Hindenburg's old regiment, the Third Foot Guards, as a subaltern in 1900. While serving in Hindenburg's old regiment, the suave Schleicher struck up a series of helpful connections that would later smooth his path to success, the most important being his close friendships with his mess-mate Oskar von Hindenburg, son of the famed future field marshal, and the future quartermaster general Wilhelm Groener. It was Groener, then an instructor at the Kriegsakademie, who would take Schleicher under his wing and promote his career, even affectionately referring to his protégé as "my adopted son."[3] During World War I, Schleicher served as a general staff officer, spending most of his time sitting behind a desk, except for a brief service in 1917 on the eastern front, which earned him the Iron Cross First Class. Near the end of the war he became aide-de-camp to General Groener, helped in organizing a Free Corps after the fall of the monarchy, and then joined the new Reichswehr. From this moment on Schleicher was always at the nerve center of power. He shared with General von Seeckt, the new chief of the army command (Heeresleitung), a passionate belief in salvaging the traditional structure of the German army; but unlike his chief, he became increasingly convinced that the army's survival in an age of intense political conflicts depended on abandoning its much-vaunted policy of neutrality (Überparteilichkeit) in favor of active involvement in politics. Under Seeckt, Schleicher's role was relatively limited, but this began to change when Seeckt was forced to resign his position in 1926. Thereafter, Schleicher's power steadily expanded, particularly after his former mentor, General Groener, became minister of defense in 1928 and appointed him to a new office in the Reichswehr Ministry. The new office gave Schleicher control over all intelligence services and empowered him to serve as the military's chief liaison person between the Reichswehr and the government. When his personal friend, General Kurt von Hammerstein-Equord, succeeded General Wilhelm Heye as chief of army command, Schleicher's influence became even more powerful. Given the fact that Schleicher had also cultivated his social connections with the Hindenburg family, enjoying the confidence of the field marshal, who was now president of the republic and commander in chief of the armed forces, it is safe to say that in 1930 Schleicher was one of the most powerful men in Germany. With his spies roaming the corridors of power and his spooks tapping the telephones of friends and foes alike, Schleicher knew every secret in Germany. He also shamelessly manipulated the press by leaking selective information or planting sly insinuations.

Unfortunately, Schleicher did not use his extensive power for constructive purposes; he was often more interested in using it on behalf of personal intrigues or various treacherous manipulations. He eventually undercut every man he had once supported, giving rise to a widely mentioned joke that any chancellor who had Schleicher's support could expect sooner or later to be sunk by a Schleicher torpedo.[4] Seeking power without accepting its responsibility, the vain, unscrupulous, and devious Schleicher now began to fish in troubled political waters. He saw himself increasingly as the king-maker behind the throne, making and breaking friends and enemies alike until, at length, facing a political wasteland strewn with the victims of his own making, he had to confront his greatest fear — personal responsibility. Not surprisingly, that fear was well founded. Having been a *Schreibtischoffizier* (desk officer) all of his career, ill-prepared for building a broad consensus beyond his own professional world, Schleicher was not suited for the politicized world of the fading Weimar Republic. In fairness, it should be said that Schleicher was by no means a right-wing reactionary; on the contrary, he saw himself as somewhat of a democratic general who upheld the old Prussian spirit of military socialism, even dreaming of constructing a coalition of comradeship between soldiers and workers. Despite his fondness for intrigue, his arrogance, and his vanity, Schleicher was also a very gracious, charming, and cultivated man. However, Germany was ill-served by his machinations because, directly or indirectly, they would contribute to the destruction of the republic and the rise of Adolf Hitler.

As a consequence of Schleicher's growing influence, the Reichswehr began to abandon its political neutrality. In John Wheeler-Bennett's words, "From being the guardian of the State and its ultimate source of power, the Army descended to the status of political broker and Party boss."[5] Working behind the scenes, Schleicher torpedoed the Müller government by persuading Hindenburg to withdraw his support and by choosing Heinrich Brüning as Müller's successor. In the opinion of Schleicher and the military, Brüning was a far more acceptable candidate than the lackluster and ailing Müller. It was the hope of the military that Brüning, a prominent Center politician, might be able to forge a solid coalition that would consist entirely of middle-class parties. Brüning was also known as a fiscal conservative, a supporter of military appropriations, and a staunch opponent of the Versailles Treaty. Finally, he had a sterling war record — a sure sign to the military that he must be a fine fellow.

On March 27, 1930, the Müller government, which had been based on a broad coalition of five parties (SPD, Center, DVP, Democrats, and Bavarian People's Party), resigned and was replaced by a cabinet of the bourgeois middle, headed by Heinrich Brüning (1885–1970). The new chancellor was a bald, bespectacled, and ascetic-looking patrician who projected the persona of an austere Jesuit priest, which may explain why the crafty Schleicher referred to him as "Ignaz." Born in Münster, the son of a Catholic vinegar merchant, Brüning had studied law, philosophy, and political economy at various German universities, graduating with a doctoral degree in political economy from the University of Bonn in 1914. He spent his formative years not only in the academy but also in the trenches, serving his country during the war as a commander of a small machine-gun unit on the western front. The experience of witnessing the deaths of many men under his command instilled in him a Spartan sense of duty and a strong conviction that the greatest virtue resided in holding out in the face of even insurmountable obstacles. After the war he entered government service as an assistant to Adam Stegerwald, Prussian minister of human services and later minister president of Prussia. In 1920 he assumed leadership of the League of German Trade Unions; in 1924, he became a deputy in the Reichstag, representing the electoral district of Breslau for the Center Party; in 1929 he became chairman of his party group (*Fraktionsvorsitzender*) in the Reichstag; and on March 28, 1930, Hindenburg appointed him chancellor.

Although Brüning was an honorable man, he was not an inspiring leader. A confirmed bachelor, the new chancellor was by temperament a taciturn and suspicious man who avoided the glare of publicity and shied away from intimate human contacts. Brüning was, at best, a competent midlevel civil servant, comfortable in the world of party caucuses and small political circles. As Heinz Höhne has pointed out, his natural impulse was to solve problems in bureaucratic-authoritarian terms by relying on personal contacts and special connections, plotting his strategy in the backroom like a chess master but knowing nothing about the feelings, prejudices, phobias, and hatreds of ordinary people.[6]

The new chancellor was also politically out of touch with many ordinary Germans. Brüning was actually a romantic conservative with a fondness for lost causes such as restoring the Hohenzollern monarchy. Idolizing the aged Field Marshal von Hindenburg, perhaps more the legend than the man, he envisioned the old man as a stalking horse to a restored monarchy. He believed that this could be accomplished by extending the president's term of office for life and having him serve as a sort of interim crowned head, a *Reichsverweser,* until the day when the monarchy would be reestablished. Brüning's fantasy bore little resemblance to reality, except that Hindenburg was in fact his political raison d'être; for without the field marshal's support, his government would have quickly collapsed, as time would prove later, because it was not based on broad parliamentary support.

In terms of economics, the new chancellor was essentially a laissez-faire liberal who, like Herbert Hoover in the United States, believed that the economic crisis was merely one of those cyclical downturns that would eventually bottom out and reverse itself without active government interference. Deploring the bloated welfare state as detrimental to economic growth, Brüning favored deflationary policies aimed at reducing taxes and government spending.[7] Although this initially endeared him to big business, his actual fiscal policies, greatly modified under the pressure of competing interest groups, alienated sizable elements within both business and labor.

On April 1, 1930, just as Brüning rose to address the Reichstag, Communist deputies rose from their benches and shouted "Hunger Chancellor," an epithet that would stigmatize the new chancellor throughout his tenure of office. The Communist deputies certainly had a valid point because the new chancellor's economic plan was an extreme austerity program, bound to antagonize most sections of German society. It was also curiously inconsistent and self-defeating. Making a fetish out of a balanced budget, which he thought could be accomplished only through rigid retrenchment policies, the "Hunger Chancellor" proposed to administer some harsh medicine by slashing unemployment benefits, levying "crisis taxes," reducing the deficit, trimming the bureaucracy, and cutting government expenditures across the board. Not surprisingly, the chancellor's program was widely attacked, even within his own cabinet, as cruel and unworkable, but the austere machine-gun officer of World War I, drawing on some twisted sense of duty, stoically stood his ground and stayed the course.

By June 1930, if not earlier, Brüning had reached the conviction that Germany's economic crisis had polarized the political process to such a point that a nonpartisan, democratic solution was no longer possible. This was confirmed on July 15 when his personal appeal for support of his austerity program received an icy reception in the Reichstag. Instead of beating a retreat, modifying his economic program, or cooperating with the Social Democrats, Brüning threatened to invoke Article

48 of the Weimar Constitution, authorizing him to dismiss the Reichstag, call for new elections, and pass his program despite parliamentary
opposition. On July 16, a majority of the delegates in the Reichstag,
by a vote of 256 to 193, rejected the key elements in Brüning's fiscal
program. Brüning then bypassed the parliamentary process and implemented his program by presidential decree, thus undermining the
principle of ministerial responsibility on which the Weimar Constitution
rested.[8]

Brüning had, in any case, already persuaded himself that a nonpar-
liamentary cabinet of experts, standing above the squabble of petty
politics, was a far better instrument for solving Germany's problems
than a hopelessly polarized Reichstag. He was not alone in this conviction. Among men of Brüning's class and background there had always
existed a strong bias against parliamentary democracy, especially among
the conservative right.[9] Brüning believed that parliament was an inappropriate place to make nonpartisan decisions. The experiences of the
troubled republic seemed to prove that it was impossible to balance the
conflicting political, social, and economic interests in a parliamentary
setting. In fact, Germany never had a genuine tradition of parliamentary government. As Ernst Fraenkel observes, Germany had no tradition
of great parliamentary debates, no tradition of flexible parliamentary
tactics, no parliamentary style growing out of an esprit de corps of deputies, no grand style of manipulating rules by diverse politicians who
had a sound instinct for play-acting in the interplay of parliamentary
forces, and no memory of parliaments in which working majorities were
held together because its members shared power and saw themselves as
part of the in-group.[10]

Brüning shared the general disdain of many German politicians of
having to submit himself to the conflicting claims and counterclaims
of special-interest groups. He conceived of politics as taking place on a
higher level than mere patronage. His trust was in the civil service state
in which decision making rested in the hands of dedicated, well educated, and nonpartisan civil servants who placed the good of the country
over the good of a party or a special-interest group. The role of parliament, in this view, should be restricted to the formulation of legislative
rules, while the executive function should be in the hands of the government and its executive branch — the civil service. In other words, many
Germans of Brüning's background conceived of parliament as in some
ways existing separate from the real executive decision-making branch
of the government; its role was to be restricted to the legalistic rather
than the practical dimensions of social policy.

Despite the fact that the Weimar Constitution had created the conditions for a parliamentary democracy, old habits of relying on authoritarian methods proved to be stronger in the end. Although there is no
apodictic law that the will of the people or the majority, represented in a
parliament, is intrinsically better than a well-governed civil-service state

with authoritarian leanings, there are sound reasons to assume that Germany would have been served better by a more inclusive political system than by a sham democracy in which an increasingly dubious fiscal policy and a reactionary political agenda resided in the hands of an unrepresentative cabinet and a senile president whose real allegiance was not to the republic but to the lost monarchy.

At any rate, with the help of Hindenburg and his conservative retainers, Brüning effectively destroyed the democratic process. By resorting to the extraconstitutional device of Article 48 as a primary means of governance, Brüning tacitly accepted unconstitutionality as a preferred alternative to parliamentary democracy. At the very time of worsening economic crisis, he dissolved the Reichstag, passed his program by presidential decree, and recklessly called for new elections, to be held in September 1930. With the benefit of hindsight, we can see that Brüning had committed several fatal errors: first, he had relegated parliament and parties to the political periphery and thus reduced the chances of collective decision making; second, by sanctioning governance by emergency decree, he tied himself dangerously close to the mercurial whims of the aging field marshal; and third, by calling elections at a time of heightened radicalism and widespread alienation, he was inviting the further growth of political extremism, as was born out by the fateful election of September 14, 1930.

The Nazi Upsurge and the End of Brüning

Hitler knew that his hour had struck with the coming of the Great Depression. Relying on his uncanny political intuition, he tirelessly built up a close psychological rapport with those who had been hurt by the depression. He did this by presenting himself as an ordinary and caring man who empathized with the suffering of the German people and promised them radical change. His appeal was not to a particular class or ideology but to the German people as a whole. He soothed middle-class fears of lawlessness by promising to restore law and order, gratified conservatives with promises of a national resurgence, pleased the military by evoking visions of a splendid new army, and confidently reassured the workers that no one would ever face poverty and unemployment under National Socialism. Above all, he reminded all of his audiences that they were not to blame for the crisis because they were victims of the system. He knew the agents of their suffering, could identify the culprits, and with the aid of the German people would wage a war of liberation, ridding the German people of their tormentors and leading them to a glorious future.

With all the remarkable energy he could muster, Hitler began to woo the German people in speech after speech, traveling the length and breadth of Germany; and behind him was the ubiquitous Nazi Party, a veritable perpetual motion machine that was drowning out all other parties in the intensity of its propaganda, the commitment of its rank and file members, and the organizational talents of its leaders.

Young people were particularly attracted by the movement's visionary zeal; they identified with its radical approaches and admired its innovative tactics of building mass support. They joined in droves. Membership in the SA increased by leaps and bounds, and it attracted Germans from all walks of life — the unemployed, students, former veterans, workers, and farmers. Its reputation began to acquire a certain magical quality because those who joined believed that the SA would groom the future saviors of Germany. By 1930, thanks to the mythmaking genius of Dr. Goebbels, the SA was also beginning to produce martyrs who could serve as shining examples to future storm troopers.

In February 1930 a young Berlin SA leader, Horst Wessel, was killed by a Communist. Wessel was the son of a prominent Protestant minister, then deceased, who had defied his mother by joining the SA, abandoning his legal studies at the University of Berlin, and consorting with a prostitute with whom he had fallen in love.[11] On January 14, 1930, the prostitute's former pimp, accompanied by several Red Front comrades, broke into Wessel's apartment and shot him in the mouth during a scuffle. Mortally wounded, Wessel lingered on for several days in a hospital. Joseph Goebbels, among others, made a daily pilgrimage to his hospital bed. It turned out that Wessel had published a stirring poem in Goebbels's newspaper, *Angriff;* the poem, entitled "Die Fahne Hoch" (Raise high the flag), would become the battle hymn not only of the SA but of the Nazi movement as a whole.[12] When Wessel finally succumbed to his injuries, Goebbels staged an elaborate funeral for the dead SA man and transfigured him into a national martyr. The carefully arranged solemnity of the funeral, replete with a roll call for the dead, lugubrious rhetoric, and sentimental pathos, turned into a bloody brawl as Communists threw stones over the cemetery wall and sent the mourners ducking for cover behind the tombstones. Yet all this was grist for Goebbels's propaganda mill. Now he could really "beat the living shit out of the murderers," as he had previously written, and excoriate the red mob: "As the coffin came to rest in the cool ground there went up outside the gates the depraved cry of the subhuman.... The departed, still with us, raised his weary hand and beckoned into the shimmering distance: Forward over the graves! At the end of the road lies Germany."[13] Such sentimental schmaltz for the dead would later became standard fare by which the Nazis tried to pull at the heartstrings of gullible Germans.

Despite the party's dynamic expansion, internal frictions continued to cause problems. The depression reopened a debate within the party that Hitler thought had been laid to rest some time ago — namely, the party's position on economic issues. The debate came to a head when Otto Strasser and his followers threatened to bolt the party because they had come to the conclusion that Hitler had sold out to the capitalists.

Strasser had stubbornly clung to his terrorist tactics and continued to preach a gospel of violent class war and the necessity of an alliance with the Soviet Union. On the evening of May 21, 1930, Hitler had a final confrontation with Otto Strasser at the Hotel Sanssouci in Berlin (with Strasser's brother Gregor, Hess, and Amann also present), making it quite clear that he wanted nothing to do with Strasser's program. In a heated, seven-hour discussion, Hitler lambasted Strasser for not turning over the resources of his Kampf Verlag to the Nazi Party and for stubbornly clinging to his Marxist program. Depicting himself as a national rather than a Marxist Socialist, Hitler insisted that his real goal was to restore Germany to national greatness — a goal that could not be achieved by resorting to crude egalitarianism or class warfare. Harking back to his ideological instincts — race, elitism, the "laws of nature" — Hitler once more revealed his innermost intentions in a torrent of words.[14] When the session ended, the breach between Hitler and Strasser was beyond repair; and when Strasser shortly afterward attacked Hitler in a vicious broadside, accusing him of betraying socialism, Hitler ordered Strasser and his followers expelled from the party.

Although Otto Strasser wielded considerable influence in certain working-class circles, having bombarded Berlin and northern Germany with Socialist propaganda through the various publications of his Kampf Verlag, it turned out that few members of the Nazi Party, including his brother Gregor, followed his apostasy. The Strasser revolt, however, was indicative that not everything was well with the Nazi Party. With the influx of thousands of new SA members, who were often motivated as much by money as they were by ideological zeal, dissatisfactions soon developed, exploding in an open mutiny in the spring of 1930. The rebellion centered on the Berlin SA leader Walter Stennes, who demanded immediate independence from the heavy hand of Joseph Goebbels, *Gauleiter* of Berlin, and better salaries for himself and his storm troopers. Stennes underscored the seriousness of his demands by announcing a general strike until various grievances had been met. The SA mutiny was primarily a reaction on the part of the rank and file toward favoritism, low wages, and "bossism" rather than a reflection of ideological divisions. Many ordinary storm troopers received a pittance for their tireless efforts and resented what they perceived to be corruption and high living among the party's elite. The situation in Berlin deteriorated to such an extent that Goebbels had to call upon Hitler himself to restore order. Knowing that a mutinous SA could seriously undermine Nazi prospects in the upcoming September elections, Hitler hurried to Berlin and visited countless beerhalls, trying to talk good sense into disenchanted storm troopers. By his very presence he managed to restore order. On September 2 he replaced Pfeffer and took personal charge of the SA, compelling all SA members to swear that they would faithfully obey his orders. After briefly relying on the advice of Otto Wagener, who had served with Pfeffer as chief of staff of the SA, Hitler then contacted Röhm in Bolivia and asked him to take charge of the day-to-day operations of the SA. On January 5, 1931, Röhm became chief of staff of the SA. Although the SA crisis had been temporarily settled, Stennes continued to be a source of friction and had to be removed in April 1931. However, Hitler had shown once again that he could use the dynamism and revolutionary potential of the SA for his own ends. In this case that end was served by using the SA as an instrument of electoral intimidation and persuasion. Without the help of some seventy thousand foot soldiers, the outcome of the September 14 election might have been much different for the Nazis.

The election of September 14, 1930, represented a turning point in the fortunes of the Nazi Party. When the votes were in, the Nazis had scored a major breakthrough, receiving 6.4 million votes (18 percent of the total vote) and seating 107 out of 577 deputies in the Reichstag. This made the Nazi Party the second largest party in the Reichstag. The Social Democrats were still the largest party, but their representation in the Reichstag since the last election in 1928 had dropped from 153 to 143 seats. The third largest party was the Communist Party, which also increased its representation by polling 4.6 million votes and receiving 77 seats in the Reichstag. The liberal parties of the middle, except for the Center Party, were all seriously crippled by the election. The Center Party held its own and even slightly increased its mandates from 62 to 68. The smaller parties on the right, on whom Brüning had been counting, lost heavily also. Hugenberg's DNVP lost 2 million votes since the last election and saw its Reichstag representation slip from 73 to 41 votes.

The election clearly mirrored the extreme polarization of German politics and also indicated that the enemies of the republic were gaining the upper hand over its defenders. Simple arithmetic ruled out the construction of some form of prorepublican government coalition.[15] With the growth of extremism on both the left and the right it was impossible for Brüning to command a majority in the Reichstag.

The Nazi upsurge can be attributed primarily to the depression that had ruined many German businesses and led to a tragic increase in unemployment. The depression, in turn, stirred up a pervasive fear of impending political chaos leading to an acute crisis in confidence in the democratic system. Many Germans blamed the system for the crisis, laying the depression squarely at the feet of what they perceived to be a failing democracy. As a result, the German middle class, already alienated from the republic by the crisis of 1923, stigmatized the "system" as criminal and incompetent. All sorts of antidemocratic ideas, articulated in bold and urgent terms by conservative pundits, came thundering down on perplexed Germans from all sorts of newspapers, books, and journals. These spokesmen of the conservative right argued that the coming of the masses in politics signaled what Edgar J. Jung called the "Herrschaft der Minderwertigen" (rule by the inferior) and the institutionalization of mediocrity and vulgarity.[16] They indicted the whole range of democratic forms — constitutions, parties, elections — as unsuited to Germany's traditions. They scorned democratic principles as empty shibboleths fabricated by parties or demagogues to disguise their self-interest or their lust for power. Democracy, according to these spokesmen, was inherently contradictory because an amorphous mass of people could not actually define goals, set policies, or literally govern itself. Elitism, they insisted, was a fact of life that could not be covered up by rhetorical fig leaves pleasing to the masses. Societies have been and always will be governed by elites, by the stronger, more powerful, and more gifted sort of people. Even in democracies we find that the wealthy few usually pull the real levers of power. It follows, as Oswald Spengler put it, that "the fundamental right of the mass to choose its own representatives remains pure theory, for in actuality every developed organization recruits itself."[17] For replacements for this corrupt Western-type of democracy, these antidemocratic spokesmen looked variously to a restoration of the monarchy, a dictatorial presidential government, a military junta, an authoritarian model based on Spengler's notion of "Prussian socialism," or a "German-type" of plebiscitarian democracy in which the mass entrusts its fate to a charismatic dictator.

The Nazis were undoubtedly beneficiaries of popular antidemocratic theories that they themselves did not create. The election of September 14, 1930, had shown the existence of a totalitarian mood on both the right and the left in the form of a longing for charismatic leadership, a wish to dismantle the egalitarian welfare state, a desire for an autocratic state run by civil-servant experts, a craving for left-wing class dictatorship of the proletariat, and a longing for a harmonious folk community (*Volksgemeinschaft*) based on racial utopias. Hitler exploited these fears and longings; he did not create them.

Nor did Hitler alone create the preconditions that led to the collapse of democracy. As previously seen, the use of extraparliamentary dictatorship was initiated by Brüning and Hindenburg and subsequently enlarged by Papen and Schleicher. In other words, Germany had been well prepared for dictatorial rule before Hitler became chancellor.

The September election produced an immediate band-wagon effect on the Nazi movement. As Joachim Fest observed, it even became chic to join the party, particularly after one of the kaiser's sons, Prince August Wilhelm ("Auwi"), became a member.[18] Would such parlor Nazis undermine the revolutionary fervor of the movement? More seriously, would the influx of Socialists and even Communists, later referred to as "beefsteak Nazis" (brown on the outside and red on the inside), pose a problem of reliability? Although it was obvious that many of these new recruits had joined the party or the SA for purely expedient reasons, the party was resilient enough to accommodate and make use of them. The new famous members simply lent respectability or legitimacy to the party; they did not moderate its underlying radicalism. Hitler welcomed new converts. He knew that the movement would change them without being changed by them.

Although the hotheads in the party were thirsting for bloody revolution following the September victory, Hitler stuck to his path of legality. However, he made it unmistakably clear that the Nazis were not a parliamentary party trafficking with others in a multiparty system but a revolutionary party aiming at sole dictatorial control of the state. On September 25, 1930, Hitler explicitly expounded this argument at a trial of several Reichswehr officers who had violated the so-called Watch Decree; issued in February of that year by General Groener, this decree warned against attempts by radicals to infiltrate the officers' corps and promised any soldier who detected and reported subversive activities an immediate gift in the form of an engraved watch. Hitler unburdened himself quite openly at the Leipzig trial of the officers accused of disseminating Nazi propaganda within the Reichswehr by informing the court that he was only bound to the constitution during the struggle for power. Once having seized power, he declared under oath, he would replace the constitution and "set up state tribunals which will be empowered to pass sentences by law on those responsible for the misfortunes of our nation. Possibly, then, quite a few heads will roll legally."[19]

Such contempt for the constitution and the rule of law would become emblematic of Nazi behavior over the next two years. On October 13, 1930, when the Reichstag met for the first time after the September election, the Nazis showed their contempt for the parliamentary process by insolently marching to their seats in their brown uniforms, hissing and howling during the proceedings. Outside the Reichstag, Goebbels was orchestrating the first attack on Jewish businesses. Meanwhile, one hundred thousand metal workers, supported by both the Communists and the Nazis, went on strike and paralyzed Berlin. The sinews of law and order were beginning to snap.

On the belief that "possession of the streets is the key to power in the state," Röhm threw himself energetically into the task of positioning his storm troopers for the coming fray. He reorganized the SA along strict military lines, dividing the country into five *Obergruppen* (supreme groups) and eighteen *Gruppen*. The highest units of the SA, the *Standarten*, were tailored to military regiments and received numbers corresponding to former imperial regiments. A system of special units for air, naval, medical, and engineering functions further underscored the military nature of the new SA. An important part of this system was the NSKK (National Socialist Motor Corps), headed by Adolf Hühnlein, a former imperial staff officer and since 1923 a member of the SA. In the summer of 1931 the SA also developed its own training college for new SA/SS recruits in Munich. The SS, headed since 1929 by Heinrich Himmler, was still subordinate to Röhm and the SA.

As was to be expected, the depression drove thousands into the ranks of the SA, particularly after the SA set up a national network of SA homes and kitchens for the unemployed. As before, the SA also continued to attract its share of deviants, men with sociopathic tendencies who looked for a supportive umbrella under which they could give free vent to their violent and sadistic impulses. The SA was not a homogeneous or elitist organization because it welcomed almost anyone who superficially pledged allegiance to its principles. People joined for different reasons: to find some shelter or security, to escape from boredom, to find authentication for violent tendencies, to save Germany from Communism, to shape a new model army, and so forth. Behind the standard brown uniform, as Peter Merkl has shown, there were several SA types — marcher-proselytizers, marchers, electioneers, marcher-fighters, and marcher-fighter-proselytizers.[20] What they all had in common was their youth and the fact that they had gone through a process of militarization and politicization whose aim was to prepare them as political foot soldiers for the Nazi Party.

When Röhm took over the SA in January 1931, its membership stood roughly at one hundred thousand men; one year later, that figure had doubled. By the end of 1932 the SA had swelled to half a million men.[21] The officers and men of this growing army increasingly saw themselves as harbingers of the new mass army of the future. Their aim, still inchoate in 1931, was to graft themselves on the regular Reichswehr and eventually to replace it by sheer force of numbers. In the meantime, the SA tried to cultivate friendly relations with the Reichswehr by playing down its radical aims and by offering itself as an auxiliary force to the Reichswehr in case of left-wing violence or foreign danger. This supportive posture lulled the leadership of the Reichswehr into a false sense of security and explains its inconsistent activities toward the SA during the last two years of the republic.

Many of these hidden agendas were drowned out by the SA's involvement in a vicious cycle of agitation and violence. Efforts to stop it seemed futile. In March 1931 Brüning issued an emergency decree prohibiting any member of a political party from wearing a uniform. The Nazis simply responded by temporarily replacing their brown shirts with white shirts. Hitler took action against the SA and its members only when his own directives were clearly violated. Thus, when Stennes defied his "law-abiding" orders, he was promptly sacked in April 1931. However, when informed about the scandalous private life some of his storm troopers were leading, Hitler made it clear that this was nobody's business. The SA, he said, was not a moral institution grooming young daughters, but a club for rough fighters. Anyone who took an interest in the private lives of SA leaders could expect to be excluded from the SA and the party.[22] This appeared to be a tacit sanction of the scandalous private lives of Röhm and the top SA leadership, for it was well known within and without the SA that Röhm had replaced Pfeffer's officers with his own homosexual friends. Hitler himself had replaced Stennes with Edmund Heines, a convicted murderer who had also been expelled previously from the SA for homosexual practices. It goes without saying that such official encouragement of deviancy would breed more deviancy.

In the meantime, Germany's economic condition continued to worsen. In March 1931, following a lengthy and secretive period of negotiations, the Brüning government signed a customs union with Austria that was designed to alleviate the depression by working out mutually beneficial tariffs. Although the treaty was a purely economic arrangement between two sovereign states and not even exclusively bilateral — for it encouraged other nations to join — the French regarded the agreement as a violation of the Versailles Treaty and a stepping-stone toward political annexation. Mobilizing their financial and diplomatic resources to squash it, the French recalled their loans in both Austria and Germany, thereby precipitating the collapse of Austria's largest bank, the Kreditanstalt, and also provoking such a "flight of capital" from Germany that two of its superbanks — the Donat and Darmstädter banks — were forced to close their doors. By the summer of 1931 the economic crisis had worsened, and complete fiscal collapse was staved off only by help from the United States in the form of the Hoover moratorium that suspended reparations and war debts for one year. Although national bankruptcy had been narrowly avoided, the Brüning government had failed miserably in its foreign policy by having to abandon the Austro-German customs union. Additionally, the "Hunger Chancellor" continued to compound the crisis with further tax increases, salary cuts, and reductions in unemployment benefits.

No wonder that extremists continued to score impressive gains. In May the Nazis scored victories in local elections in Schaumburg-Lippe and Oldenburg. Almost tasting victory, marching storm troopers now began to chant all over Germany: "Hitler at the gates." The führer himself was supremely confident, telling the editor of the *Leipziger Neueste Nachrichten* on May 4 that he would

> thump the drum until Germany wakes up.... They call me a stateless corporal and a housepainter. Is there anything improper in having earned one's daily bread by manual labor?... The day of reckoning is not far off. An increasing number of industrialists, financiers, intellectuals and officers are now looking for a man who will at last bring some order into affairs at home, who will draw the farmers, the workers and the officials into the German community once more.[23]

In the summer of 1931 Hitler thumped the financial drum by going on a fund-raising tour to convince big business to support the Nazi Party.[24] Although he did not succeed in raising a great deal of money, he was able to make contact with some very influential people in the business community.[25] In July he had an interview with Hugenberg at Berlin;

he then meet with Franz Seldte and Theodor Duesterberg, the two chief leaders of the paramilitary Stahlhelm, and agreed to join them in their new "National Opposition" against the government. Shortly afterward, he met with General Schleicher and von Hammerstein, while also communicating with Brüning and again rejecting the government's offer for cooperation.

Then on September 18, 1931, a seminal event occurred in Hitler's private life that almost wrecked his political career — the suicide of his niece Geli Raubal in the apartment they shared on Prinzregentenstrasse in Munich. For some time now Hitler had developed an infatuation for his niece Geli, smothering her with a surfeit of attention that at once delighted and frightened the young woman. Although Hanfstaengl referred to Geli as "an empty-headed slut,"[26] the truth is that she was simply a pretty, uncomplicated, vivacious, and immature young woman who fantasized about being the center of attention in the world of the rich and famous. Initially awe-struck by her uncle's influence and power, she increasingly resented his overbearing demands, which made her feel like an enslaved prisoner. From the available evidence it is also quite clear that this was no ordinary uncle-niece relationship but a sexual liaison of some sort.[27]

Although we will never know the real story behind their relationship, we do know that Geli was one of the few people who succeeded in touching Hitler's inner being and breaking down his artificial defenses, making him more human but therefore also more vulnerable. While in her company, Hitler showed qualities that he otherwise despised in himself and others — softness, gentleness, relaxation, spontaneous joy, and empathy. Even his warped sense of masculinity, which he had elevated into a personal religion, was temporarily suspended in her company; but in the end his love for her was not strong enough to change it. It did not take Geli very long to recognize that her uncle was robbing her of her own will and purpose, and that under his oppressive control she would never have a life of her own. She may have even overreacted to Hitler's jealous control with brazen promiscuity with Hitler's staff, including Emil Maurice, while at the same time flying into rages about Hitler's developing romance with Eva Braun.

On the morning of September 17, 1931, as Hitler was about to leave on an election tour, Geli had a final confrontation with her uncle, demanding that he allow her to go to Vienna, ostensibly for further voice training but more probably to resume a relationship with a young artist — a relationship that Hitler, with the connivance of his half-sister Angela (Geli's mother), had managed to undermine.[28] Hitler was adamant and forbade her to go to Vienna. It was probably a combination of Hitler's oppressive control and the feelings of shame she had buried in herself regarding their sexual liaison that drove her to suicide. On the night of September 17 Geli locked herself in her room and killed herself with Hitler's pistol. The next morning, September 18, Hitler received the shattering news, hurried back to Munich, and was so disconsolate in his grief that close friends feared that he might take his own life.

The Geli Raubal affair is significant for several reasons. First, it represents another turning point in Hitler's private life, reinforcing his warped sense of masculinity with corresponding attitudes of hardness and brutality. His belief that a great man must never show any feelings, towering serenely above the grey mass of ordinary people, appeared validated and was now easier for him to follow in the wake of the one woman, next to his mother, whom he really loved. Although Hitler's grief was intense, as is to be expected in such an explosive personality, it was not the sort of grief that led to insight or positive change. He turned Geli's memory into an unwholesome cult, which included sealing off her room and transforming it into a personal shrine. He grasped at every straw of evidence that might suggest that her death was not a suicide but a tragic accident. Possibly to atone for his guilt in her death, he became a confirmed vegetarian who never touched meat again. The second major reason for the profound importance of this event is that it briefly illuminated Hitler's obscure, secretive, and possibly aberrant private life. It is for this reason that Hitler and his trusted entourage immediately moved to hush it up by every possible means — they feared it might reveal too much about the real Hitler behind the carefully constructed image of him as a charismatic "leader-pope." Franz Gürtner, among others, sprang into action and succeeded not only in controlling ugly rumors but also in preventing a public investigation of the whole mysterious affair. Geli was secretly buried in Vienna out of harm's way without an inquest or a coroner's report.

In sum, Hitler's treatment of his niece provides us with important insights that go far beyond a sordid private scandal. It reveals, in miniature, what Germany, Hitler's future bride, could expect from a liaison with this man. The Geli Raubal affair, in other words, gives us a snapshot of Hitler's relationship with women, revealing once more his inability to form loving ties and his obsessive-compulsive need to dominate and control everyone. Although there would be other women in his life, Hitler was unable to sustain any single loving relationship because his capacity for hate, including self-hate, was far stronger than his ability for love. Deep down, he feared women for wielding seductive powers that threatened his exaggerated sense of manhood. Perhaps this is why he wanted his ideal woman to be "a cute cuddly naive little thing — tender, sweet, and stupid."[29] If the record is any indication, Hitler was not able to love a woman in a normal physical and emotional sense. Of the women he knew intimately, seven tried to commit suicide and four actually succeeded in killing themselves.[30]

If these facts about Hitler had been publicly known, the full extent of his destructive and deviant tendencies been widely circulated, his career would have come to an abrupt halt. As it was, he succeeded in drawing

a veil of secrecy around his obscure Austrian background and his erratic
private life. Nothing was allowed to penetrate the public persona — not
Geli's death; not insinuations, even by his own relatives, that he might
have Jewish blood in his veins; not rumors about his abnormal sexual
relations; not even stories about his real relationships with women. Any
signs that did not fit the emerging führer image were omitted, removed,
or appropriately sanitized. Germans did not even know of the existence
of Eva Braun until the end of World War II because Hitler tried to foster
the legend that Germany was his only bride.

Only three weeks after Geli's suicide, Hitler had his first meeting with
President Hindenburg. It went poorly. Accompanied by Göring, who
had abandoned his dying wife, Karin, in Sweden to make the meeting,
Hitler felt ill at ease in the company of a man who embodied an important part of German history and resented being lectured to by a former
corporal from what he mistakenly regarded as Bohemia. After the meeting Hindenburg told his entourage: "This Bohemian corporal wants to
become Reich chancellor? Never! At most he could be my Postmaster
General. Then he can lick me on the stamps from behind."[31]

A day later, on October 11, 1931, Hitler attended a huge rally,
staged by various formations of the right-wing "National Opposition,"
at Bad Harzburg in Brunswick. Hitler was distinctly uncomfortable in
the company of prominent army officers, industrialists, and members
of the former ruling houses who had gathered there in opposition to
the republic and its policies. Sullen and uncooperative, he turned down
Hugenberg's invitation for dinner and left the rostrum shortly after his
SA formations had passed by in review.

A week after the Harzburg meeting Hitler presided over a far more
satisfying occasion — a big rally in Brunswick that lasted six hours and
featured close to one hundred thousand SA men from northern Germany. Hitler was in good fettle. The party was on the march. By the end
of 1931, it had risen to 800,000 members. The SA numbered 225,000
and the SS 15,000. In addition, the party controlled thirty-six newspapers with a circulation of 431,000 readers. Landtag elections in the
State of Hesse on November 15, 1931, gave the Nazis 37 percent of the
vote and twenty-seven out of seventy mandates in the state legislature.

However, Hitler's boast at the Brunswick rally that the party was
within a meter of its goal was too optimistic. The road to power, as
it would turn out, was going to be longer and harder. Shortly after the
Brunswick rally, the Hesse authorities came into possession of highly
compromising Nazi documents drafted by the Hesse *Gauleitung* at a
farmstead, the Boxheimer Hof, outlining the emergency measures that
were to be put in operation when the Nazis came to power. Given to the
chief of the Frankfurt police by a Nazi renegade, these "Boxheim" documents revealed to the public what might be in store for Germans once
the Nazis had seized power: tight totalitarian control, seizure of state
ministries by the SA, and death penalties for a variety of infractions.[32]

Although Hitler penalized the Hesse *Gauleitung* and disavowed all personal knowledge, his fury was motivated by the embarrassing public exposure rather than the content of the documents itself.[33] Being on the verge of success, Hitler could ill afford revelations of the truth. The illusions of the path of legality had to be maintained at all costs. Important sections of German society — the military, the civil service, business — had to be carefully stroked into seeing National Socialism as the only vital alternative to the political left.

On January 8, 1932, Joseph Goebbels noted in his dairy that "the chess game for power has begun,"[34] a judgment that was certainly vindicated by subsequent events. The year 1932 was densely packed with momentous events, but the real chess moves — the ones that would propel Hitler into power — took place behind the scenes in government offices or private drawing rooms. Hitler turned out to be a superb chess player on both the public and the private level; and when the year was over, his goal of checkmating his opponents was within his grasp.

On January 27, 1932, Hitler addressed the Industry Club of Düsseldorf, whose wealthy members included some of the most powerful businessmen in Germany. Appearing in a dark suit and playing the role of a conservative nationalist, Hitler gave one of his most convincing performances. Many businessmen in the audience heard him speak for the first time and expected a clumsy pitch by a reputed lower-class agitator. They were in for a complete surprise. After breaking down their mental resistance with long-winded philosophical observations, Hitler followed through with scare tactics that were bound to perk up the interest of his listeners. He evoked the fear of the Communist bogeyman and warned that 50 percent of all Germans were leaning toward Communism. If the National Socialist movement did not exist, he reminded them, the German middle class would already be history.[35] His party, he insinuated, stood for the same productive values that had made German big business, and therefore Germany, great, namely, hard work, competition, struggle, and individual merit. He opposed the political left for its levelling principles, its degradation of great personalities or achievers. The greatness of a people, he said, does not consist in the sum of its achievement but rather in the sum of its supreme achievements (*Spitzenleistungen*).[36] This is exactly what his audience wanted to hear. He was not ashamed, he said, to be a mere drummer for a nationalistic Germany, for it is a far more statesmanlike achievement to drum once more into the German people a new faith than gradually to squander the only faith they have. His final appeal to a revitalized national faith was received with "stormy, long-sustained applause."[37] Absent from his speech were anti-Semitic and anticapitalist admonitions; even his usual stock-in-trade slogans were suitably moderated.

The business moguls were impressed, but not enough to loosen their purse strings, as many traditional accounts of this meeting have claimed. As Henry Turner has shown, Hitler had gained an entrée into big business but not a source of free-flowing funds.[38] His aim, in any case, had never been to turn big businessmen into confirmed Nazis; his aim was a more modest and realizable one, namely, to neutralize their influence on other sections of the political right. Given the radical nature of his movement, including its Socialist elements, Hitler had to steer clear from too close of an embrace with big business if he wanted to avoid alienating those elements of the working class who were receptive to his nationalistic message. On the other hand, he needed big business for financial and political reasons. It was a fine balancing act that called for subtle political skills.

The year 1932 would test Hitler's political skills on many occasions, especially in the public limelight. There were no less than five grueling elections in 1932 — four Reichstag elections and one important state election in Prussia — exerting further strains on the democratic process at a time when most German voters were more concerned with the cancerous growth of unemployment than the electoral process. By the end of the year German voters were thoroughly tired of the machinations of parties, the dissimulations of politicians, and the whole democratic process itself. They longed for an end to the political squabbles; and sadly, many Germans now looked to the Nazis to liberate them from further political involvement. As one perceptive observer put it:

> National Socialism was a revulsion by my friends against parliamentary politics, parliamentary debate, parliamentary government — against all the higgling and the haggling of the parties, their coalitions, their confusions, and their connivings. It was the final fruit of the common man's repudiation of "the rascals." Its motif was, "Throw them all out."[39]

President Hindenburg's term of office was scheduled to expire on May 5, 1932. It took considerable pressure by his immediate entourage to persuade the eighty-four-year-old president, now in failing health and showing disturbing signs of senility, to run again for public office for the good of the fatherland. The old man at first demurred, citing old age and failing vigor, but eventually saw merit in the argument that he was probably the last bulwark against political anarchy. However, his hope to be spared another election was dashed when Brüning failed to gain the support of the Reichstag for his plan to extend the president's term of office without new elections. Accordingly, Germans geared up for a major presidential election, to be held on March 13, 1932. The Communists fielded their leader Ernst Thälmann, a former transportation worker and dedicated Moscow operative for Joseph Stalin, while the nationalists chose Theodor Duesterberg, second-in-command of the paramilitary Stahlhelm. It was not until three weeks before the elections were scheduled that a fourth candidate stepped forward — Adolf Hitler. As previously mentioned, Hitler had been a "stateless" person since 1925 and was therefore ineligible for public office unless he obtained German citizenship. He did this by first finding a law that stated that

Reich citizenship was automatically conferred on all those who held a state citizenship. Next, on February 26, Hitler finagled an appointment for himself as a councillor (*Regierungsrat*) in the Nazi-controlled State of Brunswick; because the appointment automatically carried with it citizenship in that state, Hitler was now also a full-fledged citizen of the Reich.

The campaign was bitter and divisive. Hitler toured Germany by car from one end to the other, promising to wage a campaign "such as the world has never seen before." His stamina was remarkable. In fact, during 1932 he gave a total of 209 public speeches, something no candidate has ever done before or since.[40] Fifty thousand phonograph records of Hitler's speeches were made and distributed; propaganda movies were quickly unloaded on theater owners throughout Germany. Joseph Goebbels, who had been the driving force behind Hitler's effort to run for the presidency, brought out a special illustrated magazine highlighting the campaign issues. Needless to say, columns of the SA marched up and down the streets of Germany singing, chanting, brawling, and drowning the country in a sea of posters and banners.

Despite such unparalleled agitation, which dwarfed anything the opposition was able to muster, Hindenburg won an impressive victory over Hitler on March 13, 1932. The aging president received 18,651,497 votes (49.7 percent), while Hitler garnered 11,339,446 votes (30.2 percent). Thälmann, the Communist candidate, received 4,983,341 (13.3 percent) and Duesterberg 2,547,729 (6.8 percent). Since Hindenburg had not received the necessary majority, the constitution called for a runoff election that would decide the issue by a simple plurality.

Thus, a second election was scheduled for April 10. In view of the violent intensity of the last campaign, the government limited actual campaigning to only one week (April 3–10), making it difficult for Hitler to marshal the full force of his movement. However, Hitler managed to use the short time available to him in a very effective and clever manner: he chartered a plane and, accompanied by a carefully picked entourage that included Schreck, Schaub, Brückner, Hanfstaengl, Dietrich, and Hoffmann, he began his famous "flights over Germany," visiting twenty-one cities in just one week.[41]

These grandstanding gestures brought much publicity, but they did not bring electoral victory. Hindenburg won 19,359,983 votes (53 percent), while Hitler came in a strong second with 13,418,547 (36.8 percent) votes. Hindenburg had gained more than one-half of the votes and was reelected for another seven years, although few expected him to live out the full tenure of his office. Hitler had received more than a third of the votes — an impressive achievement — but it now appeared that his popularity had reached its peak. Gregor Strasser, among others, warned Hitler that the party had reached its apex and that Hitler should therefore abandon his "all or nothing" tactics in favor of a more conciliatory approach, perhaps involving cooperation with other parties. He also advised Hitler to concentrate more on rationalizing the party bureaucracy and strengthening its grassroots organizations, the *Gaue*, as well as improving the channels of communications between the *Reichsleitung* and the many local units of the party throughout Germany.

Strasser was not the only one who sensed that the Nazis were unlikely to gain power quickly by electoral victories. Three days after the presidential elections (April 13), the Reich government seized the opportunity to regain political control by outlawing the SA and SS, including the Hitler Youth, and prohibiting the wearing of uniforms by any political group. Members of the government, notably Groener and Brüning, had looked aghast for some time at the spectacle of civil disorders tearing apart the fabric of the nation. These civil disorders were largely the result of what Peter Merkl has aptly called the "ignorant armies of the night," well-armed paramilitary organizations of close to five million spanning the whole political spectrum and raising a constant hue and cry against the republic.[42] No state can tolerate within itself competing armies and still hope to survive. Groener's ban against the SA was therefore a sound first step, but for political reasons it did not go far enough because it did not outlaw other paramilitary organizations such as the Reichsbanner, the Stahlhelm, and the Eiserne Front. Moreover, little did Groener suspect how unpopular the ban against the SA would turn out to be among the very group that he thought might welcome it most — the military. The majority of the officers opposed the ban, and Schleicher, forever ready to fish in troubled political waters, began to whisper into Hindenburg's ear that the ban was a mistake and that Groener should be replaced. Schleicher also enjoyed informing Hindenburg about Groener's private life — the fact that the sixty-two-year-old general had recently married his much younger secretary, and that their new baby boy, born only a few months after the marriage, was widely called "Nurmi," in honor of the famous Finnish sprinter.

By this time Schleicher was also creeping in the company of all sorts of intriguers, including Röhm; Count Wolf Heinrich Helldorf, a renegade noble and since 1931 leader of the Berlin SA; and other high-ranking Nazis. On April 22 and again on May 8 Schleicher saw Hitler and outlined the shabby intrigues he was planning against Brüning's government. The government was to fall piecemeal, starting with Groener. His dismissal, in turn, would serve as a catalyst for the fall of Brüning himself. With this accomplished, a presidential cabinet would be assembled, the Reichstag dismissed, and the prohibition against the SA would be rescinded. The cleverness by which these secret machinations were conducted surprised even Goebbels, who noted in his diary how happy he felt that nobody had the slightest inkling about these plans, least of all Brüning himself.[43]

As Groener's future was hanging in the balance, Hitler did his best to prevent his restless SA forces, now estimated at four hundred thousand, from getting out of control and challenging the ban on the streets of

Germany. He swore them to observe the party's oath of legality, referred to SA members as party comrades (*Parteigenossen*), and reminded them that the "day of revenge" was just around the corner in the impending state elections of April 24.[44]

However, Hitler's hope of conquering the Reich government by capturing control over the individual state governments turned out to be as misplaced as his earlier plan to seize control of the top through the office of the presidency. The outcome of the state elections was quite similar to that of the second presidential election. The Nazis gained a leading position in all states except Bavaria, but they were unable to capture sole control of any major German state. They participated in the governments of Anhalt, Brunswick, Thuringia, Mecklenburg-Strelitz, and Thuringia. As a result of later state elections, they would gain sole control of the small governments of Oldenburg and Mecklenburg-Schwerin. In the State of Prussia, where three-fifths of the German people resided, the ruling SPD government of Otto Braun was badly mauled by spectacular Nazi gains and could maintain itself in power only as a caretaker government until a majority could be obtained in a runoff election.[45] As in many other state governments, the Nazis on the right and the Communists on the left controlled a majority of mandates, effectively paralyzing the democratic process by preventing the formation of a viable republican coalition. In other words, the "Nazicommunists" were holding the nation at ransom.[46]

On May 10, 1932, during the first session of the reconvened Reichstag, Groener rose to rebut an angry attack Göring had launched against the SA ban. Although Groener scored some valid points against "the state within a state," he was constantly hissed and shouted down by noisy delegates from the right, causing him to lose the thread of his argument and fumble so badly that he was reduced to a confused, nervous wreck. Even his friends were embarrassed for him, and Goebbels later gleefully wrote in his diary: "Such an example of incompetence and impotence was never before seen. We covered him with such catcalls that the whole house began to tremble and shake with laughter. In the end one could have only pity for him. That man is finished. He sang his own requiem."[47] Goebbels was right. After Schleicher brutally informed his former mentor that he no longer enjoyed the support of the Reichswehr, Groener resigned on May 13.

Schleicher's next victim was Brüning, whose government was hanging on the thin thread of Hindenburg's support. The "Hunger Chancellor" was still stubbornly pursuing his conservative retrenchment policies; but far from improving Germany's dire economic situation, the measures he chose to mend the economy were self-defeating and contradictory. By raising taxes, cutting wages, and slashing government spending, he discouraged investments, undermined the creation of new jobs, lowered consumer spending, and further fueled unemployment and public suffering. The impact of these policies continued to be devastating, especially on the unemployed. At the time of the Nazi upsurge in September 1930, there were roughly 3 million unemployed; one year later, that figure had risen to 4.35 million; and in 1932, it stood at 5.1 million.[48] Brüning blamed the depression on reparations and hoped that his government would be able to convince the Western powers to abolish them. Much of his efforts were therefore directed toward foreign policy, but these efforts did not come to fruition until reparations were abolished in July 1932 — too late to benefit the Brüning government. At any rate, reparations were only part of Germany's economic problems. Brüning accomplished nothing in dealing with these problems; on the contrary, he exacerbated them by a dogged pursuit of self-defeating remedies without a mandate from anyone other than a mercurial and senile president who was about to cave in to Brüning's enemies.

It was again General Schleicher who sang loudest in this chorus of Brüning detractors. Schleicher warned Hindenburg that Brüning was a weak leader because he had failed miserably in containing the radicals on both the right and the left; he also insinuated that the chancellor was becoming too socialistic. The industrialists had already bitterly complained about Brüning's labor minister, Adam Stegerwald, whose prounion background and policies they condemned as antibusiness. Brüning also faced determined opposition from East Elbian landowners who were greatly dependent on government subsidies and now feared that their subventions might be either severely cut or abolished altogether, resulting in massive bankruptcies. Since 1930 the government had poured millions of marks into *Osthilfe* (eastern aid) in order to strengthen eastern agriculture. A substantial portion of this money, however, was syphoned off by a few greedy landowners who proceeded to buy yachts, luxury cars, new homes, and horses or gamble away large sums in the casinos of Monte Carlo. Now that Brüning threatened to break up their crooked game, many of these Prussian landowners went crying, first to Oskar Hindenburg and through him to his father, President Hindenburg himself. As mentioned earlier, it turned out that President von Hindenburg had just recently become a Prussian landowner himself. Although the Hindenburgs came from an old Prussian family, they did not own any land. After Hindenburg became president, a group of prominent East Elbian Junkers decided to tie Hindenburg more closely to their vested interests by persuading several industrialists to underwrite the purchase of a large estate at Neudeck in West Prussia. On Hindenburg's eightieth birthday they presented this estate to the old soldier on behalf of a "grateful nation." Few people, however, knew that this estate was actually deeded to Hindenburg's son Oskar for the express purpose of evading inheritance taxes after the death of Hindenburg Sr.

It is difficult to determine to what extent Hindenburg's recent and financially dubious elevation to the ranks of the landed gentry influenced his decision making in the *Osthilfe* scandals or the dismissal of

Brüning. The old man had never really liked Brüning because of his aloof manners and his Catholicism. He also blamed his chancellor somewhat irrationally for failing to extend his presidential term of office, thus forcing him twice into a humiliating popularity contest with a Communist (Thälmann) and a Bohemian corporal (Hitler). Although he had won this contest, Hindenburg knew that a large number of Germans had voted against him, including the citizens of Tannenberg and the Masurian Lake district, where he had won his legendary victories in World War I.

By the end of May, Hindenburg had made up his mind to get rid of Brüning. The chancellor, lulled by favorable signs abroad, had no inkling what was in store for him. On May 29, 1932, Brüning was summoned to a meeting with Hindenburg and told in a harsh tone of voice that no further emergency decrees or cabinet changes would be approved because the present government was unpopular. When Brüning recovered from the shock, he asked whether this meant that the president wanted the cabinet to resign. The old man replied: "Yes, this government must go because it is unpopular."[49] There were no thanks or regrets. The interview was over. Next day, May 30, Brüning tendered his resignation, though strictly speaking the president had no authority to dismiss the chancellor. Brüning could have gone to the Reichstag and appealed for support. Instead, he saw himself as serving Hindenburg, his idol and substitute monarch, and was so stunned by his cruel dismissal that he saw no other course of action but to resign along with his whole cabinet. As Golo Mann put it, "He was dismissed because he felt himself dismissed; the ex-lieutenant felt that he could not remain in command if the Field-Marshal did not wish him to remain."[50]

The Papen and Schleicher Periods

In picking a successor to Brüning, President von Hindenburg relied again on the dubious advice of Schleicher, who had persuaded him that Franz von Papen (1879–1969) was the best man for the post. Most Germans had trouble placing the new chancellor's name, and the *Frankfurter Zeitung* was not exaggerating when it reported that Papen's appearance would cause widespread "rubbing of the eyes." The new chancellor came from an ancient Westphalian family of aristocrats and followed in his father's footsteps by joining the Westphalian Fifth Uhlan Regiment as a cadet. His military career was unremarkable, but his charm and conviviality opened important doors to success. In 1911 he became a general staff officer and in the autumn of 1914 he received a post as military attaché in Washington, D.C. While attached to the German embassy in Washington, his natural proclivities for intrigue got him involved in espionage activities. In 1916 he was expelled from the United States for sabotage, and on his way to Germany he carelessly carried secret documents with him that were seized by the British. He spent the rest of the war primarily as chief of staff with the Turkish Fourth Army in Palestine. After the war, he resigned his commission and entered politics as a member of the Center Party's right wing representing the agrarian interests of his constituency in the Prussian Landtag (1920–32).

The new chancellor's natural habitat was that of the old aristocratic elite — exclusive clubs, hunting events, social functions for the rich and famous. Papen was a passionate and skillful equestrian and a leading voice of the conservative Herrenklub, whose influential members of industrialists, military officers, politicians, and high-ranking civil servants had their club rooms in the Friedrich-Ebert-Strasse just opposite the Reichstag. Papen was also coeditor of the Catholic newspaper *Germania,* mouthpiece of conservative and monarchist views.

Intellectually, the new chancellor was bereft of any realistic plans for solving Germany's staggering socioeconomic problems, other than proposing to form a solid block of upper-middle-class interests against the forces of the left. Since Papen was a clever socialite whose network of acquaintances gave him access to a host of different interests — higher clergy, military leaders, industrialists, landed aristocracy, intellectuals — Schleicher concluded that the new chancellor might be able to neutralize the left and perhaps even co-opt the better elements of the Nazi movement. In addition, Papen was a witty and amusing raconteur — qualities that endeared him to Hindenburg, who affectionately took to calling him by the diminutive "Fränzchen."

Many thoughtful Germans, however, were shocked by the appointment of Papen; they could not help but wonder about a system that had given them a series of undistinguished and unrepresentative leaders. The chancellors of the 1920s, with the exception of Stresemann, had been grey, colorless, flat, and eminently forgettable. Brüning had been a bony ascetic with little parliamentary standing. Papen was worse: he was fatuous, pretentious, intellectually empty, and enjoyed no parliamentary support whatsoever. The French ambassador, André François-Poncet, famous for his astute and pithy maxims about various political characters, informed his government shortly after Papen's appointment that the new chancellor "enjoyed the peculiarity of being taken seriously by neither his friends nor his enemies. He gave the impression of an incorrigible levity of which he was never able to rid himself.... He was reputed to be superficial, blundering, untrue, ambitious, vain, crafty and an intriguer."[51] These negative qualities, well known to most insiders, did not seem to have worried the wire-puller behind the scenes, General Schleicher, who brushed off the objection by a close friend that Papen did not have a strong head by saying: "He doesn't have to have. He's a hat!"[52]

The dashing Papen immediately went to work and assembled a cabinet of aristocratic top hats so unrepresentative that it was dubbed the "cabinet of barons," for five of its members were aristocrats and two were industrialists. Schleicher, who had jobbed Papen into power, took over the Ministry of Defense. Papen had as little backing and even less popular support than Brüning. Worse, he had undermined his own standing with the Center Party, whose leader, Monsignor Ludwig Kaas, was outraged by the manner in which Brüning had been treated and was also offended by Papen's acceptance of the chancellorship after having been personally assured by him that he would not succeed Brüning. Thus, having no standing with his own party, facing the hostility of the whole left, and enjoying, at best, lukewarm support from the nationalists, Papen's government was almost entirely at the mercy of the president. The Nazis temporarily agreed to support Papen provided that he rescinded the ban against the SA, dissolved the Reichstag, and called for new elections.

On June 4, 1932, Papen dissolved the Reichstag and scheduled new elections for July 31. On June 15, he lifted the ban on the SA. This is precisely what Hitler had been counting on. He knew that Papen would never be anything more than an interim chancellor who would pave the way for his own candidature. The general mood in the Nazi movement was cheerful, and everyone looked forward to the coming elections. Goebbels noted in his diary that plans for the election had been so meticulously worked out that one only needed to push the button and the avalanche would begin to roll.[53] Indeed, with the lifting of the SA ban the streets of Germany were once more in the hands of the storm troopers, who clashed with their opposition in such violent encounters that a virtual state of siege existed in much of Germany. To the Communist catcall: "If you don't want to be a brother of mine, I'll kick your head in," the Nazis replied: "SA marches! Clear the streets! Croak the Jew!" The storm troopers positively relished the idea of seeing blood flow in profusion, singing:

> Blut muss fliessen, Blut muss fliessen!
> Blut muss fliessen Knüppelhageldick!
> Haut'se doch zusammen, haut'se doch zusammen
> Diese gottverdammte Juden-Republik!
>
> [Blood must flow, Blood must flow!
> Blood must flow as cudgel thick as hail!
> Let's smash it up, Let's smash it up
> That god-damned Jewish Republic!]

Not surprisingly, such incendiary rhetoric resulted in blood flowing in the streets of Germany in the summer of 1932. During the first three weeks of June there were 461 clashes in the State of Prussia alone, as a result of which eighty-two people died. It would be misleading to blame the Nazis for all of these excesses, for the Communists held their own in these street battles. As Arthur Koestler remembered:

> During that long, stifling summer of 1932 we fought our ding-dong battles with the Nazis. Hardly a day passed without one or two dead in

Berlin. The main battlefields were the *Bierstuben,* the smoky little taverns of the working-class districts. Some of these served as meeting-places for the Nazis, some as meeting-places (*Verkehrslokale*) for us. To enter the wrong pub was to venture into the enemy lines. From time to time the Nazis would shoot up one of our *Verkehrslokale.* It was done in the classic Chicago tradition: a gang of SA men would drive slowly past the tavern, firing through the glass-panes, then vanish at breakneck speed. We had far fewer motorcars than the Nazis, and retaliation was mostly carried out in cars either stolen or borrowed from sympathizers. The men who did these jobs were members of the RFB, the League of Communist War Veterans. My car was sometimes borrowed by comrades whom I had never seen before, and returned a few hours later with no questions asked or explanations offered.... The RFB who came to fetch the car for their guerilla expeditions were sometimes rather sinister types from the Berlin underworld.... Once the RFB men who came to fetch the car disguised themselves in my flat before starting out. They stuck on mustaches, put on glasses, dark jackets and bowler hats. I watched them from the window driving off — four stately, bowler-hatted gents in the ridiculous little red car, looking like a party in a funeral procession.[54]

One of the bloodiest clashes, appropriately called "Bloody Sunday," took place on July 17, 1932, when the Nazis invaded the predominantly Communist-controlled areas of Altona, a working-class community lying just to the west of Hamburg. The Communists fired on the marching Nazis and their police escort from windows and rooftops. The marchers, in turn, fired back. At least seventeen people, including several policemen, were killed. Such were the consequences of Papen's policy of lifting the ban on the murderous SA.

The self-deluded chancellor, however, drew the opposite conclusion, invoking the Communist bogeyman and blaming the state government of Prussia, especially its police force, for being unable to maintain law and order. Using "Bloody Sunday" as a pretext, Papen moved against the Social Democratic caretaker government of Otto Braun and Carl Severing. Invoking Article 48 of the Weimar Constitution, Hindenburg authorized Papen to assume the role of Reich commissioner for Prussia, depose Braun and his ministers, and replace them with his own appointees.

The Prussian Landtag, as previously mentioned, had been as hopelessly paralyzed by the recent elections as the Reichstag, making it impossible to form a stable, republican government. The Nazis and the Communists exercised a powerful stranglehold on the Landtag and reduced its proceedings to a complete mockery. On May 24, the day the Landtag was reconvened, Braun announced the resignation of his government. The next day, the Prussian parliament elected the Nazi Hanns Kerrl as its new president. It was during this session that a wild brawl broke out between the Nazis and Communists, with the numerically larger Nazis beating the Communists out of the assembly and celebrating their victory by singing the Horst Wessel song.[55] Although Braun continued as a shadow caretaker until elections could be held to elect a new minister president, he was so disillusioned and disgusted by the antics of the Nazicommunists that he refused to enter the Landtag again, later admitting that his nerves had snapped.[56] In the meantime, the gridlock continued, and pressing government business suffered. Interestingly enough, the same gridlock existed in other German states — Bavaria, Saxony, Württemberg, Hesse, Hamburg, attesting to the failure of parliamentary government on the state as well as the federal level.

On July 20, 1932, Papen moved quickly and unilaterally and deposed the Braun government. Papen assumed executive powers in Prussia as *Reichkommissar,* appointing Franz Bracht as his chief deputy with authority to take over the Prussian Ministry of the Interior. General Rundstedt imposed martial law on Greater Berlin and Brandenburg and moved to take over the Berlin police force, arresting its police president, Albert Grzesinski, and his deputy Bernhard Weiss, whom Goebbels and the Nazis had been lambasting for years as the Jew "Isidor Weiss."[57] Papen cited three reasons for his action: the Prussian police had failed to preserve law and order, the leadership of the police had been lax and uncoordinated, and the Prussian government had lost the confidence of the people. The first two reasons were false and therefore did not justify federal intervention. The third was true but also did not merit federal action. The truth is that Papen and his reactionary henchmen had despised the Social Democratic government of Braun from the beginning and used this opportunity to get rid of it. Papen later nonchalantly wrote off the whole affair as a reasonable act of statesmanship rather than a coup d'état or an act of violence, arguing that the decree was really aimed at the Communists because "they were in a key position and had acquired a dominant role in Prussian affairs."[58] Such insulting logic, gliding annoyingly over the fact that the Nazis controlled the Landtag and the Reichstag, cannot conceal the obvious, namely, that Papen's actions played straight into the hands of the Nazis because it eliminated the strongest republican party from its major seat of power and also set the stage for the eventual *Gleichschaltung* (coordination of power) that was to come eight months later under the Nazis. Hitler was only too happy to let Papen do his dirty work for him and begin the process of disassembling the democratic state.

Papen was right in one respect: his coup did not end the Weimar coalition in Prussia.[59] The German voters were responsible for that. The Social Democrats also share some blame for meekly accepting this constitutional outrage. The best they could do was to initiate a futile legal action with the Supreme Court that dragged on for three months, ending in a two-faced decision that questioned the legal propriety of the action but refused to change the new arrangement. The major reason why the Social Democratic leaders did not take decisive action in the form of mustering their paramilitary formations or calling a general strike is that they were exhausted by years of political struggles and genuinely feared the prospect of civil war. Facing the Reich government, supported by the Reichswehr, along with the hostility of all the right-wing parties and their howling newspapers, the Social Democrats had no real supporters. Braun went on "sick leave," and the other leaders of the SPD drew in their horns, gradually fading from the political scene and ending up either in exile or in Nazi concentration camps.

After July 20, 1932, the coming of some kind of authoritarian government was inevitable; it was simply a question of from which end of the political spectrum it would be mounted and the degree of coercion it would involve. Few astute observers expected the likelihood of a left-wing dictatorship of the proletariat. The German left was deeply at odds with itself and could neither cooperate politically nor make its rigid Socialist ideology compelling to the majority of the German people. In 1932 most Germans still lived in small cities and rural areas. They were a markedly conservative people with strong right-wing ideologies. Communism could have succeeded only if the German people had been chafing under severe conditions of economic and political oppression. Only Communist wishful thinking, however, could view Germany, for all its economic problems, as a country of exploited peasants or workers. A coal miner turned Nazi expressed it succinctly when he wondered why "socialism had to be tied up with internationalism — why it couldn't work as well or better in conjunction with nationalism,"[60] a sentiment echoed by a railroad employee who remarked that "the slogan 'Workers of the World Unite!' made no sense to me. At the same time, however, National Socialism, with its promise of a community of blood, barring all class struggle, attracted me profoundly."[61]

Eleven days after Papen's coup against the Prussian government, the country's democratic future received another staggering blow in the election of July 31, 1932. The Nazis pulled off a stunning victory, polling 13.7 million popular votes and receiving 230 seats in the Reichstag, thus replacing the SPD as the largest party in Germany. The two other major antirepublican parties, the Communists and the nationalists, also gained heavily, making it impossible to form a workable coalition government. The three major antidemocratic parties — Nazis, nationalists, and Communists — now controlled 356 seats or more than one-half of the total 608 seats in the German Reichstag.

Since the Nazis were now the largest party in the Reichstag, it became clear to both their friends and enemies that they could not be excluded from some or even all share in governing Germany. For the next six months the conservative clique around the president tried to negotiate some kind of accommodation with Hitler that would stop just short of giving him the chancellorship or to fob him off with a few cabinet posts; but true to his ideological convictions, Hitler rejected all of these offers. He wanted everything or nothing. Sooner or later, he believed, the sheer gravitational pull of his movement would overwhelm all of his opponents. He knew that after the July elections the Papen government, or any similar government, not only lacked popular standing but could not even count upon firm support from the conservative right. Its only support, in fact, continued to be the approval of the president; but, as Brüning had discovered to his great disappointment, that support was precarious. Alan Bullock put Germany's dilemma in sharp relief when he said that "with a voting strength of 13,700,000 electors, a party membership of over a million and a private army of 400,000 S.A. and S.S., Hitler was the most powerful political leader in Germany, knocking on the doors of the Chancellery at the head of the most powerful political party Germany had ever seen."[62]

On August 5 Hitler met General Schleicher in Fürstenberg near Berlin and frankly told him what he wanted: the chancellorship for himself and three cabinet posts for his party (Interior, Justice, and Agriculture). In addition, Hitler wanted the premiership of Prussia and control over its Ministry of the Interior. Schleicher's attitude, though noncommittal, was friendly and encouraging, giving Hitler the impression that the general would use his influence to help him secure the chancellorship. On the morning of August 13, Hitler had a meeting with Schleicher and Papen that revealed that the conservative establishment was not quite ready to give Hitler what he wanted. When he heard that they were willing to give him only the vice-chancellorship along with the Prussian Ministry of the Interior, Hitler flew into a rage and shocked the two leaders with wild rantings about mowing down Marxists, staging a St. Bartholomew's Night, and setting his storm troopers loose for three days of freedom on the streets of Germany.[63] In the afternoon, Hindenburg summoned Hitler to a meeting at which Papen, Frick, and Röhm were also present and asked him if he was ready to join the existing government. Hitler replied that he would join the government only if he were given full control. Hindenburg not only rejected this proposal but also proceeded to give Hitler a stern dressing down, demanding from Hitler and the Nazis more respect for the constitution and more civilized treatment of their political opponents. The president's office followed this up by an immediate release of information about the meeting to the press, so that Germans could be reassured that the president would not hand over power to a man who wanted complete control of the state and had broken his previous promises of cooperation.[64] Hitler was humiliated, temporarily drew in his horns, and retired to the Obersalzberg to reflect on what he should do next.

On September 12, 1932, the Reichstag reconvened for a few turbulent hours. Even before it opened, Papen had already secured Hindenburg's approval for its dissolution, setting November 6 as the date for new elections. No sooner had the session begun than the leader of the Communists, Ernst Torgler, introduced a motion calling for a vote of no-confidence in the Papen government. Papen was visibly shaken; he had expected several days of debates on his economic program and therefore had not brought the necessary emergency papers that would authorize him to dissolve the Reichstag. Fortunately, Papen gained time when Wilhelm Frick rose on behalf of the Nazi delegation and asked for a half-hour's adjournment to confer with his deputies. This narrow breathing space allowed the frantic Papen to send a messenger to the Reich chancellery and obtain the documents.[65] When the session resumed, Papen waived his red dispatch case but was pointedly ignored by Hermann Göring, chairman of the Reichstag, who insisted on taking a vote on the motion of no-confidence introduced by Torgler. As the voting proceeded amid much merriment, the irate Papen slapped the decree on Göring's desk and, followed by his ministers, marched out of the Reichstag. The vote, however, continued amid gales of laughter from the benches. The final vote of 512 to 42 against the Papen government was moot from a legal point of view but devastating in its political implications because it showed how impotent German parliamentary government had become. German voters could be forgiven for being disgusted, for the Reichstag they had just elected lasted little more than a few hours. President Hindenburg, who was furious with Göring's behavior in the Reichstag, decisively rejected Göring's claim that the vote was legal since it was taken before the dissolution order was formally presented.

The dissolution of the Reichstag meant yet another election for a weary and disillusioned electorate. Even the Nazis had difficulty in maintaining the fever pitch of their previous efforts; they were also running desperately short of financial resources to wage the sort of campaigns they had been fighting throughout 1932. Dissenting voices in the party, notably Strasser, once again called for compromise, condemning Hitler's stubborn policy of "all or nothing." Papen, grasping at every straw, hoped that the Nazis would exhaust themselves in frequent elections, a danger that Goebbels himself had recognized earlier when he lamented that if the National Socialists did not come to power in the immediate future, they would win themselves to death in elections.[66]

There were, in fact, several encouraging signs that the Nazis not only had peaked in popularity but had overstepped the line of public decency to such an extent that many Germans were beginning to wonder whether they should ever be entrusted with political power. Probably the most revolting incident that revealed what many Nazis storm troopers were really like came on August 10 when five SA men broke into the home of a Communist in the village of Potempa in Upper Silesia and literally trampled him to death in plain sight of his horrified mother. Caught and sentenced to death, the five murderers were instantly elevated into martyrs by the Nazis, and Hitler himself sent the five condemned men a telegram, stating: "My Comrades! I am bound to you in unlimited loyalty in the face of this most hideous blood sentence. From this moment on your freedom is a question of honor for us. It is our responsibility to fight against the government which made this possible."[67] Some, like Harry Graf Kessler, were shocked not only by the despicable murder but even more by the prospect that the Nazis who were condoning it stood a real chance of running the government — a truly alarming prospect since it obviously implied that they would murder for the sake of their beliefs.[68]

The reputation of the Nazis had also been tarnished by Hitler's arrogant behavior with Hindenburg and by Göring's antics in the Reichstag on September 12. On November 2, shortly before the impending Reichstag election, the Nazis lost further public support when they combined with the Communists and approved a crippling strike by transport workers in Berlin.

Taken together these incidents would explain, in part, why the Nazis did not perform as well in the November 6 election as they had in the three previous elections. When the votes were in, Papen's strategy of weakening the Nazis in elections appeared to be partially vindicated. For the first time since September 1930, the Nazi tide was receding. The NSDAP lost two million votes and thirty-four Reichstag seats; its national standing declined from 37.4 percent to 33.1; percent and its representation in the Reichstag dropped from 230 to 196.

However, the November 6 elections had not resolved anything because the Nazis and the Communists were still controlling half of the Reichstag seats. Moreover, Papen's position was steadily deteriorating despite some encouraging successes his government had scored at the Lausanne Conference in June, which scrapped the Young plan and ended reparations. Papen's minority government was still despised and had virtually no support. After being stalemated by the refusal of the major parties to support his government, Papen resigned from his office on November 17, though he accepted Hindenburg's request to carry on for another two weeks until a new government could be formed.

On November 19 and 21 Hitler and Göring conducted confidential discussions with president Hindenburg about the possibility of a Hitler chancellorship. The old gentleman appears to have been willing to entertain the idea of appointing Hitler as chancellor, provided that he could form a workable majority in the Reichstag. Knowing that this would be difficult, if not impossible, Hitler countered with a proposal of governing the country as a presidential rather than a parliamentary chancellor, backed up by the same emergency powers as Papen. Through Meissner, Hindenburg later replied in writing that he could not accept Hitler's plan because "a presidential cabinet led by you would necessarily evolve into a one party dictatorship."[69]

The old president, bending like a willow back and forth under various prevailing winds, now turned again to Papen. During a decisive meeting on the evening of December 1, attended by Hindenburg, his son Oskar, State Secretary Meissner, Schleicher, and Papen, two opposing plans were proposed by Papen and Schleicher as to how the current impasse might be resolved. Papen's plan was the most radical because it called for a clear-cut break with the Weimar Constitution. Papen proposed to remain in office, eliminate the recalcitrant Reichstag, repress all political parties and interest groups by the Reichswehr and the police, and formulate a new constitution, to be ratified by either a plebiscite or a newly convened constituent assembly.[70] By contrast, Schleicher outlined a more moderate solution that, he felt, would avoid a violation of the constitution and the possibility of civil war that was entailed by Papen's plan. Schleicher tried to persuade the president that he could break the political stalemate by forming a grand coalition that would cut across the political spectrum, uniting moderate elements in the army, the bourgeois parties, the SPD, the unions, and even the moderate groups in the Nazi Party. He felt sure that he could split the ranks of the Nazis by involving Strasser and his people in his new government, thus defusing the threat posed by Hitler. When Papen objected that these machinations would amount to little more than a repetition of the failed policies of the past, the old man reluctantly threw his support behind Papen and asked him to form a new government.

Although Papen appeared to have won a victory with the old man, he was handed a stunning defeat the next morning (December 2) when his cabinet, whose members had been skillfully massaged for the past two weeks by Schleicher, refused to participate in a new Papen government on the grounds that its projected policies might cause serious public disorders, perhaps even civil war. The cabinet's opposition to Papen was clinched by a surprise Schleicherian move in the form of Lieutenant Colonel Eugen Ott, one of Schleicher's colleagues in the Defense Ministry, who informed the cabinet that a study just concluded, posing the question whether the Reichswehr was able in a state of emergency to counter the terror from both the right and the left, had shown that the army would be unable to cope with public disorders of the sort that had recently been provoked by the combined Nazi-Communist transportation strike. In the event of a simultaneous attack by Poland in the east, the Colonel added, the army would be completely helpless.[71]

Deserted by his whole cabinet, Papen rushed back to Hindenburg and whined that Schleicher had betrayed him, but the old man, tears in his eyes, told the flustered Papen that he had changed his mind in favor of Schleicher. Papen recalled the scene:

> "My dear Papen," he said, "you will not think much of me if I change my mind. But I am too old and have been through too much to accept the responsibility for civil war. Our only hope is to let Schleicher try his luck." Two great tears were rolling down his cheeks as I shook his hands and turned to go. Our months of co-operation were at an end. The measure of our mutual trust and confidence can perhaps be judged by the inscription on the photograph he sent me a few hours later as a parting present: *'Ich hatt' einen Kameraden!'*[72]

On December 2, 1932, Schleicher became chancellor, while at the same time retaining his post as minister of defense and automatically inheriting Papen's position as Reich commissioner for Prussia. Few German military leaders had ever enjoyed so much power, but in this case it had been acquired at great cost and at the expense of a long line of victims — Müller, Groener, Brüning, and Papen. Now that the scheming *Schreibtischoffizier* was out in the open playing field, he soon discovered that his influence did not reach very far beyond his offices in the Bendlerstrasse. However, the general had bold plans. He intended to split the ranks of the Nazis by offering the vice-chancellorship to Gregor Strasser and to build up under his leadership a broad coalition aimed at uniting all the constructive forces from the Stahlhelm on the right to the unions and the SPD on the left. Schleicher also planned to defuse the militant spirit of the SA by separating it from the Nazi Party and merging it with other paramilitary groups in a government controlled auxiliary force that could be used to safeguard the borders of the Reich.

In a secret meeting in Berlin on December 3 the devious Schleicher formally offered Gregor Strasser the vice-chancellorship and the minister presidency of Prussia. As leader of the party's organizational wing, Strasser had opposed Hitler's inflexible tactics for several years, citing each electoral setback as confirmation that he had been right about reaching a compromise with other friendly forces. Unlike Hitler, Strasser was not an ideological fanatic; moreover, his belief in National Socialism did not revolve around one man or around inflexible doctrines backed up by even more inflexible tactics. Although he would remain inexplicably loyal to Hitler to the end, he was becoming very disenchanted by the men who were gaining Hitler's trust, confiding to Hans Frank: "It seems to me that Hitler is completely in the hands of his Himmler and Himmlers.... Göring is a brutal egotist, Goebbels is a lame devil.... Röhm a filthy creature. That is the Führer's guard. It is terrible!"[73] When Hitler got wind of Schleicher's ploy, he summoned Strasser and other party leaders to a special meeting at the Kaiserhof Hotel in Berlin on December 5, reaffirming his rigid tactics against joining any government not headed by himself. This must have struck Strasser as an act of self-castration because only a day earlier the Nazis had received a devastating setback in local elections in Thuringia, registering losses of up to 40 percent over the recent Reichstag election in November.[74] Yet after careful reflection, Strasser decided neither to challenge Hitler nor to accept Schleicher's offer. The only alternative, as he saw it, was to resign his post as Reich organization leader as well as his parliamentary seat and to remove himself, at least for the time being, from politics altogether by taking a vacation in Italy. Before going on his vacation, Strasser prophetically confided to a friend: "I am a man marked by death.... Whatever happens, mark what I say: From now on Germany is in the hands of an Austrian, who is a congenital liar, a former officer, who is a pervert, and a clubfoot. And I tell you the last is the worst of them all. This is Satan in human form."[75]

Although the immediate impact of Strasser's resignation was devastating on some of the rank and file members, the Nazi Party had become so strongly oriented around Hitler that Strasser's defection was quickly neutralized. The top leadership quickly rallied to Hitler, issued misinformation about Strasser's recent actions, and eventually managed to turn him into a "nonperson." Schleicher had expected that at least sixty Nazi Reichstag deputies would follow Strasser's defection, but none did, illustrating what many Nazi watchers had known all along, namely, that there had never been a "Nazi left" or a "Strasser wing."[76]

There undoubtedly was a pall of gloom and doom over the Nazi leadership in December. Besides Strasser's defection, there were other serious problems. Party finances were depleted, party stalwarts, especially in the SA, were depressed and restive, and Nazi support, even in traditional strongholds such as Thuringia, was slipping badly. Goebbels cursed the year 1932 as one of "perpetual bad luck," with future prospects looking bleak and hopeless.[77] Even Hitler confessed in a letter to Winifred Wagner that his political dreams would not be fulfilled because his enemies were too powerful; once he knew for sure that everything was lost, he would end his life with a bullet.[78] Outside the Nazi Party, too, there was a feeling that Hitler's star was descending. On January 1, 1933, the *Frankfurter Zeitung* editorialized that the gigantic assault on the state by the Nazis had been beaten back.[79]

The Fatal Embrace:
The Conservative Elite Picks Hitler

The turnabout for the Nazis came from an unexpected source in the form of the disgruntled Papen, who was now more than willing to undermine his former nemesis, General Schleicher. On December 16, 1932, Papen addressed the conservative Herrenklub in Berlin and criticized Schleicher's tactics with the Nazis, implying that the appropriate thing to do was not to split or destroy them but to involve them responsibly in the government. After the meeting, Papen was approached by Kurt von Schröder, a Cologne banker, who proposed to mediate between Hitler and Papen by inviting them to a private meeting at his Cologne house. As president of the Cologne Herrenklub, Schröder had built up a network of political connections in the Nazi Party as well as the government. Politically, Schröder was a right-wing conservative who had just left the DNVP and was seriously thinking of joining the Nazi Party, having already been in close contact with Hitler's two major economic advisers — Robert Ley and Wilhelm Keppler.

In fact, it was Keppler who set in motion the steps that would lead to the fateful Papen-Hitler meeting on January 4, 1933. On the advice of Heinrich Himmler, who was just visiting him, Keppler dispatched a letter by personal messenger to Munich, informing Hitler that Papen was ready to support a Hitler chancellorship and was willing to discuss the details, provided the meeting was kept strictly secret.[80] Although Hitler was still smarting from earlier humiliations at the hands of Hindenburg and his conservative retainers, he decided to swallow his pride and accept the invitation for the meeting with Papen.

Despite elaborate precautions, involving a secretive night journey by train from Munich to Bonn and a change of cars at Bad Godesberg, the Nazi trio of Hitler, Hess, and Himmler, accompanied by Keppler as a go-between, was surprised that upon their arrival at Schröder's villa a photographer, sitting next to the entrance, was avidly snapping pictures of them. It turned out that an informant in Hitler's entourage had divulged information about the secret meeting to Hans Zehrer, an influential newspaper editor, who, in turn, reported it to General Schleicher and the public at large.[81]

It is not entirely certain what was discussed at Schröder's house on January 4, 1933, since Papen and Schröder gave conflicting views of the meeting at the Nuremberg war trials in 1946. Papen claimed that he did not want to undermine the Schleicher government but to strengthen it by persuading Hitler to serve in it as vice-chancellor. This high minded but self-serving account cannot be trusted. Why would Papen arrange such a secretive meeting and negotiate behind Schleicher's back if not to outfox his former nemesis? Schröder himself left little doubt that Papen was angry with Schleicher and expected his government to fall within a short period of time, proposing a new government headed by Hitler as chancellor and himself as vice-chancellor. Of course, this is precisely what would happen later that month, and it is highly likely that by January 4 Papen was already toying with this strategy. This also fits in with other evidence suggesting that Papen's machinations were clearly part of a campaign of revenge against Schleicher, for how else do we explain the fact that Papen dragged the crisis-ridden Nazi Party back into the political limelight if not to use it as an instrument of his own ambitions?[82]

The meeting at Schröder's house, which Karl Dietrich Bracher has called "the hour of birth of the Third Reich,"[83] marked the opening round of lengthy and secretive negotiations between the conservative camarilla around Hindenburg and the Nazis. One immediate result of the Schröder meeting was a noticeable improvement in the morale of the Nazi leadership. Hitler now had reasons to believe that if he could not gain power through the front door of free elections perhaps he could attain it through the back door of secret deals and manipulations. However, the Schröder meeting did not produce major monetary benefits for the financially strapped Nazi Party, as most traditional accounts of the episode have claimed. The coffers of the industrialists did not open up and disgorge large funds to the Nazis; on the contrary, contributions by big business continued to be relatively paltry.[84]

If the Schröder meeting did not succeed in accomplishing a financial turnabout, it definitely produced a psychological change in Hitler and his immediate entourage because everyone now strongly felt that the political momentum had been regained. It was for this reason that Hitler intensified his efforts to persuade the German people that National Socialism was the wave of the future. The test for this claim was to be the upcoming Landtag elections of January 15 in the tiny agricultural state of Lippe. Since few major parties planned to campaign extensively in Lippe, the Nazis decided to saturate the state with propaganda in hopes of pulling off a stunning victory, thus confirming their claim of being on the ascendancy. Although the electoral results recorded only a modest increase of 4.8 percent since November 1932, the Nazis inflated this modest gain into a gigantic victory, claiming that the German people (all one hundred thousand of them!) had spoken. Yet propaganda, which made the Third Reich, shapes its own reality. Many Germans were convinced by the Nazi press. Even Hindenburg and his conservative retainers were favorably impressed, and this is what really counted in Hitler's equation of political success. Hitler knew that success depended on his ability to exploit the differences between Papen and Schleicher and to worm his way into the circle where the key to power really resided — the circle around President Hindenburg, including the president's son Oskar, State Secretary Meissner, and Papen.

By the middle of January, Schleicher's position was steadily deteriorating. His failure to split the Nazi Party was followed by other failures, the most notable being his inability to forge a broad multiparty coalition. On January 11 agrarian leaders, representing the influential Reichslandbund, a five-million-member organization that had been heavily infiltrated by Nazi sympathizers, visited President Hindenburg and roundly condemned Schleicher's agricultural policies as communistic, thereby greatly alarming the president. Two days later, when Schleicher turned down Hugenberg as minister of economics, he lost the support of Hugenberg and the Nationalists. In the meantime, the Center Party and the Social Democrats persisted in their determined opposition to the Schleicher government. The general's time was running out.

What happened next was a series of private meetings between Hitler and the conservative clique surrounding the president. In retrospect, these meetings appear Byzantine and lurid, with many of them taking place in the house of Joachim von Ribbentrop, an empty and pretentious social climber who was trying to graft himself onto the Nazi bandwagon through his wealthy social connections. Papen met Hitler at Ribbentrop's house in Dahlem on January 10, 18, and 22.[85] The third meeting was the most decisive because Papen now decided to enmesh Hindenburg's son, who was widely regarded as an incompetent and insensitive pretender, along with the spineless but obedient bureaucrat Meissner in his machinations to form a Hitler-Papen government. To keep the meeting absolutely secret, the participants went through an elaborate charade to conceal their activities. Hindenburg and Meissner, accompanied by their wives, spent part of the evening at the Prussian state opera, pretending to enjoy Wagner's *Das Liebesverbot*. During the intermission they made themselves especially conspicuous, but when the lights went down for the final act they left their wives and the theater by a side entrance and jumped into a taxi. Just to be on the safe side, they waited until they were inside the taxi before they gave the driver Ribbentrop's address in Dahlem, nervously peering through the back window to see whether they were being followed. Although satisfied that no one tailed them, the two schemers still got out of the car some distance from their intended goal, trudging the rest of the way to Ribbentrop's villa through darkness and heavy snowfall.[86] Papen was already there, and so were Hitler, Frick, and Göring. After a few pleasantries, Hitler headed straight for Hindenburg, separated him from Meissner, and ushered him into another room for a discussion without eavesdroppers. While Hitler and Hindenburg talked for about an hour, an expansive Göring tried to put the rest of the company at ease by reassuring them that Hitler's demands were quite reasonable: the chancellorship and perhaps two cabinet posts, not including foreign affairs and defense.

No one to this day knows exactly what Oskar Hindenburg and Hitler discussed that evening since neither of them ever revealed any information about it. After World War II Meissner reported that after the meeting had concluded, he shared a taxi ride with Hindenburg during the course of which a dejected and self-absorbed Hindenburg remarked that it would now be impossible to work around Hitler.[87] The fact that Oskar Hindenburg was promoted from colonel to general shortly after Hitler came to power and that thousands of acres were added to the Neudeck estate strongly suggests that Hitler must have got to Hindenburg personally on that evening, probably threatening to publicize the details of the *Osthilfe* scandals and intimating that he might support impeachment proceedings against President Hindenburg.

The next morning, January 23, the well-informed Schleicher called State Secretary Meissner and asked him what the president's son had discussed the previous evening. Presumably not receiving a satisfactory answer, he then marched into President Hindenburg's office, admitted that he had failed to gain broad support for his government, and requested presidential support for four emergency measures — dissolution of the Reichstag, postponement of elections for three months, declaration of a state of emergency, and prohibition of the Nazi and Communist parties. Hindenburg objected that these measures were likely to provoke civil war and reminded the general that he himself had opposed a similar plan by Papen in December. Schleicher responded by saying that the situation had greatly deteriorated since that time and that only a concerted attack on the Nazis and the Communists could stave off a political catastrophe.[88] After discussing Schleicher's proposals with Meissner, Hindenburg made up his mind to reject the proposals; he was determined that he would not even give Schleicher authorization to dissolve the Reichstag, a request he had granted without compunction to the previous two chancellors. It was clear that Schleicher was finished, but the old gentleman still vacillated for another seven days about the choice of a successor.

For the next seven days intensive negotiations took place aimed at bringing Hitler into the government with certain restrictions. A key meeting, which conceptualized the idea of a right-wing "National Front" government led by Hitler as chancellor and Papen as vice-chancellor, was held on January 24 at Ribbentrop's house in Dahlem.[89] The next evening, Oskar Hindenburg stopped by again at Ribbentrop's and apparently was won over to the scheme concocted the previous evening. In the meantime, Papen arranged a meeting with Hugenberg and the two chief Stahlhelm leaders, Franz Seldte and Theodor Duesterberg, and asked them to support a Hitler government. Hugenberg accepted on condition that he would be included in the new government as minister of economics, that Papen would serve as vice-chancellor, and that Seldte would assume control over the Ministry of Labor. Papen would later excuse his manipulative deals by arguing that he was trying to construct a genuinely representative government headed by Hitler that at the same time was carefully balanced by responsible conservative forces. Of course, Hitler had no trouble seeing through Papen's transparent strategy of blocking his power by appointing his own men to important cabinet posts. Thus, when he learned that Hugenberg opposed the idea of a Nazi appointment to the Prussian Ministry of the Interior, he almost had a falling out with Hugenberg on January 27. On that same day, Papen called on both Hindenburg and Ribbentrop, while Göring tried to assure Hindenburg that the Nazis respected the inviolability of the presidency and the Reichstag. By this time, even the public was becoming annoyingly aware of the fact that their top politicians were little more than key-hole listeners and shabby plotters. The Communist newspaper *Vorwärts* aptly summed up the mood when it reported:

> Hitler is with Papen, Strasser is with Schleicher, Hugenberg is with Hitler, Papen is with Hugenberg, Hugenberg is with Hindenburg. Alvensleben is pushing from the front, Thyssen from the back. Strasser will be Vice-Chancellor, Hitler wants the Defense Ministry, Schleicher wants this, Hindenburg that. Who can still find his way through such a secretive politics that is being played without the German people?[90]

Hindenburg was now a torn man, but he gradually succumbed to the arguments of the men he thought he could trust — his son Oskar, Papen, and Meissner. Yet as late as January 27, he could still tell several high-ranking generals who came to see him: "Surely gentlemen, you would not credit me with appointing this Austrian corporal Chancellor."[91] What troubled the old man more than anything else was the danger that Hitler could gain control over the Reichswehr. If he could be assured that a Hitler appointment was checked and balanced by trusted conservatives, especially in the Defense Ministry, he might be willing to support a Hitler government after all. It so happened that he had already decided upon a candidate who was to succeed Schleicher in the Defense Ministry — Werner von Blomberg (1878–1946), an enemy of Schleicher who was currently a delegate to the disarmament conference in Geneva. Blomberg had been commander of the army district for East Prussia, and so was well known to Hindenburg; but what the old man did not know was that Blomberg was a strong Nazi sympathizer.

On January 28, Schleicher met his cabinet, and a unanimous decision was made to resign if the president refused to dissolve the Reichstag. Schleicher then went to the president and repeated his previous proposals. The old man flatly turned him down. In a moment of rare poetic justice, Schleicher had received his comeuppance. He was nonetheless deeply hurt, accusing the old president of betraying his trust by secretly negotiating behind his back. The weary president, his finger pointing heavenward, said: "I have already one foot in the grave, and I am not sure that I shall not regret this action in Heaven later on." Schleicher's parting reply was: "After this breach of trust, Sir, I am not sure that you will go to Heaven."[92]

After Schleicher left the president's office, still not knowing that he had also been replaced as defense minister, Papen, Oskar Hindenburg, and Meissner worked on the old man to move quickly and appoint a Hitler-Papen government. The old man relented and urged Papen to firm up the new government. Hitler used this opportunity to up the ante, demanding four major positions: Reich minister of the interior, Reich minister for civil air transport, Reich commissioner for Prussia, and Prussian minister of the interior. These "go-for-broke" techniques, so typical of Hitler's later diplomatic maneuvers, almost wrecked Papen's delicate negotiations because Hindenburg went through another surge of doubt about appointing the Bohemian corporal. The old man finally relented when Hitler agreed to let Papen serve as Reich commissioner for Prussia.

At the eleventh hour, on January 29, a false rumor was floating through Berlin that Schleicher and General Hammerstein planned to call out the Posdam garrison, arrest Hindenburg, and seize the reins of power. Although Schleicher did not have the slightest intentions of staging a Putsch, he did encourage his agents, notably Hammerstein and Werner von Alvensleben, to scare the Nazis with insinuations that Hindenburg and Papen were just leading them by the nose. Alvensleben, in fact, alarmed Hitler with rumors of an impending coup and suggested that cooperation with Schleicher, who only wanted to retain his post as defense minister, was bound to be more productive for the Nazis than relying upon a senile president who was under the thumb of the scheming Papen.

In a curious way, these rumors actually benefited Hitler, for when the president got wind of what Schleicher was supposedly up to, his mind was made up: he was now ready to give his blessing to a Hitler-Papen government. On the morning of January 30, Oskar Hindenburg was dispatched to the Anhalter railroad station to pick up Blomberg and to rush him to the presidential palace for his swearing in as new defense minister, thus averting the possibility that the desperate Schleicher might still resort to a Putsch. Oddly enough, upon his arrival Blomberg was met also by General Hammerstein's adjutant, who wanted to usher him to the Bendlerstrasse instead. The perplexed Blomberg did what every good German would have done in his place: he bowed to Hindenburg and superior authority.

After Blomberg had been sworn in as new defense minister, the stage was set for the arrival of Hitler, Hugenberg, Papen, and the other members of the new government. Hugenberg almost wrecked the final arrangement when he declared himself opposed to new elections and brushed off the threat of a so-called Schleicher coup as false and meaningless. In the end, however, he was won over, and by 12:40 the word of Hitler's appointment was out. Watching the presidential palace from the Kaiserhof Hotel, Hitler's entourage could see the beaming Hermann Göring proclaim the news to a cheering crowd. Hitler's car emerged from the driveway shortly afterward. Joining his entourage at the Kaiserhof, tears in his eyes, Hitler celebrated his remarkable triumph — a triumph, however, that would not have been possible without the intrigues of Schleicher and Papen, the political myopia of German voters and parties, the narrow self-interest of the military-industrial leaders, and the senility of the "Wooden Titan," Paul von Hindenburg.

Who Supported Hitler?

With the appointment of Adolf Hitler as chancellor, Germany would be plunged into an abyss, a dark age of unprecedented evil. Although Hitler's much-heralded Thousand-Year Reich would last for only twelve years, the world has never witnessed the perpetration of so much evil in such a short period. The historiographic effect has been to produce a series of optical illusions in the eyes of many historians who have described the rise and fall of the Third Reich. The evil that Hitler unleashed had the effect of magnifying the Twelve-Year Reich within the stream of history, prompting many historians to postulate fallacious or misleading theories of political causation and psychological motivation. Since the amount of destruction the Nazis unleashed on the world was so great, historians have assumed that such evil must be rooted deeply in German history and in the German character, an assumption that, ironically, inspired some slanderous explanations of the sort that Nazi racialists had developed as their own stock-in-trade during the Third Reich.[1] For some Germanophobic historians the Nazi experience still serves as *the* pivot around which explanations about German history as a whole are formulated. At its most extreme, this has resulted in the practice of twisting many personalities or events in German history into a prefiguration of Adolf Hitler and Auschwitz. And what has been perpetrated on the past has also been extended into the future, for Hitler's shadow is still stretching beyond the present into the future.

The opposite of the Germanophobic approach is the exculpatory, which holds that the Nazi experience was an aberration unrelated to previous events or institutions in German history. Some even claim that it was a unique event, an eruption of evil whose roots reside outside historical time and place. These arguments are as inauthentic as their opposite, though they may satisfy some Germans who would like to believe that they were unwitting and innocent victims of Hitler's lust for aggression. Dodging behind various covers — ignorance (we knew nothing), obeying orders, comparative trivialization (you were as bad as we were), or simple denial — some revisionist historians have tried to whitewash the record by claiming that the Nazis, though perhaps misguided, wanted the best for Germany and did not commit most of the heinous crimes attributed to them by their opponents.

This study has tried to steer clear of these two extremes, attributing the rise of Nazism to special conditions within a sixty-year span — anti-Semitism, nationalism, imperialism, defeat in war, the Versailles Treaty, the vindictive attitude of the Western powers, catastrophic economic circumstances, Germany's unstable political institutions and parties, the myopia of Hindenburg and his conservative clique, and the charismatic genius of Adolf Hitler. In connection with Hitler, this study endorses Gordon Craig's judgment that "Adolf Hitler was *sui generis,* a force without a real historical past, whose very Germanness was spurious because never truly felt and in the end, repudiated.... Both the grandiose barbarism of his political vision and the moral emptiness of his character make it impossible to compare him in any meaningful way with any other German leader. He stands alone."[2]

It is important to remind ourselves that Hitler was not Germany and Germany was not Hitler, as one ridiculous Nazi slogan insisted. If this is the case, who supported Hitler and what was the nature of the movement he inspired? In answering the first question, it is important at the very outset to break it down into two distinct, and not always related, questions: Who were Hitler's followers? and Who voted for Hitler? Broadly speaking, there were three types of followers: followers by conviction, followers by socioeconomic self-interest, and opportunistic or bandwagon followers (especially after January 1933).

The followers by conviction represented the hard core of the Nazi movement. They were overwhelmingly male, and there is some justification to the famous Nazi boast that National Socialism was "a male event."[3] The hard core consisted largely of recalcitrant and demobilized soldiers who could not reconcile their inherited militarism with the democratic beliefs of the Weimar Republic. For them "the hour of birth of National Socialism was in the *Fronterlebnis* and only by understanding the *Fronterlebnis* can one understand National Socialism."[4] If there was an archetypal "Nazi" or "Fascist," he was neither bourgeois nor proletarian but a socially dispossessed outsider who identified himself with reactionary and *völkisch* ideologies. Although coming from a middle-class background, he had no genuine rapport with middle-class values, which he despised as decadent and materialistic. At the same time, he also despised the vulgar masses and their identification with egalitarian ideologies. The archetypal Nazi saw himself as a third force between middle-class conservatism and working-class socialism. Dialectically, he tried to synthesize the two positions by depriving both adversaries of what they treasured most — nationalism or socialism. Fascism was a hybrid of both attitudes, and its German variant was defined by Hitler's articulation of it in terms of his own conflicts and obsessions.

If economic stability had been restored and maintained during the Weimar Republic, the Nazi movement would have never amounted to anything more than a small, xenophobic group of unregenerate misfits, but with the economic collapse, first of 1923 and then of 1929, it began to amalgamate misguided sympathizers who joined out of economic self-interest because they had been frightened into believing that the only alternative was the destruction of the middle class and the triumph of Communism. In order of precedent, the following groups were amalgamated step-by-step into the Nazi movement — the lower middle classes, who were afraid of being deprived of their social status; substantial elements of the more prosperous *Mittelstand* who fell victim to scare tactics that their businesses or possessions were subject to immanent expropriation by Communism; and disenchanted workers whose loyalty to nation exceeded their loyalty to class.

In the end, however, it was Hitler's organizational and charismatic genius that made it possible for the Nazi Party to attract a broad segment of the German population. Party membership lists and electoral data reveal that the Nazi Party was able to appeal beyond its hard-core followers and attract apparently incompatible social groups.[5] Hitler seems to have known intuitively that voting patterns are shaped not only by class affiliation but by group prejudices. Hitler reasoned that if he could successfully nationalize the masses, indoctrinating them with ethnic prejudices, he could effectively diffuse economic divisions and reintegrate heterogeneous elements into one national community (*Volksgemeinschaft*). He was right. Between 1923 and 1933 he created the basis for such a mass party (*Sammelpartei*), a concept so novel that it eluded the comprehension of most observers at the time: "The idea that a fanatical petty bourgeois could, by claiming to be socialist, labour, and nationalist all in one, direct a mass movement and that he might be victorious, was sociologically too novel and politically too unwanted to be readily comprehended."[6]

Questions about the social composition of the Nazi movement are therefore less important than questions relating to the movement's ability to broaden its base beyond the typical splinter parties of the Weimar Republic and attract mass support. Since electoral strength constitutes one of the chief instruments of measuring mass support, the question arises: Who voted for Hitler? Several studies, marshaling impressive and exhaustive data, have broken down election returns into specific components, trying to show how Germans from different socioeconomic or religious backgrounds voted in various elections between 1924 and 1933. These studies have cast serious doubts on traditional explanations that Hitler received most of his support from an anxiety-ridden lower middle class that panicked into supporting the Nazis because it dreaded being pushed into the grey mass of the working population.[7] Indeed, careful analysis of voting patterns has revealed that Hitler's appeal cut across class boundaries. Contrary to traditional interpretations, which held that the Nazis swept most lower-middle-class communities, some recent studies have failed to locate pure lower-middle-class communities for electoral purposes; and since there were no purely lower-middle-class voting districts, how could they have been swept by the Nazis? These studies have also shown that the highest levels of support for the Nazis came from the upper-class and upper-middle-class districts — the more affluent, the greater the likelihood for Nazi support, especially in some urban areas.[8] Another myth that has been exploded by careful empirical studies is that the key to electoral success in Germany resided in the cities. As previously mentioned, most Germans in the interwar period lived in the country or in small towns, a fact well known to Nazi strategists who targeted the countryside, especially in the Protestant north where party loyalties had faded and Nazi prospects for success were excellent. This is why the Nazis gained most heavily in Protestant villages and middle-sized Protestant towns.[9]

Who, then, voted for Hitler? A broad but not a majority segment of the German electorate. The highest vote that Hitler received in a free election (July 31, 1932) was 37.3 percent — that is, only three out of every eight votes. But given the polarization of German politics, that margin was higher than that of any other party, making the Nazi Party "the long-sought party of the middle-class concentration."[10] The Nazi victory of July 1932 generated enough momentum for the Nazis to be able to exploit the weaknesses of their opponents and capitalize on their own organizational strengths. What came to Hitler's aid was the mediocre leadership of opposition parties, the defects of the Weimar Constitution, the universal hatred of the Versailles Treaty, a growing mood of totalitarianism, and the gradual defection of key members of the ruling elite. Capitalizing on the tactical and managerial superiority of the Nazi Party and his own manipulative talents, Hitler simply outwitted the only group that could still block him in 1932 — the conservative clique around President Hindenburg.

The Weimar Republic failed because there were not enough strongly committed republicans to save it. In normal times, the republic might have been able to muddle through, as illustrated by its modest resurgence in the middle years (1924–29); but in times of turbulent and chaotic changes, its weaknesses became fatal liabilities. Amid a climate of mutual fear and paranoia, many Germans regressed to a "quick-fix," authoritarian solution; and given the predominance of right-wing, nationalistic attitudes, such a solution was bound to originate from the political right.

National Socialism was therefore a form of right-wing totalitarianism with strong populist and millenarian overtones. It was right-wing because the key support came from the conservative and nationalistic sections of the broad middle class, from the traditional elites, and from the military. The chief element in its ideology, which was largely the creation of Hitler, was a clever German synthesis of the most potent forces of the nineteenth century — ethnocentric (*völkisch*) nationalism and state socialism. Hitler often disguised the more unbridled and militaristic features of these forces under idealistic rhetoric, so appealing to German audiences, but in reality he steadily reached deeper and deeper into the cesspool of totalitarianism.

Although thousands of Germans cheered his triumph on January 30, 1933, the record also shows that many Germans of all walks of life were gripped by fear and apprehension, strongly suspecting that Hitler would unleash a flood of sewage all over Germany and the world at large. Few stories express the eerie feeling of impending Nazi terror quite as well as the gruesome joke that circulated in the editorial rooms of the Ullstein Publishing Company, where Arthur Koestler worked in 1932:

> Under the reign of the second Emperor of the Ming Dynasty there lived an executioner by the name of Wang Lun. He was a master of his art and his fame spread through all the provinces of the Empire. There were many executions in those days, and sometimes there were as many as fifteen or twenty men to be beheaded at one session. Wang Lun's habit was to stand at the foot of the scaffold with an engaging smile, hiding his curved sword behind his back, and whistling a pleasant tune, to behead his victim with a swift movement as he walked up the scaffold.
>
> Now this Wang Lun had one secret ambition in his life, but it took him fifty years of strenuous effort to realize it. His ambition was to be able to behead a person with a stroke so swift that, in accordance with the law of inertia, the victim's head would remain poised on his trunk, in the same manner as a plate remains undisturbed on the table if the tablecloth is pulled out with a sudden jerk.
>
> Wang Lun's great moment came in the seventy-eighth year of his life. On that memorable day he had to dispatch sixteen clients from this world of shadows to their ancestors. He stood as usual at the foot of the scaffold, and eleven shaven heads had already rolled into the dust after his inimitable master-stroke. His triumph came with the twelfth man. When this man began to ascend the steps of the scaffold, Wang Lun's sword flashed with such lightning speed across his neck that the man's head remained where it had been before, and he continued to walk up the steps without knowing what had happened. When he reached the top of the scaffold, the man addressed Wang Lun as follows:
>
> "O cruel wang Lun, why do you prolong my agony of waiting when you dealt with the others with such merciful speed?"
>
> When he heard these words, Wang Lun knew that the work of his life had been accomplished. A serene smile appeared on his features; then he said with exquisite courtesy to the waiting man:
>
> "Just kindly nod, please."[11]

Arthur Koestler adds: "We walked along the hushed corridors of our citadel of German democracy, greeting each other with a grinning 'kindly nod, please.' And we fingered the backs of our necks to make sure that the head was still solidly attached to it."[12] Many more Germans would perform this gesture over the next twelve years, many losing their heads and many never able to screw them on right again.

Friedrich Ebert

Field Marshal von Hindenburg

Karl Liebknecht

Rosa Luxemburg

Hitler's mother, Klara Pölzl
(1860-1907)

Hitler's father, Alois Hitler
(1837-1903)

Hitler as an infant

Lance Corporal Hitler

Hitler, Luddendorff, and accomplices after the Munich trial, April 1924

The Adolf Hitler Shock Troops leaving for German Day in Bayreuth, September 2, 1933

Hitler fraternizing with storm troopers

Braunschweig Party Day, October 1931

Hitler's Cabinet. From left to right: Seldte, Gürtner, Goebbels, Eltz-Rübenach, Hitler, Göring, Darre(?), Blomberg, Frick, Neurath, Schacht, Schwerin von Krosigk, Popitz(?), Papen.

Reich Marshal Hermann Göring

Propaganda Minister Josef Goebbels

Alfred Rosenberg, Nazi racial philosopher and Reich Minister

Ernst Röhm, Chief of the SA

Hans Lammers, Chief of the Reich Chancellery

Rudolf Hess, Deputy Führer and Chief of the Central Committee of the NSDAP

Heinrich Himmler, Reichsführer SS and architect of the Holocaust

Martin Bormann, Hitler's personal secretary and Director of the Party Chancellery

Julius Dorpmüller, Reich
Transportation Minister

Franz Gürtner, Reich
Minister of Justice

LEFT: Otto Meissner, Chief of the Presidential Chancellery
RIGHT: Hjalmar Schacht, Reich Minister of Economics,
President of the Reichsbank, and Plenipotentiary for War
Economy

Field Marshal Werner
von Blomberg, Reich
Minister of Defense

General Werner von
Fritsch, Commander in
Chief of the German
Army

Hitler at the Nuremberg Party rally, 1936

League of German Girls (Bund deutscher Mädel or BDM)

Hitler Youth (Hitlerjugend or HJ)

Hitler with a group of children

Rudolf Hess, Albert Speer, and Hitler

Hitler with Leni Riefenstahl and
Viktor Lutze, who succeeded Röhm
as head of the SA

Hitler with Eva Braun

Nazi Party rally in Nuremberg, September 1934

Benito Mussolini with
Adolf Hitler, during the
Duce's visit to Germany,
September 1937

Hitler greets the Duke
and Duchess of Windsor
at Berchtesgaden,
October 23, 1937

Neville Chamberlain with Hitler
during the Czechoslovakian crisis,
September 1938

Students of an Ordensburg (one of the elite academies of the Nazi Party) on a march

Kristallnacht (Crystal Night or Night of Broken Glass), November 9-10, 1938, when the Nazis instigated widespread destruction of Jewish synagogues, businesses, and homes

Book burning on the Franz-Josephs-Platz near the Staatsoper in Berlin, May 1933

Poster for the *Eternal Jew* exhibition, 1937. Artist: Philippe Ruprecht (?)

"Germans beware! Do not buy from Jews" read the posters which Nazi storm troopers paste on the windows of Berlin's Jewish-owned businesses.

Jews are forced to clean the pavement with toothbrushes.

The sign worn by the young woman: "At this place I am the greatest swine; I take Jews and make them mine." The sign worn by the young man: "As a Jewish boy I always (*immer*) take German girls up to my room (*zimmer*)."

The High Command of the Wehrmacht salute their Führer.

Field Marshal Fedor
von Bock

General Alfred Jodl

Field Marshal Erwin
Rommel

Field Marshal Wilhelm
Keitel

Field Marshal Ewald
von Kleist

General Heinz Guderian

General Franz Halder

Field Marshal
Erich von Manstein

Field Marshal
Friedrich Paulus

Field Marshal Gerd
von Rundstedt

"Help Hitler Build. Buy German goods." 1930s. Artist: Gunther Nagel

"Build youth hostels and homes." 1938/39. Artist: Hermann Witte.

"Victory will be ours." 1942. Artist unknown.

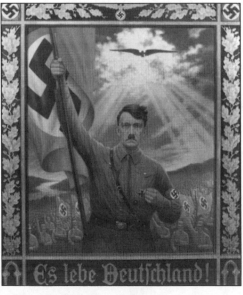

"Germany lives." 1930s. Artist: K. Stauber.

Jubilant Viennese greet the annexation of Austria
to Germany, March 1938.

Hitler declares war on the United States, December 11, 1941.

"Give me ten years and you will not recognize Germany."
—Adolf Hitler, 1933.

A family in Mannheim escapes an air raid with their lives.

The destruction of Stuttgart

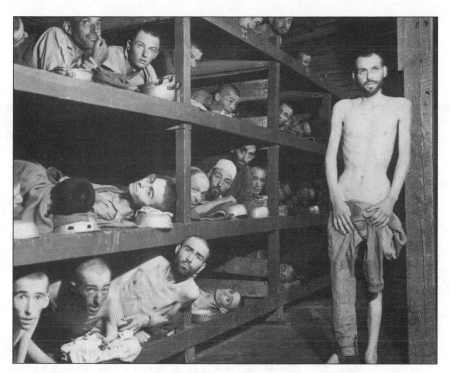

Slave laborers at Buchenwald concentration camp

On the way to the gas chamber

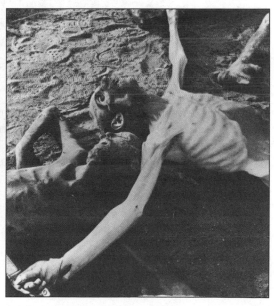

Concentration camp victims as photographed by American liberators

"Turn your gaze to the hill of corpses, spectator of contemporary history; turn for a moment within and think: This poor residue of flesh and bone is your father, your child, your wife, the person dear to you! See yourself and the one closest to you, on whom your mind and heart depend, thrown naked in the filth, tortured, starved, killed."

— Eugen Kogon

Part Two

THE FRUITS
1933–45

The Consolidation of Power, 1933-34

The Nazi Assault on the Government

Once the Nazis had insinuated themselves into the German government under the guise of a national uprising, evil results began to appear almost immediately. It took Adolf Hitler a mere eighteen months to eliminate his most serious opposition by a combination of tactics ranging from manipulation of public opinion to behind the scenes settling of private scores and the conquest of the means of totalitarian control — police, government institutions, mass media, the economy, and the armed forces. One by one, Hitler's opponents fell. The Social Democrats, Communists, liberals, and conservative nationalists alike had long ago undermined their own effectiveness through ideological wishful thinking and civic cowardice. The triumph of Nazism was accomplished on the broken backs of failed ideologies and timid men. For this reason, Klaus Epstein's judgment about Weimar politics is irrefutable: "It will always remain a reproach to the parliamentary parties that they produced, with very few exceptions, neither heroes nor martyrs but only a plentiful crop of mediocrities, and that all attempts to penetrate the German political consciousness with a positive image of Weimar are forever doomed to failure."[1]

The contour of the period under review, beginning with Hitler's appointment on January 30, 1933, and ending with President Hindenburg's death on August 1, 1934, had a curious double face of *Schein* (illusion) and *Sein* (reality), of public excitement over the "national uprising" and pervasive private fears of Nazi terror. In his domestic as in his later diplomatic policies, Hitler played with smoke and mirrors, saying one thing in public and another in private. Publicly he spoke of freedom and peace while preparing secretly for tyranny and war. He manipulated these mirrors so well that many people inside as well as outside Germany deluded themselves about Hitler's real intentions.

Hitler came to power legally as chancellor of what appeared to be just another government in which decisions were made by passing laws through executive (presidential) decree. Between January 30 and March 24, the day when the Enabling Law on which Hitler's dictatorship would rest was passed by a cowed Reichstag, a flood of bills was passed by executive decree. This appeared to be a mere continuation of the policies of the three previous chancellors, except that this time Hitler would use Article 48 to strip the German people of their democratic rights.

The conservatives were tricked into believing that Hitler was orchestrating a conservative and nationalistic revolution; they also fooled themselves into believing that they could control or moderate the Nazi leader. Those conservatives who had been directly responsible for jobbing him into power — Papen and his conservative camarilla — reasoned that they commanded the confidence of Hindenburg, who was not only president but also commander in chief of the armed forces. Papen, as vice-chancellor, was required to be present whenever the chancellor reported to the president; he was also minister president of Prussia, a position that gave him control over the Prussian police and civil service.

Hitler's conservative partners also salved their consciences by arguing that the Nazis held only two ministerial appointments — Frick as minister of the interior and Göring as minister without portfolio and Prussian minister of the interior. Surely, only one major cabinet post would not be enough to overcome the power combined in the eight other cabinet posts. The rest of the cabinet appointments appeared solidly conservative. Baron Konstantin von Neurath (1873–1956), a distinguished diplomat of the old school, became foreign minister; Werner von Blomberg (1878–1946), another conservative nationalist, became minister of defense; Alfred Hugenberg, head of the DNVP, news media mogul, and dyed-in-the-wool reactionary, took over commerce and agriculture; while Franz Seldte (1882–1947), chief of the paramilitary Stahlhelm, assumed control over the Ministry of Labor. The remaining three cabinet appointments — Franz Gürtner (justice), Eltz von Rübenach (transportation), and Count Lutz von Schwerin-Krosigk (finance) — were all in the hands of respectable nationalists and supporters of the traditional military-industrial complex. It appeared as though Hitler had been successfully "framed in," as the fatuous Papen so smugly suggested to his conservative friends. In fact, Papen was so proud of his role in assembling the cabinet and in "engaging" Hitler that he told a nervous conservative critic: "What do you want? I have Hindenburg's confidence. Within two months we will have pushed Hitler so far into a corner that he'll squeak."[2]

Papen's statement ranks as one of the most lamentable errors in judgment ever made about Adolf Hitler and the Nazi movement. Papen and his deluded cronies not only believed that they could control the volatile Hitler but also swallowed Nazi slogans about a "national uprising" or a "national revolution" as implying a "conservative" uprising or revolution. They lined up behind Hitler firmly convinced that the national uprising was really aimed, not at themselves, but only at the political left. When Hitler quickly disabused them of such fantasies, they pretended to be shocked, drawing back in horror at the excesses of his dictatorship. Hitler had never disguised his dictatorial ambitions; he had made it clear that he would not abide by parliamentary procedures, and it is curious why the Hindenburg-Papen-Hugenberg trio, which itself had no commitment to parliamentary government, would expect Adolf Hitler to set up anything other than an authoritarian state — the very thing they had pined for in their own hearts since 1919.

The conservatives actually began to lose control even before the new government was sworn in by President Hindenburg. As previously mentioned, despite Hugenberg's vocal protests, Hitler had convinced the new cabinet members that the Reichstag should be dissolved and new elections should be held in March, which would allow the Nazis, now in control of government agencies, to broaden their popular standing with the German people and thus set the stage for the elimination of their political enemies. With these steps taken, Hitler swore the oath that all his predecessors had sworn, namely, to apply his energy for the good of the German people, to uphold the constitution and laws of the Reich, and to carry out his duties in a bipartisan and just manner.

Lending credibility to such public pieties, Hitler's government proceeded, on February 1, to announce a sweeping program aimed at reestablishing the spiritual and political unity of the German people, respecting and defending pillars of German society such as Christianity and the family, revitalizing the economy by means of two mighty four-year plans, and regaining for Germany rights as an equal power in a peaceful community of nations. This, of course, was smoke and mirrors. Hitler used such pious sentiments only to disguise his dictatorial and warlike intentions. Those became apparent when he attended a secret gathering on February 3, hosted in his honor by the leading commanders of the Reichswehr. On this, as on similar occasions, he promised his military chiefs a complete domestic transformation in the form of an authoritarian government that would, once and for all, eradicate (*ausrotten*) Marxism and the cancer of democracy.[3] He also proclaimed that he would destroy the Versailles Treaty, revitalize the German army, and conquer territory in the east to give Germans more living space.

Hitler's aim was clear: to send out an unequivocal message that he was here to stay. Echoing Goebbels's promise, made in the summer of 1932, that "once we have power, we will never surrender it unless we are carried out of our offices as corpses,"[4] Hitler also prophesied that "once I enter the government I do not intend to leave it."[5]

Hitler's immediate aim was to use Article 48 of the Weimar Constitution to whittle away at the democratic features of the republican system of government. One aim, devised by the radicals within the party, that he assuredly did not seek was the notion of ushering in a social or economic revolution. Hitler preferred to work through the established institutions of the Reich — the regular army, big business, the civil service — to attain his ultimate geopolitical objective of military expansion and conquest. As long as these institutions could be made to bend to his will, he had no intention of changing or even revolutionizing them. His preferred tactic was infiltration and coordination rather than revolution.

The new chancellor's first objective was to neutralize the Reichstag and to divest himself of the parliamentary system altogether. Hitler could have governed at the head of a coalition government that enjoyed a parliamentary majority. To do so, he would have had to involve the Center Party in his government; but anticipating that the Center would want concessions in return for its support, Hitler sabotaged all efforts to form a coalition government. His next step was to dissolve the Reichstag and call for new elections. There is no doubt that he was getting impatient with playing what he considered to be a democratic charade; he wanted to dismantle the Weimar Constitution and get on with the business of rebuilding Germany along authoritarian lines. Hitler told a group of prominent industrialists that the election, scheduled for March 5, 1933, was to be the last German election, and if it was not decisive, "the decision must be brought about in one way or another by other means."[6] Göring seconded these sentiments by going one step further, saying that the coming election "would certainly be the last for the next ten years, probably even for the next hundred years."[7]

The control of Prussia, the largest and most important political state, was a precondition of control of the other German states. As will be recalled, the government of Prussia had already been revamped along more authoritarian lines by Papen in 1932, but its complete domination had been blocked to some degree by a Supreme Court decision that allowed the Social Democratic government of Braun-Severing to exercise provisional supervision pending new elections. However, in the meantime, the Reich government had appointed a provisional government of its own, headed by Papen as minister president and Göring as minister of the interior.[8] On February 6, 1933, Papen obtained a presidential decree that abruptly transferred to the provisional government the powers that were still in the hands of the Braun administration. This effectively violated the Supreme Court decision of October 25, 1932, and represented another coup d'état — a coup benefiting not just conservative nationalists but the more ruthless Nazis, who would exploit this opportunity for their own purpose.[9]

It was at this moment that the ebullient and brutal Hermann Göring came into his own because he knew "when he was handed the keys to his new office in the Prussian Justice building he held in his hands the keys to power."[10] Göring had two immediate aims: to purge the Prussian Interior Ministry of political unreliables and to gain control over the police force. Göring completely bypassed his weak nominal superior, Franz von Papen, and ruthlessly Nazified the Prussian police force. He retired fourteen Prussian police presidents, fired numerous subordinate officials, and appointed SS-Oberführer Kurt Dalugue, a pugnacious thug who was nicknamed "Dummi-Dummi" (dumb-dumb) for his limited intelligence, as "Commissioner for Special Duty," assigned to purge the police of political opponents.[11] Göring also created his own body-guard, the Special Duty Police Squad, and turned the Interior Ministry upside-down.[12] Göring's eye was on a small section of the ministry called Department 1-A, located in Berlin police headquarters, which dealt with political matters and served as a sort of political-police intelligence-gathering service for the whole country. In charge of this office he appointed Rudolf Diels, a capable official with strong conservative and anti-Communist convictions who later became related to him when he married Ilse Göring, the widow of Göring's younger brother Karl. When Diels took this office, which would involve him in dangerous political infighting with Himmler, he promised that he would turn Department 1-A into an instrument of power such as had never been seen before in Prussia. His boast turned out to be a modest one because Department 1-A would soon be removed from the jurisdiction of the police presidium and transformed into a secret state police (*Geheime Staatspolizei*), the future Gestapo, subservient to the minister of the interior. By the middle of April the Gestapo moved to a building complex of its own in the Prinz Albrechtstrasse.

To those who had survived his purge and reorganization of the Interior Ministry, Göring revealed his agenda, namely, to encourage all levels of government to support National Socialism and to implement the strongest measures against political opponents, particularly against the political left. In an order to all police authorities, Göring made it clear that police officers did not have to be squeamish when dealing with Communist terrorism, and that they should use their revolvers without regard to consequences: "Police officers who use weapons in carrying out their duties will be covered by me.... [W]hoever misguidedly fails in this duty can expect disciplinary action."[13] This virtually amounted to a "fire at will" order. Worse was to come on February 22 when Göring drafted SA, SS, and Stahlhelm members into "auxiliary police" service in order to combat the purported growing excesses of the political left. All that these paramilitary members of the Reich had to do was to put a white armband, bearing the words "auxiliary police," on their brown or black uniforms and they were transformed into instant police officials with a license to bully, beat, or even kill "political undesirables." It was the equivalent, as Allan Bullock observed, "of handing over police powers to the razor and cosh gangs"[14] or, to update an analogy, to the Mafia or gangs in America's urban jungles.

On the night of February 27, 1933, the German Reichstag went up in flames; and while the building was still burning, the police arrested a deranged Dutch Communist, Marinus van der Lubbe, who was found on the deserted premises. Many books and articles have been written about the Reichstag fire, some blaming van der Lubbe, some implicating the Communists themselves, others finding that the Nazis under the direction of Hermann Göring or SA group leader Karl Ernst actually set the Reichstag ablaze and conveniently used van der Lubbe, a known arsonist who happened to be on the Reichstag premises, as a pretext for general reprisals against Communists throughout Germany.[15] At the subsequent trial, attempts were made to implicate not only van der Lubbe but also the German Communist leader Ernst Torgler and three Bulgarian Communists (Georgi Dimitroff, Wassil Taneff, and Blagoi Popoff), but it resulted only in the conviction and eventual execution of van der Lubbe as the sole perpetrator. The trial, held from September 21 to December 23, 1933, before the Reichsgericht (Superior Court) featured many fire experts and eye-witnesses but failed to come up with any evidence that the fire was the result of a Communist plot. Whoever was ultimately responsible for burning down the Reichstag — and we suspect it was probably the Nazis — there is no doubt that the Nazis quickly exploited the situation for their own ends by claiming that van der Lubbe was merely the figurehead of a vast Communist conspiracy, and that radical measures were needed to crush the impending Bolshevik insurrection. Hitler himself referred to the Reichstag fire as "a beacon from heaven" and on February 28, 1933, the day after the fire, promulgated a decree entitled "Decree of the Reich President for the Protection of the People and State," a document that suspended the seven sections of the Weimar Constitution that guaranteed civil liberties. The decree sanctioned restrictions on a whole range of civil rights:

> Thus, restrictions on personal liberty, on the right of free expression of opinion, including freedom of the press, on the rights of assembly and association, and violations of the privacy of postal, telegraphic and telephonic communication, and warrants for house searches, orders for confiscations as well as restrictions on property rights are permissible beyond the legal limits otherwise prescribed.[16]

In addition, this document sharply curtailed the autonomy of the states by insisting that "if in any German state the measures necessary for the restoration of public security and order are not taken, the Reich government may temporarily take over the powers of the supreme authority in such a state in order to restore security."[17] Although the decree was thought to be a temporary emergency measure only, it was never rescinded.

Coming shortly before the March 5 election, the decree allowed the Nazis to marshal the whole force of the law against their political opponents. The political campaign, which culminated in a rousing speech (the "Day of the Awakening of the Nation") by Adolf Hitler on March 4 in Königsberg, was the most frenetic and violent to-date. Political opponents were rounded up, their headquarters ransacked, and their meetings disrupted; hair-raising accounts of "Red blood-baths" served as pretexts for mass arrests, as SA and SS auxiliaries rounded up numerous left-wing opponents and introduced them to the new Nazi methods of political education.

It is astonishing that despite their strong-arm methods, the Nazis still did not win a majority of votes on March 5, 1933. The Nazis polled 17,277,180 votes out of a total of 39,343,300 — an increase of 5.5 million since the last election but still less than a majority (43.9 percent). With the help of the Nationalists, who garnered 3,138,800 votes (52 seats), Hitler scraped together a majority in the Reichstag. In addition to the 288 Nazi seats, the 52 Nationalists seats yielded 340 seats out of a total of 647 — a bare majority of 17 seats.

The election victory gave Hitler and his followers powerful momentum by which to break down the constitutional wall that still separated them from dictatorial control of the government. In the days following the elections, the Nazis capitalized on their electoral gains by occupying local and state governments and subjecting them to the control of Nazi appointed "Reich commissioners." In view of the "total" victory in the March 5 election, as Göring brazenly characterized the situation, there was no further need for state governments! Within hardly a week, the duly elected state governments meekly surrendered to coup d'états carried out by local Nazi thugs. Even in Bavaria, where Prime Minister Held had let it be known earlier that he would arrest any Reich commissioner who set his foot on Bavarian soil, the Nazi takeover proceeded with minimal disruptions. The Bavarian takeover, in Karl Dietrich Bracher's judgment, was a perfect illustration of a "stage-managed revolution from above and a manipulated revolution from below."[18] The Nazis knew only too well that in Bavaria, as in some other German states, they would be unable to come to power by attaining a parliamentary majority. Using the government state of emergency decree as a pretext, they stage-managed the politics of the coup from above and used local SA and SS shock troops to implement the revolution from below.

Thus, on March 9, the Nazi *Gauleiter* for Bavaria, Adolf Wagner, accompanied by Ernst Röhm, marched into Held's office in full regalia and demanded the appointment of Ritter von Epp as Reich commissioner. Abandoned by Hindenburg and the military, Held could do nothing to stop the dismantling of his office. Leaving nothing to chance, the Nazis dispatched a commando of SS men to the Munich telegraph office to fetch the cable from Berlin that appointed Epp to the post of Reich commissioner of Bavaria. The tall, blond SS officer who picked up the telegram at pistol point was Reinhard Heydrich. Held thereupon capitulated and temporarily fled to Switzerland. When he returned, he secretly entered a Munich hospital to undergo an operation; in June, one of his sons was thrown into a new camp for political opponents at Dachau for his refusal to disclose the whereabouts of his father.

Such unconstitutional outrages were now becoming the rule rather than the exception in the new Nazi state. One by one, the other German states fell to this pattern of "planned terror." Local Nazi organizations would set in motion violent protests and unrest. This, in turn, would be followed by the appointment of Nazi Reich commissioners who would take over local governments in order to restore public safety and order. In Württemberg, Baden, Saxony, Hesse, Hamburg, Bremen, and Lübeck the same pattern developed.[19] In Prussia, the Nazis were already consolidating rule under the stage management of Hermann Göring and Wilhelm Frick. All over Germany Nazi storm troopers implemented their triumph in a thoroughly revolting manner, torturing their opponents and grabbing power for themselves.

There was a certain luridness about the first phase of this chaotic and still largely uncoordinated assault on Germany's traditions and institutions. In fact, this first wave of terror was largely spontaneous and badly organized. Political enemies were herded into abandoned army barracks, factories, and various remote sites and brutally manhandled. Most of the first concentration camps sprang up in the vicinity of Berlin, a smaller number in central Germany, and the most notorious, Dachau, near Munich in the south.[20] In Berlin the most notorious Gestapo prison was Columbia-Haus, where hundreds of Communists, Social Democrats, and Jews were tortured and beaten before being sent on to concentration camps. Only later were these wildcat camps brought under the supervision of government agencies, significantly reduced, standardized, and transformed into permanent institutions of terror. Dachau and Oranienburg were two of the most infamous camps that remained. Other major camps added were Sachsenhausen near Berlin and Buchenwald near Weimar. Although Hitler encouraged these actions, he did not plan most of them. The eruption of this form of terror was the inevitable outcome of years of pent-up Nazi aggression. Even behind Hitler's back, among his top leaders, there was a mad scramble to gain control over the instruments of state power — a scramble that would lead to the Röhm purge and the emergence of the Hitlerian hydra with its various heads of police terror (Himmler), institutional lying (Goebbels), and "scented Neroism" (Göring). The Nazi disease had started in Bavaria, and it was from there that Himmler and Heydrich, supported in Berlin by Göring, captured the police, set up concentration camps, and ultimately cast their net of surveillance, control, intimidation, torture, and "legalized" murder all over Germany.

By the middle of March, Nazi thugs, camouflaged as "auxiliary police" or quasi-legal representatives of the state, rounded up political opponents of all hues — rich and poor, famous or obscure — put them under "protective custody," tortured them, and in numerous cases killed them. The mayor of Magdeburg, Ernst Reuter, who was revolted by such Nazi treatment, which had led to his own ouster from office, sent an urgent telegram to President Hindenburg protesting such actions. The senile president, insulated from the reality of the growing Nazi terror, never responded, and Reuter disappeared from public view, thrown into a concentration camp. In Munich, Fritz Gerlach, the editor of the Catholic magazine *Der Gerade Weg* (The straight path), was beaten to a bloody pulp in his office by Nazi thugs, thrown into a concentration camp, and finally murdered in the wake of the Röhm purge on July 1, 1934. Fritz Busch, conducting the Dresden state opera, was hissed and shouted down because of his anti-Nazi views and his support of Jews. In May he joined a growing number of Germans leaving the country. Wilhelm Sollmann, former Reich minister of the interior, was also brutally beaten by SA men. Konrad Adenauer, the Catholic mayor of Cologne and future chancellor of West Germany, was unceremoniously removed from his mayoral post and forced into retirement. Bruno Walter, the Jewish conductor of the Leipzig Gewardhaus orchestra, was debarred from further musical activity. The same fate befell other non-Aryan musicians, including Otto Klemperer, Artur Schnabel, and Emil Feuermann.

On March 13, the government announced the creation of a new Ministry for Public Enlightenment and Propaganda, headed by Joseph Goebbels. Its function was to cleanse German life and culture of undesirable elements and to put a gloss on the new Nazi racial state. It was a measure of Hitler's cunning and suspicious mind that he did not give Goebbels or any of his high-ranking subordinates carte blanche in any field of operation, appointing rivals to head competing organizations. Although Goebbels would try to expand his power and influence over the minds of Germans, he always faced competition: Bernhard Rust as head of the Ministry of Science, Education, and Folk Nurture; Max Amann as Reich leader of the press; Otto Dietrich as Reich press chief; and Rosenberg as "führer representative for the monitoring of the whole spiritual schooling and education of the NSDAP."

On March 21, Goebbels helped Hitler stage a grand spectacle of reconciliation that was designed to put a nationalistic veneer on the brutal tactics the Nazis were using to subvert law and order and human decency in Germany. The event was the opening of the Reichstag in the Potsdam Garrison Church.[21] March 21 was not only the beginning of spring, and thus symbolized renewal, but had also been the day when Otto von Bismarck opened the first Reichstag of the unified Second Reich in 1871. The "Day of Potsdam" was an imposing spectacle of delusory (*Schein*) politics designed to lull Germans into the belief that the Nazis were merely carrying out the best features in Germany's conservative past. The day began with religious services in the Protestant St. Nicholas Church where Otto Dibelius preached on the text: "If God is with us, who will be against us?" Catholic delegates from the Center Party along with several Nazis like Himmler and Epp attended service in the Municipal Parish Church of Potsdam. A seat was reserved for Hitler, but the chancellor along with his propaganda chief decided to occupy himself instead with laying wreaths on the graves of various Nazi martyrs. At noon occurred the solemn opening of the Reichstag at the Garrison Church in which the bodies of Frederick William I and his son Frederick the Great were entombed. The glockenspiel chimed out the famous German hymn "Üb immer Treu und Redlichkeit" (Always exercise loyalty and decency). When Hitler and Hindenburg entered the church, the former dressed in a frock coat and the latter in his resplendent field marshal's uniform, the spectators got precisely the impression Hitler wanted to create: the old Prussian military tradition, embodying old-fashioned German values of honor, loyalty, and love of country, was now linking up with a new dynamic Germany that was symbolized by the simple front-line soldier Adolf Hitler. Subsequent picture postcards and posters, depicting the "marshal and the corporal," tried to evoke the unification of the old Germany with the new.

After entering the church, Hindenburg bowed to the royal box occupied by the crown prince and his wife; the seat of the former kaiser, who followed the speeches on the radio from his Dutch exile at Dorn, was deliberately left empty. Following the playing of a popular chorale associated with Frederick the Great's victory at Leuthen — "Now Let Us All Thank God" — Hindenburg gave a short address in which he urged the Reichstag deputies to support the new government. Hitler spoke in turn, reminding his audience of the humiliating years of Weimar but in the same breath announcing that a remarkable rebirth had already taken place since he had become chancellor. Most people present or listening to the proceedings on the radio were profoundly stirred by this mock ceremony. The public was only dimly aware of the fact that behind this charade the Nazis were constructing a new totalitarian state based on cynical manipulation of public opinion and brutal force.

Only three days later, on March 24, the new Reichstag assembled in the Kroll Opera House, where only weeks earlier the great tenor Richard Tauber had sung the gay tunes of the musical "The Land of Smiles," and ratified a new law Hitler had submitted to dispense with the Reichstag and with democracy in general.

The scene that greeted the delegates, especially the non-Nazi deputies, as they approached and then entered the building has been faithfully captured by Wilhelm Hoegner, a Bavarian SPD deputy:

> The wide square in front of the Kroll Opera House was crowded with dark masses of people. We were received with wild choruses: "we want the Enabling Act!" Youth with Swastikas on their chests eyed us insolently, blocked our way, in fact made us run the gauntlet, calling us names like "Center Pig," "Marxist Sow." The Kroll Opera House was crawling with SA and SS men.... The assembly hall was decorated with swastikas and similar ornaments.... When we Social Democrats had taken our seats on the extreme left, SA and SS men lined up at the exits and along the walls behind us in a semicircle. Their expression boded no good.[22]

The euphemistically entitled document submitted to the delegates in this highly volatile atmosphere, called the Law for Terminating the Suffering of People and Nation, usually referred to as the Enabling Law (Ermächtigungsgesetz), was the legal foundation on which Hitler would base his authority for the next twelve years. Since the Enabling Law fundamentally altered the Weimar Constitution, it required a two-thirds majority. The Communists, of course, had already been eliminated, but Hitler still needed thirty-one votes to pass the bill. He did this by persuading the Center Party to vote for the bill by agreeing to its demand that he rescind the edict of February 28, which had gone further than the proposed Enabling Law.[23] The Center leadership reasoned that they could probably not block the passage of the law one way or the other, but they hoped that if they supported Hitler, he would respect the integrity of the Center Party and Catholic interests in Germany and would restore the basic rights that had been suspended by the edict of February 28. Hitler gave his verbal approval to these conditions and even promised to put it in writing. On the day of the voting, no letter by Hitler had been received by the Center. Only when Frick personally assured the chairman of the Center, Ludwig Kaas, that the letter was on its way, did the party agree to vote for the bill. Needless to say, no letter ever arrived, nor would Hitler respect the integrity of either the Center Party or the church it represented.

The proposed Enabling Law[24] gave the government the right to pass laws without the consent of the Reichstag; to deviate from the constitution, if necessary; to conclude treaties with foreign powers; and to place the right of issuing a law into the hands of the chancellor. Although the document insisted that the powers of the president would remain inviolate, it put enough power into the hands of the chancellor to enable the Nazis to bypass both Hindenburg and his now impotent conservative go-betweens — von Papen and Hugenberg. When the cowed delegates passed the Enabling Law on that day, March 24, 1933, by a vote of 441–94, German democracy had been trampled under Hitler's jackboot. Only the Social Democrats had the courage to vote en bloc against the measure.

The Enabling Law was Hitler's decisive victory over his political opponents; it was a triumph that he savored with a kind of malicious glee that was typical of his character. We always catch the truest glimpses of him in moments of triumph and defeat; for he was arrogant in victory but self-pitying and vindictive in defeat. When the leader of the Social Democrats, Otto Wels, gave his final speech during the deliberations on the Enabling Law — a courageous and impassioned attack on Nazi gangster methods — Hitler was so aghast with anger that he mounted the rostrum a second time and savagely attacked Wels and the Social Democrats as obsolete, reminding them with mocking tone that "Germany's star is in the ascendent, yours is about to disappear, your death-knell has sounded."[25]

These rhetorical threats were soon to become reality. Wels's compatriots were either under attack, in prison, or in exile. Otto Braun, the former minister president of Prussia, was already in exile; Wilhelm Sollmann had been savagely manhandled by Nazi thugs; Carl Severing, prominent SPD leader, was under arrest; Julius Leber, SPD member

of the Reichstag, had been tied and gagged by the Nazis as he entered the Reichstag; and even Wels himself, who courageously stood
up to Hitler in a final fruitless gesture, had frittered away precious
time in the previous months by restraining his own paramilitary shock
troops, the Schufo, because he did not want to commit the SPD to
antiparliamentary activity as long as Hitler abided by the constitution.
Checkmated by Hitler, Wels knew nothing better to do than to escape
abroad in vain hopes of carrying on the good fight from the safety of
his exile. Others were not so lucky; the brutal ways of the "rising star"
began to take a grim toll as the Nazis began to assemble the instruments
of control, terror, and intimidation. In Allan Bullock's judgment, "The
street gangs had seized control of a great modern state, the gutter had
come to power."[26]

The Ways and Means of *Gleichschaltung*

On March 31, the central government passed a law called Temporary
Law for Coordination of the States with the Reich, which decreed that
the state parliaments must conform to the new party strength in the
Reichstag and authorized state governments to issue laws that did not
accord with their state constitutions. This was the first time that the term
Gleichschaltung appeared in official usage,[27] a term that the Nazis used
to describe the process by which German institutions were synchronized
to conform to National Socialism. The German word *Gleichrichter*
refers to a device that allows electric current to flow in only one direction, thus changing alternating into direct current.[28] Similarly, the führer,
representing the will of the people, directed the flow of policy through
the institutions of state and party down to the people. This mechanistic analogy, with its Orwellian image of Big Brother directing the will of
the people, was typical of the new Nazi mentality. Helmut Krausnick has
rightly observed that "coordination" was not just a Nazi revolutionary
tactic but was the Nazi revolution itself, for the ideal of National Socialism was to infiltrate, capture, and coordinate German institutions and
thereby all of German life.[29]

Gleichschaltung proceeded along two related paths: synchronization
of all government institutions and mass mobilization of all citizens for
the National Socialist cause. The first approach involved the eradication
of all political opponents and parties and the second the creation of mass
organizations for mass control.

The government was first brought into line when prominent Nazis
were put into the highest offices on both the state and federal level. Since
Hitler had carefully laid the ground work for this takeover, he already
had a prefabricated staff of loyalists in place that moved into predesignated positions. Armed with the decree of February 28, 1933, which
permitted the central government to take over the powers of the states,

the Nazis had already replaced the democratic representatives of the various state governments by putting their own "commissioners" into key positions. During the first week of April 1933, Hitler legalized and institutionalized the Reich commissioners by converting them into Reich governors (*Reichstatthalter*).

These Reich governors exercised sweeping discretionary powers such as appointing and removing state governments, preparing state laws, and appointing and dismissing state officials. Their mission was to assume control of the state governments and force them to observe the directives of the chancellor; they were Adolf Hitler's instruments for stripping the states of their independent authority with the aim of abolishing the federal system of the Weimar Constitution. All eighteen Reich governors were Nazis, and most of them were also *Gauleiter*. Thus, the *Gauleiter* often doubled as Reich governors — a curious aspect of the emerging regime in which state and party would often run on parallel tracks. In order to safeguard his own undisputed sovereignty, Hitler refrained from merging state and party and often encouraged rival agencies. To the average German citizen the emerging system of control appeared outwardly innocuous because the old authoritarian civil service seemed to adapt itself quickly to the new order. However, alongside the regular system of law and order there emerged, as will be seen, more sinister institutions — the system of protective custody (*Schutzhaft*), the Gestapo, and the concentration camp.

This duality of state and party would create overlapping jurisdictions, intense professional rivalries, and bureaucratic mismanagement. On the other hand, it successfully removed most of the vestiges of the Weimar system because it ruthlessly eliminated all political opposition. By the decree of January 30, 1934, entitled Law for the Reconstitution of the Reich, all state governments were subjected to the authority of the central government. Coinciding with the first anniversary of Hitler's seizure of power, the document solemnly announced that the German people had transcended all inner political conflicts and had been welded into an indissoluble unity. Although the law of January 30, 1934, did not abolish state governments, it did outlaw popularly elected state legislatures and made the remaining state governments mere instruments of the central government.

Hitler's policy of *Gleichschaltung* also meant the elimination of all powerful rival organizations, of which the labor unions were the most conspicuous. If *Gleichschaltung* meant mass organization for mass control, then the broad thrust of political domination had to be exerted over the most vital area of citizens' existence — their place of work.

Since the core of the German working class had not defected to National Socialism, remaining loyal to the SPD and KPD (Kommunistische Partei Deutschlands [Communist Party of Germany]), it was crucial for the regime to gain control over this key segment of the population. In order to accomplish this goal, the regime adopted a kind of Bismarckian

approach of *Zuckerbrot und Peitsche* (sugarbread and whip), of alternately bribing and intimidating the workers. In the aftermath of the
Reichstag fire and the various emergency decrees aimed at "protecting"
the German people from imaginary enemies, labor organizations were
systematically attacked in a veritable reign of terror by forces of the SA
and the police. Raids on suspect workers' housing estates all over Germany, illegal arrests and torturing of workers, banning of newspapers,
and seizure of the labor union buildings — all these became the order of
the day beginning in March 1933.

Following the whip came the bribe. On Goebbels's advice, Hitler
declared May Day the "Day of National Labor" and made it a paid
holiday, something that German workers had long dreamed about and
supported. Having created a mood of confidence, the Nazis then struck
on the very next day, May 2, and occupied union offices all over Germany and confiscated all their property. Those major trade unionists
not already under "protective custody," such as Paul Theodor and Peter
Grassmann, who had criticized Hitler for declaring war on the organized
workers, were arrested and imprisoned.[30] All workers' organizations
were merged into the German Labor Front (Deutsche Arbeitsfront
[DAF]) headed by Robert Ley, an alcoholic (later nicknamed Reich-
strunkenbold [Reich drunkard]) and megalomaniac. German workers
and employers were now forced to work through this single mass trade
union, which served the needs of the state rather than the needs of the
workers.

Coordination of agriculture paralleled that of industry. The major instrument of control in agriculture was the Agrarian-Political Apparatus
(Agrarpolitischer Apparat), founded earlier by "Blood and Soil" expert
Walther Darré, whose reactionary peasant ideology would often turn
out to be diametrically opposed to the regime's emphasis on industrial
expansion and technological innovation. Although other economic institutions such as employees' associations or handicraft, commercial, or
industrial organizations were coordinated or, in the euphemism of the
time, "coordinated themselves," the German economy as a whole, as
will be seen later, remained in large part subject to market forces and
private control.

On July 14, 1933, ironically on Bastille Day, the government issued a
law entitled Law against the Formation of New Parties, which declared
that "in Germany there is only one political party, the National Socialist German Workers' Party," and prohibited all other existing parties as
well as the formation of new ones.[31] This was the death certificate of
German parties, and it is both amazing and appalling how meekly the
German parties surrendered to Hitler's tyranny. The two left-wing parties, the KPD and the SPD, had long labored under ideological wishful
thinking, tragically underestimating the Nazis and overestimating their
own infallibility, supposedly based on the "laws of history," their belief that fascism was just a temporary stage in the history of monopoly

capitalism that would inevitably give rise to socialism. They thought of Hitler as a capitalistic stooge, doing the bidding of big business, who would quickly ruin the country as well as his party and thus ring the death knell of capitalism.

The Center Party, under the weak leadership of Ludwig Kaas, who left Germany for Rome in April 1933 and never returned, cared more for the freedom of the Catholic Church than it did for the freedom of German Catholics and believed that the church could function just as well under a Nazi regime. The Vatican, too, was primarily interested in safeguarding the church under National Socialism and was quite willing to sacrifice the Center Party for a concordat. Thus, on July 4, 1933, the Center Party voluntarily dissolved itself. On July 8 Vice-Chancellor von Papen and Cardinal Pacelli signed a concordat between Germany and the Holy See by which the Nazi government promised to protect the integrity of the Roman Catholic Church in Germany and to allow German Catholics the free and public practice of their religion. As Klaus Epstein put it, "All that remained of once mighty political Catholicism was a gaping vacuum — the natural consequence of a half-decade of impotence, opportunism, and insufficient devotion to democracy and parliamentary government."[32]

The surrender of the political right was just as swift. The DVP (German People's Party) had been declining since the late 1920s; its representation dwindled from a high of fifty-one seats under Stresemann to only two in the March 5, 1933, election. The last leader of the DVP, Eduard Dingeldey, had to contend with a noisy extremist wing, a declining membership, an alarming defections of his members to the Nazis. Although he tried to carry on after the official ban, Dingeldey reluctantly agreed to dissolve the party when Hitler refused to give DVP members the pledge of government nondiscrimination. By contrast with the relatively untarnished DVP, the role played by the DNVP between 1928 and its dissolution in June 1933 was disastrous for both the party and Germany. The blame for this must squarely rest on the shoulders of its stiff-necked and narrow-minded leader, Alfred Hugenberg, who dragged the party down to Hitler's level and destroyed himself and the party in the process. Hugenberg and many of his conservative followers were little more than upper-class parlor Fascists who wanted to replace parliamentary democracy with a new authoritarian government based on a "national movement." They labored under the illusion that the Nazis were camp followers who believed that a national movement meant a conservative national movement; worse, they thought that they could control Hitler and transform him into a conservative. Hitler quickly checkmated Hugenberg in a few moves. Isolated in the cabinet, Hugenberg resigned on June 27 and dissolved the party on the same day. In Klaus Epstein's judgement, "This was the inglorious end of the party whose irresponsible policies throughout most of the Weimar period had prevented German democracy from consolidating itself.... [W]hile never subjectively wishing the establishment of Nazi tyranny, its policy objectively contributed to this end. It fell as one of the first victims of the Frankenstein monster it had helped to create."[33]

The law passed by Hitler's government on July 14 prohibiting all political parties except the NSDAP was only one of several significant laws passed on that day that further strangled freedom in Germany.[34] Thus, the government could confiscate property belonging to any organization deemed inimical to the state; revoke anyone's citizenship without having to specify the grounds for revoking it; control rural settlements and the establishment of farms; and hold plebiscites in order to ascertain public opinion regarding proposed measures. Furthermore, the government began meddling in the internal affairs of the Evangelical Church by centralizing its structure and subordinating it to the control of a Lutheran "Reich bishop." Finally, and ominously, the government passed a law, entitled Law for the Prevention of Progeny with Hereditary Diseases, which legalized sterilization and set in motion a chain of biological measures that would result in the euthanasia program involving the gassing of over one hundred thousand "lives not worth living."

After July 14, there remained only a parliamentary shell in the form of a coordinated Reichstag that, obediently doing the bidding of Adolf Hitler, would pass any law, no matter how outlandish or unjust. To make certain that justice itself was coordinated, the Nazis also moved against the legal system. By the terms of the Law for the Restoration of the Career Civil Service, the Nazis had already removed those civil servants "who on the basis of their past political activity" had not given enough assurance that they fully supported the new state.[35] This meant that all political unreliables were arbitrarily expelled from the civil service. The new law also introduced the concept of the "Aryan Clause," which excluded all Jews from the civil service — that is, the courts, the legal profession, teaching, and government service. The first phase of legalized racism, officially encouraged by a boycott against Jewish stores on April 1, 1933, had thus begun, as Nazi Germany was moving steadily toward a policy of legalized expulsion, ghettoization, and extermination of Jews.

On the day this shameful ordinance pertaining to the civil service was released, Karl Linz, chairman of the German Federation of Judges, proudly announced after a meeting with Hitler that "we have placed everything in his (The Führer's) hand with complete confidence."[36] Bringing lawyers into the Nazi-controlled Front of German Law and the Academy of German Law, headed by Hans Frank, was next. Frank's mission was to coordinate justice in all of the German states and to "revitalize" German law on a sound National Socialist foundation. Armed with a few fundamental axioms such as "Law is what is useful to the German people" or "Law must be interpreted through healthy folk emotions," Frank and his legal team began to subvert the rule of law (*Rechtstaat*). As will be shown later, such efforts to Nazify the whole German legal system were not completely successful, and they encountered stubborn, passive-aggressive resistance from the legal establishment. Many lawyers and judges tried to continue interpreting the law honestly and objectively, though this became increasing difficult in political cases because the Nazis simply bypassed the regular judiciary by creating extralegal institutions such as the People's Court (Volksgerichtshof) and the Special Courts (Sondergerichte) — the latter established in the wake of the Reichstag fire on March 21, 1933. How far legal *Gleichschaltung* had gone may be illustrated by the oath taken at a mass meeting held in front of the Supreme Court building in Leipzig in October 1933. On that day, ten thousand lawyers, with their arms raised in the Hitler salute, publicly swore, "by the soul of the German people," that they would "strive as German jurists to follow the course of our Führer to the end of our days."[37]

The subversion of the law by the highest authorities may be further illustrated by the case of Sophie Handschuch, wife of a Munich businessman, who initiated a formal complaint with the State Assize Court (Landesgericht München II) demanding to know the details of her son's death of a "heart attack" in the concentration camp of Dachau. After annoying and petty delays, her son's coffin was finally released with the understanding that it not be opened. The court, however, continued its investigation because it was clear that a young man had been arrested without due process, had been committed to a concentration camp, and had died under questionable circumstances. Conducting an examination on the corpse, the court discovered that the young man had died of severe bludgeoning to the head by a blunt instrument. The court then asked the Bavarian political police for further information. Shortly thereafter, the police released information that two prisoners had committed suicide at Dachau by hanging, one on October 17 and the other on October 18. The Office of the State Prosecutor (Staatsanwaltschaft) investigated these two cases and discovered that both men were probably tortured and killed. Dr. Hans Frank, Bavarian minister of justice, referred the Handschuch case and the other two cases to Reich Commissioner Epp and through him to Adolf Wagner, Bavarian minister of the interior, arguing that he did not know how to handle these three cases! The Handschuch case had already gone too far for comfort, and the other two cases, if pursued with equal tenacity, would inevitably lead straight to what Shlomo Aronson has called the "triangle of SS–Police–Concentration Camp."[38] Frank suggested hushing up the whole affair under the pretext that it would tarnish the reputation of the state; he suggested finding a suitable legal pretext and directed Himmler to initiate the suspension of the criminal investigation through formal petition to the relevant authorities. However, the legal authorities handling the case pressed on with the investigation and even announced that they would use all the means at their disposal to prevent any obstruction of justice. It looked like the Bavarian authorities had won the day against

Himmler and Heydrich. They won for only one day, however. Himmler went straight to Hitler who, in turn, ordered the suspension of the whole affair. The law had lost and murder had been legitimized by the highest authority of the land.[39]

Operation Hummingbird: The Röhm Purge

By the summer of 1933 Hitler was in full control except for three major obstacles: the growing radicalization of the SA under the leadership of Ernst Röhm; the power still wielded by President von Hindenburg; and the influence of the traditionalists within the German army. These three obstacles to dictatorial control were interrelated. The revolutionary zeal of the SA was directed against many respectable elements in German society — capitalists, generals, Junkers, and what Röhm called the whole crowd of "cowardly Philistines." Such belligerent rhetoric, heard all too often from Röhm and his loud-mouthed storm troopers, threatened to disturb the tenuous rapprochement that Hitler was attempting to establish between his own regime and the traditional military-industrial complex. With absolute power within his reach, Hitler understandably worried about Röhm acting out his own brand of dictatorship by brownshirted storm troopers. If Röhm had been an asset during the years of struggle, he was now a liability on two counts: his unwillingness to become an obedient camp follower threatened to split the party, and his resentment of the traditional military-industrial complex could spell ruin for the Nazi movement itself.

As his Nazi rivals scrambled for key posts in the government, Röhm concentrated on developing his own organization by increasing its size to almost four million men and then making alarming noises to the effect that a "second revolution" was needed on the grounds that the first one — Hitler's seizure of power — had not gone far enough. Little did he suspect how far Hitler's revolution would go in the end, but by the summer of 1934 Röhm saw enough signs to convince himself that the Nazi movement was betraying its principles.

As previously shown, Röhm belonged to that growing band of mercenaries whose entire existence had been molded by war and military adventurism — the "lost generation" that neither could nor would adapt itself to the routine of civilian life. Members of Röhm's group had joined the proliferating right-wing organizations that sprang up right after World War I; they had offered their military expertise to "the vanguards of fascism" — that is, to paramilitary groups such as the Free Corps, hoping that this would enable them to continue fighting, brawling, and drinking. Ideology meant little, if anything, to such types; their life's oxygen was soldiering. In practical terms this meant fighting; and it mattered little what sort of fighting it was or against whom it was to be directed — Communists, pacifists, democrats, Jews, weaklings, or just plain civilians. Joachim Fest has aptly characterized this attitude as "Nihilism marching in step" because these agents of permanent revolution had no ideological commitment, no long-range political goal except to keep on marching and fighting.[40]

Röhm himself typified this mentality: "From my childhood," he said in the first sentence of his memoirs (appropriately entitled *The Story of a Traitor*), "I had only one thought and wish — to be a soldier."[41] He was a very good soldier, a daredevil who relished a good fight and felt at home in the company of tough characters, especially in his intimate circle of homosexual friends. Unlike Hitler, he lacked the gift for dissimulation, preferring to be blunt and naively straightforward. By temperament Röhm was a jovial bruiser who disliked pretentious attitudes or refinement. Anything that reeked of sophistication, of manners, of refinement — in short, anything that appeared to be "civilized" — was incompatible with his nature. His preferred home was the barracks, mess halls, and raucous beerhalls.

Sentimentally attached to Hitler, whom he mistook as one of his friends, Röhm had supported the party since its halcyon days of sacrifice and struggle. After Hitler had recalled him from Bolivia, he had thrown himself into the task of rebuilding the SA. His relationship with Hitler was very close; in fact, Röhm was one of the few members of the Nazi party who was allowed to address the führer with the familiar word "du." The SA's expansion was partly due to Röhm's leadership and organizational talent, partly to the growing number of unemployed and desperate men who roamed the streets of Germany searching for employment. It was this private army that ruthlessly captured the streets of Germany and was one of Hitler's trump cards in his bid for power.

By the summer of 1934, however, this boisterous private army and its fiercely independent leader were becoming political liabilities to Hitler's chances of gaining control over the levers of power. Röhm's army was still poised for yet another fight, this time against the old order itself, specifically against the traditional army, the aristocrats, and the business moguls (*Bonzen*) — the hated "old farts" who stood for law and order, respectability, and Philistine values. Hitler saw in this approach nothing but chaos. He was finished with the romance of the revolution and now hoped to get on with the practical business of running the country. Röhm sensed that Hitler was about to sell out to the conservative establishment; and in the private circle of his trustworthy cronies, he lashed out bitterly against the mealy-mouthed führer:

> Adolf is rotten. He's betraying all of us. He only goes around with reactionaries. His old comrades aren't good enough for him. So he brings in these East Prussian generals. They're the ones he pals around with now. . . . Adolf knows perfectly well what I want. I've told him often enough. Not a second pot of the Kaiser's army, made with the same old grounds. Are we a revolution or aren't we? . . . Something new has to be brought in, understand? A new discipline. A new principle of organiza-

tion. The generals are old fogies. They'll never have a new idea....But Adolf is and always will be a civilian, an "artist," a dreamer. Just leave me be, he thinks. Right now all he wants to do is sit up in the mountains and play God. And guys like us have to cool our heels, when we're burning for action.... The chance to do something really new and great, something that will turn the world upside down — it's a chance in a lifetime. But Hitler keeps putting me off. He wants to let things drift. Keeps counting on a miracle. That's Adolf for you. He wants to inherit a ready-made army all set to go. He wants to have it knocked together by "experts." When I hear that word I blow my top. He'll make it National Socialist later on, he says. But first he's turning it over to the Prussian generals. Where the hell is revolutionary spirit to come from afterwards? From a bunch of old fogies who certainly aren't going to win the new war? Don't try to kid me, the whole lot of you. You're letting the whole heart and soul of our movement go to pot.[42]

The real fact was that Hitler did not plot to destroy Röhm or the SA; he simply did not know what to do with this displaced paramilitary army. As long as he needed the SA on his way to power, he did not mind its excesses. Even after his seizure of power, the SA was a useful billy club against political opponents. It could be allowed to play a dramatic role in the opening phases of the revolution as an auxiliary police, but once the country had been coordinated there was no need for a private political army.[43] In fact, a mass of SA troopers, intent upon converting itself into a revolutionary people's army, constituted the worst nightmare to the traditional conservative army. And so it came to pass that the SA and its leader found themselves without a clear-cut mandate, caught between the state, party, and the regular Reichswehr.[44] By making common cause with Hitler, the Reichswehr hoped to escape *Gleichschaltung,*[45] which to some extent it did, as Hitler would later discover through his interminable conflicts with the German military complex. The Nazi revolution would not, like the Russian or Chinese revolutions, produce a revolutionary mass army. Hitler succeeded in Nazifying the police, capturing the chief officers of the state, but he would fall significantly short of Nazifying the armed forces, the state bureaucracy, the courts, and the school system.

Yet Röhm seriously and tragically underestimated Hitler's cunning and misunderstood the ideological convictions that shaped his character. The truth was that Hitler had decided to throw in his lot with the regular army because he realized that without the organizational talents of the conservative generals, his long-range military plans could never be fulfilled. As much as he prized Röhm's past contributions to the movement, he disliked the idea of facing Röhm, heading a revolutionary mass army, as a coequal in the new Nazi state. For its part, the Reichswehr was also horrified of being submerged in a proletarian mass army.

In his attempt to resolve the troublesome dilemma of Röhm and the SA, Hitler was finally goaded into taking action by two major groups:

the army command and Röhm's political opponents. The top military men, notably Defense Minister von Blomberg, chief of staff Colonel Walter von Reichenau, army commander in chief General Werner von Fritsch, and the aging President von Hindenburg all demanded that Hitler take decisive action against Röhm.

On April 11, 1934, Hitler joined the top leaders of the military on the cruiser *Deutschland*. Although the occasion was ostensibly a purely military one — naval maneuvers — the amiable meeting between Hitler and the military resulted in a gentlemen's agreement concerning Röhm's fate.[46] In return for their support of his dictatorship, the military leaders extracted two major promises from Hitler: suppression of Röhm's plans and a guarantee to uphold the traditional nature of the German military.

Röhm's opponents within the party were as formidable as those within the army. Among his most deadly foes were Hermann Göring and Heinrich Himmler; both stood to gain by his removal. As will be recalled, Göring had been instrumental in assembling the skeleton outlines of a police state in 1933. With his Gestapo (Geheime Staatspolizei), a force that at first was little more than a personal terror squad, Göring had already paved the way for Hitler's dictatorship by smashing his political opponents. Having been elevated to the rank of general by Hindenburg himself, the vainglorious Göring, eager to attain legitimacy, now began to gravitate toward the traditional military elite. On April 1, 1934, Göring appointed Heinrich Himmler head of the Prussian Gestapo, a reluctant decision motivated by a combination of indolence and lack of political staying power. In 1934 Himmler was slowly setting the stage for enlarging his own fiefdom within the party. He was already head of the Bavarian police and chief of the SS; and with the help of his unscrupulous second-in-command, Reinhard Heydrich, he was planning to cast his spider's web over all of Germany. In order to do so, however, he had to eliminate Röhm because the SS was still a part of the SA and thus subject to Röhm's command. Himmler went to work with painstaking care, collecting complaints and scandals about the SA leadership. When the blood purge began, his black-shirted minions went into action as firing squads against their brownshirted comrades.

Although Hitler was leaning toward Röhm's enemies, he was genuinely torn by his feelings for one of the oldest fighters (*Kämpfer*). His outward facade of camaraderie toward Röhm was not entirely insincere; the troubled führer even tried to dissuade his old comrade from continuing his self-defeating policy of revolt against the old order. On June 4, 1934, Röhm and Hitler had a five-hour private discussion in which Hitler probably warned Röhm to scale down SA actions but otherwise gave the SA chief no inkling about the exact role of the SA in the Nazi state. The meeting, however, produced two surprises: Röhm declared himself willing to undergo a "personal-illness vacation" (*Krankheitsurlaub*) at Bad Wiessee and to send the whole SA on a kind of vacation or leave of absence during the entire month of July. With historical hindsight we now know that Röhm did not plan a revolt against the army in 1934; he also did not realize that he was about to fall into Hitler's trap. Yet with a force of close to four million men behind him, Röhm was clearly sitting on a powder keg; and by continuing to encourage monster parades, military maneuvers, and vast stockpiling of weapons, the SA leader was about to light the fuse. As Joachim Fest observed, this growing tension, in turn, gripped the public: "For a year Hitler had continued to keep the population breathless by fireworks, speeches, appeals, coups, and histrionics. Now both the public and the producers seemed equally exhausted."[47] Moreover, perceptive Germans, as yet untouched by years of Nazi techniques of mind control, could clearly see what one year of Nazi control had accomplished — ruthless suppression of political parties, intimidation and harassment, difficulties with the churches, the renewed specter of inflation, threats from the SA, and growing distrust from abroad. Even the senile President von Hindenburg sensed that there was something rotten in the state of Germany, saying to Vice-Chancellor von Papen: "Things are going badly, Papen. Try to straighten them out."[48]

Reduced to political impotence, Papen now pulled himself together for a belated and, as it would turn out, pointless act of opposition. Egged on by two of his political advisers, Edgar Jung and Herbert von Bose, he delivered a speech, written by Jung, at the University of Marburg on June 17, 1934, in which he strongly denounced the excesses of the new government and warned his audience that "elements of selfishness, lack of character, mendacity, beastliness and arrogance" were spreading under the guise of a German revolution.[49] The speech caused a mighty furor. Although Goebbels managed to prevent the speech from being broadcast on German radio and kept it out of German newspapers, the damage had been done. Jung urged Papen to follow through by going to Hindenburg and personally putting in a protest against the government's suppression of the Marburg speech.

On June 19 Papen confronted Hitler, protested against Goebbels's censorship of his speech, and threatened to resign from the government. This put Hitler in a serious bind. The prospect of having to answer to the president for sabotaging the conservative coalition government and for engaging in widespread illegalities filled him with mounting apprehension. As president and commander in chief, Hindenburg could still derail his government, perhaps even put an end to his political career. News from Neudeck, however, indicated that the senile and ailing president was not expected to live more than two months. Hitler, therefore, turned his attention to Papen and promised to accompany him to see Hindenburg at Neudeck. It was clear to Hitler that decisive action had to be taken. With Hindenburg's death approaching, the question of the succession had to be addressed. The conservatives around Papen favored a restoration of the monarchy. Hitler seems to have been toying with two possibilities for some time: taking the presidency for himself and appointing a prominent National Socialist as chancellor or, more simply, combining the two offices of president and chancellor in his own role of führer of the German nation. There is persuasive evidence that Hitler had already opted for combining the two governmental offices well before July 30, 1934.[50]

On June 21, Hitler broke his promise to Papen and went to Neudeck by himself, ostensibly to report to the president on his recent trip to Italy but actually to see for himself how Hindenburg's health was holding up. The president, confined to a wheelchair, made it clear that if Hitler could not maintain law and order, he would declare marshal law and let the army run the country. Hitler returned to Berlin realizing that he had no time to waste.[51] After mulling things over at Berchtesgaden for several days, he returned to the capital on June 26 and ordered the arrest of Edgar Jung, pointedly ignoring Papen's protests. Behind the führer's back, Röhm's enemies were now itching for action, already drawing up lists of people who were to be arrested and shot. These lists made the rounds among the chief conspirators — Göring, Blomberg, Himmler, Heydrich — with each competing to add candidates or debating whether to remove them.[52] These sinister machinations, taking place in a shadow world of their own, seemed to indicate that Hitler was being manipulated into getting rid of Röhm. Even during the week before the Röhm Purge, Hitler was still indecisive, telling various SA leaders that he planned to arrest Röhm, that he would fire him, and even that he would make up with him.[53]

Röhm's opponents, however, were grimly determined to remove him. Armed with the flimsiest evidence, they whipped themselves and Hitler into a hysterical state of paranoia about a supposed SA plot against the government. Herbert von Bose and Günther von Tschirsky, two of Papen's advisors who were monitoring the developing Nazi plot from the vice-chancellery, urged Papen to intervene personally with Hindenburg as soon as possible. They suspected the worst, especially after they discovered a hastily scrawled message on a medicine chest in Jung's apartment which said "Gestapo."[54] The two men pleaded with Papen to pressure Hindenburg into declaring martial law, curbing the power of the SA and the Nazi Party, dismissing Hitler from his post as chancellor, and changing the government.

Hitler's henchmen now felt compelled to act because they could not allow Papen to work on the old president and force him to take measures against Hitler. Himmler realized that the men around Papen meant business. Further inspection of Jung's flat had yielded some interesting papers that led straight to Bose. Among the various items found by the SS sleuths was a wish list of future non-Nazi ministers, including the names of General Ferdinand von Bredow, Bose, Erich Klausener, a high-ranking official in the Transport Ministry, and Jung's own name.

On June 28, the two leading chiefs of the army, Blomberg and Reichenau, put the troops on alert and then gingerly moved to the sidelines to let the Nazi conspirators do the dirty work for them. Both the army chiefs and the Nazi plotters sent out unmistakable signals to Hitler that he was facing two potential threats: a conservative cabal instigated either by Papen or the men around him and an impending SA coup orchestrated by the disloyal Röhm. Perhaps to lull the supposed conspirators into a sense of false security, Hitler left the capital on June 28 to attend Gauleiter Josef Terboven's wedding in Essen. It was apparently in Essen that Hitler, still fed alarming misinformation, finally swallowed the bait of an impending Putsch; he was now ready to move against both the SA and the conservative clique around Papen. He sent Göring, who had accompanied him to Essen, back to Berlin to be ready to strike against the SA and the conservatives as soon as he had given the code word. Orders were also given to put all SS and SD commands on alert. This order had an immediate ripple effect, spreading waves of fear among the rank and file of the SA, who sensed that something sinister was in the offing. Some SA officers alarmed their men by shouting hysterically: "The Führer is against us. The Reichswehr is against us. SA, out into the streets!"[55]

The plot around both Hitler and Röhm was thickening. On the afternoon of June 28, Hitler visited the Krupp works; the next day, he inspected various Westphalian work camps. Untouched photographs show him dressed in a rumpled leather coat with hair unkempt, giving the wild impression of a "murderer just before committing his deed."[56] Late in the afternoon of June 29, Hitler arrived at Bad Godesberg on the Rhine and checked into the Hotel Dreesen. He was accompanied by Viktor Lutze, Goebbels, his adjutants Wilhelm Brückner and Julius Schaub, and his chauffeur, Julius Schreck. Word was sent to SS-Gruppenführer Sepp Dietrich to come to Godesberg at once. Hardly had Dietrich arrived, when Hitler ordered him to fly to Munich immediately and await further orders. Scarcely able to catch his breath, Dietrich did what he was told; and when he reported back from Munich, he was ordered to take charge of two SS companies at Kaufering on Lake Tegernsee, a small railroad station near Landsberg on Lech, and take the troops to Bad Wiessee, the resort town where Röhm's minions, blissfully ignorant of what was in store for them, were having a fine time for themselves.

While these events were unfolding in the south, thirteen hundred SS men belonging to Hitler's special guard, the SS-Leibstandarte Adolf Hitler, were alerted and made combat ready at the Berlin cadet school at Lichterfelde. Their destination was to link up with Sepp Dietrich at Kaufering. The Berlin-Lichterfelde barracks were also to be the main place of executions during the Röhm Purge.

At 2 A.M. on July 1, Hitler left Bonn by plane to Munich, landing at Oberwiesenfeld Airport. Gauleiter Wagner and two Reichswehr officers reported that the SA had attempted an unsuccessful Putsch in Munich. This was an outright lie, but it threw the agitated Hitler into a state of frenzy. He swore right then and there that he would personally drive to Bad Wiessee and carry out stern justice. Hitler was then driven to the

Ministry of the Interior, where he worked himself into righteous anger, demanding to see the two highest-ranking SA leaders in Munich, August Schneidhuber and Wilhelm Schmid. When Schmid arrived, Hitler immediately pounced on him, tore off his insignia of rank and screamed, "You are arrested and will be shot."[57] Along with Schneidhuber, Schmid was dragged off to Stadelheim Prison, where SS executioners were waiting for them.

Hitler and company then sped off to Bad Wiessee in three black Mercedes-Benzes, apparently unconcerned whether they arrived there before Sepp Dietrich's troops had secured the area. Hitler, Hess, and Lutze were in the lead car, followed by police officials, SS men, and Goebbels. Hitler saw himself as a white knight charging into a den of conspirators. By the time they arrived at Bad Wiessee, it was 6:30 in the morning. Most of the guests at the resort hotel Hanselbauer, where Röhm and his men were staying, were still fast asleep. Hitler's men, pistols cocked, stormed into the hotel, brushed past the landlady, who mumbled something about how pleased she was to see such illustrious guests, and burst into the rooms where Röhm and his men were sleeping. Hitler arrested Röhm himself, called him a traitor, and ordered him to get dressed. Edmund Heines was found in bed with another SS man, a tidbit that Goebbels would subsequently sensationalize as one of the many disgusting scenes encountered at Bad Wiessee. Hitler was overheard as screaming: "You pigs [*Schweinekerle*], you should be shot."

Meanwhile, in Munich, Gauleiter Wagner was busily rounding up "suspected" SA men, many of them at the railroad station. When Hitler returned to Munich, Goebbels immediately phoned Göring in Berlin and gave him the secret code word *Kolibri* (Hummingbird), setting in motion a wave of terror unheard-of in living memory.[58] Murder squads at Stadelheim Prison in Munich, Berlin-Lichterfelde, and other places tortured and executed people whose names had been placed on the death lists by Göring and Himmler, the former playing the role of murder manager and the latter the role of executioner.

Ritter von Kahr, Hitler's nemesis in the Beerhall Putsch of 1923, was arrested and killed; his body was found hacked to pieces in the moors of Dachau. Father Bernhard Stempfle, the man who knew too much about the führer's private life, was found with three bullet wounds in the heart and a severed spinal cord. One SA leader after another, dumbfounded by his arrest and supposed treason, was thrown into Stadelheim Prison and shot by Dietrich's execution squad. In Berlin, Papen and Tschirsky were summoned to Göring's office and held under house arrest. Papen was lucky to escape from the whole affair with his life. At the same time, thirty SS men, armed with machine-gun pistols, invaded the vice-chancellery in search of Bose. As soon as they discovered him, they gunned him down in cold blood. All over Berlin, SS assassins were busy rounding up and dispatching political enemies. Kurt von Schlei-

cher, working at his desk, was shot down by a Gestapo assassin and
so was his horrified wife, who was in the room with him. General Bredow was shot after answering his door bell. Edgar Jung was tortured in
an underground Gestapo cell and then shot. Gregor Strasser, one of the
original masterminds of the party, was killed in an adjoining cell. Erich
Klausener was gunned down in the Transport Ministry. One of the most
sought after SA leaders, Karl Ernst, who was on his way to his honey-
moon in Madeira, was arrested under vocal protest and put in front of
a firing squad.

Death also caught up with the chief character of this Germanic melodrama — Ernst Röhm. After some soul-searching and indecision, Hitler
was finally badgered by Göring and Himmler into putting a quick end to
Röhm. Himmler gave the execution order to Theodor Eicke, the psychopathic commandant of Dachau whose motto was "Toleration is a sign
of weakness." Shortly before 6 P.M. on July 1, 1934, Eicke went into
Röhm's cell at Stadelheim Prison, gave him a copy of the *Völkischer
Beobachter* with the headlines: "Röhm Arrested and Deposed: Extensive Cleansing of SA," and placed a revolver loaded with a single bullet
on the table. Eicke told Röhm, "Your life is over; the Führer is giving
you one more chance to draw the consequences."[59] He gave Röhm ten
minutes to shoot himself. When Röhm did not oblige, Eicke and his assistant, SS-Sturmführer Michael Lippert, pushed open the cell door and
pumped two bullets into Röhm, who, falling over backward, managed
to murmur pathetically: "Mein Führer, Mein Führer." Eicke's cynical reply was: "You should have thought of this before; it is too late now."[60]
One of the killers then fired another shot into Röhm's chest to finish
him off.

How many people died during the "Night of the Long Knives," as
this sordid event was subsequently called, has never been conclusively
established. This was due, in part, to secret orders by Göring and Himmler to destroy all records relating to the bloodbath. The final death toll,
subsequently inflated into hundreds and even thousands, was probably
around eighty-five.[61] The German people were told that Röhm had been
plotting against the party and the government, had involved himself in
treasonable activities with General Schleicher, and, most damagingly,
had secretly trafficked with representatives of a foreign power. These
were all lies, especially the insinuation that Röhm had negotiated with
representatives of a foreign power. The newspapers had a field day depicting how the brave führer cleared out the homosexual pigsty at Bad
Wiessee. The implication was clear: Germans should not feel any pity
for the death of such traitors and "sexual deviants."

Hitler, who had been clearly prodded into this action by Göring,
Himmler, Goebbels, and the leadership of the army, tried to convince
himself and the country that he had saved the nation and prevented the
possible loss of thousands of innocent lives. In an address to the Reichstag on July 13, a tired-looking Hitler, "clutching the podium as if for

balance,"[62] gave an emotional speech justifying his actions before the nation and sending out an unmistakable signal to future opponents that anyone who would strike against the state would find certain death.[63] The delegates wildly applauded his words that he had taken personal responsibility for the bloodbath and proudly accepted his role as the "highest judge of the German people." The members of the army, who were listening to the speech with special satisfaction, were delighted when Hitler declared that "in the state there is only one bearer of arms, and that is the army."[64] The Reichstag then unanimously approved a law that legalized the murders as "emergency defense measures of the state."

Most Germans were highly relieved, naively believing that the end of the SA terror meant a return to law and order. Goebbels, Göring, and Himmler were in great spirits. The barracks resounded with hurrahs, and in the officers' clubs champagne glasses were clinking.[65] Even President Hindenburg, regretting the death of Schleicher and the arrest of Papen, sent Hitler a telegram congratulating him for having "nipped treason in the bud and having saved the nation from serious danger."[66]

On August 2, 1934, the senile president died at Neudeck. One hour after his death it was announced that the office of president would be merged with that of the chancellor, which meant that Adolf Hitler had become head of state as well as supreme commander of the armed forces. On that same day all German soldiers swore the following personal oath to Adolf Hitler: "I swear before God this sacred oath: I will render unconditional obedience to Adolf Hitler, the Führer of the German nation and people, Supreme Commander of the Armed Forces, and will be ready as a brave soldier to risk my life at any time for this oath."[67] The unlimited nature of Hitler's dictatorship had thus been established.

Chapter 9

The Totalitarian Racial State

A number of descriptive labels have been used to characterize the National Socialist state. In the 1930s and 40s the term "Fascist" was in fashion, followed in the 1950s and 60s by the term "totalitarian," and lately by such designations as the "polycratic state" or "racial state." Some historians have described the Nazi state as a dual state, an old-fashioned tyranny, an oriental court, and even a nonstate. We have chosen the term "totalitarian racial state" because the essence of Hitler's political program consisted in the institutionalization of racism and the use of totalitarian means to accomplish it. It is also our conviction that the essence of all totalitarian regimes consists in molding a new, homogeneous type of human being, conceptualized either in racial or ideological terms. Totalitarianism therefore entails human standardization, conceived in our case in racial (ethnic) terms. "The aim of the National Socialist Revolution," said Joseph Goebbels, "must be a totalitarian state, which will permeate all aspects of public life."[1] The aim of this totalitarian state, Hitler told Hermann Rauschning, was to produce a new godlike human being. This is why National Socialism, according to Hitler, was more than just a political movement, even "more than a religion: it is the will to create a new man."[2]

The dynamics of the new totalitarian state between 1933 and 1945 consisted in the formation of the instruments of control through appropriate party and state machineries, the institutionalization of racial programs, and the mobilization of the German masses for war and conquest.

The Nazi state can be viewed roughly as an equilateral triangle with Hitler at the apex and the state and party forming two equal sides. Of course, such a geometrical analogy serves only a figurative purpose because the three angles of the Nazi triangle were hardly equal, nor were state and party always sharply delineated. Party and state offices sometimes overlapped and duplicated each other, making the system, in the eyes of some, a chaos of competing authorities. This was only partly true. The system may have been a Behemoth, a monstrous animal, but its component parts, despite showing periodic malfunctions, operated relatively smoothly and efficiently. It is, of course, true that the Nazi state was a rule of men rather than a rule of law, but the men who staffed the party and state machinery conducted their business, for the most part, in line with tested German habits of order, efficiency, and obedience to authority. In fact, the most remarkable thing about Nazi Germany was the loyalty that Nazi leaders and the German people as a whole invested in Adolf Hitler. It is for this reason that any analysis of the Nazi state must start with Adolf Hitler and only then proceed to a discussion of his party (NSDAP), the state machinery, and the most powerful institution that straddled them both — the SS.

The Führer and the *Führerprinzip*

Hitler was Nazi Germany and Nazi Germany was Hitler. This means that the personality, leadership style, and ideological convictions of Hitler would shape the nature of government and life during the Third Reich. Hitler believed in the rule of men and not the rule of law, which in practice often meant that decision making was inspired by personal fiat or desire rather than by administrative procedures or formal laws. Indeed, the Nazi regime defined itself by what it rejected — the democratic foundations of the Weimar Constitution and the legal tradition that informed it. Philosophically, the spirit of the new regime was embodied in Hitler's remark, repeated in different variations over the years, that there could be only one will in Germany, his own, and that all others had to be subservient to it.

However, it was not always clear what the führer's will, or as was often the case, "whim," was on any given question, except on those issues — race and territorial expansion — on which he held unshakable convictions. His natural indolence and habit of decision making by fits and starts caused considerable confusion in the Nazi hierarchy and compelled the stronger and more ruthless men to act on their own initiative. The result was often a kind of "authoritarian chaos,"[3] which has misled some historians into believing that Hitler was a "weak dictator" who was relatively absent in his government, was unable to deal with routine bureaucratic tasks, encouraged competition and conflict, and thus caused "unending strife, vast amounts of wasted energy, and perhaps sufficient confusion to have cost [him] his victory."[4]

There is undoubtedly some truth to the argument that Hitler was little seen in his government in the sense of involving himself in the daily routine of government work. As will be shown, this was the result of his Bohemian temperament and his contempt for bureaucrats in general. His relative absence from government could serve as evidence of weakness only if his role had been questioned or if his major decisions had been defied. Neither of these two things happened. As Norman Rich rightly points out, "Hitler was master in the Third Reich."[5] It was an axiomatic belief among the ruling elite that Adolf Hitler was the incarnation of the popular will and always sensitive to the deepest needs of the German people. Given the presumed closeness of ruler and ruled — what the Nazis touted as "German democracy" — it was unnecessary to rely on institutions of popular sovereignty, except for occasional plebiscites, usually held after the fact, to determine how the people felt on any given issue.

Hitler conceived government along the lines of an ecclesiastical order and, doffing his hat to the Roman Catholic Church, viewed himself as an infallible pope. As one young Hitler admirer put it, "If the Catholic Church is convinced that on all matters of faith and morals, the Pope is infallible, then we National Socialists declare, with the same inmost conviction, that for us, too, the Führer is flatly infallible on all matters political as well as on other matters which affect the national and social interests of the people."[6] Rarely in history had public values been so completely identified with the values of one man, whose will and caprice constituted Germany's supreme law.[7]

It is also indisputable that the will of Hitler was never seriously challenged. He may have often operated without written instructions, preferring to communicate his orders in oral form, but the fact is that these orders had the force of law. After the Röhm Purge, Hitler declared himself supreme lord (*Höchster Richtsherr*) of the land, and while he did not often intrude into the legal process, relying on his henchmen to do it, he reserved the right to intervene anytime he chose to do so. After Pastor Niemöller was found not guilty by a court on charges of sedition, Hitler said that "this is the last time a German court is going to declare someone innocent after I have declared him guilty."[8] Hitler made good on this promise by personally reversing decisions that had been made by duly constituted legal authorities.

In short, Hitler's power was inviolable. German soldiers, civil servants, and all those who were involved in any Nazi organization, and that included a sizeable majority of the German people, swore a personal oath of allegiance to Adolf Hitler. As Hans Buchheim put it, the supremacy of *Führergewalt* (führer power) over *Staatsgewalt* (state power) was an accepted principle of statecraft, the result being a virtual decertification of state administrative power in favor of individual powers, a power not bound by the norms of positive law and public morality.[9] In this way, the Nazis actually believed that they had overcome the impersonal nature of the state as it existed in the Western world.[10]

All this being the case, it is crucial to gain a clear understanding of Hitler's personality and leadership style because his visions and obsessions became public policy. What is true of Hitler is equally true of the men who supported him because they represented, in their own peculiar way, a particular part of the führer's personality.

Hitler's leadership style was based on the conviction that individuals must be empowered with strong authority to do what they have to

do. This was referred to as the *Führerprinzip*, the leadership principle.
One man rules the whole, but that one man empowers his subordinates
with the *Führergewalt* they need in order to accomplish the goals set for
them by their overlords and so on down the line of the chain of command, an arrangement that some have labeled as neofeudal. The analogy
is apt in the sense that the leadership selection and style were sometimes
based on a "ludicrous series of subinfeudations via oaths extorted by
'little Führers,' "[11] but it would be wrong to conclude that the Nazi system as a whole was therefore one of feudal decentralization rather that
totalitarian centralization. Although the Nazi state was fragmented by
rival empires run by powerful personalities, it was a modern technological and bureaucratic state that aimed at the total control of a citizen's
life through governmental agencies. Hitler practiced broad and sweeping leadership, unencumbered by administrative policy or precedent.[12]
He gave his officials equally broad authority to carry out their duties,
encouraging fierce competition among top subordinates in the belief that
the best men would gain the upper hand in a natural process of selection.
If the right man was in the right position, this principle could accomplish
miracles; but if the wrong man was in the wrong place, the result could
be confusion, chaos, and disaster. As a result of this Darwinian principle, fierce conflicts and turf battles raged from the beginning to the very
end of the Nazi regime. A few examples will suffice. Göring orchestrated
a systematic takeover of the Prussian Ministry of the Interior, reorganized the political police, and then went on to expand various empires;
but in so doing, he clashed with rivals who were also enlarging their
fiefdoms. In his role of plenipotentiary of the Four-Year Plan, Göring
clashed with Hjalmar Schacht, president of the Reichsbank, minister
of economics, and plenipotentiary for military economy. There is compelling evidence that Hitler encouraged this conflict because he wanted
to use Göring as a means of breaking up the alliance that had formed
between Schacht, on the one hand, and big business and the military,
on the other.

Turf battles abounded in other fields. Heinrich Himmler took over as
Munich police chief in 1933 and used this base of operation to encroach
on the other German police forces. Allying himself with Göring and
Goebbels, he managed to eliminate his chief rival, Ernst Röhm, and built
up the SS as an independent power providing the institutional foundation of totalitarian control. Joachim von Ribbentrop, before becoming
foreign minister, set up an independent office, Dienststelle Ribbentrop,
that competed with the foreign office; and to make matters worse, Alfred
Rosenberg set up his own foreign policy office (Aussenpolitisches Amt)
and opened a diplomatic school to groom ideologically trained candidates for the foreign service. During World War II, Dr. Hans Luther
tried to eliminate Ribbentrop from his position on the grounds that
the foreign minister was mentally incompetent. Luther lost this conflict
and was sent to a concentration camp. Joseph Goebbels, who shifted

his alliances according to the exigencies of the moment, was by all accounts the undisputed Svengali of German propaganda. In practice, however, the diminutive Goebbels was constantly feuding with fellow Nazis who labored in the same vineyard — with Max Amann, Otto Dietrich, Rosenberg, and Ribbentrop. Although Goebbels cleverly set up a system of Reich propaganda offices, he quickly found out that these offices fell under the jurisdiction of the *Gauleiter* who, in turn, were solely responsible to Hitler.

There is no doubt that Hitler preferred such ongoing conflicts because this made everybody dependent on him. As Karl Dietrich Bracher pointed out, Hitler used this method of making everyone dependent on him with "matchless virtuosity."[13] Yet the picture of Nazi rule as chaotic — a picture some have painted — is misleading and mistaken. Hitler was at heart a planner and an architect. True, he preferred to work eccentrically, paying little attention to time or routine, but he could work with surprising discipline and tenacity. Hitler also preferred to do his planning in solitude, away from the disruptive atmosphere of Berlin. This is why he often removed himself to the Berghof near Berchtesgaden on the northern slope of the Obersalzberg, where, overlooking the valley from his mountain home, he would play the role of a godlike architect and visionary, promulgating bold plans and expecting his subordinates to carry them out unconditionally.

Hitler had an aversion to systematic work all of his life, preferring instead to reach decisions intuitively and spontaneously in the manner of an artist rather than an administrator. This explains, in part, why he despised bureaucrats, except those, like Frick, who cut through red tape and did what he wanted them to do. It follows that little administrative leadership could be expected from Hitler because he had no respect for administrative procedures. Albert Speer, Hitler's favorite architect, often wondered whether Hitler actually worked in the ordinary sense of the word.[14] He got up late, disposed of one or two conferences, but from noon on he more or less idled away his time until early evening. Another observer noted that Hitler was completely unfamiliar with the daily workings of government, and for good reason: he had never spent a single day of his life employed in a government post.[15]

Besides being a visionary or artistic planner, Hitler was also very much an amateur. In fact, Speer insisted that "amateurishness was one of Hitler's dominant traits. He had never learned a profession and basically had always remained an outsider in all fields of endeavor. Like many self-taught people, he had no idea what real specialized knowledge meant."[16] But this did not mean that he was ill informed; on the contrary, he had a stupendous memory and a quick mind that astounded and often terrorized the experts. Speer noted, however, that when Hitler was confronted by an out-and-out expert he felt uncomfortable and insecure. Moreover, his technical knowledge, especially relating to military affairs, was very much limited by his experiences in World War I.

As subsequent events would prove, he had little feeling for new technological developments, especially for radar, atomic research, jet fighters, or rockets.[17]

Hitler's style, of course, was a reflection of his character. In order to understand his anfractuous personality, aspects of which will never be understood by rational minds, it is important not to demonize the man, to portray him as a raging, uncontrollable maniac. As Albert Speer puts it, "If the human features are going to be missing from the portrait of Hitler as a dictator, if his persuasiveness, his engaging characteristics, and even the Austrian charm he could trot out are left out of the reckoning, no faithful picture of him will be achieved."[18]

Although poorly educated, Hitler possessed a high degree of intelligence. He read voraciously and could talk about hundreds of subjects with convincing expertise. In social situations, Hitler could be extremely charming and ingratiating, particularly with women. In fact, he loved to surround himself with beautiful women, though he kept contact with them to a superficial level. His admiration for women was in the abstract; he idealized them as types, being incapable of loving a single woman in the flesh.

Contrary to public belief, Hitler did have a sense of humor, though, as Speer points out, it was all too often at the expense of others, as when he remarked: "Do you know when the war will be over? When Göring can get into Goebbels's trousers."[19] He was also a superb mimic who could imitate different characters and act out various roles. Hitler enjoyed listening to jokes rather than telling them himself. When a particularly good joke was told, he would "laugh loudly, sometimes literally writhing with laughter, often he would wipe tears from his eyes during such spasms."[20] However, he was uncomfortable when his more earthy companions told off-color jokes.

Another positive trait was his sense of loyalty to those who showed loyalty to him. He sent flowers to his secretaries on their birthdays; showed the utmost courtesy to chauffeurs and servants, often insisting that their needs be taken care of before his; generously rewarded loyalty or outstanding service; even remembered his family and servants in his will.[21] His old fighters could do no wrong as long as they did not defy him personally; he would often turn a blind eye to their misdeeds, rationalizing them as "justified corruption."[22]

Hitler loved children and was never so completely relaxed as when he was in their company.[23] The many pictures that show him in the company of children, the majority being undoubtedly staged, captured rare moments of sincerity in a man who himself was infantile in so many ways and found it easier to relate to children than to adults. Hitler also loved animals, particularly dogs and wolves. During his hard days in Vienna, he always saved a little bread that he would then feed to birds or squirrels.[24] This is why he hated hunters, whom he roundly condemned as murderers of nature's most beautiful creatures.[25]

Hitler also had a passionate devotion to the arts — the theater, painting, sculpture, opera, and above all architecture. He took out endless time from important political business at hand to attend the opera, visit museums, thumb through art books, and cultivate the company of artists. During the war, he repeatedly protected artists from military service because he was horrified by the thought that they might be killed in combat. Hitler enjoyed immersing himself in the music of Richard Wagner, Edvard Grieg, and Anton Bruckner. "When he listened to music," his friend Kubizek had observed years before Hitler rose to power, "he was a changed man; his violence left him, he became quiet, yielding and tractable."[26]

Although Hitler enjoyed living in luxury, his personal tastes were simple and frugal. He neither smoked nor drank. After the death of his niece Geli, he also gave up meat and became a vegetarian. Hitler avoided personal ostentation. He had only a few civilian suits, and even his military uniforms were simple and austere. Unlike Göring, who was obsessed with private wealth and gaudy uniforms, Hitler was not interested in personal possessions. On the contrary, he kept the same suits, raincoats, shoes, and hat year after year; he wore a necktie until it disintegrated.[27]

Allan Bullock said of Hitler that "if he was in the right mood, he could be an attractive indeed fascinating companion."[28] Hundreds of people have attested to the fact that the force of his personality could not only attract but convert those who fell under its spell. Seasoned generals, determined to straighten him out on the "real" military situation, would, in his presence, change their minds and bow to the führer's superior wisdom. Hitler's histrionic personality was always playing a role, and often convincingly. Even the famous führer outbursts, which could make generals tremble and break out in cold sweat, were usually theatrical. The truth is that, except for a few occasions, Hitler's rages were not spontaneous but self-induced and calculated to produce a desired effect.[29] Hitler used these theatrical talents well, especially his hypnotic eyes. His eyes fascinated those who came under their influence. They were unusually light blue with a faint tinge of greenish-grey.[30] Hitler himself confessed that he had inherited them from his mother, whose eyes he compared to those of the Greek Medusa, whose piercing glance could turn a man into stone. Hitler spoke with his eyes, and he tried to stage-manage a whole state by means of his theatrical talents.

On the surface, the result was an impressive spectacle. Yet, beneath the glittering facade of führer state and führer cult, we discover on closer examination a man with serious personality disorders and decidedly criminal tendencies. Historians are still divided about Hitler's personality. Even fifty years after his death, public and private perceptions of him continue to be blurred and indistinct. Although universally condemned, he still fascinates and even enthralls the curious, while his personality continues to defy the experts. The führer's personality, it seems, was so chameleonlike as to discourage definitive judgments; and even when the sinister and malicious intentions that inspired his policies became quite obvious, few experts could agree on the sort of monster the German dictator had really been. One thing was certain to all but the most unregenerate Nazis: Hitler had been a malignant force in world history, a calculating, willful, and brutal leader. Yet our images of him are still hazy, attesting to our inability to define evil or malignant destructiveness.

Over the years, many interpretations of Hitler's character have been offered by historians, sociologists, psychologists, and journalists. Some have argued that he was a Machiavellian who adjusted his policies to the exigencies of the moment,[31] but who also lusted after absolute power and would stop at nothing to attain it. Some historians, taking a psychological approach, have described him as a borderline personality, exhibiting narcissistic, paranoid, and neurotic traits that made him extremely volatile and unpredictable.[32] Psychologists have gone so far as to label him a malignant sadomasochistic personality,[33] perhaps schizophrenic.[34] Medical historians have argued that Hitler was a drug addict who suffered from amphetamine toxicity[35] or that he was a victim of organic brain disease such as Parkinson's syndrome.[36] There is truth in some of these theories but not the whole truth. Few experts would quarrel with the contention that Hitler suffered from one or several personality disorders, although no unanimity exists about the precise disorders in question. It is possible, however, using certain diagnostic and historical (empirical) evidence, to reconstruct a profile of symptoms, some of which have a direct bearing on public policy in Nazi Germany. These symptoms fall into seven categories:

1. Acute anxiety state
2. Depressed suicidal ideation
3. Malignant aggression
4. Mental confusion
5. Persecutory ideas
6. Somatic symptoms
7. Antisocial (criminal) attitude

1. *Acute anxiety state:* There is almost universal agreement among historians that Hitler was high-strung and habitually anxious about everything. He was a rigid and infantile character who felt himself deeply unworthy and was afflicted by neurotic fears and obsessions. Some of his compulsions were intrinsically life-denying: he was obsessed by morbid themes such as putrefaction, decapitation, strangulation, impurities of the blood, and venereal disease.[37] This may account for his excessive cleanliness and his ascetic lifestyle. Hitler was inordinately preoccupied with health foods, and one of the probable reasons for his becoming a vegetarian and a teetotaler was to cure a stomach disorder that often rendered him all but helpless. He was also so afraid of his body odor that he constantly popped pills against flatulence, pills

that contained strychnine and atropine and may well have had deleterious side effects. His fears and anxieties were so many and varied that he found it necessary to combine them into one big fear he could readily identify and combat — that fear being the pernicious influence of the Jews. Joachim Fest observed that "fear was the overwhelming experience of his formative years" and that "states of exaltation alternated frequently with moods of deep depression in which he saw nothing but injustice, hatred, hostility."[38] It is a measure of his rigidity that the young Hitler that Kubizek knew in 1905 was the same man as the ailing führer who railed against the whole world deep within the bunker in 1945.

2. *Depressed suicidal ideation:* Although Hitler cultivated a brave facade of unshakable will, he was insecure to the core of his being and castigated himself for being worthless. Like many sociopaths, he dreaded being reduced to a nothing; and if he could not be great, he preferred the "zero state" or even annihilation — an attitude that is common among deviants who dichotomize reality into sharp opposites.[39] Suicidal themes are present throughout Hitler's career. Whenever failures threatened, he would plunge into a profound despair followed by convulsions and rages. As will be recalled, when the Putsch of 1923 began to go awry, he told his astonished listeners: "If it comes off, all's well, if not, we'll hang ourselves." Later, after repeatedly failing to capture the chancellorship, he threatened suicide again. On the very day that he announced to the German people that war had been declared on Poland, he mentioned, almost in the same breath, that if the war failed, he would not live to see the end of it — hardly a reassuring message to the German people from their iron-willed führer.[40]

3. *Malignant aggression:* Hitler's actions demonstrate that he was malignantly destructive. Even in conversation, he delighted in touting masculine virtues he considered to be important: strength, hardness (*Härte*), brutality, power. His thoughts along those lines moved in patterns of polarization: what was hard was a sign of strength, what was soft was a sign of weakness; what was powerful was right, what was powerless was weak and wrong. A recurring phrase in his speech was *So oder So* (either or), by which he meant that there were only two choices — right or wrong, victory or retreat, strength or weakness. Such thought patterns are typical of rigid personalities unable to let go or show their feelings, who retreat from human emotions into a world of abstract notions. Hitler admired aggressive people who asserted themselves brutally without showing emotion. Until he fell from favor, Göring was the man he liked to recommend as an example of someone who acts brutally in a crisis while remaining ice cold (*eiskalt*) as he dispatches his victims.[41] He even held up one of his greatest enemies, Joseph Stalin, as one of the most extraordinary figures in world history and a "hell of a fellow" (*Scheisskerl*). Genghis Khan, the Mongol chief whose hordes destroyed entire cities and exterminated enemy populations — men, women, and children — with ruthless efficiency, was

another leader Hitler identified himself with and commended to his generals.[42] Reading about his free-flowing monologues, faithfully recorded by various reluctant hearers at führer headquarters, one cannot miss, in Allan Bullock's judgment, the "vulgarity of Hitler's mind, cunning and brutal in its sophistries, forceful but devoid of human feeling, as unabashed as it was ignorant."[43]

From his earliest encounter with hardship in Vienna, Hitler had developed brutal and callous attitudes toward others — attitudes he later intellectualized in pseudo-Darwinian terms, claiming that life was a ceaseless struggle for existence in which only the strongest could survive. Hitler equated strength with aggression and assault on the opposition; he admired cruelty as a method of showing one's superiority. He once confessed to Rauschning: "Cruelty is impressive. Cruelty and raw brutality. People want holy terror. They need the thrill of terror to make them shudderingly submissive.... I do not want concentration camps to become old age pensioners homes. Terror is the most effective way of politics."[44]

4. *Mental confusion:* Hitler was a profoundly miseducated man who lacked a solid foundation in any field. As we have seen, he read voraciously as a young man, but without discipline and discrimination. His knowledge of the world was pathetically distorted and ethnocentric; he spoke no foreign languages and never traveled extensively outside Germany or Austria. He preferred fantasy to reality, a trait already highlighted by his friend Kubizek. In his analysis of Hitler's malignant form of aggression, Erich Fromm observes that "if one connects Hitler's behavior in these youthful years with the data from his later life, a pattern emerges, that of a highly narcissistic, withdrawn person for whom phantasy is more real than reality."[45] Yet when Hitler's unrealistic views were challenged or questioned, he reacted by becoming angry and resentful, or, alternately, he would insist that he knew better because he had a special "sixth sense." It is a well-known fact that Hitler believed that he possessed the rare gift of prophetic sight (*Vorsehung*) and based some crucial decisions on this presumed insight. It will be recalled that his political conversion itself was probably based on some hallucinated vision in which a voice exhorted him to avenge the shame of defeat and save the German people. He trusted in this inner voice throughout his career, enjoining his followers to believe, as he did, that "whoever proclaims his allegiance to me, is by this very proclamation and by the manner in which it is made, one of the chosen."[46] He sensed invisible demonic forces all around him and objectified them as fleshly malefactors in the form of the Jews. It is no wonder that he was always thinking the unthinkable and that in his "statements an element of bitter refusal to submit to reality invariably emerged."[47]

5. *Persecutory ideas:* A persecution complex was one of the cornerstones of Hitler's flawed personality structure. Fundamentally ill informed and confused about the nature of complex events, Hitler

would externalize his anxieties or fears by blaming vast amorphous forces beyond his immediate control. His whole oratorical genius was directed toward persuading the German people that in his diagnosis the ills of German society were the results of sinister machinations by world Jewry. As shown earlier, his language increasingly took on the coloration of religion: evil forces were lurking everywhere, threatening to "rape," annihilate, or enslave the German people. Salvation therefore consisted in following the "call of the blood" and listening to one's inner racial conscience. The Jews, who were persecuting the Germans, must in turn be persecuted and annihilated. There is no choice; either annihilate or be annihilated.

6. *Somatic symptoms:* All of his life Hitler was obsessed by somatic symptoms and bodily functions, endlessly complaining about undefined aches or pains. He was an anxiety-ridden hypochondriac who constantly checked his bodily functions, taking his pulse, consulting medical books, eagerly seeking advice and information on illnesses, and taking fistfuls of pills — cold medicines, vitamins, stimulants, antigas medications, and so on. Trusting no one, he treated himself before consulting doctors, and when he sought help, he preferred unorthodox practitioners like Dr. Theodor Morrell, an obese and balding medical quack who used exotic medications to invigorate his führer, but by so doing probably gradually poisoned his patient during the later phase of World War II.

Hitler was particularly afraid of cancer; his mother had died of the disease and there is compelling evidence that Hitler thought he too was dying of cancer. In fact, after having a polyp removed from his vocal chords in 1930, Hitler increasingly believed that he would have a short life, telling Albert Speer: "I shall not live much longer.... I must carry out my aims as long as I can hold up, for my health is growing worse all the time."[48] His decision to go to war was largely based on his belief that he would not live very long and therefore had to complete his great work before passing away. As Henry Kissinger remarks, "History offers no other example of a major war being started on the basis of medical conjecture."[49]

7. *Antisocial (criminal) attitude:* Hitler had a lifelong hatred of respectable, established, or "normative" institutions. In the words of Hans Frank, he was an "insensitive psychopath" who was moved by "sheer primitive, wilful egotism, unrestricted by form or convention. That's why he hated all legal, diplomatic, religious, or bourgeois conventions — all the social values that represented restrictions to his impulsive ego-expressions."[50] If any clinical label applies to Hitler it is that of sociopathic (criminal) personality. Admittedly, Hitler was afflicted by several other possible disorders; he was certainly obsessive-compulsive, histrionic, narcissistic, and paranoid, but none of these labels captures his quintessential style. In the final analysis, his habitual style was reflected in his behavior, and that behavior was, above all, deviant. Our primary diagnosis is therefore that Hitler was a sociopathic personality

who exhibited all the antisocial tendencies generally associated with this kind of character disorder.

The chief characteristic of this personality disorder is a deep-seated emotional antipathy toward authority; it can usually be traced to a person's experiences in childhood and family life. Invariably, such antisocial personalities carry within themselves the marks of "betrayal suffered in childhood within the family."[51] Although generally intelligent, spontaneous, and likeable, they are in reality callous, deceitful, and manipulative.

As previously noted, Hitler habitually lived in the shadow of illegality and spent much of his first thirty years in "obscure asocial circumstances."[52] His rise to power, marked by constant clashes with constituted authority and by nine months of imprisonment, would strengthen and validate his criminal tendencies. Hitler's close followers reflected his tendencies: Göring was a clever sociopath and morphine addict who shamelessly plundered the wealth and possessions of others; Goebbels was a psychopathic liar and cheat who crowned his career by ordering his wife to kill his six small children in cold blood; Ernst Röhm, the SA chief, was a brutal soldier of fortune with decided antisocial tendencies; Robert Ley, head of the Labor Front, was an alcoholic and a megalomaniac; Hess, his deputy, was mentally disturbed, possibly schizophrenic; Martin Bormann, Hitler's private secretary and grey eminence, had been involved in the murder of his former teacher in elementary school; Julius Streicher, editor of the pornographic magazine *Der Stürmer*, was a malignant racist and sexual pervert; Heinrich Himmler, the führer's SS chief, was a neurotic hypochondriac, self-appointed grand inquisitor, and cold-blooded murderer of six million Jews; and Reinhold Heydrich, Himmler's right-hand man, was a brutal psychopath who had been cashiered from the German navy for conduct unbecoming an officer.

It is no accident that such personality types were attracted to Hitler. These men were made from the same cloth; they were "little Hitlers." Yet neither they nor their führer could be said to be, with the exception of Hess, mentally deranged. It is a serious error to assume that flawed personalities cannot succeed in imposing their will on entire communities. Concentrated viciousness has triumphed too many times in history to make us believe otherwise. Hitler and his men, however flawed, were intense fanatics, with all the amazing psychic energy entailed by that; and they would fling themselves on the institutions of Germany and try to bend them to their will.

The Nazi Party

In January 1933 it was not only Hitler who came to power in a highly industrialized country — the Nazi Party, which made his triumph possible, had also ascended. The NSDAP had a dual function when it was in power: it was a mass party intending to represent all Germans; it also adhered to an elitist ideology and leadership style.[53] Its ideal was to serve as a vanguard of believers, and, following certain elitist principles, it organized itself, at least on paper, in a strictly hierarchical manner. As Dietrich Orlow has shown, the NSDAP functioned on three levels: the *politische Organisation,* or territorial cadre organization; the *Gliederungen,* or divisions; and the *angeschlossene Verbände,* or affiliated associations. The political organization comprised its leadership cadre. The führer was both head of the party and head of state. On the party side, his immediate subordinate was Rudolf Hess, his deputy and "the conscience of the party," who as a Reich minister possessed the right to assist any government ministry in the formulation of policy or law. Hess's chief of staff, and the man who would gradually overshadow him, was Martin Bormann, an intensely ambitious and calculating man who has been referred to as the "Machiavellian of the office desk."[54]

The top political organization also included the head of the party chancellery, Philipp Bouhler; the party treasurer, Franz Xaver Schwarz, and his staff; the Reich organizational leader (ROL), concerned primarily with job descriptions and jurisdictional delineations; and the intraparty judiciary system. Next in importance came the *Reichsleiter* (Reich leaders), eighteen in all by the late 1930s, who held specific posts with territorial jurisdiction or were assigned tasks formulating the political goals of the German people. In general, the *Reichsleiter* executed policies that were not territorially restricted and pertained to a major social or economic interest throughout the Reich. The most important of the eighteen *Reichsleiter* were Goebbels (propaganda), Frank (law), Rosenberg (foreign policy), Schwarz (finance), and Buch (arbitration court). This group also included the heads of paramilitary organizations such as Viktor Lutze (SA) and Heinrich Himmler (SS) and a few, like Hermann Göring, who held no major party office.

Below the *Reichsleiter* were the *Gauleiter* (*Gau* leaders), the regional leaders of the Nazi Party who administered the *Gaue.* Responsible directly to Hitler, who appointed them, the *Gauleiter,* in turn, commanded the *Kreisleiter* (district leaders), who commanded the *Ortsgruppenleiter* (local group leaders), who gave orders to the *Zellenleiter* (cell leaders). Each *Zellenleiter* supervised between four to eight blocks in city or town, about forty to sixty households.[55] The thirty-five *Gauleiter* were feudal princes within their domains and ultimately answered only to the führer. The grunts of the system were clearly the *Zellen-* and *Blockleiter,* whose morale was never very high. The *Blockleiter,* serving as party town clerk, town crier, and mailman,[56] were not popular with most ordinary Germans because they were perceived as bumbling tyrants and inquisitive busybodies.[57]

The divisions of the party included the Hitler Youth (HJ), led by Baldur von Schirach; the National Socialist Women's Organization (NSF), headed by Gertrud Scholtz-Klink; the National Socialist German Student League (NSDSTB); the National Socialist Motor Corps (NSKK), a special motorized unit with paramilitary duties; the National Socialist Pilots' Corps (NSFK); the SS, led by Himmler; and the SA, headed after Röhm's execution by Viktor Lutze.

The third tier of the party included various affiliated organizations relating to professional or interest groups. These associations of the party were tasked with the responsibility of immersing all Germans not otherwise reached by the party divisions in the Nazi experience. The most important of these affiliate organizations was the German Labor Front (DAF), an organization that was sponsored by the National Socialists and headed by Robert Ley. The DAF, with its membership of over twenty million workers, had replaced the various labor unions and groups of the Weimar Republic and was supposed to bring about a lasting harmony between contending socioeconomic interest groups. Operating with a large budget, the DAF also developed various branches such as the Strength through Joy (Kraft durch Freude) organization, trying to enrich the cultural life of workers, and the Beauty of Labor (Schönheit der Arbeit) branch, seeking to improve conditions in the work place. Other affiliated organizations were the National Socialist Welfare Organization (NS-Volkswohlschaft [NSV]), National Socialist War Victims' Relief Organization (NS-Kriegsopferversorgung), National Socialist Physicians' League (NS-Ärztebund), National Socialist Teachers' League (NS-Lehrerbund), Reich League for Civil Servants (Reichsbund der Deutschen Beamten), and National Socialist Lawyers' League (NS-Rechtswahrerbund).

Having become the sole state party on July 14, 1933, the NSDAP faced a number of serious challenges that were never successfully met, the result being that the party became a hollow shell behind the real emerging power centers, including Hitler and the men who built their own empires (Himmler, Göring, Goebbels). In addition, the party fought prolonged battles with various state authorities, a conflict it neither won nor lost and that ended, at best, in a kind of stalemate detrimental to both institutions. As soon as the NSDAP had pushed Adolf Hitler into power it faced a serious identity crisis. Should it become the sole power dominating the state or should it subordinate itself to the state by becoming a supportive and purely auxiliary institution? The issue was largely decided by Hitler in the beginning of July 1933 when he made it quite clear that the revolutionary phase was over and that the emphasis from now on should be on evolution rather than revolution. This effectively removed whatever impetus there may still have been in some sections of the party that aimed at a revolutionary transformation of German society by using the party as a spearhead of radical change, as happened in Russia following the Bolshevik Revolution. Nothing of the kind happened in Germany, for several reasons.

In the first place, the Nazi Party could never compete with the führer in asserting authority and charisma.[58] This was due, to some degree, to the feeble leadership of Rudolf Hess, a shy and introverted man whose one article of faith was complete submission to Adolf Hitler. According to Joachim Fest, "Hess was the type of the passively totalitarian man with whom it is possible to do anything because he loves to feel he is wax in the hands of another."[59] To Hess the führer was and always would be right, a faith that remained with him throughout his bizarre career as the führer's feeble deputy who labored on dead-end tasks in his master's shadow and was allowed into the public limelight only to announce his appearances at mass meetings where he would cast adoring glances at him. Just as Hitler had put the ineffective Rosenberg in charge while he served his prison term at Landsberg, so he picked the basically decent but totally indecisive Hess as his deputy führer. Of course, in Nazi Germany one man's weakness was exploited by another man's strength. In this case, it was Hess's sinister chief of staff, Martin Bormann, who would wait in the wings, hone his technical and manipulative skills, undermine his chief and the old guard, and increasingly make himself indispensable to Hitler. When Hess, already showing signs of mental disorder, embarked on his futile secret mission to Scotland, ostensibly to initiate peace talks, Bormann quickly took control of the party. Although the party regained some momentum under Bormann, its inherent weaknesses had taken their toll, and time was running out for Nazi Germany.

In addition to Hess's feeble leadership, the NSDAP was troubled by internal conflicts. Its chief leaders were constantly feuding, fighting turf battles, and disagreeing on the party's social program, which created "monumental inefficiencies."[60] It must be recalled that the type of men who had succeeded in capturing major positions in the party were aggressive and often unprincipled fighters who were validated in their aggression by the warlike nature of Nazi ideology. Moreover, their talents were limited by their education and social backgrounds. They were generally disappointed petit bourgeois types from rural areas or small towns. According to Karl Dietrich Bracher, "A provincial, petty bourgeois background, limited education, military service, and job problems were common to almost all of them."[61] Nor were they agreed on the party's social mission. One faction around the labor leader Robert Ley desired a genuinely egalitarian society in which socioeconomic conflicts would be resolved in favor of social harmony and communalism. The social goal of the party, they argued, should be the creation of a genuine *Volksgemeinschaft* or people's community, and the chief strategy to bring it into being should be through government "caring" (*Betreuung*) — that is, in the form of generous welfare programs. This position, however, was rejected by key leaders of the party, notably by Hess, Bormann, and Schwarz, who were not opposed to meeting the needs of *Volksgenossen* (fellow Germans) but stressed the primacy of control over welfare.[62] Both sides, as was the rule in Nazi Germany, looked to Hitler to take a stand, only to discover that the führer, though appearing to support both sides, refused to take a final stand.[63]

Feuds and inconsistencies of leadership, combined with programmatic ambiguities, contributed to what Dietrich Orlow has aptly termed "monumental inefficiency" because the major functionaries tried to secure their own autonomous empires and staff them with many incompetent office holders.[64] Corruption often flourished because internal mechanisms of self-correction ran up against the resistance of entrenched forces, a tendency that was greatly reinforced during World War II when the Nazi empire expanded and outran an administrative apparatus already ill equipped to serve it.

These inherent weaknesses prevented the party from taking over Germany completely, let alone revolutionizing its socioeconomic substructure. The NSDAP took power in a highly industrial country whose major institutions, except for its dysfunctional political system, functioned relatively well. As previously mentioned, Hitler wanted domination rather than social revolution; he wanted to leave Germany's major institutions intact because he knew that a social revolution, with its attendant chaos and disruption of services over many years, would undermine his goal of territorial expansion and conquest.

The history of the Nazi Party was no history at all but a series of dead ends and arrested developments. By mid-1933, when Germany was in the throes of social turbulence, Hitler began to muzzle the party in order to remove its revolutionary sting. By mid-1934, when he had crushed the last flicker of radical impetus by emasculating the SA, a ripple effect stymied efforts by the party to achieve major transformations of Germany's social institutions. Although the party continued to infiltrate the traditional institutions of the state, including the civil service, the reverse was also the case. The traditional elites grafted themselves onto the NSDAP, partly to retain their old positions of influence or to gain new powers that the regime made possible in its years of expansion and victory. Several studies have shown that there was no leveling in the Nazi Party; the reverse was actually the case: the higher the rank, the greater the proportion of the elite class in it.[65] It is surely a significant fact that there were no ordinary workers in the families of the *Reichsleiter*.[66]

By 1939 the Nazi Party had 1.7 million members, most of them men.[67] Although it called itself National Socialist, workers were underrepresented, whereas the elites were overrepresented.[68] Nevertheless, its core was predominantly lower-middle-class. The party never succeeded in becoming an elite order, having admitted too many untrained and untested members, and was led from its inception by a professionally handicapped group of petit bourgeois fighters with an excess of aggression and few moral principles. In all events, the NSDAP remained a very dangerous party because, although incapable of constructing anything positive for the ages, it was in a position to annihilate the social structure through its inherent nihilistic tendencies.

The Institutions of the State

Side by side with the party were the institutions of the state. As early as the 1930s observers were intrigued by the complicated relationships that were developing between these two institutions. The first systematic study that explored this relationship, Ernst Fraenkel's *Dual State* (1941), focused on the existence of two governments — the prerogative state in which Hitler and his Nazi functionaries made ad hoc decisions and the established legal order that carried out the routine business of government. Fraenkel was quite explicit in arguing that it was the prerogative state that held the upper hand on major policy decisions to the end of the Third Reich.

However, the label "dual state" is misleading and perhaps even a contradiction in terms. There was only one state, and Hitler controlled it. Fraenkel's terminology, however, is useful if it is applied to the functions of government because these often resided in the hands of officials who not only belonged to the party but also held positions and administered offices of a similar nature in both the party and the state. Thus, Goebbels was a *Reichsleiter* and chief of propaganda in the NSDAP, but he also occupied the post of Reich minister for public enlightenment and propaganda. Walther Darré was a party *Reichsleiter* who headed the party's Office of Agrarian Policies and the SS Race and Settlement Main Office (RuSHA), while at the same time holding two state offices — Reich food minister (1933) and Reich agricultural leader (1934). Hans Frank was a *Reichsleiter* responsible for legal affairs in the party but simultaneously held state offices — Reich minister of justice, Reich minister without portfolio, governor-general of Poland. Himmler was *Reichsleiter SS* and chief of German police within the Ministry of the Interior, administering an increasingly complex system of institutional terror and racism that spread through both party and state; in the end he captured the Ministry of the Interior, replacing Frick (1943). The relationship between state and party was further complicated by the fact that Adolf Hitler, impatient with the slow pace of government bureaucracy, encouraged the creation of special positions or organizations in order to speed up a particular process that he regarded as crucial to his policies. Dr. Fritz Todt, for example, was appointed as general inspector for German roads and charged with building a new network of interstate highways (*Autobahnen*), but his position was not housed in the Ministry of Transport; instead, it was attached directly to the Reich chancellery and Hitler. As Martin Broszat has argued, this became a typical pattern for the emergence of special organizations directly subordinate to Hitler and functioning outside the Reich government.[69] A similar example was offered by the appointment of Konstantin Hierl as director of labor service, a position nominally subject to the Reich minister of labor, Franz Seldte, but in practice developing independently into a separate organization that was supposed to implement a plan for a new Reich Labor Service (RAD), a work-conscription plan by which all men between the ages of eighteen and twenty-five were required to perform six months of community labor.

The development of dual and overlapping functions, exercised by various state or party offices, hardly seems to justify the monolithic picture of totalitarian control the Nazis projected to the rest of the world and that some historians have uncritically perpetuated to this very day. Martin Broszat has therefore suggested that the term "polycracy" is more appropriate in describing the Nazi state.[70] By "polycracy" is meant a pluralism of forces and the existence of different and often competing power centers held loosely together by their subservience to the führer. Like the term "dual state," the term "polycracy" is a useful heuristic concept because it captures a significant reality of how the Nazi state often functioned in practice. However, the term does not express the essence of the Nazi system or its habitual style. The National Socialist state was a highly bureaucratized and technologically sophisticated system and its ultimate aim was the total control of a citizen's life. In practice, this intended control fell short of its goal because it was hampered by centrifugal forces operating within it. Yet its habitual style, adopted in varying degrees by both the party and the machinery of state, was totalitarian because it aimed not at encouraging individual selfhood but at the exploitation of human beings for their usefulness to the state.

At the helm of the state, as of the party, was Adolf Hitler. He was assisted by two chancelleries: a presidential chancellery he inherited from Hindenburg and his own office as chancellor. Otto Meissner (1880–1953), an Alsatian who had served as an infantry officer in World War I and had briefly worked for the German state office that administered the Ukraine, was the chief of the Reich presidential chancellery, faithfully serving under Ebert, Hindenburg, and Hitler. In 1937 Hitler also appointed him to the post of Reich minister. As previously noted, Meissner was a conservative monarchist and career bureaucrat of the old school who exercised considerable influence on President Hindenburg. After Hitler merged the offices of president and chancellor, Meissner's position, strictly speaking, became superfluous. He was kept on out of deference to the old conservative elite; in actual practice, his office became a powerless appendage relegated largely to the processing of appeals for clemency.

The more significant link between Hitler and his state institutions was the office of the Reich chancellery, headed by Dr. Hans Lammers (1879–1962), a lawyer and judge by profession. Lammers, too, was at heart a conservative monarchist with strong nationalistic commitments. This is why, as a homeless conservative, he had initially joined Hugenberg's

DNVP and then, after recognizing that the DNVP was a dead end, attached himself to the NSDAP (1932). Hitler picked him essentially to serve as his secretarial rubber stamp, preparing proposed laws, handling personnel matters relating to the ministerial bureaucracy, serving as a liaison between the various ministries, and basically informing him of ongoing state business. Lammers was essentially an obedient technician (*Fachmann*) who did what he was told so well that he became, next to Bormann, Hitler's alter ego.[71] With the beginning of the war, his influence receded rapidly, partly because his chief donned the mantle of warlord and partly because Bormann muscled in so successfully on his bureaucratic territory as to reduce him to a mere messenger boy. When asked after the war whether he was privy to any information about the fate of the Jews, Lammers responded by saying quite innocently that he had once asked Hitler what was meant by the "final solution" and was told that Hitler refused to discuss it, other than saying that he had given Himmler an order to evacuate the Jews.[72] For such moral obtuseness, coupled with his readiness to put his legal rubber stamp on Hitler's criminal decrees, Lammers was sentenced at Nuremberg to twenty years in prison, but served only five years.

Instead of formulating or drafting legislation, Lammers's Reich chancellery was limited primarily to legislative procedures. It was also only one of several institutions that served as a conduit between Hitler and the agencies that proliferated in the Third Reich. Issues relating to military affairs were assigned at first to the Ministry of Defense and then in 1938 to the Oberkommando der Wehrmacht (High Command of the Armed Forces [OKW]), organized as a quasi-military chancellery under the leadership of General Wilhelm Keitel. Party–state questions generally involving personnel matters were funnelled through the party chancellery.

Directly below the führer and these institutions were the Reich ministries with their jurisdictional competencies. Under the Weimar Constitution, Reich ministries exercised considerable power and influence through the cabinet — an institution that often served as a counterpoise to the chancellor. Before he had consolidated his power, Hitler felt obliged to work through the cabinet, most of whose members were conservative nationalists; but once he had concentrated most decision-making powers in his own hands, he divested himself of the conservatives and then let the cabinet die a natural death.[73] The last cabinet of the Third Reich met on February 5, 1938.

Hitler rejected the notion of having to reach a collective decision through anything resembling a democratic process. There was to be no shared governance in the Third Reich. Hitler dealt directly with his ministers and empowered them to rule as führers within their respective domains. They could draft legislation and sign decrees, subject to approval by Hitler, without the consent of the cabinet, the Reichstag, or any other corporate body. In return, he expected them to be uncondi-

tionally loyal, to adhere strictly to their own fields of competency, and
never to initiate discussions with other ministers without clearing them
through the Reich chancellery or himself.

The sixteen Reich ministers were responsible for the following fields:
(1) foreign policy (first under Konstantin von Neurath and then, after
1938, under Joachim von Ribbentrop); (2) the interior (Wilhelm Frick);
(3) public enlightenment and propaganda (Joseph Goebbels); (4) aviation (Hermann Göring); (5) finance (Lutz von Schwerin-Krosigk);
(6) justice (Franz Gürtner and, after his death in 1942, Otto Thierack);
(7) economics (Hjalmat Schacht and then Walther Funk); (8) agriculture (Walther Darré and, after 1942, Herbert Backe); (9) labor
(Franz Seldte); (10) science, education, and culture (Bernhard Rust);
(11) church affairs (Hanns Kerrl and, after his death in 1941, defunct);
(12) transport (Julius Dorpmüller); (13) postal service (originally Paul
von Eltz-Rübenach and, after 1937, Wilhelm Ohnesorge); (14) armaments (Dr. Fritz Todt and, after his death in February 1942, Albert
Speer); (15) eastern territories (Alfred Rosenberg); and (16) defense
(Werner von Blomberg, and then amalgamated into the new High Command of the Armed Forces in 1938). The least powerful and glamorous
of these ministries were finance, agriculture, labor, education, church
affairs, post, transport, and eastern territories. Several reasons account
for their low standing in the institutional hierarchy. To begin with, Hitler enthusiastically supported those organizations that could show the
quickest and most effective results in areas that were closest to his heart:
domestic mobilization for territorial conquest. Possessing little understanding of technical issues, he showed, at best, a dilettantish interest in
such fields as finance, agriculture, science, post, or transport. Another
reason was the type of men who headed some organizations. Some ministries (finance, education, church affairs, and eastern territories) were
led by weak or incompetent officials, others (agriculture, labor) were run
by ideologically suspect men, while still others (post and transport) were
administered by competent yet lackluster bureaucrat-technicians who
were unable to assert themselves strongly enough to raise the prestige
of their departments or to ward off encroachments by more aggressive
competitors.

The Finance Ministry was under the overall supervision of Count
Schwerin von Krosigk, a competent, honest, efficient but also weak official whose chief liability resided in his traditional elitist background.
Despite Krosigk's weaknesses, the department itself remained relatively
immune from external party interference for two reasons: first, few Nazi
functionaries understood complex tax and budgetary procedures, and
second, State Secretary Fritz Reinhardt, the party functionary in the Finance Ministry, always defended the institution from party attacks. The
result was that Krosigk was generally left alone to do his business, even
managing on some occasions to stymie excessive spending on military
or police operations. Krosigk's counterpart in the Prussian Finance Min-

istry, Johannes Popitz (1884–1945), was more aggressive in this effort and would pay for his active opposition with his life. Bernhard Rust (1883–1945), the head of the Ministry of Science, Education, and Culture, was a former high school teacher (*Oberlehrer*) who was dismissed from the school system ostensibly for health reasons, but more likely for a serious sexual transgression. A member of the NSDAP since 1925, he was appointed *Gauleiter* of Hannover and South Hannover-Brunswick in 1925 and 1928, respectively. In April 1933 Hitler appointed him to his new and important post, hoping that he would transform German education to fit the new National Socialist mold. He could not have picked a worse candidate, for Rust was a pompous and insecure bungler with a serious drinking problem. Since the actual operation of school systems remained in the hands of the states, Rust never got very far in extending his sphere of influence, being told by state education or party functionaries, notably Wagner in Bavaria, to mind his own business. One of Rust's major achievements was the creation of a system of elite schools, the National Political Institutes of Education (Napolas), intended to train future functionaries of the Third Reich. However, as was the annoying custom in the Third Reich, Rust came into constant conflict with rivals also interested in building up their own empires, in this case Baldur von Schirach and Robert Ley, who established a rival system, the Adolf Hitler Schools (AHS). Even within his own ministry, Rust became entangled in an ugly power struggle with the aggressive Wilhelm Stuckart, a conflict that had to be resolved by Hitler personally and ended in a compromise by which Stuckart was transferred to a comparable position in the Ministry of the Interior. Rust lingered on, insecure and neglected until the end, the butt of malicious jokes about his administrative shortcomings. The most popular jibe was: R (Rust) = the minimum time span between the promulgation of a decree and its cancellation.[74]

The Ministry of Church Affairs, which was the personal creation of Hanns Kerrl (1887–1941), former president of the Prussian Landtag and chief of the Prussian Ministry of Justice, was probably the least effective ministry in the Reich government because of the effort to co-opt the Evangelical Church. Alternatively trying to unite the church under a National Socialist Reich bishop or to exploit its sectarian differences, the government, each time, encountered determined opposition. Not only did Kerrl fail to unite the Evangelical churches into a unified National Socialist Church, but he also failed to neutralize the influence of the Confessional Church in opposition under the courageous leadership of Pastor Niemöller. Early in 1938 Kerrl abandoned his efforts to co-opt the church, lost the confidence of the führer, and faded into obscurity. When he died, his ministry became largely defunct.

Another weak office, which came into being in November 1941, was Rosenberg's Central Political Bureau for the East (or Eastern Territories). Rosenberg, who had sunk into obscurity during the peaceful years of the Third Reich, was able to regain a measure of prominence when Hitler attacked the Soviet Union. Born in Russia and claiming to possess special insights into the Slavic mind, most of them tinged by racism, Rosenberg was able to persuade Hitler to appoint him as an expert on eastern territories and their administration. His poor leadership qualities quickly became apparent when the Reich commissariats, ostensibly responsible to Rosenberg, ignored his orders and rejected his pragmatic proposal for more humane treatment of the eastern populations in favor of repression and annihilation, upon which Himmler insisted. Rosenberg was not able to compete in the ruthless arena of Nazi infighting. Like Himmler, he was a racial utopian, but unlike Himmler, he believed that extermination was counterproductive. Yet he spinelessly went along with Himmler's bestial policies in the east.

The Ministry of Agriculture was in the hands of the Argentinean-born Walther Darré, the "blood and soil" ideologue who believed that agriculture should be understood through the blood rather than through economic principles. According to Darré, it was the peasant who represented the economic foundation of Germany. The state had the responsibility of expanding its peasant base through resettlement plans, increasing the birth rate in rural areas, and discouraging the rural population from moving to urban areas. Between 1931 and 1938, Darré was head of the SS Office for Race and Settlement. However, his reactionary convictions were increasingly questioned by those who supported a strong industrial policy. Darré was hampered by increasing opposition not only from big business but also from millions of independent, resistant, and disorganized peasants.[75] After openly criticizing Heinrich Himmler's brutal methods in the eastern territories and even questioning Hitler's war aims in general, Darré was relieved of his office in 1942.

The Labor Ministry was run by Franz Seldte (1882–1947), former Stahlhelm leader and conservative nationalist, who increasingly recognized that he did not enjoy the full support of Hitler, whom he began to dislike intensely and only referred to as "Adolf." The feeling was mutual, according to Goebbels, who noted that the führer did not think Seldte was "worth a hoot."[76] More powerful Nazis began to encroach on his turf — Göring as plenipotentiary of the Four-Year Plan, Sauckel as plenipotentiary of manpower allocation, and even Ley as head of the DAF. This was another example, as even Goebbels later admitted, "of a Ministry being hollowed out bit by bit without the head being removed.... [W]e are living in the form of state in which jurisdictions are not clearly defined. From this fact stem most quarrels among leading personalities and in the departments. In my opinion it would be best if Sauckel or, better still, Ley were put in the place of Seldte."[77]

The Ministry of Post and Transport, originally in the hands of Elz von Rübenach, was split up into separate ministries under the leadership of Wilhelm Ohnesorge (1872–1962) and Julius Heinrich Dorpmüller

(1869–1945), respectively. Ohnesorge, a mathematician and physicist by training, had made important contributions to the field of communications as a scientist. Since the German postal system also handled all telegraph and telephone transmissions, Ohnesorge first joined the Berlin postal system and then in 1933 took over the Reich postal system. A member of the Nazi Party since 1920, Ohnesorge was strongly motivated by National Socialist ideology; he was also a proponent of Philipp Leonard's "Aryan physics," which accounts for his straying into the field of atomic research and providing government funds to Manfred Ardenne for the purpose of fission studies.[78] Although Hitler was impressed by *Wunderwaffen* (miracle weapons), he undercut efforts in this field because it did not promise immediate results. Many German scientists, including Ohnesorge, had become insulated from the larger world of international research; they had allowed ideology to distort their work and lacked the aggressive attitudes needed to mobilize political support in the Nazi system.[79] In the case of Ohnesorge, as with most Nazi administrators, there was the additional problem of having to contend with internally and externally encroaching competitors, in this case the Ministry of Transport, which had formerly been connected to the Ministry of Post.

Before he was put in charge of the Transport Ministry in 1937, Julius Dorpmüller had had a colorful past as a railroad expert in the service of the Chinese government, had been general director of the Reichsbahn since 1926, and had been appointed by Hitler to head Operation Reichs-Autobahn in 1933. An exceedingly capable administrator, Dorpmüller had inherited a staff of impartial and largely unpolitical experts and meant to keep it that way. However, the winds of ideological changes were also blowing into his ministry, especially after the agents of Göring's Four-Year Plan began to intrude at will in the internal affairs of various ministries. The war accelerated this development and involved the Transport Ministry in the odious task of doing the bidding of Himmler's Reich Main Security Office (RSHA) in evacuating millions of Jews to the eastern territories. It has been taken for granted that Dorpmüller knew about the ultimate fate of the people his railroads were transporting to their deaths.

The most intense battles were fought out in those ministries to which Hitler looked for the fulfillment of his grand design — the institutionalization of National Socialism and racial purity and the mobilization of resources for territorial expansion. The Ministries of Public Enlightenment and Propaganda, Justice, and Interior were those whose primary mission was to wage propaganda and legalize the racial tenets of the party. Responsible for mobilizing resources for the purpose of territorial expansion were the Ministry of Economics, the Ministry for Armaments and War Production (from 1940), the Foreign Ministry, the Ministry of Aviation, and the Ministry of Defense, later called the High Command of the Armed Forces (OKW). An institution that would become a state within a state, the SS, along with the various coordinating and planning agencies and liaison-adjutants, will be described later.

The new Ministry of Public Enlightenment and Propaganda was the personal fiefdom of Joseph Goebbels. Its grandiose mission, typical of totalitarian systems, was to win the people over to the idea of National Socialism "so spiritually, so vitally, that in the end they succumb to it utterly and can never again escape from it."[80] Goebbels was one of the true creative geniuses of the Third Reich, but his talents were hostage to a twisted personality that was bruised by feelings of inadequacy, self-hatred, and cynicism. Out of these character flaws emerged a twisted vision of self-transcendence through National Socialism and the führer cult. Goebbels more than anyone else created the führer cult with all its attendant pseudoreligious props, for it was from him, as Joachim Fest has observed, that "der Führer, the term by which Hitler appeared as redeemer, demiurge and blessed savior, received its visionary content."[81] With the help of the German people, who were willing to believe his propaganda as long as it was spouted in happy times, Joseph Goebbels enthusiastically threw himself into the task of perfecting the black art of government lying. From an institutional point of view, however, Goebbels was constantly beset by obstacles because, though respected for his razor-sharp intellect, the "little doctor" was also resented and despised by some members of the party and the state. His diaries are laced with complaints and cynical observations about the faults and stupidities of fellow colleagues. His ministry, which he tried to staff with young enthusiasts of his own stripe, encountered persistent objections from the traditional civil service, which was committed to strict rules of qualification and seniority for appointment and promotion.[82] Goebbels constantly tried to buck this system, insisting on out-of-line promotions and rapid advancement of candidates who were considered to be, by traditional standards, untrained and unqualified. By 1942 two-fifths of his senior civil servants lacked professional training, and the number of *Angestellte* (employees) had grown large and was disproportionately unqualified.[83] But Goebbels's real battle was with members of his own party. Although Hitler had given him control over propaganda, which included publications, he had also appointed Max Amann as *Reichsleiter* of the entire National Socialist press as well as head of the Reich Press Chamber, while at the same time elevating Otto Dietrich to the position of National Socialist press chief and state secretary to the Propaganda Ministry responsible for reporting the Nazi point of view to the rest of the world. Given the personalities involved, such ill-defined and overlapping positions were bound to cause bitter feuds between the men who occupied them. To make matters worse for Goebbels, he had to fight intramural battles with Rosenberg over culture, Göring over art, and Bouhler over literature.[84] Propaganda was also considered an important function by other ministries, chiefly education and foreign affairs. In fact, Goebbels fought an exceedingly ugly and drawn out conflict with the arrogant and aggressive Ribbentrop who, without Goebbels's knowledge, had talked Hitler into letting him have a free rein over propaganda activities outside Germany.[85]

Between 1934 and the outbreak of the war Goebbels's authority steadily diminished, and two events even threatened to jeopardize his standing with the führer. One of these events had to do with Goebbels's marital infidelities in general — for the diminutive Goebbels was an addicted philanderer — and one passionate love affair in particular: namely, the propaganda chief's liaison with the Czech actress Lida Baarova. Hitler was extremely fond of Goebbels's wife, Magda, a tall, blonde, and attractive woman who had been built up by Nazi propaganda as the archetype of German womanhood; she also appears to have been really in love with Hitler rather than with her husband.[86] For a long time Goebbels stood by Baarova, even considering emigration, but then he bowed to Hitler's will and abandoned her; Baarova discreetly returned to Czechoslovakia.[87] The second event was a response to the first. In order to rehabilitate himself with the führer, Goebbels instigated the events that triggered the widespread violence against the Jews during the infamous Kristallnacht — the Night of Crystals (November 8–9, 1938). Far from rehabilitating him, the event actually further eroded his credibility because of the strong backlash he had unleashed abroad. The episode is significant because each time Goebbels's reputation ebbed, he would use anti-Semitism as a ploy to ingratiate himself with the führer.

The war initially saw a further erosion of Goebbels's powers, as Dietrich began to undermine his position. Only when defeat appeared a possibility, and then an inevitability, did his stock rise again to the level it had occupied in the early days of struggle, to which Goebbels had always looked back with great nostalgia. With an enemy to hate and a faltering cause to support, Goebbels's adroitness became valuable in the desperate effort to convince the German people, by threats and persuasion, that victory was still just around the corner. It is in this light that his famous speeches in February and March 1943, calling for total war, must be seen. Once again enjoying the favor of the führer, who had newly empowered him with the grand title of "general plenipotentiary for the mobilization of total war," Goebbels was a reborn man, and the Propaganda Ministry became a mill churning out wishful thinking and lies. Telling the German people that they were all on a moving train, with no one being able to exit, he also tried to delude them that this train was headed toward victory.

The Ministries of Justice and the Interior, charged respectively with dispensing and enforcing justice, instead dispensed injustice and terrorized citizens. On February 16, 1934, the government passed a law, entitled Law for the Transfer of the Administration of Justice to the Reich, by which the Ministry of Justice absorbed the former Prussian Ministry of Justice and assumed supreme control over all judges and courts throughout Germany. The man who administered this centralized system was Hitler's long-time supporter Franz Gürtner, a conservative Bavarian who came from a small town, petit bourgeois background. Gürtner had been a frontline officer in World War I and then worked his way up in the legal profession, first in Bavaria as minister of justice (1922–32) and then as minister of justice for the Reich (1932–41). Although a conservative who had turned a blind eye to the excesses of the Nazis and other right-wing organizations, Gürtner was not a reactionary or a true believer in National Socialism. Like von Papen, who had brought him to Berlin, Gürtner was a Catholic conservative with strong authoritarian leanings, but not a Fascist or a murderous racist. However, his powers were negligible, and his efforts to moderate the regime ineffectual. "You cannot imagine," he remarked to a close associate, "how happy, eternally happy I would be, if I didn't have to go into this (justice) building."[88] Of Hitler, he said: "He lets me say one sentence. Then he talks, without pause...like a torrent, which inundates everything in its path. The preconceived opinion against justice is insurmountable. His very nature is anarchy without any sense for the necessity of political order."[89] Gürtner was serving a sinking ship and he knew it. The only thing he was able to do was to fight rearguard actions by imposing petty delays and obstructions. The man, however, who risked his life in this effort was his assistant Hans von Dohnanyi, the brother-in-law of the theologian and resistance fighter Dietrich Bonhoeffer. Behind Gürtner's and Dohnanyi's backs, other men in new offices of Nazi justice steadily undermined even the vestiges of conservative authoritarian justice in Germany. One was Gürtner's successor, Otto Thierack (1889–1946), president of the new Nazi tribunal, the People's Court (Volksgerichtshof), and president of the Academy of German Law. Thierack, an aggressive Nazi, was constantly sniping at decisions coming out of the Justice Ministry, which he denounced as being too "liberal" and motivated by a staff that was too "unpolitical"! And behind Thierack came his successor in the People's Court, Roland Freisler (1893–1945), a former Bolshevist commissar who had converted to National Socialism. He totally degraded German justice as a foul-mouthed advocate of the principle that German judges in reaching their decisions should always put themselves in the shoes of the führer and judge as he might judge. The real political-legal battles, however, were being fought out in the ministry that was responsible for liaison work with the individual states, civil service affairs, and law enforcement—the Ministry of the Interior. Under the Weimar Constitution, the Ministry of the Interior possessed, at best, supervisory authority, having to share the bulk of its administrative responsibility with the individual states. Wilhelm Frick was determined to change this federalist approach in favor of a centralized authoritarian system by which Germany would become a truly unitary state.[90] In 1934 Frick brought about the merger of the Prussian Ministry of the Interior with the Reich Ministry of the Interior, thus potentially setting up the most powerful centralized political institution in Germany. The merger also meant a further "Prussification" of the Ministry of the Interior; hundreds of Prussian civil servants, overwhelmingly Protestant, streamed into the new ministry and put their conservative stamp on it.[91]

On paper, the Ministry of the Interior had been given extensive powers by the Law for Reconstruction of the Reich (Neuaufbaugesetz), which abolished representative state assemblies, transferred the sovereign rights of the states to the central government, and subordinated the Reich governors to the Reich minister of the interior. Frick was a happy man, publicly announcing that a "centuries' old dream has been fulfilled. Germany is no longer a weak federal state but a strong national, centralized country."[92] However, if this dream was to be realized in practice, Frick needed a comprehensive plan for standardizing government administration throughout Germany and delimiting the jurisdiction and function of party and state offices. Indeed, Frick made several efforts to solve the vexing problem of overlapping jurisdictions and competencies that had arisen since the National Socialists had seized power. The reforms Frick envisioned to solve this problem, however, ran up against two major obstacles — the entrenched powers of the Reich governors (*Reichsstatthalter*) and the *Gauleiter* as well as the authority of Hitler himself. The Reich governors were not happy with the idea of being reduced to mere representatives of the Interior Ministry and thereby losing their special sovereignty. Bypassing Frick, they protested to Hitler and confidently waited for a resolution of the problem.[93] When the oracle finally spoke, it was in Delphic double-talk, pronouncing that, generally speaking, he did not want to get involved whenever differences of opinion arose between the Reich minister (i.e., the minister of the interior) and the Reich governors over the interpretation of the law, but that nevertheless exceptions must be made in matters of political importance. As Martin Broszat has observed, this insistence on what would amount to arbitrary interpretation of matters considered "political" completely undermined the Reich ministry's superiority over the Reich governors or other functionaries who wanted to operate in a sphere of autonomy subject only to control by the führer. What Hitler clearly did not want was a system in which complete control was lodged in any particular organization or person except his own.

The relationship between the Reich Ministry of the Interior and the states remained in a kind of suspended animation. Reich governors were generally held to a line of communication that ended up in the Interior Ministry, but a chain of command that ended up with Adolf Hitler. In practice, these governors retained extensive powers; they had the right to nominate the members of state governments, to appoint state civil servants, and to be informed on any political issue by subordinate Reich or state agencies.[94] Their positions vis-à-vis the traditional state authorities (*Oberpresident, Regierungspresident, Landrat*) also remained unresolved. For the sake of administrative efficiency, Frick suggested the merging of the office of Reich governor and *Oberpresident* (minister president), but he was never given a clear-cut mandate to do so. Only in the states of Hesse and Saxony were the offices of Reich governor and minister president combined in the hands of the *Gauleiter.*

Frick had even less control over the intrusion of the party into the state machinery. He did succeed in reserving the nominal right to exercise the final decision on ratifying appointments of local officials, but only with the proviso that the right of nomination resided in the hands of the local party representative the first time an appointment was made. If no agreement between state authority and party over a given appointment could be reached, the state authority was given the right to decide the second time around.

Frick also became entangled with the party on matters pertaining to the civil service. Frick's ideal was an authoritarian civil service state in which parliamentary democracy had been replaced by a unitary state with all field administrative units incorporated into the Ministry of the Interior.[95] This, as we saw, never materialized because it was undercut by party functionaries, by Hitler, and by the whole system of improvisational planning that was to become the hallmark of Nazi Germany. If Frick was unable to amalgamate the party into the state machinery, was the party able to capture the civil service administration? The civil service, an elite system of professionally trained administrators, was the pride of Germany. Access to the *Beamtenstand* (estate of civil servants) was limited to candidates who possessed a university education and acceptable social backgrounds and passed appropriate state examinations. Once having passed their probationary periods, all civil servants were tenured for life and unaffected by any changes in government. Most higher civil servants came from middle- or upper-middle-class backgrounds; they were bookish, conservative, and legalistic in mentality. Trained in the canons of a narrowly focused humanistic or classical education and an equally narrowly focused legal tradition, the *Beamten* stood aloof, in the form of German mandarins, from the rest of the population, which perceived them as arrogant (*hochnässig*) and elitist. This being the case, it should not come as a great surprise that the *Beamten,* though to some degree attached to the elitist and nationalistic pretensions of the Nazis, were intellectually and socially repelled by them and did not welcome them into their ranks.

For their part, the Nazis definitely wanted to storm this fortress of German power and respectability. The general consensus by historians is that the Nazis, although they infiltrated the system on the lower levels, did not make any headway in changing it.[96] It is true that many *Beamten* were dismissed from specific posts, some through forced retirement and some through simple transfers, but the majority remained in their jobs. The Law for the Restoration of the Civil Service changed little in this connection because its exclusionary measures were directed against groups (Jews, Socialists) that had never constituted a significant element in its composition in the first place. While it is also true that initially party members were able to capture civil service posts, and even suspended important civil servants, the system weathered the period of chaos, adjusted, and even managed to co-opt some of the radicalism it met in party zealots. Places that were specifically created for old party fighters were invariably lower civil service positions. The old elite dug in behind its wall of strict rules on qualification and seniority for promotions; and though some Nazis tried to chip away at this wall, like Goebbels and Göring in their respective ministries, the system proved quite resilient in protecting itself. Even civil servants who were Nazis, including Frick, had been trained in the culture of the old system and were professionally and temperamentally unable to abandon it in favor of a freewheeling system based largely on political correctness.

A debureaucratizing of the government, as favored by some hotheads in the party, therefore never took place. The Nazis may have infiltrated and even partially corrupted the system, but they did not change it. The war gave the civil service a reprieve from further assaults.

Although the final word on the German civil service has not been written, several judgments can be made with some certainty. The major reason the German state machinery continued to function at all was its dedicated civil service cadre. Not only did the civil servants continue to run their affairs efficiently, they cooperated sufficiently with their National Socialist masters to enable them to rule and conquer. The Nazis always found support in an older generation of "depoliticized" civil servants with similar authoritarian tendencies.[97] Radical Nazi functionaries and the depoliticized specialists reluctantly did each other's bidding. It could be argued that National Socialist rule was indeed the product of "authoritarian cultural lag" in which an authoritarian state administration, fearful of democratic change and mistaking radicalism for conservatism, enabled a nihilistic movement to function and even to thrive amid apparent chaos.

Frick's ministry was also responsible for law enforcement and for putting the legal imprimatur on racial legislation, a subject to be discussed in the next chapter. On the matter of police centralization, Frick at first believed that his ministry had scored a victory on behalf of totalitarian centralism, but he discovered quickly that by allowing Himmler to take over all the police forces throughout Germany and to build up the SS as an increasingly autonomous institution, he was letting the reins of power slip from his hands. Although he loudly protested to Hitler about Himmler's unrelenting power grab, he was unable to prevent the SS leader's appointment as German chief of police and as state secretary in the Ministry of the Interior. In other words, Frick now had Himmler mucking about in his own ministry and casting his net over various departments, especially those dealing with the press, arms, traffic control, passports, and personnel policies pertaining to police officials.[98] Neither Himmler nor his brutal sidekick, Reinhard Heydrich, provided Frick, their ostensible superior, with any insight into their secret machinations, hiding their activities, deflecting protests by invoking the authority of the führer, and producing quick-witted lawyers who covered their illegalities with clever sophisms.[99] By the late 1930s Frick had been reduced to a pliant ministerial rubber stamp for Hitler and Himmler. During the war, he fell out of favor with Hitler and was dismissed from his position and fobbed off with a minor post as Reich protector of Bohemia and Moravia (1943). The Ministry of the Interior was turned over to Heinrich Himmler and the SS.

Next to the party, the state bureaucracy, and the armed forces, the economy and its management constituted one of the main elements of the Nazi system. In the beginning, the Ministry of Economics was headed by Kurt Schmitt (1886–1950), a former executive of one of Germany's insurance firms who had been introduced to Hitler in 1931. When Schmitt turned out to be overly cautious, unimaginative, and passive, Hitler replaced him in 1935 with Hjalmar Schacht, president of the Reichsbank and one of the few economic talents in Germany with an international reputation. Schacht exercised a major role in the first economic phase of National Socialism (1933–36) as minister of economics, president of the Reichsbank, and general plenipotentiary for war economy. Enjoying the confidence of big business as well as the armed forces, Schacht pushed through a three-pronged policy of revitalizing the economy through massive rearmament, government deficit spending, and a close government-business partnership aimed at opening up new markets in southeastern Europe.

Although Schacht agreed with Hitler and the party on massive rearmament and public works projects, using the financial resources of the Reichsbank to support these programs, he began to have increasing doubts about National Socialism on both economic and moral grounds. He was horrified by the Röhm blood purge and by the attacks on Jews and Jewish businesses throughout Germany. From an economic point of view, he opposed the party's reactionary and largely romanticized ideal of an economy based on peasants, small shop keepers, and craftsmen. He also thought that the attack on Jewish businesses and on big department stores was a tragic error rooted in economic ignorance and ideological fanaticism. Schacht's break with the Nazis came in 1936 when Hitler demanded a major shift in economic direction, a change that would usher in the second economic phase (1936–39). Hitler demanded that the economy be switched over to total war mobilization and abandoned Schacht's emphasis on foreign trade in favor of economic self-sufficiency (autarky), especially in the field of synthetics. For this purpose, he put Göring in charge of the Four-Year Plan, giving him dictatorial powers to accomplish his goals.

Until 1936 Schacht had been able to safeguard a strong measure of independence for big business; he also worked in close partnership with more cautious elements in the armed forces (Blomberg), thus acting as a restraint against reckless plans for imperial expansion. This block restraining Hitler was essentially broken by 1938 when Hitler divested himself of cautious nay-sayers in both the army and in businesss and got rid of Blomberg and Schacht. This coincided with several looming economic crises — a serious foreign exchange shortage, an alarming shrinkage in monetary and gold reserves, mounting problems of taxation, consumer dissatisfaction, and problems created by overlapping economic offices. Some historians have suggested that these crises formed a syndrome that may well have motivated Hitler to choose war as a solution to economic problems.[100]

Having divested himself of the able and independent-minded Schacht, keeping him only as president of the Reichsbank (to 1943), Hitler picked the pliant Walther Funk (1890–1960) as his new economics minister and plunged into a third economic phase involving territorial expansion and the brutal economic exploitation of foreign countries. Funk was a shrewd, affable, and accommodating party man who had served Hitler as a personal business adviser and could always be counted on to toe the line. When Hitler appointed him to head the Ministry of Economics, he basically referred him to Göring for the future direction of his office, and that involved working closely with the offices carrying out the Four-Year Plan. Funk did this tolerably well but resented Göring's inconsistent and heavy-handed policies. Funk was also to be implicated in plundering the wealth of conquered territories and hoarding personal possessions (gold, jewels, currency) extracted from millions of murdered Jews.

Funk's Ministry of Economics worked closely with a technical ministry created in 1940, the Ministry of Armaments, headed by one of Hitler's favorite experts, Dr. Fritz Todt (1891–1942). As mentioned above, Todt, who had joined the party as early as 1923, had built the führer's freeways (*Autobahnen*); he also served as a major organizational leader of the Four-Year Plan and in 1938 constructed the fortifications of the West Wall. Todt had operated for some time very independently outside the regular machinery of government, answerable primarily to Adolf Hitler, who always gave him enthusiastic support. He largely continued operating this way even as Reich minister, building up a huge organization whose offices spanned a very broad spectrum of economic activities that increasingly became the controlling force behind the whole war economy.[101] When Todt died in a plane accident, Hitler picked Albert Speer, his favorite architect, to succeed him. Under Speer, the Ministry of Armaments became the directing force of the German war effort between 1943 and 1945.

By 1938 Adolf Hitler looked to his government to support him in his grand design — the waging of war in order to secure *Lebensraum* (living space) for the German people. Insofar as the Foreign Ministry could support him in this goal, he was not adverse to working with it. However, the ministry, as will be described later, was solidly staffed by diplomats of the old school who resisted his aggressive policies. Hitler referred to the ministry as "an intellectual garbage heap" and tried to bypass the old guard whenever possible by encouraging the efforts of rival organizations or aggressive upstarts of the stripe of Ribbentrop. In 1938, he dismissed his foreign minister, Konstantin von Neurath, and replaced him with Ribbentrop, a man without intellectual substance or moral integrity.

Hitler also neutralized the Ministry of Defense by purging it of its obstreperous and cautious leaders. Blomberg, Hindenburg's old protégé, was disgraced as a result of his marriage to a former prostitute, and Werner von Fritsch, commander in chief of the German army, whose patient and cautious attitudes also did not fit the new spirit, was removed from his position by wrongful accusations of homosexual activities. Hitler then reorganized the whole Defense Ministry under a new umbrella called Oberkommando der Wehrmacht (High Command of the Armed Forces [OKW]) and put the pliant Wilhelm Keitel in charge. Under Keitel, the OKW would do Hitler's bidding to the bitter end, although it would continue to harbor dissidents who were not convinced by Hitler's aims or capabilities. All in all, the German military leaders, alternately duped by success, rendered ineffective by blind adherence to authority, no matter how criminal, and lacking in civil courage, usually trotted obediently behind their criminal leaders, clicked their heels, and did what they were told to do.

The perfect example to round out our account of the German government and its leadership was a man who straddled both the party and the traditional military establishment, Hermann Göring, minister of aviation, commander in chief of the Luftwaffe, general plenipotentiary for the Four-Year Plan, Reich minister without portfolio, and Reich marshal.

Of the major Nazi leaders, only Göring was genuinely popular with the German people. Hitler was too aloof and godlike, Goebbels too intellectual, and Himmler too cold and impassive to make a positive impression. It was otherwise with the jovial and ebullient Hermann Göring, who managed to give the new totalitarian machine a human face. Göring was at heart a romantic royalist, and his own upper-class background, which had enabled him to move in high military and social circles, always prompted him to cultivate connections with the former conservative elite. Göring was also not a committed anti-Semite. His godfather, whom he genuinely loved and admired, had been partly Jewish, as were some close friends and associates, particularly his secretary of state for aviation. Göring judged people by first impression, emotional rapport, and usefulness to his purpose, but not by their racial characteristics, which explains his famous quip "I decide who is a Jew" in response to a subordinate who had pointed out that some visitors to his house had been Jewish.[102]

Yet the many undoubtedly positive characteristics that Göring possessed — high intelligence, creativity, loyalty, charisma, and daring —

were undercut by his shameless opportunism, greed, vanity, and moral sloth. Göring was, in fact, deeply divided by bipolar opposites: generous to friends and magnanimous to opponents, he could also be vindictive and appalling selfish. His life alternated between compulsive work and self-indulgent gluttony; after a period focused on a specific task, he would lapse into indolence and rapid weight gain. Joachim Fest has described him as a "mixture of *condottiere and sybarite*,"[103] and H. R. Trevor-Roper, as mentioned previously, has called him "a perfumed Nero,"[104] descriptions that undoubtedly capture certain aspects of his complex personality.

The fact is that Göring, like Hitler, was a sociopathic personality with all the characteristics associated with this kind of deviancy — lack of conscience, impulsive behavior, cultivation of a good front, and rejection of normative authority. Unlike Hitler, whose deviancy expressed itself as complete defiance of all authority for the sake of fulfilling a personal racial utopia, Göring's deviancy was more mundane in its aim, namely the gratification of personal vanities and material needs. Even his notorious brutality, which Hitler always commended as an example to others, was the result of opportunistic calculation rather than sadistic predilection. His manner of living was one of Byzantine splendor; he owned four mansions, a hunting lodge (Karinhall), two castles, his regal palace in the Leipziger Platz in Berlin, his own industrial combine (the Hermann Göring Werke), hundreds of uniforms, priceless jewels, a yacht, and assorted automobiles. During the war, he shamelessly stripped the museums of conquered countries of their art treasures and other priceless objects for his personal use, shrugging off all objections by saying that he was, after all, a Renaissance type (*Renaissanztyp*).[105] Side by side with such greed went a shameless exhibitionism of his private wealth that many Germans, at least during the peaceful years, could excuse as a pardonable weakness in their good old "Hermann." Even his coarseness was held to be funny, as when stories were told about his uproarious laughter after one of his lions urinated on a lady's dress or when he horrified his guests at his country estate by having a bull and a cow mate before them. Such antics and his jovial public persona were much admired by many Germans.

From a political point of view, however, it was fatal for Germans that their fate rested, to a large degree, in the hands of a man who was fundamentally opportunistic and self-serving in his aims and habitual behavior. His two greatest flaws in this respect were his nauseating submissiveness to Hitler and his lack of moral courage at critical junctures. Under Hitler's magnetic personality, his own ego, inflated as it was, shrivelled astonishingly: "I have no conscience," he once confessed; and rationalizing such moral emptiness, he would sometimes lamely add that "my conscience is Adolf Hitler."[106] Yet he retained enough self-respect to recognize how intolerably dependent he had become on the will of one man. Such slavish obeisance to the führer's will began to gnaw on him to the point of physical distress; he confessed to Schacht that every time he confronted Hitler his heart fell into his trousers. Even his subordinates reported that he had to "psyche himself up" (*aufgepustet*) for his encounters with Hitler.

Göring had been instrumental to Hitler on the road to power and in its subsequent consolidation. He was also instrumental in expanding the German air force (Luftwaffe), though not, as some still mistakenly believe, in creating it from the ground up. In his new position as minister of aviation and later as Reich marshal, he showed unmistakable flair, but his choice of personnel was not always sound. Moreover, his own experience was out-of-date, and advancements in aviation technology and engineering had passed him by. Although he had built up a large force of slightly over 4,000 aircraft, including 1,176 bombers, 408 twin-engined and 771 single-engined fighters, and 552 Ju-52 transports, its capacity was limited. It was a short-range combat unit whose fighters were designed to provide local air superiority and whose bombers were designed to provide tactical support for the army. The Luftwaffe's weaknesses, revealed even during the early stages of the war, when flashy victories tended to mask underlying problems, would turn into major liabilities. The Luftwaffe suffered from shortages in aviation fuel, machine-gun ammunition, and bombs. Training facilities and aircraft production barely provided adequate replacements for initial losses, problems that continued to worsen when Germany found itself at war with Russia and the United States. At this point Göring's bluster about the invincibility of the Luftwaffe would come home to haunt him. His failure to destroy the British expeditionary force at Dunkirk, his defeat in the Battle of Britain, his inability to destroy the Soviet air force, and, above all, his impotence in preventing round the clock saturation bombing of German cities — all these failures discredited him in the eyes of his führer and the German people. At this critical juncture of his life, he relinquished control to his rivals — Himmler, Bormann, Goebbels, and Speer — and escaped into hedonism and drug dependency. No one was amused any longer by his earthy humor, and he was publicly ridiculed for an earlier boast that if a single enemy plane would ever penetrate German air space, the people could call him Müller (a common German name) rather than Göring.

In addition to the Reich ministries, the Nazi state also spawned various organizations with specific mandates that operated largely independent of each other and answered directly to Hitler via the Reich chancellery. These "supreme Reich authorities" (*Oberste Reichsbehörden*), as they were called, included, besides the chancelleries and ministries already mentioned, such planning and coordinating agencies and positions as the general inspector of roads, the Office for Territorial Planning, the Reich Youth Directorate, the general inspector of the Reich capital, the General Construction Council for the City of the Movement (Munich), the Reich Construction Council for the City of Linz, the general plenipotentiary for the Four-Year Plan, the Private Cabinet on Foreign Policy (it never met!), and the Reich protector of Bohemia-Moravia. Included in these supreme Reich authorities were also the highest law courts and major financial institutions, especially the Reichsbank.

A State within a State: The SS

Within these institutions of the state, but also increasingly autonomous and separate from them, developed the most sinister hybrid institution of them all — the SS. Straddling both the party and the state, this organization, originally subject to the SA, began as a small elite bodyguard protecting the führer and developed into a party police force; a terrorist Reich police force; a regular army within the army commanding its own forces, the Waffen-SS; a huge economic conglomerate with its tentacles reaching deeply into big business in Germany and later in the conquered territories; and a gigantic murder machine that supervised a far-flung system of concentration camps in which people were tortured and annihilated. Without this shadow empire, the Nazis would have been unable to exercise sustained and unopposed control over the German people. The SS incubus, like the Nazi Party itself, had its origins in Bavaria in the 1920s, and it was a pudgy, short, unathletic, myopic, and balding Bavarian, Heinrich Himmler, who built up this initially small force into the much-dreaded criminal organization of the Third Reich.

Heinrich Himmler, *Reichsführer SS,* was Adolf Hitler's alter ego and ruthless bloodhound, the personification, as some have claimed, of "Nazism" itself. With meticulous skill and single-minded dedication, this cold and calculating busybody, aptly described by Albert Speer as "half school master and half crank,"[107] systematically assembled the major instruments of Nazi terror — SS, police, and concentration camp. His goal, however, was not to administer or mete out terror for its own sake but to use it for the sake of building up and expanding a pure racial state. In the service of this racial utopia, which involved sterilization, euthanasia of "lives not worth living," medical experiments, and the annihilation of racial "subhumans," Heinrich Himmler would marshal the power and resources of his growing empire. His terror machine, in other words, was the product of his and Hitler's racial beliefs. Heinrich Himmler was one of those dangerous human beings who, like the grand inquisitors of the past, was a true believer in his religion, even if that religion was absurd.

Historians have understandably tried to find an explanation for the end of this man's career by examining its beginning. Surely, a man of such evil must have had many dark corners in his background and upbringing, but when nothing dramatic (child abuse, sexual traumas, etc.) was turned up by busy investigators, some historians threw up their hands in exasperation and reluctantly admitted that Himmler's youth was "depressingly normal";[108] he came, they said, from the most ordinary of Bavarian middle-class families, and therefore it is futile to invent some psychological explanation to explain the inexplicable.[109] Not only are such judgments a retreat from reason, but they also express a lack of confidence in psychology as a science capable of explaining human behavior. It may be true that no psychological concept or set of concepts can ever explain malignant destructiveness, but it therefore does not follow that such theories cannot discover useful clues for understanding aggression and finding ways to cope with it.

In the case of Heinrich Himmler, it is true that he came from an outwardly "normal" middle-class family, but closer scrutiny reveals that the family dynamics in Himmler's upbringing were not conducive to the development of a mature, autonomous, and flexible personality.[110] His father, Gebhard Himmler, was an extremely rigid, pedantic, and compulsively legalistic school teacher who exemplified the much-dreaded authoritarian type that was so common in the German school system up to the end of World War II and even beyond.[111] Professor Himmler's father had been a police president with decidedly rigid authoritarian habits, and it was on the basis of the same principles that the professor brought up his own children, teaching them to be meticulously clean, orderly, and obedient. Since Gebhard Himmler had at one time been the teacher of Prince Heinrich of Bavaria, who graciously consented to be Heinrich Himmler's godfather, the children, including besides Heinrich his two brothers Gebhard (b. 1898) and Ernst (b. 1905), were always taught to show respect for the nobility. What about respect for his mother? In the diaries that his father urged him to keep, Himmler mentions his mother only twice. Yet from other sources, including his letters, it appears that his mother spoiled him considerably, to the point that some psychologists have called him a "mother's boy,"[112] seeking obvious relief from the heavy hand of his father who would remain, until he met Adolf Hitler, his essential role model.

Having a prince for a godfather, young Heinrich dreamed of becoming an officer who would fearlessly lead his men into battle for the fatherland. Several obstacles worked against this dream. In the first place, although Himmler was an excellent student, who dared not to be otherwise, he was too young to serve in World War I, and, in the second place, he was too unathletic and unassertive to be a great officer. In fact, it took all of his father's connections to have him accepted into officers' training school, and the war was over by the time he was ready to be sent to the front. When the war ended, Himmler was only eighteen, without specific goals for a career, and he was insufficiently mature to face both the chaotic postwar period and the identity crisis he was experiencing as a rootless young man. The riddle of his flawed personality resides in the way in which he tried to resolve this identity crisis.

Disappointing his caste-conscious parents, he chose to study agriculture rather than a traditionally prestigious field leading to a professional position. We see him at this time as an ordinary student at the Technical University of Munich, moving within a very restricted social circle, pedantically recording the most mundane routines in his diaries (shaving, bathing, sleeping), keeping immaculate records by saving lists, stubs, drafts, and ticket-stubs that would survive the Holocaust,[113] and rarely venturing outside the safety of his tidy routine. Although fascinated and, indeed, obsessed by his developing sexuality, he did not commit himself to a single woman, usually retreating behind a mask of conventionality and formality.[114] This did not prevent him, however, from meddling in other people's affairs, for behind the cover of a conventional authoritarian morality, he passed merciless and vindictive judgments on everyone. For example, he took it upon himself to carry on a vindictive campaign against his prospective sister-in-law because he thought he knew that she was the wrong woman for Gebhard. At the same time, he was steeping himself in *völkisch*-racial literature and beginning to consort with the right-wing movements that were proliferating in Munich in the troubled postwar years.

In 1922, Himmler gained his agricultural diploma, but job prospects were few and far between. He worked for a while as a technical assistant doing research on manure; he was lonely, adrift, and insecure. In August 1923, however, he joined the Nazi Party, just before the abortive Putsch in which he was to play a minor part as a member of the Röhm contingent. With the failure of the Putsch and Hitler's imprisonment at Landsberg, his life and the party he had joined seemed to fall apart. Again he toyed with the idea of emigrating to Russia or Latin America and dedicating his life to farming; but after Hitler's release and the reconstruction of the party, there was renewed hope for Himmler. Serving as Gregor Strasser's deputy as district organizer in Lower Bavaria, his fortunes began to improve, for Hitler appointed him also as second-in-command of a new and small elite corps called the Schutzstaffel (Protective Squad [SS]), a group of about two hundred shock troops who guarded the führer and kept order at various party meetings. Himmler had now reached the crossroads of his life. Already doubting his Roman Catholic beliefs, carrying within himself little more than insubstantial ideas or habits imposed by his rigid upbringing, the anxiety-ridden young man resolved his identity crisis by attaching himself to a new authority and substitute religion — Adolf Hitler and National Socialism. In other words, rather than opting for freedom in the form of individual questioning and spontaneous experimentation, Himmler escaped from freedom into another form of bondage. There is no doubt that his commitment to Hitler and the party was in the form of a conversion; he had found his savior and would follow him, like many other Nazis, to the bitter end. At about the same time in the summer of 1928, he also opted for a safe marriage to a nurse of Polish origins, Margarete (Marga) Concerzowo, eight years his senior, Protestant, and divorced, hardly the sort of woman his parents would have expected him to marry. Although the two were similar in temperament, being excessively thrifty, neat, and hard-working, their marriage was not happy. Despite his outward obeisance to middle-class values, which he cultivated to the point of caricature, Himmler would later keep a mistress and father two illegitimate children.

In January 1929 Himmler was appointed *Reichsführer SS,* still a minor position in the shadow of the SA and its commander. However, Himmler envisioned his black-shirted soldiers to be more than just ordinary street brawlers; his dream was to transform them into an elite racial cadre, carefully picked from the brightest and physically strongest segments of the population. They would be the vanguard of the new effort to purify the race. At this time, Himmler fell under the spell of the racial theories of Walther Darré, whom he met in the ranks of the Artamans, a group of young German utopians who believed in the back-to-the-soil movement that had been spawned by *völkisch* youth organizations in the early 1920s. The Artamans called for new eastern settlements, the subjugation of inferior Slavs, and the cultivation of a new Teutonic peasant class that would usher in a biological-spiritual revitalization of German blood and soil. Out of the Artamans would emerge some well-known SS racists — Himmler, Darré, and Höss, future commandant of Auschwitz.[115]

In the years of struggle, the colorless, emotionally flat, but intensely focused Himmler slowly built up his elite order. New members were screened according to height (at least 5'8"), pure Aryan descent back to 1750 for officers and 1800 for enlisted men, and appropriate health and hygienic considerations. Himmler, thus obsessed with racial purity, preferred tall, blond, and blue-eyed specimens, the very opposite of his own rather Mongoloid mixed features that were a caricature of his own racial ideal. His obsession with physical stamina, Nordic beauty, or racial purity — whatever that meant — undoubtedly exposed in him feelings of intense insecurity. He suffered from various illnesses, possibly psychosomatic, with all their attendant physical overtones — acute headaches, colitis, stomach cramps, sore muscles. The diary of Felix Kersten, Himmler's later Swedish masseur who tended to the sore muscles of his anxiety-ridden client, bears testimony to Himmler's fantasies and obsessions. Like Hitler, Himmler was a neurotic hypochondriac who was at home in the world of cranky herbalists or vegetarians.

It may be true, as some have argued, that Himmler was "schizoid,"[116] an "anal-hoarding sado-masochist,"[117] or an "obsessive-compulsive" personality, but these terms do not capture the man's essential historical nature. He was, as H. R. Trevor-Roper noticed long ago, the prototype of the grand inquisitor, the mind-numbing fanatic who, though personally kind, fastidious, austere, and incorruptible, could murder millions for the sake of some abstract ideal.[118] Himmler's ideal was a racial utopia in which history would be redeemed by a new Aryan God-man. He stared endlessly at the photographs of prospective candidates, pried into the lives of his members, and even strictly prohibited them from marrying their prospective brides until they had been racially screened. Each SS member was required to keep a genealogical clan book (*Sippenbuch*) recording specific family facts and relationships, thus safeguarding racial purity for future generations. As early as 1931 Darré joined Himmler's staff and organized the Office of Race and Settlement (Rasse und Siedlungshauptamt) charged with setting racial norms, conducting research into European ethnicity, and developing plans for resettling German colonists in eastern territories.

What clearly emerged from these early efforts was Himmler's belief that the human race could be biologically improved and that he knew the standards and techniques by which this could be accomplished. Having been, for a short time, a chicken farmer in Waldtrudering near Munich, Himmler seems to have believed that human breeding was essentially just like animal husbandry and that "on the basis of Mendel's Law" the German people could in 120 years once more become "authentically German in appearance."[119] By weeding out undesirable characteristics in the German gene pool through sterilization or strict racial laws prohibiting Germans to consort with Jews and other racially inferior breeds, it should be possible to breed a superrace of fair-haired, blue-eyed, tall, and athletic-looking Aryans. In June 1931, such a specimen, looking for a job in the SS, came to see Himmler at his farm at Waldtrudering, became his closest and most ruthless henchman, and helped to perfect his evolving SS empire. This man was Reinhard Heydrich, a twenty-five-year-old ex-naval officer who had been dismissed from the German navy for conduct unbecoming an officer. Heydrich was the son of a well-known tenor and director of a conservatory of music in Halle. The young man, who was himself musically talented and athletically gifted, grew up in a strict Catholic family in which cleanliness, order, discipline, and high achievement were the order of the day. Introspective and somewhat shy, Heydrich had difficulties in finding close friends, often compensating for his shortcomings through arrogant behavior and aggressive self-assertion.[120] Usually going his own way, he was frequently shunned by schoolmates and later by naval comrades, all the more so when rumors began to circulate that his father was Jewish. In school Reinhard was sometimes mocked by schoolmates as "Isi," an allusion to his Jewishness.[121] No credible evidence has yet surfaced that Heydrich's father was in fact Jewish, but the allegation of Jewishness would follow Heydrich throughout his murderous career and may account for the remarkable self-hatred he often demonstrated. Out of his background and his adolescent struggles emerged a twisted personality, deeply ambiguous about his identity, craving approval and recognition. Throughout his relatively short life, Heydrich was a torn and insecure man.

Of all the major Nazi leaders, Heydrich conformed most closely to the much-touted Aryan ideal: he was tall, slender, blond, and good-looking, although his horselike head, long nose, and brutal mouth with protruding teeth tarnished otherwise handsome features. His voice and laugh were so high pitched and bleating that his comrades nicknamed him "goat" (*Ziege*). He was highly intelligent and athletically gifted, especially in running, swimming, and fencing. Such abilities, however, were not matched by strength of character. His dismissal from the navy was the result of throwing over one young lady in favor of another, and doing it in such an ungentlemanly way as to drive the jilted young lady into a nervous breakdown. The affair illustrates the unscrupulous nature of Heydrich's treatment of others. People were instruments but never ends for Heydrich; he used them unscrupulously to get what he wanted. This is why some historians have described him as totally amoral, comparable only to the great criminals of the Renaissance.[122] Like Hitler, he was always thinking the unthinkable, unrestrained by law or social convention. Indeed, he could well have been Hitler's favorite son, but even the führer was slightly intimidated by the young man's overweening ambition, brash arrogance, and brazen unscrupulousness, and had to keep him in his place by using veiled threats of exposing his alleged Jewishness. At his funeral Hitler referred to Heydrich as the "man with the iron heart,"[123] an epithet equaled only by Burckhardt's remark that he was "a young, evil god of death."[124]

The Himmler-Heydrich partnership was unique because it accentuated the destructive potential in both men — Himmler's mind-numbing attention to detail and Heydrich's suave viciousness and unscrupulous aplomb. Working like moles inside the institution of party and state, these two men aimed at nothing less than the subversion of the law and control over the instruments of power. These methods consisted of insinuating themselves into the regular bureaucracy, planting their own men in key positions, eliminating rivals through extortion and arrests, and all the while playing the role of dedicated, innocent, and unknowing public officials who were simply trying to do what was best for Germany.

In the spring of 1933, when Himmler and Heydrich began their grab for power, they were two young men, thirty-three and twenty-nine years of age, respectively, who were still largely unknown to the public. On March 9, 1933, Himmler became police president of Munich, a position that he used as a base of operations for his expanding SS and police system. On April 1, Himmler was promoted to the post of political police commander of Bavaria, which put him in charge of a statewide network of police agencies and the concentration camp of Dachau. Heydrich, who was implementing Himmler's grand design, made sure that the key positions were in the hands of the most ruthless and effective police officials, preferable in the hands of proven Nazis or competent opportunists. One of Heydrich's most capable officials, previously not affiliated with the Nazis, was Heinrich Müller (1900–1945), later nicknamed "Gestapo Müller," a man of driving ambition who would quickly earn his new master's trust through his blind obedience and unscrupulous behavior. As head of Department IV (Gestapo) in the later Reich Main Security Office, Müller would participate in numerous crimes against humanity and become one of the most feared officials in Europe. Although Müller had previously worked against the Nazis as had colleagues of his such as Franz Josef Huber and Josef Meisinger, Heydrich recognized his own kind — control technicians willing to serve any regime that would promote them and allow sufficient scope to their talents and predilections. Müller and men of his type often came from solid middle-class parents, were brought up religiously, served in World War I, joined the Free Corps, ended up in the Bavarian civil service, and later served as obedient henchmen to their Nazi masters.[125]

While helping Himmler gain increasing control over the police in Bavaria and in most of Germany, Heydrich also solidified the apparatus that helped make it possible — the Security Service Branch (SD) of the Nazi Party, which he had built up since 1931. At first, the SD was little more than a small group of young and well-educated idealists who had been occupationally uprooted by hard times and, as desocialized drifters, were looking for some ideological commitment in their lives.[126] For example, Heydrich's second-in-command, Carl Albrecht Oberg (1897–1965), son of a Hamburg professor of medicine, joined the army, the Free Corps, and then drifted through much of the 1920s without steady employment until, at length, he found his way into the NSDAP and its security service. Somewhat similar types were Heydrich's senior officials, many of them amateurs in a field that still had not defined itself. Dr. Werner Best, Otto Ohlendorf, Professor Reinhard Höhn, Professor Franz Six, and Dr. Herbert Mehlhorn were all lawyers, while Dr. Helmut Knochen was a man with literary ambitions, Gunter d'Alquen a journalist, and Walter Schellenberg an aspiring James Bond. In fact, it was the aura of adventure, surveillance, and ferreting out spies that attracted a host of young men to the SD. As Walter Schellenberg, future spy master and espionage chief, recalled: "The better type of people preferred to join the SS rather than one of the other party formations."[127] What these men did not know was that, once trapped in the system, they would have to work with some very unsavory types and follow orders that were unethical and illegal; but rather than disengaging themselves from a murderous machine, they found justifications for their activities and allowed themselves to become the state's hired murderers.

At first, it was not entirely clear what the mission of the SD should be, that of an information service, a secret service, a party watchdog, or a quasi-police unit. At one time or another, the SD was all of those things, concerning itself broadly with fighting "opposition." By 1937, it had three thousand members and an army of fifty thousand informers.[128] What were these inquisitional fighters trying to unearth? Alternately fighting with but also against the Gestapo, the SD sleuths turned first against "primary enemies" — mostly political opponents or suspects,

Communists and Socialists, trade unionists, clergymen, and so on. After the elimination of primary enemies (1933–35) came phase two or the assault on "racial enemies" — that is, Jews and, later, "Asiatic inferiors."[129] The SD Department on Jewish Affairs, which had attracted one Adolf Eichmann, who became an "expert" on Zionism and was put in charge of Jewish emigration, drew up a monster list of Jewish groups throughout the world on the assumptions that they constituted a unified entity and that there existed a worldwide Jewish conspiracy. In other words, ideological thinking fabricated an amorphous force of enemies that had to be unmasked and ruthlessly eliminated, an attitude reminiscent of the beliefs of members of the Inquisition about whom it is said that they invented witches in order to justify the proliferating bureaucracy that had developed to combat them. From 1933 to 1938 the SD labored mightily with other organizations to eliminate the Jews from German public life by depriving them of their civil rights and undermining their means of livelihood. Enforced emigration followed from 1938 to 1941; and this, in turn, led to the final phase — the physical extermination of the Jewish people. The final solution had already been visualized before the war even though the plans and the means of implementing them had not been formulated.

In constructing their system of control, Himmler and Heydrich not only built up the SS, especially its Security Service, but also expended much effort on infiltrating the German police. After amalgamating the police forces in all the German states except Prussia, Himmler was on the verge of capturing the whole German police. The Gestapo, still under Göring's control, eluded him until the spring of 1934. On April 20, 1934, Göring, who had been feuding with Frick and the SA over the direction of the Gestapo, allied himself with Himmler by appointing him "inspector of the Gestapo," sacrificing his previous Gestapo chief Rudolf Diels. Himmler, of course, was still subordinate to Göring as minister president of Prussia, to Frick as minister of the interior, and to Röhm as chief of the SA and SS. During the Night of the Long Knives, Himmler's black-shirted SS assassins liquidated Röhm and thus broke the back of the SA; as a reward for its part in eliminating Röhm, the SS was made an autonomous organization and allowed to gain complete control over the Gestapo. After a year-long conflict with Frick, who attempted to bring the Gestapo under the more effective supervision of the minister of the interior, a new Gestapo law was issued in February 1936 that made the various Gestapo offices responsible to the minister of the interior, but it also stipulated that the Gestapo regional offices were responsible to the head Gestapo office in Berlin; this left open the question which main office (Interior or Gestapo-Berlin) had the ultimate authority in jurisdictional conflicts. Four months later, on June 17, Hitler placed all police powers in Himmler's hands, making him chief of German police in the Ministry of the Interior. Frick was still nominally in charge; in practice, however, Himmler and Heydrich operated the police as they saw fit. On

June 28, Himmler reorganized the German police system and formed a new "security police."

The term "security police" had previously been broadly applied to the police as a whole. Under the Weimar Republic, the police had been divided into two branches: the administrative police and the executive police, the former dealing with routine personnel procedures and traffic, the latter with four major enforcement and political branches — the Kripo (crime), the Schupo (urban constabulary), the political police, and the gendarmerie. Himmler managed to split off from the more important executive police its two most significant branches — the criminal police and the political police — and formed the security police (Sipo) under Heydrich. The remainder he left to Kurt Dalugue, merged into a new *Ordnungspolizei* (ordinary police [Orpo]). This security police thus consisted of the Gestapo, which Himmler had taken over from Göring in April 1934, the criminal police (Kripo) and the gendarmerie.

In full possession of the instruments of control and terror, Himmler's forces steadily infiltrated the German state machinery, neutralized the efforts of honest and law-abiding officials, and constructed what has been aptly called the triangle of SS, police, and concentration camp. Himmler's unscrupulous tactics paralyzed the traditional civil service, especially in Prussia.[130] Müller was transferred to Berlin and became head of the Gestapo and later a key figure in the final solution to the Jewish question. The murderous personnel that would carry out the annihilation of millions of innocent people were being assembled. Besides "Gestapo Müller," there were Bruno Streckenbach, former chief of the Hamburg police, who would set up the first ghettos in Poland and put together the infamous *Einsatzgruppen* that rounded up and murdered Jews and "Asiatic inferiors"; SS-Obergruppenführer Oswald Pohl, destined to build up a huge economic conglomerate of SS business enterprises based on slave labor, extortion, and murder; Dr. Walter Stahlecker, who was until his death the commander of Einsatzgruppe A, which followed Army Group North through the Baltic states to Leningrad, killing mercilessly as it went along; Arthur Nebe, head of Kripo, who was the first to volunteer enthusiastically to exterminate Jews in Poland under the cover of "employment duty to the east"; Erich von dem Bach-Zelewski, who had earned his badge of honor by exemplary brutality during the Röhm Purge and was assigned by Himmler to combat partisans on the whole eastern front, which involved him in liquidating countless opponents including many Jews; Otto Ohlendorf, chief of Einsatzgruppe D, who was responsible for the liquidation of at least ninety thousand civilians, mostly Jews, in southern Russia between Bessarabia and the Crimea; and Theodor Eicke, the sadistic sociopath who ran the whole system of concentration camps.

Behind these brutal men were the lawyers with nimble minds who tried to put a shiny legal veneer on extortion, torture, and state killing — men like Werner Best, Reinhard Höhn, Franz Six, and Herbert Mehlhorn. Intellectuals were also not lacking in glamorizing the mission of the SS. The most interesting was Gunter d'Alquen, a young journalist of outstanding ability who became the chief editor of the SS journal *Das Schwarze Korps* (The black corps), a slick and sophisticated weekly periodical of propaganda and investigative journalism that was widely read and feared. Benefiting from a huge SD network of informants, the paper engaged in some biting criticism including titillating insights into the behavior of highly placed party members. The favorite targets, however, were Jews, church officials, and bumbling officials. Since the journal showed traces of self-criticism and based its investigative reports on at least a grain of truth, it was widely read. In 1937, it sold 189,317 copies, and by the end of the war its circulation had reached about 750,000.[131]

It is important to recognize that the SS was perceived by most Germans, including those who joined its various branches, as a noble elite order that accepted only the best and the brightest. This was part of the Nazi policy of *Schein*, of enshrouding aggressive and immoral goals in the noblest idealism, and what could be more idealistic than to join an elite guard, draped from head to foot in puritanical black, whose mission consisted in defending the führer and the institutions of state and party? The desire to join was therefore understandably strong, especially among the upper classes. In the beginning the SS consisted largely of ex–Free Corps soldiers, but after 1933 there was a steady influx from the upper classes and the old aristocratic elite.[132] After the summer of 1933 Himmler not only stopped recruiting but steadily weeded out opportunists, alcoholics, homosexuals, and men of uncertain origins. He wanted an elite order, rigorously trained and imbued with esprit de corps. Using the Jesuit order as a model, Himmler aimed at remolding the entire being of his novices. Candidates had to undergo a grueling two-year training program before they were allowed to swear the "Sippeneid," or "Kith and Kin Oath." The whole training was based on pseudoreligious notions that made a fetish of honor, loyalty, and unconditional obedience to authority. The motto "Meine Ehre ist Treue" (My honor is loyalty) was pounded into the heads of all SS members and was inscribed on all SS daggers.

The SS faith amounted to little more than a belief in the führer, a distorted sense of Germanic greatness, and the inoculation of racial ideas under the guise of scientific truth. These shallow doctrines, in turn, were shrouded by their cranky chief with the trappings of a perverted spirituality. Only those candidates survived in the order who had withstood the worst psychic assaults on their human dignity a military organization could devise, but succeeding, they felt themselves reborn as part of a unique fraternity entrusted with a special mission. As members of this special fraternity, they were not responsible to any court of German justice. The SS had its own court of honor, and Heinrich Himmler made it a principle that no one trained in the law served on it. It was no wonder that members of the SS saw themselves as the chosen ones and that they treated each other like comrades in a special bond. However, as Hans Buchheit has observed, these bonds were not based on strength of character, which respects the dignity of the individual, but rather often fed on weaknesses concealed, transgressions overlooked, and failures covered up, by superiors as well as outsiders.[133] The cruelties of their own training resembled the tortures they inflicted on others and made the infliction of cruelty easier because it had been experienced by themselves. The glorification of hardness (*Härte*) of character, written in the faces of robotlike SS men, expressed itself in the utter contempt and brutality with which these specimens of Aryan superiority mistreated their opponents. For the SS man the word "impossible" was not supposed to exist; his life's oxygen was struggle, unconditional obedience to authority, suppression of feelings or emotions because they implied softness, contempt for inferiors, arrogant behavior toward outsiders, and internal bonding with his own kind.[134]

It would naturally follow that the centerpiece of totalitarian terror, the concentration camp, could be entrusted only to such technicians of inhumanity. Himmler groomed a special volunteer unit of SS men for long-term service as concentration camp guards. These units were called the Death's-Head Units (Totenkopfverbände), whose members wore a special insignia of skull and crossbones on their black caps. The man Himmler put in charge of this system was Theodor Eicke, a brutal psychopath who standardized a set of cruel and unusual punishments in all of his camps. He insisted that each prisoner be treated with fanatical hatred as an enemy of the state. He also routinized a system of graded punishment, consisting of solitary confinement of eight, fourteen, twenty-one, and forty-two days with warm "meals" served only after every fourth day. Corporal punishment (*Prügelstrafe*) was routinely administered by SS men on a rotating basis so that every guard had a chance to whip prisoners in the presence of fellow inmates. Prisoners were constantly bullied and harassed, especially while urinating or defecating.[135] Some were thrown into the cesspool if they were too slow. In October 1932 ten prisoners suffocated in excrement at Buchenwald. Every conceivable indignity was inflicted on inmates, especially Jews, homosexuals, and Jehovah's Witnesses. It was common for prisoners to be urinated upon from head to foot; to be made to roll around in the mud; to be hung from tree limbs and forced to croak "cuckoo"; to squat, hours on end, in the "Saxon Salute" with arms laced behind the head and in deep knee-bend; or to rot and suffocate in sadistically designed torture chambers.

The concentration camp made no pretense to rehabilitating anyone; its mission was to inflict punishment, to exploit inmates by working them to death under the euphemistic motto, inscribed on all concentration camp gates, "Arbeit macht Frei" (Work liberates), and ultimately to annihilate certain targeted groups — Jews, Gypsies, and "Asiatic inferiors." One concentration camp commandant made that clear to every new group of arrivals when he barked at them: "Forget your wives, children and families, here you will die like dogs."[136]

Although four specific groups were targeted for the concentration camp — political opponents, members of "inferior races," criminals, and asocial elements — every German had reason to be apprehensive about his or her own safety. This sense of potential police terror, much encouraged by Himmler, probably far exceeded the reality presen·ed by the small number of camps in use before the war (Dachau, Buchenwald, Sachsenhausen, Flossenbürg, Mauthausen). Nevertheless, there undoubtedly existed a haunting sense that an invisible and sinister empire was metastasizing in the German political system.

The reality actually matched the perception. By the fall of 1939, the SS was organized into four major branches: (1) the General SS, consisting largely of part-timers who combined their regular occupations with evening and weekend service in the SS on a voluntary basis; (2) the SD or Security Service; (3) the SS Military Formations (Verfügungstruppen), renamed Waffen-SS in the winter of 1939–40; and (4) the concentration camp guard units called Death's-Head Units. On September 27, 1939, state police and Gestapo agencies were all merged under one roof, administered by Heydrich and called Reich Main Security Office (Reichssicherheistshauptamt [RSHA]). This monstrous bureaucratic apparatus contained seven main departments: (1) Personnel (Streckenbach), (2) Legal Affairs (Best), (3) SD and, later, Domestic Information Service (Ohlendorf), (4) Gestapo (Müller), (5) criminal police, or Kripo (Nebe), (6) Foreign News Service (Jost and later Schellenberg), and (7) Ideological Research and Evaluation (Drittel). In addition to the RSHA department (Hauptamt), Himmler's empire comprised no fewer than eight other main departments, the last four growing up during World War II. These included Himmler's Private Office, headed by his chief of staff and liaison man with Hitler, Brigadeführer Karl Wolff; the Race and Settlement Main Office (Rasse und Siedlungshauptamt [RuSHA]) under Obergruppenführer Darré; the SS court under Brigadeführer Paul Scharfe; the SS Main Office (SS-Hauptamt), responsible for administrative affairs, and run by August Heissmeyer; the Operational Department (Führungshauptamt), housing the headquarters for the Waffen-SS and administered by Hans Jüttner; the Personnel Department (Personalhauptamt), dealing with SS commandos; the Economic and Administrative Department (Wirtschafts-und Verwaltungshauptamt [WVHA]) under Gruppenführer Pohl, which oversaw a vast conglomerate of business ventures and also administered the financial affairs of the concentration camps; and a reorganized SS-Hauptamt, now called Duty Station Obergruppenführer Heissmeyer, which took over the inspection of the elite NS schools called National Socialist Educational Institutions (NPEA).

Such a proliferation of SS institutions, overlapping as well as infiltrating other institutions of the Third Reich, gave the SS a menacing aura, made all the more sinister by the fact that no outsiders knew anything in detail about Himmler's empire. However, despite the fact that Himmler dropped a veil of secrecy over his empire, his power was not absolute because, as Heinz Höhne has shown, power was constantly shifting among Hitler's major paladins and also because the army continued to exercise its privileges as Germany's major fighting unit.[137] There was the additional factor that Heinrich Himmler, whose authority was never seriously challenged within the SS, remained doggedly devoted to his führer, as did his organization, whose raison d'être was contained in the oath sworn to him by each of its members:

> I swear to thee Adolf Hitler,
> As Führer and Chancellor of the German Reich, Loyalty and Bravery.
> I vow to thee and to the superiors whom thou shalt appoint
> Obedience unto death
> So help me God.[138]

We have come full circle in the Nazi totalitarian state, where everything began and ended with Adolf Hitler.

Chapter 10

Life in Nazi Germany

The Aesthetics and Psychology of Mass Seduction

Many years after Nazi Germany had passed into history, those who were old enough to remember what it was like to live in Hitler's Third Reich invariably recalled that they were emotionally touched by the movement's public spectacles and the dynamic force that compelled people into some form of shared participation. The regime drew people out of themselves and involved them as coactors in a continuous series of grand spectacles arranged and conducted by a man with a flair for the dramatic. It must be remembered that Hitler was not only a soldier-politician but also an artist with a keen eye for the aesthetic who knew that persuasion required conversion, and that conversion, at its deepest level, was emotional rather than cerebral. As a passionate Wagnerian, Hitler encouraged mass-produced celebrations of such emotional intensity that those who participated in them would undergo "a kind of metamorphosis from a little worm into part of a big dragon," feeling revitalized, empowered, and redeemed.

Even today as we watch Leni Riefenstahl's brilliant documentary of the 1934 Nuremberg party rally, entitled *Triumph of the Will*, we can still vicariously experience the pull of the intense feelings that swept the crowd into wild outbursts of enthusiasm and into a collective, almost religious, adoration of a man who had come to redeem Germany. Hitler knew the Germans.[1] The safest way to their hearts was by appeal to their religious and romantic sensibilities. No politician in Germany, before or after Hitler, has been able to build up such intimate emotional bonds with the people.

Life in Nazi Germany was dominated by sharp and unexpected alternations of moods and emotions; Germans rarely felt stable, relaxed, or at peace with themselves. They were always pushed into being publicly active. Some have compared the style of life in Nazi Germany to that of a mobilized soldier called upon to do his public duty by marching, singing, parading, or otherwise joining in activities designed to strip him of his private persona. In Richard Grunberger's words, "The regime's immense thrust stemmed from its capacity to make increasing numbers of Germans regard themselves as anonymous combatants with leave-passes revokable at a moment's notice, rather than as individuals rooted in their civilian existence."[2] Goebbels put it more bluntly by saying that in the Third Reich no German felt himself to be a private citizen. Under the steady pressure of government cajoling, harassment, and outright threats, the life of Germans, young and old alike, was being coordinated to produce perfect group-think — the ideal of all totalitarian states.

Ingenious rituals were devised to break down individuality: marching columns, mass rallies, making public fetishes of flags and uniforms, public commemorations, and the ubiquitous "Heil Hitler" greetings. The most famous, of course, were the carefully staged mass rallies, often held at night, in which the führer or other Nazi leaders would address crowds of varying sizes. Torchlight parades were often staged so that individual differences would melt into group harmony. These were orgiastic group intoxications, stripping individuals of their own reason and will. In its grandiose spectacles, held under Albert Speer's lofty "cathedrals of light" — searchlights that would light the sky at night and produce the illusion of being in a cathedral — or in the bright sun amid perfectly aligned formations of storm troopers, the Nazi regime succeeded in replicating its highest ideal, that of a predator nation showing no pity for the weak. It was a gleam of sinister beauty the world had not seen since the days of the ancient Assyrians.

Another means of stripping away individuals' private personas was to isolate or separate them from family ties by calling upon them periodically to attend a party camp (*Lager*) where they were particularly susceptible to propaganda. Grunberger reminds us that many of these public meetings began with a ritual called the *Appell* — a word with a double meaning since it could mean roll call or appeal to conscience or both.[3] Putting people into uniforms was another way of stripping them of their individuality. From a psychological or aesthetic point of view, the uniform represents a symbol of conformity and enforced group identity. In German life, the uniform with its impressive insignia or medals had always been an object of veneration. The Nazis reinforced this habit and produced some of the most attractive regalia in modern times. Public rituals, shrouded in pseudoreligious trappings, were another means of fostering group identity. Like the French revolutionaries, the Nazis revamped the calendar in order to bring it into line with new national commemorations or holidays. The first major event of the year was January 30, the day when Hitler was appointed chancellor. On February 24, an important day in Nazi hagiography, party faithful celebrated the anniversary of the Twenty-Five-Point Program and the founding of the NSDAP. In March, the regime marked Heroes Remembrance Day and conducted the initiation of fourteen year olds into the Hitler Youth (HJ) or the League of German Girls (BDM). On April 20, the whole country celebrated the führer's birthday, an occasion that was usually marked by effusive outpourings of praise to his genius and leadership abilities. May started with a work-free holiday, something German workers had been asking for in vain until the Nazis came to power. In May, Germans were reminded of the importance of motherhood for the future of the Thousand-Year Reich. The observance of summer and winter solstices, representing pagan elements in the Nazi movement, was popular among the ranks of the SS but generally ignored by the population at large. The greatest display came in September with the elaborately choreographed party congresses at Nuremberg. In October, harvest festival was celebrated by thousands of peasants from all over Germany, parading in traditional folk costumes on the Bückelberg near Hamelin in Westphalia. The Nazi year ended not with Christmas but with a solemn reenactment of the failed November 9, 1923, putsch, staged by the original participants. The old fighters marched to the Feldherrnhalle, where Adolf Hitler privately communed with the fallen heroes of the event.[4] The regime also constantly urged people to work for the public good, to be involved in party activities. Joseph Goebbels was the undisputed master of exploiting genuine benevolent impulses for ulterior, political ends. One famous ritual was Sunday Stew Day (Eintopfsonntag), designed to encourage a sense of common sharing and benefit the Winter Relief Campaign (Winterhilfswerk), a charitable organization founded to help the unemployed and the needy. The Nazis used public charities for their own propagandistic aims, staging public eatings (*Schau-Essen*) featuring famous personalities such as Hitler and Goebbels partaking of the meal.

The most famous ritual, of course, was the Nazi salute, which, in its most exaggerated form, consisted in clicking one's heels, standing rigidly at attention, thrusting one's right arm upward at an angle so that the palm of the hand became visible, and shouting resolutely, "Heil Hitler." Not all Germans were overjoyed by the prospect of having to perform this ritual on a regular basis, and only eager beavers engaged in it with anything resembling real enthusiasm. Some Germans devised ingenious strategies for avoiding this embarrassing display of public chauvinism, ranging from inaudible mumbles and feeble hand gestures to elaborate tricks of avoiding public encounters with friends or acquaintances.[5] Comic exaggerations were legend. In 1933, a Dresden woman was observed telling her young daughter to "go over to the Auntie on the other side of the road and make a nice little Heil Hitler" (und mach hübsch dein Heil Hitlerchen).[6] Yet despite certain annoying features involved in these acts of public conformity, most Germans felt a closer rapport with the Nazi government than they did with the republic or even the Kaiserreich. In fact, the Nazi regime tapped a genuine sense of democratic camaraderie; it touched the average German in a way no other regime had ever done. Perhaps this was because Hitler himself appeared to be the epitome of the ordinary man, who had been put in power by equally ordinary men. The American journalist Dorothy Thompson, upon meeting Hitler for the first time, described him as "formless, almost soulless, a man whose countenance is a caricature....He is the very prototype of the little man."[7]

This is why the regime's constant appeal to the people, *das Volk,* was not simply a clever Machiavellian ploy but represented its firm belief in harmonizing the one (the führer) with the many (*das Volk*), of linking ruler and ruled in some mystical bond of leadership. It was, of course, an illusion based on a political impossibility. The Nazi ideal of creating an organic *Volksgemeinschaft* (community of the people) was not in itself negative or impractical had it been based on life-enhancing values. Hitler debased the ideal of organic community life by tarnishing it with the brush of crude racial and national prejudices. In fact, Hitler built his evil empire by completely debasing certain German traditions that had already become liabilities in the life of the nation. He channelled the idealism embodied in the nation's youth movements into brutal warlike ends, further exploited an already pervasive militarism, revitalized tribal nationalism by grafting on it a biological-racist dimension, romanticized cruelty and irrationality, and carried German authoritarianism to its ultimate conclusion — blind obedience.

The veneer he put upon these perversions, however, was in the form of the noblest rhetoric. Hitler and the Nazis outdid each other publicly in appealing to the loftiest ideals, but the motives that shaped the words "honor," "sacrifice," "courage," "strength," and "selflessness" were dishonest. Hitler's trick, it has been said, was to distort positive values in German life by the use of "crazy house" mirrors "patterned after his own warped and twisted soul."[8] In Howard Becker's clever perception:

> Love of things German has become hatred of everything non-German; romantic idealism has become contempt for thought; allegiance to the values close at hand has become scorn of the values held by the rest of mankind; sturdy independence has become swash-buckling, truculent aggression; loyalty to the chosen leader has become blind subservience to a despot; reverence to the sound body has become the avowed anti-rationality of "we think with our blood"; devotion to children...has become the breeding of cannon-fodder.[9]

To outsiders, then and now, life in Nazi Germany appeared to be a regression to primitive tribalism. One author has argued that aspects of National Socialism reminded him of life in a central African tribe,[10] and another held that the Third Reich reminded him of William Golding's *Lord of the Flies,* in which civilized boys, stranded on an island, revert to primitivism by following the perverse childish fantasies of their leader, Jack. Was Adolf Hitler an adult Jack who showed contempt for the weak, murdered the innocent, enjoyed gratuitous cruelty, decreed his own brand of happiness, demanded total commitment to primitive symbols, and required incessant marching and singing?[11]

There can be no doubt that the relationship between Hitler and Germany was one of seduction. The German people allowed themselves to be tricked and seduced by a clever sociopath who knew how to exploit both their strengths and their weaknesses. Of course, no one is seduced without active participation; an act of surrender implies the suspension or abdication of the will. Blaming Hitler for every wrong is inauthentic; it is a convenient externalization of Germany's guilty conscience and inner weaknesses onto the Hitlerian scapegoat. Germans were willing participants; they would have never been taken in so completely, as Carl Jung reminds us, "if this figure had not been a reflective image of the collective hysteria."[12]

Curiously, when it was all over and sober reflection could finally replace unbridled emotion, many Germans, now released from the spell, were dumbfounded by what had happened to them. Karl Jaspers summed it up well by confessing that "during the past twelve years something has happened to us that seems like the remolding of our entire being. To put it in the form of an image: Devils have been raining blows upon us and have swept us away, together with themselves, into a chaos which has robbed us of sight and hearing. . . . We have experienced something like the witchcraft madness of the later Middle Ages."[13]

Youth and Education

The mobilization of German youth was one of the most important goals of National Socialism. Ever since Germany had experienced rapid industrialization, young people, especially of middle-class backgrounds, had organized into youth groups to voice their opposition to the Philistine mores and values of their elders and to the materialistic imperatives spawned by modern industrial civilization. From a larger cultural perspective, the various German youth movements, dating back to the Wandervögel of the Kaiserreich, must be seen as countercultural protest movements against mainstream, bourgeois, industrial civilization. Such protest movements were not unique to Germany, but seem to represent recurring outbursts of romantic protest; they are ultimately based on a perpetual tension between established mainstream cultures, with their anti-instinctual rigidity and classical order, and countercultural forces, with their inherent instinctualism and romantic striving.

Outwardly, youthful protest expressed itself primarily in escapist activities. These took the form of hiking trips, singing folk songs around a campfire, and shared interests and rites used for gender bonding. Included was also a cultivation of a sense of ethnic German heritage. Albert Speer expressed his generation's feelings when he said:

> Many of our generation sought such contact with nature. This was not merely a romantic protest against the narrowness of middle-class life. We were also escaping from the demands of a world growing increasingly complicated. We felt that the world around us was out of balance. In

nature, in the mountains and the river valleys, the harmony of Creation could still be felt.[14]

The other side to such innocent protest was its profoundly reactionary thrust, for many of these young people did not want to confront the reality of life in the modern world, but to run away from it into utopian fantasies that somehow could be made into a model for the future. World War I had also spawned new and more martial youth groups such as the Bündische Jugend, which glorified the soldier and morbid ideas of self-immolation for the glory of the fatherland.[15]

The Nazis exploited such youthful protests, idealistic or reactionary, for their own ends. When Hitler seized power in 1933, the Hitler Youth organization had a total of only 107,956 members, but this was about to change drastically under the leadership of Baldur von Schirach, whose ambition was to bring all German youth movements under the umbrella of the Hitler Youth (HJ). By the end of 1933 Schirach had coordinated most youth movements and steadily encroached on the few remaining nonconformists such as Catholic organizations. On December 1, 1936, Schirach succeeded in detaching his organization from the Ministry of the Interior and turning it into a supreme Reich authority (*Reichsbehörde*) directly responsible to Hitler. The law of December 1, 1936, stated that "the whole of German youth within the borders of the Reich is organized in the Hitler Youth," that "all German Young People, apart from being educated at home and at school, will be educated in the Hitler Youth physically, intellectually, and morally in the spirit of National Socialism to serve the nation and the community," and that "the task of educating German Youth in the Hitler Youth is being entrusted to the Reich Leader of the German Youth in the NSDAP."[16] This first Hitler Youth Law did not make membership in the HJ compulsory, but a second law, issued on March 25, 1939, made participation mandatory.

Membership in the Hitler Youth rose to 8,870,000 at the beginning of 1939.[17] In its organizational structure, the Hitler Youth was divided into two main branches (one for boys, the other for girls), with two subdivisions in each:

1. The German Young Folk (Deutsches Jungvolk [DJ]) for boys aged ten to fourteen. These young boys were usually referred to as *Pimpf* (cub).

2. The Hitler Youth (Hitlerjugend [HJ]) for boys aged fifteen to eighteen.

3. The League of Young Girls (Jungmädelbund [JM]) for girls aged ten to fourteen.

4. The League of German Girls (Bund deutscher Mädel [BDM]) for girls aged fifteen to eighteen.

All young people had to be registered by their parents or guardians; noncompliance was punishable by fine or imprisonment. The regime enshrouded admissions ceremonies with oaths and invocations, replete with solemn exhortations of loyalty and obedience to the führer and fatherland. The motto of the HJ was: "Führer, command — we follow!"

It became increasingly clear to many German parents who still thought for themselves that the Hitler Youth was a state organization designed to indoctrinate young people in the mind-set of their führer, Adolf Hitler. Young people were deceived by a smoke screen of youthful idealism. The reality was that the Hitler Youth was a very different organization from the more innocent and somewhat boy scoutish groups of the past. Although the motto "Youth must be led by youth" was largely honored by Nazi leaders, youth leaders were representatives of a Nazi state more interested in instilling an aggressive party spirit than in fostering individual growth. There were no more informal or carefree outings. Everything now assumed a military tone, which, in the words of one historian, made this generation of young Germans intolerably loutish and belligerent.[18] Young people were exhorted endlessly to fall in for roll call (*Appell*); they reported for duty like obedient soldiers. Their outings were semimilitary: marching, pitching tents in perfect order and symmetry, playing quasi-military games, singing ideologically tinged songs ("On, Raise Our Flags," "Holy Fatherland," "Soldiers Carry Rifles," "Unroll the Blood-red Flags"), and chanting passwords and catchphrases ("Heil Hitler," "Hitler is Germany and Germany is Hitler," "Blood," etc.).

What were these young Germans being taught, especially in school? The chief aim of education under the Nazis, as under all totalitarian regimes, was to produce a new type of person — in the case of the Nazis, a strong, self-conscious racial type who was proud of country and loyal to the führer. Since the German educational system had been traditionally authoritarian, there was little need to alter its structure in a revolutionary sense other than to give it a strong racist dimension. Still, the regime initially engaged in widespread purges of the teaching profession at all levels. Spearheaded primarily by Bernhard Rust, the minister of culture, this purge resulted in widespread dismissals of ideologically unreliable teachers, especially Jews. Teachers were also obligated to join the National Socialist Teachers' League (NSLB), which served as the official watchdog of the regime monitoring the behavior of teachers throughout Germany. The NSLB also assumed the responsibility for indoctrinating teachers in mandatory eight- to fourteen-day courses, held in special camps all over Germany, which focused on the duties of German teachers under National Socialism. Nazi control over German education also assumed the form of rigid centralization of the school system and reorganization of secondary schools into three broad models emphasizing specializations in science, modern languages, or the classics. On the university level, the League of German Students had spearheaded the coordination of university life and thought in the spirit of the new system. The Aryan paragraph, demanding "Aryan" racial screening as a prerequisite for public office, had eliminated a host of outstanding

Jewish teachers by the middle of 1933. In 1935 the *Führerprinzip* was officially inflicted on the universities. In the spirit of this principle, the party, whenever possible, put in charge a new Nazi rector, who, in turn, appointed politically correct deans (*Dekane*), and these appointed the appropriate department heads. Under this system, the German universities, world renowned for their great teaching staffs, suffered a steady and appalling decline in quality, but such considerations were not always primary to a regime that prided itself on its anti-intellectualism.

After these assaults on the teaching profession, teachers on all levels, with a few, all too few, notable exceptions, conformed so well and toed the party line so obediently that the regime did not have to spy extensively on teachers. It goes without saying that the content of German education under the Nazis underwent significant changes both in its broad philosophy and its curricular framework.

Philosophically, Nazi educators wanted young Germans to acquire a strong racist and aggressive mode of thinking.[19] Since loyalty, obedience, and service to the state constituted the chief virtues of the new regime, habits of mind had to be developed that fostered and rewarded these educational priorities. Analytical habits of mind were automatically suspect since they taught young people to be skeptical, open-minded, or tolerant. This explains the widespread distrust of purely analytical thinking (*Verstandesdenken*) by Nazi educators. It was the education of the will rather than the mind (*Verstand*) that now received primary consideration.[20]

The aim of education was to produce the wholesome racial type for whom knowledge is merely a means to an end. Cleverness was seen as a mark of flippancy and was discouraged. The same was true of individual initiative and the "Western" habit of encouraging youngsters to think for themselves. In *Mein Kampf,* Hitler expressed himself unequivocally on this issue of mass education for mass obedience:

> The folkish state...has to direct its entire education primarily not at pumping in mere knowledge, but at the breeding of absolutely healthy bodies. Of secondary importance is the training of mental abilities. But here again first of all the development of the character, especially the promotion of will power and determination, connected with education for joyfully assuming responsibility, and only as the last thing, scientific schooling.[21]

Hitler was convinced that the influence of intellectuals on the masses was insidious because it always subverts group cohesion. Intellectuals destroy faith; they are therefore incapable of inspiring the community to great actions or deeds. It follows that "a man, though scientifically little educated but physically healthy, who has a sound, firm character, filled with joyful determination and will power, is of greater value to the national community than an ingenious weakling."[22] To Hermann Rauschning, Hitler said:

My pedagogy is hard. Everything weak must be eliminated. My Ordensburgen [Castles of Order] will mold a youth from which the world will
shrink in terror. I want a brutal, domineering, fearless, and cruel youth.
...They must endure pain; they cannot be weak and tender. The glow
of the free and magnificent predatory animal must thunder from their
eyes. I want my youth strong and beautiful. I will train them in all of the
athletic sciences. I want an athletic youth. That's the first and most important thing. It's in this way that I am going to eliminate two thousand
years of domestication. Then I'll have a pure, noble material of nature
before me of which I can create the New.

I don't want intellectual education. I spoil my youth with knowledge.
I would prefer to let them learn what their own playful impulse freely
chooses to acquire. They shall show me in the most difficult trials how to
conquer the fear of death. That's the step up for a heroic youth....My
Ordensburgen will form the cult image of the beautiful, creative human,
the self-commanding God-man, who will prepare the coming stage of
human maturation.[23]

Since the aim of Nazi education was to produce obedient followers
and to further expansion and conquest, it logically followed that indoctrination and sports were two of the twin pillars of the Nazi temple.
The aim of education was not to aid self-discovery but to indoctrinate
young people to think like National Socialists.[24] This is why the teacher
is not just an instructor and a transmitter of knowledge, but a soldier
who serves the aims of National Socialism on the cultural-political front.
True, the battle on this front is of a different nature and is fought with
different weapons, but it is no less important because the struggle is for
the soul of the people.[25]

The new Nazi superman was to be, above all, physically strong. This
is why the time allotted for physical education in German schools was
increased from two to three hours a week in 1936 and to five hours in
1938.[26] The whole physical education curriculum was also revamped to
reflect the importance that the regime attached to discipline and good
health. Cross-country running, soccer, and boxing were added to the
list of activities because they promoted the spirit of attack (*Angriffs-
geist*) and physical superiority. Students had to pass stringent standards
of physical proficiency as a prerequisite for both entrance and graduation requirements. Persistently poor performance in sports constituted
sufficient grounds for dismissal from school itself. The importance of
sports as a core requirement also implied the academic respectability,
even superiority, of the physical education instructors, whose comments
on the grade report cards often outweighed other entries.[27]

Academic subjects were also Nazified. German history, for example,
was blatantly distorted to fit the National Socialist mold. One leading
educator even urged students to interpret German history through "German blood," whatever that meant. The emphasis in teaching history was
to be put less on textual sources or objectivity and more on the dramatic and inspirational aspects of the past. Similarly, German teachers

were badgered to stress Nordic legends, sagas, and heroic personalities in their teaching. The nature of reading materials also underwent a dramatic change, especially in the lower grades, where war stories and heroic exploits displaced fairy tales or animal stories. In a book aimed at teenagers, entitled *Battle of Tannenberg,* we read the following bloodthirsty passage: "A Russian tried to bar the infiltrator's way, but Otto's bayonet slid gratingly between the Russian's ribs, so that he collapsed groaning. There it lay before him, simple and distinguished, his dream's desire, the Iron Cross."[28]

Textbooks interspersed pictures of hardened combat troops marching in formation with stories of rabbits, robins, and flowers. Whenever possible, pictures or stories of the führer were used in order to arouse enthusiasm for the Nazi cause. In one story, entitled "The Führer Comes," a young lad by the name of Klaus eagerly awaits the arrival of the führer in his town:

> Today Klaus' mother does not need to wake him. He springs from bed on his own. Today is an important holiday. From the windows the Swastika flags wave. . . . In the shop windows stand pictures of the Führer. . . . The boys climb up trees. . . . When a flag-bearer passes, Klaus raises his right arm in salute. All at once Klaus hears Heil salutes from afar. The shouts sound even nearer, and then Klaus sees the Führer. He stands in the car and waves in a friendly manner. Heil! Heil! calls Klaus as loud as he can. What a pity, the Führer is already past! But Klaus continually calls: Heil Hitler! Heil Hitler![29]

Some of the most disturbing changes in the German school system, however, dealt with the introduction of racial studies. "No boy or girl," the führer was quoted, "shall leave school without having been fully instructed in the need for and nature of racial purity. This will create the prerequisite for the racial foundations of our nationhood and, in turn, provide a secure grounding for later cultural development."[30] Starting in September 1933, racial instruction became mandatory in German schools, but few German teachers knew exactly how they should teach this arcane subject because there were no official texts. Many teachers simply put together notes extracted from Nazi racial philosophers (Rosenberg, Günther) and introduced "cranial measurements" into the classroom.[31]

In education, just as in other spheres of German society, the regime created a dual-track system of training — one for ordinary Germans and the other for future Nazi leaders whose eyes "glow with the freedom and splendor of the beast of prey." The new system reflected the haphazard planning and coordination so characteristic of the personal style of leadership in Nazi Germany. In theory, the führer envisioned his young birds of prey being groomed for their heroic tasks by being snatched from their parents at an early age. They would join the Hitler Youth and then move, step-by-step, through the prescribed chain of Nazi maturation — elite Nazi schools, labor service, army service, marriage, followed by further political instruction in one of the party's Ordensbur-gen, capped by final immersion in a party university. The purpose of all this was to tie every German so closely to the state and to Nazi ideology that he or she would never be free again. In one of Hitler's most appalling speeches, a recording of which has survived, the führer explained his ideal of the "unfree" German youth, and when he spoke the words, "And they will not be free again for the rest of their lives," he said them with such a mixture of joy and mendacity that any freedom-loving person would have shuddered with apprehension. However, those who were present on December 4, 1938, cheered with great enthusiasm at the following words:

> These young people learn nothing else but to think as Germans and to act as Germans; these boys join our organisation at the age of ten and get a breath of fresh air for the first time, then, four years later, they move from the Jungvolk to the Hitler Youth and here we keep them for another four years. And then we are even less prepared to give them back into the hands of those who create our class and status barriers; rather we take them immediately into Party, into the Labour Front, into the SA or into the SS, into the NSKK and so on. And if they are there for eighteen months or two years and have still not become real National Socialists, then they go into the Labour Service and are polished there for six or seven months, and all of this under a single symbol, the German spade. And if, after six or seven months, there are still remnants of class consciousness or pride in status, then the Wehrmacht will take over the further treatment for two years and when they return after two or four years then, to prevent them from slipping back into the old habits once again we take them immediately into SA, SS etc., *and they will not be free again for the rest of their lives*.[32] (emphasis added)

In practice, this ideal model of enslavement never fully materialized because the führer's leadership style was too mercurial in character to encourage a coordinated approach. However, three major elite schools, the brainchild of different Nazi leaders, were actually developed — the National Political Institutes of Education (Napolas), the Adolf Hitler Schools, and the Ordensburgen. A fourth elite school, a party Hoch-schule or University, conceived by the Nazi philosopher Rosenberg, never got beyond the planning stage. On April 20, 1933, the führer's birthday, the education minister, Bernhard Rust, officially presented Hitler with an unusual birthday gift in the form of an elite school system called National Political Institutes of Education, known largely by their acronym "Napolas." The first three Napolas were simply the Nazified Prussian cadets schools at Potsdam, Plön, and Köslin. By 1938, there were 21 Napolas, including four in Austria and one in the Sudetenland. In 1943 they reached their peak of 39.

Although the Napolas were originally run by Rust's Reich Ministry of Education, they were taken over by Himmler's SS as early as 1936. Their primary mission was to train political soldiers destined to become future government leaders.[33] Great emphasis was therefore placed on political indoctrination and physical training. Academic subjects emphasized the practical or applied side of learning. Technical and military subjects predominated, and instruction was given by Hitler Youth leaders, SS, and other politically trustworthy young men. Subjects deemed particularly useful for future leaders were boxing, war games, rowing, sailing, gliding, shooting practice, and learning how to handle motorized vehicles of all sorts. The curriculum was organized along strictly military lines. Classes were called platoons, and daily activity involved frequent drills, communal activities, reveille, and other related military activities. Students were urged to discuss ideological issues under close supervision; they were also forced to interact with ordinary Germans by spending six to eight weeks in the general population, helping farmers with the harvest, or toiling alongside factory workers or coal miners. The idea behind these token concessions to egalitarianism was to acquaint the future elite with the needs of ordinary Germans and, indirectly, to counterbalance the elitism inherent in the new Nazi schools.

In practice, such contradictory aims proved to be as impossible as squaring the circle. The Napolas, in fact, turned out to be little more than breeding grounds for arrogant, half-educated technicians, who fancied themselves born leaders of men. Admission to the new Napolas was theoretically open to all German boys, but in practice youngsters had to be recommended by party district chiefs. In addition to intellectual ability, physical fitness, and political reliability, young cadets or *Jungmannen* were selected for their "racial purity." This vague appellation, with its mystical appeal to blood and soil, permeated the whole educational experience of Napola students. Romanticized events around the campfires at night or highly charged ceremonials, celebrating manhood, fatherland, and führer, were an intimate part of Napola students' lives. These occasions were accompanied by songs such as "Wo wir stehen, steht die Treue" (Where we stand, stands loyalty) and "Lever dod as Slav" (Better dead than enslaved), by readings from the *Edda,* and by music from Handel. The purpose behind these rituals was to kindle latent idealism in the boys and to instill in them an esprit de corps worthy of the institute's motto: "Believe, Obey, Fight."

On April 20, 1937, once again on the führer's birthday, a second type of elite school, appropriately named Adolf Hitler Schools (AHS), made their appearance at Crössinsee in Pomerania. This project was the result of a joint effort by Robert Ley and Baldur von Schirach, who wanted to establish special leadership schools for the party and Hitler Youth that would function outside the regular structure of German education.[34] Since Rust did not want Ley to interfere in his management of the Napolas, Ley and Schirach proceeded, with Hitler's blessings, to establish an alternate system.

The mission of the Adolf Hitler Schools was to groom future leaders for the party and the Hitler Youth. Originally, Ley and Schirach envisioned one Adolf Hitler School for each *Gau,* but party funds proved to be insufficient for this project, so that by 1942 only eleven schools had been established. Although candidates were supposed to be drawn from the brightest twelve year olds, the actual crop of Adolf Hitler students was recruited from diverse and educationally uneven backgrounds. Socially, most of the students came from petit bourgeois origins. The curriculum was similar to the Napolas, with heavy emphasis being placed on ideological subjects and premilitary training.

A third type of elite school was the Ordensburg. The idea behind this school was to take candidates who had already gone through the Hitler Youth, received their diplomas from the Adolf Hitler School, performed their duty in the labor service and the army, and put them through a kind of capstone experience in political indoctrination. Alfred Rosenberg even dreamed of taking the best Ordensjunker and forcing them to undergo further indoctrination at a party university, but the plans for this grandiose project never materialized.

Three colossal Ordensburgen, however, made their appearance in Pomerania (Crössinsee), Upper Bavaria (Sonthofen), and the Eifel (Vogelsang). These colossal castles of knightly order were designed to accommodate one thousand Junkers or cadets each. The entrance requirements were minimal: candidates had to be "sound fellows" (Ley's phrase) between the ages of twenty-five and thirty and possess experience in the Nazi Party. Recruits came from relatively humble social backgrounds and even humbler educational programs. Their training was suitable for clerical or, at best, midlevel careers in the party, but not for real leadership positions in the higher echelons of party, state, or armed services. Outsiders, in fact, poked fun at the limited abilities of Ordensburg graduates by calling them "golden pheasants" — a jibe at their brown uniforms and limited mentalities.

On the whole, the Napolas were the only successful Nazi schools, primarily because they were more rooted in the tradition of German military education. Emulating also the English public school, including its authoritarian system of prefect and fagging, it proved highly attractive to the parents of the upper classes who saw these schools as successors to the old military cadet schools with their emphasis on elitism and military esprit de corps. The other Nazi elite schools were far too improvisational and uncoordinated to make a major difference in the German educational system.

In fact, Nazi educational efforts as a whole turned out to be poorly thought out and lacking in substance. At best, the Nazis put a thin ideological veneer on German education. It is not surprising that twelve years were not enough to break down "two thousand years of European cultural heritage."[35] However, Nazi indoctrination was able to miseducate and misuse a whole generation of young people, a generation that, on the whole, felt happy and empowered under the Third Reich, but one that also came to realize, in the words of one former young man, that they were "used up and destroyed as a generation by Adolf Hitler."[36]

Women and the Family

The Nazis looked upon the family primarily as a reproductive unit furnishing future soldiers for the Reich. Of course, such blatantly crude ideas were rarely publicized. Nazi art evoked the traditional image of the clean-cut sheltering family whose members relate to each other in loving support and perform their assigned roles without question. Thousands of posters or picture postcards idealized the image of well-groomed, blond children who are lovingly supported by their protective Aryan parents. This was playing with smoke and mirrors. What the Nazis wanted from German parents was more children. The birth rate, which had been at an all-time high around the turn of the century, had leveled off substantially by the 1930s, causing much alarm among Nazi leaders.

In order to win the battle of demographics and plant the German seed throughout Europe, the Nazis encouraged large families by curtailing women's access to equal opportunities, criminalizing abortion, clamping down on homosexuality, and discouraging prostitution. The Nazis also offered all sorts of monetary incentives to encourage reproduction such as marriage loans, child subsidies, and generous family allowances.[37] The regime constantly inveighed against selfish couples who did not want children, an attitude officially condemned as decadent or "Western." Exhibitions were staged to show that great Germans such as J. S. Bach had fathered dozens of children. The phrase "blessed with children" — *Kindersegen* — was constantly used.[38] In addition, a veritable mother's cult was launched. Each year, the birthday of Hitler's mother, August 12, became an occasion of effusive sentiments surrounding the German mother and the handing out of awards to the most fertile mothers. The "Honors Cross" of the German mother came in three classes — gold, for more than eight children; silver, for more than six; and bronze, for five.

Behind this facade lingered malignant and destructive objectives: in fact, the Nazis saw families as incubators of future soldiers of the Reich. Nazi rhetoric about the family was, in other words, pious double-talk concealing malevolent intentions. Families, in the normal and healthy sense, are sturdy islands of autonomy, sheltering their members from the heavy hand of the state. It is for this reason that totalitarian governments cannot tolerate such islands of institutional separateness.[39] They recognize the cultural and psychological importance of the family unit because it is the primary source of the acculturation process; at the same time, totalitarian states attempt to transform the family unit by making it an extension of state policy. Under totalitarian rule, the state tries to co-opt the family as an independent unit by undermining biological ties in favor of new surrogate relationships, even if it requires setting one family member against another. Once the living blood is drained from the family, all that remains is a hollow shell, its place having been taken by Big Brother. That this did not happen in Germany is a living testimonial to the historical strength of this institution and its resilience.

Large families presupposed that women stay at home rather than go to work. For this reason, the image of women cultivated by the Nazis was a traditional one of mother and homemaker. Magda Goebbels, a blonde, tall, and attractive woman, became the officially promoted ideal of womanhood in the Third Reich. Her husband, the propaganda chief, had this to say about the role of women in the Third Reich: "The mission of women is to be beautiful and to bring children into the world. This is not at all as rude and unmodern as it sounds. The female bird pretties herself for her mate and hatches the eggs for him. In exchange, the mate takes care of gathering the food, and stands guard and wards off the enemy."[40] The female bird, of course, was not expected to preen herself too much: lipstick, powder, and other makeup were widely condemned as unnatural and decadent. Such "war-paint" was regarded as a regression to the decadent values of the Weimar Republic and the whole Western atmosphere of sham and artificiality in general. In their official pronouncements on this subject, the Nazis were always fond of juxtaposing the refreshingly simple Aryan beauty with the liberated, conniving, and heavily made-up female of the Western democracies.

Behind these solemn declarations praising German womanhood lurked reactionary male biases that sought to arrest female development by rigidly maintaining an outdated, one-dimensional stereotype. What most Nazi leaders really thought about women may be gauged by Hitler's condescending and indeed insulting comment that "a woman must be a cute, cuddly, naive little thing — tender, sweet, and stupid."[41] In a family speech to the National Socialist Women's Organization in September 1936 he revealed what he really expected from women — children he could use for cannon fodder. "If today a female jurist accomplishes ever so much and next door there lives a mother with five, six, seven children, who are all healthy and well-brought-up, then I would like to say: From the standpoint of eternal value of our people the woman who has given birth to children and raised them and who thereby has given back our people life for the future has accomplished more and does more."[42] This is why females were henceforth excluded from the legal profession and strenuous propaganda efforts were launched to keep women out of other traditionally male-oriented professions such as medicine and teaching. Women were even declared ineligible for jury duty on the grounds that "they cannot think logically or reason objectively, since they are ruled only by emotion."[43] For politically involved women, National Socialism had few opportunities since, as mentioned above, "the German resurrection" was seen as "a male event."[44]

In Hitler's world, women were decorative thrills, admissible to a man's world only in moments of light relaxation. Since he lacked the ability to form loving, intimate ties with women, he preferred the company of males, the world of seriousness and purpose. The role of women, first and foremost, was to produce children for the führer. Such degradation of women to the role of obedient reproducers of the race may be illustrated, time and again, by the treatment accorded to women in the Nazi hierarchy. Martin Bormann's wife, for example, soberly accepted her husband's revelation — triumphantly recounted in a letter to her in January 1944 — that he had finally succeeded in seducing the actress Manja Behrens. Bormann's wife was neither jealous nor upset by this moral indiscretion; in fact, she suggested a ménage à trois on the grounds that such an arrangement would set an example for other Germans since a ménage à trois was more likely to produce more children. Manja, she opined, was too valuable, racially and biologically, not to bear children; and with perfect sincerity, Gerda Bormann suggested to her husband: "You can certainly be helpful to Manja, but you have to see to it that Manja has a child one year and I have one the next, so that you always have one woman around who's in good shape (so dass du immer eine Frau hast, die gebrauchsfähig ist)."[45] One historian has called this the Nazi principle of crop rotation.[46]

Students of Nazi Germany have generally overlooked the supporting role played by German mothers in bolstering the aggressive drive of German men.[47] Why this omission of the role of German mothers could have existed for such a long time is probably due to the fact, as Erik H. Erikson once remarked, that "students of society and history . . . blithely continue to ignore the simple fact that all individuals are born by mothers; that everybody was once a child; that people and peoples begin in their nurseries; and that society consists of generations in the process of developing from children into parents, destined to absorb the historical changes of their lifetimes and to continue to make history for their descendants."[48] The hand that rocks the cradle rules the world. Nurturing mothers can nurture killers. If German males found it relatively easy to commit aggressions with a good conscience, the nurturing process must have provided the psychic support for it.

The Nazis inherited certain cultural patterns from preceding generations in Germany that strongly shaped aggressive and authoritarian personalities. Six of these patterns are especially worth noting. First, males were considered culturally more valuable to the community than females because they safeguarded the nation and fought for its livelihood. Second, the father was regarded as the extension of the king in every German home, ruling by divine right and expecting the rest of the family to obey him unconditionally. Third, the primary role of women was to bear children and accept their roles as homemakers. Fourth, German women were expected to move within a small *Lebensraum* of their own, the home, but in this limited space they were allowed to hold sway with a very firm hand. Their aim was to maintain an immaculately clean and ordered household. Fifth, marriage roles were strictly dichotomized on most issues. Responsibilities thus devolved on either the husband or the wife, the former being the breadwinner, the latter the homemaker. Shared responsibilities were the exception rather than the norm. Finally, the upbringing of children was equally stratified since the boys were destined to compete in the world, and the girls were preordained to be homemakers.

In nurturing their children, German women actively fostered these traits. The further Nazi perversion of already exaggerated authoritarian values accentuated their destructive potential in personality development. Claudia Koonz has gone so far as to assign a large share of the responsibility for Nazi aggression to German mothers who, wittingly or unwittingly, made the "murderous state possible in the name of concerns they defined as motherly."[49] Their complicity, she argues, can also be verified statistically because they voted for Hitler in great numbers and enthusiastically cheered for him. Why they would have supported a party that was so blatantly chauvinistic can be answered only by saying that many German women suffered from a remarkably high degree of self-deception.[50] Just like the men, women were taken in by false promises and empty slogans, a point that can be illustrated by the career of Gertrud Scholtz-Klink, the lady führer who officially spoke for the concerns of millions of German women.

The future lady führer entered politics in her early twenties when her husband, a storm trooper, died of a heart attack during a demonstration. She became determined to fight on in his place, believing, as she would later urge, that the guiding principle of German women should be "not to campaign against men but to campaign alongside them."[51] She joined the party in 1928 and became leader of the National Socialist Women's Organization (NSF) in Baden (1930) and Hesse (1931). In January 1934 she took over the labor service for women, and one month later, she was appointed Reich leader of the National Socialist Women's Organization (NSF) and the German Women's Work (DFW). Later that year, she was promoted to the largely symbolic top post of Reich women's leader (*Reichsfrauenführerin*), representing the interests of women in the spirit of National Socialism.

At this time Scholtz-Klink was only thirty-two years of age and had already had eleven children. Physically, she was the stereotype of the Nazi woman: tall and blonde; she was unassuming yet highly opinionated on every subject, proud, and, above all, fertile. She believed her own slogans about women, namely, that they are *gleichwertig* (of equal value), but not *gleichartig* (equal in kind), without realizing that the male Nazi leadership, despite its platitudes, held entirely reactionary views of the role of women. When Claudia Koonz interviewed her in 1981, she was still a confirmed Nazi offering pious excuses for her involvement and claiming that under her rule women functioned as "one happy family," that no one ever resigned, and that the Nazi leaders were all perfect gentlemen.[52] Such massive denial was found in many of those who, like Gertrud Scholtz-Klink, obediently carried out Hitler's orders.

Religion and the Churches

Germany had always suffered from internal religious and political divisions. By the end of the Middle Ages, Germany was a geographic expression, and its ramshackle empire — the Holy Roman Empire of the German Nation — was torn apart by centrifugal forces that left the real political power in the hands of feudal princes safeguarding a decentralized state administration at the very time other European countries had moved in the direction of centralized control. The Protestant Reformation added religious divisions that further weakened the development of a homogeneous nation-state. When Germany was finally unified by the Protestant state of Prussia, the inner divisions were not healed by power alone. The new Prussianized Germany was essentially Protestant because the Hohenzollern dynasty worked hand in glove with the Lutheran Church. Only one-third of Germany was Catholic because Roman Catholic Austria, which had been defeated in the Wars of Unification, was excluded from the new Germany. Catholics within the empire, painfully aware of their minority status, organized along political lines, especially after Bismarck launched his *Kulturkampf* (cultural battle) against the Roman Catholic Church and its influence on German life. This led to the development of the Roman Catholic Center Party, which tried to safeguard the interests of the church in Germany.

While these religious divisions continued in a state of uneasy tension, Christianity itself came under increasing attack by the forces of modernity — materialism, secularism, and scientific rationalism. At the same time and in reaction to modernity, Christianity was also undermined by racist and pagan ideologies that were aggressively promoted by various *völkisch* groups and authors (Richard Wagner, Felix Dahn, Julius Langbehn, Paul de Lagarde). Within the *völkisch*-inspired movements two religious branches began to predominate before World War I — a "German" form of Christianity devoid of "Jewish" or "Roman" features, and a new paganism (*Neuheidentum*) emphasizing Wotan or nature-sun worship. In the new German Christianity, Jesus was transformed into a staunch Aryan who wielded the sword rather than wearing a crown of thorns.[53]

It must be plain that such adulteration of the Christian spirit of love, humility, charity, and goodwill to all by these subversive forces made it difficult to challenge a rising totalitarian movement that was itself based on anti-Christian ideas. A strong component within the established churches continued to embrace belligerent, warlike policies throughout the postwar period, a remarkable attitude, coming as it did from the very section of German society that should have been most revolted by the death of millions of young Germans. Nor was this the only anomaly in the flawed structure of the German churches; the other was a persistent anti-Semitism. Perhaps the strongest manifestation of such anti-Semitism occurred in Bavaria, where religious prejudices against Jews formed a long-standing tradition. The Oberammergau passion play, with its emphasis on the Jews as Christ-killers, was only one of several disturbing signs of official church-sponsored events that reflected a pervasive mood of anti-Semitism. Others were the pilgrimages to Deggendorf, which commemorated a medieval ritual murder, and a noxious anti-Semitic newspaper, the *Miesbacher Anzeiger,* edited by a Catholic priest. In short, officially as well as unofficially, the established churches tended to reinforce certain aspects of the rising Nazi movement without fully understanding to what extent this behavior undermined their own autonomy. Few believers realized that their Christian faith was fundamentally at odds with Nazi ideology.

The Nazis, on the other hand, had no illusions about the fundamental incompatibility between Christianity and party ideology. Martin Bormann once captured the essence of the problem of the Nazi state versus religion when he said that "National Socialism and Christianity are irreconcilable,"[54] a position fully endorsed by Hitler, who pronounced that "one day we want to be in a position where only complete idiots (*Deppen*) stand on the pulpit and preach to old women."[55] The Nazis had a metaphysical hatred of Christianity because they saw it as a Jewish-derived faith that had been reinforced by money-grubbing clerics (*Pfaffen*). The Nazi campaign was a reflection of the sort of anti-Catholicism that had been promoted by secular ideologies since early modern times and can only be explained as "a sign of the grave sickness in the so-called Christian West."[56] The metaphysically exhausted soul of the West had made the genuine will to believe impossible, and in its place appeared ersatz religions of blood and soil, secular substitutes for Christianity that centered ultimate meaning in the here-and-now (the Thousand-Year Reich) rather than the hereafter. In this sense the Nazis were simply latter-day Jacobins who planned to de-Christianize the Western world even further and to replace it with a new and more genuine gospel of "Aryan supremacy."

In practice, the regime failed to articulate a coherent body of spiritual doctrines of a positive nature. Those Nazis who still felt a need for spiritual transcendence subscribed to a vague faith called *Gottgläubig* (God Believing) — a kind of minimal faith heavily embellished with neopagan practices. The *gottgläubig* movement was officially endorsed by the party as a genuine alternative to the established Christian churches. By 1939 the number of God Believers was officially listed as 3,481,000.[57]

The Nazi Party was clearly paving the way toward the eventual elimination of rival faiths; but the pages of the past could not be torn out overnight. In the meantime, the spiritualists in the party encouraged romantic neopaganism, substitution of religious ritual by Nazi practices, and continuous pressure and persecution of the established Christian churches. As part of the internal subversion of Christianity, Nazi zealots encouraged the de-Christianizing of rituals related to birth, marriage, and death. Other efforts to undermine the psychic bonds that had been built up between Christianity and the German people involved, as they did during the French Revolution, an attack on the Christian calendar and on Christian holidays. In 1938 carols and nativity plays were forbidden in the schools, and the word "Christmas" itself was replaced by the word "Yuletide."

The role of the two major churches, Catholic and Lutheran, in relation to the new regime was ambivalent. The churches had survived *Gleichschaltung* because the Nazis were too busy eliminating their opponents and also because they did not have a long range plan concerning the role of the churches in the future Third Reich. It is true that the more zealous Nazis dreamed of a new "German" religion under a new Reich bishop. Even before the seizure of power, a number of Evangelical supporters of the NSDAP joined forces and demanded that the Evangelical Church — splintered into three confessions (Lutheran, Reformed, and United) and twenty-eight land churches (*Landeskirchen*) — be homogenized into one *Reichskirche* (Reich church). These Nazi Protestants claimed to represent what they called "Positive Christianity," which was little more than a thinly disguised racial ideology dressed up in theological terminology. They held that God had sanctified the Aryan way of life, that racial mongrelization was immoral, and that appropriate laws should be passed in order to prevent further racial pollution, especially by Jews.

These Positive German Christians, as they called themselves, demanded immediate *Gleichschaltung* of all Evangelical churches during their meeting of April 3–4, 1933. It appeared that the motto "One Volk, one Reich, one führer" was to be amended to include also one church. Churches in each state (*Landeskirchen*) were to be autonomous in regard to creed or ritual, but the overall administration of the church was to be placed into the hands of the national government. If this proposal had been implemented, the spiritual autonomy of the church would have been compromised. The Positive Christians also demanded a *Reichsbischof* (Reich bishop) and a national synod; and after rancorous internal bickering, they elected Ludwig Müller, Hitler's adviser on Protestant church affairs, as their new Reich bishop in September 1933.

However, these attempts by a minority of evangelical Christians to impose their racial-xenophobic doctrines on the majority met with determined opposition. When the Prussian general synod, in which the Positive Christians held a two-thirds majority, ratified a proposal that required Aryan origin as a basis for clerical office, Pastor Martin

Niemöller exhorted his brethren to form a Pastoral emergency union (*Pfarrernotbund*).

It was out of this emergency union that the Confessional Church (Bekennende Kirche) originated. Its leader, Pastor Niemöller, after initially supporting the Nazi government, had become one of its staunchest opponents once he saw the unfolding of Nazi tyranny. A former World War I submarine commander, he had found his way to Christ during the chaotic postwar period and became one of the most popular preachers in Berlin. Niemöller rightly perceived that the Positive Christians were racists and nationalists first and Christians second. Indeed, the Positive Christians claimed that God revealed himself not only in sacred scriptures but also in historical events or personalities. Thus, for National Socialists, Hitler was manifestly an instrument of God sent into this world to save Germany. The idea that "Jesus Christ was sent to us in the form of Adolf Hitler," as one zealous believer expressed it, was abhorrent to the members of the Confessional Church.

On November 13, 1933, the Positive Christians convened a mass assembly at the Berlin Sportspalast and publicly called for an emancipation from Jewish bondage. Dr. Reinhold Krause, leader of German Christians for greater Berlin, exhorted the faithful to reject the Old Testament and those elements of the New Testament that he ascribed to Saint Paul, whose inferior theology and moral scapegoatism he roundly condemned. However, Krause's obscurantism clearly discredited the Positive Christian movement in the eyes of most German Protestants; and even Reich Bishop Müller believed that Krause had gone too far and relieved him of his offices. The influence of the Positive Christians subsequently declined steadily. On May 31, 1934, the confessional synod of the Evangelical Church drew a sharp distinction between the demands of National Socialism and those of the Christian church, explicitly denying that God's word was embodied in any other document or event than divine revelation.

On October 20, 1934, the Confessional synod of Dahlem pronounced an ecclesiastical emergency law because the Nazi government had suspended the church's constitutional foundation. The synod called upon all pastors to resist the rule of the new church authorities. In November 1934, the Confessional Church went on to develop a provisional church leadership and declared it to be the legitimate representative of the Evangelical Church, disavowing Müller's group. Hitler made one more effort to assimilate the Evangelical Church by force, appointing Hanns Kerrl, chief of the Prussian Ministry of Justice, as minister for church affairs, but Kerrl, like Müller before him, failed. Hitler's attempt at *Gleichschaltung* had failed, but this did not prevent the Nazis from taking the next step: vindictive reprisals against courageous opponents within the church, including Niemöller, who was subsequently arrested and spent seven years in various prisons and concentration camps. When the church went on record in 1935 as rejecting the whole racial-folkish

Weltanschauung, the Nazi regime arrested seven hundred ministers and severely restricted the civil liberties of the clergy, exposing many members to humiliating indignities. By the late 1930s the Protestant churches gave up open resistance and bowed to Hitler's dictatorship.

Unlike the Evangelical Church, which faced Nazification within its own ranks, the Roman Catholic Church presented a more organized opposition to Nazi rule. This did not imply, however, that the Catholic Church was any more successful or courageous in resisting Nazi tyranny. Two factors gave the Catholics greater strength than the Protestants: the church was international and therefore less likely to be intimidated, and the Catholics initially had a political party to promote its mission — the Center Party.

Yet the Catholics, like the Protestants, thought they could parley with Hitler and wring important concessions from him. In return for supporting Hitler's Enabling Law, the Catholic Center Party hoped that the Nazi regime would not interfere in the internal affairs of the church. Looking back, it is hard to see why the church would have expected to be left alone after it permitted Hitler to subvert its political power-base in Germany — that is to say, its political party, its unions, and its numerous youth organizations. It appears that the church was lulled by Hitler's conciliatory phrases and by his pious declarations about the inviolability of church doctrine and church institutions. Indeed, these peaceful gestures were underscored on July 20, 1933, when Franz von Papen negotiated a concordat with the Vatican.

The more astute observers in the church, including Cardinal Pacelli, the future Pius XII who had signed the treaty in his capacity as the Vatican state secretary, realized that Hitler was negotiating with the church primarily to consolidate his domestic control. Such critics suspected that Hitler would probably go to great lengths to eliminate the influence of any organization in Germany besides the Nazi Party. Still, few people suspected that he would come so close to succeeding. In the meantime, German believers were pacified by his public assurances that as long as the churches kept to otherworldly and metaphysical matters, he would not interfere in their business; but he added ominously, that in worldly or political matters the Nazi regime had absolute control over the lives of German citizens. Most German Catholics or Protestants were not alert enough to realize that Nazi ideology was all-embracing and made an absolute claim on every German regardless of his or her religious affiliation.

Indeed, it was not very long before the Nazi regime began to subvert the influence of the Roman Catholic Church, prompting a number of concerned protests from church officials that the Nazi government was violating the provisions of the concordat that had guaranteed the public exercise of religious freedom. When these protests failed to achieve their desired effects, Cardinal Faulhaber arranged for a personal interview with Hitler on November 9, 1936. Faulhaber found the führer quite expansive and even amiable on the subject of religion in general, but when the two men came to the topic of the racial laws of 1935 and sterilization of those who suffered from genetic diseases — two issues that had given rise to fundamental differences on both sides — the führer became angry and told the cardinal that he would not tolerate church interference on such matters.

Faulhaber's meeting, though cordial, did not improve the relationship between the church and the Nazi regime because official harassment against Catholics continued unabated — so much so that only five months after Faulhaber's interview with Hitler the pope felt compelled to release a general encyclical, entitled *With Burning Anxiety* (*Mit Brennender Sorge*), condemning National Socialist attacks on the church. The encyclical was read throughout Germany from church pulpits. The Nazis responded by increasing their attacks on the church and vilifying its members. Hundreds of monks and nuns were pilloried in the press and then arraigned in the courts on trumped-up charges ranging from financial malfeasance to sexual aberrations. Joseph Goebbels, himself a former Catholic, orchestrated a smear campaign and, in the process, highlighted sensational charges of clerical immorality. This set the stage for several "immorality trials" that satisfied the salacious tastes of the public and were designed to break the influence of the "black clergy" on German life.[58] Hundreds of nuns and priests were convicted and sent to concentration camps.

No other issue united the two Christian churches in Germany more than their determined opposition to the Nazi euthanasia program that began in September 1939. This program dated back to a law of July 14, 1933, and ultimately culminated in enforced sterilizations and "mercy" deaths for the incurably insane. What was at issue here was not only an elementary principle of the sanctity of human life but also the evil of a murderous state institutionalizing mass killings. We now know that these mercy killings paved the way for the extermination of inferior races, especially the Jews. Unfortunately only a few clergymen, notably Archbishop Clemens von Galen, protested publicly against such evils.

Although many acts of heroism by individual clergymen can be documented during the Third Reich, the institutions of the church, both Protestant and Catholic, failed tragically in mustering the sort of Christian courage it would have required to stop the Nazis from committing their unspeakable crimes against God and humankind. Such institutional failure of nerve, especially on the part of the Vatican, will forever be a stain on the historical record of Christianity, for when the church was confronted with unmistakable evidence of Nazi evil, it chose, at best, to respond with feeble protests rather than aroused mass protests. Such moral myopia, individual and collective, has never been captured more poignantly than by a memorable comment attributed to Pastor Niemöller:

First the Nazis went after the Jews, but I was not a Jew, so I did not object. Then they went after the Catholics, but I was not a Catholic, so I did not object. Then they went after the trade-unionists, but I was not a trade-unionist, so I did not object. Then they came after me, and there was no one left to object.[59]

The State of Culture under the Nazis

Although the Nazis were fond of touting the superiority of German *Kultur*, the quality of cultural achievements suffered an immediate and alarming decline in the Third Reich. Göring reportedly said, "Whenever I hear the word 'culture,' I reach for my revolver." Whether apocryphal or not, this vulgar outburst certainly expresses the prevailing mood among the Nazi elite. Göring was, in fact, only repeating the crudities of his führer, who on one occasion actually toyed with the idea of eliminating intellectuals but then thought the better of it after recognizing the obvious, namely, that great intellects actually promoted cultural and scientific progress.[60]

Despite the official crudities voiced by major Nazi leaders on the subject of culture, it is surprising how many leading intellects, at least initially, gave their official blessing to the new regime. Of course, many intellectuals, especially those of Jewish backgrounds, voiced their opposition to the Nazi cause early on. As soon as Hitler seized power, many intellectuals rushed to the exits. The writers Thomas and Heinrich Mann, Arnold and Stefan Zweig, Franz Werfel, and Jakob Wassermann went into exile. The masters of the Bauhaus school — Walter Gropius, Mies van der Rohe, Marcel Breuer — now condemned as decadent, relocated to America. Painters like Max Beckmann, Oskar Kokoschka, and Kurt Schwittens went to more hospitable countries. Film directors like Fritz Sternberg and Fritz Lang went to America, as did Marlene Dietrich and a host of lesser-known actresses and actors. Musicians and composers left in droves, too, including Paul Hindemith, Otto Klemperer, Kurt Weill, Hanns Jelinek, Ernst Toch, Arnold Schönberg, and Richard Tauber. Psychologists like Max Wertheimer, William Stern, and Sigmund Freud also abandoned their homelands, as did philosophers and theologians such as Paul Tillich, Ernst Bloch, Theodor Adorno, Ernst Cassirer, Kurt Goldstein, and Erich Fromm. German science lost Albert Einstein, Fritz Reiche, Hans Bethe, Richard Courant, James Frank, and Max Born, and many others.

All in all, an estimated twenty-five hundred writers left Germany,[61] either voluntarily or under duress — the effect being a serious intellectual hemorrhage in German culture.[62] However, many German writers, artists, musicians, and scientists not only stayed but flourished under the Nazis, including some famous names such as Werner Heisenberg, Otto Hahn, Max Planck, Gerhart Hauptmann, Gottfried Benn, Martin Heidegger, and many others. Why did these men, at least initially, react positively to Hitler's movement?[63] To begin with, German intellectuals had been traditionally uninvolved in politics on the ground that politics profanes the life of the spirit. Some could not resist the temptation of being bathed in public admiration by a regime that bribed them into lending their names to what they thought was a new revolutionary movement. Still others were deluded or self-deceived about the possibilities of culture in the Third Reich.

Those who sang the praises of the Nazi regime, hailing it as a creative experiment, soon found out that culture, far from being free, was to be put to the good uses of the state. Culture was to be *gleichgeschaltet* like everything else. In March 1933, Joseph Goebbels, the minister of propaganda, announced that culture and politics were henceforth to be synonymous, and in September of that year the Reichskulturkammer (Reich Cultural Chamber) was established to achieve that aim. This Reich Cultural Chamber dealt with various branches of cultural life — painting and sculpture, literature, music, theater, film, radio, and press. German artists, writers, or musicians were forced to join this organization if they wanted to practice their creative craft; but non-Aryans were not permitted to join. Goebbels assumed the presidency of the Reichskulturkammer himself.

Goebbels's Cultural Chamber was by no means the only agency involved in monitoring cultural activity. Just as Hitler encouraged intramural conflicts in the field of economics or foreign policy, he allowed other departments to involve themselves in cultural matters. Rosenberg's Office for the Supervision of Ideological Training and Education of the NSDAP, which had grown out of his earlier Kampfbund für Deutsche Kultur, became another official watchdog of the state, spying on writers, developing black lists, encouraging book burnings, and emptying museums of "non-German" works of art.

Goebbels and Rosenberg were particularly eager to purge the Prussian Academy of Arts of Jewish and modernist elements. In February 1933, both Heinrich Mann, head of the literature section, and Käthe Kollwitz, a member of the arts section, signed and circulated a petition calling upon the Communist and Socialist parties to combine forces in the upcoming March election in order to prevent Germany from "sinking into barbarism."

In response to this challenge the Nazi commissioner for culture in Prussia, Bernhard Rust, informed the academy's president, Max von Schilling, that he would abolish the academy unless the recalcitrant members were silenced. Kollwitz and Mann promptly resigned. Gottfried Benn was chosen to head the new literature section. Benn drafted a general resolution calling upon the members to abstain from all further political activities and to devote themselves fully to the task of national regeneration. The majority of the academy signed the Benn resolution, although several members (Alfred Döblin, Thomas Mann, Ricarda Huch) resigned rather than put their names on such a document.

Those who still objected were subsequently removed from the academy by ministerial decree. By the end of 1933, half of the members of the 1932 literature section had been expelled. The same happened in other sections of the academy. Those who replaced the expelled members were not always inferior in talent, but they were certainly vocal supporters of the Nazi regime. This enthusiasm, however, soon waned because free creative expression had to be channeled into a Procrustean bed, and those who failed to follow the aesthetic canons established by the watchdogs of the regime were subject to harsh treatment ranging from censorship to incarceration in a concentration camp. Those who failed to adhere to Nazi ideology were branded un-German or cultural Bolsheviks, and their works were censored, destroyed, or held up to public ridicule.

On May 10, 1933, an appalling event in the history of German culture took place — the burning of the books. The poet Heinrich Heine once observed prophetically that it was but a small step from burning books to burning people. This particular "cleaning action" (*Säuberung*) was carried out by the German Student Union (Studentschaft); it was aimed at eliminating un-German or foreign writings, especially Jewish, from libraries and bookstores. Convocations were held at all German universities during which students, professors, and party officials outdid each other in paying homage to Nazi political correctness. Goebbels marshalled the whole communications monopoly to record this memorable event for posterity, rationalizing the act of burning books by saying:

> Fellow students, German men and women! the age of extreme Jewish intellectualism has now ended, and the success of the German revolution has again given the German spirit the right of way.... You are doing the proper thing in committing the evil spirit of the past to the flames at this late hour of the night. This is a strong, great, symbolic act, an act that is to bear witness before all the world to the fact that the November Republic has disappeared. From these ashes there will arise a phoenix of a new spirit.... The past is lying in flames. The future will rise from the flames within our hearts.... Brightened by these flames our vow shall be: The Reich and the Nation and our Führer Adolf Hitler: Heil! Heil! Heil![64]

The event was crowned by the actual burning of the books. Nine student representatives, who had been given works belonging to nine categories, raised their accusatory voices and then flung the discredited books into the flames.

Another method of humiliating creative spirits was to exhibit their works under the pejorative title "Degenerate Art" (Entartete Kunst). This took the form of Schandeausstellungen or of exhibitions of shameful art, the most notorious being the one staged in Munich in 1937 and later in Berlin. Here spectators were shown examples of degenerate art, mostly modern art, which did not conform to Hitler's bland neo-classical taste. The Nazis prized art that conformed as close as possible to the pictorial; they also preferred "ennobling" or "heroic" figures. The Munich exhibition featured expressionistic works under the most unfavorable conditions, poor lighting, and with condemnatory descriptions by the high priests of Nazis taste.

The Nazis revealed their own artistic preferences in the House of German Culture in Munich, a building touted as the first beautiful work of the new Reich, but referred to by Müncheners as "Railroad Station Athens" (Hauptbahnhof Athen). Here the German public was treated to samples of the new culture of raw power and eroticized sentimentality. The building itself, inspired by Hitler, was starkly neoclassical; its ranked columns, unadorned and spaced in good military order, conveyed the feeling of sanitized beauty. Inside, spectators were treated to the grand muscular, monumental nudes of Arno Breker and the sexually enticing maidens of Adolf Ziegler.

Such state-approved art represented the fondest hopes and deepest passions of the führer himself, the architect manqué and frustrated artist who preferred "the biggest of everything to glorify his works and magnify his pride."[65] In his artistic fantasies, in which Albert Speer freely indulged him, Hitler conceived of a new and colossal capital, a model of which was prominently displayed in the Berlin Academy of Arts. When Speer's father first saw this orgiastic indulgence of architectural megalomania, he exclaimed: "You've all gone completely crazy."[66] Near the Reichstag, Hitler wanted a huge meeting hall, a domed structure dwarfing St. Peter's, with a dome 825 feet in diameter and large enough to house 125,000 adoring spectators. There was also to be a massive triumphal arch; a huge new chancellery, the only major project that was in fact completed; an Adolf Hitler Square, which would have accommodated one million people; Hitler's private palace, which would have outstripped Nero's legendary Golden House; and broad boulevards connecting these monumental structures.

As to the social dimensions of such architectural projects, the Nazi leadership had little to offer in a humane sense. Where people actually lived, congregated, worked, played, or socialized was an afterthought because in Hitler's frozen world, the buildings, designed for a thousand years, mattered more than the needs of living human beings. If people mattered, they mattered only in the mass. Public buildings all over Germany were to reflect this architectural vision. One of the most awe-inspiring architectural places was the colossal party rallying grounds at Nuremberg, with its frontal colonnade behind the speaker's platform framed by a concrete stadium designed to seat four hundred thousand. Even public entertainment during the Nazi period always aimed at colossality, as illustrated by the Olympic stadium in Berlin constructed for the games of 1936. Designed by Werner March, the huge stadium emphasized large inner spaces to accentuate a sense of *Volksgemein-schaft* (people's community). Despite the stadium's grandeur, Hitler felt that the Olympic grounds were too small, a defect he was determined to avoid with the new Nuremberg Reich Sports Field, which was designed to hold four times as many people as the Berlin stadium and which would become, if Hitler had anything to say about it, the Olympic stadium for all times to come.[67]

Nazi art, in short, was colossal, impersonal, and stereotypical. People were shorn of all individuality and became mere emblems expressive of assumed eternal truths. In looking at Nazi architecture, art, or painting one quickly gains the feeling that the faces, shapes, and colors all serve a propagandistic purpose; they are all the same stylized statements of Nazi virtues — power, strength, solidity, Nordic beauty.

What transpired in the fields of visual arts and architecture soon permeated other art forms. Academies of music also fell under the influence of the Reichskulturkammer. Here, as elsewhere, the aim was much the same: to liberate German music from Jewish, foreign, and modernist influence. Wagnerian opera was the führer's musical passion, but the watchdogs of musical purity were suspicious of anyone who wanted to go beyond Wagner. Anything that went beyond Bruckner or Pfitzer was condemned as "futuristic depravity." Richard Strauss was barely tolerated for this reason, particularly after he cooperated with Stefan Zweig, the Jewish writer, in producing the comic opera *Die Schweigsame Frau* (1934). It was only Strauss's worldwide reputation that saved him from harsh treatment. Paul Hindemith, a modern composer of great versatility, was censored repeatedly for his works and ultimately emigrated to the United States. In 1934, the Reichsmusikkammer refused to allow performances of his new opera *Mathis der Maler* on the grounds that it maligned the regime in a scene that purported to indict Nazi book burnings. Hindemith was also accused of collaborating with Jewish musicians and of having written an immoral comic work, *Neues vom Tag* (1929), in which the heroine was shown in a bathtub. The conductor Kurt Furtwängler came to Hindemith's defense, but subsequently apologized to Goebbels personally for having done so. This did not save him from Nazi reprisals because he lost his position as leader of the Berlin Philharmonic Orchestra and his post as director of the state opera.

Having driven out first-rate talent or discouraged novel ideas that were inconsistent with official views, the Nazis offered an embarrassment of inferior accomplishments in almost every field of cultural activity. In Thomas Mann's opinion: "It may be superstitious belief, but in my eyes, any books which could be printed at all in Germany between 1933 and 1945 are worse than worthless and not objects one wishes to touch. A stench of blood and shame attaches to them. They should all be pulped."[68] The range of permissible literary expression was largely limited to four subjects — war, race, soil, and the Nazi movement. One of the most popular themes concerned the heroics of front-line soldiers in

World War I. This was "war as a spiritual experience" (*Fronterlebnis*) —
a remarkable genre in the interwar period. Ernst Jünger had elevated this
genre to great heights of brilliance, celebrating the thrill of combat and
the sacredness of death when it is in the service of the fatherland. The
popularity of war stories, despite the appalling losses of the war, attest
to the ingrained love of militarism in German life. Of the *Fronterlebnis*
writers, one of the most popular, besides Jünger, was Werner Beumel-
burg, an ex-officer who evoked brutal images of combat and sanctified
them with what one critic has called "bathos-dripping" comradeship.[69]

What all of these authors shared in common was a rejection of modernism and an affirmation of conservative German values assumed to
reside in preurban feudal ideologies, suitably embellished by an aesthetic preference for monumental pseudoclassicism or pale realism. In
literature, the paradigm was the blood and soil (*Blut und Boden,* or
"Blubo") novel in which an instinctive and soil-bound peasant community wards off alien outsiders who seek to destroy its way of life. One
of the most popular novels of this kind was Hermann Löns's *Wehrwolf*
(1910), a book that established the blood and soil genre and served as
an inspiration for the murderous activities of Free Corps soldiers after
World War I.

One of the main themes embodied in Nazi literature was that of
historical ethnicity — that is, how a group of people defines itself in
a process of historical growth. Writers tried to highlight prominent
episodes in the history of the German people; they stressed the German
mission for Europe, analyzed the immutable racial essence of Nordic
man, and warned against subversive or un-German forces — the Jews,
Communists, or Western liberals. The most prominent writers of this
tendency were Erwin Guido Kolbenheyer, whose *Die Bauhütte: Ele-
mente einer Metaphysik der Gegenwart* (The building hut: Elements of a
contemporary metaphysics [1925]) is generally considered a forerunner
to Rosenberg's book *Der Mythus des 20. Jahrhunderts* (The myth of the
twentieth century [1930]); Josef Weinheber, a pan-German nationalist
rooted in the cultural traditions of the Austro-Hungarian empire; Hans
Grimm, whose best-seller, *Volk ohne Raum* (People without living space
[1926]), contained views on race and space that strongly converged with
those of Hitler's in *Mein Kampf;* Ernst Jünger, the German Maurice
Barrès, who lifted the Fascist way of life to great heights of aesthetic
brilliance in a series of novels, poems, essays, and diaries, most notably *Storm of Steel* (1920), *Struggle as Inner Experience* (1922), *Storms*
(1933), *Fire and Blood* (1925), *The Adventurous Heart* (1929), and *Total Mobilization* (1931); and Joseph Goebbels, who was not only Hitler's
stage manager and propagandist but an author of some merit, producing in his novel *Michael* (1929) a paradigmatic work of Nazi literature
that contained all of the relevant Fascist themes — the camaraderie of
the trenches in World War I; the postwar chaos; the ideal German youth
characterized by iron will; the superiority of the blood over the brain;

the mystic relationship between *Volk* and führer; the corrosive power of Communists and Jews; the ideal of motherhood and the home; and the need to counter the decadent way of life under capitalism with a heroic way of life under National Socialism.

Works on German ethnicity always stressed a close relationship between blood and soil, an outcome of the neoromantic belief that a people's destiny is linked to its organic rootedness in a given geographical space. A vast literature of blood and soil arose to meet this officially sponsored need to celebrate the unique elements associated with Germanness.

If the Nazis left little of any value on the higher cultural level, they were real innovators in what Dwight MacDonald has called masscult — that demimonde of cheap ostentation, ornamental kitsch, and swaggering in the colossal. Moreover, the Nazis were also on the cutting edge of developing the technical means of merchandising the products of masscult by way of such media as radio and film.

The chief technological instrument of disseminating masscult was radio, which fell under the control of Goebbels's Propaganda Ministry in 1933. Already operated by the state during the Weimar Republic, under the postal system, radio stations were quickly incorporated into the Nazi propaganda machine. All regional stations were expropriated and made subordinate to a new organization called Reichsrundfunk Gesellschaft (Reich Broadcasting Company [RRG]), while news-gathering was placed in the hands of the Drahtlose Dienst (Wireless Service) headed by Hans Fritzsche. The manufacture of most radio sets was placed under the aegis of the Reichsrundfunkkammer (Reich Broadcasting Chamber). In order to reach as many listeners as possible, the regime encouraged the manufacture of inexpensive radio sets, notably the *Volksempfänger* (people's receiver), which sold for seventy-six marks, the "labor front receiver" designed to take Nazi messages into the factories, and a miniature receiver, popularly referred to as Goebbels's *Schnauze* (Goebbels's big mouth), which sold for a mere thirty-five marks. German radio owners had to pay two marks a month for the privilege of listening to such state-controlled broadcasts that, in the words of Eugen Hademowski, the chief of the Radio Chamber, were designed to set in motion a "fantastic wave of political manipulation, agitation, and propaganda in every form."[70]

This is exactly what happened. Germans were inundated by a veritable blitzkrieg of verbal and musical clutter. Daily programming generally fell into three categories: political broadcasts, music, and radio plays or *Hörspiele*. In political broadcasting the Nazis made two notable innovations — the *Gemeinschaftsempfang* (community reception) and special announcements. The *Gemeinschaftsempfang*, which has the ring of God's word descending to his people, was designed to bring people together around publicly stationed radio sets so that they could share in the Nazi experience. All work stopped as people gathered in factories, taverns, party offices, and public squares to listen to government broadcasts, an act that the propaganda chief regarded as the modern counterpart to the ancient Germanic popular assemblies (*Thinge*). The Propaganda Ministry even arranged for the erection of six thousand "loud speaker pillars" in public squares all over Germany.[71] Another innovation was special announcements, heralded by horn music from a one-hundred-man orchestra, followed by the unctuous delivery of the great message, usually of another Nazi triumph, and polished off by a thanksgiving hymn, the national anthem, three minutes of silence, and more marching music. When the great Nazi victories faded after 1941, funeral marches became the order of the day.

Musical fare alternated between light music in the form of folk songs or popular hits (*Schlager*) and such acceptable classical music as Bach, Mozart, Beethoven, and Italian opera. Jazz, "the forbidden fruits" of the Third Reich, was strictly taboo for four major reasons: it was too improvisational to fit the totalitarian mold; it was disseminated by degenerate blacks or Jews and thus expressive of vulgar sexuality; it did not lend itself to the steady marching beat required for the transmission of repetitive propaganda messages; and it was too individualistic to fit the ideal of groupthink.[72] Yet despite official condemnations, jazz records and orchestras continued to be in high demand, especially among the educated upper middle class and among members of the "Swing Youth" who were bored by the dull fare offered by the Nazi regime.

The political benefits of radio became apparent during the course of 1934 when the Nazis transmitted regular weekly broadcasts to the Saar and also distributed some four thousand *Volksempfänger* to Saarländer in an effort to influence the outcome of the plebiscite. Although the Saar would have been returned to Germany in any case, the remarkably high vote of over 90 percent may well have been in part the result of this campaign. The same was probably true of the annexation of Austria. The Nazis also targeted foreign countries. At Seesen near Berlin, they erected a colossal broadcasting station, operating at one hundred thousand kilowatts, that beamed out Nazi propaganda to six geographic areas: North America, South America, Africa, East Asia, South Asia, and Australia.

Starting on September 1, 1939, Germans were prohibited from listening to foreign newscasts. In May 1940 all Reich stations were synchronized, broadcasting only one program under the auspices of the Grossdeutscher Rundfunk (Great German Broadcasting). The typical fare consisted of "news," military situation reports, political commentaries, news magazines, and music. In the occupied countries, the Nazis found it difficult to establish an efficient method of control because of the competition among rival agencies such as the military, the Propaganda Ministry, and the Foreign Office. Goebbels's role diminished in scope, and Reich commissioners or military commands generally controlled radio broadcasting. A network of stations working under the code name "Concordia" was set up to jam foreign broadcasts and track down their listeners. Concordia's most notorious station, named New British Broadcasting Station (NBBC), beamed out the voice of "Lord Haw-Haw" (William Joyce), a renegade Englishman who broadcast Nazi propaganda to his countrymen.

The Nazis also made extensive use of film because they recognized, in Goebbels's words, that film was one of the most influential means of reaching a mass audience. In July 1933, Goebbels set up a new film office and later incorporated it into a branch of the Reich Cultural Chamber. As head of his own film credit bank, he advanced considerable sums of money to filmmakers who spoke the language of National Socialism. In addition, the government coordinated the four major film studios — UFA, Bavaria, Terra, and Tobis — by bringing them under the control of a new government-controlled UFA, headed by Fritz Hippler.

During the Third Reich, 1,363 feature films were made.[73] These fell into two broad categories: propaganda and entertainment pictures. Generally, all of them were accompanied by the *Deutsche Wochenschau* (German weekly newsreel), which was the only visual source of information the Germans received of the outside world. The majority of the films were simple entertainment that served escapist purposes. Goebbels strongly believed that too much propaganda, especially bad propaganda, was counterproductive. This is why he allowed directors, script writers, and actors considerable freedom to produce their own films as long as they stayed away from political topics. The result, however, was bland uniformity. Most entertainment films presented a sanitized image of carefree life under the protective umbrella of the Nazi regime. The big box-office hits were usually romances, comedies, adventure stories, or musicals. Some of the most popular female stars, interestingly enough, were foreigners such as the Hungarian actress and singer Marika Rökk, particularly popular among the troops; the dark and passionate Swedish star Zarah Leander; the romantically vulnerable, blonde Swedish actress Kristina Söderbaum; and Goebbels's Czechoslovakian beauty Lida Baarova. Other German perennial female stars were Paula Wessely, Heidemarie Hatheyer, and Ilse Werner. The most popular male stars were Emil Jannings, Heinrich George, Willy Birgel, and Willy Fritsch. Perennial comic actors, some outliving the Nazi period, were Theo Lingen, Hans Moser, Heinz Rühmann, and the indestructible Hans Albers, who continued playing carefree sailors and noble or madcap daredevils such as Baron von Münchhausen.

The Nazis produced a number of outright propaganda pictures, most of them box-office failures. One genre revolved around the glorification of the party and its early martyrs. Three elaborate productions stand out in this field: *SA-Mann Brand,* a tribute to the exploits of storm troopers; *Hitlerjunge Quex,* the story of a Hitler youth, Herbert Norkus, who was murdered by the Communists; and *Hans Westmar,* which recounts the life and heroic death of the Nazi hero Horst Wessel. The Nazis also produced four major anti-Semitic films, some of them so vile that the public was widely revolted by them: *Robert und Bertram* (1939), *Die Rotschilds* (1940), *Jud Süss* (1940), and *Der Ewige Jude* (1940). In the case of *Jud Süss*, even though an English version had already been made of Leon Feuchtwanger's novel about a man who is half-Christian and half-Jew, Goebbels was sold on producing a vicious anti-Semitic version and literally intimidated the director, Veit Harlan, and several well-known stars into making it. The picture made such a powerful statement that, after it was shown, Jews were beaten up and in Vienna an old Jew was trampled to death by a Hitler Youth group that had just seen it.[74] *Der Ewige Jude,* a documentary directed by Fritz Hippler, was an obscene hate picture that depicted the Jews as cellar rats who scurry out of their holes and proceed to take over the world. The analogy, rubbed in by the unctuous voice of the narrator, is that Jews are like rats who, if not eradicated (*ausrotten*), will take over the world's economy.

Such scurrilous pictures played largely to empty theaters, as did some of the more lavishly produced propaganda epics. One of the most famous was *Ohm Krüger* (1941), an embarrassingly clumsy film about English mistreatment of the Boers in South Africa. There were also some opulent historical films, centering around such German heroes as Frederick the Great and Bismarck. The actor Otto Gebühr, who had made a good living out of playing Frederick roles, starred in two productions — Johannes Meyer's *Fredericus* (1936) and Veit Harlan's *Der Grosse König* (1942). There were also two nationalistic epics on Bismarck by the director Wolfgang Liebeneiner — *Bismarck* (1940) and *Die Entlassung* (1942). Probably the most spectacular epic was Goebbels's last hurrah, *Kolberg* (1945), a picture, directed over three years by Veit Harlan, that re-created the heroic resistance of the Prussian town of Kolberg against the Napoleonic hordes. Concluded toward the end of the war with a cast of thousands of German soldiers dressed in ancient uniforms and within earshot of the advancing Russian forces, the picture was intended to instill in the German people a spirit of fanatical resolve.

The only great artistic masterpieces of Nazi propaganda, great because the director intended them to be a kind of cinema verité in documentary form, were Leni Riefenstahl's two spectacular films, *Triumph des Willens* (1935) and *Olympia* (1938). Hitler had personally talked Leni Riefenstahl into producing a documentary of the 1934 Nuremberg party congress, telling her that he wanted an artistically visual document rather than a boring party film.[75] Against great odds and great opposition, notably in the form of Goebbels, who hated her because of her close relationship with Hitler, Riefenstahl managed to produce an artistic and technical masterpiece in which she showed the world the charisma that radiated from Hitler and the effect it had on his audiences. Her ingenious camera work exploited dynamic movement and technical innovations, producing the illusion of participation in a flowing panorama of marching columns, endless permutations of uniforms, and banners on the move. Riefenstahl brought the same artistic drama and flair to the Olympic games of 1936 in Berlin in a two-part visual feast of athletic beauty, strength, and endurance. Here she was courageous enough to emphasize the triumphs of Jesse Owens, the black American runner.

Whether artistically superb or crude, film in the Third Reich always had a propagandistic dimension, even when it pretended to be nothing more than sentimental escapism. As Siegfried Kracauer has written, German films persistently tried to inculcate "the authoritarian credo that the major spell of authority protects society from decomposition."[76] So while the world was in flames, one could still be sheltered from reality, at least for a few hours, through cinematic illusion. Nazi culture, like Nazi film, was an empty pretense based on empty promises and cruel deceptions.

The Economy and the Workforce

The Nazi economy, as it developed in the 1930s, represents an anomaly among the general models that were then in existence. Although the regime called itself National Socialist, the record clearly reveals that the economy was only marginally socialistic, since big business and private ownership in general remained untouched. At the same time, the German economy was not capitalistic either because the state increasingly usurped the means of production. The truth is, as Franz Neumann noted long ago, that the Nazi economy was neither socialistic nor capitalistic; it was a curious hybrid of both systems.[77] The best way of characterizing it is to call it a war economy (*Kriegswirtschaft*) in peacetime.

Having rejected the notion that Germany could support its people through increased productivity and peaceful coexistence with other nations, Hitler had long ago opted for a warlike policy of conquest of new living space (*Lebensraum*) in eastern Europe. The German economy, therefore, had to be tailored to this political imperative. In any case, Hitler had always insisted on the primacy of politics: the state drives the economy by means of its geopolitical imperatives. Hitler contradicted Marx's postulate that the economic substructure of a society determined its ideological superstructure. It made no difference to the German dictator what sort of economic system was needed to carry out his ideological objective as long as it was successfully carried out. This explains Hitler's ideological flexibility in such matters and accounts for the existence of several types of economies in Nazi Germany: a competitive economy, a monopolistic economy, and a command economy.[78] As Neumann observed, the organization of the Nazi economic system was pragmatic; it was directed solely "by the need for the highest possible efficiency and productivity required for the conducting of war."[79] If this meant encouraging big business, supporting powerful entrepreneurs (Krupp, Siemens, Thyssen, Borsig, Krauss, Maffei), advocating enforced cartelization, the elimination of inefficient small businesses, subsidizing industries — policies that in many ways appeared mutually contradictory — then the regime was willing to risk the charge of ideological inconsistency.

Hitler's opportunism on economic matters revealed itself almost immediately after his seizure of power. The most pressing issue in January 1933 was how unemployment could be reduced. Unlike the believers in true socialism, who still thought in terms of expropriating large industrial enterprises, Hitler had no intention of dismantling successful business for purely ideological reasons; he was too much of an opportunist to cripple economic organizations at a time of extreme economic distress. He believed that this would neither promote his long-range war plans nor resolve the short-range problem of unemployment.

Accordingly, in order to reassure big business, Hitler appointed Hjalmar Schacht, a financial expert, as president of the Reichsbank. He also made it clear to different interest groups that he was willing to experiment in economic matters as long as it did not undermine efficiency and productivity. In order to stimulate the economy, Hitler abandoned Brüning's deflationary policies and resorted to a daring plan of "priming the pump" — that is, of government deficit spending. The Reinhart Plan, named after the secretary of state of the Finance Ministry, allocated well over a billion marks for various public work projects, the most famous being the construction of a network of national freeways (*Autobahnen*); granted state subsidies to private construction firms for the renovation of old buildings and the expansion of new housing units; and offered tax remissions for plant expansions to industrial or agricultural businesses.

Of all these projects, it was the construction of the *Autobahnen* that captured the enthusiasm of most Germans. Although plans for the construction of these freeways had been laid during the Weimar Republic, Hitler quickly capitalized on the usefulness and popularity of this project and converted it into a propaganda triumph for his regime. Under the organizational talents of Hitler's minister of armaments, Dr. Fritz Todt, three thousand kilometers (1,860 miles) were completed between 1933 and 1938. Official pictures showing thousands of eager workers constructing the "führer's roads" created the impression of a homogeneous community of all the people in which class or privilege had been subordinated to the good of the whole.

The construction of the *Autobahnen* undoubtedly stimulated the economy because it provided jobs and revitalized the automotive industries. It also buoyed the morale of the working population and captured the loyalties of those who were impressed by the idea that the new freeways were open to everyone. This sentiment was reinforced by a government announcement in 1938 that it would shortly market a "people's car" (Volkswagen) at a modest cost of 990 Reichsmark ($235 at the time). Designed by Professor Ferdinand Porsche, the projected Volkswagen was to be within the financial reach of "every German, without distinction of class, profession, or property."[80] Although one hundred thousand Volkswagens were promised by 1940, none were delivered to prospective buyers because the factory that produced them switched to war production.

Deficit spending by itself would not have solved the problem of unemployment, but in conjunction with massive rearmament, steady progress in achieving Hitler's goal of full employment was made in the 1930s. Only three days after gaining power, Hitler promised his military chiefs that he would drastically increase the size of the armed forces in order to be able to smash the Versailles Treaty and gain his ultimate objective — the Germanization of eastern Europe. Expenditures for rearmament rose steadily between 1933 and 1938.

Hitler's immediate economic goal was self-sufficiency (autarky), a goal that was dictated by Germany's lack of crucial resources such as India rubber, copper, base metals, mineral, and fuel oils. In order to achieve this goal, Hitler authorized his special adviser on economics, Wilhelm Keppler, to establish an agency that would look into the possibility of developing substitute (ersatz) or synthetic goods. Keppler's agency soon began research on substitute rubber (Buna), synthetic fats, and cheap metals.

These initial steps were vastly expanded when two major corporate giants, I. G. Farben and Wintershall, received lucrative offers from the government to develop synthetic products for the armed forces. I. G. Farben was the first major firm to receive a state subsidy for the development of synthetic fuels. In 1934, Wintershall, a large potash company, along with several leading producers of brown coal, formed a state-supported corporation called Braunkohle Benzin A. G., whose mission was to produce synthetic gasoline. Other firms explored the development of synthetic textiles and metals. The development of synthetic material was of critical importance to the armed forces, especially to Major Georg Thomas of the Wehrmachtsamt, who became the most vociferous advocate of autarky within the armed forces.

Although rearmament undoubtedly bolstered the economy by reducing unemployment and stimulating business and industry, not all sectors benefited equally from these measures. Consumer goods were not promoted with the same zeal as tanks or airplanes. Another negative side-effect of rearmament was the further increase in the centralization of the economy and its control by the government. A third problem caused by rearmament was an unfavorable balance of trade. Since Germany still relied heavily on imports, especially in crucial raw materials such as rubber, fuel, and metals, large sums of capital had to be spent abroad. The losses incurred from these extensive imports could have been recouped if Germany had succeeded in strengthening its export market. However, German exports diminished steadily due to the economic priorities set by the government, the decline in prices of finished goods at a time of rising costs in raw material, the prohibitive tariff quotas set by foreign governments, and the reluctance of foreigners to buy Nazi goods.

In the summer of 1936, at a time when the eyes of the world were focused on the Olympic Games in Berlin, Adolf Hitler composed a top secret memorandum in his aerie at Obersalzberg on economic strategy and armament.[81] The document, which was greatly at odds with the Olympic spirit of peace and international goodwill, reflected Hitler's impatience with the slow pace of German rearmament and his insistence that "the German economy must be fit for war within four years."[82]

Hitler appointed Hermann Göring as director of a new Four-Year Plan and empowered him with "the authority to issue legal decrees and general administrative regulations" and to "issue instructions to all authorities, including the Supreme Authorities of the Reich, and all agencies of the party, its formations and affiliated organizations."[83] Although Göring had no understanding of economics, he threw himself into this new task with customary vigor, because he realized that the führer's decree could make him the economic dictator of Germany.

Under Göring's heavy-handed methods, imports were sharply curtailed, wage and price controls were instituted, and dividends restricted to 6 percent. In order to bring about self-sufficiency, Göring alternately cajoled and bullied big businesses into expanding factories geared toward the production of synthetic rubber, textiles, fuel, and other scarce products. The culmination of this policy was the establishment of the Hermann Göring Werke — industrial plants set up to exploit low-grade iron ores in central Germany. Seventy percent of this quasi-socialized project, capitalized at four hundred million marks, was owned by the government, while the private sector was forced to buy the remaining shares at 4.5 percent and obligated to hold them for at least five years.

The Hermann Göring project has been aptly labeled a gangster organization to steal and rob as many German businesses as possible because it forced the private sector into making unfavorable loans.[84] In this sense it is reminiscent of the "forced loans" exacted by seventeenth-century British monarchs, who intimidated bankers into underwriting their costly ventures and thus provoked both bankruptcy and revolution. Given the tight control exerted by the Nazi regime, the likelihood of revolution seemed remote in the 1930s, particularly since the regime was highly popular among the German people, but the possibility of national bankruptcy was a real danger. Schwerin von Krosigk, the Reich finance minister, later estimated that public expenditures between 1933 and September 1939 reached 101.5 billion marks, of which 60 percent were spent on rearmament.[85] During the same period government revenues accounted for only 62 billion marks, with a further 20 billion additional income generated by the state-owned railroad and postal service. The remaining deficit was cosmetically covered by so-called state credits, the most ingenious being the *Mefo-wechsel* (Mefo Exchange), named after a fictitious institution called Metallurgische Forschungs-

GmbH. The Mefo exchange, underwritten by four of the major defense contractors with one billion marks, enabled government contractors to receive payments in Mefo notes that would be discounted by the Reichsbank. The system was kept strictly secret by Schacht in order to hide the fact that Germany was massively rearming.

Although exact statistical evidence is lacking, it is commonly agreed that Göring's efforts fell far short of the expectations Hitler had set in his secret memorandum of August 1936. The reasons for Göring's failures were many and varied, some residing in his mercurial personality, some in the complex nature of the German bureaucracy. Rather than building up an effective organization that could cooperate and coordinate policies with already existing institutions, Göring fought intramural battles with rival agencies.

These conflicts were not merely jurisdictional, but expressed different views of how the German economy should be managed. Hjalmar Schacht had originally been a strong supporter of financing rearmament through government loans and taxation, but he increasingly questioned the economic feasibility of pursuing a policy based on both guns and butter. Imposing a permanent war economy in peacetime had raised serious problems such as mounting foreign debts, balance of payment deficits, and shortage of raw materials. Although Schacht had made progress in reducing foreign debts and trade deficits through a combination of policies ranging from a moratorium on foreign debts to a "New Plan" by which the government regulated imports and initiated bilateral trade agreements with southeastern European countries, it turned out that this was not enough to deal with a developing crisis of economic priorities in 1935. Schacht, now minister of economics and general plenipotentiary for war economy, did not have sufficient resources to pay for the massive importation of raw material and foodstuffs Germany required to continue the policy of "guns and butter." The advocates of autarky, led by Göring, argued that Germany could achieve self-sufficiency in both foodstuffs and raw material. With Hitler's support, they gained the upper hand over Schacht and those who spoke for export-minded sections of industry. On November 26, 1937, Schacht resigned as minister of economics and was replaced by the more pliant party man Walther Funk, whose ministry was now closely tied to Göring's office.

There is a general consensus that the German economy lacked the resources for a "guns and butter" policy. However, it does not follow from this conclusion or from other economic problems that were looming in 1939 that Hitler chose war to escape from an impending economic collapse. By 1939 Hitler was better armed than anyone else in the world; he had also managed to keep consumer satisfaction relatively high. Moreover, there was no serious inflation, and wages had been kept stable. Hitler's decision to go to war in 1939 was based on ideological reasons and, to some extent, on irrational fears relating to his health.

In surveying how the Nazis managed the economy, it is important to note how various social groups were affected by it. There is no doubt that massive rearmament was a bonanza for big business and to a lesser extent for the German middle class. For big business, rearmament opened many new opportunities for industrial expansion and profits, made all the more lucrative by the fact that the unions had been destroyed, thus giving employers the upper hand over their employees. However, these benefits were accompanied by corresponding government intrusions into the affairs of business. Government now told business what and how much should be produced, what profits should be reaped, how much should be paid in wages, and where business should build new plants. Except for suppliers or subcontractors to the large defense contractors, small business owners gained fewer benefits. Many businesses also reaped windfalls when Jewish business were "Aryanized" — that is, confiscated and sold at bargain prices. Despite Nazi propaganda about breaking up Germany's big department stores, many owned by Jews, very few were in fact broken up. The biggest store, the Hermann Tietz Concern, was left intact through Hitler's personal intervention and merely renamed "Hertie" to obscure the fact that it continued to be managed for some time by its Jewish proprietors.

Skilled craftsmen generally benefited from Nazi economic policies, partly because there was a great shortage of skilled workers, especially in the construction and defense industries, and partly because Nazi ideology had always extolled the independent artisan. In order to protect themselves from competition in an open capitalist market, German artisans had persistently lobbied for a craft estate (*Stand*) composed of compulsory guilds representing various crafts. In November 1933, the Nazis passed a crafts trade bill that mandated that artisan businesses could operate only if their owners belonged to the appropriate guild, possessed a "major certificate of qualification," and were politically reliable. The guilds were then reorganized vertically by being divided into Reich guilds for each trade and horizontally by being linked at district levels in chambers of trade (*Handelskammer*).[86] In theory, the system resembled the medieval corporate estate model; in practice, however, it was subject to tight political control because party functionaries supervised the system on all levels.

Farmers were the poor cousins in the German economy. When the Nazis seized power, agriculture had gone through five years of crisis. The Nazis set themselves three goals in their effort to reverse this situation: self-sufficiency through protectionism, revitalization of agriculture through the development of a new peasant order, and a better organization to represent farmers' interests.[87] The government passed a series of laws aimed at a total control of markets and prices and tried to stabilize land ownership through the Reich Entail Farm Law (Reichserbhofgesetz), designed to protect indebted farmers from impending bankruptcies, regulate inheritance in favor of one heir in the male line, and prohibit the sale of entailed farms. Furthermore, the regime instituted a land-planning program designed to encourage new homesteads with an eye toward redistributing population. All of these ambitious goals spawned a huge bureaucracy in the form of a Reich Food Estate (Reichnährstand) under the control of Darré and supported by peasant leaders at the state, district, and local levels. Despite such massive planning and financial and protectionist measures, German agriculture did not meet the goals set by Darré and other agricultural planners. As was to be expected, self-sufficiency was not achieved because Darré's reactionary ideology combined protectionism with a self-defeating antimarket policy.

Agricultural shortages quickly developed, particularly in the area of fats. Some minor successes were achieved in helping financially strapped farmers, but the money spent on farm relief redounded primarily to the benefit of the larger farmers. The regime's resettlement schemes, on the other hand, were a dismal failure because the big estates remained untouched and also because only a small amount of arable land was available for homesteading. Moreover, despite the regime's efforts to boost the image of the farmer, Germans continued to migrate to the cities in large numbers. By 1939 agriculture had lost about 1.4 million people who took higher-paying jobs in industry,[88] causing a serious farm labor shortage that was only partially alleviated by impressing young people into agricultural service during the summer months. No one went hungry in Nazi Germany, but affluence was the exception rather than the norm.

Unlike agricultural workers, Germans who were employed in business or industry generally benefited economically under National Socialist rule. Although the workers lost their right to strike and collective bargaining, they found gainful employment. In the minds of most German workers, their political losses were offset by what they perceived to be tangible rewards. Skilled laborers, as previously indicated, were in great demand, especially in the defense industries, where technical skills were at a premium. In addition, the government did much to improve working conditions under the Kraft durch Freude (Strength through Joy [KdF]) program called "Beauty of Labor" (Schönheit der Arbeit) and provided generous incentives and awards for outstanding achievements. Workers were courted by recreational opportunities provided by the KdF program administered by Ley's office.

The KdF program, aimed at ordinary laborers, represented the regime's effort to capture the hearts and minds of workers by offering inexpensive holiday excursions, both in Germany and abroad; subsidized theater performances; exhibitions; sports and hiking activities; dances; films; and adult education courses. The KdF organization gradually developed into a big business, acquiring two ocean liners and venturing into the automobile industry by promoting the subsidized Volkswagen, originally called the "KdF Wagen."[89] In 1938, approximately 180,000 Germans went on cruises, and ten million participated in various Strength through Joy activities. This meant that out of a workforce of twenty million, one worker in two hundred took a sea cruise, and one out of every three workers left his or her home environment on some kind of KdF activity.[90] A typical one-week holiday, including travel expenses, meals, accommodations, and tourist guides, might cost 43 marks round-trip from Berlin to the Mosel, 39 marks from Berlin to Upper Bavaria. A two-week round-trip package from Berlin to Bodensee was advertised for 65 marks, and a two-week excursion throughout Italy cost only 155 marks.

According to official pronouncements, the KdF organization, in contrast with the unfulfilled promises of Marxism, offered deeds rather than rhetoric. Although this may have been self-serving, the fact is that the regime could justifiably refer to itself as "socialism of deeds." Moreover, the regime even made attempts to foster a certain degree of egalitarianism among all members of the workforce, some of it well meaning and some of it inept and ridiculous. Dr. Robert Ley, head of the Labor Front and the leading light behind Strength through Joy, promised to liberate the German worker from feelings of inferiority and to promote a sense of *Volksgemeinschaft*. German industries, he predicted, would become fortresses of communal thought with its work battalions serving as watchtowers. These noble sentiments, aiming at a kind of enforced communal happiness, were alternatively shrugged off or resented as meddlesome intrusions into the lives of German workers.

The fact is that government had emasculated the independence of workers. With the destruction of labor unions, their interests had been placed in the hands of state officials called trustees of labor. By a new law, entitled Law for the Ordering of National Labor, passed on January 20, 1934, a different system of labor relations, based on a quasi-feudal model, was put into effect. The new arrangement replaced free collective bargaining between workers and employers with the concept of "plant community" (*Betriebsgemeinschaft*), in which the plant leader (employer) and his retinue (employees) worked for the common good on the basis of mutually accepted ties and obligations. Instead of conflict between employer and employee, the norm under capitalism, there was to be, under this neofeudal system, mutual trust and confidence. Conflicts, if they arose, were to be worked out internally by Councils of Trust and Labor Courts of Honor. Neither of these had any real independent authority; they consisted largely of pliant Nazis who did the bidding of the employer. Even the Reich trustees of labor, who acted as the final court of appeal, were agents of the government who usually sided with the employer.

Further measures to regiment the workforce were taken in February 1935 with the introduction of the "work book" (*Arbeitsbuch*); this severely restricted workers in choosing their own jobs and made their movements subject to close governmental control. Without a work book, which contained details of a worker's qualifications and work history, no German worker could be gainfully employed.

In the summer of 1935 all German males between the ages of eighteen and twenty-five were made subject to six months of compulsory labor service. Until 1939, women had the option of volunteering. Compulsory labor service provided the regime with cheap labor and yet another opportunity of indoctrinating young people. Labor service was dreaded by most young people, especially by young men of the upper classes who resented having to spend six months of doing busy work in the company of their social inferiors.

Important questions have been raised about the social policies of the Third Reich. To what extent, if any, did the Nazis bring about a "social revolution"? Did they pursue "modernizing" or "reactionary" policies?[91] Germany's problem was that of an arrested bourgeois-industrial society, though the ideologically tainted term "arrested" should be viewed with considerable suspicion since no one knows what a "normal" society is really like. The development of society is not like the development of a biological organism in which stages are normative and predictive. When Western sociologists or historians have used the term "arrested" in reference to social-industrial development, they have used the "advanced" or fully "modernized" industrial systems of the Anglo-American world as a normative guide; by contrast, less industrialized societies, are therefore judged as "arrested" or lacking "maturity" or "modernity," the mistaken assumption being that we can extract an apodictic method of social development from the growth of one society or culture and then apply it to all societies or cultures.

Since no clear-cut answer can be reached on the question of Germany's "arrested" development, perhaps it is possible to provide a more compelling answer to the questions: To what extent was the Third Reich socially dysfunctional? Was it a society so deeply at odds with itself that it could not work? The answer is clearly negative. Although Nazi propaganda about Germany having achieved a harmonious *Volksgemeinschaft* was clearly exaggerated, the social reality, as one historian has rightly pointed out, was one of "surprising tranquility" on the social front,[92] illustrating the effectiveness of Hitler's carrot-and-stick approach to social policies. On the other hand, Germany still had not found a viable alternative to the Western model of industrial democracy, which its major political groups had rejected. Until 1933 the political left aimed at a Marxist revolution, conceived in either democratic or totalitarian form, while the political right pursued a variety of hybrid models ranging from Arcadian racial utopias to authoritarian mercantile systems. The extreme *völkisch* notions of some Nazis like Darré and Himmler, harking back to preurban and even feudal socioeconomic conditions, which David Schoenbaum has rightly labeled a "Peter Pan ideology for a society that did not want to grow up,"[93] were never seriously entertained. Hitler stifled such reactionary utopias because he knew that wars in the modern world could not be fought with potatoes or cabbages but only with iron and steel.

From a social point of view, National Socialism had little inner substance: in Martin Broszat's judgment, it was parasitic in that it fed on fond and often illusory dreams of many Germans. It drew its ideals from "romantic pictures and clichés of the past, from war-like heroic patriarchal or absolutist ages, social and political systems which, however, were translated into the popular avant-garde, into the fighting slogans of totalitarian nationalism. The elitist notion of aristocratic nobility became the *völkisch* 'nobility of blood' of the 'master race,' the princely theory of divine right gave way to the popular national Führer."[94]

This ideological snapshot captures, in part, the real essence of National Socialism, namely, its aim to produce a racial rather than a social revolution. If National Socialism had a genuine revolutionary thrust, it resided in its efforts to transform Germany biologically and replace class with race. It has only been in the last ten years that historians have focused on Nazi racial policies from anthropological rather than sociological perspectives, pointing out that earlier sociological categories dealing with class, social status, distributive justice, and so on, have failed to penetrate to the essence of National Socialism.[95] Such anthropological interpretations should be welcomed because they shed important light on Nazi policies; they illustrate that no matter how contradictory in theory or practice, the Nazi leadership pursued "biological policies," so that no account of Nazi Germany would be complete if it omitted the institutionalization of racism in the Third Reich — the only real revolution the Nazis were able to carry out, grotesque as it was.

Racism and Anti-Semitism

In Nazi Germany race and politics were closely linked. The state and all its institutions pursued a policy aimed at transforming Germans into a higher, purer, and healthier race. The Nazis proceeded ruthlessly along several largely untrodden paths: enforced sterilization, prohibition of racial miscegenation, euthanasia, and, in general, persecution of groups perceived to be racially and morally inferior — Jews, Gypsies, the asocial, homosexuals, and the mentally ill.

Linked to the belief that race rather than class was the primary determinant of national greatness was the notion that a society could improve its racial stock through sound eugenic measures. Many German racial thinkers had sounded shrill notes of alarm, warning that the population of Germany was being degraded by biological inferiors — the poor, the weak, the insane, the asocial — who were multiplying in far greater numbers than the gifted few upon whom progress depended. A host of "racial hygienists" had influenced public debate on this subject. At first, their concern was less with race or ethnicity than with the declining birthrate and the growing number of patients in mental institutions.[96] Although the early racial hygienists were not all racists or devoted to a particular political ideology, their sympathies leaned to the nationalistic and conservative right. Among these racial hygienists, as previously shown, were well-known publishers, geneticists, and anthropologists, including the publisher Julius Friedrich Lehmann; Alfred Ploetz, the father of racial science; and well-known biologists such as Fritz Lenz, Eugen Fischer, Hermann Muckermann, and Otmar von Verschuer. Their intellectual center was the Kaiser Wilhelm Institute for Anthropology, Human Genetics, and Eugenics, headed by Eugen Fischer, who professed a passionate, even religious, belief in the importance of racially perfecting the German people.

The Nazis absorbed some of these doctrines of racial hygiene and transformed the subject into a field of radical political action. If Fritz Lenz, the editor of the *Archiv für Rassen- und Gesellschaftsbiologie* and professor of racial hygiene at the University of Munich, could still sound a cautious note when he observed in 1921 that no race as such could be ranked as "higher or lower" than another because of the absence of scientific standards that would allow such a determination, the Nazis had no compunction in supplying the necessary *political* criteria by which such a judgment might be made.[97]

In the words of Rudolf Hess, National Socialism was basically "applied racial science" (*Angewandte Rassenkunde*).[98] The first major racial law, which came on the heels of new racial offices, racial journals, and racial societies, was the sterilization law of July 14, 1933. Entitled Law for the Prevention of Progeny with Hereditary Diseases (Gesetz zur Verhütung erbkranken Nachwuchses), this law mandated that individuals could be sterilized if, in the opinion of a genetic health court, they suffered from certain specified illnesses. The categories of hereditary illnesses, however, were so sweeping and scientifically ambiguous that many people, otherwise quite healthy, could be sterilized. Nine types of "illnesses" were listed: congenital feeblemindedness, schizophrenia, manic-depressive insanity, hereditary epilepsy, Huntington's chorea, heredity blindness, deafness, serious physical deformities, and, as an addendum to the basic list — chronic alcoholism.

The radical nature of this law becomes apparent when it is remembered that sterilization was illegal up until its passage.[99] The establishment of hereditary health courts, composed of supposedly neutral and benign medical experts, scarcely concealed the radicalism of the new program, particularly since these courts were immune to public scrutiny. Although the doctors who served on these health courts pretended to lend a sense of objectivity and dignity to the proceedings, flagrant injustices were committed by zealous doctors who ferreted out numerous individuals, more women than men, who supposedly suffered from "feeblemindedness."[100] The provision that sterilization was to be performed only on homozygous rather than recessive carriers was next to useless because of the mistaken assumption that the disorders to be purged were inherited according to the Mendelian rule of single rather than multiple gene transmission. It is estimated that close to four hundred thousand received the so-called "Hitler cut" — vasectomy for men and tubal ligation for women — between the beginning of the new program in 1933 and its essential termination in the fall of 1939.[101]

The seminal year for racial hygiene was 1935, which saw the passage of three laws, often called the Nuremberg Laws, which redefined citizenship, prohibited "racial pollution," and required couples to undergo medical examination and counseling before being allowed to marry. The first two of these laws came about as the result of a last-minute decision by Hitler to include something dramatic in the 1935 Nuremberg party congress; he felt that the planned program was too thin and lacking in impact. This followed a year of relative calm on racial issues, especially anti-Semitism. Now party stalwarts, egged on by racial experts such as Gerhard Wagner, pushed for a new law banning mixed marriages. On September 13, Bernard Lösener, head of the "Jewish Office" in the Ministry of the Interior, was ordered to take a plane to Nuremberg to help formulate the new law. Upon his arrival Lösener and two colleagues from the Ministry of the Interior, Hans Pfundtner and Wilhelm Stuckart, hammered out a preliminary draft, which was rejected. On September 14, the drafters met at Frick's residence, where they crowded into the music room, Pfundtner working on the grand piano and Stuckart on the sofa, and eventually came up with several optional drafts, differing in toughness. Just as the exhausted team had finished its work about midnight, Hitler asked for another law dealing with citizenship, which they produced quickly on the back of a menu. At 2:30 A.M., September 15, Hitler accepted the milder version of the law on mixed marriages, the one recommended by the ministry team, as well as the Reich citizenship draft.

The law on mixed marriages, entitled Law for the Protection of German Blood and German Honor (Gesetz zum Schutze des deutschen Blutes und der deutschen Ehre), prohibited marriage and sexual relations between Germans and Jews, forbade Jews to display the national flag, prohibited Jews from employing female citizens of German or kindred blood under forty-five years of age, and prescribed various penalties for violation of these rules ranging from hard labor to imprisonment with a fine.[102] The Reich Citizenship Law (Reichsbürgergesetz) distinguished between citizens and subjects (*Reichsbürger* and *Staatsangehörige*), the former being of German or kindred blood with full political rights and the latter being residents belonging (*angehörig*) to the state but only enjoying protection rather than political rights. Jews were initially relieved by this classification, which designated them as subjects with certain rights. Interestingly enough, single women were also relegated to the status of subjects! In justifying the distinction between Jew and German, Wilhelm Stuckart and his legal adviser Hans Globke, a man who would later resurface as one of Adenauer's chief aides in the Bonn chancellery, provided the following official commentary:

> National Socialism opposes to the theories of the equality of all men and of the fundamentally unlimited freedom of the individual vis-à-vis the State, the harsh but necessary recognition of the inequality of men and of the differences between them based on the laws of nature. Inevitably, differences in the rights and duties of the individual derive from the differences in character between races, nations, and people.[103]

The Citizenship Law, however, still left unclear the issue of who was "a full Jew," a question that caused intense debates among racial and legal "experts" in the wake of the Nuremberg party congress and ultimately resulted in an addendum to the law that tried to specify exactly who was a Jew. These legal experts defined a "full Jew" as someone who had three Jewish grandparents. Those who had smaller fractions of Jewishness were labeled as *Mischlinge* or half-breeds, divided into half-breeds first degree (two Jewish grandparents) and second degree (one Jewish grandparent). Those who were classified as half-breed first degree could still be considered full Jews if they (1) belonged to a Jewish religious community, (b) were married to a Jew, (3) were offspring of marriages contracted with Jews after June 15, 1935, or (4) were born out of wedlock to Jews.

It goes without saying that the exact determination of who was a Jew, now also influenced by religious criteria, produced a bureaucratic nightmare because it involved scores of "family researchers" hunting down uncertain records. The determination of who was a *Mischling*, nevertheless, was of vital importance because it could mean life or death once the decision had been made to exterminate the Jews.

On October 18, 1935, a third major racial law was passed, entitled Law for the Protection of the Genetic Health of the German People (Gesetz zum Schutze der Erbgesundheit), which required that prospective marriage couples submit themselves to a medical examination before marriage. The reason behind this piece of legislation was to catch potential racial damage before it occurred. The law also prohibited marriage between individuals who suffered from either hereditary or contagious diseases. If prospective couples passed the required medical examination, they received "Certificates of Fitness to Marry" from public health authorities. Marital counseling centers were set up all over Germany as part of an extensive system of public health. These centers were staffed by physicians and nurses who examined couples and issued the certificates. Without such certificates couples could not receive their marriage licenses.[104]

These racial laws represented the deepest wishes of the Nazi leadership; they expressed, above all, the paranoid thinking of a group of racists who were obsessed with people of "inferior blood" who might "pollute" the German gene pool. Hitler's insane rantings in *Mein Kampf* were now transformed into law as new categories of crime were erected such as *Rassenverrat* (betrayal of race) or *Rassenschande* (dishonor to the race). It was racial treason to sleep with a Jew or to consort with other "carriers of non-German or related blood." It was also racial treason to curb the natural fertility of the German people by artificial means. Abortion was defined as a crime against the body of the German people.[105]

The defilers of German blood fell into several and often vague ethnic, social, or medical categories: Gypsies, "Rhineland bastards," the "asocial," homosexuals, the mentally ill, and the Jews. People of different ethnicities had always been suspect in Germany, and few of them, except the Jews, had been treated with more brutality than the Gypsies.[106] Two major groups of Gypsies, the Sinti and Roma, had migrated to Germany (and other European countries) in the fifteenth century. Originally from northern India, many Gypsies had converted along the way to Christianity, but this did not prevent them from being mistreated because they were perceived as un-German and therefore inferior. Everything about them — their unkempt appearance, their nomadic habits, their language and customs — made them unfit to be in the presence of good Germans. According to a new Nazi academic field, "criminal biology," the Gypsies were also increasingly seen as habitual thieves and criminals. For all of these reasons the Nazis eventually rounded up as many Gypsies as they could lay their hands on and threw them into concentration camps. It was probably at a conference in Berlin on September 21, 1939, chaired by SD Chief Heydrich, that a decision was made to carry out the measures that would lead to the "final solution" of the Gypsy question. During World War II entire Sinti and Roma families were exterminated along with the Jews in the annihilation camps in Poland.

Although Germany did not contain any indigenous blacks, there were about five hundred so-called "Rhineland bastards" (*Rheinlandbastarde*), children from black French occupation troops and their native German mothers.[107] Even under the Weimar Republic, the presence of such children had been referred to by none other than President Friedrich Ebert as the black disgrace (*Schwarze Schmach*). As soon as the Nazis seized power, they ordered that *Rheinlandbastarde* be registered with the appropriate health authorities. The next step, which involved much secret machination, was enforced sterilization.

Homosexuals were also singled out for discrimination because they, too, defiled German blood. Paragraph 175 of the Reich criminal code, dating back to 1871, specified that sexual relations between men constituted a criminal act punishable by imprisonment. Although Paragraph 175 was never changed, it was not as harshly enforced during the Weimar Republic as it had been during the Kaiserreich. Hitler himself had always turned a blind eye to the homosexuality that was rampant in the ranks of the SA, but after the Röhm Purge, with its attendant horror stories of perverse sexuality, Hitler gave his support to the harshest treatment for homosexual conduct. The new line may be gleaned from a remark made by Himmler that every SS homosexual "will be sent on my instruction to a concentration camp and shot while attempting to escape."[108] It was also Himmler who set up a central registry of all known homosexuals and an office to combat them. Persecution of homosexuals picked up speed in the late 1930s, and many were sent to concentration camps where they were humiliated, tortured, and killed. Probably close to fifteen thousand homosexuals were imprisoned in concentration camps during the Third Reich.[109]

In 1938 the Reich Criminal Office, in an effort to find the broadest category by which it could criminalize human behavior, defined the term "asocial" as anyone who does not want to fit in to the people's community (*Volksgemeinschaft*). Asocial persons included vagabonds, Gypsies, beggars, whores, alcoholics, or anyone who was, in another favorite epithet the Nazis used to stigmatize people, a "work-shy" (*arbeitscheu*) drifter or eccentric. Anyone labeled as "asocial" could be taken into "protective custody," sent to a concentration camp, and, by the terms of the Law for the Prevention of Progeny with Hereditary Diseases, also sterilized. It is surely one of the supreme ironies that the criminals who gained control over the German state were now defining criminality not by reference to higher legal norms or procedures but by whether someone chose or did not choose to belong to their criminal community. And the Nazi response was not rehabilitation but imprisonment and even annihilation. With such radical measures, the Nazis actually believed that they could root out "asocial" elements. In 1942, the minister of justice, Otto Thierack, in order to solve the problem of keeping "asocial elements" imprisoned, handed over all asocials to the SS so that they might be exterminated through labor.[110] Nazi justice had joined hands with its SS executioner.

Besides Gypsies, homosexuals, and asocials there were two other categories of innocent and largely helpless "racial inferiors" the Nazis chose to eradicate — the mentally ill and the Jews. Nazi racialists had pontificated for some time about the necessity of ridding Germany of the mentally ill, but Christian sensibilities were still strong enough to prevent the public implementation of a euthanasia program. The term "euthanasia" could mean, as it does in the Greek, an easy or merciful death; on the other hand, it could also mean, as some racial biologists saw it, the elimination of the "useless eater." The Nazis, in fact, confused these two meanings, focusing on one or the other as the spirit moved them. The elimination of "lives not worth living" or "nature's mistakes" was a favorite theme in Nazi propaganda. In 1936, a German physician, Dr. Helmut Unger, published a best-selling novel called *Sendung und Gewissen* (Mission and conscience), in which a beautiful young woman, a talented pianist suffering from multiple sclerosis, begs her husband, a loving doctor, to relieve her of her suffering through an easy death. No longer emotionally able to see her suffer and waste away, the husband administers a lethal dose of morphine, while a friend accompanies her last moments by playing a soothing romantic tune on the piano. Tried for murder, the doctor is acquitted because his act constituted an act of mercy and not of homicide. The novel, in turn, was followed by a motion picture, entitled *Ich Klage an!* (I accuse! [1941]), which further raised the issues in the public arena.[111]

While public opinion appeared to shift in favor of the romanticized notion of administering easy deaths to hopelessly suffering individuals, the Nazi leadership still believed that it was premature to move more radically on the euthanasia front. In 1935 Hitler purportedly told Dr. Wagner, the Reich physician leader, that large-scale euthanasia would have to wait until wartime because it would then be easier to administer.[112] In the winter of 1938 a petition, which in retrospect would serve as a catalyst for the euthanasia program, reached Hitler from a German father who requested that the life of his deformed child be terminated. Hitler turned over the decision to one of his personal physicians, Dr. Karl Brandt; the result was the creation of an ad hoc committee called Reich Committee for the Scientific Registration of Serious Hereditary and Congenital Illnesses. This committee served as a clearinghouse for reports sent in by physicians and midwives asking what to do about cases involving serious deformities. The reports were then scored by three doctors with a red plus sign (= death), a blue minus sign (= survival), or a question mark in doubtful cases requiring further assessment. Children who had been marked with a red plus sign were then killed by lethal injection.

In the summer of 1939 Hitler asked Dr. Leonardo Conti, Wagner's successor as Reich physician leader, to organize a euthanasia program for adults, but the initiative was taken out of his hands by Philipp Bouhler, head of the party chancellery, and his assistant, Viktor Brack. The two men worked out the organizational plans along with elaborate covers so that the program, which had been personally authorized by Hitler, could not be traced to its source. Code named "Aktion T4" after the relevant government department of the Reich chancellery located on Tiergarten Street 4 in Berlin, the euthanasia program followed the essential program of earlier child murders. Forms were sent out to all hospital asylums identifying prospective candidates. As in the child murder operation, patient forms were marked with life or death symbols or a question mark for further analysis by higher "assessors."

The actual killings were carried out at six selected asylums: Grafeneck near Stuttgart, Hadamar near Limburg, Bernburg on Saale, Brandenburg on Havel, Hartheim near Linz, and Sonnenstein near Pirna. In each case, specially trained SS teams of physicians and nurses moved into the facilities and prepared the way for the actual exterminations. Patients were killed in gas chambers disguised as shower rooms or in mobile vans into which carbon monoxide was pumped.[113] The corpses were then incinerated in specially constructed crematoria. Since these actions took place inside Germany, word quickly leaked out and local authorities were alerted to the gruesome activities in the asylums or the "killer boxes" seen driving around the countryside. Ugly scenes also occurred at some of the asylums where the regular staff often desperately tried to protect their patients from the clutches of the SS murderers.[114] Relatives of the victims notified clergymen and judicial authorities, demanding that immediate action be taken against the perpetrators. One judge even initiated criminal charges against Bouhler and paid for it by being prematurely retired. Bishop Clemens von Gehlen, one of the few clergymen in the upper echelons of the Catholic Church who voiced opposition, delivered several powerful sermons against the euthanasia program. In August 1941 Hitler terminated the program, possibly because of the adverse opinions it was generating but more likely because the program had met its original target figure.[115] By August 1941, when the killings stopped, 70,273 people had been exterminated. But the methods of killings, perfected in the euthanasia program, were now extended to a new and much larger target population — the Jews.

Anti-Semitism was the hate that fueled the Nazi movement. From the moment Hitler took power, Jews were under siege throughout Germany. There were only two brief periods when the Jews were afforded a little respite — the year 1934, when Hitler was busy purging his own forces, and the summer of 1936, when the Nazis hosted the Olympic Games in Berlin and temporarily suspended anti-Jewish activities for propaganda reasons. Four distinct phases of Hitler's war against the Jews can be identified: (1) legalized discrimination, (2) forced emigration, (3) resettlement and forced ghettoization, and (4) annihilation. From a chronological point of view, the first two phases spanned the years 1933 to the outbreak of World War II in 1939, while the last two phases encompassed the war years 1939–45.

As previously mentioned, attacks against the Jews occurred both spontaneously and in organized form with the beginning of Nazi rule. On April 1, 1933, Goebbels, on Hitler's instructions, organized a boycott against Jewish businesses throughout Germany, ostensibly to teach international Jewry a lesson for supposedly maligning the new government. Hitler's perverse reasoning was that the best way of hurting international Jews was to attack their "racial comrades" in Germany. A flood of laws followed in 1933, aimed at depriving Jews of their rights and their livelihood. Dismissals and forced resignations of Jews from positions as judges, lawyers, and teachers had commenced immediately after Hitler came to power in January. The Law of the Restoration of the Civil Service (April 7, 1933), introducing "Aryanism" as a prerequisite for holding civil service positions, automatically excluded all Jews from the civil service and led to the dismissal or forced retirement of Jews holding such positions.

In rapid succession came similar laws aimed at excluding Jews from other professional positions — lay assessors, jurors, commercial judges

(April 7); from serving as patent lawyers (April 22); and from being associated with state insurance institutions as panel physicians (April 22), dentists, or dental technicians (June 2).[116] A law against the overcrowding of German schools (April 25) severely limited Jewish enrollment in German public schools. On May 6, the Law of the Restoration of Civil Service was amended to close loopholes in order to exclude honorary university professors, university lecturers, and notaries from civil service employment. In late September and early October 1933 three additional measures struck the Jews: the first prohibited government employment of non-Aryans and persons married to them (September 28); the second excluded Jews from cultural and entertainment enterprises such as art, literature, theater, and film (September 29); and the third was the National Press Law, which placed all newspapers under government control and, by applying the "Aryan paragraph," effectively excluded Jews from the Fourth Estate.

After a period of relative calm in 1934, government attacks on the Jews resumed in 1935 and led, as we have seen, to the Nuremberg racial laws, decreeing that Germans could not marry Jews or engage in sexual relations with them. Jews were also politically disenfranchised, although in Nazi Germany this did not mean very much; what meant a great deal was that plans were also in the offing for stripping them systematically of their property. These measures began with the appointment of Hermann Göring as plenipotentiary of the Four-Year Plan and picked up speed after Hjalmar Schacht's resignation as minister of economics and his replacement by the more pliable Walther Funk. In the case of war, the Four-Year Plan envisioned the expropriation of all Jewish property in Germany. The preliminary steps for this were already taken on April 22 by a decree that prohibited camouflaging a Jewish business under Aryan or pseudo-Aryan ownership. The decree defined a business as Jewish if its owner was a Jew.

Although by 1938 the Nazis thought they had finally nailed down the problem of who was a Jew, they continued to dream up more strategies by which the Jews could be flushed out into the open. Heydrich's SD had established a special branch, Section II/112 (Jewish Affairs), dedicated exclusively to the identification of Jewish businesses and organizations. The Ministry of the Interior, in the meantime, was also busy keeping an eye on Jews, making sure that they kept their Jewish names. This issue of Jewish surnames had been a continuous subject of debate. Efforts had been made even before the Nazis came to power to prevent Jews from concealing their Jewish descent by changing the names previously forced upon them to Germanic-sounding names. For purposes of "easy" identification, the Nazis prohibited such name changes and, to add insult to injury, specified that all male Jews must assume the given name of Israel, while all female Jews had to take the given name of Sarah. In October 1938 passport restrictions came into effect.

The harvest of hate, fueled by many Nazi sources, especially Streicher's obscene publications, was now being gathered. Practically excluded from most economic activities, Jews were harassed whenever they tried to go to cinemas, theaters, swimming pools, hotels, or resorts. Villages competed for the honor of being "Jew-free," proudly advertised this fact, and posted signs reading "Jews are not wanted here" ("Juden sind hier unerwünscht"). Park benches were also clearly marked "Aryan" or "Jew." German Jews were being transported into a frightening and shadowy no-man's-land of great vulnerability; they could be arrested without due process and imprisoned in concentration camps. Their property could be seized and confiscated for the flimsiest of reasons. They had no legal recourse.

In November 1938 came an unexpected opportunity for the Nazis to tighten the screws. On November 7, 1938, a secretary in the German embassy in Paris, Ernst vom Rath, was assassinated by a seventeen-year-old Polish student named Herschel Grynszpan in response to the mistreatment of his parents and fifty thousand others by the Nazi government. In March 1938, Poland had passed a law that proposed to denaturalize Polish nationals who had been living outside Poland for a period of five years. The law was specifically aimed at about fifty thousand Polish Jews who had been residing in Germany and whom the Polish government did not wish to return to Poland. Grynszpan's parents, who had been living in Hannover since 1914, became automatically stateless and were herded by the Gestapo into camps near the Polish border where, in a kind of no-man's-land, they were kept in protective custody under deplorable conditions. Young Grynszpan wanted to send a message of protest to the world through his desperate deed.

The Nazis were quick to retaliate. On November 9, the day they celebrated the anniversary of the Beerhall Putsch, Hitler approved Goebbels's proposal to set in motion "spontaneous" demonstrations against Jews throughout Germany, slyly suggesting that the "SA should be allowed to have a fling."[117] The result was the infamous pogrom later referred to as the "Night of Crystals" (Kristallnacht) when fires were ignited all over Germany and the shattered glass of synagogues and Jewish businesses littered the streets of Germany. Nazi thugs went berserk and destroyed close to one thousand Jewish businesses, killed about one hundred Jews, and rounded up, all in all, twenty-six thousand Jews and herded them into concentration camps. In the wake of Kristallnacht came several measures that intensified discrimination against the Jewish population. The government, in an act of brazen insolence, blamed the Jews for having caused the outrages of November 9 and 10 and seized the money insurance companies were paying out for the damage inflicted on Jewish property. In addition, the Jews were forced to pay a "contribution" of 1 billion marks. Jews were prohibited from attending theaters, cinemas, concerts, and public exhibitions; Jewish children were forbidden to attend public schools.

The Nazis now began to usher in phase two, enforced emigration, in their effort to rid Germany of its Jewish population. Actually, Jews had begun to emigrate as soon as Hitler came to power in January 1933. Between 1933 and November 1938 more than 150,000 Jews had already left Germany of their own accord. After Kristallnacht, however, forced evacuations, which had been going on since the annexation of Austria, were greatly intensified, forcing another 150,000 to leave the country.[118] One of the chief instruments of these enforced evacuations was Adolf Eichmann (1906–62), who had joined the SS in 1933 and then moved into Heydrich's SD service, where he worked as an "expert" in the Department of Jewish Emigration. In 1938 Heydrich tasked him with setting up a central office for Jewish emigration in Vienna, which actually succeeded in expelling over a hundred thousand Austrian Jews into forced emigration, many of them to Palestine, while others found refuge in other countries — Czechoslovakia, Holland, Belgium, Britain, the United States, France, Australia, Canada, or South Africa. Eichmann's office did such a brisk business driving Jews out of Austria and relieving them of their money and possessions that Eichmann was transferred to Berlin in 1939 and put in charge of Jewish deportation in the Reich Main Security Office (RSHA) as chief of Section IV /B-4. This office was to round up well over three million Jews during the war and drive them into eastern ghettos and concentration camps (phase three) and finally set them up for physical extermination as a result of Hitler's order in the spring of 1941 to annihilate the Jews (phase 4).

That Hitler meant to declare war on the Jews is obvious from his public statements as well as his words in *Mein Kampf*. On January 21, 1939, he told the Czech foreign minister that he was planning to destroy the Jews; that they would not get away with what they did on November 9, 1918, a reference to the beginning of the German political collapse, which he had always attributed to the Jews.[119] Only a week later, speaking to the Reichstag on the anniversary of his appointment to the chancellorship, Hitler publicly issued the following threat to the Jews:

> In the course of my life I have very often been a prophet, and have usually been ridiculed for it. During the time of my struggle for power it was in the first instance only the Jewish race that received my prophecies with laughter when I said that I would one day take over the leadership of the State, and with it that of the whole nation, and that I would then among other things settle the Jewish problem. Their laughter was uproarious, but I think that for some time now they have been laughing on the other side of their face. Today I will once more be a prophet: if the international Jewish financiers in and outside Europe should succeed in plunging the nations once more into a world war, then the result will not be the Bolshevizing of the earth, and thus the victory of Jewry, but the annihilation of the Jewish race in Europe![120]

Chapter 11

The Road to War, 1933–39

The Great Powers between the Wars

Hitler's great diplomatic triumphs in the 1930s were not only the result of his cunning and reckless strategies but also the product of historical consequences of World War I, namely, the destruction of the traditional great power system, the weaknesses of the Western democracies, U.S. isolationist policies, and the opportunistic tactics of a paranoid Soviet Union. World War I had changed the traditional constellation of great powers, leaving a vacuum that Hitler was quick to exploit.

Before the war, the great European powers had been Britain, France, Russia, Italy, Austro-Hungary, and Germany. Of these five only France and Britain had emerged from the devastating conflict as major powers. Weakened by revolution and civil war, Russia had fallen into the hands of a group of Communists who were as suspicious of the Western democracies as they were of the rising Fascist states. Austro-Hungary had collapsed; Italy was torn apart by socioeconomic conflicts and felt cheated of the fruits of victory; Germany was defeated and disarmed. Only France and England maintained a semblance of stability; their political effectiveness, however, was impaired by two major weaknesses: lack of common purpose and the absence of support from the United States. Laurence Lafore observed that *"never before had even one Great Power been eliminated by a European war."*[1] If the United States had moved in concert with the two great European democracies after the war, Fascist aggression might have been stopped. Unfortunately, America's wartime idealism turned out to be little more than an ideological justification for fighting the war; it was of little effect in waging the peace. This would have required a long-range commitment that America was not willing to make. Few Americans realized that without the enormous resources of the New World there was little chance that the Old World could be reconstructed peacefully or democratically.

Upon seizing power in 1933, Hitler was determined to revise the course of European politics. Germany therefore became the catalyst of change, whereas Britain and France, paralyzed by insecurity and the horror of war, pursued an essentially defensive strategy.[2] Although both Britain and France planned to extend their wartime coalition into the postwar period and to cooperate in the preservation of peace, they differed about strategy. The French believed that only an overwhelming military preponderance and a powerful diplomatic security arrangement aimed at isolating a weakened Germany could preserve the peace. The British, on the other hand, sought to address the underlying causes that had produced international conflict in the first place. They increasingly felt that Germany's treatment at Versailles had been unworthy of a great power and that no amount of humiliation, however successful in the short-run, would ever make it a stable power in central Europe. The French, of course, also recognized that Germany could not be permanently reduced to vassalage, but they were less willing to modify the harsher terms of the Versailles Treaty without compelling evidence of Germany's peaceful intentions. When these peaceful signals failed to materialize, especially after Hitler seized power in 1933, the French maintained their hard-line approach.

Unfortunately, French resolve had been weakened by events in the early 1920s. In 1920 the U.S. Senate rejected the Versailles Treaty, and the country withdrew into isolation. This retreat from European involvement not only destroyed the Anglo-American preponderance, which alone could have stabilized Europe, but also placed an intolerable burden on France. The French were the most vociferous defenders of the Versailles settlement and advocated decisive action against violations. In 1923, as shown in chapter 2, the French invaded the Ruhr in order to enforce the treaty's provisions on reparations, which they accused the Germans of having violated. This unilateral action, launched without the support of its wartime partners, exposed France to widespread criticism; it was also self-defeating because the German response of "passive retaliation" destroyed the German economy and made future reparations payments increasingly difficult. The French never forgot this disastrous foray into Germany, and they resolved to desist from such interventions unless they had overwhelming support. There was also an increasing recognition that the encouragement of Germany's "artificial inferiority," which required the permanent crippling of German strength and the occupation of key German territory, only served to heighten German hostility.[3] The French found themselves on the horns of a dilemma: crippling the Germans actually undermined their sense of security in the sphere that counted most — the psychological. Facing a more populous nation of seventy million Germans and criticized and abandoned by their one-time friends for failed and inappropriate aggressive strategies, they next sought to develop an intricate web of security arrangements aimed at isolating Germany. This was the famous cordon sanitaire — a safety zone designed to envelop Germany on all sides. Finally, to crown this baroque strategy, the French built their own defensive wall, the Maginot Line, as a further deterrence to German aggression. Even this marvel of defensive engineering proved inadequate to bolster French security. It seemed that the level of insecurity increased with the growth of revenues expended on defense: the more money the French spent on defense, the less secure they felt about Germany. If the Maginot Line was a physical line of defense, France's intricate alliance system with smaller European powers represented its psychological line of defense against Germany. A large part of French foreign policy, according to Arnold Wolfers, centered around the negotiation of mutual assistance pacts and alliances.[4] The French literally dug themselves in not only behind walls of mortar but also behind a closely knit network of legal trenches.[5] With France's foreign policy thus unnaturally focused on the fear of a future German attack, French diplomats found themselves squirming in a straitjacket that prevented the implementation of more creative responses and transformed an obsession into a self-fulfilling prophecy.

The British were far more willing to make concessions in order to "redress legitimate grievances" — the key phrase of British diplomatic language between the wars. British receptivity to negotiations, it has been argued, was based on a widely shared belief that Germany had been unjustly treated at Versailles and that the harsher aspects of the treaty had to be either moderated or rescinded. Some historians have attributed Britain's revisionist position to its long-standing conviction, grounded in its evolutionary empirical tradition, that all human laws or customs are ultimately provisional and therefore subject to change.

Although the British supported France, they also felt uneasy about reducing Germany to a minor power and actively supported the new republic's efforts to get back on its feet, a policy that may have also been inspired by the fact that an impotent Germany tilted the balance of power on the continent too much to the French side.

Thus Britain and France often marched at cross purpose with resultant uncertainty and mutual distrust between the two powers in the 1930s. They were also at odds when it came to eastern Europe. France had fashioned a network of alliances with countries such as Poland, Czechoslovakia, and Yugoslavia, treating their territorial integrity as equally as important as its own borders.[6] In contrast, many British statesmen seemed amazingly blasé about Hitler's territorial ambitions in eastern Europe, in some cases regarding that area as a proper sphere of German expansion; they undoubtedly hoped that Hitler, by expanding eastward, would be less of a threat to Britain's maritime and imperial position. That this might endanger French continental interests or undermine Anglo-French cooperation against Nazi aggression did not particularly concern these British armchair strategists.

Hitler's Foreign Policy

Hitler's foreign policy was based on rigid racial and expansionist ideas. Nothing is more misleading than A. J. P. Taylor's assertion that Hitler was merely a traditional continental statesman, no more wicked or unscrupulous than many other contemporary statesmen, who wanted to promote Germany's interests as a great power and proceeded far more patiently than is commonly supposed by historians.[7] The facts are otherwise. Hitler's modus operandi was the use of ruthless terror on behalf of bestial policies of race supremacy, subjugation of inferior "breeds," and the conquest of "living space." As previously noted, he believed that the Aryan race, at the apex of biological-cultural evolution, was destined to conquer the world under German leadership. He envisioned a stage-by-stage diffusion of Aryan people throughout Europe and ultimately the whole world. In Hitler's mind the concept of race was intimately linked to that of space. A people's greatness, he felt, depended not only on its racial stock but also on its ability to reproduce more prodigiously than inferior races. This, in turn, required the availability of land. Confining a race to a limited space was to foreclose the possibility of historical greatness. The German people, he warned, were doomed to vassalage if they limited themselves to the borders of 1914. Hitler favored a ruthless policy of expansion reminiscent of that advocated by the pan-German nationalists and similar annexationist groups. In this sense it is perfectly legitimate to speak of a basic continuity in German foreign policy between 1890 and 1933.[8] Imperial foreign policy was also aggressive and expansionist, but those who conducted it — the conservative prewar elite — worked within the traditional framework of European diplomacy and with a caution that Hitler would have regarded as contemptible. Even such militarists as Admiral von Tirpitz spoke in favor of calculated risks; and though the concept of "preventive war" was much in the air — as evidenced by the kaiser's bellicose exclamation of "now or never" in June 1914 — few German diplomats favored war as an inherently desirable strategy over peaceful approaches.

For Hitler war was not the last resort of foreign policy; it was the preferred means of achieving Germany's ends. Gerhard Weinberg has shown the consequences of this war-oriented strategy.[9] Reliance on war rather than peace meant that opponents were expected to give in completely. In negotiations, the Nazis always seemed to operate with a psychological advantage because, unlike their opponents, they regarded war as an acceptable, even preferred, risk. It is for this reason that in the process of negotiation Hitler's demands would constantly be raised as deadlock approached, not reduced to move the parties toward compromise. Hitler also regarded treaties with foreign powers as merely short-range measures aimed at either partitioning enemy territory or fending off a specific threat. In either case, the process of negotiation should be strictly limited to unilateral agreements rather than complicated multilateral treaties that bound a nation too tightly. A treaty was a means to a specific end; once the end was obtained, the treaty could always be torn to pieces. Finally, the policy of expanding Germany's space and race brought about a noticeable change in the German diplomatic service, for it required a new breed of aggressive statesmen who thought and acted like Adolf Hitler.

In *Mein Kampf* Hitler had announced that "Germany will either be a world power or there will be no Germany" — a statement that was emblematic of his character.[10] If Germany was to become a world power, it logically followed that it had to conquer the necessary *Lebensraum* (living space). A small country, he believed, could aspire to historical greatness only by dedicating all its energies to the will to power. Hitler saw himself as catalyst of the will to Germanic greatness, and he believed that the task of national regeneration could be accomplished by institutionalizing warlike impulses. All humane values had to be rooted out because humane people do not embark on world conquest. He envisioned a hard, callous, obedient, and determined youth that would delight in war and conquest. A good general, he once remarked, should be like a mad dog held on a leash by his führer. In a revealing discussion with Hermann Rauschning he insisted that one of the chief educational goals of National Socialism was to teach all Germans the habit of being brutal with a good conscience.[11]

Ribbentrop and the New Nazi Foreign Policy

When Hitler became chancellor, the German Foreign Office was staffed by traditionalists who had grown up in imperial Germany and still reflected the monarchist beliefs of the old Kaiserreich. Many of them came from families that had deep roots in German history and some, like Secretary of State Bernhard von Bülow, refused to believe that a mere corporal could ever become chancellor of Germany.[12] When Hitler did become chancellor, an atmosphere of apprehension hung over the Foreign Office, although there was some hope that Hitler would surely listen to expert advice. The führer quickly disabused them of such expectations. As a corporal and a declassed Austrian petit bourgeois, Hitler had always harbored deep resentments against the traditional conservative elite. He was repelled by their upper-class mannerisms, but at the same time he grudgingly recognized their importance in carrying out his ambitious foreign policies. By the middle of 1934, however, Hitler began replacing some of the more cautious diplomats who had been dominating the Wilhelmstrasse. Preoccupied as he had been with consolidating his power and purging his political opponents, and at the same time trying to mend the economy, only then did Hitler reveal his own ideas on foreign policy. He relied on the same interim solutions that he was using with great effect in the domestic field, namely, bypassing traditional channels through the use of special appointments of officials who were not responsible to any traditional chain of command but owed their allegiance only to him personally.

It was in this way that Joachim von Ribbentrop insinuated himself into the field of foreign policy as "special commissioner for disarmament questions," and that Franz von Papen would later assume the post of minister to Vienna "free from the jurisdiction of the Foreign Office but...responsible to Hitler alone."[13] In addition, Hitler encouraged rival organizations in the field of foreign policy just as he encouraged them in the domestic field. This is how Ribbentrop's own foreign policy agency, the Dienststelle (Büro) Ribbentrop (Bureau Ribbentrop), came into being as a direct rival to the Foreign Office. This also happened when the Nazi Party Foreign Organization (Auslandsorganisation), established in 1931, began to dabble in matters of foreign policy traditionally reserved for the Foreign Office. In short, in foreign as in domestic affairs the Nazis bypassed, isolated, weakened, and often destroyed the effectiveness of traditional institutions. The head of the German Foreign Office, Count Konstantin von Neurath, was a quiet and somewhat unassuming gentleman of the old diplomatic school who had served as a professional diplomat since World War I in a variety of ministerial and ambassadorial posts — minister to Copenhagen (1919–22), ambassador to Rome (1922–30), ambassador to Britain (1930–32), and foreign minister since Papen's chancellorship in June 1932.

In contrast to the old-fashioned Neurath, the new Nazi foreign diplomat was epitomized by Ribbentrop, an aggressive and unprincipled parvenu who would direct the course of Nazi foreign policy. Ribbentrop was born in 1893 in Wesel, the son of a professional soldier and a consumptive mother, who died when Joachim was only nine years of age. Joachim would also lose his oldest brother to tuberculosis and was most likely infected by the disease himself, for at the age of eighteen one of his kidneys had to be removed to prevent the disease from spreading.[14] Joachim attended school in Metz, a famous garrison city in Lorraine. His performance there was unremarkable, but he was described by one of his teachers, Otto Meissner, the future presidential secretary, as "full of vanity and very pushy."[15] Joachim never finished his *Abitur* (school-leaving examination), but persuaded his father to let him travel abroad and study foreign languages instead.

Joachim found support for his youthful plans from his aunt Gertrude von Ribbentrop, who came from the titled side of the family and would later adopt Joachim and thus invest him with the much sought after honorific "von." Through his aunt's generous financial support Joachim and his brother Lothar went to study at a boarding school in Grenoble in 1907. One year later, his father, now a lieutenant colonel and only recently remarried, resigned his commission because of a long-standing difference with the kaiser's foreign policy and retired on his pension and savings. Richard Ribbentrop had always been a man of grace and polish, leading a very active social life and cultivating a broad circle of friends and acquaintances — a habit that his son Joachim imitated.

During the last few years before the war, Joachim and his brother Lothar spent several years in Canada. Joachim worked at several jobs, including that of clerk-timekeeper for the Canadian Pacific Railroad. When war broke out Ribbentrop returned to Germany and managed to join the Twelfth Hussars despite the fact that one of his kidneys had been removed. Little is known about his war record except that he served on the eastern front as an officer, was wounded several times, and was assigned to staff duty, first in Berlin and then as a language specialist at the War Ministry in Constantinople.

When the war was over, Ribbentrop found himself unemployed. Yet he had a number of assets: he was handsome, charming, witty, and superficially knowledgeable about many different things. A compulsive socializer, he wormed his way into high society and into the heart of Annelies Henkell, daughter of a wealthy manufacturer of sparkling champagnes. Shortly after his marriage to Annelies, a "chic" but not a beautiful woman,[16] Ribbentrop was offered a partnership in the Henkell firm, a position that took him all over Europe and enabled him to build up important contacts.

Ribbentrop came to Hitler through Franz von Papen, with whom he had long been acquainted. Papen had used Ribbentrop as a go-between to persuade Hitler to serve as a vice-chancellor in his government. When Ribbentrop relayed this plan to Hitler, the Nazi leader had launched into a two-hour harangue, making it unmistakably clear that he wanted sole power or nothing. Ribbentrop appears to have been so spellbound by Hitler's histrionics that from this moment on he would remain a totally "convinced, converted, and devoted" Hitlerite.[17] He joined the Nazi Party and began to devise strategies to catch the attention of his hero. Ribbentrop's tenacity in the art of parlor games, which he had fine-tuned during ten years in the company of the nouveau riches, did not miss their mark with Adolf Hitler, although in the wild scramble for positions that followed Hitler's accession to power Ribbentrop was almost overlooked.

However, Ribbentrop used every contact he could find to promote himself steadily and aggressively as a genuine Nazi. His political instincts told him that Himmler and the SS would play a key role in the future Nazi state. So he joined the SS and made sure that he was noticed by high-ranking members of the emerging Nazi elite. Ironically, all of his life Ribbentrop felt that he had to prove that he was "better" than his conservative companions, but now he tried to show that he could be just as crude and aggressive as the new horde of Nazi job seekers.

His first appointment in April 1934 was as plenipotentiary for disarmament. Although ostensibly accountable to Neurath and the Foreign Office, Ribbentrop was expected to report to Hitler before discussing matters with Neurath. In 1934 Ribbentrop set up his own foreign policy office, the Bureau Ribbentrop, headquartered in the old Bismarck palace opposite the Foreign Ministry at Wilhelmstrasse 74–76. Ribbentrop staffed this office with ambitious and untrained amateurs like himself. The mission of this hybrid institution of amateur journalists, businessmen, and party hopefuls consisted in collecting and evaluating foreign intelligence, but the agency very quickly began to intrude into matters within the proper domain of the Foreign Office.

Hitler was impressed enough by Ribbentrop's activities to appoint him "extraordinary ambassador of the German Reich on special mission," which gave Ribbentrop the right to bypass Neurath. His star now appeared to rise, particularly after negotiating the favorable Anglo-German Naval Agreement in 1935. In 1936 Hitler appointed Ribbentrop ambassador to Great Britain. Although pretending to like the English upper-class style, Ribbentrop had no real understanding of the English temperament or character, and he seriously underestimated their capacity to stand up to aggressors.

It is generally admitted that Ribbentrop's ambassadorship to England was an embarrassment to Germany. Ribbentrop offended English sensibilities by his own imperious brand of Teutonic bluster. His behavior was the noisy and embarrassing grandstanding of a social climber. German embassy ladies were told no longer to curtsy to royalty, and Ribbentrop himself reportedly presented himself to the king by saluting him with "Heil Hitler." The British press gleefully reported: "The Nazi Salute to the King; Ribb Heils King."[18]

At one point a cocky Ribbentrop, sure that his star with Hitler was on the ascendancy, indiscreetly told high-placed Nazis that he would be Germany's next foreign minister. When Hitler got wind of this, he called Ribbentrop on the carpet and gave him a vintage führer dressing-down that began with a put-down, "Was bilden Sie sich eigentlich ein?" (Who the hell do you think you are?), and ended with stern advice to behave better, especially in front of foreigners. Ribbentrop was devastated; he thought his career was shattered.

The winds of change, however, favored Ribbentrop. By 1938 Hitler was pursuing a more and more aggressive foreign policy, but felt himself restrained by the traditionalists in the Foreign Office and the army. He felt that he needed a foreign minister who was more flexible and aggressive than the cautious, tongue-tied, and stodgy Neurath. This was Ribbentrop's opportunity. He had already discovered the secret to Hitler's black heart. He would intently hang on Hitler's every word, especially regarding his pet projects; he filed away for future reference the führer's monologues and then, when the moment was ripe, he presented these ideas as his own.[19] This convinced Hitler that Ribbentrop was a man of vision and deserving the utmost support and respect. Ribbentrop used another strategy to great effect by acting more Hitlerian than Hitler and contradicting the führer's doubts with the führer's own aggressions. In the course of several years Ribbentrop had adapted himself so well to

Hitler that he literally became his alter ego. Joachim Fest observed that Ribbentrop had no inner substance whatsoever, and that Hitler's views, however irrational, were for him correct and plausible for the simple reason that Hitler proposed them. To Ribbentrop, we are told, an issue was interesting only if it had been judged interesting by Hitler; if Hitler lost interest in it, so did Ribbentrop. Totally subservient to Hitler, Ribbentrop spent his waking hours forever trying to anticipate his master's views, to adjust himself to his master's whims, and then to spout perfect Hitlerisms in his presence.

Even within the Nazi inner circle, where flattery was rampant, Ribbentrop was generally held in contempt. Goebbels once maliciously remarked that every leading party member had at least one praiseworthy quality with the exception of Ribbentrop, adding that "he bought his name, married his money, and swindled himself into his job."[20] Considering its source, this judgment should be taken with great caution, but it certainly indicates that Ribbentrop was in the company he deserved. Besotted by Hitler's presence, captivated by wealth and power, Ribbentrop sold out whatever genuine virtues, if any, he may have possessed. When Hitler appointed him foreign minister on February 4, 1938, Ribbentrop immediately went to work to change the Foreign Ministry. Under his leadership the Foreign Office was completely stripped of all policy-making functions, which were the prerogative of Hitler and himself. In Gordon Craig's judgement, the Foreign Office became little more than a stenographic bureau, and its members were expected simply to do what they were told.[21] At the time of the Polish crisis Ribbentrop reportedly warned his staff that if any member dared to express a view other than his own, "he would personally shoot him and assume responsibility for this action before the Führer."[22]

Slipping through the Risky Zone, 1933–37

When Hitler came to power in January 1933 problems of foreign policy had to be subordinated to more pressing economic and political issues. His domestic position was too precarious for anything but conciliatory gestures toward his neighbors. Accordingly, he adopted a clever policy of delay and negotiations abroad, while consolidating his rule at home. This strategy was essentially the same one he had used after the disastrous Beerhall Putsch of 1923 when he tricked the Weimar establishment into believing that he was a respectable politician who sought power entirely by legitimate or constitutional means. Now he used the same smoke screen on foreign powers. This dissimulation was as effective in foreign as it had been in domestic affairs. Goebbels wrote:

> Up to now we have succeeded in leaving the enemy in the dark concerning Germany's real goals, just as before 1934 our domestic foes never saw where we were going or that our oath of legality was a trick. We

wanted to come to power legally, but we did not want to use power legally.... They could have arrested a couple of us in 1925 and that would have been that, the end. No, they let us through the danger zone. That's exactly how it was in foreign policy too.... In 1933 a French Premier ought to have said (and if I had been the French Premier I would have said it): "The new Reich Chancellor is the man who wrote *Mein Kampf,* which says this and that. This man cannot be tolerated in our vicinity. Either he disappears or we march!" But they didn't do it. They left us alone and let us slip through the risky zone, and we were able to sail around all dangerous reefs. And when we were done, and well armed, better than they, then they started the war.[23]

Hitler's blatant policy of double-dealing, of saying one thing in public and another in private, can be observed soon after he became chancellor. Three days after his appointment he attended a meeting with his military chiefs. After dinner the commander in chief of the army, General Kurt von Hammerstein, and a select group of high-ranking officers listened to a two-hour address by Hitler; and while the führer talked, Major Horst von Mellenstein, who was concealed behind a curtain, jotted down the key points of the führer's address. Hitler informed his skeptical audience that he planned to reverse the whole course of domestic policy even if it meant twisting the arms of those who refused to convert voluntarily to National Socialism. He said that Germany could only be saved by force of arms. For this reason a strong military was absolutely essential. Politically, the new chancellor called for the toughest authoritarian orders and the eradication of such domestic cancers as Marxism and democracy. Internationally, Hitler stressed the importance of breaking the Versailles Treaty and achieving full equality at Geneva. He also promised the military chiefs that he would restore conscription and see to it that the size of the army was substantially increased.[24] He confessed that, given Germany's current vulnerable position, such a course was fraught with dangers but insinuated that he would negotiate at Geneva under the pretense of seeking equality of arms, while secretly preparing a larger force. He mentioned the possibility that France might attack Germany in order to prevent it from achieving military parity. Time would tell, he said, whether France had real statesmen who were not afraid to attack Germany during this preparatory period. To reassure his chiefs, he quickly added that this was most unlikely. France would probably not attack Germany directly, relying instead on its vassal states in eastern Europe to do its bidding. Hitler ended this highly revealing discussion by informing the military chiefs that living space (*Lebensraum*) was the ultimate objective of his government's foreign policy. He spoke in no uncertain terms about Germanizing eastern Europe in order to settle Germany's excess population and to revitalize its sagging economy. Although Hitler had not succeeded in converting all of his skeptical chiefs, one of them was overheard to reply to a snide remark about the "Bohemian corporal" that, at any rate, "no Chancellor has ever expressed himself so warmly in favor of defense."[25]

While Hitler privately prepared the stage for rearmament, conscription, and war, publicly he reassured both the German people and the Western world that he only desired peace and justice. Appealing to the latent guilt feelings of the Western powers, he used the rhetoric of Wilsonian idealism against them by giving the world the impression that he, too, stood for self-determination and a just and lasting peace. On May 17, 1933, Hitler delivered a carefully prepared peace speech (*Friedensrede*) to the Reichstag in which the whole bag of tricks for public deception that he repeated with such great effect throughout the 1930s was revealed to an unsuspecting world. He began by blaming the Versailles Treaty for the current state of international uncertainty and reminded the world that the spirit and letter of the treaty had not been applied equitably to Germany and that even Germany's former enemies were now acknowledging this injustice. He reminded his Western audience that the Versailles Treaty, which stamped the German nation as an international pariah and used "war guilt" as a thinly disguised policy of economic exploitation, was neither equitable nor economically prudent. The politics of reparation, he averred, had wreaked havoc on international money markets, artificially distorted export-import patterns, retarded the recovery of domestic industry, and led to worldwide depression and unemployment. In addition to causing specific economic problems, the Versailles Treaty had unjustly perpetuated the odious stereotype of "victor and vanquished" indefinitely into the future.[26]

In concluding his "peace speech," Hitler once more insisted that Germany would observe the disarmament provisions of the Versailles Treaty. He accused those who charged that Germany actually possessed an army much larger than the one hundred thousand force permitted under treaty provisions of maligning its honor. Paramilitary forces such as the SS, SA, Stahlhelm, or auxiliary police were political organizations; their purpose was limited to the restoration of domestic law and order. As long as France or England possessed armed forces that disproportionately dwarfed those of Germany, there was no reason the National Socialist government should submit itself to the charade of disarmament negotiations at Geneva. In essence, Hitler was telling the Western powers that he would not arm (*aufrüsten*) if they disarmed (*abrüsten*).[27] He followed this up with a veiled threat that a continuing policy of discrimination against Germany would result in Germany's withdrawal from both the Geneva Conference and the League of Nations.

Although Rudolph Nadolny, Germany's chief negotiator at Geneva, was making substantial progress in persuading the Allies to make major concessions, Hitler did not really want to negotiate seriously at Geneva. On October 14, 1933, when he realized that France was not about to disarm, he announced Germany's withdrawal from the Disarmament Conference and also terminated its membership in the League of Nations. Although he expected few foreign repercussions, Hitler was still clever enough to shroud his decision in the halo of democratic consent by announcing on the very day of his withdrawal from Geneva that he would submit his decision to the German people in a plebiscite. On November 12, the German people ratified Hitler's policy by an overwhelming margin of 95.1 percent for and 4.9 percent against.

On January 26, 1934, Hitler stunned the diplomatic community by announcing a nonaggression pact with Poland. Ever since Germany had been forced to cede territories to Poland as a result of the Versailles Treaty, it had been its axiomatic policy to prepare for war with Poland to reclaim Danzig, Silesia, Posen, and other lost territories. Popular hatred of Poland had inspired a series of incidents in Danzig and the corridor, and every Weimar government had pursued an irredentist policy. Hitler's reversal of traditional policy toward Poland, however, was more apparent than real. In January 1934 Hitler was genuinely worried that Poland, a strong dictatorship under the leadership of Josef Pilsudski, might use the provocative incidents staged by Germans in Danzig and elsewhere as a pretext for intervention when he was least prepared to counter it. As he cynically told Hermann Rauschning, the president of the Danzig Senate, "All of our agreements with Poland have a purely temporary significance. I have no intention of maintaining a serious friendship with Poland."[28]

Though Hitler's rapprochement with Poland exposed him to widespread criticism in German diplomatic and military circles, his decision was diplomatically and psychologically brilliant. He had demonstrated his peaceful intentions, reduced tensions on his eastern frontier, and cracked France's security system in eastern Europe. Poland, Czechoslovakia, Romania, and Yugoslavia were France's major allies in eastern Europe. The Poles, however, were beginning to have serious doubts about collective security arrangements in general and Poland's pivotal role against German aggression in particular. The man who veered Poland off the course of collective security was Pilsudski's right-hand man, Jozef Beck, a brilliant if neurotic colonel who pursued a quixotic policy of "even balance" between Germany and Russia, underestimating the danger in Hitler and overestimating that of Communism.[29]

The French foreign minister, Jean-Louis Barthou, a shrewd realist who had no illusions about Hitler's ultimate goals in foreign policy, tried to counter Hitler's assault on the French collective security system by concluding a series of mutual defense treaties. Barthou's policy contained two features: resolute resistance to potential German aggression; and defensive alliances moderated by gestures of conciliation aimed at binding Germany to a regional security pact. The French foreign minister approached both Russia and Poland in the hope of securing this agreement, but the Poles adamantly rejected his idea and the Russians temporized. In the end Barthou's plans were cut short by his assassination at Marseilles in October 1934. His successor at the Quai d'Orsay,

Pierre Laval, was also unsuccessful in building a wall of isolation around Hitler.

Just as Hitler was about to break through Germany's diplomatic isolation, two events in 1934 brought the real nature of his regime into sharp focus. The first was the Röhm Purge in June, and the second was the unsuccessful attempt by the Austrian Nazis in July to overthrow the Austrian government. Although the Röhm Purge was a purely domestic affair, it revealed the Nazis as cold-blooded killers and, at least fleetingly, showed the world what might be expected of them in the absence of proper restraints. More serious, as regards foreign policy, was the abortive Nazi Putsch in July, which accelerated the deterioration of German-Italian relations.

Hitler had already tried in 1933 to bring about a closer relationship with Italy. As mentioned previously, in *Mein Kampf* he had insisted that Germany had two natural allies in Europe — Italy and England. He saw in Mussolini a man close to his heart, a man of will and destiny who put the democratic midgets in Germany to shame.[30] At this time, Mussolini did not return the compliment; in fact, he was downright hostile to Hitler personally and publicly opposed the führer's plans in foreign policy. The Duce knew that Hitler's intention, announced in the opening passage of *Mein Kampf* and also embodied in the Nazi Party program of 1919, of merging people of German blood into Germany proper would include Austrians living in the South Tyrol. This area had been transferred to Italy by the Treaty of St. Germain in 1919.

Such pronouncements posed a serious threat to Italian sovereignty, and Mussolini therefore vigorously opposed German rearmament and publicly denounced Hitler's withdrawal from the World Disarmament Conference. Ulrich von Hassell, the German ambassador to Italy, spoke of a deterioration in German-Italian relations and warned that Italy saw in German rearmaments an overt threat and was campaigning against the German actions almost as energetically as was France. Mussolini set himself up as a staunch defender of Austrian independence and adamantly opposed German annexation (*Anschluss*) of Austria. On March 17, 1934, Mussolini concluded the Roman Protocols with Austria and Hungary that called for closer economic relations and frequent consultations.

Out of concern for Mussolini's opposition to German policies, Hitler later publicly renounced any German claim on the South Tyrol. He despatched both Franz von Papen and Hermann Göring to see Mussolini and even sent him a personal letter in which he explained that German rearmament was a moral imperative, a necessary step in casting off the shackles of Versailles that had rendered Germany defenseless. When Mussolini was not impressed by these overtures, Hitler decided to appeal to the Duce in person, and in June 1934 he traveled to Venice to see him. This first encounter between the two dictators was extremely cool and formal. Hitler's mind was on Röhm and the SA rather than on Italy or international relations. Moreover, Hitler made a very poor personal impression on the Duce. Dressed in a black business suit and fidgeting constantly with his grey felt hat, Hitler conveyed the impression of a minor clerk in the German bureaucracy; by contrast, the Duce, who strutted about in his splendid Fascist uniform, cut a far more regal appearance than Hitler.

The nadir of German-Italian relations occurred one month after the Venice meeting when a group of Austrian Nazis, financed and supported from Germany, attempted to stage a Putsch in Vienna. Although the Austrian Nazis succeeded in murdering the Austrian chancellor Engelbert Dollfuss, they were quickly crushed by the police and the armed forces. Mussolini, suspecting German involvement, was so infuriated by these developments that he ordered Italian troops to the Austrian frontier. Apart from safeguarding Austria's independence, Mussolini had a personal interest in the abortive affair. He liked Dollfuss and felt extremely embarrassed when he had to break the news of the chancellor's death to his wife, who, at the time of her husband's death, was staying in Rome as his personal guest. The Duce blamed Hitler personally for this outrage, calling him a "horrible sexual degenerate" and a "dangerous fool."[31]

Hitler may not have been personally involved in the Austrian Putsch, but he had encouraged his Nazi followers in Austria in their subversive activities against the Dollfuss government.[32] The diplomats he had sent to Austria were little more than fifth columnists who were expected to subvert the Austrian government as a prelude to the Nazis' final takeover. Remote from the internal affairs of Austria and preoccupied with consolidating his rule in Germany, Hitler had simply allowed the situation in Austria to get out of hand. However, on being informed of the unsuccessful Putsch, he quickly repudiated all German complicity.

Hitler's strategy in Austria revealed the sinister nature of his foreign policy, exposing its use of subversion as a means of advancing Germany's interests. Hitler never wavered from this aggressive policy, though he often obscured it under a smoke screen of outraged disclaimers and pious gestures of peace and goodwill, as after the abortive Austrian Putsch. He repudiated the whole affair in outraged moral terms, turned over the escaped assassins of Dollfuss to the Austrian government, dismissed Theo Habicht, the inspector of the Austrian National Socialist Party, and recalled the German ambassador to Vienna, Dr. Karl Rieth. Finally, in a gesture of conciliation he appointed Franz von Papen, who had barely escaped with his own life during the Röhm Purge, as ambassador to Vienna, undoubtedly hoping that the suave intriguer would help him gain power in Austria just as he had earlier helped him seize power in Germany.

Hitler's setbacks in the summer of 1934 were only temporary. Although the Röhm Purge and the Austrian Putsch had revealed a glimpse of Hitler's regime, the Western powers failed to agree on a consistent policy of collective security. Mussolini was too mercurial in his foreign policy to define strategy and unwilling to submit himself to French or English leadership. The French were badly shaken by a series of domestic upheavals leading to the fall of the Daladier government and subordinated foreign affairs to domestic issues. The English refused to take any action against Germany at all. In fact, prominent members of the Conservative Party, notably Lord Allen of Hurtwood and Lord Lothian, called for a rapprochement with Germany because they were alarmed by French negotiations with Russia. Sir John Simon, the foreign secretary, opposed the Barthou plan for isolating Germany and reviving the prewar Franco-Russian Alliance. Now that Russia was in the hands of Communists it was politically imprudent for any Western government to align itself with the Bolshevik pariah. Hitler made effective use of the red bogeyman until his own alliance with Russia made such a strategy impossible.

The year 1935 brought with it a great improvement in foreign affairs. On January 13, the citizens of the Saar Valley, an area that had been detached from Germany for fifteen years by the Versailles Treaty, voted overwhelmingly for reunion with Germany. Although the pro-German vote was a foregone conclusion in an area that was predominantly German, Hitler nevertheless hailed the result as a great Nazi victory, telling the German people that fifteen years of injustice had come to an end.

In February the British and French governments tried again to negotiate a more equitable treaty on armaments and other issues relating to security, but Hitler cleverly equivocated, and when Sir John Simon and Lord Anthony Eden wanted to discuss these issues with Hitler in person, the führer suddenly excused himself by catching a cold. He had no intention of limiting himself on matters of armament or tying Germany to multilateral treaties. Besides, Hitler had only recently been informed about the British white book of March 4, which, among other things, recommended increased armaments on the grounds that "Germany was ... rearming openly on a large scale, despite the provisions of Part V of the Treaty of Versailles."[33] This was a perfectly correct evaluation of German military activities. On March 8, 1935, in one of his famous Saturday surprises, Hitler announced that Germany had established an air force. This served as a kind of a trial balloon for his proclamation, scheduled for the following weekend, that Germany would restore conscription. On the same day Neurath informed the British ambassador that the führer was taking a fourteen-day vacation in Bavaria and that he would be pleased to meet with John Simon and Anthony Eden afterward. This gave him an additional fortnight to heighten the psychological impact of conscription and rearmament. On March 16, in another Saturday surprise, Hitler announced that he was reinstating universal military service and that he was expanding the army to thirty-six divisions with a numerical strength of 550,000 men.

Reaction to Hitler's announcement varied from mixed feelings to enthusiastic support. On March 17, Heroes Memorial Day (Heldenge- denktag), a splendid military parade was arranged to celebrate Ger- many's military revitalization. Accompanied by Field Marshal August von Mackensen, the only living marshal of the old imperial army, and other top-ranking officers, Hitler walked along Unter den Linden to the terrace of the castle, where he pinned honorary crosses to the banners of the army. Afterward, amid jubilant cheers by thousand of spectators, Hitler held a review of the army.

The initial reaction to Hitler's violation of the Versailles Treaty was surprisingly mild, amounting to little more than solemn protestations and appeals to the League of Nations. When Hitler finally deigned to meet John Simon and Anthony Eden, he was surprised by their con- ciliatory attitude. He spoke of himself as a savior who would defend Europe from Bolshevism and compared himself to Blücher at Water- loo. He laughingly added: "Did Wellington, when Blücher came to his assistance at Waterloo, first ask the legal experts of the Foreign Of- fice whether the strength of the Prussian forces was in accordance with valid treaties?"[34] Hitler's official interpreter, Dr. Paul Schmidt, recalls that only two years before the sky would have fallen in at Geneva if a German statesman had made such demands as Hitler did in these discus- sions with Simon and Eden.[35] Yet Hitler presented Germany's case with conviction and logic, reminding his guests that Germany was a great power and therefore morally entitled to build up a force that was pro- portional to its international standing. Although Simon and Eden were cautious, they accepted Hitler's argument with remarkable equanimity.

The Western powers were concerned enough, however, to convene a conference on April 11 at Stresa on Lake Maggiore. Mussolini took the lead and demanded resolute action, but the British made it clear from the beginning that they did not favor sanctions against Germany. The governments of Italy, France, and England formally condemned Ger- many's violation of the Versailles Treaty, pledged their support of the Locarno Treaty, and agreed to safeguard the independence of Austria. A week later, on April 17, 1935, the League of Nations also condemned Germany's violation of the Versailles Treaty but failed to impose either economic or military sanctions.

The brave show of solidarity at Stresa was essentially hollow. Only two months later it became embarrassingly obvious how little the Stresa powers had in common and how half-hearted their attempts to oppose Hitler turned out to be in practice. In June 1935 Ribbentrop went to London to negotiate a naval agreement with Great Britain that tacitly permitted Germany to begin naval rearmament. By the terms of this agreement, the ratio of the German surface fleet was to be limited to 35 percent of the British fleet, but the German submarine fleet could be as large as the British. The British made major concessions to Hitler by tacitly allowing him to rearm, and thus Hitler made the first step in winning the support, if not the confidence, of a great power he had always regarded as Germany's natural ally.

In order to win the support of Germany's second "natural" ally, Mussolini's Italy, Hitler had only to sit back and let events decide his next move. On October 3, 1935, to the consternation of the civilized world, Mussolini began the invasion of Ethiopia. The Duce had enticed the Italian people for some time with the glorious vision of an extended overseas empire. Neither the French nor the British had much interest in Addis Ababa; in fact, the French had indicated tacit approval of Mussolini's designs on several occasions. Thus, when England astonished the world at Geneva by demanding that the League of Nations impose sanctions against the Duce, the French openly balked at Britain's inconsistent foreign policy. The French saw no reason why they should jeopardize their good relations with Italy and come to the aid of a country that only recently had shown its bad faith as an ally by concluding a naval agreement with Germany. As Allan Bullock observed, "The British appeared to be standing on their heads and looking at events upside down"; they made an enemy of Mussolini, strained relations with France, and, most importantly, made it difficult to establish a common front against any future German aggression.[36]

The ultimate beneficiary of these events was Hitler, who was quick to exploit the Ethiopian crisis for his own purposes. By refusing to join the chorus of world denunciation against Italy, Hitler won the gratitude of the Italian dictator. Hitler knew that the Ethiopian adventure would divert Italy's attention from Austria. Being thus busily engaged overseas, Mussolini would relegate continental problems to a minor role in his strategic agenda. Hitler's calculations proved to be correct. By acquiescing in Italy's Ethiopian adventure, he improved relations between Germany and Italy almost immediately. Moreover, the Italian aggression split the Stresa front beyond repair, alienated Mussolini from the Western powers, and allowed Hitler to save himself from hostile encirclement.

Hitler increasingly became convinced that the Western powers would do almost anything to avoid war. He was sure that as long as he did not attack them directly, he would be immune from serious reprisals. His strategy was now clear: to push an aggressive agenda relentlessly and expose the point of least resistance in his war-weary, timid, and security-conscious opponents. Hitler's great psychological edge was his complete lack of scruples; he was willing to use any means to gain his ends.

Hitler's first real gamble in foreign policy came on March 7, 1936, when he reoccupied the Rhineland. Both the French and the British knew that Hitler was planning a military coup in the Rhineland, and frantic but ineffectual maneuvers took place behind the scenes to organize resistance. The French, along with their Czech and Polish allies, could have countered the German invasion by mobilizing at least ninety divisions, whereas the Germans, who were just beginning to rearm, had a very meager force at their disposal. This is why Hitler's generals were in a state of high tension; unlike Hitler they thought in conventional military terms rather than in psychological or political terms. Hitler, on the other hand, based his judgement on intuition; he sensed that international crises were battles of will rather that battles of war. He was right. When the Germans marched into the Rhineland with a mere twenty-two thousand troops and a contingent of local policemen, the French stood passively by. The Germans reoccupied a key military position from which the French could have struck at the heart of Germany's power.

Even Hitler was highly agitated as the military adventure unfolded. He later referred to the forty-eight hours after the march into the Rhineland as "the most nerve-racking in my life. If the French had then marched into the Rhineland we would have had to withdraw with our tails between our legs, for the military resources at our disposal would have been wholly inadequate for even a moderate resistance."[37] His apprehensions persisted even after it became obvious that the Western powers would not take any military countermeasures. This is why Hitler orchestrated a skillful propaganda campaign aimed at putting his shocked opponents at ease. He insisted that his action had been inspired by the recent alliance between France and Russia, an alliance, he argued, that had completely upset the European balance of power and undermined the Locarno Pact. The occupation of the Rhineland, he contended, was merely a reoccupation of German territory and therefore entirely in accord with justice and equity. He underscored this remarkable assertion of moral rectitude with a conciliatory gesture that was as pathetic as it was transparent, offering a pact of nonaggression to France and Belgium, proposing a new demilitarized zone on both sides of the western frontier, and offering a nonaggression pact to Germany's eastern neighbors; he even proposed to reenter the League of Nations. As André François-Poncet, the French ambassador to Germany, aptly summed it up, "Hitler struck his adversary in the face, and as he did so declared: 'I bring you proposals for peace!'"[38]

When it was all over Hitler had his way without serious opposition. To be sure, Western capitals rung with anxious consultation and feeble protestations, but in the end nothing was done. Hitler's cause, after all, appeared just. The Rhineland was German and not French. Lord Lothian summed up the typical British view of Germany's action: "After all, they are only going into their own back-garden."[39] In the meantime, Hitler submitted his remilitarization of the Rhineland to the German people for approval. On March 29, 1936, a plebiscite was held in which the German people approved of Hitler's action by a majority of 98.8 percent.

Four months after Hitler reoccupied the Rhineland, civil war broke out in Spain. Mussolini gave massive support to Franco; Hitler made a more modest commitment by sending a few token forces such as the

Condor Air Legion, a tank battalion, and some technical advisers. Germany was able to show solidarity with a struggling Fascist movement and also to test its pilots, planes, and military tactics in a kind of dress rehearsal for World War II. The Condor Air Legion later distinguished itself by pulverizing the Spanish town of Guernica and its civilian population, thus giving the world a preview of saturation bombing from the air as was so poignantly captured in the powerful images of Picasso's mural for the Pavilion of the Spanish Republic at the Paris International Exposition in 1937.

The crisis over Spain was an important turning point in Western diplomacy because it sealed Mussolini's decision to align himself with Hitler. Twice now the two dictators had found themselves joined against the Western powers, the first time when Hitler supported Mussolini over Ethiopia and the second in making common cause in Spain. The ground work was set for the Rome Berlin axis.[40] When the Fascists consolidated their victory in Spain, France found itself facing three Fascist powers on three borders — Spain, Germany, and Italy. Hitler had achieved a major strategic victory with minimal expenditure of resources,[41] bought himself the goodwill of Franco and Mussolini, tested new military equipment, and diverted Mussolini's attention from the Brenner Pass to the Mediterranean.

By late 1936 the Fascist powers were drawing closer together. Ribbentrop also began negotiating, behind the back of the Foreign Office, with the Japanese military attaché in Berlin regarding a common front against the Soviet Union. On November 25, 1936, a formal agreement, the Anti-Comintern Pact, was signed by Germany and Japan. This agreement, which Ribbentrop regarded as a personal triumph, meant Germany's abandoning support for Chiang Kai-shek and the recognition of Japan's puppet regime in Manchuria.

In 1937 the tone of Hitler's public speeches began to change dramatically as he cast off his pious pretensions for peace in favor of bellicose diatribes. In September 1937 Nazi Germany and Fascist Italy consolidated their friendship. Official visits between members of the two totalitarian states increased noticeably, culminating in a spectacular state visit by the Duce to Germany in late September (25–30) and Italy's adherence to the Anti-Comintern Pact. Hitler pulled all the stops of his propaganda machine and managed to spellbind his guest with a combination of unabashed flattery — you are "one of those lonely men of the ages on whom history is not tested, but who themselves are the makers of history"[42] — and awesome displays of military might. The result was the beginning of what F. W. Deakin has so aptly described as the "brutal friendship" between the two men, a friendship that was destined to destroy the Duce.

Only five days after a dazed Mussolini departed Germany, Hitler convened an important conference with his military and diplomatic chiefs, including Werner von Blomberg (defense), Werner von Fritsch (commander in chief of the army), Erich Raeder (commander in chief of the navy), Hermann Göring (commander in chief of the air force), and Konstantin von Neurath (foreign minister). The records of the conference were kept by Colonel Friedrich Hossbach and were later introduced in evidence at Nuremberg as illustrating Germany's premeditated decision to wage war of aggression on the world.[43]

Hitler unburdened himself by saying openly that his goal was to bolster the German racial community by expanding its territories into eastern Europe and Russia. Repeating his long-held convictions, already expressed twelve years before in the pages of *Mein Kampf* and only recently in a second but unpublished book, Hitler told his aides that Germany's greatest gains at the lowest cost would be obtained by the acquisition of living space rather than through economic autarky or economic competition with other nations. The immediate objective was the annexation of Austria and Czechoslovakia in order to secure Germany's eastern and southern flanks.

Far too much significance has been attributed to this document by the prosecution at Nuremberg and by later historians searching for a "smoking gun."[44] The conference was not the catalyst for Hitler's war of aggression; it was simply Hitler's means of clearing the air and testing the waters with his military chiefs. Judging by their cautious, if not downright alarmed, responses, Hitler knew that he had to shake up his high command in order to get the sort of generals who would obediently do his bidding as his "mad dogs."

Hitler's opportunity to shake up his obstreperous military staff was provided by the intrigues of Himmler and Heydrich, the self-appointed Nazi inquisitors who had been busy for some time in compiling secret dossiers on high-ranking military leaders because they wanted to bring the military under control of the SS. After the Röhm Purge, Himmler had been granted the right to form three SS regiments for the purpose of performing the sort of unsavory police duties the SS had engaged in during the Night of the Long Knives. Fritsch, however, regarded any further intrusion by the SS in army affairs as unacceptable, and he strenuously opposed Himmler's plans to convert his SS forces into fighting units. Himmler thereupon became Fritsch's sworn enemy and began to whisper into Hitler's ear that Fritsch and the army were conspiring against him.

Two scandals helped Hitler in purging his military command.[45] In January 1938 Hitler received information that Defense Minister Blomberg's second marriage, which he had personally attended only the previous month, was a great social embarrassment. It turned out that the general's much younger wife, his former secretary Eva Grühn, had once been a registered prostitute. Fritsch went to Hitler and persuaded him that Blomberg should be dismissed for the good of the army. The obvious successor to Blomberg was Fritsch himself, but the plot now thickened because Hitler had been sitting for two years on information supplied to him by Himmler that Fritsch was guilty of homosexual practices. Since he had not bothered to act on this information for two years, it was obvious that Hitler thought that Fritsch was innocent, as was subsequently proven, but the information could be highly useful to him as a means of getting rid of Fritsch. In a dramatic scene at the chancellery, Fritsch was confronted by his accuser, a stool pigeon who had been carefully put up to this charade by Himmler and Heydrich. Fritsch, generally a man of great composure, lost his temper, a pretext that Hitler used to declare him guilty. Fritsch was then asked to resign. Although Fritsch was later exonerated by a military court of honor, he was not reinstated.

On February 4, 1938, Hitler announced the resignation of Blomberg and Fritsch, the appointment of Walter von Brauchitsch as commander in chief of the army, and the promotion of Hermann Göring to the rank of field marshal. Blomberg's successor was none other than Hitler himself, who declared himself in personal command over the whole armed forces and promptly proceeded to replace the old Wehrmachtsamt with the Oberkommando der Wehrmacht (High Command of the Armed Forces [OKW]), putting himself in overall charge and delegating the routine management of the new OKW to a pliant yes-man named Keitel, later renamed by cynical Germans as "Lakeitel," a play on the German word *Lakei* (lackey).

The Fritsch and Blomberg affair was not the first nor would it be the last episode exposing an alarming failure of nerve among the German generals. Despite periodic gestures of sluggish self-assertion, usually followed by abject submission, the generals would always bow obediently to the will of the führer. With an obedient and compliant army behind him, Hitler could embark on a series of risky adventures in foreign policy. The first was the crisis over Austria, and it was surely no accident that it occurred only one week after Hitler shook up his military command and replaced the mild-mannered Neurath with the aggressive Ribbentrop.

The Annexation of Austria

Hitler was an Austrian who had always insisted that his native homeland was German and that "common blood belongs in a common Reich."[46] After seizing power in 1933 he actively supported the Nazi Party in Austria and urged his followers to engage in clandestine operations against the Austrian government. As previously noted, this policy backfired in 1934, when Chancellor Dollfuss was murdered and the Putsch was put down by the Austrian authorities. Dollfuss was replaced by Kurt von Schuschnigg, a member of the Dollfuss cabinet, and the assassins were tried and executed by the Austrian government. Hitler was temporarily embarrassed, disavowed all knowledge of the Putsch, and publicly pledged to respect the political and territorial integrity of Austria.

Privately, however, Hitler was merely biding his time before attempting to extract further concessions from the Austrian government. In July 1936 Franz von Papen, Hitler's ambassador to Vienna, concluded a "gentlemen's agreement" with Austria by which Hitler promised to respect Austrian sovereignty.[47] The two countries pledged close cooperation in foreign policy since they were both "German" states. The agreement also called for relaxation of the propaganda war waged by both sides, amnesty for political prisoners, and removal of economic restrictions against tourists. Most importantly, the Austro-German Agreement obliged the Austrian government to allow members of the National Opposition a share in political responsibility. Since the members of the National Opposition were proannexationists, Hitler had scored a major political concession. One of the proannexationists was Dr. Artur Seyss-Inquart, Hitler's inside man in the Austrian government.[48] Seyss-Inquart, who had come from Moravia, had served as a highly decorated officer in World War I and held a doctoral degree in law from the University of Vienna. After the war he had established a successful law practice in Vienna and joined several nationalistic organizations including the Styrian Home Guard. When Hitler came to power the Styrian Home Guard was taken over by the Austrian Nazi Party and Seyss-Inquart became closely associated with the Nazi cause. However, he did not formally join the party until after the annexation of Austria by Germany in 1938. In 1937, Seyss-Inquart was appointed to the Federal State Council, Austria's cabinet. In this position he would become a key player in subverting Austria for Hitler.

Hitler's decision to force a timely resolution of the Austrian problem took shape in November 1937. By that time the führer was relatively certain that Mussolini would not lift a finger to save Austria, and he strongly suspected that the other major powers would not come to its defense either. On November 6, 1937, the Duce informed Ribbentrop that he had told the French that Italy would not move against Germany if a crisis should arise in Austria. On November 19, Lord Halifax, the future British foreign minister, met Hitler at the Berghof in order to sound him out on various political issues. Although Halifax had gone to Germany to visit Göring's International Hunters' Exhibition, he had been charged by Prime Minister Chamberlain to use this occasion to gauge Hitler's intentions. Halifax found out very quickly what was on Hitler's mind — Austria and Czechoslovakia.[49] A close relationship between Germany and Austria, Hitler insisted, must be brought about because both peoples desired it. Furthermore, the brutal treatment accorded to the Sudeten Germans had to stop forthwith. Germany's intentions, Hitler suggested, were entirely peaceful; he strongly rejected foreign criticism that he had ulterior motives in southern Europe. Moved by Hitler's solemn promises to preserve peace, Halifax made an extraordinary admission, namely, that Great Britain was ready to explore any solution as long as it was not based on force. He specifically mentioned

Austria, Czechoslovakia, and Danzig, conveying the unmistakable impression that the British government saw no reason why Germany's grievances in these areas could not be appeased. Since Halifax presumably reflected the thinking of Chamberlain, Hitler inferred that he could expect neutrality from Britain if he chose to annex Austria. French thinking on this subject did not markedly differ from that of the British, as evidenced by a revealing remark from Yvon Delbos, France's foreign minister, to the effect that France had no essential objection to a further assimilation of certain of Austria's domestic institutions with Germany's.[50]

This is all that Hitler needed to know before tightening the noose around Austria's neck. The question was merely how the subversion of Austria's independence should be accomplished. Hitler clearly preferred a peaceful solution; he had no intention of provoking a military confrontation, thinking that a strategy of harassment and intimidation would just as well serve his aim of replacing Schuschnigg's government with a more pliable pro-Nazi regime.

In the meantime, Schuschnigg's choices were diminishing rapidly. Abandoned by his fickle allies, he could not even be sure of the support of his own people, most of whom had been exposed to a barrage of Nazi propaganda for years and secretly pined to be incorporated into the German Reich. In January, Schuschnigg agreed reluctantly to Papen's suggestion of a personal meeting with Hitler at Berchtesgaden. It was the beginning of the end of Austrian independence.

On a cold winter morning, February 12, 1938, the Austrian chancellor and his secretary of state for foreign affairs, Guido Schmidt, embarked on their fateful journey to the Obersalzberg. As they reached the border, they were met by Papen, who briefed them on their upcoming discussion with the führer and told them not to be apprehensive about the presence of high-ranking generals. When they arrived at the Berghof, Hitler met them personally and ushered them into his private study. The Austrian chancellor barely managed to utter some small talk about the breathtaking view when Hitler impatiently waived aside such remarks and launched into a prolonged attack against Austria's treacherous past:

> The whole history of Austria (Hitler bitterly complained) is just one uninterrupted act of high treason. That was so in the past, and is no better to-day. This historical paradox must now reach its long-overdue end. And I can tell you here and now, Herr Schuschnigg, that I am absolutely determined to make an end of all this. The German Reich is one of the Great Powers, and nobody will raise his voice if it settles its border problems.[51]

As Hitler droned on, working himself into a frenzy of self-induced anger, Schuschnigg squirmed uncomfortably in his seat, his nervousness heightened by the fact that, as a chain-smoker, he was not allowed to light up in the führer's presence. He meekly submitted himself for two hours to a stream of abuse. Describing himself as the "greatest German of all times," Hitler told the Austrian chancellor that he was unstoppable and could walk into Austria at any time he pleased. This is why he was particularly offended by Austria's feeble efforts to fortify the frontier. Neither border defenses nor meaningless pledges by foreign powers would deter him from settling the Austrian problem once and for all. Unless the Austrian government acceded to all of his demands, he would settle his account by force. Of course, being a reasonable man, he preferred peaceful solutions; but unless Schuschnigg acted immediately, not even he could prevent German revenge from taking its just toll:

> Think it over, Herr Schuschnigg, think it over well. I can only wait until this afternoon. If I tell you that, you will do well to take my words literally. I don't believe in bluffing, all my past is proof of that.[52]

After having delivered this blatant threat to another head of state, Hitler suddenly reverted to his role of the charming host and entertained the Austrian chancellor for lunch. He held forth on a variety of subjects in his usual monologue style, astonishing Schuschnigg with outlandish boasts about building the greatest skyscrapers the world had ever seen. After lunch, Hitler excused himself and left his Austrian visitors guessing about the next surprise he had in store for them. In the middle of the afternoon, Schuschnigg was ushered into the company of Ribbentrop and Papen and presented with a draft document relating to his country's future. As he read the document, he realized that it was really an ultimatum; the Austrian government was to lift the ban against the Nazi Party, release all imprisoned pro-Nazi agitators, and appoint Seyss-Inquart as minister of the interior with full authority to enforce the provisions of these demands. In addition, Edmund von Glaise-Horstenau, another pro-Nazi, was to be appointed minister of war, and the German and Austrian armies were to cooperate closely on a number of common issues, most notably exchange of officers. Finally, Hitler's ultimatum insisted on merging Austria into the German economic system and designated Dr. Hans Fischböck, another pro-Nazi, as the future minister of finance.

Schuschnigg gasped at the implications of these proposals, for he knew that they would lead to the destruction of an independent Austria. Ribbentrop strongly begged Schuschnigg to accept Hitler's demands or accept the consequences; and when the addled Austrian chancellor found himself in Hitler's presence a little later, his worst suspicions were confirmed. Hitler flatly informed him that he had no intention of changing a single iota in the draft document and that if Schuschnigg did not sign it, he would march into Austria. The bluff worked. Schuschnigg agreed to sign the document, but he told Hitler that under the Austrian constitution only the president, Dr. Wilhelm Miklas, possessed the legal power to ratify such an agreement. Schuschnigg added that he would do his best to persuade the president to accept the demands, but unfortunately he could not guarantee ratification. "You have to guarantee it," Hitler shouted at the Austrian chancellor in a fit of anger. When Schuschnigg replied that he could not give such a guarantee, Hitler flung open the door of his study and shouted: "General Keitel." To Schuschnigg he said menacingly: "I shall have you called later," ushering him out of the room. When Keitel trotted obediently into the führer's study ready to await his orders, Hitler merely grinned at him and said, "There are no orders, I just wanted you here."[53] Outside the führer's study, however, the anxious Austrian visitors, overawed by the presence of German generals, were intimidated and expected to be arrested at any moment. Half an hour later Schuschnigg was called into Hitler's presence again. This time, Hitler pretended to be magnanimous: "I have decided to change my mind," he announced dramatically, "for the first time in my life. But I warn you this is your very last chance. I have given you three additional days to carry out the agreement."[54]

The psychological pressure told on the young Austrian chancellor, and he meekly agreed to sign Hitler's document. As a final humiliation, Hitler brushed aside Schuschnigg's suggestion that the press release of their meeting should mention a confirmation of the 1936 agreement. "Oh no," Hitler insisted, "first you have to fulfill the conditions of our agreement. This is what is going to the press: 'To-day the Fuehrer and Reichskanzler conferred with the Austrian Bundeskanzler at the Berghof.' That's all."[55]

Declining the führer's invitation for supper, Schuschnigg and Schmidt drove down the mountain and back to Salzburg. As the Austrians brooded in silence about their humiliation, the garrulous von Papen, who had decided to accompany them to the border, chatted amiably about the days events: "Well, now," he fatuously remarked to Schuschnigg, "you have seen what the Fuehrer can be like at times. But the next time I am sure it will be quite different. You know, the Fuehrer can be absolutely charming."[56]

When Schuschnigg began to implement the provisions of his agreement with Hitler, appointing Seyss-Inquart as minister of the interior, he recognized what he had known all along: the control of the government was slipping away from him. During the first week of March, he seized upon a desperate and eventually fatal expedient: he determined to call a plebiscite, asking the voters whether they favored a free, independent, and Christian Austria. By thus consulting the voters, Schuschnigg hoped that the electorate would return a favorable verdict and thereby undercut Hitler's assertion that the majority of Austrians favored annexation. This would give him the sort of moral victory he could use to thwart further attempts on Hitler's part to resolve the Austrian question by force. Schuschnigg knew that, as it stood, Austria's position was politically untenable because no foreign power would lift a finger to save it. But he also believed that a victory at the polls would give him a moral edge by which he could oppose Hitler. The electorate, of course, might conceivably return an unfavorable verdict, in which case the whole exercise would turn out not only futile but self-defeating. This is why Schuschnigg bent every effort to rig the election in order to produce a favorable result. The proposition he intended to put in front of the voters ("With Schuschnigg for Austria, we want a free and a German Austria, an independent and a social Austria, a Christian and a united Austria") was patently self-serving as well as confusing. Austrians were informed on March 9 that the plebiscite would be held only four days later, on March 13; they were given two choices — to vote either yes or no. In addition, Schuschnigg's own political party, the Fatherland Front, a pale replica of the Nazi Party, was to be in charge of the election committees overseeing the plebiscite. Since elections had not been held and registries of eligible voters had not been kept in Austria since 1930, Schuschnigg was confident that he could produce a favorable result.

Hitler seems to have been seriously taken aback by Schuschnigg's announcement of a plebiscite, but he quickly recovered from the shock and acted because he could not take the risk of being defeated at the polls. The plebiscite could not be permitted unless the outcome was a foregone conclusion, and that presupposed the annexation of Austria.

The plebiscite, planned for March 13, therefore never occurred. Early on March 11, Schuschnigg was informed by Seyss-Inquart and Glaise-Horstenau, the two pro-Nazi ministers in his cabinet who were taking their orders directly from Berlin, that Hitler demanded a postponement of the plebiscite. After some soul searching, Schuschnigg accepted the Nazi demands. The two Nazi stooges immediately rushed back to the telephone, an act that they would repeat many times throughout that fateful day, to inform Göring of Schuschnigg's decision. From Berlin, Göring directed the Viennese Nazis in carrying out Hitler's orders. When Göring heard that Schuschnigg had consented to the postponement of the plebiscite, he knew that he could press his demands even further. With the insolence of the reckless political gambler he was, he demanded Schuschnigg's resignation within one hour and the appointment of Seyss-Inquart as his successor. These orders were backed up by the threat of force, made all the more humiliating by the fact that they were relayed to Schuschnigg by his designated successor — the pliable go-between, Seyss-Inquart.

Such provocative behavior demanded determined opposition by Schuschnigg and the Austrian government. Faced by naked force, however, Schuschnigg was the first to cave in by announcing that he was ready to resign. Although Schuschnigg turned out to be an easy target, the story was somewhat different when it came to President Miklas, upon whom the task of appointment and removal from office depended. He accepted Schuschnigg's resignation, but he opposed the appointment of Seyss-Inquart to the office of chancellor. He held out until midnight; by this time, seeing that everyone had deserted him, he, too, grudgingly surrendered. Austria had thus been taken over by the Nazis.

Throughout the day Göring had been busy assigning jobs over the telephone. These telephone conversations, whose taped records were uncovered after the war, are extremely revealing because they illustrate the cynical disregard for law and justice of the Nazi leadership. By the end of the day the coup had been completed. Seyss-Inquart was now chancellor, but he had been given no choice in the selection of his staff. These positions had been preselected in Berlin by Göring, who was barking out his orders over the telephone to his brother-in-law, Dr. Huebner, in Vienna. In this amazing telephone conversation, which was not without its lighter side, Göring conferred appointments while birds could be heard twittering in the background:

> Now listen, Franz. You take over the Department of Justice, and on the expressed desire of the Fuehrer, you also take Foreign Affairs for the time being.... Of the cabinet posts he [Fischböck] is to reserve Commerce for himself; Kaltenbrunner gets Security.[57]

Although Göring engineered the *Anschluss* by remote control, the local Austrian Nazis were by no means idle. Even before President Miklas had approved the appointment of Seyss-Inquart, they made themselves at home in the chancellery, cleaning out other people's desks and acting as though they already owned the building. As Schuschnigg pathetically observed later:

> Suddenly I noticed a number of young people in the hall again with that close-cropped haircut. One young man brushed past me without an apology. He turned round and looked me up and down with a purposely offensive, superior smile. Then he went on and slammed the door as if he were at home. I stared after him, and suddenly I realized: Invasion! Not at the borders as yet but here, in the Chancellery: the Gestapo.[58]

The fate of Austria was sealed. Seyss-Inquart, who had been chosen to play the role of Judas, hoped to secure at least some semblance of independence. In this he was seriously mistaken, for two days later, the day on which the original plebiscite was to have taken place, a law went into effect that proclaimed Austria a province of the German Reich, to be referred to no longer as Austria (Österreich), a name Hitler hated, but simply Ostmark.[59]

Hitler had violated treaties and promises and, most amazingly, he had achieved his goal again without bloodshed. Indeed, when he entered Austria, the enthusiasm of the Austrians knew no bounds. With streets adorned with swastikas and flowers, he entered Vienna like an oriental potentate, eagerly accepting the resounding cheers of eighty thousand Viennese.

Why was Hitler able to achieve this act of aggression without a single, determined protest from the Western powers? Schuschnigg had labored under the illusion that Mussolini was still the protector of Austrian independence when in reality he had long shifted his focus from Austria to the Mediterranean. As a result of this shift, Mussolini had drawn closer to Germany and initiated the Rome-Berlin axis. Thus, when Austria's day of reckoning came, Italy deserted it. By the spring of 1938 Mussolini had become convinced that the *Anschluss* was inevitable and that it would be unwise for Italy to get involved in a conflict between Austria and Germany. Asking the Italians for advice, Schuschnigg was told to act according to his own conscience.[60]

Italy clearly had abandoned Schuschnigg to his own devices. Hitler had been quite right when he told Schuschnigg at Berchtesgaden that he saw eye to eye with Mussolini; yet he seems to have had considerable qualms on the day of the Austrian *Anschluss,* dispatching a personal letter to Mussolini in which he tried to justify his action and promised he would never reopen the issue of the South Tyrolians who had been living in Italy since 1919. When Prince Philip of Hesse, who had been sent to hand deliver Hitler's message to Mussolini, telephoned Hitler that the Duce accepted the whole thing in a very friendly manner, Hitler was literally choked up with gratitude, pledging to support the Duce through thick and thin:

HITLER: Then please tell Mussolini I will never forget him for this.

HESSE: Yes.

HITLER: Never, never, never, whatever happens.... As soon as the Austrian affair is settled, I shall be ready to go with him through thick or thin, no matter what happens.

HESSE: Yes, my Führer.

HITLER: Listen, I shall make any agreement — I am no longer in fear of the terrible position which would have existed militarily in case we had got into a conflict. You may tell him that I thank him ever so much; never, never shall I forget.

HESSE: Yes, my Führer.

HITLER: I will never forget, whatever may happen. If he should ever need any help or be in any danger, he can be convinced that I shall stick to him, whatever may happen, even if the whole world were against him.

HESSE: Yes, My Führer.[61]

With Italy staying aloof from this conflict, there were still France and Great Britain to whom Schuschnigg could appeal for help. This he did, but the answer in both cases was negative. French politicians uttered many platitudes, but failed to act when the time came. Describing the general atmosphere in Paris during this crisis, the German embassy reported to Berlin that "the attitude prevailing to date has been characterized by a feeling of impotence in the face of the closer union of the two German states which is being initiated diplomatically and legally."[62] Frenchmen had risked their necks twice before in a war with Germany; they had no intentions of plunging head-on into another one. Thus the German embassy reported that "in many places [Frenchmen] are saying

'Finis Austriae!' "[63] Aside from general apathy in France, there was another incident that paralyzed any prospects for French intervention. On March 10, a day before the Austrian *Anschluss,* the Camille Chautemps cabinet had fallen from power. France therefore did not even have a government on March 11.

The situation was somewhat different in Great Britain. Anthony Eden had vigorously protested the Berchtesgaden Agreement and, along with several other leaders, most notably Churchill, had attempted to revive the Stresa Declaration. Unfortunately, in their communications with the British, the Austrians were minimizing the seriousness of their problem with Hitler. This attitude, as Gordon Brook-Shepherd has said, actually pulled the carpet from under Eden's feet.[64] Eden resigned, causing a cabinet crisis over the Austrian question. On its own accord, Great Britain would not act, as Ribbentrop correctly informed Hitler.

The *Anschluss* and the methods that brought it about had far-reaching consequences. Hitler had gambled successfully again. He became convinced that his strategy of ruthless power politics had been vindicated and that it was the only effective policy against his war-weary and vacillating opponents. Aside from reinforcing Hitler's belief in the effectiveness of international blackmail and intimidation, the *Anschluss* also had far-reaching consequences in the field of diplomacy. It promoted the friendship of the two Fascist tyrants — Hitler and Mussolini, and this further polarized European powers. Another consequence of the *Anschluss* was that Germany's strategic position was greatly enhanced. With Vienna at his disposal Hitler had acquired direct access to the whole of southeastern Europe. From Vienna it was only a footstep to Czechoslovakia, Hungary, and Yugoslavia.

The Sudeten Crisis and Appeasement at Munich

Ever since Hitler had outlined his aggressive plans to his military chiefs in November 1937, the German dictator was convinced that the Western powers would not lift a finger for Austria and Czechoslovakia. Every private conversation with Western diplomats seemed to confirm him in this judgment; and when the Austrian plum fell into his hands without difficulty in March 1938, he decided to escalate his aggressive ambitions. Although prepared to go to war over the Sudetenland issue, Hitler fully expected that his war-weary opponents would cave in to his demands. His strategy was to create a warlike atmosphere that would galvanize the Western powers into diplomatic initiatives aimed at forcing the Czechs to make concessions. His trump card was national self-determination; his ultimate aim was the destruction of the Czechoslovakian state.

The new state of Czechoslovakia, as previously noted, was given the boundaries of the ancient provinces of Bohemia, Moravia, and part of

Austrian Silesia. These territories included a mountainous ring around the core of the new Czech state, made up predominantly of about three million German-speaking inhabitants, who resented their new status as Czechoslovakian subjects. Known as the Sudeten Germans, they represented a special threat to the new democratic government in Prague because they constituted a potential state within a state. Political resentment was exacerbated by economic hardship, producing a volatile atmosphere the Nazis could exploit for their own ends.

Czechoslovakia was a well governed, progressive state; its people were hard-working and proud of their national heritage. Moreover, in Thomas Masaryk and Edward Benes, the two architects of the republic, the Czech people possessed statesmen of the highest caliber and foresight. Cherishing few illusions about Germany, the Czechs had entered into a series of pacts and alliances, notably with France (1924) and Russia (1935), in the hope of deterring German aggression. Czechoslovakia was a member of the League of Nations and had been the chief catalyst in the establishment of the Little Entente. Unlike the Western powers, who were eager to appease Hitler, the Czechs consistently refused to negotiate with the Nazis, preferring instead to put their trust in a sound military defense and the word of their allies.

In Hitler's jaundiced view, however, Czechoslovakia represented everything he despised: Slavic inferiors, a commitment to democracy, and friendship with France and Russia.[65] After the annexation of Austria he made it clear that he would "smash the Czechs in the near future" — not because Czechoslovakia harbored three million Sudeten Germans but because it was a stepping stone on the way to achieving his ultimate territorial intention — the conquest of living space in the east. Hitler, of course, found it useful to disguise this goal behind a rhetorical smoke screen of self-determination for three million Sudeten Germans.

In the meantime, he banked on the war-weariness of the Western powers and their suspicion of the Soviet Union. He suspected that the Western powers would exert strong pressure on Prague before they even seriously entertained military intervention; he also suspected that Czechoslovakia's allies — France and Russia — were fair-weather friends who would abandon their Czechs allies when their own security was endangered. Russian support of Czechoslovakia hinged on the stipulation that the guarantees offered to Prague would not go into effect unless the French government first carried out its obligation to Czechoslovakia. France was not likely to do this without the support of England.

The key to Czech security, therefore, resided in Britain. One would assume that a nascent democratic government, imperiled on all sides by totalitarian states, would have found in Britain a strong defender of its territorial and political integrity. In practice, the opposite happened. The Conservative government in Britain, headed by Neville Chamberlain, distrusted the Czech government because its political influence far exceeded the small size of its territory. Europe had been dragged into world war by a small power before, and Chamberlain was determined to prevent this from happening again. As early as April 1938 he told Daladier that he did not believe that Hitler wanted to destroy Czechoslovakia, but if it happened, he did not see what Britain could do to prevent it.[66]

The truth is that many Western statesmen increasingly viewed Czechoslovakia as a political liability, a sort of indiscretion against geography. In fact, the centrifugal forces within the new state of Czechoslovakia were so strong that not only the Germans but also the Slovaks, Poles, and Hungarians demanded increasing autonomy within the new federation, lending credence to Hitler's assertion that Czechoslovakia was a historical mistake. Czechoslovakia thus appeared to be a doomed nation, torn apart by centrifugal forces within, menaced by predatory powers without, and increasingly abandoned by its own friends.

Hitler's Trojan horse within Czechoslovakia was the Sudeten German Party (Sudetendeutsche Partei) under the leadership of Konrad Henlein (1898–1945), an ex-serviceman and gymnastics instructor who had been on the Nazi payroll since 1935. In a secret meeting with Hitler on March 28, 1938, Henlein was instructed always to demand more from the Prague government than it was willing to concede and to keep up a relentless campaign of propaganda and agitation. Upon his return, Henlein rejected several reasonable offers from the Czech government to alleviate ethnic tensions and countered with an eight-point program of his own called the Karlsbad Program. This document essentially proposed to establish a state within a state, calling upon the Czech government to revise its whole foreign policy and to right the historical injustices perpetrated against the Sudeten Germans through monetary restitution.[67] The Czech government contemptuously rejected this "reasonable" offer because it would have meant the end of Czech sovereignty.

The rejection of the Karlsbad Program by the Czech government forced Hitler to pursue alternate strategies of subverting Czech independence. On April 21, Hitler and Keitel discussed a number of alternatives, and they sketched out a plan (Operation Green), to be implemented by October 1, which called for an invasion of Czechoslovakia. Hitler even explored the possibility of creating a convenient incident such as the assassination of the German minister at Prague as a pretext for a military attack on Czechoslovakia. This was not the first time that he had entertained such criminal notions. A few months before the annexation of Austria, he had toyed with the idea of assassinating the German ambassador and his military attaché, blaming the Austrians for it, and using the incident as a pretext for invading Austria. These dark ruminations about assassinating one's own ambassador (Papen!), as John Wheeler-Bennett sardonically observed, gave a new and added unpleasantness to the term *traveiller pour le roi de Prusse.*[68]

The climate of political opinion, especially in some circles of the German military, was not favorable to the kind of aggression Hitler was planning. General Ludwig Beck, chief of staff of the army, and several other high-ranking officers opposed Hitler's bellicose territorial demands because they felt that Germany was inadequately prepared for war. Although Beck resigned as chief of staff of the army after receiving half-hearted support from General Brauchitsch, commander in chief of the army, he continued to intrigue against Hitler along with several conspirators. These formed the original nucleus of the later German resistance movement. Besides Beck, the men involved were Carl Goerdeler, former mayor of Leipzig; Ulrich von Hassell, ambassador to Rome until February 1938; Generals Erwin von Witzleben and Erich Hoepner; Colonel Hans Oster, a member of the secret service (Abwehr); and Ewald von Kleist, an East Elbian landowner. The group wanted to arrest Hitler as soon as he attacked Czechoslovakia and put him on trial in front of the People's Court.

In the meantime, Czech president Eduard Benes was essentially willing to meet most of Henlein's earlier demands, but in accordance with Hitler's policy of always increasing demands at the very moment they were about to be met, Henlein suddenly broke off negotiations and left for Germany to await further instructions. Here he found Hitler engaged in a battle of wills with his generals. There were also signs that the Western powers would back up Czechoslovakia. Henlein was therefore sent back to continue his game until the moment was ripe. Throughout the summer of 1938 the Nazis created a constant atmosphere of crisis. German newspapers and radio broadcasts talked in hysterical terms about terrible outrages committed by the Czechs against the Sudeten Germans. Hitler redrafted his directive for Operation Green, which now opened with the words: "It is my unalterable decision to smash Czechoslovakia by military action in the near future."[69] The attack, after being postponed several times, was now set for October 1, 1938. Propaganda attacks were also increased, and Hitler's campaign against the Czechs culminated in a venomous speech in front of a huge audience on the final day of the Nuremberg Party congress.[70]

Hitler's speech was meant to be a signal for a general rising in Czechoslovakia, but relatively few incidents occurred because the Czech government declared marshall law and promptly put down Nazi acts of terrorism. It was clear that if Czechoslovakia was to fall, it was not going to be from within. Indeed, as Allan Bullock observed, "The failure of nerve came, not in Prague but in Paris,"[71] where chaos and confusion were the order of the day. Daladier and his cabinet argued bitterly over the right course of action, some pleading for active resistance to Hitler's aggression, while others insisted that France should not risk a war over Czechoslovakia. The appeasers pointed out that Britain's support of Czechoslovakia was at best lukewarm, that Russia would never fight, that Germany was too powerful, that military preparations were inadequate, and that, in any case, Czechoslovakia would be overrun long before France could come to its aid. Unable to reconcile these insistent pleas, Daladier put the onus not on Hitler but on Chamberlain, urging him to negotiate an acceptable settlement with Hitler.

On September 13, Chamberlain dispatched a telegram to Hitler suggesting a personal meeting with the führer in hopes of peacefully resolving the Czechoslovakian crisis. The prospect of being visited by a British prime minister, twenty years his senior, making his first flight to see him, immensely appealed to Hitler's vanity: "Ich bin vom Himmel gefallen" (I fell from heaven), he reportedly exclaimed after receiving Chamberlain's telegram.[72] On September 15, Chamberlain met Hitler at the Berghof. Hitler was friendly but insistent that the Sudeten Germans had to be returned to the Reich. Chamberlain came away from this meeting convinced that Hitler meant business; he also seems to have made up his mind to put strong pressure on the Czechs to release the Sudeten Germans. Upon his return to England, Chamberlain immediately went to work on the French and the Czechs and tried to convince them to meet Hitler's demands.

On September 22, Chamberlain flew to Germany again, this time meeting Hitler at Godesberg on the Rhine. When he arrived in Cologne he was accorded the highest diplomatic honors, being greeted by an SS guard and a band that played "God Save the King." On his way to the Petersburg Hotel at Godesberg, he was greeted by Union Jacks and swastikas fluttering in the wind and jubilant crowds cheering him as the harbinger of peace. After conferring with his ambassador, Chamberlain was ferried across the Rhine to meet Hitler at the Hotel Dreesen; he was confident that war had been averted. He had good reason to feel optimistic because since his Berchtesgaden meeting a week before he had cajoled and pressured the Czechs into surrendering to Hitler's demands. Between his first and second meeting with Hitler, Chamberlain had in fact procured an Anglo-French agreement, imposed as a fait accompli on the disillusioned Czechs, which specified that the Sudetenland was to be transferred to Germany without a plebiscite. He was obviously pleased with his accomplishment, but when he met Hitler he was informed by the petulant dictator: "I'm exceedingly sorry, but after the events of the last few days the solution is no longer any use."[73]

Having staked his political career on this peace proposal, Chamberlain was angry and puzzled by Hitler's capricious behavior. After all, he had given him everything he thought that Hitler wanted — the Sudetenland — but it now turned out that Hitler wanted to occupy the Sudetenland by a specific time, October 1, claiming that the Czechs would take advantage of a longer process. He now demanded an immediate withdrawal by the Czechs from the Sudetenland or he would send in his army to expel them.

The whole meeting was vintage Hitler: theatrical outbursts followed by appeals to reason and commonsense. As Chamberlain prepared to leave the meeting place in the Hotel Dreesen, Hitler followed him out to the terrace and in a soft voice told the prime minister: "I'm sorry; I had looked forward to showing you this beautiful view of the Rhine, but now it is hidden by the mist."[74] The next day, September 23, Chamberlain tried once more to appeal to Hitler's reason, writing him a letter in which he pointed out the danger of German troops moving into the Sudetenland immediately upon the ceding of these territories. He added that this would almost certainly force the Czechs to take measures and further undermine "the basis upon which a week ago you and I agreed to work together."[75]

Hitler flew into a rage upon receipt of this letter and replied by repeating his previous demands. Chamberlain responded with a cool and courteous note, directed Sir Horace Wilson and Sir Neville Henderson to draw up a memorandum of the German proposals for transmission to Prague, and prepared to leave Germany. Apparently impressed by Chamberlain's determination, Hitler arranged for a further meeting at 10:30 P.M., September 23. During this meeting Chamberlain was presented with a memorandum that required that the Czechs start evacuating the predominantly German territories by 8·00 A.M. on September 26 and complete such operations two days later. The British prime minister correctly pointed out that this was not a memorandum but an ultimatum, to which Hitler sheepishly replied, pointing to the title, that the document was called a memorandum. At this point Chamberlain cast aside his British reserve and accused Hitler of undermining his sincere efforts to preserve the peace. Impressed by Chamberlain's outburst, Hitler amended the memorandum in his own hand, extending the time limit to October 1, a token gesture that did not alter the content of the proposal since Hitler still insisted on military occupation. Hitler was obviously pleased with this magnanimous "compromise" and confessed to Chamberlain: "You are the only man to whom I have ever made a concession."[76] Chamberlain's spirits revived, and he came away from the meeting with renewed hope; he even expressed the feeling that a special confidence had grown up between himself and Hitler. As to the führer, he made a hypocritical statement that would later incriminate him in the eyes of the world: the Czech problem, he asserted, was the last territorial demand he would make in Europe.

However, when Chamberlain returned to England with his "memorandum," which he had earlier described as really being an ultimatum, his cabinet decisively rejected it. War now seemed imminent. In a final appeal to Hitler, Chamberlain sent Sir Horace Wilson to Germany with a personal letter to the führer, informing him that although the Czech government had rejected the Godesberg proposals, there was still some hope that the issue could be resolved by direct German-Czech negotiations with Britain serving as neutral arbitrator.

Hitler was in an ugly mood when Wilson met him on September 26; and when Dr. Schmidt, his translator, read the words "The Czech government regarded the proposal as wholly unacceptable," Hitler jumped up from his chair and shouted: "Then there is no point at all in going on with negotiations,"[77] and made his way toward the door. The diplomatic discourtesy of leaving his guests stranded in his own study must have struck Hitler by the time he reached the door and he returned "like a sulking adolescent" to listen to the rest of the letter. When Schmidt finished, Hitler ranted and raved, complaining that the Germans were being treated like "niggers"; he didn't care a farthing whether England or France struck at him over Czechoslovakia. He would negotiate with the Czechs on the basis of the Godesberg proposals, he said, but nothing would deter him from occupying the Sudetenland by October 1. If Sir Horace Wilson really wanted to know how Germany felt, he remarked shortly before the British envoy left, he should listen to his upcoming speech at the Berlin Sportspalast.[78]

When Wilson called on Hitler a second time on Tuesday, September 27, the day following the Sportspalast speech, he found Hitler even more intransigent and belligerent, screaming that he would smash Czechoslovakia no matter what the French or British threatened to do. Wilson came away from this meeting with the firm conviction that, unless appeased, Hitler would really go to war over the Czechoslovakian question. In reality, Hitler had not completely foreclosed the possibility of a negotiated settlement, particularly since his military chiefs were almost unanimously opposed to fighting a war with France and England. Public opinion in Germany was also running against war, which was brought home personally to Hitler by the lack of enthusiasm that the crowds showed to a mechanized division in full field equipment that rumbled through Berlin on the afternoon of September 27.

As Hitler's deadline approached, the governments of Europe braced themselves for war. As this point, Mussolini became the key man who kept everybody from fighting. Apprehensive about a general European war, which Italy was ill equipped to fight, the Duce put considerable pressure on Hitler to extend his deadline and examine the proposals put forward by London and Paris. He sent Bernardo Attolico, his ambassador in Berlin, with a personal appeal to Hitler. Meanwhile, Chamberlain sent his final reply to Hitler's letter of September 27, suggesting an international conference in order to adjudicate the Czech-German problem. The Duce urged Hitler to agree to this proposal and volunteered Italy's willingness to participate in such a conference. In the early afternoon on September 28, Hitler agreed to Chamberlain's proposal and, on Mussolini's advice, picked Munich as the location for the conference, sending out invitations to London and Paris, but not Prague or Moscow.

The Munich Conference is generally regarded as the apogee of Neville Chamberlain's ill-fated policy of appeasement.[79] In retrospect, this strategy of appeasement appears politically indefensible and even cowardly, but at the time it was widely hailed as an act of sapient statesmanship.

What motivated it was not so much ignorance or cowardice but fear and guilt — fear of another senseless war and guilt of having stripped Germany of its status as a great power and humiliating it in the process. Additionally, the appeasers were painfully aware of their own lack of military preparedness. In addition, their fear of Communism was far stronger than their fear of Hitler, a psychological fact that the passage of time tends to obscure for us today.

Among the ranks of the British appeasers were the prime minister, Neville Chamberlain, Sir John Simon, Sir Samuel Hoare, and Lord Halifax, while the French appeasers included, among others, Edouard Daladier, the French premier, and George Bonnet, his foreign minister. None of these men, though they might have been politically naive, could be described as pro-Nazi or even pro-German. The best that can be said of them — and that is perhaps not very much — is that they were sincere. In fairness to the appeasers, no one could have anticipated the degree of infamy with which statesmen had to contend in their dealings with Hitler, but John Wheeler-Bennett is undoubtedly right in saying that "there is something tragically hideous and pathetic in this belief of Mr. Chamberlain that he could match wits and exchange troths with Hitler" and that "with the past record of broken Nazi pledges before him, he was culpably credulous in his dealings with Hitler."[80] The same may be said of Daladier, "the patriot without strength of will," who had fought bravely and gallantly in World War I but emerged from the struggle with the firm conviction, shared by most of his compatriots, that France must never be drawn into a similar holocaust. The French premier also had the misfortune of being surrounded by advisers of dubious moral quality and competence.

The Munich Conference, which took place on September 29 and 30, was an anticlimax, a ratification of Hitler's nonnegotiable demands vis-à-vis Czechoslovakia. Hitler had met Mussolini's train on the German-Austrian frontier early on September 29 and made no secret of his belligerent attitude, informing the Duce that he was prepared to launch a lightning attack on Czechoslovakia followed by a campaign against France. Mussolini tried to temporize his ally's recklessness and suggested that Hitler give the conference a chance before resorting to war. It was, in fact, Mussolini who set the tone and provided the leadership of the Munich Conference. Since he spoke the languages of the participants, he was able to ease some of the social pressures to which the excitable and awkward Hitler was exposed. The two dictators presented themselves in martial splendor; it was their moment to show the world the contrast between Fascist strength of will and democratic weakness.

The basis of discussion at Munich was a memorandum submitted by Mussolini, but actually prepared by the Germans.[81] The document was a mere copy, with slight variation, of the Godesberg proposals. Hitler's only concession was that he would not occupy all of the Czechoslovakian areas that were to be surrendered to Germany until October 10. An international commission, composed of the four signatory powers, was to determine which territories were predominantly German and to draw the borders accordingly.

On September 30 the agreement was signed, and on the next day German troops marched into the Sudetenland. Being in control of the actual implementation of the agreement, Hitler could effectively brush aside the few obstacles placed in his way at the conference. The provision to hold plebiscites was ignored, and the frontiers were drawn along strategic military lines rather than according to ethnographic considerations. As a result, a quarter of a million Germans were left living in Czechoslovakia, while close to a million Czechs remained in the territory occupied by Germany. All in all Czechoslovakia lost sixteen thousand square miles of territory, including its richest industrial sites, surrendered its impressive fortifications, and saw its communications network entirely disrupted. President Benes was forced to resign and went into exile; his successor, Dr. Emil Hacha, renounced the Czechoslovakian alliance with Russia and also gave in to Polish demands to surrender the Teschen district on October 10. On November 2 the Czech-Hungarian frontier was altered in Hungary's favor at a conference in Vienna — a conference presided over by Italy and Germany.

The end for Czechoslovakia was clearly in sight, and pious declarations by Britain and France to safeguard the rump Czechoslovakia were hollow and unconvincing. Hitler had achieved a major triumph; he had seized the Sudetenland, shattered the French security system, excluded Russia from the European alliance systems, and isolated his next victim — Poland. No wonder that his prestige was at an all-time high in Germany — so much so that the military conspiracy that had been formed against him broke up before it could gather serious strength. General Jodl represented the majority view of the German high command when he wrote in his diary:

> The Pact of Munich is signed. Czechoslovakia as a power is out. . . . [T]he genius of the Führer and his determination not to shun even a world war have again won victory without the use of force. The hope remains that the incredulous, the weak and the doubters have been converted and will remain that way.[82]

While the Germans were celebrating their victory at Munich, a pall of despair hung over those who knew what the consequences would be for the future of Europe. Winston Churchill described the Munich Agreement as an act of abject surrender, "a disaster of the first magnitude which has befallen Great Britain and France." He likened Hitler's method of negotiating to a series of extortions. At Berchtesgaden, Godesberg, and Munich he said, the ante was progressively raised: "One pound was demanded at the pistol's point. When it was given, two pounds were demanded at the pistol's point. Finally, the dictator consented to take one pound seventeen shillings and six pence and the rest in promises of good will for the future."[83] Churchill added prophetically that "you will find that in a period of time which may be measured by years, but may be measured only by months, Czechoslovakia will be engulfed in the Nazi regime."[84]

The Destruction of Czechoslovakia

Ironically, the man who was least satisfied by the Munich Agreement was the one who had gained most — Adolf Hitler. The führer had whipped himself into a war-like state and felt emasculated by his dwarfish appeasers. He also realized that he could have extorted more concessions if he had stuck to his original strategy. Chamberlain, he believed, had upstaged him at Munich and deprived him of his victorious entrance into Prague. Hitler's goal after Munich was never in doubt — the full dismemberment of Czechoslovakia.

Throughout the winter of 1938–39 Hitler explored the possibility of breaking up the Anglo-French alliance. When the French ambassador, François-Poncet, paid his final farewell after receiving another diplomatic post, Hitler used this occasion to offer a joint declaration between the two countries aimed at normalizing relations. Conversing with François-Poncet atop the pavilion he had built on his personal six-thousand-foot mountain, which could be reached only by an elevator that had been blasted into solid rock, Hitler mused about the greatness of "white civilization," the intransigence of the British, and the importance of ending traditional Franco-German differences. Hitler even declared his willingness to respect the existing Franco-German frontiers and urged consultations between the two countries on matters of mutual interest. Seeing him perched high atop the world, suspended in his immense circular room with panoramic views of the mountains, the whole view "bathed in the chiaroscuro of autumn dusk,"[85] the French ambassador labored under no illusions about Hitler's character:

> I knew him to be changeable, dissimulating, contradictory, and uncertain. The same man, good natured in appearance and sensitive to the beauties of nature, who across a tea table expressed reasonable opinions of European politics, was capable of the wildest frenzies, the most savage exultation, and the most delirious ambition.... This much is certain: he was no normal being. He was, rather, a morbid personality, a quasi-madman, a character out of the pages of Dostoevsky, a man possessed![86]

All the same, on December 6, 1938, the proposed declaration between France and Germany was signed when Ribbentrop visited Paris. While seeking to drive a wedge between France and Britain, Hitler was also engaged in paving the way toward a firm military alliance with Italy.

At Munich, Ribbentrop had already proposed a military alliance between Germany, Italy, and Japan, and when he visited Rome at the end of October 1938, he urged Mussolini to sign the treaty. The Duce was still reluctant to commit himself to such a close dependence on Germany, but by the beginning of the new year his mind was made up, although it was not until May 22, 1939, that the Pact of Steel, as the military alliance between Germany and Italy was called, was finally signed.

Hitler's strategy for the destruction of the rest of Czechoslovakia hinged on exploiting the separatist tendencies within the multiethnic and multilinguistic Czech state. The Sudeten Germans had served their purpose in paving the way for Hitler's destruction of Czechoslovakia, but after Munich it was the turn of the Slovaks and Ruthenians to complete the process. Under pressure from Germany, the Czechs were forced to grant virtual autonomy to both Ruthenians and Slovakians, including the right to establish their own quasi autonomous parliaments owing little allegiance to the central government in Prague. Even this surrender of centralized authority was not enough for Hitler, and he egged the Slovaks on in their demands for complete autonomy. On February 12, 1939, Hitler received the leader of the Slovak National Party, Dr. Bela Tuka, and the spokesman of the German minority in Slovakia, Franz Karmasin, for a meeting at the Reich chancellery. The participants reached a quick and mutually satisfactory decision: Slovakia was to secede from Czechoslovakia, and the führer was to be given a free hand in arranging it. In a groveling and submissive tone Tuka said: "I lay the destiny of my people in your hands, my Führer; my people await their complete liberation from you."[87]

In a desperate effort to prevent the total breakup of his state, the Czechoslovakian president, Dr. Emil Hacha, dismissed the Ruthenian and the Slovak governments and declared martial law. This action was an annoying surprise to Hitler. On the evening of March 13, 1939, Hitler reminded the two Slovak puppet leaders that the future of Slovakia would be grim indeed unless it declared its independence from Czechoslovakia. If not, he would leave the country at the mercy of events. In Bratislava on March 14 the majority of the deputies in the Slovak government proclaimed an independent Slovakia.

On the same day that the independence of Slovakia was proclaimed, Dr. Hacha and his foreign minister, Frantisek Chvalkowski, made a last-ditch effort to salvage the integrity of the Czechoslovakian state by making a personal appeal to Hitler. Hacha's visit to Berlin was a sad reenactment of Schuschnigg's meeting with Hitler at Berchtesgaden a little over a year before.[88] Hacha's performance was especially pitiful and pathetic. A man of advanced years with little experience in politics, Hacha arrived in Berlin not knowing what to expect, let alone what to do. Hacha tried to humor his powerful host. Knowing how Hitler felt about Benes and Masaryk, he purposely distanced himself from their position, claiming that he hardly knew the two men and disagreed with their political points of view. He even mused whether the establishment of Czechoslovakia had been a good idea in the first place and admitted that Slovakian independence was probably unavoidable. He hoped, however, that Hitler would allow the Czechs to live a free and independent national existence.

Hitler hardly allowed Hacha to state his case fully before revealing his decision to invade Czechoslovakia one way or the other (*so oder so*). If the Czechs resisted they would be squashed; if not, he would be generous to the Czechs by giving them a measure of autonomy. The only reason he had asked Hacha to Germany was to avoid needless bloodshed. The Czech premier was then handed over to Ribbentrop and Göring for some additional intimidation. When Göring threatened to destroy Prague with his Luftwaffe if the Czechs did not lay down their arms, Hacha suffered a heart attack. He was quickly revived by Hitler's private physician, Dr. Morrell, who gave him an injection and then handed him back to his tormentors so that he could complete the surrender of his country. Hacha called Prague and persuaded his cabinet not to resist Hitler's impending invasion. He then signed an already prepared communique that dressed up this despicable treatment of an honorable man and his country in the following unctuous lies:

> The conviction was unanimously expressed on both sides that the aim of all efforts must be the safeguarding of calm, order and peace in this part of central Europe.... The Czechoslovak President declared that, in order to serve this object and to achieve ultimate pacification, he confidently placed the fate of the Czech people and country in the hands of the Führer of the German Reich. The Führer accepted this declaration and expressed his intention of taking the Czech people under the protection of the German Reich and of guaranteeing them an autonomous development of their ethnic life as suited to their character.[89]

Hitler, beside himself with excitement, burst into his secretaries' room, invited them to kiss him, and exclaimed: "Children, this is the greatest day of my life, I shall go down in history as the greatest German."[90] Two hours later the German army rolled into Czechoslovakia. By late afternoon March 15, Hitler was on his way to Prague, where he spent the night in the Hradschin Castle, proudly surveying his new possession. Czechoslovakia had ceased to exist. Western statesmen were overwhelmed by the speed of Hitler's action and barely managed to voice a few feeble protests. These were brushed aside by Hitler with the comment that he had occupied Czechoslovakia on the advice of its president. A protectorate of Bohemia and Moravia was set up with Neurath as its first "protector." However, the real power of administering the new protectorate was placed into the hands of Konrad Henlein and Karl Hermann Frank, the two leaders of the Sudeten German Party.

One day after the establishment of Bohemia-Moravia as a German protectorate, Slovakia asked to be taken under German protection. The führer gladly obliged by sending German troops into Slovakia. As to

Ruthenia, the Nazis allowed the Hungarians to take it over. These events occurred so rapidly that they caught the Western powers completely by surprise.[91] Before the British or French ambassadors could even protest, Hitler had already returned from his triumphal visit to Prague, the protectorate had been set up, and the treaty with Slovakia had been concluded.

Hitler had paralyzed and outwitted the Western powers, but he had now also reached the limits of what they were willing to tolerate from him. In Western eyes, Hitler stood revealed as a liar and a menace to world peace. Czechs were not Germans, and swallowing a foreign state was not national self-determination. Even the high priests of appeasement saw the handwriting on the wall.

The Final Crisis: Poland

Only four days after Emil Hacha "placed the fate of Czechoslovakia into the Führer's hands," Ribbentrop sent an ultimatum to the government of Lithuania demanding the return of Memel, a strip of territory that Germany had lost to Lithuania in 1919. Hitler's demand was accepted and on March 23, 1939, Memelland was annexed by Germany.

Danzig was the next item on Hitler's diplomatic agenda. Ribbentrop had broached the question of Danzig's return to the Reich with the Polish ambassador, Josef Lipski, in October 1938. The discussions with Lipski and later with Colonel Beck, the Polish foreign minister, were relatively friendly but inconclusive. The Poles regarded the Danzig issue as nonnegotiable; they were willing to work toward better relations with Germany, but unwilling to make major concessions. After the Czechoslovakian crisis was over, pressure on the Polish government was stepped up. Ribbentrop told Beck that the future existence of Poland depended on its relationship with Germany, and he followed up with a new demand that Poland turn over Danzig and allow the Germans to build an extraterritorial road across the corridor to link it with Germany.[92] In return Ribbentrop promised that Germany would guarantee Poland's western frontier and hinted at future territorial compensations in the Ukraine. Ribbentrop's approach was consistent with previous Nazi policy relating to Poland. Hitler saw Poland as an ally against the Soviet Union because its government was strongly authoritarian and its people exhibited markedly anti-Communist, anti-Russian, and even anti-Semitic tendencies. Unfortunately, Polish diplomacy, conducted by the mercurial Jozef Beck, was too inconsistent and opportunistic to safeguard Poland's sensitive geopolitical position as a buffer state between Germany and the Soviet Union. Beck dreamed of a "third Europe" with a resurgent Poland as leader of a neutral bloc of nations stretching from the Baltic to the Black Sea. Although apparently leaning toward Germany, Beck dreamed of gains at Germany's expense, of amalgamating

Danzig into Poland proper and eventually even annexing East Prussia, Silesia, and Pomerania. Such ambitions, however, would require more than the support of small nations; they presupposed powerful friends who could transform Poland into a real fulcrum between Germany and the Soviet Union. When Beck turned down Hitler's offer, however, he set the stage for a rapprochement between Germany and Russia — an event he had been working hard to prevent. In the meantime, Beck looked for new Western support.

It was at this point that the British unexpectedly came to Poland's aid. Ominous reports about an impending action against Danzig, which had been reaching London for some time, galvanized the British prime minister into making an extraordinary commitment to the Poles. On March 31, 1939, Chamberlain announced in the House of Commons that Britain would unconditionally guarantee the territorial integrity of Poland.[93] When Hitler got wind of it, he flew into a rage, swearing that he would "cook them a stew that they'll choke on."[94] On April 3, 1939, Hitler issued a new directive to his military chiefs that considerably broadened earlier plans for seizing Danzig. Operation White, one of three contingency plans envisioned by Hitler against Poland (the others involved defending the frontier and seizing Danzig), aimed at the destruction of the Polish armed forces. Plans for this operation were to be ready by September 1, 1939.[95]

On April 28, following the invasion of Albania by Italy, Hitler delivered a scathing speech to the Reichstag in response to a message from President Roosevelt to Hitler and Mussolini, asking whether the two dictators could give their personal assurance to safeguard the independence of about thirty countries. It is commonly agreed that this was one of Hitler's most effective speeches, biting in its sarcasm and brilliant in its demagogic appeal. The aroused Nazi puppets who crowded the Reichstag on that day, led by the ebullient Hermann Göring, roared in unison as Hitler intoned the name of every single country on Roosevelt's list, implying the ridiculousness of the idea that Germany would want to invade the likes of Palestine, Iceland, Turkey, Switzerland, and so on.[96]

The four months following Hitler's speech to the Reichstag on April 28 were a lull before the storm. Hitler spent most of his time in seclusion at Berchtesgaden. Behind the scenes, however, military preparations proceeded rapidly as Hitler's military chiefs readied their plans for the attack on Poland. Two major diplomatic coups were also in the offing — the Pact of Steel with Italy and the Nazi-Soviet Nonaggression Pact.

On May 6, Ribbentrop was invited to Italy by Foreign Minister Ciano to reassure the concerned Italians about Germany's future intentions. Ciano had been alarmed for some time by Germany's belligerent policy toward Poland, rightly concluding that Poland was going to be the next victim of Nazi aggression. Mussolini's concern was that Hitler would launch a general European war at a time when Italy was least prepared to support it. Ciano rushed off to the meeting with Ribbentrop armed with a memorandum from the Duce indicating that Italy would not be prepared for war for another three years.[97] Ribbentrop dissembled so well at this meeting, insisting that Germany, too, required an extensive period of peace before further claims could be pursued, that Ciano was greatly relieved. When Ciano telephoned the Duce and told him how well the conversations were going, the Italian dictator ordered Ciano to publish the news that a German-Italian alliance had been reached. Two weeks later Ciano went to Berlin for the formal signing of the Pact of Steel.

The Pact of Steel embodied all the martial sentiments one would expect from the two Fascist states.[98] The two countries pledged themselves to present a common front against opponents and to come to each other's aid in case they should find themselves involved in hostilities with another power or powers. Just how steel-like the pact would turn out to be in practice would remain to be seen, but those who read it obviously could not fail to be struck by its militaristic purpose. It is true that the preamble spoke of the maintenance of peace, but it coupled peace with the acquisition of living space — two incompatible goals. In any case, the agreement was ratified with great diplomatic pomp in Berlin, and Hitler was delighted with it.

For several months after his speech of April 28 Hitler stayed out of the limelight, waiting to see whether the Western powers were serious about their commitment to Poland. The signals he received, while not conclusive, seemed to indicate that Britain and France might honor their pledges to Poland. This made Hitler pause because an attack on Poland might embroil him in a conflict with the Soviet Union on the eastern front, while at the same time exposing him to a combined Anglo-French attack on the western front. Britain's unconditional guarantee to Poland and Beck's rejection of his proposals had forced a change in Hitler's diplomatic design. Temporarily, at least, he had to swallow his ideological pride and come to terms with the Soviets. This became all the more necessary after he received signals that the Western powers were trying to negotiate a settlement of their own with the Soviet Union in order to isolate Germany. Negotiations had been under way since the middle of April between Britain and the Soviet Union; on April 16, Maksim Litvinov, the Soviet foreign minister, suggested a triple pact of mutual assistance to be signed by the Soviet Union, Britain, and France. However, these negotiations dragged on because Britain was less than enthusiastic about a strong assistance pact and rejected Litvinov's original version without pushing another agreement. Then Litvinov, a Western-oriented diplomat, whom the Nazis denounced as the "Jew Finkelstein," was replaced by Vyacheslav Molotov, a man who was far less interested in a collective security arrangement with the Western powers.

Stalin himself had repeatedly voiced the view that the Soviet Union should not allow itself to be maneuvered by the Western powers into a war with Germany. This and other signals led Hitler to believe that perhaps a pragmatic deal could be struck with the Soviets after all. He later admitted to Mussolini that making common cause with a Communist "seems to me to be a break with my whole origin, my concepts, and my former obligations";[99] but this admission did not blind him to the short-range benefits of a Nazi-Soviet agreement. In the first place, a partnership with the Soviet Union would enable Germany to avoid a war on two fronts. Such a policy had, in fact, long been advocated by certain members of the German army, notably by General von Seeckt, and by members of the Weimar Foreign Office who negotiated the Treaty of Rapallo in 1922 between Russia and Germany. With Russia on his side, Hitler believed that he could effectively isolate Poland and paralyze the will of the Western powers to such an extent that they would not come to its aid because that would mean war with both Germany and the Soviet Union. In the second place, an alliance with Russia might bring with it important economic benefits in the form of scarce resources without which Germany could not wage war or withstand another economic blockade.

Hitler pursued his negotiations with Stalin with great reluctance; the same was true on Stalin's side. Two months of secret negotiations, marked by mutual suspicions, passed without a settlement. As the deadline for the attack on Poland drew closer, Hitler pressed the Soviets for a decision. Finally, in the second week of August, Hitler authorized Ribbentrop to go to Moscow with full authority to negotiate a treaty. The Russians, however, made such a visit contingent on a prior agreement on trade relations and spheres of influence in eastern Europe. Stalin and Molotov obviously recognized Hitler's impatience. Being wooed by both the Germans and the Western powers, the Russians could afford to wait and see who might deliver greater gifts.

On August 20, after further delays and reservations on the part of the Soviets, Hitler reluctantly subordinated ideology to practical necessity and sent a personal telegraph to Stalin asking him to receive his foreign minister, who would be fully empowered to sign a nonaggression pact as well as a special protocol on questions of foreign policy. On August 21, after Hitler had spent a restless night wondering whether Stalin would go along with his urgent request, the Nazi ambassador to Moscow, Count Schulenberg, cabled Stalin's reply: it thanked Hitler for his letter and intimated that the German-Soviet Nonaggression Pact was as good as signed. Ribbentrop was welcomed to Moscow on August 23. The terms of the pact were not publicly revealed until the German archives fell into American hands in 1945. At the time, the public was told only that the Nazis and the Soviets had signed a nonaggression pact effective for ten years. In actuality, the two powers pledged to come to each other's aid in case of a war with Poland, and they agreed to split the conquered country with a designated area in the east going to Russia and the rest to Germany. In a secret protocol, Estonia, Latvia, Finland, and Bessarabia were assigned to the Soviet sphere.[100]

Word of the pact shook the capitals of the world, including Tokyo, where the Japanese, implacable enemies of the Russians, were stunned that a Fascist leader could make common cause with a Communist. The same consternation reigned among left-wing intellectuals and Communists in the West who were trying, in vain, to square this political circle with their own consciences. In the end, many gave up and resigned themselves to a politics of passivity, which may well explain, in part, why France collapsed so quickly under Hitler's onslaught in 1940.

While Ribbentrop was winging his way to Moscow, a euphoric Hitler decided to entertain the senior commanders of the armed forces at the Berghof. There had been frank meetings between Hitler and his military chiefs in the past, but this one was the most blatant display of war-mongering by a major head of state in modern times.[101] He spoke in egotistical terms about himself and mocked the Western powers as being led by little worms rather than by true men of action. Wagging his finger repeatedly, he boasted that he had been right every time in predicting what his opponents would do. Britain and France could not possibly help Poland because of his alliance with Stalin. Now he had Poland where he wanted it. Everything, however, depended on his existence and his political abilities. He was at the height of his political authority, commanding the absolute and undisputed confidence of the German people. There were other favorable conditions: the presence of strong-willed personalities such as the Duce and Franco on the side of the Fascist powers and conversely the political weakness of the Western powers. Two to three years from now the situation might reverse itself; there was, perhaps, even the chance that he might be eliminated by a criminal or a lunatic. For all these reasons, Hitler argued, the best time for conflict was now.

Militarily, Hitler continued, neither France nor Britain was prepared for war; they were in no position to aid Poland. Being psychologically war-weary they would be unlikely to strike first, and certainly not through neutral countries such as Belgium, Holland, or Switzerland. Furthermore, Germany need not fear an economic blockade because he expected the Soviet Union to supply needed wheat, cattle, coal, lead, and zinc. The only thing he feared, said the führer, was "that at the last moment some *Schweinehund* will present me with a mediation plan."[102]

Hitler's generals were stunned by this performance, especially the news of an impending alliance with the Soviet Union, and their mood was not as upbeat as Hitler expected it to be. This is why, after lunch, he gave them another pep talk, reminding them that victory was inevitable, provided that Germany closed ranks behind the war effort, showed no pity to its opponents, and proceeded brutally with a good conscience. The strongest, he said, are always right. He would find a convenient pretext to ignite the war, regardless of whether it was convincing or not; in the end, the victor is never asked whether he had spoken the truth. Judgments about the origin and conduct of war always depend upon the end result — victory or defeat — not right or wrong:

> Act brutally, 80,000,000 people must obtain what is their right.... Genghis Khan has sent millions of women and children into death knowingly and with a light heart...for the goal to be obtained in the war is not that of reaching certain lines but of physically demolishing the opponent. And so for the present only in the East I have put my death's head formations in place with the command relentlessly and without compassion to send into death many women and children of Polish origin and language.... Poland will be depopulated and settled with Germans.... As for the rest...the fate of Russia will be exactly the same.... After Stalin's death — he is a very sick man — we will break the Soviet Union. Then there will begin the dawn of the German rule of the earth.[103]

One participant who sat through this incendiary address tells us that after Hitler had exclaimed that he would kill without pity all men, women, and children "of Polish origin and language," Hermann Göring jumped on the table, offered "bloodthirsty thanks and bloody promises and proceeded to dance around like a savage."[104] Such unbridled display of war-mongering should have convinced the more astute generals present on that day that the Nazi regime was bent upon a course of aggression so vast and extensive that the outcome could only be the destruction of Germany. Yet they bowed to the will of their führer and, in Halder's case, pedantically noted the key features of Hitler's address, omitting the irrelevant remarks about wiping out men, women, and children of inferior quality.

After the conclusion of the Nazi-Soviet Nonaggression Pact, nothing was to deter Hitler from attacking Poland. Between August 21 and the outbreak of World War II on September 1, 1939, there was a flurry of diplomatic activity designed to avert military conflict, but such activity was utterly futile. Interestingly enough, Halifax and the Western appeasers still believed that a new Munich was possible and that giving Hitler Danzig would satisfy his appetite.[105] Not even Mussolini could have stymied Hitler in August 1939; in fact, Ciano had already warned the Duce before the Nazi-Soviet Pact that Germany was bent on war and would drag Italy into it. He had reached this inevitable conclusion after private discussions with Ribbentrop at Salzburg: "Ribbentrop, what is it that you want? Danzig? The Corridor?" Ribbentrop replied without a moment's hesitation: "We want war."[106]

While Ambassador Henderson in Berlin tried to convince Hitler that the British government was prepared to resist him over Poland and while Birger Dahlerus, a Swedish friend of Göring, was on a futile mission of shuttle diplomacy between Germany and England in an attempt to avert war,[107] the führer's SS minions were carefully working out Hitler's promise of August 22 to his generals of giving "a propagandist reason for starting the war, no matter whether it is plausible or not."[108] This propagandistic reason was in the form of a faked attack on a German radio station at Gleiwitz near the Polish border. On the night before the attack on Poland, Heydrich ordered SD detachments, dressed as Polish soldiers, to engineer "incidents" along the German-Polish border. In one of these incidents these fake Polish soldiers seized a German radio station at Gleiwitz, shouted some anti-German slogans into the microphone, and then withdrew. To lend "realism" to this staged attack, the SD men littered the area with actual bodies dressed in Polish uniforms. The bodies were those of concentration camp prisoners who had been killed by lethal injections to play their part in the drama.[109]

On September 1, 1939, Hitler announced to the Reichstag that he had "resolved to speak to Poland in the same language that Poland for months past has used toward us; this night for the first time, Polish regulars fired on our own territory. Since 5.45 A.M. we have been returning the fire, and from now on bombs will be met with bombs."[110] On September 3, after receiving no reply to their demands that Germany call off the attack on Poland, Britain and France declared war on Germany. One month later, but symbolically backdated to September 1, 1939, Hitler signed a memorandum empowering specific doctors to grant mercy deaths to the incurably ill. This set in motion the so-called euthanasia programs for the "destruction of unproductive lives" that would result in the killing of over one hundred thousand persons and that would also serve as the prototype for the gassing of Jews and other people considered subhuman. Two wars were thus launched simultaneously — a military and a biological-racial war.

Chapter 12

Blitzkrieg: The Expansion of German Power, 1939–41

The Psychology and Capacity for War

World War II was Hitler's war: he provoked it, he expanded it, and he desperately kept it going to the bitter end. Even the date was of his choosing. Since the führer believed himself to be a dying man, all of his visions began to take on a desperate urgency. In the early days he believed that time was on his side, that he could postpone weighty matters and temporize with his enemies. Starting in 1937 Hitler came to believe that his time was running out. In 1939, he turned fifty; it was now or never. In his meeting with his military chiefs the week before war broke out, as previously mentioned, he said that war must not be delayed because "essentially all depends on me, on my existence, because of my political talents.... But I can be eliminated at any time by a criminal or lunatic. No one knows how much longer I shall live. Therefore, better a conflict now."[1] Hitler's military chiefs shared neither Hitler's prescience about the fullness of time nor his enthusiasm for conflict. They were apprehensive about fighting a European war because they knew that Germany, heavily dependent on foreign sources for crucial war matériel, could not fight a prolonged war. Yet, trained to keep their mouths shut on political issues, they obediently followed Hitler into a war that they privately doubted he could win. Hjalmar Schacht's characterization of Hitler's military lackeys probably comes close to the truth:

> The generals are really the most to blame. I really cannot understand that militaristic mentality. Hitler says, "Let's go to war!" and they all click their heels and say, "War? Why yes, indeed, naturally, let's go to war!" Take General Halder, for instance. He did not have any use for Hitler. He was going to help me kick him out in 1938. Then Hitler says we are going to war, and all of a sudden Halder snaps to and says, "War? Oh, yes fine, anything you say!" — Never a thought about the reasons, the alternatives — nothing.[2]

Hitler's grip on German politics was so strong that few dared to oppose his will. It was therefore no exaggeration when he claimed that no one in German history had ever commanded such confidence and authority. Hitler's immense popularity not withstanding, the German people were not psychologically prepared for war. When the attack on Poland was announced, there were no wild cheers. Unlike 1914, as one American correspondent noted, there was "no excitement, no hurrahs, no cheering, no throwing of flowers, no war fever, no war hysteria."[3] Love of country compelled most Germans to support the war, though many undoubtedly shared Hermann Göring's sentiment, "Heaven have mercy on us if we lose this war."[4] Even the führer was temporarily speechless when he was informed that England and France had declared war on Germany, asking his foreign minister with an accusing tone of voice: "What now?"[5] What transpired now was a tragedy of unprecedented proportions in world history that would cost the lives of fifty-five million people. Hitler drew the German people into such a quagmire of crimes and atrocities that the very name "German" is still anathema to many people around the world.

World wars in the twentieth century are won not only on the battlefield but also in the factories, laboratories, schools, and logistical centers on the home front. Hitler claimed to have understood this salient fact when he wrote that "modern warfare is above all economic warfare, and the demands of economic warfare must be given priority."[6] Yet as chief warlord he often acted on the assumption that victory depended primarily on inflicting a series of quick crushing blows on enemies that would so terrorize and cripple their confidence that they would never be able to fight again. This strategy, of course, suited Hitler's temperament perfectly because this is how he had overwhelmed his political enemies on his way to power. Hitler's approach was essentially terroristic because it focused primarily on psychological intimidation and the use of brutal force. The use of terror and force as exclusive means of military strategy was self-defeating. Hitler did not seem to understand that if the threat of terror has only terror as its objective, the enemy's will to resist will be strengthened rather than weakened. He also did not seem to understand that quick "smash and grab" tactics, unaccompanied by long-range logistical planning and humane treatment of the conquered peoples, might contain the seeds of future defeat, particularly if the war turned into one of attrition.

Hitler, then, opted for cheap, quick campaigns that did not require mobilization for total war. Initially, this boosted morale on the home front, as it was intended to do, because it fostered the illusion that war could be waged relatively painlessly with an economy geared to both "guns and butter." As long as Germany was employing blitzkrieg tactics on one front at a time, its chances of success were excellent, but those same tactics were doomed to failure against the two great powers with whom Germany became entangled by 1941 — Russia and the United States. Although the Soviet Union was not a great economic giant in 1941, it did possess in manpower, in concentration of political authority, and in a fierce love of the motherland a powerful potential to wage war. America's power, which Hitler never grasped, resided primarily in its economic resources, but its strength also went beyond that with its highly developed technological and scientific capacity and a certain spirit of self-righteous determination that, once aroused, could be a powerful psychological force. Even Hitler was forced to change his strategy in face of such overwhelming power, but it is astonishing that it was only after Stalingrad and even as late as 1944 that he abandoned his blitzkrieg tactics. By then it was too late; Hitler had drawn Germany into a war that could not be won.

In the fall of 1939 the world looked upon the Wehrmacht as the most effective and disciplined fighting force in the world, and its spectacular victories in Poland, Norway, Denmark, Holland, Belgium, and France reinforced the perception of its invincibility as a "magnificent machine."[7] Yet behind the facade all was not well with the German army, the way it was run, and the resources on which it depended for its tenuous lifeline.

On paper, the German military-industrial complex looked like a superbly organized machine; in reality, it was a chaos of competing organizations and personalties. Hitler's own paranoid style added to the confusion. However, throughout the war he remained the undisputed authority of the Nazi system. The war even increased his authority because, as it encouraged rivalries, everyone was obliged to look to him as the ultimate arbiter. One historian has described the Nazi war machine as a "lumpish hexagonal pyramid with Hitler at its summit,"[8] another as an oriental "court as negligible in its power of ruling, as incalculable in its capacity for intrigue, as any oriental sultanate."[9] The dynamics of its organizational behavior were therefore characterized by competing fiefdoms, overlapping jurisdictions, intense jealousies, and inconsistent decision making from the top.

The striking thing about how Germany waged war was the absence of centralized coordination. Germany never coordinated the war effort through anything like a joint chiefs of staff. Command decisions were made by Hitler himself through "führer directives," written instructions that were simply passed on to the appropriate institution. It is true that a special executive organ, called the Cabinet Council for the Defense of the Reich, was created on August 30, 1939; its permanent committee, the Council for the Defense of the Reich (RVR), consisted of Hermann Göring, Wilhelm Frick, Rudolf Hess, General Wilhelm Keitel, Walther Funk, and Hans Heinrich Lammers. However, animosities among these men and lack of coordination prevented the efficient implementation of strategy.[10] Göring, who presided, proved mercurial and unreliable; his vanity and increasing drug dependency made him singularly unsuited for sustained bureaucratic work.

The formal machinery of waging war had gradually crystalized since Hitler combined the office of president, with its power over the armed forces, with his own office of chancellor. The day after Hindenburg's death, Hitler compelled all German soldiers to swear a personal oath to himself. In 1938 he also assumed personal control over the War Ministry, replacing the old Ministry of Defense with a new organization called the High Command of the Armed Forces (Oberkommando der Wehrmacht [OKW]). This new organization or functioned as Hitler's executive cabinet on all military matters; it was through the OKW that all führer directives were funnelled to the appropriate Reich departments without legal restraints.[11]

Established in February 1938, the OKW, as previously mentioned, was headed by Wilhelm Keitel, a good administrator but a spineless character whom Hitler could easily control. Although Keitel held the title of chief of OKW and was the equivalent of a Reich minister, he had no command. The OKW consisted of four departments: the Wehrmachtsführungsamt, responsible for operational orders; the Amt Ausland/Abwehr, dealing with foreign intelligence; the Wirtschafts-und Rüstungsamt, concerned with supply; and the Amtsgruppe Allgemeine Wehrmachtsangelegenheiten, involved with general military purposes. Of these four departments, the most important was the Wehrmachtsführungsamt (WFA), headed throughout the war by Alfred Jodl, an ambitious, capable, and exceedingly loyal officer who possessed a wealth of military knowledge and was widely respected for his keen eye for detail. Jodl's department was the pivot of Hitler's military machine because it was here that the details of all operations were carefully worked out and from which orders were sent to the high commands of the army, navy, and air force for conducting the war. Under Jodl's aegis were the following departments: Landesverteidigung, or Defense of the Reich (under Walter Warlimont); Armed Forces News Relations (Erich Fellgiebel); Wehrmachtspropaganda, or Armed Forces Propaganda (Hasso von Wedel); Law (Rudolf Lehmann); and Military History (Walter Scherff).

The home of the OKW was on the banks of the Tirpitz in Berlin, though both Jodl and Keitel soon moved into the new Reich chancellery, where, along with Colonel Rudolf Schmund, Hitler's personal liaison adjutant, and Göring's personal liaison officer, General Karl Heinrich Bodenschatz, they constituted the German Pentagon.

Directly below the OKW were the high commands of the various services — the Oberkommando des Heeres, or High Command of the Army (OKH); the Oberkommando der Luftwaffe, or High Command of the Air Force (OKL); and the Oberkommando der Kriegsmarine, or High Command of the Navy (OKM). These branches, in turn, had their own departments and administrative procedures.

These military branches were staffed by well-trained, competent, and dedicated officers, who still reflected the military values of the Kaiserreich, although many junior officers, soon to distinguish themselves on the battlefield, had already been converted to National Socialism. It is commonly agreed by military historians that the structure, personnel, and training of the German Wehrmacht was superior to most other armies. Morale was extraordinarily high in 1939, and so was the technical competence of enlisted men and officers alike. If this system had a weakness, it resided in a long-standing German habit of obedience, the overestimation of German ability, and, conversely, the underestimation of the enemy, especially the Russians and the Americans.

The weaknesses of Germany's military were not, however, what ultimately determined its defeat: the Achilles heel of the German war effort was the inadequate resources on which it was based.[12] The truth is that Hitler simply did not have the resources to wage all-out war for long. Despite the progress that was being made in the field of synthetic energy, Germany was still dependent on foreign imports for more than half of its energy supply. The supply of individual resources varied: two months for rubber, four months for magnesium, seven months for copper, twelve months for aluminum, eighteen months for manganese, thirty months for cobalt. Almost 45 percent of Germany's iron ore supply still had to be imported from Sweden. In the field of metallurgy, dependency on foreign sources was striking in certain areas: zinc 23 percent, lead 50 percent, copper 70 percent, tin 40 percent, nickel 96 percent, bauxite 99 percent. In certain areas, notably in the supply of chromium, tungsten, molybdenum, and vanadium, Germany was wholly dependent on foreign imports.[13]

Although Germany was one of the major industrial powers in the world and had rearmed on a massive scale since 1933, its capacity for armament production was limited. There was a high degree of armament readiness but a low degree of armament-producing potential. General Georg Thoma had advocated a policy of armaments in depth, which would have meant a major expansion of heavy industry in order to ensure a continuous output of munitions for a long, drawn-out war. However, Hitler opted for a high degree of armaments readiness in support of his strategy of "lightning war" (blitzkrieg). Blitzkrieg tactics did not require an extensive buildup of the productive capacities of German industry except in the area of synthetic oil and rubber. Such warfare also guaranteed the security of the "home front." Consumer goods would continue to be purchased, and social disruptions would be kept to a minimum to create the illusion of peacetime normality. When Hitler ran out of cheap victories and found himself in a war of attrition with the major powers of the world, he belatedly switched to total war production, but by this time it was too late.

Little thought was given to the financing of the war. Germany's gold and foreign currency reserves were nearly exhausted in September 1939. The financial measures taken to support the war included a wage freeze and the assessment of supplementary taxes on alcohol, cigarettes, theater tickets, as well as a graduated tax on income.[14] By controlling spending through cutbacks in consumer goods, the regime directed spending into savings and promised savers that their sacrifices would help to finance a mighty postwar construction project that would enable every German family to own a house.

Summarizing German prospects for victory in 1939, the following picture emerges. Germany had an initial advantage because the Nazis had regimented the people for war and aggression. As a result of massive rearmament, the Germans had caught up with and surpassed the major Western powers. From the point of view of military tactics, the Germans were also more advanced in their logistical and strategic thinking, as was subsequently demonstrated in Poland and on the western front. At first Hitler faced opponents of Germany's own size or smaller, Poland, France, Britain, Belgium, and they were at the time, for the most part, reluctant and poorly prepared combatants. He was allied with Italy, Japan, and the Soviet Union and still free from interference by the United States. These advantages eventually changed under the impact of his strategic errors, notably the invasion of Russia and the declaration of war on the United States. Germany's weaknesses then became fatal liabilities: poor military-political coordination, shortages of crucial resources, inconsistent and irrational leadership, and, eventually, deliberate obstructionism and resistance. As B. H. Liddell Hart observed, Hitler had strategy but not a rational grand-strategy.[15] His mission was expansion, conquest, the ruthless subjugation of conquered people, and the physical extermination of racially inferior breeds. No matter how much skill and competence was brought to this task by ordinary Germans, such a bestial mission was bound to arouse the world into determined opposition. If we add the inherent weaknesses of the Nazi system and its sociopathic personalities, it does not require a great deal of hindsight to understand why the Nazis' house of cards had to collapse in the long run.

Blitzkrieg and *Sitzkrieg:*
September 1, 1939–May 10, 1940

In the meantime the Germans tested their blitzkrieg tactics on the unfortunate Poles. This involved the use of swiftly moving mechanized spearheads, employment of assault teams of infantry, and a sophisticated system of air-to-ground coordination of fighter planes supporting the advanced ground forces. Hitler's reliance on lightning war was motivated as much by political as it was by tactical considerations. When he invaded Poland, he knew that his western flank was dangerously overexposed. The war against Poland required a million infantry, fifteen hundred fighter planes, and close to a thousand tanks, leaving only a skeleton force on the western front, which was outnumbered by the French and English by seventy-six to thirty-two divisions. Hitler suspected that his Western enemies lacked the will to launch a well-coordinated and swift invasion of Germany, and he banked on the efficiency of the German army to achieve a quick victory in Poland. The vast, open Polish plain was ideally suited for tank warfare, and it was across this open terrain that the German army swept to a quick victory. By September 15, 1939, the German force had penetrated so deeply into Poland that the Russians, who were afraid of being denied the fruits of victory, attacked the Poles from the east. As an American journalist described it, the Poles were crushed "like a soft-boiled egg."[16] Warsaw was captured, the Polish government fled to London, and the victors proceeded to divide the spoils.

Hitler took the Polish Corridor and the city of Danzig. The rest of central Poland was turned into a German "protectorate" under a so-called Government General administered by the brutal Hans Frank, who was later hanged at Nuremberg for crimes against humanity. As expected, Stalin annexed most of eastern Poland and soon occupied the Baltic states of Lithuania, Estonia, and Latvia, thus extending the Soviet border significantly into eastern Europe. Hitler considered these Russian gains a provisional trade-off until he had either pacified or defeated the Western powers. To help accomplish that goal, he concluded a series of economic agreements with the Soviets that involved a massive exchange of Russian raw materials for German manufactured goods, an exchange that would provide the basis of his economic security for waging war on the western front.[17]

The quick defeat of Poland reinforced Hitler's belief in Germany's invincibility and emboldened him to rely on blitzkrieg as his chief strategy for winning the war. He calculated that the use of quick strikes aimed at disorganizing and crushing his immediate enemy would enable him to expand his economic resource base and buy enough time for a protracted war if it came. In the early stages of the war this strategy so paralyzed the will of the Anglo-French side that it obscured German weaknesses: an inadequate supply system, poor replacement procedures, and frequent breakdown in communications.

Having subdued Poland in only three weeks, Hitler suddenly portrayed himself as an apostle of peace, approaching the Western powers on October 6 with a humane peace offer; but just in case such an offer would be rejected, as he probably expected it to be, Hitler had already laid the groundwork for an attack on France. In a hastily formulated directive, followed by a lengthy memorandum to General Keitel, chief of the OKW, Hitler called for an attack on France through Luxembourg, Belgium, and Holland. The possibility of a winter attack on France, which appeared to be an unimaginative repeat of the 1914 campaign, so alarmed the generals that some of them seriously toyed again with ideas of resistance. However, lack of confidence in each other along with the postponement of the attack until spring caused the disgruntled generals to drop their conspiratorial plans.

The rapidity of Hitler's blitzkrieg tactics caught the Western powers completely by surprise, scarcely knowing what to do. The French decided that perhaps the best response was to do nothing, to dig in behind their impregnable Maginot Line and wait for the Germans to attack. After an initial panic in Western capitals, which brought about massive evacuations of women and children into the countryside, everyone gradually relaxed and life appeared to return to normal. The bombs had not fallen; the dreaded poison-gas attacks, which most people expected, had not come to pass. The blitzkrieg had turned into a *sitzkrieg* (sitting war), with the Germans, ensconced behind their Siegfried Line, facing the French, dug in behind their Maginot Line.

After Hitler had crushed Poland he was in a perpetual state of nervous tension, knowing that the war he had unleashed would not be won until France and Britain had been decisively defeated. Several years of intensive military preparations, capped by invaluable experience in Poland, bolstered Hitler's belief that the German armed forces were tactically superior to anything the Allied powers could put into the breach. However, Hitler also suspected that Germany's military edge would not last indefinitely and that he would have to strike quickly before his opponents brought their military strength up to par with his own.

It was at this point that Hitler's generals, notably Brauchitsch and Halder, tried to dissuade him from an immediate attack on the west by marshaling a variety of technical arguments to convince him that the German army was not ready to fight a combined Anglo-French force. Behind Brauchitsch and Halder the old 1938 resistance group against Hitler was also gathering momentum again, and there was renewed talk of a possible coup d'état. Hitler quickly disposed of this challenge by calling Brauchitsch on the carpet in the chancellery and giving him such a dressing-down that the cowed commander in chief of the army, nearly suffering a nervous breakdown, immediately disassociated himself from any conspiratorial parties; he also resigned himself to the fact that the OKH would have to submit to Hitler's military dictates. When Hitler postponed the offensive against France, originally set for the second week in November, because of poor weather conditions, the gathering plot against Hitler collapsed.

While high-ranking generals were discussing the possibility of removing Hitler, a humble cabinetmaker named Johann Georg Elser was actually at work on a bomb to blow him up in the Bürgerbräukeller on November 8, 1939.[18] Elser was a quiet and unassuming itinerant craftsman who repaired furniture and clockwork machinery. Although he had briefly joined a militant Communist group in the 1920s, he was a moderate trade unionist who strongly believed in human dignity and social equality. Alarmed by the aggressive policies of the Nazis, which he felt would plunge Germany into another tragic war, Elser decided that the only way to prevent this catastrophe was to assassinate Hitler. He knew that every year Hitler celebrated the anniversary of the 1923 Beerhall

Putsch by speaking at the Bürgerbräukeller and later participated in a remembrance to the fallen heroes of November 9, 1923. Carefully inspecting the beerhall, Elser decided to plant a bomb in a pillar with wooden paneling behind the speaker's rostrum. He moved to Munich, ate his meals at the beerhall, and shortly before closing time hid in a storeroom, emerging after everyone had left and then working for several hours on the pillar. Every night he bored an ever larger hole in the cement filling of the pillar and carefully removed the rubble in bags. At the same time, he covered up his work with such expertise that no one noticed that the pillar had been tampered with. Elser began his work on August 5, 1939; on November 6, he placed the charges and set them for 9:20 P.M., November 8, the time Hitler was scheduled to speak. Bad weather, however, had led to a cancellation of Hitler's flight to Berlin, forcing him to take the train instead. For this reason Hitler decided to cut short his visit, spoke for little over an hour, and left just thirteen minutes before the bomb exploded. Six old fighters and a waitress were killed, and sixty-three people were injured, one of them dying later.

Hitler had escaped his first of several serious assassination attempts. Elser was captured on his way to the Swiss border and confessed that he was the lone assassin. Hitler and the Gestapo, however, did not believe him; they suspected a broader plot involving the British Secret Service because two of its agents, Captain S. Payne Best and Major R. H. Stevens, had just been captured on the Dutch border and were thought to be implicated in the plot against Hitler's life. However, this was not the case. Elser was sent to Sachsenhausen concentration camp as a "special prisoner," and so were the two British agents. It was hoped that, sooner or later, Elser would confess having been in the pay of the British. After a cat and mouse game that went on for years, Elser was finally murdered at Dachau concentration camp on April 9, 1945.

In the meantime, Hitler's preoccupation with the impending attack on the western front continued, and the German high command was buzzing with conferences and plans about the invasion. The original plan, formulated by the general staff under the aegis of General Halder, directed the main German attack through central Belgium. This frontal attack was assigned to Army Group B under the leadership of Fedor von Bock, while Army Group A under Gerd von Rundstedt was to deliver a secondary attack on von Bock's left through the Ardennes Forest. However, Rundstedt's chief of command, Erich von Manstein, argued passionately that this plan was a pale replica of the Schlieffen plan of World War I and would therefore be almost inevitably anticipated by the French. In a brilliant reformulation of the whole plan he argued that the main thrust (*Schwerpunkt*) should be made through the Ardennes Forest — a thickly wooded area that was widely considered to be impenetrable by armor.[19]

While the arguments about the Manstein proposal continued unabated, an extraordinary event forced the issue in favor of the Ardennes.

On January 10, 1940, Major Helmut Reinberger, a Luftwaffe commander who had been detailed to General Kurt Student's staff to help plan airborne operations in Holland and Belgium, was compelled to make a forced landing in a heavy snowstorm near the Belgium town of Mechelen-sur-Meuse. Reinberger was carrying top secret maps and orders pertaining to the impending airborne landings in the west.[20] Although he tried to burn the documents, he only partially succeeded before he was arrested by Belgium authorities. His captors recovered enough evidence to reconstruct the main thrust of the German plans, though they also suspected that they might be a deliberate plant.

Hitler finally decided to throw his support behind Manstein's unconventional plan by shifting the center of gravity to Army Group A rather than to Army Group B. In retrospect, this was the correct decision because a major thrust through Belgium would have run straight into the most powerful Anglo-French forces and a host of other obstacles that would have slowed down such an attack — rivers, canals, forts, and cities.[21] Such an assault might have given the Germans the fields of Flanders, but it would have failed in its most decisive objective, namely, that of cutting Allied communications and blocking the retreat of Allied troops. The war would have stabilized, rigid lines reminiscent of World War I would have been established, a deadly series of attacks and counterattacks would have ensued, and Germany would probably have been worn down again in a war of attrition.

Conventional military wisdom discounted the possibility of a successful breakthrough in the Ardennes area, but Manstein and Guderian argued that the terrain was not impassable and that any difficulties would be offset by surprise and light opposition. Once the mass of German tanks had emerged from the forested Ardennes and crossed the Meuse, they would find themselves in the open plains of Flanders, an ideal terrain for tank warfare and only a short step away from the coast.

In contrast to these offensive German plans, French strategic thinking was wholly defensive and reactive. General Maurice Gamelin, the French commander in chief, proposed to come to the aid of Belgium with a strong reinforced left wing, thus countering what he assumed would be the major German thrust with an equally strong riposte of his own. In the south, he placed a mere token force of low-grade divisions. Thus, Gamelin left the hinge of his defense so weakened that the German drive, if it pierced it at the edge of the Ardennes, could easily swing into the rear of the Allied forces, disrupt their communications, and trap them.

In November 1939 the Russians, in an attempt to extend their sphere of influence in the Baltic, attacked Finland. However, the Finns offered stubborn resistance and repelled the inadequately prepared Russian forces. Finland was a Western democracy with strong ties to other Scandinavian countries. Despite moral and material support the Finns gradually had to bow to superior Russian numbers and signed a peace treaty that ceded such strategic bases as the Karelean Isthmus, the city of Viipuri (Viborg), and a naval base at Hango. This effectively moved the Russian frontier seventy miles westward and relieved pressure on Leningrad.

Up until this time, the Allied powers had followed a wholly reactive and passive path, looking more like bystanders than belligerents. While Hitler annihilated the Poles in the east, the English and French did nothing militarily to relieve their Polish ally. If they had struck at the Ruhr with all the power at their command while Hitler was preoccupied in Poland, they could have seriously crippled Germany, perhaps to the point of forcing Hitler to sue for peace. Nothing of the sort happened. Moreover, Hitler's sweeping victory in eastern Europe created a belief in the West that the German army was unbeatable and this reinforced, certainly in France, latent defeatist views that another devastating war was inevitable. Again and again, the Western powers were to find themselves in the train of events, reacting to the initiatives of their enemies. Finland offered another example. There had been discussions about aiding the Finns in their conflict with the Soviets and using this opportunity for seizing the Norwegian port of Narvik and the Swedish ore fields — essential to German procurement of iron ore. Opponents of the idea, however, argued that attacking neutral countries was a violation of international law and that Finland had never asked for help in the first place. When Finland asked the Soviet Union for an armistice, the project was abandoned. The Western powers then pursued a plan, suggested earlier by Winston Churchill, to mine the waters off the coast of Norway, but by that time Hitler had already laid plans of his own to beat his opponents to the punch.

While the Finnish war was still raging, Admiral Erich Raeder and the German navy kept a close watch on the Norwegian seacoast, anticipating a possible Allied invasion of Norway in order to assist the Finns and also to cut off the Germans from their primary iron ore supplies at Kiruna-Gällivare in Sweden. So far, Hitler had not given the German navy a major role in the war. In August 1939 he had allowed the battleship *Graf Spee* and the *Deutschland* to sally forth into the North Atlantic, but the two ships did not engage the British fleet for some time. Hitler also kept his submarines in abeyance, ordering them not to attack Allied shipping. However, when the Western powers refused to negotiate, he gave the green light for an all-out attack on all Allied naval forces.

Hitler had no real feeling for the sea; he was also wholly unfamiliar with naval warfare and thus less apt to interfere in naval affairs.[22] In December 1939 he ordered a secret study on how an invasion of Norway might be launched by sea. Through Alfred Rosenberg, Admiral Raeder had been put in touch with Vidkun Quisling, head of the Norwegian Nazi Party, who confided that with German help he would be able to carry out a coup in Norway. Hitler saw Quisling on several occasions in December. At that time, however, Hitler's attention was focused on other issues; then came a big blow to his pride that would change his mind about Norway. On December 13, 1939, the *Graf Spee* was cornered off the coast of Uruguay by three British cruisers and so badly mauled that its captain, Hans Langsdorff, after receiving only three days of refuge in pro-British Montevideo, decided to scuttle the ship, much to the glee of the Western powers. In February 1940, the supply ship *Altmark,* which had accompanied the *Graf Spee,* was captured by a British destroyer in Norwegian waters, and the three hundred British seamen it was carrying as prisoners captured earlier by the *Graf Spee* were liberated. Hitler now ordered the invasion of Norway and Denmark as well, assigning overall command to General Nikolaus von Falkenhorst.

On April 9, 1940, German troops, emerging from coal barges that had anchored in Copenhagen harbor, took over the city and with it the country. At the same time German "coal ships," accompanied by much of the German navy, set out for Narvik, Trondheim, and Stavanger. While German ships landed troops at strategic points on the coast, airplanes dropped parachutists into major Norwegian cities such as Oslo, Trondheim, Bergen, Stavanger, and Narvik. By the evening of April 9, most of Norway was in the hands of the German forces. At Narvik, however, the German navy suffered grievous losses when the ten destroyers that had landed General Eduard Dietl's two thousand mountain troops were engaged by the British navy. In a blinding snowstorm five British destroyers penetrated the fjord in which the German destroyers were anchored and sank them all. Hitler ordered Dietl to hold Narvik at all costs, but Dietl eventually broke out of the trap laid by Allied troops and retreated to Sweden. When it became clear that Hitler was defeating the Allied forces in France, the British expeditionary force in Norway was evacuated through Narvik, Dietl returned to Narvik, and all of Norway and Denmark were now under the control of the Nazis. In Norway the government was eventually given to Quisling, whose name was to become synonymous with traitorous collaboration with the enemy. The Norwegian royal family fled the country, but in Denmark the royal family remained captive to the German occupation. Among Scandinavian nations, only Sweden managed to maintain a tenuous neutrality throughout the war.

The War against the West

At 5:35 on the morning of May 10, 1940, Hitler launched his offensive in the west, attacking Belgium, Holland, and Luxembourg without a formal declaration of war. The formation of tanks and motorized infantry that had been amassed close to the frontiers of these nations was staggering. In the words of General von Kleist, "If this Panzer group had advanced on a single road its tail would have stretched right back to Königsberg in East Prussia when its head was at Trier."[23] In his daily orders to the troops poised on the western frontier Hitler said: "The hour of the decisive battle for the future of the German nation has come....The battle beginning today will decide the future of the German nation for the next thousand years."[24]

The opening thrust of the German campaign, designed as a distraction, was directed against Holland by both land and air. German parachutists swooped down on the main nerve centers, including The Hague and Rotterdam, capturing important bridges, towns, and airports. In order to terrorize the Dutch people into a quick surrender, the Luftwaffe carried out several devastating raids, most notably against Rotterdam. The world paused in shock as wave after wave of Stuka dive bombers obliterated much of the city. While the Luftwaffe pounded Dutch defenses and parachutists seized strategic positions, regular German forces rolled into Holland from the east, causing widespread panic, confusion, and demoralization. By the third day of the invasion German armored divisions had linked up with the airborne troops at Rotterdam. Two days later, on May 15, the Dutch surrendered to the Germans and Queen Wilhelmina and the Dutch government fled into English exile.

The conquest of Belgium proceeded almost as smoothly as that of Holland. Between 1920 and 1936, Belgium had been allied with France, but Hitler's unopposed remilitarization of the Rhineland had convinced the Belgians that France was a dubious ally and that perhaps neutrality might be the safest means of avoiding another German attack. Although the French had given every indication that they would come to Belgium's aid, French support depended on the ability of the Belgians to withstand the initial German attack. However, the Belgians were poorly prepared and the Maginot Line, which was designed to protect the French frontier, was never extended along the Belgian frontier.

The attack on Belgium was carried out by the Sixth Army under General Walter von Reichenau; its chief task was to capture the two bridges over the Albert Canal along with Eben-Emael, Belgium's newest and strongest frontier fortress, which was situated a few miles south of Maastricht near the junction of the Meuse and the Albert Canal. The Belgians hoped to stop the German attack behind fixed fortifications for at least two weeks. As in Holland, however, both the bridges and fortifications such as Eben-Emael were captured in daring night-time operations by parachutists. The bridges were secured intact, and Eben-Emael was taken by a glider detachment consisting of only eighty men that landed on top of the fortress and trapped its twelve hundred defenders until the regular German infantry forced its surrender. Having secured the key of Belgium's defensive position, the Germans now poured into western Belgium toward the Dyle Line, where the retreating Belgians were linking up with French and British forces. To the Allied military commanders, German strategy appeared to be a reenactment of the 1914 offensive by which Germany had swung through the flatlands of the Low Countries into France. The attack on western Belgium, however, was merely a feint; the real assault was launched in the hilly and wooded terrain of the Ardennes in southern Belgium. Thus, while the Allied forces prepared to meet the major thrust of the German attack on the Dyle Line in central Belgium, the spearheads of Rundstedt's Army Group A, notably Guderian's armored divisions, were racing through the wooded hill-belt of southern Belgium. When Hitler's messengers brought him the news that the Allied forces had taken the bait, he was thrilled, later recalling that "when the news came that the enemy was advancing along the whole front I could have wept for joy! They'd fallen right into my trap! It was a crafty move on our part to strike toward Liege — we had to make them believe we were remaining faithful to the old Schlieffen Plan."[25]

On the fourth day of the offensive the armored divisions of General von Kleist, spearheaded by the audacious Guderian, crossed the French border and headed toward the banks of the Meuse near Sedan. Conventional strategy would have counseled a temporary respite until the mass of infantry and artillery could be brought up from the rear to ensure a successful crossing. Guderian, however, decided to cross the Meuse immediately, as did a small force under the command of Erwin Rommel forty miles to the west of Guderian at Dinant. By May 14, Guderian's three Panzer divisions had safely crossed the Meuse and fought off a weak French counterattack; Guderian then wheeled westward and smashed through the last defensive line on the Meuse. The road to the Channel coast was now open.

The German high command, including Hitler, was euphoric but at the same time made apprehensive by this unexpected good fortune. Rundstedt expected a heavy thrust again his left flank, but none was delivered. Guderian heatedly argued in favor of resuming the drive and keeping the French on the run, and he succeeded to the extent that Hitler allowed him to widen his bridgehead. This was the excuse Guderian was waiting for to push ahead. On May 16, he extended his bridgehead and drove fifty miles westward to the Oise; his daring initiative, in turn, served as a signal for other commanders who followed in his train. German tanks now rolled in an open corridor behind the Allied left wing in Belgium.[26]

Apart from ineffectual jolts by French armored forces, most of which were poorly coordinated, the German tank divisions encountered little resistance. The French were immobilized; the speed of the German assault threw them completely off balance, and they still did not know whether the attack was aimed at Paris or the Channel coast. In some cases the confusion would have been comic if it had not been so tragic. General Kleist, for example, reported:

> I was half-way to the sea when one of my staff brought me an extract from the French radio which said that the commander of their 6th Army on the Meuse had been sacked, and General Giraud appointed to take charge of the situation. Just as I was reading it, the door opened and a

handsome French General was ushered in. He introduced himself with the words "I am General Giraud." He told me that he had set out in an armoured car to look for his Army, and had found himself in the midst of my forces far ahead of where he expected them to be.[27]

The paralysis and demoralization of the French high command filtered to the troops in the field. British General Alan Brooks called the French army a rabble without the slightest discipline, perhaps a somewhat unkind assessment but not without justification in view of the appalling deterioration of the fighting spirit of the French army. Not only did the German tanks slash through the French lines, but the German Luftwaffe completely dominated the air, strafing the retreating French forces at will. French roads were littered with abandoned and destroyed equipment and congested with thousands of refugees pouring south and impeding the movement of their own troops. Liaison between the Allied armies virtually broke down, particularly after the French moved their headquarters to Briare, where only a single telephone line linked the French high command to its troops and to the outside world, and that line was shut down between twelve and two o'clock in the afternoon because the postmistress went to lunch at this time.[28]

The major reason the French were caught by surprise was that they still thought in terms of fixed lines and holding the Germans on the northern rivers. As Liddell Hart put it so incisively, "The French, trained in the slow-motion methods of World War I, were mentally unfitted to cope with the new tempo, and it caused a spreading paralysis among them. The vital weakness of the French lay, not in quantity nor in quality of equipment, but in their theory."[29] Even the Germans did not entirely trust the success of their armored divisions; they suspected that there must be something wrong when things were going so well. On May 17, Hitler temporarily ordered a halt to the westward advance until the Twelfth Army could draw up and form a protective shield on the Aisne. By taking concerted counteraction, the French might yet have stabilized the front, but they were incapable of doing so. By May 20, Guderian, who had almost resigned his command after receiving orders to stop his advance, captured Amiens and reached the coast beyond Abbeville.

As Guderian drew closer to the Channel port, his tanks rolled unopposed in the rear of the British army, which was still fighting Bock's infantry forces in Belgium. On May 22, Boulogne was isolated by the German drive; on May 23, Calais was also secured. In only five days the Germans, driving through the Somme Valley to the Channel coast, had closed the ring around the trapped Allied armies in Belgium. The French, Belgians, and British armies were being pushed against the sea, where only two ports, Dunkirk and Ostend, remained open as avenues of escape. Guderian was already within ten miles of Dunkirk, and Reinhardt's Panzer corps, supporting him on his right, arrived on the canal line Aire–St. Omer–Gravelines, where they established three bridge-heads. Just as Guderian was poised for his final assault on Dunkirk, the last escape port for the trapped Anglo-French forces, Hitler canceled the attack, thus allowing the doomed enemy to slip away, perhaps to fight again on another day.

What accounted for this inexplicable order by the führer? Hitler was reluctant to drive to the Channel coast until infantry could be brought up to cover the exposed flank. He was also afraid that the French might succeed in forming a new front on the Somme. He told his generals that the battle in Flanders was as good as won and that they should now concentrate on the battle of France.

On May 24, Hitler called von Brauchitsch to his western command post at Münstereifel, about twenty-five miles from the Belgium frontier, and informed him that Rundstedt, who was in agreement with his plan, was to halt his tanks and reorganize them for an advance on Paris. Brauchitsch protested vigorously, pointing out that Rundstedt's tanks were within fifteen miles of Dunkirk and thus in excellent position to trap the British forces, while von Bock's forces were still thirty-five miles from Dunkirk. Hitler, however, minimized the potential seriousness of letting over two hundred thousand Anglo-French troops slip away by reminding Brauchitsch that the real battle for France was not at Dunkirk.

Hitler believed that Bock's troops could do the job just as well at Dunkirk and that there was no use in jeopardizing his armor in a country honeycombed with canals. He referred to his own experience in World War I, which had convinced him that tanks were of no use in Flanders. Besides, Hermann Göring had assured him that the Luftwaffe would prevent any large-scale escape of the trapped Anglo-French armies at Dunkirk. A small British counterstroke with two tank battalions at Arras against the flank of the German drive toward Dunkirk, according to Liddell Hart, may also have reinforced Hitler's belief that he should keep his heavy armor in reserve.[30] Finally, Hitler's halt order has also been interpreted by some historians as a ploy to enable him to negotiate a compromise with the British at some future time. It seems more likely, however, that Hitler's halt order was primarily motivated by military reasons, though the wrong ones. The Luftwaffe proved incapable of destroying the British expeditionary force on the beaches of Dunkirk. It was grounded for some time because of bad weather, and when it attacked, most of its bombs plunged into the soft sand and inflicted minimal damage. Additionally, the British fighter command flew massive patrols over the area, shooting down scores of German planes. Thus, Hitler's halt order, together with the feeble performance of the Luftwaffe, enabled the British to evacuate men using every manner of vessel — regular navy vessels, lifeboats from liners in the London docks, tugs from the Thames, yachts, fishing craft, lighters, barges, pleasure boats — anything, as Churchill observed, that could be of use along the beaches.[31] Close to 860 ships were involved in rescuing the trapped Allied forces at Dunkirk.

All in all 338,000 British and Allied troops were evacuated at Dunkirk, a sizable number of them being French; only 2,000 were lost in ships sunk en route.[32] If Dunkirk was not exactly an Allied miracle, it certainly represented the first of several missed opportunities that contributed to Germany's eventual defeat. True, Hitler made much of the captured equipment of the British expeditionary force littering the beaches, but what was that "compared with saving the army, the nucleus and structure upon which alone Britain could build her armies of the future"?[33]

The final phase of the German campaign in France took place on June 5, 1940, just one day after the capture of Dunkirk. In a brilliant reformulation of the entire front, the Germans rapidly refocused their attack from the northwest to the south, where the new French commander in chief, Maxime Weygand, who had replaced Gamelin, had attempted to build up a long front along the Somme and the Aisne. The French had managed to scrape up sixty-six divisions, but seventeen of them were ensconced in the heavily fortified Maginot Line, which was intended as the final link of the new front. The new Allied front was much longer and less fortified than the old one. Moreover, the French had lost thirty divisions and could count on only two British divisions for support.

The Germans used all of their three army groups for the final assault on France. Army Group B, under Bock, was singled out to strike first on the lower Somme; Army Group A, under Rundstedt, would then drive across the Aisne; and finally Army Group C, commanded by Wilhelm Ritter von Leeb, would emerge from behind the Siegfried Line and attack the Maginot Line defenses, containing the surviving French forces in the far eastern sector of the front. The Panzer corps were reemployed, with six of the ten corps going to Bock. On the lower Somme, Hoth commanded the Fifth and Seventh (Rommel) Panzer divisions; in the center, facing the Peronne-Amiens section, were Kleist's four Panzer divisions, while Guderian faced the Aisne sector with four Panzer divisions.

Bock's Army Group B started the attack on June 5, 1940, on the lower Somme, but a stubborn French resistance held the line for two days. On Bock's extreme right, however, Rommel's Panzer division cut right through the French defenses on the third day. In a daring operation, combining ingenuity and flexibility, Rommel crossed the Somme with his tanks on two narrow rail bridges, which the French had left intact with an eye toward future counterattacks, assuming the bridges to be impassable to heavy tanks. Rommel simply pulled the rails and cross ties and ran his tanks and transport along the narrow embankments straight across the two rail bridges, suffering the loss of only one tank. Rommel's tanks now poured through this hole followed by other German divisions. By June 8, Rommel reached the Seine south of Rouen, after having thrust forty miles into a confused French defense that was thrown off balance by the swiftness of his attack. Brushing aside a hastily mounted French defense, Rommel ordered his division toward the Channel coast. On June 10, he reached the coast near St. Valery, cutting off the retreating French Tenth Army and forcing it to surrender on June 12.

While Rommel's breakthrough had been relatively easy, the right wing attack from the Somme ran into more determined opposition. It was not until June 8 that the right pincer of Kleist's Panzer corps broke through the French line at Amiens and wheeled south toward the lower reaches of the Oisne. Since Rundstedt's Army Group A had achieved a quicker breakthrough on the Aisne line, the German high command decided on June 9 to reinforce Guderian's breach of the Aisne by transferring Kleist's Panzer corps to Guderian's sector. Eight Panzer divisions were now boring their way south on both sides of Rheims. Guderian's right wing took Chalons-sur-Marne on June 12, Vitry-le-François on June 13, Chaumont on June 14, and the river Saone on June 15. On June 17, Guderian had reached Pontarlier on the Swiss frontier. When Guderian radioed the fall of Pontarlier to OKW, the response was one of incredulity: "Your signal based on error," the reply indicated, "assume you mean Pontailler-sur-Saone." Since Pontarlier was sixty miles beyond the river Saone, which Guderian had crossed only the previous day, the German high command could well be excused for questioning the general's claim. Guderian, however, wired back with incontrovertible evidence: "No error. Am myself in Pontarlier on Swiss border."[34] Guderian's audacity and independence had again triumphed over the cautiousness of OKW. Along with Rommel, who had also covered incredible distances with his tanks, Guderian became one of the major heroes of the western campaign, justifiably earning the nickname of "schnelle Heinz" (Hurrying Heinz).

Guderian's capture of Pontarlier isolated the French forces still defending the Maginot Line. He now ordered his tanks northeastward into the Vosges and Alsace, working closely with Leeb's Army Group C against the Maginot Line. On June 19 Kirchner's First Panzer Division linked up with General Friedrich Dollmann's Seventh Army and trapped four hundred thousand French troops in the Vosges.

With the collapse of Weygand's fragile Somme and Aisne front, the French government abandoned Paris, which was occupied by the Germans on June 14. On the evening of June 16 the French premier Paul Reynaud resigned and asked Marshal Pétain to form a new government whose primary aim was to negotiate an armistice with Germany.

When Hitler heard the news that Marshal Pétain desired an armistice, he was so delighted that he made a little hop; but this momentary exhilaration quickly gave way to stronger feelings for revenge. He was determined to make the French go through the same humiliation that the German delegation had been forced to endure at Compiegne in November 1918. Accordingly, he gave instructions that the wooden dining car in which Marshal Ferdinand Foche had dictated the armistice terms to the German delegation in 1918 be taken from its museum in Paris and placed in exactly the same spot in the forest of Compiègne, near the French armistice memorial.

For Hitler this victory was a moment of personal triumph and revenge. As he stepped out of his limousine on that warm June day in the little clearing of great elms and pine trees in the forest of Compiègne, he felt a surge of satisfaction at the prospect of dictating humiliating terms to the French. William Shirer, the CBS correspondent who saw the event, captured Hitler's moment of triumph in his diary, describing how Hitler, surrounded by his staff, strutted about and in a gesture of magnificent defiance "threw his whole body into harmony with his mood," by snapping his hands on his hips, arching his shoulders, and planting his feet wide apart. Shirer was right: Hitler had "reached a new pinnacle in his meteoric career" and avenged the defeat of 1918.[35]

The actual terms of the armistice were extremely Draconian, though they provided a glimmer of hope because not all of France was to be occupied by Germany. Only northwestern France was to be occupied, while the rest would remain under the control of Marshal Pétain. Hitler was even willing to renounce any German claim over the French fleet and to leave the French colonies untouched. France was to disarm and demobilize its army, to agree to pay for the German army of occupation, and to wait until peace had been concluded for the release of prisoners of war. Pétain's government, which sought a suitable capital in the unoccupied zone, eventually moved to the health resort of Vichy. Once Britain had been defeated, the French government was supposed to move back to Paris.

In the meantime, Paris was under German occupation, as the swastika fluttered on top of the Eiffel Tower. On June 23, Adolf Hitler, accompanied by his three favorite artists — the architects Albert Speer and Hermann Giesler and the sculptor Arno Breker — arrived in Paris to visit the chief sights.[36] The führer's entourage visited the modern baroque opera, the Eiffel, and the Arc de Triumph; lingered for some time in awe at the tomb of Napoleon in the Invalides; and enthusiastically praised the majestic backdrop of the Place de la Concorde. Finally, the sightseers went to Montmartre, but Hitler found Sacre Coeur quite dreadful.[37] After three hours Hitler was finished with his tour; he was now lord and master of the continent and at the height of his power. Opposition within Germany, which had temporarily welled up since the beginning of the war, was now largely silenced. In the eyes of most Germans, Hitler was not only a brilliant politician, but, in Keitel's sweeping appellation of June 1940, "Grösster Feldherr aller Zeiten" (the greatest military leader of all times).[38] It may be true that the Allied forces were weak and poorly led, that Manstein conceptualized the Ardennes campaign, and that mobile tank warfare was the brainchild of avant-garde military theorists, but the truth remains that Hitler had long ago recognized the political and military weaknesses of his enemies, had given his enthusiastic support to Manstein, and had seen to it that the German army was supplied with the Panzer divisions at a time when there was still considerable opposition to reliance on armored warfare within the German army itself. As Allan Bullock put it, "If Hitler, therefore, is justly to be made responsible for the later disasters of the German Army, he is entitled to the major share of the credit for the victories of 1940: the German Generals cannot have it both ways."[39] This is a point well taken, but Bullock's logic about the generals not being entitled to have it both ways is refutable; the generals could in fact have been right in both respects: that the army was responsible for the early victories and that Hitler's interference and mismanagement were to blame for later defeats.

The sudden and calamitous defeat of France spread dismay among the ranks of the Western powers. How was it possible, they asked, for a great nation to suffer such a humiliating defeat, to be crushed so completely within just a few weeks? In seeking scapegoats, many Frenchmen reacted like the Germans had done after World War I: they insisted that they had not really been defeated but betrayed. The facts, however, were more mundane. The French were led by incompetent generals and lackluster politicians; and when the German military hammer came down unexpectedly and overwhelmingly on the French anvil, the result was panic, retreat, and military defeat.

The Battle of Britain

In the second week of May 1940, the inept government of the appeaser Neville Chamberlain fell in disgrace; and Winston Churchill, whose prophetic warnings about Nazi Germany had been proved all too correct, became prime minister and war leader of an isolated and troubled England. In Winston Churchill, a man of courage, tenacity, great statesmanship, and unsurpassed eloquence, Hitler had found his nemesis.

In the summer of 1940 England was a beleaguered island fighting for its very existence. Standing alone, there was little chance that it could survive; its only hope lay in weathering the immediate wrath of Hitler and then finding powerful allies. As to Hitler, the sudden collapse of France left him without a war to fight. As early as 1924, when he published *Mein Kampf,* he had insisted that England was Germany's natural ally and that, in return for a free hand on the Continent, he was willing to give the English free rein overseas. This attitude of the führer's might explain, in part, the half-hearted measures to assemble an invasion force and the inconsistent manner in which German fighter bombers attacked England in the summer and fall of 1940. Hitler was never committed to an all-out war with Britain; he hoped that the British would eventually recognize the futility of continuing this no-win war and conclude peace with Germany.

But just in case they did not, he ordered the German high command to draw up a plan called "Operation Sea Lion," which called for an invasion of England by a force of ninety thousand men who would land on the beaches of England in some thousand craft of various sizes. The problem with this fantasy was that in the summer of 1940 the German navy had no surface fleet at all, having lost most of its larger vessels in the Norwegian campaign. Moreover, the German navy had almost no experience in amphibious landings. Although Hitler envisioned a big navy, construction proceeded by fits and starts. In the meantime, Hitler directed that the initial attack on England be made by the Luftwaffe, the idea being that it was necessary first to soften up English defenses before an invasion could be attempted. Accordingly, in the summer of 1940 Reich Marshal Göring assembled a huge force of fighter airplanes and long-range bombers with the intention of destroying the British war industry and terrorizing the population into submission. Although the German force outnumbered the British by almost two to one, the psychological advantage in this famous Battle of Britain (August–November 1940) clearly lay with the British. The British were defending their homeland against a foreign aggressor. This attitude was best immortalized by an unknown cockney on a London bus, who is said to have reminded his fellow passengers: "Ere, wot ye grousin' about? we're in the finals, ain't we? we're playin' at 'ome, ain't we?" The British enjoyed other advantages: they had radar, which gave their fighter command advance warning of impending attacks; they were producing as many aircraft as the Germans (over six hundred a month), and their aircraft, especially the Spitfires and the Hurricanes, were technically superior to the German Messerschmidts or Stukas; and finally, in Sir Hugh Dowding, the British air marshal, the British were fortunate to have a brilliant strategist, whose patience, courage, and quickness of mind contrasted favorably to the mercurial character of Reich Marshal Göring.

Had the Germans concentrated all their efforts on British airfields and planes, they might have broken the back of the RAF (Royal Air Force). Instead, Göring shifted the German attack from airfields to ports and shipyards and to some of the major cities. The final assault on England by air, know as the Blitz (September 7–November 13), was launched primarily on major industrial centers such as London and Coventry. During the whole month of September, German fighter bombers struck London and other British cities every night; but far from breaking the will of the population, the terror attacks actually strengthened British resistance.

It became increasingly apparent to the German high command that England could not be subdued by air and that the daily loss of life and matériel was too costly. According to postwar British figures, the RAF had brought down a total of 1,733 German fighters and bombers by the end of October as compared to a loss of 915 British fighters.[40] Such losses were prohibitive to the German high command and furnished a convenient excuse to the navy chiefs for recommending a postponement of the invasion. Thus, on October 12 Hitler shelved Operation Sea Lion indefinitely. In retrospect, the Battle of Britain was a heroic effort on the part of all Englishmen but especially the few thousand fighter pilots who, day after day, fought grueling dogfights, pushing their resources to the limit and bringing down Germans in a ratio of nearly two to one. As Winston Churchill so eloquently put it, "Never in human history have so many owed so much to so few."

The Mediterranean Theater:
The Balkans and North Africa, 1940–41

Although Hitler still believed that Russia could be attacked and defeated only if Germany had vanquished the West, he now persuaded himself that Britain's removal from the Continent meant that Germany had nothing more to fear on its western flank. Unable to subdue the British by air, he would bring them to their knees by conquering the Soviet Union and using its immense resources to strike at the heart of the British Empire. Even while the Battle of Britain was still raging, there was never any doubt in Hitler's mind that Russia rather than Britain was Germany's primal enemy. In mid-June 1940, the Soviets occupied the Baltic provinces, which Hitler saw as a threat to Finland and the Baltic. On June 28, Stalin also annexed Bessarabia and northern Bukovina from Romania. It was clear to Hitler that a reckoning with the Soviet Union was inevitable. On August 14, 1940, when his fourteen new field marshals came to collect their batons at the chancellery, he frankly informed them to be prepared to fight the Soviet Union.

On September 27, 1940, Germany, Italy, and Japan signed the Tripartite Pact in Berlin, which aimed at establishing the "New Order" in Europe and "Greater East Asia" in the Far East. The three powers agreed to assist each other against any additional country that joined the British side, specifically excluding the Soviet Union from the potential list of pro-British nations. That this provision involved primarily the United States was clearly understood. Although the Germans informed the Soviets about the Tripartite Pact at the last moment, Stalin was understandably alarmed, suspecting that the three powers might sooner or later turn against him. To trick Stalin, Hitler indicated that there was no reason why the Soviets could not join the Tripartite Pact. Molotov was invited to Berlin to discuss the pact and other outstanding matters regarding German-Soviet relations. In reality, Hitler was already busy behind the scenes with preparations to attack the Soviet Union. When Molotov arrived in Berlin on November 12, 1940, his German hosts pretended that the war with Britain was as good as won. They hoped that the Soviet Union would join the Tripartite powers in dividing the world into specific geopolitical spheres of influence. The Italians and Germans, according to this fantasy, would drive southward toward Africa, the Soviets would drive toward the Near East and the Indian Ocean, and the Japanese would take over South and Southeast Asia.[41] Molotov was not convinced by these lofty visions, and he stubbornly stuck to specific realities, namely, what the Germans were up to in Finland and the Balkans and what they meant by the "New Order" in Europe. The meeting accomplished nothing other than to deepen already existing suspicions. It ended in a curious session between Ribbentrop and Molotov, held in an air-raid shelter during an RAF night raid on Berlin. When the two men were alone together, Ribbentrop reportedly said to Molotov: "Now here we are together. Why should we not divide?" Molotov's reply was: "What will England say?" Ribbentrop responded that Britain was no longer a power, to which Molotov gave the famous riposte: "If this is so, why are we in this shelter, and whose are these bombs which fall?"[42] Neither Molotov nor Stalin believed in these German fantasies about Africa, but Stalin did not suspect that Hitler was preparing rapidly to attack him. Right up to the invasion of Russia in June 1941, Stalin did everything to appease Hitler; he even accelerated delivery of economic supplies by running extra trains to Germany.

While Hitler's imagination was gazing eastward, there was still a war to fight in the west. His military advisers argued that there were other ways of striking at England than by air. Admiral Raeder, for example, repeatedly urged Hitler to strike at Britain in a more favorable theater of operations such as the Mediterranean, where Spain, Italy, and Vichy France could be enlisted as allies in delivering a deathblow to Britain's imperial position. Accordingly, in October 1940, Hitler embarked on a personal diplomatic mission to see Franco, Pétain, and Mussolini. However, he failed to forge a Mediterranean alliance because he had no intention of treating these nations as coequals and saw them simply as weak satellites whose destiny lay in serving German war aims. On October 23, Hitler met Franco at the Spanish frontier town of Hendaye, where he had traveled by private railroad car. His promise to return Gibraltar to Spain in return for joining the war on Germany's side did not impress the Caudillo, who refused to be awed by Hitler and, in a grueling conversation that lasted for nine hours, achieved the amazing distinction of being the first man who actually dominated the führer in a personal encounter. Afterward, Hitler admitted that he would never go through anything like that again, claiming that he would rather have three or four of his teeth taken out. Upon Franco's shrewd evasions followed Marshal Pétain's equivocations, aptly summarized by the old soldier's cynical remarks to a friend: "It will take six months to discuss this programme and another six months to forget it."[43] When the tired führer reached Mussolini he received another shock: on October 28, the day Hitler's private train rolled into Florence, the Duce met Hitler at the train station with the news that early that morning victorious Italian soldiers had crossed the Albanian border on their way to Greece — an initiative the führer had attempted to prevent, suspecting correctly that Italian military weakness might drag Germany into a Balkan quagmire it could ill afford. As Allan Bullock rightly observed, "Since the defeat of France nothing had gone right for Germany: the British had refused to come to terms; the Spaniards and the French had proved elusive and unreliable; Gibraltar remained untaken and the French colonial empire remained unsecured."[44]

Mussolini's attack on Greece proved to be an embarrassing failure. The Italian army was poorly equipped, and the morale of its troops was low. Diplomatically, the Duce's aggression was not only ill advised — it was stupid. Hitler had just succeeded in pacifying the Balkan states when Mussolini stirred up renewed turmoil. Both Yugoslavia and Bulgaria had claims on Greece; Russia might be tempted into taking sides; and Britain might counter the Italian move by occupying Greece and thus gaining a foothold in the western Mediterranean. What made matters worse was the dismal performance of the Italian army, which met determined opposition by Greek fighters and had to withdraw to the mountains of Albania in December, where it was stuck until the spring of 1941.

Hitler never regarded the Mediterranean as his major theater of operation; and Mussolini's invasion of the Balkans forced him to delay fulfilling his real intention — the invasion of Russia. In the spring of 1941, therefore, he moved with impatient speed on both the diplomatic and military fronts hoping to settle the Balkan problem quickly so that he could move against the Russians.

The Duce had arrogantly referred to the Mediterranean as "our sea" (*mare nostrum*) and made outrageous demands that were far out of keeping with his actual military power. Thus, he demanded Nice, Corsica, Tunis, and eastern Algeria from France and the Suez from Great Britain. Already in possession of Libya and Cyrenaica, he attacked Egypt on September 12, 1940. Looking to the Balkans for further conquest, he moved from Albania toward Yugoslavia and Greece. However, the Greek king George II rejected the Duce's demands for strategic military outposts in northern Greece and, aided by British troops and supplies, chased the invading Italians out of Greece within fourteen days. On December 9, 1940, the English launched a counterattack in Egypt, retaking Sidi Barrani, Sollum, and Bardia. Capturing over two hundred thousand Italian prisoners between December 1940 and February 1941, the British threatened Libya and Cyrenaica, reestablished their Indian waterways, and liberated Ethiopia, returning Haile Selassie to the throne. For the first time, a country that had been conquered by one of the Axis powers had been liberated.[45] Having also established a small air force presence on the island of Crete, the British were close enough to threaten the oil fields of Romania, singled out by Hitler as vital to the German war effort.

With the Italians in defeat in Greece and North Africa, Hitler was afraid that the British might dominate the whole Mediterranean, which would threaten Vichy-controlled French colonies in North Africa and the Italian mainland from the south. Accordingly, Hitler issued several orders in December 1940 aimed at propping up his weak Italian ally. He ordered Göring to transfer several units of the Luftwaffe to southern Italy, from where they were to launch attacks on British positions in Africa and the Mediterranean. He also gave orders for the creation of a special desert tank division, later placed under the command of Erwin Rommel. On December 13, 1940, Hitler issued Directive Number 20, entitled "Operation Marita," which called for establishment of a strong force in southern Romania, and, after the return of favorable weather conditions in March 1941, this Romanian base of operations was to serve as a springboard for securing, by way of Bulgaria, the north coast of the Aegean and, if necessary, the whole Greek mainland.[46] Hitler's directive was based on friendly cooperation by the four major countries that separated Germany from Greece — Hungary, Romania, Yugoslavia, and Bulgaria. All four states had already been diplomatically and economically intimidated by Germany to the point that it would have been self-defeating to resist. In Hungary, a still semifeudal country, Admiral Horthy ruled in an authoritarian manner; he admired Hitler, joined the Tripartite Pact, and permitted German troops to march to Romania through his country. Romania was a monarchy under the young King Michael, but in actuality it was ruled by the Fascist dictator Marshal Antonescu, who also joined the Tripartite Pact and invited seventy thousand German "teaching corps" to Romania, ostensibly to train the Romanian army but in reality to occupy the Romanian oil fields and to pass into Bulgaria. On February 28, 1941, these German "advisers" marched into Bulgaria, whose ruler, King Boris, a supporter of the führer, pledged his cooperation and joined the other members of the Tripartite Pact a day after German troops had occupied his country. In March 1941, Hitler invited the Yugoslavian prime minister (Dragisa Tsetkovitch) and his foreign minister (Cincar Markovitch) to the Berghof and offered them Saloniki, which belonged to Greece, in return for joining the Axis powers. On March 25, 1941, Tsetkovitch signed the pact in Vienna; and the elated Hitler, pleased with his diplomatic efforts, told Ciano that the Greek situation would be resolved in a matter of days, provided that the weather was favorable. However, when Tsetkovitch and Markovitch returned to Belgrade, they were immediately arrested by high-ranking Serbian officers who had overthrown the regent, Prince Paul, replaced him with the young boy King Peter II, and repudiated the German alliance.

Hitler hastily summoned a war council at the chancellery to determine what sort of punishment should be meted out to the intransigent Yugoslavs. Whenever situations did not conform to his expectations, Hitler would lash out at everyone in sight and take impulsive action merely to satisfy his urge for revenge. This is exactly what happened in the Yugoslavian crisis. Hitler was so enraged by Belgrade's "treachery" that he was willing to postpone the Russian invasion by a whole month in order to deal with it. He ordered the destruction of Yugoslavia militarily and as a national unit; and so great was his fury that he insisted on destruction even in case of "any possible declarations of loyalty from the new government."[47] During the night of April 5–6, German forces marched into Yugoslavia, while squadrons of bombers headed toward Belgrade to carry out "Operation Capital Punishment," killing over seventeen thousand people and destroying a sizeable part of the city. Simultaneously other German forces invaded Greece from their bases in Bulgaria. As soon as April 12, German troops reached Belgrade from the south and north, forcing the small and poorly prepared Yugoslavian army to capitulate on April 17. The Greek campaign, fought with equal speed, lasted only four days longer. The Greek army capitulated and the swastika flew over the Athenian Acropolis. On May 4, 1941, Hitler gave his victory speech to the Reichstag — an address notable for its attempts to exculpate Mussolini for dragging Germany into the Balkan theater. Hitler asserted that the Balkan campaign was really inspired by England's efforts to gain a foothold in the area and by Yugoslavia's unpardonable insults to the Reich. In reality, the führer was drawn into the Balkans by Mussolini's failures; and the consequences of these blunders continued to consume his efforts in a theater of war that held little interest to him. Thus, after disposing of Yugoslavia, which he imperiously divided up between himself and Mussolini, Hitler continued to overextend himself by trying to recoup Mussolini's losses in Africa. The German corps sent to Africa under the command of General Rommel, operating with insufficient motorized equipment, opened its attack against British positions on March 24 and in twelve days reconquered the territories the Italians had lost the previous months. In late May (May 20–27) German parachutists captured the island of Crete from the British, thus acquiring a splendid air base in the Mediterranean from which they could attack British positions in Egypt, Palestine, and Iraq. In fact, had Hitler poured additional forces into the Mediterranean theater of war, as Admiral Raeder and General Rommel persistently urged him to do, Germany might well have struck a fatal blow to Britain's imperial position in the Middle East — "a deadlier blow than the taking of London."[48] As Allan Bullock argued, Hitler's intuition failed him badly at this crucial junction in the war.[49]

His deputy and designated successor also failed him. On May 10, 1941, Rudolf Hess embarked on his secret and, as it would turn out, futile flight to Scotland to convince the British to make peace with Germany. Endless speculation has surrounded this bizarre mission, but this much is certain: Hess had been fading in the Nazi hierarchy for some time and decided to regain his credibility with the führer by doing something unusual, which his daring flight certainly was. There is also some evidence that Hess was already showing signs of serious mental problems. Precisely what the British did with him, other than locking him up and informing the world that they would try him as a war criminal after the war had been won, is not known in detail. It is safe to assume that the British broke him and that Hess told them about Hitler's plan to invade the Soviet Union. Goebbels tells us that Hitler was in tears and looked ten years older when he heard the news, but this did not prevent the führer from announcing that Hess, after already showing traces of serious mental problems, had finally gone mad. This was hardly reassuring to those Germans who still remembered quite vividly that on September 1, 1939, Hitler had publicly told them that they should have blind trust in his designated successor.

The possibility that Hess might have revealed information about the invasion of Russia did not seem to have made any difference to Hitler's determination to press ahead with the project. Even in the fall of 1940, when he was bogged down in the Mediterranean, his real focus had been on Russia all along. The destruction of Bolshevism and world Jewry constituted Hitler's central aim. Conversely, ideological reasons had always prompted him to avoid a prolonged war with the British, a nation he admired much but understood little. With his resources stretched to the utmost, Hitler knew that he could not pursue a war of attrition on two fronts simultaneously and that the defeat of the Russians on the eastern front dwarfed every other consideration. It may be objected that Hitler was already fighting on two fronts in 1941, but this is not how the führer perceived the situation in the spring of that year. In a series of brilliant campaigns he had overrun Poland and Norway in four and eight weeks, respectively; Holland and Belgium in five days; France in six weeks; Yugoslavia in eleven days; and Greece, including the island of Crete, in three weeks. Much of North Africa was under his control as well. With these conquests he was already master of the Western world, hailed by most Germans, including his generals, as the greatest military commander of all times. Why should the conquest of Russia be any different? Those who caught him musing about this subject in late 1940 and the spring of 1941 report that he repeatedly tried to persuade himself that he would have a quick and easy victory in Russia. So persistent was his need to justify his impending action that it amounted to a kind of auto-intoxication, manifesting itself in grandiose or sweeping judgments about the "clay colossus without a head; the Bolshevized wasteland."[50] He decided it would all be over in a matter of weeks, and he expostulated to Jodl: "We have only to kick in the door and the whole rotten structure will come crashing down."[51] The rewards of such a conquest, he had convinced himself, would be colossal, as immense riches would flow into the fatherland from the vast resources of the Ukraine; all of Russia would eventually become Germany's breadbasket, the new frontier of proud Aryan colonists who would reenact in the east what the American pioneers had achieved in the west. Naturally, there would be obstacles in the way, just as there had been unfamiliar terrain and native redskins in the American West, but these barriers would be ruthlessly brushed aside by his conquering knights.

Operation Barbarossa: The Invasion of Russia

At 7:00 A.M. on June 22, 1941, Joseph Goebbels read over the radio the following proclamation by the führer to the German people:

> Weighed down with heavy cares, condemned to months of silence, I can at last speak freely — German people! At this moment a march is taking place that, for its extent, compares with the greatest the world has ever seen. I have decided again today to place the fate and future of the Reich and our people in the hands of our soldiers. May God aid us, especially in this fight.[52]

This proclamation, like most surprises Hitler had sprung on the German people, was a fait accompli because the invasion against the Soviet Union had already been underway for several hours. Hitler had massed on the Russian frontier the most terrifying arsenal of arms that had ever been assembled in the history of human warfare: 153 divisions (over three million men), 600,000 motorized vehicles, 3,580 tanks, 7,184 artillery pieces, and 2,740 airplanes.[53] The German force was buttressed by twelve Romanian divisions, eighteen Finnish divisions, three Hungarian divisions, and two and a half Slovak divisions. Later, the invaders were joined by three Italian divisions and a Spanish "blue division."

This massive force had been assembled in great secrecy, and when the flash of over seven thousand artillery pieces lit the sky in the early morning of June 22, raining fire and destruction on the thinly manned Russian line, German listening posts again and again picked up the Russian message: "We are being fired on; what shall we do?"[54] The immediate Russian response was to run, regroup, and sort out the tremendous confusion that followed in the wake of the German invasion.

Hitler's attack on Russia followed the familiar pattern of his earlier blitzkrieg campaigns. After a swift surprise assault of the Luftwaffe, which resulted in a stunning loss of over four thousand Russian airplanes, mostly on the ground, armored columns carved up the Soviet army in battles of pincerlike encirclement. The German force was divided into three army groups: Army Group North, led by Field Marshal Ritter von Leeb; Army Group Center, commanded by Field Marshal Fedor von Bock; and Army Group South, directed by Field Marshal Gerd von Rundstedt. As in France and Poland, the German tank forces were kept separate from the general infantry and organized into four groups, headed by outstanding tank commanders — Field Marshal Ewald von Kleist, Colonel General Heinz Guderian, General Hermann Hoth, and

General Erich Hoepner. Hitler's directive on Operation Barbarossa, as the invasion was called, never clearly outlined a specific geographical target, although the German army groups were targeted toward Leningrad in the north, Moscow in the center, and the Ukraine in the south. The ultimate aim, however, was the destruction of the Soviet army rather than the occupation of Soviet cities.

The military attack on the Soviet Union by the German Wehrmacht overshadowed the gruesome reality of a second attack on civilians carried out simultaneously by Himmler's special extermination squads (*Einsatzgruppen*). Few people realized that Hitler's war against the Soviet Union was more than a conventional war: it was also a racial-biological war whose ultimate goal was the extermination of the "Jewish-Bolshevik intelligentsia." In a military conference, held three months before the invasion of Russia began, Hitler had given the following forewarning to the senior commanders who had been chosen to conduct the campaign against Russia:

> The war against Russia will be such that it cannot be conducted in a chivalrous fashion. This struggle is one of ideologies and racial differences and will have to be conducted with unprecedented, merciless and unrelenting harshness. All officers will have to rid themselves of obsolete ideologies. I know that the necessity for such means of waging war is beyond the comprehension of you generals but I...insist absolutely that my orders be executed without contradiction. The [Russian] commissars are the bearers of ideology directly opposed to National Socialism. Therefore the commissars will be liquidated.[55]

According to General Halder, Hitler rationalized these brutal measures by pointing out to his generals that Russia had not signed the Hague Convention and therefore was not entitled to receive humane treatment at the hands of its enemies. In actuality, Hitler regarded the Russians as subhuman and the Soviet territory as a Bolshevized wasteland. The Russian people, he believed, were fit only to be slaves, and once they had come under German rule they had to be ruthlessly subjugated. "Nothing would be a worse mistake," he asserted, "than to seek to educate the masses there. It is in our interest that the people should know just enough to recognise the signs on the roads. At present they can't read, and they ought to stay like that."[56] Similarly, little if anything should be done by the German conquerors to improve the health of the Russians. Hitler preferred the Russians dirty and unsanitary. He claimed that, in any case, the Russians "scarcely get beyond fifty or sixty. What a ridiculous idea to vaccinate them. In this manner, we must resolutely push aside our lawyers and hygienic experts. No vaccination for the Russians, and no soap to get the dirt off them."[57]

The subjugation of the Russian people, particularly the extermination of its leadership, was assigned to Heinrich Himmler and four special task forces (*Einsatzgruppen*) of security police and SD men. Additionally, special Reich commissioners were appointed to administer the rear areas in the official spirit of "conquer, rule, and exploit." The tone of this bestial policy had been set by Himmler and Heydrich, who orally gave the leaders of the eastern task forces their blessing to murder all Jews, Asiatic inferiors, Communist functionaries, and Gypsies.[58] Several decrees by Hitler reinforced this policy. In one decree, he made the military personally immune to prosecution against crimes committed against civilians; and in the infamous Commissar Order, first formulated on March 31, 1941, he gave unit commanders carte blanche to liquidate Soviet commissars.[59] Hitler's views, in turn, permeated the thinking of numerous commanders who often sanctioned, if only by their silence, the radical measures of Nazi zealots. A guideline issued by the German high command to three million soldiers shortly before the attack of June 22 demanded "ruthless and energetic measures against Bolshevistic agitators, guerrillas, saboteurs, Jews, and total elimination of all active and passive resistance."[60]

With all eyes focused on the spectacular advance of the German juggernaut, few people perceived the atrocities that were being committed in the rear areas. The gruesome truth, however, was that Himmler's henchmen, following upon the heels of the Wehrmacht, systematically rounded up Communist functionaries, Jews, intellectuals, and other "subversives," herded them into makeshift concentration camps, and murdered them in cold blood.

The speed of the German Panzers, the total domination of the air by the Luftwaffe, the buoyant morale of the German *Landser* (GI), and the brilliant coordination of all arms — all these gave the German attack an aura of invincibility.[61] The first three months of the invasion seemed to bear out all of Hitler's predictions. In early July, Army Group North reached Riga on the Baltic; a month later, Army Group Center conquered White Russia and captured Smolensk, thus drawing within two hundred miles of Moscow; finally, in the south the Germans captured the Ukrainian capital of Kiev, taking 665,000 prisoners and enormous amounts of matériel. The road to Moscow was now open because the southern attack had eliminated the flank threat to the central sector. This is why the High Command of the Army urged Hitler to concentrate the major thrust in the center, pressing on to Moscow. If Hitler had concentrated on one goal and coordinated strategy coherently with his commanders in the field, Russia might have been knocked out of the war in the autumn of 1941. However, Hitler vacillated between several objectives. He dawdled away precious time and endlessly frustrated his generals. When the campaign against Russia began, he emphasized the urgency of capturing the Baltic states and the city of Leningrad; a little later, he became enthusiastically involved in the southern strategy aimed at encircling the Soviet army in the Ukraine. When this appeared to be accomplished, he left his general hanging on a final decisive thrust against Moscow, emphasizing the importance of capturing Leningrad, linking up with the Finns, and cutting the Murmansk railroad. Although his generals unanimously recommended a frontal attack against Moscow, Hitler deliberately held Army Group Center in abeyance until Rundstedt had destroyed the Russian armies between the Dnieper and the Volga, clearing the Black Sea coast along the way and fanning out toward both the Volga and the Caucasus. Hitler's strategy was based on von Clausewitz's dictum that ultimate victory depends not on political or even geographical considerations but upon the methodical destruction of enemy armies in the field. The trouble was that by October 1941 Hitler's Russian campaign was anything but methodical. He had switched his objectives repeatedly, overextended himself on a thousand-mile front stretching from the Baltic to the Black Sea, and failed to deliver a knockout blow in any single sector.

Despite hints of potential trouble, the Germans were euphoric about their victories. Having virtually destroyed the Russian air force and delivered devastating blows on the Russian army, capturing well over a million prisoners, the invaders were confident of final victory before the year was out. On October 3, one day after Field Marshal von Bock finally directed his attack on Moscow, Hitler delivered a sanguinary speech in the Berlin Sportspalast in which he boasted that Russia was as good as knocked out of the war and would never rise up again.[62] Inflating his figures, he told his audience:

> The number of Soviet prisoners has grown to 2.5 million. The number of captured or destroyed cannon in our possession amounts to about 22,000. The number of destroyed or captured tanks in our possession totals over 18,000. The number of destroyed, damaged, and shot down aircraft is 14.5 thousand. And behind our troops the space is twice as large as that of the German Reich of 1933 when I assumed leadership, or four times as large as England.[63]

However, Hitler made a deadly mistake in assuming that the Red Army was finished, and he was wrong in predicting that he would be in Leningrad in three weeks. Hitler's misjudgments were by no means unique to himself; they were shared by most members of the German high command. These misjudgments rested on faulty intelligence, biased assumptions about "inferior" Russians, and anti-Communist wishful thinking about the ineffectiveness of the Bolshevik government and its armed forces.[64] German expectations of an inferior Russian military performance had been nurtured by the poor performance of the Russian army in World War I, the Soviet purge of the officers' corps in the 1930s, the lackluster Soviet campaign against the Finns in the winter of 1939–40, and the Soviets' inability to withstand the Germans' massive invasion in the first summer of the war.

Unable to withstand the initial German thrust, the Russians simply retreated and drew the Germans deeper and deeper into the vast Russian interior. At the same time, the Russians fought furious rearguard actions that noticeably slowed down the German advance, making many

German commanders wonder just how strong the Russians really were. German apprehensions about Russia's seemingly endless supply of manpower have been aptly characterized by Alan Clark in his dramatic reconstruction of Operation Barbarossa:

> First, exultation; the Germans counted heads, measured the miles of their advance, compared it with their achievements in the west, and concluded that victory was around the corner. Then, disbelief: such reckless expenditure could not go on, the Russians must be bluffing, in a matter of days they would exhaust themselves. Then, a certain haunting disquiet: the endless, aimless succession of counterattacks, the eagerness to trade ten Russian lives for one German, the vastness of the territory, and its bleak horizon.[65]

One German commander, Colonel Bernd von Kleist, prophetically likened the German army to an elephant attacking a multitude of ants: "The elephant will kill thousands, perhaps even millions of ants, but in the end their numbers will overcome him, and he will be eaten to the bone."[66] It was not only the disparity in human resources but also the weather that came to the aid of the Soviet Union. Only four days after Hitler delivered his euphoric speech in the Berlin Sportspalast, the autumn rains began in Russia, slowing down the German advance as soldiers, horses, tanks, and mechanized vehicles struggled through the heavy rain, swampy woodlands, and muddy roads. Not until November, when frost and ice made the roads more passable, did the German advance slowly resume, only to come to a dead halt when early winter — the worst in living memory — depressed the temperature to thirty degrees and later even sixty degrees below zero. Since Hitler had based his Russian campaign on a blitzkrieg victory, the prospect of a long conflict left the Germans unprepared. Panic began to spread throughout the German ranks. Guderian wrote to his wife that "the icy cold, the lack of shelter, the shortage of clothing, the heavy losses of men and equipment, the wretched state of our fuel supplies, all this makes the duties of a commander a misery, and the longer it goes on the more I am crushed by the enormous responsibility which I am to bear."[67]

Although the vanguard of the German offensive reached the suburbs of Moscow, seeing "the towers of the Kremlin reflecting the setting sun,"[68] the whole German advance had in fact ground to a halt. In addition, Stalin had acquired a strategic piece of information that would help turn the tide. Unknown to Hitler, Stalin had a German mole, Richard Sorge, in the German embassy in Tokyo who on October 4 or 5 had reported to Stalin that Japan had rejected a German proposal to attack Russia and that plans were afoot in Japan to attack the United States. Acting on this report, Stalin transferred his whole far eastern force — thirty-four Siberian divisions (250,000 men) with seventeen hundred tanks and fifteen hundred airplanes — to the Moscow front, thereby staving off almost certain defeat.[69] During the night of December 4–5, 1941, the Russians mounted a heavy counterattack with these fresh Siberian troops, employing seventeen armies, led by first-rate commanders whose names have gone down in history for their tactical acumen — Ivan Koniev, Andrei Vlasov, Vladimir Govorov, Konstantin Rokossovski, Mikhail Katukov, Vasili Kuznetsov, Lev Mikhailovich Dovator. The Soviets threw back the Germans with heavy losses. For a moment it appeared that the whole German front was about to cave in. Army Group Center under von Bock was on the verge of disintegration. Harassed commanders, engaged on a two-hundred-mile front on either side of Moscow, were suddenly haunted by the specter of Napoleon's disastrous campaign of 1812 and recommended an immediate tactical withdrawal. Göring's Luftwaffe was grounded. Tanks were largely immobilized because it took hours to thaw out the engines; guns and cannons jammed; oil congealed in the tank tracks; telescopic sights were frozen blind; thousands of soldiers froze to death because they had not been issued any winter clothes, and their tight boots, with nailed leather soles measured too closely to actual foot size, were ideal cold conductors.[70] Plagued by alarming casualties, regimental strength sank below 50 percent along the whole front. Seasoned officers and noncommissioned officers melted away and were replaced by less experienced men, so that it was not unusual to see lieutenants take command of battalions and sergeants lead companies.[71]

By contrast, the Russians were better prepared to fight winter campaigns. Their soldiers were routinely issued boots that were two sizes too large, enabling the wearer to insulate them with straw or newspapers. The Russians also used special winter motor oils and lubrications; their troops were more familiar with the terrain and more strongly motivated to protect Mother Russia from imminent collapse. After an initial failure of nerve, which had lasted for several days, Stalin had rallied the Russian people into defending their homeland, fortifying the capital, and stripping the southern and eastern fronts of their defenses and hurling everything they had at the advanced German positions. No wonder that one aghast OKW officer, who felt the brunt of the onslaught of these forces, exclaimed: "From the depths of Russia, undreamed-of masses of humanity were hurled against us....I can still see the situation maps of the next days and weeks: where until now the blue of our own forces had dominated the picture, with the enemies' red only sparsely sketched in, now from Leningrad right down to the sea of Azov thick red arrows had sprung up on every sector of the front, pointing at the heart of Germany."[72] Worse yet, the Russians were using superior military weapons. For the first time, the Russians poured a large number of new T-34 tanks into the breach. Against the heavy armor of the T-34, conventional German thirty-seven-millimeter antitank shells were useless.

As the führer contemplated this disaster-in-the-making from his wolf's lair in Rastenburg on December 7, 1941, another fateful message was received. Toward midnight, a press officer burst into Hitler's company and announced Japan's sneak attack on the American fleet at Pearl Harbor. The führer's immediate reaction was one of joy; he slapped his thighs in delight and exclaimed: "The turning point!" To Walter Hewel, his liaison officer at headquarters, he later confided: "Now it is impossible for us to lose the war; we now have an ally who has never been vanquished in three thousand years, and another ally (Italy) who has constantly been vanquished but always ended up on the right side."[73]

Hitler was clearly facing the most important crossroad in the war. Having attacked the Soviet Union, he was about to become fatally entangled with the United States. Although the Roosevelt government had officially declared a policy of neutrality, the American president had no illusions about the Nazi menace. In September 1940, Roosevelt gave the British fifty destroyers for convoy duty in return for a ninety-nine-year lease on British naval bases in Newfoundland and in the Caribbean. At the same time, the United States resumed military conscription and raised seventeen billion dollars for military purposes. In December 1940, President Roosevelt asked Congress for an approval of the Lend-Lease Act to aid all countries fighting to preserve freedom; he also described the United States as the arsenal of democracy. On March 11, the Lend-Lease Act was passed by Congress. By March 1941, Germany and the United States were moving closer and closer to war, although Hitler still reacted with some caution to American provocations. These included the seizure of German vessels in American ports; the occupation of Greenland by America and its use as an advance base for sending aid to Britain; the freezing of all Axis assets in America; the proclamation of the Atlantic Charter, announcing American cooperation with Britain in securing peace; and orders to American ships on convoy to shoot on sight all Axis ships encountered in the American neutrality zone.

Although Hitler had a low opinion of America, he was not oblivious to its vast resources and its productive capacity; and it was for this reason that he counseled a cautious role toward the United States when war began in September 1939. Attacks on the United States and its leaders in the German press were kept at low key, and instructions were given to the navy, especially German submarines, to avoid any incidents that might provoke American intervention. In October 1939, Hitler turned down a complete submarine blockade around the British Isles. However, Roosevelt did not make it easy for Hitler to pursue a cautious policy. The American president had made it clear on numerous occasions that he despised the Nazi regime and intended to support its victims by every possible means. Roosevelt's interventionist attitude, however, was limited by the terms of the Neutrality Act and by vocal isolationists in and out of Congress. In November 1939, the Neutrality Act was amended to permit the sale of arms to the Allies, but only on a "cash and carry basis."

On December 9, 1941, Roosevelt announced that he considered Germany just as guilty for attacking Pearl Harbor as Japan. Hitler gave immediate orders to his submariners to attack all American ships that could be found. On December 11, 1941, Hitler declared war on the United States. Most historians have described Hitler's declaration of war as an act of lunacy and a monumental blunder, arguing that by attacking the most powerful economic country in the world, while at the same time being bogged down with his army in the second most powerful country in the world, he virtually guaranteed Germany's defeat.[74]

Hitler's declaration could hardly be explained as an act of loyalty to Japan. In fact, Japan had concluded a neutrality act with Russia in April 1941 and gave every appearance of respecting it. Moreover, Japan gave no assistance to Hitler and by its neutrality could even be accused of sabotaging Hitler's effort to take Moscow. Stalin, after all, had held off the German offensive in front of his capital with Siberian troops that he had transferred from the Russo-Japanese military frontier. Furthermore, Hitler could have procrastinated on his commitment to Japan, demanding that the Japanese attack Russia in return for his declaration of war on America.

Why, then, did Hitler promptly declare war on the United States after Japan attacked Pearl Harbor? Shortly after the war, the U.S. State Department sent a special delegation of experts to Germany to interrogate Nazi leaders about Hitler's conduct of the war; and on the question of Hitler's declaration of war on the United States the commission drew a complete blank.[75] No one, it seemed, had a real clue about this baffling issue.

Although the definitive answer will probably never be known, buried forever in irrational motivation, some answers to the question can at least be advanced. First and foremost, it seems that Hitler's declaration of war on the United States was an act of willful defiance on the part of the vainglorious führer who was delighted after a year of provocations by the United States to smack the "lout" Roosevelt publicly in the face.[76] His speech to the Reichstag on December 11, in which he justified his decision, reveals all of his stock-in-trade clichés about Satanic American Jews goading Roosevelt into an interventionist course with Germany and using him as an instrument for saving their European counterparts.[77] Yet behind these clichés Hitler's real motives stood revealed: his declaration of war on the United Stated was the logical culmination of his racial policies. The führer now saw himself confronted by two interrelated foes: the United States and the Soviet Union, and the link between them was the Jew. In the conclusion of his speech on December 11, 1941, he made this quite clear when he said that the common front between the Anglo-Saxon-Jewish-capitalist world and the Bolshevist world was no surprise to him. It may be true, as Gerhard Weinberg speculated, that Hitler had long intended to wage war on the United States, but he knew that he first needed a big navy to do it. In the absence of such a navy, the Japanese provided him with that opportunity; they would fight the naval war with the United States by proxy until he was ready to battle America with his own mighty navy.[78] It may also be true, as some historians have suggested, that Hitler's declaration of war on the United States was rooted in his unconscious urge for self-destruction. Deeply aware that he could no longer win the war or even continue Germany's conquests, his pathological urge toward destruction now turned against his own people. If Germany could not win the war, it meant that he had been betrayed by Germany and that total destruction was merited.

On December 11, 1941, Hitler may not have suspected the fatal consequences of his monumental blunder of declaring war on the United States. Besides, his attention was focused on the crumbling front before Moscow and on countering the defeatist attitude of some commanders who recommended a tactical retreat. Hitler recognized that a precipitate withdrawal, however smoothly organized and executed, would create a devastating psychological impression of defeat, and it is for this reason that he resolutely prohibited commanders in the field to yield an inch of territory to the Soviets. In a directive of December 16, he gave orders that the defensive positions on the whole front had to be held and that violations would be severely punished. Commanders who still thought that they could act independently were summarily dismissed or court-martialed. Field Marshal von Rundstedt was dismissed from his post after his withdrawal from his unsuccessful attack on Rostov; von Brauchitsch, who had borne the brunt of Hitler's wrath on several occasions, resigned the day after the Russian counteroffensive; General Otto Forster was dismissed for withdrawing his Sixth Corps; General von Sponeck, the last German commander who called a retreat from Kerch in the Crimea after being faced with almost certain annihilation, was sentenced to death (later commuted); General Hoepner was sacked and cashiered from the army after withdrawing his Panzers; Field Marshal Leeb was retired after he failed to conquer Leningrad; and General Strauss was relieved of his command of the Ninth Army. Before the war had run its bloody course almost half of the German generals in top positions were sacked, transferred, humiliated, or disciplined. Despite the rumbling avalanche of disasters, the Generalität was never able to mount serious opposition to Hitler's destructive blunders. Despite their self-serving apologies, the German generals not only lacked moral courage but also betrayed their own tradition of protecting the national interest, for it should have been obvious to them that Hitler was not acting in Germany's best interest.

Hitler's winter offensive of 1940–41 had been reckless in both manpower and supplies. Over a million lives had been lost, and invaluable material had been squandered. Out of the 153 divisions that Hitler had hurled at the Soviets, only eight were operational in the spring of 1942. These stark realities, however, did not prevent Hitler from launching new offensive plans on all fronts in 1942. In the Mediterranean, Hitler formulated two broad operations: Operation Hercules, the capture of

Malta in order to secure Rommel's supply line in North Africa, and Operation Aida, the conquest of Egypt, the Suez, and the Middle East — a grandiose strategy, appropriately called the "Great Plan," aimed at a vast encirclement of the British Empire by Germany and Japan. On the eastern front Hitler ordered a major offensive in the south; its major targets were the Caucasus, with its vast oil supplies, and the industrial areas of the Donbass and of Stalingrad on the Volga. In this way, Hitler reasoned, he would smash the Russian economy and then deliver the coup de grâce in a final assault on the heart of the Bolshevik enemy — Moscow.

Although in retrospect these offensive plans proved to be Hitler's last, the year 1942 appeared to favor the German cause. In the spring of 1942 Rommel's Afrika Korps, which had been stopped by the British Eighth Army in December, began a spectacular offensive against the British that threw the Western powers into panic. In May, Rommel captured Tobruk, and in the third week of June he crossed the border into Egypt, threatening the whole Allied position in the Middle East with imminent collapse. Rommel came to a halt at El Alamein, only seventy miles from Cairo, where the British dug in and regrouped under the new command of one of the great generals of World War II — Sir Bernard Montgomery.

Britain's losses in North Africa were overshadowed by a savage and relentless attack on its supply lines in the Atlantic by German submarines. When it became obvious that Britain could not be subdued by air, Hitler concentrated all his efforts on starving Britain into submission by sinking as many ships as America could send to keep the island alive. Hitler had started the war with only fifty-six U-boats, but production was dramatically increased in the summer of 1940. By January 1942, the number of U-boats had increased to 249, menacing the delivery of vital supplies of munitions, raw materials, and food stuffs from America to Britain. Operating from relatively safe harbors in Norway and France, the U-boats inflicted heavy losses on Allied shipping to England. Moreover, the Japanese attack on Pearl Harbor had forced the United States to divert a part of its fleet to the Far East, thus further stripping an already overextended convoy force in the Atlantic. During the first half of 1942 German submarines destroyed 4.5 million tons of shipping, including essential supplies to the Russians by way of the northern seas to Murmansk.

In the beginning of 1942, the Russian prospects for victory were no better than those of the English, although the winter of 1941–42 had given the Soviets a temporary reprieve. Not only had the Soviets lost 4,500,000 people, but their richest territories and industrial resources had fallen into German hands. In a remarkable effort of improvisation involving a massive transfer of threatened industries from the western regions to the Volga areas and the Urals, the Soviets gradually recouped their initial losses. By the end of 1941, according to Gordon Wright, "1,360 large enterprises and some 200 smaller ones were disassembled,

hauled eastward by rail (along with most of their workers), and reassem-
bled in new buildings hastily put up for the purpose."[79] In 1942, Soviet
war production steadily rose again, reaching impressive figures in most
areas, especially in the production of tanks (two thousand per month)
and aircraft (three thousand per month).

In the spring of 1942, however, the Soviet counteroffensive, begun
in December 1941, gradually petered out; and a poorly planned thrust
by Marshal Timoshenko before Kharkov in April almost destroyed the
offensive capability of the Red Army. In the south, a Soviet attack on
German positions in the Crimea turned out to be an unmitigated disaster, leading to the capture of General Vlasov and his entire staff. General
von Manstein, who had been promoted to the command of the Eleventh
Army in the fall of 1941, received a marshall's baton for overrunning
the Crimean Peninsula and capturing the fortress of Sevastopol. Hitler
was so pleased with these German successes that he decided to move
his military headquarters from Rastenburg to Winniza in the Ukraine,
where he personally conducted the eastern campaign between July 17
and October 31, 1942. In a directive to his commanders, Hitler wrote
optimistically that "the unexpectedly rapid and favorable development
of the operations against the Timoshenko Army Group entitles us to
assume that we may soon succeed in depriving Soviet Russia of the Caucasus, with her most important source of oil, and of a valuable line of
communication for the delivery of English and American supplies. Coupled with the loss of the entire Donets industrial area, this will strike
a blow at the Soviet Union which would have immeasurable consequences."[80] Two days later Army Group South captured Rostov, and
its Panzer groups were closing in on Stalingrad.

Chapter 13

The New Nazi Racial Order
in Europe

Nazi Occupation of the Continent

Hitler's blitzkrieg campaigns were so rapid, the defeat of his enemies so unexpectedly precipitate, that the Nazis had no long-range plans to administer their conquered territories. Yet in little more than a year after the start of the war, Hitler was lord and master of the European continent. Only six nations — Ireland, Switzerland, Sweden, Spain, Portugal, and Turkey — managed to retain their neutrality and independence. All the other nations of Europe fell into the German orbit in one way or another. The Danubian states of Hungary, Romania, and Bulgaria retained a measure of autonomy as satellite nations, while Finland, after a brief period of neutrality, became a quasi-partner in Hitler's alliance. Even Italy slipped increasingly into a position servile to the Nazi regime, especially after a series of humiliating military defeats from which Mussolini had to be rescued by Hitler.

The Germans used three methods of ruling their conquered territories: outright annexation, occupation and administration, and indirect control through Nazi henchmen.[1] After Hitler had conquered Poland, he annexed the old Polish Corridor outright, merged Polish Silesia into German Silesia, and incorporated other parts of Polish territory into East Prussia. The rump of Poland, called "Government General" (Generalgouvernement), was ruled by Hans Frank, who referred to himself as the "king of Poland" and only granted the Poles a limited degree of self-government. The annexed territories were divided into two new provinces (*Reichsgaue*): West Prussia (later renamed Danzig-Westpreussen), including Danzig, Marienwerder, and Bromburg; and Posen (later called Wartheland), including Posen, Hohensalza, and Kalisch. Additionally, the Nazis annexed the two Polish districts of Kattowitz and Zichenau, incorporating the former into Silesia and the latter into East Prussia. In all of these Polish areas the Nazis extended the whole panoply of German law, administration, police, and education, depriving non-German groups of their civil rights and severely curtailing their economic and cultural activities. Recalcitrant Poles who resisted their new masters were imprisoned or dumped in the Government General.

In the west, Hitler annexed the Belgian border areas of Eupen, Malmedy, and Moresnet that had been transferred to Belgium after World War I. The grand duchy of Luxembourg, having initially resisted the Nazi invaders, was first ruled by a military government and was then placed under a civilian administration. In August 1940 Hitler appointed Gustav Simon, *Gauleiter* of Koblenz-Trier, as head of a civilian administration in Luxembourg and assigned him the task of incorporating the ancient duchy into Germany and "Germanizing" its inhabitants, which meant rooting out all non-German cultural traditions and forcing its young people to serve in the German armed forces. In August 1942 Luxembourg was incorporated into Simon's administrative fiefdom and renamed "Moselland."

The same fate befell Alsace and Lorraine, two areas subject to centuries of disputes between Germany and France; following recent wars, the areas had been transferred in 1871 to Germany and then in 1919 back to France. After an initial military government, the two provinces were placed under two *Gauleiter*: Robert Wagner, *Gauleiter* and *Reichstatthalter* of Baden, who took Alsace, and Josef Bürckel, *Gauleiter* and *Reichstatthalter* of the Saar-Palatinate, who received Lorraine. As in Luxembourg, the German authorities proceeded to Germanize the new territories without respect for their non-German inhabitants: French officials were dismissed; judicial, financial, and educational institutions were revamped; and the German "mother tongue" was "reintroduced."[2] Although prevented by the armistice terms with France from annexing Alsace-Lorraine outright, the two *Gauleiter* proceeded to treat the two provinces as German possessions, a reality underscored by the fact that Strasbourg became the capital of Alsace and Saarbrücken that of Lorraine.

Hitler's vicious retaliation against Yugoslavia for defying his plans in the spring of 1941 served as a pretext for detaching two-thirds of Slovenia from Yugoslavia, thus extending German territory close to the Adriatic. These territories, former crown lands of the Austrian Habsburgs, were Lower Styria, Corinthia, and Upper Carniola (Untersteiermark, Kärnten, and Oberkrain). They were attached to already existing *Gaue* of Corinthia and Styria. Finally, when Hitler invaded Russia, he annexed Bialystok, the Polish territory that had been seized by the Soviet Union in 1939.

As long as Germany was at war, Hitler preferred to occupy and administer conquered foreign territories as dependencies. Thus, as mentioned above, the rump of Poland was occupied, administered, and looted by Hans Frank. In Denmark and Norway, German occupation forces, working hand in glove with German civilian officials, initially played a relatively mild and unobtrusive role in government because

Hitler regarded the Scandinavians as Aryan kinsmen. In Denmark the royal family remained, whereas the Norwegian king and parliament had fled to Britain. The Danes retained a greater degree of political autonomy and were fortunate to be monitored by several good German administrators, although this began to change in the summer of 1942 when serious unrest resulted in harsher control, notably under the rule of SS-Gruppenführer Werner Best. In Norway the Germans initially ruled directly through a Reich commissioner, Josef Terboven, former *Gauleiter* of Essen. Belgium and two northwestern departments of France — Nord and Pas de Calais — were ruled by German authorities headquartered in Brussels. Hitler considered this area of great strategic importance because offensively it could serve as a springboard to Britain and defensively it was a buffer protecting the industrial Ruhr.[3] In Belgium the German military government, headed by General Alexander von Falkenhausen, a strong anti-Nazi, protected the people from the worst excesses of zealous Nazi functionaries until July 13, 1944, when Hitler finally gave in to Himmler's persistent demands to establish a civilian administration. The same cannot be said for Holland, where Artur Seyss-Inquart, the Nazi Reich commissioner, proposed an aggressive policy of Germanization and exploited the Netherlands for the German war economy. Occupied France, apart from the departments of Nord and Pas de Calais and a "closed zone" (*Sperrzone*) of border areas that ran from the mouth of the Somme to Lake Geneva, was governed by the office of the chief of the military administration headquartered in Paris, first under the command of General Otto von Stülpnagel and then of his cousin General Karl Heinrich Stülpnagel; the latter was one of the plotters of the July 20 attempt to assassinate Hitler. In addition to the military government, France was also subject to control by the armistice commission that was supposed to monitor provisions of the armistice until a final peace treaty was concluded, the influence of the German Foreign Office, and the meddlesome intrusion of Nazi functionaries representing the offices of Himmler, Göring, Sauckel, and Speer. There was a steady increase of partisan activities in France that culminated in the outburst of violence on both sides in the summer of 1944.

Nazi occupation of conquered Soviet territories constituted the most ambitious part of the New Order.[4] Four major Reich commissariats were planned: Ostland, the Ukraine, Moscovy, and the Caucasus, but only the first two of these were actually established. The Reich Commissariat Ostland, administered by Hinrich Lohse, *Gauleiter* of Schleswig-Holstein, included the three Baltic states of Lithuania, Latvia, and Estonia as well as White Russia. In view of its enormous size, the area was subdivided into four general commissariats, each named after its major territory: Lithuania was placed under the control of Dr. Adrian von Ranteln, Latvia under Dr. Otto Drechsler, Estonia under SS-Obergruppenführer Karl Sigismund von Litzmann, and White Russia under Wilhelm Kube. The most disorganized of these areas was White

Russia, where Kube constantly battled powerful Nazi functionaries and made himself so hated that if a Russian partisan had not blown him up by placing a bomb under his bed, he would have been fired or executed by the Nazis. The Ukraine, which was also subdivided into general commissariats, including Kiev, Volhynia-Podolia, Zhitomir, Nikoloev, Dnepropetrovsk, and Taurida, was considered the key to Germany's success in Russia because it was expected to serve as the potential breadbasket for the Reich. Rosenberg urged an alliance with the Ukrainians, but he was overruled by Hitler, Himmler, and Erich Koch, the civilian head of the Ukraine. Koch was arguably the most venal and incompetent administrator the Nazis could have put in charge of the area, "monumentally stupid" and brutal.[5] His brutalization and exploitation gave rise to a widely told joke that "Stalin, in awarding a medal for supreme service to the Soviet state, regretted that the man who deserved it most (i.e., Koch) was not yet in a position to receive it personally."[6]

This could be said of German rule in Russia as a whole, which was almost universally grim and ill advised. Although the Germans were greeted by the people as liberators, especially in the Ukraine, their brutality invariably elicited savage reactions of terrorism and partisan activities. Refusing to enlist the despised Slavic people in the campaign against Communism and adamantly rejecting the idea of arming them, the Germans deprived themselves of important support that very possibly might have made the difference between victory and defeat. Furthermore, starving prisoners of war or ruthlessly working them to death served no useful purpose, quite apart from the fact that it was criminal as well as immoral. Germany almost certainly lost the war when Hitler made Heinrich Himmler his executive officer in Russia and assigned him a twofold task — to settle ethnic Germans in the conquered territories and to enslave the subhuman Slavs. Himmler went about his task so ruthlessly, ignoring moral, military, and even economic considerations, that the Germans earned the utter hatred of the Russians and could look forward to the same treatment from them when the tide of war turned in 1942.

The other areas in Russia envisioned for occupation, the Crimea, the area around Moscow, and the Caucasus, were on the periphery of German conquest and therefore subject to the limitations entailed by remoteness and changing military fronts. The Caucasus oil fields were crucial to the German war effort, but the military administration established in the region, though competent and popular among the native ethnic groups, lasted only a little over a year. The Crimea, also in German hands for only a brief period, was to be completely Germanized and transformed into a tropical paradise, and for that reason Himmler's SS held sway there until 1944.[7]

In the other parts of Hitler's world, the emphasis was on indirect control and reliance on native henchmen to serve the needs of the Nazis. Czechoslovakia, as previously seen, had been dissolved as an autonomous state before the war and furnished the Germans with a model they could use after their rapid conquest added further acquisitions to the Reich. The western half of former Czechoslovakia became a German protectorate with some measure of local autonomy; the eastern part of Slovakia, however, became a virtual vassal state under a pro-Nazi regime headed by a Catholic priest, Josef Tiso. Nazi reliance on pliant henchmen was most notorious in Norway, where Vidukun Quisling had paved the way for Nazi control until he was eventually jobbed into office as prime minister; he then outlawed opposition parties and ruled exclusively through his Fascist Nasjonal Samling Party and the German military. In Vichy France, where Marshal Pétain ran a basically authoritarian but not Fascist government, Hitler allowed a measure of autonomy in hopes of enlisting France in his cause. Despite its loss to Germany, France still commanded the resources of an overseas empire, a navy, and a merchant marine fleet. However, Pétain refused to be drawn into active participation in Hitler's New Order; and against great pressure, especially from internal collaborationists such as Pierre Laval and Admiral Jean François Darlan, he succeeded in resisting Hitler's designs. By the end of 1942 Hitler had lost his opportunity in France; the French overseas empire was beyond his grasp, and the French navy had been scuttled. In the spring of 1943 Hitler had also lost his bases in North Africa; and to protect his southern flank, he proceeded to occupy all of France and placed it under German military administration, appointing Field Marshal Gerd von Rundstedt as supreme military governor of France.

In southeastern Europe, Hitler relied primarily on local pro-Fascist rulers in the three satellite states of Hungary, Romania, and Bulgaria — Admiral Miklos Horthy in Hungary, Marshal Mihai Antonescu in Romania, and King Boris of Bulgaria. In general, Hitler preferred to leave Mussolini the illusion of control in the Balkans under cover of a strong German military presence. Yugoslavia was carved up into three puppet regimes in the spring of 1941: Croatia, led by the Fascist Ante Pavelić; Serbia, ruled by a military collaborator, General Milan Nedić; and the state of Montenegro, governed by a council of local pro-Fascists largely under Italian control. The Croatian nationalists were fanatical and murderous killers who tried to expel or exterminate all Serbs, Muslims, and Jews, plunging the country into a bloodbath under Pavelić's Ustasa movement. Serbian rule was no better. The Germans were primarily interested in exploiting the Bor copper mines, showed little interest in governing the country humanely, and cooperated with the anti-Communist Nedić in tyrannizing a population that would soon retaliate against their oppressors under partisan leaders like Marshal Tito and Draža Mihajlović. In Greece, Hitler opted for a supportive role, with Mussolini in command as a figurehead. In reality, the Nazis retained real political control over Greece and the Balkans. Although the coastal areas of northwestern Yugoslavia, Dalmatia, Montenegro, and

Albania had been awarded to Italy, the Balkans as a whole were in reality under the control of the Wehrmacht. This, however, turned out to be an administrative fiasco.[8] Ostensibly, Field Marshal Wilhelm List was the supreme commander of the southeast, administering the area from his headquarters in Salonika; but his jurisdiction was not always recognized by General Ludwig von Schröder, whom Hitler had appointed commander of Serbia. Nor was the situation improved by the fact that List had to supervise two commanders in Greece — one commanding the Salonika-Aegean area and the other southern Greece and Crete. Although various administrative changes were made to rationalize the situation, German policy in the Balkans remained a muddle of overlapping commands and obstructions caused by intrusive Nazi functionaries promoting their agendas (Himmler, Göring, Ribbentrop).

In summarizing the Nazi occupation and administration of Europe, several common features can be identified. The first one is that Hitler consciously chose not to set up a uniform system of government in the occupied countries because he feared that someone might build up a strong power base in the field that could represent a serious challenge.[9] In his new empire, as in the old Reich, Hitler employed the same manipulative political strategies that had by now become second nature to him — that is, to encourage rival offices and functionaries, to set them against each other in order to promote competition, and to retain for himself the final power on all decisions. This management style, based as it was on secrecy and lack of trust, caused the same problem abroad as it did at home, seriously hampering the conduct of the war and therefore contributing to the defeat.

Another common feature followed from this lack of uniformity and organizational confusion. In all of the occupied countries the Nazis reenacted the same internecine conflicts that had been going on for years on their home turf. Hitler's chief paladins extended their rivalries into the new territories. The conflict of personal or organizational agendas was nowhere more blatant than it was in Russia, where Rosenberg, Himmler, Sauckel, Göring, and the Wehrmacht were constantly fighting turf battles.

On one common goal, however, the Nazis were all agreed, and that was to dominate, administer, and exploit. It is true that the Nazis treated some conquered people (Scandinavians, Dutch, Belgians, Greeks) better than others, but that was only a matter of degree. The Nazis also encouraged local Fascist movements such as Quisling's Nasjonal Samling in Norway, the National-Socialistische Beweging in Holland, the Danish Nazis under Frits Claussen, Staf de Clercq's Vlaamsch National Verbond, and Leon Degrelle's Rexist Party, representing the Walloons, in Belgium; but here again, these groups were never regarded as coequals, partly because the Nazis were inherently ethnocentric and partly because Hitler was afraid that they might build up their own autonomous Fascist nations with expansionist policies. The most he was willing to give his foreign followers was a subsidiary role within the Nazi New Order as co-belligerents or, as in the case of Leon Degrelle, allowing them to command their own legions within the Waffen-SS (SS-Division blinde Wallonie).

In the end, the Nazi New Order was little more than a slave empire, a vast system of organized oppression, exploitation, and extermination. Not a single humane ideal inspired it. All it left was a trail of hideous and unspeakable crimes.

Nazi Crimes

The crimes the Nazis committed against conquered people are too numerous to be listed in detail. In general terms, they can be divided into crimes involving organized plunder of property and liquid assets and crimes against individuals and targeted ethnic groups. The nature of the crimes varied according to the geographical location of the conquered territory and the ethnic composition of its population. Eastern and southeastern European countries were subjected to a far greater degree of inhumanity than the northern or western countries. The Nazis viewed the Scandinavians, Dutch, and Flemish as racial kinsmen who would eventually share dominance in the new German order. The populations living to the west and south of the Germanic people — the French, Spaniards, Italians — were considered to be of inferior racial quality but worthy of being potential allies. The eastern and southeastern peoples, on the other hand, were regarded as racially inferior and fit only to be slaves. The Poles, for example, were to be uprooted at will to make room for new Germanic settlers. The remainder of Poland was to be subjected to a policy of spoliation that Hitler himself called the devil's work (*Teufelswerk*).[10] In Poland, Russia, and the Balkan countries the German authorities plundered at will. Although the rest of Europe was not treated quite as shamelessly, the pattern was similar. German financial agents seized the major assets of a country's wealth, levied high occupation costs, and indiscriminately confiscated or sequestered land or real estate for German use. In order to assure a steady supply of raw material and foodstuffs from the conquered territories, the Germans seized their banking systems and manipulated them for their own purposes. The German mark was set excessively high in relation to other currencies, which allowed the Germans to purchase goods at favorable exchange rates. The economies of all occupied countries were carefully monitored and controlled by German financial agents who, under the cover of practicing a *Grossraumwirtschaft* (greater territorial economy), claimed to work for "a mutual integration and linkage of interest" between the German economy and the conquered territories.

The phrase "mutual integration and linkage" comes from Hermann Göring, who meant by it little more than plunder and exploitation. In fact, the sybaritic Göring was one of the biggest looters, especially of the art treasures of Europe. Göring either personally or through his agents rounded up prized art objects from museums, private art dealers, or wealthy owners in conquered territories.[11] His collection was large enough to fill several museums and had to be distributed all over Germany. At the end of the war works of famous masters such as Hals, Van Dyck, Goya, Rembrandt, Velázquez, Rubens, Titian, Raphael, David, the Cranach School, Boucher, and Vermeer were found in Göring's villa and various castles, monasteries, and caverns. Göring and other party collectors like Rosenberg justified such looting as in line with Hitler's official policy that many of the world's greatest treasures were to be displayed after the war in Linz, where Hitler planned to create the biggest museum in the world. According to an interim report of itemized "acquisitions" made in July 1944, around 22,000 art objects had been seized by German authorities, including 5,281 paintings.[12]

Crimes against persons can be grouped into five broad categories: (1) slave labor, (2) abuse of prisoners of war, (3) torture and execution of hostages, (4) cruel and unusual medical experiments, and (5) organized atrocities.

Once the possibility of a protracted conflict had become reality, the Nazi leadership decided to wage an economic war as brutal as the military one they had been fighting. The tactics varied, but they generally can be summed up by the phrase "smash and grab."[13] This involved smashing the enemy in a quick lightning war, stripping the conquered territory of its raw material, and ruthlessly exploiting any manpower available to serve the needs of the Reich. Göring, who had been entrusted with the economic exploitation of conquered territories, stated the official German view when he callously observed that "in the old days, the rule was plunder. Now, outward forms have become more humane. Nevertheless I intend to plunder, and plunder copiously."[14] In a similar vein Heinrich Himmler expressed the official policy of the SS when he addressed a group of SS major generals at Posen in October 1943 and declared that "whether nations live in prosperity or starve to death interests me only insofar as we need them for slaves for our *Kultur*. Otherwise it is of no interest to me."[15] Göring and Himmler, in turn, had taken their cue from Hitler, whose feelings about conquered territories were no secret. In his endless monologues at führer headquarters he set the tone on the subject of conquered territories, outdoing everyone in calculated brutality. Marveling at the vast spaces of the eastern territories, he envisioned a policy of systematic exploitation: "Our guiding principle must be that these people have but one justification for existence — to be of use to us economically. We must concentrate on extracting from these territories everything that is possible to extract."[16] As for the "ridiculous hundred million Slavs," Hitler suggested molding "the best of them to the shape that suits us, and we will isolate the rest of them in their own pig-sties; and anyone who talks about cherishing the local inhabitant and civilising him, goes straight off into a concentration camp!"[17]

Of all the resources desired by the Nazi conquerors, manpower was the most vital because the war had seriously depleted the available labor pool in the Reich. In the Allied nations, women filled the gap created by conscription, but Hitler resolutely opposed conscripting women into war industries. Instead, the Nazi masters recruited foreign labor among the able-bodied prisoners and civilians of all occupied territories. This policy was started right after the Polish campaign, and it continued until the end of the war. By the end of 1941 almost four million foreigners worked in Germany, most of them Poles who had been ruthlessly rounded up by press-gang methods in Hans Frank's Government General. Despite these impressive gains in manpower, it became increasingly clear that a war fought on many fronts simultaneously required twice as many workers as were available in 1941. Accordingly, in March 1942 Hitler established a new office entitled Plenipotentiary for Labor Allocation and put Fritz Sauckel, *Gauleiter* of Thuringia, in charge of the new manpower department. Sauckel's job was to procure, allocate, and exploit all foreign labor, and he did so with efficient cruelty. Sauckel's agents filled their quotas by rounding up foreigners in town squares, churches, cinemas, or other places where people congregated in great numbers and shipping them back to Germany in freight cars.

Within only a year Sauckel managed to round up close to 2.1 million foreign workers, bringing the total to 7 million by the middle of 1944.[18] In addition to these 7 million foreign workers in Germany, there were 7 million men and women who worked for the German war economy in their own countries producing munitions, goods, or building fortifications. Although German employers did not universally mistreat their foreign workers, especially those from western countries, they showed little concern for their basic human needs. As to workers from eastern Europe, the German conquerors treated them essentially like slaves. Thousands of Russian prisoners had been herded into makeshift camps following the German invasion, and many of these prisoners died from malnutrition or disease. Only gradually did the Nazis subordinate ideology to economic necessity and mobilize these prisoners for wartime work. Even so, Nazi policy toward conquered people was calculated to incite opposition and obstruction.

One of the four major charges at the Nuremberg trials was "war crimes" — that is, specific violations of international agreements such as The Hague or Geneva Conventions and of basic principles of national or international law. War crimes included murder, mistreatment of civilians, execution of hostages, crimes involving prisoners of war, and massacre of civilian populations. The Nazis were judged guilty of all these offenses, and specific organizations were singled out as being major culprits — the SS, SA, the general staff and OKW, the Reich cabinet, the leadership cadre of the NSDAP, and the Gestapo and SD. Of these organizations, the leadership cadre of the NSDAP, the SS, Gestapo, and SD were branded "criminal organizations," a decision that has been and continues to be subject to considerable debate and controversy.

What cannot be challenged, however, is that many crimes against persons of all ages and nationalities were committed and sanctioned by Nazi authorities. Violations of The Hague and Geneva Conventions, safeguarding the rights of prisoners, were routinely violated on the eastern front, less commonly on the western front. As previously noted, Hitler regarded the war against the Soviets as a war of ideologies, a war of biological extermination, and in the infamous Commissar Order of June 6, 1941, he ordered the immediate executions of Communist functionaries, justifying this brutal measure not only on ideological grounds but also on the flimsy pretext that the Russians had never signed the Geneva Convention. The consequence was unspeakable atrocities against Polish and Russian prisoners of war. In cooperation with the Wehrmacht, SD and police officials would screen prisoners and execute Communist functionaries on the spot. Wounded or sick prisoners were also turned over to these so-called police officials and then shot as "useless eaters." The rest were either incarcerated in concentration camps, sent to the Reich as slave laborers, or simply allowed to starve to death. Of at least five and a half million Soviet prisoners of war, half died. This grotesque treatment, of course, was not only criminal but stupid because thousands of Soviet prisoners, especially in the Ukraine, initially welcomed the Germans as liberators and were willing to assist them in what they regarded as a fight against Communist oppression. Yet Hitler consistently rejected the idea of using captured Soviet troops, some of whom had been organized by General Andrei Vlaasov into a national army of liberation, because he distrusted all Russians and saw such renegades as useful only as propaganda tools.[19]

Western prisoners were treated better, but many cases of mistreatment and outright criminality occurred. Sadistic camp commandants often mistreated and shot prisoners "while trying to escape." On October 18, 1942, Hitler issued a top secret commando order that directed that all enemies on commando missions in or out of uniform "are to be slaughtered to the last man."[20] In response to constant Allied saturation bombings, captured flyers were often set upon by irate Germans and lynched on the spot. In March 1944, seventy-five Royal Air Force officers escaped from Stalag Luft III at Sagan in Silesia. Some were captured almost immediately, others gradually rounded up by the police; the latter were shot on Hitler's order. In the same month two British officers were shot in a camp at Eichstätt in Bavaria for leaving their barracks and cheering when they saw Allied planes fly over the camp.[21] One month later, on May 21, 1944, Hitler decreed that enemy aviators who machine-gunned German transport, civilians, or parachutists could be executed on the spot.[22] In September 1944 forty-seven Allied flyers were worked to death at Mauthausen. One of the most notorious murders of prisoners occurred at Malmedy during the Battle of the Bulge (December 17, 1944) when SS troops machine-gunned seventy-one American soldiers in cold blood.

Mistreatment of civilians was often as bad, if not worse, than that of prisoners of war. In eastern Europe, the official policy toward the civilian population was to seize their property and make them "work, work, and work again." This was justified on the grounds that "we are the master race, which must remember that the lowest German worker is racially and biologically a thousand times more valuable than the population here."[23] Anyone who resisted was severely punished. Attacks by civilians on German troops were answered promptly by rounding up hostages and executing them. At Nuremberg, Keitel and other army commanders were confronted with dozens of orders detailing crimes relating to the torture of hostages. Almost thirty thousand hostages were killed in France during the occupation, eight thousand in Poland, three thousand in Holland, thousands in the Balkans, and close to a thousand in Greece. In every country occupied by the Germans, hostages were taken and shot. This was either openly publicized or secretly carried out. The scope of these operations varied from country to country. In eastern Europe, the policy was to shoot fifty to one hundred or more hostages for every German killed or for other acts of sabotage. One local German official in Poland frankly admitted that "I did not hesitate to say that for every German killed, up to 199 Poles would be shot."[24] Torture often preceded the execution of hostages:

> The use of torture in the interrogations was almost a general rule. The tortures usually applied were beating, whipping, chaining for several days without a moment of rest for nourishment or hygienic care, immersion in ice water, drowning in a bath tub, charging the bath water with electricity, electrification of the most sensitive parts of the body, burns at certain places on the body and the pulling out of fingernails.[25]

One of the most fiendish acts of terrorism visited upon civilian populations living under German control was Hitler's *Nacht und Nebel* (night and fog) decree of December 7, 1941, under which persons who committed offenses against the German occupation forces could be killed or secretly snatched during "night and fog" so that loved ones would never know what happened to them.[26]

At Auschwitz and other German concentration camps prisoners were abused for every conceivable reason. One of the most sinister practices was the use of human beings for medical experiments by Nazi doctors. Mengele and men of his stripe used people because they were, in the words of one physician, the cheapest experimental animals, cheaper than rats.[27] From August 1942, at Dachau, Dr. Sigmund Rascher conducted freezing experiments on about three hundred prisoners — Jews, Gypsies, Poles, Russians — dumping them, some naked and others dressed in aviators' uniforms, into icy water to observe how their bodies would react to extreme cold and to see what might be done to revive them. Rascher and his assistants carefully recorded every detail of the prisoners' reactions to the experiments, noting they foamed at the mouth, writhed in pain, went into death rattles, or faded into semiconsciousness. When the temperatures of prisoners' bodies went below 79.7 degrees, Rascher tried various methods of reviving them, ranging from rapid heat in bathtubs, heated blankets, diathermy of the heart, and drugs, to the outlandish treatments involving the use of prostitutes to excite and rewarm the frozen prisoners through sexual intercourse.

Rauscher's experiments on hypothermia were sponsored by Himmler and the armed forces in an effort to find better ways of dealing with exposure to extreme cold, and for that reason the Nazi doctors had no ethical objections, arguing that these experiments were done to save lives. The fact that lives were lost apparently did not faze them; these were "lower lives." Rauscher and his colleagues also conducted experiments for the Luftwaffe on human reactions to high-altitude flight. Prisoners were thrown into a decompression chamber provided by the Luftwaffe and exposed to extreme pressure or vacuum conditions; and as they screamed or writhed in agony, the physicians dispassionately recorded the reactions:

> I have personally seen, through the observation window of a chamber, when a prisoner inside would stand in a vacuum until his lungs ruptured. Some experiments gave men such pressures in the heads that they would go mad and pull out their hair in an effort to relieve the pressure. They would tear heads and faces with their fingers and nails in an attempt to maim themselves in their madness. They would beat the walls with their hands and head and scream in an effort to relieve pressure on the eardrums. These cases...generally ended in the death of the subject. The experiments were generally classified into two groups, one known as the living experiment and the other simply as the "X" experiment, which was a way of saying execution experiment.[28]

Doctor Rauscher was not the only ghoulish experimenter, for he worked closely with two professors at the University of Kiel, Dr. Holzloehner and Dr. Finke, who produced a lengthy research report entitled "Freezing Experiments with Human Beings" and delivered their findings to a receptive audience of physicians at a medical conference at Nuremberg in October 1942. Other experiments involved using Gypsies in various tests: at Sachsenhausen they were used to determine whether seawater was drinkable, were pumped full of poison bullets, and were injected with contagious jaundice; at Ravensbrück concentration camp they were inflicted with gangrene wounds, and Polish female inmates, laughingly called "rabid girls," were given bone grafts. One of the most extensive experiments involved sterilization. One approach, pursued by a Dr. Maudas, was to inject or administer liquid doses of the juice of the plant *Caladium seguinium;* another was X-ray sterilization. The most notorious program for mass sterilization and castration was conducted in Block 10 in Auschwitz where hundreds of human guinea pigs, mostly women, were injected with various caustic substances by Professor Carl Clauberg, an expert on fertility whose preparations are still used today. Dr. Horst Schumann, a key figure in the previous euthanasia program, also sterilized hundreds of subjects by a kind of assembly-line method that was quick and innocuous: prisoners were told to fill out a form at a counter, and while they did so they were irradiated by a hidden X-ray device. In this way Schumann hoped to sterilize three thousand to four thousand persons a day.[29] Mutilations and overdoses were common, causing acute swelling and genital deterioration. But it was all worthwhile because "the thought alone that the 3 million Bolsheviks now in German captivity could be sterilized, so that they would be available for work but precluded from propagation, opens up the most far-reaching perspectives."[30]

A brisk trade also occurred in the collection of human body parts, especially well-preserved heads of "subhumans," for the purpose of anthropological and racial research. A ghoulish professor at the University of Strasbourg, Dr. August Hirt, claimed that he was conducting important anthropological and anatomical studies on human heads and requested carefully preserved heads of "Jewish-Bolshevik commissars," which he received in great numbers from a delighted Himmler, who was personally fascinated by the anatomical traits of subhumans.[31] Himmler turned over the task of selecting good candidates to Wolfram Sievers, an SS colonel and head of the SS Ahnenerbe or Ancestral Heritage Society. Also nicknamed "bluebeard," Sievers scoured Auschwitz for good candidates, ordered them killed, and sent the bodies to Professor Hirt, later claiming that he "simply carried through a function of a postman."[32]

The ultimate degeneration was the collection of human skins for pleasure and decoration. The most notorious example concerned Frau Ilse Koch, the "Bitch of Buchenwald," wife of the camp commander, whose hobby was to collect the skins of dead inmates, especially those marked with tattoos, and turn them into lamp shades, gloves, or book covers.

In addition to the genocidal crimes committed in Russia and Poland, which will be discussed in the next two sections, there were two organized atrocities that the Nazis perpetrated in Czechoslovakia and France that must be remembered. On the morning of May 27, 1942, Reinhard Heydrich, "protector" of Bohemia-Moravia, was chauffeured, as he was every morning, to his office in Prague in his open Mercedes-Benz convertible. Two Czech resistance fighters, who had been flown into Czechoslovakia by British intelligence, were waiting for him at the outskirts of Prague, where they had positioned themselves at a hairpin curve where the car was expected to slow down. When Heydrich's car approached, one of the assassins lobbed a grenade at the back of the car and wrecked it. Surprisingly, Heydrich, apparently unhurt, jumped out of the car, drew his revolver, fired, and set out after the assassins. He then collapsed, mortally wounded by steel springs from the upholstery that had ripped into his body. A week later, the "Butcher of Prague" and the brain behind the Holocaust was dead. In retaliation, the Nazis wreaked havoc on Bohemia and Moravia, arresting ten thousand people and killing thirteen hundred of them.[33] Special treatment was reserved for the village of Lidice, which had supposedly aided Heydrich's assassins. The village was surrounded by SD and security police on the evening of June 9. The women and children were transported to Germany, the women to concentration camps and the children to foster homes. The men and older boys, 172 of them, were executed on the spot. The whole village was then completely destroyed, and its name was erased from the official records. Oblivious to world opinion, the Nazis openly admitted responsibility for the massacre. Heydrich's place was taken by Ernst Kaltenbrunner, a replica of the fallen SD chief.

A similar fate befell the French village of Oradour sur Glane near Limogne. In reprisal for partisan activities, a detachment of SS troops from the elite Das Reich Division, commanded by Major Otto Dickmann, who later died at Normandy, surrounded the village on June 10, 1944, and ordered the population to assemble in the central square. The men were locked into six barns and shot there in cold blood. All the women and children were locked up in the village church. Once the men had been murdered, every building, including the church, was set on fire. The SS murderers finished off the women and children in the church by machine-gunning them and blowing them up with hand grenades. Only a few people survived; several villagers who returned by train from a shopping trip to Limogne were also murdered.

Prelude to the Holocaust: Genocidal Policies in the East

Nazi racial policies have been described in general as genocidal, while the term "Holocaust" has been reserved for Hitler's greatest crime — the extermination of five million Jews. The following account adopts this distinctive usage of the two terms. The term "genocide," which denotes the deliberate and systematic extermination of a national or racial group, must be kept separate from the term "Holocaust," a word that has been derived from a Greek translation of an Old Testament term signifying a "burnt offering" or sacrifice to God. The term will be used in this book as denoting a uniquely monstrous crime in world history, a crime sui generis and without parallel, against an ancient and maligned religious community by a criminal Nazi leadership, aided and abetted by the German people and by an indifferent world. The Nazi regime practiced genocide against Poles, Russians, homosexuals, Gypsies, and Jehovah's Witnesses, but these efforts fell far short of their goal and altogether lacked the coordinated, fanatical, and even "spiritual" zeal that the Nazis reserved for the Jews. This, of course, does not lessen the devastating impact on these "secondary victims"; but, by comparison, the horrors visited on the "primary victims," the Jews, deserve special and separate treatment in any historical account.

It is not difficult to visualize the ultimate fate that would have been in store for most of Hitler's occupied and indirectly controlled nations. In fact, German wartime policies and practices furnished unmistakable evidence about the ultimate nature of Hitler's New Order. The key feature of Hitler's geopolitical goal was the acquisition of *Lebensraum* (living space) so that Germany's excess population could be settled in the fertile territories of eastern Europe. Hitler envisioned a vast plan of colonization that involved a massive resettlement of people comparable to the colonization of the New World. If Germans were to be settled in eastern Europe, the native population would have to be displaced by brutal subjugation and resettlement to less attractive land, or liquidated altogether.

As we have seen, Hitler's demand for living space had resulted in the establishment of a Race and Settlement Office under Himmler's auspices in 1935. Shortly after the outbreak of the war, Hitler appointed Himmler to head the new Reich Commissariat for the Strengthening of Germandom (RKFVD); its primary purpose was to colonize the conquered eastern territories with German settlers. The defeat of Poland in the fall of 1939 opened the first cycle of this massive resettlement policy. Over a million Poles and Jews who had lived in annexed territories were forcibly evacuated in October 1939 and dumped in the Government General. The property of these displaced people was confiscated by Himmler's agents and placed at the disposal of German settlers. Throughout the fall of 1939 Himmler's "racial experts" carefully scrutinized potential settlers in regard to their Nordic blood and their character before allowing them to settle in the eastern territories. Many candidates for colonization were drawn from the ethnic Germans (*Volksdeutsche*) who had been living in various parts of eastern and southern Europe. Over two hundred thousand ethnic Germans were "invited" to settle in Poland at the expense of the German government. It is estimated that the total number of settlers in Poland, *Reichsdeutsche* as well as *Volksdeutsche*, reached approximately a million by 1943.

The second cycle of German colonization opened with the invasion of Russia in the summer of 1941. Shortly after Hitler invaded Russia, he expostulated to one and all about the fabulous vistas of the Russian frontier, foreseeing a day when the area would be settled by a hundred million Germans:

> This Russian desert, we shall populate it.... We'll take away its character of an Asiatic steppe, we'll Europeanize it. With this object we have undertaken the construction of roads that will lead to the southernmost part of the Crimea and to the Caucasus. These roads will be studded along their whole length with German towns and around these towns our colonists will settle.

As for the two or three million men whom we need to accomplish this task, we'll find them quicker than we think. They'll come from Germany, Scandinavia, the Western countries, and America. I shall no longer be here to see all that, but in twenty years, the Ukraine will already be a home for twenty million inhabitants, besides the natives....

We shan't settle in the Russian towns and we'll let them go to pieces without intervening. And above all, no remorse on this subject! We're absolutely without obligations as far as these people are concerned. To struggle against the hovels, chase away the fleas, provide German teachers, bring out newspapers — very little of that for us! We'll confine ourselves, perhaps, to setting up a radio transmitter, under our control. For the rest, let them know just enough to understand our highway signs, so that they won't get themselves run over by our vehicles.

For them the word "liberty" means the right to wash on feast days. ...There's only one duty: to Germanize this country by the immigration of Germans and to look upon the natives as Redskins.[31]

Nazi racial policies in the eastern territories were governed not only by Hitler's personal visions, which he freely shared with his cohorts in rambling monologues, but by a top secret document, written by Heinrich Himmler, entitled "Some Thoughts on the Treatment of Foreign Populations in the East."[35] This nightmarish paper, filled with the stench of Orwellian double-talk and the rantings of a racial lunatic, recommended ethnic cleansing in the eastern areas by appropriating racially valued elements of Aryan stock and then either letting the rest vegetate in substandard conditions or driving them further eastward. As to the Jews, they were to be completely eliminated, preferably through enforced emigration eastward or to Africa. What Himmler was proposing was nothing less than the elimination of whole races, preserving whatever elements would be "valuable" or useful to the conquerors and discarding the rest. Himmler even provided a model of what constituted a "racially valuable" element. He proposed to identify and then to eliminate the upper classes in the eastern territories and "screen" their children in regard to their value. Those children who had been identified as racially valuable would be kidnapped and sent to Germany for Germanization; the rest would be left to subsist in the east as subjects of the new Aryan elite.

Himmler's bizarre racial project found an enthusiastic supporter in Hitler, who had been given to such racial fantasies for some time. The conquered living space would be settled by carefully screened and armed Aryan peasants who would constitute new Teutonic knights: the Germans were once a farming people and must essentially become one again. The east would help to strengthen this agricultural bent inherent in the German nation—it would become the everlasting fountain of youth replenishing the lifeblood of Germany whence it will, in its turn, be continuously renewed.[36]

The tragedy of this policy of ethnic cleansing began to unfold in Poland, where Himmler's *Einsatzgruppen* (task forces) implemented their bestial policy of decimating the ranks of the upper classes and screening for racial elements considered valuable. In the initial stages of this genocidal policy, Himmler's *Einsatzgruppen* encountered considerable resistance from the regular army (Wehrmacht) because the army had been given the responsibility of maintaining order in the occupied territories. It did not take very long before members of the armed forces realized what Hitler's assassins were really up to, namely, murdering Polish teachers, doctors, aristocrats, priests, and businessmen. Although many ordinary German soldiers as well as officers were horrified by the exterminations conducted all around them, few dared to stand up and oppose this organized massacre.

It will forever be a stain on the German military that it did not resist Hitler's program of genocide. Except for a few individual acts of heroism, there was no organized resistance by the Wehrmacht to these exterminations or the atrocities committed later against the Jews. One of the few acts of outraged opposition came from General Johannes Blaskowitz, commander in chief in the east, who, "in language unparalleled in German military history,"[37] condemned the acts of the SS murderers and called for a full-scale investigation into the atrocities. Blaskowitz, however, did not get very far in his protest. Hitler reassigned him to the west and with him went the whole army in the Government General. As Heinz Höhne observed, although the generals shuddered at the ghastly atrocities, they were "only too glad for the Dictator to relieve them of responsibility for murder."[38] By mid-October 1939, Hitler established a different system of occupation for Poland in which Danzig and West Prussia constituted a new *Gau* under the leadership of Albert Forster; other areas were carved up into *Gaue* as political payoffs to Nazi loyalists, and the remainder of central Poland, called Government General, was placed in the hands of Hans Frank.

In the meantime, Himmler threw himself with great vigor into his task of missionizing the east with Aryan peasants. He began to call himself "Reich commissioner for the strengthening of Germanism" and labored endlessly over the complex task of settling ethnic Germans from the Baltic region, eastern Poland, Romania, Yugoslavia, and Slovakia in his newly acquired eastern territories. When the Russian campaign began in June 1941, well over a million Poles had been expelled from their homes and farms. In their place came ethnic Germans who had been lured to their new homes by slick "home-to-the-Reich" appeals. Hand in hand with these resettlement programs went Himmler's manic search for valued Aryan racial stock in Poland and Russia. Writing to Gauleiter Arthur Greiser, Himmler said: "Racially pure children of Poles should be brought up by us in special kindergartens or children's homes. The parents can be told that this is being done for the children's health."[39] Not stopping with small-scale measures, Himmler involved the Lebensborn or "Life Springs" organization in this project. The Lebensborn organization, as previously mentioned, was an SS mating or stud farm officially disguised as an SS maternity home. These homes now took in Polish and Russian children of Nordic or Aryan appearance, some orphaned but many brutally taken from their parents. Under the code name "Haymaking," thousands of children were kidnapped and sent to Germany.[40]

The Russian campaign removed whatever constraints the Nazi racists may have had up to this time. SS planners conceptualized wild racial fantasies of how they were going to settle the vast Russian steppes. The blueprint for this was called "Master Plan East." This plan had been worked out six months before the invasion of Russia at Himmler's SS castle of Wewelsburg. Coming together in Group III/B of the Race and Settlement Main Office (RuSHA), the SS racial utopians began to plan the future German empire in the east. Their starting point was the assumption that thirty million Slavs had to be killed. The new German empire was to extend deep into western Russia, with its border extending from Leningrad in the north to the bend of the Dnieper in the south.

Among plans for the colonization of Russia was Hitler's pet project of annexing the Crimea, settling it with Germans, and linking it by a one-thousand-mile *Autobahn* with the Reich. Both Hitler and Rosenberg planned to settle Ukrainian Germans and possibly even the South Tyrolians in the Crimean Peninsula. In one of his rambling monologues at Rastenburg, Hitler was excited by the prospect of resettling ethnic Germans in the Crimea. As he told his audience at headquarters, compared to the Tyrol the Crimea was a "real land of milk and honey.... [A]ll they have to do is to sail down just one German waterway, the Danube, and there they are."[41]

Most of these grandiose plans were postponed by the exigencies of war, but they reflect the Assyrian nature of German policy toward conquered peoples. The Nazi New Order was bereft of a single humane principle of conduct; it consisted of nothing more than brutality, exploitation, and extermination — a policy as stupid as it was brutal because it inflamed hatred against Germany and resulted in widespread opposition to German rule throughout Europe.

Even with the eventual elimination of thirty million Slavs, it would be impossible for the new German settlers to assert themselves numerically in a sea of "substandard ethnicities." Professor Konrad Meyer-Hetling of the SS had an answer for this problem: the new territory was to be divided into settlement provinces (*Marks*) under the overall authority of Himmler, the new feudal lord of the east, who would, like medieval lords of old, assign fiefs of various types (life fiefs, hereditary fiefs) to the settlers. These settlements were to be defended by twenty-six strong points in the form of small towns situated at the intersections of German communications arteries.

The SS man Himmler put in charge of implementing this fantasy was Brigadeführer Odilo Globocnik, one of the most volatile and cranky members of the SS elite. Globocnik had been a district and SS police commander in Lublin and, while serving in this capacity, had run into traces of early German settlements there. This induced him to turn the Lublin district into one vast resettlement area, a plan that fitted in perfectly with Himmler's vision of Master Plan East. However, Globocnik's plan clashed with the ideas of Hans Frank, the governor of central Poland, who had come to the conclusion that the country under his rule could not be administered by brutality alone but had to become a model of economic development for the Reich. Draining millions of Poles from the Government General by driving them eastward was bound to weaken the country beyond repair. A prolonged and vicious struggle between Frank and Himmler began to unfold, revealing as it did so the inherent instability of the Nazi regime. Frank's valiant efforts, which culminated in a public explosion of criticism of the SS police state, came to nothing when Hitler sided with Himmler, stripped Frank of all his party offices, and dismissed him as minister of the Reich. Yet Hitler could not quite bring himself to let Frank go. He seems to have valued his many past services and admired his personal courage. Frank thus stayed on as governor of Poland, but shorn of influence on what was about to unfold — the murder of a whole race of people.

The Holocaust

Responsibility and Chain of Command

Anti-Semitism is still so strong that some writers persist in maintaining that the Holocaust never occurred and that the records of the atrocities committed by the Nazis are fabrications designed for Jewish self-aggrandizement.[42] These must be grouped with the sort of persons who insist that America never actually went to the moon, that it was all a deception staged at some Hollywood studio. Since no one denies that Hitler marched into Poland, why is it that some people still refuse to believe that millions of Jews were murdered in cold blood by the Nazis? Surely, it is not because of any dearth of evidence. The grisly details of the concentration camps had been known during the war by more people than is commonly supposed.[43] When the war ended, the concentration camps disgorged thousands of victims who lived to tell the tale. The victorious powers subsequently bent every effort to ferret out the murderers; and at Nuremberg the perpetrators, most notably the notorious commandant of Auschwitz, Rudolf Höss, recounted their heinous crimes in despicable detail.[44] One victim after another came forward to bear witness against the perpetrators of modern history's most dastardly deed. The Holocaust is an incontrovertible fact, and the reality of its truth, however painful it may be to our collective memory, must be accepted as a blot on the human record in general and on the German conscience in particular.

No one knows when Hitler gave the order to annihilate the Jews. No written document has ever been discovered. Clues from various sources indicate that sometime in the spring of 1941 Hitler gave a personal order to Himmler that the Jews had to be eliminated. It is also highly likely that Hitler even suggested the precise nature of getting rid of the Jews — extermination by poison gas. After all, he had made allusions to this subject since the early days of the party; and in *Mein Kampf,* he wrote that many German lives would have been saved in World War I if "these Hebrew corruptors of the people had been subjected to poison gas."[45]

As will be recalled, Hitler had publicly warned the Jews on January 30, 1939, that he would annihilate them in case of war. When World War II began, Hitler learned that Chaim Weizmann, head of the World Zionist movement, had written a letter to Prime Minister Chamberlain, published in the *Jewish Chronicle* of September 8, 1939, in which he declared that the Jews would be fighting on the side of Britain and the democracies. Hitler seems to have not only regarded this statement as a declaration of war by the Jews on Germany but also seized on it as a rationale for interning Jews as Germany's enemies. As late as July 24, 1942, Hitler personally referred to Weizmann's letter in reminding his dinner guests that in World War II "one should never forget that world Jewry, after its declaration of war by the Zionist Congress and its leader Chaim Weizmann, was National Socialism's enemy number one."[46] It is interesting to note that when Hitler made this and other remarks about the Jews, he never revealed what was actually done to them. When he made the above-cited reference to Weizmann, Hitler was still maintaining the illusion that the Jews were being deported eastward or that he would pack them off to Madagascar.

Apparently some concern for possible public reaction, combined with a mania for secrecy and perhaps some psychological need to maintain this atrocity at a distance, kept Hitler from revealing the awful secret and his role in it to anyone but a few trusted henchmen (Himmler, Goebbels, Bormann, Göring).[47] But the fact is that Hitler had been step-by-step the guiding spirit of what happened to the Jews since he gained power in 1933.

From the very beginning the machinery for the implementation of the war on the Jews was effected through a chain of command that began with Hitler, moved to Himmler, to Heydrich's Reich Main Security Office, to Section IV of the SD (Gestapo Müller), to Section IV-B-4 (Eichmann and Jewish affairs), and finally to the *Einsatzgruppen* and Death-Head's Units in the concentration camps. As previously mentioned, treatment of the Jews had gone through two major phases between 1933 and 1939 — legalized discrimination and emigration. World War II brought two further phases: first, ghettoization and mass shootings, and, finally, systematic annihilation in the death camps (the "final solution").

In 1933 approximately 503,000 Jews were living in Germany (0.76 percent of the population). By 1939 the Jewish population in Germany had shrunk to 234,000. When Hitler invaded Poland, two million Jews came under his rule and three million more when he invaded the Soviet Union.[48] These approximately five million Jews were an important economic and cultural factor in eastern Europe; they lived, for the most part, in such urban and industrial centers as Lodz, Warsaw, Kiev, Kharkov, and such ancient cultural cities as Cracow, Vilna, Lublin, and Riga. Hitler's conquest of western Europe added another three million. Heydrich's estimate was that over eleven million Jews eventually resided within the reach of German authorities.

Ghettoization and Mass Shootings

The first steps were taken against the Polish Jews and then, starting with the invasion of Russia, against the Russian Jews. Ghettoization and mass shootings were carried out simultaneously. The ghettos were not permanent places of settlement, as the murderous SS made the Jews believe, but mere round-up centers that would make it more convenient to exterminate large numbers of them later. Herded into overcrowded ghettos, the Jews lived under the administration of their own councils (*Judenräte*), which was a particularly fiendish trick devised by Heydrich, who ordered the establishment of Jewish councils by Jews in each community. These councils were to carry out the instructions of the special SS task forces (*Einsatzgruppen*), for instance compiling accurate lists of persons and their assets. In other words, the Jews were to organize their own destruction and pay for every penny of it — a scheme worthy of the worst of sadists.

The murderous *Einsatzgruppen*, which set in motion the mass killings of Jews, dated back to Hitler's annexation of Austria and Czechoslovakia.[49] Their actual transformation into killer troops, however, did not begin until the invasion of Poland under the code name of "Tannenberg." At the time of the Polish campaign, about twenty-six hundred SD and police officials accompanied the regular army and carried out "security activities" in the conquered areas. In addition to mass shootings of Communists, Jews, and others, the *Einsatzgruppen* seized Communist Party archives, drew up lists of suspect groups or organizations, and tried to round up saboteurs. Unit commanders sent back detailed reports of their activities, many of which survived the war as valuable documents incriminating the participants in mass murders. The invasion of the Soviet Union called for even more extensive operations by the *Einsatzgruppen*. Before Operation Barbarossa began, Heydrich set up four major *Einsatzgruppen* of three thousand men he had recruited from all over Germany and trained in the border police school of Pretzsch on the Elbe northeast of Leipzig.[50] These four groups were labeled A, B, C, and D, corresponding to the German army groups that invaded Russia on June 22, 1941. Einsatzgruppe A, led by Brigadeführer Dr. Walter Stahlecker, followed Army Group North through the Baltic states to Leningrad; Einsatzgruppe B, led by Arthur Nebe, was attached to Army Group Center between the Baltic and the Ukraine; Einsatzgruppe C, headed by SS-Brigadeführer Dr. Otto Rasch, operated in the western areas (Lwow, Rowne, Zhitomir, Kiev, Kursk, Poltava, Kharkov); and Einsatzgruppe D, commanded by Dr. Otto Ohlendorf, head of the inland SD, followed the Eleventh Army and was active in Bessarabia and the Crimea (Nikolayev, Odessa, Taganrog, Rostov, Krasnodar).

The leaders of these units were well-educated police officials, three of whom held doctoral degrees (Ohlendorf, Stahlecker, Rausch). Nebe, head of the criminal police (Kripo) in the Reich Main Security Office (RSHA), was at first an enthusiastic volunteer for this new task but eventually asked to be relieved of his murderous duties, went into opposition, and was executed in March 1945. Dr. Stahlecker had been chief of the Württemberg police and advanced rapidly through the ranks of the SD, holding a variety of important posts in Vienna, Bohemia-Moravia, Norway, and in Berlin as ministerial secretary. Dr. Otto Rasch, with two doctoral degrees, had been the former lord mayor (*Oberbürger-Meister*) of Wittenberg, the city where Martin Luther had ushered in the Protestant Reformation.[51] Dr. Otto Ohlendorf was an economist and legal scholar. All of them were true believers and fanatical anti-Semites. The same was true of other *Einsatzgruppen* leaders — the SS *Sturmbannführer* and *Obersturmbannführer* who came from the ranks of academics, ministerial officials, and lawyers. There were even a Protestant minister and an opera singer among them.[52] An analysis of Einsatzgruppe A reveals that its leadership cadre consisted of highly motivated young men, most of them under forty years of age, who came from middle-class backgrounds, were well educated, had served in the Free Corps or various postwar paramilitary groups, experienced unemployment some time before 1933, and proudly rejected their former religious affiliations.[53]

Although there were some sadists among the leaders of the *Einsatzgruppen* and among the commanders and men of the *Sonderkommandos* (special details) and *Einsatzkommandos* into which each *Einsatzgruppe* was divided, the majority of these men were killers by ideological conviction. Few ever questioned their orders or asked from what source they ultimately derived.

Between June 22, 1941, and the end of the year, the *Einsatzgruppen* went on a bloody rampage hunting down Jews wherever they could find them. Typically, they would round up Jews in the larger towns, march them outside the town, and shoot them alongside ditches or antitank trenches, where they would be buried. In most cases, the Jews had to dig their own graves before they were shot:

The condemned people were not only brought in trucks but also on foot in groups of 70 and 80 and beaten mercilessly along the way. The 20 to 25 who were to be shot were taken to a spot 50 meters from the execution site, where they were guarded until they were ready to be shot. They undressed near the graves. . . . Completely undressed, they were driven into the graves and forced to lie face down. The Germans shot them with rifles and machine pistols. In this way, one party after another was driven to their grave and shot, each forced to lie face down on the corpses of those who had already been shot.[54]

There was fierce competition among the leaders of the various *Einsatzkommandos* to report the highest body counts, and some commandos proudly reported back that their areas were "Jew free":

I can now state that the aim of solving the Jewish problem for Lithuania has been achieved by *Einsatzkommando* 3. There are no more Jews in Lithuania apart from work-Jews and their families. . . . I wanted to bump off these work-Jews and their families but this brought me smack up against the civil administration and the Wehrmacht and prompted a ban on the shooting of these Jews and their families.[55]

Although the army sometimes intervened or pretended to be shocked, the *Einsatzkommandos* encountered little opposition from army authorities. In fact, reports by *Einsatzgruppen* commanders often commended the army for its cooperation: "From the first day onwards," one report declared, "the *Einsatzgruppe* (C) has succeeded in establishing an excellent understanding with all sections of the *Wehrmacht*."[56] Field Marshal Walter von Reichenau, commander of Army Group South, was particularly insistent in reminding his troops that the Russian campaign was aimed at wiping out the "Jewish-Bolshevist" system and that therefore "soldiers must show full understanding for the necessity for the severe but just atonement being required of the Jewish subhumans."[57] Since mass executions were so common, German soldiers frequently observed these atrocities and often managed to snap pictures of the gruesome events. In several towns the local population itself participated in pogroms against helpless Jews, as they did in Kaunas, Lithuania, where local thugs clubbed Jews to death with crowbars in plain sight of cheering crowds, with mothers holding up their children to enjoy the spectacle and soldiers milling around to watch the fun like a football match.[58]

The shootings set in motion what could only be described as a frenzy as the killer troops went after their prey without conscience or opposition and often in plain sight of unsuspecting bystanders. One of the most shocking accounts of such a mass killing was reported by a German engineer, Hermann Friedrich Graebe, who along with his foreman stumbled upon a ghastly mass execution:

Moennikes and I went directly to the pits. Nobody bothered us. Now I heard rifle shots in quick succession, from behind one of the earth mounds. The people who had got off the trucks — men, women, and children of all ages — had to undress upon the order of an SS man, who carried a riding or dog whip. They had to put down their clothes in fixed places.... I saw a heap of shoes of about 800 to 1000 pairs, great piles of under-linen and clothing. Without screaming or weeping these people undressed, stood around in family groups, kissed each other, said farewells and waited.... During the 15 minutes that I stood near the pit I heard no complaint or plea for mercy.... An old woman with snow-white hair was holding the one-year old child in her arms singing to it, and tickling it. The child was cooing with delight. The couple were looking on with tears in their eyes. The father was holding the hand of a boy about 10 years old and speaking to him softly; the boy was fighting his tears. The father pointed toward the sky, stroked his head, and seemed to explain something to him. At that moment the SS man at the pit shouted something to his comrade. The latter counted off about 20 persons and instructed them to go behind the earth mound. Among them was the family which I have mentioned. I well remember a girl, slim and with black hair, who, as she passed close to me, pointed to herself and said "23." I walked around the mound, and found myself confronted by a tremendous grave. People were closely wedged together and lying on top of each other so that only their heads were visible. Nearly all had blood running over their shoulders from their heads. Some of the people shot were still moving.... I looked for the man who did the shooting. He was an SS man, who sat at the edge of the narrow end of the pit, his feet dangling into the pit. He had a tommy gun on his knees and was smoking a cigarette. The people, completely naked, went down ... the pit and clambered over the heads of the people lying there.... Then I heard a series of shots. I looked into the pit and saw that the bodies were twitching.... Blood was running from their necks.[59]

Only the most sadistic or hardened executioners could stomach such barbaric horrors indefinitely. Some SS men, it is true, enjoyed killing Jews for fun, and many incidents of such blood lust have been recorded. A few examples may suffice. Major Rösler, commanding the 528th Infantry Regiment, came upon a mass execution near Zhitomir and was horrified by the picture of an execution pit in which bodies were still twitching; he ordered a policeman to kill an old man with a white beard clutching a cane in his left hand who was still writhing in agony. The policeman laughed and said: "I have already shot him seven times in the stomach. He can die on his own now."[60] In one town the Jews had gone into hiding and when the SS swept through the town they discovered a woman with a baby in her arms. When the woman refused to tell them where the Jews were hiding, one SS man grabbed the baby by its legs and smashed its head against a door. Another SS man recalled: "It went off with a bang like a bursting motor tire. I shall never forget that sound as long as I live."[61] At Riga an SS man saw two Jews carrying a log; he shot one of them, saying, "One's enough for that job."[62] Jews were often shot for sport or recreation. Some SS men believed that they made great targets for marksmanship.[63]

The culmination of mass shootings came at Babi-Yar on the outskirts of Kiev where thirty-three thousand Jews were killed. The first wave of mass killings came to an end by the winter of 1941. By that time seven hundred thousand Jews had been murdered.[64] The men of the *Einsatzgruppen,* however, were physically and psychologically drained. Some sought refuge in alcohol, some became physically ill, a few committed suicide. Under these circumstances, the question arose of how to maintain the pace of murder and even to expand the killings that were being planned in order to eradicate the remaining Jews of Europe. So far, the killings had been random and personal; they were messy and nerves were frayed. It became necessary to find a more efficient and less personal method of murdering the remaining Jews. Discussions, in fact, had been underway for some time as to how this "final solution" to the Jewish problem might be accomplished.

The Final Solution to the Jewish Question

From various statements by Hitler and his close subordinates between the spring and winter of 1941, we can trace the planning of the "final solution" with reasonable accuracy. On March 3, 1941, Hitler issued a directive to Jodl for the impending war on Russia that insisted, among other things, that "the Bolshevik/Jewish intelligentsia must be eliminated." On March 31, Hitler informed a sizable group of high-ranking officers about the activities of Himmler's *Einsatzgruppen* in the rear areas of the fighting Wehrmacht and of their future role in the impending conflict with the Soviet Union. On April 2, Alfred Rosenberg had a two-hour meeting with Hitler during which he learned of the scope of mass exterminations already committed and still planned in the eastern territories. He appears to have been so stunned that he could only note the following in his diary: "What I do not write down today, I will none the less never forget."[65] In the summer of 1941 Himmler called Rudolf Höss (1900–1947), the commandant of Auschwitz concentration camp, to Berlin and told him: "The Führer has ordered that the Jewish question be solved once and for all and that we, the SS, are to implement that order."[66] Himmler then spelled out that "every Jew that we can lay our hands on is to be destroyed now during the war, without exception." He also explained that such a task could only be done "by gassing, since it would have been impossible by shooting to dispose of the large number of people that were expected, and it would have placed too heavy a burden on the SS men who had to carry it out, especially because of the women and children among its victims."[67]

By the end of July 1941 the Nazi leadership had reached a definite decision that the eastern territories would be used for solving the Jewish question and that the principal instrument of destruction was to be the SS. Lest it be thought that Himmler acted on his own initiative, as some have argued, it is well to recall that Himmler himself admitted that "I do nothing that the Führer doesn't know."[68] Was the SS, headed by Himmler, the only institution involved in the "final solution"? The evidence points to widespread involvement of the Reich commissioners, the state bureaucracy, the Foreign Office, and the Wehrmacht. On July 31, 1941, Göring, as plenipotentiary of the Four-Year Plan, ordered Heydrich to "present to me, as soon as possible, a draft setting out details of the preliminary measures taken in the organizational, technical, and material fields for the achievement of the 'Final Solution of the Jewish question.' "[69] By November all the necessary steps for exterminating the Jews under Hitler's control had been taken. Himmler's Swedish masseur, Felix Kersten, noted in his diary for November 11, 1941: "Today Himmler is very depressed. He has just come from the Führer's chancellery. I gave him treatment. After much pressure and questions as to what was the matter with him he told me that the destruction of the Jews is being planned."[70] On November 18, 1941, Himmler told German journalists at a confidential briefing that "the biological extermination of all Jews in Europe" had begun, that no details could be reported other than the use of certain phrases such as "definite solution" or "total solution of the Jewish question."[71]

Himmler's emphasis on "biological extermination" provides the clue for the change in the methods by which Jews were to be annihilated. Although some mass shootings continued throughout the war, the SS leadership decided that execution by poison gas in remote annihilation camps was the most efficient and "humane" method of murdering the Jews. The euthanasia program provided the model and even the crew for early experiments in gassing Jews. Poison gas killings started in December 1941 in a forest near Kulmhof (Chelmno) in the Wartheland, forty miles from Lodz, where Jews from the Lodz ghetto were gassed in mobile vans by means of engine exhaust gas. Since those vans could accommodate only a limited number of victims, they were never regarded as anything but makeshift killing machines. Near the end of 1941 a new camp, the first annihilation camp, was set up at Belzec near Lublin and became operational in the spring of 1942. It was here that the first gassings using stationary gas chambers took place. The architect and chief exterminator of Belzec was Dr. Christian Wirth, who had previously served as an exterminator in the euthanasia program and was one of about one hundred people who were transferred from the euthanasia program to the annihilation camps in Poland. Wirth pumped exhaust fumes into the death chambers by using diesel engines: his first chambers opened in March 1942 and could dispose of fifteen thousand Jews a day. A second death camp opened in the same month at Sobibor in eastern Poland, a third one a little later at Treblinka (seventy-five miles northeast of Warsaw), and a fourth one at Majdanek, located just a mile from Lublin. The fifth and arguably the most gruesome camp was Auschwitz in Upper East Silesia, formerly Oswiciem, Poland. Wirth administered the exterminations at the Polish annihilation camps. At Auschwitz, as will be seen, a new and more effective chemical agent, Zyklon-B, was introduced.

The continuation of shootings and the emergence of new death camps, along with technical problems relating to transportation, the confiscation of Jewish property, and liaison work with foreign powers who were asked to surrender their Jewish populations, necessitated a more coordinated strategy for the final solution. For this purpose, Heydrich called a meeting at a villa in a posh Berlin suburb located on Lake Grosser Wannsee. On January 20, 1942, major representatives of various agencies involved in the final solution of the Jewish question assembled to discuss the technical details of murdering the remaining Jews of Europe. The meeting was hosted in a very genial atmosphere by Heydrich; the minutes were kept by Adolf Eichmann, who had also sent out the invitations.[72] Besides Heydrich and Eichmann, the other major SS representatives were Gestapo Chief Heinrich Müller; Dr. Otto Hoffmann of the Race and Settlement Office; Karl Eberhard Schöngarth, SD chief for the Government General; Dr. Rudolf Lange, commander of the SD for Latvia. Representing various important government agencies were several state secretaries, ministerial directors, and party functionaries: Dr. Wilhelm Stuckart from the Ministry of the Interior, Dr. Josef Bühler from the office of the governor-general, Erich Neumann representing the Four-Year Plan, Dr. Roland Freisler from the Ministry of Justice, Dr. Martin Luther from the Foreign Office, Dr. Friedrich Wilhelm Kritzinger from the Reich chancellery, Oberführer Dr. Gerhard Klopfer from the party chancellery, Gauleiter Dr. Alfred Meyer representing the Ministry of the Occupied Eastern Territories, and Dr. Georg Leibrandt, the chief Reich administrative officer. Of the fifteen participants eight held doctoral degrees. The final minutes of the conference are written in the Orwellian double-speak that had been adopted for discussion of the final solution, using terms such as "legalized removal," "evacuation to the east," "emigration," "natural diminution," "resettlement," "sanitary measures," "change of residence," and so on. The participants all agreed that war had to be waged on the Jews because they represented a health hazard to the Reich. Heydrich unfolded a monstrous demographic chart listing over eleven million Jews living in the various countries of Europe. A lively discussion then ensued as to how these Jews could be rounded up, stripped of their possessions, transported eastward, and ultimately annihilated. The minutes, couched in revolting bureaucratic euphemisms, reveal little of these gruesome realities; however, according to Eichmann's testimony at Jerusalem, the members of the conference discussed "the subject quite bluntly; quite differently from the language which I had to use later in the record. During the conversation they minced no words about it at all."[73]

The overall plan outlined at Wannsee was to conduct sweeps of Jews throughout the whole of Europe, starting with Germany and Bohemia-Moravia. Jews were to be rounded up and sent to "transit ghettos"

(*Durchgangsghettos*) in the east and then transported farther eastward. Jews over sixty-five or highly decorated Jewish war veterans, rather than being executed, were to be interned at Theresienstadt, the showcase ghetto in Bohemia-Moravia where prominent Jews like Leo Baeck were sent. No definitive decision was reached about half-Jews (*Mischlinge*), especially whether exceptions should be made to the general rule that first-degree half-Jews (*Mischlinge* 1) should be treated as full Jews in regard to the final solution. The decision was postponed for the next meeting, though the general consensus was to sterilize such Jews in order to prevent further racial pollution of the German people.

The Wannsee conference lasted for only an hour and a half. After the formal session the members broke into groups for further discussion of technical details. Everyone endorsed the general policy of exterminating the Jews of Europe, although no complete consensus had been reached about one single method of accomplishing this goal — shootings, gassings, or death through slave labor. This decision was out of the hands of the participants; it would define itself outside the conference rooms in the killing fields of eastern Europe. The significance of the Wannsee conference was not the initiation of the final solution — that had already begun with the mass shooting of Jews two years before — but the fact that a broad segment of the German government (not just Hitler and the SS) had endorsed the final solution and worked out common procedures and methods for its implementation.[74]

The systematic roundup of Jews began almost immediately all over Hitler's empire. Working through satellite governments or occupational administrations, the German authorities sequestered Jewish property and liquid assets. Legislation was drawn up to turn the Jews into stateless persons because then it became impossible or irrelevant for any country to enquire into the fate of its former Jewish inhabitants.[75] Moreover, any state that had transformed its Jews into stateless persons could then lay claim to their property. Stripped of their nationality and relieved of their assets, the Jews were allowed to keep only one hundred reichmarks (forty dollars) and fifty kilograms (110 pounds) of personal baggage. Before being removed (*abgeschoben*) to the east, the Jews also had to turn over an itemized list of their assets, which the Gestapo graciously accepted as payment rendered for the services about to be provided.

Dorpmüller's trains now went into action, regardless of bad weather, Allied bombings, or urgent needs of the Wehrmacht. Jews were herded like cattle into sealed freight cars and dispatched to the five eastern annihilation camps — Auschwitz, Belzec, Sobibor, Treblinka, and Majdanek. By the spring of 1942 these camps had installed stationary gas chambers that could exterminate up to twenty-five thousand people a day. Early methods of using exhaust gasses from diesel engines gave way to hydrocyanide (prussic acid) that had been marketed under the trade name of Zyklon-B by a firm called Degesch, an acronym that stands for Deutsche

Gesellschaft für Schädligungsbekämpfung (German Vermin-Combating Corporation).[76] We know a great deal about this company and the use of its chemical agents in exterminating human beings from the testimony of Kurt Gerstein, the chief disinfection officer in the Department of Hygiene in the Waffen-SS. Gerstein has left us with a graphic account of how he was ordered by Eichmann's office to accompany Rolf Günther, Eichmann's right-hand man, to transport prussic acid to a secret place. When they arrived at the secret place, Belzec concentration camp, Gerstein witnessed an extermination under the direction of Dr. Christian Wirth, the architect of human gassing. During this particular operation, the diesel engine refused to fire. Wirth was beside himself — not because seven hundred men, women, and children had to suffer two hours and forty minutes of agony stuffed into a small gas chamber (Gerstein had a stopwatch) — but because of the embarrassment such a malfunction had caused in the presence of visitors. Gerstein was so horrified by what he saw that he told Wirth that the gas he had brought with him was no longer useable and had to be buried. He later claimed that the only reason that he stayed in his position was to work against it and to bear witness to mass murder.

At any rate, at Auschwitz, Höss decided to use Zyklon-B, strongly believing that through the use of this chemical agent he could attain a better kill-ratio than Wirth, who continued using his diesel method. Zyklon-B consisted of bluish pellets that could be carried in a small canister. The operator, wearing a mask, only had to drop the pellets into the gas chamber through a hole, whereupon they turned into deadly gas that killed people within twenty to thirty minutes. Auschwitz became the most monstrous death factory of the whole Nazi annihilation system.

Outside a bleak Polish village, Höss and Himmler had transformed a small site consisting of twenty-seven abandoned, single-storey, brick barracks into a massive complex housing 150,000 prisoners. Auschwitz started out as a camp for political prisoners, mostly Polish, but it was rapidly expanded as a work camp and then as a major site for the annihilation of Jews, Gypsies, and "Asiatic inferiors." By the middle of 1942 the camp was divided into three sites: Auschwitz 1 was the original camp; Auschwitz 2 at Birkenau, built to accommodate two hundred thousand victims, was the annihilation camp; and Auschwitz 3 was the industrial center at Monowitz. Auschwitz had its own soccer stadium, library, photographic laboratory, symphony orchestra, medical facility of sixty doctors and more than three hundred nurses, a large bakery, a tannery, and a tin-smithy. There were also thirty barracks, nicknamed "Canada" by the Polish prisoners, which stored the loot taken from the prisoners. These barracks were chock-full of clothing, shoes, spectacles, jewelry, watches, silk underwear, gold and diamond rings, and the finest liquors. In short, it was a bestial city where men who were once members of a civilized community degraded helpless victims and themselves to the lowest level human beings could ever sink.

Whether at Auschwitz or at Belzec, Sobibor, Majdanek, or Treblinka, arriving Jewish prisoners encountered the same reality. Upon arrival, they were driven out of their freight cars, often leaving behind them "human excrement and trampled infants," and assembled on the ramp for the "welcome" (*Begrüssung*). A selection officer, with the simple wave of a hand, directed each new prisoner into one of two lines: on the right for those who were sentenced to hard labor and on the left for those who were condemned to death. Old men, women, and children were usually condemned to death. Those marked for death were ordered to undress and told that they would have to take a shower. A number of psychological ploys were used to conceal the horrible reality that awaited the condemned. At Auschwitz people were told to tie their shoes together and hang their clothes on numbered hooks so that they could easily find them after they had taken their showers. They were even given soap to take into the gas chambers. Women were shorn of all their hair. Prodded and hurried along like a herd of cattle by special commandos wielding whips, sticks, or rifle butts, the victims were then driven into the gas chambers. The special commandos included Ukrainians and even Jewish helpers, a particularly horrible device that had Jews serving as executioners of their own kind. "I have never known," Höss later wrote, "of any of its members giving these people who were about to be gassed the slightest hint of what lay ahead of them. On the contrary, they did everything in their power to deceive them.... Though they might refuse to believe the SS men, they had complete faith in these members of their own race."[77]

Yet even such fiendish deceptions did not fool everybody, and there were anguished cries and heartrending scenes of indescribable horror. Once the victims had been shoved into a gas chamber, which could hold close to eight hundred people when tightly packed, the doors were sealed and the gas was released through vents in the ceiling:

> It could be observed through the peephole in the door that those who were standing nearest to the induction vents were killed at once.... The remainder staggered about and began to scream and struggle for air. The screaming, however, soon changed to the death rattle and in a few minutes all lay still. After twenty minutes at the latest no movement could be discerned.[78]

It took at least thirty minutes to extract the mass of bodies, which were glued together "like pillars of basalt, still erect, not having any space to fall"; legs were covered with feces and menstrual blood.[79] Another special crew, the "tooth commandoes," sprang into action and extracted the fillings from the victims. Such valuables were collected by Odilo Globocnik, one of the chief agents of Aktion Reinhard, as the gassings of the Jews were now called after the assassination of Reinhard Heydrich; Globocnik was responsible for rounding up the loot (money, gold, diamonds, watches, and so on) and sending it to the Deutsche Reichsbank (German Reichsbank).[80]

After the gold fillings had been extracted, the bodies were cremated, either in the open air or in gigantic crematoria. The stench could be smelled for miles around. German manufacturers competed for government contracts to build the most automated and efficient incinerators. The top contract went to I. A. Topff and Sons of Erfurt, which eventually perfected a unit that contained an underground gas chamber (*Leichenkeller*) together with electric elevators for hauling up the bodies.[81] Given time, the technicians of mass murder would undoubtedly have perfected a completely self-contained unit in which people entered as living human beings and were processed, efficiently and cleanly, so that they could exit as smoke through the belching chimneys.

For those who were not marked for immediate extermination, life in the death camps was hell on earth. Many survivors have borne witness to the inhuman conditions in these camps. These range from the sophisticated voices of Elie Wiesel, Primo Levi, Viktor Frankl, and Todeusz Borowski to hundreds of heartrending stories by ordinary men and women. The perpetrators, too, have left many traces of their dastardly activities in personal diaries, testimony at Nuremberg, and official reports to superiors. Knowledge of camp life can also be reconstructed with great accuracy from extant records kept with typical German precision by the prison bureaucracy.[82]

For purposes of identification, prisoners at all camps were forced to display markings of different colors on their uniforms, consisting of a serial number and a colored triangle. At Auschwitz the number was tattooed on the left forearm. A red triangle meant a political prisoner, a green one a criminal, purple a Jehovah's Witness, black a "shiftless element," pink a homosexual, brown a Gypsy. Jews wore a regular triangle that had a second yellow triangle superimposed on it in order to create the Star of David. The German guards rarely dirtied their own hands, assigning a great deal of supervision to carefully picked trustees, most of them criminals. These bully inmates were called *Kapos,* named after the Italian word *capo,* or head. As in most brutal prisons, inmate control took place on many levels. Informants were numerous, and this compounded the atmosphere of distrust and fear.

Prisoners were awakened at dawn and had to report to roll call (*Appell*), which might last for hours. They were then driven out to work by the guards amid constant screams, insults, and harassment. Most work was petty manual labor in quarries or brickyards, but at some of the larger camps like Auschwitz prisoners worked in a cement plant, a coal mine, a steel factory, a shoe factory, and in the large I. G. Farben plant that produced synthetic rubber. At all the camps rations were inadequate and the food atrocious; in the death camps, where the object was to work people to death, the daily food allowance, usually given to the prisoners after they returned from work, included a watered-down soup and a little bread, augmented by a little extra allowance of margarine, a slice of bad sausage, a piece of cheese, or a bit of honey or watery jam.[83] Survival depended on the black market and on sheer ingenuity.

It goes without saying that this regimen reduced people to a whimpering half-human state. Emaciation set in quickly, followed by loss of energy and a general feeling of apathy. When viewed from a distance these half-dead humans, who tended to huddle on the ground in clump-like configurations, looked like zombies. Such prisoners were invariably exterminated. For this reason prisoners did everything in their power to look healthy. "If you want to stay alive," Viktor Frankl was told, "look fit for work."[84] Few were able to do so under conditions that were designed to work people to death. People wasted away because of the excruciatingly harsh labor, which only the strongest could withstand, poor nutrition, vicious forms of punishment, and hideously unsanitary conditions that caused frequent epidemics. The process of human deterioration, physically and psychologically, has been graphically detailed by Viktor Frankl:

> When the last layers of subcutaneous fat had vanished, and we looked like skeletons disguised with skin and rags, we could watch our bodies beginning to devour themselves. The organism digested its own protein, and the muscles disappeared. Then the body had no resistance left. One after another the members of the little community in our hut died.... After many observations we know the symptoms well,... "He won't last long," or "This is the next one" we whispered to each other, and when, during our daily search for lice, we saw our own naked bodies in the evening, we thought alike: "This body here, my body, is really a corpse already. What has become of me? I am but a small portion of a great mass of human flesh ... of a mass behind barbed wire, crowded into a few earthen huts; a mass of which daily a certain portion begins to rot because it has become lifeless."[85]

Yet it is a testimony to the strength of the human spirit that even under these conditions men and women could rise to a higher spiritual and aesthetic plane and gain a heightened insight into the human condition, that children could continue to laugh and draw the most touching pictures of great beauty and innocence. Life holds its own meaning, and it draws upon mysterious sources of strength. But "woe to him who saw no more sense in life," as Viktor Frankl observed, for "he was soon lost." Life is redeemed by purpose; and even at Auschwitz a man who had a *why* to live for could bear almost any how."[86] It may be true, as Elie Wiesel said, that we may never understand the Holocaust, which was embodied for him in the insane project of Auschwitz, but we will be forever condemned to try to understand, knowing that in it is concealed part of the riddle of human nature.

Gassings at the five major annihilation camps, which began in the spring of 1942, continued until the fall of 1944. By the summer of 1944, most of the Jews in eastern Europe had been annihilated, as was true of most of the Jews from the rest of Europe, except for countries that had deliberately obstructed Hitler's genocidal policies. One such country was Hungary, where Jews had found a refuge until Hitler deposed Admiral Miklos Horthy in October 1944 and set up a puppet regime he could fully control. Himmler's bloodhounds then immediately descended on Hungary and rounded up as many Jews as they could find. Eichmann personally supervised the operation, sending three trainloads of the country's Jews to Auschwitz. The Nazis also halfheartedly experimented with a new technique — selling Jews to the Western world, a plan, unfortunately, that, as a result of Nazi duplicity and the indifference and bureaucratic obstructionism of Western governments, never really worked. Sweden was one of the few countries that made an effective effort to help by sending Raoul Wallenberg to Hungary as a special envoy to assist Hungarian Jews in emigrating to Sweden; he later disappeared into the bowels of the Soviet police state. The courageous Wallenberg handed out as many special visas as he could to save as many Jews as possible. However, this made only a slight dent in the mass deportations. Himmler and his murderous agents, now working under the cloud of impending military defeat, intensified their efforts to make Europe "Jew-free." The killers combed areas and camps previously overlooked. It was in this way that thousands of Jews who had been interned at Theresienstadt were gassed at Auschwitz. Leo Baeck, who miraculously survived, accidentally ran into Eichmann in the Gestapo office. Baeck recalled: "He was visibly taken aback at seeing me. 'Herr Baeck, are you still alive?' He looked me over carefully, as if he did not trust his eyes, and added coldly, 'I thought you were dead.' " Baeck's reply was: "Herr Eichmann, you are apparently announcing a future occurrence."[87]

By November 1, 1944, the gassings stopped, but the dying would continue until the liberation in 1945. With defeat and retribution staring them in the eyes, the perpetrators did their best to hide every trace of their evil deed, blowing up the gas chambers and destroying as much of the incriminating evidence as they could. A special detachment called Commando 1005, headed by SS-Standartenführer Paul Blobel, was assigned to reopen mass graves and burn the corpses on stacks of oil-soaked railroad ties and grind up the bones in special machines.[88] The team started in Russia in the spring of 1943, moved to Poland, and ended up combing the killing fields as far as southeastern Europe. Blobel assigned the job of digging up the decomposed bodies to Jews and to other men in the area. Once the grave diggers had performed their gruesome tasks, they were murdered.

The number of Jews killed can never be precisely known. Estimates range from four to six million. Raul Hilberg's estimate[89] probably comes closest to the truth. Its breakdown by country is given in Table 1.

Apart from the general question of how the Holocaust was possible, four specific questions have often been asked: (1) Who were the perpe-

Table 1
Jews Killed per Country

Poland	up to	3,000,000
USSR	over	700,000
Romania		270,000
Czechoslovakia		260,000
Hungary	over	180,000
Lithuania	up to	130,000
Germany	over	120,000
Netherlands	over	100,000
France		75,000
Latvia		70,000
Yugoslavia		60,000
Greece		60,000
Austria	over	50,000
Belgium	over	24,000
Italy (including Rhodes)		9,000
Estonia		2,000
Norway	under	1,000
Luxembourg	under	1,000
Danzig	under	1,000
	Total	5,113,000

trators, and why did they murder millions of innocent people? (2) How secret was the Holocaust? (3) Why were the Allied powers largely silent and knowing bystanders? and (4) Why did the Jews not revolt? The first of these questions deserves the most extensive treatment.

The Perpetrators

What type of human being, it has been asked, could commit such horrors? One answer has been to label the perpetrators as sadists, but the evidence shows that only a small percentage of the murderers were actually sadistic killers. Even among the Nazi doctors who dispatched thousands of helpless victims with dispassionate efficiency, few were sadistic in any clinical sense. As Dr. Ella Lingens-Reiner, a survivor physician of Auschwitz observed: "There were few sadists. Not more than five or ten percent were pathological criminals in the clinical sense. The others were all perfectly normal men who knew the difference between right and wrong. They all knew what was going on."[90] If sadism played only a minor role, the focus must be shifted to certain larger cultural patterns in German society that furnished the motives and the institutional mechanisms that made it possible to kill millions of people by state mandate. Four such patterns, which have been regarded as central in the analysis presented in this book, must be highlighted again: (1) a virulent form of anti-Semitism with strong biological and religious components; (2) a powerful tradition of institutionalized authoritarianism in family, school, and everyday life; (3) belligerent nationalism based on lack of identity, insecurity, and the trauma of defeat in war; and (4) rule by a criminal leadership.

A knowledge of causes is not always adequate to account for the explosive impact of the effects, especially in the case of mass murder. It may be that what drove these men to mass murder was a defect in their way of *thinking* rather than in their way of *being*. Did they go wrong in their brains rather than in their psyches? If the former, cultural factors are of great importance. The Germans have demonstrated an extraordinary capacity for creative accomplishment that is in part the product of a way of thinking peculiar to themselves and characterized by unusual consequentiality. They have put convictions into practice with impressive energy and consistency that, in other realms, when it has gone wrong, can be blamed for some of the less attractive qualities often attributed to German character: rigidity, excessive orderliness, aggression, and arrogance. The Nazis put into practice a great anti-intellectual force, and they did it with religious zeal and Germanic consequentiality.

The cultural causes, however, do not sufficiently explain the psychological dimensions of the acts of mass murder. These can be known only in their graphic details and through the examination of the personalities and motives of those who perpetrated them. In general terms, there were two types of murderers — those who sat behind the desks and gave the orders — the desk murderers such as Hitler, Himmler, Heydrich, Müller, and Eichmann; and the men who carried out the actual executions or gassings — Höss, Wirth, Mengele, the men of the *Einsatzgruppen,* and the concentration camp guards. Here, again, there were relatively few sadists. Men like Himmler or Eichmann saw themselves as decent men who were doing important work in the service of a noble cause. Addressing a group of SS men at Posen in 1943, Himmler referred to the annihilation of the Jews as a necessary and noble task: "To have stuck this out and — excepting cases of human weakness — to have kept our integrity, this is what has made us hard. In our history, this is an unwritten and never-to-be written page of glory."[91] Similarly, Globocnik insisted: "Gentlemen, if there is ever a generation after us which is so weak-kneed that it does not understand our great task then the whole of National Socialism will have been in vain. On the contrary, in my view bronze tablets ought to be buried, on which it is reported that we had the courage to carry out this great work which is so vital."[92] At Jerusalem, Eichmann denied that he had had anything to do with killing Jews, that he had never killed a single Jew, and that he was not an "*innerer Schweinehund* — or dirty bastard in the depth of his heart."[93] Psychiatrists testified that Eichmann was a "normal" human being from a lower-middle-class family who followed orders without question and served his employer loyally and efficiently.

If Eichmann or Himmler saw themselves as decent men, then why did they order mass killings? The answer lies in their motivation and their rigid, almost robotic, personality structure. Eichmann, Himmler, Höss, and Mengele were true believers with all the strength and intensity that accompanies the will to believe. They were also blind believers, exhibiting the same mind-numbing rigidity, the sort that seals off all access to alternative information and refuses to see the world from any other perspective than its own. As Hannah Arendt pointed out in her assessment of Eichmann, he was the sort of man who lacked the ability to think independently; his thoughts moved entirely within the confines of his narrow ideology. Both Eichmann and Himmler could serve as textbook cases of "bad faith, of lying self-deception combined with monumental stupidity."[94] This may be illustrated in Himmler's case when he greeted the representative of the World Jewish Congress on April 21, 1945, with the incredible words: "Welcome to Germany, Herr Masur. It is time you Jews and we National Socialists buried the hatchet."[95]

In attempting to understand these technicians of mass murder, Robert Jay Lifton has drawn attention to a key psychological principle — that of doubling or dividing the self into two functioning wholes so that either one (the cold-blooded killer) or the other (the good doctor, family man, or conscientious employee) can function separately as needed.[96] The opposing self can become a usurper from within. Guilt is avoided by transferring conscience to the Auschwitz self that justifies murder as racial hygiene. Similar forms of behavior can be observed in Mafia or terrorist death squads. Lifton correctly adds that doubling is often a choice rather than a long-standing character disorder. The choice may have been made in response to entrapment in a criminal situation or lifestyle. Doubling is therefore a defense mechanism to protect the self from the voice of a higher morality or consciousness. Associated syndromes are numbing and "derealization."[97]

In short, most of those who killed did so out of conviction, and they repressed one part of the self in order to allow a murderous self to operate. They then asserted that the killing process was really a healing process — that is, they insisted that in order for Germany to live another group had to die. Within their delusional system, this made a kind of "mad sense." As previously seen, this form of thinking, which defined men such as Hitler, Himmler, Eichmann, and hundreds of Nazi racists, was the culmination of *völkisch* ideology, Christian anti-Semitism, and perverted biology. As Lifton justly and correctly points out, the Nazis made use of a culture that had a tendency toward death-haunted, apocalyptic historical visions and for that reason seized upon the relationship between killing and healing.[98]

The concentration camp doctors exemplified this killing–healing syndrome more than most other Nazis. They believed that by killing they were actually healing, as did those who burned heretics. A Jewish physician who survived the Holocaust once asked a Nazi physician, Dr. Fritz Klein, how he could reconcile his murderous activity with his Hippocratic Oath as a doctor. His answer was: "Of course I am a doctor and want to preserve life, and out of respect for human life, I would remove a gangrenous appendix from a diseased body. The Jew is the gangrenous appendix in the body of mankind."[99]

Such perverted racial hygiene found its highest expression in the infamous Dr. Josef Mengele, the "Angel of Death" at Auschwitz. Most Auschwitz survivors remembered Mengele as a dapper, immaculately dressed German officer, frigid and ruthless, who met new arrivals as they stepped down from the squalid boxcars to meet their fate. Like an operatic stage director, sometimes whistling tunes from Wagner's operas, he would point his cane at each person and order them to the right or the left.[100] He immensely enjoyed these "selections," and in his various medical experiments killed many patients, especially children, without blinking an eye — "willfully and with blood lust."[101] As in Himmler's case, his upbringing did not seem to predict his murderous activities at Auschwitz. He came from an upper-class Bavarian family that owned a business selling farm equipment in Günzburg. His youth followed a pattern we have previously encountered with the sons of middle-class parents — rigidly pedantic educations in the gymnasia, those breeding grounds of mindless authoritarianism, rejection of religion in favor of *völkisch* racial ideologies, and a marked predilection for nationalistic and military ideas. Mengele joined the Stahlhelm in 1931 and the SA in 1934, though it was not until 1938 that he joined the Nazi Party. After receiving his *Abitur,* he studied physical biology and genetics at the Universities of Munich, Bonn, Vienna, and Frankfurt. In 1935 he completed his Ph.D. at the University of Munich; in his doctoral dissertation, which focused on the lower jaw sections of four racial groups, he claimed that it was possible to identify specific racial groups by studying their jaws. In 1936 he passed his state medical examination and took up his first position at the University of Leipzig medical clinic. What changed his life, however, was his appointment as research assistant at the Third Reich Institute for Hereditary Biology and Racial Purity at the University of Frankfurt, where he worked under the direction of Otmar von Verschuer, one of Germany's foremost geneticists and racial hygienists. In fact, Mengele became Verschuer's favorite understudy. The circle of racist utopianism that had begun two generations before (see chapter 1) was now closed with Mengele, who would implement the theory in practice. It was Verschuer who encouraged Mengele's career, secured his appointment as chief medical researcher at Auschwitz, and, as director of the Kaiser Wilhelm Institute for Anthropology, Human Heredity Teaching, and Genetics in Berlin, helped marshal funds for Mengele's research at Auschwitz. The grateful Mengele repaid the professor's services by periodically sending him perfectly preserved body parts from Auschwitz.[102]

When war broke out, Mengele joined the medical corps of the Waffen-SS and served with great distinction on the eastern front, receiving the Iron Cross first- and second-class. In May 1943, at the height of the gassings, he arrived at Auschwitz to take advantage of the rare opportunity offered there to experiment on human beings, especially twins. Mengele was convinced that by experiments on twins, abnormal genetic transmissions could be identified and controlled. He collected about 250 sets of twins and treated them as any laboratory researcher might treat frogs, mice, or rats. According to Lifton, Mengele brought a "murderous scientific fanaticism" to Auschwitz.[103] Yet his murderous activities were conducted within constraints of fanatical order and with mind-numbing pedantry, for, according to him, this research had a noble purpose, namely, to breed a higher form of human being. As one of his unwilling Polish assistants, Dr. Martina Puzyna, put it:

> I found Mengele a picture of what can only be described as a maniac. He turned the truth on its head. He believed you could create a new super-race as though you were breeding horses. He thought it was possible to gain absolute control over a whole race....He was a racist and a Nazi. He was ambitious up to the point of being completely inhuman. He was mad about genetic engineering. I believe he thought that when he'd finished with the Jewish race, he'd start on the Poles, and when he finished with them, he'd start on someone else. Above all, I believe that he was doing this...for his career. In the end I believed that he would have killed his own mother if it would have helped him.[104]

For the sake of his utopian dream, Mengele tortured and murdered with a good conscience. Yet to his associates he was one of the most decent colleagues (*anständigste Kollegen*) — correct, congenial, and "cultured." This, of course, is the Auschwitz syndrome of doubling with attendant rationalizations of noble research and removing poisoning abscesses from the world. Mengele is better known as the fanatical true believer, the mad professor with a utopian vision of human perfection. Auschwitz was his ideal world, his dream come true. Here he could live out his racial fantasy and justify dissecting twins, injecting methylene blue directly into his victims' eyes, collecting body parts, and giving vent to his explosive anger by shooting, injecting (*abspritzen*), or sending his victims to the gas chambers. If in ordinary times he would probably have been a slightly sadistic German professor, as one colleague speculated, Auschwitz transformed him into the archetype of Nazi evil. In the eyes of his Jewish victims he became the embodiment of their deepest collective fears — the key to their "sense of fear from everything that is German."[105]

Secrecy, Indifference, and Resistance

How secret was the Holocaust? The answer, as painful as it still may be to some Germans, is that it was an open secret. It was known not only to the circle of direct perpetrators — Hitler, Himmler, Heydrich, the SS executioners — but also to high-ranking members of the government (Göring, Luther, Stuckart, Dorpmüller, Rosenberg, Sauckel, Goebbels, and so on), the party, and the Wehrmacht. Soldiers returning from the

front who were exposed to the "terrible secret" spilled their knowledge to loved ones, friends, and acquaintances. By the middle of 1944
the secret was widely known. A German reporter, visiting the Ukraine
in 1943, wrote that he had been fully briefed on the Jewish question
and that of the 1.1 million Jews that used to live there all had been
liquidated "like roaches."[106] As previously shown, Himmler informed
German journalists as early as November 1941 that the "biological extermination of all Jews in Europe had begun." In 1943 he celebrated the
crime as a noble chapter in German history. In 1944, the Nazi regime
actually planned to hold a big international anti-Jewish congress, to be
held in Cracow, to explain and commemorate what had been done to
the Jews.[107]

The rest of the world learned about the Holocaust almost as soon
as it began. There was, of course, some initial skepticism, particularly
since similar atrocity stories relating to World War I had turned out
afterward to be a hoax. The Polish underground, supplied with very
accurate information from concentration camp prisoners and escapees,
relayed the truth to Western governments as early as 1942. The Vatican was one of the first institutions to learn about the Holocaust and
decided to take no public action.[108] The same was true of the Allied
powers. Atrocities against Jews were reported in the Anglo-American
press as early as 1942. Both Churchill and Roosevelt knew the truth.
Although a War Refugee Board was established by Roosevelt in January
1944 in order to do everything possible to rescue the victims of Nazism, the board came up against massive institutional indifference and
entrenched anti-Semitism, especially in the State Department. The truth
is that the world stood idly by and either doubted or shrugged off what
was happening. As Walter Laqueur pointed out, the whole story was beyond human imagination. It was also the result of a basic ignorance of
Nazism, the sort of ignorance that was compounded by the sad fact that
neither Britain nor the United Stated showed much interest in the fate
of the Jews.[109]

The question of why the Jews did not resist can be answered by saying that they did resist. They fought in the Warsaw ghetto, tried to break
out at Sobibor, staged a revolt at Auschwitz, committed sabotage, established underground presses, and joined partisan groups. These acts
of resistance were admittedly few in number and made little difference
in the end.[110] Although the Jews could appeal to certain international
organizations, they were unorganized and unrepresented by any government in the world. With no single country behind them and no army
to fight for them, they were helpless to withstand the onslaught of a
racist totalitarian state that believed its mission was to destroy them and
that was assisted in this mission by anti-Semitic governments and an
indifferent world.

Chapter 14

The Defeat of Nazi Germany, 1942-45

The Hinge of Fate Turns: Stalingrad and "Tunisgrad"

In the fall of 1942 the course of the war turned in favor of the Western powers as a result of three major offensives: Rommel's Afrika Korps was defeated at El Alamein on November 2 and retreated headlong toward Tunisia; powerful Anglo-American forces landed in Morocco and Algeria on November 8; and the Russians mounted attacks north and south of Stalingrad on November 19–20. These battles raged until May 1943; and when it was all over, Germany had been driven out of North Africa, and the beginning of the end was in sight on the eastern front. Additionally, Germany was losing the war in the air and on the seas. Starting in March 1942 German cities were subjected to devastating air attacks by huge formations of fighter bombers dropping incendiary bombs that caused frightful damage to lives and property. The German people gradually realized that the war might be lost, and not even Goebbels's clever lies could conceal the reality of round-the-clock air raids and the never-ending stream of casualty reports that came in from all fronts.

The battle of Stalingrad, fought with unprecedented ferocity for eight months, was the turning point of the war on the eastern front.[1] In retrospect, Stalingrad illustrates all the fatal flaws of the German campaign in Russia: "the chronic underestimation of enemy capabilities,"[2] as the German general Franz Halder aptly called it; the lack of coordination and concentration on attainable objectives; and the disruptive and ultimately irrational interference by Adolf Hitler. If Hitler had concentrated all of his efforts on Stalingrad, he might have been able to cripple the Russians decisively. Instead, he decided to launch simultaneous attacks on the Caucasus, thus seriously dividing his forces and exposing them to potentially disastrous counterattacks. When Halder reminded him that Germany could ill-afford such campaigns of attrition, and pointed out that the Russians were producing well over twelve hundred tanks a month, Hitler was so beside himself with fury that he forbade his chief of staff to utter "such idiotic twaddle."[3]

The attack on Stalingrad was entrusted to the now legendary Sixth Army under the command of General Friedrich von Paulus, a capable staff officer but an unimaginative and even slow-witted commander in the field.[4] When the offensive began on June 28, General von Bock, commander of Army Group South, held the Sixth Army in abeyance until the Don had been cleared at Voronezh. Russian strategy was based on holding the two hinges on either end of the front — at Voronezh in the north and Rostov in the south — allowing the Germans to break through the gate into the Donetz Basin and the large bend of the Don, hoping once more to trade space for time.[5] The German thrust caught the Soviets by surprise. By July 5 Paulus's tank divisions reached the Don on both sides of Varonezh, but the Russians reinforced the Voronezh front and were still holding out by the middle of July. Von Bock decided to deal with Voronezh first before pressing on into the void, correctly pointing out the danger of leaving Russian forces undisturbed on his flank, but it was at this point that the impatient Hitler interfered personally in the course of events on the battlefield. He angrily accused von Bock of "wasting time" at Voronezh and sacked him; and compounding this ill-advised removal of a good commander, Hitler committed two additional blunders by dividing the offensive into two separate operations and ordering general Hoth's Fourth Panzer Army, originally slated to capture Stalingrad, south in order to help Kleist's drive for the Caucasus. The two army groups, A and B, that made up Army Group South were detached from each other and given independent action: Army Group A was to destroy the enemy armies near Rostov and march (six hundred miles!) along the eastern coast of the Black Sea toward Baku on the Caspian Sea; Army Group B was to take Stalingrad and move toward Astrakhan on the Caspian Sea. As Joachim Fest pointed out, this enlargement of the Southern Operation meant that "the forces that at the beginning of the offensive had occupied a front of about 500 miles would, at the end of the operations, have to cover a line more than 2,500 miles long against an enemy whom they have been unable to engage in battle, let alone defeat."[6]

The attack on Stalingrad did not begin until the end of July 1942 because General von Paulus was waiting for Hoth's Fourth Panzer Army, which had been diverted southward, to wheel to the northeast and attack the city from the south. By July 22, the left-wing corps of the Sixth Army had reached the suburbs of Stalingrad; a day later the Luftwaffe savagely blanketed the city with incendiary bombs. The Soviet armies, having been ordered by Stalin to hold the city at every cost, refused to yield under the onslaught of the Wehrmacht. It became clear that this battle was not going to be a conventional military conflict, but a clash of political will power and prestige. The city held a special place in Stalin's heart because it was here that the Soviet leader had earned a great mil-

itary victory during the civil war, prompting the citizens of the city of
Tsaritsin to rename it in honor of Stalin. Located on the Volga close to
where the Don river makes a bend, Stalingrad was the last great southern city in Russia, quite apart from being one of the great industrial
centers of the Soviet Union.

As the Germans inched forward to take the city, they encountered
an enemy who was grimly determined to fight and die for every house,
factory, water tower, cellar, and shattered ruin. It was a new experience
to the previously victory-flushed German soldiers. One of them, Wilhelm
Hoffmann of the 267th Regiment, who had confidently expected the
city to surrender in late August, has left us a revealing insight into the
progressive demoralization of the German troops:

September 1st: "Are the Russians really going to fight on the very Bank of
                    the Volga? It's madness."

September 8th: "...Insane stubbornness."

September 11th: "...Fanatics."

September 13th: "...Wild beasts."

September 16th: "...Barbarians, they use gangster methods."

October 27th: "...The Russians are not men but devils."

October 28th: "...Every soldier sees himself a condemned man."[7]

After round-the-clock bombardment, the Germans finally reached the
heart of the city, but the Russians continued fighting in the rubble and
refused to give up. Marshal Chuikov, who had been entrusted with the
overall Soviet strategy by Stalin, realized the German advance had dangerously overexposed their long-drawn-out northern flank. This segment
of the German line along the upper Don was held by Germany's satellite nations — Hungary, Italy, and Romania. These armies were ineptly
led, and their troops were poorly fed and equipped; they represented
the weak link in the German line. In the event of a counterattack it was
highly unlikely that these armies could hold the left flank while the Sixth
Army was preoccupied at Stalingrad.

General Halder repeatedly warned Hitler that Stalingrad was not
worth such heavy losses, but Hitler impatiently shrugged off his dire
warnings as a case of nerves on Halder's part. He was getting tired of
obstreperous officers who failed to see the merit of his grand designs.
When the southern advance did not proceed as rapidly as he had expected, he fired Field Marshal List and assumed command of Army
Group A himself. At the end of September he relieved General Halder,
accusing him of infecting everyone with his cautious and pessimistic
attitude. He even berated the general for being too professional: "We
need National Socialist ardor now, not professional ability."[8] Halder
was replaced by General Zeitzler, a younger and apparently more pliable
officer.

World War II in Europe and Africa

Legend:
- Axis Powers and their allies
- Axis-held, early Nov. 1942
- Allied Powers and their allies
- Neutral nations
- ← Allied advances
- ■ Major battles

Map labels:
N. IRELAND, IRELAND, ATLANTIC OCEAN, GREAT BRITAIN, London, D-Day June 6, 1944, Dunkirk, Paris liberated Aug. 25, 1944, FRANCE, VICHY FRANCE occupied Nov. 1942, PORTUGAL, SPAIN, SP. MOROCCO, MOROCCO, Casablanca, FRENCH NORTH AFRICA (Vichy France) joined Allies Nov. 1942, Kasserine Pass Feb. 14-22, 1943, TUNISIA, July 1943, LIBYA (It.)

NORTH SEA, DENMARK, Battle of the Bulge Dec. 16, 1944– Jan. 31, 1945, BELG., NORWAY, SWEDEN, BALTIC SEA, Berlin captured May 2, 1945, April 1945, GERMANY, SWITZ., ITALY, Corsica, Rome liberated June 4, 1944, Sardinia, Salerno, Monte Cassino, ADRIATIC SEA, SICILY, ALB. (It.), GREECE, Crete (Greece), Rhodes (It.), MEDITERRANEAN SEA

FINLAND, Leningrad besieged Sept. 1941– Jan. 19, 1944, EST., LATVIA, LITH., E. PRUSSIA (Ger.), POLAND, Warsaw, July 1944, SLOVAKIA, HUNGARY, Danube R., ROMANIA, YUGOSLAVIA, BULGARIA, March 1944, UKRAINE, Yalta, BLACK SEA, BULGARIA

Moscow Germans repulsed Dec. 1941, Stalingrad Aug. 21, 1942– Jan. 31, 1943, Volga R., Don R., CAUCASUS

TURKEY, SYRIA (Fr.), LEBANON, PALESTINE (Br.), Cyprus (Br.), Alexandria, El Alamein Oct. 23–Nov. 5, 1942, Suez Canal, Nile R., EGYPT (Br.), TRANS-JORDAN (Br.), RED SEA

Nov. 1942, Nov. 1942

Scale: 0   250   500 Miles / 0   250   500 Kilometers

On November 19, 1942, the Russians began a major attack on over-extended German lines. In a classic pincerlike movement reminiscent of Hannibal's victory over the Romans at Cannae, the Russians hurled two powerful groups at the weakest points north and south of Stalingrad. The Russian armies, commanded by Konstantin Rokossovski and Andrei Yeremenko, crushed the Romanian Third and Fourth Armies on Paulus's flank and closed the pincers behind him, trapping 220,000 men of the Sixth Army with one hundred tanks, eighteen hundred guns, and ten thousand vehicles between the Volga and the Don.

Hitler's response to the entrapped troops at Stalingrad was "stand your ground." Von Paulus cabled back that the annihilation of the Sixth Army was virtually certain unless he were allowed to evacuate immediately and attempt a breakout through the western and southern sides of the pocket. Hitler adamantly rejected these pleas and cabled back that a breakout was unnecessary because he would send General von Manstein's new "Army Group Don" to "break in" and relieve the beleaguered Sixth Army. He also promised to supply the Sixth Army by a massive airlift. Neither of these objectives proved feasible, for Manstein's frantic efforts came too late, and Göring's airlift fell far short of the bare minimum of five hundred tons of supplies needed daily to sustain the entombed army.

In the meantime, the noose tightened. Situation conferences at führer headquarters, dramatically recorded by General Engel, provide a stark commentary on the doomed army and on Hitler's criminal negligence:

November 24: Big discussion of radio message from General Paulus... Führer crassly rejects proposal, though Zeitzler supports it, ...[and] stresses repeatedly that Stalingrad under no circumstances is to be given up.

November 26: Führer is and remains calm, but rejects everything. Reasons: it all would be interpreted as weakness; vital living space would be lost once more; impossible impact on our allies; loss of time, since one could never tell what might happen in the west, Africa, or elsewhere.

December 19: Agitated discussion, since von Manstein had renewed request for breakout of army. Führer is implacable, always with the same arguments, does not believe in saving the army [through retreat].[9]

Near the end of January 1943 the Sixth Army had been reduced to isolated units of half-crazed soldiers who fought on by sheer instinct. Thousands of soldiers either starved or froze to death. The wounded pleaded with their comrades to shoot them on the spot. In a final desperate appeal von Paulus asked for permission to lay down his arms. Hitler was not moved. His reply was as brutal as it was clever: "Capitulation is impossible," he informed von Paulus. "The 6th Army will do its historic duty at Stalingrad until the last man, in order to make

Germany, the Axis Allies, and Axis-occupied Territory

possible the reconstruction of the eastern front";[10] and dangling a bribe in front of von Paulus, which he hoped would spur him on to further resistance, he made him a field marshal. Since no German field marshal had ever been taken prisoner, Hitler hoped that this meaningless gesture would somehow alter a predetermined course of events. Apparently unimpressed by his elevation in rank, von Paulus surrendered to the Russians on January 31, 1943. Of the ninety thousand soldiers who were taken prisoner with von Paulus only five thousand returned to Germany many years later.

When the news of the capitulation reached führer headquarters, Hitler immediately washed his own hands clean by launching a pathetic attack against von Paulus:

> How easy he had made it for himself! ... The man should shoot himself as Generals used to fall upon their swords when they saw that their cause was lost. That's to be taken as granted. Even a Varus commanded a slave: Kill me now! ... What does life mean? Life is the nation; the individual must die. ... Paulus will be speaking on the radio in no time — you'll see. ... How can anyone be so cowardly. I don't understand it. ... What hurts me personally is that I promoted him to field marshal. I wanted to give him that last pleasure. That's the last field marshal I appoint in this war. Best not to count your chickens before they're hatched. That's as ridiculous as anything can be. So many people have to die, and then one man like that comes along and at the last moment defiles the heroism of so many others. He could free himself from all misery and enter into eternity, into national immortality, and he prefers to go to Moscow. How can there be any choice. There's something crazy about it.[11]

The German defeat at Stalingrad emboldened the Russians to continue their offensive, and during the first three weeks of January 1943 it appeared that nothing could resist the Red Army as it reached the Dnieper and was about to cut off the German army in the Caucasus. But then a remarkable German commander, General von Manstein, developed a brilliant strategy to catch the Russians off balance. Von Manstein knew that it was futile to fight for every inch of territory because the Russians outnumbered the Germans in both resources and manpower. The best strategy, he reasoned, was to rely on the tactical experience and quality of the Panzer forces and to avoid costly battles of attrition along rigid lines. His strategy, aptly named "backhand" offensive,[12] allowed the Russians to penetrate deeply into the German lines and then enveloped them with concentrated Panzer attacks. By the middle of March von Manstein's strategy had proved so successful that the Russian advance had been halted. Moreover, the Germans threw the Russians back across the Donetz River, recaptured Karkhov, and restored the front. This remarkable reversal in fortune revealed that the German army was still a formidable fighting machine.

Had Hitler followed von Manstein's advice by fighting "backhand" battles, which might have demoralized the Red Army, the Russian juggernaut might have been prevented for a time from embarking relatively unopposed on its relentless drive toward the German Reich. Instead, Hitler and the majority of his generals determined to hold what they had already won and to strengthen the weakest points in their two-thousand-mile line that stretched from Leningrad in the north to Mariupol on the Sea of Azov. One of the weakest points was the Kursk salient, a hundred-mile bulge that extended into the German line and threatened to separate the fronts of Manstein and Kluge. For several months Hitler and his generals heatedly debated the feasibility of attacking the Kursk salient. Zeitzler and Kluge favored the attack while Jodl and Guderian were adamantly opposed. In truth, as Guderian told Hitler, there was no reason to launch an offensive in 1943, and certainly not one that threatened to turn into a kind of Verdun on the eastern front. Hitler himself admitted that the thought of "Operation Zitadelle," as the projected offensive was labeled, made his stomach churn,[13] but in the end Zeitzler and Keitel's argument that a German attack was necessary for political reasons decided the issue in favor of the assault.

The attack on the Kursk salient began on July 5, 1943, with the greatest concentration of armor ever assembled by the German army. Army Group South sent nine Panzer divisions, including SS Corps Totenkopf, Leibstandarte, and Das Reich, while Army Group Center attacked from the north with Model's Ninth Army, which also included nine Panzer divisions and two supporting corps. Poised north and south of the salient stood the best divisions and the most up-to-date equipment the German army could muster. Hitler had in part delayed the battle in order to supply the offensive with 324 new Panzer tanks. In addition, every army on the eastern front was stripped of tanks and armored equipment, which seriously depleted reserves. Despite this massive arsenal of arms, the Russians withstood the German attack in twelve days of furious fighting. Only small dents had been driven into the Russian defenses; the decisive breakthrough was not achieved. The highlight of the battle came on July 12 when the badly mauled Fourth Panzer Army engaged the Soviet Fifth Army in a titanic eight-hour battle involving as many as three thousand tanks on the move at the same time.

Since Russian intelligence had long anticipated the attack, and Hitler and his generals had dawdled away weeks in indecision and mutual bickering, the Kursk offensive appeared doomed before it even got underway. In addition, the Germans attacked with several different tanks — Panthers, Tigers, Elephants — each of which suffered from serious defects. The massive Elephant tanks with their 100 mm, L-70 guns in fixed mountings proved to be easy targets because they did not have any machine guns to protect them against Russian infantry. The Panther tanks experienced teething problems and were easily set aflame because the oil and gasoline systems were inadequately protected. Breakdowns on the battlefield were almost always permanent because of a lack of spare parts and the variety of equipment. By contrast, the Russians relied on less complicated but equally impressive armor. Finally, the Russians had prepared an almost impregnable defense system of eight belts, an incredible wall that contained over twenty thousand artillery pieces, supported by antitank and personnel mines packed in a density of over four thousand per mile.[14] On July 15 Hitler called off the Kursk attack, informing his commanders that the Allied landings in Sicily had to be stopped, and that this required stripping the armies of the east in order to reinforce those of the west.

In the meantime, the tide was also turning against Germany in North Africa and the Mediterranean. Seriously overextended and having lost control of the air, Rommel's Afrika Korps, despite valiant rearguard actions, was doomed to be caught in a great pincer movement of the Anglo-American forces. While the war hung in the balance at Stalingrad, the African campaign was being decided at El Alamein. Throughout the summer of 1942 the new commander of the British Eighth Army, Sir Bernard Montgomery, had painstakingly reorganized his forces and re-equipped them with tough new Sherman tanks from America. In late October the British opened their offensive with a massive barrage of artillery. The German Panzer Army fought bravely and for a short time without a commander because General Georg Stumme, Rommel's temporary replacement, died of a heart attack during the battle. When Rommel, who had been recuperating from liver and blood-pressure troubles, hurried back to Africa to take charge of the German forces, he recognized that his lines could not hold the British offensive. On November 3, 1942, Rommel, like Paulus before him, received a discouraging "stand your ground and fight to the death" telegram from Hitler. This appalling cable, which was as heartless and negligent as the cables later received by Paulus at Stalingrad, stated:

> In the situation in which you now find yourself there can be no other thought but to hold out, keep your ground and commit every last man and weapon that can be spared into the battle.... Despite his superiority, the enemy can be expected to reach the end of his strength. It would not be the first time in history that the stronger will triumphed over the stronger battalions. You cannot show your troops any other way but victory or death.[15]

When the British breached the German lines on November 4, the Desert Fox decided to save his troops for another day rather than to lead them into almost certain death, as Hitler expected him to do. On November 8, Anglo-American troops, under the command of Dwight D. Eisenhower, were landing in Morocco and Tunisia. Rommel's troops, now in headlong retreat along the Egyptian and Libyan shore, found themselves squeezed between two Allied forces — Montgomery's Eighth Army in the east and Eisenhower's in the west. Although the German troops fought on for another six months, after reinforcing a strong front in Tunisia, the end came on May 12, 1943, with the surrender of a quarter of a million German and Italian troops. Since the German defeat in

Africa came only two months after the disaster in Stalingrad, soldiers began to refer to the German defeat in Africa as Tunisgrad.

The Invasion of Italy and the Fall of Mussolini

Having expelled the Germans from North Africa, the Allied powers now kept up their momentum by carrying the fight to the European continent itself. In January 1943, Churchill and Roosevelt discussed Allied strategy at Casablanca, where they agreed to step up the Pacific war, to invade Sicily as a prelude to the invasion of what they called the Italian "soft underbelly," and to insist upon the "unconditional surrender" of the enemy, a phrase borrowed from General Grant, who had used it during the American Civil War.

Only two months after defeating the Axis powers in North Africa, the Allies landed in Sicily and cleared the island in little over a month. Although the Germans fought valiantly, their Italian allies offered little more than token resistance. Three years of war, marked by constant defeats and by a humiliating dependency on German military might, had taken its toll on the Italian people. Hitler had been receiving ominous reports that Mussolini's political fortunes in Italy were declining rapidly, and when he met the Duce in April 1943 he was shocked by his physical and mental deterioration. The truth was that the Italian people were sick and tired of the war and of Mussolini's mindless dependency on Nazi Germany. Nine days after the Allies had landed in Sicily, Hitler summoned Mussolini for another meeting to discuss joint strategy at Feltre in northern Italy.

Mussolini hoped to be released from the alliance with Germany, but Hitler would not even allow him the dignity of presenting the Italian case. Instead, he rambled on for hours about the necessity of fighting on until victory or doom. Only five days after his meeting with Hitler at Feltre, Mussolini was toppled from power. On the night of July 24, 1943, the Fascist Grand Council arraigned him for mismanaging the war and for dragging Italy into an endless quagmire of defeat and arbitrary dictatorship. The next evening Mussolini was dismissed from office by the king and placed under arrest. His successor was Marshal Badoglio, conqueror of Ethiopia, who was now charged by the crown to form a new non-Fascist government. The Fascist Party was dissolved, Fascist officials were dismissed from their posts, and control of the Italian government passed firmly into the hands of the king and the army.

In the meantime, Marshal Badoglio was squirming uncomfortably on the horns of a dilemma: while he was secretly negotiating with the Allies for a favorable armistice, he was also trying to keep the Germans ignorant of his double-dealing. Both maneuvers, however, backfired badly because the Germans were undeceived and the Allies, following the formula set down at Casablanca, demanded unconditional surrender.

Badoglio chose unconditional surrender, but his secret negotiations did not escape the gaze of Hitler, who was preparing all the while to move swiftly against his unreliable ally.

Although Hitler had anticipated grave problems for Mussolini, he was shocked when he received the news of the Duce's downfall. Only hours after Mussolini's fall from power Hitler summoned a major conference of all the Nazi leaders and quickly drew two conclusions from the events of July 24, namely, that Badoglio was merely stalling for time before capitulating to the Allies, and that it was imperative to seize the initiative by occupying all of Italy, arresting Badoglio and the king, and restoring Mussolini to his rightful position. When Jodl counseled delay until more exact reports could be studied, Hitler brushed him aside:

> There can be no doubt about one thing: in their treachery they will announce that they are going to stick with us; that is perfectly obvious. But that is an act of treachery, for they won't stick with us.... Sure that what's-his-name [Badoglio] declared right away that the war would be continued, but that changes nothing. They have to do that, it's what treachery does. But we'll go on playing the same game, with everything prepared to take possession of that whole crew like a flash, to clean up the whole riff-raff. Tomorrow I'm going to send a man down there who'll give the commander of the Third Armored Grenadiers Division orders to drive straight into Rome with a special group and immediately arrest the whole government, the King, the whole lot, especially the Crown Prince, get our hands on that rabble, especially Badoglio and the rest of the crew. Then you'll see they'll turn limp as a rag, and in two or three days there'll be another overthrow of the government.[16]

While the Badoglio government wasted a month in negotiating with the Allies, Hitler increased his forces in Italy to sixteen divisions, waiting to strike at his treacherous ally. On September 2, the British made their initial landing at Calabria on the toe of the Italian peninsula. A week later came the main thrust of the Allied invasion at Salerno, south of Naples. At the same time, Italy formally surrendered to the Allied powers. The invasion and the Italian surrender were the signal for Hitler's swift counterstrike. The German forces disarmed Italian formations, seized the city of Rome, and occupied northern and central Italy. Badoglio and the king fled south to find protection among their liberators, but the Allies, after bloody fighting on the beaches of Salerno, barely managed to hold their own ground. Although Naples was captured on October 1, 1943, the Allied offensive petered out with the arrival of the autumn rains. Field Marshal Albert Kesselring, who had been put in charge of the Italian theater, displayed an amazing genius for anticipating Allied plans and developing a flexible and innovative response. Originally, Hitler had anticipated the loss of southern Italy, so that his defensive plans called for a stand at the Apennines above Florence. Kesselring's delaying actions, however, enabled the Germans to move their defensive line south of Rome, where they established a powerful line at Cassino.

Italy was, therefore, effectively cut into two parts — the north and the south. The north was in the hands of the Germans, whose SS commandoes under the leadership of Otto Skorzeny dramatically rescued the Duce from his captivity in the Abruzzi Mountains and set him up as puppet ruler of a new "Italian Social Republic." In the south, Marshal Badoglio and the king were virtual prisoners of the Allies. The rest of the Italian people were precariously wedged between the two warring factions, having to endure another fifteen months of misery, cold weather, and starvation.

With the Allied landings in Italy, Hitler now realized that he was facing a coordinated enemy on more than one front. There was every indication that, sooner or later, he would face a major invasion in France. In the fall of 1943, Hitler was already fighting on four fronts: Italy, the high seas, the air, and the eastern front. Moreover, unlike the Allies, who began to pool resources and coordinate strategy, Hitler took everything into his own hands without seriously consulting his experts. There was a lack of coordination between the different theaters of war and between the different branches of the armed forces. Hitler's paranoid style, which had encouraged competing institutions and kept commanders ignorant of matters that did not fall into their exclusive sphere of interest, now began to bear bitter fruit. Addressing a group of staff college graduates in Berlin in 1941, the future mastermind of the July plot to kill Hitler, Count Claus von Stauffenberg, acerbically remarked that "if our most highly qualified General Staff officers had been told to work out the most nonsensical high level organization for war which they could think of, they could not have produced anything more stupid than that which we have at present."[17]

Hitler and the Germans in Defeat

Several fatal flaws in the German war effort could be seen in late 1943: Hitler's behavior became increasingly erratic and therefore unpredictable; the confident professionals in the German general staff, most notably General Halder, were replaced by pliant and subservient yes-men of the stripe of Keitel and Jodl; the chaos of competing administrative empires impeded the successful coordination of policy, administration, and production; and the bestial racial policies of Himmler and the SS provoked revulsion and finally widespread resistance throughout Europe. When the fortunes of war turned against Germany, Adolf Hitler increasingly retreated into his shell and avoided publicity. He traveled through Germany like a thief in the night because he could not bring himself to view the devastation of his shattered cities. On one occasion, when his special train pulled up beside a hospital train of wounded soldiers at Berchtesgaden, Hitler became so agitated that he immediately ordered the blinds drawn. After Stalingrad his nerves were on the verge of breaking, and only his remarkable self-discipline prevented him from suffering a complete breakdown. In addition, his physical condition gradually deteriorated under the impact of his unhealthy style of life, his intense need to control every aspect of the war, and his increasing drug dependency. Those who saw him after some prolonged absence were appalled by his physical deterioration. Göring observed that in three years of war he had aged fifteen years; and Goebbels, always oversolicitous in his concern for his idol, records the führer's gradual physical deterioration, sadly noting that "it is a tragic thing that the Führer has become such a recluse and leads so unhealthy a life, he doesn't get out into the fresh air. He does not relax. He sits in his bunker, 'fusses and broods.' "[18]

Under the influence of intense and persistent stress, Hitler's pathologies manifested themselves openly and further clouded his perception of reality. Joachim Fest has aptly drawn attention to a "galloping process of regression" on Hitler's part.[19] Confined in his solitary headquarters, surrounded by sycophants and toadies, he regressed to infantile fantasies reminiscent of his Linz period. Instead of touring the bombed cities and encouraging the German people by example, he withdrew into fantasies about building magnificent cities, planting German colonies in eastern Europe, resettling entire populations, creating a new racial nobility, and wiping out people of inferior blood.

From the summer of 1941 Hitler spent most of his time at the Wolfschanze (Wolf's Lair) — his remote headquarters located in a heavily wooded, drab, mountainous, and gloomy part of East Prussia. Visitors have described this outpost of barbed wire, bunkers, and barracks as a "blending of monastery and concentration camp."[20] In this atmosphere of self-enforced isolation, his physical and mental well-being steadily deteriorated; he began to complain of nausea, weakness, chills, and constant bouts of insomnia. His hair grayed rapidly, and his left arm and left leg began to tremble intermittently, giving rise to the suspicion that he was suffering from Parkinson's disease.[21]

As previously shown, Hitler was obsessed most of his life by somatic symptoms, complaining about acid stomach, headaches, tingling or crawling feelings, ringing or buzzing in the ears, insomnia, and a host of other undefined aches or pains. He worried so much about his health that he began to adjust his political plans to his anticipated physical condition. His phobia about cancer influenced his long-range goals, forcing him to adjust his timetable repeatedly; and as his physical health disintegrated under the impact of military defeat, Hitler resorted more and more to a frightening variety of drugs to sustain his flagging energy. His medical staff pandered to his needs and indulged his superstitions. Hitler preferred quick fixes in medicine as well as on the battlefield.

Although a staff of medical experts attended the führer, the physician who had his undivided confidence was Dr. Theodor Morrell, a medical quack who had operated a fashionable practice for skin and venereal diseases on the Kurfürstendamm in Berlin. Hitler met him when he needed a dermatologist to cure him of eczema of the leg. Morrell's willingness to experiment with unorthodox treatments impressed Hitler so much that he decided to make him his personal physician. Under Hitler's patronage, Morrell's stock rose rapidly; not only did he enrich himself by manufacturing patent medicines, but he also seems to have had few qualms in using the führer as a guinea pig.

Among the various drugs administered by Morrell were Dr. Koester's antigas pills for flatulence, a compound of strychnine and belladonna; a sex hormone preparation called Testoviran concocted out of pulverized bulls' testicles; stimulants and pep pills such as Coramine, Cardiazol, caffeine, Pervitin, and Kolz-Dallman tablets; application of cocaine to clear the head; tranquilizers and hypnotics such as Brom-Nervacit; and a variety of pills or injections aimed at relaxing the muscles, stimulating appetite, and preventing headaches or colds.[22] During the last three years of Hitler's life, Dr. Morrell gave his patient daily injections containing a variety of these drugs, and the cumulative effect, according to medical experts, was such that Hitler's personality would undergo a complete change. His eyes would flash dangerously; his language would become even more wildly exaggerated than usual; his moods would alternate between psychic exultation and extreme testiness.[23] According to Dr. Giesing, who sampled Hitler's antigas pills himself, Hitler often consumed near lethal doses of these little black pills.

These and other findings have led some scholars to conclude that Hitler's hypochondria resulted in serious drug abuse and that the German dictator probably suffered, among other things, from chronic amphetamine poisoning since the summer of 1942.[24] Yet, amazingly, Hitler kept functioning to the point of retaining control over the machinery of government, and he did so to the very last moment of his life. More amazingly still, the German people as a whole continued to have faith in his leadership, which illustrates that the will not to believe the truth is often as strong as, if not stronger than, the will to believe it.

As previously mentioned, neither Hitler nor the German people were pleased when Germany found itself at war with Britain. It was one of Hitler's firmest beliefs, mentioned several times in *Mein Kampf,* that Germany had lost World War I at home and not on the battlefield. For that reason Hitler did his utmost to prop up the home front, to the point of initiating self-defeating policies of keeping the German population pacified — policies that may well have contributed significantly toward his ultimate defeat. One strategic decision, motivated to prevent the home front from collapsing, was not to convert the German economy for total war. Hitler hoped that reliance on blitzkrieg tactics would not only assure final victory on the battlefield but also guarantee his popularity on the home front. In other words, instead of arming "in-depth," which would have meant an unpopular war economy with serious shortages of consumer goods, Hitler hoped that quick victories, bringing massive war matériel from conquered territories, would accomplish the same objective. Hitler's initial victories in the west seemed to confirm these expectations. Trainloads of confiscated raw material, foodstuffs, and machinery from the conquered territories arrived in Nazi Germany and disgorged booty for the "master race." The Nazis also made the conquered territories pay heavily for the privilege of being occupied, using the money thus derived to buy additional foodstuffs and matériel that were then hauled off to Germany.

By the end of 1941, however, Germany was facing a much wider war with the addition of the Soviet Union and the United States — powers with immense material resources and manpower. It now turned out that Germany was facing a lengthy war of attrition with both inadequate resources and misguided planning strategies. The Ministry for Armaments and War Production, set up in 1940 under the leadership of the trusted and energetic Fritz Todt, quickly stepped up war production and tried to control the whole war economy. When Fritz Todt died in a plane accident in 1942, Hitler made one of his best appointments by turning to his favorite architect, Albert Speer.

Under Speer's able leadership, war production soared. Slashing waste, reducing duplication of effort, and rationalizing policies, Speer was able to increase production dramatically — even in the face of constant air raids by Allied bombers. In the meantime, consumer goods production continued relatively uncurtailed. It soon became obvious, however, that not even Speer's organizational brilliance could stem the inevitable tide of defeat. Although Speer enjoyed Hitler's confidence, he quickly found himself entangled in the web of the Nazi bureaucracy, forced to fight encroaching and competing interest groups. He quarreled with Fritz Sauckel over the use of foreign labor and battled Bormann and the *Gauleiter* because they were unwilling to covert the economy to total war, which would have meant shifting millions of workers from consumer to War industries. Afraid of the wrath of the population, the *Gauleiter* protested to Hitler and the plan was temporarily shelved.

With defeat staring the Nazis in the face, a desperate plan for "total mobilization" was finally authorized in the summer of 1944, and Joseph Goebbels was appointed Reich Plenipotentiary for Total War. Goebbels had not entirely deluded himself into believing that the war could be won by words alone. He sprung into action with some far-reaching decisions which would affect the lives of many Germans. He began by inducting young people into service, forcing ten to fifteen year old children into farm service or becoming anti-aircraft helpers. Men and women not already engaged in service to the nation were required to register for compulsory labor duty. A Volkssturm, or People's Army, consisting largely of either very young or very old men, including any man between the ages of sixteen and sixty-five who was not already serving the country, was scratched together in a last desperate effort to avert defeat. Theaters, schools, and coffeehouses were closed. Penalties for defeatism were stiffened.

Total mobilization also involved a change in Nazi policies regarding the use of women. Unlike Britain or even the United States, Germany had not fully mobilized its women during the first three years of the war, preferring to rely primarily on foreign labor.[25] It was not until 1943 that conscription was introduced, but this was accompanied by numerous exceptions that allowed many women to stay at home. Now, at the eleventh hour, the Nazis tightened the rules, and they also raised the age limit for the compulsory labor of women from forty to fifty, terminating family subsidies for any woman who did not work.

The possibility of ignominious defeat, underscored by daily terror bombing from the air that pulverized many German cities, brought with it a climate of despair, fear, and widespread defeatism. Party members and others such as entrepreneurs and business managers continued to support the regime, but the traditional elites, the upper middle classes, and many ordinary Germans who had lost loved ones on far-flung battlefields began to lose hope. The Nazi Party, now decimated by war losses, relied largely on youth volunteers and became increasingly unpopular. This created a serious leadership crisis, especially at a time when it became necessary to organize the People's Army.

The heart and soul of the party continued to be the "old fighters" (alte Kämpfer) who had joined the party during the 1920s and were later rewarded with positions for which they showed little ability, ending up as Gauleiter or Kreisleiter. These men were often asocial types with markedly brutal and venal tendencies. The war gave them many opportunities for corruption. Germans were familiar with stories about Gauleiter who embezzled party funds and lived regally while the rest of the population had to listen to their hypocritical appeals to the virtue of sacrifice. The population also resented their increasingly brutal methods of propping up the sagging home front — methods that ranged from irritating harassment to outright murder. When the end came, many party leaders tried to save themselves by leaving Germany or hiding their identity.

Public morale was a major concern to the Nazi regime, and elaborate efforts were made by various agencies to canvas public opinion. The Security Service (SD) of the SS sent agents all over Germany to listen as objectively as possible to what ordinary Germans were actually saying about the war; and what they heard was unmistakably critical. The reaction was predictable: the SD reduced its agents and limited access to reports on German public opinion to only a few top leaders, including Goebbels and his propaganda machine.

Among the many complaints registered by field agents was public grumbling (nörgeln) about rationing. Germany had instituted a very mild system of rationing in the beginning of the war, but shortages in certain goods (butter, fats, meats, textiles, leather, coal, cosmetics, and cigarettes) became increasingly serious. This stimulated an existing and growing black market and a horde of opportunistic racketeers who managed it. An SD report stated:

> In the early stages of the war black marketeering was rejected as a form of sabotage, but since then there has grown up a practice of evading rationing regulations without any consciousness of wrong-doing. Catch phrases like "he who has one thing has everything" or "everybody swaps with everyone else" are in circulation, and folk comrades who do not join in these practices are considered stupid.[26]

As Richard Grunberger has aptly observed, the black market, like any nonregulated market, is usually able to provide very accurate information about people's perceived needs. Thus, in the spring of 1945 several remarkable items became available on the Berlin black market such as hammer-and-sickle badges and even six-pointed Stars of David.[27] There was also a brisk trade in faked documents; for eighty thousand marks one could purchase a complete set of documents legitimizing one's whole existence in Nazi Germany: passport, army pass, work book, ration card, and Volkssturm Z-card.[28] The German people had been inured against physical suffering and war losses for decades, but World War II brought a new form of suffering, allied bombing. Germany had been subjected to light bombing since the beginning of the war, but heavy attacks, launched by British (Halifax, Lancaster) and American (B-17) strategic bombers, did not begin until 1942 when Air Marshal Arthur "Bomber" Harris began to implement his policy of round-the-clock saturation bombing of German urban-civilian centers in hopes of breaking German morale or perhaps even provoking a class uprising of enraged German workers against their Nazi overlords.[29] Although these expectations turned out to be based largely on wishful thinking — for German morale was actually strengthened and there was no widespread cry to overthrow the Nazis — the Allied bombing attacks proved to be physically devastating and economically disruptive.

The first "thousand-bomber raid" was launched by the British on May 31, 1942, on the city of Cologne, consuming the whole center of the city in a hellish firestorm that left nothing standing except the cathedral. Similar raids were launched on Essen and Bremen in June. Combined British and American raids were also staged in 1943 and continued unabated until the end of the war. In July 1943 Harris unleashed a four-night raid on Hamburg that caused a firestorm that fed on oxygen drawn from the periphery by winds and suffocated thousands in air-raid shelters or cellars and reduced large stretches of the city to a fiery mass reaching fifteen hundred degrees Fahrenheit; it destroyed 80 percent of the city's buildings and killed thirty thousand of its inhabitants. Similar horrors were visited upon Kassel, Würzburg, Darmstadt, Heilbronn,

Wuppertal, Weser, and Magdeburg. All German cities of over one hundred thousand inhabitants were bombed repeatedly during the last two years of the war. Beginning in November 1943 the battle of Berlin began in the air and would continue until the end of the war, pulverizing much of Greater Berlin into a desolate landscape. But perhaps the most horrifying raid against a German city occurred on the night of February 14, 1945, when the picturesque, rococo city of Dresden, a city of no strategic value but overcrowded that night by refugees, was incinerated in apocalyptic fashion, at the cost of nearly one hundred thousand human lives.[30]

To counteract the bad news that was now streaming in from all fronts, Joseph Goebbels cranked up his propaganda machine and sent out a message of hope as well as fear — hope in the form of powerful secret weapons under development and fear in the form of gruesome reminders of what was in store for Germany if the Russian hordes would overrun the fatherland. Goebbels knew that the Germans were not stupid. The early victories, heralded as deathblows to the enemy, had not resulted in final victory or peace. The war in Russia, which continued unabated even after Hitler's public announcement in 1941 that it was as good as won, convinced many Germans that the future was indeed bleak. The disastrous defeat at Stalingrad, however, was the real clincher for many Germans that the war was lost. Not even Goebbels's ubiquitous propaganda machine could fool thoughtful Germans of all walks of life about the nearing end; and yet Goebbels still had several means for keeping up public morale. Goebbels exploited the propaganda potential inherent in the Allied demand for unconditional surrender; he reminded the German people that such a policy, allowing for no face-saving or mercy, was calculated to annihilate them. Goebbels also continued to touch up the führer's image, for he knew that despite the horrible suffering the German people were experiencing, they still trusted their leader. They had followed him obediently into the war, sacrificed their sons and daughters to him, and even now, as bombs burst all around them, many Germans were still under his spell — a spell that would not be broken until his ignominious death. The extent of collective wishful thinking about the führer is poignantly captured by Speer's account of a discussion he had with several ordinary farmers shortly before the end of the war:

> In Westphalia a flat tire forced us to stop. Unrecognized in the twilight, I stood in a farmyard talking to the farmers. To my surprise, the faith in Hitler which had been hammered into their minds all these last years was still strong. Hitler could never lose the war, they declared! The Führer is still holding something in reserve that he'll play at the last moment. Then the turning point will come. It's only a trap, his letting the enemy come so far into our country![31]

However, there were Germans who had always resisted Hitler's tyranny — Social Democrats, religious opponents, academics, Commu-

nists, conservatives, and military leaders. As previously mentioned, the
consolidation of Hitler's tyranny by the triangle of SS, police, and concentration camp made organized opposition very difficult. The war saw
an intensification rather than a lessening of totalitarian control. The
concentration camp system was greatly expanded inside and outside
Germany. People were rounded up before they had committed offenses;
they were judged guilty because of their group affiliation as Communists, Social Democrats, Jews, homosexuals, shiftless elements, and so
on. In 1940 new camps were added in Germany and other western
locations at Neuengamme near Hamburg, Bergen Belsen near Celle,
Gross-Rosen in Lower Saxony, Stutthof near Danzig, and Natzweiler
in Alsace. In addition to the major concentration camps there were ten
times as many labor camps where people were sent for the most trivial
offenses. In April 1944 there were 20 concentration camps and 165 affiliated labor camps. Whereas in 1939 German law had recognized only
3 capital offenses, that number had risen to 46 by 1942. In the Reich the
number of individuals who were put to death rose from 926 in 1940 to
3,002 in 1942. Those who still argue that there was no real opposition
to Nazi tyranny would have to explain why over 1,000,000 Germans
were incarcerated in concentration camps.

Despite a massive network of police surveillance, there were many
Germans who voiced their dissent, some openly and some in muted
form. As Detlev Peukert has shown, there was a mood that ran counter
to the officially sponsored picture of delirious Germans rallying around
the führer.[32] In the absence of opinion polls, of course, it is difficult to
gauge just how Germans really felt on most issues. There are, however,
two interesting sources that shed a great deal of light on how ordinary
Germans reacted to the Nazi regime. Heydrich's agents, as previously
noted, submitted regular reports called *Meldungen aus dem Reich* (reports from the Reich) that provide a fairly accurate picture of public
opinion. Another fascinating set of documents are reports by Social
Democratic agents in Germany reporting what they saw and heard to
the Social Democratic Party in exile (SOPADE). Although both SPD and
KPD cells had been crushed, small groups continued their active opposition. The most effective of these groups was called the Rote Kapelle (Red
Orchestra), a group of about one hundred Communist sympathizers
that engaged in widespread espionage activities by infiltrating important
civilian and military agencies and reporting its findings to Moscow. The
network was finally broken up in 1942, and many of its leaders, including Harro Schulze-Boysen and Arvid Harnack, were executed. Another
source of opposition formed at the universities, where disenchantment
with the regime, though belated, became more widespread as the war
continued. The most significant of these groups was the White Rose, a
code name for a student resistance network at the University of Munich.
This group was headed by Sophie and Hans Scholl, sister and brother,
and their mentor, Professor Kurt Huber. This little group organized an

underground network in Munich and at several other universities, distributing leaflets and trying to galvanize their fellow students to resist the Nazis. Reported to the Gestapo, the Scholls along with Huber were arrested, tortured, humiliated in front of the People's Court, and executed. Sophie Scholl went bravely to the scaffold on crutches and was beheaded by a gruesomely attired executioner in evening dress of top hat, white tie, and tails.[33]

Given such savage treatment for resisting, it is not surprising that opposition was scattered, poorly organized, and uncoordinated, for vigilant Gestapo bloodhounds constantly traced its movements. Moreover, war placed a troublesome moral burden on resistance fighters because they felt that their activities would undermine the war effort. Yet as the tide of war turned against Germany, the old opposition to Hitler that had formed among high-ranking military and civilian leaders in 1938 now redoubled its efforts.[34]

In 1943 it became increasingly obvious to many military leaders that the war could not be won. But even now, when total defeat and ruin were virtually certain, most officers could not bring themselves to overthrow Hitler. With no tradition of opposition to tyranny to guide them, the generals found it difficult to overcome inherent moral scruples. They reasoned that Germany was engaged in total war and that the majority of Germans still supported their führer. All soldiers had sworn a personal oath to Hitler. What right did they have to remove the head of state at a time of dire peril to the fatherland? Such moral scruples deeply gnawed on the consciences of some of Hitler's opponents, paralyzing their will to action and preventing them from organizing resistance on a broader front.

However, by the middle of 1943, three major centers of opposition to Hitler existed: the members of the Kreisau Circle, named after the Silesian country estate of Count Helmuth James von Moltke; the conservative circle gathered around Carl Goerdeler, ex-mayor of Leipzig, and General Ludwig Beck, former army chief of staff; and a group of younger military officers such as Claus von Stauffenberg, Henning von Tresckow, and Friedrich Olbricht. These groups consisted of high-minded and patriotic Germans who abhorred Hitler's tyranny and hoped to redeem Germany by eliminating the dictator. The problem was that these men were unable to develop a coherent plan of action. Their opposition to Hitler was also stymied by the pervasive net of totalitarian terror, making organized resistance extremely difficult, and by a pervasive fear that their fellow Germans might condemn their opposition as unpatriotic and traitorous. Finally, several feelers abroad revealed that the German resistance could not expect much help from the Western powers because most Allied statesmen saw little difference between the German resistance fighters and the Nazis, considering the former to be either disgruntled Nazis or reactionary conservatives.[35]

The hornet's nest of conspiracy against Hitler centered around Colonel Hans Oster and the counterintelligence department of the OKW, the Abwehr. Colonel Oster was the assistant to the enigmatic head of the Abwehr, Admiral Canaris, who had already predicted the end of Germany at the time of the Polish invasion.[36] Canaris provided intelligence cover for Colonel Oster's conspiratorial activities. Through hard work and clever secrecy, Oster had gathered a group of coconspirators around him that included Hans von Dohnanyi, Franz Gürtner's assistant in the Ministry of Justice; Klaus Bonhoeffer, Dohnanyi's brother-in-law; Dietrich Bonhoeffer, a well-known Lutheran theologian and brother of Klaus Bonhoeffer; the merchant Justus Delbrück; and Dr. Josef Wirmer, a Berlin lawyer and former member of the Center Party. Supplied with documents forged by the German Abwehr, Dietrich Bonhoeffer was sent to Stockholm in May 1942 to make contact with Bishop Bell of Chichester on behalf of the German resistance. Bishop Bell passed on Bonhoeffer's information to the British government. Similar contacts were made through Allen Dulles, head of the American Office of Strategic Services in Switzerland. These contacts, however, produced no positive response and only reinforced the pall of despair that hung around the conspirators.

German resistance fighters eventually reached the conclusion that only the removal of Hitler could bring an end to Germany's troubles. The first attempt against Hitler was planned in February 1943 by General Friedrich Olbricht, chief of the General Army Office and deputy to the commander of the Ersatzheer (Home Army). The Ersatzheer consisted largely of recruits in training; its only active troops consisted of garrisons in several German cities, including Berlin. Nevertheless, Olbricht hoped to use the Home Army as an instrument of control; he seems to have believed that the confusion following the death of the führer would enable him to seize power with a relatively minor force. Olbricht assigned the actual task of killing Hitler to General Henning von Tresckow, a senior operations officer in Kluge's Army Group Center, and to Fabian von Schlabrendorff, a young lieutenant on his staff.[37] When Hitler visited Kluge's headquarters at Smolensk on March 13, 1943, Tresckow and Schlabrendorff succeeded in placing a time bomb in the plane that carried the führer back to his East Prussian headquarters. However, the bomb, hidden in a package along with two bottles of brandy, failed to explode; and the desperate Schlabrendorff, who had earmarked the package for a friend, had to race to East Prussia and reclaim his dangerous "gift."[38]

Only a week after this incident, Colonel von Gersdorff planned to blow himself up in Hitler's presence at the Berlin Arsenal, but again luck came to Hitler's aid. For some inexplicable reason, Hitler simply cut his visit to ten minutes — not enough time to set off the fuses required to blow up the arsenal and everybody in it. A plan to blow up Hitler during a military conference, hatched by Colonel von Stieff, also failed because the bomb exploded prematurely.

In November 1943, Axel von dem Bussche-Streithorst, a young captain in the infantry, offered to sacrifice himself during an inspection of new army uniforms that Hitler was scheduled to attend. Bussche planned to transform himself into a walking time bomb, leap on the führer, and blow himself and the führer to smithereens. A day before the assassination, however, the building that housed the uniforms was bombed by the Allies and Hitler's inspection was canceled. Although von dem Bussche devised a new plan for December, it failed because Hitler suddenly went to Berchtesgaden. This shift in Hitler's travel plans also neutralized another plot by a young colonel named Claus von Stauffenberg, who tried to plant a bomb concealed in his briefcase in Hitler's conference room. Shortly afterward, von dem Bussche was seriously injured and therefore could not be expected to carry out further plans. An attempt by Ewald von Kleist, scheduled for February 1944, came to nothing because Hitler unexpectedly canceled a military presentation. Several other attempts on Hitler's life were equally thwarted, reinforcing the impression that the führer enjoyed magical protection.

In the meantime, the Gestapo was closing in on the conspirators. General Oster had been forced to resign as early as December 1943, and the conspirators he had encouraged were being arrested one by one. In February 1944, von Moltke was arrested and the Kreisau Circle was broken up. Two months later, Dietrich Bonhoeffer, Joseph Müller, and Hans von Dohnanyi were arrested. After lengthy interrogations of these and other suspects, the Gestapo and SS intelligence agencies began to close in on the Abwehr.

It is at this point that Stauffenberg revitalized the resistance movement almost single-handedly. Scion of an ancient family of Württemberg nobles, Stauffenberg was a conservative monarchist who had originally supported the Nazi movement. He had served with great distinction on several fronts during the war, losing an eye and half of his left hand while fighting in North Africa in 1943. By that time, however, he had become a determined opponent of Hitler, whom he saw as the Antichrist. He established connections with the Kreisau Circle through his cousin Count Peter Yorck von Wartenburg and after the arrest of Moltke he took personal charge of the conspiracy against Hitler.

Two major events appeared to galvanize the conspirators into a frenzied plan of action in the summer of 1944: Himmler's agents were on the trail of the chief conspirators, and the Allied invasion of Normandy along with the rapid collapse of the eastern front made it imperative to conclude peace if any further unnecessary loss of life was to be avoided. By a stroke of good fortune, Stauffenberg had been appointed chief of staff to General Friedrich Fromm, who commanded the Home Army. His new post gave him access to the military conferences at Hitler's headquarters, an opportunity Stauffenberg was determined to use in order to assassinate Hitler. The code name the conspirators chose to launch their coup was Operation Valkyrie. By this plan the Home Army was to take over Berlin and other major cities, neutralize major Nazi institutions and functionaries, and proclaim a new government headed by Ludwig Beck and Carl Goerdeler. It was a brilliant plan because Hitler had used the same code name for a plan he had devised to use the Home Army to put down a potential revolt by foreign workers against the German government. It almost worked. (See p. 551 below for further details.)

Nazi Defeats at Sea, in the Air, and in the Laboratories

Apart from the gradual disintegration of the Russian front and the Allied invasion of Italy, the year 1943 also saw grave German defeats in the Atlantic and in the air. In February 1943, Hitler replaced Admiral Raeder for his failure to sink Allied convoys on their way to Russia. In Raeder's place, he appointed Admiral Karl Dönitz, an expert in submarine warfare. The fact that the new commander in chief of the navy was a submarine expert signaled a major shift in German naval policy. Hitler had originally envisioned a big navy, surpassing the navies of Britain and the United States. However, construction proceeded in fits and starts. In the summer of 1940 construction on two huge battleships, the *Bismarck* and the *Tirpitz,* was just being completed. Although Hitler and his naval chiefs were agreed on strangling Britain's supply line, they could not work out a uniform plan of attack, particularly in regard to the role the big battleships were to play. On May 27, 1941, the British sunk the *Bismarck*. This convinced Hitler to hold whatever big ships he had in reserve because he expected the British to launch an invasion of Norway in order to attempt to relieve pressure on the Soviet Union. Since the submarine component of the navy had been sinking more ships than the surface vessels, Hitler decided to wage war on the high seas primarily by using submarines. Starting in the spring of 1942, Dönitz threw everything he had against the Anglo-American forces in the Atlantic, managing to sink as many as ninety-seven ships totaling more than half a million tons during the first three weeks of March. Time, however, was running against the German effort because American shipyards built ships faster than the Nazis were able to sink them. On the seas, as well as in the air, Germany was also losing the battle of science and technology. America built long-range bombers that could patrol the length and breadth of the Atlantic with new microwave systems capable of locating U-boats.

Convoys no longer sallied forth without protection. On their long trips they were now accompanied by convoy escorts and special vessels specializing in hunting down U-boats. By the end of 1943, Germany was sustaining such prohibitive losses in the Atlantic — as many as forty-one U-boats were lost in the month of May alone — that Dönitz had to call a temporary halt to the U-boat offensive.

Hitler was losing the war not only on land and on the high seas but also in the air. After the battle of Britain in September 1940, the Luftwaffe was increasingly incapable of challenging the enemy in the air or defending the homeland against Anglo-American saturation bombing. Its last success was in the Balkan campaign, culminating in the conquest of Crete. Thereafter, the Luftwaffe was unable to prevent the Allied landings in North Africa, Italy, and France. It also failed in Russia, and Göring's promise to supply Stalingrad by air proved to be one of its most costly undertakings, resulting in the loss of 488 aircraft and about 1,000 airmen.[39] Despite great efforts to increase production, especially the new ME-262 jet planes, the Luftwaffe could not overcome a host of insurmountable problems such as lack of fuel, shortage of trained pilots, and the growing domination of the air by the Allied forces. In the judgment of military historians, by 1943 the Luftwaffe was simply overwhelmed and outclassed by the combined Allied air forces.[40]

Finally, Hitler was also defeated in the scientific and intelligence fields. German scientists fell significantly behind the Allies in technological advancements, notably in the field of radar technology and atomic research.[41] The Nazi seizure of power, as previously shown, had led to a serious hemorrhaging of German science, resulting in a veritable brain drain from Germany.[42] Some of the finest scientific and technical minds, including Albert Einstein, sought refuge abroad and volunteered their talents in the service of the Allied cause. In addition, Hitler was a poor judge of scientific possibilities. Until the tide of battle turned, Germany made no systematic efforts to organize its scientific resources. In 1940, for example, the general staff even went so far as to suspend all scientific projects that did not promise tangible military results within four months.[43] When military defeat stared him in the face, Hitler encouraged crash projects, but by then it was too little and too late.

By contrast, the Allies developed long-range plans involving manpower needs and technological requirements almost from the beginning of the war. Joseph Goebbels once remarked to Speer that Britain had been luckier in having had a Dunkirk at the beginning of the war.[44] What he meant by this paradoxical remark was that Germany's cheap victories created the deceptive belief that long-range planning, especially in the scientific and industrial fields, was unnecessary.

The Allies enjoyed a clear-cut advantage in the field of radar technology; they also quickly learned to tie their radar systems to an equally effective ground-control system, thus directing their fighter planes to the right target. This was a crucial advantage during the battle of Britain; and Germany's backwardness in radar technology is clearly demonstrated by the fact that German bombers ignored English radar stations on their way to their targets. It is true that the Germans had developed effective devices — such as the Freya device — to detect approaching aircraft. They also developed a radio directional beam that could be used to direct their bombers to their targets, but the British quickly learned to "bend" the radio beam, thus causing many bombs to fall harmlessly into open fields. The Germans countered with the development of the "X-Gerät," a complex beam that could be operated at various frequencies and was therefore less prone to be jammed by British signals.[45] During the blitz on London and other English cities the Germans used this new device with great effect, but British radar proved to be a more potent weapon because it still enabled Royal Air Force fighter planes to locate their targets with remarkable precision.

In the meantime, Hitler's plans to invade Russia caused the postponement of most scientific projects, including those associated with the electronics war that had been raging throughout 1939–40. When Germany reentered the contest in late 1942, the Allies had taken a decisive and unbeatable lead. When the Allied Bomber Command decided to strike at Germany around the clock, it became necessary to equip airplanes with devices that could lead them to their targets in all kinds of weather conditions. In the early part of 1942 the British developed a navigational system called "Gee," which sent out an invisible grid of signals telling navigators where they were at any given point in their flight. The British also developed more and more sophisticated bombing devices such as the "Oboe" and the "H2S system," the former being a remote-control system for dropping bombs and the latter an airborne radar set that allowed the bombardier to "see" through the clouds or the darkness beneath him.

The H2S navigation system was used with devastating effect in a mass raid of one thousand bombers on Hamburg in January 1943. Later, the H2S device was used by British planes in the Atlantic searching for U-boats. Although German scientists countered these radar systems with some effective jamming devices, they failed to regain the lead in producing new systems of their own. In July 1943 the British found a remarkably effective means of stymieing German radar defenses by dropping massive strips of tin or aluminum over enemy targets. These strips produced a welter of blips on German radar screens, giving the deceptive impression that each strip represented an enemy plane. The Allies succeeded for over a year in disorienting the Nazis with this simple method before countermeasures were taken.

Germany had entered the war with an impressive lead in weapons technology. Visitors to Germany before the war had been awed by its latest tanks, planes, artillery pieces, and guns. These weapons not only were new but had been put to practical use in the Spanish Civil War. As the war unfolded, Germany fielded some additional weapons of destruction: magnetic mines, rocket launchers, jet fighter planes, and supersonic rockets.

Hitler had put great stock in the development of rockets, a field in which the Germans were significantly more advanced than the Allies. Four major weapons, designated V-1 to V-4, the V standing for *Vergeltungswaffe* (reprisal weapon), were planned by German scientists under the direction of Wernher von Braun and Walter Dornberger at Peenemünde. The V-1 was a small, remote-controlled plane propelled by a jet engine and guided by a gyroscope; it could reach speeds of up to four hundred miles an hour and unload a ton of explosives on a particular target. These "buzz bombs," as they were called, were unleashed from their bases in France on London a week after D-Day. Although more than eight thousand were launched and caused considerable damage, the Royal Air Force shot down many of them, and their launching sites were soon overrun by Allied troops. Starting on September 2, 1944, the Nazis hurled an even more lethal missile at the British — the V-2. Unlike the V-1, which was essentially a pilotless plane, the V-2 was a supersonic rocket, forty-six feet long and weighing more than thirteen tons; it could reach thirty-five hundred miles an hour with a range of 225 miles and was capable of delivering a ton of explosives. More than one thousand V-2 rockets fell on England before their launching sites were destroyed. The V-3 was to be a piece of artillery with a barrel 150 yards long in which a shell would be increasingly propelled by a series of explosions until it reached such a high degree of velocity that it could reach targets fifty miles away. The V-4 was a four-stage rocket propelled by powder instead of liquid fuel; it carried a warhead of one hundred pounds and had a range of one hundred miles. Only a few of these rockets were launched against Antwerp in late 1944, but most of them missed their mark by as much as thirty-five miles.[46] The Nazis were also at work on a long-range ballistic missile, the A-9, which was designed to reach New York in thirty-five minutes and could also be launched from submarines.

Although the Germans were advanced in rocketry, they were not even close to developing an atomic bomb, as the Allied powers mistakenly believed they were. Through exiled scientists, it had come to the attention of Albert Einstein that the Germans had discovered the secret of nuclear fission, which set in motion Einstein's famous letter to President Roosevelt urging that the U.S. government investigate the feasibility of developing atomic weapons. While the scientists working on the Manhattan Project made great progress in isolating the material needed in the process of nuclear fission (Uranium 235) and also determined how much of it was needed to build a bomb, the German scientists, though working along similar lines, made several miscalculations that persuaded them that years were needed for research and development. The Germans also believed that Anglo-American scientists were not capable of developing an atomic bomb, so that there was no need to develop a crash program. By the spring of 1942, the Germans had opted against using critical resources for atomic research.[47] Hitler expected to win the war quickly, as previously shown, and his scientists (Heisenberg, Hahn, and so on) saw nuclear weapons as a *postwar* development and not as a means of winning the war.[48]

Finally, the Germans were no match for the combined Allied forces in the field of espionage. In no other area have historians been so stymied in presenting accurate accounts as in the field of espionage, a field inherently difficult to penetrate because it consists of deceptions, exaggerated claims, and much bravado. Nor has it been any easier to assess the impact of espionage on the outcome of battles or wars in general. However, a few facts and generalizations about the role of Nazi espionage can be ventured with some assurance. German intelligence was poorly coordinated and riddled with internal conflict. The Abwehr, headed by Admiral Canaris, who played a double game for and against Hitler, reflected the virtuosity of its deceptive chief but was therefore not an effective organization. Canaris's competitor, Walter Schellenberg, who headed the Inland SD and Foreign Intelligence Service of the SS, was a shallow romantic visionary who believed that he could replicate the British Secret Service within the Nazi system. Far from building up an effective intelligence network that could have challenged the Allied powers, Schellenberg spent most of his time battling the Abwehr; his only major success was smashing the Red Orchestra.

Intelligence consists of spies and cryptographers, popularly referred to as "Humint" (human intelligence) and "Sigint" (signal intelligence),[49] the former being more glamorous but the latter more effective. Nazi agents and spies were generally effective in German occupied countries, especially France, Holland, and Belgium, but less so where it really counted — the Soviet Union, the United States, and Britain.[50] Probably the most effective German spy was a valet to the British ambassador in Turkey called Cicero, who leaked a series of top secret documents to the Germans. The reputations of many other German spy masters, including that of Reinhard Gehlen, have been greatly exaggerated; but what the Germans lacked in subtlety, they generally made up for in brutality.

The final word on code breaking has not been written because the relevant German documents captured by the Anglo-American side have not been released.[51] One fact, however, is clear: the Germans were badly beaten in this field. As is now well known, the Allies, chiefly the Poles and the British, broke *Enigma,* the German military's machine cipher. Ultra, the British organization of leading cryptographers, was able to decipher Germany's top-secret military codes, so that by late 1940 Churchill could read Hitler's most secret directives. In 1943 the British cryptographers also broke into the German *Geheimschreiber,* a different encoding system from *Enigma.* As a result, the Allies were well informed about Hitler's military intentions, while at the same time succeeding in keeping their own secrets much better than the Germans. The only major success on the German side, it would appear, involved the breaking of British naval ciphers, which allowed Dönitz's submarines to inflict devastating losses on Anglo-American convoys between 1940 and 1943. In 1943, however, the British changed their convoy ciphers. In contrast, the Germans refused to change their machine codes on the arrogant assumption that they were unbreakable. Here is one of the keys to the German defeat in this as in other areas of military combat: the Nazi habit of arrogant superiority repeatedly undermined actual performance. The Germans were less intelligent in the intelligence game because they refused to acknowledge the possibility that their codes had been broken by more clever enemy cryptographers, that the Americans were smart enough to build an atomic bomb, and that the Russians could build more and better tanks.

The Encirclement of the Reich: D-Day to the Battle of the Bulge

In the spring of 1944 southern England was one vast encampment of arms and men, giving rise to a frequently heard quip that the whole island might sink into the sea under such a massive weight. Besides hundreds of ammunition dumps and parking lots for tanks and vehicles, the country teemed with troops — the Americans had twenty divisions; the British, fourteen; the Canadians, three; and the French and the Poles had one each; there were also hundreds of thousands of special forces and logistical personnel.[52] On June 6, 1944, the Allies disgorged this massive force in thousands of ships and hurled it onto the beaches of Normandy in one of the most brilliantly conceived and executed operations (Overlord) in world history.[53] When this great armada appeared through the thinning mist at daybreak on June 6, 1944, one German defender, Major Werner Pluskat, who had been peering through the narrow slits of his pillbox overlooking Omaha Beach, was so awe-struck and devastated by this sight that he could only think that "this was the end for Germany."[54] Knowing that this must be the invasion, Werner Pluskat rang up his divisional headquarters, excitedly informing his superior, Major Block, that the invasion had begun and that there were ten thousand ships out there. Not surprisingly, Block told Pluskat to get hold of himself, pointedly reminding him that "the Americans and British together don't have that many ships. Nobody has that many ships!" Pluskat was undeterred and told Block to come there to see for himself. After a short pause, the quizzical voice of Block came back on the line, enquiring what way the ships were heading? Pluskat's memorable reply was: "Right for me."[55]

Pluskat and Block were not the only Germans taken by complete surprise that day. Many hours and even days after the Allies landed their troops on a sixty-mile arc between Cherbourg and La Havre, the Germans were still wondering whether it was *an* invasion or *the* invasion. The Allies had played a superb guessing game with brilliant counterintelligence operations that deceived the Germans about the precise landing places. Hitler's intelligence services failed badly, and not even the führer's gift of prophecy was of much use. In fact, while the landings were in progress Hitler was asleep at the Berghof; his chief of operations, Jodl, who had been informed about the landings, told urgent callers that there was no reason to awaken the führer until the situation had become clearer in France.

The German defenses in France were inadequate to repel such a gigantic armada. It is true that the Germans had expected an Allied invasion since the fall of Tunis, and frantic efforts had been made to construct an "Atlantic Wall" to seal off "Fortress Europe" from an Anglo-American invasion. In reality, what Hitler called a "gigantic bastion" was merely a linear coastal defense, consisting of a chain of thinly manned bunkers and fortifications. Given the fact that the Germans had to protect a three-thousand-mile coastline stretching from Holland around the French shorelines all the way to the Italian mountain frontier, it is hardly surprising that they could not fortify a given sector in depth without compelling reason to suspect that the invaders would strike it. Field Marshal Rommel, who had been entrusted with the defense of France, correctly thought that the most dangerous area lay between the mouth of the Seine in the east and the Cotentin Peninsula in the west. The Desert Fox initiated desperate eleventh-hour efforts to fortify these areas, but on the day of the invasion the "Atlantic Wall" turned out to be largely an illusion of Nazi propaganda; it extended inland for no more than a few miles. Rommel had, at any rate, always propounded the view that anyone who wanted to defend everything defended nothing and that the only effective strategy was to defeat the enemy on the beaches. Rommel fought bitter arguments on this issue with the chief commander of the western forces, Gerd von Rundstedt, who wanted to smash the Allied forces with highly mobile tank reserves from the rear areas. Although Rommel seems to have swayed Rundstedt to his point of view, the commander of the Panzer forces in the west, General Geyr von Schweppenburg, flew personally to Berchtesgaden to dissuade Hitler from accepting Rommel's plan and to hold the main body of the German tank forces under camouflage in the forests northwest or south of Paris. Seeking a compromise, Hitler ordered four Panzer divisions to the Paris area as a strategic reserve, a disastrous decision because the Germans, if they were to have any chance of success against the Allies, required the tanks immediately available in the battlefield area. Thus, on June 6, only one Panzer division was within the reach of the beaches.

The coastal areas of Normandy, then, were poorly manned; moreover, they were held mostly by young, inexperienced troops, by conscripts from the eastern territories, and by reservists. Although 60 infantry divisions were used to defend the coastal areas, they were thinly spread. Also, German defense was poorly coordinated. On the Allied side, General Eisenhower was in supreme command, unobstructed strategically by any civilian interference; and in his coordination of Operation Overlord a general consensus of strategy, despite internal bickering, was always reached in practice between the commands of Allied naval forces (Admiral Bertham Ramsey), air forces (Air Vice-Marshal Troffard Leigh-Mallory), and land forces (General Bernard Montgomery). No such unity of command existed on the German side. Field Marshal von Rundstedt, the supreme German commander of the west, was given control of two Army groups — Army Group B (Rommel) and Army Group C (Blaskowitz). However, Rundstedt had no direct control over either naval or air forces, whose western commanders took their orders from Dönitz and Göring, respectively. One German military historian characterized the German operation as being flawed by veritable chaos of command (*Befehlswirrwar*), with each of the three services fighting its own war.[56] And looming ominously in the background was an enraged führer taking inappropriate actions at the most inopportune times. When the battle of Normandy was over, Hitler had sacked Rundstedt; driven his successor, Hans von Kluge, into committing suicide; fired General Schweppenburg; had Rommel murdered for his complicity in the July 20 plot on his life; and driven General Dallmann, commander of the Seventh Army, into committing suicide for the loss of Cherbourg. Nor did these heavy-handed actions exhaust Hitler's self-destructive decision-making repertoire. Worse was still to come.

On June 6, the Anglo-American forces landed on five beaches, extending from Quineville in the west to the mouth of the river Orne in the east. The American forces under the command of General Omar Bradley, comprising the U.S. First Army and the 82nd and 101st Airborne Divisions, were to land in the west on Utah and Omaha Beaches, while the English-Canadian forces under the overall command of General Montgomery were to invade the eastern beaches designated as Gold, Juno, and Sword. The goal for D-Day was to establish at least a ten-mile beachhead on a line running from Ste. Mère-Église by way of Carentan and Bayeux all the way east to Caen. The invading troops were supported by over two thousand bombers and by naval bombardment from offshore battleships. Despite complete air control, the invading troops still had to contend with heavy German artillery and machine-gun fire from undamaged bunkers and pillboxes, barbed wire, land and sea mines, and other lethal obstacles planted slightly below high- and low-tide water marks.[57]

The British and Canadian forces encountered fierce opposition, but they were to establish a foothold on the eastern beaches (Gold, Juno, Sword). However, all hopes for a quick dash inland toward Bayeux and Caen were disappointed. In the American sector, the invaders of Utah Beach encountered almost no opposition from the Germans. Ironically, this may have been because strong currents had driven the invaders south of their intended landing places, which made it difficult to establish a strong link between the landing forces and the airborne troops that had been dropped over the fields of the Cotentin early in the morning of June 6. Eastwards on Omaha Beach, a fierce German defense caused such chaos on the beaches that Bradley feared an "irreversible catastrophe."[58] Inch by inch, the invaders, facing German gunners looking down on them from high cliffs, worked their way up west of the beach with bayonets and toggle ropes and, having overwhelmed the stubborn defenders in hand-to-hand combat, finally succeeded in securing the high ground.

On the evening of June 6, the Allied armies were established on the beaches of Normandy. Poor intelligence and a failure of nerve among the German high command now seriously hampered the German defensive effort. The führer was asleep when the invasion began and brushed off early reports with a remarkable air of self-confidence, exclaiming later that morning that "the news couldn't be better! As long as they were in England, we couldn't touch them. Now we have them where we can beat them."[59] Unfortunately, the führer did not make it clear just how this armada, supported by complete air supremacy, could be hurled back into the sea. On the day of the landings there was only one Panzer division in Normandy; Field Marshal Rommel was in Germany; the commander of the army in that part of Normandy was away directing an exercise in Brittany; the commander of one of the reserve Panzer corps was in Belgium; and another key commander is said to have been unavailable because he was sleeping with a French girl.[60]

Clearly, the Germans had been caught napping; and even when they grasped the seriousness of the situation, they still could not make up their minds whether the Normandy invasion was *the* invasion or a feint. In fact, Hitler was so obsessed with the idea that the enemy was poised for a second invasion east of the Seine that he was reluctant to release the tank reserves for the Normandy sector. A deadly race now began as both sides tried to build up their forces, but the German effort was seriously hampered by Allied air superiority. Although the British seized Bayeaux and linked the beachheads, they failed to break through the German defenses. Three German Panzer divisions poured into the breach — the Twenty-first Panzer Division, the Twelfth SS, and Panzer Lehr Division. They fought brilliant defensive battles that dismayed the Allied high command.

In the east, the British-Canadian forces hoped to form a strong shield to hold off the German Panzers, enabling the Americans in the west to break through the German defenses. However, repeated attacks on Caen between June 6 and the end of the month failed to achieve the Allied objective. Two direct attacks on the German line and one pincer assault launched by the best British forces — the Fifty-first Highlanders and Seventh Armored Division (the famous "Desert Rats") — failed to smash through the German defenses west of Caen. The three German divisions that had rushed into this sector fought brilliant battles at Tillysur-Seulles and Villers-Bocage, but not even the daredevil colonel Kurt "Panzer" Meyer, who had described the enemy as "small fish" that he would shortly hurl back into the ocean, could do anything except temporarily plug the holes of a slowly crumbling front.

The Allied high command was so worried by the slow progress in the eastern sector that Winston Churchill personally flew to Normandy to consult with General Montgomery. Churchill left somewhat reassured after Montgomery told him his forces were designed to serve as a strong pivot supporting a projected American breakthrough. In fact, during the second week of June, the eyes of the world were focused on the American thrust through the Cotentin Peninsula, particularly on the superb performance of the U.S. airborne divisions and the hard-driving commander General J. Lawton Collins, who defeated the Germans as they fell back on Cherbourg. On June 26, the Germans surrendered Cherbourg, but its harbor had been demolished by the German defenders and would not be fully operational for two months.

The second American thrust, aimed toward St. Lô in the south, faltered badly, costing the Americans ten thousand lives, and advanced only seven miles. Bradley's quick blitz to Avranche had failed; the Germans continued to hold a tenuous line in Normandy, stretching from Lessay in the Cotentin to Caen in Normandy. On June 26, the British launched Operation Epsom toward the thickly wooded banks of the river Odon. Attacking with sixty thousand men and more than six hundred tanks supported by seven hundred guns on land and sea, the Allied forces still did not succeed in their objective — the capture of Caen by yet another envelopment. Military historians still marvel at the Wehrmacht fighting off these attacks in view of the fact that it faced overwhelming air and fire power with a weak force that had already been bled of two million men in Russia long before it ever showed up to fight the Anglo-Americans in Normandy.[61]

The valiant and even desperate efforts of the German forces in Normandy obscured a deep crisis in the German high command. As early as June 17, Hitler had personally traveled to battle headquarters near Margival, north of Soissons.[62] General Speidel, who described the meeting, characterized the führer as being pale and worn out, nervously playing with his spectacles and colored crayons that he held between his fingers. He repeatedly criticized Rommel and Rundstedt for not defeating the Allied forces, but Rommel countered with a remarkably frank and accurate analysis of the situation. Hitler, however, did not want to deal with these predictions, preferring to counter Rommel's arguments with promises of stemming the tide with the new V-1 miracle weapons, which he said would rain death and destruction upon England. Curiously enough, Hitler's meeting with his commander had to be resumed in one of the main air-raid shelters of the Margival command post because a defective V-1 rocket reversed its course and ended up exploding near the führer's bunker.

Rommel prophesied the collapse of the invasion front and the Allied breakthrough into the German Reich itself, drawing the inevitable conclusion that the time had come to end the war. Hitler was furious and cut off the discussion with the remark: "Don't concern yourself with the continuation of the war but with your invasion front."[63] The seven-hour meeting was at an end. It had been interrupted only by a curious lunch during which Hitler devoured a pretasted plate of vegetables and rice, while alternately swallowing a variety of pills and liquid medicines from the liquor glasses that had been lined up in front of him. The generals probably wondered whether their commander in chief was still in complete possession of his faculties. Although a follow-up visit with frontline commanders was promised for June 19 in the La Roche-Guyon area, Hitler returned to Berchtesgaden and, in so doing, probably escaped a potential arrest or a plot on his life.

The June 17 meeting between Hitler and his field marshals was symptomatic of a rapidly disintegrating relationship. On June 28, another acrimonious meeting was held at Berchtesgaden, with Hitler holding forth on miracle weapons like the V-1 bomber and offering self-serving historical analogies in which he depicted himself as a latter-day Frederick the Great whose fortunes were bound to change. Shortly after this meeting, a heated telephone discussion ensued between Rundstedt and Keitel, in which Rundstedt supposedly responded to Keitel's exasperated question, "What should we do?" with the enraged answer, "Make peace, you fools!"[64] When Keitel relayed the content of this conversation to Hitler, Rundstedt's days as commander in chief of the western forces were numbered. On July 3, Rundstedt was replaced by Field Marshal von Kluge, who had just recovered from a car accident. At the same time, Hitler also replaced General Geyr von Schweppenburg, commander of the western Panzer group.

Field Marshal Günther Hans von Kluge, a veteran Prussian soldier of the old school who was referred to by his colleagues as "der Kluge Hans" (clever Hans), was a skillful tactician but a vacillating conspirator in the developing plot to remove Hitler. Although he had been receptive to the arguments of the plotters, his obedience to Hitler proved too strong. The führer had made him a field marshal after the fall of France, appointed him commander of Army Group Center in Russia, and gave him a lavish sum of money on the occasion of his sixtieth birthday. Like numerous other commanders, Kluge was still susceptible to Hitler's powerful psychic influence, and when he assumed command in the west, he was determined to execute the will of the führer. Thus, when he arrived at the castle of La Roche-Guyon, Rommel's headquarters in France, he made it known in no uncertain terms that he would not tolerate the pervasive mood of defeatism that he sensed to be spreading among the commanding officers in the west. To underscore this point, the new commander turned to Rommel and told him: "You, too, Herr Field Marshal Rommel, will have to obey unconditionally. I strongly urge you to do this!"[65] Rommel, however, was not the man to be addressed in this high-handed manner, and he laid into Kluge with such force that Kluge had to ask everyone to clear the room. According to Speidel, Rommel demanded a written and oral apology from Kluge for making such unfounded accusations against him.[66] Kluge, a military realist, soon discovered that Rommel had been correct about the desperate military situation in Normandy.

The crisis within the German high command now began to pick up speed. Rommel himself had been in touch with the anti-Nazi conspirators for some time, but he could not make up his mind upon the right course of action. On July 15, Rommel sent a telegram to Hitler warning him of the imminent collapse of the Normandy front and again urged him to draw the political consequences. After sending his report, he purportedly told Speidel: "I gave him his last chance. If he does not draw the consequences, we will have to act."[67] Two days later, on July 17, Rommel was severely wounded when his open car was attacked by British fighter planes on the streets near Livrot-Vimoutier. Three days later the conspirators, led by Colonel Claus von Stauffenberg, struck against Hitler. Rommel was to pay with his own life for his remote association with the conspirators.

On July 20, 1944, Colonel Stauffenberg, carrying a British time bomb in his briefcase, walked into a large wooden building at führer headquarters at Rastenburg in East Prussia, where Hitler had scheduled an important conference. After he entered the conference room, he greeted Hitler and the already assembled military dignitaries, including such high-ranking generals as Keitel, Jodl, Bodenschatz, Heusinger, and Warlimont, placed the briefcase on the floor close to Hitler, and then excused himself on the grounds that he had to make an important telephone call. Colonel Brandt, who was leaning over the table, felt the briefcase and moved it under the table so that it leaned on the upright support some distance away from Hitler. As it turned out, this would save Hitler's life. At 12:42, a huge explosion rocked the building, shattering the conference table, collapsing the roof, and sending glass in all directions. Stauffenberg, who was watching the explosion from some distance away, convinced himself that no one could have survived the impact and bluffed his way through three control posts and then took off by plane to Berlin to orchestrate Operation Valkyrie.

What Stauffenberg did not know was that Hitler was only slightly injured, suffering from superficial cuts and abrasions. When Stauffenberg arrived at the Bendlerstrasse in Berlin, where the conspirators were supposed to initiate the coup, he was shocked to learn that nothing had been done in his absence because General Olbricht, deputy commander of the Home Army and his key man at the Bendlerstrasse, had heard that Hitler was alive. Olbricht's superior, General Friedrich Fromm, who had been sitting on the fence to see which side would gain the upper hand, decided to follow the safe and expedient course, as the majority of the

Generalität had always done, and that was to support their commander in chief. Although the conspirators arrested Fromm, officers loyal to Hitler turned the tables on them by the end of the day. Through Goebbels's deft intervention, Hitler had also managed to get through to Major Otto Remer, whose Guard Battalion had been ordered into Berlin by the conspirators to cordon off all government buildings in the Wilhelmstrasse. These troops — which were to have spearheaded the conspiracy — were now used to crush the revolt. In the meantime, General Fromm, eager to disassociate himself from the conspirators, quickly arrested the ringleaders and had them taken down into the courtyard and executed in light shed by the headlights of vehicles parked there. General Beck had already shot himself; the others, one by one, were stood against a wall and shot. Colonel Stauffenberg's last words were: "Long live holy Germany."[68]

The last effort to remove the tyrant had failed; the Germans were destined to descend into the abyss with him. Very few Germans supported the plot, and Hitler's claim later that day in a radio address that the plotters represented a tiny clique of officers was essentially correct. The coup not only lacked popular support but also was limited to a small group of exceptionally courageous officers who were able to transcend the amoral military code that had made a fetish out of absolute obedience.

Hitler had always distrusted the old military elite even while making use of its talents. In the wake of the July plot, he was now determined to purge as many of them as he could implicate in the plot. A few hours after the failed plot, while hosting Mussolini, who had just arrived at Rastenburg, he flew into an uncontrollable rage that stunned his guest and deeply embarrassed others who were present to witness it, threatening bloody vengeance on the perpetrators and their loved ones.[69] What followed was one of the most despicable chapters in the history of German justice. Those who had been implicated were tortured and dragged in front of the People's Court, presided over by Roland Freisler, who ridiculed, belittled, and screamed at the defendants, whose sentences had been decided before the trial began.[70] The grotesque proceedings were duly captured on film, as were the ghastly executions at Plötzensee Prison where the first batch of prisoners (Erwin von Witzleben, Erich Hoepner, Helmuth von Moltke, Paul von Hase, Helmuth Stieff, Albrecht von Hagen, Friedrich Klausing, Robert Bernardis) were hanged with thin chicken wire from meat hooks, squirming and wiggling in agony until they died. The executions continued until the end of the Third Reich, as additional plotters, real or imagined, found their death — Admiral Canaris, Carl Goerdeler, Ulrich von Hassell, Julius Leber, Hans Oster, Johannes Popitz, Dietrich Bonhoeffer, Hans von Dohnanyi, and thousands of others. The attempt to destroy the old ruling elite, as Joachim Fest has observed, was indeed the final and radical consummation of National Socialism,[71] whose final end was already clearly in sight.

Four days after the abortive attempt on Hitler's life, the American Seventh Corps (Collins) broke through weak German defenses near St. Lô (Operation Cobra) and found itself in the open country. The whole western front was wavering as the Americans cut off the Germans caught in the Cherbourg Peninsula. In early August, General George Patton was in open country heading west into Brittany. A weak German counterattack at Mortain, aimed at separating the American lines at Avranche, was mercilessly devastated by air. Except for a few fanatical SS units, fighting on without hope of victory, German morale collapsed all over Normandy.

The American breakthrough put an end to the static nature of the Normandy campaign. In the north, where the British and Canadians had been tied down by Kluge's formations, Montgomery surrounded eight German divisions in a pocket near Falaise. Field Marshal von Kluge, now a marked man under increasing suspicion of seeking to negotiate with the Western powers, dawdled away precious time in authorizing a German retreat. On August 15, his staff car was destroyed, and he found himself cut off from OKW as well as his own troops. Hitler, suspecting treason, relieved him of his command and replaced him with Field Marshal Walter Model.[72] On his way back to Germany, Kluge committed suicide.

In the meantime, the German army in Normandy was doomed to a grisly fate in the Falaise pocket. Although a few units escaped eastward after Hitler finally authorized a retreat, the bulk was devastated by artillery as well as by fighter bombers. The carnage was unspeakable:

> The roads were chocked with wreckage and the swollen bodies of men and horses. Bits of uniform were plastered to shattered tanks and trucks and human remains hung in grotesque shapes on the blackened hedgerows. Corpses lay in pools of dried blood, staring into space and as if their eyes were being forced from their sockets....Strangely enough it was the fate of the horses that upset me most. Harnessed as they were, it had been impossible for them to escape, and they lay dead in tangled heaps, their large wide eyes crying out to me in anguish. It was a sight that pierced the soul, and I felt as if my heart would burst.[73]

The German army had received its worst defeat since Stalingrad. In August 1944, however, the end seemed much closer than in 1943. A second Allied invasion was taking place in the south of France. Seven French and three American divisions landed on the Riviera beaches, took Nice and Marseille two weeks later, and pushed up the Rhone Valley. All over southern, southwestern, and central France, the Germans were in headlong retreat toward the Reich, harassed by partisans as they went. The road to Paris lay open, and the honor of taking it was given to Charles De Gaulle's elite armored division under the command of General Leclerk de Hauteclocque. Paris fell on August 25. Six days later, Patton's tanks crossed the Meuse, arriving at Metz on the Moselle on September 1. To the west, Montgomery's forces crossed the Seine and swept up to the Belgium frontier, liberating Brussels during the first week of September and taking the port of Antwerp intact. By the middle of September, Montgomery's forces were advancing into Holland. By the end of September the western front ran from the banks of the Scheldt in the north to the source of the Rhine near Basel in the south.

It looked like the Allied forces might still leapfrog across the Rhine into Germany in 1944. That this did not happen was due to two major reasons. One was the inability of the Allies to clear the Scheldt estuary at the time they took Antwerp, preventing them from supplying their armies directly through the port of Antwerp. The other reason was a daring but badly executed operation (Market Garden), conceived by Montgomery, that involved massive parachute landings behind German lines aimed at seizing bridges at Eindoven and Nijmegen by American forces and more remote bridges on the Rhine at Arnhem by British paratroopers. Although the Americans made excellent progress, the British ran into two SS Panzer divisions that were refitting in the area after their retreat from Normandy. After ten days of heavy fighting, the trapped British paratroopers in the Arnhem perimeter either surrendered or fled across the river. Montgomery's goal of establishing a foothold across the Meuse and lower Rhine and penetrating into the north German plain had gone "a bridge too far."

The noose, however, was tightening on Hitler's empire on both the eastern and western fronts. Stalin had opened a major offensive against Army Group Center on June 22, the third anniversary of Hitler's attack on the Soviet Union! Within two weeks, the Soviets smashed twenty-eight German divisions and destroyed the operational effectiveness of Army Group Center. Hitler had squandered another 350,000 men; 57,600 were triumphantly paraded through the streets of Moscow.[74] The Russians now relentlessly pushed their advantage, reconquering the Ukraine and the Crimea, driving the Finns out of the war and reaching East Prussia. When the Russian armies crossed the Vistula and moved into Poland, Polish resistance fighters rose in Warsaw against their German oppressors, hoping the Russian army would liberate them from German control; instead, Stalin halted his armies in order to let the Germans rid him of a potential threat to his own Communist-controlled government at Lublin. Despite anguished appeals by Churchill and Roosevelt to support the Warsaw Uprising, Stalin held his armies back while the Germans wiped out the Polish resistance. In an act of wanton savagery, the SS systematically razed the Polish capital to the ground.[75]

On the southern Russian front, Soviet armies under Marshal Malinovski were pouring into Romania. The corrupt regime of Marshal Antonescu was removed by King Michael II, who abandoned his German ally and defected to the Soviet side. Cut off from retreat, sixteen German divisions were lost, not to speak of the Romanian oil fields that had provided invaluable fuel for the Wehrmacht. On September 8, the Russians marched into Bulgaria. Only now did Hitler allow a tactical retreat out of the Balkans, too late for most of the German forces in Romania and Bulgaria. Only the troops of Army Group E, fleeing from the British who had landed in Greece and captured Athens, fought their way back through partisan country. In Yugoslavia, Tito's guerrillas inflicted frightful damage on the retreating Germans. Soviet units, working with Tito's forces, pushed into Yugoslavia and liberated Belgrade.

In a desperate attempt to prevent the whole Balkans from falling into Russian hands, Churchill personally flew to Moscow to arrange for an agreement on spheres of influence, spelling out precisely who should have dominant influence in the various Balkan countries. Churchill knew that Bulgaria and Romania were already in Stalin's pocket since his armies were in full control there. He therefore suggested that the two go fifty-fifty on Yugoslavia and Hungary, giving the Western Allies a 90 percent preponderance in Greece alone. Stalin ratified this informal agreement without blinking an eye when Churchill pushed the breakdowns across the conference table on a half-sheet of paper.[76] Nothing was said about Poland; perhaps nothing had to be said since the Soviets were already in virtual control there. The hard sheet of Communism was now being spread over the Balkans and over all of eastern Europe in the wake of the conquering Soviet armies. The Soviets now had what the Nazis had always denied them — a foothold in the eastern part of the Balkan Peninsula.

In actual fact, the Russians appeared to be in possession of a far greater part of the Balkans; they had made common cause with Tito, captured Belgrade, and pushed up the Danube toward Hungary. Since Hungary was the last southeastern buffer of Hitler's shrinking empire, concerted efforts were made to strengthen it against the impending Soviet onslaught. Hitler rightly suspected that the Hungarian government would follow in the train of the Romanian and Bulgarian governments by defecting to the enemy or, at the very least, arranging a separate peace. The Hungarians had fought valiantly on the German side, and it was for this as well as for geopolitical reasons that Hitler was not about to release such an ally. He built up the Hungarian buffer by stripping his already weak reserves on the eastern front and sending them south of the Carpathians. Hand in hand with this action, he moved against the increasingly vacillating government of Admiral Miklos Horthy. Suspecting treason, he arrested Horthy, had his son kidnapped, and forced the establishment of a new pliable government that would continue the war on the German side. By these moves, Hitler temporarily delayed the inevitable loss of Hungary until February 1945.

On the day that Hitler carried out his coup in Hungary, it was made public that Rommel had died as a result of the head wounds he had suffered in Normandy. In reality, Hitler had forced Rommel to take his own life after evidence surfaced that he had been implicated in the July 20 plot. The whole despicable affair of Rommel's death had been carefully sanitized by Goebbels's propaganda machine. Rommel received a magnificent state funeral in the cathedral of Ulm, where Rundstedt, who represented Hitler, piously exclaimed that Rommel's "heart belonged to the Führer."[77]

Although Hitler had managed to build up his Hungarian buffer and temporarily gained some breathing room as the Russian advances slowly ebbed in the Balkans and on the eastern front, time was rapidly running out for the Third Reich. The loss of the Balkans, with its oil and raw materials, meant that Hitler's arms factories would be unable to function much longer. Yet, amazingly, German industry under Speer's brilliant direction at this time still supplied the faltering German armies fighting on a two-thousand-mile front from Scandinavia in the north to the Balkans in the south.

In the fall of 1944 it appeared that Germany would be defeated before the year was out. On the eastern front the Russians, though overstretched as a result of their summer offensive, were poised to strike at the heart of the Reich from their Polish bases in the east and their Balkan positions in the southeast. In the west, General Patton's forces had drawn close to Germany itself, but lack of gasoline for his tanks prevented him from piercing the frontier.

Germany still had nine million men under arms, but they were scattered over several far-flung fronts. Prudent military strategy would have dictated a general withdrawal to more defensible positions, but Hitler's egomania prevented the implementation of such ideas. Hitler's options were running out fast; he could gather all his forces in the east or attempt one quick knockout blow in the west. He decided on both psychological and strategic grounds to launch an assault in the west. The huge open spaces on the eastern front had sucked up one German army after another. Hitler had also come to the conclusion that the Russians were far better and tougher soldiers than the Anglo-American troops. Attacking the west had another advantage, namely, that of attacking from well-established fortifications along shorter stretches of territory. Hitler reasoned that this would require less fuel and less material. Meeting his commanders, notably Field Marshals Rundstedt and Model, at the Adlerhorst (Eagle's Nest) near Bad Nauheim, he revealed his last and exceedingly desperate gamble. The plan called for a surprise attack on the weakest point in the Ardennes aimed at Antwerp, the major supply port for the Allies. He hoped to demoralize and disorganize the Allied rear, split Eisenhower's forces in two, and trap the British army. To support this desperate fantasy, Hitler had scraped together his last reserves: two hundred thousand troops, six hundred tanks, and about nineteen hundred artillery pieces. He clearly hoped for a repeat of 1940, but this time he was facing a determined and much better led Allied command.

Operation Wacht am Rhein, known to the Allies as the battle of the Bulge, began on December 16 with an attack on the weakest link in the Allied front held by unprepared American troops in the Ardennes. Spreading panic and confusion in its wake, the Sixth SS Panzer Army slashed its way through the Ardennes and approached St. Vith, a major junction from which a mountain road led to the Meuse. But the American Seventh Armored Division, quickly reinforced by the Eighty-second Airborne Division, held St. Vith for several days and slowed the main thrust of the advance well before it could even get close to the Meuse, let alone the approaches to Antwerp a hundred miles away.[78] One SS unit, the First Panzer Division, apparently desperately wanted to make up for this lack of progress and did so by murdering seventy-one American soldiers at Malmedy.

In the southern section of the battle, the Fifth Panzer Army destroyed two American army divisions and, protected by dense winter fog and mist that kept Allied planes grounded, approached the road junction of Bastogne. Although both advances in the north and south had opened up a big "bulge" in the Allied front, the Germans, already spread thin by lack of manpower, supply, and fuel, failed to penetrate any farther. Bastogne was quickly reinforced by paratroopers from the 101st Airborne Division and refused to surrender. Montgomery rushed forces to the northern sector, and Patton sent several divisions of the Third Army from the south to break the ring around Bastogne. On December 26, the weather cleared and Allied planes inflicted heavy losses on the German forces in the bulge and on their choked-up supply lines in the rear areas. A secondary thrust by the Germans toward Alsace during the last days of December also petered out quickly, though on the Allied side the battle led to a bitter confrontation between Eisenhower and General Charles de Gaulle over the possible evacuation of Strasbourg. On January 1, 1945, Hitler ordered a massive air attack on Allied airfields, which destroyed about 180 Allied planes, but cost the Germans 277 planes, thereby making it impossible to deliver another major air offensive in the war.[79] By January 16, the Allied powers had driven the Germans out of the bulge and restored the front. Seventy thousand Germans had died, and the last reserves had been depleted. Hitler's last gamble had failed.

The Allied Invasion of Germany: January–May 1945

On New Year's Day, 1945, Hitler addressed the German people and exhorted them to fight to the bitter end. While he was calling for a last-ditch effort, ten million enemy soldiers were closing in on the Reich on all frontiers. In the east, three Russian formations moved toward the German capital. Koniev's armies struck at the German front in southern Poland, quickly swept over the open terrain of Poland, and invaded the industrial sections of Upper Silesia, thus further reducing Germany's war-making ability. Although Koniev was poised on the Oder River above Breslau and had gained several crossings, the Germans temporarily rallied and prevented the extension of the Russian bridgeheads. On the Russian right wing, Rokossovski's forces moved toward East Prussia; on January 26, they reached the Baltic coast east of Danzig, isolating twenty-six German divisions in the Baltic states. Hitler had once more rejected urgent pleas by his Baltic commanders for an ordered retreat.

The third Russian attack came at the center, where Georgy Zhukov's armies launched a north to west drive toward the German frontier, bypassing the two important communication centers of Torun and Posen. Zhukov reached the Oder near Küstrin on January 31, 1945; his forces were now within sixty miles of Berlin.

As the Russian forces advanced, a red terror descended on the German population from Königsberg in the north to Breslau in the south. Russian troops exacted a terrible price for what they had endured at the hands of the Nazi invaders since the summer of 1941. The roads were jammed with German civilians who, leaving their homes and possessions behind them, joined the retreating German troops. Those unfortunate enough to remain behind, mostly old men, women, and children, were quickly taken by the Russians and tortured, shot, crushed by tanks, or, in the case of the women, brutally raped and left to die.[80] Even Goebbels, who could not be accused of being squeamish, ordered that these horrifying atrocities should not be reported in detail.[81] In retrospect, the Russian invasion into east German territory resulted in one of the largest mass expulsions of Germans in modern history. It is estimated that almost fourteen million Germans were dispossessed as they fled from the wrath of the Soviet army and the vengeance of eastern people who set upon the fleeing refugees. The German navy managed to rescue over two million civilians by transporting them from Pillau along the Baltic coast to the west or to Finland, Sweden, and Denmark. Many refugees, however, lost their lives because the Soviets sunk several large rescue ships such as the *Wilhelm Gustloff,* the *General Steuben,* and the *Goya,* resulting in the death of 14,300 people.[82]

In the west, Eisenhower's forces closed in on Germany's last defensive line — the Rhine. Not since Napoleon had a foreign army succeeded in crossing the Rhine frontier. The Rhine is broad and swift, and on its eastern side the German defenders could observe any invader from the high ground offered by the steep banks of the river. On March 7, a small American tank spearhead reached the old medieval city of Remagen, located between Bonn and Koblenz, and found the bridge over the Rhine intact. The German commander had failed to blow up the bridge, a failure that would cost him his life in front of a firing squad. Within forty-eight hours, more than eight thousand Allied soldiers had gained a foothold on the other side of the Rhine. Eighteen days later all the Allied troops had breached the Rhine frontier. Germany was now without any natural defenses.

After the Allied forces crossed the Rhine, they struck toward three goals — the north, the industrial Ruhr, and the south. Montgomery's forces broke into the Westphalian plain and moved toward the Danish frontier and the Baltic; Bradley's forces enveloped the Ruhr; and another Allied force wheeled southeast toward Karlsruhe and Stuttgart. Of these attacks, the encirclement of the Ruhr, which required eighteen American divisions, was the most decisive battle on the western front in the spring of 1945. Allied planes savagely pounded the Ruhr and devastated it into a wasteland. Over 400,000 German troops were trapped; their commanding officer, Walter Model, ordered a general capitulation and then shot himself in a forest near Düsseldorf. Around 325,000 German soldiers fell into Allied hands. The heart of the Reich was mortally pierced.

After the Ruhr battle, the American forces set off to the east to cut Germany in half. On April 11, they reached the Elbe. The American forces were within sixty miles of Berlin, linking up for the first time with the Russian forces at Torgau. There was no German defense to stop them from taking the German capital.

During the Cold War considerable controversy swirled around the question of why the Anglo-American forces had not taken Berlin. There are three compelling reasons for it. First, it had always been Eisenhower's policy to defeat the remaining German forces in the west and to let the Russians have the dubious honor of taking the German capital, an operation that, according to his calculations, was likely to result in at least a quarter of a million casualties. Second, Berlin was in the occupation zone assigned to the Soviets by the European Advisory Committee and reaffirmed at the Yalta Conference. Third, Allied intelligence had mistakenly warned that Hitler would make a last stand in his "Alpine Redoubt" in the south, a fantasy that assumed the existence of a vast network of mountainous fortifications the Nazis planned to use as a final bulwark against the Allied powers.[83] The remaining campaigns of the Americans, mostly mopping up operations, were therefore in the south. In the meantime, the battle for Berlin was on.

The End of Hitler and the Third Reich

When the German Reich was at last encircled by the Russians in the east and the Anglo-American powers in the west, Adolf Hitler and his entourage were confronted with their inevitable fate — ignominious defeat. Although the Nazi leadership was maintaining a grim facade of iron strength, defiantly repeating Hitler's motto, "We shall never capitulate," only a few diehards seriously believed that Germany could still win the war or even negotiate an acceptable peace. The Allied forces had made it abundantly clear that they would never parley with Hitler and his gang; they expected the Nazis to surrender unconditionally. Moreover, they also planned to make good on Churchill's earlier promise that they would rid the world of Hitler's shadow.

Allied demands of an unconditional German surrender stiffened Nazi resistance and also demoralized whatever was left of the German resistance movement. There is enough evidence to show that the Nazi leaders actually welcomed Allied intransigence because it provided them with a powerful rationale for bolstering the home front and intimidating the German people with horror stories about the brutal treatment that would be in store for them in the event of an Allied victory.

"Aprèes nous le déluge" (After us the flood) — that slogan seemed to reflect the prevailing cynical attitude of the high priests of National Socialism. Some Nazi leaders promised that they would immolate themselves in the flames of the impending *Götterdämmerung* (twilight of the gods). The fanatical Goebbels, in fact, actually looked forward to more destruction by Allied bombers on the perverse grounds that the "bomb-terror spares the dwellings of neither rich nor poor; before the labor offices of total war the last class barriers have had to go down."[84] Only twisted personalities can derive a noble meaning from such devastating destruction instigated by themselves. The propaganda minister may have derived a grim satisfaction from the fact that the terror-bombing was a universal leveler, and thus a consummation of National Socialism, but ordinary Germans, cowering in cellars, air-raid shelters, or just plain holes in the ground, did not find anything ennobling or redeeming about the destruction of their country. Yet, having entrusted their future to a criminal leadership, they had no choice, certainly not after July 20, 1944, except to follow their leaders into the abyss. Besides, the Nazi leadership had seen to it that all bridges were burned behind the whole nation.

After the failure of the Ardennes offensive and the beginning of the great Soviet push toward Berlin on January 16, Adolf Hitler returned to the German capital to make his last stand. The magnificent chancellery, intended to be the visible emblem of Hitler's power, was now a battered shell; its windows were shattered and boarded up, its marble and porphyry cracked, and several wings badly damaged. Only Hitler's private section was largely undamaged, but more and more frequent air raids forced the führer to seek refuge in the bunker beneath the garden of the Reich chancellery. Continuous and unrelenting attacks finally persuaded Hitler to move permanently into his inevitable tomb.[85] Built only in 1944, the führer's bunker was located about sixty feet beneath the garden of the chancellery. Reachable from within the chancellery, it consisted of an upper and a lower level. The upper level housed storerooms, servants' quarters, and Hitler's private kitchen, aptly called Dietküche (diet kitchen) because it specialized in vegetarian meals. A deeper bunker, called Führerbunker, consisting of eighteen cramped rooms, housed Hitler's study, living room, bedroom, and a tiny bedroom for Eva Braun. There was also provision in the cramped space for a conference room; a bedroom and living room occupied by Dr. Morrell and later by the Goebbels family; toilets; switchboard and guard room;

machine room for heating, light, and ventilation; and a small dressing room used by Dr. Stumpfegger.

It was from this small underground "submarine," increasingly isolated from the world above, that Hitler and the remaining Nazi leaders fought the last three months of the war. Goebbels used every trick of propaganda to frighten the German people into continuing the war, widely circulating the details of the Morgenthau Plan, which proposed to turn most of postwar Germany into a purely agrarian country and recommended the sterilization of German men. In April 1945, Hitler was shown a captured British manual, ominously called *Eclipse,* which identified many Germans as war criminals and contained maps showing how Germany and Berlin were to be divided into occupation zones by the victorious powers.[86] Hitler also saw a copy of Stalin's "Order Number Five," which left little doubt what the Soviet dictator had in mind for Germany: "The German people," the document said, "is to be destroyed. All German factories and property are to be laid waste. The German animal must be battered to death in its hovels."[87]

These ominous threats from the encroaching enemy may have persuaded many of the rats that they should leave the sinking Nazi ship. Speer was one of the most straightforward, telling the führer bluntly that the war was lost. In a March 15 memorandum, Speer laid the facts on the table with unmistakable frankness. Hitler gave him a day to think over his statement, almost pleading with him to tell him that there was still hope for a final victory, and that if he could tell him that, he could keep his position. When Speer returned to the Führerbunker the next day, he could not bring himself to repeat the same judgment, but merely said, *"Mein Führer,* I stand unreservedly behind you."[88] Hitler was visibly moved, his eyes filling with tears, saying that then all was well. Of course, all was not well. Moreover, Hitler's parting with other high-ranking Nazis was far more unpleasant than his final parting with Speer.

Many of the führer's closest subordinates started to disassociate themselves from him in a desperate attempt to save their skins. The top leadership had always been subject to petty jealousies and malicious back-biting. With the end in sight, these tendencies now multiplied. Göring, Himmler, and Speer were already acting largely on their own. Hitler sent away Heinrich Lammers and Otto Dietrich, accepted Milch's resignation, transferred Warlimont, and, after heated confrontations, retired Guderian and replaced him with General Hans Krebs. Hundreds of lesser government officials also found compelling reasons to leave the city. Berliners referred to this exodus as the "flight of the golden pheasants."

The atmosphere in the bunker became increasingly surrealistic. Under the impact of the impending defeat, Hitler's sociopathic tendencies began to manifest themselves with stark brutality. He alternated between lengthy periods of brooding, hysterical outbursts, and wishful fantasies.

He saw himself betrayed by everyone, including his closest subordinates. His daily situation conferences degenerated into interminable monologues.

Although Hitler must have known that the war was lost — and he admitted this to a few intimates — he still clung to wholly unrealistic visions of a magical turnaround. He banked on the new secret weapons, especially jet fighter planes that were just now being mass produced, hoping that they would sweep the enemy from the sky. He also placed hopes on the V-1 and V-2 rockets and the new Mark XXI submarines that could travel submerged to the shores of the United States. The realities, however, belied such wishful thinking: entire armies were melting away; aircraft production came to a virtual standstill; the most important industrial parts of Germany were being overrun by the enemy. When these facts sunk in, Hitler's "Vandal nature," as Fest aptly described it, asserted itself in its ugliest form. He blamed everyone for betraying him: "I'm lied to on all sides," he told his secretary; "I can rely on no one, they all betray me, the whole business makes me sick. If I had not got my faithful Morrell I should be absolutely knocked out — and those idiot doctors wanted to get rid of him.... If anything happens to me, Germany will be left without a leader. I have no successor. The first, Hess, is mad, the second, Göring, has lost the sympathy of the people; and the third, Himmler, would be rejected by the party."[89]

It was everybody's fault but his own. He had been jockeyed into the war by the Western powers, especially by the Jews. The two-front war was not his mistake either; it was forced upon him by Soviet occupation of eastern territories and by Stalin's refusal to furnish enough raw materials for Germany's war effort. The British, in their stubborn and willful opposition to Germany's geopolitical rights, were also to blame. By conquering Russia, and therefore its immense resources, he wanted to show the British that they could not win a war of attrition. The declaration of war against the United States, which sealed his doom, was also not his fault. True, he had instigated it, but Hitler saw the actual declaration as a mere formality, a necessary one since the United States had been waging an undeclared war against Germany all along.

Even the overwhelming obstacles presented by so many enemies could have been overcome if internal reactionaries had not blocked his policies, if the generals had not been so incompetent or traitorous, if the miracle weapons had been available sooner, if Germany's allies, especially the Italians, had not been such a source of embarrassment. The führer's mind was feverishly preoccupied with such distorted chains of hypothetical causes and effects; and when he was not so preoccupied, he lashed out furiously against friend and foe alike.

Increasingly, Hitler's fury expressed a malignantly destructive intention. He saw no reason why anyone should survive him. The enemy, he ordered, was to find nothing but a desolate wasteland. Speer was instructed to engage in a scorched-earth policy, destroying everything,

including not only industrial plants and supplies but also all the basic
elements of life and civic order: food supplies, public utilities, communication centers, medical supplies, bank records, public records, and
so on.[90] He even demanded the destruction of the remaining historical monuments in the form of theaters, castles, churches, and historical
buildings. When it was pointed out to him that such wanton destruction would deprive the German people of the means of survival, Hitler
revealed his real nature, that of malignant destructiveness:

> If the war is to be lost, the people will be lost also. It is not necessary
> to worry about what the German people will need for elemental survival.
> On the contrary, it is best for us to destroy even these things. For the
> nation has proved to be the weaker, and the future belongs solely to
> the stronger eastern nation. In any case only those who are inferior will
> remain after this struggle, for the good have already been killed.[91]

If it had not been for Speer and others, who deliberately sabotaged
and countermanded Hitler's insane "Nero Command," Germany might
have been crippled for generations to come. By April, Hitler was convinced that the end was near; his last gamble in the Ardennes had failed,
the miracle weapons had not achieved their purpose, and Germany had
been invaded and cut in half. His only remaining hope was that the
Grand Alliance would fall apart. In early February, however, the Allied powers reaffirmed their wartime coalition at Yalta. The Big Three
pledged to continue the war against Nazi Germany and reasserted their
demand for unconditional surrender. They also agreed in principle on
the partition of Germany into zones of occupation, to be administered
by the Soviet Union, the United States, Great Britain, and France. Stalin
was the clear-cut winner at Yalta, wringing important concessions out of
the Western powers, especially in regard to Poland. Stalin succeeded in
gaining a seal of approval for his Communist-controlled government at
Lublin, making a few token concessions to put some "democratic" leaders in it. He also succeeded in having the Polish frontier redrawn to his
advantage and further extending it at Germany's expense once the war
had been won. President Roosevelt, who was already a dying man, was
in no condition to resist Stalin, as Churchill was, and certainly not at
this crucial juncture in the war. Roosevelt believed that the alliance was
more important and that it would be futile to deprive Stalin of what he
had already conquered.

Hitler was obviously disappointed that the Grand Alliance did not
crack, but he privately wondered how far the Western powers would
allow the Bolsheviks to penetrate into the heart of Europe. In a remarkably prophetic observation, he predicted:

> With the defeat of the Reich and pending the emergence of the Asiatic,
> the African, and perhaps the South American nationalisms, there will re-
> main in the world only two Great Powers capable of confronting each
> other — the United States and Soviet Russia. The laws of both history

and geography will compel these two powers to a trial of strength, either military or in the fields of economics and ideology. These same laws make it inevitable that both powers should become enemies of Europe. And it is equally certain that both these powers will sooner or later find it desirable to seek the support of the sole surviving great nation in Europe, the German people.[92]

What Hitler did not want to admit to himself was that he, like Napoleon 130 years before him, was the major unifying agent of the Grand Alliance. As long as he was alive, the alliance would hold; and yet Hitler still hoped that some miracle might deliver him from inevitable defeat. That hope appeared fulfilled on April 12, 1945, when President Roosevelt died of a stroke at his desk in Warm Springs, Georgia. Only a few days earlier Goebbels had read Hitler the passages in Carlyle's *History of Frederick the Great* in which the Prussian king, on the verge of certain defeat, was ready to commit suicide, only to be miraculously saved when Czarina Elizabeth, who hated the Prussian king, suddenly died and was succeeded by the pro-Prussian Czar Peter III. The alliance against Prussia fell apart, and the House of Brandenburg was saved. We are told that Hitler had tears in his eyes when Goebbels read him these passages. Roosevelt's death seemed like a prophecy fulfilled. When Goebbels learned of it, he called for champagne and excitedly rang up Hitler: "My Führer, I congratulate you! Roosevelt is dead. It is written in the stars that the second half of April will be the turning point for us. This is Friday 13th April. It is the turning point."[93]

The excitement was short-lived: President Harry Truman, who succeeded Roosevelt, was also an implacable enemy of Nazism. Even Goebbels sadly admitted that "perhaps fate has again been cruel and made fools of us."[94] Three days after Roosevelt's death the Russians mounted their final assault on Berlin. On April 20, Hitler's fifty-sixth birthday, the leadership of the declining Nazi empire met for the last time to pay homage to the führer and to reminisce about the good old days. Present were Goebbels, Himmler, Göring, Bormann, Speer, Ley, Ribbentrop, and leaders of the Wehrmacht. Eva Braun, Hitler's mistress, had also joined the führer, presumably to be with him to the bitter end.

Hitler had planned to leave Berlin and conduct the war from his "National Redoubt" in the Bavarian Alps near Berchtesgaden, but Goebbels and others persuaded him that the battle of Berlin would be meaningless without his commanding presence. Such appeals to leadership heroics clinched the argument for Hitler. On the eve of his birthday, he had made up his mind to go down fighting for "fortress" Berlin. Many of his closest followers, however, did not feel this need to immolate themselves in the flames of Berlin; they joined a growing exodus toward the south. Those who stayed with him in the cramped quarters of the bunker were Eva Braun; the Goebbels with their six children; his valet, Heinz Linge; his surgeon, Dr. Ludwig Stumpfegger; his adjutant Otto Günsche; his two secretaries, Gerda Christian and Gertrud Junge; and his vegetarian cook, Constanze Manzialy.[95] Visitors from other bunkers would frequently join this group, notably Martin Bormann; General Krebs, the man who succeeded General Guderian as army chief of staff; General Burgdorf, Hitler's chief military adjutant; Artur Axmann, leader of the Hitler Youth; and scores of liaison officers, adjutants, and SS guards.

During the last ten days of his life, Hitler was frantically engaged in moving about imaginary armies and ranting against those who were betraying him. The Russians had swept from the Oder to the suburbs of Berlin and were relentlessly moving in on the heart of the city, which was now cut off on three sides. Hitler called upon SS-General Steiner to mount a counterattack northwest of the city, but Steiner's force of less than eleven thousand men and fifty-odd tanks was totally inadequate to repel the red tide. Steiner could not possibly attack even if he had wanted to do so. When Hitler found this out during the conference of April 22, he went into a paroxysm of rage, accusing his elite SS forces of betraying him. Hitler lost all control and blurted that the war was lost; that he would give up his command, sending Keitel and Jodl to direct resistance in the south; and that he would hold out to the last and then commit suicide.[96] He also gave permission to those present in the bunker to leave if they chose to do so. On that same day, Berliners were surprised to learn by radio that the führer was in their midst conducting the battle of Berlin. The last time they had heard his voice was three months earlier on January 30, 1945.

On April 23, Hitler received a radio transmission from Göring asking whether he could take over the leadership of the Reich with full freedom of action at home and abroad. Bormann, who relayed this message to Hitler, cleverly twisted its meaning as representing an ultimatum and infringement on the führer's power. Hitler had lost all respect for Göring long before this incident, but that anyone would question his authority, insinuate that he was incapable of exercising his authority properly — that was clearly a blatant insult and had to be severely punished. Hitler fired off an immediate telegraphic message to Göring, accusing him of treason and invalidating the decree of June 1941 that had named Göring his successor. He then expelled the field marshal from the party. In Göring's place he appointed General Ritter von Greim, who was obliged to fly into the embattled capital with his copilot Hanna Reitsch in order to be invested with his new office. Reitsch later reported that Hitler was pale and drooping, still reeling from Göring's "ultimatum," and muttering that nothing was spared him. Two days later, the führer received another blow. His personal valet, Heinz Linge, brought him a copy of a Reuter's news release that reported that Heinrich Himmler was negotiating a surrender in the west through Swedish diplomatic circles. This was the final blow. Hitler turned purple and ranted like a madman. Göring's defection had been expected, but the notion that the *Reichsführer SS,* loyal Heinrich, would betray him was beyond comprehension. Hitler gave orders to arrest Himmler's liaison man, Hermann

Fegelein, who had married Eva Braun's sister, and to shoot him by firing squad in the chancellery garden. He then commanded Greim to leave Berlin and arrest Himmler.

The final Soviet assault on Berlin began on April 26, 1945; it was launched by close to half a million troops supported by 12,700 guns and mortars, 21,000 multiple rocket launchers called "Stalin organs," and 1,500 tanks.[97] The spearheads of this invading army had surrounded Berlin on all sides; they were also within four miles of Hitler's chancellery. Confronting them were only two cohesive military forces: the Fifty-sixth Panzer Corps and the Waffen-SS group defending the chancellery. The rest of the defenders of fortress Berlin consisted of a badly organized, poorly trained collection of men with barely sixty tanks, led by a commander, General Helmuth Weidling, who knew nothing of the city's defense plans. All in all, the commander of Berlin had about sixty thousand men, including old men from the Volkssturm, Hitler Youth volunteers, and assorted units thrown together from police, SS, and factory defense groups.[98] The last known newsreel of Adolf Hitler shows him reviewing teenagers whom he was about to send back into combat against seasoned Soviet troops.

Chuikov, the hero of Stalingrad, mercilessly pounded the city by land and air before sending in his forces for the kill; and while Chuikov's forces slugged their way to the center of the city from the south and southeast, seven other Soviet armies pounded their way through all the other sections. The first wave of invading Russian soldiers, many of them speaking German, were well-disciplined and orderly, but subsequent troops went berserk, killing and raping as they advanced. This orgy of destruction by out-of-control Russians would persist for a whole week. Fanatical Nazis, too, in wanton acts of self-destruction, blew up bridges, rounded up and shot supposed "deserters," destroyed installations, and even blew up a four-mile tunnel running under the river Spree and the Landwehr Canal, a tunnel that had served as both a railroad link and a shelter. As water began to flood into the tunnel, a wild scramble for the high ground ensued, causing many to drown.[99]

Despite stubborn street-to-street fighting, the Soviets overran district after district, drawing closer and closer to the Reich chancellery and the Reichstag. The switchboard operator in the Führerbunker was already picking up Russian voices at the other end of various lines. One daring young Russian officer, Victor Boëv, who spoke excellent German, dialed Berlin information service and asked to be connected to the Ministry of Propaganda and actually succeeded in getting Dr. Goebbels on the line:

> "I am a Russian officer, speaking from Siemensstadt," Boëv told him. "I should like to ask you a few questions."
>
> Goebbels showed no surprise. "Please go ahead," he replied in a calm, matter-of-fact voice....
>
> "How long can you hold out in Berlin?" Boëv asked.
>
> Goebbels's reply was distorted by a crackle on the line.

"Several . . ."

"Several what? Weeks?"

"Oh, no. Months. Why not? Your people defended Sevastopol for nine months. Why shouldn't we do the same in our capital?"

"Another question. When and in what direction will you escape from Berlin?"

"That question is far too insulting to deserve an answer."

"You must remember that we shall find you, even if we have to comb the ends of the earth. And we have prepared a scaffold for you."

There was a confused jumble of voices at the other end. Boëv shouted: "Is there anything you would like to ask me?"

"No," Goebbels said, and hung up.[100]

The truth was that Goebbels knew very well that a scaffold would be waiting for him, his führer, and all those who had instigated the war. Hitler knew it too. The pounding of artillery and the bursting of shells came closer and closer. On the day of Chuikov's final assault, the Führerbunker received several direct hits by heavy shells. The roof withstood the shelling, but showers of concrete particles fell from it. The bunker inmates almost suffocated when the ventilators drew in sulphurous fumes from the fire that was raging above. Even to Hitler, it was clear that the end was near.

At 2 A.M. on April 29, 1945, Hitler sent for his secretary Traudl Junge and dictated his last will and testament, in which he noted that the "glorious seed" he had sown would eventually blossom forth in a glorious rebirth of National Socialism. The war, he said, had not been his fault but had been forced on him by the machinations of international Jewry. Hitler's pathological anti-Semitism thus held firm to the very end. He then named a new government, appointing Grand Admiral Karl Dönitz as president and commander in chief, Joseph Goebbels as Reich chancellor, and Martin Bormann as party chancellor. He made a special point of pronouncing anathema on Göring and Himmler, expelling the two former paladins from their posts and from the party. Finally, coming to a personal matter, which made Traudl Junge look up from her notes, Hitler announced his intention to marry Eva Braun and then die with her, adding that it was his "wish that our bodies be burnt immediately in the place where I have performed the greater part of my daily work during the course of my twelve years' service to my people."[101] Hitler's statement about wanting to be cremated reflected his grave concern of not ending up like Mussolini, who, with his mistress, had been killed only the day before and then hanged upside down in a public square, taunted, cursed, and spat upon by an angry crowd. When he heard the report of the Duce's death, Hitler swore that all traces of his body must vanish completely (*spurlos verschwinden*).

Later that day, Hitler arranged one of the most bizarre wedding ceremonies ever held. An obscure municipal councillor, Walter Wagner, was fetched by Goebbels to perform the civil ceremony, with Goebbels and

Bormann as witnesses. Afterward, in the company of a private party, the couple celebrated the "happy" event with champagne and food. The bride, dressed in a long silk gown, chatted away amiably while the gramophone played sentimental music.

The next day, April 30, 1945, with the Russians closing in on the Reich chancellery but still not knowing exactly where the German dictator was hiding out, Hitler decided that the time had come to end his life. After having lunch with his two secretaries and his vegetarian cook, Hitler and his new bride solemnly said goodbye to the staff and withdrew to their private quarters. Hitler's last words were to his private valet, Linge, whom he directed to join the breakout group; when the startled Linge asked, "Why, my Führer," his master's last reply was, "To serve the man who will come after me."[102] The vaultlike door to Hitler's private apartment then clanged shut. A frantic Magda Goebbels, brushing past Major Otto Günsche, who blocked the way to Hitler's inner sanctum, burst into Hitler's quarters and tried to plead with the Hitlers not to take their lives but escape instead to Berchtesgaden. Hitler refused to discuss it and ordered her to leave.

At about 3:30 P.M. on Monday April 30, 1945, Hitler and his mistress committed suicide. The physical evidence, as reported inconsistently by eyewitness observers such as Linge and Günsche, seems to suggest that Hitler bit down on a cyanide capsule and simultaneously shot himself in the right temple with his 7.6 millimeter Walther pistol.[103] Sitting on the sofa next to him, Eva Braun was physically unmarked, apparently also having swallowed poison. Although it is theoretically conceivable that Hitler could have taken poison while at the same time shooting himself in the head, this author accepts Robert G. L Waite's hunch that Hitler took poison and was then shot as a coup de grâce by the only person he trusted — Eva Braun, the woman he had married after divorcing Germany, his other wife that he had rejected as unworthy of him.[104] This was his last defiant, most selfish, and also his most cowardly act; by it he evaded responsibility for the horrors he had unleashed on his country and the world at large.

The couple's bodies, wrapped in blankets, were then carried upstairs and placed in a shallow ditch located about ten meters from the bunker entrance. The bodies were doused with several Jerry cans of gasoline and set afire. The participants in this macabre Wagnerian scene — Goebbels, Bormann, Hewel, Linge, Axmann, Johann Rattenhuber, Stumpfegger, Franz Schaedle, and Günsche — stood at rigid attention and give the Hitler salute, while artillery shells from Russian "Stalin organs" provided the funereal background music.[105] The bodies burned for several hours, and their remains were then buried in a nearby six-foot trench.

As a final act of institutional deceit, the remaining Nazi leaders informed the German people by radio on the evening of May 1, 1945, that "our Führer, Adolf Hitler, fighting to the last breath against Bolshevism, fell for Germany this afternoon in his operational command post in the Reich Chancellery."[106] The voice of Dönitz, relayed by a Hamburg radio station, for the admiral was speaking from a remote hideout in northern Germany, then came on and added further lugubrious lies.[107] The regime had stayed true to its lying self until the very end.

With Hitler dead, the Nazi house of cards quickly fell apart. After vainly seeking an advantageous accommodation with the Russians, Goebbels also made his inglorious exit from the stage of history by allowing his wife Magda to murder all of his six children and then committing suicide with her. The rest of the bunker inmates broke out, some into Russian captivity, death, or suicide. The commander of Berlin, General Weidling, arranged a cease-fire and capitulated to the Russians. The battle of Berlin had resulted in 125,000 German and well over 100,000 Russian casualties. The Dönitz regime, after trying to carry on the war from its headquarters at Flensburg in Schleswig-Holstein, capitulated to the Allied forces. On May 7, 1945, Dönitz sent Jodl and Keitel to General Eisenhower's headquarters at Rheims in France to sign the terms of unconditional surrender. Three days later, the surrender terms were confirmed at an inter-Allied meeting in Berlin on May 10, 1945.

Zero hour had struck in Germany. It was an eerie moment of unreality, of emptiness, experienced by many Germans as a feeling of betrayal and hopelessness. Not since the Thirty Years War had Germany been so utterly devastated. Adolf Hitler had almost made good on his promise that if Germany did not become the world's greatest power there would be no Germany. That prophecy was not fulfilled. Hitler's fantasy of Germany becoming the greatest power in the world died with him, but the German people, shamed, humiliated, conquered, and occupied, would endure to build a better Germany out of the ruins of defeat.

Conclusion

The Question of German Guilt

In April 1946, Hans Frank confessed his war crimes to the Nuremberg tribunal, which had been convened by the Allied powers to judge the major Nazi leaders, by declaring: "A thousand years will pass and this guilt of Germany will not be erased."[1] When Frank spoke these words, the heinous crimes perpetrated by the Nazis were fresh in everybody's mind, and there was a universal outcry to punish the guilty. This worldwide revulsion was directed not only at the top Nazis but also at the German people as a whole; they stood condemned in the eyes of the world as the most bestial murderers in history. This was in 1946. Time erases memories and heals wounds; but Nazi Germany continues to haunt our collective memory and disturbs our sleep. The specter of Hitler is still abroad in the world, and Germans in particular are still living, in part, under his dark shadow. When Germans visit foreign countries, they still evoke unpleasant memories; bitterness toward Germans is still very strong in some countries, and a heavy German accent is still perceived and exploited by our public image-makers as a sign of either arrogant bluster or unbridled aggression.

Given the unspeakable crimes committed by the Nazis, such reactions were to be expected in 1946. Should they still be expected today? One historian has asked: Has the time come to stop blaming the Germans for the crimes of Nazism? The question hides two assumptions, namely, that it would be the task of people other than the Germans to persuade the world of this and that the Germans are either incapable or unqualified to speak for themselves.

In 1946 there was every reason to assume that the Germans were incapable of honestly coming to terms with the crimes in which their Nazi leaders had implicated them. The problem then was one of identifying the guilty and punishing them. Twenty-one major Nazi leaders were tried before the Nuremberg tribunal, an Allied legal machine whose responsibility was to ferret out those who had committed war crimes and crimes against humanity. In order to lend respectability and credibility to the proceedings, this trial was presided over by a lord justice of Great Britain, flanked by eight Allied judges and assisted by a judge of the United States Supreme Court who served as chief prosecutor. The defendants were well treated during their incarceration, and they were accorded legal rights that were consistent with the actual practices then standard in Western societies. Despite the claims of Göring and others that the proceedings were a sham and the outcome a foregone conclusion, the trial was conducted fairly by judges who, though not brilliant, were professional and honest.[2]

Nuremberg was only one of many trials, held inside and outside Germany, that were conducted to judge those who had committed crimes during World War II. Although the Germans would eventually be able to judge their own people, this option was not available in 1945 because Germany's institutions had collapsed and its people lacked the moral strength to confront the problems of guilt and punishment. The three major Nazi leaders who were responsible for the decisions that led to the tragedy of World War II — Hitler, Himmler, and Goebbels — had committed suicide. All the twenty-one defendants at Nuremberg pleaded innocent, and only a few of them admitted that they were guilty of serious transgressions. They also questioned the legality of being tried by non-Germans and by legal principles and procedures for which they claimed there was no precedent. Confronted by incriminating evidence, many dodged behind a series of rationalizations. The most popular was that they merely followed orders and that Hitler or Himmler was really the guilty one. It was, of course, convenient for the top Nazis, as it was to some degree for all Germans, to blame everything on Hitler, for with Hitler dead and unable to speak for himself, they could claim ignorance or innocence or both. Almost to a man, the Nazi leaders also claimed that they were ignorant of what went on beyond their own spheres of competence. Keitel explained that as an assistant to Hitler he had nothing to do with the political motives or backgrounds of the operations he planned. He or Jodl, he said, "never discussed with the Führer the question of aggression or defensive war. According to our concept that was not our job."[3] That his signature was on immoral orders resulting in mass murder was also not his official concern. When the consequences of such decisions were brought home to the defendants, they often used another defense mechanism by downplaying the crime and defusing its sting by what Peter Gay has called "comparative trivialization," which consists in acknowledging brutality but also pointing indignantly at crimes committed by others that were just as bad.[4] Thus, Rosenberg told Dr. Gilbert, one of the Nuremberg prison psychiatrists, "The Russians have the nerve to sit in judgement — with 30 million lives on their conscience! Talk about persecution of the church! Why they are the world's greatest experts. They killed priests by the thousands in their revolution."[5] Ribbentrop also parroted the same line: "Haven't you heard about how the Americans slaughtered the Indians? Were they an inferior race too? — Do you know who started the concentration camps in the first place? — The British."[6] As to those atrocity films, Göring shrugged them off by saying, "Anybody can make an atrocity film if they take corpses out of their graves and then show a tractor shoving them back in again."[7]

When not indulging in massive denial or comparative trivialization, Göring and other dyed-in-the-wool Nazis engaged in mutual accusations, which took the form of casting blame on one another for having lost battles or failed to perform duties as administrators or military leaders. Such mutual recrimination, which had been endemic throughout the Nazi period, was as irrelevant as it was unproductive because it foreclosed genuine dialogue and thus blocked the truth. A few Nazi leaders did acknowledge their culpability, even dramatically confessing their crimes in the courtroom, as did Hans Frank, the butcher of Poland. The Allies, however, were not convinced by dramatic confessions, suspecting that such belated urges to confess harbored ulterior motives aimed at enhancing self-importance and pleasing the accuser.

If the highest leaders of Germany did not come clean in 1945, it should not be surprising that the German people, still traumatized by war and economic ruin, were unable to confront the problem of culpability. Ordinary people, too, dodged into convenient excuses, claiming that they were insignificant cogs caught in a totalitarian system where opposition was difficult to organize and invariably resulted in imprisonment or death. Having undergone tremendous suffering at the hands of their own criminal regime and those of their enemies, many Germans came to believe that the suffering already inflicted on them relieved them of the stigma of responsibility or collective guilt. But even if the German people had desired to grapple with the legal or ethical problem of guilt and punishment, circumstances made this increasingly difficult. The country was occupied and administered by the victorious powers that began to impose their own political and ideological agenda on them. For a second time in the twentieth century, the course of Germany's future had been taken out of the hands of Germans and placed in the hands of foreigners. As Friedrich Meinecke justly observed, this made it difficult, if not impossible, to accomplish the task of assigning guilt and meting out punishment from a position of autonomy and strength.[8] It was the Allied powers that instituted, each in its own peculiar ways, what became known as "denazification" — that is, identifying those who had been seriously implicated in the Nazi regime, punishing them, and excluding them permanently from public office. Five categories were drawn up: (1) major offenders, punishable by death or life imprisonment; (2) offenders, sentenced to a maximum of ten years; (3) lesser offenders, to be placed on probation; (4) followers who went along with the NSDAP; and (5) exonerated persons. Although denazification was placed in the hands of German tribunals (*Spruchkammer*), the Allied powers supervised the process. Denazification was part of a larger effort by the Allied powers to destroy German militarism and National Socialism, to hold war criminals to account, to force the Germans to pay for war damages, and to embark upon a policy of reeducating the Germans along the political lines deemed appropriate by the occupying powers.

Denazification proceeded by fits and starts between 1945 and 1950. It was clouded over by conflicting ideological aims; the Soviets, who had occupied most of eastern Germany, saw Nazism as rooted largely in socioeconomic conditions associated with capitalism and amenable to Communist treatment, whereas the Anglo-Americans believed that the establishment and acceptance of democratic institutions and practices, combined with major efforts in social rehabilitation, would eventually root out Nazism in a capitalist state. Although many guilty Nazis were punished and imprisoned, as many, if not more, got off scot-free. Many Germans mocked the process, especially the elaborate questionnaires (Fragebogen) that they had to fill out before judgment in every case was rendered. Some later privately admitted that too many of them had been whitewashed by what they called Persilscheine — testimonials obtained by many Germans from priests, anti-Nazis, or Jews who attested to the sterling quality of the holder and were then given to the tribunals as affidavits. A contemporary joke compared the tribunals to laundries that one entered with a brown shirt and exited with a white one.

The coming of the Cold War and the division of Germany into a Communist East and a capitalist-democratic West put an end to any real soul-searching about what would later be called the unmastered past. The question of German guilt remained in a kind of suspended animation. Both the Germans and their guardians were preoccupied with economic reconstruction and the ideological battle between two different ways of life.

The economic miracle of the 1950s, which saw a remarkable resurgence of economic prosperity in West Germany, stifled criticism and reinforced a kind of collective amnesia about the Nazi past that had set in right after the collapse of Nazism in 1945. Although the Bonn government instituted a program of reparations called Wiedergutmachung, aimed at compensating the victims of Nazism, particularly the Jews, for damages to life, health, freedom, or property incurred at the hands of the Nazis, most Germans (East or West) refused to grapple with the Nazi legacy. Important work on Hitler and National Socialism took place in Britain and the United States rather than in Germany, where historians were still reluctant to reopen old wounds and where the relevant documents were difficult to obtain because they had been appropriated by the victorious powers and stored in faraway places. Until the late 1960s German schools continued past practices of neglecting the importance of contemporary history in favor of more remote historical periods, thereby making it conveniently impossible to confront the recent Nazi past.

As the tranquil Adenauer years began to fade by the mid-1960s, giving way to a decade of social conflict, Germans were once more confronted with the dark shadow of Adolf Hitler. The younger generation of Germans, too young to have participated in the crimes of the Third Reich, demanded better answers from their parents about the Third Reich and their involvement in it. In West Germany the younger generation was becoming increasingly Americanized and radicalized, which caused acute generational conflicts and led to widespread criticism of government institutions, particularly the universities where conservatism was strongly entrenched. For better or worse, the social tensions of the 1960s prepared the way for a more open forum of ideas, which unfortunately also erupted into violence and sorely tested West Germany's democratic institutions. Yet, despite a certain shrillness that colored the intellectual climate of opinion in the late 1960s, the Germans made undeniable progress in coming to terms with their recent past. Several tenacious historians, social scientists, and journalists such as Werner Maser, Helmut Heiber, Max Domarus, Ernst Nolte, Martin Broszat, Karl Dietrich Bracher, and Joachim Fest wrote or edited incisive and comprehensive studies on Adolf Hitler and National Socialism. Elementary and secondary schools revamped their outmoded curricula and began to instruct their students more honestly regarding Germany's recent past. Meanwhile, a flood of newspaper and magazine articles, records, and films began to appear on Nazi Germany, which further stimulated public discussion. In 1960 Adolf Eichmann was tried in Jerusalem; from December 1963 to August 1965 Germans followed the Auschwitz proceedings of twenty major offenders who were tried for war crimes at Frankfurt. Information about Nazi atrocities was therefore widely available to ordinary Germans who were receptive to the truth.

Unfortunately, many chose not to watch documentaries such as Claude Lanzmann's film *Shoah* but preferred instead to listen to the fabrications, half-truths, and plain lies that were still being disseminated by neo-Nazis and fellow travelers, aided and abetted by foreign racists, who wanted to whitewash Nazi crimes. Even in 1969, the author of the first comprehensive German work on National Socialism, Karl Dietrich Bracher, had to admit the persistence of such ideas, again camouflaged under the guise of "National Opposition," which were widely promoted by elite journals, newspapers, a flood of pamphlets, and a steady stream of exculpatory memoirs or sanitized biographies of fallen idols of World War II.[9] Moreover, Bracher's judgment that this revisionist literature was being handed down to a new generation of politically ignorant youthful followers is as true now as it was then. On the other hand, very few young Germans identified with Nazism; the vast majority supported the democratic way of life. The truth is that most Germans surely wanted to get along with their lives in a resurgent economy, unburdened by the weight of historical crimes.

Yet the ghost of Hitler continues to spook the Germans and the world at large: "Hitler is today all around us — in our loathings, our fears, our fantasies of power and victimization, our nightmares of vile experience and violent endings."[10] In 1983, Gerd Heidemann, a journalist for the German magazine *Stern,* presented a stunned world with the "discovery" of Hitler's diaries, which he claimed had been fully authenticated by scholarly experts, including H. R. Trevor-Roper, and would disclose exciting new information about Nazi Germany. The "Hitler diaries" became a media event, dwarfing most other newsworthy stories and making 1983 one of the best years the führer ever had. However, it turned out that these sixty volumes were outright forgeries and that Heidemann had worked closely with the forger, Konrad Kujau, and had almost conned the world into believing that the führer had confided his innermost thoughts over many years to his secret diaries. The Hitler diary affair disclosed some ugly truths about Germans, neo-Nazis, and a world obsessed by sordid scandals and revolting people.[11]

Several years later, a red-hot controversy, involving some foremost German historians, erupted in the German press and quickly assumed ugly political overtones. The debate was set off by several conservative historians, notably Ernst Nolte, who argued that the time had come to view the Third Reich in proper historical perspective, by which he meant liberating historical consciousness from the collective images of horror and barbarism by which Nazi Germany had been perceived. According to Nolte, perceptions of the Third Reich had hardened into a mythology of absolute evil, residing outside historical space and time, which made it impossible to view the period in comparison to any other period and prevented the historian from drawing comparisons between the deeds of Nazism and those of other totalitarian systems that engaged in similar genocidal activities. Nolte had written a comparative study of fascism in the 1960s in which he described fascism as a metaphysical system whose broad aim was to usurp the radicalization of the left, also based on metaphysical assumptions of social reality, and usher in a new homogenized community of the people. Nolte was quite properly describing the clash of absolute ideologies that had plagued the twentieth century with wars of annihilation. In the 1970s and 1980s Nolte left the plane of abstract thought and began to examine how and to what extent the clash of ideologies resulted in genocidal activities on all sides; by so doing, he stirred up a hornet's nest because it was his contention that Hitler's extermination of the Jews was not a unique act but was to be expected from a political religion that presupposed extermination as a necessary element of its worldview. After all, the Communists had long accepted the view that their enemies, the bourgeois, had to be liquidated. To the Bolsheviks, class membership determined whether individuals were either saved or damned. The Soviets had made it unmistakably clear that they intended to exterminate a whole class. Nolte's point was that the Nazis were no different except that they aimed to exterminate races rather than classes. So far, so good, but when Nolte next proceeded to draw causal connections between Bolshevik genocide and the Nazi Holocaust, claiming that the latter was in response to the former, he began to skate on thin ice indeed. It may be true to some extent,

as has been argued in this study, that the Nazis thought they were using exterminatory measures out of self-defense against an enemy who
was also waging a war of annihilation. Hitler undoubtedly linked Communism with the Jews, which, in his view, justified exterminating them
both. But this way of thinking is mad, and by stepping into this pattern
of irrational reasoning, if perhaps only to understand it, Nolte created
some very unfortunate impressions, namely, that Hitler's policies were
understandable and to some extent justified, and that the Holocaust,
however unfortunate, was not unique at all but part of a dynamic of
hate that was deeply rooted in history.

Nolte is not a racist and neither are the conservative historians who
come to his aid, but the cumulative effect of relativizing Nazism was to
diminish the uniqueness of the Holocaust and, by extension, to minimize
the guilt and responsibility of the generation of Germans who shaped
the Third Reich. Very little is served by arguing that the biological extermination of the Jews was a copy of the class extermination practiced
by the Communists[12] and that "Auschwitz did not result in the first
place from inherited anti-Semitism and was at its core not a mere genocide (*Völkermord*), but was really a reaction born out of the anxiety of
the annihilating occurrences of the Russian Revolution."[13] Such speculations can only trivialize the Nazi experience and, by so doing, play into
the hands of racist revisionists who argue that German policies toward
the Jews were standard in world history because societies always tend
toward biological ethnic homogeneity and are therefore justified in removing alien forces. In this view, ethnic cleansing is a necessary measure
in order to maintain public health and hygiene.

The *Historikerstreit* (historians' conflict), pitting conservative against
liberal or left-wing historians, was conducted on all sides with such ve-
hemence that the purpose was largely obscured for the public.[14] The
controversy illustrates how sensitive the issue of Nazism still is fifty years
after its ignominious defeat. It hangs over the Germans, obscuring the
past and clouding the future. Even the assertion of minimal national
pride has been a problem for Germans because it has frequently evoked
paranoia abroad about the rise of a "Fourth Reich." In fact, the *Historikerstreit* quickly expanded beyond its German forum when foreign
pundits began to inject their own tendentious opinions. German historians were accused of whitewashing history and promoting an ominous
political agenda aimed at political unification and teaching Germans to
get off their knees and learn to walk tall again.

Can Germans walk tall again, or is the burden of Nazi Germany so
great that they will always be held under its weight? This question goes
to the heart of the problem of guilt. It also goes to the heart of the problem of national identity that is connected to it. As long as Germans lived
in a divided nation, these two problems were less acute than they are today in the context of a reunified Germany. A divided nation did not have
to worry unduly about a national identity, but with the recent reunifica-

tion of East and West, the problem of German identity cries out for a workable solution, and we suspect that the answer, in turn, depends on how Germans deal with the question of guilt and responsibility.

In 1947, the German philosopher Karl Jaspers, who had a clear conscience, a good heart, and great moral vision, provided a compass that can still serve us in finding our way out of the moral wilderness of Nazism. In trying to examine "German guilt," it is first necessary to define the wrong that was committed that should precipitate guilt. Jaspers and most moral Germans would agree that in the case of Nazism such wrongdoing involved committing war crimes and crimes against humanity. Other crimes included imperialist expansion, the manner in which war was fought, and even the crime of starting the war. There can be no denying that Hitler's Germany was indeed guilty of these crimes. There are, however, as Jaspers points out, types of guilt, which he labels as criminal guilt, political guilt, moral guilt, and metaphysical guilt.[15] Criminal guilt involves anyone who committed a crime under unequivocal laws, with jurisdiction resting with the court. Political guilt attaches to all citizens who tolerated what was done under the name of the state. We are all co-responsible for the way in which we are governed and therefore liable for the consequences of the deeds done by the state, although not every single citizen is liable for the criminal actions committed by specific individuals in the name of the state. Jurisdiction for political guilt rests ultimately with the victor. Moral guilt involves the individual's awareness of serious transgressions or participation in unethical choices that resulted in specific wrongdoing. Jaspers argued that "moral failings cause the conditions out of which both crime and political guilt arise."[16] Jurisdiction of moral guilt rests with one's individual conscience. Finally, there is metaphysical guilt, which arises when we transgress against the general moral order and violate the archetypal moral bonds that connect us to each other as human beings. As humans we are co-responsible for every wrong and injustice that is committed; and by inactively standing by, we are metaphysically culpable. The jurisdiction with metaphysical guilt ultimately rests with God.

Although Jaspers was willing to admit that Germans were morally and metaphysically culpable in the sense of tolerating conditions that gave rise to criminal activities on a large scale, he denies that all Germans were collectively guilty of the crimes committed by the Nazis. For crimes one can punish only individuals; a whole nation cannot be charged with a crime.[17] The criminal is always an individual. Moreover, it would be tragic to repeat the practice of the Nazis and judge whole groups by reference to some abstract "trait" or character. There is no national character that extends to every single individual. This would be committing the fallacy of division that holds that what is true of some presumed whole must be true of all its members. One cannot make an individual out of a people without falling victim to the same disease that afflicted the Nazis. People are not evil; only individuals are.

In rejecting collective guilt, Jaspers by no means excluded the notion of collective responsibility. Adult Germans who lived through the Third Reich and served as active participants in Hitler's world were coresponsible for what happened, perhaps not from a criminal point of view but from a political, moral, and metaphysical one. Indeed, it has been suggested by various philosophers that, as part of a social contract, we are all corporately responsible, even for what was done by others before us because we are the recipients of decisions, good or bad, that have been made for the social group by those who preceded us — decisions, of course, that can and sometimes must be reversed if they are demonstrably unworkable or harmful. Most decent Germans today have seen the need of accepting a corporate responsibility for what was done in the name of Germany by the Nazis, which does not involve collective guilt but a moral obligation to prevent the recurrence of criminal actions that are undertaken in the name of Germany.

If one accepts, as Jaspers did, that Germans were guilty in the sense just described, how far does that guilt extend? This is a question that Jaspers did not examine, but on January 24, 1984, West German chancellor Helmut Kohl, who was visiting Israel, said:

> The young German generation does not regard Germany's history as a burden but as a challenge for the future. They are prepared to shoulder their responsibility. But they refuse to acknowledge a collective guilt for the deeds of their fathers. We should welcome this development.[18]

Accepting as a fact that Nazi Germany committed horrendous crimes against humanity in general and against the Jewish people in particular; accepting as given that Germans carry varying degrees of guilt, as postulated by Karl Jaspers; and further agreeing with Chancellor Kohl that the degree of guilt diminishes with distance, it appears that the question of German guilt can be likened to the concentric circles formed by ripples when a rock is dropped into a still pond. The rock is the act, the crime, that stirs the pool to movement; the first circle holds those criminally responsible; the second, those politically responsible; the third, those morally responsible; and the fourth and all circles after that are those metaphysically guilty. Just as the ripples formed in water eventually lose their momentum and fade back into the stillness of the pond, so should the ripples of guilt be allowed to subside so that quiet and peace can be attained. The political ramifications of not allowing the German people to work through the question of guilt by themselves, especially now that they are again one people and can face such problems on a basis of strength — in short, keeping the issue as alive and pressing in 1995 as it was in 1945 — could be grave not only for the Germans but for the world at large. It will only be when the Germans have rediscovered a sense of humane statehood that Nazi Germany will have passed into history.

Notes

Part One
THE ROOTS, 1870-1933

Chapter 1: The Origins of Totalitarianism

1. The term "totalitarian" was first used by Giovanni Gentile, Italy's foremost theorist of fascism, who along with Mussolini began to use the word *totalitario* to refer to the structure and goals of the new Italian state. Although the literature on totalitarianism is extensive, the single most comprehensive study is still that of Carl J. Friedrich and Zbigniew K. Brzezinski, *Totalitarian Dictatorship and Autocracy* (New York: Praeger, 1962). Besides the work of Friedrich and Brzezinski, the following are also indispensable for an understanding of totalitarianism: Hannah Arendt, *The Origins of Totalitarianism* (New York: Meridian, 1958); Dietrich Bracher, *Zeitgeschichtliche Kontroversen: Um Faschismus, Totalitarismus, Demokratie* (Munich: Piper, 1976); Erich Fromm, *Escape from Freedom* (New York: Avon Books, 1965); Franz Neumann, *Behemoth: The Structure and Practice of National Socialism* (New York: Harper & Row, 1966); Barrington Moore, *Social Origins of Dictatorship and Democracy* (Boston: Beacon, 1966); Ernst Nolte, *Three Faces of Fascism* (New York: Holt, Rinehart and Winston, 1966); José Ortega y Gasset, *The Revolt of the Masses* (New York: Norton, 1932); J. L. Talmon, *The Origins of Totalitarian Democracy* (New York: Praeger, 1960); W. Wippermann, *Faschismustheorien: Zum Stande der gegenwärtigen Diskussion* (Darmstadt: Wissenschaftliche Buchgesellschaft, 1975).

2. Zevedei Barbu, *Democracy and Dictatorship: Their Psychology and Patterns of Life* (New York: Grove Press, 1956), 122.

3. Carlton J. Hayes, *A Generation of Materialism* (New York: Harper & Row, 1941), 242.

4. Gerhard Masur, *Prophets of Yesterday: Studies in European Culture, 1890–1914* (New York: Harper & Row, 1961), 13–14.

5. Geoffrey G. Field, *Evangelist of Race: The Germanic Vision of Houston Stewart Chamberlain* (New York: Columbia Univ. Press, 1981), 206.

6. Bernard Semmel, *Imperialism and Social Reform: English Social-Imperial Thought, 1895–1914* (New York: Doubleday, 1960), 27.

7. Field, *Evangelist of Race*, 173–74.

8. For this shift in the axis of European consciousness, see H. Stuart Hughes, *Consciousness and Society: The Reorientation of European Social Thought, 1890–1930* (New York: Random House, 1958).

9. See Fritz Stern, *The Politics of Cultural Despair: A Study in the Rise of the Germanic Ideology* (New York: Doubleday, 1965).

10. Stanley G. Payne, *Fascism: Comparison and Definition* (Madison: Univ. of Wisconsin Press, 1980), 32.

11. See H. Stuart Hughes's treatment of the "recovery of the unconscious" in *Consciousness and Society,* chap. 4.

12. Arthur Schopenhauer, *The World as Will and Idea*, trans. R. B. Haldane and J. Kemp, 2 vols. (London: Routledge & Kegan Paul, 1883), 2:409.

13. Walter Kaufmann, ed., *The Portable Nietzsche Reader* (New York: Viking, 1968), 570.

14. Ibid., 572.

15. See Joseph Campbell's sympathetic works on mythology, especially *The Masks of God,* 4 vols. (New York: Viking, 1964) and *The Hero with a Thousand Faces* (Princeton, N.J.: Princeton Univ. Press, 1949).

16. On propaganda in World War I, see H. C. Peterson, *Propaganda for War* (Norman: Univ. of Oklahoma Press, 1939); J. D. Squires, *British Propaganda at Home and in the United States from 1914–1917* (Cambridge, Mass.: Harvard Univ. Press, 1935); J. M. Read, *Atrocity Propaganda* (New Haven: Yale Univ. Press, 1941); George Creel, *How We Advertised America* (New York: Harper and Brothers, 1920).

17. Friedrich and Brzezinski, *Totalitarian Dictatorship and Autocracy,* 9.

18. Nolte, *Three Faces of Fascism,* 20–21.

19. Friedrich Meinecke, *The German Catastrophe*, trans. Sidney Fay (Boston: Beacon Press, 1963), 10.

20. Alfred Vagts, *A History of Militarism* (reprint, Westport, Conn.: Greenwood Press, 1981), 14.

21. J. W. Wheeler-Bennett, *The Nemesis of Power: The German Army in Politics* (London: Macmillan, 1964), 9.

22. Quoted by Richard Hanser, *Putsch! How Hitler Made Revolution* (New York: Pyramid, 1970), 74.

23. Gordon Craig, *Germany, 1866–1945* (New York: Oxford Univ. Press, 1978), 39–40.

24. Ralf Dahrendorf, *Society and Democracy in Germany* (New York: Doubleday, 1969), 33.

25. Ibid., 37.

26. Oswald Spengler, *Selected Essays*, trans. Donald O. White (Chicago: Henry Regnery, 1967), 47–48.

27. I owe this analogy to Fritz Stern. See *The Failure of Illiberalism: Essays on the Political Culture of Modern Germany* (New York: Alfred A. Knopf, 1972), xxiii.

28. Kaufmann, *Portable Nietzsche Reader,* 570.

29. Klemens von Klemperer, *Germany's New Conservatism* (Princeton, N.J.: Princeton Univ. Press, 1957), 47–69.

30. Ibid., 69.

31. For the most penetrating account of Germany's imperialistic aims, see Fritz Fischer's work, *Germany's Aims in the First World War* (New York: Norton, 1967), especially his introductory account of German imperialism.

32. Ibid., 155–62.

33. Klaus Hildebrand, *The Foreign Policy of the Third Reich,* trans. Anthony Fothergill (Berkeley: Univ. of California Press, 1973), 2, 77, 136.

German historians in the last decades have increasingly stressed such a basic continuity in both domestic and foreign policy between 1871 and 1945. The most important relevant works are Hans-Ulrich Wehler, *Das deutsche Kaiserreich 1871–1918* (Göttingen: Vandenhoeck & Ruprecht, 1973); Helmuth Böhme, *Deutschlands Weg zur Grossmacht* (Cologne: Kiepenheuer & Witsch, 1966); Dirk Stegmann, *Die Erben Bismarcks: Parteien und Verbände in der Spätphase des Wilhelminischen Deutschlands. Sammlungspolitik 1871–1918* (Cologne: Kiepenheuer und Witsch, 1970); Michael Stürmer, ed., *Das Kaiserliche Deutschland: Politik und Gesellschaft, 1870–1918* (Düsseldorf: Droste, 1970); Peter Christian Witt, *Die Finanzpolitik des Deutschen Reiches von 1903–1913: Eine Studie zur Innenpolitik des Wilhelminischen Deutschlands* (Hamburg: Mattiessen, 1970).

34. Erich Kahler, *The Jews among the Nations* (New York: F. Ungar, 1967), 99.

35. See Horst von Maltitz, *The Evolution of Hitler's Germany: The Ideology, the Personality, the Moment* (New York: McGraw-Hill, 1973), 86.

36. Quoted by Maltitz, *Evolution of Hitler's Germany,* 86–87.

37. Kahler, *Jews among the Nations,* 99–102.

38. Walter Laqueur, *Out of the Ruins of Europe* (New York: Library Press, 1971), 479.

39. Quoted in Maltitz, *Evolution of Hitler's Germany,* 85.

40. Walter Laqueur, *Weimar: A Cultural History* (New York: Putnam, 1974), 45–46, 68–71.

41. Quoted in Maltitz, *Evolution of Hitler's Germany,* 148.

42. Ibid., 148.

43. Ibid., 117.

44. Ibid., 115.

45. Adolf Hitler, *Mein Kampf* (New York: Reynal & Hitchcock, 1941), chap. 11, esp. 419–20. All subsequent citations of *Mein Kampf* are from this edition.

46. Wolfgang Scheffler, *Judenverfolgung im Dritten Reich* (Berlin: Colloquium Verlag, 1964), 15–16.

47. Arendt, *Origins of Totalitarianism,* 37.

48. See Fritz Stern, *Gold and Iron: Bismarck, Bleichröder, and the Building of the German Empire* (New York: Alfred A. Knopf, 1977), esp. chap. 18.

49. Ibid., 495.

50. Paul W. Massing, *Rehearsal for Destruction* (New York: Harper & Brothers, 1949), 12.

51. See Peter Pultzer, *The Rise of Political Anti-Semitism in Germany and Austria* (New York: Wiley, 1964).

52. Hitler, *Mein Kampf,* 72.

53. Wilfried Daim, *Der Mann, der Hitler die Ideen gab* (Munich: Isar Verlag, 1958), 20–21.

54. Leon Poliakov, *The Aryan Myth: A History of Racist and Nationalist Ideas in Europe* (New York: Meridian, 1971), 296. For just how these racist ideas turned into "racial hygiene" under the Nazis, see Robert N. Proctor, *Racial Hygiene: Medicine under the Nazis* (Cambridge, Mass.: Harvard Univ. Press, 1988).

55. Poliakov, *Aryan Myth,* 296.

56. Ibid.

Chapter 2: The Trauma of Military Defeat and Economic Ruin

1. Quoted by Alan Palmer, *The Kaiser: Warlord of the Second Reich* (New York: Scribner's, 1978), 175.

2. Gordon Craig, *War, Politics, and Diplomacy* (New York: Praeger, 1966), 46–57.

3. Georg Alexander von Müller, *Regierte der Kaiser? Kriegstagebücher, Aufzeichnungen und Briefe des Chefs des Marine-Kabinetts Admiral Georg Alexander von Müller 1914–1918,* ed. Walter Görlitz (Göttingen: Muster-schmidt, 1959), 68.

4. For the origins of the stab-in-the-back legend (*Dolchstosslegende*), see John W. Wheeler-Bennett, *Wooden Titan: Hindenburg* (New York: W. Morrow, 1938), 238.

5. Erich Eyck, *A History of the Weimar Republic,* trans. Harlan P. Hanson and Robert G. L. Waite, 2 vols. (Cambridge, Mass.: Harvard Univ. Press, 1962), 1·37–39.

6. A good summary of scholarly views on the German revolution of 1918–19 is contained in Reinhard Rürup, "Problems of the German Revolution of 1918–19," *Journal of Contemporary History* 3 (1968) 109–35. The most acute analysis of the survival of prewar institutions (armed forces, civil service, education) into the postwar period is Dietrich Bracher, *Die Auflösung der Weimarer Republik: Eine Studie zum Problem des Machtverfalls in der Demokratie* (Villingen, Schwarzwald: Ring-Verlag, 1960).

7. Scheidemann quoted by Karl W. Meyer, *Karl Liebknecht: Man without a Country* (Washington D.C.: Public Affairs Press, 1957), 127.

8. Golo Mann, *The History of Germany since 1789,* trans. Marian Jackson (New York: Praeger, 1968), 332.

9. Philipp Scheidemann, *The Making of New Germany: The Memoirs of Philipp Scheidemann,* trans. J. E. Mitchell (New York: Appleton, 1929), 2:262.

10. Ibid., 2:264.

11. Ibid.

12. Wheeler-Bennett, *Nemesis of Power,* 21.

13. Friedrich Ebert, *Schriften, Aufzeichnungen und Reden* (Dresden: C. Reissner, 1926), 2:127–30.

14. On the Free Corps, see Robert G. L. Waite, *Vanguard of Nazism: The Free Corps Movement in Germany, 1918–23* (Cambridge, Mass.: Harvard Univ. Press, 1952).

15. Richard M. Watt, *The Kings Depart: The Tragedy of Germany: Versailles and the German Revolution* (New York: Simon & Schuster, 1968), 248.

16. See especially Ernst Jünger's autobiographical account of the "Fronterlebnis" in *Krieg als inneres Erlebnis* (Bielefeld: Velhagen und Klasing, 1933).

17. Quoted by Watts, *Kings Depart,* 238.

18. Ibid., 219.

19. For Noske's own account, see *Von Kiel bis Kapp* (Berlin: Verlag für Politik und Wirtschaft, 1920).

20. Watt, *Kings Depart,* 314.

21. Dietrich Bracher, *The German Dictatorship,* trans. Jean Steinberg (New York: Praeger, 1970), 75.

22. Hajo Holborn, *A History of Modern Germany*, 3 vols. (New York: Alfred A. Knopf, 1969), 3:542.

23. William S. Halperin, *Germany Tried Democracy: A Political History of the Reich from 1918 to 1933* (New York: Norton, 1965), 160.

24. Ibid., 155.

25. On the practice and shortcomings of proportional representation, see Eyck, *History of the Weimar Republic,* 1:70–71.

26. Halperin, *Germany Tried Democracy,* 160.

27. Quoted by Eyck, *History of the Weimar Republic,* 1:66.

28. On the range of historical judgments of the Versailles Treaty, see Ivo J. Lederer, ed., *The Versailles Settlement: Was It Foredoomed to Failure?* (Boston: D. C. Heath, 1960).

29. Mann, *History of Germany,* 343.

30. Jacques Chastenet, *Histoire de la Troisieme Republique,* 4 vols. (Paris: Librairie Hachette, 1955), 4:340–44.

31. Mann, *History of Germany,* 343.

32. Watt, *Kings Depart,* 408.

33. Ibid., 418.

34. Scheidemann quoted by Gordon Craig, *Germany, 1866–1945,* 425.

35. U.S. Senate, *Treaty of Peace with Germany,* 66th Cong., 1st sess., 1919, Senate Doc. 49.

36. John Maynard Keynes, *The Economic Consequences of the War* (New York: Harcourt, Brace & Howe, 1920), 15–16.

37. Ibid., 187.

38. Ibid., 51.

39. For the fate of the German navy, see Langhorne Gibson and Paul Schubert, *Death of a Fleet* (New York: Coweard-McCan, 1932).

40. On the Kapp Putsch, see Wheeler-Bennett, *Nemesis of Power,* chap. 1; Waite, *Vanguard of Nazism,* chap. 4; Johannes Erger, *Der Kapp-Lüttwitz Putsch: Ein Beitrag zur deutschen Innenpolitik 1919–20* (Düsseldorf: Droste, 1967).

41. On Seeckt's role in the Kapp Putsch, see Wheeler-Bennett, *Nemesis of Power,* 76–82; and Gordon Craig, *The Politics of the Prussian Army* (New York: Oxford Univ. Press, 1955), 375–81.

42. Craig, *Politics of the Prussian Army,* 379–80.

43. On the Bavarian situation, see Georg Franz-Willing, *Ursprung der Hitlerbewegung: 1919–22* (Preussisch Oldendorf: Schütz, 1975); Werner Maser, *Der Sturm auf die Republik: Frühgeschichte der NSDAP* (Stuttgart: Deutsche Verlags-Anstalt, 1973); Allan Mitchell, *Revolution in Bavaria 1918–1919: The Eisner Regime and the Soviet Republic* (Princeton, N.J.: Princeton Univ. Press, 1965); and Karl Schwend, *Bayern zwischen Monarchie und Diktatur* (Munich: R. Pflaum, 1954).

44. Craig, *Germany, 1866–1945,* 433.

45. Quoted by Peter Gay, *Weimar Culture: The Outsider as Insider* (New York: Harper & Row, 1968), 153.

46. Robert G. L. Waite provides an excellent account of Organization "C" and similar murder societies in his *Vanguard of Nazism.* For a good German account, see Emil J. Gumbel, *Vom Vememord zur Reichskanzlei* (Heidelberg: L. Schneider, 1962).

47. See, Emil J. Gumbel's painstaking indictment in *Vier Jahre politischer Mord* (Berlin: Verlag der Neuen Gesellschaft, 1922).

48. On the complexities of the German economic collapse of 1923 there is an excellent summary of views in Fritz Ringer's documentary collection entitled *The German Inflation of 1923* (New York: Oxford Univ. Press, 1969).

49. On the Ruhr question, see Paul Wentzcke, *Ruhrkampf: Einbruch und Abwehr im Rheinisch-westfälischen Industriegebiet* (Berlin: R. Hobbing, 1930).

50. Konrad Heiden, *Der Fuehrer: Hitler's Rise to Power* (Boston: Houghton Mifflin, 1944), chap. 7.

51. Ibid., 127.

Chapter 3: The Rise of Adolf Hitler

1. The decisions leading to the destruction of Döllersheim are still disputed by historians. Werner Maser (*Adolf Hitler: Legende, Mythos, Wirklichkeit* [Munich: Bechtle Verlag, 1971], 7–8) argues that Döllersheim and surrounding areas were not declared military training areas until 1941 and that most houses purchased by the Wehrmacht remained intact until 1945, when the Russians systematically stripped the properties of usable material and destroyed the rest. This account, however, is challenged by a statement from General Knittersched, commander of Military District 17, that in May 1938 he was given a direct order to make the area "ready as soon as possible." Relevant documentation can be found in the archives of the Oberösterreichische Landesarchiv (Linz), folder 161. In general, I have followed Robert G. L. Waite's hunches in his reconstruction of Hitler's pathology in *The Psychopathic God Adolf Hitler* (New York: Basic Books, 1977), 150–51. Waite's account also agrees with a similar one by Franz Jetzinger, *Hitler's Youth* (London: Hutchinson, 1958), 24. There is also an unpublished dissertation by Karl Merinsky in the Vienna Institut für Zeitgeschichte, entitled "Das Ende des Zweiten Weltkrieges und die Besatzungszeit im Raum vom Zwettl und in Niederösterreich," in which the author focused, among other things, on Wehrmacht troop encampments in the Waldviertel, showing that Döllersheim was pulverized by Hitler's big guns.

2. Werner Maser, *Hitler,* trans. Peter and Betty Ross (London: Allen Lane, 1973), chap. 1. On Hitler scholarship in general, see Andreas Hillgruber, "Tendenzen, Ergebnisse und Perspektiven der gegenwärtigen Hitler-Forschung," *Historische Zeitschrift* 226, no. 3 (June 1978). The most factual account of Hitler's childhood is by Bradley Smith, *Adolf Hitler: His Family, Childhood and Youth* (Stanford, Calif.: Hoover Institution Press, 1967).

3. Hans Frank, *Im Angesicht des Galgens* (Munich: A. Beck, 1953).

4. Ibid., 330.

5. Ibid.

6. Ibid., 320–21.

7. On Hitler's fear of being tainted by Jewish blood, see Waite, *Psychopathic God,* 146–52.

8. Franz Jetzinger, *Hitler's Youth,* trans. Lawrence Wilson (London: Hutchinson, 1958; reprint, Westport, Conn.: Greenwood Press, 1976), 25.

9. Quoted by Joachim Fest, *Hitler,* trans. Richard and Clara Winston (New York: Harcourt, Brace & Jovanovich, 1973), 16.

10. Maser, *Hitler,* 19.

11. Hitler, *Mein Kampf*, 6.

12. Maser, *Hitler*, 19.

13. Bridget Hitler, "My Brother-in-Law Adolf," unpublished manuscript in the New York Public Library. Bridget's account of Hitler's visit to Liverpool in the autumn of 1912 has never been corroborated and is probably pure fantasy. However, one of Hitler's biographers, Robert Payne, accepted her story and even based an entire chapter of his book *The Life and Death of Adolf Hitler* (New York: Praeger, 1973), 93–102, on Hitler's supposed "journey to England."

14. Waite, *Psychopathic God*, 154.

15. Various allegations about Alois Hitler's rough treatment of his wife and children have come long after the fact from neighbors and are purely anecdotal. The story about Alois beating his wife, children, and dog comes from Bridget Hitler (interviews in OSS Source Book, 924, quoted by Waite, *Psychopathic God*, 155).

16. Waite, *Psychopathic God*, 156.

17. Ibid., 168–70.

18. Such retroactive psychological judgments, though unverifiable in principle, are nevertheless legitimate aids to further discovery as long as they are based on factual data. Unfortunately, such data do not exist when it comes to much of Hitler's childhood. For example, we know nothing about Hitler's toilet training and therefore cannot claim that an alleged need to retain and control his feces would account for his later preoccupation with feces, filth, or manure. Similarly, we cannot assume that Hitler had only one testicle and that the absence of one testicle had a significant impact on his psychosexual maturation. This theory rests on a Russian autopsy report on the charred body presumed to have been that of Adolf Hitler (Lev Bezymenski, *The Death of Adolf Hitler* [New York: Pyramid, 1969], 44–45). Some historians have erected a series of bold speculative theories around this dubious report, arguing that Hitler suffered from either congenital monorchidism or from cryptorchidism. Perhaps he did, but it is conjecture and not established fact.

19. Waite, *Psychopathic God*, 187–94.

20. Maser, *Hitler*, 25.

21. Hitler, *Mein Kampf*, 10–15.

22. Fest, *Hitler*, 20.

23. *Hitler's Table Talks* (London: Weidenfeld and Nicolson, 1953), 698–99.

24. Quoted by Jetzinger, *Hitler's Youth*, 68–69.

25. Hitler, *Mein Kampf*, 24.

26. August Kubizek, *The Young Hitler I Knew*, trans. E. V. Anderson (New York: Tower Publications, 1954), 166–67, 168.

27. Hitler, *Mein Kampf*, 46–47.

28. Ortega y Gasset, *Revolt of the Masses*, 73–74.

29. Kubizek, *Young Hitler*, chap. 10.

30. Ibid., 86–89.

31. Ibid., 90–94.

32. Ibid., chap. 7.

33. Werner Maser, *Hitlers Briefe und Notizen: Sein Weltbild in handschriftlichen Dokumenten* (Vienna: Econ Verlag, 1973), 12–13.

34. Fest, *Hitler*, 3.

35. Hitler, *Mein Kampf*, 27.

36. Rudolph Binion, *Hitler among the Germans* (New York: Elsevier, 1976), 17.

37. Eduard Bloch, "Erinnerungen an den Führer und dessen verewigte Mutter," *NSDAP Central Archives, Federal Archives, Coblenz,* N.S. 26/65 (dated November 7, 1938). Dr. Bloch gave this account to a party archivist who had asked him to write down his memories of Hitler and his mother. Dr. Bloch gave an almost identical account from the safety of his American exile in 1943 (*Colliers,* March 15, 1943).

38. Maser, *Hitler,* 43.

39. Hitler, *Mein Kampf,* 29–30; also 161–62.

40. J. Sydney Jones, *Hitler in Vienna, 1907–13* (London: Blond & Briggs, 1983), 133.

41. Ibid., 144.

42. Fest, *Hitler,* 46.

43. Hitler, *Mein Kampf,* 29.

44. Ibid., 33.

45. Ibid., 397.

46. Quoted by Alan Bullock, *Hitler: A Study in Tyranny* (New York: Harper & Row, 1962), 158.

47. Wilhelm Reich, *The Mass Psychology of Fascism,* trans. Vincent R. Carfagno (New York: Farrar, Strauss & Giroux, 1970), 47.

48. Kubizek, *Young Hitler,* 21.

49. Winston S. Churchill, *The Second World War,* 6 vols. (Boston: Houghton Mifflin, 1948–53), 1:52.

50. Hitler, *Mein Kampf,* 52.

51. Ibid., 113.

52. Maser, *Hitler,* 173.

53. Jones, *Hitler in Vienna,* 149, 163.

54. Fest, *Hitler,* 37.

55. W. A. Jenks, *Vienna and the Young Hitler* (New York: Columbia Univ. Press, 1960), 118–20.

56. Ibid.

57. Hitler, *Mein Kampf,* 73.

58. Ibid., 75.

59. Ibid.

60. Ibid., 78.

61. Ibid., 448.

62. Waite, *Psychopathic God,* 421.

63. Ibid., 412–25.

64. See *Diagnostic and Statistical Manual of Mental Disorders,* 3rd. ed., revised (DSM-III-R) (Washington, D.C.: American Psychiatric Association, 1987), 346–47.

65. Ibid., 342–46.

66. Hitler, *Mein Kampf,* 160.

67. On the political, social, and cultural situation of Bavaria in general and Munich in particular, see Kristian Bäthe, *Wer wohnte wo in Schwabing?* (Munich: Süddeutscher Verlag, 1965); Ludwig Hollweck, *Unser München* (Munich: Süddeutscher Verlag, 1967); Ludwig Hümmert, *Bayern vom Kaiserreich zur Diktatur* (Pfaffenhofen: Verlag W. Ludwig, 1979); and Karl Schwend, *Bayern zwischen Monarchie und Diktatur* (Munich: R. Pflaum Verlag, 1954).

68. On Kurt Eisner and Erich Mühsam, the two major coffeehouse low brows, there is a vivid account in Hanser, *Putsch*. On Eisner's place in Bavarian politics, see Mitchell, *Revolution in Bavaria*, and Franz Schade, *Kurt Eisner und die bayerische Sozialdemokratie* (Hannover: Verlag für Literatur und Zeitgeschehen, 1961).

69. Fest, *Hitler*, 61–62.

70. Ibid., 62.

71. Hitler, *Mein Kampf*, 210.

72. Hanser, *Putsch*, 81.

73. The most reliable and the most detailed account of Hitler's wartime service can be found in Maser, *Hitler*, chap. 4.

74. Quoted by Hanser, *Putsch*, 89.

75. Quoted by Fest, *Hitler*, 69.

76. Ibid., 68; also Bullock, *Hitler*, 53.

77. Jünger, quoted in Hanser, *Putsch*, 85.

78. Fest, *Hitler*, 69–70.

79. Ibid., 70.

80. Hitler, *Mein Kampf*, 250.

81. In 1932, Hitler sued a Hamburg newspaper that tried to cast aspersions on his war record, suggesting that he really was a coward. His former commanding officer testified to his bravery, and Hitler won the case. See Bullock, *Hitler*, 52, and Maser, *Hitler*, 83, 363, and n. 42, chap. 2.

82. Hitler, *Mein Kampf*, 266–67.

83. Ibid., 268.

84. Ibid., 268–69.

85. Binion, *Hitler among the Germans*, 14–35.

86. Ibid., 33–34.

87. Ibid., 34.

88. John Toland, *Adolf Hitler*, 2 vols. (New York: Doubleday, 1976), 1:88–89.

89. Quoted by Heinrich Beneke, *Hitler und die S.A.* (Munich: Olzog Verlag, 1962), 15.

90. Bullock, *Hitler*, 65.

Chapter 4: The Rise of the NSDAP, 1919-23

1. Allan Mitchell, *Revolution in Bavaria, 1918–1919* (Princeton, N.J.: Princeton Univ. Press, 1965), 78–79.

2. Ironically, Eisner's cell no. 70 at Stadelheim Prison was later occupied by his own assassin, Count von Arco Valley, and in 1923 by Adolf Hitler. Ernst Röhm was executed in the same cell on Hitler's orders in 1934. See Mitchell, *Revolution in Bavaria*, 69.

3. Ibid., 94.

4. Quoted by Richard M. Watt, *Kings Depart*, 283.

5. Gerhard Schmolze, ed., *Revolution und Räterepublik in München 1919/19, in Augenzeugenberichten* (Düsseldorf: Karl Rauch Verlag, 1969), 104.

6. For a comprehensive and readable account of the Wittelsbach dynasty, see Ludwig Hüttl, *Das Haus Wittelsbach: Die Geschichte einer europäischen Dynastie* (Munich: Wilhelm Heyne Verlag, 1980).

7. Ernst Müller-Meiningen, *Aus Bayerns schwersten Tagen* (Berlin, 1923), 46.

8. Watt, *Kings Depart,* 286.

9. Mitchell, *Revolution in Bavaria,* 231.

10. Richard Grunberger, *Red Rising in Bavaria* (London: Arthur Barker, 1973), 62.

11. Mitchell, *Revolution in Bavaria,* 232.

12. Ibid., 212.

13. Quoted by Grunberger, *Red Rising in Bavaria,* 64.

14. Ibid., 68.

15. This little-known rebellion of the Hereros illustrates our previous contention (chap. 1) that imperialism was a significant factor in the rise of totalitarianism, reinforcing aggressive military habits, stimulating racial and ethnic prejudices, and encouraging in its practitioners a messianic sense of imperial authority. General von Trotha, the German commander in southwest Africa, ordered an extermination policy against the rebellious Hereros and condoned an orgy of bloodletting. The Germans took no prisoners and systematically butchered men, women, and children. These criminal practices foreshadowed later Nazi treatments of subjugated peoples — torture, "resettlement" plans, concentration camps, slave labor. As a result of these genocidal policies, the Hereros were practically wiped out. At the time of the rebellion in 1904, they numbered 80,000; by 1911 only 15,130 were still alive. For this little-known episode in the prehistory of German totalitarianism, see Jon M. Bridgman, *The Revolt of the Hereros* (Berkeley: Univ. of California Press, 1981), and Horst Drechsler, *Let Us Die Fighting: The Struggle of the Herero and Nama against German Imperialism* (London: Zed Press, 1980).

16. Of particular importance to the rise of National Socialism is the role played by the junior officers in the postwar period. As Robert G. L Waite points out, these men, more than their commanders, formed the backbone of the Free Corps and later also of the developing Nazi Party. When the Free Corps were ostensibly disbanded, these junior officers joined the various military and semimilitary organizations sponsored by National Socialism. See Waite, *Vanguard of Nazism,* 45–49.

17. On the Thule Society, see Reginald H. Phelps, "Before Hitler Came: Thule Society and Germanen Orden," *Journal of Modern History* 35 (1963) 245–61.

18. Bracher, *German Dictatorship,* 81.

19. See Phelps, "Before Hitler Came," 245.

20. Ibid., 247.

21. Toland, *Adolf Hitler,* 1:90–91.

22. Like Arco-Valley, Auer survived the attempt on his life as a result of the heroic surgical intervention by Professor Sauerbruch.

23. Watt, *Kings Depart,* 295.

24. Georg Franz, "Munich: Birthplace and Center of the National Socialist German Workers' Party," *Journal of Modern History* 29, no. 4 (December 1957), 322–23.

25. Fest, *Hitler,* 110.

26. Waite, *Vanguard of Nazism,* 82–83.

27. Ibid., 83.

28. Ibid.

29. See Werner Maser, *Sturm auf die Republik,* 38–41.

30. Grunberger, *Red Rising in Bavaria,* 152.

31. Ibid.

32. Ibid., 153.

33. Thomas Mann, *Diaries, 1918–1939,* trans. Richard and Clara Winston (New York: Harry N. Abrams, 1982), 55.

34. Maser, *Sturm auf die Republik,* 148. See also the detailed discussion of the founding of the DAP in Franz-Willig, *Ursprung.*

35. Dietrich Orlow, *The History of the Nazi Party, 1919–1933* (Pittsburgh: Univ. of Pittsburgh Press, 1969), 11.

36. Maser, *Sturm auf die Republik,* 145.

37. David Schoenbaum, *Hitler's Social Revolution: Class and Status in Nazi Germany, 1933–1939* (New York: Doubleday, 1966), 15.

38. Richard Hofstadter, *The Paranoid Style in American Politics and Other Essays* (New York: Random House, 1960), esp. chap. 1. For the millenarian colorations of this style, the most compelling account is by James M. Rhodes, *The Hitler Movement: A Modern Millenarian Revolution* (Stanford, Calif.: Hoover Institution Press, 1980).

39. Hitler, *Mein Kampf,* 287.

40. Robert Cecil, *The Myth of the Master Race: Alfred Rosenberg and Nazi Ideology* (New York: Dodd Mead, 1972).

41. Joachim Fest, *Das Gesicht des dritten Reiches* (Munich: R. Piper, 1980), 230.

42. Cited by Cecil, *Myth of the Master Race,* 45.

43. Ibid., 52.

44. On Ludendorff, see Roger Parkinson, *Tormented Warrior: Ludendorff and the Supreme Command* (New York: Stein & Day, 1978).

45. On the exiles from Bolshevism, see Robert C. Williams, *Culture in Exile: Russian Émigrés in Germany, 1881–1941* (Ithaca, N.Y.: Cornell Univ. Press, 1972). There is also a very colorful chapter ("A Welter of Tears and Vodka") of these Russian exiles in Otto Friedrich's book *Before the Deluge: A Portrait of Berlin in the 1920s* (New York: Avon Books, 1972), 102–21.

46. Konrad Heiden, *Der Fuehrer* (Boston: Houghton Mifflin, 1944), 253–54.

47. Bruce Mazlish, *The Revolutionary Ascetic: Evolution of a Political Type* (New York: McGraw-Hill, 1976).

48. Ibid., 24.

49. Orlow, *History of the Nazi Party,* 1:15.

50. Ibid., 1:18.

51. Hitler, *Mein Kampf,* 511–14.

52. Ibid., 512.

53. J. P. Stern, *Hitler: The Führer and the People* (Glasgow: William Collins Sons, 1975), 36–37.

54. Ibid., 10.

55. Eberhard Jäckel, ed., *Hitler: Sämtliche Aufzeichnungen, 1905–1924* (Stuttgart: Deutsche Verlags-Anstalt, 1980), 110.

56. Ibid., 110.

57. Ibid.

58. Joachim Remak, ed., *The Nazi Years: A Documentary History* (Englewood Cliffs, N.J.: Prentice-Hall, 1969), 28–30.

59. Jäckel, *Sämtliche Aufzeichnungen,* 96.
60. Remak, *Nazi Years,* 28.
61. Jäckel, *Sämtliche Aufzeichnungen,* 88–90.
62. Fest, *Hitler,* 122.
63. Orlow, *History of the Nazi Party,* 1:23.
64. Ibid., 28.
65. Ibid., 31.
66. See Maser, *Sturm auf die Republik,* 324; also Hitler, *Mein Kampf,* 735.
67. Hitler, *Mein Kampf,* 737.
68. Fest, *Hitler,* 128.
69. Maser, *Sturm auf die Republik,* 325.
70. Ibid., 327–28.
71. Fest, *Hitler,* 150.
72. Maser, *Sturm auf die Republik,* 328.
73. Michael Kater, *The Nazi Party: A Social Profile of Members and Leaders, 1919–1945* (Cambridge, Mass.: Harvard Univ. Press, 1983), 23–24; also 242–43.
74. Ibid., 242–43.
75. Schoenbaum, *Hitler's Social Revolution,* 5.
76. Kater, *Nazi Party,* 242–43.
77. See Seymour Lipset, *Political Man: The Social Bases of Politics* (Garden City, N.Y.: Doubleday, 1960).
78. For Otto Strasser's account of this meeting, see his *Hitler und Ich* (Säckingen/Brombach: Hermann Stratz, 1948), 17–30.
79. Randall L. Bytwerk, *Julius Streicher* (New York: Dorset Press, 1983), 1.
80. Ibid., 15.
81. Ibid., 49.
82. Ibid., 105.
83. Hanser, *Putsch,* 277.
84. Ernst Hanfstaengl, *Unheard Witness* (New York: J. B. Lippincott, 1957), esp. chaps. 2, 3, 4.
85. John Dornberg, *Munich 1923: The Story of Hitler's First Grab for Power* (New York: Harper & Row, 1982), 326–27.
86. Personal interview, August 1984.
87. After Henry A. Turner's impressive work on the role of big business and the rise of Hitler, this judgment must now be accepted as conclusive. See Henry A. Turner, *German Big Business and the Rise of Hitler* (New York: Oxford Univ. Press, 1985).
88. Jäckel, *Sämtliche Aufzeichnungen,* 642.
89. Turner, *Big Business and the Rise of Hitler,* 59.
90. Quoted in ibid., 51.
91. Ibid., 51–52.
92. Ibid., 59.
93. Fest, *Hitler,* 167.
94. Ibid., 129.
95. Foreword to Jetzinger, *Hitler's Youth,* 10.
96. Stern, *Hitler,* 35.
97. Hjalmar Greeley Schacht, *Account Settled* (London: Weidenfeld and Nicolson, 1949), 206.
98. Fest, *Hitler,* 161.

99. Ibid., 145.

100. On the SA, see Heinrich Bennecke, *Hitler und die S.A.* (Munich: Olzog, 1962), and Peter Merkl, *The Making of a Stormtrooper* (Princeton, N.J.: Princeton Univ. Press, 1980).

101. Konrad Heiden, *A History of National Socialism* (New York: Alfred A. Knopf, 1936), 73.

102. Quoted by Heinz Höhne, *The Order of the Death's Head* (New York: Ballantine, 1971), 21.

103. Hitler, *Mein Kampf,* 748.

104. Fest, *Hitler,* 162.

105. Bennecke, *Hitler und die S.A.,* 28–29.

106. Höhne, *Order of the Death's Head,* 22.

107. Hans Kallenbach, *Mit Hitler auf Festung Landsberg* (Munich: Verlag Kress und Hornung, 1939), 13–15.

108. Höhne, *Order of the Death's Head,* 22.

109. Bullock, *Hitler,* 94.

Chapter 5: The Beerhall Putsch and Its Aftermath

1. Quoted by Friedrich von Rabenau, *Hans von Seeckt. Aus seinem Leben, 1918–1936.* 2 vols. (Leipzig: Hase und Koehler, 1941), 2:342.

2. Ernst Deuerlin, ed., *Der Hitler Putsch: Bayerische Dokumente zum 8./9. November 1923* (Stuttgart: Deutsche Verlags-Anstalt, 1962), 74–76.

3. Ibid., 79.

4. Ibid., 238.

5. Ibid.

6. Bullock, *Hitler,* 104.

7. Deuerlin, *Der Hitler Putsch,* 257–58.

8. Wheeler-Bennett, *Nemesis of Power,* 171.

9. Dornberg, *Munich 1923,* 6.

10. Bullock, *Hitler,* 101–4.

11. Dornberg, *Munich 1923,* 161.

12. Ibid., 162.

13. Wheeler-Bennett, *Nemesis of Power,* 105–6.

14. Ibid., 108.

15. Craig, *Politics of the Prussian Army,* 416–18.

16. Quoted by Wheeler-Bennett, *Nemesis of Power,* 108. Class subsequently plotted with other right-wing extremists to have Seeckt assassinated. The plot was uncovered and the ringleaders, former followers of von Lüttwitz, were arrested, tried, and convicted, although Class managed to extricate himself during the trial.

17. Dornberg, *Munich 1923,* 50–51.

18. Hanfstaengl, *Unheard Witness,* 101.

19. Ibid.

20. Hanser, *Putsch,* 320.

21. Jäckel, *Sämtliche Aufzeichnungen,* 1052.

22. Hanser, *Putsch,* 321.

23. Dornberg, *Munich 1923,* 70.

24. Ibid., 89.

25. Ibid., 95.

26. Ibid., 174.

27. Hanser, *Putsch,* 328.

28. Ibid., 335–36.

29. Ibid., 336.

30. Ibid., 337.

31. Ibid.

32. Maser, *Sturm auf die Republik,* 435.

33. Fest, *Hitler,* 87.

34. Hanser, *Putsch,* 351.

35. Dornberg, *Munich 1923,* 293.

36. Ibid., 295.

37. Harold J. Gordon, *Hitler and the Beer Hall Putsch* (Princeton, N.J.: Princeton Univ. Press, 1972), 475–85.

38. Ibid., 479–80.

39. *The Hitler Trial before the People's Court in Munich,* trans. H. Francis Freniere, Lucie Karcic, and Philip Fandek, with an introduction by Harold J. Gordon, Jr., 3 vols. (Arlington, Va.: Univ. Publications of America, 1976), 1:61.

40. Ibid., 1:71.

41. Ibid., 1:72.

42. Ibid., 2:144–45.

43. Ibid., 2:137–39.

44. Ibid., 2:445.

45. Ibid., 3:366.

46. Fest, *Hitler,* 193.

47. Bullock, *Hitler,* 120.

48. Kallenbach, *Mit Hitler auf Festung Landsberg,* 96–100.

49. Hanfstaengl, *Unheard Witness,* 119.

50. Quoted by Werner Maser, *Hitlers Mein Kampf: Entstehung, Aufbau, Stil Änderungen, Quellen, Quellenwert kommentierte Auszüge* (Munich: Bechtle Verlag, 1966), 13.

51. This reconstruction of Hitler's daily activities comes from Maser's *Hitlers Mein Kampf,* 13–36, and Hans Kallenbach's *Mit Hitler auf Festung Landsberg.*

52. Hanfstaengl, *Unheard Witness,* 145.

53. Maser, *Hitlers Mein Kampf,* 27–29.

54. Ibid., 34–35.

55. Waite, *Psychopathic God,* 82.

56. Bullock, *Hitler,* 121–22.

57. Eberhard Jäckel, *Hitlers Weltanschauung: Entwurf einer Herrschaft* (Stuttgart: Deutsche Verlags-Anstalt, 1981), 129.

58. Hitler, *Mein Kampf,* 580; subsequent references to *Mein Kampf* in this chapter are given in the text.

59. The term *Lebensraum,* popular among pan-German writers before World War I, was rarely used by Hitler in *Mein Kampf.* Hitler used such terms as "soil and territory," "space," or "roots" (*Scholle*), terms that would later evoke a whole Nazi ideology of "blood and soil." The most popular work on this theme of *Lebensraum,* published in the same year as Hitler's second volume of *Mein Kampf* (1926), was Hans Grimm's best-seller *Volk ohne Raum* (People without space).

60. Quoted by David Jablonsky, *The Nazi Party in Dissolution: Hitler and the Verbotzeit, 1923-1925* (London: Frank Cass, 1989), 53.

61. Bullock, *Hitler*, 125.

62. Ibid., 124; also Orlow, *History of the Nazi Party*, 51-64.

63. Jablonsky, *Nazi Party in Dissolution*, 82.

64. Ibid., 85.

65. Jäckel, *Sämtliche Aufzeichnungen*, 1238-39.

66. Jablonsky, *Nazi Party in Dissolution*, 150-51.

Chapter 6: The Years in the Political Wilderness, 1924-29

1. Detlev J. K. Peukert, *The Weimar Republic: The Crisis of Classical Modernity*, trans. Richard Deveson (New York: Hill & Wang, 1992), 120-21.

2. Bullock, *Hitler*, 133-35.

3. On political parties in Germany, see Ludwig Bergsträsser, *Geschichte der politischen Parteien in Deutschland*, 11th ed. (Munich: Olzog, 1965).

4. On the record of the German judiciary in handling political cases, consult the authoritative works of E. J. Gumbel, *Zwei Jahre Mord* (Berlin: Verlag Neues Vaterland, 1921); *Vier Jahre politischer Mord; Verräter verfallen der Feme* (Berlin: Verlag der Neuen Gesellschaft, 1929).

5. There is an excellent study on law enforcement agencies in Berlin during the Weimar Republic by Hsi-Huey Liang, entitled *The Berlin Police Force in the Weimar Republic* (Berkeley: Univ. of California Press, 1970). Liang points out that the Berlin police force was never democratized and that its officers and officers' associations remained largely in the hands of conservatives and reactionaries (71, 84-85).

6. Wolfgang Zorn, "Student Politics in the Weimar Republic," *Journal of Contemporary History* 5 (1970) 128-43.

7. Karl Dietrich Bracher, *Die Auflösung der Weimarer Republik* (Villingen/Schwarzwald: Ring Verlag, 1960), 259.

8. Peukert, *Weimar Republic*, 134.

9. Turner, *German Big Business and the Rise of Hitler*, 103-4.

10. Laqueur, *Weimar*, 225. There are several other books that faithfully capture the mood of the Roaring Twenties in the Western world and Germany: Frederick Lewis Allen, *Only Yesterday: An Informal History of the 1920s* (New York, 1931); Robert Graves and Alan Hodge, *The Long Week-end: A Social History of Great Britain 1918-1939*, 2nd ed. (New York, 1963); Bruno Werner, *Die Zwanziger Jahre von Morgens bis Mitternachts* (Munich, 1962); Friedrich, *Before the Deluge;* and Christopher Isherwood, *The Berlin Stories* (New York: New Directions, 1945).

11. Laqueur, *Weimar*, 225.

12. Ibid., preface. See also Gay, *Weimar Culture*.

13. On the conservative critique of modernity, which some historians have mistakenly referred to as a "revolution," see the following works: von Klemperer, *Germany's New Conservatism;* Arnold Mohler, *Die Konservative Revolution in Deutschland 1918-1932* (Stuttgart: Cotta, 1950); Jean Neurohr, *Der Mythos vom Dritten Reich* (Stuttgart: Cotta, 1957); and Kurt Sontheimer, *Anti-Demokratisches Denken in der Weimarer Republik* (Munich: Nymphenburger, 1962).

14. Mary Fulbrook, *The Divided Nation: A History of Germany 1918–1990* (New York: Oxford Univ. Press, 1992), 40.

15. Thomas Childers, *The Nazi Voter: The Social Foundations of Fascism in Germany, 1919–1933* (Chapel Hill: Univ. of North Carolina Press, 1983), 266.

16. Peukert, *Weimar Republic,* 90.

17. Quoted by Merkl, *Making of a Stormtrooper,* 16–17.

18. Peukert, *Weimar Republic,* 149–50.

19. *Ibid,* 150.

20. Liang, *Berlin Police Force,* 6.

21. Christopher Isherwood, *The Berlin Stories* (New York: New Directions, 1954), 86.

22. Bullock, *Hitler,* 257.

23. Craig, *Germany, 1866–1945,* 484.

24. Ibid.

25. For the most astute discussion of the psychological dimensions of German films, see Siegfried Kracauer, *From Caligari to Hitler: A Psychological History of the German Film* (Princeton, N.J.: Princeton Univ. Press, 1947).

26. For a more detailed discussion of this topic, consult Friedrich's brilliant account in *Before the Deluge,* chap. 15, on which I have relied.

27. Ibid., 383.

28. Waite, *Psychopathic God,* 303–4.

29. Dahrendorf, *Society and Democracy in Germany,* 331.

30. Ibid.

31. Quoted by Friedrich, *Before the Deluge,* 396.

32. Bracher, *German Dictatorship,* 139.

33. Kurt Lüdecke, *I Knew Hitler* (London: Jarrolds, 1938), 217–18.

34. Fest, *Hitler,* 224.

35. *Völkischer Beobachter,* March 7, 1925; also in Fest, *Hitler,* 227.

36. Orlow, *History of the Nazi Party,* 1:52–53.

37. Fest, *Hitler,* 225.

38. Two days after Hindenburg appointed Hitler as chancellor, Ludendorff sent the field marshal a telegram in which he accused him of having put the fatherland into the hands of "one of the greatest demagogues of all times." Quoted in Parkinson, *Tormented Warrior,* 224.

39. Jeremy Noakes, "Conflict and Development in the NSDAP 1924–1927," *Journal of Contemporary History* 1, no. 4 (1966) 16–17.

40. Ibid., 17.

41. Orlow, *History of the Nazi Party,* 1:56, 67.

42. Noakes, "Conflict and Development," 20.

43. Helmut Heiber, ed., *The Early Goebbels Diaries, 1925–1926,* trans. Oliver Watson (New York: Praeger, 1962), 29–30.

44. Detlef Felken, *Oswald Spengler: Konservativer Denker zwischen Kaiserreich und Diktatur* (Munich: C. H. Beck, 1988), 188–89.

45. Noakes, "Conflict and Development," 24.

46. Ibid., 26–27.

47. Afraid that he might be deported to Austria, Hitler approached the Austrian government and formally renounced his citizenship (April 7, 1925). On April 30, 1925, the request was granted, and Hitler became a stateless person

for the next seven years. On February 25, 1932, Hitler found a loophole in the law and, by a political sleight of hand, became a German citizen overnight.

48. Strasser, *Hitler and I*, 97; also in Curt Ries, *Joseph Goebbels* (New York: Ballantine, 1948), 25.

49. Orlow, *History of the Nazi Party*, 1:69.

50. Ibid., 1:69–71.

51. Helmut Heiber, *Goebbels*, trans. John K. Dickinson (New York: Da Capo Press, 1972), 41.

52. Heiber, *Early Goebbels Diaries*, 67.

53. Ibid., 72.

54. Ibid., 77–78.

55. Heiber, *Goebbels*, 5.

56. Ibid., 6.

57. Ibid., 15.

58. Ibid., 36.

59. Ibid., 38.

60. Heinz Höhne, *Die Machtergreifung: Deutschlands Weg in die Hitler-Diktatur* (Hamburg: Spiegel Verlag, 1983), 116.

61. Peter D. Stachura, *Gregor Strasser and the Rise of Nazism* (London: George Allen & Unwin, 1983), 106.

62. Fest, *Hitler*, 243.

63. Orlow, *History of the Nazi Party*, 1:87.

64. Heiber, *Goebbels*, 55.

65. Joseph Goebbels, *Der Angriff: Aufsätze aus der Kampfzeit* (Munich: Eher Verlag, 1940), 71.

66. Orlow, *History of the Nazi Party*, 1:102–3.

67. The thesis that the Nazi Party was a "lower-middle-class" party of small shopkeepers, teachers, preachers, lawyers, doctors, farmers, and craftsmen has had a long history, starting with its original formulation by Harold Lasswell in 1933 ("The Psychology of Hitlerism," *Political Quarterly* 4 [1933] 373–84) and subsequently repeated as historical orthodoxy by historians who were trained to explain social change in terms of class affiliation or economic status. In its most sophisticated form, this thesis has been advanced by Karl Dietrich Bracher (*German Dictatorship*, 152–67), who argues that the NSDAP was a lower-middle-class party of merchants, artisans, military adventurers, and youthful romantic activists, and that their distress and panic account for the breakthrough of 1930–33. Although this thesis has some merit, it is inadequate as an explanatory model. As a result of some compelling studies on German voting patterns (Richard Hamilton, *Who Voted for Hitler?* [Princeton, N.J.: Princeton Univ. Press, 1982]; and Childers, *Nazi Voter*) and biographic-statistical profiles of Nazi members (Peter Merkl, *Political Violence under the Swastika: 581 Early Nazis* [Princeton, N.J.: Princeton Univ. Press, 1975]), it has become increasingly obvious that "class analysis" must be supplemented by other approaches. It has also become obvious that the appeal of the Nazi Party, although perhaps having its roots in middle-class disaffection, was far broader than has been previously assumed. Unlike other German parties, the NSDAP was a new and broadly based populist party that appealed to diverse social groups — from the petit bourgeoisie to "military adventurers" (who were hardly bourgeois!) to "youthful romantic activists" (also not necessarily bourgeois) to former nobility as well as urban workers.

68. Orlow, *History of the Nazi Party*, 1:130–31.

69. On the role and function of the *Gauleiter*, see Peter Hüttenberger, *Die Gauleiter* (Stuttgart: Deutsche Verlags-Anstalt, 1970), and Karl Höffkes, *Hitlers politische Generale: Die Gauleiter des Dritten Reiches* (Tübingen: Grabert Verlag, 1986).

70. Orlow, *History of the Nazi Party*, 1:80.

71. Bennecke, *Hitler und Die S.A.*, 131–32.

72. Höhne, *Machtergreifung*, 120.

73. Bennecke, *Hitler und die S.A.*, 139.

74. Fest, *Hitler*, 261.

75. Turner, *German Big Business and the Rise of Hitler*, 90–92.

76. See Schoenbaum, *Hitler's Social Revolution*, 2.

77. Peukert, *Weimar Republic*, 119.

78. Ibid., 252.

79. Bracher, *German Dictatorship*, 169.

80. Peukert, *Weimar Republic*, 253.

Chapter 7: The Nazi Seizure of Power

1. Höhne, *Machtergreifung*, 63–65.

2. The following studies provide an excellent guide to the role of the Reichswehr in undermining parliamentary government: Craig, *Politics of the Prussian Army*; Walter Goerlitz, *History of the German General Staff, 1657–1945*, trans. Brian Battershaw (New York: Praeger, 1957); Wheeler-Bennett, *Nemesis of Power*; and Thilo Vogelsang, *Reichswehr, Staat und NSDAP* (Stuttgart: Deutsche Verlags-Anstalt, 1962).

3. Craig, *Politics of the Prussian Army*, 431.

4. Wheeler-Bennett, *Nemesis of Power*, 250.

5. Ibid., 201.

6. Höhne, *Machtergreifung*, 96–97.

7. Turner, *German Big Business and the Rise of Hitler*, 160.

8. Halperin, *Germany Tried Democracy*, 431.

9. On the thunder of the political right against democracy during the Weimar Republic, see Sontheimer, *Antidemokratisches Denken in der Weimarer Republik*.

10. Ernst Fraenkel, "Historical Obstacles to Parliamentary Government in Germany," in *The Path to Dictatorship, 1918–1933: Ten Essays by German Scholars*, trans. John Conway (New York: Doubleday, 1966), 26–27.

11. For a detailed reconstruction of Wessel's case, including the trial of his murderers, see Imre Lazar, *Der Fall Horst Wessel* (Munich: Wilhelm Heyne Verlag, 1980).

12. Wessel's poem is this:

> Die Fahne hoch! Die Reihen dicht geschlossen!
> SA marschiert mit mutig festem Schritt.
> Kameraden, die Rotfront und Reaktion erschossen,
> Marschier'n im Geist in unseren Reihen mit.
>
> Die Strasse frei den braunen Bataillonen,
> Die Strasse frei dem Sturmabteilungsmann!

Es schau'n aufs Hakenkreuz voll Hoffnung schon Millionen,
Der Tag für Freiheit und für Brot bricht an!

Zum letzten Mal wird nun Appell geblasen!
Zum Kampfe steh'n wir alle schon bereit!
Bald flattern Hitlerfahnen über alle Strassen,
Die Knechtschaft dauert nur noch kurze Zeit!

Die Fahne hoch! Die Reihen dicht geschlossen!
SA marschiert mit mutig festem Schritt,
Kameraden, die Rotfront und Reaktion erschossen,
Marchier'n im Geist in unseren Reihen mit.

13. Quoted by Heiber, *Goebbels,* 70.

14. Otto Strasser has left an interesting account of this meeting in a pamphlet he wrote shortly afterward, in 1930; the pamphlet is entitled *Ministersessel oder Revolution? Eine wahrheitsgemässe Darstellung meiner Trennung von der NSDAP.* Otto Strasser was not always a trustworthy source on Hitler, but his account of this meeting probably comes fairly close to the truth.

15. Peukert, *Weimar Republic,* 209.

16. Edgar J Jung, *Herrschaft der Minderwertigen* (Berlin: Deutsche Rundschau, 1927).

17. Oswald Spengler, *Politische Schriften* (Munich: Beck, 1932), 189. For Spengler's political views, see also Klaus P. Fischer, *History and Prophecy: Oswald Spengler and the Decline of the West* (New York: Peter Lang, 1989), and Detlef Felken, *Oswald Spengler: Konservativer Denker zwischen Kaiserreich und Diktatur* (Munich: Beck, 1988).

18. Fest, *Hitler,* 289.

19. Quoted by Fest, *Hitler,* 292.

20. Merkl, *Political Violence under the Swastika,* 383–407.

21. Wolfgang Sauer in *Die nationalsozialistische Machtergreifung: Studien zur Errichtung des totalitären Herrschaftssystems in Deutschland, 1933/34* (Berlin: Ullstein, 1962), 3:223.

22. Ibid., 3:222.

23. Edouard Calic, *Unmasked: Two Confidential Interviews with Hitler in 1931* (London: Chatto and Windus, 1971), 17–46.

24. Unfortunately much of the information on Hitler's movements comes from Otto Dietrich's self-serving recollections, which Henry Turner has aptly described as "a sycophantic codification of the myths of the NSDAP" (Turner, *German Big Business and the Rise of Hitler,* 171). However, Dietrich's general account of Hitler's efforts that summer is accurate; it is only in his exaggerated claims that Hitler won over the leaders of big business that Dietrich cannot be trusted (see Dietrich's memoirs, *Mit Hitler in die Macht* [Munich: Eher Verlag, 1934]).

25. That Hitler received very little in financial contributions from big business was confirmed by none other than Dietrich himself, who changed his tune after the war by stating that the leaders of big business were still decidedly reserved and that Hitler had to rely on membership dues and fees for rallies in his efforts to raise funds for Nazi propaganda (Dietrich, *Zwölf Jahre mit Hitler* [Munich: Isar, 1955], 185). See also Turner, *German Big Business and the*

Rise of Hitler, 171–72. There is also a very balanced account in Bullock, *Hitler,* 171–75.

26. Hanfstaengl, *Unheard Witness,* 169.

27. Several commentators on Hitler insist that the relationship was definitely aberrant. See Walter Langer, *The Mind of Adolf Hitler* (New York: Basic Books, 1972), 188–89; Waite, *Psychopathic God,* 274–75; and Norbert Bromberg and Verna Volz Small, *Hitler's Psychopathology* (New York: International Universities Press, 1983), 247–49. These three sources, however, base their judgments on hearsay, primarily derived from Otto Strasser's revelation in an interview in Montreal in 1943 in which he said that Geli had told him that Hitler made her undress and "squat over his face where he could examine her at close range and this made him very excited. When the excitement reached its peak, he demanded that she urinate on him and that gave him physical pleasure" (Quoted by Waite, *Psychopathic God,* 275). Coming from Otto Strasser, this account is practically worthless. However, the persistence of dark hints and insinuations by people close to Hitler, combined with other indirect evidence, seems to lend weight to the argument that Hitler was a sexual pervert.

28. Toland, *Hitler,* 1:265.

29. Quoted by Waite, *Psychopathic God,* 57.

30. The women in question were Mimi Reiter, a pretty, blonde clerk in her mother's dress shop on the ground floor of Hitler's hotel in Berchtesgaden; Geli Raubal; Eva Braun; Inge Ley, last wife of the Labor Front leader; the actress Renate Müller; and Unity Mitford, daughter of Lord Redesdale. All tried to commit suicide; four succeeded in killing themselves (Raubal, Braun, Müller, and Ley). Several other relationships, probably platonic, have also been noted by historians, including Hitler's friendship with the film director Leni Riefenstahl (see Waite, *Psychopathic God,* 258–69).

31. Hans Otto Meissner and Harry Wilde, *Die Machtergreifung: Ein Bericht über die Technik des nationalsozialistischen Staatsstreiches* (Stuttgart: J. G. Cotta'sche Buchhandlung, 1958), 49.

32. Bracher, *Auflösung,* 431–32.

33. Interestingly enough, the chief author of the Boxheim Paper, Dr. Werner Best, was not expelled from the party. On the contrary, he enjoyed a very successful career as a high legal official in the Nazi Ministry of the Interior.

34. Joseph Goebbels, *Vom Kaiserhof zur Reichskanzlei: Eine historische Darstellung in Tagebuchblättern* (Munich: Eher, 1934), 20.

35. Max Domarus, ed., *Hitler: Reden und Proklamationen 1932-1945,* 4 vols. (Wiesbaden: R. Löwit, 1973), 1:87.

36. Ibid., 1:71.

37. Ibid., 1:90.

38. Turner, *German Big Business and the Rise of Hitler,* 216–18.

39. Milton Mayer, *They Thought They Were Free* (Chicago: Univ. of Chicago Press, 1955), 101.

40. Consult the excellent chronicle of Hitler's activities in Milan Hauner, *Hitler: A Chronicle of His Life and Time* (New York: St. Martin's Press, 1983).

41. Fest, *Hitler,* 320.

42. Merkl, *Making of a Stormtrooper,* chap. 2.

43. Goebbels, *Vom Kaiserhof zur Reichskanzlei,* 93.

44. Bracher, *Auflösung,* 490.

45. See Otto Braun's account of the devastating consequences of the Nazi upsurge in Prussia, especially the revolting antics of Nazis and Communists in undermining democracy and human decency (Braun, *Von Weimar zu Hitler* [Hamburg: Hammonia Norddeutsche Verlagsanstalt, 1949], 218–42).

46. Bracher, *Auflösung,* 503–4.

47. Goebbels, *Vom Kaiserhof zur Reichskanzlei,* 95.

48. Bracher, *German Dictatorship,* 169.

49. Heinrich Brüning, *Memoiren 1918–1934* (Stuttgart: Deutsche Verlags-Anstalt, 1970), 599.

50. Mann, *History of Germany,* 403.

51. Quoted by Wheeler-Bennett, *Nemesis of Power,* 246.

52. Gottfried Reinhold Treviranus, *Das Ende von Weimar: Heinrich Brüning und seine Zeit* (Düsseldorf: Econ Verlag, 1968), 334.

53. Goebbels, *Vom Kaiserhof zur Reichskanzlei,* 119.

54. Arthur Koestler in *The God That Failed* (1949; reprint, New York: Bantam Books, 1965), 46–47.

55. Braun, *Von Weimar zu Hitler,* 232; also Bracher, *Auflösung,* 573–74.

56. Braun, *Von Weimar zu Hitler,* 244.

57. For the impact of these actions on the Berlin police, see Liang, *Berlin Police Force in the Weimar Republic,* chap. 5.

58. Franz von Papen, *Franz von Papen: Memoirs* (London: Andre Deutsch, 1952), 192.

59. Ibid., 192–93.

60. Theodor Abel, *Why Hitler Came into Power* (1938; reprint, Cambridge, Mass.: Harvard Univ. Press, 1986), 139.

61. Ibid.

62. Bullock, *Hitler,* 218.

63. Ibid., 220–21.

64. Ibid., 222.

65. Different versions of this burlesque have been given by historians, the most creditable being that of Meissner and Wilde (*Die Machtergreifung,* 100–101), which argues that State Secretary Meissner himself quickly wrote out the dissolution, obtained Hindenburg's signature, wrote and crossed out Neudeck, replacing it with Berlin, and rushed back to the Reichstag in the fastest Mercedes available to the presidential office.

66. Goebbels, *Vom Kaiserhof zur Reichskanzlei,* 87.

67. Domarus, *Hitler: Reden und Proklamationen,* 1:130. On March 21, 1933, the Nazis freed the five murderers under a general amnesty for crimes committed "for the good of the Reich during the Weimar period."

68. Harry Graf Kessler, *Tagebücher 1918–1937* (Frankfurt: Insel Verlag, 1961), 684. Kessler's diary, the work of a highly civilized and humane author and statesman, is an important document by a man who had no illusions about the Nazis and the barbarity to which they would descend.

69. Quoted by Bracher, *Auflösung,* 666.

70. Ibid., 672.

71. Ibid., 674.

72. Papen, *Memoirs,* 223.

73. Quoted by Stachura, *Gregor Strasser and the Rise of Nazism,* 106.

74. Ibid., 108.

75. Toland, *Hitler,* 1:294–95.

76. Ibid., 111.
77. Goebbels, *Vom Kaiserhof zur Reichskanzlei,* 229.
78. Toland, *Hitler,* 1:296. Hitler had expressed the same sentiments to Goebbels in early December: "If the party should collapse one day, then I will end it in three minutes with a pistol" (*Vom Kaiserhof zur Reichskanzlei,* 220). It will be recalled that Hitler had threatened to commit suicide several times before and would continue to do so again in the future.
79. Editorial by Rudolf Kirchner in the *Frankfurter Zeitung,* January 1, 1933.
80. Höhne, *Machtergreifung,* 239.
81. Eliot Barculo Wheaton, *The Nazi Revolution: 1933–1935* (New York: Doubleday, 1969), 150.
82. Bracher, *Auflösung,* 691–92.
83. Ibid., 691.
84. For an exhaustive refutation of traditional, especially Marxist, views, consult Turner, *German Big Business and the Rise of Hitler,* 313 39, and the relevant citation of documents on 459–71. Also Höhne, *Machtergreifung,* 244–45.
85. In order to dispel the charges of being a shabby intriguer, Papen denied having seen Hitler from January 4 to 22 (*Memoirs,* 236). But this is contradicted by Ribbentrop's later recollections (*Zwischen London und Moskau: Erinnerungen und letzte Aufzeichnungen,* 38–39). See also Höhne, *Machtergreifung,* 247–48, 250–51; and John Weitz, *Hitler's Diplomat: The Life and Times of Joachim von Ribbentrop* (New York: Ticknor & Fields, 1992), 53–55.
86. For the Hitler–Hindenburg meeting, see Meissner, *Die Machtergreifung,* 161–63. There is also a good reconstruction by Toland, *Hitler,* 1:299–300.
87. Meissner, *Die Machtergreifung,* 166–67.
88. Ibid.
89. It should be of more than passing interest to note that Papen does not mention this key meeting in his *Memoirs,* confirming our view that he was the one who greased the path to power for Adolf Hitler.
90. Quoted by Bracher, *Auflösung,* 705.
91. Ibid., 714.
92. Quoted by Wheeler-Bennett, *Nemesis of Power,* 280.

Conclusion: Who Supported Hitler?

1. Omitting obvious wartime propaganda, the worst examples of Germanophobia are William Shirer, *The Rise and Fall of the Third Reich* (New York: Simon & Schuster, 1960); A. J. P. Taylor, *The Course of German History* (New York: Capricorn, 1962); and Edmond Vermeil, *Germany in the Twentieth Century* (New York: Praeger, 1956).
2. Craig, *Germany, 1866–1945,* 543.
3. George L. Mosse, ed., *Nazi Culture: Intellectual, Cultural and Social Life in the Third Reich* (New York: Grosset & Dunlap, 1966), 47.
4. Merkl, *Making of a Stormtrooper,* 118; also Able, *Why Hitler Came into Power,* 142.
5. Childers, *The Nazi Voter,* 13–14.
6. Pierre Aycoberry, *The Nazi Question: Essay on the Interpretations of National Socialism, 1922–1975* (New York: Pantheon, 1981), 15.

7. Hamilton, *Who Voted for Hitler?* 6.

8. Ibid., 72, 110–12.

9. Ibid., 364.

10. Childers, *The Nazi Voter,* 262.

11. Arthur Koestler, *Arrow in the Blue: An Autobiography* (New York: Macmillan, 1952), 254.

12. Ibid.

Part Two

THE FRUITS, 1934-45

Chapter 8: The Consolidation of Power, 1933–34

1. Klaus Epstein, "The End of the German Parties in 1933," *Journal of Central European Affairs* 23 (1963) 76.

2. Quoted by Bracher, *German Dictatorship,* 195. Papen's nervous friend, later executed by the Nazis for his wartime opposition to the regime, was Ewald von Kleist-Schmenzin.

3. Domarus, *Hitler,* 1:197–98.

4. Goebbels, *Vom Kaiserreich zur Reichskanzlei,* 139.

5. Domarus, *Hitler,* 1:207.

6. J. Noakes and G. Pridham, eds., *Nazism: A History in Documents and Eyewitness Accounts, 1919–1945* (New York: Schocken Books, 1983), 1:135.

7. Ibid.

8. Martin Broszat, *The Hitler State,* trans. John W. Hiden (London: Longman, 1981), 63.

9. Ibid.

10. Leonard Mosley, *The Reich Marshal: A Biography of Hermann Göring* (New York: Dell, 1974), 186.

11. Höhne, *Order of the Death's Head,* 69.

12. Ibid., 96.

13. Mosley, *Reich Marshal,* 189; also Broszat, *Hitler State,* 65.

14. Bullock, *Hitler,* 261.

15. The most trustworthy account is still Fritz Tobias, *Der Reichstagsbrand: Legende und Wirklichkeit* (Rastatt, Baden: Grote, 1962), and the excellent recapitulation by Hans Mommsen, "Der Reichstagsbrand und seine politische Folgen," *Vierteljahreshefte für Zeitgeschichte* 4 (1964) 350–413. Other useful sources are Alfred Berndt, "Zur Entstehung des Reichtagsbrands," *Vierteljahreshefte für Zeitgeschichte* 23 (1975) 77–90; Martin Broszat, "Zum Streit um den Reichstagsbrand," *Vierteljahreshefte für Zeitgeschichte* 8 (1960) 275–79; H. Schulz-Wilde, "Legenden um den Reichstagsbrand," *Politische Studien* 13 (1962) 295–312. The evidence and credibility offered by Walter Hofer et al., *Der Reichstagsbrand: Eine Wissenschaftliche Dokumentation* (Berlin: Arani, 1972), have been seriously challenged and cannot be fully trusted. See Uwe Backe et al., *Reichstagsbrand — Aufklärung einer historischen Legende* (Munich: Piper, 1986).

16. Noakes and Pridham, *Nazism,* 1:142.

17. Ibid.

18. Bracher, *German Dictatorship*, 206.

19. Ibid., 208–9.

20. On the emerging system of concentration camps, the best book is still the gripping account by one of its victims and survivors, Eugen Kogon, *The Theory and Practice of Hell: The German Concentration Camps and the System behind Them*, trans. Heinz Norden (1950; reprint, New York: Berkeley Publishing, 1958), 22–33.

21. For a detailed description of the event, see Wheaton, *Nazi Revolution*, 283–85.

22. Noakes and Pridham, *Nazism*, 1:159–60.

23. Hermann Mau and Helmuth Krausnick, *German History, 1933–1945* (New York: Ungar, 1967), 25–27.

24. For the text, see Noakes and Pridham, *Nazism*, 1:161–62.

25. Domarus, *Hitler*, 2:245–46.

26. Bullock, *Hitler*, 270.

27. Helmuth Krausnick, "Stages of Coordination," in *The Path to Dictatorship*, 140.

28. Ibid., 136.

29. Ibid.

30. Wheaton, *Nazi Revolution*, 236.

31. For the text, Noakes and Pridham, *Nazism*, 1:167.

32. Epstein, "The End of the German Parties," 65.

33. Ibid., 68.

34. See, Wheaton, *Nazi Revolution*, 365–67.

35. Krausnick, "Stages of Coordination," 143.

36. *Deutsche Richter Zeitung* 25 (1933) 156; also Ingo Müller, *Hitler's Justice: The Courts of the Third Reich*, trans. Deborah Lucas Schneider (Cambridge, Mass.: Harvard Univ. Press, 1991), 37.

37. Müller, *Hitler's Justice*, 38.

38. Shlomo Aronson, *Reinhard Heydrich und die Frühgeschichte von Gestapo und SD* (Stuttgart: Deutsche Verlags Anstalt, 1971), 129.

39. Ibid., 130–31.

40. Fest, *Gesicht des dritten Reiches*, 191.

41. Ernst Röhm, *Die Geschichte eines Hochverräters* (Munich: Eher, 1931), 1.

42. Quoted by Fest, *Hitler*, 451–52.

43. Hermann Mau, "Die Zweite Revolution — Der 30. Juni 1934," *Vierteljahreshefte für Zeitgeschichte* 2 (1953) 125.

44. Aronson, *Reinhard Heydrich*, 191.

45. Ibid., 192.

46. Bullock, *Hitler*, 290.

47. Fest, *Hitler*, 457.

48. Ibid.

49. Heinz Höhne, *Mordsache Röhm: Hitlers Durchbruch zur Alleinherrschaft, 1933–1934* (Hamburg: Spiegel Verlag, 1984), 235.

50. Mau, "Die Zweite Revolution," 130.

51. Fest, *Hitler*, 460.

52. Höhne, *Mordsache Röhm*, 243.

53. Ibid., 246.

54. Ibid., 247.

55. Ibid., 262.

56. Domarus, *Hitler,* 1:394.

57. Höhne, *Mordsache Röhm,* 266–67.

58. Ibid., 270.

59. Ibid., 294.

60. Ibid., 295.

61. See, Höhne, *Mordsache Röhm,* 296, 319–21; Bennecke, in his book on the SA, *Hitler und die S.A.,* mentions eighty-three deaths.

62. Toland, *Hitler,* 1:367.

63. Domarus, *Hitler,* 1:409.

64. Ibid., 1:417.

65. Höhne, *Mordsache Röhm,* 303.

66. Bullock, *Hitler,* 304.

67. Noakes and Pridham, *Nazism,* 1:186.

Chapter 9: The Totalitarian Racial State

1. Cited in Franz Neumann, *Behemoth: The Structure and Practice of National Socialism, 1933–1944* (1944; reprint, New York: Harper & Row, 1966), 48.

2. Hermann Rauschning, *Gespräche mit Hitler* (New York: Europa, 1940), 232.

3. Fest, *Hitler,* 419.

4. Edward Peterson, *The Limits of Hitler's Power* (Princeton, N.J.: Princeton Univ. Press, 1969), 4.

5. Norman Rich, *Hitler's War Aims: Ideology, the Nazi State, and the Course of Expansion* (New York: Norton, 1973), 11.

6. Remak, *The Nazi Years,* 68.

7. Stern, *Hitler,* 60.

8. Quoted by Friedrich and Brzezinski, *Totalitarian Dictatorship,* 35.

9. Hans Buchheim et al., *Anatomie des SS-Staates* (Freiburg: Walter-Verlag, 1965), 1:20–21.

10. Ibid., 21.

11. Robert Koehl, "Feudal Aspects of National Socialism," *American Political Science Review* 54 (1960), 925.

12. Rich, *Hitler's War Aims,* 12.

13. Bracher, *German Dictatorship,* 212.

14. Albert Speer, *Inside the Third Reich,* trans. Richard and Clara Winston (New York: Macmillan, 1970), 131.

15. Percy Ernst Schramm, *Hitler: The Man and the Military Leader,* trans. Donald S. Detwiler (Chicago: Quadrangle Books, 1971), 57.

16. Speer, *Inside the Third Reich,* 230.

17. Ibid., 232.

18. Albert Speer, *Spandau,* trans. Richard and Clara Winston (New York: Pocket Books, 1977), 44.

19. Henry Picker, ed., *Hitlers Tischgespräche im Führerhauptquartier* (Stuttgart: Goldmann, 1981), 140.

20. Speer, *Inside the Third Reich,* 123.

21. Waite, *Psychopathic God,* 44.

22. Fest, *Hitler,* 421.

23. Waite, *Psychopathic God,* 45.

24. Ibid.

25. David Irving, *Hitler's War* (New York: Viking, 1977), 1:250.

26. Kubizek, *The Young Hitler I Knew,* 175.

27. Waite, *Psychopathic God,* 15.

28. Bullock, *Hitler,* 396–97.

29. Fest, *Hitler,* 518.

30. Waite, *Psychopathic God,* 5.

31. The Machiavellian argument that depicts Hitler primarily as either an opportunist or an old-fashioned tyrant is largely associated with the works of British historians such as A. J. P. Taylor (*The Origins of the Second World War* or *The Course of German History*), Alan Bullock (*Hitler*), and H. R. Trevor-Roper (*The Last Days of Hitler* [New York: Macmillan, 1947]).

32. See Langer, *Mind of Adolf Hitler;* Waite, *Psychopathic God;* and Bromberg and Small, *Hitler's Psychopathology.*

33. See Erich Fromm, *Anatomy of Human Destructiveness* (New York: Holt, Rinehart & Winston, 1973), 369–433.

34. See Wolfgang Treher, *Hitler, Steiner, Schreber: Ein Beitrag zur Phäno-mologie des kranken Geistes* (Emmendingen/Breisgau: Selbstverlag, 1966), 101–236.

35. See Leonard L. Heston and Renate Heston, *The Medical Casebook of Adolf Hitler* (New York: Stein & Day, 1979), a work to be balanced, however, by David Irving, ed., *The Secret Diaries of Hitler's Doctor* (New York: Macmillan, 1983).

36. See, J. Recktenwald. *Woran hat Adolf Hitler gelitten? Eine neuropsy-chiatrische Deutung* (Munich: Reinhardt, 1963); also Irving, *Secret Diaries.*

37. Waite, *Psychopathic God,* chap. 1.

38. Fest, *Hitler,* 60.

39. See Samuel Yochelson and Stanton Samenow, *The Criminal Personality* (New York: Jason Aronson, 1977), 1:265–68.

40. Domarus, *Hitler,* 3:1318.

41. Waite, *Psychopathic God,* 440.

42. Note his bloodthirsty speech to his generals on August 22, 1939, in Domarus, *Hitler,* 3:1234–39.

43. Bullock, *Hitler,* 673.

44. Rauschning, *Gespräche,* 81.

45. Fromm, *Anatomy of Human Destructiveness,* 383.

46. James M. Rodes, *The Hitler Movement: A Modern Millenarian Revolution* (Stanford, Calif.: Hoover Institution Press, 1980), 60.

47. Fest, *Hitler,* 376.

48. Speer, *Inside the Third Reich,* 106.

49. Henry Kissinger, *Diplomacy* (New York: Simon & Schuster, 1994), 290.

50. Quoted in G. M. Gilbert, *Nuremberg Diary* (1947; reprint, New York: Signet, 1961), 25.

51. Norman Cameron, *Personality Development and Psychopathology* (Boston: Houghton Mifflin, 1963), 65.

52. Fest, *Hitler,* 511.

53. Bracher, *German Dictatorship,* 233.

54. Fest, *Gesicht des dritten Reiches,* 178.

55. Kater, *The Nazi Party*, 191.
56. Ibid., 193.
57. Ibid., 208.
58. Buchheim, *Anatomie des SS-Staates*, 1:27.
59. Fest, *Gesicht des dritten Reiches*, 259.
60. Orlow, *History of the Nazi Party*, 2:487.
61. Bracher, *German Dictatorship*, 276.
62. Orlow, *History of the Nazi Party*, 2:14–16.
63. Ibid., 2:16.
64. Ibid., 2:487.
65. Kater, *The Nazi Party*, 194.
66. Ibid., 196.
67. Ibid., 190.
68. Ibid., 235–36.
69. Broszat, *Hitler State*, 265.
70. Ibid., esp. 276, 294–327, 348.
71. Peterson, *Limits of Hitler's Powers*, 27.
72. Ibid., 30.
73. Broszat, *Hitler State*, 280–82.
74. Richard Grunberger, *The Twelve-Year Reich* (New York: Holt, Rinehart & Winston, 1971), 334.
75. Peterson, *Limits of Hitler's Powers*, 51–52.
76. Louis P. Lochner, ed., *The Goebbels Diaries* (1948; reprint, New York: Popular Library, n.d.), 420.
77. Ibid., 346.
78. Thomas Power, *Heisenberg's War: The Secret History of the German Bomb* (New York: Alfred A. Knopf, 1993), 96–97.
79. For an excellent treatment of German science under the Nazis, see Allan Beyerchen, *Scientists under Hitler: Politics and the Physics Community in the Third Reich* (New Haven Conn.: Yale Univ. Press, 1977).
80. Fest, *Gesicht des dritten Reiches*, 138.
81. Ibid., 120.
82. Jane Caplan, *Government without Administration: State and Civil Service in Weimar and Nazi Germany* (Oxford: Oxford Univ. Press, 1988), 171.
83. Ibid., 172.
84. Heiber, *Goebbels*, 171–72.
85. Peterson, *Limits of Hitler's Powers*, 56–57.
86. See the interesting account in Leni Riefenstahl's *Leni Riefenstahl: A Memoir* (New York: St. Martin's Press, 1992), 140–41.
87. See Heiber, *Goebbels*, 240–46.
88. Quoted by Peterson, *Limits of Hitler's Powers*, 67.
89. Ibid., 67.
90. Caplan, *Government without Administration*, 134–37.
91. Broszat, *Hitler State*, 116.
92. Quoted by Broszat, *Hitler State*, 112.
93. Caplan, *Government without Administration*, 155.
94. Ibid., 156–57.
95. Ibid., 136.

96. See Hans Mommsen, *Beamtentum im Dritten Reich* (Stuttgart: Deutsche Verlags-Anstalt, 1966), 13ff.

97. Gerhard Schulz, *Die Nationalsozialistische Machtergreifung* (Berlin: Ullstein, 1974), 2:139–54.

98. Höhne, *Order of the Death's Head,* 219–20.

99. Ibid., 224.

100. See Tim Mason, "Labour in the Third Reich," *Past and Present* 33 (1966) 112–41, and *Sozialpolitik im Dritten Reich: Arbeiterklasse und Volksgemeinschaft* (Opladen: Westdeutscher Verlag, 1977).

101. Broszat, *Hitler State,* 304.

102. Mosley, *Reich Marshal,* 270.

103. Fest, *Gesicht des dritten Reiches,* 105.

104. Trevor-Roper, *Last Days of Hitler,* 15.

105. Mosley, *Reich Marshall,* 324.

106. Fest, *Gesicht des dritten Reiches,* 108.

107. Ibid., 157.

108. Gerald Reitlinger, *The SS: Alibi of a Nation, 1922–1945* (Englewood Cliffs, N.J.: Prentice-Hall, 1981), 16.

109. Höhne, *Order of the Death's Head,* 35.

110. See Bradley F. Smith, *Heinrich Himmler: A Nazi in the Making, 1900–1926* (Stanford, Calif.: Hoover Institution Press, 1971), and Peter Loewenberg's excellent essay, "The Unsuccessful Adolescence of Heinrich Himmler," in his *Decoding the Past* (Berkeley: Univ. of California Press, 1985).

111. In the case of Himmler's father, and perhaps many others like him, the term "sadistic" may not be too inappropriate. There is a telling episode, recounted by Peter Padfield (*Himmler: Reichsführer SS* [New York: Henry Holt], 1990], 16–17), in which a student in Professor Himmler's school recalls a particularly nasty form of mental torture he had to endure at the hand of the sadistic professor in front of his class.

112. Fromm, *Anatomy of Human Destructiveness,* 304–5.

113. Roger Manvell and Heinrich Fraenkel, *Himmler* (New York: Paperback Library, 1968), 20ff.

114. Smith, *Heinrich Himmler,* 113.

115. See George L. Mosse, *The Crisis of German Ideology: The Intellectual Origins of the Third Reich* (New York: Grosset & Dunlap, 1964), 116–20.

116. Loewenberg, "The Unsuccessful Adolescence of Heinrich Himmler," 213.

117. Fromm, *Anatomy of Human Destructiveness,* 301.

118. Trevor-Roper, *Last Days of Hitler,* 18–19.

119. Quoted by Fest, *Gesicht des dritten Reiches,* 160.

120. Shlomo Aronson, *Reinhard Heydrich und die Frühgeschichte von Gestapo und SD* (Munich: Oldenbourg, 1971), 17.

121. Ibid., 19.

122. Fest, *Gesicht des dritten Reiches,* 139.

123. Ibid.

124. Ibid., 142.

125. Aronson, *Reinhard Heydrich,* 97–98.

126. Höhne, *Order of the Death's Head,* 236–54.

127. Quoted by Höhne, *Order of the Death's Head,* 150.

128. Ibid., 246.

129. Aronson, *Reinhard Heydrich*, 204.

130. Ibid., 225.

131. Höhne, *Order of the Death's Head*, 249–50.

132. Ibid., 1522–53.

133. Buchheim et al., *Anatomie des SS Staates*, 2:308.

134. Ibid., 2:276–77.

135. Kogon, *Theory and Practice of Hell*, 58.

136. Höhne, *Order of the Death's Head*, 227.

137. Ibid., 464.

138. Ibid., 167–68.

Chapter 10: Life in Nazi Germany

1. For a fascinating account of the making of this documentary, see Leni Riefenstahl's autobiography, *Leni Riefenstahl*, esp. 156–66.

2. Grunberger, *Twelve-Year Reich*, 75.

3. Ibid., 77.

4. Norbert Frei, *National Socialist Rule in Germany*, trans. Simon B. Steyne (Oxford: Blackwell, 1993), 84.

5. Grunberger, *Twelve-Year Reich*, 82.

6. Ibid.

7. Dorothy Thompson, "Good Bye to Germany," *Harper's Magazine*, December 1934, 12–14.

8. Howard Becker, *German Youth: Bond or Free* (London: Kegan, 1946), preface.

9. Ibid.

10. Stern, *Hitler*, 21.

11. Waite, *Psychopathic God*, 12.

12. Carl G. Jung, *Collected Works of C. G. Jung* (Princeton, N.J.: Princeton Univ. Press, 1964), 10:204.

13. Quoted by Wheaton, *Nazi Revolution*, 123.

14. Speer, *Inside the Third Reich*, 10.

15. See Joachim Fest's indictment of such youthful protests in *Das Gesicht des Dritten Reiches*, 300–18. Although in many ways a just indictment, it misses the positive cultural protest by accentuating the extreme reactionary side.

16. Noakes and Pridham, *Nazism*, 1:419.

17. Ibid., 1:421.

18. Frei, *National Socialist Rule*, 87.

19. Kurt Zentner, *Illustrierte Geschichte des Dritten Reiches* (Cologne: Lingen Verlag, n.d.), 2:321.

20. See Hitler's rantings on the subject in *Mein Kampf*, 625ff.

21. Ibid., 613.

22. Ibid.

23. Rauschning, *Gespräche*, 237.

24. Mosse, *Nazi Culture*, 127.

25. Ibid.

26. Grunberger, *Twelve-Year Reich*, 287–88.

27. Ibid.

28. Ibid.

29. Gilmer W. Blackburn, *Education in the Third Reich: A Study of Race and History in the Nazi Textbooks* (Albany: State Univ. of New York Press, 1985), 41.

30. Hitler quoted as a motto in Emil Jörns and Julius Schwab, *Rassenhygienische Fibel* (Berlin: A. Metzner, 1933); also Hans Peter Bleuel, *Sex and Society in Nazi Germany*, trans. J. Maxwell Brownjohn (New York: Bantam, 1974), 141.

31. Michael Burleigh and Wolfgang Wippermann, *The Racial State: Germany 1933–1945* (Cambridge: Cambridge Univ. Press, 1991), 213.

32. Speech by Hitler on December 4, 1938, in Reichenberg, quoted by Burleigh and Wippermann, *Racial State*, 206–7.

33. H. W. Koch, *The Hitler Youth: Origins and Development, 1922–45* (New York: Dorset, 1975), 180.

34. Ibid., 196.

35. Ibid., 199.

36. Horst Krüger, "Das Grunewald-Gymnasium: Eine Erinnerung an die Banalität des Bösen," in Marcel Reich-Ranicki, ed., *Meine Schulzeit im Dritten Reiche* (Cologne: Kiepenheuer & Witsch, 1982), 49.

37. Grunberger, *Twelve-Year Reich*, 234–35.

38. Ibid., 235.

39. This aptly chosen phrase comes from Friedrich and Brzezinski *Totalitarian Dictatorship*, 239.

40. Quoted by Mosse, *Nazi Culture*, 41.

41. Quoted by Waite, *Psychopathic God*, 57.

42. Mosse, *Nazi Culture*, 39.

43. Quoted by Grunberger, *Twelve-Year Reich*, 260.

44. Mosse, *Nazi Culture*, 47.

45. Jochen von Lang, *The Secretary: Martin Bormann: The Man Who Manipulated Hitler*, trans. Christa Armstrong and Peter White (Athens: Ohio Univ. Press, 1979), 276.

46. H. R. Trevor-Roper, ed., *The Bormann Letters: The Private Correspondence between Martin Bormann and His Wife* (London: Weidenfeld and Nicolson, 1954), xx.

47. An excellent groundbreaking work in this connection is Claudia Koonz, *Mothers in the Fatherland: Women, the Family and Nazi Politics* (New York: St. Martin's Press, 1981).

48. Erik H. Erikson, *Identity, Youth and Crisis* (New York: Norton, 1968), 45.

49. Koonz, *Mothers in the Fatherland*, 5.

50. Even decades later, German women who grew up during the Nazi period still tended to cling to self-deceptive attitudes and widespread denials. For a splendid piece of oral history on this subject, see Alison Owings, *Frauen: German Women Recall the Third Reich* (New Brunswick, N.J.: Rutgers Univ. Press, 1993).

51. Quoted by Jill Stephenson, *Women in Nazi Germany* (New York: Barnes & Noble, 1975), 8.

52. Koonz, *Mothers in the Fatherland*, xxiii.

53. Grunberger, *Twelve-Year Reich*, 435.

54. Quoted by John S. Conway, *The Nazi Persecution of the Churches, 1933–1945* (London: Weidenfeld & Nicolson, 1968), 330.

55. Picker, *Hitlers Tischgespräche,* 80.

56. Ibid., 329.

57. Grunberger, *Twelve-Year Reich,* 444.

58. Ibid., 159.

59. Klemens von Klemperer, *German Resistance against Hitler: The Search for Allies Abroad, 1938–1945* (Oxford: Clarendon, 1992), 39.

60. Domarus, *Hitler,* 2:975–76.

61. Grunberger, *Twelve-Year Reich,* 341.

62. J. M. Ritchie, *German Literature under National Socialism* (Totowa, N.J.: Barnes & Noble, 1983), 187.

63. For a fair assessment of why men of great talent and achievement initially supported the Nazis, see Craig, *Germany, 1866–1945,* 639–45.

64. Ritchie, *German Literature,* 70.

65. Speer, *Inside the Third Reich,* 64.

66. Ibid., 132.

67. Richard D. Mandell, *The Nazi Olympics* (New York: Ballantine, 1971), 329–30.

68. Quoted by Ritchie, *German Literature,* 115. See also Ernst Loewy's general assessment in *Literatur unter dem Hackenkreuz* (Frankfurt: Europäische Verlagsanstalt, 1966), which is less condemnatory than Mann's, but nevertheless as severe.

69. Grunberger, *Twelve-Year Reich,* 341.

70. Heiber, *Goebbels,* 148.

71. Ibid., 147.

72. Michael Kater, "Forbidden Fruit: Jazz in the Third Reich," *American Historical Review* 94, no. 1 (February 1989) 13.

73. David Stewart Hull, *Film in the Third Reich* (New York: Simon & Schuster, 1973), 8.

74. Hull, *Film in the Third Reich,* 169.

75. Riefenstahl, *Leni Riefenstahl,* 158.

76. Kracauer, *From Caligari to Hitler,* 100.

77. Neumann, *Behemoth.*

78. Ibid., 291.

79. Ibid., 228.

80. Remak, *Nazi Years,* 76.

81. Noakes and Pridham, *Nazism,* 1:281–87; for the German text, Hans-Adolf Jacobsen and Werner Jochman, eds., *Ausgewählte Dokumente zur Geschichte des Nazionalsozialismus* (Bielefeld: Verlag Neue Gesellschaft, 1961), 8:1936.

82. Noakes and Pridham, *Nazism,* 1:287.

83. Ibid., 1:289.

84. Friedrich and Brzezinski, *Totalitarian Dictatorship,* 206.

85. Cited by Dietmar Petzina, *Die deutsche Wirtschaft in der Zwischenkriegszeit* (Wiesbaden: Franz Steiner Verlag, 1977), 119.

86. Noakes and Pridham, *Nazism,* 1:306.

87. Schoenbaum, *Hitler's Social Revolution,* 156ff.

88. Frei, *Der Führerstaat,* 77.

89. Schoenbaum, *Hitler's Social Revolution,* 104–5.

90. Grunberger, *Twelve-Year Reich,* 198.

91. See, Schoenbaum, *Hitler's Social Revolution*. Schoenbaum appears to argue that the Nazis tried to destroy bourgeois industrial society by using the bourgeoisie to do it (preface). No coherent argument can be based on such a contradiction, nor is it clear what kind of social revolution Schoenbaum had in mind. It would presumably have been a nihilistic revolution. Only the lunatic "blood and soil" fringe of the NSDAP wanted to deemphasize industrialism in favor of large-scale agriculture.

92. Frei, *National Socialist Rule,* 80.

93. Schoenbaum, *Hitler's Social Revolution,* 13.

94. Broszat, *Hitler State,* 21–22.

95. Two groundbreaking works in English stand out in particular: Burleigh and Wippermann, *Racial State;* and Proctor, *Racial Hygiene.*

96. Proctor, *Racial Hygiene,* 20.

97. Ibid., 56.

98. Ibid., 64.

99. Ibid., 101.

100. Burleigh and Wippermann, *Racial State,* 138.

101. Proctor, *Racial Hygiene,* 101–2, 108.

102. For the law, Noakes and Pridham, *Nazism,* 1:535–36.

103. Ibid., 1:537.

104. Proctor, *Racial Hygiene,* 138–39.

105. Ibid., 120–21.

106. For an excellent discussion of this little-known topic of the Gypsies and their treatment by the Nazis, see Burleigh and Wippermann, *Racial State,* 113–35.

107. On the *Rheinlandbastarde,* another neglected topic, see Proctor, *Racial Hygiene,* 112–14.

108. Höhne, *Order of the Death's Head,* 162.

109. Burleigh and Wippermann, *Racial State,* 196.

110. Müller, *Hitler's Justice,* 181–82.

111. Hull, *Film in the Third Reich,* 200–203; also Proctor, *Racial Hygiene,* 182–83.

112. Burleigh and Wippermann, *Racial State,* 142.

113. Ibid., 150.

114. Ibid., 152.

115. Ibid., 153.

116. Lucy S. Dawidowicz, *The War against the Jews, 1933–1945* (New York: Bantam Books, 1976), 77–78.

117. Ibid., 134–35.

118. Ibid., 252.

119. Helmut Krausnick, in Buchheim, *Anatomie des SS Staates,* 2:340.

120. Noakes and Pridham, *Nazism,* 2:1049. For the German text, Domarus, *Hitler,* 3:1058.

Chapter 11: The Road to War, 1933–39

1. Laurence Lafore, *The End of Glory: An Interpretation of the Origins of World War II* (New York: J. B. Lippincott, 1970), 39.

2. On the diplomacy of the Western powers between the wars, see Arnold Wolfers, *Britain and France between the Wars* (New York: Norton, 1966);

E. H. Carr, *International Relations between the Two World Wars, 1919–1939* (New York: Harper & Row, 1966); Gordon Craig and Felix Gilbert, eds., *The Diplomats, 1919–1939*, 2 vols. (New York: Atheneum, 1963); Pierre Renouvin, *World War II and Its Origins: International Relations 1919–1945*, trans. Remy Inglis Hall (New York: Harper & Row, 1969); and Taylor, *Origins of the Second World War.*

3. Wolfers, *Britain and France*, 12.

4. Ibid., 25–27.

5. Ibid., 27.

6. Ibid., 382–83.

7. Taylor, *Origins of the Second World War*, 72.

8. Hildebrand, *Foreign Policy of the Third Reich*, 12, 136.

9. Gerhard L. Weinberg, *The Foreign Policy of Hitler's Germany: Diplomatic Revolution in Europe, 1919–1936* (Chicago: Univ. of Chicago Press), 1:8–9.

10. Hitler, *Mein Kampf*, 950.

11. Rauschning, *Gespräche*, 22.

12. Craig and Gilbert, *Diplomats*, 2:407–8.

13. Papen, *Memoirs*, 340–41.

14. Weitz, *Hitler's Diplomat*, 5.

15. Ibid., 6

16. Ibid., 27.

17. Ibid., 42.

18. Ibid., 122.

19. Craig and Gilbert, *Diplomats*, 2:420.

20. Quoted by Fest, *Das Gesicht des Dritten Reiches*, 246.

21. Craig and Gilbert, *Diplomats*, 2:436.

22. Ibid.

23. Quoted by Andreas Hillgruber, *Germany and the Two World Wars*, trans. William C. Kirby (Cambridge, Mass.: Harvard Univ. Press, 1981), 56–57.

24. Jacobsen and Jochman, *Ausgewählte Dokumente*, doc. no. 4; also Weinberg, *Foreign Policy of Hitler's Germany*, 1:26–27.

25. Herbert Rosinski, *The German Army* (New York: Praeger, 1966), 188.

26. Domarus, *Hitler*, 1:272.

27. Ibid., 1:277.

28. Rauschning, *Gespräche*, 113.

29. There is an excellent portrait of Beck by Henry L. Roberts in Craig and Gilbert, *Diplomats*, 2:579–614.

30. Hitler, *Mein Kampf*, 908.

31. For the series of invectives Mussolini hurled at Hitler, see E. R. Starhemberg, *Between Hitler and Mussolini* (London: Hodder & Stoughton, 1942), 164–68.

32. Weinberg, *Foreign Policy of Hitler's Germany*, 1:102–4.

33. Bullock, *Hitler*, 332.

34. Paul Schmidt, *Statist auf Diplomatischer Bühne, 1923–1945* (Bonn: Athenäum Verlag, 1952), 300. Also Domarus, *Hitler*, 2:498.

35. Schmidt, *Statist*, 302.

36. Bullock, *Hitler*, 340.

37. Schmidt, *Statist*, 320; Bullock, *Hitler*, 345.

38. André François-Poncet, *The Fateful Years* (London: Gollancz, 1949), 193.

39. Quoted by Churchill, *The Second World,* 1:197–98.

40. Bullock, *Hitler,* 350.

41. *Documents on German Foreign Policy, 1918–1945* (Washington D.C.: U.S. Department of State, 1949–), series D, 3:783. Hereafter cited as *DGFP.*

42. Quoted by Bullock, *Hitler,* 361.

43. For the relevant document, *DGFP,* series D, 1:29

44. Weitz, *Hitler's Diplomat,* 141–42.

45. For a detailed discussion of these military "scandals," see Wheeler-Bennett, *Nemesis of Power,* pt. 3, chaps. 2 and 3.

46. Hitler, *Mein Kampf,* 3.

47. *DGFP,* series D, 1:282.

48. On Seyss-Inquart, see H. J. Neumann, *Arthur Seyss-Inquart* (Utrecht: Nederlandsche Boekhandel, 1967).

49. See Schmidt, *Statist,* 377–78.

50. *DGFP,* series D, 1:448–49, 463–64.

51. Kurt von Schuschnigg, *Austrian Requiem,* trans. Franz von Hildebrand (London: Gollancz, 1947), 21.

52. Ibid.

53. This comes from Papen's account in *Memoirs,* 417; also Bullock, *Hitler,* 424.

54. Schuschnigg, *Austrian Requiem,* 30.

55. Ibid., 131.

56. Ibid., 32.

57. Ibid., 251–52.

58. Ibid., 51.

59. *DGFP,* series D, 1:374.

60. Galeazzo Ciano, *Ciano's Hidden Diary, 1937–1938,* trans. Andreas Mayor (New York: E. P. Dutton, 1953), 87.

61. Quoted by Bullock, *Hitler,* 431–32.

62. *DGFP,* Series D, 1:302.

63. Ibid.

64. Gordon Brook-Shepherd, *The Anschluss: The Rape of Austria* (New York: Lippincott, 1963), 91.

65. Bullock, *Hitler,* 439.

66. *Documents on British Foreign Policy, 1919–1939* (London: H.M. Stationary Office, 1949), series 3, 1:198–325.

67. Wheeler-Bennett, *Munich,* 46–47.

68. Ibid., 48.

69. Noakes and Pridham, *Nazism,* 2:712.

70. This speech, reprinted in Domarus (*Hitler,* 2:924–32), was probably his most compelling performance as a political demagogue. Even Hitler was intoxicated by his performance, gazing at the sky and being absolutely delighted by his own words.

71. Bullock, *Hitler,* 454.

72. Domarus, *Hitler,* 2:907.

73. Wheeler-Bennett, *Munich,* 132; also Schmidt, *Statist,* 401.

74. Wheeler-Bennett, *Munich,* 134.

75. Ibid., 135.

76. Ibid., 137.

77. Schmidt, *Statist*, 407.

78. Domarus, *Hitler*, 2:922–23; also Kirkpatrick's recollection in *DGFP*, series 3, 2:1118.

79. On the Munich Conference and appeasement in general, Wheeler-Bennett, *Munich*; K. Eubank, *Munich* (Norman, Okla.: Univ. of Oklahoma Press, 1963); Andrew Rothstein, *The Munich Conspiracy* (London: Lawrence and Wishart, 1958); Martin Gilbert, *The Roots of Appeasement* (London: Weidenfeld and Nicolson, 1966). For a fresh reexamination of British motives and policies, R. A. C. Parker, *Chamberlain and Appeasement: British Policy and the Coming of the Second World War* (New York: St. Martin's, 1994).

80. Wheeler-Bennett, *Munich*, 16.

81. For the text of the memorandum, see Noakes and Pridham, *Nazism*, 2:718–20.

82. Quoted by Bullock, *Hitler*, 469.

83. *Parliamentary Debates*, 5th series, vol. 339 (October 5, 1938).

84. Ibid.

85. François-Poncet, *Fateful Years*, 280–91.

86. Ibid.

87. *DGFP*, series D, 4:68.

88. For Hacha's ordeal, see Schmidt, *Statist*, 427–31.

89. *DGFP*, series D, 4:270.

90. Quoted by Bullock, *Hitler*, 485.

91. Ibid., 486–87.

92. Weitz, *Hitler's Diplomat*, 195.

93. *Parliamentary Debates*, vol. 345, col. 2415.

94. Fest, *Hitler*, 578.

95. For the text of Operation White, Noakes and Pridham, *Nazism*, 2:735–36.

96. For the entire text, see Domarus, *Hitler*, 3:1148–79.

97. Bullock, *Hitler*, 507–8.

98. For the text of the treaty, see Walther Hofer, ed., *Der National Sozialismus: Dokumente, 1933–1945* (Frankfurt: Fischer, 1957), 227–29.

99. Quoted by Craig, *Germany, 1866–1945*, 711.

100. For the full text, see Noakes and Pridham, *Nazism*, 2:743–44.

101. There are several versions, taken from notes by various military commanders who were present at this unusual meeting. The most reliable is the one by Admiral Canaris, *DGFP*, series D, 7:200–206, which is reprinted in Noakes and Pridham, *Nazism*, 2:739–43. See also Domarus, *Hitler*, 3:1233–38; Bullock, *Hitler*, 525–27.

102. *International Military Tribunal: Trial of the Major War Criminals before the International Military Tribunal: Proceedings and Documents*, 42 vols (Nuremberg, 1947–49), 26:798-PS; also Fest, *Hitler*, 594.

103. *International Military Tribunal*, 26:1014-PS.

104. Ibid.

105. Lafore, *End of Glory*, 247.

106. Quoted by Craig, *Germany, 1866–1945*, 712–13.

107. Birger Dahlerus, *The Last Attempt* (London: Hutchinson, 1947).

108. Noakes and Pridham, *Nazism*, 2:743.

109. Höhne, *Order of the Death's Head,* 294ff.
110. Domarus, *Hitler,* 3:1315.

Chapter 12: Blitzkrieg: The Expansion of German Power, 1939-41

1. Noakes and Pridham, *Nazism,* 1:740.
2. Quoted by Gilbert, *Nuremberg Diary,* 205.
3. William L. Shirer, *Berlin Diary* (1941; reprint, New York: Popular Library, 1961), 151.
4. Domarus, *Hitler,* 2:1334.
5. Schmidt, *Statist,* 464.
6. Quoted by Gordon Wright, *The Ordeal of Total War, 1939–1945* (New York: Harper & Row, 1968), 44.
7. Shirer, *Berlin Diary,* 281.
8. Alan Clark, *Barbarossa: The Russian-German Conflict, 1941–45* (New York: Signet, 1966), 25.
9. Trevor-Roper, *Last Days of Hitler,* 1.
10. Helmuth Günther Dahms, *Die Geschichte des Zweiten Weltkriegs* (Munich: F. A. Herbig, 1983), 65–66.
11. For a detailed account of the German high command, see Helmut Greiner, *Die Oberste Wehrmachtsführung, 1933–1943* (Wiesbaden, 1951); Walther Hubatsch, ed., *Hitlers Weisungen für die Kriegsführung* (Frankfurt: Bernard & Graefe, 1962); and W. Warlimont, *Im Hauptquartier der deutschen Wehrmacht* (Frankfurt: Bernard und Graefe, 1962). For the most lucid English account, H. R. Trevor-Roper, ed., *Blitzkrieg to Defeat: Hitler's War Directives 1933–1945* (New York: Holt, Rinehart & Winston, 1964).
12. For an excellent account of Germany's economic preparedness for war, see Alan S. Milward, *The German Economy at War* (London: Oxford Univ. Press, 1965).
13. These figures are taken from Dahms, *Geschichte des Zweiten Weltkriegs,* 79–80.
14. Frei, *National Socialist Rule,* 113–14.
15. B. H. Liddell Hart, *Strategy* (New York: Praeger, 1960), 236.
16. O. D. Tolischus, in *New York Times,* Sept. 12, 1939; Wright, *Ordeal of Total War,* 17.
17. Gerhard Weinberg, *A World at Arms: A Global History of World War II* (Cambridge: Cambridge Univ. Press, 1994), 63.
18. On the real facts pertaining to Elser, see Anton Hoch, "Das Attentat auf Hitler im Münchner Bürgerbräukeller," *Vierteljahreshefte für Zeitgeschichte* 17 (1969) 383–413.
19. For an excellent discussion of Manstein's plan, see B. H. Liddell Hart, *History of the Second World War* (New York: Putnam, 1970), 33–41; also idem, *The German Generals Talk* (New York: William Morrow, 1964), chap. 10.
20. Liddell Hart, *History of the Second World War,* 37.
21. Ibid., 40.
22. Irving, *Hitler's War,* 1:68.
23. B. H. Liddell Hart, *The German Generals Talk* (New York: Morrow, 1948), 124–25.

24. Domarus, *Hitler*, 3:1502–3.
25. Quoted by Irving, *Hitler's War*, 1:125.
26. Liddell Hart, *German Generals Talk*, 129.
27. Ibid., 130.
28. Fest, *Hitler*, 631.
29. Liddell Hart, *Strategy*, 247.
30. Ibid., 248.
31. Churchill, *Second World War*, 2:101.
32. Liddell Hart, *History of the Second World War*, 79–80.
33. Churchill, *Second World War*, 2:76.
34. Quoted by Richard Humble, *Hitler's Generals* (New York: Kensington, 1973), 68.
35. Shirer, *Berlin Diary*, 311–15.
36. Irving, *Hitler's War*, 1:143; also Fest, *Hitler*, 636.
37. Fest, *Hitler*, 636.
38. Craig, *Germany, 1866–1945*, 714.
39. Bullock, *Hitler*, 588.
40. *The Cambridge Modern History* (Cambridge: Cambridge Univ. Press, 1968), 12:757.
41. Weinberg, *World at Arms*, 200.
42. Churchill, *Second World War*, 2:586.
43. Quoted by Bullock, *Hitler*, 606.
44. Ibid., 610.
45. Weinberg, *World at Arms*, 211.
46. Trevor-Roper, *Blitzkrieg to Defeat*, 46–48.
47. Bullock, *Hitler*, 635.
48. Fest, *Hitler*, 645.
49. Bullock, *Hitler*, 638.
50. Fest, *Hitler*, 646.
51. Bullock, *Hitler*, 652.
52. Quoted by Clark, *Barbarossa*, 65.
53. Fest, *Hitler*, 648.
54. Clark, *Barbarossa*, 65.
55. Quoted by Bullock, *Hitler*, 640–41.
56. *Hitler's Secret Conversations, 1941–44* (1953; reprint, New York: Octagon Books, 1972), 13.
57. Ibid., 259; also Picker, *Hitlers Tischgespräche*, 107.
58. Richard Breitman, *The Architect of Genocide: Himmler and the Final Solution* (New York: Knopf, 1991), 169–70; also Fest, *Hitler*, 649–50.
59. Domarus, *Hitler*, 3:1683–84.
60. Quoted by Fest, *Hitler*, 650.
61. Clark, *Barbarossa*, 70.
62. Domarus, *Hitler*, 3:1758.
63. Ibid., 1764.
64. Hillgruber, *Germany and the Two World Wars*, 80–81.
65. Clark, *Barbarossa*, 76.
66. Ibid.
67. Ibid., 200.
68. Ibid., 206.

69. Paul Carell, *Unternehmen Barbarossa: Der March nach Russland* (Berlin: Ullstein, 1963), 276.

70. Ibid., 157.

71. Ibid., 275.

72. Irving, *Hitler's War,* 1:383.

73. Ibid., 1:385.

74. For an excellent discussion of Hitler's declaration of war on the United States, see Rich, *Hitler's War Aims,* chap. 20.

75. See Waite, *Psychopathic God.,* 468–76.

76. Irving, *Hitler's War,* 1:386.

77. For the text of Hitler's December 11, 1941 speech, see Domarus, *Hitler,* 3:1797–1811.

78. Weinberg, *World at Arms,* 250–51.

79. Wright, *Ordeal of Total War,* 58.

80. Trevor-Roper, *Blitzkrieg to Defeat,* 127.

Chapter 13: The New Nazi Racial Order in Europe

1. The definitive account of Hitler's "New Order" is still Norman Rich's impressive work *Hitler's War Aims,* vol. 2: *The Establishment of the New Order.* There is also an excellent treatment of German occupied Europe in Wright, *Ordeal of Total War,* chap. 6.

2. Rich, *Hitler's War Aims,* 231–39.

3. Ibid., 172.

4. The best study of Nazi rule in Russia is still Alexander Dallin's *German Rule in Russia, 1941–1945* (London: Macmillan, 1957).

5. Rich, *Hitler's War Aims,* 376.

6. Ibid., 377.

7. Ibid., 383.

8. Ibid., 283.

9. Ibid., 142.

10. Helmut Krausnick and Hans-Heinrich Wilhelm, *Die Truppe des Weltanschauungskrieges: Die Einsatzgruppen der Sicherheitspolizei und des SD 1938–1942* (Stuttgart: Deutsche Verlags-Anstalt, 1981), 86.

11. See David Irving, *Göring* (New York: William Morrow, 1989), 298–306; also Mosley, *Reich Marshal,* 318–25.

12. *Nazi Conspiracy and Aggression* (Washington, D.C.: US Government Printing Office, 1946), 3:666–74, 1015–B-PS, and 1015–I-PS; hereafter cited as NCA.

13. Wright, *Ordeal of Total War,* 117.

14. *International Military Tribunal,* 39:390–91.

15. Ibid., 22:480.

16. *Hitler's Secret Conversations,* 343.

17. Ibid., 501.

18. Wright, *Ordeal of Total War,* 121.

19. Irving, *Hitler's War,* 2:526.

20. NCA 3:416–17, 498–PS.

21. Martin Broszat et al., eds., *Bayern in der NS-Zeit* (Munich: Oldenbourg, 1977), 1:584–85.

22. Irving, *Göring*, 423.

23. *NCA* 7:798–99, 1130–PS.

24. *International Military Tribunal*, 7:47.

25. *The Trial of German Major War Criminals*, 22 parts (London: H.M.S.O., 1946–50), pt. 4 (1946), 360. This collection was published in Britain and contains a verbatim record of the Nuremberg proceedings; they are hereafter cited as *NP* (Nuremberg proceedings).

26. Domarus, *Hitler*, 4:1790.

27. Robert Jay Lifton, *The Nazi Doctors: Medical Killing and the Psychology of Genocide* (New York: Basic Books, 1986), 301.

28. *NP*, pt. 21, 3.

29. Lifton, *Nazi Doctors*, 279.

30. *NP*, pt. 21, 11.

31. Lifton, *Nazi Doctors*, 285–86.

32. *NP*, pt. 20, 402.

33. Höhne, *Order of the Death's Head*, 560.

34. *Hitler's Table Talks*, 68–69.

35. For the text, Noakes and Pridham, *Nazism*, 2:932–34. Also Helmut Krausnick et al., "Denkschrift Himmlers über die Behandlung der fremdvölkischen im Osten," *Vierteljahreshefte für Zeitgeschichte* 4 (April 1957).

36. Quoted by Höhne, *Order of the Death's Head*, 334.

37. The words are Krausnick's, "Hitler und die Morde in Polen, *Vierteljahreshefte für Zeitgeschichte* 4 (1963) 204.

38. Höhne, *Order of the Death's Head*, 344.

39. Ibid., 355.

40. Ibid., 355–56.

41. *Hitler's Secret Conversations*, 513.

42. The best comprehensive study of the Holocaust deniers is Deborah E. Lipstadt, *Denying the Holocaust: The Growing Assault on Truth and Memory* (New York: Free Press, 1993).

43. As to who knew about the holocaust and when, there are two indispensable books: Walter Laqueur, *The Terrible Secret: Suppression of the Truth about Hitler's "Final Solution"* (New York: Penguin Books, 1982), and Gerald Fleming, *Hitler and the Final Solution* (Berkeley: Univ. of California Press, 1984).

44. Rudolf Höss, *Commandant of Auschwitz*, trans. Constantine FitzGibbon (London: Weidenfeld & Nicolson, 1951; paperback ed., New York: Popular Library, n.d.). This autobiography, written by Höss in a Polish prison, constitutes a harrowing yet important document describing his role in the final solution.

45. Hitler, *Mein Kampf*, 984.

46. Picker, *Tischgespräche*, 456.

47. Fest, *Hitler*, 681.

48. Dawidowicz, *War against the Jews*, 265.

49. For a detailed study of these murder squads, the most scholarly work is by Helmut Krausnick and Hans-Heinrich Wilhelm, *Die Truppe des Weltanschauungskrieges* (Stuttgart Deutsche Verlags-Anstalt, 1981). There are also two brief but chilling studies of the murder mentality of these forces by Christopher R. Browning, *Ordinary Men: Reserve Police Battalion 101 and the*

Final Solution in Poland (New York: HarperCollins, 1992) and Heinz Artzt, *Mörder in Uniform: Organisationen, die zu Vollstreckern nationalsozialistischer Verbrechen wurden* (Munich: Kindler, 1979).

50. Krausnick and Wilhelm, *Die Truppe des Weltanschauungskrieges,* 141.

51. Ibid., 628.

52. Höhne, *Order of the Death's Head,* 405.

53. Krausnick and Wilhelm, *Die Truppe des Weltanschauungskrieges,* 281–85.

54. Ibid., 597.

55. Quoted by Noakes and Pridham, *Nazism,* 2:1094; also Krausnick and Wilhelm, *Die Truppe des Weltanschauungskrieges,* 536–37.

56. Noakes and Pridham, *Nazism,* 2:1095.

57. Ibid., 2:1096.

58. This and similar atrocities are recorded in a book of chilling documents collected by Ernst Klee, Willi Dreesen, and Volker Riess and called *The Good Old Days: The Holocaust as Seen by Its Perpetrators and Bystanders,* trans. Deborah Burnstone (New York: Free Press, 1991). For the gruesome visual documents, see Yitzhak Arad, ed., *The Pictorial History of the Holocaust* (New York: Macmillan, 1990).

59. *NCA* 5:696–98, 2992–PS.

60. Höhne, *Order of the Death's Head,* 409.

61. Ibid.

62. Ibid.

63. Leni Yahil, *The Holocaust: The Fate of European Jewry* (New York: Oxford Univ. Press, 1990), 325.

64. Ibid., 256.

65. Quoted by Richard Breitman, *The Architect of Genocide: Himmler and the Final Solution* (New York: Alfred A. Knopf, 1991), 147.

66. Höss, *Commandant of Auschwitz,* 173.

67. Ibid., 174.

68. Breitman, *Architect of Genocide,* 112.

69. *NCA,* 3:525–26.

70. F. Kersten, *The Kersten Memoirs, 1940–45* (London: Hutchinson, 1956), 119; also Padfield, *Himmler,* 353.

71. Breitman, *Architect of Genocide,* 219; also Fleming, *Hitler and the Final Solution,* 50–60.

72. For a copy of the German document, see Jacobsen and Jochman, *Ausgewählte Dokumente,* DH Dokument, Wannsee-Protokoll from 20 January 1942; for a partial English translation, see Noakes and Pridham, *Nazism,* 2:1127–34

73. Raul Hilberg, ed., *Documents of Destruction: Germany and Jewry, 1933–1945* (Chicago: Quadrangle Books, 1971), 102–3.

74. Yahil, *The Holocaust,* 312.

75. Hannah Arendt, *Eichmann in Jerusalem: A Report on the Banality of Evil* (New York: Viking Press, 1965), 115.

76. On the use of *Zyklon-B,* see Hilberg, *Documents of Destruction,* 219–21; also Raul Hilberg, *The Destruction of the European Jews,* rev. ed. (New York: Holmes & Meier, 1985), 3:885–93.

77. Höss, *Commandant of Auschwitz,* 139.

78. Ibid., 187–88.

79. Dawidowicz, *War against the Jews,* 199.

80. Yahil, *The Holocaust,* 367–68.

81. Hilberg, *Destruction of the European Jews,* 3:883–85.

82. Yahil, *The Holocaust,* 375.

83. Viktor Frankl, *Man in Search of Meaning* (New York: Washington Square Press, 1963), 46–47.

84. Ibid., 29.

85. Ibid., 47–48.

86. Ibid., 164–65.

87. Quoted by Leonard Baker, *Days of Sorrow and Pain: Leo Baeck and the Berlin Jews* (New York: Macmillan, 1978), 315.

88. Artzt, *Mörder in Uniform,* 70–72; also Höhne, *Order of the Death's Head,* 422.

89. Hilberg, *Destruction of the European Jews,* 3:1120.

90. Quoted by Otto Friedrich, *The End of the World: A History* (New York: Coward, McCann & Geohegan, 1982), 292.

91. For the whole document, *International Military Tribunal,* 29:110–173, 1919–PS.

92. Noakes and Pridham, *Nazism,* 2:1150.

93. Arendt, *Eichmann in Jerusalem,* 22–25.

94. Ibid., 51.

95. Quoted by Fest, *Gesicht des dritten Reiches,* 172.

96. Lifton, *Nazi Doctors,* chap. 19.

97. Ibid., 442.

98. Ibid., 481.

99. Quoted by Lifton, *Nazi Doctors,* 15–16.

100. Gerald L. Posner and John Ware, *Mengele* (New York: Dell, 1986), 27–28.

101. Lifton, *Nazi Doctors,* 341.

102. Posner and Ware, *Mengele,* 12.

103. Lifton, *Nazi Doctors,* 351.

104. Quoted by Posner and Ware, *Mengele,* 46.

105. Lifton, *Nazi Doctors,* 381.

106. Weinberg, *World at Arms,* 474.

107. Ibid.

108. Laqueur, *Terrible Secret,* 56, 201.

109. Ibid., 202.

110. Hilberg, *Destruction of the European Jews,* 3:1030.

Chapter 14: The Defeat of Nazi Germany, 1942-45

1. The best and most gripping account of the battle of Stalingrad is still William Craig, *Enemy at the Gates: The Battle of Stalingrad* (New York: E. P. Dutton, 1973).

2. Hans-Adolf Jacobsen, ed., *Generaloberst Halder, Kriegstagebuch,* 3 vols. (Stuttgart: Kohlhammer, 1962), 3:489.

3. Franz Halder, *Hitler as Warlord* (New York: Putnam, 1950), 57.

4. This is also Clark's assessment in *Barbarossa,* 267. For a good snapshot of von Paulus, see Martin Middlebrook, "Paulus," in Correlli Barnett, ed., *Hitler's Generals* (New York: Grove Weidenfeld, 1989), 361–73.

5. Clark, *Barbarossa,* 236.

6. Fest, *Hitler,* 659.

7. Quoted by Clark, *Barbarossa,* 250.

8. Halder, *Hitler as Warlord,* 55–56.

9. Quoted by Percy Ernst Schramm, *Hitler: The Man and the Military Leader* (Chicago: Quadrangle Books, 1971), 114–16.

10. Paulus's testimony at Nuremberg, *NP,* pt. 6, 262; also Bullock, *Hitler,* 690.

11. Quoted by Fest, *Hitler,* 665.

12. Clark, *Barbarossa,* 345.

13. Toland, *Hitler,* 2:849.

14. Clark, *Barbarossa,* 360.

15. Domarus, *Hitler,* 4:1931.

16. Quoted by Fest, *Hitler,* 692.

17. Joachim Kramarz, *Stauffenberg: The Architect of the Famous July 20th Conspiracy to Assassinate Hitler,* trans. R. H. Barry (New York: Macmillan, 1967), 87.

18. Lochner, *Goebbels Diaries,* 306–7.

19. Fest, *Hitler,* 668.

20. Ibid., 667.

21. This is what David Irving suspects after discovering the journals of Theodor Morrell, Hitler's private physician. See, Irving, *Secret Diaries,* 17.

22. Waite, *Psychopathic God,* 408–9; also Irving, *Secret Diaries.*

23. Maser, *Hitler,* 215.

24. Heston and Heston, *Medical Casebook,* 113, 134.

25. Jill Stephenson, *The Nazi Organization of Women* (Totowa, N.J.: Barnes & Noble, 1981), 180–81.

26. Grunberger, *Twelve-Year Reich,* 214.

27. Ibid., 215.

28. Ibid., 214–15.

29. John Keegan, *The Second World War* (New York: Viking, 1989), 421.

30. For a graphic reconstruction of the event, see David Irving, *The Destruction of Dresden* (New York: Holt, Rinehart and Winston, 1963).

31. Speer, *Inside the Third Reich,* 446.

32. Detlev J. K. Peukert, *Inside Nazi Germany: Conformity, Opposition and Racism in Everyday Life,* trans. Richard Deveson (New Haven: Yale Univ. Press, 1987). There is also a splendid collection of documents and articles on everyday life (*Alltagsgeschichte*) entitled *Bayern in der NS-Zeit,* edited in six volumes by Martin Broszat and others.

33. Terry Charman, *The German Home Front, 1939–45* (London: Barrie-Jenkins, 1989), 142.

34. The most comprehensive account on the German resistance is still Peter Hoffmann, *The History of the German Resistance, 1933–1945,* trans. Richard Barry (Cambridge, Mass.: MIT Press, 1977). Other useful works are Gerhard Ritter, *The German Resistance: Carl Goerdeler's Struggle against Tyranny,* trans. R. T. Clark (New York: Praeger, 1958); Joachim Kramarz, *Stauffenberg* (New York: Macmillan, 1967); Hans Rothfels, *Die deutsche Opposition gegen Hitler* (Frankfurt: Fischer, 1958), Bodo Scheuerig, ed., *Deutscher Widerstand: Fortschritt oder Reaktion* (Munich: Deutscher Taschenbuch Verlag, 1969); and

Fabian von Schlabrendorff, *Offiziere gegen Hitler* (Zurich: Europa Verlag, 1951).

35. See Helmut Krausnick and Hermann Graml, *Der deutsche Widerstand und die Aliierten* (Koblenz, 1962).

36. Ritter, *German Resistance,* 139.

37. For the details, see Hoffmann, *History of the German Resistance,* 263–300.

38. For a gripping account of this and other conspiratorial events, see Schlabrendorff, *Offiziere gegen Hitler.*

39. Irving, *Hitler's War,* 2:526.

40. Keegan, *Second World War,* 430.

41. On the role of German science and scientists, Beyerchen, *Scientists under Hitler;* Mark Walker, *German National Socialism and the Quest for Nuclear Power, 1933–1949* (Cambridge: Cambridge Univ. Press, 1989); David Irving, *The Virus House: Germany's Atomic Research and Allied Countermeasures* (London: Kimber, 1967); Karl-Heinz Ludwig, *Technik and Ingenieure im Dritten Reich* (Düsseldorf: Droste, 1974).

42. See Donald Fleming and Bernard Bailyn, eds., *The Intellectual Migration: Europe and America, 1930–1960* (Cambridge, Mass.: Harvard Univ. Press, 1969), and H. Stuart Hughes, *The Sea Change: The Migration of Social Thought, 1930–1965* (New York: McGraw-Hill, 1975).

43. Wright, *Ordeal of Total War,* 82.

44. Speer, *Inside the Third Reich,* 254–55.

45. Wright, *Ordeal of Total War,* 84–85.

46. Weinberg, *World at Arms,* 563–64.

47. Walker, *German National Socialism,* 51. Also Powers, *Heisenberg's War,* 478–84.

48. Ibid., 51–52.

49. Keegan, *Second World War,* 496.

50. Weinberg, *World at Arms,* 544.

51. Ibid., 549.

52. Max Hastings, *Overlord: D-Day and the Battle for Normandy* (New York: Simon & Schuster, 1984), 46.

53. With the recent fiftieth anniversary of D-Day, the literature on the invasion has been mounting steadily. Some of the better guides are Hastings, *Overlord;* Stephen Ambrose, *D-Day June 6, 1944: The Climatic Battle of World War II* (New York: Simon and Schuster, 1994); Gerald Astor, *June 6, 1944: The Voices of D-Day* (New York: St. Martin's, 1994); John Keegan, *Six Armies in Normandy: From Normandy to the Liberation of Paris* (New York: Penguin, 1983); and Cornelius Ryan's great classic *The Longest Day* (New York: Fawcett, 1959).

54. Ryan, *Longest Day,* 150–51.

55. Ibid., 151.

56. Gert Buchheit, *Hitler der Feldherr* (Rastatt: Grote, 1958), 396–97.

57. Ryan, *Longest Day,* 28.

58. Hastings, *Overlord,* 42.

59. Domarus, *Hitler,* 4:2104.

60. Liddell Hart, *History of the Second World War,* 550.

61. Hastings, *Overlord,* 144.

62. For this curious conference see Buchheit, *Hitler der Feldherr,* 416–19; also Domarus, *Hitler,* 4:2106–7.

63. Quoted by Buchheit, *Hitler als Feldherr,* 418–19.

64. Chester Wilmot, *The Struggle for Europe* (London: Collins, 1952), 347. Some historians have questioned this remark as apocryphal, but whether it is or not, it certainly expresses how Rundstedt felt at the time.

65. Buchheit, *Hitler als Feldherr,* 422.

66. Ibid.

67. Domarus, *Hitler,* 4:2121.

68. Hoffmann, *History of the German Resistance,* 508.

69. For a superb re-creation of this incident, see Trevor-Roper, *Last Days of Hitler,* 31–32.

70. Ibid., 524.

71. Fest, *Hitler,* 715.

72. Keegan, *Second World War,* 408–9; also Irving, *Hitler's War,* 2:762–63.

73. Quoted by Hastings, *Overlord,* 311.

74. Dahms, *Geschichte des Zweiten Weltkriegs,* 510.

75. For the details, see Weinberg, *World at Arms,* 710–11. On the Warsaw Uprising, see Janusz K. Zawodny, *Nothing but Honor: The Story of the Warsaw Uprising, 1944* (London, 1978), and Hans von Krannhals, *Der Warschauer Aufstand, 1944* (Frankfurt: Bernard und Graefe, 1962).

76. Churchill, *Second World War,* 6:226–28.

77. David Fraser, *Knight's Cross: A Life of Field Marshal Erwin Rommel* (New York: HarperCollins, 1993), 554.

78. Weinberg, *World at Arms,* 766–67.

79. Ibid., 769.

80. Since German atrocities, especially those committed against Jews, so dwarfed everything else, historians have tended to ignore atrocities committed against Germans. For a correction of the record, see Theodor Schieder, ed., *Dokumentation der Vertreibung der Deutschen aus Ost-Mitteleuropa,* 8 vols. (Bonn: Ministry for Expelled Persons, Refugees, and War Injured, 1953–62). There is also an excellent account of what happened to those who were fleeing from the Russian invaders by G. Böddeker, *Die Flüchtlinge* (Munich: F. Herbig, 1980).

81. Hugh Trevor-Roper, ed., *Final Entries 1945: The Diaries of Joseph Goebbels* (New York: Avon Books, 1979), 20.

82. Dahms, *Geschichte des Zweiten Weltkriegs,* 583.

83. For the details of this Allied fantasy, see Rodney G. Minott, *The Fortress That Never Was: The Myth of Hitler's Bavarian Stronghold* (New York: Holt, Rinehart and Winston, 1964).

84. Trevor-Roper, *Last Days of Hitler,* 50.

85. For a gripping reconstruction of Hitler's last four months in his bunker, see James P. O. O'Donnell, *The Bunker: The History of the Third Reich Chancellery Group* (New York: Bantam, 1979).

86. Irving, *Hitler's War,* 2:857.

87. Ibid.

88. Speer, *Inside the Third Reich,* 455.

89. Quoted by Bullock, *Hitler,* 769.

90. Speer, *Inside the Third Reich,* 400–406.

91. Ibid., 440.

92. Quoted by Bullock, *Hitler,* 772–73.

93. Trevor-Roper, *Last Days of Hitler,* 100.

94. Quoted by Bullock, *Hitler,* 781.

95. For the reminiscences of some of these bunker diehards, see Pierre Galante and Eugene Silianoff, eds., *Voices from the Bunker* (New York: Doubleday, 1989).

96. O'Donnell, *The Bunker,* 117.

97. Anthony Read and David Fisher, *The Fall of Berlin* (New York: Norton, 1992), 385.

98. Ibid., 387.

99. Cornelius Ryan, *The Last Battle* (London: Collins, 1966), 379–80.

100. Quoted by Read and Fisher, *The Fall of Berlin,* 412–13.

101. Trevor-Roper, *The Last Days of Hitler,* 182.

102. O'Donnell, *The Bunker,* 227.

103. Ibid., 236, 329. Trevor-Roper argues that Hitler shot himself in the mouth (*Last Days of Hitler,* 201), a version also accepted by Bullock (*Hitler,* 799). The Russian version, supposedly based on a careful autopsy of the body of Hitler, concluded that Hitler poisoned rather than shot himself (Bezymenski, *Death of Adolf Hitler,* 66–69), but this report cannot be trusted for political reasons. According to all the eyewitness observers who saw the body, there was blood from a bullet wound, the question to this very day being what kind of wound it was and its precise location.

104. Waite, *Psychopathic God,* 489–90.

105. O'Donnell, *The Bunker,* 241.

106. Quoted in ibid., 368.

107. Ibid.

Conclusion: The Question of German Guilt

1. Gilbert, *Nuremberg Diary,* 253.

2. Telford Taylor, *The Anatomy of the Nuremberg Trials: A Personal Memoir* (New York: Alfred A. Knopf, 1992), 632.

3. Quoted by Werner Maser, *Nuremberg: A Nation on Trial.* Trans. Richard Barry (New York: Charles Scribner's Sons, 1979), 140–41.

4. Peter Gay, *Freud, Jews, and Other Germans* (New York: Oxford Univ. Press, 1978), xi.

5. Gilbert, *Nuremberg Diary,* 110.

6. Ibid., 143.

7. Ibid.

8. Meinecke, *German Catastrophe,* 102–3.

9. Bracher, *German Dictatorship,* 476.

10. Alvin Rosenfeld, *Imagining Hitler* (Bloomington: Indiana Univ. Press, 1985), 43.

11. For a good summary of the affair, see Robert Harris, *Selling Hitler* (New York: Penguin Books, 1987).

12. Ernst Nolte, *Der europäische Bürgerkrieg, 1917–45* (Frankfurt: Ullstein, 1987), 517.

13. Ernst Nolte, "Zwischen Geschichtslegende und Revisionismus?" in *Historikerstreit* (Munich: Piper, 1987), 32.

14. For a summary of the debate in English, see Richard J. Evans, *In Hitler's Shadow: West German Historians and the Attempt to Escape from the Nazi Past* (New York: Pantheon, 1989). On the German side, Ernst Nolte, *Das Vergehen der Vergangenheit: Antwort an meine Kritiker im sogenannten Historikerstreit* (Berlin: Ullstein, 1988); Hans-Ulrich Wehler, *Entsorgung der deutschen Vergangenheit?* (Munich: Beck, 1988); Jürgen Habermas, *Eine Art Schadensabwicklung* (Frankfurt: Suhrkamp, 1987); and *Historikerstreit.*

15. Karl Jaspers, *The Question of German Guilt,* trans. E. B. Ashton (1947; reprint, New York: Capricorn Books, 1961), 31–32.

16. Ibid., 34.

17. Ibid., 40.

18. *LA Times,* January 25, 1984.

Chronology

April 20, 1889	Birth of Adolf Hitler in Braunau on the river Inn, Austria.
September 16, 1919	Hitler joins the German Workers' Party (DAP).
February 24, 1920	Proclamation of the party's Twenty-Five-Point Program.
August 8	Founding of the National Socialist German Workers' Party (NSDAP).
November 8–9, 1923	Hitler's Beerhall Putsch in Munich fails.
April 1, 1924	Hitler is sentenced to five years imprisonment at Landsberg.
December 20	Hitler is released after serving only eight months. While in prison, he completes the draft of volume 1 of *Mein Kampf*.
February 24, 1925	Reestablishment of the NSDAP.
April 26	Hindenburg is elected president of the Weimar Republic after Friedrich Ebert's death.
November 11	Founding of the SS (Schutzstaffel [Protective Squads]), an elite personal guard protecting Hitler.
May 20, 1928	Reichstag elections. The Nazis poll a mere 810,000 (2.6 percent) popular votes and receive just twelve seats in the 491-member Reichstag.
October 29, 1929	"Black Tuesday." The stock market collapses in the United States, triggering a widespread economic depression that also tragically affects Germany.
September 14, 1930	Reichstag elections. The Nazis stage a spectacular breakthrough by receiving 6,409,600 votes (18.3 percent) and seating 107 deputies in the new 577-member Reichstag.
December 1931	Unemployment reaches 5.6 million in Germany.
March 13 and April 10, 1932	Hitler is defeated by President Hindenburg in two Presidential elections.

April 13	Chancellor Brüning prohibits the SA and the SS.
May 30	Brüning is replaced as chancellor by Papen.
June 16	Papen lifts the ban on the SA/SS.
July 31	Reichstag elections. The Nazis poll 13,745,800 votes (37.4 percent) and receive 230 seats in the new 608-member Reichstag. This makes the NSDAP the largest party in Germany.
August 13	Hindenburg turns down Hitler as chancellor.
November 6	Reichstag elections. The Nazi vote declines to 11,737,000 votes (33.1 percent) and to 196 out of 584 members in the new Reichstag.
December 2	General Schleicher becomes chancellor.
December 18	A crisis develops in the Nazi Party between Gregor Strasser and Hitler over the future direction of the NSDAP. Strasser resigns.
January 4, 1933	Secret meeting between Hitler and Papen in the house of the Cologne banker Schröder.
January 15	The Nazis score election gains in the state of Lippe.
January 23	Schleicher resigns as chancellor.
January 30	Hindenburg appoints Hitler chancellor in a coalition government.
February 27	The German Reichstag burns down. The Communists are blamed.
February 28	A Reichstag fire decree, entitled Protection of the People and State, is passed by presidential decree; it suspends civil liberties, allows the police to place suspects in "protective custody," and prepares the way for an extended state of emergency.
March 5	Last Reichstag election in a multiparty state. The NSDAP gains a slim majority (43.9 percent of the vote).
March 21	Day of Potsdam.
March 24	Passage of Enabling Law, on which Hitler's dictatorship for the next twelve years would be based.
April 1	Boycott against Jewish businesses and professionals. Himmler is appointed police commander of Bavaria.
May 2	Destruction of labor unions and arrest of labor leaders. Creation of the German Labor Front (DAF), headed by Robert Ley.

July 14	Law against the establishment of new parties, which bans all existing parties and prohibits the forming of new ones.
July 20	Conclusion of a concordat with the Catholic Church.
September 29	Establishment of the Reich Chamber of Culture headed by Joseph Goebbels.
October 14	Germany withdraws from the League of Nations.
November 12	First Reichstag elections in the new one-party state. Predictable result: 95.2 percent cast their votes for the NSDAP!
January 20, 1934	Law for the Regulation of National Labor.
January 30	Law for the Reconstruction of the Reich suspends state or land governments and their jurisdictions.
June 17	Papen delivers a speech at the University of Marburg in which he strongly criticizes the excesses of the Nazi revolution.
June 30–July 2	Röhm Purge. Hitler helps orchestrate a purge against Röhm as well as his political opponents, chiefly members of the conservative right. SS and Gestapo are used to murder the supposed plotters.
July 20	The SS becomes an independent organization
August 2	President Hindenburg dies. Hitler immediately merges the offices of chancellor and president, thus becoming head of state as well as commander in chief.
January 13, 1935	Saar plebiscite results in the reincorporation of the Saarland into the Reich.
March 16	Reintroduction of military conscription.
June 18	Anglo-German Naval Agreement.
June 26	Introduction of compulsory labor service for young men aged eighteen to twenty-five.
September 15	Proclamation of the Nuremberg Race Laws.
March 7, 1936	Hitler marches into the demilitarized Rhineland and reclaims it for Germany.
March 29	Plebiscite on Hitler's policies; 99 percent approve of those policies.
June 17	Himmler becomes *Reichführer SS* and chief of the German police.
August 1	Hitler opens the Olympic Games in Berlin.

September 8–14	Party congress. Four-Year Plan is proclaimed.
October 25	Rome-Berlin Axis comes into effect through the treaty between Italy and Germany.
November 25	Anti-Comintern Pact between Germany and Japan.
January 30, 1937	Extension of the Enabling Law for four years.
March 14	Papal encyclical *With Burning Concern* denounces Nazi policies toward the church.
September 25–29	State visit by Mussolini.
November 5	Hossbach memorandum records secret military meeting between Hitler and his military chiefs in which the führer reveals his aggressive territorial designs.
November 26	Schacht resigns as Reich economics minister and is replaced by Walther Funk.
February 4, 1938	Fritsch and Blomberg crisis and the formation of the High Command of the Armed Forces (Oberkommando der Wehrmacht [OKW]).
March 12–13	Annexation of Austria.
August 27	Chief of the army general staff, Ludwig Beck, resigns.
September 29–30	Munich Conference "appeases" Hitler by awarding him the Sudeten region of Czechoslovakia.
November 8–9	Kristallnacht (Night of Crystals) resulting in pogroms against Jews all over Germany.
March 14–16, 1939	Germany invades the rest of Czechoslovakia and establishes the Reich Protectorate of Bohemia and Moravia.
March 23	Germany invades and reincorporates the Memel region.
April 22	The Pact of Steel, a military alliance, is concluded between Germany and Italy.
August 23	The Nazi-Soviet Nonaggression Pact.
September 1	Germany invades Poland.
September 3	Britain and France declare war on Germany.
September 27	Establishment of the Reich Main Security Office (RSHA) under the leadership of Heydrich combines the security police (Gestapo and Kripo) with the Security Service (SD), making this office the most powerful instrument of police terror.

October	Hitler signs a written note, backdated to September 1, 1939, authorizing the "mercy killing" of "lives not worth living," thus ushering in the euthanasia program.
October 8–12	Hitler divides up Poland by incorporating its western areas into the Reich and setting up the rump or rest of Poland as a vassal state called Government General, headed by Hans Frank.
November 8	Major assassination attempt by Georg Elser against Hitler fails.
April 9, 1940	German invasion of Denmark and Norway.
May 10	Hitler's attack against the west begins with the invasion of Holland, Belgium, Luxembourg, and France.
June 22	Franco-German armistice.
August 13	The battle of Britain begins and extends into late September.
October 23	Hitler meets Franco at Hendaye.
October 24	Inconclusive meeting between Hitler and Pétain.
October 28	Mussolini attacks Greece.
December 18	Hitler formalizes plans (Operation Barbarossa) for the invasion of Russia.
February 1941	Formation of the Afrika Korps under the command of General Rommel.
April 6	German invasion of Yugoslavia and Greece.
May 10	Rudolf Hess flies on a secret mission to Scotland, ostensibly to bring about peace between Britain and Germany. Stamped "mad" by Hitler, Hess is replaced by Bormann.
June 6	Hitler releases the infamous "Commissar Order" calling for the liquidation of all Communist Party functionaries in the impending war against Russia.
June 22	Hitler invades the Soviet Union. Behind the regular army (Wehrmacht) special police units (*Einsatzgruppen*) systematically round up Jews, Communists, and Gypsies and murder them in cold blood.
July 31	Göring requests Heydrich to present a draft setting out the details of the measures to be taken for the achievement of the "final solution" to the Jewish question.

September 1	Jews in Germany must wear the yellow Star of David and are prohibited from emigrating as of October 1, 1941.
September 3	First experimental gassing with Zyklon-B at Auschwitz.
September 29–30	Mass shootings of 33,771 Jews at Babi Yar, a ravine near Kiev.
December 5	Battle of Moscow. Soviet counteroffensive begins.
December 7	*Nacht und Nebel* (Night and Fog) decree. Japan attacks Pearl Harbor.
December 11	Hitler declares war on the United States.
December 16	Hitler sacks General Brauchitsch and assumes supreme command of the army himself.
January 20, 1942	Wannsee Conference finalizing the measures to be taken for the "final solution" to the Jewish problem.
February 8	Albert Speer replaces Fritz Todt as minister of armaments.
March 21	Fritz Sauckel is appointed as general plenipotentiary for labor allocation.
May 27	Heydrich is assassinated in Prague.
May 30–31	First "one-thousand-bomber attack" on a German city (Cologne).
June	Beginning of mass gassings at Auschwitz.
June 10	Destruction of the town of Lidice and liquidation of its inhabitants in reprisal for the death of Heydrich. June Beginning of mass gassings at Auschwitz.
November 11	The British break through at El Alamein. Rommel's Afrika Korps retreat headlong toward northeast Africa.
November 19	The Soviets launch their counteroffensive at Stalingrad. Four days later, the Soviets close the ring around Stalingrad and trap the Sixth Army.
January 31, 1943	The Sixth Army surrenders at Stalingrad.
February 18	Goebbels delivers his "Do you want total war?" speech at the Berlin Sportspalast.
February 22	Execution of the Scholls (Hans and Sophie) and the smashing of the "White Rose" resistance group.
March 13	Failed plot against Hitler by the officers of Army Group Center.

April 19	Warsaw Ghetto uprising. On May 16, the uprising is smashed.
May 12	The last Axis troops capitulate in North Africa.
July 25	The fall of Mussolini and fascism in Italy.
September 2	Speer is authorized to centralize all war industries; he forms a new Ministry for Armaments and War Production.
September 8	Hitler occupies north and central Italy.
June 6, 1944	D-Day: The Allied invasion of Normandy.
June 10	Destruction of the French town of Oradour-sur-Glane and liquidation of its inhabitants in reprisal for partisan activities.
June 20	Opening of Soviet offensive against Army Group Center.
July 20	Colonel Stauffenberg attempts unsuccessfully to assassinate Hitler at his headquarters in Rastenburg, East Prussia.
July 24	Soviets liberate concentration camp at Majdanek.
July 25	Himmler is appointed as commander in chief of the Reserve Army, and Goebbels becomes general plenipotentiary for total war.
September	V-2 rockets are launched against London.
September 1	Beginning of the Warsaw Uprising.
September 25	All men between sixteen and sixty who are not already called up are required to serve in the Volkssturm (Home Guard).
October 2	Warsaw Uprising is crushed, and the city is destroyed.
October 21	Aachen is occupied by American troops.
November 1	Himmler stops the gassings at Auschwitz.
December 16–24	Battle of the Bulge.
January 27, 1945	Auschwitz is liberated by the Russians.
January 30	Hitler's last broadcast to the German people, urging them to hold out to the last.
February 4–11	Yalta Conference.
February 13–14	The destruction of Dresden.
March 7	Americans cross the Rhine at Remagen.

March 19	Hitler's Scorched-Earth or Nero Command.
April 25	American and Soviet troops meet at Torgau on the Elbe.
April 30	Hitler commits suicide. Dönitz assumes command.
May 2	Berlin capitulates to the Soviets.
May 7–9	Unconditional surrender terms are signed in the American headquarters at Rheims and repeated in the Soviet headquarters in Berlin.

Glossary of Key Names, Terms, and Abbreviations

Abwehr. German espionage and news service agency. The office originated in 1920; its title, stressing defensiveness, was chosen with an eye to the tragic losses of human life in World War I. Attached to military command (OKW) under the Nazis, the office was headed by Admiral Wilhelm Canaris and served as a refuge for various civilian and military opponents of the Nazi regime. Its independent role ended with the dismissal of Canaris in February 1944 and its subordination to the SS.

Afrika Korps. The various military formations sent by Hitler to aid the Italians in North Africa. Under the command of General Rommel since February 1941, the Afrika Korps fought valiant battles against the British and later against combined Anglo-American forces, but was decisively beaten by the spring of 1943.

Aktion Reinhard. Code name for the annihilation of Jews in the Polish territory (Government General) administered by the Nazis. The operation was named in "honor" of SD chief Reinhard Heydrich, who was assassinated in Prague on May 27, 1942.

Aktion T4. Code name for the actions taken in the euthanasia program that led to the killing of one hundred thousand "lives not worth living" (mentally retarded men, women, children). It was named after the relevant government department of the Reich chancellery located on Tiergarten Strasse 4 in Berlin.

Alte Kämpfer (old fighters). Refers to the group of loyal and dedicated Nazis who had joined the NSDAP and its affiliated paramilitary formations (SA, SS) before the seizure of power in January 1933. Particularly prized by the führer were those party members who had joined before November 9, 1923, were involved in the Putsch, and were incarcerated with him at Landsberg Prison.

Amann, Max (1891–1957). Hitler's regimental sergeant during World War I. In 1921 he became the first business manager of the Nazi Party, and in 1922 he was appointed director of the party's publishing house, the Franz Eher Verlag. In 1933 he became president of the Reich Press

Chamber and was instrumental in coordinating the German press, making it a pliant tool of Nazi ideology. His close relation with Hitler enabled him to amass a sizeable fortune.

Anschluss. The annexation of Austria by the Nazis in February 1938 and its incorporation as a province (Ostmark) into the German Reich.

Auschwitz. The largest Nazi concentration and annihilation camp. Located in Upper East Silesia (formerly Oswiecim, Poland), Auschwitz started out as a camp for political prisoners, mostly Polish, but was rapidly expanded as a work camp and then as a site for the annihilation of Jews. The camp was divided into three sites: Auschwitz 1 was the original camp; Auschwitz 2 at Birkenau, built to accommodate two hundred thousand victims, was the annihilation camp; and Auschwitz 3 was the industrial center in Monowitz. Starting in the summer of 1941, Himmler targeted Auschwitz as one of the main sites for the annihilation of Jews by poison gassing (Zyklon-B) and put Rudolf Höss (1900–1947), the camp's later commandant, in charge of preparing the annihilation site. It is estimated that about two million Jews perished at Auschwitz.

Barbarossa. Code name for the German attack on the Soviet Union on June 22, 1941.

BDM (Bund deutscher Mädel, or League of German Girls). A subdivision of the Hitler Youth. The Hitler Youth had a male and female division. The latter was subdivided into the League of Young Girls (ages ten to fourteen) and the League of German Girls (ages fifteen to eighteen).

Beck, Ludwig (1880–1944). Colonel general who served as general staff officer in World War I. Hitler appointed him chief of the general staff in 1933, but when Beck realized the full implications of Hitler's warlike policies, especially during the Czech crisis, he tried unsuccessfully to organize resistance among high-ranking army officers. In 1938 he retired from active duty and became, over the next six years, a focal point of the resistance. In July 1944 he took his life after being implicated in the plot against Hitler's life.

Berghof. Adolf Hitler's Bavarian home at the Obersalzberg, northeast of Berchtesgaden.

Blomberg, Werner von (1878–1946). General staff officer in World War I, high-ranking official in the Reich Ministry of Defense, and, on Hindenburg's recommendation, Hitler's first minister of defense. In this position he actively supported Hitler's rearmament policies and was rewarded in 1936 by being made a field marshal. In 1938 Blomberg was forced into retirement as a result of a scandal involving his marriage to a prostitute.

Blut und Boden (blood and soil). A term used to describe the fundamental Nazi belief that a healthy nation presupposes a people of common blood living on its own soil. The overuse of the term by Nazi ideologues prompted many Germans to refer to such blood and soil propaganda as "Blubo."

Bonhoeffer, Dietrich (1906–45). Protestant theologian and member of the German resistance. Arrested by the Gestapo in 1943, he was executed at Flossenbürg shortly before the liberation.

Bormann, Martin (1900–1945). Hitler's grey eminence and personal secretary. A "walking cabinet file," the indefatigable, single-minded, scheming Bormann wormed his way into Hitler's inner party circle by becoming Rudolf Hess's chief of staff and Reich leader (*Reichsleiter*) of the NSDAP. After Hess's flight to Scotland in 1941, Bormann became director of the party chancellery, Reich minister, and member of the Cabinet Council for Defense. He was at Hitler's side during most of the war and personally screened all communications and contacts with the führer. He remained with Hitler to the end and was killed while trying to escape from Berlin.

Bouhler, Philipp (1899–1945). Loyal NSDAP business manager and later director of the relatively powerless office of the NSDAP chancellery. On September 1, 1939, Hitler assigned him responsibility for the euthanasia program whose murderers were later used to annihilate the Jews. Bouhler evaded responsibility for his activities by committing suicide in May 1945.

Brauchitsch, Walter von (1881–1948). German general and later field marshal who succeeded von Fritsch as commander in chief of the army in 1938. Apolitical and cautious, he was not held in high esteem by his fellow officers. When the German drive toward Moscow was repelled in the winter of 1941, Hitler singled him out as a scapegoat, sacked him, and assumed command of the army himself.

Braun, Eva (1912–45). Hitler's secret mistress and bride for one day. Since Hitler gave the public the impression that Germany was his only bride, Eva Braun's role was not publicly revealed. Although Hitler allowed her to move to the Berghof, she could socialize only within a very restricted circle of initiates. She committed suicide with Hitler on April 30, 1945.

Brüning, Heinrich (1885–1970). Leading Christian trade union leader and Center Party politician. In 1930 he was appointed by President Hindenburg to lead a presidential cabinet at a time of heightening economic depression. Brüning's conservative fiscal policies, which exacerbated the economic hardships, earned him the epithet "Hunger Chancellor." He emigrated to the United States.

Canaris, Wilhelm (1887–1945). Admiral and head of the German secret service, the Abwehr. His initial enthusiasm for the Nazi movement gave way to determined opposition after he watched firsthand how Hitler maneuvered Germany into World War II. For years he played a clever double game of pretending to support the regime while secretly encouraging active opposition to it. His cat-and-mouse game ended when important Abwehr agents defected to Britain in 1944. Arrested in the wake of the July 20 plot against Hitler, Canaris was sent to a concentration camp and executed shortly before Allied troops closed in.

Chamberlain, Houston Stewart (1855–1927). British writer and racial philosopher whose work *Foundation of the Nineteenth Century* became one of the ideological cornerstones of National Socialism. In 1885 he took up residence in Germany, married one of Richard Wagner's daughters, and became an apostle of Aryan supremacy and German nationalism.

Dachau. The site of the first National Socialist concentration camp located about ten miles northwest of Munich. Opened in March 1933, it housed a variety of prisoners — Socialists, Communists, Jews, Gypsies, homosexuals — who were held in "protective custody." The camp expanded steadily and became one of the most notorious camps in Germany. During World War II the number of inmates grew to about seventeen thousand, some of them being used for cruel medical experiments.

DAF (Deutsche Arbeitsfront, or German Labor Front). Labor organization, sponsored by the National Socialists, that replaced the various labor unions of the Weimar Republic. Headed by Robert Ley, the DAF encompassed all of German labor, reaching a membership of more than twenty million. Its function was to bring about a lasting harmony between contending socioeconomic interest groups and to protect the rights of labor. It provided financial assistance to workers, set wages, and used its funds to improve the lives of German workers. Operating with a large budget, the DAF also developed various branches such as the Strength through Joy (Kraft durch Freude) movement, which provided holidays to workers at inexpensive rates, and the Beauty of Labor (Schönheit der Arbeit) office, which tried to improve working conditions in plants and factories.

Dalugue, Kurt (1897–1946). SS officer and lieutenant general of the Prussian state police who helped Göring pave the way for the Nazification of the police in Prussia. He participated in the Röhm Purge and then became director of the police department in the Ministry of the Interior. Once Himmler had captured the police forces of the Reich, Dalugue was neutralized by being kicked upstairs, becoming the director of the ordinary police (Orpo). During the war, he replaced the martyred Heydrich as "Reich protector" of Bohemia and Moravia. Held responsible for the massacres associated with the destruction of Lidice, Dalugue was tried and executed in 1946.

Darré, Richard Walther (1895–1953). NSDAP agronomist and expert in animal husbandry, famous for his "blood and soil" ideology based on *völkisch* racial convictions. As head of the Office of Agrarian Policies of the NSDAP, Darré was charged with the mission of organizing the peasants. Between 1931 and 1938 he was head of the SS Office for Race and Settlement. In 1933 he also became Reich minister of food and agriculture. His reactionary convictions were increasingly questioned by those who supported a strong industrial policy. After openly criticizing Himmler's methods of dealing with eastern settlements and questioning Hitler's war aims, Darré was relieved of his office in 1942.

Diels, Rudolf (1900–1957). German jurist who was appointed by Göring to head Department 1-A, secret police, in the state of Prussia. This department would become the dreaded Gestapo. As chief of the secret police, Diels was instrumental in developing the theory and practice of "protective custody" and launching attacks on Jews. During Göring's power struggle with Himmler, Göring ultimately sacrificed Diels, who was married to his cousin, by fobbing him off with minor posts.

Dietrich, Joseph ("Sepp," 1892–1966). Former butcher and SS officer who helped establish Hitler's bodyguard regiment, the Leibstandarte-SS Adolf Hitler. During the Röhm Purge, Dietrich and his SS men served as the executioners of high-ranking SA officers, many of them Dietrich's friends. As part of the Waffen-SS (Armed SS), Dietrich's regiments fought bravely on many fronts during World War II, but also participated in the massacre of Allied troops during the battle of the Bulge (Malmedy). After the war Dietrich was tried and imprisoned first by the Allies (serving seven years) and then by a German court for his participation in the Röhm Purge (serving nineteen months).

Dietrich, Otto (1897–1952). National Socialist press chief who played a key role in the coordination of the German press. In 1937 Hitler appointed him Reich press chief and state secretary to the Propaganda Ministry responsible for reporting the Nazi weltanschauung to the rest of the world. He fed Germans a steady diet of misinformation, first by inflating the Nazis' victories and then deflating their defeats.

Dönitz, Karl (1891–1980). Grand admiral and commander of the U-boat branch of the German navy. A devout follower of Hitler, he succeeded Admiral Raeder in 1943 as commander in chief of the German navy. In the closing days of the war, Hitler appointed Dönitz as his successor, but the new führer served less than one month in his new office before he was arrested by the Allies. Tried at Nuremberg as a war criminal, he was sentenced to ten years in prison.

Drexler, Anton (1884–1942). Munich locksmith who founded the Deutsche Arbeiterpartei (German Workers' Party), which later became the Nationalsozialistische deutsche Arbeiterpartei (National Socialist German Workers' Party [NSDAP]). Initially encouraging Hitler, Drexler was soon pushed out of the way and fobbed off with an honorary title. In 1925 he broke with Hitler and founded the National Socialist People's League. Although Drechsler later reconciled with Hitler, he never played another role in the party he helped to found.

Ebert, Friedrich (1871–1925). Politician and leader of the Social Democratic Party who became the first president of the Weimar Republic. As president, he tried to chart a middle course between the left and the right and was savagely attacked by both. His agreement in November 1918 to work with the traditional military establishment may have staved off a social revolution, but it also foreclosed the possibility of democratizing German institutions, especially the military.

Eckart, Dietrich (1868–1923). Poet, journalist, and mentor of the young Hitler. Known for his anti-Semitic views, best expressed in his weekly paper *Auf gut Deutsch* (In plain German), Eckart served as an important catalyst of the rising Nazi Party, which he supported financially. He was also the first editor-in-chief of the *Völkischer Beobachter,* the Nazi Party's official newspaper. Hitler thought so highly of Eckart that he dedicated *Mein Kampf* to his memory.

Eichmann, Adolf (1906–62). *SS-Obersturmbannführer* who joined the SS in 1933 and then moved to Himmler's SD (Security Service), where he worked in the Department of Jewish Emigration. In 1938 he was tasked with setting up a central office for Jewish emigration in Vienna, which succeeded in driving 150,000 Austrian Jews into forced emigration. Transferred to Berlin in 1939, he was put in charge of Jewish deportation in the Reich Main Security Office (RSHA) as chief of Section IV B-4. This office rounded up well over three million Jews in all German-controlled territories and drove them into the annihilation camps as part of Hitler's "final solution (*Endlösung*) to the Jewish question." As an unobtrusive "desk murderer," Eichmann was overlooked after World War II and managed to escape to Argentina. Israeli secret agents caught up with him there, kidnapped him, and returned him to Israel to stand trial on charges of crimes against humanity. Found guilty, he was executed in 1962.

Eicke, Theodor (1892–1943). Brutal, sociopathic SS officer and head of the German concentration camps. His first major post, which he owed to Himmler, was as commandant of Dachau concentration camp. In this post he instituted methods of control and punishment that would later be replicated throughout all concentration camps — vicious corporal punishment, the use of the Kapo system, and so on. Eicke played a prominent role in the Röhm Purge, personally murdering the SA chief.

IIis star in the SS rose rapidly thereafter. The SS Death's-IIead Units he had used as executioners during the Röhm Purge would later form the core of the Waffen-SS divisions called Death's-Head Divisions, infamous for their brutal actions against their enemies. Eicke died in a plane crash in 1943.

Einsatzgruppen. Special battalion-sized mobile units of security police and SD officials that conducted police and terroristic actions behind and alongside the regular German army. During the Russian campaign four *Einsatzgruppen* were attached to Army Group North, Center, South, and the Eleventh Army. Their function was to round up Communist functionaries, "Asiatic inferiors," and Jews and herd them into concentration camps or conduct brutal liquidations on the spot. It is estimated that these killer troops murdered close to one million people, mostly Jews in mass executions and later helped to murder five million additional Jewish victims in annihilation camps.

Enabling Law (Law for Terminating the Suffering of People and Reich). The law on which Hitler's dictatorship was based from 1933 until 1945. The law enabled the chancellor and his cabinet to pass laws, to deviate from the constitution, and to pass treaties with foreign powers without the consent of the Reichstag.

Endlösung (final solution). Euphemistic code word for the "final solution of the Jewish question," or the program involving the annihilation of six million Jews.

Epp, Franz Xaver Ritter von (1868–1947). General and early supporter of the Nazi Party. After serving as a Reichstag deputy for the NSDAP, Epp took an active part in coordinating the state of Bavaria for the National Socialists. On Hitler's order, he dissolved the Bavarian government and made himself a *Reichstatthalter* (governor), a post he retained along with that of *Reichsleiter* until the collapse of the Nazi regime in 1945.

Esser, Hermann (1900–1981). One of the original founders of the NSDAP and a close comrade of Adolf Hitler. A "demon speech-maker," notorious womanizer, and rabid anti-Semite, he was often an embarrassment even to the Nazis, though Hitler always valued him as an old fighter and rewarded him with various posts after 1933 — Bavarian minister of economics, chief of the Bavarian state chancellery, and president of the Bavarian Landtag. His quarrel with Adolf Wagner, *Gauleiter* of Bavaria, and additional private scandals (Esser was a notorious cad) finally caused Hitler to relieve him of his post in 1935. Only three years later, however, Hitler gave him another chance by appointing him secretary of state for tourist traffic. During World War II, Esser faded into obscurity — so much so that even the Allies overlooked him in 1945. A

Munich court, however, convicted him in 1949 as a major offender and sentenced him to five years at hard labor.

Feder, Gottfried (1883–1941). One of the original members of the NS-DAP and Hitler's adviser on economic issues. Although not opposed to productive capitalism, Feder constantly attacked "interest slavery," which he associated with stock-exchange capitalism and the people who supported it — the Jews. Feder succeeded in embodying some of his populist and reactionary notions into the party's Twenty-five Point Program. Hitler later divested himself of Feder because he needed the support of big business. After the seizure of power, Feder was fobbed off with a minor post as undersecretary in the Ministry of Economics, but protests by Schacht and others led to his dismissal after only one year. Feeling deeply betrayed by the course Hitler had charted for the movement, Feder retired and died in obscurity in 1941.

Frank, Hans (1900–1946). Member of the old Nazi guard, Frank joined the German Workers' Party at the age of nineteen, participated in the Beerhall Putsch of 1923, and then served as Hitler's personal attorney for many years. As head of the party's legal division, he was privy to the inner workings of the party as well as Hitler's personal history. When Hitler became chancellor in 1933, Frank rose rapidly in both party and state, holding a variety of offices — Bavarian minister of justice, Reich minister of justice, and *Reichsleiter* of the party. After the conquest of Poland, Hitler appointed Frank as governor-general of Poland. Known as the "king of Poland," Frank governed so brutally and venally, plundering the nation's treasures and sending thousands of Poles and Jews to their deaths, that he was later tried as a war criminal and executed.

Frick, Wilhelm (1877–1946). Hitler's favorite bureaucrat and comrade-in-arms since the early 1920s. Between 1919 and 1923, Frick was Hitler's inside man in the Munich police department who protected the interests of the NSDAP. He participated in the Beerhall Putsch, managed to avoid being legally implicated, and helped in reconstructing the party in the late 1920s. He became the first Nazi to hold a major state position as minister of the interior in Thuringia, where he proceeded to Nazify the police force. When Hitler came to power, he appointed Frick as Reich minister of the interior. In this post he was instrumental in coordinating justice throughout the Reich, dissolving the governments of the individual states, and drawing up the Nuremberg racial laws of 1935. Frick was an authoritarian nationalist with decidedly anti-Semitic tendencies, but he was not a murderous racist. Unable to assert himself against the more persistent and aggressive Himmler, who constructed his own police empire, Frick's Ministry of the Interior was increasingly emasculated and eventually taken over by Himmler. Frick was tried at Nuremberg, found guilty, and executed as a war criminal in 1946.

Fritsch, Werner von (1880–1934). Commander in chief of the German army whose patient and cautious attitudes did not fit into Hitler's conception of what a commanding officer should be in the Third Reich. Wrongly accused by Himmler of a homosexual liaison, Fritsch was removed from his position in 1938, though later cleared by an army court of honor. Recalled to active duty just before the outbreak of World War II, Fritsch died on the battlefield near Warsaw in September 1939.

Führer (leader). Term chosen by the Nazi Party and later by all German authorities to describe their supreme leader, Adolf Hitler.

Führerprinzip (leadership principle). Antidemocratic belief that efficiency in government or businesses can be achieved only when leaders (führers) are fully empowered to do what they are assigned to do by their immediate supervisors. Only the highest führer is responsible to the people through plebiscitarian measures, but otherwise delegates strong führer power (*Führergewalt*) to his subordinates who, in turn, delegate it to their subordinates.

Funk, Walther (1890–1960). Economist, journalist, and later minister of economics under Hitler. As chief editor of the *Berliner Börsenzeitung*, a Berlin business newspaper, he made contacts with the Nazi Party and became Hitler's personal adviser on economic issues, helping him gain an entrée into big business. After the Nazis came to power, he held several posts, including press chief for the Reich government and undersecretary in the Ministry of Propaganda. His real opportunity came in 1938 when he replaced Schacht as minister of economics and general plenipotentiary for war economy as well as president of the Reichsbank. During the war he became implicated in exploiting the wealth of conquered territories and hoarding the personal wealth (gold, jewels, currency) extracted from millions of murdered Jews. At Nuremberg he was sentenced to life imprisonment but was released for health reasons in 1957.

Gauleiter (party district leader[s]). The highest ranking Nazi official below the *Reichsleiter*. Directly responsible to Hitler, the *Gauleiter* were responsible for all economic and political activities in their districts (*Gaue*). During the war they were also responsible for civil defense. Many *Gauleiter* also served as *Reichsstatthalter*, or provincial governors, thus fusing state and party offices.

Gestapo (Geheime Staatspolizei). The terrorist police force developed out of the Prussian police department called "security police" (Sipo); it was greatly expanded under Göring's tutelage by his assistant Rudolf Diels. When Himmler coordinated all of the police forces of Germany under his control in 1933–34, he also took charge of the Gestapo and transformed it into one of the most dreaded organizations of intimidation and terror. Putting Heydrich in charge, Himmler managed to detach the Gestapo from any effective control by constituted legal authorities. The primary mission of the Gestapo was to identify enemies of the state, put them into "protective custody" (*Schutzhaft*), use any methods deemed necessary to extract information, and consign such enemies to prison or concentration camp.

Gleichschaltung (coordination). The term the Nazis used to describe the process by which German institutions were synchronized to conform to the policies of National Socialism. Named after an electronic device called *Gleichrichter,* which allows electric current to flow in only one direction, *Gleichschaltung* was really a policy of Nazifying all German institutions while at the same time eliminating political opponents, parties, unions, and so on.

Globocnik, Odilo (1904–45). One of the most brutal and unscrupulous henchmen of Heinrich Himmler. For his help in subverting the independence of his native Austria, he was made *Gauleiter* of Vienna. When World War II broke out, he served as an *SS-Brigadeführer* and police chief in Lublin, Poland. Instrumental in opening three major concentration camps in Poland — Belzec, Maidanek, and Sobibor — he was eventually put in charge of all the annihilation camps in 1941. After his arrest in Austria in 1945, he committed suicide.

Goebbels, Joseph (1897–1945). Hitler's minister of propaganda and alter ego who created the theory and practice of the führer cult. Next to Himmler and Göring, he was the most powerful henchman of Adolf Hitler. Diminutive and clubfooted, Goebbels made up for his physical shortcomings with his nimble mind (Ph.D University of Heidelberg) and sharp tongue. As an unemployed intellectual, he had found his way into the NSDAP as early as 1922, but did not commit himself, heart and soul, to Hitler until 1926. From *Gauleiter* of Berlin and NSDAP Reichstag deputy, he rose to become one of the most powerful and sinister figures in the Third Reich, perfecting the black arts of government deception that made and destroyed Nazi Germany. He never wavered in his almost religious devotion to Adolf Hitler and immolated himself upon the death of his führer on May 1, 1945.

Goerdeler, Carl Friedrich (1884–1945). Mayor of Leipzig and prominent opponent of National Socialism. His association with the men who planned the July 20, 1944, plot against Hitler led to his arrest and execution.

Göring, Hermann (1893–1946). Next to Hitler, the most powerful man in the Third Reich. The swashbuckling hero of the famed Richthofen flying squad had joined the NSDAP in the fall of 1922, organized the SA, participated in the Beerhall Putsch of 1923, and then helped Hitler gain and consolidate his power. As Reich minister without portfolio and Prussian minister of the interior, he ruthlessly expanded the police force by building up the state secret police (Gestapo). Between 1933 and 1939 he greatly expanded his powers; his various titles included Reich minister, aviation minister, commander in chief of the air force, Reich forest master, Reich hunting master, general plenipotentiary of the Four-Year Plan, and Reich marshal. Witty, affable, charming, and intelligent, he was also vain, selfish, greedy, brutal, and venal. The German people admired Göring's apparent bonhomie, but lost confidence in his leadership during World War II. His failure to destroy the Allied forces at Dunkirk, his bungling of the battle of Britain, his inability to destroy the Soviet air force, and his impotence in preventing the round-the-clock saturation bombing of German cities — all these earned him the contempt of Hitler, and his standing in the Nazi hierarchy diminished rapidly. To escape from his failures, he increasingly retreated into drugs and hedonistic living. Arrested in 1945, he was tried as a war criminal at Nuremberg, found guilty, but escaped execution by committing suicide.

Groener, Wilhelm (1867–1939). General and politician during the Weimar Republic. As general quartermaster of the army, he was instrumental in organizing the successful withdrawal of German troops at the end of World War I and in solidifying an alliance between the Social Democrats and the armed forces, which earned him the lasting enmity of right-wing nationalists. He served as transport minister (1920–23), minister of defense (1928–32), and minister of the interior. His decisive actions against the NSDAP, including the prohibition of the SA and the SS in the spring of 1932, exposed him to widespread criticism and led to his dismissal in May 1932.

Guderian, Heinz (1888–1954). General and foremost German expert on modern tank warfare. His tank forces were instrumental in bringing about Hitler's early blitzkrieg victories in Poland and France. His relationship with Hitler was generally stormy. Hitler relieved him of his command during the winter of 1941 but then reappointed him as inspector general of German tank forces in 1943 and then as chief of staff of the army in 1944. When he called for an armistice in the spring of 1945, Hitler dismissed him for good.

Günther, Hans F. K. (1891–1968). Next to Alfred Rosenberg, Günther was the chief racial philosopher in the Third Reich. His major work, *Rassenkunde des deutschen Volkes* (Racial ethnology of the German people [1922]), sold more than a quarter of a million copies and became one of the seminal works of Nazi racial views. Appointed to a major chair of racial anthropology at the University of Jena in 1930 by Wilhelm Frick, he rose rapidly in the academic world after Hitler's seizure of power, holding the position of director at the Institute of Racial Studies in Berlin and then a professorship at the University of Freiburg (1940). He never abandoned his racial beliefs and continued to republish some of his works after World War II.

Gürtner, Franz (1881–1941). Conservative and antidemocratic jurist and politician. As Bavarian minister of justice, he tended to overlook right-wing extremism, especially on the part of the NSDAP, while dealing harshly with left-wing extremism. In 1932 Papen appointed him as Reich minister of justice, a post he continued to hold under National Socialist rule. Although opposed to the brutalities of National Socialism, he was unable to prevent the perversion of the law that Hitler demanded of his ministry.

Halder, Franz (1884–1972). General staff officer and commander in chief of the army from 1938 to 1942. He was instrumental in planning Hitler's campaigns in Poland, France, the Balkans, and Russia. He began to have increasing doubts about Hitler's reckless strategy in Russia, particularly after Hitler decided to commit himself to the disastrous campaign that led to the battle of Stalingrad. Hitler sacked him in September 1942. Although he opposed Hitler, he did not participate in the resistance against him. In the wake of the July 20, 1944, plot against Hitler, Halder was arrested and sent to a concentration camp.

Henlein, Konrad (1898–1945). Leader of the Sudeten Germans and Hitler's Trojan Horse in Czechoslovakia. As head of the Sudeten German Party, the second largest party in Czechoslovakia, he paved the way for the subversion and eventual destruction of Czechoslovakia. After the Munich Conference, Henlein was appointed *Gauleiter* and then *Reichsstatthalter* (Reich governor). In 1945 he was tried, sentenced to death, and committed suicide in Allied captivity.

Hess, Rudolf (1894–1987). Adolf Hitler's deputy and leader of the party. The introverted Hess, born to a German merchant in Alexandria, Egypt, had been a member of the party since 1920, participated in the Beerhall Putsch, and spent eighteen months at Landsberg Prison, where Hitler dictated *Mein Kampf* to him. Overshadowed by more aggressive Nazis, especially his own chief of staff, Martin Bormann, he steadily receded into the background as a mere figurehead. It may have been because of his increasing isolation from Adolf Hitler, whom he worshipped with doglike devotion, that Hess embarked on his futile mission to Scotland during World War II (May 10, 1941), ostensibly to initiate peace talks but more likely to regain the führer's favor and save him from destruction. While Hess was in English captivity, his mental condition seriously deteriorated, but he was declared sane by the Allied powers and tried along with other major Nazi members at Nuremberg. Found guilty, he was sentenced to life imprisonment at Spandau where, a lonely and tragic figure, he was the last Nazi prisoner to be guarded by the Allied powers. In 1987, at the age of 93, he committed suicide.

Heydrich, Reinhard (1904–42). *SS-Obergruppenführer* and Himmler's alter ego in creating the Nazi police state. Son of a well-known tenor and director of a conservatory, the musically and athletically gifted Heydrich had joined the navy but was cashiered for conduct unbecoming an officer. Through connections the unprincipled young man found his way into the SS, becoming Himmler's chief of the Security Service (SD) in 1932. Together with Himmler he captured the police forces throughout Germany, becoming the executive authority over the security police (Sipo) and the secret state police (Gestapo). In 1939 he was appointed as head of the Reich Main Security Office (RSHA), which combined all state police and SS branches. Cold, brutal, and egotistic, he managed the Nazi system of terror, including the administrative plans leading to the extermination of six million Jews. He chaired the infamous Wannsee Conference, which led to the formulation of specific methods by which Jews throughout Europe were to be transported to their annihilation camps. In September 1941 he was appointed, in addition to his other positions, as deputy Reich protector of Bohemia and Moravia, where he was assassinated by Czechoslovakian resistance fighters in May 1942.

Himmler, Heinrich (1900–1945). *Reichsführer SS* and Hitler's ruthless bloodhound who built up the Nazi system of institutional control and terror: SS, police, and concentration camp. Born into a respectable and pious Roman Catholic family, Himmler had studied at the Technical University of Munich and received a diploma in agriculture. His contact with various *völkisch* groups and paramilitary organizations led him to adopt a worldview in which the ideal of a new German racial utopia was combined with extreme nationalistic and anti-Semitic prejudices. He found his way into the Nazi Party as early as 1923, participated in the Beerhall Putsch, and then dedicated himself to the reconstruction of the NSDAP. In 1929 Hitler appointed him *Reichsführer SS*, at this time the SS being a small, elite cadre that guarded the führer and kept order at party meetings. Subject to the control of the larger SA, Himmler's Blackshirts were instrumental in helping Hitler consolidate his power and ridding him of the SA threat. In 1934 Himmler gained control of the Gestapo, and in 1936 he was appointed chief of the German police. With his second-in-command, Reinhard Heydrich, Himmler extended his network of SS, police, and concentration camp all over Germany. With the outbreak of World War II, Himmler's SS empire, now consisting of large fighting units (Waffen-SS), business conglomerates, and concentration camps, exploited the whole continent. In the spring of 1941 Hitler gave Himmler a personal order to annihilate the Jews, making Himmler the architect of genocide, responsible for the deaths of six million Jews. The pinnacle of Himmler's power came in 1943 when Hitler appointed him minister of the interior. Although Hitler expelled him from the party in April 1945 for negotiating behind his back with the Allied powers, Himmler remained personally loyal to his führer. Arrested by the British in May 1945, he committed suicide by swallowing poison.

Hindenburg, Paul von (1847–1934). Germany's legendary military leader in World War I who became a national icon in the interwar period. In 1925, already retired, Hindenburg was reluctantly persuaded to run for the presidency of the Weimar Republic. After his election, he served faithfully for the next turbulent nine years. His increasing senility and lack of political acumen caused him to misjudge the radical nature of National Socialism. On January 30, 1933, goaded by his myopic conservative advisers, he appointed Adolf Hitler as chancellor and gave him a series of emergency powers to break down the wall of constitutional order that stood in the way of the Nazi dictatorship. On the day of his death, August 2, 1934, Hitler combined the office of chancellor with that of the president, thus becoming the most powerful man in Germany.

Hitler, Adolf (1889–1945). Sociopathic leader (führer) of the Third Reich who was instrumental in establishing a totalitarian dictatorship, institutionalizing racism, and mobilizing the German people for war and conquest. Born in Austria, the son of a minor postal official, he spent some of his earlier years as a minor painter on the fringes of Austrian and German society, acquiring a set of interrelated prejudices — anti-Semitism, social Darwinism, and extreme pan-German nationalism. World War I, in which he served bravely as a German corporal, provided the social conditions that would make his rise to power possible. Drawing upon festering inner rages and prejudices, acquired as a failed social outsider before the war and now normalized during the chaotic postwar period, he discovered a gift for oratory and political demagoguery.

In 1919, he joined a small, nationalistic, and anti-Semitic party, the German Workers' Party (DAP), and found in this racist beerhall club the instrument by which he would rise to power. He quickly assumed dictatorial control over this small party, and, with the help of committed fanatics, many of whom came from military or paramilitary backgrounds and shared his pathologies, he turned the German Workers' Party, now rechristened the National Socialist German Workers' Party (NSDAP), into a rising force in Bavarian politics.

On November 8–9, 1923, Hitler, in cooperation with affiliated right-wing organizations, tried to overthrow the Bavarian government as a prelude to a national takeover of the hated Weimar government. When the Putsch failed, Hitler was arrested and tried for treason, but he turned failure into triumph by grandstanding as a martyred hero in front of a confused nation. A friendly Bavarian legal system, dominated by right-wing conservatives, sentenced him to only five years in prison with the possibility of parole after eighteen months. While at Landsberg Prison, he wrote his major work, *Mein Kampf* (My battle), a distorted autobiographical account of his life, a justification of his political activities, and an ideological statement of his political prejudices.

After release from prison in December 1924, he patiently reconstructed his party and decided to abandon insurrectionary tactics in favor of legal and democratic means, going on record that he would destroy democracy through democratic means. He spent six years in the political wilderness (1924–30), but then his fortunes dramatically improved as a result of the Great Depression, the weaknesses of his opponents, and the political myopia of German voters, enabling the NSDAP to make a remarkable breakthrough. From a low of 810,000 popular votes and a mere 12 seats in the Reichstag in the election of 1928, the Nazi Party scored 6.4 million votes and seated 107 delegates in the Reichstag in the September 14, 1930, election, making the Nazi Party the second largest party in the country. Two years later, on July 31, 1932, the NSDAP became the largest mass party in Germany. With a private army of close to one million paramilitary forces of SA and SS and the party behind him, Hitler wore down his political opponents and converted a substantial segment of the German people, who increasingly saw him as a national savior. These facts persuaded President Hindenburg, who was also goaded on by his deluded reactionary advisers, to appoint Hitler as chancellor with a mandate to lead a presidential cabinet that was empowered to pass legislation by presidential decree.

Between January 30, 1933 and August 2, 1934, Hitler orchestrated a systematic takeover of the government, using the Reichstag fire of February 27, 1933, as an excuse to force a pliant parliament to give him broad emergency powers enabling him to rule by dictatorial decree (Enabling Law). He used this power to bring about a systematic coordination (*Gleichschaltung*) of German institutions with the political aims of National Socialism. By the summer of 1933, he was in complete control except for the still growing power of the SA under its independent-minded chief Ernst Röhm, who commanded an army of almost four million storm troopers, the traditional German army, and the senile President Hindenburg. Allying himself for tactical and opportunistic reasons with the traditional army and members of the party who stood to gain from Röhm's removal (Goebbels, Göring, Himmler), Hitler eliminated his former SA chief in a bloody purge (June 30–July 1, 1934) and emasculated the power of the SA. Only one month later, on August 2, President Hindenburg died; on that same day Hitler merged the office of chancellor with that of the president, which made him not only the supreme political authority but also commander in chief of the armed forces.

Between 1933 and 1939 Hitler was able to pull Germany out of the economic depression through government deficit spending, extensive public works projects, and massive rearmament. Through the use of sophisticated government propaganda, which involved the skillful manipulation of mass opinion and mass emotions, Hitler immersed the German people in a collective fantasy that they could overcome any obstacle, no matter how staggering, and become the greatest power in the world. He promoted the idea that the Germanic (Aryan) race, being at the apex of biological evolution, was destined to govern the world; but to do so, it had to undergo internal racial purification, involving sterilization of the unfit, euthanasia of "lives not worth living," and elimination of inferior races, chiefly the Jews. In Hitler's mind, the concept of race was intimately linked to the concept of space because a people's greatness depended upon sufficient living space (*Lebensraum*). As long as sixty-five million Germans were limited to a small geographic space, they would remain small and insignificant. He promised to change this situation by rearming the German people and providing living space for them in eastern Europe. In order to make Germany a world power, it was necessary to mobilize its entire resources and to promote in the German people aggressive and warlike tendencies. For this reason, Hitler wanted to breed a hard and callous youth that would delight in war and conquest. The aim of National Socialism, he insisted, should be to teach all Germans to be brutal with a good conscience.

Between 1933 and 1939, his volatile, unstable, and sociopathic personality dominated European diplomacy, for he was able to manipulate the war-weary Western democracies into dismantling the Versailles settlement. At first, he pretended to speak as a man of peace and as a statesman whose nation had been tragically wronged by the Versailles Treaty. Appealing to the latent guilt feelings of the Western powers, he cleverly used the rhetoric of Wilsonian idealism against them by giving the world the impression that he, too, stood for national self-determination and a just and lasting peace. Secretly, however, he was preparing the way for conscription, rearmament, and war.

One brilliant success after another, giving Hitler an aura of invincibility, followed: the reoccupation of the Rhineland (March 7, 1936), the annexation (*Anschluss*) of Austria (March 13, 1938), the annexation of the Sudetenland (September 29, 1938), the destruction of Czechoslovakia and its conversion into a German "protectorate" (Bohemia-Moravia, March 15, 1939), and the incorporation of Memel into the Reich (March 23, 1939). By the spring of 1939, it had become obvious that Hitler was insatiable and that his goals went far beyond national self-determination, for Czechs were not Germans and swallowing up a foreign state was not national self-determination. Yet, regarding himself as the greatest German of all times, his ego inflated to the point of megalomania, Hitler continued to push his aggressive agenda, this time demanding the Polish Corridor and the city of Danzig from Poland as a prelude to his ultimate aim — the conquest of Poland and Russia. In order to forestall having to fight a two-front war and still dismember Poland, Hitler allied himself with his archenemy, the Soviet Union, and signed a Nazi-Soviet Nonaggression Pact on August 23, 1939. One week later, he attacked Poland. Honoring their commitment to Poland, Britain and France declared war on Germany two days later. World War II had begun.

Hitler saw himself waging two world wars: a conventional military war and a biological war aimed at exterminating Germany's greatest enemy — the Jewish race. Between 1939 and 1942 his armies, relying on blitzkrieg (lightning war) tactics, appeared invincible on all fronts. Poland was defeated in three weeks and destroyed as an independent state by Germany and Russia. After a period known as the phoney war or *Sitzkrieg* (sitting war), Hitler resumed his conquests in April 1940, invading and defeating Denmark and Norway in rapid succession. On May 10, he attacked the Western powers; in one month he defeated Holland, Belgium, and France and drove the British expeditionary force from the Continent. By the summer of 1940 he was lord and master of the continent, but the British continued to hold out stubbornly and could not be subdued either by air or sea. After being side-tracked into conquering the Balkans and parts of North Africa as a result of Mussolini's military failures, Hitler committed his greatest and most fatal strategic error. In order to fulfill his racial utopia, which required the defeat of what he regarded as a Bolshevized and Jew-infested Russia, Hitler invaded the Soviet Union on June 22, 1941. On December 11, 1941, following the Japanese attack on Pearl Harbor, he also declared war on the United States.

Hitler was now at war with the major powers of the world: the British Empire, the United States, and Russia, a war of attrition that could not be sustained by the limited resources and manpower at his command. For the next three and a half years, Hitler would wage war on five fronts: the home front, the air, the high seas, the eastern front, and the western front. Over seven million German and associated troops were stationed on far-flung fronts from Scandinavia in the north to the suburbs of Leningrad and Moscow, the Ukraine, and the Crimea in the east; to Holland, Belgium, and France in the west; to Italy and the Balkans in the southeast; and to North Africa and the Atlantic Ocean. At the same time, Hitler's brutal occupation of conquered people and territories, combined with his bestial extermination policies of "inferior races" — Jews, Gypsies, "Asiatic inferiors" — turned his empire into a charnel house and caused a savage backlash against Germany. His crowning achievement, what his henchman Heinrich Himmler called "a glorious page" in German history, was the extermination by poison gas of over five million Jews in annihilation camps in Poland (Auschwitz, Belzec, Chelmno, Maidanek, Sobibor, Treblinka).

With his cities pulverized by air and his armies in retreat on all fronts, Hitler increasingly withdrew from reality into vengeful recrimination, psychosomatic illnesses, and drug dependency. In January 1945, he went underground, directing the war from the safety of his bunker fifty feet under the Reich chancellery. When the Russians mounted their final attack on Berlin, closing in on the chancellery itself, Hitler made out his last will and testament, in which he blamed the Jews for everything and exhorted the Germans to keep the blood pure; he then married his mistress, Eva Braun, and committed suicide along with his new bride on April 30, 1945.

HJ (Hitlerjugend, or Hitler Youth). A youth organization of the NS-DAP that forcibly amalgamated all youth groups in the Third Reich. Under the leadership of Baldur von Schirach, the HJ encompassed the Deutsches Jungvolk, or German Young Folk (ten- to fourteen-year-olds); the Jungmädelbund, or League of Young Girls (ten- to fourteen-year-olds); the Bund deutscher Mädel, or League of German Girls (BDM); and the HJ of fifteen- to eighteen-year-olds. The HJ was further divided into forty areas and subdivided into *Banne* (regiments), *Stämme* (clans), *Gefolgschaften* (followers), *Scharen* (troops), and *Kammeradschaften* (comradeships).

Holocaust. A term derived from an ancient Greek translation signifying "a burnt offering" or sacrifice to God. Although the term can have ambiguous meanings, for it is not clear whether Nazis made a burnt offering to God, God demanded that the Jews be sacrificed as a burnt offering, or the Jews sacrificed themselves as a burnt offering, the term is now generally used to describe the Nazi policy of physically annihilating the Jewish people.

Höss, Rudolf Franz (1900–1947). The SS commandant of Auschwitz who was responsible for seeing to it that over 2.5 million inmates, mostly Jews, were exterminated in his concentration camp. He was sentenced to death for his crimes in 1947.

Hossbach, Friedrich (1894–1980). General and author of the Hossbach Memorandum of November 5, 1937, in which he recorded Hitler's secret comments to his military chiefs that clearly articulate his warlike intentions. His criticisms of Hitler's treatment of Fritsch caused him to lose his position as adjutant representing the armed forces with the führer. Hossbach later served on the eastern front and was dismissed for his independent actions in East Prussia in January 1945.

IMT (International Military Tribunal). A public trial of twenty-two major Nazi leaders by the victorious powers at Nuremberg from November 1945 to October 1946.

Jodl, Alfred (1890–1946). General and chief of staff of operations in the German high command. Responsible for formulating the operational aspects of all military plans and for advising Hitler personally, Jodl became one of the most important military planners in the Third Reich. Conscientious and loyal to Hitler, he later paid for his uncritical and apolitical attitude with his life at Nuremberg.

Kaltenbrunner, Ernst (1903–46). *SS-Obergruppenführer* and successor to Reinhard Heydrich as chief of the Security Service (SD) of the SS from

1943 to 1945. An Austrian lawyer, he was instrumental in helping subvert his country for the *Anschluss* and was rewarded for his efforts by being appointed state secretary for internal security in a cabinet headed by Seyss-Inquart. He was responsible for building up the Gestapo in his native Austria and the concentration camp at Mauthausen. As successor to Heydrich, he distinguished himself in rounding up Jews for the gas chambers and using the Abwehr, which he took over in February 1944, as a tool to combat partisans. The tall and thuggish-looking Kaltenbrunner, his face disfigured by a huge scar, was sentenced to death at Nuremberg for crimes against humanity.

KdF (Kraft durch Freude, or Strength through Joy). Government subsidized program to support recreational activities for German workers. Consisting of five offices — evening leisure, sports, beauty of labor, armed forces homes, and travel — the KdF arranged cheap trips for workers at home and abroad, sponsored concerts and theater productions, organized sports events and hiking trips, and promoted adult education programs. In order to prove its commitment to the German worker, the government lavishly subsidized the KdF. The KdF acquired two ocean liners and tried to market a much-touted people's car (Volkswagen), originally called the KdF Wagen, under the jingle "5 Mark die Woche musst du sparen willst du im eigenen Wagen fahren" (If your own car you want to drive, save the weekly sum of five). Although 336,000 orders for the beetle were placed, none was delivered because the factory switched over to war production.

Keitel, Wilhelm (1882–1946). General field marshal and head of the High Command of the Armed Forces (Oberkommando der Wehrmacht [OKW]). Keitel, also called "Lakaitel" (Toady), was part of all military plans under Hitler; as such, he was later implicated in war crimes and crimes against humanity and sentenced to death at Nuremberg.

Kerrl, Hanns (1887–1941). Politician and jurist. After joining the NSDAP in 1923, Kerrl was elected to the Prussian Landstag in 1928 and in 1932 became its president. When the Nazis seized power, Kerrl became chief of the Prussian Ministry of Justice and served as minister without portfolio in Hitler's government. In 1935 Hitler appointed him minister for church affairs, responsible for all church and state relations. His inability to unite all evangelical churches in one German Evangelical Church, together with his failure to reduce the influence of the Confessional Church, forced him to give up the attempt to coordinate the churches with National Socialism. Kerrl thereafter lost his influence with Hitler, and when he died in 1941, his position was not refilled.

Kesselring, Albert (1885–1960). General field marshal. Kesselring joined the new Aviation Ministry in 1933 and was appointed in 1936 chief of the general staff of the Luftwaffe. In World War II he commanded Air Fleet I in Poland and Air Fleet II in the western campaign and in the east.

In 1941 Hitler appointed him commander in chief of the south, responsible for liaison work between the Italian high command and Rommel's Afrika Korps. After Italy's withdrawal from the war, Kesselring was appointed commander in chief of the Mediterranean theater of war, and in March, Hitler put him in charge of the overall command of the west. Captured by the Allied forces, he was tried for having condoned the execution of 335 Italian partisans and was sentenced to death. His sentence, however, was commuted to life in prison. In 1952 he was pardoned.

Kleist, Ewald von (1881–1954). General field marshal who distinguished himself by commanding a Panzer group on the western front that broke through the French lines at Abbeville. In 1940 he captured Belgrade, and in 1941 he led the first Panzer group in the invasion of Russia, but he made little progress toward Rostov. In 1942 Kleist was ordered to capture the valuable oil reserves in the Caucasus. Although the Nazis used vicious tactics in treating eastern people, Kleist tried to cooperate with the people of the Caucasus; in so doing, he earned not only their respect but also their cooperation in fighting Communism. At the end of the war, Kleist was taken prisoner in Yugoslavia and later transferred to the Soviet Union, where he died in a prison camp for war criminals in 1954.

Kluge, Günther Hans (1882–1944). General field marshal. He was a career soldier who had been retired in 1938 for his support in the Fritsch affair, but was recalled to active duty in September 1939, serving in the Polish and western campaigns. In 1940 Hitler promoted him to general field marshal and then gave him control of Army Group Center during the Russian campaign. Kluge was an indecisive officer who was easily spellbound by Hitler, who always managed to convince him with his histrionic performances. On July 2, 1944, Hitler turned to Kluge to stem the Normandy invasion, but when Kluge was no more successful than Rundstedt, he was replaced by Field Marshal Walther Model. Unable to face his failure on the western front and being suspected of negotiating with the Allied powers, he committed suicide.

Koch, Erich (1896–1986). Brutal *Gauleiter* and later Reich commissioner of the Ukraine. His brutal rule in Russia, which shocked even the SS, provoked intense partisan opposition from a population that was originally friendly toward the German troops. He was personally responsible for sending thousands of Ukrainians to Germany as slave laborers and ensured that countless Jews were transported to annihilation camps. Near the end of the war he organized resistance against the Red Army at Königsberg and then disappeared from view, not to surface until 1949 when he was arrested by the British and turned over to the Poles for trial.

Kristallnacht (Night of Crystals). Refers to the night of November 9–10, 1938, when the Nazis instigated widespread attacks on Jewish synagogues, businesses, and homes throughout Germany in retaliation for the assassination of Ernst vom Rath, secretary to the German legation in Paris, by a young Jewish protester, Herschel Grynszpan, whose parents along with many former Polish Jews in Germany were being forcibly evicted. The Nazis used this assassination as a pretext to instigate pogroms that resulted in the deaths of ninety-one Jews, the incarceration of twenty-six thousand Jews in concentration camps, and the destruction of seventy-five hundred Jewish businesses. In the wake of Kristallnacht came several measures that further intensified Nazi discrimination against the Jewish population. The government blamed the Jews for the outrage it instigated and brazenly seized the money German insurance companies were paying for damaged Jewish property. In addition, the Jews were forced to pay a "contribution" of one billion RM. On November 12, 1938, a decree was passed by which Jews were prohibited from attending theaters, cinemas, concerts, and public exhibitions. Jewish children were forbidden to attend public schools. Shortly thereafter, the Nazis ushered in Phase 2 in their attacks on the Jews, opening a Reich Central Office for Jewish Emigration under Heydrich's overall command.

K2. German abbreviation for *Konzentrationslager* or concentration camp.

Lammers, Hans Heinrich (1879–1962). Head of the Reich chancellery. A lawyer and judge by profession, Lammers was a cautious, conservative bureaucrat who essentially functioned as Hitler's secretarial rubber stamp, preparing laws, handling personnel matters relating to the ministerial bureaucracy, serving as a liaison between the various ministries, and informing Hitler of ongoing state business. His "hear no evil, see no evil, and speak no evil" attitude, coupled with his readiness to put his legal rubber stamp on Hitler's criminal decrees, earned Lammers a twenty-year prison sentence at Nuremberg.

Lebensborn (Life Springs). An SS organization, founded in 1935, that provided safe homes for women, married or unmarried, who had children by SS men. Located in out of the way places, these homes also functioned as stud farms where suitable German women could mate with equally suitable SS "assistants of conception." By 1944 almost eleven thousand children were born in thirteen Life Springs homes. In addition, these homes served as conduits for Himmler's criminal program of kidnapping Aryan-type children in the eastern territories and finding adoptive parents for them in Germany.

Leeb, Ritter von (1876–1956). General field marshal whose career is in many ways paradigmatic of the German Generalität — general staff officer in World War I, continuation of service in the Reichswehr, retired in the wake of the Fritsch crisis, and recalled on active duty during the Sudeten crisis. He commanded Army Group C in France and then Army

Group North in Russia. Dismissed by Hitler for his lack of progress in taking Leningrad, he spent the rest of the war in retirement.

Ley, Robert (1890–1945). One of the early leaders of the Nazi Party. As *Gauleiter* and NSDAP Reichstag deputy, Ley fought periodic bouts with alcoholism that caused him to fade in and out of favor with Hitler. For a time, he was deputy party organization leader under Strasser, a post to which he succeeded when Röhm was murdered. After the seizure of power, Hitler appointed Ley as leader of an Action Committee for the Protection of German Labor. Ley used this position to destroy the unions and replace them with the German Labor Front (DAF), one of the largest mass organizations under the Nazis. Ley increased his empire by developing the Strength through Joy Movement within the DAF and also by establishing two major Nazi elite educational institutions — the Adolf Hitler Schools and the Ordensburgen. During the war his influence began to diminish under the impact of rival empires (Todt, Speer, Sauckel). Arrested by Allied troops, Ley committed suicide before he could be tried as a war criminal at Nuremberg.

Ludendorff, Erich (1865–1937). Legendary World War I hero and Hindenburg's chief of staff. After the war Ludendorff drifted into right-wing nationalistic causes and teamed up with Hitler in the abortive Beerhall Putsch of November 8–9, 1923, to overthrow the Reich government. Acquitted at the subsequent trial, he became a National Socialist delegate to the Reichstag (1924–28). Under the influence of his second wife, Ludendorff became increasingly eccentric, cultivating neopagan and conspirational beliefs. He also distanced himself from Hitler and the Nazis and even declared that Hindenburg, by having appointed Hitler chancellor, "had put the fate of the fatherland into the hands of one of the greatest demagogues of all time."

Mein Kampf (My battle). Hitler's autobiographical and ideological account of his struggles and hopes for Germany. Dictated to Rudolf Hess at Landsberg Prison in the summer of 1924, the book was originally entitled "Four and a Half Years of Struggle against Lies, Stupidity, and Cowardice," but Hitler's publisher and business manager, Max Amann, shortened it to *Mein Kampf*. Until 1930, the book appeared in two separate volumes, but then it was combined in a one-volume, Bible-like people's edition selling at eight marks a copy. By 1945, roughly ten million copies had been sold, and the book had been translated into sixteen languages. After 1945, publication rights reverted to the state of Bavaria, whose official policy has been to prohibit publishing the book. *Mein Kampf* has been unavailable to German readers through bookstores.

Meissner, Otto (1878–1968). German jurist and chief of the presidential chancellery under Ebert, Hindenburg, and Hitler. Meissner was a key figure in the secret negotiations that led to Hitler's appointment as chancellor. A conservative monarchist and a career bureaucrat of the old school, Meissner found himself isolated under the Nazis. After Hitler merged the office of president and chancellor, Meissner's position became essentially superfluous; his office became a powerless appendage relegated largely to processing appeals for clemency.

Mengele, Josef (1911–79). SS physician and infamous "Angel of Death" at Auschwitz. As a strong believer in racial science, Mengele joined the Waffen-SS in 1940 and served as a medical officer in France and Russia. In 1943 Himmler appointed him as chief doctor at Auschwitz where he conducted gruesome "scientific experiments," especially on twins, and presided over the daily selections of incoming Jews, picking some for hard labor and others (old people, women, children) for extermination. After the war, he managed to flee Germany for Argentina, always eluding the law by moving from country to country (Argentina, Paraguay, Brazil). He probably died of a heart attack in Brazil in 1979.

Morrell, Theodor (1886–1948). Hitler's favorite private physician. Before meeting Hitler, he had operated a fashionable practice for skin and venereal diseases on the Kurfürstendamm in Berlin. Hitler met him when he needed a dermatologist to cure him of eczema of the leg. Morrell's willingness to experiment with unorthodox treatment methods, usually in the form of injections (hence his nickname, "Reich Injection Master"), commended him to Hitler. Under the führer's patronage, Morrell's stock rose rapidly. Not only did he enrich himself but he also seems to have had few qualms in using Hitler as a guinea pig, possibly turning him into a drug addict during the later stages of World War II.

Müller, Heinrich (1900–?). *SS-Gruppenführer* and head of the Gestapo (1939–45). Nicknamed "Gestapo Müller," he was feared throughout Germany and occupied Europe for his brutal treatment of the people under his control. He rounded up countless opponents and personally participated in organizing mass liquidations of Jews. His fate after he fled the Reich chancellery bunker in May 1945 remains unknown.

Napolas (National Political Institutes of Education). Elite party schools designed to train future government leaders.

Nebe, Arthur (1894–1945). German police official and chief of the criminal police (Kripo) in the Reich Main Security Office. During the Russian campaign, he headed Einsatzgruppe B, but could not tolerate the mass murders committed under his command and returned to his former position in the criminal police. Implicated in the July 20, 1944, plot against Hitler's life, he was tried and executed in March 1945.

Neurath, Konstantin von (1873–1956). German diplomat and Nazi foreign minister from 1933 to 1938. A diplomat of the old school, Neurath proved to be too cautious and conservative for the aggressive path Hitler was charting for Germany. In 1938 Hitler replaced Neurath with the more aggressive Ribbentrop, retaining Neurath as a minister without portfolio and in 1939 appointing him to the largely symbolic post of Reich protector of Bohemia and Moravia. In 1943 Neurath was retired for good. At Nuremberg he was sentenced to fifteen years in prison but was released on account of his poor health in 1954.

Niemöller, Martin (1892–1984). Lutheran pastor and staunch opponent of the Nazis after they tried to coordinate the Lutheran Church. Mercurial and enigmatic, Niemöller had been a submarine commander in World War I but decided to dedicated his life to Christ upon his return to civilian life. After studying theology he was ordained in the Lutheran Church and became one of the most popular pastors in Berlin. When the Nazis tried to coordinate the church, he took over leadership of the Confessional Church, set up the Pastors' Emergency League, and bravely stood up to Nazi intimidation. In 1937, he was arrested and imprisoned for many months before being tried on charges of sedition and sentenced to seven months. Hitler was furious with this "lenient sentence," had Niemöller rearrested almost immediately after his release, and had him sent to a concentration camp, where he remained until the end of the Third Reich.

NSBO (National Socialist Factory Cell Organization). A protounion wing of the NSDAP whose aim was to wage propaganda in business and industrial plants in order to win the workers over to National Socialism.

NSDAP (Nationalsozialistische deutsche Arbeiter Partei, or National Socialist German Workers' Party). The Nazi Party.

Obersalzberg. A one-thousand-meter mountain northeast of Berchtesgaden on which Adolf Hitler constructed his private villa, the Berghof.

Ohlendorf, Otto (1907–51). *SS-Obergruppenführer* and head of Einsatzgruppe D in Russia. He was responsible for the deaths of one hundred thousand victims, mostly Jews, and was sentenced to death at Nuremberg.

OKH (Oberkommando des Heeres, High Command of the Army).

OKL (Oberkommando der Luftwaffe, High Command of the Air Force).

OKM (Oberkommando der Kriegsmarine, High Command of the Navy).

OKW (Oberkommando der Wehrmacht, High Command of the Armed Forces). Refers to the new command structure, established in February 1938, of the armed forces that replaced the old Reich War Ministry.

Operation Barbarossa. *See* **Barbarossa.**

Ordensburgen (Castles of Order). The highest elite academies of the Nazi Party, located in rustic settings at Sonthofen in the Allgäu,

Crössinsee in Pomerania, and Vogelsang in the North Eifel. Candidates, called Ordensjunker, were to undergo three and a half years of training in political and administrative subjects qualifying them as party functionaries. Only a two-year course actually took place between 1937 and 1939. Candidates were about twenty-five years of age and had already attended six years in the Adolf Hitler Schools, had spent two and a half years in the Labor Service (Abeitsdienst), and had done several years of party work. Emphasis was on athletics and military training rather than demanding intellectual work.

Orpo (*Ordnungspolizei,* order police). Police branch that had been separated by Himmler from the Gestapo and the criminal police. Led by Kurt Dalugue, the order police forces handled routine business such as traffic, patrols, and other police matters in both city and rural areas. Some of the "order police" units, however, were involved in mass atrocities in Poland and Russia, functioning like the *Einsatzgruppen.*

Oster, Hans (1888–1945). General and chief of staff of the Abwehr, the German espionage and news agency service. A determined opponent of Hitler, he worked hand in glove with his superior, Admiral Canaris, in spearheading the military resistance against the Nazis. In April 1944 he was dismissed from his post and in the wake of the failed plot against Hitler on July 20, 1944, he was arrested, sent to Flossenbürg concentration camp, and hanged along with Canaris shortly before the end of the war.

Papen, Franz von (1879–1969). Conservative Catholic politician, Weimar chancellor (1932), vice-president in the initial Hitler (1933–34) cabinet, minister and then ambassador to Austria (1934–38), and ambassador to Turkey (1939–44). The dashing, suave, and opportunistic Papen was one the most important stalking horses that Hitler used to gain access to the ruling elites of Germany and through them made his leap into power. Although a clever intriguer, Papen lacked the psychological acumen to recognize Hitler's ruthlessness and destructiveness. Cleared of any wrongdoing at Nuremberg, he was subsequently found guilty by a German denazification court and sentenced to eight years of hard labor in 1949 but released for time already spent. If Papen was guilty of anything, it was a monumental ignorance of the destructive power of Adolf Hitler and his opportunistic willingness to do his bidding to the very end.

Pfeffer, Franz (1888–?). World War I officer, Free Corps leader, and Röhm's successor as head of the SA from 1926 to 1930. Unable to work smoothly with Hitler, who replaced him briefly as chief of the SA, Pfeffer faded into the background, particularly after Röhm's reappointment to the top SA post. His only rule during the Third Reich was to serve as a member of the Reichstag (1933–42). What happened to him after the war has never been fully established.

Pohl, Oswald (1892–1951). *SS-Obergruppenführer* and chief of administration in the SS Main Office (SS-Hauptamt). As chief financial administrator of the SS, Pohl managed a huge economic empire that included the administration and supply of the Waffen-SS, all concentration and labor camps, and all economic enterprises. Unscrupulous, slick, and intensely ambitious, he ruthlessly exploited his massive army of close to seven hundred thousand slave laborers and obediently carried out Himmler's order to annihilate concentration camp inmates through hard work. Captured in 1946, Pohl was tried and sentenced to death.

RAD (Reichsarbeitsdienst, or Reich Labor Service). Starting on June 26, 1935, labor service for German males between the ages of eighteen and twenty-five became mandatory and after 1939 for females as well. Originally intended as a means of reducing unemployment, compulsory labor service was increasingly used to indoctrinate young people after they had already been brainwashed by the Hitler Youth. Under the leadership of Konstantin Hierl, a retired colonel, the RAD was organized according to strict military principles and thus served the regime as a training ground for future soldiers of the Reich.

Raeder, Erich (1876–1960). Grand admiral and supreme commander of the navy. Although a strong supporter of Hitler's rearmament program, he warned against a conflict between Germany and Britain, strongly believing that the German navy was inadequately prepared to support Hitler's grand ideological goals. Raeder became increasingly frustrated after Hitler subordinated his Mediterranean strategy, aimed at breaking the back of the British Empire, to his eastern (Russian) campaign. Raeder's break with Hitler occurred when the latter insisted on changing Germany's naval strategy from building up a large surface fleet to massive expansion of U-boats. In March 1943, Raeder was replaced by Dönitz as supreme commander of the navy. Raeder was found guilty of having participated in the planning and waging of aggressive war and was sentenced to life in prison. He was released in 1955.

Reichenau, Walter von (1884–1942). General field marshal who supported Hitler's aggressive military goals. Hitler made him a field marshal after he had served in the Polish and French campaigns. Reichenau was one of the few German commanders who enthusiastically supported the campaign against Russia, including the brutal treatment of "Asiatic inferiors" and Jews. In December 1941 Hitler gave him the command of Army Group South, but he died shortly afterwards of a stroke.

Reichsleiter (Reich leader). The highest functionary in the Nazi Party, who exercised sweeping powers in his particular field. Appointed by Hitler, the *Reichsleiter* formed the highest level of the party, collectively called the *Reichsleitung*.

Reichstatthalter (Reich governor). Agent or commissioner of the Reich government who was responsible for supervising a state government. These officials were empowered to appoint and dismiss state officials and to monitor whether individual state governments were in compliance with the Reich government. Most Reich governors were also *Gauleiter* and thus directly responsibly to Hitler.

Ribbentrop, Joachim von (1893–1946). An opportunistic and intensely ambitious social climber, Ribbentrop had grafted himself on the rising Nazi movement in the early 1930s and used his social connections and his villa in Dahlem to bring together Hitler and the conservative political elite around President Hindenburg. After the Nazi seizure of power, he served Hitler as an adviser on foreign affairs and, on his own initiative, created a new foreign service institution (Dienststelle Ribbentrop), which concentrated primarily on Anglo-German relations. In 1935 Ribbentrop helped to negotiate the favorable Anglo–German Naval Agreement, which served as a springboard to his appointment as ambassador to Great Britain (1936–38). In 1938 Hitler appointed him to the post of foreign minister. In this position, he became Hitler's willing instrument in the conspiratorial policies that would lead to World War II. The Nazi-Soviet Nonaggression Pact, negotiated by Ribbentrop in Moscow in August 1939, was his crowning achievement. During the war, which he had helped to initiate, his influence steadily diminished, but he involved the Foreign Office in the final solution to the Jewish question by putting intense pressure on Allied or occupied countries to turn over Jewish citizens. For this as well as his role in triggering the war, Ribbentrop was found guilty on all counts at Nuremberg and hanged in 1946.

Riefenstahl, Leni (1902–). German dancer, actress, and filmmaker. The strikingly beautiful and vivacious Riefenstahl began her career as a dancer employed by Max Reinhardt in the early 1920s and became a motion picture idol by the time Hitler seized power. In 1933 Hitler "persuaded" her to direct a film on the Nazi Party annual congress at Nuremberg. The result was the most famous documentary of Nazi propaganda called *Triumph of the Will,* a clever masterpiece of cinematic illusionism that tried to show the world the power and charisma of Hitler and his movement. Riefenstahl brought the same artistic flair to the Olympic Games of 1936 in a two-part visual feast of athletic beauty and drama.

Röhm, Ernst (1887–1934). Chief of the SA and one of the earliest supporters of Hitler and the Nazi Party. A dyed-in-the-wool militarist, Röhm belonged to the "lost generation," hardened by war and disillusioned by a dishonorable peace. He was instrumental in helping launch the NSDAP, participated in the Beerhall Putsch of 1923, and then drifted without a clear purpose through the late 1920s, ultimately going to Bolivia as a military adviser. In late 1930, Hitler recalled him and asked him to take charge of the SA. In little over two years, Röhm built up the SA into a mass army of brownshirted storm troopers that Hitler could use as an instrument of electoral intimidation and persuasion. After the seizure of power, however, Röhm and Hitler increasingly came to a parting of the ways over how this mass army should be used. Röhm saw the SA as a revolutionary people's army of the future that would incorporate the regular German army. Since this conception threatened to derail Hitler's own political plans, he decided to purge the SA along with its independent-minded chief. On June 30, 1934, Röhm and the top SA leaders were arrested and killed.

Rommel, Erwin (1891–1944). General field marshal and one of Hitler's most effective and popular generals of World War II. Highly decorated as an officer in World War I (Pour le Mérite), Rommel made the army his career, serving in the Reichswehr as an instructor at the infantry school in Dresden (1929–33). Rommel strongly supported the National Socialist movement and was identified early on by Hitler as an outstanding talent. He served as liaison officer to the Reich Youth Leadership and participated as commandant at führer headquarters in the Sudeten crisis, in the second Czechoslovakian crisis of March 1939, and in the invasion of Poland. His first field command was as leader of the Seventh Panzer Division on the western front, but his legendary reputation was earned as commander of the Afrika Corps in northern Africa. In a series of brilliant tank battles, which earned him the title of "Desert Fox," he threw the British back to El Alamein, just sixty miles from Alexandria. Because of lack of support from Hitler, who had shifted his major military resources to the eastern front, Rommel was ultimately defeated by the British at El Alamein and driven out of Africa by combined British and American forces. After commanding Army Group B in Italy, Rommel was put in charge of an army in northern France, responsible for fortifying the coast against an Allied invasion. After D-Day, Rommel urged Hitler to end the war; he also established contact with the resistance group that planned to eliminate Hitler. When the plot failed on July 20, 1944, Rommel was in the hospital recuperating from a serious car accident. When Hitler learned of his complicity in the July 20 plot, he gave Rommel two choices: committing suicide or facing trial in front of the People's Court with all the attendant consequences for his family. Rommel took poison on October 14, 1944, and was given a hero's state funeral. The German people were told that he had succumbed to his automobile injuries but that his "heart had always belonged to the führer."

Rosenberg, Alfred (1893–1946). Foremost Nazi racial philosopher and politician. Born in Reval, Estonia, and educated in Riga and Moscow, Rosenberg belonged to the Auslandsdeutsche, to those persons of German ethnicity who lived outside Germany in various tight-knit communities whose members acted more German than the Germans. His ideology, culled primarily from ethnic-racial tracts and conspiratorial theories, became an important element in Nazi doctrines. Hitler leaned heavily on Rosenberg in the formative years of the party (1919–23) and made him chief editor of the *Völkischer Boelbachter.* Rosenberg participated in the putsch of 1923 and unsuccessfully tried to keep the party afloat during Hitler's imprisonment. Only peripherally involved in the political machinations that would lead to Hitler's seizure of power, Rosenberg tried to assert himself as an intellectual, publishing a monumentally turgid and nebulous work called *Myth of the Twentieth Century,* which was widely ridiculed even by the Nazis. After the seizure of power, Rosenberg was put in charge of the party office for foreign politics and also served as the führer's deputy for monitoring the spiritual education of the NSDAP. In both posts he was overshadowed and outmatched by more powerful rivals (Goebbels, Rust, Ribbentrop). The same was true during World War II when Hitler appointed him as Reich minister for the occupied eastern territories. In his effort to implement a more diplomatic and even humane policy toward ethnic groups in Russia, he was stymied by Himmler and ultimately Hitler himself. Caught in a web of conflicts with the army, the SS, Göring, and the Reich commissioners, he ended up being ignored by everyone. At Nuremberg he was found guilty on all charges and hanged.

RSHA (Reichssicherheitshauptampt, or Reich Main Security Office). The super security agency of the SS created on September 27, 1939, and headed by Reinhard Heydrich.

Rundstedt, Gerd von (1875–1953). General field marshal and, next to Rommel, one of the most respected German generals. A strong believer in the old-school Prussian tradition, Rundstedt, like Rommel, had a checkered relationship with Hitler and National Socialism. A career officer, he served as a general staff officer in World War I and continued to advance rapidly through the ranks of the Reichswehr. Hitler retired him after learning of his critical attitude during the Czech crisis of 1938. However, he was recalled for the Polish campaign as supreme commander of Army Group South. In France as well as in Russia he commanded a major army group. When he withdrew his troops from Rostov in December 1941 he was retired again. But Rundstedt came out of retirement yet again, serving as supreme commander of the western forces from March 1942 to March 1945. Although aware of the plot against Hitler's life, even supporting some of the men who spearheaded it, Rundstedt decided to remain on the sidelines. He even served on the army's court of honor in weeding out officers who had participated in the plot. He was kept in British captivity until 1949 on charges of lesser war crimes but released for health reasons in 1949.

RuSHA (Rasse und Siedlungshauptamt, Race and Settlement Main Office of the SS).

SA (Sturmabteilung, or Storm Detachment). Hitler's private army of brownshirted storm troopers who safeguarded Nazi meeting halls, served as bodyguards to party leaders, fought street battles with members of the opposition, and acted as political foot soldiers distributing leaflets, begging for donations, and pounding the pavement for votes in support of the führer.

Sauckel, Fritz (1894–1946). National Socialist politician and during World War II general plenipotentiary for labor allocation. Sauckel was an early party member and devoted follower of Adolf Hitler. In 1927 Hitler appointed him *Gauleiter* and in 1933 *Reichstatthalter* of Thuringia. When World War II broke out, Hitler made him Reich defense commissioner and general plenipotentiary of labor allocation. In 1942 Sauckel was given supreme authority to mobilize German and foreign workers. He performed his duties of recruiting foreign labor with great brutality. His protection squads scoured all of Europe for slave labor; they kidnapped their prey and shipped them to Germany in freight cars under appalling conditions. By the end of 1944, there were more than seven million foreign laborers in Germany. Sauckel was found guilty and hanged at Nuremberg in 1946.

Schacht, Hjalmar (1877–1970). One of the most important financial experts during the interwar period. As currency commissioner in the Finance Ministry in 1923, he was instrumental in stabilizing the mark and bringing an end to inflation. From 1924 to 1929 he was president of the Reichsbank, Germany's most important financial institution. In the late 1920s Schacht moved increasingly to the political right and saw merit in some elements of National Socialism. In 1933, after being reappointed as president of the Reichsbank, he initially supported Hitler's massive rearmament policy, which led to his appointment as Reich finance minister (1935–37) and general plenipotentiary for war economy. He began to develop serious doubts about the nature of National Socialism on both political and moral grounds, particularly after the Röhm Purge and the relentless attacks on the Jews. In 1936, after Hitler appointed Göring as head of the Four-Year Plan, he openly criticized Hitler's economic policies and resigned all of his posts except that of minister without portfolio, which he retained until 1943. His connections with the resistance led to his imprisonment in the wake of the July 20, 1944, plot against Hitler's life. To his great disgust, he was tried at Nuremberg with the other major Nazis but was acquitted on all counts.

Schirach, Baldur von (1907–74). German youth leader and politician. Son of a well-known Weimar theater director and his American wife, young Schirach became involved in the Nazi movement while he was an art and German language student at the University of Munich. In 1931

Hitler appointed the idealistic Schirach as Reich youth leader and then tasked him with the responsibility of coordinating all youth movements after 1933. Carried away by the empty shibboleths of Nazi propaganda, the fatuous and morally obtuse Schirach deluded himself and many young people into believing that the Nazi state was a new dawn for young Germans. The war quickly disabused him of these illusions. Unable to assert himself against his unprincipled rivals, he was replaced as youth leader in 1940 by Arthur Axmann and was pushed out of the way by being appointed *Gauleiter* and *Reich Statthalter* of Vienna. In 1943, during a visit to the Berghof, Schirach and his wife, Henriette, protested to Hitler about the brutal occupation policies and the treatment of Jews. After this encounter, Hitler no longer trusted Schirach and totally ignored him. Interestingly enough, as *Gauleiter* of Vienna, Schirach was responsible for rounding up and deporting 185,000 Austrian Jews to the east. Although he later claimed at Nuremberg that he did not know of the annihilation camps to which these Jews were sent, he was found guilty and sentenced to twenty years in prison.

Schleicher, Kurt von (1882–1934). General and politician. Of the handful of men who determined the course of German politics between 1930 and 1933, none was more perniciously influential than this scheming desk general whose name (Schleicher suggests "creeper" or "crawler" in German) was in many ways an index to his character. Holding an important liaison position in the Reichswehr Ministry and advising the minister of defense, Schleicher strongly believed that the army had to abandon its nonpartisan position and actively involve itself in politics. He did so on behalf of right-wing conservative causes and acted as a kingmaker who enjoyed power without responsibility. After manipulating the downfall of Brüning, Groener, and Papen, he was called on by President Hindenburg to form what would turn out to be the last government of the Weimar Republic. Schleicher lasted less than two months (December 3, 1932–January 28, 1933). Neither his plan to form a broad multiparty coalition nor his effort to split the ranks of the Nazis by wooing Strasser worked out. With his resignation, the way was open for Adolf Hitler. On June 30, 1934, Schleicher and his wife were murdered during the Röhm Purge.

Scholtz-Klink, Gertrud (1902–). Nazi women's leader. Mother of eleven children, the blonde, tall, and fertile Scholtz-Klink actively entered politics when her husband, an SA man, died of a heart attack during a demonstration. She joined the party in 1928 and became leader of the National Socialist Women's Organization in Baden (1930) and Hesse (1931). In January 1934 she took over the Labor Service for Women and then became Reich leader of the National Socialist Women's Organization (NSF) and the German Women's Work (DFW). Later in 1934 Hitler promoted her to the top post of Reich women's leader (*Reichsfrauenführerin*). As "lady führer," she officially spoke for the concerns of millions of German women, and she did so by putting a sentimental veneer on the male reactionary views of the Nazi leadership.

SD (Sicherheitsdienst, or Security Service). The intelligence service of the SS headed by Reinhard Heydrich. Its function was to discover the enemies of National Socialism and ideally arrest them before they had done anything wrong. Mushrooming into a grotesque bureaucracy of professionals, informants, and sadists, this terroristic police and "thought control" agency became not only an instrument of totalitarian control but also one of the chief executive organs of the annihilation of Jews, Gypsies, Communists, and "Asiatic inferiors."

Seyss-Inquart, Arthur (1892–1946). Austrian lawyer and councilor of state who helped Hitler in paving the way for the *Anschluss* (annexation) of Austria in March 1938. Hitler rewarded him for his service in subverting Austria by making him Reich governor (*Reichstatthalter*) of the Ostmark, as Austria was now called. He served briefly as Hans Frank's deputy in Poland (October 1939–May 1940) and was then promoted to Reich commissioner of the Netherlands, a post he held until the end of the war. For sanctioning the deportation and liquidation of Jews and hostages, he was found guilty and executed at Nuremberg in 1946.

Sipo (Sicherheitspolizei, or security police). The security police force consisting of the Gestapo, the criminal police, and border police. Heydrich fused the Sipo with the SD when he became head of the Reich Main Security Office (RSHA).

Speer, Albert (1905–81). Hitler's favorite architect and minister of armaments (1942–45). As a young and idealistic architectural student, Speer had joined the Nazi Party after listening to a speech by Hitler. Various minor architectural commissions for the party ultimately brought the unknown Speer to Hitler's notice. Hitler seems to have seen in the young man a reflection of what he might have been had he succeeded as painter and architect, and he used Speer as the instrument of his own monumental aesthetic visions. Speer's rise under Hitler's tutelage was meteoric. He designed the various theatrical props that made the Nuremberg party congresses such impressive spectacles; he also designed the new Reich chancellery and several other buildings. In 1942, after Fritz Todt's death, Hitler appointed Speer as minister of armaments. Despite constant saturation bombings, Speer substantially increased production between 1942 and 1944, making him one of the few effective Nazi administrators. In the spring of 1945 Speer told Hitler that the war was lost and obstructed his irrational orders (Nero Order) to obliterate German industries. At Nuremberg he was one of the few leading Nazis who accepted full responsibility for his actions and denounced the crimes of the Nazi regime. He was sentenced to twenty years in prison,

where he wrote two of the most important works on Nazi Germany —
Inside the Third Reich (memoirs) and *Spandau Diaries.*

Spengler, Oswald (1880–1936). Conservative monarchist and philosopher of history whose epochal work, *Decline of the West,* a comparative
study of the rise and fall of world civilizations, established him as one
of the most prophetic minds of the twentieth century. Although initially
attracted by National Socialism, Spengler became increasingly repelled
by the movement's bombastic utopianism and virulent racism. His last
book, *The hour of Decision* (1933), portrayed the Nazis as dangerous extremists, intoxicated by their bombastic rhetoric and unhistorical
views. Officially prohibited from publishing anything in Germany, Spengler withdrew into inner exile, throwing such barbs at the Nazis as,
"Only racial inferiors preach racism"; "the Nazi Party is an organization of the unemployed by those who shirk work"; or the Nazis are
not "barbarians like the ancient Germans but cannibals who torture,
murder, and rob." True to his prophetic gifts, he predicted the coming
of a second world war in which Germany would face the same powers as in World War I. Death by heart attack in 1936 spared him from
experiencing the truth of his gloomy predictions.

SS (Schutzstaffel, or Protective Squads). An elite paramilitary organization, formed in 1923, that began as a small group of bodyguards
protecting the führer and developed into a party police force, a terrorist Reich police force, a regular army within the army (Waffen-SS), a
huge economic conglomerate with its tentacles reaching into German
businesses, and a gigantic murder machine that supervised a far-flung
system of concentration camps in which people were tortured and annihilated. Under Heinrich Himmler, the SS became a state within a state,
and its blackshirted members formed a tight-knit fraternity of racial true
believers.

Stauffenberg, Claus Graf Schenk von (1907–44). Colonel and catalyst
of Operation Valkyrie, the plan to assassinate Hitler and topple the
Nazi government. Member of an ancient family of Württemberg nobles,
young Stauffenberg was a conservative monarchist who initially supported the Nazi movement and served with great distinction on several
fronts during the war, losing an eye and half of his left hand while fighting in North Africa in 1943. By that time he had become a determined
opponent of Hitler, whom he described as the Antichrist. He established
connections to the Kreisau Circle through his cousin Count Peter Yorck
von Wartenburg, and after the arrest of Moltke he took personal charge
of the conspiracy against Hitler. On July 20, 1944, he carried a bomb
in his briefcase to the conference room at Rastenburg in East Prussia,
Hitler's military headquarters. Although the device exploded and Stauffenberg was able to fly to Berlin to lead the projected coup, Hitler was

only slightly injured and ordered the arrest and execution of its ring leaders. Stauffenberg was shot at the Bendlerstrasse on the same day.

Strasser, Gregor (1892–1934). Pharmacist and one of the earliest leaders of the NSDAP. Strasser joined the Nazi Party in 1921, served as *Gauleiter* of Lower Bavaria, and participated in the Munich Beerhall Putsch of 1923. As a member of the Bavarian legislature, he received an amnesty for his participation in the coup and was able to carry on as one of the major organizational leaders of the party while Hitler was incarcerated at Landsberg. From 1925 to 1932 Strasser was instrumental in building up the party organization and served as its organizational leader. However, his strong socialistic beliefs eventually put him at odds with Hitler, whose support of Strasser began to diminish, particularly after Gregor's brother Otto openly bolted the party. In December 1932 Hitler drummed Strasser out of the party after learning that General Schleicher had offered Strasser the vice-chancellorship in his government. Strasser then retired from active politics; he was murdered by Nazi assassins during the Röhm Purge.

Strasser, Otto (1897–1974). German politician and journalist. Like his brother Gregor, he joined the Nazi Party believing that it represented the working population. Between 1925 and 1930, he promoted the cause of National Socialism through his publishing company called Kampf Verlag. When he noticed that Hitler was turning his back on socialism, he accused him of betraying the basic principles on which he believed the NSDAP was founded, bolted the party, and formed the Black Front, consisting of disenchanted Socialists and assorted Communists. After the seizure of power, he left Germany, not to return until 1955.

Stülpnagel, Karl Henrich von (1886–1944). German general and resistance fighter. As supreme military commander of France, Stülpnagel became the focal point of the military resistance against Hitler. When the coup against Hitler began, Stülpnagel arrested SS, SD, and Gestapo leaders in France, but when the plot failed, he was recalled to Germany, where, after an unsuccessful suicide attempt, he was tried by the People's Court and executed.

Stürmer, der. Nauseous anti-Semitic newspaper published by Julius Streicher from 1923 to 1945 in Nuremberg. At its height, the paper reached close to an average of six hundred thousand copies per year (1933–40). The paper served up a steady stream of abusive anti-Semitic stories, stereotyping Jews as rapists of Aryan women, financial shysters, ritual murderers of innocent children, and so on. In depersonalizing Jews as vermin, toads, bacilli, rats, and other maligned animals, Streicher greatly contributed to the harvest of hate that led to the Holocaust.

Thierack, Otto (1889–1946). German jurist, chief of the People's Court, and minister of justice. Thierack was indicted for his efforts to subvert justice and use the judicial system as an instrument of totalitarian terror. He escaped his impending trial by committing suicide in 1946.

Thule Society. Conspiratorial racial society founded in 1918 by Rudolf von Sebattendorf (Rudolf Glauer). The society became a focal point for right-wing, nationalistic, and anti-Semitic agitators such as Dietrich Eckart, Alfred Rosenberg, Hans Frank, Gottfried Feder, and Rudolf Hess. Although the Thule Society was a kind of midwife to the NSDAP, its own future was short-lived because it could never rise above the role of a small conspiratorial sect with distinct elitist pretensions.

Thyssen, Fritz (1878–1951). German industrialist and steel magnate who helped finance the Nazi Party but eventually quarrelled with the party's rearmament and anti-Semitic policies. After the Nazi-Soviet Nonaggression Pact, which he strongly denounced, Thyssen left Germany but was later turned over to the Nazis by the Vichy government, ending up in a concentration camp. In 1948 he left Germany and emigrated to Argentina.

Todt, Fritz (1891–1942). German engineer and politician. In 1933 Hitler appointed Todt, an early party member, to the post of general inspector of German roads, responsible for the construction of the *Autobahnen* (freeways). Todt rose rapidly in the Nazi hierarchy because Hitler personally liked him. In 1938, he became general plenipotentiary for all public construction projects, particularly the construction of the West Wall. In 1940 he was appointed minister of armaments in addition to his other duties. Operating largely on a very independent basis outside the regular machinery of government, answerable only to Hitler, Todt built up a huge organization that spanned a very broad spectrum of economic activities and that became the controlling force behind the war effort. When Todt died in a plane accident, Hitler replaced him with Albert Speer.

Völkisch (National- or ethnic-mindedness). The term denotes a sense of Germanic ethnocentrism, cultivated by hosts of nationalistic movements before and after World War I. An important part of this Germanic ethnocentrism was anti-Semitism. The Nazis represented the extreme expression of such tribal feelings and beliefs.

Völkischer Beobachter (Ethnic/racial observer). The official newspaper of the NSDAP, published with only a short interruption (1924) from 1919 to 1945 and edited throughout much of this period by Alfred Rosenberg.

V-1/V-2 (*Vergeltungswaffen,* or reprisal weapons). These *Wunderwaffen,* or "miracle" weapons, were missiles developed by German scientists such as Wernher von Braun and Colonel Walter Dornberger at Peenemünde. The V-1 was basically a remote-controlled airplane that could reach speeds of four hundred miles per hour and unload a ton of explosives at a particular target. The V-2, the first supersonic rocket, was a much larger missile, forty-six feet long and weighing more than thirteen tons, that could reach thirty-five hundred miles per hour and deliver a ton of explosives over a distance of 225 miles. The V-1 bombs were launched against London from their bases on the French coast in June 1944, causing as much fear as they did damage. It is estimated that eight thousand V-1 and more than one thousand V-2 were launched against England before their launching sites were destroyed.

VW (Volkswagen, or People's Car). Designed by Ferdinand Porsche, the People's Car was designed to be affordable for ordinary Germans and represented the regime's efforts to win over the hearts and minds of the German working population. The suggestion for its beetlelike shape supposedly came from Hitler; the promise of mass production, however, was not fulfilled because the factory that was supposed to produce the VW switched over to war production.

Waffen-SS (Armed SS). Term used to describe the fighting arm of the SS.

Wannsee Conference (January 20, 1942). A top-secret government conference, chaired by Heydrich and attended by major representatives involved in Jewish affairs (Eichmann, Stuckart, Luther, Freisler). It was during this conference that the technical means of bringing about the "final solution" to the Jewish question were discussed. The participants all agreed that the Jews represented a deadly biological health hazard and therefore had to be exterminated. The overall plan was to conduct a thorough sweep of Jews in the whole of Europe and transport them to the five major annihilation camps at Auschwitz, Belzec, Treblinka, Sobibor, and Majdanek. The Wannsee Conference was not the initiation of the final solution — that had already begun with mass shootings two years before — but a cooperative effort by which major state organizations agreed on common procedures of implementing the annihilation of European Jews.

Wehrmacht (Armed Forces). Term first used in 1935 to refer collectively to the branches of the German military — army, navy, air force.

Wessel, Horst (1907–30). A young university student and early martyr of the Nazi Party who is best known for the stirring lyrics that became part of the party's anthem, the "Horst Wessel Lied." Wessel was killed by Communists in a personal brawl in February 1930.

White Rose. Code name for a student resistance group at the University of Munich, headed by Sophie and Hans Scholl, sister and brother, and their mentor, Professor Kurt Huber. The little group organized an underground network in Munich and at several other German universities, protesting Nazi rule. Reported to the Gestapo, the Scholls along with Huber were arrested and executed in February 1943.

Witzleben, Erwin von (1881–1944). German field marshal and one of the military leaders who attempted to remove Hitler on July 20, 1944. Witzleben had served with great distinction during the early phases of the war on both the western and the eastern fronts and retired as a field marshal in 1942. As commander in chief of the armed forces he worked behind the scenes in organizing opposition against Hitler within the military and became a key figure in the 1944 plot. Witzleben, like the other plotters, was arrested, tried, and executed for his participation in the plot.

Zeitzler, Kurt (1895–1963). Chief of staff of the army who replaced Halder in September 1942 and held that office until 1944. A career soldier of the old school, Zeitzler was a capable and energetic officer who supported Hitler to the limits of his professional loyalty, but finally asserted himself against Hitler's risky operations. In January 1945, Zeitzler retired from the army.

Bibliography

Original Sources

I. Archives
II. Autobiographies, Diaries, Memoirs, Speeches
    1. German
    2. Non-German
III. Bibliographic Aids
IV. Ideological Works
V. Newspapers and Periodicals
VI. Published Documents and Collections

Secondary Sources

I. The European Background
II. The German Background
III. General Surveys and Interpretive Works
IV. The Nazi Movement during the Weimar Republic
V. Adolf Hitler
VI. Major Nazi Leaders
    1. Martin Bormann
    2. Karl Dönitz
    3. Joseph Goebbels
    4. Hermann Göring
    5. Rudolf Hess
    6. Reinhard Heydrich
    7. Heinrich Himmler
    8. Ernst Kaltenbrunner
    9. Robert Ley
    10. Franz von Papen
    11. Joachim von Ribbentrop
    12. Alfred Rosenberg
    13. Albert Speer
    14. Julius Streicher
VII. Domestic Politics under National Socialism
    1. The Nazi Party
    2. Totalitarian Control: Propaganda and Terror
    3. Youth and Education

Original Sources

I. Archives

Bayerisches Hauptstaatsarchiv, Munich (BHSA)
Berlin Document Center (BDC)
Bibliothek für Zeitgeschichte, Stuttgart
Bundesarchiv Freiburg (BA Freiburg)
Bundesarchiv Koblenz (BA Koblenz)
The Hoover Institution on War, Revolution and Peace (HI), Stanford, California.
Institut für Zeitgeschichte, Munich (IfZ)
Leo Baeck Institute, New York
National Archives, Washington D.C.

II. Autobiographies, Diaries, Memoirs, Speeches

1. German

Bormann, Martin. *The Bormann Letters: The Private Correspondence between Martin Bormann and His Wife.* Ed. H. R. Trevor-Roper. London: Weidenfeld and Nicolson, 1954.

Braun, Otto. *Von Weimar zu Hitler.* Hamburg: Hammonia Norddeutsche Verlagsanstalt, 1949.

Brecht, Arnold. *Mit der Kraft des Geistes: Lebenserinnerungen, 1927–1967.* Stuttgart: Deutsche Verlags-Anstalt, 1967.

Brüning, Heinrich. *Memoiren: 1918–1934.* Stuttgart: Deutsche Verlags-Anstalt, 1970.

Diels, Rudolf. *Lucifer ante Portas.* Zurich: Internaverlag, 1969.

Dietrich, Otto. *Mit Hitler an die Macht.* Munich: Eher, 1934.

———. *Zwölf Jahre mit Hitler.* Munich: Isar, 1955.

Dönitz, Karl. *Memoirs.* London: Weidenfeld and Nicolson, 1958.

Frank, Hans. *Im Angesicht des Galgens.* Munich: Beck, 1953.

Gisevius, Hans. *Bis zum bitteren Ende.* 2 vols. Zurich: Fretz & Wasmuth, 1946.

Goebbels, Joseph. *Der Angriff: Aufsätze aus der Kampfzeit.* Munich: Eher, 1940.

———. *The Early Goebbels Diaries: 1925–1926.* Ed. Helmut Heiber. New York: Praeger, 1963.

————. *Final Entries 1945: The Diaries of Joseph Goebbels*. Ed. H. R. Trevor-Roper. New York: Avon Books, 1979.

————. *The Goebbels Diaries*. Ed. Louis P. Lochner. New York: Popular Library, 1948.

————. *Goebbels-Reden*. Ed. Helmut Heiber. Düsseldorf: Droste, 1971–72.

Die Tagebücher von Joseph Goebbels: Sämtliche Fragmente. Ed. Elke Fröhlich. 4 vols. Munich: Saur, 1987.

————. *Vom Kaiserhof zur Reichskanzlei*. Munich: Eher Verlag, 1937.

Göring, Emmy. *An der Seite meines Mannes*. Göttingen: K. W. Schütz, 1967.

Göring, Hermann. *The Political Testament of Hermann Göring: A Selection of Important Speeches and Articles by Field-Marshal Hermann Göring*. Ed. H. W. Blood-Ryan. London: John Long, 1939.

————. *Gespräche mit Hermann Göring während des Nürnberger-Prozesses*. Ed. W. Bross. Flensburg-Hamburg: C. Wolff, 1950.

Guderian, Heinz. *Erinnerungen eines Soldaten*. Heidelberg: Kurt Vowinckel, 1951.

Halder, Franz. *Hitler as Warlord*. New York: Putnam, 1950.

————. *Kriegstagebuch: Tägliche Aufzeichnungen des Chefs des Generalstabs des Heeres, 1939–1942*. 3 vols. Stuttgart: Kohlhammer, 1962–64.

Hanfstaengl, Ernst. *Unheard Witness*. New York: Lippincott, 1957.

Hassell, Ulrich von. *Vom andern Deutschland: Aus dem nachgelassenen Tagebüchern, 1938–44*. Frankfurt: Fisher, 1946.

Heusinger, Adolf. *Befehl im Widerstreit: Schicksalstunden der deutschen Armee, 1923–1945*. Tübingen: R. Wunderlich, 1950.

Himmler, Heinrich. *Diaries of Heinrich Himmler's Early Years*. Ed. W. T. Angress and B. F. Smith. *Journal of Modern History* 31 (1959).

————. *Heinrich Himmler: Geheimreden 1939–1945*. Ed. Bradley F. Smith and Agnes Peterson. Frankfurt: Propyläen, 1974.

————. *Reichsführer! Briefe an und von Himmler*. Ed. H. Heiber. Stuttgart: Deutsche Verlags-Anstalt, 1968.

Hitler, Adolf. *Blitzkrieg to Defeat: Hitler's War Directives, 1939–1945*. Ed. H. R. Trevor-Roper. New York: Holt, Rinehart & Winston, 1964.

————. *Hitler: Reden und Proklamationen, 1932–1945*. Ed. Max Domarus. 2 vols. in 4. Wiesbaden: R. Löwit, 1973.

————. *Hitler: Sämtliche Aufzeichnungen, 1905–1924*. Ed. Eberhard Jäckel. Stuttgart: Deutsche Verlags-Anstalt, 1980.

————. *Hitlers Briefe und Notizen*. Ed. Werner Maser. Düsseldorf: Econ Verlag, 1973.

————. *Hitler's Secret Book*. Trans. Salvator Attanasio. New York: Grove Press, Inc., 1961.

————. *Hitlers Tischgespräche im Führerhauptquartier*. Ed. Henry Picker. Stuttgart: Goldmann Verlag, 1981.

————. *Mein Kampf*. New York: Reynal & Hitchcock, 1941.

————. *The Speeches of Adolf Hitler: April 1922–August 1939*. Ed. Norman H. Baynes. 2 vols. London: Oxford Univ. Press, 1942.

Höss, Rudolf. *Kommandant of Auschwitz*. Ed. Martin Broszat. New York: World, 1961.

Hossbach, Friedrich. *Zwischen Wehrmacht und Hitler*. Wolfenbüttel: Wolfenbütteler Verlagsanstalt, 1949.

Jünger, Ernst. *Der Kampf als inneres Erlebnis*. Berlin: Mittler, 1925.

Kehrl, H. *Krisenmanager im Dritten Reich: 6 Jahre Frieden, 6 Jahre Krieg. Erinnerungen.* Düsseldorf, 1973.

Kersten, Felix. *The Kersten Memoirs.* London: Hutchinson, 1956.

Kessler, Count Harry. *Tagebücher, 1918–1937.* Frankfurt: Insel-Verlag, 1961.

Kordt, Erich. *Nicht aus den Akten: Die Wilhelmstrasse in Frieden und Krieg.* Stuttgart: Deutsche Union Verlagsgesellschaft, 1950.

————. *Wahn und Wirklichkeit.* Stuttgart: Deutsche Union Verlagsgesellschaft, 1948.

Kubizek, August. *The Young Hitler I Knew.* Trans. E. V. Anderson. New York: Tower Publications, n.d.

Leber, Julius. *Ein Mann geht seinen Weg: Schriften, Reden und Briefe von Julius Leber, herausgegeben von seinen Freunden.* Berlin: Mosaik, 1952.

Mann, Klaus. *Heute und Morgen.* Munich: Nymphenburger, 1969.

Mann, Thomas. *Diaries, 1918–1939.* Trans. Richard and Clara Winston. New York: Abrams, 1982.

Manstein, Erich. *Aus einem Soldatenleben.* Bonn: Athenäum, 1958.

————. *Verlorene Siege.* Bonn: Athenäum, 1955.

Meinecke, Friedrich. *Augewählter Briefwechsel.* Ed. Ludwig Dehio and Peter Classen. Stuttgart: Koehler, 1962.

Meissner, Otto. *Staatssekretär unter Ebert-Hindenburg-Hitler: Der Schicksalsweg des deutschen Volkes von 1918–1945, wie ich ihn erlebte.* Hamburg: Hoffmann & Campe, 1951.

Niemöller, W. *Aus dem Leben eines Bekenntnispfarrers.* Bielefeld: Bechauf, 1961.

Papen, Franz von. *Der Wahrheit eine Gasse.* Munich: P. List, 1952. Translated as *Franz von Papen: Memoirs.* London: Andre Deutsch, 1952.

Raeder, Erich. *Mein Leben.* 2 vols. Tübingen: Fritz Schlichtenmayer, 1960.

Rauschning, Hermann. *Gespräche mit Hitler.* New York: Europa, 1940.

————. *Men of Chaos.* New York, 1942.

Reck-Malleczewen, Friedrich Percyval. *Diary of a Man in Despair.* Trans. Paul Rubens. New York: Macmillan, 1970.

Ribbentrop, Joachim. *The Ribbentrop Memoirs.* London: Weidenfeld & Nicolson, 1962.

Riefenstahl, Leni. *A Memoir.* New York: St. Martin's Press, 1993.

Röhm, Ernst. *Geschichte eines Hochverräters.* Munich: Eher, 1931.

Rommel, Erwin. *The Rommel Papers.* Ed. B. H. Liddell Hart. London: Collins, 1953.

Rosenberg, Alfred. *Letzte Aufzeichnungen.* Göttingen: Plesse, 1955.

————. *Das Politische Tagebuch Alfred Rosenbergs aus den Jahren 1934/35 und 1939/40.* Ed. Hans-Günther Seraphim. Göttingen: Musterschmidt, 1956.

————. *Portrait eines Menschenverbrechers, nach den hinterlassenen Memoiren des ehemaligen Reichsministers Alfred Rosenberg.* Ed. S. Lang and E. von Schenck. St. Gallen: Zollikofer, 1947.

Schacht, Hjalmar Greeley. *Account Settled.* London: Weidenfeld and Nicolson, 1949.

————. *Confessions of the Old Wizard.* Boston: Houghton Mifflin, 1956.

Schirach, Baldur von. *Ich glaubte an Hitler.* Hamburg Mosaik, 1967.

Schmidt, Paul. *Statist auf diplomatischer Bühne, 1923–1945.* Bonn: Athenäum Verlag, 1952.

Schuschnigg, Kurt. *Austrian Requiem.* Trans. Franz von Hildebrand. London: Gollancz, 1946.

———. *Im Kampf gegen Hitler.* Vienna: Molden, 1969.

Severing, Carl. *Mein Lebensweg.* 2 vols. Cologne: Greven, 1950.

Speer, Albert. *Infiltration.* Trans. Joachim Neugroschel. New York: Macmillan, 1981.

———. *Memoirs.* Trans. Richard and Clara Winston. New York: Macmillan, 1970.

———. *Spandauer Tagebücher.* Berlin: Propyläen, 1975.

Spengler, Oswald. *Briefe, 1913–1936.* Ed. Anton Koktanek and Manfred Schröter. Munich: Beck, 1963.

Strasser, Otto. *Hitler and I.* Boston Houghton Mifflin, 1940.

Thomas, Georg. *Geschichte der deutschen Wehr-und Rüstungswirtschaft, 1918–45.* Ed. Wolfgang Birkenfeld. Boppard am Rhein: Boldt, 1966.

Thyssen, Fritz. *I Paid Hitler.* London: Hodder & Stoughton, 1941.

Treviranus, Gottfried Reinhold. *Das Ende Von Weimar: Heinrich Brüning und seine Zeit.* Vienna: Econ-Verlag, 1968.

Warlimont, Walter. *Inside Hitler's Headquarters.* London: Weidenfeld and Nicolson, 1954.

2. Non-German

Beck, Józef. *Dernier Rapport.* Neuchatel: Baconniere, 1951.

Benes, E. *From Munich to New War and New Victory.* Boston: Houghton Mifflin, 1954.

Burckhardt, Carl J. *Meine Danziger Mission, 1937–1939.* Munich: Callwey, 1960.

Chamberlain, Neville. *In Search of Peace.* New York: Putnam, 1939.

Churchill, Winston S. *The Second World War.* 6 vols. Boston: Houghton Mifflin, 1950.

Ciano, Galeazzo. *The Ciano Diaries, 1939–1943.* New York: Doubleday, 1946.

———. *Ciano's Diplomatic Papers.* Ed. Malcolm Muggeridge. London: Odhams, 1948.

———. *Ciano's Hidden Diary, 1937–1938.* New York: Dutton, 1953.

Cooper, Alfred Duff. *Old Men Forget.* London: Ruppert Hart Davis, 1953.

Dahlerus, Birger. *The Last Attempt.* London: Hutchinson, 1948.

Dodd, William, and Martha Dodd, eds. *Ambassador Dodd's Diary, 1933–1938.* London: Gollancz, 1941.

Eden, Anthony. *The Eden Memoirs: Facing the Dictators.* London: Cassell, 1962.

François-Poncet, André. *The Fateful Years.* London: Gollancz, 1949.

Gilbert, G. M. *Nuremberg Diary.* New York: New American Library, 1947.

Henderson, Neville. *Failure of a Mission.* New York: Putnam, 1940.

Hoare, Samuel. *Nine Troubled Years.* London: Collins, 1954.

Jones, Thomas. *A Diary with Letters.* Oxford: Oxford University Press, 1954.

Kennan, George F. *Memoirs, 1925–1950.* Boston: Little, Brown & Co., 1967.

Lipski, Josef. *Diplomat in Berlin, 1933–1939.* Ed. W. Jedrzejewicz. New York: Columbia University Press, 1968.

Nicolson, Harold. *Diaries and Letters of Harold Nicolson.* 2 vols. Ed. Nigel Nicolson. New York: Atheneum, 1967.

Shirer, William. *Berlin Diary: The Journal of a Foreign Correspondent, 1934–1941*. New York: Alfred Knopf, 1941.
———. *20th Century Journey: A Memoir of a Life and the Times*. 3 vols. New York: Bantam, 1976–90.
Simon, John. *Retrospect*. London: Hutchinson, 1952.
Vansittart, Robert. *The Mist Procession*. London: Hutchinson, 1958.

III. Bibliographic Aids

American Historical Association, Committee for the Study of War Documents. *Guides to German Documents Microfilmed at Alexandria, Virginia*. Washington D.C.: National Archives, 1958–.
Aycoberry, Pierre. *The Nazi Question: An Essay on the Interpretations of National Socialism*. New York: Pantheon, 1988.
Facius, Friedrich, et al. *Das Bundesarchiv und seine Bestände*. Boppard am Rhein: Boldt, 1961.
Freeman, Michael. *Atlas of Nazi Germany*. New York: Macmillan, 1987.
Hüttenberger, Peter. *Bibliographie zum Nationalsozialismus*. Göttingen: Vandenhoeck & Ruprecht, 1980.
Kehr, Helen, and Janet Langmaid. *The Nazi Era 1919–1945: A Select Bibliography of Published Works from the Early Roots to 1980*. London: Mansell, 1980.
Kent, George O. *A Catalogue of the Files and Microfilms of the German Foreign Ministry Archives, 1920–1945*. 3 vols. Stanford, Calif.: Stanford University Press, 1962–66.
Lötzke, Helmut. *Übersicht über die Bestände des deutschen Zentralarchivs Potsdam*. East Berlin: Rutten & Loening, 1957.
Snyder, Louis L. *Encyclopedia of the Third Reich*. New York: Paragon, 1976.
Statistisches Jahrbuch für das Deutsche Reich. Berlin, published annually.
Whiteside, Andrew G. "The Nature and Origin of National Socialism." *Journal of Central European Affairs* 17 (1957) 48–73.
Who's Who in Nazi Germany. London: British Ministry of Economic Warfare, 1944.
Wistrich, Robert S. *Who's Who in Nazi Germany*. London: Weidenfeld and Nicolson, 1982.
Zentner, Christian, and Friedemann Bedürftig, eds. *Das Grosse Lexikon des Dritten Reiches*. Munich: Südwest, 1985.

IV. Ideological Works

Bürgel, Bruno. *Das Weltbild des modernen Menschen: Das All, die Erde, der Mensch, der Sinn des Lebens*. Berlin: Ullstein, 1937.
Chamberlain, Houston S. *Die Grundlagen des neunzehnten Jahrhunderts*. Munich: Bruckmann, 1906.
Clauss, Ludwig F. *Eine Einführung in die Rassenkunde*. Munich: Lehmann, 1934.
Darré, Walther R. *Neuadel aus Blut und Boden*. Munich: Lehmann, 1930.
———. *Um Blut und Boden*. Munich: Eher, 1942.

Dcisz, Robert. *Das Recht der Rasse: Kommentar zur Rassengesetzgebung.* Munich: Zentralverlag der NSDAP, 1938.

Drexler, Anton. *Mein politisches Erwachen,* Munich: Deutscher Volksverlag, 1923.

Eckart, Dietrich. *Der Bolshevismus von Moses bis Lenin: Zwiegespräch zwischen Adolf Hitler und mir.* Munich: Hoheneichen, 1924.

Feder, Gottfried. *Der deutsche Staat auf nationaler und sozialer Grundlage.* Munich: Eher, 1923.

————. *Kampf gegen die Hochfinanz.* Munich: Eher, 1933.

————, ed. *Nationalsozialistische Bibliothek.* Munich: Eher, n.d.

Goebbels, Joseph. *Der Angriff. Wetterleuchten: Aufsätze aus der Kampfzeit.* Munich: Zentralverlag der NSDAP, 1939.

————. *Das eherne Herz: Reden und Aufsätze aus den Jahren 1941/42.* Munich, Zentralverlag der NSDAP, 1943.

————. *Michael: Ein deutsches Schicksal in Tagebuchblättern.* Munich: Eher, 1929.

————. *Die Zeit ohne Beispiel: Reden und Aufsätze aus den Jahren 1939/40/41.* Munich: Zentralverlag der NSDAP, 1941.

Günther, Hans F. R. *Rassenkunde des deutschen Volkes.* Munich: Lehmann, 1935.

————. *Rassenkunde Europas.* Munich: Lehmann, 1929.

Hartner, Herwig. *Erotik und Rasse: Eine Untersuchung über sittliche und geschlechtliche Frage.* Munich: Deutscher Volksverlag, 1925.

Jung, Rudolf. *Der nationale Sozialismus, seine Grundlagen, sein Werdegang und seine Ziele.* Munich: Deutscher Volksverlag, 1922.

Meister, Wilhelm. *Judas Schuldbuch: Eine deutsche Abrechnung.* Munich: Deutscher Volksverlag, 1919.

Moeller van den Bruck, Artur. *Das Dritte Reich.* Hamburg: Hanseatische Verlagsanstalt, 1931.

Passow, H., ed. *Ja aber, was sagt Hitler selbst?* Munich: Eher, n.d.

Retcliffe, Sir John (Hermann Goedsche). *Biarritz.* Munich: Deutscher Volksverlag, 1929 (originally published in 1868).

Rosenberg, Alfred. *Der Mythos des 20. Jahrhunderts.* Munich: Hoheneichen, 1934.

————. *Wesen, Grundsätze und Ziele der Nationalsozialistischen Deutschen Arbeiterpartei.* Munich: Deutscher Volksverlag, 1929.

————, ed. *Die Protokolle der Weisen von Zion und die jüdische Weltpolitik.* Munich: Deutscher Volksverlag, 1923.

Zöberlein, Hans. *Der Befehl des Gewissens: Ein Roman von den Wirren der Nachkriegszeit und der ersten Erhebung.* Munich: Eher, 1937.

————. *Der Glaube an Deutschland: Ein Kriegserleben von Verdun bis zum Umsturz.* Munich: Eher, 1931.

V. Newspapers and Periodicals

Berliner Tageblatt
Frankfurter Allgemeine
Die H. J. Das Kampfblatt der Hitlerjugend
Münchner Neueste Nachrichten

Münchner Post
Nationalsozialistische Monatshefte
Nationalsozialistisches Bildungswesen
Neues Deutschland
The New York Times
Das Reich
Das Schwarze Korps
Der Stürmer
Süddeutsche Zeitung
The Times of London
Völkischer Beobachter
Vorwärts
Wille und Macht: Führerorgan der H. J.

VI. Published Documents and Collections

Deuerlin, Ernst, ed. *Der Aufstieg der NSDAP in Augenzeugenberichten.* Munich: DTV, 1974.

————. *Der Hitler Putsch: Bayerische Dokumente zum 8./9. November 1923.* Stuttgart: Deutsche Verlags-Anstalt, 1962.

Documents diplomatiques francais, 1932–1939. Paris: Imprimerie Nationale, 1963–86.

Documents on British Foreign Policy, 1919–1939. London: H.M. Stationary Office, 1949.

Documents on German Foreign Policy, 1918–1949. Washington, D.C.: U.S. Department of State, 1949–.

Documents on International Affairs. Royal Institute of International Affairs. London: Oxford University Press, 1929–.

Dokumente der deutschen Politik. 9 vols. Berlin: Junker & Dünnhaupt, 1937–44.

Fuehrer Conferences on Matters Dealing with the German Navy, 1939–1945. 8 vols. Washington D.C.: U.S. Government Printing Office, 1946–47.

The Hitler Trial before the People's Court in Munich. Trans. H. Francis Freniere, Lucie Karcic, and Philip Fandek. 3 vols. Arlington, Va.: University Publications of America, 1976.

Hofer, Walther, ed. *Der Nationalsozialismus: Dokumente 1933–1945.* Frankfurt: Fischer, 1957.

International Military Tribunal: Trial of the Major War Criminals before the International Military Tribunal: Proceedings and Documents. 42 vols. Nuremberg, 1947–49.

Jacobsen, Hans-Adolf and Werner Jochman, eds. *Ausgewählte Dokumente zur Geschichte des Nationalsozialismus.* Bielefeld: Verlag Neue Gesellschaft, 1961.

Junker, Detlef, ed. *Deutsche Parlamentsdebaten.* 2 vols. Frankfurt: Fischer, 1971.

Kriegstagebuch des Oberkommandos der Wehrmacht, 1940–1945. Ed. Percy E. Schramm, et al. 4 vols. Frankfurt Bernard Graefe, 1961–65.

Meldungen aus dem Reich: Auswahl aus dem geheimen Lageberichten des Sicherheitsdienstes der SS, 1933 bis 1944. Ed. H. Boberach. Berlin: Luchterhand, 1965.

Michaelis, Herbert, and Ernst Schraepler, eds. *Ursachen und Folgen: Vom deutschen Zusammenbruch 1918 und 1945 bis zur staatlichen Neuordnung Deutschlands in der Gegenwart.* 21 vols. Berlin: Wandler, 1958–.

Mosse, George L., ed. *Nazi Culture: Intellectual, Cultural and Social Life in the Third Reich.* New York: Grosset & Dunlap, 1966.

Nazi Conspiracy and Aggression. 8 vols. and 2 supplements. Washington, D.C.: U.S. Government Printing Office, 1946–48.

Noakes, Jeremy, and Geoffrey Pridham, eds. *Nazism: A History in Documents and Eyewitness Accounts, 1919–1945.* 2 vols. New York: Schocken, 1988.

Pross, Harry, ed. *Die Zerstörung der deutschen Politik: Dokumente, 1871–1933.* Frankfurt: Fischer, 1959.

Remak, Joachim, ed. *The Nazi Years.* Englewood Cliffs, N.J.: Prentice-Hall, 1969.

Schmolze, Gerhard, ed. *Revolution und Räterepublik in München 1918/19, in Augenzeugenberichten.* Düsseldorf: Karl Rauch, 1969.

Sontag, Raymond J., and J. S. Beddie, eds. *Nazi-Soviet Relations, 1939–41.* Washington, D.C.: U.S. Government Printing Office, 1948.

Secondary Sources

I. The European Background

Arendt, Hannah. *The Origins of Totalitarianism.* New York: Meridian, 1958.

Barbu, Zevedei. *Democracy and Dictatorship: Their Psychology and Patterns of Life.* New York: Grove, 1956.

Carsten, Francis. *Fascist Movements in Austria: From Schönerer to Hitler.* London: Sage, 1977.

———. *The Rise of Fascism.* Berkeley: University of California Press, 1967.

Cassel, Alan. *Fascism.* New York: Crowell, 1975.

De Felice, Renzo. *Interpretations of Fascism.* Cambridge, Mass.: Harvard University Press, 1977.

Drucker, Peter. *The End of Economic Man: A Study in the New Totalitarianism.* New York: John Day, 1939.

Friedrich, Carl J., and Zbigniew K. Brzezinski. *Totalitarian Dictatorship and Autocracy.* New York: Praeger, 1962.

Fromm, Erich. *Escape from Freedom.* New York: Avon Books, 1965.

Gregor, James A. *The Fascist Persuasion in Radical Politics.* Princeton, N.J.: Princeton University Press, 1974.

———. *Interpretations of Fascism.* Morristown, N.J.: General Learning Press, 1974.

Halevy, Elie. *The Era of Tyrannies.* Trans. R. K. Webb. New York: Doubleday, 1965.

Hayes, Carlton J. H. *A Generation of Materialism.* New York: Harper & Row, 1941.

Hoffer, Eric. *The True Believer: Thoughts on the Nature of Mass Movements.* New York: Harper & Row, 1966.

Hughes, H. Stuart. *Consciousness and Society: The Reorientation of European Social Thought, 1890–1930.* New York: Vintage, 1958.

Kornhauser, William. *The Politics of Mass Society.* London: Routledge and Kegan Paul, 1960.

Laqueur, Walter, ed. *Fascism: A Reader's Guide.* Berkeley: University of California Press, 1976.

Laqueur, Walter, and George L. Mosse, eds. *International Fascism, 1920–1945.* New York: Harper & Row, 1966.

Larsen, Stein Ugelvik, et al. *Who Were the Fascists? Social Roots of European Fascism.* New York: Columbia University Press, 1981.

Le Bon, Gustave. *The Crowd.* New York: Viking Press, 1960 (originally published in 1895).

Ledeen, Michael. *Universal Fascism.* New York: Fertig, 1972.

Masur, Gerhard. *Prophets of Yesterday: Studies in European Culture, 1890–1914.* New York: Harper & Row, 1961.

Mayer, Arno J. *Dynamics of Counter-Revolution in Europe, 1870–1956.* New York: Harper & Row, 1971.

Mazlish, Bruce. *The Revolutionary Ascetic: Evolution of a Political Type.* New York: McGraw-Hill, 1976.

Moore, Barrington, Jr. *Social Origins of Dictatorship and Democracy.* Boston: Beacon, 1966.

Nagy-Talavera, N. M. *The Green Shirts and the Others: A History of Fascism in Hungary and Rumania.* Stanford, Calif.: Stanford University Press, 1970.

Nolte, Ernst. *Three Faces of Fascism.* Trans. Leila Vennewitz. New York: Holt, Rinehart & Winston, 1966.

————, ed. *Theorien über Faschismus.* Königstein/Ts: Athenäum, 1984.

Ortega y Gasset, José. *The Revolt of the Masses.* New York: Norton, 1960 (originally published in 1932).

Payne, Stanley G. *Fascism: Comparison and Definition.* Madison, Wis.: University of Wisconsin Press, 1980.

Reich, Wilhelm. *The Mass Psychology of Fascism.* Trans. Vincent R. Carfagno. New York: Strauss & Giroux, 1970.

Remon, René. *The Right-Wing in France from 1815 to de Gaulle.* Philadelphia: University of Pennsylvania Press, 1966.

Rogger, Hans, and Eugen Weber, eds. *The European Right: A Historical Profile.* Berkeley: University of California Press, 1966.

Sorel, Georges. *Reflections on Violence.* Trans. T. E. Hulme and J. Roth. New York: Collier Books, 1961 (originally published in 1906).

Talmon, J. L. *The Origins of Totalitarian Democracy.* New York: Praeger, 1960.

Thamer, H. U., and Wolfgang Wippermann, eds. *Faschistische und Neofaschistische Bewegungen.* Darmstadt: Wissenschaftliche Buchgesellschaft, 1977.

Tuchman, Barbara. *The Proud Tower: A Portrait of the World before the War: 1890–1914.* New York: Macmillan, 1966.

Turner, Henry A., ed. *Reappraisals of Fascism.* New York: Viewpoints, 1975.

Vagts, Alfred. *A History of Militarism.* Reprint. Westport, Conn.: Greenwood, 1981.

Weber, Eugen. *Varieties of Fascism.* Princeton, N.J.: Van Nostrand, 1964.

Wippermann, Wolfgang. *Faschismustheorien.* Darmstadt: Wissenschaftliche Buchgesellschaft, 1975.

II. The German Background

Becker, Howard. *German Youth: Bond or Free?* London: Kegan Paul, Trench, Trubner & Co., 1946.

Bergsträsser, Ludwig. *Geschichte der politischen Parteien in Deutschland.* 11th ed. Munich: Olzog, 1965.

Böhme, Helmuth. *Deutschlands Weg zur Grossmacht.* Cologne: Kiepenheuer & Witsch, 1966.

———. *The German Dilemma.* Trans. Richard Berry. London: Weidenfeld & Nicolson, 1974.

Bridgman, Jon M. *The Revolt of the Hereros.* Berkeley: University of California Press, 1981.

Chickering, Roger. *We Men Who Feel Most German: A Cultural Study of the Pan-German League, 1886–1914.* London: Allen & Unwin, 1984.

Craig, Gordon A. *The Germans.* New York: New American Library, 1982.

———. *Germany, 1866–1945.* New York: Oxford University Press, 1978.

Dahrendorf, Ralf. *Society and Democracy in Germany.* New York: Doubleday, 1969.

Dehio, Ludwig. *Germany and World Politics.* Trans. Dieter Pevsner. New York: Norton, 1959.

———. *The Precarious Balance: Four Centuries of the European Power Struggle.* Trans. Charles Fullman. New York: Vintage, 1962.

Drechsler, Horst. *Let Us Die Fighting: The Struggle of the Herero and Nama against German Imperialism.* London: Zed, 1980.

Felken, Detlef. *Oswald Spengler: Konservativer Denker zwischen Kaiserreich und Diktatur.* Munich: Beck, 1988.

Field, Geoffrey G. *Evangelist of Race: The Germanic Vision of Houston Steward Chamberlain.* New York: Columbia University Press, 1981.

Fischer, Fritz. *Germany's Aims in the First World War.* New York: Norton, 1967.

Fischer, Klaus P. *History and Prophecy: Oswald Spengler and the Decline of the West.* New York: Peter Lang, 1989.

Holborn, Hajo. *A History of Modern Germany.* 3 vols. New York: Alfred A. Knopf, 1959–69.

Jarausch, Konrad H. *Students, Society, and Politics in Imperial Germany.* Princeton, N.J.: Princeton University Press, 1983.

Klemperer, Klemens von. *Germany's New Conservatism.* Princeton, N.J.: Princeton University Press, 1957.

Kohn, Hans. *The Mind of Germany: The Education of a Nation.* New York: Harper & Row, 1960.

Krieger, Leonard. *The German Idea of Freedom.* Chicago: University of Chicago Press, 1957.

Mann, Golo. *The History of Germany since 1789.* Trans. M. Jackson. New York: Praeger, 1968.

Massing, Paul W. *Rehearsal for Destruction.* New York: Harper & Brothers, 1949.

Meinecke, Friedrich. *The German Catastrophe.* Trans. Sidney B. Fay. Boston: Beacon, 1963.

Mosse, George L. *The Crisis of German Ideology: The Intellectual Origins of the Third Reich.* New York: Grosset & Dunlap, 1964.

————. *The Nationalization of the Masses: Political Symbolism and Mass Movements in Germany from the Napoleonic Wars through the Third Reich*. New York: Fertig, 1975.

Palmer, Alan. *The Kaiser: Warlord of the Second Reich*. New York: Scribner's, 1978.

Poliakov, Leon. *The Aryan Myth: A History of Racist and Nationalist Ideas in Europe*. New York: Meridian, 1971.

Pultzer, Peter. *The Rise of Political Anti-Semitism in Germany and Austria*. New York: Wiley, 1964.

Reinhardt, Kurt F., Gerhart Hoffmeister, and Frederic C. Tubach. *Germany: 2000 Years*. 3 vols. New York: Frederick Ungar, 1950; new expanded edition (vol. 3, 1992) by Hoffmeister and Tubach.

Ringer, Fritz. *The Decline of the German Mandarins*. Cambridge, Mass.: Harvard University Press, 1969.

Schorschke, Carl E. *Fin-de-Siècle Vienna: Politics and Culture*. New York: Alfred A. Knopf, 1980.

Stern, Fritz. *The Failure of Illiberalism: Essays on the Political Culture of Modern Germany*. New York: Alfred A. Knopf, 1972.

————. *Gold and Iron: Bismarck, Bleichröder, and the Building of the German Empire*. New York: Alfred A. Knopf, 1977.

————. *The Politics of Cultural Despair: A Study in the Rise of the German Ideology*. New York: Doubleday, 1965.

Struve, Walter. *Elites against Democracy: Leadership Ideals in Bourgeois Political Thought in Germany, 1990–1933*. Princeton, N.J.: Princeton University Press, 1973.

Stürmer, Michael. *Das Kaiserliche Deutschland: Politik und Gesellschaft, 1870–1918*. Düsseldorf: Droste, 1970.

Wehler, Hans-Ulrich. *Das deutsche Kaiserreich 1871–1918*. Göttingen: Vandenhoeck & Ruprecht, 1973.

III. General Surveys and Interpretive Works

Baumont, Maurice, et al. *The Third Reich*. New York: Praeger, 1955.

Bracher, Karl Dietrich. *The German Dictatorship: The Origins, Structure, and Effects of National Socialism*. New York: Praeger, 1970.

————, et al. *Nationalsozialistische Diktatur, 1933–1945: Eine Bilanz*. Düsseldorf: Droste, 1983.

Broszat, Martin. *The Hitler State*. New York: Longman, 1981.

————, et al., eds. *Bayern in der NS-Zeit*. 6 vols. Munich: Oldenbourg, 1977–83.

Buchheim, H. *The Third Reich: Its Beginning, Its Development, Its End*. Munich: Kösel, 1961.

Burleigh, Michael, and Wolfgang Wippermann. *The Racial State: Germany 1933–1945*. Cambridge: Cambridge University Press, 1991.

Caplan, Jane. *Government without Administration: State and Civil Service in Weimar and Nazi Germany*. Oxford: Oxford University Press, 1988.

Childers, Thomas, and Jane Caplan, eds. *Reevaluating the Third Reich*. New York: Holmes & Meier, 1993.

Fest, Joachim. *Das Gesicht des Dritten Reiches*. Munich: Piper, 1963.

Frei, Norbert. *National Socialist Rule in Germany: The Führer State, 1933–1945.* Trans. Simon B. Steyne. Oxford: Blackwell, 1993.

Glaser, Hermann. *Das Dritte Reich: Anspruch und Wirklichkeit.* Freiburg: Herder, 1961.

Grunberger, Richard. *The Twelve-Year Reich: A Social History of Nazi Germany, 1933–1945.* New York: Holt, Rinehart & Winston, 1979.

Heberle, Rudolf. *From Democracy to Nazism: A Regional Case Study on Political Parties in Germany.* New York: Grosset & Dunlap, 1970.

Heiden, Konrad. *A History of National Socialism.* New York: Alfred A. Knopf, 1936.

Hildebrand, Klaus. *Das Dritte Reich.* Munich: Oldenbourg, 1980.

Hofer, Walther. *Die Diktatur Hitlers bis zum Beginn des Zweiten Weltkrieges.* Konstanz: Akademischer Verlag Gesellschaft Athenaion, 1959.

Huber, Heinz, and Arthur Müller, eds. *Das Dritte Reich: Seine Geschichte in Texten, Bildern und Dokumenten.* 2 vols. Munich: Kurt Desch, 1964.

Kershaw, Ian. *The Nazi Dictatorship: Problems and Perspectives of Interpretation.* Baltimore: Edward Arnold, 1985.

Maltitz, Horst von. *The Evolution of Hitler's Germany: The Ideology, the Personality, the Moment.* New York: McGraw-Hill, 1973.

Mau, Hermann, and Helmut Krausnick. *German History, 1933–45.* New York: Frederick Ungar, 1963.

Mommsen, Hans. *Beamtentum im Dritten Reich.* Stuttgart: Deutsche Verlags-Anstalt, 1966.

Mosse, George L. *Nazism: A History and Comparative Analysis of National Socialism.* New Brunswick, N.J.: Transaction Books, 1978.

Neumann, Franz. *Behemoth: The Structure and Practice of National Socialism, 1933–1944.* New York: Harper & Row, 1966.

Peterson, Edward N. *The Limits of Hitler's Powers.* Princeton, N.J.: Princeton University Press, 1969.

Rauschning, Hermann. *The Revolution of Nihilism: Warning to the West.* New York: Longman, Green & Co., 1939.

Rhodes, James M. *The Hitler Movement: A Modern Millenarian Revolution.* Stanford, Calif.: Hoover Institution Press, 1980.

Sauer, Wolfgang. "Nation Socialism: Totalitarianism or Fascism?" *American Historical Review* 73, no. 2 (December 1967) 404–22.

Schoenbaum, David. *Hitler's Social Revolution: Class and Status in Nazi Germany, 1933–1945.* New York: Doubleday, 1966.

Shirer, William. *The Rise and Fall of the Third Reich.* New York: Simon & Schuster, 1959.

Snell, John L., ed. *The Nazi Revolution: Germany's Guilt or Germany's Fate?* Boston: Heath, 1959.

Spielvogel, Jackson J. *Hitler and Nazi Germany: A History.* Englewood Cliffs, N.J.: Prentice-Hall, 1992.

Thamer, Hans-Ulrich. *Verführung und Gewalt: Deutschland 1933–1945* Berlin: Siedler, 1986.

Waite, Robert G. L., ed. *Hitler and Nazi Germany.* New York: Holt, Rinehart & Winston, 1965.

IV. The Nazi Movement during the Weimar Republic

Abel, Theodor. *Why Hitler came to power.* Cambridge, Mass.: Harvard University Press, 1986 (originally published in 1938).

Allen, William Sheridan. *The Nazi Seizure of Power: The Experience of a Single German Town, 1930–35.* New York: Franklin Watts, 1973.

Bennecke, Heinrich. *Hitler und die SA.* Munich: Olzog, 1962.

Bracher, Karl Dietrich. *Die Auflösung der Weimarer Republik: Eine Studie zum Problem des Machtverfalls in der Demokratie.* Villingen, Schwarzwald: Ring-Verlag, 1960.

———, et al. *Die Nationalsozialistische Machtergreifung: Studien zur Errichtung des totalitären Herrschaftssystems in Deutschland, 1933/1934.* 3 Vols. Berlin: Ullstein, 1983.

Childers, Thomas. *The Nazi Voter: The Social Foundations of Fascism in Germany, 1919–1933.* Chapel Hill: University of North Carolina Press, 1983.

———. "The Social Language of Politics in Germany: The Sociology of Political Discourse in the Weimar Republic." *American Historical Review* 95, no. 2 (April 1990) 331–58.

Dornberg, John. *Munich 1923: The Story of Hitler's First Grab for Power.* New York: Harper & Row, 1982.

Eschenburg, Theodor, et al. *The Path to Dictatorship, 1918–1933: Ten Essays by German Scholars.* Trans. John Conway. New York: Doubleday, 1966.

Eyck, Erich. *A History of the Weimar Republic.* Trans. Harlan P. Hanson. 2 vols. Cambridge, Mass.: Harvard University Press, 1962.

Franz, Georg. "Munich: Birthplace and Center of the National Socialist German Workers' Party." *Journal of Modern History* 29, no. 4 (December 1957) 319–34.

Franz-Willing, Georg (same as Georg Franz). *Krisenjahr der Hitlerbewegung 1923.* Preussich Oldendorf: Schütz, 1975.

———. *Ursprung der Hitlerbewegung: 1919–22.* Preussich Oldendorf: Schütz, 1974.

Friedrich, Otto. *Before the Deluge: A Portrait of Berlin in the 1920s.* New York: Avon Books, 1973.

Gay, Peter. *Weimar Culture: The Outsider as Insider.* New York: Harper & Row, 1968.

Gordon, Harold J., Jr. *Hitler and the Beer Hall Putsch.* Princeton, N.J.: Princeton University Press, 1972.

———. *The Reichswehr and the German Republic, 1919–26.* Princeton, N.J.: Princeton University Press, 1957.

Grunberger, Richard. *Red Rising in Bavaria.* London: Arthur Barker, 1973.

Halperin, William S. *Germany Tried Democracy: A Political History of the Reich from 1918–1933.* New York: Norton, 1965.

Hamilton, Richard. *Who Voted for Hitler?* Princeton, N.J.: Princeton University Press, 1983.

Hanser, Richard. *Putsch: How Hitler Made Revolution.* New York: Pyramid, 1971.

Höhne, Heinz. *Die Machtergreifung: Deutschlands Weg in die Hitler Diktatur.* Hamburg: Spiegel, 1983.

———. *Die Mordsache Röhm: Hitlers Durchbruch zur Alleinherrschaft.* Hamburg: Spiegel, 1984.

Isherwood, Christopher. *The Berlin Stories.* New York: New Directions, 1945.

Jablonsky, David. *The Nazi Party in Dissolution: Hitler and the Verbotzeit, 1923–1925.* London: Frank Cass, 1989.

Keynes, John Maynard. *The Economic Consequences of the War.* New York: Harcourt, Brace & Howe, 1920.

Laqueur, Walter. *Weimar: A Cultural History, 1918–1933.* New York: Putnam, 1974.

Lederer, Ivo, ed. *The Versailles Settlement: Was It Foredoomed to Failure?* Boston: Heath, 1960.

Liang, Hsi-Huey. *The Berlin Police Force in the Weimar Republic.* Berkeley: University of California Press, 1968.

Maser, Werner. *Der Sturm auf die Republik: Frühzeit der NSDAP.* Stuttgart: Deutsche Verlags-Anstalt, 1973.

Meissner, Hans Otto, and Harry Wilde. *Die Machtergreifung: Ein Bericht über die Technik des nationalsozialistischen Staatsstreiches.* Stuttgart: J. G. Cotta'sche Buchhandlung, 1958.

Merkl, Peter. *The Making of a Stormtrooper.* Princeton, N.J.: Princeton University Press, 1980.

———. *Political Violence under the Swastika: 581 Early Nazis.* Princeton, N.J.: Princeton University Press, 1975.

Mitchell, Allan. *Revolution in Bavaria, 1918–1919.* Princeton, N.J.: Princeton University Press, 1965.

Mitchell, Otis C. *Hitler over Germany: The Establishment of the Nazi Dictatorship, 1918–1934.* Philadelphia: ISHI, 1983.

Mommsen, Hans. *Die Verspielte Freiheit: Der Weg der Republik von Weimar in den Untergang 1918 bis 1933.* Berlin: Propyläen, 1990.

Müller-Meiningen, Ernst. *Aus Bayerns schwersten Tagen.* Berlin, 1923.

Noakes, Jeremy. "Conflict and Development in the NSDAP 1924–1927." *Journal of Contemporary History* 1, no. 4 (1966) 3–36.

Peukert, Detlev J. K. *The Weimar Republic: The Crisis of Classical Modernity.* Trans. Richard Deveson. New York: Hill & Wang, 1992.

Phelps, Reginald H. "Before Hitler Came: Thule Society and Germanen Orden." *Journal of Modern History* 35 (1963) 245–61.

Ringer, Fritz, ed. *The German Inflation of 1923.* New York: Oxford University Press, 1969.

Rürup, Reinhard. "Problems of the German Revolution of 1918–19." *Journal of Contemporary History* 3 (1968) 109–35.

Sontheimer, Kurt. *Anti-Demokratisches Denken in der Weimarer Republik.* Munich: Nymphenburger, 1962.

Stachura, Peter. *Gregor Strasser and the Rise of Nazism.* London: George Allen & Unwin, 1983.

Turner, Henry A. *German Big Business and the Rise of Hitler.* New York: Oxford University Press, 1985.

Vogelsang, Thilo. *Reichswehr, Staat und NSDAP, Beiträge zur deutschen Geschichte 1930–32.* Stuttgart: Deutsche Verlags-Anstalt, 1962.

Waite, Robert G. L. *Vanguard of Nazism: The Free Corps Movement in Germany, 1918–23.* Cambridge, Mass.: Harvard University Press, 1952.

Watt, Richard M. *The Kings Depart: The Tragedy of Germany, Versailles and the German Revolution.* New York: Simon & Schuster, 1968.

Werner, Bruno. *Die Zwanziger Jahre von Morgens bis Mitternachts.* Munich: Bruckmann, 1962.

Wheaton, Eliot B. *The Nazi Revolution, 1933–35: Prelude to Calamity.* New York: Doubleday, 1969.

Zorn, Wolfgang. "Student Politics in the Weimar Republic." *Journal of Contemporary History* 5 (1970) 128–43.

V. Adolf Hitler

Bezymenski, Lev. *The Death of Adolf Hitler.* New York: Pyramid, 1969.

Binion, Rudolph. *Hitler among the Germans.* New York: Elsevier, 1979.

Bloch, E. "My Patient, Hitler." *Colliers,* March 15 and 22, 1941.

Bromberg, Norbert, and Verna Volz Small. *Hitler's Psychopathology.* New York: International Universities Press, 1983.

Buchheit, Gert. *Hitler der Feldherr: Die Zerstörung einer Legende.* Rastatt: Grote, 1958.

Bullock, Alan. *Hitler: A Study in Tyranny.* New York: Harper & Row, 1962.

———. *Hitler and Stalin: Parallel Lives.* New York: Alfred A. Knopf, 1992.

———. "The Schickelgruber Story." *New York Review of Books,* July 7, 1977.

Carr, William. *Hitler: A Study in Personality and Politics.* New York: St. Martin's, 1979.

Cross, Colin. *Adolf Hitler.* New York: Berkeley Publishing, 1973.

Deakin, F. W. *The Brutal Friendship: Mussolini, Hitler and the Fall of Italian Fascism.* New York: Doubleday, 1966.

Dorpalen, Andreas. "Hitler 12 Years After." *Review of Politics* 9 (1957) 695–710.

Fest, Joachim. *Hitler.* Trans. Richard and Clara Winston. New York: Harcourt, Brace & Jovanovich, 1973.

Filmer, Werner, and Heribert Schwan, eds. *Was von Hitler blieb: 50 Jahre nach der Machtergreifung.* Berlin: Ullstein, 1983.

Graml, H. "Probleme einer Hitler-Biographie." *Vierteljahreshefte für Zeitgeschichte* 22 (1974) 76–92.

Günther, H. F. K. *Mein Eindruck von Adolf Hitler.* Pähl: Franz von Bebenburg, 1969.

Haffner, Sebastian. *Anmerkungen zu Hitler.* Düsseldorf: Tholenaar, 1973.

Harris, Robert. *Selling Hitler.* New York: Penguin Books, 1987.

Hauner, Milan. *Hitler: A Chronology of His Life and Time.* New York: St. Martin's Press, 1983.

Heer, Friedrich. *Der Glaube des Adolf Hitler: Anatomie einer politischen Religiosität.* Munich: Bechtle, 1968.

Heiber, Helmut. *Adolf Hitler: Eine Biographie.* Berlin: Colloquium, 1960.

Heiden, Konrad. *Der Führer: Hitler's Rise to Power.* Boston: Houghton Mifflin, 1944.

———. *Hitler.* 2 vols. Zurich: Europa, 1936.

Heston, Leonard L., and Renate Heston. *The Medical Casebook of Adolf Hitler.* New York: Stein & Day, 1979.

Infield, Glenn B. *Eva and Adolf.* New York: Ballantine, 1974.

Jäckel, Eberhard. *Hitlers Herrschaft: Vollzug einer Weltanschauung.* Stuttgart: Deutsche Verlags-Anstalt, 1986.

———. *Hitlers Weltanschauung. Entwurf einer Herrschaft.* Stuttgart: Deutsche Verlags-Anstalt, 1983.

———. "Rückblick auf die sogenannte Hitler-Welle." *Geschichte in Wissenschaft und Unterricht* 28 (1977) 695–710.

Jenks, W. A. *Vienna and the Young Hitler.* New York: Columbia University Press, 1960.

Jetzinger, Franz. *Hitler's Youth.* Trans. Lawrence Wilson. London: Hutchinson, 1958.

Jones, Sydney J. *Hitler in Vienna, 1907–13: Clues to the Future.* London: Blond & Briggs, 1983.

Kallenbach, Hans. *Mit Hitler auf Festung Landsberg.* Munich: Kress & Hornung, 1939.

Kershaw, Ian. *The "Hitler Myth": Image and Reality in the Third Reich.* New York: Oxford University Press, 1987.

Kurth, Wolfram. *Genie, Irrsinn und Ruhm.* Munich: Reinhardt, 1956.

———. "The Jew and Adolf Hitler." *Psychoanalytical Quarterly* 6 (1947) 28–29.

Langer, Walter C. *The Mind of Adolf Hitler.* New York: Basic Books, 1972.

Maser, Werner. *Hitler.* Trans. Peter and Betty Ross. London: Allen Lane, 1973.

———. *Mein Kampf: Der Fahrplan eines Welteroberers.* Esslingen: Bechtle, 1974.

Müller-Schönhausen, J. *Die Lösung des Rätsels Adolf Hitler.* Vienna: Verlag zur Förderung der Wissenschaft, n.d.

O'Donnell, James R. *The Bunker.* New York: Bantam, 1979.

Payne, Robert. *The Life and Death of Adolf Hitler.* New York: Praeger, 1973.

Pemsel, Richard. *Hitler: Revolutionär, Staatsmann, Verbrecher?* Tübingen: Grabert-Verlag, 1986.

Rauschning, Hermann. *Gespräche mit Hitler.* New York: Europa, 1940.

Recktenwald, J. *Woran hat Adolf Hitler gelitten? Eine neuropsychiatrische Deutung.* Munich: Reinhardt, 1963.

Rich, Norman. *Hitler's War Aims.* 2 vols. New York: Norton, 1973.

Rosenfeld, Alvin. *Imagining Hitler.* Bloomington: Indiana University Press, 1985.

Schramm, Percy. *Hitler: The Man and the Military Leader.* Trans. Donald S. Detwiler. Chicago: Quadrangle, 1971.

Schreiber, Gerhard. *Hitler Interpretationen, 1923–1983.* Darmstadt: Wissenschaftliche Buchgesellschaft, 1984.

Smith, Bradley F. *Adolf Hitler: His Family, Childhood and Youth.* Stanford, Calif.: Hoover Institution Press, 1967.

Stein, George H., ed. *Hitler.* Englewood Cliffs, N.J.: Prentice-Hall, 1968.

Stern, J. P. *The Führer and the People.* Glasgow: William Collins Sons, 1975.

Stierlin, Helm. *Adolf Hitler: A Family Perspective.* New York: Psychohistory Press, 1976.

Toland, John. *Hitler.* 2 vols. New York: Doubleday, 1976.

Treher, Wolfgang. *Hitler, Steiner, Schreber: Ein Beitrag zur Phänomologie des kranken Geistes.* Emmendingen/Breisgau: Selbstverlag, 1966.

Trevor-Roper, H. R. *The Last Days of Adolf Hitler.* New York: Macmillan, 1947.

Tyrell, Albrecht. *Vom "Trommler" zum Führer*. Munich: Wilhelm Fink, 1975.
Vernon, W. H. "Hitler, the Man: Notes for a Case History." *Journal of Abnormal Psychology* 37 (1942) 295–308.
Waite, Robert G. L. *The Psychopathic God Adolf Hitler*. New York: Basic Books, 1977.
Zitelmann, Rainer. *Hitler: Selbstverständnis eines Revolutionärs*. New York: Berg, 1987.

VI. Major Nazi Leaders

1. Martin Bormann

Lang, Jochen von. *The Secretary, Martin Bormann, the Man Who Manipulated Hitler*. Trans. Christa Armstrong and Peter White. Athens: Ohio University Press, 1981.
MacGovern, J. *Martin Bormann*. New York: Morrow, 1968.
Wulf, J. *Martin Bormann, Hitlers Schatten*. Gütersloh: Mohn, 1962.

2. Karl Dönitz

Görlitz, W. *Karl Dönitz: Der Grossadmiral*. Göttingen: Musterschmidt, 1972.
Padfield, Peter. *Dönitz: The Last Führer*. London: Gollancz, 1984.

3. Joseph Goebbels

Bramsted, Ernest K. *Goebbels and National Socialist Propaganda*. East Lansing: Michigan State University Press, 1965.
Frankel, H., and R. Manvell. *Dr. Goebbels: His Life and Death*. New York: Simon & Schuster, 1960.
Heiber, Helmut. *Goebbels*. Trans. John K. Dickinson. New York: Da Capo, 1972.
Reimann, Victor. *Dr. Joseph Goebbels*. Trans. Stephen Wendt. New York: Doubleday, 1976.
Ries, Kurt. *Joseph Goebbels*. New York: Ballantine, 1948.

4. Hermann Göring

Asher, Lee. *Göring: Air Leader*. London: Duckworth, 1972.
Bewley, Charles. *Hermann Göring and the Third Reich*. New York: Devin-Adair, 1962.
Frischauer, Willi. *The Rise and Fall of Hermann Göring*. New York: Ballantine, 1951.
Gritzbach, Erich. *Hermann Göring: Werk und Mensch*. Munich: Eher, 1940.
Irving, David. *Göring: A Biography*. New York: Morrow, 1989.
Martens, Stefan. *Hermann Göring: "Erster Paladin des Führers," und "Zweiter Mann im Reich."* Paderborn: Schöningh, 1985.
Mosley, Leonard. *The Reich Marshal: A Biography of Herman Goering*. New York: Dell, 1974.

5. Rudolf Hess

Leaser, James. *Rudolf Hess: The Uninvited Envoy*. London: Allen & Unwin, 1962.

Manvell, R., and H. Fraenkel. *Rudolf Hess: A Biography.* London: MacGibban and Kee, 1971.
Schwarzwälder, Wulf. *Der Sellvertreter des Führers: Rudolf Hess.* Munich: Delphin, 1974.

6. Reinhard Heydrich

Calic, Edouard. *Reinhard Heydrich.* Trans. Lowell Bair. New York: Morrow, 1982.
Deschner, G. *Reinhard Heydrich: Statthalter der Totalen Macht.* Esslingen: Bechtle, 1977.

7. Heinrich Himmler

Breitman, Richard. *The Architect of Genocide: Heinrich Himmler and the Final Solution.* New York: Alfred A. Knopf, 1991.
Loewenberg, Peter. "The Unsuccessful Adolescence of Heinrich Himmler." *American Historical Review* 76 (1971–72) 612–41.
Manvell, Roger, and H. Fraenkel. *Himmler.* New York: Paperback Library, 1968.
Padfield, Peter. *Himmler: Reichsführer SS.* New York: Henry Holt, 1990.
Smith, B. F. *Heinrich Himmler: A Nazi in the Making, 1900–1926.* Stanford, Calif.: Hoover Institution Press, 1971.
Wulf, Josef. *Heinrich Himmler: Eine Biographische Studie.* Berlin: Arani, 1960.

8. Ernst Kaltenbrunner

Black, Peter R. *Ernst Kaltenbrunner: Ideological Soldier of the Third Reich.* Princeton, N.J.: Princeton University Press, 1984.

9. Robert Ley

Smelser, Ronald. *Robert Ley: Hitler's Labor Front Leader.* New York: Berg, 1988.

10. Franz von Papen

Adams, Henry M., and Robin K. Adams. *Rebel Patriot: A Biography of Franz von Papen.* Santa Barbara, Calif.: McNally & Loftin, 1987.

11. Joachim von Ribbentrop

Schwarz, Paul. *This Man Ribbentrop.* New York: Julian Messer, 1943.
Weitz, John. *Hitler's Diplomat: The Life and Times of Joachim von Ribbentrop.* New York: Ticknor & Fields, 1992.

12. Alfred Rosenberg

Cecil, Robert. *The Myth of the Master Race: Alfred Rosenberg and Nazi Ideology.* New York: Dodd Mead, 1972.

13. Albert Speer

Bracher, Karl Dietrich. "Die Speer Legende." *Neue Politische Literatur* 15 (1970) 429–431.
Schmidt, Mathias. *Albert Speer: The End of a Myth.* Trans. Joachim Neugroschl. New York: St. Martin's Press, 1984.

14. Julius Streicher

Bytwerk, Randall L. *Julius Streicher.* New York: Dorset, 1983.

VII. Domestic Politics and Culture

1. The Nazi Party

Diehl-Thiele, Peter. *Partei und Staat im Dritten Reich.* Munich: Beck, 1969.
Hüttenberger, Peter. *Die Gauleiter.* Stuttgart: Deutsche Verlags-Anstalt, 1970.
Kater, Michael H. *The Nazi Party: A Social Profile of Members and Leaders, 1919–1945.* Cambridge, Mass.: Harvard University Press, 1983.
Koehl, Robert. "Feudal Aspects of National Socialism." *American Political Science Review* 54, no. 4 (December 1960) 921–33.
Orlow, Dietrich. *The History of the Nazi Party.* 2 vols. Pittsburgh: University of Pittsburgh Press, 1969.
Schäfer, Wolfgang. *NSDAP, Entwicklung und Struktur der Staatspartei des Dritten Reiches.* Hannover: Norddeutsche Verlagsanstalt, 1957.

2. Totalitarian Control: Propaganda and Terror

Aronson, Shlomo. *Reinhard Heydrich und die Frühgeschichte von Gestapo und SD.* Stuttgart: Deutsche Verlags-Anstalt, 1971.
Baird, J. W. *The Mythical World of Nazi War Propaganda, 1939–45.* Minneapolis: University of Minnesota Press, 1974.
Bennecke, Heinrich. *Hitler und die S.A.* Munich: Olzog, 1962.
Buchheim, Hans, et al. *Anatomie des SS-Staates.* 2 vols. Freiburg: Walter-Verlag, 1965.
Combs, William L. *The Voice of the SS: A History of the SS Journal Das Schwarze Korps.* New York: Peter Lang, 1986.
Crankshaw, Edward. *Gestapo.* New York: Jove, 1956.
Graber, G. S. *The History of the SS.* New York: David McKay, 1978.
Hale, Oren J. *The Captive Press in the Third Reich.* Princeton, N.J.: Princeton University Press, 1964.
Höhne, Heinz. *The Order of the Death's Head.* Trans. Richard Berry. New York: Ballantine, 1971.
Koehl, Robert Lewis. *The Black Corps: The Structure and Power Struggles of the Nazi SS.* Madison: University of Wisconsin Press, 1983.
Kogon, Eugen. *The Theory and Practice of Hell: The German Concentration Camps and the System behind them.* Trans. Heinz Norden. New York: Berkeley Publications, Inc., 1958.
Merkl, Peter. *The Making of a Storm Trooper.* Princeton, N.J.: Princeton University Press, 1980.
Müller, Ingo. *Hitler's Justice: The Courts of the Third Reich.* Trans. Deborah Lucas Schneider. Cambridge, Mass.: Harvard University Press, 1991.
Reiche, Eric G. *The Development of the S.S. in Nürnberg, 1922–34.* New York: Cambridge University Press, 1986.
Reitlinger, Gerald. *The SS: Alibi of a Nation, 1922–1945.* Englewood Cliffs, N.J.: Prentice-Hall, 1981.
Snydor, Charles W. *Soldiers of Destruction: The SS Death's Head Division, 1933–1945.* Princeton, N.J.: Princeton University Press, 1977.

Stein, George H. *The Waffen SS.* Ithaca, N.Y.: Cornell University Press, 1966.

Weinrich, Harold. *Linguistik der Lüge.* Heidelberg: L. Schneider, 1966.

Wulf, J. *Presse und Funk im Dritten Reich: Eine Dokumentation.* Gütersloh: Sigbert Mohn, 1964.

Zeman, Z. A. B. *Nazi Propaganda.* Oxford: Oxford University Press, 1973.

3. Youth and Education

Assel, H. G. *Die Perversion der politischen Pädagogik im Nationalsozialismus.* Munich: Ehrenwirth, 1969.

Becker, Howard. *German Youth: Bond or Free?* London: Kegan Paul, Trench, Trubner & Co., 1946.

Blackburn, Gilmer W. *Education in the Third Reich: A Study of Race and History in the Nazi Textbooks.* New York: State University of New York Press, 1985.

Bleuel, H. P., with A. Klinert. *Deutsche Studenten auf dem Weg ins Dritte Reich.* Gütersloh: Mohn, 1967.

Boberach, H. *Jugend unter Hitler.* Düsseldorf: Droste, 1981.

Erdmann, Karl Dietrich. *Wissenschaft im Dritten Reich.* Kiel: Hirt, 1967.

Gamm, Hans-Jochen. *Der braune Kult: Das Dritte Reich und seine Ersatzreligion.* Hamburg: Rutten & Loening, 1962.

Hamilton, Alastair. *The Appeal of Fascism: A Study of Intellectuals and Fascism, 1919–1945.* New York: Macmillan, 1971.

Hofer, Walther, ed. *Wissenschaft im totalen Staat.* Bern: Haupt, 1964.

Kantorowicz, A. *Deutsche Schicksale: Intellektuelle unter Hitler und Stalin.* Vienna: Europa, 1964.

Klönne, A. *Hitlerjugend: Die Jugend und ihre Organisation im Dritten Reich.* Hannover: Goedel, 1955.

Koch, H. W. *The Hitler Youth: Origins and Development, 1922–45.* New York: Dorset, 1975.

Laqueur, Walter. *Young Germany: A History of the German Youth Movement.* London: Routledge & Kegan Paul, 1962.

Loewenberg, P. "The Psychohistorical Origins of the Nazi Youth Cohort." *American Historical Review* 76 (1971) 1475–1502.

Rempel, Gerhard. *Hitler's Children: The Hitler Youth and the SS.* Chapel Hill: University of North Carolina Press, 1989.

4. Women and the Family

Bleuel, Hans Peter. *Sex and Society in Nazi Germany.* Trans. J. Maxwell Brownjohn. New York: Bantam, 1973.

Evans, Richard. "German Women and the Triumph of Hitler." *Journal of Modern History* (March 1976).

Kirkpatrick, Clifford. *Nazi Germany: Its Women and Family Life.* New York: Bobbs-Merrill, 1938.

Klinksiek, Dorothea. *Die Frau im NS-Staat.* Stuttgart: Deutsche Verlags-Anstalt, 1982.

Koonz, Claudia. *Mothers in the Fatherland: Women, the Family and Nazi Politics.* New York: St. Martin's Press, 1987.

Owings, Alison. *Frauen: German Women Recall the Third Reich.* New Brunswick, N.J.: Rutgers University Press, 1993.

Scholtz-Klink, Gertrud. *Die Frau im Dritten Reich.* Tübingen: Grabert, 1978.

Stephenson, Jill. *The Nazi Organisation of Women.* London: Croom Helm, 1981.

———. *Women in Nazi Society.* New York: Barnes and Noble, 1975.

5. Nazi Culture

Aley, Peter. *Jugendliteratur im Dritten Reich.* Hamburg: Verlag für Buchmarkt-Forschung, 1967.

Berglund, Gisela. *Der Kampf um den Leser.* Worms: Verlag Georg Heinz, 1980.

Brenner, Hildegard. *Die Kunstpolitik im Dritten Reiche.* Hamburg: Rowohlt, 1963.

Denkler, Horst, and Karl Prümm, eds. *Die Deutsche Literatur im Dritten Reich.* Stuttgart: Reclam, 1976.

Furhammer, Leif, and Folke Isakson. *Politics and Film.* Trans. Kersti French. New York: Praeger, 1971.

Gray, Ronald. *The German Tradition in Literature, 1871–1945.* Cambridge: Cambridge University Press, 1965.

Hull, David Stewart. *Film in the Third Reich: Art and Propaganda in Nazi Germany.* New York: Simon & Schuster, 1973.

Kater, Michael H. "'Forbidden Fruit': Jazz in the Third Reich." *American Historical Review* 94, no. 1 (1989) 11–43.

Klemperer, Victor. *Die unbewältigte Sprache: Aus dem Notizbuch eines Philologen LTI.* Darmstadt: Melzer, 1966.

Lane, Barbara Miller. *Architecture and Politics in Germany, 1918–1945.* Cambridge, Mass.: Harvard University Press, 1968.

Loewy, E. *Literatur unterm Hakenkreuz: Das Dritte Reich und seine Dichtungen.* Frankfurt: Europäische Verlagsanstalt, 1966.

Mandell, Richard D. *The Nazi Olympics.* New York: Ballantine, 1971.

Mosse, George L., ed. *Nazi Culture: Intellectual, Cultural and Social Life in the Third Reich.* New York: Grosset & Dunlap, 1966.

Muschg, Walter. *Die Zerstörung der deutschen Literatur.* Bern: Francke, 1956.

Ritchie, J. M. *German Literature under National Socialism.* Totowa, N.J.: Barnes & Noble, 1983.

Roh, Franz. *German Art in the Twentieth Century.* London: Thames & Hudson, 1968.

Sternberger, D., et al. *Aus dem Wörterbuch des Unmenschen.* Hamburg: Claasen, 1968.

Taylor, R. R. *The World in Stone: The Role of Architecture in National Socialist Ideology.* Berkeley: University of California Press, 1974.

Vandrey, Max. *Der politische Witz im Dritten Reich.* Munich: Goldmann, 1967.

Wulf, J. *Die bildenden Künste im Dritten Reich: Eine Dokumentation.* Gütersloh: Mohn, 1963.

———. *Literatur und Dichtung im Dritten Reich: Eine Dokumentation.* Gütersloh: Mohn, 1963.

———. *Musik im Dritten Reich: Eine Dokumentation.* Gütersloh: Mohn, 1963.

———. *Theater und Film im Dritten Reich: Eine Dokumentation.* Gütersloh: Mohn, 1964.

6. The Churches

Conway, John S. *The Nazi Persecution of the Churches, 1933–1945.* London: Weidenfeld & Nicolson, 1968.

Helmreich, Ernst Christian. *The German Churches under Hitler.* Detroit: Wayne State University, 1979.

Löwy, Günter. *The Catholic Church and Nazi Germany.* London: Weidenfeld & Nicolson, 1966.

Meier, Kurt. *Kirchen und Judentum: Die Haltung der Evangelischen Kirche zur Judenpolitik des dritten Reiches.* Düsseldorf: Droste, 1972.

Müller, Hans, ed. *Katholische Kirche und Nationalsozialismus: Dokumente.* Munich: Deutscher Taschenbuchverlag, 1965.

Niemöller, Wilhelm. *Die Evangelische Kirche im Dritten Reich.* Bielefeld: Bechauf, 1956.

Scholder, Klaus. *Die Kirchen und das Dritte Reich.* Berlin: Ullstein, 1972.

7. Racism, Anti-Semitism, Holocaust

Arad, Yitzhak. *The Pictorial History of the Holocaust.* New York: Macmillan, 1990.

Arendt, Hannah. *Eichmann in Jerusalem.* New York: Viking, 1963.

Barzun, Jacques. *Race: A Study in Superstition.* New York: Harper & Row, 1965.

Baker, Leonard. *Days of Sorrow and Pain: Leo Baeck and the Berlin Jews.* New York: Macmillan, 1978.

Cohn, Norman. *Warrant for Genocide: The Myth of the Jewish World Conspiracy.* Chico, Calif.: Judaic Studies, 1981.

Dawidowicz, Lucy. *The War against the Jews, 1933–1945.* New York: Bantam, 1975.

Fleming, Gerald, *Hitler and the Final Solution.* Los Angeles: University of California Press, 1982.

Gay, Peter. *Freud, Jews and Other Germans.* New York: Oxford University Press, 1978.

Gilbert, Martin. *The Holocaust: A History of the Jews of Europe during the Second World War.* New York: Holt, Rinehart & Winston, 1985.

Gordon, Sarah. *Hitler, Germans, and the Jewish Question.* Princeton, N.J.: Princeton University Press, 1984.

Hilberg, Raul. *The Destruction of the European Jews.* 3 vols. New York: Holmes & Meier, 1985.

———, ed. *Documents of Destruction: Germany and Jewry, 1933–45.* Chicago: Quadrangle, 1971.

Hillel, Marc, and Clarissa Henry. *Of Pure Blood.* Trans. Eric Mossbacher. New York: McGraw-Hill, 1976.

Klee, Ernst, et al. *The Good Old Days: The Holocaust as Seen by Its Perpetrators and Bystanders.* Trans. Deborah Burnstone. New York: Free Press, 1991.

Laqueur, Walter. *The Terrible Secret: Suppression of the Truth about Hitler's "Final Solution."* New York: Penguin, 1982.

Lifton, Robert J. *The Nazi Doctors: Medical Killing and the Psychology of Genocide.* New York: Basic Books, 1986.

Lilienthal, Georg. *Der "Lebensborn e.V.": Ein Instrument nationalsozialistis-cher Rassenpolitik*. Mainz: Akademie der Wissenschaften und der Literatur, 1985.

Lipstadt, Deborah E. *Denying the Holocaust: The Growing Assault on Truth and Memory*. New York: Free Press, 1993.

Luel, Steven A., and Paul Marcus, eds. *Psychoanalytic Reflections on the Holo-caust: Selected Essays*. Denver: Holocaust Awareness Institute, Center for Judaic Studies, University of Denver; New York: Ktav, 1984.

Marrus, Michael R. *The Holocaust in History*. Hanover, N.H.: University of New England Press, 1987.

Massing, Paul W. *Rehearsal for Destruction: A Study of Political Anti-Semitism in Imperial Germany*. New York: Harper, 1949.

Mendelssohn, John, ed. *The Holocaust*. 18 vols. New York: Garland, 1982.

Mosse, George L. *Toward the Final Solution: A History of European Racism*. New York: Harper & Row, 1978.

Poliakov, Leon. *The Aryan Myth*. Trans. Edmund Howard. New York: New American Library, 1977.

———. *The History of Anti-Semitism*. Trans. Richard Howard. New York: Schocken, 1974.

Proctor, Robert N. *Racial Hygiene: Medicine under the Nazis*. Cambridge, Mass.: Harvard University Press, 1988.

Pulzer, Peter. *The Rise of Political Anti-Semitism in Germany and Austria*. New York: Wiley, 1964.

Reitlinger, Gerald. *The Final Solution: The Attempt to Exterminate the Jews of Europe*. New York: Beechhurst, 1953.

Saller, K. *Die Rassenlehre des Nationalsozialismus in Wissenschaft und Propa-ganda*. Darmstadt: Progress, 1961.

Sartre, Jean-Paul. *Anti-Semite and Jew*. Trans. George J. Becker. New York: Schocken, 1948.

Scheffler, Wolfgang. *Judenverfolgung im Dritten Reich, 1933–45*. Berlin: Collo-quium, 1964.

Schleunes, Karl A. *The Twisted Road to Auschwitz*. Chicago: University of Illinois Press, 1990.

Schmuhl, Hans-Walter. *Rassenhygiene, Nationalsozialismus, Euthanasie: Von der Verhütung zur Vernichtung "lebensunwerten Lebens," 1890–1945*. Göttingen: Vandenhoeck & Ruprecht, 1987.

Weindling, Paul. *Health, Race, and German Politics between National Unifi-cation and Nazism, 1870–1945*. New York: Cambridge University Press, 1989.

Yahil, Leni. *The Holocaust: The Fate of European Jews*. New York: Oxford University Press, 1990.

8. Economic Policies

Caroll, Berenice. *Design for Total War: Arms and Economics in the Third Reich*. The Hague: Mouton, 1968.

Milward, Alan S. *The German Economy at War*. London: Oxford University Press, 1965.

Mollin, Gerhard. *Montankonzerne und "Drittes Reich": Der Gegensatz zwi-schen Monopolindustrie und Befehlswirtschaft in der deutschen Rüstung und Expansion, 1936–1944*. Göttingen: Vandenhoeck & Ruprecht, 1988.

Pfahlmann, Hans. *Fremdarbeiter und Kriegsgefangene in der deutschen Kriegs wirtschaft, 1939–45*. Darmstadt: Wehr & Wissen, 1968.

Schumann, Hans-Gerd. *Nationalsozialismus und Gewerkschaftsbewegung*. Hannover: Goebel, 1958.

Schweitzer, Arthur. *Big Business in the Third Reich*. Bloomington: Indiana University Press, 1964.

Turner, Henry A., Jr. "Big Business and the Rise of Hitler." *American Historical Review* 75 (1969) 56–70.

————. *German Big Business and the Rise of Hitler*. New York: Oxford University Press, 1985.

9. Military

Correlli, Barnett. *Hitler's Generals*. New York: Grove Weidenfeld, 1989.

Craig, Gordon. *The Politics of the Prussian Army, 1640–1945*. New York: Oxford University Press, 1955.

Geyer, M. "Aufrüstung oder Sicherheit: Reichswehr und die Krise der Machtpolitik, 1924–1936." Ph.D. diss., Freiburg/Breisgau, 1976.

Gordon, Harold J. *The Reichswehr and the German Republic, 1919–1926*. Princeton, N.J.: Princeton University Press, 1957.

Görlitz, Walter. *History of the German General Staff, 1657–1945*. Trans. Brian Battershaw. New York: Praeger, 1957.

Hubatsch, Walther. *Der Admiralstab und die obersten Marinebehörden in Deutschland, 1848–1945*. Frankfurt: Bernard & Graefe, 1958.

O'Neil, Robert J. *The German Army and the Nazi Party*. London: Cassell, 1966.

Salewski, M. *Die deutsche Seekriegsleitung, 1935–1945*. 3 vols. Frankfurt: Bernard & Graefe, 1970–75.

Taylor, Telford. *Sword and Swastika: Generals and Nazis in the Third Reich*. New York: Quadrangle, 1952.

Vagts, Alfred. *A History of Militarism*. Westport, Conn.: Greenwood, 1981 (originally published in 1959).

Vogelsang, Thilo. *Reichswehr, Staat und NSDAP*. Stuttgart: Deutsche Verlags-Anstalt, 1962.

Wheeler-Bennett, John W. *The Nemesis of Power: The German Army in Politics, 1918–1945*. London: Macmillan, 1964.

VIII. Foreign Policy: The Road to War

Baumgart, Winfried. "Zur Ansprache Hitlers vor den Führern der Wehrmacht am 22. August 1939. Eine Quellenkritische Untersuchung." *Vierteljahresschrift für Zeitgeschichte* 6 (1969) 120–49.

Brook-Shepherd, Gordon. *The Anschluss: The Rape of Austria*. New York: Lippincott, 1963.

Bullock, Alan. "Hitler and the Origins of the Second World War." *Proceedings of the British Academy* 53 (1967) 259–87.

Carr, E. H. *German-Soviet Relations between the Two World Wars, 1919–1939*. New York: Harper & Row, 1966.

————. *International Relations between the Two World Wars, 1919–1939*. New York: Harper & Row, 1966.

Craig, Gordon A. *From Bismarck to Adenauer: Aspects of German Statecraft.*
   New York: Harper & Row, 1965.
Craig, Gordon A., and Felix Gilbert, eds. *The Diplomats, 1919–1939.* 2 vols.
   New York: Atheneum, 1963.
Denne, Ludwig. *Das Danziger-Problem in der deutschen Aussenpolitik, 1934–*
   1939. Bonn: Rohrscheid, 1959.
Eichstädt, Ulrich. *Von Dollfuss zu Hitler: Geschichte des Anschlusses östereichs,*
   1933–1938. Wiesbaden: Steiner, 1955.
Eubank, Keith. *Munich.* Norman, Okla.: University of Oklahoma Press, 1963.
———. *The Origins of World War II.* New York: Crowell, 1969.
Freund, Gerald. *Unholy Alliance.* London: Chatto & Windus, 1957.
Hildebrand, Klaus. *The Foreign Policy of the Third Reich.* Trans. Anthony
   Fothergill. Berkeley: University of California Press, 1970.
———. *Vom Reich zum Weltreich: Hitler, NSDAP und koloniale Frage, 1919–*
   1945. Munich: Wilhelm Fink, 1969.
Hillgruber, Andreas. *Germany and the Two World Wars.* Trans. William C.
   Kirby. Cambridge, Mass.: Harvard University Press, 1981.
———. *Kontinuität und Diskontinuität in der deutschen Aussenpolitik von*
   Bismarck bis Hitler. Düsseldorf: Droste, 1969.
———. *Staatsmänner und Diplomaten bei Hitler.* 2 vols. Frankfurt: Bernard &
   Graefe, 1967.
Hofer, W. *Die Entfesslung des Zweiten Weltkrieges: Eine Studie über die in-*
   ternationalen Beziehungen im Sommer 1939 mit Dokumenten. Frankfurt:
   Fischer, 1964.
Hoggan, David. *Der erzwungene Krieg.* Tübingen: Grabert, 1961.
———. *Frankreichs Widerstand gegen den zweiten Weltkrieg.* Tübingen: Verlag
   der Deutschen Hochschullehrer-Zeitung, 1963.
Holborn, Hajo. *The Political Collapse of Europe.* New York: Alfred A. Knopf,
   1957.
Jäckel, Eberhard. *Frankreich in Hitlers Europa.* Stuttgart: Deutsche Verlags-
   Anstalt, 1966.
Jacobsen, Hans-Adolf. *Nationalsozialistische Aussenpolitik, 1933–1938.* Frank-
   furt: Alfred Metzner, 1968.
———. *Der Weg zur Teilung der Welt: Politik und Strategie 1939 bis 1945.*
   Koblenz: Wehr & Wissen, 1977.
Kissinger, Henry, *Diplomacy.* New York: Simon & Schuster, 1994.
Lafore, Laurence. *The End of Glory: An Interpretation of the Origins of World*
   War II. New York: Lippincott, 1970.
Martin, Bernd. *Deutschland und Japan im Zweiten Weltkrieg.* Göttingen:
   Musterschmidt, 1969.
Mason, W. T. "Some Origins of the Second World War." *Past and Present* 29
   (1964) 67–87.
McSherry, James E. *Stalin, Hitler and Europe, 1933–1939: The Origin of World*
   War II. Cleveland: World, 1968.
Renouvin, Pierre. *World War II and Its Origins: International Relations 1929–*
   1945. Trans. Remy Inglis Hall. New York: Harper & Row, 1969.
Rich, Norman. *Hitler's War Aims.* 2 vols. New York: Norton, 1973–74.
Robertson, Esmonde M. *Hitler's Pre-War Policy and Military Plans, 1933–*
   1939. London: Longman, 1963.

————. *The Origins of the Second World War: Historical Interpretations.* London: Macmillan, 1971.

Schustereit, Helmut. *Vabanque: Hitlers Angriff auf die Sowjetunion als Versuch durch den Sieg im Osten den Westen zu bezwingen.* Herford, F. R. G.: Mittler und Sohn, 1988.

Seabury, Paul. *The Wilhelmstrasse: A Study of German Diplomats under the Nazi Regime.* Berkeley: University of California Press, 1954.

Sontag, Raymond J. "The Last Months of Peace." *Foreign Affairs* 35 (1957) 507–24.

————. "The Origins of the Second World War." *Review of Politics* 25 (1963) 497–508.

Taylor, A. J. P. *The Origins of the Second World War.* New York: Fawcett, 1961.

Thorne, Christopher. *The Approach of War, 1938–1939.* London: Macmillan, 1967.

Toscano, Mario. *The Origins of the Pact of Steel.* Baltimore: Johns Hopkins University Press, 1968.

Watt, D. C. "The Anglo-German Naval Agreement of 1935: An Interim Judgment." *Journal of Modern History* 28 (1956) 155–75.

————. "The Rome-Berlin Axis, 1936–1940: Myth and Reality." *Review of Politics* 22 (1960) 519–43.

Weinberg, Gerhard L. *The Foreign Policy of Hitler's Germany: Diplomatic Revolution in Europe, 1933–1936.* Chicago: University of Chicago Press, 1970.

————. *The Foreign Policy of Hitler's Germany: Starting World War II, 1937–1939.* Chicago: University of Chicago Press, 1981.

————. *Germany and the Soviet Union, 1939–41.* Leiden: Brill, 1972.

Wheeler-Bennett, John W. *Munich: Prologue to Tragedy.* New York: Viking, 1963.

Wiskemann, Elizabeth. *Europe of the Dictators, 1919–1945.* New York: Harper & Row, n.d.

————. *The Rome-Berlin Axis.* London: Collins, 1966.

Wolfers, Arnold. *Britain and France between the Wars.* New York: Norton, 1966.

IX. World War II

Artzt, Heinz. *Mörder in Uniform.* Munich: Kindler, 1979.

Baldwin, Hanson W. *Battles Lost and Won: Great Campaigns of World War II.* New York: Harper & Row, 1966.

Beyerchen, A. D. *Scientists under Hitler: Politics and the Physics Community in the Third Reich.* New Haven: Yale University Press, 1977.

Boelcke, Willy, ed. *Deutschlands Rüstung im Zweiten Weltkrieg.* Frankfurt: Akademische Verlagsgesellschaft, 1969.

Broszat, Martin. *Nationalsozialistische Polenpolitik, 1939–1945.* Stuttgart: Deutsche Verlags-Anstalt, 1961.

Browning, Christopher R. *Ordinary Men: Reserve Police Battalion 101 and the Final Solution in Poland.* New York: HarperCollins, 1992.

Chapman, Guy. *Why France Fell.* New York: Holt, Rinehart & Winston, 1969.

Churchill, Winston. *The Second World War.* 6 vols. New York: Houghton Mifflin, 1948–53.

Clark, Alan. *Barbarossa: The Russian-German Conflict, 1941–45.* New York: Signet, 1966.

Collier, Basil. *The Battle of Britain.* London: Macmillan, 1962.

————. *The Battle of the V-Weapons, 1944–45.* Morely, England: Elmfield, 1976.

————. *The Second World War: A Military History.* New York: William Morrow, 1967.

Carrell, Paul. *Sie kommen.* Oldenburg: Stalling, 1961.

————. *Unternehmen Barbarossa: Der Marsch nach Russland.* Frankfurt: Ullstein, 1963.

————. *Die Wüstenfüchse.* Hamburg: Nannen, 1958.

Craig, William. *Enemy at the Gate: The Battle of Stalingrad.* New York: Reader's Digest, 1973.

Creveld, Martin van. *Hitler's Strategy, the Balkan Clue.* Cambridge: Cambridge University Press, 1973.

Dahms, Helmuth Günther. *Die Geschichte des Zweiten Weltkriegs.* Munich: Herbig, 1983.

Dallin, Alexander. *German Rule in Russia, 1941–45.* London: Macmillan, 1957.

Derry, T. K. *The Campaign in Norway.* London: H.M. Stationary Office, 1952.

Deutsch, Harold C. *The Conspiracy against Hitler in the Twilight War.* Minneapolis: University of Minnesota Press, 1968.

Dornberger, Walter. *V-2.* New York: Viking, 1954.

Erickson, John. *The Road to Berlin.* Boulder, Colo.: Westview, 1983.

————. *The Road to Stalingrad.* New York: Harper & Row, 1975.

————. *The Soviet High Command, 1918–1945.* London: Macmillan, 1962.

Feis, Herbert. *Churchill, Roosevelt, Stalin: The War They Waged and the Peace They Sought.* Princeton, N.J.: Princeton University Press, 1957.

————. *The Spanish Story: Franco and the Nations at War.* New York: Norton, 1966.

Fenyo, M. D. *Hitler, Horthy and Hungary: German-Hungarian Relations, 1941–44.* New Haven: Yale Univ. Press, 1972.

Fleming, Peter. *Operation Sea Lion.* New York: Simon & Schuster, 1957.

Frankland, Noble. *The Bombing Offensive against Germany.* London: H.M. Stationary Office, 1951.

Hahn, Fritz. *Waffen und Geheimwaffen des deutschen Heeres 1933–1945.* 2 vols. Koblenz: Bernard & Graefe, 1986–87.

Hasting, Max. *Bomber Command.* London: Pan, 1972.

————. *Overlord: D-Day and the Battle for Normandy.* New York: Simon & Schuster, 1984.

Hillgruber, Andreas. *Hitlers Strategie: Politik und Kriegsführung 1940 bis 1941.* Frankfurt: Bernard & Graefe, 1965.

————. *Der 2. Weltkrieg: Kriegsziele und Strategie der grossen Mächte.* 3rd ed. Stuttgart: Kohlhammer, 1983.

Hinsley, F. H., et al. *British Intelligence in the Second World War.* 2 vols. Cambridge: Cambridge University Press, 1979–1981.

Hoffmann, Peter. *The History of the German Resistance, 1933–1945.* Cambridge, Mass.: MIT Press, 1977.

Horne, Alistair. *To Lose a Battle, France 1940*. Boston: Little, Brown and Co., 1969

Hubatsch, Walther, ed. *Hitlers Weisungen für die Kriegsführung*. Frankfurt: Bernard & Graefe, 1962.

———. *"Weserübung": Die deutsche Besetzung von Dänemark und Norwegen 1940*. Göttingen: Musterschmidt, 1960.

Irving, David. *Hitler's War*. 2 vols. New York: Viking, 1977.

———. *Mare's Nest*. London: Kimber, 1964.

———. *The Virus House*. London: Kimber, 1967.

Jackson, W. G. F. *The Battle for North Africa, 1940–43*. New York: Mason/Charter, 1975.

Jacobsen, Hans-Adolf. *Dünkirchen: Ein Beitrag zur Geschichte des Westfeldzugs, 1940*. Neckargemund: Vowinckel, 1958.

———. *Fall Gelb: Der Kampf um den deutschen Operationsplan zur Westoffensive, 1940*. Wiesbaden: Steiner, 1957.

———. *1939–1945: Der Zweite Weltkrieg in Chronik und Dokumenten*. Darmstadt: Wehr & Wissen, 1960.

———, ed. *Dokumente zum Westfeldzug*. Göttingen: Musterschmidt, 1960.

———, ed. *Dokumente zur Vorgeschichte des Westfeldzugs 1939–40*. Göttingen: Musterschmidt, 1956.

Keegan, John. *The Second World War*. New York: Viking, 1990.

———. *Six Armies in Normandy: From D-Day to the Liberation of Paris*. New York: Penguin, 1983.

Kehrig, M. *Stalingrad: Analyse und Dokumentation einer Schlacht*. Stuttgart: Deutsche Verlags-Anstalt, 1974.

Kennedy, Robert M. *The German Campaign in Poland*. Washington D.C.: GPO, 1956.

Krausnick, Helmut, and Hans-Heinrich Wilhelm. *Die Truppe des Weltanschauungskrieges: Die Einsatzgruppen der Sicherheitspolizei und des SD, 1938–1942*. Stuttgart: Deutsche Verlags-Anstalt, 1981.

Liddell Hart, B. H. *The German Generals Talk*. New York: Morrow, 1948.

———. *History of the Second World War*. New York: Putnam, 1970.

———. *The Red Army, 1918 to 1945*. New York: Harcourt, Brace & Co., 1956.

———. *Strategy*. New York: Praeger, 1960.

Middleton, Drew. *The Sky Suspended*. New York: Mckay, 1960.

Petrow, Richard. *The Bitter Years: The Invasion and Occupation of Denmark and Norway*. New York: Morrow, 1974.

Powers, Thomas. *Heisenberg's War: The Secret History of the German Bomb*. New York: Alfred A. Knopf, 1993.

Ritter, Gerhard. *The German Resistance: Carl Goerdeler's Struggle against Tyranny*. Trans. R. T. Clark. New York: Praeger, 1958.

Ryan, Cornelius. *A Bridge Too Far*. New York: Simon & Schuster, 1974.

———. *The Last Battle*. London: Collins, 1966.

———. *The Longest Day: June 6, 1944, D-Day*. New York: Fawcett, 1959.

Schulte, Theo J. *The German Army and Nazi Policies in Occupied Russia*. New York: Berg, 1989.

Snyder, Louis L. *The War: A Concise History*. New York: Dell, 1960.

Steinert, Martin G. *Hitlers Krieg und die Deutschen: Stimmung und Haltung der deutschen Bevölkerung im Zweiten Weltkrieg*. Düsseldorf: Econ, 1970.

Taylor, Telford. *The Breaking Wave: The Second World War in the Summer of 1940*. New York: Simon & Schuster, 1967.

———. *The March of Conquest: The German Victories in Western Europe, 1940*. New York: Simon & Schuster, 1958.

Trevor-Roper, H. R. *Blitzkrieg to Defeat: Hitler's War Directives*. New York: Holt, Rinehart & Winston, 1964.

———. *The Last Days of Hitler*. New York: Macmillan, 1947.

Welchman, Gordon. *The Hut Six Story: Breaking the Enigma Codes*. New York: McGraw-Hill, 1982.

Walker, Mark. *German National Socialism and the Quest for Nuclear Power*. New York; Cambridge University Press, 1989.

Weinberg, Gerhard L. *A World at Arms: A Global History of World War II*. Cambridge: Cambridge University Pres, 1994.

———. *World in the Balance: Behind the Scenes of World War II*. Hanover, N.H.: University Press of New England, 1981.

Wheatley, Ronald. *Operation Sea Lion*. Oxford: Clarendon, 1958.

Wilmot, Chester. *The Struggle for Europe*. London: Collins, 1952.

Wright, Gordon. *The Ordeal of Total War, 1939–1945*. New York: Harper & Row, 1968.

X. The Aftermath: Nuremberg and the Question of German Guilt

Augstein, Rudolph, ed. *Historikerstreit: Die Dokumentation der Kontroverse um die Einzigartigkeit der Nationalsozialistischen Judenvernichtung*. Munich: Piper, 1987.

Belgion, Montgomery. *Victor's Justice*. Hinsdale, Ill.: Henry Regnery, 1949.

Conot, R. E. *Justice at Nuremberg*. New York: Harper & Row, 1983.

Davidson, E. *The Trial of the Germans*. New York: Macmillan, 1967.

Diner, Dan, ed. *Ist der Nationalsozialismus Geschichte? Zur Historisierung und Historikerstreit*. Frankfurt: Fischer, 1987.

Evans, Richard J. *In Hitler's Shadow*. New York: Pantheon, 1989.

Fischer, Klaus P. "The Liberal Image of German History." *Modern Age* 22, no. 4 (fall 1978) 371–83.

Geiss, Immanuel. *Die Habermas-Kontroverse: Ein deutscher Streit*. Berlin: Siedler, 1987.

Gilbert, G. M. *Nuremberg Diary*. New York: Signet, 1961 (originally published in 1947).

Habermas, Jürgen. *Eine Art Schadensabwicklung*. Frankfurt: Suhrkamp, 1987.

Hartman, Geoffrey H., ed. *Bitburg in Moral and Political Perspective*. Bloomington: Indiana University Press, 1986.

Hoffmann, Hilmar, ed. *Gegen den Versuch, Vergangenheit zu verbiegen*. Frankfurt: Athenäum, 1987.

Jaspers, Karl. *The Question of German Guilt*. Trans. E. B. Ashton. New York: Capricorn, 1961.

Kelley, Douglas M. *22 Cells in Nuremberg*. New York: Greenberg, 1947.

Koch, H. W., ed. *Aspects of the Third Reich*. London: Macmillan, 1985.

Maier, Charles S. *The Unmasterable Past: History, Holocaust, and German National Identity*. Cambridge, Mass.: Harvard University Press, 1988.

Maser, Werner. *Nuremberg: A Nation on Trial.* Trans. Richard Barry. New York: Scribner's, 1979.

Mayer, Arno J. *Why Did the Heavens not Darken?* New York: Pantheon, 1990.

Mommsen, Hans. *Auf der Such nach historischer Normalität: Beiträge zum Geschichtsbildstreit in der Bundesrepublik.* Berlin: Argon, 1987.

Nolte, Ernst. *Der Europäische Bürgerkrieg 1917–1945: Nationalsozialismus und Bolshevismus.* Frankfurt: Ullstein, 1987.

———. *Das Vergehen der Vergangenheit. Antwort an meine Kritiker im sogenannten Historikerstreit.* Berlin: Ullstein, 1988.

Pross, Harry. *Vor und nach Hitler: Zur deutschen Sozialpathologie.* Olten: Walter, 1962.

Schneider, Peter. "Hitler's Shadow: On Being a Self-Conscious German." *Harper's Magazine,* September, 1987, 49–54.

Schulze, Hagen. *Wir sind was wir geworden sind. Vom Nutzen der Geschichte für die deutsche Gegenwart.* Munich: Piper, 1987.

Smith, Bradley F. *The Road to Nuremberg.* New York: Basic, 1981.

Stern, Fritz. *Dreams and Illusions: National Socialism in the Drama of the German Past.* New York: Vintage, 1987.

Stürmer, Michael. "Weder Verdrängen noch bewältigen. Geschichte und Gegenwartsbewusstsein der Deutschen." *Schweizer Monatshefte* 66 (September 1986) 690.

Taylor, Telford. *The Anatomy of the Nuremberg Trials.* New York: Alfred A. Knopf, 1992.

Tusa, A., and J. Tusa. *The Nuremberg Trial.* New York: Atheneum, 1984.

Wechsler, Herbert. "The Issue of the Nuremberg Trial." *Political Science Quarterly* 62 (1947) 1–26.

Wehler, Hans-Ulrich. *Entsorgung der deutschen Vergangenheit? Ein polemischer Essay zum "Historikerstreit."* Munich: Beck, 1988.

Index

immigrant illegally entering. Anarchists and prostitutes added to the list of excluded persons.

1906. Establishment of the Bureau of Immigration to keep records and statistical data.

1906–24. JAPANESE EXCLUSION. No significant Japanese immigration appeared until the decade 1891–1900, during which period 25,942 Japanese entered the U.S., a total which rose to a peak of 129,797 in the following decade. By the first "Gentlemen's Agreement" (Aug. 1900) Japan agreed to inaugurate a policy of voluntary limitation of emigration through refusal to issue passports to emigrant laborers. On 7 May 1905 the Japanese and Korean Exclusion League was organized on the West Coast. On 11 Oct. 1906 the San Francisco School Board ordered that Chinese, Japanese, and Korean children attend a separate public school. As a result of a conference with President Theodore Roosevelt the board rescinded this action (13 Mar. 1907), and in a series of notes, 1907–08 (the **"Gentlemen's Agreement"**), Japan affirmed her intention of stopping the emigration of laborers. This arrangement continued until superseded by the Immigration Act of 1924, excluding Japanese immigrants as "aliens ineligible to citizenship." Meantime, state laws, notably in California, had limited the right of the Japanese to own (1913) and then to lease (1920) farm lands; upheld by the Supreme Court, 1923. The result was "Humiliation Day" in Tokyo, 1 July 1924, marked by "Hate American" mass meetings.

1917–20. LITERACY TEST AND FURTHER BARS. Bills imposing a literacy test were vetoed by Cleveland (1896) and Taft (14 Feb. 1913). On 28 Jan. 1915 President Wilson vetoed such a bill on the ground that it constituted a fundamental reversal of historical policy without popular mandate. Again, on 29 Jan. 1917, Wilson vetoed a similar measure on the ground that it was "not a test of character, of quality, or of personal fitness." The act, passed over the president's veto, required aliens over 16 years of age to read "not less than 30 nor more than 80 words in ordinary use" in the English language or some other language or dialect. As a war measure, an act of 16 Oct. 1918 excluded alien anarchists and others advocating the overthrow of the government. An act of 10 May 1920 provided for the deportation of alien enemies and anarchists.

1921, 19 MAY. FIRST "QUOTA LAW" limited immigration in any year to 3% of the number of each nationality according to the **Census of 1910**, with a maximum quota of 357,000.

1924, 26 MAY. NEW QUOTA LAW halved 1921 quota (1923, 357,803; 1924–25, 164,447) and limited immigration in any year to 2% of the **Census of 1890** (in order to reduce quotas from Eastern and Southern Europe); to remain in force until 1927, when an apportionment on the basis of 1920 distribution of "national origins" would serve as the basis for a maximum quota of **150,000** per annum. Owing to opposition this law did not go into effect until 1 July 1929, since which date the annual quota of any nationality for each fiscal year has been a number which bears the same ratio to 150,000 as the number of inhabitants in 1920 having that origin bears to the total number of inhabitants in the U.S. in 1920. Under an act of 1929 consuls were empowered to refuse visas to all applicants who may become "public charges." The quota laws did not apply to immigration from Canada or Latin America, and provided a few minor exceptions for ministers, professors, and bona fide college students.

1945–52. DISPLACED PERSONS. Under directive of President Truman, 22 Dec. 1945, measures were taken to facilitate the entrance under quota of displaced persons. Under the directive 42,000 persons were admitted to the country. By act of 25 June 1948, visas were authorized for the admission of 205,000 European displaced persons, including 3,000 nonquota orphans; the number of visas authorized was increased by act of 16 June 1950 to 341,000 to be issued by 30 June 1951. Certain discriminatory provisions were eliminated and new categories of expellees and war orphans added with total visas of 54,744 and 5,000 respectively to be issued by 30 June 1952. By act of 28 June 1951, issuance of visas to displaced persons was extended to 31 Dec. 1951.

1951–65. IMPORTATION OF "BRACEROS." Under "temporary" laws Congress permitted controlled annual importation of farm workers (*braceros*) from Mexico (renewed 1951, 1956, 1958, but terminated 31 Dec. 1961). In Feb. 1962 the *braceros* became subject to the provisions of the minimum wage law, and in 1965 the importation of workers under the *bracero* program ended.

1952, 30 JUNE. McCARRAN-WALTER ACT, passed over the veto of President Truman (House vote, 278–133; Senate, 57–26), codified U.S. immigration laws and generally retained the provisions of the 1924 act on maximum immigration and the quota system, but removed the ban against immigration of Asian and Pacific peoples. Screening measures to keep out "subversives" and other undesirables were incorporated and the Attorney General empowered to deport immigrants for "Communist and Communist-front" affiliations even after they acquired U.S. citizenship.

1953, 7 AUG. REFUGEE RELIEF ACT provided for entry into the U.S., on an emergency basis outside regular immigration quota, of 186,000 escapees from Communist persecution, as well as selected persons in other groups up to a total of 214,000. Under accelerated procedure adopted late in 1956 to cope with a mass influx of refugees from Hungary into Austria, 21,500 Hungarian refugees were admitted into the U.S., with an emergency air- and sea-lift instituted by the Defense Department. Total displaced persons admitted, 1948–55, 406,028; refugees, 1954–59, 234,145.

1965. IMMIGRATION AND NATIONALITY ACT. The McCarran-Walter Act was revised (1 Dec.) and the national quota system substantially altered. Effective 1 July 1968, a limit of 170,000 was set for immigrants from countries outside the Western Hemisphere, with a 20,000 annual maximum for any one country. At the same time, an annual ceiling of 120,000 was set for the Western Hemisphere, on a first-come basis with no limitations set for a country.

1966. STATUS OF CUBANS. Effective 2 Nov. Cubans admitted or paroled into the U.S. after 1 Jan. 1959 and present in the U.S. for at least 2 years were made eligible for permanent resident status.

1951–70. CHANGING IMMIGRATION PATTERNS. The altered quota system, with special exceptions, was reflected in the changing immigration flow.

1951–60. Total (by country of birth): from **Europe:** 1,492,215 (Germany, 345,-450; United Kingdom, 208,872; Italy, 187,904; Poland, 127,985); from **Asia,** 157,081; from **North America,** 769,147 (Mexico, 319,312; Canada, 274,926; Cuba, 78,330); from **South America,** 72,166 (Colombia, 17,581); from **Africa,** 16,569.

1961–70. Total: from **Europe,** 1,238,-553 (United Kingdom, 230,452; Italy, 206,650; Germany, 199,980; Greece, 90,-235); from **Asia:** 445,269 (Philippines, 101,656; China, incl. Taiwan, 96,702); from **North America:** 1,351,099 (West Indies, 519,499, incl. Cuba, 256,769;

Mexico, 443,301; Canada, 286,667); from **South America**, 228,475 (Colombia, 70,327; Argentina, 42,135); from **Africa**, 39,262.

1965–70. AWAKENING OF LA RAZA. A shift of Mexican-American population from the farms to the cities (80% by 1970), along with affirmative support for *La Raza* in a context of American cultural pluralism and militant organizing of migrant workers, opened up a new era for the Mexican-American. In 1965 the grape-pickers under **Cesar Chavez** (1927–   ), who had founded the National Farm Workers Association (1963), later transposed to United Farm Workers, struck against the growers of Delano, Calif. and called for an International Boycott Day (10 May 1969) of California table wines. In 1966 Cesar Chavez's force affiliated with the AFL-CIO, and on 29 July 1970 the 5-year-long strike was ended by a pact with the growers. By 1974, however, the UFW had suffered severe setbacks as the Teamsters sought to represent migrant agricultural workers. Other militant civil rights leaders have been Rodolfo ("Corky") Gonzalez, founder in Denver, Colo. (1965) of the Crusade for Justice, and Reies Lopez Tijerina, founder in the 1960s of the Alliance of Land Grants (later named Alliance of Free City-States), whose purpose was to reopen the question of Spanish and Mexican land grants.

1970. AMERICANS OF ASIATIC DESCENT in U.S. estimated as 591,000 of Japanese ancestry, 435,000 of Chinese ancestry, and 343,000 of Filipino ancestry.

1972. AMERICANS OF SPANISH DESCENT in U.S. estimated at 9,178,-000, of whom 5,254,000 were of Mexican origin and 1,518,000 of Puerto Rican origin.

Black Americans Since the Civil War:
A Chronological Conspectus[1]

1865–77. BLACKS AND RECONSTRUCTION (see pp. 292–302).

1879. Start of black migration from South in large numbers, notably to the Middle West. Black population, Chicago, 1870, c.4,000; 1880, 7,400; 1890, 14,800.

1881. First Jim Crow law segregating railroad coaches passed by Tennessee; similarly, Florida, 1887; Texas, 1889.

Tuskegee Institute, headed by Booker T. Washington (p. 1117), founded.

1883. CIVIL RIGHTS CASES (p. 671).

[1] The role of blacks and the institutions with which they were associated is discussed at further length at appropriate places throughout this book. This section is intended to serve as a point of reference for major political developments.

1892. Lynching of blacks on the rise: 160 (1892); 1,400 since 1882.

1896. "Separate but Equal." See *Plessy* v. *Ferguson* (p. 672), upholding segregation in railroad carriages.

1898. Literacy tests and poll tax upheld in *Williams* v. *Mississippi* (170 U.S. 213).

"Grandfather clause" added by Louisiana to state constitution, waiving other voting requirements if a man's father or grandfather had voted on 1 Jan. 1867; also adopted by North Carolina (1900), Alabama (1901), Virginia (1902), Georgia (1908); upset by Supreme Court in *Guinn* v. *U.S.* (1915), (238 U.S. 497).

1903. General Education Board, endowed by John D. Rockefeller, supported improved preparation of teachers of black schools in the South.

1905. Niagara Conference, called by W. E. B. Du Bois (p. 1017), founded Niagara Movement, asserting equal political rights, economic opportunity, education, justice, and end to segregation.

1906–19. BROWNSVILLE AFFAIR touched off allegedly by riotous conduct of unidentified black soldiers in Brownsville, Tex., 13 Aug. 1906, resulting in dishonorable discharges of 167 privates and noncommissioned officers, 5 Nov. 1906. In 1972 the army cleared the soldiers of guilt and changed the discharges to honorable.

1909. NATIONAL ASSOCIATION FOR THE ADVANCEMENT OF COLORED PEOPLE (NAACP) founded; originally advocated extending industrial opportunity and greater police protection for blacks.

1910. National Urban League formed to aid adjustment of migrant blacks to cities, focusing on economic and social problems.

1911. Peonage declared unconstitutional, *Bailey* v. *Alabama* (219 U.S. 219 [1911]).

1920, Aug. Marcus Garvey (p. 1038) opens National Convention in Harlem of Universal Negro Improvement Association (UNIA); adopts bill of rights and advocates emigration of blacks to Africa.

Ku Klux Klan revival, with 100,000 members in 27 states (est. 4–4.5 million by 1924).

HARLEM RENAISSANCE, black cultural movement, continues for a decade.

1927. Texas law barring blacks from voting in the Democratic primaries invalidated in *Nixon* v. *Herndon* (273 U.S. 536). See also *Smith* v. *Allwright* (1944, p. 678).

1931. First Temple of Islam for Black Muslims founded in Detroit (p. 829).

1931. 25 Mar. Nine Scottsboro boys arrested in Alabama, charged with rape. Found guilty in 3 controversial trials; convictions reversed by U.S. Supreme Court, 1 Apr. 1935.

1935. 19 Mar. Harlem, N.Y., rioting with 3 killed, property damage est. $200 million.

1939. 2 Apr. Marian Anderson (1902–   ) gave concert on Easter Sunday at the Lincoln Memorial after having been denied Constitution Hall, Washington, due to racial policies of Daughters of the American Revolution. Anderson made her debut at Metropolitan Opera as Ulrica in *The Masked Ball* (7 Jan. 1955).

1941. 25 June. President Franklin D. Roosevelt issued Executive Order 8802, forbidding discrimination in employment in government and defense industries.

1941–60. BLACK MIGRATION. 43 cities outside the South doubled their black population as against 2 in the South, 1941–50. Black increase was greater in central part of cities, showing 48.3% increase, 1940–50, as against 10.1% for whites. Nonwhite population was 10% of central parts of cities (1940), 33½% (1950). In the period 1950–58, nonwhite population increased 21.9% in U.S. as against 14.2% for white, with greatest nonwhite percentage gains in Pacific (53.3%), Northeast (49.7%), East North Central (47.6%), Middle Atlantic (38.2%), and the lowest in the East South Central (4.9%). The South contained 6% less of the nation's nonwhite population in 1958 than in 1950.

1942. Congress of Racial Equality (CORE) founded by James Farmer.

1943. Spring. Race riots in Detroit, Mich., and Mobile, Ala., over employment of blacks. A Harlem riot (Aug.) left 5 persons killed, 400 injured, and property damage of some $5 million.

1946. 5 Dec. President Truman issued Executive Order 9802 creating Presidential Committee on Civil Rights; issued report, 1947, urging a civil rights section in the Department of Justice and a permanent Fair Employment Practices Commission (also p. 452).

1948. 30 July. President Truman's Executive Order 9981 barred segregation in armed forces, and a federal law (1949) barred discrimination in federal civil service positions (p. 515).

1951. 12 July. Cicero, Ill., riots over segregated housing led to calling out of National Guard.

1954. 17 May. *Brown* v. *Board of Education of Topeka* and other school and college desegregation tests (p. 679).

1955. 1 Dec. Montgomery bus boycott begins (p. 523).

1956. 11 Mar. Southern Manifesto (p. 521).

1957. 9 Sept. CIVIL RIGHTS ACT (p. 527).

Southern Christian Leadership Conference (SCLC) organized by Martin Luther King, Jr., Bayard Rustin, and others to achieve full citizenship rights for blacks and their integration in all aspects of life.

24 Sept. Little Rock desegregation incident (p. 527).

1960, 1 Feb. Sit-in at F. W. Woolworth lunch counter in Greensboro, N.C., set off a national movement of nonviolent protest.

15 Apr. Student Non-Violent Coordinating Committee (SNCC) formed at Shaw Univ., to win political power for Southern blacks.

1960–70. BLACK MIGRATION. U.S. Census showed for first time more than half the nation's blacks living outside the South, with 1,457,000 nonwhites moving from the South in the previous decade. Black migration, 1960–70: Mid-

dle Atlantic, 540,000; East North Central, 356,000; Pacific, 286,000; South Atlantic, 538,000; East South Central, 560,000; West South Central, 282,000. In official 1970 Census black population, 22,580,000, being 11.1% of total population, but apparently underestimation of 1.9 million. As of 1970 black population was located 39% in North, 53% in South, 8% in West; 16.8 million lived in metropolitan areas (74%) of which 13.1 million lived in central cities (58%).

1961, 4 May. Freedom Ride campaign initiated by CORE, testing integration by bus rides through the South.

1961–68. Civil rights under Kennedy-Johnson administrations, including Civil Rights Law of 2 July 1964 (pp. 528, 529).

1963, 12 June. Medgar Evers, state desegregation leader, fatally shot in Jackson, Miss.

1965, 21 Feb. Assassination in New York City of Malcolm X (b. 1925), founder of the Organization of Afro-American Unity and proponent of a philosophy of black unity.

7 Mar. Protest march from Selma to Montgomery, Ala., led by Martin Luther King, Jr.

1964–68. URBAN RACE RIOTING (p. 531).

1965–67. BLACK APPOINTEES to high federal positions, include **Thurgood Marshall** (p. 1098), Solicitor General of the U.S. (1965–67), justice of the U.S. Supreme Court (1967–   ); **Robert Weaver,** Secretary of Housing and Urban Development (1966–69), **Andrew Brimmer,** member of Federal Reserve Board (1966–74).

1966. The Black Panthers, a black revolutionary party, founded by Bobby Seale and Huey P. Newton. The Black Panthers subsequently were involved in many violent confrontations with the police and many of their leaders were killed or imprisoned.

JUNE. "Black Power" popularized as a slogan by Stokely Carmichael, leader of SNCC, during march to Jackson, Miss., led by James Meredith. Richard Wright authored *Black Power* (1954) writing about blacks on the Gold Coast of Africa, and Rep. Adam Clayton Powell, Jr., used the term at a Chicago rally (May 1965). The Black Power movement, rejecting the nonviolent, integrationist, coalition-building approach of traditional civil rights groups, advocated black control of black organizations—black self-determination.

1967. Carl Stokes elected mayor of Cleveland, Ohio, the first black mayor of a major U.S. city. Others included: Richard Hatcher (Gary, Ind., 1967); Kenneth A. Gibson (Newark, N.J., 1970); Thomas Bradley (Los Angeles, Calif., 1973); Maynard Jackson (Atlanta, Ga., 1973).

1968, 4 APR. Assassination of Martin Luther King, Jr., in Memphis, Tenn. (also p. 1076); SCLC leadership assumed by Rev. Ralph Abernathy.

2 MAY–24 JUNE. "Poor People's March" on Washington led by Rev. Ralph Abernathy.

5 Nov. Presidential election: 51.4% of registered nonwhites voted compared with 44% in 1964. Black registration, of voting-age black population, in 11 Southern states rose from 1,463,000 (1960) to 3,449,000 (1971), or from a total of 29.1% (1960) to 58.6% (1971).

1970–73. BLACK MIGRATION from North to South (198,000) outnumbered those moving from South to North (117,000), largely reflecting economic factors.

1971. The 13 black members of the U.S. House of Representatives formed the Congressional Black Caucus.

LEADING SUPREME COURT DECISIONS

The unanimous decision of the United States Supreme Court in *United States of America* v. *Richard M. Nixon* reminds us not only that almost all major issues of domestic policy arrive at the high court in the form of constitutional questions but also that it is a basic tenet of American governance that the Supreme Court is the final arbiter of the American Constitution. It is a remarkable paradox that the American republic refers some of its most difficult policy decisions to non-elected "wise elders" for resolution by interpretation of a document drawn up two centuries ago. Perhaps even more remarkable is the evolution of the court in the past thirty-five years as the most egalitarian branch of government and the one most protective of the individual citizen.

Although the docket of the court was light during its very first decade, the justices encountered cases raising substantial political controversy in their capacity as circuit justices. The first great era of the court was that dominated by John Marshall, who in thirty-four years left a heritage of broad nationalist decisions, laying the foundation for modern American federalism. Closer to his own time, those decisions assisted the growth of American capitalism. For the next three decades the able Roger Taney presided over a court which reconciled the approach of Marshall with the spirit of Jacksonian democracy.

The court rebounded rapidly from the tragic *Dred Scott* decision; from 1878 to 1937 it emerged as the protector of capital from most regulation of either the national or the state governments. Concurrently, the court strayed from the spirit of the 14th and 15th Amendments and ultimately, in *Plessy* v. *Ferguson*, sustained state-sponsored segregation.

Another great crisis, the court-packing fight of 1937, was triggered by the unwillingness of a majority of the Supreme Court, confronted by New Deal legislation aimed at pulling the nation out of the great depression, to depart from their constitutional gloss of sixty years. But once again the court was resilient, abandoning its role as chief economic arbiter, and assuming another, that of protector of civil liberties.

Remarkable indeed were the court's accomplishments under Chief Justice Earl Warren. Then the court struck down not only the segregation of schools but all state-imposed segregation, ordered the reapportionment of state legislatures and the redrawing of congressional district lines on the basis of "one man, one vote," and read into the 14th Amendment the protections of the Bill of Rights, greatly expanding the rights of the individual facing criminal prosecution.

Since then the Burger Court, responsive to growing public conservatism, has engaged in a partial retreat. It has, on the one hand, circumscribed the implementation of desegregation of Northern school systems and given freer rein to police procedures. On the other, it has invalidated all criminal abortion and capital punishment statutes then existing on the books; it resisted Nixon administration pressures by refusing to enjoin publication of the Pentagon Papers and by ordering the president to turn the Watergate tapes over to the lower federal courts.

1793. CHISHOLM v. GEORGIA (2 Dallas 419). The Constitution (Art. III, Sec. 2) gave the federal courts explicit jurisdiction over "controversies between a state and citizens of another state." As executors for a British creditor, 2 South Carolina citizens brought suit in the Supreme Court against the state of Georgia for the recovery of confiscated property. Georgia denied the court's jurisdiction, and refused to appear. The court decided in favor of Chisholm. Opinions of 4 majority justices (notably John Jay and James Wilson) elaborated on the sovereignty and the nature of the Union. Dissenting Justice James Iredell held that no constitutional sanction superseded the right (under English common law) of a sovereignty not to be sued without its consent. As a result of the decision, the 11th Amendment was proposed and ratified (p. 151).

1796. WARE v. HYLTON (3 Dallas 199). By the peace treaty with Great Britain (1783), no legal impediment was to be placed on recovery of debts owed by Americans to British creditors. In this test case, the court invalidated a Virginia statute (1777) providing for the sequestration of debts owed to British subjects before the outbreak of the Revolution, on the ground that under the Constitution treaties are the supreme law of the land; hence paramount over state laws.

1796. HYLTON v. U.S. (3 Dallas 171) involved the question of whether a tax on carriages enacted in 1794 was an excise or a direct tax within the meaning of the Constitution. Holding that only land and capitation levies were direct taxes, the court ruled that the carriage tax was indirect and hence could be levied without apportionment among the states. This was the first time the court passed on the constitutionality of an act of Congress.

1798. CALDER v. BULL (3 Dallas 386). The court interpreted that provision of the Constitution (Art. I, Sec. 10) prohibiting state leigslatures from enacting *ex post facto* laws as extending only to criminal, not civil, laws.

1803. MARBURY v. MADISON (1 Cranch 137), p. 158.

1810. FLETCHER v. PECK (6 Cranch 87) involved the claims arising under the Yazoo land frauds (p. 166). The Georgia legislature, many of its members having been bribed by land speculators, granted large tracts along the Yazoo River to land companies

(1795). The grant was rescinded by the succeeding legislature on the ground that its enactment had been attended by fraud and corruption. Chief Justice Marshall rendered the opinion for a unanimous court, upholding the original grant on the grounds that (1) it was not within the province of the court to inquire into the motives actuating a legislature, and (2) the rescinding act impaired the obligation of contracts, Marshall ruling that the contract clause made no distinction between public and private contracts. This was the first time the court invalidated a state law as contrary to the Constitution.

1816. MARTIN v. HUNTER'S LESSEE (1 Wheaton 304) arose from the litigation over Virginia's confiscation of the Fairfax land grants and its statute prohibiting an alien from inheriting land, and involved the crucial question of the court's appellate jurisdiction over the decisions of state courts. The first court decision (1813), rendered against Virginia, stirred the defiance of the state court of appeals, which refused to obey the mandate and held that Sec. 25 of the Judiciary Act was unconstitutional. When the case was again brought to the Supreme Court, Justice Story vigorously affirmed the court's right to review decisions of state courts. Asserting the court's role as the harmonizer of decisions emanating from inferior courts, Story ruled that the constitutional grant of concurrent jurisdiction in specified cases did not deprive the Supreme Court of its appellate jurisdiction. The decision renewed the opposition of the Virginia Republicans led by Judge Spencer Roane and set off a lively pamphleteering war.

1819. TRUSTEES OF DARTMOUTH COLLEGE v. WOODWARD (4 Wheaton 518), p. 189.

1819. STURGES v. CROWNINSHIELD (4 Wheaton 122) involved the constitutionality of a New York statute (1811) relieving insolvent debtors of obligations contracted before the passage of the act. While Chief Justice Marshall held that state bankruptcy laws were permissible in the absence of congressional legislation, he declared that the New York statute impaired the obligation of contracts and was therefore unconstitutional. The decision served to restrict state action on bankruptcy during a period of financial chaos.

1819. M'CULLOCH v. MARYLAND (4 Wheaton 316), pp. 189–190.

1821. COHENS v. VIRGINIA (6 Wheaton 264) arose from the conviction of the Cohens for selling lottery tickets in violation of a state law. The larger issues involved were the constitutionality of Sec. 25 of the Judiciary Act, under which the Cohens had appealed to the Supreme Court, and the interpretation of the 11th Amendment, under which Virginia claimed exemption from federal jurisdiction in this instance. On the merits, the court decided in favor of Virginia, but Chief Justice Marshall issued a firm reply to the Virginia Republicans who denied that state court decisions were subject to court review. His comprehensive interpretation of the court's scope of jurisdiction was based squarely on the doctrine of national supremacy.

1823. GREEN v. BIDDLE (8 Wheaton 1). Ruling that the contract clause applied to contracts between 2 states as well as those between private persons, the Court nullified a Kentucky law pertaining to land titles on the ground that it impaired the obligation of contracts deriving from a political agreement that Kentucky made with Virginia when the former state was organized. The court also denied Kentucky's claim that agreement was invalid because Congress had not consented.

1824. GIBBONS v. OGDEN (9 Wheaton 1) involved a monopoly granted by the New York legislature

(1808) for the operation of steamboats in state waters. Aaron Ogden, successor to the exclusive right granted to Robert Fulton and Robert R. Livingston, sued Thomas Gibbons (who operated under a federal license) to restrain him from engaging in steam navigation between New York and New Jersey. The court invalidated the New York grant. The opinion of Chief Justice Marshall was the first broad construction of the nature and scope of congressional power under the commerce clause. Rejecting a narrow definition of commerce as "traffic" or simple exchange, Marshall construed it as embracing "every species of commercial intercourse," including navigation and other agencies of commerce. While he conceded that the regulation of wholly intrastate commerce was reserved to the state, he asserted that congressional power to regulate interstate and foreign commerce "does not stop at the jurisdictional lines of the several states." This curb on state authority, coming at a time when many states had granted similar monopoly privileges, freed transportation from state restraints.

1824. OSBORN v. BANK OF THE U.S. (9 Wheaton 738) involved the validity of a circuit court decree restraining an Ohio tax and outlaw act directed against branches of the U.S. Bank within the state, and was a direct result of the opposition to the court's decision in **M'Culloch v. Maryland.** The state auditor, Ralph Osborn, and other Ohio officials who seized bank funds were sued for damages. The court decision was in favor of the bank. Chief Justice Marshall held that the agent of a state, when executing an unconstitutional statute, was personally responsible for damages caused by his enforcement of the act, and that a state could not invoke the protection of the 11th Amendment.

1827. MARTIN v. MOTT (12 Wheaton 19). During the War of 1812 state authorities in New England employed various means for effectively denying the authority of the Congress or president to call out the state militia. Justice Story held that the president, acting under congressional authority, was the sole judge of the existence of those contingencies prescribed in the Constitution upon which the militia might be called out; that the president's decision was binding on state officials; and that state militia in federal service were subject to the authority of officers commissioned by the president.

1827. OGDEN v. SAUNDERS (12 Wheaton 213). The court ruled 4 to 3 that a New York bankruptcy law (1801) did not violate the obligation of contracts entered into *after* the enactment of the law. Justice William Johnson of the majority, anticipating the later doctrine of the state's police power, declared that "all the contracts of men receive a relative, and not a positive interpretation: for the rights of all must be held and enjoyed in subserviency to the good of the whole." But the majority also declared that a state insolvency law could not discharge a contract of a citizen of another state. This was the first time Chief Justice Marshall was in a minority on the interpretation of a constitutional provision. He and Justice Story dissented on the ground that the contract clause protected all contracts, future as well as past, from impairment.

1827. BROWN v. MARYLAND (12 Wheaton 419) invalidated a Maryland law requiring a special license for wholesalers dealing in foreign goods. Marking out the line between state and federal control of commerce, Chief Justice Marshall laid down the **"original package"** doctrine: imported goods which became "incorporated and mixed up with the mass of property in the country" were subject to the state taxing power, but those which remained "in the original form or package" (i.e., the property of the importer) were still imports and hence subject to congressional regulation.

1830. CRAIG v. MISSOURI (4 Peters 410). The court, 4 to 3, upset a Missouri law authorizing the issuance of loan certificates receivable in discharge of taxes and debts due the state. Marshall narrowly construed the constitutional clause prohibiting states from emitting bills of credit, while the dissenting justices held the law to be a justifiable use of the state's borrowing power.

1831. CHEROKEE NATION v. GEORGIA (5 Peters 1), p. 204.

1832. WORCESTER v. GEORGIA (6 Peters 515), pp. 204, 205.

1833. BARRON v. BALTIMORE (7 Peters 243). Chief Justice Marshall held that the amendments included in the Bill of Rights were protection against infringement by the federal government, but not binding upon the state governments.

1837. BRISCOE v. BANK OF KENTUCKY (11 Peters 257) upheld a Kentucky law creating a state-owned bank empowered to issue notes for public circulation on the ground that the state had not pledged the redemption of the notes but had established for this purpose a public corporation capable of suing and being sued; hence, the state bank notes could not be construed as bills of credit. Story dissented. The decision paved the way for increased state regulation of currency and banking.

1837. CHARLES RIVER BRIDGE v. WARREN BRIDGE (11 Peters 420). The Massachusetts legislature authorized (1785) the Charles River Bridge Co. to construct and operate a toll bridge over the Charles River, and in 1792 extended the charter to 70 years. The grant did not confer exclusive privileges. The charter of the Warren Bridge (1828) provided that the structure (built a short distance from the Charles Bridge) should be turned over to the state upon the recovery of construction costs. The Charles River Bridge Co. brought suit for an injunction on the ground that the erection of the Warren Bridge constituted an impairment of the obligation of contracts. Rejecting the doctrine of vested rights invoked by the Charles River counsel, Chief Justice Taney ruled that the competing bridge was no such impairment, that a legislative charter must be construed narrowly, that no implied rights could be claimed beyond the specific terms of a grant, and that ambiguous clauses must operate against the corporation in favor of the public. Taney's first pronouncement on a constitutional issue, the decision substantially modified Marshall's earlier contract doctrines.

1837. NEW YORK v. MILN (11 Peters 102) upheld the constitutionality of a New York statute requiring masters of coastwise or transoceanic vessels entering New York to furnish prescribed information concerning all passengers brought in, as a legitimate use of the state police power for purposes of internal health and welfare, not in conflict with the federal commerce power. In a dissenting opinion, Story maintained that the statute infringed upon the exclusive congressional power to regulate foreign commerce.

1839. BANK OF AUGUSTA v. EARLE (13 Peters 519) was the chief of the 3 Comity Cases of 1839, which arose from the attempt of Alabama to exclude corporations chartered by other states. A citizen of Alabama refused to honor the bills of exchange of a Georgia bank, contending that a "foreign" corporation had no lawful right to enter into a contract within a "sovereign" state. Chief Justice Taney recognized the general right of a corporation to do business under interstate comity with other states, but also upheld the right of states to exclude corporations by positive action. Taney rejected the argument that a corporation possessed all the legal rights guaranteed to natural persons under the Constitution.

1842. PRIGG v. PENNSYLVANIA (16 Peters 539) involved the constitutionality of the federal fugitive slave law of 1793 and of a Pennsylvania "personal liberty" law of 1826 banning forcible seizure and removal of a fugitive. For the majority, Story held (1) the state law unconstitutional, and (2) the execution of the fugitive slave clause in the Constitution exclusively a federal power, hence no state was obliged to undertake the enforcement of the law. As a result, Northern states enacted a series of "personal liberty" laws forbidding state authorities from assisting in the return of fugitive slaves.

1847. LICENSE CASES (5 Howard 504). These 3 cases involved the legality of state laws restricting and taxing the sale of alcoholic liquors. The Massachusetts and Rhode Island statutes were upheld as not contrary to the "original package" dictum. The New Hampshire case, however, involved a tax upon liquor in the original and unbroken package. From the 9 opinions written by 6 justices emerged agreement on the view that a tax imposed as an exercise of the state police power is valid, even though the levy impinges on interstate commerce. Four justices (including Taney) indicated that in the absence of federal legislation the states had a concurrent right to regulate interstate commerce unless they came in conflict with a law of Congress.

1849. LUTHER v. BORDEN (7 Howard 1) arose from the Dorr Rebellion in Rhode Island (p. 222) and involved the validity of the declaration of martial law by the existing state legislature. The court decided that Congress

had power under Art. IV, Sec. 4 of the Constitution to guarantee republican government in the states and to recognize the lawful government; the president by Act of Congress must decide in case of an armed conflict within a state which is the lawful government. Neither decision could be questioned by the court as they turn upon "political questions."

1849. PASSENGER CASES (7 Howard 283). These 2 cases involved the legality of New York and Massachusetts acts authorizing a head tax on each alien brought into the ports of these states and directing the tax collections to be used for internal welfare. The court (5–4) held the acts unconstitutional on the ground that the power to regulate foreign commerce belonged exclusively to the federal government and could not be exercised even in the absence of congressional legislation. The dissenting justices maintained that the laws were a legitimate exercise of state police power. Taney contended that, failing positive congressional regulation, the states had a concurrent power in this domain.

1851. COOLEY v. BOARD OF WARDENS (12 Howard 299) upheld the validity of a Pennsylvania law regulating the employment of pilots in the port of Philadelphia. Justice Benjamin R. Curtis ruled that where commerce was national in character, the federal power was exclusive; but where local, the states had a concurrent power to legislate in the absence of federal action.

1857. DRED SCOTT v. SANDFORD (19 Howard 393), p. 263.

1859. ABLEMAN v. BOOTH (21 Howard 506). This case arose when the Wisconsin Supreme Court (1854) freed the abolitionist editor Sherman M. Booth, who had been convicted in federal district court of violating the fugitive slave law of 1850. U.S. District Marshal Ableman obtained a writ of error in the U.S. Supreme Court to review the state court's findings. In an opinion notable for its affirmation of national supremacy and its analysis of divided sovereignty, Taney denied the right of the state judiciary to interfere in federal cases and, in a brief obiter dictum, upheld the constitutionality of the fugitive slave law. His pronouncement led the Wisconsin legislature to adopt resolutions defending state sovereignty in the spirit of the Kentucky and Virginia resolutions.

1861. EX PARTE MERRYMAN (Fed. Cases No. 9487) involved military suspension of the privilege of the writ of habeas corpus, authorized in exceptional instances by President Lincoln. John Merryman, a Baltimore secessionist, arrested by military authority, successfully petitioned Chief Justice Taney (sitting as a circuit judge) for a writ of habeas corpus. That writ was rejected by the military commander. Taney, who cited the commander for contempt, filed an opinion denying that the executive had the power to suspend the writ, holding such power to be vested in Congress, and condemning the suspension of constitutional rights by military order. Lincoln justified his course in his message to Congress (July 1861).

1863. PRIZE CASES (2 Black 635). Before Congress recognized a state of war, neutral shipping was seized under Lincoln's proclamations (19, 27 Apr. 1861) which authorized a blockade of Confederate ports. The court (5–4) sustained the legality of the seizures, declaring that the president could not initiate war, but was fulfilling his lawful duties in resisting insurrection, and that insurrection was in fact war.

1864. EX PARTE VALLANDIGHAM (1 Wallace 243) involved arrests and trials of civilians by military commissions. Upon rejection of Vallandigham's petition for a writ of habeas corpus by a U.S. circuit court, his counsel appealed to the Supreme Court. The court refused to review the case on the ground that its authority did not embrace the proceedings of a military commission.

1866. EX PARTE MILLIGAN (4 Wallace 2) involving the trial and conviction of civilians by military commission at Indianapolis, unanimously held the military commission authorized by the president to be void and released Milligan. A majority held that neither Congress nor the president had legal power to institute a military commission to try civilians in areas remote from the actual theater of war, stating that the Constitution "is a law for rules and people equally in war and in peace, and covers with the shield of its protection all classes of men, at all times, and under all circumstances." Four justices argued in an opinion by Chief Justice Chase that Congress could have authorized the military commission under the war powers.

1867. TEST-OATH CASES: Cummings v. Missouri (4 Wallace 277), **Ex parte Garland** (4 Wallace 333). The **Cummings** case involved a Missouri constitutional (1865) provision requiring an oath of past allegiance from teachers, preachers, voters, and many others. The **Garland** case arose from a federal loyalty oath requirement (1865) demanded of attorneys practicing in the federal courts. Heard simultaneously, the court split 5–4 in both decisions. The majority held such tests of past fidelity ex post facto and bills of attainder. The dissenters maintained that such requirements were valid expressions of a government's right to protect itself by laying down certain qualifications of its officers and voters.

1867. MISSISSIPPI v. JOHNSON (4 Wallace 475) concerned an attempt by Mississippi to enjoin President Johnson from enforcing the 1867 Reconstruction Acts. Unanimously, the court refused the injunction on the ground that purely executive and political functions were not subject to judicial restraint, although mere ministerial acts might be. Similarly, a suit to enjoin the Secretary of War from enforcing these acts was dismissed as involving political questions over which the court had no jurisdiction; **Georgia v. Stanton** (6 Wallace 50).

1869. EX PARTE McCARDLE (7 Walker 506), p. 297.

1869. TEXAS v. WHITE (7 Wallace 700) involved the legality of financial actions of the Confederate government of Texas. The court held that, secession being inadmissible, the Confederate state authorities had never legally existed. Chief Justice Chase, for the majority, analyzed the nature of the Union and the theories of secession and Reconstruction in a manner consistent with the Union's constitutional arguments during the war. "The Constitution," he said, ". . . looks to an indestructible Union, composed of indestructible states." While refraining from passing on the validity of the Reconstruction Acts of Congress, the court declared that Congress had the duty to provide guarantees of republican governments in the states.

1869. VEAZIE BANK v. FENNO (8 Wallace 533) dealt with the prohibitive 10% tax levied by Congress on state bank notes to promote the national banking system initiated during the Civil War. Chief Justice Chase, for the majority, upheld the tax as a legitimate exercise both of Congress' taxing power and of its authority to provide for a sound national currency.

1870. 1ST LEGAL TENDER CASE: Hepburn v. Griswold (8 Wallace 603). By a 5–3 decision, the court held unconstitutional the Legal Tender Acts (1862, 1863), insofar as fulfillment of contracts made before their passage was concerned, as violating the obligation of contracts and due process clauses of the 5th Amendment. The minority held these acts to be legitimate exercises of the war power.

1871. 2D LEGAL TENDER CASE: Knox v. Lee, Parker v. Davis (12 Wallace 457). Two new justices, J. P. Bradley and W. Strong, appointed by Grant, joined the minority of the **Hepburn** case to reverse the latter ruling. Legal tender was validated as a justifiable exercise of the national government's powers in time of emergency, not limited to war. While there is no evidence that Grant "packed the court," he made no secret of his disapproval of the **Hepburn** decision, and was aware how his appointees stood on the issue.

1871. COLLECTOR v. DAY (11 Wallace 113). By an 8–1 decision, the court held invalid a federal income tax on the salary of a state official. From this decision there grew a large area of intergovernmental tax immunities, which was not ended until the **Graves** case (1939).

1873. SLAUGHTERHOUSE CASES (16 Wallace 36) were the first judicial pronouncement on the 14th Amendment. A monopoly grant of the Louisiana legislature was contested as a violation of the privileges and immunities clause of that amendment. By a 5–4 decision, the court upheld the grant. For the majority, Justice Miller distinguished between state and national citizenship. Only the rights deriving from federal citizenship were protected by the 14th Amendment, and those rights were narrowly defined. This interpretation placed the great body of civil rights under the protection of the state governments. The court refused to consider the due process clause as a general substantive limitation upon the regulatory powers of the states, and held that the equal protection clause applied solely to state laws which discriminated against Negroes. The dissenting jurists held that the 14th Amendment was a safeguard against state violations of the privileges and immunities of U.S. citizens, and that impairment of property rights by statute violated due process.

1877. GRANGER CASES: Munn v. Illinois (94 U.S. 113). This case (one of a group known collectively as the Granger cases) involved an Illinois law (1873) fixing maximum rates for grain storage. Chief Justice Waite, for the court, upheld the law as a legitimate expression of the state's police power in regulating **businesses affected with "... a public interest."** He declared that appeal was "to the polls, not to the courts," and denied that the due process clause was substantively violated or that state regulation of intrastate commerce impaired Congress' unilateral control over interstate commerce. In dissent, Justice Field asserted that procedural due process was insufficient protection for property rights.

1881. SPRINGER v. U.S. (102 U.S. 586) upheld the constitutionality of the federal income tax adopted during the Civil War on the ground that it was not a direct tax within the meaning of the Constitution, and did not require apportionment among the states in proportion to population.

1883. CIVIL RIGHTS CASES (109 U.S. 3) were 5 cases where Negroes had been refused equal accommodations or privileges, allegedly in defiance of the 1875 Civil Rights Act. That act was declared invalid for protecting social rather than political rights. The court held that the 14th Amendment prohibited invasion **by the states** of civil rights, but did not protect the invasion of civil rights **by individuals** unaided by state authority. This ruling virtually ended for 80 years federal attempts to protect the Negro against discrimination by private persons.

1884. JUILLIARD v. GREENMAN (110 U.S. 421). In issue was the 1878 Act of Congress which provided that Civil War legal tender notes should not be retired, but kept in circulation. Justice Gray for the court upheld the act on the ground that the power of Congress to make notes legal tender was derived from its constitutional authority to provide a uniform national currency and did not rest solely on the war power. Dissenting, Justice Field stressed the alleged dangers of a doctrine which gave to government ". . . the power to alter the conditions of contracts."

1884. KU KLUX KLAN CASES: Ex parte Yarbrough (110 U.S. 651) upheld Congress' power to punish as a crime against federal law private interference with the right of an American citizen to vote in a federal election. Such right, held Justice Miller, is dependent on the Constitution and laws of the U.S., and not exclusively on state law.

1886. SANTA CLARA CO. v. SOUTHERN PACIFIC R.R. CO. (118 U.S. 394). In 1882 in **San Mateo Co. v. Southern Pacific R.R. Co.** (116 U.S. 138), Roscoe Conkling, counsel for the railroad and ex-senator from New York, contended that in congressional committee the word "persons" in the 14th Amendment had been chosen to extend the protection of the due process clause to legal persons, i.e., corporations. In the **Santa Clara Co.** case Chief Justice Waite, for the court, by way of dictum, announced acceptance of this doctrine, and thereby encouraged the substantive interpretation of the due process clause as a defense of corporate property rights.

1886. WABASH, ST. LOUIS & PACIFIC R.R. CO. v. ILLINOIS (118 U.S. 557) involved the validity of an Illinois statute prohibiting long-short-haul clauses in transportation contracts. The court invalidated the law as an infringement on Congress' exclusive control over interstate commerce. The decision gravely weakened the ruling in the

Granger Cases (1877) and created a "twilight zone" where neither the states nor the federal government could operate.

1890. CHICAGO, MILWAUKEE & ST. PAUL R.R. CO. v. MINNESOTA (134 U.S. 418) invalidated a Minnesota law (1887) providing for a rate-setting railroad and warehouse commission, to have final rate-fixing powers without permissible appeal to the courts, on the ground that denial of recourse to the courts was, substantively, deprivation of property without due process of law. The decision posed the question of the possibility of judicial review of rates prescribed by legislative bodies rather than by quasi-judicial commissions.

1894. REAGAN v. FARMERS' LOAN AND TRUST CO. (154 U.S. 362) upheld the right of the courts to review the fixing of rates by a Texas commission, acting under state law. Justice Brewer declared: "It has always been a part of the judcial function to determine whether the act of one party . . . operates to divest another party of any rights of person or property."

1895. U.S. v. E. C. KNIGHT CO. (156 U.S. 1) involved the first judicial interpretation of the Sherman Antitrust Act. The government charged defendant with a near monopoly of sugar refining. In an 8–1 decision against the government Chief Justice Fuller, for the majority, drew a sharp line between commerce and manufacturing. "Commerce succeeds to manufacture," he asserted, "and is not a part of it." The Sherman Act was held inapplicable to intrastate manufacturing combinations. The effect of this decision was to impair seriously enforcement of the antitrust laws, and to place most monopolies beyond the reach of federal control.

1895. INCOME TAX CASES: Pollock v. Farmers' Loan and Trust Co. (157 U.S. 429, 158 U.S. 601). These cases involved the validity of the federal income tax clauses of the Wilson-Gorman Tariff Act (1894). In the first case the Court, 6–2, declared invalid that part of the tax statute imposing a tax on income from realty and municipal bonds. Such a tax, according to the court, was a direct tax, and must be levied by apportionment among the states, while its incidence on income from municipal bonds was held a tax on an instrumentality of a state. Since no decision resulted on the issue of whether the income tax as a whole was voided, a rehearing was held. By 5–4 the court invalidated the entire tax law, holding that taxes on personal property were direct taxes. As a result, the 16th Amendment was adopted to enable the federal government to enact the income tax.

1895. IN RE DEBS (158 U.S. 564). The 1894 Pullman strike resulted in an injunction under the Sherman Antitrust Act against the union leaders. Debs, president of the American Railway Union, was cited for contempt in violating that injunction, and sued out a writ of habeas corpus in the Supreme Court. The writ was denied. The court rested its judgment not on the Sherman Act, but on the broader ground that the relations of the federal government to interstate commerce and the transportation of the mails authorized the use of the injunction to prevent forcible obstruction.

1896. PLESSY v. FERGUSON (163 U.S. 537) upheld a Louisiana law requiring segregated railroad facilities. As long as equality of accommodation existed, the court held, segregation did not constitute discrimination, and the Negro was not deprived of equal protection of the laws under the 14th Amendment.

1897. U.S. v. TRANS-MISSOURI FREIGHT ASSOCIATION (166 U.S. 290). The court ruled (5–4) an association of 18 railroads which existed to fix transportation rates to violate the Sherman Antitrust Act. The counsel for the railroads pleaded the "rule of reason"—that only those combinations were illegal which were in unreasonable restraint of trade. Although rejected in this instance, this doctrine was later to rule the court.

1898. HOLDEN v. HARDY (169 U.S. 366) upheld (7–2) the validity of a Utah law (1896) limiting maximum work hours in mining industries as a reasonable exercise of the state's police functions. The right of freedom of contract must be modified when inequalities of bargaining power exist, the majority held. In addition, the court stressed the peculiarly hazardous nature of the mining industry. This case served as a precedent for state regulation of labor conditions.

1898. SMYTH v. AMES (169 U.S. 466) invalidated a Nebraska act of 1893 which had fixed railroad rates, on the ground that it constituted a deprivation of property without due process as guaranteed by the 14th Amendment. In order to be reasonable the rates fixed must yield a "fair" return on a "fair value" of the property involved. The rule was so vague as to leave to the courts for determination in each case the fairness of the rates contested.

1899. ADDYSTON PIPE AND STEEL CO. v. U.S. (175 U.S. 211) invalidated a market-allocation scheme as an infringement of the Sherman Act and as directly affecting interstate commerce. The ruling restored a degree of effectiveness to the Sherman Act, which had been impaired by the ruling in the **Knight** case (1895).

1901. INSULAR CASES: De Lima v. Bidwell (182 U.S. 1). The court ruled (5–4) that Puerto Rico ceased to be a foreign nation at the formal close of the Spanish-American War. Thus, duties could not be levied upon goods im-

ported from Puerto Rico without congressional authority. **Dooley v. U.S.** (182 U.S. 222) held that U.S. goods shipped into Puerto Rico were free of duty. But **Downes v. Bidwell** (182 U.S. 244) asserted the principle that the Constitution did not automatically and immediately apply to the people of an annexed territory, nor did it confer upon them all the privileges of U.S. citizenship, but that it was for Congress specifically to extend such constitutional provisions as it saw fit.

1903. LOTTERY CASE: Champion v. Ames (188 U.S. 321) upheld (5–4) a federal law prohibiting the dissemination of lottery tickets through the mails under the commerce power, which, according to the majority, implied the power to prohibit as well as to regulate. For the minority, Chief Justice Fuller attacked the intent of the law as an infringement upon the police powers of the states under the guise of regulating interstate commerce. What was to become known as a "federal police power" was given judicial sanction by this case.

1904. NORTHERN SECURITIES CO. v. U.S. (193 U.S. 197) rejuvenated the dormant Sherman Antitrust Act and upheld (5–4) the government in its suit against the railroad holding company. The majority held that stock transactions constituting an illegal combination (whether reasonable or unreasonable) in restraint of interstate commerce came within the scope of the Sherman Act. Justice Holmes, in dissent, pleaded for the "rule of reason."

1905. SWIFT & CO. v. U.S. (196 U.S. 375) upheld unanimously the government's antitrust prosecution of the "Beef Trust." For the court, Justice Holmes expounded the "stream of commerce" concept, according to which certain local business agreements are regarded as integral parts of interstate commerce.

1905. LOCHNER v. NEW YORK (198 U.S. 45) involved the validity of a New York maximum-hours law for bakers. A bare majority of the court held the law invalid as an unreasonable interference with the right of free contract, and an excessive use of the state's police powers. In a notable dissent, Justice Holmes criticized the majority's decision as based ". . . upon an economic theory which a large part of the country does not entertain. . . . The 14th Amendment does not enact Mr. Herbert Spencer's Social Statics." He insisted that the Constitution "is not intended to embody a particular economic theory, whether of paternalism . . . or of *laissez-faire.*"

1908. ADAIR v. U.S. (208 U.S. 161). The Erdman Act (1898) prohibited railroads engaged in interstate commerce from requiring as a condition of employment an agreement ("yellow-dog" contract) by workers not to join a labor union. The court (6–2) invalidated this provision as an unreasonable violation of freedom of contract and property rights guaranteed by the 5th Amendment. Union membership, according to the majority, was not a subject of interstate commerce.

1908. LOEWE v. LAWLER (208 U.S. 274). This **"Danbury Hatters Case"** resulted in a unanimous decision by the court that a **secondary boycott** (initiated 1902) by a labor union was a conspiracy in restraint of trade within the meaning of the Sherman Act. This was the first time the act was applied to labor organizations.

1908. MULLER v. OREGON (208 U.S. 412) upheld an Oregon law limiting maximum working hours of women and denied that it impaired the liberty of contract guaranteed by the 14th Amendment. Notable was the use by Louis D. Brandeis, counsel for the state, of a brief (**"Brandeis Brief"**) which amassed statistical, historical, sociologi-cal, and economic data to support his contentions, rather than traditional legal arguments.

1911. U.S. v. GRIMAUD (220 U.S. 506) upheld the validity of federal laws (1891, 1905) relating to the disposition and administration of public lands which vested the executive with a substantial measure of administrative discretion. The court distinguished between "administrative discretion" and outright delegation of legislative power (the latter declared unconstitutional).

1911. STANDARD OIL CO. OF NEW JERSEY ET AL. v. U.S. (221 U.S. 1) upheld the dissolution of the company, applying the "rule of reason" to the Sherman Act. Harlan, in dissent, denounced the ruling as judicial usurpation.

1911. U.S. v. AMERICAN TO-BACCO CO. (221 U.S. 106) ordered the reorganization of the "tobacco trust" rather than its complete dissolution on the basis of the "rule of reason" (White).

1913. MINNESOTA RATE CASES (230 U.S. 252) sustained the validity of an order by a state commission setting intrastate railroad rates. The court held that, while Congress' authority over interstate commerce was exclusive, a state might properly act in a field where it did not conflict with federal laws.

1917. WILSON v. NEW (243 U.S. 332). Chief Justice White, for a bare majority of the court, upheld the constitutionality of the Adamson Eight-Hour Act (1916), which specified 8 hours as a day's work on railroads operating in interstate commerce. Despite the fact that this was in effect a wage-fixing measure, the court held that in an emergency Congress might establish a temporary standard.

1918. ARVER v. U.S. (245 U.S. 366), among the **Selective Draft Law Cases**, sustained the World War I conscription act. The power of a nation to secure military service from its residents was an incidence of sovereignty, the court found, as well as a direct result of the Constitutional authorization to Congress "to declare war . . . to raise and support armies" (Art. 1, Sec. 8). Similarly, in 1919, in the **War Prohibition Cases** (251 U.S. 146), the court upheld the wartime prohibition measure as a legitimate exercise of the war power of the government. Again in 1919, the power granted the president to seize and operate the railroads in wartime was upheld under the war power in **Northern Pacific Railway Co. v. North Dakota** (250 U.S. 585).

1918. HAMMER v. DAGENHART (247 U.S. 251). The Keating-Owen Child Labor Act (1916) forbade interstate shipment of products of child labor. The court split 5–4 on the issue of mutually restrictive areas of federal-state operations. Justice Day, for the majority, declared the act invalid as a regulation of local labor conditions rather than commerce. Holmes' dissent upheld Congress' right to regulate interstate commerce in unqualified terms, including the power to prohibit. **Bailey v. Drexel Furniture Co.** (259 U.S. 20), in 1922, involved the second Child Labor Act (1919), which levied prohibitive taxes upon the products of child labor in interstate commerce. Chief Justice Taft spoke for the majority of the court in holding the law invalid on much the same grounds as in the **Hammer** decision.

1919. SCHENCK v. U.S. (249 U.S. 47). For a unanimous court, Justice Holmes upheld the wartime Espionage Act as not violating the 1st Amendment. Applying the "clear and present danger" test, Holmes found that Schenck's pamphlets encouraged real resistance to the draft; that free speech is always under restraint, especially in time of war.

1919. ABRAMS v. U.S. (250 U.S. 616) upheld the 1918 Sedition Law. Applying the "bad tendency" test, Justice Clarke, for the majority, found pamphlets which criticized the U.S. expeditionary force to Siberia as falling within the scope of that act and held that the invoking of disaffection during wartime was not protected by the 1st Amendment. Holmes' dissenting opinion became a classic philosophical argument for freedom of speech ("the best test of truth is the power of the thought to get itself accepted in the competition of the market").

1920. MISSOURI v. HOLLAND (252 U.S. 416), involving the constitutionality of the Migratory Bird Treaty of 3 July 1918, which sought to enforce a convention between the U.S. and Canada, held (7–2) that a treaty conferred powers upon Congress which it might not possess otherwise. Holmes for the majority asserted that treaties are made under the authority of the U.S., while acts of Congress are enacted under the authority of the Constitution. By implication, the powers of the central government are almost limitless if written into a treaty.

1921. DUPLEX PRINTING PRESS CO. v. DEERING (254 U.S. 443), the first court pronouncement on the labor provisions of the Clayton Act, held that secondary boycotts were still enjoinable despite the anti-injunction provision of that act. As a result, the Clayton Act furnished meager protection in the 1920s for labor union practices held by the courts to constitute illegal obstructions to interstate commerce and violations of the antitrust laws. In **Truax v. Corrigan** (257 U.S. 312), 1921, the court invalidated a state statute forbidding the granting of injunctions against picketing as violating the due process and equal protection clauses of the 14th Amendment.

1923. MASSACHUSETTS v. MELLON (262 U.S. 447) involved the validity of the grants-in-aid provisions of the Sheppard-Towner Maternity Act, which the state attacked as coercion upon the states by the central government. While denying jurisdiction, the court (Justice George Sutherland) impliedly upheld the legitimacy of such grants. Since that date grants-in-aid have formed a vast complex of federal-state-municipal relationships.

1923. ADKINS v. CHILDREN'S HOSPITAL (261 U.S. 525) invalidated, as infringing upon the 5th Amendment, an act of Congress (1918) authorizing the Wage Board for the District of Columbia to fix minimum wages for women. In dissent Holmes stated: "The criterion of constitutionality is not whether we believe the law to be for the public good."

1923. WOLFF PACKING CO. v. COURT OF INDUSTRIAL RELATIONS (262 U.S. 522) restricted the concept of public interest to the narrow monopoly definition. A mere declaration by a legislature that a business is affected with a public interest is not conclusive of the question whether its regulation is justified, declared Chief Justice Taft. Holmes' dissent in 1927 in **Tyson and Bros. v. Banton** (273 U.S. 418), where the court invalidated a New York law regulating resale theater ticket prices, attacked the doctrine of public interest and insisted that the state legislature could do whatever it saw fit unless specifically restrained by the Constitution. By 1934, in **Nebbia v. New York** (291 U.S. 502), involving a state law fixing retail milk prices, the majority (Roberts) upheld the right of the state to correct maladjustments in industries subject to regulation in the public interest, following Holmes' view that there is no closed category of business affected with a public interest.

1925–1932. GITLOW v. NEW YORK (268 U.S. 652), 1925; **WHITNEY v. CALIFORNIA** (274 U.S. 357), 1927; **STROMBERG v. CALIFORNIA** (283 U.S. 359), 1931; **NEAR v. MINNESOTA** (283 U.S. 697), 1931; **POWELL v. ALABAMA** (1ST SCOTTSBORO CASE [287 U.S. 45]), 1932—all extended the 14th Amendment to cover the 1st as well as an uncertain number of the remaining sections of the Bill of Rights.

1935. GOLD CASES—Perry v. U.S. (294 U.S. 330), **U.S. v. Bankers Trust Co.** (294 U.S. 240), **Norman v. Baltimore & Ohio R.R. Co.** (294 U.S. 240), **Nortz v. U.S.** (294 U.S. 317)—involved the constitutionality of the congressional joint resolution of 5 June 1933 which nullified the gold clause in private and public contracts. The government's power to so act in private contracts was affirmed in the **Bankers Trust, Norman,** and **Nortz** cases. In the **Perry** case Chief Justice Hughes held that government bonds were contractual obligations of the U.S. government. Hence, the joint resolution was unconstitutional. But since the plaintiff had suffered no more than nominal damages he could not sue in the Court of Claims. In effect, the government was upheld.

1935. SCHECHTER v. U.S. ("Sick Chicken Case" [295 U.S. 495]) unanimously invalidated the NIRA on 3 grounds (Chief Justice Hughes): (1) the excessive delegation of legislative power to the executive, (2) the lack of constitutional authority for such legislation, and (3) the regulation of businesses wholly intrastate in character.

1935. RETIREMENT BOARD v. ALTON R.R. Co. (295 U.S. 330) invalidated (5–4) the Railroad Retirement Act as violating due process and the 5th Amendment and involving matters (pensions) outside the federal commerce power (Justice Roberts).

1936. U.S. v. BUTLER (297 U.S. 1) invalidated (6–3) the AAA on the ground (Justice Roberts) that the processing tax in issue was not really a tax but a part of a system for regulating agricultural production and not within the purview of the welfare clause. Justice Stone in dissent attacked the trend toward judicial legislation. By the Soil Conservation and Domestic Allotment Act (1936) and the Second AAA (1938) the court's objections were met.

1936. U.S. v. CURTISS-WRIGHT EXPORT CORP. (299 U.S. 304) upheld an embargo imposed on arms destined for nations at war in the Chaco (Paraguay and Bolivia) under authorization of a Congressional joint resolution. Justice Sutherland deemed the resolution a proper delegation of legislative power to the president, holding further that the power of the U.S. to conduct foreign relations did not derive from the enumerated powers of the Constitution, but that the transfer of external sovereignty had been effected by the American Revolution.

1936. ASHWANDER v. TVA (297 U.S. 288) upheld the dams built under the TVA as legitimate exercise of the federal government's power to control navigable streams and provide for adequate national defense.

1937. NEW DEAL CASES. During the struggle over President Roosevelt's court reorganization plan (p. 420) the court upheld a series of important New Deal measures. **West Coast Hotel Co. v. Parris** (300 U.S. 379) upheld (5–4) a Washington minimum wage law, overruling the **Adkins** precedent. The National Labor Relations Act was upheld (5–4) in **NLRB v. Jones and Laughlin Steel Corp.** (301 U.S. 1), where the majority stressed the broadest definition of the "stream of commerce" concept, and (5–4) in **NLRB v. Friedman-Harry Marks Clothing Co.** (301 U.S. 58), de-

spite the local nature of the respondent's operations. The social security laws were upheld in **Steward Machine Co. v. Davis** (301 U.S. 548) and **Helvering v. Davis** (301 U.S. 619), by 5–4 in each instance. The **Steward** case upheld both the employer tax and the conditional federal grant-in-aid. Justice Cardozo found no coercion of the states involved in such grants. The **Helvering** case upheld the old-age and benefit provisions.

1937–43. CIVIL LIBERTIES CASES. De Jonge v. Oregon (299 U.S. 253), 1937, voided a conviction under an Oregon criminal syndicalist law by insisting that there was not a "clear and present danger" in a speech at an orderly meeting. **Herndon v. Lowry** (301 U.S. 242), 1937, reversed a Georgia conviction of a Communist organizer, with the court squarely applying the "clear and present danger" doctrine. The **Flag Salute Cases: The Gobitis Case** (310 U.S. 586), 1940, sustained a state flag salute law; but this decision was reversed in **West Virginia State Board of Education v. Barnette** (319 U.S. 624), 1943, where a state law was invalidated as infringing the 1st Amendment.

Palko v. Connecticut (302 U.S. 319), 1937, held that the 14th Amendment did not include the double jeopardy provision of the 5th Amendment (a state could retry a person on criminal charges after he had been found innocent), but opened the way for the court to investigate the scope of basic liberties which the states by the 14th Amendment were forbidden to infringe: (1) Peaceful picketing—**Thornhill v. Alabama** (310 U.S. 88), 1940. (2) Peaceable assemblage—**Hague v. C.I.O.** (207 U.S. 496), 1939. (3) the **Jehovah's Witnesses Cases** generally reaffirmed the right to disseminate religious literature without a license (**Lovell v. Griffin** [303 U.S. 444], 1938), and to solicit funds for religious ends (**Cantwell v.**

Connecticut [310 U.S. 396], 1940) and without being subject to a tax (**Murdock v. Pennsylvania** [319 U.S. 105], 1943).

1938. MISSOURI EX REL. GAINES v. CANADA (305 U.S. 337) upheld the "equality" of educational opportunity for Negroes in segregated Missouri, specifically the petitioner's right to be admitted to the law school of the state university in the absence of other provision for his legal training; reaffirmed in **Sipuel v. University of Oklahoma** (332 U.S. 631), 1948.

1939. GRAVES v. NEW YORK EX REL. O'KEEFE (306 U.S. 466) put an end to intergovernmental tax immunities, which had deprived federal and state governments of large potential sources of revenue, by holding that a state tax on federal employees was no unconstitutional burden upon the federal government.

1941. U.S. v. CLASSIC (313 U.S. 299) upheld the power of the federal government to regulate a state primary where such an election was an integral part of the machinery for choosing a candidate for federal office, reversing a previous decision that party primaries were private affairs.

1941. EDWARDS v. CALIFORNIA (314 U.S. 160) invalidated California's anti-"Okie" law designed to exclude indigent immigrants as a barrier to interstate commerce. In **Morgan v. Virginia** (328 U.S. 373), 1946, a Jim Crow law was voided as a barrier upon interstate commerce.

1941. U.S. v. DARBY (312 U.S. 100) unanimously overruled the **Hammer** case (1918) by upholding the Fair Labor Standards Act of 1938. Commerce was held a complete function, controllable by Congress to the point of prohibition. This decision repudiated the doctrine of mutually exclusive spheres of federal and state activities.

1943. HIRABAYASHI v. U.S. (320 U.S. 81) upheld military curfew regula-

tions on the West Coast under the war powers, but refused to consider the issue of Japanese exclusion from that area.

1944. KOREMATSU v. U.S. (323 U.S. 214) upheld the exclusion of Japanese from the West Coast. The dissenters (Roberts, Murphy, and Jackson) termed the relocation program unconstitutional. In **Ex parte Endo** (323 U.S. 283), 1944, however, it was held that the War Relocation Authority could not detain a person whose loyalty had been established.

1944. SMITH v. ALLWRIGHT (321 U.S. 649) involved the exclusion of Negroes from voting in a primary in Texas, where Democratic party membership was restricted to whites. The court held that in Texas political party membership was equivalent to suffrage; hence, exclusion from the party on grounds of race violated the 15th Amendment.

1947. FRIEDMAN v. SCHWELLENBACH (330 U.S. 838). The court here refused to review a lower court decision involving the dismissal of a federal civil servant on disloyalty charges, and in effect upheld the president's 1947 Loyalty Order authorizing such removal.

1947. U.S. v. CALIFORNIA (332 U.S. 19) rejected California's claim to the 3-mile marginal belt along its coast, Justice Black holding that protection and control of the belt was a function of national external sovereignty. Similarly, Louisiana's seaward claims were denied in **U.S. v. Louisiana** (339 U.S. 699), 1950, as well as those of **Texas** (339 U.S. 706), 1950, despite the latter's claim that it had enjoyed control over the marginal sea when it was an independent sovereign state. Such claims, the court held, were impliedly relinquished as a condition of statehood.

1948. ILLINOIS EX REL. McCOLLUM v. BOARD OF EDUCATION (333 U.S. 203) involved the "released time" plan (in this instance permitting public school students to receive religious instruction during school hours on school property but with private teachers). The court held this particular program violated the 1st Amendment prescribing separation of church and state, but left open the larger question of public aid to religious instruction. A New York released-time law was upheld (**Zorach v. Clauson,** 1952).

1948. SHELLEY v. KRAEMER (334 U.S. 1) held that a racially restrictive covenant violated the equal protection clause of the 14th Amendment.

1950. AMERICAN COMMUNICATIONS ASSN., C.I.O., ET AL. v. DOUDS (339 U.S. 382) upheld Sec. 9h of the Taft-Hartley Act (1947), requiring a non-Communist affidavit from labor union officers under penalty of denying to the union involved certain statutory privileges. The majority denied that the oath was ex post facto, a bill of attainder, or an abridgment of the 1st Amendment. Justice Black in dissent stigmatized test oaths as "instrument[s] for inflicting penalties and disabilities on obnoxious minorities."

1951. DENNIS ET AL. v. U.S. (341 U.S. 494) upheld the Smith Act (1946), which made it a criminal offense to advocate the forceful overthrow of the government. Implicit in the majority opinion of Chief Justice Vinson was a revival of the "bad tendency" test criticized by Holmes. Dissenting, Justice Black called for a return to the "clear and present danger" doctrine and declared the Smith Act violated the 1st Amendment, and Justice Douglas differentiated between a "conspiracy to overthrow" the government and the teaching of "Marxist-Leninist doctrine."

1952. SAWYER, PETITIONER v. YOUNGSTOWN SHEET & TUBE CO., ET AL. (STEEL SEIZURE CASE, [343 U.S. 579]) invalidated (6–3) the seizure of the steel companies by President Truman. Justice Black, for the majority, held that the president's power "must stem either from an act of Congress or from the Constitution itself." Chief Justice Vinson, for the minority, argued that there was no statute prohibiting seizure "as a method of enforcing legislative programs."

1954. BROWN v. BOARD OF EDUCATION OF TOPEKA (347 U.S. 483) reversed **Plessy v. Ferguson** (1896), with its "separate but equal" doctrine. In 1950 **McLaurin v. Okla. State Regents** (339 U.S. 637) and **Sweatt v. Painter** (339 U.S. 629) had struck down state laws for the higher or professional education of Negroes as failing to meet the requirements of equality. In the Brown case, involving elementary education, the court (Warren, Chief Justice) held unanimously that segregation in public education was a denial of the equal protection of the laws. The court (349 U.S. 294), 1955, directed the lower courts to admit Negroes to public schools on a racially nondiscriminatory basis "with all deliberate speed." Reactions ranged from compliance in some border states to hostile gestures toward the court. On 19 Jan. 1956, the Alabama Senate passed a "nullification" resolution; the Virginia legislature adopted (1 Feb.) an "interposition" resolution asserting the right of the state to "interpose its sovereignty" against the decision of the court. On 11 Mar., 19 senators and 81 representatives issued a "**Southern Manifesto**" declaring their purpose to use "all lawful means" to reverse the desegregation decision. **Cooper v. Aaron** (358 U.S. 1), 1958, held that no scheme of racial discrimination against Negro children in school attendance can stand the test of the 14th Amendment if "there is state participation through any arrangement, management, funds or property."

1956. PENNSYLVANIA v. NELSON (350 U.S. 497) found Pennsylvania's antisubversive legislation, to the extent that it punished subversion against the U.S., to be unconstitutional, on the ground that Congress had preempted antisubversion enforcement. Since this is a field in which national interest is dominant, the federal system must be assumed to preclude enforcement of state laws on the same subject.

1957. WATKINS v. U.S. (354 U.S. 178) reversed a contempt conviction of a labor union official who had testified before the House Committee on Un-American Activities about his earlier activities with respect to the Communist party, but refused to name others on the ground that such questions were not relevant to the work of the committee. The court sustained Watkins on the ground of the lack of pertinency of the subject under inquiry and held that the resolution setting up the committee in 1938 was too vague and uncertain to give Watkins sufficient indication of the matter under inquiry.

1957. YATES v. U.S. (354 U.S. 298) held that the government had too broadly construed its powers under the Smith Act to prosecute Communist leaders. Since the **Dennis Case** (1951), nearly 100 convictions and many more indictments had been obtained for Smith Act violations. The court ruled that the Smith Act did not forbid advocacy and teaching of forcible overthrow as an abstract principle, divorced from any effort to incite action to that end.

1958. NAACP v. ALABAMA (357 U.S. 449). In reversing a contempt conviction by an Alabama court the Supreme Court held that the NAACP had a constitutional right to claim protection for its membership and to refuse to divulge its membership list.

1959. ABBATE v. U.S. (359 U.S. 187) and **BARTKUS v. ILLINOIS** (359 U.S. 121) held that neither the constitutional prohibition against double jeopardy nor the guarantee of due process prevented the federal and state governments from successively prosecuting the same man for the same criminal act.

1959. BARENBLATT v. U.S. (360 U.S. 109) upheld the conviction (under 2 U.S. Code 192) of a university teaching fellow who refused to answer questions on Communist affiliation asked by the House Committee on Un-American Activities on the ground that the balance of defendant's and the government's interest is struck in favor of the government, and that the conviction does not transgress the 1st Amendment. Contrariwise, 3 justices (Justice Black) held that the committee was improperly seeking to try, convict, and punish, powers denied a legislative body.

1960. BOYNTON v. VIRGINIA (81 Sup. Ct. Rep. 182) extended **Morgan v. Va.** (1946) in holding that a bus terminal operated as an "integral" part of interstate bus service may not segregate passengers who are on a trip across state lines.

1961–72. CRIMINAL CASES extended coverage of 14th Amendment to include: (1) Federal Exclusionary Rule (evidence secured by state officers through unreasonable search and seizure must be excluded from the trial): **Mapp v. Ohio** (367 U.S. 643), 1961, overturning **Wolf v. Colo.** (338 U.S. 25), 1949; (2) right to court-appointed counsel in state felony prosecution of indigent defendant: **Gideon v. Wainright** (372 U.S. 335), 1963, overturning **Betts v. Brady** (316 U.S. 455), 1942; **Gideon** extended by **Argersinger v. Hamlin** (407 U.S. 25), 1972, to all offenses potentially punishable by a jail sentence; (3) 5th Amendment protection against compelled self-incrimination: **Malloy v. Hogan** (378 U.S. 1), 1964; (4) statements obtained by the police when a suspect is in custody are inadmissible as evidence unless the suspect prior to interrogation is clearly informed (a) of his right to remain silent, (b) that anything he says may be used against him, (c) of his right to consult with an attorney, and (d) of his right, if indigent, to a lawyer appointed for him. Counsel may be present during questioning, **Miranda v. Arizona** (384 U.S. 436), 1966.

1962. ENGEL v. VITALE (370 U.S. 421), considering New York State Board of Regents' prayer, held that "it is no part of the business of government to compose official prayers to be recited as a part of a religious program carried on by government." Readings of the Lord's Prayer and daily Bible readings were struck down in **School Dist. of Abington Township v. Schempp** (373 U.S. 930), 1963.

1962–64. REAPPORTIONMENT DECISIONS. Baker v. Carr (369 U.S. 186), 1962, held that federal courts must consider on merits suits challenging apportionment of state legislatures as allegedly violating equal protection clause of 14th Amendment. In disposing of 14 such suits in June, 1964, the court held that those states did not meet the requirements of the clause; that both houses of the state legislature must be apportioned on basis of equal protection as nearly as possible (**Reynolds v. Sims** [377 U.S. 533]). Not even the electorate's approval by referendum of an apportionment plan can validate it if it is discriminatory (**Lucas v. Colo. Gen. Assembly** [377 U.S. 713]). Court also held that congressional districts must be equal in population "as nearly as practicable" (**Westberry v. Sanders** [376 U.S. 1], 1964).

1964. NEW YORK TIMES v. SULLIVAN (376 U.S. 254) held that public officials acting in their public capacity could recover in libel actions only by proof of publication of defamatory falsehood with actual malice. The rule was extended in later cases to encompass suits brought by public figures: **Curtis**

Publishing Co. v. Butts (388 U.S. 130), 1967, and to private persons, if the statements concerned matter of public interest: **Rosenbloom v. Metromedia, Inc.** (403 U.S. 29), 1971. In **Gertz v. Robert Welch, Inc.** (418 U.S. 323), 1974, the court moved away from *Rosenbloom*, refusing to apply the **New York Times v. Sullivan** rule to private individuals where an interest of general or public concern is involved.

1964. HEART OF ATLANTA MOTEL, INC. v. U.S. (379 U.S. 241) upheld constitutionality of Public Accommodations Title of 1964 Civil Rights Act.

1964. GRISWOLD v. CONNECTICUT (381 U.S. 479) held unconstitutional the Connecticut birth control statute, which banned the use of contraceptives and the giving of medical advice as to their use as a violation of marital privacy emanating from the 1st, 3rd, 5th, 9th, and 14th Amendments. **Griswold** was expanded by **Eisenstadt v. Baird** (405 U.S. 438), 1972, holding state ban on distribution of contraceptives violated equal protection clause.

1966. SOUTH CAROLINA v. KATZENBACH (383 U.S. 301) upheld the constitutionality of provisions of the Voting Rights Act of 1965 (p. 531).

1966. SHEPPARD v. MAXWELL (384 U.S. 333) reversed the murder conviction of Dr. Samuel Sheppard on grounds that he was deprived of a fair trial because of the massive prejudicial newspaper publicity which had taken place during the trial.

1966. A BOOK NAMED "JOHN CLELAND'S MEMOIRS OF A WOMAN OF PLEASURE" v. ATTORNEY-GENERAL OF MASSACHUSETTS (383 U.S. 413) continued the court's trend of hostility to the censorship of books by reversing the Massachusetts Supreme Judicial Court's holding that Cleland's *Fanny Hill* was obscene. The book was deemed not to be "utterly without redeeming social value," the test of **Roth v. United States** (345 U.S. 476), 1957.

1966–67. ANTI-MERGER CASES. Mergers and other centralizing business practices were attacked in a series of cases: (1) **U.S. v. Pabst Brewing Co.** (384 U.S. 546), 1966, where Pabst acquisition of Blatz Brewing Co. was held to have violated Sect. 7 of the Clayton Act. (2) **Federal Trade Commission v. Brown Shoe Co.** (384 U.S. 316), 1966, where the franchise program of the nation's largest shoe manufacturer was held to have violated Sect. 5 of the Federal Trade Commission Act barring unfair trade practices as well as sections of the Sherman and the Clayton acts. (3) **Federal Trade Commission v. Borden Co.** (383 U.S. 637), 1966, held that Borden's practice of marketing its milk under its own name and private brand names for customers was price discrimination tending to lessen competition substantially, thus violating Sect. 2(a) of the Robinson-Patman Act. (4) **Federal Trade Commission v. Procter & Gamble Co.** (386 U.S. 568), 1967, held that the acquisition of Clorox, a leading manufacturer of household liquid bleach, by Procter & Gamble might have substantially anticompetitive effects and therefore violated Sect. 7 of the Clayton Act.

1967. IN RE GAULT (387 U.S. 1) struck a blow at widespread juvenile court practices by finding that the Arizona Juvenile Court violated the 14th Amendment by failing to provide adequately for notice of hearings, right of counsel, right of confrontation, cross-examination of witnesses, and exercise of the privilege against self-incrimination.

1967. LOVING v. VIRGINIA (388 U.S. 1) held the Virginia antimiscegenation statute unconstitutional. Such schemes, said Chief Justice Warren, to prevent the marriage of persons solely on the basis of racial classifications violated the 14th Amendment.

1968. PENN CENTRAL & N&W INCLUSION CASES (389 U.S. 486) upheld the merger between the Pennsylvania R.R. Co. and the New York Central R.R. Co. and the inclusion of 3 small lines in the N&W system.

1969. STANLEY v. GEORGIA (394 U.S. 557) held unconstitutional statutes making it a crime to privately possess obscene material as a government intrusion into the privacy of one's home and an impermissible inquiry into what one might read or see.

1969. POWELL v. McCORMICK (395 U.S. 486). The House of Representatives voted to exclude Rep. Adam Clayton Powell, Jr. of New York from the 90th Congress (1 Mar. 1967) for misconduct. The Supreme Court held (1) that Powell had been improperly excluded; (2) that a suit was properly maintainable only against the employees of the House of Representatives as the representatives themselves were immune from suits for their legislative actions; (3) that the case did not present a "political question" as it required only a constitutional adjudication by the court. Powell was sworn in (3 Jan. 1969) at the beginning of the 91st Congress but fined $25,000. A later court decision refused to award Powell back pay or lost seniority.

1969–71. DESEGREGATION DECISIONS. Alexander v. Holmes County Board of Education (396 U.S. 19), 1969, turned down Nixon administration request for delay in desegregation of 33 Mississippi school systems holding that "the obligation of every school district is to terminate dual systems at once and to operate now and hereafter only unitary schools." **Swann v. Charlotte-Mecklenburg Board of Education** (402 U.S. 1), 1971, held that busing, balancing ratios, and gerrymandered school districts were all permissible methods of ending state-imposed segregation.

1969–72. ANTITRUST DECISIONS included (1) **Citizen Publishing Co. v. United States** (394 U.S. 131), 1969, applied to merger between advertising and circulation departments of newspapers where price-fixing, market control, and pooling of profits were involved: (2) **Federal Trade Commission v. Sperry and Hutchinson Co.** (405 U.S. 233), 1972, held FTC empowered to protect consumer and judge business practice against standards of fair competition; (3) **Flood v. Kuhn** (407 U.S. 258), 1972, held that Congress has acquiesced in exemption of baseball and its reserve clause from the antitrust laws; (4) **United States v. Topco Associates** (405 U.S. 596), 1972, held that territorial allocations among distributors are unlawful.

1969–73. POVERTY-WELFARE DECISIONS. The court generally expanded the rights of the poor in a series of decisions holding (1) that a state cannot constitutionally allow garnishment without prior notice and hearing: **Sniadach v. Family Finance Corp.** (395 U.S. 337), 1969; (2) state laws requiring residence for 1 year prior to eligibility for welfare assistance were held to violate right to interstate travel: **Shapiro v. Thompson** (394 U.S. 618), 1969; (3) a welfare recipient is entitled to full hearing prior to termination of welfare payments: **Goldberg v. Kelly** (397 U.S. 254), 1970; (4) summary seizure of goods sold on installment purchase without prior notice and hearing is unconstitutional: **Fuentes v. Shevin** (407 U.S. 67), 1972. However, in **Wyman v. James** (400 U.S. 309), 1971, court upheld right of a state to condition welfare assistance to dependent children upon onsite visits by caseworkers, and in **United States v. Kras** (409 U.S. 434), 1973, a $50 filing fee required for filing for bank-ruptcy was held not to violate due process or equal protection of the laws.

1970–72. JURY TRIALS. The court held in **Williams v. Florida** (399 U.S. 78), 1970, that states could use a 6-man jury in noncapital cases. In **Johnson v. Louisiana** (406 U.S. 356) and **Apodaca v. Oregon** (406 U.S. 404), 1972, the jury trial guarantee was held not to encompass jury unanimity, 4 justices dissented. State laws providing for verdicts by votes of 11–1, 10–2, and 9–3 were upheld.

1970. OREGON v. MITCHELL (400 U.S. 112) held that Congress had power to lower the voting age in federal but not state elections. Justice Black's opinion constituted that of the court, although 4 justices held that Congress had power to accomplish both objectives, and 4 justices held that Congress lacked the power to do either. The 18-year-old vote was subsequently achieved by the 26th Amendment (1971).

1970. WALZ v. TAX COMMISSION (397 U.S. 664) upheld property tax exemptions for church-owned land used solely for religious purposes as evidence of the "benevolent neutrality" of the states and not unconstitutional under 1st Amendment, as there was but a "minimal and remote involvement between church and state" which reinforced the desired separation.

1971. ABSTENTION. In a series of cases the doctrine of **Dombrowski v. Pfister** (380 U.S. 479), 1965, permitting federal injunctions where state officials threatened or were about to commence prosecution under statutes challenged as unconstitutional, was limited and the power of federal courts to enjoin state trials was limited to (1) great and immediate threat of irreparable injury; (2) where state law is flagrantly unconstitutional on its face; (3) where there has been official lawlessness: **Younger v. Harris** (401 U.S. 37), **Perez v. Ledesma**

(401 U.S. 82), **Samuels v. Mackell** (401 U.S. 66).

1971. PENTAGON PAPERS CASE. New York Times v. United States, United States v. Washington Post (403 U.S. 713). In 1 *per curiam* and 9 separate opinions, the court by a 6–3 vote held that the government had failed to show sufficient justification for an injunction against the publication of the Pentagon Papers (p. 537). Justices Black and Douglas stated that all attempts to enjoin publication would violate the 1st Amendment; Justice Brennan argued that even temporary stays and restraining orders to block publication would in the future be improper. Dissenting, Justice Harlan objected to the haste with which the litigation had been considered by the Supreme Court (one week) and Chief Justice Burger argued that the *New York Times* had the duty to return the purloined documents. The "swing" justices, White and Stewart, found no immediate and irreparable damage sufficient for an injunction but indicated that criminal prosecutions for the publication under the **Espionage Act of 1917** might be proper.

1972. WIRETAPPING CASES. United States v. U.S. District Court (407 U.S. 297) rejected in a unanimous opinion written by Justice Powell the Justice Department claim of inherent power to wiretap without warrant domestic groups suspected of being subversive, as a reasonable exercise of the president's power to protect national security. The court held the surveillance violative of the 4th Amendment. Addressing the **Omnibus Crime Control and Safe Street Act** (p. 536), which authorizes court-approved electronic surveillance, and noting that the act does not delimit the president's constitutional power, the court held (1) that this did not constitute a grant of authority to the president to conduct warrantless national security surveillance;

(2) that the 4th Amendment contemplates a prior judicial judgment; (3) that the president's domestic security role must be exercised in a manner compatible with the 4th Amendment. In an earlier case, **Alderman v. United States** (399 U.S. 165), 1969, the court ruled that the federal government must turn over for examination to a defendant all material obtained by illegal electronic surveillance even if the surveillance involved national security. **Olmstead v. United States** (277 U.S. 438), 1929, was reversed by **Katz v. United States** (389 U.S. 347), 1967, which held that any electronic surveillance not court approved ahead of time was unreasonable search and seizure, except in national security matters.

1972. FURMAN v. GEORGIA (408 U.S. 234), a 5–4 decision, held unconstitutional the imposition of the death penalty in the cases before the court, and invalidated the death penalty throughout the nation as then imposed, sparing the lives of almost 600 condemned persons. There was a *per curiam* opinion for the court and one opinion for each of the 9 justices. Justices Brennan and Marshall argued that executions are *per se* cruel and unusual punishment in violation of the 8th Amendment prohibition. Justice Douglas stated that the discretionary application of punishment affected the "poor and despised" unequally and therefore violated equal protection of the laws. Justices Stewart and White found the system as then operating "so wantonly and freakishly imposed" as to be unconstitutional under the 8th and 14th Amendments. Chief Justice Burger's dissent emphasized that capital punishment laws which did not mete death out in a random and unpredictable manner might ultimately be held constitutional.

1972. BRANZBURG v. HAYES (408 U.S. 665) denied that reporters were constitutionally privileged under the 1st Amendment to refuse to divulge their sources to grand juries investigating a crime, stating that the public has the right to every man's evidence.

1972–73. CONGRESSIONAL IMMUNITY CASES. The court held that congressional immunity did not protect Sen. Daniel B. Brewster from bribe prosecution, **United States v. Brewster** (408 U.S. 501), 1972, but that it did protect Sen. Mike Gravel and his aides from having to testify before a grand jury about conduct or preparations for a subcommittee meeting at which Gravel read the Pentagon Papers. However, the immunity did not protect Gravel from testifying as to his source for the papers. **Gravel v. United States** (408 U.S. 606), 1972. In **Doe v. MacMillan** (412 U.S. 306), 1973, it was held that the immunity of committee members was limited to legislative activities and not to non-legislative functions.

1973. ROE v. WADE struck down state abortion laws as a violation of privacy in the woman's decision as to whether or not to terminate her pregnancy. According to Justice Blackmun's decision, government interference with abortion was unconstitutional during the first 3 months of pregnancy; during the next 3 months the state may regulate to the extent that bears reasonable relation to protection of maternal health; in the last 3 months the state could bar abortions.

1973. SAN ANTONIO INDEPENDENT SCHOOL DISTRICT v. RODRIGUEZ (411 U.S. 1) upheld the state financing of public schools through property tax revenues.

1973. COMMITTEE FOR PUBLIC EDUCATION v. NYQUIST (413 U.S. 756) struck down reimbursement of tuition and tuition tax credits for parochial schools.

1974. UNITED STATES v. RICHARD M. NIXON (418 U.S. 683). Special Prosecutor Leon Jaworski subpoenaed tape recordings and other data involving 64 conversations of the president and his aides for use in the Watergate coverup trial of 6 former White House aides. The president refused to turn over the recordings, citing the doctrine of executive privilege. In the district court Judge John J. Sirica ordered the president to turn over the tapes. The Supreme Court heard appeals from Judge Sirica's decision on an expedited procedure bypassing the Court of Appeals. On 24 July 1974, the Supreme Court held unanimously in an opinion written by Chief Justice Burger (1) that Jaworski had standing to bring the action against his nominal superior; (2) that while certain conversations in the White House were undoubtedly privileged, especially where military and national security issues were involved, the president must surrender evidence for use in a criminal proceeding; (3) the Supreme Court rather than the president is the final judge of the Constitution (citing **Marbury v. Madison**). The court took no action on the president's request to expunge the grand jury citation of R. M. Nixon as a co-conspirator in the Watergate coverup.

1975. U.S. v. MAINE et al. upheld the federal government's exclusive rights to the continental shelf beyond the 3-mile limit along the Atlantic coast, denying the validity of the claims of 11 Atlantic states resting on colonial charters, and holding that the Submerged Lands Act of 1953 "embraced" the paramount rights of the federal government.

THE AMERICAN ECONOMY

Agriculture

Once America was a nation of farmers, with agriculture the most important economic activity. By the mid-nineteenth century, agriculture's share in the national product was steadily declining—from 69% (1839) to 49% (1879). Yet even as industry grew in the nineteenth century, by the 1880s replacing agriculture as the principal contributor to national product, farming also expanded. Farm employment reached an all-time high of 13.6 million persons in 1916. For the rest of the twentieth century, agriculture came to attract a decreasing number of persons. Agricultural employment had sunk to 3.5 million persons in 1972 (and the farm population was down to 9.5 million). Of the civilian labor force in 1972, only 4% were employed in agriculture. While farm employment was dropping, for a while the amount of land in farming continued to increase, peaking with 1,183 million acres in farmland in 1959; subsequently, this figure too has declined, and in 1972 American farmland comprised 1,114 million acres. From a labor-intensive activity, agriculture became highly capital-intensive. The application of mechanization and biochemical products as well as scientific and managerial methods sharply increased agricultural productivity. In 1916 a single farm worker provided food and farm products to 7 Americans; in 1972, each farm worker served 60 persons. Over the years, land tenure, ownership relationships, and the nature of the farm labor force have sharply altered. Crops have varied in importance, with tobacco and cotton showing relative declines and soybeans becoming in the post-World War II years a leading crop. Corn and wheat were important from the colonial period to the present. Americans have come to consume more meat relative to food grains and vegetables.

IMPACT OF LAND TENURE. The organization of farm production was determined not alone by soil, climate, technology, and labor, but also by land-tenure and land-grant policies. **Free and common socage** (the tenure of the Eng- lish peasant proprietors) was generally established by colonial charters. Land was held in **freehold,** which by 1607 had come to mean for an indefinite period of time. In New Netherlands (later New York) and Maryland, where manorial systems were established, this tenure appeared in somewhat more feudalized form than in New England, but feudal services were generally limited to the reservation of a specific **quitrent** (in Pennsylvania, by 1775, 4s for 100 acres). Owing to the opposition to quitrents on the ground that they constituted a source of private income instead of being devoted to public purposes, they were abolished (Virginia and Pennsylvania, 1779; New York, 1786).

In New England and eastern Long Island grants of land were made to towns, generally 36 square miles (a figure later adopted for the rectangular surveys of the U.S. public lands of the Northwest), and group settlement was fostered (by the 18th century the descendants of the original grantees [proprietors] were generally able to acquire ownership of the undistributed lands [against the noncommoners]). Except in Rhode Island, New England land was inherited by the children equally, saving a double portion for the eldest son (held illegal by the Privy Council in *Winthrop* v. *Lechmere*, 1728; but reversed in *Phillips* v. *Savage*, 1737). New York, both under Dutch (patroonship of Rensselaerswyck [1630–37 and 1685], 1 million acres) and English rule, fostered large grants to proprietors and promoters, discouraging settlement. In the period, 1760–75, at least 6,000 tenant farmers dwelt in the colony, many of whom engaged in antirent demonstrations (1751–62), especially in Westchester, Dutchess, and Albany counties (culminating in the uprising under Pendergrast, Apr.–Aug. 1766). Although New Jersey followed a more democratic system of land distribution, uprisings broke out between squatters and proprietors (1745–48), finally quelled by 1755. The squatter problem was especially serious in western Pennsylvania.

In the Southern colonies large land accumulation was fostered by **headrights,** generally 50-acres per head to each person who transported an emigrant at his own expense. This system fostered land accumulation and speculation in land warrants which often raised the price of land beyond the means of servants who had worked out their time. As a result of modification of the system in 1705, after which date headrights were sold for cash, the system was in effect abolished and direct land purchases substituted.

Land accumulation in New York and the South was fostered by the **entail, a** legal device to make land inalienable (Georgia, 1750, enlarged all entails previously granted to absolute inheritances; Virginia, as a result of Jefferson's efforts, abolished entails, 1776; followed by the vast majority of states), and **primogeniture,** descent of land to the eldest son (abolished, Ga.; 1777; N.C., 1784; Va., 1785; Md. and N.Y., 1786; S.C., 1791; R.I., 1798, with the New England states and Pa. abolishing the eldest son's double portion). Two instances where huge land grants were conferred without rights of government (unlike Maryland and Pennsylvania) were the holdings of Lord Fairfax of 5 million acres between the Potomac and Rappahonnock rivers, Virginia, and of Lord Granville, North Carolina (1744); confiscated, 1777. The **confiscation of Loyalist estates** (p. 131) contributed eventually to the establishment of more moderate-sized farm holdings.

ABORIGINAL FARMING. Aside from hunting, fishing, and gathering, the Indians along the Atlantic seaboard generally engaged in hoe-type agriculture, utilizing natural clearings or clearing forest land by girdling, felling, or burning trees. Main products were **maize** (Indian corn), peas, and beans (cultivated in mounds—**hill culture**), squash, pumpkins, and tobacco. Fish was used as fertilizer along the Northern coast. The Indians lacked draft animals.

1607–1700. CEREAL CULTIVA-TION. European grains were initially unsuccessful. Because of its rapid ripening, its higher yield per acre (c.40% more), and its ease of cultivation (Indian-fashion) in stump-filled fields, **corn** quickly became the principal grain. **Wheat** was raised successfully in New Netherland by 1626, and by 1640 proved to be a close competitor to corn in the Connecticut Valley. The appearance of the wheat blast (black stem rust, 1660) served to check the introduction of the crop into other areas. **Rye,** better adapted to sandy soils, was successfully raised in eastern New England (1636), and by 1700 ranked second to corn. The Swedes and Finns on the Delaware preferred rye to wheat (from 1644), but later migrations into the area imposed a wheat culture (by 1680). Barley (for beer) was raised in scattered areas, and oats occasionally for feed (among the New Jersey Scots for human consumption). By 1696 a **rice** crop had been successfully raised in South Carolina from seed imported from Madagascar.

Livestock. Imported from Europe into Virginia, New Netherland, and Massachusetts, livestock was largely uncared for (especially in the South), with wild herds of cattle, horses, and swine roaming in droves, subsisting on roots and herbs. By 1682 cattle grazing had become a major economic activity in South Carolina, and early expansion southward along the coast was primarily to secure greater ranges. Since native grasses in the North (wild rye, broom straw) were not nutritious when dry, English grasses were introduced into New England by 1663 and spread to the Middle Colonies (direct importations from England to Pennsylvania, 1689).

1612–1700. EXPANSION OF TO-BACCO CULTIVATION. After a short period of experimentation (1612–15), tobacco quickly became the cash crop of Virginia. Exports rose from 20,000 lbs. (1618) to 500,000 lbs. (1627). The crop was raised in Maryland shortly after settlement. By the 1680s tobacco exports from the 2 colonies averaged 28 million lbs.

Other Crops. Virginia experimented with viniculture (1612–22), silk culture (1613–22; bounties offered, 1658), hemp and flax (1611–21), indigo (c.1622), various exotic fruits, nuts, and spices (1609–21), as well as West Indies cotton (1607, 1611–12, 1622–23), without commercial success; although flax, hemp and, to a lesser degree, cotton were cultivated for domestic consumption. Flax production, encouraged by Connecticut (1640), was inconsequential in this period. The cultivation of fruits from England and northern Europe, better adapted to the country north of Cape Hatteras, proved successful, especially apples, while peaches did well in the warmer coastal regions (particularly Virginia), where they were used to fatten hogs. European vegetables were introduced at settlement, with the largest varieties in New Netherland by 1650. However, pumpkins, squash, and native beans were still favored for human consumption. Potatoes were first introduced into Pennsylvania in 1685.

1701–75. SOUTHERN TRENDS. The farm economy of South Carolina and Georgia came to be based upon two staples, **rice** and **indigo** (especially after the successful experiments of **Eliza Lucas [Pinckney]** of St. Andrews' Parish, S.C., 1739–44, in producing indigo profitably with slave labor). Charleston rice exports mounted: 1699–1700, 1,800 barrels; 1734–35, 45,000 bbls; 1755–56, 90,000 bbls; 1772–73, 110,000 bbls.

Savannah shipments: 1755–56, 2,000 bbls; 1772–73, 24,000 bbls. With the introduction of irrigation in rice cultivation (c.1724), the crop, originally confined to the inland river swamps, was by 1750 introduced into the tidal swamps. Indigo, especially adapted to the sandy uplands of the coastal region (by 1744), made sensational gains as a Charleston export: 1747–48, 138,334 lbs.; 1756–57, 393,531 lbs.; 1772–73, 720,591 lbs.; 1774–75, 1,122, 218 lbs. (highest figure). Shipments from Savannah rose from about 5,000 lbs. (1755–56) to an annual average of 16,000 lbs. (1768–73). **Silk** production was constantly encouraged by bounties (South Carolina acts of 1736 and 1755; Georgia Trustees established a nursery of mulberry trees at Savannah and 4 public filatures). Results were meager: Virginia, 300 lbs. of raw silk exported (1730); South Carolina, 651 lbs., 1742–55. High point of Georgia exports, 1766–67, 1,087 lbs.; declined, 1772–73, to 485 lbs. **Tobacco** exports rose sharply: 1709, 29 million lbs.; 1744–46, 47 million lbs. (annual average); 1771–75, 100 million lbs. Production techniques showed no substantial change from the colonial period to the Civil War. Exhaustion of the soil (after 3 years fields generally turned over to other crops) required large holdings and the acquisition of newer acreage, with geographical shifts westward characteristic of tobacco farming. In some Tidewater areas grain displaced tobacco, but the substantial rise in grain exports (especially in wheat after 1742) in Maryland and Virginia was at least in part the result of the settlement of the Piedmont. **Livestock:** North Carolina became the chief Southern meat-producing colony. Swine and cattle were driven to Virginia and even as far north as Philadelphia to be fattened for slaughter (a practice introduced, c.1705, but not generally adopted in the South).

1701–75. NORTHERN TRENDS. Corn remained the chief cereal product of the North. **Wheat** cultivation shifted in New England from the eastern region and the Connecticut Valley to western Massachusetts. In the Middle Colonies the heavily fertilized (fish) lands on Long Island, the Hudson and Mohawk valleys, and the Delaware and Susquehanna regions became the chief wheat-producing centers. **Flax** became a commercial crop, first in New England, and later in New York (1740–60). The **plow** was used in grain growing, already having been introduced into corn cultivation in Connecticut (before 1700), with oxen extensively employed. **Livestock:** yellow oxen (Danish) and a hardy breed of red milch cattle had been introduced by 1700. The Conestoga horse was raised in Pennsylvania (by 1750) as a general work animal, and the Narragansett pacer was raised in Rhode Island, largely for the West Indies trade. By 1749 the practice of sowing grasses on tilled land had become widespread, with timothy widely adopted in the Middle Colonies. Sheep raising was general in New England, where there was an average of 7 to 10 sheep per farm, but the Narragansett country specialized in livestock raising. Along the Delaware, in northern New Jersey and around Hadley, Massachusetts (by 1750), stall feeding for the Philadelphia, New York, and Boston export markets had developed.

1789–1854. SCIENTIFIC AGRICULTURE. Although European scientific developments in agriculture had been called to the public's attention by **Jared Eliot** (1685–1763) with his *Essay upon Field Husbandry in New England* (1760) and by such agronomists as Jefferson and Washington, and modern techniques (rotation of crops, already practiced in eastern Pa., cultivation of legumes, use of fertilizer, and control of soil erosion) were already known, widespread adoption by American farmers proceeded slowly (rotation of crops in New England by 1800; in eastern N.Y., N.J., Va., and the older South by the 1840s). Public attention was called to the utility as fertilizers of lime, marl, gypsum, and other calcareous materials by **Edmund Ruffin** (1794–1865), Virginia planter, through his *Essay on Calcareous Manures,* published in 1831, and the columns of the *Farmer's Register* (1836–42). Publication (1841) of Liebig's *Chemistry in Its Application to Agriculture and Physiology* promoted soil chemistry studies in the U.S. A further stimulus was given by **agricultural societies** (Philadelphia Society founded 1785); by **fairs,** a movement sponsored by **Elkanah Watson** (1758–1842), beginning in Pittsfield, Mass., 1807, with an exhibit of Merino sheep; and by **farm journals** (*American Farmer,* established by John P. Skinner, 1819; *Cultivator,* founded at Albany by Jesse Buel, 1834, was the first to attain national circulation). In 1839 the U.S. Patent Office received an appropriation of $1,000 for work with agricultural statistics; budget increased to $35,000 by 1854.

1789–1860. SOUTHERN AGRICULTURE. Cotton: Sea Island or smooth-seed cotton was cultivated in South Carolina as early as 1767, but the importation of Bahama strains (1786–87) caused production to expand along the Carolina coast. Exports rose from 9,840 lbs. (1789–90) to 8 million lbs. (1800–01). Short-staple or green-seed cotton was also grown in scattered areas before the Revolution. Rising British cotton imports (1784, 12 million lbs.; 1800, 56 million) combined with the loss of the British indigo market turned South Carolina planters to this crop. The **invention of the cotton gin** (1793, p. 793) facilitated processing and encouraged extraordinary expansion. Out of the total national output of 100,000 bales (1801), South Carolina produced half; Georgia, a

quarter; with the remainder largely raised in North Carolina and Virginia. **Geographical Expansion:** Cultivation spread into the Yazoo delta region (by 1795), to Louisiana (by 1802), and to central Tennessee (by 1796). National production rose from 171,000 bales (1810), to 731,000 bales (1830), to 2,133,000 (1850), and reached 5,387,000 bales (1859). States in order of production (1859): Mississippi, 1,203,000 bales; Alabama, 990,000; Louisiana, 778,000; Georgia, 701,000; while Texas by 1860 already grew more cotton than South Carolina, as land values declined in the Southeast. The large **plantation system** developed in the rich lands along the Mississippi and in Alabama, with 2% of the planters holding estates of more than 50 slaves. However, the intermediate planter and the yeoman farmer were more truly characteristic of the Southern landholding class. In 1850 only 18% of the farms and plantations of the South could be described as "plantations." Even in the Black Belt of Alabama almost 80% of the nonslaveholding landowners, who in 1850 constituted 44% of the region's farm population, owned farms ranging up to 200 acres. The small planters and yeoman farmers of the Black Belt owned 75% of the landed wealth. **Rice** production remained stable during the period and was confined largely to the coastal districts of South Carolina and Georgia. **Cane sugar** production, after some experimentation (1791–95), rose from 20,000 tons (1823) to 270,000 tons (1861), of which Louisiana produced 95%. **Tobacco** production, after reaching a new high (average of 110,000 hogsheads, 1790–92), stabilized until 1840, with exports rising on the eve of the Civil War to 160,000 hhds. Cultivation spread to Kentucky (by 1783) and Tennessee (by 1789), and receipts at New Orleans rose from 24,000 hhds. (1818) to 25,500 hhds. (1831–34), and an average of 74,000 hhds. (1842–46). Virginia remained the chief tobacco state (1839, 75 million lbs.; 1859, 124 million), with Kentucky 2nd (1839, 53 million; 1859, 108 million). Corn was the only grain grown extensively in the lower South (274,-762,000 bu. out of U.S. total of 838,-793,000, 1859). The border states (including Missouri) produced c.25% of the nation's wheat, c.17% of its rye, 19% of its oats. In addition to a more varied grain economy, the border states raised livestock (especially mules and horses in Ky. and Mo.) for the Southern market, and participated actively in the improvement of American breeds.

1789–1860. NORTHERN AGRICULTURE AND WESTERN COMPETITION. During the first quarter of the 19th century New York and Pennsylvania led in wheat production, but a westward shift was taking place even within their borders. The Genesee country supplanted the Hudson-Mohawk Valley (1810–25), but by the 1830s lost ground to Ohio, which became an important wheat producer. By 1860 the top-ranking wheat states were Illinois, Indiana, and Wisconsin. During 1850–60 production in the Northeast remained stabilized (around 30 million bu.), while increasing from 43,842,000 bu. to 95 million in the North Central states. Corn production in the North Central states, occupying a belt directly south of the wheat region, doubled from 222,209,000 bu. (1850) to 406,107,000 (1860), or about 50% of the total crop. In 1840, Kentucky, Tennessee, and Virginia were the leading corn states; in 1860, Illinois, Ohio, Missouri and Indiana. The North Atlantic states expanded dairy production, and by the end of this period produced about 70% of the nation's cheese, 50% of its butter, and continued to lead the country in the production of the lesser grains (rye, over 60%; barley, c.35%, buckwheat, c.75%) as well as Irish potatoes (c.58%).

Cattle Raising and Meat Packing. Hog raising in the Middle West was closely related to corn production. By 1818 a meat-packing industry had been established at Cincinnati (founded 1788), which was the leading center until 1860, when it was surpassed by Chicago (established at Fort Dearborn, 1830). In 1833 Cincinnati firms packed 85,000 hogs; in 1848, 500,000.

1820–60. INTRODUCTION OF AGRICULTURAL MACHINERY (also pp. 793–795). The cradle was introduced in the North (c.1820) as a substitute for the sickle in reaping; in general use by 1840. The cast-iron plow replaced the wooden moldboard plow between 1825–40, and the steel plow (manufactured by John Lane, 1833, and John Deere [1804–86], 1837) replaced the iron plow on the prairies by 1845. The Hussey and McCormick reapers came into use in the East (c.1846) and the West (c.1848), and replaced the cradle by 1860. Mowing (patented 1844), threshing, and haying machines, as well as seed drills and cultivators, were widely adopted in the 2 decades before the Civil War. The first grain elevator was constructed in Buffalo, 1842.

1841–63. RISE OF PACIFIC AND MOUNTAIN STATES AGRICULTURE. The arrival of settlers in Willamette Valley (Ore.), 1841–43, opened the Pacific coast to the American farmer, and the settlement of the Salt Lake Valley, 1846, opened the Mountain States. The California gold rush (1849–50) created a demand for food products. Cattle increased from c.250,000 head (1849) to over 2 million head (1860). After being obliged to import 740,000 bags of grain (1853), California became self-sufficient by 1855, even producing a surplus the next year, while garden crops and viniculture expanded rapidly. The Pikes Peak rush (1859) had a similar effect on farm conditions in the Denver region.

1861–70. SOUTHERN AGRICULTURAL PROBLEMS. During the Civil

**PER ACRE MAN-HOUR REQUIREMENTS
IN WHEAT PRODUCTION
(U.S. Dept. of Agriculture, *Yearbook*, 1941)**

Date	Man-Hours 20 bu. per acre	Implements
1822	50–60	Walking plow, bundle of brush for harrow, hand broacast of seed, sickle harvesting, flail threshing
1890	8–10	Gang plow, seeder, harrow, binder, reaper, harvester, thresher, wagons, and horses
1930	3–4	3-bottom gang plow, tractor, 10-ft. tandem disk, harrow, 12-ft. combine, and trucks.

War, with the dislocation of foreign markets, cotton production dropped from an annual average of 4,500,000 bales (1859–61) to 1,597,000 (1862), reaching a low in 1864 of 299,000. Southern planters were further impoverished by the depreciation of Southern currency and securities, the wartime confiscatory policies of the federal government, the instability of the labor market, and the effects of 2 drought years (1865, 1867). In 1870 cotton production was only 51% of prewar figures, cattle and swine 60%, rice 40%, sugar under 50%. While average holdings in the Cotton Belt declined from 402 to 230 acres (1870–80), the holdings of sharecroppers and tenants were included in the census, distorting the nature of the breakup. By 1869 the gang labor system, the first approach to tillage under free labor, was largely superseded by **sharecropping** (a seasonal arrangement where the landlord determines the crop and arranges the market, with division of the proceeds: one third for labor, one third for land, one third for implements, seeds, fertilizer, etc.); **tenancy**, a leasehold arrangement; and the **crop-lien** system, under which the small farmer pledges his crop to be marketed by the merchant-creditor.

1862–1916. EXPANSION OF FEDERAL ACTIVITIES. The U.S. Department of Agriculture was established 15 May 1862 to expand and continue the activities of the agricultural division of the Patent Office. Chemical, entomological, statistical, and forestry divisions were set up (by 1881), and a Bureau of Animal Husbandry, 1884. Appropriations rose from $64,000 (1862) to over $1 million (1889). The commissioner was raised to cabinet rank (1889) and entrusted with the protection of national forests (1905), enforcement of the Pure Food and Drug Act (1906), Meat Inspection Act (1907), the inspection of dairy products for export (1908), and the Warehouse, Cotton Futures, and Grain Standards Acts (1916).

1866–1900. AGRICULTURAL EXPANSION. With the expansion of both domestic and foreign markets, the number of farms increased from around 2,660,000 to 5,377,000; total farm acreage from 493 million to 839 million (1870–1900).

**AGRICULTURAL EXPANSION
(in million acres)**

	corn	wheat	oats	cotton	hay
1866–75	40	22	11	9	20
1896–1901	91	47	30	24	42

**LIVESTOCK EXPANSION
(in million head)**

	cattle	milk cows	hogs	horses	mules
1870	24	8.9	25	7	1
1900	52	17	63	17	3

1870–90 GROWTH OF REGIONAL SPECIALIZATION. Rise of production (in million bu.) in west North Central States from 67 (1869) to 307 (1899) accounted for almost half of U.S. total **wheat** crop. Production in Pacific states rose from 19 to 72 and in Oklahoma and Texas to 33 by 1899. **Wool** production (in million lbs.) rose in the Mountain States from 1 (1869) to 123 (1899). **Corn** remained the most widely distributed of the grains, but the west North Central States produced over 40% of the national crop (1899), as well as 50% of the **barley** and over 95% of the **flaxseed.**

Illinois and Iowa produced over 35% of the **oats,** Pennsylvania and New York 70% of the **buckwheat,** Virginia and North Carolina 70% of the **peanuts,** and 4 states (Kentucky, North Carolina, Virginia, and Tennessee) over 70% of the **tobacco,** with Kentucky accounting for 35%. **Rice** production moved from South Carolina and Georgia to Louisiana, which by 1899 produced almost 70% of the national crop. Four states (New York, Wisconsin, Iowa, and Illinois) produced over 50% of the whole **milk,** with over 20% from New York.

1870–1900. TECHNOLOGICAL ADVANCES. Total value of farm implements and machinery increased from $271 million (1870) to $750 million (1900), or from $102 per farm to $130. Efficiency was promoted by the twine binder (1878), spring-tooth harrow (after 1877), disc harrow (after 1892 in the Prairie States), gang plow (after 1880 in the Pacific States), cotton seed planters and special plows (by 1900), corn shucking and fodder shredding machine (1890), corn binder (1892), and giant combine harvester thresher (1880s in Pacific States). The centrifugal cream separator (1879) became common in all dairy regions (40,000 in use, 1900). Consumption of commercial fertilizer increased from 321,000 short tons (1870) to 2,730,000 (1900).

1870–1900. FARM DIFFICULTIES. In the face of vast expansion the wholesale price index of farm products generally declined:

FARM PRODUCTS WHOLESALE PRICE INDEX
(Warren and Pearson)
(1910–14 = 100)

1866	140
1870	112
1876	89
1880	80
1882	99
1886	68
1890	71
1896	56
1900	71

Mortgages and Tenancy. Estimated average equity of farm operators in land they farmed was 62% (1880). This figure declined at an average rate of 4% each decade until 1935. In some prairie counties 90% of the farms changed hands during the 1890s; 11,000 foreclosures in Kansas (1889–93). Tenancy increased from 26% of total farms (1880) to 35% (1900), with marked rises in the cotton and wheat states.

GRANGER MOVEMENT (pp. 295, 313).

1900–14. AGRICULTURAL TRENDS. Agriculture stabilized in this period. Farms increased from 5,737,000 to 6,480,000; wheat acreage expanded from an average of 7 million bu. to c.8 million; and corn expanded gradually but steadily. Notable production gains were scored in (1) **cotton** (from 10 million bales, 1900, to 16 million, 1914), (2) **tobacco,** and (3) **citrus fruits;** while a sharp decline occurred in the exports of beef (352 million lbs., 1898, to 194 million, 1913) and bacon (from 650 million lbs., 1898, to 194 million, 1913), largely the result of increase in world production of these products.

1914. SMITH-LEVER EXTENSION ACT, providing for a nationwide extension of the county-agent system (p. 327).

1914–18. EFFECT OF WORLD WAR I. Wheat production rose to an average of c.870 million bu., although corn production was relatively stable. Beginning with 1918 grain production reached into the most arid sections of the Great Plains. Wholesale price index of farm products (Warren and Pearson; 1910–14 = 100) rose from 100 (1914) to 208 (1918) and continued to rise until 1920 (211).

1920–69. RISE AND DECLINE OF TENANCY. Tenancy rose during the farm depression: 38.1% of farm holdings (1920) to 42.2% (1935). World War II and postwar farm prosperity brought general declines: 24% (1954) to 12.9% (1969).

1920–39. SOME TECHNOLOGICAL CHANGES: (1) First hybrid corn involving inbred lines sold in 1921; (2) mills for extracting oil from soybeans first built about 1920; between 1930 and 1940, hybridization in breeding soybeans; (3) developments in livestock breeding: hogs with more meat, since lard was being replaced with vegetable oils; sheep-breeding; artificial breeding of cattle (first in New Jersey in 1938); and (4) increasing mechanization.

1921–33. FARM DEPRESSION. Wholesale price index of farm products dropped to 121 (1921), rising slightly to 138 (1923), but even in the prosperous years 1926–29 it never exceeded 149 (1928), and with the depression dropped to 68 (1932), lowest since 1899. Wheat hit an all-time low of 32 cts. per bu. Total farm receipts declined by 1932 to one third of the amount of 1918, while farm mortgage debt rose from $7,857 million (1920) to a high of $10,785 million (1923). Forced sales (bankruptcies, foreclosures, tax delinquencies) rose from an average of 12 per 1,000 (1921–24) to 21 per 1,000 farms (1926–30) and 54 per 1,000 (1933), and were exceptionally heavy in the Dakotas and Iowa. The estimated equity of farm operators in their farm land dropped from 62% (1880) to 39% (1935).

1924–32. FARM RELIEF. For the **Farm Loan Act** (1916), see p. 329. Under the **Agricultural Credits Act** (24 Aug. 1924) loans were granted dealers and cooperative groups to permit them to hold farm goods for domestic and foreign trade in an effort to prevent bankruptcies and dumping; $304 million loaned, 1924–32. For the **Agricultural Marketing Act** (1929), see p. 396.

1933–40. NEW DEAL FARM PROGRAM. By the **Agricultural Adjustment Act** (p. 405), the **Cotton Control Act** (p. 411), and the **Tobacco Control Act** (p. 413), the federal government sought to curtail farm production. Contributing to crop curtailment was a **severe drought,** even more severe than in the late 1880s, in the Prairie and Plains states (1934), as a result of which one third of the nation's grain crop was lost and "Okies" abandoned their Oklahoma farms to seek work in California. Total acreage in 52 major crops harvested fell from an average of 358 million (1929–32) to 321 million (1933–35). After these acts were declared unconstitutional (p. 676), the federal government continued its curtailment program through the **Soil Conservation and Domestic Allotment Act** (1936, p. 418), modified by the **2nd AAA** (1938, p. 423). Cash receipts for farm products rose from $4,743 million (1932) to $7,659 million (1935) and remained over $8 billion (1936–40). Wholesale price index of farm products (Bureau of Labor Statistics; 1926 = 100) rose from 48.2 (1932) to 86.4 (1936), then declined until World War II to 65.3 (1939). Farm mortgage debt declined from $8,466 million (1933) to $6,586 million (1940), and forced sales dropped from 54 per 1,000 farms (1933) to 16 per 1,000 (1940).

1940–52. WORLD WAR II AND POSTWAR EXPANSION. The index of gross farm production (1935–39 = 100) rose from 108 (1940) to 126 (1946), with a further high to 131 (1948), as cash receipts for farm products rose from $9,132 million (1940) to $22,286 million (1945). Value of farm implements and machinery rose from $2,153 million (1935) to an all-time high of $12,166 million (1950). Expenditures for fertilizer and lime in 1945 approximated $508 million, more than treble the 1934 figure. Farm prices soared in this period: No. 1 wheat, $.90 per bu. (1940) to a high of $2.88 (1948); cotton from an average of $.096 per lb. (1936–40) to

$.319 (1947) as production decreased. Beef cattle prices per 100 lbs. continued to soar in the postwar period: $7.46 (1940) to $23.30 (1950), as did hog prices: $5.39 (1940) to $23.10 (1948). The farm mortgage debt was reduced from $6,586 million (1940) to $4,681 million (1946), rose to $5,413 million (1950), but the ratio of mortgage debt to total farm value declined from 41.5% (1940) to 25% (1956).

1950–72. FARM POPULATION AND NUMBER AND TYPE OF FARMS. The farm population declined sharply in absolute and relative terms from 23 million or 15.2% of the population in 1950, to 15.6 million or 8.7% (1960), to 9.7 million or 4.7% (1970), to 9.5 million or 4.5% (1972 prel.). So too, the number of farms decreased: 5.65 million (1950), 3.96 million (1960), 2.92 million (1970), to 2.83 million (1972 prel.). While many small farms remained, the trend was for existing farms to grow both larger and more specialized. Over the years, a larger percentage of the major agricultural products came from a smaller proportion of the farms. The corporate form came to farming. By 1969 1,586 farms had annual sales of more than $1 million. Of these, 239 were corporations with more than 10 shareholders, while 731 were "small" corporations, having fewer than 10 shareholders; 287 were partnerships and 300 were individual proprietorships.

1950–72. FARM INCOME, PRODUCTION, AND PRODUCTIVITY. Gross realized income from farming rose steadily: $32.3 billion (1950), $38.1 billion (1960), $57.8 billion (1970), $68.8 billion (1972). But production expenses rose, so the net to the farmer actually went down in the 1950s: $12.9 billion (1950), $11.7 billion (1960), and then rose slowly in the 1960s and 1970s: $16.8 billion (1970), $19.7 billion (1972). Farm incomes did not increase as much as incomes in other sectors. Direct government payments supplemented farm income, rising from $283 million (1950) to $702 million (1960), $3,717 million (1970), $3,961 million (1972), as agricultural subsidies shifted further away from high price supports toward cash payments from the government to farmers. The **Omnibus Farm Bill** (5 Nov. 1965) utilized cash payments as incentives for the diversion of planted acreage of cotton, wheat, and food grains to conservation and other uses. The **Agricultural Act of 1970** increased direct payments to the farmer and gave him greater freedom in his planning decisions. Price support was not, however, abandoned; milk price supports increased 50% (1965–71). Quotas limited imports of sugar and thus supported high internal prices.

Despite fewer farmers and farms, farm production mounted. Based on 1967 = 100, indices of farm production rose from

FARM MECHANIZATION, 1930–73[1]
(Historical Statistics of U.S. to 1957; U.S. Dept. of Agric., Economic Research Service)

Year	Tractors	Motor Trucks	Grain Combines	Corn Pickers	Farms with Milking Machines
1930	920,000	900,000	61,000	50,000	100,000
1941	1,665,000	1,095,000	225,000	120,000	210,000
1950	3,394,000	2,207,000	714,000	456,000	636,000
1960	4,685,000	2,825,000	1,042,000	792,000	660,000
1970	4,618,000	2,984,000	790,000	635,000	[1965: 500,000]
1973 (prel.)	4,387,000	2,915,000	703,000	607,000	

[1] Declining numbers of farms and the acquisition of larger, more efficient machines were the principal reasons for the declines in the *number* of major machinery items 1960–73.

73 (1950) to 90 (1960), 102 (1970), 112 (1972 prel.); farm output per man-hour jumped from 35 (1950) to 93 (1960), 113 (1970), 122 (1972 prel.); while crop production per acre showed a less dramatic rise: 69 (1950), 88 (1960), 102 (1970), 116 (1972 prel.). These figures reflected the increasing efficiency of American agriculture. Contributing were mechanization; the use of fertilizer; superior seed; improved breeding stock; protection against insects, diseases, parasites, and weeds; irrigation and drainage techniques; better livestock feeds; the application of electronic data processing; and more professional general management of equipment, skills, land, and livestock to obtain higher yields.

INDEX NUMBERS OF INPUTS—MECHANIZATION AND FERTILIZER (1967 = 100)

Year	Mechanical Power and Machinery	Fertilizer and Liming Materials
1930	40	11
1941	44	15
1950	79	32
1960	91	54
1970	102	113
1972 (prel.)	103	122

1950–73. PRINCIPAL CROPS

Year	Corn	Soybeans	Wheat	Production Oats	Cotton	Rice	Hay
	in million bushels[1]				in 000 bales	in 000 cwt	in 000 short tons
1950	3,075	299	1,019	1,369	10,014	38,820	103,820
1957	3,422	484	950	1,301	10,964	42,935	120,977
1973 (est. as of 8/1/73)	5,661	1,540	1,716	707	12,740	99,270	125,948

[1] In *value* of production (in billions of dollars) in 1972 (prel.), the principal four crops were **corn** ($7.1), **soybeans** ($5.3), **hay** ($3.7), and **wheat** ($2.7).

FARM PRODUCTION INDICES (1967 = 100)

Year	Total Farm Output	Meat Animals	Dairy Products	Poultry & Eggs
1950	73	74	93	56
1960	90	85	101	75
1970	102	102	100	106
1972 (prel.)	112	112	103	110

International Trade and Investment, Tariffs, Domestic Commerce

From being an exporter principally of raw materials in the colonial period, America became over time an exporter of manufactured products (although agricultural output still constituted an important part of U.S. exports); once an importer of manufactured goods, America became an importer of a range of raw materials (oil, copper, lead, zinc, iron ore) along with manufactured products. From the colonial period to 1875, America was in most years a net *importer* of goods; from 1875 to 1970 (with only two years excepted), America was a net *exporter*. In 1971–72, America was again a net importer (for the first time since 1893).

Until 1914, the United States was a debtor nation in international accounts (that is, we owed more than was owed to us); after 1914, America became the creditor nation of the world. In 1933, the dollar was overpriced relative to other currencies and gold, and in 1934, the dollar was set at $35.00 an ounce of gold (the former price was $20.67 an ounce). When the Bretton Woods international monetary system was established in 1944 the dollar was a foundation currency. After the United States had experienced about two decades of balance of payments problems, the dollar was again devalued, once in 1971–72 and again in 1973, emerging at $42.22 an ounce. The entire international monetary system as a consequence would need to be revised.

When America was part of the British empire, the colonies were subject to imperial, protectionist policy. After independence, out from under the British cloak, the U.S. developed national tariff policies. In broad terms, tariffs mounted until 1828, declined through 1857, rose from 1861 to 1897 to new heights, to be reduced in 1909 and 1913; from 1921 to 1930 rates increased, especially in 1930; since 1934 there has been an attempt at liberalization of trade policy and a tendency toward freer trade.

In the colonial period, domestic trade within, between, and among the colonies had begun, but transatlantic and West Indian trade was greater. After independence, as the nation became settled, internal transactions mounted and attention shifted to domestic commerce. Navigable rivers, roads, canals, railroads, and in the twentieth century, trucks and airplanes all contributed to the expansion of national commerce. Regional specialization increased trade. As products traded multiplied, so the outlets to sell these products became more numerous and over time their character changed.

International Trade and Investment

MERCANTILISM. The economic controls for the regulation of commerce, industry, and labor which were introduced into the English colonies were rooted in English experience and stemmed from a body of doctrine called "mercantilism," which had as its objective the creation of a prosperous and powerful national state or self-sufficing empire. Such prosperity and power were to be secured by (1) maintaining an adequate stock of precious metals; (2) protecting home industries against foreign competition; (3) making it possible for home industries to compete successfully in foreign markets through the assurance of necessary raw materials (from the colonies) and low production costs (subsistence labor). The **Acts of Trade and Navigation** (1650–1767) provided for the external regulation and control of foreign trade and the subordination of colonial interests to those of the mother country. The principal regulatory trade measures relating to the colonies:

1620. EARLY ATTEMPTS. Under the early Stuarts Parliament left colonial economic development to the crown. By agreement between the crown and the Virginia Co., in return for a duty of 1s. per lb. on tobacco, English tobacco growing was to be prohibited (carried out by proclamation 29 June 1620).

1650–60. LEGISLATION DURING THE INTERREGNUM. To liberate English trade from Dutch control Parliament (1) forbade foreign ships from trading in the colonies without special license (3 Oct. 1650); (2) enacted (9 Oct. 1651) that no goods from Asia, Africa, or America could be imported into England, Ireland, or the colonies except in ships of which the owner, the master, and the **major** part of the crew were English (including colonials); (3) that no European goods could be imported into England, Ireland, or the colonies except in **English** ships or ships of the **country of origin;** (4) prohibited foreign goods from being imported into England except from the place of production; (5) prohibited the importation of fish by aliens; and (6) excluded all foreign ships from the English coasting trade. These comprehensive acts depended for enforcement upon (1) informers and (2) colonial governors. Complaints arose of the hardships of enforcement owing to England's lack of shipping to replace the Dutch. The governors of Barbados and Antigua complained of supply shortages (1652, 1656) and the former colony petitioned for repeal of the Act of 1650. The Virginia Assembly declared that freedom of trade would be maintained and all merchants protected (1655), demanding bond of all sea captains not to molest foreign ship-

ping (Mar. 1660). Massachusetts (1655), Rhode Island (1657), and Connecticut (1660) publicly announced their intention of continuing trade with the Dutch.

1660. NAVIGATION ACT OF 1660, passed by the Convention Parliament, approved by the crown, 1 Oct. 1660, and confirmed by the first regular Restoration Parliament (27 July 1661), (1) provided that no goods or commodities, regardless of origin, could be imported into or exported out of any English colony except in English-built or owned ships (of which the master and **three fourths** of the crew were English); (2) required that **enumerated articles** (including **sugar, tobacco,** and **indigo**) of colonial growth and manufacture be shipped only to England or her colonies, with ships sailing from the colonies required to give bond that they would unload enumerated commodities in the realm.

1662. ACT OF FRAUDS provided that only **English-built** ships were to enjoy the privileges under the Act of 1660 (except ships bought before 1662).

1663. NAVIGATION ACT OF 1663 (passed to benefit English merchants) provided that, with the exception of certain specified commodities (salt for the New England and Newfoundland fisheries, wine from Madeira and the Azores, and provisions, servants, and horses from Scotland and Ireland), European goods destined for the colonies must be shipped from England and on English-built ships. Enforcement duties were placed upon colonial governors, who customarily delegated responsibility to a **naval officer** (in practice appointed in England).

1673. NAVIGATION ACT OF 1673 assessed duties at the **ports of clearance** upon enumerated products when shipped from one plantation to another (in order to prevent colonial shippers from evading English duties by stopping at a colonial port en route to Europe) and provided for the appointment of **customs commissioners** to collect the duties.

1696. NAVIGATION ACT OF 1696 (1) confined all colonial trade to English-built ships; (2) gave the provincial customs officers the same powers as in England, including the right of forcible entry; (3) required that bonds be posted on enumerated commodities, even where plantation duties were paid; (4) enlarged the direct responsibility of the colonial naval officer; and (5) voided colonial laws contrary to the Navigation Acts.

1699. WOOL ACT (passed to meet competition from Ireland and potential competition from the American colonies) restricted woolen manufacture in Ireland and forbade the export of wool products from any American colony either overseas or in the intercolonial trade.

1705. ENUMERATED ARTICLES (to be shipped only to English ports) expanded with the broadening of colonial economic activity: **rice** (now an established crop in Carolina) and **molasses,** mainstay of the West Indies economy; **naval stores,** not only enumerated but also given **bounties** per ton as follows: pitch and tar, £4; rosin and turpentine, £3; hemp, £6; masts, yards, and bowsprits, £1.

1709–74. FURTHER NAVAL STORES ACTS. Bounties continued for 11 years after expiration (1713) of Act of 1705; on hemp continued for another 16 years (1725); but on the other naval stores were allowed to lapse (1725–29). When renewed in 1729 the rates were changed per ton: pitch, £1; turpentine, £1 10s.; masts, £1; tar, £2 4s. Under this act the cutting of white pines was restricted to those standing on private property; of white pines 24 in. in diameter or greater was permitted only on lands granted before 7 Oct. 1692 (such a restriction had been included in the Massachusetts charter of 1692). Bounties

on naval stores were continued to 1774, except for hemp, which was allowed to lapse in 1741 (renewed 1764). Bounty payments totaled, 1706–74, £1,438,702.

1721. BEAVER SKINS, FURS, AND COPPER ENUMERATED and the duties on beaver skins lowered. Prior to this enactment 30–40% of New York's fur exports went to Continental Europe. In 1721 copper ore shipments had been made both to England and Holland from a newly opened New Jersey mine.

1730–35. Rice shipments were permitted from South Carolina to Europe south of Cape Finisterre (1730), and the privilege extended to Georgia (1735).

1732. HAT ACT. As a result of pressure upon Parliament from London felt makers, already suffering from French competition and fearing the effects of an expanding hat industry in the Northern colonies, Parliament (1) prohibited the exportation of hats from one colony to another; (2) limited the pursuit of this trade in the colonies to those who had served a 7-year apprenticeship and (3) the number of apprentices to 2 per shop; and (4) barred the employment of Negro apprentices. Enforcement sporadic.

1733. MOLASSES ACT, passed to protect the British West Indies planters from competition of the foreign West Indies, levied an almost prohibitive duty of 9d. per gallon on rum and spirits, 6d. on molasses, and 5s. per hundredweight on sugar imported to the continental colonies from the foreign West Indies. The act proved unenforceable.

1748–63. INDIGO BOUNTIES of 6d. per lb. granted to encourage production of a dye used in the woolen industry; lowered (1763) to 4d. Bounties paid to 1776 exceeded £185,000 (chiefly to Carolina and Georgia planters).

1750, 1757. IRON ACTS. To maintain the colonial supply of bar and pig iron for the iron and steel industry of the English Midlands but check the expansion in the colonies of the iron-finishing industry, Parliament (1) forbade the erection henceforth in the colonies of rolling and slitting mills, tilt-hammer forges, and steel furnaces; (2) allowed pig and bar iron to enter England free of duties under certain special conditions, which were removed (1757), after which date plantation iron was admitted free into England.

1764. SUGAR ACT (also p. 85) (1) forbade the importation of rum and spirits from the foreign West Indies into the continental colonies; (2) lowered the duties on molasses; (3) placed on the enumerated list hides and skins, pot and pearl ashes (a newly produced commodity), iron and lumber for Europe, and two minor products, whale fins and raw silk.

1767. ALL NONENUMERATED GOODS destined for any part of Europe north of Cape Finisterre were required to be first shipped to England. Only about 4.3% of colonial exports were affected by this act, for by 1770 it is estimated that, from the time of first enumeration, 96% of the tobacco exported from the colonies had been reexported from England, 79% of the rice, 40% of the indigo, 58% of the beaver skins, 95% of other furs, 26% of hides and skins, 13% of pot and pearl ashes. On the other hand, colonial naval stores (except for tar, 5% of which was reexported) and pig and bar iron were almost entirely utilized in English industry (L. A. Harper).

PATTERNS OF COLONIAL TRADE. Handicaps to Overseas Trade. In addition to (1) the **Acts of Trade**, which, while encouraging shipping, shipbuilding, and naval stores, were especially detrimental to the tobacco trade and to a lesser degree to certain branches of manufacturing, other obstacles existed, including (2) **piracy** (robbery committed

upon ships of friendly nations). Under Act of 28 Hen. VIII, c.8 (1536), providing that pirates be tried in England before a commission specially named, the accused were sent from the colonies to England for trial. Most notable instance was the trial of Capt. **William Kidd** (c.1645–1701) for murder and piracy in Old Bailey (hanged 23 May 1701). By 11 Wm. III, c.7 (1699), pirates could be tried by commission in any colony. Under this act **Stede Bonnet** (S.C., 1718) was tried, convicted, and hanged. By proclamation, 1717, pirates who surrendered were pardoned (including a large contingent on Providence Island, Bahamas). **Robert Teach** ("Blackbeard") was killed in an attack by a Virginia expedition (1718). Thereafter a major hazard was (3) **privateering** (authorized attacks and seizures of enemy ships in wartime). (4) **Lack of Money and Credit Facilities:** Since the exportation of coin from Great Britain was forbidden, the colonists in the early period were dependent upon **wampum** (Indian shell bead money); **barter; commodity money** or "country pay" (notably tobacco crop notes [warehouse receipts] in Md. and Va. and rice crop notes in S.C.); **local coinage,** confined to the Massachusetts "pine-tree shillings" coined between 1652–84; **foreign coins,** which were consistently overvalued to attract importation (despite Royal Proclamation, 1704, limiting such overvaluation to 33⅓%, and the Parliamentary Act of 1704 providing a prison term and fine for violations); **bills of exchange** (especially those secured in trade with the British West Indies); and **paper money** (begun by Mass., 1690). In the early stages paper money was lawful only in **public** payments; after 1720 it was used as legal tender in all payments. Inflation arose, primarily in New England, 1730–50, as a result of the failure to support such

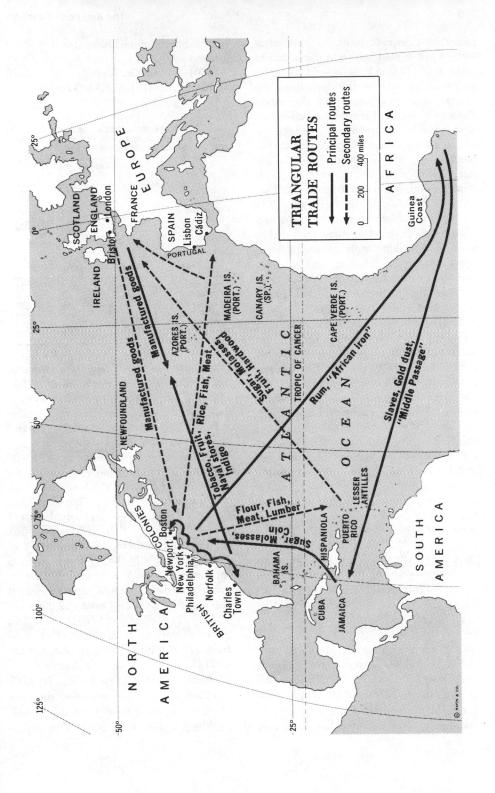

TRIANGULAR
TRADE ROUTES

Principal routes
Secondary routes

0   200   400 miles

NORTH AMERICA

SCOTLAND
IRELAND
ENGLAND
  London
Bristol
FRANCE
EUROPE
SPAIN
PORTUGAL
Lisbon
Cádiz

AFRICA

Guinea
Coast

AZORES IS.
(PORT.)

MADEIRA IS.
(PORT.)

CANARY IS.
(SP.)

CAPE VERDE IS.
(PORT.)

NEWFOUNDLAND

Manufactured goods
Manufactured goods

Sugar, Molasses,
fruit, Hardwood

Tobacco, Fruit, Rice, Fish, Meat,
Naval stores, Indigo

TROPIC OF CANCER

ATLANTIC   OCEAN

Rum, "African Iron"

Slaves, Gold dust,
"Middle Passage"

BRITISH COLONIES
Boston
Newport
New York
Philadelphia
Norfolk
Charles
Town

BAHAMA
IS.

CUBA

JAMAICA

HISPANIOLA

PUERTO
RICO

LESSER
ANTILLES

Flour, Fish,
Meat, Lumber

Sugar, Molasses, Coin

SOUTH
AMERICA

© RAND & CO.

issues by adequate taxes. In Massachusetts, 1740, a **land bank** was organized to issue £ 150,000 in bills secured by mortgages at 3% interest. In opposition the Boston merchants organized the Silver Bank, which issued notes based on silver. The operations of the land bank were declared illegal and void by Act of Parliament, 1741, which extended the Bubble Act, 1720, outlawing joint-stock companies operating without special authority of Parliament. By Act of 1751 Parliament prohibited the New England colonies from erecting new land banks and from making bills of credit legal tender except in times of war or other emergency, and by Act of 1764 (p. 86) forbade the further issuance of paper money throughout the colonies.

1621–1700. NORTHERN OVERSEAS TRADE. The "Triangular Trade" was in fact a series of geometrical patterns which were largely the result of the necessity of the Northern colonies (in the absence of English demand for their products) to raise enough money to pay England for imported manufactured goods (textiles and hardware). Among the "triangles": (1) New England (fish and lumber) or Middle Colonies (flour) to the English (or foreign) West Indies, in exchange for sugar, molasses, or rum, with a final haul to London or Bristol, returning with English goods; (2) New England to the West Indies for rum, shipped to West Africa for slaves, with numerous variations in these 2 patterns.

1607–1700. SOUTHERN OVERSEAS TRADE. Tobacco shipments from Virginia after 1616 increased rapidly: 1619, 20,000 lbs.; 1627, 500,000 lbs. With the spread of cultivation to Maryland and North Carolina, exports rose: 1663, 7,367,140 lbs.; 1669, 9,026,046 lbs.; and in the 1680s averaged 28 million lbs. Trade of the Carolinas (forest products and hides) was still at a low level and

in the hands of outsiders (chiefly New Englanders).

1701–74. EXPANSION OF THE COLONIAL OVERSEAS TRADE.

TRADE WITH GREAT BRITIAN
(Annual averages in thousands of £ sterling; D. Macpherson, *Annals of Commerce*)

Colony	Exports to England		
	1701–10	1731–40	1761–70
New England	37	64	113
New York	10	16	62
Pennsylvania	12	12	35
Md.-Va.	205	394	468
Carolinas	14	177	330
Georgia	—	—	36

Colony	Imports from England		
	1701–10	1731–40	1761–70
New England	86	197	358
New York	28	92	349
Pennsylvania	9	52	295
Md.-Va.	128	207	491
Carolinas	22	94	262
Georgia	—	3	40

Chief export to Britain was **tobacco** (c. £ 900,000 out of a total of £ 1,750,-000 in 1770). Other principal exports in 1770 were **rice** (£ 170,000), indigo (£ 130,000), whale products, naval stores, pot and pearl ashes, furs and skins, and iron. In the years 1700–20 Virginia and Maryland accounted for about 75% of exports; 1760–70, 50%, with the proportion of the Carolinas and Georgia (rice, indigo, and naval stores) growing from less than 10% to over 35% in the same periods. The proportion of the export trade of the Northern colonies increased, 1770–75, as a result of heavier grain shipments. Philadelphia's wheat shipments increased from 52,000 bu. (1771) to 182,000 (1773), while all grain shipments from New York rose from 110,000 bu. (1766) to 350,000 bu. (1774).

Trade with the West Indies. In 1769 the Northern colonies provided the bulk of the exports (New England, c.40%; Middle Colonies over 30%). The importance of the foreign West Indies is indicated by the following figures for imports of gallons of **molasses** (Harper):

	From Foreign West Indies	From British West Indies
1768–70	9,625,426	853,229

The relative importance to Great Britain of the West Indies trade as compared with that of the continental colonies is evidenced by the fact that the annual average combined British imports and exports to the former, 1761–70, amounted to £3,406,000; to the continental colonies, £2,843,000. By 1772 Philadelphia was first in the overseas trade (in tonnage cleared), with Boston, New York, and Charleston rivals for second place.

1700–73. UNFAVORABLE BALANCE OF TRADE of the continental colonies with Great Britain is revealed by statistics of imports and exports showing excess of imports from England over exports rising from £50,680 (1700) to £754,000 (ann. av., 1761–70). While the sterling gap was greatest in the Northern colonies, all thirteen except the Carolinas had an unfavorable balance, 1761–70. For the period, 1700–73, the unfavorable trade balance amounted to £20,195,568.

1775–89. COMMERCE DURING THE REVOLUTION AND IN THE CONFEDERATION. During the war trade between Great Britain and the U.S., restricted generally to the area held by British troops, shrank to less than 5% of its former level. As a result of large-scale "dumping" of manufactured goods, imports from Britain, 1783–89, averaged only 10% less than the prewar level, while exports, on the other hand, amounted to only 50% of the prewar figure. The export industries lost their preferential treatment in the British market, and restrictions on trade with the West Indies (1783–1828) deprived the

Northern states of a major outlet for their goods, only in part compensated for by direct shipments to the Continent of Europe; by the opening of the China trade (*Empress of China* entered New York from Canton, 1785); and by the beginning of trade between New England and the Pacific Northwest for fur products (then traded in China for Oriental goods), opened as a result of the voyage of Captain **Robert Gray** (1755–1806) to Oregon and China (1787–90).

1789–1815. FOREIGN TRADE. After averaging $20 million annually (1790–92), U.S. exports rose sharply, reaching $94 million (1801), and, after a temporary setback (1802–04), made a new high of $108 million (1807). Imports rose from $23 million (1790) to $110 million (1801) and, after suffering contraction along with exports, reached a new high of $138.5 million (1807). The rise, in large measure the result of the position of the U.S. as a major neutral shipping nation, represented in appreciable degree reexports ($6.5 million, 1794; $47 million, 1801; $60 million, 1806). The British Continental blockade, Napoleon's retaliatory acts, and the Embargo (1807) negated this advantage. Exports shrank to $22 million (1808), rising gradually until the War of 1812 (averaging $60 million annually, 1809–11). During the war exports sank to an all-time low of $7 million (1814) and imports to $13 million. **Cotton** exports, increasing throughout the period ($5 million, 1802; $15 million, 1810), surpassed tobacco as early as 1803. Lumber and potash replaced fur and naval stores as major forest products exported.

1789–1830. INTERNATIONAL INVESTMENT. America was a debtor in international accounts. The country hoped to attract foreign capital. Alexander Hamilton sought to pay off foreign loans to establish national credit. Under the Jay Treaty (1794), the U.S. guaranteed payment to Great Britain, in sterling, of bona fide private debts incurred before 1783, and in 1802, the U.S. agreed to pay the British £ 600,000 sterling to settle private British claims. Foreign capital entered the U.S., investing in government securities, canals, and land. Both the First and Second National Banks had foreign stockholders. Some foreign investors profited, but many did not. In the years 1816–19, some $50 million in U.S. securities held by foreigners were in default. This retarded the entry of foreign capital in the 1820s.

NET LIABILITIES OF THE U.S. TO FOREIGNERS
1789–1830
(in millions of dollars)

Year	Amount	Year	Amount	Year	Amount
1830	75	1816	118	1802	74
1829	83			1801	81
1828	85	1815	80		
1827	74	1814	65	1800	83
1826	84	1813	56	1799	81
		1812	71	1798	96
1825	81	1811	50	1797	94
1824	88			1796	83
1823	89	1810	85		
1822	91	1809	92	1795	79
1821	83	1808	104	1794	66
		1807	87	1793	75
1820	88	1806	82	1792	77
1819	89			1791	69
1818	104	1805	75		
1817	109	1804	65	1790	61
		1803	77	1789	60

There were some U.S. investments abroad by traders and individual investors in commercial and producing activities, and by individuals in securities, but the total was small. The inflow of capital far exceeded the outflow.

1815–60. FOREIGN COMMERCE. Imports rose after the War of 1812 to an annual average of nearly $100 million (1815–20), declined to $72 million (1821–30), rising again in the following decades to $284 million (1851–60), with the greatest advances after 1850. Despite the growth of the domestic textile industry, **woolen and cotton manufactures** were the leading imports, amounting to 20% of the total, 1860, as against 29%, 1821, but rising in value from $12.7 million (1821) to $69.2 (1860). **Sugar** was the principal commodity imported, rising from 5% of the total imports (1821) to 9% (1860), with **coffee** in second place (6%, both years). **Exports** averaged $70 million (1815–20), remained steady during the next decade, but rose gradually to an average of $249 million (1851–60). **Cotton** remained the No. 1 export, rising in value from $321 million (1836–40) and 43% of exports to $744.6 million and 54% of total, 1856–60. Domestic manufactures amounted to 12% of total exports, 1856–60, wheat and flour 11%, while tobacco declined from 15% (1816–20) to 6% (1856–60). Beef and pork products rose from 2% of the total, 1812–20, to 6% (1856–60). **New York** and **New Orleans** shared first position among export ports, but 70% of imports entered New York. The bulk of exports went to the European market, with the West Indies declining in importance.

1830–60. INTERNATIONAL INVESTMENT. During the 1830s, British capital entered the U.S. in quantity, investing in canals, railroads, land, state bonds. That the U.S. government was able to pay off the national debt encouraged the inflow of British capital. The U.S. seemed a secure place for investment. But by the late 1830s, the British had become wary of U.S. investment. In 1841–42 there were U.S. defaults. Thus, America in the 1840s did not attract new investments. Its net foreign obligations were less in 1849 than in 1839. With the booming American economy in the 1850s, once again foreign (mainly British) capital entered the U.S.

There were U.S. direct and portfolio investments in foreign countries. The first "branch" plant of an American industrial company was started in England

NET LIABILITIES OF THE U.S. TO FOREIGNERS
1830–60
(in millions of dollars)

Year	Amount	Year	Amount
1860	377	1845	200
1859	384	1844	213
1858	358	1843	217
1857	381	1842	239
1856	364	1841	257
1855	352	1840	261
1854	337	1839	292
1853	295	1838	243
1852	239	1837	240
1851	223	1836	218
1850	217	1835	159
1849	188	1834	129
1848	191	1833	110
1847	189	1832	96
1846	208	1831	89

(Colt, 1852–53). The flow abroad of American capital was negligible compared with the influx of foreign capital into the U.S.

1789–1860. MERCHANT MARINE. U.S.-owned tonnage entering U.S. ports increased from 127,000 (1789) to 1,116,-000 (1807), but declined sharply during the War of 1812 to 60,000 (1814). Thereafter U.S. tonnage entering showed a steady growth (784,000, 1819; 1,577,-000, 1840; 5,921,000, 1860), but its proportion of the total tonnage of all vessels cleared in foreign trade declined from 90% (1821) to 71% (1860), reflecting rising' U.S. shipbuilding costs and U.S. cost disadvantage in building **iron** ships. **Transatlantic packet lines** were inaugurated by New York merchants, 1818. By 1845, 52 transatlantic packets were sailing regularly from New York (three sailings weekly). Average time (Liverpool-New York), 1818–22, 39 days; 1848–52, 33.3 days (reflecting improved efficiency of ship design). **Clipper ships,** especially 1843–60, set numerous speed records: Boston to San Francisco, 89 days, 8 hrs. (*Flying Cloud*, 1854). **Steamboats** in transatlantic trade were used from 1838, but were not competitive with the packets until 1848. In 1840 a Canadian, Samuel Cunard, with the aid of a British government mail subsidy, established a steamboat line, Liverpool to Boston; challenged by Collins Line (U.S.) in 1850–57. Speed increased to 13 knots by 1860, but by that date steam navigation was largely in European hands. Factors leading to the decline of U.S. shipping: (1) reluctance of Americans to shift from sails to steam; (2) federal subsidies for mail carrying, inaugurated 1845, were less liberal than the British and were discontinued by Congress in 1858; revived 1862; (3) U.S. shops were unable to produce large iron frames and large steam engines.

1861–65. FOREIGN COMMERCE DURING THE CIVIL WAR. Value of exports declined from $400 million (1860) to an average of $248 million (1861–65), reflecting decline of cotton exports. Imports showed a much smaller decline, from $362 million (1860) to an average of $275 million (1861–65). Net tonnage of American vessels entering U.S. ports declined from 5,024,000 (1861) to 2,944,000 (1865), while foreign tonnage increased from 2,218,000 (1861) to 3,217,000 (1865).

1866–1914. EXPANSION OF FOREIGN TRADE. Value of exports more than trebled from $434 million (1866) to $1,499 million (1900), while imports more than doubled (from $445 million, 1866, to $929 million, 1900). **Chief Exports: Baled cotton** remained No. 1 export item ($192 million, 1860; $243 million, 1900), but its proportion declined from c.60% to c.17%. Meat exports rose to $176 million (1900) and exports of grain and grain products rose to $159 (1900). Both petroleum products and machinery ($84 million and $78 million respectively in 1900) became major exports during the period. Europe bought 80% of U.S. exports (1860) as against 76.7% (1901–05), while imports from Europe declined from 61.3% to 52.6% in the same period, during which exports to South America rose from 9.9% to 13.2% and to Asia from 8.3% to 14.6%.

The value of U.S. exports rose from $1.6 billion (1901) to $2.5 billion (1914); U.S. imports increased from $.9 billion (1901) to $2 billion (1914). Unmanufactured cotton continued as No. 1 export ($610 million, 1914).

In 1866, 72% of American exports were crude materials and crude foodstuffs; in 1914, 60% of U.S. exports were manufactured foodstuffs, semi-manufactures, and finished manufactures. In 1866, 75% of U.S. imports were manufactured goods; in 1914, 47% of U.S. imports were crude materials and crude foodstuffs (53% were manufactured goods).

1866–1914. U.S. MERCHANT MARINE. In 1860 American ships carried two thirds of U.S. ocean-bound commerce, but this figure declined to 10% in 1914. Decline was due to unfavorable cost differentials in ship construction, repair, and operation, and the American policy of limiting registration of the national merchant marine to American-built ships.

1866–1914. GROWTH OF INTERNATIONAL INVESTMENT. Foreign (in large part British) capital flowed into the U.S. (with reversals in the late 1870s and 1890s); a large amount of the funds went into financing U.S. railroads. Most British investment in the U.S. was in securities that did not carry management. Far more slowly, U.S. investment abroad also rose; U.S. foreign stakes were predominantly in direct investment that carried with the investment managerial

INTERNATIONAL INVESTMENT POSITION
OF THE U.S. 1869 TO 1914
(in billions of dollars)

Year	Foreign Investments in the U.S.	U.S. Investments Abroad
1869	1.5	.1
1897	3.4	.7
1908	6.4	2.5
1914	7.2	3.5

control. Large American industrial corporations from their origins participated in international investment.

1914–45. FOREIGN TRADE FROM WORLD WAR I THROUGH WORLD WAR II. U.S. merchandise exports rose from 1914 to 1920 ($2.3 billion, 1914; $8.1 billion, 1920); they fell sharply with the recession of 1921 and fluctuated in the 1920s between a low of $3.8 billion (1922) and a high of $5.2 billion (1929); with the depression they sank to $1.6 billion (1932); then they rose slowly, reaching $3.3 billion in 1937, to decline in 1938, increase slightly in 1939; with World War II, U.S. exports once more soared (1940, $3.9 billion; 1941, $5 billion; 1942, $8 billion; 1943, $12.8 billion; 1944, $14.2 billion; 1945, $9.6 billion).

U.S. merchandise exports every year exceeded U.S. merchandise imports. But imports grew too from 1914 to 1920 ($1.9 billion to $5.3 billion); dropped in 1921 to $2.5 billion, and remained in the 1920s in the range of $3.1 billion (1922) to $4.4 billion (1926). 1930–32 saw a sharp dip in imports to a nadir of $1.4 billion (1932); slowly imports recovered, reaching $3 billion (1937), but then declining to $2 billion in 1938. Imports then moved slowly upward (1942 excepted), peaking in 1945 at $4.1 billion.

In 1914, America's principal exports had been crude materials (34% of U.S. exports); in 1945 finished manufactured goods accounted for 65% of U.S. exports (crude materials accounted for only 9%). In 1945 major exports by value were machinery, petroleum and petroleum products, and automobiles. In 1914 crude materials (including hides and skins, silk, and rubber) represented the largest single category of imports; in 1945, the largest single category of imports remained crude materials (raw materials of all kinds were imported to support the U.S. war effort).

In 1914 America's principal trading partner remained the U.K. Germany and Canada ranked second and third. 1945: Canada became America's key trading partner (taking $1,178 million in U.S. exports and sending the U.S. $1,125 million in merchandise, making a total trade of $2,303 million); the U.K. obtained from the U.S. $2,193 million in exports but sent the U.S. only $90 million in merchandise, making a total trade of $2,283 million.

1914–45. U.S. MERCHANT MARINE. Expansion of the merchant marine during World War 1 was the result of (1) the activity of the U.S. Shipping Board (est. by act of Congress, Sept. 1916); (2) seizure by the U.S. of German vessels (600,000 tons) upon U.S. entry into the war; (3) chartering by by Congress of the Emergency Fleet Corporation to build, own, and operate a merchant fleet for the U.S. government. Some 700 vessels (300 of them wooden) were completed by the armistice. Subsequently the Shipping Board disposed of c.1,100 vessels to U.S. citizens (for Merchant Marine Act [1920], see p. 390). In view of the decline of U.S. shipping from 18 million tons (1923) to 16 million (1928), Congress passed the **Jones-White Act** (1928, p. 397), providing for loans to private shipowners for new shipbuilding and for subsidies for mail carrying. The act failed to stimulate substantial ship construction, but $176 million in mail subsidies were paid out by 1937. The **Merchant Marine Act** (1936, p. 418) continued low-interest construction loans and inaugurated a policy of encouraging a merchant marine for national defense. The program expanded with the outbreak of World War II. U.S. tonnage entered rose to a record high (61,465,000) in 1945, but subsequently declined to 35,376,000 (1950).

1914–45. VICISSITUDES OF INTERNATIONAL INVESTMENT. America was a debtor nation in 1914; by 1919, America had become the greatest creditor nation in the world. In the 1920s, Americans made extensive direct foreign investments, carrying management, and also portfolio investments in foreign securities. U.S. foreign investments exceeded $15 billion (1929). In the 1930s, with the depression, Americans retreated from foreign investments; the devaluation of the dollar (1933) made foreign investment in the U.S. more attractive; in the late 1930s, Europeans were sending funds to the U.S. for safety. While the book value of U.S. investments abroad in 1940 was less than in 1929, foreign investment in the U.S. had risen 1934–40 and was higher in 1940 than in 1930.

During World War II, U.S. private foreign investment increased but not dramatically. The major element in the changing U.S. foreign investments related to the U.S. government's financing of the war effort. The Lend-Lease program (p. 434) involved a massive outflow of U.S. funds. The U.S. government became involved in international financial transactions as never before in history. In 1944, the U.S. participated in the **Bretton Woods Conference,** out of which emerged the **International Bank for Reconstruction and Development** (the World Bank) and the **International Monetary Fund** (IMF). The World Bank and later its associated agencies would play an important role in postwar development financing. The monetary arrangements set the basis for the free world monetary system for more than 25 years. The agreement that established the IMF provided for a pool of currencies and gold, drawn from member nations' reserves, to be available for aiding countries with short- and medium-term balance of payments problems.

Member currencies were valued according to a dollar-gold standard based on a fixed value of gold of $35 an ounce.

1945–73. FOREIGN TRADE. U.S. merchandise exports rose: 1945, $9.5 billion; 1950, $10.1 billion; 1960, $19.6 billion; 1970, $42 billion; 1972 (prel.), $47.4 billion. (The selected figures obscure periods of slumping exports, 1948–50, 1954, 1958–59.) U.S. imports rose more dramatically: 1945, $4.1 billion; 1950, $8.7 billion; 1960, $14.7 billion; 1970, $39.8 billion; 1972 (prel.), $54.4 billion. In 1971–72, for the first time in the 20th century, the U.S. had a deficit in its international trade accounts. America, once a large exporter of raw materials, became an importer of oil, copper, lead, and zinc. But America also became a leading importer of manufactured products. In fact, by the 1970s, the bulk of U.S. imports were manufactured goods.

FOREIGN TRADE 1960–70
(percentages by category)

	1960 Exports	1960 Imports	1970 Exports	1970 Imports
Food & beverages (incl. tobacco)	15.6	22.5	11.8	15.6
Crude materials (except fuel)	13.7	18.3	10.8	8.3
Mineral fuels & related materials	4.1	10.5	3.7	7.7
Chemicals	8.7	5.3	9.0	3.6
Machinery & Transport	34.3	9.7	42.0	28.0
Other Manufactured Goods	18.7	30.3	17.9	33.3

In 1960 by value the 4 leading U.S. exports (in $ billions) were nonelectrical machinery (3.4), transporation equipment (2.5), grains and preparations (1.8), metals and manufactures (1.6); leading imports: petroleum and products (1.6), metals and manufactures (1.5), coffee (1.0), and ores and metal scrap (.8). In 1970 the leading exports: non-

electrical machinery (8.7), transportation equipment (6.2), electrical machinery (3.0), metals and manufactures (3.0); leading imports: transportation equipment (5.8), metals and manufactures (4.5), nonelectrical machinery (3.1), petroleum and products (2.8). In 1972 the leading exports: nonelectrical machinery (9.5), transportation equipment (8.2), electrical machinery (3.7), grains and cereals (3.5); leading imports: transportation equipment (9.6), metals and manufactures (6.0), nonelectrical machinery (4.4), petroleum and products (4.3).

1972, JULY–AUG. The Soviet Union made arrangements to buy U.S. grain, the largest order in U.S. history of grain exporting. The exports were U.S. government subsidized, under a wheat export subsidy that had been in effect since 1949. The size of the order pushed up domestic prices, contributing to inflation in the U.S.

1973. The 2 devaluations of the dollar (p. 711) improved the competitive position of U.S. exports and the U.S. trade balance once more became positive.

1945–72. Canada was U.S.'s key trading partner (1972: U.S. exports to Canada, $12.4 billion; U.S. imports from Canada, $14.9 billion). The U.K. ranked 2d through 1959; in 1960 Japan became the U.S.'s 2d most important trading partner (1972: U.S. exports to Japan, $4.9 billion; U.S. imports from Japan $9.1 billion). In 1961, the German Federal Republic surpassed the U.K. as the U.S.'s 3d most important trading partner (1972: U.S. exports to Germany, $2.8 billion; U.S. imports from Germany, $4.2 billion). In 1972, as a region, Western Europe was the major trading partner with the U.S. (1972: U.S. exports to Western Europe, $15.3 billion; U.S. imports from Western Europe, $15.4 billion).

1945–72. FOREIGN TRANSACTIONS OF THE U.S. GOVERNMENT.

From 1945 to 1947, the U.S. government participated in limited foreign aid programs; with the Marshall plan (p. 468) postwar foreign aid began on scale; in the 1950s U.S. foreign aid was shifted from Europe to less developed countries. By the 1960s and early 1970s, the U.S. was giving financial aid and technical assistance through the Agency for International Development (AID), the Export-Import Bank (p. 410), the Food for Peace Program, the Peace Corps (p. 492), and through contributions and subscriptions to such international lending organizations as the International Bank for Reconstruction and Development, the International Development Association, the Inter-American Bank, and the Asian Development Bank. U.S. foreign economic loans and grants (obligations and loan authorizations) averaged 1962–71 $4.7 billion per annum. 1972: Loans, $3.4 billion; grants $2.3 billion; total, $5.7 billion. In addition, unilateral outflows for military transactions were made by the U.S. government in connection with stationing of U.S. troops abroad, support to friendly governments, and fighting the Korean and Vietnam wars. The net outflow from the U.S. on military transactions was $.5 billion in 1946; it rose to $.8 billion in 1948 and declined in the next 2 years; with the Korean War the outflow increased and when the war was over the ascent continued; 1951, $1.3 billion; 1952, $2.1 billion; 1953, $2.4 billion; 1954, $2.5 billion; 1955, $2.7 billion; by 1958 it was up to $3.1 billion; then it declined slowly to reach a low of $2.1 billion in 1965, after which with the Vietnam War the figure moved steadily upward, peaking at $3.4 billion in 1970. A small decline in 1971 ($2.9 billion outflow) was offset when the outflow in 1972 reached a new all-time high of $3.6 billion.

1946–72. PRIVATE INTERNATIONAL INVESTMENTS.

American interest in foreign investment revived slowly after the war; by the mid-1950s, U.S. private foreign investment had started to accelerate. The bulk of the private foreign investment was by large U.S. corporations that developed and enlarged multinational operations. They built plants near their major customers around the world. Some of the private foreign investment involved overflow of funds from the U.S.; other investment involved the reinvestment of profits earned abroad.

U.S. DIRECT INVESTMENTS ABROAD
(book value at year's end—in $ billions)

1950	11.8
1960	31.8
1970	78.2
1972 (prel.)	94.0

The bulk of the U.S. direct investment was in industrial countries, for that was where the main markets were located. 1972 (prel.): $64.1 billion of the $94.0 billion total direct investment was in developed countries. The leading countries for U.S. direct investment abroad (book value at the end of 1972) were: Canada, which had $24.7 billion, the U.K., $9.0 billion, and Germany, $5.2 billion (prel. figures). Sales by U.S. multinational corporations abroad far exceeded U.S. exports.

Foreign investments in the U.S. also mounted—and now the investments were mainly in industrial activities. European, and by the early 1970s Japanese, firms established businesses in the U.S.

1946–72. BALANCE OF PAYMENTS PROBLEMS.

In the immediate postwar period, Europeans were short on dollars; American aid gave Europeans the opportunity to buy dollar goods. Gold flowed into the U.S. U.S. gold stocks *increased* from \$20.7 billion to \$24.6 billion, 1946–49. After the devaluation of the pound sterling in Sept. 1949 (from \$4.86 to \$2.80), a change occurred: the U.S. began to run balance of payments deficits. In 1950, U.S. gold stock was down to \$22.8 billion.

1958–60. Balance of payments and gold drain. As a result of a sharp decline in exports, 1958–59, higher spending abroad by U.S. tourists, increased U.S. private investment abroad, foreign economic aid, and U.S. military expenditures overseas, the U.S. lost over \$4 billion in gold in 1958–60, with gold stock dropping below \$18 billion by Dec. 1960. To stem the deficit in balance of payments President Eisenhower ordered (16 Nov. 1960) substantial reduction in total number of dependents of military personnel abroad, to go into effect 1 Jan. 1961, as well as cuts in staffs of civilian agencies abroad and purchases of foreign goods.

Kennedy administration efforts to stem the deficit in balance of payments included a rise in the rediscount rate (1963) from 3 to 3.5% by the Federal Reserve Board.

2 SEPT. 1964. Interest Equalization Tax became law, designed to discourage U.S. investment abroad. Early in 1965, France decided to exchange \$200 million of its dollar holdings for gold. President Johnson recommended new measures to cope with the now chronic balance of payments difficulties. He urged tourists to travel in the U.S. and called for voluntary curbs on foreign investments by bankers and businessmen.

Speculation in the dollar increased after the devaluation of the pound sterling by Great Britain (18 Nov. 1967) from \$2.80 to \$2.40 and with the concurrent rise in the interest rate to 8%. The Federal Reserve increased the dis-

count rate from 4% to 4.5% while banks raised the prime interest rate to 6% from 5.5%. President Johnson imposed mandatory curbs on most direct investments abroad by U.S. corporations (1 Jan. 1968) and ordered a 10% reduction in the overseas staffs of U.S. agencies (18 Jan.).

Following a wave of speculative buying in the world gold markets (1–14 Mar.), the U.S. and 6 Western European nations agreed to supply no more gold to private buyers, and established a 2-price system in gold, the official \$35/oz. and a free-market fluctuating price (17 Mar. 1968). Congress eliminated the requirement that 25% of U.S. currency be backed in gold (19 Mar.), freeing \$10.4 billion in gold reserves for use in meeting international demands for gold.

The U.S. payments position improved in 1968. Measured on a net liquidity basis the balance was less negative, while on an official reserve transactions basis there was a positive balance. The improvement was, however, temporary; the trade deficit in 1971 put new and more serious strains on the U.S. balance of payments. Confidence in the dollar deteriorated. From the start of 1971 to mid-August, the U.S. Treasury paid out over \$3 billion in reserve assets—about 40% of this in early August. **15 Aug. 1971,** President Nixon announced new methods to curb inflation (p. 752), suspension of the convertibility of the dollar into gold, a 10% surcharge on goods imported into the U.S., and a 10% reduction in foreign aid.

With the suspension of convertibility, the dollar lost ground in relation to the major foreign currencies. The dollar had been the key currency in the international monetary system established at Bretton Woods in 1944. This system had served as a basis for international monetary transactions throughout the postwar

period. It had proved relatively successful, but since about 1965, with the dollar
under fire, the system had showed signs
of strain. There had been adaptations;
the introduction, for example, of Special
Drawing Rights (SDRs), first issued in
1970, had added a new reserve currency
and served to increase international
liquidity. Nonetheless, with the vast expansion of the world economy, a system inaugurated in 1944 clearly needed
major revisions in order to apply to the
1970s. **17–18 Dec. 1971,** meeting of the
Group of Ten (made up of representatives of major industrial nations) at the
Smithsonian Institution, Washington,
D.C. 18 Dec. Smithsonian Agreement included a new set of exchange rates (the
dollar would be devalued in terms of
gold to $38.00 an ounce, from $35.00 an
ounce); provisions were made for a wider
band that let market rates move to 2.25%
above or below the new central rates;
the U.S. agreed to lift the surtax on imports imposed on 15 Aug. The way was
opened for discussions of major modifications in the Bretton Woods system. **31
Mar. 1972,** the new price of gold at
$38.00 an ounce was signed into law in
the U.S.

In 1972, as the U.S. trade deficit
worsened, confidence in the dollar
weakened. **12 Feb. 1973,** after c.$6
billion of unwanted dollars flooded
Europe and Japan, the U.S. announced it
was again devaluing the dollar; the new
rate was set at $42.22 an ounce of gold.
22 Feb., the free market price of gold
reached $90 an ounce as speculators
dumped dollars. Despite steps taken by
the Group of Ten, confidence was not
restored. In June, Germany revalued the
Deutsche mark; the dollar declined in
value. In July the free market price of
gold reached a record $127 an ounce,
and then declined. Prospects of an improving U.S. trade balance—made possible by the devaluation—and the energy
crisis (p. 731) that affected Europe and
Japan more than the U.S. together served
to strengthen the dollar. **13 Nov.,** the
U.S. and 6 Western European nations
terminated their 1968 agreement prohibiting the sale of gold on the free
market by monetary authorities. The
gold price dropped, closing 14 Nov. at
$90 an ounce. In Dec., gold was again
selling at over $100 an ounce, rising to
c.$195.50 in U.S. on 30 Dec. 1974.

U.S. BALANCE OF PAYMENTS 1960–72
(billions of dollars)

	1960–64 average	1965–69 average	1968	1969	1970	1971	1972
Net Liquidity Balance	−2.8	−3.4	−1.6	−6.1	−3.8	−22.0	−13.8
Official Reserve Transactions Balance	−2.2	*	1.6	2.7	−9.8	−29.8	−10.3

* Less than $.05 billion

U.S. Gold Stock
(billions of dollars)*

1950	1960	1970	1972
22.8	17.8	11.1	10.5

* U.S. reserve assets are greater than the gold
stock, since they include Special Drawing Rights
(as of 1970), convertible foreign currencies, and a
reserve position in the International Monetary Fund.

Tariffs

**1607–1789. COLONIAL PERIOD
AND THEREAFTER.** The American
colonies were subject to British imperial
rules (pp. 697–700) and were not
allowed to establish their own tariffs.

After the revolution, various states erected tariffs. The Constitution gave Congress the sole power to impose national tariffs; there could be no tariffs established by the states.

1789–1816. EARLY TARIFFS. Tariff of 1789 (4 July), designed chiefly for revenue, with moderately protectionist features, provided for (1) specific duties on 30 commodities including molasses, hemp, steel, and nails; (2) ad valorem rates (from 7½% to 15%, averaging 8½%) on listed articles; (3) 5% duty on all other goods (increased, 1792, to 7½%). A 10% reduction in duties was permitted on articles imported in U.S.-built or -owned shipping. Ad valorem duties rose to c.12½% (by 1812) and later (during War of 1812) to c.25%. **Tonnage Act** (20 July 1789) taxed U.S.-built and -owned vessels 6 cents per ton; U.S.-built but foreign-owned shipping, 30 cts.; foreign-built and -owned shipping, 50 cts.

1816–28. RISE OF PROTECTION. Tariff of 1816 (27 Apr.) placed a duty of 25% on most woolen, cotton, and iron manufactures (reduced, 1819, to 20%). Cheap cottons were virtually excluded by setting a minimum valuation on cotton cloth of 25 cts. a sq. yd. Ad valorem rate of 30% on certain goods including paper, leather, and hats; 15% on all other commodities. Chief opposition came from New England shipping interests. **Tariff of 1818** (20 Apr.) increased rates on iron manufactures; 25% duty on cotton and woolens was extended to 1826 instead of being reduced to 20% in 1819, as provided in Act of 1816. **Tariff of 1824** (22 May) increased protection for iron, lead, glass, hemp, and cotton bagging. The 25% minimum duty on cotton and woolens was increased to 33⅓%, but rates for raw wool advanced 15%. New England commercial and shipping interests joined with the South in opposition. In the "**Tariff of Abominations**" (19 May 1828) protection reached its highest

point before the Civil War. An ad valorem duty of 50% as well as a specific duty of 4 cts. per lb. were imposed on raw wool; 45% ad valorem on most woolen; duties on pig and bar iron and hemp sharply increased.

1832–60. LOWERING OF DUTIES. The **Tariff of 1832** (14 July) eliminated the features of the Tariff of 1828 objectionable to the manufacturers and commercial East; increased the duty on woolens, but admitted cheap raw wool and flax free. Hence, it was viewed in the South as a sectional measure. The **Compromise Tariff** (2 Mar. 1833) expanded the free list (including worsted goods and linens), and provided for a gradual reduction of all duties above 20% by removing, at 2-year intervals (from 1834 to 1842), one tenth from each impost in excess of that level. Chief opposition came from New England and the Middle States. The **Tariff of 1842** (30 Mar.), a Whig measure, returned the tariff to the level of 1832 with duties averaging (1842–45) between 23% and 35%. The **Walker Tariff** (30 July 1846), a Democratic measure, essentially for revenue, reversed the trend (since 1816) of substituting specific for ad valorem duties and dropped the minimum valuation principle. A few commodities were duty free. The **Tariff of 1857** (3 Mar.), another Democratic measure, reduced the tariff to a general level of 20%, the lowest rate since 1850, and enlarged the free list.

1861–97. TRIUMPH OF PROTECTION. The **Morrill Tariff** (2 Mar. 1861) once more substituted specific for ad valorem duties and raised duties generally from (5% to 10%). Subsequent revision (16 July 1862, 30 June 1864, 2 Mar. 1867, 24 Feb. 1869) increased duties to an average rate of 47%. The **Tariff of 1870** (14 July) reversed the trend, placing 130 articles, mostly raw materials, on the free list and provided for some small reductions in rates on other commodities. The **Tariff of 1872** (6 June) continued this trend, reducing by 10% the rates on all manufactured goods. Most of these reductions, however, were restored by the Act of 1875 (3 Mar.). The **Tariff of 1883** (3 Mar.), lowered schedules 5% but retained the protectionist principle. The **McKinley Tariff** (1 Oct. 1890) raised the average level to 49.5% and provided for reciprocal raising of duties to meet discrimination by foreign nations. Its successor, the **Wilson-Gorman Tariff** (28 Aug. 1894), which became law without President Cleveland's signature, put wool, copper, and lumber on the free list and lowered duties to the average level of 39.9%. The **Dingley Tariff** (7 July 1897) raised rates to a new high (average level 57%), imposed high duties on raw and manufactured wool, and restored hides to the dutiable list.

1909–21. PERIOD OF MODERATION. The **Payne-Aldrich Tariff** (9 Apr. 1909) lowered duties to c.38%. Its successor, the **Underwood Tariff** (3 Oct. 1913) lowered duties yet further to c.30% and put iron, steel, raw wool, and sugar (the latter in 1916) on the free list.

1921–34. RETURN TO PROTECTION. The **Emergency Tariff** (27 May 1921) reversed the downward trend of the Wilson administration by raising rates on most agricultural products. Its successor, the **Fordney-McCumber Tariff** (21 Sept. 1922) exceeded the rates of 1909 up to 25% on manufactured goods, with high duties imposed on farm products. The tariff introduced the "American selling price," a valuation of duties on chemical products based not on foreign market value but on the selling price of U.S. domestic output, which in effect increased the duties. The **Smoot-Hawley Tariff** (17 June 1930) raised rates upon agricultural raw materials from 38% to 49% and on other commodities from 31%

to 34%, with special protection given to sugar and textile interests. Under the Fordney-McCumber Act the president was authorized to change individual tariff rates on recommendation of the **Tariff Commission** (est. 1916), but such changes were limited to 50% of the congressional rates.

1934–60. TOWARD FREER TRADE. The **Trade Agreements Act** (12 June 1934) authorized the president to enter into agreements with other governments for the reduction of specific duties by as much as 50%. Such agreements (1) did not require congressional ratification; (2) were to be based on the unconditional most-favored-nation principle. By 1951 agreements had been concluded with 53 nations with which the U.S. did more than 80% of its normal foreign trade. The act was extended for 3-year periods down to 1951 and by Act of 16 June 1951 for a 2-year period, with certain restrictions imposed on the president's power to make concessions and the requirement that "escape clauses" be included in all agreements. On 1 Aug. President Truman proclaimed cancellation of tariff concessions to countries under Soviet control. Three major international tariff conferences were held after World War II: (1) **Geneva,** where, 30 Oct. 1947, a **General Agreement on Tariffs and Trade** (**GATT**) was concluded by 28 nations, with some two thirds of the trade items between the participating countries covered by concessions; (2) **Annecy,** France, 1949, where additional nations entered the Geneva Agreement and the U.S. granted concessions on about 400 items; (3) **Torquay,** England (Sept. 1950–Apr. 1951), where the U.S. received concessions on an estimated half billion dollars of 1949 exports. The effect of the Trade Agreements program had been to reduce U.S. tariffs from an average of 53%, 1930–33, to less than 15% by 1951.

Modifications of the New and Fair Deal tariff policy were introduced during the Eisenhower administration. On 21 June 1955 the Trade Agreements Act was extended for 3 years, with authority granted to the president to reduce tariffs 5% a year in return for foreign concessions, and on duties in excess of 50% ad valorem. On 20 Aug. 1958 the act extended the president's authority for 4 years, but also authorized increasing rates 50% above rates in effect on 1 July 1934 (instead of previously specified date of 1 Jan. 1945). Quota restrictions were proclaimed (22 Sept.) on imports of lead and zinc to 80% of average for preceding 5 years. Mandatory quotas on oil imports were imposed (Mar. 1959). Japan was encouraged to continue to ʼextend its practice of establishing quotas on its shipment of certain items to the U.S.

1962. TRADE EXPANSION ACT (11 Oct.) contained unprecedented tariff-cutting authority for the president, authorizing him to reduce existing tariff of 1 July 1962 by 50% in 5 years. Further authority was granted to eliminate duties (1) on categories for which U.S. and European Economic Community together account for 80% of free world exports, (2) on selected agricultural commodities where such modification would assure some level of increase of U.S. exports of like goods, (3) on tropical agricultural or forestry products not produced in U.S. if EEC would reciprocate, (4) on articles for which ad valorem rate was 5% or less. Any industry, firm, or group of workers threatened with or experiencing serious injury as a result of tariff concession and increased imports can apply for assistance to be given in various forms such as loans, tax relief, technical assistance, unemployment allowances, and retraining or relocation allowances for workers.

1964–67. KENNEDY ROUND. Extensive negotiations began 1964 in Geneva among 50 countries accounting for 80%

of world trade for reduction of trade duties. The 6th round, under GATT, concerned itself with multilateral trade negotiations. Unlike the earlier negotiations, the Kennedy Round was conducted on a linear, across-the-board basis rather than item-by-item. It dealt with agricultural as well as industrial products, considered nontariff as well as tariff barriers to trade, and provided special negotiation procedures for developing countries. The principal result of the round was a tariff reduction of 50% by major participants on most industrial products and reductions of 30% to 50% on others. The average reduction of duties on industrial articles was about 35%.

1967–73. TARIFF AND TRADE POLICY. General U.S. policy continued to be toward freer trade; nonetheless, as imports rose (p. 708), protectionist sentiment grew. With the exception of the temporary 10% surcharge on imports (introduced 15 Aug. 1971 and removed 18 Dec. 1971), no new tariffs were imposed. But there were nontariff barriers to trade. The U.S. and Japan agreed that Japan would limit its steel and textile exports to the U.S. Until 1 May 1973 petroleum imports remained subject to quotas. Sugar, meat, and dairy products were under quantitive restrictions.

Efforts were made to stimulate U.S. exports, including: (1) extension of export credits; (2) under the Revenue Act of 1971, U.S. exporters could establish a Domestic International Sales Corporation (DISC); taxes on 50% of a DISC's income could be deferred indefinitely if 95% of DISC's receipts and assets were export-related; (3) attempts to increase East-West trade; and (4) most important, the devaluations of the dollar (pp. 710, 711).

1973 (12–14 Sept.). The 7th round of international trade discussions under the auspices of GATT opened in Tokyo, with 103 countries participating. The goal was to liberalize world trade still further, although developing nations were demanding preferential treatment. The U.S. sought to open European and Japanese markets to larger U.S. farm exports.

Domestic Commerce

1607–1775. INTERNAL AND INTERCOLONIAL COMMERCE. Aside from furs, the only frontier product that could bear the cost of overland haulage was **potash,** exchanged with the Middle Colonies for grain, primarily wheat (after 1720). Other New England ports depended on Boston for their European products, as did many Southern regions, notably North Carolina. Tonnage clearing Boston for the coastal trade (1714–17, 11,589) roughly equal that clearing for Great Britain. As late as 1769 Boston still led in the coastal trade, with New York and Philadelphia close rivals for 2nd place. In that year tonnage of vessels engaged in the coastal trade entering and clearing at colonial ports amounted to 213,000 tons as against 189,000 to and from Great Britain and Ireland, and 191,000 to and from the British and foreign West Indies.

1607–1789. RETAIL TRADE. Little specialization existed: in trade with Indians or settlers, in rural or urban areas, merchants handled a variety of staples, cotton and woolen cloth, gunpowder, kitchenware, sugar, rum, drugs, axes, and trinkets; this was true of the trading post, the peddler, and the general store. Exceptions related to goods produced by craftsmen (the blacksmith, for example). The reason for the typical lack of specialization lay in the small, segmented markets and sometimes in the shortage of money (barter was not uncommon and the retailer resold the goods obtained).

1789–1830. INTERNAL COMMERCE. The rapidly increasing population of the Ohio and Mississippi valleys (150,000, 1790; 1 million, 1810) utilized the interior river systems for shipment of commodities to **New Orleans,** especially after 1803. Receipts at the Gulf port rose from $5 million (1807) to $10 million (1816) and $22 million (1830). **Cincinnati** (population 10,000, 1818) became a principal shipping point for provisions (grain and hogs) and **Louisville** for tobacco. The introduction of the steamboat on Western waters (*Enterprise,* 1815, also p. 602) proved a great boon to this trade, and by 1825 half the river traffic was carried on steamboats. The Great Lakes region, slower in development, tended to ship to Montreal. Land haulage from the West continued ($18 million from Pittsburgh to Philadelphia, 1820).

1831–60. DOMESTIC COMMERCE. The completion of the Erie Canal (p. 602) promoted the eastward flow of commerce. Ohio (by 1830), Indiana (by 1835), Michigan (by 1836), Illinois (by 1838), and Wisconsin (by 1841) shipped grain to the Erie Canal, and, later, to the Lakes termini of the railroads. Pork, lumber, copper (after 1845), and iron (after 1855) moved eastward. Chicago, drawing from more westerly farmlands from 1849), became the chief grain-shipping center (20 million bu. by 1858), and its meat trade surpassed Cincinnati (by 1863). Cincinnati's trade, still oriented toward the South as late as 1850, switched to the East (by 1860). Mississippi traffic continued to grow, with receipts at New Orleans rising from $50 million (1840) to $185 million (1860). Cotton was the chief commodity handled, with livestock and provisions for the cotton and sugar plantations major items of river traffic. The tonnage moved through the Erie Canal increased one fourth over 1856–60 as trade between the East and Midwest expanded.

Opening the way for the trade expansion was the growth of the railroad network (pp. 606, 610).

1800–60. RETAIL AND WHOLESALE TRADE. The general merchant continued in rural areas and on the frontier, but in cities specialization in retailing occurred. By the 1850s the general merchant had disappeared from the city and in his place were groceries, dry goods, hardware, house furnishing stores, as well as bookstores, hosiery stores, tobacco shops, and so forth. Small stores proliferated, each confined to a specialized line of merchandise. The retail and wholesale functions became clearly separable. But even as specialization occurred, the pendulum swung back, and certain retailers once again started to buy directly from the manufacturer, eliminating the middleman. Other innovations in retailing included (1) cash-only sales, adoption began c.1806 and (2) a one-price policy used by Arthur Tappan in the 1820s; Lord & Taylor by 1838; at least 2 Boston firms before 1850; R. H. Macy (1822–1877) in 1851.

1860–1900. INTERNAL TRADE. Canal and railroad traffic increased during the Civil War years. Subsequently, industrial and agricultural growth and specialization of era were accompanied by a great expansion of internal trade. The railway network expanded from 36,801 miles (1866) to 193,346 miles (1900). Railroad freight rose from c.39 billion ton-miles (1861) to c.142 billion (1900). Tonnage of vessels engaged in coastwise and internal trade increased from c.2,720,000 (1866) to c.4,286,000 (1900), Great Lakes tonnage alone from 408,000 (1870) to 1,446,000 (1900), including, in addition to grain shipments, the now expanded output of Lake Superior copper and iron mines.

1862–1900. WHOLESALE MARKETING TRENDS IN MANUFACTURED GOODS: (1) shift from general commission merchant to sales through brokers or manufacturers' agents (representing more specialization in wholesaling); (2) manufacturing companies often integrated forward into handling their own wholesale trade, thus bypassing wholesalers.

1860–1900. CHANGING RETAIL PATTERNS. (1) The **department store** was developed by **Alexander Turney Stewart** (1807–76) in New York (1862), by R. H. Macy and Lord & Taylor in New York (1860–74), by **John Wanamaker** (1838–1922) in Philadelphia (1876) and in New York (1896), and by **Marshall Field** (1834–1906) in Chicago (1865–81). (2) **Mail order houses:** Montgomery Ward & Co., opened in Chicago, 1872, to sell to the Grangers, and Sears Roebuck (1895) revolutionized rural retailing. (3) **Chain stores:** Great Atlantic & Pacific Tea Co. (1859); **Frank Winfield Woolworth** (1852–1919), who opened his first "5-and-10-cent" store in Utica, N.Y., 1879; United Cigar Stores (1892). (4) **Advertising:** Participation of nationally advertised brands began with patent medicines on eve of the Civil War; business consolidations in the postwar period promoted large-scale advertising.

1901–73. INTERNAL TRADE. Railroad mileage (first-line track) continued to expand until 1929 (260,570 miles); declined gradually, 230,169 miles (1960) to 222,164 miles (1969). Ton-miles of freight carried fluctuated as follows (in billions): 1920, 414; 1929, 450; 1931–35, 270 (annual average); 1936–40, 341; 1941–45, 655; 1960, 675; 1972, 800. Percentage of total freight traffic measured in ton-miles hauled by railroads declined from 62.34 (1939) to 44.73 (1960) to 38.64 (1971), during which period freight carried by water declined from 17.71 to 16.61 to 15.90%; motor vehicular freight percentage rose from 9.72 to 21.46 to 22.28, oil pipelines from 10.23

to 17.14 to 23.00, and airplanes from .002 to 0.06 to .18%. Rail passenger revenue dropped from wartime peak of $915 million (1944) to $412 million (1957) to $257 million (1972). In same period total domestic airline revenues rose from $160 million to $1,515 million to $11,163 million.

In terms of **ton-miles**, although their percentage of the business declined, railroads remained the chief freight carriers. Piggyback service (trailer-on-flatcar) in the 1960s was an exceptional innovation. **1960–73**: railroad mergers multiplied. **1966**: ICC approved merger of the Pennsylvania R.R. and the New York Central into the Penn Central. **2 March 1970**: merger of the Great Northern Railway Co., the Northern Pacific Railway Co., the Chicago, Burlington & Quincy R.R. Co.; these were the railroads separated in the Northern Securities Case of 1904 (p. 673). Railroad bankruptcies were frequent, the most spectacular being that of Penn Central in 1970. **21 Dec 1973**: Congress approved $1.5 billion in guaranteed loans to create a new system uniting 7 bankrupt railroad lines. While continuing to be important as freight carriers, rail passenger service declined drastically. **1971, May**: Amtrak (est. by Rail Passenger Service Act of 1971), a quasi-governmental corporation, began operating most intercity passenger trains. Trucks provided more flexibility than railroads in freight transportation. In terms of **operating revenues**, from 1967 motor carriers of freight had higher revenues than the railroads. Automobiles, buses, and airplanes captured passenger traffic from the railroads.

1901–73. CHANGING MARKETING PATTERNS. Wholesaling. (1) Wholesalers services changed from trading to distribution, as more manufacturers marketed trademarked goods and handled advertising. (2) Specialization increased in wholesaling. The number of wholesale establishments rose (in thousands): 1929, 168; 1954, 252; 1963, 308; 1967, 311. The kinds of business engaged in changed in importance. Number of establishments in leading businesses, 1929 (in thousands): petroleum bulk stations (20), groceries, incl. meat (15), farm products (9), dry goods and apparel, (8); 1967: machinery, equipment, supplies (52), groceries and related products (40), petroleum, petroleum products (34), motor vehicles and automotive equipment (31). Wholesale trade, 1973, $357.8 billion (est.).

Retailing. Changes in retailing were related to the spread of the automobile and the spread of affluence. The automobile enlarged the consumer's trading area and changed the contents of his retail purchases. Affluence extended the demand for numerous differentiated consumer products. Related changes in retailing: (1) Chain stores: 1919, 4% of all retail sales; 1933, 27%. Chains with 11 or more stores increased their percentage of the retail trade from 18.2% (1951), 25.8% (1965), 30.7% (1972). Mail-order houses, Sears Roebuck (1925) and Montgomery Ward (1926), began to open retail stores. (2) Chain franchises: in the 1920s, automobile dealers to fast-food stands (A & W Root Beer began one of the earliest fast-food franchises in 1925). In the 1950s and 1960s, franchised retail outlets assumed even greater importance and came to include motels, car rentals, and other service industries. (3) Shift of country stores to towns: in the 1920s, as automobiles extended the trading areas; the trend accelerated in later years. (4) As suburbs grew, the suburban department store first appeared in the 1920s. (5) The supermarket developed in the 1930s: 6,175 food supermarkets (1940); 11,885 (1948); chain store organizations opened supermarkets. (6) Discount stores emerged in the 1950s and rapidly became incorporated in chain operations. (7) 1950–73. Expansion of suburban shopping centers, including both chain and independent stores. Supermarkets and discount stores were included in shopping centers. There was a move away from shopping in the central city. (8) 1972–73. a number of department stores accepted bank-issued credit cards, a major policy change. Large department store chains began to install computerized credit verification and automated point-of-sale cash registers, providing more detailed information, improved inventory control, and faster credit authorization. Total retail sales (in billions): 1929, $48.3; 1954, $170; 1959, $215.4; 1972, $448.4; 1973, $488.0 (est.). Number of retail establishments (in millions): 1929, 1.5; 1954, 1.7; 1967, 1.8. The figures indicate that the sales per retail establishment have grown substantially over the years.

Advertising expenditures rose steadily until 1929, slumped in the depression, and from 1933 onward generally moved upward. Expenditures (in billions): 1900, $.5; 1920, $2.9; 1929, $3.4; 1933, $1.3; 1940, $2.1; 1950, $5.7; 1957, 10.3; 1967, $16.8; 1973, $25.8 (est.). Brand names came to dominate many branches of retailing. Index of national advertising expenditures (1957–59 = 100): 19 (1940), 162 (1970); by media: magazines, 24 (1940), 162 (1970); network radio, 206 (1940), 104 (1970); network TV, 12 (1950), 249 (1970); newspapers, 20 (1940), 127 (1970); outdoor, 25 (1940), 109 (1970)

Consumer credit expanded, reaching $7.1 billion (1929) about one-half in installment credit and one-half in charge accounts, single-payment loans, and service credit; it equaled 9.2% of personal consumption expenditures in 1929. By 1972 (prel.) consumer credit had mounted to a new high of $156.4 billion, of which 81.1% was in installment credit; this represented 21.7% of personal consumption expenditures (1972 prel.).

Industry

From a country with small-scale, mostly workshop or home manufacture, American industry in the nineteenth century moved into the factory. Steam began to replace horsepower, waterpower, and often manpower. Business ownership was primarily by individuals or partnerships. Gradually, in the nineteenth century in some industries mass production began, using standardized, interchangeable parts. In the late nineteenth and early twentieth centuries new sources of power emerged: electricity and the internal-combustion engine. Industrial enterprise grew in scale. The corporation became dominant in industry. The twentieth century saw new ways of organizing work. True mass production was realized with the assembly line; scientific management made production more efficient. By the 1920s, American industrial companies were becoming more diversified in their output, using technology based on science, becoming more international, and developing new methods to administer large-scale multiproduct industrial organizations. After World War II, new power sources for industry emerged, principally nuclear power plants.

Growth industries were science- and technology-related. Processes of production became more efficient with the use of automated techniques, particularly the application of computers. Business organization grew in complexity, with the rise of conglomerates and vast multinational operations; business management became more sophisticated.

Products in the colonial period related to basic needs—eating, clothing, housing, and transportation. Since then, the number of products has risen sharply. In the nineteenth century more producer goods (products used to produce other goods) came to be made; new consumer goods were presented (canned milk, fresh beef transported over distances, bananas, Coca-Cola, cigarettes, and also consumer durables such as sewing machines and washing machines). The twentieth century saw a multiplication of both producer and consumer products. Consumer durables such as telephones, automobiles, radios, and refrigerators—and later, TV sets and dishwashers—spread. Synthetic products were new to the 1920s, and numerous by the post-World War II years. Science-based industry created a panoply of both producer and consumer goods.

By 1900, American industrial production held world leadership, a leadership that began to be challenged in the 1970s by the growth of industry in Germany and Japan. In the 1970s unfamiliar concerns over the environment and sources of energy began to plague U.S. industry.

CAPITAL INVESTMENT to 1789. Both European and colonial sources furnished capital for industry. English capital financed the colonial fisheries, control of which soon passed into the hands of settlers; as well as a large part of the New England shipbuilding industry, the Lynn Iron Works (1643–44), the Principio Co. in Maryland (1715), and the projects in New Jersey and New York of Peter Hasenclever, Prussian-trained ironmaster (c.1764). Government subsidies in various forms also aided industry. Colonial capitalists (with considerable fortunes acquired between 1750–83) generally preferred more conservative investments—real estate or British government securities—to industrial risks. Notable exceptions at the end of this period were **Robert Morris** and **William Duer.**

FOREST INDUSTRIES TO 1775. (1) **Lumbering** (white pine abundant in New England) prospered despite royal conservation measures (p. 699). British navy sought a source of forest products to lessen dependence upon Baltic countries. (2) **Shipbuilding** (fostered by Navigation Act of 1660, p. 698): By 1760 one third of the total British tonnage (398,-000) was colonial-built; 1765–75, 25,000 tons built yearly in the colonies. Except during period of New England inflation (1730–50), ships were constructed in the colonies 20%–50% below European costs. (3) **Naval stores:** Tar, pitch, turpentine, and potash favored by British bounties (p. 699). Exports rose (1770) to 82,000 barrels of tar, 9,000 pitch, 17,000 turpentine (value £175,000).

MARITIME INDUSTRIES TO 1775. Fishing. From the presettlement period down to the present day, codfishing from New England to Labrador has been steadily pursued. There were three grades: (1) best—traded down the coast for flour and tobacco; (2) medium—sent to Southern Europe (Catholic) in exchange for salt and wine; (3) "refuse" —shipped to sugar isles to feed the slaves (H. A. Innis). **Whaling** flourished to supply demand for spermaceti (for important candlemaking industry begun in Rhode Island, c.1750, with attempted intercolonial monopoly and price-fixing agreements, 1761–75), sperm oil, whalebone, and ambergris (for drugs, confectionery, and perfumery). By 1774 a fleet of 360 ships collected 45,000 barrels of sperm oil, 75,000 lbs. of whalebone.

TECHNOLOGY AND ORGANIZA-TION TO 1789. (1) **Workshop crafts** made custom-made goods, with the leather and hat industries (beaver felt hats despite restrictions under the Hat Act [p. 699] outstanding examples), and with high standards obtaining among silversmiths (e.g., Jeremiah Dummer of Boston, Simeon Soumaine and Myer Myers of New York), cabinetmakers (Joshua Delaplaine of New York, William Savery, Philadelphia), and clockmakers (the Claggetts and Willards of New England). (2) **Domestic or putting-out system,** notably in weaving (chiefly homespuns), encouraged by the Nonimportation Agreements (pp. 88, 91, 99) and shoemaking (organized in Lynn, Mass., for wholesale operations by 1760). (3) **Mills and factories:** Flourmilling, especially in the vicinity of New York and Philadelphia, produced for export. Oliver Evans' mill elevator (p. 792), with its conveyor belt and labor-saving, cost-cutting features, was introduced shortly after 1783 by Ellicott brothers on the Patapsco River. Notable strides took place in **iron manufacture** despite restrictions of Iron Act of 1750 (p. 699), with **Henry William Stiegel** (1729–85) outstanding (after 1760) as an ironmaster and glassware maker (after 1764). In 1700 the colonies produced one seventieth of the world's iron supply; in 1775, **one seventh,** with pig and bar iron production exceeding England and Wales combined. Bar iron exports, 1771, 2,234 tons. Other outstanding ironmasters include, for the 17th century, John Winthrop, Jr. (1606–76), in Massachusetts (at Lynn, 1643) and Connecticut; for the 18th, Alexander Spotswood (1676–1740), who established iron furnaces on the Rapidan River (1714), Robert Carter (1663–1732), Peter Hasenclever (1716–93), John Jacob Faesch (1729–99), William Alexander ("Lord Stirling," 1726–83), Charles Carroll (1737–1832), and Philip Livingston (1716–78).

1789–1807. EXPANSION OF FAC-TORY PRODUCTION. Textiles. Samuel Slater, copying Arkwright machinery, first spun cotton by power, 20 Dec. 1790, at Pawtucket, R.I., a venture financed by **Moses Brown** (1738–1836), a Quaker merchant. By 1800, 7 Arkwright mills, containing 2,000 spindles, were in operation. Attempts to apply power carding and spinning to wool had proved abortive as late as 1801.

Arms Manufacturing. Eli Whitney (p. 1182), turning in 1798 to arms production for the U.S. government, succeeded in developing a system of interchangeable parts. **Simeon North** (1765–1852) of Connecticut devised tools and machinery for the production of interchangeable parts in the manufacture of pistols, 1799. Many of the ideas came from techniques already worked out in woodworking and reproductive metal industries. Cards and nails were manufactured in uniform shapes by automatic mechanisms in the 1790s. **Eli Terry** (1772–1852) and **Seth Thomas** (1785–1859) began the manufacture of clocks at Plymouth Hollow, Conn., and the basis of interchangeable parts and quantity production (1807–12). Seth Thomas Clock Co. organized, 1853.

1808–18. Nonintercourse and the War

of 1812 boomed domestic manufacturing. Gallatin's report (1810) listed 14 woolen mills and 87 cotton mills. By 1816 it was estimated that $12 million was invested in the woolen industry, which produced an annual product worth $19 million. The **Boston Manufacturing Co.** (also called the Waltham Co.), established at Waltham, Mass., 1813, was the first textile factory to conduct **all** operations for converting cotton into cloth by power under a single management (the "**Waltham System**"). Other features: large capital investment, recruitment of New England farm girls housed in dormitories, and the production of standardized coarse cloth requiring minimum skills of operatives.

1816–30. IRON INDUSTRY REORGANIZES. (1) The production of bar iron by **puddling and rolling** as a continuous process in western Pennsylvania (at Plumstock), 1817; soon adopted by the iron industry at **Pittsburgh.** (2) Introduction in urban rolling mills of coal for refining pigs while rural blast furnaces continued to use charcoal.

Machinery Production. Although the manufacture of machinery as a separate branch of industry dates back as early as 1803, when **Oliver Evans** (1755–1819) established a shop to fabricate steam engines (**Mars Iron Works**), a **specialization** trend is more decided in this period. Among the largest units were the Allaire Works, 1816; the Merrimac Co. (textile machinery), 1820; and the Novelty Works, 1830. By 1830, 9 textile machinery works existed in Worcester, Mass., alone, with the Lowell and Lawrence shops among the largest. The founding of mills at **Lowell**, Mass., the "Manchester of America," 1822, by Jackson and Lowell, marked the rapid extension of the Waltham System in cotton manufacturing. By 1830 belt transmission of power, dating back to the 1790s,

began to be widely employed in textile manufacturing.

Paper Manufacture. Thomas Gilpin is credited with manufacturing the first machine-made paper in the U.S. (1817) near Wilmington, Del. **Fourdrinier process** of paper manufacture was introduced into the U.S. c.1825; placed in large-scale operation at Holyoke, Mass. (1853), by Parson Paper Co.

1830–50. STEAM ENGINES AND STEAM POWER. As steam engines came into common use, locomotive building was transferred from general machine shops to specialized works—Baldwin Works (1832), Norris Works (1834). Steam power, however, was not widely introduced in manufacturing until 1850. The expansion of steam utilization as well as puddling and rolling created a demand for **anthracite coal.** Anthracite production rose from 215,272 tons to over 1 million tons by 1837. Although Frederick W. Geisenheimer conducted successful experiments in smelting iron ore with anthracite, 1830, and the hot blast was introduced, 1834, charcoal remained practically the sole fuel used for smelting.

Textiles. Power weaving and the Waltham System were extended in wool manufacture, beginning at Lowell, Mass. (1830), and at Lawrence, Mass. (1845). A loom for the manufacture of figured woolens was successfully demonstrated, 1840, by William Crompton (1806–91), and the process improved by his son, George (1829–86). As a result, hand weaving in New England practically disappeared, but in frontier areas household manufactures actually expanded down to 1830. During this period the cotton industry about doubled its capacity, the number of spindles exceeding 2,280,000.

1840–50. RAPID PROGRESS IN THE IRON INDUSTRY resulted from (1) substitution of mineral coal for charcoal, (2) replacement of open forge by reverberatory-type closed furnace, (3) advances in refining and rolling (heavy rails successfully rolled, 1845), (4) large-scale adoption of steam power, and (5) expansion of the railroad system. On 4 July 1840 David Thomas (1794–1884) made the first successful attempt to produce pig iron by the use of anthracite coal in hot-blast furnace of the Lehigh Crane Ironworks at Catasauqua, Pa. Output of anthracite quadrupled, exceeding 4 million tons.

Machine shop products multiplied in variety on the basis of standardized parts and quantity production: plows, threshing machines, harvesters, reapers (McCormick factory, Chicago, 1847), revolving pistols, stoves, metal clocks, sewing machines (first practical sewing machine produced by the Singer factory, 1850).

Textiles. Installation of steam power operation in textile mills at Salem and New Bedford, Mass., 1847, freed the industry from the limitations of water power.

Household manufactures throughout the U.S. declined: Per capita value 1840, $1.70; 1850, $1.18; 1860, $.78.

1850–60. In 1859 the value of the products of U.S. industry ($1,885,862,-000) exceeded for the first time the value of agricultural products. In gross value of products flour milling ranked first (first commercial flour mill began operations at Minneapolis, 1854), followed by the iron industry. Anthracite iron held first place, followed in order by charcoal iron, and bituminous coal and coke iron. Lake Superior ores were beginning to be used by 1860. In the 20 years ending in 1860 the consumption of raw cotton by the textile industry had almost quadrupled, and the number of spindles more than doubled (exceeding 5,235,000). In capital invested, labor employed, and net value of product, the cotton industry was first in the U.S. by 1860.

This period is also marked by the emergence of **machine toolmaking** as a separate industry. The manufacture of the **vernier caliper** (1851) by J. R. Brown of Providence (later known as Brown and Sharpe Mfg. Co.), making possible measurements in thousandths of an inch, inaugurated true precision manufacturing. The **turret lathe** manufactured by Robbins and Laurence at Windsor, Vt., 1854, proved essential to mass production techniques.

Expansion of Steam-Powered Factories. By 1860 almost one fourth of the Fall River spindles were steam-driven.

MANUFACTURING BY SECTIONS, 1860

Section	Number of Establishments	Capital Invested	Average Number of Laborers	Annual Value of Products
New England	20,671	$257,477,783	391,836	$468,599,287
Middle States	53,387	435,061,964	546,243	802,338,392
Western States	36,785	194,212,543	209,909	384,606,530
Southern States	20,631	95,975,185	110,721	155,531,281
Pacific States	8,777	23,380,334	50,204	71,229,989
Territories	282	3,747,906	2,333	3,556,197
Total	140,533	$1,009,855,715	1,311,246	$1,885,861,676

Phenomenal increase in manufacturing output since 1860: the result of technological developments which have revolutionized (1) **mineral production** through deeper mining (improved ventilation and air-conditioning) and deeper drilling of oil wells (made possible by rotary drill and steel alloys); improved blasting techniques; the pneumatic rock drill, increasing drilling speed; power shovels; the cyanide process in gold and silver mining; the electrolytic process in aluminum, copper, zinc, and lead refining; the open-hearth method in steel production (man-hour production in mineral industry, 1902–39, multiplied 3.67 times, in oil and gas 5-fold); (2) **chemical industry** (rayon, rubber, oil, leather, plastics); (3) **alloyed metals** production; (4) **electric power** and the **internal-combustion engine** (cheapening transportation and promoting farm production and marketing); (5) **large-scale organization** promoting industrial efficiency.

1861–65. IMPACT OF THE CIVIL WAR was variously felt, wool production expanding, cotton manufacturing being severely curtailed. The introduction of power-driven sewing machines in the manufacture of military uniforms and boots and shoes brought these industries into the factory system. Agricultural machinery output spurted, but locomotive production fell off sharply. Extensive use of condensed milk processed by **Gail Borden** (1801–74) on the basis of a patent (1856) encouraged development of food processing industry. Demands for iron for military use expanded, while curtailment was marked in structural iron and railroad equipment, in building construction, and in most types of raw-material production. The war encouraged technological developments by creating a demand for rolled-iron plates of considerable thickness. The Rodman process was successfully utilized in casting large cannon hollow, and progress was made in crucible steel.

1866–73. THE BESSEMER PROCESS IN MANUFACTURE OF STEEL started, 1864, at Troy, N.Y. (also p. 795), to meet demand for rails was principal achievement. By 1873, 115,000 tons of Bessemer rails were rolled, but as yet nearly 7 tons of iron rails were rolled for every ton of Bessemer rails. With **Bethlehem Steel Co.** beginning operations in 1873 and the Edgar Thompson Steel Works under construction, the Bessemer industry was on a firm basis by the end of this period. The **Lake Superior** region (U.S. government surveyors discovered ore deposits near Marquette, Mich., 1844) became the most important single source of iron ore, with annual shipments exceeding 1 million tons by 1873 (ultimately a number of ranges were opened up in Michigan and Minnesota, including the Menominee, Gogebic, Vermilion, Mesabi, and Cuyuna). While the Pittsburgh district continued to maintain its leadership, new establishments on a large scale were constructed on the Great Lakes with convenient access to the ore (notably at Gary, Ind., and Chicago district). Other trends: (1) **steam power** now surpassed water power as a source of industrial energy; (2) **coal production** almost doubled, with bituminous surpassing anthracite in physical output by 1870; (3) the **worsted industry** rapidly expanded.

1867–1911. PETROLEUM INDUSTRY AND STANDARD OIL. As a result of a scientific report by **Benjamin Silliman, Jr.** (1816–85), refining and drilling operations were begun in Pennsylvania. Oil was successfully drilled by **Edwin L. Drake** (1819–80) near Titusville, 1859, leading to an **oil boom,** as petroleum quickly ousted whale oil and burning fluids as an illuminant. After 1884 drilling became nationwide, with production in Ohio and West Virginia, in the 1890s in Wyoming, and by the early 1900s in Texas, Indian Territory (Okla.), Kansas, Louisiana, and Illinois. First oil pipeline completed from Pithole, Pa. (1866). **John D. Rockefeller** (p. 1138), concentrating on control of (1) **refining,** merged the interests of the Rockefellers, Harkness, and Flagler, organizing, 1870, the **Standard Oil Co. of Ohio** (capital $1 million). (2) By special **rate agreements** with Eastern railroads Rockefeller secured a competitive transportation advantage over rivals. (3) Control of **pipelines.** As a result of these 3 factors, by 1879 Standard Oil controlled 90–95% of the oil refined. Trust agreement, 1879; formally organized (1882) as one unit in Trust; Trust Jersey Standard became the leading Standard Oil Co.; trust broken by Ohio Courts (1892). **Standard Oil Co. of N.J.** became the leading Standard Oil Co.; acting as holding and operating company (1892, 1899); dissolved, 1911 (p. 674); since that date the business has been controlled by a number of corporations with competition appearing in the industry from Gulf Oil, Shell, Texas, as well as between the old Standard Oil companies.

1873–1904. CONCENTRATION OF ECONOMIC POWER. Devices employed: (1) **Pools** (1873–87), a combine of business units to control prices by apportioning markets; forbidden to railroads by Interstate Commerce Act, 1887 (p. 309), and by Supreme Court, 1897 (p. 672). For *Addyston Pipe and Steel Co.* v. *U.S.* (1899), which forbade pools among manufacturers shipping across state lines, see p. 673. (2) **Trusts,** a device whereby stockholders under a trust agreement deposit their stock with trustees—Standard Oil Co. (1879–82); "Cotton-Oil" Trust (1884); "Whisky Trust," "Sugar Trust," and "Lead Trust" (1887); illegal under the Sherman Act, 1890, p. 312; for Supreme Court interpretation, p. 672. (3) **Holding companies** (esp. 1892–1904) controlling stock in other corporations. Laws of states like New Jersey encouraged this device. The most notable example was the **U.S. Steel Corporation,** organized, 1901, by a group of financiers headed by **Elbert H. Gary** (1846–1927), Chicago, and **J. P. Morgan,** New York, who bought out **Andrew Carnegie's** (p. 998) interest in the Carnegie Steel Co. (resulting from a series of consolidations of iron and steel

works, ore properties, and shipping facilities, 1874–99). Capitalized at $1.4 billion, U.S. Steel was for many years the largest holding company in the U.S. Holding companies were partially curbed by the dissolution of the Northern Securities Co., 1904 (p. 673); the dissolution of the Standard Oil Co. (p. 674) and the American Tobacco Co. (p. 674); and New Deal legislation (p. 417). **Operating companies** combined merged enterprises and on their own integrated horizontally and vertically. Often large companies acted as both holding and operating units. **International corporations:** most of the giant U.S. enterprises were interested in foreign business. Use of the **corporate form** became typical for industrial enterprises (p. 739).

1874–80. Bessemer plant capacity increased. By 1880 Pittsburgh blast furnaces produced 1,200 tons a week as against a maximum output of 600 tons in the previous decade. As a result Bessemer steel output exceeded 1 million tons for the first time, with pig iron production, 1880, attaining a new high of 4,295,000 tons, a one-third increase over the boom year, 1873. Other developments included (1) application of **refrigeration** to transportation, with the meat-packing industry now producing for a national market on a year-round basis; (2) expansion of machine manufacture of shoes, especially marked after the merger of firm established by Charles Goodyear (1833–96) with his competitor, Gordon McKay (1880).

1881–90. EXPANSION IN THE STEEL INDUSTRY. The **Open-Hearth Process** (introduced into the U.S. by **Abram S. Hewitt** at Trenton, N.J., 1868), removing sulfur and especially phosphorus, and consequently opening up a larger portion of the ore reserve of the U.S. (including scrap metal) than the Bessemer process, expanded its operatives 5-fold, especially after 1886. At the same time Bessemer steel ingots and castings rose from 1,074,262 to 3,658,871 long tons. By 1885 iron rails accounted for only 15,000 out of over 1 million tons, with the proportion devoted to other products constantly increasing. Structural iron, wire, pipe, tubes, and armored plate faced heavy competition from steel. Reflecting the marked growth in size per unit, the number of blast furnaces in Pennsylvania, chief U.S. producer, fell from 269 to 211. The northern Alabama and adjacent Tennessee district (center: **Birmingham**), with resources of coal as well as iron ore, spurted to second place in pig iron production. By 1890 iron ore production amounted to 4 million tons, or 25% of the national total, but this area did not keep up the pace, 1893–1914. Lake Superior ore shipments rose from 2 million to 9 million tons, accounting for 56% of the total U.S. output.

Other developments: (1) **rise of Southern textile production** (number of cotton spindles increased from 542,000 to 1,554,000, but in 1890 New England still accounted for 76% of total U.S. spindles); (2) **ready-made clothing industry** expanded as a result of the introduction of cutting machines and mechanical pressers, with the organization largely characterized by **subcontract system** and **sweat shops**; (3) **shoe industry** expanded, with annual output of Goodyear welt shoes amounting to 12 million pairs by 1890.

1891–1900. ELECTRIC POWER AND INTERNAL-COMBUSTION ENGINES. The introduction of steam turbines (1890) to drive dynamos for the generation of electric power and the development of the internal-combustion engine were the chief industrial developments. The Niagara Falls plant (1894) inaugurated the era of hydroelectric power. Utilization of such power was still in its infancy. By 1899 horsepower of electric motors run by purchased current amounted to merely 1.8% of the total installed primary power in manufacturing industries, while installed horsepower of internal-combustion engines amounted to 1.3%. The introduction (1891) of the electrolytic process of copper refining speeded up the complete displacement of steel wire by copper wire in the conduction of electricity. Other trends: (1) Southern cotton industry aided by the perfection of the Northrop loom (1889–95). By 1900, Southern mills consumed 1.5 million bales of cotton as against slightly under 2 million spun in Northern mills. (2) Meat-packing industry became centralized in the Middle West as receipts of live cattle in the East began to decline absolutely, beginning in 1890, and shipments of slaughtered cattle expanded. (3) Kerosene production declined relatively, amounting to one half of all petroleum refining in 1900 as against three quarters, 1890. During the same period petroleum output increased 40%. (4) Decline of relative importance of rails in the steel industry. By 1891 steel used for structural and other rolled products exceeded rails, with the ratio widening to 2–1 by 1896. In forging, hydraulic presses supplanted steam hammers. Open-hearth steel production outstripped Bessemer in rate of expansion. (5) American industrial output was the largest in the world by 1900.

1901–09. (1) Output of steel products rose from 10 million to almost 24 million tons, with open-hearth steel exceeding Bessemer output by 1908. In 1909 open-hearth accounted for 14,493,000 tons, Bessemer 9,330,000 tons. **Coke** (of major importance as a blast-furnace fuel after 1890) became the principal fuel in the steel industry. (2) Heavy chemical industry rapidly expanded as a result of the **Solvay** process and the electrolytic process. (3) Machine tool industry introduced electrically driven and high-speed cutting tools, power presses, heavy portable machine tools, and compressed air tools. (3) The **automobile industry,** not listed separately in the Census of 1900, rose rapidly by 1909, its output increasing 3,500% during the decade, with a corresponding increase in demand for alloys, glass, steel, rubber, and petroleum products. (4) Fuel oil production rose from 300 million gallons to 1.7 billion gallons. (5) Lagging industries included wheat flour milling, forest products (dropped 36%), and cotton and wool manufacturing, which kept pace with the population rise but not at the rate of knit goods and silk production.

1909–14. Steel Industry Trends. Bessemer production declined from 9.5 million tons to 6.2 million tons annually, while open-hearth steel totaled 21.5 million in 1914, setting a trend which continued through the first half of the 20th century. 1945: Bessemer, 3,844,034 long tons; open-hearth, 64,231,788 long tons. Ore from the Mesabi Range (about 100 miles long in N.E. Minn.) virtually supplanted ore from Wisconsin and Michigan fields, constituting over 70% of all Lake Superior region shipments in 1914.

Automotive expansion from 21st to 6th place in relation to value of output. In 1913–14 the **Ford Motor Co.** started reorganizing the assembly process, including the manufacture of its own motors and other important parts, and the utilization of "continuous flow production." A corresponding expansion was recorded in the rubber industry, largely due to a 4-fold increase in the value of tire and inner-tube production.

Textiles. Cotton manufacturing in the Southern Piedmont was accelerated by the utilization of hydroelectric power. By 1914 the South had almost 13 million spindles as against less than 11 million for Massachusetts. The former produced coarse cotton goods; New England specialized in finer cloth. Rapid advances were recorded in silk and knit goods. The value of silk products reached $254 million in 1914. The introduction of rayon in 1909 inaugurated a new **era of synthetics,** but production remained small in 1914.

Electric power installed in manufacturing rose from 1.7 to 3.8 million horsepower. By 1914 energy run by purchased current reached 17.3% of all installed primary power in manufacturing.

Scientific management ideas associated with **Frederick Winslow Taylor** (p. 1166), **Henry Lawrence Gantt** (1861–1919), and **Frank B. Gilbreth** (1868–1924) were introduced in certain industries; efficiency experts began to apply systems to plant management.

1914–19. WORLD WAR I increased the demands for alloys and accelerated the rise of the **aluminum industry.** To meet the needs for special alloys, electric furnace production increased conspicuously, rising from 27,000 long tons, 1914, to 511,693 long tons, 1918. In the tool industry electrically produced steel displaced crucible steel. During the war period total steel ingots and castings rose from 23,513,030 long tons (1914) to 45,060,607 (1917). Shipbuilding rose from $211,319,000 (1914) to $775,093,-000 (1918). The enlarged demands for munitions placed a premium upon the construction of **by-product coking ovens** to supply coal tar for explosives, the number of such ovens doubling by 1919, by which date by-product coke amounted to 56.9% of 44.2 million tons total. Installed primary power represented by purchased current more than doubled, reaching 9,347,556 horsepower, or 31.6% of total horsepower of manufacturing industries. New construction expenditures rose from $3.3 billion (1915) to $6.7 billion (1919). The **War Industries Board** (p. 331) supported increases in productive capacity, standardization and simplification of products and processes, and scientific management.

1920–29. RATE OF GROWTH IN MANUFACTURING. In terms of distribution of the national income and employment, manufacturing remained relatively constant, while advances were scored in aggregate physical output far greater than in nonmanufacturing industries. Rate of growth **uneven**, with a **recession** in older basic industries—coal, textiles, lumber, wheat flour milling. Expansion in steel and iron leveled off. **Marked expansion** in **automotive industry,** which now took 1st rank in terms of value of product as well as value added by manufacture, with 2,798,737 passenger cars manufactured in 1929. Output of tires and inner tubes doubled. Gasoline production increased 4-fold, accounting for 48% of all refined products, while fuel oil output doubled but declined from 52% to 42% of petroleum refining. **Chemical industry** expansion, given a fillip by World War I, made spectacular gains, especially in the fields of dyes (formerly imported from Germany) and synthetic fibers (rayon production rose from 3 million lbs., 1919, to 33 million lbs., 1929) and plastics. **Electrical equipment** manufacturing enjoyed boom conditions, with the value of heavy household appliances rising from $109 million to $268 million; portable household electric appliances, from $71 million to $106 million; **radios** and related apparatus, from $15 million to $338 million; and industrial electrical appliances, from $46 million to $976 million. By 1929 the rated capacity of horsepower equipment of motors run by purchased energy exceeded the rated horsepower capacity of all other prime movers in manufacturing. New construction expenditures rose from $6.7 billion (1919) to $12.1 billion (1926), declining to $10.8 billion (1929). Corporations grew in size, diversified their

product lines, and frequently enlarged their business in foreign countries. Novel managerial methods were developed to administer multiproduct and, often, multinational companies. Enterprises emerged with central staffs and multidivisional structures (General Motors, Standard Oil of New Jersey, du Pont).

1929–39. DEPRESSION AND TRANSITION. The index of physical output of all manufacturing rose from 364 in 1929 to 374 in 1939 (1899 = 100; 1865 = 8.5), but in only 2 years of the entire decade was the 1929 output exceeded. Physical production rose 2.8%, while population increased about 6%, with one half of all industries declining absolutely and over one half declining in relation to population. New construction expenditures, $10.8 billion (1929), $2.9 billion (1933), $8.1 billion (1939). **Growth industries** included **chemicals** (plastics output rose from 50,000 tons, 1935, to 170,000 tons, 1939), **electrical equipment** (household refrigerator output rose from 890,000 units, 1929, to 2,824,000, 1937), and **petroleum** (gasoline production rose almost 50%, and the catalytic "cracking process" was developed). **Uneven trends** were marked in **textiles** (rayon used in the silk and rayon goods industry increased 4-fold, 1929–35, while silk consumption declined 50%, and by 1939 was relegated to full-fashioned hosiery only; cotton goods dropped from 22% of total physical output in textiles, 1929, to 16%, 1937) and in **clothing** (men's ready-made clothing showed a net rise in output of about 2%, while women's clothing advanced by almost 50%, 1929–37). Other trends: the introduction of cemented tungsten carbide (1928), followed by tantalum carbide, for cutting tools permitted "super-speed" cutting and practical cutting speeds on materials formerly unmachinable. Developments in synthetic abrasives, electric drive and control, hydraulic feed, and pneumatic accessories led to widespread redesigning of **machine tools.** Such processes as electrical welding and such substitutes for metal cutting as pressing, stamping, and punching were increasingly applied in the auto and other mass production industries and, during World War II, in the aircraft and shipbuilding industries. Purchased power used in manufacturing rose from 48% to almost 60% of total primary power utilized.

1938–52. ECONOMIC CONCENTRATION. By 1929, 69.2% of the products of manufacturing were produced by firms doing a business in excess of $1 million as against 1.1% ($5,000–$20,000) by small firms (*Statistical Abstract*, 1933). The depression accelerated this trend, according to the TNEC *Hearings and Final Report* (p. 424). In 1935 less than 6% of the tobacco corporations owned 92% of the assets; 3% of the chemicals, 86%; 4% of the rubber concerns, 80%; 2% of the metal and metal products concerns, 74%. In 1937 one company produced 100% of the virgin aluminum (Aluminum Co. of America); 3 companies, 86% of the autos; and 4 companies, 58% of the whisky (1938). By 1938, 30 corporations had assets in excess of $1 billion. The leaders:

Corporation	Assets in Billion Dollars
Metropolitan Life Insurance	4.23
Amer. Tel. & Tel. Co.	3.99
Prudential Insurance Co.	3.12
Pennsylvania R.R. Co.	2.86
N.Y. Central R.R. Co.	2.35
Chase National Bank	2.33
New York Life Insurance Co.	2.22
Standard Oil Co. (N.J.)	1.89
National City Bank of N.Y.	1.88
Guaranty Trust Co.	1.84
Equitable Life Assurance Co.	1.82
U.S. Steel Corp.	1.82
Allegheny Corp.	1.73
Southern Pacific R.R. Co.	1.67
General Motors Corp.	1.49
Consolidated Edison Co.	1.38
Bank of America	1.27

By 1952 the number of corporations with a billion or more in assets rose to 59 (24 industrial, utility, and railroad companies; 21 banks; 13 insurance companies; 1 finance company). Assets of Standard Oil Co. of N.J. rose to $4.7 billion; General Motors, to $3.67 billion; U.S. Steel, to $3.14 billion.

1940–52. WORLD WAR II, RECONVERSION, AND COLD WAR. As a result of a shift from civilian to military production (military production rose from 2% of total national output, 1939, to 40%, 1944), plant expansion, and labor mobilization, industrial production rose from 100 (1935–39) to **239** by 1943, and durable manufactured goods to **360.** Mineral production rose to 148 (1942), fuels to 145 (1944). Steel ingots and castings reached a peak output in 1944 of 80,037,130 long tons, almost 50% above 1929 output ("turbo-hearth," new steelmaking technique, introduced, 1949). Most striking industrial gains occurred in (1) **alloys and light metals** (aluminum production increased 6-fold; magnesium output rose from 2,500 tons, 1939, to a peak of 170,000 tons, 1943); (2) **synthetics** (synthetic rubber production rose from 2,000 tons, 1939, to 930,000 tons, 1945, meeting most of U.S. needs, and compared with prewar annual imports of natural rubber ranging from 550,000–650,000 tons); and (3) **plastics** (output expanded 5-fold as light-metal shortages developed, equaling by 1945 nearly one half the tonnage of aluminum produced. **U.S. government financed five sixths of the new plant** construction ($160 million through the Defense Plants Corp.). By the end of World War II the government owned 90% of the plants for synthetic rubber, aircraft, magnesium, and shipbuilding; 70% of the aluminum capacity; and 50% of the machine tool facilities. In addition, 3,800 miles of oil pipes ("Big Inch" and "Little Inch") were constructed by the government to carry petroleum to the East Coast.

The reconversion shift at the end of the war was virtually completed by mid-1947. Civilian production sought to meet shortages in **autos** (5 million units produced annually by end of 1948), **consumers' durable goods** (6,200,000 refrigerators, 14.6 million radios, and 7.4 million television sets manufactured, 1950), and **residential dwellings** (curtailed by high construction costs and material and labor shortages, with peak construction, 1950, $11,525 million). Production was further augmented by the European Recovery Program (p. 468). The Cold War, beginning 1949, curtailed industrial reconversion and led to restrictions upon civilian production (autos, one third from 1950 levels by 1952; radios and television sets, 40%) in favor of rearmament requirements. Nevertheless, peak output figures were achieved in this period. Iron and steel production rose to approximately 260 by 1951 (1935–39 = 100) as against 208, highest war year (1943); petroleum and coal products to 267 as against a record war output of 236 (1945); chemical products to 242 as compared with 228 (1943); and aircraft manufacturing was accelerated to reach, by July 1952, a production rate of 250 military planes monthly, considerably below earlier estimates.

Income originating from manufacturing (1949) amounted to $62.8 billion out of total national income of $216.8 billion as against $7.5 billion (manufacturing) out of $39.5 billion total national income in 1933.

1950–73. RATE OF GROWTH. Index of industrial production (1967 = 100) continued to rise from 45 (1950) to 66 (1960), 107 (1970), to 128 (Oct. 1973), with largest percentage increases in utilities output, 27 (1950), 158 (Oct. 1973). Overall, America's economic rate of growth (average annual increase in gross national product per capita in constant 1954 dollars), 1950–59, was 1.4%, considerably behind the rates of growth of Western Europe and the U.S.S.R. for the same period. In 1960–70, America's economic performance improved. The average annual increase in gross domestic product per capita (in constant dollars) was 3.3%, which nonetheless still compared unfavorably with the growth performance in the European Economic Community (4.1%), the U.S.S.R. (6.0%, net material product per capita), and Japan (9.7%).

1950–73. INDUSTRIAL TRENDS marked by greater regional diversification of industry. There was a relative decline of the Northeast and rise of Southern (esp. South Atlantic) and Pacific states.

VALUE ADDED BY MANUFACTURING
(percentage distribution by geographical area)

Area	1950	1963	1969
U.S.	100.0	100.0	100.0
New England	8.3	7.1	6.9
Middle Atlantic	26.2	22.7	21.3
East North Central	33.2	29.3	28.6
West North Central	5.7	6.1	6.5
South Atlantic	9.4	11.0	11.3
East South Central	3.8	4.8	5.5
West South Central	4.3	5.7	6.5
Mountain	1.2	1.0	1.8
Pacific	7.9	11.5	11.6

Technological innovation included (1) the spread of automation, aided by automatic high-speed computers; (2) development of computers (first production model of a large-scale general-purpose computer delivered to Census Bureau, 14 June 1951); IBM became the world leader in computers; by 1973 computers, serving a wide variety of functions, had become commonplace in American industry; 1972–73, mini-computers, developed for process and industrial controls, opened vast new markets for computers; as of summer 1973, est. 125,000 general- and special-purpose computers installed in the U.S.; (3) photocopying machines: the trademark Xerox entered the language; by 1973 over 1 million photocopiers in use; (4) TV sets became universal; by 1972, 99.8% of American households had TV sets; (5) the transistor (p. 801) came to substitute for the vacuum tube in radios, TVs, computers, etc.; (6) the electronics industry was stimulated by the development of defense and space industries, which encouraged research geared to military technology, notably in the fields of spacecrafts, electronics (guidance, control, and communication), instrumentation, along with expanded use of lightweight metals (beryllium, titanium, molybdenum) and the refractory metals; space missions made operational the fuel cell, a converter of the energy of hydrogen and oxygen into electricity; (7) electronics penetrated traditional industries, 1970s. Textiles: introduction of electronic knitting machines; electronic signals drive the needles; instead of taking 8 hours to change a pattern, the switch is made in minutes; production is one third more per day than by the mechanical counterpart; (8) electronic calculators appeared in the 1960s for office use and by 1972–73 for home use; (9) new chemical and petrochemical products related to agriculture proliferated: weed and brush killers, insecticides, fungicides, soil conditioners, mold inhibiters, fertilizers, synthetic hormones for animals; (10) chemical and petrochemical revolution in clothing, with acrylic and polyester fibers; durable press garments; new cleaning substances from detergents to solvents; (11) the chemical industry also presented new paints and pigments, new insulation materials, synthetic carpeting, heavy-duty construction materials, higher octane gasoline, new lubricants, nylontire cord, new plastics for the automobile industry, new synthetic rubber compounds, new tools and equipment, manmade industrial diamonds, new packaging materials (polyethylenes); (12) the electrochemical industries witnessed product and process innovations; (13) pharmaceuticals: new antibiotics, antihistamines, synthetic hormones, tranquilizers, vaccines, oral contraceptives; (14) processed food industry: new lines of frozen foods and premixed products; (15) the aircraft industry produced for civilian requirements a range of new planes; defense and space age industry had spinoffs for the aircraft industry; in the 1960s, the jet plane replaced the prop plane in commercial transportation; (16) automobile industry: cars grew in size and comfort; 1957–60, introduction of "compact" cars to meet rise in small-car imports, with greatly expanded production as the energy crisis loomed (1973). 1972, Japanese Mazda car with Wankel (rotary) engine introduced in U.S.; G.M. declared it would bring out a car with a Wankel engine; energy crisis stimulated production and sales of compact cars while sales of larger cars dropped sharply; (17) other consumer durables: expanded output of refrigerators and freezers, washing and drying machines, dishwashers, self-cleaning ovens helped simplify the life of the housewife; (18) 1961–73, modernization of steel industry occurred due in part to competition from West Germany and Japan. Among the improved techniques were widespread adoption of the basic oxygen process of steel making (1972: 56% of raw steel output) by which steel of open-hearth quality is produced in a rotary oxygen converter using high phosphorus molten iron obtained from the blast furnace; continuous casting facilities, eliminating the ingot stage and **primary** rolling mill; new high-speed computer-controlled rolling mills; development of "ultrahigh strength" steels for space industry; (19) 1969–72, shipments of 1.9 million mobile homes equaled the number shipped in the previous 2 decades; (20) the construction industry boomed, from $33.6 billion of new construction (1950) to $123.8 billion (1972); (21) research and development expenditures by private business grew: $3.5 billion (1953) to $19.2 billion (1972 est.).

1950–73. ENERGY. Energy consumption expanded rapidly. Electrical energy production rose from 389 billion kwh (1950) to 1,747 billion kwh (1972 prel.). Production and consumption rose with affluence.

SELECTED APPLIANCES IN THE HOME

PERCENT OF HOUSEHOLDS WITH SELECTED APPLIANCES (1972)

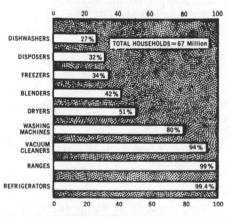

SOURCE: Merchandising Week,
Bureau of Competitive Assessment and Business Policy

With the exception of the ranges (which used gas as well as electricity), these appliances typically used electricity.

Americans came to depend on oil to run their cars, to heat their homes, to produce electricity (in power plants), and for numerous other uses; oil exceeded natural gas and coal in energy consumption.

The U.S., once a net exporter of petroleum and petroleum products, by 1953 came on a regular basis to be an importer of oil. In an attempt to protect the domestic producer, from 1959 to 1 May 1973, the U.S. had quotas on imported oil. American oil reserves dropped, to be boosted only by the discovery of oil in commercial quantities in Alaska (Feb. 1968, Prudhoe Bay discovery announced). Alaskan oil did not, however, enter the U.S. market at once, for transportation was required. Fear about the impact on the environment delayed approval of the Alaska pipeline until 1973. Clean-burning natural gas—unlike oil and coal—does not pollute the environment; new use was made of natural gas; 1966–73, U.S. natural gas reserves decreased by one fifth; shortages began to develop. Despite abundant American coal, ecological and pollution considerations limited its use; states passed legislation requiring that coal operators restore land after mining; concern over the unpleasantness of burning high-sulfur coal curbed its consumption and added extra cost when employed. Fears over oil spills retarded the development of offshore oil resources. With import quotas, oil companies did not build refinery capacity to process large-scale crude oil imports. Widespread apprehension delayed the spread of nuclear power plants (in 1957, the Shippingport, Pa. Atomic Power Station was America's first nuclear power plant; 1973, Sept., 37 such plants in operation in the U.S.). After the 1973 Arab-Israeli war (6–22 Oct.), Arab nations embargoed oil shipments to the U.S. Embargo announced 17 Oct. President Nixon's energy crisis address (7 Nov.) presented temporary measures, involving personal, business, and government reduction in energy use and also long-run steps: the licensing of new nuclear plants, more utilization of coal relative to oil, increased oil production from naval

42% oil 31% domestic; 11% imported	34% natural gas 33% domestic; 1% imported	20% coal * all domestic

* Other 4% hydroelectric power; less than 1% nuclear power.

reserves, approval of the Alaska pipeline, and greater energy research and development efforts, designed to make U.S. self-sufficient in energy resources by 1980. Nixon asked for authority to suspend environmental standards. States lowered speed limits to 50 mph. 16 Nov., Nixon signed the controversial Alaska pipeline enactment; 27 Nov., Nixon signed Emergency Petroleum Allocation Act, requiring president to establish a program for oil allocation. 14 Dec., Congress passed year-round daylight savings time (for 2 years) to save energy. Other measures of Nov.–Dec. to curb energy consumption included Sunday gas station closings, cutbacks in heating fuel deliveries, a ban on display and outdoor ornamental lighting, reductions in jet fuel deliveries (causing reduction in scheduled flights). Plans were made for accelerated research on solar, geothermal, nuclear, and numerous other possible sources of energy.

1953–73. TRENDS IN BUSINESS ORGANIZATION. (1) **Conglomerate mergers.** The late 1960s saw more mergers than ever in U.S. history. The peak year was 1968, when 2,407 manufacturing and mining firms disappeared through mergers. Many mergers joined companies in unrelated industries. Among the leading conglomerates were Ling-Temco-Vought (originally in electronics and aircraft), the majority stockholder in Jones & Laughlin Steel Corp.; Litton Industries (typewriters to ships); ITT acquired Avis (car rentals), Sheraton (hotels), Levitt & Sons (home construc-

tion), and Hartford Fire Insurance, rising from country's 80th (1955) to 8th ranking firm in terms of dollar volume of sales (1970). Because of antitrust action (controversial settlement announced 31 July 1971), ITT divested Avis and Levitt, but it retained Hartford Insurance and most other of its many acquisitions. Conglomerates appeared to reach their crest c.1970. The general decline of stock prices put them in a poor position to purchase new subsidiaries by offering own shares in exchange for those of smaller companies. (2) **Multinational enterprises.** Companies added production facilities worldwide. Industrial leaders at home, GM, Exxon (the old Standard Oil of N.J.), Ford, IBM, ITT took the lead abroad (p. 709, on distribution of foreign investments). (3) **Management.** In response to more diversified and more multinational corporations, management methods became more sophisticated. The central staff, multidivisional organization, an innovative structure in the 1920s, became a common means of organizing multiproduct, multiplant, multinational enterprises.

1965–73. ENVIRONMENT. The consequences of industrial and technological expansion concerned Americans as they worried about nuclear fallout; chemical products that resisted natural degradation and remained to pollute waters and countryside; chemical products that killed birds as they killed insects; and automobiles and smokestacks that dirtied the atmosphere (pp. 639–643 for legislation).

National Public Finance

From the origin of the U.S. federal government to the twentieth century, national public finance simply meant raising money to pay the expenses of government and paying those expenses. To meet special government needs, the government issued bonds; it was accepted that the public debt should be repaid. In 1836–37, for the only time in American history, there was no public debt. The principal source of federal government revenues until World War I was customs duties. Before the Civil War, typically over 50% of the expenditures went to the War and Navy departments; after the Civil War, veterans' benefits constituted an important part of government expenditures. Until well into the twentieth century, the total federal government budget was small—small relative to the national product as well as to later government budgets.

During the twentieth century the size of the federal budget grew. From World War I on, personal income taxes provided the most important single source of federal revenue. Government expenditures over the years became more diversified as they became more substantial. Until the 1930s, it was almost universally accepted that a balanced budget was desirable; from the 1930s onward, this idea—while it continued to be held—began to be replaced by the view that the budget should be used as an instrument of economic policy; deficit financing might be wise to spur recovery from depression and encourage economic growth. After World War II, as the government role expanded, it became accepted that the budget was an important economic tool.

1789–1800. Hamilton's "Report on Public Credit" (9 Jan. 1790) placed the total public debt outstanding at **$77,-124,564** (foreign debt, $11,710,379; domestic debt, $40,414,086; state debts, $25 million, of which **$18,271,786** was actually assumed). Customs duties constituted the principal source of revenue, as a number of excise taxes and, in 1798, a direct tax on houses, land, and slaves apportioned among the states on the basis of population proved unproductive.

1791. Bank of U.S. chartered (p. 147).

1792, 2 APR. Mint Act (1) provided for decimal system of coinage; (2) val-ued U.S. dollar at 24.75 grains of gold; (3) established bimetallism, with silver and gold legal tender at a ratio of 15 to 1; (4) established a mint at Philadelphia. New discoveries of Mexican silver resulted in silver being overvalued at this ratio.

1801–11. The Jeffersonian Republicans were committed to **retrenchment.** Increasing customs receipts made it possible to repeal all excises (1802), except tax on salt (eliminated 1807), and to reduce the debt of $83 million inherited from the Federalist administration by almost 50%.

1812–15. The War of 1812 undid the

economy moves of the preceding years. Heavy government borrowing (loans, c.$80 million; Treasury notes, c.$37 million) brought the debt to $127,335,000 ($15 per capita). Prewar annual expenditures of c.$11 million rose to $35 million, 1814, in which year Congress increased tariff rates; doubled the tax of 1813 on land, dwelling houses, and slaves; and increased items subject to internal revenue.

1816. Second Bank of U.S. chartered (p. 184).

1816–18. Large revenues permitted the retirement or funding into stock of Treasury notes outstanding and the removal by 1817 of most war taxes.

1819–21. Annual deficits handicapped Treasury fiscal operations.

1822–29. The accrual of surpluses was used to liquidate the public debt by the purchase in the open market of government securities. In 1826 a Senate committee complained of "the serious inconvenience of an **overflowing Treasury**."

1830–35. Land speculation made receipts from the sales of public lands an important source of government revenue. Reduced to only $7 million by 1832, the entire debt was paid off by Jan. 1835.

1834, 28 JUNE. Second Coinage Act authorized ratio of 16–1 between silver and gold and reduced weight of gold to 23.22 grains. Discovery of gold in California (p. 247) led to overvaluation of gold at this ratio.

1836. Income from land sales totaled $25 million, exceeding customs receipts for the first and only time. The government surplus exceeded $40 million.

11 JULY. Specie Circular (p. 211).

1837. $28 million of the surplus was distributed among the states in the form of a loan.

1837–43. Declining revenues brought deficits totaling $46.4 million. To finance

government expenditures, over $47 million of Treasury notes were issued.

1840. Independent Treasury system established (p. 217), discontinued 1841 (p. 219), reestablished 1846 (p. 233), continuing until merged with Federal Reserve System (1913, p. 326), and finally abolished (1921) by Act of 1920.

1844–46. Reappearance of annual surpluses.

1846–49. The War with Mexico was financed almost entirely by borrowing. The total deficits for the 3-year period amounted to $53.2 million. 1847 marked the record federal expenditure to date of **$57 million.**

1850–57. A period of large surpluses.

1853, 21 FEB. Coinage Act reduced silver in all small coins except the dollar and authorized coinage of $3 gold pieces.

1858–60. The Panic of 1857 was followed by annual deficits, annual expenditures increasing to $74 million in 1858, with government credit at low ebb.

1861–65. CIVIL WAR led to the introduction of a variety of taxes. An **income tax,** for the first time, was enacted, 5 Aug. 1861; its rates (3% on incomes in excess of $800) increased in succeeding years. 31 Dec. 1861 government suspended specie payments. Internal revenue surpassed customs duties as a source of government revenue. By 1865 the income tax produced almost 20% of the total federal receipts, and the manufacturers' and sales taxes amounted to some 23%. However, the major portion of the war expenditures was financed by paper money issues and loans. In Aug. 1865 the public debt reached a peak of $2,845,900,000 (in excess of $75 per capita), while some $450 million of U.S. legal tender notes or "**greenbacks**" had been issued (authorized Feb. 1862).

1866–70. With certain exceptions, excise taxes were gradually removed and the inheritance tax expired in 1870. Yet revenue exceeded expenditures by $133 million, 1867. Most of the debt was converted into long-term bonds, and the greenbacks outstanding were moderately contracted to c.$356 million.

1871–74. The U.S. Treasury issued $26 million legal tender notes by purchasing bonds. The income tax expired in 1872.

1873. Fourth Coinage Act ("Crime of '73"), p. 299.

1875. Specie Resumption Act. Under this act the dollar became convertible into gold in 1879.

1875–93. Every single year showed an excess of revenue over expenditures (1881, $145 million). The major source of government income was customs duties unrelated to fiscal needs. In order not to drain off currency by retaining in the Treasury the mounting surpluses, the government applied the surplus to debt reduction at an unprecedented rate, the net debt falling to $839 million and the bonded debt from about $1,800 million to less than $600 million.

1878–94. The struggle to monetize silver—bimetallism (pp. 303, 304, 312)—**Bland-Allison Act,** 28 Feb. 1878 (p. 303), **Sherman Silver Purchase Act,** 14 July 1890 (p. 312), repealed 1 Nov. 1893 (p. 314).

1894. Federal revenue failed to exceed expenditures (deficit $61 million) for the first time since the Civil War. Income tax passed 1894 (declared unconstitutional 1895, p. 672).

1895–99. Each year showed a deficit, which rose to $89 million in 1899. The war with Spain created no serious fiscal problem, although borrowing constituted the major source of government receipts, with the deficit rising to only $127 million for the war period.

1900. Gold Standard Act (p. 317).

1900–13. Government expenditures increased, but frequently lagged behind revenue, with surpluses in 6 years and deficits in 7 years. The gross national debt was slightly reduced and the per capita debt fell from $16.60 to **$12.27.**

1913. 16th Amendment to Constitution authorized Congress to impose taxes on income (p. 326); an income tax was included in the Underwood Tariff (3 Oct. 1913, p. 713).

1914–16. Slightly heavier spending for military purposes increased the annual deficit to over $62 million in 1915.

1917–20. U.S. entry into World War I brought drastic tax increases. The largest revenue producer was the excess profits tax, yielding over $2 billion in 1918, in which year income taxes amounted to $663.1 million. Of the c.$35.5 billion expended, including $9 billion loans to the Allies, approximately 25% was raised by taxes, the rest by borrowing. Public debt rose from $1,300 million in Apr., 1917, to a peak exceeding $26 billion in Aug., 1919 (**$242** per capita).

1921–29. With "economy" the watchword of fiscal policy, tax reductions were effected, especially in the higher income brackets, and budgetary surpluses were applied to debt reduction. The national debt was reduced to $16 billion by 1930 (**$131** per capita). However, expenditures after World War I remained permanently higher than before the war, averaging in this period around $3 billion.

1931–32. Owing to falling revenues and declining incomes annual deficits occurred (1932, $2,529 million).

1933–36. In Mar. 1933 the gross national debt amounted to $20.9 billion. In 1936 it was in excess of $33 billion (**$263** per capita). Revenue rose ($3,-100 million, 1934, to $4,115 million, 1936), but expenditures mounted even more rapidly (from $6 billion, 1934, to $8,600 million, 1936). Relief expenditures constituted the largest single item in the "emergency" budgets. For **abandonment of gold standard** (19 Apr. 1933), see p. 405; **gold devaluation** (25 Oct. 1933), p. 409; and **silver purchase proclamation** (9 Aug. 1934), p. 412.

1937. With recovery under way, President Roosevelt's budget message recommended sharp reductions in expenditures in the expectation of a balanced budget; but the acute business slump in the latter part of the year brought about a resumption of government spending to combat the down trend: 1937, $8,177 million; 1938, $7,238 million.

1938–40. The public debt rose from $37 billion to $43 billion (**$325** per capita), while the launching of an armament program in 1940 presaged larger deficits in the future.

1940–45. U.S. expenditures, 1 July 1940–30 June 1946, **$370 billion.** Despite the heaviest taxation in U.S. history revenue amounted to only $169 billion. The Treasury borrowed the remainder. The national debt exceeded $258 billion (**$1,852.74** per capita), and

annual interest payments to maintain the debt structure exceeded $5 billion.

1946, 20 Feb. Employment Act (p. 614).

1946–52. Slight surpluses were recorded in 1947–48, but military and diplomatic exigencies brought a return of deficits: $1.8 billion (1949), $3.1 billion (1950), $4 billion (1952), $9.4 billion (1953). As a result of continuing high tax rates (1951 record receipts, $48.1 billion) the national public debt remained virtually stabilized at peak levels, with per capita debt, 1951, **$1,693.80**; total public debt, 30 June 1952, $259.1 billion.

1953–60. Total **budget expenditures** in billions: 74.2 (1953), 67.7 (1954), 64.5 (1955), 66.5 (1956), 69.4 (1957), 71.9 (1958), 80.6 (1959), 77.2 (1960). **Deficits** were incurred in 5 out of 8 years, 1953–60, rising to record for peacetime of $12,427 million (1959). **Public debt** of U.S. subject to statutory debt limit rose to $286.3 billion (1960).

1961. With the Kennedy administra-

SOURCES OF FEDERAL REVENUE
(U.S. Treasury, *Annual Report*, 1945 and U.S. Bureau of the Budget)

1800	%	1836	%	1845	%
Customs	82.7	Customs	45.9	Customs	91.85
Int. Rev.	7.5	Public lands	48.9	Public lands	6.9
All others	10.8	All others	5.2	All others	1.25

1890	%	1925	%	1945	%
Customs	61.7	Customs	14.4	Individ. income	39.9
Liquor & tobacco	38.0	Tobacco	9.1	Corp. income	10.2
All others	3.0	Individ. income	22.4	Excess profits	23.3
		Corp. income	24.2	Liquor	4.8
		Foreign debt	4.9	Tobacco	1.9
		Estate and gifts	2.9	All others	19.7
		All others	18.4		

1960	%	1972	%
Individ. income	44.0	Individ. income	45.4
Corporate income	23.2	Corporate income	15.4
Social ins. &		Social ins. &	
contributions	15.9	contributions	25.8
Excise tax	12.6	Excise tax	7.4
All others	4.2	All others	6.0

EXPENDITURES OF THE FEDERAL GOVERNMENT
(in percentages)

Purpose	1800	1836	1845	1890	1926
War Dept.	23.7	39.4	25.1	14.0	11.8
Navy Dept.	32.0	18.8	27.4	6.9	10.1
Interest on Public Debt	31.3	—	4.6	11.4	26.9
Veterans' Benefits*	.1	9.3	10.4	33.6	23.3
Other	12.9	32.5	32.5	34.1	27.9

	1945**	1960†	1972†
National Defense	82.5	49.8	33.8
International Affairs and Finance	3.4	3.3	1.6
Space Research and Technology	—	.4	1.5
Agriculture and Rural Development	1.6	3.6	3.0
Natural Resources and Environment		1.1	1.6
Commerce and Housing	4.0		
Commerce and Transportation		5.2	4.8
Labor and Welfare	1.1		
Community Development and Housing		1.0	1.8
Education and Manpower		1.4	4.2
Health			7.4
Income Security	***	20.3	28.0
Veterans' Benefits*	2.1	5.9	4.6
Interest on Public Debt	3.7	8.9	8.9
General Government	.9	1.4	2.1

* Includes only veterans' compensation and pensions 1880–90; all veterans' services and benefits 1926 +.
** Percentages do not add up to 100% because of rounding.
*** 1945 totals do not include transfer payments for social security, etc.; subsequent figures do.
† Percentages total over 100% because of intragovernmental transactions (−2.5% 1960; −3.4% 1970) and rounding.

tion economic growth became a prime object; a balanced budget was secondary.

1961–70. Unified Budget. Total budget receipts (in billions): $94.4 (1961); $99.7 (1962); $106.6 (1963); $112.7 (1964); $116.8 (1965); $130.9 (1966); $149.6 (1967); $153.7 (1968); $187.8 (1969); $193.8 (1970). Total budget outlays (in billions): $97.8 (1961); $106.8 (1962); $111.3 (1963); $118.6 (1964); $118.4 (1965); $134.6 (1966); $158.2 (1967); $178.8 (1968); $184.6 (1969); $196.6 (1970). With the exception of 1969, when the budget showed a surplus of $3.2 billion, in every year there were deficits, reaching $25.1 billion (1968), the largest deficit since 1943–45. The public debt of U.S. rose to $382.6 billion in 1970 (30 June).

Tax Reduction Act of 1964 (see p. 529) was designed to promote private demand and reduce unemployment, and it did so. The 10% tax surcharge of June 1968 was designed to slow spending and curb inflation but did not prove successful due in part to the overheating of the economy by high government military spending.

1971–73. Unified Budget. Budget receipts (in billions): $188.4 (1971); $208.6 (1972); $232.2 (1973). Budget outlays (in billions): $211.4 (1971); $231.9 (1972); $246.5 (1973). Deficits were recorded each year. Public debt rose (1973) to $458.1 billion.

Faced with high unemployment along with inflation (an unprecedented situation), **15 Aug. 1971,** President Nixon proposed tax changes designed to stimulate the economy, including repeal of the excise tax on automobiles, a tax credit on investment, and a reduction of income taxes on individuals. With some revisions, the president's proposals were enacted into law (1971, 10 Dec.). Nixon increased public spending. Fiscal policy continued to be expansionary in 1972, with the stimulus from rising expenditures. (See p. 752 for measures taken to try to cope with inflation.) **1972, 20 Oct.,** $5.2 billion **revenue-sharing bill** became law, providing for federal gov-

PER CAPITA NATIONAL DEBT

1790	(beginning of national govt.)	$19	1958		$1,630
1816	(after War of 1812)	15	1960		1,582
1866	(after Civil War)	78	1970		1,806
1919	(after World War I)	240	1973		2,177
1948	(after World War II)	1,720			

ernment grants to state and local governments. **1973:** expansionary fiscal policy
continued; 3 Dec. Bill extending the
debt limit to $475.7 billion (through
30 Dec. 1974) was sent to President
Nixon for signature. The former debt
ceiling of $465 billion expired midnight
30 Nov. and the ceiling had automatically reverted to $400 billion (the per-
manent statutory limit, set in 1971),
which was $64.9 billion below the
existing outstanding debt.

Banking and Capital Markets

To mobilize capital the corporate form began to be used on a limited scale in
the colonial period. America's first private commercial bank appeared in 1781.
National banking began with the first national bank (1791). The first security
exchange was organized that year. From 1812 onward, life insurance companies
and savings banks also provided for capital mobilization. The second national
bank was chartered for 20 years (1816–36) and when the charter expired it
was not renewed. Meanwhile, state banks began to proliferate. The period
between 1836 and the Civil War was characterized by a laissez-faire approach
to banking, moderated by some state regulations. The national banking acts
of 1863–65 attempted to provide a safer and uniform currency.

The post-Civil War years witnessed the rise in investment banking houses.
These promoted mergers in railroads, utilities, and industrials and provided
capital resources for expansion. Commercial banking also flourished, although
there was a high rate of bank failures. In 1913, the Federal Reserve System
was established to correct the deficiencies in the national banking acts and
state banking legislation. The Federal Reserve Act created the basis for
modern banking, developing payments mechanisms that made dollars anywhere
applicable to payments of dollar debts across the nation, influencing credit
availability, and providing a means by which the national government could
attempt to use monetary policy to correct business fluctuations. Hopefully, the
Federal Reserve would provide effective supervision of national banking.

The 1920s witnessed a rapid expansion of the securities market, the growth
of investment trusts, and bank consolidations. Bank failures persisted. Industrial
corporations served as important mobilizers of capital. With the crash, 1929–33,
bank failures soared. New Deal measures attempted to reform the banking
system and the securities market. The U.S. government also came to play a
more direct role in the extension of credit, a role enlarged during the war years.

From 1945 to 1973 commercial banking expanded, and branch banking
increased in importance; the bank holding company in the late 1960s and early
1970s took on new significance. The growth of life insurance firms and savings
and loan associations was rapid. Pension funds became increasingly important

as holders of personal savings. The stock market did not play as significant a role in corporate financing as it had in the 1920s. For nonfinancial corporate business, internal sources of finance (profits and depreciation) were in every year—from 1951 onward—greater than all external financing. Throughout, the Board of Governors of the Federal Reserve System sought to employ monetary policy to avoid sharp economic fluctuations; the controls of the Federal Reserve over the entire banking system were extended.

1607–1810. CORPORATE form of organization developed very slowly. Early joint-stock companies (each member liable for the obligations of the joint enterprise) were principally **nonprofit** corporations for religious worship, philanthropy, education, or **land companies.** Commercial corporations make their appearance with a Connecticut trading corporation (1723), a Massachusetts wharf company (1772), a number of early fire insurance (notably Philadelphia Contributionship, 1768) and water supply companies, and the United Co. of Philadelphia (1775), organized to promote manufactures. For the Massachusetts Land Bank (1740), see p. 702. During the period 1783–89 numerous corporations were organized for building roads, canals, and bridges, and for banking (the **Bank of North America,** chartered by Congress, 31 Dec. 1781, the first private commercial bank in the U.S., and the **Bank of New York** and the **Bank of Massachusetts,** 1784). Such banks were localized and limited in scope (an exception was Aaron Burr's **Manhattan Co.** [1799], chartered as a water company but with broad enough powers to permit banking), paying out their notes on loans, with customers mainly merchants and bank stock subscribers.

1791. 1ST BANK OF THE U.S. (p. 147) opened its main office at Philadelphia, 12 Dec. 1791. Its 8 branches, located in the principal commercial towns, acted as clearing agencies. The bank acted as fiscal agent for the government, its notes had general acceptance, and its specie holdings made it a bank of last resort.

STOCK EXCHANGES. The first securities exchange was informally organized at **Philadelphia,** 1791, followed, 1792, in **New York.** Both dealt mainly in federal "stock." Most **domestic** enterprise was financed by **local capital.** Local merchants and storekeepers maintaining open accounts were still important sources of commercial credit. **Foreign commerce,** in large proportion, was financed by British merchants extending liberal credit.

1801–11. EXPANSION OF STATE-CHARTERED BANKING. The number of state banks rose from 30 to 88, while their total capital increased about 3-fold. In Feb. 1811, Congress failed to recharter the Bank of the U.S. State-owned banks ("mixed" enterprises in which private banks owned stock) started in Vermont (c.1800) and reached their highest development in Indiana, Ohio, and Virginia.

1811–60. EXPANSION OF CORPORATE DEVICE. Limitation of liability, almost invariably conferred in the early charters, was made general by judicial decisions and statutes limiting the risks of investors (Massachusetts between 1809–30, general acceptance by 1856). Beginning with the New York law of 1811 general incorporation laws were substituted for the previous practice of negotiating with the state legislature for a charter. After the restraints of the Jacksonian period had been lifted (in New York by the Constitution of 1846), general incorporation laws became increasingly loose (especially in Delaware, Maryland, and later Nevada). Down to 1860 only a minority of corporations were in manufacturing; in Pennsylvania over 60% chartered, 1790–1860, were in transportation. By 1900, however, two thirds of all manufacturing was done by corporations, a percentage which rose to 69.2%, 1929.

1812–15. WAR OF 1812 induced a banking boom (120 new banks chartered).

1812–60. LIFE INSURANCE AND SAVINGS BANKS. Pennsylvania Co. for Insurance on Lives and Granting Annuities, first company specializing in life insurance, incorporated Philadelphia, 1812. Rapid development of life insurance companies after 1843. By 1860, $160 million life insurance in force. First incorporated savings bank chartered, Boston, 1816; New York, Baltimore, and Philadelphia inaugurated policy of paying interest on deposits (1819). Total savings deposits: 1835, $7 million; 1850, $43 million; 1860, $150 million (278 savings banks).

1816–18. 2ND BANK OF THE U.S. (p. 184), chartered, Apr. 1816, as a result of the efforts of **Alexander J. Dallas, Stephen Girard** (1750–1831), and **John Jacob Astor** to aid government fiscal operations and support government securities, functioned, as did its predecessor, as a central bank. Under the direction of **William Jones** (1760–1831), a Republican politician, the bank was mismanaged and came close to bankruptcy.

1819–22. Administration of **Langdon Cheves** of South Carolina, second president of the Bank of the U.S., pursued a conservative and restrictive policy, restoring the bank to a sound condition.

1820–40. RAPID EXPANSION OF STATE BANKS to meet demand for loans of persons without capital or credit resulted in basic weaknesses: (1) lack of adequate specie reserve to redeem bank notes; (2) legal office for redemption purposely located in inaccessible spots ("wildcat banks").

1823–36. BIDDLE AND THE BANK. On the resignation (fall 1823) of Cheves, **Nicholas Biddle** succeeded to the presidency. During his regime the bank's operations and influence were aggressively expanded. Bank notes issued, 1823, averaged $4.5 million; 1831, $19 million. The bank advanced necessary loans to the U.S. government and made credit and currency more abundant in the West and South. The bank's expansion of operations in domestic exchange led to the rise of documentary bills rivaling the promissory note as a type of short-term commercial paper. Such short-term paper in effect provided the nation with an "elastic" currency. However, after 1832 the bank sought to check inflation and contributed markedly to the business contraction which occurred (pp. 213, 747). The bank's federal charter expired, 1836.

1825–40. "SUFFOLK SYSTEM," in full operation by 1825, by the Suffolk Bank, Boston (founded 1818), required country banks to keep deposits in the Suffolk Bank to insure honoring their notes. Result: discount on country bank notes disappeared. A similar system was set up by the Metropolitan Bank of New York (1851). However, this system of *de facto* clearing houses did not operate on a nationwide basis until the establishment of the National Banking System, 1863 (p. 285). In this period country banks began depositing surplus funds with correspondent banks in leading financial centers. In 1840 bankers' balances held by New York City banks reached nearly $8 million. These funds were increasingly concentrated (1857–72) in 6 or 7 out of a total of 50 banks (M. G. Myers).

1829. Safety Fund Act of New York, passed for the protection of bank creditors, established the principles of (1) insurance and (2) control by bank commissioners.

1830–40. NEW YORK'S FINANCIAL PREEMINENCE. New York Stock Exchange passed Philadelphia in volume of trading, beginning with the 1820s with the successful flotation of Erie Canal bonds. With the expiration of the Second Bank's charter, New York also supplanted Philadelphia in the commercial credit field. Other trends: Boston Stock Exchange, 1834, facilitated security transactions of New England manufacturing companies. The **Anglo-American merchant bankers,** a group of British houses led by Baring Bros. & Co., floated large issues of state bonds for internal improvements. Until the 1830s lotteries were also extensively used for this purpose; prohibited by state laws, 1821–33. By this period commercial credit dealing had become a major phase of banking, with rates on commercial paper quoted regularly in leading financial journals.

1837–48. PANIC OF 1837 (p. 213) and the wholesale failures of state banks with deposits of federal funds led to the establishment of the **Independent Treasury** on 4 July 1840; repealed 13 Aug. 1841, but reenacted in Aug. 1846. As a number of states repudiated their maturing obligations, American credit suffered abroad and foreign capital was curtailed.

1838. N.Y. FREE BANKING ACT introduced competition in the banking field by no longer requiring special legislation to obtain a charter. However, the state law required banks to keep a specie reserve of 12.5% against note issues. Louisiana, 1842, and Massachusetts, 1858, introduced similar reserve requirements.

1841. Establishment by Lewis Tappan of the Mercantile Agency, the first credit-rating agency, which became Dun & Co., 1859; Bradstreet's est. 1855.

1847–48. U.S. government loans for the War with Mexico were handled by Corcoran & Riggs, Washington, D.C., outbidding New York firms.

1849–60. INVESTMENT OPERATIONS. Renewed foreign investments, particularly in railroads, raised U.S. foreign indebtedness (p. 734). Nevertheless, the U.S. money market had now become the chief source of capital funds. Out of a total exceeding $2 billion of corporate securities outstanding, 1860, **over three fourths** were owned by Americans. The expansion of security dealings led to the rise of "investment houses," particularly in New York, as well as brokerage firms, and firmly established the preeminent position in security trading of the New York Stock Exchange.

1853, Oct. Establishment of New York Clearing House formalized clearing operations. (Clearing houses also established at Boston, 1855; Philadelphia, Baltimore, and Cleveland, 1856.)

1857. PANIC OF 1857. Bankers' balances held in New York City surged from $17 million, 1850, to over $30 million. The withdrawal of balances during the fall, coupled with the failure of the Ohio Life Insurance and Trust Co., precipitated a panic (p. 265), during which specie payments were temporarily suspended.

1862. Employing new retail marketing techniques and stressing patriotic appeal, **Jay Cooke** successfully floated U.S. Civil War loan.

1863–65. National banking legislation (1863–64, p. 285) bore a striking resemblance to the New York Free Banking Act, but provided a safer currency. With the first national bank organized at Philadelphia by Jay Cooke, 20 June 1863, some 450 banks were established by 1863, of which one third constituted former state banks. The enactment, 1865, of a prohibitory tax on state bank note issues (p. 285) forced an additional 700 state banks to become national banks and brought about a **uniform currency** (national bank notes).

1869, 24 SEPT. Black Friday (p. 298).

1873. The failure of Jay Cooke & Co. contributed to the increased prominence in the investment banking field of the house of **J. P. Morgan** (associated with the Drexels since 1871). The practice now emerged of bankers demanding a share in management control before granting credit (financing of N.Y. Central R.R., 1879, although the general practice was not conspicuous until the 1890s). Concentration of bankers' balances in a few New York banks continued (Sprague), making possible the development of the **call loan market.** For Panic of 1873, see p. 748. Bank suspensions, 1873–75: 104 (17 national, 87 state).

1879–90. Investment bankers undertook a larger share of railroad financing, as they began to exert influence on management and to promote combinations.

1891–1900. Investment bankers promoted consolidations in the railroad, utility, and industrial field. Bank suspensions, 1893: 491 (69 national). State-chartered **trust companies** rose from 251 to 290, with their investments increasing from $192 million to $326 million.

1901–12. TRUST COMPANY EXPANSION: number, 6-fold; capital, 4-fold; investments, $1.5 billion.

1907–8. Bank suspensions, which had averaged 100 a year, rose to well over 200 in the years of the depression.

1913. FEDERAL RESERVE SYSTEM established (p. 326) to remedy defects of the National Banking System: inelasticity of the currency; need for a "lender of last resort" to come to the aid of commercial banks when there was a drain on reserves (demonstrated by Panic of 1907).

1914–18. Financing World War I. Investment market handled unprecedented volume of securities, including loans to Allies (nearly $2 billion by 1916), as well as **Liberty Loans,** which encouraged widespread public acquaintance with security issues.

1917–20. Modifications of Federal Reserve System: (1) Federal Reserve banks authorized to issue Federal Reserve Notes on the basis of gold as well as discounted paper; (2) gold reserves of Reserve banks raised from approximately $600 million to nearly $1,300. The effort of the Federal Reserve Board to hold down interest rates had an inflationary impact.

1921–29. Corporations increasingly applied their earnings to satisfying capital needs, adopting a conservative dividend policy. The expansion of the securities market and the rapid growth of **investment trusts** led to bypassing established investment bankers. The business practices of reducing accounts outstanding, and stressing smaller inventories and rapid turnover, left commercial banks with idle funds. The volume of **call loans** on security collateral dangerously expanded, and commercial banks branched into other fields—real estate, time-deposit banking, and investment banking through investment affiliates. This period is also noted for large banking consolidations and the spread of branch banking. Bank failures totaled 5,411.

1929–33. Following the initial phase of stock market decline and leveling off of industrial production, European financial stringency (p. 384) led to large withdrawals from the U.S. of foreign bank deposits. Decline of agricultural prices led to farm mortgage deterioration, with rapid increase in the mortality of country banks in 1930 and the undermining of the whole rural credit structure, 1931–32. Liquidation of collateral by banks caused a demoralization of security values. **Bank suspensions, 1929–33: 9,765** (member, 2,391), or over a third of all banks.

1933–39. For New Deal reforms relating to banking and capital markets including deposit insurance, see pp. 404–411. New Deal banking legislation forced investment bankers to choose between deposit banking and underwriting. Between 1934–39, 20 New York City investment firms managed 78.6% of securities registered with the SEC, with **Morgan, Stanley & Co.** in first position. The U.S. government, especially through the medium of the RFC (p. 400) and various farm and mortgage credit agencies (pp. 401–422), became increasingly a supplier of capital funds for long and short terms, and Treasury officials largely supplanted the Federal Reserve Board as formulators of credit policy.

1940–45. The war years were marked by an enormous expansion of the government's role as supplier of capital needs. On 25 June 1940 the RFC was authorized to make loans for acquiring, producing, or stockpiling strategic raw materials and for constructing, expanding, and operating plants. Under an executive order of 26 Mar. 1942 the government began to guarantee or participate in loans made by banks to finance war production. By 31 Dec. 1945, Federal Reserve banks had executed 7,999 agreements for credits, totaling $9.9 billion, 80% of which were loans of $1 million and above. The Smaller War Plants Corp. was set up by the government to provide funds for small businesses with war contracts; its functions were taken over by the RFC in 1945. As a result of the government's desire to issue its securities at low interest, the Federal Reserve Board acted as an agency to support the bond market, and temporarily abdicated control over the money market.

1946–60. NEW INVESTMENT TRENDS. As a result of a marked increase in the assets of life insurance companies (500% by 1938 over 1910; by 1948, assets of legal reserve companies, $56 billion), such companies began to purchase whole issues of securities direct from the borrowing corporation in competition with investment bankers. Other corporations, owing to high taxes, proceeded to finance themselves out of profits in lieu of increasing dividends. In decade of 1950s investment companies, notably **mutual funds,** greatly expanded, with the number of shareholders exceeding 2.5 million (1960). Savings-bank deposits rose from $63.2 billion (31 Dec. 1952) to $100.8 billion (31 Dec. 1959); life insurance in force, $276 billion (1 Jan. 1953), $542 billion (1 Jan. 1960). Commercial banks in 1946 held 70% of the assets of the 4 major financial intermediaries—commercial banks, life insurance companies, savings and loan associations, and mutual savings banks; in 1955, they held only 54%. The competition from the so-called nonbank intermediaries was thus severe. 1956, 9 May, Bank Holding Company Act made it unlawful for any bank holding company to acquire bank stocks or take certain other actions without prior approval of the Federal Reserve System. Bank holding companies were required to divest themselves of interests in nonbanking organizations with certain specified exceptions.

Stock Market. Prices rose on the stock market; in 1954, the market passed its

1929 Dow-Jones high of 381.17; the bull market of the 1950s bore some resemblance to the 1920s market, *except* (1) with new margin requirements, stock trading was mainly in cash and thus the exchange was a relatively minor force in the money market and (2) since capital requirements of business were financed primarily from internal sources (profits and depreciation), the market did not play the role in corporate financing that it had in the 1920s. Mutual funds, trusts, pension funds, insurance portfolios, and foundations became important in the 1950s market; in 1949, such institutions held $9.5 billion in New York Stock Exchange securities; by the end of 1960 the figure was $70.5 billion; institutional holdings had risen from 12.5% to 20% of all equities.

Rising Interest Rates. To meet the record-breaking expansion of credit and bank loans (beg. fall 1950), the Federal Reserve Board increased bank reserve requirements (1951). 1951 accord between the Federal Reserve and Treasury gave the former independence in policy-making; the Federal Reserve was relieved of the responsibility to support government securities at a set price. U.S. government bonds sold below par for the first time in more than a decade, with long-term interest rates showing a tendency to rise. As an anti-inflationary step, bank rates on loans rose gradually in the 1950s—short-term business loans (average) from 2.7% (1950) to 5% (1959), the highest level in 28 years.

1960–73. TRENDS IN BANKING included: (1) Decline of the unit bank and increase in branch banking. 1960, the number of banks exceeded the number of branches (13,472 banks; 10,472 branches). 1966, branch bank offices accounted for almost 65% of total banking offices, and branch banks controlled almost 70% of the country's banking re-

sources. 1972, 31 Dec., 13,928 commercial banks, which had 24,414 branches and offices. (2) Increase in bank holding companies. In 1960 there were 42 bank holding companies and most of the major ones were organized between 1925 and 1930. They had 1,463 offices (6% of all commercial bank offices) and controlled c.8% of the deposits in commercial banks. The number rose in the 1960s, especially after a 1966 amendment to the Bank Holding Company Act of 1956. Then, under the authority granted by a 1970 amendment to that act, the Federal Reserve permitted bank holding companies to engage in a wider range of activities. 1972, 31 Dec., 1,607 bank holding companies owned 2,720 banks and 13,441 branches, a total of 42.1% of the nation's banking offices; they controlled 61.5% of total commercial bank deposits and 63.2% of total commercial bank assets; (3) commercial banks gave competition to nonbank intermediaries, offering full-service banking; (4) banking became more international, as banks established foreign branches, subsidiaries, and affiliates. 1968–73, American banks joined with foreign banks of industrial nations to participate in consortia, to create specialized institutions for Eurodollar lending, in part a response to the vast development of multinational industrial enterprises (p. 732). (5) The Federal Re-

LARGEST U.S. COMMERCIAL BANKS
(includes banks with deposits over $20 billion, 6/30/73)

Name	Deposits 6/30/73 (in billions)
Bank of America, S.F.	$36.86
First National City, N.Y.	29.55
Chase Manhattan, N.Y.	26.18

serve Board played an increasingly active role in monetary policy, concerning itself with the growth of the stock of money, with counter-cyclical responses to credit conditions, and with the outflow of gold (p. 710).

Interest Rates. Despite declines in 1960–61, 1967, 1970–72, the trend was upward. 3-month treasury bills, 1960, 2.9%; 1973 (Oct.), 7.2%; 3–5 year government securities issues, 1960, 3.5%; 1973 (Oct.), 6.8%; prime commercial paper, 4–6 months, 1960, 3.5%; 1973 (Oct.), 8.9% (the rate reached a new peak in Sept., 10.23%). FHA mortgages, 1960, 6.2%; 1973 (Oct.), 9%. 1973, with high interest rates and inflation combined, the efficacy of monetary policy was subject to numerous questions.

Life Insurance and Pensions. Life insurance became a principal private absorber of savings. In 1972 total life insurance in force was $1,628 billion; assets of life insurance companies equaled $240 billion. The investments of such insurance companies included corporate securities ($113 billion), mortgages ($77 billion), and government securities ($11 billion). Private pension funds multiplied; unlike insurance companies, which were subject to state regulations, the pension funds were not regulated. In 1959 Congress passed the Welfare and Pension Fund Disclosure Act, which required pension funds to register with the U.S. Department of Labor; by 1972, 34,000 such funds had registered. The law established no rules or checks, or provisions for insurance and safety, of the pension funds. By 1972, c.$135 billion in assets had accumulated in private pension plans.

Stock Market. Sharp gyrations characterized the stock market, especially in 1962 and 1973. In 1960, the Dow-Jones range had been between 560 and 685; in 1962, the Dow-Jones index slumped to 535. 1973, 11 Jan., it reached a new high of 1,050, only to drop as low as 788 (5 Dec.). Between 26 Oct. and 5 Dec. the market fell 198¾ points—the largest point decline in any 3 months of market history. (But the drop was only 20.1% compared with the 193-point decline of 50.6% in 1929.) The decline was associated with the energy crisis and general economic uncertainty. In 1960–73, as in the 1950s, with capital requirements in large part—always over 50%—financed from internal sources (profits and depreciation) and with the margin requirements, the market gyrations did not have the economic consequences of the collapse of 1929. In 1960, est. gross proceeds from new corporate issues totaled $10.15 billion; in 1972, $41.96 billion. Such proceeds went as high as $46.02 billion in 1971. In the early 1970s, the small investor got out of the market; in 1970, an estimated 30% of U.S. families owned stock; in 1973, 21%. In 1972, 17% of the families in a Harris Poll survey said they would probably or certainly buy stock in the next 6 months; in 1973, the figure was down to 8%. Institutions, pension funds, insurance portfolios, mutual funds, trusts, foundations, dominated the market; the sharp fluctuations of 1973 were blamed on institutional trading of large blocks of stock.

Business Cycles and Price Trends

Economic fluctuations (business cycles) have characterized American economic history. Each business cycle has a trough, a peak, and a trough. Until the depression of the 1930s, in the main market forces acted to correct the ups and downs of the economy. From the 1930s onward, the U.S. government played a major role in pursuing countercyclical policies (that is, in times of downturn to promote recovery; in times of inflation to try to dampen it). Countercyclical measures include fiscal, monetary, and incomes policies. In post-World War II years such policies were successful in that a downturn of the severity of the 1930s has not occurred; cyclical fluctuations have been moderated. On the other hand, the policies have not been effective in curbing the inflationary spiral. But the efficacy of government policies has been severely challenged during recession-inflation (stagflation) which began toward the end of 1972.

For most of U.S. history, prices have risen in wartime and then dropped; indeed, in 1790 and 1900, the price levels were about the same; the price level was actually higher in 1800 than in 1900. In the 20th century, prices rose during World War I, declined in the 1930s (but not below the 1900 level) and then climbed with World War II, the Korean War, the Vietnam War, and continued upward.

1760. Peak of the French and Indian War boom. CP[1]: **79.**

1762–65. Low point of business slump early 1765. CP: 1762, **87**; 1765, **72**; 1766, **73.**

1768. Currency contraction precipitated a business slump, especially acute

DURATION OF MAJOR DEPRESSIONS
(Sachs-Thorp)

Years	Months' duration
1762–65	36
1768–69	12
1772–75	30
1784–88	**44**
1796–98	36
1802–03	24
1807–09	27
1815–21	**71**
1825–26	13
1833–34	9
1837–43	**72**
1857–58	18
1866–67	18
1873–78	**66**
1882–85	36
1890–91	9
1893–97	**48**
1907–08	12
1913–14	20
1920–21	18
1929–33	**42**
1937–38	10

1. CP represents commodity prices down to 1860, based on Warren-Pearson wholesale price index for all commodities, New York—1910–14 = 100.

in New York and Philadelphia. CP: **74.**

1770–71. The termination of nonimportation agreements, combined with rising prices and favorable exchange rates, fostered speculation and large importations of British goods. CP: 1770, **77**; 1772, **89.**

1772. The British banking crisis of the summer, with the ensuing credit contraction, brought widespread inventory liquidation and distress to colonial importers.

1773–75. Business sagged. CP: 1773, **84**; 1775, **75.**

1776–83. The American Revolution produced a business boom, with a sharp price rise caused in large measure by sizable emissions of paper money and deficit financing. CP: 1776, **86**; 1779, **226**; 1781, **216** (in depreciated currency the percentage rise was far greater).

1784–88. Excessive importations of British goods after the war, combined with an unstable currency and fiscal situation, set off a downturn, with the British banking crisis of 1784 precipitating a sharp deflation in the U.S. Although the business decline was arrested in the course of 1787, the drop in commodity prices was not halted until late 1788. CP: 1785, **92**; 1789, **86** (Bezanson, Philadelphia prices, puts decline at c.30% for same period).

1789–1800. While previous business fluctuations were mainly associated with external factors, cyclical factors inherent in business now became faintly discernible. Except for a minor recession, 1796–98, the period was one of substantial prosperity. The European wars created a large demand for U.S. farm commodities and shipping. Prices climbed steadily until 1797. CP: 1790, **90**; 1797, **131**; 1800, **129**.

1801–02. The peace of Amiens halted the war boom. CP: 1801, **142**; 1802, **117**.

1803–07. Another wave of prosperity followed renewal of the European war, only to be terminated by the Embargo Act, 22 Dec. 1807. CP: 1804, **126**; 1806, **134**; 1807, **130**.

1808–09. Depression spread inland, followed by revival, 1810–11. CP: 1810, **131**.

1812–14. The War of 1812 curbed foreign trade, but most other branches of economic activity enjoyed an uneven war boom, with manufacturing especially benefiting by the curtailment of British imports and the South depressed, 1813–14. Heavy government borrowing stimulated banking expansion. CP: 1813, **162**; 1814, **182**.

1815–21. Resumption of importations hurt U.S. manufacturing, but the downtrend was checked by European demand for American farm staples. As farm commodities soared and bank credit was liberalized, a wave of land speculation occurred. CP: 1815, **170**. However, with the collapse of foreign markets prices broke in the fall (1819) (CP: **125**), land values sank rapidly, and numerous banks and mercantile houses failed in

the **first major banking crisis** in U.S. history, with general business depressed until 1822. CP: 1821, **102**; 1822, **106**.

1823–34. Slow business recovery with minor fluctuations (downturns, 1825–26, 1833–early 34). CP ranged from **103** down to **95**. The recession of 1833 resulted from the removal of government deposits from the Second Bank of the U.S., with subsequent credit curtailment by the bank (pp. 213, 740).

1834–36. Brisk business activity returned by the spring of 1834. Land speculation was fostered by (1) a boom in canal and railroad building, (2) the transfer of U.S. deposits to state banks, (3) an inflow of foreign capital. The Specie Circular (July 1836, p. 211) resulted in a sharp downturn in land sales by the latter part of that year. CP: 1834, **90**; 1836, **114**.

1837. The collapse in real estate was followed in the 2d quarter of 1837 by a precipitate fall in stock and commodity prices and an acute banking crisis attributed to (1) Specie Circular; (2) distribution legislation of 1836, leading to government drafts on state banks; (3) high interest rates and calling in of loans by British bankers; (4) crop failures in 1835 and 1837; (5) mounting state debts; (6) unfavorable balance of trade which increased flow of specie to Europe. CP: 1838, **110**.

1838–43. The decline was briefly halted in 1838 as business activity appeared to be building toward a secondary boom, but a major break came in 1839 when the Bank of the U.S., now a Pennsylvania-chartered bank, closed its doors after an unsuccessful attempt to sustain cotton prices. The crisis was followed by a protracted depression, with its low point near Feb. 1843. CP: 1839, **112**; 1843, **75**.

1844–48. Gradual recovery with mild fluctuations. CP: 1848, **82**.

1849–56. A marked expansion of business fed in part by the inflow of foreign (particularly British) capital, which revived railroad building, and by the discovery of gold in California, which facilitated payments of international balances, stimulated foreign trade, and encouraged loans by domestic banks. Prosperity was briefly interrupted by a panic on the New York Stock Exchange in the fall of 1854. CP: 1850, **84;** 1854, **108;** 1855, **110;** 1856, **105.**

1857–58. The failure of the Ohio Life Insurance and Trust Co. (Aug.) touched off a sharp, though shortlived, financial panic, basically caused by overspeculation in railroad securities and real estate. CP: 1857, **111;** 1858, **93.**

1859–65. Recovery set in quickly, with prosperity continuing until the outbreak of the Civil War. Business wavered with the coming of war (1861), but heavy government spending and an inflationary price rise produced a war boom. The collapse of currency and finance in the Confederacy (Mar. 1865) brought temporary chaos to the South. CP[2]: 1861, **61.3;** 1862, **71.7;** 1863, **90.5;** 1864, **116;** 1865, **132.**

1866–72. Postwar readjustment (1866–67) brought little distress to the North as a railroad boom steadily gained momentum; violent stock market fluctuations, mainly the result of speculative activity, had only a limited nationwide impact. Most spectacular incident was "Black Friday," 24 Sept. 1869 (p. 298). CP: 1868, **97.7;** 1870, **86.7.**

1873–78. The failure of the banking house of Jay Cooke and Co., 18 Sept. 1873, revealed the weakened speculative structure resultant upon overextension in railroad securities. With bankruptcies among banks and brokers multiplying, prices fell precipitately, as did national income. CP: 1874, **81.0;** 1879, **58.8.** SP[3]: 1872, **39.8;** 1877, **24.8.**

1873–96. Economists not infrequently characterize this period as a "long-wave" depression. The price level declined steadily (CP: 1885, **56.6;** 1896, **46.5),** with only 8 partly or wholly prosperous years. Nevertheless, vigorous business upswings occurred, with enormous extension of investment in industrial plants and equipment. Recovery began in 1878 and continued until 1882, when a depression, 1883–85, primarily financial in origin, occurred, followed by quick recovery again, 1885–90, a short recession (1890–91), then a further upturn particularly in heavy industry (1892). The failure of the Philadelphia and Reading R.R. and the National Cordage Co. early in 1893 gave warning that the boom was over. Uncertainty over the status of the gold standard was a further depressing factor as foreign investors proceeded to sell U.S. securities, capital left the country, the reserve fell, and wholesale liquidation was set in motion. Before 1893 had ended, 491 banks and over 15,000 commercial institutions were reported to have failed. Before the turning point was reached by 1897, almost one third of the total railroad mileage was in the hands of receivers. SP: 1892, **43.9;** 1896, **33.5.**

1897–1914. Recovery followed rapidly, with relative continuing prosperity save for brief financial crises in 1903 and 1907, a recession, 1910–11, and a downturn on the eve of World War I (1913–14). CP: 1897, **46.6;** 1900, **56.1;** 1910, **70.4;** 1913, **69.8.** SP: 1897, **35.2;** 1912, **75.5,** with a decline, 1913–14, to **63.8.**

1914–19. A financial reaction following the outbreak of war was succeeded by a war boom fed by Allied orders. The peak of business activity was reached

2. After 1860, CP is based on wholesale price index, all commodities, Bureau of Labor Statistics (1926 = 100).

3. Index of Common Stock Prices, all stocks (1926 = 100) U.S. Bureau of the Census, *Hist. Stat. of U.S., 1789–1945.*

EFFECT OF U.S. WARS ON WHOLESALE PRICES, 1770-1972*

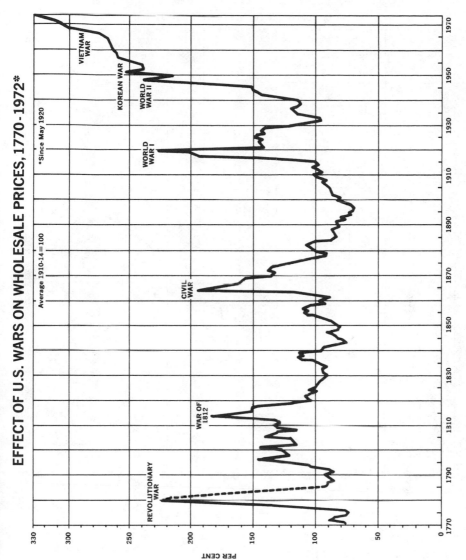

*From *Our National Debt*, prepared by the Committee on Economic Policy, copyright, 1949, by Harcourt, Brace and Company, Inc. and *Statistical Abstract*, 1960; *Economic Report of the President*, 1973.

CONSUMER PRICE INDEX: 1913-1973

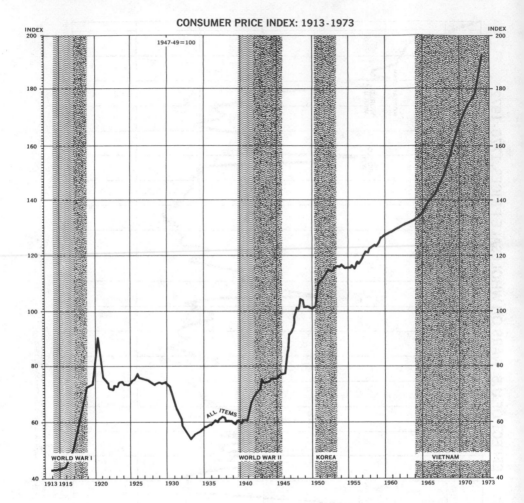

in 1916, and sustained by America's participation in the war. Temporary hesitation after the Armistice gave way to soaring prices, sales, and production, resulting from credit expansion and speculation in inventories. CP: 1916, **85.5**; 1917, **117.5**; 1918, **131.3**; 1919, **138.8**. SP: 1914, **63.8**; 1920, **64.2**.

1920–21. Sharp deflation after May 1920. CP: 1920, **154.5**; 1921, **97.6**; 1922, **96.7**.

1922–29. A rising tide of prosperity was sustained by conspicuous expansion of the consumers' durable goods industry. A boom in construction and real estate also developed (**Florida real estate boom** collapsed in 1926). By 1927 residential construction, auto output, purchases of consumers' durable goods, and new investment in producers' durable goods had begun to decline; but the boom continued, fed almost entirely by **unprecedented securities speculation not reflected in commodity prices.** CP: 1923, **100.6**; 1929, **95.3**, as contrasted with SP: 1922, **67.7**; 1929, **190.3**. The spectacular crash of stock prices occurred in Oct.–Nov. 1929.

1930–33. The depression deepened despite efforts to ease money market and extend credits (pp. 399, 727). Low point of depression: **Mar. 1933**, with industrial production rising 15%, July–Oct. 1932, but declining sharply by Mar. 1933 as the **banking crisis** deepened and bank holidays blanketed the nation. Industrial output almost halved, unemployment mounted to about 15 million, one third of the nation's railroad mileage was thrown into bankruptcy, and farm mortgage foreclosures were widespread. CP: 1930, **86.4**; 1931, **73.0**; 1932, **64.8**; 1933, **65.9**. SP: 1930, **149.8**; 1932, **48.6**.

1933–37. New Deal intervention to halt the downward spiral took a variety of forms (pp. 403–422), including **deficit financing.** Business activity and

prices rose. SP: 1934, **72.4**; 1937, **111.8**.

1935–37. The business recovery was interrupted by a brief, but acute, recession, Aug. 1937. CP: 1935, **80**; 1937, **86.3**.

1938–39. Deficit financing on an increasing scale contributed to recovery. Yet in Aug. 1939, about 10 million persons were still unemployed. Based on 1929 national income of $81 billion, the estimated loss of national income, 1930–38, totaled $132,600,000,000 (TNEC *Hearings*). CP: 1938, **78.6**; 1939, **77.1**.

1939–45. The outbreak of World War II in Europe was followed by a sudden spurt in economic activity. The index of industrial production standing at **105** (1935–39 = 100) in Aug. 1939 leaped to **125** in Dec., with unemployment falling 10%. By 1940 the effects of the U.S. military program were being felt in government expenditures, industrial output, and national income. The entry of the U.S. into the war brought large-scale mobilization of manpower and resources, with economic activity making giant strides. Peak levels were attained by 1944–45. The index of industrial production by 1944 reached **235**, and national income increased 2½ times. Despite wartime price and wage controls (p. 451) wholesale CP rose from **78.6** (1940) to **105.8** (1945).

CURRENCY IN CIRCULATION
(Hist. Statistics of U.S.)

1932	$5,695,171,000
1940	7,847,501,000
1945	26,746,438,000
1957	31,081,913,000

1946–60. The inflationary upturn was accelerated by the removal of government economic controls, deferred postwar demand, and financing (in part deficit) for defense and foreign expenditures.

BOOM AND RECESSION. Period of general business expansion interrupted by 4 recessions: (1) 1948–49, decline in gross national product from $259.4 billion (1948) to $258.1 billion (1949), chiefly as a result of shift in inventory accumulation; unemployment reached 3.4 million in 1949; (2) 1953–54, resulting from inventory liquidation and decline in federal expenditures for defense purposes, with 3.7 million persons unemployed by spring of 1954, and decline of gross national product from $364.9 billion (1953) to $356 billion (1954); (3) 1957–1958, resulting from overexpansion of plant capacity and drop in exports, with durable goods production chiefly hit; followed by rapid recovery until steel strike (15 July 1959); (4) beginning midsummer 1960, accompanied by falling off of demand for steel (below 40% capacity, Jan. 1961), autos, and appliances. Unemployment rose contraseasonally to 4 million (Nov. 1960) and est. 5.25 million (Jan. 1961). CP (1947–49 = 100) continued to rise, from 83.4 (1946) to 114.4 (1953) to 127.4 (Nov. 1960), with especially sharp increases in cost of housing, apparel, transportation, and medical care. (Care went from 90.6, 1947, to 155.0, Mar. 1960.)

Business cycle peak and trough dates (as determined by the National Bureau of Economic Research): **troughs:** Oct. 1945, Oct. 1949, Aug. 1954, Apr. 1958, Feb. 1961, Nov. 1970; **peaks:** Nov. 1948, July 1953, July 1957, May 1960, Nov. 1969, Nov. 1973.

1961–68. PROSPERITY. Period of increasing prosperity and high employment marked by moderate price rises (1958–65) and balance of payments problems. The gross national product reached $864 billion (1968). Corporate profits increased after taxes to $47.8 billion (1968). Profits before taxes, $87.6 billion (1968). The seasonally adjusted unemployment rate of 3.3% (Dec. 1968) was the lowest since the Korean War: 75.4 million employed, 2.45 million unemployed.

Balance of payments problems eased in 1968 (p. 710), although the surplus of exports over imports, $726 million, was the lowest since 1937.

The consumer price index rose 6% (1968) to 148.6 (1947–49 = 100), the worst inflationary year since the Korean War, as the high rate of federal spending overheated the economy. Wage increases in major industries (1968), involving 3.4 million workers, amounted to 7.5%, not including fringe benefits and cost of living increases.

1969–73. INFLATION. The inflationary spiral continued upward; at the same time, the rate of unemployment rose from 3.5% of all workers (1969), to 4.9% (1970), 5.9% (1971), and rose steeply by 1974 to 7.1%. Fiscal and monetary policy steps to curb inflation also tended to raise unemployment. In 1969, the administration, seeking to control inflation, attempted to hold back economic expansion. By the end of 1969 and early 1970, the rise in demand had slowed and output fell. Policy goals then aimed at expansion. Recovery was impeded by a long strike at General Motors at the end of 1970. 1971 saw output begin to mount. 1971, 15 Aug., Nixon imposed a 90-day freeze on prices, wages, and rents to try to halt inflation. The freeze was followed (14 Nov.) with **Phase II,** a broad, mandatory system of controls, directed by a Price Commission and a Pay Board, under the general coordination of a Cost of Living Council (CLC). Concurrently, Nixon took steps to stimulate the economy with an eye to increasing employment. 1972 was the first peacetime year in American history of national, general price and wage controls; despite them, consumer prices continued to rise (see p. 750). Food prices that were excluded from the controls rose most rapidly. 1973, 11 Jan., the more permissive **Phase III** was announced; prices spurted upward and 5 months later (13 June) **Phase III½** — a new freeze was imposed; this lasted until 18 July, when **Phase IV** began with restraints in between those of Phases II and III. In Phase IV, companies could raise prices as long as the increase did not exceed the average rise set by the CLC. Prices continued to climb. Nov.–Dec.; the energy crisis created new higher prices.

1960–73. GROWTH OF MONEY STOCK.

CURRENCY PLUS DEMAND DEPOSITS
Averages of daily figures in billions of dollars

1960, Dec.	$141.7
1965, Dec.	168.0
1970, Dec.	214.8
1972, Dec.	246.9 (prel.)

1972–75. STAGFLATION. The inflationary spiral was joined by a recession. Real economic growth declined approximately 2% in 1974 while inflation continued at about 12%. 7.1% of the workforce was unemployed by the end of 1974. New car sales dropped off approximately 35% and new housing construction dropped nearly 40%. The net loss of the stock market was approximately 28% (1974); largely recouped by 30 June 1975.

Labor, Slavery, and Social Reform

In preindustrial America the labor force comprised slaves, bound, and free labor. White bound labor gradually died out, in large part the result of insolvency and bankruptcy laws ending imprisonment for debt. The American Revolution proved a fillip to ending slavery, either immediately or by gradual stages, in most of the Northern states, but the "peculiar institution" remained the basis of plantation labor in the South as that region gradually shifted to cotton cultivation for a world market. While the Civil War and the 13th Amendment brought about the abolition of slavery throughout the United States, the black farm population, through sharecropping, tenancy, and peonage, remained for more than a generation thereafter in a semi-servile condition.

While sporadic strikes by free white labor took place in colonial and Revolutionary times, it was not until the post-Revolutionary and early National periods that more permanent trade unions appeared, notably in such skilled trades as the cordwainers, printers, and house carpenters. Moving from individual unions to city centrals in the Age of Jackson, the roots of national trade unions were nurtured in the 1850s, and assumed a large significance in post–Civil War industrial society.

Before the Civil War the amelioration of laboring conditions was closely tied to the reform movement. That movement pressed for an end to imprisonment for debt, prison reform, public education, temperance, women's rights, and a cluster of other issues, but, notably, its most sustained effort was directed toward abolition.

A landmark in the history of the labor movement was the organization in 1886 of the American Federation of Labor; its efforts were expended largely in behalf of craft unions and its objectives were chiefly business unionism. Its great rival, the Congress of Industrial Organizations, which concentrated on industrial workers and the organization of vertical unionism, came into being in 1935. Both labor organizations were beneficiaries of the New Deal reforms, the rivals finally merging in 1955.

For years, higher wages and shorter hours were the principal goals of labor unions; these goals broadened considerably in post-World War II years, to include job security, supplementary benefits, protection against inflation, and retirement pay. Union membership peaked at 35.8% of the nonagricultural labor force in 1945, and thereafter in percentages declined, although in recent years considerable attention has been devoted to organizing farm workers.

Real wages in America rose over time; income distribution tended to become more equitable. Although blacks shared in rising incomes, the gulf between the real incomes of white and black families remained wide.

Occupational shifts were dramatic. In 1820, only 28% of the labor force was in nonagricultural pursuits; by the twentieth century the bulk of the labor force was in nonagricultural activities. Employment in manufacturing gained vis-à-vis agriculture, but the service sector gained even more. In the years 1950–72, employment in the service sector (especially in trade, services, and government) witnessed substantial growth. In 1900 women constituted 20% of the labor force; in 1972, 44%.

Slavery to 1789

1619, AUG. First Negroes (20) imported into Virginia as **bound servants,** while in Spanish Florida, as in other Spanish colonies, black slavery had been long established.

1619–90. Importations of African Negroes continued on a moderate scale (only 3,000 Negroes estimated in Virginia, 1681), as white servants continued to perform bulk of farm labor.

1650–70. Judicial decisions and legislation in the tobacco provinces established slavery. Virginia act of 1661 assumed that some Negroes served for **life;** act of 1670 declared that "all servants not being Christian" brought in by sea were slaves for life, the issue following the status of the **mother.** Laws passed between 1667–71 authorizing conversion of Negroes to Christianity did not bring release from servitude. Black Code, 1705, severely restrained the mobility of slaves and forbade miscegenation under heavy penalties, evidencing a racial as well as a legal differentiation between Negroes and whites. Maryland, 1663, provided life servitude for Negroes.

1672–1760. SLAVE TRADE. Royal African Co., a reorganized trading company, was granted a monopoly of the English slave trade, 1672; but owing to the protests of independent traders, the monopoly was lost, 1698. In the 18th century New England traders were active in the slave trade, with **Newport, R.I.**, a principal port of entry. For the relation of the slave trade to the Triangular Trade (in which the trip from Africa to the West Indies was called the "**Middle Passage**"), see p. 702. Colonial legislatures imposed duties on slave importations, but royal instructions, 1731, forbade governors consenting to such acts. The action of South Carolina, 1760, in prohibiting the slave trade entirely was disallowed by the king in council. After 1690, slave importations mounted sharply. Virginia had 12,000 Negroes by 1708, with about 1,000 Negroes being imported annually for the 3 preceding years. By 1715, the total had risen to 23,000 Negroes, to 42,000 by 1743, 120,156 by 1756, and 259,230 by 1782. Slave importations to the continental colonies increased from an annual average of 2,500 (1715–50) to 7,450 (1760–70), with South Carolina averaging 2,800 (1753–73).

1712–40. NEGRO PLOTS AND INSURRECTIONS. Apr. 1712, the militia were called out to suppress a Negro insurrection in New York City; 21 Negroes executed. In 1739, 3 Negro uprisings broke out in South Carolina, most serious being the **Cato Conspiracy** (9 Sept.), which occurred at Stono, about 20 miles southwest of Charleston, with 30 white and 44 Negro fatalities. As the result of uncovering a Negro plot in Charleston, Jan. 1740, 50 Negroes were hanged. Beginning with a burglary committed in **New York City, 28 Feb. 1741**, followed by a series of fires, panic seized the city as rumors spread that Negroes and poor whites had conspired to seize control. Despite insufficient evidence, 101 Negroes were convicted (18 Negroes and 4 whites were hanged, 13 Negroes burned alive, and 70 banished).

1749. Trustees' prohibition against slavery in Georgia was repealed and a fixed ratio of 4 male Negroes to 1 white servant adopted. As early as 1741, settlers had hired slaves for 100-year terms.

1776. Slavery and the Declaration of Independence. Jefferson's attack on the role of the crown in the slave trade ("He has prostituted his negative for suppressing every legislative attempt to prohibit or to restrain this execrable commerce") was unacceptable to the Southern delegates at the Continental Congress and was stricken from the document.

1776–89. ANTISLAVERY AND MANUMISSION MOVEMENTS. (1) The first antislavery society in the U.S. was organized by the Quakers in 1775, but their fight goes back to Apr. 1688 when **Francis Pastorius** and the German Friends at Germantown declared that slavery was contrary to Christian principles. In 1696 the Yearly Meeting cautioned members against importing Negroes, and in 1755 ruled that all Friends who should thereafter import slaves would be excluded from the denomination. Antislavery societies spread in the Revolutionary era. (2) The New York Society for Promoting Manumission, with John Jay as president, was established in 1785, with other states from Massachusetts to Virginia following between 1788–92. The movement to manumit (free) slaves by will or deed continued in strength in the South during this period and down to c.1800. (3) The movement against the slave trade (prohibited in Maryland, 1783; curbed in North Carolina by imposing a heavy duty on every Negro imported; repealed, 1790) culminated in the antislave-trade provision of the federal Constitution (p. 570) as well as the provision relating to interstate fugitive slaves (p. 573). (4) Legislation was enacted, gradually abolishing slavery: Pennsylvania, 1780; Connecticut and Rhode Island, 1784; New York, 1785; New Jersey, 1786. By judicial decision, 1783, the Massachusetts Constitution of 1780, which held that "all men are born free and equal," was construed as having abolished slavery. In 1787 slavery was prohibited in the Northwest Territory (p. 139).

1790. POPULATION OF U.S. CLASSIFIED BY COLOR. White, 3,172,444; Free Negro, 59,557; Slaves, 697,624; Total, 3,929,625.

SLAVE DISTRIBUTION

Virginia	292,627
South Carolina	107,094
Maryland	103,036
North Carolina	100,783
Georgia	29,264
New York	21,193
Kentucky	12,430
New Jersey	11,423
Delaware	8,887
Pennsylvania	3,707
Southwest Terr.	3,417
Connecticut	2,648
Rhode Island	958
New Hampshire	157

In no state did the slave population exceed the white, but the ratio was higher in South Carolina, which had 140,178 white persons, and the highest average number of slaves per slaveholding family (12.1), as against 8.5 (est.) for Virginia and 7.5 for Maryland (W. S. Rossiter).

Slavery and the Negro, 1789–1860

1789–1831. MANUMISSION AND COLONIZATION PROJECTS. Chief impulse in this period for slavery reform came from the South. Out of 143 emancipation societies in the U.S. in 1826, 103 were in the South, including 4 abolition papers (1819–28). As far back as 1776, Jefferson proposed a plan for African colonization of the Negroes. Pro-colonization resolutions were passed by the Virginia Assembly (1800, 1802, 1805, 1816). As a result, the **American Colonization Society** was established in 1817, headed at various times by Monroe, Madison, and John Marshall, and supported by **Henry Clay.** Free Negroes were first sent to Sierra Leone, and finally in 1821 a permanent location was purchased at Monrovia (settled, 1822); established 1847 as independent Republic of **Liberia** (named by **Robert Goodloe Harper** [1765–1825]). The **Mississippi Colonization Society** (founded, 1831) set up a separate African colony for Negro emigrants from that state. The colonization movement declined in the South after 1831. Total Negroes colonized by 1860 estimated at 15,000, of whom 12,000 were transported through the efforts of the American Colonization Society.

1790, 11 FEB. First petition to Congress for emancipation (presented by the Society of Friends). Many such petitions were presented prior to 1820.

1793. Invention of the **cotton gin** by Eli Whitney, displacing the existing method of manual extraction of seed and increasing 50-fold the average daily output of clean short-staple cotton, promoted the rapid expansion of the **cotton kingdom,** firmly established the **plantation system** (also used for the cultivation of such staples as sugar cane, rice, and tobacco), and led to concentration of slaveholding. Of the more than 8 million whites in the South in 1860 only 383,637 were slaveholders. Of these, only 2,292 were large planters (holding 100 or more slaves).

1801, 30 AUG. GABRIEL PLOT in Richmond and elsewhere in Henrico County, Va., was suppressed by Governor Monroe; estimates of executions range from 16 to 35. Jefferson's comment: "We are truly to be pitied."

1808–60. SLAVE TRADE, FOREIGN AND DOMESTIC. Although Congress in 1808 prohibited the further importation of slaves, the illicit trade persisted, even after Congress declared it piracy (1820). Between 1854–60 every Southern commercial convention advocated reopening the trade. One estimate of the slaves brought into the U.S. illegally, 1808–60, places the total at 250,000. But the chief source of supply was the domestic slave trade, which by 1800 had already become regularized in response to the increasing demand for slaves. The upper South found that the sale of surplus slaves in soil-exhausted areas was more profitable than crop cultivation. Chief marketing and distribution points: Richmond, Louisville, Charleston, Mobile, and New Orleans. A substantial part of the domestic trade was in prime field hands, ranging from 18 to 30 in age. Next in order of demand were the full hands used for household and industrial tasks. As a rule slave prices rose continuously after the closure of foreign trade, but were subject to considerable fluctuation in periods of agricultural prosperity and depression. The approximate price of a field hand in 1795 was $300; in 1860 it ranged between $1,200 and $1,800. **Slave hiring** supplemented slave purchases, and made possible the seasonal use of slaves in iron, lead, and coal mines and in factories (notably in tobacco and textile mills). Slave-hiring wages (paid to owners, but bonuses and incentive payments to slaves in addition) rose from $100 (1800) to $500–$600 per annum for a skilled artisan (1860).

1820. Missouri Compromise (p. 190).

1821, JAN. Publication of the *Genius of Universal Emancipation,* antislavery journal edited by **Benjamin Lundy** (1789–1839), advocate of colonization, who published first in Ohio, then in Tennessee, and finally in Baltimore, where (1829) **William Lloyd Garrison** served as associate editor.

1822, 30 MAY. VESEY SLAVE PLOT in Charleston, S.C., led by a free Negro,

Denmark Vesey, and urban slave artisans, was revealed by an informer and crushed; 37 executed (18 June–9 Aug.).

1826. Nashoba, a Utopian community near Memphis, Tenn., established by **Frances Wright** for the training of Negroes and their eventual resettlement outside the U.S. It was active until 1828.

1831, 1 JAN. First number of *The Liberator,* edited and published by **William Lloyd Garrison:** the organ of the militant abolitionist movement. "I will not retreat a single inch—AND I WILL BE HEARD."

13–23 AUG. NAT TURNER INSURRECTION in Southampton County, Va., led by Turner (1800–31), a Negro preacher, in the course of which 57 whites—men, women, and children—were killed. Tracked down in a sensational manhunt (possibly 100 Negroes killed), 20 Negroes (including Turner) were executed after trials.

1831–32, WINTER. VIRGINIA CONVENTION, after debates covering every phase of the slavery problem, defeated by a small majority various proposals for emancipation. These debates mark a turning point in the handling of the slave problem by the South. Immediately thereafter, beginning with North Carolina, and spreading to all the slave states, the **slave codes were tightened** to curb the mobility of slaves (through a strict system of patrols and passes), prohibit their attendance at meetings, curtail their education, drastically restrict manumissions, and impose special disabilities on free Negroes. By 1860, 10 states had constitutional provisions curbing either statutory or voluntary emancipation or both.

1832–40. Organization by Garrison of the New England Anti-Slavery Society, which, with a New York group led by **Arthur** (1786–1865) and **Lewis Tappan** (1788–1873), merchants and philanthropists, formed the **American Anti-**

slavery Society (1833). The Lane Theological Seminary debate at Cincinnati (1832) on colonization and abolition was followed by withdrawal (May 1833) of most of the students, led by **Theodore Dwight Weld** (Ohio, 1803–95), when the trustees ordered a halt to such discussions. After its organization (1833) Oberlin College (Ohio) was visited by Weld, who converted it into the center of Western abolitionism. The trustees of Oberlin, first college to admit women, voted (1835) to admit Negro students. Shortly afterward it became an important station on the Underground Railroad. In 1837 **James G. Birney** (Kentucky, 1792–1857) became secretary of the American Anti-Slavery Society. By 1838 a Garrisonian group in New England came out for passive resistance rather than physical force. With the Tappans and the **Grimké sisters** (Sarah Moore, 1792–1873; Angelina Emily, 1805–79), Weld launched the non-Garrisonian wing of the organized abolition movement—the **American and Foreign Antislavery Society,** which broke with the Garrison group in 1840.

1836. Adoption of the "gag rule" (p. 213).

1837, 7 Nov. A mob in Alton, Ill., attacked the office of **Elijah P. Lovejoy** (1802–37), an antislavery editor. In the ensuing battle Lovejoy was killed. Several persons were indicted, but found not guilty.

1839. *American Slavery As It Is,* by Theodore Weld and his wife, the former Angelina Grimké, was published. Consisting of extracts from Southern newspapers and the testimony of abolitionists who had seen slavery at first hand, this volume presented evidence of oppression. Additional eyewitness testimony was provided by a number of Negroes who participated in the abolition movement as speakers and agents, notably

Frederick Douglass (p. 1015), who escaped from slavery in 1838, and was active in Negro conventions and the Underground Railroad.

Formation of the **Liberty party** (p. 216).

1840. UNDERGROUND RAILROAD, a secret and shifting network of hiding places and routes for helping fugitive slaves escape to the North or Canada, was well established by this date. Without formal organization, it is known to have existed as early as 1786 and to have flourished in the Western Reserve after the War of 1812, but its spread through 14 Northern states did not come until 1830. The name (originally "Underground Road") supposedly dates from the time (1831) the Kentucky master of a fugitive slave named Tice Davids unsuccessfully pursued him across the Ohio River at Ripley, Ohio, and remarked that Davids "must have gone off an underground road." At least 3,200 active workers have been identified (Siebert), outstanding among whom was the Quaker **Levi Coffin** (1789–1877) and the escaped slave **Harriet Tubman** (c.1821–1913), known as "Moses." At the most liberal estimate some 50,000 slaves escaped to freedom via the Underground Railroad, c.1830–60. A number of Northern states, including Pennsylvania, Connecticut, New York, Vermont, and Ohio, passed a series of **"personal liberty laws"** (1820–40) which impeded the enforcement of the federal fugitive slave law of 1793.

1848. "Free Soil" Convention (p. 249).

1850. COMPROMISE (p. 250) and **FUGITIVE SLAVE ISSUE.** 1850–58 (p. 255).

1952. *Uncle Tom's Cabin* (p. 256). *The Pro-Slavery Argument,* a collection of essays by **William Harper** (1790–1847), **Thomas R. Dew** (1802–46),

James H. Hammond (1807–64), and others, defended slavery as a positive good on the basis of (1) the Scriptures, (2) its role in the prosperity of the South, (3) the alleged biological inferiority of the Negro, (4) slavery as the foundation for a culture based on white supremacy, and (5) as an agency for the education and adjustment of a barbarian people.

1854. *Sociology for the South; or, the Failure of Free Society,* by George Fitzhugh (1806–81), who also wrote *Cannibals All! or, Slaves Without Masters* (1857), praised the slave economy and social order of the South as superior to the laissez-faire capitalism of the North.

Kansas-Nebraska Act (p. 258).

1857. Dred Scott Decision (p. 263).

1859. John Brown's Raid (p. 268).

GROWTH OF SLAVE SYSTEM, 1790–1860*

1790	697,624
1800	893,602
1810	1,191,362
1820	1,538,022
1830	2,009,043
1840	2,487,355
1850	3,204,313
1860	3,953,760

* Chief expansion was in the New South, where increase over 1810 was over 1,000% as against less than 100% in the Old South. Greatest increases: Ala., Miss., La., Tex., and Ark.

DISTRIBUTION OF SLAVES IN THE SLAVE STATES (1860)

Delaware	1,798
Maryland and Washington, D.C.	90,374
Virginia	472,494
West Virginia*	18,371
North Carolina	331,059
South Carolina	402,406
Georgia	462,198
Kentucky	225,483
Tennessee	275,719
Alabama	435,080
Mississippi	436,631
Louisiana	331,726
Arkansas	111,115
Missouri	114,931
Florida	61,745
Texas	182,566

* Comprises counties set off from Virginia to form West Virginia, 1863–66, demonstrating marked difference in the regions with respect to slavery.

Free and Bound Labor to 1789

Demand was met by (1) **free labor,** (2) **bound labor,** (3) **slaves.**

1621–1773. MAXIMUM WAGE AND PRICE CONTROLS, adopted in certain periods because of labor shortages.

1621–40. Tobacco Provinces. Virginia (1621–23) set specific wage and price scales. Maryland (Oct. 1640) authorized county courts to regulate wages; expired in 2 years.

1630–75. New England. Massachusetts set maximum wages in the building trades (1630); repealed, 1631; revived and extended to farm labor, 1633; turned over to towns, Oct. 1636. Proposals to reestablish sweeping wage scales, 1670, 1672, defeated; but act of 1675, passed at time of King Philip's War, authorized selectmen to impose double penalty upon takers of excessive wages. Similar legislation enacted in Connecticut (prior to 15 June 1640, and in 1641; repealed 1650; scales set in specific crafts, 1677) and New Haven (1640–41).

1671–1741. Rice and Sugar Colonies. In British West Indies **minimum** wage scales adopted to ensure adequate supply of white labor (e.g., Barbados, 1696); but **maximum** scales were drafted by South Carolina authorities, 1671, and in Georgia, 1739, 1741, for servants and laborers employed by the Trustees.

1690–1773. General wage scales and fees fell into disuse, but specific wages, fees, or prices were fixed by local authority in monopoly trades—carmen, porters, butchers, bakers, innkeepers, teachers, ministers, etc.

1774–83. REVOLUTIONARY WAGE AND PRICE CONTROLS. Congress and local committees set prices for scarce commodities as early as 1774. Major activity: **Providence, R.I., Convention,** 31 Dec. 1776, adopted sweeping wage and price regulations for New England states. **York, Pa., Convention,** Mar. 1777, failed to agree on schedules. **New Haven Convention,** Jan. 1778 (New England and Middle States), set up revised schedules. Subsequently town conventions in New England and Middle States continued to revise schedules to curb inflationary spiral (to 1780). Last regional convention, **Philadelphia,** 1790. Action of Congress, 18 Mar., fixing the value of Continental bills at not more than one fortieth of their face value (also p. 123), contributed ultimately to price and wage stabilization.

1636–1789. LABOR COMBINATIONS prior to permanent trade unionism fall into distinct categories: (1) **Combinations of master workers to maintain monopoly: Massachusetts,** shipbuilding guild, 1644; shoemakers, 1648; **New York,** coopers, 1675; Westchester, weavers, 1702; **Philadelphia,** cordwainers and tailors, 1718; **Carpenters' Co.,** 1724; **New York,** building-trades workers, 1747, 1769; ship carpenters, 1784. (2) **Combinations of white servants to redress grievances by strikes or insurrections:** Virginia, York Co., 1659, 1661; Gloucester, Sept. 1663 (4 executed for high treason); **Bacon's Rebellion,** 1676 (p. 33); **East Florida,** revolt of Minorcan immigrants at New Smyrna, 19 Aug. 1768 (2 leaders executed). (3) **Combinations of free white labor to bar their trades to Negroes:** Charleston, shipwrights, 1744; **North Carolina,** river pilots, 1773. (4) **Joint political action by workmen and employers,** 1765–75: Sons of Liberty (p. 87), Sons of Neptune (mariners); Boston Massacre, 5 Mar. 1770, p. 93; strikes of mariners on British transports, New York, 1768; of workers on British fortifications, Boston, 1774. (5) **Strikes by journeymen to secure better working conditions:** Rare prior to 1775, but occur at least as early as 1636 when fishermen struck on Richmond Island off the Maine coast. Boston

calkers, 1741, agreed not to accept notes in payment of wages; Savannah carpenters struck, 1746; New York tailors struck for higher wages, 1768; printers, 1778, for raise of $3 a week, successful; Philadelphia seamen, 1779.

1783–89: Increasing frequency of strikes and trade union organization: New York shoemakers, 1785; Philadelphia printers, 1786 (permanent organization by 1802); cordwainers, 1789 ("Federal Society," 1794).

WAGE SCALES. Statistics, fragmentary and without data on supplementary income derived by labor from farming, indicate that wages exceeded English scale—skilled workers by up to 100%, unskilled about 50%. Except during periods of inflation colonial real wages exceeded English by 30% to 100%. The differential was noted by Alexander Hamilton, "Report on Manufactures," 1791. High wage scale favored land purchases by labor, contributing to maintaining labor shortages in this period. **Per diem wages: Carpenters** (Massachusetts), 1701, 58.4–61 cts.; 1712, 83.3 cts.; 1735–40, 45.6 cts. (specie); 1743, 40 cts. (specie); 1751–75, 67 cts. **Common (unskilled) labor** (Massachusetts), 1752–57, 33 cts.; 1758–61, 25 cts.; 1762, 17.8 cts.; 1777, 22 cts.; 1779, 79 cts.

1619–1789. BOUND LABOR OR INDENTURED SERVITUDE, used principally in the Middle Colonies and the tobacco provinces, fell into 2 categories: (1) **voluntary,** (2) **involuntary.** The former were either (a) **redemptioners** or "free willers," white immigrants who, in return for passage to America, bound themselves as servants for from 2 to 7 years (4 years average), estimated at from 60% to 77% of total immigration down to 1776; (b) **apprentices,** minors who were provided training in return for services in specified trades (in addition, poor children were bound out by public authority—1619, London Common Council sent to Virginia 100 poor children as "bound apprentices"). The involuntary workers comprised (a) **British convict servants** transported to the colonies (principally Maryland, Virginia, or the West Indies) in commutation of death sentence—1655–99, 4,500 transported; 1750–70, 10,000 to Maryland alone. Total to continental colonies to 1775: approximately **50,000** (Butler). Terms of service fixed by Act of Parliament, 1718: **7 years** for lesser crimes within benefit of clergy; **14 years** for nonclergyable felonies (actually a number were transported for **life**). After the Revolution Britain continued convict dumping in the U.S. illegally as late as Aug. 1787, but eventually Australia replaced America for this purpose. (b) **Victims of kidnaping,** mostly cases of forcible detaining of prospective emigrants prior to taking passage for England committed by overzealous recruiting agents (called "spirits" or "crimps" in England; "newlanders" on the Continent). (c) **Servitude in satisfaction of criminal sentences imposed by colonial courts,** particularly for **larceny** (usually punished in the colonies by multiple restitution, as contrasted with England, where larceny from the person above 12d was capital) and **unlawful absence** from employer's service (punishable **10-fold** in Maryland by act of 1661); continued in Delaware to 1839 for whites; to 1867 for Negroes. (d) **Servitude for debt,** gradually eliminated by legislation abolishing imprisonment for debt, chiefly in the period, 1820–60 (below), with survivals in the form of post–Civil War **peonage,** or debt bondage, in the South.

Labor and Social Reform, 1789–1860

1794–1815. ORIGINS OF TRADE UNIONS. Federal Society of Journeymen Cordwainers, Philadelphia (1794–

1806), was the longest-lived of the early U.S. trade unions; struck, 1799. New York, printers struck (1794), cabinetmakers (1796); Pittsburgh, shoemakers (1809); Boston, printers (1809), and in other cities (1810–15). Objectives: higher wages, shorter hours, union control of apprenticeship, closed shop.

1806–15. CONSPIRACY CASES. Trade unions were prosecuted for strikes as illegal conspiracies at common law. Issue drawn between Federalists (antilabor) and Jeffersonian Republicans (pro-trade unions). Major cases: Philadelphia Cordwainers (1806), New York Cordwainers (1809–10).

1817–48. DEBTOR RELIEF AND PRISON REFORM. New York legislature (1817) made $25 minimum debt for which a man could be imprisoned. Kentucky (1821) abolished imprisonment for debt; Ohio followed, 1828; Vermont and New Jersey, 1830; New York, 1832; Connecticut, 1837; Louisiana, 1840; Missouri, 1845; Alabama, 1848. Prison reform stems from prison societies (Philadelphia, 1787; Boston, 1825; New York, 1845). Auburn (N.Y.) Penitentiary instituted (1824) **Auburn System—** cell blocks, silence, group labor. Opposing **Pennsylvania System** (exemplified by Eastern State Penitentiary, erected 1829) provided completely solitary confinement and solitary labor. By 1840, 12 Auburn-type prisons erected in the U.S. For treatment of the insane and role of **Dorothea Dix,** see p. 1014.

1824. First recorded strike of women workers—Pawtucket, R.I., weavers.

1825. Establishment at **New Harmony,** Ind., by **Robert Owen** (1771–1858), British social reformer, of a short-lived collectivist colony.

1827. CITY CENTRALS, or central trade councils in cities, first established in Philadelphia with Mechanics' Union of Trade Associations. By 1836, 13 cities had centrals.

762 The American Economy

1828–34. LABOR PARTIES. Participation of workers in politics was accelerated by **removal of property qualifications for voting** (new Western constitutions and Connecticut, 1818; Massachusetts, 1820; New York, 1821; in Rhode Island not until 1843, after rebellion led by **Thomas W. Dorr** [1805–54]). First U.S. "labor" party organized in Philadelphia (May 1828); gained balance in the city council in the fall election. New York and Boston quickly followed. Leadership primarily not laborers but reformers and small businessmen. In Jacksonian period Eastern workers were divided in their allegiance. New York labor voted for Jackson; Philadelphia labor voted National Republican-Whig; Baltimore closely divided, as were the New Jersey towns. Jackson drew greater support from the small Eastern farmers than from industrial areas. Labor platforms demanded (1) 10-hour day; (2) abolition of imprisonment for debt (75,000 debtors in jail, 1829); (3) abolition of prison contract labor; (4) enactment of mechanics' lien laws (piecemeal extension beg. Pennsylvania, 1803; New York, 1830; Virginia, 1843; Maine, 1848); (5) abolition of discriminatory militia system; (6) curbs on licensed monopolies, particularly banks; (7) universal education. **Leadership:** New York: **Thomas Skidmore,** agrarian radical, and **William Leggett** (1801–39), editor and social reformer, as well as such extremists as **Robert Dale Owen,** son of Robert Owen, and Scottish-born **Frances Wright,** pioneer agitator in U.S. for women's rights, who coedited (with Owen) the *Free Enquirer.* Philadelphia: **John Ferral** and **William English.** New England: **Seth Luther,** labor agitator, **Charles Douglas,** and **George Bancroft,** historian, who feared the effects of industrialization on labor. By 1834 the "labor" parties were defunct, being absorbed by the 2 major parties or reorganized as factions like **Loco-Focos** or Equal Rights faction, radical wings of the Democratic party in New York and Pennsylvania.

1834, 29 JAN. FIRST USE OF FEDERAL TROOPS to intervene in a labor dispute (closed shop). President Jackson ordered the War Department to put down "riotous assembly" among Irish laborers constructing Chesapeake and Ohio Canal near Williamsport, Md.

1834–37. NATIONAL FEDERATIONS. City central movement spread from Philadelphia to New York (14 Aug. 1833), Baltimore, Boston, Louisville, Pittsburgh, and Cincinnati, with emphasis on nonpolitical, trade-union objectives. In 1834, New York General Trades Union called a convention of delegates from other city centrals, which organized the **National Trades Union,** headed by **Ely Moore** (1798–1861), elected to Congress on Tammany ticket. A number of trades held national conventions during this period, but the movement was aborted by the Panic of 1837 (p. 213). Mounting number of strikes in this period. In the decade 1831–40, 126 strikes have been uncovered in Pennsylvania alone (W. A. Sullivan).

1835–42. In *People* v. *Fisher,* New York court declared strikes illegal; but in Massachusetts in *Commonwealth* v. *Hunt* (1842), Chief Justice Lemuel Shaw (p. 1150) ruled that trade unions were lawful and strikes for a closed shop legal.

1836–60. 10-HOUR MOVEMENT. Building trades workers in Eastern cities had obtained 10-hour day by 1834, and the Whig municipal government of Philadelphia had prior to 1836 put the 10-hour day into effect. As a result of a memorial to Congress by Ely Moore on behalf of the National Trades Union, and a local strike, President Jackson's Secretary of the Navy, Mahlon Dickerson, issued an order for a 10-hour day in Philadelphia Navy Yard (31 Aug.

1836). Executive order of President Van Buren, 31 Mar. 1840, extended "10-hour system" to all laborers and mechanics employed on federal public works. Average daily hours of factory workers in 1840 estimated at 11.4. New England Convention (Oct. 1844) urged 10-hour legislation; enacted: New Hampshire, 1847; Maine, 1848; Pennsylvania, 1848; Ohio, 1852; Rhode Island, 1853; California, 1853; Connecticut, 1855; no action in Massachusetts. Such laws were subject to evasion by contract. By 1860, the 10-hour day was standard among most skilled workers and common laborers, but had not yet been adopted in Lowell and Salem mills.

1840–52. SOCIAL REFORMS affected the labor movement, particularly the **Association** movement, an effort to draw men into cooperative programs: (1) Most notable example was the **Fourierist system** inspired by a French reformer, Charles Fourier (1772–1837), and endorsed in the U.S. by **Albert Brisbane** (1809–90), who expounded his ideas in Horace Greeley's N.Y. *Tribune*. This system provided for the setting up of **phalanxes,** communities of about 1,500 persons devoted to an agrarian-handicraft economy based upon voluntarism. Goods produced were the property of the phalanx, but private property and inheritance were not abolished. More than 40 phalanxes were established, from Massachusetts to Wisconsin, all disappearing by 1860. Best known: **Brook Farm,** West Roxbury, Mass. (1841–47), established by **George Ripley** (1802–80), a Unitarian minister and Transcendentalist (p. 854), and numbering among its members Nathaniel Hawthorne, Charles A. Dana, and John S. Dwight; in 1845 it was converted into a Fourierist phalanx but failed to survive a major fire in 1846. The short-lived **Sylvania Phalanx** in Pennsylvania was organized, 1842, by Greeley and others. The

North American Phalanx near Red Bank, N.J., was established by Brisbane; disbanded, 1854. (2) **Owenite societies,** highly paternalistic collectivist communities, combining agriculture and factory production. In 1848 an Icarian community was settled in Texas by European workingmen under the leadership of **Étienne Cabet** (1788–1856), whose *Le Voyage en Icarie* (1840) projected a social order on communist principles. The Texas colony, like the one at Nauvoo, Ill. (1849), was unsuccessful. (3) **Cooperative societies** or protective unions (both producers' and consumers'). New England Protective Union, 1845, set up central agency to buy for retail stores; iron molders, Cincinnati, 1848; especially strong in New York City by 1851; more than 800 organized, 1845–60. (4) **Agrarian reform** agitated by the National Reform Association led by **George Henry Evans** (1805–56), editor of N.Y. *Working Man's Advocate* (1829–37, 1844–47), advocated free homesteads, exemption of homesteads from seizure for debt (p. 635), and foreshadowed Henry George's "single-tax" program (p. 1039). (5) **Temperance crusade,** with roots in the colonial period, was stimulated by the writings of Dr. Benjamin Rush, the preaching of Lyman Beecher, and popularized by Timothy Shay Arthur (p. 856), as well as by the activities of the General Conference of the Methodist Church (1780, 1816), the American Temperance Union (first national convention, 1836), and the Washingtonian Temperance Society (reformed drunkards, 1840). Under the leadership of **Neal Dow** (1804–97), Maine passed first statewide prohibition law in 1846; revision of 1851 served as model. Vermont, Rhode Island, and Minnesota Territory followed, 1852; Michigan, 1853; Connecticut, 1854; and 8 other states by 1855. (6) **Peace movement,** led by **William Ladd** (1778–

1841), who organized the American Peace Society (1828), and the "learned blacksmith," **Elihu Burritt** (1810–70), who founded the League of Universal Brotherhood (1846) and promoted the 2d Universal Peace Congress held at Brussels (1848).

1852–60. RISE OF NATIONAL TRADE UNIONS stressing business objectives: National Typographical Union, 1852; Hat Finishers, 1854; Journeymen Stone Cutters Assn., 1855; United Cigarmakers, 1856; Iron Molders (led by **William Sylvis** (1828–69) and Machinists and Blacksmiths, 1859. The weaker nationals were shattered by the Panic of 1857. In decade 1851–60 cost of living rose 12%; money wages rose 4%.

1860, 22 FEB. Strike of shoemakers in Lynn and Natick, Mass., for higher wages spread throughout New England and involved 20,000 workers, including women. Major demands won.

INDEX OF REAL WAGES
(Hansen)

Years	(Index 1913 = 100)
1820–29	46
1830–39	48
1840–49	56
1850–59	52

Labor and Occupational Trends Since 1860

1861–65. IMPACT OF THE CIVIL WAR. Few strikes during war years, although by 1865 real wages had declined one third from 1860 level. Expansion of **city centrals** and **national** organizations was countered by the organization of **employers' associations** (as in Mich., 1864; N.Y. Master Builders Assn., 1869). Louisville Convention, Sept. 1865, representing 8 city centrals, attempted unsuccessfully to form a national labor federation. **Consumers' cooperatives** mul-

tiplied, inspired by the **Rochdale** pioneers in England (1844).

1864, 4 JULY. Passage of the federal emigrant **contract labor** act, pledging wages of emigrants for terms not exceeding 12 months, resulted in the setting up of the **American Emigrant Co.** to import laborers.

1864–73. NATIONAL TRADE UNION MOVEMENT. Organization of 26 national unions, with 6 previously established. Total trade union membership, 1870–72: 300,000. Most influential national was the **Molders.** Defeated in its fight against organized employers (1867–68), that union organized **cooperative stove foundries,** but the cooperators quickly became "capitalists." **Railway brotherhoods** originated in this period: **Locomotive Engineers** (1863), **Railway Conductors** (1868), **Firemen** (1873). Widespread utilization of shoe machinery, 1861–70, led to displacement of skilled mechanics by unskilled labor and prompted the organization of the **Order of the Knights of St. Crispin** (7 Mar. 1867). By 1870 its membership was estimated at 50,000. Major objective: protection of members against competition of "green hands" and apprentices. By the end of this period the shoeworkers' union had already begun to decline in membership.

1866, 20 AUG.–1872. NATIONAL LABOR UNION organized at Baltimore. Original objective: the **8-hour day,** a movement led by **Ira Steward** (1831–83), a Boston machinist, and **George E. McNeill** (1837–1906). As early as July 1862, Congress had provided that the hours and wages of employees in federal navy yards should conform to those of private firms. Illinois, New York, and Missouri, 1867, enacted 8-hour day laws; not enforced; Wisconsin for women and children, but with loopholes. Failure of the 8-hour demands led the **National Labor Union,** under the presidencies of

Sylvis (1868) and **Richard F. Trevellick** (1869), head of Ship Carpenters and Caulkers Intl., to concentrate on **political reform**. In 1872 the federation was transformed into the **National Labor Reform party**, with Judge David Davis (Ill.) its nominee for president (22 Feb.). The withdrawal of Davis caused the collapse of both party and federation. The period 1868–72 was also marked by the establishment of numerous **producers' cooperatives** under union auspices.

1868. First federal 8-hour day enacted by Congress; confined to laborers and mechanics employed by or on behalf of the U.S. government.

1873–78. DEPRESSION AND LABOR TURBULENCE. National unions dropped from 30 to 9 (1877), and unionized labor from 300,000 to c.50,000. Knights of St. Crispin disappeared by 1878. Outstanding manifestations of labor unrest: (1) **Tompkins Square Riot,** New York City, 13 Jan. 1874, where police charged radical labor meeting. (2) **"Molly Maguires,"** a secret organization of miners, an outgrowth of the **Ancient Order of Hibernians**, organized in Ireland to oppose encroachments of landlords, promoted labor violence in eastern Pennsylvania, beg. 1862. As a result of prosecution instituted by Philadelphia & Reading R.R. and evidence gathered by a Pinkerton detective, 24 Molly Maguires were convicted (fall 1875), 10 hanged for murder, the others sentenced to jail terms of 2–7 years (1876), and the order was crushed. (3) **General Strike.** Railroad strikes, beg. 17 July 1877 on the B.&O. in protest against wage cuts, spread quickly to other lines east of the Mississippi and eventually to Western lines, with rioting in Baltimore, Pittsburgh, Chicago, and St. Louis. **President Hayes sent federal troops** to restore order at **Martinsburg,** W.Va., after strikers had repulsed militia (9 persons killed), and at **Pittsburgh,**

where, after resisting Philadelphia militia in a pitched battle (21 July, 26 killed), a mob tore up railroad tracks and burned down machine shops, the Union Depot, and other property, with damage estimated at from $5–$10 million. As a result of strike violence legislatures revived conspiracy laws.

EUROPEAN REVOLUTIONARY LABOR PROGRAMS made their appearance in this period. Three major groups: (1) **Marxian Socialists,** who split in 1872 with (2) the **Anarcho-Communists,** followers of Mikhail Bakunin, and moved the headquarters of the **First International** to New York City, under the leadership of a lieutenant of Karl Marx, **Friedrich A. Sorge** (1827–1906); formed Workingmen's party, 1876; name changed to **Socialist-Labor party,** 1877; worked in the trade-union movement especially through the **Cigarmakers Union,** headed by **Adolph Strasser.** (3) **Lassallean Socialists,** mostly German immigrants, followers of Ferdinand Lassalle, who favored **political action.**

1878, Jan.–1893. KNIGHTS OF LABOR organized on a national basis. The Knights originated, 1871, as a **secret order** at a tailors' meeting in Philadelphia called by **Uriah Stephens** (1821–82), who headed the Knights until 1879, when he was succeeded by **Terence V. Powderly** (p. 1131), who held the post until 1893 (elected, 1878, mayor of Scranton on a labor ticket). The Knights was an **industrial union** headed by a General Assembly to which workers belonged as individuals, regardless of sex, race, or color. All gainfully employed persons, **including unskilled workers** (except certain professional groups) were eligible, but three fourths of each assembly were required to be wage earners. In the West farmers dominated; in the East trade unionists. Local assemblies rose from 484 (1882) to 5,892

(1886), with membership in excess of 700,000. Knights supported (1) 8-hour day; (2) boycotts and arbitration (rather than strikes); (3) various political reforms, including adoption of **graduated income tax;** (4) consumers' and producers' cooperatives (135 set up, including the ownership and operation of a coal mine). Hard times, 1884–85, led to widespread boycotts and strikes, notably by railway shopmen of Union Pacific and the Southwest System (1884), both successful, and against the Wabash (1885), forcing Jay Gould to negotiate with the Knights and agree to end discriminatory practices. Decline after 1886 peak due to (1) **failure of strike against Southwest R.R. System** (1 Mar.–3 May 1886) led by **Martin Irons,** which Powderly sought to terminate by negotiation, and to unsuccessful results of strike waves in the latter half of 1886, including **collapse of 8-hour-day general strike** at Chicago (begun 1 May 1886), and the packinghouse lockout of 1887; (2) **Haymarket incident** (below). Agrarian control led to Powderly being replaced, 1893, by James R. Sovereign of Iowa.

1882, SEPT. First Labor Day celebration held in New York City. By Act of Congress, 1894, first Monday in Sept. made an annual legal holiday. Two labor leaders, Peter J. McGuire and Matthew Maguire, share honors as cosponsors of the holiday.

1886, 4 MAY. HAYMARKET MASSACRE resulted when, after police broke up an Anarcho-Communist meeting at Haymarket Square, Chicago, a bomb exploded among the front rank of police, who then opened fire (7 police fatally injured; 70 wounded). The trial (19 June–20 Aug.) of **August Spies, Albert Parsons, Samuel J. Fielden,** and other radical agitators before Judge **Joseph E. Gary** resulted in convictions (7 sentenced to death; 1 to 15 years in prison). Conviction affirmed by Illinois

Supreme Court, 14 Sept. 1887. As a result of petitions circulated by **William Dean Howells** (p. 1063), **Henry Demarest Lloyd** (1847–1903), and labor groups for commutation of the death sentence, 2 prisoners were commuted by Gov. Richard J. Oglesby to life terms. Remaining 4 executed on 11 Nov. 1887. Gov. **John Peter Altgeld** (1847–1902) freed 3 others, charging that the trial had been unfair (June 1893). The actual bomb thrower was never identified. The incident damaged the labor movement.

1886, 8 DEC.–1914. AMERICAN FEDERATION OF LABOR organized at Columbus, Ohio, by some 25 labor groups representing about 150,000 members. First president, **Samuel Gompers** (p. 1042), who, with Strasser, had reorganized the Cigarmakers Union (by 1879) and had participated at the founding of the **Federation of Organized Trades and Labor Unions** (Pittsburgh, Nov. 1881), formed to protect the legislative interests of trade unions. The A.F. of L. immediately declared war on the Knights and accepted members and locals also in the latter body. Recognizing the **autonomy of each trade,** it confined its objectives chiefly to **business unionism.** After the depression, 1893–97, large gains in trade union membership took place. Despite antiunion campaign of **National Association of Manufacturers** (org., 1895), the A.F. of L. claimed, 1904, 1,676,200 out of 2,072,700 union members. After a brief decline, 1905–09, union membership rose again, 1910–14, by which date the A.F. of L. claimed 2,020,671 out of 2,687,100 union members (Wolman)— the greatest gains among **coal miners, railroad workers,** and in the **building trades.** The bulk of the unskilled and semiskilled workers were still unorganized. A.F. of L. unions, 1900–14, (1) stressed "job ownership," (2) favored immigration curbs, (3) demanded relief from **technological unemployment,** (4) enactment of **labor legislation**, and (5) **collaboration** with employers, as evidenced by labor participation (with employers and the public) in the **National Civic Federation** (1900) to promote mediation of labor disputes (particularly effective between 1900–05).

1892, 6 JULY. HOMESTEAD MASSACRE occurred when strikers at the Carnegie Steel Co. plant at Homestead, Pa., fired upon 2 barges being towed up the Monongahela with 300 **Pinkerton detectives** engaged by the company's general manager, **Henry Clay Frick** (1849–1919); 7 killed. Strike, broken by strikebreakers as state militia took over on 12 July, ended 20 Nov. On 23 July **Alexander Berkman** (1870–1936), a Russian-born anarchist, shot and stabbed Frick, in an assault planned with **Emma Goldman** (1869–1940). Berkman was sentenced to 21 years. No effective steel union was organized until the 1930s.

14 JULY. Martial law declared in Coeur d'Alene silver mines in Idaho as result of violence between striking miners and strikebreakers. Federal troops dispatched to the area.

1894, 21 JUNE–20 JULY. PULLMAN STRIKE called by **American Railway Union** (independent under **Eugene V. Debs**), with a boycott on Pullman cars. By the end of June the strike had tied up every Midwestern railroad. Attorney General Richard Olney had 3,400 men sworn in as special deputies to keep trains running. When violence broke out, railroad association appealed to **President Cleveland,** who (over the protest of Gov. **John Peter Altgeld,** p. 974) **sent federal troops** to restore order, safeguard the mail, and protect interstate commerce. On 2 July, a federal court issued an **injunction** forbidding interference with the operation of the mails or interstate commerce. Debs was jailed for contempt and the strike was smashed. The incident dramatized the increasing use of the

labor injunction (since 1883). Between 1901–28, 118 applications were officially reported for the federal courts; 116 unreported (Frankfurter and Greene)— most of which ended strikes before a final decree was needed. State injunctions were widespread, and the courts frequently circumvented curbs imposed by legislatures.

1898–1934. ADJUSTMENT OF RAILROAD LABOR DISPUTES. Although an act of Congress of 1888 provided for arbitration by special boards set up by the parties in interest and for a presidential commission to investigate and report where one of the parties refused the offer of the other to arbitrate, such machinery was ineffective in the Pullman strike. The **Erdman Act** (1 June 1898) provided for mediation by the chairman of the ICC and the commissioner of the Bureau of Labor, although neither official had legal power to initiate proceedings. Between 1906 and 1913, 61 railroad labor controversies were settled (26 by mediation). The **Newlands Act** (15 July 1913) created a Board of Mediation and Conciliation consisting of 4 members. Between 1913 and end of 1917 the board settled 58 out of the 71 controversies which came before it. The **Adamson Act** (3 Sept. 1916) provided for an 8-hour day and time and a half for overtime on interstate railroads. While the railroads were under federal operation during and after World War I, 3 national adjustment boards were established, representing management and unions, to settle grievances. Under the **Esch-Cummins Act** (28 Feb. 1920; p. 390) a Railroad Labor Board was established, comprising 9 members (3 each from the companies, the employees, and the public), whose authority stopped short of compulsory arbitration. Under the **Act of 1926** (20 May) the Labor Board was replaced by a Board of Mediation, an independent agency consisting of 5 members appointed by the president. By the **Railway Labor Act** of 1934 (27 June) a National Railroad Adjustment Board, with offices in Chicago, was established. The act upheld the right of employees to organize and bargain collectively through representatives of their own choosing.

1902. ANTHRACITE COAL STRIKE, called (12 May) by United Mine Workers of America (UMW) President John Mitchell, when mine owners declined offer of arbitration, led to intervention (3 Oct.) by President Theodore Roosevelt, who (16 Oct.) appointed a commission to mediate the dispute. The strike was called off on 21 Oct., and on 22 Mar. 1903 the commission awarded the miners a wage increase of 10% but refused union recognition.

1902–08. DANBURY HATTERS' CASE (p. 674).

1905, June–1920. INDUSTRIAL WORKERS OF THE WORLD (I.W.W.), launched at Chicago convention, comprising Western Federation of Miners (1893) and the American Labor Union (org. 1898 as a rival of the AFL), emphasized revolutionary program: (1) **abolition of wage system,** and (2) **industrial unionism.** After eliminating the Socialist Labor faction headed by Daniel De Leon, the "Wobblies" stressed the organization in the West of **unskilled and migratory workers** in lumber, shipping, fruit growing, and textiles (largely the result of a successful strike at Lawrence, Mass., 1912). Most active organizer: **William D. ("Big Bill") Haywood** (1869–1928). Convicted in Salt Lake City on an allegedly trumped-up murder charge, and executed (1915), the Swedish immigrant **Joe Hill** became part of the movement's folklore. As a result of vigilante action and federal prosecutions, 1918–20, notably at **Centralia,** Wash., Chicago, Sacramento, and

Wichita, the I.W.W. was eliminated as an effective power in the Northwest.

1909–11. INTERNATIONAL LADIES GARMENT WORKERS UNION (ILGWU), organized in 1900, made notable strides in eliminating evils in sweatshops in the shirtwaist trade, particularly after the **Triangle fire** (25 Mar. 1911), with 146 fatalities (proprietors indicated, 11 Apr.; acquitted, 7 Dec.), which led to enactment in New York of a drastically revised and stringent building code and a revision of the labor laws.

1910–12. ARBITRATION, as a result of ILGWU's 2 successful strikes (1909–11), set up in **protocol** (1910) in New York cloak and suit industry (initiated by Louis D. Brandeis) and in agreement negotiated (1911) by Sidney Hillman of the United Garment Workers with **Hart, Schaffner & Marx,** Chicago; latter developed into **impartial chairman** machinery (1912).

1912. First minimum wage act for women and minors passed in Massachusetts.

1913. U.S. Department of Labor established.

1914. Clayton Act (p. 327).

1915. 4 Mar. La Follette Seamen's Act regulated conditions of employment for maritime workers.

1914–20. WORLD WAR I AND LABOR. Union membership increased by 2,350,000, with A.F. of L. gaining 2,068,000 (Wolman). Strikes were successful during the "seller's market." A.F. of L. strongly supported the war; the Socialist party and I.W.W. opposed U.S. entry. For prosecution of radicals, see p. 391. To maintain production schedules President Wilson set up a **Mediation Commission,** 1917, and the **National War Labor Board,** 8 Apr. 1918 (p. 332). Government agencies' general insistence that suppliers bargain collectively led to the rapid rise of company unions. After federal labor agencies ceased operations strikes increased, with the number of wage earners involved rising from 1,239,989 (1918) to 4,160,348 (1919). Most notable was the steel strike, 1919. The refusal of Judge Elbert H. Gary (1846–1927), chairman of the board, U.S. Steel, to confer with the strike leaders brought on a strike call by the A.F. of L. at the urging of radical labor organizer William Z. Foster (1881–1961). Strikers sought (1) union recognition, (2) collective bargaining rights, (3) abolition of the 12-hour day and (4) of company unions, (5) wage increases. The strike began 22 Sept. 1919 and was abandoned 9 Jan. 1920.

1916, 1 SEPT. FEDERAL CHILD LABOR LAW (Keating-Owen Act) barred from interstate commerce the products of child labor; declared unconstitutional 3 June 1918; Act of 24 Feb. 1919 declared unconstitutional 15 May 1922; 2 June 1924, **Child Labor Amendment** to the Constitution was submitted to the states for ratification. By 1950 only 26 of the necessary 36 states had ratified. For **Fair Labor Standards Act,** 1938, restricting child labor, see p. 425.

1921–32. LABOR SETBACKS. The sharp recession of 1921–22, strong opposition by employer associations, and unfavorable decisions by federal courts weakened organized labor. Real wages and per capita income rose after 1923 (except in textiles and coal mining). Total union membership, 1929, 3,442,-600 as against 5 million in 1921; A.F. of L., 2,961,096 against almost 4 million in 1921. Further drop by 1933 to 2,973,000, of whom 2,126,796 belonged to A.F. of L. **United Mine Workers** under **John L. Lewis** shrank from 500,-000 to 150,000.

Communist Agitation (**Trade Union Education League** headed by W. Z. Foster) within trade unions (particularly the ILGWU, Furriers, Amalgamated Clothing, and United Mine Workers) resulted in dual unions and forced progressives into alignments with conservative leaders against Communists.

Judicial Setbacks: See pp. 675, 676.

Major Labor Gains: Railway Labor Act, 1926 (p. 767); **Norris–La Guardia Anti-Injunction Act,** 23 Mar. 1932, forbade injunctions to sustain antiunion employment contracts or to prevent strikes, boycotts, and picketing.

For A.F. of L. support of **La Follette** for president in 1924, see p. 395. **William Green** (1873–1952), of United Mine Workers, succeeded to the presidency of the A.F. of L. on the death of Gompers (1924), and kept the organization along **craft union** lines. **Company unions** expanded to over 400 by 1926, with a membership of 1,369,000, continuing to expand until 1935 to about 2,500,000. Chief violence occurred in textile strikes: Gastonia and Marion, N.C.; Elizabethtown, Tenn.; and Paterson, N.J.

1932. First Unemployment Insurance law in the U.S. enacted in Wisconsin.

1933–51. LABOR GAINS UNDER THE NEW DEAL AND FAIR DEAL. As a result of New Deal labor policies (pp. 415–425) total noncompany union membership approximated 4,400,000 in 1935, of which the A.F. of L. claimed 3,045,347. Further expansion was due in large measure to the **Wagner Act** (p. 416) and to the activities of industrial unions largely as the result of the formation, 9 Nov. 1935, within the A.F. of L. of the **Committee for Industrial Organization** (**CIO**). In May 1938, leaders expelled from the A.F. of L. (**John L. Lewis** had resigned as vice-president of the A.F. of L., 23 Nov. 1935) set up a rival organization under the leadership of Lewis—spectacularly successful in increasing the membership of the United Mine Workers—and **Sidney Hillman** (p. 1058) of the

Amalgamated Clothing Workers. The CIO was reorganized, 1938, as the **Congress of Industrial Organizations**. **Philip Murray** (1886–1952) succeeded to the presidency of the CIO in Nov. 1940. By 1936 CIO began to organize the motor and steel industries. On 31 Dec. 1936 a few hundred workers seized a number of General Motors plants at Flint, Mich., staging a spectacular **sit-down strike** which lasted 44 days; involved 40,000 workers directly and 110,000 indirectly. Sit-down strikes spread to rubber, steel, textiles, oil refining, shipbuilding, and involved a half million workers. Following the Supreme Court decision in **Hague v. CIO**, 1939, declaring sit-down strikes illegal, this technique was discredited by organized labor.

1937, 30 MAY. MEMORIAL DAY MASSACRE. In the spring of 1937, the Steel Workers' Organizing Committee secured recognition by U.S. Steel as the bargaining agency, a wage boost of 10%, and a 40-hour week with time and a half for overtime. Other employers challenged the constitutionality of the Wagner Act (upheld by Supreme Court, 1937, p. 677). "Little Steel" under the leadership of **Republic Steel,** headed by **Tom M. Girdler** (1877–1965), was adamant. The issue came to a head when a group of union demonstrators before the gates of the Republic plant in South Chicago were fired upon by police, with 10 killed, 84 injured. Finally, in 1941, virtually all of the independent steel companies signed agreements with the CIO.

Dec. Publication of a report of a Senate subcommittee, headed by **Robert M. La Follette, Jr.** (1895–1953), disclosed antilabor techniques employed to fight unions (1933–37), including blacklists, espionage, vigilante groups to curb labor organizers (**Mohawk Valley formula**), recruiting of strikebreaking services, private armed forces, and private arsenals (in the possession of Youngstown Sheet and Tube Co. and Republic Steel Corp.). The report singled out terrorism in Harlan Co., Ky.

1938. FAIR LABOR STANDARDS ACT (p. 425).

LABOR IN WORLD WAR II (p. 449).

SMITH-CONNALLY ACT (1943, p. 451). For formation of CIO–PAC (1944), see p. 454.

UNION EXPANSION. A.F. of L. membership by 1943 had increased to almost 9 million; CIO claimed 5,285,000, with a total of 13 million union members in the U.S. by early 1944 out of a total employment of 54 million. By 1945 union membership rose to 14.8 million (35.8% of the nonagricultural labor force as against 11.5% in 1933). In percentage terms this was an all-time high.

1946, 20 FEB. Employment Act (p. 514) committed federal government to take steps to create and to maintain employment opportunities and to promote full employment.

1946, 1 APR. United Mine Workers' strike of 400,000 bituminous coal miners began. President Truman seized the mines; the government retained control when the operators refused to accept a contract with the union negotiated by federal authorities. A second strike call on 21 Nov. by John L. Lewis in defiance of a government injunction led to his being held in contempt of court by a federal district court (4 Dec.) and fined $10,000; United Mine Workers fined $3,500,000 (sustained by Supreme Court, 6 Mar. 1947, but fine subsequently reduced to $70,000). On 7 Dec. 1946 Lewis ordered the miners back to work.

1947, 23 JUNE. TAFT-HARTLEY ACT (p. 514).

1947–52. STRIKES AND WORK STOPPAGES increased in response to the inflationary cycle. By 1949 labor stressed pension plans and other "fringe" demands rather than higher wages. Work stoppages, relative to size of labor force, were lower in the postwar period (4,750 in 1945; 4,843 in 1950) than in 1903 (3,600) or 1917 (4,450), but were substantially higher than for the exceptional period, 1921–26 (c.1,500). When steel companies refused to abide by a Wage Mediation Board award (20 Mar. 1952) of higher wages to workers without rise in steel prices, President Truman under emergency powers seized the steel mills (8 Apr.). A preliminary injunction was granted 29 Apr. to nullify the seizure; on 2 June the Supreme Court ruled the seizure unconstitutional. The United Steel Workers Union called another strike, which was settled as a result of the intervention of President Truman (24 July), with the union obtaining a 16-ct. increase in wages, a rise of $5.20 per ton of steel, and a modified union shop.

1948. Mississippi became the 48th state to enact **workmen's compensation** legislation; first act, Maryland, 1902.

1952. Both A.F. of L. and CIO endorsed Adlai E. Stevenson, the Democratic party's unsuccessful candidate for president, who favored repeal of the Taft-Hartley Act.

Upon the deaths of William Green and Philip Murray, **George Meany** (p. 1101) and **Walter P. Reuther** (p. 1137) succeeded to the presidency of the A.F. of L. and CIO respectively.

1954. **"Right-to-work"** laws (outlawing union shop), on books of 13 states at beginning of year, adopted in Utah and Kansas, but new bills defeated in 31 states.

1955. GUARANTEED ANNUAL WAGE. Provisions for payments during layoff periods were obtained by UAW in a compromise settlement with Ford and General Motors; similar contracts were obtained by the CIO–Steelworkers.

5 DEC. MERGER OF A.F. OF L. AND CIO made official, with **George Meany** elected president. Under charter of the consolidated union, craft and industrial organizations were to have equal rank.

1957–73. RACKETEERING AND CRIME. A special Senate committee under the chairmanship of Sen. **John L. McClellan** to investigate racketeering in labor-management relations held hearings, largely concerned with the Teamsters Union and the activities of its president, **Dave Beck.** In May, Beck was expelled as vice-president of the AFL–CIO. He was convicted of embezzlement in a state court in Seattle, Dec. 1957. In addition, the Teamsters vice-president, **James R. Hoffa,** was also charged with misappropriation of funds and close connections with gangsters (and eventually jailed for jury tampering, 1967–71). The disclosure led to the adoption by the AFL–CIO of a Code of Ethics, the resignation of a number of union officials, and the suspension of several national affiliates in Oct. In Dec. the AFL–CIO convention expelled the Teamsters Union, the Bakery Workers Union, and the Laundry Workers Union. Previously, 22 Sept. 1954, the International Longshoremen's Association had been expelled from the A.F. of L. for refusing to rid itself of racketeering elements. Frank Fitzsimmons was elected president after Hoffa relinquished the office from prison (1971). Fitzsimmons and the Teamsters were among the leading labor supporters of President Nixon's reelection bid in 1972. Although granted clemency by Nixon (1971), Hoffa was prohibited from participating in union activity until 1980.

1959, 14 Sept. LABOR MANAGE-MENT REPORTING AND DISCLO-SURE ACT (LANDRUM-GRIFFITH), (p. 526).

15 July. Steel strike lasted until 7 Nov. when a federal court issued an 80-day injunction under the Taft-Hartley Act, ordering the men back to work. The strike was settled by year end at an estimated increase of 41 cts. per hour over 30 months. Previous steel strike of 1956 ended with a wage rise of c.50 cts. per hour by 1958 and rise in steel prices.

1929–59. TRENDS IN INCOME DISTRIBUTION.

PERCENTAGE OF INCOME AFTER FEDERAL TAX
(in percentages)

To:	1929	1941	1950–54	1955–59
Top 5%	29.5	21.5	18.0	18.0
Top 20%	54.0	47.0	43.0	44.0
Lowest 60%	26.5	30.0	34.0	34.0

Source: Department of Commerce

1960. UNIONS, concerned about unemployment and automation, stressed security in their bargaining. Under terms of the 5½-year contract between the Pacific Maritime Association and the International Longshoremen's and Warehousemen's Union, the unions agreed to relax work rules and accept labor-saving devices. In return, the employers agreed to reimburse workers for wages lost because of the effects of automation. Supplementary wages and retirement benefits were to be drawn from a $27.5 million automation fund supported by the employers.

1961–68. NATIONAL LABOR POLICY. The Kennedy and Johnson administrations attempted to combat unemployment by (1) increasing overall economic activity without inflation and (2) promoting manpower development programs. Beginning in 1962 the Eco-

nomic Report of the President contained "guideposts" for noninflationary wage and price behavior—suggesting that wage increases (including fringe benefits) in each industry equal the rate of increase in productivity in the economy as a whole. By 1966, a time of high employment and inflation, a number of major agreements exceeded recommended limits despite government pressures.

Manpower development programs aimed particularly at the hard-core unemployed were stressed in such legislation as the **Area Redevelopment Act** (1961), **Manpower Development and Training Act** (1962), and the **Economic Opportunity Act** (1964) and took the form of programs such as the Job Corps and Job Opportunities in the Business Sector (JOBS). Outlays for such programs increased from $735 million (1964) to an estimated $3.5 billion (1970).

MINIMUM WAGE LEGISLATION. The **Fair Labor Standards Act** (p. 425) was amended to increase the federal minimum wage to $1.25 per hour and extended to cover 3,624,000 new workers (5 May 1961). The minimum wage was increased (24 Sept. 1966) to $1.60 per hour (effective 1 Feb. 1968) with the coverage extended to approximately 8 million more workers, for whom the minimum of $1.60 was to be reached by 1971. The **Equal Pay Act** required equal wages for equal work in industries engaged in commerce or producing goods for commerce (10 June 1963).

1961–68. EMPLOYMENT. The size of the civilian labor force rose from 69 million (1960) to 79 million (1968). Unemployment rates for Negroes, teenagers, and the unskilled persistently were higher than the national average (1967, Oct.: Negroes, 8.8%; teenagers, 15.1%; nonfarm labor, 9.2%).

1964. EQUAL EMPLOYMENT OPPORTUNITY. Title VII of the Civil Rights Act of 1964 provided the first federal fair employment practices law, prohibiting discrimination on the basis of race, color, religion, national origin or sex by employers, employment agencies, and unions. An Equal Opportunity Commission was established to investigate and judge complaints.

1966–68. STRIKES. Inflation, high employment levels, and the growth of corporate profits rose more rapidly than aggregate labor income in the early 1960s. In addition, the efforts of skilled workers to restore wage differentials, contributed to the increase in time lost because of strikes. Public service employees began to show increased willingness to strike or take other "job action." The first official strike in the history of the New York City transit system lasted 12 days (1966). Teachers unions displayed increasing militancy as did police and firemen. New York City schools were closed for 36 days (1968).

1969–74. UMW SCANDALS. W. A. "Tony" Boyle won reelection as president of the United Mine Workers over reformer Joseph A. Yablonski in an election (1969) marked by intimidation and vote fraud. Yablonski and his wife and daughter were murdered (30–31 Dec. 1969) and Boyle found guilty (11 Apr. 1974) of first-degree murder in ordering the assassination. The election was set aside by federal court (June 1972) and when held in Dec. 1972 under Labor Department supervision, Boyle was defeated by Arnold Miller. Boyle was convicted (31 Mar. 1972) of illegal use of UMW funds in 1968 national elections. The union was held liable (1971, 1972) for $11.5 million for improper handling of its pension fund and Boyle ordered to step down as trustee of the fund.

1969–73. UNIONIZATION. Unions attempted to organize the service trades (from college professors to government employees), Southern workers, Kentucky coal miners, and agricultural employees. After 5 years of strikes and nationwide boycotts, in 1970 (Apr.–July) grape workers obtained contracts from California grape growers, a victory for **Cesar Chavez,** head of AFL–CIO United Farm Organizing Committee; early 1973, when the contracts expired, the International Brotherhood of Teamsters signed with the owners and a dispute between the 2 unions ensued. **1973, Nov.,** Chavez called for a new boycott of grape and lettuce growers. Despite continued attempts at unionization, the U.S. labor force grew far more rapidly than the spread of unions. Union membership totaled 19.76 million in 1970, up slightly from earlier years, but as a percent of nonagricultural employment, union membership was 27.9%, a new low for the post–World War II years.

1969–73. STRIKES. Man-days lost from strikes: 1969, 42,869,000; 1970, 66,414,000; 1971, 47,589,000; 1972 (prel.), 26,000,000. **1970, 15 Sept.,** 67-day General Motors strike began, which slowed nation's economic growth. Issues were pay, inflation protection, and early retirement; **12 Nov.,** UAW accepted contract with an est. 30% increase in wages and fringe benefits for 3 years. Major league baseball players struck for 2 weeks in 1972. **1973, Mar.** Major steel producers signed an innovative labor agreement with the steel workers, involving no strikes, no lockouts, binding arbitration, and at least a 3% pay rise per annum when the current contract expired.

1969–73. INFLATION. Real spendable earnings dropped in 1969–70, but rose in 1971–72 (real spendable earn-

AVERAGE HOURLY EARNINGS IN MANUFACTURING	
Year	Earnings
1909	$0.193
1919	0.477
1929	0.566
1933	0.442
1937	0.624
1945	1.023
1957	2.070
1972	3.810
1973 (Oct.)	4.130

PRODUCTIVITY AND COMPENSATION COMPARED
(Private Nonfarm)
(1967 = 100)

Year	Output per man-hour	Compensation per man-hour
1950	59.7	42.8
1960	88.6	73.9
1970	103.4	123.1
1972 (prel.)	112.1	140.3

SELECTED UNEMPLOYMENT RATES, 1961–70 (Percent)[1]

Group of Workers	1961–65 average	1966	1967	1968	1969	1970	1971	1972	1973
All workers	5.5	3.8	3.8	3.6	3.5	4.9	5.9	5.6	4.9
Sex and age:									
Both sexes 16–19 years	15.9	12.8	12.8	12.7	12.2	15.3	16.9	16.2	14.5
Men 20 years and over	4.4	2.5	2.3	2.2	2.1	3.5	4.4	4.0	3.2
Women 20 years and over	5.4	3.8	4.2	3.8	3.7	4.8	5.7	5.4	4.8
Race:									
White	4.9	3.4	3.4	3.2	3.1	4.5	5.4	5.0	4.3
Black and other races	10.4	7.3	7.4	6.7	6.4	8.2	9.9	10.0	8.9

Source: Statistical Abstract of the U.S.
[1] Percent of civilian labor force in specified group.

ings are calculated after social security and income taxes have been deducted as average weekly earnings in constant dollars in private nonagricultural businesses). By 1973, 40% of all workers under union contracts had escalator clauses in their contracts, which automatically increased their pay when the cost of living rose.

1969–73. GOVERNMENT POLICIES. With Nixon's new economic policy of 15 Aug. 1971 (p. 752) wage controls were imposed. Measures to stimulate the economy sought to reduce unemployment. New concern emerged to promote equality of opportunity for women. 1972. Equal Employment Opportunity Act gave the Equal Opportunity Commission (est. 1964) enforcement power through the courts in sex-discrimination cases. Unemployment affected teenagers far more severely than those over 20, blacks to a far greater extent than whites, women more than men.

Government policies did little to solve the problems of the high teenage and black unemployment.

1946–72. UNEMPLOYMENT INSURANCE. The total unemployment insurance benefits paid was a function of the amount of unemployment and the extension of coverage. Total benefits paid under all programs was $2.9 billion in 1946; the figure declined in 1947–48; rose in 1949 ($2.3 billion); declined with the Korean War to a low for the entire period in 1951 ($.9 billion); the figure increased slightly in 1952–53, and with the end of the Korean War in 1954 was $2.3 billion. The sum declined again in 1955–56, rose moderately in 1957, and with the recession of 1958 reached a new high of $4.3 billion; in 1959, the figure dropped to $2.8 billion and then moved upward in 1960–61 (reaching $4.4 billion in 1961); from 1962 to 1966 benefits paid went down annually (1966: $1.9 billion); 1967–69, benefits were in the range of \$2.2–\$2.3 billion; they soared 1970–72 (1970: \$4.2 billion; 1971: \$5.5 billion; 1972 [prel.] \$5.0 billion).

1947–71. FAMILY INCOMES.

MEDIAN FAMILY INCOMES
(in 1971 dollars)

Year	All Families	White	Black and Other Races
1947	\$5,483	\$5,714	\$2,930
1950	5,594	5,811	3,142
1960	7,688	8,109	4,321
1970	10,289	10,674	6,806
1971	10,285	10,672	6,714

PERCENTAGE OF FAMILIES WITH INCOMES UNDER \$3,000
(in 1971 dollars)

Year	All Families	White	Black and Other Races
1947	21.2%	18.4%	51.2%
1950	21.6	19.3	47.8
1960	14.6	12.5	34.8
1970	8.3	7.0	19.0
1971	8.3	6.9	19.4

OCCUPATIONAL TRENDS. Shift of population from rural to urban life (cf. p. 650) and technological progress were accompanied by far-reaching shifts in occupations:

LABOR FORCE STATUS
Number of Persons Engaged in Agricultural and Nonagricultural Pursuits
(1820–1970: 10 yrs. old and over)

(U.S. Bureau of Census, *Hist. Stat. of U.S., 1789–1945;* 1950–60: 14 yrs. and over, *Stat. Abstract, 1970:* 16 and over, Dept. of Labor.)

	Nonagri-cultural	%	Agri-cultural	%
1820	812,042	28.2	2,068,958	71.8
1860	4,325,116	41.1	6,207,634	58.9
1900	18,161,235	62.5	10,911,998	37.5
1940	42,985,704	82.4	9,162,547	17.6
1950	52,450,000	83.1	7,500,000	16.9
1960	59,702,000	92.9	4,565,000	7.1
1970	75,165,000	95.6	3,462,000	4.4

DISTRIBUTION OF GAINFUL WORKERS
(in thousands of persons)

	1870	1900	1940
All gainful workers	12,920	29,070	53,300
Agriculture	6,730	10,950	9,000
Forestry and fisheries	60	210	140
Mining	190	750	1,110
Manufacturing and hand trades	2,130	6,250	11,940
Construction	700	1,640	3,510
Transportation and other public utilities	580	2,020	4,150
Trade	850	2,870	7,180
Finance and real estate			1,550
Education	190	650	1,680
Other professional services	140	510	2,320
Domestic service	940	1,740	2,610
Personal service	270	1,020	3,100
Govt., not elsewhere classified	100	300	1,690
Not allocated	40	160	3,330

EMPLOYEES IN NONFARM ESTABLISHMENTS
1950–1972
(in thousands)

	1950	1960	1970	1972
Total Wage and Salary Workers	45,222	54,234	70,593	72,764
Manufacturing	15,241	16,796	19,349	18,933
Mining	901	712	623	607
Construction	2,333	2,885	3,381	3,521
Transportation and Public Utilities	4,034	4,004	4,493	4,495
Wholesale and Retail Trade	9,386	11,391	14,914	15,683
Finance, Insurance, and Real Estate	1,919	2,669	3,688	3,927
Services	5,382	7,423	11,612	12,309
Government (federal, state, local)	6,026	8,353	12,535	13,290

In the years 1870–1970, divided by sector, there were profound changes in employment patterns.

PERCENTAGE PARTICIPATION OF LABOR FORCE BY SECTOR 1870–1970

Year	Agriculture*	Manu-facturing**	Services***
1870	52	23	25
1970	4	32	64

* Includes forestry and fishing; ** includes mining and construction; *** includes all other activities not under agriculture or manufacturing.

As agriculture declined, manufacturing increased, but services expanded even more. In 1970, the service sector—augmented by the giant increase in government employment—was by far the most significant employer of American labor.

1900–72. The composition of the labor force changed as more women became employed.

WOMEN IN LABOR FORCE OR GAINFULLY OCCUPIED, 15 YRS. AND OVER

	Total No.	Married* No.	%
1890	3,712,144	515,260	13.9
1920	8,346,796	1,920,281	23.0
1940	13,840,000	5,040,000	36.4
1960	23,270,000	7,097,960	30.5
1972	33,320,000	13,827,800	41.5

* 1960, 1972 figures are for married with husband present. 1960: 14 yrs. and over; 1972: 16 yrs. and over.

WOMEN IN THE LABOR FORCE, SELECTED YEARS, 1900–72

Year	Women in Labor Force (thousands)	Women in labor force as percent of	
		Total labor force	All women of working age
1900	5,114	18.1	20.4
1910	7,889	20.9	25.2
1920	8,430	20.4	23.3
1930	10,679	22.0	24.3
1940	12,845	24.3	25.4
1945	19,270	29.6	35.7
1950	18,412	28.8	33.9
1955	20,584	30.2	35.7
1960	23,272	32.3	37.8
1965	26,232	34.0	39.3
1970	31,560	36.7	43.4
1972	33,320	37.4	43.8

Note.—Data for 1900 to 1940 are from decennial censuses and refer to a single date; beginning 1945 data are annual averages.
For 1900 to 1945 data include women 14 years of age and over; beginning 1950 data include women 16 years of age and over.
Labor force data for 1900 to 1930 refer to gainfully employed workers.
Data for 1972 reflect adjustments to 1970 Census benchmarks.
Sources: Department of Commerce, Bureau of the Census, and Department of Labor, Bureau of Labor Statistics.

WOMEN AS A PERCENT OF PERSONS IN SEVERAL PROFESSIONAL AND MANAGERIAL OCCUPATIONS, 1910–70
(Percent)

Occupational Group	1910	1920	1930	1940	1950	1960	1970
Clergymen	0.6	1.4	2.2	2.4	4.0	2.3	2.9
College presidents, professors, and instructors[1]	18.9	30.2	31.9	26.5	23.2	24.2	28.2
Dentists	3.1	3.3	1.9	1.5	2.7	2.3	3.5
Editors and reporters	12.2	16.8	24.0	25.0	32.0	36.6	40.6
Engineers	[2]	[2]	[2]	.4	1.2	.8	1.6
Lawyers and judges	.5	1.4	2.1	2.5	3.5	3.5	4.9
Managers, manufacturing industries	1.7	3.1	3.2	4.3	6.4	7.1	6.3
Physicians	6.0	5.0	4.4	4.7	6.1	6.9	9.3

[1] Data for 1920 and 1930 probably include some teachers in schools below collegiate rank. The Office of Education estimates the 1930 figure closer to 28 percent.
[2] Less than one tenth of 1 percent.
Note.—Data are from the decennial censuses. Data for 1910 and 1920 include persons 10 years of age and over; data for 1930 to 1970 include persons 14 years of age and over.
Source: Department of Commerce, Bureau of the Census.

SCIENCE, INVENTION, AND TECHNOLOGY

★ ★
★

General Science

The discovery of the New World opened up a treasure-house of natural phenomena for scientific study and classification. The settlers of British North America, however, were more than mere collectors of data. From the seventeenth century on, they were members of the transatlantic scientific community, and some, notably Benjamin Franklin, made universally acclaimed contributions to theoretical science. But this promising start was cut short by the American Revolution. The ensuing cultural nationalism weakened the institutional base for scientific endeavor, threw open the field to gifted amateurs and hobbyists, and ushered in an exploitative economic order that set a premium on applied rather than basic science. In the mid-1870s the distinguished mathematician and astronomer Simon Newcomb, lamenting the state of science in America, contrasted its "beggarly and humiliating showing" to the progress of European science and asked: "Why, with our numerous educational institutions, and our great crowd of professors, should our contributions to the exact sciences be so nearly zero?" He detected "nothing worthy of the name of national science." Yet even as Newcomb delivered this harsh indictment, new and auspicious developments were visible.

The wave of scientific discoveries in the nineteenth century had a major impact upon America after the Civil War, when the rise of the modern research-oriented university, and its panoply of graduate schools, was accompanied by the rapid professionalization and specialization of the scientific community, the separation of religious and metaphysical speculation from the intrinsic concerns of scientific thought and inquiry, and increasing financial support for science from the private accumulations of wealth under the new industrialism, such as the large foundations. By 1910 American scientists were speaking confidently of "pure research." The role of science in the two great wars of the twentieth century endowed it with an unprecedented and even decisive importance in the affairs of mankind, and the increasing complexities of scientific knowledge stressed the necessity of cooperative investigation. Massive federal funding between 1950 and 1970 stimulated enormous progress in basic and experimental work, but also raised serious questions concerning the involvement of scientists with research and development goals laid down by the political and military establishment. Shaped in large measure by its relations with government and corporate enterprise, American science by the mid-1970s was marked by bureaucratic organization and increasingly centralized control seemingly at odds with the traditional patterns of self-directed basic research.

1665–1735. EARLY ASTRONOMY AND SEISMOLOGY. John Winthrop, Jr. (1606–76), probably the first colonial member of the Royal Society of London (Brasch), made the first systematic astronomical observations in the colonies (before 1665). Advanced astronomical knowledge was revealed by **Thomas Brattle** (1658–1713) in his *Almanack* (1678). His observations of Halley's comet (1680) were utilized and credited to him by Newton in his landmark *Principia mathematica* (1687). His account of a solar eclipse of 1694 was published in the *Philosophical Transactions* of the Royal Society (1704). He made significant observations of a later (1703) solar eclipse, 3 lunar eclipses (1700, 1703, 1707), and of variations of the magnetic needle (1708). **Thomas Robie** (1689–1729), Harvard astronomer and mathematician, described a meteor (1719) as a natural phenomenon. **Paul Dudley's** (1675–1751) report of an earthquake in New England (1727) and further data on such phenomena appeared in *Transactions* (1735).

1680–1725. NATURAL HISTORY. John Banister (c.1648–92) transmitted (1680) 52 species of American insects to Petiver, the English naturalist, and contributed a paper on American molluscs to the Royal Society (1693). His *Catalogus Plantarum in Virginia Observatarum* (published in Ray's *Historia Plantarum*) is probably the first systematic paper upon natural history written in the colonies. **Cotton Mather** contributed 13 letters on natural history and biology to *Transactions* (1712) and was credited by Petiver (1717) with specimens of bones and dried plants. **Paul Dudley** contributed data on the swamp sumac, bees, and the rattlesnake to the *Transactions* (1720–23). Work on New England fruit trees (1724) established him as the first colonial horticulturist. His *Natural History of Whales* (1725), with its account of the source of ambergris, became a standard work.

1708–51. PHYSICS AND MATHEMATICS. James Logan (1674–1751) is generally credited with formally introducing Newton's *Principia* into the colonies (1708), although information was already available through the *Transactions*. Cotton Mather's *Christian Philosopher* (1721) contained the first lengthy explanation of Newtonian physics (in the colonies). The first colonial chair in philosophy and mathematics was filled (1717) at William and Mary by Rev. Hugh Jones (c.1670–1760). More significant was the endowment of a chair in mathematics and natural philosophy at Harvard (1727); the first incumbent, **Isaac Greenwood** (1702–45), offered a course in fluxions (calculus) and proposed (1727) to the Royal Society a plan for ocean charts, anticipating M. F. Maury's much later work.

1716–68. BOTANY AND ZOOLOGY. Cotton Mather wrote the earliest known account of plant hybridization (24 Sept. 1716)—hybridization of Indian corn and squash (Zirple); more details provided by **Paul Dudley** (1724). The correspondence between **John Bartram** (1699–1777) and Peter Collinson, English botanist, developed a channel for transmission of colonial plants and data abroad. Bartram, who established (1728) the first botanical garden in the colonies at Philadelphia, traveled widely through the colonies collecting specimens of rare plants and cultivating in North America plants received from abroad. He published (1751) his *Observations* of his trip to Lake Ontario. Together with his son, **William** (1739–1823), he explored the St. John's River, Fla., and there discovered the royal palm. William's list of 215 American birds (*Travels*, 1791) was the most complete published up to that time. Other pioneers in botany include **John Clayton** (1694–1773), best known for his *Flora Virginica*, revised and published by Gronovises (1739); **John Mitchell** (1680–1768), who pioneered in applying the Linnaean system of plant classification; **James Logan**, who performed the first colonial experiments in physiological botany—on the fructification of maize (reported 1734, 1736); **Cadwallader Colden** (1688–1776), whose work on the flora of New York was published in **Acts** of the Royal Society of Uppsala (1744); **Alexander Garden** (1728–92), who from 1752, collected the flora of South Carolina and discovered the mud iguana (1765) and the Congo snake (an eel, before 1775), correcting Linnaeus's classification of American flora and fauna; Rev. **Jared Eliot** (1685–1765), who published the first colonial work in the field of scientific

agriculture (1760), and **Adam Kuhn** (1741–1817), who offered (1768) the first course in botany as professor of materia medica at the College of Philadelphia.

1739–69. ASTRONOMY. John Winthrop IV (1714–79), who succeeded Greenwood as professor of mathematics and natural philosophy at Harvard, wrote papers on sunspots (1739), on a transit of Venus and a lunar eclipse (1740), and on Halley's comet (1759), with pioneer studies regarding the density of comets (1767) and the undulatory character of earthquakes (1756). He journeyed to Newfoundland to record the transit of Venus (1761; also transit of 1768), and observed the transits of Mercury (1740, 1743, 1769). **Ezra Stiles** (1727–95), applying Newton, calculated the true position of the sun and moon (1745). **David Rittenhouse** (1732–96), Philadelphia clock and instrument maker, built the first orrery in the colonies (1767); made notable observations of the transits of Venus and Mercury (1769), and of Lexell's comet (1770).

1743–71. AMERICAN PHILOSOPHICAL SOCIETY. Although Cotton Mather formed a group interested in natural history (1681) and Franklin organized the **Junto** (1727), the first truly scientific society was the American Philosophical Society, organized in Philadelphia, with Thomas Hopkinson (1737–91) as first president and Franklin as secretary. Its meetings were held irregularly until it was reorganized (1769) with Franklin as president (until his death, 1790). *Transactions* first published, 1771.

1746–52. ELECTRICITY. John Winthrop IV gave the first lectures on electricity in the colonies (at Harvard, 1746). **Benjamin Franklin** began his first experiments in electricity (1747), discovered the phenomenon of plus and minus charges (1747–48), suggested (1749) that thunder and lightning could be explained electrically, and performed an experiment proving the electrical nature of lightning (1752). His pamphlet, *Experiments and Observations on Electricity,* went through 11 editions (1751–76), 5 in English, 3 in French, 1 in German, 1 in Latin and 1 in Italian. **Ebenezer Kinnersley** (1711–78) refined and added to Franklin's electrical discoveries, noting (1762) that lightning and electricity melt metals by hot rather than cold fusion, while **James Bowdoin** corrected Franklin's notion that electricity was gathered into clouds of the sea (1756).

1746–56. MATHEMATICS. Cadwallader Colden's *Principles of Action in Matter* (1745–51), a highly original supplement to Newton, propounded the theory that gravitation was a force exerted by an elastic, contractive form of matter. Winthrop at Harvard is reputed to have been the first to teach a course in Newtonian fluxions (calculus).

1780–94. SCIENTIFIC SOCIETIES. American Academy of Arts and Sciences founded 1780 at Boston largely through the efforts of John Adams; published *Memoirs* (1785). New Jersey Society for the Promotion of Agriculture, Commerce, and Art (1781), with agricultural societies founded in South Carolina and Pennsylvania (1785), and the Chemical Society of Philadelphia (1792). Charles Willson Peale's Philadelphia Museum (1794) was the first independently established museum in the U.S.

1785. DESCRIPTIVE BOTANY. Publication of **Humphry Marshall's** (1722–1801) *Arbustrum Americanum,* a notable botanical essay based on the Linnaean system, and in the *Memoirs* of a paper by **Manasseh Cutler** (1742–1823), marked the beginning of systematic botany in New England.

1794–1860. DESCRIPTIVE ZOOLOGY. A paper on fish taken near Piscataqua, N.H., by **William Peck** (1763–1822) is considered the first paper on systematic zoology published in America (Coe). **Samuel Latham Mitchill** (1764–1831), professor of natural history at Columbia (1792–1801), established himself as a foremost zoologist with his work on the fish of New York (1814). **Thomas Say** (1787–1834) published a paper (1817) and 2 books (1824–28) on entomology, followed by *American Conchology* (1830), both illustrated by Charles Alexander Leseur (1778–1846). **Constantine Samuel Rafinesque** (c.1783–1840) contributed papers on sponges, Western fishes, foxes, and on salivation of horses to Silliman's *Journal of Science* (1819–20). His *Ichthyologia Ohiensis* (1820) was notable in its field. **John D. Godman** (1794–1830) published his 3-vol. *American Natural History* (1826–28). With the encouragement of William Bartram, **Alexander Wilson** (1766–1813) began his *American Ornithology* (9 vols., 1808–13). **John James Audubon's** (p. 976) *Birds of America* began to appear in 1827; completed with publication of 5th vol., *Ornithological Guide* (1838). With John Bachman (1790–1874) he began work on the *Viviparous Quadrupeds of North America* (5 vols., 1842–54). **Louis Agassiz** (p. 973) became professor of zoology at Harvard (1848), founded the Museum of Comparative Zoology at Harvard (1859), and also established a pioneer marine station at Buzzard's Bay (1873).

1794–1860. CHEMISTRY. Arrival in U.S. of **Joseph Priestley** (1733–1804) stimulated interest in the field. First separate chair established at Princeton (1795) with **John MacLean** (1771–1814) as first incumbent. **Thomas Cooper** (1759–1839), as professor of chemistry and mineralogy at Dickinson College (1811–16), at the Univ. of Pennsylvania (1817–19), and the Univ. of South

Carolina (1819–34), acted as a missionary for the new .chemistry of Priestley, Lavoisier, and Davy. **Benjamin Silliman** (p. 1152), first professor of chemistry and natural history at Yale (1802–53), discovered that carbon was vaporized in an electric arc (1822), prepared hydrofluoric acid for the first time in the U.S. (1823), and detected bromine in a natural American brine (1830), was also founder of *American Journal of Science and Arts* (1818), which he edited to 1846. Other advances in chemical analysis: detection of boric acid in tourmaline (1822) and of beryllium in chrysoberyl (1824) by **Henry Seybert**, and development by **J. Lawrence Smith** of a method for determining alkalies in minerals and destroying ammonium salts with aqua regia (1853). *Memoir on the Ammonia Cobalt Bases* (1857) by **Oliver Wolcott Gibbs** (1822–1908) and **Frederick A. Genth** (1820–93) constituted a solid achievement.

1797–1859. PALEONTOLOGY. **Thomas Jefferson** described a fossil found in Virginia (1797) and in the remains of Proboscidea and other finds at Big Bone Lick, Ky. (1808). **Rembrandt Peale** wrote an account of the mastodon ("mammoth," 1802). **Edward Hitchcock** (1793–1864) pioneer in the detection of fossil footprints in the Connecticut Valley (1836), continued his work in his *Final Report on the Geology of Massachusetts* (1841) and *Ichnology* and *Supplement* (1858, 1865). The arrival in the U.S. (1846) of **Louis Agassiz,** followed (1847) by work on fossils by Hiram A. Prout and S. D. Culbertson, focused attention on the prairie regions. Other notable contributions include the series of papers on the paleozoic vertebrates (1849) by **Isaac Lea** (1792–1886) and *The Ancient Fauna of Nebraska* (1853) by **Joseph Leidy** (1823–91), based on the findings of an expedition sent out by Spencer F.

Baird (1823–87) of the Smithsonian Institution.

1798. BENJAMIN THOMPSON (Count Rumford, 1753–1814), a Loyalist exile who did all his scientific work abroad, reported the results of his experiments on the nature of heat as a form of motion. He endowed medals of the Royal Society (first awarded, 1802) and the American Academy of Arts and Sciences (first award, 1839) as well as the Rumford professorship of physics at Harvard (Jacob Bigelow, 1816, first incumbent).

1799. Publication of *Practical Navigator* by **Nathaniel Bowditch** (p. 990), still a standard work of reference for mariners. Bowditch translated Laplace's *Mécanique céleste* (1814–17) and made observations on a meteor (1815).

1799–1804. WILLIAM DUNBAR (1749–1810) took the first important meteorological recordings in the Southwest and gave the first scientific account and analysis of the waters of Hot Springs.

1806–55. BENJAMIN SILLIMAN founded (at Yale) a notable school of geologists, including Benjamin Silliman, Jr. (1816–85), who made valuable investigations into the uses and preparation of petroleum products and wrote a report on petroleum in Pennsylvania; **Edward Hitchcock,** who published notable reports on the geology of New England (1818, 1823); **Amos Eaton** (1776–1842), who published his *Index* to the geology of the North (1815); **Denison Olmstead** (1791–1859), whose report on the geology of North Carolina (1824–25) was the first official state geological survey in the U.S.; and, most notable, **James Dwight Dana** (1813–95), who, on his return from the Wilkes expedition (p. 1184) described for the first time 230 species of zoophytes and 636 of Crustacea, and published basic manuals on geology (1837, 1848, 1863). Other important geologists: **William Maclure** (1763–1840), whose

Observations on the Geology of the U.S.
(1809) contained the first geological map
of America; revised, 1817; **Thomas Say,**
the first American to point out the chro-
nogenetic value of fossils (1819). The
final integration of European and American chronologies was achieved through
the efforts of **Isaac Lea, T. A. Conrad**
(1803–77), and **James Hall** (1811–98).

1818–60. DESCRIPTIVE BOTANY.
Notable work in this period contributed
by **Gotthilf Muhlenberg** (1753–1815),
with his catalogue of 2,800 species of
North American plants (1813); **Thomas
Nuttall** (1786–1859), *Genera of North
American Plants* (1818); **John Torrey**
(1796–1873), on flora of North and Middle States (1824); **Lewis David von
Schweinitz** (1780–1834), on fungi
(1831). For the work of **Asa Gray** both
before and after 1860, see p. 1045.

1829–46. ELECTRICITY. Following
Franklin, electrical research was actively
pursued in Europe (Galvani, current
electricity, 1790; Volta, electric battery,
1800; Oersted, Ampère, Arago, electromagnetism, c.1820; Schweigger, galva-
nometer, 1820; Sturgeon, electromagnet,
1825). **Joseph Henry** (p. 1056) began experiments in electricity (1827); improved
the electromagnet (1829) and, independent of Faraday, discovered the method
for producing induced currents of electricity (1830–32); aided Morse in his
experiments in telegraphy; discovered the
oscillatory nature of electrical discharge
of Leyden jar (1842); and anticipated
later discoveries in radio and light waves
(to 1846).

**1831–61. METEOROLOGY. William
C. Redfield's** (1789–1857) pioneer observations (1831–37) and papers on
wind motion during storms (1842, 1846)
were challenged by **James P. Espy**
(1785–1860), whose *Law of Cooling of
Atmospheric Air* (1843) was one of the
great U.S. contributions to the field.
Further contributions in this field were

made by **James H. Coffin** (1806–73) and
William Ferrel (1817–91), who propounded (1856) Ferrel's Law, which
expressed the fact that on account of
the earth's rotation bodies on its surface
are deflected to the right in the Northern
Hemisphere and to the left in the Southern Hemisphere.

**1836–1902. ETHNOLOGY AND AN-
THROPOLOGY.** Earliest work in Ameri-
can ethnology directly related to the
study and classification of North American Indians by linguistic families. **Albert
Gallatin** (p. 1037) published pioneer contribution, "A Synopsis of the Indian
Tribes . . .," in American Antiquarian
Society *Transactions,* II (1836), drew
up first good ethnographical map of
North America, founded (1842) the
American Ethnological Society, and in its
Transactions (1845, 1848) published
important essays on the Indians of the
New World. Gallatin's writings prepared
the ground for an American science of
ethnology. **Henry Rowe Schoolcraft**
(1793–1864), an explorer and Indian
agent who lived among frontier tribes
for many years, compiled the monumental *Historical and Statistical Informational Respecting the . . . Indian Tribes
of the United States,* 6 vols. (1851–57).
Lewis Henry Morgan (p. 1106) published
in his account of the Iroquois (1851),
the first scientific study of an Indian
tribe; his analysis of Iroquois social and
political organization, as well as kinship
systems and marriage customs, constituted one of the significant steps in the
emergence of an American anthropology.
John Wesley Powell (p. 1132) founded
and served as first director (1879–1902)
of the U.S. Bureau of Ethnology of the
Smithsonian Institution, and in *An Introduction to the Study of Indian Languages*
(1877) and in a paper on North American Indian linguistic families (1891)
devised a system of nomenclature that
was later generally adopted for studies of

Amerindian languages. **Daniel G. Brinton** (1837–99) was one of the pioneers of American anthropology; although many of his hypotheses were subsequently discarded, his paper on the Mound Builders (1866) correctly identified them as Amerindian, while his *The American Race* (1891) was the first attempt to classify systematically the aboriginal languages of the New World Indians. He complied *Aboriginal American Authors and Their Productions* (1882–90). **American Anthropological Association** founded (1902) at Washington, D.C.

1840–59. ASTRONOMY. Astronomical observatory erected at Harvard (1840) by **William Cranch Bond** (1789–1859), its first director. With his son, **George Phillips Bond** (1825–65), he discovered 8th satellite of Saturn and first moon of Neptune, and invented electrochronograph for determining longitude. The Great Comet, which appeared in 1843, stimulated astronomical investigation. Notable work on the planet Neptune (discovered 1846) and the rings of Saturn done in this period by **Benjamin Peirce** (1809–80). **Maria Mitchell** (1818–89), of Nantucket, Mass., discovered a comet (1847) and became the first woman professor of astronomy in the U.S. (Vassar, 1865).

1846. SMITHSONIAN INSTITUTION founded by Act of Congress (1846), utilizing bequest (c. £100,000) of James Smithson, an English chemist and mineralogist; Joseph Henry named first director. **American Association for the Advancement of Science** organized, with William C. Redfield, president.

1847–56. HYDROGRAPHY AND OCEANOGRAPHY. Of great aid to worldwide exploration were the various *Wind and Current Charts* compiled by **Matthew Fontaine Maury** (p. 1100), appointed (1842) superintendent of Department of Charts and Instruments (later U.S. Naval Observatory and Hydrographic Office); cut sailing time from New York to San Francisco (by 1855) from 180 to 130 days, with similar reductions in many other parts of the world. His *Physical Geography of the Sea* (1856) was widely translated.

1864–1903. CHEMISTRY. M. Carey Lea (1823–97): platinum metals (1864); photochemistry (1865–93); discovery of photosalts (by 1880); notable work on colloidal suspensions, especially with silver (from 1889). Technics in volumetric analysis improved by **Josiah Parsons Cooke** (1827–94). Electrolytic analysis introduced by **Oliver Wolcott Gibbs** (1865) was improved by **Frank Austin Gooch** (before 1903) by the introduction of the rotating cathode. Completion by **Josiah Willard Gibbs** (p. 1041) of his *On the Equilibrium of Heterogeneous Substances* (1875), followed by a further paper (1877–78), established him as the founder of "chemical energetics." He extended the method of thermodynamics, applying it to chemical problems, and introduced the "phase rule." **Ira Remsen** (1846–1927), who founded U.S. graduate research in chemistry at Johns Hopkins (1876), obtained benzoic sulfinide (saccharin) and enunciated "Remsen's Law" determining the protection of methyl and other groups from oxidation.

1864–1903. GEOLOGY. California survey proved the presence of Upper Triassic (1864); found in Idaho (1877) and subsequently over most of the West. **F. V. Hayden** found marine Jurassic fossils in "Red Beds" of Rocky Mountain area, but it was not until the Jurassic strata were found in California (1885) that the outlines of this formation could be drawn. Work of **Robert T. Hill** (on Texas Cretaceous, 1887) and of **W. M. Gabb** and **J. D. Whitney** (on California Cretaceous, 1869) contributed to rounding out the geological map of the U.S. Glacial formations described by Hilgard (Miss., 1866), Stevens (Va., 1873), Hall

(Pa., 1876), and Rogers (Va. and N.C., 1876), with outstanding work (1873–82) by **Thomas C. Chamberlain** (1843–1928). **Grove K. Gilbert** (1843–1918) reported on extinct Lake Bonneville (1879). **William H. Dall** (1845–1927) made major contributions to stratigraphy (1885–1903). See also p. 613.

1864–1952. ASTRONOMY. Lewis M. Rutherfurd (1816–98) built astronomical camera and photographed the moon (1864), and invented micrometer to measure stars. **Henry Draper** (1837–82) obtained first successful photograph of the spectrum of a star (1872) and introduced photography of nebulae (1880). Using telescopes built by **Alvan Clark** (1808–87), **Asaph Hall** (1829–1907) discovered the moon of Mars (1877) and **James E. Keeler** (1857–1900) the composition of Saturn's rings (1886). **Samuel P. Langley** (1834–1906) devised the bolometer to detect temperatures and demonstrated a new way to test variations in surface temperatures of the sun (1881). **William H. Pickering** (1858–1938) discovered Phoebe, 9th satellite of Saturn (1898). As a result of prediction and research originated in 1905 by **Percival Lowell** (1855–1916), the planet Pluto was discovered (1930) by **Clyde W. Tombaugh** (1906–   ). **George Ellery Hale** (1868–1932) invented the spectroheliograph, with which he took the first successful photograph of solar prominence (1891). Through Hale's efforts the Mt. Wilson Observatory was opened (1906). Hale Telescope at Mt. Palomar opened in 1948. **Seth B. Nicholson** (1891–1963) discovered 9th, 10th, 11th moons of Jupiter 1914, 1938; 12th, 1952.

1866–1941. PALEONTOLOGY. Othniel Charles Marsh (1831–99), first professor of paleontology in the U.S. (Yale, 1866), led organized bone-hunting expeditions for Yale, and later (1881) for U.S. Geological Survey (discovered 500 new species, 225 new genera, 64 new families, 19 new orders). **Edward D. Cope** (1840–97) published 3 notable studies (1875, 1877, 1883) as a result of field expeditions he organized; his work on herpetology and ichthyology prepared the way for modern classification of North American reptiles, amphibians, and fishes. **Henry Fairfield Osborn** (1857–1935), professor of zoology at Columbia (1896–1910) and curator of vertebrate paleontology at American Museum of Natural History (1891–1910), popularized knowledge of the field. Dinosaur National Monument (Utah and Colorado) established (1915) to preserve area of great finds. The largest footprints yet found (4½ x 3 ft.) discovered in the Texas Big Bend country (1941).

1870–84. MATHEMATICS. At Johns Hopkins, **James J. Sylvester** (1814–97), the British mathematician, advanced the studies in this field and founded the *American Journal of Mathematics*. At Yale **Josiah Willard Gibbs** published his *Elements of Vector Analysis* (c.1881–84).

1881–1920. VELOCITY OF LIGHT. Albert A. Michelson (p. 1102) determined the velocity of light (1878–80) and invented the interferometer, by which length of standard meter was ascertained in terms of wave length of cadmium light (1887), and began investigations on existence of hypothetical ether (1881). Famous experiment with **Edward W. Morley** (1838–1923) in 1887 served as starting point for Einstein's Special Theory of Relativity (1905).

1902–60. ANTHROPOLOGY AND CULTURAL ANTHROPOLOGY. Franz Boas (p. 988) was the principal figure in establishing an American science of anthropology. He organized (1902) the Jesup Expedition to study the Indians of the Canadian Pacific Northwest; the expedition's reports on the Kwakiutl and other Indians reinforced the "culture-area" approach as distinguished from the geographical-diffusionist viewpoint. Clark Wissler (1870–1947), associated with the American Museum of Natural History, stressed the historical-diffusionist approach and was influential in defining Indian culture areas in the New World. Boas, who introduced cultural objectivity and scientific method into field work, and stressed the functional interconnection of group institutions, trained in his seminars at Columbia Univ. a number of anthropologists who made important contributions to theory and knowledge and were instrumental in shaping the direction of cultural anthropology in the U.S. Among his students were (1) **Alfred L. Kroeber** (1876–1960), who in 1902 received the first Ph.D. in anthropology awarded by Columbia. Kroeber studied the diffusion of tribal cultures in North and South America; gave standing to cultural anthropology in such books as *Handbook of the Indians of California* (1925), *Cultural and Natural Areas of Native North America* (1939), and *Configurations of Culture Growth* (1944); and, after Boas, was the major force in professionalizing anthropology in the U.S. and in fostering it as an academic discipline; (2) **Alexander A. Goldenweiser** (1880–1940), who wrote on totemism and contributed suggestive insights into theory and methodology in the study of magic, religion, and social organization, as in his *History, Psychology, and Culture* (1933); (3) **Robert H. Lowie** (1883–1957) wrote many monographs on North American Indians, especially the Crows (1912, 1935); his *Primitive Society* (1920) strongly influenced social organization theory, while his *Primitive Religion* (1924) expounded a diffusionist hypothesis; (4) **Edward Sapir** (1884–1939) drew links between personality and culture and wrote the innovative

paper "Time Perspective in Aboriginal American Culture: A Study in Method" (1916); he devoted much of his work to investigating American Indian languages and cultures, and was one of the trailblazers of an American science of linguistics; (5) **Ruth F. Benedict** (1887–1948), in her *Patterns of Culture* (1934), applied the findings of Gestalt psychology to the Kwakiutl, Pueblo, and Dubu societies. (6) **Margaret Mead** (1903–) used the insights of Freudian psychoanalysis and made the relations between personality and culture the central theme of such works as *Coming of Age in Samoa* (1928), *Growing Up in New Guinea* (1930), and *Sex and Temperament in Primitive Societies* (1935). Other cultural anthropologists of note were **Ralph Linton** (1883–1953) and **Robert Redfield** (1897–1958). A trained anthropologist, **William Lloyd Warner** (1898–1970), used the techniques of the discipline in studying an American community (Newburyport, Mass.) in his "Yankee City" series (1941–59).

1909–26. STUDIES IN INHERITANCE. Thomas Hunt Morgan (p. 1107) at Columbia used the fruit fly (drosophila) to test Mendel's laws of inheritance; first to use "gene" (1909) to describe individual parts of chromosomes controlling particular characteristics; discovered the phenomenon of sex-linked characteristics (1910) and later (1911, 1913) characteristics of different linkages. His students elaborated work on mutants and the gene theory. Work by **R. A. Emerson** (1873–1947) on mutations in corn (from 1914) tended to confirm Morgan. **Hermann J. Muller** (p. 1111) found that with X rays he could artificially increase the rate of mutation in the fruit fly (by 1926). Confirmation of findings provided by experiments with barley by **Lewis J. Stadler** (1896–1954) and with tobacco by **T. H. Goodspeed** (1887–1966).

1910. Trivalent carbon discovered by **Moses Gomberg** (1866–1947).

1910–25. ROBERT A. MILLIKAN (p. 1104) announced (1910) he had measured the charge of an electron as a definite constant; elaborated results in his *The Electron* (1912; 2d ed., 1925). He succeeded in proving Einstein's hitherto unproven photoelectric equation and in evaluating Planck's Constant (h).

1911–70. LINGUISTICS. The major influence on linguistics in the U.S. in the 20th century was the concern of anthropologists with the indigenous languages of North America. The introduction by Franz Boas to *Handbook of American Indian Languages* (1911), a volume he edited, set forth a method of systematic description that challenged traditional grammatical theory by holding that each language had its own unique grammatical structure. This view, although not originated by Boas or restricted to him, became the point of departure for the "structuralist" approach with which the American school of linguistics has been associated. This school had 2 periods of development: (1) **1920–40.** The Linguistics Society of America was established in 1924. The professionalization of linguistics developed around the 2 seminal scholars of the period, **Edward Sapir** and **Leonard Bloomfield** (1887–1949), both of whom were initially trained in Germanic philology but turned to linguistics as a result of their studies of American Indian languages. Sapir, as an anthropologist, did field work in many American Indian languages, and produced 2 notable works: *Language* (1921), a discussion of basic principles that was destined to be influential for more than 2 generations; and the paper "Sound Patterns in Language" (1925), which set down the fundamentals of structural analysis for American linguistics. While insisting on the interdependence of linguistics with other disciplines, Sapir stressed the autonomy of grammatical form. Emphasis on the autonomy of linguistics was reinforced by Bloomfield, whose *Language* (1933), embodying an approach based on the behaviorist psychology of John B. Watson, became a central work of the new structuralist school. Bloomfield established (1940) a department of linguistics at Yale that became a center of American linguistic scholarship. (2) **1940–70.** By 1945, linguistics was rapidly being distinguished from philology, and became generally accepted as an independent, scientific, and academic discipline. In this period a leading exponent of structuralism was **Zellig S. Harris** (1909–   ), of the Univ. of Pennsylvania, author of *Methods in Structural Linguistics* (1951), *Mathematical Structure of Language* (1968), and *Papers in Structural and Transformatinal Linguistics* (1970). His most gifted pupil, and the single most influential figure in American linguistics in this period, is **Noam Chomsky** (1928–   ), who since 1955 has been on the faculty of MIT. Initially a structuralist, Chomsky later rejected the mechanistic implications of the Bloomfieldian approach, and came to view linguistics as a branch of cognitive psychology. He has brought to the investigation of language a rigorous scientific method based on mathematics and logic. His chief contribution has been the formal syntactic theory associated with his universal models of generative and transformational grammar. Among his works are *Syntax Structures* (1957), *Aspects of the Theory of Syntax* (1965), *Cartesian Linguistics* (1966), and *Language and Mind* (1968).

1912–48. MEASURING THE UNIVERSE. Henrietta Leavitt (1868–1921) at Harvard announced her "period-luminosity" law; i.e., the period of fluctuation of brightness of a Cepheid star is directly proportional to its candlepower. **Harlow Shapley** (1885–1972), applying this law to globular clusters, was able (1917) to measure distances in the Milky Way. Data accumulated (by 1928) by **Vestro M. Slipher** (1875–1969), Lowell Observatory, on 43 spiral nebulae, using spectroscope and working with the "Doppler shift," showed that these nebulae were moving away from the earth at speeds increasing with distance. **Edwin Powell Hubble** (1899–1953), in conjunction with Milton L. Humason (1891–1972), at the Wilson Observatory, by adding the period-luminosity law to Slipher's technic (1929–43), worked out quantitative measurements of distance and speeds confirming Slipher.

1914–51. ATOMIC RESEARCH. Gilbert N. Lewis (p. 1083) set forth new theory of the structure of the atom (1916); expanded by **Irving Langmuir** (p. 1080) into the concentric shell theory (1919), which explained chemical activity of an element in terms of the completeness of its outer shell of electrons. **Theodore W. Richards** (1868–1928) at Harvard discovered an isotope of lead (1914, 2 isotopes of neon had been found in England, 1913). **William D. Harkins** (1873–1951), working on the problem of nuclei of atoms (1914–21), found that nitrogen bombarded by helium nuclei produced an oxygen isotope (atomic wt. 17) and predicted the neutron (1920), which was discovered in England (1932). **Arthur H. Compton** (p. 1004) discovered the Compton effect, which showed that X rays had a corpuscular structure (1923). **Clinton J. Davisson** (p. 1010) and **Lester H. Germer** (1896–1971) found that electrons shot against a nickel crystal were reflected in the same way as light waves, thus showing for the first time that matter has wavelike characteristics (1927). **Ernest O. Lawrence** (p. 1081) constructed the first cyclotron, which made possible the acceleration of nuclear particles to

energies of millions of volts for smashing atoms (1930). **Harold C. Urey** (p. 1173) discovered hydrogen isotope of mass 2 (deuterium, or heavy hydrogen, 1931). **Arthur J. Dempster** (1886–1950) built improved mass spectrograph and isolated isotope uranium 235, later found to be the only natural fissionable element existing in relatively large quantities (1935). **Enrico Fermi** (1901–1954), **John R. Dunning** (1907–1975), and **George B. Pegram** (1876–1958) repeated uranium fission experiment of Otto Hahn and Fritz Strassman in Germany and Otto Frisch and Lise Meitner in Denmark, in which vast amounts of nuclear energy are released by the splitting of uranium 235 atoms with fast or slow neutrons, the discovery which led to the production of the atomic bomb and to the utilization of atomic energy. **Edwin M. McMillan** (p. 1094) and **Philip H. Abelson** (1913–) isolated neptunium (element 93), first transuranic element (1940). **Glenn T. Seaborg** (p. 1148) and **Emilio Segre** (1905–) produced plutonium, (element 94), first man-made fissionable element (1941). First self-perpetuating nuclear chain reaction, demonstrating practicability of atomic bomb and industrial atomic power, on 2 Dec. 1942. Electromagnetic and gaseous diffusion plants for separation of isotope uranium 235 built at Oak Ridge, Tenn., 1943–44. Nuclear reactors for producing plutonium built at Hanford, Wash., 1943–44. **First atomic bomb** designed and constructed at Los Alamos, N.M., 1945; tested at Alamogordo, N.M., 16 July 1945. McMillan announced discovery of principle of synchrotron (1945). Seaborg *et al.* produced americium, curium, berkelium, and californium, elements 95, 96, 97, and 98 (1944–50). First production of electric power from nuclear reactor, Arco, Ida. (1951). Cosmotron at Brookhaven National Laboratory generated 2,250 million volts (10 June 1952).

1916–53. ALBERT EINSTEIN (p. 1022), continuing (1933) his life work at the Institute for Advanced Study, Princeton, N.J., disclosed (30 Mar. 1953) formulas as last step in his quest for a Unified Field Theory, a single mathematical system embracing electromagnetism and gravitation in one universal law, and eventually uniting the Relativity and Quantum theories.

1921–51. COSMIC RAYS. Millikan, with **Ira S. Bowen** (1898–1973) began investigations in California on nature and origin of cosmic rays from outer space. **Arthur H. Compton** (p. 1004) organized worldwide study (1931). **Carl D. Anderson** (1905–   ) discovered the positron particle with mass of negative electron but with a positive charge of equal magnitude in cosmic rays (1932). Anderson with **Seth H. Neddermeyer** (1907–   ) discovered in the cosmic rays a new charged particle, intermediate in mass between the proton and the electron, which was named the meson (1936). **Jabez C. Street** (1906–   ) and **E. C. Stevenson** discovered same particle independently (1937). **Robert Marshak** (1916–   ) predicted on theoretical grounds the existence of heavier type of meson to account for nuclear forces, in accordance with earlier prediction by **Hideki Yukawa** of Japan (later at Columbia). Heavier meson, named pi-meson, later found in cosmic ray in British studies. Pi-meson produced artificially (1948) in giant synchrocyclotron at Univ. of California, marking first time that matter was created out of energy in accordance with famous Einstein formula ($E = mc^2$).

1941, 28 June. Office of Scientific Research and Development (p. 435).

1954–57. NEW ELEMENTS. 99 (einsteinium, atomic weight 247) and 100 (fermium, atomic weight 254)—AEC's Argonne National Laboratory and Univ.

of California (1954); 101 (mendelevium) —Univ. of California (1955); 102 (nobelium)—Nobel Institute and Argonne Laboratory (1957).

1955. Nobel prize awards in physics to **Polykarp Kusch** (1911–   ), Columbia, for precision determination of the magnetic moment of the electron, proving that energy level calculations of P. A. M. Dirac, British physicist, did not agree with experimental evidence, and to **Willis E. Lamb** (1913–   ), Stanford, for discoveries regarding the hyperfine structure of the hydrogen spectrum.

18 Oct. ANTI-PROTON, a new atomic particle, discovered by Emilio Segre and associates at Univ. of California.

1956. ANTI-NEUTRON identified at Bevatron Laboratory of U. of California.

1957. SPONTANEOUS GENERATION. Amino acids, the basic substance of proteins, produced by exposing mixtures of methane, ammonium, water, and hydrogen to electrical charges comparable to lightning in experiment performed by **Stanley L. Miller** of Columbia Univ. College of Physicians and Surgeons.

1957, July 1–1958, Dec. 31. INTERNATIONAL GEOPHYSICAL YEAR, an 18-month period of intensive study of the earth, the oceans, the atmosphere, and the sun. U.S. scientists participated, with an appropriation of $39 million from Congress to National Science Foundation.

1960–70. NEW ELEMENTS. 103 (lawrencium)—Lawrence Radiation Laboratory, Univ. of California, 1960; the Laboratory also created the heaviest known nucleus, the isotope mendelevium, 258 (1963); 104 (rutherfordium)—identified by Albert Ghiorso and others of the Lawrence Radiation Laboratory, 1969 (discovery disputed by Soviet scientists who claim precedence and named element kurchatovium); 105 (hahnium)—discovered in 1970 by A. Ghiorso and associates.

1960–73. NOBEL PRIZES IN PHYSICS: 1960, Donald A. Glaser (1918–) for invention of bubblebath chamber for photographing atomic particles; **1961, Robert Hofstader** (1915–) shared prize for providing evidence that the proton has complex structure; **1963, Eugene Wigner** (1902–) shared prize for formulation of the symmetry principles governing the interaction of nuclear particles in accordance with their direction of spin; **1964, Charles H. Townes** (1915–) for work on masers which helped produce lasers, light amplification by stimulated emission of radiation; **1965, Richard P. Feynman** (1918–) and **Julius S. Schwinger** (1918–) for their fundamental work in quantum electrodynamics with deep-plowing consequences for the physics of elementary particles; **1967, Hans Bethe** (1906–) for his theoretical studies of the processes from which the sun devises its energy; **1968, Luis W. Alvarez** (1911–) for his work on subatomic particles and techniques for their detection; **1969, Murray Gell-Mann** (1929–) for his discoveries and contributions concerning the classification of elementary particles and their interactions; **1972, John Bardeen** (1908–), who shared a Nobel prize in physics, 1956, thus becoming the first laureate to win twice in the same field; **Leon N. Cooper** (1924–) and **John R. Schrieffer** (1931–) for joint research and development of the theory of superconductivity in ultracold metals, a property causing them to lose resistance to electric current; **1973, Leo Esaki** (1925–) and **Ivar Giaever** (1929–) for theories concerning "tunneling," or the superconducting behavior of electrons in solids, whose application underlies revolutionary progress in miniature electronics.

1960–72. NOBEL PRIZES IN CHEMISTRY: 1960, Willard F. Libby (1908–) for inventing atomic time clock; **1961, Melvin Calvin** (1911–) for contributions to the discovery of the chemical reactions involved in photosynthesis; **1965, Robert Burns Woodward** (1917–); see p. 1188 for the synthesis of organic structures; **1966, Robert S. Mulliken** (1896–) for theoretical studies of the chemical bonds that hold atoms together in a molecule; **1968, Lars Onsager** (1903–) for system of equations that show reciprocal reactions of activities such as the interaction of voltage and temperature in the transfer of heat (work done in 1931). **1972 prize** (p. 817).

1960–71. ELEMENTARY PARTICLE RESEARCH. Larger atom smashers such as the Brookhaven Synchotron (1960) and the Brookhaven High-Flux Beam research reactor (HFBR) (1965) and Stanford University's 2-mile, 20-billion-volt linear accelerator (1966) facilitated research into the atom or "nuclear zoo." Among the observed particles were the omega meson (1961, Lawrence Rad. Lab.); rho meson (1961, many labs); anti-xi-xero (1963, Brookhaven); omega minus (1964, Brookhaven); the anti-neutron (1965, Brookhaven team led by Leon M. Lederman); the phi-meson was confirmed (1963, Lawrence Lab. and Brookhaven). A team at Lawrence Radiation Laboratory identified (1971) the anti-omega-minus baryon, one of a basic group of subatomic particles comprising the principal constituents of atomic nuclei.

1962–74. DEVELOPMENTS IN ASTRONOMY spurred by space program. **Ranger 4** hit far side of moon 23 Apr. 1962. **Mariner 2** space probe (launched 22 Aug. 1962) discovered Venus temperature at 800° and indicated that there was no break in the planet's cloud cover; U.S. spacecraft **Ranger 7** took 4,316 photographs of lunar surface before hitting moon, 31 July 1964, discovering more small craters and reporting the slight depth of moon dust. Further lunar photographs by **Ranger 8** (moon hit 20 Feb. 1965) and **Ranger 9** (24 Mar. 1964), as well as **Surveyor 1** (2 June 1966). U.S. lunar orbiter launched 14 Aug. 1966. Sun-orbiting **Pioneer 6** launched 16 Dec. 1965. **Mariner 4** spacecraft photographs of Mars (15–24 July 1965) after 7½ month flight detected no trace of canals or seas. **Mariner 5** launched for Mars 14 June 1967. **Surveyor 5** landed on moon (10 Sept. 1967) and relayed analysis of moon area consisting of basaltic materials, primarily oxygen and silicon, very earthlike in composition. **Mariner 6** (launched 24 Feb. 1969) and **Mariner 7** (launched 27 Mar. 1969) passed within 2,000 miles of Mars on different orbits and sent back many photos of the planet's varied terrain; once more these did not confirm the existence of canals on Mars. Infrared spectrometer aboard Mariner 7 detected features of the southern polar ice-cap, found to consist of frozen carbon dioxide. Information was obtained on Phobos, one of the planet's two moons. **Mariner 8** having failed shortly after takeoff in May, 1971, **Mariner 9** was launched on 30 May 1971, and entered orbit about Mars on 13 Nov. 1971. On 14 Nov. it began transmitting the first of many thousands of photos, resulting in the first systematic photomapping of the planet's surface. An infrared spectrometer measured the atmospheric and surface characteristics. This information, in addition to the photos, materially altered scientists' conceptions of Mars. It was indicated that many of the surface formations are possibly of volcanic origin, and that liquid water may have existed on the planet. On 27 Oct. 1972 **Mariner 9,** after making its 698th orbit around Mars and transmitting 7,329 photos, exhausted its supply of altitude control gas, and the mission was terminated. **Mariner 10,** launched 3 Nov. 1973, provided views of Venus (5 Feb. 1974) and first closeup information on Mercury (closest approach, 29 Mar. 1974). **Pioneer 10,** a nuclear-powered 570–pound unmanned interplanetary probe, was launched from Cape Kennedy, Fla. at 8:50 PM EST on 2 Mar. 1972. Traveling faster and farther than any other man-made object (it attained speeds as high as 82,800 mph, or 23 miles per second), it was the first to pass the orbit of Mars and to journey safely through the asteroid belt. On 3 Dec. 1973, after a voyage of 620 million miles lasting 21 months, Pioneer 10 flew within 81,000 miles of Jupiter; the spacecraft's sophisticated communications enabled the first closeup inspection of the largest planet in the solar system, and transmitted to earth color pictures and scientific data on Jupiter's radiation belts, magnetic field, atmosphere, satellites, and other features. Accelerated by Jupiter's gravitational force, Pioneer 10 sped toward Pluto, continuing a voyage that in 1987 should make it the first earth-launched spacecraft to leave the gravitational field of the solar system and enter interstellar space.

1962–73. QUASARS. Identification of quasars (quasi-stellar radio sources) by **Allan R. Sandage** (1926–), **Jesse L. Greenstein** (1909–), and **Maarten Schmidt** (1929–), led to discovery by U.S. and other astronomers of approximately 200 of these extragalactic phenomena, generally considered to be more distant (possibly 12 billion light-years) than any other class of space object. One hypothesis holds that quasars constitute the "edge of the universe," and it is believed by some that the basic assumptions of physics and cosmology may require radical revision to account for quasars. The enormous amount of infrared light emitted by quasars suggests that some of them may have energy ranging from an equivalent of 100 million suns to possibly 10 trillion suns.

1973, 2 Aug. Scientists of Lamont-Doherty Geological Observatory made the 1st successful prediction of an earthquake in the U.S., a very small one in the Adirondack area.

Invention and Technology

The course of American technological development was set by the conditions of the colonial and early national period, during which the economic potential of an ever-expanding continental domain rich in natural resources was constrained by a sparse population in an underdeveloped country with a chronic scarcity of investment capital. A people largely devoted to agriculture and extractive industries in 1789, the Americans employed technology as an avenue to national power, social modernization, and a broader diffusion of abundance, prefiguring the road that other underdeveloped nations would take in the twentieth century. At first the United States borrowed its technology, chiefly from Great Britain. The British textile industry, the vanguard of the First Industrial Revolution, was quickly adapted and improved in the United States, where the social and economic climate was generally more receptive to technological innovation than in Europe. Between 1840 and 1890 the completion of the basic rail transportation network helped create a national market economy in which competitive advantage in the emerging large industries, among them oil and steel, came to depend more and more upon the cost-benefits yielded by technology. Moreover, the dynamic development of railroading, America's first example of big business, stimulated ancillary industries, and levied fresh demands for advanced technology.

The rise of an industrial economy based upon the intensive exploitation of technology gave impetus to the trend toward the integrated manufacturing enterprise and industrial consolidation and concentration in the late nineteenth century. At the same time, the first industrial laboratories came into existence; it is suggestive that the pioneer laboratory for the systematic "invention of invention" was set up in 1876 at Menlo Park, N.J., by the individualist inventor Thomas A. Edison. The period 1880–1914 saw the culminating result of the "American system" of manufacturing evolved by Eli Whitney and others in the early nineteenth century. Using a broad array of semiautomatic and automatic machine tools, of which Americans were the foremost makers by 1900, factories producing bicycles, typewriters, and other complex articles made from a multiplicity of diverse components, Americans gained rich experience in the manufacture of articles assembled from standardized interchangeable parts. The advent of the automobile, and the revolutionary innovation of the moving assembly line by Ford Motor Co. production engineers in 1913–14, opened the way for the central role of technology in the consumer economy of modern America. Not until the Great Depression of the 1930s, with its widespread unemployment, did public opinion begin to question the relentless pace of labor-saving industrial mechanization; but the technological feats that helped to bring a U.S. military victory in World War II, and the successive bursts of postwar prosperity marked by new or expanding industries like electronics and petrochemicals, restored a popular faith in the beneficence of technology. That faith would not be qualified until ecological concerns in the late 1960s pointed to the urgent need for restraining man's technological capability both to create his own environment and to alter, exhaust, or destroy the natural one.

1730–35. MARINER'S QUADRANT improved by **Thomas Godfrey** (1704–49), the mathematician. The theodolite, an instrument for measuring horizontal angles, improved by Roland Houghton (1735).

1730–40. LONG RIFLE (also Pennsylvania and, later, Kentucky Rifle) developed by Pennsylvania gunsmiths by elongating barrel, narrowing and improving the rifling of bore, and adding grease patch. Prototype was introduced by German immigrants (1710–20).

1742–52. BENJAMIN FRANKLIN invented Franklin stove (Pennsylvania fireplace), an adaptation of the German stove which permitted ventilation (1742), and the lightning rod (1752).

1750. FLATBOAT for inland navigation invented by Jacob Yoder (Pa.).

1750–60. CONESTOGA WAGON, adapted to frontier travel, made its first appearance in Pennsylvania.

1762. REV. JARED ELIOT (1685–1763) of Killingworth, Conn., developed a process for smelting iron from black magnetic sand (*Transactions*, 1762).

1775. DAVID BUSHNELL (c.1742–1824) built first American submarine, *American Turtle;* nearly succeeded in blowing up a British frigate in New York Harbor (1776).

c.1777–85. OLIVER EVANS (1755–1819) invented a card-making machine (c.1777–78) which could complete 150 pairs of cotton or wool cards from wire per day. During the same period he invented an **automatic flour mill** (cutting labor requirements by one half), which was first put into operation c.1785.

1781–87. STEAM ENGINES. First multitubular boiler (**John Stevens,** 1749–1838; patented, 1783). Noncondensing, high-pressure steam engine (**Oliver Evans,** 1787).

1783. Bifocal spectacles invented by Benjamin Franklin.

1785–87. FIRST STEAMBOATS. Steamboat invented by **John Fitch** (1743–89) franchised for New Jersey waters, 1786; launched on Delaware, 1787; patented, 1791. Second steamboat built by **James Rumsey** (1743–92), launched on Potomac, 1787; patented, 1791.

1790, 10 APRIL. FIRST PATENT LAW. A Patent Board consisting of the Secretary of State (who was entrusted with administering the law), the Secretary of War, and the Attorney General was given responsibility for granting patents on "useful and important" inventions. First federal patent, 31 July 1790, granted to **Samuel Hopkins** (Vt., 1721–1803) for a process for the manufacture of pot and pearl ash. Machine to cut and head nails in one operation invented by **Jacob Perkins** (Mass., 1766–1849). In the first 3 years (1790–92) 47 patents were issued. Under the patent law of 21 Feb. 1793, the system was changed. The duty of granting patents was conferred on the Secretary of State, and the requirement for investigating the originality and usefulness of inventions was discarded, thus substituting mere registration for evaluative examination. The term of a patent, as in the act of 1790, remained at 14 years.

1790–91. SAMUEL SLATER (p. 1152) reproduced Arkwright machinery, employing water power at Pawtucket, R.I.

1793–99. FARM INVENTIONS. Eli Whitney invented the **cotton gin**, cheapening the most costly process in refining cotton (1793). **Thomas Jefferson** invented the moldboard plow (1793). **Charles Newbold** patented the first cast-iron plow (1797). **Eliakim Spooner** invented a seeding machine (1799).

1798. Jig for guiding tools in operation invented by **Eli Whitney.**

1804–49. STEAM ENGINE ADVANCES. Steam dredge by **Oliver Evans.** Jacob Perkins embodied experiments with steam of high pressure (1823) in numerous inventions down to 1849, including bathometer (to measure depth of water), plenometer (to record speed of vessel through water), piezometer (to measure compressibility of water).

1805. ROBERT FULTON (p. 1036) built the first marine torpedo.

1807–08. PRACTICAL STEAMBOATS. Although **John Stevens** designed a screw propeller (1802) and with it operated *Phoenix* to Philadelphia by sea (1808, first steam vessel in the U.S. to navigate the ocean), **Robert Fulton** built the first successful steamboat (*Clermont* sailed, 17 Aug. 1807, New York to Albany, 32 hrs.). The first ironclad vessel was built by Stevens (1813).

1807–54. MACHINERY. Manufacture of tacks (Jesse Reed, Conn., 1807), screw-cutting machine (Abel Stowel, Mass., 1809), circular saw (David Melville, 1814), profile lathe (1818, **Thomas Blanchard,** Mass. [1788–1864]); commercial vernier caliper by Brown and Sharp (1851); turret lathe, Robbins and Lawrence (Vt., 1854).

1816–27. PRINTING PRESS IMPROVEMENTS. Hand printing press: George Clymer, Pa., 1816; with a toggle joint, Samuel Rust, 1827; improved, 1829.

1819–22. PLOW IMPROVEMENTS. Cast-iron 3-piece plow (standardized interchangeable parts), **Jethrow Wood** (N.Y., 1819); lock colter devised by John Conant (Vt., 1822).

1819. Breech-loading flintlock (John Hall).

1822. ARTIFICIAL TEETH. First patent to C. M. Graham.

1826–37. LOCOMOTIVE with multitubular boiler (John Stevens, 1826; first patent to William Howard (1828). **Robert L. Stevens** (1788–1856), son of John Stevens, invented the balance valve for steam engines and the T-rail (1830). Other railroad improvements included pilot truck and bogie and double-slide cutoff for locomotives. **Peter Cooper** (p. 1006) built first U.S. locomotive (1830). Swivel truck for locomotives devised by John B. Jervis (1831), equalizing lever by Joseph Harrison (1837).

1827–31. JOSEPH HENRY (p. 1056) insulated wire; invented multiple coil magnet; built first magnetic and acoustic telegraph.

1831–34. REAPER invented by **Cyrus H. McCormick** (p. 1092), 1831; patented, 1834; similar machine invented independently (1832–33) by **Obed Hussey** (1792–1860).

1833. STEEL-BLADE PLOWSHARE (John Lane, Ill.).

1834–39. ELECTRICAL MACHINERY. First actual electric motor invented by **Thomas Davenport** (1802–51), who also invented electric commutator (1835) and electric printing press (1839).

1835. REVOLVER patented by **Samuel Colt** (1814–62).

1836, 4 JULY. Inauguration of the **patent system.** A fundamental revision of the patent laws, the Act of 1836 reestablished the examination requirement for determining the novelty and usefulness of an invention. It created the Patent Office as a separate and distinct bureau in the Department of State, and placed it under a Commissioner of Patents. In 1849 the Patent Office was transferred to the Department of the Interior, and on 1 April 1925 was placed under the Department of Commerce. The term of a patent, as set under the act of 2 Mar. 1861, is 17 years. Since 1880 a model has no longer been required as part of the patent application.

1836–43. JOHN ERICSSON (b. Sweden, 1803–89) improved screw propeller for steamships (1836). Going to U.S. (1840), designed *Princeton,* first warship to have propelling machinery below waterline (1843). Other inventions in U.S.: telescopic smokestack, recoil mechanism for gun carriages, instrument for measuring distances at sea, gauges for fluids under pressure, alarm barometer, pyrometer, and self-registering deep-sea lead. For the *Monitor* (1861–62), see p. 281.

1837–40. FARM AND MILLING. Steel plow introduced (1837) in the U.S.

by **John Deere** (1804–86); thresher fanning mill (prototype of later improved threshers) built by Hiram A. and John Pitts (Me.).

1839. VULCANIZATION OF RUBBER discovered by **Charles Goodyear** (p. 1043); patented (France, 1844).

1840–44. ADVANCES IN IRON AND COAL TECHNOLOGY. Hot-blast iron furnace for anthracite coal (David Thomas, Conn.), anthracite coal breaker (Gideon Bast, 1840), roller and crusher for coal (J. and S. Battin, 1844).

1846–80. STEAM ENGINE IMPROVEMENTS. Valve gear and drop cut-off, central features of a 4-valve control system invented by **George H. Corliss** (1817–88), reduced condensation and enabled substantial fuel economies in the operation of reciprocating steam engines. Incorporating this and subsequent improvements constituting the most significant innovation in the art of the steam engine since that of James Watt, the Corliss engine was manufactured at the Corliss works at Providence, R.I., and was universally adopted. The spectacular 680-ton, 10-foot-stroke Corliss engine that provided the power for some 8,000 machines in Machinery Hall at the Philadelphia Centennial Exposition (1876) was one of the mechanical marvels of the age of steam.

1843–68. TYPEWRITER. Machine invented by **Charles Thurber** (Conn., 1843). First practical typewriter constructed, 1867, by **Christopher L. Sholes** (1819–90) in collaboration with Carlos Glidden and Samuel W. Soulé. Working alone, Sholes made numerous improved models and secured patents (1868); sold rights (1873) to E. Remington & Sons, who marketed it as Remington typewriter.

1844. TELEGRAPH. Samuel F. B. Morse (p. 1109) developed the first practical telegraph (1832), following a large number of experiments; put into operation (24 May 1844) with message from **Alfred Vail** (1807–59) in Baltimore to Morse in Washington, D.C. Morse invented Morse code (1838). Telegraphic printing technique invented by Vail (1844); patented by Royal E. House (1846).

1846–54. SEWING MACHINE invented by **Elias Howe** (p. 1063); improved (1849–54) by **Allen B. Wilson** (1824–88) and (1851) by **Isaac Merritt Singer** (1811–75), who, with the aid of Edward Clark, opened plant in New York City (1853).

1846. ROTARY PRINTING PRESS invented by **Richard M. Hoe** (p. 1058).

1847–64. FARM IMPLEMENTS. Revolving disc harrow (G. Page, 1847), agricultural binder (John E. Heath, 1850), chilled plow (**James Oliver,** 1855; improved by Marsh brothers, 1857), twine knotter (John F. Appleby, 1858), checkrower corn planter (John Thompson and John Ramsey, 1864).

1849. MODERN SAFETY PIN invented by Walter Hunt.

Pendulum press for can tops invented by Henry Evans.

1851–60. IRON AND STEEL ADVANCES. William Kelly (1811–88), Kentucky ironmaster, developed a process for converting pig iron into steel by directing a current of air upon molten metal (1851), independently of Henry Bessemer in England, who perfected the technic (1856). First Bessemer converter built at Troy, N.Y. (1864); Kelly process at Wyandotte, Mich., same year. Rival claims compromised 1866. Wrought-iron I-beams rolled (1860) by **Peter Cooper** at Trenton, N.J.

1852. ELISHA G. OTIS (p. 1120) invented first passenger elevator (making skyscraper possible).

1853. Sluicing process in mining perfected by E. E. Matteson.

1858–99. SHOE MACHINERY. Lyman R. Blake (1835–83) patented (1858) a machine capable of sewing soles of shoes to the upper; promoted by **Gordon McKay** (1821–1903), who patented improved version (1862). The Blake-McKay machines were widely adopted by 1876. Charles Goodyear (1833–96), who acquired (1864–67) the welt-sewing machine, joined forces with McKay by 1880. Centralization of machine ownership brought about by formation (1899) of United Shoe Machinery Co.

1859. Successful **oil drilling** at Titusville, Pa., by **Edwin L. Drake** (1819–80).

1860. REPEATING RIFLE introduced by **Oliver F. Winchester** (1810–80).

1862. REVOLVING MACHINE GUN perfected by **Richard J. Gatling** (1818–1903).

1864. GEORGE M. PULLMAN (1831–97) built "Pioneer," first especially constructed sleeping car, and organized Pullman Palace Car Co. (1867).

1865. COMPRESSION ICE MACHINE invented by **Thaddeus Lowe** (1832–1913), who made first artificial ice in U.S., and in 1873 invented carbureted water-gas process.

1865–75. WEB PRINTING PRESS (using a web or role of paper) invented by **William A. Bullock** (1813–63). **Rotary press** (printing on both sides of a sheet at the same time) attributed to Andrew Campbell and Stephen D. Tucker (1875).

1868–72. AIR BRAKE patented by **George Westinghouse** (p. 1180); improved, 1872.

1869–99. CARPET SWEEPERS AND VACUUM CLEANERS. Suction-type vacuum cleaner patented by I. W. McGaffey (1869). Melville R. Bissell invented practical carpet sweeper (1876). First motor-driven vacuum cleaner patented by John Thurman (1899).

1869. ELECTRIC VOTING MACHINE invented by **Thomas A. Edison**

(p. 1021). First voting machine authorized for use, 1892.

1870–78. MOTION PICTURES: PIONEER STAGE. Experiments in depicting motion followed invention of zoetrope (designed in France, 1860), a series of pictures whirled on a drum to give effect of motion. Applying similar principle to magic lantern, Henry R. Heyl showed projected animated pictures (1870). Eadweard J. Muybridge set up a series of coordinated cameras to take successive photographs of a horse in motion (1878).

1871–74. TRANSPORTATION. Andrew S. Hallidie (1836–1900) invented cable streetcar (1871; in use in San Francisco, 1873). First electrically powered streetcar invented by **Stephen Dudley Field** successfully run in New York City, 1874. Railroad coupler patented by **Eli H. Janney** (1831–1912).

1872. CELLULOID. Commercial production developed by **John W. Hyatt** (1837–1920).

1872–85. CACULATING MACHINES. Edmund D. Barbour invented adding machine with printed totals and subtotals (1872). **Dorr Eugene Felt** (1862–1930) made first accurate comptometer (1884). First successful recording adding machine (1888) by **William S. Burroughs** (1857–1898).

1874. BARBED WIRE (p. 614).

1875–81. DYNAMOS. William A. Anthony (1835–1908) constructed first dynamo for outdoor lighting (1875, at Cornell Univ.); C. F. Brush (1876). Edison Machine Works constructed first successfully operating dynamo (27 tons, 1881).

1876–84. TELEPHONE invented by **Alexander Graham Bell** (p. 982) prior to 14 Feb. 1876; patent granted, 7 Mar.; first distinguishable conversation, 10 Mar.; outdoor transmission, 9 Oct.; first private home installation, 1877; New York to Boston, 1884.

1877–95. DISCOVERIES BY NIKOLA TESLA (p. 1168). Telsa dis-covered the principle of the rotary magnetic field, applying it in a practical form to the induction motor and making possible the alternating current motor and the transmission of power by such current, employing what became known as 2-phase, 3-phase, multiphase, and polyphase systems, particularly on long distance lines (later used extensively). Also p. 1168. Edison system of central power production introduced (1882) at New York City.

1878–83. ELECTRIC LIGHTING. Practical application of electric arc lamps (Philadelphia, 1878; Cleveland, 1879). Although Moses Gerrish of Salem had built an incandescent lamp as early as 1859, **Thomas A. Edison** invented the first practical incandescent bulb (1879); established factory (1880).

1878–1948. PHONOGRAPH patented by **Edison** (1878); practical machine made by firm of Bell and Tainter (1886). Electronic phonograph introduced 1924 by Western Electric Co., manufactured 1927 by RCA; 33⅓ rpm. microgroove record invented by Dr. Peter C. Goldmark, marketed 1948.

1879. CASH REGISTER patented by **James Ritty** (4 Nov.).

1880–88. CAMERA ADVANCES. **George Eastman** (p. 1020) patented first successful roll film (1880); perfected first "Kodak" hand camera (1888), resulting in popularization of photography.

1880–1931. RAZORS. Safety razor developed by Kampfe Bros., New York. First modern type with throwaway blades invented (1895) by **King C. Gillette** (1855–1932). Jacob Shick patented electric dry shaver 1928; marketed, 1931.

1882–1910. ELECTRIC APPLIANCES. Electric fan invented by **Schuyler Skaats Wheeler** (1860–1923). Patents granted for electric flatiron (1882, Henry W. Seely), electric stove (1896, William S. Hadaway), separable electric attachment plug (1904, Harvey Hubbell). Electric sewing machine developed

(Singer Mfg. Co., 1889). Completely self-contained electric washing machine developed (1907, Hurling Machine Co.).

1884. FOUNTAIN PEN perfected by **Lewis E. Waterman** (1837–1901).

1884–89. LINOTYPE MACHINE invented by **Ottmar Mergenthaler** (p. 1102); used commercially, 1886. **Mono-type** machine patented 1887 by **Tolbert Lanston** (1844–1913).

1886. ELECTRIC WELDING MACHINE patented by **Elihu Thomson** (1853–1937), widely applied in auto industry and as a substitute for riveting in construction work; also patented cream separator, 1881.

Electrolytic process of refining aluminum discovered by **Charles Martin Hall** (1863–1914).

1890. PNEUMATIC HAMMER patented by Charles B. King.

1891. CARBORUNDUM (abrasive) discovered by **Edward G. Acheson** (1856–1931).

1893–1923. AUTOMOBILE. First successful U.S. gasoline-powered car, built by the brothers **Charles E.** (1862–1938) and **J. Frank Duryea** (1870–1967), was operated by the latter in its initial run (Springfield, Mass., 21 Sept., 1893). George B. Selden, of Rochester, N.Y., applied (1879) for first gasoline auto patent; granted 1895. Patent issued (1902) to Packard Motor Car Co. for "H" slot gearshift (sliding gear transmission); soon became standard on most American automobiles. Steering knuckle invented (1902) by Sterling Elliott; by allowing both front wheels to turn while axle remains stationary, it introduced steering wheel principle and led to replacement of tiller. Pneumatic tire (1892) followed by clincher-type tire (1899), standard quick-demountable tire rims (1904), the nonskid tire (1908), the cord tire (1910), and the balloon tire (1922). Automatic lubrication (1904); front bumpers (1906); first V-8 engine in production model

(1907 Hewitt, made by Hewitt Motor Co., N.Y.C.); left-hand steering (1908). Electric self-starter developed (1911) by **Charles F. Kettering** (p. 1076), introduced in 1912 Cadillac. All-steel automobile body (1912) by Edward G. Budd; 4-wheel hydraulic brakes (1918) by Malcolm Loughead (later Lockheed). Introduction of ethyl gasoline, 1923, developed by Thomas Midgley, Jr., and Charles F. Kettering.

1893–1953. MOTION PICTURES. Invention of photographic gun (E. J. Marey, France) and development of celluloid film (introduced by John Carbutt, 1883) led to invention of Edison's Kinetoscope (peepshow, 1893), which, employing a continuous roll of film, could be viewed by but one person at a time. Woodville Latham demonstrated the Pantoptiken (1895), a combination of the Kinetoscope with magic-lantern projection (simultaneously with the Cinematographe by the Lumières in France, the best projector at that time). **C. Francis Jenkins** (1867–1934) perfected the phantascope, modification of Edison's Kinetoscope, and with Thomas Armat demonstrated the Vitascope (1896), prototype of the modern motion picture projector. Cameraphone, first sound moving picture, developed by Edison, 1904. For later developments see p. 885. For wide screen processes see p. 891.

1896–1913. AIRPLANE. Orville and **Wilbur Wright** (p. 1189) made first heavier-than-air flight at Kitty Hawk, N.C., 17 Dec. 1903; previously, 8 Dec., Samuel P. Langley had made an unsuccessful attempt in a power-driven airplane. First American monoplane invented by Henry W. Walden (1909). **Gyroscope** stabilizer by **Elmer A. Sperry** (1860–1930) demonstrated on an airplane (1913), foreshadowing later instrument developments.

1897–1912. DIESEL ENGINES. Adolphus Busch (1839–1913) bought Diesel rights for the U.S. (1897); built first engine (1898); applied to submarine (1912, Vickers 4-cylinder).

1901. MERCURY VAPOR LAMP patented by **Peter C. Hewitt** (1861–1921).

1901–24. RADIO. Early American experiments in wireless communication were conducted (1866) by Dr. Mahlon Loomis (1826–86), Prof. Amos Dolbear (patent for "induction" system of wireless telegraphy, 1866), and Nathan B. Stubblefield (1892). Predicted by James Maxwell (1865), major research was undertaken abroad (Marconi, Fleming) until **Reginald A. Fessenden** (1866–1932) superimposed voice on continuous wave (1901). His improved transmitter, demonstrated 24 Dec. and 31 Dec. 1906 at Brant Rock, Mass., was heard by ships as far away as the West Indies. **Lee De Forest** (p. 1011) invented the 3-element vacuum tube (1906, triode amplifier) and applied the microphone (ordinary telephone-type mouthpiece, 1907) to broadcasting. **Irving Langmuir** (p. 1080) and associates developed the high vacuum tube for the General Electric Co. (1912–14). For **Edwin H. Armstrong's** regenerative circuit, 1912, and superheterodyne circuit, 1918, see p. 975. **Ernst F. W. Alexanderson's** (p. 974) high frequency alternator (1917), patented by General Electric, was supplanted by shortwave broadcasting, pioneered at Westinghouse and GE, 1923–24.

1902–10. SYNTHETICS AND PLASTICS. Rayon (cellulose ester) patented (1902) by **Arthur D. Little** (1863–1935), with William H. Walker and Harry S. York; same group patented artificial silk (1902). First commercial production by American Viscose Co. (1910). **Leo H. Baekeland** (p. 978) patented thermosetting plastic, 1909 (Bakelite).

1911. GYROCOMPASS patented by Elmer A. Sperry (another pat. abroad by Anchütz-Kämpfe, 1908), who also

perfected the gyroscope (invented by Foucault, 1852) and invented the automatic steersman.

1913. X RAY. Development by William D. Coolidge of new X-ray tube capable of sustained operation at 140,000 volts (later designed for 200,000 volts) revolutionized making of radiographs.

CRACKING PROCESS for gasoline patented by **William M. Burton.**

1914–26. EARLY ROCKETS. **Robert H. Goddard** (p. 1041) patented liquid fuel rocket (1914), using liquid ether and oxygen; demonstrated lifting force of rockets (1920); directed first rocket flight (1926).

1916. THOMPSON SUBMACHINE GUN invented by **John T. Thompson** (1860–1940). **National Research Council** organized 20 Sept. 1916 to promote wartime research; perpetuated by order of President Wilson 11 May 1918 to stimulate scientific research, programs, and information.

1918–52. HELICOPTER. First to rise successfully from ground built by Peter C. Hewitt and F. B. Crocker (1918). Developments in U.S. largely due to **Igor Sikorsky** (1889–1972), who arrived in U.S. in 1918. Improved product (VS-300) produced by Vought-Sikorsky Aircraft (1939).

1922. TECHNICOLOR process successfully developed by **Herbert T. Kalmus** (1881–1963).

1922–26. TELEPHOTO. C. Francis Jenkins sent photos over telephone wires; transcontinental photo (1925); transatlantic service (1926).

1922–46. RADAR. Based on studies of Hertz (1888), radio detection was first developed by **Albert H. Taylor** (1879–1961) and **Leo C. Young** (1922) for the U.S. Navy. True radar detection, using pulse-ranging technic, employed by **Gregory Breit** (1899–) and **Merle A. Tuve** (1901–) for ionospheric research (c.1926), and for naval detection by

Taylor and Young (1930). Radar system developed by Naval Research Laboratory (1934–39) and U.S. Army Signal Corps (1936–38). By 1935 Great Britain had 5 radar detector stations in operation. Research accelerated under National Defense Research Committee (from July 1940). During World War II radar was employed both to direct artillery fire and to detect enemy submarines and aircraft. Radar signals sent to the moon and reflected back (from Belmar, N.J., 10 Jan. 1946).

1923–51. TELEVISION. Background work on television largely European (Senlecq, France; Nipkow and Braun, Germany; Rosing, Russia; Swinton, England) until **Vladimir Zworykin** (p. 1191) demonstrated for Westinghouse executives a partly electronic television system (Dec. 1923). In 1925 Zworykin invented the iconoscope, basis of the electronic television camera, and **C. Francis Jenkins** demonstrated television with the Nipkow system (1925). Philo Farnsworth patented dissector tube (1927). First transmission of television, New York City to Washington, D.C. (1927) by American Telephone and Telegraph. First televised drama (11 Sept. 1928), "The Queen's Messenger," the result of experiments of Ernst F. W. Alexanderson at Westinghouse. Radio Corp. of America demonstrated electronic transmission (using iconoscope and cathode ray tube, 1933). **Peter C. Goldmark** (1906–   ) of Columbia Broadcasting System (CBS) demonstrated "sequential method" of **color television** (1940). CBS and RCA evolved independent systems by 1949. Hearings by FCC (1949–50) found CBS sytem sufficiently advanced to permit general transmission; production curtailed in interest of national defense (1951).

1926–57. AUTOMOBILE. Hypoid gears, introduced by Packard, 1926, fa-cilitated design of lower-slung bodies. Carl Breer, Chrysler Corp., began work, 1927, on "Airflow" streamlined body design (introduced 1933–34). Aerocar (1929), first production-type house trailer. Free-wheeling, introduced by Studebaker, 1930, widely adopted for its gasoline economy, but subsequently abandoned after a number of states prohibited it as a safety hazard. Synchronized transmission, developed by Earl A. Thompson, offered by Oldsmobile, 1931. Independent front-wheel suspension (1939); tubeless tires introduced by Goodrich, 1948; puncture-sealing tires, 1950. High-compression V-8 engine (1949). Hardtop convertible introduced by Buick, 1949. Power steering, 1951. Improved sealed-beam headlamps became standard equipment, 1954–55; dual headlamps, introduced by Cadillac, 1954, became standard equipment in 1957–58. Seatbelts and padded dashboards first offered as optional equipment, by Ford (1955–56).

1927. MECHANICAL COTTON PICKER invented by **John Daniel Rust** (1892–1959) and **Mack Donald Rust** (1900–1966).

1928–34. AUTOGIRO first brought to U.S. from England (1928) by Harold F. Pitcairn; manufactured with closed cabin (1931) and applied to military uses (1934).

1930–31. TRACTORS. Diesel engine tractor manufactured (steam tractor, 1886; gasoline, 1892). Caterpillar tractor developed (1931).

1932. POLAROID GLASS invented by **Edwin H. Land** (p. 1080); polaroid camera 1947.

PARKING METER patented by Carl C. Magee.

1934. RAILROAD DEVELOPMENTS. First streamlined high-speed train (2 Mar.), followed by all-steel Diesel-motored train (11 Nov.) and streamlined steam locomotive (14 Dec.).

1934–39. FREQUENCY MODULA-TION. Early experiments by **Edwin H. Armstrong** (p. 975) led to patents (1933), public demonstration (Nov. 1935). Experimental 50,000-watt station W₂XMN built by Armstrong at Alpine, N.J. reached full power operation in 1939, and first regularly scheduled FM broadcast occurred 18 July 1939. Commercial operation of FM authorized by FCC, May 1940.

23 May. NYLON. Wallace H. Carothers synthesized a superpolymer; marketed (1938) by Du Pont as nylon.

1935. SPECTROPHOTOMETER patented by **Arthur C. Hardy** (1895–).

1935–39. SYNTHETICS. Casein fiber developed by **Earl O. Whittier** (1891–) and **Stephen P. Gould** (1897–1939); patented, 1938. **Nylon:** commercial production begun (toothbrush bristles, Du Pont, 1938; followed by nylon yarn, 1939). **Fiberglas** technics patented (1938) by **Games Slayter** (1896–1964) and John H. Thomas.

1940. XEROGRAPHY ("dry writing") patented by its inventor, **Chester F. Carlson** (p. 997), who developed this widely used duplicating process with the assistance of Roland M. Schaffert, a research physicist at the Batelle Memorial Institute. Utilizing electrostatics and photoconductivity, xerography produces an image by heat-fusing powder particles in the charged areas of a sensitized paper. In 1947 the Haloid Corp., Rochester, N.Y., was licensed to develop xerography commercially; it subsequently became the Xerox Corp., makers of the Xerox mechanized office copying machine. The first Xerox automatic copier was introduced in 1959. Xerography using different processes has also been developed by other companies.

1942–45. ROCKETS IN WORLD WAR II. "Bazooka," first U.S. rocket gun, developed by Capt. L. A. Skinner and C. N. Hickman; standardized, 1942.

Germans first used V-1, 250–400-mph pilotless aircraft, 12 June 1944, 6 days after D-Day; shot down by Allied gunners aided by radar, M-9 director, and proximity fuse. V-2 (long-range rocket, 3,400 mph) first struck London on 12 Sept. 1944. Rocket and guided-missile experiments pushed in postwar period. U.S. navy guided missiles reported used in combat in Korea (1 Sept. 1952).

1942–60. JET PLANES. Jet engine first produced by British inventor, Frank Whittle, 1937. Jets first tested in U.S., 1942. In June 1944 a Lockheed P-80 with jet motor flew over 500 mph. Jet-propelled fighters were ordered by U.S. air force (1947); bombers developed (1947). By 1952, U.S. had developed B-52 bomber, with 8 turbojet engines, ceiling 50,000 ft., speed c.600 mph.; B-47, c.700 mph. B-70 supersonic heavy bomber (designed for speeds exceeding 2,000 mph) program drastically restricted by government 1 Dec. 1959. Bell X-2 rocket-powered research airplane set speed record in excess of 2,100 mph (1956); North American X-15 rocket plane made first successful flight under own power 17 Sept. 1959. Commercial jet transport initiated 15 Aug. 1958 with Boeing 707 (transatlantic service by Pan American Airways, 26 Oct. 1958), followed by Douglas DC-8 (1959), and Convair 880 (TWA, 1961).

1944–51. ELECTRONIC DIGITAL COMPUTER. The "Automatic Sequence Controlled Calculator," known also as the Harvard Mark I, was built (1939–44) and operated at Harvard by the International Business Machines Corp. It was conceived principally by **Howard H. Aiken,** who in 1937, while a graduate student in physics at Harvard, distinguished between punched-card accounting machinery and the computer as required in scientific work, pointing out that the computer must be able to handle positive and negative numbers, use various mathematical functions, perform calculations in the natural sequence of mathematical events, and be completely automatic in operation. The Harvard Mark I was an electromechanical computer with external storage. Eight ft. high and 51 ft. long, it was slow and cumbersome by later standards, and, although not a true electronic computer, was nevertheless the pioneer information-processing device of the computer age. It could multiply two 11-place numbers at 3-second intervals. **1940–46. ENIAC** (Electronic Numerical Integrator and Computer), the first truly automatic electronic computer, was based mainly on the work of Dr. John Mauchly and Dr. John Presper Eckert, Jr., both of the Moore School of Electrical Engineering at the Univ. of Pennsylvania. Although large in size (ENIAC contained 18,000 vacuum tubes), its internal storage represented an important advance. It could multiply two 10-decimal numbers in less than three-thousandths of a second, and could complete 5,000 additions a second. **28 June 1946–16 August 1948.** Series of papers, "Preliminary Discussion of the Logical Design of an Electronic Computing Instrument," a report by **John L. von Neumann** (p. 1174), Herman H. Goldstine (1913–), and Arthur W. Burks (1915–), was the result of a project initiated by von Neumann in 1945 at the Institute for Advanced Study, Princeton, N.J., "to develop and construct a fully automatic, digital, all-purpose electronic calculating machine" controlled by orders formulated in a binary digital code and handling a wide range of problems at extremely high speeds. This landmark report became fundamental to the theory of computer logic and design; its conceptualization of stored programs and conditional transfer were later embodied in computer hardware. **1951. UNIVAC** (Universal Automatic Computer), a stored program computer made by the Eckert-Mauchly Corp. (later absorbed by the present Sperry Rand), was installed at the Bureau of the Census. The state of the art was subsequently improved by printed circuits, magnetic drums and magnetic-core storage, and the replacement of radio tubes by transistors. Miniaturized components made it possible to reduce the size of computers while increasing their information-handling capability.

1945–60. ATOMIC AND NUCLEAR DEVELOPMENTS. Atomic bomb completed and exploded (16 July 1945, p. 452). For **cyclotron,** see p. 1081; **cosmotron,** p. 787. First **atomic-powered submarine, U.S.S.** *Nautilus,* commissioned 30 Sept. 1954, made first undersea crossing of the North Pole (5 Aug. 1958), submerging near Point Barrow, Alas., 1 Aug. and sailing under 50-ft.-thick icecap for 96 hours before surfacing. Six days later submarine **Skate** covered same route from east to west. On 6 Oct. **Seawolf** surfaced after remaining submerged 60 days. Atomic-powered submarines were equipped (1960) with **Polaris** missiles, with nuclear warheads and range of 1,200 nautical miles. **Atomic-power projects,** p. 731. Controlled thermonuclear reaction created in Univ. of California laboratories, 3 Nov. 1960.

1948. TRANSISTOR invented at Bell Telephone Laboratories by Walter Brattain, John Bardeen, and William Shockley (p. 1151)—awarded Nobel prize in physics, 1956.

1954. SOLAR BATTERY developed by 2 different laboratories—Bell Telephone and the Air Research and Development Command, Baltimore, Md.

1955, 18 MAY. NUCLEAR REACTOR patent issued to **Enrico Fermi** (p. 1027) and **Leo Szilard.**

4 OCT. 1957. DAWN OF THE SPACE AGE. The world's first artificial satellite (Sputnik I) was launched as part of the Soviet participation in the International Geophysical Year 1957–58. On 3 Nov. a second artificial satellite (Sputnik II), carrying a dog, was launched. Sputnik III, a 2,925-lb. satellite, was launched 15 May 1958. In 1959 the U.S.S.R. launched 3 cosmic rockets: Lunik I, 2 Jan., reported 3 Jan. to have gone into permanent orbit around the sun as "first artificial planet"; Lunik II, 12 Sept., making contact with the moon 14 Sept.; and Lunik III, 4 Oct., which circled the moon. A photograph of the hidden side of the moon was released 27 Oct. Sputnik IV was launched 15 May 1960, and space ships 14 May, 1 Dec.

1958–60. U.S. SATELLITE, ROCKET, AND MISSILE EFFORT. The first U.S. artificial earth satellite (Explorer I) was placed in orbit by a modified Jupiter-C rocket, 31 Jan. 1958, followed 17 Mar. by the orbiting of a 3¼-lb. navy satellite (Vanguard I), and 26 Mar. by a 3¼-lb. satellite (Explorer III). On 11 Oct. an air force Pioneer rocket failed to go into orbit around the moon but achieved a penetration of 79,-173 statute miles into space. On 28 Nov. an Atlas intercontinental ballistic missile was successfully test-fired for a distance of 6,325 miles. On 18 Dec. an Atlas missile weighing c.8,700 lbs. was placed in orbit around the earth. In 1959 space exploration was achieved by Vanguard II (17 Feb.), Vanguard III (18 Sept.), Discoverer I (28 Feb.), and other Discoverer satellites (13 Apr., 13 Aug., 19 Aug., 7 Nov.).

1960–67. NONMANNED SPACE ACHIEVEMENTS include: (1) space probes taking photographs and performing other experiments (p. 790); (2) camera-bearing weather satellites: Tiros 1, Tiros 2 (1 Apr., 23 Nov. 1960), Nimbus 1 (28 Aug. 1964), Tiros 9 (22 Jan. 1965), Essa 1 (3 Feb. 1966), Essa 2 (28 Feb. 1966), replaced by Essa 3 (launched 2 Oct. 1966 in sun synchro-

nous polar orbit); (3) orbiting Solar Observatory (3 Mar. 1962); (4) communications satellites: Telstar 1, Telstar 2 (7 May 1963); Syncom (26 July 1963), stationary above the earth; Early Bird (6 Apr. 1965); Lanibird (11 Jan. 1967), launched by International Telecommunications Satellite Consortium; (5) Biosatellite 2 (7–8 Sept. 1967), studying the effect of weightlessness on various kinds of activities under controlled laboratory conditions, discovered that seedlings grew faster in space.

1961–74. U.S. MANNED SPACE FLIGHTS: 5 May 1961, U.S. Navy Cmdr. Alan B. Shepard, Jr.; 21 July, Capt. Virgil I. Grissom; 20 Feb. 1962, Lt. Col. John H. Glenn, Jr. (3 orbits); 24 May, Lt. Cmdr. M. Scott Carpenter (3 orbits); 3 Oct., Cmdr. Walter M. Schirra, Jr. (6 orbits); 15 May 1963, Maj. L. Gordon Cooper (22 orbits).

Gemini Series, launched by Titan 2 rocket. Gemini 3 (23 Mar. 1965, Virgil I. Grissom and John W. Young; 3 orbits) showed spacecraft could be maneuvered for docking purposes. Gemini 4 (3–7 June 1965, James A. McDivitt and Edward H. White 2d; 62 orbits) marked by 20 minute space walk of White. Gemini 5 (21–29 Aug. 1965, L. Gordon Cooper, Jr., and Charles Conrad; 120 orbits) 8 days in orbit, displayed ability of astronauts to endure; apogee of 219 miles. Gemini 6A (15–16 Dec. 1965, Walter M. Schirra, Jr., and Thomas P. Stafford; 16 orbits) rendezvoused with Gemini 7 (4–18 Dec., Frank Borman and James A. Lovell, Jr.; 206 orbits). Gemini 8 (16–17 Mar. 1966, Neil A. Armstrong and David R. Scott; 6.5 orbits) achieved the docking of 2 vehicles in space. Gemini 9A (3–6 June 1966, Thomas A. Stafford and Eugene A. Cernan; 44 orbits) featured 2-hour 9-minute walk in space. Gemini 10 (18–21 July 1966, John W. Young and Michael Collins; 43 orbits) rendezvous with 2 targets. Gemini 11 (12–15 Sept. 1966, Charles Conrad, Jr., and Richard F. Gordon, Jr.; 44 orbits) record apogee of 851 miles. Gemini 12 (11–15 Nov. 1966, James A. Lovell, Jr., and Edwin E. Aldrin, Jr.; 59 orbits) photographs of 7 second total solar eclipse.

Apollo Program. Saturn 5 rocket and Apollo capsule. Crew of Apollo 1, Virgil I. Grissom, Edward H. White, and Roger Chaffee killed when a flash fire swept their craft, Cape Kennedy (27 Jan. 1967). First flight test of Saturn 5 rocket (9 Nov. 1967). Apollo 7 (11–22 Oct. 1968, Walter M. Schirra, Jr., Donn F. Eisele, R. Walter Cunningham; 163 orbits); Apollo 8 (21–27 Dec. 1968, Frank Borman, James A. Lovell, Jr., William A. Anders; orbiting of moon 10 times), "vast, lonely and forbidding sight"; live telecast from lunar orbit, Christmas Eve, 69.8 miles above moon. Apollo 9 (3–13 Mar. 1969, James A. McDivitt, David R. Scott, Russell L. Schweickart; 151 orbits) included test flight of the lunar module.

U.S. (13 Mar. 1969) led the U.S.S.R. in manned flights, 19 to 12; in moon orbital flights, 1 to 0; manned hours in space, 3,938 to 868; space "walks," 10 to 3; rendezvous missions, 8 to 3; space link-ups, 9 to 1.

Moon Landings. On 18 May astronauts Thomas P. Stafford, Eugene A. Cernan, and John W. Young descended in Apollo 10 to within 9 miles of the moon. Climaxing 8 years of manned space flight competition between the U.S. and the Soviet Union, U.S. astronauts Neil A. Armstrong and Col. Edwin E. Aldrin, Jr., taking off 16 July in Apollo 11, touched down on the moon with their lunar module. Armstrong's first step on the moon was taken 20 July at 10:56:20 AM, EDT. After taking rock and soil specimens, the pair successfully rendezvoused with Lieut. Col. Michael Collins, navigator of the Apollo craft,

and splashed down 950 miles S.W. of Hawaii, 24 July. Apollo 12 was launched 14 Nov.; Cmdrs. Charles Conrad, Jr., and Alan L. Bean in lunar module *Intrepid* landed on moon, 500 feet from Surveyor 3 spacecraft, 19 Nov., 1:54 AM, EST. After 31½ hours on lunar surface (2 moon walks), and 3 hours 20 minutes later, the *Intrepid* docked with command ship *Yankee Clipper*, Cmdr. Richard F. Gordon, Jr., pilot, at 12:45 PM, EST, 20 Nov. Splashdown in Pacific: 24 Nov., 3:58 PM, EST, 1,950 miles S.W. of Hawaii, less than 3 miles from target. Apollo 13, launched 11 Apr. 1970, was aborted 13 Apr. Apollo 14 launched from Cape Kennedy 31 Jan. 1971 at 6:30 PM EST, with astronauts Navy Capt. Alan B. Shepard, Jr., Navy Cmdr. Edgar D. Mitchell, and Air Force Maj. Stuart A. Roosa. It went into lunar orbit 4 Feb. In their lunar module *Antares*, Shepard and Mitchell landed on the target site at Fra Mauro, and remained on the surface of the moon for 33½ hours. They made 2 surface excursions lasting a total of some 9 hours, using a 2-wheeled cart, cameras, a magnetometer, hand tools, and a sample bag in which they collected corings and 97 pounds of rocks. The mission returned to earth at 1:37 PM EST on 9 Feb. Apollo 15 launched from Cape Kennedy 26 July 1971 at 9:34 AM EDT. Maj. Alfred M. Worden was at the controls of the command module *Endeavour* and Col. David R. Scott and Lt. Col. James B. Irwin, Jr., were in the lunar module *Falcon*. The target area was Hadley Rille, a deep canyon in the Apennine Mts., 465 miles north of the lunar equator. An innovation on this mission was the Lunar Rover, a 2-man, 4-wheeled, battery-operated vehicle which the astronauts used for exploring the surface for a distance of several miles from the touchdown area. In their 3 surface excursions, accounting for 21 of the 57 hours they spent on the moon, the crew covered more terrain than in any previous manned mission, making this the most productive of the Apollo flights. They obtained valuable data with special equipment that included an X-ray spectrometer, a gamma-ray spectrometer, and a TV color camera. The mission returned to earth at 4:46 PM EDT on 7 Aug. Apollo 16 launched from Cape Kennedy 16 Apr. 1972 at 12:54 PM EDT, with Cmdr. Thomas K. Mattingly 2d in the command module. Astronauts Capt. John W. Young and Lt. Col. Charles M. Drake, in the lunar module *Orion,* reached a landing site 45 miles north of the Descartes Crater on the Kant Plateau in the central lunar highlands. In 3 surface excursions lasting a total of 20 hours 14 minutes, they used an electric-powered Lunar Roving Vehicle to gather rock and soil samples that provided important data concerning the age and composition of the moon's surface. The astronauts spent about 71 hours on the moon, brought back 214 pounds of rocks, and returned to earth at 2:45 PM EST on 27 April. Apollo 17, launched from Cape Kennedy 7 Dec. 1972 at 12:33 AM EST, carried astronauts Capt. Eugene A. Cernan, Cmdr. Ronald E. Evans, and the civilian geologist Dr. Harrison H. Schmitt, the first scientist to journey to the moon. With Evans aboard the command module *America,* Cernan and Schmitt landed the lunar module *Challenger* in the Taurus-Littrow Valley, an area ringed by high mountains southeast of the Sea of Serenity. In 2 explorations that lasted a total of 7 hours 49 minutes, the astronauts used a 2-wheeled Lunar Rover with a wide array of equipment to gather data on geological formations, surface radiation, lunar gas, and gravity waves, and returned with a collection of rocks and soil samples. The discovery of soil containing iron oxide was especially significant, for it suggested that the moon's interior occasionally produced

water and gases. The astronauts returned to earth on 19 Dec. at 2:24 PM EST. Apollo 17, the 6th successful manned lunar mission by the U.S., concluded the $25 billion Project Apollo. President Richard M. Nixon announced (14 Dec.): "This may be the last time in this century that men will walk on the moon." Cernan was the 11th astronaut to walk on the moon, and Schmitt the 12th.

Skylab Program. The first U.S. space station project, Skylab cost $2.6 billion and was designed to test man's ability to live and work effectively in outer space for prolonged periods under conditions of weightlessness. The project consisted of 3 successive missions, each manned by a different crew of astronauts. **Skylab 1.** The 85-ton Skylab, an orbiting space laboratory and workshop, was launched from Cape Canaveral (formerly Cape Kennedy), Fla., on 14 May 1973 at 1:30 PM EDT. One minute and 3 seconds after its unmanned liftoff, Skylab was damaged. The loss of the micrometeoroid and thermal shielding caused overheating, and the jammed solar-power wings threatened loss of half of the space station's power capacity. On 25 May, at 9 AM EDT, 3 astronauts were launched in an Apollo spacecraft from Cape Canaveral, carrying 400 pounds of tools, heat-shielding devices, and other materials. Locking their spacecraft with Skylab, the astronauts made emergency repairs that cooled the interior of Skylab and salvaged the station. The crew members were Capt. Charles Conrad, Jr.; Cmdr. Joseph P. Kerwin, the first American M.D. to make a space flight; and Cmdr. Paul Weitz, an aeronautical engineering expert. The Skylab astronauts spent an unprecedented 28 days and 50 minutes in space, making 395 trips around the earth, performing scientific experiments, and taking 16,000 photographs of the earth and 30,000 solar telescope pictures of the sun. The 3 astronauts returned to earth in the Apollo spacecraft at 9:50 AM EDT on 22 June. Skylab 2. This mission was launched in an Apollo spaceship from Cape Canaveral at 7:11 AM EDT on 28 July 1973, bearing aloft astronauts Capt. Alan L. Bean, Maj. Jack R. Lousma, and Dr. Owen K. Garriott, a civilian solar physicist. Despite technical difficulties in their Apollo module, and severe motion sickness at the outset, the astronauts successfully completed their mission, spending a record 59 days and 11 hours in space, making 859 trips around the earth, and covering a total of 24 million miles. One of their accomplishments was a record 6 hour 31 minute space walk (6 Aug.). The Apollo spacecraft returned to earth on 25 Sept. at 6:20 PM EDT with a vast amount of scientific information, including 16,800 pictures and 18 miles of magnetic tape data on observations of the earth, 77,600 solar telescope photos of the sun's corona, samples of metals welded and shaped in space, and biomedical specimens whose analysis promised to advance the knowledge of changes attributable to sustained exposure to weightlessness. Skylab 3. The final mission was launched in an Apollo spacecraft from Cape Canaveral at 9:01 AM EST on 16 Nov. 1973, carrying astronauts Lieut. Col. Gerald P. Carr, Lieut. Col. William R. Pogue, and Dr. Edward G. Gibson, a civilian scientist specializing in plasma physics. The longest manned space flight, it lasted 84 days; in addition to providing further information on the physiological and psychological adjustments required for protracted confinement to a space vehicle, the mission made observations and photographs of the comet Kohoutek. The astronauts returned to earth on 8 Feb. 1974 at 11:17 AM EDT. Skylab 3 terminated manned spaceflight by the U.S. until the summer of 1975, when U.S. astronauts were scheduled to participate in a joint mission with Soviet counterparts and link up their Apollo with a Soyuz space vehicle.

Medicine and Public Health

Epidemiology was the major concern of public health authorities in both the colonial and Revolutionary War years, with the decision to introduce smallpox inoculation truly a turning point in public health in that era. Prior to the introduction of medical education in some of the colleges in the late colonial period, physicians attained their education abroad, notably at Edinburgh, or by apprenticeship. In the nineteenth century American medical science kept abreast of European developments, and in the case of anesthesia and puerperal fever initiated important experiments and discoveries.

Since World War II vast advances in medical education, public health, vitamin research, chemotherapy, open heart surgery, and electronic devices for detection and diagnosis propelled the U.S. to the front rank in the fields of medicine and public health. As epidemic diseases declined in importance (notably with the recent development of vaccines for polio and measles) the principal areas of medical research came to be devoted to detecting the cause and treatment of cancer and circulatory diseases and in finding a cure for narcotics addiction. Birth control and abortion involved the medical profession in new ethical and moral issues, while spiraling medical costs posed the necessity of national health care, the need for paramedical training to supplement a shortage of physicians and hospital personnel, and raised the possibility of a complete transformation in the traditional goals of the profession.

1618–1776. EARLY EPIDEMICS. Smallpox: 1618–19, Mass. Indians, probably; 1631, 1635, 1638, 1648–49, 1666, N.E.; 1667, 1679–80, Va.; 1677–78, N.E.; 1689–90, Canada, N.E., N.Y.; 1696, Jamestown, Va.; 1702–03, 1721, Boston (over 50% infected, 1 in 7 deaths); 1730–31, Boston, N.Y., Phila.; 1737–38, N.E., Va., S.C.; 1746–47, Middle Colonies; 1751–52, Boston; 1756–57, Phila., Annapolis; 1758, N.Y.; 1759–60, Indians in S.C. and Ga.; 1760–61, 1764, N.E.; 1765, Md.; 1768, Reading, Pa. and Va.; 1774–76, throughout colonies. **Diphtheria:** 1659, N.E.; 1686, Va.; 1724, S.C.; 1735, N.H.; 1736–40, 1744–45, N.E., N.Y.; 1750–51, S.C.; 1754–55, N.E., N.Y.; 1763, Phila.; 1765, Boston; 1769, N.Y. **Scarlet fever:** 1702, 1735–36, Boston, Newport; 1764, Phila., N.C., S.C. **Measles:** 1657, Boston; 1687–88, N.E.; 1713–15, N.E. to Pa.; 1717, Va.; 1747–48, Conn., N.Y., Pa.; 1759, S.C., 1772–73, colonies generally. **Influenza:** 1647, N.E.; 1688, Va.; 1697–98, N.E.; 1722–23, colonies generally; 1756–57, 1761, 1767, 1770–72. **Pneumonia:** 1753–54, Mass. **Malaria:** 1658, 1668, 1683, N.E.; 1687, Va. Rising incidence in 18th cent., esp. in N.C. and S.C. **Dysentery:** 1669, N.E.; 1715, S.C.; 1731, Middle Colonies; 1751, S.C.; 1756, N.E.; 1757, Phila.; 1769, N.E. **Typhoid fever:** 1607, possibly, Jamestown; 1658, New Amsterdam; 1727, 1734, 1737, Conn. and Mass.; 1734, S.C.; 1741, N.E.; 1746, Albany, N.Y. By 1760 widely prevalent. **Typhus:** 1759, N.C.; 1764, 1766, Md. **Yellow fever:** first reported in Barbados,

1647; first clearly described in Phila., 1699, when it killed one-sixth of population; also Charleston; 1702, N.Y.; 1703, 1728, 1732, 1739, 1740, Charleston; 1741, Phila.; 1745, Charleston; 1747–48, Phila., Charleston; 1762, Phila.

1607–1750. EARLY PHYSICIANS, in addition to company physicians and ships' surgeons, included ministers like Revs. Gershom Bulkeley and Jared Eliot (Conn.) and emigrant physicians—**Cadwallader Colden, William Douglass** (c.1691–1752), the elder **John Moultrie** (d.1771), **Alexander Garden** (1730–91). Native physicians in this period received their training through apprenticeship.

1716–66. SMALLPOX INOCULATION (serum from mildly infected human patients) was advocated by **Cotton Mather** through readings of the *Transactions* (1714, 1716) and successfully put into practice (1721) by Dr. **Zabdiel Boylston** (1679–1766) prior to general acceptance in Europe (British royal children inoculated, 1722). Opposition led by **William Douglass** (died in smallpox epidemic, 1752), but practice spread to Philadelphia (1730) and South Carolina (1738). Results reported by Benjamin Gale (Conn.) in *Translations* (1766).

1735. First medical society in colonies founded at Boston.

First work describing lead poisoning from rum distilled with lead pipes published by **Thomas Cadwallader** (1708–79).

1736. First description of scarlet fever in the colonies by William Douglass.

1749–75. EUROPEAN MEDICAL TRAINING. Starting with **John Moultrie**, the younger (1729–98), Americans began to study abroad, particularly at the Univ. of Edinburgh (41 colonials in period), at private London lectures, and at the universities of Leyden and Paris.

1752. EARLY HOSPITALS. Pesthouses were established at Boston (1717), Philadelphia (1742), Charleston (before 1752), New York (before 1757). A hospital for chronically ill patients was established at Charleston (1738). The first general hospital was established by **Thomas Bond** (1712–84) in Philadelphia (1752). New York Hospital, sponsored by Dr. **Samuel Bard** (1742–1821), was chartered 1771, but not opened until 1791. The first publicly supported mental hospital opened at Williamsburg, Va., 1773.

1754. *Opishotonus and Tetanus* by Lionel Chalmers (d.1777), the most important work on tetanus produced in the course of the century.

1765–68. MEDICAL SCHOOLS. Medical faculty of College of Philadelphia (1765, largely through efforts of **John Morgan** [1725–89] and **William Shippen** [1736–1808] and King's College [1768]).

1775. First surgical textbook written in the colonies by **John Jones** (1729–91), *Remarks on the Treatment of Wounds and Fractures.*

1778. First American pharmacopoeia published by **William Brown** (1748–92).

1783–1810. MEDICAL SCHOOLS. Massachusetts Medical School, 1783. Faculties at Dartmouth (1798), Transylvania (1799), and Yale (1810). College of Medicine (Md.) organized, 1807; associated with Univ. of Maryland, 1812. College of Physicians and Surgeons (1807) joined by the medical faculty of Columbia (1813); reorganized as Medical Department of Columbia (1860).

1786–91. DISPENSARIES. Philadelphia Dispensary, opened, 1785, by Dr. **Benjamin Rush** (p. 1143); New York Dispensary, 1791.

c.1788–90. SURGERY. Dissection provoked serious rioting in New York City (1788). Dr. **John Jeffries** (1745–1819)—Loyalist physician who made a cross-Channel balloon ascension with François Blanchard, 1785—had his first public lecture on anatomy (on return to Boston, 1789) broken up by a mob.

1793, AUG.–OCT. YELLOW FEVER EPIDEMIC in Philadelphia, worst in history of any U.S. city, led to improvement of urban sanitary conditions and water-supply systems. Croton Aqueduct for New York City's water supply built 1837–42. **Other major epidemics:** cholera (New York City, June–Oct. 1832; South, 1849; Middle West, 1850); smallpox, typhoid fever, typhus (Northern cities, 1865–71); yellow fever, cholera, and smallpox (Southern cities, 1873).

1797–1820. MEDICAL PERIODICALS. *Medical Repository* (quarterly, edited by **Samuel Latham Mitchill** [1764–1831]), followed in this period by 11 journals, including *New England Medical Review and Journal* (1812, now *New England Journal of Medicine*) and *Philadelphia Journal of Medical and Physical Sciences* (1820, now *American Journal of Medical Sciences*).

1800–02. COWPOX VACCINATION introduced by Dr. **Benjamin Waterhouse** (Philadelphia, 1754–1846). Experiment by Boston Board of Health (Oct.–Nov. 1802) proved its efficacy and safety.

1808–20. PHARMACOPOEIAE. Massachusetts Medical Society published first official pharmacopoeia (1808; followed by New York Hospital, 1816). *U.S. Pharmacopoeia* prepared by representatives of state medical societies (1820), first to be nationally accepted.

1808. First work on **naval medicine** in U.S.: **Edward Cutbush's** (1772–1843)

Observations on the Means of Preserving the Health of Soldiers and Sailors.

1809. First **ovariotomy** anywhere in the world performed by **Ephraim McDowell** (1771–1830) at Danville, Ky.

1810–40. MEDICAL EDUCATION. In this period 27 new medical schools were founded in U.S., foreshadowing later overexpansion. Middle Western pioneer was **Daniel Drake** (1785–1852).

1811. John Syng Dorsey (1783–1818) was the first in U.S. to ligate the external iliac artery for inguinal aneurism.

1812. *Diseases of the Mind* by **Benjamin Rush,** a pioneer work on mental disorders, earning for its author the sobriquet, "Father of American Psychiatry."

1817–50. CARE OF THE INSANE. Asylum opened at Frankford, Pa., 1817, and Boston (McLean) and New York (Bloomingdale), 1818, with general adoption by 1850. For work of **Dorothea L. Dix,** see p. 1014.

1829. Publication of first U.S. textbook on pathology, by **William E. Horner** (1793–1853).

1831. CHLOROFORM discovered by **Samuel Guthrie** (1782–1848) simultaneously with, but independently of, von Liebig in Germany and Soubeiran in France. First used as anesthetic in England (1847); popularized in U.S. (1863) by **Gardner Q. Colton** (1814–98).

1833. GASTRIC PHYSIOLOGY. Publication of experiments by **William Beaumont** (p. 982).

1837. Typhus and typhoid fever clinically differentiated by **William W. Gerard** (1809–72).

1839. PATHOLOGY. *Elements of Pathological Anatomy* by **Samuel D. Gross** (1805–84), first comprehensive work on the subject in English; also wrote significantly on intestinal lesions (1843), urinary bladder conditions (1851), respiratory organs (1854), and surgery (1859).

1839–41. DENTISTRY. *American Journal of Dental Science* (1839), College of Dental Surgery (Baltimore, 1840), American Society of Dental Surgeons (1840). Alabama introduced licensing of dentists (1841).

1842–46. ANESTHESIA. Although nitrous oxide (laughing gas) had been discovered by Joseph Priestley (1772) and its effects recognized by Humphry Davy and William Allen (1800), neither it nor ether (whose effects were observed by Faraday, 1818) was used in surgery until William E. Clarke, a medical student, administered ether for a tooth extraction by Dr. Elijah Pope (Rochester, N.Y., Jan. 1842). For the claims of Long, Wells, and Morton, see pp. 1109–1110.

1843. *Contagiousness of Puerperal Fever,* a paper by **Oliver Wendell Holmes** (p. 1058), anticipated Semmelweis in Vienna (1847; the latter's definitive report, 1861).

1844–47. NATIONAL MEDICAL ASSOCIATIONS. Assn. of Medical Superintendents of Amer. Institutions for the Insane (1844; now known as Amer. Psychiatric Assn.). Amer. Medical Assn. founded, 1847. Membership 1974, c.200,000).

1844–85. MEDICAL JOURNALS. *American Journal of Psychiatry,* first (1844) among others; *American Journal of Obstetrics* (1868) considered to be first specialized medical journal; *Annals of Surgery* (1885).

1846. LARYNGOLOGY introduced into the U.S. by **Horace Green** (1802–66) with his *Treatise on Diseases of the Air Passages.* Introduction into U.S. of laryngoscope (1858) by **Ernest Krackowizer** (1821–75) expanded field.

1849. James M. Sims (1813–83) devised original operative treatment of vesicovaginal fistula.

1849–55. WOMEN IN MEDICINE. Elizabeth Blackwell (1821–1910), first woman medical graduate in the world, received M.D. degree from Medical School at Geneva, N.Y. Women's Medical College of Pennsylvania, first school of medicine entirely reserved for women (1850); Woman's Hospital, New York (1855).

1850–54. ADVANCES IN PUBLIC HEALTH. Monumental *Report of Massachusetts Sanitary Commission* by **Lemuel Shattuck** (p. 1149). No action in Massachusetts until 1869 when a Board of Public Health was established; New Orleans, 1855. Daniel Drake's *Systematic Treatise* (1850–54) also aroused interest in subject.

1852. American Pharmaceutical Assn. founded.

1853. PEDIATRICS. Arrival in U.S. of **Abraham Jacobi** (1830–1919) promoted work in the field, as did **Job Lewis Smith** (1827–97) and **Thomas Morgan Rotch** (1849–1914).

1861. Kidney successfully removed by **Erastus B. Wolcott** (1804–80).

1867–68. ADVANCES IN ANESTHESIA. Gas inhaler covering nose and mouth introduced by S. S. White Dental Mfg. Co. (1867). **Edmund Andrews** (1824–1904) introduced use of oxygen with nitrous acid.

1869–72. PUBLIC HEALTH. First state board of health established in Massachusetts (1869). Amer. Public Health Assn. (1872) promoted work in field.

1872. Silas Weir Mitchell (1829–1914), pioneer U.S. neurologist, published his *Injuries of Nerves and their Consequences;* introduced "Weir Mitchell" treatment for certain types of nervous diseases. **Willard Parker** (1800–84) had distinguished (1856) between concussion of nerves and conclusion of nerve centers.

1873. NURSING. Bellevue Hospital (N.Y.) established school of nursing following principles of Florence Nightingale; rapidly spread: 15 schools by 1880; 432 schools by 1900.

1873–95. MEDICAL EDUCATION. From 1873–90, 112 medical schools were founded. Faulty distribution: Missouri first with 42; Cincinnati, 20; Chicago, 14; Louisville, 11. In an effort to raise professional level states tightened licensure; boards of examination by 1895 and the modern type in almost every state. Model was the Medical School at Johns Hopkins (founded 1893), with **William Henry Welch** (1850–1934) in pathology; **William S. Halsted** (1852–1922), surgery; Sir **William Osler** (1849–1919), the clinician.

1874–1930. OSTEOPATHY (emphasizing placement of bones in the body as key to health) founded by **Andrew Taylor Still** (1828–1917). Amer. Assn. of Advanced Osteopathy established, 1897. Three schools and 7,644 osteopaths in U.S. (1930).

1879–80. "INDEX MEDICUS" AND "INDEX-CATALOGUE." John Shaw Billings (1838–1913), curator of Army Medical Museum and Library, founded *Index Medicus* (1879), monthly list of newly published medical literature, and compiled great *Index-Catalogue to the Library of the Surgeon-General's Office* (1880), monumental bibliography of medical literature.

1884–99. ADVANCES IN ANESTHESIA. William Halsted injected cocaine into nerves to anesthetize peripheral regions (1884); **J. Leonard Corning** (1855–1923), using cocaine as spinal anesthetic, induced epidural anesthesia (1885) and used cocaine as local anesthetic (1887); spinal anesthesia used by Dudley Tait and Guido Caglieri in San Francisco and Rudolph Matas in New Orleans (1899).

1885–1913. ADVANCES IN SURGERY. Joseph O'Dwyer (1841–98) improved technic for intubation of the larynx in diphtheria (1885). Peroral endoscopy improved and modified by **Chevalier Jackson** (Philadelphia, 1865–1958). **Reginald Heber Fitz** (1843–1913) established "appendicitis" as a definite lesion (1886). First appendectomy following correct diagnosis of appendicitis performed by **Thomas George Morton** (1835–1903); technic improved by **John B. Murphy** (1857–1916), inventor of "Murphy Button" (1892), and **Charles McBurney** (1845–1913), who originated short incision. First successful removal in U.S. of brain tumor performed by **William W. Keen** (1837–1932; done in London, 1884). **William Steward Halsted** introduced the use of rubber gloves (c.1890), was the first to ligate the subclavian artery (1891), and perfected operations for hernia and breast removal. Founding of the **Mayo Clinic** (1889) at Rochester, Minn. by the brothers **William James Mayo** and **Charles Horace Mayo** (p. 1100) opened a new era in U.S. surgery, with stress on diagnosis as well as advanced technics. Advances in prevention of surgical shock and in operations for toxic goiter were made by **George W. Crile** (1864–1943). **Hugh H. Young** (1870–1945), urologist, devised a technic of prostatectomy. First thoracoplasty (1893) performed by **George Ryerson Fowler** (1848–1906). **American College of Surgeons** originated 1913 by **Franklin H. Martin** (1857–1935).

1885–1941. FIGHT AGAINST TUBERCULOSIS. Sanitarium at Saranac Lake, N.Y., founded (1884) by **Edward L. Trudeau** (1848–1915); established Saranac Laboratory for study of tuberculosis (1894). Early diagnosis aided by Roentgen's discovery of X ray (1895). For contribution of **Theobald Smith**, see p. 1155. National Association for Study and Prevention of Tuberculosis founded, 1904.

1889–1910. PREVENTIVE MEDICINE. Basic research in hog cholera, swine plague, and Texas fever in cattle by **Theobald Smith. William Henry Welch** (1850–1934) discovered the bacillus of gas gangrene (1892). For the work in yellow fever of **Walter Reed** and associates, see p. 1136. Col. **William Gorgas** (p. 1043), applying technics worked out by Reed, eliminated yellow fever from the Panama Canal Zone (1904–06). **Howard Taylor Ricketts** (1871–1910) demonstrated (c.1910) that typhus fever was caused by a new class of organisms now known as Rickettsiae (including Rocky Mountain fever, by a tick; trench fever, by a louse).

1895. CHIROPRACTICS founded by **Daniel D. Palmer** (1845–1904), emphasizing position of joints (especially of the spine) as key to health. Illegal in some states, there were 21 schools and 16,000 practitioners by 1930. Its gradual rise to respectability is recognized by Medicare legislation (1973).

1896–1905. RADIUM AND X RAY IN THERAPY. X-ray treatment of breast cancer by **Emil H. Grube** (29 Jan. 1896) followed immediately upon publication of Roentgen's findings (5 Jan. 1896). Radium treatment for cancer used by **Robert Abbe** (1903); also first to treat cancer of womb with radium (1905).

1898–1927. HORMONES. Basic work on isolating adrenalin done by **John J. Abel** (1857–1938); completed by **Jokichi Takamine** (1854–1922) on basis of Abel's finding (1901). For isolation of thyroxine by **Edward C. Kendall**, see p. 1074. Work on insulin of Sir Frederick G. Banting and J. J. R. MacLeod (1922) utilized findings of **Moses Baron** on the pancreas. Isolation of substance in bull testes (later, androsterone and testosterone) accomplished (1927) by **Lemuel McGee.**

1901. ROCKEFELLER INSTITUTE OF MEDICAL RESEARCH founded.

William W. Welch first head; succeeded, 1904, by **Simon Flexner** (1863–1946), who discovered (1905–07) serum for treating cerebrospinal meningitis and was first to transmit poliomyelitis to monkeys and to show it is caused by a virus (1909).

1906. "TYPHOID MARY," discovered by G. A. Soper, documented role of healthy carriers as sources of disease.

1908–50. MEDICAL EDUCATION. Report (1910) by **Abraham Flexner** (p. 1030) for the Carnegie Foundation exposed abuses in medical education and proposed reforms. Large grants for medical schools and centers to Duke, Vanderbilt, George Washington, and universities of Chicago, Rochester, and Iowa. Number of medical schools declined: 148 (1910), 76 (1932), 77 (1950). Number of graduates declined: Over 5,000 per annum (1900–06) to a low of 2,529 (1922), with a gradual rise to above 5,000 (1934–43). Number of physicians fluctuated slightly from 1 per 750 to 1 per 800. Studies abroad by many students (1,481 in 1931–32) cut off by World War II. Dental schools declined: 54 (1910), 39 (1945).

1909–52. PSYCHIATRY AND PSYCHOTHERAPY. Adolf Meyer (1866–1950), a founder (after 1892) of the mental hygiene movement in the U.S., enunciated the dynamic conception of dementia praecox, and with his associates discovered that serious mental disorders might yield to treatment involving introduction of malarial organisms into the blood stream. **Clifford W. Beers** (1876–1943) founded mental hospital movement (1909); **Elmer Ernest Southard** (1876–1920) made notable contributions in the field of neuropsychiatry and its social implications. Later U.S. psychiatrists (since 1930) confirmed European discovery that dementia praecox could be cured by insulin or other shock treatment. First concerned with treatment of persons in asylums and mental hospitals,

psychiatrists broadened their scope to include the origin of criminal behavior (with pioneer work on juvenile delinquency by Dr. **William Healy,** 1869–1962) and child guidance. Since 1940 considerable advances in psychotherapy and psychosomatic medicine have been achieved by **Franz Alexander** (1891–1964) and Dr. **William C. Menninger** (1899–1966) at the Menninger Clinic, Topeka, and as director of neuropsychiatry, Surgeon General's Office, U.S. Army, 1943–46. Lectures by **Sigmund Freud** and **Carl G. Jung** at Clark Univ. (1909) advanced psychoanalysis in U.S. *Psychoanalytic Review* established (1913) by **William Alanson White** (1870–1937) and S. E. Jelliffe. Recent psychoanalysis (since 1930) has emphasized social and cultural factors in neurosis and interpersonal aspect of analyst-patient relationship (**Karen Horney** [1885–1952], **Erich Fromm** [1900–], **Harry Stack Sullivan** [1892–1947]).

1912–32. NEUROLOGICAL SURGERY. Contributions of greatest U.S. figure in field, **Harvey Cushing,** see p. 1009.

1913. Bela Schick (1877–1967) devised "Schick test," a skin test to determine susceptibility to diphtheria. Mass surveys, first in New York City, followed by immunization of Schick-positive children by inactive toxin, drastically cut incidence of disease.

1914–48. VITAMIN RESEARCH. Beginning 1888, early work was conducted abroad (Eijkmann, Dutch East Indies; Funk and Hopkins, England; Frohlich and Holst, Norway; Pekelharing, Holland; Lunin, Switzerland). Vitamin A discovered (1912–14) by **Elmer V. McCollum** (1879–1967); Vitamin B (1915–16); Vitamin D (1922). **Joseph Goldberger** (1874–1929), of U.S. Public Health Service, discovered (1915) that pellagra was a deficiency disease. **Harry Steenbock** (1886–1968) at the Univ. of

Wisconsin and Alfred Hess at Columbia announced almost simultaneously (1924) methods for irradiating Vitamin D. Vitamin E isolated from wheat germ (1922) by **Herbert M. Evans** (1882–1958). Vitamin C isolated by Dr. Charles G. King (1932). R. J. Williams reported pantothenic acid (1933). Vitamin K discovered (1934) by **Edward A. Doisy** (1893–   ), simultaneously with Dam and Schønheyder in Denmark; synthesized (1939). Medical use of niacin discovered by **Conrad Elverhjem** (1901–1962). Thiamin synthesized (1936); pyridoxine isolated (1938); biotin's complex structure determined (1942). Para-amino benzoic acid synthesized (1943), in which year folic acid was discovered. By 1941 vitamin B was shown to be a complex of at least 5 distinct vitamins. Vitamin B_{12} shown to be effective in treatment of pernicious anemia (1948).

1918–19. INFLUENZA PANDEMIC spread from Western Front, with estimated 500,000 deaths in U.S. alone.

1920–43. TREATMENT OF EPILEPSY. Phenobarbital (discovered by Hauptmann, Germany, 1911) introduced in treatment by **Julius Grinker** (1920). Work of **William G. Lennox** (1884–1960) and **Tracy J. Putnam** (1894–   ) led to dilantin being synthesized and applied (1936). Tridione synthesized at Abbott Laboratories (1940); applied (1943).

1923–34. ANESTHESIA. Ethylene demonstrated by Arno B. Luckhardt; Sodium Amytal used on animals by F. J. Fulton and on humans intravenously by Leon G. Zerfas (1923). Cyclopropane (by Neff, Rovestine, and Waters) and Nembutal (by R. H. Fitch, Waters, and Tatum) used as anesthetics (1930). Divinyl oxide, fastest yet devised, produced by Chauncey D. Leake (1930). Sodium Pentothal administered (1934) intravenously by John S. Lundy; also to permit free questioning by psychiatrists.

1927–28. IRON LUNG invented by Philip Drinker and Louis A. Shaw; used for poliomyelitis (1928).

1936–39. SULFA DRUGS. Perrin H. Long and Eleanor A. Bliss at Johns Hopkins proved the effectiveness of both prontosil (discovered by Domagk, Germany, 1932) and sulfanilamide (discovered by Fourneau and Trèfouëls, France) on peritonitis, scarlet fever, tonsillitis, blood poisoning, and impetigo. These drugs were displaced, first by sulfapyridine (proved effective in the Sudan, 1939), and later by sulfathiazole, sulfadiazine, and other sulfa compounds.

1939–52. ANTIBIOTICS. René J. Dubos (1901–   ) at Rockefeller Institute discovered tyrothricin in soil bacteria (effective in eye infections, ulcer, impetigo). **Selman Waksman** (p. 1175) discovered astinomycin (1940), streptothricin (1941)—both too destructive—and streptomycin (with Schatz, 1944; Nobel prize for discovery, 1952), the last effective in meningitis, tuberculosis, dysentery, and bladder and kidney infections. Other antibiotics followed: chloromycetin (Ehrlich *et al.*, 1947); aureomycin (Duggar, 1948); terramycin (Finlay *et al.*, 1950); magnamycin (Pfizer Lab., 1952).

1941–43. PENICILLIN. Discovered by Dr. Alexander Fleming in London (1929); experiments by Dr. Howard W. Florey (1938) led to use on a human patient (1941). At beginning of World War II production of penicillin transferred to the U.S. under the wartime direction of Dr. Chester Keefer. Due to findings of Robert D. Coghill, production rose to 300 billion units (c.15 lbs.) per month (1945). Tests made by Florey abroad, and by Keefer, Leo Lowe, and John Mahoney, revealed effectiveness in most sulfa-resistant streptococcus and straphylococcus infections, including syphilis and subacute bacterial endocarditis (1943). **Synthetic penicillin** developed in Beecham Laboratories, England (1959), and Bristol-Myers, U.S.; introduced in U.S., 1960.

1943–50. ANTIHISTAMINES. Paralleling work at Pasteur Institute, U.S. researchers began work in field (1943). Benadril discovered by George Rieveschl, Jr. (1943); Pyrobenzamine (1946); Neohetramine (1948). Dramamine shown to be effective for control of seasickness (1948). Antihistamines used in treatment of allergies; promoted for common cold (1949–50), with debatable results.

1946–52. CORTISONE, a hormone of the cortex of the adrenal gland, synthesized by several groups (Sarett; Kendall, Mason, and Mattox; Julian; Gallagher, 1946; from carbon, oxygen, and hydrogen by Sarett, 1952). First used (1949) for rheumatic arthritis by Edward C. Kendall (p. 1074) and Philip S. Hench (1896–1965). ACTH, a hormone from the pituitary gland, was concentrated at Armour Laboratories and used by Hench *et al.* for rheumatoid arthritis.

1950–70. INDEX OF MEDICAL CARE PRICES
(U.S. Bureau of the Census, *Statistical Abstract*, 1973.)

	Total Medical Care	Drugs and Prescriptions	Physician Fees	Dentist Fees	Hospital Daily Charges
1950	53.7	88.5	55.2	63.9	28.9
1960	79.1	104.5	77.0	82.1	56.3
1970	120.6	103.6	121.4	113.5	143.9

1951–60. DRUG TRENDS. Tranquilizers: Miltown first synthesized 1950, in widespread use by 1955. Isolation (1952) of reserpine from old Indian shrub, along with introduction (1954) of thorazine, or chlorpromazine (synthesized in France), with dramatic effects in treatment of patients with mental disorders. **Steroids:** In addition to corticosteroids (for arthritis), research and development progressed rapidly in field of sex steroids for treating endocrine deficiencies, of applying steroids as an anabolic agent for reconstruction of body and muscle tissues, and as cardiovascular agents. Synthesis of polypeptide hormone, oxytocin, by **Vincent du Vigneaud** (1901–), who also synthesized hormone vasopressin (1956), won him Nobel prize in chemistry (1955). ACTH equivalent synthesized (1960) by Dr. Klaus Hofmann and associates. **Diabetes control:** Introduction (1957) of a nonbactericidal sulfonamide (Orinase) for treatment of mild diabetes of old age. **Fatreducing diets:** Rockefeller Institute an-

nounced (1956) liquid formula based on glucose and corn oil, which served as basis of proprietary products, widely marketed beginning 1959.

1953. CANCER AND CIGARETTE SMOKING. Increase of incidence of cancer of the lung due to cancer-producing factor in cigarette smoking reported 8 Dec. 1953 by Dr. Alton Ochsner; statistical confirmation by Drs. Evarts A. Graham and Ernest L. Winder, 2 Feb. 1954; by British government study, 12 Feb.; and by statistical report of American Cancer Society, 21 June.

1955, 12 APR. SALK VACCINE. Widespread field tests of use of gamma globulin during polio epidemics in Utah, Texas, and Iowa, 1952, showed only short-term protection (c. 5 weeks). Earlier (1949) Drs. **John F. Enders** (p. 1025), **Thomas H. Weller** (1915–), and **Frederick C. Robbins** (1916–) of Harvard Medical School found that polio virus could be grown in clusters of non-nervous human and monkey tissues in test tubes, for which they were awarded the Nobel

Prize in medicine and physiology (1954). This discovery paved the way for growth of the virus in quantities massive enough for use as vaccine. Using 3 strains of inactivated polio, Dr. **Jonas E. Salk** (p. 1145) of Pittsburgh Univ. Medical School reported (26 Mar. 1953) hopeful results from a vaccine he prepared. In the largest medical field test in history, 1,830,000 school children participated in program to evaluate Salk vaccine. Evaluation report (12 Apr. 1955) disclosed that active immunity was provided for at least 6 months, with more permanent protection by use of booster injections. As a result of a number of fatalities in the early stages, due to accidental inclusion of live virus in certain batches of vaccine, both the method of preparation and the strains of virus were modified for greater safety. The Poliomyelitis Vaccination Act (12 Aug. 1955) provided that the Public Health Service should allocate $30 million to the states to help them buy the vaccine, of which about 20% was given free. Rise and decline in U.S. polio cases: (annual average) 1938–42, 6,400; 1942–47, 16,800; 1947–51, 34,000; 1952, c. 60,000; 1955, 37,771; 1957–58, c. 5,700; 1960, 3,277 (lowest since 1938).

Building on the work of **Hilary Koprowski** (1916–), Dr. **Albert Sabin** (1906–) developed a live (attenuated) virus poliomyelitis vaccine during the late 1950s. Licensed in 1962, with the advantages of ease of administration, rapidity, and high degree of effectiveness, the oral vaccine has become widely used in the U.S. and the Soviet Union, largely supplanting Salk vaccine. Reported polio cases declined to 72 (1965), 21 (1971).

1957. Pandemic of "Asian flu," a new strain of Type A influenza, spread from northern China and reached the U.S. in June, where it quickly became epidemic, although death rate remained low.

1958–72. NOBEL PRIZES IN MEDICINE AND PSYCHOLOGY were dominated by American doctors: 1958, **Joshua Lederberg** (p. 1082) for discoveries concerning genetic recombination and organization of genetic material of bacteria, and **George Wells Beadle** (1903–) and **Edward Lawrie Tatum** (1909–) for discovery that genes act by controlling specific chemical reactions; **1959,** Drs. **Arthur Kornberg** (1918–), Stanford Univ., and **Severo Ochoa** (1905–), New York Univ., for the synthesis of nucleic acid; **1961, Georg von Békésy** (1899–1972), Harvard, for discoveries concerning physical mechanisms of stimulation within the cochlea which opened the way for major advances in diagnosis and correction of damaged hearing; **1962,** Dr. **James Watson** (1928–), Harvard, shared the prize with British biophysicists Francis Crick and Maurice Wilkins for determination (1953) of the molecular structure of deoxyribonucleic acid (DNA), the device by which genetic information is transmitted from one generation to the next; 1964, **Konrad Bloch** (1912–) (shared with Feodor Lynen, of Germany), for research into the relation between heart disease and cholesterol and fatty acids; **1966, Charles B. Huggins** (1901–), Univ. of Chicago, for cancer research, and **Frances Peyton Rous** (1879–1970), Rockefeller Univ., for demonstrating in 1910 that animal cancer can be transmitted by virus; **1967, Haldan Keffer Hartline** (1903–), Rockefeller Institute, **George Wald** (1906–), Harvard, with Ragnar Granit of Sweden, for research into processes of the eye; **1968, Robert W. Holley** (1922–), Salk Institute, **Marshall W. Nirenberg** (1927–), National Institutes of Health, and **H. Gobind Khorana** (1922–), Univ. of Wisconsin, for "breaking the genetic code"; **1969, Max Delbruck** (1906–), **Salvador E. Luria** (1908–), and **Alfred D. Hershey** (1912–) for work in the "replication mechanism and genetic structure of virus"; **1970, Julius Axelrod** (1912–   ) (shared with Bernard Katz, England, and Ulf Svante vol Euler, Sweden), for studies in the chemistry of nerve transmission; **1971, Earl Wilbur Sutherland, Jr.** (1915–   ), for studies in the mechanism of hormones; **1972, Gerald Edelman** (1929–   ) (shared with Rodney Porter, England), for studies of the chemical structure of antibodies.

1960. KIDNEY DISEASE, treatment by transplantation and routine dialysis initiated.

1961–68. BIRTH CONTROL. Research on oral contraceptives ("the pill") began in the 1950s. Drs. **Gregory Goodwin Pincus** (p. 1128), **M. C. Chang,** and **John Rock** led in development of means of birth control dependent for the first time upon physiological action. A synthetic progesterone (hormonelike substance) suppresses ovulation. Believed to be 100 percent effective, the pill was first marketed in 1960. Initial popularity was later limited by side effects such as nausea and the gaining of weight, which were reduced by later research. By 1968 more than 6 million American women (nearly ⅕ of those of child-bearing age) had adopted the use of the pill, which was also credited with influencing changes in sexual mores.

A United States grant of $500,000 to the World Health Organization for research into human reproduction (1963) was the first official recognition of the need to provide technical assistance on population control to those nations requesting it.

1961–71. HEART SURGERY AND TRANSPLANTS. Dramatic advances were made in the treatment of abnormalities of the heart, blood vessels, and circulation. New instruments were employed for diagnosis, treatment, and observation; radioactive isotopes to estimate blood flow through the heart muscle; miniaturized "pacemakers" inserted to correct abnormal heartbeat; artificial pumps applied temporarily. First artificial heart surgery by Dr. **Michael E. De Bakey** (1908–   ) employing ventricle bypass pump to assist the heart. The discovery of new drugs effective in suppressing antibodies made possible the dramatic heart transplant operations. Dr. Christiaan N. Barnard, Groote Shur Hospital, Capetown, South Africa, performed the first heart transplant 3 Dec. 1967, the patient surviving 18 days. Dr. Barnard transplanted a heart for Dr. Philip Blaiberg (2 Jan. 1968), who survived over 19 months. The first American transplant, 6 Dec. 1967, was performed by Dr. Adrian Kantrowitz (1918–   ), Maimonides Hospital Center, New York City; the patient surviving only a few hours. Dr. Norman E. Shumway (1923–   ), Stanford Univ., devised the standard transplant technique and Dr. Denton A. Cooley (1920–   ), St. Luke's Hospital, Houston, Tex., employed a streamlined technique, reducing the length of surgery from over 2 hours to about 25 minutes. Drs. Shumway, Cooley, and De Bakey, St. Luke's and Houston Methodist Hospitals, performed close to half of the 80 transplants which had taken place in 15 countries throughout the world as of Dec. 1968; 36 persons with new hearts were surviving (28 Nov. 1968). While heart transplants decreased by 1971, new techniques included completely artificial heart device inserted by Cooley (4 Apr. 1969) and patch booster, a partially mechanical heart driven by an air pump outside the body, inserted by Kantrowitz (11 Aug. 1971).

1962. Thalidomide Scare, caused by abnormal births to pregnant women taking drug in Europe (9 such births in U.S.), led to strong safety provisions of **Drug Amendments** of 1962 (10 Oct.) to assure that new drugs were safe and effective.

1963. Measles Vaccine. Vaccines against common ("red") measles introduced.

1964–67. CANCER AND CIGARETTE SMOKING. After 14 months of study, the U.S. Surgeon General's Special Advisory Committee on Smoking and Health reported that smoking was the chief cause of lung cancer (11 Jan. 1964). Although the causative role of smoking in coronary artery disease was not considered proven, risk of death from coronary artery disease was 70 percent greater for middle-aged men who smoked. A mandatory health warning on cigarette packages became effective 1 Jan. 1966 (bill signed 19 July 1965). Although numerous further studies, including *The Health Consequences of Smoking* by the U.S. Public Health Service (1967), reinforced and amplified the earlier warning, controversy over restrictions on cigarette advertising continued and smoking in the U.S. increased.

1965. Rubella Virus strain HPV-77 developed by Dr. Harry M. Meyer, Jr. and Dr. Paul D. Parkman of the National Institutes of Health, based upon isolation of rubella virus (1961) separately by Drs. Thomas H. Weller and Franklin A. Nevas of Harvard, and Drs. Parkman, Edward L. Buescher, and Malcolm S. Artenstein of Walter Reed Army Medical Center, led to rubella vaccine as developed by Drs. Maurice R. Hilleman and Eugene B. Buynak of Merck, Sharp, and Dohme (licensed 1969).

1965. MEDICARE. Social Security Amendments (30 July 1965), Medical Care for the Aged Program, were enacted more than 12 years after President Truman's Commission on the Health Needs of the Nation recommended a federal health insurance plan under social security. The Medicare program consists of (1) a basic hospital insurance program covering hospital and posthospital services for those 65 and over, paid for from a special contribution through social security, (2) supplementary (voluntary) medical insurance program providing payment for physicians' and surgeons' services, home health and other Medicare services for those aged 65 and more, (3) **Medicaid,** Title 19, a measure to assist the needy and disabled not covered by social security to meet expenses covered by the other two programs, plans to be implemented by individual states, with costs divided between the state and federal governments. 19.7 million persons were enrolled in the hospital insurance program (June 1968). By Jan. 1968, 30 states were participating in Medicaid programs.

1965–68. AIR AND WATER POLLUTION. Growing concern over air and water pollution was reflected in the increasing federal role (see pp. 639–643).

1966. L-DOPA, as a nonsurgical treatment of Parkinson's disease, introduced, proving highly effective in alleviating symptoms but not slowing the underlying progression of the disease.

1968. RH FACTOR. Reverse vaccination at the time of a woman's first delivery to ward off future Rh incompatibility crisis introduced.

1968–73. DEFINING DEATH AND MEDICAL ETHICS. Increasing transplantation of organs engendered concern over the definition of death. A new definition involving the use of the electroencephalograph was developed (1968) by a committee at Harvard Medical School in which the ceasing of brain function as detected by the electroencephalograph represented the death of the patient.

During the 1960s and reaching a high level of concern in the 1970s, physicians and society examined the ethics of medical practices. Noteworthy was the debate over defining informed consent for patients undergoing medical care and as subjects in experiments, the use of heroic measures to forestall death, and the treatment of the dying patient.

1969–72. MEDICAL SCIENCE AND GENETICS. 1972 Nobel prize in chemistry to Christian B. Anfisen (1916–   ), Stanford Moore (1913–   ), and William H. Stein (1911–   ) for studies in the composition and functioning of enzyme ribonuclease, the first synthesis of which was achieved by Merck, Sharp, and Dohme Research Laboratories and by the Rockefeller Institute. Isolation of a single gene by Harvard Medical School team (22 Nov. 1969) headed by Dr. Jonathan Beckwith. Major contribution to gene isolation also made by Dr. David Kohne of the Carnegie Institute. First synthetic gene by H. G. Khorana and group, Univ. of Wisconsin (1970).

Watson and Crick's detailed description of DNA as a double helix was confirmed by photographic evidence of Jack Griffith (1942–   ), Univ. of California, Berkeley.

Amniocentestis began to attract wide medical attention for prenatal diagnosis of Down's Syndrome and other inherited disorders characterized by chromosome abnormalities or enzyme deficiencies. The procedure involved piercing the uterus with a needle to withdraw some of the fluid surrounding the fetus and thus invading the hitherto sacrosanct uterine cavity for diagnosis during pregnancy.

1969–72. MEDICAL PROFESSION developments included (1) increasing interest in family practice, group practices, prepaid medical plans; (2) experiments in cutting one year from medical school; (3) postgraduate residencies in social medicine and in family practice; (4) employment of paramedics. New specialty, family medicine, announced by AMA, 10 Feb. 1969.

1969–73. DRUG USE AND ENVIRONMENTAL ISSUES. Society's alarm at the growing number of students taking drugs like marijuana, LSD, and dex-

edrine increased penalties for drug use and narcotics traffic (with life sentence being the enacted maximum penalty in New York state [1973]). Scientific studies expanded on the effect of certain drugs, particularly marijuana, on human beings.

In the face of increased concern about the quality of the American environment, the U.S. government banned the use of DDT in gradual stages, to be completely prohibited by 1971. President Nixon announced (1970) the establishment of the Council on Environmental Quality and the Environmental Protection Agency, but a number of programs were suspended as a result of the growing energy crisis beginning in 1973.

1970. LINUS PAULING'S (p. 1123) claim that vitamin C in massive amounts would ward off the common cold stirred considerable controversy in the medical profession.

1970–74. WOMEN STUDENTS in U.S. medical schools increased dramatically from 3,894 (1970–71) school year, 9.6% of total enrollment, to 7,824 or 15.4% (1973–74). Percentage first-year female medical students: 7.8% (1963–64), 11.1% (1970–71), 19.7% (1973–74).

1971. ACUPUNCTURE. Thaw in political relationship with Mainland China led to visits by doctors and journalists whose enthusiastic reports of the success of the ancient Chinese practice of inserting needles into various parts of the body as anesthetic and for relief of pain and cure of illness led to experimentation in U.S.

1970–72. ABORTION. Colorado was the 1st state to adopt liberalized model penal code abortion statute (1967). By 1970, 13 states had followed. The U.S. Supreme Court in *Roe* v. *Wade* (1972, p. 685) defined the rights of the mother and fetus in the case of abortion, striking down all existing state laws making abortion a crime. The decision followed several years of liberalized abortion laws in a number of states (1967–71).

1972. 2 JAN. Cigarette advertising ban on radio and TV effective following act of Congress (1970).

1973. PATIENTS' BILL OF RIGHTS issued by American Hospital Association included right to complete and current information regarding diagnosis, treatment, and progress, as well as the right to refuse treatment.

THOUGHT AND CULTURE

Religion

The fact that the American religious experience has been pluralistic has contributed substantially to the complete separation of church and state, while at the same time fostering religious liberty. Although the Roman Catholic faith had maintained an establishment on the North American continent some two centuries before the arrival of Protestantism, it was the latter, in diverse forms, which dominated the Thirteen English Colonies. Formally separating from the Church of England were the Congregationalists, Presbyterians, and Baptists, along with a number of more radical sects such as the Quakers, and to this latter group were added various Pietist sects that migrated to America from central Europe, starting in the 1680s. While the Church of England was established in the Southern colonies and in the 4 lower counties of New York, the Puritan Congregationalists effectively established their churches throughout New England save for Rhode Island.

Organized religion felt the thrust of the great revivals of the colonial period and the nineteenth century, with a quasi-establishment of evangelical Protestantism emerging, dominated by Methodists and Baptists, along with other indigenous groups, and the black churches having a separate and distinctive experience. More recently, the religious scene has responded to the powerful neo-orthodox impulse, with its thoroughgoing reconsideration of judgments rendered by a previous generation of liberal churchmen. Nineteenth- and twentieth-century immigration has given increasing prominence in numbers and influence to Roman Catholicism, Judaism, and the Eastern Orthodox churches, while mystical cults have recently emerged in response to youthful disillusionment and malaise.

c.1000. CHRISTIANITY IN THE NEW WORLD. According to the Icelandic *Saga of Eric the Red,* Leif Ericson (pp. 16, 17) introduced Christianity in Greenland and along the North American coast.

1492–1769. CATHOLICISM IN NEW SPAIN. Spanish explorers and conquistadores, supported by the church, introduced Catholicism into the Caribbean islands and the continents of North and South America as a culmination of a long campaign in Spain against Jews and Moors. In what is the continental U.S. the Catholic faith was spread by Spanish missions from Florida (1565), New Mexico (1598), Arizona (1680s), Texas (1690), and California, the last through the efforts of Father Junipero Serra (p. 27) starting in 1769. All these areas constituted borderlands of New Spain where Catholicism had been long entrenched.

1632–1774. CATHOLICISM IN NEW FRANCE. For the role of the Recollect and Jesuit missions, see pp. 72–73. For the treatment of the Catholic Church in Canada by the British government, 1763–1774, see pp. 97–98.

1609. CHURCH OF ENGLAND was established by law in Virginia. A statute (1610), reenacted when Virginia became a royal colony, but never rigidly enforced, provided for compulsory church attendance. The Anglican Church was also established in the lower counties of New York (1693), and in Maryland (1702), South Carolina (1706), North Carolina (nominally, 1711), and Georgia (1758). The first Anglican church in New York City, Trinity Church, was founded in 1697, with Rev. William Vesey as rector. In Massachusetts Anglican worship was introduced by Governor Andros (1686). In Pennsylvania Christ Church, Philadelphia, was organized in 1694 and gained ground following the Quaker schism. Anglicanism was introduced in New Jersey (1702) and in Connecticut (1706). The influence of the church was restricted by the predominantly mediocre quality of the colonial clergy, by oversized parishes, low salaries, neglect of discipline, and lay control. In the absence of a resident bishop confirmation and ordination could not be administered in the colonies. The latter served to discourage the growth of a native ministry. The **Bishop of London** was placed in charge of colonial churches in 1635, and was represented in the colonies by **commissaries,** notably by **James Blair** (1655–1743) in Virginia, 1689–1743, and **Thomas Bray** (1656–1730) in Maryland. The latter founded (1701) the **Venerable Society for the Propagation of the Gospel in Foreign Parts** (S.P.G.), which engaged in missionary activities and founded churches (notably in the Carolinas). After the first quarter of the 18th century the Anglican Church gained ground as a result of a split among Calvinists. In 1722 a great defection from Yale College and the Congregational ministry to Anglicanism was led by **Samuel Johnson** (1696–1772), a follower of Bishop Berkeley's idealistic system of philosophy. Repeated agitation for an **American episcopate** (1700–70) failed because of the opposition of governmental officials, dissenters, and Southern laymen who insisted on the right to choose their own curates. The first bishop in America was **Samuel Seabury** (1729–96), consecrated in Aberdeen by nonjuring bishops (1784).

1620. THE CONGREGATIONAL CHURCH was introduced by the Pilgrims in Plymouth (1620) and by the Puritans in Massachusetts Bay (1630). The principal difference was that the former (Independents) repudiated the Church of England; the latter (Nonconformists) did not openly break with the Established Church. The Puritan theological system stressed 3 covenants—between God and man, between the church and its members, and between the state and its citizens. Since the church never controlled the state officially, Massachusetts never achieved a true theocracy, but rather a "Bible Commonwealth" in which the civil rulers, seeking to rule in accordance with the will of God, sought counsel of the divines (Calvinist "consociation"). Factors contributing to the decline of the church in New England were (1) the disappearance of the distinction in civil matters between the "elect" and all others, (2) gradual dispersal of the population on farms, and (3) the growth of rationalism. The **Halfway Covenant** (1657–62), which admitted to baptism the children of baptized persons who themselves had not experienced conversion, served to erase the distinction between the "elect" and all others, and marked an effort to return to the original New England way when evidence simply of purity of faith and life was required. Rationalist influences: (1) the revulsion against the **Salem witchcraft trials** (1692–93), (2) the ouster of the orthodox Increase Mather as president of Harvard College (1701); (3) the founding of the Brattle Street Church in Boston (1699), the first Puritan church not to require a public confession of faith for admission to communion. The religious monopoly of the Congregationalists was challenged by the Baptists under **Roger Williams** (p. 1185) and **Henry Dunster** (1609–59), who was forced to resign (1654) the presidency of Harvard College because of his opposition to infant baptism; by the Presbyterians, as evidenced in the remonstrance of Dr. Robert Child (1646), the later attempt of Increase Mather to Presbyterianize the church, resisted by Rev. **John Wise** (1710–17), and the **Saybrook Platform** (1708), by which Connecticut Congregationalists placed themselves under a Presbyterian-type government; and by the Quakers (p. 822); and was terminated as a result of the revocation of the old charter (1684).

1628. THE DUTCH REFORMED CHURCH (a Calvinist, Presbyterian group) was organized in New Amsterdam by Rev. Jonas Michaëlius (1628), placed under the jurisdiction of the Classis of Amsterdam, and established by the Freedoms and Exemptions (1640). A Coetus or synod of ministers and elders was formed in 1747. Between 1755 and 1771 a cleavage developed between the **Coetus** (demanding virtual self-government) and the **Conferentie** (conservative), which was settled by Rev. **John Henry Livingston** (1770–1825), with substantial independence for the Coetus. The organization of a General Synod, 1792, made the American church independent.

1633. THE ROMAN CATHOLIC CHURCH. The first group of Catholics to arrive in the English colonies came to Maryland, which had been founded (1632) to provide refuge for that denomination. Instructions from the proprietor, Cecilius Calvert, allowed freedom of religion to all Christians, and bid Roman Catholics to worship "as privately as may be." For the Toleration Act (1649) and its repeal (1654), see p. 35. The Revolution of 1689 in Maryland, leading to Protestant ascendancy, resulted in the passage of anti-Catholic legislation (1) imposing poll tax on Irish Catholic immigrant servants; (2) requiring that children of mixed marriages be reared as Protestants; (3) imposing a fine for sending children to Catholic schools abroad. Thenceforward to the American Revolution the Roman Catholic Church subsisted on a clandestine basis. In New York Roman Catholics enjoyed toleration under the administration of the Catholic Governor, Thomas Dongan (1682–88), but between 1691 and 1776 they were deprived of both political rights and religious freedom. In the beginning of the 18th century Rhode Island and Pennsylvania were the only colonies in which Roman Catholics enjoyed religious and civil rights. St. Joseph's Church, Philadelphia, 1733, was the first completely public Catholic church in the English colonies. For Protestant opposition to the Quebec Act, 1774, see p. 98. By 1775 public worship by Roman Catholics was confined to Pennsylvania (with Jesuit churches and chapels in Philadelphia, Conewago, Goschenhoppen, Lancaster, and Reading).

1639. BAPTISTS (opposed to infant baptism and stressing the separation of church and state) were organized as a church by **Roger Williams** (p. 1185) at Providence, R.I., followed by Newport (1644). Large gains were made in the Middle Colonies among the Welsh and as a result of the Quaker schism. In addition, their membership expanded as a result of (1) the Great Awakening and (2) the American Revolution, with substantive gains among the rural population of the South. Under such leaders as **Isaac Backus** (1724–1806) and **John Leland** (1754–1841), they were active on behalf of religious liberty and the separation of church and state.

1640. LUTHERAN CHURCH. Rev. **Reorus Torkillus**, first Lutheran minister to serve in the New World, arrived in New Sweden (spring 1640). In 1649 Dutch Lutherans organized a congregation in New Netherland. Large immigration of German Lutherans to New York began in 1708; after 1722, main stream flowed to Pennsylvania. The first synod was organized (1748) under Rev. **Heinrich Melchior Mühlenberg** (1711–87). The organization of the Ministerium of Pennsylvania led ultimately to the independence of the Lutheran Church in the U.S., with some 130 congregations, chiefly in Pennsylvania, at the outbreak of the Revolution.

1654. JEWS. Despite the efforts of Stuyvesant to deprive them of civil rights, the first group of Jews, arriving in New Amsterdam (1654) from Curaçao, induced the Dutch West India Co. (7 Jews were among the 167 stockholders) to permit them to reside and engage in wholesale trade (1655–56). In 1657 they were admitted to the retail trades. In 1685 they demanded the right of public worship, denied under Dutch rule, and a synagogue (Shearith Israel, "Remnant of Israel") was known to exist in New York City in 1695. In 1737 their right to vote for the N.Y. Assembly was denied. Admitted in Rhode Island to the freemanship (1665), they were later denied political rights (1728), which were restored by the state constitution (1777). Similarly, in South Carolina voting was confined to Christians (1721), but at least one Jew was elected to public office—Francis Salvador, Jr., to the first provincial congress. In Savannah, Ga., Jews held minor public office (1765–88), with David Emanuel elected governor (1801). The disqualification of the Maryland constitution of 1776, barring Jews from public office, was finally removed in 1826; in North Carolina, not until 1868. The Jews prior to 1789 were mainly **Sephardim** (of Spanish, Portuguese, and Dutch origin).

1656. QUAKERS (SOCIETY OF FRIENDS), founded by George Fox (1624–91), stressed "inner light," separation of church and state, opposition to war and oaths. Except in Rhode Island, they were persecuted in the period, 1656–70 (p. 44). Expansion of this sect is attributed to the visit of Fox to America (1671) and to Penn's "Holy Experiment" (1681, pp. 57, 1125). As a result of a schism in 1692 between Penn and **George Keith** (c.1638–1716), principal of the Penn Charter School, the latter founded a sect known as Christian, or Baptist, Quakers, or "Keithians," and then was ordained in the Church of England (1700).

1683. MENNONITES, led by **Francis Daniel Pastorius** (1651–c.1720), settled in Germantown, Pa. They advocated separation of church and state, religious liberty, adult baptism, a church of the elect, pacifism, refusal to take oaths, and drew up the first protest against slavery (1688). Most conservative of this group were the **Amish.** The Old Amish Order still uses the German language exclusively and is opposed to innovation.

1706. PRESBYTERIANS. The first presbytery was organized in Philadelphia by **Francis Makemie** (1658–1708); the first synod in 1718. The Adopting Act, the first constitution of American Presbyterianism, was adopted (1729). Expansion was due to the founding of "log colleges," especially the one by Rev. **William Tennent, Sr.** (c.1673–1746) at Neshaminy (1736), and by the establishment of the College of New Jersey (1746). Synod of 1786 provided for a General Assembly, the first meeting of which was held in Philadelphia (1789).

1721. Hollis Chair in Divinity, the first professorship in theology, was established at Harvard.

1723. DUNKARDS, OR GERMAN BAPTISTS, were organized under the leadership of **Alexander Mack.** Their distinctive features were triple immersion, pacifism, and agape feasts.

1726–56. GREAT AWAKENING, a series of revivals, usually dates from the preaching of Domine **Theodorus Frelinghuysen** (1691–1748), a Dutch Reformed minister in New Jersey, the establishment of Tennent's log college (1736), and the first visit of **George Whitefield** (p. 1181) to Georgia (1738) and his later itinerant preaching from Maine to Georgia (1739–40). In New England, undisputed leadership in the movement was assumed by **Jonathan Edwards** (p. 1021), beginning with his sermons of 1734. In Virginia it attained its peak, 1748–49, under Rev. **Samuel Davies** (1723–61). Stubal Stearns and Daniel Marshall spread the movement among the Virginia Baptists. The Methodist phase, under Rev. Devereux Jarrett, reached its climax, 1775–85. Among Presbyterians, the Great Awakening led to a schism between "New Side" (revivalists, who organized an independent synod, 1745) and "Old Side" (conservatives), which was healed in 1758. Among Congregationalists a similar division developed, with the more conservative joining the Anglican Church. The Awakening heightened back-country opposition to religious restriction, intensified the Protestant tradition to set limits to governmental power, and promoted the democratization of society.

1732. EPHRATA SOCIETY, an offshoot of the German Baptists, was founded by **Johann Conrad Beissel.** The group stressed the monastic life, chastity, and the 7th-day sabbath. For contributions to music, see p. 915.

1734. SCHWENKFELDERS, followers of the radical mystic Kaspar Schwenkfeld (1489–1561), made their first appearance in Pennsylvania, but lacked formal organization until 1782.

1735. MORAVIANS, OR UNITED BRETHREN, comprising Hussites and German Pietists, came to Georgia in 1735, under the leadership of **Augustus Gottlieb Spangenberg** (1704–92), to convert the Indians. Then, after impressing John Wesley with their pietist faith, they removed to Pennsylvania, where, under Count **Nikolaus Zinzendorf** (1700–60), they founded a settlement at Bethlehem (1741). Spangenberg was consecrated bishop of the Church in America (1744). In that year a semi-communistic General Economy was established at Bethlehem (at Winston-Salem, N.C., 1753), but was dissolved, 1762, when the crafts and trades returned to private management. Control was exercised from Herrnhut, Saxony. Not until 1857 was the American Church given a constitution with relative independence from German control. Renowned for church music, notably part-singing of congregations.

1747. THE GERMAN REFORMED CHURCH, organized by **Michael Schlat-**

ter (1716–90) as a subordinate body of the Dutch Reformed Church, made large gains among the Pennsylvania Germans. The church remained under Dutch control until 1793.

c.1750. RISE OF RATIONALISM. Influenced by John Locke (1632–1704), who applied the scientific method to problems of human understanding, the need for toleration, and the basis of government, were such seminal figures as Rev. Jonathan Mayhew (1720–66) and Charles Chauncey (1705–87), who, by stressing the function of reason apart from revelation (p. 847), laid the foundation for Unitarianism.

1766. METHODISM began in America, as in England, as a movement within the Church of England. It appeared first in New York City (1766) with the organization by **Philip Embury** (1728–73) of the John Street Church, and was expanded by the activities of itinerant preachers sent out by Wesley (1771), notably **Francis Asbury** (1745–1815). In Virginia, Rev. **Devereux Jarratt** (1733–1801), an Anglican minister, acted as unofficial chaplain to the Methodists. Centered first in Dinwiddie Co., Va., Jarratt (beginning in 1777) spread the Methodist faith through a dozen counties of Virginia and North Carolina, with a circuit some 500 miles long.

1774. SHAKERS, OR "MILLENNIAL CHURCH," a Protestant monastic group, first arrived in the colonies, led by Mother **Ann Lee** (1736–84). Settling at Watervliet, N.Y., they set up a socialistic Christian community. Scored gains in Kentucky and Ohio, with greatest growth, 1830–50.

1775–83. CHURCHES AND THE REVOLUTION. The Anglican clergy throughout the colonies were Loyalist, the Southern laity overwhelmingly Patriot. The Congregational and Presbyterian clergy took a Patriot stand. The Methodist missionaries were Loyalist.

Lutherans and Roman Catholics were divided in loyalty. The Quakers, officially neutral, leaned toward the Loyalists, as did the Shakers.

RELIGIOUS CENSUS, 1775 (Based on Rough Estimates—3,105 Religious Organizations and Congregations)	
Congregationalists	575,000
Anglicans	500,000
Presbyterians	410,000
Dutch Reformed	75,000
German Churches (incl. German Reformed, 50,000, and Lutheran in Pa., 75,000)	200,000
Quakers	40,000
Baptists	25,000
Roman Catholics	25,000
Methodists	5,000
Jews	2,000

1776–89. DISESTABLISHMENT. Under the leadership of Baptists and Presbyterians the movement for religious freedom and separation of church and state gained headway in Virginia in the Revolutionary period. Mainly the work of **George Mason** (1725–92) and **James Madison,** the Virginia **Declaration of Rights** (12 June 1776) advocated "free exercise of religion." An act of 1776 suspending payment of tithes (becoming effective 1 Jan. 1777) really disestablished the Church of England, although final steps were taken in Jefferson's Bill for Establishing Religious Freedom, passed through Madison's efforts (1785), and preceded by the latter's "Memorial and Remonstrance against Religious Assessments" (1784). Elsewhere the church was disestablished: 1776, Pa., Del., and N.J.; 1777, N.Y., N.C., and Ga. (partially, completely in 1789); 1790, S.C.; 1818, Conn.; 1833, Mass.

1780. UNIVERSALISTS. The first American Universalist church, built by Rev. John Murray (1741–1815) in Gloucester, Mass., favored separation of church and state. Its leading spokesman, **Hosea Ballou** (1771–1852), stressed Unitarian theology combined with evangelical conviction. "Winchester Program" adopted, 1803. General Convention, governing body, established 1833; incorporated, 1866; merged with Unitarians (1961).

1782. FIRST PAROCHIAL SCHOOL erected by St. Mary's Church, Philadelphia ("Mother School"). The system was officially sanctioned in Baltimore (1829). By 1840, there were 200 parochial schools in the U.S. In 1951, there were 236 colleges with 236,636 students, 1,628 high schools (diocesan and parochial) with 337,414 students, and 8,202 elementary schools (parochial) with 2,575,329 students.

1784. THEOLOGICAL SCHOOLS. The first theological college in the U.S. was established at New Brunswick, N.J. Other important seminaries were. Andover (founded to oppose Unitarian trends at Harvard, 1808), Princeton (1812), General (1817), Auburn (1818), Virginia (1823), Hartford (1834), and Union Theological (1836).

1784. Sixty **Methodist** preachers convened in Baltimore (Nov.) and organized an Episcopal Church independent from Anglicanism, with Francis Asbury (consecrated bishop, 1784) as its head. A schism led by James O'Kelley, who opposed Asbury's appointive powers, resulted in the organization of the Republican Methodist Church (1792). The Methodist Protestants seceded (1830).

1789. PROTESTANT EPISCOPAL CHURCH, depleted by Loyalist emigration, now independent of the Church of England, was organized at its first triennial convention in Philadelphia, and adopted canons along with revised prayers. By 1792 five bishops had been named.

1790. ROMAN CATHOLIC EPISCOPATE was established with the consecration of Rev. **John Carroll** (1735–1815); nominated, 1788; previously, 1784, appointed superior with power to administer confirmation. Political discrimina-

tion against Catholics continued until 1835 (N.C.).

1792. RUSSIAN ORTHODOX CHURCH began missionary activities in Alaska, wtih a resident bishop at Sitka, 1798. The episcopal see was moved to San Francisco (1872), and in 1905 to New York City.

1794. DEISM gained ground after the publication of Tom Paine's *Age of Reason*. Previously such views had been expounded in Ethan Allen's *Reason the Only Oracle of Man* (1784), but deism's most influential exponent in America was **Elihu Palmer,** ex-Baptist preacher, whose *Principles of Nature* (1797) attacked the orthodox tenets of Christianity. Deists established ties with pro-Jacobin democratic societies after 1794.

1797. GREAT REVIVALS began on the frontier with the preaching of **James McGready** (c.1758–1817). His camp-meeting movement was climaxed by the **Cane Ridge Meeting** (Aug. 1801). A schism among revivalists resulted in the organization of the Cumberland Presbyterian Church (1810). In Kentucky, the revival of **Barton W. Stone** (1772–1844) led to the New Light ("Stoneite") schism (1803; ultimately merging with Methodist and Baptist groups as the "Christian Church"). In New England the revival was led by the **Edwardseans,** centered at Yale under **Timothy Dwight** (1752–1817) and **Lyman Beecher** (1775–1863), and opposed by the rationalists and Unitarians.

1800. UNITED BRETHREN IN CHRIST, an Arminian group, was founded by **Martin Boehm** (1725–1812) and **Philip W. Otterbein** (1726–1813), first bishops; merged (1946) with the Evangelical Church, founded, 1800, by **Jacob Albright** (1769–1808).

1801. Adoption of the Presbyterian-Congregational Plan of Union to eliminate competition in regions where one or the other was already established.

1805. RAPPISTS, a group of German pietists led by **George Rapp** (1755–1847), was organized in Pennsylvania, founded New Harmony, Ind. (1815), sold to Robert Owen (1824), and then moved to Economy, near Pittsburgh. A celibate, authoritarian sect, it declined following Rapp's death, and its affairs were terminated (1905).

1810. Organization of the **AMERICAN BOARD OF COMMISSIONERS FOR FOREIGN MISSIONS** (Congregational), which became interdenominational (1812), marked the beginning of American missionary interest. The American Bible Society (1816), the Home Missionary Society (1826), and the American Tract Society (1825) followed. In 1814 the General Missionary Convention of the Baptists for Foreign Missions initiated home missions movement. In 1832 the Baptist Home Missionary Society was organized to operate in the South and West. American Board's missionary activity in Hawaii (beginning 1820) had profound cultural, economic, and political results. Foreign mission movements penetrated India, China, Japan, and Africa.

DISCIPLES OF CHRIST, a group of progressive Presbyterians opposed to closed communion, founded the Independent Church of Christ at **Brush Run, Pa.** Two groups, 1 founded by Rev. **Barton Warren Stone** (1774–1844) and the other by Rev. **Thomas Campbell** (1763–1854) and his son, Alexander (1788–1866) united at Lexington, Ky. (1832).

1813–17. BLACK CHURCHES. Large Negro groups formed independent churches, including African Methodist Episcopal Church (Philadelphia, 1816). The first Negro Baptist church was founded in Georgia (1773). In 1861 there were 200,000 Negro members of the Methodist Episcopal Church, South; 150,000 Negro Baptists.

1818. Connecticut constitution disestablished the Congregational Church.

1819. UNITARIAN CHURCH (stressing unity of God and denying Trinitarianism) founded by **William Ellery Channing** (p. 1000), but the transformation of Boston's King's Chapel from an Anglican to a Unitarian church occurred 18 Nov. 1787. The Dedham Case (Mass., 1820) allowed Unitarians, even though a minority, to retain church property they were occupying after a majority of orthodox had withdrawn, thereby strengthening the denomination.

1820–60. General Synod of the Lutheran Church held at Hagerstown, Md. (Oct. 1820). German (Missouri) Synod established 1847; Norwegian Synod, 1853, ultimately Norwegian Lutheran Church of America. Augustana, Swedish Synod, established 1860.

1824–50. REVIVALISM in Pennsylvania, New York, and Massachusetts led by **Charles G. Finney** (1792–1875), licensed to preach as a Presbyterian. The Broadway Tabernacle was established for him in New York City (1834). His followers withdrew from Presbyterianism (1836) and adopted Congregationalism. In the Middle West revivalism was led by such itinerant preachers as **Peter Cartwright** (1785–1872) and **James B. Finley** (1781–1856).

1827–28. Schism between **Orthodox** and **Hicksite** Quakers.

1828. Presbyterian schism between Old School (orthodox Calvinists) and New School (Western liberals).

1829–54. ANTI-CATHOLIC AGITATION, following the founding of the Society for the Propagation of the Faith (Lyons, France, 1822) and the Leopold Association (Vienna, 1829) to promote Roman Catholic missions in America (with Catholic laity increasing from 200,000 [1829] to 1.75 million [1850]— to which the Irish exodus after 1845 contributed substantially) resulted in such publications as *The Protestant* and *Priestcraft Unmasked,* of anti-Catholic sermons by Rev. **Lyman Beecher** and writings by **Samuel F. B. Morse** and of acts of violence, such as the burning of the Ursuline Convent at Charlestown, Mass. (11 Aug. 1834). For nativism and the Know-Nothing movement of the 1840s and 1850s, see pp. 223, 259.

1830. LATTER-DAY SAINTS, OR MORMONS, owe their origin to the publication of the *Book of Mormon,* based on a revelation claimed by **Joseph Smith** (p. 1154), followed by the founding of the church at Fayette, N.Y., the same year. As a result of opposition, the Mormons left New York (1831) for Kirkland, Ohio, and Independence, Mo. Expelled from Missouri, they settled at Nauvoo, Ill. Violence followed them, culminating in the lynching of Smith in the jail at Carthage. Driven from Nauvoo (1846), the Saints settled in the valley of the Great Salt Lake in Utah (1848) under the leadership of **Brigham Young** (p. 1190). Smith's pronouncement (1848) that polygamy was divinely sanctioned aroused intense opposition by non-Mormons, and led to the passage in Congress of anti-polygamy laws (1862, 1882, 1884). Finally, the church prohibited the practice (1890), and 6 years later Utah gained statehood.

1832–69. SLAVERY AND THE CHURCHES. The issue of abolitionism came to a head when Theodore Dwight Weld, a student at Lane Theological Seminary, Cincinnati, was dismissed from that institution when the trustees suppressed an antislavery society (1834). In the North abolitionism quickly became part of revivalism. The issue divided the Protestant churches. The Southern Baptists withdrew (1843) to organize the Southern Baptist Convention. The Methodist Church, South, set up a separate organization (1844). An abolitionist group of New School Presbyterians organized the Synod of Free Presbyterian Churches, Ohio (1847), followed by a major schism in the New School (1857), when the United Synod of the South was established. Old School Presbyterians split (1861), and the Presbyterian Church in the Confederate States was founded. The Ohio Synod and the New School Presbyterians united in 1862. In 1864 the Southern groups united as the Presbyterian Church in the U.S. The Northern groups united as the Presbyterian Church in the U.S.A. (1869). Division on this issue was avoided in the Protestant Episcopal Church.

1833. Massachusetts disestablished the church by constitutional amendment, ratified by popular vote of 32,234 to 3,273.

1840–60. REFORM AND CONSERVATIVE JUDAISM. Rabbis Isaac Mayer Wise (1819–1900), through *The Israelite,* established in Cincinnati, and **David Einhorn** (1809–79), in Baltimore (1855), transplanted from Germany the notion of reform (including vernacular worship, sermons, and hymns). In 1873 Wise organized the Union of American Hebrew Congregations, followed (1875) by Hebrew Union College in Cincinnati (merged with the Jewish Institute of Religion, New York City, 1948) and (1889) the Central Conference of American Rabbis. A conservative movement in opposition was headed by Rabbis **Isaac Leeser** (1806–68) and **Sabato Morais** (1823–97) of Philadelphia. The Jewish Theological Seminary (conservative) was founded (1886). Ashkenazi Orthodoxy reflected waves of immigration of Eastern European Jews from 1880s to World War I.

c.1840–60. GOSPEL OF INDIVIDUALISM, combining rationalism and evangelical Protantism, was expounded by **Francis Wayland** (1796–1865), president of Brown University, and author of *Elements of Moral Science* (1835).

1843. MILLERISM, an Adventist movement, resulted from the preaching of **William Miller** (1782–1849), who prophesied the second coming of Christ between 1843–44. His followers founded the Adventist Church (1845). The **Seventh-Day Adventists** separated from the parent body (1846), with headquarters at Battle Creek, Mich. (1855), and later (1903) near Washington, D.C., where Ellen Harmon White (1827–1915) organized a united and rapidly growing movement, stressing legalism, Sabbatarianism, and strong views on health, medicine, and diet.

RISE OF THE BLACK CHURCHES. In the Revolutionary era black congregations appeared, notably the Baptists at Silver Bluff, S.C. 1773–75, with dozens of others, mostly Baptist, by 1800. By 1821 2 independent African Methodist Episcopal churches had been formed. The antislavery movement spurred Southern missionary activity, which sought to counter the antislavery movement. At the start of Civil War formal membership of Southern blacks (est.): Methodists, 225,000; Baptists, 175,000. After the Civil War blacks organized separate churches: Colored Primitive Baptists, 1866; National Baptist Convention, 1895; Colored Presbyterian Church, 1874; Methodists, 1870.

1847. THEOLOGICAL LIBERALISM was exemplified by the publication of Rev. **Horace Bushnell's** (1802–76) *Christian Nurture*, stressing mysticism, free will, and Christian nurture, rather than election, as the road to salvation.

1874. The publication of *Outlines of Cosmic Philosophy* by **John Fiske** (1842–1901), with its attempt to reconcile theism with Darwinian evolution, brought theological liberalism (advocated by

Rev. **Henry Ward Beecher** [p. 982], Rev. **Lyman Abbott** [1835–1922], **Washington Gladden** [1836–1918], Rev. **Phillips Brooks** [p. 992], **John William Draper** [1811–82], and **Andrew D. White** [1832–1918]) into open conflict with orthodoxy.

1875–86. Archbishop **John McClosky** became the first American cardinal. Archbishop **James Gibbons** (p. 1040) was elected to the same rank (1886). The Catholic Univ. of America was founded at Washington, D.C., by the third plenary council (1884).

1875–92. CHRISTIAN SCIENCE textbook, *Science and Health,* by **Mary Baker Eddy** (p. 1020), was published and the Christian Science Association organized. The first church was established at Boston, 1879; reorganized, 1892.

1876. SOCIETY FOR ETHICAL CULTURE established in New York by **Felix Adler** (1851–1933).

1880. SALVATION ARMY, evangelistic organization, after being first established by Gen. **William Booth** in England, was organized in the U.S.

1892. HIGHER CRITICISM resulted in several heresy trials, notably that of **Charles A. Briggs** (1841–1913), professor at Union Theological Seminary. Tried (1892) and acquitted, he was suspended from the Presbyterian ministry and subsequently entered the ministry of the Protestant Episcopal Church.

1898. ZIONISM. Following first Zionist Congress in Basel (1897), Zionism, a movement for Jewish colonization of the Bible homeland in Palestine, spurred Federation of American Zionists (1898), with Rabbi Stephen S. Wise (1874–1949) as secretary. Antisemitism of the 1930s served to advance Zionist cause in U.S., a movement culminating in the establishment of the state of Israel (1948).

1902. Five Years Meeting (a loose confederation) formed by 13 Yearly

Meetings of the Society of Friends. Kansas and Oregon have since withdrawn. Three Yearly Meetings from outside the U.S. have joined.

1905. The Federal Council of Churches of Christ in America, first major interdenominational organization, was founded; succeeded (1950) by the National Council of Churches of Christ in the U.S.A.

1907. SOCIAL GOSPEL. Publication of *Christianity and the Social Crisis* by **Walter Rauschenbusch** (p. 1135), with its criticism of capitalism and the industrial revolution and its stress on cooperation rather than competition. His views had been anticipated as far back as 1876 with the publication by **Washington Gladden** (1836–1918) of *Working People and their Employers,* and other works aiming to Christianize the social order.

1908. Home Missions Council established to direct noncompetitive missionary activity.

1909–25. FUNDAMENTALIST REACTION, inspired by such traveling evangelists as William Jennings Bryan (p. 992), William A. ("Billy") Sunday, and John Alexander Dowie, reached its climax at Dayton, Tenn. (10–21 July 1925), in the trial and conviction of **John Scopes,** a Tenn. schoolteacher, for teaching evolution contrary to a state law enacted 21 Mar. 1925 (Okla. first state to pass anti-evolution act [1923]). Scopes was opposed by Bryan; defended by Clarence Darrow and Dudley Field Malone.

1918. United Lutheran Church in U.S. formed, placing 45 synods on the same doctrinal basis.

1918. RECONSTRUCTIONISM, expounded at the Jewish Center (N.Y.) by **Mordecai M. Kaplan** (1881–   ), stressed the totality of Jewish civilization.

1931. BLACK MUSLIMS founded in Detroit, Mich., by Wali Farad, considered messenger from Allah to **Elijah Muhammad** (b. Elijah Poole, 1897–1975). Religion stressed black supremacy and separatism.

1931. JEHOVAH'S WITNESSES, under the leadership of Judge J. F. Rutherford (originating with the Russellites, incorporated by Pastor Charles T. Russell, 1884), were incorporated (1939) as The Watch Tower Bible and Tract Society. For Jehovah's Witnesses cases, see p. 677.

c.1935. NEO-ORTHODOXY, a synthesis of the socioeconomic liberalism of the Social Gospel and a rediscovery of Biblical theology, with stress on the fall of man and the judgment of God, secured a wide following among American Protestants under the leadership of **Paul Tillich** (1886–1965) and **Reinhold Niebuhr** (p. 1115).

1939. Methodist Episcopal Church, Methodist Episcopal Church, South, and the Methodist Protestant Church were reunited.

1952. Bible, Revised Standard Version (Natl. Council, Churches of Christ, U.S.A.), best seller; also Roman Catholic Confraternity translation, vol. I.

1950–60. PROTESTANT CHURCH UNITY TREND. National Council of the Churches of Christ in the U.S.A. formed 29 Nov. 1950 by 25 Protestant denominations and 5 Eastern Orthodox bodies embracing 37 million church members. Congregational Christian Churches and the Evangelical Reformed Church united (June, 1957) to form the United Church of Christ. Presbyterian Church in the U.S.A. and United Presbyterian Church joined 28 May, 1958 to form the United Presbyterian Church in the U.S.A. On 4 Dec. 1960 the chief executive officer of the United Presbyterian Church proposed a merger into a new church of the Methodist, Protestant Episcopal, and United Presbyterian

Churches and the United Church of Christ, with total membership of 12,-250,000 for the 4 churches.

1954–57. Evangelist **Rev. Dr. Billy Graham** (1918–   ), who began a series of popular evangelistic campaigns in 1946, toured Great Britain and western Europe in 1954–55, and conducted a 16-week campaign in New York City, culminating 27 Oct. 1957.

1960s–1970s. NON-WESTERN RELIGIOUS UPSURGE. Various mystical and occult cults gained in popularity, including **theosophy** (org. N.Y., 1875), and spread by Madame Helena Petrovna Blavatsky (1831–91) and Annie Wood Besant (1847–1933), with its concern for the Hindu and Buddhist tradition; **Vedanta,** with Transcendantal Meditation, spread by Maharishi Mashesh Yogi, a notable offshoot; and **Bahaism,** from a messianic sect of the Shiite Islam of Iran (beg. in U.S. 1893), centered at Wilmette, Ill. Similarly, **Zen Buddhism** enjoyed surging popularity among college students.

1960–74.   ECUMENISM.   Secular trends tended to undermine old confessional commitments and interchurch cooperation burgeoned. The Consultation on Christian Churches (COCU) proposed highly acceptable terms of reunion for 10 major Protestant denominations while Catholic-Protestant dialogue expanded. In Dec. 1973 the Anglican-Roman Catholic International Commission reported it had reached "basic agreement" on the nature of the Christian ministry. A joint commission of U.S. Roman Catholic theologians in a study issued 3 Mar. 1974 declared that papal primacy need no longer be a "barrier to reconciliation of their churches," the first time since the 16th century that the 2 creeds agreed on crucial aspects of papal authority, thus clearing the way for Christian unity. The U.S. Roman Catholic hierarchy was also engaged in separate

dialogues with 4 other Protestant groups as well as with the Orthodox churches. **Church affiliation in 20th century** rose from est. 43% (1910) to 62.4% (1970).

CHURCH MEMBERSHIP 1970
(Yearbook of American Churches, 1970)
(summary in millions)

Roman Catholic Church	47.9
Southern Baptist Convention	11.3
United Methodist Church	11.0
National Baptist Convention, USA, Inc.	5.5
Episcopal Church	3.4
United Presbyterian Church, USA	3.2
Lutheran Church in America	3.2
Lutheran Church—Missouri Synod	2.8
National Baptist Convention of America	2.7
American Lutheran Church	2.6
Churches of Christ	2.4
Church of Jesus Christ of Latter-Day Saints	2.1
United Church of Christ	2.0
Greek Orthodox Archdiocese of North and South America	1.9
Christian Churches (Disciples of Christ)	1.6
National Primitive Baptist Convention, Inc.	1.4
American Baptist Convention	1.4
Russian Orthodox Greek Catholic Church of America (now the Orthodox Church in America)	1.0

1960–74. CHALLENGES TO TRADITION. Reexamination of religious values and structures was sparked by such writings as **H. Richard Niebuhr's** *Radical Monotheism* (1960), **Gabriel Vahanian's** *The Death of God: The Culture of Our Post-Christian Era* (1961), **Peter Berger's** *The Noise of Solemn Assemblies* (1961), **Martin Marty's** *The Second Chance for American Protestantism* (1963), **Thomas O'Dea's** *The Catholic Crisis* (1968), and other provocative works giving a secular interpretation of the gospel, stripping the Bible of mythology, and laying bare the moribund state of religious institutions and traditions. Reaction to these critiques took a variety of forms. The United Presbyterian Church of the U.S., making the first major change in the Presbyterian position in 320 years, adopted a new confession of faith (1967). The widespread support for family planning, along with recently enacted liberalized abortion laws and judicial decisions in the U.S., prompted unprecedented resistance to Pope Paul's manifesto *Humanae Vitae* (July 1968), condemning artificial methods of birth control.

1963. Elizabeth Ann Bayley (**Mother**) Seton (1774–1821), founder of the Sisters of Charity of St. Joseph at Emmitsburg, Md., in 1809, was the first native-born American to receive beatification (17 Mar. 1963). John Nipomucene Neumann (1811–60), fourth bishop of Philadelphia, was beatified 13 Oct.

1965. PAPAL VISIT. Pope Paul VI became the first Pontiff to visit the United States (4 Oct.). During his one-day visit to New York City, he spoke at the United Nations, talked privately with President Johnson, and conducted a mass at Yankee Stadium.

1967–73. Responding to the Six-Day Arab-Israeli War (1967) and the Yom Kippur War (1973) American Jews sent extraordinary aid to Israel, setting new records for U.S. private philanthropy.

1961–73. REFORM, ECUMENISM, AND SOCIAL INVOLVEMENT. Changing evaluations of the role of religious leaders contributed to the increased participation of clergymen in social and political conflicts. In 1960 the Southern Christian Leadership Conference (Rev. Martin Luther King, Jr.) and the Alabama Christian Movement for Human Rights . (Rev. Frederick L. Shuttlesworth) were formed to act as Christian instruments for the promotion of better treatment of Negroes. As the civil rights movement gained momentum, the active participation of religious leaders of all faiths was enlisted. Religious leaders spoke out against the war in Vietnam and religious organizations acted to combat the problems of poverty. The 62nd General Convention of Episcopal Churches in the U.S. allocated nearly $2 million to aid in solving urban ghetto problems. The "Women's Lib" movement was reflected in a steady pressure to ordain women to the ministry.

The church unification movement continued as the American, Evangelical, and United Evangelical Lutheran churches joined in 1960, with a total membership of 2,225,000; the 10-million-member Methodist Church merged with the 750,-000-member Evangelical United Brethren Church to become the United Methodist Church, the largest Protestant church in the U.S. (1966), while other religious reunions were spurred by the Consultation on Christian Union (COCU).

Within both Catholic and Protestant religious bodies there were reexaminations and protests against traditional structures of authority combined with reforms, reflecting in part the worldwide influence of Pope John XXIII and Vatican Council II.

Education

The American educational tradition was the result of the confluence of four distinct streams of thought which had their sources in widely scattered parts of Europe and which reached America during the colonial and early national periods. Perhaps the widest stream flowed from the Protestant Reformation, with the Reformers' emphasis on education for religious and moral purposes. A second stream, with tributaries coming from Central Europe and England, introduced the utilitarian principle of education, the ideal of the Czech philosopher-educator-theologian John Amos Comenius and the English pioneer of the inductive method, Francis Bacon. The third stream had its origins in the Renaissance tradition and carried with it the ideal of the well-rounded gentleman scholar. The last stream, which joined the others somewhat later, came from John Locke and was to be replenished by French Enlightenment thought, stressing the role of education for civic and moral purposes. Until late in the nineteenth century, Renaissance and Reformation ideals dominated the colleges, but at the lower levels the other traditions proved far more influential.

Educational reform was the most popular and widely supported of all the reform movements of the period 1830–60. The reformers held that education was the responsibility of the community and that elementary education should be required of all children. As the fight for public schools was being won, reformers turned their attention to the conditions of the educational system itself, with such resultant innovations as the broadening of the school curriculum beyond the "three R's," the study of modern languages instead of Latin and Greek, and a gradual secularization of the ends of education.

After the Civil War public support and private philanthropy in combination stimulated an enormous expansion in higher education, with the enactment in 1862 of the Morrill Act, setting up the land-grant colleges, a major factor. New directions in education transformed the college curriculum. Notable among such reforms was the introduction of the elective system, associated with President Charles W. Eliot of Harvard, and the rise of graduate schools, modeled at the start largely on the German examples. By the third quarter of the twentieth century issues of desegregation, government support for private and parochial education, and a revolution in the career expectations of young people commanded increasing attention. Those who would reappraise the traditional role of teacher, student, and administrator and advocate for education a responsibility to be involved in community and societal problem solving were countered by traditionalists concerned with the decline of discipline and intellectual values.

1636–1775. ELEMENTARY SCHOOLS. Diversity in the 3 major regional systems was the result of (1) religious differences at the time of settlement and (2) divergences in the economic and social structure of the areas. New England (influenced by Calvinist emphasis upon individual responsibility for salvation and the concomitant necessity of each individual's reading the Bible) was committed to the compulsory maintenance program as developed in 2 Massachusetts laws:

1642. Act imposed fines for neglect of education.

1647. Act required all towns of 50 families to provide a teacher for instruction in reading and writing; all towns of 100 families to establish a Latin grammar school (already set up in Boston, 1636). The act made it optional whether the school was to be tax-supported or fee-supported, and imposed a penalty of £5 (raised in 1671 to £10) for noncompliance. Similar acts passed by Connecticut, 1650; Plymouth, 1671; New Hampshire, 1689; with Rhode Island only exception. Although historians disagree as to the extent of enforcement of this law, statistical evidence points to a higher degree of literacy in New England than elsewhere (1640–1700, 95% literacy [Shipton] as against 54%–60% for males in Virginia [Bruce]).

1692. Disallowance of Massachusetts statute reviving compulsory education laws resulted in adoption of policy whereby selectmen or overseers of poor were empowered to bind out as apprentices "any poor children."

1765. At least 48 out of the 140 Massachusetts towns with a population of 100 families or more were maintaining Latin schools.

The **Middle Colonies** adopted a **parochial school** program, both as a result of private and church efforts. New Amsterdam: 1638, first school under Adam Roelantsen, Dutch Reformed auspices but town-supported; 1659, classical school established. New York: despite act of 1702 to encourage a free grammar school in New York City, activity was left to the Venerable Society (S.P.G.), which in 1710 founded the Trinity School. Chief emphasis thereafter was upon charity and private schools. Pennsylvania: 1689, Friends' School, Philadelphia (chartered, 1697, later known as William Penn Charter School). In the Northern and Middle colonies **apprenticeship** generally imposed educational requirements, such as one quarter's schooling each year, necessitating the establishment in the 18th century of **evening schools** in the larger towns.

In the **South** apprenticeship was the leading method for educating the poor (in Virginia book education provided by

act of 1705), supplemented by the establishment of **pauper schools** (county pauper schools established in Maryland, 1723). Children of planters were educated by tutors or through private fee-supported schools.

1750–1860. ACADEMY (with a broader and more practical curriculum) came to supplant the Latin grammar school. **Franklin's Academy** (1751) had 3 curricula: English, mathematical, and classical; **Phillips Andover** (1778); **Phillips Exeter** (1783) 2 curricula: classical and English. Although especially popular in the South, the academy was by no means confined to that area (Massachusetts, 1840, had 112 chartered academies).

1636–1775. HIGHER EDUCATION. Nine colleges founded before the Revolution.

1636. Harvard (Congregational) established by bequest of John Harvard and a grant from the Massachusetts General Court.

1693. William and Mary (Anglican) through efforts of Rev. **James Blair** (1655–1743).

1701. Yale (Congregational), located at New Haven, 1716; named in honor of benefactor, Elihu Yale, 1718.

1746. College of New Jersey (Presbyterian); name changed to Princeton 1896.

1751. Franklin's Academy (originally nonsectarian), chartered 1754; reorg. as University of Pennsylvania, 1779.

1754. King's College (nonsectarian under Anglican control), largely suspended activities, 1776–84; reopened 1784 as Columbia College.

1764. Rhode Island College (Baptist); renamed Brown University, 1804, in honor of Nicholas Brown, benefactor.

1766. Queen's College (Dutch Reformed); renamed Rutgers, 1825, in honor of benefactor, Col. Henry Rutgers.

1769. Dartmouth College (Congregational), named for Lord Dartmouth, patron; originally Rev. **Eleazar Wheelock's** (1711–79) Indian school, established at Lebanon, Conn.; moved to Hanover, N.H., 1770.

1765–1817. PROFESSIONAL TRAINING was first provided in **medicine** by the College of Philadelphia, 1765 (affiliated with the Univ. of Pennsylvania, 1791), and by the medical department of King's College, 1767. The first **law** lectures were offered by Chancellor **George Wythe** (1726–1806) at William and Mary, 1779–89. In the post-Revolutionary period law schools were established by Judge Tapping Reeve at **Litchfield,** Conn. (1784–1833), and Peter Van Schaack at **Kinderhook,** N.Y. (1786–1830s), and law lectures at Pennsylvania (1790), Columbia (1797), and Transylvania (1799). A law faculty was organized at the Univ. of Maryland (1812) and a law school was opened at Harvard (1817).

1776, 5 Dec. Phi Beta Kappa (national scholarship fraternity) founded at William and Mary, Williamsburg, Va.

1779–86. Introduction by **Thomas Jefferson** of a school bill into the Virginia legislature containing the first definite proposal for a modern state school system (free tuition to all free children for 3 years, with attendance voluntary; outstanding students to be given grammar school education, with superior scholars furnished an additional 3 years at William and Mary). No action by the legislature.

1805–67. ORIGINS OF THE FREE PUBLIC SCHOOL:

1805. Establishment of Free School Society (later known as Public School Society) of New York, a private philanthropic body, opposed to the pauper school system. **De Witt Clinton** first president of board of trustees.

1806. First Bell-Lancastrian school in

the U.S. (employing monitorial system of mass instruction) established at New York City; reduced teaching costs.

1834–67. Free School vs. Pauper School. Pennsylvania Free School Act, 1834, created school districts with option (supplanting act of 1802 for educating paupers at public expense); attempted repeal, 1835, blocked through efforts of **Thaddeus Stevens;** fully adopted, 1873. New York held two referenda, 1849–50 —cities (majority) favored having state assume rate bills by general tax; rural districts opposed. Result: a compromise (poor children entitled to free education with local option) adopted; in force until 1867, by which date public schools were free to all. Connecticut, Rhode Island, Michigan, and New Jersey followed by 1871.

1837–39. Major school reforms effected by **Horace Mann** (p. 1096), secretary of the newly established Massachusetts State Board of Education (first state normal school in U.S. established at Lexington, Mass., 1839) and by **Henry Barnard** (p. 980), appointed secretary of the Connecticut Board of School Commissioners, 1838.

1816–1902. EDUCATIONAL EXTENSION:

1816–73. Infant school introduced in Boston, 1816, and included in the public school system, 1818; admitted children at 4 years; New York, 1827. First German **kindergarten** (Froebel) introduced in the U.S. at Watertown, Wis., 1855, by Mrs. Carl Schurz; first English kindergarten at Boston, 1860, by **Elizabeth Peabody** (1804–94); first public school kindergarten by Susan Blow at St. Louis (1873) under sponsorship of **William Torrey Harris** (1835–1908), superintendent of schools (national Commissioner of Education, 1889–1906).

1821–27. First **high school** in U.S. established in Boston, 1821, with broad, liberal curriculum. Massachusetts act of 1827 required every town of 500 families to establish a high school.

1826–83. Josiah Holbrook (1788–1854) instituted adult education and self-improvement courses at Millbury, Conn., where he established the Millbury Lyceum No. 1, branch of the American Lyceum, thus inaugurating the **lyceum** movement. The National American Lyceum was organized at New York in 1831. By 1834 there were 3,000 town lyceums in 15 states. In 1874 Bishop **John H. Vincent** (1832–1920) and Lewis Miller organized the first **Chautauqua Assembly.** Home reading program established by 1878. **William Rainey Harper** (1856–1906, later president of the University of Chicago) appointed educational director, 1883; attracted outstanding lecturers. Young Men's Christian Assn. set up evening classes in the 1880s. In 1888 the New York City Board of Education established public lectures for working people. Other public lectures provided by Lowell Institute of Boston (inaugurated by Benjamin Silliman, 1839); Peabody Institute, Baltimore (1857); Cooper Union, New York (1857–59), endowed by **Peter Cooper** (p. 1006).

1821–36. WOMEN'S EDUCATION:
1821. The Troy (N.Y.) Female Seminary, the first women's high school in the U.S., established by **Emma Willard** (p. 1184).

1833. Oberlin College (Oberlin, Ohio) opened its doors to women, thus becoming the first coeducational college in the U.S.

1836. Mount Holyoke Female Seminary (later Mount Holyoke College), South Hadley, Mass., first permanent women's college, founded by **Mary Lyon.**

By 1902 women made up 25% of the undergraduates, 26% of graduate students, 3% of professional enrollment, with 128 women's colleges founded by 1901.

1789–1860. RISE OF STATE UNIVERSITIES. Univ. of North Carolina (1789) first state university to begin instruction (1795). Univ. of Georgia first state university to be chartered (1785), but not established until 1801. Other early state universities: Vermont, 1800; Univ. of South Carolina, 1801; Univ. of Virginia, 1819, a project conceived by Jefferson. Although the national government, beginning with Ohio, 1802, granted 2 townships to each new Western state for a university, there were only 17 state universities out of a total of 246 in 1860.

1862–1952. FEDERAL LEGISLATION. Morrill Act (p. 636) provided for grants of land to states to aid the establishment of agricultural colleges. Resulted in vast expansion of agricultural and engineering schools and served as the keystone of higher education in the Middle West and Far West. Extension of federal aid provided by Hatch Act (1887, p. 310), Smith-Lever Act (1914, p. 327), Smith-Hughes Act (1917, p. 330).

1944–66. "G.I. Bill" (Servicemen's Readjustment Act) of 1944 provided payments for tuition fees, books, and living expenses for up to 4 years of education for World War II veterans. Similar education benefit programs were provided (1952) for Korean War veterans and for post-Korean War and Vietnam War veterans (1966).

1861–1952. MAIN TRENDS IN HIGHER EDUCATION. Elective system fully in effect at Harvard under the administration of President **Charles W. Eliot** (p. 1023); swing to free electives accelerated, 1885–1918. Eliot's ideas supported by Presidents **Andrew Dickson White** (1832–1918) of Cornell, **James Burrill Angell** (1829–1916) of Michigan, **David Starr Jordan** (1851–1931) of Stanford, and **Arthur T. Hadley** (1856–1930) of Yale; opposed by Hadley's predecessor, **Noah Porter** (1811–92) and by **James McCosh** (1811–84) of Princeton. After 1918 free elective trend was checked, with emphasis placed upon a prescribed core of basic study for early college years. **Graduate study:** First Ph.D. degree in U.S. awarded at Yale, 1861. Graduate work organized at Yale and Harvard, 1870. In 1876 Johns Hopkins (under presidency of **Daniel Coit Gilman,** 1831–1908) opened as an institution of purely graduate study, followed by Clark Univ. (1887), Worcester, Mass., especially under the presidency of the eminent psychologist **Granville Stanley Hall** (p. 1047). Other leaders in the expansion of graduate instruction and research were **Charles Kendall Adams** (1835–1902) at Michigan, **John W. Burgess** (1844–1931) at Columbia, and Presidents **Frederick Augustus Porter Barnard** (1809–89) and **Nicholas Murray Butler** (p. 995) of Columbia. **General education,** with emphasis upon orientation courses, was established at Columbia 1918–19 with the course in Contemporary Civilization, and there were notable innovations in the Univ. of Chicago Plan, 1931.

1885–1974. PHILANTHROPY AND FOUNDATION SUPPORT FOR HIGHER EDUCATION. Among the more notable endowments were those of Stanford Univ. (1885), by Leland Stanford, of the Univ. of Chicago (1891) by John D. Rockefeller, and of Duke Univ. (1924, formerly Trinity College) by James B. Duke. Endowed institutions (notably in the South) have been the recipients of large grants from such foundations as the Peabody Education Fund, established by George Peabody (1795–1869); the Julius Rosenwald Fund (1917; dissolved, 1948); the Rockefeller Foundation (1913), including the Rockefeller Institute for Medical Research (University, 1965), the Gen-

eral Education Board, and the Laura Spelman Rockefeller Memorial; the Carnegie Endowment, including the Carnegie Institution of Washington (1902), the Carnegie Foundation for the Advancement of Teaching (1905), the Carnegie Endowment for International Peace (1910), and the Carnegie Corporation of N.Y. (1911); and the Commonwealth Fund, established by Mrs. Stephen V. Harkness (1918).

Foundations expanded rapidly after 1940, with only 600 reporting up to 1939 as against 3,564 reporting, 1940–55. They were the subject of an investigation by a special committee of the House of Representatives in 1954, and their policies subject to U.S. government control under the Tax Reform Act of 1969. A record educational grant of $550 million was made in 1955 by the Ford Foundation (chartered 1936) to 4,157 privately supported colleges, universities, and hospitals, to help raise salaries and improve services, with an additional $455.5 million granted in 1956, including $8 million for educational TV. Through 1973 Ford grants for educational and charitable projects totaled $4.5 billion.

1903–50. EDUCATIONAL TRENDS. Educational testing, the application of statistical measurement to mental and other human traits, developed in the U.S. notably by **Edward Lee Thorndike,** chiefly after 1902. **Progressive Education,** largely inspired by the instrumentalist philosophy of **John Dewey** (p. 1012), with emphasis on **problems** instead of rote learning (Progressive Education Association organized, 1918); opposed by National Council of American Education, Allan A. Zoll, director. **Modern School Plans** include the **Gary,** or platoon, school, first brought to public notice at Gary, Ind., by W. A. Wirt, 1908; the **Dalton** plan (individual instruction on laboratory plan), first used extensively by Helen Parkhurst at Dalton, Mass.

1920; the **Winnetka** plan (individual instruction supplemented by group activity), introduced by F. L. Burke of the San Francisco Normal School (1913) and C. W. Washburne at Winnetka, Ill. **Junior High School,** organized in Richmond, Ind., 1896, spread to Columbus, Ohio, 1908, and elsewhere. Numbers increased from 387 (1922) to 2,372 (1938). **Junior College,** organized by President Harper in Joliet, Ill., 1902. Numbers increased from 74 (1915) to 584 (1945). **Community colleges** multiplied in 1950s to meet postwar population bulge.

1929–74. INTERCOLLEGIATE ATHLETICS AS "ROMAN CIRCUS." In 1929 the Carnegie Foundation for the Advancement of Teaching reported that the college sports establishment was "sodden" with commercialism and professionalism. Reforms proved sporadic and ineffectual. Recruiting violations burgeoned in the 1970s as TV greatly increased the viewing public and superstadia attracted vast throngs to athletic events. A *New York Times* exposé (Mar. 1974) set off new calls for reform.

1946–74. FULBRIGHT PROGRAM. An amendment (1946) to the Surplus Property Act of 1944, sponsored by Sen. J. William Fulbright to establish educational exchange programs with funds in foreign currencies accruing to the U.S. from the sale abroad of surplus property after World War II, supplemented by enabling legislation authorizing the appropriation of dollar funds, led to the setting up of exchange programs with some 40 nations (by 1960). Under this program thousands of Americans have gone abroad to teach, study, or engage in research and an even greater number of foreigners have visited the U.S. A presidentially appointed Board of Foreign Scholarships supervised the program in Washington while binational foundations were responsible for the operation of the programs abroad. Among other fields, the program stimulated American studies abroad and foreign area studies in the U.S.

SCHOOL ATTENDANCE (% of population): 1910, 59.2; 1920, 64.3; 1930, 69.9; 1940, 70.8.

ENROLLMENT IN ELEMENTARY AND SECONDARY SCHOOLS, 1870–1972

	1870	1900	1972
% of total population— 5–17-yr.-olds	31.3	28.3	24.7
Pupils enrolled—% of population 5–17 yrs.	57.0	72.43	83.6

1947–1969. ILLITERACY (persons unable to read or write any language). **1947:** total, 14 years of age and over: 2.7% of population (urban, 2%; rural nonfarm, 2.4%; rural farm, 5.3%), as compared with 20.0% (1870), 10.7% (1900), 4.3% (1930). **1959:** total 2.2% (white, 1.6%; black, 7.5%); **1969:** total 1.0% (white 0.7%; black 3.6%), figures documenting improving educational facilities for blacks.

1955, 28 Nov.–1 Dec. WHITE HOUSE CONFERENCE ON EDUCATION focused attention on educational goals as well as needs, teacher training and recruitment, and school financing, with the participants approving, 2–1, the proposition that the federal government should increase its financial participation in public education.

1957, 11 Nov. IMPACT OF SPUTNIK. U.S. Office of Education released 2-year study of Soviet educational system, revealing vast strides being made in secondary and technical education in U.S.S.R., with stress on science subjects; findings confirmed by government-sponsored study of Soviet education by U.S. educators, May–June, 1958, pointing out widespread teaching of foreign languages.

1958. NATIONAL DEFENSE EDU-CATION ACT (p. 525).

1959–73. DESEGREGATION. The initial impact of *Brown* v. *Board of Education of Topeka* (1954) was slight and its implementation marked by sporadic violence (see pp. 521, 524). As of the 1962–63 school year, only .4% of black school children were attending integrated schools in the 11 states of the Deep South, with Alabama, Mississippi, and South Carolina still maintaining complete segregation except in colleges. The **Civil Rights Act of 1964** (p. 529), combined with massive new programs of federal aid to education, stimulated desegregation as each school district had to state its intention to integrate in order to share in federal funds for public schools. By Dec. 1966, 4,653 out of 7,072 school districts in 17 Southern states were "in compliance" with the federal regulations of the U.S. Office of Education; 965,000 black students (25.8% of black enrollment) were in schools with white students, with sharp gains continuing through 1973.

Outside the South efforts to end de facto segregation by busing school children to schools outside their neighborhoods or by redrawing the borders of school districts met with intense opposition. With a busing program begun Sept. 1968, Berkeley, Calif., became the first city with a population of over 100,000 to totally desegregate its school system. Racial imbalance and tensions contributed to the mounting problems of urban school systems. Attempts to begin the decentralization of the New York City school system resulted in a lengthy strike (1968).

1969–73. BUSING ISSUE. The directive of the Department of Health, Education, and Welfare restricting "freedom of choice" for school children if it had the practical result of maintain-ing a dual school system fueled the flames of controversy over the issue of busing to attain desegregation. While the federal courts and the U.S. Supreme Court (April, 1971) approved widespread busing to assure an integrated education for black children, President Nixon formally asked Congress (Mar. 1971) to call a temporary halt to all further court-ordered busing until 1 July 1973 or until broad legislation to control busing could be enacted. Congress agreed to prohibit the implementation of federal court orders for busing to achieve racial balance until all appeals had been exhausted or until the time for such appeals had expired, effective only until 31 Dec. 1973 (signed by the president, June 1972). In possible reaction to a rising tide of opposition to busing for integration the 4th U.S. Circuit Court of Appeals overruled (6 June 1972) a U.S. District Court order that would have required the merger of the Richmond, Va., city school system (70% black) with 2 suburban counties of Henrico and Chesterfield (each more than 90% white). As late as Feb. 1974 the New York City Board of Education admitted that the exodus of white residents to the suburbs was continuing de facto segregation in core areas of the city.

1961–71. EDUCATIONAL TECH-NIQUES AND INNOVATIONS. Among the innovations in teaching methods and curricula at all levels were (1) the "new" mathematics, with greater emphasis on understanding of abstract concepts; (2) widespread application of team teaching, the nongraded primary unit, teaching machines (programed teaching), and audio-visual aids, including educational TV; (3) increased attention to both the gifted and the disadvantaged; (4) increasing regard for preschool education exemplified by the federally subsidized **Operation Head**

Start program, assisting environmentally deprived preschoolers; (5) bilingual programs, notably in Spanish-speaking areas (Florida, California, Texas, New York City); (6) **Open Classroom**, a British innovation, introduced in Watts section of Los Angeles, and in some schools in New York City and Atlanta, as well as in middle-class communities like Andover, Mass., and Culver City, Calif.; (7) multi-ethnic textbooks widely introduced to provide a more representative and positive image of blacks and other minorities; (8) "open admission" policies in colleges to encourage entry by minority groups.

1961–73. CHANGING ROLE OF FEDERAL, STATE, AND LOCAL GOVERNMENTS IN EDUCATION. Down through 1968 an unparalleled growth in federal support for education took place. Federal funds appropriated for education and related activities rose from $5,437.9 million (1963) to $12,-198.2 million (1967). As the revenue of public elementary and secondary schools increased from $14,747 million (1960) to $25,481 million (1966), the percentage accounted for by federal sources rose from 4.9% to 7.9%. Among the numerous legislative measures pertaining to education were the **Vocational Educational Act** (1963, with amendments 1968), the **Elementary and Secondary Education Act** (1965), the **Higher Education Act** (1965), and **Higher Education Act Amendments** (1968). The enactment in 1972 of the **Revenue-Sharing Bill** (p. 538) had the effect of shifting responsibility for certain funding for health, welfare, and education from the federal government to the states, and resulted in a substantial decline in government-supported funding for education. The **Education Amendments Act of 1972** (23 June) set up a new government-sponsored private corporation, the

Student Loan Marketing Assn., but the funding proved inadequate and student loan funds increasingly difficult to obtain. The system of financing schools by local property taxes was ruled unconstitutional by the California Supreme Court (30 Aug. 1971) as constituting discrimination against the poor. However, the Supreme Court upheld such financing as a matter of U.S. constitutional law in *San Antonio Independent School District* v. *Rodriguez* (1973, p. 685). State reimbursement of tuition and tuition tax credits to parents whose children attended nonpublic schools held unconstitutional by Supreme Court, *Committee for Public Education* v. *Nyquist* (1973; p. 685).

1961–74. TRENDS IN SCHOOL ENROLLMENT. A reversal of expanding trends marked the latter portion of this period. Down to 1970 enrollments in institutions of higher education expanded rapidly from 3,570,000 (fall 1960) to 6,963,687 (fall 1967); 32% of all males 19 to 24 were enrolled in colleges (1967). Between 1960 and 1965 junior colleges and community colleges increased at an unprecedented rate both in number and size. By the start of the 1970s, however, a leveling of enrollments was evident. Total school enrollment declined from 56.4% of the population (1960) to 54.9% (1972). From a high of 34 million (1970) public school enrollment dropped to 31.5 million (fall, 1973), falling 1972–73 by 500,000, with private enrollment off 200,000. These figures, combined with tightened budgets and drastically reduced job openings for teachers, were reflected in declining enrollments in graduate schools, except in the fields of law and medicine.

1964–73. STUDENT RIOTS AND COUNTERMOVES. College campuses were swept by a wave of activism, demonstrations, sit-ins, strikes. Contributing to unrest were the size and impersonality of the multiversity, the impact of such issues as civil rights, the Vietnam War, and the quest by black and other minority students for recognition. The student upheavals gained national attention first at the Univ. of California at Berkeley (1964) and at Columbia (1968), with riots spreading to high schools, this time touched off by news of the assassination of Martin Luther King (4 April, 1969). A student strike closed San Francisco State College for months, with bombings and loss of life at the Univ. of Wisconsin. Announcement by President Nixon (30 April 1971) of the movement of U.S. troops into Cambodia rekindled campus flames. Tragedies occurred at **Kent State Univ.** (Kent, Ohio), 4 May 1970, when the National Guard opened fire on activist demonstrators, with 4 students slain and 9 others wounded, and at **Jackson State** (Miss.), 14 May, when police fired upon a women's dormitory, with 2 students dead and 12 wounded. After the Jackson incident some 130 colleges suspended classes for a week, and some, like Princeton, for the remainder of the spring semester. The President's Commission on Campus Unrest headed by former Gov. William Scranton (Pa.) reported Sept.–Oct., condemning alike fanatical student tactics, complacent campus officials, and brutal law-enforcement officers. Following the Vietnam truce, the U.S. military withdrawal from that area, and the ending of the draft, order once more prevailed on American campuses (1973–74).

1967–74. GROWING MILITANCY OF TEACHERS. Teachers' unions displayed a new militancy, as some hundred strikes were called over both salaries and teaching conditions in 1968, a trend that continued in this period, with long stoppages of classroom activity in some of the nation's leading cities. Toward the end of this period the National Education Association and the American Federation of Teachers seemed poised for a power struggle to organize teachers nationwide.

1968–74. IMPACT OF "WOMEN'S LIB." Teaching Patterns. A 1968 survey revealed that, while 86% of teachers in elementary schools were women, 78% of the principals were men; in high schools, 47% were women, as against 95% male principals, while only 2 women held school superintendencies out of 13,000. A 1969 survey of women teaching in colleges and universities: instructors, 34.8%; assistant professors, 28.7%; associate professors, 15.7%; full professors, 9.4%, with salaries for women almost always less than those of their male counterparts. As a result of complaints of "patterns of discrimination" brought against numerous colleges and universities, combined with "affirmative action" directives of the Department of Health, Education, and Welfare, the teaching status of women in

1972. TOP UNIVERSITY ENDOWMENTS

Harvard	$1,350,000,000
Univ. of Texas[1]	630,000,000
Yale	600,000,000
Rochester	555,000,000
Princeton	542,000,000
M.I.T.	440,000,000
Columbia	425,000,000
Univ. of Chicago	360,000,000
Stanford	332,000,000
Univ. of California	328,000,000

[1] Does not include oil properties.

1972. TOP RECIPIENTS OF FEDERAL SUPPORT (awards to individual institutions)

M.I.T.	$89,574,000
Univ. of Minnesota	72,534,000
Univ. of Michigan	60,881,000
Univ. of Wisconsin (Madison)	57,320,000
Univ. of Washington	56,535,000
Stanford	54,648,000
Harvard	54,037,000
Univ. of California (Los Angeles)	54,030,000
Univ. of California (Berkeley)	52,279,000
Columbia	52,219,000

colleges and universities showed some improvement by 1974. In addition, courses on women and even women's studies programs were widely initiated. Passing of the Education Amendments Act of 1972 (23 June) prohibited discrimination in all federally assisted educational programs, with some exceptions.

Coeducation. Beginning with 1968 coeducation at colleges accelerated, soon even penetrating the all-male citadels of "Ivy League" institutions, while the number of exclusively women's colleges declined sharply. Experiments in mixed dormitories were initiated in this period.

1971–74. REVIVAL OF TRADITIONAL APPROACHES spurred by results of testing, which showed a decline in achievement in fundamental subjects, prompted a reconsideration of reading and "new" mathematics programs as well as countermoves against informal "learning-through-joy" approaches and a reevaluation of "open admission" policies.

Literature

American letters during the seventeenth and eighteenth centuries were primarily records of the colonists' confrontation with a new continent and slavish imitations of European literature; the insularity of the first tradition and the derivativeness of the second prevented either from reaching an audience outside the United States. Histories of colonial settlements, chronicles of Indian tribes, and travel writings abound in the pre-Revolutionary era, but not much of it transcended its provincial heritage. On a slightly more formidable plane are the intensely Calvinistic documents of Puritan theologians such as Increase Mather, his prolific son Cotton, and Jonathan Edwards. Transcending parochial boundaries, however, was the Revolutionary political literature—notably the literary efforts of Thomas Jefferson and of that inspired pamphleteer Thomas Paine.

Side by side with such undeniably American work stand authors who are easily recognizable tintypes of the European masters of the period. In poetry this included the neoclassicist Philip Freneau and the pseudo-Augustan "Hartford Wits"; in the novel Charles Brockden Brown, a follower of Mrs. Radcliffe's school of gothic horror, is a good example. At the same time, a sui generis status must be accorded to Benjamin Franklin's *Autobiography*, with its plainspoken charms.

The real flowering of American literature came in the nineteenth century with the emergence of figures like Washington Irving, who brought a European narrative skill to his tales of headless horsemen and twenty-year slumbers. It was this fusion of Continental forms, philosophy, and technique with native American subject matter that accounted for such widely differing contributions as the nature poetry of William Cullen Bryant, the austere yet lyrical verse of Emily Dickinson, and the bardic chants of Walt Whitman. In the American novel this same amalgam was evident in the works of James Fenimore Cooper—a disciple of Walter Scott—whose *Leatherstocking Tales* chronicled the frontier; Nathaniel Hawthorne, whose New England romances were often a mating of English gothic formulas to Puritan themes and settings; Herman Melville, a post-Romantic who schooled himself on Byron and poured his lessons into *Moby Dick;* and Mark Twain, a journeyman in the racy, picaresque, colloquial tradition of Daniel Defoe. Even the Transcendentalism of philosophers like Henry David Thoreau and Ralph Waldo Emerson, derived from Rousseau and others, is given a characteristically (and memorably) American cast. Of the major American authors of the nineteenth century, only Edgar Allan Poe remained largely aloof from American experience, locking himself exclusively into the gothic mode.

The late nineteenth and early twentieth centuries brought a still more obvious European influence on American letters, the naturalism that Frank Norris, Stephen Crane, and others borrowed from Emile Zola. Concurrently, however, another American author had initiated a school of psychological realism that was to make him one of the prime movers of twentieth-century fiction. This was Henry James, whose *Portrait of a Lady* and *The Ambassadors* made their impact felt across the Atlantic with the force of Balzacian or Dickensian works. From this point on, American writing pulled abreast of its European rivals, especially in poetry, where T. S. Eliot and Ezra Pound—with their combination of traditionalism and experimentalism—literally rang up the curtain on modern verse. Other American poets who were leaders rather than followers were Wallace Stevens, Robert Frost, and Edwin Arlington Robinson. In fiction, the so-called Lost Generation, American expatriates centered in Paris, were also highly influential. The outstanding figures in this set were F. Scott Fitzgerald and Ernest Hemingway, the latter of whom created a whole new literary style. Even more substantial was William Faulkner, who, with his rich sagas of Southern life, captivated Europe long before his stature was fully recognized in America.

American literature since World War II has continued to produce works of interest, though it is too soon to make predictions about its durability. As poets have gradually faded from view, the works of Theodore Roethke and Robert Lowell have nevertheless continued to command respect. In fiction, some major developments have been the rise of black novelists like Ralph Ellison; the popularity of the "Jewish novel," particularly in the hands of such practitioners as Saul Bellow, Bernard Malamud, and Philip Roth; and the "new journalism," a mode of highly personalized reportage that makes use of fictional techniques (e.g., the works of Norman Mailer).

Pioneer Period, 1607–60

Best Seller: *Bay Psalm Book* (1640); reached 27 editions before 1750.

REPORTERS, ANNALISTS, AND HISTORIANS. 1608–29. **Capt. John Smith** (p. 1054), adventurer, explorer, and Virginia pioneer, 1607–09, published an account of the founding of Jamestown: *A True Relation of Occurrences in Virginia* (1608); subsequently recounted his exploring expedition along the New England coast in *A Descrption of New England* (1619) and *New England's Trials* (1620). His account of his rescue by Pocahontas first appeared in *The Generall Historie of Virginia* (1624), and its authenticity has been questioned. Despite embroidery, Smith's narration is unsurpassed for vivid and dramatic description of pioneer struggles. **1622–47. William Bradford** (p. 990) is generally believed to have collaborated with **Edward Winslow** (1595–1655) in compiling materials subsequently published in England (1622) by **George Morton** (1585–1624) and known because of its preface (signed "G. Mourt") as "*Mourt's*" *Relation,* a journal of events in Plymouth, 1620–21. Bradford's major historical work was his *History of Plimouth Plantation,* written 1630–47, but not published until 1856 (although drawn upon by **Nathaniel Morton** [1613–86] in his *New England's Memorial,* 1669). **Edward Winslow** (1595–1655) added further light on early New England history in his *Good News from New England,* 1624, and *Brief Narration,* 1646. **1630–49:** Comparable in importance for the early history of Massachusetts with the Pilgrim Bradford's *History* was the Puritan **John Winthrop's** (p. 1187) *Journal* (or *History of New England*), a diary record from Mar. 1630 to 1649, which remained unpublished until 1790 (subsequently revised,

1825, and again, 1929–31). In addition to accounts of the relations of the Massachusetts authorities with such major critics as Roger Williams and Anne Hutchinson, the *Journal* includes Winthrop's General Court speech, 1645, on the nature of liberty (which he maintained must be under authority and restraint). While en route to the Bay Colony, Winthrop wrote his *Model of Christian Charity* (1630), emphasizing self-denial and cooperation ("We must be knit together in this work as one man"). A leading critic of affairs in Plymouth and Massachusetts, **Thomas Morton** (1575–1647) satirized colonial policy in his *New English Canaan* (1637). **1654:** To counteract hostile reports of the Puritan colonization, which he considered a sacred crusade, **Edward Johnson** (1598–1672) wrote his *Wonder-Working Providences of Sion's Saviour in New England* (1654), an apologia for theocratic rule.

THEOLOGICAL AND RELIGIOUS WRITERS. "Chief stewards of the theocracy." **1638–40: Thomas Hooker** (?1586–1647), in his *Survey of the Summe of Church Discipline* (1648), postulated the principle of divine absolutism. This book and his orthodox Calvinist sermons reveal literary power and the author's conviction that it was his duty to "fasten the nail of terror deep" into the hearts of sinners. **1641–60: Thomas Shepard** (1605–49), "soul-melting preacher," whose *Sincere Convert* (1641) preached a gospel of love; *Theses Sabbaticae* (1649), Sabbath origin and observance; *Parable of the Ten Virgins* (1660). **1642–48: John Cotton** (1584–1652), major spokesman of theocracy, preeminent as scholar and theologian ("They could hardly believe God would suffer Mr. Cotton to err"— Roger Williams). His numerous writings include *The Keyes of the Kingdom of*

Heaven (1644), stressing consociation of church and state; *Milk for Babes, Drawn out of the Breasts of Both Testaments* (1646), for the religious instruction of children; and *The Bloudy Tenent, Washed and Made White in the Bloud of the Lamb* (1647), in refutation of Roger Williams and opposing freedom to "sinful error." **Minor figures** of the period include **Nathaniel Ward** (?1578–1652), author of the first Massachusetts Code of Laws, the Body of Liberties (1641), and a humorist and satirist (*Simple Cobbler of Aggawamm*, 1647); and **John Eliot** (1604–90), Puritan missionary, translator of the Bible into the Indian tongue, 1663, and author of *The Christian Commonwealth* (1659) and an Indian grammar (1666) and primer (1669).

Critic of the Established Order: Roger Williams (c.1603–83), radical in religious and political outlook; advocated separation of church and state as early as 1635; as ardent in polemics as his opponents. Writings include *A Key into the Language of America* (1643); *The Bloudy Tenent of Persecution for the Cause of Conscience* (1644), attack on the conservative ideas of Cotton. The latter's vindictive reply elicited from Williams *The Bloudy Tenent Made Yet More Bloudy* (1652). His *George Fox Digged out of his Burrowes* (1676) was a criticism of Quaker views.

POETS. 1641: *The Bay Psalm Book* (*The Whole Book of Psalms Faithfully Translated into English Metre*), the first book printed in the colonies,[1] was a translation of the Psalms purposefully sacrificing beauty to accuracy by **Thomas Welde, Richard Mather** (1596–1669), and **John Eliot,** an uninspired rendition. **1650:** Publication in London of *The Tenth Muse,* a collection of didactic poems by **Anne Bradstreet** (?1612–72),

[1] The first piece of printing was "The Freeman's Oath," followed by an almanac, both in 1639.

influenced by Spenser, Quarles, and Du Bartas. Emancipated from her literary models, she produced her most distinguished poem, *Contemplations,* written late in life (pub. 1678).

First Century of Native Literature, 1661–1760

BEST SELLERS BY COLONIAL WRITERS[2]

1640.	*Bay Psalm Book*
1662.	Michael Wigglesworth, *Day of Doom*
1682.	Mary Rowlandson, *Captivity and Restoration*
1683?	*New England Primer,* comp. and pub. by Benj. Harris (total sales estimated at 6 to 8 million)
1699.	Jonathan Dickinson, *God's Protecting Providence*
1707.	John Williams, *The Redeemed Captive*
1719.	*Mother Goose's Melodies for Children*
1725–64.	Nathaniel Ames, comp., *Astronomical Diary and Almanac*
1732–57.	Benjamin Franklin, *Poor Richard's Almanac*
1741.	William Penn, *No Cross, No Crown*

NARRATIVES OF INDIAN WARS AND CAPTIVITIES. c.1670: Capt. **John Mason** (1600–72) wrote *A Brief History of the Pequot War* (partly published by Increase Mather, 1677; completely, 1736). **1674: Daniel Gookin** (1612–87), *Historical Collections of the Indians in New England* (1792), a description of Indian mores, and *An Historical Account of the Doings and Sufferings of the Christian Indians* (completed 1677, published 1836), a vindication of their role in King Philip's War. **1676: Increase Mather** (1639–1723), *A Brief History of the War with the Indians* (1676). **1677: William Hubbard** (1621–1704), *A Narrative of the Troubles with the Indians* (hostile toward the Indians); also wrote *A General History of New England* (to 1680), not published until 1815. **1682: Mary White Rowlandson**

[2] Best-seller lists based upon A. D. Dickinson, *One Thousand Best Books* (1924); F. L. Mott, *Golden Multitudes* (1947); James D. Hart, *The Popular Book* (1950); Alice P. Hackett, *Fifty Years of Best Sellers* (1945; with *Supplement,* 1952). Best sellers' list hereinafter confined to works by American writers.

(c.1635–c.1678), captured by the Indians in a raid on Lancaster, 1676, wrote the most popular captivity account, *The Sovereignty and Goodness of God*, republished many times by its subtitle, *The Narrative of the Captivity and Restoration of Mrs. Mary Rowlandson.* **1699:** A straightforward, graphic account of captivity in Florida was told by an English Quaker merchant who later became chief justice of Pennsylvania, **Jonathan Dickinson** (1663–1722), *Journal, or God's Protecting Providence.*

1698: Gabriel Thomas. *An Historical and Geographical Account of the Province of Pennsylvania and West New Jersey,* a Quaker's humorous and favorable account.

TRAVELERS AND EXPLORERS. **1704: Sarah Kemble Knight** (1666–1727), Boston schoolmistress, wrote a lively account of a horseback journey to New York (*Journal*, published for the first time, 1825), with refreshing sidelights on rural conditions. **1728–33:** Col. **William Byrd, 2d** (1674–1744) of Westover, a great Virginia estate owner, educated abroad, left a collection of manuscripts of absorbing interest, consisting of both travels and explorations (not published until 1841), and a shorthand diary, a frank and racy document, deciphered and published in part, 1709–12 (1941), 1739–41 (1942). His major work of exploration was *History of the Dividing Line Run in the Year 1728,* an account of experiences with a party surveying the Virginia–North Carolina boundary line. A satirical version, *The Secret History of the Dividing Line* (not published until 1929) is the most interesting and uninhibited travel book of the colonial period. His other works include *A Journey to the Land of Eden* (1732) and *A Progress to the Mines* (1736), published 1841. **1744:** Dr. **Alexander Hamilton** (1712–56), of Annapolis, whose *Itinerarium* describing his journey

from Annapolis, Md., to Portsmouth, N.H., is one of the most entertaining and informative travel books of the colonial period. **1751: John Bartram** (1699–1777), the Pennsylvania botanist, published an account of a scientific expedition to western New York and Lake Ontario in 1751 (*Observations*).

REPORTERS, ANNALISTS, DIARISTS, AND HISTORIANS. **1666:** George Alsop (1638–?), who served a term as an indentured servant in Maryland, wrote a colorful and humorous defense of that colony, *A Character of the Province of Maryland.* **1670: Daniel Denton** (d.1696), in his *Brief Description of New York,* provided a graphic account of a "terrestrial Canaan." **1673–1729:** Samuel Sewall (1652–1730) left the fullest diary of the period (1674–1729), with gaps 1677–85), invaluable for the social historian (not published until 1879–82). His tract *The Selling of Joseph* (1700) was an early antislavery appeal. **1676:** The *Burwell Papers*, attributed to **John Colton** (published 1814; revised, 1866), a spirited, if affected, account of the course of Bacon's Rebellion, closing with an eloquent eulogy of Bacon. **1676–93: Increase Mather** (p. 1099), president of Harvard, 1685–1701, upholder of the theocratic tradition of John Cotton, wrote *A Brief History of the War with the Indians in New England* (1676) and an uncritical compilation of other people's narratives of providential events, published, 1684, as *An Essay for the Recording of Illustrious Providences* (commonly known as *Remarkable Providences*). **1693–1702:** His son, **Cotton Mather** (p. 1099), the most prolific colonial author (over 400 published works), served as annalist of the Salem witchcraft episode (1692) in his book *The Wonders of the Invisible World* (1693). His apologia for the trial and execution of the accused was effectively answered by **Robert Calef** (1648–

1719), a Boston merchant, whose *More Wonders of the Invisible World* (1700) was publicly burned in the Harvard Yard upon order of Increase Mather. Cotton Mather's major work is his *Magnalia Christi Americana, or, The Ecclesiastical History of New England, 1620–98* (1702), which set forth the splendor of government by God's elect, combining accurate information with fable and gross misrepresentation. For his scientific contributions, see pp. 778, 806.

1697: Rev. James Blair (1655–1743), an Anglican clergyman, collaborated with **Henry Hartwell** and **Edward Chilton,** on a report, *The Present State of Virginia and the College* (published 1727).

1705: Robert Beverley (1675–1716), *The History and Present State of Virginia* (revised 1722), a lucid account of a land where "nobody is poor enough to beg or want food." **1724: Hugh Jones** (c.1670–1760), clergyman, *The Present State of Virginia,* a frank and factual account, with a dismal picture of educational standards at William and Mary College, where he was a teacher of mathematics.

1727–47: Cadwallader Colden (1688–1776), scientist and later lieutenant governor of New York, wrote a valuable account of the Iroquois tribes, *The History of the Five Indian Nations,* the most substantial colonial treatise on the Indians. **1736–56: Thomas Prince** (1687–1758), *Chronological History of New England,* arid but scholarly annals. **1740:** Patrick Tailfer's *A True and Historical Narrative of the Colony of Georgia,* a documented history attacking Oglethorpe. **1747: William Stith** (1689–1755), president of William and Mary, 1752–55, *History of the First Discovery and Settlement of Virginia* (from Jamestown to 1624), drew heavily upon Captain John Smith. **1748–53: William Douglass** (1691–1752), Scottish physician who settled in Boston, 1718, and

wrote innumerable pamphlets against religious revivalism, paper money, etc., produced a caustic, partisan, and disorganized *Summary, Historical and Political, of the First Planting, Progressive improvements and Present State of the British Settlements in North America.* **1756: William Livingston** (1723–90), educator, statesman, governor of New Jersey (1776–90), *A Review of the Military Operations in North America, 1753–56,* frank and significant history. **1757: William Smith** (1728–93), jurist and later Loyalist, *The History of the Province of New York* (to 1732), reprinted (1829) with his continuations to 1762, an able, if partisan, historical account, with valuable insights on contemporary New York society (supplemented by his massive unpublished diary in the New York Public Library).

THEOLOGICAL AND RELIGIOUS WRITERS. 1669–1717: Representative of the conservative theological tradition were **Increase Mather** and **Cotton Mather.** The former, a great pulpit orator, published 92 titles (1669–1723), mostly sermons. The latter, a child prodigy, published innumerable sermons and religious and moral tracts, one of the most notable being *Bonifacius* (1710), endorsing the performance of good deeds on business principles—a work which influenced Benjamin Franklin. Representative of liberalism and opposition to the Mather hierarchy was **John Wise** (1652–1725), minister at Ipswich, who, in addition to his notable fight against Governor Andros over the payment of unauthorized taxes, was the author of 2 pamphlets opposing the plan of the Mathers for reorganizing the churches along Presbyterian lines, and favoring democratic Congregationalism: *The Churches' Quarrel Espoused* (1710), and *A Vindication of the Government of the New England Churches* (1717).

1720–54: Jonathan Edwards (p. 1021),

pastor at Northampton, was a major writer on theological and moral questions, a logical thinker who devoted his energies to a regeneration of religious values, defended the "revival" as a legitimate device for quickening spiritual values, and opposed Locke's idealism with emphasis on mystical experience. His "Notes on the Mind" was a venture in Berkeleyan idealism. Typical of his later revivalist sermons emphasizing hell-fire and brimstone was *Sinners in the Hands of an Angry God* (Enfield, 9 July 1741). His greatest intellectual effort was *A Careful and Strict Enquiry into the Modern Prevailing Notions of Freedom of the Will* (1754), an exposition of his understanding of Calvinist predestination, followed 4 years later by the posthumous publication of *The Great Christian Doctrine of Original Sin Defended*. In his second dissertation, "Concerning the End for Which God Created the World" (written 1755), he returned to the mystic pantheism of his youth and foreshadowed Transcendentalism. Foremost opponents of revivalism were **Charles Chauncy** (1705–87), Boston Congregationalist pastor, whose notable sermon *Seasonable Thoughts on the State of Religion in New England* (1743), stressing divine benevolence assuring man a rational place in a world of free choice, dates the start of the controversy between the **New** and **Old Lights**; and **Samuel Johnson** (1696–1772), convert to Anglicanism and first president (1754–63) of King's College (Columbia), who became the chief exponent in the colonies of the doctrines of the English philosopher George Berkeley, as exemplified by *Elementa Ethica* (1746), republished by Benjamin Franklin in enlarged form as *Elementa Philosophica* (1752), stressing rationalism in religion and the concepts of the Enlightenment. Very different in form and spirit were the works of the New Jersey Quaker

John Woolman (1720–72), whose *Journal*, written 1756–72, published 1774, reveals his simplicity and purity. Sensitive to social injustice, he criticized the institution of slavery in *Some Considerations on the Keeping of Negroes* (1754–62), a plea for racial equality; and his *Considerations on the True Harmony of Mankind* (1770) revealed his concern about growing antagonisms between labor and capital.

POETS include **Michael Wigglesworth** (1631–1705), whose *Day of Doom* (1662), in jog-trot ballad measure, was a Calvinist version of the last judgment (unbaptized infants assigned to the "easiest room in hell"); **Edward Taylor** (c.1644–1729), English-born pastor of Westfield, Mass., whose sensuous poetry, rich in imagery, imaginative and dramatic, and the most inspired American verse of the 17th century, was discovered (1937) with the publication of some of his poems from MS.; the anonymous author ("Eben. Cook, Gent.") of *The Sot-Weed Factor* (1708) and *Sot-Weed Redivivus* (1730), satirical burlesques on the inhabitants of Maryland; and 2 Massachusetts Loyalists who produced poetry in the pre-Revolutionary era— **Mather Byles** (1707–88), an imitator of Pope (*Elegy addressed to Governor Belcher on the Death of his Lady*, 1732, and *The Conflagration*, 1744) and **Benjamin Church** (1734; lost at sea, 1776), whose *The Choice* (1757) was modeled upon a poem of Pomfret (1700), who also influenced the poetry of **William Livingston** (*The Philsophic Solitude*, 1747).

1696–1760. EARLY LIBRARIES. Dr. **Thomas Bray** (1656–1730), cofounder of the Society for the Propagation of the Gospel in Foreign Parts (1701), on becoming Commissary in Maryland (1696), established free circulating libraries in most of the 30 parishes in that province, beginning with Annapolis. Other libraries were established under his auspices in New York (Trinity Parish, 1698) and Charleston (1699). Although the largest libraries prior to 1789 were either those of private individuals (Cotton Mather, 3,000 vols.; William Byrd II, 4,000, 1788) or of colleges, the semipublic **subscription library** was the most common. Between 1731–60, 21 were founded, notably:

1731. Library Co. of Philadelphia, an outgrowth of the Junto, a debating society organized by Benjamin Franklin, 1727.

1747. Redwood Library, Newport, R.I. (Ezra Stiles librarian, 1755–75).

1748. Charleston Library Society.

1754. New York Society Library.

Revolutionary Generation, 1763–89

BEST SELLERS

1768. John Dickinson, *Letters from a Farmer in Pennsylvania*
1775–76. John Trumbull, *McFingal* (1st complete ed. 1782)
1776. Thomas Paine, *Common Sense*
1776–83. Thomas Paine, *The American Crisis*
1783. Noah Webster, *American Spelling Book* (*Blue-Backed Speller*—estimated total sale 70 million copies by 1883)
1787–88. Alexander Hamilton, James Madison, and John Jay, *The Federalist*

LITERATURE OF POLITICS: 1762: A year after his renowned arguments against the issuance of writs of assistance (24 Feb. 1761), **James Otis,** Boston lawyer, published his first political pamphlet, *A Vindication of the Conduct of the House of Representatives* (Mass.), in which he affirmed the privileges of the colonies under the British constitution. **1764:** His ablest effort, called forth by the Sugar Act, was *The Rights of the British Colonies Asserted* (July), in which he raised the argument of no taxation without representation. Other critics of the new imperial policy in-

cluded **Oxenbridge Thacher,** *Sentiments of a British American;* and Rhode Island's governor, **Stephen Hopkins** (1707–85), *The Rights of the Colonies Examined* (1765); answered by Martin Howard, a Newport lawyer, *A Letter from a Gentleman at Halifax*). **1765:** The Stamp Act prompted a series of articles by **John Adams** in the Boston *Gazette,* republished, 1768, in revised form, as *A Dissertation on the Canon and Feudal Law;* and 2 notable pamphlets, one by **John Dickinson** (1732–1808), *Considerations upon the Rights of the Colonists to the Privileges of British Subjects,* the other by **Daniel Dulany** (1722–97), a Maryland lawyer and later Loyalist, *Considerations on the Propriety of Imposing Taxes* (p. 87). **1766:** Most vigorous of the New England clergy in opposing parliamentary measures was **Jonathan Mayhew** (1720–66), a rationalist who anticipated later Unitarian doctrines. As early as 1750 in his *Discourse Concerning Unlimited Submission* he had asserted: "Britons will not be slaves." On the repeal of the Stamp Act he wrote his last published sermon, *The Snare Broken.* **1767–68:** The passage of the Townshend Acts prompted the issuance by Dickinson of a widely distributed pamphlet (at least 12 editions in the colonies and abroad), *Letters from a Farmer in Pennsylvania to the Inhabitants of the British Colonies* (p. 90). **1773:** The qualities of **Benjamin Franklin** as a political satirist are exemplified by his imaginary "An Edict of the King of Prussia" (*Gentleman's Mag.,* Oct.) and his renowned *Rules for Reducing a Great Empire to a Small One.* **1774:** The Loyalist argument was forcefully presented by Rev. **Samuel Seabury** (1729–96), later first bishop of the Protestant Episcopal Church in the U.S., in a series of four *Westchester Farmer* pamphlets attacking the aims and policy of the first Continental Congress (answered effectively by young **Alexander Hamilton,** in *A Full Vindication of the Measures of Congress* [1774] and *A Farmer Refuted*) and by **Daniel Leonard** (1740–1829), in a series of 17 letters to the newspapers under the pen name of "Massachusettensis," in which the unconstitutional character of the Revolutionary position was stressed. For **John Adams'** refutation, see p. 99. The plan of union proposed by **Joseph Galloway** (1731–1803; p. 1037) was published the following year in *A Candid Examination of the Mutual Claims of Great Britain and the Colonies.* The development of Patriot thinking by this date was best exemplified in **James Wilson's** (1742–98) *Considerations of the Nature and Extent of the Legislative Authority of Great Britain* (p. 99), and **Thomas Jefferson's** *A Summary View of the Rights of British America* (p. 99). **1776:** Most influential of all Revolutionary pamphlets was **Thomas Paine's** *Common Sense* (p. 106), which was followed by a series of 16 irregularly issued (1776–83) essays called *The Crisis,* designed to lift Patriot morale, the first words of the first number being "These are the times that try men's souls." **1782–87:** Thomas Jefferson's *Notes on Virginia,* a reply to a series of questions by the Marquis de Barbé-Marbois, is representative of his political thought. Written, 1782, it was first printed privately in Paris, 1785, then in London, 1787.

1787–88: The ratification of the Constitution was opposed in a considerable number of pamphlets, most notably by **Richard Henry Lee** (Va., p. 1082), (*Observations Leading to a Fair Examination* [1787] and *An Additional Number of Letters* [1788]) and **George Mason** (Va., 1725–92), (*Objections to the Proposed Federal Constitution*). Supporters of ratification included the lexicographer **Noah Webster** (1758–1843), *An Examination into the Leading Principles of the*

Federal Constitution; the political economist **Pelatiah Webster** (1725–95), *The Weakness of Brutus Exposed;* **Tench Coxe** (1755–1824), political economist and industrialist, *An Examination of the Constitution,* and **John Dickinson** (*Letters of Fabius*); but most influential were the papers produced by **Hamilton, Madison,** and **Jay,** published as *The Federalist* in book form 1788 (p. 140).

FRANKLIN'S AUTOBIOGRAPHY. Ranking as an American classic is Franklin's *Autobiography* (covering the events of his life to the end of 1759), written between 1771 and 1789, published in part in France, 1791, and not in complete form until 1867, and exemplifying the Yankee-Puritan spirit which could accept the Enlightenment and follow the literary models of Defoe and Addison. For Franklin's journalistic enterprises, see p. 941; for his scientific contributions, p. 779. Franklin wrote for the amusement of his friends urbane bagatelles: *The Ephemera* (1778), *The Morals of Chess* (1779), *The Whistle* (1779), *The Dialogue between Franklin and the Gout* (1780).

HISTORIANS. 1764–67: **Thomas Hutchinson** (1711–80), lieutenant governor of Massachusetts, produced the major historical writing of the period. The 1st volume of *The History of the Colony of Massachusetts Bay* (1628–91) appeared in 1764; the 2nd (down to 1750) appeared in 1767; and the 3rd (1750–74) was published posthumously in 1828. The earlier volumes are marked by more detachment than the last, which is in part a defense of his own administration. Although an outstanding Loyalist he managed in the main to make judicious and objective valuations. **1780:** Another Loyalist, **George Chalmers** (1742–1825), published an account of colonial history down to 1763 (*Political Annals*) which largely reflects the official British attitude. **1782:** Chalmers' *Intro-*

duction to the History of the Revolt of the American Colonies was a legalistic and unsympathetic approach to colonial problems based largely on official records. **1784:** **Jeremy Belknap** (1744–98) wrote a scholarly *History of New Hampshire* (2nd vol. to 1790, pub. 1791) based upon prodigious research. **1788:** A more biased, but nevertheless notable, firsthand account of Shays' Rebellion was **George Minot's** (1758–1802) *History of the Insurrections in Massachusetts in the Year 1786*, a conservative's view of the issues and events.

MR. PENROSE: THE JOURNAL OF PENROSE, SEAMAN, a first-person picaresque narrative written by **William Williams** (1717–91) probably between 1745–75 and published posthumously in England (1815) is now credited as being the first American novel.

TRAVELERS. 1778: **Jonathan Carver** (1710–80), a New Englander, wrote a travel book based upon an exploring expedition to the Great Lakes and the Upper Mississippi, containing much information on natural history and Indian mores, *Travels through the Interior Parts of North America*. **1782:** A fresh recorder of rural life was **J. Hector St. John de Crèvecoeur** (1735–1813), born in France, served under Montcalm, traveled through the Great Lakes and Ohio Valley, and settled down on a farm in Orange Co., N.Y. (1769). His book of impressions of America, which attained wide popularity abroad, was published as *Letters from an American Farmer*. Crèvecoeur saw the American environment transforming the European from a peasant to a freeholder. To him the American was an amalgam of all nations, and his ultimate role in world affairs was dimly foreseen. **1784:** A Kentucky pioneer, **John Filson** (c.1747–88), prepared an account of *The Discovery, Settlement, and Present State of Kentucke*, to which was appended a pur-

ported autobiography of **Daniel Boone.**

POETS. 1776–88: The major poet of the period was **Philip Freneau** (1752–1832), whose poetry reflects 18th-century deism, love of nature, idealization of the "noble savage," the idea of progress, and hostility to tyranny. His more notable efforts include "The Beauties of Santa Cruz" (1776), lyric; "The House of Night" (1779), a powerful poem in the graveyard tradition; an elegy to the war heroes, "To the Memory of Brave Americans" or "Eutaw Springs" (1781); perhaps his most beautiful lyric, "To a Wild Honeysuckle" (1786); "The Indian Burying Ground" (1788); and a number of sea poems, including "The Memorable Victory of Paul Jones" and "The Battle of Lake Erie." For his pro-Jefferson paper, *National Gazette,* see p. 943.

1778: "The Battle of the Kegs," a satirical poem by **Francis Hopkinson** (1737–91), also the author of several satirical essays as well as musical compositions (p. 917), was one of the most popular poems of the war period.

CONNECTICUT (HARTFORD) WITS patterned themselves after the Augustan wits. Essentially conservative, opposing deism and egalitarianism and clinging to Calvinism and Federalism, they celebrated America's independence by extolling its history and society. Members included **John Trumbull** (1750–1831), *The Progress of Dullness* (1772–73), a Hudibrastic satire on education, and the enormously popular *McFingal,* an epic satire on the Tories (1775–82). **Joel Barlow** (1754–1812), land speculator, diplomat, and later an ardent democrat, whose most ambitious patriotic poem was *The Vision of Columbus* (1787), subsequently (1807) enlarged as *The Columbiad,* who is best remembered for his charming poem *Hasty Pudding* (1796). His volume of political essays, *Advice to the Privileged Orders* (1792), a radical defense of the

French Revolution, was proscribed by the British government. **Timothy Dwight** (1752–1817), a Congregational minister and president of Yale, 1795–1817, whose *Triumph of Infidelity* (1788) was a defense of orthodoxy, also wrote an important multivolume work on theology (1818–19) and a book of *Travels in New England and New York* (1821–22). Two of the minor Connecticut wits, **David Humphreys** (1752–1818) and **Lemuel Hopkins** (1750–1801), in collaboration with Barlow and Trumbull, pilloried New England radicals in the *Anarchaiad* (1786–87), a satire on mob rule, currency inflation, and other nostrums.

1789–1860

BEST SELLERS, 1789–1815

1971. Susanna Rowson, *Charlotte Temple*
1792. Hugh H. Brackenridge, *Modern Chivalry*
1794. Benjamin Franklin, *Autobiography*
1794–95. Thomas Paine, *Age of Reason*
1800. Mason L. Weems, *Life of Washington*
1809. Washington Irving, *History of New York*

NOVELISTS. 1789: *The Power of Sympathy* by **William Hill Brown** (1765–93) is generally considered the seminal American novel. **1790: Susanna Haswell Rowson** (c.1762–1824), English-born actress, dramatist, novelist, and Boston schoolteacher, wrote an exceptionally popular sentimental novel, *Charlotte Temple*. **1789–1801: Charles Brockden Brown** (1771–1810) wrote a series of Gothic romances revealing some of the moral purpose of Godwin, the sentimentalism of Richardson, and above all the horrors of the school of Mrs. Radcliffe: *Weiland* (1798), an attack on superstition; *Arthur Mervyn* (1799), a realistic picture of the yellow fever epidemic in Philadelphia; *Ormond* (1799); *Edgar Huntley* (1799), crimes committed by a sleepwalker; *Clara Howard* (1801); and *Jane Talbot* (1801). His *Alcuin* (1798) was a treatise on women's rights. **1792–**

1815: Hugh Henry Brackenridge (1748–1816), editor and jurist, wrote *Modern Chivalry* (1792), a satire, realistically depicting frontier conditions and reflecting the influence of Cervantes.

BEST SELLERS, 1816–60

1819. Washington Irving, *Sketch Book**
1821. James Fenimore Cooper, *The Spy**
1823. James Fenimore Cooper, *The Pilot**
1823. James Fenimore Cooper, *The Pioneers**
1824. James Everet Seaver, *Life of Mrs. Jemison* (Indian captivity)
1826. James Fenimore Cooper, *The Last of the Mohicans**
1827. James Fenimore Cooper, *The Prairie**
1832. Rev. Jacob Abbott, *The Young Christian*
1836. Maria Monk, *Awful Disclosures* (as novice in a Montreal nunnery, an imposture)
1837. Robert Montgomery Bird, *Nick of the Woods** (forerunner of dime-novel thrillers); Nathaniel Hawthorne, *Twice-Told Tales**; Hannah Farnham Lee, *Three Experiments of Living*
1839. Henry Wadsworth Longfellow, *Voices of the Night**; Jared Sparks, *Life of Washington*; Daniel Pierce Thompson, *The Green Mountain Boys**
1840. Richard Henry Dana, Jr., *Two Years before the Mast**; James Fenimore Cooper, *The Pathfinder**
1841. James Fenimore Cooper, *The Deerslayer**; Ralph Waldo Emerson, *Essays**
1842. Rufus Wilmot Griswold, ed., *Poets and Poetry of America* (outstandingly popular anthology)
1843. Robert Sears, *The Wonders of the World*; William Hickling Prescott, *Conquest of Mexico**
1844. George Lippard, *The Monks of Monk Hall*, printed 1845 as *The Quaker City*
1845. Edgar Allan Poe, *The Raven and Other Poems**
1846. Joel Tyler Headley, *Napoleon and His Marshals**
1849. John G. Whittier, *Poems**
1850. Nathaniel Hawthorne, *The Scarlet Letter**; Ik Marvel (Donald Grant Mitchell), *Reveries of a Bachelor**; Susan Bogert Warner, *The Wide, Wide World**
1851. Nathaniel Hawthorne, *The House of the Seven Gables**; Herman Melville, *Moby-Dick**
1852. Mrs. E. D. E. N. Southworth, *The Curse of Clifton**; Harriet Beecher Stowe, *Uncle Tom's Cabin**
1854. Phineas T. Barnum, *Struggles and Triumphs*; Maria Susanna Cummins, *The Lamplighter**; Mary Jane Holmes, *Tempest and Sunshine**; Timothy Shay Arthur, *Ten Nights in a Bar-Room*; Henry D. Thoreau, *Walden**
1855. Joseph Holt Ingraham, *The Prince of the House of David*; Walt Whitman, *Leaves of Grass**
1856. Mary Jane Holmes, *Lena Rivers**
1859. Augusta Jane Evans [Wilson], *Beulah*; Mrs. E. D. E. N. Southworth, *The Hidden Hand**
1860. Edward Sylvester Ellis, *Seth Jones* (a dime novel); Miriam Coles Harris, *Rutledge*; Ann Sophia Stephens, *Malaeska* (1st of the Beadle Dime Novels)

* Best sellers after their period, including cheap reprints.

1809–60. KNICKERBOCKER SCHOOL. For some 2 decades after 1815 the foremost native literary figures were **Washington Irving** (p. 1066), **James Fenimore Cooper** (p. 1006), and **William Cullen Bryant** (p. 993). Irving and Bryant were identified with the Knickerbocker School of writers at New York, a group which took its name from Irving's satirical *A History of New York . . . by Diedrich Knickerbocker* (1809). Cooper's conventional association with the school is based almost wholly upon geographical circumstances.

Leaving the U.S. in 1815, Irving produced in 1819–20 *The Sketch Book*, which included such tales as "Rip Van Winkle" and "The Legend of Sleepy Hollow." His literary activity on the Continent resulted in *Bracebridge Hall* (1822), *The Life and Voyages of Columbus* (1828), *The Conquest of Granada* (1829), *Tales of a Traveller* (1829), and *The Alhambra* (1832). He returned to the U.S. in 1832 and maintained his popularity with *A Tour on the Prairies* (1835), *Astoria* (1836), and *The Adventures of Captain Bonneville* (1837), the U.S. army officer who led an expedition into the Rocky Mountain region. The most important of Irving's later works was the *Life of Washington* (1855–59), facilitated by the publication of *The Writings of Washington* (1833–39), edited by **Jared Sparks** (1789–1866).

Cooper's first novel, *Precaution* (1820), portrayed English society life. In *The Spy* (1821), the first of his works using an American theme and setting, Cooper displayed his capacity for picturing forest life and creating authentic American character. With *The Pioneers* (1823), Cooper inaugurated the *Leatherstocking Tales* for which he is best remembered, completing the series with *The Last of the Mohicans* (1826), *The Prairie* (1827, last in narrative order),

The Pathfinder (1840), and *The Deerslayer* (1841). Almost single-handed Cooper established the historical romance of the American scene and made American fiction's greatest statement about the clash between primitive and civilized values on the frontier. He is also noted for his sea tales, e.g., *The Pilot* (1823) and *The Red Rover* (1827–28), and his novels of social criticism, e.g., the Antirent series begun with *Satanstoe* (1845). Unlike Irving's continued popularity, Cooper's waned after 1833 when his aristocratic social ideals expressed in *A Letter to His Countrymen* (1834), *The American Democrat* (1839), and many novels antagonized his fellow citizens.

Bryant's fame began with the publication of "Thanatopsis" in the *North American Review* (1817, enlarged version in 1821), a poem notable for its handling of the theme of death and for its lyrical treatment of nature; and "To a Waterfowl" (1818), generally considered his masterpiece. In 1825 Bryant left Massachusetts and settled at New York City, joining (1828) the staff of the N.Y. *Evening Post,* of which he was editor (1829–78). He published *The Fountain* (1842), *The White-Footed Deer* (1844), and *A Forest Hymn* (1860), but his absorption in newspaper work weakened his powers as a poet.

Among the other members of the Knickerbocker School were **James Kirke Paulding** (1778–1860), author of *The Diverting History of John Bull and Brother Jonathan* (1812), the historical novels *Koningsmarke* (1823) and *The Dutchman's Fireside* (1831), and *The Book of St. Nicholas* (1836); **Fitz-Greene Halleck** (1790–1867), author of *Alnwick Castle, with Other Poems* (1827), who collaborated with another Knickerbocker writer, **Joseph Rodman Drake** (1795–1820), on the "Croaker Papers" (1819), a set of satirical verses; **Gulian C. Ver-**

planck (1786–1870), who divided his time between politics and literature; **Nathaniel P. Willis** (1806–67), writer of popular verse and travel sketches; and **Charles Fenno Hoffman** (1806–84), journalist and novelist.

1815–60. NEW ENGLAND RENAISSANCE. The community of thought which drew its vitality from New England Transcendentalism made the most fruitful and enduring contributions to American letters before the Civil War. After the War of 1812 the focal point of national literature gradually shifted to Boston, Cambridge, and the New England hinterland, where the successive ferments of Unitarianism and Transcendentalism gave to the nation that period later characterized as the "flowering of New England." Boston remained the intellectual capital of the country until after the Civil War. The **"Unitarian Controversy,"** which came to a climax in 1815 under the leadership of **William Ellery Channing** (p. 1000), was a spiritual revolt against the confinements of orthodox Congregationalism which exerted a potent liberating influence over the New England mind.

1836–50. When Unitarianism in turn fell into the ways of orthodoxy, it was challenged by **Transcendentalism,** whose doctrines received their most comprehensive exposition in *Nature* (1836), by **Ralph Waldo Emerson** (p. 1024). *Nature* appeared in the year when the Transcendental Club became active at Boston and Concord. Transcendentalism was a mood or cast of mind rather than a systematically articulated philosophy. Despite their diversity of outlook, the Transcendentalists agreed on the sacredness, uniqueness, and authority of the individual apprehension of experience. Man was of the divine essence. His insights, drawn from a conception of the mystic unity of nature, might enable the discovery of truth without reference to dogma and established authority. The self-reliance and self-determination exalted by Transcendentalism gave to American writers a freedom that vitalized the first great period in national letters.

Emerson was the seer of Transcendentalism. Between 1826 and 1832, when he held a Unitarian pulpit, he formulated the basic elements of his moral vision. His retirement from the church formalized his revolt against orthodoxy. After his journey to Europe in 1833 he became the spokesman of his generation. *The American Scholar,* delivered as the Phi Beta Kappa address at Harvard (1837), was an eloquent expression of the Emersonian creed of individualism, independence, and self-sufficiency. His address (1838) before the Harvard Divinity School challenged conservative Unitarianism. The luminous passages of the *Essays* (1841, 1844) contained the mature fruits of his thought. In the years before the Civil War, Emerson also expounded Transcendentalism from lecture platforms throughout the North and West. This period witnessed the publication of his *Poems* (1847), *Representative Men* (1850), *English Traits* (1856), and *The Conduct of Life* (1860).

In **Henry David Thoreau** (p. 1170) the individualism of the Transcendentalist movement reached its most intense and uncompromising form. Thoreau's views, molded by a long and extraordinary process of self-discipline, had already become confirmed principles by the time he went to live at Walden Pond in 1845. His 2-year sojourn was a criticism by example of the materialism of a social order that he regarded as a block to man's capacity for free development. Thoreau's first book, *A Week on the Concord and Merrimack Rivers* (1849), was received coldly by the public and by the few critics who noticed its appearance. *Walden* (1854) fared somewhat better, but general recognition of Thoreau came only after his death. Thoreau's literary artistry attained its high point in *Walden*. His philosophy of nature, supported by concrete instance, showed how man's rediscovery of himself could bring his freedom. The essay on "Civil Disobedience" (1849), which posed the sovereign rights of conscience against the claims of the state, was one of Thoreau's most moving utterances of an individualism grounded on high moral conviction.

Among the other members of the Transcendentalist movement were **Margaret Fuller** (p. 1035), editor of *The Dial;* **Bronson Alcott** (1799–1888); **Jones Very** (1813–80); **George Ripley** (1802–80); **Theodore Parker** (1810–60); **Orestes A. Brownson** (1803–76); **James Freeman Clarke** (1810–88); and **Christopher P. Cranch** (1813–92).

One of New England's most popular writers, and a leader of literary society in the Boston he christened the "hub of the Universe," was the Harvard medical professor **Oliver Wendell Holmes** (p. 1058). Mingled with his charming wit and light touch was a rationalism that appeared in his humorous parable of orthodox Calvinism, "The Deacon's Masterpiece; or, The Wonderful 'One-Hoss Shay,'" included (1858) in *The Autocrat of the Breakfast-Table* (1831–32 in the *New England Magazine* and 1857 as an installment in the initial number of the *Atlantic Monthly*). Holmes also published *The Professor at the Breakfast-Table* (1860), another collection of intimate and congenial essays; 3 psychiatric novels (including *Elsie Venner*, 1861); and poems ("Old Ironsides") and humorous ballads.

1837–52. HAWTHORNE, MELVILLE, WHITMAN, AND POE. The currents of Transcendentalism touched **Nathaniel Hawthorne** (p. 1053) and **Herman Melville** (p. 1101), although at a divergent angle. They did not share Emerson's optimism; for them the problem of evil was the most meaningful and enduring element in life.

Hawthorne's focus was relatively narrow, but it was intense. With a craftsmanship of the first order, he gave a somber portrayal of the Puritan mind of New England, searching out the play of evil and the ramifications of sin, guilt, and remorse. His finest achievement is embraced by *Twice-Told Tales* (1837), *The Scarlet Letter* (1850), *The House of the Seven Gables* (1851), *The Blithedale Romance* (1852), and *The Snow-Image* and *Other Twice-Told Tales* (1852).

Melville, who had been a sailor, set his great romances against the background of the sea. *Typee* (1846), *Omoo* (1847), and *Mardi* (1849) were based on experiences in the South Seas. *Redburn* (1849) drew upon his experiences on the Atlantic and in England. In *White-Jacket* (1850) and in *Billy Budd* Melville's portrayal of the brutality that prevailed aboard the warships of the Navy ranked with the revelation of stern treatment in *Two Years Before the Mast* (1840) by **Richard Henry Dana, Jr.** (1815–82). Melville's masterpiece was *Moby Dick* (1851), a novel of a whaling voyage allegorically conceived as a great tragedy imbued with philosophic significance.

Together with *Leaves of Grass* (1855; enlarged in successive editions to 1892) by **Walt Whitman** (p. 1182), *Moby Dick* was proof that American writers had shaped their own idiom. Whitman utilized a simple poetic style devoid of the ordinary usages of rhyme, meter, or ornament, and distinguished by a natural organic growth. Whitman had a profound belief in the perfectibility of man and in democracy. Among his later poems inspired by the events of the Civil War were "The Wound-Dresser" and 2 poems called forth by grief over Lincoln's death—"When Lilacs Last in the Dooryard Bloom'd" and "O Captain! My Captain!" (1865). His poetry is also marked by the frank though frequently symbolic treatment of sex—"Children of Adam" and "Calamus" (1860). His most important prose works were *Democratic Vistas* (1871) and *Specimen Days and Collect* (1882).

The greatest literary figure produced by the South during this period was **Edgar Allan Poe** (p. 1129), but his productive years were passed in Philadelphia and New York after 1837 and his art was independent of historical and geographical association. One of the most complex personalities in American letters, Poe is remembered as an innovator in fields as different as poetry and the detective story. He did pioneer work as a literary critic. His "The Philosophy of Composition," "The Rationale of Verse," and "The Poetic Principle" revealed his conception of poetic unity to be one of mood or emotion, with emphasis upon the beauty of melancholy. He preferred the short story to the novel on the same basis that he preferred the short poem to the long. These stories were either of horror or of careful reasoning. The latter set the standard for the modern detective story. Poe's aesthetic principles had a marked influence upon the French *Symbolistes* as well as upon such Americans as Ambrose Bierce and Hart Crane and such Englishmen as Rossetti, Swinburne, Dowson, and Stevenson. Among his works are *Tales of the Grotesque and Arabesque* (1840), "The Murders in the Rue Morgue" (1843), and *The Raven and Other Poems* (1845).

SOUTH. The representative Southern writers of the time concentrated on local themes. In *Swallow Barn* (1832), **John Pendleton Kennedy** (1795–1870) wrote a series of sketches portraying plantation life in Virginia. Working in a more realis-

tic vein, **Augustus Baldwin Longstreet** (1790–1870) produced *Georgia Scenes, Characters, and Incidents* (1835), dealing with life in the backwoods. It was notable for its handling of dialect. The most prolific Southern writer was **William Gilmore Simms** (p. 1152), who published poetry, historical romances, history, and biography. His best works include *Guy Rivers* (1834), one of his Border Romances; *The Partisan* (1835), one of his Revolutionary Romances; and *The Yemassee* (1835), a panel in the series of romances dealing with the colonial period. In the first rank of the Southern poets of this period were **Henry Timrod** (1828–67) and **Paul Hamilton Hayne** (1830–86), both born in South Carolina.

1838–58. POETS. Henry Wadsworth Longfellow (p. 1089) was the most popular American poet of his day. Many of his lines, for all of their lack of originality and firsthand observation, quickly became American household favorites. His popularity was based on such works as *Voices of the Night* (1839), *Evangeline* (1847), the *Song of Hiawatha* (1855), and *The Courtship of Miles Standish* (1858). When **John Greenleaf Whittier** (p. 1183) did not turn his hand to antislavery agitation, as in *Poems Written During the Progress of the Abolition Question* (1838) and in individual pieces like "Massachusetts to Virginia" (1843) and "Ichabod" (1850), he produced ballads and narrative poems based on New England life and legend, as in "The Barefoot Boy" and "Maud Muller" (both 1856). **James Russell Lowell** (p. 1089) used Yankee dialect to good advantage in offering a Northern Whig's satirical view of the Mexican War in the *Biglow Papers* (1st series, 1848) and attacking slavery (2nd series, 1867). Other antislavery poems include "Prometheus" (1843), "The Present Crisis" (1845), and "On the

Capture of Certain Fugitives near Washington" (1845). Lowell characterized contemporary authors in *A Fable for Critics* (1848) and reached a wide audience with *The Vision of Sir Launfal* (1848).

1834–60. HISTORIANS. William Hickling Prescott (p. 1132), author of the *History of the Reign of Ferdinand and Isabella* (1838), *History of the Conquest of Mexico* (1843), *History of the Conquest of Peru* (1847), and *History of the Reign of Philip the Second* (1855–58), worked in the dramatic vein of William Robertson and Sir Walter Scott. **George Ticknor** (1791–1871), **George Bancroft** (p. 978), and **John Lothrop Motley** (p. 1111) were schooled in high standards of historical scholarship at German universities. Ticknor's *History of Spanish Literature* was published in 1849. In 1834 Bancroft brought out the first volume of his *History of the United States*, a work which ultimately ran to 11 volumes and concluded with the establishment of the national government. It was noteworthy both for its patriotic tone and its research in original materials. In 1856 Motley published *The Rise of the Dutch Republic*. Motley's concept of the vitalizing influence of Protestantism was shared by **Francis Parkman** (p. 1122), who began the grand design of his epic of France and England in North America to 1763 with the *History of the Conspiracy of Pontiac* (1851). Parkman did not write the bulk of his work until after the Civil War, but he had already won fame with his travel account, *The California and Oregon Trail* (1849). In conscious contrast to Bancroft's oratorical prose, **Richard Hildreth** (1807–65) employed a sparse, dry style in his *History of the United States*, whose 6 volumes covering the period 1492–1821 appeared between 1849 and 1852. Virtually ignored by contemporary readers, Hildreth's work has a high degree of factual accuracy and penetrating insights into economic interests. Two collections of source materials published at government expense were important in encouraging the writing of American history: the *Debates, Resolutions, and Other Proceedings in Convention on the Adoption of the Federal Constitution*, brought out between 1827 and 1845 under the editorship of **Jonathan Elliot** (1784–1846); and the *American Archives* (covering the years 1774–76), edited by **Peter Force** (1790–1868) and brought out between 1837 and 1853.

1848–60. REFORM NOVEL. The novel of propaganda, instruction and uplift flourished during this period of reform. *Uncle Tom's Cabin* (1852), by **Harriet Beecher Stowe** (p. 1161), was the most successful of the many tracts for the times largely because its publication coincided with the national impact of the antislavery crusade. Her second novel in this genre was *Dred, A Tale of the Great Dismal Swamp* (1856). Where *Uncle Tom's Cabin* (p. 256) fixed its attention on the evils of slavery as an institution, and was remarkably free from attacks upon Southerners, *Dred* sought to show the mark the institution left upon those who lived by it. Supposedly the first novels based on the antislavery theme were *Northwood, or Life North and South* (1827), by Sarah Josepha Hale (1788–1879), and *The Slave; or, Memoirs of Archy Moore* (1836), by Richard Hildreth.

Another reform impulse that was embodied in literature was the temperance movement, which reached its height in the 1850s. **Timothy Shay Arthur** (1809–85), best known for *Ten Nights in a Bar-Room and What I saw There* (1854), published some 100 tracts and stories of which 1,000,000 copies had been printed by 1860. Also popular as a temperance writer was Lucius Manlius Sargent (1786–1867), whose *Temper-*

ance Tales (1848) included such best-selling stories as "My Mother's Gold Ring" and "Groggy Harbor," originally issued between 1833 and 1843.

1840–60. POPULAR LITERATURE. The growth of the middle class, along with the extension of free public education, the establishment of subscription libraries, and the lyceum movement, had a direct influence on book publishing and literary standards. The mass audience widened the market for books of practical social instruction and sentimental novels of moral uplift. In addition to the best sellers listed above, etiquette books, juveniles (notably the moralistic *Peter Parley* juveniles, which sold approximately 7 million copies from 1827–60 and were written on a mass production basis by authors employed by **Samuel G. Goodrich** [1793–1860]), and anthologies were widely sold in this period. Two anthologist-editors, **Rufus W. Griswold** (1815–57) and **Evert A. Duyckinck** (1816–78), editor of the *Literary World,* had a substantial impact on reading taste. With **Park Benjamin** (1809–64), Griswold began in 1839 to serialize pirated fiction in *Brother Jonathan.* The first dime novel, *Malaeska* by **Ann Sophia Stephens** (1813–86), appeared in 1860. The last decade of this period is often called the "Feminine Fifties," a tribute to the number of women authors who wrote best sellers, easily outselling the works by Emerson, Hawthorne, Melville, and Whitman.

1802–60. BOOK PUBLISHING. **Matthew Carey** (1760–1839), Philadelphia publisher and economist, and founder of Carey and Lea (1785), promoted the American Co. of Booksellers, which managed 5 book fairs, 1802–06. More effective distribution was achieved by Harper & Bros. (est. New York City, 1817, as J. & J. Harper), with the adoption in 1830 of the stereotyping of plates for "omnibus editions" of English reprints, and in the 1840s with the issuance of 25-ct. English novels. Carey & Hart (Philadelphia, 1829) followed suit. Scott, Dickens, and other foreign authors were printed in enormous pirated editions before the International Copyright Law (1891). Other major publishing houses included D. Appleton & Co. (1825); J. B. Lippincott & Co. (Philadelphia, 1836); Dodd, Mead & Co. (1839, 1870); the Boston firms of Little, Brown (1847), Houghton, Mifflin (1852) and E. P. Dutton (1852; moved to New York City, 1869); and Charles Scribner's Sons (Baker & Scribner, 1846).

1800–60. PUBLIC LIBRARY MOVEMENT. Library of Congress, Washington, D.C., established 1800 with the library of Thomas Jefferson as a nucleus. Its greatest expansion occurred under the librarianship of **Herbert Putnam** (1861–1955), 1899–1939. In 1951 its holdings totaled 9,400,000 books and pamphlets. **Beginning of Tax-Supported Local Libraries. 1803:** Founding of a childen's library in Salisbury, Conn., by a gift from Caleb Bingham, Boston publisher, supplemented by occasional grants of town money. **1833:** Under the leadership of Rev. Abiel Abbot a social library was established at Peterborough, N.H., supported by a small membership fee and a portion of the state bank tax set aside by the town to purchase books. **1850:** Public library at Wayland, Mass., established by gift of President Francis Wayland (1796–1865) of Brown University, matched by town donation and supported by regular tax funds. **1851:** Enactment in Massachusetts of a law permitting towns to tax inhabitants for the support of free libraries. Founding of the **Boston Public Library,** largely as a result of the activities of **Edward Everett** (1794–1865), orator, statesman, and scholar, and **George Ticknor,** with private book donations, money gifts, and a city appropriation.

Trends since 1860

BEST SELLERS

1862. William G. Brownlow, Parson Brownlow's Book
1863. Mrs. E. D. E. N. Southworth, The Fatal Marriage*; Mrs. A. D. T. Whitney, Faith Gartney's Girlhood
1864. Mrs. E. D. E. N. Southworth, Ishmael*
1865. Mary Mapes Dodge, Hans Brinker and His Silver Skates*
1867. Horatio Alger, Jr., Ragged Dick*; Augusta J. Evans Wilson, St. Elmo
1868. Elizabeth S. P. Ward, The Gates Ajar*; Louisa May Alcott, Little Women*
1869. Mark Twain, Innocents Abroad*
1870. Bret Harte, The Luck of Roaring Camp*
1871. Louisa May Alcott, Little Men*; Edward Eggleston, The Hoosier Schoolmaster*
1872. Edward Payson Roe, Barriers Burned Away; Mark Twain, Roughing It*
1874. Edward Payson Roe, Opening a Chestnut Burr
1876. John Habberton, Helen's Babies*; Mark Twain, Tom Sawyer*
1878. Anna Katharine Green, The Leavenworth Case*
1879. Henry George, Progress and Poverty*
1880. Joel Chandler Harris, Uncle Remus*; Harriet Lothrop (Margaret Sidney), Five Little Peppers and How They Grew*; Lew Wallace, Ben-Hur*
1883. James Whitcomb Riley, The Old Swimmin'-Hole*; Mark Twain, Life on the Mississippi* (chief sales in 1940's in pocket size)
1885. Mark Twain, Huckleberry Finn*; Ulysses S. Grant, Personal Memoirs
1886. Frances Hodgson Burnett, Little Lord Fauntleroy*
1887. Archibald C. Gunter, Mr. Barnes of New York*
1888. Edward Bellamy, Looking Backward*
1894. William Hope Harvey, Coin's Financial School (free-silver argument)
1895. Opie Read, The Jucklins; Stephen Crane, The Red Badge of Courage*
1896. Harold Frederic, The Damnation of Theron Ware
1897. Charles Monroe Sheldon, In His Steps* (sales c.8 million to 1945)
1898. Edward Noyes Westcott, David Harum*
1899. Charles Major, When Knighthood Was in Flower; Winston Churchill, Richard Carvel; Paul Leicester Ford, Janice Meredith; Elbert Hubbard, A Message to Garcia*
1900. Mary Johnston, To Have and to Hold; Irving Bacheller, Eben Holden
1901. George Barr McCutcheon, Graustark; Alice Hegan Rice, Mrs. Wiggs of the Cabbage Patch; Winston Churchill, The Crisis
1902. Owen Wister, The Virginian*
1903. John Fox, Jr., The Little Shepherd of Kingdom Come; Kate Douglas Wiggin, Rebecca of Sunnybrook Farm; Jack London, The Call of the Wild*
1904. Jack London, The Sea Wolf*; Gene Stratton Porter, Freckles

1906. Zane Grey, The Spirit of the Border*
1907. Harold Bell Wright, The Shepherd of the Hills*
1908. John Fox, Jr., The Trail of the Lonesome Pine; Mary Roberts Rinehart, The Circular Staircase
1909. Gene Stratton Porter, A Girl of the Limberlost; Harold Bell Wright, The Calling of Dan Matthews*
1911. Kathleen Norris, Mother; Gene Stratton Porter, The Harvester; Harold Bell Wright, The Winning of Barbara Worth*
1912. Zane Grey, The Riders of the Purple Sage*
1913. Eleanor Hodgman Porter, Pollyanna; Gene Stratton Porter, Laddie
1914. Edgar Rice Burroughs, Tarzan of the Apes*; Booth Tarkington, Penrod*; Harold Bell Wright, The Eyes of the World*
1915. Gene Stratton Porter, Michael O'Halloran
1916. Edgar A. Guest, A Heap o' Livin'*; Harold Bell Wright, When a Man's a Man*
1918. Edward Streeter, Dere Mable; Henry Adams, The Education of Henry Adams; Zane Grey, The U.P. Trail*
1920. Edward W. Bok, The Americanization of Edward Bok; Sinclair Lewis, Main Street*
1921. Dorothy Canfield, The Brimming Cup
1923. Emily Post, Etiquette*
1924. Edna Ferber, So Big
1925. John Erskine, The Private Life of Helen of Troy; Anita Loos, Gentlemen Prefer Blondes; Bruce Barton, The Man Nobody Knows
1926. Sinclair Lewis, Elmer Gantry; Will Durant, The Story of Philosophy*; Thorne Smith, Topper*
1927. Thornton Wilder, The Bridge of San Luis Rey
1929. Lloyd C. Douglas, The Magnificent Obsession; Robert L. Ripley, Believe It or Not*
1930. Edna Ferber, Cimarron
1931. Pearl Buck, The Good Earth*; Ellery Queen, The Dutch Shoe Mystery*
1932. Ellery Queen, The Egyptian Cross Mystery*
1933. Hervey Allen, Anthony Adverse; Erle Stanley Gardner, The Case of the Sulky Girl*
1934. Erle Stanley Gardner, The Case of the Curious Bride*; Ellery Queen, The Chinese Orange Mystery*
1935. Lloyd C. Douglas, Green Light; Erle Stanley Gardner, The Case of the Counterfeit Eye*
1936. Dale Carnegie, How to Win Friends and Influence People*; Erle Stanley Gardner, The Case of the Stuttering Bishop*; Margaret Mitchell, Gone with the Wind*
1937. Erle Stanley Gardner, The Case of the Dangerous Dowager*; The Case of the Lame Canary*
1938. Marco Page, Fast Company; Marjorie K. Rawlings, The Yearling; Max Brand (Frederick Faust), Singing Guns*; Erle Stanley Gardner, The Case of the Substitute Face*; Damon Runyon, The Best of Damon Runyon*
1939. John Steinbeck, The Grapes of Wrath*
1940. Ellery Queen, New Adventures of Ellery Queen*; Ernest Hemingway, For Whom the Bell Tolls*
1942. Lloyd C. Douglas, The Robe; Marion Hargrove, See Here, Private Hargrove
1943. Ernie Pyle, Here Is Your War; Betty Smith, A Tree Grows in Brooklyn; Wendell Willkie, One World
1944. Ernie Pyle, Brave Men; Kathleen Winsor, Forever Amber; Lillian Smith, Strange Fruit
1945. Thomas Bertram Costain, The Black Rose; Betty MacDonald, The Egg and I; Samuel Shellabarger, Captain from Castile

1946. Joshua Loth Liebman, *Peace of Mind;* Frank Yerby, *Foxes of Harrow;* Taylor Caldwell, *This Side of Innocence*
1947. John Gunther, *Inside U.S.A.;* Laura Z. Hobson, *Gentleman's Agreement;* Sinclair Lewis, *Kingsblood Royal;* Samuel Shellabarger, *The Prince of Foxes*
1948. Frank Yerby, *The Golden Hawk;* Alfred C. Kinsey, *Sexual Behavior in the Human Male;* Frances Parkinson Keyes, *Dinner at Antoine's;* Thomas Costain, *High Towers;* Norman Mailer, *The Naked and the Dead*
1949. Lloyd C. Douglas, *The Big Fisherman;* Frank Yerby, *Pride's Castle*
1950. Henry Morton Robinson, *The Cardinal*
1951. Rachel Carson, *The Sea Around Us;* Herman Wouk, *The Caine Mutiny;* James Jones, *From Here to Eternity;* Gaylord Hauser, *Look Younger, Live Longer*
1952. Thomas B. Costain, *The Silver Chalice**; *The Holy Bible: Revised Standard Version**
1953. Lloyd C. Douglas, *The Robe* (reissue); Catherine Marshall, *A Man Called Peter*
1954. Norman Vincent Peale, *The Power of Positive Thinking*
1955. Herman Wouk, *Marjorie Morningstar;* Anne Morrow Lindbergh, *Gift from the Sea*
1956. Edwin O'Connor, *The Last Hurrah;* Grace Metalious, *Peyton Place*;* Morey Bernstein, *The Search for Bridey Murphy*
1957. James G. Cozzens, *By Love Possessed;* Meyer Levin, *Compulsion;* Vance Packard, *The Hidden Persuaders*
1958. Robert Traver, *Anatomy of a Murder;* James Jones, *Some Came Running*
1959. Leon Uris, *Exodus;* Moss Hart, *Act One;* Harry Golden, *Only in America;* D. C. Jarvis, *Folk Medicine*
1960. Allen Drury, *Advise and Consent;* James A. Michener, *Hawaii*
1961. *The New English Bible: The New Testament*;* William Shirer, *The Rise and Fall of the Third Reich;* Irving Stone, *The Agony and the Ecstasy;* J. D. Salinger, *Franny and Zooey*
1962. Katherine Anne Porter, *Ship of Fools;* Dr. Herman Taller, *Calories Don't Count;* Allen Drury, *A Shade of Difference*
1963. Charles M. Schulz, *Happiness Is a Warm Puppy;* Morris L. West, *The Shoes of the Fisherman;* J. D. Salinger, *Raise High the Roof Beam, Carpenters* and *Seymour—An Introduction*
1964. American Heritage & UPI, *Four Days;* John F. Kennedy, *Profiles in Courage;* Terry Southern and Mason Hoffenberg, *Candy*
1965. Dan Greenberg, *How to Be a Jewish Mother;* James A. Michener, *The Source;* Saul Bellow, *Herzog*
1966. Norman F. Dicey, *How to Avoid Probate;* William Howard Masters and Virginia E. Johnson, *Human Sexual Response;* Truman Capote, *In Cold Blood;* Jacqueline Susann, *Valley of the Dolls*
1967. Eric Berne, *Games People Play;* Thornton Wilder, *The Eighth Day;* Jacqueline Susann, *Valley of the Dolls*
1968. Stephen Birmingham, *"Our Crowd": The Great Jewish Families of New York;* Leon Uris, *Topaz;* William Styron, *The Confessions of Nat Turner*
1969. *"Adam Smith," The Money Game;* John Updike, *Couples;* Arthur Hailey, *Airport;* Gore Vidal, *Myra Breckenridge*

1970. Joe McGinniss, *The Selling of the President;* Chaim Potok, *The Promise;* Philip Roth, *Portnoy's Complaint;* Mario Puzo, *The Godfather*
1971. *The New York Times* Staff, *The Pentagon Papers;* Dee Brown, *Bury My Heart at Wounded Knee;* Sylvia Plath, *The Bell Jar;* Frederick Forsyth, *Day of the Jackal*
1972. Larry Collins and Dominique LaPierre, *O Jerusalem!;* Roger Kahn, *The Boys of Summer*
1973. Richard Bach, *Jonathan Livingston Seagull;* Alex Comfort, *The Joy of Sex*

---

* Also best sellers after their period, including cheap reprints (but not dictionaries, almanacs, manuals, textbooks, cookbooks, comic books, or government publications).

ALL-TIME PAPERBACK BEST SELLER LIST (1968)

Benjamin Spock, *Baby and Child Care*
The Merriam-Webster Pocket Dictionary
Grace Metalious, *Peyton Place*
Erskine Caldwell, *God's Little Acre*
Harper Lee, *To Kill a Mockingbird*
Jacqueline Susann, *Valley of the Dolls*
Webster's New World Dictionary of the American Language
University of Chicago English-Spanish, Spanish-English Dictionary
Charles Sheldon, *In His Steps*
Leon Uris, *Exodus*
Roget's Pocket Thesaurus
Harold Robbins, *The Carpetbaggers*

1865–1900. LITERATURE OF AMERICA'S REDISCOVERY. The West: Samuel Langhorne Clemens (Mark Twain, also p. 1002), the great voice of the West of his generation, won a worldwide reputation by his defiantly American outlook, his uncompromising democracy (hostility to slavery, snobbery, and the tyrannies of chivalry), and his pungent colloquial style. Of all contemporary humorists (including **John Phoenix** [George Horatio Derby, 1823–61], **Josh Billings** [Henry Wheeler Shaw, 1818–85], **Maj. Jack Downing** [Seba Smith, 1792–1868], **Bill Arp** [Charles Henry Smith, 1826–1903], **Petroleum V. Nasby** [David Ross Locke, 1833–88], and **Artemus Ward** [Charles Farrar Browne, 1834–67]), Clemens alone created great literature. His experience on the frontiers in the Old Southwest and the Far West (the latter depicted in *Roughing It,* 1872) prepared him to use regional tall tales and realism with his own idiom, as in *The Celebrated Jumping Frog of Calaveras County* (1865), a brilliant reworking of a California folk tale. His frontier irreverence for ancient culture, displayed in *The Innocents Abroad* (1869), the first of several travel books, is in contrast to his enthusiasm in the first part of *Life on the Mississippi* (1883). *The Gilded Age* (1873), written with Charles Dudley Warner (1829–1900), was his first novel, marked like others by its episodic improvisation, but it lacks the distinction of *The Adventures of Tom Sawyer* (1876) and particularly *The Adventures of Huckleberry Finn* (1884), picaresque portrayals of regional character and frontier experience centered on the adventures of 2 boys. His later pessimism is seen in *The Man That Corrupted Hadleyburg* (1900) and *The Mysterious Stranger* (1916). The Western **Local-Colorists** (concerned with commonplace local scenes, utilizing regional dialects, and presenting character types) include **Bret Harte** (1836–1902), who, using stock characters and plots, created a romantic legendary view of California in stories and sketches (notably *The Luck of Roaring Camp*, 1870, called "the father of all Western local color stories," and *Mrs. Skagg's Husbands*, 1873), as well as poems, the most popular being the satiric comic ballad, "Plain Language from Truthful James" (1870), familiarly known under the pirated name "The Heathen Chinee." The vogue for vernacular Western poetry was further solidified by *The Pike County Ballads* (1871) of **John Hay** (p. 1054), whose prose works include *Castilian Days* (1871), an attack upon the Catholic Church; *The Bread-Winners* (1883), an antilabor novel; and, in collaboration with J. G. Nicolay, the classic 10-vol. *Abraham Lincoln: A History* (1890); and by **Joaquin Miller** (Cincinnatus

Hiner Miller, c.1839–1913). Miller romanticized some of his early experiences in *Life Amongst the Modocs* (1873), but in Oregon and California he was by turn horse thief, lawyer, newspaperman, and Indian fighter. His extravagantly romantic poems, e.g., *Songs of the Sierras*, were first hailed as products of a primitive, but he dwindled into a hack writer although the late *Songs of the Soul* (1896) includes his well-known "Columbus." Other balladists of the West: Will Carleton (1845–1912), *Farm Ballads* (1873), including the poem "Over the Hills to the Poor House"; **James Whitcomb Riley** (1849–1916), Indiana poet; and **Eugene Field** (1850–95), Chicago *Daily News* columnist, whose best-known poem was "Little Boy Blue." **Edward Eggleston** (1837–1902), in addition to writing pioneer historical works on American cultural history, notably *The Transit of Civilization* (1901), founded the **Hoosier School** with his novels of the middle border, notably *The Hoosier Schoolmaster* (1871), *The Circuit Rider* (1874), *Roxy* (1878), and *The Graysons* (1888).

The South: Joel Chandler Harris (p. 1052), creator of many "Uncle Remus" stories, a humorous animal legendary reflecting Negro folk life, furnished a memorable picture of the Georgia Negro under slavery and Reconstruction, notably in *Free Joe and Other Georgian Sketches* (1887), and of the "cracker" or "poor white" (*Mingo and Other Sketches in Black and White*, 1884). Other Southern Local-Colorists included **George Washington Cable** (1844–1925), with short stories (*Old Creole Days*, 1879) and novels of Creole life (*The Grandissimes*, 1880; *Dr. Sevier*, 1885; *Bonaventure*, 1888); **Thomas Nelson Page** (1853–1922), who idealized Tidewater Virginia of antebellum days (*Red Rock*, 1898, a study of the Negro problem); and **James Lane Allen** (1849–

1925), who used the central Kentucky plateau around his native Lexington for the locale of his novels (*A Kentucky Cardinal*, 1894; *Summer in Arcady*, 1896; *The Choir Invisible*, 1897; *The Reign of Law*, 1900).

New England: Regional fiction found its most accomplished exponent in **Sarah Orne Jewett** (1849–1909), who revealed social and psychological problems in the declining Maine seaport settlements, beginning with *Deephaven* (1877) and culminating in her masterpiece, *The Country of the Pointed Firs* (1896). Another exponent of the Local-Colorist School was **Mary Eleanor Wilkins** (Freeman) (1852–1930), whose early short stories (*A Humble Romance*, 1887, and *A New England Nun*, 1891) represent her most important work.

1865–1892. RISE OF REALISM. An early realist was **John William De Forest** (1826–1906), whose Civil War novel, *Miss Ravenel's Conversion from Secession to Loyalty* (1867), and story of a South Carolina feud, *Kate Beaumont* (1872), are frank accounts of the seamy, brutal, and corrupting aspects of life. Most popular exponent of the realists was **William Dean Howells** (also p. 1063), with his masterpiece, *The Rise of Silas Lapham* (1885), a sympathetic study of the *nouveaux riches*. Howells' novels provide a penetrating analysis of the post–Civil War American economy. His sympathy with socialism (by 1887) is evident in such novels of social protest as *A Hazard of New Fortunes* (1890). His critical theories are summarized in *Criticism and Fiction* (1891), in which he championed realism, whose sources he ascribed not only to science but to democracy. He insisted that art must serve morality. His economic novels showed the influence of the Utopian socialist novel of **Edward Bellamy** (1850–98), *Looking Backward, or 2000–1887* (1888). Howells' realistic approach was adopted by Garland, Stephen Crane, Frank Norris, and Robert Herrick. **Hamlin Garland** (1860–1940), an advocate of "veritism," or honest realism (*Crumbling Idols*, 1894), wrote a number of propaganda novels of prairie life and agrarian conditions (1887–94). His major work was *Main-Travelled Roads* (1891), stories of the burdens of farm life. His autobiography, *A Son of the Middle Border* (1917), presents the everyday life of a group of migrating families to the prairies and the plains (1840–95).

1875–1941. HENRY JAMES AND THE NOVELISTS OF MANNERS. A detached observer contrasting American and European cultures and moral standards in relation to social conventions, James (also p. 1069) was a leader in psychological realism, a sensitive interpreter of subtle characters, and a master of a complex style and the formal architecture of fiction. His many novels of contrasting characters developed in subtlety from *The American* (1877) through *The Portrait of a Lady* (1881) to the later major period of *The Wings of the Dove* (1902), *The Ambassadors* (1903), and *The Golden Bowl* (1904). His short stories (e.g., "The Turn of the Screw," 1898) and his criticism (e.g., the prefaces to his revised collected novels and tales, 1907–09) are as distinguished as his longer fiction. James' most articulate disciple in portraying upper-class American society was **Edith Wharton** (1862–1937), whose major novels of New York's social elite include *The House of Mirth* (1905), *The Age of Innocence* (1920), and *The Old Maid* (1924). In *Ethan Frome* (1911), a tale of sordid misery in the New England hills, she produced a work of dignified simplicity. **Ellen Glasgow** (1874–1945) dealt with the ironies of a decaying Virginia society (*Barren Ground*, 1925; *The Romantic Comedians*, 1926; *In This Our*

Life, 1941), and **Willa Cather** (p. 1000) produced chronicles in which environment and character are deftly interwoven: *O Pioneers!* (1913), *My Antonia* (1918), *A Lost Lady* (1923), *Death Comes for the Archbishop* (1927), and *Shadows on the Rock* (1931).

1893–1949. NATURALISM AND THE PROPAGANDA NOVEL. 19th century theories of biological and economic determinism shaped the literary theory of naturalism, with its frankness, objectivity, determinism, and fatalism. Notable among the fiction writers of this school were **Stephen Crane** (p. 1007), **Frank Norris** (1870–1902), **Robert Herrick** (1868–1938), and **Jack London** (1876–1916). The influence of Zola was found in Crane's *Maggie: A Girl of the Streets* (1893), an impressionistic novelette; but his masterpiece was *The Red Badge of Courage* (1895), a lyrical and intense novel of the Civil War, influenced by both Zola and Tolstoi. Among his most successful short stories were "The Open Boat" and "Blue Hotel." *McTeague* (1899) by Norris was a major naturalistic American novel, a study in character disintegration under economic pressure. *The Octopus* (1901), the first of his "Epic of the Wheat" trilogy, a struggle between the wheat growers and the Southern Pacific Railroad, was followed (1903) by *The Pit* (Chicago grain market). *The Wolf*, last of the trilogy, was never written. Social protest against the forces of acquisitiveness found expression in Herrick's novels, notably in the *Memoirs of an American Citizen* (1905), *Clark's Field* (1914), and in *Waste* (1924), where the engineer, Thornton, finds "a sense of corruption working at the very roots of life." Most widely read in the U.S. and abroad of any of these writers was London, among whose 49 vols. of fiction, drama, and essays are *The Call of the Wild* (1903), the story of a dog in the far North who escapes from civilization to lead a wolf pack; *The Sea Wolf* (1904), a ruthless captain of a sealing ship; *Martin Eden* (1909), a writer's struggle; and *The Valley of the Moon* (1913), in which economic problems are solved by a return to the land.

Other problem novelists of the period who diverged from the path of naturalism and produced straight propaganda novels include **Winston Churchill** (1871–1947), a middle-class progressive, who, in addition to historical romances like *Richard Carvel* (1899) and *The Crisis* (1910), wrote political and economic novels—*Coniston* (1900), *Mr. Crewe's Career* (1908), *A Far Country* (1915), *The Dwelling Place of Light* (1917); **Ernest Poole** (1880–1950), *The Harbor* (1915); **David Graham Phillips** (1867–1911), *The Great God Success* (1901) and *Susan Lenox: Her Fall and Rise* (written 1908, pub. 1917), an epic of slum life and political corruption; and **Upton Sinclair** (1878–1968), whose major novels include *The Jungle* (1906, corruption in meat packing and labor exploitation) and a series of expository and propagandist works: *The Profits of Religion* (1918), on the church; *The Brass Check* (1919), the press; *The Goose Step* (1923) and *The Goslings* (1924), on the schools; *Mammonart* (1925) and *Money Writes* (1927), on the arts. Other exposé novels include *Oil!* (1927), a story of corruption in the Harding era; *Boston* (1928), based on the Sacco-Vanzetti case; and the "Lanny Budd" series (1940–49), a personal interpretation of the two World Wars (1940–49).

1899–1901. FIN-DE-SIÈCLE ROMANCE was exemplified in the works of **Paul Leicester Ford** (1865–1902), *Janice Meredith* (1899); **Mary Johnston** (1875–1936), *To Have and to Hold* (1900); and **Booth Tarkington** (1869–1946), *Monsieur Beaucaire* (1900).

Tarkington's best work dates from the end of World War I and includes *The Magnificent Ambersons* (1918) and *Alice Adams* (1921).

1900–25. NATURALISM OF THEODORE DREISER (p. 1016). *Sister Carrie* by Dreiser, the story of the realization of her own personality by a poor young girl (1900), remained largely unread until its 3d edition, 1912, a year after the appearance of *Jennie Gerhardt*, on a similar theme. Dreiser's preoccupation with Social Darwinism is given expression in the notable trilogy *The Financier* (1912), *The Titan* (1914), and *The Stoic* (1947), with the masterly character delineation of Cowperwood, prototype of worldly success. Another victim of social and biological forces is Clyde Griffiths in *An American Tragedy* (1925). Objective, amoral, Dreiser, despite lack of style and undistinguished language, achieved a powerful projection of reality.

1918–39. BETWEEN WORLD WARS. "Lost generation" was the name applied by **Gertrude Stein** (1874–1946) to the disillusioned intellectuals and aesthetes of post-World War I years. This group was typified by **F. Scott Fitzgerald** (p. 1029), whose *This Side of Paradise* (1920) is an expression of jazz-age cynicism, and *The Great Gatsby* (1925) of disillusion about quickly acquired riches. That cynicism and disillusionment were also reflected in the writings of **Sinclair Lewis** (p. 1084) in a revolt against small-town meanness (*Main Street*, 1920) and the dullness of the businessman (*Babbitt*, 1922). His writing is closer to caricature than to photographic realism. Other novels include *Arrowsmith* (1924), an exposé of the medical profession; *Dodsworth* (1929), a sympathetic portrayal of a retired American manufacturer; *It Can't Happen Here* (1935), concerned with a future fascist revolt in the U.S.; and

Kingsblood Royal (1947), a novel about race prejudice. Lewis became (1930) the first American author to be awarded the Nobel Prize for literature. This period was also marked by the literature of the **escapists,** including **James Branch Cabell** (1879–1958), with *Jurgen* (1919) and *Figures of Earth* (1921); **Joseph Hergesheimer** (1880–1954), with *The Three Black Pennys* (1917) and *Java Head* (1919); **Elinor Wylie** (1885–1928), poet and novelist; and **Thornton Wilder** (1897–   ), *The Bridge of San Luis Rey* (1927), *Ides of March* (1948) (also p. 879); and by experiments with words rather than ideas carried on by **Gertrude Stein** in many books written between *Three Lives* (1909) and *The Autobiography of Alice B. Toklas* (1933). The most powerful literary impact upon the new generation of American writers was that of **Ernest Hemingway** (p. 1055), with his plain, factual, but evocative style (*The Sun Also Rises,* 1926, a depiction of an expatriate group; and *A Farewell to Arms* [1929], the best American novel of World War I). Other writers of the period include **Sherwood Anderson** (1876–1941), with *Winesburg, Ohio* (1919), stories of small-town life, a naturalistic interpreter of America; and **Ring Lardner** (1885–1933), a sardonic humorist exposing foibles through conversational speech—*How to Write Short Stories* (1924), a collection; *What of It* (1925); *Round Up* (1929); *First and Last* (1934).

Bridging the decades of the 1920s and 1930s was **Thomas C. Wolfe** (1900–38), whose first novel, *Look Homeward, Angel* (1929), was a recognizably autobiographical account of his early years. In *Of Time and the River* (1935) he attempted to capture the variety and vastness of American life. His lyric passages, his brooding depths, and his mastery of satirical portraiture combine to give him a unique place in American letters. Other writings: *The Web and the Rock* (1939), *You Can't Go Home Again* (1940), and *The Hills Beyond* (1941).

The pervasive economic depression of the 1930s resulted in a revitalized social problem novel, as exemplified by such writers as **James T. Farrell** (1904–   ), whose *Studs Lonigan* trilogy (1932–35) constitutes a naturalistic portrayal of squalor among the Chicago Irish; **Erskine Caldwell** (1903–   ), whose most popular novel, *Tobacco Road* (1932), recreates the contemporary Jukes and Kallikaks of the South; and **John Dos Passos** (1896–1970), whose outlook and style reached maturity in *Manhattan Transfer* (1925). His *U.S.A.* trilogy (1930, 1932, 1936), a Domesday Book of economic malpractices, employs several distinctive fictional devices, including a panoramic background, or "newsreel," and the "Camera Eye," the author's point of view toward his subject matter expressed in stream-of-consciousness passages. **John Steinbeck's** (1902–1968) *The Grapes of Wrath* (1939) is a memorable recreation of the economic dislocation of the Okies and the tragedy of the Dust Bowl. Other outstanding novels: *Tortilla Flat* (1935), *Of Mice and Men* (1937), *East of Eden* (1952). **William Faulkner** (p. 1026) wrote a series of novels constituting a bitter comedy of plantation family decadence (*The Sound and the Fury*, 1929, decadence as seen through the eyes of an idiot son; *As I Lay Dying*, 1930, psychology of a subnormal poor-white family with its use of naturalism to highlight the dominance of the irrational in human nature; *Sanctuary*, 1931, a sadistic horror story; *Light in August*, 1932, the ordeal of a pregnant girl; *Intruder in the Dust*, 1948).

1919–30. HARLEM RENAISSANCE. The post-World War I period brought an upsurge of black literary activity that culminated in the Harlem Renaissance of the 1920s. Under the influence of **W. E. B. DuBois** (p. 1017) and poet and novelist **James Weldon Johnson** (1871–1938), the movement was characterized by racial pride and interest in African culture and protest against bigotry and discrimination. **Langston Hughes** (1902–67), author of *Weary Blues* (1926), was the most popular poet, but equally accomplished verse was produced by **Countee Cullen** (1903–46) and **Claude McKay** (1889–1948). The latter also won renown as a novelist with *Home to Harlem* (1926), as did **Jean Toomer** (1894–1969), best known for his collection of rural sketches, *Cane* (1923).

1861–1950. CHANGING FASHIONS IN POETRY. Despite her individualism, the influence of **Emily Dickinson** (p. 1013), whose pieces were distinguished by sharp and unexpected imagery and poignant feeling, has been profound. Her metaphors made her seem to Amy Lowell a precursor of the Imagist School. Among the **conservative** poets of the earlier period were **Bayard Taylor** (1825–78); **Edmund Clarence Stedman** (1833–1908); **Thomas Bailey Aldrich** (1836–1907), editor of the *Atlantic* (1881–90); **Richard Watson Gilder** (1844–1909), reflecting the influence of Rossetti and other Pre-Raphaelites; **Edward Rowland Sill** (1841–87), whose *Poems* (1902) are marked by a classic finish and stoic idealism; **John Banister Tabb** (1845–1909), poet-priest whose poetry has been compared to Emily Dickinson and to the 17th-century English metaphysical poets; **Sidney Lanier** (1842–81), the outstanding Southern poet of the period, who attempted to produce in verse the sound patterns of music, revealing in his poetry exceptional melodic gifts and a fine rhythmical feeling ("The Song of the Chattahoochee,"

"The Symphony," and "The Marshes of Glynn"). Others in the period include **Richard Hovey** (1864–1900), whose poetry reveled in the joys of the open road (*Songs from Vagabondia*, 1894), **William Vaughan Moody** (1869–1910), best known for his verse dramas (p. 878), whose poetry combined lyrical treatment with attention to political questions treated along anti-imperialist lines; **Edwin Markham** (1852–1940), whose most popular poem, "The Man with the Hoe" (1899), was inspired by Millet's painting; and **Joyce Kilmer** (1886–1918), *Trees and Other Poems* (1914); **Paul Laurence Dunbar** (1872–1906), black poet whose verse suggested both apprehension and aggressive feelings about emancipation (*Lyrics of Lowly Life*, 1896).

The **revolt against traditionalism** was led by **Ezra Pound** (p. 1131), who served as an editor of *Poetry* (founded Chicago, 1912), a leader of the Imagists, and a sponsor of diverse authors. His disciplined metrical experiments, concern with a continuum of culture, and use of medieval and Chinese literature brought powerful new forces to play on modern poetry. His works include *Personae* (1926) and *Cantos* (1930–69). Pound's impact was especially notable in the work of **T.[homas] S.[tearns] Eliot** (1888–1965), American-born poet who became a British subject in 1927, with *The Waste Land* (1922), his major poetic effort, an epic compressed into 400 lines. In *Ash-Wednesday* (1930) he made clear his allegiance to the Church of England, and its value as a medium of social action is affirmed in *Murder in the Cathedral* (1935), a latter-day morality play. Eliot considered poetry as an escape from emotion and personality. His influence in turn was felt in the work of **Hart Crane** (1899–1932).

Other principal poets of the post-World War I period (many of whom published major works prior to 1914) include **Edwin Arlington Robinson** (p. 1138), heir to the New England tradition of Puritanism and Transcendentalism, who dealt primarily with ethical conflicts within the individual; **Amy Lowell** (1874–1925), a free-verse Imagist; **Robert Frost** (p. 1034), whose lyrics are marked by an intense but restrained emotion and a brilliant insight into New England character; **Vachel Lindsay** (1879–1931), known for his vivid imagery, vigorous rhythm, and dramatic conception (*Congo and Other Poems*, 1914); **Carl Sandburg** (1878–1967), also author of a monumental biography of Lincoln (1926–43), whose realism captures the American idiom; **Edgar Lee Masters** (1869–1947), *Spoon River Anthology* (1915), a bitter commentary on American urban standards; **Robinson Jeffers** (1887–1962), *Tamar* (1924), *Roan Stallion* (1925), poems of violence set in the headlands and valleys of California; **Conrad Aiken** (1889–1973), whose subjective poetry is marked by subtle musical rhythms; **Stephen Vincent Benét** (1898–1943), *John Brown's Body* (1928), a narrative poem of the Civil War; **Edna St. Vincent Millay** (1892–1950), whose *Renascence and Other Poems* (1917) exhibited technical virtuosity, freshness, and a hunger for beauty —her mastery of the sonnet form was demonstrated by *The Buck in the Snow* (1928) and *Fatal Interview* (1931); **Marianne Moore** (1887–1972), *Collected Poems* (1951); and **Wallace Stevens** (1879–1955), whose poems exhibit intensity, precision, and command of imagery; *Collected Poems* (1954); **William Carlos Williams** (1883–1963), who found a highly colloquial poetry in commonplace objects and everyday experience (*Patterson*, 1946); **John Crowe**

Ransom (1888–1974), whose hard, dry modern verse is typified by *Chills and Fevers* (1924); **Archibald MacLeish** (p. 1094), blank-verse drama, *Fall of the City* (1937).

1890–1970. LITERATURE AND SOCIAL CRITICISM. Chief critics of the period who considered literature from the point of view of social values were **Randolph Bourne** (1886–1918), *Youth and Life* (1913) and *Untimely Papers* (1919); and **Van Wyck Brooks** (1886–1963), who, in *The Wine of the Puritans* (1909), developed the thesis that the Puritan tradition crushed American culture, views which have been altered in later works, notably his 5 studies in cultural history, *Movers and Makers*, begun in 1936. His *America's Coming of Age* (1915) affirmed the prewar idealism of the younger generation. The most notable achievement in socioliterary criticism was *Main Currents in American Thought* (1927–30) by **Vernon Louis Parrington** (1871–1929). **Henry L. Mencken** (1880–1956), founder with **George Jean Nathan** (1882–1958) of *The American Mercury* (1924), which he edited to 1933, is best known for his aggressive iconoclasm toward American democracy and the cultural gaucheries of the American scene. His most important scholarly work is *The American Language* (1919–48). Leaders of **conservative criticism** were **Paul Elmer More** (1864–1937), **Irving Babbitt** (1865–1933), **Stuart Pratt Sherman** (1881–1926), and **William Crary Brownell** (1851–1928), with a neohumanist movement launched (1930) by **Norman Foerster** (1887–) and supported by More and Babbitt. Among the critics who rose to prominence in the 1930s were **Edmund Wilson** (p. 1186), whose wide-ranging interests were evident in works such as *Axel's Castle* (1931), and **Lionel Trilling** (1905–), whose *The Liberal Imagination* (1950) contained a number of seminal essays. Other important critical voices during this period were **Lewis Mumford** (1895–), **Kenneth Burke** (1897–), and **Allen Tate** (1899–).

1861–1951. HISTORIANS. The major impact on historical writing in the post-Civil War period derived from the "scientific school," as evidenced in the writings of **Henry Harisse** (1829–1910) and **Justin Winsor** (1831–97) and in the introduction of the seminar method in the universities by **Charles K. Adams** at Michigan (1869), by **Henry Adams** at Harvard (1871), and notably after 1880 at Johns Hopkins under **Herbert Baxter Adams** (1850–1901) and at Columbia under **John W. Burgess** (1844–1931). The founding of the American Historical Association, 1884 (with its *Review* appearing 1895), and the establishment of the *Political Science Quarterly*, 1886, were early evidences of the new trend. Major historians of the period include **Henry Adams** (p. 970); **James Ford Rhodes** (1848–1927), with his multivolume history of the U.S. since 1850; **John Fiske** (1842–1901), notable as well for his fight for Spencerian evolution (*The Outlines of Cosmic Philosophy*, 1874) as for his vitalizing early American history and stressing the European genesis of American institutions; **John Bach McMaster** (1852–1932), first of the important social historians; and a new group of objective analysts of (1) the colonial period: **Herbert Levi Osgood** (1855–1918), **George Louis Beer** (1872–1920), and **Charles McLean Andrews** (1863–1943), and (2) Reconstruction: **William Archibald Dunning** (1857–1922) and his disciples. But the chief impulse to the newer group of 20th-century historians came from the writing of **Frederick Jackson Turner** (p. 1172) and **Charles Austin Beard** (p. 980). In a paper entitled "The Significance of the Frontier in American History"

(1893) Turner pointed out that the frontier has been the one great determinant of American civilization, a point of departure from previous writers who stressed continuity of American institutions with Europe. Despite significant correctives of this thesis, it has had an exceptional impact upon the study of the roles of environment and geographical sections in U.S. history. The widest reading public in the post-World War period was achieved by Beard, whose major research was embodied in 2 early monographs, *An Economic Interpretation of the Constitution* (1913) and *The Economic Origins of Jeffersonian Democracy* (1915). *The Rise of American Civilization* (2 vols., pub. in 1927 with Mary Beard; vol. 3, *America in Midpassage*, 1939) revealed that Beard was no longer an economic determinist and stressed pluralism in historical causation. **James Harvey Robinson** (1863–1936) in *The New History* (1912) insisted that the historian had a duty to explain how things came to be as they are, to study all kinds of social facts, and to make "syntheses." Although Beard in later life distinguished between **history as actuality** and the **historical record** (involving selection and interpretation of the facts), and Robert L. Schuyler cautioned against the "present-mindedness" of recent historians, the prevailing trend down to the mid-century was to stress social, economic, and intellectual history and to relate historical data to contemporary problems.

In the 1930s and 1940s historical biography reacted from the earlier muckraking school, as well as from the critical and psychoanalytical studies of the 1920s (W. E. Woodward's Grant; Van Wyck Brooks, *Ordeal of Mark Twain*) to providing fuller and more sympathetic factual biographies (Carl Van Doren's Franklin, Douglas S. Freeman's Lee, Allan Nevins' Grover Cleveland, Carl Sandburg's and James G. Randall's multivolume Lincoln, and Dumas Malone's Jefferson).

1861–1952. LIBRARIES: MAJOR TRENDS. System and Technique: In 1876 the American Library Association held its first convention; established *Library Journal*, 1876. The introduction of methods of business efficiency and cataloguing was largely the result of the efforts of **Melvil Dewey** (1851–1931), who founded the New York State Library School (1887) and originated the Dewey "decimal classification." **Free Library Movement:** in 1881 **Andrew Carnegie** (p. 998) made his original offer to donate buildings for public libraries provided that each municipality would establish and adequately finance such a library by annual tax appropriations. By 1900 there were 1,700 free libraries in the U.S. with over 5,000 vols.; by 1947 there were more than 7,100 public libraries and 4,200 libraries of other kinds. The free library movement was further accelerated by the enactment in 1893 of the first state law (in New Hampshire) requiring townships to create libraries. **Founding of the New York Public Library**, 23 May 1895, out of the consolidation of the Astor (1848) and Lenox (1870) Libraries, and the Tilden Trust created by the will of Samuel J. Tilden (d. 1886). By 1952 it had in excess of 5 million volumes and was the largest public library in the U.S. **Growth of University and Reference Libraries:** Among the largest university libraries at the end of the period were Harvard, 5,400,000 vols.; Yale, 3,980,000; California (including branches), 2,717,000; Illinois, 2,384,000; Columbia, 2,000,000. Notable among the specialized reference libraries: American Antiquarian Society, Worcester, Mass. (older newspapers); Henry E. Huntington Library and Art Gallery, San Marino, Calif. (English and U.S. literature and history); Smithsonian Institution (1846), Washington, D.C., scientific and learned societies publications; Library of the Surgeon General's Office, U.S. Army, Washington, D.C. (beg. 1818), medical science; Folger Shakespeare Library, Washington, D.C., English books, 1475–1640.

1861–1960. PUBLISHING TRENDS. Dime novels had a sensational vogue, 1860–1900, inspired by the success of the "penny dreadfuls" in England and published by such firms as Beadle & Adams and Street & Smith. The pen name "Nick Carter" was used by such writers as John Russell Coryell, Frederick William Davis, Frederick Van Rensselaer Day, and others. **Juveniles:** Conspicuously successful down to World War I were the works of **Louisa May Alcott** (p. 973); **Frances Hodgson Burnett** (1849–1924), *Little Lord Fauntleroy* (1886); and **Booth Tarkington,** *Penrod* (1914). Despite serious competition from comic books, juveniles came to command an increasing share of publishers' attention after 1940, constituting in 1950, after fiction, the largest single category. **Consolidation** among major firms took place throughout the period, notably in the formation, 1890, of the American Book Co. to publish school texts. Greater centralization of publishing in the New York area developed. Other firms founded prior to 1901 included Henry Holt & Co. (1866 as Leypoldt & Holt); Macmillan Co., 1870; Doubleday, 1900 (merged with Doran, 1927). Of considerable advantage to U.S. writers was the enactment, 3 Mar. 1891, of an international **copyright law** to prevent pirating the works of foreign authors; revised 4 Mar. 1909 (amended through 3 June 1949). New literary and distribution trends were encouraged by the rise of new publishing houses in the 20th century, notably B. W. Huebsch, 1905 (absorbed by Viking, 1925); Alfred A. Knopf, 1915, with emphasis upon books by outstanding European authors; Boni & Liveright, 1917, with the moderate-priced "Modern Library" series (acquired by Bennett A. Cerf, 1925; since 1927 by Random House); Harcourt Brace, 1919; Simon & Schuster, 1924; Random House, 1927; and, in the field of scholarly and scientific works, by the establishment of **university presses,** notably Columbia, Harvard, Chicago, Yale, Princeton, and North Carolina. Two major distributing trends after World War I were the establishment of **book clubs** (Book-of-the-Month Club and Literary Guild both began distribution in 1926), with over 50 different clubs by 1947; and the successful distribution of reprints of popular books in the 25 ct.–35 ct. range, with Pocket Books (1939), Bantam Books (1946), and Signet-Mentor (New American Library) the 3 major organizations in the field by 1952.

1960 witnessed a rash of mergers in the book publishing business, including Henry Holt & Co. with Rinehart and Winston, the acquisition of Meridian by World, of the New American Library by the Los Angeles *Times-Mirror,* of Macmillan by Crowell-Collier, of Appleton-Century-Crofts by Meredith, and of Alfred A. Knopf, Inc., by Random House. Financing was chiefly done by public sale of stock, in most cases mergers being prompted by desire to expand in the textbook field.

1930–73. AMERICAN NOBEL PRIZE WINNERS in literature: Sinclair Lewis (1930), Eugene O'Neill (1936), Pearl S. Buck (1938), William Faulkner (1949), Ernest Hemingway (1954), John Steinbeck (1962).

1945–73. FICTION. Major novelists of the prewar era continued to produce work of merit, especially Faulkner (*Intruder in the Dust,* 1948), and Hemingway (*The Old Man and the Sea,* 1952). At a somewhat lower level, John

Steinbeck also remained productive (*East of Eden*, 1952).

Among the writers who established themselves with novels about World War II were **Norman Mailer** (p. 1095), with *The Naked and the Dead* (1948), and **Irwin Shaw** (1913–), with *The Young Lions* (1948). Simultaneously, the Southern school of writing continued to flourish with *All the King's Men* by **Robert Penn Warren** (1905–), *A Member of the Wedding* by **Carson McCullers** (1917–1967), both published in 1946, and the short stories and novels of **Eudora Welty** (1909–). In this school one might also mention **Flannery O'Connor** (1925–1964) and **Katherine Anne Porter** (1890–). Still other novelists who made their mark in this decade were **James Gould Cozzens** (1903–) with *Guard of Honor* (1948), **Nelson Algren** (1914–) with *The Man With the Golden Arm* (1949), and **Saul Bellow** (1915–) with *The Victim* (1947).

The 1950s produced diverse trends in American fiction, among them free-flowing picaresque narratives such as *The Catcher in the Rye* (1951), by **J. D. Salinger** (1919–) and *The Adventures of Augie March* (1953) by Bellow; the understated domestic tragedies of **John Cheever** (1912–) and **John Updike** (1932–), the most polished of which were, respectively, *The Wapshot Chronicle* (1957) and *Rabbit, Run* (1960); the anti-establishment "Beat" novels of **Jack Kerouac** (1922–1969), e.g., *On the Road* (1957); and the cold-eyed satires of the Russian émigré **Vladimir Nabokov** (p. 1112), of which *Lolita* (1958) was typical.

Most of these writers continued to produce fiction in much the same vein in the 1960s and 1970s, a period marked by 2 new schools of writing—"black humor" and "new journalism." The former, represented by such novelists as **Joseph Heller** (1923–), author of *Catch-22* (1961), was fiercely comic in its treatment of formerly serious or taboo subjects. Other "black humorists" who caught the critics' fancy were **Bruce Jay Friedman, Thomas Pynchon,** and **Donald Barthelmé**. The new journalism stressed a loose, fictionalized approach to reporting, as in the later works of Norman Mailer (e.g., *Miami and the Siege of Chicago*, 1968). **Truman Capote**'s "nonfiction novel" *In Cold Blood* (1965), based on a set of murders in Kansas, seems to have been the most lucrative of these works.

Ethnic writing was also prominent at this time. Fiction by black authors had attracted a considerable national audience as far back as 1940, when **Richard Wright** (1908–60) published *Native Son*. The real outpouring came in the 1950s and 1960s, however, with **James Baldwin** (1924–) and **Ralph Ellison** (1915–) leading the way. Ellison's complex, subtly textured *Invisible Man* (1952) created a high standard of excellence for black writing. Some of those who attempted to equal it were Willard Motley, Ismael Reed, and John A. Williams.

Jewish culture also received considerable attention in the postwar period. The best-known practitioners of the "Jewish novel" were **Bellow, Philip Roth** (*Portnoy's Complaint*) and **Bernard Malamud** (1914–), whose *The Magic Barrel* (1958) was widely praised.

The short stories and novels of **Joyce Carol Oates** (1938–) such as *Them* (1969) captured critical attention in the 1960s. Major contemporary novelists include **Thomas Pynchon** (*V*, 1963; *Gravity's Rainbow*, 1973) and **John Gardner** (*The Sunlight Dialogues*, 1972).

1945–1973. POETRY. Poetry in America has been generally less memorable than fiction since the war. Still, noteworthy contributions were made by

Robert Lowell (1917–), **Theodore Roethke** (1908–63), and **Richard Wilbur** (1924–), all of whom abandoned the experimentalism of Eliot and Pound, creating instead a verse that followed traditional poetic forms. They were modest in their choice of subject matter, which was frequently personal and immediate, in contrast to the sweeping issues of cultural decline that occupied Pound and Eliot. Lowell's work is best exemplified in *Lord Weary's Castle* (1946) and *Life Studies* (1959), Roethke's in *Collected Poems* (1966), and Wilbur's in *Things of This World* (1957).

Simultaneously, senior American poets continued to produce work of some merit. Robert Frost's *In the Clearing* (1963) was a hard, crystalline, occasionally coy collection of verse. A naturalized American, **W. H. Auden** (1907–1973) brought out a number of volumes of highly uneven work, including *Collected Shorter Poems* in 1967. The same year saw the publication of Marianne Moore's *Complete Poems*.

Revolting against the "academicism" of poets like Lowell, the "Beat" poets tried to return to the colloquial, bardic manner of Whitman, whose influence they traced through William Carlos Williams to Charles Olson. Some followers of this school were Robert Duncan, Gregory Corso, and the flamboyant **Allen Ginsberg** (1926–), who produced the most publicized work of the movement, "Howl" (1955).

Though better known as a novelist, **Robert Penn Warren** has won praise for such poetic efforts as *Selected Poems* (1966). Of about equal stature is **John Berryman** (1915–72), whose rather obscure *Seventy-Seven Dream Songs* (1964) is his most substantial work. Later figures of note included a talented group of women poets such as Denise Levertov, Anne Sexton and, most memorably, **Sylvia Plath** (1932–63), author of the brilliant collection *Ariel* (1965).

Schools and trends were hard to discern in the 1960s and early 1970s, but there were many individual poets of ability, though rarely of genius. Robert Bly, James Merrill, and Robert Creely were typical figures. Among black poets, **Gwendolyn Brooks** (1917–), remained the most highly regarded; *In the Mecca* (1968) is representative of her racially oriented work. **Imamu Baraka** (LeRoi Jones), the black playwright, has also evoked a certain degree of enthusiasm for his poetry.

1951–74. HISTORIANS. Since World War II historians like Perry Miller (1905–63) and Richard Hofstadter (1916–72) have stressed intellectual history and ideological issues, while at the same time subjecting the Populist-Progressive historians to a critical reassessment. Stressing agreement rather than conflict, the "consensus historians" have argued that the American Revolution wrought no basic change in the life of the community (Daniel J. Boorstin), have stressed the divergence of the American from the European experience on the ground of the absence in America of feudal institutions and the relative freedom from poverty (Louis Hartz), have denied that the American Revolution was fought to achieve democracy, as a comparatively broad suffrage already existed (Robert E. and B. Katherine Brown), and have defended the constitutional and ideological arguments of the Whigs as sincerely held and not opportunistic (Edmund S. Morgan). To the "consensus historians" the Constitution was not the repudiation of the Revolution, as the Populist-Progressive historians viewed it, but the fulfillment of the aspirations of its leadership.

One of the major contributions of American historians since the 1950s has been the issuance of definitive editions of the writings of American statesmen and other figures (Julian P. Boyd's Jefferson; Leonard W. Labaree *et al.*'s Franklin; Lyman H. Butterfield's John Adams; Harold C. Syrett's Hamilton; William T. Hutchinson, William M. E. Rachal, Robert A. Rutland, *et al.*'s, Madison), editions published in accordance with the canons of modern scholarship. These editorial labors have rekindled a nationwide concern for collecting, preserving, and microfilming historical manuscripts and public records long neglected, a concern most appropriate to the commemoration of the Bicentennial of the American Revolution.

In the 1960s and 1970s a group of "New Left" revisionists, of whom William Appleman Williams may be considered a spokesman, have traced the roots of alleged U.S. neocolonialism back to post-Civil War years, while challenging the standard view of the origins of the Cold War, shifting the blame for obstinacy and myopia from Soviet to American leadership. "Cliometrics," the wedding of history and quantification, has been exemplified by a number of distinguished demographic and family monographs for the colonial period along with a notable, if controversial, analysis of the institution of slavery: *Time on the Cross: the Economics of Negro Slavery, I,* by R. W. Fogel and S. L. Engerman (1974).

1962–73. LIBRARIES: MAJOR TRENDS. University libraries pioneered in the adoption of new techniques, making use of developments in systems analysis, computers, data processing, xerography. The automation of bibliographic processing, catalog search, and document retrieval began. The National Library of Medicine employed computer process for *Index Medicus* (1963). Florida Atlantic Univ. opened (1964) with a computer-based library operation involving (1) automated ordering, cataloging, and circulation, (2) methods of handling and disseminating information made possible by data processing but without an electronic information-retrieval system. The Univ. of Chicago Library received $500,000 from the National Science Foundation (1967) for development of integrated modular (building-lock) system of library data that will include bibliographic processing, catalog searching, and circulation control, while M.I.T. received $250,000 from the Council on Library Resources for Project Intrex, a study of remote access to centrally stored information.

Federal assistance to university libraries was expanded by the Higher Education Act of 1965, which authorized $70 million per year for 5 years for purchase of textbooks and materials to train students. By the period 1969–73, however, rising costs and declining federal support had left most American libraries in serious financial trouble. The New York Public Library, for example, reported a deficit of $1 million in 1972.

Other developments in the late 1960s and early 1970s included the opening of the Lyndon B. Johnson Library at the Univ. of Texas in Austin; a firm stand by the American Library Association against attempts by the government to obtain records of who had checked out books; a drive to unionize librarians; a U.S. court of claims decision (1972) prohibiting photocopying of copyrighted materials; an increase in the number of library schools offering accredited graduate programs to 57.

1960–73. PUBLISHING TRENDS. A sharp increase in book sales in the first part of this period was spurred in part by federal funds for education and library programs. The gross national book product jumped from $1 billion (1960) to $2.7 billion (1966); 28,762 new titles were published in 1967. By the early 1970s the book industry's gross was in excess of $3 billion, but the number of new titles had dropped to 26,000, while curtailment of funds for schools and libraries, along with a decline of leisure-time reading (from 21%, 1938, to 14%, 1974, according to a 1974 Gallup poll), combined with inflationary factors slowed sales of college and school texts, and were reflected in declining publishing profits.

Consolidation among major firms continued with the merger of Harper & Brothers with Row, Peterson, becoming Harper & Row (1962), and the purchase of G. & C. Merriam Co. by Encyclopaedia Britannica (1964). Publishing houses acquired by giant conglomerates included Random House, part of the RCA communications combine (1966); Bobbs-Merrill, which became an affiliate of ITT (1966); Holt, Rinehart and Winston, which was acquired by CBS (1967); American Book Co. and D. Van Nostrand Co., Inc., absorbed by Litton Industries (1968).

In the period 1968–73, sales in certain areas—notably fiction and textbooks—fell off markedly. Paperback titles soared but overall publishing experienced financial difficulties. University presses were especially hard hit, though a $2 million grant from the Mellon Foundation helped.

Technical breakthroughs in these years included the introduction of audiovisual cassettes, on which even the lengthiest literary works could be "recorded." One of the first of these to be undertaken in the new process was the 12-vol. *Oxford English Dictionary*. Posing a serious challenge to traditional school texts and library book sales were various types of "teaching machines," combining audio and visual materials, often supplanting and frequently supplementing the printed book in the elementary and secondary schools.

Theater

Theatrical performances in America date from 1665, when *Ye Bare and Ye Cubb*, an English play, was presented in Virginia. A formal theatrical unit, the company founded by Thomas Kean and Walter Murray, existed as early as 1749 in Philadelphia, and the Hallam Company, formed in England, toured the colonies for two years (1752–54). The Revolution interrupted most activity on the stage, but it quickly resumed in the 1790s. Landmarks in the evolution of the American theater include the emergence of Negro minstrelsy (about 1799); the establishment of repertory companies in most major American cities during the early part of the nineteenth century; the creation of theatrical syndicates (especially the one founded by Charles Frohman in 1896, which controlled booking throughout the U.S. for a number of years); the "little theater" movement (1900–19), which sought to reduce the scale of stage productions and increase the quality; the Group Theater founded in New York City in the 1930s to bring social consciousness onto the American stage; and the off-Broadway movement of the late fifties and early sixties. The preeminence of the actor was established early in American theatrical history. Some of the notable stars of the past, with the dates of their debuts, are: Edwin Forrest (1820), Charlotte Cushman (1836), Edwin Booth (1849), Ethel Barrymore (1896), and Katherine Cornell (1917).

As one might expect, American playwrighting followed the English lead for some time, producing the comedies of Royall Tyler, the blank-verse tragedies of William Dunlap, and, later in the nineteenth century, the comparatively realistic dramas of Augustus Daly and Clyde Fitch. There was no work of lasting merit, however, until the arrival of Eugene O'Neill, whose gloomy but poetic family tragedies reach from *All God's Chillun Got Wings* (1924) to *Long Day's Journey into Night* (1956). After O'Neill, American drama at least became a distinct entity, rather than a facsimile of European work. Its entertaining, occasionally profound, efforts in different modes include the brittle sophistication of the Broadway team of George S. Kaufman and Moss Hart; the ambitious poetic dramas of Maxwell Anderson; the social realism of Clifford Odets; the earnest humanism of Arthur Miller; and the romanticized Southern dramas of Tennessee Williams. Despite repeated comments voiced in the sixties and seventies about the ill health of theater in America, specifically its declining audience appeal and the lack of major playwrights, new companies were still being formed (often with the help of foundations), and newer dramatists like Edward Albee and David Rabe indicated the continued vitality of the creative side of the American theater.

1665. *Ye Bare and Ye Cubb,* the first English play known to have been performed in the colonies, was written and produced by 3 amateurs of Accomac Co., Va.; prosecuted but acquitted.

1714. *Androborus,* a satirical farce by Gov. Robert Hunter (N.Y., d.1734), printed but not produced.

1716. First theater in the colonies was erected at Williamsburg. Foreclosed 1723, it became the Town Hall in 1745.

1749–50. First American acting company was organized in Philadelphia by Thomas Kean and Walter Murray. Staged Addison's *Cato.* The company opened in New York (1750) in *Richard III* with Kean in the title role. Fourteen other Shakespearean plays were produced in the colonies. In addition to *Richard III,* the most popular were *King Lear* and *Katharine and Petruchio* (*The Taming of the Shrew*). The Kean-Murray company's New York repertoire included 24 plays (by Addison, Cibber, Congreve, Dryden, Farquhar, Fielding, Garrick, Lillo, and Otway). The company also performed in Williamsburg, Fredericksburg, and Annapolis.

1752. HALLAM COMPANY, sent to America by William Hallam and headed by his brother, **Lewis,** opened at Williamsburg with *The Merchant of Venice.* This company had a repertoire of over 40 plays, chiefly from Elizabethan and Restoration dramatists. Played also in New York and Philadelphia; disbanded in Jamaica, 1754.

1758. David Douglass, organizer of the American Company, opened in New York with Rowe's *Jane Shore.*

1766. Southwark Theater in Philadelphia, the first permanent theater built in the colonies, opened with Shakespeare's *Katharine and Petruchio.*

Ponteach; or The Savages of America, by Maj. **Robert Rogers**; first tragedy written on a native subject; unproduced.

1767. *The Prince of Parthia,* a tragedy (written before 1763) by **Thomas Godfrey** (1736–63), pioneer American dramatist, performed at Southwark Theater, Philadelphia; first native play to be professionally staged.

1775–83. REVOLUTIONARY THEATER. During the war most theatrical companies moved to Jamaica. Resolutions of the Continental Congress (24 Oct. 1774 and 12 Oct. 1778) recommended legislation prohibiting public entertainments. However, regular performances were given by the British troops in occupied towns. Howe's Thespians, an amateur group directed by Surgeon General Beaumont, opened its season in New York in 1777 and in Philadelphia in 1778. Clinton's Thespians gave their first performance at the John Street Theater (built 1767), New York, and continued intermittently until 1782. A number of propaganda plays were written in this period. Tory plays included *A Dialogue between a Southern Delegate and His Spouse on His Return from the Grand Continental Congress* (anon., 1774), Jonathan Mitchell Sewell's *Cure for the Spleen,* and General Burgoyne's *The Blockade of Boston* (both in 1775). The Patriot playwrights included Mrs. **Mercy Warren** (1728–1814), whose first play, *The Adulateur,* a satire on Gov. Hutchinson (1773), was followed by *The Group* (1775), based on the revocation of the Massachusetts charter (neither play produced). Other Patriot plays included *The Fall of British Tyranny* (1776), attributed to John or Joseph Leacock (1776);

an anonymous farce, *The Blockheads* (1776); and 3 plays by **Hugh Henry Brackenridge** (1748–1816), *The Battle of Bunker's Hill* (1776), *The Rising Glory of America* (1771), and *The Death of General Montgomery* (1777).

1787. *The Contrast,* by **Royall Tyler** (1757–1826; later chief justice of Vermont), the first American comedy to be produced by a professional company, performed in New York.

1789–97. EARLY AMERICAN PLAYWRIGHTS of this period included **William Dunlap** (1766–1839)—*The Father, or American Shandyism* (1789), *The Fatal Deception* (1794; published, 1806, as *Leicester*) and *Fontainville Abbey,* a Gothic drama (1795); **Samuel Low**—*The Politician Outwitted,* Federalist satire, published 1789; **Susanna Haswell Rowson** (c.1762–1824)—*Slaves in Algiers* (1794) and *The Volunteers,* a play dealing with the Whisky Insurrection (1795); **John Daly Burk** (c.1775–1808)—*Bunker Hill,* patriotic drama (1797); **Royall Tyler**—*A Georgia Spec, or Land in the Moon,* based on the Yazoo land frauds (1797).

1797. The tragedy *Douglas,* performed at Washington, Ky., the first recorded performance of an English-language drama west of the Alleghenies.

1799. NEGRO MINSTRELSY. At the close of the 2d act of *Oroonoko,* a play produced in Boston, Gottlieb Graupner, said to have been made up in Negro character, sang "The Gay Negro Boy," accompanying himself on the banjo; one of the earliest known origins of Negro minstrelsy, subsequently developed and popularized by Andrew Jackson Allen, Thomas Dartmouth Rice, Bob Farrell, and George Washington Dixon.

1806–18. Leading American playwrights included **John Howard Payne** (1791–1852)—*Julia, or the Wanderer* (1806, at New York's leading theater,

Park Theater, built, 1798; destroyed by fire, 1820); Payne wrote 64 plays; including *Brutus, or the Fall of Tarquin,* a tragedy produced at the Drury Lane, London (1818; N.Y., 1819). **James Nelson Barker** (1784–1858)—*Tears and Smiles* (1807); *The Indian Princess,* first Indian play by a native American to be performed (Philadelphia, 1808); its production at the Drury Lane, London (1820), under the title of *Pocahontas,* made it the first American play performed overseas after initial production at home; *Marmion,* based on Scott's poem (1812).

1817–32. ACTING DEBUTS. Noah Miller Ludlow (1795–1886), a leading figure in the theatrical history of the West, embarked on his career as actor-manager (1817); **Edwin Forrest** (p. 1031), first native-born actor to attain top rank, made his debut at the Walnut Street Theater, Philadelphia, as Young Norval in the tragedy *Douglas* (1820); **Edmund Kean** (1787–1833), the English tragedian, made his American debut in New York as Richard III (1820); **Junius Brutus Booth** (1796–1852), English actor, made his American debut at the Richmond (Va.) Theater as Richard III (1821). **James H. Hackett** (1800–71) made his New York debut in *Love in a Village* (1826); **William Charles Macready** (1793–1873), English actor, made his American debut at the Park Theater, N.Y., in the role of Virginius (1826); **Fanny Kemble** (1809–93), British actress, made her American debut at the Park Theater, N.Y., as Bianca in *Fazio* (1832).

1823–35. Notable American plays of this period included *Clari, or The Maid of Milan,* by John Howard Payne (1823, Covent Garden, London; N.Y., 1823; included the song "Home, Sweet Home"); *Superstition,* James Nelson Barker's best play (1824); *Charles the Second, or the Merry Monarch,* a comedy by John Howard Payne in collaboration with Washington Irving (London and N.Y., 1824); *Metamora, or the Last of the Wampanoags,* a tragedy by **John Augustus Stone** (1800–34), N.Y., 1829; first surviving dramatization of Rip Van Winkle by John Kerr (1829); *The Triumph of Plattsburgh,* by **Richard Penn Smith** (1799–1854), a play celebrating McDonough's victory in 1814 (1830); *Pocahontas,* by **George Washington Parke Custis** (1781–1857), 1830; *The Gladiator,* by **Robert Montgomery Bird** (1806–54), a drama of democracy, including antislavery sentiments (1831); *The Broker of Bogota,* a domestic tragedy by Bird (1834); *Jack Cade,* a play by Robert T. Conrad, dealing with a Kentish peasant uprising in 1450.

1828. The minstrel character and song *Jim Crow* introduced in Louisville, Ky., by **Thomas Dartmouth** ("Daddy") **Rice** (1808–60).

1832. Publication of *A History of the American Theatre* by **William Dunlap,** a pioneer work.

1836. CHARLOTTE CUSHMAN (p. 1009), American tragedienne and first native-born actress to attain top rank, made her New York debut (1836) at the Bowery Theater (opened 1826) as Lady Macbeth.

1837–48. Notable American plays included *Bianca Visconti* (1837), tragedy by **Nathaniel P. Willis** (1806–67), and Willis' romantic comedy, *Tortesa the Usurer* (1839); *The People's Lawyer* (1839), by **Joseph Stevens Jones** (1809–77), with the central character the Yankee type, Solon Shingle; *Fashion* (1845), an outstandingly popular social comedy by Mrs. **Anna Cora Mowatt** (1819–70); *Witchcraft, or the Martyrs of Salem* (1846), historical drama by **Cornelius Mathews** (1817–89); *The Bucktails; or, Americans in England* (pub., 1847), a satirical play by **James Kirke Paulding** (1778–1860); *A Glance at New York* (1848), one of the first "city" plays, by **Benjamin A. Baker** (1818–90).

1842. PHINEAS T. BARNUM (p. 980) opened Barnum's American Museum at New York.

1843. Virginia Minstrels, a quartette that included **Daniel Decatur Emmett** (1815–1904), appeared at the Masonic Temple, Boston, in what is regarded as the first accurately dated public performance of a genuine full-length minstrel show. Among the popular minstrel companies of the following 2 decades were the Dixie Minstrels, the Columbia Minstrels, the Christy Minstrels, Bryant's Minstrels, White's Serenaders, the Congo Minstrels, the Kentucky Rattlers, and the Nightingale Serenaders.

1849, 10 MAY. ASTOR PLACE RIOT, which took lives of 22 persons and caused injuries to 36 others, occurred outside the Astor Place Opera House, New York City. A manifestation of revived anti-British sentiment, it involved the partisans of Edwin Forrest and William Charles Macready.

1849–60. Notable plays included *Calaynos,* a tragedy by **George Henry Boker** (1823–90), produced at the Sadler's Wells Theater, London (1849); in the U.S., 1851. Other plays of Boker: *The Betrothal,* a comedy (1850); *Leonor de Guzman,* a tragedy (1853); *Francesca da Rimini,* a tragedy and his most highly esteemed work (1855). In addition, *Uncle Tom's Cabin* (1852), dramatized by **George L. Aiken** (1830–76); *Ten Nights in a Bar-Room* (1858), a play by William W. Pratt based on the novel of Timothy Shay Arthur.

1849–60. NOTABLE DEBUTS. Edwin Booth (p. 989) at the Boston Museum as Tressel in Cibber's version of *Richard III* (1849); **Joseph Jefferson** (1829–1905) at the National Theater, N.Y., as Jack Rackbottle in *Jonathan Bradford* (1849); **Lola Montez** (1818–61), American debut in *Betty the Tyrolean* at the Broadway Theater, N.Y.; **Edward Askew Sothern** (1826–81), American debut at National Theater, Boston, as Dr. Pangloss in *The Heir at Law;* achieved fame as Lord Dundreary in *Our American Cousin* (1858); **Laura Keene** (c.1826–73), British actress, made her American debut at Wallack's Theater, N.Y.; subsequently became the first woman manager in the U.S. **Dion Boucicault** (1820–90), Irish actor-playwright, made his American debut at the Old Broadway Theater as Sir Charles Coldstream in his own farce, *Used Up;* several of his plays produced in this period, including *The Poor of New York* (1857), *The Octoroon* (1859), *The Colleen Bawn* (1860); organized the **road show** (1860). **Lotta Crabtree** (1847–1924) made her first stage appearance at the mining camp of Rabbit Creek, Calif.

1856. First copyright law passed protecting dramatists against literary piracy.

1861–1900. VOGUE OF DION BOUCICAULT. After 1860 his most important plays included *Arrah-no-Pogue* (London, 22 Mar. 1865), *The Shaughraun* (New York, 14 Nov. 1874), and the revision of Charles Burke's version of Washington Irving's *Rip Van Winkle* (London, 4 Sept. 1865).

1867–75. IMPACT OF (JOHN) AUGUSTIN DALY (1838–99), both as playwright and theatrical manager. His first play was *Leah the Forsaken* (1862). *Under the Gaslight* (a realistic drama of New York life) produced in New York 12 Aug. 1867. Original plays include *Divorce* (5 Sept. 1870), *Horizon* (25 Mar. 1871), and *Pique* (14 Dec. 1875). Daly organized a stock company (1867) and opened his own theater in New York,

1869, starring **John Drew** (1853–1927), Adelaide Neilson (1848–1880), and **Maurice Barrymore** (1847–1905).

1870–89. COMEDY OF MANNERS. The influence of the French drama was reflected in the popular plays of **Bronson Howard** (1842–1908), including *Saratoga* (21 Dec. 1870), *The Banker's Daughter* (30 Sept. 1870), *The Young Mrs. Winthrop* (9 Oct. 1882), *The Henrietta* (26 Sept. 1887), and *Shenandoah,* the first successful drama of the Civil War (9 Sept. 1887). Other exponents of the social comedy form were **Augustus Thomas** (1875–1934), whose most notable plays include *Alabama,* a romance of Reconstruction (1891); *In Mizzoula* (1893); *The Earl of Pawtucket* (1903); *Mrs. Leffingwell's Boots* (1905); *The Witching Hour* (1907), the first of his realistic dramas; *The Harvest Moon* (1909); *As a Man Thinks* (1911); and *The Copperhead* (1919), starring Lionel Barrymore; and **William Clyde Fitch** (1865–1909), with his first success, *Beau Brummel* (1890), written for Richard Mansfield. His 30 plays include *The Climbers* (1901); *The Girl with the Green Eyes* (1902), generally considered his best play; *Truth Again* (1907); *The City* (1909). Best known of his 17 adaptations was *Sappho.*

1872–79. THE WEST IN THE DRAMA. *Davy Crockett* (1872), a frontier drama by **Frank Hitchcock Murdock;** Daly's *Big Bonanza* (1875), satire on speculation; Bret Harte's *The Two Men of Sandy Bat* (1876); Joaquin Miller's *The Danites in the Sierras* (1877); Bartley Campbell's *My Partner* (1879).

1880–1930. ERA OF THE THEATRICAL MANAGER. Dramatist, actor, and producer, **David Belasco** (1854–1931) wrote or adapted 75 plays and made pioneer contributions to realistic staging. His successful plays include *The Darling of the Gods* (1902),

Madam Butterfly (1900, in collaboration with John Luther Long), *The Return of Peter Grimm* (1911), and *The Girl of the Golden West* (1905). Coming to New York in 1880, he became stage manager of the Madison Square Theater, was later an associate of Daniel Frohman, and opened the Belasco Theater in 1902. Other notable theatrical managers of the period include **Charles Frohman** (1860–1915), who organized a stock company in 1890, opened the Empire Theater in 1893, and formed in 1896 the first theatrical syndicate, including Sam Nixon, Fred Zimmerman, Al Hayman, Marc Klaw, and Abraham Erlanger, which gradually extended its control throughout the U.S. From 1897 until his death (on the *Lusitania*) Frohman was the leading American manager, placing emphasis upon the "star system" (Maude Adams, Ethel Barrymore, and Otis Skinner) and the productions of established British dramatists. His brother, **Daniel Frohman** (1851–1940), opened the Lyceum Theater, N.Y. (1885), and was an exponent of the stock company. More commercialized was the impact of J. J., Lee, and Sam S. Shubert, who, beginning with the Herald Square Theater, N.Y., controlled some 70 theaters in N.Y. and other principal cities by 1924. During the period 1905–13 a **vaudeville empire** was erected by Benjamin F. Keith and Edward F. Albee, although the most conspicuously successful managers in that field were Oscar and William Hammerstein. Marcus Loew and William Fox rapidly accumulated theater chains.

1880–92. EARLY REALISM was exemplified in the plays of **James A. Herne** (1839–1901), notably his *Hearts of Oak* (1880), with David Belasco; *Margaret Fleming* (1890); and *Shore Acres* (1892).

1895–1913. Notable plays at the turn

of the century included **William Gillette's** (1855–1937) *Secret Service* (1895), a Civil War theme, and *Sherlock Holmes* (1899); **William Vaughan Moody's** (1869–1910) *The Great Divide* (1906); **Langdon Mitchell's** (1862–1935) *The New York Idea* (1906), critical of the marriage institution; **Eugene Walter's** (1874–1941) *The Easiest Way* (1909); and **Edward Sheldon's** (1886–1946) *The Nigger* (1909), *The Boss* (1911), and *Romance* (1913), with Doris Keane as Madame Cavallini.

1900–19. LITTLE-THEATER MOVEMENT. The first "little theater" in the U.S. was constructed (1900) for the Hull House Players, Chicago; the first in the academic world was **G. P. Baker's** (1866–1935) **47 Workshop** at Harvard (1912), later at Yale. Civic theaters developed rapidly, beginning (1919) with the Théâtre du Vieux Carré in New Orleans.

1908–48. MUSICALS. *The Black Crook* (1866) was the first long-run musical extravaganza produced in the U.S. **Florenz Ziegfeld** (1869–1932) originated a series of revues called the *Ziegfeld Follies,* featuring beautiful girls ("glorifying the American girl"), scenic invention, and comic sketches, and including such actors as W. C. Fields, Eddie Cantor, Fannie Brice, and Bert Williams. The **musical comedy,** a highly developed form in the U.S., combining opera, comedy, and ballet, flourished in the early 1900s with *The Merry Widow* and *The Chocolate Soldier,* but major innovations appeared in the 1920s largely as a result of the efforts of **Jerome Kern** (1885–1945), with his notable *Show Boat* (1928); **George** and **Ira Gershwin; Cole Porter;** and the team of **Richard Rodgers** and **Lorenz Hart** (beg. with *Garrick Gaieties,* 1925). An outstanding success was *Of Thee I Sing* (1931), book by George S. Kaufman and Morrie Ryskind. An innovation in

the field was *Pal Joey* (1941), a modern *Beggar's Opera,* music by Rodgers, lyrics by Hart, and book by John O'Hara. The most striking success was the presentation in 1943 of *Oklahoma!* by **Richard Rodgers** (p. 1140), and **Oscar Hammerstein II** (p. 1048), followed in 1949 by *South Pacific* (with Mary Martin and Ezio Pinza). The introduction of **ballet** by **Agnes De Mille,** dancer and choreographer, in such productions as *Oklahoma!, Bloomer Girl* (1944), *Carousel* (1945), and *Brigadoon* (1947) gave to the musical comedy of the 40s its major innovating feature.

1915–52. SCENIC DESIGN. Chief impact upon modern scenic design in the U.S. stems from 1915, with the designs of **Robert Edmond Jones** (1887–1954) for *The Man Who Married a Dumb Wife;* later *Hamlet* (1922), *Richard III, Othello* (1936), and *The Philadelphia Story* (1939). Other notable contributors in this field: **Norman Bel-Geddes** (1893–1958), *The Miracle* (1923), *Dead End* (1935); **Lee Simonson** (1888–1967), *Lilliom,* O'Neill's *Dynamo;* **Jo Mielziner** (1901–), *Winterset* (1935), *High Tor* (1937).

1916–46. EUGENE O'NEILL (p. 1118), the most notable American playwright, whose works were first performed at the Provincetown Playhouse, New York (*S.S. Glencairn*), a group interested in experimental drama. His plays varied from the naturalism of *Anna Christie* (1921) to the expressionism of *The Hairy Ape* (1922), and from the symbolism of *The Great God Brown* (1926) to experiments in combining Greek tragedy and Freudian psychology, as in *Mourning Becomes Electra* (1931).

1919, 19 APR. First production of the **Theater Guild,** Jacinto Benavente's *The Bonds of Interest,* at the Garrick Theater, followed by St. John Ervine's *John Ferguson.* Under the direction of **Theresa Helburn** the Guild, a subscription

PULITZER PRIZE PLAYS, 1918–51

1918. *Why Marry?* By Jesse Lynch Williams
1920. *Beyond the Horizon.* By Eugene O'Neill
1921. *Miss Lulu Bett.* By Zona Gale
1922. *Anna Christie.* By Eugene O'Neill
1923. *Icebound.* By Owen Davis
1924. *Hell-Bent Fer Heaven.* By Hatcher Hughes
1925. *They Knew What They Wanted.* By Sidney Howard
1926. *Craig's Wife.* By George Kelly
1927. *In Abraham's Bosom.* By Paul Green
1928. *Strange Interlude.* By Eugene O'Neill
1929. *Street Scene.* By Elmer L. Rice
1930. *The Green Pastures.* By Marc Connelly
1931. *Alison's House.* By Susan Glaspell
1932. *Of Thee I Sing.* By George S. Kaufman, Morrie Ryskind, and George and Ira Gershwin
1933. *Both Your Houses.* By Maxwell Anderson
1934. *Men in White.* By Sidney Kingsley
1935. *The Old Maid.* By Zoe Akins
1936. *Idiot's Delight.* By Robert E. Sherwood
1937. *You Can't Take It With You.* By Moss Hart and George S. Kaufman
1938. *Our Town.* By Thornton Wilder
1939. *Abe Lincoln in Illinois.* By Robert E. Sherwood
1940. *The Time of Your Life.* By William Saroyan
1941. *There Shall Be No Night.* By Robert E. Sherwood
1943. *The Skin of Our Teeth.* By Thornton Wilder
1945. *Harvey.* By Mary Chase
1946. *State of the Union.* By Russel Crouse and Howard Lindsay
1948. *A Streetcar Named Desire.* By Tennessee Williams
1949. *Death of a Salesman.* By Arthur Miller
1950. *South Pacific.* By Richard Rodgers, Oscar Hammerstein II, and Joshua Logan
1951. No award

group dedicated to raising the level of the American stage, scored brilliant successes in the 20s with Du Bose Heyward's *Porgy*, Shaw's *St. Joan*, O'Neill's *Strange Interlude*, Molnar's *The Guardsman* (Alfred Lunt and Lynn Fontanne), and Sidney Howard's *They Knew What They Wanted*.

1924–48. POETIC AND IMAGINATIVE DRAMA. Maxwell Anderson (1888–1959), coauthor, with Laurence Stallings, of the most popular U.S. war play of the 20s, *What Price Glory?* (1924), wrote such notable tragedies as *Elizabeth the Queen* (1930), *Mary of Scotland* (1933), *Winterset* (1935), *Key Largo* (1939), *The Eve of St. Mark* (1942, war play), and *Joan of Lorraine* (1947). In addition, he wrote a romantic verse comedy, *High Tor* (1937), and a musical comedy, *Knickerbocker Holi-*

day (1938). Other exemplars of the imaginative drama were **Paul Green** (1894–   ), whose plays include *In Abraham's Bosom* (1926), *The Field God* (1927), *The House of Connelly* (1931), *Tread the Green Grass* (1932), *Roll, Sweet Chariot* (1934), and *The Common Glory* (1948); **Marc Connelly** (1890–   ), who, in addition to collaborating with **George S. Kaufman** (1889–1961) on satires and comedies (*Dulcy*, 1921; *Beggar on Horseback*, 1924), wrote *The Green Pastures* (1930); and **Thornton Wilder** (1897–   ), *Our Town* (1938), *The Skin of Our Teeth* (1942).

1924–39. TRENDS. Drawing-room comedy done with wit and craftsmanship was notably exemplified by **S. N. Behrman** (*The Second Man*, 1927; *Rain From Heaven*, 1934; and *No Time for Comedy*, 1939) and by **Philip Barry** (*Holiday*, 1928; *Animal Kingdom*, 1932; and *The Philadelphia Story*, 1939). **Sidney Howard** (1891–1939) contributed to realism with *They Knew What They Wanted* (1924), *Ned McCobb's Daughter* (1926), and *The Silver Cord* (1926). **Elmer Rice** (1892–1967), who had contributed an expressionistic play, *Adding Machine* (1923), wrote a naturalistic drama, *Street Scene* (1929). An individualistic approach is found in **William Saroyan's** (1908–   ), *The Time of Your Life* (1940).

1935–39. WPA FEDERAL THEATER PROJECT, under the national direction of Mrs. **Hallie Flanagan** of Vassar College, brought back the theater to the road with low-priced productions of T. S. Eliot's *Murder in the Cathedral*, the Negro *Macbeth*, Orson Welles' and John Housman's *Doctor Faustus*, and *Pinocchio*. Most notable was its contribution of a new form to the American theater, the Living Newspaper, in which headlines were dramatized, including *Triple A Ploughed Under* (1936),

Power (1937), *One Third of a Nation* (1938).

1935–47. PLAYS OF PROPAGANDA AND SOCIAL CRITICISM were especially popular during the depression and in the early years of World War II. Representative were **Clifford Odets** (1906–63), *Awake and Sing*, 1935; *Waiting for Lefty*, 1935; *Golden Boy*, 1937; *Rocket to the Moon* (1938), **Lillian Hellman** (1907–   , *The Children's Hour*, 1934; *The Little Foxes*, 1939; *Watch on the Rhine*, 1941; *Another Part of the Forest*, 1947), and **Robert E. Sherwood** (1896–1955), *The Petrified Forest*, 1934; *Idiot's Delight*, 1936; *There Shall Be No Night*, 1940).

1951–60. OFF-BROADWAY THE-ATER continued its remarkable growth, stressing daring and experimental plays (*The Threepenny Opera* and the revival of O'Neill's *The Iceman Cometh*) and attracting performers of rank.

PULITZER PRIZE PLAYS, 1952–75

1952. *The Shrike.* By Joseph Kramm
1953. *Picnic.* By William Inge
1954. *The Teahouse of the August Moon.* By John Patrick
1955. *Cat on a Hot Tin Roof.* By Tennessee Williams
1956. *The Diary of Anne Frank.* By Frances Goodrich and Albert Hackett
1957. *Long Day's Journey Into Night.* By Eugene O'Neill
1958. *Look Homeward, Angel.* By Ketti Frings
1959. *J. B.* By Archibald MacLeish
1960. *Fiorello!* By Jerry Bock, Sheldon Harnick, Jerome Weidman, and George Abbott
1961.   *All the Way Home.* By Tad Mosel
1962. *How to Succeed in Business Without Really Trying.* By Abe Burrows and Frank Loesser
1965. *The Subject Was Roses.* By Frank Gilroy
1967. *A Delicate Balance.* By Edward Albee
1968. No award
1969. *The Great White Hope.* By Howard Sackler
1970. *No Place to Be Somebody.* By Charles Gordone
1971. *The Effect of Gamma Rays on Man-in-the-Moon Marigolds.* By Paul Zindel
1972. No award
1973. *That Championship Season.* By Jason Miller
1974. No award
1975. *Seascape.* By Edward Albee

1944–1962. IMPORTANT DRAMA-TISTS. O'Neill solidified his position as the preeminent American dramatist with *The Iceman Cometh* (1947) and the posthumous *Long Day's Journey into Night* (1957). After O'Neill, the most notable American playwrights were **Tennessee Williams** (p. 1185), whose poetic, heavily symbolic dramas included *The Glass Menagerie* (1944) and *A Streetcar Named Desire* (1947), and **Arthur Miller** (p. 1103), whose concern with ethical and moral dilemmas, particularly in family situations, found powerful expression in *Death of a Salesman* (1949) and *A View From the Bridge* (1955). The most highly regarded new dramatists to emerge in the 50s were **William Inge** (1913–73) and **Edward Albee** (1928–   ). Inge made his reputation with dramas of Midwestern sensibility, such as *Come Back, Little Sheba* (1950), a study of domestic conflict. Albee's masterpiece, *Who's Afraid of Virginia Woolf?* (1963), was also a story of marital strife. Some others who rose to prominence simultaneously or during the 60s were Jack Gelber, Arthur Kopit, Lorraine Hansberry, Murray Schisgal, Jack Richardson, and William Gibson.

1948–73. THE AMERICAN MUSI-CAL. The musical continued to flourish in this period. Among the most notable were *Kiss Me Kate* (1948), by **Cole Porter;** *The King and I* (1951), by **Rodgers** and **Hammerstein;** *Guys and Dolls* (1949), by **Frank Loesser;** *My Fair Lady* (1956), by **Alan Jay Lerner** and **Frederick Lowe;** *The Music Man* (1958), by **Meredith Willson;** and *West Side Story* (1958), by **Leonard Bernstein** and **Stephen Sondheim.** In the 60s and 70s the trend toward musicals with serious, even ponderous books was evident from *Fiddler on the Roof* (1964), *Man of La Mancha* (1965), *Cabaret* (1966), *Follies* (1971), and *A Little Night Music* (1973). Concurrently, however, shows like *The Fantasticks* (1960), *Man With a Load of Mischief* (1966), and *You're a Good Man, Charlie Brown* (1968) exhibited a lighter touch. Important also in this period was the emergence of a new permutation of the musical form, the "rock musical," commencing with *Hair* (1968), and including *Jesus Christ Superstar* (1970) and *Godspell* (1972).

1961–73. GROWTH OF COMMUNITY THEATERS. The appearance of regional theater throughout the country, though it was heavily dependent on foundation grants, was one of the healthiest signs in the American theater. The Association of Producing Artists (APA) became the first professional theater company backed entirely by university funds (subsidized by the Univ. of Michigan, 1962). The APA began Broadway seasons in 1966. By 1965, 24 cities other than New York had professional resident companies recognized by Actors Equity, including the Minnesota Theater Co. (1 May 1963) with Sir Tyrone Guthrie as director. Companies in 8 cities were aided by Ford Foundation grants. The Lincoln Center Repertory Co. opened with the premiere of Arthur Miller's *After the Fall* in the ANTA-Washington Square Theater, New York (23 Jan. 1964), moving (1965) to a permanent home, the Vivian Beaumont Theater in Lincoln Center for the Performing Arts. The American Conservatory Theater found a permanent home in San Francisco (1967). Among the major repertory successes were the APA's *You Can"t Take It With You* (1966), Minnesota's *The House of Atreus* (1967), based on the Greek *Oresteia* (1967), Arena Stage (Washington, D.C.), *The Great White Hope* by Howard Sackler (1967).

1964–72. PLAYS OF POLITICAL AND SOCIAL CRITICISM. A substantial number of plays offering a radical view of American life were produced during the 60s and early 70s. Barbara Garson's *MacBird* (1966), a blank-verse parody, took on the entire political establishment; Megan Terry's *Viet Rock*

(1966) questioned America's role in Vietnam; Jean Claude Van Itallie's *American Hurrah* (1966) satirized contemporary American mores; and Arthur Kopit's *Indians* (1969) promulgated a revisionist view of the American West.

New theater groups stressed political radicalism (peace, civil rights, sexual freedom) and dramatic radicalism (spontaneity, involvement of audience through dialogue and panel discussion, sensory communication, Eastern mysticism, and ritual). Among them were the San Francisco Mime Troup, the Living Theater, the Open Theater, and Cafe La Mama. The experimental new work of these groups soon became known as Off-Off-Broadway.

1967–73. CONTINUED GROWTH OF OFF-BROADWAY. In New York artistic hopes shifted from Broadway to the small Off-Broadway houses. The most exciting Off-Broadway producer in the 60s was **Joseph Papp** (1921–), whose New York Shakespeare Festival provided free Shakespearean productions during the summer at the Delacorte Theater; in 1967 it found a permanent home, the New York Public Theater. There it offered the works of provocative new dramatists such as David Rabe (1941–), e.g., *Sticks and Bones* (1971), and Jason Miller (*That Championship Season*, 1972). Papp assumed control of the 2 theaters at Lincoln Center in 1973.

1962–75. DECLINE OF BROADWAY. Broadway during this period suffered from ongoing financial woes and an increasing tendency toward slick, commercial offerings, especially grandiose musicals and lightweight comedies. The master of this latter mode was the phenomenally successful **Neil Simon** (1927–), of whose slight but entertaining work *The Odd Couple* (1966) is representative. However, several new theaters, including the Circle in the Square and the Uris opened in 1972–73, and Broadway was infused with new vigor during the 1974–75 season.

1964–72. BLACK PLAYS. The concerns of black Americans were brought to the attention of theatergoers in a series of plays by young black dramatists. *A Raisin in the Sun* (1959) by **Lorraine Hansberry** (1930–65) led the way and was soon followed by **James Baldwin's** *Blues for Mr. Charlie* (1964), **LeRoi Jones'** *The Toilet* and *The Slave* (1967), **Charles Gordone's** *No Place to Be Somebody* (1970) and **Joseph A. Walker's** *The River Niger* (1972). The cause of black theater was further advanced by the establishment of the Negro Ensemble Co. (1968) under the direction of Douglas Turner Ward.

1962–72. BRITISH IMPORTS. The 60s and early 70s were noteworthy for bringing a steady stream of British imports to America. *Oliver* (1962), a musical based on *Oliver Twist;* John Osborne's *Luther* (1963); Peter Shaffer's historical extravaganza *The Royal Hunt of the Sun* (1967); Harold Pinter's *The Homecoming* (1967); Tom Stoppard's *Rosencrantz and Guildenstern Are Dead* (1968)—these were a few of the many English works that made the Atlantic crossing successfully.

1972. OFF-OFF-BROADWAY ALLI-ANCE of 50 experimental companies, largely located in New York's Soho and Lower East Side, was formed and received financial assistance from the Theater Development Fund.

LONGEST RUNS ON BROADWAY
5 Jan. 1975
(*Variety*, 8 Jan. 1975)

Plays	No. of Performances
Fiddler on the Roof	3,242
Life with Father	3,224
Tobacco Road	3,182
Hello Dolly	2,844
My Fair Lady	2,717
Man of La Mancha	2,329
Abie's Irish Rose	2,327
Oklahoma!	2,212
Harvey	1,775
Hair	1,742
South Pacific	1,694
Born Yesterday	1,642
Mary, Mary	1,572
The Voice of the Turtle	1,557
Barefoot in the Park	1,532
Mame	1,508
Arsenic and Old Lace	1,444
The Sound of Music	1,443
How to Succeed in Business Without Really Trying	1,417
Hellzapoppin	1,404

LONGEST RUNS OFF-BROADWAY
1 July 1973

Plays	No. of Performances
The Fantasticks*	5,578
The Threepenny Opera	2,611
Jacques Brel Is Alive and Well and Living in Paris	1,847
You're a Good Man, Charlie Brown	1,597
This Was Burlesque	1,509
The Premise	1,490
The Blacks	1,408
Little Mary Sunshine	1,143
The Boys in the Band	1,001
One Flew Over the Cuckoo's Nest*	951

* Still running 1 July 1973.

The longest continuous run for a play in the U.S. was *The Drunkard,* which ran 20 years in Los Angeles and 9,477 performances, from 6 July 1933 to 6 Sept. 1953.

Film

Motion pictures in America have continually manifested the extraordinary diversity of their origins—Yankee technology, theatrical tradition, the visual arts, and even European experimentalism. By common consent, the most significant film pioneer in the U.S. was D. W. Griffith, who revolutionized film technique with devices like montage. The "giants of the earth" like Griffith quickly gave way (c. 1920) to the "studio system," in which films were the result of group efforts and studio executives held (and exercised, often brutally) final control. The major studios—MGM, Warner Brothers, Paramount, etc.— quickly followed the example of the stage by creating a star system. Soon the financial fate of movies was tied to names like Rudolph Valentino, Gloria Swanson, Clark Gable, Gary Cooper, and Elizabeth Taylor. Competition from TV, spiraling production costs, and a new breed of independent producers dissolved the old movie empires. In their place, very frequently at least, were low-budget productions that ignored the importance of "name players."

In the absence of individual genius and high artistic goals, the most distinctive American film contribution during the first half-century was the "genre" film. At their best, though, these films were very good indeed, high-spirited and entertaining. American Westerns (*High Noon*), musicals (*Singin' in the Rain*), gangster melodramas (*Little Caesar*), and detective stories (*The Maltese Falcon*) attained worldwide popularity. The situation altered a good deal in the sixties and early seventies with the shift to a younger and more literate audience and the rise of independent producers. It became possible once more for American directors to experiment and to use films as a medium for personal expression. Some of the more striking examples of these new tendencies are Peter Bogdanovich's *The Last Picture Show* and Martin Scorsese's *Mean Streets*.

The Silent Screen Period. 1889–1927

1889–1903. THE BEGINNINGS. Early efforts at developing moving pictures culminated in Thomas Edison's Kinetoscope, a machine with a light source and a peephole; pictures were produced by photographic film—a recent invention of George Eastman—which ran continuously in front of the hole.

1896. VITASCOPE, a mechanism for projecting film on a wall or screen, was developed by **Thomas Armat** of Washington, D.C. On 23 Apr. the first commercially exhibited motion picture was shown at Koster and Bial's Music Hall, New York. It used Armat's projector and Edison's Kinetoscope film.

1900. CINDERELLA, the first film to use "artificially arranged scenes" in progressive continuity, was produced by **George Méliès**, French producer.

1903. THE GREAT TRAIN ROBBERY, the first film narrative, was produced by **Edwin S. Porter.**

1905. NICKELODEON, an early movie house, was established in Pittsburgh by John P. Harris and Harry Davis. By 1908 between 8,000 and 10,000 were in operation, augmenting the need for expansion of film production facilities.

1909–14. EARLY STUDIOS. The pioneer film studios were Edison, Biograph, and Vitaphone, which, along with several others, formed the Motion Picture Patents Co. in 1909. However, a lawsuit by **William Fox** (1879–1952), independent distributor, broke the power of the monopoly. Subsequently, independent producers burgeoned, establishing Hollywood as the home of American movies.

1912. The first feature films to be shown in America, Italian spectacles, were imported by Adolph Zukor (1873–   ).

1913 SERIALS. *What Happened to Mary?* evidenced growing interest in serial films. Queens of the serial were Pearl White (*Perils of Pauline*) and Ruth Roland (*Ruth of the Rockies*).

1913–27. MAJOR FILM GENRES OF THE SILENT SCREEN.

Comedies. The earliest screen comedies were those of Mack Sennett, whose 2-reel films, featuring the Keystone Cops in a variety of burlesque situations, launched a new school of "slapstick" comedians. Sennet was soon transcended, however, by 2 of his protégés, **Charles Chaplin** (1889–   ) and **Buster Keaton** (1895–1966), who brought real genius to comedy of the silent period. Chaplin's "little tramp," a tragicomic small fry in baggy pants, endeared himself to the world in films like *Shoulder Arms* (1918) and *The Kid* (1921). Keaton's deadpan style, humanistic but unsentimental, was no less inspired and achieved equal popularity. *The General* (1927) and *The Playhouse* (1921) are among his best films. Other notable comedians of this era were **Fatty Arbuckle, Harry Langdon,** and the team of **Stan Laurel** and **Oliver Hardy.**

Westerns. From *The Great Train Robbery* (1903), the Western was one of Hollywood's liveliest and best-loved genres. The open spaces, the clear-cut conflicts, the heroic qualities had a wide appeal—even in Europe. The leading cowboy star in this period was **William S. Hart,** who portrayed a thin-lipped, 2-gunned protector of American virtues in such films as *The Return of Draw Egan* (1916). *The Covered Wagon* (1923), directed by **James**

Cruze, was another highly successful Western of the silent era.

Swashbucklers. A mode perfected and dominated by **Douglas Fairbanks,** the swashbuckler brought the swaggering romance and excitement of Dumas and other adventure writers to the screen. Fairbanks was particularly famous for daring athletics, virile charm, and faint self-parody, qualities that he exhibited most brilliantly in *The Black Pirate* (1926) and *The Three Musketeers* (1921).

Sentimentalism. Producers of the silent era found a rich vein of popular interest in sentimental tales of lost waifs and pure-hearted farm girls. The leading player in this mode was **Mary Pickford,** "America's sweetheart," whose boyish figure and wholesome face became an international symbol of virginal innocence. Among her most popular films was *Pollyana* (1920).

Exoticism. A rage for movies with faraway settings and glamorously swarthy leading men brought 2 "Latin lovers" to the summits of fame—**Ramon Novarro** (1899–1968) and **Rudolph Valentino** (1895–1926). Valentino, whose films included *The Sheik* (1921) and *Blood and Sand* (1922), was perhaps the preeminent matinee idol of silent films.

1912–27. MAJOR CHARACTERISTICS OF THE SILENT FILM ERA.

Star System. From about 1912 on, producers gave greater and greater prominence to their leading players, who became household names throughout the world. The result was the "star system," in which the presence of a Chaplin or a Valentino was deemed a form of box-office security. Other silent film stars included **Lillian** and **Dorothy Gish, Gloria Swanson,** and **Greta Garbo.**

Directors. With his first film, *The Squaw Man* (1913), **C. B. DeMille** (1881–1959) established himself as an immensely skillful entertainer and held this reputation through a series of spectacles (*Ben Hur*, 1926; *King of Kings*, 1927) which employed a formulaic blend of sex, pomp, and piety. Far more talented was **D. W. Griffith** (1875–1948), almost universally regarded as the father of the American cinema. Using hackneyed Victorian melodramas, Griffith nevertheless managed to develop a set of revolutionary film techniques in such classics as *Birth of a Nation* (1915) and *Intolerance* (1919). **Erich von Stroheim** (1885–1957) was second only to Griffith as an innovator in the silent film period. His ambitious, experimental movies, often dealing with bizarre subject matter, included *Greed* (1923) and *Foolish Wives* (1922). Stroheim was one of a series of foreign directors who brought their imagination and intelligence to Hollywood in the 20s. Particularly influential were exponents of the "German school," which emphasized unnatural but poetic lighting and other expressionistic effects they had borrowed from the German stage. Ernst Lubitsch and F. W. Murnau (*Sunrise*, 1928) were 2 of these.

Technical Innovations. The best-known technical breakthrough of the silent era was montage, a method popularized by D. W. Griffith in which different shots were spliced together to achieve a dramatic effect. An approach diametrically opposed to montage, the "long take," in which continuous shots were used, was developed by the German school.

Although films were predominantly black and white until the 1930s, experimentation with color began as early as 1908, when Charles Urban and G. Albert Smith developed Kinemacolor. In 1915 Dr. Herbert Kalmus founded Technicolor Motion Corp., whose first film was *Toll of the Sea* (1922).

Early Critiques of Film. During the silent era, most serious critics of the arts regarded movies as strictly a form of popular entertainment and, as such, inherently vulgar and inartistic. The leading exception to this tendency was **Gilbert Seldes** (1893–1970), who wrote perceptively and sympathetically on the infant medium. The poet **Vachel Lindsay** also contributed an enthusiastic full-length work on the movies, *The Art of Moving Pictures* (1915).

Censorship. Regulation of movies became an issue as early as 1907 when the Chicago police department was invested with power to suppress offensive films. Other cities, such as New York and Boston, showed that they too regarded the supervision of movies as a municipal prerogative. To provide self-regulation of the industry, the Patents Co. founded the National Board of Censorship, renamed the National Board of Review in 1915. In the same year the Supreme Court held that moving pictures were not covered by the First Amendment. Later efforts at self-regulation were led by Will H. Hays, who organized Motion Picture Producers and Distributors of America (1922). For 23 years the "Hays office" policed movie morals.

Studio System. The studio system originated in Hollywood with the formation of the Famous Players Films Co. (reorganized as Paramount) in 1912 and innovated "block booking." Loew's (Metro-Goldwyn-Mayer, 1924) followed in 1920, Warner Bros. in 1923, Columbia in 1924, and Radio-Keith-Orpheum in 1928. Last of the major combines was 20th-Century-Fox (1935).

The Sound Era, 1927–74

SOUND FILMS were developed by Lee De Forest (p. 1011), transcribing sound waves into electric impulses which could be photographed on celluloid and, when passed around a photoelectric cell in a projector, transformed back into natural sound. De Forest's Phonofilms (1923) were commercially distributed. The Vitaphone system, which coupled a phonograph record synchronized to projector motors, was used by Warner Brothers in *Don Juan* (6 Aug. 1926), starring John Barrymore, to produce sound effects. *The Jazz Singer* (6 Oct. 1927), produced by Warner and starring Al Jolson, was the first movie in which singing and spoken dialogue were heard. Talkies quickly replaced silents and comparatively few of the silent screen idols succeeded in making the transition to the new medium. Such stars as John Gilbert, Emil Jannings, and Douglas Fairbanks saw their careers blighted overnight. The survivors included Ronald Colman and Greta Garbo.

MAJOR FILM GENRES OF THE SOUND ERA.

Social Protest. The most serious and ambitious films turned out in Hollywood during the 30s were in the area of social protest. *I Am a Fugitive From a Chain Gang* (1932) criticized the prison system in the South; *Black Fury* (1935) dealt sympathetically with the labor movement; *Fury* (1936) indicted mob violence; *The Grapes of Wrath* (1940) focused on the problems of migrant farm workers.

Social protest all but disappeared from American films during World War II, but the postwar era brought attacks on antisemitism (*Crossfire*, 1947) and racial intolerance (*Intruder in the Dust*, 1949). Exposés of racial injustice continued to appear throughout the 50s and 60s (e.g., *Island in the Sun*, 1957; *Guess Who's Coming to Dinner?*, 1967).

Escapism. For the most part, however, American studio heads seemed reluctant to test the endurance of a mass audience and were most successful at producing enjoyable escapism, with Frank Capra's *It Happened One Night* (1934), starring **Claudette Colbert** and **Clark Gable**,

a highly popular example. Films that aspired to be serious drama tended to disintegrate into melodrama (*Detective Story*, 1951) or sentimentality (*How Green Was My Valley*, 1942). And even among the exceptions, most were taken directly from the stage (e.g., *A Streetcar Named Desire*, 1951).

The Musical. The only new genre of the sound era was the musical, but to many this represented Hollywood's major contribution to film culture. The first of these "all talking, all singing, all dancing" extravaganzas was *The Broadway Melody* (1929). In general, early musicals did little more than exploit the novelty of sound; revues (*The King of Jazz*, 1930), operettas (*The New Moon*, 1930), and Broadway shows (*Cocoanuts*, 1929) poured forth, nearly all of them clumsy and static. *Forty-Second Street* (1933) proved to be a major landmark, establishing the highly successful "backstage" formula, in which the characters were generally performers preparing a show. Later versions of this proven paradigm were *Gold Diggers of 1933*, *Dames* (1934), and *Babes in Arms* (1939). The outstanding innovator in this mode was the choreographer **Busby Berkeley** (1895–   ). Lasting popularity was achieved by *The Wizard of Oz* (1939).

A second musical tradition in the 30s was born when **Fred Astaire** and **Ginger Rogers** first appeared together in *Flying Down to Rio* (1933). Their intricate, swirlingly elegant dancing kept their fans entertained in *Top Hat* (1935) and *Swing Time* (1936), among other films. Yet another popular musical series in this decade was the operettas of **Jeanette MacDonald** and **Nelson Eddy**, commencing with *Naughty Marietta* (1935).

In the 40s, **Gene Kelly** became a dominant figure in musicals, introducing imaginative effects like animation (*Anchors Aweigh*, 1945) and extended ballet sequences (*American in Paris,* 1951). However, by the late 50s, original musicals had become virtually extinct, and only carefully packaged Broadway hits (e.g., *Oklahoma!,* 1955) were being produced. During the 60s even these dwindled, though a resurgence occurred with the remarkably lucrative *My Fair Lady* (1964), *Mary Poppins* (1964), and *The Sound of Music* (1965).

Gangster Movies. Though gangland subject matter had been seen in the silent period (e.g., *Underworld,* 1927), it did not become an important genre until the appearance of 3 classic efforts—*Little Caesar* (1930), *Scarface* (1932) and *Public Enemy* (1931)—which made their respective stars (Edward G. Robinson, Paul Muni, and James Cagney) world famous. These movies were fast, tough, laconic, and always reminded the audience that "crime does not pay." The host of imitations, all inferior to the originals, included *Manhattan Melodrama* (1934) and *The Roaring Twenties* (1939). The 40s brought *High Sierra* (1941) and *Johnny Eager* (1941), the 50s *New York Confidential* (1954) and the 60s *The Brotherhood* (1968), but these films lacked the fresh vigor of the first 3. *Bonnie and Clyde* (1967), *The Godfather* (1972), and *Godfather II* (1974) were among the few latter-day gangster films to be well reviewed and widely seen.

Westerns. The Western genre was well established by the time of sound movies, and such films as *The Virginian* (1929) and *In Old Arizona* (1928) perpetuated and amplified the traditions of pictorialism, simple frontier values, and ritualistic showdowns. A major plateau was reached with *Stagecoach* (1939), directed by **John Ford,** an archetypal Western that was copied for years afterward. The 40s brought a more psychological thrust to the prairie, particularly

in *The Ox-Bow Incident* (1942), *Duel in the Sun* (1946), and *Red River* (1948). In the 50s this trend continued with the immensely successful *High Noon* (1952), though *Shane,* released the following year, was a return to the old heroic, legendary format. Since the early 50s, Westerns have evoked less critical praise, but they have never lost their hold on the public, as witnessed by the success of *The Professionals* (1968). One of the few to find general critical favor was *Ride the High Country* (1962).

Comedies. Of the major silent screen comedians, only Laurel and Hardy and Chaplin succeeded in talkies. The former retained their vast following with *The March of the Wooden Soldiers* (1934). Chaplin reached new heights in the 30s with *Modern Times* (1936), a satirical treatment of technology, and *The Great Dictator* (1940), a devastating burlesque of Hitler. Later Chaplin films included *Limelight* (1952) and *Monsieur Verdoux* (1947).

The 30s were perhaps Hollywood's richest era in comedy. The inspired nonsense of the **Marx Brothers** was displayed in such hilarious farces as *Duck Soup* (1933) and *A Night at the Opera* (1935). More restrained was the cynical and misanthropic **W. C. Fields,** whose movies (e.g., *You Can't Cheat an Honest Man,* 1939) took deadly aim at the cherished beliefs of the American bourgeoisie. Simultaneously, **Mae West** enjoyed a brief reign as the movie's leading comedienne (e.g., *I'm No Angel,* 1933) before her risqué jokes brought the wrath of censorship groups down on her.

Side by side with these comedians was a group of excellent light actors, whose films provided yet another facet of American screen humor, urbane and sophisticated comedy. Known as "screwball comedies," these movies included *Design for Living* (1933), *Trouble in*

Paradise (1932), and *My Man Godfrey* (1936). The "screwball" mode tended to focus on the foibles of the upper class and to utilize the same performers— among them, **Cary Grant, Melvyn Douglas, Irene Dunne,** and **Carole Lombard.**

On the whole, comedy in the 40s was blander and less creative, though there were a number of bright spots: *The Man Who Came to Dinner* (1942) with Monty Woolley; the lively teaming of Katharine Hepburn and Spencer Tracy (e.g., *The Woman of the Year,* 1941); the topical humor of *Mr. Blandings Builds His Dream House* (1948). Also of interest were the witty social satires of Preston Sturges—e.g., *Sullivan's Travels* (1941). In addition, the movies produced one major comedian in this decade, the versatile **Danny Kaye,** whose foremost screen successes included *Up in Arms* (1944) and *The Secret Life of Walter Mitty* (1947).

The 50s and 60s did little to improve the state of American comedy. Exceptions to the general mediocrity were *The African Queen* (1951), a comedy-adventure with **Humphrey Bogart** and **Katharine Hepburn,** and *How to Marry a Millionaire* (1953) and *Some Like It Hot* (1959), in which **Marilyn Monroe** graduated from a sex goddess to a talented comedienne. Stanley Kubrick's black comedy *Dr. Strangelove* (1963) commanded attention, as did *A Thousand Clowns* (1965) and *Mash* (1968).

Detective Movies. Another movie genre that came to fruition in the 30s was the detective film. *The Thin Man* (**Dashiell Hammett**) (1934) presented the sophisticated husband-and-wife team Nick and Nora Charles. The hardboiled school, created by the fiction of Hammett and **Raymond Chandler,** surfaced in the 40s with *The Maltese Falcon* (1941), in which Bogart played and immortalized the tough Sam Spade. Bogart, the epitome of the detective hero, was equally tough as Philip Marlowe in *The Big Sleep* (1946). In the 50s, the detective tradition was carried on, not too memorably, in the Mike Hammer films (e.g., *I, the Jury,* 1953), from the popular novels by Mickey Spillane. However, by the end of the 50s this genre was more or less moribund.

War Movies. The first significant war film of the sound period was the celebrated *All Quiet on the Western Front* (1930), a powerful indictment of militarism in World War I. The gallantry of war was dealt with in 2 versions of *Dawn Patrol* (1930, 1938) and its boisterous, jovial aspects were featured in *The Fighting Sixty-Ninth* (1940). Not unexpectedly, production of war movies was particularly intense in the period 1941–45, when Hollywood turned out such morale-boosting efforts as *The Immortal Sergeant* (1943), *The Purple Heart* (1944), and *Back to Bataan* (1945). The most respected war film to emerge after World War II was probably *Paths of Glory* (1957), which was fiercely antiwar in its treatment of the French army during World War I. An interest in expensive, spectacular recreations of famous World War II battles during the 60s brought *The Longest Day* (1962) and *The Battle of the Bulge* (1965). In 1971 **George C. Scott** scored a great personal success in the title role of *Patton.*

Animated Films. Although some animated movies were produced in the silent era, they are primarily associated with the sound period. The giant in this field was unquestionably **Walt Disney** (p. 1013), who formed his own company in 1928 and brought out the first talking cartoon, *Steamboat Willie,* the same year. In addition to inventing such famous cartoon characters as Mickey Mouse, Goofy, and Donald Duck, Disney introduced feature-length animation in such films as *Snow White and the Seven*

Dwarfs (1937) and *Fantasia* (1940). Another important figure in the cartoon world was **Walter Lantz** (1900–), creator of Woody Woodpecker. Animation of a more offbeat, even avant-garde nature was produced by the UPA Studios.

1946–74. INDEPENDENT PRODUCERS. Hit hard by the rise of television in the 50s, the movie industry saw weekly attendance drop from an all-time high of 90 million in 1946 to a nadir of 40 million in 1960. Symbolic of the decline were RKO's sale of pre-1948 movies to TV and MGM's auction of sets and properties used in its most famous films. A new breed of independent producers began to appear, while simultaneously the role of the studios shrank to that of distributors and financial backers.

A positive outcome of the shattering of big-studio control was that American filmmakers suddenly found themselves with far more artistic freedom than ever before. The lifting of restrictions on content and treatment was evident from such independently produced, low-budget films as *Easy Rider* (1969), a savage attack on American conformity, and *Bonnie and Clyde,* an unorthodox biography of 2 bank robbers that impressed critics with its combination of humor and violence. Other attempts to deal honestly and intelligently with American life were *The Last Picture Show* and *Desperate Characters,* both 1972.

Black Films. One of the major phenomena of American films during the early 70s was the appearance of films created by blacks and aimed specifically at black audiences. Though damned by most critics, the financially successful *Cotton Comes to Harlem* (1970) and *Shaft* (1971) have given considerable impetus to this movement and created a place in the industry for black directors like **Ossie Davis** and **Gordon Parks.**

1946–74. THE DIMMING OF THE STAR SYSTEM. The star system continued to be a major factor in Hollywood after the advent of sound and the names of well-known players were generally billed over the title of the picture. MGM acquired the most impressive galaxy, boasting "more stars than there are in the skies." Prior to World War II most leading men were either rugged types cast in a heroic mold, such as Gary Cooper and John Wayne, or suave sophisticates like Melvyn Douglas and William Powell. These matinee idols often played opposite such equally glamorous actresses as Greta Garbo, Joan Crawford, and Ann Sheridan.

Following the war, a new acting style, called "method acting," developed in New York's Actors Studio, and spread to Hollywood. Stressing a more naturalistic approach to acting, it found its outstanding practitioner in **Marlon Brando,** whose studied inarticulateness and emotional turbulence became world-famous, especially through his powerful characterization of Stanley Kowalski in *A Streetcar Named Desire.* Other method actors who gained celebrity in the postwar era were Montgomery Clift, Rod Steiger, and the short-lived James Dean.

The star system declined somewhat in the 60s when many producers found themselves unable to afford expensive performers and had to rely on unknowns. The result was films like *Mash* and *Easy Rider,* which managed to turn a handsome profit without benefit of big-name actors. Frequently, however, graduates of these modestly produced ventures— e.g., **Elliott Gould**—became high-priced stars themselves.

DIRECTORS. American directors of the sound period were notoriously subject to the restrictions (and interference) of the studios they worked for. Still, the best of them managed to create films of imagination, energy, and beauty. None was more widely respected than **John Ford** (1895–1973), best known for his Westerns, beginning with *Stagecoach* and including *Wagonmaster* (1956). Of similar stature was **Orson Welles** (1915–   ), who at the age of 25 produced, directed, and starred in what many critics regard as the finest American film of the sound era—*Citizen Kane* (1941). Also highly esteemed were the versatile **John Huston** (1906–   ), director of *The Maltese Falcon* (1941) and *The African Queen,* and the clever satirist **Preston Sturges** (1898–1959). Another of the ablest products of the studio system was **Howard Hawks** (1896–   ), a superb craftsman who was at his best in the comedies *Twentieth Century* (1934) and *His Girl Friday* (1940) and in the Western *Red River.* Equally craftsmanlike but more sophisticated was **Fred Zinnemann** (1907–   ), whose feeling for character was evident in *High Noon* and *From Here to Eternity* (1953). As in the silent epoch, foreign directors of note brought their talents to America, among them the Englishman **Alfred Hitchcock,** whose long series of ingenious thrillers included *Foreign Correspondent* (1940) and *North by Northwest* (1959).

1934–73. CENSORSHIP. The early talkies made frequent use of fairly racy material and a storm of protest by concerned moralists frightened the Hays office into creating a highly restrictive code (1934) governing permissible language and subject matter in films. Eric Johnson succeeded Hays in 1945 and perpetuated the code. When Johnson was replaced by Jack Valenti in 1966, the old system of puritanical restraints was lifted from movies in favor of a rating system that labeled each film according to the frankness of its content (1968). The result was a marked increase in candor, obscenity, violence, and frank, even sordid, subject matter in American movies. In particular, pornography such as *Deep Throat* has thrived alongside attempts to deal maturely with formerly forbidden subjects (e.g., *Carnal Knowledge,* 1971).

In a landmark decision, the Supreme Court ruled that films are protected by the First Amendment (1952). A later (1959) high court ruling on a French version of *Lady Chatterley's Lover* established the principle that film material must be "utterly without redeeming social value" to be regarded as pornographic. However, in 1973 the more conservative Burger court decreed that local community standards were sufficient to determine whether censorship should be imposed, opening the way for more official, if highly inconsistent, suppression of films.

CRITICAL RESPONSES. The American film continued to receive little in the way of serious critical attention during the 30s and early 40s. A voice in the wilderness during this period was **James Agee** (1909–55), whose sensitive and impassioned critiques in *The Nation* are still looked on as the pinnacle of American movie criticism. Following World War II, critics writing in the French journal *Cahiers du Cinema* began to explore American films with great interest and enthusiasm. One of the most influential was **François Truffaut,** later a director of note, who helped originate the *auteur* theory of film criticism, which holds that a great director will impose his style and vision on his movies, even when working with poor actors or an inferior script. The auteur theory took hold in America, where its foremost proponent is **Andrew Sarris** (1928–   ), and helped to bring about a reappraisal of American films during the 60s and a recognition of movies as an art form. Among the critics who have helped to put them there are Stanley Kauffmann, Dwight Macdonald, and Pauline Kael.

1935–74. TECHNICAL INNOVA-TIONS. The major technical innovation of the 30s was the perfection and general adoption of color in American movies. Walt Disney's *Flowers and Trees* (1935) was the first picture to utilize successfully the 3-color process of **Technicolor,** while such films as *The Wizard of Oz* and *Gone With the Wind* (both 1939) brought the use of color to a high level of effectiveness. During the 50s, the crippling competition of TV sent the movie industry in search of splashy new techniques and it came up with various wide-screen processes, the first being *Cinerama* by Fred Waller (1952) and the most famous was CinemaScope, introduced by 20th Century-Fox in *The Robe* (1953). 3-D, a method requiring that the viewer wear special glasses to create a 3-dimensional effect, had its brief, spectacular day in films like *House of Wax* (1953).

SCREENWRITERS. Although for most critics, the director is the primary creative force behind a movie, the contribution of scenarists cannot be ignored. The most famous of these was undoubtedly **Ben Hecht** (1894–1964), author of *Nothing Sacred* (1937), *Gunga Din* (1939), and dozens of other films. Hecht, with his crisp, workmanlike approach, personified the smooth professionalism of Hollywood scenarists. Others who made important contributions were **Nunnally Johnson, Dudley Nichols,** and **Jules Furthman.**

ALL-TIME FILM LEADERS
(Estimated gross film rentals from U.S. and Canada, *Variety,* 8 Jan. 1975*)

Title and Release	
The Godfather (Paramount, 1972)	$85,747,184
The Sound of Music (20th Century-Fox, 1965)	83,891,000
Gone With the Wind (Selznick-MGM, 1939)	70,179,000
The Sting (Universal, 1973)	68,450,000
The Exorcist (Warner, 1973)	66,300,000
Love Story (Paramount, 1970)	50,000,000
The Graduate (Avco-Embassy, 1968)	49,978,000
Airport (Universal, 1970)	45,300,000
Doctor Zhivago (MGM, 1965)	44,390,000
Butch Cassidy and the Sundance Kid (Fox, 1969)	44,000,000
The Ten Commandments (Paramount, 1957)	43,000,000
The Poseidon Adventure (20th Century-Fox, 1972)	42,500,000
Mary Poppins (Disney-Buena Vista, 1964)	42,000,000
American Graffiti (Universal, 1973)	41,200,000
Mash (20th Century-Fox, 1970)	40,500,000
Ben-Hur (MGM, 1959)	36,550,000
Fiddler on the Roof (United Artists, 1971)	35,550,000
My Fair Lady (Warner, 1964)	01,000,000
Billy Jack (Warner, 1971)	31,000,000
Thunderball (Eon-United Artists, 1965)	28,300,000

* The Birth of a Nation (Griffith, 1915), which may have grossed as much as $50,000,000, is omitted because of unreliable data.

Fine Arts and Architecture

The American colonies produced no Rembrandt or Rubens, no Palladio or Sir Christopher Wren, but they did develop skilled craftsmen with integrity and imagination, and artists with a special gift for realistic portraiture. The earliest

American painters, the self-taught limners, whose portraits made up in qualities of innocence and vigor what they lacked in technique, were supplanted as the early eighteenth century began by European-trained artists, who spawned a school of painting that included such masters as Robert Feke and John Singleton Copley, and artists who used a broad historical canvas like Benjamin West and his protégé, John Trumbull. Romanticism in the early national period was exemplified by Washington Allston, and during the antebellum period an authentic native school of landscape painting emerged called the Hudson River School. In the post-Civil War years two expatriates, John Singer Sargent and James A. McNeill Whistler, attained international reputations by their facile brushwork and experimentation with light and color, while George Inness and Winslow Homer captured the American land- and seascape and Thomas Eakins demonstrated his profound mastery of the human form. The early twentieth century was marked by a revolt against the genteel tradition in the arts, signalized by the Armory Show (1913), and, by the 1920s, American artists were running the gamut of Cubism, Expressionism, and Abstractionism. The Federal Art Project of the New Deal era encouraged mural painting and provided the means of survival for a generation of talented painters, including Jackson Pollock, Willem de Kooning, and Mark Rothko, who were to make their mark as Abstract Expressionists.

Architecture in the colonies was influenced by the building style and techniques of the countries of the colonists' origin, and by the end of the seventeenth century prosperous planters and merchants reflected the affluent Renaissance taste of Europe. Dominating the east coast was the English Renaissance style, developed much earlier by Inigo Jones, and introduced by talented amateur architects like Thomas Jefferson and Peter Harrison, while French and Spanish architectural styles were introduced in areas under the control of these two powers. The early national and antebellum years were marked, first, by the dominance of the classical style in public buildings, then by the Gothic style, used not only for churches, but also for mansions, factories, and prisons. In the years 1860–1920 structural and mechanical developments made possible spectacular architectural advances, including the introduction of the steel skeleton, the elevator, and electricity. By the 1920s enthusiasm for the skyscraper became an obsession. In the 1930s the International style was in competition with the streamlined moderne, but the former dominated the urban scene for more than a decade after World War II, reaching its peak in the early 1960s, until such innovative architects as Louis I. Kahn and Robert Venturi broke away from the rectangular, International-style boxes, and founded the new movement of supermannerism, a rebellion against the stilted formality of the International style.

1650–1721. EARLY AMERICAN PAINTING. The **limners,** the earliest American painters, were probably self-taught. Their portraits are characterized by an excess of realistic detail and a refreshing naïveté (*The Mason Children,* c.1670; *Mrs. Freake and Baby Mary,* c.1674). Among the earliest known limners were John Foster (1648–81) and **Thomas Smith** (active c.1650–85), a sea captain, whose paintings shared the Puritan obsession with death. Later New England limners after 1700 reflect English influence more directly. The earlier rugged energy is replaced by shallow elegance and a looser technique (Pierpont limner, 1711; Nathaniel Emmons [d. 1740]; J. Cooper [active c.1714–18]; the Pollard limner, 1721). In New Netherland and New York the **patroon painters,** 1660–c.1710 (Stuyvesant limner, Provoost limner [c.1700]; *Grootje Vas,* 1723, possibly by Pieter Vanderlyn), portrayed the upper class in an attempted style of elegance after European models.

1708–17. German-born Justus Englehardt Kühn introduced at Annapolis a provincial translation of the European tradition of aristocratic portraiture (*Eleanor Darnall,* c.1712).

1729–50. NEW ENGLAND REVIVAL was inaugurated by **John Smibert** (1688–1751), who staged the first art exhibition in the American colonies in Boston, 1730. His severe middle class realism, variant of the English portrait tradition (*Bishop Berkeley and his Entourage*), created a school that was to include the colonial masters **Robert Feke** (c.1705–c.1750) and **John Singleton Copley** (p. 1007). Feke, the first supposedly American-born painter of recognized talent, painted chiefly in Newport (R.I.), Boston, and Philadelphia, between c.1741 and c.1750. He was a skillful draftsman with a fine sense of color (*Isaac Royall*

and Family, 1741; *Rev. Thos. Hiscox,* 1745; *Mrs. Charles Willing,* 1746; *Charles Apthorp,* 1748), but no naturalist.

1740–74. In Charleston, S.C., the Swiss Jeremiah Theüs dominated local portraiture with his version of the "international" style derived from Lely and Kneller.

1760–63. BENJAMIN WEST (1738–1820) left Philadelphia for Rome to study, setting up his studio 3 years later in London.

1760–74. In Boston **Copley** painted his early realistic masterpieces (*Boy with Squirrel* [Henry Pelham], c.1765).

1761. John Hesselius (1728–78), son of the Swedish-born painter Gustavus Hesselius, painted *Charles Calvert and His Colored Slave;* had a wide patronage from Philadelphia to Virginia.

1765–81. In his famous London studio **West** played host to American artists, determining in large measure the character of American painting. His group included Matthew Pratt (1734–1805; returned to America, 1768), Earl, Charles Willson Peale, Copley, Stuart, and Trumbull. His romanticized characterization of *The Death of Wolfe* (1771), containing recognizable portraits, achieved wide popularity. In 1772 West became historical painter to George III.

1778–92. RALPH EARL (1751–1801), after whose paintings Amos Doolittle made popular engravings of 4 scenes of the early Revolution, went to London to study (probably with West); returned to the U.S., 1785. His mature portraits (*Chief Justice Oliver Ellsworth and His Wife,* 1792) are notable for the importance of placing setting and landscape in a personal relationship to his sitters.

1781–93. The highly successful London period of **Gilbert Stuart** (p. 1162). In this period also **Charles Willson Peale** (p. 1123) established himself at Philadelphia (*Benjamin Franklin,* 1787).

1792. Benjamin West succeeded Sir Joshua Reynolds as president of the Royal Academy.

c.1681–1789. EARLY SCULPTURE. Seventeenth-century efforts were chiefly in the field of gravestone carving in New England (Thomas Child, 1655–1706). Native sculptors were slow in appearing; 18th-century activity was chiefly the carving of ship figureheads (Senior Simeon Skillin, c.1741) and weathervanes (Sherm Drowne). **Patience Lovell Wright** (1725–86), a wax sculptress, was a U.S. secret agent in Great Britain during the Revolution (modeling George III, Queen Charlotte, and other notables), and her son, **Joseph** (1756–93), who studied under Trumbull and West, was commissioned to make a statue of Washington, but all that survived are 2 medallions based on a life mask (1783–84). Appointed (1792) diesinker of the U.S. Mint, he designed numerous coins and medals. When Franklin was commissioned by Congress, 1776, to find a sculptor to carve the memorial tablet to Gen. Richard Montgomery, he selected Jean-Jacques Caffieri; and Jefferson subsequently selected **Jean-Antoine Houdon** (1741–1828) to make a marble effigy of Washington, which he executed from a life mask (1785).

EARLY ARCHITECTURE. In their early architecture the colonists attempted to duplicate in their new homes the forms and atmosphere of those they had left, in areas with different materials and different climates. Three European countries provided the chief models—Spain, in Florida, later in the Southwest and California; France, in the Mississippi Valley; and England, along the Atlantic coast—with 3 diverging types developing: **Spanish** (Saint Augustine: Castillode San Marcos, 1672; the Cathedral [1793–97]; and a few early houses), **French** (New Orleans, planned 1721; Ste. Genevieve, early houses; Cahokia, Ill., *Courthouse,*

c.1737), and **English** (which eventually became the major influence).

1607–c.1640. EARLIEST ENGLISH HOUSES were shacks based either on Indian "wigwams" (round-roofed structures of oblong plan) or palisadoed dwellings (reconstruction of old Salem); but in Virginia timber-framed and even brick houses were built in urban fashion by 1612, and in the more northern areas permanent timber-framed houses were the rule by the 1630s or 40s. **Log cabins** (logs laid around **horizontally**) were unknown in England, and were introduced by the Swedes on the Delaware (*Lower Log House,* Darby, Pa., 1640); ultimately the Scotch-Irish made them the prevailing frontier dwelling.

1641–1700. Evolution of the "Colonial" Style. Seventeenth-century architecture remained largely medieval, a product of unsophisticated craftsmanship, but with variants from European standards, chiefly caused by the more severe climate. Characteristic clapboard or shingle-covered walls (found occasionally in southeastern England) were used, rather than typical English "half-timber" filled with brick or plaster, because they were more weather-proof. Windows were small leaded casements. Early examples of this type (upper story overhang, small windows, inconspicuous doorways, central chimney, and often characteristic "salt box" roof sloping to the rear) have survived in Connecticut, Rhode Island, and Massachusetts. The smaller houses of the less well-to-do settlers were frame structures of from 1 to 1½ stories, with relatively tall and simple gable or gambrel roofs. Roof slopes tended to become less steep in accordance with weather conditions.

The current English **Jacobean** style was introduced in details, especially in the South, notably in Bacon's Castle (c.1655), Surrey Co., Va., a good example of full Jacobean design, with its geometrical gables, clustered chimneys, and stair tower, and in **Fairfield,** or Carter's Creek, Va. (1692). The style was also found in Middleton Place, Ashley River, S.C.; in the old *Landgrave Smith Back River* plantation house; and in the *Peter Sergeant House* (*Province House*), Boston. *Malvern Hill,* Va., represents the transition from Jacobean to more classic Renaissance. Timber construction continued to prevail in New England; brick, stone, and wood were used in the Middle Colonies (with stone predominating in portions of Pennsylvania, New Jersey, and Delaware); and brick houses were generally constructed in the South (in Virginia as early as 1636), becoming the prevailing material for the better dwellings. The brick was sometimes stuccoed in Charleston; wood was more general in North Carolina).

1700–50. Increasing prosperity, greater numbers of skilled craftsmen, and the increased importation of architectural books and building details rapidly modified the earlier trends, and permitted a more sophisticated following of the fashions of the mother country. The English **baroque** style (of Wren and Gibbs) was now adopted for more pretentious homes, with symmetrical façades, the double-hung window (replacing the casement type), and the elimination of overhangs. Pediments and pilasters were added in the later period to embellish the central doorway. The better houses were in brick or stone, but wooden houses often imitated stone details.

c.1751–89. Growing national feeling and closer commercial and political contacts produced increasing similarities in colonial architecture and a greater freedom in using English precedent. An American architecture was being created. The term **Georgian** came to be applied to houses of 2 or 3 stories built upon a strictly rectangular plan, with windows regularly spaced, the use of dormers, with horizontal lines emphasized, the small entry, or porch, replaced by a spacious center hall, with 2 chimneys, one on each side of the hall, in place of the central chimney (*Hooper House,* Marblehead, 1745; *Longfellow House,* Cambridge, Mass., 1759).

In New York the earlier **Dutch** style of New Amsterdam and the Hudson Valley (stepped gables, *Widow Sturtevant House,* Albany) and the **Flemish** style (projecting roof curved or flared at the ends) of parts of Long Island and New Jersey were ultimately supplanted by the Georgian. Classicism was evident in *Johnson Hall,* Johnstown, 1762, and the *Morris* (*Jumel*) *Mansion,* N.Y.C., 1765. In the Hudson River Valley simple houses of stone masonry, long low rectilinear structures with chimneys at either end, were built after the English conquest (*Senate House,* Kingston, 1676–95; *Freer House,* New Paltz, 1720). Until 1750 the simple Quaker style dominated the Philadelphia area, but Georgian rapidly came into vogue (*Mt. Pleasant,* 1761, brick, stone, and stucco; *Woodford,* c.1750, brick, both with Doric doorways; *Cliveden,* Germantown, 1770, American Palladian style). **Pennsylvania-Dutch** architecture of the Upper Rhine Valley immigrants radiated from Bethlehem, Pa., down the Great Valley into South Carolina, with its generally stone construction and its square plan for a number of rooms clustered about a central flue (*Miller's House,* Milbach).

In the South the baroque style of colonial Georgian was adopted in such plantation houses as the *Hammond House,* Annapolis, 1770, designed by **William Buckland,** who came from England in 1755; in Virginia at *Stratford Hall,* Westmoreland Co. (c.1725), and at *Westover,* Charles City Co. (c.1730), with the Palladian influence notably present in *Mount Airy,* Warsaw (1755–58), and in *Mount Vernon* (1758–86).

Charleston's brick and stucco mansions adapted the West Indian style of long porches or piazzas, with houses often standing endwise to the street. The galleries (most existing galleries are post-Revolutionary additions) faced the gardens, rooms were high-ceilinged and spacious, and the ground-floor story was raised several feet above the ground, with curving wrought-iron stair rails. Outstanding examples: *Izard House* (before 1757); the *Miles Brewton House* (1765–69), with its double portico, Doric columns on the 1st floor and Ionic on the 2nd, evidencing the growing classical influence. The **Huguenot** type, based on French architectural styles, was also found in South Carolina, c.1690–1800 (*The Mulberry*, Berkeley Co., with its mansard roof; *Brick House*, Edisto Island, (c.1725).

Churches. Early churches were simple, in the South following English Gothic small parish churches (*St. Luke's*, Smithfield, Va., 1682); in the North, because of the Puritan religious-government system, taking the form of meeting houses—large rectangular structures with entrance on 1 long side, galleries on 3 sides, and the high pulpit on the long side opposite the entrance (*"Old Ship" Meeting House*, Hingham, Mass., 1681). By 1750, however, English influence, introducing the type of towered church developed by Sir Christopher Wren and James Gibbs, almost completely effaced the earlier types, even for dissenting churches (*St. Michael's Church*, Charleston, S.C., 1752–61, possibly the work of **Peter Harrison** [1716–75], patterned after James Gibbs' St. Martin's-in-the-Fields; Harrison's *King's Chapel*, Boston, 1749–54, also after Gibbs; and his *Touro Synagogue*, Newport, 1759–63, influenced by Inigo Jones and Gibbs).

Public Buildings were notably represented by the *Old State House*, Boston (1712–28); *Carpenters' Hall*, Philadel-

phia (1724); *Independence Hall*, designed by Andrew Hamilton, Philadelphia (1732–41); the *Pennsylvania Hospital* (1755); and the *Maryland State House*, Annapolis (1772), which helped to set the domed type which had become almost universal in state capitol buildings. The *Capitol* (1701–05) and the *College of William and Mary* (1695–1702) at Williamsburg (restoration begun 1927) show, in reconstructed and restored fashion, the most highly developed types; the latter was built from drawings supplied by Wren.

1793–1828. PAINTING. Portraiture. After his return from England in 1792 **Gilbert Stuart** was active in New York, Philadelphia, Washington, and Boston, producing a gallery of life-size bust portraits limning worthies of the Federal and Republican eras. His canvases, bearing the strong impress of the British tradition of Reynolds, Gainsborough, and Raeburn, possessed a high technical finish and a mastery of color tones. Among his portraits are many of *George Washington*, and those of *Mrs. Richard Yates, Mrs. Timothy Pickering, Mrs. Perez Morton* (c.1802), and *Nathaniel Bowditch*.

At Philadelphia, **Charles Willson Peale**, who had made his mark before 1789, finished *The Family Group* (1809) and also painted *The Staircase Group* (c.1795), *Exhuming the Mastodon* (1806), and *Self-Portrait in His Museum* (1824). These works were all innovations in American painting, possibly because Peale's interest in the Natural History Museum gave him an objective approach to nature. Because he believed anyone could learn to paint he taught many of his family to follow his trade, including his brother James (1749–1831) and his sons, Rembrandt (1778–1860) and Raphaelle (1774–1825).

Stuart's work helped make the life-size portrait bust in oil the favorite medium of the age. Active at New York were

Samuel Lovett Waldo (1783–1861) and William Jewett (1795–1874), and at Philadelphia, Thomas Sully (1783–1872).

c.1800–25. Miniature painters included Edward Green Malbone (1777–1807) and Benjamin Trott (c.1790–c.1841).

1830–50. Among portrait painters active near the midcentury, many of whom show the mark of their competition with **photography** from its rise, c.1840, were Henry Inman (1801–46), John Neagle (1796–1865), Charles Loring Elliott (1812–68), Thomas Hicks (1823–90), George P. A. Healy (1812–94), and Chester Harding (1792–1866). Mention should also be made of the Negro painter, Robert S. Duncanson (1821–71).

1790–1860. HISTORICAL PAINTING. The genres of historical, religious, and panoramic painting were developed about 1789. **John Trumbull** (1756–1843) painted *The Battle of Bunker's Hill* in West's studio in London in 1785 and *The Declaration of Independence*, one of the 4 murals in the National Capitol, between 1786–94. **John Vanderlyn** (1776–1852) painted the *Panorama of Versailles, The Death of Jane McCrea, The Landing of Columbus, Marius Musing Amid the Ruins of Carthage*, and his *Ariadne* (1810), one of the early nudes in American painting, and thought to be in such poor taste that it blighted his career. Edward Savage (1761–1817), who did a canvas of Washington's family, also painted a panorama of London. Henry Sargent (1770–1845) painted *The Landing of the Pilgrims* and *Christ Entering Jerusalem*. The versatile **William Dunlap** (1766–1839) painted *Calvary, The Bearing of the Cross*, and *The Attack on the Louvre*. Dunlap's *History of the Rise and Progress of the Arts of Design in the United States* (1834) was the first treatment of that subject.

Washington Allston (1779–1843) struck the first vibrant note of romanticism in American painting. His poetic-philosophic bent for religious themes was exhibited in the famous unfinished *Belshazzar's Feast, The Deluge, Uriel in the Sun*, and *The Dead Man Restored to Life by the Bones of Elijah*. A pupil of Allston was **Samuel F. B. Morse,** who made his mark as a portraitist before his association with the development of the telegraph. Among his portraits are those of De Witt Clinton, Lafayette, and President James Monroe. His *Exhibition Gallery of the Louvre* is a *tour de force*.

The school of historical painting that emerged by the midcentury included Robert Walker Weir (1803–89), *Embarkation of the Pilgrims;* John Gadsby Chapman (1808–89), *Baptism of Pocahontas;* James Walker (1819–89), *Battle of Chapultepec;* William Henry Powell (1823–79), *Perry's Victory on Lake Erie;* Emmanuel Leutz (1816–68), *Washington Crossing the Delaware* and *Westward the Course of Empire Takes Its Way;* Daniel Huntington (1816–1906), *Mercy's Dream* and *Pilgrim's Progress;* and Thomas P. Rossiter (1818–71), *Washington and Lafayette at Mount Vernon, 1776.* Perhaps the most deliberate of the historical-genre painters was George Caleb Bingham (1811–77), who recorded contemporary river and frontier life in *Daniel Boone Coming Through Cumberland Gap, Fur Traders Descending the Missouri, The Jolly Flatboatmen,* and *The Verdict of the People.*

1830–60. LANDSCAPE PAINTING. The early landscape painters included Alvan Fisher (1792–1863), Thomas Birch (1779–1851), James Hamilton (1818–78), and Robert Salmon (fl. 1800–40). A distinctive school of American landscape emerged only with the achievement of **Thomas Doughty** (1793–1856), the first American painter who made a successful career in this genre; **Asher Brown Durand** (1796–1886), and **Thomas Cole** (1801–52). These 3 pioneers were the leaders of the **Hudson River School,** which also included John W. Casilear 1811–93), John Frederick Kensett (1818–72), the early work of **George Inness** (p. 1066), Jasper F. Cropsey (1828–1900), Sanford R. Gifford (1823–80), Worthington Whittredge (1820–1910), Frederick Edwin Church (1826–1900), Jervis McEntee (1828–91), William M. Hart (1823–94), and James M. Hart (1828–1901).

ANECDOTAL GENRE PAINTING. The work of such early storytelling painters as Charles Cattron (1756–1819) and John Lewis Kimmel (1789–1821) became more fully developed in the anecdotal paintings of William Sidney Mount (1807–68), the first American to establish himself in this genre; also James Henry Beard (1812–93), William Holbrook Beard (1824–1900), William Ranney (1813–57), Tompkins M. Matteson (1813–84), and David Gilmor Blythe (1815–65). The life of the North American Indian and the Far West was recorded in the paintings of **George Catlin** (1796–1872), **Alfred Jacob Miller** (1810–74), Seth Eastman (1808–75), John Mix Stanley (1814–72), Frank B. Mayer (1827–99), and Carl Wimar (1828–62). Among the most popular of the later painters of Western scenes was **Frederic Remington** (p. 1137).

In the field of art reproductions, **John James Audubon** issued his superb aquatint plates of the *Birds of America* (1827–38). On a popular level, the prints of Currier & Ives were based on the work of such artists as George Henry Durrie (1820–63) and Arthur Fitzwilliam Tait (1819–1905). The development of commercial lithography created a wide market for art reproductions in the medium of the "chromolith."

1789–1830. SCULPTURE. The work of the early artisan carvers displays technical ingenuity and artistic integrity, notably William Rush (1756–1833), who enjoyed a busy career as a woodcarver of ships' figureheads, among them *The Genius of the United States* and *Nature,* both of which were mounted on U.S. frigates. His Indian figures, e.g., the *Indian Trader* (on the ship *William Penn*), were among his best works. Another woodcarver, who later worked in marble, was Hezekiah Augur (1791–1858), whose best-known work is *Jephthah and His Daughter.* John Frazee (1790–1852) began as a New Jersey stonecutter, was wholly self-taught as a sculptor, and did not carve his first marble bust until c.1825. Among his marble portraits are those of John Jay, John Marshall, and Daniel Webster. Although the work of John Henri Isaac Browere (1792–1834) may be classified as life masks rather than sculpture, his portraits of prominent Americans are valuable as authentic historical records.

1830–60. ITALIAN NEOCLASSICISM. In the 1830s U.S. sculptors began to pursue professional training abroad (particularly in Italy). The first American who deliberately chose sculpture as a profession was **Horatio Greenough** (1805–52), best known for the heroic, half-draped statue of Washington that stands on the Capitol grounds. Other sculptors who performed all or most of their work in Italy were William Wetmore Story (1819–95) and Harriet G. Hosmer (1830–1908). Among Story's works were a statue of his father, Justice Joseph Story, and *Saul, Moses, Cleopatra,* and *Medea.* Those by Hosmer include *Beatrice, Zenobia,* and the statue of *Thomas Hart Benton* at St. Louis.

Hiram Powers (1805–73) shares with Greenough the distinction of being the first professionally trained native sculptor. He did many portrait busts of American statesmen in an age when the marble bust predominated, but his best-known work is the *Greek Slave,* which created a sensation in its time. Powers was the first American sculptor to win a European reputation.

Other sculptors noted for their busts and figures in white marble include Erastus D. Palmer (1817–1904) and Thomas Ball (1819–1911). Palmer is best known for *Indian Girl, White Captive*, and the bust of Washington Irving. Ball did the equestrian statue of Washington at the Boston Public Gardens and the *Emancipation* group at the national Capitol. William Rimmer (1816–79), whose works include *Falling Gladiator* and *Head of Saint Stephen*, was noted for his mastery of anatomical knowledge.

Thomas Crawford (1813–57) was one of the outstanding pioneers of American sculpture. Among his works are the statue of *Armed Freedom* on the dome of the Capitol, the group called *Past and Present of America* on the pediment of the Senate wing, and the *Washington Monument* at Richmond.

Henry Kirke Brown (1814–86) is best known for his equestrian statue of *Washington* in Union Square, New York City, where his statue of *Lincoln* also stands. Clark Mills (1815–83) made the first equestrian statue cast in the U.S., that of *Gen. Andrew Jackson* (erected 1853) which stands near the White House.

Randolph Rogers (1825–92) did the bronze doors of the Capitol rotunda and the *Genius of Connecticut* on the dome of the State House at Hartford, as well as *Nydia* and *Lost Pleiad*. John Rogers (1829–1904) gained wide popularity with his "Rogers groups," the mass-produced plaster statuettes that found their way into thousands of American homes. His folk artistry and sharp delineation are displayed in such representative works as *Checkers up at the Farm, Town Pump, The Fugitive's Story, Union Refugees, Council of War,* and *The Wounded Scout.*

1789–1860. ARCHITECTURE: CLASSIC REVIVAL. The American Revolution brought with it a demand (recognized by Jefferson in his *Notes on Virginia*) for a new American architecture, expressive of the new nation. Yet for some time the older building ways and the older dependence on England continued. Thus the **Adam** style continued as a major influence for 2 or 3 decades. Jefferson saw the source of inspiration for the new work in the ancient classic architecture of Rome and Greece, and eventually a **Roman Revival** (1789–c.1820) and a **Greek Revival** (c.1820–60) became dominant. One of the foremost practitioners in the persisting Adamesque manner was **Samuel McIntire** (1757–1811), who built houses and mansions for the Salem merchants, among them the Derbys and Crowinshields. Other adapters of this mode were **Asher Benjamin** (1773–1845), who worked at the beginning of his career in the Connecticut Valley and was the author of the popular handbook *The Country Builder's Assistant* (1797) and many other similar books; and **Charles Bulfinch** (p. 994), who embodied it in many distinguished houses in Boston. It was characteristic of the time that McIntire and Benjamin practiced as carpenter-builders rather than professional architects.

1789–c.1820. ROMAN REVIVAL saw the emergence of the professional architect in the U.S. Its vogue was due to (1) direct importation from Europe; (2) the analogy with the Roman Republic drawn by Americans of the early national period. Chiefly influential in this initial phase were **Thomas Jefferson** and **William Thornton** (1759–1828). Jefferson's design for the *Virginia Capitol* at Richmond (1785–89), the first American structure after the Roman style, was based on the ancient Roman temple at Nîmes, France, known as the Maison Carrée. His plan for the *University of Virginia* at Charlottesville, with its systematic use of the various orders, represents the high mark of the Roman Revival. Charles Bulfinch, among the first native professional architects, later shifted to the style of the Roman and, rarely, the Greek Revivals. In houses, the new classicism shows chiefly in the creation of a restrained, clear simplicity, with a diminution in decorative adjuncts. These are often called **Federal** in style. French influence appears occasionally. Perhaps the finest example of this type is the New York *City Hall* (1803–12), whose design was shared by **John McComb, Jr.** (1763–1853), and **Joseph F. Mangin** (fl.1794–1818).

1793–1830. NATIONAL CAPITOL expressed the idealism of the new nation. After Maj. **Pierre Charles L'Enfant** (1754–1825) had designed the Washington city plan, President Washington, as the result of a competition, selected **William Thornton** as architect of the Capitol. **Stephen Hallet** (fl.1789–65), who succeeded Thornton, shares the credit for the basic conception—the large central dome and the flanking Senate and House wings. Beginning in 1803, **Benjamin Henry Latrobe** (p. 1081) modified the somewhat impractical original design and used Greek inspiration in the details, working on the Capitol (which was burned by the British in 1814) until 1817. **Charles Bulfinch** brought Latrobe's plans to completion (1817–30). The architect of the **Executive Mansion** was **James Hoban** (c.1762–1831), who also designed the State House at Charleston, S.C. In the White House the east and west porticoes were built from Latrobe's designs. After the British burned the White House, Hoban rebuilt it with Latrobe's modifications.

c.1820–60. GREEK REVIVAL is attributable to the renewed Continental interest in classic forms, to the influx of foreign architects, and to American enthusiasm for the Greeks in their struggle for independence. This period saw the dominance of the carpenter-builder, when handbooks came into use, e.g., Asher Benjamin's widely reprinted *The Practical House Carpenter* (1830) and the 3 books by **Minard Lefever** (1797–1854): *Young Builder's General Instructor* (1829), *Modern Builder's Guide* (1833), and *Beauties of Modern Architecture* (1835), even more important in spreading the Greek Revival throughout the country. Many federal and state government buildings, merchants' exchanges, banks, and churches were designed in this style, generally a free inventive rendering of Greek forms based on such Greek structures as the Parthenon, the Erectheum, and the monument of Lysicrates. Among the prominent characteristics of the style were the use of the Greek orders, doors and mantels with creative versions of Greek inspiration, great variety in house plans, and, in public buildings, magnificent fireproof masonry-vaulted construction. Chiefly responsible for introducing the Greek Revival was **Benjamin Henry Latrobe.** The first Greek building in America was his Bank of Pennsylvania at Philadelphia, characteristic in its free adaptation of ancient precedent and in its fireproof vaulted construction. Two of his pupils were **Robert Mills** (1781–1855) and **William Strickland** (c.1787–1854). Mills, the designer of many houses, customhouses, and other federal buildings, is best known for the *Treasury Building, Patent Office,* and *Washington Monument* (begun 1836). Strickland built the *Merchants Exchange,* Philadelphia, and the *Capitol,* Nashville, Tenn. A pupil of Strickland was **Thomas U. Walker** (1804–87), who designed *Girard College,* Philadelphia, and brought the U.S. Capitol to final completion (1850–65). Others identified with this style include **Minard Lefever; Gideon Shryock** (1802–80); **Isaiah Rogers** (1800–69), who created the modern hotel concept in the *Tremont House* (Boston, 1828), and built the *Merchants Exchange* at New York; and **Alexander Jackson Davis** (1803–92), in partnership with **Ithiel Town** (1784–1844) until 1844, who designed the New York *Custom House* (1832) and several state capitols.

1840–60. BEGINNING OF THE GOTHIC REVIVAL. Groundwork was laid by **A. J. Davis; Richard Upjohn** (1802–78), first president of the American Institute of Architects, founded, 1857, who designed the new Trinity Church and Trinity Chapel; and **James Renwick** (1818–95), Grace Church, 1843–46, and St. Patrick's Cathedral, 1850–79, all in New York. The many-times-republished books of **Andrew J. Downing** (1815–52), dealing with landscape and rural architecture, had great influence in spreading the Gothic Revival, as well as in stimulating romantic gardens; he is also one of the fathers of the city park in the U.S. The eclecticism of the period did not go unchallenged. In 3 important works on architecture Horatio Greenough attacked current trends (*American Architecture* [1843], *Aesthetics at Washington* [1851], and *Structure and Organization* [1852]), anticipating by a half century Louis Sullivan's functional approach.

1861–1910. PAINTING. Portrait and Figure. Still active after 1860 were many of the portraitists, among them Daniel Huntington and Charles Loring Elliott, who before the Civil War shaped a technique of sober and almost photographic realism. The Lincoln theme made its early appearance in a series of studies by Francis Bicknell Carpenter (1830–1900), including *The Lincoln Family in 1861* and *The Reading of the Emancipation Proclamation*. Portraits of public figures

were a specialty of Alonzo Chappell (1828–87), whose pictures reached a wide audience through the medium of the steel engraving.

The absorption of Continental influences appeared in the work of a later generation: Gustave H. Mosler (1841–1920), Francis D. Millet (1846–1912), Frank Duveneck (1848–1919), William Merritt Chase (1849–1916), Wyatt Eaton (1849–96), and Kenyon Cox (1856–1919). The most successful portrait painter of the time was **John Singer Sargent** (p. 1147), who did most of his work abroad. His technical finish is evident in such characteristic portraits as those of *Ada Rehan, Ellen Terry, Mrs. John L. Gardner, Coventry Patmore, Madame X, The Four Doctors,* and *The Misses Hunter*. Another American portraitist who did virtually all of his work in Europe was **James A. McNeill Whistler** (p. 1180), whose work includes *Portrait of the Artist's Mother, Thomas Carlyle,* and *Miss Alexander*. Whistler's *Nocturnes* and *Symphonies* used color and mass with fresh inventiveness, and his etchings of Venetian and London waterside subjects exhibit a brilliant Impressionist technique.

Figure painting in the U.S. reached a new level with the work of Eastman Johnson (1824–1906), *Old Kentucky Home* and *In the Fields;* William Morris Hunt (1824–79), *The Bathers;* George Fuller (1822–84); Robert L. Newman (1827–1912); Abbott H. Thayer (1849–1921); Thomas Dewing (1851–1938); **Frederic Remington,** and John W. Alexander (1856–1915).

Historical, Mural, Anecdotal, and Still Life. The pre–Civil War tradition of historical painting was continued by Constantino Brumidi (1805–80), whose work at the national Capitol includes *Apotheosis of Washington;* and by William De La Montagne Cary (1840–

1922), Henry F. Farny (1847–1916), and John Mulvaney (1844–1906). Among the outstanding mural painters were **John La Farge** (p. 1078), who was also a prolific worker in stained glass; Kenyon Cox; Edwin Austin Abbey (1852–1911); Elihu Vedder (1836–1923); Edwin H. Blashfield (1848–1936); John W. Alexander; and Robert F. Blum (1857–1903). Anecdotal painters of the time included John George Brown (1831–1913), *The Music Lesson;* Thomas Waterman Wood (1823–1913), *The Village Post Office;* and Edward Lamson Henry (1841–1919), *The 9:45 Accommodation.* Among the still-life painters were George Henry Hall (1825–1913), Andrew J. H. Way (1826–88), William Michael Harnett (?1848–92), William Merritt Chase, John Frederick Peto (1854–1907), and John Haberle (1856–1933).

Landscape. Those who continued to produce repetitions or variations of the Hudson River School included William Rickaby Miller (1818–93), Frederick Edwin Church (1826–1900), **Albert Bierstadt** (p. 986), Samuel Colman (1832–1920), James David Smillie (1833–1909), Thomas Moran (1837–1926), George Henry Smillie (1840–1921), and Robert Swain Gifford (1840–1905). **George Inness,** who before the Civil War had been a follower of the Hudson River School, shaped a fresher idiom in such canvases as *Peace and Plenty, Autumn Oaks, Delaware Water Gap,* and *Home of the Heron.* Other landscape painters included Alexander H. Wyant (1836–92), *Falls of the Ohio and Louisville, Mohawk Valley,* and *An Old Clearing;* Homer D. Martin (1836–97), *View of the Seine* (best-known as *Harp of the Winds*); Ralph Albert Blakelock (1847–1919), *Brook by Moonlight;* and Abbott H. Thayer, *Monadnock.*

1860–80. TRANSITION TO OBJECTIVE REALISM: Homer and **Eakins.** American painting took on a greater power, resourcefulness, and maturity with the work of **Winslow Homer** (p. 1060) and **Thomas Eakins** (p. 1019).

Homer, who began as a magazine illustrator, first came to prominence in 1866 with *Prisoners from the Front,* a canvas based on his Civil War experience as a pictorial reporter; this reminiscent phase was continued in *Rainy Day in Camp* and *Sunday Morning in Virginia.* After 1880, when he began living in Maine, Homer abandoned illustrative and anecdotal subjects. Along the Maine seacoast, and during his stay in the Caribbean, Homer developed an original vein which appears in *All's Well, Winter Coast, Rowing Home, The Gulf Stream,* and *After the Tornado, Bahamas.* As a watercolorist, Homer is of the first rank.

Eakins brought to portrait and figure painting a strength and character based on a profound study of the human form and an intimate acquaintance with the work of the French and Spanish masters. His choice and treatment of subject signaled the rise of a new realism reflected in such paintings as *The Swimming Hole, The Agnew Clinic, The Gross Clinic, The Thinker, Max Schmitt in a Single Scull, The Concert Singer,* and *Katherine.*

1877. Opening of the first American Salon des Réfusés by the Society of American Artists (early exhibitors included La Farge, Inness, Ryder, and Eakins); amalgamated with the Academy in New York, 1906, to form the present National Academy of Design.

1880–1910. MYSTICISM. The poetic intensity of **Albert Pinkham Ryder** (p. 1144) produced canvases weighted with heavy yet luminous color and with strange masses and forms drawn from an imaginary world. A solitary worker during his lifetime, it was only after his death that Ryder won general recognition. Among his paintings are *Macbeth and the Witches, The Flying Dutchman, Jonah and the Whale, Toilers of the Sea,* and *Pegasus.*

1880–1910. IMPRESSIONIST MOVEMENT. French Impressionism, a school preoccupied with the subtle and iridescent play of light over forms, developed c.1871, *et seq.,* with the work of such painters as Claude Monet, Berthe Morisot, Camille Pissarro, and Alfred Sisley. American painting's first direct acquaintance with Impressionism began with **Mary Cassatt** (p. 1000), known for such characteristic pieces as *Caresse Maternelle* and *Mother and Child.* The only American invited to exhibit with the French Impressionists, she did all of her work abroad. It remained for Theodore Robinson (1852–96) to introduce Impressionism into America. The influence of Monet is apparent in Robinson's *Spring in Giverny.* Impressionism combined with American themes in the work of J. Alden Weir (1852–1919), *A Factory Village, Visiting Neighbors, Ploughing for Buckwheat,* and *Nocturne, Queensboro Bridge;* John H. Twachtman (1853–1902), *The White Bridge, Snowbound, Waterfall, Summer,* and *October;* and Childe Hassam (1859–1935), *Union Square in Spring, Church at Old Lyme, The 17th of October,* and *Central Park from the Plaza.* In 1898 Hassam, Twachtman, Weir, and others banded together as "Ten American Painters" and held the first exhibition of U.S. Impressionists.

1900–1910. REALISTS. In the early 20th century there emerged a group of painters who concentrated on homely incident, subject, and character, basing their content on direct observation and their technique on European masters such as Hals, Goya, Hogarth, and Daumier. Known as "The Ash Can School"

(and sometimes, with Maurice Prendergast [1859–1924] and others, as "The Eight"), this group included **Robert Henri** (p. 1056), *Martche in a White Dress* and *Boy with a Piccolo;* George Luks (1867–1933), *The Old Duchess, The Little Milliner,* and *The Spielers;* William Glackens (1870–1938), *Chez Mouquin* and *Roller Skating Rink;* John Sloan (1871–1951), *The Wake of the Ferry, Dust Storm, Election Night,* and *McSorley's Bar* (organizer of the Society of Independent Artists, 1917, in protest against the conservatism of the National Academy of Design); **George Bellows** (p. 983), *Stag at Sharkey's, Edith Cavell,* and *Day in June;* and Everett Shinn (1876–1953), best known for his treatments of stage subjects, as in *Revue* and *White Ballet.*

1913. ARMORY SHOW, which opened at the 69th Regiment Armory in New York on 17 Feb. 1913, was organized by the Association of Painters and Sculptors, whose president was Arthur B. Davies (1862–1928). It had a twofold purpose: to introduce to an American audience in coherent and integrated form the origins and evolution of the modern European art tradition, and to create a more favorable atmosphere for the reception of artists working outside the established academic tradition. In addition to exhibiting works by Ingres, Delacroix, Courbet, and the French Impressionists, the Armory Show included the post-Impressionists (Cézanne, Van Gogh, Seurat, and others), and Cubist and abstractionist painters like Picasso, Matisse, Duchamp, and Kandinsky. In the work of Brancusi, Maillol, and Lehmbruck, Americans saw new experiments in sculpture.

A landmark in the history of American art, the Armory Show signified a definite break in the hold exerted by the academic school and had a lasting influence over a wide range of media, including interior design and advertising art. Its notes were heard in the art criticism of Willard Huntington Wright, Leo Stein, and Walter Pach. The Armory Show paved the way for the acceptance of a new generation of American painters, among them Louis M. Eilshemius (1864–1941), Jerome Myers (1867–1940), George ("Pop") Hart (1868–1933), Alfred Maurer (1868–1932), **John Marin** (p. 1097), Eugene Higgins (1874–1958), Kenneth Hayes Miller (1876–1962), Maurice Sterne (1877–1957), Marsden Hartley (1877–1943), Arthur G. Dove (1880–1946), Walt Kuhn (1880–1965), Max Weber (1881–1961), Rockwell Kent (1882–1971), Edward Hopper (1882–1967), Charles Demuth (1883–1935), Charles Sheeler (1883–1965), Guy Pène du Bois (1884–1958), and Georgia O'Keeffe (1887–   ).

1861–85. SCULPTURE. The sculptors of the post–Civil War era alternated between realism and classicism until c.1885, when the influence of the Italian Renaissance began to make itself strongly felt in monumental and ornamental sculpture. The leading sculptors up to c.1880 included Launt Thompson (1833–94), who executed *Rocky Mountain Trapper*, the statue of *Abraham Pierson* at Yale University, and the equestrian statues of *Gen. John Sedgwick* at West Point and of *Gen. Winfield Scott* at Washington, D.C.; Larkin G. Mead (1835–1910), *Lincoln Monument* at Springfield, Ill., the statue of *Ethan Allen* at the national Capitol, and *The Father of Waters;* George Bissell (1839–1920), statues of *Chancellor James Kent* at the Congressional Library, *President Arthur* in Madison Square Park, New York, and *Chancellor James Watts* at Trinity Church, New York; Franklin Simmons (1839–1913), the *Naval Monument* at Washington, D.C., and statues of *Roger Williams* and *Gov. William King* at the nation Capitol; Martin Milmore (1844–

83), *Soldiers' and Sailors' Monument* on Boston Common; and Olin L. Warner (1844–96), known for his portrait busts of *J. Alden Weir* and *William Crary Brownwell*, the statue of *William Lloyd Garrison* at Boston, and a series of relief portraits of North American Indians.

1885–1938. American sculpture attained a new mark of craftsmanship and conception with the work of the Irish-born **Augustus Saint-Gaudens** (p. 1144) and that of **Daniel Chester French** (1850–1931) and **George Grey Barnard** (1863–1938). Saint-Gaudens executed the statue of *Lincoln* at Lincoln Park, Chicago; the *Adams Memorial* (the noted hooded figure sometimes called *Grief*) in Rock Creek Cemetery, Washington, D.C.; the *Shaw Memorial* at Boston; the *Sherman* and *Farragut Memorials,* both at New York; *Amor Caritas;* and *Diana* (the figure on the tower of the old Madison Square Garden at New York). Among French's many works are *The Minute-Man* and *Ralph Waldo Emerson* at Concord, Mass.; the statue of *Lincoln* at the Lincoln Memorial, Washington, D.C.; the statue of *John Harvard* and the *Longfellow Memorial* at Cambridge, Mass.; the statue of *Lewis Cass* at the national Capitol; the massive figure of *The Republic* at the World's Columbian Exposition; *Gallaudet and His First Deaf-Mute Pupil* at Washington, D.C.; the *Parkman Memorial* at Boston; and *Death and the Young Sculptor* at Roxbury, Mass. Barnard's works include *The Two Natures, The Prodigal Son, The Hewer,* the group at the state Capitol at Harrisburg, Pa., and the uncompleted colossal World War I memorial.

Other leading sculptors of the period were Frederick W. MacMonnies (1863–1937), who executed *Civic Virtue,* formerly at City Hall Park, New York, the site of his statue of *Nathan Hale; Bacchante,* at Boston; *Victory,* at West Point,

N.Y.; the *Soldiers' and Sailors' Memorial* at Grand Army Plaza, Brooklyn, N.Y., on which Thomas Eakins collaborated; the statue of *Shakespeare* at the Congressional Library; and the *Columbian Fountain* at the World's Columbian Exposition; Herbert Adams (1858–1945), best known for his polychrome portrait busts, including *Primavera, The Rabbi's Daughter,* and *Julia Marlowe;* Paul Wayland Bartlett (1865–1925), *The Ghost Dancer, The Bear Tamer, The Genius of Man,* and statues of *Michelangelo* and *Columbus* at the Congressional Library; Karl Bitter (1867–1915), *Carl Schurz Memorial* at New York, monumental reliefs at the Broad Street Station, Philadelphia, and *The Standard Bearers* at the Pan-American Exposition held at Buffalo; and James Earle Fraser (1876–1953), *End of the Trail, Alexander Hamilton* at the Treasury Department Building, Washington, D.C., group for the Theodore Roosevelt Memorial at New York, figures of *Thomas Jefferson* and *Lewis and Clark* at the Missouri State Capitol, and the statue of *Franklin* at the Franklin Institute, Philadelphia.

c.1861–c.1885.   ARCHITECTURE. Rapid industrialization profoundly changed older ideas; cast iron came into wide use in commercial buildings, and glass in large sheets became available for the first time. New fortunes placed a premium on lavish, showy design. This period witnessed the first practical passenger elevators (p. 795), and the beginnings of the typical city office building as well as the large department store.

VICTORIAN GOTHIC (English), marked by an Italianate strain, appeared in numerous guises, ranging from the filigree jigsaw detail of "carpenter's Gothic" to polished careful designs that reflected the influence of John Ruskin. Used for public buildings and in many town and country houses, the style featured polychrome masonry, squat pointed arches, high ceilings, arcaded windows, and elaborate bays and oriels. Among the best examples: old *Boston Museum of Fine Arts* (1872–75), designed by **Russell Sturgis** (1836–1909; better known for his critical writings and *A History of Architecture,* 4 vols., 1906–15); library and *Memorial Hall* at Harvard University (completed 1874), designed by **William Robert Ware** (1832–1915) and **Henry Van Brunt** (1832–1903); and the *State House,* Hartford, Conn. (completed 1885), designed by **Upjohn.**

FRENCH RENAISSANCE REVIVAL was the architectural hallmark of the "Gilded Age." Among its prominent characteristics were mansard roofs, lavish and heavy ornamentation, coupled columns and pilasters, large cornices, and an undiscriminating use of the architectural orders. This style was employed in many types of buildings—churches, hotels, hospitals, schools, railroad stations, and public buildings. One of the most active exemplars was A. B. Mullett (?–1890), who as government architect designed the *State, War and Navy Building,* Washington, D.C., and the old *Post Offices* at Boston and New York. An important offshoot of this mode was the **brownstone-front house,** adopted on a wide scale in New York City during the 1870s and 1880s. The style achieved a fresh delicacy in the work of **Richard Morris Hunt** (1828–95), trained in Paris, designer of numerous houses for merchant princes at New York, Newport, R.I., and elsewhere, including those for the Vanderbilts.

COLLEGIATE ARCHITECTURAL EDUCATION began in the U.S. in this period. The first architectural school was opened at the Massachusetts Institute of Technology (1866) under the direction of William Robert Ware. Architectural courses were subsequently introduced at the University of Illinois (1870), Cornell (1871), Columbia (1883), and Harvard

(1890). The influence of the École des Beaux Arts in Paris, where many Americans were trained in the 1870s, was dominant in the majority.

1876. PHILADELPHIA CENTENNIAL EXPOSITION (U.S. International Exposition), with its 249 buildings occupying 465 acres of Fairmount Park, constituted a grandiose summation of the architectural styles of the period; its dominant modes were the Queen Anne variation of Victorian Gothic, French mansard, and Swiss châlet derivations. In it, however, the influence of new constructional ideas gave rise to a few prophetic and independent exteriors important as reflecting the new forms industrialized engineering might produce. Foreign art exhibits, particularly in the crafts, left a deep mark on public taste.

c. 1876–c.1894. ROMANESQUE REVIVAL. Although derived from the Romanesque of southern France, it was not based on any current European revival; its leading force was **Henry Hobson Richardson** (p. 1138), who received his training at the École des Beaux Arts. At the outset of his career he employed Victorian Gothic (design for the *Church of the Unity,* Springfield, Mass.), but turned to his own adaptation of French Romanesque in his plans for the *Brattle Square Church,* Boston. His integrated use of mass, space, and line, and his imaginative treatment of ornament, rank him among the foremost U.S. architects. His most famous work is *Trinity Church* at Boston (opened 1877). His other outstanding designs include *Crane Library,* Quincy, Mass.; the libraries at Malden, Mass., and Burlington, Vt.; the *Allegheny Courthouse and Jail,* Pittsburgh; the *Marshall Field Wholesale Store,* Chicago; the now demolished *Hay-Adams* houses at Washington, D.C.; and railroad stations for the Boston and Albany line. Especially influential in New England and the West, the Romanesque Revival was frequently employed in the latter area by the partners, **Daniel H. Burnham** (1846–1912) and **John Wellborn Root** (1850–91), who designed the old *Chicago Art Institute* and the *Montauk, Phoenix, Rookery,* and *Rialto* buildings, all at Chicago.

1884–1914. COMING OF THE SKYSCRAPER. An indigenous American contribution, the skyscraper was made possible by cheap and abundant structural steel, the passenger elevator, inexpensive fireproofing, and resourceful solutions of the structural problems of foundations. Because its problems were new, the skyscraper induced architects to work out solutions based on function rather than style. Customarily accredited as the first tall structure embodying in part the basic principles of metal frame construction is the *Home Insurance Building* at Chicago (built 1884–85), designed by **William LeBaron Jenney** (1832–1907), who used cast-iron columns and wrought-iron beams. The first building erected completely of wrought-iron skeleton construction was the 13-story *Tacoma Building* at Chicago (built 1887–88), designed by Holabird and Roche. Precursors of the functional form were the *Wainwright Building* at St. Louis (1890), the characteristic nontraditional skyscraper design of the early 20th century, and the horizontal emphasis in the *Carson, Pirie, and Scott Building* at Chicago (1899), both by **Louis H. Sullivan** (p. 1163). Prevailing eclecticism governed architectural style at the turn of the 20th century. Characteristic of this style, all in New York City: *Singer Building,* by **Ernest Flagg** (1857–1947); *Metropolitan Life Insurance Co. Tower* (1906), by N. LeBrun & Sons; the *"Flatiron" Building* (1902), by Daniel H. Burnham; and the *Woolworth Building* (1911–13), with its overlay of Gothic motifs, by **Cass Gilbert** (1859–1934).

1893–1917. NEW CLASSICAL REVIVAL AND ECLECTICISM.

The Chicago World's Fair (World's Columbian Exposition, 1893) provided the major impetus for the general adoption of Greek, Roman, and Renaissance forms and the gradual abandonment of the Romanesque. The Roman Classical mode for the grounds and buildings on 686 acres of Jackson Park, along Lake Michigan, was chosen by a group of architects working under the direction of Daniel H. Burnham, including Richard M. Hunt, McKim, Mead & White, and George B. Post. The most important building at the "White City" which did not bear the classic stamp was the *Transportation Building* by Sullivan. The classic-eclectic tradition of exposition architecture was continued at the **Pan-American Exposition** (1901) and the **Louisiana Purchase Exposition** (1904) at St. Louis. Among leading exponents of classic eclecticism was the firm of **McKim, Mead & White,** of which the most important members were **Charles F. McKim** (1849–1909) and **Stanford White** (1853–1906). Their work includes the *Henry Villard House* (1885), the *Century Club* (1890), *Low Memorial Library,* Columbia University (1893), the *Herald Building* (1894), the *J. Pierpont Morgan Library* (1906), all at New York City, and the *Boston Public Library* (1888). Other exemplars were Carrère and Hastings, who designed the *New York Public Library* and the *Senate* and *House Office Buildings,* Washington, D.C.; and **Cass Gilbert,** who designed the *Minnesota State Capitol,* the *U.S. Custom House* at New York City, the *U.S. Treasury Annex,* and the *Supreme Court Building,* Washington, D.C. Eclecticism marked the work of **Henry J. Hardenbergh** (1847–1918), who designed the old *Waldorf-Astoria Hotel* (1891–96) and the *Plaza Hotel* (1907), both at New York City, and the *Copley Plaza* (1910) at Boston; and the work of **George B. Post** (1837–1913), who designed the *Pulitzer Building* (1889–92), the *New York Produce Exchange* (1881–85), the *New York Cotton Exchange* (1883–86), the *St. Paul Building* (1897–99), the *College of the City of New York* (1902–11), the *New York Stock Exchange* (1904), and the *Wisconsin State Capitol.* Gothic eclecticism found its most brilliant expression in **Ralph Adams Cram** (1863–1942), member of the firm of Cram, Goodhue & Ferguson. Among the structures which bear his distinctive mark are *St. Stephen's Church,* Cohasset, Mass.; major buildings at the U.S. Military Academy, West Point (1904); *St. Thomas's Church,* New York City (1911–13); *Calvary Church,* Pittsburgh (1907); and the *Fourth Presbyterian Church,* Chicago (1912). In his latter days **Bertram Grosvenor Goodhue** (1869–1924) broke with the Gothic style. His plan for the *Capitol* at Lincoln, Neb., marked a new expression of the classic tradition, with a free and daring use of decorative sculpture.

SULLIVAN AND WRIGHT. During the Classical Revival the quest for a functional, indigenous style was carried forward by **Louis H. Sullivan** and his disciple **Frank Lloyd Wright** (p. 1189). Sullivan was in partnership with Dankmar Adler at Chicago (1881–1900), and here Wright served his apprenticeship. Among Sullivan's most notable structures: *Chicago Auditorium* (1889), *Chicago Stock Exchange Building* (1894), *Bayard Building,* New York City (1898), and the *National Farmers Bank,* Owatonna, Minn. (1908). Toward the turn of the 20th century Wright began to develop his distinctive **"prairie house"** style in the Midwest. His first important commercial structure was the *Larkin Administration Building,* Buffalo, N.Y. (1904). One of his most successful suburban dwellings was the *Robie House,* Chicago (1908).

1914. World War I found U.S. architecture in a confused state. The brilliance of the planning in many of the great classic-eclectic monuments blinded many to the basic superficiality of its approach. Office buildings, department stores, mass housing, and factories of undreamed-of complexity and size constituted pressing challenges to which rational and beautiful answers were still rare. Industrial production of building materials was breaking down hand craftsmanship and curtailed building appropriations discouraged lavishness on the earlier scale. Only a completely new creative architecture, then only in its infancy, could provide the answer.

1905-73. GROWTH OF PHOTOGRAPHY AS ART. During this period, photography developed as an independent art form. Formalism, abstraction, and realism were approaches used by photographers who tried to capture on film the forms and textures of nature and the harsh social reality of the depression years. **Edward Steichen** (1879-1973), **Alfred Stieglitz** (p. 1159), **Edward Weston** (1886-1958), **Ansel Adams** (1902-), **Paul Strand** (1890-), **Dorothea Lange** (1895-1965), and **Walker Evans** (1903-75) are among the earliest photographers to capture the concentrated sense of reality available through the medium of still photography. Most challenging of the photographic undertakings during these years was Steichen's notable exhibition, "The Family of Man" (1953), representing the work of 273 photographers and shown in more than 70 countries.

1914-29. REIGN OF PARIS ABSTRACTION. With the outbreak of World War I French artists (Gleizer, Picabia, and Duchamp) came to the U.S. and spread ideas of **cubism,** which in the period 1919-29 was changed into a purist style by Demuth, Sheiler, and Preston Dickinson (1891-1930). The mid-20s saw the apogee of Paris Abstractionism in the work of such artists as Weber, Maurer, and **John Marin** (p. 1097).

1914-60. DEVELOPMENT OF FORMALISM IN SCULPTURE. A revived interest in the archeotonic and expressive aspects of sculpture developed after 1914. Works displayed concern with the integrity of materials and questions of weight and balance as well as of texture and overall contour. Important work in direct carving and modeling was done by **Jacob Epstein** (1880-1959), U.S.-born expatriate who lived in London. **William Zorach** (1887-1966), *Mother and Child, Affection;* **Gaston Lachaise** (1882-1935), *Figure of a Woman;* and **Elie Nadelman** (1882-1946), *Seated Woman, Head in Marble,* simplified anatomical forms and captured a classical sense of monumentality and power in their work. In contrast to the rugged quality of Jo Davidson's (1883-1952) creations, *Gertrude Stein, Dr. Albert Einstein,* were the works of **Paul Manship** (1885-1966) reflecting Renaissance, archaic, and Oriental influences, *Centaur and Dryad, The Indian Hunter.* Outstanding for his animal sculpture was John B. Flannagan (1898-1942), *Chimpanzee.*

In general, concerns similar to those of the painters are reflected in the sculpture of this period. Abstract sculpture goes back to Cubism—**Max Weber,** *Spiral Rhythm* (1915); John Storrs (1885-1956), *Seated Gendarme* (1925). **Alexander Calder** (p. 995) created sculptures and suspended mobiles which owe much to the surrealists but break with the representational tradition. **David Smith** (p. 1153) created abstract sculptures of welded metal which bridge the gap between 2-dimensional and 3-dimensional art. Other sculptors, more concerned with shapes, voids, and masses than with representation were David Hare (1917-), Seymour Lipton (1903-), Herbert

Ferber (1906–), Theodore Roszak (1907–) and Richard Lippold (1915–). Richard Stankiewicz (1922–) and **Louise Nevelson** (p. 1113) used crude everyday "found objects" to construct their sculptures. Less affected by changing aesthetic style were such realists as William Zorach, Robert Laurent (1890–1970), José de Creeft (1884–), and Chaim Gross (1904–), who continued to work in their own respective styles throughout most of this period.

1918–60. SOME ARCHITECTURAL TRENDS. The confused state of taste in 1914 yielded to more creative tendencies, despite the widespread wave of "colonialism" in domestic architecture—final manifestation of eclecticism. Shortly after World War I strong influences from the new architecture of Europe (especially of France and Germany) were dominant. The form this new architecture took in the 1920s was primarily ascetic, geometrical, and antihistorical, even deliberately avoiding the use of traditional building materials and techniques. This is sometimes called the **International style.** It influenced domestic, school, and factory architecture profoundly, but its disregard of regional and national differences in materials, climate, and ways of living proved it too limited for wide U.S. application, although some of its basic ideals of truth to structure and material and its geometrical quality were absorbed into the U.S. tradition. The **Chicago World's Fair** (1933) and the **New York** and **San Francisco World's Fairs** (1939) were important chiefly as indicating public acceptance of the objectives of modern architecture. By 1940 its dominance was at an end. Instead, the best U.S. architecture sought much freer, though equally new and logical, solutions, using the traditional brick, stone, and wood in new ways, with marked regional differences (e.g., houses in Florida compared to California). In

this development the influence of **Wright,** who had always stood for a humane and nonmechanized ideal, was of primary importance.

In the 1950s, in protest against the neoclassicism of **Ludwig Mies van der Rohe** (1886–1964), with its stress on form rather than site (860 Lake Shore Dr., Chicago; Seagram Building, New York), new forms emerged—**Hugh Stebbins'** Congress Hall in Berlin, **Eero Saarinen's** (1910–61) auditorium for MIT and hockey rink for Yale; or texture was stressed—**Edward D. Stone's** U.S. Embassy at New Delhi and **Harry Weese's** U.S. Embassy at Accra. **Louis I. Kahn's** (p. 1074) Yale Univ. *Art Gallery* (1951) and *Richards Medical Research Laboratories* (1961), Univ. of Pennsylvania, gave the mechanical and service areas of modern buildings equal prominence with the other, more public, aspects of the structure. The use of exposed reinforced concrete as a building material became popular. Nevertheless, the boxlike curtain-wall office building became the most common form of urban architecture. The best example is *Lever House,* 1952, New York City, by Skidmore, Owings, and Merrill. These buildings have their roots in the International style but became popular due to their relatively low cost and easy method of construction.

1919–29. FROM REALISM TO SOCIAL REALISM. The influence of Robert Henri in emulating the work of Manet and Velasquez is found in the works of such students as **George Bellows** (p. 983), notable for his career as an illustrator and lithographer and for his prizefight scenes (*Dempsey and Firpo,* 1923); Edward Hopper, who classicized the facts of daily life in the U.S. (*Automat; The City; Compartment C, Car 293*); Edward Speicher (1883–1962; *Katharine Cornell, Graziana*); Alexander Brook (1898– ; *Morning*); and Rockwell Kent, with his Alaskan and marine scenes. During the same period Georgia O'Keeffe and Charles Burchfield (1898–1967) painted objective records of the local scene.

1930–40. The social realism of the "Ash Can School" was intensified by the depression and by the organization in 1935 of the **WPA Federal Art Projects.** The newer artists, powerfully influenced by the Mexican school of muralists, divested slum scenes of poetry or sentimentality and used them as a medium of social protest. Robert Gwathmey (1903– ; *End of Day*) projected his message through complex semi-abstract types; Jack Levine (1915–) caricatured the privileged (*The Reluctant Ploughshare*); Mitchell Siporin (1910–) portrayed the heroes of the class struggle in allegorical groupings. Among the most effective exponents of social realism were William Gropper (1897–1973); *The Opposition*), Philip Evergood (1901– ; *Suburban Landscape*), and Ben Shahn (1898–1969; *Vacant Lot, Sunday Football*). A sympathetic treatment of working people was notably expressed in the work of the three Soyer brothers, Moses, Raphael, and Isaac.

1930–40. REGIONALISTS OR ISO-LATIONISTS. In reaction to the influence of Picasso, Matisse, and the Parisian school, a trio of U.S. artists stressed native Midwestern scenes, particularly after 1932: Grant Wood (1892–1942; *Dinner for Threshers, Return from Bohemia, American Gothic*), John Steuart Curry (1897–1946; *My Mother and Father, Baptism in Kansas, Roadworkers' Camp*), and Thomas Hart Benton (1889–1975; *First Crop*). Ultimately the trend ran its course and revealed its sterility.

1930–40. Abstract traditions were maintained by Stuart Davis (1894–1964), Karl Knaths (1891–1971), and Arthur G. Dove. When the **Bauhaus** closed in 1934, some of its leaders came

to the U.S. (Walter Gropius [1883–1969], Laszlo Moholy-Nagy [1895–1946], and Josef Albers [1888–]), as well as the expressionist George Grosz (1893–1959), and the American Lyonel Feininger (1871–1956).

1939–48. With the rise of fascism many European artists found refuge in the U.S. (Marc Chagall [1887–], Chaim Lipschitz [1912–], Pavel Tchelitchew [1898–1957], and Salvador Dali [1904–]). Socially conscious painting declined after the Nazi-Soviet pact (the American Artists Congress, a left-wing group founded in 1936, broke up in 1940), and abstractions and surrealist works enjoyed an increase in popularity (Peter Blume, *The Eternal City*). New experimentation appeared in the "magic realism" of Byron Thomas (1902–), *Night Ball Game*, and the abstractionism of German-born Max Beckmann (1884–1950). In addition, the WPA Index of American Design revived interest in U.S. primitives and encouraged self-taught artists, including in this period **Grandma Moses** (p. 1110), with her anecdotal detail, and the black artist **Horace Pippin** (1888–1946), *The Trial of John Brown*. A personal art form was still being developed by **Yasuo Kuniyoshi** (p. 1078).

1945–60. DEVELOPMENT OF AB-STRACT EXPRESSIONISM. The most significant aspect of the postwar period was the full development of Abstract Expressionism. American artists strove to create a new style, free of provincialism and the social preoccupation which marked much of prewar painting, and to find a form of expression different from that offered by the European movements of Cubism and Surrealism. **Ashile Gorky** (1905–48), *Agony* (1947), relied upon the biomorphic forms of the Surrealist tradition. **Willem de Kooning** (1904–), *Woman* (1950–51), used abstracted and torn-apart images of women in which the gesture and action of the painting process assumes great importance. The art of **Jackson Pollock** (p. 1131), *Mural on Indian Red Ground* (1950), broke new ground with his paintings made by dripping and splashing paint on canvas in order to create an all-over image free of recognizable subject matter and associations. The problem for painters became primarily to resolve the relationship of painted figures or forms to the ground of the canvas itself and to have the expressive content of the work carried by this relationship. **Franz Kline** (1910–62), *Ninth Street* (1951), and **Philip Guston** (1913–   ), *Passage* (1957–58), are other artists who practiced "action painting." **Mark Rothko** (1903–70), *Tundra* (1950), and Adolph Gottlieb (1903–74), *Counterpoise* (1959), concentrated more on specific shapes and relationships of image masses to explore the same kinds of problems. These and other artists composed the New York School of painting and achieved international prominence to the point where American painting became trend-setting for the rest of the world. Other important Abstract Expressionists are Robert Motherwell (1915–   ), *At Five in the Afternoon* (1949), Hans Hoffmann (1880–1966), *Cathedral* (1959), Clyfford Still (1904–   ), *1948-D* (1948), and Mark Tobey (1890–   ), *New Life* (*Resurrection*) (1957). At the same time, Andrew Wyeth (1917–   ) achieved great popularity through his evocative but highly representational paintings of subjects closely associated with rural America (*Christina's World*, 1948).

1959–73. EXPANDING INTEREST IN ART museums and galleries proliferated and established ones built new homes (Solomon R. Guggenheim Museum, 1959; Whitney Museum, 1966; Los Angeles County Museum of Art, 1964; Museum of Fine Arts, Houston, 1973). Numerous contemporary and retrospective exhibitions of importance were mounted; the volume of published art books skyrocketed. Paintings of both contemporary artists and recognized old masters sold for record prices (Rembrandt's *Aristotle Contemplating the Bust of Homer*, in 1961, for $2,234,000; Velasquez's *Juan de Parcja*, over $5 million [1970]) as museums competed for new acquisitions and private collectors speculated. American artists fetched record prices (Andrew Wyeth, Jackson Pollock, $2 million [1973]). Museum attendance figures shot up during the late 60s and museums became the center of social controversies as part of the protest movements of the times. Antiwar and antiestablishment attacks by artists extended to strikes and challenges to prevalent museum exhibitions and private collecting attitudes (sit-in at the Museum of Modern Art, 1970, the Art Workers Coalition). In the 70s attention was focused on the practice of paying high prices for works which had been surreptitiously exported from their place of creation or historic preservation (a portrait attributed to Raphael returned to Italy after purchase by the Museum of Fine Arts, Boston, 1971; controversy raged over the source of the Euphronios Vase purchased for over $1 million by the Metropolitan Museum of Art, 1972). The UN passed a resolution designed to restrict illicit traffic in art objects and archaeological artifacts (1973). Generally, museum operating policies became a matter of public concern as works of art were bought and sold for great sums of money, often works received as bequests.

The increased importance of art in public life was evidenced by the White House Festival of the Arts (14 June 1965), the reproduction of works of modern art on postage stamps (designed by Stuart Davis [1894–1964], 1964, and by Robert Indiana [1928–   ] 1973), the establishment of the National Foundation on the Arts and Humanities (1965), and the proliferation of state Arts Councils. The influence of American artists abroad became more firmly established as American art dominated the principal international art events such as the Venice Biennale and the Documenta held in Kassel, W. Germany. Showings of American sculpture occurred on a major scale in Paris for the first time in 1960, and the Tate Gallery, London, established an American wing in the same year. News magazines gave instant publicity to events in the art world and heralded each new artistic development: the creation of Pop Art, Self-destroying Art, Happenings, and Op Art. Auction prices shot up for American art and Madison Avenue art dealers and auction houses attained the stature of big business (Marlborough, André Emmerich; Parke-Bernet merged with Sotheby of London), while new galleries devoted to less well-established talents, sprung up in the SoHo (South Houston Street) district of New York City.

1960–73. PROLIFERATION OF STYLES IN PAINTING AND SCULPTURE. Abstract Expressionism began to wane as artists looked for new principles to govern their work. The emotional and subjective aspect of action painting was replaced by a carefully considered intellectual analysis of forms, colors, and subject matter. Owing something to Marcel Duchamp and the European tradition of Dada, **Pop** (popular) **Art** took advertising art and everyday objects and monumentalized them as if to draw attention to artistic qualities that could be found in mundane and commercial aspects of the environment. **Andy Warhol's** (1930–) Campbell's soup cans, **Roy Lichtenstein's** (1923–) blown-up comic-strip-like pictures, **Jasper Johns'** (1930–) *Pointed Bronze Beer Cans* sculpture, and **Claes Oldenburg's**

(1929–) *Hamburger with Pickle and Tomato Attached,* transformed objects commonly taken for granted. Other artists, such as **James Rosenquist** (1933–) and **Robert Rauschenberg** (1925–), whose work bridges the art of de Kooning with the Pop school, recombined everyday images into new compositions, which question assumptions about them. The sculptor George Segal (1924–), who made lifelike figures out of plaster and put these into actual settings, reminds one of the art of Edward Hopper, with nostalgic references to the 1930s, but in a very contemporary idiom. **"Happenings"** were events supposedly designed—or "allowed to happen"—to reveal the artistic significance of things that occur in experience (Al Hansen, Claes Oldenburg). Concern with more formal issues was evidenced by the **Op** (optical) artists who experimented with the perceptual process in combining and recombining colors in geometrically abstract shapes. This trend, which also has European precedents in the work of Victor Vasarely and Bridget Riely, develops from Josef Albers' experiments and studies. Gene Davis (1920–), Larry Poons (1937–), Richard Anuszkiewicz (1930–), and Nicholas Krushenick (1929–) associated with this movement and are also called "post-painterly abstractionists." The use of "hard edge" images is related to this style and relates as well to the concept of **"Minimal Art."** Minimal works, proceeding from the dictum that "Less is more," reduced the complexity of works to basic geometric shapes, subtle modifications of tone and brushwork or flat areas of color (Barnett Newman [1925–70], Ad Reinhardt [1913–67]). More lyrical color field paintings were made by Morris Louis (1912–62), *Saraband* (1962), and Jules Olitski (1922–). These involve the interaction of blended colors with each other to the canvas support and its edge. The paintings of Frank Stella (1936–   ) and Kenneth Noland (1924– ·) deal with the relationship of flat areas of color in geometric configurations to the rectangular or shaped picture surface. The analysis of picture making led to new media and to multimedia works such as shaped canvases in 3 dimensions (Charles Hinman, 1932–   ), the fluorescent-light works of Dan Flavin (1933–   ), neon works by Chryssa (1933–   ), painted wooden satirical sculptures by Escobar Marisol (1930–   ), kinetic art based on movement (*The Party*, 1965–66), laser-light-beam works, and those using a variety of other materials and processes. Earthworks and environmental constructions, too large to house in a museum or private home, were created in an attempt to treat new questions of scale, materials, and the definitions of art (Richard Serra [1939–   ], Ronald Bladen [1918–   ]). With the death (1965) of **David Smith** (p. 1153), whose large stainless steel sculptures (Cubi Series, 1961–65) culminate the line of development through Cubism and Abstract Expressionism to geometric abstraction, sculpture becomes more diverse. Surrealism survives in the work of Edward Kienholz (1927–   ) and Escobar Marisol, but it is transformed by modern concerns and realizations. Formalism continues in the work of Robert Morris (1931–   ) and Donald Judd (1928–   ). By the end of the 60s definitions between painting and sculpture had become indistinct and the arts overlapped considerably. Videotape (Keith Sonnier [1941–   ]) and movie film (Stan Brachage, Michael Snow) are 2 of the latest media being explored by artists.

1960–73. ARCHITECTURE. New materials were exploited for their expressive and structural potential. **Paul Rudolph's** (1918–   ) *Art and Architecture Building* at Yale (1963) was a harsh example of the power of raw concrete. **Eero Saarinen's** *TWA Terminal Building* (1956–62) at the John F. Kennedy International Airport, a concrete structure suggesting a bird in flight, while expressing the potential of this material, marks a triumph of style over convenience and function. **I. M. Pei** (1917–   ), **Skidmore, Owings, and Merrill,** and **Philip Johnson** (1906–   ) continued in the International style in major office buildings and public projects, and Edward Durrell Stone (1902–   ) and **Minoru Yamasaki** (1912–   ) allude to historical types in a romantic or evocative manner. **Louis I. Kahn's** dramatic buildings for the Salk Institute for Biological Research, La Jolla, Calif., 1965, and for the Library at Phillips Exeter Academy, Exeter, N.H., 1972, achieve monumentality and classical harmonies through novel structural systems, giving full expression to the functional and mechanical realities of modern construction. By contrast, **Robert Venturi** (1925–   ), Yale's *Mathematics Building*, 1970, and **Charles W. Moore** (1925–   ) avoid monumentality as unsuitable to the modern age of mass production and economic necessity. With reference to the imagery of Pop Art, these architects rely upon humble vernacular building types and distinguish their structures by the use of signs and graphic decoration, their unorthodox approach often arousing storms of protest. Office buildings continued to dominate construction, as residential housing sharply declined in the early 1970s, the skyscrapers still conforming to the curtain-wall techniques evolved during the postwar period, with little if any regional variation. New heights were reached in the *Sears Tower*, Chicago, and the *World Trade Center*, New York City, but in brash disregard of demographic and environmental considerations.

Music

The colonial period was a time when song rather than instrumental music was the prevailing mode of musical expression. The colonists sang psalms, hymns, ballads, plantation work songs, sea chanteys, tavern songs, and, in the Revolutionary years, patriotic songs to English ballad tunes. What little professionalism existed was restricted to a few European performers and such religious groups as the Moravians. Versatile statesmen like Franklin, Jefferson, and Francis Hopkinson displayed a more than amateur interest in music, and by the early national period Americans were familiar with the works of such European giants as Handel, Gluck, and Haydn.

Professionalism took hold in the United States in the first half of the nineteenth century, with the founding of orchestras, choral societies, and music schools, with the distribution of sheet music by music publishers, and the manufacture of musical instruments on a large scale. Individual Europeans, notably Lorenzo Da Ponte at the start of the period, later Ole Bull, Jenny Lind, and Adelina Patti, provided a fillip to musical life, as did the immigration of many musicians as a result of the revolutions of 1848 in Europe. Theodore Thomas and other distinguished symphonic conductors played major roles in bringing the best European music and the most talented performers to the United States.

It was not until the twentieth century, however, that America's contribution both to popular and serious music gained wide recognition. Jazz, a distinctively American idiom, attained worldwide popularity, and its influence internationally has burgeoned with the years. As the quality of music conservatories improved so did the achievements of individual performers, symphonic orchestras, and opera companies. American composers have proliferated in numbers, performances of their music are less rare than in the past, and avant-garde experimentation has won a discriminating, if small, following.

Pioneer Period, 1640–1800

1640–1787. RELIGIOUS MUSIC. Psalmody, 1640–1764. *Bay Psalm Book* (also p. 844) published at Cambridge, Mass.; the first hymn book printed in the English colonies; adopted throughout New England and as far south as Philadelphia. This psalm collection was printed without tunes, leaving choice of psalmody to the individual congregation, with the result that psalm singing became a confused cacophony. The 9th edition (1698) included 13 tunes (first book with music printed in the colonies). 1712. Rev. John Tufts of Boston published *A Very Plain and Easy Introduction to the Whole Art of Singing Psalm Tunes*, containing 28 tunes in 3-part harmony, the first instruction book on singing to be compiled in the colonies. **1721.** Rev. Cotton Mather of Boston published *The Accomplished Singer,* while his nephew, Rev. Thomas Walter of Boston, published *Grounds and Rules of Music Explained.* **1764.** Josiah Flagg of Boston published *A Collection of Best Psalm Tunes,* engraved by Paul Revere. **1771.** *New England Psalm Singer* published by **William Billings** (1746–1800), first New England composer, organizer of singing societies, composer of *Fuguing Tunes, Chester,* and numerous Revolutionary patriot songs.

Hymns, 1703–39. Hymns or hymnody began to replace psalmody as a result of the influence of the "singing dissenters." **1737.** John Wesley, influenced by Moravian hymn singing, was arraigned by the Savannah, Ga., grand jury, charged, among other counts, with introducing unauthorized psalms and hymns into the Anglican church service. The folk hymnody of the Methodists and Baptists on the frontier continued this tradition. **1739.** First American edition of Isaac Watts' famous *Hymns and Spiritual Songs* (pub. in England, 1707).

1720–30. EPHRATA CLOISTER, founded by German Dunkers, 50 miles west of Philadelphia. Women copied and illuminated hymn books. Hymns were sung in 4-, 5-, 6-, and 7-part harmony (while in the rest of the colonies congregations sang only in unison). *Ephrata Hymnbook* (*Gottliche Lieben und Lobes Gethöne*) published by Benjamin Franklin (1730). More than 1,000 of the hymns are attributed to **Johann Conrad Beissel** (1690–1768), reputedly the first composer in the colonies whose works were published.

1742. MORAVIAN MUSIC. First **singstunde** in **Bethlehem, Pa.** (settled, 1741, by Moravians). **Collegium musicum,** founded 1744; continued until 1820, when it was succeeded by the Philharmonic Society. Most notable among the Revolutionary generation of Moravian musicians was **John Frederick Peter** (1746–1813), a composer of chamber music as well as organist of the Moravian congregation.

1787. CATHOLIC HYMNS. First hymnal published for the use of Catholics in the U.S., *A Compilation of the Litanies and Vesper Hymns and Anthems as They Are Sung in the Catholic Church,* adapted to voice and organ by John Aitkin, Philadelphia (2 parts treble and bass; 3d part added later).

1627–1787. INSTRUMENTS. 1627. Pilgrims assembled by use of **drum. 1633.** Shipment of **recorders** and **hautboys** (oboes) received at New Hampshire plantations of Newitchwanke and Pascattaquack. **1635.** Shipment of **jewsharps** at Roxbury, Mass. **1638. Trumpet** used for assembly at Windsor, Conn. **1660. Viol** requested by Harvard College students. **1678.** Bequest of **bass viol** in Sudbury, Mass. **1694.** German Pietists settling in Wissahickon, Pa. (near Philadelphia) used **trombones** in quartets. **1699. Virginals** used and tuned in Boston. **1703–87. Organ.** First recorded use in a colonial church, Gloria Dei Church (Swedish) in present Philadelphia, accompanied by viols, oboes, trumpets and kettledrums. First organ built in the colonies was constructed by Dr. Thomas Witt of Philadelphia (1704). The first imported into New England was in 1711 by Thomas Brattle of Boston (still in existence in Portsmouth, N.H.). The first to be constructed (1745–46) by a native American was built by Edward Bromfield, Jr., of Boston. In 1756 the new organ constructed by Gilbert Ash was dedicated at City Hall, New York. A pipe organ was used for the first time in a colonial Congregational Church in Philadelphia, 1770. The first pipe organ west of the Alleghenies was built (1787) in Cookstown (now Fayette City), Pa., by Joseph Downer of Brookline, Mass.; instrument now at Carnegie Institute, Pittsburgh. **1716.** Shipment of **flageolets** and **flutes** advertised in Boston newspaper. Most of the previously named instruments were believed to have been in use by this time in the other colonies, including the **French horn** and **bassoon. 1736. Harpsichord** used in recital given in New York by **Karl Theodore Pachelbel,** son of the famous organist (first European musician of note to visit Boston). **1761. Benjamin Franklin** invented his improved version of the glass harmonica, the **glassychord.** (Franklin is known to have played the guitar, harp, and dulcimer.) **1769–74. Spinet** and **pianoforte.** First American spinet made by John Harris in Boston; first pianoforte by John Behrent, Philadelphia.

1731–1800. PERFORMANCE. 1731–32. Early concerts. First authentic record in the English colonies of public concert at Mr. Pelham's (*Boston News-Letter,* 16, 23 Dec. 1731). First recorded concert in Charleston, S.C., a few months later.

1735–50. Ballad Operas. The ballad opera *Flora, or Hob in the Well* at the Courtroom, Charleston, S.C. (1735), the first recorded operatic performance in the colonies. *The Mock Doctor* (1750), the first performed ballad opera in New York, was followed that year by *The Beggar's Opera.*

1744. Collegium musicum founded by Moravians, credited with early performance of parts of oratorios, later of chamber music of **John Frederick Peter,** of Haydn quartets and symphonies, the first performance in America of *The Creation* and of Handel's *The Seasons.*

1752. First use of an orchestra in an operatic performance in the colonies: *The Beggar's Opera,* given in Upper Marlboro, Md., by the Kean and Murray Co.

1753. William Tuckey (1708–81), on arrival in New York, became organist and choirmaster of Trinity Church.

1754–69. Concert Halls and Outdoor Concerts. First concert hall in Boston opened by Stephen Deblois (1754). Ranelagh Gardens' series of open-air summer concerts announced in *N.Y. Mercury* (1765); continued for 4 years.

1757. Dr. Arnes' *Masque of Alfred* performed by students in Philadelphia. **1770.** Milton's *Masque of Comus* performed by Hallam Co., Philadelphia.

1761–87. MUSICAL SOCIETIES. St. Cecilia Society, oldest musical society, founded at Charleston, S.C.; continued until 1912; gave several concerts each year, including St. Cecilia's Day, 22 Nov. The orchestra was composed of "gentlemen performers," supplemented by professional musicians engaged by the season. **Harmonic Society,** New York, gave concert series (1773–74) presenting first French and Italian virtuosi. **Handel Society** (Dartmouth College, 1780), **Harmonic Society** (Fredericksburg, Va., 1784), **Musical Society of Boston** (1785–89) performed excerpts from Handel's works. **Stoughton** (Mass.) **Musical Society** organized by William Billings, probably the oldest singing society still in existence in the U.S.; held first singing contest in U.S. at Dorchester (1790), competing against First Parish of Dorchester. **Uranian Society** established (Phila., 1787–1800) to improve church music.

1763. EARLY MUSIC SCHOOL. James Bremner opened a music school in Philadelphia; subsequently active in city's musical life; pupils reputed to have included **Francis Hopkinson.**

1619–1800. POPULAR MUSIC. Black people's music, 1619–1776. First transported to Virginia as servants and later as slaves, black people from Africa introduced native African dances and songs into the colonies, to which were added elements borrowed from church and white folk music. Utilizing utensils and other materials at hand, they improvised primitive percussion, wind, and string instruments, invented the banjo (named "banjar" by Thomas Jefferson), and showed proficiency in the use of sophisticated European instruments. Notable performers included Sy Gilliat, a slave of Gov. Botetourt, and official fiddler at Williamsburg balls, and London Brigs.

c.1715. MOTHER GOOSE rhymes composed by "Mother Goose," mother-in-law of Thomas Fleet, Boston printer, who came to live with Thomas and her daughter Elizabeth after the birth of their baby, and sang to him. Fleet published the nursery rhymes under the title, *Songs for Nursery or Mother Goose Melodies for Children.*

c.1754–98. PATRIOTIC SONGS. "YANKEE DOODLE," attributed to Dr. Richard Schuckburg, a British army physician, whose original version written during the French and Indian War was a parody of the colonial soldier. It was set to a *Mother Goose* tune called "Lucy Locket Lost Her Pocket." It is mentioned in the first American comic ballad opera libretto, **Andrew Barton's** *The Disappointment, or the Force of Credulity* (Philadelphia, 1767; music by **James Ralph** [d. 1762]). First American printing, as part of an instrumental medley, in *Federal Overture* (1794), arranged by Benjamin Carr (1769–1831) and published by him in Philadelphia and New York (1795). First American edition to use words and music published by G. Willig (1798).

1767. *The Psalms of David,* the 1st book of music printed in the colonies from type (New York).

1768. John Dickinson wrote "American Liberty Song" to the tune of "British Grenadiers."

1775. Dr. Joseph Warren wrote "Free Amerikay" and Thomas Paine composed the ballad "Liberty Tree."

c.1776. "Chester" by **William Billings,**

one of the most inspiring patriotic tunes.

c.1793. "The President's March," variously attributed to Philip Roth and Philip Phile.

1798. "Adams and Liberty," words by Robert Treat Paine; "Hail Columbia," words by Joseph Hopkinson, set to tune of "The President's March."

1759–88. SECULAR SONGS. First secular song by a native American, "My Days Have Been So Wondrous Free," music by **Francis Hopkinson** (1737–91), poem by Thomas Parnell. Hopkinson, a Philadelphian and the first native composer, was later a signer of the Declaration of Independence, a member of the Constitutional Convention, the first judge of the Admiralty Court of Pennsylvania, and author of many pamphlets and poems; his *Seven Songs,* 1788.

1781–96. EARLY AMERICAN OPERAS. *The Temple of Minerva,* libretto and music by **Francis Hopkinson,** 1st attempt at grand opera, performed in Philadelphia (11 Dec. 1781) in the presence of George Washington. *Tammany,* by **James Hewitt** (1770–1827), produced at New York under the auspices of the Tammany Society (1794). *The Archers, or the Mountaineers of Switzerland,* libretto by **William Dunlap,** music by **Benjamin Carr** (1768–1831); and *Edwin and Angelina,* libretto by Elihu H. Smith, music by Victor Pelissier (both New York, 1796).

1769–96. FOREIGN COMPOSITIONS IN AMERICA. John Gualdo (Italian immigrant, d. 1771), *Symphony,* Philadelphia, 1769; **Handel:** *Messiah,* first performance in colonies (overture and 16 numbers) at Trinity Church, New York, conducted and arranged by William Tuckey; **Gluck:** overture to *Iphigenie en Aulide,* performed by an orchestra of some 30 instruments, Charleston, S.C., 1796; **Haydn:** *Stabat Mater,* Charleston, S.C., 1796.

1791–94. EARLY SONG AND HAR-

MONY BOOKS. *Harmonia Americana,* by Samuel Holyoke (1791); *The American Harmony,* by Oliver Holden (1792), and Holden's *The Union Harmony* (1793), with first printing of "Coronation" (later the hymn "All Hail the Power of Jesus' Name"); *Rural Harmony,* by Jacob Kimball (1793); *The Continental Harmony,* by **Willam Billings** (1794).

Early National and Antebellum Years, 1800–60

1803–53. INSTRUMENTS. First authentic American **piano** made by Benjamin Grehorne of Milton, Mass. (1803). Firm of Stewart & Chickering, piano manufacturers, established at Boston, 1823. **Jonas Chickering** (1798–1853) patented first successful casting of a full iron piano frame capable of withstanding powerful tension without deflecting pitch. **Wilhelm Knabe** (1803–64) established at Baltimore the firm of Knabe & Co. (1837). Henry Steinway & Sons established by **Henry E. Steinway** (1797–1871), at New York (1853), exhibiting there (1855) a square piano with cross- or over-strung strings, and a full cast-iron frame.

1805. DA PONTE. Lorenzo Da Ponte (1749–1838), Italian poet who wrote the libretti for Mozart's *Don Giovanni* and *The Marriage of Figaro,* arrived in the U.S. (1805); held professorship of Italian literature at Columbia College; was active (1825–26) in establishing Garcia's Opera Co.; and backed the French tenor Montrésor in opening a season in New York with Rossini's *La Cenerentola* (1832). He also promoted the building of the Italian Opera House in New York (1833).

1810–50. MUSICAL PERFORMING GROUPS. Orchestras. Boston Philharmonic Society founded by **Gottlieb Graupner** (1767–1836); credited as the first genuine and regular orchestra in

the U.S.; gave its last concert, 1824. Philharmonic Society of New York founded (1842) chiefly through the efforts of Ureli C. Hill, its first president; first concert 7 Dec. Chicago Philharmonic Society, 1850; disbanded c.1854.

1815–56. Choral Societies. Handel and Haydn Society, organized at Boston (1815) under the leadership of Gottlieb Graupner, Thomas Smith Webb, and others. Lowell Mason president and conductor beginning 1827. German Männerchor organized by Philip Wolsifer at Philadelphia (1835); oldest German singing society in the U.S. Chicago Sacred Music Society established 1842. Deutsche Liederkranz, New York, 1847. Milwaukee Musikverein, 1849. *Saengerfest* held at Cincinnati (1849) brought together for the first time the German singing societies of the Midwest. Chicago Männergesang-Verein (1852; disbanded, 1859). Arion Society, a German choral group (New York, 1854; merged, 1918, with the Liederkranz Society). Cecilia Society and Harmonic Society (Cincinnati, 1856).

1837. Harvard Musical Assn. founded by John S. Dwight.

c.1840. "Singing Family" Troupes (the Hutchinsons, Cheneys, Bakers, Harmoneons, and Father Kemp's Old Folks), group performers of popular choral and instrumental music.

1849. Ensembles. Mendelssohn Quintet Club, the first important string chamber music group in the U.S., established at Boston.

1825–60. MUSIC SCHOOLS AND EDUCATION. Musical Fund Society established a music school at Philadelphia (1825); first important institution of its kind in the U.S. Music school of Boston Academy of Music (established by Lowell Mason, 1832) introduced first significant advances in musical education in the U.S. First music school in Chicago, 1834. Lowell Mason introduced (1838) the teaching of music into the Boston public schools. Boston Music School established (1850) by Benjamin F. Baker; dissolved, 1868. Class system of pianoforte instruction begun (1851) by Eben Tourjéc at Providence, R.I.

1827–35. MUSIC PUBLISHERS. Carl Fischer (New York, 1827); Oliver Ditson (Boston, 1835).

1800–81. MUSIC PERIODICALS. *American Musical Magazine* (Northampton, Mass., 1800; disc. 1801); *Boston Musical Gazette* (1838; disc. 1846); *Musical World* (N.Y., 1849; disc. 1860); *American Monthly Musical Review* (N.Y., 1850; disc. 1852); *Dwight's Journal of Music* (Boston, 1852; pioneered in musical criticism; disc. 1881).

1809–60° FOREIGN COMPOSITIONS IN AMERICA. Haydn: Haydn societies org. Phila., 1809; Cincinnati, 1819; first complete perf., *Creation*, Boston, 1819. **Handel:** *Messiah*, Univ. of Pa. (1801); 1st complete performance, probably HH (1818); oratorio, *Israel in Egypt*, Seguin Opera Co., N.Y. (1842). **Beethoven:** *1st Symph.*, MFSP (1821); *6th* (Pastoral) and *2nd* Boston (1842); *5th*, PS (1843); *Egmont Overture*, Boston (1844); *9th*, PS (1846); *3d* (*Eroica*) PS (1847); *7th Symph.*, MFSB (1859); *Leonore Overture*, No. 3 (Boston, 1850); *Egmont*, music complete (Boston, 1859). **Mozart:** *Jupiter Symph.*, No. 41, PS (1844); Mozart Society org., Chicago (1847); *G minor Symph.* (No. 40), MFSB (1850); *Requiem*, HH (1857); *E flat maj. Piano Concerto* (Boston, 1859); **Rossini:** *Stabat Mater*, HH (1843). **Mendelssohn:** oratorio, *St. Paul*, N.Y. (1838); oratorio, *Elijah*, HH (1840); *Hebrides Overture*, PS (1844); *Scotch Symph.*, PS (1845); Mendelssohn Festival, Castle Garden, N.Y. (1847); *Mid-*

summer Night's Dream, Germania Orch. (N.Y., 1848); *Italian Symph.* (Boston, 1851). **Schumann:** *1st Symph.*, MFSB (1841); cantata, *Paradise and the Peri*, Musical Institute, N.Y. (1848); *Symph. in D.*, PS (1857); *Manfred Overture*, PS (1857); *A minor Piano Concerto* (op. 54), PS (1859). **Berlioz:** *King Lear Overture*, PS (1846); *Roman Carnival Overture* (1857). **Donizetti:** *Il Poliuto*, performed as oratorio, HH (1849). **Schubert:** *C maj. Symph.*, PS (1851). **Wagner:** Overture to *Rienzi* played from manuscript by Germania Orch. (Boston, 1853); *Faust Overture* (Boston, 1857); Prelude to *Lohengrin*, PS (1857).

1819–59. FOREIGN OPERA. Rossini: *Barber of Seville* (English, N.Y., 1819; Italian, by Manual Garcia troupe, N.Y., 1825; 6 operas given at Italian Opera House, N.Y., 1833, including *La Gazza Ladra*). **Mozart:** *Marriage of Figaro* (Bishop's English version, N.Y., 1823; in Italian, N.Y., 1858); *Don Giovanni* (N.Y., 1825); *Die Zauberflöte* (Phila., 1832). **Weber:** *Der Freischütz* (English, N.Y., 1825); *Oberon* (Phila., 1827). **Meyerbeer:** *Roberto il Diavolo* (English, N.Y., 1834); New Orleans productions of *Les Huguenots* (1839), *L'Étoile du Nord* (1850), *Il Profeta* (1850). **Bellini:** *La Straniera* (N.Y., 1834); *La Sonnambula* (English, N.Y., 1834); *Norma* (Phila., 1841); *I Puritani* (N.Y., 1844). **Donizetti:** *L'Elisir d'Amore* (N.Y. 1838); *Lucia di Lammermoor* (New Orleans, 1841); *La Favorita* and *The Daughter of the Regiment* (New Orleans, 1843); *Gemma di Vergi* (N.Y., 1843); and 8 others by 1850. **Verdi:** Havana Opera Co. productions of *I Lombardi* and *Ernani* (N.Y., 1847); *Nabucco* (N.Y., 1848); *Attila* (N.Y., 1848); *Macbeth* (N.Y., 1850); *Luisa Miller* (Phila., 1852); *Il Trovatore* (N.Y., 1855); *La Traviata* (N.Y., 1856); *Rigoletto* (New Orleans, 1860). **Wagner:** *Tannhäuser* and *Lohengrin* (N.Y., 1859).

° *Abbreviations*

HH   Handel and Haydn Society, Boston (1815)
MFSP   Musical Fund Society, Philadelphia (1820)
MFSN   Musical Fund Society, New York (c.1828)
MFSB   Musical Fund Society, Boston (1847)
PS   Philharmonic Society of New York (1842); now New York Philharmonic

Halévy: New Orleans operatic season, 1858–59, probable first performances of *Jaquarita l'Indienne, La Juive,* and *Reine de Chypre.*

1845. AMERICAN OPERA. *Leonora,* an opera by **William H. Fry** (?1815–64), Phila., the first **grand opera** to be composed by a native American.

1847–52. OPERA HOUSES AND CONCERT HALLS. Astor Place Opera House opened in New York (1847). New York Academy of Music and Boston Music Hall (1852). Academy of Music, Philadelphia (1856).

1835–59. MUSICAL DEBUTS. Charlotte Cushman, actress, made her debut as a singer in *The Marriage of Figaro* (Boston, 1835). **Ole Bull,** Norwegian violinist (N.Y., 1843); **Jenny Lind,** Swedish soprano (Castle Garden, N.Y., 11 Sept. 1850); **Henriette Sontag,** German dramatic soprano (N.Y., 1853); **Louis M. Gottschalk** (1829–69), native-born composer and pianist (N.Y., 1853); **Marietta Alboni,** Italian operatic soprano (U.S. tour, 1853); **Adelina Patti** (in *Lucia,* N.Y., 1859).

1848. REVOLUTIONS OF '48 led to the migration of many musical artists to the U.S. The Germania Orchestra (N.Y., 1848) introduced Wagner's music into the U.S. Counterparts were organized at Boston, Philadelphia, and other cities. Among the composers and instrumentalists of the Germania group who later became well known were **Carl Bergmann** (1821–76), **Carl Zerrahn** (1826–1909), **Theodor Eisfeld** (1816–82), and **Otto Dresel** (1826–90).

1853–58. CONDUCTORS. American debut of the French conductor **Louis Antoine Jullien,** who toured the U.S. with his orchestra (1853–54), conducting 200 concerts, and directing a "Grand Musical Congress" made up of 1,500 instrumentalists and 16 choral societies performing oratorios and symphonies (1854). **Carl Zerrahn** named conductor

of the Handel and Haydn Society at Boston; later (1865–82) conducted the concerts of the Harvard Musical Assn. **Theodore Thomas** (p. 1170), who arrived in the U.S. from Germany in 1845, joined **William Mason** (1829–1908) in organizing a string quartet, which introduced music of Schumann and Brahms into the U.S.; Thomas named conductor of N.Y. Academy of Music (1858).

1814–60. POPULAR SONGS. 1814–43. Patriotic Songs. "Star-Spangled Banner." "The Defence of Fort McHenry," by **Francis Scott Key** (1779–1843), published (1814) in the Baltimore *Patriot.* This poem, based on the author's observation of the British bombardment of Ft. McHenry (13–14 Sept. 1814), was issued in handbill form almost immediately after its composition. On or about 19 Oct. 1814 the title was changed to "The Star-Spangled Banner," which by Act of Congress (1931) was designated as the national anthem. The tune, a familiar one in post-Revolutionary days, is that of "To Anacreon in Heaven," variously credited to the British composers Samuel Arnold and John Stafford Smith. Words of the national hymn "America" written by Rev. Samuel Francis Smith (1808–95); first performed at the Park St. Church, Boston (1831). The tune is that of the English national anthem, "God Save the King." "Columbia, the Gem of the Ocean" (1843) is usually credited to Thomas A. Beckett, but sometimes claimed for David T. Shaw.

1827–60. POPULAR SONGS. "The Minstrel's Return from the War," by John Hill Hewitt (1827). "Jim Crow" (1828) by Thomas Rice, Louisville, Ky., an international hit as well as the source of an unfortunate connotation implying racial segregation. "The Old Oaken Bucket" (1834), words by Samuel Woodworth, who wrote the poem in 1818. "Zip Coon" (c.1834, later known as "Turkey in the Straw"). "Woodman,

Spare That Tree" (1837), words by George P. Morris, music by Henry Russell. "Tippecanoe and Tyler, Too" (1840), political campaign song used by the Whig party; words by Alexander C. Ross to the tune of "Little Pigs." "We Won't Go Home Till Morning" (1842), words by William Clifton; based on the old French melody "Malbrouck." "Old Dan Tucker" (1843), generally credited to **Daniel D. Emmett** (1815–1904), also thought to be the composer of "The Blue Tail Fly" (also called "Jim Crack Corn," 1846). By **Stephen C. Foster** (p. 1032): "Oh! Susanna" (1848); "Ben Bolt" (1848), words by Thomas Dunn English; "De Camptown Races" (1850); "Old Folks at Home" (1851, often called "Swanee River"); "Massa's in de Cold, Cold Ground" (1852). Original version of "Frankie and Johnny" (1850); later reputedly sung at siege of Vicksburg (1863); more than 100 different versions uncovered, chiefly after 1899. "My Old Kentucky Home" (1853) by Foster. "Listen to the Mocking Bird" (1855), music by Septimus Winner (1826–1902). "Darling Nelly Gray" (1856) by Benjamin Russel Hanby. "Jingle Bells" (1857) by J. S. Pierpont. "Dixie's Land" (written 1859, commonly called "Dixie") by Daniel D. Emmett; first performed by Bryant's Minstrels (N.Y., 1859); played at the inauguration of Jefferson Davis, Montgomery, Ala., 18 Feb. 1861, it quickly became the symbol of the Confederacy. "Old Black Joe" (1860) by Foster.

Civil War and Postbellum Years, 1861–1900

1861–65. CIVIL WAR SONGS. "John Brown's Body," most widely sung Federal song, has been credited to Thomas B. Bishop, the musical adaptation of a Negro Carolina low-country melody to James E. Greenleaf. A ribald parody, beginning "Hang Jeff Davis on a sour apple tree," appeared in 1865. "Battle Hymn of the Republic," written by **Julia Ward Howe** (1819–1910) to the tune of "John Brown's Body" (pub. Feb. 1862). Next to Emmett's "Dixie" (1859), the most popular Southern marching song was "The Bonnie Blue Flag" (1862), words by Mrs. Annie Chambers-Ketchum, music by Henry McCarthy. "Maryland, My Maryland" (1861), by James Ryder Randall, sung to German folksong "O Tannenbaum." "We Are Coming, Father Abraham" (1862), by James Sloan Gibbons, abolitionist writer in answer to a plea to the states by Lincoln to raise "300,000 more" soldiers; musical settings by Orlando Emerson (1820–1915) and Stephen Foster. Walter Kittredge's "Tenting Tonight" (1862). "When Johnny Comes Marching Home" (1863), by **Patrick Sarsfield Gilmore** (1829–92). "Tramp, Tramp, Tramp" (1864), by George Root. "Marching Through Georgia" (1865), by **Henry Clay Work** (1832–84), who also wrote "Father, Dear Father, Come Home with Me Now."

1861–1900.[*] FOREIGN COMPOSITIONS IN AMERICA. Verdi: *Un Ballo in Maschera* (N.Y., 1861); *La Forza Del Destino* (1865); *Aida* (1873); *Requiem Mass,* Italian Opera Co. (N.Y., 1875); *Don Carlo,* Havana Opera Co. (1877); *Otello,* Campanini, conduct. (N.Y., 1888); *Falstaff,* MO (1895). **C. P. E. Bach:** *Symph. in D maj.* (N.Y., 1862); *Symph. in C* (N.Y., 1866); **J. S. Bach:** *Toccata in F* and *Passacaglia,* Theo. Thomas (N.Y., 1865); *Suite in D,* PS (1869); *St. Matthew Passion,* in part, HH (1874), complete (1879); *Christmas Oratorio,* pts. 1 & 2, HH, with

[*] *Abbreviations*
BS   Boston Symphony Orchestra (1881)
CO   Chicago Opera Assn. (1910)
HH   Handel and Haydn Society, Boston (1815)
MO   Metropolitan Opera, New York (1883)
PH   Philadelphia Orchestra (1900)
PS   Philharmonic Society of New York (1842); now New York Philharmonic
SS   Symphony Society of New York (1878)

Emma Thursby (1877); *Mass in B min.,* Bach Festival, Bethlehem, Pa. (1900). **Beethoven:** *2nd Piano Concerto,* Brooklyn Philharmonic Society (1865); *Choral Fantasia* (1866); *Prometheus music,* Theo. Thomas (1867); *Grand Quartet* (op. 131), scored for full orchestra by Carl M. Berghaus, BS (1884). **Tchaikovsky:** frequent performances beginning with *1st Piano Concerto,* Hans von Bülow, soloist (Boston, 1875); *Romeo and Juliet Overture,* PS (1876). First complete performance of *Violin Concerto,* Maude Powell (N.Y., 1889); *4th Symph.,* SS (1890); *Nutcracker Suite,* Chicago Symphony Orchestra (1892); *1812 Overture,* Theo. Thomas (Chicago, 1893). **Wagner:** *Flying Dutchman music,* Theo. Thomas (N.Y., 1862); prelude to *Tristan,* PS (1866); "Ride of the Valkyries," Theo. Thomas (N.Y., 1872); "Wotan's Farewell" and "Magic Fire Scene" from *Die Walküre,* Thomas (Phila., 1865); "Centennial March," Centennial Exposition, Thomas (Phila., 11 May 1876); "Good Friday Spell" from *Parsifal,* SS (1883). *Die Meistersinger,* MO (1886); *Tristan,* MO (1886); *Der Ring des Nibelungen,* MO (1888). **Brahms:** *German Requiem,* N.Y. Oratorio Society (1877); *1st Symph.,* Damrosch and Thomas (1877); *2d,* Thomas (1878); *3d* (BS, 1884); *4th* (BS, 1886); *Academic Festival Overture,* Thomas (Boston, 1881); *2nd Piano Concerto,* PS, Rafael Joseffy soloist (1882); *Violin Concerto* (BS, 1889). **Gounod:** *Faust* (Phila. and N.Y., 1863). **Bizet:** *Carmen* (N.Y., 1878). **Johann Strauss:** *Die Fledermaus* (N.Y., 1885). **Leoncavallo:** *I Pagliacci* (N.Y., 1894). **Humperdinck,** *Hansel and Gretel* (English, N.Y., 1895). **Richard Strauss:** *F min. Symph.,* Thomas (N.Y., 1884); tone poem, *Don Juan,* BS, A. Nikisch (1891); *Tod und Verklärung,* PS, Thomas (1892); *Ein Heldenleben,* Chicago Symphony (1900). **Dvořák:** *Carnival* and *Otello* overtures at concert honoring composer's first U.S. appearance, National Conservatory of Music (N.Y., 1892); *New World Symph.,* PS (1893); *Concerto for Violin,* SS (1894). **Schubert:** Overture to *Fierabras,* Harvard Music Assn. (Boston, 1866); extracts from *Rosamunde,* Theo. Thomas (N.Y., 1867); *Unfinished Symph.,* Theo. Thomas (1867); *Octet for Strings; C maj. Symph.,* Theo. Thomas (N.Y., 1875). **Berlioz:** *Symphonie Fantastique,* N.Y. (1866); *Damnation of Faust,* N.Y. Symph. (1880). **Franck:** *D min. Symph.,* BS (1899). **Puccini:** *Manon Lescaut* (Phila., 1894); *La Bohème,* Royal Italian Opera (San Francisco, 1898).

1861–1905. PERFORMANCES OF AMERICAN COMPOSITIONS. John Knowles Paine (1839–1906); *Oratorio* (Portland, Me., 1873); *1st Symph.,* Theo. Thomas (Boston, 1876); *Spring Symph.* (Cambridge, Mass., 1880); symphonic poem, *An Island Fantasy,* BS (1889). George W. Chadwick (1854–1931): Overture to *Rip Van Winkle* (Boston, 1879); royalty of $13 by BS for performance of *2nd Symph.* (1886) established a precedent; *3rd Symph.,* BS (1894); *Judith,* choral work (Worcester, 1901); *Cleopatra,* symphonic poem, Chicago Orch. (1905). George F. Bristow (1825–98): *Arcadian Symph.,* PS (1874). Arthur Foote (1853–1937): Overture *In the Mountains,* BS (1887); *Suite for Strings* (1889). Edward A. MacDowell (p. 1093); *1st Piano Concerto* Theo. Thomas (N.Y., 1889); symphonic poem, *Lancelot and Elaine,* BS (1890); *Suite in A min.,* Worcester Festival (1891); *Indian Suite,* BS (N.Y., 1896). Dudley Buck (1839–1909): prize symphonic cantata, *Golden Legend,* Cincinnati Festival (1880); *Romance for 4 Horns and Orch.* (N.Y., 1891); *Star-Spangled Banner Overture* (N.Y., 1891). Victor Herbert (1859–1924): dramatic cantata, *The Captive,* Worcester Festival (1891); also composer of operas and numerous comic operas. **Charles M. T.**

Loeffler (1861–1935): *Concerto Fantastique*, BS (1894); *La Mort de Tintagiles* (1898). **Amy M. Beach** (Mrs. H. H. A.; 1867–1944): *Gallic Symph.*, BS (1896).

1862–1900. DEBUTS OF MUSICAL ARTISTS. Teresa Carreño, Venezuelan pianist (N.Y., 1862); **Carlotta Patti** in *La Sonnambula* (N.Y., 1862); **Christine Nilsson** (N.Y., 1870); **Anton Rubinstein**, pianist, and **Henri Wieniawski**, violinist (N.Y., 1872); **Hans von Bülow**, pianist (Boston, 1875); **Marcella Sembrich** as Lucia in *Lucia di Lammermoor*, MO (1883); gave violin, piano, and vocal concert 21 Apr. 1884; **Lillian Norton** (**Nordica**) as Margaret in *Faust* (N.Y., 1883); **Lilli Lehmann**, as Carmen in *Carmen*, MO (1885); **Maude Powell**, American violinist (Orange, N.J., 1885); **Josef Hofmann**, pianist (N.Y., 1887); **Francesco Tamagno** as Arnold in *William Tell*, MO (1889); **Adelina Patti** as Juliet in *Romeo and Juliet*, MO (1889); **Jean de Reszke** (tenor) as Lohengrin and **Edouard de Reszke** (bass) as King Henry in *Lohengrin*, MO (1891); **Emma Calvé** as Santuzza in *Cavalleria Rusticana*, MO (1893); **Nellie Melba** as Lucia in *Lucia di Lammermoor*, MO (1893); **Ernestine Schumann-Heink** as Ortrud in *Lohengrin* (Chicago, 1898); **Antonio Scotti** as Nevers in *Les Huguenots*, MO (1898); **Louise Homer** as Amneris in *Aïda*, MO (1900); **Ossip Gabrilowitsch**, pianist (N.Y., 1900).

1861–85. MUSIC PUBLISHERS. Beer and Schirmer took over C. Breusing; after 1866, G. Schirmer; Thomas B. Harms (N.Y., 1881), after 1922, Harms, Inc.; Theo. Presser (Phila., 1884); M. Witmark & Sons (N.Y., 1885).

1865–1900. CONSERVATORIES. Oberlin Conservatory (1865); Boston Conservatory, New England Conservatory, Cincinnati Conservatory, Chicago Academy of Music (later Chicago Musical College)—all 1867; Illinois Conservatory of Music, Jacksonville (1871);

Northwestern Univ. (1873); Cincinnati College of Music, Theo. Thomas dir. (1878); Chicago Conservatory (1884); American Institute of Applied Music, Kate Chittenden (N.Y., 1885); American Conservatory of Music, J. J. Haffstaedt (1886).

1865–92. OPERA COMPANIES. Performance of 24 operas in San Francisco (1865); Crosby Opera House (Chicago, 1865); French *opéra bouffe* (N.Y., 1867), Offenbach's *La Grande Duchesse de Gérolstein* ran 180 nights); 6 nights of Russian opera given at Théâtre Française (N.Y., 1869); Col. Henry Mapleson's first operatic tour of U.S. (1878–79); opening of **Metropolitan Opera House** (23 Oct. 1883; destroyed by fire, 27 Aug. 1892; new opera house opened 1893); American Opera Co. (N.Y., 1886–87), Theo. Thomas conduct.; Tivoli Opera House (San Francisco, 1877); grand opera given in U.S. by Henry E. Abbey Co. (1883–84), with cast including Nilsson and Sembrich; Abbey and Schoeffel (1890), with cast including Patti, Nordica, Tamagno (1890). **Oscar Hammerstein** (1847–1919) opened first Manhattan Opera House (1892).

1862–95. EXPANSION OF THE SYMPHONY ORCHESTRA. First concert by **Theodore Thomas'** own orchestra (N.Y., 1862); summer night concerts at Terrace Gardens, N.Y., begun by Thomas (1866); first of 22 annual tours by Thomas orchestra (1869). Germania Orch. (Pittsburgh, 1873). Symphony Society of N.Y., **Leopold Damrosch** (1832–85), conductor (1878); **Walter Damrosch** (1862–1950) succeeding his father (1885); merged with the N.Y. Philharmonic, 1928. Boston Symphony Orch., est. (1881) by Henry L. Higginson, with Georg Henschel conducting first concert; Chicago Symphony Orch. under Hans Balatka (1886), Frederick Stock, conduct., beg. 1905; Pittsburgh Symphony under Frederick Archer

(1893), Victor Herbert conduct., 1898; Cincinnati Orchestra Assn., Frank von der Stucken, conduct. (1895).

1865–1900. FESTIVALS. Peabody concerts (Baltimore, Md., 1865); World Peace Jubilee, org. Boston (1869) by Patrick S. Gilmore, employed chorus of 10,000 and orchestra of 1,000 pieces; imported Johann Strauss to conduct *Blue Danube Waltz.* First annual Cincinnati Festival, dir. Theo. Thomas (1873); Bach *B min. Mass,* Bach choir, Bethlehem, Pa., as part of Bach Festival begun 1900.

1872–99. MUSICAL SOCIETIES. Mendelssohn Society (N.Y., 1863–72), Cecilia Society (Boston, 1874), Music Teachers National Assn. (1876). Society of American Musicians and Composers (1899).

The Twentieth Century

1900–45. POPULAR MUSICAL TRENDS. Ragtime, with catchy melodies, syncopated rhythm, played "hot," originated before the turn of the century with Scott Joplin's (?1868–1917) "Maple Leaf Rag" (c.1897), and was developed by **J. Rosamund Johnson** and his brother **James Weldon Johnson.** "Under the Bamboo Tree" (1902) was the most significant ragtime song before 1910. Ragtime attained its acme of popularity with **Irving Berlin's** "Alexander's Ragtime Band" (1911). **Blues,** sad words set to a special pattern (12 bars), using "blue" notes (off pitch, usually 3d and 7th notes), best exemplified by **W. C. Handy's** (1873–1958) "St. Louis Blues" (1914). **Jazz,** innovative dance music style, with varied instruments, individual solos, and syncopated ragtime melodies. Dixie Jass [*sic*] Band of New Orleans opened at Reisenweber's Cabaret, Chicago (26 Jan. 1917); jazz band reported in New York by *Variety* (2 Feb. 1917). **Paul Whiteman's** (1891–1968) concert

at Aeolian Hall, New York (1924), to bring artistic respectability to jazz, introduced **George Gershwin's** (p. 1039) *Rhapsody in Blue.* **Swing,** using large bands and "planned out" music, was the rage of the 1930s, exemplified by **Louis Armstrong** (1900–71), **Duke Ellington** (p. 1023), and **Count Basie,** with **Benny Goodman** (1909–   ), "King of Swing," giving a sensational concert at Carnegie Hall (1938). **Country Music,** commercial popular music favored in the hinterlands, has a remote origin. Accompanied in early times by dulcimer, fiddle, guitar, or banjo, country music in more recent times has utilized larger instrumental groups. Its great vogue dates from 1926, when "Grand Ole Opry," the leading country music program, began to broadcast from Nashville, Tenn., which still remains the center of the movement. Its leading exponents have been Johnny Cash (1932–   ) and Elvis Presley (1935–   ).

1900–46°. NON-OPERATIC WORKS BY FOREIGN COMPOSERS. Bach: *Brandenburg Concerto, F maj.* (1901); *1st Violin Concerto,* BS (1902); *2d,* BS (1904). **Mahler:** *4th Symph.,* SS (1903); *5th Symph. (Giant),* Cincinnati Symph. (1905); *1st Symph.,* PS (1909); *8th Symph.,* PH with more than 1,000 performers (1916). **Rachmaninoff:** *2nd Symph.,* composer conduct., Russian Symph. Orch. (N.Y., 1909); *2nd Piano Concerto,* composer soloist, SS (1909); *Isle of the Dead* (tone poem), Chicago Symph. (1909). **Sibelius:** *2nd Symph.,* BS, 1904; *1st,* BS, 1907; *Finlandia,* BS, 1908; *Swan of Tuonela,* BS, 1911. On visit to the U.S. he conducted *Pohjala's Daughter, King Christian II, Swan of Tuonela,* Litchfield, Conn., Choral Union (1914). **Stravinsky** (p. 1161): *Feuerwerk,* Russian Symph. Orch., N.Y. (1910); BS (1914); Orch. suite from *Petrouchka,* BS (1920); *Le Sacre du Printemps,* PH

° For abbreviations, see footnote, p. 921.

(1922); *Symph. of Psalms* for orch. and chorus, BS (1930). Schoenberg: *5 Pieces for Orch.*, BS (1914); *Verklärte Nacht*, sextet, BS (1921). Prokofieff: *Concerto for Violin and Orch.*, BS (1924); *Concerto No. 3*, piano and orch., BS (1926); *Classical Symph.*, BS (1927); *Concerto No. 2*, piano and orch., BS (1930). Ravel: *Rhapsodie Espagnole*, BS (1914); *Daphnis et Chloë*, 1st suite, BS (1918); 2d suite, BS (1917); *Bolero*, Toscanini, PS (1929). Hindemith: *Nusch-Nuschi Dances*, PH (1924–25); *Concerto for Orch.*, BS (1926); *Konzertmusik for String and Brass Instruments*, BS (1931). Milhaud: *2d Orch. Suite*, BS (1921): *Le Carnaval d'Aix*, BS (1926). Vaughan Williams: *London Symph.*, N.Y. Symph. (1920); *Fantasia on a Theme by Thos. Tallis*, N.Y. Symph. (1922); *Norfolk Rhapsody No. 1*, BS (1926). Shostakovich: *1st Symph.*, BS (1928); *7th*, Toscanini, NBC Orch. (1942); *8th*, PS (1944); *9th* (Tanglewood, 1946).

1900–74. CONTINUED EXPANSION OF THE SYMPHONY ORCHESTRA. Leopold Stokowski (1887–   ) named conductor of Cincinnati Orchestra Assn. (1909); Fritz Reiner replaced (1922) Eugène Ysaye as conduct.; Philadelphia Orch., Fritz Scheel, conduct. (1900), succeeded by Stokowski (1914–36); St. Paul Symph., Walter Rothwell conduct. (1905); St. Louis (1907), Max Zach conduct.; Rudolph Ganz, 1921–27; Seattle, Michael Kegrizi conduct. (1908), Henry K. Hadley (1909); Kansas City, Mo., Carl Busch (1911); San Francisco, Henry K. Hadley (1911), reorg. under Alfred Hertz (1915); Baltimore, Gustav Strube (1915); New Orleans (1917); Detroit, Gabrilowitsch (1917); Cleveland, Nikolai Sokoloff (1918). Decade 1921–30 marked by **phenomenal increase** in professional orchestras, with notable conductors engaged: **Pierre Monteux** (1875–1964) to conduct Boston (1920), succeeded (1924) by **Serge Koussevitsky**

(1874–1951); **Willem Mengelberg** from Amsterdam as guest conductor of Bodanzky's National Symphony Orch. (1921), succeeding Josef Stransky when the N.Y. Philharmonic merged with Bodanzky's Symphony (1922); **Wilhelm Furtwängler** of Leipzig Gewandhaus and Berlin Philharmonic to conduct N.Y. Philharmonic (1925), with **Arturo Toscanini** (1867–1957) made regular conductor (1928–36), inaugurating the orchestra's most successful decade. Toscanini was organizer and conductor of National Broadcasting Co. (NBC) Symphony Orch., beg. 1937. **Eugene Ormandy** began his tenure as conductor and music director of the Philadelphia Orch. (1936–   ). **Leonard Bernstein** (p. 985), who replaced (14 Nov. 1943) **Bruno Walter** as guest conductor of the N.Y. Philharmonic upon the latter's illness, succeeded Stokowski as conductor of the New York City Symphony (1945–48); became co-conductor with **Dimitri Mitropoulos**, 1957–58; music director, 1958–59; succeeded by **Pierre Boulez**, 1971. **Erich Leinsdorf**, music director, Boston (1962–69), succeeded by William Steinberg (1969), Seiji Ozawa (1972). **Georg Solti** named music director, Chicago (1968) and **Lorin Maazel**, Cleveland (1971) after the death of **George Szell**. **Henry Lewis,** first black to be named music director of a major orchestra, appointed to New Jersey Symphony, and in 1970 Dean Dixon became the first black to conduct New York Philharmonic.

1900–73. FESTIVALS. MacDowell Festival est. Peterborough, N.H. (1910). Music festival at Pittsfield, Mass., est. by Elizabeth Sprague Coolidge (1918), marking the beginning of her active participation in chamber music; Elizabeth Sprague Coolidge Foundation for sponsoring festivals of music at the Library of Congress est. 1925; first Festival of Chamber Music, 28 Oct. First Festival of

Contemporary American Music, Yaddo, Saratoga Springs, N.Y. (1932); first annual summer Berkshire Music Festival, Lenox (Tanglewood), Mass. (1934); Koussevitzky Music Foundation est. by Serge Koussevitzky (1942); first annual Festival of Contemporary American Music, sponsored by Alice M. Ditson Fund, Columbia Univ. (1945). American Jazz Festival began (1954) annual summer concerts at Newport, R.I. Pablo Casals moved to Puerto Rico (1956) and directed annual festivals at San Juan. During the 1950s other festivals, some long established, flourished, including Berkshire (Tanglewood, Mass.); Aspen, Colo.; Blossom (Cuyahoga Falls, Ohio); Caramoor (Katonah, N.Y.); Empire State (Ellenville, N.Y.); Eastman School (Rochester, N.Y.); Hollywood Bowl (Los Angeles, Calif.); Lewisohn Stadium Concerts (N.Y.C.); Marlboro, Vt.; Robin Hood Dell Concerts (Phila.); Ravinia Park (Chicago); Saratoga, N.Y.; Cincinnati Zoo; Central City, Colo. Woodstock rock festival (Bethel, N.Y.) drew more than 400,000 (1969); Newport Jazz Festival moved to New York City (1972); Watkins Glen, N.Y., festival (1973), attendance 600,000, largest on record.

1903–45. DEBUTS OF MUSICAL ARTISTS IN THE U.S.[*] **Enrico Caruso** as the Duke in *Rigoletto* (1903); **Geraldine Farrar** as Juliette in *Romeo et Juliette* (1906); **Feodor Chaliapin** as Mefistofele in *Mefistofele* (1907); **Emmy Destinn** as Aïda, Toscanini conduct. (1908); **Pasquale Amato** as Germont in *La Traviata* (1908); **Leo Slezak** as Otello in *Otello* (1909); **Alma Gluck** as Sophie in *Werther* (1909); **Lucrezia Bori** as Manon in *Manon Lescaut* (1910); **Luisa Tetrazzini** as Lucia in *Lucia di Lammermoor* (1911); **Frieda Hempel** as Marguerite in *Les Huguenots* (1912); **Giovanni Mar-**

[*] Metropolitan Opera for operatic performers unless otherwise indicated.

tinelli as Cavaradossi in *Tosca* (1913); **Amelita Galli-Curci** as Gilda in *Rigoletto*, Chicago Opera (1916); **Jascha Heifetz,** violinist (N.Y., 1917); **Rosa Ponselle** as Leonora in *La Forza del Destino* (1918); **Beniamino Gigli** as Faust in *Mefistofele* (1920). Last appearance of **Caruso,** *La Juive* (24 Dec. 1920; d. Naples, 2 Aug. 1921); farewell appearance of **Farrar** in *Zaza* (22 Apr. 1923). **Lawrence Tibbett** as Lovitsky in *Boris Godunov* (1923); **Yehudi Menuhin,** violinist, San Francisco Orch. (1923); PS (1926); **Lauritz Melchior** as Tannhauser in *Tannhäuser* (1926); **Ezio Pinza** as Pontifex in *La Vestale* (1926); **Vladimir Horowitz,** pianist (PS, 1928); **Lotte Lehmann** as Sieglinde in *Die Walküre* (1934); **Kirsten Flagstad** as Sieglinde in *Die Walküre* (1935); **Jussi Bjoerling** as Rodolfo in *La Bohème* (1938); **Leonard Warren** as Paolo in *Simon Boccanegra* (1939); **Jan Peerce** as Alfredo in *La Traviata* (1941); **Richard Tucker** as Enzo in *La Gioconda* (1945); **Robert Merrill** as Germont in *La Traviata* (1945).

1903–59. FOREIGN OPERAS IN AMERICA. Wagner: *Parsifal,* 1st performance in German outside of Bayreuth, Alfred Hertz, conduct., MO (1903). **Richard Strauss:** *Salome,* MO (1907), aroused storm of protest; barred for 27 years from MO repertory; banned in Boston (1909); *Elektra,* MO (1910); *Der Rosenkavalier,* MO (1913). **Puccini:** *Tosca,* MO (1901); *Madame Butterfly,* English, Washington, D.C. (1908); world premiere of *Il Tabarro, Gianni Schicchi,* and *Suor Angelica,* MO (Farrar, Easton, De Luca, 1918); *Turandot,* MO (1926). **Debussy:** *Pelléas et Mélisande,* Manhattan Opera (Mary Garden, 1908); *L'Enfant Prodigue,* Boston (1910). **Tchaikovsky:** *Eugene Onegin* in concert form, SS (1908); operatic version, MO (1910). **Mussorgsky:** *Boris Godunov,* MO (Anna Case, Louise Homer, 1913). **Prokofiev:**

Love for Three Oranges, Chicago Opera Assn. (1921). **Berg:** *Wozzek,* Philadelphia Grand Opera Co. (1931). **Gian-Carlo Menotti:** *Amelia Goes to the Ball,* Philadelphia (1937); MO (1938); *The Old Maid* and *The Thief* broadcast over NBC (1939), first stage performance, Philadelphia Opera (1941); *The Medium* and *The Telephone,* N.Y. (1947); *The Consul,* N.Y. (1950); *Amahl and the Night Visitors,* TV (1950). **Benjamin Britten:** *Peter Grimes, Tanglewood* (1946); *Billy Budd,* TV (1952).

1896–1952. OPERA BY AMERICAN COMPOSERS. Walter Damrosch: *Scarlet Letter,* Boston (1896); *Cyrano de Bergerac,* MO (1913); **Frederick Converse:** *Pipe of Desire,* first American opera to be performed MO, with entirely American cast (1910); **Victor Herbert:** *Natoma* (Phila., 1911), *Madeleine,* MO (1914); **Horatio T. Parker:** *Mona,* MO (1912, awarded $10,000 prize); **Reginald de Koven:** *Rip Van Winkle,* Chicago Opera Assn. (1920); **Deems Taylor:** *King's Henchman,* libretto by Edna St. Vincent Millay, MO (1927), *Peter Ibbetson,* MO (1931); **Howard Hanson:** *Merrymount,* MO (1934); **George Gershwin:** *Porgy and Bess,* setting of DuBose Heyward play, *Porgy,* with an all-Negro cast (Boston, 1935); **Douglas Moore:** *Devil and Daniel Webster* (1939), *Giants in the Earth* (N.Y., 1951); **Virgil Thomson:** *Four Saints in Three Acts,* based on text by Gertrude Stein, with Negro cast (Hartford, Conn., 1934), *The Mother of Us All* (1947); **Bernard Rogers:** *The Warrior* (book by Norman Corwin), awarded $1,500 Ditson prize (1946); MO (1947); **Leonard Bernstein:** *Trouble in Tahiti* (Tanglewood and TV, 1952).

1905–40. CONSERVATORIES. Institute of Musical Art (1905), Frank Damrosch, financed by a $500,000 bequest; Eastman School of Music (1918), est. by George Eastman as an affiliate of Univ. of Rochester (Howard Hanson,

dir., 1924–64). Juilliard Graduate School est. (1924) with an endowment of $15 million, Ernest Hutcheson, dean. In 1926 the Institute of Musical Art became the preparatory school of the Juilliard. Curtis Institute of Music (Phila., 1924) by an endowment of $12,500,000 from Mrs. Mary Louise Curtis Bok (Josef Hofmann, dir., 1927). Berkshire Music Center org. at Tanglewood (1940) by Koussevitzky.

1906–74. OPERA COMPANIES. Second and better-known **Manhattan Opera House** opened by **Oscar Hammerstein,** 1906, with such artists as Melba, Nordica, Tetrazzini, and Garden, to become a serious rival of the Metropolitan; sold out to Metropolitan (1910). **Giulio Gatti-Casazza** (1869–1940) appointed manager of Metropolitan (1908). Boston Opera House (1909). Chicago Opera Co. (1910), Andreas Dippel, dir. Mary Garden (1874–1967) succeeded (1919) Campanini as impresario of the Chicago Opera, to become the first woman impresario; in turn succeeded (1923) by Giorgio Polacco. Edward Johnson, tenor, became manager MO (1935), and Rudolf Bing (1950). Schuyler Chapin named (1972) to succeed Goeran Gentele after latter's death in auto accident; Rafael Kubelik named music director; resigned (1974). New York City Center Opera Co. founded 1944; Julius Rudel named managing director (1957).

1907–52. PIONEER RADIO AND TV MUSICAL PERFORMANCES. Lee De Forest (p. 1011) transmitted (5 Mar. 1907) Rossini's *William Tell* overture by wireless from the Telharmonic Hall, N.Y., to the Brooklyn Navy Yard, the first broadcast of a musical composition. First broadcast from the stage of the Metropolitan (20 Jan. 1910), when portions of *Cavalleria Rusticana* and *Pagliacci,* both with Caruso, were picked up by radio amateurs. First major orchestral broadcast, BS over NBC (1926). First regular series of opera broadcasts from stage of Chicago Civic Opera (1927). In the same year concerts broadcast from BS and PS. Regular Sunday broadcasts inaugurated by PS (1929). First broadcast of a full opera from MO, *Hänsel and Gretel* (25 Dec. 1931). First opera written expressly for radio, *The Willow Tree*, by Charles W. Cadman, broadcast, NBC (1931); for television, Gian-Carlo Menotti's *Amahl and the Night Visitors*, NBC (Christmas eve, 1951; again 1952). First telecast of a major symphony concert, Ormandy, PH (20 Mar. 1948); Toscanini, NBC Orch., 1 hour later. Texaco sponsorship of MO broadcasts began with *Le Nozze di Figaro* (7 Dec. 1940). By conclusion of 35th season (19 Apr. 1975), 698 operas had been broadcast. **Milton Cross** (1897–1975) was announcer for over 34 years.

1913–41. MUSICAL SOCIETIES. Friends of Music Society (N.Y.), first concert 7 Dec. 1913; produced Schoenberg, Bloch, and Bach; disc. after 1931. Organization (1914) of American Society of Composers, Authors, and Publishers (ASCAP) by Victor Herbert, **John Philip Sousa,** Witmark, and others to protect musical copyright interests. Organization (1923) of League of Composers to promote contemporary compositions. New Friends of Music founded (N.Y., 1936), "to give the best in the literature of chamber music and lieder." Founding of the American Composers' Alliance (1938). ASCAP, after a struggle with radio networks and rival organization, Broadcast Music, Inc., over royalties, reached settlement (1941).

1935. FEDERAL MUSIC PROJECT of the WPA established to relieve unemployment among musicians, under direction of Nikolai Sokoloff; 1935–39, $50 million expended, 225,000 performances financed, 700 projects launched, 15,000 musicians employed. Among its most significant achievements was the establishment (1935) of the Composers' Forum-Laboratory devoted to the works of living American composers.

1919–49. PERFORMANCES OF AMERICAN COMPOSITIONS. Charles T. Griffes (1884–1920), *Pleasure Dome of Kubla Khan,* BS (1919); *Three Songs,* soprano and orch., PH (1919); *Clouds* and *White Peacock,* BS (1922). **Henry K. Hadley** (1871–1937): symph., *The Four Seasons* (Chicago, 1902); *The Culprit Fay* (Grand Rapids, Mich., 1909), *5th Symph.* (1949). **John Alden Carpenter** (1876–1951): orchestral suite, *Adventures in a Perambulator,* Chicago Symph. (1915); *Concertino* (1916). **Ernest Bloch** (1880–1959); came to U.S. 1917; naturalized, 1924): *Israel Symph.* and *Schelomo,* Society of Friends of Music (N.Y., 1916); *Three Hebrew Poems,* BS (1917); *Symph. in C sharp min.,* PS (1918); *Piano Quartet,* inaugural concert, League of Composers (N.Y., 1923); *America,* epic rhapsody, PS (1928). **George Gershwin** (p. 1039): *An American in Paris,* symphonic poem (N.Y., 1928). **Aaron Copland** (1900–): *1st Symph.,* SS (1925); *Concerto for Piano and Orch.,* BS (1927); *Symphonic Ode,* BS (1932); ballet, *Billy the Kid* (1938); *Appalachian Spring* (1945), *3rd Symph.,* BS (1946). **Douglas Moore** (1893–1969): *2nd Symph.,* Paris Radio Orch. (1946). **Charles Ives** (p. 1067): *3rd Symph.,* (1946). **Frederick Jacobi** (1891–1952): *Symph. in C,* San Francisco Symph. (1948). **Walter Piston** (1894–): *2nd Symph.* (1943), *3rd Symph.,* BS (1948). **Roger Sessions** (1896–): *1st Symph.,* BS (1927), *2nd Symph.,* PS (1951). **William Schuman** (1910–): *1st Symph.* (1936), *2nd Symph.* (1937), *3rd Symph.* (1938), *Symph. for Strings,* BS (1947). **Howard Hanson** (1896–): *Nordic Symph.* (1924), *4th Symph.* (*Requiem*) (1943), *Piano Concerto,* BS (1948). **Samuel Barber** (1910–): *Adagio for Strings* and *Essay for Orch.,* NBC Orch., Toscanini (1938), *Symph. in One Movement* (Rome, 1936), *Violin Concerto* (1940), *2nd Essay for Orch.*, PS (1942), *2nd Symph.*, BS (1944), *Capricorn Concerto* (1944), *Concerto for Violoncello and Orch.*, BS (1946). **Virgil Thomson** (1896–): *Suite for Orch.*, PH (1948); **Lukas Foss** (1922–): *Song of Songs*, BS (1947), *Recordare*, orch. threnody, BS (1948). **David Diamond** (1915–): *2nd Symph.*, BS (1944), *Rounds for Orch.* (1944). **Roy Harris** (1898–): *3rd Symph.*, BS (1939), *6th Symph.*, BS (1944). **Leonard Bernstein** (p. 985): *Jeremiah Symph.*, PS (1944); symph., *The Age of Anxiety*, awarded $1,000 BS prize (1949). **William Grant Still** (1895–): *Afro-American Symph.* (1931), *Symph. in G min.* (1937). **Marc Blitzstein** (1905–64): *Airborne Symph.* (1946).

1945–74. POPULAR MUSICAL TRENDS. Bop, chamber jazz using thrumming "bop" sound, took hold in the 1940s, with such exemplars as **Charles "Bird" Parker** (1920–55), and **"Dizzy" Gillespie** (1917–). **Cool** marked the reaction to Bop and utilized French horns, trumpet, trombone, and tuba in dance bands, introduced (1948) by Miles Davis (1927–) with a 9-piece band. **Hard Bop,** which came out of folk music, using more traditional jazz forms, and **Funky,** more primitive and earthy, combining "blues" and "hot gospel," were in turn the reaction to Cool. An outstanding exponent of Funky was the black folk singer **Mahalia Jackson** (1911–72). Transforming "pop" music was **Rock 'n' Roll,** combining black beat and white sentiment, producing a great volume of sound. Among its most successful proponents were Fats Domino, Ray Charles, The Platters, Bo Diddley, and Bill Haley. The tremendously popular British group "The Beatles" made its U.S. debut (1964) using electrified instruments. Among the most popular figures in folk

music in the early 1960s were Pete Seeger, The Kingston Trio, Joan Baez, and Peter, Paul and Mary. **Folk Rock** took hold by 1965, popularized by **Bob Dylan** (1941–), composer and performer, whose return to the stage in 1974 after a long absence proved a sensational success. **Soul,** the black people's "pop," is perhaps best exemplified by such black singers as **Aretha Franklin** (1942–). Major trends (1965–71) were exemplified by (1) Hard Rock: "The Doors," "Jefferson Airplane"; (2) Folk Rock: "The Band," "Country Joe and the Fish"; (3) Blues Rock: "Blood, Sweat, and Tears," and Janis Joplin. Difficult to classify but enormously popular were "The Mamas and the Papas," with their distinctive harmonies, Simon and Garfunkle, "The Beach Boys," identified with the "California Sound." Most of these artists performed their own material.

1950–74. PERFORMERS. Debuts: **Cesare Siepi** as Philip II in *Don Carlo*, MO (1950); **Marian Anderson,** contralto, made her debut at MO as Ulrica in *Un Ballo in Maschera* (7 Jan. 1955), first black singer in its 71-year history. **Beverly Sills** as Rosalinda in *Die Fledermaus*, New York City Opera (1955), MO debut as Pamira in *The Siege of Corinth* (1975); **Renata Tebaldi** as Desdemona in *Otello*, MO (1955); MO debut of **Maria Callas** as Norma in *Norma* (1956); **Birgit Nilsson** as Isolde in *Tristan und Isolde*, MO (1959); **Sviatoslav Richter,** Soviet pianist, N.Y. (1960); **Joan Sutherland** in Handel's *Alcina*, Dallas Opera (1960); MO debut as Lucia (26 Nov. 1961); **Jon Vickers** as Canio in *Pagliacci*, MO (1960); **Leontyne Price's** and **Franco Corelli's** debuts as Leonora and Manrico in *Il Trovatore*, MO (27 Jan. 1961); American Symphony Orch., **Leopold Stokowski,** conductor (1st concert, N.Y., 15 Oct. 1962); Moscow Philharmonic, N.Y. (1965); **Montserrat Caballé** as Lucrezia Borgia in *Lucrezia Borgia*, N.Y. (1965), MO debut as Marguerite in *Faust* (1965); **Sherrill Milnes** as Valentin in *Faust*, MO (1965); Orchestre de la Suisse Romande, N.Y. (1966); Hamburg State Opera, N.Y. (1967); **Herbert von Karajan's** MO debut, conductor and director, new production of *Ring* cycle, *Die Walküre* (2 Nov. 1967); **Martti Talvela** as Grand Inquisitor in *Don Carlo*, MO (1968). European orchestras appearing in U.S. for first time in 1968 included Helsinki, Stockholm, Orchestre de Paris, English Chamber Orch.; in addition, Hamburg State Opera performed at MO (1967), Rome Opera (1968); **Placido Domingo** MO debut as Maurizio in *Adriana Lecouvreur* (1968); **Marilyn Horne** MO debut as Adalgisa in *Norma* (1971); **Kiri Te Kanawa** as Desdemona in *Otello*, MO (1974).

1954, 4 Apr. TOSCANINI RETIRED as conductor of NBC Symphony Orch.; reorganized as Symphony of the Air, with first concert, New York (27 Oct.).

1955, 19 Nov. LEONARD BERNSTEIN named musical director of PS to succeed Dimitri Mitropolous; in Sept. his musical *West Side Story* opened on Broadway, followed by *Candide* (1956); presented TV shows on music (*Omnibus*, 1954–58).

1965. VLADIMIR HOROWITZ returned to concert stage (Carnegie Hall, 9 May) after 12 years of self-imposed retirement.

1950–73. PERFORMANCES OF AMERICAN COMPOSITIONS. Roger Sessions, *2d Symphony*, PS (1950); **Roy Harris:** *Symph. Fantasy* (Pittsburgh, 1954); **Darius Milhaud:** *6th Symph.*, BS (1955); **Walter Piston:** *5th Symph.*, BS (1955); *Concerto for Violin and Orch.* (1958); **Ives:** *He Is There*, Norwalk, Conn. (1959); *2d Symph.*, PS (1951), Stravinsky: *Canticum Sacrum* (Los Angeles, 1957), ballet score *Agon*, New York City Ballet (1957)—both on occasion of 75th birthday, *Threni*, Schola

Cantorum, N.Y. (1959), *Movements for Piano and Orch.*, Columbia Symphony Orch., N.Y. (1960); *4th Symph.* (completed 1916), American Symphony Orch., N.Y. (1965), *Variations*, Chicago Symphony (1965), *Introitus: T. S. Eliot in Memoriam*, Chicago Symphony (1965); **Peter Mennin:** *Piano Concerto*, Cleveland Symphony, N.Y. (1958); **Barber:** *Toccata Festifa*, PH (1960); **Foss:** *Time Cycle, for Soprano and Orchestra*, PS (1960); **Vittorio Giannini:** *4th Symph.*, Juilliard School of Music, N.Y. (1960); **Carl Ruggles:** *Sun Treader* (composed 1933), BS at Festival of Carl Ruggles, Bowdoin College (1966); **Elliott Carter:** *Piano Concerto*, BS (1967), *Concerto for Orchestra*, PS (1970); **Louis M. Gottschalk:** *Montevideo*, American Symphony Orch., N.Y. (1969), *Concerto for Orchestra*, PH (1970); **Charles Wuorinén:** *Concerto for Amplified Violin and Orchestra*, BS (Tanglewood, 1972); **Alan Hovhaness:** *And God Created Whales*, PS (1970); **Louis W. Ballard:** *Devil's Promenade*, Tulsa Philharmonic (1973). **George Rochberg,** *Concerto for Violin and Orchestra*, Pittsburgh Symphony (1975).

1954–73. SOME EXPERIMENTAL TRENDS, including electronic music and mixed media, gained ground in this period. Pioneers include **John Cage** (1912–), who utilized tape recorder in *Imaginary Landscape No. 5* (duration 4 mins., 1952); **Otto Luening** (1900–) and **Vladimir Ussachevsky** (1911–), who collaborated on works for tape recorder and orchestra (1954); Lejaren Hiller and Leonard Isaacson used computer for producing music at Univ. of Illinois (1955); **Columbia-Princeton Electronic Music Center** est. (1959), produced Ussachevsky's *Creation-Prologue*. In the late 60s and early 70s music workshops and laboratories proliferated at such institutions as Hunter

College, Univ. of Illinois, Buffalo, etc. John Cage and Lejaren Hiller produced (1967–69) *HPSCHD* for 7 harpsichords and 52 computer-generated tapes. **Moog synthesizer,** invented by Robert A. Moog (1969), turned interest of "pop" enthusiasts toward Bach.

1953–74. NEW YORK PRO MUSICA, founded by Noah Greenberg, brought vitality to Medieval and Renaissance music.

1953–72. OPERAS BY AMERICAN COMPOSERS. Igor Stravinsky: *Rake's Progress,* MO (1953); **Aaron Copland:** *Tender Land,* New York City Opera Co. (1953); **Norman Dello Joio:** *Trial at Rouen,* NBC–TV (1956), *The Ruby* (N.Y., 1957); **William Bergsma:** *Wife of Martin Guerre* (N.Y., 1956); **Douglas Moore** and **J. Latouche,** *Ballad of Baby Doe,* New York City Opera Co. (1958); **Carlisle Floyd:** *Susannah,* Univ. of Florida, Tallahassee (1955), New York City Opera Co. (1959). **Leonard Kastle:** *Deseret,* NBC Opera Co., TV (1961); **Robert Ward:** *The Crucible,* New York City Opera Co. (1961); **Jack Beeson:** *Lizzie Borden,* New York City Opera Co. (1965); **Douglas Moore:** *Carry Nation,* Univ. of Kansas (1966); **Samuel Barber:** *Vanessa,* MO (1958), *Antony and Cleopatra,* first opera performed in new Metropolitan Opera House (16 Sept. 1966); **Martin David Levy:** *Mourning Becomes Electra,* Metropolitan Opera (1967); **Hugo Weisgall:** *Nine Rivers from Jordan,* New York City Opera Co. (1968); **Gunther Schuller** (John Updike, librettist): *Fisherman and His Wife,* Boston Opera Co. (1970); **Carlisle Floyd:** *Of Mice and Men* (based on John Steinbeck's novel), Seattle Opera Co. (1970); **Ezra Pound:** *Le Testament du Villon* (music written 1921–22), Western Opera Theater (1971); **Scott Joplin:** ragtime opera, *Treemonisha* (written 1907–11), 1 performance, Harlem (1911),

Morehouse College, Atlanta (1972), Carnegie Hall (1972); **Virgil Thomson:** *Lord Byron,* Juilliard, American Opera Co. (1972).

1953–71. PERFORMANCES OF FOREIGN COMPOSERS. Shostakovich: *10th Symph.,* PS (1954), *13th Symph.,* PH (1970); **Menotti:** *2nd Piano Concerto,* PS (1958); *Saint of Bleecker St.* (N.Y., 1954); *Maria Golovin,* NBC Opera Co. at Brussels World's Fair (1958); **Prokofiev:** *War and Peace,* NBC Opera Co., TV (1957); **Pablo Casals:** *El Pesebre,* San Francisco Symph. (1962), *Hymn to the United Nations* (UN, 1971); **Benjamin Britten:** *War Requiem,* BS, Tanglewood (1963); **Gustav Mahler:** *10th Symphony,* recons. by Deryck Cooke, PH (1965); **Krzysztof Penderecki:** *The Passion and Death of Jesus Christ According to St. Luke,* Minneapolis Symphony Orch., Minneapolis (1967), N.Y.C. (1969); **Hans Werner Henze:** *Essay on Pigs,* Los Angeles Philharmonic (1971).

1954–65. FOUNDATION GRANTS. Through a grant from the Rockefeller Foundation (Apr. 1953) the Louisville Orch. initiated (2 Jan. 1954) series of commissioned works by 65 American and foreign composers. Grants broadened to include other orchestras (1957). In spring of 1958 New York City Opera Co. presented 5-week season of 10 American operas under Ford Foundation grant. Four opera companies shared 1959 Ford grant to foster American opera, and in 1965 orchestras throughout U.S. shared $80.2 million in Ford grants.

1955–63 MUSICAL THAW IN COLD WAR. Exchange of visits of Soviet and American musicians included visits to U.S. of Emil Gilels and David Oistrakh (1955); Moiseyev Dance Co. (1958); Bolshoi Ballet; Soviet composers, including D. Shostakovich (1959); Moscow State Symph.; Leonid Kogan; Sviatoslav Richter (1960), Leningrad Kirov Ballet

(1961), Mstislav Rostropovich (1963). U.S. and U.S.S.R. signed a 2-year cultural exchange pact, 1962. U.S. artists who toured U.S.S.R. included Isaac Stern and Jan Peerce (1956), Boston Symphony (1956), New York Philharmonic (1959, 1960). In addition, Louis ("Satchmo") Armstrong (1900–71), Dixieland trumpeter and jazz-band leader, made a triumphal tour of the Middle East, Mediterranean countries, and Western Europe (1956) and of Africa (1960). **Harvey K. ("Van") Cliburn, Jr.,** 23-year-old Texan, won first prize at International Tchaikovsky Piano Competition in Moscow (1958); on return to the U.S. he drew huge audiences at Chicago's Grant Park, Hollywood Bowl, and New York's Lewisohn Stadium.

1960–75. OPERAS BY FOREIGN COMPOSERS. Handel: *Hercules,* American Opera Society, N.Y. (1960); **Britten;** *A Midsummer Night's Dream,* San Francisco Opera Co. (1961), *The Burning Fiery Furnace,* Caramoor, N.Y. (1967), *The Prodigal Son,* Caramoor (1969), *Death in Venice,* MO (1974); **Berg:** *Lulu,* Santa Fe Opera Co. (1963); **Shostakovich:** *Katerina Ismailova,* New York City Opera Co. (1965); **Hans Werner Henze:** *Elegy for Young Lovers,* Juilliard (1965), *The Stag King,* Santa Fe Opera Co. (1965), *The Young Lord,* Santa Fe (1967); **Alberto Ginastera:** *Don Rodrigo,* New York City Opera Co. (1966), *Bomarzo,* New York City Opera Co. (1968); *Beatrix Cenci,* Opera Society of Washington (1971); **Janacek:** *The Makropulos Affair,* San Francisco Opera Co. (1966); **Schoenberg:** *Moses and Aaron,* Boston Opera Co. (1966); **Rameau:** *Hippolyte and Aricie,* Boston Opera Co. (1966); **Mozart:** *Lucio Silla,* Baltimore Opera Co. (1968); **Carl Orff:** *Ballad of Agnes,* Univ. of Missouri (1968); Richard Rodney Bennett: *Mines of Sulphur,* Juilliard (1968); **Penderecki:** *The Devils of Lou-*

don, Santa Fe Opera Co. (1969); **Luciano Berio:** *Opera,* Santa Fe Opera Co. (1970); **Villa-Lobos:** *Yerma,* Santa Fe Opera Co. (1971); **Berlioz:** *Les Troyens,* Boston Opera Co. (1972), MO (1973), *Benvenuto Cellini,* Boston Opera Co. (1975); **Delius,** *A Village Romeo and Juliet,* Opera Society of Washington (1972), New York City Opera Co. (1973).

1960–74. GOVERNMENT AND THE ARTS. Among the signs of the federal government's increasing interest in the arts were (1) the successful intervention as arbitrator of Secretary of Labor Arthur Goldberg after labor-management negotiations had broken down and the N.Y. Metropolitan Opera season had been announced as canceled (28 Aug. 1961); (2) a White House state dinner in honor of Luis Muñoz Marín (13 Nov. 1961), featuring a program by Pablo Casals, Alexander Schneider, and Mieczyslaw Horszowski; (3) the establishment of the National Foundation on the Arts and Humanities (29 Sept. 1965), whose appropriations increased to $81.5 million (fiscal 1973) and which announced, Mar. 1974, a grant of $1 million to Metropolitan Opera on matching basis.

1962–73. BURGEONING OF PERFORMING ARTS CENTERS. Lincoln Center for the Performing Arts, a $178 million project, includes Philharmonic Hall (opened 23 Sept. 1962), renamed Avery Fischer Hall (1973), home of New York Philharmonic; the New York State Theater (23 Apr. 1964), where New York City Opera Co. and New York City Ballet Co. are resident; and the Metropolitan Opera House (16 Sept. 1966). **The John F. Kennedy Center for the Performing Arts,** Washington, D.C., whose construction was funded in part by federal money, opened (8 Sept. 1971) with a performance of Leonard Bernstein's *Mass.* Other newly built performing arts centers included the Music Center, Los Angeles (fully opened 1967); Memorial

Arts Center, Atlanta, Ga. (1968), and Centers in San Antonio, Tex.; Jackson, Miss.; Garden State Arts Center in New Jersey (all in 1968), and at Indiana Univ. (1972), with new auditoriums for symphonic performance in Miami, Fla., and Norfolk, Va. (1972).

ALL-TIME SONG HITS, 1892-1970

Daisybelle (On a bicycle built for 2), w., m., Harry Dacre	1892
The Sidewalks of New York, w., m., Charles B. Lawler and James W. Blake	1894
The Stars and Stripes Forever, m., John Philip Sousa	1897
Sweet Adeline, w. Richard H. Gerard [Husch]; m., Harry Armstrong	1903
Kiss Me Again, w., Henry Blossom; m., Victor Herbert	1905
Shine on Harvest Moon, w., m., Nora Bayes and Jack Norworth	1908
Ah! Sweet Mystery of Life, w., Rida Johnson Young; m., Victor Herbert	1910
A Perfect Day, w., m., Carrie Jacobs Bond	1910
Alexander's Ragtime Band, w., m., Irving Berlin	1911
When Irish Eyes Are Smiling, w., Chauncey Olcott and George Graff, Jr., m., Ernest R. Ball	1912
St. Louis Blues, w., m., W. C. Handy	1914
Swanee, w., Irving Caesar; m., George Gershwin	1919
Yes, We Have No Bananas, w., Frank Silver; m., M. Irving Cohn	1923
Tea for Two, w., Irving Caesar; m., Vincent Youmans	1924
Dinah, w., Sam M. Lewis and Joe Young; m., Harry Akst	1925
Ol' Man River, w., Oscar Hammerstein 2nd; m., Jerome Kern	1927
Star Dust, w., Mitchell Parish; m., Hoagy Carmichael	1929
Dancing In The Dark, w., Howard Dietz; m., Arthur Schwartz	1931
Easter Parade, w., m., Irving Berlin	1933
Begin the Beguine, w., m., Cole Porter	1935
September Song, w., Maxwell Anderson; m., Kurt Weill	1938
God Bless America, w., m., Irving Berlin	1939
White Christmas, w., m., Irving Berlin	1942
Some Enchanted Evening, w., Oscar Hammerstein 2d; m., Richard Rodgers	1949
I Could Have Danced All Night, w., Alan Jay Lerner; m., Frederick Loewe	1956
Mack the Knife, German w., Berthold Brecht; English w., Marc Blitzstein; m., Kurt Weill	1959
We Shall Overcome, new w., m., Z. Horton, F. Hamilton, G. Caravan, Peter Seeger[1]	1960
Blowin' in the Wind, w., m., Bob Dylan[1]	1962
Sunrise, Sunset, w., Sheldon Harnick; m., Jerry Bock[1]	1964
The Impossible Dream, w., Joe Darion; m., Mitch Leigh[1]	1965
Aquarius, w., James Rado and Gerome Ragni; m., Galt MacDermot[1]	1966
Mrs. Robinson, w., m., Paul Simon[1]	1968

[1] A projection, as time insufficient to determine all-time-hit status.

Dance

Social dancing and folk dancing have long been an important part of American life. However, widespread interest in dance as a serious art form is a relatively new phenomenon. The seminal forces in modern dance—Duncan, St. Denis, Graham, and Humphrey—were American. So are a substantial proportion of contemporary choreographers of modern dance. But it has been only the last ten years that have seen modern dance attract an audience of reasonable size.

The visits of great foreign performers, such as Pavlova and Nijinsky early in the century, as well as Diaghilev's Ballets Russes and the later Ballet Russe de Monte Carlo, laid a foundation for the tentative establishment of indigenous ballet companies in the 1930s which were to last. Later visits of stars, such as Fonteyn and Nureyev, and great companies, the Royal, Bolshoi, and Stuttgart, usually under the aegis of Sol Hurok, vastly expanded the size of the ballet audience in America. The past two decades have witnessed the rise to international stature of two American ballet companies, tremendous growth of regional companies, and the acclaimed choreography of Balanchine, Robbins, and others.

1607–1700. SOCIAL DANCING. Puritan laws discouraged dancing in New England except where instruction could teach coordination and poise. Despite the laws, people danced; dancing masters were common by the 1670s. Laws were less restrictive in other colonies. Dancing was considered an essential part of life among the aristocratic Southerners.

1701–1800. SOCIAL AND FOLK DANCING. Dancing masters, who generally taught country dances, jigs, cotillions, the minuet, courante, and other European imports were well established in the social life of the colonies. Toward the end of the century balls and assemblies were common in the large cities. Dancing was considered an important form of socializing on the frontier, where dances were less formal than in the Eastern cities and included versions of the square dance and the Virginia reel.

c.1727–94. BALLET. The first ballet performances in America were given by amateur and semiprofessional groups and by individual dancing masters. An English group, headed by Lewis Hallam, was the first truly professional company to dance in the colonies (c. 1750), performing harlequinades, spectacles, and incidental dances.

1767. John Street Theater opened in New York City for visiting European companies.

1774. First Continental Congress forbade theatrical activity in the colonies but Revolutionary War inspired patriotic pageants, which reawakened interest in the dance.

1785. Debut of John Durang, the first native American performer of repute, with the Hallam Company in Philadelphia. Durang's popularity increased throughout the 1790s.

c.1790. French Revolution stimulated the immigration of dancers from the continent who offered performances and instruction.

1794. *La Forêt Noire,* the first seriously regarded ballet in the U.S., performed in Philadelphia, featuring Anne Gardie and John Durang.

1801–1900. SOCIAL DANCING became increasingly popular in the 19th century. The rich continued to hold formal assemblies, cotillions, and society balls in larger cities and various organizations began to sponsor annual balls. Smaller cities and towns held public balls. The poor danced in concert saloons, beer gardens, and dance halls. On the frontier informal dancing such as the Virginia reel, country jigs, shakedowns, and plankdances, occurred at country fairs, logrollings, quilting parties, husking bees, and holidays. The Shakers, using a variety of movements in their religious services, structured and refined them into group dances. The waltz and polka were introduced from Europe (c. 1830). Other popular 19th-century dances included the cakewalk, the Washington Post, and the barn dance.

1801–1900. THEATRICAL DANCING, performed in musical variety shows and vaudeville, derived from many sources, a primary one being American Negro dance. By 1810 the singing and dancing "Negro Boy" (usually a blackened white man) was an established part of stage productions, dancing a jig or clog, accompanied by songs with allusions to Negroes. **Juba,** who imitated popular dancers and performed traditional Negro dances, became the first black to achieve fame as a stage performer (c. 1840). The black influence upon American dance forms included the buck-and-wing, tap dancing (a combination of the Irish clog and black shuffle dances), and the cakewalk. *Clorindy: The Origin of the Cake Walk* was performed on Broadway by a black company (1898).

1801–1850. POPULARITY OF BALLET led to increasingly frequent performances by visiting European artists.

1827. Mme. Francisque Hutin introduced Americans to the *pointe* footwork and multiple pirouettes of the romantic ballet.

1837. Debuts, in *The Maid of Cashmere,* Chestnut Street Theatre, Philadelphia, of American ballerinas **Mary Ann Lee** and **Augusta Maywood,** the first American to dance at the Paris Opera (1839), and as prima ballerina at La Scala.

1838. Debut of **George Washington Smith,** first American *danseur noble.*

1835–1887. FOREIGN BALLET PREMIERES IN AMERICA. *La Sylphide,* Philadelphia (1835) by M. Celeste; *La Fille Mal Gardée,* Park Theatre, New York (6 July 1839); *Giselle,* Howard Atheneum, Boston (1 Jan. 1846); *Coppélia,* Metropolitan Opera House (11 Mar. 1887).

1839–40. PERFORMANCES OF FOREIGN ARTISTS. Marius Petipa with Ballet Company of Madame Lacomte (1839); **Paul** and **Marie Taglioni,** Park Theatre, New York (21 May 1839); **Fanny Elssler,** New York (14 May 1840).

c.1855. Decline of ballet due to lack of major theaters, opera houses, state-supported schools, or other government subsidy.

1866. Premiere of *The Black Crook,* major dance phenomenon of Victorian Age, performed for forty years and featuring one ballet number in which performers danced almost nude.

1885–87. American Opera Co., formed in New York, made effort to present high-quality ballet.

c. 1890. Waning of popularity of ballet, with excessive emphasis upon technical virtuosity generating artistic stagnation.

1900–26. MODERN DANCE: THE BEGINNINGS. Modern dance in America developed as a reaction against the increasing sterility of classical ballet. The technical, mechanical, and elaborate aspects of the ballet were rejected for greater freedom of movement and emotional involvement. Subject matter of dances began to reflect contemporary interests as well as concurrent developments in art and music. Major concerns of dancers were simplicity, functionalism, and expressiveness. American choreographer-dancers dominated early developments; among them: **Isadora Duncan** (p. 1018), established the idea of dance as a means of personal expression; **Ruth St. Denis** (1877–1968) and her husband, **Ted Shawn** (1891–1972), established a school, Denishawn, which trained students in Eastern and other dance forms, introduced theatrical appeal and a religious mysticism, while creating new audiences. The Denishawn School produced **Martha Graham,** Doris Humphrey, and Charles Weidman.

1908–29. BALLET popularity revived with visits of leading European artists and companies. Major arrivals included **Adeline Genée** (1908), **Cid Fornaroli** (1910), and **Anna Pavlova** (1881–1931), whose debut occurred in *Cop-*

pélia, MO,* with Mikhail Mordkin (28 Feb. 1910). Pavlova toured the U.S. (1910–1925). **Serge Diaghilev's Ballets Russes** arrived, New York (1916), introducing **Vaslav Nijinsky** in *Le Spectre de la Rose* and *Petrouchka*, MO (12 Apr. 1916), **Michel Fokine, Léonide Massine** (1894–) and **Adolph Bolm**. 2d N.Y. season opened Manhattan Opera House with Nijinsky (*Tl Eulenspiegel*).

1910–29. SOCIAL DANCES attaining great popularity included the tango (introduced c. 1910) and the fox-trot, devised by **Harry Fox** for the *Ziegfeld Follies* (1913). **Vernon** and **Irene Castle** refined and popularized these dances, as well as the Boston waltz, the hesitation waltz, the turkey trot, and their own Castle Walk. Ragtime music inspired the grizzly bear and the bunny hug, popular in the 1910s. Dixieland jazz, whose roots were in African rhythms imported by slaves, was reflected in popular dances of the 1920s, especially the Charleston, noted for wildly flailing legs, the Black Bottom, with twisted contortions, and the Shimmy, with frenetic shaking.

1911–49. PERFORMANCES OF FOREIGN BALLETS.† *Les Sylphides*, New York (1911); *Swan Lake* (4 acts), MO (20 Dec. 1911); *Firebird*, BR, New York (1916); *The Rite of Spring*, Academy of Music, Philadelphia (11 Apr. 1930; danced by Martha Graham); *The Nutcracker*, MC, New York (17 Oct. 1940); *The Sleeping Beauty*, Philadelphia Ballet (12 Feb. 1937), Sadler's Wells' version, MO (9 Oct. 1949); *Les Patineurs*, BT, New York (2 Oct. 1946); *Symphonic Variations*, SW, MO (12 Oct. 1946).

* MO—Metropolitan Opera House, New York City
† *Abbreviations*
BR   Serge Diaghilev's Ballets Russes
BT   Ballet Theatre
MC   Ballet Russe de Monte Carlo
MO   Metropolitan Opera
SW   Sadler's Wells

1921. Fokine School opened in New York (1 Jan.).

1924–25. Pavlova and company make last American tour.

1926–63. MODERN DANCE. Martha Graham (p. 1043) gave her first independent dance recital, 48th St. Theatre, New York (18 Apr. 1926). Developing a nonballetic dance vocabulary expressive of inner tensions, Graham was the teacher of most of the important modern dancers-choreographers for five decades, including Merce Cunningham, Erick Hawkins, Donald McKayle, Glen Tetley, Paul Taylor, Anna Sokolow, and Pearl Lang. **Doris Humphrey** (1895–1958) based her style on "falls and recoveries," exploiting the drama of the falling body as well as the pressures and tensions of a balanced body in repose. More socially committed than Graham, Humphrey worked closely with choreographer **Charles Weidman** (1901–1975). Humphrey's major students included José Limon and Ruth Currier. Both Humphrey and Graham integrated the spoken word into their dances. **José Limon** (1908–72) was noted for symmetry in composition and a flair for theater, combining formal discipline with dramatic passion; *The Moor's Pavane* (1949) was one of the first modern dance pieces to enter the repertory of ballet companies. **Alwin Nikolais** (1912–) has developed a mass media theater where as choreographer-composer-designer he fuses sound, color, lighting, unusual props, music, and dance. A major work is *Imago* (1963). **Merce Cunningham** (1919–) works with dance-by-chance or random methods of composition, exemplified in *Suite by Chance* (1953), as well as in developing dance without either drama or music. **Paul Taylor** (1930–), who studied under Graham and danced under Balanchine, exemplifies a style close to ballet (*Aureole*, 1962), ofttimes spiced with humor. **Alvin Ailey** (1931–

) and **Donald McKayle** (1930–)
are black dancers–choreographers, who
successfully combine modern dance techniques with African and West Indian
dance elements. Ailey's *Revelations*
(1960) is perhaps the most popular
of all works of modern dance. *Cry*
(1971), written for Judith Jamison, is a
major solo. The Alvin Ailey City Center
Dance Theater is virtually unique in having a repertory embracing works of other
major modern dance choreographers including McKayle's *Rainbow Round My
Shoulder,* as well as works of Pearl
Primus and Janet Collins. Other major
creative figures in modern dance include
**Anna Sokolow, Pauline Koner, Erick
Hawkins, Ann Halprin, Lucas Hoving,
Katherine Litz, Pearl Lang, Glen Tetley,
Ruth Currier,** and **Katherine Dunham.**

1930–74. SOCIAL DANCING. Jazz
inspired the swing era of the 1930s and
dancing to the music of "big bands." It
led to the Lindy hop, which featured
gymnastics and wild footwork, as well
as other popular dances like the Big
Apple, the Shag, and Trucking. The
Lindy hop was the precursor of the jit-
terbug, which became the rage throughout the 1930s and was exported all over
the world by GIs in the 1940s. Group
dances became popular in the late 1930s.
The conga, in which a line of dancers
followed a leader, and the Lambeth walk,
a strutting dance, were imported from
England. Another phenomenon of the
1930s was the dance marathon in which
couples danced nonstop for days. In the
1940s Latin American dances such as the
samba, rhumba, and mambo became
popular. These rhythms inspired the ca-
lypso and cha-cha dances of the following
decade. The rock 'n' roll phenomenon
of the 1950s was another outgrowth of
American jazz. Couples danced to rock
'n' roll music but rarely established body
contact. The dances were open to a
great deal of individual improvisation.

In the 1960s, social dances such as the
twist, the monkey, and the frug encouraged individual expression.

**1933. BALLET RUSSE DE MONTE
CARLO,** outgrowth of disbanded Diaghilev troupe, toured U.S. (1st perf. St.
James Theatre, N.Y., 22 Dec. 1933),
under sponsorship of impresario **Sol
Hurok** (1888–1974) with Léonide Massine as chief choreographer. Repeated
tours increased the popularity of ballet.

1933. The Jooss Ballet makes U.S.
debut.

**1933–69. U.S. BALLET COMPA-
NIES. San Francisco Ballet Co.** (1933–
), founded by Adolph Bolm. **School
of American Ballet,** founded by **Lincoln
Kirstein** (1907–), E. M. M. Warburg,
and **George Balanchine** (2 Jan. 1934).
American Ballet, founded by Kirstein
and Edward M. M. Warburg, with a
repertory of ballets by Balanchine, gave
2-week season at the Adelphi Theatre,
New York (1935) and became resident ballet company at MO (1935–38).
Littlefield Ballet, Philadelphia, organized
(1935) by **Catherine Littlefield** (1904–
51), became the Philadelphia Ballet
(1936). **Ballet Caravan,** organized by
Lincoln Kirstein to tour U.S. and offer
opportunities to American artists (1936).
Ballet Theatre (since 1957, American
Ballet Theatre), founded by Lucia Chase
and Richard Pleasant (1st perf., Center
Theatre, N.Y., 11 Jan. 1940), encouraged
American choreographers **Jerome Robbins** (1918–), Michael Kidd, Agnes
de Mille, Antony Tudor, and Eliot Feld.
Ballet Theatre became first U.S. company
to dance at Covent Garden (4 July
1946). It became a company in residence
at the John F. Kennedy Center for the
Performing Arts, Washington, D.C.
(1971). **Ballet Society,** created by Kirstein and Balanchine for private subscription audience (1st perf., N.Y., 20
Nov. 1946) became **New York City Ballet,** resident company of the New York

City Center of Music and Drama (1st perf., 11 Oct. 1948), and was recognized as a company of international stature after its performances at Covent Garden (1950). It moved to the New York State Theater of Lincoln Center for the Performing Arts (1964). Major companies founded in the 1960s included **Pennsylvania Ballet,** Philadelphia (1962); **City Center Joffrey Ballet** evolved from the Robert Joffrey Ballet with a well-balanced repertory combining revival of 19th and early 20th century works with contemporary multimedia ballets (1966); **Dance Theatre of Harlem,** combining classical training with black influences, established by **Arthur Mitchell** (1969).

1934–71. PERFORMANCES OF AMERICAN BALLETS.° *Serenade* (Balanchine-Tchaikovsky), School of American Ballet, Warburg Estate, White Plains, N.Y. (9 June 1934); *Orpheus* (Balanchine-Gluck, AB, MO (22 May 1936); *Billy the Kid* (Loring-Copland), BC, Chicago (16 Oct. 1938); *Pillar of Fire* (Tudor-Schoenberg), BT, MO (8 Apr. 1942); *Rodeo* (de Mille-Copland), MC, MO (16 Oct. 1942); *Fancy Free* (Robbins-Bernstein), BT, MO (18 Apr. 1944); *Orpheus* (Balanchine–Stravinsky), BS, NYCC (28 Apr. 1948); *La Valse* (Balanchine-Ravel), NYCB (20 Feb. 1951); *The Cage* (Robbins-Stravinsky), NYCB (10 June 1951); *The Concert* (Robbins-Chopin), NYCB (1956); *Les Noces* (Robbins-Stravinsky), ABT, New York (1965); *Astarte* (Joffrey-Syrcus), Joffrey, New York (1967); *Harbinger* (Feld-Prokofiev), ABT, New York (1967); *Dances at a Gathering* (Robbins-Chopin), NYCB (1969); *The River* (Ailey-Ellington), ABT, New York

° *Abbreviations*
AB   American Ballet
ABT   American Ballet Theatre
BC   Ballet Caravan
BS   Ballet Society
BT   Ballet Theatre
NYCB   New York City Ballet
NYCC   New York City Center
Joffrey City Center Joffrey Ballet

(1970); *In the Night* (Robbins-Chopin), NYCB (1970); *Trinity* (Arpino-Raph and Holdridge), Joffrey, New York (1970); *The Goldberg Variations* (Robbins-Bach), NYCB (27 May 1971); *Watermill* (Robbins-Ito), NYCB (1972).

1936–54. DANCING IN THEATER AND FILMS. Choreographers from ballet and modern dance contributed to the distinctiveness of the American musical theater as well as to the integration of dance and drama. Among the milestones were Balanchine's *On Your Toes* (1936), de Mille's *Oklahoma!* (1943), Jerome Robbins' *West Side Story* (1957). Modern dance choreographers who made major contributions to the stage musical include Hanya Holm, *Kiss Me Kate* (1948) and *My Fair Lady* (1956), Helen Tamiris, *Show Boat* (1928), and Jack Cole, *Man of La Mancha* (1965).

1930s film audiences were treated to the dance extravaganzas of Busby Berkeley (1895–   ). Fred Astaire and Ginger Rogers were an exceptionally popular dance team. Gene Kelly became the dominant dance figure in the films of the 1940s and 1950s.

1941–74. MODERN DANCE FESTIVALS of greatest influence were the Jacob's Pillow Dance Festival (Lee, Mass.), founded by Ted Shawn (1941) for presentation of modern dance, ethnic dance, and ballet, and the American Dance Festival at Connecticut College (New London, Conn.) (1948).

1949–74. POPULARIZATION OF BALLET. Annual tours by foreign companies attracted large audiences: **Sadler's Wells** (later **Royal Ballet**) (1st tour, 1949); **Royal Danish Ballet** (1st tour, 1956); **Bolshoi Ballet** (1st tour, 1959); **Leningrad Kirov Ballet** (1st tour, 1961); **Stuttgart Ballet** (1st tour, 1969); Maurice **Béjart Ballet of the 20th Century** (1st tour, 1971). Major foreign performers included **Dame Margot Fonteyn** of the Royal Ballet (debut 1949), **Erik**

Bruhn (debut, BT, 1955), **Maya Pliset-skaya** of the Bolshoi (1959), **Rudolf Nureyev** (debut Ruth Page Chicago Opera Ballet, 1962), Natalia Makarova (debut with ABT after defection, N.Y., 22 Dec. 1970), Mikhail Baryshnikov (1974). Nureyev made U.S. modern dance debut with Paul Taylor Company in *Aureole,* New York (14 Oct. 1974).

New York City Ballet offered Stravinsky Festival (18–25 June 1972) of 27 ballets, 20 of them world premieres; NYCB Ravel Festival (14–31 May 1975).

In addition to major companies in urban areas, regional companies expanded from 30 in 1955 to 200 in 1965. Books, magazines, and newspaper criticism proliferated in the late 1960s.

1964–74. MODERN DANCE DEVELOPMENTS. Differences between ballet and modern dance began to disappear in some choreography. While some of ballet's technical elements, costumes, decor, and music became incorporated by modern dance, some of the freedom and emotionality as well as abstraction of modern dance were absorbed by ballet. Innovations in modern dance in the 1960s and 1970s have included the use of eurythmy, where dancers interpret a spoken or sung accompaniment; the use of film, slide, and light projections; the introduction of social and political protest in the dance, as well as nudity and homosexuality. Among major contemporary choreographers are Twyla Tharp, Meredith Monk, Yvonne Rainer, and Eleo Pomare.

Improved financing from government and foundations led to vast expansion of the number of performances. Audiences increased, seasons lengthened, and companies added artistic and administrative personnel.

MASS MEDIA

Newspapers and Periodicals

Newspapers and pamphlets flourished on the eve of the Revolution and contributed to its genesis. During the first century after independence newspapers continued to boom, growing from 92 in 1790 to 3,725 in 1860, with the appearance of the penny newspaper a major factor in attaining a mass circulation. In the latter part of the nineteenth century intense competition between newspapers spawned such features as comics, photographs, and sensational reporting ("yellow journalism"), notoriously evident on the eve of the Spanish-American War.

Along with the growth of great newspaper chains and the wire services, the early twentieth century witnessed a concern for more factual and in-depth reportage. The economics of the industry had by the midcentury led to a monopoly situation, with most U.S. cities boasting but one newspaper and newspaper proprietors often owning local radio and TV stations. Magazines, once a flourishing industry, have been a victim of TV and economics, with recent casualties including *Life* and *Look*. News magazines, however, continue to be profitable, and a few journals low in circulation but high in quality continue to survive.

The polarization of the 1960s spurred openly subjective reporting, but more characteristic of contemporary trends in journalism is the investigative reporting of Seymour Hersh and Jack Anderson, and notably of Robert Woodward and Carl Bernstein, who contributed mightily to uncovering facts about the Watergate scandals.

Relations between the U.S. government and the press, despite First Amendment safeguards, have never been entirely free from friction, from the time of the Alien and Sedition Acts to the censorship of stories from the battlefield and the suppression or seizure of newspapers during the Civil War. Recent years have seen a heightening of tensions as a result of newspaper exposés of a credibility gap in administration statements during the Vietnam War, and relentless publication of the evidence in the Watergate scandal.

1690–1736. HARRIS TO ZENGER.

Public Occurrences (Boston; Benjamin Harris [fl.1673–1728]), suppressed by the government after 1 issue for critical comments on conduct of King William's war. First continuous colonial newspaper: Boston *News-Letter* (1704, John Campbell; discontinued, 1776), contained first illustration in colonial paper (19 Jan. 1708). Other papers: Boston *Gazette* (1719, William Brooker); Philadelphia *American Mercury* (1719, Andrew Bradford [1686–1742], employed Benjamin Franklin; disc. 1749); *New England Courant* (1721, Boston, James Franklin; issued by brother Benjamin when editor jailed for criticizing government; disc. 1726); New York *Gazette* (1725, William Bradford [1663–1752]; sold to James Parker, 1743, and merged with New York *Post-Boy or Gazette*); *New England Weekly Journal* (1727, Samuel Kneeland; merged with Gazette, 1741); *Maryland Gazette* (1727, William Parker (c.1698–1750); disc. 1734; revived, 1745, by Jonas Green; cont. to 1839); *Universal Instructor . . . and Pennsylvania Gazette* (1728, Philadelphia, Samuel Keimer; bought by **Benjamin Franklin**, 1729, continued as *Pennsylvania Gazette;* David Hall proprietor after 1766; disc. 1815). *Weekly Rehearsal* (1731, Boston, Jeremy Gridley, forerunner of Boston *Evening Post;* disc. 1775 after pursuing neutral course); *South Carolina Gazette* (1732, Charleston, Thomas Whitmarsh with Franklin's support; later edited by Peter Timothy; became *Gazette of State of South Carolina*, 1777; then *State Gazette of South Carolina;* disc. 1802); *Rhode Island State Gazette* (1732, Newport, James Franklin, disc. 1773); New York *Weekly Journal*, 5 Nov. 1733, **John Peter Zenger** (p. 1190). For **Zenger Trial** (1734–35) in which Andrew Hamilton successfully argued that truth was a defense to seditious libel, see p. 1190. Boston *Post-Boy* (1734), leading Tory organ.

Virginia Gazette (1736), Williamsburg, William Parks; disc. 1750; succeeded by 4 other weeklies of this name, in order: Hunter, 1751–78; Rind, 1766–76; Purdie, 1775–80; and Dixon & Nicholson, 1779–80.

1739–78. FOREIGN LANGUAGE PRESS.

The first foreign language newspaper in the colonies was the Philadelphia *Zeitung* (1732, Benj. Franklin); it quickly expired. The most lasting were the Germantown *Zeitung* (1739, **Christopher Sower**, 1693–1758, son 1721–1781, and Loyalist grandson, 1754–1799) and *Wöchentliche Philadelphische Staatsbote* (1762–79, Heinrich Miller).

1741–1775. EVE OF THE REVOLUTION.

American Magazine, first magazine in the colonies (Jan. 1741, Philadelphia, Andrew Bradford; disc. Mar. 1741); *General Magazine and Historical Chronicle* (Jan. 1741, Philadelphia, Benjamin Franklin; disc. June 1741); *Pennsylvania Journal* (1742, Philadelphia, William Bradford, III; later *Patriot;* disc. 1793); New York *Post-Boy* (1743, James Parker; disc. 1773); Boston *Weekly Museum* (1743, Gamaliel Rogers and John Fowle, disc. 1743); *Christian History* (1743, a weekly to report Great Awakening, disc. 1745); New York *Evening Post* (1744, Henry DeForest; disc. 1752); *American Magazine and Historical Chronicle* (1746, Boston, Rogers and Fowle; disc. Dec. 1746); *Independent Advertiser* (1748, Boston, Rogers and Fowle); New York *Weekly Mercury* (1752, **Hugh Gaine** [1727–1807]; 2 editions published during Revolution—Loyalist in New York; Patriot in Newark, N.J.); *Independent Reflector* (1752, James Parker; disc. 1753). *Pennsylvania Gazette* carried first colonial cartoon (attributed to Franklin), depicting a cut-up snake and the caption: "Join or Die" (9 May 1754). Boston *Gazette* (1755, **Benjamin Edes** [1732–1803] and John Gill), leading Patriot organ, with such contributors as Sam and

John Adams, Josiah Quincy, Jr., and Joseph Warren. *Connecticut Gazette* (1755, New Haven, James Parker; disc. 1768); *New Hampshire Gazette* (1756, Portsmouth, **Daniel Fowle** [1715–87]), still published; *American Magazine and Monthly Chronicle* (1757, Philadelphia, William Bradford, III, with Rev. William Smith, provost of College of Philadelphia, as editor), first well-edited colonial magazine; disc. 1757. *New American Magazine* (1758, Woodbridge, N.J., Judge Samuel Nevill; disc. 1760); *Newport Mercury* (1758, James Franklin, nephew of Benj. Franklin), still published; *New York Gazette* (1759, William Weyman; merged with *Mercury*, 1768); *American Chronicle* (1762, New York, Samuel Farley; disc. July); *Providence Gazette* (1762, William Goddard; disc. 1825); *Georgia Gazette* (1763, James Johnston), Loyalist; published under British occupation during Revolution as *Royal Georgia Gazette*, 1779–82. New York *Pacquet* (1763, Benjamin Mecom; disc. Aug.); *Connecticut Courant* (1764, Hartford, Thomas Green, still published); New York *Journal or General Advertiser* (1766, **John Holt** [1721–84], Patriot organ published during Revolution in Kingston and Poughkeepsie; merged, 1793, with *Greenleaf's N.Y. Journal*); *Essex Gazette* (1768, Salem; removed to Cambridge 1775 as *New England Chronicle*; to Boston, 1776, as *Independent Chronicle;* cont. as *Semi-Weekly Advertiser*, 1840–76); New York *Chronicle* (1769, James Robertson; disc. 1770); *Massachusetts Spy* (1770, Boston, **Isaiah Thomas** [p. 1169]), Patriot; removed to Worcester, 3 May 1775, carrying story of Lexington and Concord; became Worcester *Gazette*, 1781). McDougall libel case (p. 93). *Pennsylvania Packet* (1771, Philadelphia, John Dunlap; disc. 1790); *Rivington's New York Gazetteer* (1773, **James Rivington** [1724–1802], Loyalist; disc. 1775, resumed,

1777, as *Loyal New York Gazette;* disc. 1783). *Royal American Magazine* (1774, Boston, Isaiah Thomas, Patriot; disc. Mar. 1775); *Pennsylvania Magazine* (1775, Philadelphia, Robert Aitken; **Thomas Paine** (p. 1020) editor, Feb. 1775–May 1776; disc. July 1776).

1775. POLITICS AND CIRCULATION. There were 37 newspapers in the colonies (23 Patriot, 7 Loyalist, 7 neutral or doubtful in loyalty). Average weekly circulation rose from c.600 (1765) to as much as 3,500 (1775, *Massachusetts Spy*). Price ranged from 2s. 6d.–6s. per quarter. Philadelphia *Evening Post* (1775, Benjamin Towne, later Loyalist; disc. 1784), first American daily, sold for 2d. an issue.

1776–89. New York *Packet* (1776, **Samuel Loudon** [1727–1813]; pub. at Fishkill, Jan. 1777; returned to New York, 1783; became daily; disc. 1792). New York *Evening Post* (1782, Christopher Sower *et al.;* became *Morning Post,* 1783; disc. 1792); *Boston Magazine* (1783, John Eliot, James Freeman, George R. Minot; disc. 1786); New York *Independent Journal* (1783, semiweekly; later a daily as *Daily Gazette;* published *Federalist Papers;* disc. 1795); *Mass. Centinel and Republican Journal* (1784, Boston, Benjamin Russell and William Warden, supported Constitution; as *Columbian Centinel,* beg. 1790, was a leading Federalist paper; disc. 1840). New York *Daily Advertiser* (1785; disc. 1806); *New Haven Gazette and Connecticut Magazine* (1786, Josiah Meigs and Eleutheros Dana; disc. 1789); *Worcester Magazine* (1786, Isaiah Thomas; disc. 1788); *Columbian Magazine* (1786, Philadelphia, ed. by Mathew Carey *et al.;* merged 1790 with *Universal Asylum;* disc. 1792); *Pittsburgh Gazette* (1786, John Sculland and Joseph Hall; first newspaper west of the Alleghenies; Federalist; cont. after merger [1927] as *Post-Gazette*); *American Museum* (1787,

Philadelphia, **Mathew Carey** [1760–1839]; disc. 1792; *American Magazine* (1787, New York, **Noah Webster** [p. 1179]; disc. 1788); *Gazette of the U.S.* (1789, New York; Philadelphia beg. 1790; **John Fenno** [1751–98]; leading Federalist organ; known, 1804–18, as *U.S. Gazette*).

1790–1860. NEWSPAPER GROWTH. There were 92 newspapers in U.S., 1790 –8 dailies, 70 weeklies, 14 semiweekly or at other intervals; 3,725 newspapers, 1860–387 dailies, 3,173 weeklies, 79 semiweeklies, 86 triweeklies.

1790–1804. FEDERALIST AND REPUBLICAN PRESS. *General Advertiser,* 1790, Philadelphia, **Benjamin F. Bache** (1769–98); later (1794) known as *Aurora,* succeeding *National Gazette* as leading Republican organ; later ed. by **William Duane** (1760–1835); disc. 1835. *National Gazette,* 1791, Philadelphia, ed. **Philip Freneau** (1752–1832), anti-Federalist; disc. 1793. *Massachusetts Mercury* (1793, Boston); known as *New England Palladium,* 1803–14. *New Hampshire Journal* (1793, Walpole, N.H.), best known beg. 1797 as *The Farmer's Weekly Museum,* a famous village weekly; **Joseph Dennie** (1768–1812) ed., 1796–99; shared literary column with **Royall Tyler** (1757–1826), beg. 1794; disc. 1810. *Centinel of the North-Western Territory* (1793, Cincinnati); first paper in present Ohio; later known as *Freeman's Journal;* merged with *Scioto Gazette* (Chillicothe), started by Nathaniel Willis; still published. *American Minerva* (1793, New York, **Noah Webster**), Federalist; became (1797) *Commercial Advertiser;* renamed *Globe and Commercial Advertiser,* 1904; absorbed by New York *Sun,* 1923. Dunlap and Claypoole's *American Daily Advertiser,* 1793, Philadelphia; became (1800) *Poulson's American Daily Advertiser;* absorbed (1839) by the Philadelphia *North American.* New York *Argus* (1795, Thomas Greenleaf, a Burr Republican; name changed, 1800, to *American Citizen). Federal Gazette* (1796, Baltimore; disc. 1825); *Porcupine's Gazette and U.S. Advertiser* (1797, Philadelphia, **William Cobbett** [1763–1835], Federalist; disc. 1799). *Palladium* (1798, Frankfort, Ky., disc. c.1817). **Sedition Act** prosecutions, 1798 (p. 155). Baltimore *American* (1799). *Western Spy* (1799, Cincinnati; disc. 1822). Raleigh (N.C.) *Register* (1799, **Joseph Gales** [1761–1841]). *Washington Federalist* (1800, Georgetown; disc. 1809). Charleston (S.C.) *Times* (1800). *National Intelligencer* (1800, Washington, D.C.); purchased (1807) by **Joseph Gales, Jr.** (1786–1860); from 1812–60 by Gales and **William W. Seaton** (1785–1866); leading political organ (Whig); disc. 1869. New York *Evening Post* (1801), **Alexander Hamilton** *et al.,* Federalist; **William Cullen Bryant** (p. 993), editor in chief, 1829–78, supported Democratic party. Charleston (S.C.) *Courier* (1803); later as *News and Courier,* Unionist during Nullification. Richmond (Va.) *Enquirer* (1804), **Thomas Ritchie** (1778–1854) sole publisher in 1805; a leading Southern paper; disc. 1877. *Indiana Gazette* (1804, Vincennes) became (1807) *Western Sun;* later (1879) *Sun-Commercial.*

1804. CROSWELL LIBEL CASE. Harry Croswell, publisher of the Hudson (N.Y.) *Wasp,* convicted for a criminal libel upon President Jefferson. On appeal Alexander Hamilton, his counsel, reaffirmed and modified defense contention in Zenger case (p. 1190), arguing that truth published "with good motives and justifiable ends" was a defense. Although **James Kent** (p. 1075), then dominating the N.Y. Supreme Court, supported Hamilton, the motion for a new trial was denied by a divided court, but the prosecution was dropped. A New York act of 6 Apr. 1805 adopting Hamilton's formula (incorporated into constitutions of 1821 and 1846) served as a model for the press guarantees of many state constitutions.

1806–20. WESTERN EXPANSION. *Western World* (1806, Frankfort, Ky., Joseph M. Street) exposed Burr Conspiracy (p. 162); disc. 1810. *Democratic Press* (1807, Philadelphia; disc. 1829). *Argus of Western America* (1808, Frankfort, Ky., **Amos Kendall** [1789–1869] coeditor, 1816–29; disc. c.1838). *Federal Republican* (1808, Baltimore; plant destroyed by mob for opposition to War of 1812; resumed, 1816; disc. 1834). *Missouri Gazette* (1808, St. Louis; disc. 1822). *New Hampshire Patriot* (1809, Concord, **Isaac Hill** [1789–1851], Democrat; disc. c.1921). *Mobile Centinel* (1811, Fort Stoddert, first paper in present Alabama). *Ohio State Journal* (1811, Columbus; daily since 1837). *Niles' Weekly Register* (1811, Baltimore, **Hezekiah Niles** [1777–1839], Whig, with a nationwide influence; distinguished for factual reporting; disc. 1849). Albany *Argus* (1813), later organ of the "Albany Regency," disc. c.1894. Boston *Daily Advertiser* (1813, Whig; disc. 1929). *Illinois Herald* (1814, Kaskaskia); first paper in Illinois Territory. *Western Journal* (1815, St. Louis); later known as *Enquirer,* with **Thomas Hart Benton** (1782–1858) among early editors. *Ohio Monitor* (1816, Columbus); became (1838) *Ohio Statesman* Democratic. Detroit *Gazette* (1817), first successful paper in present Michigan; disc. 1830. *Texas Republican* (1819, Nacogdoches); first English-language paper in Texas. *Arkansas Gazette,* 1819, *Arkansas Post* (1822) removed to Little Rock. *National Gazette* (1820, Philadelphia; disc. 1842).

1820. Out of some 1,634 newspapers established between 1704 and 1820 only 4 had lasted 50 years or more.

1821–33. CONTINUED EXPANSION. Mobile *Register* (1821). Charleston *Mercury* (1822, Henry Laurens Pinckney ed., 1823–32; chief secessionist organ).

Richmond *Whig,* 1824, **John H. Pleasants** (1797–1846); disc. 1888. Boston *Courier* (1824, **Joseph T. Buckingham** [1779–1861]; disc. 1864). *National Journal* (1824, Washington, D.C.; disc. 1832). *U.S. Telegraph* (1826, Washington; **Duff Green** [1791–1875]; chief Jackson organ until c.1831; disc. 1837). New York *Morning Courier* (1827) became (1829) *Courier and Enquirer* (Whig) after merging with New York *Enquirer;* **James Watson Webb** (1802–84); merged with *World* (1861). Baltimore *Republican* (1827; actually Democratic; disc. 1863); Cincinnati *Daily Gazette* (1827; disc. 1883). *Journal of Commerce* (1827, New York, **Arthur Tappan** [1786–1865]). *Cherokee Phoenix* (1828, New Echota, Ga.), Indian newspaper printed in characters devised by Sequoyah (?1770–1843); disc. 1835. *Pennsylvania Inquirer* (1829; later *Philadelphia Inquirer*). Albany *Evening Journal,* 1830, **Thurlow Weed** (1797–1882), Whig; disc. 1925. *Evening Transcript* (1830, Boston, L. M. Walter, cultural organ; disc. 1941). Louisville (Ky.) *Journal,* 1830, **George D. Prentice** (1802–70); later (1868) merged with *Democrat* (1843) and *Courier* (1844) as *Courier-Journal,* ed. by **Henry Watterson** ("Marse Henry," 1840–1921). Washington *Globe,* 1830, **Francis P. Blair** (1791–1876); Jackson organ; disc. 1845. Boston *Morning Post* (1831; Democratic). Boston *Atlas* (1832; disc. 1861). *Pennsylvanian,* 1832, Philadelphia, ed. for a time by John W. Forney (1817–81); leading Democratic paper in state; disc. 1861. *Mercantile Journal* (1833, Boston); became *Evening Journal,* 1845; absorbed (1917) by Boston *Herald.* *Weekly Democrat* (1833, Chicago; disc. 1861). Green Bay *Intelligencer* (1833; first paper in Wisconsin Territory; disc. c.1836).

1828–34. EARLY LABOR PRESS. *Mechanics' Free Press* (1828, Philadelphia; first labor paper in U.S.; disc.

c.1835). *Working Man's Advocate,* 1829, New York, **George Henry Evans** (1805–56); disc. c.1851. *Man* (1834, New York, **George Henry Evans;** disc. 1835).

1834–56. GERMAN PRESS. New York *Staats-Zeitung* (1834, **Jacob Uhl**); tri-weekly, 1842; daily 1848; claimed largest German language circulation of any newspaper in the world. *Volksblatt* (1836, Cincinnati). There were 56 German newspapers in U.S., 1856.

1833–37. RISE OF THE PENNY PRESS. New York *Sun,* 1833, **Benjamin H. Day** (1810–89); first successful penny daily in the U.S.; celebrated "Moon Hoax" appeared in its papers in 1835; in 1868 purchased by **Charles A. Dana** (1819–97) and others; absorbed (1950) by New York *World-Telegram.* New York *Transcript* (1834; disc. c.1839). *New York Morning Herald,* 1835, **James Gordon Bennett** (p. 983); chief rival of *Sun;* pioneered in reporting crime and society news; following merger (1924), became *Herald Tribune.* Philadelphia *Public Ledger,* 1836; merged (1934) in the *Inquirer.* Boston *Daily Times,* 1836; merged (1857) with Boston *Herald.* Baltimore *Sun* (1837, Swain, Abell, and Simmons).

1835–60. ANTEBELLUM EXPANSION. *Telegraph and Texas Register,* 1835, San Felipe; later Houston *Telegraph;* disc. 1877. *Union* (1835, Nashville, Tenn.; supported Polk's candidacy; disc. 1875). Detroit *Free Press* (1835). New Orleans *Picayune,* 1836, **George W. Kendall** (1809–67); noteworthy coverage of War with Mexico; later the *Times-Picayune.* New York *Morning Express* (1836; Whig; disc. c.1864). Milwaukee *Advertiser* (1836; disc. 1841); Milwaukee *Sentinel,* 1837; became (1844) first daily in Wisconsin. Philadelphia *North American* (1839; Whig; disc. 1925). New York *Tribune,* 1841, **Horace Greeley** (p. 1045); Whig-Republican; *Weekly Tribune,* 1841, with wider circulation especially in Northern rural areas; merger

(1924) created *Herald Tribune.* Cincinnati *Commercial* (1843; disc. 1930). Springfield (Mass.) *Republican,* 1844, Whig, pioneer in independent journalism; est. as daily by **Samuel Bowles** (1826–77); previously a weekly since 1824; still published. *Plain Dealer* (1845, Cleveland, Ohio). New Orleans *Delta* (1845; disc. 1863). Rotary press invented by **Richard M. Hoe** (p. 1058) revolutionized newspaper printing; first used (1847) by Philadelphia *Public Ledger.* *Oregon Spectator* (1846, Oregon City; first newspaper on Pacific Coast; disc. 1855). *Californian* (1846, Monterey); first newspaper in California; became (1849) the *Alta Californian,* first daily in California; disc. 1891. *Republican* (1847, Santa Fe); first successful paper in present New Mexico. Chicago *Daily Tribune,* 1847; under **Horace White** (1834–1916) supported Lincoln in 1856 and 1860; came under control of **Joseph Medill** (1823–99) in 1874. Toledo (Ohio) *Blade* (1848). New Orleans *Crescent* (1848; disc. 1869). Organization of a group of New York newspapers later known as the **Associated Press** (1848). *Minnesota Pioneer* (1849, St. Paul; disc. 1875). *Deseret News* (1850, Salt Lake City). *Weekly Oregonian* (1850, Portland; became daily, 1861). New York *Daily Times,* 1851, **Henry J. Raymond** (1820–69); Whig-Republican; became (1857) *The New York Times.* *Missouri Democrat* (1852, St. Louis, later *Globe-Democrat*). *Columbia* (1852, Olympia, Wash.); later *Washington Pioneer;* disc. 1861. St. Paul (Minn.) *Daily Pioneer,* 1854; later (1875) *Pioneer-Press.* *Nebraska Palladium* (1854, Bellevue, Neb.); first paper printed in Nebraska; issued first number in Iowa. Chicago *Times* (1854; disc. 1895). *Kansas Weekly Herald* (1854, Leavenworth; disc. 1861). Two Free-Soil papers est. 1855 at Lawrence, Kan.: *Kansas Free State* and *Herald of Free-*

dom; latter disc. 1860. Proslavery *Squatter Sovereign* (1855, Atchison, Kan.); became (1858) *Freedom's Champion* and (1868) *Atchison Champion;* disc. 1917. San Francisco *Bulletin* (1855), **James King;** killed in 1856 for opposing lawlessness; later ed. by **Fremont Older** (1856–1935), who fought political machine; merged (1929) by **W. R. Hearst** with San Francisco *Call* (founded 1856). *Territorial Enterprise* (1858, Genoa, Nev.); later removed to Carson City and Virginia City; first newspaper in present-day Nevada; Mark Twain was reporter, 1862–63. Richmond *Examiner* (1859; disc. 1867); *Weekly Arizonian* (1859, Tubac; later removed to Tucson; disc. 1871). *Democrat* (1859, Sioux Falls, S.D.). Des Moines *Register* (1860). New York *World* (1860, Alexander Cummings); sold 1 July 1861 to August Belmont and Fernando Wood, with **Manton Marble** (1835–1917), as editor (to 1867).

1801–60. PERIODICALS. 1801: *Port Folio* (Philadelphia, **Joseph Dennie** [1768–1812]; a leading literary journal; disc. 1827). **1803:** *Massachusetts Baptist Missionary Mag.* (later *American Baptist Mag.*, Boston, disc. 1909). *Literary Mag. and American Reg.* (Philadelphia, **Charles Brockden Brown** [1771–1810]; disc. 1807). **1808:** *American Law Jl.* (Philadelphia; disc. 1817). **1813:** *Analectic Mag.* (later *Literary Gazette*, Philadelphia; disc. 1821). *Religious Remembrancer* (later *Christian Observer*, Philadelphia). **1815:** *North American Rev.* (Boston, **William Tudor** [1779–1830], a leading intellectual organ; other early editors included **Edward Everett** and **Jared Sparks;** disc. 1939): **1816:** *Portico* (Baltimore; disc. 1818); *Cobbett's American Political Reg.* (New York; disc. 1818). **1818:** *Methodist Mag.* (later *Methodist Rev.*, New York). **1819:** *American Farmer* (Baltimore; disc. 1897); *Universalist Mag.* (later *Universalist Leader*), Boston. **1821:** *Genius of Universal Emancipation*

(Mt. Pleasant, Ohio, antislavery monthly, **Benjamin Lundy** [1789–1839]; disc. 1839); *Saturday Evening Post* (Philadelphia, Charles Alexander and Samuel C. Atkinson); claims descent from *Pennsylvania Gazette*, founded, 1728; originally a newspaper, changed gradually to a weekly magazine by 1871. Bought 1897 by **Cyrus H. K. Curtis** (1850–1933). **1822:** *U.S. Catholic Miscellany* (Charleston; disc. 1832). *New England Farmer* (Boston; disc. 1846). **1823:** *Zion's Herald* (Boston); New York *Mirror* (a leading weekly; disc. c.1857); *Christian Examiner* (Boston; disc. 1869). **1825:** *Biblical Repertory* (later *Princeton Rev.*, Princeton, N.J.; disc. 1884). *New Harmony Gazette* (later *Free Enquirer*, New Harmony, Ind.; disc. 1835). **1826:** *American Journal of Education* (later *American Annals of Education,* Boston; disc. 1839). *Casket* (Philadelphia; disc. 1840); *Franklin Jl.* (later *Jl. of the Franklin Institute,* Philadelphia); *Christian Advocate* (New York). **1827:** *American Quarterly Rev.* (Philadelphia; disc. 1837). *Youth's Companion* (Boston; famous children's mag.; disc. 1929). **1828:** *Southern Agriculturalist* (Charleston; disc. 1846). *Southern Rev.* (Charleston; disc. 1832). **1829:** *American Jurist and Law Mag.* (Boston; disc. 1843). **1830:** *Lady's Book* (later *Godey's Lady's Book,* Philadelphia; most important of early women's mags.; disc. 1898). **1831:** *The Liberator,* 1 Jan., Boston, abolitionist organ, **William Lloyd Garrison** (p. 1038); disc. 29 Dec. 1865. *Biblical Repository* (Andover, Mass.; disc. 1850). *Spirit of the Times* (New York; disc. 1861). **1833:** *Knickerbocker Mag.* (New York; first popular monthly; **Lewis Gaylord Clark** [1808–73]; disc. 1865); *Parley's Mag.* (New York; disc. 1844). **1834:** *Southern Literary Messenger* (Richmond; leading Southern mag.; Poe, Simms, Matthew F. Maury among contributors; disc. 1864). **1837:** *U.S. Mag. and Democratic Rev.* (Washington, D.C.;

John L. O'Sullivan and Samuel D. Langstreet; later known as *Democratic Rev.;* jingoist; introduced term "Manifest Destiny" [p. 230]; disc. 1859). **1838:** *Pennsylvania Freeman* (Philadelphia, antislavery; disc. 1854). *Connecticut Common School Jl.* (Hartford; disc. 1866). *Common School Jl.* (Boston: disc. 1852). **1839:** *Brother Jonathan* (New York; disc. c.1845). *Merchants' Mag. and Commercial Rev.* (later *Hunts' Merchants' Mag.,* New York; disc. 1870). *Dial* (Boston; Transcendentalist organ; edited first by **Margaret Fuller** [p. 1035], then by **Ralph Waldo Emerson** [p. 1024]; disc. 1844). *Lowell Offering* (Lowell, Mass.; printed contributions by young women mill operatives; disc. 1845). *Graham's Mag.* (Philadelphia, **Edgar Allan Poe** lit. ed., 1841–42; disc. 1858). **1842:** *Pennsylvania Law Jl.* (later *American Law Jl.*), Philadephia; disc. 1852. *American Agriculturalist* (New York, now Ithaca; oldest farm jl. still published). *Peterson's Ladies National Mag.* (Philadelphia; close competitor to *Godey's;* disc. 1898). **1843:** *New Englander* (later *Yale Rev.*), New Haven, Conn. **1844:** *Brownson's Quarterly Rev.* (Boston; disc. 1875). *Littell's Living Age* (Boston; disc. 1941). **1845:** *American Rev.* (later *Whig Rev.,* New York; disc. 1852). *Harbinger* (Brook Farm, West Roxbury, Mass., **George Ripley** (1802–80), Fourierist; disc. 1849); *Scientific American* (New York). **1846:** *Commercial Rev. of the South and West* (later *De Bow's Rev.,* New Orleans; outstanding for economic coverage of antebellum South; disc. 1880). **1847:** *National Era* (Washington, D.C., **Gamaliel Bailey** [1807–59], antislavery jl.; disc. 1860). **1848:** *The Independent* (New York; disc. 1928). **1850:** *Harper's New Monthly Mag.* (later *Harper's Mag.*), New York; circulation 200,000 by 1860. *Waverly Mag.* (Boston; disc. 1908). **1851:** *New York Ledger* (**Robert Bonner** [1824–99], weekly; circulation 400,000

by 1860; disc. 1903). *Gleason's Pictorial Drawing-Room Companion* (Boston; first illustrated mag. in the U.S.; disc. 1859). **1852:** *American Law Reg. and Rev.* (later *Univ. of Pennsylvania Law Rev.,* Philadelphia). **1853:** *Putnam's Monthly Mag.* (New York; disc. 1857). *Country Gentleman* (Albany; now Philadelphia). **1855:** *Amer. Jl. of Education* (New York; disc. 1882). *Frank Leslie's Illustrated Newspaper* (later *Leslie's Weekly,* New York; disc. 1922). **1856:** *Jl. of Agriculture* (St. Louis; disc. 1921). **1857:** *Atlantic Monthly* (Boston, **James Russell Lowell** [p. 1089]). *Harper's Weekly* (New York, news weekly; disc. 1916).

1861–65. NEWSPAPERS: CIVIL WAR. The Northern press was divided in its support of the war. Only 5 out of 17 New York dailies were unquestionably loyal. To protect military secrets courts-martial were authorized where news was released considered as aiding the enemy; telegraph wires from Washington were placed under State Department censorship. For open hostility to the war effort, the New York *Daily News* lost its postal privilege (Aug. 1861; suspended 18 months). The Columbus *Copperhead* (1861), the New York *Copperhead* (1863), and the Philadelphia *Evening Journal* were suppressed for support of Vallandigham, and the Chicago *Times* and Philadelphia *Christian Observer* were seized by the federal authorities.

1861–82. SYNDICATES AND PRESS ASSOCIATIONS. First newspaper syndicate organized (1861) by Ansell N. Kellogg of the Baraboo (Wis.) *Republic,* providing "readyprint" for local papers. United Press organized (1882); expired 1893. Second United Press founded (1907, below). McClure Newspaper Syndicate organized 1884 by **Samuel S. McClure.**

1864–96. NEWSPAPER CHANGES. St. Louis *Dispatch,* 1864; acquired by **Joseph Pulitzer** (p. 1132) in 1848 and combined with St. Louis *Post,* est. by John A. Dillon, 1875. San Francisco *Chronicle* (1865, Charles and Michael De Young). Atlanta *Constitution* (1868, W. A. Hemphill). New York *Sun* acquired (1868) by **Charles A. Dana** (1819–97). Its issue of 8 Nov. 1876 (Hayes-Tilden election story) had record sale of 220,000 copies. Sold to *World-Telegram,* 1950. *Public Record* (Philadelphia, 1870, W. J. Swain). Boston *Globe* (1872, Maturin Ballou; eve. ed. begun 1877). **Whitelaw Reid** (1837–1912) succeeded Horace Greeley (1872) as editor of New York *Tribune.* New York *Daily Graphic* (1873; featuring news pictures; disc. 1889). Chicago *Daily News,* 1876, **Melville E. Stone** (1848–1929). Washington *Post* (1877; sold to John R. McLean 1905). Kansas City *Star* (1880, W. R. Nelson). New York *Evening Post* sold (1881) to **Henry Villard** (1835–1900), with **Carl Schurz** (p. 1147) as editor. **Edwin L. Godkin** (p. 1042) became editor in chief, 1883. New York *Morning Journal* (1882, Albert Pulitzer); sold, 1884, to John R. McLean; **William Randolph Hearst** (p. 1055) became owner in 1895; merged with New York *Evening Journal* (1937) to become *Journal-American.* New York *World* acquired by **Joseph Pulitzer.** News coverage innovations, editorials, and 2-ct. price boosted circulation from 20,000 (1883) to 250,-000 (1886). New York *Evening World* (1887, S.S. Carvallo; disc. 1931). Ownership of San Francisco *Examiner* (1865) transferred (1887) from George Hearst to his son, **William Randolph Hearst.** Emporia *Gazette* (1890); acquired, 1895, by **William Allen White** (1868–1944), whose editorials, e.g., "What's the Matter with Kansas?" (1896) were nationally read. **Adolph S. Ochs** (p. 1117) acquired (1896) *The New York Times.*

1880–1914. Daily circulation of German papers in St. Louis (1880) amounted to 21% of aggregate; in New York, 10%; in Cincinnati, 28%, with 80 German dailies, 466 weeklies, and 95 other German periodicals. In addition: 13 Bohemian periodicals, 49 Scandinavian, 41 French, 26 Spanish, 4 Italian, 5 Welsh. *Jewish Daily Forward* (New York, 1897), ed. **Abraham Cahan** (1860–1951). There were 1,300 foreign language newspapers and periodicals in the U.S., 1914; 140 dailies (one third German). New York had 32 (including 10 German, 5 Yiddish, 3 Italian).

1897–1933. CHAIN NEWSPAPER ERA (paralleling trends in industry and merchandising) was inaugurated with the organization (1897) by Edward Wyllis Scripps and Milton Alexander McRae of the Scripps-McRae League of Newspapers; Scripps-McRae Press Assn., 1897. Together with the Publisher's Press (1904), it was the forerunner of the second **United Press** (1907). Between 1892–1914 the Scripps chain had a controlling interest in 13 newspapers, acquired principally by establishing new papers in smaller cities. With the addition of Roy W. Howard to the board in 1922 the organization became the **Scripps-Howard** chain. The **Munsey Chain** began (1901) with the purchase by Frank A. Munsey of the Washington *Times* and New York *Daily News,* followed by the acquisition of the Boston *Journal* (1902), the Baltimore *Evening News* (1908), and the Philadelphia *Evening Times* (1908). The **Hearst Chain** acquired 30 papers (1913–34) in addition to control of 2 wire services, the King Features Syndicate, 6 magazines, a newsreel, and the *American Weekly* (a Sunday supplement). The 5 other leading chains (1933, Patterson-McCormick, Scripps-Howard, Paul Block, Ridder, and Gannett) controlled 81 dailies, with combined total circulation of 9,250,000.

1897–1907. COMIC STRIPS appeared in the comic weeklies of the 70s and 80s; color sequence in New York *Sunday*

World (1894). Real origin dates from Rudolph Dirks' "Katzenjammer Kids" (New York *Journal,* 1897). First 6-days-a-week strip was H. C. "Bud" Fisher's "A. Mutt" (San Francisco *Chronicle,* 1907); later "Mutt and Jeff."

1898. SPANISH-AMERICAN WAR. New York *Journal* and *World* outdistanced all other "yellows" in agitating for U.S. intervention in Cuba as well as in coverage of the war.

1908–12. JOURNALISM SCHOOLS. School of Journalism est. at University of Missouri (1908; courses offered as early as 1878). Columbia University School of Journalism est. (1912) by a bequest from Joseph Pulitzer.

1917. PULITZER PRIZE awards inaugurated by the trustees of Columbia Univ., granted on recommendation of the Advisory Board of the Columbia School of Journalism. Awards have been made to newspapers for meritorious public service and to working newspapermen in various branches of journalism. In addition, awards are made for (1) novel, (2) drama, (3) U.S. history, (4) biography, (5) poetry, (6) music.

1918. The *Stars and Stripes* published by the American Expeditionary Force in France; disc. 1919; revived in Washington, D.C., 1919–26.

1919–24. TABLOIDS. The New York *Daily News* est. by the McCormick-Patterson chain. A tabloid featuring sensational news, crime, and sex stories, it attained the largest daily circulation in the U.S. in 1924 (1,750,000). By 1944, 2 million daily, 4 million Sundays. Its success led to the establishment in 1924 of New York *Daily Mirror* by W. R. Hearst and the *Daily Graphic* by Bernarr Macfadden.

1940. *PM* (New York, Marshall Field; disc. 1946).

1941. Chicago *Sun* (Marshall Field).

1942–45. ARMY PAPERS. *Stars and Stripes* est. as a weekly (17 Apr.; a daily

by 2 Nov.; coined phrase "GI Joe"). *Yank,* 24-page weekly tabloid est., with ultimately 21 editions in various war theaters.

1944, Nov. Thomas E. Dewey was supported for president by 796 newspapers (68.5% of total circulation); 291 (17.7% of circulation) supported F. D. Roosevelt (lowest press support since Bryan's campaign against McKinley, 1896). Similarly proportionate press support for Dewey v. Truman, 1948, and Eisenhower v. Stevenson, 1952.

1949, 1 Oct. There were 1,780 dailies with a circulation of 52,845,551; 546 Sunday papers with a circulation of 46,498,968 (*Editor and Publisher*).

1862–1900. PERIODICALS. 1862: *The Old Guard* (New York, C. Chauncey Burr; Copperhead; disc. 1870). **1863:** *Army and Navy Jl.* (New York, William Conant Church, ed., 1863–1917). **1865:** *The Catholic World* (New York, Paulist Fathers). *The Nation* (New York, weekly jl. of politics, literature, science, the arts); first ed., **E. L. Godkin** (p. 1042), to 1881; later eds. include **Oswald Garrison Villard** (1918–32), **Joseph Wood Krutch** (1933–37), **Freda Kirchwey** (1933–55), and Carey McWilliams (1955–). **1866:** *The Galaxy* (New York, monthly literary mag., William Conant Church and Francis Pharcellus; disc. 1878). **1867:** *The Southern Rev.* (Baltimore, Albert Taylor Bledsoe; disc. 1879). *Jl. of Speculative Philosophy* (St. Louis, **William Torrey Harris;** disc. 1893). *Harper's Bazaar* (New York, weekly women's mag.; Fletcher Harper; became monthly, 1901; purchased by Hearst, 1913). **1868:** *Overland Monthly* (San Francisco; California regional mag. **Bret Harte,** ed.; suspended 1876–82; cont. again until 1935). *Lippincott's Mag.* (Philadelphia, literary monthly; John Foster Kirk ed. until 1884; 1915 moved to New York as *McBride's Mag.;* merged with *Scribner's Mag.,* 1916). *Vanity Fair* (New York, ed. for a time by **Frank Harris;** absorbed by *Vogue*, 1936, a woman's fashion mag.). **1869:** *Appleton's Jl.* (New York, literary weekly; became monthly 1876; disc. 1881). **1870:** *Christian Union* (New York, "family mag.," Henry Ward Beecher and Lyman Abbott; name changed, 1893, to *The Outlook*, with more emphasis on political commentary; disc. 1935). *Scribner's Monthly* (New York, literary jl., ed., Josiah G. Holland); after absorbing *Putnam's* (1870), it was continued as the *Century* (1881); merged 1930 with *The Forum* (est. 1886), with **Walter Hines Page,** ed., a mag. of controversy; merged with *Current History* (1940). **1872:** *Publisher's Weekly* (New York, Frederick Leypoldt); *Popular Science Monthly* (New York, Edward L. Youmans). **1873:** *The Delineator* (New York, E. Butterick & Co., fashion mag.; later of general circulation; disc. 1937). *Woman's Home Companion* (Cleveland, originally a semimonthly under name of *Home Companion;* after 1897 a monthly). *St. Nicholas* (New York, children's mag.; ed. 1873–1905 by Mrs. Mary Mapes Dodge; disc. 1940). **1876:** *Frank Leslie's Popular Monthly* (New York, name changed, 1906, to *The American Mag.*, published by a group of muckraking authors including Ida Tarbell, Lincoln Steffens, *et al.*). **1877:** *Puck* (New York, a comic mag., Joseph Keppler and A. Schwarzmann; disc. 1912). **1880:** *The Dial* (Chicago, conservative rev.; became fortnightly 1892, when it was moved to New York as a radical jl. of opinion and chief of the "little magazines"; eds. included **Conrad Aiken, Randolph Bourne, Van Wyck Brooks;** disc. 1929). **1881:** *The Critic* (New York, weekly literary rev.; Jeannette and Joseph Gilder; disc. 1906). *Judge* (New York, comic weekly by authors and artists who seceded from *Puck;* disc. 1939). **1883:** *Ladies Home Jl.* (Philadelphia, monthly; **Cyrus H. K. Curtis;** popularized by its 2d ed., **Edward**

W. Bok [1863–1930], ed. 1899–1920). **1884:** *The Christian Century* (Chicago). *The Journalist* (New York; first professional mag. for journalists; consolidated 1907 with *Editor and Publisher*). **1887:** *Scribner's Mag.* (New York, literary jl.; purchased 1939 by *The Commentator* and renamed *Scribner's Commentator*). *The Cosmopolitan* (Rochester, a conservative family monthly; but removed to New York, 1887, and became popular mag.; after 1900 entered muckraking movement; purchased by Hearst, 1925). **1888:** *Collier's* (New York, weekly; under ed. of **Norman Hapgood** [1903–12] and **Mark Sullivan** [1914–17] was a leading liberal-muckraking publication). **1889:** *The Arena* (Boston, Benjamin O. Fowler; first muckraking periodical; disc. 1909). *Life* (New York humor mag., featuring **Charles Dana Gibson,** and his "Gibson Girl"; disc., 1936, when its title was acquired by a news weekly. *Munsey's Mag.* (New York, Frank A. Munsey; merged 1929 with *Argosy All-Story Weekly*). **1890:** *The Literary Digest* (New York, newspaper and mag. of comment; its straw poll erroneously predicting the election of Landon in 1936 contributed to its demise, 1938). *Smart Set* (New York, jl. of society; Mencken and Nathan, eds., 1914–24, when purchased by Hearst; disc. 1930). **1891:** *Review of Reviews* (New York, monthly of comments on events; **Albert Shaw** ed. from 1894; merged when *Literary Digest* 1937). **1893:** *McClure's Mag.* (New York, S. S. McClure; merged, 1929, with *New Smart Set*). **1899:** *Everybody's Mag.* (New York, absorbed by *Romance*, 1929). **1900:** *World's Work* (New York, monthly record of current events; **Walter Hines Page;** absorbed, 1932, by *Rev. of Revs.*).

1905–16. 1905: *Variety* (New York, theatrical trade jl., **Sime Silverman,** 1873–1933). **1911:** *Masses* (New York, proletarian monthly; superseded, 1918, by *The Liberator; New Masses*, 1926).

1912: *Poetry* (Chicago, **Harriet Monroe,** organ for new trends in poetry). **1914:** *New Republic* (New York, **Herbert Croly** and **Walter Lippmann,** p. 1086). *The Little Review* (Chicago, moving to New York and then Paris; best known for its serialization of Joyce's *Ulysses;* disc. 1929). **1916:** *Theater Arts Mag.* (New York, quality jl., cont. since 1924 as *Theatre Arts Monthly;* disc. 1964).

1922–36. 1922: *The Reader's Digest* (Pleasantville, N.Y., condensation of reprints of other periodicals, **De Witt Wallace;** circulation, 1944, exceeded 9 million, with another 4 million among its foreign editions). **1923:** *Time* (New York, news weekly, **Henry R. Luce** (p. 1090) and **Brinton Hadden**). **1924:** *American Mercury* (New York, critical and literary, **H. L. Mencken** and **George Jean Nathan**). *The Saturday Rev. of Literature* (New York **Henry Seidel Canby** ed. to 1936). **1925:** *The New Yorker* (New York, weekly humorous mag. for the "caviar sophisticates"; **Harold Wallace Ross** [1892–1951]). **1930:** *Fortune* (New York, monthly mag. of business, finance, and industry; **Henry R. Luce**). **1933:** *Newsweek* (New York, news mag.). *Esquire* (New York, monthly, short stories and humorous illustrations). **1936:** *Life* (New York, **Henry R. Luce,** news and feaures through photos).

1951, 30 June (period ending). IN-ROADS OF COMICS revealed by the net paid circulation of leading U.S. magazines, (A.B.C. Publishers' statements):

Marvel Comic Group	11,057,832
Reader's Digest	8,500,000
National Comics Group	7,906,688
Harvey Comics Group	5,458,861
Life	5,301,331
True Story Women's Group	5,068,968
Ladies' Home Journal	4,458,219
McCall's	4,011,643
Woman's Home Companion	3,992,005
Woman's Day	3,866,062
Fawcett Comic Group	3,569,927
Archie Comic Group	3,569,927
Better Homes and Gardens	3,563,856
Look	3,260,927

1954, 27 Oct. Adoption of comic book code to be voluntarily enforced by 26 publishing firms to bar vulgar, obscene, and terror comics. By 1955, 13 states had passed laws to police comics.

1952–60 PERIODICAL TRENDS. While a few new periodicals quickly achieved success (*TV Guide, Confidential,* 1952; *Sports Illustrated, American Heritage,* 1954), the long-term trend was toward mergers and discontinuance. In 1956 *Collier's, American,* and *Woman's Home Companion* ended publication, followed (1957) by *Town Journal* (successor, 1953, to *Pathfinder*), *Omnibook,* and *Étude.*

1953, 28 Nov.–8 Dec. 11-day strike of photoengravers left New York City without a major daily newspaper for first time since 1778.

1958. United Press Assn. and International News Service merged to form United Press International.

1960–73 CONSOLIDATION. The number of daily newspapers serving many metropolitan areas decreased as economic difficulties led to mergers and to the demise of newspapers. New York City, with 15 major daily newspapers in 1900, was left with 3 in 1969. Philadelphia and Washington, D.C., had 3 newspapers; while Los Angeles, Detroit, and St. Louis had only 2 major dailies. In many cities, single corporations published both morning and evening newspapers, often the only major dailies operating in the area (i.e., San Francisco, after 1965).

There was a marked trend toward consolidation in the newspaper industry as major chains rapidly increased their holdings. Lord Thomson of Fleet, owner of 20 dailies, bought the entire Brush Moore chain (1967), 12 dailies and 4 weeklies, for $72 million, until then the biggest newspaper transaction in history. Already the largest chain in terms of circulation, the Hearst Corp. purchased the *Knicker-*

bocker News (Albany, N.Y.) in 1960, its first purchase in 32 years, and made several more acquisitions thereafter. Other evidence of consolidation was the purchase of the Montgomery *Advertiser* and the Atlanta *Journal* by the Scripps League News in 1969 and the acquisition of four Florida papers by the New York *Times* in 1972. The biggest merger, however, was brought off by the Los Angeles *Times,* which bought the Dallas *Times Herald* and its broadcasting interests for $91.5 million (1969), then taking over *Newsday* of Long Island, New York.

Concerned by this trend, the Anti-Trust Division of the Department of Justice brought suit against the Los Angeles *Times* which, in 1967, was forced to divest itself of the San Bernadino *Sun,* purchased in 1964. In further antitrust action, the Supreme Court prohibited (1970) cooperation in the production of newspapers, a practice used by 44 papers in 22 cities. Congress, however, counteracted the Court's decision with the Newspaper Preservation Act (1971).

In the magazine field, the pattern of consolidation was the same. McGraw-Hill bought *American Heritage* and *Horizon* in 1969, while simultaneously Curtis Publications was selling *Ladies' Home Journal* to Downe Communications, Inc. and Cowles was turning *Family Circle* over to the New York *Times.* In 1971 *Saturday Review* was sold to a syndicate headed by Nicholas H. Charney, who had successfully launched *Psychology Today* in 1967, but Norman Cousins reacquired *Saturday Rev.* in 1973. In the biggest of all sales and mergers, Cahners bought Conover-Mast Publications Inc. for $20 million.

The mortality rate for magazines was high in the period 1960–73. Among the most celebrated casualties were *Saturday Evening Post,* which died in 1969 after

148 years of continuous publication; *Look* (1971), which failed despite a circulation of 7 million; and *Life* (1972), which had dominated the field of photojournalism for 40 years. The causes of death were competition from TV, loss of advertising revenue, and steadily increasing postal rates.

1968–73. NEW PUBLICATIONS. Despite the problems besetting the journalistic world, new newspapers and magazines were created in the 60s and early 70s. In 1968 the Los Angeles *Times* established a new daily in Orange County, and the suburban Chicago area found itself with 2 new papers. There was far more activity, however, in the magazine world. In 1971 the *Saturday Evening Post* was reborn as a quarterly. Other notable births were *Change* (1969), an educational journal funded by the Ford Foundation; *Essence* (1970), a magazine appealing to young urban black women; *Liberty* (1971), the "Nostalgia Magazine"; and *Ms.* (1972), a feminist journal. The most successful of these new vehicles seemed to be *New York* (1968), one of a number of magazines aimed at a local audience.

Innovations and alterations were also evident among journalistic survivors. Losing circulation to *Newsweek, Time* toned down its splashy, hyperbolical style and exchanged its conservative stance for a liberal one.

1964–73. UNDERGROUND PAPERS. Spawned by the student uprisings of the 60s, underground newspapers numbered 600 by 1969 and boasted an estimated readership of 3 million. Generally they were short, economically produced, and technically inferior. They served as a conduit for radical political expression that was stifled by the mainstream press. Among the causes most commonly espoused were the movement against the war in Vietnam, the struggle for racial equality, the activities of Cesar Chavez' Farm Workers Union, the legalization of marijuana. Among the best-known of these publications were *The Berkeley Barb*, founded in 1964; the *Advocate*, a Los Angeles-based publication that first appeared in 1967; the *L.A. Free Press* (1968), modeled on New York's *Village Voice* and the most successful of all underground papers (circulation: 95,000); *Rat*, published in New York and run largely by a group of women who seized control in 1970. A group of environmentalist, how-to-do-it publications also flourished in the underground sphere, the most renowned of these being *The Whole Earth Catalog*, which was issued from 1969–71.

1967–73. UNDERGROUND COMICS. Underground comics (or "Comix") were another important journalistic phenomenon of the period. The fountainhead of this movement was Robert Crumb, who in 1967 conceived and published *Zap*, a comic book featuring offbeat artwork, unorthodox subject matter, radical politics, and a good deal of social criticism. Aimed at the counterculture, *Zap* was quickly followed by an even more provocative series called *Feds 'n' Heads*, the brainchild of Gilbert Shelton. Typical of Shelton's work was the satirical treatment of superheroes embodied in a character named the "Wonder Wart-Hog." These and other underground comics were frequently obscene in their efforts to outrage bourgeois sensibilities and became the target of censorship attempts throughout the country.

1968. THE PRESS AND THE '68 CAMPAIGN. Press coverage of the tumultuous 1968 Democratic convention in Chicago confirmed the opinions of many Americans that the political process was breaking down and convinced others that newspapermen were slanting the news

and encouraging violence. In the course of the convention, 24 reporters and photographers were beaten by the Chicago police, while attempting to observe the events. A report by a presidentially-appointed analyst, Daniel Walker, accused the police of promoting disorder and exonerated the press.

1969–73. NIXON ADMINISTRATION AND THE PRESS (p. 535). For publication of the **Pentagon Papers,** see pp. 537, 541, 684.

1961–73. STRIKES. Issues related to automation precipitated a wave of major strikes, often accompanied by sympathy lockouts by unaffected publishers, causing total printed-news blackouts. The pattern of the long strike was set in Minneapolis (117 days, 1962). Two lengthy blackouts (113 days, 1962–63; 25 days, 1965) and a strike against 3 dailies (139 days, 1966) contributed to the demise of 4 major daily newspapers in New York City, including the New York *Herald Tribune* (1966). Other cities experiencing major shutdowns included Cleveland (129 days, 1962–63), Detroit (134 days, 1964), Baltimore (74 days, 1970), Pittsburgh (129 days, 1971).

1960–73. TECHNOLOGICAL ADVANCES. Coded tape signals sent by cable to activate typesetting machines in Paris produced the first international edition of the *New York Times* (20 Oct. 1960). The idea of an overseas edition, available the same day as the original, was immediately adopted by the *Herald Tribune*, whose international edition continued beyond the demise of its New York editions and outlived the international edition of the *Times*.

During the 60s and early 70s the replacement of lead type by offset type became commonplace. Other technological changes included development of varieties of photocomposition and composition by typewriter. Perforated tapes activating lead casting machines increasingly replaced human compositors while machines were programed to edit copy, justify lines (by memorizing syllable breaks), transmit tapes steadily from plant to plant, etc.

Radio and Television

A hobby at first and then a medium for entertainment, radio, by its capability of giving immediacy to distant events, helped revolutionize news reporting, perhaps best exemplified by Edward R. Murrow's wartime broadcasts from London. Its political impact was early recognized by Franklin D. Roosevelt, whose fireside chats became a national institution. ·

Although the entertainment potential of television may never have been fully realized, its popularity sharply altered the patterns of family life. Even more than radio, TV makes the viewer a part of an event, as was most tragically brought home in the few days following the assassination of John F. Kennedy. TV's potential in civic affairs has been repeatedly demonstrated, notably in the Kefauver hearings on organized crime, the Army-McCarthy hearings, and those of the Senate Watergate Committee, and its cultural potential especially by educational TV stations.

Enjoying less than rigorous government regulation, with little consistency in the enforcement of the "public interest" criteria by the FCC, radio and TV networks came under heavy fire during the Nixon administration, but the Watergate revelations undercut drastic regulatory proposals.

1901–24. RADIO: EARLY TECHNOLOGICAL DEVELOPMENTS (p. 798).

1907–16. RADIO: EARLY BROADCASTS. Early programs by individuals and small enterprises, heard by experimenters, ship operators, and a growing number of amateurs, included musical performances (p. 927), news bulletins, phonograph records, poetry readings, and presidential election returns (De Forest, 1916).

1912. RADIO ACT OF 1912 (13 AUG.) required operator's and station licenses to be awarded by the Secretary of Commerce and Labor (after 1913 Secretary of Commerce), who had power to assign wave lengths and time limits. Ship, amateur, and government transmissions were kept apart.

1914–21. EXPANSION OF RADIO COMMUNICATIONS SYSTEMS. Consolidation of radio industry was fostered by coordination imposed by Navy during World War I. In 1919 the **Radio Corporation of America** was organized by **Owen D. Young** (1874–1962), receiving the assets and operations of the Marconi Wireless Company of America. By 1921 two-thirds of RCA stock was held by General Electric, American Telephone and Telegraph Co., Westinghouse, and United Fruit, resolving patent struggles.

David Sarnoff (1891–1971) became general manager (1921), president (1930–47), chairman of the board (1947–71).

1920–29. GROWTH OF REGULAR BROADCASTING. The first station to begin regular commercial broadcasting was WWJ, Detroit, with a formal period of testing commencing 20 Aug. 1920. Election returns were broadcast by WWJ in Detroit, 31 Aug. 1920, and by WWJ and KDKA, Pittsburgh, Pa., 2 Nov. 1920, holding a special license to launch a broadcast service in order to stimulate radio receivers manufactured by Westinghouse. WJZ, Newark, N.J., broadcast the World Series, beginning 5 Oct. 1921. KYW, Chicago, began broadcasting with the Chicago Civic Opera, 11 Nov. 1921. 500 new stations began in 1922, many established by colleges, newspapers, churches, and department stores. The first municipally owned radio station was WNYC, New York (1924). The first commercial program was aired by WEAF, New York (later WRCA, WNBC), 28 Aug. 1922.

Programing in 1920s was dominated by classical music with both professional and amateur performers. The first radio drama broadcast, WGY, Schenectady, N.Y., 3 Aug. 1922; first news analysis, **H. V. Kaltenborn** (1878–1965), WEAF, New York (1921); first syndicated radio show, **Amos 'N Andy** (1928), established the possibilities of the radio serial.

SALES OF RADIO SETS AND PARTS
(millions $s)

1922	60	1926	506
1923	136	1927	426
1924	358	1928	651
1925	430	1929	843

1922. WASHINGTON RADIO CONFERENCES of representatives of regional and industrial interests was convened by Secretary of Commerce Herbert Hoover, 27 Feb. 1922, asking for advice concerning his regulatory powers. Conferees asked for government action to regulate airwaves. Second conference (1923) declared that Secretary could regulate hours and wave lengths where necessary in order to prevent interference detrimental to the public good. Hoover reallocated broadcast band (1923). After fourth conference (1925) Hoover refused to issue further licenses.

1922–32. CREATION OF NETWORKS. WJZ, Newark, N.J., and WGY, Schenectady, N.Y., joint broadcast of World Series (Oct. 1922) was earliest forerunner of network broadcasting. First network, a 6-station hookup by AT&T was established in 1923. Calvin Coolidge address on election eve (1924) estimated to have reached 20 to 30 million people. **National Association of Broadcasters** was founded in 1923 to oppose demands for royalties for songs which were broadcast. **National Broadcasting Co.** (NBC), incorporated 9 Oct. 1926, a subsidiary of RCA, General Electric, and Westinghouse, absorbed AT&T's interest in active broadcasting. Competition from NBC's 2 networks, "red" and "blue," led to a decline in local production. General Electric and Westinghouse withdrew from RCA and NBC (1932). **Columbia Broadcasting System** (CBS) was formed in Apr. 1927. William S. Paley (1901–) served as president, 1928–46, chairman of the board, 1946–).

1927. Car radios first produced by Philco.

1923–51. TELEVISION: EARLY TECHNOLOGICAL DEVELOPMENTS (p. 799).

1927. RADIO ACT (23 Feb.) provided ownership of airwaves by U.S., established a bipartisan 5-man Radio Commission for 1 year, licensing by a standard of public interest, convenience, or necessity, prohibited censorship except for obscenity. Broadcasters were required to treat rival candidates for public office equally. Later amendments extended the commission's life.

1930–39. RADIO PROGRAMING.
Comedy and variety programs with stars such as Eddie Cantor, Al Jolson, Rudy Vallee, George Burns and Gracie Allen, Jack Benny, and Ed Wynn dominated programing. Serials, *The Goldbergs, Just Plain Bill, Vic and Sade,* proliferated. Mystery and crime programs such as Eno Crime Club, Charlie Chan, and Sherlock Holmes were popular as were tales of romance and adventure. Among the quizzes and game shows was *Information Please* (1938). Major programs included Archibald MacLeish's verse drama, *The Fall of the City,* broadcast by CBS, 4 Mar. 1937; first NBC Symphony broadcast led by Arturo Toscanini (1937).

1933–39. PUBLIC AFFAIRS BROADCASTING.
Franklin D. Roosevelt delivered first "fireside chat" 12 Mar. 1933. Political influence was wielded by broadcasts of Father Charles Coughlin and Sen. Huey Long. In the early days of the Spanish Civil War battle sounds were broadcast by shortwave to America by H. V. Kaltenborn as commentator on CBS. **Edward R. Murrow** (1908–65) broadcast news of the Anschluss by shortwave from Vienna on CBS, 13 Mar. 1938. During the Munich crisis (12–29 Sept.) CBS broadcast 151 pickups, NBC, 147.

1934–39. FREQUENCY MODULATION
invented by Edwin H. Armstrong (pp. 800, 975).

1934, 19 JUNE. COMMUNICATIONS ACT OF 1934
reenacted 1927 **Radio Act,** establishing 7-man Federal Communications Commission, with added telephone jurisdiction, was based upon obsolete premise that broadcasting was local responsibility exercised by individual licensees.

1938, 30 MAR. *The War of the Worlds,*
narrated by Orson Welles, on CBS, triggered nationwide panic.

1939–45. WARTIME PROGRAMING.
Edward R. Murrow's broadcasts from wartime London gained wide attention. Among other major news broadcasters during World War II: Howard K. Smith (CBS), Berlin; Charles Collingwood (CBS), England; Larry Lesueur (CBS), Moscow; Eric Sevareid (CBS), Paris; William Shirer (CBS), Berlin. Manufacture of receivers and recordings halted by war, 1942. Office of censorship created 16 Dec. 1941. Censorship was voluntary although news about troop movements and the weather was abandoned. **Voice of America** was launched (1942); placed within U.S. Information Agency (1953).

1939–41. TELEVISION: EARLY COMMERCIAL DEVELOPMENTS.
Regularly scheduled commercial TV programs by NBC began formally 30 Apr. 1939 with program including Franklin D. Roosevelt. By May 1940, 23 stations were in operation. First coverage of election returns by TV, 5 Nov. 1940 (NBC and Dumont TV stations). Full commercial TV inaugurated 1941 but TV manufacturing and programing was severely curtailed by World War II.

1943, 12 OCT. FCC
ordered the sale of NBC "Blue Network" and approved creation of American Broadcasting System (later, ABC).

1945–55. RADIO PROGRAMING.
Major trends influenced by development of the tape recorder included the growth of disc jockeys on local stations playing phonograph records and giveaway shows. In addition, schedule dominance was maintained by comedians, drama series, serials.

1948–53. TV PROGRAMING.
Among the early successes in programing was *Toast of the Town* (CBS, 1948)—later the long-lived *Ed Sullivan Show, Kukla, Fran, and Ollie, Texaco Star Theater* (starring Milton Berle), and *I Love Lucy.*

1950–73. TV NEWS COVERAGE on major political events included the Kefauver Crime Hearings (p. 517); Richard M. Nixon's "Checkers" Speech, 23 Sept. 1952 (p. 519); President Eisenhower's acceptance of B'Nai Brith's Anti-Defamation League award for contributions to civil rights (23 Nov. 1953), where he spontaneously asserted the right of everyone to confront his accuser "face-to-face" (p. 519); the Army-McCarthy Hearings (p. 520); Nikita S. Khrushchev's appearance on *Face the Nation* (CBS, 2 June 1957); the Nixon-Khrushchev "kitchen" debate (24 July 1959); Khrushchev's visits to the U.S. (1959, 1960); the Kennedy-Nixon debates (7, 13, 21, 26 Oct. 1960); live presidential press conferences (first, Kennedy, 25 Jan. 1961); the coverage of the Kennedy assassination and murder of Lee Harvey Oswald by Jack Ruby (22–25 Nov. 1963); news coverage of Vietnam (1964–72); the "Fulbright Hearings" on the Vietnam War (Feb. 1966, p. 501); coverage of the 1968 Democratic National Convention; and the Ervin Committee Hearings on Watergate (17 May–7 Aug.; 24 Sept.–15 Nov. 1973, p. 541).

1951, 18 Aug. First call placed over the microwave radio relay system, consisting of 107 steel and concrete towers, 30 miles apart, between New York and San Francisco, constructed at cost of $40 million.

1952. FCC freeze of TV licenses at 108 (1948) lifted, permitting increase in number of stations in the U.S. and territories from 108 to 2,051 by making maximum use of VHF band frequencies and opening UHF band. Two types of licenses were to be issued: for commercial stations (1,809) and for noncommercial stations (educational institutions and groups, 242). Processing of channel applications began July 1952. National Educational Television was established and supported by the Ford Foundation. First educational TV station in U.S., KUHT, operated by Univ. of Houston, Tex., began broadcasting 25 May 1953.

Amendments to Federal Communications Commission Act (16 July, 1952) prevented FCC from considering alternative applications for licenses in considering approval of sale of station.

1953–60. TV PROGRAMING encompassed (1) episodic series (*I Love Lucy, Dragnet, Gunsmoke*); (2) TV drama (*Philco Television Playhouse, Goodyear Television Playhouse, Studio One, Robert Montgomery Presents*) with scripts by authors such as Paddy Chayefsky (*Marty,* 24 May 1953), Robert Alan Arthur, Gore Vidal, Rod Serling; (3) quiz shows (*The $64,000 Question,* 1955); (4) "spectaculars" (*Peter Pan* with Mary Martin), (5) films. Sale by RKO of pre-1948 films to TV (1955), for $25 million, followed shortly by other major companies, contributed to decline of "live" and original TV, replaced not only by movies, but by more situation comedies, quiz programs, and westerns. Difficult to classify but among the best critically-received shows of this period was *Omnibus* (1952–57), a Sunday-afternoon series, with Ford Foundation support. Influential documentaries included *See It Now* report on Sen. Joseph R. McCarthy (9 Mar. 1954). First colorcast of a commercial program: *Amahl and the Night Visitors* (NBC, 21 Dec. 1953).

1957–58. FCC PROBE produced links between applicants for TV licenses and politicians and FCC commissioners (p. 525).

1958. QUIZ PROGRAM SCANDALS. Revelations (Aug.–Dec.) that contestants on *Twenty-One* and *The $64,000 Question* had been given the answers to questions led to hearings (6–10 Oct. 1959) by House Special Subcommittee on Legislative Oversight of the Commerce Committee. Further probes brought out allegations of "payola" to disc jockeys (21 Nov., 4 Dec.). The result was the passage (30 Aug. 1960) of a federal law designed to curb payola and quiz-show rigging, which required radio and TV stations to announce whether they had received money or anything of value for broadcasting material and outlawed clandestine aid to contestants in purportedly bona fide contests, with maximum penalties of $10,000 fine and 1 year imprisonment fixed.

1957–69. MAJOR TV TECHNOLOGICAL DEVELOPMENTS included the videotape (employed 1957) leading to the "instant replay," used in sports coverage (1963). Due to the legislative requirement that all TV sets shipped in interstate commerce after 30 Apr. 1964 be capable of receiving all channels, 1–13 VHF, 14–83 UHF, 51 new stations, 26 of them educational, almost all UHF, went on the air in 1967, and the 11 million TV sets sold (1967) brought to 23 million (est.) the number equipped to receive UHF (1967). Videotape recorders were perfected and marketed for recording and playing back TV pictures in the home (1965). In 1967, CBS demonstrated EVR, a new electronic video recorder, invented by **Peter Carl Goldmark** (1906–   ), that records picture and sound data originating from the TV camera, magnetic tape or motion picture films on very thin film by means of special electronic process, then converts it to radio-frequency signals to which EVR is directly connected. Color TV made rapid strides in sales and programing due to the introduction of new color studio cameras with improved resolution, definition, and more faithful color rendition. Sales of color TV sets outsold black and white for the first time in 1968.

1960–69. RADIO PROGRAMING reflected a heavy reliance upon phonograph records with stations aimed at spe-cific audience groups. Other programing included telephone "call-in shows," and all-news stations.

1960–69. TV PROGRAMING was dominated by telefilm westerns, comedy series, shows with medical background, spy and science fiction, and shows of violence. Coverage of sports events claimed an increasing amount of time. CBS paid $28 million for TV rights for the National Football League games for 1964 and 1965. Late evening talk-shows (Johnny Carson, Dick Cavett) were also popular. Running out of feature films, networks entered their own feature film production (1967). Major TV documentaries included *Harvest of Shame* (CBS, 25 Nov. 1960) and *Hunger in America* (CBS, 1968).

1961–69. FEDERAL COMMUNICATIONS COMMISSION. FCC Chairman Newton N. Minow referred to TV as a "vast wasteland" in speech to National Association of Broadcasters (May 1961). "Network option" clauses, giving networks virtual control over blocks of time on affiliate stations, were banned (1963). U.S. Court of Appeals for the District of Columbia Circuit reversed FCC decision to renew on a 1-year basis without public hearings the license of WLBT and WJTV, Jackson, Miss., accused of ignoring black viewers (1964), and later held that the black listening audience had a right to intervene in the FCC hearing (*Office of Communication of United Church of Christ* v. *F.C.C.*, 1964, 1969). The FCC ruled (1968) that in the future a holder of an AM radio license could not acquire local TV or local FM license. In 1969 license renewal was denied to Boston channel WHDH.

1962. INTERCONTINENTAL LIVE TELECASTS became possible with the launching (10 July) of Telstar 1 satellite. Live transmissions were privately received (11 July 1962). The first public transatlantic TV broadcast occurred with the launching of Telstar 2 (7 May 1963). The opening ceremonies of the 1964 summer Olympic games were transmitted live from Japan via Syncom 3 (10 Oct. 1964). The first live coverage of the recovery of a space capsule occurred via the Early Bird satellite, launched by the Communications Satellite Corporation (COMSAT) (6 Apr. 1965), with the recovery of Gemini 9 (6 June 1966). The first global hook-up, a two-hour program, *Our World*, presented originations from 19 countries on 5 continents and was seen simultaneously in 39 countries by means of 4 satellites, 3 U.S. and 1 Russian (25 June 1967). Westar I, launched 13 Apr. 1974, was first U.S. domestic communications satellite.

1962–68. EXPANSION OF EDUCATIONAL TV. The Educational Television Facilities Act (1 May 1962) provided $32 million on a matching grant basis over a 5-year period for TV equipment for new educational TV station projects. The Ford Foundation continued its strong financial support; by Oct. 1966 it had given $100 million. The **Public Broadcasting Act** (7 Nov. 1967) set up a 15-man corporation to dispense federal and private funds for educational and cultural program production and networking. A fourth TV network started live programing (5 Jan. 1969) committed to noncommercial broadcasting, made possible by the cooperation of the non-profit Corporation for Public Broadcasting and ATT.

1963. Nov. Roper Poll found for first time chief source of news for Americans was TV.

1964–73. TV-GOVERNMENT TENSIONS. Indications of political hostility to TV newsmen surfaced at 1964 Republican National Convention and deteriorated during the Vietnam War. TV cameramen were clubbed by police during demonstrations outside the 1968 Democratic National Convention in Chicago. During Nixon's first term pressures were exerted to persuade networks to give a more sympathetic treatment to the administration, with public attacks by Vice-Pres. Spiro T. Agnew and other White House spokesmen. President Nixon accused networks of "outrageous, vicious, distorted reporting" (26 Oct. 1973). In addition, FCC regulatory measures were proposed to compel networks to divest themselves of stations and antitrust actions initiated by Department of Justice prohibited networks from producing their own entertainment shows or financing motion pictures (10 Apr. 1972).

1966–70. Publication of 3-vol. definitive *History of Broadcasting in the United States* by Erik Barnouw.

1967. TV profits (3 networks and 619 stations) reported at $2,275,000,000.

1968. Expenditures by political parties for radio and TV time continued to increase, exceeding $40 million as against $2,250,000 spent by the major parties for radio time in 1940.

1968. 24 Dec. Astronauts on Apollo 8 mission read from Genesis while in the vicinity of the moon.

1969–74. CABLE TV. By 1 Jan. 1969 there were approximately 1,900 community antennae or cable television systems operating in all 50 states. Founded (1949) in Lansford, Pa., such systems were confined originally to remote localities. By 1974 it was estimated that approximately 12% of the nation's 68 million homes were connected to cable systems.

The FCC (13 Dec. 1968) announced changes in the operation of CATV, permitting and requiring the origination of programs. At the same time, subscription TV (Pay TV) was authorized subject to severe restrictions.

1969. NATIONAL PUBLIC RADIO

incorporated to provide national program service for public radio stations. First programing, 1 Apr. 1971. By 1975 National Public Radio, with primarily educational, informational, and cultural programs, was composed of over 150 members operating over 175 noncommercial public radio stations with funds provided primarily by Corporation for Public Broadcasting.

1969. 20 JULY. Neil A. Armstrong's first steps and words ("That's one small step for a man, one giant leap for mankind") telecast live from the moon followed by split-screen conversation between Armstrong and Edwin "Buzz" Aldrin, Jr. and President Nixon.

1972. 2 JAN. Cigarette Advertising Ban.

1972–74. RADIO PROGRAM developments included both an increase of the one-dimension format—all news, all country music, all hard rock stations— and the revival of recordings of serials from the 1930s and 1940s, such as *The Lone Ranger, The Shadow,* and *The Green Hornet.* Original radio dramas began to be broadcast again by the CBS radio *Mystery Theater* (Feb. 1974).

1975–76. BICENTENNIAL PROGRAMS. Extensive American Revolution Bicentennial programing initiated by CBS-TV *Bicentennial Minute* (4 July 1974).

3
Five Hundred
Notable
Americans

BIOGRAPHICAL SECTION

★ ★
★

This Biographical Section, confined by reason of space limitations to 500 eminent figures, is meant to be used as a handy reference source. It underscores the contribution that men and women of different ethnic and racial origins have made to the building of the nation, from the settlement of Jamestown to the Nuclear Space Age. The 500 are representative of top-level achievement for their own time in a range of fields crowded with significant names.

Making selections involved some arbitrary choices. Thus, Nelson W. Aldrich has been chosen to symbolize the powerful clique that controlled the U.S. Senate in the late nineteenth century, while a more extended list would have included William B. Allison. In the steel industry Andrew Carnegie was selected in preference to either Henry Clay Frick or Charles M. Schwab, likewise substantial figures. In the areas of general science, of medicine and public health, and of invention and technology an effort has been made to give representation to earlier and less creative periods of American history, but the worldwide impact of American scientific achievement in the twentieth century justifies adequate recognition. Much technical knowledge and experiments by others contributed to the range of inventions covered herein, but the persons singled out for biographical treatment were those who developed, perfected, and usually patented their inventions.

To qualify as an American on the list of the 500 one must have spent a major portion of his career in the original Thirteen Colonies (exceptions being made for William Penn and James Edward Oglethorpe as founders of colonies) or, after 1776, made substantial contributions as citizens of the U.S. On this ground Charles Chaplin has been excluded as well as such expatriates as Benjamin Thompson (Count Rumford), the physicist, and T. S. Eliot. An exception has been made in the case of Henry James, who became a British subject at the very end of his career. Naturalized citizens are included as well as natural-born. All 37 presidents receive biographical treatments, but their relative historical importance is suggested by respective space allocations. Inclusion of such significant figures as Benedict Arnold and Aaron Burr does not imply value judgments, it goes without saying.

The table preceding the biographical articles lists the subjects for convenience by major fields of activity. A word of caution, however: the allocation by categories has been done rather arbitrarily. Men as versatile as Benjamin Franklin, Thomas Jefferson, Albert Gallatin, Increase and Cotton Mather, Samuel F. B. Morse, Theodore Roosevelt, and Benjamin Rush were conspicuous in more than one field. Natural and behavioral scientists like Louis Agassiz and G. Stanley Hall, who were perhaps more effective in the diffusion of knowledge than in original and creative work, appear in the table as Educators without necessarily reflecting on the originality and quality of their scientific contributions.

Finally, it should be pointed out that a great many notable Americans not herein included are referred to elsewhere in the *Encyclopedia* and appear in the Index.

THE PRESIDENTS (37)[1]

JURISTS and LAWYERS (31)

Hugo L. Black
Louis D. Brandeis
Benjamin N. Cardozo
Salmon P. Chase
Thomas M. Cooley
Clarence Darrow
Oliver Ellsworth
William Maxwell Evarts
David Dudley Field
Stephen J. Field
Felix Frankfurter
Melville Weston Fuller
Learned Hand
John Marshall Harlan
Oliver Wendell Holmes, Jr.
Charles Evans Hughes
John Jay
William Johnson
James Kent
Edward Livingston
John Marshall
Thurgood Marshall
Samuel Freeman Miller
Lemuel Shaw
Harlan Fiske Stone
Joseph Story
Roger B. Taney

Morrison R. Waite
Earl Warren
Edward D. White
James Wilson

STATESMEN and PUBLIC OFFICIALS (87)

Dean Acheson
Charles Francis Adams
Samuel Adams
Nelson W. Aldrich
John Peter Altgeld
Stephen F. Austin
Nathaniel Bacon
Alben W. Barkley
Thomas Hart Benton
Sir William Berkeley
Albert Beveridge
James G. Blaine
William E. Borah
William Bradford
William Jennings Bryan
Aaron Burr
John C. Calhoun
Joseph S. Cannon
Lewis Cass
Henry Clay
De Witt Clinton
George Clinton
Caleb Cushing
Jefferson Davis
John Dickinson

---

1. Listed pp. 545–559. Cleveland, who served 2 nonconsecutive terms, is considered the 22nd and 24th president. Hence, Gerald Ford is technically the 38th president, but in fact the 37th.

Sanford B. Dole
Stephen A. Douglas
John Foster Dulles
Hamilton Fish
Benjamin Franklin
J. William Fulbright
Albert Gallatin
Joseph Galloway
Alexander Hamilton
John Hancock
W. Averill Harriman
Townsend Harris
John Hay
Patrick Henry
J. Edgar Hoover
Harry Hopkins
Edward M. House
Sam Houston
Thomas Hutchinson
Harold L. Ickes
Sir William Johnson
Robert F. Kennedy
Henry A. Kissinger
Robert La Follette
Fiorello La Guardia
Richard Henry Lee
Robert R. Livingston
Henry Cabot Lodge
Huey Long
Joseph R. McCarthy
George Mason
Increase Mather
Robert Moses
Luis Muñoz Marín
George Norris
James E. Oglethorpe
James Otis
William Penn
Frances Perkins
Joel R. Poinsett
John Randolph of Roanoke
Samuel Rayburn
Thomas B. Reed
Nelson A. Rockefeller
Elihu Root
Carl Schurz
William H. Seward
Roger Sherman

Alfred E. Smith
Alexander H. Stephens
Thaddeus Stevens
Adlai E. Stevenson
Henry L. Stimson
Peter Stuyvesant
Charles Sumner
Robert A. Taft
Tecumseh
Samuel J. Tilden
Henry A. Wallace
Thomas E. Watson
Daniel Webster
John Winthrop

MILITARY and NAVAL FIGURES (28)[2]

Benedict Arnold
Omar Bradley
George Rogers Clark
Stephen Decatur
George Dewey
David G. Farragut
Nathanael Greene
Thomas J. Jackson
Joseph E. Johnston
John Paul Jones
Robert E. Lee
Douglas MacArthur
George B. McClellan
Alfred T. Mahan
Francis Marion
George C. Marshall
William Mitchell
Daniel Morgan
Chester W. Nimitz
George S. Patton, Jr.
Matthew C. Perry
Oliver H. Perry
John J. Pershing
Winfield Scott
Philip Henry Sheridan
William T. Sherman
J. E. B. Stuart
George H. Thomas

2. Other notable military figures are included with the presidents: Washington, Andrew Jackson, Taylor, Grant, and Eisenhower.

BELLES LETTRES (38)

Louisa May Alcott
Willa Cather
Samuel L. Clemens
James Fenimore Cooper
Stephen Crane
Emily Dickinson
Theodore Dreiser
Ralph Waldo Ellison
William Faulkner
F. Scott Fitzgerald
Robert Frost
Joel Chandler Harris
Nathaniel Hawthorne
Ernest Hemingway
Oliver Wendell Holmes
William Dean Howells
Washington Irving
Henry James
Sinclair Lewis
Henry Wadsworth Longfellow
James Russell Lowell
Archibald MacLeish
Norman Mailer
Herman Melville
H. L. Mencken
Edna St. Vincent Millay
Vladimir Nabokov
Thomas Paine
Edgar Allan Poe
Ezra Pound
Edwin Arlington Robinson
Carl Sandburg
William Gilmore Simms
Harriet Beecher Stowe
Henry David Thoreau
Walt Whitman
John Greenleaf Whittier
Edmund Wilson

HISTORY, PHILOSOPHY, and SOCIAL SCIENCES (24)

Henry Adams
George Bancroft
Charles A. Beard
Franz Boas

John Dewey
Ralph Waldo Emerson
William James
Simon S. Kuznets
Wassily Leontief
Lewis Henry Morgan
Samuel Eliot Morison
John Lothrop Motley
Allan Nevins
Francis Parkman
Talcott Parsons
Charles S. Peirce
William H. Prescott
Josiah Royce
Paul A. Samuelson
Lemuel Shattuck
William Graham Sumner
Frederick Jackson Turner
Thorstein Veblen
Lester Frank Ward

ARTISTS (27)[3]

John J. Audubon
George W. Bellows
Albert Bierstadt
Alexander Calder
Mary Cassatt
John Singleton Copley
Thomas Eakins
Robert Henri
Winslow Homer
George Inness
Yasao Kuniyoshi
John La Farge
John Marin
Anna M. R. Moses
Thomas Nast
Louise Nevelson
Isamu Noguchi
Charles Willson Peale
Jackson Pollock
Frederic Remington
Albert P. Ryder
Augustus Saint-Gaudens
John Singer Sargent

3. Includes Photography.

David R. Smith
Alfred Stieglitz
Gilbert Stuart
James A. M. Whistler

ARCHITECTS (8)

Charles Bulfinch
Louis I. Kahn
Benjamin H. Latrobe
Frederick Law Olmsted
Henry H. Richardson
Eliel Saarinen
Louis H. Sullivan
Frank Lloyd Wright

THEATER and ALLIED ARTS (13)

George Balanchine
Phineas T. Barnum
Edwin Booth
Charlotte Cushman
Walt Disney
Isadora Duncan
Edwin Forrest
Martha Graham
D. W. Griffith
Oscar Hammerstein, 2d
Arthur Miller
Eugene O'Neill
Tennessee Williams

MUSICIANS and COMPOSERS (10)

Irving Berlin
Leonard Bernstein
Edward K. ("Duke") Ellington
Stephen C. Foster
George Gershwin
Charles E. Ives
Edward MacDowell
Richard Rodgers
Igor F. Stravinsky
Theodore Thomas

RELIGIOUS LEADERS (18)

Henry Ward Beecher
Phillips Brooks
William Ellery Channing
John Cotton
Mary Baker Eddy
Jonathan Edwards
James Gibbons
Anne Hutchinson
Cotton Mather
Dwight L. Moody
Reinhold Niebuhr
Theodore Parker
Walter Rauschenbusch
Joseph Smith
George Whitefield
Roger Williams
Issac Mayer Wise
Brigham Young

EDUCATORS (19)

Louis Agassiz
Henry Barnard
Nicholas Murray Butler
James Bryant Conant
Charles W. Eliot
Abraham Flexner
Daniel Coit Gilman
G. Stanley Hall
William Rainey Harper
Christopher C. Langdell
Mary Lyon
William H. McGuffey
Horace Mann
Benjamin Silliman
Edward L. Thorndike
Noah Webster
Andrew Dickson White
Emma Willard
John Witherspoon

SOCIAL REFORMERS and LABOR LEADERS (32)

Jane Addams
Susan B. Anthony
Clara Barton
John Brown
Peter Cooper
Eugene V. Debs

Dorothea L. Dix
Frederick Douglass
Neal Dow
W. E. B. Du Bois
Margaret Fuller
William Lloyd Garrison
Marcus Garvey
Henry George
Samuel Gompers
Sidney Hillman
Samuel Gridley Howe
Martin Luther King, Jr.
John L. Lewis
George Meany
Ralph Nader
Wendell Phillips
Terence V. Powderly
A. Philip Randolph
Walter P. Reuther
Anna Eleanor Roosevelt
Margaret H. Sanger
Elizabeth Cady Stanton
Lincoln Steffens
Norman Thomas
Booker T. Washington
Frances Willard

JOURNALISTS, EDITORS, and PUBLISHERS (12)

James Gordon Bennett
William Cullen Bryant
Herbert Croly
Edwin L. Godkin
Horace Greeley
William Randolph Hearst
Walter Lippmann
Henry R. Luce
Adolph Ochs
Joseph Pulitzer
Isaiah Thomas
John Peter Zenger

PIONEERS and EXPLORERS (10)

Daniel Boone
Richard E. Byrd
John C. Frémont

Meriwether Lewis and William Clark
Robert E. Peary
Zebulon M. Pike
John Wesley Powell
John Smith
Charles Wilkes

BUSINESS LEADERS (20)

John Jacob Astor
Nicholas Biddle
Andrew Carnegie
Jay Cooke
James B. Duke
Eleuthère Irénée du Pont
Cyrus W. Field
Marshall Field
Henry Ford
Daniel Guggenheim
Marcus A. Hanna
James J. Hill
Cyrus H. McCormick
J. Pierpont Morgan
Robert Morris
John D. Rockefeller
Samuel Slater
Leland Stanford
Cornelius Vanderbilt
Aaron Montgomery Ward

MEDICINE (incl. Psychiatry) and PUBLIC HEALTH (17)

William Beaumont
Alfred Blalock
Edwin J. Cohn
Harvey William Cushing
Arnold Gesell
William Crawford Gorgas
Alfred C. Kinsey
William J. and Charles H. Mayo
William T. G. Morton
Gregory Goodwin Pincus
Walter Reed
Benjamin Rush
Jonas Salk
Theobald Smith
Harry Stack Sullivan
Selman A. Waksman

GENERAL SCIENCE (33)

Benjamin Banneker
Norman E. Borlaug
Nathaniel Bowditch
George Washington Carver
Arthur H. Compton
Clinton J. Davisson
Albert Einstein
John Franklin Enders
Enrico Fermi
Josiah Willard Gibbs
Asa Gray
Joseph Henry
Edward C. Kendall
Joshua Lederberg
Gilbert N. Lewis
Fritz Albert Lipmann
Edwin M. McMillan
Matthew Fontaine Maury
Albert A. Michelson
Robert A. Millikan
Thomas Hunt Morgan
Hermann J. Muller
J. Robert Oppenheimer
Linus Pauling
I. I. Rabi
Henry A. Rowland
Glenn T. Seaborg
Wendell M. Stanley
Edward Teller
Harold C. Urey
John von Neumann
Norbert Wiener
Robert Burns Woodward

INVENTION and TECHNOLOGY (36)

Ernst F. W. Alexanderson
Edwin H. Armstrong
Leo H. Baekeland
Alexander Graham Bell
Chester F. Carlson
Wallace H. Carothers
Willis H. Carrier
Lee De Forest
James Buchanan Eads

George Eastman
Thomas Alva Edison
John Ericsson
Robert Fulton
Robert H. Goddard
George W. Goethals
Charles Goodyear
Richard M. Hoe
Elias Howe
Charles F. Kettering
Edwin H. Land
Irving Langmuir
Ernest O. Lawrence
Ottmar Mergenthaler
Samuel F. B. Morse
Elisha Graves Otis
Michael Pupin
John Augustus Roebling
William B. Shockley
Charles Proteus Steinmetz
Frederick Winslow Taylor
Nikola Tesla
George Westinghouse
Eli Whitney
Wilbur and Orville Wright
Vladimir Zworykin

Acheson, Dean Gooderham (b. Middletown, Conn., 11 Apr. 1893; d. Sandy Spring, Md., 12 Oct. 1971), statesman, was graduated from Croton (1911), Yale (1915), and Harvard Law School (1918). After spending 2 years (1919–21) as law secretary to Supreme Court Justice Brandeis he joined the Washington law firm now known as Covington and Burling, where he became a senior partner and practiced whenever he was not in the government. A Democrat, he was appointed Under Secretary of the Treasury in 1933 but was forced to resign 6 months later because he disapproved of President Roosevelt's plan to devalue the gold content of the dollar. Maintaining a good personal relationship with the president, he became an Assistant Secretary of State (1941–45)—helping to draft the Lend-Lease program and, as liaison with Congress, aiding in the development of the UN Food and Agricultural Organization, the UN Relief and Rehabilitation Administration, the World Bank, and the International Monetary Fund. As Under—Secretary of State (1945–47) and as Secretary of State (1949–53) he was a major architect of postwar U.S. foreign policy. His activities included development of the Marshall Plan for European economic recovery, NATO, the Truman Doctrine, and the policy of support of Nationalist China. A staunch anti-Communist, he pushed for strengthening the U.S. atomic arsenal and U.S. aid to countries on the perimeter of the Soviet bloc. After resuming his Washington law practice (1953), he exercised considerable influence, advising Presidents Kennedy, Johnson, and Nixon. His books include *Power and Diplomacy* (1958) and *Present at the Creation,* which won a Pulitzer prize in 1970.

Adams, Charles Francis (b. Boston, Mass., 18 Aug. 1807; d. there, 21 Nov. 1886), diplomat and statesman, son of John Quincy Adams and father of Henry Adams, was graduated from Harvard (1825), and admitted to the bar in 1829, establishing his practice at Boston. A member (1841–44) of the Massachusetts House of Representatives, he also served (1844–45) in the state senate. His growing antislavery convictions led him to establish the Boston *Whig* as an organ of opposition to conservative Whiggery, and in 1848 he was the unsuccessful Free-Soil candidate for vice-president on the ticket with Martin Van Buren. Elected to Congress as a Republican, he served from 4 Mar. 1859 to 1 May 1861, and in the months before the outbreak of the Civil War headed the Northern forces of concession and conciliation in the House of Representatives. He re-

signed from Congress to accept appointment by President Lincoln as minister to England, a post he held until 1868. During the first half of the Civil War, when British official sympathy for the Confederacy was at its height, Adams handled with exemplary tact and firmness vital diplomatic matters such as the *Trent* affair (p. 280) and the armored rams built by the Lairds for the Confederacy. (Adams to Lord Russell: "This is war.") In 1872 the Liberal Republicans considered him for a time as a likely candidate for the presidency. He brought out the *Works of John Adams* (10 vols., 1850–56) and the *Memoirs of John Quincy Adams* (12 vols., 1874–77).

Adams, Henry Brooks (b. Boston, Mass., 16 Feb. 1838; d. Washington, D.C., 27 Mar. 1918), historian and man of letters, grandson of John Quincy Adams. He was graduated from Harvard (1858), pursued postgraduate study in Germany, and during the Civil War served as secretary to his father, Charles Francis Adams, U.S. minister to England (1861–68). He returned to Washington (1868), was active as a journalist (1869–70), and from 1870 to 1877 was assistant professor of history at Harvard, meanwhile serving during most of his period at Cambridge as editor of the *North American Review.* He married (1872) Marian Hooper, whose suicide (1885) had a tragic impact on his life. While at Harvard and Washington, D.C., he brought out the following works: *Essays on Anglo-Saxon Law* (1876) and *Documents Relating to New England Federalism, 1800–1815* (1877), both of which he edited; *The Life of Albert Gallatin* (1879), *The Writings of Albert Gallatin* (1879); 2 novels, *Democracy* (1880) and *Esther* (1884), both of which were published anonymously; *John Randolph* (1882); and the *History of the United States During the Administrations of*

Jefferson and Madison (9 vols., 1889–91), a diplomatic, political, and military account that ranks as one of the landmarks in American historical writing. The latter part of his life was spent in travel in Europe and the South Seas. He is best remembered for *The Education of Henry Adams* (1907), which, with the writings collected in *The Degradation of the Democratic Dogma* (1919), sets forth his formulation of the dynamic theory of history and expresses his doubts that technological advance reflects progress. He also wrote *Mont-Saint-Michel and Chartres* (1904).

Adams, John (b. Braintree [now Quincy], Mass., 30 Oct. 1735; d. there, 4 July 1826), 2d president of the U.S., was graduated from Harvard (1755) and admitted to the Massachusetts bar in 1758. He attacked the Stamp Act in a series of articles in the Boston *Gazette* (1765), and after removal to Boston (1768) defended the British soldiers tried for murder in the "Boston Massacre" (1770). He served in the General Court (1770–71) and the Revolutionary Provincial Congress (1774–75), and his constitutional views were expounded in *Novanglus* (1774), written in reply to the Loyalist Daniel Leonard. As a delegate to the 1st and 2nd Continental Congresses (1774–78) he helped draft the petition to the king and the petition of rights, recommended Washington for command of the army, and defended the Declaration of Independence in its passage through Congress. He served as chairman of the Board of War and Ordnance and superseded Silas Deane as commissioner to France (1778). He was a delegate to the convention which framed the Massachusetts Constitution (1780), of which he was the principal author. With Franklin and Jay he negotiated the Paris peace treaty with Great Britain (1783), and was U.S. minister to Great Britain (1785–88). He was 1st vice-president of the U.S. (1789–97), casting votes in Senate ties no less than 20 times, and succeeded Washington as president (1797–1801). His feud with Hamilton, along with the Alien and Sedition Acts, for which he had no direct responsibility, contributed to his loss of popularity and the downfall of the Federalist party. In retirement he lived in Quincy and renewed his relationship with Jefferson.

Adams, John Quincy (b. Braintree [now Quincy], Mass., 11 July 1767; d. Washington, D.C., 23 Feb. 1848), 6th president of the U.S., eldest son of John and Abigail (Smith) Adams, studied in France (1778–79) and Holland (1780), and served as secretary to Francis Dana in Russia (1781) and to his father in Great Britain (1782–83). Returning to the U.S., he was graduated from Harvard (1787), admitted to the bar (1790), and practiced in Boston. Under Washington he served as minister to the Netherlands (1794–96) and, under his father, to Prussia (1797–1801). He was defeated for Congress in 1802, but elected to the U.S. Senate the following year. As a result of his support of the administration in the Embargo of 1807, which he favored as an alternative to war, he was forced to resign (1808). He served briefly as a professor of rhetoric at Harvard; was minister to Russia, 1809–14, chairman of the peace commission that negotiated the Treaty of Ghent (1814), and minister to Great Britain, 1815–17. Appointed Monroe's Secretary of State (1817–25), he obtained the cession of Florida (1819) and shared with Monroe credit for formulating the Monroe Doctrine (1823). In the presidential election of 1824, he was 2d to Jackson in electoral votes. In the House of Representatives Clay threw his support to Adams (resulting in an unsubstantiated charge of a "corrupt bargain") and Adams was elected president. During his administration he favored a broad national program of internal improvements, but refused to build up a personal political machine. Defeated by Jackson (1828), he was elected to Congress (1831–48). He opposed the annexation of Texas (1836) and the extension of slavery. Every year (1836–44) he opposed without success the adoption of the "gag rule," forbidding discussion or action in the House on antislavery petitions, until its defeat (1844). He was further identified with the antislavery cause by his argument before the Supreme Court vindicating the right to freedom of the *Amistad* captives (1841).

Adams, Samuel (b. Boston, Mass., 27 Sept. 1722; d. there, 2 Oct. 1803), Revolutionary patriot leader, 2d cousin of John Adams (1735–1826), was graduated from Harvard (1740); joined his father in the brewery business, which he later inherited and lost; and served (1756–64) as a tax collector. A member of the Boston "Caucus Club," he was by 1764 a power in local politics. He took a leading role in whipping up opposition to the Sugar Act (1764), the Stamp Act (1765), and the Townshend Acts (1767), was one of the organizers of the Non-Importation Association (1768), and played an important part in the agitation that culminated in the Boston Massacre (1770). He helped organize the Sons of Liberty (1765) and was a member (1765–74) of the Massachusetts House of Representatives, of which he served as recording clerk (1766–74). In writings for the press he enunciated many of the basic arguments that later became familiar Revolutionary doctrine, and kept the spirit of controversy alive during the period of comparative calm and conservative ascendency (1770–72). He initiated the Massachusetts committee of correspondence (1772), drafted

the Boston declaration of rights (1772), was the leading force behind the Boston Tea Party (1773), and with John Hancock was singled out by the British government for punishment. As a delegate (1774–81) to the Continental Congress, he favored immediate independence, proposed an intercolonial confederation of independent states, voted for and signed the Declaration of Independence, and opposed compromise with Great Britain. He was a delegate to the Massachusetts constitutional convention (1779–80) and to the state convention (1788) for ratifying the federal Constitution. He served as lieutenant governor (1789–93) and governor (1794–97) of Massachusetts.

Addams, Jane (b. Cedarville, Ill., 6 Sept. 1860; d. Chicago, Ill., 21 May 1935), humanitarian and social reformer. She was graduated from Rockford College (A.B., 1882) attended the Woman's Medical College in Philadelphia, and during a trip to England (1887–88) became interested in social reform. With Ellen Gates Starr, she founded (1889) Hull-House at Chicago, a settlement house devoted to the improvement of community and civic life in the Chicago slums, the first of its kind in the U.S. Active (1915–34) as a crusader against war, she was named chairman in 1915 of the Woman's Peace party and president of the International Congress of Women at The Hague. She served as president of the Women's International League for Peace and Freedom. In 1931 she was co-recipient (with Nicholas Murray Butler) of the Nobel peace prize. Her writings on social reconstruction include *Democracy and Social Ethics* (1902), *Newer Ideals of Peace* (1907), *The Spirit of Youth and the City Streets* (1909), *Twenty Years at Hull-House* (1910), *A New Conscience and an Ancient Evil* (1912), *The Second Twenty Years at*

Hull-House (1930), and *The Excellent Becomes the Permanent* (1932).

Agassiz, Jean Louis Rodolphe (b. Canton Fribourg, Switzerland, 28 May 1807; d. Cambridge, Mass., 14 Dec. 1873), educator, zoologist, and geologist, studied at the universities of Zurich, Erlangen (Ph.D., 1829), Heidelberg, and Munich (M.D., 1830). After an early contribution to zoology (*The Fishes of Brazil,* 1829), he studied fossil fish under Cuvier in Paris (1831), publishing in that field *Recherches sur les poissons fossiles* (1833–44) and *Études critiques sur les mollusques fossiles* (1840–45). Professor of natural history at Neuchâtel Univ. (1832–46), he made extensive investigations of glacial phenomena in Europe (*Études sur les glaciers,* 2 vols., 1840). Coming to the U.S. (1846), he accepted (1848) the chair of natural history at the newly established Lawrence Scientific School at Harvard, where he founded the Harvard Museum of Comparative Zoology (1859). Interested in the natural history and geology of the western hemisphere (*Contributions to the Natural History of the U.S.,* 1857), he made extensive field trips to Brazil (1865) and to the U.S. West (1868, 1871), but his career in the U.S. was chiefly notable as teacher and lecturer and promoter of scientific study. His teleological view of natural history prompted him to take the leadership in the U.S. in opposing Darwinian evolution with its theory of natural selection, and his scientific reputation suffered as a result. He founded (1873) the Anderson School of Natural History on Penikese Island in Buzzard's Bay to train teachers of natural history.

Alcott, Louisa May (b. Germantown, Pa., 29 Nov. 1832; d. Boston, Mass., 6 Mar. 1888), author, daughter of Amos Bronson Alcott (1799–1888), was reared in Boston and Concord and received most of her education from her father. Her first book, written at the age of 16, was *Flower Fables* (1854). During the Civil War she served as a nurse in a Union hospital at Georgetown until her health was impaired. A volume of her letters, *Hospital Sketches* (1863), was followed by her first novel, *Moods* (1864). She became (1867) editor of *Merry's Museum,* a children's magazine. Her most popular work is *Little Women* (2 vols., 1868, 1869), whose familiar characters of Jo, Amy, Beth, and Meg were drawn from her family life. These books enjoyed a phenomenal sale. Among her later works are *An Old Fashioned Girl* (1870), *Little Men* (1871), *Aunt Jo's Scrap-Bag* (6 vols., 1872–82), *Work* (1873), *Eight Cousins* (1875), *Rose in Bloom* (1876), *Silver Pitchers* (1876), *Under the Lilacs* (1878), *Proverb Stories* (1882), *Jo's Boys* (1886), and *A Garland for Girls* (1888).

Aldrich, Nelson Wilmarth (b. Foster, R.I., 6 Nov. 1841; d. New York City, 16 Apr. 1915), statesman, attended public schools and the Academy of East Greenwich, R.I. Starting in the wholesale grocery business, he rapidly expanded his fortunes to include banking, sugar, rubber, gas, and electricity. As a Republican, Aldrich became state assemblyman (1875–76), a member of the U.S. House of Representatives (1879–81), and U.S. senator from Rhode Island (1881–1911). After 1890 he led a group of long-tenured Republicans including William B. Allison (Ia.), Orville H. Platt (Conn.), and John C. Spooner (Wis.) in dominating the Senate, the first effective leadership organization in the history of that body. This group dictated committee assignments, caucus positions, and decisions of standing committees. They succeeded in persuading the Senate to repeal the Silver Purchase Act (1893) and to pass the

Gold Standard Act (1900), forcing silver Republicans out of the party. Responsible for Republican administration legislation after 1897, this group forced President Theodore Roosevelt to modify the original Hepburn Rate Bill (1906) in order to stipulate how railroads could appeal rates set by the ICC to the circuit courts. Aldrich was considered a spokesman for big business and was a proponent of protective tariffs, such as the Wilson-Gorham Tariff (1894) and the Payne-Aldrich Tariff (1909). Successful passage of the latter tariff produced a split in the Republican party and a decline in the power of the leadership group. He shaped the Aldrich-Vreeland Currency Act of 1908 and headed the resulting National Monetary Commission which studied bank reform and produced a thorough and comprehensive report (8 Jan. 1912) which, although pigeonholed for a time, was to become—in modified form—the basis of the Federal Reserve Act (1913).

Alexanderson, Ernst Frederick Werner (b. Uppsala, Sweden, 25 Jan. 1878; d. Schenectady, N.Y., 14 May 1975), electrical engineer and inventor, was graduated (1900) from the Royal Institute of Technology, Stockholm, and pursued postgraduate studies at Berlin. Arriving in the U.S. in 1901, he joined the staff (1902) of the General Electric Co. at Schenectady, N.Y. His association with General Electric was unbroken for over 46 years except for service as chief engineer (1920–24) of the Radio Corp. of America, and after his retirement he became a consultant to GE. He was naturalized in 1908. The holder of patents for more than 300 inventions, many of which have revolutionized the field of radio communications, he is the inventor (1917) of the Alexanderson high frequency alternator, making worldwide wireless possible, and has also done pioneering work

in electric ship propulsion, radio electronics, railroad electrification, and television. Among his inventions are the tuned radio frequency receiver, the vacuum tube radio telephone transmitter, and the multiple tuned antenna.

Altgeld, John Peter (b. Nieder Selters, Germany, 30 Dec. 1847; d. Chicago, 12 Mar. 1902), governor of Illinois, reformer, came to Richmond County, Ohio, with his parents as an infant and was largely self-taught. Elected state's attorney for Andrew Co., Mo. (1874), he moved (1875) to Chicago, where he served as judge and chief justice of the Superior Court of Cook Co. (1886–91). Elected first Democratic governor of Illinois (1893–97), he outraged public opinion by pardoning (1893) the anarchists Fielden, Schwab, and Neebe, convicted of complicity in the Haymarket murders (1886). Conservatives were equally critical of his opposition on constitutional grounds to President Cleveland's use of regular army troops in the Pullman strike (1894). Supporter of free silver in the Democratic National Convention (1896), he was defeated that year for a 2d gubernatorial term by John R. Tanner. His treatise on crime, *Our Penal Machinery and Its Victims* (1884), expressed the view that the poor lacked equal opportunity before the law.

Anthony, Susan Brownell (b. Adams, Mass., 15 Feb. 1820; d. Rochester, N.Y., 13 Mar. 1906), social reformer and woman suffrage leader. Reared in a Quaker household, she was educated at her father's school and became a schoolteacher, serving (1846–49) as head of the Female Department of the Canajoharie (N.Y.) Academy. Abandoning education for reform activities, she devoted her first efforts to temperance, and was among the organizers of the Woman's

State Temperance Society of New York, the first body of its kind. She also took part in the abolitionist cause, being among the first to advocate Negro suffrage after the Civil War, but gradually shifted her main energies to the woman suffrage movement. She attempted to have inserted in the 14th Amendment a provision guaranteeing the franchise to women as well as to male Negroes. She was involved in a celebrated case that was touched off when she registered and voted at the Rochester city elections (1872) in a plan to test the legality of woman suffrage. She became president (1869) of the National Woman Suffrage Association and was president (1892–1900) of the National American Woman Suffrage Association.

Armstrong, Edwin Howard (b. New York City, 18 Dec. 1890; d. there, 1 Feb. 1954), engineer and inventor, studied at Columbia Univ. (E.E., 1913) under Michael Pupin (*q.v.*), succeeding him (1934) as professor of electrical engineering. His regenerative circuit (1912) won him engineering acclaim along with a patent controversy with Lee De Forest (*q.v.*). As a Signal Corps officer in World War I he developed the principles of his superheterodyne circuit (1918), basic to radio receivers. In 1920 he devised the super-regenerative circuit, used in 2-way police and aircraft radio systems. "Father of FM," Armstrong perfected (1939) his system of static-free radio through frequency modulation, widely adopted in the U.S., England, and Germany. At the time of his death by suicide he was involved in litigating claims against leading broadcasting and electronic manufacturing firms for patent infringement. In 1947 he was awarded the Medal of Merit for his contributions to military communications during World War II.

Arnold, Benedict (b. Norwich, Conn., 14 Jan. 1741; d. London, 14 June 1801), Revolutionary patriot and traitor, served in the French and Indian War, became a druggist and bookseller as well as active in the West India trade. Captain in the Connecticut militia, he undertook as colonel, with Ethan Allen of Vermont, the successful attack on Ft. Ticonderoga (1775). Heading an expedition across the Maine wilderness to Quebec, he was wounded in the assault on that city, but made brigadier general (10 Jan. 1776) for his conspicuous role. At Valcour Island he held up Carleton's invasion force on Lake Champlain (11 Oct. 1776), forcing the British to abandon the invasion of New York. Promoted major general as a result of actions at Ridgefield and Norwalk (1777), he played a leading role in frustrating Burgoyne's invasion of New York, raising the siege of Ft. Stanwix (1777), anticipated Burgoyne's movement to turn the American left at Freeman's Farm, and was wounded in a frontal assault on Breymann's redoubt at Bemis Heights. Military commander of Philadelphia (1778), he was court-martialed (1779) and found guilty of using military forces for his own private purposes. Gently reprimanded by Washington, his steadfast supporter, he was given command of West Point. Entering into treasonable correspondence with Sir Henry Clinton (in which his wife, Margaret Shippen Arnold, was involved) to surrender the key fort to the British, he was forced to flee to the British army when Major André was captured and the plot exposed. He received £6,315 for his treason and was made brigadier general of provincial troops by the British. He carried out a marauding expedition into Virginia (1780) and raided New London, Conn. (1781). He sailed for England Dec. 1781, and was held there in scorn.

Arthur, Chester Alan (b. Fairfield, Vt., 5 Oct. 1829; d. New York City, 18 Nov. 1886), 21st president of the U.S., was graduated from Union College (1848) and admitted to the New York bar (1853). An abolitionist, he was counsel for the state in the case of Jonathan Lemmon, securing a decision that slaves brought into New York while in transit between 2 slave states were thereby made free. During the Civil War he served as quartermaster general of New York, was appointed collector of the Port of New York by President Grant (1871), but was removed (1878) by President Hayes for violating an executive order (1876) forbidding federal officials from participating in party management and campaigns. Elected vice-president of the U.S. (1880), he became president following the death of Garfield (19 Sept. 1881). His administration continued the prosecution of the "Star Route" mail frauds (1882–83) and secured enactment of the Pendleton Civil Service Act (1883). In addition, he began the rebuilding of the U.S. Navy and vetoed a Chinese exclusion bill. He was denied renomination in 1884.

Astor, John Jacob (b. John Jakob Ashdour, Waldorf, Germany, 17 July 1763; d. New York City, 29 Mar. 1848), fur trader and merchant. Migrated to London, 1780; to the U.S., 1783; obtained a job in a fur store in New York City, mastered the business, and in 1786 opened his own establishment. The provisions of Jay's Treaty and the subsequent evacuation of frontier posts by the British (1796) enabled Astor to trade with the British North West Co. His business expanded rapidly; by 1800, when he had a fortune of $250,000, he was the chief factor in the fur trade. He became active in the shipping trade to the Far East and made prudent investments in New York City real estate. Fol-lowing the acquisition of Louisiana and the Lewis and Clark expedition, he made plans for penetrating the West. He established the American Fur Co. (1808) and the Pacific Fur Co. (1810). With Montreal merchants as partners, he formed the South West Fur Co. (1811) for the purpose of supplying goods to both the British and his own fur companies free of customs duties. He established Astoria at the mouth of the Columbia River (1811) for transshipment of furs to Canton. He lost the post during the War of 1812, but managed to retain the South West and American Fur Cos. and to carry on trade with the British in the Great Lakes region throughout the conflict. After 1815, he established posts in the Mississippi Valley (old North West Co. posts) and expanded his fur-trading operations by establishing the Western Dept. of the American Fur Co. (1822). After absorbing the Columbia Fur Co. (1827), he held a monopoly in the upper Missouri territory, but after failing to eliminate the Rocky Mountain Fur Co., retired from business. At his death he was the richest man in America. He left a fortune of more than $20 million.

Audubon, John James (b. Les Cayes, Santo Domingo [now Haiti], 26 Apr. 1785; d. New York City, 27 Jan. 1851), artist and naturalist, pioneer American ornithologist. Taken to France in 1789, he was educated at Nantes and arrived (1803) in the U.S., where he began his ornithological studies in the Pennsylvania countryside. He made (Apr. 1804) the first experimental banding on the young of an American wild bird. Beginning in 1807, he made his home in Kentucky, where he was a merchant at Louisville and Henderson, and there continued his paintings and sketches of birds. Following a series of business reverses, he became (1820) a taxidermist at the Western Museum in Cincinnati. In 1826 he went to England and Scotland, where he secured the first subscriptions for the projected publication of his drawings and obtained the services of Robert Havell, Jr., a London engraver who brought out Audubon's monumental work, *The Birds of America* (1827–38), containing more than 1,000 life-size figures of about 500 species. After 1827 Audubon spent much of his time at Edinburgh, where he brought out his *Ornithological Biography* (with the assistance of William MacGillivray; 5 vols., 1831–39) and *Synopsis of the Birds of North America* (1839), and in 1842 made his home at the present site of Audubon Park, New York City. He collaborated with Rev. John Bachman on the *Viviparous Quadrupeds of North America* (2 vols. of plates, 1842–45; text, 3 vols., 1846–54). The Audubon Societies were founded in his memory.

Austin, Stephen Fuller (b. Wythe Co., Va., 3 Nov. 1793; d. Austin, Tex., 27 Dec. 1836), founder of Texas, moved with his parents to Missouri (1798), to which he returned (1810) after studying near New Haven, Conn., and at Transylvania Univ. He planted the first legal settlement of Anglo-Americans in Texas (1822), obtaining confirmation of his grant when Mexico achieved independence. Until 1828 he was executive, lawmaker, supreme judge, and military commandant, and kept a steady stream of emigrants coming into Texas. In 1828 he obtained the enactment of a contract labor law permitting the continued introduction of slaves as indentured servants. In pressing the claim of the convention of 1833 for a state government (against his own judgment), he was arrested and held by the Mexican government on the baseless charge of fomenting revolution in Texas and annexation to the U.S. He was released in July 1835. When the War of the Texas Revolution broke out, Austin was called to command the army, then sent to Washington to negotiate a loan and enlist support. He returned to Texas (June 1836) and was defeated for the presidency of the Republic of Texas by Sam Houston, whose secretary of state he became for the brief period remaining until his death.

Bacon, Nathaniel (b. Suffolk, England, 2 Jan. 1647; d. Gloucester Co., Va., 26 Oct. 1676), colonial insurrectionist. Born into a wealthy and prominent family (he was a cousin of Francis Bacon), he attended Cambridge and studied law at Gray's Inn. Emigrating with his wife to Virginia (1674), he was appointed to the governor's council. Quickly at odds with the governor, his cousin, William Berkeley, Bacon sympathized with the country planters who complained of inadequate protection of the frontiers from Indian attack, a limited franchise, excessive taxation and unfair distribution of offices, tax and customs exemptions. In 1676, in defiance of Berkeley, Bacon led a small army against the Pamunkey, Susquehannock, and Occaneechee Indians. He asked the governor to summon an assembly with a wider suffrage to reform the colony's laws. Berkeley denounced Bacon as a traitor and had him arrested, but when Bacon confessed his guilt the governor quickly pardoned him and readmitted him to the council. Bacon soon assembled his supporters to form another raiding party. Again denounced by Berkeley, Bacon and his followers occupied Jamestown without a battle and the governor fled. While Bacon attacked the Pamunkeys, Berkeley returned to Jamestown, only to be forced out when Bacon and his forces, after a battle, captured Jamestown and burned it down. By this time in control of virtually all of Virginia, Bacon withdrew to Green Springs to consolidate his position, but his sudden death from illness led to the rebellion's rapid suppression.

Baekeland, Leo Hendrik (b. Ghent, Belgium, 14 Nov. 1863; d. Beacon, N.Y., 23 Feb. 1944), chemist, inventor, received his B.S. from the Univ. of Ghent (1882), where he taught until emigrating to the U.S. (1889) to serve as consultant to A. & H. T. Anthony (later Ansco) of New York City, a photographic firm. In 1888 he patented a dry plate which could be developed in water. Founding with Leonard Jacobi the Nepara Chemical Co. to produce a photographic paper (Velox) he invented, he sold his rights (1899) to Eastman Kodak for $1 million. Attacking the problem of chemical synthesis, he produced a plastic which he exhibited (Feb. 1909) as Bakelite, the first of a long series of resins to revolutionize modern economic and technological life. Organizer (1910) of the General Bakelite Co., Perth Amboy, N.J., he was president until 1939, when it was acquired by Union Carbon and Carbide Corp. He received the Franklin Medal in 1940. He wrote *Some Aspects of Industrial Chemistry* (1914).

Balanchine, George (b. St. Petersburg, Russia, 9 Jan. 1904–   ), choreographer. Born Georgi Melitonovitch Balanchivadze, son of composer Meliton Balanchivadze, at the age of 10 he entered the Imperial Academy of Dance (later the Soviet State Ballet School), graduating in 1921. He continued his studies at the Conservatory of Music and joined the Soviet State Dancers. While touring Europe with the ballet company he decided to remain in Paris (1924), where he joined (1925) Serge Diaghilev's Ballets Russes. It was Diaghilev who suggested the new name he then adopted. Until Diaghilev's death and the disbandment of his troupe (1929), Balanchine served the company less as a performer than as ballet master and choreographer. During this period he choreographed, to music by Igor Stravinsky, *Apollo, Leader of the Muses* (premiere, 12 June 1928), his first masterpiece and, because of its innovations within the classical ballet tradition, his most influential and historically significant. He choreographed Cole Porter's *Wake Up and Dream* (1929) before becoming ballet master of the Royal Danish Ballet, Copenhagen (1930). He had helped organize (1932) the Ballet Russe de Monte Carlo when Lincoln Kirstein, an American philanthropist, intellectual, and balletomane, invited him (1933) to emigrate to the U.S., where they established (1934) the School of American Ballet in New York. Until 1948, when the New York City Ballet was established as a stable institution, with Kirstein as director, Balanchine was associated with the various emanations of the School of American Ballet—American Ballet Company, Ballet Caravan, and Ballet Society—and choreographed as a freelance as well. A seminal figure who has extended the vocabulary of classic ballet, he emphasizes visual patterns and movements drawn from the music. Prolifically inventive, he has choreographed more than 100 ballets, most of them plotless in the traditional sense. His ballets include *Agon* (1957), *Brahms-Schoenberg Quartet* (1966), *Bugaku* (1963), *Episodes* (1959), *Four Temperaments* (1946), *Jewels* (1966), *Serenade* (1935), *Square Dance* (1957), *Symphony in Three Movements* (1972), *Theme and Variations* (1947), and the *Nutcracker* (1954) —the last regularly performed each Christmas season. A full-length *Coppélia* (1974) was hailed by critics.

Bancroft, George (b. Worcester, Mass., 3 Oct. 1800; d. Washington, D.C., 17

Jan. 1891), historian, diplomat, and cabinet officer, was graduated from Harvard (1817) and in 1820 received the degrees of Ph.D. and M.A. from the Univ. of Göttingen. With Joseph Green Cogswell, he founded (1823) the Round Hill School at Northampton, Mass., but abandoned teaching in 1831 to begin research for his *History of the United States* (10 vols., 1834–76), covering the span between the discovery of America and the close of the Revolutionary War. Bancroft was active in the Jacksonian movement in Massachusetts in the 1830s; in 1844, when he was an unsuccessful candidate for the governorship of Massachusetts, he was instrumental in securing the Democratic Presidential nomination for James K. Polk. As Secretary of the Navy (1845–46), he established the U.S. Naval Academy at Annapolis, giving orders to Commodore John D. Sloat which upon the outbreak of the Mexican War facilitated early American success in the California area. As acting Secretary of War (May 1845) he signed the order which sent Gen. Zachary Taylor across the Texas frontier and brought on the clash with Mexico. Bancroft served as U.S. minister to Great Britain (1846–49) and Germany (1867–74), meanwhile tirelessly searching out materials in private and public collections for use in his *History*. In 1865 he wrote President Andrew Johnson's first annual message. In 1876 he brought out a revised edition ("Centenary Edition") of his history in 6 vols. His final revision (6 vols., 1883–85) included the *History of the Formation of the Constitution* (1882). He also wrote *Poems* (1823), *Literary and Historical Miscellanies* (1855), and *Martin Van Buren to the End of His Public Career* (1889).

Banneker, Benjamin (b. Ellicott's Mills, Md., 9 Nov. 1731; d. Baltimore, Md., 25 Oct. 1806), mathematician and astronomer, was the son of free black parents and was taught to read by his maternal grandmother, Molly Welsh, who was originally an indentured servant from England. Son of a prosperous farmer, he was given an education, in which he quickly demonstrated his mechanical aptitude. Inheriting his father's farm, which he worked for many years, Banneker did not seriously turn to scientific pursuits until he was 41 years old, when some astronomical books were given him by his Quaker neighbor, the manufacturer Andrew Ellicott. Thereafter he read widely in geology, astronomy, and physics, observing the heavens with a makeshift telescope and accurately predicting an eclipse (1789). In that year he was named a member of the commission to survey the new Federal District (later D. C.). In 1791 he began issuing an annual almanac which, aside from his astronomical calculations which earned the approval of the renowned David Rittenhouse, contained his commentaries on social problems, and on bees and locusts, whose plague he calculated correctly as a 17-year cycle. On 19 Aug. 1791 Banneker forwarded a copy of his first almanac to Secretary of State Jefferson, accompanied by a letter denouncing the injustice of slavery. Jefferson courteously acknowledged the communication. In the 1793 edition of his almanac Banneker included "A Plan of a Peace Office for the U.S.," recommending what amounted to a department of the interior for the U.S. and a league of nations to achieve peace. He also came out against capital punishment. Two days after his death most of his manuscripts were accidentally burned.

Barkley, Alben William (b. Graves Co., Ky., 24 Nov. 1877; d. Lexington, Va., 30 Apr. 1956), statesman, attended rural schools and graduated from Marvin College in Clinton, Ky. (1897). After further study at Emory College and the Univ. of Virginia Law School, he was admitted to the bar (1901) and immediately began practicing law in Paducah, Ky. Barkley's political career began as prosecuting attorney for MacCracken Co., Ky. (1905–09) and he served there as judge of the county court (1909–13). He was elected in 1912 to the U.S. House of Representatives, where he served 7 successive terms. In 1926 he was elected to the U.S. Senate, to which he was reelected 3 times (1927–49). As Senate majority leader (1937–47), he was the main spokesman for the New Deal. A Democratic party regular, he vigorously fought for antilynching legislation and piloted the Lend-Lease Bill through the Senate (1941). A loyal supporter of President Roosevelt's foreign and domestic programs, Barkley broke with him briefly over his veto of a revenue law (Feb. 1944), resigning as majority leader. He was, however, unanimously reelected by his colleagues. A notable orator, he keynoted the Democratic conventions of 1932, 1936, and 1940. Truman's running mate in 1948, Barkley as vice-president cooperated closely with the president, was unusually active as congressional liaison, and participated in policy-making at cabinet meetings and on the National Security Council. Immensely popular, known as the "Veep," he sought the presidential nomination in 1952 but withdrew after labor refused support due to his age. He was reelected to the Senate (1954) and served until his death, while giving a speech at a mock political convention. He was the author of *That Reminds Me* (1954).

Barnard, Henry (b. Hartford, Conn., 24 Jan. 1811; d. there, 5 July 1900), edu-

cator. He was educated at the Monson (Mass.) Academy and at the Hopkins Grammar School in Hartford, was graduated from Yale (1830), read law privately and attended the Yale Law School (1833–34), and was admitted to the bar (c.1835). He was a member (1837–40) of the Connecticut General Assembly, where he sponsored legislation for the improvement of the common schools; secretary (1838–42) of the board of school commissioners in Connecticut; school commissioner (1843–49) of Rhode Island; superintendent (1850–54) of the Connecticut state schools; chancellor (1858–60) of the Univ. of Wisconsin; and president (1866–67) of St. John's College, Annapolis, Md. In 1867 he became the first U.S. Commissioner of Education, serving in that post until 1870. A leader in the public school movement, he published the *American Journal of Education* (1855–82) and founded the Connecticut *Common School Journal.*

Barnum, Phineas Taylor (b. Bethel, Conn., 5 July 1810; d. Bridgeport, Conn., 7 Apr. 1891), showman and promoter. Until 1834, when he came to New York City, he pursued a variety of occupations, including the editing of an abolitionist newspaper at Danbury, Conn. His career in show business began with his purchase and exhibition (1835) of Joice Heth, a Negress purported to be the nurse of George Washington and 161 years old (she was actually about 80 years old). He bought (1841) Scudder's American Museum and Peale's Museum, using their collections for his American Museum (opened at New York in 1842), where he exhibited the dwarf, Gen. Tom Thumb, and other freaks, and delighted the public with hoaxes. With Tom Thumb, Barnum made a successful tour of the Continent in 1844. In 1850 he brought the Swedish singer, Jenny Lind, to the U.S. for a concert tour, and in 1855 retired to Iranistan, his lavish home at Bridgeport, Conn. In 1871 he made his return as a showman, opening his circus ("The Greatest Show on Earth") at Brooklyn. In 1881 he combined forces with a rival to form the Barnum & Bailey Circus, and imported from the Royal Zoological Society at London the elephant known as Jumbo. One of the colorful aspects of his showmanship was the elaborate advertising he used to whet the public appetite for his bizarre exhibitions. In developing aquariums and menageries, Barnum stimulated the museum movement and popularized natural history.

Barton, Clara (b. N. Oxford, Mass., 25 Dec. 1821; d. Glen Echo, Md., 12 Apr. 1912), humanitarian. After teaching school in New Jersey, she went to Washington, D.C. (1854), where at the outbreak of the Civil War she organized supply and nursing services for sick and wounded Union troops. Without receiving compensation or accreditation, she performed her work behind the lines and on battlefields, including that of the Wilderness. In 1864, when she accompanied the Army of the James, she acted as superintendent of nurses under authority of Gen. Benjamin Butler. After the war she was in charge (1865–69) of a government-sponsored search for missing soldiers. During the Franco-Prussian War she was active in relief activities in association with the International Red Cross at Geneva. Upon her return to the U.S. she undertook a campaign to establish an American Red Cross, and it was through her efforts that a National Society of the Red Cross was organized (1881). Miss Barton served as its president until 1904. She was active in relieving suffering caused by wars

and disasters, such as the Spanish-American War, the Boer War, and the Galveston flood (8 Sept. 1900), and was responsible for the introduction of the "American Amendment" at the Geneva International Conference (1884), specifying that in extreme peacetime emergencies the Red Cross should carry out humanitarian work similar to that assumed by it during wars.

Beard, Charles Austin (b. Knightstown, Ind., 27 Nov. 1874; d. New Haven, Conn., 1 Sept. 1948), historian, political scientist, was graduated from DePauw Univ. (1898), studied English local government at Oxford, and received his M.A. (1903) and Ph.D. (1904) from Columbia. Teaching history and politics at Columbia (1904–17), he resigned (1917) on an academic freedom issue, and cofounded (1919) the New School for Social Research. He was adviser (1922) to the Institute of Municipal Research in Tokyo. With James Harvey Robinson, he coauthored *The Development of Modern Europe* (1907) and an accompanying book of readings—pioneer text and source book offering a brilliant synthesis of political, social, and cultural history. *An Economic Interpretation of the Constitution* (1913), attributing the work of the Federal Convention to the self-interest of the Founding Fathers (in line with J. Allen Smith [1907] and Arthur F. Bentley [1908]) and introducing a strong element of economic determinism, had an enormous vogue. It was followed by *Economic Origins of Jeffersonian Democracy* (1915) and *The Economic Basis of Politics* (1910). He later repudiated such economic determinism in *The Republic* (1943), and more recent critics have challenged both his methodology and his evidence. With his wife, Mary Ritter Beard, he wrote *The Rise of American Civilization* (1927) and its sequels *America in Midpassage* (1939) and *The American Spirit* (1943), a notable and popular historical synthesis, stressing the Civil War as a second American Revolution. He also wrote *The Supreme Court and the Constitution* (1912) and *President Roosevelt and the Coming of the War, 1941* (1948), an isolationist critique.

Beaumont, William (b. Lebanon, Conn., 21 Nov. 1785; d. St. Louis, Mo., 25 Apr. 1853), army surgeon, pioneer in gastric physiology. He served his medical apprenticeship under Dr. Benjamin Chandler of St. Albans, Vt., was licensed (June 1812) by the Third Medical Society of Vermont, and was commissioned (13 Sept. 1812) a surgeon's mate to the 6th Infantry at Plattsburg, N.Y. After the close of the War of 1812, he resigned from the service and established a private practice at Plattsburg. He enlisted again (1820) and was assigned to Ft. Mackinac (in present-day Michigan) as a surgeon. It was there, on 6 June 1822, that Alexis St. Martin, a Canadian youth, was accidentally shot and suffered a powder-and-shot wound that left a portion of his stomach punctured and protruding from the abdominal cavity. St. Martin was brought to the military hospital for treatment. After a time a flap of the inner stomach closed the puncture, but the lid could be pushed back to expose the interior. Early in 1825 Beaumont undertook scientific studies in digestion, observing St. Martin's stomach temperature during digestion, the movements of his stomach walls, the relative digestibility of certain foods, and the workings of gastric juice under artificial conditions. These studies eventuated in the publication of *Experiments and Observations on the Gastric Juice and the Physiology of Digestion* (1833), revolutionary in its impact upon the existing knowledge and theories of the physiology

of the stomach and the chemistry of gastric digestion, much of it still valid.

Beecher, Henry Ward (b. Litchfield, Conn., 24 June 1813; d. Brooklyn, N.Y., 8 Nov. 1887), clergyman and orator, son of Lyman Beecher (1775–1863) and brother of Harriet Beecher Stowe (*q.v.*), was graduated from Amherst (1834) and attended the Lane Theological Seminary, Cincinnati, in which city he began preaching as an independent Presbyterian. Called (10 Oct. 1847) to the Plymouth Congregational Church, Brooklyn, N.Y., he drew weekly audiences averaging 2,500, with notable sermons printed in pamphlet form and widely circulated. His influence was extended in editorials in the *Independent* (1861–64) and the *Christian Union*, which he edited 1870–81. An antislavery leader, he opposed interference in the slave states but counseled disobedience of the Fugitive Slave Law. In 1863 he visited England and defended the Union cause before hostile audiences. A modernist, he supported woman suffrage and civil service reform, accepted evolution, but clung to his belief in miracles. His Christianity stressed the love of God and the joy and glory of the religious life. His personal life became a public issue in the Beecher-Tilton adultery case (1874), in which his defense was upheld by a divided jury.

Bell, Alexander Graham (b. Edinburgh, Scotland, 3 Mar. 1847; d. Cape Breton Island, Nova Scotia, 2 Aug. 1922), inventor of the telephone and educator of the deaf. He was educated at McLauren's Academy in Edinburgh and at the Royal High School; became (c.1867) assistant in London to his father, Alexander Melville Bell (1819–1905), inventor of the Visible Speech System; accompanied his family to Canada (1870); and in 1871 began giving special instruction in his father's speech system to teachers of the deaf in cities throughout New England. He opened a normal training school at Boston (1872) and served (1873–77) as professor of vocal physiology and the mechanics of speech in the School of Oratory of Boston Univ. His work for the deaf and his interest in the science of acoustics were related to the experiments which he meanwhile pursued (1873–76) to invent a multiple telegraph and an electric speaking telegraph or telephone. These experiments led to his invention of the harmonic multiple telegraph (1874) and the telephonic telegraphic receiver (1874), in the course of which he gained a thorough knowledge of electrical wave transmission. His preoccupation with the idea of a machine for the electrical transmission of speech finally resulted in the first practical demonstration (at Boston, 10 Mar. 1876) of the first magneto-electric telephone. The Bell Telephone Co., the first organization of its kind, was founded in 1877, and thereafter the commercial development and application of the telephone proceeded rapidly. Bell became an American citizen in 1882. His career as an inventor did not interrupt his activities as an educator of the deaf. Among his other inventions were the photophone for the transmission of sound by light (1880), the telephone probe for locating metallic masses in the human body (1881), the spectrophone (1881), and the tetrahedral kite (1903). He was associated (1884–86) with the invention of the wax cylinder record for phonographs.

Bellows, George Wesley (b. Columbus, Ohio, 12 Aug. 1882; d. New York City, 8 Jan. 1925), painter, lithographer, and illustrator, was graduated from Ohio State Univ. (1903), studied painting in New York under Robert Henri (*q.v.*), and, in his early painting, was inspired by city crowds (*42 Kids*, 1907) and prizefights (*Stag at Sharkey's*, 1907), following directly in the tradition of Eakins' realism. He taught at the Art Students League, beginning in 1910, and also at the Chicago Art Institute in 1919. His paintings show the influence of Goya and Daumier, and later of El Greco and Renoir, but are stamped with his own personality. Among his larger canvases are *Edith Cavell* (1918), with dramatic use of light and dark; *The Return of the Useless* (1918); and *The Pic-nic* (1924). Turning to lithography (1916), he soon became a master of that medium.

Bennett, James Gordon (b. Newmills, near Keith, Scotland, 1795; d. New York City, 1 June 1872), editor, emigrated to Halifax, Nova Scotia (1819), thence to Boston and New York, where he wrote for the press and acquired the *Sunday Courier* (1825). He was appointed associate editor of the New York *Enquirer* (1826) and coedited the combined *Courier & Enquirer* (1829). On 6 May 1835 he founded the New York *Herald,* a penny paper. Its sensational and comprehensive news coverage (in the Civil War it employed 63 war correspondents) and personalized editorial style raised its circulation to 100,000 (by 1864). Editorially, Bennett generally supported the Democrats, Douglas against Lincoln, and secession; but after Ft. Sumter, when a mob threatened him, he executed an about-face and backed the war, although he did not give Lincoln his full support until 1864.

Benton, Thomas Hart (b. Harts Mill, near Hillsboro, N.C., 14 Mar. 1782; d. Washington, D.C., 10 Apr. 1858), statesman, studied at Chapel Hill College (now Univ. of North Carolina) and the law department of William and Mary. Tennessee state senator (1809), he was admitted to the bar at Nashville (1806), served in the War of 1812 as aide-de-camp to Jackson, then removed to St. Louis (1815), where he practiced law and edited the *Missouri Inquirer*. In 1817 he killed Charles Lucas, U.S. district attorney in a second duel after wounding him in the first. Elected (1820) to the U.S. Senate, he was the first senator to serve 30 consecutive years (1821–51). Supporting Jackson (1828) as Senate floor leader in the war against the Bank and in his advocacy of hard money, "Old Bullion" secured a change in the ratio of gold and silver from 15 to 1 to 16 to 1. He sponsored the resolution to expunge from the Senate journal the resolution of censure of President Jackson. Advocate of free homesteads of 160 acres, anticipating the later Homestead Act, he opposed the annexation of Texas but supported the War with Mexico. Preferring compromise to war over the Oregon issue, he favored the 49th parallel, the boundary finally secured. Opposing Calhoun's pro-slavery resolution of 1850 as well as Clay's compromise, he lost his seat in the Senate, but in the House (1853–55) fought the Missouri Compromise repeal, which lost him his seat and his campaign for governor (1856). He supported Buchanan for president (1856) against his own son-in-law John C. Frémont (*q.v.*). He wrote a notable autobiography, *Thirty Years' View* (1854–56) and compiled *Abridgement of the Debates of Congress, 1789–1856* (1857–61).

Berkeley, Sir William (b. at or near London, 1606; d. England, 13 July 1677), colonial governor, received his B.A. (1624) and M.A. (1629) from Oxford. Knighted by Charles I (1639), he became royal governor of Virginia (1642), where he inaugurated vigorous and constructive policies. Heading an expedition (1644) against the Indians, he established a generation of peace and encouraged crop diversification and manufactures. Anglican and Royalist, he denied toleration to nonconformists, defied Parliament after the execution of Charles I, and, confronted by a naval force dispatched to Virginia by Parliament to establish its authority, worked out a compromise but yielded his own office. Back in office with the Restoration, his 2d administration, though continuing some of his constructive policies, was increasingly arbitrary, with no new elections of the burgesses called between 1660 and 1674. The unrest stemming from tax policies, bad crops, and Indian attacks, which Nathaniel Bacon (*q.v.*) exploited, found the governor obdurate. In the ensuing insurrection (1676) he was driven out of Jamestown, but on Bacon's death returned to power, rescinded recent reform measures, and despite royal promise of pardon hanged 23 rebels. Refusing to yield office to a royal investigating commission, he resigned on ground of ill health, returned to England, and, failing to obtain an audience with Charles II, died soon after.

Berlin, Irving [Isidore Baline] (b. Temun, Russia, 11 May 1888–), songwriter and composer, came to the U.S. in 1893, studied in the New York City public schools for 2 years, then worked as a song-plugger on the Bowery and as a singing waiter (1904). His first song hit, "Dorando," was published in 1909. Graduating to Broadway, he appeared in *Up and Down Broadway* (1910) and his "Alexander's Ragtime Band" (1911) quickly became a top hit. In 1912 he wrote the score for Ziegfeld's *Follies*. During World War I he became a U.S. citizen, and as an army sergeant he wrote an all-soldier show, *Yip-Yip-Yaphank*, while stationed at Camp Upton, Yaphank, L.I. Among his top hits was his musical comedy all-soldier revue *This Is* *the Army,* which opened on Broadway (1942), with Berlin singing "Oh, How I Hate to Get Up in the Morning," and wearing his World War I sergeant's uniform. For this show, the profits of which went to Army Emergency Relief, he was awarded the Medal of Merit, and for his song "God Bless America" (1917, but introduced in 1938) he received a congressional gold medal (1954). Other stage successes include *Annie Get Your Gun* (1947), *Call Me Madam* (1950, with Howard Lindsay and Russel Crouse), *Mr. President* (1962), and the film musical *Easter Parade* (1933). Lacking formal musical instruction, he played tunes in one key, F sharp, and used a piano adapted to change keys mechanically. Among his innumerable song hits are "Remember," "Always," "What'll I Do?," "All Alone," "A Pretty Girl Is Like a Melody," "Blue Skies," "White Christmas." He was married twice. His first wife, Dorothy Goetz, died 8 months after their marriage in 1913. In 1926 he married Ellin, daughter of Clarence H. Mackay.

Bernstein, Leonard (b. Lawrence, Mass., 25 Aug. 1918–   ), received his B.A. (1939) from Harvard, studying composition with Walter Piston, and at the Curtis Institute of Music, from which he was graduated (1941; piano with Isabella Vengerova and conducting with Fritz Reiner). Assistant to Serge Koussevitsky at the Berkshire Music Center (1943–44), he achieved fame overnight when in 1943 as Asst. Conductor he conducted the N.Y. Philharmonic upon the illness of Bruno Walter. Conductor of the New York City Symph. (1945–48), co-conductor of the N.Y. Philharmonic (1957–58) and its musical director 1958 to 1969, he has been outstanding as music educator and popularizer. He headed the conducting department of the Berkshire Music Center beg. 1948,

was professor of music at Brandeis Univ., 1951–56, a frequent music interpreter on TV (*Omnibus,* 1957; children's concerts), and inaugurator of the Thursday night previews of the N.Y. Philharmonic. His compositions include *Clarinet Sonata* (1942), *Symph. No. 1* (*Jeremiah,* 1942), *The Age of Anxiety* (1949), *Kaddish Symph.* (1963), *Chichester Psalms* (1965), *Mass* (1971), and *The Dybbuk,* a ballet score (1974). A musical virtuoso, he also wrote *Trouble in Tahiti,* a 1-act opera (1952); scores for musical shows *On the Town* (1944), *Wonderful Town* (1953), *Candide* (1956), *West Side Story* (1957); and the film score for *On the Waterfront* (1954). He conducted acclaimed revivals of *Falstaff,* Met. Opera (1963), and *Der Rosenkavalier,* Vienna State Opera (1968).

Beveridge, Albert (b. Highland Co., Ohio, 6 Oct. 1862; d. Indianapolis, Ind., 27 Apr. 1927), U.S. senator and historian, graduated from DePauw Univ. (1885) and was admitted to the Indiana bar (1887). After practicing law in Indianapolis and involving himself in politics for 12 years, Beveridge was elected as a Republican to the U.S. Senate (1899–1911). A nationalist and imperialist, Beveridge believed that "the trade of the world must and should be ours," supported the strengthening of the navy, and intervention in the Philippines. A leading progressive senator and strong supporter of President Theodore Roosevelt, he drafted the Meat Inspection Act (1906) which provided for the enforcement of sanitary regulations in packinghouses and for federal inspection of all companies selling meats in interstate commerce. Not against business *per se* but rather against big business, Beveridge supported Roosevelt's legislation regulating trusts and public utilities, and supported an income tax to curb "unhealthy fortunes." He was a leader in the campaign for national legislation against child labor, making the first important appeal (23, 28, 29 Jan. 1907) for action against an evil "as brutal and horrible in its humanity as anything the pen of Dickens ever painted." He was also a promoter of conservation. In the Republican split over the Payne-Aldrich tariff bill (1909), Beveridge strongly opposed the tariff as against the public interest, particularly attacking the tobacco schedule. After his defeat for reelection (1911), he became active in the new Progressive party, running unsuccessfully for governor of Indiana (1912), and for the Senate (1914, 1922) as a Republican. During an era when many politicians were also scholars, Beveridge produced major contributions to history. He is best known for his 4-vol. *The Life of Marshall* (1916–19), which remains the standard work on the Marshall court, in spite of a Federalist bias. At his death Beveridge was completing the first 2 vols. of a biography of Abraham Lincoln, which impressively placed the pre-presidential career of Lincoln in its historical setting (published posthumously, 1928).

Biddle, Nicholas (b. Philadelphia, 8 Jan. 1786; d. "Andalusia," near Philadelphia, 27 Feb. 1844), financier and editor, was graduated from the College of New Jersey (1801) and served abroad (1804) as secretary to John Armstrong, U.S. minister to France, and to Monroe, minister to Great Britain (1806). On his return to the U.S. (1807) he settled in Philadelphia and became associate editor (1807–12) of the *Port Folio* with Joseph Dennie and sole editor (1812). In collaboration with Paul Allen he prepared the *History of the Expedition of Captains Lewis and Clark* (1814). He served in Congress (1810–11) and in the Pennsylvania state senate (1814–18). Presi-

dent Monroe appointed him a government director of the 2d Bank of the U.S., of which he became president (1823) and served in that capacity until it closed its doors (1836) on failure to secure renewal of the charter. Following a conservative policy, Biddle made the Bank of the U.S. a paramount influence in the national economy, only to arouse the enmity of advocates of an "easy money" policy. His fatal error was to make the bank an issue in the presidential election of 1832. Jackson's overwhelming victory left no doubt about the issue. Under a charter from Pennsylvania Biddle continued to act as president of the bank, which finally failed (1841), although the creditors were fully paid.

Bierstadt, Albert (b. Düsseldorf, Germany, 7 Jan. 1830; d. New York City, 18 Feb. 1902), landscape painter. At the age of 2 he accompanied his parents to the U.S. and spent his childhood in New Bedford, Mass. After early exhibitions of his work in Boston (1851, 1853), he studied art in Germany and Rome (1853–57), with summer sketching tours of Germany and Switzerland. Returning to the U.S. in 1857, he went west with Gen. W. F. Lander's surveying expedition (1858–59). Thereafter his impressions of the scenery of the Rocky Mountains and the West, based on sketches made during this and subsequent visits, were recorded on canvas. One of his first Western landscapes was *Thunderstorm in the Rocky Mountains* (1859, Boston Mus. Fine Arts). Others include *Laramie Peak* (1861, Buffalo Acad. Fine Arts), *Looking Down Yosemite Valley* (1865, W. H. Cosby), *Estes Park, Colorado* (1877, Earl of Dunraven), and *Valley of Kern's River, California* (1875), bought for the Hermitage in St. Petersburg. He also produced historic landscapes such as *The Discovery of the Hudson River* (1875), which hangs in the Capitol, as well as 4 paintings (1887–88) treating Columbus' voyages, but his romantic landscapes of Western wilderness proved his most distinctive contribution.

Black, Hugo La Fayette (b. Harlan, Ala., 27 Feb. 1886; d. Bethesda, Md., 25 Sept. 1971), jurist, received his LL.B. (1906) from the Univ. of Alabama, practiced law in Birmingham (1907), where he served as police judge (1910–11) and later as solicitor of Jefferson Co. (1915–17). Democratic senator from Alabama (1927–37), he resigned to accept appointment as associate justice of the Supreme Court (1937). When appointed, considerable criticism was aroused by the revelation that he had once been a member of the Ku Klux Klan (1923–25), although his record in the Senate had been consistently progressive, notably in his investigation of the public utility lobby. His role as a liberal activist on the bench soon silenced some of his critics. Taking an absolutist position regarding much of the Bill of Rights, especially the 1st Amendment (*Bridges* v. *Calif.*, 1941; dissent in *Yates* v. *U.S.*, 1957), he opposed setting limits to the right to picket (*Milk Wagon Drivers Union* v. *Meadowmoor Dairies*, 1941). His dissenting opinion in *Conn. Gen. Life Ins. Co.* v. *Johnson* (1938) denied the right of corporations to claim protection under the 14th Amendment. In dissent in *Adamson* v. *Calif.* (1947) he asserted that the 14th Amendment extended to all the people the complete protection of the Bill of Rights. He upheld the right to distribute religious literature in a company town (*Marsh* v. *Ala.*, 1946), and in *Everson* v. *Bd. of Education* (1947) ruled that a N.J. law expending tax money for transportation

to parochial schools did not constitute support of religion. Although he held that the exclusion order relating to Japanese-Americans during World War II was within the federal war powers (*Korematsu* v. *U.S.*, 1944), he invalidated the military courts set up in Hawaii during the war (*Duncan* v. *Kahanamoku*, 1946). His majority opinion held invalid President Truman's seizure of steel companies (*Youngstown Sheet & Tube Co.* v. *Sawyer*, 1952). He invalidated N.Y. State official school prayer (*Engel* v. *Vitale*, 1962), and upset inequitable congressional districting (*Westberry* v. *Sanders*, 1964). He refused to extend his 1st Amendment absolutism to symbolic speech (*Adderly* v. *Fla.*, 1966), and his 4th Amendment absolutism to cover electronic eavesdropping (dissent in *Berger* v. *N.Y.*, 1967). In his last major opinion he held that the U.S. could not enjoin publication of the Pentagon Papers (*New York Times* v. *U.S.*, 1971).

Blaine, James Gillespie (b. West Brownsville, Pa., 30 Jan. 1830; d. Washington, D.C., 27 Jan. 1893), statesman, was graduated from Washington College (1847); taught school (1848–54); studied law, moving to Augusta, Me., where he edited the Kennebec *Journal* (1854–57). While Republican state legislator (1859–62), he became speaker (1861–62). He served in Congress (1862–76) and was speaker of the House (1869–75). The "Mulligan letters" (1876), which accused Blaine of using his position as speaker for personal gain by giving a land grant to the Little Rock & Ft. Smith R.R., blasted his hopes for the presidential nomination that year. He again failed to secure the nomination in 1880. As Garfield's Secretary of State (1881) he planned the first Pan-American Conference and proposed to Great

Britain a modification of the Clayton-Bulwer Treaty. Republican nominee for president (1884), his defeat has been attributed in no small part to the indiscreet reference by one of his supporters to the Democratic party as the party of "Rum, Romanism, and Rebellion," which might well have lost the crucial state of New York. He supported Harrison (1888), and became Secretary of State (1889–92). His constructive achievements include the convening of the first Pan-American Conference (1889) and the settlement of the Bering seal dispute with Great Britain. He favored Hawaiian annexation.

Blalock, Alfred (b. Colloden, Ga., 5 Apr. 1899; d. Baltimore, Md., 15 Sept. 1964), surgeon, was graduated from Univ. of Georgia (B.A., 1918) and from Johns Hopkins (M.D., 1922), was on the medical faculty in surgery (1927–41) at Vanderbilt Univ. Medical School, and in 1941 became director of the department of surgery at Johns Hopkins Univ. and surgeon in chief of the Johns Hopkins Hospital. His most notable work was done in surgical shock and in regulation of the circulation. Testing a theory advanced by Dr. Helen Brooke Taussig (1898–   ), he operated (9 Nov. 1944) on a "blue baby," by-passing the pulmonary artery. As a result thousands of "blue babies" regained their health by the Blalock operation.

Boas, Franz (b. Minden, Westphalia, Germany, 9 July 1858; d. New York City, 21 Dec. 1942), anthropologist. He studied at Heidelberg and Bonn, received the degree of Ph.D. (1881) at Kiel, and as a member of a German Arctic expedition (1883–84) studied Eskimo life in Baffin Land. He served (1885–86) as an assistant at the Royal Ethnological Museum in Berlin and as *Privatdocent* in geography at the Univ.

of Berlin. Arriving in the U.S. in 1886, he was an editorial staff member (1886–88) of *Science* and instructor in anthropology (1888–92) at Clark Univ. In 1896 he was named lecturer in anthropology at Columbia Univ., where he became professor in 1899. He was curator of anthropology (1901–05) in the American Museum of Natural History; organized the Jesup North Pacific Expedition (1902), and edited its *Reports;* was president (1907–08) of the American Anthropological Society; and president (1910) of the New York Academy of Sciences. His numerous papers and studies, based upon the scientific fact-finding technique of the field survey, modified earlier concepts of cultural evolution. His publications on the Kwakiutl Indians are classics in their field. Among his writings are *Baffin Land* (1885), *The Central Eskimos* (1888), *The Mind of Primitive Man* (1911, 1938), *Anthropology and Modern Life* (1928), *General Anthropology* (1938), and *Race, Language and Culture* (1940).

Boone, Daniel (b. near Reading, Pa., 2 Nov. 1734; d. near St. Charles, Mo., 26 Sept. 1820), pioneer. Becoming a hunter at the age of 12, he settled (1751) at Buffalo Lick in the Yadkin Valley of North Carolina; served as a teamster and blacksmith in Braddock's campaign (1755); made his first trip into Kentucky (1767–69), leading a party through Cumberland Gap over a trail later known as the Wilderness Road, living and exploring in central Kentucky with his brother-in-law John Stuart Finley and others, returning to North Carolina after his 2d trip (1769–71). Serving as the agent of Col. Richard Henderson of the Transylvania Co., he returned to Kentucky with a party of settlers (1775) and established a fort at what became the site of Boonesborough. Captured and adopted by the Shawnees (1778), he escaped. After Virginia repudiated Henderson's land titles and made Kentucky a county of Virginia, Boone served as lieutenant colonel of the Fayette County militia, and was chosen a delegate to the legislature, and was made sheriff and county lieutenant (1782). He moved to Maysville in 1786 and in 1788 left Kentucky, going to Point Pleasant in what is now West Virginia. Because of failure to make proper entry of his land holdings, he lost all of his claims. After being ejected from his last holding, he moved (c.1798) to present-day Missouri, where he received a land grant and continued his hunting and trapping. One of the folk heroes of American history, Boone is popularly credited with deeds, such as the discovery of Kentucky, which have no foundation in fact.

Booth, Edwin Thomas (b. near Bel Air, Md., 13 Nov. 1833; d. New York City, 7 June 1893), actor, son of Junius Brutus Booth (1796–1852), brother of John Wilkes Booth (1838–65). He made his debut (10 Sept. 1849) at Boston as Tressel in Cibber's version of *Richard III* and up to 1856 did most of his acting in California, where he emerged as an accomplished tragedian. Returning to the East in 1856, he scored a great success at Boston (20 Apr. 1857) in the role of Sir Giles Overreach. His appearances at New York and in the South and West established him as the leading American actor of his day. Among his favorite roles were Shylock, Hamlet, Romeo, and Othello. Between 1869 and 1874 he reached the peak of his career in performances given at Booth's Theater, built by him at New York City. Because of financial difficulties brought on by the Panic of 1873, Booth went into bankruptcy (1874) and for the remainder of his life was a roving player in the U.S. and Europe. He was the founder (1888) and first president of the Players' Club, to which he gave its present building on Gramercy Park, New York City.

Borah, William Edgar (b. Jasper Township, Ill., 29 June 1865; d. Washington, D.C., 19 Jan. 1940), statesman, studied at the Univ. of Kansas (1885–86), read law, was admitted to the bar (1889), and quickly gained prominence in Boise, Ida., as a criminal lawyer as well as counsel for timber and mining interests. Special prosecutor in the trial (1907) of William D. Haywood and others for the murder of Gov. Frank D. Steunenberg, he himself was unsuccessfully prosecuted (1907) for timber frauds. Elected to the U.S. Senate (1907), he served in that body until his death. Orator, reformer, and political maverick, he supported labor reform legislation and fought for the income tax and direct election of senators. Though a supporter of Theodore Roosevelt, he refused to follow him into the Progressive party in 1912. Opposing most of Wilson's progressive legislation, including women's suffrage, he favored national prohibition. Leader of the irreconcilables opposed to the League of Nations, he refused, with Henry Cabot Lodge, to compromise on that issue. Responsible for calling the Washington Disarmament Conference (1921) he exercised, as chairman of the Senate Committee on Foreign Relations (beg. 1924), enormous influence on U.S. foreign policy, favoring recognition of Russia but opposing U.S. intervention in Latin America as well as membership in the World Court. He induced Secretary of State Kellogg to substitute a multinational for a bilateral pact outlawing war (1928). He opposed Hoover's farm and tariff policies, supported much of the New Deal domestic program, but was an outstanding critic of the NRA and Franklin D. Roosevelt's Supreme Court bill. Supporting the Neutrality Act of 1935, he remained an isolationist to the end, advocating nonintervention in World War II.

Borlaug, Norman Ernest (b. Cresco, Ia., 25 Mar. 1914–), agronomist. The son of Norwegian immigrants, he grew up on a 56-acre farm. He received a B.S. in forestry (1937), M.S. (1940) and Ph.D. (1941) in plant pathology from Univ. of Minnesota. After spending 3 years as a pathologist for the du Pont de Nemours Foundation, studying how chemicals affect plants, Borlaug joined the Rockefeller Foundation's wheat improvement project in Mexico (1944). Borlaug has remained there ever since, directing a team of experts from 17 countries, experimenting with new, higheryielding strains of wheat. Borlaug and the team's work began in 1944 when they planted 3 varieties of wheat— Japanese "Norin" dwarfs, Gaines, and Mexican—and found the only crop to resist rust was Norin. Then they crossed Norin with wheat from countries all over the world, until they developed a strain with good color and milling quality, rust resistance, high protein, a strong stem, and a very high yield. Planting seeds from Borlaug's strain of wheat, such countries as India and Pakistan have doubled their wheat production and Mexico quadrupled it. For his role in initiating the "Green Revolution," Borlaug received the Nobel peace prize (1970).

Bowditch, Nathaniel (b. Salem, Mass., 26 Mar. 1773; d. there, 17 Mar. 1838), astronomer, mathematician, was completely self-educated, learning algebra at 14 and studying Latin at 17 in order to read Newton's *Principia*. On his 5 sea voyages (1795–1803) as clerk, supercargo, or master, he perfected his knowledge of mathematics and navigation. He corrected J. H. Moore's *The Practical Navigator*, and from the 13th English edition published (with his brother William's collaboration) the 1st American edition (1799). The 3d American edition, extensively altered, appeared under his name as *The New Practical American Navigator* (1802). Nine other editions of this classic appeared in his lifetime and at least 56 more since. *Bowditch's Useful Tables* were reprinted (1844) from the work. In addition, he published (1804–20) 23 important nautical and astronomical papers in the *Memoirs* of the American Academy of Arts and Sciences and translated the first 4 vols. of La Place's *Mécanique céleste* (1828–39). In addition to his numerous scientific honors he was president of the Essex Fire and Marine Insurance Co. (beg. 1804) and actuary of the Massachusetts Hospital Life Insurance Co. (1823–38).

Bradford, William (b. Austerfield, Yorkshire, England, 1590; d. Plymouth Colony, [now Mass.], 19 May 1657), Pilgrim leader. While still a boy he attended the Separatist group meetings held at William Brewster's house in Scrooby, and in 1609 accompanied the Scrooby congregation to Amsterdam and later to Leyden. He came to America (1620) in the *Mayflower* and was elected governor (1621) of Plymouth Colony following the death of John Carver. Between 1622 and 1656 he was reelected to the governorship in every year except 1633, 1634, 1636, 1638, and 1644, when he served as an assistant. The leading statesman of the Plymouth Colony, he exercised (1622–36) broad authority in governmental and religious matters. Plymouth Colony was placed on a firm economic footing when Bradford and other Pilgrim Fathers assumed (1627) the original investment of the merchant adventurers who had financed the settlement. Bradford took part in drafting (1636) a body of laws that endowed the office of governor with a quasi-constitutional status. Although he believed in maintaining the Plymouth Colony as a separate and compact settlement, Bradford cooperated in larger undertakings such as the Pequot War and the New England Confederation. He began (c.1630) writing his *History of Plimmouth Plantation*, completing it in 1651. It was not published in full until 1856.

Bradley, Omar (b. Clark, Mo., 12 Feb. 1893–   ), soldier. A graduate of the U.S. Military Academy (1915), he also received diplomas from the Army Infantry School (1925), the Command and General Staff School (1929), and the Army War College (1934). Commissioned a second lieutenant upon graduation from West Point, he served at various posts in the West and Midwest before becoming a professor of military science and tactics at South Dakota State College (1919–20). At the U.S. Military Academy he served as an instructor of mathematics (1920–24) and a training officer and instructor of military planning and tactics (1934–38). Promoted to brigadier general in 1941, his first combat service was in 1943, when he became a deputy to Gen. Patton (*q.v.*) in North Africa. After taking over command of the 2d Corps, in North Africa, he took part in the invasion of Sicily (1943). He was sent to England to begin planning for the invasion of Europe and to take over command of the 1st Army, which he directed during Operation Overlord (1944). Assuming command (Aug. 1944) of the 12th Army Group—composed of the 1st, 3d, 9th, and 15th armies, the largest force (1.3 million combat troops) ever to serve under a single American field commander —he played a key role in engineering the offensive which led to Germany's defeat. Known as the "GI's General," he was respected for his tactical skill, courage, and refusal to waste troops. Promoted to full general (1945), after the war he served as head of the Veterans Administration (1945–47), Chief of Staff of the U.S. Army (1948–49), and the first chairman of the U.S. Joint Chiefs of Staff (1949–53). He was promoted to general of the army (1950). After his retirement from the army (16 Aug. 1953), he pursued various business interests. He published a volume of reminiscences, *A Soldier's Story* (1951).

Brandeis, Louis Dembitz (b. Louisville, Ky., 13 Nov. 1856; d. Washington, D.C., 5 Oct. 1941), jurist, studied in Germany (1873–75), was graduated from Harvard Law School (1878), and practiced in Boston until 1916. Because of his advocacy of public causes he came to be known as the "people's attorney." Attorney for the policyholders in the investigation of the Equitable Life (1906), he devised and secured enactment in Massachusetts of the issue of low-cost life insurance through savings banks (1907). His mastery of the facts and his firm grasp of economics were demonstrated in his pathmaking brief in *Muller* v. *Oregon* (1908), largely devoted to an analysis of the injurious effect of hard labor upon the physique of women. An opponent of bigness in business or government, his advice was sought by President Wilson on trust legislation, currency, and and labor problems. His appointment as associate justice of the U.S. Supreme Court (1916) was confirmed over strong opposition by the organized bar. Serving until retirement (1939), he was aligned in dissent with Holmes and (after 1932) with Cardozo and Stone. He cautioned the court against curbing social and economic experimentation by the states

(*New State Ice Co.*, 1932) and sought, in public-utility rate making, a measurement of value according to "prudent investment" (*Southwestern Bell Telephone Co.*, 1923).

Brooks, Phillips (b. Boston, Mass., 13 Dec. 1835; d. there, 23 Jan. 1893), Episcopal bishop. He attended Harvard; studied in the seminary at Alexandria, Va., where he was ordained a deacon (1859); and occupied his first ministry in the Church of the Advent in Philadelphia from 1859 to 1862. Here his eloquent and lofty preaching soon won wide attention. He served as rector (1862–69) of Holy Trinity in Philadelphia, and in 1865 made the prayer at the Harvard commemoration day. Brooks was rector (1869–91) of Trinity Church in Boston, where he brought into Episcopal preaching fresh currents of piety and conviction. His definition of preaching as "the bringing of truth through personality" was the central idea of the Lyman Beecher Lectures on Preaching given by Brooks at the Yale Divinity School (Jan.–Feb. 1877). In 1880, he preached in Westminster Abbey, winning the distinction of being the first American to preach before a crowned head in the Royal Chapel at Windsor. In 1891 he was elected and consecrated Bishop of Massachusetts, a post he held until his death.

Brown, John (b. Torrington, Conn., 9 May 1800; d. Charlestown, W. Va., 2 Dec. 1859), reformer son of an abolitionist and "underground railway" agent, Owen Brown, and Ruth Mills Brown (who died insane), had an unsuccessful business career as a tanner, land speculator, and shepherd in 10 different locations. Convinced of the need for a slave insurrection, he left Ohio in 1855 to join 5 of his sons in the Ossawatomie colony in Kansas, where he became captain of the local militia company. As Free-Soil crusaders, Brown and a party of 6 (4 of whom were his sons) planned and executed the massacre of 5 proslavery men (24 May 1856). "Old Ossawatomie Brown" and his company were eventually dispersed and the colony burned in retaliation. Supplied with arms and money by leading abolitionists, Brown and a band of 21 men, aiming to liberate the slaves, seized (16 Oct. 1859) the Harpers Ferry armory and bridges leading to the Ferry, a blow which inflamed the South. Forced to surrender to Col. Robert E. Lee, he was tried for treason to Virginia and speedily convicted. During and subsequent to the trial he conducted himself with dignity, protesting that his only desire was to free the slaves. Hanged at Charlestown, he was hailed as a martyr by antislavery elements.

Bryan, William Jennings (b. Salem, Ill., 19 Mar. 1860; d. Dayton, Tenn., 26 July 1925), political leader and orator, was graduated from Illinois College, Jacksonville, Ill. (1881), and from the Union College of Law in Chicago (1883); practiced law in Jacksonville (1883–87); and in 1887 moved to Lincoln, Neb., where he became active in Democratic politics. Elected to Congress in 1890, and reelected in 1892, he became a member of the silver bloc. An unsuccessful candidate for the Senate in 1894, he became editor in chief of the Omaha *World-Herald*, and at about this time began his long association with the Chautauqua lecture platform. Having already demonstrated in Congress his powers as an orator, he was much sought after as a public speaker advocating the free coinage of silver, and during 1894–95 went on speaking tours that augmented his reputation by the time the Democratic National Convention met at Chicago in 1896. His "Cross of Gold" speech (8 July 1896), his most famous oration, won him the presidential nomination. Conducting a brilliant and energetic campaign on the platform of the free coinage of silver in a sectional battle that saw the agrarian South and West aligned against the industrial and commercial Northeast, Bryan lost to William McKinley by 600,000 votes out of a total of 13,600,000. From 1896 until 1912 he was the virtually undisputed leader of the Democratic party. He advised Democrats in the Senate to approve the treaty of peace with Spain, but fought the presidential campaign of 1900 on the issue of anti-imperialism, receiving less votes than he had in 1896. In 1901 he established the weekly newspaper, the *Commoner*, which he edited and published until 1913, and in 1908 was again an unsuccessful presidential candidate. At the Democratic Convention of 1912, held in Baltimore, Bryan wielded considerable influence in securing the nomination of Woodrow Wilson on a liberal platform. As Secretary of State in Wilson's cabinet (1913–15) he adhered, after the outbreak of World War I, to strict neutrality. Differences with Wilson over the second *Lusitania* note led to his resignation from the cabinet (9 June 1915). A fundamentalist in religion, he drafted state legislation forbidding the teaching of evolution in public schools. When John T. Scopes, a teacher in Dayton, Tenn., was indicted for violating a state law of this nature, Bryan, on the prosecution staff, was subjected to withering examination by Clarence Darrow (*q.v.*), a defense attorney (1925).

Bryant, William Cullen (b. Cummington, Mass., 3 Nov. 1794; d. New York City, 12 June 1878), poet and editor, attended Williams College (1810–11); wrote the Federalist satire *The Embargo: or Sketches of the Times, a Satire; by a Youth of Thirteen* (1808); and in 1811 the first draft of the poem "Thanatop-

sis," first published in the *North American Review* in 1817. He studied law privately, was admitted to the bar in 1815, and finally established his practice at Great Barrington, Mass. He published *Poems* (1821), which included "The Ages," "To a Waterfowl," and "The Yellow Violet." His contributions (1824–25) to the *United States Literary Gazette* included "Monument Mountain" and the "Forest Hymn." By 1825 he had gained wide recognition as a poet. Abandoning his law practice, he moved to New York City in 1825 and for a year was coeditor of the *New York Review and Athenaeum Magazine*. In 1826 he was made assistant editor of the New York *Evening Post*; becoming its editor in 1829, he served in that capacity until his death. During his first decade as a newspaper editor he wrote relatively little poetry. A Jacksonian Democrat and a free trader, Bryant broke with the Democratic party in 1848, when he supported the Free-Soil ticket, and in 1856 became a Republican spokesman. During the Civil War, he took a radical stand on emancipation and the prosecution of the war, but afterward favored a liberal policy toward the South. He also published *Poems* (1832), *The Fountain, and Other Poems* (1842), and *The White-Footed Doe, and Other Poems* (1844). He ranks as one of the finest American lyric poets of nature.

Buchanan, James (b. near Mercersburg, Pa., 23 Apr. 1791; d. Wheatland, near Lancaster, Pa., 1 June 1868), 15th president of the U.S., was graduated from Dickinson College (1809), admitted to the Pennsylvania bar (1812), and practiced at Lancaster. Federalist state legislator (1815–16) and congressman (1820–31), he served as U.S. minister to Russia (1832–33), negotiating a commercial treaty, and was Democratic U.S. senator (1835–45). He entered Polk's cabinet as Secretary of State (1845–49), settled the Oregon dispute, and offered to purchase Cuba from Spain. Minister to Great Britain (1853–56), he joined with Mason and Soulé in drafting the "Ostend Manifesto" (1854). Democratic president of the U.S. (1857–61), he held slavery to be a moral wrong but urged acceptance of the Lecompton Constitution in Kansas (1858). Denying the right of states to secede, he failed to find the legal authority to meet secession and favored an amendment to the Constitution expressly recognizing slavery and the right to recover fugitive slaves. Although he endorsed Breckinridge in 1860, he supported the federal government during the Civil War.

Bulfinch, Charles (b. Boston, Mass., 8 Aug. 1763; d. there, 4 Apr. 1844), architect, was graduated from Harvard in 1781 and made a tour (1785–86) of England and the Continent, where, at Jefferson's suggestion, he studied the classical architecture of France and Italy that was to leave a lasting imprint on his style. He designed the old Hollis Street Church in Boston (1788), churches at Taunton and Pittsfield, the Beacon Monument (1789), the Boston Theater, the Massachusetts State House at Boston, and the State House at Hartford. His introduction of the Adamesque style (1792 *et seq.*), as in the Coolidge, Barrell, and Derby houses, led to a general adoption of that mode for New England residences during the early Federal period and influenced architect-builders such as Samuel McIntire and Asher Benjamin. Bulfinch also drew up plans for the Franklin Crescent (1793), the Harrison Gray Otis houses, India Wharf, the Boylston Market, additions to Faneuil Hall, the New South Church (1814), and the old courthouse, all at Boston; Christ Church at Lancaster (1816–17); the State Prison at Charlestown; the

Massachusetts General Hospital (1817–20); and the State Capitol at Augusta, Me. (1828–31). As chairman (1799–1817) of the Boston board of selectmen, he was largely responsible for the renovation and development of old Boston. He succeeded (1817) Benjamin H. Latrobe (*q.v.*) as architect of the Capitol Building at Washington, D.C., remaining in that post until the structure's completion in 1830.

Burr, Aaron (b. Newark, N.J., 6 Feb. 1756; d. Port Richmond, N.Y., 14 Sept. 1836), statesman, was graduated from the College of New Jersey (1772); studied theology briefly and then law. In 1775 he served in Arnold's expedition to Canada and, subsequently, on Washington's staff and then on Putnam's, becoming lieutenant colonel (1777). Admitted to the bar (1782), he moved from Albany to New York City (1783); became attorney general of New York (1789–91) and U.S. senator (1791–97). Defeated for reelection (1796), he served in the New York Assembly (1797–99). In the presidential election of 1800 he tied Jefferson. When the House of Representatives chose the latter, Burr became 3d vice-president of the U.S. He was defeated for governor of New York (1804). Provoked by published accusations made by his political foe, Alexander Hamilton, Burr mortally wounded Hamilton in a duel at Weehawken, N.J. (11 July 1804). He fled southward, but returned to preside over the impeachment trial of Supreme Court Justice Samuel Chase. In 1806 he became involved in a conspiracy which, whether to seize Mexico for the U.S. or to have the Western states secede from the Union, has never been clarified. Arrested by co-conspirator Gen. James Wilkinson, he was brought before Chief Justice Marshall (30 Mar. 1807), sitting at Richmond in the U.S. Circuit Court. Acquitted both of treason and of high misdemeanor, he resided in Europe (1808–12) and then practiced law in New York City.

Butler, Nicholas Murray (b. Elizabeth, N.J., 2 Apr. 1862; d. New York City, 7 Dec. 1947), educator and author, was graduated from Columbia (A.B., 1882; A.M., 1883; Ph.D., 1884), studied at Berlin and Paris (1884–85), and served at Columbia as an assistant (1885–86), tutor (1886–89), and adjunct professor of philosophy (1889–90). In 1889 he established the *Educational Review*, of which he was the first editor (1889–1920). He was the organizer and first president (1886–91) of Teachers College and, as president of Columbia, from 1901 until his retirement in 1945, he was outstandingly successful in expanding the university's effectiveness and prestige. Active in public affairs, Butler was Republican vice-presidential nominee in 1912. He was appointed (1905) a trustee of the Carnegie Foundation for the Advancement of Teaching, served as president (1925–45) of the Carnegie Endowment for International Peace, and was chairman (1937–45) of the Carnegie Corporation. In 1931 he shared the Nobel peace prize with Jane Addams.

Byrd, Richard Evelyn (b. Winchester, Va., 25 Oct. 1888; d. Boston, Mass., 11 Mar. 1957), naval officer, explorer, was graduated from the U.S. Naval Academy (1912), entered the Aviation Service (1917); and was commander (July–Nov. 1918) of the U.S. air forces in Canada. He made a dirigible flight across the Atlantic (1921) and was commander (1925) of the aviation unit of the Navy-MacMillan Polar Expedition. With Floyd Bennett, he made an airplane flight (9 May 1926) over the North Pole, for which he was awarded the Congressional Medal of Honor. With 3 companions, he made a 4,200-mile flight from New York to France (29 June–1 July 1927). He made his 1st expedition to the Antarctic in 1928–30, flying over the South Pole (29 Nov. 1929) from his base at "Little America." In his 2d expedition to the Antarctic (1933–35) he recorded important scientific data near the South Pole and discovered and named Maria Byrd Land and the Edsel Ford Mountains, and on his 3d (1939) he made flights that resulted in the discovery of 5 islands, 5 mountain ranges, and 100,-000 square miles of land area. He commanded the U.S. Navy Expedition (1946–47) which explored 1,700,000 square miles, tested equipment, made weather observations, and carried out a geological survey of the South Pole region.

Calder, Alexander (b. Lawton, Pa., 22 July 1898–   ), sculptor. Although the grandson and son (of Alexander Stirling Calder, 1870–1945) of well-known sculptors, Calder studied mechanical engineering, receiving a degree from Stevens Institute of Technology (1919) and worked at a variety of jobs, until he enrolled (1923) in the Art Students League of New York City, where he studied under John Sloan and George Luks, Kenneth Kayes Miller, Guy Pène du Bois, and Boardman Robinson. Du Bois, with his mannikinlike figures, and Robinson, with his background in journalistic illustrations, most directly influenced Calder. As an illustrator for the *National Police Gazette*, Calder came in contact with the circus (1925), attending performances frequently and drawing the animals and acrobats. He began to create a small circus of animals and performers out of wood and wire. In 1926 he set up a studio in Paris, displaying *Le Cirque Calder*, which was admired by Cocteau and Miro, among others. His sculptures of wood and metal (often just large sheets of steel), "stabiles," were first shown in 1931. His first "mobile," sections of wire and shaped sheets of metal in balance, suspended from a sphere, were shown the following year, and the first outdoor mobile designed in 1935. Mobiles were crafted for Martha Graham's *Panorama* at the Bennington (Vt.) School of the Dance and for other programs of hers. Calder designed the famous mobile *The Mercury Fountain* for the Spanish Pavilion at the Paris World's Fair (1937). Among his widely acclaimed mobiles are *The Whirling Ear* (Brussels Exposition, 1958), the hanging mobile for the John F. Kennedy International Airport, the *Big Sail* at MIT. Among his major stabiles are *Ticket Window* (Lincoln Center, New York City, 1965) and his largest, *Man*, standing 70 feet high, at Montreal's Expo '67. Calder's work is graceful and appealing, ofttimes humorous. He has worked on toys, jewelry, opaque watercolors, tapestries, and book illustrations.

Calhoun, John Caldwell (b. Abbeville District, S.C., 18 Mar. 1782; d. Washington, D.C., 31 Mar. 1850), statesman, was graduated from Yale (1804) and admitted to the South Carolina bar (1807). After a term in the South Carolina legislature (1808–09), he was in Congress (1811–17), where he became a leader of the "war hawks" and supported nationalistic legislation after the War of 1812, including the protective Tariff of 1816. He served as Secretary of War under Monroe (1817–25), was a candidate for president (1824), but was elected vice-president of the U.S., serving first under John Quincy Adams (1825–29) and then under Jackson (1829–32). Charged with having improperly received profits from a contract while Secretary of War, Calhoun demanded (29 Dec. 1826) a House investi-

gation. He was exonerated by a Select Committee (1827). In his "South Carolina Exposition" (1828), written in opposition to the Tariff of 1828, he postulated the principles of states' rights and nullification. Breaking with Jackson over Peggy Eaton and nullification, he resigned as vice-president (1832). As U.S. senator (1832–43) he became the leading proponent of states' rights. While Tyler's Secretary of State (1844–45), he secured the annexation of Texas. Again senator (1845–50), he opposed the Mexican War, the admission of California to statehood (because its constitution forbade slavery), and the Wilmot Proviso. In his last speech, on the Compromise of 1850, read to the Senate by Sen. James Murray Mason of Virginia (4 Mar. 1850), he approved the purpose of the act but criticized it for its failure to provide the South with adequate guarantees. In his "Discourse on the Constitution," posthumously published, he proposed a dual Executive (from North and South), each armed with a veto.

Cannon, Joseph Gurney (b. Guilford, N.C., 7 May 1836; d. Danville, Ill., 12 Nov. 1926), political leader. Raised in Indiana, he studied law under John P. Usher and for 6 months at the Cincinnati Law School and was admitted to the bar in Illinois (1858). He practiced law in Danville, Ill., and served as state's attorney for the 27th judicial district (1861–68). First elected to the U.S. House of Representatives in 1873, he served in Congress for the next 50 years except for 2 terms (1891–93, 1913–15) when first the Populists and then the Progressives defeated him. Except for sponsoring a bill granting a low rate on 2d class mail and another starting the parcel post system (1874), he sponsored little legislation. As speaker of the House (1903–11), Cannon brought the power of that office to its peak, ruling dictatorially in the interest of his fellow "Old Guard" Republicans. He instituted few parliamentary changes but fully exploited those of his predecessors. Recognition was made entirely arbitrary; usually "Uncle Joe" recognized on the floor only those who had previously secured permission to speak. He made the Rules Committee an even more potent instrument of the speaker than it had been—its clearance was normally granted only for measures which Cannon approved and procedures were followed whereby "riders" added by him and his associates in committee stood little chance of defeat on the floor. He established a network of trusted lieutenants who were given key committee assignments. Cannon was shorn of his powers (1910) by a coalition of Democrats and insurgent Republicans. In the reaction, the speaker was barred from membership on the Rules Committee, the power of appointment to standing committees was transferred from the speaker to the full House, and the speaker's powers of recognition were limited to some extent.

Cardozo, Benjamin Nathan (b. New York City, 24 May 1870; d. Port Chester, N.Y., 9 July 1938), jurist, was graduated from Columbia (1889), admitted to the New York bar (1891), practicing law in New York until his election to the state supreme court (1913). Appointed to the state court of appeals (1917) and elected its chief judge (1927), he established that court's preeminent prestige and was the obvious choice to succeed O. W. Holmes on his retirement from the U.S. Supreme Court. Appointed by Hoover associate justice (1932), he aligned himself with the liberal wing (Brandeis and Stone) on social and economic issues. Although he vigorously concurred in the *Schechter Case* (1935)

in opposition to "delegation running riot," he just as vigorously dissented from the tendency of the majority to curb distasteful governmental policies (*Carter Case,* 1936), and upheld the Social Security Act under the general welfare clause (*Stevens Machine Co.* and *Helvering* v. *Davis,* 1937). His ideas of sociological jurisprudence and his position that adherence to precedent should be relaxed in the face of changing conditions were expressed in his writings (*The Nature of the Judicial Process,* 1921; *The Growth of the Law,* 1924; and *The Paradoxes of Legal Science,* 1928).

Carlson, Chester F. (b. Seattle, Wash., 8 Feb. 1906; d. New York City, 19 Sept. 1968), physicist and inventor. The son of a barber, Carlson supported his family from the time he was 12. Graduating from the California Institute of Technology (1930), he worked for a short time at Bell Telephone Co. and then took a job in the patent department of P. R. Mallory Co., an electronics firm in New York City. Finding it difficult to get copies of drawings of patents, Carlson started experimenting, using electrostatics to produce copies (1934). Working in a tiny one-room laboratory in Queens, he produced his first electrostatic copy, or Xerox, on 22 Oct. 1938, and received his first patent (1940). About the same time (1934–39) he studied law at night at New York Law School, and was admitted to the New York bar (1940). Four years later, after being refused by more than 20 companies, Carlson persuaded the Battelle Memorial Institute, a nonprofit research organization, to make Xerox copies. In 1947, the Haloid Co., a small company in Rochester, N.Y., later named Xerox Corp., bought the first commercial rights to Xerox. In 1958, the company introduced the first Xerox office machine, the

"914," whose widespread use revolutionized photocopying.

Carnegie, Andrew (b. Dunfermline, Scotland, 25 Nov. 1835; d. Lenox, Mass., 11 Aug. 1919), industrialist and philanthropist. Coming to the U.S. with his poverty-stricken parents (1848), he began his career in Allegheny, Pa., as a bobbin boy employed at $1.20 a week, then (1849) a messenger in the Pittsburgh telegraph office. At the age of 16 he became one of the first operators in the U.S. able to take messages by sound. In 1853 he became private secretary and personal telegrapher to Thomas A. Scott, general superintendent of the Pennsylvania R.R. Upon Scott's appointment (1860) as vice-president of the road, Carnegie was named superintendent of the Pittsburgh division; and when Scott was named assistant secretary of war (1861), Carnegie became superintendent of the eastern military and telegraph lines, performing notable services for the Union forces during the Civil War. Having reorganized the Keystone Bridge Works (1862), Carnegie resigned from the Pennsylvania R.R. (1865) to devote himself to the iron, oil, and other businesses. He established (1868) the Union Iron Mills, and beginning in 1873 concentrated solely on the steel industry. In the following 3 decades, during which the U.S. took the lead over British steel production, the rapid expansion of U.S. steel manufactures was largely his creation. Carnegie progressively added to his holdings by lease or purchase, and in 1888 took over the Homestead Steel Works. By 1900, the Carnegie Steel Co., which had been organized in 1899, controlled the bulk of U.S. steel production. After selling his company to the interests that formed the U.S. Steel Corp. (1901), Carnegie retired and devoted himself to philanthropy. He set up the Carnegie trusts and foundations, among them the Carnegie Institution of Washington (1902), the Carnegie Foundation for the Advancement of Teaching (1906), the Carnegie Endowment for International Peace (1910), the Carnegie Corp. of New York (1911), and the Carnegie United Kingdom Trust (1913). He endowed numerous libraries throughout the world. He wrote *The Gospel of Wealth* (1900).

Carothers, Wallace Hume (b. Burlington, Ia., 27 Apr. 1896; d. Philadelphia, Pa., 29 Apr. 1937), chemist, inventor, received his B.S. (1920) from Tarkio College, Mo., and his M.S. (1921) and Ph.D. (1924) from the Univ. of Illinois. His first independent papers, "Isosterism of Phenal Isocynate and Diazobenzene-Imide" (1923) and "The Double Bond" (1924), revealed his creativity in the field of theoretical organic chemistry. Instructor at Harvard (1926–28), he left to direct a fundamental research program in organic chemistry at E. I. du Pont de Nemours and Co. in Wilmington, Del. His interest in unsaturated compounds led to the production of a rubberlike polymer (1930) and to the commercial development of a synthetic rubber known as neoprene. The research of Carothers and his associates (1929–37) provided a general theory of polymerization processes, culminating (23 May 1934) in the synthesizing of a superpolymer, which led (1939) to the commercial production of nylon, the first completely synthetic fiber. Despondent over the death of his sister (1937), he committed suicide.

Carrier, Willis Haviland (b. Angola, N.Y., 26 Nov. 1876; d. New York City, 7 Oct. 1950), inventor and mechanical engineer. He received his E.E. degree from Cornell Univ. (1901). While an engineer at Buffalo Forge Co. (1901–15), Carrier developed the principles of air conditioning. He found that by regulating the temperature of a spray-water conditioning machine he could control the amount of water in the air. Carrier's *Rational Psychrometric Formulae* and *Air Conditioning Apparatus* (1911) mark the beginning of scientific air conditioning design. He also invented the dehumidifier, centrifugal refrigeration, central air conditioning, in which air ducts were used to produce uniform circulation in buildings, and developed the first application of air conditioning to railroad cars (1929–30). Carrier Engineering Corp. manufactured air conditioners from 1915–30, when it merged with York Heating and Ventilating Co. and Brunswick Kruesch Co.

Carver, George Washington (b. near Diamond Grove, Mo., c.1860; d. Tuskegee, Ala., 5 Jan. 1943), Negro agricultural chemist. Born of slave parents, he was illiterate until he was almost 20 years old. He worked his way through the Minneapolis (Kan.) high school and through the Iowa State College of Agriculture and Mechanic Arts (B.S., 1894; M.S., 1896), where he was head of the college greenhouse and of bacterial laboratory work in systematic botany (1894–96). In 1896 he became director of the department of agricultural research at Tuskegee Institute, Ala., where he remained for the rest of his life. Essentially a practical chemist, he used empirical methods in his work on the diversified utilization of common agricultural products, including the peanut, sweet potato, and soybean. His achievements exercised an important influence on the shift of the Southern agricultural economy from a single-crop basis to a diversified and more prosperous foundation. From the peanut and the sweet potato he developed more than a hundred different products, including plastics, lubricants, dyes, medicines, ink, wood stains, face creams, tapioca, and molasses. He also evolved the cross between the short-stalk and tall-stalk cotton known as "Carver's Hybrid." In 1940 he gave his life savings to establish the Carver Foundation for research in creative chemistry.

Cass, Lewis (b. Exeter, N.H., 9 Oct. 1782; d. Detroit, Mich., 17 June 1866), soldier, diplomat, statesman, attended Exeter Academy. He set out on foot from Wilmington, Del., for the Northwest Territory in 1801; he studied law under Gov. R. J. Meigs in Marietta, Ohio, and was admitted to the Ohio bar (1802). In the Ohio legislature (1806), he was U.S. Marshal for Ohio (1807–12), when he resigned to enlist in the army. Colonel and brigadier general, he played an important role in Harrison's victories over the British and Indians in the War of 1812. Governor of Michigan Territory (1813–31), he concluded treaties with the Indians. Jackson's Secretary of War (1831–36), he directed the Black Hawk War. Minister to France (1836–42), he resigned because of differences with Secretary of State Webster over a 5-party treaty legalizing the right of search, which he opposed. In a bid for the Democratic presidential nomination, he urged (Hannegan Letter, 10 May 1844) annexation of Texas. A nationalist and expansionist, he backed Polk's Oregon policy and opposed the Wilmot Proviso as senator from Michigan (1845–48). He resigned to run as the Democratic nominee for president in 1848, suffering defeat by Taylor as a result of party defection in New York and Pennsylvania. Senator again (1849–57), he favored the Compromise of 1850. As Buchanan's

Secretary of State (1857–60), he resigned 12 Dec. 1860 in protest against the president's decision not to reinforce the Charleston forts.

Cassatt, Mary (b. Allegheny City, Pa., 22 May 1844; d. Mensil-Theribus, France, 14 June 1926), painter. Having spent 5 years in Paris as a child (1852–57), she returned to the U.S. and studied at the Pennsylvania Academy of Fine Arts (1861–62), but then returned to Europe where she studied the work of the old masters, especially Correggio. Her first major show was in the Paris Salon (1872). She made that city her home (1874). A disciple of Dégas, influenced by Manet and by Japanese prints, Cassatt was the only American to exhibit her paintings in Paris with the Impressionists (1877–86). Outstanding Impressionist examples were *Little Girl in a Blue Armchair* (1878, Paul Mellon), *Dans la Loge* (1879, Paris), *The Boating Party* (1893, National Gallery, Washington), and *La Toilette* (Art Institute of Chicago, 1894). Much of her work was done in pastels and she employed a richer and wider assortment of colors than other Impressionists. Her work was notable for simplicity and originality. Motherhood idealized was a major theme. While her visits to the U.S. were infrequent and Americans were slow to recognize her importance, she considered herself American and was awarded the Lippincott prize by the Pennsylvania Academy of Fine Arts (1904) for *Caress* (1902, National Collection Fine Arts, Washington), the same year she received the chevalier of the Legion of Honor from France. Her work was included in the famous Armory Show (New York, 1913). Her eyesight began to fail (1900) and she ceased to work by 1914.

Cather, Willa Sibert (b. Winchester, Va., 7 Dec. 1876; d. New York City, 24 Apr. 1947), novelist, moved with her parents to Nebraska (1884) and graduated from the Univ. of Nebraska (1895). She taught school, did newspaper work in Pittsburgh, and published her first book of stories, *The Troll Garden* (1905). Editor, *McClure's Magazine* (1907–12), she resigned to devote herself to creative writing. Her novels, poignant recollections of a pioneer past stressing the supremacy of moral and spiritual over material values, are economically constructed and marked by a graceful, lucid style. They include: *O Pioneers!* (1913), *The Song of the Lark* (1915), *My Antonia* (1918), *One of Ours* (1922, a Pulitzer prize-winner), *A Lost Lady* (1923, often regarded as her best work), *Death Comes for the Archbishop* (1927), and *Shadows on the Rock* (1931).

Channing, William Ellery (b. Newport, R.I., 7 Apr. 1780; d. Bennington, Vt., 2 Oct. 1842), Unitarian clergyman. Graduating from Harvard in 1798, he was ordained and installed (1803) as minister of the Federal Street Church at Boston, a pastorate he held until his death. His humane and liberal theology touched off the "Unitarian Controversy" that saw Channing and his followers ranged against orthodox Calvinists. The controversy reached its height c.1815. Expressing the viewpoint of members of Congregationalist and other sects who were dissatisfied with Calvinist doctrine, particularly its emphasis on the depravity of man, he preached the gospel of goodness and love, the dignity and perfectibility of man, the validity of reason, and freedom of will and moral responsibility, but accepted the supernatural in Christianity. Channing became the acknowledged head of the Unitarians, whose formal emergence was precipitated by the sermon he delivered at Baltimore (1819) at the ordination of

Jared Sparks, an address in which he formulated the Unitarian creed. Channing organized the Berry Street conference of liberal ministers (1820), the predecessor of the American Unitarian Association (1825). After 1825 his influence spread beyond religious circles. His addresses on education, literature, slavery, and war attracted wide attention; some of them were published in pamphlet form, including *Remarks on American Literature* (1830), *Slavery* (1835), *The Abolitionist* (1836), and *Duty of the Free States* (1842). The moral and religious forces which he liberated were the bases of New England Transcendentalism.

Chase, Salmon Portland (b. Cornish, N.H., 13 Jan. 1808; d. New York City, 7 May 1873), statesman, was graduated from Dartmouth (1826), admitted to the bar (1829), and commenced law practice in Cincinnati (1830). Through his defense of fugitive slaves he became a leader of the antislavery movement, an organizer (1841) of the Liberty party, and a founder (1848) of the Free-Soil party. As U.S. senator (1849–55) he opposed the Compromise of 1850 and the Kansas-Nebraska Bill. Republican governor of Ohio (1855–60), he was again elected to the U.S. Senate (1860). Unsuccessful candidate for president in that year, he became Lincoln's Secretary of the Treasury, maintaining credit and funds to prosecute the Civil War and recommending the National Banking Act (1863). Opposing Seward in the cabinet, his resignation was finally accepted (June 1864), but in Dec. of that year Lincoln appointed him Chief Justice of the U.S. Supreme Court. He reorganized the federal courts in the South, presided over the trial of Jefferson Davis and favored quashing the indictment (1867), and over the Senate

impeachment proceedings against President Johnson (1868). In the *Hepburn Case* (1870) he declared the opinion of the court invalidating the Legal Tender Act of 1862 making "greenbacks" (issued by him as Secretary of the Treasury) legal tender, and dissented from the reversal (1871). He stood with the majority of the court in decisions upholding the Republican policy of Reconstruction.

Clark, George Rogers (b. Charlottesville, Va., 19 Nov. 1752; d. Louisville, Ky., 13 Feb. 1818), conqueror of the Northwest, explored the Ohio (1772) and Kentucky rivers (1774), the latter as surveyor for the Ohio Co. Commissioned major in charge of the defense of the Kentucky area when the Revolution broke out, his plan for the conquest of the Illinois country was endorsed by Virginia's governor, Patrick Henry (*q.v.*). As lieutenant colonel he set out with a company of 175 men, capturing Kaskaskia and Vincennes (1778), soon lost to British counterattack. In a heroic winter march of 180 miles he recaptured Vincennes (1779), forcing Lt. Gov. Henry Hamilton to surrender. In 1780 he met a British threat to the Spanish outpost in St. Louis, was on the defensive in 1781, but held fast to the key bastion of Ft. Nelson on the Falls of the Ohio (1782). The close of the war found Kentucky in U.S. hands and much of Ohio and Illinois, and by the Treaty of Paris (1783) the Northwest was given to the U.S. In 1786 James Wilkinson made political capital out of Clark's seizure of Spanish goods at Vincennes (1786) in order to provision his garrison. Involved in 2 French projects (1793, 1798) to lead an expedition against the Spanish for the reconquest of Louisiana, he refused a U.S. demand to surrender his generalship in the French army, taking refuge in St. Louis. In later life he was interested in Indian history and archaeology.

Clark, William, see **Lewis, Meriwether, and Clark, William.**

Clay, Henry (b. Hanover Co., Va., 12 Apr. 1777; d. Washington, D.C., 29 June 1852), statesman, studied law in Richmond, was admitted to the bar (1797), and practiced in Lexington, Ky. Kentucky legislator (1803–06), he filled an unexpired term in the U.S. Senate (1806–07), became speaker of the state legislature (1807–09), and filled another unexpired term in the Senate (1809–10). While congressman (1811–21, 1823–25), he was speaker (1811–20 and 1823–25) and was a leader of the "war hawks." A commissioner to negotiate peace with Great Britain (1814), he urged recognition of South American republics by the U.S. (1817) and was influential in framing the Missouri Compromise (1820). As a candidate for president (1824), he was 4th in the number of electoral votes, throwing his support to John Quincy Adams, whose Secretary of State (1825–29) he became. Senator (1831–42 and 1849–52), Clay was the Whig candidate for president (1832), but was defeated by Jackson largely because of his support of the 2d Bank of the U.S. His "American System" was based upon tariff protection and federal aid for internal improvements. He sponsored the compromise Tariff of 1833, failed to secure the Whig nomination in 1840, and ran in 1844, losing because of his noncommittal stand on Texas. His sponsorship of the Compromise of 1850 earned him the title "The Great Pacificator."

Clemens, Samuel Langhorne [pseudonym **Mark Twain**] (b. Florida, Mo., 30 Nov. 1835; d. Redding, Conn., 21 Apr. 1910), novelist and humorist, was reared in Hannibal, Mo. (1839–53), where, at the age of 12, he was apprenticed to a printer. As a journeyman printer he worked (1853–57) in cities in the Old West and along the Eastern seaboard, and from 1857 to 1861 served successively as apprentice pilot and licensed pilot on Mississippi steamboats. In 1861 he became secretary to his brother Orion, who had just been named secretary to the territorial governor of Nevada. After an unsuccessful attempt at prospecting and mining, he became (1862) a reporter on the *Territorial Enterprise* in Virginia City, using for the first time the pseudonym Mark Twain (a river term indicating 2 fathoms deep), by which he is best known. This had been the nom de plume of Capt. Isaiah Sellers (d. 1863). Going to California in 1864, he wrote in the following year the humorous story "The Celebrated Jumping Frog of Calaveras County," which was reprinted in newspapers throughout the U.S. and served as the title of his first book (1867). After taking an assignment as a roving correspondent in the Sandwich Islands, he began (1866) his long career as a lecturer. A commission as a travel correspondent for a San Francisco newspaper took him to the Mediterranean and the Holy Land, a trip that provided the material for *The Innocents Abroad* (1869), a book that brought him a national reputation. He lived in Buffalo (1869–71), writing for the Buffalo *Express,* and married (1870) Olivia Langdon of Elmira, N.Y. His outstanding books include *Roughing It* (1872), *The Adventures of Tom Sawyer* (1876), *Life on the Mississippi* (1883), *The Adventures of Huckleberry Finn* (1884), *A Connecticut Yankee at King Arthur's Court* (1889), and *The Tragedy of Pudd'nhead Wilson* (1894). See also p. 860. *Mark Twain's Autobiography* was published in 1924.

A growing despair and bitterness toward the end of his life was reflected in *What Is Man?* (1906) and *The Mysterious Stranger* (1916). At his best, Twain raised to the level of universal human appeal the lusty humor of the frontier.

Cleveland, Stephen Grover (b. Caldwell, N.J., 18 Mar. 1837; d. Princeton, N.J., 24 June 1908), 22d and 24th president of the U.S., studied law in Buffalo and was admitted to the New York bar (1859). Assistant district attorney of Erie County (1863), elected Democratic sheriff (1869), mayor of Buffalo (1881–82), and governor of New York (1882–84), he was elected Democratic president of the U.S. (1885–89). He married Frances Folsom (1886) at the White House. His conciliatory attitude toward the South, his vetoes of over two-thirds of bills presented to him (mostly private pension bills), and his tariff reduction proposal (1887) contributed to his defeat by Harrison in 1888. Again elected president (1892), serving 1893–97, he took a "hard money" stand and had Congress repeal the Sherman Silver Purchase Act (1893) following the panic of that year. By sending troops into Illinois to break the Pullman strike and permitting Attorney General Olney to employ a railroad attorney as special counsel to the government (4 July 1894), he alienated labor. Cleveland intervened in the boundary dispute between Great Britain and Venezuela (1895). An anti-imperialist, he withdrew the U.S. treaty of annexation of Hawaii (1893), although he recognized the republic the following year.

Clinton, De Witt (b. Little Britain, Orange Co., N.Y., 2 Mar. 1769; d. Albany, 11 Feb. 1828), statesman, was graduated from Columbia (1786), studied law, was admitted to the New York bar (1788), and became private secre-

tary (1790–95) to his uncle George Clinton, governor of New York. State assemblyman (1797–98) and state senator (1798–1802), he is credited with introducing the "spoils system" when serving on the Council of Appointment. In the legislature he sponsored relief for prisoners for debt, the abolition of slavery, and the promotion of steam navigation. Elected to the U.S. Senate (1802), he resigned to become mayor of New York City (1803–15, except for 1807–08 and 1810–11), in which office his record was outstanding. As chief organizer of the Public School Society (1805) and sponsor of the Lancastrian school system, he laid the foundation of the public school system in New York. Candidate of the New York Republicans (1812) in the presidential race of that year, he was defeated by Madison, 128–89. Appointed (1817) commissioner to examine and survey the route for the Erie Canal, he was chiefly responsible for its successful completion in 1825. Elected governor (1817) and reelected (1820), he retired from office in 1823 when the "Albany Regency" became supreme. Public reaction to his removal from office as canal commissioner (1824) led to his reelection as governor (1825–28).

Clinton, George (b. Little Britain, N.Y., 26 July 1739; d. Washington, D.C., 20 Apr. 1812), statesman, studied law under William Smith in New York City and returned to practice in Ulster Co. In the New York Assembly (1768) and the 2d Continental Congress (1775–76), as brigadier general of militia he unsuccessfully defended Ft. Montgomery against Sir Henry Clinton (1777). Seven-term governor of New York, serving from 1777–95 and from 1801–04, he may be considered the "father" of the state. Leader of the New York Antifederalists, he was outspoken in opposition to the Constitution, unwilling to surrender either his own power or any significant vestige of state sovereignty. As "Cato" his arguments in the N.Y. *Journal* against the Constitution were answered by "Caesar" (allegedly Hamilton) in the *Daily Advertiser*. His plan (1783) for a series of canals connecting the Hudson with Lakes Ontario and Champlain (1783) were later carried out by his nephew De Witt Clinton (*q.v.*). Elected vice-president (1804 and again 1808), he registered his old animosity against Hamilton and his contempt for Madison by casting (1811) the deciding vote against the bill to recharter the Bank of the U.S.

Cohn, Edwin Joseph (b. New York City, 17 Dec. 1892; d. Boston, Mass., 2 Oct. 1953), biochemist, was graduated from the Univ. of Chicago (B.S., 1914; Ph.D., 1917), held a National Research Council fellowship (1919–22) during his studies at the Carlsberg Laboratory in Copenhagen and at Cambridge Univ., and became (1922) assistant professor of physical chemistry at the Harvard Medical School, where he served (1935–49) as professor of biochemistry and head of the department of physical chemistry, and after 1949 as director of the physical chemistry laboratory at Harvard. His most notable researches have been made in the protein fractionization of blood, particularly the isolation of albumin. Serum albumin, as precipitated by Cohn and his associates, is a nontoxic, stable, and compact blood substitute better suited to emergency conditions than stored whole blood or dried plasma and widely used in the U.S. armed services after Pearl Harbor. Gamma globulin contains antibodies which help prevent or treat diseases like measles and jaundice. Other pure plasma proteins isolated by fractionization (such as thrombin and fibrinogen, in combination as a blood-clotting agency) serve a variety of uses

in medicine and surgery. He wrote *Proteins, Amino Acids and Peptides* (with J. T. Edsall in 1943).

Compton, Arthur Holly (b. Wooster, Ohio, 10 Sept. 1892; d. Berkeley, Calif., 15 Mar. 1962), physicist and educator, was graduated from the College of Wooster (B.S., 1913) and Princeton (M.A., 1914; Ph.D., 1916); was an instructor in physics (1916–17) at the Univ. of Minnesota; research engineer (1917–19) for the Westinghouse Lamp Co.; research fellow (1919–20) at the Cavendish Laboratory, Cambridge Univ.; professor of physics (1920–23) at Washington Univ., St. Louis, and (1923–45) at the Univ. of Chicago. Chancellor of Washington Univ. (1945–53), he then became distinguished service professor of natural philosophy. His investigations (1923 *et seq.*) of the scattering of X rays by matter led to his discovery of the change of wave length known as the Compton effect. He also discovered the total reflection and (with C. H. Hagenow) polarization of X rays. With C. T. R. Wilson, he was the joint recipient (1927) of the Nobel prize in physics. He also did important work on cosmic rays, in which field he directed a worldwide study (1931–33) and showed the electrical composition of cosmic rays and their variation with altitude and latitude. As wartime director (1942–45) of plutonium research for the U.S. atomic bomb project, he guided the development of the first quantity production of plutonium.

Conant, James Bryant (b. Dorchester, Mass., 26 Mar. 1893–   ), chemist, diplomat, educator, received his A.B. (1913) and Ph.D. (1916) from Harvard, where he taught chemistry (1916–33), with an interruption during World War I for service as lieutenant, Sanitary Corps, U.S. army, and major in the Chemical Warfare Service. He did notable research in the field of organic chemistry, specifically on the structure of chlorophyll and hemoglobin. President of Harvard (1933–53), he introduced significant reforms as regards admissions and curriculum. Chairman (1941–46) of the National Defense Research Comm., he had a key role in the production of the atomic bomb, was instrumental in the creation of the National Science Foundation (1950), and was a member of the general advisory committee, AEC (1947–52). He was high commissioner to West Germany (1953–55) and U.S. ambassador there (1955–57). He made extensive investigations of U.S. high schools (1957–62) and the education of American teachers (1962–63) under Carnegie grants, publishing several works including *The American High School Today* (1959), *Slums and Suburbs* (1961), *The Education of American Teachers* (1963), *Shaping Educational Policy* (1964), *The Comprehensive High School* (1967). He wrote numerous works in organic chemistry (1928) and *The Chemistry of Organic Compounds* (1933). He authored *My Several Lives* (1970).

Cooke, Jay (b. in present-day Sandusky, Ohio, 10 Aug. 1821; d. Ogontz, Pa., 16 Feb. 1905), banker and financier, was a clerk at St. Louis and at Philadelphia, where he entered (1839) the banking house of E. W. Clark & Co., from which he retired (1857) to participate in the general banking business. In 1861 he formed with his brother-in-law the banking house of Jay Cooke & Co. at Philadelphia, which during the Civil War acted as agent for the U.S. government in floating bond issues for meeting military requirements. In 1865 he was appointed fiscal agent of the Treasury Department. During the course of the war he floated $2,500 million worth of bonds at virtually no profit to himself. His firm

became financial agent for the Northern Pacific R.R. Its connection with that enterprise led to its failure (18 Sept. 1873), precipitating the panic of that year. Compelled to go into bankruptcy, Cooke later repaid his creditors and recouped his fortune.

Cooley, Thomas McIntyre (b. near Attica, N.Y., 6 Jan. 1824; d. Ann Arbor, Mich., 12 Sept. 1898), jurist, was admitted to the Michigan bar (1846) and practiced in Tecumseh and Adrian. He compiled the state statutes (1857), became reporter for the state supreme court (1858), and published his *Digest of Michigan Reports* (1866). Professor of law (1859–84) and of American history (1884–98) at the Univ. of Michigan, he was justice of the state supreme court (1864–85) and chairman of the ICC (1887–91), where he was largely responsible for turning it into a quasi-judicial body and for formulating ruling principles of rate regulation. His most important writings were on constitutional law. *The Constitutional Limitations Which Rest upon the Legislative Power of the States of the American Union* (1868), with its doctrine of implied constitutional limitations upon the state's legislative power, was the basis for widening the scope of the doctrine of judicial review, while his concept of due process provided the courts with authority to curb government intervention in the economic and social sphere. With Story, he ranks as the most influential commentator on the Constitution. Other works include *The Law of Taxation* (1876), *Treatise on the Law of Torts* (1879), and *General Principles of Constitutional Law in the U.S.* (1880).

Coolidge, Calvin (b. Plymouth, Vt., 4 July 1872; d. Northampton, Mass., 5 Jan. 1933), 30th president of the U.S., was graduated from Amherst (1895) and practiced law at Northampton (1897). Member of the Massachusetts General Court (1907–08), mayor of Northampton (1910–11), state senator (1912–15, serving as president of that body, 1914–15), and lieutenant governor (1916–18), he came into national prominence as governor (1919–20) through his suppression of the Boston police strike (1919). Elected Republican vice-president of the U.S., he became president on Harding's death (2 Aug. 1923), and was elected president (1924), serving 1925–29. He twice vetoed the McNary-Haugen Farm Relief Bill, refused to intervene in the general coal strike (1927), and did not "choose" to run for president in 1928. On 4 Dec. 1928 he told Congress: "The country . . . can anticipate the future with optimism." He left office before the 1929 crisis.

Cooper, James Fenimore (b. Burlington, N.J., 15 Sept. 1789; d. Cooperstown, N.Y., 14 Sept. 1851), novelist, historian, and social critic, was expelled from Yale, where he was a member of the class of 1806. He shipped before the mast (1806–07), was commissioned midshipman in the U.S. Navy (1808), and resigned from the service in 1810. From 1811 to 1822 he followed the life of a country squire. His first novel, *Precaution* (1820), was a conventional story with an English background that he wrote for his own satisfaction, but in *The Spy* (1821), where Cooper used a native setting for a theme drawn from the Revolutionary period, he showed signs of his powerful narrative gift. The novel enjoyed an international success. In 1822 Cooper moved to New York to follow a literary career. His most famous work, the Leatherstocking series, includes the following novels: *The Pioneers* (1823), *The Last of the Mohicans*

(1826), *The Prairie* (1827), *The Pathfinder* (1840), and *The Deerslayer* (1841). He also wrote *The Pilot* (1824) and *Lionel Lincoln* (1825) before going to Europe (1826), where he found the themes and settings for the novels *The Bravo* (1831), *The Heidenmauer* (1832), and *The Headsman* (1833). During his European stay he also published novels with an American background, such as *The Red Rover* (1828), *The Wept of Wish-ton-Wish* (1829), and *The Water-Witch* (1831), and gathered the material for the following travel accounts: *Sketches of Switzerland* (1836), *Gleanings in Europe* (1837), *Gleanings in Europe: England* (1837), and *Gleanings in Europe: Italy* (1838). Upon his return to the U.S. in 1833 he published *A Letter to His Countrymen* (1834) and *The American Democrat* (1838), forthright criticisms of the provincialism of his native land that precipitated a quarrel between Cooper and his public that lasted for several years. The same critical viewpoint was incorporated in novels such as *Homeward Bound* (1838) and *Home as Found* (1838), and, to some extent, in *The Monikins* (1835). After 1834, when Cooper lived at Cooperstown, he enjoyed his most productive period, including the writing of a scholarly *History of the Navy of the United States of America* (1839).

Cooper, Peter (b. New York City, 12 Feb. 1791; d. there, 4 Apr. 1883), manufacturer, inventor, and philanthropist. After brief formal schooling, he was apprenticed (1808) to a New York coachmaker, and later manufactured cloth-shearing machines of his own invention, glue, and isinglass. In partnership with 2 others, he established (1828) the Canton Iron Works at Baltimore. In 1830 he designed and constructed for the Baltimore & Ohio R.R. the first steam locomotive (popularly known as "Tom Thumb") built in America. In 1845 he established at Trenton, N.J., a rolling mill where the first structural iron for fireproof buildings was rolled (1854); and in 1856 became the first U.S. iron manufacturer to use the Bessemer converter. Cooper was the chief financial supporter of Cyrus Field's Atlantic cable project and was president of the New York, Newfoundland & London Telegraph Co. He founded (1857–59) Cooper Union, an educational institute at New York City "for the advancement of science and art." He was the presidential candidate (1876) of the Greenback party and outlined his position on currency and other matters in *Political and Financial Ideas of Peter Cooper with an Autobiography* (1877) and *Ideas for a Science of Good Government* (1883).

Copley, John Singleton (b. Boston, Mass., 1738; d. London, 9 Sept. 1815), painter, probably received his early training under his stepfather, the painter and engraver Peter Pelham, and at about the age of 18 became a professional portraitist. In the 1760s and early 1770s he painted many of the prominent personages of New England. In 1766, following the exhibition in London of Copley's *The Boy with the Squirrel*, he was elected a Fellow of the Society of Artists of Great Britain. In 1771–72 he held sittings at New York and in 1774, partly at the urging of Benjamin West, left Boston. He made the Continental tour and settled (1775) in London, where he painted portraits and also historical subjects, notably *The Death of Lord Chatham*. In 1783 he was elected a member of the Royal Academy. Among his many portraits are those of John Adams, Samuel Adams, Mr. and Mrs. Thomas Mifflin, and Mr. and Mrs. Isaac Winslow.

Cotton, John (b. Derby, Derbyshire, England, 4 Dec. 1584; d. Boston, Mass., 23 Dec. 1652), Puritan divine and author. He was graduated from Cambridge (A.B., 1603; A.M., 1606), was ordained deacon and priest (1610), and served as head lecturer and dean of Emmanuel College, Cambridge. In 1613 he received his divinity degree. While serving as vicar of St. Botolph's at Boston, Lincolnshire, he was attracted (c.1615) to Puritan tenets. A friend of John Winthrop, he preached the farewell sermon at Southampton when the *Arbella* departed for America (1630). In 1633 Cotton arrived at Boston aboard the *Griffin* and became teacher of the church at Boston. His change from liberalism to orthodox conformity is evidenced in the Antinomian controversy, during which his initial defense of Anne Hutchinson (*q.v.*) gave way to support of her excommunication and banishment from Massachusetts Bay. A prolific author, he prepared a code of laws for the colony, "Moses his Judicialls" (1636), which was not adopted, and wrote treatises on Congregationalism, such as *The Keyes of the Kingdom of Heaven* (1644), *The Way of the Churches of Christ in New England* (1645), and *The Way of the Congregational Churches Cleared* (1648). He also wrote *Milk for Babes* (1646), a children's catchism which long remained standard in New England. Cotton's controversy with Roger Williams (*q.v.*), which led the latter to write *The Bloudy Tenent of Persecution* (1644), brought in reply Cotton's *The Bloudy Tenent Washed and Made White* (1647).

Crane, Stephen (b. Newark, N.J., 1 Nov. 1871; d. Badenweiler, Germany, 5 June 1900), novelist and short-story writer, worked as a newspaper correspondent in Asbury Park, N.J., and attended Lafayette College and Syracuse Univ. (1890–91). He settled in New York City, where he was a reporter for the *Tribune* and *Herald,* and in 1892 published at his own expense his first novel, *Maggie: A Girl of the Streets,* a study of New York slum life that revealed Crane's strong bent for realism. His Civil War novel, *The Red Badge of Courage* (1895), brought him instant fame. In 1896 his adventures with a filibustering expedition bound for Cuba provided him with the substance of the short story "The Open Boat." As a war correspondent he covered the Spanish-American and Greco-Turkish wars. His last 2 years were spent in England, where he formed friendships with such authors as Joseph Conrad, Henry James, and H. G. Wells. He died of tuberculosis. Among his works are *The Black Riders and Other Lines* (1895, verse), *The Little Regiment and Other Episodes of the Civil War* (1896), *George's Mother* (1896), *The Third Violet* (1897), *Active Service* (1899), *The Monster* (1899), *War Is Kind* (1899, verse), *Wounds in the Rain* (1900), *Whilomville Stories* (1900), *The O'Ruddy* (1903), and *Men, Women, and Boats* (1921).

Croly, Herbert David (b. New York City, 23 Jan. 1869; d. Santa Barbara, Calif., 17 May 1930), editor, reformer, studied intermittently (1893–99) at Harvard with William James, Josiah Royce, and George Santayana, but did not receive his B.A. until 1910. Editor of the *Architectural Record* (1900–06), he gave up the editorship to write *The Promise of American Life* (1909), a Progressive classic. Combining a Hamiltonian belief in strong central government with advocacy of a positive program for social goals, it was a source of T.R.'s New Nationalism and of Wilson's New Freedom. Editor of the *New Republic,* founded 1914, he played a significant role in bringing about U.S. entry into World War I, but broke with Wilson

after publication of the Treaty of Versailles. His opposition to treaty ratification injured the magazine's circulation and influence. Other books include *Progressive Democracy* (1914) and *Marcus Alonzo Hanna, His Life and Work* (1912).

Cushing, Caleb (b. Salisbury, Mass., 17 Jan. 1800; d. Newburyport, Mass., 2 Jan. 1879), political leader and statesman. A prodigy, he was only 13 when he began studies at Harvard, where he graduated a member of Phi Beta Kappa and Latin Salutatorian (1817). After studying law (1817–19), he tutored mathematics and natural philosophy at Harvard (1819–21). He was admitted to the bar (1822) and practiced law, wrote political essays, and served intermittently in the state legislature before being elected to the U.S. House of Representatives (1834). During his 4 terms in the House (1835–43) he joined John Quincy Adams in opposing the "gag rule" which prevented the presentation of antislavery petitions on the floor, loyally supported President Harrison and, after his death, remained a Whig but chose to stand by President Tyler rather than to follow Henry Clay in his opposition program. Appointed by Tyler as minister plenipotentiary to China, Cushing negotiated the Treaty of Wang Hiya (3 July 1844), opening 5 Chinese ports to American merchants and ensuring extraterritorial legal rights for Americans living in China. Though out of office, he continued to be prominent in politics. An expansionist, he favored increased expenditures on defense and the acquisition of Texas, Oregon, and, later, Cuba. He served on the Supreme Judicial Court of Massachusetts (1852–53). He engineered the nomination of Franklin Pierce at the Democratic Convention of 1852 and served as President Pierce's attorney general (1853–57). He led the Democrats who nominated J. C. Breckinridge (1860) but supported Lincoln after secession convinced him that conciliation was impossible. He was a Republican thereafter. He acted as counsel for the U.S. at the arbitration of the Alabama Claims (1871–72) and was minister to Spain (1874–77). He was nominated by President Grant (1874) to be chief justice but his nomination was withdrawn after political opposition.

Cushing, Harvey William (b. Cleveland, Ohio, 8 Apr. 1869; d. New Haven, Conn., 7 Oct. 1939), neurological surgeon, specialist in brain surgery. He was graduated from Yale (A.B., 1891) and Harvard (A.M., M.D., 1895), was a practicing surgeon at Cleveland (1895–1902), and served as associate professor of surgery (1902–12) at Johns Hopkins, spending the years 1901–03 abroad studying under leading Continental surgeons. In 1912 he became professor of surgery at Harvard and surgeon in chief to the Peter Bent Brigham Hospital at Boston, holding these posts until 1932. During World War I he was senior consultant in neurological surgery to the A.E.F. He was Sterling professor of neurosurgery (1933–37) at Yale, where he was director in the history of medicine from 1937 until his death. During his service at the Peter B. Brigham Hospital he evolved a notable school of brain surgery based on experimental research in neurophysiology. He did important work on the operative treatment of facial paralysis, cerebral tumors, nerve block, and the intracranial hemorrhage of newborn babies; invented surgical instruments; pioneered in using the X ray and blood-pressure determination in the U.S.; and made contributions to endocrinology. He wrote the biography, *The Life of Sir William Osler* (2 vols., 1925), which was awarded the Pulitzer prize. Among his medical writings are *The Pituitary Body and Its Disorders* (1912), *Tumors of the Nervus Acusticus* (1917), *A Classification of the Glioma Group* (1926), *Intracranial Tumors* (1932), *Pituitary Body and Hypothalamus* (1932), and *Meningomas* (1939).

Cushman, Charlotte Saunders (b. Boston, Mass., 23 July 1816; d. there, 17 Feb. 1876), actress. In 1835 she made her debut as an operatic singer, but while performing at New Orleans in that year abandoned opera for the dramatic stage, appearing as Lady Macbeth. She came to New York (c.1836) and appeared (8 May 1837) for the first time as Meg Merrilies in *Guy Mannering*, one of her best-known roles. She won acclaim as Nancy Sykes in *Oliver Twist* (1837), was stage manager (1842–44) of the Walnut Street Theater at Philadelphia, and made her London debut (14 Feb. 1845) as Bianca in *Fazio*. Emerging in England as a Shakespearean actress of the first rank, she toured the U.S. (1849–52), playing male as well as female roles, and was received as the leading actress of the American stage. She lived in England until 1857, but gave frequent "farewell performances" in the U.S., to which she returned in 1870.

Darrow, Clarence (b. Kinsman, Ohio, 18 Apr. 1857; d. Chicago, 13 Mar. 1938), lawyer and reformer, attended Allegheny College and spent a year at Univ. of Michigan Law School. Admitted to the Ohio bar (1878), he removed to Chicago (1887), where he was junior law partner of John Peter Altgeld (*q.v.*). Supporter of many reform movements and opponent of capital punishment, he won a reputation as a preeminent trial lawyer by his defense of more than 50 persons charged with 1st-degree murder, of whom only one, Robert Prendergast (1894), was lost to the executioner. His defense of Eugene Debs (*q.v.*) in the injunction proceedings and conspiracy charges resulting from the rail strike of 1894 gave him national prominence. He successfully defended Haywood, Moyer, and Pettibone (1907), charged with being accessories to the murder of Gov. Frank Steunenberg of Idaho. Undertaking the defense (1924) of Nathan Leopold and Richard Loeb, tried for the kidnapping and murder of Robert Franks, his introduction of psychiatric evidence and his masterly summation resulted in the prisoners receiving life sentences. In the Scopes evolution trial (1925) he had a celebrated courtroom encounter with William Jennings Bryant (*q.v.*), whom he subjected to a merciless cross-examination. Normally on the side of the underdog, he surprised his admirers by acting as defense counsel in the Massie case (1932), a sensational Honolulu trial for the murder and kidnapping of a Hawaiian, in which he secured for his clients a nominal sentence.

Davis, Jefferson (b. Todd Co., Ky., 3 June 1808; d. New Orleans, La., 6 Dec. 1889), president of the Confederacy, was graduated from West Point (1828) and served in the Black Hawk War (1832). Resigning his commission (1835), he married Zachary Taylor's daughter (who died within 3 months) and became a Mississippi planter (married Varina Howell, 1845). Democratic congressman (1845–46), he resigned to command the Mississippi Rifles in the War with Mexico and was wounded at Buena Vista. U.S. senator (1847–51), he resigned to run for governor (1851), being narrowly defeated by Henry S. Foote. As Pierce's Secretary of War he strengthened the army and coast defenses, directed surveys for the transcontinental Southern route, and urged the president to sign the Kansas-Nebraska Bill (1854). Again senator (1857–61), he resigned 21 Jan. 1861, when Missis-

sippi seceded. On 18 Feb. 1861 he was inaugurated at Montgomery as provisional president of the provisional Confederate government, and was then elected for a 6-year term and inaugurated at Richmond (22 Feb. 1862). His autocratic methods and interference in military affairs aroused hostility among Confederate leaders. When Richmond fell he moved the executive offices to Danville, Va., and thence to Greensboro, N.C. At final cabinet meeting held at Charlotte (24 Apr. 1865), he conceded the end of the Confederacy. He was captured at Irwinville, Ga., and imprisoned at Ft. Monroe (1865–67). In 1866 he was indicted for treason; released on bail the following year, and the trial dropped. After travel abroad he made his home at Beauvoir, Miss., and wrote *Rise and Fall of the Confederate Government* (1881).

Davisson, Clinton Joseph (b. Bloomington, Ill., 22 Oct. 1881; d. Charlottesville, Va., 1 Feb. 1958), physicist, was graduated from the Univ. of Chicago (B.S., 1908) and Princeton (Ph.D., 1911); was an instructor in physics (1911–17) at the Carnegie Institute of Technology, Pittsburgh; and (1917–46) was a member of the research staff of the Bell Telephone laboratories (originally the engineering department of the Western Electric Co.) at New York. Beginning his researches on the electron in 1923, he discovered (1927, with Dr. L. H. Germer) the principle of electron diffraction (the exhibiting by electrons of wavelike as well as corpuscular properties). In 1928 he was awarded the Comstock prize for the "most important research in electricity, magnetism, and radiant energy made in North America" during the preceding 5 years. In 1937 Davisson and Germer discovered that the wave length of electrons depends on their velocity, confirming De Broglie's law (1932). He was awarded the Nobel prize in physics in 1937.

Debs, Eugene Victor (b. Terre Haute, Ind., 5 Nov. 1855; d. Elmhurst, Ill., 20 Oct. 1926), Socialist and labor leader. In 1870 he became a worker in the shops of the Terre Haute & Indianapolis R.R., subsequently becoming a locomotive fireman, and in 1875 took part in the organization of a Terre Haute Lodge of the Brotherhood of Locomotive Firemen, becoming secretary of the lodge. Debs was named (1880) national secretary and treasurer of the Brotherhood and editor of the *Firemen's Magazine*. An advocate of industrial unionism, he participated in the organization (1893) of the American Railway Union, of which he was made president. During the Pullman strike of 1894 he and other union leaders were held in contempt of court and sentenced to 6 months in jail. He emerged from his imprisonment a convert to socialism, and in 1897 founded the Social Democratic party of America, which in 1900 was formally united with a faction of the Socialist Labor party to form the Socialist party of America. He was 5 times a candidate for president on the Socialist ticket (1900, 1904, 1908, 1912, 1920). Sentenced to jail (1918) for 10 years on charge of violating the sedition provisions of the Espionage Act, he received during his confinement in the Atlanta penitentiary more than 900,-000 votes as Socialist candidate for the presidency. Debs was released (1921) by order of President Harding, but his citizenship was not restored. He was an editor of the *Appeal to Reason*, a Socialist weekly, and editor (1925–26) of the *American Appeal*, organ of Socialist and Progressive elements.

Decatur, Stephen (b. Sinepuxent, Md., 5 Jan. 1779; d. near Bladensburg, Md., 22 Mar. 1820), naval officer. During the naval war with France he was commissioned midshipman (30 Apr. 1798) and served in West Indian waters. He won fame during his service under Commo. Edward Preble in the Tripolitan War. On the evening of 16 Feb. 1804 Decatur and a boarding party recaptured the U.S. frigate *Philadelphia,* which had been stranded off Tripoli, and destroyed it, thus denying its use to the enemy. He was commissioned a captain and took part in the bombardments (3, 7 Aug. 1804) and subsequent assaults on Tripoli. He served (1808) as a member of the court-martial that suspended Capt. James Barron following the *Chesapeake-Leopard* encounter. During the War of 1812 he commanded the *United States* and the *President,* taking several valuable prizes, and was wounded in an engagement with the British blockading force off Long Island. In 1815 he commanded the squadron which compelled the Tripolitans to end their exactions of tribute and the other Barbary pirates to make compensation for damages inflicted by them during the War of 1812. Acclaimed as a hero on his return to the U.S., Decatur responded to a toast made at a dinner given in his honor: "Our country! In her intercourse with foreign nations may she always be in the right; but our country, right or wrong." He served (1815–20) on the Board of Navy Commissioners and was killed in a duel with Capt. James Barron.

De Forest, Lee (b. Council Bluffs, Iowa, 26 Aug. 1873; d. Hollywood, Calif., 30 June 1961), radio engineer and inventor, pioneer in the development of wireless communications, received his Ph.B. (1896) and Ph.D. (1899) from Yale, joined the experimental telephone laboratory of the Western Electric Co. at Chicago, and while engaged in working on wireless telegraphy for the Armour Institute of Technology at Chicago

(1900–02) designed the alternating current transmitter. He was the first to use the electrolytic receiver (a type of telephone receiver). He established (1902) the American De Forest (later United) Wireless Telegraph Co. at Jersey City, N.J., which installed at 5 U.S. Navy bases the first high-power naval radio stations. De Forest also developed several types of antennae, including the loop and direction antennae. His invention of the Audion amplifier (1905 *et seq.*), and in its improved form the 3-electrode vacuum tube, made possible transcontinental telephony after his telephone repeater rights were sold to the American Telephone and Telegraph Co. (1912). His invention of the oscillating Audion, first demonstrated in 1913, paved the way for the developments which earned him the sobriquet, "the father of radio broadcasting." The holder of more than 300 patents, he perfected the phonofilm method of sound recording, the glow-light recording of sound films, contributed to the development of television and high-speed facsimile transmission, and invented radio-therapy and the radio knife.

Dewey, George (b. Montpelier, Vt., 26 Dec. 1837; d. Washington, D.C., 16 Jan. 1917), naval officer, was graduated (1858) from the U.S. Naval Academy and became executive officer of the *Mississippi*, which was part of Farragut's fleet at the Battle of New Orleans (1862). Dewey became (1889) chief of the Bureau of Equipment in the Navy Department, and was appointed (1895) president of the Board of Inspection. He attained the rank of commodore and was ordered (Nov. 1897) to assume command of the Asiatic Squadron, which he led during the Spanish-American War. Learning (26 Apr. 1898) that war had been declared, Dewey led his squadron,

which he had been holding in readiness for such a contingency, from Mirs Bay to Manila, 600 miles away. He entered Manila Bay at dawn on 1 May 1898 and in 7 hours of fighting destroyed 8 Spanish warships, thus eliminating the enemy's naval power in the Far East. The victory assured the U.S. possession of the Philippines and made Dewey a national hero. Congress created for him the rank of admiral of the navy. He served (1900–17) as president of the General Board of the Navy Department.

Dewey, John (b. Burlington, Vt., 20 Oct. 1859; d. New York City, 1 June 1952), philosopher and educator, was graduated from Univ. of Vermont (B.A., 1879) and Johns Hopkins (Ph.D., 1884); taught philosophy at Univ. of Michigan (1884–88, 1890–94) and Univ. of Minnesota (1889); headed the philosophy department at Univ. of Chicago (1894–1904), where he was also director of the school of education (1902–04); and in 1904 joined the faculty of Columbia. As a philosopher, Dewey was the foremost exponent of the pragmatism of William James and evolved a view of environmental and functional reality called "instrumentalism" that has been widely influential in American social thought. In the field of education, he proved a major force in the development of progressive education. Among his many works are *The School and Society* (1899), *The Child and the Curriculum* (1902), *How We Think* (1909), *The Influence of Darwin on Philosophy and Other Essays in Contemporary Thought* (1910), *Essays in Experimental Logic* (1916), *Democracy and Education* (1916), *Human Nature and Conduct* (1922), *Experience and Nature* (1925), *The Quest for Certainty* (1929), *Philosophy and Civilization* (1931), *Art as Experience* (1934), *Ex-*

perience and Education (1938), *Freedom and Culture* (1939), and *Problems of Men* (1946).

Dickinson, Emily Elizabeth (b. Amherst, Mass., 10 Dec. 1830; d. there, 15 May 1886), poet, attended Amherst Academy and Mt. Holyoke Female Seminary (1847–48). Except for a trip to Washington and Philadelphia (1854) and 2 journeys to Boston (1864, 1865), she never left Amherst, where she gradually withdrew from society. She never married. During her lifetime only 2 of her poems were published. Her intense spiritual life was expressed in poetry whose directness of vision and vivid imagery are found in posthumously published works that include *Poems* (1890), *Poems: Second Series* (1891), *Poems: Third Series* (1896), *The Single Hound* (1914), *Further Poems* (1929), and *Unpublished Poems* (1936).

Dickinson, John (b. Talbot Co., Md., 8 Nov. 1732; d. Wilmington, Del., 14 Feb. 1808), statesman, moved with his parents in 1740 to Dover, where he studied privately under a tutor. In 1750 he began the study of law in the office of John Moland of the Philadelphia bar. After 3 years at the Middle Temple in London he returned in 1757 to Philadelphia, where he began to practice law and quickly rose to eminence in his profession. Elected to the Delaware assembly (1760–62) and the Pennsylvania assembly (1762–65 and 1770–76), he opposed Benjamin Franklin and defended the proprietary system. His pamphlet *The Late Regulations Respecting the British Colonies* (1765), showing the economic injury to the British business interests resulting from the Sugar and Stamp Acts, led to his designation by the Pennsylvania legislature as a delegate to the Stamp Act Congress in New York, where he drafted the resolutions petitioning the king and Parliament for the repeal of the Stamp Act. His pamphlet *Letters from a Farmer in Pennsylvania to the Inhabitants of the British Colonies* (1768), written in opposition to the Townshend Acts, denied the authority of Parliament to tax the colonies in whatever form. It proved enormously influential in shaping colonial opinion. Thereafter he pursued an increasingly conservative course, opposing the use of force by the colonists. In the 1st Continental Congress from Pennsylvania he drew up the Petition to the King and the Address to the People of Canada; in the 2d Continental Congress as a Delaware member (1776, 1777, 1779, 1780), his 2d Petition to the King, or "Olive Branch Petition." Coauthor with Thomas Jefferson of the "Declaration of the Causes of Taking up Arms" (1775), he opposed the Declaration of Independence but stayed away from the final vote. In Congress he headed a committee which drafted (1776) the Articles of Confederation. Subsequently he served (1781) as president of the Delaware Supreme Executive Council and as president of Pennsylvania, 1782–85, and was a delegate and signer from Delaware to the Federal Convention. In the "Fabius" letters he advocated the adoption of the Constitution. His political writings in 2 vols. were published in 1801. He was a founder (1783) of Dickinson College, Carlisle, Pa., which was named for him.

Disney, Walter Elias (b. Chicago, Ill., 5 Dec. 1901; d. Los Angeles, Calif., 15 Dec. 1966), artist, film producer. He studied cartoon drawing at night at the Academy of Fine Arts, Chicago, left high school to drive an ambulance in France during World War I (1918), then worked as a cartoonist in Kansas City (1919–22). He organized his own company to make cartoons of fairy tales (1920) and moved it to Hollywood (1923), where he produced *Alice in Cartoonland* (1923–26) and *Oswald the Rabbit* (1926–28). These were the first motion pictures that combined animation with live action, a technique used successfully again in *Mary Poppins* (1964). The idea to use a rodent as a protagonist came to Disney on a train ride from New York City to Los Angeles (1927). First named Mortimer Mouse, then renamed Mickey, drawn by Ubbe Iwerks, it first appeared in *Plane Crazy* (1928), a filmed cartoon with sound track. In Mickey Mouse, Donald Duck, Pluto, Goofy, and other animated characters, he created the most popular of movie stars and the foundation of an entertainment empire. *Snow White and the Seven Dwarfs* (1937) was his first feature-length animated cartoon. It was followed by *Pinocchio* (1940), *Dumbo* (1941), *Bambi* (1942), *Cinderella* (1950), and *Alice in Wonderland* (1951). In 1943 he produced *Victory Through Air* to illustrate the importance of the airplane in modern warfare. During World War II he also produced a number of films for the government used for training in defense plants and the military. He achieved commercial success with "true-adventure" nature films (*Seal Island*, 1948; *The Living Desert*, 1953) and live-action adventure films (*20,000 Leagues Under the Sea*, 1954; *Swiss Family Robinson*, 1960). He was the first major movie producer to make shows for TV (1954). Disney was the creator of the world-famous amusement park Disneyland (1955) in Anaheim, Calif., termed "the greatest piece of urban design in the U.S. today," and of its successor, Disneyworld, near Orlando, Fla. (opened posthumously, 1 Oct. 1971). The appeal of his work is traceable in part to his evocation of simpler times, his combination of realism and fantasy, and

his ability to recreate "old-fashioned" beauty. During his career he received 29 Oscars, 4 Emmys, and the Presidential Medal of Freedom (1964). His work has captivated a new generation with the re-release of *Fantasia* (first shown, 1940) and a Disney retrospective at Lincoln Center (1973).

Dix, Dorothea Lynde (b. Hampden, Me., 4 Apr. 1802; d. Trenton, N.J., 17 July 1887), humanitarian. She operated the Dix Mansion at Boston (1821–34), a school for girls, went abroad for her health, and upon her return to Boston (1838) devoted herself to the reform of conditions in prisons, houses of correction, almshouses, and insane asylums. Her *Memorial to the Legislature of Massachusetts* (Jan. 1843), an indictment of prevailing conditions and treatment of the insane, was followed by similar investigations and exposés in other states. According to her own estimate, she visited in 3 years (c.1841–44) 18 state penitentiaries, 300 county jails and houses of correction, and more than 500 almshouses and other institutions, in addition to hospitals and houses of refuge. She was directly responsible for the enlargement or founding of state-supported hospitals for the insane in 15 states and in Canada and England. At the outbreak of the Civil War she offered her services to the surgeon general and was appointed (10 June 1861) superintendent of women nurses, in which capacity she was in charge of hospital nursing for the Union forces.

Dole, Sanford Ballard (b. Honolulu, 23 Apr. 1844; d. there, 9 June 1926), statesman, jurist, son of the missionary Daniel Dole, was educated in missionary schools, attended Williams College (1866–67), and studied law. Admitted to the Massachusetts bar, he returned to Hawaii to practice. In the legislature in 1884 and 1886, he supported the monarchy but advocated reforms. He was a leader in the revolution (1887) which ended the Gibson regime and forced King Kalakaua to grant a new constitution. Associate justice of the Hawaii Supreme Court (1887–93), he joined the 2d Hawaiian revolution aimed at overthrow of the monarchy, which failed to support the reforms, and annexation to the U.S. Heading the provisional government (1893), he refused, as minister of foreign affairs, to comply with Cleveland's demand (Dec. 1893) for the restoration of Queen Liliuokalani, denying the president's right to interfere in Hawaii's internal affairs but favoring ultimate union with the U.S. Declared president (1894) of the newly formed republic, he visited Washington (1898) in the interests of the newly negotiated annexation treaty. First governor of the Territory of Hawaii (1901), he resigned to become judge of the U.S. district court for Hawaii (1903–15).

Douglas, Stephen Arnold (b. Brandon, Vt., 23 Apr. 1813; d. Chicago, Ill., 3 June 1861), statesman. He attended the Canandaigua (N.Y.) Academy, and in 1833 set out for the Old Northwest, finally settling in Jacksonville, Ill., where he taught school and read law. Licensed to practice (1834), he became state's attorney (1835), state legislator (1835–37), secretary of state for Illinois (1840), and judge of the state supreme court (1841–43). During his 2 terms in the U.S. House of Representatives (1843–47), he was an expansionist on the Oregon issue, vigorously supported the Mexican War, and was chairman of the Committee on Territories. Elected (1847) to the Senate, where he served until his death, he was made chairman of the Committee on Territories. In the Compromise of 1850, he drafted bills providing territorial governments for

Utah and New Mexico which left those governments free to enact laws concerning slavery. Known as the "Little Giant," he led the "Young America" wing of the Democratic party in the early 1850s and zealously championed sectional compromise. His principle of "popular sovereignty," an adaptation of "squatter sovereignty," was incorporated in his Kansas-Nebraska Bill (1854) and precipitated further sectional strife. Douglas was an unsuccessful contender for the Democratic presidential nomination in 1852 and 1856. In 1857–58, during the Senate debate over the Lecompton constitution, his denunciation of that constitution as a violation of the "popular sovereignty" principle led to a break between him and the Buchanan administration and alienated the proslavery wing of the Democratic party. In the Illinois campaign of 1858, he conducted with his opponent, Abraham Lincoln, a series of 7 joint debates commonly known as the Lincoln-Douglas debates, during the course of which he formulated the "Freeport doctrine," further angering Southern Democrats, with whom he finally broke in 1859. In 1860, when Douglas won the Democratic nomination for the presidency, the Southern faction withdrew and chose John C. Breckinridge as their candidate. The rift contributed to the election of Lincoln. In the closing days of the Buchanan administration, Douglas made further attempts at compromise, but upon the outbreak of the Civil War gave his complete support to Lincoln's measures to preserve the Union.

Douglass, Frederick (b. Tuckahoe, near Easton, Md., c.Feb. 1817; d. Washington, D.C., 20 Feb. 1895), Negro abolitionist, writer, and orator. The son of a Negro slave and a white father, he was originally named Frederick Augustus Washington Bailey, taking the name of

Douglass after he escaped to freedom from Baltimore (3 Sept. 1838), where he had learned to read and write while a house servant. Going to New York, and thence to New Bedford, Mass., where he supported himself by working as a common laborer, Douglass in 1841 attended a convention of the Massachusetts Antislavery Society at Nantucket. A speech he delivered there was so moving that he was immediately named as a lecturing agent of the society. Mobbed and assaulted in the performance of his duties, he became the leading figure in the "One Hundred Conventions" of the New England Antislavery Society and published a frank account, *Narrative of the Life of Frederick Douglass* (1845). To avoid possible reenslavement, Douglass stayed in Great Britain and Ireland (1845–47), where he collected enough money to buy his freedom upon returning to the U.S. He edited an abolitionist newspaper, the *North Star* (1847–64), at Rochester, N.Y., was active as a lecturer, and supported industrial education for Negroes and woman suffrage. One of the advisers of John Brown, he fled to Canada and then to the British Isles after Brown was arrested for the raid on Harpers Ferry. During the Civil War he assisted in raising Negro regiments and agitated for Negro suffrage and civil rights. He was secretary of the Santo Domingo Commission (1871), marshal (1877–81) and recorder of deeds (1881–86) of the District of Columbia, and U.S. consul general to Haiti (1889–91).

Dow, Neal (b. Portland, Me., 20 Mar. 1804; d. there, 2 Oct. 1897), temperance reformer, was a son of Quaker parents and reared according to the principles of the Friends, although he was eventually excluded from the Society because of his views on arms. At 24 he made his first temperance speech as a clerk of the Deluge Engine Co., opposing liquor at a company dinner. In 1838 he was instrumental in founding the Maine Temperance Union, committed to total abstinance and prohibitory legislation (1845). The first law (1846) proved inadequate, and Dow, elected mayor of Portland (1851), headed a committee urging more stringent legislation. With the passage of the "Maine Law" (2 June 1851) Dow achieved world renown for temperance reform, speaking on tours, serving (1853) as president of the World's Temperance Convention in New York City. In his 2d term as mayor (1855) the "June riot," led by antiprohibitionists, caused the repeal of the "Maine Law," but it was enacted again in 1857. As opposed to slavery as he was to liquor, Dow became colonel (1861), 13th Reg. of Maine Volunteers, during the Civil War and was commissioned brigadier general (1862). He was twice wounded at Port Hudson and imprisoned for 8 months in Libby Prison and at Mobile. He ran for president (1880) as a Prohibitionist.

Dreiser, Theodore (b. Terre Haute, Ind., 27 Aug. 1871; d. Hollywood, Calif., 28 Dec. 1945), novelist. Born into a poverty-stricken family, he was reared chiefly in Warsaw, Ind., attended Indiana Univ. (1889–90), and was a newspaper reporter (1892–94) in Chicago, St. Louis, and Pittsburgh. In 1894, when he settled in New York, he began a career as a magazine editor and free-lance writer that closed with his post as editor in chief (1907–10) of the Butterick Publications. His novels bear the deep impress of a deterministic philosophy drawn from his reading of Spencer, Huxley, Tyndall, and Haeckel. His view of life as a welter of blind, amoral forces was the underpinning of his first novel, *Sister Carrie* (1900), whose bold social realism (particularly its treatment of sexual mores) brought threats of censorship. The novel was withdrawn by the publisher; its reissuance was a victory for literary realism. Dreiser's naturalism and realism permeated his other novels: *Jennie Gerhardt* (1911); the trilogy based on the career of the traction magnate, Charles T. Yerkes, *The Financier* (1912), *The Titan* (1914), and *The Stoic* (1947); *The Genius* (1915); and the novel which found Dreiser's widest audience, *An American Tragedy* (1925). *The Bulwark* (1946) showed evidences of a return to religious conviction. In the years after World War I, Dreiser embraced socialism, writing *Dreiser Looks at Russia* (1928), *Tragic America* (1932), and *America is Worth Saving* (1941).

Du Bois, William Edward Burghardt (b. Great Barrington, Mass., 23 Feb. 1868; d. Accra, Ghana, 27 Aug. 1963), writer, reformer. Of slave descent, he received his A.B. at Fisk Univ. (1888), then 3 degrees at Harvard (A.B., 1890; A.M., 1891; Ph.D., 1895). Professor of history and economics at Atlanta Univ. (1896–1910), he devoted himself to Negro sociological and historical problems. Taking a militant position on race relations, as opposed to Booker T. Washington (*q.v.*), he helped launch (1905) the Niagara Movement for racial equality and became (1910) director of publicity and research of the NAACP, a post he held for 24 years. He organized the Pan-African Congress (1919) and called the first International Congress of Colored Peoples during the Versailles Peace Conference (1918). Heading the department of sociology at Atlanta Univ. (1933–44), he returned to the NAACP as head of a department of special research (1944–48). Candidate for senator in New York on the American Labor party ticket (1948), he subsequently served as vice-chairman of the Council on African Affairs (1949–54) and was prominent in organizations favoring friendlier postwar

relations with the U.S.S.R. He renounced his American citizenship (1961) and spent his remaining years in Ghana. Du Bois' numerous writings included *The Suppression of the African Slave Trade* (1896), *The Philadelphia Negro* (1899), *The Souls of Black Folk* (1903), *The Negro* (1915), and *Black Reconstruction* (1935). In addition he edited *Encyclopedia of the Negro* (1933–45), *Crisis* magazine (1910–32), and *Encyclopedia Africana* (1961–63).

Duke, James Buchanan (b. near Durham, N.C., 23 Dec. 1856; d. New York City, 10 Oct. 1925), industrialist and philanthropist. Shortly after the Civil War, he and his brother, Benjamin Newton Buchanan (1855–1929), helped their father put up packaged leaf tobacco which they sold on the road in North Carolina. The firm of W. Duke & Sons, of which he became a member in 1884, began in 1881 the manufacturing of cigarettes by hand and shortly thereafter turned them out by machine. In 1884 the Duke firm opened a branch factory at New York City and by adroit price and advertising policies commanded by 1889 half of the total U.S. production of cigarettes. The "tobacco war," a contest among 5 chief cigarette manufacturers, led to the organization (1890) of the American Tobacco Co., which merged the rival concerns. Named president, J. B. Duke was also president of the combination of plug manufacturers known as the Continental Tobacco Co. (formed 1898). In succession, he organized the American Snuff Co. (1900), the American Cigar Co. (1901), the Consolidated Tobacco Co. (1901), and the United Cigar Stores Co. In 1911, by which year Duke's various combinations controlled 150 factories capitalized at $502 million, the U.S. Supreme Court ordered the dissolution of the American Tobacco Co. as a combination in restraint of trade. Duke was also active in forming (1905) and developing the Southern Power Co. In 1924 he created a trust fund for Trinity College, subsequently renamed Duke Univ.

Dulles, John Foster (b. Washington, D.C., 25 Feb. 1888; d. there, 24 May 1959), lawyer, statesman, received his B.A. from Princeton (1908), studied at the Sorbonne (1908–09), and obtained his LL.B. from George Washington Univ. (1911). Beginning in 1911, he spent his entire legal career with Sullivan & Cromwell, which firm he headed from 1927. An outstanding international lawyer, he was chief counsel for U.S. bondholders of Kreuger & Toll, the international match trust. During World War I, in addition to service in the armed forces, he was special agent of the State Department in Central America (1917), assistant to the chairman, War Trade Board (1918), and counsel to the American Peace Commission (1918–19). Delegate to the San Francisco Conference (1945) and to the UN (1946–50), he also served as adviser to the Secretary of State at the Council of Foreign Ministers at London (1945, 1947). Appointed interim U.S. senator from New York (1949), he acted as adviser to the State Department (1950–53) and was the chief architect of the Japanese Peace Treaty (1951). Secretary of State (1953–59) in the Eisenhower administration, he was the major force in U.S. foreign policy in that period, personally engaging in innumerable missions abroad, traveling over 500,000 miles during his term. Holding Truman's policy of "containment" of Communism to be inadequate, he espoused "liberation" of Communist-controlled areas, held firm against Red Chinese threats to seize Quemoy and Matsu, forced Britain and France to abandon the Suez Canal attack (1956),

was responsible for the Eisenhower Doctrine (1957) designed to preserve peace in the Middle East, and committed the U.S. to hold West Berlin, if necessary by force (1958). Resuming his duties after an operation for abdominal cancer (1957), he died of that disease.

Duncan, Isadora (b. San Francisco, 27 May 1878; d. Nice, France, 14 Sept. 1927), dancer, quit school at the age of 10 to devote herself entirely to dancing, and with her sister, Elizabeth, taught a system of movements interpretative of nature, music, and poetry, which had some vogue in her native city. She made her first appearance in New York (1895) in the Augustin Daly company. Disillusioned by the formalism of dance in America, she left with her family for London on a cattle boat. Joining Loie Fuller's company on tour to Germany, she went on alone to Budapest, Munich, Vienna, and Berlin, taking them by storm. Failing in her attempt to build a temple of dance on a hill outside Athens, she opened (1904) a school of the dance on the outskirts of Berlin and returned to the stage, with tours of France, Germany, Russia, and the U.S. (1906–08). Performing barefoot and in flowing costumes, she was a notable interpreter of classical music and popularized the dance as an art in the U.S., awakening an enthusiasm upon which such later figures as Martha Graham (*q.v.*) and Agnes de Mille were able to build a more solid structure. Pagan in her advocacy of free love, she had one child by Edward Gordon Craig and another by "Lohengrin," a wealthy patron. The children were both drowned in an accident. In Moscow, where she established a dance school at the invitation (1921) of the Soviet government, she finally married Sergei Yessenin, later a suicide. A moment after saying, "*Je vais à la gloire*," she came to a dramatic end when her long scarf caught in the wheel of a moving auto, breaking her neck.

du Pont, Eleuthère Irénée (b. Paris, 24 June 1771; d. Philadelphia, 31 Oct. 1834), manufacturer, son of the economist Pierre Samuel du Pont de Nemours, was given his baptismal name by Minister of Finance Turgot, his godfather. In 1788 Lavoisier, a friend of his father's, took him into the royal powder works at Essonne. He married at 20, fighting 2 duels over his fiancée. In 1797 the du Pont publishing business was suppressed, and the family left for the U.S. Here, Irénée investigated gunpowder manufacture and returned to Paris to procure machinery and designs for its manufacture in the U.S. He set up his works (1801) on the Brandywine River, near Wilmington, Del. In 1804 powder was ready for sale, and military orders, greatly increasing with the War of 1812, established the firm's position as the principal manufacturer of powder for the government. The plant also supplied South American governments. In 1833 he turned down a $24,000 cash order from the South Carolina nullifiers. In spite of opposition from his partner, Peter Bauduy, the company was called E. I. du Pont de Nemours & Co., the name by which it is still known.

Eads, James Buchanan (b. Lawrencebury, Ind., 23 May 1820; d. Nassau, Bahamas, 8 Mar. 1887), engineer and inventor. An autodidact, his formal education ended when he was 13. Using the knowledge of mechanics he gained as a purser on a Mississippi steamboat, he invented a diving bell which could retrieve sunken steamboats and their cargoes and became a partner (1842) in the first ship salvaging business on the Mississippi. He gave up this lucrative venture (1845) to start a glassworks in St. Louis but, soon heavily in debt, he returned to ship salvaging (1848) and within 9 years had acquired a fortune. He studied the geology of rivers and became a recognized authority on the Mississippi River system. At President Lincoln's request he developed (1861) plans for fortifying the Western rivers and was consulted on military operations in the region during the Civil War. At the outbreak of the war he proposed to build a fleet of ironclad, steam-propelled gunboats; the first was delivered within 45 days and the others followed rapidly. After a team of 27 leading engineers had been defeated by the project, Eads designed and constructed (1867–74) a bridge—with a center span of 520 ft. and a 50-ft. clearance—over the Mississippi at St. Louis, the largest bridge of any type built until that time and the first such bridge ever built almost entirely of steel. The bridge was a pioneering effort in the cantilevered method of constructing arches and marked the introduction in the U.S. of pneumatic caisson method of founding piers and abutments. An equally daring and successful feat was undertaken when he proposed (1874) to clear the mouth of the Mississippi. He devised and constructed (1875–79) a system of jetties which forced the river to dredge its own channel by carrying its sediment out into the Gulf of Mexico. His achievement made New Orleans an ocean port.

Eakins, Thomas (b. Philadelphia, 25 July 1844; d. there, 25 June 1916), artist and teacher, attended the Pennsylvania Academy of Fine Arts; was a student (1866–69) at the École des Beaux Arts in Paris, where he worked under Bonnat and Gérôme; in 1869 traveled in Spain, where his study of the realist painters, such as Velásquez and Goya, was influential in forming his style; and in 1870 returned to Philadelphia, where his study of anatomy at the Jefferson Medical College helped to make him a master of the human figure and resulted in two of his best compositions, *The Gross Clinic* and *The Agnew Clinic*. In 1873 he became a teacher (and subsequently dean) at the Pennsylvania Academy of Fine Arts, and also taught at the Art Students League. Among his paintings, both portrait and figure, are *The Writing Master, The Thinker, The Chess Players, Max Schmitt in a Single Scull, Whistling for Plover, Salutat, Between Rounds, The Concert Singer, The Swimming Hole,* and *Edith Mahon*. He also modeled sculpture, including 2 reliefs on the battle monument at Trenton, N.J.

Eastman, George (b. Waterville, N.Y., 12 July 1854; d. Rochester, N.Y., 14 Mar. 1932), inventor, manufacturer, philanthropist, became interested in photography at an early age. Patenting his invention of a dry-plate process in 1880, he began manufacturing dry plates in Rochester. Forming a partnership with Henry A. Strong, he invented a paper-backed flexible film (1884), soon put into production as roll film, and then a small box camera, the Kodak. Developing motion-picture film on the basis of patents he held jointly with Henry M. Reichenbach, the inventor, he formed the Eastman Kodak Co. (1892), recapitalizing and expanding its operations until by 1901 it was the world's largest industrial plant devoted to the manufacture of photographic supplies. Stressing research, Eastman's technicians constantly improved the firm's products and his welfare and profit-sharing programs built up a loyal labor force. His philanthropies by grant and bequest exceeded $100 million and included such institutions as the Univ. of Rochester, MIT, Tuskegee, and Hampton institutes, the establishment of a chair of American studies at Balliol

College, Oxford, and founding the Eastman School of Music in Rochester. Ironically, he preferred anonymity and was rarely photographed. He had no family, and leaving a note, "My work is done, why wait?" he took his own life.

Eddy, Mary Baker (b. Bow, N.H., 16 July 1821; d. Chestnut Hill, Newton, Mass., 3 Dec. 1910), founder of the Practice of Christian Science and of the Church of Christ, Scientist. She married (1843) George Washington Glover, by whom, a few months after his death, she had a son, George (born in Sept. 1844). In 1853 she married Dr. Daniel Patterson, a N.H. dentist and homeopathist, from whom she was separated in 1866 and divorced in 1873. She practiced intermittently (1866–70) a system of mental healing after undergoing treatment from Dr. Phineas P. Quimby (1802–66) of Portland, Me., in 1862. The principles later associated with Christian Science were formulated by her (c.1866), supposedly after making through "divine revelation, reason and demonstration" a remarkable recovery from a serious injury. Setting up a spiritual-healing practice at Lynn, Mass. (1870), she published *Science and Health with Key to the Scriptures* (1875, and numerous revised editions), in which she set forth the basic doctrines of Christian Science. She married (1877) Asa Gilbert Eddy, one of her disciples; he died in 1882. The Christian Scientists' Association, established in 1876, was chartered (1879) as The Church of Christ, Scientist. In 1881 Mrs. Eddy obtained a charter for the Massachusetts Medical College, a training institution for Christian Science practitioners. In 1883 she began publishing the *Journal of Christian Science*. She and 12 followers established at Boston (1892) The First Church of Christ, Scientist, the mother church of the national religious organization. In her last years she founded *The Christian Science Monitor.*

Edison, Thomas Alva (b. Milan, Ohio, 11 Feb. 1847; d. West Orange, N.J., 18 Oct. 1931), inventor. Taken out of school after a few months because he was a slow learner, he received his education at home from his mother. As a boy, he sold newspapers, candy, and other articles on trains; becoming acquainted with telegraph operators during his trips, he became one himself (1863), continuing in the meantime his keen interest in chemistry. In 1868, he joined the Western Union Telegraph Co. at Boston, patenting (1869) his first invention, an electrographic vote recorder. Moving to New York that year, he entered into partnership in the electrical engineering firm of Pope, Edison & Co. When the firm was bought out in 1870, Edison received $40,000 as his share, and with this money established his own business, early initiating his policy of hiring assistants capable of collaborating on inventions under his guidance. During the period 1870–75 he was active in the improvement of the telegraph. In 1876 he built an establishment at Menlo Park, N.J., and in 1887 transferred the Edison research laboratories to larger quarters at Orange, N.J. His ventures were ultimately combined into the Edison General Electric Co., later absorbed by the General Electric Co. In 1877 he produced one of his most important inventions, the phonograph. Beginning in 1879 he introduced improvements that made possible the commercial production of the incandescent electric lamp. During his work on this device he made his first and only significant discovery in pure science when he observed the "Edison effect," demonstrating that the incandescent lamp could be utilized as a valve admitting negative but not positive electricity. (In 1904 the principle of the "Edison effect" was employed by J. Ambrose Fleming, inventor of the electron tube.) In the field of motion pictures, Edison acquired and improved the projector invented by Thomas Armat (1895) and placed it on the market as the Edison Vitascope. Although Edison was granted a total of more than 1,000 patents, most of them were the fruit of collective effort in his research laboratories. Among the inventions or improvements produced at the Edison laboratories were the storage battery, dictaphone, mimeograph, district telegraph signal box, Sprague motor, ore separator, composition brick, compressing dies, electric safety lantern, electric dynamo, and electric locomotive.

Edwards, Jonathan (b. East Windsor, Conn., 5 Oct. 1703; d. Princeton, N.J., 22 Mar. 1758), Congregational theologian and philosopher. After his graduation from Yale (1720), he studied theology there, and in 1722 became minister of a Presbyterian church in New York, where he remained until 1723. He was a tutor at Yale (1725–26), and in 1727 became assistant pastor to his grandfather, Solomon Stoddard, in the church at Northampton, Mass. Edwards became its sole pastor in 1729. His preaching initiated the New England phase of the religious revival known as the "Great Awakening" (c.1730–50). At Northampton, Edwards expounded doctrines fusing rationalism and mysticism and aimed at stemming the rising tide of liberal thought. He stressed the rationality of Scriptural knowledge, the intuitive apprehension of spiritual experience, and the metaphysical concepts of understanding and will as moral agencies under the supreme and arbitrary power of God. In 1750, following a controversy over church doctrine and practices, he was dismissed from the Northampton pastorate. Edwards settled at Stockbridge, Mass., as pastor of the church and missionary to the Indians, and there wrote his most important treatises. In 1757 he was chosen as president of the College of New Jersey at Princeton, but died a few months after taking the post. For his principal works, see p. 847.

Einstein, Albert (b. Ulm Donnau, Germany, 14 Mar. 1879; d. Princeton, N.J., 18 Apr. 1955), physicist, was graduated (1900) from the Federal Institute of Technology at Zurich and received his doctorate (1905) at the Univ. of Zurich. His special theory of relativity (1905), his equation $E = mc^2$ (1905, keystone in the modern concept of the atom), and his contributions to quantum theory (1905) were followed by his general theory of relativity (1915) and work on the photoelectric effect of light, for which he received the Nobel prize (1921). He taught at the Federal Institute of Technology at Zurich (1912–14) and in 1914 assumed the post of director of the Kaiser Wilhelm Institute in Berlin. With the advent of Hitler he came to the U.S. (1932), accepted a post at the Institute for Advanced Study at Princeton (1933–45), and on 2 Aug. 1939 sent a historic letter to President Roosevelt stressing the urgency of research on the atomic bomb. His major work in the U.S. was his formulation (30 Mar. 1953) of a unified field theory, the mathematical expression of which appeared in 1950 as an appendix to *The Meaning of Relativity* (1922; Eng. tr., 4th ed., 1950). He also wrote *Relativity: the Special and the General Theory* (1918), and was active in the peace movement and in Zionism.

Eisenhower, Dwight David (b. Denison, Tex., 14 Oct. 1890; d. Washington, D.C., 28 Mar. 1969), 34th president of the U.S., soldier, spent his boyhood in Abi-

lene, Kan.; was graduated (1915) from the U.S. Military Academy; served (1915–17) with the 19th Infantry at Ft. Sam Houston, Tex.; and during World War I, when he organized Camp Colt for the training of tank troops, attained the rank of captain. He was graduated (1926) from the Command and General Staff School at Ft. Leavenworth, Kan.; (1929) from the Army War College, Washington, D.C.; and (1932) from the Army Industrial College. He was named (1933) special assistant to Gen. Douglas MacArthur (*q.v.*), then chief of staff, under whom he served (1935–39) as assistant military adviser to the Philippine Commonwealth. Promoted to lieutenant colonel in 1936, he returned to the U.S. in 1939 and was named (Feb. 1942) chief of the War Plans Division in the Office of Chief of Staff, subsequently became chief of the Operations Division, and in June 1942, was appointed commander of U.S. forces in the European Theater. He commanded the Allied invasion of North Africa that began on 8 Nov. 1942; was named (Jan. 1944) Supreme Commander of the Allied Expeditionary Force in Western Europe and set up his headquarters (SHAEF) near London. After the invasion of Europe (6 June 1944 *et seq.*) and the surrender of Germany (7 May 1945) he served as commander of the U.S. occupation zone of Germany. General of the army (Dec. 1944), he succeeded (Nov. 1945) Gen. George C. Marshall as chief of staff, became (7 June 1948) president of Columbia Univ., and took a leave of absence from Columbia to become (1951) Supreme Commander of the Allied Powers in Europe (SHAPE). He resigned that command in 1952 to campaign for the presidency, was the Republican nominee that year, and was elected with the largest popular vote to that time. Reelected (1956), he advocated personal top-level diplomacy, sought to contain Soviet expansion in the

Middle East, and to achieve a balanced budget. He was author of *Crusade in Europe* (1948), *Mandate for Change* (1961), *Waging Peace: The White House Years* (1965).

Eliot, Charles William (b. Boston, Mass., 20 Mar. 1834; d. Northeast Harbor, Me., 22 Aug. 1926), educator, was graduated from Harvard (1853), where he taught mathematics and chemistry (1854–63). After 2 years of study on the Continent, he was appointed (1865) professor of chemistry at Massachusets Institute of Technology. Early in 1869 he published in the *Atlantic Monthly* 2 articles on "The New Education: Its Organization," which drew wide notice, and in the same year was appointed and inaugurated president of Harvard, a post he held until his retirement in 1909. During his administration the elective system and sabbatical year were introduced at Harvard College; Harvard Univ. was expanded in enrollment and size to include units such as the graduate school of arts and sciences, applied science, and business administration; and the standards of the professional schools were raised. In 1892, as chairman of the National Education Association's Committee on Secondary School Studies, he prepared a report on the functions and curricula of public schools which led to the organization (1901) of the Board of College Entrance Examinations. He edited the *Harvard Classics* (popularly called the "five-foot shelf").

Ellington, Edward Kennedy (Duke) (b. Washington, D.C., 29 Apr. 1899; d. New York City, 24 May 1974), composer. His only formal musical education was a few piano lessons as a child and a few private music lessons as a teenager. His first composition, "Soda Fountain Rag," was written while working after school as a soda jerk. He formed his first band, The Duke's Serenaders, in 1917. A visit to New York (1922) gave Ellington the opportunity to hear the Harlem pianists Willie (The Lion) Smith, James P. Johnson, and Fats Waller, who influenced his own playing. Ellington brought his band, The Washingtonians, to New York (1923) and performed for over 4 years at the Kentucky Club and at the Cotton Club (1927–32), cutting 160 records between 1928–31 and making his first radio broadcast, introducing a signature theme, "East St. Louis Toodle Oo." During the 1930s he was associated with a large orchestra with fine sidemen, appearing in several films including *Check and Double Check* (1930). His band hit one of its peaks (1941–42) but by 1943 he was turning to extended compositions and concert presentations. *Black, Brown, and Beige*, a 50-minute work, received its first performance at Carnegie Hall (1953). The popularity of his band waned during the late 40s and early 50s when "bop" emerged and the big bands were no longer the leaders in the field. His triumph at the Newport Jazz Festival (1956) established his international reputation. For 15 years he performed throughout the world under State Department auspices. In 1965, he presented a concert of sacred music in Grace Cathedral, San Francisco, and gave sacred concerts of his compositions at the Cathedral of St. John the Divine, New York City (1968) and Westminster Abbey (1973). A prolific composer of thousands of pieces, Ellington's famous songs include "Solitude," "Sophisticated Lady," "I Got It Bad," "I Let a Song Go Out of My Heart." Short instrumental pieces include "Creole Love Call" and "Mood Indigo." As composer and arranger, his style was built upon the sounds of the instrumentalists in his band, among them Johnny Hodges, alto sax, Sam Nanton, trombone, and Bubber Miley, Cootie Williams, and Ray Nance, trumpets. His extended compositions include *Night Creatures* (1955), *Sweet Thursday* (1960), *My People* (1963). Among his film scores is *Assault on a Queen*. He also authored the theatrical score *Beggar's Holiday* (lyrics by John La Touche, 1947) and the ballet *The River* (1970).

Ellison, Ralph Waldo (b. Oklahoma City, Okla., 1 Mar. 1914–   ), author. While attending Tuskegee Institute (1933–36), where he studied musical composition, he visited New York and studied sculpture briefly, meeting Richard Wright, who inspired him to write. Ellison joined the New York City Writers' Program and began to contribute short stories, articles, and book reviews to a variety of publications and was a member of the editorial board of *The American Scholar*. *Invisible Man* (1953) has been described as a black American variation upon Dostoevski's *Notes from the Underground*. The theme of racial identity is prominent in this work which has been praised for its technical sophistication. The book won the 1953 National Book Award and was named the "most distinguished single work" published in the past 20 years by a *Book Week* poll (1965). *Shadow and Act*, a spirited, intellectual autobiography, was published in 1964. Ellison has been a lecturer on Black American culture and creative writing at Columbia, Princeton, Chicago, and Bennington, and Albert Schweitzer Professor in Humanities at New York Univ. (1970–   ).

Ellsworth, Oliver (b. Windsor, Conn., 29 Apr. 1745; d. there, 26 Nov. 1807), jurist and statesman, attended Yale for 2 years; then the College of New Jersey, where he acquired an M.A. in 1766. Admitted to the Connecticut bar (1771), he soon gained prominence, serving as state's attorney for Hartford Co. (1777–85). Member of the Connecticut General Assembly and delegate to the Continental Congress (1777–83), he served on the latter's committee on appeals from state admiralty courts and the committee dealing with army supplies. Ellsworth was a member of the Governor's Council (1780–84), a position he left to serve first on the state's newly created Supreme Court of Errors (1784) and then on its Superior Court (1784–89). Influential at the Constitutional Convention, he helped shape the Connecticut Compromise and proposed the name "the government of the United States." His *Letters to a Landholder* urged ratification by Connecticut. As senator from Connecticut (1789–96), he was a major force in the early Congresses, drafting the Judiciary Act of 1789, reporting out the proposed first 12 amendments, helping to organize the census and the army, and proposing an economic boycott of Rhode Island, which induced that state to make its belated entry into the Union. A strong Federalist, he supported Hamilton's fiscal program. Appointed chief justice of the U.S. (1796), he served for 3 years, leaving no significant imprint. He retired for reasons of ill health (1800). With William R. Davie and William Vans Murray he served as envoy to France (1799–1800), negotiating the Convention of 1800 which helped to avert war.

Emerson, Ralph Waldo (b. Boston, Mass., 25 May 1803; d. Concord, Mass., 27 Apr. 1882), philosopher, poet, essayist, and lecturer, was graduated from Harvard (1821), where he was class poet, taught school at Boston and at Roxbury, Mass., and for a brief period in 1825 attended the Harvard Divinity School. Admitted (1826) as a candidate for the Unitarian ministry, he resigned his pastorate at the Second Church of Boston (1829–31) when he decided that he could not conform in the administration of the Lord's Supper. He made a tour of

England and the Continent (1832–33), meeting Coleridge, Wordsworth, and Carlyle, through whom he became acquainted with the doctrines of German idealism which, together with infusions from neo-Platonism and the sacred books of the East, influenced the molding of Transcendentalist thought. After his return to Boston, he resumed preaching, but gradually abandoned it for the lyceum and lecture platform. Settling at Concord in 1835, he formed friendships with Thoreau, Bronson Alcott, Margaret Fuller, and Nathaniel Hawthorne. His first publication, *Nature* (1836), was a fundamental exposition of Transcendentalism, a philosophical and literary reaction against Unitarian intellectualism. His address "The American Scholar," delivered as the Phi Beta Kappa oration at Harvard (1837), called for an indigenous national culture and defined the functions of the intellectual in the light of Transcendentalism. His "Divinity School Address," also delivered at Harvard (1838), indicted orthodox Christianity and brought attacks on Emerson from the ministery. With Margaret Fuller and other Transcendentalists, he edited *The Dial* (1840–44). The quarter century after 1840 constituted the period of his greatest activity as a lecturer in the North and the West. He published the *Essays* (1st series, 1841; 2nd series, 1844), which established his reputation in the U.S. and Europe; *Poems* (1847), including "May-Day," "Threnody," and "Concord Hymn"; *Addresses and Lectures* (1849); *Representative Men* (1850); and *English Traits* (1856). Active in the antislavery movement, he wrote *The Conduct of Life* (1860) and *Society and Solitude* (1870), gave a course of lectures at Harvard that was published as *Natural History of Intellect* (1893), and published *Letters and Social Aims* (1876). The *Journals* (10 vols., 1909–14) were edited by his son, Edward Waldo

Emerson; the *Letters* (6 vols., 1939), by Ralph L. Rusk.

Enders, John Franklin (b. West Hartford, Conn., 10 Feb. 1897–), bacteriologist, received his B.A. (1920) from Yale and his M.A. (1922) and Ph.D. (1930) from Harvard, where he taught in the department of bacteriology and immunology (1929–), and served as chief of the research division of infectious diseases (1947–72), and chief of the Virus Research Unit (1972–), Children's Hospital, Harvard Medical School. Civilian consultant to the Secretary of War on epidemic diseases (1942–46), and member of the Commission on Viral Infections, Armed Forces Epidemiological Bd. (1945–49); he received the Nobel prize in medicine and physiology (1954) for culturing poliomyelitis virus in living tissue, laying the foundation for the production of the antipolio, measles, and mumps vaccine. He edited *Journal of Immunology* (1942–58).

Ericsson, John (b. Langbanshyttan, Sweden, 31 July 1803; d. New York City, 8 Mar. 1889), inventor and engineer, grew up in the midst of mining works, and at 11 designed and constructed a miniature sawmill. Adm. Count Platen, celebrated engineer, recognizing his ability, appointed him a cadet in the mechanical engineer corps. At 17 he enlisted in the Swedish army, where he was detailed to do topographical surveying. In London for 12 years, beginning in 1826, he made various marine inventions, and developed the screw propeller, which revolutionized navigation. Coming to New York in 1839, he furnished (1840) designs for the screw warship *Princeton* (which suffered an explosion on trials in 1844), the first ship to have its propelling machinery under water and out of firing range. In 1861 he designed and built for the Union the ironclad *Monitor* with a circular armored revolving turret. Following the victory of the *Monitor* over the *Merrimac* at Hampton Roads, Va. (9 Mar. 1862), he was kept busy designing and building other ironclads. He also made notable contributions to the improvement of the steam engine. After his death Ericsson's body was carried back to Sweden with great ceremony, appropriately in a new steel naval vessel.

Evarts, William Maxwell (b. Boston, Mass., 6 Feb. 1818; d. New York City, 28 Feb. 1901), lawyer and statesman, was graduated from Yale (1837), studied at Harvard Law School, and was admitted to the New York bar (1841). An assistant U.S. attorney for the Southern District of New York, 1849–53, and unsuccessful candidate for the U.S. Senate (1860), he argued in behalf of New York state the Lemmon slave case in dispute with Virginia (1860) and represented the federal government before the Supreme Court during the Civil War in asserting the right to treat captured vessels as maritime prizes. Among the preeminent leaders of the bar, he was President Johnson's chief defense counsel in the impeachment trial before the Senate (1868), winning an acquittal, and from 15 July until the close of Johnson's administration was U.S. attorney general. He was U.S. counsel in the Geneva Arbitration (1871–72) over the *Alabama* claims, chief counsel for Hayes in the presidential election dispute of 1876, and senior counsel for defendant in *Tilton* v. *Henry Ward Beecher* (1874–75). As Hayes' Secretary of State (1877–81) he asserted the "paramount interest" of the U.S. in an isthmian canal (1880). He was U.S. senator from New York (1885–91).

Farragut, David Glasgow (b. Campbell's Station, near Knoxville, Tenn., 5 July 1801; d. Portsmouth, N.H., 14 Aug. 1870), naval officer. Adopted (c.1808) by Cmdr. David Porter of the New Orleans naval station, he was appointed (1810) midshipman, and during the War of 1812 served aboard the frigate *Essex* in the Pacific. He saw duty in the Mediterranean (1815–20), and during the middle 1850s established the navy yard at Mare Island. Farragut was appointed (9 Jan. 1862) commander of the West Gulf Blockading Squadron with orders to open the Mississippi River and to attack and invest New Orleans. Departing from Hampton Roads aboard his flagship, the steam sloop *Hartford,* Farragut, with 17 ships and a mortar flotilla at his disposal, opened the Battle of New Orleans on 18 Apr. 1862. At his orders the Union warships ran by the Confederate defenses before they were reduced, destroying most of the Confederate fleet and thus hastening the fall of New Orleans (28 Apr.). In recognition of his achievement, Farragut was commissioned a rear admiral (30 July 1862), becoming the first to hold that grade. His victory (5 Aug. 1864) in the Battle of Mobile Bay, when to the warning of "Torpedoes ahead!" he replied, "Damn the torpedoes!" brought him the commission of vice-admiral (23 Dec. 1864), an office created for him, as was the commission of admiral (26 July 1866). He led the European Squadron on a goodwill tour (1867–68) of Continental ports.

Faulkner, William (b. New Albany, Miss., 25 Sept. 1897; d. Oxford, Miss., 6 July 1962), novelist and short-story writer, served as a pilot with the Canadian Royal Air Force in 1918 and attended the Univ. of Mississippi from 1919 to 1921. Most of his novels and stories comprise a saga of the Compson, Sartoris, Snopes, McCaslin, and other families living in imaginary Yoknapatawpha County, with its county seat of Jefferson, in northern Mississippi, a powerful narrative of decay and corruption portraying Southern life from early frontier days to the coming of modern industrialism. His works include *Soldier's Pay* (1926), *Mosquitoes* (1927), *Sartoris* (1929), *The Sound and the Fury* (1929), *As I Lay Dying* (1930), *Sanctuary* (1931), *These Thirteen* (1931), *Light in August* (1932), *Doctor Martino, and Other Stories* (1934), *Pylon* (1935), *Absalom, Absalom!* (1936), *The Unvanquished* (1938), *The Wild Palms* (1939), *The Hamlet* (1940), *Go Down, Moses, and Other Stories* (1942), *Intruder in the Dust* (1948), *Knight's Gambit* (1949), *Collected Stories* (1950), *Requiem for a Nun* (1951), *A Fable* (1954)—Pulitzer prize (1955), *The Reivers* (1962). In 1950 he was awarded the Nobel prize in literature.

Fermi, Enrico (b. Rome, Italy, 29 Sept. 1901; d. Chicago, 28 Nov. 1954), physicist, was graduated from the Univ. of Pisa (1922), taught physics at Florence (1924) and Rome (1926–38) before coming to the U.S. (1939). His early experiments in artificial radioactivity, using slow neutrons, led directly to the discovery of uranium fission and brought him the Nobel prize in physics (1938). In the U.S. he set the first atomic furnace into successful operation (2 Dec. 1942). The U.S. atomic bomb project was not only materially aided by his research abroad, but it benefited from his active participation in the project at Los Alamos. Professor of physics at Columbia (1939–45) and thereafter at Chicago, his numerous contributions to the new physics include his postulating the existence of an atomic particle (neutrino), his discovery of element 93 (neptunium), and his formulation of the theory of beta-ray emission in radiocativity. For work on the A-bomb he received the first Special Award

($25,000) of the AEC (1954). He wrote *Thermodynamics* (1937), *Elementary Particles* (1951).

Field, Cyrus West (b. Stockbridge, Mass., 30 Nov. 1819; d. New York City, 12 July 1892), financier, promoter of the first transatlantic cable, brother of David Dudley and Stephen Johnson Field. At the age of 15 he settled in New York City, where he became an errand boy in A. T. Stewart's dry-goods store. In 1837 he went to Lee, Mass., where he was assistant to his brother Matthew, a paper manufacturer, and about 2 years later organized his own paper mill at Westfield, Mass. Soon afterward he became a junior partner in the wholesale-paper-dealing firm of E. Root & Co. at New York. When this establishment failed (1841), he founded Cyrus W. Field & Co., and within 10 years paid all his debts and retired with a fortune of $250,-000. His interest in the project of a transatlantic cable from Newfoundland was aroused when he met (1854) Frederick N. Gisborne, a Canadian engineer. Field vigorously promoted the idea and won the support of a group of New Yorkers who subscribed $1,500,000 for the project. After surmounting many disheartening technical and financial obstacles, the company completed the laying of the telegraph cable joining Valentia, Ireland, and Trinity Bay, Newfoundland (5 Aug. 1858). On 16 Aug. 1858 Queen Victoria sent over the line a message to President Buchanan. Soon thereafter, the cable stopped working. Field suffered heavy financial loss, but continued to press for support of the project. After the Civil War he secured the *Great Eastern*, at that time the largest steamboat afloat, and with it relaid an improved cable. Subsequent investments in railroad and elevated railway stocks cost him his fortune.

Field, David Dudley (b. Haddam, Conn., 13 Feb. 1805; d. New York City, 13 Apr. 1894), lawyer and jurist, was graduated from Williams College (1825), admitted to the New York bar (1828), and practiced in New York City. A Democrat, he opposed the extension of slavery and supported Frémont (1856) and Lincoln (1860), returning to the Democratic party in 1876, with 3 months service in Congress. Although notable as a lawyer (counsel for Milligan in *Ex parte Milligan,* 1867; for McCardle in a case involving the constitutionality of the Reconstruction Act of 1867; for Jay Gould and James Fiske in the Erie R.R. litigation, 1869; chief counsel for "Boss" Tweed, 1873–78; and counsel for Tilden before the Electoral Commission, 1876), his major contribution was as a law reformer and codifier. Appointed (1847) to a commission for codification of New York State laws and to another for reform of procedure, he drafted a code of civil procedure which was enacted by the legislature (1848). Codes based on his reforms were soon passed in many states, notably in the West, and ultimately influenced English judicial reforms. Chairman of a new commission (1857) to prepare penal and civil codes, a task completed by 1865, his proposals were opposed by James C. Carter (1827–1905) and only the penal code became law (1881). His *Draft Outline of an International Code* (2 vols., 1872) gained recognition by the courts of many nations. He was a founder and first president of the Association for Reform and Codification of the Law of Nations (now International Law Association).

Field, Marshall (b. near Conway, Mass., 18 Aug. 1835; d. New York City, 16 Jan. 1906), merchant and philanthropist. His formal schooling ended when, at the age of 17, he became a clerk in a dry-goods store at Pittsfield, Mass. Moving to Chicago in 1856, he became a clerk and traveling salesman in the wholesale dry-goods establishment of Cooley, Wadsworth & Co., of which he became general manager (1861) and a partner (1862). In 1865 the store became known as Field, Palmer & Leiter, and in 1881 became Marshall Field & Co., with Field as major proprietor. He eventually bought out the other interests in the concern. Field made several pioneering innovations in retail merchandising: the making of wholesale purchases of goods in anticipation of consumer demand in order to improve his position on the open market, the segregation of wholesale and retail departments in his store, the operation of buying agencies throughout the world, the purchase of the entire output of manufacturing plants, and the establishment of his own factories as sources of supply. Among his philanthropies were the founding of the Chicago Manual Training School, the donation of the site of the Univ. of Chicago, and the Columbian Museum at the Chicago World's Fair of 1893, a structure that was later converted, through a provision in his will, into the Field Museum of Natural History.

Field, Stephen Johnson (b. Haddam, Conn., 4 Nov. 1816; d. Washington, D.C., Apr. 1899), jurist, was graduated from Williams College (1837), admitted to the New York bar (1841), and practiced in New York City with his brother, David Dudley. He went to California (1849) and was elected to the state legislature (1850), serving on the judicial committee which reorganized the judicial code of California along lines laid down by his brother, and securing passage of basic mining laws. Judge of the state supreme court (1857–59) and chief justice (1859–63), he was appointed by Lincoln associate justice of the U.S. Supreme Court (1863–97), serving 34 years and 7 months, the 2d longest term of any member of that bench. His most notable opinions were dissents, acting as a curb upon the centralizing tendencies of the majority. His dissents in the *Slaughterhouse Cases* (1873) and *Munn v. Ill.* (1876) forecast later recognized constitutional principles. He upheld Congress' paramount power over interstate commerce, even denying to the states the right to prohibit imports or exports of articles not recognized by them as legitimate subjects of commerce. With the majority in *Pollock* v. *Farmers' Loan* (1894), he opposed the income tax as an "assault upon capital." As presiding judge in his home circuit he courageously defied local sentiment on the Chinese question (*Chinese Immigration Case; Queue Case*).

Fillmore, Millard (b. Locke, N.Y., 7 Jan. 1800; d. Buffalo, 8 Mar. 1874), 13th president of the U.S., read law, was admitted to the bar (1823), practiced in East Aurora until 1830, and then moved to Buffalo. As a protégé of Thurlow Weed he was sent to the state assembly (1829–31) on the Anti-Masonic ticket. Congressman (1833–35 and 1837–43), he joined the Whig party (1834) and became its leader in the House. As chairman of the Ways and Means Committee he drafted the tariff bill of 1842. Defeated as Whig nominee for governor of New York (1844), he was elected vice-president of the U.S. (1848), having been nominated on the ticket with Zachary Taylor to placate the Clay wing of the Whig party. On Taylor's death he succeeded to the presidency (9 July 1850–4 Mar. 1853), signed the Clay Compromise of 1850, and sought to enforce the Fugitive Slave Act at the cost of much popularity in the North. He approved the Perry Treaty opening relations with Japan. Denied renomination in 1852, he was the nominee of the American (Know-Nothing) party for the presidency in 1856, running a poor third.

Fish, Hamilton (b. New York City, 3 Aug. 1808; d. there, 6 Sept. 1893), statesman. Graduated from Columbia (1827), he was admitted to the New York bar (1830), and in 1842 was elected to Congress on the Whig ticket, serving 1 term. He was lieutenant governor (1847–48) and governor (1849–50) of New York, and served (1851–57) in the U.S. Senate, during which time he moved into the Republican party. During the Civil War he was a member of the Union defense committee of New York State and was a federal commissioner for the relief of prisoners. As Secretary of State (1869–77) under President Grant, he negotiated the Treaty of Washington (1871), which settled the *Alabama* controversy and other matters of dispute between the U.S. and Great Britain; handled the *Virginius* crisis that arose (Nov. 1873) with Spain; negotiated a treaty of commercial reciprocity with Hawaii (1875); and reached a general settlement with Spain (1876) concerning American claims in Cuba.

Fitzgerald, Francis Scott Key (b. St. Paul, Minn., 24 Sept. 1896; d. Hollywood, Calif., 21 Dec. 1940), novelist, lived between the poles of success and despair, much like the lost-rich characters of his novels. Entering Princeton in 1913, he left in 1917 to enlist in the army. His first novel, rewritten for the third time in St. Paul, *This Side of Paradise* (1920), depicted the younger generation of the "Jazz Age." On the strength of its financial success he married the beautiful Zelda Sayre, and they began the life of desperate gaiety which took a heavy toll of both. In 1922 he published *The Beautiful and Damned*. In 1924 he and his wife moved to Europe, where they hoped to live more cheaply, and remained there until 1930. Zelda Sayre suffered 2 mental breakdowns from which she never recovered, and Fitzgerald began drinking heavily. His most brilliant book, *The Great Gatsby* (1925), was a critical success but a financial failure, and *Tender Is the Night* was a critical failure as well (1933). He retreated to a small Southern town, where he wrote *The Crack-Up* (1936), and then left for Hollywood, where he wrote for the movies.

Flexner, Abraham (b. Louisville, Ky., 13 Nov. 1866; d. Washington, D.C., 21 Sept. 1959), educational administrator, was graduated from Johns Hopkins (A.B., 1886). After 19 years as secondary school teacher and principal he took graduate work at Harvard (M.A., 1906) and the Univ. of Berlin (1906–07). In 1908 he joined the research staff of the Carnegie Foundation for the Advancement of Teaching. His reports, *Medical Education in the U.S. and Canada* (1910) and *Medical Education in Europe* (1912), hastened much-needed reforms in teaching, curricula, and standards of American medical schools. His pamphlet, *A Modern School* (1916), led to the founding of the Lincoln Experimental School of Teachers College, Columbia. A member of the General Educational Board, 1912–25, he was influential in guiding philanthropies of the Rockefellers, the Carnegie trusts, and George Eastman. His *Universities—American, English, German* (1930) criticized abuses of the elective system in the U.S. and the trend toward noncultural subjects. As first director of the Institute for Advanced Study, Princeton, N.J., he profoundly influenced its plan, scope, and original membership. His other works include *I Remember: An Autobiography* (1940) and biographies of H. S. Pritchett (1943) and Daniel Coit Gilman (*q.v.*) (1946).

Ford, Gerald Rudolph [Leslie King, Jr.] (b. Omaha, Neb., 14 July 1913–), 38th president of the U.S. When he was 2 years old, his mother divorced his father and left Omaha for Grand Rapids, Mich. When she remarried, her husband, Gerald Ford, Sr., president of Ford Paint and Varnish Co., adopted the boy and gave him his name. Ford attended the Univ. of Michigan, where he was a star football player (A.B., 1935) and Yale Univ. Law School (LL.B., 1941). After 4 years in the navy (1941–45), he practiced law in Michigan. Elected to the House of Representatives as a Republican (1948), he served almost 25 consecutive years (1949–72). He was a member of the House Appropriations Committee (1951–65), elected chairman of the House Republican Conference (1963), and Minority Leader (1965), deposing Charles A. Halleck. His voting record in the Congress was conservative, opposing minimum wage bills (1960, 1966, 1973), the creation of the Office of Economic Opportunity (1964), and Medicare (1965). Known for tolerance of differing opinions, he was considered for the Republican vice-presidential nomination in 1960. Ford supported Richard M. Nixon for the presidential nomination (1968) and served as permanent chairman of the Republican Convention (1968, 1972). During Nixon's first term, he was a strong supporter of controversial administration policies such as construction of the supersonic transport plane and prohibiting the busing of school children. In 1970 Ford led the unsuccessful attempt to impeach Supreme Court Justice William O. Douglas. He was nominated vice-president (12 Oct. 1972) by President Nixon in accordance with procedures of the 25th Amendment, two days after the resignation of Spiro T. Agnew. He took the oath of office the day the House of Representatives completed the confirmation process (6 Dec. 1972). While vice-president, Ford staunchly defended Nixon's innocence of involvement in the Watergate coverup. He assumed the presidency (9 Aug. 1974) upon the resignation of Nixon.

Ford, Henry (b. near Dearborn, Mich., 30 July 1863; d. Dearborn, Mich., 7 Apr. 1947), industrialist. His formal schooling at Greenfield, Mich., ended in 1878, and in the following year he moved to Detroit, where he worked (1879–84) as a machine-shop apprentice and as a traveling repairman for a farm machinery firm. After operating a sawmill for several years, he became (1887) chief engineer of the Edison Illuminating Co. in Detroit. His first automobile was developed and built by 1896. For a time he was associated with the Detroit Automobile Co., manufacturers of custom-built vehicles. After manufacturing his first racing car, the "999," Ford organized (1903) the Ford Motor Co., which in 1909 produced the first "Model T" (popularly known as the "flivver"), a standardized vehicle turned out on a mass-production assembly line. The factory assembly methods evolved by Ford engineers made him a worldwide symbol of American industrial technique. Ford's victory in the suit (1903–11) brought against him by the Association of Licensed Automobile Manufacturers (the Selden Patent Suit) freed the industry from the hold of an agreement that threatened to retard the development of automobile manufacture. In 1914 Ford attracted national attention by introducing into his plants the 8-hour day with a minimum daily wage of $5. At the same time he inaugurated a profit-sharing plan for his employees. Late in 1915, Ford chartered the *Oscar II* (commonly known as the Ford Peace Ship), which took to the Scandinavian nations a group of pacifists, feminists, and other idealists in an attempt to halt World War I by neutral mediation. During that war he manufactured a wide range of equipment for the U.S. government, including gun carriages and Liberty motors. In 1918 he was an unsuccessful candidate for U.S. senator from Michigan. He served as president of the Ford Motor Co. until 1919, when he was succeeded by his son, Edsel B. Ford; upon the death of the latter, he again became president (1943) and served until his death. The Ford Foundation was established by Henry and Edsel Ford in 1936. Its operations were conducted on a relatively modest scale until 1951, when with vastly increased assets the Ford Foundation undertook a diversified program in educational philanthropy and other fields.

Forrest, Edwin (b. Philadelphia, Pa., 9 Mar. 1806; d. there, 12 Dec. 1872), actor. He made his debut (27 Nov. 1820) at the Walnut Street Theater, Philadelphia, in the role of Young Norval, and subsequently was a member of a roving company on the frontier circuit. He played at New Orleans as a member of James H. Caldwell's company and supported Edmund Kean in an engagement at Albany (1825). He made his New York debut (23 June 1826) at the Park Theater as Othello and in the ensuing decade became a leading American actor, appearing in Shakespearean tragic roles and in plays such as John H. Stone's *Metamora* (1829) and Robert M. Bird's tragedy *The Gladiator*, both of which won prizes offered by Forrest to encourage plays by native dramatists. In 1834 Forrest went to Europe, where he was acclaimed as the first great American-born actor. His rivalry with the British actor Macready resulted in the Astor Place Riot (10 May 1849) at New York, in which 22 persons lost their lives. The last 2 decades of Forrest's life were darkened by domestic difficulties that took on the dimensions of public scandals, and by a growing personal bitterness and isolation. The house he bought at Philadelphia is now maintained as the Forrest Home for aged actors.

Foster, Stephen Collins (b. Allegheny City, Pa., 4 July 1826; d. New York City, 13 Jan. 1864), composer, for a brief period in 1841 attended Jefferson College. He worked (1846) as a bookkeeper for his brother at Cincinnati, where several Negro ballads composed by Foster, such as "O Susanna," "Away Down South," and "Uncle Ned," were used by a local publisher who brought out *Songs of the Sable Harmonists* (1848). Thereafter Foster devoted himself to songwriting, producing ballads and songs, most of them for Negro minstrels. He made an agreement (1851) with E. P. Christy giving first-performance rights to Christy's Minstrels and publication rights to himself. Among Foster's songs are "Nelly Was a Lady" (1849), "De Camptown Races" (1850), "The Old Folks at Home" (1851; also known as "Swanee River"), "Massa's in de Cold, Cold Ground" (1852), "My Old Kentucky Home" (1853), "Old Dog Tray" (1853), "Jeannie with the Light Brown Hair" (1854), and "Old Black Joe" (1860). Foster spent his last years in poverty.

Frankfurter, Felix (b. Vienna, Austria, 15 Nov. 1882; d. Washington, D.C., 22 Feb. 1965), jurist, came to the U.S. in 1894, received his A.B. (1902) from College of the City of New York and his LL.B. (highest honors, 1906) from the Harvard Law School. Assistant U.S. Attorney, southern district of New York (1906–10), he served as law officer in the Bureau of Insular Affairs (1911–14), and joined the faculty of the Harvard Law School in 1914, where he taught administrative law until 1939. During World War I he served as assistant to the Secretary of War, counsel to the president's Mediation Board (1917–18), and chairman, War Labor Policies Board (1918). He argued or filed briefs before the Supreme Court in *Bunting* v. *Oregon* (1917) and *Adkins* v. *Children's Hospital* (1923), and gained national prominence by his critique of the Sacco-Vanzetti trial (*The Case of Sacco and Vanzetti*, 1927). Close adviser to President Franklin D. Roosevelt, he was influential in recruiting personnel for the New Deal. Although officially neutral during the court-packing fight (1937), posthumous publication of his correspondence proves that he was a constant adviser to Roosevelt during the episode, remaining publicly silent at the president's request. Appointed associate justice of the Supreme Court (1939), he quickly assumed leadership in opposing the Black-Douglas position that the 1st Amendment rights were absolute, whereas he considered that amendment a generic provision requiring definition by present experience. The view that freedom is not absolute but must be weighed against legislative judgment he expressed in the *Gobitis Case* (1940), sustaining a state flag salute law. "One who belongs to the most vilified and persecuted minority in history is not likely to be insensible to the freedoms guaranteed by our Constitution," he declared in dissenting to the reversal in *W. Va. Bd. of Educ.* v. *Barnette* (1943). In setting boundaries to the right to picket (*Milk Drivers Union* v. *Meadowmoor Dairies* [1941]), he said: "Utterance in a context of violence can lose its significance as an appeal to reason and become part of an instrument of force." In the *Dennis Case* (1951) he repudiated the "clear and present danger" formula, holding that advocacy of overthrow of the government deserves little protection. He wrote numerous works in the field of constitutional and administrative law, including *The Commerce Clause under Marshall, Taney and Waite* (1937) and *Felix Frankfurter Reminisces* (1960, recorded by H. B. Phillips).

Franklin, Benjamin (b. Boston, Mass., 17 Jan. 1706; d. Philadelphia, 17 Apr. 1790), statesman, diplomat, editor, and scientist, attended school briefly; worked in his father's tallow shop and then in his brother's printing shop. In 1723 he went to Philadelphia and worked as a printer, acquiring an interest in (1729) and sole ownership of the *Pennsylvania Gazette*, which he edited until 1748, and publishing annually (1732–57) *Poor Richard's Almanack*. Leader in cultural movements, he founded the Junto, a debating club (1727) which developed into the American Philosophical Society (1743); a circulating library (1731); Philadelphia's first fire company (1736); and an academy (1751), nucleus of the Univ. of Pennsylvania. His international fame as scientist and inventor began with the invention of the Franklin stove (1742). The identity of lightning and electricity was demonstrated in France (1752) by methods he suggested, and he later confirmed it by his kite experiment. Clerk of the Pennsylvania Assembly (1736–51), he was a member of that body (1751–64), deputy postmaster at Philadelphia (1737–53), and, jointly with William Hunter, postmaster general for the colonies (1753–74). In this office he improved the postal service and placed it on a profitable basis. Delegate to the Albany Congress (1754), he drafted a Plan of Union which the Congress adopted but which both Great Britain and the colonies rejected for opposing reasons. He went to England (1757) to press the claims of the Pennsylvania Assembly to tax the proprietary estates, and acted as agent in England for Pennsylvania (1764–75), for Georgia (after 1768), and for Massachusetts (after 1770). He was instrumental in securing the repeal of the Stamp Act (1766), but was publicly censured for allowing publication of the "Hutchinson letters" (1774). Returning to Philadelphia (1775), he was a member of the 2d Continental Congress and became the first Postmaster General (1775–76). He was one of 3 commissioners sent (1776) to secure the aid of Canada, helped draft the Declaration of Independence, and was a signer. One of the 3 agents dispatched to France (1776–85), where his fame preceded him, he secured loans and concluded a treaty of alliance (1778). He was one of the negotiators of the Treaty of Peace with Great Britain (1783). President of the Executive Council of Pennsylvania (1785–88), he was a member of the Constitutional Convention (1787), where he was influential in framing the compromise between the large and small states on the question of representation in the House of Representatives. His most famous book was his unfinished *Autobiography*, 1706–59 (written between 1771 and 1789).

Frémont, John Charles (b. Savannah, Ga., 31 Jan. 1813; d. New York City, 13 July 1890), explorer, politician, and soldier. He attended Charleston (S.C.) College, 1829–31, and in 1835 became an assistant engineer in the U.S. Topographical Corps, in which he was commissioned a 2d lieutenant (1838). In 1838 he assisted Joseph N. Nicollet in exploring the plateau between the upper Mississippi and Missouri rivers. He married (1841) Jessie Benton, daughter of Sen. Thomas Hart Benton (*q.v.*), who used his influence to further Frémont's expeditions. Frémont made 3 important explorations that earned for him the sobriquet "the Pathfinder": a scientific investigation of the Oregon Trail that took him to the Wind River chain of the

Rockies and through South Pass (1842); to the Great Basin between the Rockies and the Sierras (1843–44); and to the Sierra Nevada by way of the headwaters of the Arkansas, Rio Grande, and Colorado rivers. The 3d exploration was made on the eve of the Mexican War; when he reached the Pacific Coast, Frémont played a leading and controversial role in the conquest of California. His quarrel with Gen. Stephen W. Kearny resulted in a court-martial at Washington, D.C. (Nov. 1847–Jan. 1848), that found Frémont guilty of mutiny and disobedience. A 4th expedition (1848–49) to ascertain the practicality of Sen. Benton's proposed central route to the Pacific proved a disaster. Despite President Polk's remission of the sentence, Frémont resigned from the army. Returning to California, Frémont served a brief term as U.S. senator from that state and in 1853–54 made winter expeditions for a southern railway route to the Pacific. In 1856 he was the first presidential candidate of the newly organized Republican party on an antislavery platform, losing to Buchanan by about 500,000 votes. At the outbreak of the Civil War he was appointed major general in charge of the Department of the West, with headquarters at St. Louis. When his radical policy toward slaveholders brought him into conflict with the Lincoln administration, he was removed from his post and given a command in western Virginia, but resigned when he was placed under Gen. John Pope, with whom he was on unfriendly terms. After making unsuccessful attempts at railroad promotion, he served as territorial governor of Arizona (1878–83) and in 1890 was restored to the rank of major general with retirement pay.

Frost, Robert (b. San Francisco, Calif., 26 Mar. 1874; d. Boston, Mass., 29 Jan. 1963), poet. He attended Dartmouth and Harvard; worked in New England as a shoemaker, teacher, country editor, and farmer; and in 1912 went to England, where he brought out his first volume of poetry, *A Boy's Will* (1913). Following the publication of *North of Boston* (1914), he returned to the U.S. (1915), where he soon won recognition as a poet of the first rank; he was awarded the Pulitzer prize 4 times (1924, 1931, 1937, 1943). Most of his poetry is based on themes drawn from New England rural life. His works include *Mountain Interval* (1916), *New Hampshire* (1923), *West-Running Brook* (1928), *Collected Poems* (1930, 1939), *Selected Poems* (1937), *A Further Range* (1937), *A Witness Tree* (1943), and *The Gift Outright* (1961). Among his individual poems are "Mowing," "The Death of the Hired Man," "Home Burial," "Mending Wall," "Birches," and "Fire and Ice." He was the first poet to partcipate in a presidential inaugural ceremony (1961).

Fulbright, James William (b. Sumner, Mo., 9 Apr. 1905–   ), statesman, received his B.A. from the Univ. of Arkansas (1925), studied as a Rhodes scholar at Oxford, where he received a B.A. (1928) and M.A. (1931). He attended George Washington Univ. Law School and served as an attorney for the Justice Department's Antitrust Division. He taught law at the George Washington Univ. Law School (1935) and the Univ. of Arkansas (1939), and became president of the latter institution (1939–41). Elected to the U.S. House of Representatives (1942), Fulbright, the freshman congressman from Fayetteville, Ark., introduced the Fulbright Resolution (1943) ensuring active U.S. involvement in world affairs after the war and its entrance into the UN. He was elected to the U.S. Senate (1944) and served 5 consecutive terms (1945–74). He sponsored the Fulbright Act (1946), which established an educational exchange program between the U.S. and foreign countries. Although wary of Communist aggression during the Cold War, Fulbright opposed Gen. MacArthur's attempt to escalate the Korean War against Communist China. A close friend of Adlai Stevenson, he served as his adviser during the 1952 presidential campaign. Fulbright was one of the few senators to oppose U.S. atom bomb testing at Bikini Island (1946) and to vote against funds for Sen. Joseph McCarthy's investigations. As chairman of the Senate Foreign Relations Committee (1959–74), Fulbright was one of the first senators to oppose the Vietnam War, amplifying the national debate by holding televised hearings (1966). In his later years in the Senate he led the opposition to the manner and terms of U.S. foreign aid programs, and called for a less pro-Israel stance in the Middle East, and favored legislation curbing presidential warmaking powers. Fulbright was defeated in the Democratic party primary (1974) in his bid for a 6th term. His books— *Old Myths and New Realities* (1964) and *The Arrogance of Power* (1966)— were critical of U.S. foreign policy.

Fuller, Margaret [full name **Sarah Margaret Fuller**; title **Marchioness Ossoli**] (b. Cambridgeport, Mass., 23 May 1810; d. off Fire Island, N.Y., 19 July 1850), feminist, critic, and journalist. A precocious child, she received most of her education from her father and at an early age formed friendships with New England intellectual leaders such as James Freeman Clarke and Frederic Henry Hedge. She conducted (1839–44) her "conversations" at the Boston residence of Elizabeth Peabody, drawing her pupils from leading circles of the city. The material of her "conversations" appeared in her feminist work, *Woman in the Nineteenth Century* (1845). With Ralph Waldo Emerson and George Ripley, she edited (1840–42) *The Dial*, Transcendentalist journal. Her book, *Summer on the Lakes, in 1843* (1844), drew the attention of Horace Greeley, who offered her a staff job with the New York *Tribune*. Her significant writings as literary critic of the *Tribune* from 1844 to 1846 were published as *Literature and Art* (1846). She went abroad in 1846 and while in Italy had a son (1848) by the Marquis Angelo Ossoli, whom she married in 1849. With her husband, an ardent follower of Mazzini, she took part in the Roman Revolution. She and her family died in a shipwreck while returning to America.

Fuller, Melville Weston (b. Augusta Me., 11 Feb. 1833; d. Sorrento, Me., 4 July 1910), chief justice of the U.S., graduated from Bowdoin College (1853). He studied law in the offices of his uncles (1853–54) and for 6 months at the Harvard Law School (1854–55), after which he entered practice in Bangor, Me. (1855). He became associate editor of *The Age*, a Democratic magazine (1855–56), and in 1856 became city solicitor and president of the Common Council of Augusta, Me. He soon moved to Chicago, where he established a reputation as an expert in commercial and real estate law, representing merchants and railroads. Active in politics, he was a member of the Illinois Constitutional Convention (1862), of the Illinois House of Representatives (1863–65), and a delegate to several Democratic National Conventions. As an advocate, Fuller appeared often before the U.S. Supreme Court. Fuller was appointed chief justice (1888) by President Cleveland and served on the court until his death. The Supreme Court during the period of Fuller's service developed new tools and concepts to protect property rights from government regulation—

among them substantive due process and liberty of contract. The Fuller court was noteworthy for its antilabor decisions. In *Pollock* v. *Farmers' Loan and Trust Company* (1895), a narrow majority of the court agreed with Fuller that the income tax law of 1894 was unconstitutional on the grounds that it was a direct tax, thereby reversing earlier decisions which the chief justice termed "a century of error." Fuller spoke for the majority in *United States* v. *E. C. Knight Co.* (1895), holding that sugar refining was manufacturing and not commerce, thereby drastically curbing the Sherman Anti-Trust Act. However, in the *Danbury Hatters Case* (1908) Fuller construed the Sherman Act so as to apply to labor. Believing that the Constitution followed the flag, Fuller was generally in the minority in the Insular Cases which followed the Spanish-American War. An excellent judicial administrator, he was responsible for calming tensions within the court and for persuading Congress to pass the Circuit Court of Appeals Act of 1891. Fuller declined Cleveland's offer (1892) to become Secretary of State but he did serve as arbitrator with Justice David J. Brewer of the Venezuela-British Guiana boundary dispute (1899).

Fulton, Robert (b. Little Britain, now Fulton, Pa., 14 Nov. 1765; d. New York City, 24 Feb. 1815), artist, civil engineer, and inventor, pioneer in steam navigation. During his boyhood he showed a talent for drawing and mechanical crafts, becoming an expert gunsmith in nearby Lancaster. Going to Philadelphia in 1783, he worked as an artist and draftsman; in 1786 he went abroad, where he remained for 20 years. Although his first years in London were devoted to painting, he soon shifted his interest to science and engineering. He invented an apparatus (the double inclined plane) for raising and lowering canal boats, a power

shovel for digging canal channels, a device for sawing marble, and a flax-spinning machine. His chief interest was in internal improvements, particularly inland waterways. In 1794 he settled in Paris, where he painted what is held to be the first panorama. He published *A Treatise on the Improvement of Canal Navigation* (1796), a comprehensive work of its kind, and submitted to the Board of Agriculture of Great Britain detailed plans and proposals (1796) for the construction of cast-iron aqueducts requiring simplified casting and building operations. One of these structures was later reared across the Dee near Chester. Fulton also proposed cast-iron bridges of his own design which were built at several points in England. For 9 years, beginning in 1797, he devoted himself to the development of the submarine mine and torpedo; failing to gain the financial support of the French government, he secured the aid of Joel Barlow and made short-lived experiments with a self-propelled submarine torpedo. In 1801, after Napoleon showed interest in Fulton's project, Fulton made successful experiments with his submarine boat, the *Nautilus;* but upon his failure to make a satisfactory demonstration under actual combat conditions, the French authorities quickly lost interest. In 1804 he placed his invention at the disposal of the British government, which finally refused to adopt it despite a successful test carried out in 1805. Returning to the U.S. (1805), Fulton continued the experiments with steamboats that he had begun along the Seine in 1803 with the assistance of the U.S. minister to France, Robert R. Livingston. Fulton designed the *Clermont,* a boat with 2 side paddlewheels. The *Clermont* was completed in the spring of 1807 and the Watt steam engine was installed later. During the course of its construction, he demonstrated in New York Harbor (20 July 1807) the effectiveness of his torpedo device. Starting out from New York on 17 Aug. 1807, the *Clermont* made its voyage to Albany and back in 5 days (62 hours of actual operating time). Until his death Fulton was active in organizing and managing steamboat lines. In 1814 he constructed for the U.S. government the *Fulton the First,* a huge paddlewheel steam warship, never tested in warfare.

Gallatin, Albert [full name **Abraham Alfonse Albert Gallatin**] (b. Geneva, Switzerland, 29 Jan. 1761; d. Astoria, Long Island, N.Y., 12 Aug. 1849), statesman, diplomat, and ethnologist. He was graduated (1779) from Geneva Academy; emigrated to Massachusetts (1780); settled in the Pennsylvania back country (1784), where he made unsuccessful ventures in land speculation; and as a member (1790–92) of the Pennsylvania legislature emerged as a leader of the nascent Republican forces in the western part of the state. He was elected (28 Feb. 1793) to the U.S. Senate, but a Federalist majority deprived him of his seat (28 Feb. 1794) on the ground that he had not been a U.S. citizen for 9 years. An opponent of the federal excise tax of 1791, he took a moderate stand during the Whisky Rebellion of 1794 and was instrumental in averting serious bloodshed. As a member of Congress (1795–1801), he became the recognized leader of the Republican minority in the House. His able grasp of finance and his criticism of the Federalist policy in the Treasury Department led to the creation of a standing committee on finance. As Secretary of the Treasury (1801–14) under Jefferson and Madison, he carried out a program of financial reform and economy which after 1807 was virtually destroyed by embroilments in the Napoleonic Wars and by the War of 1812. He was a member of the commission (1814) which negotiated the Treaty of Ghent, served as

minister to France (1816–23) and to England (1826–27), and from 1831 to 1839 was president of the National Bank at New York City. Called "the father of American ethnology," he wrote *Synopsis of the Indian Tribes . . . of North America* (1836) and founded (1842) the American Ethnological Society.

Galloway, Joseph (b. West River, Anne Arundel Co., Md., c.1731; d. Watford, England, 29 Aug. 1803), colonial statesman, studied law in Philadelphia, where he rose to eminence at the bar. Assemblyman (1756–76, except for 1764–65), he joined Franklin in attempts to tax the Penns' land, and eventually, with Franklin, petitioned the crown to substitute royal for proprietary government. An imperial statesman, he saw the need for a revenue for America, but opposed parliamentary taxation. Instead, he advocated a written constitution for the empire. In the 1st Continental Congress (1774) he proposed the Galloway Plan for an imperial legislature, defeated by a close vote. Refusing to be a delegate to the 2d Congress, he criticized its predecessor in *A Candid Examination of the Mutual Claims of Great Britain and the Colonies* (1775). Civil administrator of Philadelphia during Gen. Howe's occupation of the city, he left for London with the recapture of the city (1778), and became the spokesman for the Loyalists. His estates confiscated by Pennsylvania and his petition (1793) to return denied, he spent his last 20 years in exile.

Garfield, James Abram (b. Cuyahoga Co., Ohio, 19 Nov. 1831; d. Elberon, N.J., 19 Sept. 1881), 20th president of the U.S., was graduated from Williams College (1856), served as president of Western Reserve Electric Institute (later Hiram College), 1857–61, was admitted to the bar, and elected to the Ohio Senate as a Republican (1859). During the Civil War he distinguished himself in engagements at Middle Creek, Ky., Shiloh, and Chickamauga; was a member of the court of inquiry in the Fitz John Porter case (1862); and was on the staff of Gen. W. S. Rosecrans. Congressman (1863–81), his prestige as orator and parliamentarian made him Blaine's rival for influence with that body. Although charged, without proof, of corruption in connection with Crédit Mobilier, he was elected to the U.S. Senate (1880), and in that same year nominated and elected president. In the midst of involvements over appointments to office, prompting the resignation of Roscoe Conkling and T. C. Platt from the U.S. Senate, he was fatally shot in the Washington railroad station by Charles J. Guiteau, a disappointed office seeker.

Garrison, William Lloyd (b. Newburyport, Mass., 10 Dec. 1805; d. New York City, 24 May 1879), abolitionist. After brief schooling, he was apprenticed (1818) to the editor of the Newburyport *Herald;* became (1826) editor of the Newburyport *Free Press;* when that newspaper failed, he moved to Boston and became (1828) coeditor of the *National Philanthropist,* an organ devoted to reform causes. At about this time he met Benjamin Lundy, a Quaker antislavery writer and journalist, whom he joined at Baltimore (1829) as coeditor of *The Genius of Universal Emancipation.* Garrison's tirades in the columns of this paper resulted in his imprisonment for libel (1830), but he was released after the New York merchant and abolitionist sympathizer Arthur Tappan paid his fine. Returning to Boston (1830), he founded and published the *Liberator,* in which he was joined by his partner, Isaac Knapp. The first issue of this abolitionist paper, dated 1 Jan. 1831, announced the uncompromising attitude that henceforth characterized Garrison's crusade against slavery and slaveholders. He remained its editor until the last issue of the *Liberator* appeared 35 years later. Garrison demanded immediate and complete emancipation of slaves. He was one of the founders of the New England Antislavery Society (1831) and organized the American Antislavery Society (1833). Resentment in the North against the abolitionists was so strong that Garrison was dragged through the streets by a Boston mob and almost killed (21 Oct. 1835). His opposition to political action resulted in a split in the organized antislavery ranks in the late 1830s. During that period Garrison embraced disunionism, demanding that the North withdraw from a compact that sheltered slavery. Under his influence the Massachusetts Antislavery Society resolved (1843) that the Constitution of the U.S. was "a covenant with death and an agreement with hell." On 4 July 1854, before a gathering at Framingham, Mass., he publicly burned the Constitution, saying: "So perish all compromises with tyranny!" During the Civil War he gave his full support to Lincoln after the issuance of the Emancipation Proclamation. In the years after the war he was allied with reform causes, including prohibition and women's suffrage.

Garvey, Marcus (b. St. Ann's Bay, Jamaica, 17 Aug. 1887; d. London, England, 10 June 1940), social reformer. Largely self-taught, Garvey attended school in Jamaica until he was 14, and then worked for a printer, traveled in Central America, and lived in London (1912–14). After returning to Jamaica he established the Universal Negro Improvement and Conservation Association and African Communities League (UNIA, 1 Aug. 1914), whose aims were to instill racial pride, acquire economic power for blacks, and build a black-governed nation in Africa. In Mar. 1916 he arrived in Harlem where his oratory and natural leadership abilities drew thousands of blacks into the UNIA, making it the first important U.S. black nationalist movement. By 1919 there were 30 branches of the UNIA in the U.S., most in Northern urban ghettos. Garvey established (Jan. 1918) the *Negro World,* the official UNIA weekly, which was published until 1933 with an estimated circulation of from 60,000 to 200,-000. He presided over an international UNIA convention (1920), which promoted African nationalism and adopted a Declaration of the Rights of the Negro People of the World. The following year he proclaimed himself provisional president of an empire of Africa. Garvey was criticized by other black leaders, among them W.E.B. DuBois (*q.v.*) and A. Philip Randolph (*q.v.*), for his advocacy of racial purity and separatism and for his impracticality. A second convention in 1924 produced final plans for a "back-to-Africa" colonization program, which never received the necessary support from African nations. He supported an independent black economy within the framework of white capitalism and organized the Universal Black Cross Nurses, the Negro Factories Corp., as well as a chain of restaurants and grocery stores. His biggest project was the organization of the Black Star Line (1919), a steamship company owned, controlled, and operated by black people. In 1922 the line collapsed, due to faulty ships and mismanagement, and Garvey was tried, convicted, and sentenced to a maximum of 5 years in prison for using the mails to defraud shareholders. President Coolidge commuted his sentence and ordered his deportation as an undesirable alien (1927). Garvey moved the headquarters of the UNIA to London (1935) but he could never again build up a large following, and died in relative obscurity. Without Garvey the UNIA

declined, but his ideas of racial solidarity and racial enterprise were revived by the Black Power movement of the 1960s.

George, Henry (b. Philadelphia, Pa., 2 Sept. 1839; d. New York City, 29 Oct. 1897), economist and reformer. After a brief period of formal schooling, he went to sea as a foremast boy (1855), became a typesetter (1856), was a prospector in the Pacific Northwest (1858), and until 1880, when he moved to New York, was a printer and newspaperman, chiefly at San Francisco. He published (1871) a pamphlet, *Our Land and Land Policy,* which set forth the basic elements of the single-tax theory elaborated by him in *Progress and Poverty* (1879). Holding that taxes should be confined to the economic rent derived from land, George asserted that the accumulation of such unearned increment tended to impoverish society, and that the single tax, by eliminating all other government levies, would enable the unimpeded and benevolent operation of the economic mechanism. After publishing *The Irish Land Question* (1881), he served as a correspondent in the British Isles for the *Irish World.* He was also active as a lecturer. In 1886, as the liberal and labor candidate for mayor of New York, he was defeated in a contest with Abram S. Hewitt and Theodore Roosevelt. In 1897 he was the independent Democratic candidate for mayor of New York, and died while campaigning for that office.

Gershwin, George (b. Brooklyn, N.Y., 26 Sept. 1898; d. Hollywood, Calif., 11 July 1937), composer, was educated in the New York public schools, studied the piano with Charles Hambitzer and harmony with Rubin Goldmark, and worked as a song plugger in Tin Pan Alley. His first song, "When You Want 'Em You Can't Get 'Em," was published in 1916; his first musical comedy score was written for *La, La, Lucille* (1919). Gershwin's use of the native jazz idiom in serious music first appeared in *Rhapsody in Blue* (1st performance given by Paul Whiteman and his orchestra at Aeolian Hall, New York City, 12 Feb. 1924). In this vein Gershwin also wrote *Concerto in F* (1925), *An American in Paris* (1928), *Second Rhapsody* (1931), *Cuban Overture* (1932), and the opera *Porgy and Bess* (1935). Among Gershwin's popular musical comedies were *George White's Scandals* (1920–24), *Lady Be Good* (1924), *Rosalie* (1927), *Strike Up the Band* (1927), *Show Girl* (1929), *Girl Crazy* (1930), *Of Thee I Sing* (1931; 1st musical comedy awarded the Pulitzer prize), and *Let 'Em Eat Cake* (1933). His best-known songs include "I'll Build a Stairway to Paradise" (1922), "Somebody Loves Me" (1924), "It Ain't Necessarily So" (1935), and "Summertime" (1935).

Gesell, Arnold (b. Alma, Wis., 21 June 1880; d. New Haven, Conn., 29 May 1961), child psychologist, received his B.Ph. from the Univ. of Wisconsin (1903) and his Ph.D. in psychology from Clark Univ. (1906). Meanwhile he taught history, German, and psychology in Wisconsin high schools (1899–1901), was principal of Chippewa Falls high school, Wis. (1903–04), and was a settlement worker on New York's lower east side (1906–07). While an assistant professor of education at Yale, he was a full-time student at the Yale Univ. Medical School, where he received his M.D. (1915). He first became interested in child psychology when he visited Dr. Henry Goddard's training school for mentally defective children in Vineland, N.J. (1909). Dr. Gesell was director of the Yale Clinic for Child Development from its inception (1911) to his retirement (1948); professor of child hygiene at Yale Medical School (1915–48); and a research as-

sociate at the Yale Child Vision Research Center (1948–50). He became a pioneer in studying the mental growth of babies from infancy until they went to school. *The Child from Five to Ten* (1946); *Youth: The Years from Ten to Sixteen* (1956); and *Infant and Child in the Culture of Today* (1943), all written with Dr. Frances L. Ilg, were Gesell's best-known works and were widely consulted by many American parents. Gesell considered these books only as broad guides and not as exact stipulations of normal child behavior, insisting that, while the mental growth of children reveals itself in consistent behavior patterns, each child is an individual at birth. His studies emphasized that parents should rear children with "discerning guidance," with neither excessive severity nor excessive laxity.

Gibbons, James (b. Baltimore, Md., 23 July 1834; d. there, 24 Mar. 1921), Roman Catholic prelate, was graduated (1858) from St. Charles College, near Baltimore, took advanced training for the priesthood at St. Mary's Seminary, Baltimore, and was ordained (1861). He took charge of St. Bridget's Church in the suburb of Canton and during the Civil War was chaplain at Ft. McHenry. Invited to take the post of secretary to Archbishop Martin J. Spalding, he became (1866) assistant chancellor of the Second Plenary Council of Baltimore and head of the newly established Vicarate Apostolic of North Carolina. Consecrated bishop of Adramyttum (16 Aug. 1868), he was at that time the youngest of all Catholic bishops. He served (1870) as the youngest member of the Ecumenical Council of the Vatican; succeeded (1872) to the bishopric of Richmond; was appointed (May 1877) coadjutor archbishop of Baltimore; and, upon the death of Archbishop James R. Bayley (Oct. 1877), became head of the See of

Baltimore. He organized and conducted the Third Plenary Council of Baltimore (1884), over which he presided as apostolic delegate. In 1885 he was named the second American cardinal and was formally installed at Baltimore (1886) and at Rome (1887), where he made a memorable pronouncement expressing his attachment to American institutions. Sympathetic to the cause of labor, he secured at Rome ecclesiastical assurances that the Knights of Labor would not be condemned in the U.S., and was instrumental in obtaining the removal of the hierarchical ban against that body in Canada. He laid the cornerstone of the Catholic Univ. of America at Washington, D.C. (1888), and served as chancellor until his death. In 1903 he was the first American to participate in the election of a pope.

Gibbs, Josiah Willard (b. New Haven, Conn., 11 Feb. 1839; d. there, 28 Apr. 1903), mathematical physicist. He was graduated from Yale (1858), where he received the degree of Ph.D. (1863), served as tutor at Yale, and in 1866 went to the Continent, where he continued his studies at Paris (1866–67), Berlin (1867–68), and Heidelberg (1868–69). He was appointed (1871) professor of mathematical physics at Yale, holding that post until his death. His chief contribution was his theory of thermodynamics, the basis for the major part of modern physical chemistry and chemical engineering. Among the papers he published are "Graphical Methods in the Thermodynamics of Fluids" (1873), "A Method of Geometrical Representation of the Thermodynamic Properties of Substances by Means of Surfaces" (1873), and "Electrochemical Thermodynamics" (1886). His most important single paper, "On the Equilibrium of Heterogeneous Substances" (1876), contained his formulation of the phase rule, one of the

revolutionary laws of theoretical physics. Between 1880 and 1884 he evolved a system of vector analysis adapted to the needs of mathematical physicists, publishing papers such as "On the Role of Quaternions in the Algebra of Vectors" (1891) and "Quaternions and Vector Analysis" (1893). From 1882 to 1889 he devoted himself principally to theories of optics, developing an electromagnetic theory of light. In 1902 he published *Elementary Principles in Statistical Mechanics*. His *Collected Works* were published in 1928.

Gilman, Daniel Coit (b. Norwich, Conn., 6 July 1831; d. there, 13 Oct. 1908), educational administrator. He was graduated from Yale (1852), served as an attaché (1853–55) of the U.S. legation at St. Petersburg, and drew up the plan for the Sheffield Scientific School at Yale, where he served (1855–72) as librarian and professor of physical and political geography. With Eliot of Harvard and White of Cornell he was the chief maker of the modern American university, serving as president (1872–75) of the Univ. of California, and as first president (1876–1901) of Johns Hopkins, which he made into a leading center of creative study and research. He was instrumental in founding the Johns Hopkins Hospital (1889) and Medical School (1893), and raised the general level of medical training in the U.S.

Goddard, Robert Hutchings (b. Worcester, Mass., 5 Oct. 1882; d. Baltimore, Md., 10 Aug. 1945), physicist, "father of the modern rocket," attended the Worcester Polytechnic Institute (B.S., 1908) and Clark Univ. (M.A., 1910; Ph.D., 1911), where he became professor of physics (1919). In 1912 he began his work on rocketry, developing a general theory of rocket action, including the "optimum velocity" principle. Engaged in research during World War I, he developed a solid-propellant projectile which was used in World War II as the "bazooka." His paper "A Method of Reaching Extreme Altitudes" (1919) predicted the use of rockets to explore high altitudes and the lunar terrain. Other writings predicted interplanetary and intergalactic explorations. In 1926 he completed and successfully launched the world's first liquid-fuel rocket (prototype of the German V-2) and 4 years later fired a rocket to a height of 2,000 ft. at a speed of 500 mph. In 1935 one of his liquid-propellant rockets exceeded the speed of sound. During World War II he directed research in jet propulsion for the Navy.

Godkin, Edwin Lawrence (b. Moyne, County Wicklow, Ireland, 2 Oct. 1831; d. Brixham, England, 21 May 1902), editor. He was graduated (1851) from Queen's College, Belfast; worked in the London publishing house of Cassell, which brought out his *History of Hungary and the Magyars* (1853); was correspondent (1853–55) for the London *Daily News* during the Crimean War; and came to the U.S. in 1856. As the first editor (1865–1900) of the weekly *Nation,* and as editor (1883–1900) of the New York *Evening Post,* Godkin established new standards of American political journalism. An ardent exponent of civil service reform, he was an implacable foe of the spoils system. He pursued an independent liberal course in politics and in 1884 took a leading role in the Mugwump revolt against James G. Blaine.

Goethals, George Washington (b. Brooklyn, N.Y., 29 June 1858; d. New York City, 21 Jan. 1928), army officer and engineer, builder of the Panama Canal. He attended the College of the City of New York and was graduated from the U.S. Military Academy (1880). He

served (1882–1905) in the Engineer Corps of the U.S. army and (1903–07) on the Army General Staff. In the spring of 1907, when he held the rank of lieutenant colonel, he was appointed by President Theodore Roosevelt as chairman and chief engineer of the Isthmian Canal Commission. In this capacity, Goethals bore virtually sole responsibility for the successful administration of the canal project. His organizing ability overcame numerous serious difficulties involving engineering problems, employee grievances, housing and sanitation, and the establishment of a law enforcement system. He was made (1914) the first civil governor of the Panama Canal Zone, serving in that post until 1916, and was promoted to major general and received the thanks of Congress (1915). From Apr. to July 1917, he was general manager of the Emergency Fleet Corp. Although he was transferred to the retired list in 1916, he was recalled to duty (1917–19) as acting quartermaster general and director of purchase, storage, and supplies, responsible for the supply and transportation of all U.S. troops at home and abroad.

Gompers, Samuel (b. London, England, 27 Jan. 1850; d. San Antonio, Tex., 13 Dec. 1924), labor leader. Apprenticed as a cigarmaker in London, he arrived in the U.S. in 1863 and joined (1864) the Cigarmakers' Union, of which he became president in 1877. He was one of the main figures in the organization (1881) of the Federation of Organized Trades and Labor Unions of the U.S. and Canada, reorganized (1886) as the American Federation of Labor. Gompers was chosen president of the A.F. of L. and, with the exception of the year 1895, served in that capacity until his death. During that period he was the acknowledged head of the American labor movement. An exponent of craft unionism, Gompers stressed practical demands such as wages and hours, and was an avowed opponent of theorists and radicals in the labor movement. He was opposed to an independent labor party and eschewed political commitments by labor organizations to any of the existing parties. During World War I he organized a War Committee on Labor that was instrumental in maintaining national unity. Among his works are *Labor in Europe and America* (1910), *American Labor and the War* (1919), and *Seventy Years of Life and Labor* (2 vols., 1925).

Goodyear, Charles (b. New Haven, Conn., 29 Dec. 1800; d. New York City, 1 July 1860), inventor, pioneer of the rubber industry in the U.S. Until 1830, when he was declared bankrupt, he was in the hardware business at New Haven and Philadelphia. In 1834 he became interested in improving the process for curing India rubber. In the following years, despite poverty and time spent in debtors' prison, he experimented with raw rubber in an attempt to make a product that would not melt or decompose at high and low temperatures. He patented a process (17 June 1837) which he used in making articles such as shoes, tablecloths, and piano covers. From Nathaniel M. Hayward, who had devised a process that included the use of sulfur, Goodyear acquired a patent in 1839, and in the same year accidentally dropped a rubber and sulfur mixture on a hot stove, thus discovering the vulcanizing process. Borrowing a total of more than $50,000, Goodyear perfected the process and received a patent for it (15 June 1844). Financial obligations forced him to sell licenses and to establish royalties that were far less than the true value of the rights; consequently, the profits derived from his discoveries accrued to others. His subsequent years in Europe (1851–59) and America were marked by unsuccessful lawsuits and increasing debt.

Gorgas, William Crawford (b. Toulminville, Ala., 3 Oct. 1854; d. London, 3 July 1920), sanitarian, received his B.A. (1875) from the Univ. of the South. Unable to enter West Point, he was graduated from Bellevue Hospital Medical College (1879). After a year's internship at Bellevue, he was appointed (1880) to the U.S. Army Medical Corps. Surviving an epidemic of yellow fever at Ft. Brown, Tex., he was, due to his immunity, often assigned to posts where yellow fever was rampant. In 1898, following the occupation of Havana, he became chief sanitation officer of the city. Once the cause of yellow fever was established by Walter Reed, Gorgas succeeded in ridding the city of the disease by destroying the breeding places of the *Stegomyia* mosquito. Despite criticism, he introduced (1904) the same measures in the Panama Canal Zone, making Panama and Colón models of sanitation, and winning a worldwide reputation as a top sanitary expert. Appointed surgeon general of the army with the rank of brigadier general (1914), he was sent (1916) by the International Health Board to Central and South America on yellow fever missions. During World War I he served as head of the army Medical Service, and, when the war ended, on a yellow fever mission to the west coast of Africa. He wrote *Sanitation in Panama* (1915).

Graham, Martha (b. Pittsburgh, Pa., 11 May, c.1894–), dancer and choreographer, studied with Ruth St. Denis and Ted Shawn in Los Angeles and toured with their company. Her first professional appearance, with Shawn (1920), was followed by 2 years as solo dancer with the *Greenwich Village Follies* (1923–24). Her first recital with pupils came at the 48th Street Theater,

New York City (18 Apr. 1926). In 1930 Graham founded a Dance Repertory Theater. She taught at the Neighborhood Playhouse, the Juilliard School of Music, and founded Dance Studio (1928) which became the Martha Graham School of Contemporary Dance (1938). Graham was the first dancer to receive a Guggenheim Fellowship (1932). She enlarged the expressive possibilities of dance by her emotionality, her sense that movement is communicative, and by her strict technique with its distinctive vocabulary of contractions and contortions. She explored universal meanings in myth (*Alcestis*, 1960), religion (*Embattled Garden*, 1959), mystery (*El Penitente*, 1940), and in the conflicts of the individual psyche. She sought out as themes the basic forces of life—love, ecstasy, evil, and death—seen largely from the viewpoint of woman. She added to the theatrical possibilities of dance by employing dream sequences, flashbacks, symbolism, by collaborating with leading sculptors (Isamu Noguchi, *Seraphic Dialogue*, 1955), and by attention to costume and to color. A remarkable dancer, she starred in most of her own works and dominated the stage with a commanding "totemic" presence. Other major works include *Primitive Mysteries* (1931), *Letter to the World* (1940), *Appalachian Spring* (1944), *Night Journey* (1947), *Diversion of Angels* (1948), *Phaedra* (1962), *Clytemnestra* (1958). As a teacher, Graham's influence has been felt throughout contemporary dance. Her pupils have included Paul Taylor, Merce Cunningham, Erick Hawkins, Glen Tetley, and Anna Sokolow. Her company led off the Festival of Dance, 1968–69 (New York City), a turning point in the popular reception of modern dance. She retired as a dancer (1969) but reshaped her company to preserve her repertory and style. During her company's Broadway season (15 Apr.–4 May 1974) her 147th stage work, *Holy Jungle*, was premiered. The edited *Notebooks of Martha Graham* was published in 1973.

Grant, Ulysses Simpson (b. Point Pleasant, Ohio, 27 Apr. 1822; d. Mt. McGregor, near Saratoga, N.Y., 23 July 1885), 18th president of the U.S., was graduated from the U.S. Military Academy (1843). During the war with Mexico he served under Zachary Taylor and Winfield Scott (1845–48), being breveted captain for gallantry at Chapultepec. He served in California and Oregon until resigning from the army (1854), when he engaged in farming and real estate in St. Louis, Mo. (1854–60), and then clerked in his father's leather store in Galena, Ill. At the outbreak of the Civil War he was commissioned colonel, 21st Illinois Volunteer Infantry; then brigadier general of volunteers; and after capturing Forts Henry and Donelson (winning in the latter operation the sobriquet "Unconditional Surrender Grant"), he was promoted major general of volunteers (1862). Victor at Shiloh (Apr. 1862), he captured Vicksburg (4 July 1863) and won the Battle of Chattanooga (23–25 Nov. 1863). After driving the Confederates from Missionary Ridge and raising the siege of Chattanooga, he was given supreme command of the Union forces, with revived rank of lieutenant general (Mar. 1864). In a campaign of attrition (Wilderness, Spotsylvania, Cold Harbor, 5 May–3 June 1864), he wore down Lee's resistance and, finally, by capturing Petersburg forced his surrender at Appomattox, Va. (9 Apr. 1865). Commissioned general (1866), he was appointed Secretary of War ad interim (12 Aug. 1867–14 Jan. 1968). Republican nominee, he was elected and reelected president of the U.S. (1869–77). Among the constructive achievements of his administration were the funding of the national debt, the resumption of specie payments (1875), the inauguration of civil service reform, and the negotiation of the Treaty of Washington with Great Britain (8 May 1871). On the debit side were involvements in scandals, notably the Fisk-Gould attempt to corner the gold market (1869); Crédit Mobilier (1873); the resignation of Secretary of the Treasury W. A. Richardson (1874) to escape a vote of censure by Congress; the implication in the Whisky Ring of O. E. Babcock, Grant's private secretary; and the resignation of Secretary of War W. W. Belknap (1876) to escape impeachment for bribe taking. His administration also had to weather the severe depression which followed the Panic of 1873. After a world tour (1877–80) Grant lost his fortune through the bankruptcy of Grant & Ward (1884), but it was recouped by his writing his *Personal Memoirs* (1885), which earned nearly $500,000. In his later years he also served as president of the Mexican Southern R.R.

Gray, Asa (b. Sauquoit, Oneida Co., N.Y., 18 Nov. 1810; d. Cambridge, Mass., 30 Jan. 1888), botanist, received his M.D. (1831) from the Fairfield (N.Y.) Medical School, but soon he abandoned medicine for his study of plants and brought out his first independent publication, *North American Gramineae and Cyperaceae* (2 pts., 1834–35). He published his first botanical textbook, *Elements of Botany* (1836), and with John Torrey collaborated on *The Flora of North America* (2 vols., 1838–43). In 1842, when he published the first edition of his *Botanical Text-Book,* he was appointed Fisher professor of natural history at Harvard, a post he held until his retirement in 1873. The leading American botanist of his time, he was one of the founders of the National Academy of Science, president (1863–73) of the American Academy of Arts and Sciences,

and president (1872) of the American Association for the Advancement of Science. He made valuable contributions to the descriptive botany of North America, in which his most important work was *Manual of the Botany of the Northern United States* (1848 and subsequent editions). He also elaborated the botanical findings of the Wilkes Expedition in *United States Exploring Expedition during the Years 1838–42* (1854–57, 1874). It was to Gray that Charles Darwin wrote the letter (5 Sept. 1857) first outlining his theory of evolution. Gray became the chief American exponent of the Darwinian concepts, defending them against the attacks of Louis Agassiz (*q.v.*).

Greeley, Horace (b. Amherst, N.H., 3 Feb. 1811; d. New York City, 29 Nov. 1872), newspaper editor and reformer. He served his newspaper apprenticeship (c.1825–30) with the *Northern Spectator* at East Poultney, Vt.; arrived (1831) at New York City where he engaged in job printing and founded (1834) a weekly literary and news journal, the *New Yorker;* and edited and published 2 Whig journals, the *Jeffersonian* (1838) and the *Log Cabin* (1840). He founded (1841) the New York *Tribune,* which in its daily and weekly editions was influential in shaping political opinion in the Northern and Western parts of the U.S., and served as the vehicle for Greeley's social and economic views, including Fourierism, antislavery sentiment, temperance, women's rights, homestead legislation, and the protective tariff. He originated the phrase "Go West, young man." Until 1854 he maintained political alliance with William H. Seward (*q.v.*) and Thurlow Weed. One of the founders of the Republican party, he supported the nomination of Lincoln at the Chicago convention (1860), but during the war aligned himself with the radical antislavery faction and at times pursued an erratic course on the prosecution of the war. His attempt to bring about direct peace negotiations in the summer of 1864 ended in a fiasco. After the war he favored a liberal policy toward the South. In 1872, as the Liberal Republican candidate for the presidency, he made a poor showing against Grant.

Greene, Nathanael (b. Potowomut, now Warwick, R.I., 7 Aug. 1742; d. Mulberry Grove, near Savannah, Ga., 19 June 1786), Revolutionary general, served as deputy (1770–72, 1775) to the Rhode Island General Assembly, was appointed brigadier (May 1775) in charge of 3 regiments authorized by Rhode Island, and was named (22 June 1775) a brigadier general in the Continental army. He served through the siege of Boston, and after its evacuation by the British (Mar. 1776) was placed in command of the army of occupation. He was promoted (9 Aug. 1776) to major general in the Continental army, took part in the defensive operations in and around New York City, and played an important role in Washington's surprise assault on the British at Trenton (Dec. 1776). He participated in the Battle of Germantown (1777), went into winter quarters at Valley Forge, and was appointed (25 Feb. 1778) quartermaster general, in which capacity he reorganized and improved the supply system. He took part in the battles of Monmouth (1778) and Newport (1778). Difficulties with Congress and members of the "Conway Cabal" led to his resignation as quartermaster general. He was acting commander of the Continental army when Benedict Arnold's plot was brought to light, and served (1780) as president of the board of general officers which condemned Maj. John André to the gallows. Following the defeat of Gen. Horatio Gates at Camden, S.C. (1780), Washington chose Greene (14 Oct. 1780) to command the Revolutionary forces in the Southern theater. Carrying out an extensive program of reorganization and refitting, Greene assembled an army that included subordinate commanders such as Henry Lee and Francis Marion. To face Lord Cornwallis, he divided his forces. One division under Morgan defeated Tarleton at Cowpens (17 Jan. 1781). Cornwallis then turned upon Greene, who drained British strength at Guilford Court House, N.C. (15 Mar. 1781) and Hobkirk's Hill (26 Apr. 1781), forcing the British withdrawal from Camden. He defeated the British at the Battle of Eutaw Springs (8 Sept. 1781) and compelled the enemy to fall back on Charleston. The triumph of the Patriot forces in the South was largely due to his generalship.

Griffith, David Lewelyn Wark (b. La Grange, Ky., 22 Jan. 1875; d. Hollywood, Calif., 23 July 1948), motion picture director and producer. After being connected with the stage for almost a decade, he played his first movie role in *The Eagle's Nest*, made at the Edison Studio, and in 1908 joined the Biograph Co. as an assistant director, remaining with that unit until 1912. His first film was *The Adventures of Dollie*. Griffith won fame with *The Birth of a Nation*, which was made in 1914 and had its premiere at New York City on 3 Mar. 1915. Based on *The Clansman*, a novel by Thomas Dixon, Jr., *The Birth of a Nation* was produced on a $100,000 budget and earned approximately $48 million by the time Griffith died. Among the better known of the 500 pictures directed and produced by Griffith are *Intolerance* (1916), *Broken Blossoms* (1919), *Way Down East* (1920), *Orphans of the Storm* (1922), and *America* (1924). He was one of the founders of the United Artists Corp. in 1919, and retired in 1932. Among the foremost pioneers in the art of the motion picture,

Griffith introduced technical devices such as the fade-out and fade-in, cross-cutting, long shots for crowd scenes, high and low angle shots, soft focus, mist photography, the vignette, the vista backlighting and tinting. He did not introduce the close-up, but 1st used it for psychological and dramatic effects. His *Judith of Bethulia* was the first four-reeler.

Guggenheim, Daniel (b. Philadelphia, Pa., 9 July 1856; d. near Port Washington, N.Y., 28 Sept. 1930), industrialist and philanthropist, served his mercantile apprenticeship in Switzerland and upon his return to the U.S. (1884) became active in the copper mining and smelting business in which his father, Meyer Guggenheim (1828–1905), had made heavy investments. He soon became the leading figure among the 7 Guggenheim sons. It was largely due to his planning that the combination and integration of copper mining, smelting, and refining took place on a large scale. With his brothers, he took control (1901) of the reorganized American Smelting & Refining Co., of which he served as president or chairman of the board at different times between 1901 and 1919. Under his guidance the enterprise took shape as a vast industrial empire. It extended its activities to South America and Africa; developed nitrate fields in Chile, tin mines in Bolivia, and rubber plantations and diamond fields in the Belgian Congo; set up subsidiaries such as the Utah Copper Co., the Guggenheim Exploration Co., the Chile Copper Co., the Chile Nitrate Co.; and introduced mass production methods and technological improvements in mining and metallurgy. He established the Daniel and Florence Guggenheim Foundation and the Daniel Guggenheim Fund for the Promotion of Aeronautics; his brother, Simon (1867–1941), with his wife, the John Simon Guggenheim Memorial Foundation.

Hall, Granville Stanley (b. Ashfield, Mass., 1 Feb. 1844; d. Worcester, Mass., 24 Apr. 1924), psychologist, educator. He received his B.A. from Williams College (1867), and attended the Union Theological Seminary for a year before going to Germany, where he studied experimental psychology (1868–72). Returning to the U.S., he taught literature and psychology at Antioch College (1872–76), and English at Harvard (1876–77), where, studying under William James, he earned his Ph.D. (1878). After further studies in Germany, where he worked with L. F. von Helmholtz and Wilhelm M. Wundt, he became a lecturer in the new field of educational psychology at Harvard (1880–81). At Johns Hopkins, where he taught psychology and pedagogics (1881–89), he established one of the first psychology laboratories in the U.S. (1883). Applying the ideas of Darwin, Freud, Wundt, and others, his studies contributed to the development of the discipline. Among his many outstanding students were John Dewey (*q.v.*) and James McKeen Cattell. He founded and, at various times, edited journals which contributed to the growth of experimental psychology and child psychology in the U.S.: *American Journal of Psychology* (1887), *Pedagogical Seminar* (1891), *Journal of Religious Psychology and Education* (1902), *Journal of Applied Psychology* (1915). He was one of the organizers, and was first president of the American Psychological Association, founded in 1891. Author of some 490 published works, his major books include: *The Content of Children's Minds on Entering School* (1883), which gave great impetus to the new field of child psychology, *Adolescence* (1904), *Youth* (1906), *Educational Problems* (1911), *Jesus the Christ, in the Light of Psychology* (1917), and *Senescence* (1922). First president of Clark Univ. (1889–1920), he established there the first institute of child psychology in the U.S. and developed ambitious programs of graduate study in the fields of education and psychology.

Hamilton, Alexander (b. Nevis, B.W.I., 11 Jan. 1755; d. New York City, 12 July 1804), statesman. After clerking at St. Croix, left for New York in 1773, in which year he entered King's College, where he wrote pamphlets in the Patriot cause (1774–75). At the outbreak of the Revolution he organized an artillery company and gained Washington's attention by his skillful conduct in campaigns around New York City. With rank of lieutenant colonel he served as Washington's private secretary and aide-de-camp (1777–81). At his request he was given command of troops and fought at Yorktown (1781). Married (1780) Elizabeth, daughter of Philip Schuyler. After a year in Congress (1782–83), he began law practice in New York. As a delegate from New York to the Annapolis Convention (1786) he drafted report which led to the assembling of the Constitutional Convention (1787), where he advocated an extremely strong central government. He worked wholeheartedly for the ratification of the Constitution, writing some fifty-one of the *Federalist* papers (1787–88), and carrying the New York convention (1788) despite strong opposition. As first Secretary of the Treasury (1789–95), he devised the U.S. fiscal program (1790), recommending the funding of both the foreign and domestic debt at par, assumption by the federal government of Revolutionary state debts, and supplementing revenue from duties with an excise tax to bring national authority home to every citizen. He also recommended the creation of a national bank (1791), which he justified under the "implied powers" of the Constitution, and tariffs for industry, bounties for agriculture, and federally sponsored internal improvements (1791). His policies ("Hamiltonian system") were supported by the Federalists and opposed by the Jeffersonian Republicans (1792). Resigning from the cabinet, he resumed law practice in New York, interrupted by assuming command of the army, second only to Washington, when war with France appeared likely (1798–1800). Federalist leader of New York, he was in opposition to President John Adams. By throwing support to Jefferson (1800) he thwarted Aaron Burr's ambitions for the presidency and killed his chances for the governorship of New York (1804). Challenged by Burr to a duel on account of his acrimonious comments, he was fatally shot at Weehawken, N.J., and died the following day.

Hammerstein, Oscar, 2d (b. New York City, 12 July 1895; d. Doylestown, Pa., 23 Aug. 1960), librettist, was graduated from Columbia (B.A., 1916), and quickly won acclaim for the books and lyrics he wrote, often in collaboration, for many Broadway musicals. Notable among his early productions were *Rose Marie* (music by Rudolf Friml, 1924); the *Desert Song* (1926) and *New Moon* (1928), for both of which Sigmund Romberg wrote the music; and his adaptation of Edna Ferber's novel *Show Boat* (1927) to Jerome Kern's score. His collaboration with Richard Rodgers (*q.v.*) established the musical comedy, employing serious plots and sometimes serious overtones, as a distinctively American contribution to the drama. Their first smash hit, *Oklahoma!* (1943, special Pulitzer award, 1944), was followed by *Carousel* (1945), based on Molnar's *Liliom;* the international success *South Pacific* (Pulitzer prize award for drama, 1949); and *The King and I* (1951). At the time of Hammerstein's death their last joint production, *The Sound of Music,* was playing on Broadway. The songs of Rodgers and Hammerstein quickly became American classics, among them "The Surrey with the Fringe on Top," "You'll Never Walk Alone," "Bali H'ai," "I'm in Love with a Wonderful Guy," "Do-Re-Mi."

Hancock, John (b. North Braintree, now Quincy, Mass., 12 Jan. 1737; d. there, 8 Oct. 1793), merchant and Revolutionary leader, first signer of the Declaration of Independence. He was graduated from Harvard (1754) and entered the shipping trade; became (1763) a partner in the leading Boston mercantile house of Thomas Hancock & Co., and its head in 1764. He took part in the protest (1765) against the Stamp Act and in 1768 was defended by John Adams in a *cause célèbre* involving the seizure by customs officers of Hancock's sloop *Liberty* on charges of illegal trading. He was elected (1769) to the Massachusetts General Court, became (1770) head of the Boston town committee, and thereafter took a leading part in the Patriot cause. Elected (1774) president of the Massachusetts Provincial Congress, he and Samuel Adams were singled out for punishment in Gov. Gage's proclamation (12 June 1775) and expressly denied amnesty. In 1775 he was chosen delegate to the 2d Continental Congress, of which he served as president (24 May 1775–29 Oct. 1777). Alone with Charles Thomson, secretary of the Congress, he signed the Declaration of Independence 4 July 1776. The other delegates affixed their signatures later. In 1780 he was elected the first governor of Massachusetts, serving (1780–85, 1787–93) in that capacity for 9 terms. Again elected president of the Continental Congress on 23 Nov. 1785, illness prevented him from serving, and he resigned on 29 May 1786. He presided (1788) over the Massachusetts convention for ratifying the Federal Constitution.

Hand, Learned (b. Albany, N.Y., 27 Jan. 1872; d. New York City, 18 Aug. 1961), jurist, was graduated summa cum laude from Harvard (1893); returned to secure his M.A. the following year, and his LL.B. from Harvard Law School (1896). Admitted to the New York bar (1897), he clerked or practiced in Albany (1897–1902), then moved to New York City (1902), becoming a member (1904) of the firm of Gould & Wilkie. U.S. District Judge, southern district of New York (1909–24), he ran unsuccessfully (1913) as a Progressive for the post of Chief Judge of the New York Court of Appeals. He served as Judge of the U.S. Circuit Court, 2d Circuit, from 1924 until his retirement (1951), rendering notable opinions in the fields of maritime law, taxation, banking, trademarks, and labor law. In the antitrust suit against the Aluminum Co. of America he declared: "Congress did not condone 'good trusts' and condemn 'bad' ones; it forbade all." He upheld (1950) the conviction of the 11 Communist leaders under the Smith Act, interpreting Justice Holmes's "clear and present danger" test to mean that the courts must ascertain "whether the gravity of the 'evil,' discounted by its improbability, justifies such invasion of free speech as is necessary to avoid the danger." A literary craftsman and master of epigram, he made numerous addresses, including his eloquent "The Spirit of Liberty," delivered (1944) at an "I Am an American Day" ceremony in Central Park, New York (pub. with other papers, 1952). Recognizing the values of detachment, skepticism, and nonconformity, he regarded the key to his philosophy to be epitomized in Oliver Cromwell's plea before the Battle of Dunbar: "I beseech ye in the bowells of Christ, think that ye may be mistaken."

Hanna, Marcus Alonzo (b. New Lisbon, Ohio, 24 Sept. 1837; d. Washington,

D.C., 15 Feb. 1904), businessman and politician, attended Western Reserve College for a brief time, entered the grocery and commission business at Cleveland, and in 1867 transferred his interests to the coal and iron trade in that city, becoming (1885) head of the firm of M. A. Hanna & Co. He also helped establish the Union National Bank, became owner of the Cleveland Opera House and the Cleveland *Herald,* and dominated the city's street railway system. Active in local politics, he was chosen a member of the Republican state committee and soon became a power in Ohio politics. A break between him and Joseph B. Foraker in 1888 led Hanna to support Congressman William McKinley, whom he backed for the Ohio governorship (1891, 1893) and groomed as a presidential candidate. In 1894–95 Hanna withdrew from business activity to devote himself to launching a McKinley boom. A skilled and astute political manager, Hanna conducted a preconvention McKinley campaign for which he paid most of the financial cost. McKinley was nominated on the first ballot at the Republican convention in 1896. In recognition of his political ability, Hanna was chosen chairman of the Republican national committee. Chiefly by levies on businessmen and corporations, Hanna raised the unprecedented sum of $3,500,000 for the Republican national campaign. He was elected (1897) to the Senate, where he defended large corporate enterprises and supported ship subsidies and the Panama route for an isthmian canal. He was an intimate adviser to Presidents McKinley and Theodore Roosevelt. Although Hanna became in the public mind almost synonymous with big business, he supported labor's right to organize and was chairman of the executive committee of the National Civic Federation. Shortly before his death there were signs that powerful Republican elements in the East were hoping to secure

for him the presidential nomination in 1904.

Harding, Warren Gamaliel (b. Corsica, Ohio, 2 Nov. 1865; d. San Francisco, Calif., 2 Aug. 1923), 29th president of the U.S., attended Ohio Central College, Iberia (1879–82), studied law briefly, and (1884) became owner and editor of Marion *Star,* weekly, later a daily. He entered Republican politics as a protégé of Sen. Joseph B. Foraker, was elected to the state senate (1900–04), became lieutenant governor (1904–06), but was defeated in the gubernatorial election (1910). U.S. senator from Ohio (1915–21), he supported the 18th Amendment and the Volstead Act, and was known for his party regularity. At the Republican National Convention (1920) he was designated by the party leaders and nominated after a deadlock in the balloting between Gen. Leonard Wood and Frank O. Lowden. Straddling the League issue and pledging a "return to normalcy," he was elected by a landslide vote. Despite appointments to his cabinet of men of such standing as Hughes and Hoover, many of his choices were mediocrities (Attorney General Harry M. Daugherty of the "Ohio Gang" and Secretary of the Interior Albert B. Fall). The major achievement of his administration was the Washington Conference for naval limitation (1921–22). On a return trip from Alaska he died suddenly at San Francisco. Subsequent exposure of corruption in the Departments of Interior, Justice, and Navy, the Veterans Bureau, and Alien Property Custodian stamped his administration as both corrupt and incompetent.

Harlan, John Marshall (b. Boyle Co., Ky., 1 June 1833; d. Washington, D.C., 14 Oct. 1911), jurist, was graduated from Centre College (1850), studied law at Transylvania Univ. and was admitted to the Kentucky bar (1859). Adjutant general of Kentucky (1851) and judge of Franklin Co. (1858), he served in the Civil War as colonel, 10th Kentucky Infantry (1861–63). State attorney general (1863–67), unsuccessful candidate for governor in 1871 and again in 1875, he was appointed by President Hayes associate justice of the U.S. Supreme Court (1877–1911). His dissents (in 316 cases) were notable. He dissented in the sugar-trust cases (1895), opposing the majority's narrow interpretation of the commerce power; vigorously challenged the majority of the court which held the income tax unconstitutional (1895); and dissented in *Lochner* v. *N.Y.* (1905) on the ground that limiting hours of employment in an unhealthful occupation was a justifiable infringement on liberty of contract. He wrote the majority opinion dissolving the Northern Securities Co. (1904) and sustaining the Sherman Antitrust Act, maintained in the *Insular Cases* (1901) that "the Constitution followed the flag," and declared federal legislation barring "yellow-dog" contracts in railroad employment to infringe upon the 5th Amendment (1907).

Harper, William Rainey (b. New Concord, Ohio, 24 July 1856, d. Chicago, Ill., 10 Jan. 1906), educator and scholar, was graduated (1870) from Muskingum College (Ohio), where he taught Hebrew (1872–73), and in 1874, at the age of 18, received the degree of Ph.D. at Yale. He taught at Denison Univ., Granville, Ohio, from 1876 to 1879, when he became teacher of Semitic languages at the Baptist Union Theological Seminary in Chicago, and at Yale (1881–86), and was active in the Chautauqua movement, giving summer courses in Semitic languages and Biblical studies. In 1891 he assumed the presidency of the newly founded Univ. of Chicago, a post he held until his death. He introduced

such features as the university press, university extension, the summer quarter, and the division of the academic year into 4 quarters. He guided the Univ. of Chicago through the complex period of initial growth and was instrumental in assembling there a faculty that was among the most brilliant of its time. His work as a Hebraist produced *The Priestly Element in the Old Testament* (1902), *The Prophetic Element in the Old Testament* (1905), and *Critical and Exegetical Commentary on Amos and Hosea* (1905).

Harriman, William Averell (b. New York City, 15 Nov. 1891–   ), statesman and businessman, son of Edward H. Harriman of the Union Pacific R.R., graduated from Yale (1913). Vice-president of the Union Pacific and director of the Illinois Central (1915–32), he expanded his railroad inheritance—becoming chairman of the board of Merchant Shipbuilding Corp. (1917–25); founding (1921) the investment banking firm W. A. Harriman and Co.; and acquiring major interests in numerous other corporate enterprises. Originally a Republican, he became a Democrat when he supported Alfred E. Smith's presidential candidacy (1928). He first entered government service as a divisional administrator for the National Recovery Administration (1934–35). After serving as an official in the Department of Commerce (1937–40) he moved to the Office of Production Management and, after 3 months, was sent (1941) as a special representative of the president to Great Britain and the U.S.S.R. to coordinate the flow of U.S. military aid to those nations. He held the posts of ambassador to the U.S.S.R. (1943–46) and to Great Britain (1946)—relinquishing the latter after only 6 months to become Secretary of Commerce (1946–48). Resuming his diplomatic career, he was U.S. representative in Europe under the Economic Cooperation Act of 1948 (1948–50) and served as director of the Mutual Security Agency (1951–53). Entering electoral politics, he ran successfully for governor of New York (1954) but failed in his bids for the Democratic presidential nomination (1956) and for reelection as governor (1958). In 1961 President Kennedy appointed him Assistant Secretary of State for Far Eastern Affairs and 2 years later he was named Under Secretary of State for Political Affairs (1963–65). As ambassador-at-large (1965–69), he undertook a number of roving assignments—notably, that of chief negotiator (1968–69) at the Vietnam peace talks in Paris. Though never realizing his great ambition to become Secretary of State, he dealt with virtually every world leader prominent during his time and was highly respected as an effective negotiator.

Harris, Joel Chandler (b. near Eatonton, Ga., 9 Dec. 1848; d. Atlanta, 3 July 1908), journalist, author, became (1862) printer's devil for Joseph Addison Turner's *Countryman.* He worked for 6 months (1866) for the publisher of the New Orleans *Crescent Monthly,* but thereafter never left his home state except for brief trips. A growing reputation as a humorist earned him a position on the Savannah *Morning News,* and then with the Atlanta *Constitution,* His "Uncle Remus Stories," first published in the Atlanta *Constitution,* made that paper nationally famous. His first collection, *Uncle Remus, His Songs and His Sayings* (1880), was enormously popular, especially the "Tar-Baby" story (1904), and was followed by a series down to 1918. A master of dialect, he used folk tales, but the dialogue and characters of Uncle Remus and Br'er Rabbit (1907) and the world of animals were uniquely his own. In *Mingo and Other Sketches in Black and White* (1884) and *Free Joe*

and Other Sketches (1887), he captured the white Georgia cracker on printed page.

Harris, Townsend (b. Sandy Hill, N.Y., 3 Oct. 1804; d. New York City, 25 Feb. 1878), diplomat, was largely self-educated, beginning work in a dry-goods store in New York City at 13. Later he established a family partnership for importing china. Elected to the Board of Education as a Democrat (1846), he launched a vigorous campaign, against strong opposition, for a free city college, and carried through the necessary legislation to establish (1847) the College of the City of New York. Following his mother's death (1847), the bachelor Harris bought a trading ship and made trips in the Pacific and Indian oceans. In 1853 he applied for a consular post. First assigned (1855) to Ningpo, China, he managed, through the influence of Secretary of State William L. Marcy and Seward, to be named consul general to Japan (1855), a post resulting from ratification of the Perry Treaty. Responsible for the first U.S.-Japanese commercial agreement (17 June 1857) and the treaty of 29 July 1858, he exercised at Yeddo (Tokyo) great influence over the Japanese government. Resigning his post with Lincoln's election, he returned to New York and became a War Democrat.

Harrison, Benjamin (b. North Bend, Ohio, 20 Aug. 1833; d. Indianapolis, Ind., 13 Mar. 1901), 23d president of the U.S., grandson of William Henry Harrison, 9th president, was graduated from Miami Univ. (1852), admitted to the Cincinnati bar (1853), commenced practice in Indianapolis (1854), and was reporter of Indiana supreme court, 1860–62, and again, 1864–68, after service in the Civil War (commissioned 2d lt.; raised 70th Indiana Regiment and became its col.). Defeated as Republican candidate for governor of Indiana

(1876), he declined a post in Garfield's cabinet, having been elected to the U.S. Senate (1881–87), where he opposed Cleveland's pension vetoes and advocated civil service reform. Defeated for reelection, he was the Republican nominee for president (1888) and defeated Cleveland. During his administration (1889–93) the McKinley Tariff and Sherman Silver Act were passed, Civil War pensions were augmented, and imperialist policies pressed in the Pacific. Renominated (1892), he was defeated by Cleveland, and resumed his law practice, serving as chief counsel for Venezuela in arbitration of her boundary dispute with Great Britain.

Harrison, William Henry (b. Berkeley, Charles City Co., Va., 9 Feb. 1773; d. Washington, D.C., 4 Apr. 1841), 9th president of the U.S., attended Hampden-Sidney College (1787–90), studied medicine briefly at the Univ. of Pennsylvania, then entered the army, attaining a captaincy, resigning (1798) to accept appointment as Secretary of the Northwest Territory. He was elected its first delegate to Congress (1799) and was the drafter of the Land Act of 1800. Appointed by President John Adams first governor of Indiana Territory (1801–12), and as special commissioner to deal with the Indians he negotiated several boundary treaties. Confronted with Indian resistance under Tecumseh to further white encroachments, he won a nominal victory at Tippecanoe (7 Nov. 1811), and during the War of 1812, when he held the rank of major general, he decisively defeated both the British and the Indians at the Battle of the Thames (5 Oct. 1813). Congressman from Ohio (1816–19), state senator (1819–21), U.S. senator from Ohio (1825–28), he was appointed U.S. minister to Colombia (1828), but recalled by Jackson the following year. Retiring

to North Bend, Ohio, he became clerk of the common pleas court of Hamilton Co. Candidate for the presidency on one of the Whig tickets (1836), with Anti-Masonic support, he was defeated by Van Buren, but was the successful Whig nominee (1840), staging his "log cabin and hard cider" campaign. He died of pneumonia a month after his inauguration.

Hawthorne, Nathaniel (b. Salem, Mass., 4 July 1804; d. Plymouth, N.H., 18/19 May 1864), novelist and writer of tales. Born of Puritan ancestry, he was graduated from Bowdoin College (1825) and returned to Salem, where he led a secluded life devoted to the mastery of his craft. He issued at his own expense the anonymously published novel *Fanshawe* (1828), and began publishing in the *Token,* an annual brought out by Samuel G. Goodrich, the stories later collected in *Twice-Told Tales* (1837; enlarged ed., 1842). He was editor (1836) of the *American Magazine of Useful and Entertaining Knowledge,* also published by Goodrich, for whom he compiled *Peter Parley's Universal History* (1837) and wrote children's books such as *Grandfather's Chair* (1841), *Famous Old People* (1841), *Liberty Tree* (1841), and *Biographical Stories for Children* (1842). With the aid of Franklin Pierce, whom he had known at Bowdoin, he secured a post as weigher and gauger (1839–41) in the Boston Custom House. He spent several months (1841–42) at Brook Farm, which furnished him with the setting for *The Blithedale Romance* (1852); was married (9 July 1842) to Sophia Amelia Peabody of Salem; settled in the Old Manse at Concord (1842–45); and was surveyor of the port of Salem from 1846 to 1849, during which time he published *Mosses from an Old Manse* (1846). His best-known novel, *The Scarlet Letter* (1850), dealt with the moral decadence of 17th-century New England Puritanism, and was followed by *The House of the Seven Gables* (1851), *The Snow Image and Other Twice-Told Tales* (1852), *A Wonder-Book for Girls and Boys* (1852), and *Tanglewood Tales for Girls and Boys* (1853). In 1850 Hawthorne moved to Lenox, Mass., where he became acquainted with Herman Melville, but in a few years returned to Concord. As a reward for writing a campaign biography, *The Life of Franklin Pierce* (1852), he was appointed (1853) U.S. consul at Liverpool, a post he held until 1860. The last books by him published during his lifetime were *The Marble Faun* (1860) and *Our Old Home* (1863). Among his other works are *Passages from the American Notebooks* (1868), *Passages from the English Notebooks* (1870), *Septimius Felton* (1871), *Passages from the French and Italian Notebooks* (1871), *The Dolliver Romance* (1876), *Dr. Grimshawe's Secret* (1883), and *The Ancestral Footstep* (1883). Among his better-known tales are "Ethan Brand," "The Great Stone Face," "The Maypole of Merrymount," "Dr. Heidegger's Experiment," and "The Ambitious Guest."

Hay, John Milton (b. Salem, Ind., 12 Oct. 1838; d. Lake Sunapee, N.H., 1 July 1905), statesman, was graduated from Brown Univ. (1858), admitted to the Illinois bar (1861), and practiced in Springfield, where he was drawn into the Lincoln circle. Accompanying Lincoln to Washington as assistant private secretary, he served until the president's death. Subsequently he was 1st secretary of legation at Paris (1865–67) and Madrid (1868–70) and chargé d'affaires at Vienna (1867–68). On his return to the U.S. (1870), he became an editorial writer on the New York *Tribune* (1870–75), then moved to Cleveland, returning to Washington as assistant secretary of state

under William M. Evarts (1879–81). McKinley's ambassador to Great Britain (1897–98) and thereafter, until his death, McKinley's and Theodore Roosevelt's Secretary of State (1898–1905), he supported the Open Door policy in China, and concluded the Hay-Pauncefote Treaty with Great Britain (1900–01) and the Hay-Herrán and Hay-Bunau-Varilla treaties with Colombia and Panama respectively. Poet and novelist, as well as historian, he published *Pike County Ballads* and *Castilian Days* (1871), the antilabor union novel *The Bread Winners* (anon., 1883), and, in collaboration with John G. Nicolay, *Abraham Lincoln: A History* (10 vols., 1890), and *Abraham Lincoln: Complete Works* (2 vols., 1894).

Hayes, Rutherford Birchard (b. Delaware, Ohio, 4 Oct. 1822; d. Fremont, Ohio, 17 Jan. 1893), 19th president of the U.S., was graduated from Kenyon College (1842) and Harvard Law School (1845); was admitted to the Ohio bar and commenced practice at Fremont (1845), removing to Cincinnati (1849). A Whig and then a Republican (from 1854), he was city solicitor (1858–61), resigning to become governor of Ohio (1868–72). Running on a "sound money" platform, he was elected for a 3d term (1875) and established himself as the logical candidate of the anti-Blaine forces at the Republican National Convention the following year, where he won the nomination. Although Tilden, the Democratic candidate, secured a larger popular vote, Hayes was adjudged by the partisan Electoral Commission to have obtained 1 more electoral vote (185–184). Despite party factional disputes and Democratic control of the lower house (1876) and of both houses (1878), his administration ended military reconstruction by withdrawal of federal troops from South Carolina

(1877) and made indecisive efforts toward civil service reform. On issues of labor and finance he was conservative, calling out federal troops to suppress the railroad strike (1877) and vetoing the Bland-Allison Silver Coinage Act (1878), which was passed over his veto.

Hearst, William Randolph (b. San Francisco, Calif., 29 Apr. 1863; d. Beverly Hills, Calif., 14 Aug. 1951), journalist. While at Harvard (1882–85), Hearst was financial editor of the *Harvard Lampoon.* He worked as a reporter for the New York *World* for several months and then took over his father's *San Francisco Examiner* (1887). In 1895 Hearst purchased the New York *Morning Journal,* where he boosted circulation by lowering the price and introducing sensational reportage of crime, society gossip, and comic strips in color. That newspaper's coverage of Spanish atrocities in Cuba sharply aroused the public and contributed to the Spanish-American War. Between 1885–1937, Hearst built a newspaper empire, publishing and personally editing during the latter year over 20 newspapers, including the New York *Evening Journal* (1896), *Chicago Examiner* (1902), and *Los Angeles Examiner* (1903). His papers took controversial positions, favoring reforms such as the 8-hour day, public ownership of utilities, and popular election of U.S. senators. Isolationist and anti-British, the newspapers were against U.S. entry into both world wars and into the League of Nations. Hearst also established King Features Syndicate (1914), published magazines including *Good Housekeeping* and *Harper's Bazaar,* and pioneered in movie newsreels (1913). He owned gold and silver mines and, at one time, was one of the leading real-estate owners in New York City, California, and Mexico. He moved permanently to his 240,-000-acre ranch at San Simeon (1927), where he amassed art and archaeological treasures. He served in the U.S. House of Representatives from New York City (1903–07) but ran unsuccessfully for the presidential nomination (1904), for mayor of New York City (1905, 1909), for governor of New York state (1906), and for Democratic nominee for senator (1922).

Hemingway, Ernest (b. Oak Park, Ill., 21 July 1898; d. Ketchum, Ida., 2 July 1961), novelist and short-story writer. After working as a reporter on the Kansas City *Star,* he went to France as a volunteer ambulance driver in World War I and then enlisted in the Italian army, winning 2 medals for battle actions in which he was wounded. After the war he served as a newspaper correspondent in the Near East for the Toronto *Star* and then settled in Paris, where he became associated with the expatriates of the "lost generation," whose leading spokesman he became. Hemingway spent most of his life abroad, chiefly in Europe and Cuba, and was a war correspondent during the Spanish Civil War and in France during World War II. His stories and novels, most of which are concerned with the disintegration of private values in a world between wars, are marked by a high level of craftsmanship and a terse prose style that has had a wide influence on writing in the U.S. and elsewhere. Hemingway's novels include *The Sun Also Rises* (1926), *A Farewell to Arms* (1929), *To Have and Have Not* (1937), *For Whom the Bell Tolls* (1940), *Across the River and into the Trees* (1950), and *The Old Man and the Sea* (1952). His volumes of short stories are *In Our Time* (1924), *Men Without Women* (1927), and *Winner Take Nothing* (1933), collected in *The Fifth Column and the First Forty-Nine Stories* (1938). *Death in the Afternoon* (1932) deals with bullfighting and *Green Hills of*

Africa (1935) is about big-game hunting. He was awarded the Nobel prize in literature in 1954 for *The Old Man and the Sea* (1952).

Henri, Robert (b. Robert Henry Cozed, Cincinnati, Ohio, 25 June 1865; d. New York City, 12 July 1929), artist and teacher, changed his name when his father became a fugitive from justice. He studied at the Pennsylvania Academy of Fine Arts (1886–88) under Thomas Anschutz and at the Académie Julien and the École des Beaux Arts in Paris (1888–91). Returning to the U.S., he enjoyed a distinguished teaching career at the Philadelphia School of Design for Women, beginning in 1891, and after 1899 at the New York School of Art, the Henri School, the radical Ferrer Center School, and the Art Students League. Rebelling against the narrow creed of "art for art's sake," but without abandoning technical excellence, Henri was a leading spokesman for better exhibition opportunities for newer painters. Henri was a member of "The Eight," or "The Ash Can School," a group of realists whom he encouraged to record the dramas of urban life. After the National Academy refused their canvases (1908), Henri withdrew his own pictures and organized the exhibition of "The Eight." Shocking the conservative art world, they protested also the excessive Europeanization of American painting. Although his work was exhibited at the Armory Show (1913), it was not in tune with some of his more radical contemporaries. His brushwork showed the influence of Hals and Monet, and in later years drew upon the color system of Hardesty Maratta. His work was not bloodlessly refined but healthy and vigorous. The subjects for most of his portraits painted during the years 1906–14 were men and women from all over the world, including Irishmen, Indians from New

Mexico, and Yankees. Some of his best known paintings are *Young Woman in White* (1904, National Gallery, Washington), *Himself and Herself* (both 1913, Art Institute of Chicago), *The Laughing Girl* (1910, Brooklyn Museum); and *The Spanish Gypsy* (c. 1906, Metropolitan). Henri inspired and motivated many students, including such notable ones as George Bellows, Stuart Davis, Edward Hopper, Yasao Kuniyoshi, Moses Soyer, and even Leon Trotsky.

Henry, Joseph (b. Albany, N.Y., 17 Dec. 1797; d. Washington, D.C., 13 May 1878), physicist. He attended the Albany Academy, where he became (1826) professor of mathematics and natural philosophy and carried out experiments in the magnetic fields created by electrical currents. In the course of these researches he improved William Sturgeon's electromagnet, increasing the magnetic condition of its core by an arrangement that is still the basis of the modern electromagnet. In a paper published in the *American Journal of Science* (Jan. 1831), Henry described his discovery of the quantity and intensity magnets, correctly predicting that the latter type would be used in the electromagnetic telegraph. His findings were indispensable to the commercial development of the telegraph. Another paper published by him on electromagnetic induction (July 1832) paralleled contemporaneous and independent researches by Faraday and led to Henry's important discoveries in self-induction (the modern practical unit of inductance, the henry, is named after him). In 1832 he was named professor of natural philosophy in the College of New Jersey, where his continued researches foreshadowed many of the developments in the modern science of electricity. He discovered (1842) the oscillatory nature of electrical discharge. In 1846 he was appointed the first secretary and director of the Smithsonian Institution at Washington, D.C.; his first report to its Board of Regents laid down the broad policies, particularly those relating to original research and the free diffusion of knowledge, that have since guided the Smithsonian. Henry introduced (c.1850) the system of transmitting weather reports by telegraph and using them for forecasting weather conditions, thus laying the foundation for the U.S. Weather Bureau. He also made valuable researches in fog signaling. One of the organizers of the American Association for the Advancement of Science, he was chosen its president (1849) and served as president of the National Academy of Science (1868–78).

Henry, Patrick (b. Hanover Co., Va., 29 May 1736; d. at his plantation, Red Hill, Charlotte Co., Va., 6 June 1799), Revolutionary patriot, orator, and statesman. After an early career as a storekeeper and farmer, he read law, was licensed to practice (1760), and soon became one of the leading lawyers in western Virginia. His fame as an orator began in 1763, when he appeared for the defense in the "parson's cause" and invoked the theory of mutual compact in making a plea against the royal disallowance of the "twopenny act" passed by the Virginia assembly. In 1765 he became a member of the House of Burgesses and emerged as a leader of the frontier and back-country elements in their contest with the conservative Tidewater interests. With the adoption of the Stamp Act, he proposed 7 resolutions (29 May 1765), one of which contended that Virginia enjoyed complete legislative autonomy, and in their behalf made the speech later reputed to have closed with the famous injunction: "Caesar had his Brutus—Charles the first, his Cromwell— and George the third—may profit by their example. . . . If *this* be treason, make the most of it." Under his leadership the

legislators gathered at Raleigh Tavern (27 May 1774), after Lord Dunmore dissolved the colonial assembly, and issued the calls for the Virginia convention and a Continental Congress. On 23 Mar. 1775, in a speech urging resistance to British policy and in advocating the establishment of an armed force, he declared: "Give me liberty, or give me death!" He was outlawed in a proclamation issued by Lord Dunmore (6 May 1775). Henry took his seat in the Continental Congress on 18 May 1775, helped draft the Virginia constitution of 1776, and as governor of Virginia (1776– 79) dispatched in 1778 George Rogers Clark on a military mission to the Illinois country. After the war, Henry's political views changed sharply. He served again as governor (1784–86), but at the Virginia convention (1788) for ratifying the Constitution opposed its adoption as inimical to state sovereignty. A leader in the movement for the Bill of Rights, he wrote the Virginia appeal to the 1st Congress and the other states for amendments to the Constitution. In his closing years he was a Federalist.

Hill, James Jerome (b. near Rockwood, Ontario, Canada, 16 Sept. 1838; d. St. Paul, Minn., 29 May 1916), railroad builder, went to work at the age of 14 as a clerk in a village store, lost the sight of an eye by the accidental discharge of an arrow, and in 1856 became clerk in St. Paul, Minn., in a steamboat transportation firm. By 1865 he had gone into the forwarding and transportation business for himself, organized (1870) the Red River Transportation Co., and joined (1878) a syndicate that built the Canadian Pacific R.R. and purchased (1878) the St. Paul and Pacific R.R., which was expanded (1890) into the Great Northern R.R., from Lake Superior to Puget Sound. Without the aid of government land grants, Hill's line weathered financial storms. Together with J. P. Morgan, Hill was involved in a struggle with Edward H. Harriman and Jacob H. Schiff for control of the Northern Pacific R.R., which precipitated the stock market panic of 1901. The Northern Security Co., organized (1901) as a holding company of all Hill's interests, was dissolved by the U.S. Supreme Court (1904) as violating the Sherman Act. Because of his notable role in the development of the Northwest, Hill has been called the "empire builder."

Hillman, Sidney (b. Zagare, Lithuania, 23 Mar. 1887; d. Point Lookout, N.Y., 10 July 1946), labor leader, was educated at the Slobodka Rabbinical Seminary in Lithuania, and came to the U.S. in 1907, becoming a clothing worker with the Chicago firm of Hart, Schaffner, and Marx. The agreement which he negotiated with that firm (1911) formed the basis for the impartial chairman plan (1912), adopted by other industries. First president of the Amalgamated Clothing Workers (1914), he organized the New York, Rochester, Philadelphia, and Chicago industries and initiated such union activities as cooperative housing and banking. An advocate of industrial unionism, he quit the AFL (1935) to cofound the CIO, of which he became vice-president (1935–40) and headed the textile workers' organizing drive. Codirector of the Office of Production Management, later WPB (1940–42), he cofounded Labor's Non-Partisan League (1936) to support the reelection of Franklin D. Roosevelt and headed (1943) the CIO-PAC to support Roosevelt and congressmen sympathetic to labor. A central figure at the Democratic National Convention of 1944 ("Clear it with Sidney," F.D.R. told the party managers), he threw his support to Harry S. Truman for the vice-presidential nomination. Founder and chairman (1944–45) of the American Labor party, he was instrumental in setting up the World Federation of Trade Unions (1945).

Hoe, Richard March (b. New York City, 12 Sept. 1812; d. Florence, Italy, 7 June 1886), inventor and manufacturer. Educated in the public schools of New York, he entered (1827) the printing-press factory owned by his father, whom he succeeded in 1830. At about that time the Hoe Co. was manufacturing a single small cylinder press; in 1837 the double small cylinder press improved by Hoe was perfected and put into production; and during the same period Hoe designed and introduced the single large cylinder press, the first flat bed and cylinder press ever used in America. To meet the demands of newspaper publishers, Hoe invented and designed (1845–46) the rotary printing press, the first of which, capable of printing 8,000 papers an hour, was installed (1847) in the plant of the Philadelphia *Public Ledger*. This machine was the predecessor of the web press (1871) designed by Hoe and Stephen D. Tucker. First installed in the plant of the New York *Tribune*, the web press printed simultaneously from a continuous roll of paper both sides of a sheet at the rate of 18,000 papers an hour. Hoe also introduced the stop cylinder press (1853) and devised the triangular form folder (1881). The latter, in combination with the web press and the curved stereotype plate, is the foundation of the modern newspaper printing press.

Holmes, Oliver Wendell (b. Cambridge, Mass., 29 Aug. 1809; d. Boston, 7 Oct. 1894), author and physician, was graduated from Harvard (1829), studied law for a year, and then turned to medicine, graduating from Harvard Medical School (1836) and studying in Paris (1833–35). He commenced practice in Boston (1836); was professor of anatomy at Dartmouth (1838–40) and Parkman professor of anatomy and physiology at Harvard Medical School (1847–82) as well as dean (1847–53). His medical papers include "Homeopathy and Its Kindred Delusions" (1842) and, most notable, "The Contagiousness of Puerperal Fever" (1843), in which he demonstrated, statistically, that the disease was spread by contagion, a position which, despite criticism, was entirely vindicated by Semmelweis' study (1861). Accomplished as a poet ("Old Ironsides," 1830; "The Chambered Nautilus," "Wonderful One-Hoss Shay"), he was especially renowned as lecturer, conversationalist, and essayist, contributing extensively to the *Atlantic Monthly* after its founding (1857) and publishing *The Autocrat of the Breakfast Table* (1858), followed by *The Professor at the Breakfast Table* (1860) and *The Poet at the Breakfast Table* (1872). In addition, he published 3 novels of heredity and psychology (*Elsie Venner*, 1861; *The Guardian Angel*, 1867; and *A Mortal Antipathy*, 1885) and biographies of Motley (1879) and Emerson (1885).

Holmes, Oliver Wendell, Jr. (b. Boston, 8 Mar. 1841; d. Washington, D.C., 6 Mar. 1935), jurist, son of Oliver Wendell Holmes, was graduated from Harvard (1861) and served in the Civil War for 3 years, being wounded at Ball's Bluff, Antietam, and Fredericksburg, and attaining the rank of lieutenant colonel. On graduation from the Harvard Law School (1866) he practiced in Boston and became instructor in constitutional law at Harvard (1870–71), professor of law editor of the *American Law Review* (1870–73). Associate justice (1882) of the Massachusetts supreme judicial court, and chief justice (1899–1902), he was appointed by President Theodore Roosevelt an associate justice of the U.S. Supreme Court (1902), serving until his retirement at the age of 90 (12 Jan.

1932). The court's most notable dissenter and leader of its liberal wing, he sharply criticized the Sherman Anti-Trust Act (*Northern Securities' Case*), but his conception of a "current of commerce" (*Swift Case*, 1905) paved the way for increasingly broad interpretations of the commerce clause. In his dissent in *Lochner* v. *N.Y.* (1905) he declared that "the 14th Amendment does not enact Mr. Herbert Spencer's *Social Statics*." His opposition to the rule in the *Adair* (1908) and *Coppage* (1915) cases foreshadowed later reversals by the court. He also dissented in *Hammer* v. *Dagenhart* (1918), where the majority invalidated the federal child labor law. In *Schenck* v. *U.S.* (1919) he enunciated the "clear and present danger" doctrine to govern the interpretation of the 1st Amendment, although in the *Abrams Case* (1919) he made an eloquent plea for "free trade in ideas." In later opinions he attacked wiretapping as "dirty business" (*Olmstead* v. *U.S.*, 1928) and denounced the use of the 14th Amendment to "prevent the making of social experiments" (*Truax* v. *Corrigan,* 1921). He refused to accept the common law as a fundamental all-pervasive set of principles and denied that it was "a brooding omnipresence in the sky." He edited the 12th edition of Kent's *Commentaries* (1873); his published works include *The Common Law* (1881) and *Collected Legal Papers* (1920).

Homer, Winslow (b. Boston, Mass., 24 Feb. 1836; d. Scarboro, Me., 29 Sept. 1910), painter and illustrator. After serving his apprenticeship under Bufford, a lithographer in Boston, he established his studio there (1857), drew illustrations for *Ballou's Pictorial* and *Harper's Weekly,* and in 1859 moved to New York, where he continued his training at the National Academy of Design. During the Civil War he drew battlefield scenes for

Harper's Weekly and recorded these impressions in such paintings as *Rainy Day in Camp, Sharpshooter on Picket Duty,* and *Prisoners from the Front.* He gradually abandoned magazine illustration and anecdotal painting, and after 1882, when he established his home at Scarboro, Me., began work on the long line of marine pieces that occupied the rest of his life. In Maine, and during his annual journeys to the Caribbean, he produced oil paintings and watercolors marked by original design, virile draftsmanship, and vivid color. His works include *The Life Line, Eight Bells, Sun and Cloud, Summer Night, The Fallen Deer, Northeaster, Cannon Rock,* and *The Wreck* (also p. 902).

Hoover, Herbert Clark (b. West Branch, Iowa, 10 Aug. 1874; d. New York City, 20 Oct. 1964), 31st president of the U.S., moved to Oregon and was graduated from Stanford Univ. (1895) as a mining engineer. After several years in the U.S. he engaged in mining operations abroad, first in Australia, then in China, Africa, Central and South America, and Russia. During World War I he was notably effective as chairman of the American Relief Committee in London, as chairman of the Commission for Relief in Belgium, and as U.S. Food Administrator. Appointed Secretary of Commerce (1921–28), he served in both the Harding and Coolidge cabinets, expanding the activities of that department and fostering trade associations. Republican nominee, he was elected president (1928). To deal with the economic collapse which occurred in the first year of his administration, he counted upon economic forces to bring about a revival and was hesitant to extend federal activities, although at the end of his term he signed an act creating the Reconstruction Finance Corp. (1932) to extend loans to banks and large business enterprises.

On 20 June 1931 he announced a 1-year moratorium on all intergovernmental debts. Renominated, he was defeated (1932) by Franklin D. Rosevelt. He served (1947–49, 1953–55) as chairman of the Commissions on Organization of the Executive Branch of the Government (Hoover Commissions). An isolationist prior to 1941, he advocated (1952) U.S. military withdrawal from Western Europe. His works include *Memoirs* (3 vols., 1951–52) and *The Ordeal of Woodrow Wilson* (1958).

Hoover, John Edgar (b. Washington, D.C., 1 Jan. 1895; d. there, 2 May 1972), public official, was a messenger in the Library of Congress while studying law at night at George Washington Univ. (LL.B. 1916; LL.M. 1917). Hired by the Justice Department as a file reviewer (1917), he became special assistant to the attorney general of the U.S. (1919–24) and was responsible for oversight of the "Red Scare" deportation cases, helping to put together 60,000 dossiers on radicals and anarchists, a prelude to the "Palmer Raids." Assistant director of the Justice Department's Bureau of Investigation (1921–24), he was appointed director (1924) and began its reorganization. Hoover remained director for 48 years, changing the bureau from an organization notorious for its apathy and corruption to the least corruptible and most sophisticated investigatory agency in the world. During his first year as director he set up the Identification Division, including the Central Fingerprint Repository. He established a crime laboratory (1932), the FBI Academy (1935), the same year the bureau became the FBI, and set up retrieval systems such as the National Fraudulent Check File, National Typewriter File, and National Automobile Altered Number File. In 1939, responding to presidential authorization, he inaugurated wartime internal-security and counterespionage programs. In later years Hoover and the FBI came under increasing attack for their concentration on finding Communists at the expense of enforcing civil rights laws and attacking organized crime. Hoover feuded with Attorney Generals Robert F. Kennedy (1961–64) and Ramsey Clark (1967–69) while maintaining close relations with President Lyndon B. Johnson and on Capitol Hill. A superadministrator and wily bureaucrat, he refused to cooperate with the Nixon administration's "Huston Plan" for domestic intelligence-gathering operations. He was the author of *Persons in Hiding* (1938), *Masters of Deceit* (1958), and *J. Edgar Hoover on Communism* (1962).

Hopkins, Harry (b. Sioux City, Ia., 17 Aug. 1890; d. New York City, 29 Jan. 1946), social reformer and statesman, graduated from Grinnell College (1912). As a social worker, Hopkins directed a boy's camp run by Christadora House, a settlement on the lower east side of New York City (1912), worked there for a year, and then took charge of fresh-air work and unemployment relief for the New York Association for the Improvement of the Conditions of the Poor. From 1915–17 he handled widows' pensions for the New York City Board of Child Welfare. During World War I and in the early 1920s he was chairman of the southern division of the American Red Cross in New Orleans. Brought to the attention of Franklin Roosevelt by Eleanor Roosevelt, he headed the New York State Temporary Emergency Relief Administration for Gov. Roosevelt (1931–33). When Roosevelt became president, Hopkins became director of New Deal relief agencies such as the Federal Emergency Relief Administration (1933), Civil Works Administration (1933–34), and Works Projects Administration (1935–40). Called the "world's greatest spender,"

Hopkins distributed over $10 billion both in dole and the work relief. A first-class administrator who fought for his agencies, Hopkins was radical in his willingness to experiment freely with social and economic reform. He attempted to end discrimination in the administration of relief funds. As Secretary of Commerce (1938–40) Hopkins supported Roosevelt's candidacy for a 3d term, after his own aspirations failed due to ill health. F.D.R.'s closest confidant during wartime, living at the White House (1940–43), "my house guest without portfolio," he was greatly admired by the president for his common sense, quickness, sympathy, and mixture of cynicism and idealism. Roosevelt's leading adviser during the war, he acted as buffer, communications line, and sounding board. As F.D.R.'s superadministrative assistant, Hopkins was given assignments without fixed boundaries in the conduct of the Grand Alliance. He was head of the Lend-Lease Program, member of the "Little War Cabinet," of the War Mobilization Committee, of the War Production Board, and a speechwriter for the president. He served as the president's special emissary to Churchill and to Stalin, making repeated trips abroad, and attending all of the major wartime conferences with the president. Although seriously ill, he made a last trip to Moscow to see Stalin (26 May–7 June 1945) at the behest of President Truman, insuring the holding of the Potsdam Conference and the success of the San Francisco Conference. He was author of *Spend to Save* (1936).

House, Edward Mandell (b. Houston, Tex., 26 July 1858; d. New York City, 28 Mar. 1938), statesman, attended Cornell (1878–79), took over his father's cotton plantation and bank after his death. Although he never ran for public office, he was active in Texas politics, advising a series of governors, one of whom made him an honorary colonel. In 1912 he influenced the Texas delegation to support Woodrow Wilson for the presidential nomination and planned strategy during the subsequent campaign. He became Wilson's most intimate friend (1912–19), called by the president "my second personality . . . my independent self." As Wilson's unofficial but most important adviser, he helped select his cabinet and performed an important role in political fence-mending. He was also a channel through which the captains of finance could get their needs and views relayed to the president. He was sent to Europe in 1914 by Wilson to attempt to prevent the outbreak of war and again for 4 months (1915) on a secret peace mission to England, Germany, and France. His 2d mission for negotiated peace (1916) resulted in the House-Grey Memorandum (22 Feb. 1916), suggesting U.S. commitment to the Allied cause. House was pro-Ally, believing that Allied victory was vital to American national interest. He represented the U.S. at the Inter-Allied Conference in Paris (Nov.–Dec. 1917) where the coordination of Allied resources against Germany was discussed. As early as Sept. 1917 House directed research on European social and economic conditions for use at the subsequent peace conference. He influenced Wilson's decision to issue a statement of war aims as well as the substance of those aims and it was his hint that the U.S. might make a separate peace (Nov. 1918) which precipitated the Allies into acceptance of those "14 Points." He was a delegate at the negotiations of the armistice and, with Wilson, a member of the 5-man U.S. delegation at the Paris Peace Conference, working especially on the Covenant of the League of Nations and the mandates system. Wilson apparently blamed him for U.S. concessions made during the president's brief return to the U.S. (Mar. 1919) and resisted House's advice for

greater concessions to the Allies in order to achieve agreement on the League of Nations. Their friendship was strained during the peace negotiations, possibly because Wilson was ill, and House never saw Wilson again after the president left Paris (June 1919). After Wilson's stroke (2 Oct. 1919) House counseled compromise with the Senate in order to secure ratification of the League Covenant, and after Wilson persisted, urged his resignation so that vice-president Marshall could lead the fight (Nov. 1919). House's advice may never have been seen by the ill president. He advised Franklin D. Roosevelt during the 1932 campaign.

Houston, Samuel (b. near Lexington, Va., 2 Mar. 1793; d. San Antonio, Tex., 26 July 1863), soldier and statesman, removed to Blount Co., Tenn. (1807), clerked in a trader's store, left home, and lived nearly 3 years with the Cherokee. On return, he taught in a country school. In the War of 1812 he served under Andrew Jackson against the Creeks and was wounded at Horseshoe Bend (28 Mar. 1814). After assisting in the removal of the Cherokee from Tennessee to present Arkansas (1817–18), he resigned from the army, studied law in Nashville, and was admitted to the bar. Congressman, 1823–27, and governor of Tennessee, 1827–29, he resigned after his wife left him and was adopted into the Cherokee nation. Jackson sent him to Texas to negotiate a treaty with the Indians (1832) and he settled at Nacogdoches (1833). He was elected a delegate to the San Felipe constitutional convention, which petitioned for separation of Texas from Cohuila (1833). With the outbreak of the War for Texan Independence he became commander in chief of the Texan army (1835). He surprised and routed Santa Anna at San Jacinto (21 Apr. 1836), thereby achieving Texan independence. The newly founded (1836) city of Houston was named for him. Elected president of Texas (1836–38) and reelected (1841–44), he secured recognition of the republic by the U.S. After Texas was admitted to the Union (1845), he became one of the first 2 senators (1846–59). A Union Democrat, he opposed the Kansas-Nebraska Bill (1854). Elected governor of Texas (1859), he opposed secession, refused to espouse the Confederate cause, and was deposed (18 Mar. 1861).

Howe, Elias (b. Spencer, Mass., 9 July 1819; d. Brooklyn, N.Y., 3 Oct. 1867), inventor of the sewing machine. He was an apprentice (1835–37) in a cotton machinery factory in Lowell, Mass., and subsequently, while working in an instrument maker's shop in Cambridge, Mass., designed and constructed a sewing machine which he improved during the winter of 1844–45. The patent for the machine was issued on 10 Sept. 1846. Encountering indifference in the U.S., Howe marketed his machine in England to William Thomas, a London corset manufacturer, who also bought the English rights from Howe. After a quarrel that led to a break with Thomas, Howe returned to the U.S. to find that the English reputation of his machine had spread to his homeland. The lawsuits which Howe instituted against those (like Isaac M. Singer) whom he accused of infringing his patent lasted from 1849 to 1854 and ended in Howe's favor with the award of a royalty on every sewing machine that infringed his rights. His royalties for the period 1861–67 often amounted to $4,000 a week. He established (1865) that Howe Machine Co. of Bridgeport, Conn., whose perfected machine won the gold medal at the Paris Exhibition of 1867.

Howe, Samuel Gridley (b. Boston, Mass., 10 Nov. 1801; d. there, 9 Jan. 1876), humanitarian, reformer, was graduated from Brown Univ. (1821) and received his M.D. from Harvard (1824). Drawn to the Greek cause like other romantics of his time, he spent 6 years fighting against the Turks, distributing food and clothing supplies, and aiding reconstruction. Appointed (1831) to run a Massachusetts school for the blind, he established it in his father's home and later in the Perkins mansion (Perkins Institution). His work with the blind demonstrated that the sightless could be economically and socially competent. During his 45 years with the school he trained a staff in educating the blind, visiting 17 states to advance this cause. He taught the deaf and blind child Laura Bridgeman, demonstrating to an incredulous world the values of such training, and promoted the oral, as against the sign, method for instructing the deaf. From 1865–74 he headed the Massachusetts State Board of Charities, the first of its kind in the U.S. With his gifted wife, Julia Ward Howe (1819–1910), whom he married in 1843, he coedited the antislavery paper *The Commonwealth* and aided and abetted John Brown. He backed Horace Mann's fight for better schools, helped Dorothea Dix in her campaign for care of the insane, and agitated for prison reform.

Howells, William Dean (b. Martin's Ferry, Belmont Co., Ohio, 1 Mar. 1837; d. New York City, 11 May 1920), novelist and critic, spent his boyhood in several Ohio towns, including Dayton and Ashtabula, had little formal schooling, and at the age of 9 began setting type in his father's printing office. He served (1856–61) on the editorial staff of the *Ohio State Journal*, in association with John J. Piatt published *Poems of Two Friends* (1860). After writing a campaign life of Lincoln (1860) he served as U.S. consul at Venice (1861–65) and published *Venetian Life* (1866) and *Italian*

Journeys (1867). Returning to the U.S. in 1865, he worked for the *Nation* and in 1866 became subeditor of the *Atlantic Monthly,* of which he was editor in chief from 1871 to 1881. During this period he formed his friendship with Henry James and gained an intimate knowledge of Boston and New England society. The novels published during this period were *Their Wedding Journey* (1872), *A Chance Acquaintance* (1873), *A Foregone Conclusion* (1875), *The Lady of the Aroostook* (1879), *The Undiscovered Country* (1880), *A Fearful Responsibility* (1881), and *Dr. Breen's Practice* (1881). After leaving the *Atlantic* he wrote serials for the *Century Magazine,* contributed (1886–91) influential critical writings to the "Editor's Study" in *Harper's Monthly,* and in 1891 moved to New York. After the Haymarket affair, Howells developed a deep interest in social and economic problems. During his middle and later period he wrote *A Modern Instance* (1881), *A Woman's Reason* (1883), *The Rise of Silas Lapham* (1885), *Indian Summer* (1886), *The Minister's Charge* (1887), *April Hopes* (1888), *Annie Kilburn* (1889), *A Hazard of New Fortunes* (1890), *The Quality of Mercy* (1892), *An Imperative Duty* (1893), *The World of Chance* (1893), *The Coast of Bohemia* (1893), *A Traveler from Alturia* (1894), *The Landlord at Lion's Head* (1897), and *Through the Eye of the Needle* (1907). His last novel was *The Leatherwood God* (1916). He also wrote works of reminiscence, such as *Boys' Town* (1890), *My Year in a Log Cabin* (1893), *My Literary Passions* (1895), *Impressions and Experiences* (1896), *Literary Friends and Acquaintances* (1900), *My Mark Twain* (1910), and *Years of My Youth* (1916). His critical works, among them *Criticism and Fiction* (1891) and *Literature and Life* (1902), helped pave the way for the acceptance of realism in the American novel. Howells gave encouragement to such realist writers as Frank Norris, Stephen Crane, and Hamlin Garland.

Hughes, Charles Evans (b. Glens Falls, N.Y., 11 Apr. 1862; d. Osterville, Mass., 27 Aug. 1948), 10th chief justice of the U.S., was graduated from Brown Univ. (1881) and received his law degree from Columbia (1884). His practice in New York City was temporarily interrupted by his professorship of law at Cornell (1891–93). He was counsel for the Stevens Gas Commission investigating utility practices in New York (1906) and attained nationwide reputation as counsel for the Armstrong Commission, which exposed abuses in the life insurance field (1906–07). Republican governor of New York (1906–10), his administration was notable for its reforms, including the establishment of a Public Service Commission. Appointed associate justice of the U.S. Supreme Court (1910), he resigned (1916) to accept the Republican nomination for president. His close defeat by President Wilson was attributed in no small measure to tactical errors he made during an electioneering tour of California, the loss of which state gave Wilson a majority in the electoral college. After a period of law practice, he served as Secretary of State in the administrations of Harding and Coolidge (1921–25), organized the Washington Conference on Naval Limitation of Armaments, and negotiated a series of multipartite treaties. Member of the Permanent Court of Arbitration (1926–30) and judge on the Permanent Court of International Justice (1929–30), he was chosen chief justice of the U.S. Supreme Court that same year, serving until his retirement (1941). In the alignment between liberals and conservatives, he, together with Associate Justice Roberts, occupied a middle ground and contributed to a cautious reshaping of the law to meet social change. He upheld civil liberties and the freedom of the press, curbed the judicial power of administrative agencies, spoke for a unanimous court in invalidating the NIRA (*Schechter Case*, 1935), but sustained the Wagner Act (1937). He effectively opposed President Franklin D. Roosevelt's court reorganization plan (1937).

Hutchinson, Anne (b. Alford, Lincolnshire, England, 1591; d. Eastchester, N.Y., Aug. or Sept. 1643), religious leader. Born Ann Marbury, she married (1612) William Hutchinson, and in 1634 came with her husband and family to Massachusetts Bay, where her openly avowed religious views provoked keen antagonism among the orthodox. She attacked the religious polity of the Massachusetts colony as a "covenant of works" and advocated a "covenant of grace" based on a direct personal apprehension of divine grace and love. Characterized as an Antinomian by her enemies, she was backed by Rev. John Cotton, Rev. John Wheelwright, and Gov. Henry Vane; but lost her support when Cotton recanted, Wheelwright was banished, and Vane departed for England. Brought to trial for sedition and contempt of the magistrates, she was sentenced to banishment and was later formally excommunicated from the church for heresy, after refusing to make a public recantation. With her family, she emigrated (1638) to the colony on the island of Aquidneck (now part of R.I.). For her subsequent career and death, see p. 41.

Hutchinson, Thomas (b. Boston, 9 Sept. 1711; d. Brompton, England, 3 June 1780), Loyalist statesman, received his B.A. (1727) and his M.A. (1730) from Harvard, and after serving in his father's business was elected to the Massachusetts House of Representatives (1737). Serving there (1737–49), he was speaker

(1746–48). An advocate of hard money, he opposed the Massachusetts Land Bank, and sponsored legislation to redeem the colony's bills of credit. Serving in the Council (1749–66), he represented Massachusetts at the Albany Congress (1754), where he collaborated with and supported Franklin in a plan of union. Lieutenant governor beg. 1758, he also served as chief justice from 1760. In the latter capacity he granted the writs of assistance (1761). His support of enforcement of both the Sugar and Stamp Acts marked him as the leader of the Court party. On 26 Aug. 1765 his home was sacked and his books and papers scattered in reprisal. Royal governor (1770–74), he argued for the supremacy of Parliament over the colonies. Publication in Boston (1773) of letters he sent to England urging the government to assert more vigorously its authority over the colonies created a sensation. His insistence that clearance papers would not be given to the tea ships until the tea was landed brought on the Boston Tea Party (1773). Reporting personally to George III (1774), he now advocated a conciliatory policy, but remained in exile, hopeful to the last of laying his "bones in New England." His most important writings were his notably objective *History of the Colony of Mass. Bay* (3 vols., 1764–1828) and *A Collection of Original Papers Relative to the History of Mass. Bay* (1769).

Ickes, Harold LeClaire (b. Frankstown, Pa., 15 Mar. 1874; d. Washington, D.C., 3 Feb. 1952), political leader. Ickes received his B.A. (1897) and LL.B. (1907) from Univ. of Chicago. He was a reporter on the *Chicago Tribune* and the *Chicago Record* (1897–1900), and later practiced law. An active and independent political campaigner, Ickes supported C. E. Merriam for mayor of Chicago (1911) and fought the influence of business interests in municipal government there. At first a Republican, he became leader of the Illinois Progressive party (1912–15), but returned to support Hughes for president in 1916. A delegate-at-large to the Republican National Convention (1920), Ickes opposed Harding's nomination and later endorsed the Cox-Roosevelt ticket. Partially because he campaigned for Franklin D. Roosevelt in the Middle West (1932) and because of his strong views on conservation, Ickes was Roosevelt's choice for Secretary of the Interior (1933), after he had trouble filling the position. As Secretary of the Interior (1933–46) Ickes was an outspoken opponent of big business, deeply concerned for the public interest, a supporter of conservation and of comprehensive national planning. As director of the Public Works Administration for 6 years (appointed 16 June 1933), established to provide employment and stimulate business by providing purchasing power, "Honest Harold" scrutinized each contract to determine whether the project was economically justifiable, satisfied engineering requirements, and was untainted by graft, corruption, and maladministration. Insuring incorruptibility, this procedure delayed the effect of the PWA in stimulating the economy. President of the Chicago NAACP in younger days, Ickes was, with Eleanor Roosevelt, the staunchest advocate of civil rights within the New Deal, hiring blacks, seeing that they received their share of the massive low-cost housing projects he supported, integrating the cafeteria of the Interior Department, and arranging for Marian Anderson to perform from the steps of the Lincoln Memorial when denied Constitution Hall by the Daughters of the American Revolution (1939). He advised Roosevelt to "purge" opposition congressmen (1938), attacked the Dies Committee (1938), and encouraged Roosevelt

to seek a 3d term (1940). An early and outspoken opponent of Hitler, during World War II Ickes also served as Petroleum and Solid Fuels Coordinator for National Defense. In 1943 he favored the immediate release of interned Japanese-Americans. President Truman accepted Ickes' resignation, an expression of Ickes' opposition to the appointment of Edward Pauley as Under Secretary of the Navy (1946). Both before and after his resignation, Ickes campaigned for civilian administration of U.S. islands in the Pacific. Pugnacious and honest to the point of bluntness, he wrote *The New Democracy* (1934) and *The Autobiography of a Curmudgeon* (1943).

Inness, George (b. near Newburgh, N.Y., 1 May 1825; d. Bridge of Allan, Scotland, 3 Aug. 1894), painter, received brief instruction in the studio of Régis Gignoux, New York City, but was virtually self-taught. He studied in Italy (1847, 1851, and 1871) and in France (1854), but did most of his painting in Medfield, Mass., and later in Montclair, N.J., and New York City. His early work was in the tradition of the Hudson River School, but his style broadened (*Delaware Meadows*, 1867) in the direction of lyricism and subjectivity, with a feeling for light and air achieved by his color patterns. Foremost American landscapist, his paintings are in the Art Institute, Chicago; the Metropolitan Museum, New York; and the National Gallery, Washington, D.C. They include *Peace and Plenty* (1865), *Coming Storm* (1878), *Sunset in the Woods* (1883), *Niagara Falls* (1884), and *March Breezes* (1885).

Irving, Washington (b. New York City, 3 Apr. 1783; d. Tarrytown, N.Y., 28 Nov. 1859), man of letters. He began reading law in 1798 and for a short time practiced law at New York, but soon abandoned this calling for writing and travel.

Beginning in 1802 he published in New York City journals "The Letters of Jonathan Oldstyle, Gent.," and in 1807–08 brought out a collection of essays, *Salamagundi: or, the Whim-Whams and Opinions of Launcelot Langstaff, Esq. and Others*. The spirit of these lively satirical pieces was carried over into his comic account, *History of New York . . . by Diedrich Knickerbocker* (1809), which gave its name to the Knickerbocker School of writers. In 1815 he sailed for Europe, remaining there until 1832. During his stay in England he wrote *The Sketch Book of Geoffrey Crayon, Gent.* (1819–20), which included essays such as "Westminster Abbey" and "The Mutability of Literature," and tales such as "Rip Van Winkle" and 'The Legend of Sleepy Hollow." He also published *Bracebridge Hall* (1822). Leaving England in 1822, he went to Germany and France, and in 1826 went to Spain, where he served (1826–29) on the staff of the U.S. embassy. At Madrid, and in the Alhambra at Granada, he wrote *The History of the Life and Voyages of Christopher Columbus* (1828), *A Chronicle of the Conquest of Granada* (1829), and *The Alhambra: A Series of Tales and Sketches of the Moors and Spaniards* (1832). Irving served as attaché (1829–32) at the U.S. legation in London, and upon his return to the U.S. was hailed as the nation's leading man of letters. His travels to the West produced *A Tour on the Prairies* (1835), *Astoria* (1836), and *The Adventures of Captain Bonneville, U.S.A.* (1837). He settled at Sunnyside, near Tarrytown, N.Y., and, except for the years 1842–46, when he was U.S. minister to Spain, lived there until his death. Among his other works are *Tales of a Traveller* (1824), *The Crayon Miscellany* (1835), *Oliver Goldsmith* (1849), *Mahomet and His Successors* (2 vols., 1849–50), *Wolfert's Roost* (1855), and *Life of George Washington* (5 vols., 1855–59). Irving was the first American to gain an international reputation as a man of letters and to make writing his full-time profession.

Ives, Charles Edward (b. Danbury, Conn., 20 Oct. 1874; d. New York City, 19 May 1954), composer. Son of George Edward Ives, a well-known musician and bandmaster in Gen. Grant's army, Ives took his first music lessons from his father, who encouraged him to adapt the disharmonies of village bands and country fiddlers to his compositions. At Yale he studied organ under Dudley Buck and composition under Horatio W. Parker. Upon receiving his A.B. (1898), Ives realized the impracticality of a musical career and chose instead to earn his living as an insurance executive. He remained in the insurance business retiring in 1930 as a millionaire. At the same time he was active as an organist and composer. By 1918, when illness forced him to curtail composition, he had composed 4 symphonies, 4 violin sonatas, 2 piano sonatas, 3 orchestral suites, 11 volumes of chamber music, as well as choral music and numerous pieces for organ. After 1915 he composed some 200 songs. His most famous compositions are the *Second String Quartet* (1896), the *Second Piano Sonata* ("Concord") (1909–15), the *New England Symphony* (1904–13), the *Fourth Symphony* (1910–16), and the *Third Symphony* (1901–04), which won the Pulitzer Prize in 1947. Ives' works are known for their complexity. He was one of the first to experiment with polyharmonies, polyrhythms, tone clusters, exotic scales, atonal systems, and quarter tone effects. His works often contain reference to American hymns, marches, and ditties. Because of the technical complexity of his music, the tendency of others to look to European models, and his fierce independence, Ives' work was largely ignored until well after his most productive years. Recognition came with the first complete performance of the *Concord Sonata* (Town Hall, New York, 20 Jan. 1939).

Jackson, Andrew (b. Waxhaw, S.C., 15 Mar. 1767; d. near Nashville, Tenn., 8 June 1845), 7th president of the U.S., served briefly in the American Revolution (1781), when he was taken prisoner by the British, studied law in Salisbury, N.C., was admitted to the bar (1787), and began practice in Martinsville. Appointed (1788) prosecuting attorney for western district of North Carolina (now Tenn.), he moved to Nashville. Married (1791) Mrs. Rachel Robards (née Donelson), mistakenly believing that she had already obtained a divorce (actually granted 2 years later). Member of state constitutional convention (1796), first congressman from Tennessee (Dec. 1796–Mar. 1797), U.S. senator (1797), he resigned and became judge of the Tennessee supreme court (1798–1804). In one of several duels he killed Charles Dickinson (1806). Personal feuds with President Jefferson (partly growing out of his attachment to Aaron Burr) and Gov. John Sevier (Tenn.) led to his temporary retirement from public life. As major general of militia he defeated the Creeks (1813–14). Commissioned major general in U.S. army, he decisively defeated the British at New Orleans (8 Jan. 1815) after the treaty of peace had been signed at Ghent. Commanding in the Seminole War, he invaded Florida (1818), captured Pensacola, and created an international incident by having 2 British subjects, Arbuthnot and Ambrister, executed for inciting the Creeks against the Americans. Military governor of Florida (1821) and U.S. senator (1823–25), he received the largest number of electoral votes for the presidency (1824), but, failing of a majority, was defeated in the House of Representatives, which elected John Quincy Adams (1825). He won easily 4 years later. His administration (1829–37) initiated the spoils system, set up a "Kitchen Cabinet" of intimate advisers (Amos Kendall, Duff Green, William Berkeley Lewis), and checked the program of federal internal improvements (Maysville veto, 1830). He reorganized his cabinet (1831) when Mrs. Calhoun and other wives of cabinet members refused to meet Mrs. J. H. (Peggy) Eaton. He finally broke with Calhoun on learning that the latter had favored censuring him for his conduct in Florida in 1818 and over the issue of nullification, which Jackson vigorously opposed, taking military measures to enforce South Carolina's respect for federal authority (1832). Favoring hard money, he warred on the Bank of the U.S., vetoed its recharter (1832), and ordered withdrawal of U.S. funds. His Indian policy consisted of relocation on lands west of the Mississippi. His administration is notable for expansion of the presidential power. After the inauguration of Van Buren, his choice for the presidency, he retired to his home, The Hermitage, near Nashville.

Jackson, Thomas Jonathan [commonly called "Stonewall" Jackson] (b. Clarksburg, Va., now W. Va., 21 Jan. 1824; d. Guiney's Station, Va., 10 May 1863), Confederate general, was graduated (1846) from the U.S. Military Academy; was breveted major during the Mexican War; became (1851) professor of artillery tactics and natural philosophy at the Virginia Military Institute, Lexington, Va.; and resigned from the army in 1852. He commanded the cadet corps at the hanging of John Brown (2 Dec. 1859). Commissioned (17 June 1861) a brigadier general in the Confederate forces, he earned his sobriquet "Stonewall" at 1st

Bull Run when his troops held off a strong Union assault (21 July 1861). Jackson was made a major general (7 Oct. 1861) and took command (5 Nov. 1861) of Confederate forces in the Shenandoah Valley. The Valley campaign (Mar.–June 1862) demonstrated Jackson's brilliance as a field tactician. Despite numerical inferiority, he defeated the Union force under Gen. Nathaniel P. Banks at Front Royal (23 May 1862) and Winchester (24–25 May 1862), and prevented the main enemy forces from uniting. During the 7 Days before Richmond, Jackson took part in the actions at Gaines' Mill (27 June 1862) and White Oak Swamp (30 June 1862). After destroying the Union advanced base at Manassas Junction (27 Aug. 1862), he helped defeat Pope at 2d Bull Run (30–31 Aug. 1862). He also took part in the battles of Antietam (17 Sept. 1862) and Fredericksburg (13 Dec. 1862). After forcing a Union retreat at Chancellorsville (2 May 1863), Jackson was accidentally wounded by the fire of Confederate pickets and died of pneumonia shortly afterward. His death deprived Lee of the greatest of his lieutenants.

James, Henry (b. New York City, 15 Apr. 1843; d. London, 28 Feb. 1916), novelist and essayist, son of Henry James (1811–82), the theologian, and brother of William James, was educated in France, entered Harvard Law School (1862), but turned to letters, contributing to the *Nation*, the *Atlantic*, and *Galaxy*. Returning to Europe for several visits in the 1870s, he finally settled in London (1876), becoming a British subject (July 1915). A master of the fiction technique, he established himself in the forefront of the analytical school of novelists with his subtle treatment of British and American society and his romanti-

cizing of aristocratic European culture. In his early works (*The American*, 1877; *Daisy Miller*, 1878; *The Bostonians*, 1886), his leading characters are Americans, although the scene is often abroad; but in his second period (*The Princess Casamassima*, 1886; *The Sacred Fount*, 1901), his novels are confined to English society. In his third period (*The Wings of the Dove*, 1902; *The Ambassadors*, 1903; *The Golden Bowl*, 1904; and his unfinished novels), he returned to his theme of the American abroad.

James, William (b. New York City, 11 Jan. 1842; d. Chocorua, N.H., 26 Aug. 1910), psychologist and philosopher, was educated abroad. After accompanying Agassiz on the Thayer expedition to the Amazon (1865–66), he entered Harvard Medical School, then pursued medical studies in Germany, and obtained a Harvard M.D. (1869). Harvard lecturer on anatomy and physiology (1872), assistant professor of physiology (1876), he transferred to the Department of Philosophy as assistant professor (1880), becoming a full professor (1885–1907). His works include *The Principles of Psychology* (1890), *The Varieties of Religious Experience* (1907), *A Pluralistic Universe* (1909), *The Meaning of Truth* (1909), and *Essays in Radical Empiricism* (1912). A radical empiricist, he evolved the method of pragmatism (the testing of truth by practical consequences), with its emphasis upon individuality, free initiative, spontaneity, and novelty. His conception of the world as one of changes, chance, and plurality largely anticipated trends in the physical sciences.

Jay, John (b. New York City, 12 Dec. 1745; d. Bedford, N.Y., 17 May 1829), first chief justice of the U.S., was graduated from King's College (1764), studied law, was admitted to the bar (1768), and practiced in New York. Secretary of the N.Y.-N.J. boundary commission (1773), he was a member of the 1st and 2d Continental Congresses (1775–76) and of the New York Provincial Congress (1776–77). Chairman of the committee which drew up the New York state constitution (1777), he became chief justice of New York in that year and also a member of Congress, becoming its president (10 Dec. 1778). Sent to Spain as minister plenipotentiary, his mission (1780–82) failed owing to Spanish hostility to U.S. independence. Member of the U.S. delegation to negotiate peace with Great Britain, he was instrumental in the decision to deal with Great Britain independent of France (1782). Secretary of Foreign Affairs (1784–90), his agreement with Gardoqui to settle differences with Spain (1785), which involved restricting U.S. use of the Mississippi, was defeated in Congress. Advocate of the new Constitution, he wrote 5 of the *Federalist* papers. Chief justice of the U.S. (26 Sept. 1789), he was sent to Great Britain (1794) to settle outstanding differences with that country. Jay's Treaty was denounced by Jeffersonian Republicans for its concessions to England, but its averted war at that time. His most important Supreme Court decision, *Chisholm* v. *Georgia* (1793), holding that a state could be sued by a citizen of another state, led to the 11th Amendment to the Constitution. He resigned from the court (1795) to accept the governorship of New York (1795–1801). Long an opponent of slavery, he signed (1799) the act for its gradual abolition in New York.

Jefferson, Thomas (b. Shadwell, Albemarle Co., Va., 13 Apr. 1743; d. Monticello, 4 July 1826), 3d president of the U.S., was graduated from William and Mary (1762), studied law, and was ad-

mitted to the bar (1767), practicing until 1770 and managing his estate. Sent to the House of Burgesses (1769–75), he published (1774) *A Summary View of the Rights of British Amercia*. A delegate to the Continental Congress (1775–76), he drafted the Declaration of Independence. Returning to the Virginia legislature, he supported measures providing "a foundation for a government truly republican"— abolition of primogeniture and entails, separation of church and state, establishment of a public school system. He also favored discontinuing the slave trade and gradual emancipation. Succeeding Patrick Henry as governor of Virginia (1779–81), he directed without conspicuous success resistance to British invasion. Returning to Congress (1783–84), he devised a plan for a decimal monetary system and drafted the Land Ordinance of 1784, the basis for the later organization of the territories. Succeeding Franklin as minister to France (1785–89), he published his *Notes on Virginia* (Paris, 1785) and witnessed the beginnings of the French Revolution. Washington's first Secretary of State, he supported Hamilton's funding and assumption plan on condition that the national capital be located on the Potomac. He served until 1793, when he resigned in protest against Hamilton's fiscal and centralizing policies. Leader in retirement of the Democratic-Republican party, he was vice-president under John Adams (1797–1801). Opposing the Alien and Sedition Acts, he prepared, with Madison, the Virginia and Kentucky Resolutions (1798), implying that a state could nullify congressional legislation. In the election of 1800 he tied with Aaron Burr in electoral votes and was chosen president by the House of Representatives with Hamilton's support. His administration (1801–09) was marked by simplicity and economy, the successful war against the Barbary pirates (1801–05), the

Louisiana Purchase (1803), the Lewis and Clark and Pike expeditions, the Burr treason trial (1807), and the Embargo Act (1807), adopted to preserve U.S. neutral rights, but repealed (1809). In retirement at Monticello, Jefferson founded the Univ. of Virginia (1819) and contributed notably to the revival of classical architecture in the U.S. A philosopher-statesman of the Enlightenment, he favored a society of self-sufficient free farmers and decentralized governmental powers.

Johnson, Andrew (b. Raleigh, N.C., 29 Dec. 1808; d. Carter Station, Tenn., 31 July 1875), 17th president of the U.S., was self-educated, becoming a tailor in Greenville, Tenn. Soon engaging in politics, where he came to stand for a more equitable land policy, he was alderman (1828–30), mayor (1830–33), Democratic member of the state's lower house (1835–37 and 1839–41) and of the state senate (1841–43); he was elected Democratic congressman (1843–53), served as governor of Tennessee (1853–57), and U.S. senator (1857–62) where he distinguished himself as the only Southern senator to support the Union during the Civil War. Appointed by Lincoln military governor of Tennessee with the rank of brigadier general (4 Mar. 1862), he was Lincoln's running mate (1864) on the Union-Republican ticket and was elected vice-president, becoming president upon Lincoln's death (1865). His attempt to carry out Lincoln's conciliatory Reconstruction policy led him into conflict with the Radical Republicans, who passed over his veto their own Reconstruction Act (1867) which enfranchised Negroes and disfranchised ex-Confederates. Johnson violated the Tenure of Office Act (passed 2 Mar. 1867 over his veto and declared unconstitutional by the Supreme Court, 1926), by dismissing Edwin M. Stanton, Secretary

of War. Impeached by the House of Representatives, the Senate failed by one vote to convict him (May 1868, see p. 296). Reelected senator (1875), he died the same year.

Johnson, Lyndon Baines (b. nr. Stonewall, Tex., 27 Aug. 1908; d. Johnson City, Tex., 22 Jan. 1973), 36th president of the U.S., worked his way through Southwest State Teachers College, San Marcos, Tex. (B.S., 1930), and taught public speaking and debating in the Houston public schools (1930–32). He entered public service as secretary to Rep. M. Kleberg (1932–35). In 1934 he married Claudia Alta (Lady Bird) Taylor. State Director, National Youth Administration (1935–37), he was elected to fill a congressional vacancy, serving in the House of Representatives (1937–49), with a leave of absence for naval duty (1941–42). U.S. senator (1949–61), he was minority leader (1953–55) and majority leader (1955–61), cooperating closely with the Eisenhower administration. In 1955 he suffered a heart attack. Defeated by John F. Kennedy for the Democratic nomination for president (1960), he accepted the vice-presidential nomination. As vice-president (1961–63) he traveled extensively and served as chairman of the Presidential Committee on Equal Employment Opportunity, curbing racial bias by government contractors. Following the assassination of Kennedy (22 Nov. 1963), he succeeded to the presidency and secured the passage of such Kennedy legislation as a tax cut and the civil rights bill (1964). In 1964 he was elected to the presidency. His years as president were marked by extraordinary legislative accomplishment. Decisions he made to escalate American military efforts in Vietnam involved the United States in a lengthy, costly land war. The domestic unpopularity of the war led to his decision (announced 31

Mar. 1968) not to seek reelection. He wrote *The Vantage Point: Perspectives of the Presidency 1963–69* (1971).

Johnson, Sir William (b. Smithtown, County Meath, Ireland, 1715; d. Johnstown, N.Y., 11 July 1774), colonial official and diplomat, came to America in 1737, settling on the Mohawk, trading with the Indians, amassing a fortune as well as huge landholdings, and founding (1762) Johnstown. On intimate terms with the Six Nations, particularly the Mohawks, he was largely responsible for keeping them on the British side during King George's War. In 1746 he was made colonel and commissary of New York for Indian affairs, resigning the latter office in 1750. At the start of the French and Indian War, he attended, as a member of the New York Council, the Albany Congress (1754), helping to formulate Indian policy. In 1755 Braddock gave him command of the force against Crown Point and "sole management" of the Six Nations. Though he failed to capture Crown Point, he warded off the French threat to the northern colonies and was made (1755) a baronet for his achievements and superintendent of Indian affairs (1756). He advocated centralized control of the fur trade and a boundary line between white settlement and Indian hunting lands. Such a boundary he negotiated (1768) at Ft. Stanwix, opening up to settlement large tracts in New York, Pennsylvania, and Virginia. An imperialist, he secured by his policies the attachment of most of the Iroquois to the British side when the Revolution broke out (after his death).

Johnson, William (b. Charleston, S.C., 27 Dec. 1771; d. Brooklyn, N.Y., 4 Aug. 1834), jurist, graduated at the head of his class from Princeton (1790) and studied law in Charleston under Charles Cotesworth Pinckney. Admitted to the bar in 1793, Johnson was elected as a Republican member of the South Carolina House of Representatives (1794–98), serving as its speaker (1798). The legislature elected him to the South Carolina Court of Common Pleas (1799–1804). In naming Johnson to the Supreme Court of the U.S. (1804), President Jefferson expected that his appointee would counterbalance Chief Justice Marshall. These expectations were fulfilled only in part. Johnson did become the first major exponent of the dissenting tradition on the Supreme Court, opposing what were usually Marshall's majority views in 34 dissenting opinions and 21 concurring opinions during his 30 years on the court. Major dissents are exemplified by *Osborn* v. *Bank of the United States* (1824) and *Ogden* v. *Saunders* (1827). His Jeffersonian principles were reflected in his majority opinion in *U.S.* v. *Hudson and Goodwin* (1812), holding that the federal courts lacked the power to try offenses at common law—a decision which, however, terminated a criminal libel trial of 2 Federalist editors. His independence was revealed in his decision as circuit judge in *Gilchrist* v. *Collector of Charleston* (1808) declaring Jefferson's embargo illegal and asserting that "the officers of our government, from the highest to the lowest, are equally subject to legal restraint." He concurred with such typically Marshallian readings of the Constitution as *Cohens* v. *Virginia* (1821) and *Gibbons* v. *Ogden* (1824), where his interpretation of the commerce powers was even broader than Marshall's. As a justice, Johnson supported strong national powers and a powerful judiciary but not at the expense of Congress—as in *Anderson* v. *Dunn* (1821), upholding the contempt power—and looked to the states for economic and social regulation.

He vigorously opposed nullification in a pamphlet written under the pseudonym "Hamilton" (1828). He also authored *Sketches of the Life and Correspondence of Nathanael Greene* (1822) and *Eulogy of Thomas Jefferson* (1826).

Johnston, Joseph Eggleston (b. "Cherry Grove," Prince Edward Co., Va., 3 Feb. 1807; d. Washington, D.C., 21 Mar. 1891), Confederate general. Graduated (1829) from the U.S. Military Academy, he served in the Mexican War, in which he was wounded 5 times, and was promoted to lieutenant colonel in 1855 and brigadier general in 1860. With the secession of Virginia, Johnston resigned from the U.S. Army and was appointed (May 1861) brigadier general in the Confederate army. After turning back the Union forces at 1st Bull Run (21 July 1861), where he shared the field with Beauregard against McDowell, Johnston was commissioned a general and was wounded while commanding (31 May–1 June) at the Battle of Seven Pines (Fair Oaks). He was placed in command (Nov. 1862) of the Confederate forces in Tennessee and Mississippi, and after the fall of Vicksburg, which contributed to a worsening of Johnston's relations with Jefferson Davis, was assigned (Dec. 1863) to the Army of Tennessee, before Chattanooga. Late in the spring of 1864 Johnston fell back before Sherman's assault and was relieved from his command (17 July 1864) before Atlanta. The Confederate Congress passed a resolution asking his reinstatement. Restored (23 Feb. 1865), Johnston signed an armistice (18 Apr. 1865) with Sherman which the Union government rejected. When Johnston was ordered by Jefferson Davis to continue the war in the interior, he refused and surrendered his force to Sherman near Durham Station, N.C. (26 Apr.

1865). He served in Congress (1879–81) and was appointed (1885) a federal commissioner of railroads.

Jones, John Paul (b. Kirkbean, Kirkcudbrightshire, Scotland, 6 July 1747; d. Paris, France, 18 July 1792), naval officer. Until c.1773, when he arrived in America, he was known as **John Paul.** He was commissioned (7 Dec. 1775) a lieutenant in the newly organized Continental navy, captured 16 prizes as commander of the *Providence,* and in 1776 was promoted to captain. Appointed (14 June 1777) commander of the sloop *Ranger,* he carried out raids on British shipping, using Brest as a base of operations. Early in 1779 he was given command of an old East Indiaman which he christened the *Bonhomme Richard* (*Poor Richard*) in honor of Benjamin Franklin. On 14 Aug. 1779 he set out from L'Orient at the head of a small fleet to prey upon the British coast. On 23 Sept. 1779 there took place off Flamborough Head the naval engagement between the *Bonhomme Richard* and the larger and more heavily armed British warship *Serapis.* Although the *Richard* was sunk, the *Serapis* was captured by Jones, who on this occasion is reported to have said in reply to the British demand for surrender: "I have not yet begun to fight." He was made commander (26 June 1781) of the warship *America,* whose construction he supervised. When the navy was discontinued (1783), Jones went abroad. By unanimous resolve, Congress authorized (16 Oct. 1787) the presentation of a gold medal to Jones, the only Continental naval officer so honored. Late in 1787 Jones decided to enter the Russian naval service and, as a rear admiral, took command (26 May 1788) of a fleet on the Black Sea. He resigned from the Russian navy in 1789 and returned to Paris. In 1905 what are thought to be his remains were brought to the U.S. and now rest in the crypt of the chapel of the U.S. Naval Academy.

Kahn, Louis I. (b. Island of Saaremaa, Estonia, Russia, 20 Feb. 1901; d. New York City, 17 Mar. 1974), architect, came to the U.S. (1905), and graduated from the Univ. of Pennsylvania School of Architecture (1924). Though influenced by his training in the Beaux Arts tradition, Kahn was a fundamentalist who rethought the process and nature of architecture. Fitting into neither of the dominant schools of modern architecture (the abstract rationalism of the international style identified with Le Corbusier and Mies van der Rohe; the "organic" school of Frank Lloyd Wright), Kahn believed that both function and form should dictate a building's style. Rather than the modernists' steel and glass, he preferred brick, concrete, and stone. His work demonstrated an ability to create dramatic interactions of light and shadow and effective combinations of space and solid and of the grand and the intimate. Though he established his own firm in Philadelphia (1935) and was considered an excellent teacher at the Yale School of Architecture (1947–57), he did not receive recognition as a major architect until his Yale Art Gallery was completed (1951). His other major works include: the Richards Medical Research Laboratories of the Univ. of Pennsylvania (1961), the Salk Institute (La Jolla, Calif., 1965), the Kimbell Museum (Ft. Worth, Tex., 1972), and the Phillips-Exeter Academy Library (Exeter, N.H., 1972). At the time of Kahn's death, 2 major projects were under construction in Bangladesh: the capital area of Dacca, and the Institute of Ahmedabad. He was also professor

of architecture at the Univ. of Pennsylvania (1956–71).

Kendall, Edward Calvin (b. South Norwalk, Conn., 8 Mar. 1886; d. Princeton, N.J., 4 May 1972), biochemist, was graduated from Columbia (B.S., 1908; M.S., 1909; Ph.D., 1910), where he was a Goldschmidt fellow. He served as a research chemist with Parke, Davis & Co. at Detroit (1910–11) and with St. Luke's Hospital at New York (1911–14). Head of the biochemistry section at the Mayo Foundation, Rochester, Minn., and professor of physiological chemistry under the Mayo Foundation at the Univ. of Minnesota (1914–52), and at Princeton (1952–72). His first notable achievement was to isolate thyroxine from the thyroid gland (1914); then he isolated glutathione from yeast (1929). For isolating and synthesizing the principal hormone of the adrenal cortex (cortisone), he won a Nobel prize in medicine and physiology (with Phillip Hench and Tadeus Reichstein).

Kennedy, John Fitzgerald (b. Brookline, Mass., 29 May 1917; d. Dallas, Tex., 22 Nov. 1963), 35th president of the U.S., son of Joseph P. Kennedy, banker and realtor, received his B.S. cum laude (1940) from Harvard, spending six months during his junior year working in the London embassy while his father was ambassador to Great Britain. His observations inspired *Why England Slept* (1940). In the navy (1941–45), he was awarded the Navy and Marine Corps Medals and the Purple Heart for action as commander of a PT boat. After a brief period as a news correspondent, he was elected Democratic congressman from Massachusetts for 3 terms (1947–53). His defeat of Henry Cabot Lodge in the senatorial race of 1952 was a major upset. His *Profiles in Courage*

(1956) was awarded the Pulitzer prize in biography (1957). He lost a close race to Estes Kefauver for the vice-presidential nomination in 1956, but was reelected to the Senate (1958) by a 875,000-vote margin. He won the Democratic nomination for the presidency (1960) on the 1st ballot. He became the first Catholic and youngest man to be elected president. His administration strongly resisted Communist threats in Berlin (1961) and Cuba (1962), entered into a nuclear test ban (1963), and was solidly committed to civil rights. His assassination, 22 Nov. 1963, by Lee Harvey Oswald caused universal grief.

Kennedy, Robert F. (b. Brookline, Mass., 20 Nov. 1925; d. Los Angeles, Calif., 6 June 1968), political leader, received his A.B. from Harvard (1948) and his LL.B. from the Univ. of Virginia (1951). During World War II, while at Harvard, Kennedy enlisted in the U.S. Naval Reserve, and served as a seaman on the destroyer *Joseph P. Kennedy, Jr.*, named for his elder brother who had been killed in battle. Admitted to the Massachusetts bar (1951), he began his legal career as an attorney in the Criminal Division of the Department of Justice (1951–52). In 1953 he served as assistant counsel to the Hoover Commission. Later that year he was appointed assistant counsel to the Senate Permanent Subcommittee on Investigations, whose chairman was Sen. Joseph McCarthy. Kennedy served as counsel to the Democratic minority (1954) and as chief counsel and staff director of the committee (1955). He gained prominence by the vigor of his investigations of Teamster Union presidents Dave Beck and Jimmy Hoffa during his service as chief counsel to the Senate Committee on Improper Activities in Labor or Management (1957–60), writing *The Enemy Within* (1960). Campaign man-

ager for his brother, John F. Kennedy, during his 1952 senatorial and 1960 presidential campaigns, Robert Kennedy became attorney general of the U.S. (1961–64). In that position he continued the investigations of Hoffa and other union leaders. During his years in the Justice Department he actively supported reforms in criminal justice, fought for black civil rights, and strongly enforced federal voting laws. His brother's closest friend and adviser, Kennedy played a major role in deliberations during the Cuban missile crisis (1962). After the assassination of John F. Kennedy (1963), Robert Kennedy, grieving, sought his own political course. Rejected as a running mate by President Lyndon Johnson, Kennedy was elected U.S. senator from New York (1964). In the Senate he was among the earliest to oppose the Vietnam War and became increasingly associated with the causes of minorities generally lacking in power, such as migrant agricultural workers, American Indians, and Eskimos. A belated candidate for the Democratic presidential nomination in 1968, attempting to rally antiwar forces, Kennedy won major primaries in Indiana and Nebraska. He was assassinated by Sirhan Sirhan almost immediately after acknowledging his victory in the California primary.

Kent, James (b. Fredericksburg, N.Y., 31 July 1763; d. New York City, 12 Dec. 1847), jurist, was graduated from Yale (1781), admitted to the New York bar (1785), and practiced in Poughkeepsie until 1793 and thereafter in New York City until his elevation to the bench. Professor of law at Columbia (1794–98 and 1824–26), he became master in chancery (1796), justice (1798), and chief justice (1804) of the state supreme court, where he introduced much French civil law into the New York legal system as well as the practice of written opinions. Appointed chancellor (1814–23), his decisions, along with the work of Story, laid the foundations of equity jurisprudence in the U.S. His Columbia lectures, which followed the model of Blackstone, were expanded into *Commentaries on the American Law* (1826–30), called by Justice Story "our first judicial classic," and soon accepted as an authoritative exposition of the English common law in the U.S. and a standard interpretation of the Constitution. The most notable edition was the 12th by O. W. Holmes, Jr. (1873). A lifelong Federalist, Kent vigorously opposed universal suffrage at the New York Constitutional Convention (1821).

Kettering, Charles Franklin (b. Londonville, Ohio, 29 Aug. 1876; d. Dayton, Ohio, 25 Nov. 1958), inventor, received his E.E. degree (1904) from Ohio State Univ. He began work with the Star Telephone Co., Ashland, and then, with the National Cash Register Co., Dayton, he invented an electric motor for cash registers. In 1909 he organized the Dayton Engineering Laboratories Co. (Delco), and within 2 years made notable improvements in automobile ignition and lighting systems. His perfection (1911) of the self-starter, first installed in the Cadillac, enormously expanded the market for the motorcar. As general manager of General Motors' research laboratories (1925–47) he directed research on improving Diesel engines and the development of a nontoxic and noninflammable refrigerant. He also originated and guided researches resulting in higher octane gasoline, adding tetraethyl lead. In 1951 he developed a new high-compression engine. Founder and chairman of the Charles F. Kettering Foundation (1927), he directed research in the natural sciences, working on chlorophyll and photosynthesis, artificial-fever therapy, and cancer. He was cofounder of the Sloan-Kettering Institute for Cancer Research.

King, Martin Luther, Jr. (b. Atlanta, Ga., 15 Jan. 1929; d. Memphis, Tenn., 4 Apr. 1968), social reformer and clergyman, received his A.B. from Morehouse College (1948), his B.D. from Crozer Theological Seminary (1951), and his Ph.D. from Boston Univ. (1955). As pastor of the Dexter Avenue Baptist Church, he helped to direct the Negro bus boycott in Montgomery, Ala. (1955–56). His philosophy of nonviolent demonstrations, influenced by Gandhi (later expressed eloquently in *A Letter from Birmingham Jail* [1963]) was widely adopted in the rapidly growing civil rights movement. He founded (1957) and was president of the Southern Christian Leadership Conference, which first spurred voter registration activity and later helped to organize sit-ins and freedom rides. He was a leader of the demonstrations in Birmingham, Ala. (1963) which triggered Pres. Kennedy's decision to fight for a strong civil rights law. One of 8 leaders of the March on Washington by over 200,000 (28 Aug. 1963), he electrified the audience with his "I Have a Dream" address. His shrewd sense of strategy, eloquence, and moral courage proved major assets to the civil rights movement. King was awarded the Nobel peace prize (1964). He led a Freedom March from Selma to Montgomery, Ala. (1965), planned and led assaults on Chicago's de facto school desegregation (1965) and slum conditions (1966). He announced his opposition to the Vietnam War (1967). He was about to lead a nationwide campaign of the poor when assassinated in Memphis by James Earl Ray. He was the author of *Stride Toward Freedom* (1958), and *Why We Can't Wait* (1964).

Kinsey, Alfred C. (b. Hoboken, N.J., 23 June 1894; d. Bloomington, Ind., 25

Aug. 1956), sex researcher and zoologist, received his B.S. from Bowdoin College (1916) and his Sc.D. from Harvard (1920). He became a professor of zoology at Indiana Univ. (1929–56). Throughout the 1930s, Kinsey, an entomologist, studied the life and habits of the gall wasp, and his publications established him as a leading authority. Turning to research on sex (1938), he established, with financial support from the Rockefeller Foundation and the National Research Council, the Institute for Sex Research at Indiana Univ. (1942). Kinsey and 14 associates undertook the most ambitious investigation of sexual activity up to that time, interviewing 5,300 men and boys, and 5,940 women and girls. Using polling techniques, his interviews sometimes included as many as 300 questions on sex. The result of this research was the publication of *Sexual Behavior in the Human Male* (1948) and *Sexual Behavior in the Human Female* (1953). His controversial findings aroused wide national interest. Among the general conclusions, he found a wide divergence between moral codes and social mores; premarital intercourse more widespread among men and women than previously believed; a close relationship between social class and sex habits; potency among the male continuing far beyond age 60; and a far greater percentage of Americans engaged in homosexual activity than had previously been believed.

Kissinger, Henry Alfred (b. Fuerth, Germany, 27 May 1923–), statesman and scholar. Kissinger came to the U.S. (1938), becoming an American citizen (1943), and serving in the U.S. army (1943–46). He received his A.B. *summa cum laude* (1950) and his Ph.D. in government (1954) from Harvard. As professor of government at Harvard (1959–

69), Kissinger's scholarship included studies of diplomacy, nuclear strategy, and contemporary U.S. foreign policy. His Ph.D. dissertation was published as *A World Restored: Metternich, Castlereagh, and the Problems of Peace, 1812–22* (1957), and was followed by *Nuclear Weapons and Foreign Policy* (1957), *The Necessity for Choice: Prospects of American Foreign Policy* (1961), *The Troubled Partnership* (1965), and *American Foreign Policy, Three Essays* (1969). He was the founder and editor of the Harvard journal *Confluence* (1952), director of Harvard's Defense Studies Program (1951–69), and executive director of the Harvard International Seminar (1951–69). During this period Kissinger was director of the Special Studies Project of the Rockefeller Brothers Fund (1956–58), and director of Nuclear Weapons and Foreign Policy Studies of the Council on Foreign Relations (1955–58). He was consultant to the National Security Council during the Berlin crisis (1961–62), to the U.S. Arms Control and Disarmament Agency (1961–68), and to the Department of State (1965–69). As Assistant to the President for National Security Affairs (1969–), and Secretary of State (1973–), Kissinger was both a major architect and the key implementer of foreign policy during the Nixon administration. His performance, infused with energy, was characterized by personal diplomacy, secrecy, surprise tactics, and the conviction that in diplomacy momentum produces results. His major achivements were negotiating the opening of relations with mainland China and a peace agreement for Vietnam, promoting détente with the U.S.S.R. and, after the Yom Kippur War (1973), mediation in the Middle East. In 1973 Kissinger and Le Duc Tho of North Vietnam received the Nobel peace prize for their efforts towards ending the Vietnam War. During 1974 Kissinger came under increasing criticism for the style and substance of his foreign policy.

Kuniyoshi, Yasao (b. Okayama, Japan, 1 Sept. 1893; d. New York City, 14 May 1953), painter and graphic artist. He attended technical schools in Japan, emigrated to the U.S. at the age of 13, studied at the Los Angeles School of Art (1908–10), and in New York City at the National Academy of Design and the Robert Henri School (1910–14), the Independent School of Art (1914–16), and the Art Students League (1916–20). Throughout his school years, Kuniyoshi used his hobby, photography, as a means of support. His first 1-man exhibition came at the Daniel Gallery in New York (1922). When he visited Japan (1931–32), he gave 1-man shows in Tokyo and Osaka. In 1942 he had a 20-year retrospective for the United China War Relief Fund. Kuniyoshi taught at the New School for Social Research (1936–50) and at the Art Students League (1933–53). During World War II he created posters for the Office of War Information and broadcast to the Japanese. The first artist to have a 1-man show at the Whitney Museum of American Art (1948), Kuniyoshi was one of 4 artists to represent the U.S. at the 26th Biennale in Venice (1952). Among his notable paintings are *Mother and Daughter* (1945, Carnegie), *I'm Tired* (1938, Whitney), *Amazing Juggler* (1952, Des Moines). His paintings are distinguished by their iridescence, shimmering colors, witty sophistication, and inner meaning, combining Oriental sensitivity and Western sensuousness. His drawings and lithographs, like his paintings, revealed a gradual departure from his earlier soft-textured work to harshly powerful creations stressing fantasy and symbolic content.

Kuznets, Simon Smith (b. Kharkov, Russia, 30 April 1910–   ), economist. After emigrating to the U.S. (1922), Kuznets attended Columbia, where he was given advanced standing and graduated (1923). Continuing his studies in economics at Columbia, he received his M.A. (1924) and Ph.D. (1926). His first appointment as an economist was at the National Bureau of Economic Research (1926), just founded by his mentor, Prof. Wesley Clair Mitchell. There Kuznets worked on estimating and analyzing the U.S. national income, defining national income as the sum of earnings from wages, profits, interest, and rents. During the depression his work on national income and economic growth was spurred by the New Deal's need for economic statistics. He helped transform economics into a more exact science, and by developing the framework of national incomes accounting contributed much to the study of the problems of economic growth. His system eventually became the basis for the concept of gross national product. Kuznets was a professor of economics at the Univ. of Pennsylvania (1930–54) and at Johns Hopkins (1954–71). During World War II he was associate director of the Bureau of Planning and Statistics, War Production Board. In 1971 Kuznets received the Nobel prize for economics for his work on national income accounting. Among his works are *National Income and Its Composition* (1941), *National Product Since 1869* (1947), *Shares of Upper Income Groups in Income and Savings* (1953), and *Economic Growth of Nations* (1971).

La Farge, John (b. New York City, 31 Mar. 1835; d. Providence, R.I., 14 Nov. 1910), artist and writer. He was graduated (1853) from Mount St. Mary's College at Emmitsburg, Md.; in 1856 went to Paris, where he worked briefly under the painter Couture and then made studies of the old masters during a tour of northwestern Europe; returned to the U.S. in 1858, studied under William Morris Hunt, and subsequently experimented with luminism in painting, anticipating the colorist treatments of the French Impressionists. From easel work he moved into mural painting, in which his outstanding achievements are decorations for Trinity Church at Boston, *The Ascension* in the Church of the Ascension at New York, panels for the Church of the Incarnation at New York, and lunettes at the State Capitol at St. Paul, Minn. La Farge also attained eminence as a worker in stained glass, reviving that field as a craft and an industry. He invented opaline glass and designed and manufactured hundreds of windows. With Henry Adams, he visited Japan and the South Seas in 1886, recording his journey in *An Artist's Letters from Japan* (1897) and *Reminiscences of the South Seas* (1912), illustrated by his paintings and sketches.

La Follette, Robert Marion (b. Primrose, Wis., 14 June 1855; d. Washington, D.C., 18 June 1925), statesman, was graduated from the Univ. of Wisconsin (1879), studied law privately and at the university law school, was admitted to the bar in 1880, and practiced at Madison, Wis. As a Republican, he opposed the regular political leaders of Dane Co., of which he was elected (1880) district attorney, and in 1884 was elected to Congress, where he served from 1885 to 1891. His fight against the political leadership of U.S. Sen. Philetus Sawyer led to an open break between La Follette and the party bosses. Although failing to win the Republican nomination for governor in 1896 and 1898, his fight against the entrenched political groups brought him (1900) nomination by acclamation. He took office as governor

(1901) with a program that soon became known as the "Wisconsin Idea" and served as a model of progressive government: opposition to political bosses, direct appeal to the people, and the employment of technical experts; and specific proposals for direct primary legislation, railroad control, and tax reform. The primary law was enacted in 1903; a railroad commission was set up in 1905. La Follette was reelected governor in 1902 and 1904, and in 1906 took his seat in the U.S. Senate, to which he was reelected 3 times. As a Progressive leader in the Senate, he opposed the Payne-Aldrich Tariff, advocated the physical valuation of railroads as a basis for rate making, and sponsored the La Follette Seamen's Act (1915). He established (1909) *La Follette's Weekly Magazine.* In 1911 he drafted the program for the National Progressive Republican League, campaigned for the Progressive nomination in 1911–12, but lost it to Theodore Roosevelt, partly as a result of a temporary breakdown (Feb. 1912) suffered in public. He opposed Wilson's foreign policy and early in 1917, as one of the "little group of willful men" (in Wilson's phrase), prevented passage of the armed merchant ship bill. He voted against the declaration of war on Germany, but supported most of the war measures. He opposed U.S. participation in the League of Nations and the World Court. A liberal leader in the postwar years, he was the author of a resolution for a Senate inquiry into the Teapot Dome and other naval oil leases made during the Harding administration. The Progressive candidate for president in 1924, he received nearly 5 million votes. He published his *Autobiography* (1913).

La Guardia, Fiorello Henry (b. New York City, 11 Dec. 1882; d. there, 20 Dec. 1947), congressman, mayor of New

York, reformer, received his early education in Arizona, where he wrote for the Phoenix *Morning Courier*. During the Spanish-American War he was a Florida correspondent for the St. Louis *Post-Dispatch*. He worked (1901–04) for the U.S. consular service in Budapest, Trieste, and Fiume, then for the U.S. Immigration Service at Ellis Island, N.Y. (1907–10) while studying law at New York Univ. (LL.B., 1910), and was admitted to the New York bar that year. Victor over Tammany, he was elected to Congress as a Republican (1917) and joined in the successful fight for the liberalization of the House rules, but resigned to command the U.S. air forces on the Italo-Austrian front in World War I. President of the board of aldermen (1920–21), he returned to Congress (1923–33), where he fought for labor reforms and cosponsored the Norris-La Guardia anti-injunction bill (1932). Elected Fusion mayor of New York (1933) and reelected (1937, 1941), the "Little Flower" (from his first name) proved indefatigable, incorruptible, and colorful in executing a vast program of reform and public works and bringing about the adoption (1938) of a new city charter. He served (1946) as director of the UN Relief and Rehabilitation Administration.

Land, Edwin Herbert (b. Bridgeport, Conn., 7 May 1909–   ), inventor. Even before attending Harvard (1926–27, 1929–32), Land experimented with a filter which would screen out all light not moving in parallel planes. In 1929 he successfully developed a plastic sheet —called Polaroid—capable of polarizing light passed through it. He left Harvard and, with a former Harvard physics instructor, opened Land-Wheelwright Laboratories (1932). They began producing polarizing filters for cameras

(1935) and Polaroid lenses for sunglasses (1936). In 1937 Land organized the Polaroid Corp.—serving thereafter as president, chairman of the board, and director of research. During World War II Polaroid research teams worked for the U.S. army developing such optical devices as light-weight, stereoscopic range finders and searchlight filters used in signaling at night. In 1947 Land announced the invention of a camera that could produce a photograph with a minute of exposure. The Polaroid Land camera, a tremendous commercial success, was later refined to deliver color prints. Of special importance to cancer research was Land's development of a color-translating microscope (1948), which could produce full-color still and motion pictures of living cells.

Langdell, Christopher Columbus (b. New Boston, N.H., 22 May 1826; d. Cambridge, Mass., 6 July 1906), jurist and law teacher. He was graduated from Harvard (1851) and the Harvard Law School, practiced law at New York City (1854–70), and in 1870 was named Dane professor of law in the Harvard Law School, a post he held until 1900, as well as that of dean (1870–95). His fame rests on his introduction of the case method of teaching law, with its emphasis upon the formulation of legal principles from a study of specific court decisions, as expounded in his *A Selection of Cases on the Law of Contracts* (1871). He also wrote *A Summary of Equity Pleading* (1877) and works in the field of contracts.

Langmuir, Irving (b. Brooklyn, N.Y., 31 Jan. 1881; d. Schenectady, N.Y., 16 Aug. 1957), physical chemist, was graduated from the Columbia Univ. School of Mines (1903) and the Univ. of Göttingen (Ph.D., 1906), was an instructor in chemistry (1906–09) at Stevens Institute, and in 1909 joined the General Electric Co. as a research chemist and physicist. He was assistant (1909–32) and associate director (1932–51) of the General Electric Research Laboratory. In 1912 he developed a high-intensity tungsten electric lamp filled with nitrogen (later argon), a great improvement over the vacuum-type lamp. He did pioneer work in surface tension and with Gilbert N. Lewis formulated the Lewis-Langmuir theory of atomic structure and valence. He also carried out important investigations in colloid chemistry, the kinetics of gas reactions at low pressures, the production of artificial snow, the dissociation of hydrogen, acoustic devices for detecting submarines, and the vapor pressures of metals. In 1932 he received the Nobel prize in chemistry.

Latrobe, Benjamin Henry (b. Fulneck, Yorkshire, England, 1 May 1764; d. New Orleans, La., 3 Sept. 1820), architect and civil engineer. Educated in Germany, he took his professional training in England under the architect Samuel Pepys Cockerell and the civil engineer John Smeaton. He came to the U.S. in 1796; improved the navigation of the Appomattox and James rivers; designed (1797) the penitentiary at Richmond, Va.; and completed the façade of the Virginia State Capitol designed by Jefferson. The leading exponent of the Greek Revival in the U.S., Latrobe designed in that style the Bank of Pennsylvania at Philadelphia, where he also built (1799–1801) the city water works on the Schuylkill. He improved the navigation of the Susquehanna River, served as engineer of the Chesapeake & Delaware Canal, and constructed the Washington City Canal. In 1803 President Jefferson named him surveyor of

the public buildings, in which capacity Latrobe revised the plans for the national Capitol drawn up by William Thornton. He intermittently continued work on the Capitol, including its rebuilding after its destruction by fire in 1814, until his retirement from federal service in 1817. He also drew up plans for the Marine Hospital and St. John's Church, both at Washington, D.C.; the Baltimore Cathedral; the Bank of Philadelphia; the old Pennsylvania Academy of Fine Arts, the Markoe and Waln houses, and the 2d Bank of the U.S., all at Philadelphia; the Henry Clay house at Ashland, Ky.; and the Exchange (including the Bank of the U.S. and the Custom House) at Baltimore. In his last years he was engaged on the water supply system for New Orleans. Almost singlehanded, Latrobe raised architectural practice in the U.S. to the status of a profession.

Lawrence, Ernest Orlando (b. Canton, S.D., 8 Aug. 1901; d. Palo Alto, Calif., 27 Aug. 1958), nuclear physicist, inventor of the cyclotron, was graduated from the Univ. of South Dakota (A.B., 1922), the Univ. of Minnesota (A.M., 1923), and Yale (Ph.D., 1925), taught physics at Yale (1925–28), and after 1928 at the Univ. of California, where he directed the radiation laboratory beginning 1936. His major contribution was the development of the cyclotron, a mechanism which produces atomic transmutation through bombardment of matter with high-energy particles. Lawrence outlined the fundamental concept of the cyclotron as early as 1930 and, with his associates, constructed the first cyclotron in 1932, thereafter making improvements. In 1936 he transmuted other elements into gold. For his invention of the cyclotron, he was awarded (1939) the Nobel prize in physics. In World War II the cyclotron was used for separating U-235 from natural uranium during research on the atomic bomb, a project in which Lawrence took part. In 1957 he received the Fermi award given by the U.S. Atomic Energy Commission.

Lederberg, Joshua (b. Montclair, N.J., 23 May 1925–   ), geneticist, was graduated from Columbia (B.A., 1944), studied at the Coll. of Physicians and Surgeons (1944–46), receiving his Ph.D. at Yale (1947), where he worked with Dr. Edward L. Tatum (1909–   ) on sexual reproduction in bacteria. He taught genetics at the Univ. of Wisconsin (1947–57) and became (1959) professor of genetics and biology at the Stanford School of Medicine. In 1958 he received the Nobel prize in physiology and medicine for his discoveries concerning genetic recombination and organization of the genetic material of bacteria. His work in virus breeding and cross-breeding is basic to research on the control of virus diseases.

Lee, Richard Henry (b. "Stratford," Westmoreland Co., Va., 20 Jan. 1732; d. neighboring "Chantilly," 19 June 1794), Revolutionary statesman, studied under private tutors, completing his education at the academy at Wakefield, in Yorkshire, England. Entering the House of Burgesses (1758), he opposed (1764) the Sugar Act and organized (1766) the Westmoreland Association, initiating the nonimportation association movement. With Henry and Jefferson, he originated (1773) the plan for intercolonial committees of correspondence. At the 1st Continental Congress (1774) he formed close personal and political ties with Sam Adams and backed the Continental Association. In the 2d Continental Congress he introduced (7 June 1776) the resolution calling for a declaration of independence, foreign alliances, and a confederation of the American

states. To secure ratification of the Confederation he advocated the surrender by Virginia of her claims to western lands. He supported his brother Arthur in his dispute with Silas Deane, which divided Congress into 2 camps. President of Congress (1784–85), he declined to serve as a delegate to the Constitutional Convention. Leader of the opposition to ratifying the Constitution in Virginia, he urged in *Letters of the Federal Farmer* (1787) the need for a bill of rights and a more democratic lower house. Senator from Virginia (1789–92), his chief proposals were embodied in the first 10 Amendments.

Lee, Robert Edward (b. Stratford, Va., 19 Jan. 1807; d. Lexington, Va., 12 Oct. 1870), soldier, was graduated from the U.S. Military Academy (1829) and commissioned in the engineers. He married Mary Custis (1831), great-granddaughter of Martha Washington. Serving in the War with Mexico under Scott, he was superintendent of West Point (1852–53), and lieutenant colonel of cavalry on frontier duty in Texas (1855–61), with the exception of 2 years (1857–59) spent on leave at Arlington. He commanded the troops which put down John Brown's raid (1859). At the outbreak of the Civil War he declined field command of the U.S. army offered by Lincoln (18 Apr. 1861) but accepted command of Virginia's military forces, soon receiving the rank of general. When J. E. Johnston was wounded he was assigned to command the Army of Northern Virginia (1 June 1862), removing McClellan's threat to Richmond in the 7 Days' Battles (25 June–1 July 1862). He routed Pope at 2d Bull Run (29–30 Aug.), was checked at Antietam (17 Sept.), and defeated Burnside at Fredericksburg (13 Dec.) and Hooker at Chancellorsville (2–4 May 1863). His defeat and withdrawal at Gettysburg (1–3

July) constituted the turning point of the war. He opposed Grant (May–June 1864) in the battles of Wilderness, Spotsylvania, and Cold Harbor, and was appointed general in chief of all Confederate armies (Feb. 1865). He surrendered to Grant at Appomattox Court House (9 Apr. 1865) and advised the South to create a new and better section within the Union. After the war he accepted the presidency of Washington College (later renamed Washington and Lee Univ. in his honor).

Leontief, Wassily (b. Leningrad, Russia, 6 Aug. 1906–), economist. The son of a Russian economist, Leontief attended the Univ. of Leningrad (1921–25) and the Univ. of Berlin (1925–28), where he received his Ph.D. in economics. He became an economist for the Research Institut für Weltwirtschaft at the Univ. of Kiel, Germany (1927–28, 1930) and in 1929 he was an economic adviser to the Chinese government on railroad building. He emigrated to the U.S. (1931), working first for the National Bureau for Economic Research and then joining the faculty of Harvard (1935). Leontief holds the Henry Lee Chair in Economics, is director of Harvard's Economic Research Project, and is chairman of the Society of Fellows, Harvard's most elite organization for scholars. Leontief received the Nobel prize for economic science (1973) for his development of the "input-output" method of economic analysis. By using the input-output method economists can predict how changes in one sector of an economy will affect the performance of other sectors. With the advent of the computer practical application of input-output analysis became feasible; it has been employed in economic forecasting by more than 50 industrialized countries —both Communist and non-Communist. Leontief has also worked with index numbers for prices and quantities and has studied economic aspects of automation. Proud of his empirical methods, Leontief is openly critical of other economists for building theories and models little related to economic reality. His works include *Structure of the American Economy 1919–1929; An Empirical Application of Equilibrium Analysis* (1941), *Studies in the Structure of the American Economy* (with others, 1953), *Input-Output Economics* (1966), and *Collected Essays* (1966).

Lewis, Gilbert Newton (b. Weymouth, Mass., 23 Oct. 1875; d. Berkeley, Calif., 23 Mar. 1946), physical chemist. He was graduated from Harvard (A.B., 1896; A.M., 1898; Ph.D., 1899), attended the universities of Leipzig and Göttingen (1900–01), and taught chemistry at Harvard (1899–1906), the Massachusetts Institute of Technology (1907–12), and the Univ. of California (1912–46). During World War I he headed the defense division of the gas service of the A.E.F. One of the most versatile of American physical chemists, he evolved the "octet" theory of molecular structure, did important work on the absorption bands and phosphorescence spectra of dyes, improved thermodynamic methods by the concepts of "fugacity" and "activity," collaborated with Dr. Ernest O. Lawrence in inventing the cyclotron (atom-smashing machine), and with Dr. Irving Langmuir formulated the Lewis-Langmuir theory of atomic structure and valence. He wrote *Thermodynamics and the Free Energy of Chemical Substances* (with M. Randall, 1923), *Valence and the Structure of Atoms and Molecules* (1923), and *The Anatomy of Science* (1926).

Lewis, John Llewellyn (b. Lucas, Iowa, 12 Feb. 1880; d. Washington, D.C., 11 June 1969), labor leader, son of a

Welsh miner, joined his father as a laborer in a Lucas coal mine at the age of 16. As state legislative agent for District 12 of the United Mine Workers of America (1909–11), he secured the passage of workmen's compensation and mine safety laws in Illinois. Field and legislative representative of the AFL, he rose to the presidency of the UMW (1920), which post he held until his retirement (1960). A militant unionist and formidable bargainer, he called the crippling bituminous coal strikes of 1919 and 1922, scoring notable victories in each case. In a period of economic distress for the coal industry, he fought off (1930) an ouster move by insurgents. Vice-president of the AFL (1934), he resigned (1935) to form, with Sidney Hillman (q.v.) and David Dubinsky (1892–   ), the Congress of Industrial Organizations (later CIO), AFL's giant rival. With Hillman he organized (1936) Labor's Non-Partisan League, supporting the reelection of Franklin D. Roosevelt, with whom he later broke. His Apr. 1946 coal strike precipitated U.S. government seizure of the mines (21 May) and was ended by an injunction and a contempt conviction, although when the mines were returned to their owners (June 1947) Lewis secured all his demands.

Lewis, Meriwether (b. in Albemarle Co., Va., 18 Aug. 1774; d. in central Tenn., 11 Oct. 1809), and **Clark, William** (b. in Caroline Co., Va., 1 Aug. 1770; d. St. Louis, Mo., 1 Sept. 1838), explorers and territorial governors, leaders of the Lewis and Clark overland expedition to the U.S. Northwest (1803–06). Both were officers in the U.S. army, Clark being the brother of the Revolutionary soldier George Rogers Clark (1752–1818). In 1801 Lewis became private secretary to President Jefferson, who selected him as commander of an overland expedition to the Pacific. Lewis chose Capt. Clark as his companion officer, and they shared authority. The expedition was fitted out in Illinois during the winter of 1803–04 and was later transferred to St. Louis. Clark joined Lewis at St. Charles, Mo. Their party, consisting of 23 soldiers, 3 interpreters, and 1 slave, set out in the spring of 1804 and followed the Missouri River in a 1,600-mile journey to the Mandan villages in North Dakota, where it went into winter quarters near the site of present-day Bismarck, N.D. Resuming the journey on 7 Apr. 1805, the expedition reached the mouth of the Yellowstone (26 Apr.), the triple fork of the Missouri (25 July), and descended the Columbia, reaching the Pacific Ocean on 15 Nov. On the return journey (23 Mar.–23 Sept. 1806) to St. Louis, the party divided and, after exploring much of what is now the state of Montana, reunited below the mouth of the Yellowstone. The records of the Lewis and Clark expedition, including the diaries kept by both leaders and the maps and drawings made by Clark, constituted valuable scientific findings. Lewis, appointed governor of Louisiana Territory (1806), died either by suicide or killing. Clark, appointed superintendent of Indian affairs at St. Louis (1807) and governor of Missouri Territory (1813), concluded treaties with the Indians after the War of 1812.

Lewis, Harry Sinclair (b. Sauk Centre, Minn., 7 Feb. 1885; d. Rome, Italy, 10 Jan. 1951), author. He interrupted his studies at Yale (begun 1903) to join Upton Sinclair's utopian socialist community in Palisades, N.J. and to visit Panama to watch the canal construction. After graduating from Yale (1908), he pursued an unsuccessful career in journalism—at various times working as a reporter for the Waterloo (Ia.) *Courier*,

the San Francisco *Bulletin,* and the Associated Press, and as editor for *Adventure*
magazine and for the George Doran Co.
He published several minor novels, but it
was not until the appearance of his short
stories in the *Saturday Evening Post*
(1915) that his literary career began to
blossom. His first major novel, *Main
Street* (1920), an iconoclastic treatment
of the American myth of the small town,
was sensationally popular both in the
U.S. and abroad. It was followed by
such successes as: *Babbitt* (1922),
Arrowsmith (1925), *Elmer Gantry*
(1927), *Dodsworth* (1929), and *It
Can't Happen Here* (1935). His works
contributed to American thought the
concept of "Babbittry"—complacent conformity to middle-class ideas, especially
of material success. His social criticism
and satire inspired much controversy. In
1926 he refused to accept the Pulitzer
prize he was awarded for *Arrowsmith.*
With *Babbitt,* he became the first American to win the Nobel prize for literature
(1930). Lewis' oeuvre includes 23 novels and 3 plays.

Lincoln, Abraham (b. Hardin, Ky., 12
Feb. 1809; d. Washington, D.C., 15 Apr.
1865), 16th president of the U.S., moved
with his parents (Thomas and Nancy
Hanks Lincoln) to Spencer Co., Ind.
(1816), then settled in southern Illinois
(1830), where he clerked in a store at
New Salem. He became captain of volunteers in the Black Hawk War (1832),
but did not see action. He operated a
store, practiced surveying, and served as
postmaster at New Salem (1833–36)
while he studied law and was admitted
to the bar (1836). He moved to Springfield (1837), where he opened a law office and quickly obtained a reputation
on the circuit as an outstanding jury
lawyer. Whig state legislator (1834–42),
he was elected to Congress (1846), but
did not stand for reelection. In his

Peoria speech (1854) he denounced the
Kansas-Nebraska Act. Joining the Republican party (1856), he ran for the
Senate against Stephen A. Douglas
(1858), accepting the nomination (17
June) with a speech in which he declared: "A house divided against itself
cannot stand." In the course of 7 campaign debates with Douglas he forced
the latter to announce the so-called Freeport Doctrine. Losing the election, Lincoln had established himself as a national
figure. Although he won the Republican
nomination for the presidency in 1860
because of his conservative views on
slavery, his election was regarded in the
South as forecasting an attack on the
"peculiar institution." By 4 Mar. 1861,
7 states had already seceded. In his first
inaugural Lincoln reiterated his constitutional doctrine that the contract between
the states was binding and irrevocable.
Against the advice of his cabinet, he ordered the provisioning of Ft. Sumter
and when war began called out the state
militia, suspended the writ of habeas
corpus, proclaimed a blockade of Southern ports, and in other ways did not
hesitate to use the dictatorial powers
with which he was invested. He largely
countermanded Frémont's proclamation
(30 Aug. 1861) emancipating the slaves
of rebels in Missouri and proposed his
own plan for compensated emancipation
(Dec. 1861, 12 July and 1 Dec. 1862).
"My paramount object is to save the
Union, and not either to save or destroy
slavery," he stated (22 Aug. 1862). After Antietam he prepared a draft of
emancipation, proclaimed formally 1 Jan.
1863. A diplomat in the handling of
both his cabinet and his generals, his reelection in 1864, when he easily defeated
McClellan, was assured by the military
victories of Grant, Sherman, and Sheridan. His plan of Reconstruction (8 Dec.
1863) was based on the prompt restoration of the Southern states to "their

proper practical relation with the Union."
He pocket-vetoed the harsher Wade-
Davis Bill (8 July 1864). He personally
attended the Hampton Roads Conference (3 Feb. 1865) to discuss peace
terms with Confederate leaders. His
most notable speeches were his Gettysburg Address (19 Nov. 1863) and his
second inaugural (4 Mar. 1865), in
which he appealed to the nation to "finish the work we are in . . . with malice
toward none, with charity for all."
Shortly after Lee's surrender he was shot
by John Wilkes Booth in Ford's Theater,
Washington (14 Apr. 1865), and died
the next day.

Lipmann, Fritz Albert (b. Koenigsberg,
Germany, 12 June 1899–   ), biochemist, received his M.D. (1922) and Ph.D.
(1927) from the Univ. of Berlin, became
research assistant at the Kaiser Wilhelm
Institute in the laboratory of Otto Meyer-
hof, where he began investigating the
mechanism of fluoride effects and, from
1930–31, the field of tissue culture. Winner of a Rockefeller fellowship, he began
work at the Rockefeller Institute (1931)
on phosphorus mechanisms, then returned to Europe (1932), spending
7 years as research associate in the
Biological Institute of Carlsberg Foundation at Copenhagen. Returning to the
U.S. (1939) as a research fellow at the
Cornell Univ. Medical College, he became (1941) senior biochemist at the
Massachusetts General Hospital and
professor at the Harvard Medical School.
In 1957 he became a professor of the
Rockefeller Institute. He became a U.S.
citizen (1944). Experiments in 1937
started him on a series of investigations
during which he developed the idea of
phosphate bond energy. He isolated
acetyl phosphate (1942) and with his
coworkers synthesized it (1944). He received the Nobel prize in medicine and

physiology (1953) for isolating and
identifying coenzyme A (1945) as a
crucial element in providing usable energy for the body-building process and
demonstrating how coenzyme A brought
forth the construction of fatty acids and
steroids necessary to the body's renewal
and growth. He later did research in the
structure of cancer cells and investigated
pantothenic acid and the action of the
energy-regulating thyroid hormone.

Lippmann, Walter (b. New York City,
23 Sept. 1889; d. New York City, 14
Dec. 1974), journalist and author. After
graduating from Harvard (1909) he
did graduate work in philosophy there
(1909–10). Joining Lincoln Steffens
briefly on *Everybody's Magazine* (1910–
11), he wrote *A Preface to Politics*
(1913). With Herbert Croly he founded
The New Republic (1914), a liberal
weekly journal. During World War I he
left the *New Republic* to serve as an
assistant to Secretary of War, Newton D.
Baker (1917), and as a captain in the
U.S. Military Intelligence (1918), working on propaganda directed at persuading
the Germans to surrender. President Wilson selected him to help formulate the
Fourteen Points and contribute to
preparations for the peace conference at
Versailles, which he attended before rejoining *The New Republic* (1919). On
the editorial staff of the *New York
World* (1921–31), serving as editor the
last 8 years, he wrote more than 2,000
editorials. In 1931 he began his column
"Today and Tomorrow," which appeared
regularly in the *New York Herald Tribune* and was syndicated internationally
in at least 200 newspapers. The column,
for which he won 2 Pulitzer prizes
(1958, 1962), not only earned him a
wide audience (more than 38 million
readers) but established him as one of
the foremost analysts of national and

international affairs. In his commentaries on political, social, and ethical problems he sought to promote "liberal democracy" and warned against forces in society which he perceived as opposed to that end. He contributed articles to a wide variety of magazines, wrote 26 books, including 10 of political philosophy, among them: *Public Opinion* (1922), *The Phantom Public* (1927), *A Preface to Morals* (1929), *The Good Society* (1937), and *The Public Philosophy* (1955).

Livingston, Edward (b. "Clermont," Columbia Co., N.Y., 28 May 1764; d. "Montgomery Place," N.Y., 23 May 1836), jurist, statesman, and diplomat, was graduated from the College of New Jersey (1781), studied law in Albany, and was admitted to the New York bar (1785). In Congress as a Jeffersonian Republican (1795–1801), he was U.S. district attorney of N.Y. (1801). Elected mayor of New York City (1801–03), he reformed the rules of procedure of the mayor's court. When a custom-house clerk misappropriated public funds, he sold his own property to meet the deficit and moved to New Orleans (1803), where he resumed law practice. Purchaser (1808) of the Gravier estate, he improved the *batture* (an alluvial deposit or river beach), was dispossessed on Jefferson's orders, but was the ultimate victor in a celebrated litigation. In the lower house of the Louisiana legislature (1820), congressman (1822–29), U.S. senator (1829–31), he was President Jackson's Secretary of State (1831–33) and wrote the Nullification Proclamation. U.S. minister to France (1833–35), he futilely endeavored to secure payment of U.S. spoliation claims. His fame rests upon his work as a codifier of the laws. After reading Bentham he drafted a code of procedure which was adopted by the Louisiana legislature (1805), the first real code in the U.S. At the request of the legislature he began his comprehensive criminal code (1820), completed (1824), and published (1833). Although not adopted in his own state, it was acclaimed abroad and became the model of state penal codes in the U.S., foreshadowing many later reforms in penology. Sir Henry Maine called Livingston "the first legal genius of modern times."

Livingston, Robert R. (b. New York City, 27 Nov. 1746; d. "Clermont," Columbia Co., N.Y., 26 Feb. 1813), Revolutionary patriot, jurist, diplomat, was graduated from King's College (1765). Admitted to the bar (1770), he practiced law briefly with John Jay (*q.v.*). In the Continental Congress (1775–76, 1779–81, 1784–85), he was on the committee which drafted the Declaration of Independence, but, owing to lack of instructions from the New York convention, neither voted for nor signed the document. Member of the committee which drafted the New York Constitution (1777), he was Chancellor of New York (1777–1801), administering the oath to Washington in 1789. First Secretary of Foreign Affairs (1781–83), he criticized the U.S. peace commissioners for their distrust of France, but supported the treaty they negotiated. With Hamilton and Jay, he was a leading supporter of the Constitution at the New York ratifying convention, but broke with the Federalists over the patronage and used his family and public influence to oppose Jay's Treaty. Defeated by Jay for governor (1798), he was appointed by Jefferson (1801) minister to France, where his most conspicuous achievement was the successful negotiation of the Louisiana Purchase (1803). Patron of the arts, he was interested both in scientific agriculture and technology, and financed Robert Fulton's (*q.v.*) experiments in steam navigation. The steamboat *Clermont* was named for his estate. With Fulton, he secured and maintained during his lifetime a monopoly of steam navigation on the Hudson, which involved him in litigation and was terminated by *Gibbons* v. *Ogden* (1824).

Lodge, Henry Cabot (b. Boston, 12 May 1850; d. Cambridge, Mass., 9 Nov. 1924), statesman and author, was educated at E. S. Dixwell's Latin School and Harvard, graduating in 1871. After a year in Europe, Lodge attended the Harvard Law School, graduating 1874, and was admitted to the bar (1875). He was assistant editor of the *North American Record* (1874–76), under Henry Adams (*q.v.*), and completed his Ph.D. in political science (1876), the first ever given at Harvard. He was lecturer in American History at Harvard (1876) and associate editor of the *International Review* (1879). Among his historical writings were biographies for the American Statesmen Series of *Alexander Hamilton* (1882), *Daniel Webster* (1883), and *George Washington* (2 vols. 1889), as well as *Life and Letters of George Cabot* (1877), a biography of his great-grandfather. He served in the Massachusetts House of Representatives (1880–83), but was defeated in an election for the U.S. House of Representatives (1884) before serving there for 6 years (1887–93). In the House he championed civil service reform and drafted and strongly supported the controversial "Force Bill," aimed at federal supervision of voting in the South to prevent discrimination. Serving in the U.S. Senate from 1893 until his death, Lodge, a Republican, helped to draft the Sherman Antitrust Law and the Pure Food and Drug Law. A thoroughgoing protection-

ist, Lodge also strongly opposed free silver. In the area of foreign affairs, he supported a strong navy and American imperialist ambitions, exercising a profound influence upon Theodore Roosevelt. As majority leader of the Senate and chairman of the Foreign Relations Committee, Lodge led the fight against ratification of the Versailles Treaty and the Covenant of the League of Nations (1919), publishing his account of the controversy as *The Senate and the League of Nations* (1925). He served as U.S. Representative at the Washington Conference (1921–22).

Long, Huey Pierce (b. near Winnfield, La., 30 Aug. 1893; d. Baton Rouge, 10 Sept. 1935), politician, worked as a traveling salesman before studying law (1914) at Tulane Univ. Admitted to the Louisiana bar (1915), he won a reputation as a poor man's lawyer by specializing in workmen's compensation cases. Elected and reelected railroad (later public service) commissioner (1921–26), as chairman he brought about telephone rate reductions and prevented streetcar fare rises. Defeated for the governorship (1924), he won election (1928), trouncing the New Orleans Democratic machine. An oil property owner himself and long known for his vindictive opposition to the Standard Oil Co., he pushed through the legislature a constitutional amendment to tax the oil interests and use the revenue for highways and education. Impeached by the lower house .(1929) for bribery and gross misconduct, he rounded up enough state senators (the "Famous 15") to avoid conviction. Elected to the U.S. Senate (1930), he ruled Louisiana (1930–34) by alliance with the New Orleans machine, retaining the governorship and sponsoring a vast highway program and the expansion of Louisiana

State Univ. As U.S. senator, the "King-fish" failed to secure President Roosevelt's backing for his social program and organized (Jan. 1934) a Share-Our-Wealth Society, promising a homestead allowance of $6,000 and a minimum annual income of $2,500 for every American family. Meantime, to keep control in Louisiana, he reorganized the state government (1934–35), abolishing local government and creating a virtual dictatorship. Announcing his own candidacy for the presidency (Mar. 1935), he was fatally wounded on the steps of the Baton Rouge Capitol by Dr. Carl Weiss, who was shot and killed by Long's bodyguard. His death ended a threat to the New Deal of a 3d party, but his program, along with parallel proposals of Dr. Francis E. Townsend and Rev. Charles E. Coughlin, provided the impetus for the later New Deal social security legislation. Of all Southern demagogues Long posed the most serious threat to democracy.

Longfellow, Henry Wadsworth (b. Portland, Me., 27 Feb. 1807; d. Cambridge, Mass., 24 Mar. 1882), poet. He was graduated (1825) from Bowdoin College; studied modern languages in France, Spain, Italy, and Germany from 1826 to 1829; was professor and librarian at Bowdoin (1829–35); and served (1836–54) as Smith professor of modern languages and belles-lettres at Harvard. His first book of poetry was *Voices of the Night* (1839). His *Ballads and Other Poems* (1841) included "The Village Blacksmith," "Excelsior," and "The Wreck of the Hesperus." When he died he was the most popular American poet. Among other works of poetry by him are *Poems on Slavery* (1842), *Evangeline* (1847), *The Belfry of Bruges and Other Poems* (1845), *The Seaside and the Fireside* (1849), *Hiawatha* (1855),

The Courtship of Miles Standish (1858), *Tales of a Wayside Inn* (1863–74, which includes "Paul Revere's Ride"), *The Masque of Pandora* (1875), *Ultima Thule* (1880), and *In the Harbor* (1882). He translated *The Divine Comedy of Dante Alighieri* (3 vols., 1865–67).

Lowell, James Russell (b. Cambridge, Mass., 22 Feb. 1819; d. there, 12 Aug. 1891), author, editor, teacher, and diplomat. He was graduated from Harvard (1838) and from the Harvard Law School (1840), published *A Year's Life* (1841) and *Poems* (1844), and co-edited (Jan.–Mar. 1843) *The Pioneer: A Literary and Critical Magazine*. Through the influence of Maria White, whom he married in 1844, he became interested in the antislavery movement, and was an editorial writer (1845) for the *Pennsylvania Freeman* and a contributor and corresponding editor of the *National Anti-Slavery Standard*. He established himself as a writer with the following, all published in 1848: *Poems by James Russell Lowell, 2nd Series, A Fable for Critics, The Vision of Sir Launfal,* and *The Biglow Papers* (1st series), a satire on the Mexican War written in the Yankee vernacular. He succeeded Longfellow (1855), as Smith professor of modern languages and belles-lettres at Harvard, was the first editor (1857–61) of the *Atlantic Monthly,* and joint editor (with Charles Eliot Norton) of the *North American Review* from 1864 to 1872. He was minister to Spain (1877–80) and to England (1880–85). His critical and other writings include *Fireside Travels* (1864), *Biglow Papers* (2nd series, 1867), *Under the Willows* (1868), *The Cathedral* (1870), *Among My Books* (1st and 2nd series, 1870, 1876), *My Study Windows* (1871), *Heartease and Rue* (1888), *Political*

Essays (1888), *Latest Literary Essays and Addresses* (1891), and *The Old English Dramatists* (1892). One of his best-known poems is "Ode Recited at the Harvard Commemoration" (1865).

Luce, Henry Robinson (b. Tengchow, Shantung Prov., China, 3 Apr. 1898; d. Phoenix, Ariz., 28 Feb. 1967), journalist and businessman. Son of a missionary in China, Luce came to the U.S. at the age of 15 and attended Hotchkiss School, Yale (1916–20), and then spent a year doing graduate work at Oxford. His educational career was briefly interrupted by service in the army (1918). At that time he and former classmate Britton Hadden planned a weekly news magazine. After serving as reporters on the *Baltimore News* (1920–23), Hadden and Luce put their plans into effect with the publication of the first issue of *Time* (3 Mar. 1923). With Hadden's death (1929), Luce assumed ownership of the successful enterprise. From the beginning *Time* was opinionated with a conservative slant. A staunch Republican, Luce defended free enterprise and big business and supported aggressive opposition to Communism. Originated by Hadden, *Time*'s unique style was "curt, clear, and complete." The magazine was known for its coining of new words such as "tycoon," from the Japanese "taik," "GOPolitics," "Freudulent," and "socialite." In 1930 Luce established *Fortune*, a monthly magazine for business executives, known for its artistic format and articles on technology. By 1954 Luce's magazine empire included *Time*, *Fortune*, *Architectural Forum* (1932), *Life* (1936–72), *House and Home* (1952), and *Sports Illustrated* (1954). The concept of *Life*, the first photojournalism magazine, was largely inspired by Clare Boothe Brokaw, editor of *Vanity Fair* and a playwright, who became Luce's second wife (1935). Luce is considered the key figure in the development of the modern news magazine and the concept of group journalism.

Lyon, Mary (b. Buckland, Mass., 28 Feb. 1797; d. South Hadley, Mass., 5 Mar. 1849), educator. She attended seminaries at Ashfield and Amherst, Mass., and in 1821 studied at the Byfield (Mass.) Seminary. She was a teacher (1821–34) at Ashfield and Ipswich, Mass., and at Londonderry, N.H. Between 1834 and 1837 she worked on a plan to establish a seminary for the education of girls of moderate means, raising the funds for the project and shaping the curriculum (which was based on that at Amherst College). Mount Holyoke Female Seminary (later Mount Holyoke College), of which she served as principal until her death, was opened at South Hadley, Mass., on 8 Nov. 1837. It was the first permanent institution devoted to the higher education of women. Miss Lyon made valuable contributions to educational theory and wrote *Tendencies of the Principles Embraced and the System Adopted in the Mount Holyoke Seminary* (1840).

MacArthur, Douglas (b. Little Rock, Ark., 26 Jan. 1880; d. New York City, 5 Apr. 1964), soldier. Graduated (1903) from the U.S. Military Academy, he saw service in the Philippines (1903–04) and Japan (1905–06), was aide-de-camp (1906–07) to President Theodore Roosevelt and served on the army general staff (1913–15, 1916–17). In Aug. 1917 he was named chief of staff of the 42d (Rainbow) Div., on 6 Aug. 1918 commanding general of the 84th Infantry Brigade, and in Nov. 1918 commanding general of the 42d Div. He took part in the major U.S. offensives of World War I and was twice wounded in action. He served (Nov. 1918–Apr. 1919) with the army of occupation in Germany, was appointed (12 June 1919) superintendent of the U.S. Military Academy, and was promoted to brigadier general in 1920. He served in the Philippines (1922–25) as commander of the Manila District, was promoted to major general (1925) and general (1930), and in 1928 became commander of the Philippine Department. After serving as chief of staff (1930–35) of the U.S. army, he became (1935) director of the organization of national defense for the Philippine Commonwealth. Appointed (1936) a field marshal in the Philippine army, he retired (1937) from the U.S. army, but was recalled to active service (26 July 1941) as commander of the U.S. forces in the Far East, and subsequently assumed his former rank of general. Following the Japanese attack on the Philippines, MacArthur led a skillful defense, made a planned retreat to Bataan Peninsula, and set up his headquarters on Corregidor. Appointed (22 Feb. 1942) Supreme Allied Commander of forces in the Southwest Pacific, he escaped to Australia and commanded the Allied campaigns against Japanese forces in that area. He was made (Dec. 1944) a general of the army, and in Aug. 1945 was appointed supreme commander to accept the formal surrender of Japan, where he subsequently served as commander of the occupational forces. Following the Communist invasion of South Korea (25 June 1950), he was made commander of the United Nations forces fighting there. On 11 Apr. 1951 President Truman relieved him of his Far Eastern commands.

McCarthy, Joseph Raymond (b. Grand Chute, Wis., 14 Nov. 1909; d. Bethesda, Md., 2 May 1957), U.S. senator, left school at the age of 14. After working for a short time, he returned to complete 4 years of high school in one year while working as a grocery store manager and movie theater usher in Manawa, Wis. He received his LL.B. from Marquette Univ. and was admitted to the bar (1935). While practicing law in Shawaho, Wis. he became interested in politics as a Democrat, but his first successful bid for elected office, as a state circuit court judge, was as a Republican (1939). He interrupted his term of office during World War II to enlist in the Marine Corps air force as lieutenant. He was elected to the U.S. Senate from Wisconsin in a surprising upset of incumbent Robert LaFollette, Jr. (1946). Exploiting public fear of Communism, engendered by Communist control of China and Eastern Europe, McCarthy had the distinction of being one of the most popular and most hated men of his time. In a speech delivered in Wheeling, W. Va. (1950) he declared that he had with him a list of card-carrying members of the Communist party then employed by the Department of State. After subsequent speeches, he testified before a subcommittee of the Senate Foreign Relations Committee without producing the name of a single Communist working for the State Department, although he did list several "fellow travelers." Between 1951–54 McCarthy brought charges of Communist membership or leanings against civil servants, army officers, writers, actors, professors, and industrial workers. Among those accused were Gen. George C. Marshall and Adlai E. Stevenson. He charged previous administrations with "twenty years of treason" (1953) and later amended the charge to include the first year of the Eisenhower administration. As chairman of the Permanent Subcommittee on Investigations of the Senate Committee on Government Operations, McCarthy looked into disloyalty in the Voice of America and reports of spying at the Army Signal Corps installation at Ft. Monmouth. The dispute widened to include Army Secretary Robert T. Stevens. Exposure to a national TV audience (Apr.–May 1954) sharply diminished the senator's popularity. An investigation of McCarthy's activities by a senate committee resulted in his formal condemnation by the Senate for refusal to explain a financial transaction and for abuse of other senators (Dec. 1954). His influence continually declined until his death.

McClellan, George Brinton (b. Philadelphia, 3 Dec. 1826; d. Woodstock, Conn., 29 Oct. 1885), soldier, studied at the Univ. of Pennsylvania (1840–42) and was graduated from West Point (1846) No. 2 in his class. He saw service during the Mexican War at Contreras, Chirubusco, and Chapultepec. Asst. engineer for the construction of Ft. Delaware (1851), he accompanied Capt. R. B. Marcy on an exploration to trace the source of the Red River (Ark.), then did river and harbor work in Texas, and commanded an expedition to survey a railroad route across the Cascade Mts. After a year in Europe observing the siege of Sevastopol (1855), he resigned from the army (1857) to become chief engineer of the Illinois Central R.R. and then (1860) president of the Ohio and Mississippi R.R. At the outbreak of the Civil War he was commissioned major general of the Ohio volunteers, and on 3 May 1861 appointed major general of the regular army in command of the Department of Ohio. He cleared western Virginia of Confederate troops and was given command of the Division of the Potomac, succeeding (Nov. 1861) Winfield Scott (q.v.) as general in chief. His Peninsular campaign ended in the bloody Seven Days' Battles (26 June–2 July 1862). His troops were detached from him and assigned to Gen. Pope's Army of Virginia, but after Pope's defeat at 2d Manassas,

he was called upon to defend Washington. Defeating Lee at South Mountain (14 Sept.) and Antietam (17 Sept.), he allowed the Confederates to withdraw across the Potomac. Criticized 13 Oct. 1862 by Lincoln for being "overcautious," he was removed from command 7 Nov. Democratic candidate for the presidency (1864), he was defeated by Lincoln, 212–21 electoral votes. After residing in Europe (1864–68) he served as chief engineer of the Department of Docks, New York City (1870–72), and governor of New Jersey (1878–81).

McCormick, Cyrus Hall (b. in Rockbridge Co., Va., 15 Feb. 1809; d. Chicago, 13 May 1884), inventor and manufacturer. He invented and patented a hillside plow (1831) and in 1832 designed and constructed a reaper which avoided the errors of the mechanism upon which his father, the inventor Robert McCormick (1780–1846), had been engaged for 2 decades. Successfully demonstrated in 1832, the reaper had the basic components of the modern reaper: the divider, reel, straight reciprocating knife, fingers or guards, platform, main wheel and gearing, and the front-side draft traction. McCormick added improvements to his machine during the 1830s and began its commercial manufacture (c.1840) at his birthplace. In 1847 he set up his own plant at Chicago. Despite widespread competition following the expiration of his patent in 1848, he developed a nationwide business by 1850. In 1851, on the occasion of the world's fair at London, he introduced the reaper into Europe; the machine won major prizes at London, Paris, Hamburg, Lille, Vienna, and elsewhere. Not less important than McCormick's achievement as an inventor was his contribution to modern industrial and business methods. He pioneered in the use of labor-saving, mass-production factory machinery, and in the use of field trials, cash and deferred payments, and guarantees and testimonials in advertising. His reaper increased the food output of the North during the Civil War, and made possible the export grain trade to Europe that helped to bolster the finances of the Union government; it tied agriculture even closer to the market economy, accelerated the settlement of vacant Western lands, and released manpower from the farms for industrial enterprises and urban settlement.

MacDowell, Edward Alexander (b. New York City, 18 Dec. 1861; d. there, 23 Jan. 1908), composer and teacher. In 1876 he went to Paris, where he studied with Marmontel and Savard; subsequently at Wiesbaden and at the Frankfort Conservatory; and in 1881 became chief piano teacher at the Darmstadt Conservatory. By the time he returned to America (1888), he had composed his 1st and 2d *Modern Suites*, 2 concertos, and a symphonic poem, *Hamlet and Ophelia*. From 1888 to 1896 he lived in Boston, where in addition to teaching and composing he gave recitals. During these years he wrote *Woodland Sketches, Sonata Eroica, Sonata Tragica, Twelve Virtuoso Studies*, and the 1st and 2d *Indian Suites* for orchestra. He became (1896) professor of music at Columbia, but resigned in 1904 after a conflict over policy. His health declined rapidly beginning in 1905. Among the works of his last active period are *Sea Pieces, New England Idylls, Norse Sonata*, and *Keltic Sonata*. After his death, MacDowell's farm at Peterboro, N.H., was established by his widow as the MacDowell Colony for artists, writers, and composers.

McGuffey, William Holmes (b. near Claysville, Pa., 23 Sept. 1800; d. Charlottesville, Va., 4 May 1873), educator and compiler of school readers, was graduated from Washington College (1826) and served (1826–36) as professor of languages, philosophy, and philology at Miami Univ., Oxford, Ohio. He was appointed (1836) president of Cincinnati College and was instrumental in securing the enactment of the law under which the common schools of Ohio were first established. He served as president (1839–43) of Ohio Univ., as professor (1843–45) at Woodward College, Cincinnati, and as professor of moral philosophy (1845–73) at the Univ. of Virginia. He is best remembered for his *Eclectic Readers* (commonly called McGuffey's Readers), 6 schoolbooks for elementary grades that were published between 1836 and 1857 and went through numerous editions that sold an estimated total of 122 million copies. The *Readers*, in part extracts from standard English writers, were an amalgam of entertaining literature, self-improvement themes, and patriotic and moral instruction.

McKinley, William (b. Niles, Ohio, 29 Jan. 1843; d. Buffalo, N.Y., 14 Sept. 1901), 25th president of the U.S., studied at Allegheny College; served in the Union Army during the Civil War, seeing action at South Mountain, Antietam, Winchester, and Cedar Creek (breveted maj., 1865); studied law in Albany, N.Y., and was admitted to the Ohio bar, 1867, commencing practice in Canton. Elected prosecuting attorney of Stark Co. (1869), he was Republican congressman (1876–90, excepting 1882). High-tariff advocate, he sponsored the McKinley Tariff (1890). Defeated on this issue (1890), he was elected governor of Ohio in 1891 and again in 1893. With the support of Marcus A. Hanna, he was Republican nominee for president (1896) on a protective tariff, sound money (gold standard) platform, defeating Bryan. His administration was marked by revision of the tariff upward to the highest rate in U.S. history (Dingley Tariff, 1897), the passage of the Gold Standard Act (1900), and the annexation of Hawaii (7 July 1898). After the blowing up of the battleship *Maine* (15 Feb. 1898), he yielded to press clamor for war and recommended intervention in Cuba (11 Apr.), despite a note received from Spain (10 Apr.) promising to order immediate cessation of hostilities on that island. The acquisition of Puerto Rico, the Philippines, and Guam (1899) as a result of the War with Spain established the U.S. as a world power. He again defeated Bryan for president (1900) in a "full dinner pail" campaign, but was assassinated (6 Sept. 1901) by an anarchist, Leon Czolgosz, on a visit to the Pan-American Exposition in Buffalo.

MacLeish, Archibald (b. Glencoe, Ill., 7 May 1892–   ), poet and public official, was educated at Yale (A.B., 1915) and Harvard (LL.B., 1919). He served from private to captain in World War I, then practiced law in Boston (1920–23), but left the law for poetry, studying in France (1923–28). Turning from personal and subjective poetry (*Poems, 1924–33* [1933]), he won a Pulitzer prize with his narrative poem of the conquest of Mexico, *Conquistador* (1932). In a radio verse drama, *The Fall of the City* (1937), as well as in prose writings (*The Irresponsibles* [1940], *A Time to Speak* [1941]), he spoke out on behalf of democratic values and against fascism. Librarian of Congress (1939–44), his appointment aroused criticism because of his lack of special training. He resigned this post to serve as Assistant Secretary of State (1944–45). During World War II he had also served as director of the Office of Facts and Figures (1941–42) and as-

sistant director of the Office of War Information (1942–43). In the postwar period he was active in UNESCO and became Boylston Professor at Harvard (1949–62). His *Collected Poems, 1917–52* (1952) won Pulitzer prize, Bollingen and National Book awards; *J.B.* (1958) dramatic verse adaptation of story of Job, also Pulitzer. Later works include *Poetry and Experience* (1961), *Herakles* (verse play, 1967), *The Magic Prison* (libretto, 1967), *A Continuing Journey* (prose, 1967); *The Wild Wicked Old Man and Other Poems* (1968), and *Scratch* (play, 1971).

McMillan, Edwin Mattison (b. Redondo Beach, Calif., 18 Sept. 1907–   ), nuclear physicist. He was graduated from the California Institute of Technology (B.S., 1928; M.S., 1929) and received his Ph.D. in physics at Princeton in 1932. In 1934 he joined the staff of the Radiation Laboratory (director since 1958) at Univ. of California, where he has taught physics. During World War II he worked on microwave radar and on sonar (underwater sound detection) at the Navy Radio and Sound Laboratory at San Diego, Calif., and was on the staff of the Los Alamos (N.M.) Atomic Bomb Laboratory. He has made important researches in nuclear physics, particularly in the field of artificial radioactivity. The discoverer of neptunium (element 93), he laid the foundation for the production of plutonium (element 94) by Glenn T. Seaborg and others. In 1951 he and Seaborg were joint recipients of the Nobel prize in chemistry for their discoveries in the chemistry of the transuranic elements. The construction of cyclotrons, such as the synchrotron, synchrocyclotron, cosmotron, and bevatron, with an atom-smashing potential exceeding that of earlier models, was made possible by his theory of phase stability.

Madison, James (b. Port Conway, Va., 16 Mar. 1751; d. Montpelier, Va., 28 June 1836), 4th president of the U.S., was graduated from the College of New Jersey (1771), was chairman of the committee of public safety for Orange Co., Va. (1775), and helped draft the state constitution in the Virginia Convention (1776). Member of the Virginia Council of State (1778–79), he served in the Continental Congress (1780–83), drafted instructions to Jay to demand of Spain free navigation of the Mississippi, and drew up the compromise plan whereby Virginia ceded her Western lands to the U.S. A member of the Virginia House of Delegates (1784–86), he was the author of the "Memorial and Remonstrance" (1784) in which he opposed taxation to support religious teachers, and secured the enactment of Jefferson's bill for religious freedom. Active in the call for the Alexandria and Mount Vernon conferences (1785), the Annapolis Convention (1786), and the Federal Convention (1787), he played a most influential role in the adoption of the Constitution, drafting the Virginia large-state plan presented by Randolph, and acting as reporter of the proceedings. Author of 29 of the *Federalist* papers, he was largely responsible for securing ratification in Virginia. Congressman (1789–97), he proposed the first 10 amendments to the Constitution, known as the Bill of Rights. Parting with Hamilton over debt assumption and later opposing his pro-British leanings, he became a leader of the Jeffersonian Republicans. He married Dolly Payne Todd (1794). He drew up the Virginia Resolves (adopted by the state legislature, Dec. 1798), condemning the Alien and Sedition Acts. While Jefferson's Secretary of State (1801–09), he was involved in controversies with France and Great Britain over neutral rights. President (1809–17), being elected over

C. C. Pinckney (1808) and over De Witt Clinton (1812), he lost popularity largely as a result of his inept leadership of the War of 1812 ("Mr. Madison's War"), which the U.S. entered unprepared and disunited. His signing in his 2d administration of a bill chartering the 2d Bank of the U.S. and raising tariff rates marked a trend toward Hamiltonian nationalism.

Mahan, Alfred Thayer (b. West Point, N.Y., 27 Sept. 1840; d. Quogue, N.Y., 1 Dec. 1914), naval officer and historian, was graduated from the U.S. Naval Academy (1859) and an officer in the U.S. navy down to 1896, lecturer on naval history and tactics at Newport War College (1886), and its president (1886–89 and 1892–93). His monumental work, *The Influence of Sea Power upon History, 1660–1783* (1890), examined naval strategy and sea power, to which he gave pivotal importance. His *The Influence of Sea Power upon the French Revolution, 1793–1812* showed how British sea power nullified Napoleon's victories on the Continent. He also wrote *Major Operations of the Navy in the War of American Independence* (1913). His arguments in favor of a big U.S. navy, a strong merchant marine, naval bases, and colonial possessions had an enormous impact on U.S. political thought and were influential abroad, notably in Germany before World War I.

Mailer, Norman (b. Long Branch, N.J., 31 Jan. 1923–), author. He grew up in Brooklyn and, while at Harvard (1939–43), wrote for the *Advocate*, the undergraduate literary magazine, and, with "The Greatest Thing in the World" won *Story Magazine*'s college fiction contest (1941). After receiving a B.S. in engineering he served (1943–45) in the Pacific in the infantry. His first published novel, *The Naked and the Dead* (1948), a searing war story, brought him critical acclaim and was a best seller. The more philosophical and symbolic *Barbary Shore* (1951) suggested Mailer's hostility to both Communism and the authoritarianism he saw in the U.S. After a brief period as a scriptwriter in Hollywood he published *The Deer Park* (1955), a portrayal of a psychopathic Hollywood personality. With Daniel Wolf and Edwin Francher he cofounded *The Village Voice* (1955), becoming a frequent contributor to the weekly journal. His provocative essays also appeared in *Partisan Review, Commentary, Esquire, Dissent,* and other journals. He received the National Book Award (1969) and was cowinner of the Pulitzer prize for general nonfiction (1969) for *Armies of the Night*—a personal account of the 1967 march on the Pentagon by antiwar demonstrators. His other books include: *Advertisements for Myself* (1959), autobiographical and confessional essays; *The Presidential Essays* (1963), essays on President Kennedy, whom he much admired; *Cannibals and Christians* (1966), a collection of verse; *An American Dream* (1965), and *Why Are We in Viet Nam?* (1967), both allegorical novels; *Miami and the Siege of Chicago* (1969), on the 1968 presidential nominating conventions; *Of a Fire on the Moon* (1971), on the Apollo moon shot; and *Marilyn* (1973), a speculative biography of Marilyn Monroe. Mailer has also directed films—most notably *Maidstone* (1968)—and run for mayor of New York City (1967), conducting an unsuccessful Democratic primary campaign on the platform that the city should become the 51st state. Controversial, restless, turbulent, and very much a public personality, Mailer is recognized as a seminal figure in modern American literature.

Mann, Horace (b. Franklin, Mass., 4 May 1796; d. Yellow Springs, Ohio, 2 Aug. 1859), educator, pioneer in the improvement of the common school system. With little formal schooling up to his 17th year, he was graduated with high honors from Brown Univ. (1819), where he was a tutor in Latin and Greek (1819–21). He attended the Litchfield (Conn.) Law School, was admitted to the Massachusetts bar (1823), and practiced at Dedham (Mass.) and Boston until 1837, meanwhile serving in the Massachusetts house (1827–33) and senate (1833–37). He was active in humanitarian and reform movements and, as president (1836–37) of the state senate, signed the education bill (1837) providing for a state board of education. As secretary of the board (1837–48) he eliminated many of the evils of the decentralized state school-district system that had been in force for about a half century and instituted the following reforms: a minimum school year of 6 months, appropriations for public education more than doubled, about 50 new high schools established, public school-teachers' salaries increased, curriculum and methods of instruction revamped, the operations of local schools linked to a central authority, and professional training of teachers improved and regularized. During the period of his secretaryship Mann advanced the principle of nonsectarian education, established and edited the *Common School Journal,* and made illuminating surveys of existing conditions and needs in 12 annual reports that exercised a wide influence on the course of public education in the U.S. In 1839 he established at Lexington, Mass., the first state normal school in the U.S. His 7th annual report was devoted to a survey of European educational conditions made by him during a 5-month tour in 1843. He resigned his secretaryship (1848) to occupy the congressional seat made vacant by the death of John Quincy Adams. He was defeated (1852) as the Free-Soil candidate for the Massachusetts governorship, and from 1853 until his death served as president of Antioch College, Yellow Springs, Ohio.

Marin, John (b. Rutherford, N.J., 23 Dec. 1872; d. Addison, Me., 1 Oct. 1953), painter, studied at the Stevens Institute, then in an architect's office, at the Pennsylvania Academy of Fine Arts, the Art Students League, and in Paris. In 1906 he did an oil which was accepted by the Luxembourg. In New York his work was sponsored by Alfred Stieglitz (1864–1946). His annual 1-man shows of the sea (notably his Maine seascapes) and landscape, beginning 1909, brought to the attention of the art world an individual mode of painting, reflecting the influence of the Chinese school and the method both of abstract cubism and of expressionism. By 1932 he was producing important work in watercolor, and by 1936, when a 1-man show was assembled at the Museum of Modern Art, his reputation in the top rank of American artists was secure.

Marion, Francis (b. probably in St. John's Parish, Berkeley Co., S.C., c.1732; d. there, 26 Feb. 1795), Revolutionary soldier, popularly known as "the Swamp Fox." He took part (1759, 1761) in campaigns against the Cherokee; was elected to the South Carolina Provincial Congress of 1775; became a captain in the militia; and, as a lieutenant colonel of the Continental Line, commanded a regiment in the attack on Savannah (1779). When the Revolutionary forces under Gen. Horatio Gates were routed at Camden, S.C., Marion resorted to guerrilla warfare against British lines of communication, using Williamsburg as his base of operations and taking refuge

in the swamps when numerically superior enemy forces faced him. By also weakening Loyalist potential in South Carolina, Marion helped to wrest the initiative from the British in the South. In 1781, as a brigadier general of militia, Marion was instrumental in retaking South Carolina from the enemy. He served under Gen. Nathanael Greene at the Battle of Eutaw Springs (8 Sept. 1781), which forced the British to fall back on Charleston.

Marshall, George Catlett (b. Uniontown, Pa., 31 Dec. 1880; d. Washington, D.C., 17 Oct. 1959), soldier and statesman, was graduated from Virginia Military Institute (1901) and commissioned in the U.S. army (1902). With the A.E.F. (1917–19), he was detailed to the general staff, 1st Div.; was chief of operations, 1st Army; chief of staff, 8th Army Corps; and aided in planning the St. Mihiel and Meuse-Argonne offensives (1918). Aide to Gen. Pershing (1919–24), assistant commandant of the Infantry School, Ft. Benning, Ga. (1927–32), he was detailed to the general staff as chief of the war plans division (1938), and was appointed chief of staff with rank of general (1939–45), becoming general of the army (1944). As chairman of combined chiefs of staff he was the principal Allied strategist in World War II. Special ambassador to China (1945), he served as Secretary of State under President Truman (1947–49), responsible for the Marshall Plan (ERP) and in formulating the Truman Doctrine (Mar. 1947). In 1950–51 he served as Secretary of Defense, responsible for rebuilding U.S. armed forces and for overall military planning in defense of Korea. He was awarded the Nobel peace prize in 1953.

Marshall, John (b. Germantown [now Midland], Va., 24 Sept. 1755; d. Philadelphia, Pa., 6 July 1835), 3d chief justice of the U.S., served in the American Revolution (1776–79), first as lieutenant, then captain; attended law lectures at William and Mary (May–June 1780), was admitted to the bar, and began practice in Fauquier Co. and (1783) in Richmond. Member of the Virginia Assembly (1782–91 and 1795–97), delegate to the state convention which ratified the Federal Constitution (1788), he declined the attorney generalship offered by Washington (1795) and the post of minister to France (1796), but served as a member of the "X.Y.Z." mission to that country (1797–98). Federalist congressman (1799–1800) and then Secretary of State under John Adams (June 1800–Mar. 1801), he was in the meantime appointed chief justice of the U.S. Supreme Court (from 31 Jan. 1801). His 34 years on the bench established the prestige of the court. Taking upon himself the task of writing most of the important opinions, he used the court and the Constitution to curb interference by the states with vested rights. His major opinions include *Marbury* v. *Madison* (1803), with its assertion of the right of judicial review; *Fletcher* v. *Peck* (1810), the *Dartmouth College Case* (1819), and *Ogden* v. *Saunders* (dissenting opinion, 1827), sustaining the contract clause of the Constitution; *McCulloch* v. *Maryland* (1819), with its doctrine of implied powers; and *Gibbons* v. *Ogden* (1824), with its broad interpretation of the commerce clause.

Marshall, Thurgood (b. Baltimore, Md., 2 July 1908–), lawyer and jurist. The great-grandson of a slave, Marshall attended segregated public schools and worked his way through Lincoln Univ. as a grocery clerk and a waiter. Graduating from college in 1930, Marshall was ineligible because of his race to study at the Univ. of Maryland Law School. He was graduated first in his class from Howard Univ. Law School and was admitted to the Maryland bar (1933). During a brief period of private practice in Baltimore, Marshall successfully litigated a suit resulting in the admission of the first black to graduate study at the Univ. of Maryland (1935). Marshall came to New York to serve as assistant to the NAACP Special Counsel (1936–38), Counsel (1938–40), and then became head of the Legal Defense Fund, a separate litigating arm of the NAACP. Serving for 23 years as director-counsel of the NAACP (1940–62), Marshall coordinated attacks on discrimination in education, housing, public accommodations, and voting. Distinguished both as a legal strategist and as an advocate, Marshall won 29 of the 32 cases he personally argued before the U.S. Supreme Court. Among his notable victories was the decision holding unconstitutional the "white primary" (*Smith* v. *Allwright*, 1944), the decision invalidating segregation on interstate buses (*Morgan* v. *Virginia*, 1946), and the decision striking down state court enforcement of racially restrictive covenants (*Shelley* v. *Kraemer*, 1948). His most significant triumph occurred in *Brown* v. *Board of Education of Topeka* (1954, 1955), where segregation of schools was held impermissible under the Constitution. In 1961 President Kennedy appointed Marshall to the U.S. Court of Appeals for the 2d Circuit where he served until his appointment as Solicitor General of the U.S. (1965–67). On 2 Oct. 1967 Marshall became the first black justice on the Supreme Court, where he has since been recognized as a liberal and activist jurist.

Mason, George (b. near Pasbytanzy, Northern Neck, Va., 1725; d. "Gunston Hall," Va., 7 Oct. 1792), Revolutionary statesman, was educated by private tutors and studied law under John Mercer. He began his political association with Washington in the House of Burgesses (1759), joined with him in anti-Stamp Act activity (1766), and prepared the nonimportation resolutions, successfully proposed by Washington to the dissolved burgesses. Author of the Fairfax Resolves (18 July 1774), restating the colonial position toward the crown, he framed for the Virginia convention the Bill of Rights (12 June 1776), model for the first part of Jefferson's Declaration of Independence and basis of the first 10 Amendments to the federal Constitution, and the major part of the Virginia Constitution (29 June 1776). In collaboration with Jefferson, Patrick Henry, and George Wythe, he revised Virginia's legal system. Backer of George Rogers Clark's (*q.v.*) campaign, he also initiated the plan for the cession of Virginia's western lands and influenced Jefferson's first Territorial Ordinance (1784). A leading figure at the Federal Convention, he refused to sign the Constitution and campaigned against its ratification, insisting on the inclusion of a Bill of Rights and opposing especially the compromise on the slave trade, which he denounced as "disgraceful to mankind."

Mather, Cotton (b. Boston, Mass., 12 Feb. 1662; d. there, 13 Feb. 1727), clergyman, eldest son of Increase Mather and grandson of John Cotton and Richard Mather. He enrolled at Harvard at age 12, graduating in 1678. First a student of medicine, he turned to theology, receiving his M.A. from Harvard (1681). He was ordained (1685) and joined his father in the pulpit of Boston's 2d Church, where he remained for the rest of his life. While the elder Mather petitioned King James II in England for a new charter for Massachusetts, Cotton

Mather led the colony's rebellion against the governor, Sir Edmund Andros. When a new charter was granted and a new governor, William Phips, appointed (1692), he became an adviser in the government (1692–95). His *Memorable Providences, Related to Witchcrafts and Possessions* (1689) contributed to the hysteria that led to the Salem witch trials (1692). Mather had advised the judges that executions would not be necessary; however, during the trials he did not criticize the mass executions, and in *Wonders of the Invisible World* (1693) he defended the verdicts of various trials. As colonial politics became increasingly secular his political influence waned. He tirelessly devoted himself to the cause of orthodox Congregationalism and to scholarly pursuits. A prolific writer—he published some 450 works—his best-known book, *Magnalia Christi Americana* (1702), is an aggregation of materials on the ecclesiastical history of New England. A Fellow at Harvard (1690–1703), he resigned when the college became less strictly Congregationalist in its policies and his hopes for the presidency were disappointed. He promoted the establishment of Yale as a new orthodox stronghold. He organized a school for Negro children and ministered personally to his parishioners. When a smallpox epidemic broke out in Boston (1721), he led an unpopular campaign promoting inoculation. Deeply interested in science, he was the first American elected to the Royal Society (1713).

Mather, Increase (b. Dorchester, Mass., 21 June 1639; d. Boston, 23 Aug. 1723), Puritan clergyman and political leader, was graduated from Harvard (1656), and received his A.M. from Trinity College, Dublin (1658). Before returning to Massachusetts (1661), he preached at Great Torrington, Devonshire, Gloucester, and on Guernsey. Teacher of the 2d Church in Boston (1664), he ultimately (1675) supported the Half-Way Covenant. Acting president of Harvard (1685) and rector (1686–1701), he supported the study of science and sought to maintain Congregational influence. He urged Bostonians (1683) to resist the royal authorities in the *quo warranto* proceedings against the Massachusetts charter. Representing the Congregational churches, he personally appealed (1688) to James II for renewal of the charter, which he finally obtained from William III. The charter, more liberal than the Puritans expected, gave the lower house the right to elect the Council, a unique feature. In 1692 he returned to Boston with William Phips, the governor whom he had nominated. Unlike his son and supporter Cotton Mather (1663–1728), most prolific of American Puritan writers, he took a cautious attitude toward the Salem witch trials. His *Cases of Conscience Concerning Evil Spirits* (1693), disapproving of spectral evidence, induced Phips to stop the execution of the convicted "witches." Other writings include *Wo to Drunkards* (1673), an early temperance tract, *A Brief History of the Warr with the Indians* (1676), and *Remarkable Providences* (1684).

Maury, Matthew Fontaine (b. near Fredericksburg, Va., 14 Jan. 1806; d. Lexington, Va., 1 Feb. 1873), oceanographer, naval officer, went to school in Tennessee. Becoming a midshipman (1825), he made 3 extended cruises in the following 9 years. In his leisure time he worked on navigation, publishing (1836) *A New Theoretical and Practical Treatise on Navigation*. In a series of anonymous articles in the Richmond *Whig* (1838) and the *Southern Literary Messenger* (1840–41) he criticized the

Department of the Navy and proposed reforms. Permanently lamed by a stagecoach accident (1839), he was appointed superintendent of the Dept. of Charts and Instruments of the Navy Dept. (1842), devoting himself to hydrographic and meteorological research, and publishing (1847) *Wind and Current Chart of the North Atlantic* and related works (1850–51). The uniform system of recording oceanographic data which he advocated was adopted at the Brussels International Congress (1853) for worldwide use by naval vessels and merchant ships. His charts reduced the time of passage from New York to San Francisco by 47 days (1855). His *The Physical Geography of the Sea* (1855) was the first text of modern oceanography. Dropped from active service (1855), but restored (1858), he resigned (1861) to accept a commission as commander in the Confederate navy, where he began experiments with electric mines. In England as special agent, he secured ships of war for the Confederacy. After the Civil War he was involved in an abortive colonization scheme to send ex-Confederates to Mexico. After a stay in England again, he returned to the U.S. (1868) to accept a professorship of meteorology at the Virginia Military Institute.

Mayo, William James (b. Le Sueur, Minn., 29 June 1861; d. Rochester, Minn., 28 July 1939) and his brother, **Charles Horace** (b. Rochester, Minn., 19 July 1865; d. Chicago, 26 May 1939), surgeons, sons of Dr. William Worrall Mayo (1820–1911), pioneer surgeon of the Northwest, both took medical degrees, William at the Univ. of Mich. (1883), Charles at the Chicago Medical College (1888). They gradually took over their father's large practice in Rochester, and father and sons constituted the medical and surgical staff of

St. Mary's Hospital, opened in 1889. Observing clinical and surgical practice in Europe and America, they incorporated the latest surgical techniques and originated much, William in abdominal surgery, Charles in surgery of the thyroid gland. Developing a cooperative group clinic, they added general practitioners, surgeons, and laboratory scientists. Out of this grew the Mayo Clinic, a group of some 200 doctors, each a specialist, engaged in cooperative practice. The first Mayo Clinic building was constructed in 1912, and in 1915 the brothers donated $1,500,000 (increased to $2,500,000 by 1934) to establish the Mayo Foundation for Medical Education and Research, which became an affiliate of the graduate school of the Univ. of Minn. During World War I they served as chief army consultants for surgical service, receiving the rank of brigadier general (1921). They published *Collected Papers of the Mayo Clinic and the Mayo Foundation* (1932).

Meany, George (b. New York City, 16 April 1894–   ), labor leader. Educated in New York City public schools, he became an apprentice plumber in 1910, was promoted to the rank of journeyman plumber in 1915, and practiced his trade in New York City. In 1922 he was elected business agent of Local 463 of the Plumbers Union, an affiliate of the American Federation of Labor, and he was subsequently elected to the New York City Central Trades and Labor Assembly, which was the main body of the AFL in the city. He was president of the New York State Federation of Labor (1934–39), and on 1 Jan. 1940 became secretary-treasurer of the AFL. When William Green died in 1952, Meany became president of the AFL. He was an architect of that organization's merger with the Congress of Industrial Organizations. In 1955 he

was elected president of the new AFL-CIO, a position he still holds. Under his direction the AFL-CIO conducted a campaign against corruption in organized labor, which culminated in the 1957 expulsion from the federation of 3 major unions, including the International Brotherhood of Teamsters. A political moderate who espouses the tradition of Samuel Gompers, he has since 1960 actively led the AFL-CIO in support of legislation dealing with minimum wages, civil rights, public housing, aid to education, national health insurance, and election reform. A strong backer of the Vietnam War, he was lukewarm toward Sen. George McGovern's presidential candidacy (1972). He led the AFL-CIO in its call for the impeachment of President Richard M. Nixon (1973–74).

Melville, Herman (b. New York City, 1 Aug. 1819; d. there, 28 Sept. 1891), author. His only formal schooling, which he received at the Albany Academy, ended at the age of 15. He worked as a bank and store clerk, farmer, and teacher, and in 1837 shipped to Liverpool as a cabin boy. In 1841–42 he made a voyage to the South Seas aboard the whaler *Acushnet*. Deserting at the Marquesas Islands, he lived among the natives, went to Tahiti, and in 1843 enlisted as an ordinary seaman on the frigate *United States*. He was discharged at Boston in 1844 and immediately set to work on the novels that were based on his adventures: *Typee* (1846), *Omoo* (1847), *Mardi* (1849), *Redburn* (1849), and *White-Jacket* (1850). Moving (1850) to a farm near Pittsfield, Mass., he formed here his friendship with Nathaniel Hawthorne and wrote his masterpiece, *Moby Dick* (1851). This was followed by a period of uneven achievement: *Pierre: or the Ambiguities* (1852), *Israel Potter* (1855), *The Piazza Tales* (1856), and *The Confidence Man*

(1857). In 1863 he moved to New York, where he worked as a customs inspector (1866–85) and lived in obscurity. His works of poetry date from this period: *Battle-Pieces and Aspects of the War* (1866), *Clarel* (1876), *John Marr and Other Sailors* (1888), and *Timoleon* (1891). The novelette *Billy Budd,* completed in his last year, was not published until 1924, following a revival of interest in Melville.

Mencken, Henry Louis (b. Baltimore, Md., 12 Sept. 1880, d. there, 29 Jan. 1956), journalist, literary critic, was graduated from Polytechnic Institute at the head of his class. Police reporter (1899), then city editor (1903) of the Baltimore *Morning Herald,* he joined the staff of the Baltimore *Sun* (1906). In the era following World War I, Mencken's vogue was enormous. Nietzschean iconoclast and debunker, he was critical of his age and cynical about democracy and the "Boobus Americanus." His literary criticism helped bring to the fore such writers as Dreiser, D. H. Lawrence, Ford Madox Ford, and Sherwood Anderson. With George Jean Nathan, he collaborated on *The Smart Set,* later (1924) on *The American Mercury,* of which Mencken was sole editor, 1925–33. His monumental *The American Language,* published in several editions (1919–48), is a more durable contribution to letters. His popularity waned during the depression, when his former admirers sought more constructive values.

Mergenthaler, Ottmar (b. Hachtel, Germany, 11 May 1854; d. Baltimore, Md., 28 Oct. 1899), inventor of the linotype. After serving his apprenticeship (1868–72) to a watchmaker at Bietigheim, he came to the U.S. in 1872 and was engaged in the making of scientific instruments in the establishments of August Hahl at Washington, D.C. (1872–76) and Baltimore (1876–82). During the early part of this period Mergenthaler worked on the improvement of a writing machine (originated by James O. Clephane and devised by Charles Moore) aimed at the lithographic reproduction of print. A full-scale model failing to operate successfully, Mergenthaler began experimenting with a machine that would eliminate typesetting by hand and supplant stereotyping with the lithographic process. Difficulties compelled Mergenthaler to abandon the project (1879); but shortly after he opened his own establishment (1883), he secured from Clephane an order to construct a typesetting machine capable of obtaining clean type from a matrix. When this device proved to be unsatisfactory, Mergenthaler devised a plan for the stamping and casting of type metal in the same machine; by July 1884, he had successfully incorporated this principle in the first direct-casting linotype. The machine was patented on 26 Aug. 1884, and for its manufacture he and Clephane organized the National Typographic Co. of W. Va.; a subsidiary, the Mergenthaler Printing Co., was established in 1885. By the time of his death Mergenthaler had made an aggregate of more than 50 patented improvements. The linotype revolutionized mass-circulation newspaper production.

Michelson, Albert Abraham (b. Strelno, Prussia, 19 Dec. 1852; d. Pasadena, Calif., 9 May 1931), physicist. Brought to the U.S. as an infant (1854), he was educated at Virginia City, Nev., and San Francisco, Calif., and was graduated (1873) from the U.S. Naval Academy, where he served (1875–77) as an instructor in physics and chemistry. He pursued postgraduate studies (1880–81) at Heidelberg, Berlin, and Paris; taught physics at the Case School of

Applied Science, Cleveland, Ohio (1883–89), and at Clark Univ. (1889–92); and in 1892 was made chief professor in the Ryerson Physical Laboratory and head of the physics department at the newly established Univ. of Chicago, where he served until his retirement in 1931. Virtually all of his experiments and researches lay in the field of optics and were marked by skillfully designed apparatuses for attaining precise measurement. His improvements of the Foucault apparatus for measuring the speed of light enabled him to determine the velocity of light with a margin of error of less than 1 in 100,000. He designed (1887) an interferometer with which he determined linear distances in terms of the wave length of light. Using the interferometer, he made (with Edward Williams Morley) the famous experiment (1887) designed to detect the relative motion of the earth through the ether. The findings of the Michelson-Morley experiment contributed much to the development of the theory of relativity. Michelson also determined the length of the meter in terms of the wave length of lines in the cadmium spectrum, was the first to measure the angular diameter of a star, devised the echelon spectrometer, and measured the tides in the solid earth. He was awarded the Nobel prize in physics (1907). He wrote *Light Waves and Their Uses* (1903).

Millay, Edna St. Vincent (b. Rockland, Me., 22 Feb. 1892; d. Austerlitz, N.Y., 19 Oct. 1950), poet, wrote her first long poem, "Renascence," at 19. Published in *The Lyric Year*, a prize anthology (1912), it won her critical acclaim. Her education at Barnard and Vassar (A.B., 1917) was financed by a woman admirer of that poem. Entering enthusiastically into Bohemian life in Greenwich Village, New York City, she published in that period *A Few Figs from Thistles* (1920)

and *Aria da Capo* (1921), an antiwar piece. In protest against the Sacco-Vanzetti trial, she wrote the poem "Justice Denied in Massachusetts" (1927) and was arrested for participating in the "death watch" demonstration outside the Boston State House. Recognizing the Nazi threat to Western civilization, she wrote *There Are No Islands Any More* (1940), a plea for U.S. aid to Britain and France, and *The Murder of Lidice* (1942). An advocate of sexual equality for women, her love poetry is characterized by an ironic poignance and a clarity of style. Her works include *Buck in the Snow* (1928); *Fatal Interview* (1931), a collection of sonnets; *Huntsman, What Quarry?* (1939); *Collected Sonnets* (1941). She was awarded the Pulitzer prize in poetry (1923).

Miller, Arthur (b. New York City, 7 Oct. 1915–), playwright, was graduated from the Univ. of Mich. (1938). Writing plays while at college, he later joined the Federal Theater Project in New York. In 1944 *Situation Normal* examined army conditions, and *Focus* (1945), a novel, dealt with anti-Semitism. His first Broadway play, *The Man Who Had All the Luck* (1944), was followed by *All My Sons* (1947; N.Y. Drama Critics Circle award). His Pulitzer prize-winning *Death of a Salesman* (1949), depicting the drama of a small man destroyed by an empty society, has been called the modern American tragedy. Other plays include *The Crucible* (1953), *A View from the Bridge* (1955), *After the Fall* (1964), *Incident at Vichy* (1964), *The Price* (1968), *The Creation of the World and Other Business* (1972). A collection of stories, *I Don't Need You Any More*, was published in 1967. Married to movie star Marilyn Monroe (1956; divorced 1961), he wrote a screenplay, *The Misfits* (1961), for her starring role. His sentence for contempt of Congress (1957) was reversed on appeal.

Miller, Samuel Freeman (b. Richmond, Ky., 5 Apr. 1816; d. Washington, D.C., 13 Oct. 1890), jurist, was graduated from the medical school of Transylvania Univ. (1838), practiced for 12 years, then turned to the law, and was admitted to the bar (1847). Becoming an abolitionist, he moved to Keokuk, Ia. (1850), and became a state leader of the Republican party. Lincoln appointee as associate justice of the U.S. Supreme Court (1862), he was a staunch supporter of the national authority. In his dissent in the *Test-Oath Cases* (1867) he upheld the loyalty oath. In the *Slaughterhouse Case* (1873) he denied that the 14th Amendment was applicable to business corporations, but restricted it to Negroes. In dissent in *Hepburn* v. *Griswold* (1870) he upheld the legality of the Legal Tender Act, and in *Ex parte Yarbrough* (1884) he upheld the authority of the federal government to supervise congressional elections in the states (1884). He voted with the Republican majority in the Electoral Commission (1876).

Millikan, Robert Andrews (b. Morrison, Ill., 22 Mar. 1868; d. Pasadena, Calif., 19 Dec. 1953), physicist. He was graduated from Oberlin College (A.B., 1891; A.M., 1893), received the degree of Ph.D. at Columbia (1895), and studied at Berlin and Göttingen (1895–96). He was a member of the physics staff (1896–1921) at the Univ. of Chicago, and in 1921 became director of the Norman Bridge Laboratory of Physics at the California Institute of Technology at Pasadena. He received the Nobel prize in physics (1923) for his determination of the exact values of the mass and charge of the electron. He also made important investigations in the laws of

reflection of gas molecules, cosmic rays, the absorption of X rays, the polarization of light from incandescent surfaces, the effect of temperature on photoelectric discharge, and the velocities of electrons discharged from metals under the influence of ultraviolet light. He was the author of *Mechanics, Molecular Physics and Heat* (1901), *Electricity, Sound and Light* (1908), *The Electron* (1917), *Cosmic Rays* (1939), and others.

Mitchell, William Lendrum (b. Nice, France, 29 Dec. 1879; d. New York City, 19 Feb. 1936), military aviation officer and pioneer exponent of air power, popularly known as "Billy" Mitchell. He attended Racine College, Wisc., was graduated from George Washington Univ., enlisted as a private at the outbreak of the Spanish-American War (1898), and in the same year was commissioned an officer in the U.S. Army Signal Corps. He was graduated (1909) from the Army Staff College, served on the Mexican border (1912), and in 1913 became the youngest officer ever appointed to the army general staff. During World War I he was chief of air service for several units, including the U.S. 1st Corps and the U.S. 1st and 2d Armies, and after the war was promoted to the rank of brigadier general and named director of military aviation. As assistant chief of the Army Air Service from 1920 to 1924, Mitchell openly criticized national aviation policy and demonstrated his confidence in air power as a major arm of warfare by sinking target battleships with aerial bombs. He called for a unified command of the armed forces. In 1925, while serving as air officer for the 8th Corps Area, he accused the high military and naval command of "incompetency, criminal negligence, and almost treasonal administration of national defense." He was court-martialed, found guilty, and suspended for 5 years without pay or allowances. While President Coolidge upheld the suspension, he granted Mitchell half pay and restored his allowances; Mitchell, however, resigned from the service (1 Feb. 1926) and continued his criticism of official military aviation policy. He was posthumously restored to the service (1942) with the rank of major general.

Monroe, James (b. Westmoreland Co., Va., 28 Apr. 1758; d. New York City, 4 July 1831), 5th president of the U.S., left William and Mary (1774–76) to serve in the Continental army, fighting at Harlem Heights, White Plains, Trenton, Brandywine, Germantown, and Monmouth. He studied law under Jefferson (1780–83), and entered the Virginia House of Delegates (1782) and the Continental Congress (1783–86). In the Virginia convention (1788) he opposed the Federal Constitution. As U.S. senator (1790–94), he joined the Jeffersonian Republicans. Minister to France (1794–96), he was recalled for failure to allay resentment caused by the Jay Treaty. Governor of Virginia (1799–1802), he returned to France as envoy extraordinary (1802–03), joining R. R. Livingston with instructions to buy New Orleans from France and West Florida from Spain. Exceeding instructions, he acquired all Florida. Subsequently he served as minister to Great Britain (1803–06) and, with Charles Pinckney, went to Madrid (1804–05) in a futile effort to settle a boundary dispute. Again governor of Virginia (1811), he resigned to become Madison's Secretary of State (1811–17) and to serve for a time as Secretary of War (1814–15). Elected president (1816) and reelected (1820) with all but 1 electoral vote, his administration was characterized as an "Era of Good Feelings" following a quarter century of rivalry between Federalists and Republicans. He settled boundaries with Canada and eliminated border forts, acquired Florida (1819), and formulated with modifications suggested by J. Q. Adams, the Monroe Doctrine (2 Dec. 1823), which he decided to issue unilaterally.

Moody, Dwight Lyman (b. Northfield, Mass., 5 Feb. 1837; d. there, 22 Dec. 1899), evangelist, was admitted to membership in the Congregational Church at Boston (1856), but moved to Chicago, where he combined a career as a shoe salesman with church work. In 1860 he abandoned business to become an independent city missionary; in 1866, after having served with the U.S. Christian Commission during the Civil War, he was made president of the Chicago Young Men's Christian Association. He made his mark as a lay preacher dedicated to the saving of souls. In 1873–75, during his third trip to Great Britain, he and the organist and singer, Ira D. Sankey, conducted a series of revivalist meetings which were attended by an estimated total of 2,530,000 people and led to an almost unprecedented religious awakening in the British Isles. Upon his return to the U.S., he and Sankey conducted evangelistic campaigns (1875–76) in Philadelphia, New York, and Brooklyn, and between 1877 and 1881 preached in cities including Chicago, Hartford, Baltimore, St. Louis, and San Francisco. Subsequent evangelistic campaigns in Great Britain (1881–84, 1891–92) equaled the success of his British tour of 1873–75. Between 1884 and 1891 Moody was active as an evangelist in many small cities in the U.S. and Canada. He founded the Chicago Bible Institute (1889) and the Bible Institute Colportage Association (1894). The spiritual awakening he stimulated in American colleges led to the organization of the Student Volunteer Movement, a group devoted to foreign missionary service.

Morgan, Daniel (b. Hunterdon Co., N.J., 6 July 1736; d. Winchester, Va., 6 July 1802), Revolutionary soldier, ran away from home, worked as a farm laborer and teamster in the Shenandoah Valley in Virginia, was a lieutenant in Pontiac's War, and accompanied (1774) Lord Dunmore's expedition to western Pennsylvania. Commissioned (22 June 1775) captain of a company of Virginia riflemen, he traveled from Winchester to Boston in 21 days. On the march to Quebec with Benedict Arnold (*q.v.*), he took command after Arnold was wounded there, captured the first barrier, and penetrated to the lower city, but was forced to surrender to overwhelming odds. Released (12 Nov. 1776), he was commissioned colonel of a Virginia regiment and, rejoining Washington, organized a corps of 500 sharpshooters. His part at Saratoga was notable. At Freeman's Farm his riflemen checked the movement to turn the American left and at Bemis Heights he took his men on a wide circuit around the enemy's right and from the flank and rear of the British poured deadly fire on Lord Balcarre's troops. Sent (1780) by Nathanael Greene (*q.v.*) to harass British outposts, he inflicted a disastrous defeat upon Tarleton in the battle of Cowpens (17 Jan. 1781), a military classic and model for Greene at Guilford Courthouse and Eutaw Springs. In command of the Virginia militia (1794) he assisted in putting down the Whiskey Rebellion. He served 1 term in Congress (1797–99).

Morgan, John Pierpont (b. Hartford, Conn., 17 Apr. 1837; d. Rome, Italy, 31 Mar. 1913), financier. After being educated at Boston, he received further schooling at Vevey, Switzerland, and at the Univ. of Göttingen; entered (1856) his father's banking house at London; and came to New York (1857), where he established J. P. Morgan & Co. (1860), which acted as agent for his father's firm. During the Civil War he was engaged in foreign exchange and gold speculation. In 1864 he became a member of the firm of Dabney, Morgan & Co., and in 1869 won control of the Albany & Susquehanna R.R. from Jay Gould and Jim Fisk. In 1871 he established the New York firm of Drexel, Morgan & Co., which in 1895 became known as J. P. Morgan & Co. Together with its allied houses in London and Paris, this firm became one of the leading and most influential banking houses in the world. An exponent of combination, integration, and centralized financial control in the business and industrial world, Morgan played an important role in the reorganization of American railroads (1885 *et seq.*). After the Panic of 1893, the Cleveland administration called upon him to relieve the pressure on the Treasury. Morgan took part in the financing and organization of the United States Steel Corp. (1901) and the International Harvester Co. (1902). In alliance with James J. Hill, he became embroiled in a struggle with Edward H. Harriman for control of the Northern Pacific R.R. that ultimately came before the Supreme Court in the *Northern Securities Case* (1904). During the panic of 1907 he helped stabilize financial conditions. In 1912 he became the chief target of the Pujo investigation of the so-called Money Trust. Perhaps the leading private art collector of his time, he left at his death valuable collections of books, manuscripts, and art objects now housed in the Pierpont Morgan Wing of the Metropolitan Museum and in the Pierpont Morgan Library, both in New York City.

Morgan, Lewis Henry (b. Aurora, N.Y., 21 Nov. 1818; d. Rochester, N.Y., 17

Dec. 1881), ethnologist and anthropologist, was graduated from Union College (1840), studied law, and moved to Rochester, where he practiced in partnership with George F. Danforth. Member of the New York assembly (1861–68) and state senate (1868–69), he is best known for his work in ethnology and as the "father of American anthropology." His first research was an investigation of the customs and institutions of the Iroquois, inspired by his adoption (1 Oct. 1847) into the Hawk clan of the Seneca in appreciation of his services in defeating ratification of a treaty unfavorable to the Seneca. His *League of the Ho-dé-no-sau-nee, or Iroquois* (1851), written in collaboration with Ely S. Parker, was the first scientific account of an Indian tribe. In addition to his Iroquois research, he made ethnological investigations (1859–62) of the Prairie Indians and observed similarities between the kinship systems of the Iroquois and other Indian tribes in North America. These observations led to his *Systems of Consanguinity and Affinity of the Human Family* (1870), a comprehensive collection of the kinship systems of the world. In *Ancient Society* (1877) he formulated his social evolutionary scheme of culture as having developed in stages from savagery to barbarism and then to civilization. His postulate of unilateral evolution has been modified basically by later anthropology. He also wrote *Houses and Houselife of the American Aborigines* (1881). Although no Marxist, his work influenced Karl Marx and Friedrich Engels.

Morgan, Thomas Hunt (b. Lexington, Ky., 25 Sept. 1866; d. Pasadena, Calif., 4 Dec. 1945), biologist. He was graduated from the State College of Kentucky (B.S., 1886; M.S., 1888) and from Johns Hopkins (Ph.D., 1890), served as professor of biology 1891–1904) at Bryn Mawr College, was professor of experi-

mental zoology (1904–28) at Columbia, and in 1928 was named director of biological science at California Institute of Technology. After carrying out his initial researches in experimental embryology and regeneration, he made his more noted experiments and studies on heredity and mutation in the fruit fly (Drosophila). His findings made valuable contributions to the knowledge of the genes and the nature of mutations, and provided the basis for the development of the science of genetics. For his work in the phenomena of heredity, Morgan received the Nobel prize in physiology and medicine (1933). Among his publications are *Regeneration* (1901), *Evolution and Adaptation* (1903), *Heredity and Sex* (1913), *Mechanism of Mendelian Heredity* (1915), *Critique of the Theory of Evolution* (1916), *The Physical Basis of Heredity* (1919), and *The Theory of the Genes* (1926).

Morison, Samuel Eliot (b. Boston, Mass., 9 July 1887–   ), historian, received his B.A. (1908), M.A. (1909), and Ph.D. (1913) from Harvard. Instructor at the Univ. of California (1914) and at Harvard (1915), Morison enlisted as a private in the army during World War I, afterward serving as an attaché to the Russian division of the Commission to Negotiate Peace, then returning to Harvard as a professor of history. An authority on early American history, Morison has also made a major mark as a naval historian. Denying previous theories, Morison's *Builders of the Bay Colony* (1930) portrayed the Puritans not as straitlaced individuals but as men and women with human strengths and weaknesses and motivated by deep-felt religious convictions. Morison's multivolume *Tercentenary History of Harvard College and University, 1636–1936* (1935, 1936) contributed significantly to an understanding of the development of American education. Morison's major textbooks include *The Growth of the American Republic* (with Henry Steele Commager, 1930) and the *Oxford History of the American People* (1965). A lieutenant commander of the naval reserve, who saw action at sea during World War II, Morison wrote a 15-vol. *History of the United States Naval Operations in World War II* (1947–62) as well as a short history of the U.S. navy in that war, *The Two Ocean War* (1963). He won Pulitzer prizes for *Admiral of the Ocean Sea* (1942), during the writing of which he had sailed 10,000 miles retracing Columbus' course, and for *John Paul Jones* (1959). Both Morison's love of the sea and his desire to make history come alive were exemplified by his research for *The European Discovery of America, The Northern Voyages, 1500–1600* (1971), for which, in his 80s, he coasted the eastern shores of the U.S. and Canada and flew at low altitude in a small plane along the north Atlantic seaboard to obtain a better comprehension of the challenges confronting the early explorers. *The European Discovery of America, The Southern Voyages, 1492–1616* was published in 1974.

Morris, Robert (b. at or near Liverpool, England, 31 Jan. 1734; d. Philadelphia, Pa., 8 May 1806), financier of the American Revolution. He received a brief schooling at Philadelphia, where he joined the shipping and mercantile house of Charles Willing, becoming partner of the latter's son Thomas (1754), under the firm name of Willing & Morris. Morris was not definitely committed to the Patriot cause until 1775. The Pennsylvania assembly named him (30 June 1775) a member of the council of safety. He also served on the committee of correspondence and was chosen (Nov. 1775) as a delegate to the Continental Congress, in which he served until 1778. He

was a member of several committees, including the secret committee for procuring munitions. He was occasionally assigned banking business by Congress; meanwhile, he continued his private activities as a member of his Philadelphia firm in importing military supplies. Although he voted against the Declaration of Independence in July 1776 on the ground that it was premature, he signed it in Aug. When Congress fled from Philadelphia (Dec. 1776), Morris remained there to continue the work of the committee of secret correspondence to which he had been appointed in Jan. 1776. He borrowed money and purchased supplies that were of crucial importance to the weakened Revolutionary forces. During the critical financial period, 1780–81, Morris was appointed by Congress (20 Feb. 1781) as superintendent of finance. In this capacity, he wielded the powers of a financial dictator. He strengthened the public credit, instituted an economy program, and at times used notes based on his personal credit. He also served as marine agent for the government. His efforts contributed directly to the victory over Cornwallis at Yorktown. A loan he secured from the French enabled the organization (1781–82) of the Bank of North America. He resigned his government post on 24 Jan. 1783. Morris was a delegate to the Annapolis Convention (1786) and, as a delegate to the Federal Convention of 1787, supported a strong central government. He declined Washington's offer of the post of Secretary of the Treasury in the first administration, and served (1789–95) as U.S. senator from Pennsylvania. His involvement in various land speculations, including a large interest he held in the present site of Washington, D.C., brought his financial ruin. Confined to the Philadelphia debtors' prison (1798–1801), he never regained his fortune.

Morse, Samuel Finley Breese (b. Charlestown, Mass., 27 Apr. 1791; d. New York City, 2 Apr. 1872), artist and inventor. The son of the Congregational clergyman, Jedidiah Morse (1761–1826; known as the "father of American geography"), he was graduated from Yale (1810), and in 1811 accompanied the painter Washington Allston to England. Morse spent the next 4 years studying under Allston and at the Royal Academy in London. Returning to Boston (1815), he opened a studio, but the lack of sufficient portrait commissions compelled him to seek patrons elsewhere. He scored his first success at Charleston, S.C., where he passed the winters from 1818 to 1821, and in 1823 settled at New York. In 1825 he executed at Washington his 2 portraits of Lafayette. He was the chief founder of the National Academy of Design and served as its first president (1826–42). He went to Europe in 1829, and upon his return in 1832 was appointed professor of painting and sculpture in the Univ. of the City of New York (later New York Univ.). During the period 1832–35 he was active in the Native American movement and was its candidate (1836) for mayor of New York. Morse abandoned painting (c.1837) to devote himself to experimenting with the transmission of signals by electricity, an idea first broached to him during his return voyage from Europe in 1832; at that time Morse had set down his original conception of an electromagnetic recording telegraph. While working on the apparatus, which after many experiments was improved by the addition of Joseph Henry's intensity magnet, Morse devised a code of dots and dashes that was named after him (Morse code). Morse's most important contribution was his system of electromagnetic renewers or relays for the transmission of messages over great distances and through any number of stations and branch lines. In the development of the telegraph, he

received financial support from Alfred Vail, who became his partner in 1837. Although Morse filed for a patent in 1837, he did not receive it until 1844. Congress appropriated (1843) $30,000 for an experimental line from Washington to Baltimore that was constructed by Ezra Cornell. On 24 May 1844 Morse transmitted over this line the message, "What hath God wrought!" When the government refused to buy the rights to the apparatus, Morse and his associates formed a company for the manufacture of the telegraph.

Morton, William Thomas Green (b. Charlton, Mass., 9 Aug. 1819; d. New York City, 15 July 1868), dentist and pioneer in surgical anesthesia. He was educated at academies in Northfield and Leicester, entered (1840) the College of Dental Surgery at Baltimore, Md., and in 1842 began his practice at Farmington, Conn. In 1842–43 he set up a joint practice at Boston with Dr. Horace Wells of Hartford, Conn., who in 1844 was to use nitrous oxide (laughing gas) in the extraction of teeth. When the partnership was terminated in late 1843, Morton remained in Boston. He matriculated (1844) at Harvard Medical School, but attended only for a brief period. At about this time, at the suggestion of Prof. Charles T. Jackson, a chemist, Morton employed ether in drops as a local anesthetic in filling a tooth. Jackson had also demonstrated that the inhalation of sulfuric ether induced loss of consciousness; it was this method that Morton used in experiments on animals and himself. He performed the painless extraction of an ulcerated tooth (30 Sept. 1846) after using ether inhalation on the patient. Following other successful painless extractions, Dr. John Collins Warren, a Boston surgeon, arranged for the use of Morton's discovery in an operation at the Massachusetts General Hospital. On

16 Oct. 1846, with Morton administering the anesthetic in the presence of physician spectators, Warren removed a vascular tumor from the neck of a patient. Formal announcement of the discovery was made on 18 Nov. 1846 in the *Boston Medical and Surgical Journal*. Morton patented his discovery under the name of "letheon" (12 Nov. 1846). When the French Academy of Medicine awarded a joint prize of 5,000 francs (1847) to Jackson and Morton, the latter did not accept his share, asserting that the discovery was his alone. Morton's claims led Dr. Crawford W. Long (1815–1878) of Athens, Ga., to publish accounts (1848, 1853) of independent discoveries he had made with sulfuric ether in 8 operations on human beings performed between 1842 and 1846. To Morton, however, goes the major credit for the discovery, for he was the first to make a public demonstration with assumption of full responsibility for the consequences.

Moses, Anna Mary Robertson (Grandma Moses) (b. Greenwich, N.Y., 7 Sept. 1860; d. Hoosick Falls, N.Y., 13 Dec. 1961), primitive painter. The daughter of a painter, from age 12 until her marriage (1887) she worked as a hired girl. The mother of 10 children, 5 of whom died in infancy, she took over their farm when her husband died. When she could no longer farm and when arthritis made it difficult for her to use a needle to make her woolen embroideries or "worsted pictures," she took up painting (1937). Using house paints and then oils she began by copying pictures from postcards. She became more imaginative, drawing scenes of her childhood from memory. In 1938 Louis J. Caldor, an art collector, saw 3 of her paintings in a drugstore in Hoosick Falls and bought all her existing work. After the Museum of Modern Art (New York City) hung 3 of her pictures in a show entitled "Contemporary Unknown

American Painters" (1939), her fame mounted, as did the price of her art. Acclaimed as the American Henri Rousseau, her works tell the story of skating, sleighing, picnics, weddings, wash days, and quilting bees. Reflecting craft tradition, her traditional American folk art was known for brilliant use of color as well as its humor, simplicity, realism, and emotional effectiveness. Altogether she held 250 exhibits and painted over 1,500 paintings, including 25 after the age of 100. Her works include *The Old Oaken Bucket* (1939), *Catching the Thanksgiving Turkey* (1943), and *From My Window* (1946).

Moses, Robert (b. New Haven, Conn., 18 Dec. 1888–), urban planner, graduated from Yale (1909), earned B.A. and M.A. degrees from Oxford (1911, 1913) and a Ph.D. from Columbia (1914). Involved as a young man in reform politics, Moses became closely associated with New York Gov. Alfred E. Smith, serving as Chief of State of the New York State Reconstruction Commission (1919–21) and Secretary of State for New York State (1927–28). Moses persuaded Smith to form the New York State Council of Parks from 11 isolated regional parks councils (1924). Appointed president of the Long Island Park Commission, he was chosen state chairman, serving for 39 years. His remarkable record of public service included the chairmanships of the Jones Beach State Parkway and Bethpage Authorities (1934–60), New York State Power Authority (1954–63), Triborough Bridge and Tunnel Authority (1946–68). He was also coordinator of construction for New York City (1946–60) and New York City Park Commissioner (1934–60). In 1959 Moses held 12 positions at once. He wielded more influence in public works construction in New York than any other man in the 20th century, supporting vast parkway construction, bridge building, and the creation of parks, beaches, and playgrounds. He employed the device of the public authority, which raised money by issuing its own bonds and collecting tolls and fees, thus providing a source of revenue and patronage outside traditional political processes. Moses believed in accommodating the automobile. His efforts fostered suburban growth, especially the development of Long Island. Moses' approach to urban renewal emphasized high-rise public and luxury housing. His achievements have been criticized for destruction of landmarks, harm to neighborhoods, for lack of interest in the problems of the poor, and for an unwillingness to address the need for mass transit. His preference for the use of parks for recreation rather than as islands of tranquility has been criticised by recent urban planners. Moses was defeated for governor of New York as a Republican candidate in 1934. He was president of the 1964–65 New York World's Fair Corp. from 1960–67. He is the author of *Public Works: A Dangerous Trade* (1970).

Motley, John Lothrop (b. Dorchester, Mass., 15 Apr. 1814; d. in Dorsetshire, England, 29 May 1877), historian and diplomat. He was graduated from Harvard (1831), studied at Göttingen and Berlin, and after returning to Boston wrote 2 novels, *Morton's Hope* (1839) and *Merrymount* (1849). He served (1841–42) as secretary of legation at St. Petersburg and in 1847 began work on the historical subject that was to occupy the rest of his life. To further his researches in archives in Germany and Holland, he went to Europe in 1851. *The Rise of the Dutch Republic* (3 vols., 1856) indicated the main lines of Motley's history and his point of view: his dramatic narrative treatment, his preoccupation with political and religious de-

velopments, and his studied contrast of liberty and absolutism. He also published *The History of the United Netherlands* (4 vols., 1860, 1867) and *The Life and Death of John of Barneveld* (2 vols., 1874). From 1861 to 1867 Motley was minister to Austria and from 1869 to 1870 minister to Great Britain.

Muller, Hermann Joseph (b. New York City, 21 Dec. 1890; d. Indianapolis, Ind. 5 Apr. 1967), geneticist, received his degrees at Columbia (B.A., 1910; M.A., 1911; Ph.D., 1916), and taught at Cornell, Rice Inst., Columbia, and the Univ. of Texas. Senior geneticist (1933–37) of the Institute of Genetics in Moscow, he was professor of Zoology, Indiana Univ. (1945–65). His genetics research was begun in 1911 and conducted mainly by breeding experiments in the fruit fly, Drosophila. Working with Thomas Hunt Morgan (*q.v.*), he established the principle of linear linkage, accounting for the inheritance of characteristics on the basis of a linear arrangement of genes. He made a special study of mutations leading to permanently altered, hereditary characteristics, and described the gene as probably a single molecule. For his discovery of hereditary changes or mutations produced by X rays, he was awarded the Nobel prize (1946). His writings include *The Mechanics of Mendelian Heredity* (with others, 1915), *Out of the Night* (1935), and *Genetics, Medicine, and Man* (with others, 1947).

Muñoz Marín, Luis (b. San Juan, P.R., 18 Feb. 1898–   ), statesman. The son of the Puerto Rican leader Luis Muñoz-Rivera, he attended Georgetown Univ. (1912–16) and then spent 2 years as secretary to the Puerto Rican Resident Commissioner in Washington. For the next few years he spent most of his time in New York City and was an author, contributing to the *Nation, New Repub-*

lic, and *American Mercury,* and editing *La Revista de Indias,* a journal focusing on Caribbean and Latin American culture. He returned to Puerto Rico, where he edited his father's daily newspaper, *La Democracia* (1925–27), and wrote "Puerto Rico, the American Colony," an argument for complete independence, which was published in *These United States* (1925). In 1927 he was sent to the U.S. as representative of the economic committee of the Puerto Rican legislature and, later, served as member of the Pan-American Conference in Havana (1928). He was elected to the Puerto Rican Senate (1932) on the ticket of the Liberal party. While a senator he was in contact with leading New Dealers, including President Franklin D. Roosevelt and Rexford Tugwell. In reaction to the punitive independence proposed in the Tydings Bill (1936), Muñoz began to search for a different solution to the status problem. Forced to withdraw from the Liberal party (May 1936), he founded (July 1938) the Popular Democratic party, dedicated to social and economic reform, and appealing to the working population as well as the landless *jíbaros.* The PDP won a majority of votes in its first campaign, Muñoz becoming president of the Puerto Rican Senate (1941–48). He worked closely with the newly appointed governor, Rexford Tugwell, on a program for economic and land reform. Muñoz was the first elected governor of Puerto Rico and served 4 terms (1949–65). He supported Operation Bootstrap, in which industrialization and capital investment were stimulated. He was the chief architect of a Puerto Rican commonwealth as an alternative to both independence and statehood.

Nabokov, Vladimir (b. St. Petersburg, Russia, 23 Apr. 1899–), author. Born into a family of old Russian nobility, he attended Prince Tenishev Gynasium and,

after his family left Russia (1919), earned his B.A. from Trinity College, Cambridge (1922). While living in Germany (1922–37) and France (1937–40) he wrote in Russian, his poetry, plays, short stories, and novels establishing him as a major post-1917 émigré author. Among his early novels later translated into English are: *Kamera Obskura* (1932, published in the U.S. in an altered version as *Laughter in the Dark,* 1938), and *Invitation to a Beheading* (1935, English, 1964). In 1940 he emigrated to the U.S., becoming a citizen in 1945. He taught at Stanford (1940–41), was a lecturer and professor of literature at Wellesley (1941–48), a professor of Russian literature at Cornell (1948–59), and a visiting lecturer at Harvard (1952). His novels written in English include *Bend Sinister* (1947), *Lolita* (1955), the controversial best seller which deals with the love of a middle-aged European man for a 12-year-old American girl, and *Pale Fire* (1962), which is considered to be the English work in which his intricate structural effects and verbal displays are at their peak. Although some have described him as a comic novelist, since his works display a magnificent wit and contain elaborate jokes and puns, his novels ultimately deal with a contemporary sense of loss and of society's disintegration, revealing a penetrating cultural and political awareness. Among his numerous other works are: *Nikolai Gogol* (1944), a critical evaluation; *Conclusive Evidence: A Memoir* (1950) and *Speak on, Memory* (1967), autobiographical works; *Look Back at the Harlequins* (1974), a mock autobiography. He has produced poetry (*Poems,* 1959), short stories, and translated Pushkin. A noted lepidopterist, he was a research fellow at Harvard's Museum of Comparative Zoology (1942–48).

Nader, Ralph (b. Winsted, Conn., 27 Feb. 1934–), social reformer, received his A.B. *magna cum laude* from Princeton (1955) and his LL.B. with distinction from Harvard Law School (1958), and was admitted to the Connecticut bar (1958). His book *Unsafe at Any Speed* (1965) portrayed the automobile industry as placing style, horsepower, comfort, and sales over safety, and attacked industry and government secrecy. Nader argued that additional safety features could save lives lost not by the "first collision" but immediately thereafter as victims collided with parts of their car or were thrown from it. Revelations (Mar. 1966) of industry surveillance and harassment of Nader brought Nader, his book, and viewpoint prominently to the fore. The National Traffic and Motor Vehicle Safety Act of 1966 (9 Sept.) is considered to be his achievement. As consumer advocate, Nader investigated health conditions in the coal industry, severely criticizing the Bureau of Mines (1968). His campaign led to legislation on matters as removed from one another as gas pipelines and the meat industry. Establishing the Center for the Study of Responsive Law (1969) with 5 full-time lawyers and 100 students hired for the summer, he inspired his "Nader's Raiders" in their investigations of the FTC, ICC, CAB, FDA, and the pesticide division of the Agriculture Department. He also organized the Public Interest Research Group, the Center for Auto Safety, Professionals for Auto Safety, and the Project for Corporate Responsibility. His study groups have produced works on old-age homes and water pollution. The Congress Project (1971–72) produced profiles of over 475 congressmen, encompassing their voting records, campaign financing, and personal behavior. Known for honesty, candor, incredible energy, and asceticism, Nader, with his modern brand of muckraking, has been the spearhead of consumer protection in the 1960s and 1970s.

Nast, Thomas (b. Landau, Bavaria, 27 Sept. 1840; d. Guayaquil, Ecuador, 7 Dec. 1902), artist and cartoonist, came to New York in 1846, studied art under Theodore Kaufman and at the National Academy of Design, and at 15 became draftsman for *Frank Leslie's Illustrated Weekly*. He was sent to London by the New York *Illustrated News* (1860), and accompanied Garibaldi as artist of the *Illustrated London News* and *Le Monde Illustré* (Paris). Returning to New York (1861), he became a staff artist of *Harper's Weekly*, with war drawings (*Emancipation*, 24 Jan. 1863; *Compromise with the South*, 3 Sept. 1864), which influenced public opinion. His fame rests largely on his dramatic cartoons exposing the Tweed Ring in New York City (1869–72), notably *Let Us Prey* and *Tiger Loose*. His adaptation of the tiger to represent Tammany proved a potent weapon of municipal reform. He also invented the elephant for the Republican party and popularized the donkey for the Democrats. The line and texture of his bold, graphic style lost none of their bite in being engraved in wood.

Nevelson, Louise (b. Kiev, Russia, 23 Sept. 1900–), sculptor. Nevelson emigrated to the U.S. (1905). From 1928–30 she studied at the Art Students League, New York City, then spent a year in Munich studying with the abstract painter Hans Hoffman. From 1932–33 she was an assistant to the Mexican muralist Diego Rivera. As part of a WPA project, Nevelson taught art at the Educational Alliance School of Art, New York (1937). She first exhibited her sculpture at a group show at the Brooklyn Museum (1935) and at a 1-man show in New York City (1940). Her works of the 1930s and 40s reflected the influences of cubism and Picasso, as well as Aztec, Mayan, and African art. Nevelson is most famous for her wood assemblages, bits of wood put together in an abstract form and usually painted in solid black, gold, or white. The earliest such assemblages, created in the 1940s, include *Circus, Menagerie,* and *Crowded Outside.* But it was not until the 1950s, after her series of exhibitions at the Grand Central Moderns Gallery (New York), that her wood assemblages first achieved fame. One of her most notable wood constructions of this period was *Sky Cathedral,* shown at the Albright-Knox Art Gallery, Buffalo, N.Y. (1958) and purchased by the Museum of Modern Art. Nevelson has also worked with terra cotta, stone, bronze, plaster, aluminum, and most recently, steel. In 1959 she won the grand prize of the New York Coliseum's "Art U.S.A.," and in 1960 the Logan Award of the Art Institute of Chicago. Since the 1960s Nevelson's style has become simpler and sparer, as reflected in her 1974 2-floor exhibit of collages, constructions, and etchings at the Pace Gallery, New York. A major retrospective took place at the Whitney Museum (Mar.–Apr. 1967).

Nevins, Allan (b. Camp Point, Ill., 20 May 1890; d. Menlo Park, Calif., 5 Mar. 1971), historian and journalist, author of more than 50 books, editor of another 175, and innumerable articles. Son of a farmer with a large library, Nevins early became interested in books. Graduating Phi Beta Kappa from the Univ. of Illinois (1912), he went on to receive his M.A. in English (1913). Up until 1930 he pursued a career as a journalist, working as an editor at various times on the *Nation,* the *New York Evening Post,* the *Herald,* the *Sun,* and the *World.* His first history books were written during this period, including his earliest work, *Life of Robert Rogers,* about a colonial frontiersman, written while he was still an undergraduate (1913), and the well-known *The Emergence of Modern Amer-*

ica (1927). Nevins began his second career in 1927 when he accepted an appointment as professor of history at Cornell. A year later he became associate professor history at Columbia, and in 1931 De Witt Clinton Professor of History. During his tenure at Columbia (1928–58) he was known as both a dedicated teacher and scholar. Although he never received a doctorate, he actively supported his Ph.D. candidates, backing them up during their oral examinations and dissertation defenses. An indefatigable worker, his writings were characterized by intense research, objectivity, imagination, engaging style, and the ability to make history come alive. Challenging Charles A. Beard's interpretation of American history, Nevins questioned whether the politics of American leaders had been influenced by economic self-interest. Nevins believed that America's economic leaders must be treated more objectively by historians, and appreciated for their contributions to American industrialization which allowed the U.S. to successfully engage in 2 world wars. He wrote numerous biographies of entrepreneurs, including *John D. Rockefeller: The Heroic Age of Enterprise* (1940) and *Ford: The Times, The Man, The Company* (with Frank E. Hill, 1954). He was awarded the Pulitzer prize in biography for his *Grover Cleveland* (1932) and a 2d time for *Hamilton Fish* (1938). During the last 30 years of his life, Nevins completed a 6-vol. definitive study of the U.S. through the Civil War, entitled *The Ordeal of the Union* (1947, 1952, the last 2 vols. posthumously). He pioneered tape-recorded interviews, founding Columbia University's Oral History Collection (1948). He was also one of the founders of *American Heritage,* a monthly magazine of popular history, and served as chairman of the Civil War Centennial Commission (1961).

Niebuhr, Reinhold (b. Wright City, Mo., 21 June 1892; d. Stockbridge, Mass., 1 June 1971), clergyman and theologian. He was graduated from the Yale Divinity School (B.D., 1914; A.M., 1915), was ordained (1915) as a minister in the Evangelical Synod of North America, and served as a pastor at Detroit (1915–28). In 1928 he became assistant professor of the philosophy of religion at the Union Theological Seminary, New York, where he was professor of applied Christianity (1930–60). Primarily concerned with social ethics and politically oriented, Niebuhr's theology combined the political liberalism of the Social Gospel with Biblical theology, stressing original sin and God's judgment. It differs from Continental Neo-orthodoxy (Karl Barth and Emil Brunner) in its refusal to consider man as having lost contact with God. Among his works were *Does Civilization Need Religion?* (1927), *Moral Man and Immoral Society* (1932), *Reflections on the End of an Era* (1934), *An Interpretation of Christian Ethics* (1935), *Beyond Tragedy* (1937), *Christianity and Power Politics* (1940), *The Nature and Destiny of Man* (1941–43), *Faith and History* (1949), and *The Irony of American History* (1952), *Faith and Politics* (1968). He was editor of *Christianity in Crisis* (1941–66).

Nimitz, Chester William (b. Fredericksburg, Tex., 24 Feb. 1885; d. San Francisco, 20 Feb. 1966), naval officer, was graduated from the U.S. Naval Academy (1905), and served as chief of staff to the commander of the U.S. Atlantic submarine fleet during World War I. In 1939 he was made chief of the Bureau of Navigation with the rank of rear admiral. After the Pearl Harbor attack he took over command of the Pacific Fleet from Admiral Husband E. Kimmel. Commander of the Pacific Fleet and the Pacific Ocean Areas with the rank of admiral, his initial strategy was to defend the Hawaiian approaches and the lines of mainland communication. Given much of the credit for the strategy of "island hopping," he began his offensive with the amphibious landing on Guadalcanal (7 Aug. 1942) and the decisive victory in the naval Battle of Guadalcanal (12–15 Nov.). In 1943 he pursued his offensive aimed at seizing the Solomons, the Gilberts and Marshalls, and the Bonin Islands to come within effective bombing distance of Japan. At the time of Japan's surrender he commanded 6,256 ships and 4,847 combat aircraft, the largest fighting fleet in history. Nimitz accepted the Japanese surrender in Tokyo Bay. He served as U.S. Chief of Naval Operations (1945–47). He headed (1949) the UN mediation commission in the dispute over Kashmir. He edited *Sea Power, A Naval History* (with E. B. Potter, 1960).

Nixon, Richard Milhous (b. Yorba Linda, Calif., 9 Jan. 1913–), 37th president of the U.S., graduated from Whittier College (A.B. 1934) and Duke Law School (LL.B. 1937), having been elected student body president of both schools. He practiced law in Whittier, Calif. (1937–42) and spent 6 months with the Office of Price Administration (1942) before service in the navy (1942–46) where he attained the rank of lieutenant commander. Elected to the 80th Congress, he served 2 terms as a representative (1947–51). A member of the House Un-American Activities Committee, he achieved national prominence for spearheading the investigation of Alger Hiss (1948–49). After a bitter election contest with Rep. Helen Gahagan Douglas, he was elected U.S. senator from California (1950). Reaching the Senate a month ahead of schedule, having been chosen to fill a vacancy, he served until 1953. As vice-president (1953–61), he served with restraint during the 3 major disabling illnesses of President Eisenhower (heart attack, 1955; ileitis operation, 1956; stroke, 1957). Traveling to 56 countries while vice-president, his unpopular reception in Latin America (1968) demonstrated the weaknesses of U.S.–Latin-American policies. On a goodwill trip to the U.S.S.R. (1959) to open the American National Exhibition, he engaged in an extemporaneous debate with Premier Nikita Khrushchev over merits of the rural economic systems. Nominated for the presidency in 1960 by the Republican party, he was defeated by John F. Kennedy in one of the closest elections of the century. Defeated by Pat Brown for the governorship of California (1962), he moved to New York City, where he practiced law (1963–68). Maintaining his activities in the Republican party by campaigning for Sen. Barry Goldwater (1964) and congressional candidates (1964, 1966), he was nominated again for the presidency on the 1st ballot and won a close election over Hubert H. Humphrey and George C. Wallace (1968). His 1st term as president was marked by major foreign initiatives, including the change of direction of U.S. policy toward mainland China, dramatically demonstrated by his trip there (21–28 Feb. 1972). Although he won an overwhelming reelection victory (1972), his 2d term was overshadowed by the Watergate scandals. Leading members of his staff and cabinet were indicted for offenses connected with covering up the Watergate break-in. Nixon cited the doctrine of executive privilege and refused to turn over to the special prosecutor's office, the courts, and the House Judiciary Committee, transcripts or tapes of White House conversations. After the Supreme Court ordered Nixon to turn over tapes to the lower courts, and the House Judiciary Committee voted 3 articles of impeachment, Nixon released transcripts which indicated that

he had known of the Watergate coverup 9 months earlier than previously admitted and had ordered the FBI to stop its investigation. Faced with the loss of almost all support in Congress and with the imminence of impeachment and conviction, Nixon resigned on 9 Aug. 1974. He received a full and complete pardon from his successor, Gerald R. Ford, on 8 Sept. 1974. He is the author of *Six Crises* (1962).

Noguchi, Isamu (b. Los Angeles, 7 Nov. 1904–), sculptor, studied for 2 years at Columbia as a premedical student, then switched to art, serving an apprenticeship in sculpture to Gutzom Borglum, then in Paris (1927–28) as assistant to Constantin Brancusi, an abstract sculptor, where he studied the works of Picasso and the constructionists. Experimenting with constructions, he used grooved joints held together by gravity or tension, and exhibited his creations in New York (1929). In 1930 he traveled to Peking, making brush and wash drawings, and then to Japan, studying Japanese traditional techniques, which have found expression in his later works in a feeling for landscapes and natural materials. After his model "Play Mountain" (1933), featuring sculptured earth, was rejected by the New York City Parks Department, he secured big commissions, including a 65-ft.-long relief sculpture in colored cement (Mercado Rodriguez, Mexico City, 1936) and a 10-ton stainless steel work for the façade of the Associate Press Bldg. in Rockefeller Center, New York (1938). During these years he also designed costumes and 20 "stagesets" for Martha Graham, creating a series of planes for dancers to move through. Widely employed as an interior designer of leading buildings, he is renowned as well for his courtyards and gardens (Yale Library, Chase Manhattan Plaza) and for his lamps and furniture. Basically a stone carver, he combines the abstract with a deep respect for nature. Among his best known creations is the 29-ft.-high bright red cube with a hole on one side standing in front of the Marine Midland Grace Trust Co. in New York. Widely exhibited internationally, Noguchi had a retrospective at the Whitney Museum (1968).

Norris, George William (b. Sandusky, Ohio, 11 July 1861; d. McCook, Neb., 2 Sept. 1944), statesman, was graduated in law (1882) from Northern Indiana Normal School (now Valparaiso Univ.), moved to Beaver City, Neb. (1885), and served 3 terms as prosecuting attorney of Furnas Co. and then as a district judge (1895–1902). As congressman (1903–18), he was a leader in the revolt against Speaker Cannon (1910). As a progressive Republican he supported the Bull Moose movement (1912), opposed U.S. entry into World War I as well as participation in the League of Nations, but endorsed U.S. participation in World War II. U.S. senator from Nebraska (1913–43), he was sponsor of the Norris-La Guardia Anti-injunction Act (1932) and of the 20th (Lame Duck) Amendment (1933); his most notable service was his fight for federal water power regulation and for public ownership and operation of hydroelectric plants. In 1928 he secured passage of a bill providing for government operation of the dam at Muscle Shoals, but it was vetoed by Coolidge. Another bill (1931) was vetoed by Hoover. The Tennessee Valley Authority (TVA) constituted the culmination of his efforts. Norris Dam (near Knoxville) was named in his honor.

Ochs, Adolph Simon (b. Cincinnati, Ohio, 12 Mar. 1858; d. Chattanooga, Tenn., 8 Apr. 1935), newspaper publisher. He received most of his schooling from his parents and during his boyhood served his apprenticeship in the newspaper business on the Knoxville (Tenn.) *Chronicle*. In 1878 he purchased the controlling interest in the Chattanooga *Times*, then on the brink of failure, and instituted a policy of full, accurate, and reliable reporting that characterized his subsequent career (1896–1935) as publisher of *The New York Times*. Taking over the *Times* when it was on the verge of bankruptcy, Ochs reorganized the newspaper according to the canons of responsible journalism in a day when the influence of the sensational press in New York City was at its height. By 1900 he had made the *Times* a profitable venture, and under his guidance it became known as the "newspaper of record" because of its extensive coverage of public events and its intelligent specialized reporting. His view of the responsibility of a free press is expressed in the motto he selected for the *Times*: "All the news that's fit to print."

Oglethorpe, James Edward (b. London, England, 1 June 1696; d. Cranham Hall, Essex, England, 1 July 1785), founder of the colony of Georgia. Oglethorpe studied at Eton and Corpus Christi College, Oxford. He held an army commission (1713–15) and in 1717 served as an aide-de-camp to Prince Eugene of Savoy in his campaign against the Turks. Elected to the House of Commons (1722) he served as the representative of Haslemere for 32 years. As chairman of Parliament's committee on prison reform he became concerned about the plight of the debtor classes. In his pamphlet *The Sailor's Advocate* (1728) he exposed the evils of impressment. Persuaded by Oglethorpe's arguments that a colony should be established as a refuge for imprisoned debtors and as a buffer against Spanish, French, or Indian encroachment on South Carolina, Parliament granted (1732) Oglethorpe and 19 associates a charter, to expire in 21 years, making them trustees of the colony of Georgia. With 116 carefully selected colonists, he reached Charleston, S.C. and went on to found (12 Feb. 1733) Savannah. Oglethorpe encouraged the immigration of Protestants being persecuted on the European continent and proved a benefactor to the German Lutherans, Moravians, Scotch Highland Presbyterians, and Jews who came. He developed a vigorous defense program, building forts and establishing a system of military training. In 1738 he persuaded Prime Minister Robert Walpole to send him a regiment of 700 men. After England declared war on Spain (1739), Oglethorpe led an unsuccessful expedition against St. Augustine (1740). When the Spanish attacked Frederica, Georgia's southern outpost, Oglethorpe defeated them in the Battle of Bloody Marsh (9 June 1742), thereby assuring Georgia's survival. A second unsuccessful assault on St. Augustine (1743) and increasing reports from malcontents led to his recall to England. Charges brought against him were dropped but he never returned to Georgia. Promoted a general (1765), Oglethorpe was offered the command of the British army in America (1775), but declined the position because he would not have had the power of concession and conciliation.

Olmsted, Frederick Law (b. Hartford, Conn., 26 Apr. 1822; d. Waverly, Mass., 28 Aug. 1903), landscape architect and author. He attended Yale (1842–43) and from 1847 to 1857 engaged in experimental farming in Connecticut and Staten Island. In 1850 he made an overseas tour, recording his observations in *The Walks and Talks of an American Farmer in England* (1852). His 3 journeys in the South (1852 *et seq.*) were described in as many volumes, comprising one of the most valuable factual records of Southern social and economic life on the eve of the Civil War: *A Journey in the Seaboard Slave States* (1856), *A Journey Through Texas* (1857), and *A Journey in the Back Country* (1860), all 3 of which were condensed in *The Cotton Kingdom* (2 vols., 1861). In 1857 he was appointed superintendent of Central Park, New York City, and in 1858, in collaboration with Calvert Vaux (1824–95), he won the prize competition for its new design. In 1858 he was named chief architect of Central Park, a pioneer enterprise of American municipal planning. In numerous commissions, most of them executed between 1865 and 1895, Olmsted laid the foundations of American landscape architecture and made the public park a significant factor in urban life. Among his works are Prospect Park, Brooklyn; Riverside Park, New York; the grounds of the national Capitol, Washington, D.C.; the park systems of Boston, Hartford, and Louisville; Mount Royal Park, Montreal; the grounds of the World's Fair (1893) at Chicago; Roland Park, Baltimore; Belle Isle Park, Detroit; and the grounds of Stanford Univ. and the Univ. of California.

O'Neill, Eugene Gladstone (b. New York City, 16 Oct. 1888; d. Boston, Mass., 27 Nov. 1953), dramatist. The son of the actor James O'Neill, he attended Princeton (1906) and, after a period of travel and adventure, was a student (1914–15) in the 47 Workshop of George Pierce Baker at Harvard. He became associated (1916) with the Provincetown Players, who produced (1916–20) 10 of his 1-act plays, including *Bound East for Cardiff* and *The Moon of the Caribbees*. With the Broadway production of *Beyond the Horizon* (1920), which was awarded the Pulitzer prize, O'Neill took his place as the foremost American dramatist of his day. He also won the Pulitzer prize for

Anna Christie (1921) and *Strange Inter-lude* (1928), both of which were later produced as motion pictures, and in 1936 was awarded the Nobel prize in litera-ture. A resourceful and inventive drama-tist, whose work passed through several stages of development including natural-ism, expressionism, symbolism, romanti-cism, and a combination of Greek tragedy and Freudian psychology, O'Neill au-thored 45 published plays, including *The Emperor Jones* (1920), *Diff'rent* (1921), *The Hairy Ape* (1922), *All God's Chillun Got Wings* (1924), *De-sire Under the Elms* (1924), *The Great God Brown* (1926), *Lazarus Laughed* (1927), *Marco Millions* (1928), *Mourn-ing Becomes Electra* (1931), *Ah, Wilder-ness!* (1933), and *The Iceman Cometh* (1946). Unproduced before his death were *A Moon for the Misbegotten* (pub. 1952), *A Touch of the Poet* (1957), and *Long Day's Journey into Night* (1956), Pulitzer prize play, 1957. These late plays are the finest examples of the great drama O'Neil created from the stuff of his tortured spirit.

Oppenheimer, J. Robert (b. New York City, 22 Apr. 1904; d. Princeton, N.J., 18 Feb. 1967), physicist. He was gradu-ated *summa cum laude* from Harvard (A.B., 1925), studied briefly at the Cav-endish Laboratories in Cambridge under Lord Rutherford (1925–26) and at Göt-tingen (Ph.D., 1927) under Max Born. He was a National Research Fellow (1927–28) at Harvard and at the Cali-fornia Institute of Technology and continued postdoctoral studies as Inter-national Education Board Fellow (1928–29) at the Univ. of Leyden and the Technische Hochschule at Zürich. In 1929 he joined the physics faculties at both the Univ. of California, Berkeley, and the California Institute of Technol-ogy (1929–47), where he distinguished himself as a superb teacher. As a scholar

he made notable contributions to quan-tum theory (1926–27 with Max Born; 1935 with Melba Phillips), to the under-standing of cosmic rays, of fundamental particles, and did work which later led others to explain quasars (1938–39 with George M. Volkoff and others). Because of his grasp of the entire range of nuclear and quantum physics he was appointed director of the Los Alamos Science Labo-ratory (1942), where he gathered to-gether about 4,000 scientists and coordinated the effort to produce an atomic bomb by 1945. The successful effort was undoubtedly due in large measure to his administrative and diplo-matic skills. For this he has been named the "father of the atomic bomb." In 1945 he resigned his position as director at Los Alamos but served as chairman of the General Advisory Committee of the Atomic Energy Commission (1947–52). He was the principal author of the Acheson-Lilienthal Report and of the Baruch Plan, proposals for international control of atomic energy. He also served on President Eisenhower's Scientific Ad-visory Committee and as an adviser to the Departments of State and Defense, and to the National Security Council. In 1947 he became director of the Institute for Advanced Study at Princeton, a posi-tion he held until his resignation in 1966. Because of his earlier associations with left-wing groups, his misrepresenta-tion of a 1943 conversation with a friend regarding leakage of secret information to the U.S.S.R., and his cautious ap-proach to the development of a hydrogen bomb, Oppenheimer became the subject of a security hearing in 1954. There-after, the Atomic Energy Commission permanently denied him security clear-ance (June 1954), although in 1963 it awarded him the prestigious Fermi prize for his "outstanding contributions to theo-retical physics and his scientific and ad-ministrative leadership." In addition to several scientific papers, he was the author of *Science and the Common Understanding* (1954), *The Open Mind* (1955), and *Some Reflections on Science and Culture* (1960).

Otis, Elisha Graves (b. Halifax, Vt., 3 Aug. 1811; d. Yonkers, N.Y., 9 Apr. 1861), inventor and manufacturer. Educated in public school, Otis worked in construction (1830–35), the hauling business (1835–38), and owned a shop which manufactured carriages and wagons (1838–45). While operating a machine shop (1845–48) Otis built his first invention, a turbine waterwheel. In 1852, as supervisor of the construction of a bedstead factory in Yonkers, he invented a number of automatic safety devices for the installed elevator, preventing it from falling when rope or chain broke. Otis started manufacturing freight elevators. His business increased after his device was publicly exhibited at the Crystal Palace Exposition in New York City (1854). The first permanent passenger elevators were installed in the Haughwout Department Store (1857) and in the Fifth Avenue Hotel (1859). Otis' safety devices significantly increased the value of real estate by making it possible to reach towering heights by elevator and in fact underpinned the skyscraper. Demand for Otis and Sons elevators increased even further with the invention of the steam-run elevator (1861). Otis also invented railroad car trucks and brakes (1852), a steam plow (1857), a rotary oven for bread (1858), and an automatic wood-turning machine.

Otis, James (b. West Barnstable, Mass., 5 Feb. 1725; d. Andover, Mass., 23 May 1783), pre-Revolutionary leader, was admitted to the Plymouth Co. bar (1748), and 2 years later moved to Boston. He resigned his office as king's advocate general of the vice-admiralty court to appear on behalf of a group of Boston merchants to oppose (1761) as unconstitutional the issuance by the superior court of writs of assistance—general search warrants to aid the enforcement of the Sugar Act of 1733. Writing years later, John Adams asserted: "Then and there the child Independence was born." Although the court issued the writs, Otis took the battle to the general court, to which he was elected that year. Chief target of Otis was Thomas Hutchinson (*q.v.*), whose appointment as chief justice in place of Otis's father, James, senior, an active candidate, aroused the enmity of father and son. A vigorous pamphleteer, he expounded his constitutional views in *A Vindication of the Conduct of the House of Representatives* (1762) and most notably in *The Rights of the British Colonies Asserted and Proved* (1764). Participating in the Stamp Act Congress (1765), which had been summoned at his suggestion, he advocated colonial representation in Parliament and conceded the supremacy of Parliament (*A Vindication of the British Colonies*, 1765). By the time of the Townshend Acts he had become even more moderate in his political views, although he was increasingly abusive and unbalanced in personal behavior and was caned in a coffeehouse brawl by John Robinson, a customs officer. In 1771 his younger brother Samuel A. Otis was appointed his guardian, and he took no part in the Revolution. His death was dramatic; he was struck down by lightning in the Isaac Osgood farmhouse.

Paine, Thomas (b. Thetford, Norfolk, England, 29 Jan. 1737; d. New York City, 8 June 1809), Revolutionary propagandist. The son of a Quaker corsetmaker, he was engaged in a wide variety of occupations before coming to America in 1774. He settled at Philadelphia, where he contributed to the *Pennsylvania*

Magazine and wrote *Common Sense,* an anonymous pamphlet published on 9 Jan. 1776. In *Common Sense,* reputed to have sold 120,000 copies in 3 months and to have attained a total sale of 500,000, Paine advocated the immediate declaration of independence on both practical and ideological grounds. Joining the Revolutionary army, he took part in the retreat across New Jersey, writing at Newark the first of his *Crisis* papers (1776–83), of which the opening passage was: "These are the times that try men's souls. The summer soldier and the sunshine patriot will, in this crisis, shrink from the service of their country." The pamphlet, ordered read to the troops in the Revolutionary encampments, resolved by its eloquent patriotism the hesitation of many in and out of the army. In subsequent *Crisis* papers Paine favored a strong federal union and called for effective fiscal measures. He served (1777–79) as secretary to the committee on foreign affairs of the Continental Congress, and in 1779 was named clerk of the Pennsylvania assembly. After peace was concluded with Great Britain, he lived at New York and at Bordentown, N.J., until 1787, when he went to France and England. In *The Rights of Man* (1791–92), Paine defended republican government and the practical measures of the early phases of the French Revolution in reply to Edmund Burke's *Reflections on the French Revolution* (1790). *The Rights of Man,* which contained some seditious passages, was suppressed by the British government, and Paine, at that time in France, was tried for treason and was outlawed (1792). Made a citizen by the French Assembly (1792), Paine was elected to the Convention. He associated himself with the Girondist party; with the fall of the Girondins, he was stripped of his French citizenship and imprisoned (Dec. 1793). He remained in jail until Nov. 1794, when he was released through the

intervention of the U.S. minister, James Monroe. While in jail he began work on *The Age of Reason* (1794–96), a deistic work, beginning: "I believe in one God, and no more; and I hope for happiness beyond this life." In his closing years, spent in New Jersey and New York, Paine lived in poverty and obscurity. He was buried on his farm in New Rochelle, N.Y.; in 1819 William Cobbett exhumed the remains and took them to England.

Parker, Theodore (b. Lexington, Mass., 24 Aug. 1810; d. Florence, Italy, 10 May 1860), clergyman, theologian, and author, graduated (1836) from the Harvard Divinity School, was ordained (1837) at the West Roxbury (Mass.) Church, and during the course of the Unitarian controversy supported the radical wing, enunciating his position in his sermon on "The Transient and Permanent in Christianity" (1841), which endorsed the views set forth by Emerson in the "Divinity School Address" (1838). His interpretation of Christianity as the high point of evolutionary progress, and his call for a new theology based on the immanence of God in human experience and in nature, appeared in *A Discourse of Matters Pertaining to Religion* (1842). His Transcendentalist views brought him into open conflict with the orthodox Unitarians and with the liberal clergy of the Boston Association of Ministers, and led to his resignation from the West Roxbury pulpit (1852) and to his installation as minister of the newly created 28th Congregational Society of Boston. An erudite scholar, Parker was also active in humanitarian and reform movements. He wrote *A Letter to the People of the United States Touching the Matter of Slavery* (1848), aided in the escape of fugitive slaves, and played a notable role in the defense of Anthony Burns (1854). He supported the New England Emigrant Aid Society and was a member of a secret committee that abetted John Brown's raid on Harpers Ferry (1859). His writings were collected in *Theodore Parker's Works* (14 vols., 1863–70).

Parkman, Francis (b. Boston, Mass., 16 Sept. 1823; d. Jamaica Plain, Mass., 8 Nov. 1893), historian. He was graduated from Harvard (1844), received the degree of LL.B. (1846) from the Harvard Law School, and in 1846 made the journey to the Far West which he recorded in *The California and Oregon Trail* (1849; commonly called *The Oregon Trail*). The strenuous expedition taxed his already impaired health and, soon after returning from the West, he suffered a physical and nervous breakdown. Although he was for the rest of his life a semi-invalid suffering from weak eyesight bordering on blindness and from a nervous disorder that prevented unbroken concentration, Parkman eventually won a place as the leading American historian of his time. His historical series dealing with the struggle of England and France for the domination of North America is based on a scholarly use of original sources, and is marked by a sweeping narrative power and vivid descriptive passages dealing with life in the primitive wilderness. In order of their publication, the volumes of his series are *History of the Conspiracy of Pontiac* (1851), *Pioneers of France in the New World* (1865), *The Jesuits in North America* (1867), *The Discovery of the Great West* (1869), *The Old Régime in Canada* (1874), *Count Frontenac and New France under Louis XIV* (1877), *Montcalm and Wolfe* (2 vols., 1884), and *A Half-Century of Conflict* (2 vols., 1892).

Parsons, Talcott (b. Colorado Springs, Colo., 13 Dec. 1902–   ), sociologist. He graduated from Amherst College (A.B., 1924), studied at the London School of Economics (1924–25), where he was deeply influenced by Bronislaw Malinowski, and received his Ph.D. from the Univ. of Heidelberg (1927). At Harvard he taught economics (1927–31) and sociology (1931–73 retirement), and helped to establish the Department of Social Relations and served as its chairman, 1946–56. In the 1930s he changed the focus of American sociology by introducing and emphasizing the broad theoretical works of Max Weber and Emile Durkheim. A structural functionalist in approach, he pioneered in constructing a complex general theory of society. Basic to his theory is the concept that a social system's structure is governed by the way it meets 4 basic needs: goal-attainment, adaptation, integration, and pattern maintenance. He is the author of numerous books, articles, and translations, including *The Structure of Social Action* (1937), *The Social System* (1951), and *Essays in Sociological Theory* (1947, 1954).

Patton, George Smith, Jr. (b. San Gabriel, Calif., 11 Nov. 1885; d. Heidelberg, Germany, 21 Dec. 1945), soldier. Upon graduation from the U.S. Military Academy (1909), he was commissioned a 2d lieutenant in the cavalry. After taking part in Gen. John J. Pershing's expedition into Mexico (1916), he sailed to France (May 1917) as a member of Pershing's staff. He organized and directed the American Tank Center at Langues and commanded a tank brigade at St. Mihiel and Meuse-Argonne. After World War I he promoted the new tank warfare methods and commanded the 304th Tank Brigade at Camp Meade, Md., before returning to cavalry duty. He served in the Washington, D.C. office of the Chief of Cavalry (1928–31), graduated from the Army War College (1932), and served with the 3d Cavalry at Ft. Meyer, Va. (1932–35). He became brigade commander (1940) and then commanding officer (1941) of the 2d Armored Division, which became known as the toughest outfit of the army. Promoted to commanding general of the 1st Armored Corps, he organized the Desert Training Center at Indio, Calif. Under Gen. Eisenhower he was in charge of the Task Force troops in the North African campaign (1942). Then he commanded the 7th Army in the successful invasion of Sicily and the rapid capture of Palermo (1943). During the Sicilian campaign a widely publicized incident— Patton had slapped a hospitalized soldier suffering from battle fatigue whom he suspected of malingering—brought Patton a reprimand from Gen. Eisenhower, cost him his command, and delayed his promotion to the permanent rank of major general until Aug. 1944. In the summer of 1944 he prepared the 3d Army for the surprise invasion of Normandy. His brilliant sweep across the base of the Breton Peninsula, liberation of Metz (3 Oct.–22 Nov. 1944), breaking of the "Bulge" (Dec. 1944–Jan. 1945), destruction of the Nazi forces in the Saar-Palatinate region, and surprise crossing of the Rhine (22 Mar. 1945) insured his place as one of the great tactical commanders. Relieved of his command of the 3d Army (2 Oct. 1945) for putting too little emphasis on denazification, he was assigned command of the 15th Army, a paper organization devoted to the study of tactical lessons to be learned from the war. He died from injuries suffered in an automobile accident.

Pauling, Linus Carl (b. Portland, Ore., 28 Feb. 1901–   ), chemist, received his B.S. from Oregon State College (1922) and his Ph.D. from the California Institute of Technology (1925), where from 1931 to 1964 he was professor of chemistry and director of the Gates and Crellin laboratories (1937–58). Now professor of chemistry at Stanford Univ., he is renowned for his theory of resonance in the molecular structure of organic chemicals, leading to a better understanding of certain properties of the carbon compounds, especially the aromatics, and for his contributions to immunology, notably on the nature of serological reactions and the molecular structure of antitoxins. With Campbell and Pressman he produced synthetic antibodies. He has also done important work in applying the quantum theory to chemistry, in crystal structure, and in the theory of electrolytes. He was awarded the Nobel prize in chemistry in 1954 for discoveries of forces holding proteins and molecules together, and became the first man to win a 2d complete Nobel award by receiving the prize for peace (1962, awarded 1963) for his intense campaign against nuclear testing. He has stirred controversy with his theory that large doses of vitamin C prevent or ameliorate the common cold.

Peale, Charles Willson (b. Queen Anne Co., Md., 15 Apr. 1741; d. Phila., 22 Feb. 1827), portrait painter, naturalist, was apprenticed as a saddler at 13. He began portrait painting at 20, studying with John Hesselius, then in Boston under Copley (*q.v.*) and in London (1767) in Benjamin West's studio. Lieutenant in the Philadelphia militia, he fought at Trenton, Princeton, and Germantown, and served 1 term (beg. 1779) in the Pennsylvania assembly. A naturalist as well as a painter, he opened (1802) Peale's Museum of Natural History Objects and Portraits (later the Philadelphia Museum) and founded (1805) the Pennsylvania Academy of Fine Arts. Renowned as the painter of Washington, he painted the first portrait of the Virginian in 1772, 7 additional ones from sittings, and a total of 60 in all. Of all Washington's portraits, Peale's are the most faithful and uncompromising. He painted other leading patriots, faithfully reproducing their dress and manner, but adding little character interpretation. He also painted *Christ Healing the Sick at the Pool of Bethesda* (1822). His sons, Raphael, Rembrandt, Titian, and Rubens, were painters and naturalists like their father.

Peary, Robert Edwin (b. Cresson, Pa., 6 May 1856; d. Washington, D.C., 20 Feb. 1920), naval officer and Arctic explorer. Graduating from Bowdoin College (1877), he became a county surveyor, entered the U.S. Coast and Geodetic Survey in 1879, and was commissioned a lieutenant (1881) in the U.S. navy corps of civil engineers. While on leave in the summer of 1886, he explored the west coast of Greenland, at that time still unknown territory, reaching the ice cap 100 miles inland at an elevation of 7,500 feet above sea level. After further tours of duty in Nicaragua and along the Atlantic coast, he secured support from scientific and geographical societies in the U.S. for another Greenland expedition, which he made (1891–92) in the company of 5 others, including his wife. Peary made a 1,300-mile return journey to the northeast coast of Greenland from his base on the northwest coast, determining the insularity of Greenland and the northernmost limit of the ice cap. The party returned to the U.S. with valuable scientific data. He made further trips (1893–95, 1896) in order to bring to the U.S. large meteorites discovered by him. In 1898 he made a voyage on the *Windward*, a vessel presented by Lord Northcliffe; reaching the shores of the Polar Sea, he marked the region of Smith Sound and made his nearest approach yet to the North Pole, returning to the U.S. in 1902. His next trip (1905–06), made in the *Roosevelt*, saw him come within 174 miles of the North Pole,

the closest approach made up to that time. Starting out again in the *Roosevelt* (1908), Peary, with his Negro servant Matthew Henson, 4 Eskimos, and 40 dogs, reached the North Pole by sledge on 6 Apr. 1909. Shortly before Peary's ship put in at Labrador, where he announced his discovery, a similar claim was made by Dr. Frederick A. Cook, who asserted he had reached the North Pole on 21 Apr. 1908. The bitter controversy which followed was finally resolved by the scientific world in Peary's favor.

Peirce, Charles Sanders (b. Cambridge, Mass., 10 Sept. 1839; d. Milford, Pa., 19 Apr. 1914), philosopher, logician, and scientist. The son of the Harvard mathematician and astronomer Benjamin Peirce (1809–80), he was graduated from Harvard (1859), where he also received the degrees of M.A. (1862) and Sc.B. (1863). As a staff member (1861–91) of the U.S. Coast Survey, he was the first American delegate to the International Geodetic Congress (1877) and made researches in pendulum work and geodesy. During the same period he was an assistant (1869–72) at the Harvard Observatory; the astronomical observations made there by him between 1872 and 1875 provided the material for the only book by Peirce that appeared during his lifetime, *Photometric Researches* (1878). He lectured on science and logic at Harvard (1864, 1869, 1870), the Lowell Institute (1866, 1892, 1903), and Johns Hopkins (1879–84). His most significant contributions were made in formal logic and philosophy. He laid the basis for the logic of relations in mathematical logic, and made vital contributions to the theory of probability, induction, and the logic of scientific methodology. Among the concepts developed by him were tychism (theory of the reality of absolute chance) and synechism (doctrine of continuity). Peirce is best known as the creator (1877–78) of the principle of pragmatism, as well as the term itself. The latter first appeared in print in 1898, when William James used it. Peirce's views, however, differed from those of James, and Peirce later called his doctrine "pragmaticism" to stress the distinction. Most of his voluminous papers remained unpublished until after his death. His studies covered a wide range of subjects including religion, philology, psychology, meteorology, and chemistry.

Penn, William (b. London, England, 14 Oct. 1644; d. Ruscombe, England, 30 July 1718), statesman and religious leader. The son of Adm. Sir William Penn, conqueror of Jamaica, he attended Christ Church College, Oxford, where he was expelled because of his Puritan beliefs (1662). Studying and traveling on the continent and then studying law at Lincoln's Inn (1665), Penn became a staunch member of the Society of Friends while holding office in Ireland (1667). During the next 10 years his sermons and pamphlets praising the Quaker faith led to periods of imprisonment, although it was his acquittal from charges of street preaching which led to *Bushnell's Case* (1670), a landmark in British law protecting the verdict of a jury. His pamphlet *The Sandy Foundation Shaken* led to his incarceration in the Tower of London for 8 months (1669), when he wrote *No Crosses, No Crown*, a moral tract, as well as political tracts. A wealthy man for much of his life, Penn was part owner of East Jersey and trustee of the colony of West Jersey, formulating its *Laws, Concessions, and Agreements* (13 Mar. 1677), a libertarian and democratic document. The idea of a colony where religious and political freedom could flourish came to him during a trip to the Continent (1677) with George Fox,

Quaker leader. Penn was granted proprietorship of Pennsylvania ("Penn's Woods") by charter of Charles II (14 Mar. 1681) as repayment for money owed by the crown to Penn's father. He acquired the "Lower Counties" (Del.) by charter (24 Aug. 1682) from his friend, the Duke of York (later James II). He arrived 27 Oct. 1682, after the first colonists, and after he had drafted the first *Frame of Government* (5 May 1682), which bore the stamp of his Quaker faith, humanitarian views, imperial vision, and proprietary aspirations. Remaining in America (1682–84), he made a peace with the Indians (1682) which built goodwill for generations, and assisted in laying out the city of Philadelphia. He returned to the court of James II (16 Aug. 1684) to press boundary claims against Charles Calvert, 3d Lord Baltimore. After the exile of James II (1688) Penn was accused of treason and the crown held his colony (1692–94). After Penn resumed his governorship (1694), he returned to Pennsylvania (1699–1701) and formulated a new constitution, *Charter of Liberties* (1701), which permitted greater internal autonomy and provided for the voluntary withdrawal of Delaware counties (1704), which nonetheless were governed by the governor of Pennsylvania until 1776. The first plan for unifying the British colonies under one government was proposed by Penn to the Board of Trade (1697). Penn's last years were unhappy due to his dissolute and profligate son and difficulties in the colony. He authored *An Essay Towards the Present and Future Peace of Europe* (1693), a significant early plan for confederation, arbitration, and peace.

Perkins, Frances (b. Boston, Mass., 10 Apr. 1882; d. New York City, 14 May 1965), social reformer and political leader. She received an A.B. from Mt.

Holyoke (1902), taught school, and did social work before resuming her studies at the Wharton School of Finance and Commerce, the Univ. of Pennsylvania, and at Columbia, where she received her M.A. in sociology and economics (1910). Executive secretary of the Consumers' League of New York (1910–12) and of the New York Committee on Safety (1912–17), she became an authority on industrial hygiene and safety. After the Triangle Shirtwaist Factory fire (1911), in which 146 died, she lobbied for state legislation on factory safety standards and, as director of an investigation for the State Factory Commission (1912–13), promoted legislation on hours and wages. On the New York Commission of Safety she worked for industrial and labor legislation, and in her lobbying became acquainted with New York political leaders such as Alfred E. Smith and Franklin D. Roosevelt. Perkins was largely responsible for the state legislation which lowered the 54-hour work week for women to 48 hours. She served as a member of the New York State Industrial Board (1922–26) and as its chairman (1926), as a member of the State Industrial Commission (1919–29), and as its Industrial Commissioner (1929–33). She was President Roosevelt's Secretary of Labor (1933–45), the first woman to serve in a president's cabinet. She influenced passage of national legislation establishing a federal floor on wages and a ceiling on hours, unemployment compensation, the Civilian Conservation Corps, and limiting the employment of children under 16. The Department of Labor's activities were greatly expanded during her tenure as the administration's interest in the problems of labor was unprecedented. Directly responsible for implementing New Deal labor legislation, particularly the Fair Labor Standards Act, she was

often embroiled in controversy yet remained an efficient administrator. After resigning from the cabinet she became a member of the U.S. Civil Service Commission (1946–53). Thereafter she lectured on labor and industrial problems. She was the author of *The Roosevelt I Knew* (1946).

Perry, Matthew Calbraith (b. Newport, R.I., 10 Apr. 1794; d. New York City, 4 Mar. 1858), naval officer, brother of Oliver Hazard Perry. Entering the navy as a midshipman (1809), he served under his brother on the *Revenge* and took part in the War of 1812. After a varied tour of duty, he was named (1833) 2d officer of the New York navy yard, where he organized the U.S. Naval Lyceum, an educational body for naval officers, and served as its president. His plan for a naval apprentice system was adopted by Congress in 1837. Promoted to captain (1837), he took command of the *Fulton*, one of the first naval steam-powered vessels, aboard which he conducted (1839–40) the first American naval school of gun practice. He organized the first naval engineer corps and was appointed (1841) commandant of the New York navy yard. After another tour of duty that included the command (1843 *et seq.*) of the African Squadron for aiding in the suppression of the slave trade, service in the Mexican War (including command of the naval force that helped take Vera Cruz in 1847), and special duty at New York (1848–52) as superintendent of ocean mail steamship construction, he was chosen by President Fillmore to negotiate a treaty with Japan, which at that time barred all intercourse with the West. In command of the augmented Eastern Squadron, Perry anchored in Yedo Bay (8 July 1853), where he stayed 9 days; the Japanese officials, impressed with his show of naval strength, agreed to transmit Fillmore's proposals to high dignitaries. Perry sailed for China and returned to Yedo Bay (Feb. 1854), and concluded at Yokohama (31 Mar. 1854) a treaty that opened Japan to the Occidental nations. His official report is in *Narrative of the Expedition of an American Squadron to the China Seas and Japan* (3 vols., 1856).

Perry, Oliver Hazard (b. South Kingston, R.I., 20 Aug. 1785; d. along the Orinoco River, Venezuela, 23 Aug. 1819), naval officer, became a midshipman in the U.S. navy (1799), saw service in West Indian waters during the naval war with France, and was on tours of duty (1802–03, 1804–06) in the Mediterranean during the Tripolitan War. After the outbreak of the War of 1812, he was ordered (1813) to join Commodore Isaac Chauncey's force at Sackett's Harbor, N.Y., and was given command of the U.S. naval forces on Lake Erie. Perry went to Erie, Pa., where he spent the spring and summer constructing and equipping a fleet of 10 vessels, of which the largest were the *Lawrence* and the *Niagara*. The Battle of Lake Erie (10 Sept. 1813), in which Perry defeated the British fleet under Cmdr. Robert H. Barclay, was one of the decisive battles of the war. It gave the Americans control of Lake Erie and enabled Gen. William Henry Harrison (to whom Perry sent the message: "We have met the enemy and they are ours") to seize much of upper Canada. Perry was promoted to captain (1813), received the thanks of Congress (1814), and was acclaimed a national hero. He later took part in the operations against Detroit and in the Battle of the Thames. He commanded the *Java* on a Mediterranean tour (1815–16) and died of yellow fever after completing a diplomatic mission to the Venezuelan government.

Pershing, John Joseph (b. near Laclede, Linn Co., Mo., 13 Sept. 1860; d. Washington, D.C., 15 July 1948), soldier, commander of the A.E.F. in World War I, was graduated (1886) from the U.S. Military Academy, and served as a cavalry officer in operations (1886–90) against Indians in the Southwest and in South Dakota. He was a military instructor (1891–95) at the Univ. of Nebraska, from which he received the degree of LL.B. (1893), was an instructor in military tactics (1897–98) at the U.S. Military Academy, and served in the Spanish-American War. He was on a tour of duty in the Philippines (1899–1903), served on the army general staff (1903–05), was a military observer with the Japanese forces during the Russo-Japanese War, and was promoted (1906) from captain to brigadier general. He again served in the Philippines (1906–13), was named (1913) commander of the 8th Cavalry Brigade, with headquarters at the Presidio, San Francisco, commanded the Mexican border operations (1916), and was promoted (1916) to major general. He was appointed (May 1917) commander of the American Expeditionary Forces (A.E.F.), which he led in France during World War I. It was mainly through his insistence that the American forces operated as a separate command. He was promoted (Oct. 1917) to the rank of full general and received (Sept. 1919) the title of "General of the Armies of the United States." He served as army chief of staff from 1921 until his retirement from the service in 1924.

Phillips, Wendell (b. Boston, 29 Nov. 1811; d. there, 2 Feb. 1884), reformer, orator, obtained his B.A. (1831) and LL.B. (1834) from Harvard and practiced law briefly in Boston. In a speech at

Faneuil Hall (1837) he publicly identified himself with abolitionism, speaking out against the murder of Elijah P. Lovejoy, abolitionist editor. Frequent contributor to Garrison's *Liberator,* he was delegate from Massachusetts to the World Anti-Slavery Convention at London (1840) and was outspoken and uncompromising in his stand against slavery, opposing the annexation of Texas, the Mexican War, and Webster's stand on the Compromise of 1850. In the Civil War, he attacked Lincoln for his moderation on the slavery question and opposed his renomination. Succeeding Garrison (1865) as president of the American Antislavery Society, he kept it active until the adoption of the 15th Amendment. Phillips was sympathetic with the broad spectrum of reform, advocating the abolition of capital punishment, currency and Indian reform, votes for women, and the rights of labor. Gubernatorial nominee of the Labor Reform party and the Prohibitionists (1870), he drew up the Labor Reform platform (1871), advocating the overthrow of the profit system. An orator of the stature of Edward Everett and Daniel Webster (*q.v.*), although his style was easy and colloquial, his most popular lectures and orations include "The Lost Arts" (delivered over 2,000 times), "The Scholar in a Republic," and "Toussaint L'Ouverture." Two series of his *Speeches, Lectures, and Letters* were published (1863, 1891).

Pierce, Franklin (b. Hillsboro, N.H., 23 Nov. 1804; d. Concord, N.H., 8 Oct. 1869), 14th president of the U.S., was graduated from Bowdoin (1824), studied law, and was admitted to the New Hampshire bar (1827). In the state legislature (1829–32; as speaker, 1831–32), he became a Democratic congressman (1833–37) and U.S. senator (1837–42), when he resigned to resume law practice in Concord, N.H. In the War

with Mexico he became brigadier general of volunteers, serving under Winfield Scott. Democratic nominee (1852) on the 49th ballot over Buchanan, Cass, and Douglas, he defeated Scott. His administration was under proslavery influence. He extended the U.S. southern border through the Gadsden Purchase (1853), sent Perry to Japan (1853), signed the Kansas-Nebraska Act (1854), and recognized the Walker régime in Nicaragua. His "bleeding Kansas" policy lost him the support of Northern Democrats and the renomination (1856).

Pike, Zebulon Montgomery (b. Lamberton, now part of Trenton, N.J., 5 Jan. 1779; d. York, now Toronto, Canada, 27 Apr. 1813), soldier and explorer. Entering the army as a cadet (1794), he was commissioned (1805) by Gen. James Wilkinson to take an exploring party to the source of the Mississippi. His expedition, based at St. Louis, explored (9 Aug. 1805–30 Apr. 1806) the upper Mississippi region of the Louisiana Purchase, but did not find the true source of the river. Promoted to captain in 1806, Pike led a 2d expedition (1806–07) which explored what is now Colorado and New Mexico. He sighted but did not succeed in climbing the summit that was later named Pikes Peak. He explored the headwaters of the Arkansas and Red rivers; was arrested by the Spaniards in Santa Fe, but was soon set free; and published *An Account of Expeditions to the Sources of the Mississippi and through the Western Parts of Louisiana* (1810). After the outbreak of the War of 1812, he was commissioned a brigadier general (1813) and was killed in the explosion of a powder magazine while leading the assault on York.

Pincus, Gregory Goodwin (b. Woodbine, N.J., 9 Apr. 1903; d. Boston, Mass., 22 Aug. 1967), biologist. He received his

B.S. from Cornell (1924) and his M.Sc. and Sc.D. from Harvard (1927) and, as a National Research Council Fellow, did postdoctoral research at Harvard, Cambridge, and Kaiser Wilhelm Institute (1927–30). In 1930 he became an instructor in general physiology at Harvard and was an assistant professor there (1931–38). Having published some 70 research papers, he was already an authority on sex hormones and the sex of mammals when, in 1939, while a professor of experimental zoology at Clark Univ., he brought about the first fatherless mammalian birth by inducing parthenogenesis in a female rabbit. He fertilized the ovum in a test tube by using high-temperature hormone treatments and salt solutions and then implanted the fertilized ovum in the rabbit. In 1944 he founded, with H. Hoagland, the Worcester Foundation for Experimental Biology, where he was director of laboratories and later research director. In addition to his work at the foundation, he was research professor in physiology at the Tufts Medical School (1946–50) and research professor in biology at Boston Univ. (1950–67). In the late 1940s he focused his attention on the role of hormones in reproduction. His study of the properties of hydrocortisone, an adrenal hormone, involved use of progesterone, a female hormone secretion. Recognizing that progestins can inhibit ovulation, Pincus and Dr. M. C. Chang developed a synthetic progestin which prevented ovulation in laboratory animals. The development of the oral contraceptive for the human female, known as the Pill, was accomplished with the collaboration of Dr. John Rock and Dr. Celso-Ramon Garcia. After 4 years of experimentation with thousands of women, Enovid, a birth control pill, was first marketed in 1960. Believed to be 100% effective, the Pill is taken today by at least one fifth of all American women of

childbearing age. Not only did the Pill revolutionize methods of birth control, it drastically altered the nature of the worldwide debate on the problem of overpopulation. Dr. Pincus also developed estrone, a hormone used in the treatment of breast cancer and pregnancy complications. His publications include: *The Eggs of Mammals* (1936), *The Control of Fertility* (1965), and *Steroid Dynamics* (1966).

Poe, Edgar Allan (b. Boston, Mass., 19 Jan. 1809; d. Baltimore, Md., 7 Oct. 1849), poet, short-story writer, and critic. Orphaned when he was about 3 years old, he was reared by a Richmond (Va.) tobacco merchant, John Allan, whose name he used as his middle name after 1824. He was admitted (1826) to the Univ. of Virginia, but left after 1 term because of gambling debts. His first volume, *Tamerlane and Other Poems* (1827), was published anonymously at Boston. Poe served (1827–29) in the U.S. army, was admitted (1830) to West Point, and was dismissed (1831) for gross neglect of duty. His second volume, *Al Aaraaf, Tamerlane, and Minor Poems* (1829), was published at Baltimore; *Poems by Edgar A. Poe* (1831) was published at New York. He first won public notice with "A MS. Found in a Bottle," which was awarded (1833) a prize by a Baltimore publication. He contributed to the *Southern Literary Messenger*, of which he became (1835) assistant editor. He married (1836) his 14-year-old cousin Virginia Clemm, and moved to New York City (1837), where he published *The Narrative of Arthur Gordon Pym* (1838). He moved to Philadelphia (1838), where he coedited (1839–40) *Burton's Gentleman's Magazine* and was literary editor (1841–42) of *Graham's Lady's and Gentleman's Magazine*. He published *Tales of the Grotesque and Arabesque* (2 vols., 1840) and won a prize (1843) for his story "The Gold Bug." He returned (1844) to New York, where he did freelance writing (the "Balloon Hoax" was published in the New York *Sun* on 13 Apr. 1844) and published his poem "The Raven," which brought him his first fame. He became (1845) editor and proprietor of the *Broadway Journal* and published (1845) *Tales* and *The Raven and Other Poems*. His chronic poverty, alcoholism, and poor health worsened after the death of his wife (1847). He returned to Richmond (1849) and died in Baltimore after being found semiconscious in a saloon. A lyric poet of the first rank, he exerted an important influence upon poetry in the U.S. and abroad, particularly on the French Symbolists; was one of the originators of the detective story genre; and made important contributions as a literary critic, notably in his essays "The Poetic Principle" and "The Philosophy of Composition."

Poinsett, Joel Roberts (b. Charleston, S.C., 2 Mar. 1779; d. Sumter Co., S.C., 12 Dec. 1851), statesman. After studying medicine at the Univ. of Edinburgh and attending Woolwich Military Academy in England (1797–99), Poinsett studied law in the U.S. (1800). Following 10 years of travel throughout Europe and Asia, he became special U.S. agent to Rio de la Plata and Chile (1810–14), investigating for President Monroe the conditions of countries struggling for independence. He encouraged the Carrera brothers' efforts to achieve Chilean independence. When the Carrera government fell, Poinsett returned to the U.S., where he served as a member of the South Carolina state legislature (1816–20) and U.S. representative (1821–25). As the first American ambassador to Mexico (1825–30), Poinsett sought to replace British with American influence in Mexico. However, he was

regarded as an intriguer and imperialist with designs on Texas for the U.S. Mexico repeatedly asked for his dismissal. He introduced the U.S. to the Mexican flowering plant which is named for him—*poinsettia pulcherrima*. Poinsett aided his friend President Andrew Jackson during the nullification crisis as leader of the Unionist party in South Carolina (1830–33). As Secretary of War during President Van Buren's administration (1837–41) he organized a general staff and improved the artillery. He also removed 40,000 Indians to land west of the Mississippi and organized the war against the Seminole Indians in Florida. Poinsett founded the Academy of Fine Arts (South Carolina) and the museum of the National Institute for the Promotion of Science and the Useful Arts (Washington, D.C., 1840), which became a part of the Smithsonian (1862).

Polk, James Knox (b. Mecklenburg Co., N.C., 2 Nov. 1795; d. Nashville, Tenn., 15 June 1849), 11th president of the U.S., moved with his parents (1806) to central Tennessee, was graduated from the Univ. of North Carolina (1818), read law, was admitted to the bar (1820), and began practice in Columbia, Tenn. State legislator (1823–25), congressman (1825–39; served as speaker, 1835–39), he was governor of Tennessee (1839–41), but was defeated for reelection in 1841 and again in 1843. He was Democratic nominee (1844) on the 9th ballot when Van Buren failed of the necessary two thirds vote. He defeated Clay in the ensuing election. As president he accomplished all his major objectives; settled the Oregon question by a compromise on the 49th parallel (1846); achieved tariff reduction (1846) and the reestablishment of the independent treasury system originated under Van Buren. Dispute over the Texas boundary led to War with Mexico (1846–48). An expansionist rather than an imperialist, he approved the acquisition of Texas, California, and New Mexico, but opposed retaining Mexico by force. He did not seek reelection.

Pollock, Jackson (b. near Cody, Wyo., 28 Jan. 1912; d. Southampton, L.I., 11 Aug. 1956), painter, left Los Angeles high school at 17, receiving his formal training at the Art Students League, New York, under Thomas Hart Benton. On the Federal Arts Project (1939–42), he gave his first 1-man show in New York (1943). His work in his first period was characterized by violence and passion still under control (*Male and Female in Search of a Symbol, Wounded Animal*). In the mid-1940s he broke away from American realism to develop his own distinctive abstract style, abandoning the easel for drippings of color on canvas and creating "rhythmic labyrinths" or "dripped mazes" (*Sleeping Effort, Portrait with a Dream, Eastern, Totem, Scent,* and others simply given numbers). Before his death in an auto accident, he had become a leading figure among abstract expressionists, giving 1-man shows abroad, at Venice and Milan (1950) and Paris (1952). His paintings quickly acquired a phenomenal posthumous success.

Pound, Ezra Loomis (b. Hailey, Ida., 30 Oct. 1885; d. Venice, Italy, 1 Nov. 1972), poet, studied at Hamilton College (Ph.B., 1905) and the Univ. of Pennsylvania (M.A., 1906) and taught 4 months at Wabash College before leaving the U.S. (1907) to travel through Spain, France, and Italy, eventually settling in England. His *Personae* and *Exultations* (1909), followed by *Canzoni* (1911) and *Ripostes* (1912), demonstrated his poetic gifts. Leader of the Imagists, he edited (1917–19) the *Literary Review* (London) and was Paris correspondent (1920) for *The Dial*. He was a major influence upon

William Butler Yeats, whom he served as secretary and literary guide. He assisted T. S. Eliot in revising *The Waste Land* (1922), making it more intense and compact. He raised money for James Joyce and was responsible for the publication of *Ulysses*. His *Cantos* (1926–72), drawing upon legend, Oriental poetry, troubadour ballads, and modern jargon, constituted his most substantial work. Resident of Italy from 1924, he began (1941) broadcasting Fascist propaganda from Rome to the U.S. during World War II. Brought back to the U.S. on a charge of treason (1945), he was adjudged insane and hospitalized, but continued to write poetry. The award (1949) of the Bollingen prize for his *Pisan Cantos* (1948, part of the *Cantos*) evoked a storm of protest. Released from St. Elizabeth's Hospital (1958), he returned to Italy with his wife, Dorothy Shakespeare Pound, after treasons charges were dropped.

Powderly, Terence Vincent (b. Carbondale, Pa., 22 Jan. 1849; d. Washington, D.C., 24 June 1924), labor leader, reformer, attended school until 13, then worked on the railroad. Apprenticed to the machinist trade at 17, he worked at that trade until 1877. President of the Machinist and Blacksmith's National Union (1872), he was initiated into the secret order of the Knights of Labor (1874), became its Grand Master Workman (1879), and held that office until 1893. Heading the largest and most powerful labor organization of its day, he was basically a reformer, placing little stress on immediate demands for wages and hours, opposing strikes; but advocating producers' cooperatives, trust regulations, currency reform, and the abolition of child labor. He was instrumental in the passage of the alien contract labor law (1885). Elected mayor of Scranton on a Greenback-Labor ticket (1878), he was twice reelected (1880, 1882), but supported the Republican ticket beginning in 1894. Commissioner general of immigration (1897–1902), he was chief of the division of information in the Bureau of Immigration (1907–21). He wrote *Thirty Years of Labor, 1859–1889* (1889) and an autobiography, *The Path I Trod* (1940).

Powell, John Wesley (b. Mt. Morris, N.Y., 24 Mar. 1834; d. Haven, Me., 23 Sept. 1902), geologist and explorer, attended Illinois, Oberlin, and Wheaton colleges, and while still a youth made solitary botanizing trips on the Ohio and Mississippi rivers. He enlisted in the Union army at the outbreak of the Civil War, lost his right arm at the elbow as the result of a wound received at the battle of Shiloh (1862), and rose to the rank of major of artillery. He served as professor of geology in the Illinois Wesleyan College at Bloomington and as lecturer and curator of the museum of the Illinois Normal Univ. In 1869, on a grant from the federal government and the Smithsonian Institution, he led an exploring party along some 900 miles of the Green and Colorado rivers, being the first white man to make this expedition, and continued his Western explorations in 1871, 1874, and 1875. He became (1875) director of the 2d division of the U.S. Geological and Geographical Survey of the Territories, which in 1877 became known as the Survey of the Rocky Mountain Region, and in 1879 issued the *Report on the Lands of the Arid Region of the United States*, whose recommendations subsequently became a part of national land policy. When the western explorations were consolidated (1879) as the U.S. Geological Survey under Clarence King, Powell was placed in charge of anthropological investigations under the Smithsonian Institution. From 1880 to 1894 Powell served as director of the U.S. Geological Survey. His most important contributions in the field of physiographic geology were made in *Explorations of the Colorado River of the West and Its Tributaries* (1875; issued in 1895 in revised and enlarged form as *Canyons of the Colorado*).

Prescott, William Hickling (b. Salem, Mass., 14 May 1796; d. Boston, Mass., 28 Jan. 1859), historian. He was graduated from Harvard (1814), where an accidental blow blinded his left eye (1813); in 1815 an inflammation of his right eye virtually deprived him of his sight. In the research and composition of his histories, he was aided by a noctograph (a visual-aid device), by secretaries who read aloud to him, and by a tenacious memory. On the history of Spain and Spanish conquest, which he chose as his special subject, he wrote *History of the Reign of Ferdinand and Isabella* (3 vols., 1838), *History of the Conquest of Mexico* (3 vols., 1843), *History of the Conquest of Peru* (2 vols., 1847), and *History of the Reign of Philip the Second* (3 vols., 1855, 1858). His histories, narrative rather than analytical, and romantic in conception, are based on rigid standards of scholarship which justify the claim that he was the first American scientific historian. His stress on literary form popularized the reading of history by Americans.

Pulitzer, Joseph (b. Mako, Hungary, 10 Apr. 1847; d. Charleston, S.C., 29 Oct. 1911), journalist and newspaper publisher. Arriving in the U.S. in 1864, he served briefly in the Union army, became (1868) a reporter on the St. Louis *Westliche Post*, and in 1869 was elected to the Missouri legislature. He soon became a figure of some importance in St. Louis politics, served as a city police commissioner, and was active as a supporter of the Liberal Republican movement (1870–72). He was part owner (1871–73) of the *Westliche Post* and was admitted to the bar (1876) in the District of Columbia. He purchased (1878) the St. Louis *Post* and the *Dispatch,* combining them as the *Post-Dispatch,* a journal which under his leadership became one of the foremost organs in the Midwest. In 1883 he purchased the New York *World* from Jay Gould and, following a policy of sensational journalism that included recourse to large headlines, comic strips, and crime stories, converted the *World* into a profitable enterprise. The *Evening World* was established in 1887. During the period 1896–98 the *World* rivaled Hearst's *Evening Journal* in its "yellow journalism." Both newspapers shared responsibility for arousing public opinion for war against Spain. In subsequent years, however, the *World* became a responsible and politically independent journal that observed high standards. Pulitzer's announced intention (1903) to establish a school of journalism at Columbia resulted in the provision in his will of $2 million for the School of Journalism (1912) and for the Pulitzer prizes awarded annually in many fields of achievement.

Pupin, Michael Idvorsky (b. Idvor, Banat, Austria, 4 Oct. 1858; d. New York City, 12 Mar. 1935), physicist, inventor, grew up in an atmosphere supercharged with Serbian hostility to Hapsburg rule. He went to Prague (1873) to study, but left for the U.S. in 1874. He held odd jobs in Delaware and New York, picking up English, Latin, and Greek. Entering Columbia (1879), he obtained his A.B. degree and his U.S. citizenship papers in 1883. He then studied mathematics with John Edward Routh at Cambridge Univ. and physics with Helmholtz at Berlin

(Ph.D., 1889). Returning to New York, he taught mathematical physics and electromechanics at Columbia (1889–1931). Inventor of numerous electrical devices relating to long-distance telephony and multiplex telegraphy, his "pupinized" cable, transmitting sound over long distances, solved the problem of sound attenuation and distortion. He conducted research in X ray, was the first in the U.S. to obtain an X-ray photograph (1896), and discovered X-radiation. He was adviser to the Yugoslav delegation at the Peace Conference (1919). In addition to his Pulitzer prize-winning autobiography, *From Immigrant to Inventor* (1923), he wrote *Thermodynamics of Reversible Cycles in Gases and Saturated Vapors* (1894), *New Reformation* (1927), and *The Romance of the Machine* (1930).

Rabi, Isidor Isaac (b. Rymanow, Austrian Galicia, 29 July 1898–   ), physicist. He was brought to the U.S. in his infancy, was graduated from Cornell (B. Chem., 1919) and from Columbia (Ph. D., 1927), and as a fellow of the International Education Board took postgraduate study (1928–29) in Munich, Copenhagen, Hamburg, Leipzig, and Zurich. In 1929 he joined the physics faculty at Columbia, and in 1940 became associate director of the radiation laboratory at the Massachusetts Institute of Technology, where he was engaged in radar research (1940–45) during World War II. He was also wartime consultant to the Los Alamos atomic bomb laboratory. He has made notable advances in the study of magnetic properties of molecules, atoms, and atomic nuclei and in quantum mechanics, nuclear physics, and molecular beams, and was awarded the Nobel prize in physics (1944) for the general application of the resonance method to the magnetic properties of atomic nuclei. He was vice-president of the International Conference on Peaceful Uses of Atomic Energy at Geneva, 1955, 1958.

Randolph, Asa Philip (b. Crescent City, Fla., 15 Apr. 1889–   ), labor and civil rights leader. He graduated as valedictorian from the Cookman Institute (1907), moved to Harlem (1911), and attended City College (1912–16) while working at various jobs. In 1915 he met Chandler Owen and together they studied socialism and working-class politics, joining the Socialist party in 1916. In 1917 they coedited *Hotel Messenger*, the monthly organ of the Headwaiters and Sidewaiters Society of Greater New York, but were fired after 8 months for exposing a kickback scheme. They began a successful, radical magazine, *The Messenger* (1917–28), which urged blacks to join unions, preferably the Industrial Workers of the World, and to endorse Socialist candidates for office. In his journal and in his numerous addresses to Negro workers, Randolph stated his conviction that only unionization would bring them equal treatment and recognition in industry and stimulate pride among members of their race. In 1925 Randolph founded and was elected president of the Brotherhood of Sleeping Car Porters, which became partially affiliated with the American Federation of Labor in 1929 (full membership in 1937). With almost no funds, the union struggled and dwindled in numbers until 1933, when the New Deal encouraged the formation of labor unions. Reenergized, the Brotherhood fought a successful battle for recognition by the Pullman Co. (1935) and finally won a favorable contract (1937). The Brotherhood gave impetus to the revival of a strong black mass movement in the next two decades. In 1941 Randolph threatened President Roosevelt with a mass march on Washington to protest the exclusion of Negroes from jobs in defense industries. The demonstration was called off when Roosevelt, by executive order (25 June 1941), established the Fair Employment Practices Committee to prevent racial discrimination in war production and government jobs. Randolph's advice spurred President Truman to issue the executive order by which the military was desegregated (1948). In 1955 Randolph was named a vice-president of the newly merged AFL–CIO. Regarded as the elder statesman of the civil rights movement, he was principal organizer of the March on Washington for Freedom and Jobs (28 Aug. 1963). The collapse of the railroad travel industry brought about the virtual demise of the once-powerful Brotherhood, and Randolph retired as president in 1968. He was awarded the Presidential Medal of Freedom (1964).

Randolph, John, of Roanoke (b. "Cawsons," Prince George Co., Va., 2 June 1773; d. Philadelphia, 24 May 1833), statesman, orator, studied at the College of New Jersey (1787) and at William and Mary (1792–93). A restless person, his education was casual and varied, but he was widely read. Elected to Congress in 1799 as a Jeffersonian, he became at 28 chairman of the Ways and Means Committee and administration leader under Jefferson. He mismanaged the prosecution in the impeachment trial of Judge Samuel Chase and was held responsible for the failure to convict. Heading a faction called the "Quids," he blocked the bill (1804–05) awarding land to holders of Yazoo land warrants, losing his party leadership thereby. Opposing the Embargo and Madison's candidacy in 1808, he was defeated for reelection (1813) as a result of his opposition to the War of 1812. Returning to Congress (1815), he opposed chartering the 2d Bank of the U.S. and the tariff. Maligning the Adams-

Clay alliance as the combination of the "puritan and the blackleg," he fought a duel with Clay (1826). In the Senate (1825–27) and again in the House (1827–29), he headed the opposition to President J. Q. Adams. Delegate to the Virginia Convention (1829), he sided with the conservative forces. U.S. minister to Russia under Jackson, he remained there only a month because of his health. Incomparable orator and master of invective, champion of lost causes and strict constructionist, he was, with his high soprano voice and increasingly unbalanced behavior, a figure both brilliant and pathetic.

Rauschenbusch, Walter (b. Rochester, N.Y., 4 Oct. 1861; d. New York City, 25 July 1918), clergyman, was graduated from the Gymnasium of Gütersloh, Westphalia (1883), received his A.B. (1884) from the Univ. of Rochester, and 2 years later was graduated from the Rochester Theological Seminary. Ordained a Baptist minister, he took charge of the 2d German Baptist Church, New York City, working with German immigrants. Studying economics and theology at the Univ. of Berlin (1891–92) and industrial conditions in England, he was influenced by the Fabian movement and by the work of the Salvation Army and the Consumers' Cooperatives. Succeeding his father, Rev. Augustus Rauschenbusch, to the chair of New Testament interpretation at the Rochester Theological Seminary (1897), he gained prominence as an advocate of the "social gospel," the application of Christian principles to social problems, by his *Christianity and the Social Crisis* (1907). This positive reaction to social Darwinism was also expounded in *Prayers of the Social Awakening* (1910), *Christianizing the Social Order* (1912), *The Social Principles of Jesus* (1916), and *A Theology for the Social Gospel* (1917).

Rayburn, Samuel (b. Roane Co., Tenn., 6 Jan. 1882; d. Bonham, Tex., 16 Nov. 1961), political leader. Raised on a farm in northern Texas, he received his early education in a 1-room schoolhouse, was graduated from East Texas Normal College (1903), studied at the Univ. of Texas Law School, was admitted to the bar (1908), and practiced law in Bonham Co. With the stated ambition of one day becoming speaker of the House, he entered politics as a Democrat and served in the Texas House of Representatives (1907–13), becoming speaker in 1911. First elected to the U.S. House of Representatives in 1912, he was reelected 24 times, serving a record 48 years 8 months. As chairman of the Interstate and Foreign Commerce Committee he shaped such New Deal legislation as the Securities Act (1933), the Securities Exchange Act (1934), and the Public Utilities Holding Company Act (1935). He became speaker of the House in 1940 and held that position a total of 17 years —a record. A master of the legislative process and the arts of persuasion, "Mr. Sam" was a strong speaker, respected for his integrity and fairness as well as for his skills. He was able to achieve his ends by maintaining personal friendships with key members of both parties, controlling Democratic committee assignments, and bargaining with individuals. If they followed his advice—"to get along, go along" —younger Democrats generally were rewarded. He was able to push through considerable legislation in the field of foreign relations as well as several significant domestic bills, including the civil rights acts of 1957 and 1960. He worked well with Presidents Roosevelt, Truman, Eisenhower, and Kennedy, and with his legislative counterparts in the Senate.

Reed, Thomas Brackett (b. Portland, Me., 18 Oct. 1839; d. Washington, D.C., 7 Dec. 1902), political leader. After graduating from Bowdoin College (1860), he began to study law, moved to California (1861), and was admitted to the bar there two years later. He returned to Portland and, after admission to the bar in Maine (1865), he started a legal practice and soon entered politics as a Republican. He served in the state assembly (1868–69), the state senate (1870), and was state attorney general (1870–73) before he was elected to the U.S. House of Representatives (1876), in which he served continuously until 1899. A brilliant parliamentarian and an extremely able debater with a caustic wit, Reed quickly took his place among his party's top congressional leaders. A conservative, he opposed the Greenback and Free Silver movements and supported a substantial tariff, a modernized navy, and legislation securing for Negroes the right to vote. He was appointed to the Committee on Rules (1882) and, while the Republicans were in the minority, began his campaign for reform of House rules of procedure. When the Republicans gained a majority he became speaker (1889–91). In this office he had his greatest impact, instituting the "Reed Rules" for more expeditious handling of business, the most significant of which were the redefinition of the quorum (members present rather than members voting) and the granting to the speaker of discretionary power to refuse to hear dilatory motions. Reed exercised his powers so vigorously—not only using his discretionary powers to break the power of the minority to filibuster but also stacking the committees with members sympathetic to his views —that he became known as "Czar" Reed. With Reed as speaker, the 51st Congress enacted a flood of Republican legislation. The old regime returned when the Democrats regained control of the House (1891), but the "Reed Rules" were readopted with the Republican victory of

1894 and Reed's return as speaker (1895–99). Bitterly opposed to his party's imperialist policies, he resigned from the House (1899) and engaged in a lucrative law practice in New York City until his death.

Reed, Walter (b. Belroi, Va., 13 Sept. 1851; d. Washington, D.C., 22 Nov. 1902), army surgeon and bacteriologist. He was graduated from the Univ. of Virginia (1869) and the Bellevue Hospital Medical School, New York City (M.D., 1870). In 1875, after having served on the boards of health in New York and Brooklyn, he entered the Medical Corps of the U.S. army with the rank of 1st lieutenant and was assigned to duty as an assistant surgeon. Ordered to Baltimore (1890) as attending surgeon and examiner of recruits, he studied at the Johns Hopkins Hospital and was attached to the pathological laboratory, where, under Dr. William H. Welch and others, he specialized in the then emerging science of bacteriology. In 1893, he was made curator of the Army Medical Museum at Washington, D.C., and named professor of bacteriology and clinical microscopy at the newly established Army Medical School. In the years immediately preceding the outbreak of the Spanish-American War he carried out researches in the bacteriology of erysipelas and diphtheria. In 1898 he was made chairman of a committee for investigating typhoid fever, at that time rife in the volunteer camps. The commission's report (1904) pointed to the importance of transmission by flies, dust, and other hitherto ignored agencies. In 1897–99 Reed and Dr. James Carroll disproved the theory propounded by Dr. Giuseppe Sanarelli of Italy concerning the causative agency of yellow fever. Named as head of the U.S. Army Yellow Fever Commission (1900), Reed and his associates (Carroll, Lazear, and Agramonte) carried out in Cuba experiments with soldiers and other volunteers which conclusively proved the theory of mosquito transmission of yellow fever (through the agency of *Stegomyia fasciata,* later classified as *Aëdes ægypti*). The commission's findings made it possible to control yellow fever and virtually eliminate the disease in the U.S. and Cuba. The general hospital of the army medical center at Washington, D.C., is named for Reed.

Remington, Frederic (b. Canton, N.Y., 4 Oct. 1861; d. Ridgefield, Conn., 26 Dec. 1909), noted painter, illustrator, sculptor, and writer on the American West and frontier. In between attending the Yale School of Fine Arts (1878–80) and the Art Students League (1880), Remington raised sheep and cattle out west. After graduating he traveled extensively through Germany, Russia, and North Africa. While a correspondent in Cuba during the Spanish-American War, he made sketches which were later used for his painting *Charge Upon San Juan Hill*. Remington's art first gained recognition with the publication of his drawings in Theodore Roosevelt's *Ranch Life and Hunting Trails* (1888). Thereafter, Remington was commissioned to make drawings for *Harper's Weekly* and for books by Longfellow, Francis Parkman, Owen Wister, and Hamlin Garland. The *Century* published his illustrated article on Indian life. The swift action and accurate detail revealed in Remington's paintings of frontiersmen, soldiers, Indians, and their horses, contributed a unique realism to American art. A skillful journalist, Remington also wrote and illustrated the books *Pony Tracks* (1895), *Crooked Trails* (1898), *Sundown Leflare* (1899), *Men with Bark On* (1900), *John Ermine of the Yellowstone* (1902), and *The Way of an Indian* (1906). Remington's sculpture *The*

Bronco Buster was exhibited at the Pan-American Exposition in Buffalo in 1901.

Reuther, Walter Philip (b. Wheeling, W. Va., 1 Sept. 1907; d. near Pellston, Mich., 9 May 1970), labor leader and social reformer. He quit school at age 16 to work as an apprentice at the Wheeling Steel Corp. but was discharged for mobilizing a protest against Sunday and holiday work. He went to Detroit (1926), where he became a tool and die craftsman and soon a foreman at a Ford Motor Co. plant. At the same time he finished high school and went on to complete 3 years at Wayne Univ. Laid off by Ford during the depression because, according to Reuther, of his union activities, he and his brother traveled around the world (1932–35), touring auto plants in England, bicycling across Europe, working in a Ford-built plant in Gorki, and continuing on through China before returning home. Back in Detroit he found work in a General Motors plant, helped organize United Auto Workers Local 174, and actively participated in the union's Flint, Mich., sitdown strike (1936–37) that led to the UAW's recognition by the major auto companies. Reuther soon became a major union organizer and a spearhead of the fight against Communism within the UAW. During World War II he helped keep auto workers in line on the no-strike pledge. He led the 113-day UAW strike (1945–46) of 200,000 workers against General Motors which ended with the union gaining significant pay increases. He was elected president of the UAW in 1946 and president of the Congress of Industrial Organizations in 1952. Shot in the chest and right arm by a would-be assassin (1948), never identified, he never recovered full use of his arm. In 1955 he led the merger of the CIO and the American Federation of Labor and served as vice-president and executive board members of the AFL–CIO, and as head of its industrial union department, but after years of disagreement with George Meany (president of the AFL–CIO) over the direction and structure of the organization, he took the UAW out of the AFL–CIO (July 1968) and joined the Teamsters in the Alliance for Labor Action (May 1969). An expert bargainer, he pioneered in achieving for his union pensions, pay increases based on the cost of living and productivity rises, supplementary unemployment benefits, profit-sharing, and early retirement. As a progressive, he sought to involve labor in industrial planning, the fight for a guaranteed annual wage, cooperative movements, production and pricing problems, civil rights, and politics. He died in an airplane crash.

Richardson, Henry Hobson (b. St. James Parish, La., 29 Sept. 1838; d. Brookline, Mass., 27 Apr. 1886), architect. Graduated from Harvard (1859) and admitted (1860) to the École des Beaux Arts in Paris, he made his early reputation with prize-winning designs for churches at Springfield and West Medford, Mass. With the Brattle Square Church at Boston he abandoned Victorian Gothic for the style that became his hallmark and reached its flower in Trinity Church, Boston, for which he was awarded the prize commission in 1872. Richardson was the leader in introducing the Romanesque Revival into the U.S. Adapted chiefly from the forms of Southern French Romanesque, this mode was widely used in the American Northeast and West until it gave way to the Classical Revival. Toward the close of his life Richardson was evolving a functionalist architecture, as in the John H. Pray Co. Bldg. at Boston (c.1886), that foreshadowed the modernism of Louis H. Sullivan and others. For other outstanding designs, see p. 906.

Robinson, Edwin Arlington (b. Head Tide, Me., 22 Dec. 1869; d. New York City, 6 Apr. 1935), poet, attended Harvard from 1891 to 1893. His first volume of poetry, *The Torrent and the Night Before* (1896; reprinted with additions in 1897 as *The Children of the Night*), was published at his own expense. In 1899 he settled at New York, where poverty forced him to work as a timekeeper (1904) on the subway construction project. When his plight came to the attention of President Theodore Roosevelt, an admirer of Robinson's poetry, Robinson received (1905) a clerkship in the customs service at New York, a post he held until 1909. The following years brought him general recognition and fame in the U.S. and abroad. His poetry, which bears the stamp of his Calvinistic New England background, deals with traditional themes and reveals a masterly command of blank verse technique. His works include *Captain Craig and Other Poems* (1902), *The Town Down the River* (1910), *The Man Against the Sky* (1916), *Merlin* (1917), *Collected Poems* (1921), *Avon's Harvest* (1921), *Roman Bartholow* (1923), *The Man Who Died Twice* (1924), *Tristram* (1927), *Cavender's House* (1929), *Matthias at the Door* (1931), *Amaranth* (1934), and *King Jasper* (1935). He was awarded three Pulitzer prizes.

Rockefeller, John Davison (b. Richford, N.Y., 8 July 1839; d. Ormond Beach, Fla., 23 May 1937), industrialist and philanthropist, was educated in Cleveland, Ohio, where he worked as a clerk and bookkeeper and became a member of the firm of Clark & Rockefeller. Following the discovery of oil at Titusville, Pa. (1859), he became associated with

Samuel Andrews, inventor of a cheaper process of refining oil, and in 1865 joined his brother, William Rockefeller (1841–1922), in establishing the firm of William Rockefeller & Co. and the Standard Oil Works at Cleveland. The Standard Oil Co., organized in 1867 and incorporated in 1870 with John D. Rockefeller as president, became the largest unit in the American oil industry and the first great effective industrial combination of its time. By the mid-1870s it had absorbed or eliminated most of its rival concerns; by the end of that decade it exercised a virtual monopoly over oil refining and transportation. The company became known (1881) as the Standard Oil Trust, a unit that was outlawed by the Supreme Court of Ohio (1892) and dissolved in 1899. It was replaced by the Standard Oil Co. of N.J., which functioned as a holding company for the Rockefeller interests until its dissolution was ordered by the U.S. Supreme Court (1911). At about that time the active management of the business was handed over to his son, John D. Rockefeller, Jr. (1874–1960). The senior Rockefeller retired with a fortune estimated at $1 billion. The immense financial resources built up by him were devoted to a variety of philanthropies, including the endowment of the Univ. of Chicago (1892), the Rockefeller Institute of Medical Research (1901), the General Education Board (1902), and the Rockefeller Foundation (1913).

Rockefeller, Nelson Aldrich (b. Bar Harbor, Me., 8 July 1908–   ), statesman, was the third of 6 children of John D. Rockefeller, Jr., the grandson of John D. Rockefeller (q.v.) and Nelson W. Aldrich. Rockefeller was graduated from Dartmouth (1930) and served with family interests, including the Chase Manhattan Bank, Creole Petroleum Co.

–Venezuelan Exxon affiliate (1935–40), and Rockefeller Center, where he was president (1938–45, 1948–51). His career in government service began as coordinator of Inter-American Affairs (1940–44). He served as Assistant Secretary of State for Latin American Affairs (1944–45), chairman of the Development Advisory Board, where he helped to develop Point 4 aid for underdeveloped countries (1950–51), Under-Secretary of the Department of Health, Education, and Welfare, Special Assistant to President Eisenhower (1954–55) and chairman of the president's Advisory Committee on Government Organization (1953–58). Rockefeller was elected governor of New York as a Republican in 1958 and thereafter reelected 3 times. His gubernatorial career was marked by expansion of the State Univ. of New York, the building of the South Mall in Albany, considerable subsidization of the arts, development of a pure waters program as well as a land-use program for the Adirondacks, and the creation of the Urban Development Corp. to build new towns and neighborhoods. During the Attica prison uprising (1971) he refused to go to the scene and ordered a trooper raid which left 39 inmates and hostages dead. Rockefeller withdrew from active consideration for the Republican presidential nomination in 1960 and was defeated for the nomination in 1964 and 1968. He resigned as governor (Dec. 1973) to head his Commission on Critical Choices for Americans, but accepted Gerald Ford's nomination to the vice-presidency (20 Aug. 1974). He was confirmed and took office (19 Dec. 1974). Rockefeller's 4 brothers, known for their economic influence and interest in public service, are John D. 3d (1906–   ), head of the Rockefeller Foundation; Laurance S. (1910–   ), business executive and conservationist;

David (1915–   ), president of the Chase Manhattan Bank, and Winthrop (1912–73), former governor of Arkansas. Nelson Rockefeller is also a noted art collector, who served as president of the Museum of Modern Art (1939–41, 1946–53) and was the founder of the Museum of Primitive Art. He is the author of several books including *Future of Federalism* (1962).

Rodgers, Richard (b. New York City, 28 June 1902–   ), composer, studied at Columbia Univ. (1919–21) and the Institute of Musical Art, New York (1921–23). He was the first Columbia freshman to win the competition for the annual varsity show, *Fly With Me*. As an outstanding composer for musical comedy, his greatest achievements were in collaboration with Lorenz Hart (1895–1943), whom he met in 1919, and, beginning in 1943, with Oscar Hammerstein, 2d (*q.v.*). He and Hart had their first musical hit with *Garrick Gaieties* (1925). They worked together on *The Girl Friend* (1926), *A Connecticut Yankee* (1927), *I'd Rather Be Right* (1937), *Pal Joey* (1940), and *By Jupiter* (1942), in which Rodgers collaborated on the script. Among their song hits of the 20s were "Thou Swell," "With a Song in My Heart," and in the 30s, "Bewitched, Bothered and Bewildered." His association with Oscar Hammerstein started with a signal success, *Oklahoma!* (Special Pulitzer award, 1944), and was continued with *Carousel* (1945), *Allegro* (1947), the Pulitzer prize-winning *South Pacific* (1949), and *The King and I* (1951). Their song hits quickly became American classics, among them "Oh, What a Beautiful Mornin'," "People Will Say We're in Love," "Some Enchanted Evening," and "I'm Gonna Wash That Man Right Outa My Hair." Rodgers also wrote film scores for numerous motion pictures, including *State Fair* (1945).

The Sound of Music (1959) was a great success on stage and screen. After Hammerstein's death (1960), he authored *No Strings* (1962) and *Do I Hear a Waltz?* (with Stephen Sondheim, 1965).

Roebling, John Augustus (b. Mühlhausen, Thuringia, Germany, 12 June 1806; d. Brooklyn, N.Y., 22 July 1869), engineer, bridge builder, and manufacturer. He was educated at Mühlhausen and at the Royal Polytechnic Institute at Berlin, where he received the degree of civil engineer (1826), and for the next 3 years worked on road construction in Westphalia, meanwhile making special studies of bridge construction. He came to the U.S. in 1831. After a period of unsuccessful farming in western Pennsylvania, he became a state engineer in the same year (1837) that he was naturalized. His work on the Allegheny Portage R.R. provided the stimulus for his manufacture at Saxonburg, Pa. (1841), of the first wire rope made in America. The factory, subsequently transferred to Trenton, N.J., is today known as the John A. Roebling's Sons Co. He built his first suspension bridge (1846) over the Monongahela River at Pittsburgh. After constructing other bridges, including the railroad suspension span at Niagara Falls (1851–55), Roebling suggested in 1857 the possibility of an East River bridge joining lower Manhattan and Brooklyn (Brooklyn Bridge). When the charter was granted, Roebling was named chief engineer, and his plans were approved by the bridge commission in 1869. Construction was about to begin when, as the result of an accident suffered by him at the bridge site (28 June 1869), he developed tetanus and died. The bridge was completed under the general supervision of his son, Washington Augustus Roebling (1837–1926). With James Buchanan Eads (*q.v.*) J. A. Roebling ranks as the greatest American bridge builder of the 19th century.

Roosevelt, Anna Eleanor (b. New York City, 11 Oct. 1884; d. there, 7 Nov. 1962), humanitarian, was educated in private schools, and married her distant cousin, Franklin D. Roosevelt (17 Mar. 1905). Active since World War I in educational and social reform, she participated in her husband's gubernatorial campaigns (1928 and 1930) and aided him in his campaign for the presidential nomination (1932). Her notable public career after entering the White House (1933–45) was unrivaled by any other president's wife. Lecturer and newspaper columnist, champion of the underprivileged and minority groups, she served the president as an invaluable source of public opinion. During World War II she served as assistant director, Office of Civilian Defense, and toured military bases abroad. After her husband's death she accepted appointment as U.S. delegate to the UN General Assembly (1945, 1949–52, 1961–62), and served as chairman, commission on human rights, Economic and Social Council (1946). In addition to her widely syndicated newspaper column, she continued political activity in the postwar years, supporting black civil rights, campaigning for Adlai Stevenson in 1956 and heading an unsuccessful draft movement for him at the 1960 Democratic National Convention. Author of several books, her most successful was *This I Remember* (1949).

Roosevelt, Franklin Delano (b. Hyde Park, N.Y., 30 Jan. 1882; d. Warm Springs, Ga., 12 Apr. 1945), 32d president of the U.S., was graduated from Harvard (1904), studied law at Columbia Law School, was admitted to the bar (1907), and practiced in New York. Democratic state senator (1911–13), he served as Assistant Secretary of the Navy (1913–20). James M. Cox's running mate on the Democratic ticket (1920), he was defeated in the Republican landslide of that year. Stricken with infantile paralysis (Aug. 1921), he recovered partial use of his legs and established the Warm Springs (Ga.) Foundation for those so afflicted. At the Democratic conventions of 1924 and 1928 he placed in nomination Gov. Alfred E. Smith, the "Happy Warrior." Elected governor of New York (1928) and reelected (1930), he was the Democratic nominee for president in 1932, defeating Herbert Hoover. His first inaugural, in which he exhorted that "the only thing we have to fear is fear itself" and promised "direct, vigorous action," keynoted his first administration, which was largely concerned with "New Deal" economic and social legislation to overcome the depression—relief and public works (resulting in deficit financing), labor legislation to implement collective bargaining (Wagner Act), and farm legislation to support agricultural prices. Largely responsible for U.S. aid to Great Britain after the fall of France (1940), he contributed notably to achieving interallied unity during World War II and conducted his own foreign relations. His "unconditional surrender" announcement (24 Jan. 1944) and his conferences with Allied leaders at Casablanca, Cairo, Quebec, Teheran, and Yalta determined the bases of the postwar world. First president to break the 3d term tradition (1940) by defeating Wendell L. Willkie, he was elected to a 4th term (1944), winning over Gov. Thomas E. Dewey. Three months after his 4th term had begun, and on the verge of victory against Germany and Japan, he was stricken with a cerebral hemorrhage and died.

Roosevelt, Theodore (b. New York City, 27 Oct. 1858; d. Oyster Bay, N.Y., 6 Jan. 1919), 26th president of the U.S., was graduated from Harvard (1880), read law briefly, and engaged in historical writing (*The Naval War of 1812*, 1882; *The Winning of the West*, 1889–96). After a term in the state assembly (1882–84), he lived on a North Dakota cattle ranch (1884–86). Returning to New York City, he was unsuccessful candidate for mayor (1886) and a notably effective U.S. civil service commissioner (1889–95) and president of the board of police commissioners of New York (1895–97). Assistant Secretary of the Navy (1897–98), he helped prepare the navy for the war with Spain. When war broke out he resigned and, with Leonard Wood, organized the 1st U.S. Volunteer Cavalry ("Rough Riders"), and as its colonel led the charge up San Juan Hill. Elected governor of New York (1898), his reform administration alarmed the political bosses, notably T. C. Platt, who arranged to have him nominated as McKinley's running mate (1900). On McKinley's death he became president and was reelected (1904), decisively defeating Alton B. Parker. Known as a trust buster, he dissolved the Northern Securities Co., but distinguished between "good" and "bad" trusts. His most notable achievements on the domestic front were his sponsorship of conservation of natural resources and of food inspection and railway rate legislation. Hastily recognizing the Republic of Panama, he secured the right to construct the Panama Canal (1903). For his successful intervention in the Russo-Japanese War (1905) he was awarded the Nobel peace prize. He supported his Secretary of War, William Howard Taft, as his successor; but after traveling abroad (1909–10), he reentered politics. Failing to secure the Republican nomination (1912), he was the nominee of the Progressive ("Bull Moose") party, losing in a 3-cornered contest to Woodrow Wilson. On an expedition to Brazil (1914) he explored

the "River of Doubt," named Rio Teodoro in his honor. At the outbreak of World War I he favored the Allies and criticized Wilson's neutrality policy.

Root, Elihu (b. Clinton, N.Y., 15 Feb. 1845; d. New York City, 7 Feb. 1937), statesman, jurist, and diplomat, was graduated from Hamilton (1865) and in law from New York Univ. (1867). He began practice in New York, was U.S. attorney for southern district of New York (1883–85) and chairman of the judiciary committee of the state constitutional convention (1894). While Secretary of War under McKinley and Theodore Roosevelt (1899–1904) he created a general staff for the army, drew up a constitution for the Philippines, and formulated the Platt Amendment (1901) for the government of Cuba. As Secretary of State under Roosevelt (1905–09), he reorganized the consular service and negotiated the Root-Takahira Open-Door Agreement with Japan (1908). Republican senator from New York (1909–15), he served as chief counsel for the U.S. in the North Atlantic Fisheries Arbitration (1910) and was also, from 1910, a member of the Permanent Court of Arbitration at The Hague. In recognition of his services as president of the Carnegie Endowment for International Peace (1910–25) he was awarded the Nobel prize (1912). Advocate of U.S. entry into the League of Nations, he was a member of the committee of jurists at The Hague which devised the Permanent Court of International Justice (1920–21). He was a U.S. delegate to the Washington Conference on Limitation of Armaments (1921), and as a member of the commission to revise the World Court statute (1929), he devised a formula to facilitate U.S. entry.

Rowland, Henry Augustus (b. Honesdale, Pa., 27 Nov. 1848; d. Baltimore, Md., 16

Apr. 1901), physicist, was graduated as a civil engineer (1870) from the Rensselaer Polytechnic Institute at Troy, N.Y., where he taught physics (1872–75). In 1876 he became the first professor of physics in the newly established Johns Hopkins Univ., where he served for the remainder of his life. His achievements as a pioneer in the fields of optics, magnetism, the spectra of the elements, and the electron were marked by a combination of practical mechanics and mastery of theory. His researches into optics resulted in diffraction gratings which are still used in spectrum analysis. His work on the magnetic lines of force produced his paper "On Magnetic Permeability, and the Maximum of Magnetism of Iron, Steel, and Nickel," published in the *Philosophical Magazine* (1873), which served as the foundation for later researches into permanent and induced magnetization, and was essential to the design of transformers and dynamos. His experiments in electromagnetism (1875–76) in the Berlin laboratory of von Helmholtz made significant contributions to the modern theory of electrons. He made accurate measurements of the values which are still standard for the mechanical equivalent of heat, the wave lengths of various spectra and the ohm, carried out researches in the theory of alternating currents, and was consultant for the installation of equipment at the Niagara Falls power plant.

Royce, Josiah (b. Grass Valley, Nevada Co., Calif., 20 Nov. 1855; d. Cambridge, Mass., 14 Sept. 1916), philosopher and teacher, was graduated from the Univ. of California (1875) and in 1878 received the Ph.D. degree from Johns Hopkins. He taught English at the Univ. of California (1878–82) and in 1882, with the aid of William James, received an appointment at Harvard, where he taught philosophy for 34 years. His great-

est metaphysical work, *The World and the Individual* (2 vols., 1900–01), expounded his view that the life of an absolute purpose required the moral independence of the individual. His *Studies in Good and Evil* (1898) and *Outline of Psychology* (1903) provided the psychological basis for this theory. In *The Philosophy of Loyalty* (1908) and *The Hope of the Great Community* (1916) he established the metaphysical basis of loyalty.

Rush, Benjamin (b. Byberry, Pa., 24 Dec. 1745; d. Philadelphia, 19 Apr. 1813), physician, Revolutionary patriot, obtained his A.B. (1760) from the College of New Jersey, then studied medicine under Dr. John Redman (1761–66), completing his medical education at the Univ. of Edinburgh (M.D., 1768) and St. Thomas' Hospital, London (1768). Returning to Philadelphia (1769), he began the practice of medicine and served as a professor of chemistry at the College of Philadelphia, publishing (1770) the first American text on the subject. Member of the 2d Continental Congress and signer of the Declaration of Independence, he was surgeon general of the armies of the Middle Department (1777), but resigned in a dispute with Dr. William Shippen when he was not supported by Washington. In turn, he became a critic of Washington's military competence, favoring the general's replacement by Gates or Conway. With James Wilson, he led the successful fight in the Pennsylvania ratifying convention for the adoption of the Constitution, and was treasurer of the U.S. Mint (1797–1813). On the staff of the Pennsylvania Hospital from 1783, he established the first free dispensary in the U.S. (1786) and held chairs at the College of Philadelphia (1789) and the new Univ. of Pennsylvania (beg. 1792), in medical theory and practice, exercising an enormous influence as a teacher in medicine and clinical practice. Stoutly advocating the view that disease was due to spasms in the blood vessels, he favored extensive bleedings, which he practiced during the yellow fever epidemic of 1793 in Philadelphia, doubtless increasing the mortality rates. His principal works were *An Account of the Bilious Remitting Yellow Fever* (1794), where he stressed the need for sanitation, and *Medical Inquiries and Observations upon Diseases of the Mind* (1812), with its pioneer insights into mental healing and psychiatry.

Ryder, Albert Pinkham (b. New Bedford, Mass., 19 Mar. 1847; d. Elmhurst, N.Y., 28 Mar. 1917), painter. He took his early training at New York City under the painter William E. Marshall and, beginning in 1871, studied at the National Academy of Design. Although Ryder was a member of the Society of American Artists and was elected to the National Academy in 1906, he received scant recognition during his lifetime, most of which he spent as a recluse in New York. His paintings, the bulk of which were produced between 1873 and 1898, derived from an intense poetic vision and rank among the finest imaginative works of modern art. His works include *Toilers of the Sea, The Flying Dutchman, Moonlight at Sea, Death on a Pale Horse, Forest of Arden, Macbeth and the Witches, Jonah and the Whale, Ophelia, Temple of the Mind,* and *Pegasus.*

Saarinen, Eliel (b. Helsinki, Finland, 20 Aug. 1873; d. Bloomfield Hills, Mich., 1 July 1950), architect and city planner, graduated from Polytechnic Institute of Helsinki. From 1896–1907 he was associated with Herman Gesellius and Armas Lindgren, architects, designing the Finnish Pavilion at the 1900 Paris World's Fair, their own studio and

residence "Hvitträsk" (1902), the National Museum of Helsinki, and the Helsinki Railroad Station (1905–14). He published *Munksnas-Haga* (1915), a major work on city planning. Winning 2d prize in an international competition for a new office building for the *Chicago Tribune* (1922), Saarinen's design had a marked influence upon developing a more organic form for tall buildings. He came to the U.S. in 1923, and taught for a year at the Univ. of Michigan School of Architecture. After designing several art schools in Bloomfield Hills, Mich., he was named head of the Cranbrook Academy of Art. As a city planner he advocated greenbelts and satellite communities, and wrote the treatise *The City: Its Growth, Its Decay, Its Future.* His buildings were known for his ability to express the spirit of their environment. Major works include Kleinhaus Music Hall, Buffalo (1939), the opera and concert sheds, chamber music hall, and studios of the Berkshire Music Center (1941), and Christ Lutheran Church, Minneapolis (1950). He collaborated with his son **Eero Saarinen** (1910–61), also an internationally renowned architect, on the Tabernacle Church of Christ in Columbus, Ind. (1942) and other buildings. He won international prizes for city plans for Tallinn, Estonia; Riga, Latvia; Canberra, Australia.

Saint-Gaudens, Augustus (b. Dublin, Ireland, 1 Mar. 1848; d. Cornish, N.H., 3 Aug. 1907), sculptor. Brought to the U.S. in his infancy, he was apprenticed to cameo cutters during his boyhood at New York City. He studied drawing in night classes at Cooper Union and attended the National Academy of Design; went to France (1867), was admitted to the École des Beaux Arts in Paris; and then went to Rome, where he came under the influence of the Renaissance tradition and won his first commissions. His *Hiawatha, Silence,* and bust of *William Maxwell Evarts* were followed by *Admiral Farragut* (1881; in Madison Square, New York City), which demonstrated the forceful characterization and original design that appeared in later works such as *The Puritan* (1885), *Lincoln* (1887; in Lincoln Park, Chicago), the *Shaw Memorial* (1897) at Boston, the equestrian statue of *Gen. John A. Logan* (1897) at Chicago, and the equestrian statue of *Gen. William T. Sherman* (1903) in New York City. Among other works by Saint-Gaudens are *Diana* (1892; figure modeled for the tower of the old Madison Square Garden), *Amor Caritas,* reliefs of *Homer Saint-Gaudens* and *Bastien-Lepage,* the *Adams Memorial* (the figure sometimes called *Grief*) at Rock Creek Cemetery, Washington, D.C., and the *Parnell Monument* at Dublin.

Salk, Jonas (b. New York City, 28 Oct. 1914–), virologist, received his B.S. (1934) from City College, New York, and his M.D. (1939) from New York Univ. College of Medicine, where he carried on virus research under Thomas Francis, Jr. Joining Francis (1944) at the Univ. of Michigan's School of Public Health, he did research on influenza vaccine. He joined (1947) the staff of the Univ. of Pittsburgh School of Medicine and became director of its Virus Research Laboratory. With funds from the National Foundation for Infantile Paralysis, Salk began work on a polio preventive in 1951. Using a technique reported (1949) by Dr. J. F. Enders (*q.v.*) for growing polio virus in cultures of nonnervous tissues, he announced (1953) a trial vaccine against polio, made by cultivating 3 strains of virus separately in monkey tissue and killing the viruses in the vaccine with formaldehyde. Tested during a mass trial conducted by Francis in 1954, the vaccine was pronounced safe (1955) and 80–90% effective. First recipient (1955) of the Medal for Distinguished Civilian Achievement awarded by Congress, Salk became director of the Salk Institute for Biological Studies, La Jolla in 1963. He wrote *Man Unfolding* (1972).

Samuelson, Paul Anthony (b. Gary, Ind., 15 May 1915–), economist. The son of Polish immigrants, he received his A.B. from the Univ. of Chicago (1935) and his Ph.D. from Harvard (1941), where he studied under Prof. Alvin M. Hansen, at the time a leading spokesman for Keynesian economics. Upon graduating, Samuelson became a member of the faculty at the Massachusetts Institute of Technology, where, as institute professor of economics, he still remains. Samuelson's textbook, *Economics, an Introductory Analysis,* was first published in 1948. Since then it has been translated into almost every modern language, has gone through 8 revisions and has sold more than 3 million copies. Samuelson is also known for his theoretical contributions to the field of economics, his emphasis on the use of mathematics and scientific methods in economic analysis, and his willingness to discard a theory for another which proves more valid. Samuelson has proven the basic unity between such fields as international trade, production economics, consumer behavior, and business cycles. Criticizing laissez-faire capitalism as a system in which the wealthier sector of society can coerce the poorer, he believes that government in a capitalist society must be involved in regulating employment and distributing income. During the Kennedy and Johnson administrations he served as President Kennedy's economic adviser and as a consultant to the Council of Economic Advisers (1961–69). Samuelson has also served as a consultant to the National Resources Board (1941–43), the War Production Board (1945), the U.S. Treasury (1945–52, 61–   ), the RAND Corp. (1949–   ), and the Federal Reserve Board (1967–   ). Samuelson received the Nobel prize for economic science (1970) for his work both in deriving new economic theorems and for devising new applications of existing ones. In addition to his textbook, his other works include *Foundations of Economic Analysis* (1947), *Readings in Economics* (1955), *Linear Programming and Economic Analysis* (1958), and *Collected Scientific Papers* (1966).

Sandburg, Carl (b. Galesburg, Ill., 6 Jan. 1878; d. Flat Rock, N.C., 22 July 1967), poet, son of a Swedish blacksmith, left school at 13, enlisted in the army, and saw active service in Puerto Rico in the Spanish-American War. He attended Lombard College in Galesburg (1898–1902), but never graduated. He served as a private secretary to the mayor of Milwaukee (1910–12) and as a newspaperman. First recognition as a poet came to him in 1914, when *Poetry* magazine awarded him the Helen Haire Levinson prize. His *Chicago Poems* (1915) established his reputation. In his rugged poems Middle Western vernacular is mixed with lyric passages. His *Collected Poems* received the Pulitzer prize for poetry (1951). A prodigious Lincoln scholar, he published the first vol. of his multivol. Lincoln biography, *The Prairie Years* (1926), followed by *The War Years* (1939), Pulitzer prize in history. He wrote *Rootabaga Stories* for children (1922). Collector and singer of American folk music, he edited his own collection, *The American Songbag* (1927). Other works include *The People, Yes* (1936); a novel, *Remembrance Rock* (1949); his autobiography, *Always the*

Young Strangers (1953); *Harvest Poems* (1960); *Honey and Salt* (1963).

Sanger, Margaret Higgins (b. Corning, N.Y., 14 Sept. 1883; d. Tucson, Ariz., 6 Sept. 1966), social reformer. She graduated from the Nurses Training School of White Plains (N.Y.) Hospital (1902), and soon settled with her husband, William Sanger, in Hastings-on-Hudson, N.Y. Tired of suburban living, they moved back to New York City (1912) and became involved in bohemian society. She became a Socialist and developed a particular interest in the sexual theories of Havelock Ellis, Ellen Key, and Sigmund Freud. As a visiting nurse for maternity cases on the lower east side of Manhattan she saw many women die of self-induced abortions. Renouncing her career in nursing as merely palliative and futile, she began to devote herself to the cause of birth control. She left her husband (from whom she was divorced in 1921), and went to France and Scotland (1913) to study birth control conditions. Returning to New York City, she launched (16 Mar. 1914) her magazine, *Woman Rebel*, as the spearhead of her movement. While not the first in the U.S. to advocate the use of contraceptives, she coined the term "birth control" (1914) and made the cause a worldwide movement. She was indicted (Aug. 1914) for sending pleas for birth control through the mails (under New York's Comstock Act of 1873 contraceptive data was classified as obscene). The indictment was quashed (1916), but the interest in the movement which it had aroused encouraged Mrs. Sanger to open the first birth control clinic in the U.S. (Brooklyn, 16 Oct. 1916). Charged with creating a public nuisance, she served 30 days in jail, but a decision on appeal enabled doctors to give contraceptive advice "for the prevention or cure of disease." Although legal harassment continued, her work was increasingly accepted. An effective organizer, she planned the first American Birth Control Conference (New York City, 1921), the International Birth Control Conference (New York City, 1921), and the World Population Conference (Geneva, 1927). She was the founder and first president of both the Margaret Sanger Research Bureau (1923) and the American Birth Control League (1921)—which became the Planned Parenthood Federation of America in 1946 and now includes more than 250 Planned Parenthood Centers in 150 cities throughout the U.S. She launched birth control programs in Europe, India, China, and Japan. Her numerous publications include *What Every Girl Should Know* (1916), *The Case for Birth Control* (1917), *Women, Morality, and Birth Control* (1922), *My Fight for Birth Control* (1931), *Margaret Sanger: An Autobiography* (1938).

Sargent, John Singer (b. Florence, Italy, 12 Jan. 1856; d. London, 15 Apr. 1925), painter, of American parentage, studied at the Academy of Fine Arts, Florence, and, when his parents moved to Paris (1874), at the École des Beaux Arts under Carolus Duran. After a first trip to the U.S. (1876), he returned to Paris, painting *Gitana* and exhibiting at the salons (1877–81). Following Spanish and Moroccan trips (1880) and a visit to Venice, he whipped up a storm of criticism in Paris by his *Madame Gautreau*, and at 28 established a studio in London. His triumphant *Carnation, Lily, Lily, Rose* (1884–86), first of a long series of pictures of children, brought him commissions in the U.S., where (1857) he painted Mrs. H. G. Marquand, Mrs. Charles Inches, and Mrs. John L. Gardner. Exhibiting in Boston (Dec. 1887), he made many visits to that city and was commissioned to do murals for the Boston Public Library (completed 1916), the Art Museum, and Harvard's Widener Library. A brilliant technician and a stylist both exotic and elegant, he was considered by contemporaries first of all as a portraitist (*Carmencita*, the Wertheimer family, and portraits of Theodore Roosevelt, Henry James, and Woodrow Wilson), but he did original and charming work as a painter of genre (*The Weavers, Neapolitan Children Bathing*), and his swiftly executed and luminous watercolors (*Melon Boats, White Ships*), painted during his later years, were to be considered his masterpieces. Declining a knighthood (1907) on the ground that he considered himself a U.S. citizen, he was sent to the front in northern France by the British government during World War I, where he painted *Gassed* (1919).

Schurz, Carl (b. Liblar, near Cologne, Germany, 2 Mar. 1829; d. New York City, 14 May 1906), soldier, statesman, diplomat, and author. Taking part in the unsuccessful German revolutionary movement (1848–49) while a student at the Univ. of Bonn, he emigrated to the U.S. (1852) and in 1856 settled at Watertown, Wis. He became active in politics, helped organize the Republican party in Wisconsin, and, as an antislavery man, actively supported Lincoln against Douglas in the Illinois senatorial campaign of 1858. He was admitted to the Wisconsin bar (1858) and practiced law at Milwaukee. As chairman of the Wisconsin delegation to the Chicago Republican Convention (1860) he backed Lincoln's nomination, was appointed (1861) minister to Spain, returned to the U.S. (1862), and was appointed brigadier general of volunteers. He commanded a division at 2d Bull Run (1862), was promoted to major general (1863), and in 1863 took part in the battles of Chancellorsville and Gettysburg. At President Johnson's request he made a survey (July–Sept. 1865) of the postwar South, was Washington correspondent (1865–66) of the New York *Tribune,* editor (1866–67) of the Detroit *Post,* and joint editor and owner (1867–69) of the St. Louis *Westliche Post.* An anti-Grant Republican, he served (1869–75) in the Senate as a member from Missouri and was one of the chief organizers of the Liberal Republican movement (1870–72). An exponent of civil service reform and of a liberal policy toward the South, he supported Hayes in 1876 and served (1877–81) as Secretary of the Interior, carrying out signal reforms in the treatment of the Indians. He lived in New York after 1881 and was an editor (1881–83) of the New York *Evening Post,* chief editorial writer (1892–98) for *Harper's Weekly,* and president (1892–1900) of the National Civil Service Reform League. He wrote *Henry Clay* (2 vols., 1887), a penetrating essay on Lincoln (1891), and *The Reminiscences of Carl Schurz* (3 vols., 1907–08).

Scott, Winfield (b. "Laurel Branch," near Petersburg, Va., 13 June 1786; d. West Point, N.Y., 29 May 1866), soldier, popularly called "Old Fuss and Feathers." He attended the College of William and Mary; served in the War of 1812, attaining the rank of brigadier general (1814) and performing gallantly at the battles of Chippewa and Lundy's Lane (1814), for which he was breveted a major general and acclaimed as a military hero. He served in the Black Hawk War and in the campaigns against the Seminole and Creek Indians, and in 1838, following the *Caroline* crisis in

Anglo-American relations, restored peace on the Canadian border. He became (June 1841) general in chief of the U.S. army, and in the Mexican War commanded the amphibious operation that took Vera Cruz (27 Mar. 1847) and led the overland advance over mountainous terrain, winning the battles of Cerro Cordo, Churubusco, Molino del Rey, and Chapultepec, and finally taking Mexico City (14 Sept. 1847). After the war his strained relations with Polk resulted in the preferring of charges against Scott; the charges, however, were withdrawn, and in 1852 Congress passed a resolution giving Scott the pay and rank of a lieutenant general. The Whig candidate for the presidency in the campaign of 1852, he was decisively defeated by Franklin Pierce. In 1859 he again acted as peacemaker between the U.S. and Great Britain, on this occasion averting serious trouble in the dispute over the possession of San Juan Island in Puget Sound. Despite his Virginian background, he remained loyal to the Union when the Civil War broke out, and as commander of the U.S. army made preparations for defending the capital. He retired on 1 Nov. 1861.

Seaborg, Glenn Theodore (b. Ishpeming, Mich., 19 Apr. 1912–   ), physical chemist. He was graduated (1934) from the Univ. of California, where he received the degree of Ph.D. in 1937 and became a full professor in 1945. With associates, including Dr. Edward M. McMillan, with whom he shared the Nobel prize in chemistry (1951) for their work in the transuranic elements, he discovered plutonium, which supplied the fuel for the atomic bomb. The researches of Seaborg and his associates on heavier-than-uranium substances led to the discovery of 8 other elements, including americium (95); curium (96); berkelium (97);

californium (98), produced by the alpha bombardment of americium and curium; einsteinium (99); fermium (100); mendelerium (101); and nobelium (102). The instruments and methods which were devised for the determination of these transuranic elements included the use of the Berkeley 184-inch cyclotron, and virtually created the new technique of ultramicrochemistry. Chancellor of the Univ. of California at Berkeley, 1958–61, he served as chairman of the AEC (1961–70).

Seward, William Henry (b. Florida, Orange Co., N.Y., 16 May 1801; d. Auburn, N.Y., 10 Oct. 1872), statesman, was graduated from Union College (1820), admitted to the bar (1822), and commenced practice in Auburn. Affiliated with the Anti-Masonic party, he was elected to the state senate (1830–34), but defeated for reelection (1832), and was unsuccessful Whig nominee for governor (1834). After election (1838) and reelection (1840) as governor, he resumed the practice of law with notable success in criminal cases and in the patent field. Elected to the U.S. Senate (1848) and reelected (1854), he took an advanced stand against slavery. In his speech of 11 Mar. 1850 attacking the Compromise of 1850 he enunciated "a higher law" than the Constitution. Opposed to the Kansas-Nebraska Bill, he declared at Rochester on 25 Oct. 1858 that the slavery struggle was "an irrepressible conflict" between North and South. Prominent in the new Republican party, he was unsuccessful candidate for president in 1856 and again in 1860, but entered Lincoln's cabinet as Secretary of State. His advocacy of a strong foreign policy to unify the country faced with civil war was fortunately not heeded by Lincoln. His most notable achievements were his negotiations with Great Britain

of the *Trent* affair and the *Alabama* claims. At the end of the war he forced France to agree to withdrawal from Mexico within a specified time limit. Coincident with Lincoln's assassination, he was wounded by Lewis Powell, co-conspirator with John Wilkes Booth. On his recovery he continued in the cabinet of Johnson and supported him against the Radical Republicans. An expansionist, he acquired Alaska from Russia (1867) for $7,200,000 ("Seward's Folly"), negotiated a treaty for the purchase of the Danish West Indies which the Senate failed to ratify, and advocated the annexation of Hawaii.

Shattuck, Lemuel (b. Ashby, Mass., 15 Oct. 1793; d. Boston, Mass., 17 Jan. 1859), statistician. After briefly attending Appleton Academy, he taught school at Troy and Albany, N.Y., and then in Detroit. Returning to Concord, Mass., he set up a mercantile business at the age of 30 and, in addition, took a leadership role in reorganizing the school system of that town. Around 1836 he moved to Boston to become a successful publisher and bookseller, retiring at the age of 46 to devote himself to public service. A study of the local history of Concord (1835) and then a turn at genealogy suggested to him the value for vital statistics of birth, marriage, and death records. Founding the American Statistical Association (1839), he was instrumental in securing the passage in 1842 of a Massachusetts law requiring the registration of births, marriages, and deaths. Chosen to direct a census of the city of Boston in 1845, he made it one of persons rather than of families. He was instrumental in extending the scope of the U.S. Census of 1850, which marked a notable advance in information gathering. Chairman (1849) of the commission to make a sanitary survey of Massachusetts, his *Report* (1859) used newly gathered statistics for farsighted recommendations, which stamped the report a landmark in U.S. public health.

Shaw, Lemuel (b. Braintree, Mass., 9 Jan. 1781; d. Boston, 30 Mar. 1861), jurist, was graduated from Harvard (1800), was admitted to the bar (1804), and began practice in Boston. Representative in the General Court (1811–14, 1820, and 1829), he was also state senator (1821–22), and a member of the constitutional convention of 1820. He became chief justice of Massachusetts in 1830 and served for 30 years. On the bench he reshaped the state common law in accordance with changing industrial and social conditions, with especially notable contributions in the field of railway and public utility law. He invariably construed public grants in favor of the community and against private interests. His ruling (*Lombard* v. *Stearns,* 1849) that a water company was under an obligation to serve the public was a judicial landmark, as was his decision in *Comm.* v. *Hunt* (1842, p. 762), supporting legitimate trade union activity. On the other hand, in expounding the "fellow-servant rule," holding a company not liable when an employee was injured owing to the negligence of another employee, he materially delayed the expansion of workmen's compensation. Shaw presided (1850) over the trial of Prof. John W. Webster for the murder of Dr. George Parkman. Although personally opposed to slavery, Shaw upheld school segregation in Boston (*Roberts* v. *Boston,* 1849), and refused (1851) to release Sims, the fugitive slave, on habeas corpus.

Sheridan, Philip Henry (b. Albany, N.Y., 6 Mar. 1831; d. Nonquitt, Mass., 5 Aug. 1888), Union soldier, was reared in Ohio, had little schooling, clerked in a store at 14, and was appointed to West Point in 1848. Suspended a year for misconduct, he was graduated in 1853. He first saw service along the Rio Grande and against the Indians in the Northwest. When war broke out he was made captain in the 13th Infantry (1861), with service in the Corinth campaign, then (1862) colonel of the 2d Michigan Cavalry, and for his victory at Boonville, Mo., made brigadier general a little over a month later. Major general of volunteers (31 Dec. 1862), he commanded the 20th Corps, Army of the Cumberland, at Chickamauga, and his charge over Missionary Ridge at Chattanooga contributed largely to Grant's victory. Taking command (Apr. 1864) of the cavalry of the Army of the Potomac, he protected the flanks of Grant's army and attacked Confederate communications around Richmond. In Aug. 1864 he was given command of the Army of the Shenandoah, with orders to push the enemy south and destroy all supplies in the Valley. He defeated Jubal Early at Opequon Creek, Fisher's Hall, and Cedar Creek, making his renowned ride to the battlefield from Winchester 20 miles away to turn a near defeat into victory. Following this raid, he turned the flank of the Confederate army (1 Apr. 1865), forcing it to evacuate Petersburg and retreat to Appomattox. Military governor of the 5th Dist., Louisiana and Texas, with headquarters at New Orleans, he pursued stern policies and earned President Johnson's disapproval and transfer to the Dept. of Missouri, where he launched military operations against hostile Indians, whom he forced to settle on reservations allotted them. Lieutenant general (1869), he went to Europe (1870) to observe the Franco-Prussian War, and was made a full general (1888). He wrote *Personal Memoirs* (1888).

Sherman, Roger (b. Newton, Mass., 19 Apr. 1721; d. New Haven, Conn., 23 July 1793), jurist and statesman. Trained as a shoemaker by his father, Sherman nevertheless became surveyor of New Haven Co. (1745–58), studied law, and was admitted to the bar (1754). While a successful merchant, he served as justice of the peace for Litchfield Co. (1755–61) and for New Haven (1765–66), and as judge of the superior court (1766–67). As chairman of the New Hampshire Committee of Correspondence, Sherman backed a colonial boycott of English goods. By 1774, he denied Parliament's right to legislate for the colonies. A delegate to the Continental Congress (1774–81, 1783–84), he was a member of the committee which drafted the Declaration of Independence and the Articles of Confederation. At the Constitutional Convention (1787), Sherman introduced the Connecticut Compromise. Afterward he campaigned in the press for the Constitution's ratification under the pen name "A Countryman." He served in the first U.S. House of Representatives (1789–91). As U.S. senator (1791–93) he favored the federal government's assumption of state debts and opposed locating the capital on the Potomac. He was the only man to sign the Continental Association (18 Oct. 1774), the Declaration of Independence, the Articles of Confederation, and the Constitution.

Sherman, William Tecumseh (b. Lancaster, Ohio, 8 Feb. 1820; d. New York City, 14 Feb. 1891), soldier, was graduated from West Point (1840), served in the War with Mexico (1846–47), resigning from the army (1855) to engage in banking in San Francisco. After his bank failed, he practiced law briefly in Leavenworth, Kan., and then served as superintendent of the military academy at Alexandria, La. (1859–61). At the outbreak of the Civil War he rejoined the U.S. army, commanded a brigade at 1st Bull Run, was given command in Kentucky (Oct. 1861), promoted to major general for conduct at Shiloh (6–7 Apr. 1862), participated in Grant's final Vicksburg campaign, and, as commander of the Army of the Tennessee, in the Battle of Chattanooga. He succeeded Grant (Mar. 1864) in command of the military division of the Mississippi, set out from Chattanooga (May), and began his invasion of Georgia with a brilliant campaign against J. E. Johnston and later Hood. Taking Atlanta (1 Sept.), he made his "March to the Sea" with 62,000 men without supplies, capturing Savannah (21 Dec.). Under orders to live off the country and to destroy war supplies, public buildings, railroads, and factories, his army exceeded instructions by acts of pillage. In bringing the war home to civilians by destruction of goods rather than life, Sherman has been considered the first modern general. Turning northward, he marched through the Carolinas to join Grant in Virginia, receiving the surrender of J. E. Johnston at Durham, N.C. (26 Apr. 1865). In 1869 he succeeded Grant in command of the army, until his retirement (1884). His *Memoirs* (2 vols.) appeared in 1875.

Shockley, William Bradford (b. London, Eng., 13 Feb. 1910–   ), physicist and inventor, received his B.S. (1932) from the California Institute of Technology, and his Ph.D. from MIT (1936), in which year he joined the technical staff of the Bell Telephone Laboratories. During World War II he directed (1942–44) research at Columbia for the antisubmarine warfare operations program, and in the postwar period served as director of the research weapons system evaluations group, Department of Defense (1955–58). Known for his studies of semiconductivity and other aspects of solid-state physics, he shared with John Bardeen and W. H. Brattain the 1956 Nobel prize in physics for developing (1948) the transistor, a semiconductor and substitute for the vacuum tube. He is the inventor of the junction transistor (1951). He wrote *Electrons and Holes in Semiconductors* (1950) and edited *Imperfections in Nearly Perfect Crystals* (1952), *Mechanics* (with W. A. Gong, 1966). His recent exposition of alleged links between IQ, heredity, and race has aroused sharp controversy.

Silliman, Benjamin (b. Trumbull, Conn., 8 Aug. 1779; d. New Haven, Conn., 24 Nov. 1864), educator, scientist, was graduated from Yale (1796), studied law at New Haven, and was admitted to the Connecticut bar (1802), but abandoned law for chemistry and natural history. Professor of chemistry and natural history at Yale from 1802 to 1853, he was extraordinarily influential as a teacher and popularizer of science. His interest in geology was aroused on a trip to England and the Continent (1805). Utilizing the mineral collection of Col. George Gibbs, he introduced (1813) an illustrated lecture course in mineralogy and geology, and was one of the organizers of the Yale Medical School (1818). He began to give (1818) scientific lectures, utilizing experiments as demonstrations, open to the public of New Haven, and, responding to popular demand, lectured in New York, New England, and other parts of the country. He initiated the lecture series of the Lowell Institute (1839–40). He founded (1818) the influential *American Journal of Science and Arts,* which he edited for 20 years. In addition to many scientific papers, he wrote *A Journal of Travels in England, Holland and Scotland* (1810),

A Visit to Europe in 1851 (1853), and edited *The Elements of Experimental Chemistry* (1814).

Simms, William Gilmore (b. Charleston, S.C., 17 Apr. 1806; d. there, 11 June 1870), author, studied law privately and in 1827 was admitted to the Charleston bar. Writing in a Byronic vein, he produced 5 vols. of verse by 1832. Also active as a journalist, he was editor (1828–33) of the Charleston *City Gazette.* His first novel was *Martin Faber* (1833), a study of a criminal. With *Guy Rivers* (1834) and *The Yemassee* (1835), Simms inaugurated the series of romances based on South Carolina history and Southern frontier life by which he is chiefly remembered: The Border Romances, including *Richard Hurdis* (1838), *Border Beagles* (1840), *Beauchampe* (1842), *Helen Halsey* (1845), *Charlemont* (1856), *Voltmeier* (1869) and *The Cub of the Panther* (1869); and the Revolutionary Romances, including *Mellichampe* (1836), *The Kinsmen* (1841; published as *The Scout* in 1854), *Katharine Walton* (1851), *The Sword and the Distaff* (1853; published as *Woodcraft* in 1854), *The Forayers* (1855), and *Eutaw* (1856). A prolific writer who is the most representative of the men of letters of the Old South, he also wrote plays, a *History* (1840) and *Geography* (1843) of South Carolina, biographies of Francis Marion (1844) and Nathanael Greene (1849), and contributed to *The Pro-Slavery Argument* (1852).

Slater, Samuel (b. Belper, Derbyshire, England, 9 June 1768; d. Webster, Mass., 21 Apr. 1835), pioneer of cotton manufacture in the U.S. Apprenticed (1783) to Jedediah Strutt, a partner of Richard Arkwright in the development of cotton textile machinery, Slater became thoroughly skilled in all aspects of the business. At a time when the British government forbade the emigration of textile workers and the export of textile machinery or data, Slater memorized the details of the machinery made by Crompton, Arkwright, and Hargreaves, and, attracted by the bounties offered by American state legislatures, emigrated to the U.S. (1789). He met (1790) Moses Brown at Providence, R.I., and for the firm of Almy & Brown reproduced from memory Arkwright's cotton machinery, thus ushering in the American cotton industry. He became (1793) a member of the firm of Almy, Brown & Slater, which built a plant at Pawtucket, R.I. In 1798 he formed a partnership under the name of Samuel Slater & Co., which established plants at Pawtucket, Smithfield (later Slatersville), R.I.; East Webster, Mass.; Amoskeag Falls, N.H.; and Oxford (later Webster), Mass. In 1815 he began the manufacture of woolen cloth in his plants.

Smith, Alfred Emanuel (b. New York City, 30 Oct. 1873; d. there, 5 Oct. 1944), governor of New York, grew up on Manhattan's lower east side, attended parochial school, and worked in the Fulton Fish Market. Tammany assemblyman (1903–15) and majority leader of the assembly, he was identified with reform legislation, playing with Robert Wagner a leading role in the New York State Factory Investigation Comm., which secured the passage of safety laws after the Triangle fire (1911). Sheriff of New York Co. (1915–17) and president of the New York City Board of Aldermen (1917), he was governor of New York for 4 terms (1918–21, 1923–28). An outstanding state executive, he demonstrated exceptional talent for political administration and progressive legislation in the fields of labor, housing, and public works. Nominated for president by Franklin D. Roosevelt at the Demo-

cratic National Convention in 1924, he was opposed by William G. McAdoo, both withdrawing after 95 ballots, making possible the nomination of John W. Davis. First Roman Catholic nominee for president (1928) and advocate of the repeal of the 18th Amendment, he was defeated by Herbert Hoover. Failing to secure the Democratic nomination in 1932, he retired from politics and engaged in business. An organizer of the American Liberty League (1934), he aligned himself with the opponents of the New Deal.

Smith, David Roland (b. Decatur, Ind., 9 Mar. 1906; d. Albany, N.Y., 23 May 1965), sculptor, studied art at Ohio Univ. (1924), Notre Dame (1925), George Washington Univ. (1926), and at the Art Students League in New York City (1926–32). A summer job (1925) as a welder and riveter in the Studebaker plant, South Bend, Ind., gave him a feeling for industrial forms and for the handling of tools. Early sculptures (1930–39) reflected his interest in painting and his assimilation of European styles such as Cubism, Constructivism, and Surrealism (*Reclining Figure*, 1935), and specifically the influence of Picasso (*Head,* 1932) and Giacometti (*Head with Cogs for Eyes,* 1933). From 1934–40 he rented studio space at the Terminal Iron Works in Brooklyn. He participated in the art programs of the New Deal, first as technical supervisor in the mural division for the Treasury Relief Art Project (1937). Smith's first 1-man show occurred at the East River Gallery (1938). A period characterized by a unique symbolic and expressive style (1939–52) dates from *Medals of Dishonor* (completed 1940), an attack on war and social injustice. From this period are *Head of a Still Life* (1940), *Widow's Lament* (1942–43), and *The Cathedral* (1950). Beginning c.1951–52 and lasting until his death, he produced works (normally displayed outdoors) in a public, monumental sculptural style, the turning point coming with *Australia* (9 ft. high, 1951). He produced abstract sculpture in related series: *Agricola, Tank Totem, Verticals, Voltri-Bolton* (portraying the human figure in the flat planes of cubism), *Zig* (7 works, 1961–64), and his culminating achievement, the *Cubi* series (1961–65). He also produced landscape sculptures (*Hudson River Landscape,* 1951) and the lyrical *Study in Arcs* (1959). Smith's work was an amalgam of painting and sculpture. He would employ industrially fabricated units and raw materials of industrial construction (*Tank Totem,* 1955–56) or welded many small steel units together (*Raven,* 1957). Influential and prolific, Smith understood the sculptural possibilities of Cubism but developed them far beyond what Cubist sculptors had achieved. His mastery enabled the creation of a new monumental sculptural style.

Smith, John (b. Willoughby, Lincolnshire, England, c.1579; d. London, England, 21 June 1631), soldier of fortune, explorer and author, was apprenticed to a merchant, and then sought adventure as a soldier on the Continent, serving against the Turks. Returning to England (c.1604), where according to his own claim he participated in the organization of the London Co. (1606), he left for Virginia in Dec. 1606, as one of the party of 144 colonists aboard 3 ships and disembarked at Jamestown on 24 May 1607. He was made a member of the governing council, was active in exploration, and performed his most valuable services in securing food from the Indians for the hard-pressed colony. According to Smith's account in his *General Historie of Virginia* (1624), he was taken prisoner by the Indians, was condemned to death, and was saved by the intercession of Pocahontas, daughter of the chief Powhatan. When Smith returned to Jamestown (Jan. 1608), he found his enemies had seized control, was arrested and sentenced to hang, but was saved by the arrival of Capt. Christopher Newport with supplies and colonists from England. In the summer of 1608 Smith explored the Potomac and Rappahannock rivers and Chesapeake Bay. To Newport, who sailed for England in June 1608, he gave the manuscript of the account of Virginia's settlement brought out that year as *A True Relation.* Elected president by the council in late 1608, he governed the colony until 1609, returning to England in Oct. of that year. He published *A Map of Virginia* (1612). In Mar. 1614, he went on an expedition along the New England coast on behalf of London merchants. He returned with an excellent cargo of fish and furs, and in *A Description of New England* (1616), which fixed the name on that region, included a valuable map, and stressed the importance of fishing.

Smith, Joseph (b. Sharon, Vt., 23 Dec. 1805; d. Carthage, Ill., 27 June 1844), Mormon founder. Little is known about his childhood before 1820, when he claimed to have had a vision from God and then, 3 years later (21 Sept. 1823), to have been visited by the angel Moroni, who declared that the second advent was near and that Smith was to help God in these latter days. In a subsequent visit (1827), the angel directed him to buried golden plates (Palmyra, N.Y.) containing a history of the American Indians which described them as the lost tribe of Israel. With the aid of magic stones called Urim and Thummim he translated the text from "reformed Egyptian" and published it as *The Book* *of Mormon* (1830). Generally, scholars today regard the book as a combination of Indian legends, anti-Masonry, Biblical, and popular stories. Smith organized the Church of Jesus Christ of Latter-Day Saints on 6 Apr. 1830 at Fayette, N.Y., in order to restore primitive Christianity. Swelling numbers of converts followed Smith from New York to Ohio, Missouri, and Illinois, where at Commerce (renamed Nauvoo) he ruled his church of about 18,000 members and practiced polygamy (declared as a revelation 12 July 1843). Jailed for destroying the press of a heretical newspaper, he and his brother were fatally shot by an anti-Mormon mob. Smith is considered by the Church of Jesus Christ of Latter-Day Saints to be "seer, and translator, a prophet, an apostle of Jesus Christ, an Elder of the Church."

Smith, Theobald (b. Albany, N.Y., 31 July 1859; d. New York City, 10 Dec. 1934), pathologist and parasitologist. He was graduated from Cornell (Ph.B., 1881) and the Albany Medical College (M.D., 1883), and pursued postgraduate studies in biology at Johns Hopkins, Cornell, and the Univ. of Toronto. In 1884 he was named director of the newly established pathological laboratory in the Bureau of Animal Industry, Department of Agriculture. In 1886 he organized at the Columbian (later George Washington) Univ. the first department of bacteriology in any U.S. medical school, and was professor there from 1886 to 1895. With Dr. Daniel E. Salmon he made studies in the diseases of hogs, set forth in *Special Report on the Cause and Prevention of Swine Plague* (1891), and showed that the alarming mortality among pigs was caused chiefly by hog cholera and swine plague. He also demonstrated (1886) the practicability of immunizing man to cholera by injection of the filtered virus

of hogs. He published studies (1898, 1902) on the differentiation of the human and bovine types of the bacillus of tuberculosis. His researches in Texas fever of cattle resulted in the publication of *Investigations into the Nature, Causation, and Prevention of Texas or Southern Cattle Fever* (in collaboration with F. L. Kilborne, 1893), which set forth the discovery of the transmission of the protozoan parasite *Babesia bigemina* by the cattle tick *Boophilus annulatus,* a study which for the first time demonstrated the transmission of diseases by insect carriers. Smith served as director (1895–1915) of the pathological laboratory of the Massachusetts Board of Health, professor of comparative pathology (1896–1915) in the Harvard Medical School, and was director (1915–29) of the department of animal pathology of the Rockefeller Institute for Medicine. In 1933 he became president of the Rockefeller Institute. Among his many publications are *Studies in Vaccinal Immunity Towards Diseases of the Bovine Placenta Due to Bacillus Abortus* (1923) and *Parasitism and Disease* (1934). The debt of the American livestock industry to Smith is almost incalculable.

Stanford, Leland (b. Watervliet, N.Y., 9 Mar. 1824; d. Palo Alto, Calif., 21 June 1893), railroad builder, attended school at Clinton and Cazenovia, N.Y., entered an Albany law firm at the age of 21, and was admitted to the bar 3 years later. After the burning of his law office at Port Washington (1852), he followed his younger brothers to the Pacific coast, setting up in the merchandise business in El Dorado Co., and then Sacramento. Republican nominee for governor (1859), he was decisively defeated, but was elected in 1861 due to a split in the Democratic party. As governor he held California in the Union. Interested by

Theodore Dehone Judah (1826–63), engineer, in a transcontinental railroad, he joined with Mark Hopkins (1813–78), Charles Crocker (1822–88), and Collis P. Huntington (1821–1900) in organizing the Central Pacific R.R. (1861), which benefited by grants and other state assistance while he was governor. At the expiration (1863) of his term of office, he devoted himself entirely to railroad affairs, handling the financial and political interests of the Central Pacific, while Crocker took charge of construction and Huntington acted as chief railroad lobbyist back East. He was president and director of the Central Pacific R.R. from the beginning until his death and director of the Southern Pacific Co. (1885–93) and president (1885–90), as well as a shareholder in the railroad construction companies. His election as U.S. senator (1885–93) caused a break with Huntington, who succeeded in supplanting him as president of the Southern Pacific. He founded (1885) and endowed Stanford Univ. in memory of his son Leland Stanford, Jr. (d. 1884), and selected David Starr Jordan (1851–1931) as president.

Stanley, Wendell Meredith (b. Ridgeville, Ind., 16 Aug. 1904; d. Salamanca, Spain, 15 June 1971), biochemist. He was graduated from Earlham College (B.S., 1926) at Richmond, Ind., and from the Univ. of Illinois (M.S., 1927; Ph.D., 1929), where he was a research associate and instructor in chemistry (1929–30). As a National Research fellow he studied at Munich (1930–31) and was associated with the Rockefeller Institute for Medical Research (1931–48). He was professor of biochemistry and director of the virus laboratory at the Univ. of California (1948–69). He was the first to isolate and crystallize a virus (the tobacco mosaic virus) and has done notable work on the chemical na-

ture of influenza and other viruses, and in the fields of diphenyl sterochemistry and lepracidal compounds. In 1946 he shared the Nobel prize in chemistry with J. H. Northrop.

Stanton, Elizabeth Cady (b. Johnstown, N.Y., 12 Nov. 1815; d. New York City, 26 Oct. 1902), social reformer and militant feminist, was graduated (1832) from the Troy (N.Y.) Female Seminary, and in 1840 married the lawyer and reformer Henry Brewster Stanton. In 1840, while attending a London anti-slavery convention where Lucretia C. Mott and other American women were refused official accreditation because of their sex, Mrs. Stanton joined with Mrs. Mott in planning a women's rights convention in the U.S. This gathering, held at the Wesleyan Methodist Church in Seneca Falls, N.Y. (19–20 July 1848), ushered in the modern feminist movement. Mrs. Stanton was also active in the abolition and temperance movements, but devoted her chief efforts to the crusade for women's rights. After 1851 she worked in close cooperation with Susan B. Anthony. She was president of the National Woman Suffrage Association and its successor body, and was coeditor (1868 *et seq.*) of the *Revolution,* an organ of the feminist movement.

Steffens, Lincoln (b. San Francisco, 6 Apr. 1866; d. Carmel, Calif., 9 Aug. 1936), journalist, reformer, obtained a Ph.B. from the Univ. of California (1889), then studied abroad at Heidelberg, Munich, Leipzig, and the Sorbonne. Returning to New York (1892), he worked as a reporter for the *Evening Post,* covering the Lexow Committee's exposé of vice, and as city editor of the *Commercial Advertiser* (1897). Joining (1901) the staff of *McClure's Magazine,* which included Ida Tarbell and Ray

Stannard Baker, he wrote a series of articles, "Tweed Days in St. Louis" (1902), a pioneer "muckraking" article, focusing attention on municipal corruption in St. Louis, and following with an exposé of Minneapolis. His *Shame of the Cities* (1904) stressed the link between business and politics, maintaining that privilege was the enemy rather than the corruptionists. With Tarbell and Baker, he took over (1906) the *American Magazine,* which quickly became a major reform publication, but quit the following year to write as a freelance. He sponsored Walter Lippmann, whom he made his secretary, and John Reed, and after a trip to Russia (1917) he lectured in favor of a just peace. On the William C. Bullitt mission to Russia (1919), he met Lenin. ("I have seen the future; and it works.") His *Autobiography* (1931) evidenced disillusionment with the early reform efforts and a more revolutionary approach.

Steinmetz, Charles Proteus [Karl August Rudolf], (b. Breslau, Germany, 9 Apr. 1865; d. Schenectady, N.Y., 26 Oct. 1923), mathematician and electrical engineer, distinguished himself as a student in the sciences at the Univ. of Breslau, but owing to his Socialist activities was forced to flee Germany, emigrating to the U.S. in 1889 after a year in Switzerland. He worked with Osterheld and Eickemeyer Co. at Yonkers, N.Y., and, after its absorption by the General Electric Co. (1892), with G.E. at Schenectady, N.Y., serving as consulting engineer until his death, as well as professor of electrical engineering at Union College (1902–23). Concentrating on electrical engineering problems, he designed an alternating current commutator motor and determined the law of hysteresis mathematically from existing data, reporting his results in 2 papers

before the American Institute of Electrical Engineers (1892). This led to great progress in generator and motor design. He discovered a mathematical method of calculating the alternating current theory, which he presented to the International Electrical Congress at Chicago (1893), and published, with Ernest J. Berg, as a text, *Theory and Calculation of Alternating Current Phenomena* (1897). Expanded into several vols. (1901, 1911, 1916, 1917), this work established the universally adopted method in alternating current calculations which made a difficult subject more comprehensible to electrical engineers, and spawned major commercial developments. Steinmetz's work on lightning ("transient electrical phenomena," 1907–21) produced man-made lightning in the laboratory and the development of lightning arresters for the protection of electrical power lines. Steinmetz secured some 200 patents for improvements in electrical apparatus. Remaining a Socialist, he served as president of the Schenectady board of education (1912–23) and of the common council (1916–23).

Stephens, Alexander Hamilton (b. in present-day Taliaferro Co., Ga., 11 Feb. 1812; d. Atlanta, Ga., 4 Mar. 1883), statesman, author, and Confederate vice-president, was graduated (1832) from the Univ. of Georgia, admitted to the Georgia bar (1834), and practiced law at Crawfordville, Ga. He served in the state legislature (1836–42) and was a Whig (later Democratic) representative in Congress (1843–59). While he opposed the Mexican War, he resisted efforts to restrict slavery in the territory won from Mexico. In 1852 he entered the Democratic ranks. During the critical pre–Civil War years he advocated sectional moderation and conciliation, but became increasingly firm on the slavery issue. At the Georgia secessionist convention (Jan. 1861) he opposed immediate separation, but when the ordinance of secession was adopted he took part in organizing the new government and was elected (9 Feb. 1861) vice-president of the Confederate States of America. In his "cornerstone speech" delivered at Savannah (21 Mar. 1861), he termed slavery the basic foundation of the Confederate government. During the war his zeal for states' rights and civil liberties brought him into conflict with Jefferson Davis. He was head of the Confederate peace mission at the Hampton Roads Conference (1865). After the war he was held prisoner for 5 months at Ft. Warren in Boston Harbor. Although elected (1866) to the U.S. Senate, he was not permitted to take his seat. He was an editor and part proprietor (1871–73) of the Atlanta *Southern Sun*, served in Congress (1873–82), and in 1882 was elected governor of Georgia. He wrote *A Constitutional View of the Late War Between the States* (2 vols., 1868, 1870) and *The Reviewers Reviewed* (1872).

Stevens, Thaddeus (b. Danville, Vt., 4 Apr. 1792; d. Washington, D.C., 11 Aug. 1868), statesman, was graduated (1814) from Dartmouth College; moved (1814) to York, Pa., where he studied law; and after being admitted to the bar settled (1816) in Gettysburg, Pa., and practiced law, soon becoming one of the leading attorneys in his part of the state. His strong antislavery convictions led him to defend many fugitive slaves without fee. In 1826 he became a partner in the iron works of James D. Paxton & Co., which in 1828 became Stevens & Paxton. Elected on the Anti-Masonic ticket, he was a member of the Pennsylvania House of Representatives (1833–35, 1837, 1841) and served as a delegate to the state constitutional convention

(1838). In 1842 he moved to Lancaster, Pa. Elected (1848) to Congress on the Whig ticket, he served until 1853, becoming one of the leading antislavery spokesmen. He took an important part in the formation of the Republican party in Pennsylvania, and was elected (1858) as a Republican to the 36th and the four succeeding Congresses, serving from 1859 until his death. In 1860 he opposed concessions to the South. He was made chairman of the Ways and Means Committee, thus increasing his power in Congress; and during the Civil War became the foremost exponent of a stern policy toward the South, opposing Lincoln's plan of reconstruction in favor of harsh measures. As chairman of the House group of the Joint Committee on Reconstruction, he was the leader of the congressional Radical Republicans. He broke with President Andrew Johnson over the Freedmen's Bureau Bill (1866), imposed military Reconstruction on the South (1867), and was chairman of the managers appointed by the House in 1868 to conduct the impeachment proceedings against President Johnson, but was prevented by failing health from taking an important part in the trial.

Stevenson, Adlai Ewing (b. Los Angeles, Calif., 5 Feb. 1900; d. London, England, 14 July 1965), statesman, served in the U.S. Naval Reserve (1918) as apprentice seaman, was graduated from Princeton (A.B., 1922), attended Harvard Law School and received his law degree from Northwestern (1926), when he was admitted to the Illinois bar. He practiced law in Chicago (1927–41), except for the years (1933–35) when he served as special counsel to the new AAA (1933–34) and Asst. Gen. Counsel, Federal Alcohol Administration (1934). During World War II he was special assistant to the Secretary of the

Navy (1941–44). Assigned to the Foreign Economic Administration, he headed a mission to Italy (1943). Subsequently (1944) he returned to Europe for the War Department as a member of an Air Force mission. Special assistant to Secretaries of State Stettinius and Byrnes (1945), he was a member of the U.S. delegation to the UN Conference at San Francisco (Apr. 1945), Senior Adviser to the U.S. delegation to the UN (1946), and alternate delegate (1946–47). Elected Democratic governor of Illinois (Nov. 1948) by an unprecedented 572,067 plurality, he overhauled and reorganized the state administration, attacked gambling and corruption, introduced state economies, vetoed a loyalty oath bill, and fought unsuccessfully for a state FEPC. Democratic nominee for president (1952, 1956), he was defeated both times by Dwight D. Eisenhower. In 1961 he was made U.S. ambassador to the UN with cabinet rank.

Stieglitz, Alfred (b. Hoboken, N.J., 1 Jan. 1864; d. New York City, 13 Apr. 1946), photographer, studied at the College of the City of New York (1879–81) and the Berlin Polytechnic Laboratory (1881–90), where he experimented in new photographic techniques. Returning to New York (1890) after winning numerous photographic awards abroad, he edited a series of photo magazines, *American Amateur Photographer* (1892–96), *Camera Notes* (1897–1902), and *Camera Work* (1902–17), organ of the photo-secessionists. A master of the commonplace who used photographs to symbolize an extraordinary range of thoughts and feelings, he achieved for photography recognition as a fine art. Championing the newest art trends, Stieglitz, in his notable photographic and art galleries—291 Fifth Avenue (1905–07), the Intimate (1925–30),

and the American Place (1930–46)—introduced the works of Cézanne, Picasso, Matisse, Lautrec, and Brancusi, and was responsible for making known the works of such American artists as Max Weber, John Marin (*q.v.*), Charles Demuth, and Georgia O'Keeffe (1887–   ), whom he married in 1924.

Stimson, Henry Lewis (b. New York City, 21 Sept. 1867; d. Huntington, N.Y., 20 Oct. 1950), statesman, was graduated from Yale (B.A., 1888), Harvard (M.A., 1889), and the Harvard Law School (1889–90), and was admitted to the bar in 1891. He was in private practice in New York City until 1906, when President Theodore Roosevelt appointed him U.S. attorney for the southern district of New York, a post he held until 1909. The unsuccessful Republican candidate for the governorship of New York (1910), he was named (1911) Secretary of War by President Taft and served until 1913. As a delegate to the New York constitutional convention (1915), he was responsible for many of the principal reforms effected by it. During World War I he served with the A.E.F. in France as a colonel of field artillery. In 1927 he was named by President Coolidge as special representative to Nicaragua, where by arbitration he settled a political dispute that had brought on civil war. He served as governor general of the Philippines (1927–29), and as Secretary of State (1929–33) in President Herbert Hoover's cabinet was chairman of the U.S. delegations to the London Naval Conference (1930) and to the Geneva Disarmament Conference (1932). He formulated and announced the "Stimson Doctrine" (1931) of nonrecognition of territories and agreements obtained by acts of aggression. Resuming his private law practice in 1933, he supported many of President Franklin D. Roosevelt's foreign policy measures, and called for aid to Great Britain and for compulsory military training. Named Secretary of War (July 1940), he served through World War II and retired in Sept. 1945, when he resigned from Truman's cabinet. Stimson was the first American to serve in the cabinets of 4 presidents. He was the author of *American Policy in Nicaragua* (1927) and *On Active Service in Peace and War* (with McGeorge Bundy, 1948).

Stone, Harlan Fiske (b. Chesterfield, N.H., 11 Oct. 1872; d. Washington, D.C., 22 Apr. 1946), 11th chief justice of the U.S., was graduated from Amherst (1894) and Columbia Law School (1898), commenced practice in New York City, and joined the faculty of Columbia Law School (1899), serving as dean (1907 and from 1910–23, when he returned to private practice). Appointed attorney general in Coolidge's cabinet (1924), he reorganized the Federal Bureau of Investigation. As an associate justice of the U.S. Supreme Court (1925), becoming chief justice (1941), he was early identified with Holmes and Brandeis in dissents on social issues and after 1932 generally supported the New Deal program. In his dissent in *U.S.* v. *Butler* (1935), where the AAA processing tax was held unconstitutional, he declared: "Courts are not the only agencies of government that must be assumed to have capacity to govern." He sustained federal and state social security legislation. In a lone dissent in the *Jehovah's Witnesses' Case* (1940), he opposed state legislation compelling belief or expression violating religious convictions, but upheld restrictions imposed at the time of World War II upon U.S. citizens of Japanese origin as being within the war powers (1943). During the war he opposed the use of members of the court for nonjudicial activities.

Story, Joseph (b. Marblehead, Mass., 18 Sept. 1779; d. Cambridge, Mass., 10 Sept. 1845), jurist, was graduated from Harvard (1798), studied law under Chief Justice Sewall and later under Samuel Putnam, was admitted to the bar (1801), and practiced in Salem. A Jeffersonian Republican, he served in the state legislature (1805–08) and in the U.S. House of Representatives (1808–09), where he favored repeal of the embargo. Again in the state legislature (1811) he was appointed in that year by President Madison as associate justice of the U.S. Supreme Court. His decisions in admiralty and prize cases during the War of 1812 became classic expositions of international law. A nationalist along with Marshall, he went so far as to maintain that the power of Congress to regulate interstate and foreign commerce was exclusive (dissent in *N.Y.* v. *Miln,* 1837). He upheld the property rights of private corporations (*Terrett* v. *Taylor,* 1815) as well as the obligation of contracts, although outvoted by the Jacksonian majority in the *Charles River Bridge Case.* After Marshall's death (1835) he upheld, in dissent, the broad construction of the Constitution. His antislavery views were evident in the *Armistad Case* (1839), where he freed slaves as "property rescued from pirates," and in *Prigg* v. *Pa.* (1842), where he held that the enforcement of the federal fugitive slave laws vested exclusively in the national government. Appointed (1829) to the newly established Dane professorship of law at Harvard, where he taught until his death, he made a notable contribution both as a teacher and a writer on the law, particularly to the development of American equity jurisprudence (1836) and through his treatise on the conflict of laws (1834). He also published his *Commentaries on the Constitution of the U.S.* (3 vols., 1833).

Stowe, Harriet Elizabeth Beecher (b. Litchfield, Conn., 14 June 1811; d. Hartford, Conn., 1 July 1896), author, daughter of Lyman Beecher (1775–1863), sister of Henry Ward Beecher (p. 982). She was educated at Litchfield and Hartford, moved to Cincinnati (1832), where she produced her first published writings and developed anti-slavery sympathies, and married (1836) Calvin E. Stowe, professor of Biblical literature in the Lane Theological Seminary, of which her father was president. She left Cincinnati in 1850, when her husband became professor at Bowdoin College. The agitation over the Fugitive Slave Law of 1850 led her to write *Uncle Tom's Cabin, or Life Among the Lowly* (2 vols., 1852), originally published in serial form (5 June 1851–1 Apr. 1852) in the *National Era*, an antislavery newspaper brought out at Washington, D.C. The book sold 300,000 copies within a year, aroused deep hostility in the South, and won her an international reputation. She answered her critics in *A Key to Uncle Tom's Cabin* (1853). She wrote a second antislavery novel, *Dred; a Tale of the Great Dismal Swamp* (1856). Among her later works were *The Minister's Wooing* (1859), *The Pearl of Orr's Island* (1862), *Oldtown Folks* (1869), *Sam Lawson's Oldtown Fireside Stories* (1872), and *Poganuc People* (1878).

Stravinsky, Igor Fedorovitch (b. Oranienbaum, Russia, 17 June 1882; d. New York City, 6 Apr. 1971), composer. The son of an opera singer, Stravinsky started piano lessons at age 9, and although an apt pupil, was not thought to have extraordinary talent. From his earliest years he had shown a serious interest in composition, but his family having decided that he study law instead, he graduated from the Univ. of St. Petersburg (1905). Stravinsky came into contact with Rimsky-Korsakov at the university through the composer's son (1902) and a year later became his pupil. His early music such as *Symphony in E Flat* (1908) was of the traditional Russian nationalist school. It was with the music for the ballet that he achieved his first and most lasting fame—*The Firebird* (1910) and *Petrouchka* (1911) commissioned by Serge Diaghilev for the Ballets Russes—as well as *The Rite of Spring* (29 May 1913), which nearly caused a riot at its premiere, and was not recognized as a major work until Pierre Monteaux conducted an orchestral version almost a year later, again in Paris. *The Rite of Spring*, along with *Petrouchka*, opened the door to 20th-century music, offering complicated rhythms, severe melodies, polytonality, and wild dissonances. Among the other works in this style were *The Soldier's Tale* (1918) and, later, *Les Noces* (1923). In 1919 Stravinsky left his native country permanently and applied for French citizenship. With the ballet *Pulcinella* (1920) came a new phase of his work, a "neoclassical" period, utilizing past materials but aiming for clarity, brevity, and precision, thus moving from iconoclasm to formalism. Among his "neoclassical" compositions are the opera-oratorio *Oedipus Rex* (1926) and *Symphony of Psalms* (1930). Moving to the U.S. when World War II began (1939), he produced *Symphony in Three Movements* (1945), *Orpheus* (1947), and an opera, *The Rake's Progress* (1951). His music became more abstract and sparse with *Canticum Sacrum* (1956), *Agon* (1956), and *Movements for Piano and Orchestra* (1960), arriving at a "serial" technique, influenced by Webern and Schoenberg. His secretary (1947–71) and close friend Robert Craft is credited with influencing his later development, as well as assisting Stravinsky with the recording of his works, and with some of his books. Some of the latter are strictly about music, e.g. his *Poetics of Music* (1948), others are in a more personal vein, such as *Chronicles of My Life* (1956) and *Conversations with Igor Stravinsky* (1958). He became a naturalized U.S. citizen in 1945.

Stuart, Gilbert (b. North Kingston, R.I., 3 Dec. 1755; d. Boston, Mass., 9 July 1828), painter. He received his first professional training (c. 1769 *et seq.*) under Cosmo Hamilton, a Scotch painter at Newport whom he accompanied to Edinburgh. Returning to America after Hamilton's death (1772), he went to London (1775) and became the pupil (1776–c.1781) of Benjamin West. His *Portrait of a Gentleman Skating* (1782) brought him public notice, and thereafter Stuart enjoyed a wide patronage in London, where he won a place as a leading portrait painter and exhibited with the Royal Academy until 1785. In 1787 he went to Ireland to continue his success as a portraitist. He came to the U.S. (c.1793), set up a studio in New York City, and in 1794 opened a studio in Philadelphia, where he produced many notable portraits of women and his first 2 life portraits of George Washington. He moved to Germantown in 1796 and in 1803 went to Washington, D.C., where he painted his gallery of statesmen of the early republic, including Jefferson, Madison, and Monroe, by which he is best remembered. In 1805 he moved to Boston. Among his many portraits are those of Benjamin West, Colonel Isaac Barré, Rev. Joseph Stevens Buckminster, Gen. Henry Knox, James Sullivan, Joseph Story, Samuel Eliot, James Perkins, Oliver Wolcott, Albert Gallatin, Mrs. Perez Morton, John Trumbull, and John Randolph. These and many other lifelike and luminous paintings left him an unrivaled reputation in American portraiture.

Stuart, James Ewell Brown (b. Patrick Co., Va., 6 Feb. 1833; d. Richmond, Va., 12 May 1864), soldier, attended Emory and Henry College (1848–50), was graduated from West Point (1854), and joined the U.S. cavalry. He served with Lee in suppressing John Brown's raid at Harpers Ferry (1859). Resigning his commission at the outbreak of the Civil War, he was made a captain of Confederate cavalry (24 May 1861). At the 1st Battle of Bull Run he protected the Confederate left and was made brigadier general (21 Sept. 1861). He covered the Confederate withdrawal to the Chickahominy in the Peninsular campaign and rode completely around McClellan's army on reconnaissance. In a raid to the rear of Pope's forces he burned stores and captured headquarters documents disclosing the strength and position of the Union forces. Promoted major general (25 July 1862), he fought at the 2d Battle of Bull Run and in the Antietam campaign. He fought at Fredericksburg and Chancellorsville, and, after Jackson had been wounded, assumed command of the 2d Army Corps. His most controversial action took place in the Gettysburg campaign, where he allowed himself to be held up in interposing his cavalry between the Union army and Washington before attempting to make contact with Ewell, as a result of which Lee was deprived for 3 days of information about Union movements. At Yellow Tavern he turned off Sheridan's columns from the direct road to Richmond and was fatally wounded. A spectacular cavalry officer, "Jeb" Stuart was regarded by Lee as the "eyes of the army."

Stuyvesant, Petrus [Peter] (b. Scherpenzeel, Friesland, Holland, c.1610; d. New York City, Feb. 1672), colonial governor, enrolled at the Univ. of Franeker (c. 1628), then pursued a military career, followed (1635) by service with the Dutch West India Co., becoming governor of Curaçao (1644). His right leg was amputated as the result of an injury sustained in leading an expedition (Mar.–Apr. 1644) against the island of St. Martin. Commissioned (1646) director general of New Netherland, he arrived in Manhattan in 1647. His career was notable for its progressive measures and reforming zeal. He curbed the sale of liquor to the Indians, enforced Sabbath observance, and taxed imports to construct public works. He promoted intercolonial relations with the English, negotiating (1650) the Treaty of Hartford fixing a boundary line with Connecticut. He drove the Swedes from the Delaware (1655), which was incorporated into New Netherland. On the debit side, he was arbitrary and dictatorial, banished his critics, and, although instituting (1649) a Board of Nine Men to assist him, he only yielded (1653) under pressure to the demands of the burghers for municipal self-government in New Amsterdam. Devout Dutch Reformed adherent, he was intolerant toward other sects and, in a move aimed primarily against the Lutherans, forbade meetings by other religions. Reproved by the directors of the Company in Amsterdam, he was forced to back down, as he was in his efforts to bar the Jews from settlement and burgher rights (1655–56). On 6 Sept. 1664 he surrendered the colony to the English, but after returning to the Netherlands (1665) to defend his official conduct, he went back to New York (1667), living the remainder of his life on "Stuyvesant's Bouwery," the farm conveyed to him (1650) by the Company.

Sullivan, Harry Stack (b. Norwich, N.Y., 21 Feb. 1892; d. Paris, France, 15 Jan. 1949), physician and psychiatrist, worked his way through Chicago College of Medicine and Surgery (M.D., 1917). During World War I he served as a 1st lieutenant attached to the board of examiners for the Medical Corps, and after the war was medical executive officer, Federal Board for Vocational Education (1919–20), drafting policy and procedures for handling soldiers disabled by neuropsychiatric conditions. As psychiatrist, Public Health Institute (1921–22), and veterans' liaison officer at St. Elizabeth's Hospital (1922–23), where he worked in association with William Alanson White, he launched his career in psychiatry. As director of clinical research at Sheppard and Enoch Pratt Hospital, near Baltimore (1923–25), he pursued intensive studies of schizophrenic disorders. Convinced that psychoanalysis needed to be supplemented by consideration of the impact of cultural forces upon personality, he developed his theory of interpersonal relations. He taught psychiatry at the Maryland Medical School (1923–39) and became professor and head of the department at Georgetown School of Medicine (1939). Previously, he investigated schizophrenia and obsessional neurosis while practicing psychiatry in New York City, beginning 1931, and as head of both the William Alanson White Foundation (1933–43) and the Washington School of Psychiatry (1936–47). Coeditor and editor of *Psychiatry* (1938–49), he gathered a number of his papers in *Conceptions of Modern Psychiatry* (1940). During World War II he was consultant in psychiatry for the Selective Service System and medical adviser, personnel section, War Department General Staff.

Sullivan, Louis Henri (b. Boston, Mass., 3 Sept. 1856; d. Chicago, 14 Apr. 1924), architect. He attended (1872–73) the Massachusetts Institute of Technology, worked (1873) in the architectural office of William LeBaron Jenney at Chicago, and was admitted (1874) to the École des Beaux Arts at Paris. As a partner in the architectural firm of Adler and Sullivan (1881–95), he became the leading figure in the so-called Chicago school of architecture. His abandonment of the modes of Victorian Gothic and Romanesque Revival became evident in his plans for the interior of the Chicago Auditorium (built 1886–90), where he used the delicate ornamentation that became associated with his style. In his designs for the Wainwright Building at St. Louis (1890), the Schiller Building (1892) and the Gage Building (1898) at Chicago, and the Prudential Building at Buffalo, N.Y. (1895), he evolved resourceful solutions of the architectural and structural problems posed by the skyscraper, and was among the first to stress the vertical lines of steel skeleton construction. His root idea, "form follows function," established the basis of the modern organic architecture created by his disciple, Frank Lloyd Wright (q.v.). For his other notable designs, see p. 907.

Sumner, Charles (b. Boston, Mass., 6 Jan. 1811; d. Washington, D.C., 11 Mar. 1874), statesman, was graduated from Harvard (1830) and the Harvard Law School (1833). Admitted to the bar in 1834, he was appointed reporter of the U.S. circuit court and lectured at the Harvard Law School (1835–37). After a sojourn on the Continent (1837–40), he became active in the movement for outlawing war and in an address (1849) before the American Peace Society urged the establishment of a "Congress of Nations." An opponent of the Mexican War, he helped found the Free-Soil party (1848) and was the senatorial candidate of a coalition of Free-Soilers and Democrats. Following a prolonged contest in the Massachusetts legislature, he took his Senate seat in 1851, and was reelected as a Republican in 1857, 1863, and 1869,

serving until his death. An outspoken antagonist of slavery, he made a stirring indictment (1852) of the Fugitive Slave Law of 1850, opposed the Kansas-Nebraska Bill (1854), and helped organize the Republican party. After making "The Crime Against Kansas" speech (20 May 1856), Sumner was violently assaulted (22 May 1856) on the Senate floor by Rep. Preston Brooks (S.C.); the injuries he received compelled his absence from the Senate until 5 Dec. 1859. He became (1861) chairman of the Foreign Relations Committee; beginning late in 1861 he was an ardent exponent of emancipation; and in 1862 formulated the "state suicide" theory of Reconstruction, holding that the Confederate states had relinquished all rights under the Constitution. After the war, however, he gradually adopted a more sympathetic attitude toward the South. He championed equal suffrage for whites and Negroes. Differences with President Grant and Secretary of State Hamilton Fish led to his removal (1872) from the chairmanship of the Foreign Relations Committee.

Sumner, William Graham (b. Paterson, N.J., 30 Oct. 1840; d. Englewood, N.J., 12 Apr. 1910), economist, political and social scientist, and teacher, was graduated from Yale (1863), studied for the ministry in Germany and England, was a tutor at Yale (1866–69), and in 1869 was ordained a priest of the Protestant Episcopal Church. He remained in the ministry until 1872, when he was invited to occupy the newly established chair of political and social science at Yale, a post he held for the remainder of his life. An exponent of laissez-faire, he opposed trade unions, social legislation, and government regulation. As an economist, he favored free trade and opposed free silver and bimetallism. As a sociologist, he pioneered in establishing a general science of society based on the study and interrelationships of all social institutions; making his most illuminating contribution in *Folkways* (1907). Among his works are *A History of American Currency* (1874), *What Social Classes Owe to Each Other* (1883), *Protectionism* (1885), *The Financier and Finances of the American Revolution* (2 vols., 1891), *War and Other Essays* (1911), and *The Forgotten Man and Other Essays* (1919). The posthumously published *Science of Society* (4 vols., 1927) was completed by Albert G. Keller.

Taft, Robert Alphonso (b. Cincinnati, Ohio, 8 Sept. 1889; d. Washington, D.C., 31 July 1953), lawyer, statesman, son of President William Howard Taft, was graduated from Yale (1910) and studied law at Harvard (LL.B., 1913), practicing in Cincinnati with Maxwell & Ramsey, later (1923) becoming senior partner of Taft, Stettinius & Hollister. Member of the state House of Representatives (1921–26), he was elected U.S. senator from Ohio (1938) and served until his death. He consistently opposed the New Deal program, spearheaded the isolationist bloc in Congress, and fought the Lend-Lease bill, but later backed U.S. participation in the UN. Cosponsor of the Taft-Hartley Act (1947), he was 3-time candidate for the Republican presidential nomination (1940, 1948, 1952), supporting Gen. Eisenhower in return for the latter's acceptance (12 Sept. 1952) of most of Taft's program. After Eisenhower's election he became Senate floor leader.

Taft, William Howard (b. Cincinnati, Ohio, 15 Sept. 1857; d. Washington, D.C., 8 Mar. 1930), 27th president of the U.S. and 9th chief justice, was graduated from Yale (1878) and Cincinnati Law College (1880); practiced law in Cincinnati; and was assistant county prosecutor (1881–82, 1885–86), collector of internal revenue, 1st district of Ohio (1882–83), superior court judge (1887–90), and U.S. solicitor general under Harrison (1890–92). While federal judge for 6th Circuit (1892–1900), he was also dean of the Univ. of Cincinnati Law School. Appointed by McKinley president of the Philippine Commission (1900), he became the first civil governor (1901–04), credited with notable reforms, the restoration of peace, solving the problem of church lands, and establishing limited self-government. Theodore Roosevelt's Secretary of War (1904–08), he was the president's personal choice as Republican nominee (1908), defeating Bryan for the presidency. Although he continued a number of Roosevelt's policies, notably a vigorous enforcement of the antitrust laws (Standard Oil and American Tobacco trusts dissolved), he split with the progressives over the Payne-Aldrich Tariff (1909). Renominated (1912), he was defeated in a 3-cornered race with Theodore Roosevelt and Woodrow Wilson. Kent professor of law at Yale (1913–21), he was appointed by Harding as chief justice of the U.S. Supreme Court (1921–30). An intelligent conservative, he upheld the president's removal power (*Myers' Case*, 1926), and his dissent in *Adkins* v. *Children's Hospital* was later upheld by the court. However, his labor decisions curtailed the Clayton Act, permitted injunctions in secondary boycotts, made unions liable to be sued even though unincorporated, and invalidated the attempt of Congress to impose a tax on the interstate products of child labor.

Taney, Roger Brooke (b. Calvert Co., Md., 17 Mar. 1777; d. Washington, D.C., 12 Oct. 1864), 4th chief justice of the U.S., was graduated from Dickinson College (1795), read law, and was admitted to the bar (1799), practicing in Calvert Co. (1799–1801), Fredericksburg (1801–23), and Baltimore. Federalist state legislator (1799–1800), he broke with the Federalists (1812) and led a dissenting faction (the "Coodies"). State senator (1816–21), he supported Jackson (1824) and resigned his post as Maryland attorney general (1827–31) to enter Jackson's cabinet as U.S. attorney general. He drafted that part of Jackson's bank-charter veto message (10 July 1832) in which contention was made that the president was not bound by the interpretation placed upon the Constitution by the Supreme Court. When the Senate refused confirmation of his appointment as Secretary of the Treasury to succeed William J. Duane (1833), he was given a recess appointment to remove federal deposits from the 2d Bank of the U.S. and to set up a system of government depositories. On Marshall's death (6 July 1835) he was appointed chief justice of the U.S. Supreme Court over bitter Whig opposition. Reversing the court's nationalist trend, his most notable decision was the *Charles River Bridge Case* (1837), which curtailed the scope of the *Dartmouth College Case* and curbed the growth of monopolies. "We must not forget that the community also have rights," he declared on that occasion. His most fateful decision was the *Dred Scott Case* (1857), where, under cover of a discussion of jurisdiction, he declared invalid the Missouri Compromise and the Compromise of 1850, and furnished a major cause of the Civil War. In *Ex parte Merryman* (1861) he defended the rights of civilians in wartime.

Taylor, Frederick Winslow (b. Germantown, Pa., 20 Mar. 1856; d. Philadelphia, Pa., 21 Mar. 1915), efficiency engineer and inventor. After graduating from Phillips Exeter Academy (1874), Taylor became a patternmaker and machinist at Enterprise Hydraulic Works (1874–78), and afterward rose from a common laborer (1878) at Midvale Steel Co. to chief engineer (1884–90). During the same period he studied engineering at night at Stevens Institute of Technology, receiving his M.E. (1883). While at Midvale Steel Co., Taylor developed the concept of "scientific management." He believed that by scientifically studying the reasonable production capacity of man and machine, production could be raised and antagonism between worker and owner alleviated. Applying his concept, Taylor devised more powerful machinery and studied the amount of time involved in performing every operation at the plant. He was able to increase the output by 300% and pay by 25% to 100% at Midvale Steel Co. In 1893 Taylor became the first scientific management consultant, and Bethlehem Steel Co. became one of his major clients. Taylor received patents for over 100 inventions, including his design and construction of the largest successful steam hammer ever built (1890). Convinced that earning beyond one's needs was dehumanizing, Taylor volunteered his services as a scientific management expert after 1900. Among his published works were "A Piece Rate System," in *Transactions of the American Society of Mechanical Engineers* (1895), *Principles of Scientific Management* (1911), and *A Treatise on Concrete: Plain and Reinforced* (1905).

Taylor, Zachary (b. Montebello, Va., 24 Nov. 1784; d. Washington, D.C., 9 July 1850), 12th president of the U.S., moved with his family to Kentucky, was privately tutored, and served as a volunteer in the Kentucky militia (1806). His commission as 1st lieutenant, 7th U.S. Infantry (1808), inaugurated 40 years service in the U.S. army. He successfully defended Ft. Harrison, Indiana Territory

(4–5 Sept. 1812); fought in the Black Hawk (1832) and Seminole (1837) wars, with a victory at Lake Okeechobee (25 Dec.); and commanded the department of Florida, 1838–40. Commanding the Army of Occupation on the Mexican Border (1845–46), his forces engaged in hostilities which precipitated war with Mexico (Matamoras, 25 Apr. 1846). Victor at Palo Alto (8 May) and Resaca de la Palma (9 May), he was appointed major general and, ignoring Polk's order to fight on defense, advanced into Mexico, capturing Monterrey (24 Sept.). Compelled to detach many of his best troops to reinforce Winfield Scott, he continued his invasion, decisively defeating Santa Anna at Buena Vista (23 Feb. 1847). "Old Rough and Ready," now a national hero, was the Whig nominee for President (1848) and was elected over his Democratic opponent, Lewis Cass (q.v.). Opposing appeasement of the South, he died suddenly in the midst of the struggle over the Compromise of 1850.

Tecumseh (b. nr. Oldtown, Ohio, Mar. 1768; d. Moravian Town, Canada, 5 Oct. 1813), Indian statesman and warrior, distinguished himself in the rout of Gen. Arthur St. Clair (4 Nov. 1791), one of the most disastrous defeats in the history of U.S. Indian fighting. He participated (1792) in an attack on the Cumberland settlement near Nashville, Tenn., by Creeks, Cherokees, and Shawnees, and later joined with Chickasaws in raids against Tennessee settlers. He directed Shawnee scouting of Maj. Gen. Anthony Wayne in Ohio (fall, 1793). Chief of the Shawnees, who were forced west by white settlements (1805–08), finding less and less game to hunt, Tecumseh conceived of a plan at once defensive and regenerative. He attempted to establish a confederation of Indian tribes of the Old West, the South, and the Eastern Mississippi Valley, believing that this could be a separate Indian nation which white men would respect. The confederation was based upon the principle that Indian land was held in common by all tribes and could not rightly be alienated by one tribe. An orator and diplomat, courageous, and endowed with organizational ability and leadership qualities, Tecumseh and his brother, the Prophet, encouraged Indians in the confederation to keep apart from white men, till their own soil, and give up liquor. Supplied with ammunition from England in increasing quantities (1803–11), he remained unwilling to wage war against the U.S. until the alliance was solid and the entire confederation in a state of readiness. While he traveled south to obtain the allegiance of the Creek nation, his brother, who had been warned, apparently found it difficult to resist the pressures of young braves, leading his troops into battle at Tippecanoe, Ind. (7 Nov. 1811) against troops led by the governor of the Indiana Territory, William Henry Harrison. Although not a defeat on the surface, the battle proved a disaster as food supplies dwindled and the confederation almost dissolved. Tecumseh joined the British during the War of 1812 as brigadier general and led a force of Indians in the siege of Ft. Meigs, covered the British retreat after Oliver H. Perry's victory on Lake Erie, and was killed, allegedly by Col. Richard M. Johnson (1780–1850), later vice-president, at the Battle of the Thames. His death brought about the collapse of the confederacy and Indian desertion from the British cause. Known for his chivalry, he opposed massacres and the torture of prisoners.

Teller, Edward (b. Budapest, Hungary, 15 Jan. 1908–   ), physicist, obtained his Ph.D. at the Univ. of Leipzig (1930), studied at Copenhagen with Niels Bohr, and left Germany when Hitler came to power. After lecturing at the Univ. of London, he came to George Washington Univ. as visiting professor (1935), collaborating on research with Dr. George Gamow. He worked on the A-bomb project (1941–45). Joining the physics department of the Univ. of Chicago (1945), he returned to work at Los Alamos Laboratory (1949). Following Russia's successful A-bomb test and the revelations (Jan. 1950) of Klaus Fuchs' atomic espionage, he became a leading proponent of a crash program for producing a thermonuclear weapon, and has been called "the principal architect of the H-bomb," although he himself had little to do with its actual building. Placed in charge of the new H-bomb laboratory of the AEC at Livermore, Calif. (1952), he brought the H-bomb issue to national attention by testifying before the AEC's Gray Committee in the Oppenheimer case (Apr. 1954). In subsequent international controversy over the dangers of H-bomb testing, he opposed cessation of tests and advised that a "clean" bomb, with little fallout, was practicable. He has coauthored *The Constructive Uses of Nuclear Explosives* (1968).

Tesla, Nikola (b. Smiljan, Lika, Austria-Hungary, 9 July 1856; d. New York City, 7 Jan. 1943), inventor. He was educated at Karlstadt and Gratz, where he specialized in mechanics, mathematics, and physics, studied philosophy at the Univ. of Prague, and in 1881 settled in Budapest, where he invented the telephone repeater and discovered the principle of the rotating magnetic field. He arrived in the U.S. in 1884, became a naturalized citizen, and for several years was associated with George Westinghouse and Thomas A. Edison. His best-known inventions are the alternating current motor (1888) and the Tesla coil

or transformer (1891). Principally known for his researches in alternating currents of high frequency and high potential, Tesla's discoveries and inventions include an arc lighting system (1886); incandescent lamps; an alternating current power transmission system (1888); an electrical conversion and distribution system based on oscillatory discharges (1889); high frequency current generators (1890); mechanical oscillators and generators of electrical oscillations (1894–95); radiations, material streams and emanations (1896–98); and a high-potential magnifying transmitter (1897). He worked (1897–1905) on a system of transmission of power without wires and subsequently devoted himself to the fields of telephony and telegraphy.

Thomas, George Henry (b. Southampton Co., Va., 31 July 1816; d. San Francisco, 28 Mar. 1870), soldier, often called "the Rock of Chickamauga." He was graduated (1840) from the U.S. Military Academy; during service in the Mexican War was promoted to brevet captain and major for gallantry at Monterey and Buena Vista; and was an instructor in artillery and cavalry (1851–54) at West Point. Despite his Southern ties, Thomas adhered to the Union cause at the outbreak of the Civil War. He was commissioned (17 Aug. 1861) brigadier general of volunteers; as commander, 1st Div., Army of the Ohio, won the Battle of Mill Springs (19 Jan. 1862); was promoted (25 Apr. 1862) to major general of volunteers; and was a corps commander at Stone River (31 Dec. 1862–3 Jan. 1863) and in the Tullahoma campaign (June–July 1863) in Tennessee. As commander of the XIV Corps of the Army of the Cumberland, Thomas withstood a fierce assault by Bragg and Longstreet during a general Northern rout at the Battle of Chickamauga (19–20 Sept. 1863). Promoted (27 Oct.

1863) to brigadier general in the regular army, Thomas relieved Rosecrans as commander of the Army of the Cumberland and held Chattanooga against a siege. In the Battle of Chattanooga (24–25 Nov. 1863), his troops captured Lookout Mountain and Missionary Ridge. In the Atlanta campaign, the Army of the Cumberland under Thomas made up over half of Sherman's force. At Nashville (15–16 Dec. 1864) Thomas decisively defeated the Confederate army under Hood.

Thomas, Isaiah (b. Boston, Mass., 30 Jan. 1750; d. Worcester, Mass., 4 Apr. 1831), printer and publisher. He learned the printing trade at Boston during his apprenticeship to Zechariah Fowle, whose partner he became in 1770, and founded the *Massachusetts Spy*, a Patriot newspaper. He joined Paul Revere in warning the countryside (18 Apr. 1775) and as a Minuteman participated in the fighting at Lexington and Concord. Removing his printing plant to Worcester, he resumed publishing the *Spy* on 3 May, and quickly ranked as the leading publisher of the time, producing books distinguished for their typography and format. Also active as a bookseller, he maintained branches in Boston, Albany, Portsmouth, Baltimore, and elsewhere. He published the *Royal American Magazine* (1774–75), the *Worcester Magazine* (1786–88), and the *Massachusetts Magazine* (1789–96). Between 1771 and 1822 he published the almanac which, beginning in 1775, was known as *Thomas's New England Almanack*. He published the first dictionary (William Perry's) printed in America and the first English illustrated folio Bible in U.S. Included in his prolific output were editions of more than 100 children's books, including *Mother Goose's Melody* (1768). He wrote *The History of Printing in America* (2 vols., 1810), long a standard authority, and founded and incorporated (1812) the American Antiquarian Society, of which he served as first president.

Thomas, Norman (b. Marion, Ohio, 20 Nov. 1884; d. Huntington, N.Y., 19 Dec. 1968), social reformer and political leader. Son and grandson of Presbyterian ministers, he attended Bucknell for one year before transferring to Princeton, where he graduated at the head of his class (1905). He did settlement work in New York City traveled abroad before attending the Union Theological Seminary (1907–11). After receiving his divinity degree he was ordained in the Presbyterian Church (1911) and became pastor of the East Harlem Church (New York), where he worked among Italian immigrants. In his college days a self-described "progressive," Thomas had been influenced during his studies at the seminary by the writings of Dr. Walter Rauschenbusch (*q.v.*), who emphasized the Protestant churches' social responsibility. His work in the slums of New York City and his opposition to World War I converted him to Socialism. He joined (1916) the Fellowship of Reconciliation, a Christian pacifist group, and soon resigned his church post to work for the organization full-time, editing its monthly magazine, *The World Tomorrow* (1918–21). Joining the Socialist party (Oct. 1918), he lectured nationwide, often sponsored by the League for Industrial Democracy (the educational arm of the Socialist party), of which he was co-director (1922–37). He became active in the National Civil Liberties Bureau and helped found its successor, the American Civil Liberties Union (1920). He ran for office unsuccessfully as the Socialist party candidate for governor of New York (1924), for mayor of New York City (1925, 1929) and, as leader of the party after the death of Eugene

Debs (1926), for president in every election from 1928 to 1948. A brilliant orator and prolific writer, Thomas appealed to ethical values in his call for the reformation of American society. He stood for a mild brand of Socialism: public and democratic control of the means of production and long-term economic planning, denying the necessity of class conflict, and criticizing Communism and the Soviet Union. For over 40 years he effectively shaped the policies of the Socialist party and saw many of his proposals—e.g. 5-day work week, minimum wage, unemployment, accident and health insurance, old-age pensions, low-cost public housing, slum clearance—adopted by the major parties and enacted into law. He was a leading advocate of nuclear disarmament and, in his 80s, publicly assailed U.S. involvement in Vietnam. Among his 20 books are *Is Conscience a Crime?* (1927), *As I See It* (1932), *A Socialist's Faith* (1951), *Socialism Reexamined* (1963).

Thomas, Theodore [full name **Christian Friedrich Theodore Thomas**] (b. Esens, Germany, 11 Oct. 1835; d. Chicago, 4 Jan. 1905), musician and conductor. He received his musical training as a violinist under his father, arrived (1845) in New York with his parents, made a concert tour (1850) of the South, and played 1st violin (1853) with the American orchestra of Louis Antoine Jullien. He was made (1854) a member of the Philharmonic Society of New York; took part with William Mason in the Mason-Thomas chamber music concerts (1855) at New York, where he appeared (1857-58) as a violin soloist; and in 1860 became an operatic conductor at New York. He organized (1862) his own orchestra, which he took on frequent tours; became (1866) conductor of the Brooklyn Philharmonic Society; conducted the Philadelphia Centennial concerts (1876); and

was director (1878) of the College of Music in Cincinnati. He served as conductor (1877, 1880 *et seq.*) of the New York Philharmonic Society; became (1885) director of the American Opera Co.; was conductor (1891-1905) of the Chicago Symphony Orchestra and music director for the Chicago World's Fair (1893). Through his orchestral tours and astute program planning, Thomas advanced popular musical taste in America.

Thoreau, Henry David (b. Concord, Mass., 12 July 1817; d. there, 6 May 1862), poet and essayist, was graduated from Harvard (1837), taught school intermittently (1837-41), and from 1841 to 1843, when he lived in Emerson's home, became acquainted with the Transcendentalist circle. He lived at Walden Pond from 4 July 1845 to 6 Sept. 1847. His antislavery convictions led him to refuse the payment of the Massachusetts poll tax during the Mexican War, which he regarded as an expansionist scheme of the slave power. He was arrested and jailed, and later related his experiences in his essay on "Civil Disobedience," which subsequently became one of the leading works on passive resistance. Thoreau left Concord only to make his nature tours, or for lecture engagements, and toward the end of his life became an outspoken advocate of abolition. A poet-naturalist whose prose has a homely strength, Thoreau was also a social critic who believed in moral imperatives superior to the institutions fashioned by men. His works include *A Week on the Concord and Merrimack Rivers* (1849), *Walden* (1854), *Excursions* (1863), *The Maine Woods* (1864), *Cape Cod* (1865), and *A Yankee in Canada* (1866). Among his speeches and lectures are "Slavery in Massachusetts" (1854) and "A Plea for Captain John Brown," "The Last Days of John Brown," and "After the Death of John Brown" (1859).

Thorndike, Edward Lee (b. Williamsburg, Mass., 31 Aug. 1871; d. Montrose, N.Y., 9 Aug. 1949), educator, studied at Wesleyan, Harvard, and Columbia, then taught education at Western Reserve Univ. for a year before going to Teachers College, Columbia, where he taught until his retirement (1941). Starting with his early books (*Educational Psychology*, 1903; *Mental and Social Measurements*, 1904; *The Principles of Teaching*, 1905), he emphasized the application of scientific method in education, especially statistical techniques, and placed stress on practical education. His psychological testing methods employed in the U.S. army in World War I set the pattern for personnel, placement, and educational guidance. His doctrine of innate differences in the aptitudes of pupils constituted an important modification of the idea of equality of educational opportunity. His later views in educational psychology are embodied in *The Measurement of Intelligence* (1926).

Tilden, Samuel Jones (b. New Lebanon, N.Y., 9 Feb. 1814; d. Yonkers, N.Y., 4 Aug. 1886), governor of New York, reformer, spent one term at Yale (1834), studied at New York Univ. Law School (1838–41), and was admitted to the bar (1841), practicing law in New York City. Corporation counsel of the city (1843), he rose rapidly in the Democratic party, cofounding with John L. O'Sullivan the N.Y. *Morning News* to help Polk carry New York in 1844. In the subsequent party split Tilden joined the Barnburners opposing Marcy's Hunkers. Although Tilden was in the state legislature (1846), was prominent at the constitutional convention of that year, and ran unsuccessfully for attorney general (1855), his prominence in the pre-Civil War years was at the bar rather than in politics. The defense (1856) of Azariah C. Flagg

in a vote fraud case was one of his more sensational trial appearances, but more important was his huge railroad practice, which laid the foundations for his great fortune. During the Civil War he sought to build up the Democratic party as a "constitutional opposition" and supported Johnson's reconstruction policy. He gained national attention by his role as chairman of the Democratic state committee in ousting the "Tweed Ring" (1872), helping in prosecuting its members, securing legislation reforming the New York City government, and impeaching corrupt judges. Elected governor (1874) he introduced tax reforms and shattered the "Canal Ring." Democratic nominee for president (1876), he won a majority of 250,000 votes over Hayes, but lost the election when a partisan electoral commission awarded Hayes the electoral votes of all the contested states. He bequeathed the Tilden Trust, which after protracted litigation made possible the establishment of the New York Public Library.

Truman, Harry S. (b. Lamar, Mo., 8 May 1884; d. Kansas City, Mo., 26 Dec. 1972), 33d president of the U.S., was educated in the public schools; operated the family farm near Independence, Mo. (1906–17); and saw service in World War I as 1st lieutenant and captain, 129th Field Artillery, 35th Div., participating in the Vosges operation and the St. Mihiel and Meuse-Argonne offensives. He studied nights at Kansas City School of Law (1923–25); was, with the backing of "Boss" Tom Prendergast, made judge of Jackson Co. court (1922–24) and presiding judge (1926–34), and was elected U.S. senator from Missouri (1934) and reelected (1940), where he achieved prominence as chairman of the Senate Committee to Investigate the National Defense Program. Franklin D. Roosevelt's choice as compromise running mate (1944), he was elected vice-president, succeeding to the presidency on the death of Roosevelt (12 Apr. 1945). With little preparation he was forced to make decisions for carrying the war to a successful conclusion (authorizing the use of the A-bomb against Japan) and for planning the postwar world (at Potsdam, July 1945). Losing control of Congress (1946), his sponsorship of the "Fair Deal," civil rights legislation, and repeal of the Taft-Hartley Act (1947), as well as his vigorous election campaign, won him a surprise victory over Gov. Thomas E. Dewey (1948). His 2d term was largely concerned with the Cold War against the Soviet Union, the Marshall and Truman plans, the resistance (after June 1950) to North Korean and later Chinese aggression in South Korea, the organization of the defense of Western Europe, and the negotiation of the Japanese (1951) and German (1952) peace treaties. He wrote 2 vols. of memoirs (1955, 1956).

Turner, Frederick Jackson (b. Portage, Wis., 14 Nov. 1861; d. Pasadena, Calif., 14 Mar. 1932), historian, received his B.A. (1884) and M.A. (1888) from the Univ. of Wisconsin and his Ph.D. (1890) from Johns Hopkins. Rebelling against the Johns Hopkins "germ theory" (holding that American institutions descended unchanged from their European ancestors) and responding to the universally held belief in environmental determinism, he delivered a seminal paper, "The Significance of the Frontier in American History," at a congress of historians held in connection with the World's Columbian Exposition at Chicago in the summer of 1893. In it he brilliantly advanced the hypothesis that the frontier experience had strengthened American democracy, individualism, and nationalism, and altered the character traits that distinguished Americans from Europeans. Within a dozen years his thesis had transformed the nature of historical teaching and investigation as the "frontier influence" was used to explain all aspects of the nation's past. A second concept that he considered even more important—that "sections" bargained among themselves to shape the political history of the 19th century—was less favorably received. Turner published few books—the *Rise of the New West* (1906) and *The Frontier in American History* (1920) during his lifetime and *The Significance of Sections in American History* (1932) and *The United States, 1830–50* (1935; Pulitzer award) posthumously—but more than any other historian he convinced scholars to use interdisciplinary techniques to discover the underlyng economic and social forces shaping human behavior. His frontier thesis was violently attacked just after his death in 1932, but attracted renewed interest in the 1960s and 1970s. Turner taught at the Univ. of Wisconsin (1889–1910), and Harvard (1910–24), and spent his last years (1927–32) as research associate at the Huntington Library.

Twain, Mark, see **Clemens, Samuel Langhorne.**

Tyler, John (b. Greenway, Va., 29 Mar. 1790; d. Richmond, Va., 18 Jan. 1862), 10th president of the U.S., was graduated from William and Mary (1807), admitted to the bar (1809), and practiced in Charles Co., Va. State legislator (1811–16), he entered Congress as a Jeffersonian Democrat (1816–21), served as governor of Virginia (1825–27), and was U.S. senator (1827–36). He broke with Jackson over the Bank of the U.S., resigning his seat when ordered by the Virginia legislature to support Benton's resolution expunging Clay's censure of Jackson for removal of deposits from the bank. Joining the states' rights group cooperating with the Whigs, he was state legislator (1838–40) and was nominated vice-president on the Whig ticket with Harrison (1840) and elected in the "Tippecanoe and Tyler, too" campaign. He became president on Harrison's death (4 Apr. 1841). His veto of Clay's bank bill led to resignation of the entire Whig cabinet (12 Sept. 1841) except Daniel Webster, who also withdrew (May 1843) after negotiating the Webster-Ashburton Treaty. He reorganized his cabinet with both Whigs and Democrats, with Calhoun as Secretary of State (May 1844). The principal achievements of his administration were the Preemption Act (1841), a victory for the frontier, and the annexation of Texas through joint congressional resolution. Retiring to "Sherwood Forest," his Virginia home, he emerged briefly in 1861 as chairman of a peace convention at Washington, served in the Confederate Provisional Congress, and was elected to the Confederate Congress, but died before that body assembled.

Urey, Harold Clayton (b. Walkerton, Ind., 29 Apr. 1893–   ), physical chemist. He was graduated from the Univ. of Montana (B.S., 1917), where he was an instructor in chemistry (1919–21); received the degree of Ph.D. (1923) from the Univ. of California; and studied at Copenhagen (1923–24). He taught chemistry at Johns Hopkins (1924–29), Columbia (1929–45), Chicago (1945–58), and the Univ. of Calif. at La Jolla (1958–70). He was awarded the Nobel prize in chemistry (1934) for having been the first to isolate (1932) heavy water (deuterium oxide), which led to the discovery of the heavy isotope of hydrogen named deuterium. Research director (1942–45) of the Manhattan District project that produced the materials for the atomic bomb, he worked on the separation of uranium 235 and heavy water. One of the foremost authorities on the separation of isotopes, he has also done work on atomic and molecular structure, absorption spectra, the thermodynamic properties of gases, and the measurement of paleotemperatures.

Van Buren, Martin (b. Kinderhook, N.Y., 5 Dec. 1782; d. there, 24 July 1862), 8th president of the U.S., was admitted to the bar (1803) and practiced in Kinderhook (1807–16) and Albany. Surrogate of Columbia Co. (1808–13), state senator (1812–20), and state attorney general (1815–19), he headed a political organization known as the "Albany Regency." U.S. senator (1821–28), he supported Crawford in 1824 and Jackson in 1828. Governor of New York (1 Jan. 1829), he resigned (5 Mar.) to accept appointment in Jackson's cabinet as Secretary of State. After securing Great Britain's consent to opening direct trade with the British West Indies (1830), he resigned (Aug. 1831) to become minister to Great Britain, but returned from London when Calhoun blocked confirmation in the Senate. Vice-president under Jackson (1833–37), he was Jackson's choice for president, defeating Harrison (1836). His Independent Treasury policy reflected the views of the hard-money Democrats, but the Panic of 1837 undermined his popularity. Although nominated (1840), he was defeated by Harrison. His opposition to the immediate annexation of Texas cost him the nomination in 1844. Active among New York "Barnburners" opposing extension of slavery, he was the Free-Soil nominee for president (1848). He later returned to the Democratic party but opposed secession.

Vanderbilt, Cornelius (b. Staten Island, N.Y., 27 May 1794; d. New York City, 4 Jan. 1877), steamship and railroad promoter, financier, quit school after the age of 11, bought a small boat at 16, and began a freight and passenger service between Staten Island and New York. At 19 he married his cousin, Sophia Johnson, who bore him 13 children. During the War of 1812 he had a government contract to provision forts in New York harbor and in 1814 built a schooner for service to Long Island Sound. Working as a captain (1818–29) for Thomas Gibbons' shipping line, he moved to New Brunswick, where his wife ran "Bellona Hall," a stopping place for travelers between New York and Philadelphia. Competing aggressively with Daniel Drew in steamboat operations on the Hudson, he amassed over a half-million dollars by the age of 40. During the Gold Rush, he organized the Accessory Transit Co. and secured a charter from the Nicaraguan government to operate a passenger route (water and highway) across the isthmus, 2 days shorter than the Panama route, enabling him to cut the New York-San Francisco passenger fare. Selling out his Panama concern to rivals, he entered (1855) into competition for the Atlantic trade with the Cunard and Collins Lines. After the Civil War he turned his attention to railroads, winning control of the New York & Harlem R.R., then combining the Hudson River R.R. with the New York Central, and leasing the Harlem to the combination, creating a single line. At his death his fortune was estimated at $100 million. Late in life he gave $1 million to Vanderbilt (previously Central) Univ., Nashville, Tenn.

Veblen, Thorstein Bunde (b. in Cato township, Manitowoc Co., Wis., 30 July 1857; d. Palo Alto, Calif., 3 Aug. 1929), economist and writer. He was graduated (1880) from Carleton College, Northfield, Minn., and pursued postgraduate studies at Johns Hopkins, Yale (Ph.D.,

1884), and Cornell. He taught at the Univ. of Chicago (1893–1906), at Stanford (1906–09), the Univ. of Missouri (1911–18), and the New School for Social Research, New York, N.Y. (1918–20). His first published book, *The Theory of the Leisure Class* (1899), an analysis of the pecuniary values of the business and middle classes, won him public notice. It was followed by *The Theory of Business Enterprise* (1904). A seminal social thinker, he conceived of the existing economic system as a price system, whose recurrent crises testified to its inability to adjust. As an alternative he suggested in his later works a system in which production and distribution would be controlled by the engineers, foreshadowing "Technocracy." Other works by him include *The Instinct of Workmanship* (1914), *Imperial Germany and the Industrial Revolution* (1915), *An Inquiry into the Nature of Peace* (1917), *The Higher Learning in America* (1918), *The Vested Interests and the State of the Industrial Arts* (1919), *The Engineers and the Price System* (1921), and *Absentee Ownership and Business Enterprise in Recent Times* (1923).

von Neumann, John (b. Budapest, Hungary, 28 Dec. 1903; d. Washington, D.C., 8 Feb. 1957), mathematician, studied at the universities of Berlin (1921–23) and Zurich (1923–25), obtained a Ph.D. from Budapest Univ. (1926), and came to the U.S. in 1930, becoming a citizen in 1937. He taught at Princeton and after 1933 was a member of the Institute for Advanced Study. Cofounder with Oskar Morganstern of the theory of games, a mathematical approach to the study of economic behavior, sociology, and military strategy, he also made important contributions to quantum theory. He worked on the A-bomb and the H-bomb projects and was a leader in the design and development of high-speed computers, notably MANIAC (mathematical analyzer, numerical integrator, and computer) developed at the Institute, and utilized in advanced government research projects, notably in building and testing the H-bomb. He was a member of the Atomic Energy Commission (1954–57).

Waite, Morrison Remick (b. Lyme, Conn., 29 Nov. 1816; d. Washington, D.C., 23 Mar. 1888), 6th chief justice of the U.S., was graduated from Yale (1837), studied law, and began practice (1839) in Maumee, Ohio, moving to Toledo (1850). Ohio state legislator (1849–50), he was, with William M. Evarts and Caleb Cushing, counsel for the U.S. before the *Alabama* tribunal in Geneva (1871–72) and president of the Ohio constitutional convention (1873–74). Appointed chief justice of the U.S. Supreme Court (1874), his most notable opinions were rendered in the *Granger Cases* (1877), where he stated that "business affected with a public interest" must be controlled by the public for the common good; upheld state legislation fixing rates; and declared that, until Congress acted, a state regulation of railroads was valid "even though it may indirectly affect those without." This position was reversed in the *Wabash Case* (1886), with Waite dissenting. He also laid the foundation for the modern interpretation of due process as a limitation of state power, insisting on reasonable regulation (*Stone* v. *Farmers' Loan*, (1886).

Waksman, Selman Abraham (b. Priluka, Russia, 22 July 1888; d. Hyannis, Mass. 16 Aug. 1973), microbiologist, came to the U.S. (1910), receiving his B.S. from Rutgers Univ. (1915) and his Ph.D. from the Univ. of California (1918) and becoming a citizen in 1916. Microbiolo-

gist at the New Jersey Agricultural Experiment Station (1921–24), he taught soil microbiology at Rutgers (1918–58). The discoverer of streptomycin (Nobel prize in medicine and physiology, 1952), an antibiotic—a term he coined—derived from a soil fungus and effective against tuberculosis, he turned over (1948) to Rutgers the funds accruing from the patent rights, making possible the establishment of the Institute of Microbiology at Rutgers. Its first director, he retired in 1958. His writings include *Streptomycin, Its Nature and Application* (1949), *Soil Microbiology* (1952), *My Life with the Microbes* (1954), *Neomycin, Nature and Application* (1958), *The Actinomycetes* (3 vols., 1959–62), *The Conquest of Tuberculosis* (1964).

Wallace, Henry Agard (b. Adair Co., Ia., 7 Oct. 1888; d. Danbury, Conn., 18 Nov. 1965), political leader. Son of Henry C. Wallace, magazine editor and Secretary of Agriculture under Harding and Coolidge. Upon graduation from Iowa State College (1910), he became associate editor of his family's magazine, *Wallace's Farmer,* and published *Agricultural Prices* (1926). When his father became Secretary of Agriculture he became editor (1921–33) of the magazine which, after a merger (1929), was known as *Wallace's Farmer and Iowa Homestead.* Shifting from the Republican to the Democratic party in 1928, he was Secretary of Agriculture (1933–41) under President Roosevelt, and responsible for the controversial Agricultural Adjustment Acts, aiming to stabilize farm income at parity levels and to bring about a more equitable distribution of income among farmers through storage of reserves, soil conservation, and government control of prices and production. His innovations, accepted by every subsequent administration, included the establishment of a federal food stamp plan for needy people. He was also a principal spokesman for other aspects of the New Deal. As vice-president during Roosevelt's 3d term, he acted as goodwill ambassador to Latin America and served as a member of the "war cabinet," chairman of the Economic Defense Board and of the Board of Economic Welfare. Passed over for the vice-presidential nomination in 1944 because of his ultraliberal views, he served as Secretary of Commerce (1945) but was forced to resign (1946) because of differences with President Truman over foreign policy. As the presidential candidate of the newly formed Progressive party he gained more than 1 million popular votes but no electoral votes (1948). He soon broke with the Progressive party—whose machinery was largely controlled by elements of the far left—and returned to private life. As a young man he had developed successful strains of hybrid corn and at the time of his death he was conducting other significant agricultural experiments. His other books include *America Must Choose* (1934) and *The Century of the Common Man* (1943).

Ward, Aaron Montgomery (b. Chatham, N.J., 17 Feb. 1843; d. Highland Park, Ill., 7 Dec. 1913), mail-order pioneer, moved with his parents to Niles, Mich., where he attended public school until he was 14, then worked in a barrel-stave factory and later in a brickyard. His first merchandising experience was in a general store in nearby St. Joseph, then, about 1865, with Marshall Field's firm in Chicago. As a traveling salesman for a dry-goods wholesale house, he covered the rural West and learned at first hand the problems of farmers dependent upon a general store for purchases. Recognizing the advantages of purchasing direct from manufacturers and then selling for cash direct to the rural consumer, he returned to Chicago, where he laid

his plans for a mail-order business. Although most of his savings were consumed by the Chicago fire of 1871, he managed by the next year to scrape together $1,600, to which a partner added $800, sufficient to set up a small mail-order business. An original price list soon became an 8-page and then a 72-page catalog with enticing illustrations. By 1884 the catalog had swollen to 240 pages and listed nearly 10,000 items. Montgomery Ward, as the firm was known, benefited by the support of the Patrons of Husbandry, a farm organization which wished to eliminate the middleman. The savings offered to Grangers were soon extended to all buyers. The consumer was wooed by competitive pricing, ironclad guarantees, and personal correspondence. Sales of the firm reached $1 million by 1888 and some $40 million by 1913. Active in the civic life of Chicago, Ward was responsible for preserving for the public Chicago's lake frontage. In turn, his widow, the former Elizabeth J. Cobb, made notable benefactions, especially to Northwestern Univ.

Ward, Lester Frank (b. Joliet, Ill., 18 June 1841; d. Washington, D.C., 18 Apr. 1913), sociologist. He attended (1861–62) the Susquehanna Collegiate Institute at Towanda, Pa., enlisted (1862) in the Union army, was wounded at Chancellorsville (1863), and was discharged in 1864. He served (1865–81) with the U.S. Treasury Department at Washington, D.C., meanwhile attending Columbian College (later George Washington Univ., A.B., 1869; LL.B., 1871; A.M., 1872). He took posts as a geologist (1883 *et seq.*) and paleontologist (1892 *et seq.*) with the U.S. Geological Survey; served as president of the Institut International de Sociologie (1900–03) and first president of the American Sociological Society (1906–07). In 1906 he was named professor of sociology at Brown Univ., where he served until his death. A pioneer of American evolutionary sociology, Ward stressed the role of mind and education in human progress and the necessity of intelligent and systematic planning for the furthering of rational social development, in opposition both to the laissez-faire school and to the evolutionary determinism of Spencer. His works include *Dynamic Sociology* (1883), *The Psychic Factors of Civilization* (1893), *Outlines of Sociology* (1898), *Pure Sociology* (1903), and *Glimpses of the Cosmos* (6 vols., 1913–18).

Warren, Earl (b. Los Angeles, Calif., 19 Mar. 1891; d. Washington, D.C., 9 July 1974), 13th chief justice of the U.S., received his B.L. (1912) and his J.D. (1914) from the Univ. of California, was admitted to the bar in 1914, and practiced in San Francisco and Oakland. District attorney of Alameda Co. (1925–39) and attorney general of California (1939–43), he was governor of California for 3 terms (1943–53), winning both the Democratic and Republican nominations in 1946. Republican nominee for vice-president of the U.S. in 1948, he resigned the governorship to become chief justice of the U.S. Supreme Court (Sept. 1953–June 1969). He proved adept at marshalling the court during one of its most activist periods, a time of libertarian reform. Among his most notable opinions were *Brown* v. *Bd. of Education of Topeka* (1954), abolishing the separate-but-equal doctrine and upholding desegregation in public education; *Reynolds* v. *Sims* (1964), holding that states must apportion both legislative houses according to equal population; *Miranda* v. *Arizona* (1966), holding that all arrested persons had a right to an attorney before questioning by the police and to be advised of that right. He served as chairman of the

special 7-man presidential commission to investigate the assassination of President Kennedy (1963–64).

Washington, Booker Taliaferro (b. Hale's Ford, Franklin Co., Va., 5 Apr. 1856; d. Tuskegee, Ala., 14 Nov. 1915), Negro educator. The son of a Negro slave and a white father, he worked (c. 1865 *et seq.*) in a salt furnace and coal mine at Malden, W. Va., meanwhile attending school. He entered (1872) Hampton Institute, the Negro vocational school in Virginia, where he earned his board by working as a janitor, and graduated in 1875. He was a schoolteacher at Malden (1875–77) and a student (1878–79) at Wayland Seminary, Washington, D.C., and in 1879 returned to Hampton Institute, where he took charge of the Indian dormitory and night school. Chosen (1881) to organize at Tuskegee a Negro normal school that had been chartered by the Alabama legislature, Washington founded there the Normal and Industrial Institute for Negroes. He soon became the foremost advocate of Negro education and was active as a public speaker on race relations, stressing industrial education and gradual adjustment rather than political and civil rights. He wrote *The Future of the American Negro* (1899), *Sowing and Reaping* (1900), the autobiographical *Up From Slavery* (1901), and *Frederick Douglass* (1907).

Washington, George (b. Bridges Creek, Westmoreland Co., Va., 22 Feb. 1732; d. Mount Vernon, Va., 14 Dec. 1799), 1st president of the U.S. After his father's death (1743) he lived chiefly at Mount Vernon, and worked as a surveyor. He visited Barbados with his half-brother Lawrence (1751–52). Sent by Gov. Dinwiddie to warn the French from encroaching on land in the Ohio Valley (1753), he served in the French and Indian Wars (1754–58) with the rank of lieutenant colonel, was obliged to surrender Ft. Necessity (3 July 1754), distinguished himself in the engagement known as Braddock's Defeat (9 July 1755), and participated in the capture of Ft. Duquesne (1758). Inheriting Mount Vernon from Lawrence (1752), he married Martha Dandridge Custis (6 Jan. 1759), entering the Virginia House of Burgesses that same year. A leader in the movement for independence, he was a delegate to the 1st and 2d Continental Congresses. On 15 June 1775 he was chosen to command the Continental army and took up duties before Boston (3 July). When the British evacuated that city, he attempted to defend New York, but was forced to withdraw to Westchester Co. and thence into New Jersey (1776). Brilliant successes at Trenton (26 Dec. 1776) and Princeton (3 Jan. 1777) raised Patriot morale. Defeated at Brandywine (11 Sept. 1777), he evacuated Philadelphia, was thrown back at Germantown (4 Oct.) and endured a winter of semistarvation at Valley Forge (1777–78). The exposé of the alleged Conway Cabal (1777–78) to displace Washington left him secure in his command. His most brilliant achievement was his secret and rapid march from the Hudson to Chesapeake Bay, resulting in the surrender of Cornwallis at Yorktown (19 Oct. 1781), ending the war. He denounced the Newburgh Address (1783), which had hinted at monarchy, and took leave of his officers at Fraunces' Tavern, New York (4 Dec. 1783), retiring to Mount Vernon. Returning to public life, he supported the movement for more effective union and presided over the Federal Convention (1787) which adopted the Constitution. Unanimously elected first president, he was inaugurated in New York (30 Apr. 1789) and administered the office for 2 terms, during which Hamiltonian fiscal policies were followed, neutrality was observed

(1793), the Whisky Rebellion suppressed (1794), and Jay's Treaty (1795) upheld. Declining a 3d term as president, he advised his countrymen in his Farewell Address (19 Sept. 1796) "to steer clear of permanent alliances . . . [trusting] to temporary alliance for extraordinary measures." When war with France threatened (1798), he was called from retirement as commander in chief, but hostilities were averted.

Watson, Thomas Edward (b. Columbia Co., Ga., 5 Sept. 1856; d. Washington, D.C., 26 Sept. 1922), political leader and author. Following 2 years at Mercer Univ., Watson taught school and studied law (1874–76). Admitted to the Georgia bar (1875), he gained a reputation as a criminal lawyer and became a substantial property owner. As a state assemblyman (1882–83), Watson expressed distrust of "New South" leaders who were allying the South with the industrial North. In 1890 he was elected to the U.S. House of Representatives on a Farmers' Alliance platform calling for an alliance between the South and agrarian West (1891–93). A radical egalitarian, Watson favored a sweeping program of agrarian reform, a drastic shakeup in the Georgia penal system, and racial equality. He was the People's (Populist) party candidate for speaker of the House and a leader of the party (1890–92), supporting passage of the Rural Free Delivery Act. Although he opposed the fusion of Populists and Democrats with Bryan at the head of the ticket (1896), he reluctantly accepted the vice-presidential nomination on the Populist line. In 1904 and 1908 he ran for president as a Populist. He wrote a number of substantial histories, including *The Story of France* (1898), *Napoleon: A Sketch of His Life* (1902), *The Life and Times of Thomas Jefferson* (1903), and *The Life and Times of An-*

drew Jackson (1912). *Tom Watson's Magazine,* published in New York (1905), contained his reform editorials as well as articles by Gorky and Dreiser. After his defeats for president, Watson became reactionary and, in his appeals to tenant farmers and mill workers, anti-Negro, anti-Semitic, and anti-Catholic. His book *The Roman Catholic Hierarchy* (1910), virulently anti-Catholic, led to 3 indictments but no convictions. He used the Leo Frank case (1913) to attack all Jews. Watson opposed American entry into World War I and conscription. He was elected Democratic senator from Georgia (1920), with Ku Klux Klan backing, on a platform opposing the League of Nations but supporting the restoration of civil liberties.

Webster, Daniel (b. Salisbury, N.H., 18 Jan. 1782; d. Marshfield, Mass., 24 Oct. 1852), statesman and orator, was graduated from Dartmouth (1801), read law at Salisbury and Boston, and was admitted to the Boston bar in 1805. He moved (1807) to Portsmouth, N.H., where he engaged in politics as a Federalist advocate of regional interests opposing Jefferson's embargo. His "Rockingham Memorial" (Aug. 1812), a forceful condemnation of the War of 1812, led to his election (Nov. 1812) to Congress. Reelected in 1816, he opposed the protective features of the Tariff of 1816 as inimical to New England commerce and shipping, and in the same year moved to Boston. In the following years he devoted himself to his law practice, appearing before the U.S. Supreme Court in cases including the *Dartmouth College Case, M*c*Culloch* v. *Maryland,* and *Gibbons* v. *Ogden,* and gaining a reputation as one of the foremost constitutional lawyers in the country. His standing as an orator was established by his Plymouth speech (22 Dec. 1820), his speech on Greek independence (19 Jan.

1824), and his Bunker Hill oration (17 June 1825). Elected to Congress from Massachusetts in 1823, he opposed the Tariff of 1824, and in 1827 was elected to the U.S. Senate. Reflecting the shift in the economic development of New England, Webster supported the Tariff of 1828 and thereafter was an ardent protectionist. A champion of nationalism, he made one of his great orations during the nullification controversy, when he engaged Sen. Robert Y. Hayne (S.C.) in the debate that stimulated Webster's utterance, "Liberty *and* Union, now and forever, one and inseparable!" Opposed to Jackson's financial policies, he supported a national bank and fought Van Buren's subtreasury proposal. In 1836 and 1840 he was an unsuccessful contender for the Whig nomination for the presidency. He served as Secretary of State under Presidents William Henry Harrison and John Tyler, negotiated the Webster-Ashburton Treaty of 1842, and resigned from the cabinet in 1843. Elected to the Senate in 1844, he served there until 1850. Although he consistently supported the Wilmot Proviso, he held the preservation of the Union as paramount and backed the Compromise of 1850, answering secessionists and abolitionists alike in his famous 7th of March speech: "I wish to speak today, not as a Massachusetts man, nor as a northern man, but as an American. . . . I speak today for the preservation of the Union. 'Hear me for my cause.'" As Fillmore's Secretary of State, he wrote the nationalistic "Hülsemann letter." With Calhoun and Clay, he comprised the great senatorial triumvirate; and to the conservatives of New England was known as "the god-like Daniel."

Webster, Noah (b. West Hartford, Conn., 16 Oct. 1758; d. New Haven, Conn., 28 May 1843), lexicographer, philologist, and journalist. After graduating from

Yale (B.A., 1778), he read law and was admitted to the bar at Hartford, but practiced for only a short period (1789–93). While teaching at Goshen, N.Y. (1782), he prepared the first part of what later became his *Spelling Book* (*Blue-Backed Speller*) for the use of school children. Published (1783) as *A Grammatical Institute of the English Language,* and completed with a grammar (1784) and a reader (1785), the work, designed to meet American needs, was influential in standardizing spelling and pronunciation in the U.S. as distinguished from prevailing British forms. The *Spelling Book* had an estimated printing of 15 million copies by 1837; by 1890 of more than 70 million. Webster wrote *Sketches of American Policy* (1785) and was later active as a Federalist pamphleteer and journalist, editing the *American Minerva* and *Herald,* both at New York (1793–1803). He abandoned journalism for lexicography and, moving to New Haven, brought out *A Compendious Dictionary of the English Language* (1806). This small work was succeeded by the scholarly *An American Dictionary of the English Language* (2 vols., 1828), which assured Webster's reputation in the U.S. and abroad as a pioneer in the science of lexicography.

Westinghouse, George (b. Central Bridge, N.Y., 6 Oct. 1846; d. New York City, 12 Mar. 1914), inventor and manufacturer. He served in the Union army until he was honorably discharged in 1864, and for the remainder of the Civil War was an engineer in the Union navy. Interested in mechanical inventions, he abandoned his education at Union College, Schenectady, N.Y., to enter his father's agricultural implement shop. In 1865 he obtained patents for a rotary steam engine and a car replacer, and in 1868–69 developed a railroad frog. In 1869, when he secured the first air-brake patent, he incorporated the Westinghouse Air Brake Co. This compressed air apparatus had a revolutionary impact on railroad transportation, making high-speed rail travel safe, and is still used as standard equipment. Westinghouse also invented an automatic air brake for long freight trains, and next turned his attention to railroad signaling by electrical controls. He organized (1882) the Union Switch and Signal Co. and later, after he became interested in natural gas and electrical power, formed the Philadelphia Co., the Westinghouse Machine Co., and the Westinghouse Electric Co. In the field of natural gas, he developed a long-distance transmission system. His interest in electrical inventions began in 1885, when he promoted the development and construction of transformers which enabled the introduction into the U.S. of high-tension systems using single-phase alternating currents. In 1886 he purchased the patents held by Nikola Tesla (*q.v.*) and developed a 2-phase system suitable for lamps and motors. Westinghouse held more than 400 patents, among them shock absorbers, marine steam turbines, a trolley car motor, and an electrical brake for subway cars.

Whistler, James Abbott McNeill (b. Lowell, Mass., 10 July 1834; d. London, 17 July 1903), painter and etcher. During his childhood he traveled with his parents in Russia and England; entered the U.S. Military Academy (1851), from which he was dismissed in 1854; served as a draftsman (1854–55) with the U.S. Coast Survey; and went to Paris (1855), where he took professional training and brought out his first etchings (1858). After c.1870 he did most of his work in England. The famous libel suit (1878) against John Ruskin, which resulted from the latter's excoriating comments on Whistler's *Black and Gold—The Falling Rocket,* ended with a 1-farthing verdict in favor of Whistler. The 2 dominant influences in his painting were Velásquez and Japanese art patterns. For Whistler, the essence of painting was arrangement in color. Among his works are the *Portrait of My Mother,* portraits of Thomas Carlyle, Theodore Duret, Rosa Corder, and Lady Meux, and a series of *Nocturnes* and *Symphonies* (such as *Battersea Bridge*) in which he experimented with color harmonies. A brilliant etcher, his etchings and dry-points of London river scenes and Venetian subjects show a complete authority in the medium. He wrote *The Gentle Art of Making Enemies* (1890).

White, Andrew Dickson (b. Homer, N.Y., 7 Nov. 1832; d. Ithaca, N.Y., 4 Nov. 1918), educator, diplomat, and historian. He was graduated from Yale (1853), served as an attaché (1854–55) to the U.S. legation at St. Petersburg, and in 1857, after taking his master's degree at Yale, became professor of history at the Univ. of Michigan, where he remained until 1863. He was elected (1863) to the New York senate and during his incumbency (1864–67) served as chairman of the committee on education, created the state system of normal schools, and was the leading spirit in planning and securing the charter for Cornell Univ., of which he became (1867) first president, serving in that capacity until 1885. At Cornell he introduced such innovations as the non-segregation of the humanities, the natural sciences, and technical arts, and the employment of leading scholars as "nonresident professors." He also taught history at Cornell, and was one of the founders and the first president of the American Historical Association (1884).

He served as U.S. minister to Germany (1879–81), minister to Russia (1892–94), ambassador to Germany (1897–1902), and was president of the International Peace Conference at The Hague (1899). His works include *History of the Warfare of Science with Theology in Christendom* (2 vols., 1896), which accepted Darwinism, and *Autobiography* (2 vols., 1905).

White, Edward Douglass (b. Parish Lafourche, La., 3 Nov. 1845; d. Washington, D.C., 19 May 1921), 8th chief justice of the U.S., studied at Jesuit College, New Orleans, and at Georgetown, enlisted in the Confederate army at the age of 16, was taken prisoner at Port Hudson, La., and paroled. Admitted to the state bar (1868), he practiced in New Orleans, was state senator (1874–78), and judge of the state supreme court (1879–80). Democratic U.S. senator (1891–94), he was appointed by Cleveland as associate justice of the U.S. Supreme Court (1894) and made chief justice by Taft (1910). On the high court he followed a middle-of-the-road policy, taking a liberal position in his dissent in *Lochner* v. *N.Y.* (1905) and in *Wilson* v. *New* (1917), upholding the Adamson Act providing an 8-hour day for railroad workers, but he dissented in *Bunting* v. *Oregon* (1917), which upheld the Oregon 10-hour law. Dissenting in the *Northern Securities Case* (1904), he laid down the "rule of reason" opinion dissolving the Standard Oil Co. and the American Tobacco Co. (1911).

Whitefield, George (b. Gloucester, England, 16 Dec. 1715; d. Newburyport, Mass., 30 Sept. 1770), evangelist. He was graduated from Oxford, where he became associated with John and Charles Wesley and the Methodist movement. During the absence of the

Wesleys in Georgia (which Whitefield visited in May–Sept. 1738), he acted as the leader of the Methodist movement. When virtually all of the churches in England closed their doors against him, Whitefield took to preaching outdoor sermons, soon attracting large audiences and wide attention with his impassioned oratory and expert histrionics. In 1739 he returned to America, where he was the most important single influence in stirring the religious revival commonly called the Great Awakening. Upon his return to England (1741) Whitefield, who had become a Calvinist, broke with the Wesleys and assumed the leadership of the Calvinistic Methodist movement. He made subsequent visits to America in 1744–48, 1751, 1754–55, 1763–64, and 1769–70.

Whitman, Walt (b. West Hills, Huntington, Long Island, N.Y., 31 May 1819; d. Camden, N.J., 26 Mar. 1892), poet, worked as a printer's devil, taught school, and edited (1838–39) the *Long Islander*. From 1841 to 1848 he was associated with newspapers and magazines at New York, editing (1846–48) the *Brooklyn Eagle* and publishing a temperance novel, *Franklin Evans; or, The Inebriate, a Tale of the Times* (1842). He went to New Orleans (1848), where he worked for the *Crescent*, and after his return to Brooklyn wrote for the Free-Soil daily, the *Freeman*, during 1848–49, and edited (1857–59) the Brooklyn *Times*. He published *Leaves of Grass* (1855), which struck a new and indigenous note in American poetry, and to which many pieces were added in subsequent editions. During the Civil War, Whitman was a volunteer nurse at Washington, D.C., where he also worked as a clerk in the Department of the Interior. Following a paralytic stroke suffered by him in 1873, he moved to Camden, N.J., where he resided for the rest of his life. Sometimes called "the Good Gray Poet," Whitman is the bard of democracy who, in celebrating his own identity, extolled both the average man and the uniqueness of the individual. Among his works are *Drum Taps* (1865), *Passage to India* (1871), *Democratic Vistas* (1871, prose work), *Specimen Days and Collect* (1882–83, prose work), and *Good-bye, My Fancy* (1891). Among his individual poems are "Pioneers! O Pioneers!" "The Song of the Broad Axe," "Once I Pass'd through a Populous City," "When Lilacs Last in the Dooryard Bloom'd," and "O Captain! My Captain!"

Whitney, Eli (b. Westboro, Mass., 8 Dec. 1765; d. New Haven, Conn., 8 Jan. 1825), inventor. As a boy and young man he became familiar with mechanical crafts in his father's metalworking shop. He entered Yale in 1789 and was graduated in 1792. While in the South, where he began his law studies on the Georgia plantation of the widow of Gen. Nathanael Greene, his attention was called to the tedious method of cleaning green seed cotton, at that time an unprofitable crop because of the costly manual process of separating the staple. Whitney designed a cotton gin and, after successive experiments, built a large and improved model (1793) with which a single slave could maintain a daily output of 50 lbs. of cleaned cotton. Before Whitney obtained his patent (1794), many imitations were placed on the market; in the various infringement suits he undertook, Whitney did not secure a favorable verdict until 1807, and most of the little money he made from the invention went for law costs. His cotton gin revolutionized the course of Southern agriculture and territorial expansion. In New Haven, Whitney undertook the manufacture of firearms. He obtained from the federal government a contract for 10,000 muskets (1798). For their manufacture he devised a system of interchangeable parts (1800), also devised independently (before 1808) by Simeon North (1765–1852), the Connecticut gunsmith. Whitney established a factory near New Haven, at the site of present-day Whitneyville, and designed and built the machinery for producing muskets with precision parts turned out by relatively inexperienced workmen engaged in simple operations.

Whittier, John Greenleaf (b. Haverhill, Mass., 17 Dec. 1807; d. Hampton Falls, N.H., 7 Sept. 1892), poet and abolitionist, published his first poems (1826 et seq.) in the Newburyport (Mass.) *Free Press,* edited by William Lloyd Garrison. He attended (1827–28) Haverhill Academy, became (1829) editor of *The American Manufacturer* at Boston, and edited (1831) the *New England Weekly Review* at Hartford, Conn. He published *Legends of New England in Prose and Verse* (1831) and *Moll Pitcher* (1832), and under the influence of Garrison became an active abolitionist (after c.1833). He served (1835) in the Massachusetts legislature, edited (1838–40) the *Pennsylvania Freeman,* and published *Poems Written During the Progress of the Abolition Question* (1838). He helped establish the American and Foreign Antislavery Society and ran for Congress on the Liberty party ticket. He became (1847) corresponding editor of the antislavery journal the *National Era.* His volumes of poetry include *Lays of My Home* (1843), *Voices of Freedom* (1846), *Songs of Labor* (1850), *The Chapel of the Hermits* (1853), *The Panorama and Other Poems* (1856), *In War Time and Other Poems* (1864), *Snow-Bound* (1866), *The Tent on the Beach* (1867), *Ballads of New England* (1870), and *At Sun-down* (1890). His best-known individual poems include "Maud Muller," "Barefoot Boy," "Massachusetts to Virginia," "Ichabod," and "Barbara Frietchie."

Wiener, Norbert (b. Columbia, Mo., 26 Nov. 1894; d. Stockholm, Sweden, 18 Mar. 1964), mathematician and philosopher. Son of Leo Wiener, Harvard's first professor of Slavonic languages, he was a child prodigy, with a B.A. from Tufts at age 14 and a Ph.D. from Harvard at 19. His graduate study also took him to Cornell, to Cambridge, England, where he studied under Bertrand Russell, to Göttingen Univ., and to Columbia. He lectured in mathematics at Harvard (1915–16) and at the Univ. of Maine (1916–17). From 1919 to 1960 he was a member of the mathematics department at the Massachusetts Institute of Technology. He formulated a theory of Brownian movement (1920) and made far-reaching discoveries about the flow of information along a wave (1925). Working for the government during World War II, he made major contributions to the development of radar, coding, antiaircraft fire-control and gun-aiming devices but, disturbed by the destructive potential of devices based on his investigations, he renounced (1947) military research. A pioneer in computer science, he recognized computers as constituting a second industrial revolution—one with great possibilities as well as great dangers, if through intellectual sloth man relinquished control to his mechanical creations. Though technical in nature, his *Cybernetics: On Control and Communication in Animal and the Machine* (1948), in which he summarized the results of his work in information control and communication, gained popular as well as scientific attention. He coined the term cybernetics —derived from the Greek for "steersman"—to define a new science which attempts to construct a theoretical framework for the comparative study of control and communications in machines and in living organisms. Cybernetics attempts to find the common elements in the functioning of automatic information-processing machines and of the human nervous system. Known as the "father of automation," his contributions altered the face of the modern world. The author of numerous articles and books (including detective stories written under a pseudonym, W. Norbert), his other works include *The Human Use of Human Beings* (1950), *Ex-Prodigy* (1953), *I Am a Mathematician* (1956).

Wilkes, Charles (b. New York City, 3 Apr. 1798; d. Washington, D.C., 8 Feb. 1877), naval officer and explorer, was commissioned midshipman in the U.S. navy (1818) and given charge of the Department of Charts and Instruments (1833), out of which developed the Naval Observatory and Hydrographic Office. In 1838 he was given command of the first national marine exploration and surveyed routes in the Pacific Ocean and South Seas frequented by American whalers. In Jan. 1840 he claimed discovery of the Continent of Antarctica, coasting along part of the Antarctic barrier from about 150°E to 108°E, subsequently named Wilkes Land in his honor. He supervised the preparation of the 19-vol. report of the expedition and personally prepared *Narrative* (1844), *Meteorology* (1851), and *Hydrography* (1861). Commanding the *San Jacinto* in the Civil War, he stopped the British mail steamer *Trent* in the old Bahama Channel (8 Nov. 1861) and seized the Confederate commissioners, James M. Mason and John Slidell, en route to Europe. Although thanked by Congress, his action was disavowed by Lincoln as a breach of international law, and Mason and Slidell were surrendered to Britain.

Willard, Emma Hart (b. Berlin, Conn., 23 Feb. 1787; d. Troy, N.Y., 15 Apr. 1870), educator. She attended the Berlin Academy, and from 1807 until 1809, when she married John Willard, was head of the Middlebury (Vt.) Female Academy. In 1814 she established the Middlebury Female Seminary, where she made innovations in women's education. She sent to Governor De Witt Clinton of New York *An Address . . . Proposing a Plan for Improving Female Education* (1819), in which she advocated educational equality for women. Although her proposals led the New York legislature to charter (1819) the Waterford Academy established by her, the state failed to provide financial aid. At the invitation of citizens of Troy, N.Y., she established there (1821) the Troy Female Seminary, the first U.S. college-level institution for women. It provided instruction in subjects such as mathematics and philosophy from which women had been traditionally excluded. Mrs. Willard wrote history and geography textbooks that were used in many schools and trained hundreds of teachers who spread her doctrines. She retired in 1838, thereafter devoting herself to the improvement of common schools. She was the author of a volume of poetry, *The Fulfilment of a Promise* (1831), which included "Rocked in the Cradle of the Deep."

Willard, Frances (b. Churchville, N.Y., 28 Sept. 1839; d. New York City, 18 Feb. 1898), reformer, was graduated from Northwestern Female College (1859) and settled in Evanston, Ill., where she began teaching (1860) and became president of the Evanston College for Ladies (1871–74). She resigned to join the temperance crusade and served as president (from 1879) of the National Women's Christian Temperance Union (WCTU) and of the World

Woman's Christian Temperance Union (from 1887). She helped organize the Prohibition party and participated in the women's suffrage movement.

Williams, Roger (b. London, England, c.1603; d. Providence, R.I., between 26 Jan. and 25 Mar. 1683), religious leader, founder of the Rhode Island Colony. Protégé of the lawyer Sir Edward Coke, who helped Williams secure his education, he was graduated from Cambridge (B.A., 1627), took holy orders in the Church of England (c.1628), and as chaplain to Sir William Masham became acquainted with Puritan circles. Immigrating to Massachusetts (1631), he antagonized the magistracy by his contentions that the civil government was not empowered to enforce the religious precepts of the Ten Commandments and that the royal charter illegally expropriated the land rights of the Indians. After serving in churches at Plymouth and Salem, he was tried by the General Court, which ordered his banishment (1635). With some of his followers he founded (1636) the earliest Rhode Island settlement at Providence, adopting a humane policy toward the Indians. Having already taken a position more radical than Separatism, he now viewed with skepticism all established churches. After a brief period as a Baptist, he became (1639) a Seeker, i.e., one who adhered to the basic tenets of Christianity but refused to recognize any creed. First champion of complete religious toleration in America, he also espoused a liberal political order in the Rhode Island colony, which was founded on the compact theory of the state and featured a democratic land association. To safeguard his colony against the encroachments of the New England Confederation, he went to England (1643) and secured a charter (1644). During his stay in England he wrote pamphlets on behalf of the liberal wing of Puritanism, including *Queries of Highest Consideration* (1644), which opposed the establishment of a national church, and *The Bloudy Tenent of Persecution* (1644), which advocated unqualified religious and political freedom. He returned to Rhode Island (1644) to find that William Coddington of Newport had organized opposition to Williams' plans for the union of the 4 Rhode Island settlements. With John Clarke, Williams again went to England (1651) where he succeeded in having Coddington's commission withdrawn. During this period he wrote *The Bloudy Tenent Yet More Bloudy* (1652) in reply to John Cotton's *The Bloudy Tenent Washed and Made White* (1647). Upon his return to Rhode Island, Williams served for 3 terms (1654–57) as president of the colony, which in 1663 obtained a new charter from Charles II.

Williams, Tennessee [Thomas Lanier] (b. Columbus, Miss., 26 Mar. 1911–   ), playwright, moved to St. Louis at 12, attended the Univ. of Missouri (1931–33), but left during the depression to clerk with a shoe company. After a year at Washington Univ., St. Louis (1936–37), he finished his college course at the Univ. of Iowa (B.A., 1938). A Rockefeller fellow in 1940, he quickly established a reputation as a talented and prolific playwright. His early plays include *Battle of Angels* (1940) and *The Glass Menagerie* (1945). His Pulitzer prize-winning *A Streetcar Named Desire* (1947) established his reputation. His plays, often concerned with the destruction of innocence by inexorable forces and with individual depravity, reached a broad audience through adaptation for the screen. Among his later plays are *The Rose Tattoo* (1948), *Cat on a Hot Tin Roof* (1955, Pulitzer prize), *Sweet Bird of Youth* (1959),

The Night of the Iguana (1962, N.Y. Drama Critics Circle award). Screenplays of importance are *Baby Doll* and *The Fugitive Kind*.

Wilson, Edmund (b. Red Bank, N.J., 8 May 1895; d. Talcottville, N.Y., 12 June 1972), author and critic. After graduating from Princeton (1916), where he began an association with fellow student F. Scott Fitzgerald (*q.v.*) which lasted until the latter's death, Wilson spent several months as a reporter on the New York *Evening Sun*. During World War I he served as private, a hospital attendant, and a member of the Intelligence Corps. As managing editor of *Vanity Fair* (1920–21) and associate editor of the *New Republic* (1926–31), he helped launch the careers of John Dos Passos and F. Scott Fitzgerald. His publication of *Axel's Castle* (1931)—a study of the writings of Yeats, Eliot, Pound, and Joyce in the context of the French Symbolist movement—and *American Jitters* (1932)—a collection of articles with a political bent—brought him acclaim as a critic. During the depression he called for a radical approach to the nation's ills and supported the Communist party's presidential candidate in 1932. His visit to the U.S.S.R. as a Guggenheim fellow (1935) led to his writing *To the Finland Station* (1940). At the conclusion of this scholarly survey of the revolutionary tradition—which focused on Vico, Saint-Simon, Taine, Marx, Engels, Lenin, and Trotsky—Wilson expressed doubt that Marxist theories would lead to a society without exploitation. The next year he published *The Wound and the Bow*, which explored the dualism of Dickens, Kipling, Casanova, Edith Wharton, Hemingway, and Joyce. Having mastered French, Italian, German, and Greek as an adolescent, he learned Hebrew, Russian, and Hungarian later in life. He wrote with authority

and elegance on a wide variety of topics, including the Dead Sea Scrolls (1955), the Iroquois (1959), the literature of the Civil War (*Patriotic Gore,* 1962), and the income tax (1963).

Wilson, James (b. Carskerdo, Scotland, 14 Sept. 1742; d. Edenton, N.C., 21 Aug. 1798), Revolutionary statesman, jurist, attended St. Andrews, Glasgow, and Edinburgh universities (1757–63). Leaving Scotland for America, he arrived in New York during the Stamp Act crisis and obtained a post as Latin tutor at the College of Philadelphia (1766). Studying law with John Dickinson (*q.v.*), he was admitted to the bar (1767), practiced in Reading (1768), and moved to Carlisle, where by 1774 he had amassed a huge practice. Heading a Committee of Correspondence at Carlisle (1774), he published in that year his notable *Considerations on the Nature and Extent of the Legislative Authority of the British Parliament,* denying Parliament's authority over the colonies and anticipating a British Commonwealth. Signer of the Declaration, he sought in the 2d Continental Congress to strengthen the national government. An opponent of the radical Pennsylvania constitution of 1776, he became leader of the conservative forces in Philadelphia, to which he moved in 1778. Incurring animosity for his defense of the Penn family and of profiteering merchants, he and his friends barricaded themselves against a mob (4 Oct. 1779). In Congress (1785–87), he played a leading role at the Federal Convention and successfully fought for adoption of the Constitution in Pennsylvania. Law lecturer at the College of Philadelphia (1789), he was associate justice of the U.S. Supreme Court (1789–98), and wrote a notable opinion in *Chisholm* v. *Georgia* (1793), upholding the national against the states' authority. Throughout his life a heavy land speculator, he fled to North Carolina to avoid arrest for debt and died under a cloud.

Wilson, [Thomas] Woodrow (b. Staunton, Va., 28 Dec. 1856; d. Washington, D.C., 3 Feb. 1924), 28th president of the U.S., was graduated from Princeton (1879), studied law at the Univ. of Virginia (1880), was admitted to the bar (1881), and, after opening a law office in Atlanta, entered the graduate school at Johns Hopkins (1883), where he completed his notable doctoral thesis, *Congressional Government* (1885). After teaching history at Bryn Mawr (1885–88) and Wesleyan (1888–90), he became professor of jurisprudence and political economics at Princeton (1890–1902), quickly establishing himself as a preeminent authority in his field and was in wide demand as a public lecturer. Appointed first nonclerical president of Princeton (1902–10), he became second only to Eliot of Harvard as an educational leader. Defeated in his plans for the graduate school, his position became untenable, and he resigned to accept the Democratic nomination for governor of New Jersey. His term (1911–12) was marked by reforms and a courageous fight against the Democratic political machine. Put forward as a conservative Democrat to defeat W. J. Bryan, he obtained the Democratic nomination for president (1912) and was elected as a result of a split in Republican ranks. His 1st administration was notable for such reforms as the Underwood Tariff, the Federal Reserve Act (1913), the Federal Trade Commission, and the Clayton Act (1914). He sent a punitive expedition across the Mexican border (1916) and sought to maintain U.S. neutrality after the outbreak of World War I despite infringement of American rights. Reelected president (1916) on the campaign slogan "he kept us out of war," he called for war (2 Apr. 1917) after Germany renewed unrestricted submarine warfare. "The world must be made safe for democracy," he then declared. On 8 Jan. 1918 he laid down 14 Points as the basis of peace and stated (27 Sept.) that the League of Nations was the "most essential part" of the peace settlement. Heading the U.S. peace delegation, he was given an unprecedented reception in Paris (14 Dec. 1918) and in other European capitals, but became involved in disputes with Allied leaders and was forced to compromise numerous of the 14 Points in order to save the League. When the Senate refused to ratify the Treaty of Versailles without reservations unacceptable to him, he set out from Washington (3 Sept. 1919) to carry to the people his case against "the little group of willful men." He collapsed at Pueblo (26 Sept. 1919) and never fully recovered.

Winthrop, John (b. Edwardstone, Suffolk, England, 22 Jan. 1588; d. Boston, Mass., 26 Mar. 1649), colonial Puritan statesman, first governor of Massachusetts Bay. He attended Cambridge, was admitted at Gray's Inn (1613), and practiced law in London, being admitted to the Inner Temple in 1628. A country squire, his Puritan convictions led him to take an interest in the Massachusetts Bay Co., of which he was chosen governor (1629). He signed the Cambridge Agreement (1629) by which 12 members pledged that if the charter and company could be legally transferred to New England they would go there with their families. He sailed from Southampton (1630) aboard the *Arbella*, part of a fleet transporting to Salem some 700 passengers, the first large contingent of the Puritan migration, and settled at the present site of Boston. Winthrop and his Puritan associates laid the foundation of the "Bible Commonwealth." He served as governor (1629–34, 1637–40, 1642–44, 1646–49) and was deputy governor for a total of ten years. As early as 1637 he advocated a New England Confederation, particularly for reasons of defense, and was the first president of the confederation when it was formed in 1643. The first 2 vols. of his manuscript *Journal* (1630–44) appeared in 1790, and it was published in full as *The History of New England* (2 vols., 1825–26).

Wise, Isaac Mayer (b. Steingrub, Bohemia, 29 Mar. 1819; d. Cincinnati, Ohio, 26 Mar. 1900), religious leader, entered (1835) a rabbinical school in Jenikau, then attended the Univ. of Prague for 2 years and the Univ. of Vienna for a year. Admitted to the rabbinate, he was elected (1843) rabbi of the congregation of Radnitz, but opposing government control and censorship, he left Bohemia for the U.S. (1846). Rabbi in Albany, N.Y. (1846–54), he accepted a call to the Bene Yeshurun Congregation in Cincinnati, where he was rabbi (1854–1900). His weekly newspaper, the *Israelite* (later *American Israelite*), advocated adjusting Judaism to American life and institutions, including the use of English in religious services and a simplification of ritual observances. Founder of Reform Judaism in the U.S. he appealed (1848) for a union of congregations, which saw fruition in the Union of American Hebrew Congregations (1873); founded the Hebrew Union College (1875), first native institution for training rabbis; and established a rabbinical organization, the Central Conference of American Rabbis (1889), of which he was president until his death. His writings include *History of the Israelitish Nation from Abraham to the Present Time* (1854), *The Cosmic God* (1876), and *Pronaos to Holy Writ* (1891).

Witherspoon, John (b. Yester, near Edinburgh, Scotland, 5 Feb. 1723; d. New Jersey, 15 Nov. 1794), religious leader, educator, and Revolutionary patriot. He received his divinity degree (1743) from the Univ. of Edinburgh, was ordained in the Presbyterian ministry in 1745, and held pulpits in Scotland until 1768, when he came to America to occupy the presidency of the College of New Jersey (now Princeton). As an educator, he revamped methods of instruction and the college curriculum, and was an exponent of the Scottish "common sense" philosophy. As a religious leader, he closed the factional breach between the "Old Side" and "New Side" Presbyterians in the colonies, was partly responsible for the rapid growth of the Presbyterian Church in America on the eve of the Revolution, and was a staunch advocate of religious liberty. Delegate to the Continental Congress in 1776, he favored the Declaration of Independence, of which he was a signer. He served intermittently in Congress until 1782, and was a signer of the Articles of Confederation. He was a member (1783, 1789) of the New Jersey legislature and of the state convention that ratified (1787) the Federal Constitution, and was active (1785–89) in furthering the national organization of the Presbyterian Church. He coined the term "Americanism" in an article on language in the *Pennsylvania Journal* (1781). His *Works* (4 vols.) were published in 1800–01.

Woodward, Robert Burns (b. Boston, 10 Apr. 1917–   ), chemist, obtained his B.S. (1936) from MIT and his Ph.D. a year later. Joining the Harvard faculty that year, he achieved, with Dr. William E. Doering, the first total synthesis of quinine (1944). His synthesis, with C. H. Schramm, of protein analogues (1947), materials resembling natural proteins found in animal and plant life, came closer than ever before to duplicating a natural growth process, and proved valuable in plastics, antibiotics, and medical research. First to synthesize a steroid (1951), he announced later that year the total synthesis of cortisone. He synthesized cholesterol (1951), strychnine (1954), chlorophyll (1960), and tetracycline (1962). He received the Nobel prize in chemistry (1965).

Wright, Frank Lloyd (b. Richland Center, Wis., 8 June 1867; d. Phoenix, Ariz., 10 Apr. 1959), architect. He studied civil engineering (1884–88) at the Univ. of Wisconsin and was a draftsman (1889–94) with architectural firms at Chicago, including Adler & Sullivan, for whom he worked on plans for the Transportation Building at the Chicago World's Fair (1893) and the James Charnley house at Chicago. In 1894 he established independent practice at Oak Park, Ill., and in 1911 moved to Spring Green, Wis., where he designed his own residences, Taliesin I and Taliesin II. His "prairie house" style appeared as early as c.1894 in the W. H. Winslow house at River Forest, Ill. A disciple of Louis H. Sullivan (*q.v.*), Wright became the foremost American innovator and exponent of an organic architecture based on the integration of form, function, building site, and materials, and on the subordination of style to human needs. His preoccupation with the social relations of architecture is expressed in his model for the projected community of Broadacre City. His designs have exerted a pervasive influence on modern European architecture, particularly in France, Holland, Germany, and the Scandinavian countries. Among his works are Unity Temple, Oak Park, Ill.; the Larkin Administration Bldg. and the Darwin Martin house, both at Buffalo, N.Y.; the Coonley Playhouse and Kindergarten,

Riverside, Ill.; the Ward H. Willits house, Highland Park, Ill.; the F. C. Robie house, Francisco Terrace, and Midway Gardens, all at Chicago; the Aline Barnsdall house, Los Angeles, Calif.; the Imperial Hotel at Tokyo, which withstood the earthquake of 1923; Taliesin West at Paradise Valley, Phoenix, Ariz.; the Johnson Wax Co. Administration Bldg., Racine, Wis.; the Jacobs house, Madison, Wis.; the Jones house, Tulsa, Okla.; and the Kaufmann house (Falling River) at Bear Run, Pa. In 1956 he completed work on the Price Tower in Bartlesville, Okla. The Solomon R. Guggenheim Museum (New York) was completed posthumously (Oct. 1959).

Wright, Wilbur (b. Millville, near New Castle, Ind., 16 Apr. 1867; d. Dayton, Ohio, 30 May 1912), and his brother, **Orville** (b. Dayton, Ohio, 19 Aug. 1871; d. there, 30 Jan. 1948), aviation pioneers and inventors. The sons of Bishop Milton Wright of the United Brethren in Christ, they had only brief formal schooling, neither completing high school. In 1892 they established a bicycle shop at Dayton, where they began (1895) the manufacture of bicycles. Their interest in aviation having been aroused (c.1898), they read articles and books on aeronautics, built a biplane kite (1899), and conducted two man-carrying glider experiments (1900, 1901) at Kitty Hawk, N.C. Finding a relative paucity of scientific information in the field of aircraft design and construction, they built a wind tunnel (1901) in which they tested and verified the operation of some 200 wing and biplane surfaces. They worked out major innovations in aircraft control systems and, on the basis of their painstaking compilation of scientific data, began (Oct. 1902) the construction of a powered aircraft with a total weight of 750 lbs.

and carrying a 170-lb., 12-hp gasoline engine. This machine was completed at Kitty Hawk, where, on 17 Dec. 1903, Orville Wright made the first piloted flight in a powered airplane, remaining aloft for 12 seconds over a distance of about 120 ft. Of the 4 flights made on that day, Wilbur flew the longest one: 59 seconds over a distance of 852 ft. Returning to Dayton, the Wright brothers improved their machine. Toward the close of 1905 they made in it a flight of about 38 minutes over a distance of more than 24 miles around Huffman Field, Dayton. They obtained a patent for their aircraft on 22 May 1906. In 1908–09 Wilbur toured England, France, and Italy, setting records for altitude and distance. Their machine, after being subjected to tests at Ft. Myer, Va., was accepted by the U.S. Army (2 Aug. 1909). The commercial development and manufacture of the Wright airplane was begun in 1909 with the organization of the Wright Co.

Young, Brigham (b. Whitingham, Vt. 1 June 1801; d. Salt Lake City, 29 Aug. 1877), Mormon leader and colonizer. In his infancy he was taken by his family to the "burnt-over" district in western New York, a region of intense evangelical activity. After working as a house painter and glazier, he settled (1829) on a farm at Mendon, N.Y., about 40 miles from Palmyra, N.Y., where Joseph Smith (*q.v.*) published *The Book of Mormon* and founded the Church of Jesus Christ of Latter-Day Saints. Young became a convert to Mormonism (1832) and devoted the rest of his life to the upbuilding of the Mormon Church. In 1835 he became the 3d ranking member of the Quorum of the 12 Apostles, the administrative body of the church, and by 1838 was its senior member. During these years he was active as a Mormon missionary. Upon the death of Joseph

Smith at Carthage, Ill., he became head of the church. In this role Young demonstrated his brilliance, energy, and determination as a practical organizer. He led the Mormon mass migrations to the Valley of the Great Salt Lake and directed the settlement of Deseret, which in 1850 was organized by Congress as Utah Territory. Young was named territorial governor, and although removed from his post (1857) during the Mormon controversy with the federal government, remained the effective leader of the community. His lasting contribution was the shaping of an administrative machinery that enabled the survival and development of the Mormon Church. He adopted polygamy, had about a score of wives, and fathered 56 children.

Zenger, John Peter (b. in Germany, 1697; d. New York City, 28 July 1746), printer and journalist. He arrived at New York in 1710 and served his apprenticeship (1711–19) to the printer William Bradford, with whom he formed (1725) a short-lived partnership. In 1726 Zenger established an independent business. In 1733, after Gov. Cosby adopted arbitrary measures, Zenger became the editor and publisher of the *New-York Weekly Journal,* set up by him and prominent New Yorkers in opposition to the provincial administration and its organ, Bradford's *New York Gazette.* The polemical articles which appeared in the *Weekly Journal* were probably written by Zenger's associates; under existing law, however, the publisher was held responsible. In 1734 Zenger was arrested and imprisoned, and held incommunicado for about 10 months. Brought to trial (1735) for seditious libel, he was defended by Andrew Hamilton of Philadelphia. Despite the court's refusal to admit evidence establishing the truth of the libel, Hamilton succeeded in securing Zenger's acquittal. The case is a landmark in the history of the freedom of the press in America. Zenger became public printer for the colony of New York (1737) and the colony of New Jersey (1738).

Zworykin, Vladimir (b. Mourom, Russia, 30 July 1889–   ), electronics engineer, pioneer in the development of television. He was graduated from the Petrograd Institute of Technology (E.E., 1912), came to the U.S. in 1916, was naturalized in 1924, and served as research engineer (1920–29) with the Westinghouse Electrical and Manufacturing Co. He applied (1925) for the patent on the iconoscope (the essential basis of the electronic television camera), the first practical application and predecessor of modern television. He served as director of electronic research (1929–42) for the RCA Manufacturing Co., and was associate director (1942–45) of the RCA Laboratories, of which he was named director of electronic research (1946) and vice-president and technical consultant (1947). In 1933, employing the iconoscope and the cathode-ray tube, he made a successful demonstration of television over a radio-wave relay between New York and Philadelphia. He has also done work in the fields of electron optics and the electron microscope. He is the author of *Photocells and Their Applications* (1932), *Television* (1940), and *Television in Science and Industry* (1958).

INDEX

IN CONGRESS, JULY 4, 1776.

The unanimous Declaration of the thirteen united States of America,

When in the Course of human events, it becomes necessary for one people to dissolve the political bands which have connected them with another, and to assume among the powers of the earth, the separate and equal station to which the Laws of Nature and of Nature's God entitle them, a decent respect to the opinions of mankind requires that they should declare the causes which impel them to the separation.

We hold these truths to be self-evident, that all men are created equal, that they are endowed by their Creator with certain unalienable Rights, that among these are Life, Liberty and the pursuit of Happiness.—That to secure these rights, Governments are instituted among Men, deriving their just powers from the consent of the governed,—That whenever any Form of Government becomes destructive of these ends, it is the Right of the People to alter or to abolish it, and to institute new Government, laying its foundation on such principles and organizing its powers in such form, as to them shall seem most likely to effect their Safety and Happiness. Prudence, indeed, will dictate that Governments long established should not be changed for light and transient causes; and accordingly all experience hath shewn, that mankind are more disposed to suffer, while evils are sufferable, than to right themselves by abolishing the forms to which they are accustomed. But when a long train of abuses and usurpations, pursuing invariably the same Object evinces a design to reduce them under absolute Despotism, it is their right, it is their duty, to throw off such Government, and to provide new Guards for their future security.—Such has been the patient sufferance of these Colonies; and such is now the necessity which constrains them to alter their former Systems of Government. The history of the present King of Great Britain is a history of repeated injuries and usurpations, all having in direct object the establishment of an absolute Tyranny over these States. To prove this, let Facts be submitted to a candid world.

He has refused his Assent to Laws, the most wholesome and necessary for the public good.

He has forbidden his Governors to pass Laws of immediate and pressing importance, unless suspended in their operation till his Assent should be obtained; and when so suspended, he has utterly neglected to attend to them.

He has refused to pass other Laws for the accommodation of large districts of people, unless those people would relinquish the right of Representation in the Legislature, a right inestimable to them and formidable to tyrants only.

He has called together legislative bodies at places unusual, uncomfortable, and distant from the depository of their public Records, for the sole purpose of fatiguing them into compliance with his measures.

He has dissolved Representative Houses repeatedly, for opposing with manly firmness his invasions on the rights of the people.

He has refused for a long time, after such dissolutions, to cause others to be elected; whereby the Legislative powers, incapable of Annihilation, have returned to the People at large for their exercise; the State remaining in the mean time exposed to all the dangers of invasion from without, and convulsions within.

He has endeavoured to prevent the population of these States; for that purpose obstructing the Laws for Naturalization of Foreigners; refusing to pass others to encourage their migrations hither, and raising the conditions of new Appropriations of Lands.

He has obstructed the Administration of Justice, by refusing his Assent to Laws for establishing Judiciary powers.

He has made Judges dependent on his Will alone, for the tenure of their offices, and the amount and payment of their salaries.

He has erected a multitude of New Offices, and sent hither swarms of Officers to harass our people, and eat out their substance.

He has kept among us, in times of peace, Standing Armies without the Consent of our legislatures.

He has affected to render the Military independent of and superior to the Civil power.

He has combined with others to subject us to a jurisdiction foreign to our constitution, and unacknowledged by our laws; giving his Assent to their Acts of pretended Legislation:

For quartering large bodies of armed troops among us:

For protecting them, by a mock Trial, from punishment for any Murders which they should commit on the Inhabitants of these States:

For cutting off our Trade with all parts of the world:

For imposing Taxes on us without our Consent:

For depriving us in many cases, of the benefits of Trial by Jury: